GODKNOWY
PUBLISHERS

~ THE MOST COMPLETE ~
ETHIOPIAN BIBLE

ONE-OF-A-KIND EDITION IN ENGLISH

180 BOOKS

Table of Contents

THE COMPLETE APOCRYPHA

The bonus includes over 20 Apocrypha books, completing this as the full 180-book Ethiopian Bible. You'll also get exclusive video lectures, inspiring audio content, beautifully illustrated books, and much more for a truly immersive experience.

~ ETHIOPIAN BIBLE ~
FREE BONUS

GODKNOWY PUBLISHERS

Introduction

We are honored to introduce you to the Ethiopian Bible, a sacred compilation that is not only expansive in content but also deeply rich in history, spirituality, and cultural significance. This Bible, with its 180 books—more than any other Christian biblical collection—carries the heartbeat of Ethiopian Christianity, preserving a wealth of writings that offer insight into our faith's journey over centuries. As members of a tradition that treasures these texts as our spiritual inheritance, we see this Bible as more than a compilation of divine teachings; it is our story, our guidance, and our bond with the divine and with each other. For us, this Bible is both a spiritual anchor and a cultural treasure, unique in its canon and unmatched in its breadth. These books have been the guiding light of Ethiopian Christians, not only in church services but also in the daily lives of our people. They carry teachings on morality, justice, wisdom, and divine mysteries that have shaped our families, communities, and the values that we hold close. When we open this Bible, we don't merely read its words—we encounter the voices of those who came before us, who devoted their lives to preserving and passing down these sacred texts.

A Bible Rooted in Faith and Heritage

The Ethiopian Bible is more than a scripture; it is a testament to the resilience of our faith. From the earliest days of Christianity's arrival in Ethiopia in the 4th century CE, this Bible has been our companion and our guide. Through centuries of political shifts, foreign invasions, and times of hardship, we have clung to these texts with reverence and dedication. To us, the Ethiopian Bible is not just an ancient relic but a living document, one that we turn to for answers, for wisdom, and for connection with God.

Unlike other biblical traditions, the Ethiopian Bible includes books that have long been forgotten or left out in other parts of the world. The Book of Enoch, the Books of Meqabyan, and the Book of Jubilees, to name a few, are part of our sacred canon. These texts carry themes of divine mystery, cosmic order, and the battles of good and evil, all resonating with a mystical depth that speaks to the soul. For us, these books do not simply supplement our faith; they form an integral part of it, offering perspectives that inspire awe and humility, reminding us of the vastness of God's wisdom.

The Journey of Translating a Monumental Collection

Bringing this Bible into modern English was no simple task. We undertook this endeavor not merely as a translation project but as a mission to share our heritage and to honor the depth of the original language, Ge'ez, in which these texts were first recorded. For centuries, Ge'ez has been the language of our liturgy and scripture, a language that embodies layers of meaning that can be difficult to capture in translation. Every phrase, every word, carries weight and nuance that reflects our cultural and spiritual worldview. We knew that the translation process would require not only linguistic expertise but also a sensitivity to the spiritual resonance that these words carry for us. As we worked on this translation, we collaborated closely with Ethiopian Orthodox clergy, scholars, and language experts who could help us convey not just the words but the heart of the text.

For us, translating the Ethiopian Bible was as much about faithfully sharing our faith as it was about remaining true to the integrity of the original writings. We carefully balanced the need for clarity with a respect for the sacred, rhythmic nature of Ge'ez. Our aim was to bring readers as close as possible to the essence of these words, to help them experience not just the teachings, but the reverence, awe, and devotion that these scriptures inspire in us.

Preserving the Sacredness: A Matter of Faithful Responsibility

Our goal has always been to protect the sacredness of these texts, to ensure that they are not merely read but felt, and that their spiritual depth is preserved. This is why we paid close attention to the structure, cadence, and poetic nature of the original language, attempting to recreate a sense of the divine rhythm that we experience in Ethiopian liturgy. This translation required patience, humility, and a deep respect for what these words mean to our people.

Every line we translated reminded us that we were handling something holy, something that has shaped lives and inspired countless generations. In Ethiopia, scripture is not confined to the church; it is part of our home, our community, and our daily lives. Our Bible is a moral compass that guides us, a source of wisdom that we turn to in moments of joy and sorrow alike. We see this Bible as a bridge between heaven and earth, a book that invites us into a relationship with God that is both profound and personal. In translating it, we wanted to invite others into this relationship, to share with the world a text that is so dear to our hearts and so central to our identity.

A Unique Canon, a Universal Message

One of the most distinctive aspects of the Ethiopian Bible is its broad canon, which includes works not found in other Christian Bibles. This canon reflects our belief in an inclusive faith, a faith that embraces wisdom from various sources, each offering a unique perspective on life, morality, and our relationship with the divine. Texts like the Book of Enoch reveal mysteries of the cosmos and the angelic realm, inviting us to ponder the vastness of God's creation. The Books of Meqabyan echo themes of resilience and courage, reflecting the Ethiopian experience and our long history of faithfulness through adversity. Our Ethiopian canon includes teachings that honor both the known and the unknown, the seen and the unseen, encouraging us to embrace a fuller picture of faith. We view these writings as windows into God's multifaceted revelation, a revelation that doesn't limit itself to a single form but manifests in stories, parables, laws, and prophecies. Each book in this Bible serves a purpose, offering us wisdom, warning, or comfort, and together they create a cohesive vision of a faith that is as diverse as it is unified.

Safeguarding Our Spiritual Heritage Through Turbulent Times

The Ethiopian Bible is a witness to our resilience and faithfulness as a people. Ethiopia has faced challenges from foreign invasions to internal conflicts, yet we have held onto these texts with unwavering dedication. Our monasteries and churches have served as sanctuaries for these manuscripts, where monks and scribes painstakingly copied and preserved them by hand, often under difficult conditions. To us, safeguarding these texts has always been a sacred duty, a way to protect our heritage and honor the divine teachings that have guided us through times of struggle and change.

In recent years, we have taken steps to further preserve these manuscripts through digitalization and high-resolution imaging, ensuring that future generations will have access to these precious writings. These preservation efforts are a testament to our commitment to keep our heritage alive, not just for ourselves but for the global community. By sharing this Bible with the world, we are inviting others to understand our journey, our faith, and our values, and to see the beauty of a tradition that has survived through love, devotion, and faith.

A Bridge from the Ancient to the Modern

As we bring the Ethiopian Bible into modern English and make it available to a wider audience, we see it as an opportunity to connect the ancient with the modern. We believe that the message of our Bible is timeless, resonating with themes of justice, compassion, humility, and divine love that are as relevant today as they were centuries ago. In sharing this text, we hope to offer a perspective on Christianity that is deeply rooted in a tradition that embraces diversity, spirituality, and a profound sense of mystery. For us, the Ethiopian Bible is not just a collection of texts but a testament of God's love for all people, a call to live with integrity, humility, and devotion. This Bible invites us to explore our faith more fully, to ask questions, and to seek answers within a rich tapestry of teachings that honor both the known and the unknown. It reminds us that faith is a journey, one that we walk together, guided by the wisdom and stories passed down through the ages.

Conclusion: Inviting the World into Our Faith

The Ethiopian Bible is our sacred legacy, a treasure that we hold dear and that we now share with the world. It is a Bible that speaks not only to us as Ethiopians but to anyone seeking a deeper understanding of faith, resilience, and divine mystery. By opening this Bible, we invite you to experience a tradition that values both the mystical and the practical, both the communal and the personal. We hope that as you read these words, you will feel the same awe, reverence, and inspiration that we feel, and that you too will be drawn into the divine truths and timeless wisdom within.

To us, the Ethiopian Bible is not simply a book; it is a journey of faith, a guide for life, and a bridge between us and God. As we share this Bible with you, we are sharing a part of ourselves, our history, and our devotion. It is our hope that this introduction to the Ethiopian Bible will inspire you to delve deeper, to reflect on the messages within, and to find in these pages a source of hope, strength, and spiritual fulfillment. Welcome to our world of faith, history, and devotion—welcome to the Ethiopian Bible.

Notes by the Author

Welcome to this remarkable journey through the Ethiopian Bible! This book is not just another translation; it's an invitation to explore a vast and rich biblical tradition, one that holds a unique place in the spiritual heritage of Christianity. As you dive into these pages, you'll discover that the Ethiopian Bible has its own voice, its own structure, and an expansive collection of books that make it unlike any other. We're delighted to bring you this modern English translation of such a historically significant text, crafted with the intent to make these ancient writings accessible and engaging for readers today.

Reading Tips to Enhance Your Experience

To help you navigate this translation and appreciate the unique elements of the Ethiopian Bible, here are some reading tips to guide you along the way:

- **Ethiopic Canon:** The Ethiopian canon is often cited as containing either 81 or 88 books; however, in Ethiopia today, the canon comprises 81 books. This 180-book collection includes all significant Ethiopic texts that have been either discovered or hold special importance within Ethiopian Christianity.

- **An Original Yet Familiar Experience:** This is a modern English translation, which means you'll encounter familiar phrases and passages from the Bible, but with a unique Ethiopian twist. While some sections might feel reminiscent of other modern Bibles, it's crucial to read with an open mind. The Ethiopian Bible includes books and verses not found in Western Bibles, so take your time and explore these differences. You may find verses, stories, and details that add new dimensions to familiar biblical themes, providing a broader understanding of the text.

- **Understanding the Three Dots (...):** As you read, you may occasionally encounter three empty dots (...) within the text. This notation indicates that part of a sentence was missing during the translation process. However, there's no need to worry—these are small omissions that do not alter the overall meaning of the passages. These gaps are an inevitable part of translating such an ancient and extensive text. Rest assured that we're committed to refining this translation, and these minor issues will be addressed in future editions as more manuscripts and resources are discovered.

- **Missing Verses:** Similar to the three-dot symbol, you may notice missing verses in some chapters. These omissions occurred because the source text was unavailable or incomplete at the time of translation. While it's natural to wonder about these gaps, know that they don't detract from the overall message of the Bible. Like the three-dot omissions, these missing verses will be added and refined in future editions as our team continues its work on this project.

- **Exploring Hypothetical Books:** The Ethiopian Bible is home to several extraordinary texts, some of which are known as hypothetical books—meaning they are referenced but don't have complete surviving content. These include titles like the Books of Mysteries, Covenant, Order, and Herald, among others. Since we don't have full texts for these books, we've done our best to provide a biblical format for each, using other historical and biblical references to reconstruct their message. As you read, remember that these books reflect a deep cultural and spiritual heritage that has been meticulously preserved, even if parts remain hypothetical.

- **Navigating the 160 Books and Digital Content:** This print volume includes 160 books, but to make this edition more accessible and portable, we have placed 20 additional books in digital format. You can download these books using the QR code provided on the bonus page after table of content, which will give you access to the full collection without overwhelming the printed version. These additional texts were separated to keep this Bible compact and easy to carry, and because they are classified as Ethiopian texts but have origins in other biblical traditions. By downloading these digital texts, you'll also gain access to over 1,000 terms in the Ethiopian Bible glossary, audiobooks, video lectures, and beautifully illustrated copies to enrich your understanding.

- **Stay Updated with Future Editions:** This Ethiopian Bible is an evolving project, and we are constantly working to improve and update it as new findings come to light. After downloading the bonus materials, we invite you to subscribe to our newsletter to receive free updates of future editions. By subscribing, you'll be among the first to know about new revisions, expanded content, and any newly available manuscripts. This way, you can continue your journey with us and stay connected as we work to perfect this extraordinary Bible.

Thank you for choosing to read this translation of the Ethiopian Bible. We are thrilled to share this sacred text with you, and we hope it brings you inspiration, knowledge, and a deeper connection to this rich tradition. May your journey through these pages be enlightening and transformative.

Here's a brief introduction for each book in the Ethiopian Bible also known as the Mäṣḥafä Kedus (መጽሐፈ ቅዱስ), which follows the Old & New Testament and then Apocrypha as commonly understood but includes unique perspectives rooted in Ethiopian Orthodox tradition.

THE OLD TESTAMENT

- **Genesis:** Known as the መጽሐፈ ምሕረት (Mäṣḥafä Məḥərät), Genesis recounts the beginnings of creation, humanity, and the patriarchs Abraham, Isaac, and Jacob, establishing the covenant between God and His people and setting the stage for Israel's history.
- **Exodus:** In መጽሐፈ ውግዕ (Mäṣḥafä Wəgä'), Exodus narrates the liberation of the Israelites from Egyptian bondage, the journey through the wilderness, and the giving of the Law on Mount Sinai, emphasizing divine deliverance and covenantal law.
- **Leviticus:** መጽሐፈ ካህናት (Mäṣḥafä Kahənat) provides detailed priestly laws and rituals for worship, cleanliness, and atonement, emphasizing holiness as the Israelites' means of preserving their relationship with God.
- **Numbers:** መጽሐፈ ጥምርት (Mäṣḥafä Ṭəmərt) records the Israelites' wanderings in the desert, detailing census data, priestly instructions, and the community's challenges as they prepare to enter the Promised Land.
- **Deuteronomy:** In መጽሐፈ አንትምና (Mäṣḥafä Antəmna), Moses delivers final teachings and exhortations, reaffirming the Law for a new generation and underscoring Israel's commitment to faithfulness before entering Canaan.
- **Joshua:** መጽሐፈ ዮስዋ (Mäṣḥafä Yoswa) follows Joshua as he leads the Israelites into the Promised Land, conquering and dividing territories, while emphasizing God's faithfulness and the importance of obedience.
- **Judges:** Known as መጽሐፈ ዳኞች (Mäṣḥafä Dännəwoch), Judges covers a period of tribal leadership, where God raises judges to deliver Israel from oppression, revealing cycles of sin, repentance, and redemption.
- **Ruth:** In መጽሐፈ ሩት (Mäṣḥafä Rut), Ruth tells a touching story of loyalty and redemption, highlighting God's providence in the lives of ordinary people, which ultimately leads to King David's lineage.
- **1 Samuel:** መጽሐፈ ሳሙኤል አንዲተኛ (Mäṣḥafä Samu'el Andətäñña) details Israel's transition from tribal confederacy to monarchy under Saul and David, exploring themes of leadership, prophecy, and divine sovereignty.
- **2 Samuel:** In መጽሐፈ ሳሙኤል ሁለተኛ (Mäṣḥafä Samu'el Hulatäñña), the narrative continues with David's reign, his triumphs and failures, and God's covenant promise to establish an everlasting dynasty.
- **1 Kings:** Known as መጽሐፈ ነገሥታት አንዲተኛ (Mäṣḥafä Nägäśtat Andətäñña), this book chronicles the reigns of Solomon and subsequent kings, focusing on the division of Israel, idolatry, and prophetic intervention.
- **2 Kings:** መጽሐፈ ነገሥታት ሁለተኛ (Mäṣḥafä Nägäśtat Hulatäñña) continues the story of Israel's decline, documenting the spiritual and political deterioration that led to exile, emphasizing the consequences of covenant unfaithfulness.
- **1 Chronicles:** In መጽሐፈ ዜናታት አንዲተኛ (Mäṣḥafä Zénatat Andətäñña), the genealogies and reign of David are emphasized, aiming to inspire post-exilic Israel with a renewed sense of identity and purpose.
- **2 Chronicles:** መጽሐፈ ዜናታት ሁለተኛ (Mäṣḥafä Zénatat Hulatäñña) revisits Israel's history from Solomon to the Babylonian exile, underscoring the importance of temple worship and faithfulness to God.
- **Ezra:** Known as መጽሐፈ ዕዝራ (Mäṣḥafä 'Ezra), Ezra recounts the Jews' return from Babylon and the rebuilding of the temple, emphasizing covenant renewal and religious reform under Ezra's leadership.
- **Nehemiah:** In መጽሐፈ ነህምያ (Mäṣḥafä Nəhəmya), Nehemiah leads the reconstruction of Jerusalem's walls, focusing on the community's spiritual and physical restoration after the exile.
- **Esther:** መጽሐፈ ኢስጠር (Mäṣḥafä 'Estər) presents the story of Queen Esther, who courageously saves the Jewish people from genocide, celebrating God's hidden yet active providence.
- **Job:** Known as መጽሐፈ ኢዮብ (Mäṣḥafä Iyob), Job explores profound questions of human suffering and divine justice, ultimately affirming God's wisdom and sovereignty.
- **Psalms:** In መጽሐፈ መዝሙር (Mäṣḥafä Məzmur), the Psalms offer prayers, praises, and laments that express a deep relationship with God, serving as a cornerstone for worship in the Ethiopian Church.
- **Proverbs:** መጽሐፈ ምሳሌ (Mäṣḥafä Məsäle) contains wise sayings and instructions, traditionally attributed to Solomon, guiding readers on ethical living and the pursuit of wisdom.
- **Ecclesiastes:** Known as መጽሐፈ ሰቆቃ (Mäṣḥafä Səqoqä), Ecclesiastes reflects on life's fleeting nature and the search for meaning, concluding that reverence for God is humanity's ultimate purpose.
- **Song of Solomon:** መጽሐፈ ዘማሪት (Mäṣḥafä Zämarit) celebrates the beauty of love, often interpreted allegorically in Ethiopian tradition as symbolizing the relationship between God and Israel.
- **Isaiah:** In መጽሐፈ ኢሳያስ (Mäṣḥafä 'Isayas), Isaiah delivers prophecies of judgment, hope, and messianic salvation, emphasizing God's holiness and the restoration of Israel.
- **Jeremiah:** መጽሐፈ ኤርምያስ (Mäṣḥafä 'Erəmyas) recounts Jeremiah's prophetic mission to call Judah to repentance and prophesy impending exile, conveying a profound message of God's covenantal faithfulness.
- **Lamentations:** Known as መጽሐፈ ነቃቒት (Mäṣḥafä Näqaqit), this poetic book mourns Jerusalem's fall, expressing sorrow, yet clinging to hope in God's compassion and steadfast love.
- **Ezekiel:** መጽሐፈ ኢዝኪኤል (Mäṣḥafä 'Eziqi'el) contains prophetic visions and warnings, revealing God's glory and foretelling Israel's eventual restoration after exile.
- **Daniel:** In መጽሐፈ ዳኒኤል (Mäṣḥafä Dani'el), Daniel's visions and stories of resilience in exile illustrate God's sovereignty and foreshadow messianic deliverance.
- **Hosea:** Known as መጽሐፈ ሆሴአ (Mäṣḥafä Hose'a), Hosea's prophetic life and message symbolize Israel's unfaithfulness and God's steadfast love and willingness to restore His people.
- **Joel:** መጽሐፈ ዮኤል (Mäṣḥafä Yo'el) warns of impending judgment and promises a future outpouring of God's Spirit, emphasizing repentance and divine mercy.
- **Amos:** In መጽሐፈ አሞጽ (Mäṣḥafä 'Amoṣ), Amos condemns social injustice and idolatry in Israel, reminding the people of their covenant obligations to justice and righteousness.
- **Obadiah:** መጽሐፈ አብዲዮ (Mäṣḥafä 'Obadya) prophesies judgment against Edom for its role in Judah's downfall, assuring Israel of God's ultimate justice.
- **Jonah:** In መጽሐፈ ዮናስ (Mäṣḥafä Yonäs), Jonah's reluctant mission to Nineveh reveals God's compassion for all nations and the possibility of repentance and mercy.
- **Micah:** Known as መጽሐፈ ሚካኤል (Mäṣḥafä Mika'el), Micah speaks against social injustice, foretelling the fall of Samaria and Jerusalem but also a future messianic ruler.
- **Nahum:** መጽሐፈ ናሁም (Mäṣḥafä Nahom) focuses on Nineveh's impending judgment, celebrating God's justice and His concern for those oppressed by violent empires.

- **Habakkuk:** In መጽሐፈ አበቆም (Mäṣḥafä 'Abak'om), Habakkuk wrestles with the problem of evil and God's justice, concluding with a profound expression of faith.
- **Zephaniah:** መጽሐፈ ዘፍንያስ (Mäṣḥafä Zäfənyas) warns of the "Day of the Lord" bringing judgment but also a promise of restoration and refuge for the faithful.
- **Haggai:** Known as መጽሐፈ ሐጌ (Mäṣḥafä Hagge), Haggai encourages the rebuilding of the temple, inspiring spiritual renewal and emphasizing God's presence among His people.
- **Zechariah:** መጽሐፈ ዘከርያስ (Mäṣḥafä Zäkarəyas) contains visions and prophecies that offer hope and future messianic expectations, stressing God's faithfulness.
- **Malachi:** In መጽሐፈ ማላኪ (Mäṣḥafä Malaki), Malachi addresses spiritual complacency, calling for renewed devotion and foreshadowing a coming "messenger" of God.

THE NEW TESTAMENT

- **Matthew:** Known as መጽሐፈ ማቴዎስ (Mäṣḥafä Matéwos), the Gospel of Matthew presents Jesus as the fulfillment of Hebrew prophecy, emphasizing His role as the Messiah and Teacher, with a focus on His teachings, parables, and the Kingdom of Heaven.
- **Mark:** In መጽሐፈ ማርቆስ (Mäṣḥafä Marqos), the Gospel of Mark portrays Jesus as a powerful, action-oriented figure, highlighting His miracles and authority while also exploring the nature of discipleship through His journey to the Cross.
- **Luke:** መጽሐፈ ሉቃስ (Mäṣḥafä Luqas) presents a compassionate narrative of Jesus' life, emphasizing His ministry to marginalized and universality of His message, with a strong focus on prayer, the Holy Spirit, and Jesus as Savior of all.
- **John:** Known as መጽሐፈ ዮሐንስ (Mäṣḥafä Yoḥannəs), the Gospel of John offers a deeply theological portrait of Jesus as the Logos and Son of God, emphasizing His divinity and the transformative power of belief in His name.
- **Acts:** In መጽሐፈ ሥራዊተ ሐዋርያት (Mäṣḥafä Sərawit Ḥawaryat), Acts narrates the early Church's formation and growth through the work of the Apostles, focusing on the spread of the Gospel, the role of the Holy Spirit, and the mission to both Jews and Gentiles.
- **Romans:** መጽሐፈ ሮሜያን (Mäṣḥafä Romyan) is a theological exposition by Paul on the righteousness of God, exploring themes of sin, grace, faith, and the transformative power of Christ's salvation for both Jews and Gentiles.
- **1 Corinthians:** Known as መጽሐፈ ቆሮንቶስ አንዳተኛ (Mäṣḥafä Qorontos Andətäñña), this letter addresses various moral and doctrinal issues within the Corinthian church, emphasizing unity, spiritual gifts, and the resurrection of the dead.
- **2 Corinthians:** In መጽሐፈ ቆሮንቶስ ሁለተኛ (Mäṣḥafä Qorontos Hulatäñña), Paul defends his apostolic authority, speaks of the challenges of ministry, and encourages generosity, reconciliation, and faithfulness amid adversity.
- **3 Corinthians:** Unique to the Ethiopian canon as መጽሐፈ ቆሮንቶስ ሶስተኛ (Mäṣḥafä Qorontos Sosäñña), this epistle addresses heretical teachings and reinforces Paul's message on the resurrection, divine grace, and doctrinal purity.
- **Galatians:** Known as መጽሐፈ ገላትያስ (Mäṣḥafä Galatyas), Galatians is Paul's passionate defense of justification by faith, warning against legalism and emphasizing freedom in Christ and the fruits of the Spirit.
- **Ephesians:** In መጽሐፈ ኤፌሶን (Mäṣḥafä Efeson), Paul writes on unity in the body of Christ, the Church as God's mystery, and encourages believers to live in holiness, emphasizing spiritual maturity and the armor of God.
- **Philippians:** Known as መጽሐፈ ፊሊጰስዩስ (Mäṣḥafä Filipəsyus), Philippians is a letter of joy and encouragement, focusing on humility, unity, and perseverance in faith despite adversity, epitomized in the example of Christ.
- **Colossians:** መጽሐፈ ቆሎስይን (Mäṣḥafä Qolosyas) emphasizes the supremacy of Christ over all creation and warns against false teachings, encouraging believers to live according to the divine knowledge found in Christ.
- **1 Thessalonians:** In መጽሐፈ ቴሰሎንቄያ (Mäṣḥafä Ṭesalonqya) Paul encourages the church to remain steadfast in faith, addresses eschatological concerns, and exhorts believers to live in holiness and love in anticipation of Christ's return.
- **2 Thessalonians:** Known as መጽሐፈ ቴሰሎንቄያ ሁለተኛ (Mäṣḥafä Ṭesalonqya Hulatäñña), this letter addresses misunderstandings about the second coming of Christ and encourages perseverance and discernment.
- **1 Timothy:** መጽሐፈ ጢሞቴዎስ አንዳተኛ (Mäṣḥafä Ṭimotéwos Andətäñña) is a pastoral letter offering guidance for church leadership, emphasizing sound doctrine, moral integrity, and the qualities of a faithful servant.
- **2 Timothy:** In መጽሐፈ ጢሞቴዎስ ሁለተኛ (Mäṣḥafä Ṭimotéwos Hulatäñña), Paul encourages Timothy to stand firm in faith amid trials, stressing perseverance, scripture's power, and the responsibilities of ministry.
- **Titus:** Known as መጽሐፈ ቲቶስ (Mäṣḥafä Titoṣ), this pastoral letter advises Titus on establishing order and sound teaching within the Cretan church, highlighting moral conduct, community guidance, and faithfulness.
- **Philemon:** መጽሐፈ ፊሊሞን (Mäṣḥafä Filimon) is a personal letter advocating for the reconciliation of a runaway slave, Onesimus, to his master Philemon, emphasizing forgiveness and the transformative power of Christian brotherhood.
- **Hebrews:** In መጽሐፈ ኪብሪዮስ (Mäṣḥafä Hebrəyos), the unknown author explores Christ's supremacy as the eternal High Priest and mediator, encouraging perseverance and faith amidst persecution and trials.
- **James:** Known as መጽሐፈ ያዕቆብ (Mäṣḥafä Ya'qob), this epistle emphasizes practical wisdom, moral integrity, and the importance of faith manifesting in righteous actions and care for the poor.
- **1 Peter:** መጽሐፈ ጴጥሮስ አንዳተኛ (Mäṣḥafä Peṭros Andətäñña) addresses suffering Christians, encouraging them to endure trials and remain faithful, reflecting Christ's example of humility and hope in salvation.
- **2 Peter:** In መጽሐፈ ጴጥሮስ ሁለተኛ (Mäṣḥafä Peṭros Hulatäñña), Peter warns against false teachers, emphasizes the importance of knowledge, and assures believers of Christ's promised return.
- **1 John:** Known as መጽሐፈ ዮሐንስ አንዳተኛ (Mäṣḥafä Yoḥannəs Andətäñña), this letter underscores God's love and light, encouraging believers to love one another and maintain a faithful relationship with God.
- **2 John:** In መጽሐፈ ዮሐንስ ሁለተኛ (Mäṣḥafä Yoḥannəs Hulatäñña), John writes a brief exhortation on truth, love, and caution against false teachings, emphasizing fidelity to Christ's commands.
- **3 John:** Known as መጽሐፈ ዮሐንስ ሶስተኛ (Mäṣḥafä Yoḥannəs Sosäñña), this short letter encourages hospitality and support for true missionaries, contrasting the behaviors of faithful and self-centered church leaders.
- **Jude:** መጽሐፈ ይሁዳ (Mäṣḥafä Yəhuda) warns against false teachers and calls for perseverance, urging believers to uphold the faith entrusted to them while awaiting God's judgment on the wicked.
- **Revelation:** In መጽሐፈ ትንቢት (Mäṣḥafä Tənbət), Revelation presents apocalyptic visions of cosmic conflict, divine judgment, and ultimate salvation, symbolically portraying final victory of God's kingdom and the renewal of creation.

THE APOCRYPHA

- **The Book of Tobit:** Known as መጽሐፈ ጦቢት (Mäṣḥafä Ṭobit), this book recounts the pious life and trials of Tobit and his family, emphasizing themes of faith, divine guidance through the angel Raphael, and the rewards of righteousness.
- **The Book of Judith:** In መጽሐፈ ዩዲት (Mäṣḥafä Yudit), Judith is a courageous widow who delivers Israel from the Assyrian general Holofernes, underscoring God's deliverance through faithful and resourceful individuals.
- **The First Book of Esdras:** መጽሐፈ ኤስድራስ አንዳተኛ (Mäṣḥafä 'Esdras Andətäñña) retells parts of Israel's return from exile and the rebuilding of the temple, focusing on themes of repentance and restoration.

- **The Second Book of Esdras:** Known as መጽሐፈ ኢስድራስ ሁለተኛ (Mäṣḥafä ʾEsdras Hulatäñña), this book explores questions of divine justice, human suffering, and eschatology through visions granted to the prophet Ezra.
- **The Book of Baruch:** መጽሐፈ ባሩክ (Mäṣḥafä Baruk) contains Baruch's reflections on Israel's exile, encouraging repentance and hope in God's mercy, followed by the *Epistle of Jeremiah*, warning against idolatry.
- **The Paralipomena of Jeremiah:** In ዘይዞማውያን ኤርምያስ (Zäyizomawiḵana ʾErəmyas), this text expands on Jeremiah's life and trials, emphasizing his struggles and unwavering dedication as a prophet of God.
- **The History of Bel and the Dragon:** Known as ታሪከ ቤልand እና አዝያድራን (Tarik Bel ena Azəyadaran), this addition to Daniel tells of Daniel's exposure of idolatry in Babylon, highlighting God's protection over the faithful.
- **The History of Susanna:** ታሪከ ሱሳና (Tarik Susana) is a story of virtue and justice, where Daniel defends the falsely accused Susanna, demonstrating God's providence and the value of righteousness.
- **The Prayer of Manasseh:** In መንፈስ ማናሴ (Mänfäs Manase), this penitential prayer attributed to King Manasseh exemplifies heartfelt repentance and God's readiness to forgive the humble.
- **The Prayer of Azariah:** መንፈስ አዛርያስ (Mänfäs ʾAzaryas) includes a prayer by Azariah and the song of the three youths in the fiery furnace, celebrating God's deliverance and faithfulness to His servants.
- **The Wisdom of Sirach:** Known as መጽሐፈ ሲራቅ (Mäṣḥafä Siraq), this wisdom text offers ethical teachings, honoring the law, and practical counsel on righteousness, humility, and divine wisdom.
- **The Wisdom of Solomon:** In መጽሐፈ ሰሎሞን (Mäṣḥafä Selomon), Solomon's reflections address the rewards of wisdom, the dangers of idolatry, and the role of divine wisdom in guiding human lives.
- **The Psalms of Solomon:** መዝሙራተ ሰሎሞን (Mäzmuratä Selomon) is a collection of psalms emphasizing trust in God, hope for deliverance, and the expectation of a messianic figure to restore Israel.
- **The Odes of Solomon:** Known as ኦዶተ ሰሎሞን (Odətä Selomon), this collection of hymns is rich in mystical and spiritual imagery, celebrating God's love, salvation, and the believer's union with the divine.
- **The Rest of Esther:** In ተቀረውት ኢስጦር (Täqärawət ʾEstər), additional passages to Esther provide prayers and elaborations that reflect Esther's reliance on God and the deliverance of Israel.
- **The Rest of Psalms:** Known as ተቀረውት መዝሙር (Täqärawət Mäzmur), this section includes additional psalms focusing on praise, repentance, and the continued expressions of faith and devotion.
- **The First Book of Meqabyan:** መጽሐፈ መቃብያን አንዲተኛ (Mäṣḥafä Mäqabyan Andətäñña) recounts the struggle of righteous Jews against foreign oppression, honoring faithfulness and courage.
- **The Second Book of Meqabyan:** In መጽሐፈ መቃብያን ሁለተኛ (Mäṣḥafä Mäqabyan Hulatäñña), further narratives of the Maccabees emphasize their faith, the protection of Israel, and God's intervention in times of trial.
- **The Third Book of Meqabyan:** Known as መጽሐፈ መቃብያን ሶስተኛ (Mäṣḥafä Mäqabyan Sosäñña), this book continues with accounts of heroism, moral lessons, and the assurance of God's justice and deliverance.
- **The History of Joseph the Carpenter:** ታሪከ ዮሴፍ አንደ አናገለ ክርስቶስ (Tarik Yosef ʾənda Anägälä Krəstos) tells of Joseph's life and death, emphasizing his role as Jesus' guardian and his devotion to the Holy Family.
- **The Testament of Our Lord in Galilee:** Known as መስተዋልው ጌታችን በጊሊላ (Mästäwaläw Gétachən bä-Galila), this text records Jesus' final instructions to His disciples in Galilee, focusing on faith, humility, and mission.
- **The Testament of Joseph of Arimathaea:** In መስተዋልው ዮሴፍ አንደ አሪማታያ (Mästäwaläw Yosef ʾända Arimatäya), this book narrates the testimony of Joseph, who buried Jesus, reflecting on his encounter with Christ and faith.
- **The Testaments of the Twelve Patriarchs:** መስተዋልው ዘ አሥራ ሁለት አባቶች (Mästäwaläw zä ʾAsra Hulat ʾabatotch) contains ethical and spiritual teachings from the twelve sons of Jacob, guiding the Israelites on piety and moral conduct.
  - *The Testament of Reuben*: Reuben's testament warns against lust and urges self-control and repentance.
  - *The Testament of Simeon*: Simeon emphasizes envy's dangers, calling for love and brotherhood.
  - *The Testament of Levi*: Levi reflects on priestly duties, holiness, and spiritual wisdom.
  - *The Testament of Judah*: Judah highlights bravery, justice, and repentance for sin.
  - *The Testament of Issachar*: Issachar teaches simplicity, humility, and labor's virtue.
  - *The Testament of Zebulun*: Zebulun advocates compassion, integrity, and service to others.
  - *The Testament of Dan*: Dan warns against anger and urges forgiveness and self-discipline.
  - *The Testament of Naphtali*: Naphtali extols the beauty of God's creation and obedience to Him.
  - *The Testament of Gad*: Gad advises against hatred, stressing love, and reconciliation.
  - *The Testament of Asher*: Asher teaches about truthfulness, patience, and kindness.
  - *The Testament of Joseph*: Joseph reflects on purity, forgiveness, and God's providence.
  - *The Testament of Benjamin*: Benjamin advocates peace, honesty, and unity among brethren.
- **The Martyrdom of Ignatius:** In መስቀላው ኢግናጥዮስ (Mäskäläw ʾIngənatyos), Ignatius' martyrdom exemplifies devotion to Christ, courage in persecution, and the ultimate sacrifice for faith.
- **The Martyrdom of Polycarp:** Known as መስቀልው ፖሊካርፖስ (Mäskäläw Polikarpos), Polycarp's story highlights steadfast faith, emphasizing loyalty to Christ even unto death.
- **The First Epistle of Clement:** መጽሐፈ ክለመንት አንዲተኛ (Mäṣḥafä Klémənt Andətäñña) is a letter advocating for unity, love, and order in the Church, addressing conflicts within the Corinthian community.
- **The Second Epistle of Clement:** In መጽሐፈ ክለመንት ሁለተኛ (Mäṣḥafä Klémənt Hulatäñña), Clement calls for repentance, humility, and perseverance in Christian faith.
- **The Epistle of Barnabas:** Known as መጽሐፈ በርናባስ (Mäṣḥafä Bärnabas), this letter contrasts the Old and New Covenants, emphasizing the spiritual interpretation of the Law and Christian moral instruction.
- **The Epistles of Ignatius:** ደብረ ኢግናጥዮስ (Däbrä ʾIngənatyos) includes Ignatius' letters to early Christian communities, stressing obedience to bishops, unity, and the importance of Christ's divinity.
- **The Epistle of Polycarp to the Philippians:** In መጽሐፈ ፖሊካርፖስ ወደ ፊልጵስዩስ (Mäṣḥafä Polikarpos wäda Filipəsyus), Polycarp urges perseverance, righteousness, and harmony within the Church.
- **The Epistle of Peter to Philip:** ደብረ ጴጥሮስ ወደ ፊሊጵስዮስ (Däbrä Peṭros wäda Filipəsyus) focuses on spiritual wisdom, the Apostles' mission, and encouragement to remain true to Christ's teachings.
- **The Epistle of Paul to the Laodiceans:** ደብረ ጻውለስ ወደ ላዶቤሳይን (Däbrä Pawlos wäda Ladobesayn) addresses unity, thanksgiving, and growth in knowledge of Christ.
- **The Epistle of Jesus Christ and King Abgarus:** Known as ደብረ ኢየሱስ ክርስቶስ እና አብጋሩስ (Däbrä Iyäsus Krəstos ʾəna Abgarus), this letter preserves an early tradition where Jesus offers healing and guidance to King Abgar of Edessa.
- **The Apostles' Creed:** In ዘአሳተሩ ሐዋርያት (Zä ʾasatäru Ḥawaryat), the Apostles' Creed outlines core Christian beliefs, emphasizing faith in God, Christ's mission, and the hope of eternal life.
- **The Tales of the Patriarchs:** Known as ታሪከተ አባቶች (Tarikat ʾabatotch), this collection recounts stories of the forefathers of Israel, offering insights into their lives, faith, and the promises God made to them, providing a deeper context for the covenantal relationship.

- **The Book of Giants:** In መጽሐፈ አዳነት በታላቅ (Mäṣḥafä 'adanät bä-Talaq), this text elaborates on the pre-flood world, focusing on the Nephilim and their transgressions, which led to divine judgment and helped set the stage for the flood narrative.
- **The First Book of Enoch:** Known as መጽሐፈ ሄኖከ አንዲተኛ (Mäṣḥafä Henok Andətäñña), this book presents a series of visions attributed to Enoch, exploring themes of divine judgment, cosmic order, and angelic interactions, structured into multiple sections:
  - *The Book of Watchers*: Describes the fall of Watchers, angels who descended to Earth and corrupted humanity.
  - *The Book of Parables*: Contains visions of the "Son of Man" and prophecies of final judgment.
  - *The Astronomical Book*: Discusses celestial phenomena, offering an ancient perspective on astronomy.
  - *The Book of Dreams*: Enoch's symbolic dreams represent future events, including the flood and redemption.
  - *The Epistle of Enoch*: Addresses ethical instructions and prophecies about the last days.
  - *The Fragment of the Book of Noah*: Focuses on the character of Noah and the coming flood.
- **The Second Book of Enoch:** መጽሐፈ ሄኖከ ሁለተኛ (Mäṣḥafä Henok Hulatäñña) presents Enoch's journey through the seven heavens, revealing secrets of creation, the angelic realm, and moral teachings that emphasize the rewards for righteousness and punishment for sin.
- **The Third Book of Enoch:** In መጽሐፈ ሄኖከ ሶስተኛ (Mäṣḥafä Henok Sosäñña), Enoch is transformed into the angel Metatron and receives mystical revelations about the structure of heaven, offering insight into divine mysteries and the angelic hierarchy.
- **The Fragment of Ascension of Moses:** Known as አንስቶነው ሙሴ (Ansətonäw Musé), this text recounts Moses' vision before his death, revealing hidden knowledge about the future of Israel and his ascension to divine presence.
- **The First Book of Adam and Eve:** In መጽሐፈ አዳምና ኢይብ አንዲተኛ (Mäṣḥafä 'Adamna 'Eyəv Andətäñña), the story explores Adam and Eve's life after expulsion from Eden, emphasizing themes of repentance, struggle, and God's continued care for humanity.
- **The Second Book of Adam and Eve:** መጽሐፈ አዳምና ኢይብ ሁለተኛ (Mäṣḥafä 'Adamna 'Eyəv Hulatäñña) continues with the narrative of their descendants, highlighting spiritual battles, the persistence of sin, and the promise of redemption.
- **The Third Book of Adam and Eve:** Known as መጽሐፈ አዳምና ኢይብ ሶስተኛ (Mäṣḥafä 'Adamna 'Eyəv Sosäñña), this text elaborates on Adam's legacy and the moral lessons he imparts to his progeny about faithfulness and obedience to God.
- **The Book of Jubilees:** መጽሐፈ ዮብልያን (Mäṣḥafä Yobəlyan) recounts biblical history from creation to Moses, structured around "jubilee" cycles, providing additional details and interpretations that underscore covenant faithfulness.
- **The Book of Jasher:** In መጽሐፈ ኢታዕር (Mäṣḥafä 'Ita'ər), or "The Upright Book," this text supplements Genesis and Exodus narratives, giving detailed accounts of patriarchal history, battles, and moral lessons.
- **The Book of Eldad and Modad:** Known as መጽሐፈ ኢልዳድና ሞዳድ (Mäṣḥafä 'Eldadna Modad), this book contains prophetic visions of Eldad and Modad, who are gifted with divine insight to instruct and warn the people of Israel.
- **The Book of Jannes and Jambres:** መጽሐፈ ያንነስና ጄምብራስ (Mäṣḥafä Yannisna Jämbras) recounts the lives of two Egyptian magicians who opposed Moses, illustrating themes of spiritual warfare, deceit, and the power of God.
- **The Book of the Order:** In መጽሐፈ ሥርዓት (Mäṣḥafä Sərä'at), this text details liturgical and ecclesiastical practices within the Ethiopian Orthodox Church, emphasizing order, discipline, and reverence in worship.
- **The Book of the Sinodos:** Known as መጽሐፈ ሲኖዶስ (Mäṣḥafä Sinodos), this collection of canonical decrees and ecclesiastical guidelines defines the practices, doctrinal stances, and governance of the Ethiopian Orthodox Church.
- **The Book of the Covenant:** መጽሐፈ ኪዳን (Mäṣḥafä Kidän) contains covenantal laws, promises, and theological reflections that define the spiritual and moral obligations of believers in their relationship with God.
- **The Book of the Mysteries:** In መጽሐፈ ምስጢራት (Mäṣḥafä Məstirat), mystical teachings and revelations explore divine secrets, angelic realms, and the unseen spiritual realities central to Ethiopian monastic tradition.
- **The Book of the Herald:** Known as መጽሐፈ አሳሰይ (Mäṣḥafä 'asasay), this prophetic text announces eschatological events and calls for repentance, urging believers to prepare for the final judgment.
- **The Miracles of Mary:** ተአምረ ማርያም (Tä'amrä Maryam) recounts miraculous deeds attributed to the Virgin Mary, emphasizing her intercessory role and the special reverence given to her within Ethiopian Orthodox devotion.
- **The Questions of Esdras:** In መጽሐፈ ጥያቄያተ ኢስድራስ (Mäṣḥafä Ṭəyaqəyatä 'Esdras), Esdras poses questions about divine justice, human suffering, and the fate of Israel, revealing answers that affirm God's wisdom and compassion.
- **The Revelation of Esdras:** መጽሐፈ ራእይ ኢስድራስ (Mäṣḥafä Ra'əy 'Esdras) offers visions of the end times, apocalyptic imagery, and eschatological prophecies that provide insight into the final events of history.
- **The Book of John the Evangelist:** Known as መጽሐፈ ዮሐንስ እንተ አርኣየቱ (Mäṣḥafä Yoḥannəs 'ənta 'ara'yatu), this text elaborates on John's visions and teachings, focusing on his unique theological perspectives and revelations about Christ's nature.
- **The Teaching of the Twelve Apostles:** In ምኣንተ ዐሥረ ሁለተ ሐዋርያተ (Mə'əntä 'Asra Hulat Ḥawaryat), this instructional text, also known as the *Didache*, provides early Christian guidance on ethics, worship, and community life.
- **The Avenging of the Saviour:** Known as መቀበል ማዕዶ እንተ መድኃኔተ (Mäqäbäl Ma'ədo 'ənta Mädhanit), this account focuses on the events following Jesus' crucifixion, including the fate of those involved in His death, underscoring divine justice.
- **The Ethiopic Creed:** ኢትዮጵያዊው መንበረ ሃይማኖት ('Ityopyawew Mänbärä Haimanot) outlines the core beliefs of the Ethiopian Orthodox faith, affirming key doctrines about the Trinity, Christ's nature, and salvation.

~ THE OLD ~
TESTAMENT

The First Book of Moses, called Genesis

{1:1} In the beginning, God created the heavens and the earth. {1:2} The earth was formless and empty, and darkness covered the deep waters. The Spirit of God was moving over the waters. {1:3} Then God said, "Let there be light," and there was light. {1:4} God saw that the light was good, and He separated the light from the darkness. {1:5} God called the light "Day" and the darkness "Night." Evening came, and then morning—the first day. {1:6} God said, "Let there be a firmament (sky) to separate the waters," and it was so. {1:7} God made the firmament and separated the waters below from the waters above. {1:8} God called the firmament "Heaven." Evening came, and then morning—the second day. {1:9} God said, "Let the waters under the heavens be gathered into one place, and let dry land appear," and it was so. {1:10} God called the dry land "Earth," and the gathered waters He called "Seas." God saw that it was good. {1:11} God said, "Let the earth produce grass, herbs that yield seeds, and fruit trees that bear fruit with seeds in them." And it was so. {1:12} The earth brought forth grass, herbs yielding seeds, and fruit trees with seeds in their fruit, all according to their kinds. God saw that it was good. {1:13} Evening came, and then morning—the third day. {1:14} God said, "Let there be lights in the firmament of the heavens to separate day from night. They will serve as signs for seasons, days, and years. {1:15} Let them be lights in the firmament to give light on the earth." And it was so. {1:16} God made two great lights—the greater light to govern the day and the lesser light to govern the night. He also made the stars. {1:17} God set them in the firmament of the heavens to give light on the earth, {1:18} to govern the day and the night, and to separate the light from the darkness. God saw that it was good. {1:19} Evening came, and then morning—the fourth day. {1:20} God said, "Let the waters swarm with living creatures and let birds fly above the earth in the open firmament of the heavens." {1:21} God created the great sea creatures and every living thing that moves in the waters, each according to its kind, and every winged bird according to its kind. God saw that it was good. {1:22} God blessed them, saying, "Be fruitful, multiply, and fill the waters in the seas, and let birds multiply on the earth." {1:23} Evening came, and then morning—the fifth day. {1:24} God said, "Let the earth bring forth living creatures according to their kinds: livestock, creeping things, and beasts of the earth, each according to its kind." And it was so. {1:25} God made the beasts of the earth according to their kinds, the livestock according to their kinds, and everything that creeps on the ground according to its kind. God saw that it was good. {1:26} Then God said, "Let us make man in our image, in our likeness, and let them have dominion over the fish of the sea, the birds of the air, the livestock, and all the earth, and every creeping thing." {1:27} So God created man in His own image; in the image of God, He created him; male and female, He created them. {1:28} God blessed them and said, "Be fruitful, multiply, fill the earth, and subdue it. Have dominion over the fish of the sea, the birds of the air, and every living thing that moves on the earth." {1:29} God said, "Look, I have given you every herb that yields seeds on the face of the whole earth, and every tree that has fruit with seeds; it will be your food. {1:30} And to every beast of the earth, every bird of the air, and everything that creeps on the earth, I have given every green herb for food." And it was so. {1:31} God saw everything that He had made, and indeed, it was very good. Evening came, and then morning—the sixth day.

{2:1} Thus, the heavens and the earth were completed, along with all their hosts. {2:2} On the seventh day, God finished His work, and He rested on the seventh day from all the work He had done. {2:3} God blessed the seventh day and made it holy, because on it He rested from all His work of creation. {2:4} These are the generations of the heavens and the earth when they were created, on the day that the LORD God made the earth and the heavens. {2:5} Every plant of the field had not yet appeared, and every herb had not yet grown, because the LORD God had not sent rain on the earth, and there was no man to work the ground. {2:6} But a mist came up from the earth and watered the whole surface of the ground. {2:7} Then the LORD God formed man from the dust of the ground and breathed into his nostrils the breath of life, and man became a living being. {2:8} The LORD God planted a garden in Eden, in the east, and there He placed the man He had formed. {2:9} Out of the ground, the LORD God made every tree that was pleasing to the eye and good for food, including the tree of life in the middle of the garden and the tree of knowledge of good and evil. {2:10} A river flowed out of Eden to water the garden, and from there it divided into four headwaters. {2:11} The name of the first is Pishon; it encircles the entire land of Havilah, where there is gold. {2:12} The gold of that land is good; it also has aromatic resin and onyx stone. {2:13} The name of the second river is Gihon; it encircles the entire land of Cush (Ethiopia). {2:14} The name of the third river is Hiddekel; it flows east of Assyria. The fourth river is the Euphrates. {2:15} The LORD God took the man and put him in the garden of Eden to cultivate it and keep it. {2:16} The LORD God commanded the man, saying, "You may freely eat from any tree in the garden, {2:17} but you must not eat from the tree of knowledge of good and evil, for when you eat of it, you will surely die." {2:18} The LORD God said, "It is not good for man to be alone; I will make a helper suitable for him." {2:19} Out of the ground, the LORD God formed every beast of the field and every bird of the air, and brought them to Adam to see what he would call them. Whatever Adam called each living creature, that was its name. {2:20} Adam named all the livestock, the birds of the air, and every beast of the field; but for Adam, no suitable helper was found. {2:21} So the LORD God caused Adam to fall into a deep sleep, and while he was sleeping, He took one of his ribs and closed up the place with flesh. {2:22} Then the rib that the LORD God had taken from man, He made into a woman and brought her to the man. {2:23} Adam said, "This is now bone of my bones and flesh of my flesh; she shall be called 'Woman,' because she was taken out of Man." {2:24} For this reason, a man will leave his father and mother and be united with his wife, and they will become one flesh. {2:25} The man and his wife were both naked and felt no shame.

{3:1} Now the serpent was more cunning than any of the wild animals the LORD God had made. He said to the woman, "Did God really say you must not eat from any tree in the garden?" {3:2} The woman replied to the serpent, "We may eat the fruit from the trees in the garden, {3:3} but about the fruit of the tree in the middle of the garden, God said, 'You must not eat it or touch it, or you will die.'" {3:4} The serpent said to the woman, "You will not surely die. {3:5} For God knows that when you eat from it, your eyes will be opened, and you will be like God, knowing good and evil." {3:6} When the woman saw that the tree was good for food, pleasing to the eye, and desirable for gaining wisdom, she took some of its fruit and ate it. She also gave some to her husband, who was with her, and he ate it. {3:7} Then the eyes of both of them were opened, and they realized they were naked; so they sewed fig leaves together and made themselves loincloths. {3:8} They heard the LORD God walking in the garden in the cool of the day, and Adam and his wife hid themselves from the LORD God among the trees of the garden. {3:9} The LORD God called to Adam and said, "Where are you?" {3:10} He answered, "I heard you in the garden, and I was afraid because I was naked; so I hid." {3:11} God said, "Who told you that you were naked? Have you eaten from the tree that I commanded you not to eat from?" {3:12} The man replied, "The woman you put here with me—she gave me some fruit from the tree, and I ate it." {3:13} Then the LORD God said to the woman, "What is this you have done?" The woman said, "The serpent deceived me, and I ate." {3:14} The LORD God said to the serpent, "Because you have done this, you are cursed more than all livestock and wild animals; you will crawl on your belly and eat dust all the days of your life. {3:15} And I will put enmity (hostility) between you and the woman, and between your offspring and hers; he will crush your head, and you will strike his heel." {3:16} To the woman He said, "I will greatly increase your pain in childbearing; with pain, you will give birth to children. Your desire will be for your husband, and he will rule over you." {3:17} To Adam He said, "Because you listened to your wife and ate from the tree about which I commanded you, 'You must not eat from it,' cursed is the ground because of you; through painful toil (work) you will eat food from it all the days of your life. {3:18} It will produce thorns and thistles for you, and you will eat the plants of the field. {3:19} By the sweat of your brow you will eat your food until you return to the ground, since from it you were taken; for dust you are, and to dust you will return." {3:20} Adam named his wife Eve because she would become the mother of all the living. {3:21} The LORD God made garments of skin for Adam and his wife and clothed them. {3:22} The LORD God said, "The man has now become like one of us, knowing good and evil. He must not be allowed to reach out his hand and take also from the tree of life and eat, and live forever." {3:23} So the LORD God expelled him from the Garden of Eden to work the ground from which he had been taken. {3:24} After He drove the man out, He placed cherubim (angels) at the east of the Garden of Eden and a flaming sword that turned every way to guard the way to the tree of life.

{4:1} Adam had relations with his wife Eve, and she became pregnant and gave birth to Cain. She said, "I have received a man from the LORD." {4:2} Later, she gave birth to his brother Abel. Abel was a shepherd, while Cain was a farmer. {4:3} After some time, Cain brought an offering of the fruits of the ground to the LORD. {4:4} Abel also brought an offering—he gave the best portions from some of the firstborn of his flock. The LORD looked favorably on Abel and his offering, {4:5} but He did not look favorably on Cain and his offering. This made Cain very angry, and his face fell. {4:6} The LORD said to Cain, "Why are you angry? Why has your face fallen? {4:7} If you do what is right, will you not be accepted? But if you do not do what is right, sin is crouching at your door; it desires to have you, but you must rule over it." {4:8} Cain spoke to his brother Abel. While they were in the field, Cain attacked his brother Abel and killed him. {4:9} The LORD asked Cain, "Where is your brother Abel?" "I don't know," he replied. "Am I my brother's keeper?" {4:10} The LORD said, "What have you done? Your brother's blood cries out to me from the ground. {4:11} Now you are under a curse and driven from the ground, which has opened its mouth to receive your brother's blood from your hand. {4:12} When you work the ground, it will no longer yield good crops for you. You will be a restless wanderer (fugitive) on the earth." {4:13} Cain said to the LORD, "My punishment is more than I can bear. {4:14} Today you are driving me from the land, and I will be hidden from your presence; I will be a restless wanderer on the earth, and anyone who finds me will kill me." {4:15} But the LORD said to him, "Not so; anyone who kills Cain will suffer vengeance seven times over." Then the LORD put a mark on Cain so that no one who found him would kill him. {4:16} So Cain went out from the LORD's presence and lived in the land of Nod, east of Eden. {4:17} Cain knew his wife, and she became pregnant and gave birth to Enoch. Cain built a city and named it after his son Enoch. {4:18} To Enoch was born Irad; Irad was the father of Mehujael; Mehujael was the father of Methusael; and Methusael was the father of Lamech. {4:19} Lamech took two wives; one was named Adah and the other Zillah. {4:20} Adah gave birth to Jabal; he was the father of those who live in tents and raise livestock. {4:21} His brother's name was Jubal; he was the father of all who play stringed instruments and pipes. {4:22} Zillah also gave birth to Tubal-cain, who forged all kinds of tools out of bronze and iron. Tubal-cain's sister was Naamah. {4:23} Lamech said to his wives, "Adah and Zillah, listen to me; wives of Lamech, hear my words: I have killed a man for wounding me, a young man for injuring me. {4:24} If Cain is avenged seven times, then Lamech seventy-seven times." {4:25} Adam knew his wife again, and she gave birth to a son and named him Seth, saying, "God has granted me another child in place of Abel, since Cain killed him." {4:26} Seth also had a son, and he named him Enosh. At that time, people began to call on the name of the LORD.

{5:1} This is the account of the descendants of Adam. When God created mankind, He made them in His own likeness. {5:2} He created them male and female, blessed them, and named them Adam when they were created. {5:3} Adam lived 130 years and became the father of a son in his own likeness, named Seth. {5:4} After Seth was born, Adam lived 800 years and had other sons and daughters. {5:5} Altogether, Adam lived 930 years, and then he died. {5:6} Seth lived 105 years and became the father of Enosh. {5:7} After Enosh was born, Seth lived 807 years and had other sons and daughters. {5:8} Altogether, Seth lived 912 years, and then he died. {5:9} Enosh lived 90 years and became the father of Cainan. {5:10} After Cainan was born, Enosh lived 815 years and had other sons and daughters. {5:11} Altogether, Enosh lived 905 years, and then he died. {5:12} Cainan lived 70 years and became the father of Mahalaleel. {5:13} After Mahalaleel was born, Cainan lived 840 years and had other sons and daughters. {5:14} Altogether, Cainan lived 910 years, and then he died. {5:15} Mahalaleel lived 65 years and became the father of Jared. {5:16} After Jared was born, Mahalaleel lived 830 years and had other sons and daughters. {5:17} Altogether, Mahalaleel lived 895 years, and then he died. {5:18} Jared lived 162 years and became the father of Enoch. {5:19} After Enoch was born, Jared lived 800 years and had other sons and daughters. {5:20} Altogether, Jared lived 962 years, and then he died. {5:21} Enoch lived 65 years and became the father of Methuselah. {5:22} Enoch walked faithfully with God for 300 years after the birth of Methuselah and had other sons and daughters. {5:23} Altogether, Enoch lived 365 years. {5:24} Enoch walked faithfully with God; then he was no more because God took him away. {5:25} Methuselah lived 187 years and became the father of Lamech. {5:26} After Lamech was born, Methuselah lived 782 years and had other sons and daughters. {5:27} Altogether, Methuselah lived 969 years, and then he died. {5:28} Lamech lived 182 years and became the father of a son. {5:29} He named him Noah and said, "He will comfort us in our labor and painful toil of our hands because of the ground the LORD has cursed." {5:30} After Noah was born, Lamech lived 595 years and had other sons and daughters. {5:31} Altogether, Lamech lived 777 years, and then he died. {5:32} Noah was 500 years old when he became the father of Shem, Ham, and Japheth.

{6:1} When humans began to multiply on the earth and daughters were born to them, {6:2} the sons of God saw that the daughters of men were beautiful, and they took wives from among all those they chose. {6:3} Then the LORD said, "My Spirit will not contend with humans forever, for they are mortal; their days will be 120 years." {6:4} In those days, there were giants on the earth, and also afterward, when the sons of God had children with the daughters of men. These children became the mighty men of old, men of renown. {6:5} The LORD saw how great the wickedness of the human race had become on the earth, and that every inclination of the thoughts of the human heart was only evil all the time. {6:6} The LORD regretted that He had made humans on the earth, and His heart was deeply troubled. {6:7} So the LORD said, "I will wipe from the face of the earth the human race I have created—and with them the animals, the creatures that move along the ground, and the birds in the sky—because I regret that I have made them." {6:8} But Noah found favor in the eyes of the LORD. {6:9} This is the account of Noah: Noah was a righteous man, blameless among the people of his time, and he walked faithfully with God. {6:10} Noah had three sons: Shem, Ham, and Japheth. {6:11} Now the earth was corrupt in God's sight and was full of violence. {6:12} God saw how corrupt the earth had become, for all the people on earth had corrupted their ways. {6:13} So God said to Noah, "I am going to put an end to all people, for the earth is filled with violence because of them; I am surely going to destroy both them and the earth. {6:14} So make yourself an ark of cypress wood; make rooms in it and coat it with pitch inside and out. {6:15} This is how you are to build it: The ark is to be 450 feet long, 75 feet wide, and 45 feet high. {6:16} Make a roof for it and finish the ark to within 18 inches of the top. Put a door in the side of the ark and make lower, middle, and upper decks. {6:17} I am going to bring floodwaters on the earth to destroy all life under the heavens; every creature that has the breath of life in it will die. Everything on earth will perish. {6:18} But I will establish my covenant with you, and you will enter the ark—you and your sons and your wife and your sons' wives with you. {6:19} You are to bring into the ark two of all living creatures, male and female, to keep them alive with you. {6:20} Of every kind of bird, of every kind of animal, and of every kind of creature that moves along the ground, two of every kind will come to you to be kept alive. {6:21} You are to take every kind of food that is to be eaten and store it away as food for you and for them." {6:22} Noah did everything just as God commanded him.

{7:1} The LORD said to Noah, "Come into the ark, you and your whole family, because I have found you righteous in this generation. {7:2} Take with you seven pairs of every kind of clean animal, a male and its female, and one pair of every kind of unclean animal, a male and its female. {7:3} And take seven pairs of every kind of bird, male and female, to keep their species alive on the face of the earth. {7:4} For in seven days, I will send rain on the earth for forty days and forty nights, and I will wipe from the face of the earth every living creature I have made." {7:5} And Noah did all that the LORD commanded him. {7:6} Noah was six hundred years old when the floodwaters came on the earth. {7:7} Noah and his sons and his wife and his sons' wives entered the ark to escape the waters of the flood. {7:8} Pairs of clean and unclean animals, birds, and every creeping thing went in with Noah into the ark. {7:9} Two by two they entered, male and female, as God had commanded Noah. {7:10} After seven days, the floodwaters came on the earth. {7:11} In the six hundredth year of Noah's life, on the seventeenth day of the second month, all the springs of the great deep burst forth, and the floodgates of the heavens were opened. {7:12} And rain fell on the earth for forty days and forty nights. {7:13} On that very day, Noah and his sons—Shem, Ham, and Japheth—together with his wife and the three wives of his sons, entered the ark. {7:14} They had with them every kind of wild animal, livestock, and creeping thing, and every kind of bird. {7:15} They entered the ark in pairs of all living creatures that have the breath of life. {7:16} Those that entered were male and female of every living thing, as God had commanded Noah. Then the LORD shut him in. {7:17} The floodwaters came on the earth for forty days, and the waters rose, lifting the ark above the earth. {7:18} The waters rose and increased greatly on the earth, and the ark floated on the surface of the waters. {7:19} The waters rose higher and higher, covering all the high mountains under the entire heavens. {7:20} The waters rose fifteen cubits above the mountains, covering them completely. {7:21} Every living thing that moved on the earth perished—birds, livestock, wild animals, and all the creatures that swarm over the earth, as well as all mankind. {7:22} Everything on dry land that had the breath of life in its nostrils died. {7:23} Every living thing on the face of the earth was wiped out; people and animals alike, and the creatures that move along the ground, and the birds were destroyed. Only Noah and those with him in the ark were left. {7:24} The waters flooded the earth for a hundred and fifty days.

{8:1} God remembered Noah and all the animals and livestock that were with him in the ark. He made a wind blow over the earth, and the waters began to recede. {8:2} The fountains of the deep and the windows of heaven were closed, and the rain stopped falling from the sky. {8:3} The waters steadily returned from the earth, and after one hundred and fifty days, they began to lower. {8:4} The ark came to rest on the seventeenth day of the seventh month on the mountains of Ararat. {8:5} The waters continued to decrease until the tenth month; on the first day of that month, the tops of the mountains became visible. {8:6} After forty days, Noah opened the window he had made in the ark. {8:7} He sent out a raven, which kept flying back and forth until the waters had dried up from the earth. {8:8} Then he sent out a dove to see if the waters had receded from the ground. {8:9} But the dove found no place to rest and returned to him in the ark, because the waters still covered the earth. He reached out his hand, took her, and brought her back into the ark. {8:10} He waited another seven days and then sent the dove out again. {8:11} In the evening, the dove returned to him with an olive leaf in her beak, so Noah knew the waters had receded. {8:12} He waited another seven days and sent the dove out again, but this time it did not return. {8:13} In the six hundred first year, on the first day of the first month, the waters had dried up from the earth. Noah removed the covering of the ark and saw that the ground was dry. {8:14} By the twenty-seventh day of the second month, the earth was completely dry. {8:15} God said to Noah, {8:16} "Come out of the ark, you and your wife, your sons, and your sons' wives. {8:17} Bring out every living creature that is with you—birds, livestock, and all the creatures that crawl on the ground—so they can reproduce and fill the earth." {8:18} So Noah came out with his sons, his wife, and his sons' wives. {8:19} Every animal, every creeping thing, and every bird, came out of the ark, each kind after its own kind. {8:20} Noah built an altar to the LORD and took some of every clean animal and clean bird, and offered burnt offerings on the altar. {8:21} The LORD smelled the pleasing aroma and said in his heart, "I will never again curse the ground because of man, even though the inclination of his heart is evil from childhood. I will never again destroy every living creature as I have done. {8:22} As long as the earth endures, seedtime and harvest, cold and heat, summer and winter, day and night will never cease."

{9:1} God blessed Noah and his sons, saying, "Be fruitful, multiply, and fill the earth. {9:2} The fear and dread of you will be upon every animal on the earth, every bird in the air, every creature that moves on the ground, and all the fish in the sea; they are all delivered into your hands. {9:3} Every living creature that moves is food for you; just as I gave you the green plants, I now give you everything. {9:4} But you must not eat meat that has lifeblood still in it. {9:5} I will require a reckoning for your lifeblood; I will require it from every animal and from every human; I will hold every person accountable for another's life. {9:6} Whoever sheds human blood, by humans shall their blood be shed, for in the image of God has God made mankind. {9:7} As for you, be fruitful, multiply, and fill the earth abundantly. {9:8} Then God spoke to Noah and his sons, saying, {9:9} "I am establishing my covenant with you and your descendants after you, {9:10} and with every living creature that is with you, including birds, livestock, and every beast that came out of the ark. {9:11} I establish my covenant with you: never again will all flesh be cut off by the waters of a flood, and never again will there be a flood to destroy the earth." {9:12} God said, "This is the sign of the covenant I am making between me and you and every living creature for all generations: {9:13} I set my rainbow in the clouds, and it will be the sign of the covenant between me and the earth. {9:14} Whenever I bring clouds over the earth, the rainbow will appear in the clouds. {9:15} I will remember my covenant between me and you and all living creatures; the waters will never again become a flood to destroy all flesh. {9:16} When the rainbow appears in the clouds, I will see it and remember the everlasting covenant between God and all living creatures on earth." {9:17} God said to Noah, "This is the sign of the covenant I have established between me and all flesh on the earth." {9:18} The sons of Noah who came out of the ark were Shem, Ham, and Japheth. Ham was the father of Canaan. {9:19} These three were the sons of Noah, and from them the whole earth was populated. {9:20} Noah became a farmer and planted a vineyard. {9:21} He drank some of the wine and became drunk, and he lay uncovered inside his tent. {9:22} Ham, the father of Canaan, saw his father's nakedness and told his two brothers outside. {9:23} So Shem and Japheth took a garment, laid it across their shoulders, walked backward, and covered their father's nakedness; their faces were turned away, so they did not see their father's nakedness. {9:24} When Noah woke up from his wine and found out what his youngest son had done, {9:25} he said, "Cursed be Canaan! A servant of servants shall he be to his brothers." {9:26} He also said, "Blessed be the LORD, the God of Shem! Canaan will be his servant. {9:27} God will enlarge Japheth, and he will dwell in the tents of Shem, and Canaan will be his servant." {9:28} Noah lived three hundred fifty years after the flood. {9:29} The total lifespan of Noah was nine hundred fifty years, and then he died.

{10:1} These are the generations of Noah's sons: Shem, Ham, and Japheth. Sons were born to them after the flood. {10:2} The sons of Japheth were Gomer, Magog, Madai, Javan, Tubal, Meshech, and Tiras. {10:3} The sons of Gomer were Ashkenaz, Riphath, and Togarmah. {10:4} The sons of Javan were Elishah, Tarshish, Kittim, and Dodanim. {10:5} Through these, the islands of the nations were divided in their lands, each according to their language, family, and nation. {10:6} The sons of Ham were Cush, Mizraim, Phut, and Canaan. {10:7} The sons of Cush were Seba, Havilah, Sabtah, Raamah, and Sabtecha. The sons of Raamah were Sheba and Dedan. {10:8} Cush fathered Nimrod, who became a mighty warrior on the earth. {10:9} He was a great hunter before the LORD, which is why people say, "Like Nimrod, a mighty hunter before the LORD." {10:10} The beginning of his kingdom was Babel, Erech, Accad, and Calneh in the land of Shinar. {10:11} From that land, Asshur went out and built Nineveh, the city Rehoboth, and Calah, {10:12} and Resen, which is between Nineveh and Calah; this is the great city. {10:13} Mizraim fathered Ludim, Anamim, Lehabim, and Naphtuhim, {10:14} Pathrusim, Casluhim (from whom the Philistines came), and Caphtorim. {10:15} Canaan fathered his firstborn Sidon and Heth, {10:16} as well as the Jebusite, Amorite, and Girgasite, {10:17} the Hivite, Arkite, and Sinite, {10:18} the

Arvadite, Zemarite, and Hamathite. Later, the families of the Canaanites spread out. {10:19} The border of the Canaanites extended from Sidon toward Gerar, to Gaza; then toward Sodom, Gomorrah, Admah, and Zeboim, even to Lasha. {10:20} These are the sons of Ham, according to their families, languages, countries, and nations. {10:21} To Shem, the father of all the children of Eber and brother of Japheth the elder, children were also born. {10:22} The children of Shem were Elam, Asshur, Arphaxad, Lud, and Aram. {10:23} The children of Aram were Uz, Hul, Gether, and Mash. {10:24} Arphaxad fathered Salah, and Salah fathered Eber. {10:25} Eber had two sons: the name of one was Peleg, for in his days the earth was divided, and his brother's name was Joktan. {10:26} Joktan fathered Almodad, Sheleph, Hazarmaveth, and Jerah, {10:27} Hadoram, Uzal, and Diklah, {10:28} Obal, Abimael, and Sheba, {10:29} Ophir, Havilah, and Jobab. All these were the sons of Joktan. {10:30} Their dwelling was from Mesha, as you go toward Sephar, a mountain in the east. {10:31} These are the sons of Shem, according to their families, languages, lands, and nations. {10:32} These are the families of Noah's sons, according to their generations and nations; through these, the nations were divided on the earth after the flood.

{11:1} The whole earth had one language and one speech. {11:2} As people traveled east, they found a plain in the land of Shinar and settled there. {11:3} They said to each other, "Come, let's make bricks and bake them thoroughly." They used bricks instead of stone and tar (a sticky substance) for mortar. {11:4} They said, "Come, let's build a city and a tower that reaches to the heavens. Let's make a name for ourselves so we won't be scattered across the earth." {11:5} The LORD came down to see the city and the tower that the people were building. {11:6} The LORD said, "Look, the people are united and they all speak the same language. This is only the beginning of what they will do; now nothing they plan to do will be impossible for them. {11:7} Come, let's go down and confuse their language so they won't understand each other." {11:8} So the LORD scattered them from there across the earth, and they stopped building the city. {11:9} That is why it was called Babel, because there the LORD confused the language of the whole earth, and from there the LORD scattered them across the earth. {11:10} These are the generations of Shem: Shem was one hundred years old when he fathered Arphaxad two years after the flood. {11:11} Shem lived five hundred years after he fathered Arphaxad and had other sons and daughters. {11:12} Arphaxad lived thirty-five years and fathered Salah. {11:13} Arphaxad lived four hundred and three years after he fathered Salah and had other sons and daughters. {11:14} Salah lived thirty years and fathered Eber. {11:15} Salah lived four hundred and three years after he fathered Eber and had other sons and daughters. {11:16} Eber lived thirty-four years and fathered Peleg. {11:17} Eber lived four hundred and thirty years after he fathered Peleg and had other sons and daughters. {11:18} Peleg lived thirty years and fathered Reu. {11:19} Peleg lived two hundred and nine years after he fathered Reu and had other sons and daughters. {11:20} Reu lived thirty-two years and fathered Serug. {11:21} Reu lived two hundred and seven years after he fathered Serug and had other sons and daughters. {11:22} Serug lived thirty years and fathered Nahor. {11:23} Serug lived two hundred years after he fathered Nahor and had other sons and daughters. {11:24} Nahor lived twenty-nine years and fathered Terah. {11:25} Nahor lived one hundred and nineteen years after he fathered Terah and had other sons and daughters. {11:26} Terah lived seventy years and fathered Abram, Nahor, and Haran. {11:27} These are the generations of Terah: Terah fathered Abram, Nahor, and Haran; and Haran fathered Lot. {11:28} Haran died before his father Terah in the land of his birth, Ur of the Chaldeans. {11:29} Abram and Nahor took wives for themselves: the name of Abram's wife was Sarai, and the name of Nahor's wife was Milcah, the daughter of Haran, who was the father of Milcah and Iscah. {11:30} Sarai was barren; she had no children. {11:31} Terah took his son Abram, his grandson Lot (the son of Haran), and his daughter-in-law Sarai (Abram's wife), and they left Ur of the Chaldeans to go to the land of Canaan. They came to Haran and settled there. {11:32} Terah lived two hundred and five years and died in Haran.

{12:1} The LORD had said to Abram, "Leave your country, your relatives, and your father's house, and go to a land that I will show you. {12:2} I will make you into a great nation, I will bless you, and I will make your name great; you will be a blessing. {12:3} I will bless those who bless you and curse those who curse you; all families on earth will be blessed through you." {12:4} So Abram left, as the LORD had instructed him, and Lot went with him. Abram was seventy-five years old when he left Haran. {12:5} He took his wife Sarai, his brother's son Lot, and all the possessions they had accumulated, along with the people they had acquired in Haran, and they set out for the land of Canaan. They arrived in Canaan. {12:6} Abram traveled through the land as far as the site of Shechem, near the oak of Moreh. At that time, the Canaanites were in the land. {12:7} The LORD appeared to Abram and said, "To your descendants, I will give this land." So Abram built an altar there to the LORD, who had appeared to him. {12:8} From there, he moved to a mountain east of Bethel, where he pitched his tent, with Bethel on the west and Ai on the east. He built an altar there to the LORD and called on the name of the LORD. {12:9} Abram continued his journey southward. {12:10} There was a famine in the land, so Abram went down to Egypt to live there for a while, because the famine was severe. {12:11} As he was about to enter Egypt, he said to Sarai, his wife, "I know you are a beautiful woman. {12:12} When the Egyptians see you, they will say, 'This is his wife,' and they will kill me but let you live. {12:13} Please say that you are my sister, so it will go well for me because of you, and my life will be spared." {12:14} When Abram arrived in Egypt, the Egyptians noticed that Sarai was very beautiful. {12:15} Pharaoh's officials saw her and praised her to Pharaoh, and she was taken into his palace. {12:16} He treated Abram well for her sake, and Abram received sheep, cattle, male and female donkeys, male and female servants, and camels. {12:17} But the LORD inflicted serious diseases on Pharaoh and his household because of Sarai, Abram's wife. {12:18} So Pharaoh summoned Abram and asked, "What have you done to me? Why didn't you tell me she was your wife? {12:19} Why did you say, 'She is my sister,' so that I took her to be my wife? Now, here is your wife; take her and go!" {12:20} Then Pharaoh gave orders to his men about Abram, and they sent him away, along with his wife and everything he had.

{13:1} Abram went up from Egypt with his wife and all that he had, along with Lot, into the southern region. {13:2} Abram was very wealthy, with many cattle, silver, and gold. {13:3} He journeyed from the south to Bethel, to the place where his tent had been at the beginning, between Bethel and Ai. {13:4} This was the place where he had built an altar before, and there Abram called on the name of the LORD. {13:5} Lot, who traveled with Abram, also had flocks, herds, and tents. {13:6} The land could not support both of them living together, for their possessions were too great, and they could not dwell together. {13:7} There was strife between the herdsmen of Abram's cattle and the herdsmen of Lot's cattle, and the Canaanites and Perizzites were living in the land at that time. {13:8} Abram said to Lot, "Let there be no strife between us or between our herdsmen, for we are brothers. {13:9} Is not the whole land before you? Please separate from me: if you go left, I will go right; or if you go right, I will go left." {13:10} Lot looked up and saw the entire plain of the Jordan, well watered everywhere (this was before the LORD destroyed Sodom and Gomorrah), like the garden of the LORD, like the land of Egypt, as you go toward Zoar. {13:11} So Lot chose the whole plain of the Jordan for himself and journeyed east; they separated from each other. {13:12} Abram settled in the land of Canaan, while Lot settled in the cities of the plain and pitched his tent near Sodom. {13:13} The men of Sodom were wicked and sinned greatly against the LORD. {13:14} After Lot had separated from him, the LORD said to Abram, "Lift up your eyes and look from where you are: northward, southward, eastward, and westward. {13:15} All the land you see, I will give to you and your descendants forever. {13:16} I will make your descendants like the dust of the earth; if anyone could count the dust, then your descendants could be counted. {13:17} Get up and walk through the land in its length and width, for I am giving it to you." {13:18} So Abram moved his tent and settled near the oak trees of Mamre in Hebron, where he built an altar to the LORD.

{14:1} During the days of Amraphel, king of Shinar, Arioch, king of Ellasar, Chedorlaomer, king of Elam, and Tidal, king of the nations, {14:2} these kings went to war against Bera, king of Sodom, Birsha, king of Gomorrah, Shinab, king of Admah, Shemeber, king of Zeboiim, and the king of Bela (which is Zoar). {14:3} All these kings joined together in the valley of Siddim, which is near the Salt Sea. {14:4} They had served Chedorlaomer for twelve years, but in the thirteenth year, they rebelled. {14:5} In the fourteenth year, Chedorlaomer and the kings who were with him attacked the Rephaim in Ashteroth Karnaim, the Zuzim in Ham, and the Emims in Shaveh Kiriathaim, {14:6} as well as the Horites in their mountains of Seir, all the way to Elparan, which is near the wilderness. {14:7} They returned to Enmishpat (which is Kadesh) and attacked all the territory of the Amalekites and the Amorites living in Hazezontamar. {14:8} The kings of Sodom, Gomorrah, Admah, Zeboiim, and Bela (also known as Zoar) went out to battle against them in the valley of Siddim. {14:9} They faced Chedorlaomer, king of Elam, Tidal, king of the nations, Amraphel, king of Shinar, and Arioch, king of Ellasar—four kings against five. {14:10} The valley of Siddim was full of tar pits, and the kings of Sodom and Gomorrah fled and fell there; the others escaped to the mountains. {14:11} They took all the goods of Sodom and Gomorrah and all their food and left. {14:12} They also captured Lot, Abram's nephew, who lived in Sodom, along with his possessions, and left. {14:13} A survivor came and told Abram the Hebrew, who was living in the plain of Mamre the Amorite, brother of Eshcol and Aner; they were allies of Abram. {14:14} When Abram heard that his relative had been taken captive, he armed his trained servants, born in his household—318 of them—and pursued the captors as far as Dan. {14:15} During the night, he divided his men and attacked them, pursuing them to Hobah, which is north of Damascus. {14:16} He recovered all the goods and brought back his relative Lot, along with his possessions, the women, and the other people. {14:17} After his return from defeating Chedorlaomer and the kings who were with him, the king of Sodom went out to meet Abram in the valley of Shaveh (the King's Valley). {14:18} Melchizedek, king of Salem, brought out bread and wine; he was the priest of God Most High. {14:19} He blessed Abram, saying, "Blessed be Abram by God Most High, Creator of heaven and earth. {14:20} And blessed be God Most High, who has delivered your enemies into your hand." Abram gave him a tenth of everything. {14:21} The king of Sodom said to Abram, "Give me the people, and you can keep the goods for yourself." {14:22} But Abram said to the king of Sodom, "I have raised my hand to the LORD, God Most High, Creator of heaven and earth, {14:23} and I will not take anything, not even a thread or a sandal strap, so that you cannot say, 'I made Abram rich.' {14:24} I will accept nothing but what my men have eaten and the share that belongs to the men who went with me—Aner, Eshcol, and Mamre—let them have their share."

{15:1} After these events, the word of the LORD came to Abram in a vision, saying, "Do not be afraid, Abram; I am your shield and your very great reward." {15:2} Abram replied, "Sovereign LORD, what can you give me since I remain childless, and the one who will inherit my estate is Eliezer of Damascus?" {15:3} He continued, "You have given me no children, so a servant in my household will be my heir." {15:4} Then the word of the LORD came to him, saying, "This man will not be your heir, but a son who is your own flesh and blood will be your heir." {15:5} He took Abram outside and said, "Look up at the sky and count the stars—if indeed you can count them." Then he said to him, "So shall your offspring be." {15:6} Abram believed the LORD, and he credited it to him as righteousness. {15:7} He also said to him, "I am the LORD who brought you out of Ur of the Chaldeans to give you this land to take possession of it." {15:8} But Abram asked, "Sovereign LORD, how can I know that I will gain possession of it?" {15:9} The LORD said to him, "Bring me a three-year-old heifer, a three-year-old female goat, a three-year-old ram, a dove, and a young pigeon." {15:10} Abram brought all these to him, cut them in two, and arranged the halves opposite each other; the birds, however, he did not cut in half. {15:11} Then birds of prey came down on the carcasses, but Abram drove them away. {15:12} As the sun was setting, Abram fell into a deep sleep, and a thick and dreadful darkness came over him. {15:13} Then the LORD said to him, "Know for certain that for four hundred years your descendants will be strangers in a country not their own and that they will be enslaved and mistreated there. {15:14} But I will punish the nation they serve as slaves, and afterward they will come out with great possessions. {15:15} You, however, will go to your ancestors in peace and be buried at a good old age. {15:16} In the fourth generation, your descendants will come back here, for the sin of the Amorites has not yet reached its full measure." {15:17} When the sun had set and darkness had fallen, a smoking firepot and a blazing torch appeared and passed between the pieces of the animals. {15:18} On that day the LORD made a covenant with Abram and said, "To your descendants, I give this land, from the river of Egypt to the great river, the Euphrates— {15:19} the land of the Kenites, Kenizzites, and Kadmonites, {15:20} the Hittites, Perizzites, and Rephaims, {15:21} the Amorites, Canaanites, Girgashites, and Jebusites."

{16:1} Now Sarai, Abram's wife, had not borne him any children, but she had an Egyptian servant named Hagar. {16:2} Sarai said to Abram, "The LORD has kept me from having children. Please go to my servant; perhaps I can build a family through her." Abram agreed to what Sarai said. {16:3} So after Abram had been in the land of Canaan for ten years, Sarai, his wife, took her servant Hagar and gave her to Abram to be his wife. {16:4} He slept with Hagar, and she became pregnant; and when she saw that she was pregnant, she began to despise her mistress. {16:5} Then Sarai said to Abram, "You are responsible for the wrong I am suffering. I put my servant in your arms, and now that she is pregnant, she despises me. May the LORD judge between you and me!" {16:6} Abram replied, "Your servant is in your hands; do with her whatever you think best." Then Sarai mistreated Hagar, so she fled from her. {16:7} The angel of the LORD found Hagar near a spring in the desert; it was the spring that is beside the road to Shur. {16:8} He said, "Hagar, servant of Sarai, where have you come from, and where are you going?" She said, "I'm running away from my mistress Sarai." {16:9} The angel of the LORD told her, "Go back to your mistress and submit to her." {16:10} The angel added, "I will increase your descendants so much that they will be too numerous to count." {16:11} The angel of the LORD also said to her, "You are now pregnant and will give birth to a son. You shall name him Ishmael (meaning 'God hears'), for the LORD has heard of your misery." {16:12} He will be a wild donkey of a man; his hand will be against everyone and everyone's hand against him, and he will live in hostility toward all his brothers." {16:13} She gave this name to the LORD who spoke to her: "You are the God who sees me," for she said, "I have now seen the One who sees me." {16:14} That is why the well was called Beer Lahai Roi; it is still there, between Kadesh and Bered. {16:15} So Hagar bore Abram a son, and Abram named him Ishmael. {16:16} Abram was eighty-six years old when Hagar bore him Ishmael.

{17:1} When Abram was ninety-nine years old, the LORD appeared to him and said, "I am God Almighty; walk before me and be blameless. {17:2} I will establish my covenant between you and me and will greatly increase your numbers." {17:3} Abram fell facedown, and God said to him, {17:4} "As for me, this is my covenant with you: you will be the father of many nations. {17:5} No longer will you be called Abram; your name will be Abraham, for I have made you a father of many nations. {17:6} I will make you very fruitful; I will make nations of you, and kings will come from you. {17:7} I will establish my covenant as an everlasting covenant between me and you and your descendants after you for generations to come, to be your God and the God of your descendants after you. {17:8} The whole land of Canaan, where you now reside as a foreigner, I will give as an everlasting possession to you and your descendants after you; and I will be their God." {17:9} Then God said to Abraham, "As for you, you must keep my covenant, you and your descendants after you for the generations to come. {17:10} This is my covenant with you and your descendants: Every male among you shall be circumcised. {17:11} You are to undergo circumcision, and it will be the sign of the covenant between me and you. {17:12} For the generations to come, every male among you who is eight days old must be circumcised, including those born in your household or bought with money from a foreigner—those who are not your offspring. {17:13} Whether born in your household or bought with your money, they must be circumcised. My covenant in your flesh is to be an everlasting covenant. {17:14} Any uncircumcised male who has not been circumcised in the flesh will be cut off from his people; he has broken my covenant." {17:15} God also said to Abraham, "As for Sarai your wife, you are no longer to call her Sarai; her name will be Sarah. {17:16} I will bless her and will surely give you a son by her. I will bless her so that she will be the mother of nations; kings of peoples will come from her." {17:17} Abraham fell facedown; he laughed and said to himself, "Will a son be born to a man a hundred years old? Will Sarah bear a child at the age of ninety?" {17:18} And Abraham said to God, "If only Ishmael might live under your blessing!" {17:19} Then God said, "Yes, but your wife Sarah will bear you a son, and you will call him Isaac. I will establish my covenant with him as an everlasting covenant for his descendants after him. {17:20} And as for Ishmael, I have heard you: I will surely bless him; I will make him fruitful and will greatly increase his numbers. He will be the father of twelve rulers, and I will make him into a great nation. {17:21} But my covenant I will establish with Isaac, whom Sarah will bear to you at this time next year." {17:22} When he had finished speaking with Abraham, God went up from him. {17:23} On that very day Abraham took his son Ishmael and all those born in his household or bought with his money—every male in his household—and circumcised them, as God told him. {17:24} Abraham was ninety-nine years old when he was circumcised. {17:25} His son Ishmael was thirteen years old when he was circumcised. {17:26} Abraham and his son Ishmael were both circumcised on that very day. {17:27} And every male in Abraham's household, including those born in his household or bought from a foreigner, was circumcised with him.

{18:1} The LORD appeared to Abraham near the oaks of Mamre while he was sitting at the entrance of his tent in the heat of the day. {18:2} Abraham looked up and saw three men standing nearby. When he saw them, he ran from the entrance of his tent to meet them and bowed low to the ground. {18:3} He said, "If I have found favor in your eyes, my lord, do not pass your servant by. {18:4} Let a little water be brought, and then you may all wash your feet and rest under this tree. {18:5} And let me get you something to eat so you can be refreshed and then go on your way, now that you have come to your servant." "Very well," they answered, "do as you say." {18:6} So Abraham hurried into the tent to Sarah. "Quick," he said, "get three measures of the finest flour and knead it and bake some bread." {18:7} Then he ran to the herd and selected a choice, tender calf and gave it to a servant, who hurried to prepare it. {18:8} He then brought some curds and milk and the calf that had been prepared and set these before them. While they ate, he stood near them under a tree. {18:9} "Where is your wife Sarah?" they asked him. "There, in the tent," he said. {18:10} Then the LORD said, "I will return to you at the appointed time next year, and Sarah will have a son." Sarah was listening at the entrance to the tent, which was behind him. {18:11} Abraham and Sarah were already very old, and Sarah was past the age of childbearing. {18:12} So Sarah laughed to herself as she thought, "After I am worn out and my lord is old, will I now have this pleasure?" {18:13} Then the LORD said to Abraham, "Why did Sarah laugh and say, 'Will I really have a child now that I am old?' {18:14} Is anything too hard for the LORD? I will return to you at the appointed time next year, and Sarah will have a son." {18:15} Sarah was afraid, so she lied and said, "I did not laugh." But he said, "No, you did laugh." {18:16} When the men got up to leave, they looked down toward Sodom, and Abraham walked along with them to see them on their way. {18:17} Then the LORD said, "Shall I hide from Abraham what I am about to do? {18:18} Abraham will surely become a great and powerful nation, and all nations on earth will be blessed through him. {18:19} For I have chosen him so that he will direct his children and his household after him to keep the way of the LORD by doing what is right and just, so that the LORD will bring about for Abraham what he has promised him." {18:20} Then the LORD said, "The outcry against Sodom and Gomorrah is so great and their sin so grievous {18:21} that I will go down to see if what they have done is as bad as the outcry that has reached me. If not, I will know." {18:22} The men turned away and went toward Sodom, but Abraham remained standing before the LORD. {18:23} Then Abraham approached him and said: "Will you sweep away the righteous with the wicked? {18:24} What if there are fifty righteous people in the city? Will you really sweep it away and not spare the place for the sake of the fifty righteous people in it? {18:25} Far be it from you to do such a thing—to kill the righteous with the wicked, treating the righteous and the wicked alike. Far be it from you! Will not the Judge of all the earth do right?" {18:26} The LORD said, "If I find fifty righteous people in the city of Sodom, I will spare the whole place for their sake." {18:27} Then Abraham spoke up again: "Now that I have been so bold as to speak to the LORD, though I am nothing but dust and ashes, {18:28} what if the number of the righteous is five less than fifty? Will you destroy the whole city for lack of five people?" "If I find forty-five there," he said, "I will not destroy it." {18:29} Once again he spoke to him, "What if only forty are found there?" "I will not do it for forty's sake," he said. {18:30} Then he said, "May the Lord not be angry, but let me speak. What if thirty can be found there?" "I will not do it if I find thirty there," he said. {18:31} Abraham said, "Now that I have been so bold as to speak to the Lord, what if twenty can be found there?" "I will not destroy it for the sake of twenty," he said. {18:32} Then he said, "May the Lord not be angry, but let me speak just once more. What if ten can be found there?" "I will not destroy it for the sake of ten," he said. {18:33} When the LORD had finished speaking with Abraham, he left, and Abraham returned home.

{19:1} Two angels arrived at Sodom in the evening, and Lot was sitting at the city's gate. When Lot saw them, he stood up to greet them and bowed with his face to the ground. {19:2} He said, "Please, my lords, come into your servant's house, spend the night, wash your feet, and then you can rise early and go on your way." But they said, "No, we will stay in the street tonight." {19:3} Lot insisted strongly, so they turned aside and entered his house. He made a feast for them, baking unleavened bread, and they ate. {19:4} Before they went to bed, the men of the city—both young and old from every part of Sodom—surrounded the house. {19:5} They called to Lot and said, "Where are the men who came to you tonight? Bring them out to us so we can know (in this context, "know" means to engage in sexual relations with) them." {19:6} Lot went out to meet them, closing the door behind him. {19:7} He said, "Please, my brothers, don't do such a wicked thing." {19:8} "Look, I have two daughters who have never been with a man. Let me bring them out to you, and you can do with them as you see fit, but don't do anything to these men, for they are under the protection of my roof." {19:9} But they replied, "Get out of our way!" They said, "This man came here as a foreigner, and now he wants to judge us! We will treat you worse than them." They pressed hard against Lot and came near to break down the door. {19:10} But the men (angels) inside reached out and pulled Lot back into the house, shutting the door. {19:11} Then they struck the men outside the door with blindness, both young and old, so that they couldn't find the door. {19:12} The angels said to Lot, "Do you have anyone else here—sons-in-law, sons, daughters, or anyone in the city? Get them out of this place. {19:13} We are going to destroy this city because the cries against its people have become so great before the Lord, and He has sent us to destroy it." {19:14} Lot went out and spoke to his sons-in-law, who were pledged to marry his daughters. He said, "Hurry and get out of this place, because the Lord is about to destroy the city!" But his sons-in-law thought he was joking. {19:15} At dawn, the angels urged Lot, saying, "Hurry! Take your wife and your two daughters who are here, or you will be swept away when the city is punished." {19:16} When Lot hesitated, the men took hold of his hand, the hands of his wife and his two daughters, and led them safely out of the city, for the Lord was merciful to them. {19:17} As soon as they had brought them out, one of the angels said, "Flee for your lives! Don't look back, and don't stop anywhere in the plain. Flee to the mountains, or you will be swept away!" {19:18} But Lot said to them, "No, my Lord, please! {19:19} Your servant has found favor in your eyes, and you have shown great kindness to me by sparing my life. But I can't flee to the mountains; disaster will overtake me, and I'll die. {19:20} Look, there is a town nearby, small enough to flee to, and it's not far. Let me escape there—it's just a little place—and my life will be spared." {19:21} The angel said, "Very well, I will grant this request too; I will not overthrow the town you speak of. {19:22} But flee there quickly, because I cannot do anything until you reach it." (That is why the town was called Zoar, meaning "small.") {19:23} By the time Lot reached Zoar, the sun had risen over the land. {19:24} Then the Lord rained down burning sulfur (a compound like brimstone) on Sodom and Gomorrah—from the Lord out of the heavens. {19:25} He overthrew those cities, the entire plain, and all the people living in the cities, as well as everything growing on the ground. {19:26} But Lot's wife looked back, and she became a pillar of salt. {19:27} Early the next morning, Abraham went to the place where he had stood before the Lord. {19:28} He looked down toward Sodom and Gomorrah, toward all the land of the plain, and saw dense smoke rising from the land, like smoke from a furnace. {19:29} So when God destroyed the cities of the plain, He remembered Abraham and brought Lot out of the catastrophe that overthrew the cities where Lot had lived. {19:30} Lot and his two daughters left Zoar and settled in the mountains, for he was afraid to stay in Zoar. He and his two daughters lived in a cave. {19:31} One day, the older daughter said to the younger, "Our father is old, and there is no man around here to give us children, as is the custom all over the earth. {19:32} Let's get our father to drink wine and then sleep with him so we can preserve our family line through our father." {19:33} That night, they got their father to drink wine, and the older daughter went in and slept with him. He was not aware of it when she lay down or when she got up. {19:34} The next day, the older daughter said to the younger, "Last night I slept with my father. Let's get him to drink wine again tonight, and you go in and sleep with him so we can preserve our family line through our father." {19:35} So they got their father to drink wine that night also, and the younger daughter went in and slept with him. Again, he was not aware of it when she lay down or when she got up. {19:36} So both of Lot's daughters became pregnant by their father. {19:37} The older daughter had a son, and she named him Moab; he is the father of the Moabites of today. {19:38} The younger daughter also had a son, and she named him Ben-Ammi; he is the father of the Ammonites of today.

{20:1} Abraham journeyed from there toward the southern region and settled between Kadesh and Shur, sojourning in Gerar. {20:2} He said about Sarah, his wife, "She is my sister," and Abimelech, the king of Gerar, sent for Sarah and took her. {20:3} But God came to Abimelech in a dream at night and said, "You are a dead man because of the woman you have taken; she is a married woman." {20:4} Now Abimelech had not approached her, so he said, "Lord, will you destroy a nation that is righteous?" {20:5} "Did he not say to me, 'She is my sister'? And she herself said, 'He is my brother.' In the integrity of my heart and innocence of my hands, I have done this." {20:6} God replied to him in the dream, "Yes, I know you did this with a clear conscience. That is why I kept you from sinning against me. I did not let you touch her. {20:7} Now return the man's wife, for he is a prophet, and he will pray for you, and you will live. But if you do not return her, know that you will surely die, you and all your people." {20:8} Early the next morning, Abimelech got up, called all his servants, and told them everything that had happened, and they were very afraid. {20:9} Abimelech then called Abraham and said to him, "What have you done to us? How have I offended you that you have brought such great sin upon me and my kingdom? You have done things to me that should not be done." {20:10} Abimelech asked Abraham, "What were you thinking when you did this?" {20:11} Abraham answered, "I thought, 'Surely there is no fear of God in this place, and they will kill me because of my wife.' {20:12} Besides, she really is my sister; she is the daughter of my father, though not the daughter of my mother, and she became my wife. {20:13} When God caused me to wander from my father's house, I told her, 'This is your kindness to me: wherever we go, say of me, "He is my brother."'" {20:14} Then Abimelech took sheep, oxen, male and female servants, and gave them to Abraham, and he returned Sarah, his wife, to him. {20:15} Abimelech said, "Look, my land is before you; settle wherever you like." {20:16} To Sarah he said, "I have given your brother a thousand pieces of silver. This is to cover your honor before all who are with you; you are vindicated." {20:17} So Abraham prayed to God, and God healed Abimelech, his wife, and his female servants, so they could have children. {20:18} For the LORD had closed all the wombs in Abimelech's household because of Sarah, Abraham's wife.

{21:1} The LORD visited Sarah as He had promised, and He did for Sarah what He had spoken. {21:2} Sarah conceived and gave Abraham a son in his old age, at the time God had set for him. {21:3} Abraham named his son, who was born to him by Sarah, Isaac. {21:4} Abraham circumcised his son Isaac when he was eight days old, as God had commanded him. {21:5} Abraham was one hundred years old when his son Isaac was born to him. {21:6} Sarah said, "God has brought me laughter, and everyone who hears about it will laugh with me." {21:7} She added, "Who would have said to Abraham that Sarah would nurse children? Yet I have given him a son in his old age." {21:8} The child grew and was weaned, and Abraham made a great feast on the day Isaac was weaned. {21:9} But Sarah saw the son of Hagar, the Egyptian, whom she had borne to Abraham, mocking. {21:10} So she said to Abraham, "Cast out this slave woman and her son, for the son of this slave woman shall not be heir with my son Isaac." {21:11} The matter distressed Abraham greatly because it concerned his son. {21:12} But God said to Abraham, "Do not let it be displeasing in your sight because of the lad and your slave woman. Listen to everything Sarah says to you, for it is through Isaac that your offspring will be reckoned. {21:13} And I will make a nation of the son of the slave woman because he is your offspring." {21:14} Early the next morning, Abraham took bread and a skin of water and gave it to Hagar, placing it on her shoulder along with the child, and sent her away. She went on her way and wandered in the wilderness of Beersheba. {21:15} When the water in the skin was gone, she put the child under one of the shrubs. {21:16} Then she went and sat down across from him, about a bowshot away, for she said, "Let me not see the death of the child." And as she sat there, she raised her voice and wept. {21:17} God heard the voice of the lad, and the angel of God called to Hagar from heaven and said, "What troubles you, Hagar? Do not be afraid, for God has heard the voice of the lad where he is. {21:18} Get up, lift the lad, and hold him in your hand, for I will make him a great nation." {21:19} Then God opened her eyes, and she saw a well of water. She went and filled the skin with water and gave the lad a drink. {21:20} God was with the lad as he grew up; he lived in the wilderness and became an archer. {21:21} He lived in the wilderness of Paran, and his mother took a wife for him from Egypt. {21:22} At that time, Abimelech and Phichol, the commander of his army, spoke to Abraham, saying, "God is with you in all that you do. {21:23} Now swear to me here by God that you will not deal falsely with me or with my descendants or with my posterity. Treat me with the same faithfulness that I have shown you and the land where you have sojourned." {21:24} Abraham said, "I will swear." {21:25} Then Abraham reproved Abimelech because of a well of water that Abimelech's servants had violently seized. {21:26} Abimelech replied, "I do not know who has done this; you did not tell me, and I heard about it only today." {21:27} So Abraham brought sheep and oxen and gave them to Abimelech, and the two men made a covenant. {21:28} Abraham set seven ewe lambs apart from the flock. {21:29} Abimelech asked Abraham, "What is the meaning of these seven ewe lambs you have set apart?" {21:30} He replied, "You will accept these seven ewe lambs from my hand as a witness that I dug this well." {21:31} Therefore, he called that place Beersheba, because there they swore an oath. {21:32} They made a covenant at Beersheba, and Abimelech and Phichol, the commander of his army, rose up and returned to the land of the Philistines. {21:33} Abraham planted a tamarisk tree in Beersheba and called on the name of the LORD, the everlasting God. {21:34} And Abraham stayed in the land of the Philistines for a long time.

{22:1} After these things, God tested Abraham and called to him, "Abraham!" He replied, "Here I am." {22:2} God said, "Take your son, your only son Isaac, whom you love, and go to the land of Moriah. Offer him there as a burnt offering on one of the mountains that I will show you." {22:3} Early the next morning, Abraham got up, saddled his donkey, took two young men with him, and Isaac his son. He chopped the wood for the burnt offering, set out, and went to the place God had told him about. {22:4} On the third day, Abraham looked up and saw the place in the distance. {22:5} He said to his young men, "Stay here with the donkey; I and the boy will go over there to worship, and we will come back to you." {22:6} Abraham took the wood for the burnt offering and laid it on Isaac his son. He carried the fire and the knife, and the two of them went on together. {22:7} Isaac spoke to Abraham, his father, saying, "My father!" Abraham replied, "Here I am, my son." Isaac said, "Here is the fire and the wood, but where is the lamb for the burnt offering?" {22:8} Abraham answered, "God will provide for Himself the lamb for the burnt offering." So they both went on together. {22:9} When they reached the place God had told him about, Abraham built an altar there, arranged the wood, bound Isaac his son, and laid him on the altar on top of the wood. {22:10} Then Abraham stretched out his hand and took the knife to slay his son. {22:11} But the angel of the LORD called to him from heaven, saying, "Abraham! Abraham!" He answered, "Here I am." {22:12} The angel said, "Do not lay a hand on the boy, or do anything to him, for now I know that you fear God, since you have not withheld your son, your only son, from me." {22:13} Abraham looked up and saw a ram caught in a thicket by its horns. He went and took the ram and offered it up as a burnt offering instead of his son. {22:14} Abraham named that place Jehovahjireh (The LORD Will Provide), and it is said to this day, "On the mountain of the LORD it will be provided." {22:15} The angel of the LORD called to Abraham from heaven a second time {22:16} and said, "By Myself I have sworn, says the LORD, because you have done this thing and have not withheld your son, your only son, {22:17} I will surely bless you and multiply your descendants as the stars in the sky and as the sand on the seashore. Your descendants will possess the gates of their enemies, {22:18} and through your offspring all nations on earth will be blessed because you have obeyed my voice." {22:19} So Abraham returned to his young men, and they got up and went together to Beersheba. Abraham stayed in Beersheba. {22:20} After these things, it was reported to Abraham that Milcah had also borne children to your brother Nahor. {22:21} His firstborn was Huz, and his brother was Buz, along with Kemuel, the father of Aram, {22:22} Chesed, Hazo, Pildash, Jidlaph, and Bethuel. {22:23} Bethuel became the father of Rebekah. These eight Milcah bore to Nahor, Abraham's brother. {22:24} His concubine, named Reumah, also bore Tebah, Gaham, Thahash, and Maachah.

{23:1} Sarah was one hundred and twenty-seven years old; these were the years of her life. {23:2} Sarah died in Kirjatharba, which is Hebron in the land of Canaan. Abraham came to mourn for Sarah and weep for her. {23:3} Abraham stood up from beside his deceased wife and spoke to the Hittites, saying, {23:4} "I am a stranger and a foreigner among you. Please sell me a burial site so I can bury my dead out of my sight." {23:5} The Hittites replied to Abraham, {23:6} "Listen to us, my lord. You are a mighty prince among us. Bury your dead in the best of our tombs; no one will refuse you a tomb for burying your dead." {23:7} Abraham stood up and bowed to the people of the land, the Hittites. {23:8} He said to them, "If you agree that I should bury my dead out of my sight, please ask Ephron son of Zohar {23:9} to sell me the cave of Machpelah, which is at the end of his field. Let him sell it to me at its full price for a burial site among you." {23:10} Ephron lived among the Hittites and replied to Abraham in front of the Hittites who had come to the city gate, saying, {23:11} "No, my lord, listen to me. I give you the field and the cave that is in it; I give it to you in the presence of my people. Bury your dead." {23:12} Abraham bowed down before the people of the land {23:13} and spoke to Ephron in front of them, saying, "If you will give it, please listen to me. I will pay you for the field; accept it from me so I can bury my dead there." {23:14} Ephron replied to Abraham, {23:15} "My lord, listen to me: the land is worth four hundred shekels of silver; what is that between you and me? Bury your dead." {23:16} Abraham agreed to Ephron's offer and weighed out for him the silver he had named in the hearing of the Hittites, four hundred shekels of silver according to the merchant's standard. {23:17} So Ephron's field in Machpelah, near Mamre, along with the cave that was in it and all the trees in the field and the borders all around, was confirmed {23:18} as Abraham's possession in the presence of the Hittites, before all who went in at the city gate. {23:19} After this, Abraham buried Sarah his wife in the cave of the field of Machpelah near Mamre, which is Hebron in the land of Canaan. {23:20} The field and the cave that was in it were confirmed to Abraham as a burial site by the Hittites.

{24:1} Abraham was old and well advanced in age, and the LORD had blessed him in every way. {24:2} So Abraham said to his oldest servant, who was in charge of all he owned, "Put your hand under my thigh. {24:3} I want you to swear by the LORD, the God of heaven and the God of the earth, that you will not get a wife for my son from the daughters of the Canaanites, among whom I live. {24:4} Instead, go to my country and my own relatives and get a wife for my son Isaac." {24:5} The servant asked him, "What if the woman is unwilling to come back with me to this land? Shall I then take your son back to the country you came from?" {24:6} Abraham said to him, "Make sure that you do not take my son back there. {24:7} The LORD, the God of heaven, who brought me out of my father's household and my native land and who spoke to me and promised me, saying, 'To your offspring I will give this land,' will send his angel before you so that you can get a wife for my son from there. {24:8} If the woman is unwilling to come back with you, then you will be released from this oath of mine. But do not take my son back there." {24:9} So the servant put his hand under the thigh of his master Abraham and swore an oath to him concerning this matter. {24:10} Then the servant took ten of his master's camels and left, taking with him all kinds of good things from his master. He set out for Mesopotamia and went to the city of Nahor. {24:11} He made the camels kneel down near the well outside the city at the time when the women go out to draw water. {24:12} Then he prayed, "LORD, God of my master Abraham, make me successful today and show kindness to my master Abraham. {24:13} See, I am standing beside this spring, and the daughters of the townspeople are coming out to draw water. {24:14} May it be that when I say to a young woman, 'Please let down your jar that I may have a drink,' and she says, 'Drink, and I'll water your camels too,' let her be the one you have chosen for your servant Isaac. By this I will know that you have shown kindness to my master." {24:15} Before he had finished praying, Rebekah came out with her jar on her shoulder. She was the daughter of Bethuel, son of Milcah, who was the wife of Nahor, Abraham's brother. {24:16} The girl was very beautiful, a virgin; no man had ever slept with her. She went down to the spring, filled her jar, and came up. {24:17} The servant hurried to meet her and said, "Please give me a little water from your jar." {24:18} "Drink, my lord," she said, and quickly lowered the jar to her hands and gave him a drink. {24:19} After she had given him a drink, she said, "I'll draw water for your camels too, until they have had enough to drink." {24:20} So she quickly emptied her jar into the trough and ran back to the well to draw more water and drew enough for all his camels. {24:21} The man watched her closely to see if the LORD had made his journey successful. {24:22} When the camels had finished drinking, the man took out a gold earring weighing a half shekel and two gold bracelets weighing ten shekels. {24:23} Then he asked, "Whose daughter are you? Please tell me, is there room in your father's house for us to stay?" {24:24} "I am the daughter of Bethuel, the son of Milcah, who bore to Nahor," she answered. {24:25} "We have plenty of straw and fodder, as well as room for you to stay." {24:26} Then the man bowed down and worshiped the LORD, {24:27} saying, "Praise be to the LORD, the God of my master Abraham, who has not abandoned his kindness and faithfulness to my master. As for me, the LORD has led me on the journey to the house of my master's relatives." {24:28} The girl ran and told her mother's household about these things. {24:29} Now Rebekah had a brother named Laban, and he hurried out to the man at the spring. {24:30} As soon as he had seen the earrings and the bracelets on his sister's arms and heard Rebekah tell what the man said to her, he went out to the man and found him standing by the camels near the spring. {24:31} "Come, you who are blessed by the LORD," he said. "Why are you standing out here? I have prepared the house and a place for the camels." {24:32} So the man went to the house, and the camels were unloaded. Straw and fodder were provided for the camels, and water was brought to wash his feet and the feet of the men who were with him. {24:33} Then food was set before him, but he said, "I will not eat until I have told you what I have to say." "Then tell us," Laban said. {24:34} So he said, "I am Abraham's servant. {24:35} The LORD has blessed my master abundantly, and he has become wealthy; he has given him sheep and cattle, silver and gold, male and female servants, and camels and donkeys. {24:36} My master's wife Sarah bore him a son in her old age, and he has given him everything he owns. {24:37} And my master made me swear an oath and said, 'You must not get a wife for my son from the daughters of the Canaanites, in whose land I live, {24:38} but go to my father's family and to my own clan and get a wife for my son.' {24:39} Then I asked my master, 'What if the woman will not come back with me?' {24:40} He replied, 'The LORD, before whom I have walked, will send his angel with you and make your journey a success, so that you can get a wife for my son from my own clan and from my father's family. {24:41} Then you will be released from my oath if, when you go to my clan, they refuse to give her to you.' {24:42} "When I came to the spring today, I said, 'LORD, God of my master Abraham, if you will, please grant success to the journey on which I have come. {24:43} I will stand by this spring and if a young woman comes out to draw water and I say to her, "Please let me drink a little water from your jar," {24:44} and she says to me, "Drink, and I'll draw water for your camels too," let her be the one the LORD has chosen for my master's son.' {24:45} "Before I finished praying in my heart, Rebekah came out with her jar on her shoulder. She went down to the spring and drew water, and I said to her, 'Please give me a drink.' {24:46} She quickly lowered her jar from her shoulder and said, 'Drink, and I'll water your camels too.' So I drank, and she watered the camels as well. {24:47} "I asked her, 'Whose daughter are you?' She said, 'I am the daughter of Bethuel, Nahor's son, whom Milcah bore to him.' Then I put the earring on her nose and the bracelets on her arms. {24:48} And I bowed down and worshiped the LORD. I praised the LORD, the God of my master Abraham, who had led me on the right road to get the granddaughter of my master's brother for his son. {24:49} Now if you will show kindness and faithfulness to my master, tell me; and if not, tell me, so I may know which way to turn." {24:50} Laban and Bethuel answered, "This is from the LORD; we can say nothing to you one way or the other. {24:51} Here is Rebekah; take her and go, and let her become the wife of your master's son, as the LORD has directed." {24:52} When Abraham's servant heard what they said, he bowed down to the ground before the LORD. {24:53} Then the servant brought out gold and silver jewelry and articles of clothing and gave them to Rebekah; he also gave costly gifts to her brother and her mother. {24:54} Then he and the men who were with him ate and drank and spent the night there. When they got up the next morning, he said, "Send me on my way to my master." {24:55} But her brother and her mother replied, "Let the girl remain with us ten days or so; then you may go." {24:56} But he said to them, "Do not hinder me, now that the LORD has granted success to my journey. Send me on my way so I may go to my master." {24:57} Then they said, "Let's call the girl and ask her about it." {24:58} So they called Rebekah and asked her, "Will you go with this man?" "I will go," she said. {24:59} So they sent their sister Rebekah on her way, along with her nurse and Abraham's servant and his men. {24:60} And they blessed Rebekah and said to her, "Our sister, may you increase to thousands upon thousands; may your offspring possess the cities of their enemies." {24:61} Then Rebekah and her maids got ready and mounted their camels and went back with the man. So the servant took Rebekah and left. {24:62} Now Isaac had come from Beer Lahai Roi, for he was living in the Negev. {24:63} He went out to the field one evening to meditate, and as he looked up, he saw camels approaching. {24:64} Rebekah also looked up and saw Isaac. She got down from her camel {24:65} and asked the servant, "Who is that man in the field coming to meet us?" "He is my master," the servant answered. So she took her veil and covered herself. {24:66} Then the servant told Isaac all he had done. {24:67} Isaac brought her into the tent of his mother Sarah, and he married Rebekah. So she became his wife; and he loved her; and Isaac was comforted after his mother's death.

{25:1} Abraham took another wife, whose name was Keturah. {25:2} She bore him Zimran, Jokshan, Medan, Midian, Ishbak, and Shuah. {25:3} Jokshan was the father of Sheba and Dedan. The descendants of Dedan were the Asshurites, Letushites, and Leummites. {25:4} The children of Midian were Ephah, Epher, Hanoch, Abida, and Eldaah. All these were the children of Keturah. {25:5} Abraham gave everything he had to Isaac. {25:6} But he gave gifts to the sons of his concubines and sent them away from his son Isaac while he was still alive, sending them eastward into the eastern country. {25:7} These are the years of Abraham's life: he lived a total of one hundred seventy-five years. {25:8} Then Abraham died at a good old age, an old man full of years, and was gathered to his people. {25:9} His sons Isaac and Ishmael buried him in the cave of Machpelah, near the field of Ephron, the son of Zohar the Hittite, facing Mamre. {25:10} This field was purchased from the Hittites; there Abraham was buried, along with Sarah his wife. {25:11} After Abraham's death, God blessed his son Isaac, who then lived near the well Lahairoi. {25:12} Now this is the account of Ishmael, Abraham's son, whom Hagar the Egyptian, Sarah's maidservant, bore to Abraham. {25:13} These are the names of the sons of Ishmael, listed in the order of their birth: Nebajoth (the firstborn), Kedar, Adbeel, Mibsam, {25:14} Mishma, Dumah, Massa, {25:15} Hadar, Tema, Jetur, Naphish, and Kedemah. {25:16} These are the sons of Ishmael and their names, by their settlements and encampments; they became twelve tribal leaders according to their nations. {25:17} Ishmael lived a total of one hundred thirty-seven years; he breathed his last and died, and was gathered to his people. {25:18} His descendants settled from Havilah to Shur, near Egypt, as you go toward Assyria. He died in the presence of all his brothers. {25:19} This is the account of Isaac, Abraham's son: Abraham was the father of Isaac. {25:20} Isaac was forty years old when he married Rebekah, the daughter of Bethuel the Aramean from Paddan Aram and sister of Laban the Aramean. {25:21} Isaac prayed to the LORD on behalf of his wife because she was childless; the LORD answered his prayer, and his wife Rebekah became pregnant. {25:22} The babies jostled each other within her, and she said, "Why is this happening to me?" So she went to inquire of the LORD. {25:23} The LORD said to her, "Two nations are in your womb, and two peoples from within you will be separated; one people will be stronger than the other, and the older will serve the younger." {25:24} When the time came for her to give birth, there were twin boys in her womb. {25:25} The first to come out was red, and his whole body was like a hairy garment; so they named him Esau. {25:26} After this, his brother came out, with his hand grasping Esau's heel; so he was named Jacob. Isaac was sixty years old when Rebekah gave birth to them. {25:27} The boys grew up, and Esau became a skillful hunter, a man of the open country, while Jacob was content to stay at home among the tents. {25:28} Isaac, who had a taste for wild game, loved Esau, but Rebekah loved Jacob. {25:29} Once when Jacob was cooking some stew, Esau came in from the open country, famished. {25:30} He said to Jacob, "Quick! Let me have some of that red stew! I'm starving!" (That is why he was also called Edom, which means "red.") {25:31} Jacob replied, "First sell me your birthright." {25:32} "Look, I am about to die," Esau said. "What good is the birthright to me?" {25:33} But Jacob said, "Swear to me first." So he swore an oath to him, selling his birthright to Jacob. {25:34} Then Jacob gave Esau some bread and lentil stew. He ate and drank, and then got up and left. So Esau despised his birthright.

{26:1} There was a famine in the land, besides the first famine that occurred during Abraham's time. Isaac went to Abimelech, the king of the Philistines, in Gerar. {26:2} The LORD appeared to him and said, "Do not go down to Egypt; live in the land I will show you. {26:3} Stay in this land, and I will be with you and bless you; for I will give you and your descendants all these lands and fulfill the oath I swore to your father Abraham. {26:4} I will make your descendants as numerous as the stars in the sky and give them all these lands, and through your offspring all nations on earth will be blessed. {26:5} This is because Abraham obeyed my voice and kept my charge, my commandments, my statutes, and my laws." {26:6} So Isaac stayed in Gerar. {26:7} The men of that place asked him about his wife, and he answered, "She is my sister," because he was afraid to say, "She is my wife," thinking the men there might kill him for Rebekah, since she was very attractive. {26:8} After Isaac had been there a long time, Abimelech, the king of the Philistines, looked out a window and saw Isaac caressing Rebekah, his wife. {26:9} Abimelech called Isaac and said, "Surely she is your wife. Why did you say she is your sister?" Isaac replied, "I said this because I thought I might die because of her." {26:10} Abimelech said, "What is this you have done to us? One of the men might easily have slept with your wife, bringing guilt upon us." {26:11} So Abimelech ordered all his people, saying, "Anyone who touches this man or his wife shall surely be put to death." {26:12} Isaac planted crops in that land and reaped a hundredfold that same year, and the LORD blessed him. {26:13} The man became rich and continued to grow richer until he became very wealthy. {26:14} He had many flocks, herds, and servants, and the Philistines envied him. {26:15} The Philistines had stopped up all the wells his father Abraham's servants had dug, filling them with dirt. {26:16} Abimelech said to Isaac, "Move away from us; you have become too powerful for us." {26:17} Isaac left that place and camped in the valley of Gerar, where he settled. {26:18} Isaac dug again the wells of water that had been dug in the days of his father Abraham, which the Philistines had stopped up after Abraham died, and he named them after the names his father had given them. {26:19} Isaac's servants dug in the valley and discovered a well with fresh water. {26:20} The herdsmen of Gerar quarreled with Isaac's herdsmen, saying, "The water is ours." So Isaac named the well Esek (which means "contention") because they contended with him. {26:21} Then they dug another well, but they quarreled over that one too, so he named it Sitnah (which means "hostility"). {26:22} He moved on from there and dug another well, and they did not quarrel over it. He named it Rehoboth (which means "room"), saying, "Now the LORD has given us room and we will flourish in the land." {26:23} From there he went up to Beersheba. {26:24} That night, the LORD appeared to him and said, "I am the God of your father Abraham. Do not be afraid, for I am with you; I will bless you and increase the number of your descendants for the sake of my servant Abraham." {26:25} Isaac built an altar there and called on the name of the LORD. He pitched his tent there, and his servants dug a well. {26:26} Then Abimelech came to him from Gerar, along with Ahuzzath, one of his friends, and Phichol, the commander of his army. {26:27} Isaac asked them, "Why have you come to me, since you were hostile to me and sent me away?" {26:28} They answered, "We saw clearly that the LORD was with you; so we said, 'There ought to be a sworn agreement between us'—between us and you. Let us make a treaty with you. {26:29} Promise that you will not harm us, just as we did not harm you but always treated you well and sent you away in peace. And now you are blessed by the LORD." {26:30} Isaac prepared a feast for them, and they ate and drank. {26:31} Early the next morning, they swore an oath to each other. Then Isaac sent them on their way, and they departed from him in peace. {26:32} That same day, Isaac's servants came and told him about the well they had dug, saying, "We have found water!" {26:33} He named it Shebah (which means "oath"), and to this day, the city is called Beersheba. {26:34} Esau was forty years old when he married Judith, the daughter of Beeri the Hittite, and Bashemath, the daughter of Elon the Hittite. {26:35} These women brought grief to Isaac and Rebekah.

{27:1} When Isaac was old and his eyesight had faded so that he could not see, he called for Esau, his eldest son, and said to him, "My son." Esau replied, "Here I am." {27:2} Isaac said, "Look, I am old and I do not know the day of my death. {27:3} Therefore, take your weapons, your quiver and your bow, and go out to the field to hunt me some game. {27:4} Prepare a delicious meal, the kind I love, and bring it to me so that I may eat and bless you before I die." {27:5} Rebekah overheard Isaac speaking to Esau. So Esau went to hunt for game to bring back. {27:6} Rebekah said to her son Jacob, "I heard your father telling your brother Esau, {27:7} 'Bring me game and prepare a delicious meal so that I may eat and bless you before the LORD before I die.' {27:8} Now, my son, listen to me and do what I say. {27:9} Go to the flock and bring me two choice young goats. I will prepare them as a delicious meal for your father, the kind he loves. {27:10} Then you can take it to your father to eat so he can bless you before his death." {27:11} Jacob said to Rebekah, his mother, "But my brother Esau is a hairy man, and I am smooth-skinned. {27:12} What if my father touches me? He will see that I am deceiving him and I will bring down a curse on myself instead of a blessing." {27:13} His mother said to him, "Let the curse fall on me, my son. Just obey my voice and go get the goats." {27:14} He went and got them, and brought them to his mother, and she prepared a delicious meal for his father. {27:15} Rebekah took some of Esau's best clothes that were in the house and put them on Jacob, her younger son. {27:16} She covered his hands and the smooth part of his neck with the skins of the goats. {27:17} Then she gave Jacob the delicious meal and the bread she had prepared. {27:18} He went to his father and said, "My father." Isaac replied, "Here I am. Who are you, my son?" {27:19} Jacob answered, "I am Esau, your firstborn. I have done what you asked. Now sit up and eat some of my game so that you may bless me." {27:20} Isaac asked, "How did you find it so quickly?" Jacob replied, "The LORD your God brought it to me." {27:21} Then Isaac said, "Come here, so I can feel you, my son, to see if you are really my son Esau or not." {27:22} Jacob went closer to Isaac, who touched him and said, "The voice is Jacob's voice, but the hands are the hands of Esau." {27:23} He did not recognize him because his hands were hairy like his brother Esau's. So he blessed him. {27:24} Isaac asked, "Are you really my son Esau?" Jacob answered, "I am." {27:25} Isaac said, "Bring me the meal so I can eat and bless you." Jacob brought it to him, and he ate; and he brought him wine, and Isaac drank. {27:26} Isaac said, "Come here and kiss me, my son." {27:27} Jacob went to him and kissed him. Isaac smelled his clothes and blessed him, saying, "The smell of my son is like the smell of a field that the LORD has blessed. {27:28} May God give you the dew of heaven and the richness of the earth, abundance of grain and new wine. {27:29} May nations serve you and peoples bow down to you. Be lord over your brothers, and may the sons of your mother bow down to you. Cursed be anyone who curses you, and blessed be anyone who blesses you." {27:30} As soon as Isaac finished blessing Jacob and Jacob had scarcely left his father's presence, Esau returned from hunting. {27:31} He also prepared a delicious meal and brought it to his father, saying, "Let my father arise and eat of his son's game so that you may bless me." {27:32} Isaac asked, "Who are you?" Esau replied, "I am your son, your firstborn, Esau." {27:33} Isaac trembled violently and said, "Who was it then that hunted game and brought it to me? I ate it just before you came, and I blessed him, and indeed he will be blessed!" {27:34} When Esau heard his father's words, he cried out with a great and bitter cry and said to his father, "Bless me, too, my father!" {27:35} Isaac said, "Your brother came deceitfully and took your blessing." {27:36} Esau said, "Isn't he rightly named Jacob? He has deceived me these two times: he took my birthright, and now he's taken my blessing!" He asked, "Haven't you reserved any blessing for me?" {27:37} Isaac answered, "I have made him your lord and have given him all his relatives as servants. I have sustained him with grain and new wine. What can I do for you, my son?" {27:38} Esau said to his father, "Do you have only one blessing, my father? Bless me, too, my father!" Esau wept aloud. {27:39} Isaac answered, "Your dwelling will be away from the richness of the earth, away from the dew of heaven above. {27:40} You will live by the sword and you will serve your brother. But when you grow restless, you will throw his yoke off your neck." {27:41} Esau held a grudge against Jacob because of the blessing his father had given him and said to himself, "The days of mourning for my father are near; then I will kill my brother Jacob." {27:42} When Rebekah was told what Esau said, she sent for Jacob and said, "Your brother Esau is planning to avenge himself by killing you. {27:43} Now then, my son, do what I say: flee to my brother Laban in Haran. {27:44} Stay with him for a while until your brother's anger subsides. {27:45} When your brother is no longer angry and forgets what you did to him, I will send for you and bring you back. Why should I lose both of you in one day?" {27:46} Rebekah said to Isaac, "I am disgusted with my life because of the Hittite women. If Jacob marries a Hittite woman like these, my life will not be worth living."

{28:1} Isaac called for Jacob, blessed him, and instructed him, saying, "You must not marry a woman from the daughters of Canaan. {28:2} Go to Padanaram, to the house of Bethuel, your mother's father, and take a wife from there, from the daughters of Laban, your mother's brother. {28:3} May God Almighty bless you, make you fruitful, and multiply you, so that you may become a multitude of people. {28:4} May He give you the blessing of Abraham, to you and your descendants with you, so that you may inherit the land where you are a foreigner, which God gave to Abraham." {28:5} Isaac sent Jacob away, and he went to Padanaram to Laban, the son of Bethuel the Aramean, the brother of Rebekah, Jacob's and Esau's mother. {28:6} When Esau saw that Isaac had blessed Jacob and sent him away to Padanaram to find a wife, {28:7} and that Jacob had obeyed his father and mother and gone to Padanaram, {28:8} he realized that Isaac did not approve of the daughters of Canaan. {28:9} So Esau went to Ishmael and added Mahalath, the daughter of Ishmael Abraham's son and the sister of Nebajoth, to his wives. {28:10} Jacob left Beersheba and headed toward Haran. {28:11} He came to a certain place and spent the night there because the sun had set. He took some stones from that place and used them as pillows, lying down to sleep. {28:12} He dreamed of a ladder set up on the earth, with its top reaching to heaven, and saw the angels of God ascending and descending on it. {28:13} The LORD stood above it and said, "I am the LORD, the God of Abraham your father and the God of Isaac. The land where you lie I will give to you and your descendants. {28:14} Your descendants will be like the dust of the earth and will spread out to the west, the east, the north, and the south. All the families of the earth will be blessed through you and your descendants. {28:15} I am with you and will protect you wherever you go, and I will bring you back to this land; I will not leave you until I have done what I promised you." {28:16} Jacob woke up from his sleep and said, "Surely the LORD is in this place, and I wasn't aware of it!" {28:17} He was afraid and said, "How awesome is this place! This is none other than the house of God, and this is the gate of heaven." {28:18} Early the next morning, Jacob took the stone he had used as a pillow and set it up as a pillar, pouring oil on top of it. {28:19} He named that place Bethel, although the city was previously called Luz. {28:20} Jacob made a vow, saying, "If God will be with me and protect me on this journey I am taking, and if He gives me food to eat and clothing to wear, {28:21} so that I return safely to my father's house, then the LORD will be my God. {28:22} This stone I have set up as a pillar will be God's house, and of all that You give me, I will give You a tenth."

{29:1} Jacob continued his journey and arrived in the land of the eastern people. {29:2} He looked and saw a well in the field, with three flocks of sheep lying by it, because the flocks were watered from that well. A large stone covered the mouth of the well. {29:3} All the flocks gathered there, and they would roll the stone from the well's mouth, water the sheep, and then put the stone back in place. {29:4} Jacob asked them, "Brothers, where are you from?" They replied, "We are from Haran." {29:5} He then asked, "Do you know Laban, the son of Nahor?" They said, "Yes, we know him." {29:6} Jacob asked, "Is he well?" They said, "He is well, and look, his daughter Rachel is coming with the sheep." {29:7} Jacob said, "It is still broad daylight; it is not the time to gather the cattle. Water the sheep and then go feed them." {29:8} They replied, "We can't until all the flocks are gathered and we roll the stone from the well's mouth; then we water the sheep." {29:9} While he was still talking with them, Rachel arrived with her father's sheep, for she was a shepherdess. {29:10} When Jacob saw Rachel, the daughter of Laban, his mother's brother, and the sheep of Laban, Jacob went up, rolled the stone from the well's mouth, and watered Laban's flock. {29:11} Jacob kissed Rachel and raised his voice, weeping. {29:12} He told Rachel that he was her father's brother and Rebekah's son, and she ran and told her father. {29:13} When Laban heard the news about Jacob, his sister's son, he ran to meet him, embraced him, kissed him, and brought him to his house. Jacob told Laban all these things. {29:14} Laban said to him, "You are certainly my own flesh and blood." Jacob stayed with him for a month. {29:15} Laban then said to Jacob, "Since you are my relative, should you work for me for nothing? Tell me what your wages should be." {29:16} Laban had two daughters: the older was named Leah, and the younger was Rachel. {29:17} Leah had weak eyes, but Rachel was beautiful and well-favored. {29:18} Jacob loved Rachel and said, "I will work for you seven years for your younger daughter Rachel." {29:19} Laban replied, "It is better that I give her to you than to another man; stay with me." {29:20} Jacob worked for seven years to get Rachel, but they seemed like just a few days to him because of his love for her. {29:21} Jacob said to Laban, "Give me my wife, for my time is complete, and I want to be with her." {29:22} So Laban gathered all the men of the place and made a feast. {29:23} In the evening, he took Leah, his daughter, and brought her to Jacob, and Jacob went in to her. {29:24} Laban gave Leah his maid Zilpah as a servant. {29:25} In the morning, Jacob saw that it was Leah! He said to Laban, "What have you done to me? Did I not work for you for Rachel? Why have you deceived me?" {29:26} Laban replied, "It is not our custom to give the younger before the firstborn. {29:27} Fulfill her week, and we will give you this one also for the work you will do for me for another seven years." {29:28} Jacob agreed and fulfilled Leah's week, and Laban gave him Rachel, his daughter, as a wife as well. {29:29} Laban also gave Rachel his maid Bilhah to be her maid. {29:30} Jacob went in to Rachel and loved her more than Leah, and he served Laban for another seven years. {29:31} When the LORD saw that Leah was unloved, He opened her womb, but Rachel was barren. {29:32} Leah conceived and gave birth to a son, and she named him Reuben, saying, "Surely the LORD has looked upon my affliction; now my husband will love me." {29:33} She conceived again and gave birth to another son, saying, "Because the LORD has heard that I am unloved, He has given me this son also." She named him Simeon. {29:34} She conceived again and gave birth to a son, saying, "Now my husband will be joined to me because I have borne him three sons." Therefore, she named him Levi. {29:35} She conceived again and gave birth to another son, saying, "Now I will praise the LORD." So she named him Judah and stopped having children.

{30:1} When Rachel saw that she wasn't giving Jacob any children, she became jealous of her sister and said to Jacob, "Give me children, or I'll die!" {30:2} Jacob became angry with Rachel and said, "Am I in the place of God, who has withheld children from you?" {30:3} Rachel said, "Here is my maid Bilhah; go to her, and she will bear children for me, so I can have a family through her." {30:4} So she gave Bilhah, her maid, to Jacob as a wife, and he went in to her. {30:5} Bilhah conceived and bore Jacob a son. {30:6} Rachel said, "God has vindicated me; He has listened to my voice and given me a son." Therefore, she named him Dan. {30:7} Bilhah, Rachel's maid, conceived again and bore Jacob a second son. {30:8} Rachel said, "I have struggled hard with my sister and have won." So she named him Naphtali. {30:9} When Leah saw that she had stopped having children, she took her maid Zilpah and gave her to Jacob as a wife. {30:10} Zilpah bore Jacob a son. {30:11} Leah said, "What good fortune!" and named him Gad. {30:12} Zilpah, Leah's maid, bore Jacob a second son. {30:13} Leah said, "I am so happy; the other women will call me blessed." So she named him Asher. {30:14} During the wheat harvest, Reuben found mandrakes in the field and brought them to his mother Leah. Rachel said to Leah, "Please give me some of your son's mandrakes." {30:15} Leah replied, "Is it enough that you have taken my husband? Would you take away my son's mandrakes too?" Rachel said, "I will let him sleep with you tonight for your son's mandrakes." {30:16} When Jacob came in from the field that evening, Leah went out to meet him and said, "You must come to me, for I have hired you with my son's mandrakes." So he slept with her that night. {30:17} God listened to Leah, and she conceived and bore Jacob a fifth son. {30:18} Leah said, "God has rewarded me for giving my maid to my husband." So she named him Issachar. {30:19} Leah conceived again and bore Jacob a sixth son. {30:20} Leah said, "God has granted me a good gift; now my husband will honor me, for I have borne him six sons." So she named him Zebulun. {30:21} Later, she bore a daughter and named her Dinah. {30:22} Then God remembered Rachel; He listened to her and opened her womb. {30:23} She conceived and bore a son and said, "God has taken away my disgrace." {30:24} She named him Joseph and said, "May the LORD add to me another son." {30:25} After Rachel had given birth to Joseph, Jacob said to Laban, "Send me on my way so I can return to my own homeland. {30:26} Give me my wives and children, for whom I have served you, and let me go, for you know my service that I have given you." {30:27} Laban said, "If I have found favor in your eyes, please stay; I have learned by experience that the LORD has blessed me because of you." {30:28} Jacob replied, "Name your wages, and I will pay them." {30:29} Jacob said to him, "You know how I have served you and how your livestock has thrived under my care. {30:30} The little you had before I came has increased greatly, and the LORD has blessed you wherever I have been. But now, when will I provide for my own family?" {30:31} Laban asked, "What can I give you?" Jacob answered, "Don't give me anything. But if you will do this one thing for me, I will continue to tend your flocks and watch over them: {30:32} Let me go through all your flocks today and remove every speckled or spotted sheep, every dark-colored lamb, and every spotted or speckled goat. These will be my wages. {30:33} My honesty will testify for me in the future. When you check on my wages, any goat that is not speckled or spotted and any lamb that is not dark will be considered stolen." {30:34} Laban agreed, "Good! Let it be as you have said." {30:35} That same day, he removed the male goats that were streaked and spotted and all the female goats that were speckled and spotted, and every one that had any white in it, along with all the brown sheep, and gave them to the care of his sons. {30:36} Then he put a three-day journey between himself and Jacob, while Jacob continued to tend Laban's remaining flocks. {30:37} Jacob took fresh branches from poplar, almond, and plane trees and peeled white strips in them, exposing the white inside the branches. {30:38} He placed the peeled branches in the watering troughs where the flocks came to drink, so they would conceive when they came to drink. {30:39} When the flocks were in heat and came to drink, they conceived in front of the branches, and they bore young that were streaked, spotted, and speckled. {30:40} Jacob separated the lambs and made the flocks face the streaked and dark lambs of Laban's flock. He kept his own flocks separate and did not mix them with Laban's.

{30:41} Whenever the stronger sheep were in heat, Jacob laid the branches in front of them at the troughs, so they would conceive near the branches. {30:42} But he did not put the branches in front of the feebler animals; so the feebler ones belonged to Laban, and the stronger ones were Jacob's. {30:43} In this way, Jacob became exceedingly prosperous and had large flocks, maidservants, menservants, camels, and donkeys.

{31:1} Jacob heard Laban's sons saying, "Jacob has taken everything that belonged to our father, and he has gained all this wealth from our father's belongings." {31:2} Jacob noticed that Laban's attitude toward him was not the same as before. {31:3} Then the LORD said to Jacob, "Go back to your homeland and to your relatives, and I will be with you." {31:4} Jacob sent for Rachel and Leah to meet him in the field where his flocks were. {31:5} He said to them, "I can see that your father's attitude toward me is not the same as it was before, but the God of my father has been with me. {31:6} You know that I have worked hard for your father. {31:7} Yet your father has deceived me and changed my wages ten times, but God did not let him harm me. {31:8} If he said the speckled animals would be my wages, then all the animals gave birth to speckled ones; and if he said the ringstraked ones would be my wages, then all the animals gave birth to ringstraked ones. {31:9} In this way, God has taken your father's livestock and given it to me. {31:10} At the time when the animals were mating, I had a dream in which I saw that the rams that mated were ringstraked, speckled, and spotted. {31:11} The angel of God spoke to me in the dream, saying, "Jacob!" and I replied, "Here I am." {31:12} He said, "Look up and see that all the rams that mate are ringstraked, speckled, and spotted, for I have seen all that Laban is doing to you. {31:13} I am the God of Bethel, where you anointed a pillar and made a vow to me. Now get up, leave this land, and return to your relatives." {31:14} Rachel and Leah replied, "Is there any inheritance left for us in our father's house? {31:15} Are we not considered strangers? He has sold us and taken what was our price. {31:16} All the wealth that God has taken from our father belongs to us and our children. So do whatever God has told you." {31:17} Then Jacob got up and placed his children and wives on camels. {31:18} He took away all his livestock and goods that he had acquired in Padanaram to go to his father Isaac in the land of Canaan. {31:19} While Laban was away shearing his sheep, Rachel stole her father's household gods. {31:20} Jacob deceived Laban the Aramean by not telling him he was running away. {31:21} So he fled with everything he had and crossed the Euphrates River, heading toward the hill country of Gilead. {31:22} Three days later, Laban was told that Jacob had fled. {31:23} He took his relatives with him and pursued Jacob for seven days, overtaking him in the hill country of Gilead. {31:24} God came to Laban the Aramean in a dream at night and said, "Be careful not to say anything to Jacob, either good or bad." {31:25} Laban caught up with Jacob, who had pitched his tent in the hill country, and Laban and his relatives pitched their tents in the hill country of Gilead. {31:26} Laban said to Jacob, "What have you done? You've deceived me and carried off my daughters like captives taken in war. {31:27} Why did you run away secretly and deceive me? Why didn't you tell me, so I could send you away with joy, singing and playing music? {31:28} You didn't even let me kiss my grandchildren and daughters goodbye. You have acted foolishly! {31:29} I have the power to harm you, but the God of your father said to me last night, 'Be careful not to say anything to Jacob, either good or bad.' {31:30} Now you have gone off because you longed to return to your father's house, but why did you steal my gods?" {31:31} Jacob answered Laban, "I was afraid you would take your daughters away from me by force. {31:32} If you find your gods with anyone here, that person shall not live. In the presence of our relatives, see for yourself what is yours and take it." (Jacob did not know that Rachel had stolen the gods.) {31:33} So Laban went into Jacob's tent, Leah's tent, and the tents of the two maidservants, but he found nothing. Then he went into Rachel's tent. {31:34} Rachel had taken the household gods and put them in the saddle of her camel and was sitting on them. Laban searched the whole tent but found nothing. {31:35} She said to her father, "Please don't be angry, my lord, that I cannot stand up in your presence; I am having my period." (This was a custom of women.) He searched but found the household gods. {31:36} Jacob became angry and confronted Laban. He said, "What is my crime? How have I wronged you that you hunt me down? {31:37} Now that you have searched through all my things, what have you found that belongs to you? Set it here in front of my relatives and yours, and let them judge between the two of us. {31:38} I have been with you for twenty years. Your sheep and goats have not miscarried, and I have not eaten rams from your flock. {31:39} I did not bring you animals torn by wild beasts; I bore the loss myself, and you demanded payment from me for whatever was stolen, whether by day or night. {31:40} This is my situation: The heat consumed me in the daytime and the cold at night, and sleep fled from my eyes. {31:41} It has been twenty years since I came to your service. I served you fourteen years for your two daughters and six years for your flocks, and you have changed my wages ten times. {31:42} If the God of my father, the God of Abraham, and the Fear of Isaac had not been with me, you would surely have sent me away empty-handed. But God has seen my hardship and the toil of my hands and last night rebuked you." {31:43} Laban answered Jacob, "These daughters are my daughters; these children are my children; these flocks are my flocks, and all you see is mine. What can I do today about these daughters or the children they have borne? {31:44} Come now, let's make a covenant, you and I, and let it serve as a witness between us." {31:45} So Jacob took a stone and set it up as a pillar. {31:46} He said to his relatives, "Gather some stones." So they took stones and piled them in a heap, and they ate there by the heap. {31:47} Laban called it Jegarsahadutha, and Jacob called it Galeed. {31:48} Laban said, "This heap is a witness between you and me today." So he named it Galeed {31:49} and Mizpah, saying, "The LORD watch between us when we are away from each other. {31:50} If you mistreat my daughters or take other wives besides my daughters, even though no one is with us, remember that God is a witness between us." {31:51} Laban said to Jacob, "Look at this heap and this pillar I have set up between you and me. {31:52} This heap is a witness, and this pillar is a witness, that I will not cross this heap to you, and that you will not cross this heap and this pillar to me for harm. {31:53} May the God of Abraham and the God of Nahor, the God of their father, judge between us." And Jacob swore by the Fear of his father Isaac. {31:54} Then Jacob offered a sacrifice on the mountain and invited his relatives to eat. They ate and spent the night there on the mountain. {31:55} Early the next morning, Laban kissed his grandchildren and daughters and blessed them. Then Laban left and returned home.

{32:1} Jacob continued on his journey, and the angels of God met him. {32:2} When Jacob saw them, he said, "This is God's camp," and he named that place Mahanaim. {32:3} Jacob sent messengers ahead to his brother Esau in the land of Seir, the country of Edom. {32:4} He instructed them, saying, "Tell my lord Esau that your servant Jacob says: I have been staying with Laban and have remained there until now. {32:5} I have oxen, donkeys, flocks, and servants. I am sending this message to find favor in your eyes." {32:6} The messengers returned to Jacob, saying, "We went to your brother Esau, and he is coming to meet you, and he has four hundred men with him." {32:7} Jacob was very afraid and distressed, so he divided the people who were with him, along with the flocks, herds, and camels, into two groups. {32:8} He said, "If Esau comes to one group and attacks it, the other group that is left will escape." {32:9} Jacob prayed, "O God of my father Abraham and God of my father Isaac, LORD, you said to me, 'Return to your country and your relatives, and I will do well by you.' {32:10} I am not worthy of all the kindness and faithfulness you have shown your servant. When I crossed the Jordan with just my staff, I now have become two groups. {32:11} Please deliver me from my brother, from Esau, for I am afraid he will come and attack me, along with the mothers and their children. {32:12} But you said, 'I will surely do you good and make your descendants like the sand of the sea, which cannot be counted.'" {32:13} He stayed there that night and took a portion of what he had on hand as a gift for Esau, {32:14} including two hundred female goats, twenty male goats, two hundred ewes, and twenty rams, {32:15} thirty nursing camels and their young, forty cows, ten bulls, twenty female donkeys, and ten foals. {32:16} He entrusted them to his servants, each herd by itself, and instructed his servants, "Go ahead of me and keep a distance between the herds." {32:17} He commanded the first servant, saying, "When my brother Esau meets you and asks, 'Whose are you? Where are you going? Whose animals are these in front of you?' {32:18} you are to say, 'They belong to your servant Jacob. They are a gift sent to my lord Esau, and he is right behind us.'" {32:19} He also instructed the second and third servants, and all who followed the herds, saying, "This is what you are to say to Esau when you find him. {32:20} And be sure to say, 'Your servant Jacob is coming behind us,' for he thought, 'I will appease him with the gift that is going ahead of me. After that, I will see his face; perhaps he will accept me.'" {32:21} So the gift went on ahead, but Jacob stayed that night in the camp. {32:22} He got up that night and took his two wives, his two maidservants, and his eleven children and crossed the ford of Jabbok. {32:23} After he had sent them across the stream, he sent over all his possessions. {32:24} So Jacob was left alone, and a man wrestled with him until daybreak. {32:25} When the man saw that he could not overpower Jacob, he touched the socket of Jacob's hip so that his hip was wrenched as he wrestled with him. {32:26} Then the man said, "Let me go, for it is daybreak." But Jacob replied, "I will not let you go unless you bless me." {32:27} The man asked, "What is your name?" "Jacob," he answered. {32:28} Then the man said, "Your name will no longer be Jacob, but Israel, because you have struggled with God and with humans and have overcome." {32:29} Jacob asked him, "Please tell me your name." But he replied, "Why do you ask my name?" Then he blessed him there. {32:30} Jacob named the place Peniel, saying, "I have seen God face to face, and yet my life was spared." {32:31} The sun rose above him as he passed Peniel, and he was limping because of his hip. {32:32} Therefore, the Israelites do not eat the tendon attached to the socket of the hip, because the man touched the socket of Jacob's hip near the tendon.

{33:1} Jacob looked up and saw Esau coming with four hundred men. He divided the children among Leah, Rachel, and the two maidservants. {33:2} He put the maidservants and their children first, Leah and her children next, and Rachel and Joseph last. {33:3} Jacob went ahead of them and bowed to the ground seven times as he approached his brother. {33:4} Esau ran to meet him, embraced him, fell on his neck, and kissed him, and they both wept. {33:5} Esau looked up and saw the women and children and asked, "Who are these with you?" Jacob replied, "They are the children God has graciously given your servant." {33:6} The maidservants came near with their children and bowed down. {33:7} Leah and her children also approached and bowed down, and finally, Joseph and Rachel came near and bowed down. {33:8} Esau asked, "What was the meaning of all those animals I met?" Jacob answered, "These are a gift to find favor in your eyes, my lord." {33:9} Esau said, "I have enough, my brother; keep what you have for yourself." {33:10} Jacob replied, "No, please, if I have found favor in your eyes, accept this gift from me. Seeing your face is like seeing the face of God, and you are pleased with me. {33:11} Please take my blessing that has been brought to you, because God has been gracious to me, and I have everything I need." He urged Esau, and Esau accepted it. {33:12} Esau said, "Let us be on our way; I will accompany you." {33:13} Jacob said to him, "My lord knows that the children are fragile, and the flocks and herds are nursing. If they are driven too hard for just one day, all the animals will die. {33:14} Please let my lord go ahead of his servant, and I will follow slowly, according to the pace of the animals and the children, until I reach my lord in Seir." {33:15} Esau said, "Let me leave some of my men with you." Jacob replied, "What for? I just want to find favor in your eyes." {33:16} So Esau returned home that day on his way to Seir. {33:17} Jacob traveled to Succoth, built a house, and made shelters for his livestock; that's why the place is called Succoth (meaning "shelters"). {33:18} Jacob arrived safely in Shalem, a city in Shechem in the land of Canaan, after coming from Padanaram, and he pitched his tent near the city. {33:19} He bought a plot of land where he had pitched his tent from the sons of Hamor, Shechem's father, for a hundred pieces of money. {33:20} There he set up an altar and called it Elelohe-Israel (meaning "God, the God of Israel").

{34:1} Dinah, the daughter of Leah, whom she had borne to Jacob, went out to visit the women of the land. {34:2} When Shechem, the son of Hamor the Hivite, the ruler of the area, saw her, he seized her, lay with her, and violated her. {34:3} His heart was deeply attached to Dinah, the daughter of Jacob; he loved the young woman and spoke tenderly to her. {34:4} So Shechem said to his father Hamor, "Get me this young woman as my wife." {34:5} Jacob heard that Shechem had defiled his daughter Dinah, but since his sons were in the fields with the livestock, he remained silent until they returned. {34:6} Then Hamor, Shechem's father, went to speak with Jacob. {34:7} Meanwhile, Jacob's sons came in from the field as soon as they heard what had happened. They were filled with grief and anger, because Shechem had committed a disgraceful act against Israel by lying with Jacob's daughter, something that should not be done. {34:8} But Hamor spoke with them, saying, "My son Shechem longs for your daughter. Please give her to him as his wife. {34:9} Intermarry with us; give us your daughters and take our daughters for yourselves. {34:10} You can live among us; the land is open to you. Live in it, trade in it, and acquire property in it." {34:11} Then Shechem said to Dinah's father and brothers, "Let me find favor in your eyes, and I will give you whatever you ask. {34:12} Demand as great a bride price (a traditional payment) and gift as you like, and I will pay whatever you ask of me. Just give me the young woman as my wife." {34:13} Because Shechem had defiled their sister Dinah, Jacob's sons replied deceitfully to Shechem and his father Hamor. {34:14} They said to them, "We cannot do such a thing; we cannot give our sister to a man who is uncircumcised, for that would be a disgrace to us. {34:15} We will only consent on the condition that you become like us by circumcising all your males. {34:16} Then we will give you our daughters and take your daughters for ourselves. We will live among you and become one people. {34:17} But if you do not agree to be circumcised, we will take our sister and leave." {34:18} Their proposal seemed good to Hamor and his son Shechem. {34:19} The young man, who was more respected than anyone in his father's household, lost no time in doing what they asked, because he was delighted with Jacob's daughter. {34:20} So Hamor and his son Shechem went to the gate of their city to speak to the men of their city. {34:21} They said, "These men are at peace with us. Let them live in our land and trade in it; the land has plenty of room for them. We can marry their daughters, and they can marry ours. {34:22} But the men will consent to live with us as one people only if every male among us is circumcised, as they are. {34:23} Won't their livestock, their property, and all their animals become ours? So let us agree to their terms, and they will settle among us." {34:24} All the men who went out of the city gate agreed with Hamor and his son Shechem, and every male in the city was circumcised. {34:25} Three days later, while all of them were still in pain, two of Jacob's sons, Simeon and Levi, Dinah's brothers, took their swords, boldly attacked the city, and killed all the males. {34:26} They also killed Hamor and his son Shechem with their swords, took Dinah from Shechem's house, and left. {34:27} The sons of Jacob came upon the dead bodies and looted the city because their sister had been defiled. {34:28} They seized their flocks, herds, donkeys, and everything else of theirs, both in the city and in the fields. {34:29} They carried off all their wealth, their women, and children, taking as plunder everything in the houses. {34:30} Then Jacob said to Simeon and Levi, "You have brought trouble on me by making me a stench among the inhabitants of the land—the Canaanites and Perizzites. We are few in number, and if they join forces and attack me, I and my household will be destroyed." {34:31} But they replied, "Should he have treated our sister like a prostitute?" (here "harlot" refers to a prostitute).

{35:1} God said to Jacob, "Get up and go to Bethel and settle there. Build an altar to God, who appeared to you when you fled from your brother Esau." {35:2} Jacob then said to his household and all who were with him, "Get rid of the foreign gods among you, purify yourselves, and change your clothes. {35:3} Let's go to Bethel, where I will build an altar to God, who answered me in my time of trouble and has been with me wherever I have gone." {35:4} They gave Jacob all the foreign gods they had and the earrings they were wearing, and Jacob buried them under the oak near Shechem. {35:5} They set out, and God caused the towns around them to fear, so they did not pursue the sons of Jacob. {35:6} Jacob arrived at Luz, in the land of Canaan, also known as Bethel, with all the people who were with him. {35:7} There he built an altar and named the place Elbethel because it was there that God appeared to him when he fled from his brother. {35:8} Deborah, Rebekah's nurse, died and was buried beneath Bethel under an oak, and the place was called Allonbachuth (meaning "oak of weeping"). {35:9} God appeared to Jacob again after he had come from Padanaram and blessed him. {35:10} God said to him, "Your name is Jacob, but you will no longer be called Jacob; your name will be Israel." So he named him Israel. {35:11} God said to him, "I am God Almighty. Be fruitful and multiply; a nation and a community of nations will come from you, and kings will come from your descendants. {35:12} The land I gave to Abraham and Isaac, I now give to you and your descendants after you." {35:13} God went up from him in the place where he had spoken with him. {35:14} Jacob set up a stone pillar in the place where God had talked with him, and he poured out a drink offering and anointed it with oil. {35:15} Jacob named the place where God spoke with him Bethel. {35:16} They traveled from Bethel, and while they were still some distance from Ephrath, Rachel went into labor and had a difficult delivery. {35:17} As she was having great difficulty, the midwife said to her, "Don't be afraid; you will have another son." {35:18} As she breathed her last, for she was dying, she named her son Benoni (meaning "son of my sorrow"), but his father named him Benjamin (meaning "son of the right hand"). {35:19} Rachel died and was buried on the way to Ephrath, that is, Bethlehem. {35:20} Jacob set up a pillar on her grave; it marks Rachel's grave to this day. {35:21} Israel traveled on and pitched his tent beyond the Tower of Edar. {35:22} While Israel was living in that region, Reuben went in and slept with Bilhah, his father's concubine, and Israel heard about it. The sons of Jacob were twelve: {35:23} The sons of Leah were Reuben, Jacob's firstborn, Simeon, Levi, Judah, Issachar, and Zebulun. {35:24} The sons of Rachel were Joseph and Benjamin. {35:25} The sons of Bilhah, Rachel's maidservant, were Dan and Naphtali. {35:26} The sons of Zilpah, Leah's maidservant, were Gad and Asher. These were the sons of Jacob, born to him in Padanaram. {35:27} Jacob went to his father Isaac in Mamre, near Kiriath Arba (that is, Hebron), where Abraham and Isaac had stayed. {35:28} Isaac lived one hundred eighty years. {35:29} Then Isaac breathed his last and died, and was gathered to his people, old and full of years. His sons Esau and Jacob buried him.

{36:1} These are the generations of Esau, who is also known as Edom. {36:2} Esau took wives from the daughters of Canaan: Adah, the daughter of Elon the Hittite, and Aholibamah, the daughter of Anah, the daughter of Zibeon the Hivite; {36:3} and Bashemath, the daughter of Ishmael, and sister of Nebajoth. {36:4} Adah bore Esau a son named Eliphaz, and Bashemath bore Reuel. {36:5} Aholibamah bore Jeush, Jaalam, and Korah. These are the sons of Esau, born to him in the land of Canaan. {36:6} Esau took his wives, sons, daughters, and all the members of his household, along with his livestock and all his possessions that he had acquired in Canaan, and he moved away from his brother Jacob. {36:7} Their wealth was too great for them to live together, and the land where they had settled could not support them because of their livestock. {36:8} So Esau settled in the hill country of Seir; Esau is Edom. {36:9} These are the generations of Esau, the father of the Edomites, in the hill country of Seir. {36:10} The names of Esau's sons are as follows: Eliphaz, the son of Adah, Esau's wife, and Reuel, the son of Bashemath, Esau's wife. {36:11} The sons of Eliphaz were Teman, Omar, Zepho, Gatam, and Kenaz. {36:12} Timna was a concubine of Eliphaz, Esau's son, and she bore him Amalek. These were the sons of Adah, Esau's wife. {36:13} These are the sons of Reuel: Nahath, Zerah, Shammah, and Mizzah. These were the sons of Bashemath, Esau's wife. {36:14} The sons of Aholibamah, the daughter of Anah and Esau's wife, were Jeush, Jaalam, and Korah. {36:15} These were the chiefs (or dukes) among the sons of Esau: the sons of Eliphaz, Esau's firstborn: chief Teman, chief Omar, chief Zepho, chief Kenaz, {36:16} chief Korah, chief Gatam, and chief Amalek. These are the chiefs that descended from Eliphaz in the land of Edom; these were the sons of Adah. {36:17} The sons of Reuel, Esau's son, were: chief Nahath, chief Zerah, chief Shammah, and chief Mizzah. These are the chiefs that descended from Reuel in the land of Edom; these were the sons of Bashemath, Esau's wife. {36:18} The sons of Aholibamah, Esau's wife, were: chief Jeush, chief Jaalam, and chief Korah. These were the chiefs that came from Aholibamah, the daughter of Anah, Esau's wife. {36:19} These are the sons of Esau, who is Edom, and these are their chiefs. {36:20} These are the sons of Seir the Horite, who lived in the land: Lotan, Shobal, Zibeon, Anah, {36:21} Dishon, Ezer, and Dishan. These are the chiefs of the Horites, the descendants of Seir in the land of Edom. {36:22} The children of Lotan were Hori and Hemam; Lotan's sister was Timna. {36:23} The children of Shobal were Alvan, Manahath, Ebal, Shepho, and Onam. {36:24} The children of Zibeon were Ajah and Anah. This is the Anah who found the mules in the wilderness while feeding his father Zibeon's donkeys. {36:25} The children of Anah were Dishon and Aholibamah, the daughter of Anah. {36:26} The children of Dishon were Hemdan, Eshban, Ithran, and Cheran. {36:27} The children of Ezer were Bilhan, Zaavan, and Akan. {36:28} The children of Dishan were Uz and Aran. {36:29} These are the chiefs that descended from the Horites: chief Lotan, chief Shobal, chief Zibeon, chief Anah, {36:30} chief Dishon, chief Ezer, and chief Dishan. These are the chiefs that descended from Hori, among their chiefs in the land of Seir. {36:31} These are the kings who reigned in the land of Edom before any king ruled over the Israelites. {36:32} Bela, the son of Beor, was king in Edom; his city was named Dinhabah. {36:33} Bela died, and Jobab, the son of Zerah from Bozrah, succeeded him as king. {36:34} Jobab died, and Husham from the land of Temani succeeded him as king. {36:35} Husham died, and Hadad, the son of Bedad, who defeated Midian in the field of Moab, became king in his place; his city was named Avith. {36:36} Hadad died, and Samlah from Masrekah succeeded him as king. {36:37} Samlah died, and Saul from Rehoboth by the river became king. {36:38} Saul died, and Baalhanan, the son of Achbor, succeeded him as king. {36:39} Baalhanan, the son of Achbor, died, and Hadar became king in his place; his city was named Pau, and his wife's name was Mehetabel, the daughter of Matred, the daughter of Mezahab. {36:40} These are the names of the chiefs that descended from Esau, according to their families and places: chief Timnah, chief Alvah, chief Jetheth, {36:41} chief Aholibamah, chief Elah, chief Pinon, {36:42} chief Kenaz, chief Teman, chief Mibzar, {36:43} chief Magdiel, chief Iram. These are the chiefs of Edom, according to their settlements in the land they possessed. Esau is the father of the Edomites.

{37:1} Jacob lived in the land where his father had been a stranger, in the land of Canaan. {37:2} These are the generations of Jacob. Joseph, at seventeen years old, was tending the flock with his brothers; he was with the sons of Bilhah and the sons of Zilpah, his father's wives, and Joseph brought a bad report about them to his father. {37:3} Israel loved Joseph more than all his other children because he was the son of his old age, and he made him a beautiful coat. {37:4} When his brothers saw that their father loved him more than them, they hated him and couldn't speak to him kindly. {37:5} Joseph had a dream, which he told to his brothers, and they hated him even more. {37:6} He said to them, "Please listen to this dream I had: {37:7} We were binding sheaves in the field, and my sheaf rose and stood upright, and your sheaves gathered around it and bowed down to my sheaf." {37:8} His brothers replied, "Are you really going to reign over us? Will you really have authority over us?" They hated him even more because of his dreams and what he said. {37:9} He dreamed another dream and told it to his brothers, saying, "Look, I had another dream! The sun, the moon, and eleven stars were bowing down to me." {37:10} He told it to his father and his brothers, and his father rebuked him, saying, "What is this dream you have dreamed? Shall I, your mother, and your brothers actually come and bow down to you on the ground?" {37:11} His brothers were jealous of him, but his father kept the matter in mind. {37:12} His brothers went to feed their father's flock in Shechem. {37:13} Israel said to Joseph, "Aren't your brothers feeding the flock in Shechem? Come, I will send you to them." Joseph answered, "Here I am." {37:14} He said, "Go and see if all is well with your brothers and with the flocks, and bring me word." So he sent him from the Valley of Hebron, and Joseph went to Shechem. {37:15} A certain man found him wandering in the field and asked, "What are you looking for?" {37:16} Joseph replied, "I'm looking for my brothers. Please tell me where they are feeding their flocks." {37:17} The man said, "They have gone away, for I heard them say, 'Let us go to Dothan.'" Joseph followed his brothers and found them in Dothan. {37:18} When they saw him from a distance, before he came near, they plotted to kill him. {37:19} They said to one another, "Look, here comes that dreamer. {37:20} Let's kill him and throw him into one of the pits, and we'll say a wild animal has devoured him. Then we'll see what becomes of his dreams." {37:21} Reuben heard this and rescued him from their hands, saying, "Let's not kill him." {37:22} Reuben said to them, "Shed no blood; throw him into this pit in the wilderness, but don't lay a hand on him," intending to rescue him later and return him to his father. {37:23} When Joseph arrived, they stripped him of his coat, the beautiful coat he was wearing, {37:24} and they took him and threw him into the pit, which was empty and had no water in it. {37:25} They sat down to eat a meal, and as they looked up, they saw a caravan of Ishmaelites coming from Gilead with their camels carrying spices, balm, and myrrh to take to Egypt. {37:26} Judah said to his brothers, "What profit is there if we kill our brother and conceal his blood? {37:27} Come, let's sell him to the Ishmaelites and not lay our hands on him, for he is our brother, our own flesh." His brothers agreed. {37:28} Then the Midianite merchants passed by, and they drew Joseph up and lifted him out of the pit and sold him to the Ishmaelites for twenty pieces of silver. So they brought Joseph into Egypt. {37:29} Reuben returned to the pit and saw that Joseph was not in it; he tore his clothes in despair. {37:30} He went back to his brothers and said, "The boy isn't there! What am I going to do?" {37:31} They took Joseph's coat, killed a goat, and dipped the coat in the blood. {37:32} They sent the beautiful coat to their father, saying, "We found this; please identify whether it's your son's coat or not." {37:33} Jacob recognized it and said, "It is my son's coat; an evil beast has devoured him. Joseph is surely torn to pieces." {37:34} Jacob tore his clothes and put on sackcloth, mourning for his son for many days. {37:35} All his sons and daughters came to comfort him, but he refused to be comforted, saying, "I will go down to the grave mourning for my son." Thus his father wept for him. {37:36} Meanwhile, the Midianites sold Joseph in Egypt to Potiphar, an officer of Pharaoh, the captain of the guard.

{38:1} At that time, Judah left his brothers and went to stay with a man from Adullam named Hirah. {38:2} There, Judah saw the daughter of a Canaanite man named Shuah. He married her and slept with her. {38:3} She conceived and gave birth to a son, whom Judah named Er. {38:4} She conceived again and gave birth to another son, and she named him Onan. {38:5} She gave birth to yet another son and named him Shelah. She was in Chezib when she gave birth to him. {38:6} Judah found a wife for his firstborn son Er, and her name was Tamar. {38:7} But Er, Judah's firstborn, was wicked in the sight of the Lord, so the Lord put him to death. {38:8} Then Judah said to Onan, "Go and sleep with your brother's wife, fulfill your duty as her brother-in-law, and raise up offspring for your brother." {38:9} But Onan knew the offspring would not be his, so whenever he slept with his brother's wife, he wasted his seed on the ground to avoid providing offspring for his brother. {38:10} What he did was evil in the sight of the Lord, so the Lord put him to death as well. {38:11} Judah then said to his daughter-in-law Tamar, "Live as a widow in your father's house until my son Shelah grows up," for he thought, "He may die too, just like his brothers." So Tamar went to live in her father's house. {38:12} After a long time, Judah's wife, the daughter of Shuah, died. After Judah was comforted, he went up to Timnath to his sheepshearers, along with his friend Hirah the Adullamite. {38:13} When Tamar was told, "Your father-in-law is going up to Timnath to shear his sheep," {38:14} she took off her widow's clothes, covered herself with a veil to disguise herself, and sat by the roadside at a place called Enaim, which is on the way to Timnath. She realized that although Shelah had now grown up, she had not been given to him as a wife. {38:15} When Judah saw her, he thought she was a prostitute because she had covered her face. {38:16} He went over to her by the roadside and said, "Come now, let me sleep with you" (not knowing that she was his daughter-in-law). She asked, "What will you give me to sleep with you?" {38:17} He answered, "I'll send you a young goat from my flock." She said, "Will you give me something as a pledge until you send it?" {38:18} He asked, "What pledge should I give you?" She replied, "Your signet, your bracelets, and your staff." So he gave them to her and slept with her, and she became pregnant by him. {38:19} Afterward, she got up, left, took off her veil, and put on her widow's clothes again. {38:20} Judah later sent the young goat by his friend the Adullamite to retrieve his pledge from the woman, but he couldn't find her. {38:21} He asked the men of that place, "Where is the prostitute who was by the roadside at Enaim?" They replied, "There hasn't been any prostitute here." {38:22} So he returned to Judah and said, "I couldn't find her. Besides, the men of the place said there hasn't been any prostitute." {38:23} Then Judah said, "Let her keep what she has, or we'll become a laughingstock. After all, I did send her this goat, but you couldn't find her." {38:24} About three months later, Judah was told, "Your daughter-in-law Tamar has played the harlot, and now she's pregnant because of it." Judah said, "Bring her out and burn her to death!" {38:25} As she was being brought out, she sent a message to her father-in-law: "I am pregnant by the man who owns these," she said. "See if you recognize whose signet, bracelets, and staff these are." {38:26} Judah recognized them and said, "She is more righteous than I, since I didn't give her to my son Shelah." And he did not sleep with her again. {38:27} When the time came for Tamar to give birth, there were twins in her womb. {38:28} As she was giving birth, one of them put out his hand, and the midwife tied a scarlet thread around it, saying, "This one came out first." {38:29} But as he drew back his hand, his brother came out, and she said, "What a breach (breaking through) you have made for yourself!" So he was named Perez (which means "breach"). {38:30} Then his brother, who had the scarlet thread on his hand, came out, and he was named Zerah.

{39:1} Joseph was taken down to Egypt, where Potiphar, an officer of Pharaoh and captain of the guard, an Egyptian, bought him from the Ishmaelites who had brought him there. {39:2} The LORD was with Joseph, and he became a successful man while serving in the house of his Egyptian master. {39:3} His master noticed that the LORD was with him and that the LORD made everything he did successful. {39:4} Joseph found favor in his master's sight and served him; Potiphar made him overseer of his house and entrusted everything he owned to Joseph. {39:5} From the time Joseph was made overseer, the LORD blessed Potiphar's house for Joseph's sake, and the blessing of the LORD was on everything he had, both in the house and in the field. {39:6} Potiphar left everything he had in Joseph's care; he didn't even worry about what he had except for the food he ate. Joseph was well-built and handsome. {39:7} After a while, his master's wife looked at Joseph and said, "Sleep with me." {39:8} But he refused, saying to her, "My master doesn't know what is in the house. He has entrusted everything he owns to my care. {39:9} No one in this house is greater than I am; he has withheld nothing from me except you, because you are his wife. How could I do this great evil and sin against God?" {39:10} She spoke to Joseph day after day, but he refused to listen to her or be with her. {39:11} One day, he went into the house to do his work, and none of the household servants were there. {39:12} She grabbed him by his garment and said, "Sleep with me!" But he left his garment in her hand and ran outside. {39:13} When she saw that he had left his garment in her hand and had fled, {39:14} she called to the men of her house and said, "Look, he has brought a Hebrew in here to mock us! He came in to me to sleep with me, and I screamed loudly. {39:15} When he heard me scream, he left his garment with me and ran away." {39:16} She kept his garment with her until her husband came home. {39:17} Then she told him the same story: "The Hebrew servant whom you brought in here came in to me to mock me. {39:18} But when I screamed, he left his garment with me and fled." {39:19} When Joseph's master heard the words of his wife, which she spoke to him, saying, "Your servant did this to me," his anger was aroused. {39:20} Joseph's master took him and put him in prison, where the king's prisoners were confined, and there he remained in prison. {39:21} But the LORD was with Joseph and showed him mercy, giving him favor in the sight of the prison keeper. {39:22} The prison keeper put all the prisoners in Joseph's care, and he was responsible for everything that was done there. {39:23} The prison keeper paid no attention to anything under Joseph's care because the LORD was with him, and whatever he did, the LORD made it succeed.

{40:1} After these events, the king of Egypt's butler and baker offended their lord, the king of Egypt. {40:2} Pharaoh was angry with his two officials, the chief butler and the chief baker. {40:3} He put them in custody in the house of the captain of the guard, in the same prison where Joseph was confined. {40:4} The captain of the guard assigned Joseph to serve them, and they remained in custody for some time. {40:5} Both men dreamed dreams on the same night, each according to his own interpretation; the butler and the baker of the king of Egypt were imprisoned together. {40:6} Joseph came to them in the morning and saw that they were upset. {40:7} He asked Pharaoh's officers who were with him in custody, "Why are you looking so sad today?" {40:8} They replied, "We have dreamed dreams, and there is no one to interpret them." Joseph said to them, "Do not interpretations belong to God? Tell me your dreams, please." {40:9} The chief butler told his dream to Joseph, saying, "In my dream, I saw a vine in front of me; {40:10} and on the vine were three branches. As it budded, its blossoms came out, and its clusters produced ripe grapes. {40:11} Pharaoh's cup was in my hand; I took the grapes, pressed them into Pharaoh's cup, and gave the cup to Pharaoh." {40:12} Joseph said to him, "This is the interpretation: The three branches represent three days. {40:13} Within three days, Pharaoh will lift up your head and restore you to your position, and you will put Pharaoh's cup in his hand as you did before. {40:14} But when it goes well for you, please remember me and show me kindness. Mention me to Pharaoh and get me out of this prison. {40:15} I was forcibly taken from the land of the Hebrews, and here, I have done nothing to deserve being put in the dungeon." {40:16} When the chief baker saw that the interpretation was favorable, he said to Joseph, "I also had a dream: I had three white baskets on my head. {40:17} In the top basket were all kinds of baked goods for Pharaoh, and the birds were eating them out of the basket on my head." {40:18} Joseph replied, "This is the interpretation: The three baskets are three days. {40:19} Within three days, Pharaoh will lift up your head and hang you on a tree, and the birds will eat your flesh." {40:20} On the third day, which was Pharaoh's birthday, he gave a feast for all his servants. He lifted up the head of the chief butler and the chief baker among his servants. {40:21} He restored the chief butler to his former position, and he put the cup in Pharaoh's hand. {40:22} But he hanged the chief baker, just as Joseph had interpreted to them. {40:23} Yet the chief butler did not remember Joseph; he forgot him.

{41:1} After two full years, Pharaoh had a dream: he was standing by the river. {41:2} Suddenly, seven healthy and fat cows came up out of the river and grazed in a meadow. {41:3} Then, seven other cows came up after them, looking poor and thin, and they stood beside the other cows at the riverbank. {41:4} The thin and ugly cows ate the seven healthy and fat cows, and Pharaoh woke up. {41:5} He fell asleep again and dreamed a second time: seven ears of corn came up on one stalk, full and good. {41:6} Then, seven thin ears, scorched by the east wind, grew up after them. {41:7} The seven thin ears swallowed the seven full ears. When Pharaoh awoke, it was just a dream. {41:8} In the morning, he was troubled, so he sent for all the magicians and wise men of Egypt. Pharaoh told them his dream, but no one could interpret it. {41:9} Then the chief butler said to Pharaoh, "I remember my mistakes today. {41:10} Pharaoh was angry with his servants and put me and the chief baker in custody in the captain of the guard's house. {41:11} We both had dreams on the same night, each according to the interpretation of his own dream. {41:12} There was a young Hebrew man with us, a servant of the captain of the guard. We told him our dreams, and he interpreted them for us, giving each man the interpretation of his dream. {41:13} Just as he interpreted, it happened: I was restored to my position, and the chief baker was hanged." {41:14} Then Pharaoh sent for Joseph, and they quickly brought him out of the dungeon. He shaved, changed his clothes, and came to Pharaoh. {41:15} Pharaoh said to Joseph, "I had a dream, and no one can interpret it. I've heard that you can understand a dream and interpret it." {41:16} Joseph answered, "It's not in me; God will give Pharaoh a favorable answer." {41:17} Pharaoh told Joseph, "In my dream, I was standing on the bank of the river. {41:18} Suddenly, seven healthy and fat cows came up out of the river and grazed in a meadow. {41:19} Then seven other cows came up after them, very poor and thin, worse than any I've seen in all of Egypt. {41:20} The thin and ugly cows ate the first seven fat cows. {41:21} After they had eaten them, no one could tell that they had eaten them; they still looked just as bad as before. Then I woke up. {41:22} I saw in my dream that seven ears of corn grew on one stalk, full and good. {41:23} Then seven thin ears, withered and scorched by the east wind, sprouted up after them. {41:24} The thin ears swallowed the seven good ears. I told this to the magicians, but no one could explain it to me." {41:25} Joseph said to Pharaoh, "Your dream is one: God has revealed to Pharaoh what he is about to do. {41:26} The seven good cows are seven years, and the seven good ears are also seven years; the dream is one. {41:27} The seven thin and ugly cows that came up after them are seven years, and the seven empty ears, scorched by the east wind, will be seven years of famine. {41:28} This is what I told Pharaoh: God is about to do this. {41:29} There will be seven years of great abundance in all the land of Egypt. {41:30} After that, there will be seven years of famine, and all the abundance will be forgotten in the land of Egypt, and the famine will consume the land. {41:31} The abundance will not be remembered because of the famine that follows, for it will be very severe. {41:32} Since the dream was repeated to Pharaoh twice, it means that this thing has been firmly decided by God, and God will bring it about soon. {41:33} Therefore, let Pharaoh find a wise and discerning man and put him in charge of the land of Egypt. {41:34} Let Pharaoh appoint officers to collect one-fifth of the harvest during the seven years of abundance. {41:35} They should gather all the food produced in those good years and store it under Pharaoh's authority, keeping it in the cities. {41:36} This food will be a reserve for the land during the seven years of famine, so the land will not perish during the famine." {41:37} The proposal seemed good to Pharaoh and all his officials. {41:38} Pharaoh asked them, "Can we find anyone else like this man, in whom is the Spirit of God?" {41:39} Then Pharaoh said to Joseph, "Since God has made all this known to you, there is no one as wise and discerning as you. {41:40} You will be in charge of my palace, and all my people will submit to your orders; only with respect to the throne will I be greater than you." {41:41} Pharaoh said to Joseph, "I hereby put you in charge of all Egypt." {41:42} He took his signet ring from his hand and put it on Joseph's finger. He dressed him in fine linen and put a gold chain around his neck. {41:43} He had Joseph ride in the second chariot he owned, and they shouted before him, "Make way!" He made him ruler over all Egypt. {41:44} Pharaoh said to Joseph, "I am Pharaoh, and without your approval, no one will lift a hand or foot in all Egypt." {41:45} Pharaoh gave Joseph the name Zaphnath-Paaneah and gave him Asenath, daughter of Potipherah, priest of On, as his wife. Joseph went throughout the land of Egypt. {41:46} Joseph was thirty years old when he entered the service of Pharaoh, king of Egypt. Joseph left Pharaoh's presence and traveled throughout Egypt. {41:47} During the seven years of abundance, the land produced large quantities of food. {41:48} He collected all the food produced during the seven years in Egypt and stored it in the cities, putting the food from the fields surrounding each city in the same place. {41:49} Joseph collected so much grain, it was like the sand of the sea; he stopped keeping track because it was beyond measure. {41:50} Before the years of famine came, two sons were born to Joseph by Asenath, daughter of Potipherah, priest of On. {41:51} Joseph named his firstborn Manasseh, saying, "God has made me forget all my troubles and all my father's household." {41:52} The second son he named Ephraim, saying, "God has made me fruitful in the land of my suffering." {41:53} The seven years of abundance in Egypt came to an end. {41:54} The seven years of famine began, just as Joseph had said. The famine was in every land, but in all of Egypt, there was food. {41:55} When the people of Egypt cried out to Pharaoh for food, he said to them, "Go to Joseph; do what he tells you." {41:56} The famine spread across the whole earth, and Joseph opened all the storehouses and sold grain to the Egyptians, for the famine was severe in Egypt. {41:57} People from all over the world came to Egypt to buy grain from Joseph because the famine was severe in every land.

{42:1} When Jacob saw that there was grain in Egypt, he said to his sons, "Why are you looking at each other? {42:2} I have heard that there is grain in Egypt. Go down there and buy some for us, so that we may live and not die." {42:3} So Joseph's ten brothers went to buy grain in Egypt. {42:4} But Jacob did not send Benjamin, Joseph's brother, with them because he said, "What if some harm comes to him?" {42:5} The sons of Israel went to buy grain among those who came, for the famine was in the land of Canaan. {42:6} Joseph was the governor of the land and was the one who sold grain to all the people. When Joseph's brothers came, they bowed down to him with their faces to the ground. {42:7} Joseph saw his brothers and recognized them, but he pretended to be a stranger and spoke harshly to them. "Where do you come from?" he asked. They replied, "From the land of Canaan to buy food." {42:8} Although Joseph recognized his brothers, they did not recognize him. {42:9} Then he remembered the dreams he had about them and said, "You are spies; you have come to see where our land is unprotected." {42:10} "No, my lord," they said. "Your servants have come to buy food. {42:11} We are all the sons of one man. Your servants are honest men; we are not spies." {42:12} "No!" he insisted. "You have come to see where our land is unprotected." {42:13} They replied, "Your servants are twelve brothers, the sons of one man in the land of Canaan. The youngest is with our father today, and one is no longer with us." {42:14} Joseph said to them, "It is just as I told you: you are spies! {42:15} This is how you will be tested: As surely as Pharaoh lives, you will not leave this place unless your youngest brother comes here. {42:16} Send one of your number to get your brother; the rest of you will be kept in prison so that your words may be tested to see if you are telling the truth. If you are not, then as surely as Pharaoh lives, you are spies!" {42:17} And he put them all in custody for three days. {42:18} On the third day, Joseph said to them, "Do this and you will live, for I fear God. {42:19} If you are honest men, let one of your brothers stay here in prison while the rest of you go and take grain back for your starving households. {42:20} But you must bring your youngest brother to me so that your words may be verified and you may not die." They agreed to this. {42:21} They said to one another, "Surely we are being punished because of our brother. We saw how distressed he was when he pleaded with us for his life, but we would not listen; that's why this distress has come upon us." {42:22} Reuben replied, "Didn't I tell you not to sin against the boy? But you wouldn't listen. Now we must give an accounting for his blood." {42:23} They did not realize that Joseph could understand them, since he was using an interpreter. {42:24} He turned away from them and wept. Then he turned back and spoke to them again. He had Simeon taken from them and bound before their eyes. {42:25} Joseph gave orders to fill their sacks with grain, to put each man's silver back in his sack, and to give them provisions for their journey. And this was done for them. {42:26} They loaded their donkeys with the grain and left. {42:27} At the place where they stopped for the night, one of them opened his sack to get feed for his donkey, and he saw his silver in the mouth of his sack. {42:28} "My silver has been returned!" he said to his brothers. "Here it is in my sack!" Their hearts sank and they turned to each other, trembling and said, "What is this that God has done to us?" {42:29} When they came to their father Jacob in the land of Canaan, they told him all that had happened to them. They said, {42:30} "The man who is lord over the land spoke harshly to us and treated us as though we were spying on the land. {42:31} But we said to him, 'We are honest men; we are not spies. {42:32} We are twelve brothers, sons of one father. One is no more, and the youngest is now with our father in Canaan.' {42:33} Then the man who is lord over the land said to us, 'This is how I will know whether you are honest men: Leave one of your brothers here with me, and take food for your starving households and go. {42:34} But bring your youngest brother to me so I will know that you are not spies but honest men. Then I will give you back your brother, and you can trade in the land.'" {42:35} As they were emptying their sacks, there in each man's sack was his pouch of silver! When they and their father saw the bundles of silver, they were frightened. {42:36} Their father Jacob said to them, "You have deprived me of my children. Joseph is no more, Simeon is no more, and now you want to take Benjamin. Everything is against me!" {42:37} Then Reuben said to his father, "You may put both of my sons to death if I do not bring him back to you. Entrust him to my care, and I will bring him back." {42:38} But Jacob said, "My son will not go down there with you. His brother is dead, and he is the only one left. If harm comes to him on the journey you are taking, you will bring my gray head down to the grave in sorrow."

{43:1} The famine was severe in the land. {43:2} When they had eaten all the grain they had brought back from Egypt, their father said to them, "Go back and buy us a little more food." {43:3} Judah said to him, "The man warned us solemnly, 'You will not see my face unless your brother is with you.' {43:4} If you will send our brother with us, we will go down and buy food for you. {43:5} But if you don't send him, we won't go down, because the man said, 'You will not see my face unless your brother is with you.'" {43:6} Israel asked, "Why did you tell the man you had another brother?" {43:7} They replied, "The man questioned us closely about ourselves and our family. He asked, 'Is your father still alive? Do you have another brother?' We simply answered his questions. How could we know he would say, 'Bring your brother down'?" {43:8} Judah said to his father Israel, "Send the boy with me, and we will go at once so that we and you and our children may live. {43:9} I will guarantee his safety; you can hold me responsible for him. If I do not bring him back to you and set him here before you, I will bear the blame before you forever. {43:10} If we had not delayed, we could have gone and returned twice by now." {43:11} Their father Israel said to them, "If it must be so, then do this: Take some of the best products of the land in your bags and carry them down to the man as a gift—a little balm and a little honey, some spices and myrrh, nuts and almonds. {43:12} Take double the amount of money with you, for you must return the silver that was put back into the mouths of your sacks. Perhaps it was a mistake. {43:13} Take your brother also and go back to the man at once. {43:14} May God Almighty grant you mercy before the man so that he will let your other brother and Benjamin come back with you. As for me, if I am bereaved of my children, I am bereaved." {43:15} So the men took the gift and double the amount of money, along with Benjamin. They hurried down to Egypt and presented themselves to Joseph. {43:16} When Joseph saw Benjamin with them, he said to the steward of his house, "Take these men to my house, slaughter an animal and prepare a meal; they are to eat with me at noon." {43:17} The steward did as Joseph told him and took the men to Joseph's house. {43:18} Now the men were frightened when they were taken to his house. They thought, "We were brought here because of the silver that was put back into our sacks the first time. He wants to attack us and seize us as slaves and take our donkeys." {43:19} So they went up to Joseph's steward and spoke to him at the entrance to the house. {43:20} "We beg your pardon, our lord," they said. "We came down here the first time to buy food. {43:21} But when we came to the place where we lodged, we opened our sacks and each of us found our silver—the exact amount we had paid—back in our sacks. So we have brought it back with us. {43:22} We have also brought additional silver to buy food. We don't know who put our silver in our sacks." {43:23} "It's all right," he said. "Don't be afraid. Your God, the God of your father, has given you treasure in your sacks; I received your silver." Then he brought Simeon out to them. {43:24} The steward took the men into Joseph's house, gave them water to wash their feet, and provided fodder for their donkeys. {43:25} They prepared their gift for Joseph's arrival at noon, for they had heard that they were to eat there. {43:26} When Joseph came home, they presented to him the gifts they had brought into the house, and they bowed down before him to the ground. {43:27} He asked them how they were, and said, "Is your father well, the old man you told me about? Is he still alive?" {43:28} They answered, "Your servant, our father, is still alive and well." And they bowed down, prostrating themselves before him. {43:29} Joseph looked up and saw his brother Benjamin, his mother's son. "Is this your youngest brother, the one you told me about?" he asked. "God be gracious to you, my son." {43:30} Deeply moved at the sight of his brother, Joseph hurried out and looked for a place to weep. He went into his private room and wept there. {43:31} After he had washed his face, he came out and, controlling himself, said, "Serve the food." {43:32} They served him by himself, the brothers by themselves, and the Egyptians who ate with him by themselves, because Egyptians could not eat with Hebrews, for that is detestable to Egyptians. {43:33} The men had been seated before him in the order of their ages, from the firstborn to the youngest, and they looked at each other in astonishment. {43:34} When portions were served to them from Joseph's table, Benjamin's portion was five times larger than anyone else's. So they feasted and drank freely with him.

{44:1} He commanded the steward of his house, "Fill the men's sacks with as much food as they can carry, and put each man's money in the mouth of his sack. {44:2} Also, put my silver cup in the sack of the youngest, along with his money for the grain." The steward did as Joseph instructed. {44:3} As soon as morning came, the men were sent away with their donkeys. {44:4} When they had left the city and were not far off, Joseph said to his steward, "Go after the men; when you catch up with them, ask them, 'Why have you repaid good with evil? {44:5} Isn't this the cup my master drinks from and uses for divination (foretelling the future)? You have done wrong in doing this.'" {44:6} He caught up with them and said these same words. {44:7} They replied, "Why does my lord say such things? Far be it from your servants to do anything like that! {44:8} We even brought back the money we found in our sacks from Canaan. How could we steal silver or gold from your master's house? {44:9} If any of your servants is found with it, let him die, and we will become my lord's slaves." {44:10} "Very well," he said, "let it be as you say: whoever is found with it will become my slave; the rest of you will be free from blame." {44:11} Each of them quickly lowered his sack to the ground and opened it. {44:12} The steward searched, beginning with the oldest and ending with the youngest, and the cup was found in Benjamin's sack. {44:13} At this, they tore their clothes, loaded their donkeys, and returned to the city. {44:14} Judah and his brothers went to Joseph's house; he was still there, and they fell to the ground before him. {44:15} Joseph said to them, "What have you done? Don't you know that a man like me can surely practice divination?" {44:16} Judah said, "What can we say to my lord? What can we speak? How can we clear ourselves? God has uncovered your servant's guilt. We are now my lord's slaves, we and the one in whose possession the cup was found." {44:17} "Far be it from me to do that," Joseph replied. "The man who was found with the cup will become my slave; the rest of you can go in peace to your father." {44:18} Then Judah approached him and said, "Please, my lord, let your servant speak a word in your ears, and do not let your anger burn against your servant, for you are like Pharaoh himself. {44:19} My lord asked his servants, 'Do you have a father or a brother?' {44:20} We answered, 'We have an aged father, and there is a young boy born to him in his old age. His brother is dead, and he is the only one left of his mother, and his father loves him.' {44:21} Then you said to your servants, 'Bring him down to me so I can see him.' {44:22} But we said to my lord, 'The boy cannot leave his father; if he leaves him, his father will die.' {44:23} You said to your servants, 'Unless your youngest brother comes down with you, you will not see my face again.' {44:24} When we went back to your servant, our father, we told him what you had said. {44:25} Then our father said, 'Go back and buy us a little more food.' {44:26} But we said, 'We cannot go down. Only if our youngest brother goes with us will we go down; we cannot see the man's face unless our youngest brother is with us.' {44:27} Your servant, my father, said to us, 'You know that my wife bore me two sons. {44:28} One of them went away, and I said, "Surely he has been torn to pieces," and I have not seen him since. {44:29} If you take this one away from me and harm comes to him, you will bring my gray head down to the grave in misery.' {44:30} Now, if I go to your servant, my father, and the boy is not with us—seeing that his life is bound up with the boy's life— {44:31} when he sees that the boy is not there, he will die, and your servants will bring the gray head of your servant, our father, down to the grave in sorrow. {44:32} I guaranteed the boy's safety to my father, saying, 'If I do not bring him back to you, I will bear the blame before you, my father, all my life.' {44:33} Now, please let your servant remain here as my lord's slave in place of the boy, and let the boy go back with his brothers. {44:34} How can I go back to my father if the boy is not with me? I could not bear to see the misery that would come upon my father."

{45:1} Joseph could no longer control himself in front of all those standing around him, so he cried out, "Make everyone leave me!" No one remained with him as Joseph revealed his identity to his brothers. {45:2} He wept loudly, and the Egyptians and Pharaoh's household heard him. {45:3} Joseph said to his brothers, "I am Joseph! Is my father still alive?" His brothers were too terrified to answer him. {45:4} Joseph then said, "Come closer to me." They approached, and he said, "I am your brother Joseph, whom you sold into Egypt. {45:5} Don't be upset or angry with yourselves for selling me here, because God sent me ahead of you to save lives. {45:6} The famine has been in the land for two years, and there are still five years to come when there will be neither plowing nor harvesting. {45:7} God sent me ahead of you to ensure that you would have descendants on earth and to save your lives through a great deliverance. {45:8} So it wasn't you who sent me here, but God. He has made me a father to Pharaoh, lord of all his household, and ruler over all the land of Egypt. {45:9} Hurry and go to my father and say to him, 'This is what your son Joseph says: God has made me lord of all Egypt. Come down to me right away! {45:10} You will live in the land of Goshen, and you will be near me, you, your children, and your grandchildren, along with your flocks, herds, and everything you have. {45:11} I will provide for you there, because there are still five years of famine, otherwise you and your household and everything you have will become destitute.' {45:12} Look, your own eyes and the eyes of my brother Benjamin see that it is my mouth speaking to you. {45:13} You must tell my father about all my glory in Egypt and everything you have seen, and hurry to bring my father down here." {45:14} Then he threw his arms around his brother Benjamin and wept, and Benjamin embraced him, weeping. {45:15} He kissed all his brothers and wept over them, and afterward, his brothers talked with him. {45:16} The news reached Pharaoh's house that Joseph's brothers had come, and it pleased Pharaoh and his servants. {45:17} Pharaoh said to Joseph, "Tell your brothers this: Load your animals and go back to the land of Canaan; {45:18} take your father and your households and come back to me. I will give you the best of the land of Egypt, and you will eat from the fat of the land. {45:19} You are also commanded to take wagons from Egypt for your little ones and your wives, and bring your father back here. {45:20} Don't worry about your belongings, for the best of all Egypt will be yours." {45:21} The Israelites did this; Joseph gave them wagons as Pharaoh had commanded and provided them with provisions for the journey. {45:22} To each of them, he gave a change of clothes, but to Benjamin, he gave three hundred pieces of silver and five changes of clothes. {45:23} For his father, he sent the following: ten donkeys loaded with the good things of Egypt and ten female donkeys loaded with grain, bread, and meat for the journey. {45:24} Then he sent his brothers away, and as they left, he said, "Don't quarrel on the way!" {45:25} They went up from Egypt and came to their father Jacob in the land of Canaan. {45:26} They told him, "Joseph is still alive! He is governor over all the land of Egypt." Jacob was stunned, for he did not believe them. {45:27} But they told him everything Joseph had said to them, and when he saw the wagons Joseph had sent to carry him, the spirit of their father Jacob revived. {45:28} Israel said, "It's enough! My son Joseph is still alive. I will go and see him before I die."

{46:1} Israel set out with everything he had and arrived at Beersheba, where he offered sacrifices to the God of his father Isaac. {46:2} God spoke to Israel in visions during the night and said, "Jacob, Jacob!" He replied, "Here I am." {46:3} God said, "I am God, the God of your father. Do not be afraid to go down to Egypt, for I will make you into a great nation there. {46:4} I will go down with you to Egypt, and I will surely bring you back again, and Joseph will close your eyes when you die." {46:5} Jacob left Beersheba, and his sons carried their father Jacob, their little ones, and their wives in the wagons that Pharaoh had sent to transport them. {46:6} They took their livestock and the possessions they had acquired in the land of Canaan and came to Egypt, Jacob and all his descendants with him. {46:7} His sons, grandsons, daughters, and granddaughters, all his descendants, went with him into Egypt. {46:8} These are the names of the Israelites who went to Egypt with Jacob and his sons: Reuben, Jacob's firstborn. {46:9} The sons of Reuben were Hanoch, Phallu, Hezron, and Carmi. {46:10} The sons of Simeon were Jemuel, Jamin, Ohad, Jachin, Zohar, and Shaul, the son of a Canaanite woman. {46:11} The sons of Levi were Gershon, Kohath, and Merari. {46:12} The sons of Judah were Er, Onan, Shelah, Perez, and Zerah; but Er and Onan died in Canaan. The sons of Perez were Hezron and Hamul. {46:13} The sons of Issachar were Tola, Phuvah, Job, and Shimron. {46:14} The sons of Zebulun were Sered, Elon, and Jahleel. {46:15} These are the sons of Leah, whom she bore to Jacob in Padan-aram, along with his daughter Dinah. The total number of his sons and daughters was thirty-three. {46:16} The sons of Gad were Ziphion, Haggi, Shuni, Ezbon, Eri, Arodi, and Areli. {46:17} The sons of Asher were Jimnah, Ishuah, Isui, Beriah, and their sister Serah; the sons of Beriah were Heber and Malchiel. {46:18} These are the sons of Zilpah, whom Laban gave to his daughter Leah, and she bore these to Jacob, a total of sixteen souls. {46:19} The sons of Rachel, Jacob's wife, were Joseph and Benjamin. {46:20} In Egypt, Joseph had two sons: Manasseh and Ephraim, born to him by Asenath, the daughter of Potipherah, priest of On. {46:21} The sons of Benjamin were Bela, Becher, Ashbel, Gera, Naaman, Ehi, Rosh, Muppim, Huppim, and Ard. {46:22} These are the sons of Rachel born to Jacob, totaling fourteen souls. {46:23} The sons of Dan were Hushim. {46:24} The sons of Naphtali were Jahzeel, Guni, Jezer, and Shillem. {46:25} These are the sons of Bilhah, whom Laban gave to Rachel, and she bore these to Jacob, totaling seven souls. {46:26} All the souls that came with Jacob to Egypt, besides his sons' wives, were sixty-six. {46:27} The sons of Joseph, born to him in Egypt, were two souls. Therefore, the total number of the household of Jacob that came into Egypt was seventy. {46:28} He sent Judah ahead of him to Joseph to get directions to Goshen, and they arrived in the land of Goshen. {46:29} Joseph prepared his chariot and went to meet his father Israel in Goshen. When Joseph saw him, he embraced him and wept on his neck for a long time. {46:30} Israel said to Joseph, "Now that I have seen you and know you are alive, I can die in peace." {46:31} Joseph said to his brothers and his father's household, "I will go up and inform Pharaoh, saying, 'My brothers and my father's household, who were in Canaan, have come to me. {46:32} They are shepherds, for they raise livestock, and they have brought their flocks and herds and everything they own.' {46:33} When Pharaoh calls you and asks, 'What is your occupation?' {46:34} you should say, 'Your servants have been keepers of livestock from our youth until now, both we and our fathers,' so that you may dwell in the land of Goshen, because every shepherd is an abomination to the Egyptians."

{47:1} Joseph went and informed Pharaoh, saying, "My father and my brothers, along with their flocks, herds, and everything they own, have come from the land of Canaan, and they are now in the land of Goshen." {47:2} He took five of his brothers and presented them to Pharaoh. {47:3} Pharaoh asked his brothers, "What is your occupation?" They replied, "We are shepherds, both we and our fathers." {47:4} They added, "We have come to live in this land because your servants have no pasture for their flocks; the famine is severe in Canaan. Please let your servants settle in the land of Goshen." {47:5} Pharaoh spoke to Joseph, saying, "Your father and your brothers have come to you. {47:6} The land of Egypt is before you; settle your father and brothers in the best part of the land. Let them live in Goshen. If you know of any capable men among them, put them in charge of my livestock." {47:7} Joseph brought his father Jacob and presented him to Pharaoh, and Jacob blessed Pharaoh. {47:8} Pharaoh asked Jacob, "How old are you?" {47:9} Jacob replied, "The years of my pilgrimage are one hundred thirty. Few and hard have been the days of my life, and I have not reached the years of the lives of my fathers during their pilgrimages." {47:10} Then Jacob blessed Pharaoh and left his presence. {47:11} Joseph settled his father and brothers in Egypt, giving them property in the best part of the land, in the region of Rameses, as Pharaoh had commanded. {47:12} Joseph provided for his father, brothers, and all his father's household, giving them food according to their families. {47:13} There was no food in all the land because the famine was severe; both Egypt and Canaan were exhausted from hunger. {47:14} Joseph collected all the money that was found in Egypt and Canaan for the grain they bought and brought it into Pharaoh's palace. {47:15} When the money ran out in Egypt and Canaan, the Egyptians came to Joseph and said, "Give us food! Why should we die in your presence? Our money is gone." {47:16} Joseph replied, "If your money is gone, bring me your livestock, and I will give you food in exchange for your cattle." {47:17} They brought their livestock to Joseph, and he gave them food in exchange for horses, flocks, herds, and donkeys, feeding them for that year with bread in exchange for their animals. {47:18} At the end of that year, they came to him the next year and said, "We will not hide from my lord that our money is spent; my lord has our herds of cattle. There is nothing left in your sight except our bodies and our land. {47:19} Why should we die before you, both we and our land? Buy us and our land for bread, and we will be Pharaoh's servants. Give us seed so that we may live and not die, and that the land won't become desolate." {47:20} So Joseph bought all the land in Egypt for Pharaoh; the Egyptians sold their fields because the famine was overwhelming, and the land became Pharaoh's. {47:21} Joseph relocated the people to cities from one end of Egypt to the other. {47:22} He did not buy the land of the priests because they had a portion assigned to them by Pharaoh, and they received food from that portion; thus, they did not sell their land. {47:23} Then Joseph said to the people, "Look, I have bought you and your land for Pharaoh. Here is seed for you, and you may sow the land. {47:24} When the harvest comes, you must give a fifth of it to Pharaoh, and the other four-fifths will be yours for seed and for food for your households and for your little ones." {47:25} They replied, "You have saved our lives; may we find favor in your sight, and we will be Pharaoh's servants." {47:26} Joseph established it as a law in Egypt that Pharaoh would receive a fifth of the produce, except for the land of the priests, which did not become Pharaoh's. {47:27} Israel settled in Egypt, in the region of Goshen; they acquired property there, grew, and became exceedingly numerous. {47:28} Jacob lived in Egypt for seventeen years, so the total lifespan of Jacob was one hundred forty-seven years. {47:29} As the time drew near for Israel to die, he called for his son Joseph and said to him, "If I have found favor in your eyes, please put your hand under my thigh and promise to show me kindness and faithfulness; do not bury me in Egypt. {47:30} When I rest with my ancestors, carry me out of Egypt and bury me in their burial place." Joseph answered, "I will do as you have asked." {47:31} Jacob said, "Swear to me." So Joseph swore to him. Then Israel bowed down at the head of his bed.

{48:1} After these events, someone informed Joseph that his father was sick, so he took his two sons, Manasseh and Ephraim, with him. {48:2} Someone told Jacob, "Your son Joseph is coming to see you," and Israel strengthened himself and sat up on the bed. {48:3} Jacob said to Joseph, "God Almighty appeared to me at Luz in the land of Canaan and blessed me. {48:4} He said to me, 'I will make you fruitful and multiply you; I will make you a multitude of people and give this land to your descendants after you as an everlasting possession.' {48:5} Now your two sons, Ephraim and Manasseh, who were born to you in Egypt before I came to you, are mine; they will be as Reuben and Simeon to me. {48:6} Any children you have after them will be yours, and they will be named after their brothers in their inheritance. {48:7} As for me, when I came from Padan, Rachel died near me in the land of Canaan on the way when there was still a distance to Ephrath, and I buried her there on the way to Ephrath, which is Bethlehem." {48:8} Israel looked at Joseph's sons and asked, "Who are these?" {48:9} Joseph replied, "They are my sons, whom God has given me here." Israel said, "Bring them to me, and I will bless them." {48:10} Israel's eyes were dim with age, and he could not see well. Joseph brought them near, and he kissed and embraced them. {48:11} Israel said to Joseph, "I never expected to see your face, and now God has allowed me to see your children too." {48:12} Joseph removed them from between his knees and bowed down with his face to the ground. {48:13} He positioned Ephraim in his right hand toward Israel's left hand and Manasseh in his left hand toward Israel's right hand, bringing them near to him. {48:14} Israel stretched out his right hand and placed it on Ephraim's head, even though he was the younger, and his left hand on Manasseh's head, crossing his hands intentionally, for Manasseh was the firstborn. {48:15} Then he blessed Joseph, saying, "God, before whom my fathers Abraham and Isaac walked, the God who has been my shepherd all my life to this day, {48:16} the Angel who has redeemed me from all evil, bless these boys. May my name and the names of my fathers Abraham and Isaac be named on them, and may they grow into a multitude in the midst of the earth." {48:17} When Joseph saw that his father placed his right hand on Ephraim's head, he was displeased, so he held up his father's hand to move it from Ephraim's head to Manasseh's head. {48:18} Joseph said to his father, "Not so, my father! This one is the firstborn; put your right hand on his head." {48:19} But his father refused, saying, "I know, my son, I know. He too will become a people, and he too will be great. However, his younger brother will be greater than he, and his descendants will become a multitude of nations." {48:20} He blessed them that day, saying, "In you will Israel bless, saying, 'May God make you like Ephraim and Manasseh.'" Thus he placed Ephraim before Manasseh. {48:21} Israel said to Joseph, "Look, I am about to die, but God will be with you and will bring you back to the land of your fathers. {48:22} Furthermore, I give you one portion more than your brothers, which I took from the hand of the Amorite with my sword and my bow."

{49:1} Jacob called his sons together and said, "Gather yourselves so that I may tell you what will happen to you in the last days. {49:2} Gather together and listen, sons of Jacob; listen to your father Israel. {49:3} Reuben, you are my firstborn, my strength, and the first sign of my power, the peak of dignity and the peak of honor. {49:4} Unstable as water, you will not excel, for you went up to your father's bed and defiled it; he went up to my couch. {49:5} Simeon and Levi are brothers; they use weapons of violence. {49:6} O my soul, do not join their company; do not unite with their assembly, for in their anger they killed a man, and in their self-will they tore down a wall. {49:7} Cursed be their anger, for it was fierce, and their wrath, for it was cruel. I will divide them in Jacob and scatter them in Israel. {49:8} Judah, your brothers will praise you; your hand will be on the neck of your enemies; your father's children will bow down before you. {49:9} Judah is a lion's cub; you return from the prey, my son. He crouches down like a lion, and like an old lion; who dares to rouse him? {49:10} The scepter will not depart from Judah, nor a lawgiver from between his feet until Shiloh comes, and to him will be the gathering of the people. {49:11} He ties his foal to the vine and his donkey's colt to the choice vine; he washes his garments in wine and his robes in the blood of grapes. {49:12} His eyes will be red with wine, and his teeth white with milk. {49:13} Zebulun will dwell by the sea and will be a haven for ships, and his border will extend to Sidon. {49:14} Issachar is a strong donkey lying down between the saddlebags. {49:15} He sees that rest is good, and that the land is pleasant; so he bows his shoulder to bear burdens and becomes a servant to forced labor. {49:16} Dan will judge his people as one of the tribes of Israel. {49:17} Dan will be a snake on the path, a viper along the road, that bites the horse's heels, so that its rider falls backward. {49:18} I wait for your salvation, O LORD. {49:19} Gad will be attacked by a band of raiders, but he will attack them at their heels. {49:20} From Asher, his food will be rich, and he will provide royal delicacies. {49:21} Naphtali is a doe set free; he gives beautiful words. {49:22} Joseph is a fruitful vine, a fruitful vine near a spring, whose branches climb over the wall. {49:23} The archers have bitterly attacked him; they shot at him and harassed him. {49:24} But his bow remained steady, and his hands were made strong by the hands of the Mighty One of Jacob; from there is the Shepherd, the Stone of Israel. {49:25} By the God of your father, who helps you, and by the Almighty, who blesses you with blessings from the heavens above, blessings from the deep below, blessings from the breasts and the womb. {49:26} The blessings of your father surpass the blessings of my ancestors, up to the utmost bound of the everlasting hills. They will be on the head of Joseph, on the brow of the prince among his brothers. {49:27} Benjamin is a ravenous wolf; in the morning he devours the prey, and in the evening he divides the spoils. {49:28} All these are the twelve tribes of Israel, and this is what their father said to them and blessed them; he blessed each one according to his blessing. {49:29} He instructed them, saying, "I am about to be gathered to my people; bury me with my fathers in the cave in the field of Ephron the Hittite, {49:30} in the cave in the field of Machpelah, near Mamre, in the land of Canaan, which Abraham bought as a burial place from Ephron the Hittite. {49:31} There they buried Abraham and Sarah, his wife; there they buried Isaac and Rebekah, his wife; and there I buried Leah. {49:32} The field and the cave in it were purchased from the Hittites." {49:33} When Jacob finished commanding his sons, he drew his feet into the bed, took his last breath, and was gathered to his people.

{50:1} Joseph fell on his father's face, weeping over him and kissing him. {50:2} He commanded his servants, the physicians, to embalm his father, and the physicians embalmed Israel. {50:3} Forty days were required for this, for that is how long it takes to embalm, and the Egyptians mourned for him for seventy days. {50:4} When the days of mourning were over, Joseph spoke to the house of Pharaoh, saying, "If I have found favor in your eyes, please speak to Pharaoh for me, saying, {50:5} 'My father made me swear an oath, saying, "I am about to die; bury me in the tomb I dug for myself in the land of Canaan."' Now let me go up and bury my father, and I will return." {50:6} Pharaoh said, "Go up and bury your father as he made you swear." {50:7} So Joseph went to bury his father, and with him went all the servants of Pharaoh, the elders of his household, and all the elders of the land of Egypt, {50:8} as well as all the house of Joseph, his brothers, and his father's household; only their little ones, flocks, and herds were left in the land of Goshen. {50:9} They also took chariots and horsemen, and it was a very large company. {50:10} They came to the threshing floor of Atad, which is beyond the Jordan, and there they mourned with a great and very bitter lamentation, making a mourning for his father for seven days. {50:11} When the Canaanite inhabitants of the land saw the mourning at the threshing floor of Atad, they said, "This is a grievous mourning for the Egyptians." Therefore, the place was named Abel-mizraim, which is beyond the Jordan. {50:12} Joseph's sons did as he commanded them. {50:13} They carried him to the land of Canaan and buried him in the cave of the field of Machpelah, which Abraham had bought as a burial place from Ephron the Hittite, near Mamre. {50:14} After burying his father, Joseph returned to Egypt, along with his brothers and all who had gone up with him. {50:15} When Joseph's brothers saw that their father was dead, they said, "Joseph might hold a grudge against us and pay us back for all the wrong we did to him." {50:16} So they sent a message to Joseph, saying, "Your father instructed us before he died, {50:17} 'Say to Joseph: "I ask you to forgive the sins and wrongs of your brothers who treated you so badly."' Now, please forgive the sins of the servants of the God of your father." When Joseph heard this, he wept. {50:18} His brothers also came and threw themselves down before him, saying, "We are your servants." {50:19} Joseph said to them, "Don't be afraid. Am I in the place of God? {50:20} You intended to harm me, but God intended it for good to accomplish what is now being done, the saving of many lives. {50:21} So don't be afraid; I will provide for you and your children." He reassured them and spoke kindly to them. {50:22} Joseph stayed in Egypt, along with his father's household, and he lived a hundred and ten years. {50:23} Joseph saw the children of Ephraim to the third generation; the children of Machir, the son of Manasseh, were also brought up on Joseph's knees. {50:24} Joseph said to his brothers, "I am about to die, but God will surely come to your aid and take you out of this land to the land he promised on oath to Abraham, Isaac, and Jacob." {50:25} Joseph made the Israelites swear an oath and said, "God will surely come to your aid, and then you must carry my bones up from this place." {50:26} So Joseph died at the age of a hundred and ten, and they embalmed him and placed him in a coffin in Egypt.

The Second Book of Moses, called Exodus

{1:1} These are the names of the Israelites who came to Egypt; each man and his family came with Jacob. {1:2} Reuben, Simeon, Levi, and Judah, {1:3} Issachar, Zebulun, and Benjamin, {1:4} Dan, Naphtali, Gad, and Asher. {1:5} All the descendants of Jacob who came to Egypt numbered seventy; Joseph was already in Egypt. {1:6} Joseph died, along with all his brothers and that entire generation. {1:7} The Israelites were very fruitful, grew rapidly, multiplied, and became exceedingly strong; the land was filled with them. {1:8} Then a new king arose over Egypt who did not know Joseph. {1:9} He said to his people, "Look, the Israelites are more numerous and stronger than we are. {1:10} Let us deal wisely with them; otherwise, they may multiply further, and if a war breaks out, they might join our enemies, fight against us, and leave the land." {1:11} So they put slave drivers over them to oppress them with heavy burdens. They built treasure cities for Pharaoh, Pithom and Raamses. {1:12} But the more they oppressed them, the more they multiplied and spread. The Egyptians came to dread the Israelites. {1:13} The Egyptians forced the Israelites to work hard, {1:14} making their lives bitter with harsh labor in mortar and brick, and in all kinds of work in the fields. Their work was rigorous. {1:15} The king of Egypt spoke to the Hebrew midwives, one named Shiphrah and the other Puah: {1:16} He said, "When you help the Hebrew women give birth and see them on the birthing stools, if it's a boy, kill him; but if it's a girl, let her live." {1:17} But the midwives feared God and did not do what the king of Egypt commanded; they let the boys live. {1:18} The king of Egypt summoned the midwives and asked them, "Why have you done this and let the boys live?" {1:19} The midwives answered Pharaoh, "The Hebrew women are not like the Egyptian women; they are vigorous and give birth before the midwives arrive." {1:20} So God was kind to the midwives, and the people multiplied and became very numerous. {1:21} Because the midwives feared God, he gave them families of their own. {1:22} Then Pharaoh commanded all his people, "Every boy that is born, you must throw into the Nile River, but let every girl live."

{2:1} A man from the tribe of Levi married a Levite woman. {2:2} She became pregnant and gave birth to a son. When she saw that he was a beautiful child, she hid him for three months. {2:3} When she could no longer hide him, she made a basket from bulrushes, coated it with tar and pitch, and placed the child inside. She set it among the reeds at the riverbank. {2:4} His sister stood at a distance to see what would happen to him. {2:5} The daughter of Pharaoh came down to bathe in the river, and her maidens walked along the riverbank. When she saw the basket among the reeds, she sent her maid to fetch it. {2:6} When she opened it, she saw the baby, and he was crying. She felt sorry for him and said, "This is one of the Hebrew children." {2:7} Then his sister asked Pharaoh's daughter, "Shall I go and get a Hebrew woman to nurse the child for you?" {2:8} Pharaoh's daughter replied, "Yes, go." So the girl went and called the child's mother. {2:9} Pharaoh's daughter said to her, "Take this child and nurse him for me, and I will pay you." The woman took the child and nursed him. {2:10} When the child grew, she brought him to Pharaoh's daughter, and he became her son. She named him Moses, saying, "I drew him out of the water." {2:11} One day, when Moses had grown up, he went out to see his people and noticed their hard labor. He saw an Egyptian beating a Hebrew, one of his own people. {2:12} Looking around to make sure no one was watching, he killed the Egyptian and hid him in the sand. {2:13} The next day, he went out again and saw two Hebrews fighting. He asked the one in the wrong, "Why are you hitting your fellow Hebrew?" {2:14} The man replied, "Who made you a ruler and judge over us? Are you planning to kill me like you killed the Egyptian?" Moses was afraid and thought, "What I did must be known." {2:15} When Pharaoh heard about this, he tried to kill Moses. But Moses fled from Pharaoh and went to live in Midian, where he sat down by a well. {2:16} The priest of Midian had seven daughters. They came to draw water and fill the troughs to water their father's flock. {2:17} Some shepherds came and drove them away, but Moses stood up and helped them, watering their flock. {2:18} When they returned to their father Reuel, he asked, "How did you come back so soon today?" {2:19} They answered, "An Egyptian rescued us from the shepherds and drew enough water for us to water the flock." {2:20} He said to his daughters, "Where is he? Why did you leave the man behind? Invite him to have something to eat." {2:21} Moses agreed to stay with the man, who gave him his daughter Zipporah as a wife. {2:22} She bore him a son, and he named him Gershom, saying, "I have been a stranger in a foreign land." {2:23} After a long time, the king of Egypt died. The Israelites groaned in their slavery and cried out; their cry for help rose up to God because of their slavery. {2:24} God heard their groaning and remembered his covenant with Abraham, Isaac, and Jacob. {2:25} God looked on the Israelites and was concerned about them.

{3:1} Moses was tending the flock of Jethro, his father-in-law, the priest of Midian. He led the flock to the far side of the desert and came to the mountain of God, known as Horeb. {3:2} There, the angel of the LORD appeared to him in a flame of fire coming from the middle of a bush. Moses looked, and saw that the bush was on fire but not burned up. {3:3} So Moses said, "I will turn aside and see this amazing sight—why the bush is not burning up." {3:4} When the LORD saw that he had turned aside to look, God called to him from the middle of the bush, saying, "Moses, Moses!" He replied, "Here I am." {3:5} God said, "Do not come any closer. Take off your sandals, for the place where you are standing is holy ground." {3:6} Then He said, "I am the God of your father, the God of Abraham, the God of Isaac, and the God of Jacob." At this, Moses hid his face because he was afraid to look at God. {3:7} The LORD said, "I have indeed seen the suffering of my people in Egypt. I have heard their cries because of their slave drivers, and I am aware of their pain. {3:8} So I have come down to rescue them from the hand of the Egyptians and to bring them up out of that land to a good and spacious land, a land flowing with milk and honey— to the places of the Canaanites, Hittites, Amorites, Perizzites, Hivites, and Jebusites. {3:9} Now the cry of the Israelites has reached me, and I have seen how the Egyptians are oppressing them. {3:10} So now, go. I am sending you to Pharaoh to bring my people, the Israelites, out of Egypt." {3:11} But Moses said to God, "Who am I that I should go to Pharaoh and bring the Israelites out of Egypt?" {3:12} God answered, "I will be with you, and this will be the sign to you that it is I who have sent you: When you have brought the people out of Egypt, you will worship God on this mountain." {3:13} Moses said to God, "Suppose I go to the Israelites and say to them, 'The God of your fathers has sent me to you,' and they ask me, 'What is his name?' What shall I tell them?" {3:14} God said to Moses, "I AM WHO I AM. This is what you are to say to the Israelites: 'I AM has sent me to you.'" {3:15} God also said to Moses, "Say to the Israelites, 'The LORD, the God of your fathers—the God of Abraham, the God of Isaac, and the God of Jacob—has sent me to you. This is my name forever, the name you shall call me from generation to generation.' {3:16} Go, gather the elders of Israel together and say to them, 'The LORD, the God of your fathers, the God of Abraham, Isaac, and Jacob, has appeared to me and said: I have watched over you and have seen what has been done to you in Egypt. {3:17} And I have promised to bring you up out of your misery in Egypt to the land of the Canaanites, Hittites, Amorites, Perizzites, Hivites, and Jebusites, a land flowing with milk and honey.' {3:18} The elders of Israel will listen to you. Then you and the elders are to go to the king of Egypt and say to him, 'The LORD, the God of the Hebrews, has met with us. Let us take a three-day journey into the wilderness to offer sacrifices to the LORD our God.' {3:19} But I know that the king of Egypt will not let you go unless a mighty hand compels him. {3:20} So I will stretch out my hand and strike the Egyptians with all the wonders that I will perform among them. After that, he will let you go. {3:21} And I will make the Egyptians favorably disposed toward this people, so that when you leave, you will not go empty-handed. {3:22} Every woman is to ask her neighbor and any woman living in her house for articles of silver and gold, and for clothing, which you will put on your sons and daughters. And so you will plunder the Egyptians."

{4:1} Moses answered, "But what if they don't believe me or listen to me? They might say, 'The LORD did not appear to you.'" {4:2} The LORD asked him, "What is that in your hand?" He replied, "A staff." {4:3} The LORD said, "Throw it on the ground." So he threw it down, and it became a snake, and Moses ran away from it. {4:4} Then the LORD said to Moses, "Reach out your hand and grab it by the tail." Moses reached out and caught it, and it turned back into a staff in his hand. {4:5} This is so they will believe that the LORD, the God of their ancestors—the God of Abraham, Isaac, and Jacob—has appeared to you. {4:6} The LORD said, "Now put your hand inside your coat." He did so, and when he took it out, his hand was leprous (a skin disease) like snow. {4:7} Then the LORD said, "Put your hand back inside your coat." He did so, and when he took it out again, it was restored like the rest of his flesh. {4:8} If they do not believe you or pay attention to the first sign, they will believe the second sign. {4:9} If they do not believe even these two signs or listen to you, take some water from the Nile and pour it on dry ground. The water you take from the river will become blood on the dry ground. {4:10} Moses said to the LORD, "Pardon your servant, Lord. I have never been eloquent (fluent in speaking), neither in the past nor since you have spoken to your servant. I am slow of speech and tongue." {4:11} The LORD said to him, "Who gave humans their mouths? Who makes them deaf or mute? Who gives them sight or makes them blind? Is it not I, the LORD? {4:12} Now go; I will help you speak and will teach you what to say." {4:13} But Moses said, "Pardon your servant, Lord. Please send someone else." {4:14} Then the LORD's anger burned against Moses, and He said, "Isn't Aaron, your brother, the Levite, a good speaker? He is coming to meet you, and he will be glad to see you. {4:15} You shall speak to him and put words in his mouth; I will help both of you speak and will teach you what to do. {4:16} He will speak to the people for you, and it will be as if he were your mouth and you were God to him. {4:17} Take this staff in your hand so you can perform signs with it." {4:18} Moses went back to Jethro, his father-in-law, and said to him, "Let me go back to my people in Egypt to see if they are still alive." Jethro said, "Go in peace." {4:19} The LORD said to Moses in Midian, "Go back to Egypt, for all the men who wanted to kill you are dead." {4:20} So Moses took his wife and sons, put them on a donkey, and started back to Egypt. He took the staff of God in his hand. {4:21} The LORD said to Moses, "When you return to Egypt, see that you perform before Pharaoh all the wonders I have given you the power to do. But I will harden his heart so that he will not let the people go. {4:22} Then say to Pharaoh, 'This is what the LORD says: Israel is my firstborn son, {4:23} and I told you, 'Let my son go so he may worship me.' But you refused to let him go; therefore, I will kill your firstborn son.'" {4:24} At a lodging place on the way, the LORD met Moses and was about to kill him. {4:25} But Zipporah took a flint knife, cut off her son's foreskin, and touched Moses' feet with it. She said, "Surely you are a bridegroom of blood to me." {4:26} So the LORD let him go. At that time, she said, "You are a bridegroom of blood," referring to the circumcision. {4:27} The LORD said to Aaron, "Go into the wilderness to meet Moses." So he met Moses at the mountain of God and kissed him. {4:28} Then Moses told Aaron everything the LORD had said to him and all the signs He had commanded him to perform. {4:29} Moses and Aaron gathered all the elders of the Israelites, {4:30} and Aaron spoke all the words the LORD had spoken to Moses. He also performed the signs before the people. {4:31} And they believed. When they heard that the LORD was concerned about them and had seen their misery, they bowed down and worshiped.

{5:1} Afterward, Moses and Aaron went to Pharaoh and said, "This is what the LORD, the God of Israel, says: Let my people go so they may hold a feast for me in the wilderness." {5:2} Pharaoh replied, "Who is the LORD that I should obey him and let Israel go? I do not know the LORD, and I will not let Israel go." {5:3} They said, "The God of the Hebrews has met with us. Please let us go three days' journey into the desert to sacrifice to the LORD our God, or he may strike us with a plague or the sword." {5:4} Pharaoh said, "Moses and Aaron, why are you distracting the people from their work? Get back to your tasks!" {5:5} Pharaoh continued, "Look, the people of the land are now many, and you want them to stop working." {5:6} That same day, Pharaoh commanded the taskmasters and officers, {5:7} "You are no longer to provide straw for the people to make bricks as you did before. Let them go and gather straw for themselves. {5:8} But require them to make the same number of bricks as before; do not reduce their quota. They are lazy, and that's why they keep saying, 'Let us go and sacrifice to our God.' {5:9} Make them work harder so they pay no attention to false promises." {5:10} The taskmasters went out and spoke to the people, saying, "Pharaoh says I will not give you straw. {5:11} Go and get your own straw wherever you can find it, but your work will not be reduced at all." {5:12} So the people scattered throughout Egypt to gather stubble instead of straw. {5:13} The taskmasters pressed them, saying, "Complete your work, the daily quota, just as you did when there was straw." {5:14} The officers of the Israelites, whom Pharaoh's taskmasters had set over them, were beaten, and asked, "Why haven't you met your quota for making bricks yesterday and today as you did before?" {5:15} Then the Israelite officers went to Pharaoh and cried out, "Why are you treating your servants this way? {5:16} No straw is being given to your servants, and yet they tell us, 'Make bricks.' Look, we are being beaten, but the fault is with your own people." {5:17} Pharaoh said, "You are lazy, lazy! That's why you say, 'Let us go and sacrifice to the LORD.' {5:18} Now go and work. No straw will be given to you, yet you must produce the full quota of bricks." {5:19} The Israelite officers realized they were in trouble when they were told they could not reduce their daily brick quota. {5:20} They met Moses and Aaron as they were leaving Pharaoh, {5:21} and they said to them, "May the LORD look on you and judge you; you have made us a stench to Pharaoh and his officials, and have put a sword in their hand to kill us." {5:22} Moses returned to the LORD and said, "Lord, why have you brought trouble on this people? Why did you send me? {5:23} Ever since I went to Pharaoh to speak in your name, he has brought trouble on this people, and you have not rescued your people at all."

{6:1} Then the LORD said to Moses, "Now you will see what I will do to Pharaoh: he will let them go with a strong hand, and he will drive them out of his land with a strong hand." {6:2} God spoke to Moses and said, "I am the LORD. {6:3} I appeared to Abraham, Isaac, and Jacob as God Almighty, but I did not make my name known to them as JEHOVAH. {6:4} I also established my covenant with them to give them the land of Canaan, the land where they were foreigners. {6:5} I have heard the groaning of the Israelites whom the Egyptians are enslaving, and I have remembered my covenant. {6:6} Therefore, say to the Israelites: 'I am the LORD. I will bring you out from under the burdens of the Egyptians, and I will free you from their bondage. I will redeem you with an outstretched arm and with great judgments. {6:7} I will take you as my people, and I will be your God. You will know that I am the LORD your God, who brings you out from under the burdens of the Egyptians. {6:8} I will bring you into the land I swore to give to Abraham, Isaac, and Jacob, and I will give it to you as a heritage. I am the LORD.' {6:9} Moses spoke this to the Israelites, but they did not listen to him because of their broken spirit and harsh slavery. {6:10} The LORD spoke to Moses, saying, {6:11} "Go and speak to Pharaoh, king of Egypt, that he let the Israelites go out of his land." {6:12} Moses said to the LORD, "The Israelites have not listened to me; how then will Pharaoh listen to me? I am unskilled in speech." {6:13} The LORD spoke to Moses and Aaron, giving them a charge to the Israelites and to Pharaoh, king of Egypt, to bring the Israelites out of the land of Egypt. {6:14} These are the heads of their fathers' houses: The sons of Reuben, the firstborn of Israel: Hanoch, Pallu, Hezron, and Carmi; these are the families of Reuben. {6:15} The sons of Simeon are Jemuel, Jamin, Ohad, Jachin, Zohar, and Shaul, the son of a Canaanite woman; these are the families of Simeon. {6:16} These are the names of the sons of Levi according to their generations: Gershon, Kohath, and Merari; Levi lived for one hundred thirty-seven years. {6:17} The sons of Gershon are Libni and Shimi, according to their families. {6:18} The sons of Kohath are Amram, Izhar, Hebron, and Uzziel; Kohath lived for one hundred thirty-three years. {6:19} The sons of Merari are Mahali and Mushi; these are the families of Levi according to their generations. {6:20} Amram married his father's sister, Jochebed, and she bore him Aaron and Moses. Amram lived for one hundred thirty-seven years. {6:21} The sons of Izhar are Korah, Nepheg, and Zichri. {6:22} The sons of Uzziel are Mishael, Elzaphan, and Zithri. {6:23} Aaron married Elisheba, the daughter of Amminadab and sister of Naashon, and she bore him Nadab, Abihu, Eleazar, and Ithamar. {6:24} The sons of Korah are Assir, Elkanah, and Abiasaph; these are the families of the Korhites. {6:25} Eleazar, Aaron's son, married one of the daughters of Putiel, and she bore him Phinehas; these are the heads of the fathers' houses of the Levites according to their families. {6:26} These are the Aaron and Moses to whom the LORD said, "Bring the Israelites out of Egypt according to their divisions." {6:27} They spoke to Pharaoh, king of Egypt, to bring the Israelites out of Egypt; these are the same Moses and Aaron. {6:28} It happened on the day when the LORD spoke to Moses in the land of Egypt, {6:29} that the LORD said to Moses, "I am the LORD; speak to Pharaoh, king of Egypt, all that I say to you." {6:30} But Moses said before the LORD, "I am unskilled in speech, so how will Pharaoh listen to me?"

{7:1} The LORD said to Moses, "See, I have made you like a god to Pharaoh, and your brother Aaron will be your prophet. {7:2} You will speak all that I command you, and Aaron will speak to Pharaoh to let the Israelites go out of his land. {7:3} I will harden Pharaoh's heart and multiply my signs and wonders in the land of Egypt. {7:4} But Pharaoh will not listen to you, so that I can bring my judgments upon Egypt and free my armies, the Israelites, from the land of Egypt. {7:5} The Egyptians will know that I am the LORD when I stretch out my hand over Egypt and bring the Israelites out from among them. {7:6} Moses and Aaron did as the LORD commanded them; they did exactly that. {7:7} Moses was eighty years old, and Aaron was eighty-three years old when they spoke to Pharaoh. {7:8} The LORD spoke to Moses and Aaron, saying, {7:9} "When Pharaoh speaks to you and says, 'Show a miracle,' you shall say to Aaron, 'Take your rod and throw it before Pharaoh,' and it will become a serpent." {7:10} So Moses and Aaron went to Pharaoh and did just as the LORD commanded: Aaron threw down his rod before Pharaoh and his servants, and it became a serpent. {7:11} Then Pharaoh called for the wise men and sorcerers; the magicians of Egypt did the same with their enchantments. {7:12} Each one threw down his rod, and they became serpents, but Aaron's rod swallowed up their rods. {7:13} Yet Pharaoh's heart was hardened, and he did not listen to them, just as the LORD had said. {7:14} The LORD said to Moses, "Pharaoh's heart is hardened; he refuses to let the people go. {7:15} Go to Pharaoh in the morning; he will be by the water. Stand by the river's edge when he comes, and take in your hand the rod that turned into a serpent. {7:16} Say to him, 'The LORD God of the Hebrews has sent me to you, saying, "Let my people go so they may serve me in the wilderness." But up until now, you have not listened. {7:17} This is what the LORD says: "By this, you will know that I am the LORD: I will strike the waters of the river with the rod that is in my hand, and they will turn to blood. {7:18} The fish in the river will die, and the river will stink, and the Egyptians will not want to drink the water of the river." {7:19} The LORD said to Moses, "Tell Aaron to stretch out his hand over the waters of Egypt—over their streams, rivers, ponds, and all their pools—so that they may become blood. There will be blood throughout all the land of Egypt, in both wooden and stone vessels." {7:20} Moses and Aaron did as the LORD commanded; he raised the rod and struck the waters in the river, in front of Pharaoh and his servants, and all the waters in the river turned to blood. {7:21} The fish in the river died; the river stank, and the Egyptians could not drink the water of the river. There was blood throughout all the land of Egypt. {7:22} The magicians of Egypt did the same with their enchantments, and Pharaoh's heart was hardened; he did not listen to them, as the LORD had said. {7:23} Pharaoh turned and went into his house, and he did not pay attention to this either. {7:24} All the Egyptians dug around the river for water to drink, for they could not drink the water of the river. {7:25} Seven days passed after the LORD struck the river.

{8:1} The LORD said to Moses, "Go to Pharaoh and tell him, 'This is what the LORD says: Let my people go so they may serve me. {8:2} If you refuse to let them go, I will strike all your borders with frogs. {8:3} The river will produce frogs in abundance, and they will come into your house, your bedroom, your bed, the houses of your servants, your people, your ovens, and your kneading bowls. {8:4} The frogs will be everywhere, affecting you, your people, and all your servants." {8:5} The LORD said to Moses, "Tell Aaron to stretch out his hand with his rod over the streams, rivers, and ponds to bring frogs upon the land of Egypt." {8:6} Aaron stretched out his hand over the waters of Egypt, and the frogs came up and covered the land. {8:7} The magicians did the same with their enchantments and brought frogs upon the land. {8:8} Then Pharaoh called for Moses and Aaron and said, "Pray to the LORD to take away the frogs from me and my people, and I will let the people go so they can sacrifice to the LORD." {8:9} Moses said to Pharaoh, "You can have the honor of deciding: when shall I pray for you, your servants, and your people to remove the frogs, so they only remain in the river?" {8:10} Pharaoh said, "Tomorrow." Moses replied, "It will be as you said, so you may know that there is no one like the LORD our God. {8:11} The frogs will leave you, your houses, your servants, and your people; they will remain only in the river." {8:12} After Moses and Aaron left Pharaoh, Moses cried out to the LORD because of the frogs he had brought against Pharaoh. {8:13} The LORD did what Moses requested; the frogs died in the houses, villages, and fields. {8:14} They piled them up in heaps, and the land stank. {8:15} But when Pharaoh saw that there was relief, he hardened his heart and did not listen to them, as the LORD had said. {8:16} The LORD said to Moses, "Tell Aaron to stretch out his rod and strike the dust of the land so that it may become lice throughout all the land of Egypt." {8:17} They did this; Aaron stretched out his hand with his rod and struck the dust of the earth, and it became lice on both people and animals; all the dust turned to lice throughout Egypt. {8:18} The magicians tried to bring forth lice with their enchantments, but they could not. So there were lice on people and animals. {8:19} The magicians said to Pharaoh, "This is the finger of God," but Pharaoh's heart was hardened, and he did not listen to them, as the LORD had said. {8:20} The LORD said to Moses, "Get up early in the morning and stand before Pharaoh when he goes to the water. Say to him, 'This is what the LORD says: Let my people go so they may serve me. {8:21} If you will not let them go, I will send swarms of flies upon you, your servants, your people, and into your houses. The houses of the Egyptians will be full of flies, and the ground will be affected. {8:22} On that day, I will distinguish the land of Goshen, where my people live, so that no swarms of flies will be there. This way, you will know that I am the LORD in the midst of the earth. {8:23} I will set apart my people from your people; tomorrow this sign will occur." {8:24} The LORD did so; a grievous swarm of flies invaded Pharaoh's house, his servants' houses, and all of Egypt. The land was ruined because of the flies. {8:25} Pharaoh called for Moses and Aaron and said, "Go and sacrifice to your God in the land." {8:26} Moses replied, "It would not be right to do that, for we would be sacrificing what the Egyptians consider an abomination to the LORD our God. If we sacrifice what they see as abominable in front of them, they will stone us! {8:27} We will travel three days into the wilderness to sacrifice to the LORD our God, as he has commanded us." {8:28} Pharaoh said, "I will let you go to sacrifice to the LORD your God in the wilderness, but you must not go very far. Plead for me." {8:29} Moses said, "I will go out from you and plead with the LORD that the swarms of flies may leave Pharaoh, his servants, and his people tomorrow. But let Pharaoh not deceive us again by not letting the people go to sacrifice to the LORD." {8:30} Moses went out from Pharaoh and prayed to the LORD. {8:31} The LORD did what Moses asked and removed the swarms of flies from Pharaoh, his servants, and his people; not one remained. {8:32} But Pharaoh hardened his heart at this time also and would not let the people go.

{9:1} The LORD said to Moses, "Go to Pharaoh and tell him, 'This is what the LORD God of the Hebrews says: Let my people go so they can serve me. {9:2} If you refuse to let them go and continue to hold them, {9:3} I will bring the hand of the LORD upon your cattle in the field—the horses, donkeys, camels, cattle, and sheep—with a very severe plague. {9:4} The LORD will make a distinction between the cattle of Israel and the cattle of Egypt; none of the Israelites' animals will die. {9:5} The LORD has set a time: tomorrow the LORD will do this in the land." {9:6} The next day, the LORD did what He said, and all the cattle of Egypt died, but not one of the cattle belonging to the Israelites died. {9:7} Pharaoh sent to check and found that none of the Israelites' cattle were dead. Yet his heart was hardened, and he did not let the people go. {9:8} The LORD said to Moses and Aaron, "Take handfuls of ashes from the furnace and have Moses sprinkle it toward heaven in front of Pharaoh. {9:9} It will become fine dust throughout all Egypt, and it will cause festering boils on people and animals throughout the land." {9:10} They took the ashes and stood before Pharaoh. Moses sprinkled it toward heaven, and festering boils broke out on people and animals. {9:11} The magicians could not stand before Moses because of the boils; they were afflicted too, just like all the Egyptians. {9:12} The LORD hardened Pharaoh's heart, and he did not listen to them, as the LORD had told Moses. {9:13} The LORD said to Moses, "Get up early in the morning and stand before Pharaoh. Say to him, 'This is what the LORD God of the Hebrews says: Let my people go so they can serve me. {9:14} For this time I will bring all my plagues upon your heart, your servants, and your people, so you may know that there is no one like me in all the earth. {9:15} By now, I could have struck you and your people with a plague and wiped you off the earth. {9:16} But I have raised you up for this purpose: to show my power, so my name may be proclaimed in all the earth. {9:17} Are you still holding out against my people by refusing to let them go? {9:18} Tomorrow at this time, I will send a hailstorm unlike any that has occurred in Egypt since it became a nation. {9:19} Therefore, send word now to gather your livestock and all you have in the field, for every person and animal found in the field and not brought home will die when the hail comes down on them." {9:20} Those among Pharaoh's servants who feared the word of the LORD hurried to bring their servants and livestock indoors. {9:21} But those who ignored the word of the LORD left their servants and livestock in the field. {9:22} The LORD said to Moses, "Stretch out your hand toward heaven so hail may fall on all Egypt, on people, animals, and every plant in the field throughout the land." {9:23} Moses stretched out his rod toward heaven, and the LORD sent thunder and hail, and fire ran down to the ground; the LORD rained hail upon the land of Egypt. {9:24} The hail was so severe and mixed with fire that there had never been anything like it in all Egypt since it became a nation. {9:25} The hail struck everything in the field throughout Egypt, both people and animals; it beat down every plant in the field and shattered every tree. {9:26} Only in the land of Goshen, where the Israelites lived, was there no hail. {9:27} Pharaoh summoned Moses and Aaron and said to them, "I have sinned this time; the LORD is righteous, and I and my people are wicked. {9:28} Pray to the LORD for us, for the thunder and hail are enough. I will let you go, and you won't have to stay any longer." {9:29} Moses replied, "As soon as I leave the city, I will spread my hands toward the LORD. The thunder will cease, and there will be no more hail, so you will know that the earth is the LORD's. {9:30} But I know that you and your servants still do not fear the LORD God." {9:31} The flax and barley were destroyed, for the barley was in the ear and the flax was in bloom. {9:32} But the wheat and spelt were not destroyed because they were not yet ripe. {9:33} Moses left Pharaoh and went outside the city. He spread his hands toward the LORD, and the thunder and hail ceased, and rain no longer fell on the earth. {9:34} When Pharaoh saw that the rain, hail, and thunder had stopped, he sinned again and hardened his heart, he and his servants. {9:35} Pharaoh's heart was hardened, and he would not let the Israelites go, just as the LORD had said through Moses. Despite the severity of the plagues, Pharaoh's pride and defiance led him to reject God's command, further sealing his fate.

{10:1} The LORD said to Moses, "Go to Pharaoh, for I have hardened his heart and the hearts of his servants so that I can show these signs before him. {10:2} You will tell your children and grandchildren about what I have done in Egypt and the signs I performed among them, so that you may know that I am the LORD." {10:3} Moses and Aaron went to Pharaoh and said to him, "This is what the LORD God of the Hebrews says: How long will you refuse to humble yourself before me? Let my people go so they can serve me. {10:4} If you refuse to let them go, tomorrow I will bring locusts into your country. {10:5} They will cover the surface of the land so that no one will be able to see the ground. They will eat the remaining crops that survived the hail and every tree that grows in the fields. {10:6} They will fill your houses and the houses of all your servants and all the Egyptians—something your ancestors have never seen from the day they settled in this land until now." Then he turned and left Pharaoh. {10:7} Pharaoh's officials said to him, "How long will this man be a snare to us? Let the men go so they can serve the LORD their God. Do you not realize that Egypt is destroyed?" {10:8} Moses and Aaron were brought back to Pharaoh, and he said to them, "Go, serve the LORD your God, but who exactly will go?" {10:9} Moses answered, "We will go with our young and old, with our sons and daughters, and with our flocks and herds; we must hold a feast for the LORD." {10:10} Pharaoh replied, "The LORD be with you if I let you and your children go! Look, you have some evil plan in mind. {10:11} No! Only the men may go and serve the LORD, since that is what you asked for." And they were driven out from Pharaoh's presence. {10:12} The LORD said to Moses, "Stretch out your hand over the land of Egypt for the locusts so they may come up on the land and eat every plant left after the hail." {10:13} So Moses stretched out his staff over Egypt, and the LORD sent an east wind that blew all day and all night. When morning came, the east wind brought the locusts. {10:14} The locusts swarmed over the entire land of Egypt and settled in every area. They were extremely numerous; before them there had never been such locusts, nor will there be again. {10:15} They covered the surface of the whole land, making it dark, and they ate every plant in the land and all the fruit on the trees that the hail had left. Nothing green remained on the trees or in the fields throughout all Egypt. {10:16} Pharaoh quickly summoned Moses and Aaron and said, "I have sinned against the LORD your God and against you. {10:17} Please forgive my sin this time and pray to the LORD your God to take this death away from me." {10:18} Moses left Pharaoh and prayed to the LORD. {10:19} The LORD sent a strong west wind that took away the locusts and threw them into the Red Sea; not a single locust remained in all Egypt. {10:20} But the LORD hardened Pharaoh's heart, and he would not let the Israelites go. {10:21} The LORD said to Moses, "Stretch out your hand toward heaven so that darkness spreads over Egypt—darkness that can be felt." {10:22} So Moses stretched out his hand toward heaven, and there was thick darkness throughout Egypt for three days. {10:23} No one could see each other or move from their places for three days, yet all the Israelites had light in their homes. {10:24} Pharaoh summoned Moses and said, "Go, serve the LORD, but let your flocks and herds remain behind. Even your children may go with you." {10:25} Moses replied, "You must provide us with sacrifices and burnt offerings to offer to the LORD our God. {10:26} Our livestock must go with us; not a hoof will be left behind, for we will need some of them to serve the LORD our God. We won't know how we are to serve the LORD until we arrive there." {10:27} But the LORD hardened Pharaoh's heart, and he would not let them go. {10:28} Pharaoh said to him, "Get away from me! Watch yourself! Don't let me see your face again; the day you see my face, you will die." {10:29} Moses replied, "You are right; I will never see your face again."

{11:1} The LORD said to Moses, "I will bring one more plague upon Pharaoh and Egypt; after that, he will let you go. When he does let you go, he will drive you out completely. {11:2} Speak to the people and have each man ask his neighbor, and each woman ask her neighbor for silver and gold jewelry. {11:3} The LORD made the Israelites favorable in the eyes of the Egyptians. Also, Moses was very respected in the land of Egypt, both by Pharaoh's servants and by the people. {11:4} Moses said, "This is what the LORD says: About midnight, I will go throughout Egypt. {11:5} Every firstborn in the land of Egypt will die, from the firstborn of Pharaoh sitting on the throne to the firstborn of the female servant grinding grain, and all the firstborn of the livestock. {11:6} There will be a loud wail throughout all Egypt, such as has never been before and will never be again. {11:7} But among the Israelites, not even a dog will bark at any person or animal, so you will know that the LORD distinguishes between the Egyptians and Israel. {11:8} All your officials will come to me, bowing down and saying, 'Get out, you and all the people who follow you!' After that, I will leave." He left Pharaoh's presence in anger. {11:9} The LORD said to Moses, "Pharaoh will not listen to you, so that my wonders may be multiplied in the land of Egypt." {11:10} Moses and Aaron performed all these wonders before Pharaoh, but the LORD hardened Pharaoh's heart, and he would not let the Israelites leave his land.

{12:1} The LORD spoke to Moses and Aaron in the land of Egypt, saying, {12:2} "This month will be the beginning of months for you; it will be the first month of the year. {12:3} Tell the entire congregation of Israel that on the tenth day of this month, each man should take a lamb for his family, a lamb for each household. {12:4} If a household is too small for a lamb, he and his neighbor next to his house should share it, according to the number of people; each person should eat according to what they can handle. {12:5} Your lamb must be a year-old male without blemish; you may take it from the sheep or the goats. {12:6} You must keep it until the fourteenth day of the month, and then the whole assembly of the congregation of Israel must kill it at twilight. {12:7} They should take some of the blood and put it on the two doorposts and the top of the doorframe of the houses where they will eat it. {12:8} They will eat the meat that night, roasted over the fire, along with unleavened bread and bitter herbs. {12:9} Do not eat it raw or boiled in water, but roast it over the fire, including the head, legs, and inner organs. {12:10} Do not leave any of it until morning; whatever remains until morning must be burned in the fire. {12:11} This is how you are to eat it: with your clothes tucked in, sandals on your feet, and a staff in your hand; you are to eat it in haste. It is the LORD's Passover. {12:12} For I will pass through the land of Egypt that night and strike down every firstborn in Egypt, both people and animals, and I will bring judgment on all the gods of Egypt. I am the LORD. {12:13} The blood will be a sign for you on the houses where you are; when I see the blood, I will pass over you, and no destructive plague will touch you when I strike Egypt. {12:14} This day will be a memorial for you, and you must celebrate it as a festival to the LORD for generations to come; you are to celebrate it as a lasting ordinance. {12:15} For seven days you must eat unleavened bread; on the first day, remove the yeast from your houses. Anyone who eats leavened bread from the first day through the seventh must be cut off from Israel. {12:16} On the first and seventh days, you are to hold a sacred assembly; no work may be done on those days except to prepare food for everyone to eat. {12:17} You must observe the Festival of Unleavened Bread, because it was on this very day that I brought your divisions out of Egypt. Celebrate this day as a lasting ordinance for generations to come. {12:18} In the first month, on the fourteenth day at twilight, you must eat unleavened bread until the twenty-first day of the month at twilight. {12:19} For seven days, no yeast is to be found in your houses; anyone who eats anything with yeast must be cut off from the congregation of Israel, whether they are a foreigner or native-born. {12:20} You must not eat anything with yeast; wherever you live, you must eat unleavened bread. {12:21} Then Moses called for all the elders of Israel and said to them, "Go and select a lamb for your families, and kill the Passover lamb. {12:22} Take a bunch of hyssop, dip it in the blood in the basin, and put some of the blood on the top and sides of the doorframe; none of you should go out of the door of your house until morning. {12:23} The LORD will pass through to strike down the Egyptians, and when he sees the blood on the top and sides of the doorframe, the LORD will pass over that doorway and will not permit the destroyer to enter your houses and strike you down. {12:24} You must observe this as an ordinance for you and your descendants forever. {12:25} When you enter the land the LORD will give you as he promised, you must keep this service. {12:26} When your children ask you, 'What does this ceremony mean to you?' {12:27} tell them, 'It is the Passover sacrifice to the LORD, who passed over the houses of the Israelites in Egypt and spared our homes when he struck down the Egyptians.' Then the people bowed down and worshiped. {12:28} The Israelites did just as the LORD had commanded Moses and Aaron. {12:29} At midnight, the LORD struck down all the firstborn in Egypt, from the firstborn of Pharaoh who sat on the throne to the firstborn of the prisoner in the dungeon, and the firstborn of all the livestock as well. {12:30} Pharaoh and all his officials and all the Egyptians got up during the night, and there was loud wailing in Egypt, for there was not a house without someone dead. {12:31} During the night, Pharaoh summoned Moses and Aaron and said, "Up! Leave my people, you and the Israelites! Go, worship the LORD as you have requested. {12:32} Take your flocks and herds, as you have said, and go. And also bless me." {12:33} The Egyptians urged the people to hurry and leave the country, for otherwise, they said, "We will all die!" {12:34} So the people took their dough before the yeast was added and carried it on their shoulders, wrapped in clothing. {12:35} The Israelites did as Moses instructed and asked the Egyptians for articles of silver and gold and for clothing. {12:36} The LORD made the Egyptians favorable toward the Israelites, and they gave them what they asked for; so they plundered the Egyptians. {12:37} The Israelites journeyed from Rameses to Succoth, about six hundred thousand men on foot, besides women and children. {12:38} A mixed crowd also went up with them, along with a large number of livestock, both flocks and herds. {12:39} They baked the dough they had brought out of Egypt into unleavened bread because it had not been leavened; they were driven out of Egypt and did not have time to prepare food for themselves. {12:40} The time the Israelites had lived in Egypt was 430 years. {12:41} At the end of that time, on the very day, all the LORD's divisions left Egypt. {12:42} Because the LORD kept vigil that night to bring them out of Egypt, on this night all the Israelites are to keep vigil to honor the LORD for generations to come. {12:43} The LORD said to Moses and Aaron, "This is the ordinance of the Passover. No foreigner is to eat of it. {12:44} Any slave you have bought may eat it after you have circumcised him. {12:45} But a temporary resident or a hired worker may not eat it. {12:46} It must be eaten inside one house; take none of the meat outside the house. Do not break any of the bones. {12:47} The whole community of Israel must celebrate it. {12:48} If an alien resides among you and wants to celebrate the LORD's Passover, all the males in his household must be circumcised, and then he may take part like one born in the land. No uncircumcised male may eat it. {12:49} The same law applies to the native-born and to the alien residing among you." {12:50} All the Israelites did just what the LORD had commanded Moses and Aaron. {12:51} And on that very day, the LORD brought the Israelites out of Egypt by their divisions.

{13:1} The LORD spoke to Moses, saying, {13:2} "Consecrate (set apart as holy) to me every firstborn male among the Israelites, both human and animal; they belong to me." {13:3} Moses said to the people, "Remember this day when you came out of Egypt, out of the land of slavery, because the LORD brought you out with a mighty hand. Do not eat any leavened bread. {13:4} You came out on this very day in the month of Abib. {13:5} When the LORD brings you into the land of the Canaanites, Hittites, Amorites, Hivites, and Jebusites, the land he promised to give your ancestors, a land flowing with milk and honey, you must observe this ceremony in this month. {13:6} For seven days, eat unleavened bread, and on the seventh day, hold a festival to the LORD. {13:7} For seven days, you must eat unleavened bread; there must be no leavened bread or yeast seen anywhere in your territory. {13:8} On that day, tell your child, 'This is done because of what the LORD did for me when I came out of Egypt.' {13:9} It will be a sign for you on your hand and a reminder on your forehead so that the LORD's law may be on your lips, because with a mighty hand the LORD brought you out of Egypt. {13:10} You must keep this ordinance at the appointed time from year to year. {13:11} When the LORD brings you into the land of the Canaanites, as he promised you and your ancestors, {13:12} you must set apart for the LORD every firstborn male that opens the womb, and every firstborn male animal; the males belong to the LORD. {13:13} You must redeem every firstborn donkey with a lamb, but if you do not redeem it, you must break its neck. Redeem every firstborn among your children. {13:14} In the future, when your son asks you, 'What does this mean?' tell him, 'With a mighty hand, the LORD brought us out of Egypt, out of the land of slavery. {13:15} When Pharaoh stubbornly refused to let us go, the LORD killed all the firstborn in Egypt, both people and animals. That is why I sacrifice to the LORD the firstborn males of everything that opens the womb, and redeem each of my firstborn sons.' {13:16} This will serve as a sign on your hand and as frontlets (small boxes containing scripture) between your eyes, because with a mighty hand the LORD brought us out of Egypt." {13:17} When Pharaoh let the people go, God did not lead them through the road that goes through the Philistine country, although it was shorter. For God said, "If they face war, they might change their minds and return to Egypt." {13:18} So God led the people around by the desert road toward the Red Sea, and the Israelites went up out of Egypt armed for battle. {13:19} Moses took the bones of Joseph with him, because Joseph had made the Israelites swear an oath, saying, "God will surely come to your aid, and you must carry my bones up from this place." {13:20} After leaving Succoth, they camped at Etham on the edge of the wilderness. {13:21} The LORD went ahead of them in a pillar of cloud to guide them on their way, and by night in a pillar of fire to give them light, so they could travel by day or night. {13:22} Neither the pillar of cloud by day nor the pillar of fire by night left its place in front of the people.

{14:1} The LORD spoke to Moses, saying, {14:2} "Tell the Israelites to turn back and camp near Pihahiroth, between Migdol and the sea, across from Baalzephon. They should camp by the sea. {14:3} Pharaoh will think the Israelites are wandering around the land, trapped by the wilderness. {14:4} I will harden Pharaoh's heart so he will pursue them, and I will gain glory over Pharaoh and all his army. Then the Egyptians will know that I am the LORD." And they did as instructed. {14:5} When the king of Egypt was told that the people had fled, he and his officials changed their minds about the Israelites, saying, "What have we done? We let Israel go, freeing them from serving us!" {14:6} So he prepared his chariot and took his army with him. {14:7} He took six hundred of his best chariots and all the other chariots of Egypt, each with its commander. {14:8} The LORD hardened Pharaoh's heart, and he pursued the Israelites, who were marching out boldly. {14:9} The Egyptians chased after them, all of Pharaoh's horses and chariots, along with his horsemen and troops, and caught up with them as they camped by the sea near Pihahiroth, opposite Baalzephon. {14:10} As Pharaoh approached, the Israelites looked up and saw the Egyptians marching after them. They were terrified and cried out to the LORD. {14:11} They said to Moses, "Did you bring us out here to die in the wilderness because there were no graves in Egypt? What have you done to us by bringing us out of Egypt? {14:12} Didn't we tell you in Egypt to leave us alone so we could serve the Egyptians? It would have been better for us to serve the Egyptians than to die in the wilderness." {14:13} Moses answered the people, "Do not be afraid. Stand firm and see the deliverance the LORD will bring you today. The Egyptians you see today, you will never see again. {14:14} The LORD will fight for you; you need only to be still." {14:15} Then the LORD said to Moses, "Why are you crying out to me? Tell the Israelites to move on. {14:16} Raise your staff and stretch out your hand over the sea to divide the waters so the Israelites can go through the sea on dry ground. {14:17} I will harden the hearts of the Egyptians so they will go in after them, and I will gain glory through Pharaoh and all his army, through his chariots and horsemen. {14:18} The Egyptians will know that I am the LORD when I gain glory through Pharaoh, his chariots, and his horsemen." {14:19} Then the angel of God, who had been traveling in front of Israel's army, withdrew and went behind them. The pillar of cloud moved from in front and stood behind them. {14:20} It came between the armies of Egypt and Israel. The cloud brought darkness to the one side and light to the other side, so neither went near the other all night. {14:21} Then Moses stretched out his hand over the sea, and the LORD drove the sea back with a strong east wind all night and turned it into dry land; the waters were divided. {14:22} The Israelites went through the sea on dry ground, with walls of water on their right and left. {14:23} The Egyptians pursued them and went after them into the sea, all of Pharaoh's horses, chariots, and horsemen. {14:24} During the last watch of the night, the LORD looked down from the pillar of fire and cloud at the Egyptian army and threw it into confusion. {14:25} He jammed the wheels of their chariots so they had difficulty driving. The Egyptians said, "Let's get away from the Israelites! The LORD is fighting for them against Egypt." {14:26}

Then the LORD said to Moses, "Stretch out your hand over the sea so the waters may flow back over the Egyptians and their chariots and horsemen." {14:27} Moses stretched out his hand over the sea, and at daybreak, the sea went back to its place. The Egyptians were fleeing toward it, and the LORD swept them into the sea. {14:28} The water flowed back and covered the chariots and horsemen—the entire army of Pharaoh that had followed the Israelites into the sea. Not one of them survived. {14:29} But the Israelites went through the sea on dry ground, with the waters a wall on their right and on their left. {14:30} That day, the LORD saved Israel from the hands of the Egyptians, and Israel saw the Egyptians lying dead on the shore. {14:31} When the Israelites saw the great power the LORD displayed against the Egyptians, the people feared the LORD and put their trust in him and in Moses, his servant.

{15:1} Then Moses and the Israelites sang this song to the LORD: "I will sing to the LORD, for he has triumphed gloriously; he has thrown the horse and its rider into the sea. {15:2} The LORD is my strength and my song; he has become my salvation. He is my God, and I will praise him; he is my father's God, and I will exalt him. {15:3} The LORD is a warrior; the LORD is his name. {15:4} He has hurled Pharaoh's chariots and army into the sea; his elite troops were drowned in the Red Sea. {15:5} The depths have covered them; they sank to the bottom like a stone. {15:6} Your right hand, LORD, is glorious in power; your right hand, LORD, shatters the enemy. {15:7} In the greatness of your majesty, you overthrow those who rise up against you; you unleash your burning anger, and it consumes them like stubble. {15:8} With the blast of your nostrils, the waters were piled up; the floods stood upright like a wall, and the depths congealed in the heart of the sea. {15:9} The enemy boasted, 'I will pursue, I will overtake them, I will divide the spoils; I will be satisfied with them; I will draw my sword; my hand will destroy them.' {15:10} But you blew with your wind, and the sea covered them; they sank like lead in the mighty waters. {15:11} Who among the gods is like you, LORD? Who is like you—glorious in holiness, awesome in praise, doing wonders? {15:12} You stretched out your right hand, and the earth swallowed them. {15:13} In your unfailing love, you will lead the people you have redeemed; in your strength, you will guide them to your holy dwelling. {15:14} The nations will hear and tremble; anguish will grip the people of Philistia. {15:15} The chiefs of Edom will be terrified; the leaders of Moab will be seized with trembling; all the inhabitants of Canaan will melt away. {15:16} Terror and dread will fall on them; by the power of your arm, they will be as still as a stone until your people pass by, LORD, until the people you bought pass by. {15:17} You will bring them in and plant them on the mountain of your inheritance, the place, LORD, you made for your dwelling, the sanctuary, LORD, your hands established. {15:18} The LORD will reign forever and ever. {15:19} For Pharaoh's horse went into the sea with his chariots and horsemen, but the LORD brought the waters of the sea back over them; however, the Israelites went through the sea on dry ground. {15:20} Then Miriam the prophetess, Aaron's sister, took a tambourine in her hand, and all the women followed her with tambourines and dancing. {15:21} Miriam sang to them, "Sing to the LORD, for he has triumphed gloriously; he has thrown the horse and its rider into the sea." {15:22} So Moses led Israel from the Red Sea, and they went into the wilderness of Shur. They traveled for three days in the wilderness without finding water. {15:23} When they came to Marah, they could not drink the water there because it was bitter; that is why the place was called Marah. {15:24} The people grumbled against Moses, saying, "What are we to drink?" {15:25} Moses cried out to the LORD, and the LORD showed him a piece of wood. When he threw it into the water, the water became sweet. There the LORD issued a ruling and instruction for them, and there he tested them. {15:26} He said, "If you listen carefully to the LORD your God and do what is right in his eyes, if you pay attention to his commands and keep all his decrees, I will not bring on you any of the diseases I brought on the Egyptians, for I am the LORD who heals you." {15:27} Then they came to Elim, where there were twelve springs and seventy palm trees, and they camped there near the water.

{16:1} They set out from Elim, and the entire Israelite community arrived at the wilderness of Sin, which is between Elim and Sinai, on the fifteenth day of the second month after leaving Egypt. {16:2} The whole Israelite community complained against Moses and Aaron in the wilderness. {16:3} They said to them, "If only we had died by the LORD's hand in Egypt! There we sat around pots of meat and ate all the bread we wanted. But you have brought us out into this wilderness to starve this entire assembly to death." {16:4} Then the LORD said to Moses, "I will rain down bread from heaven for you. The people are to go out each day and gather enough for that day. In this way, I will test them to see whether they will follow my instructions. {16:5} On the sixth day, they are to prepare what they bring in, and it will be twice as much as they gather on the other days." {16:6} So Moses and Aaron said to all the Israelites, "In the evening you will know that it was the LORD who brought you out of Egypt, {16:7} and in the morning you will see the glory of the LORD because he has heard your grumbling against him. Who are we, that you should grumble against us?" {16:8} Moses also said, "You will know that it was the LORD who gave you meat to eat in the evening and all the bread you want in the morning, because he has heard your grumbling against him. You are not grumbling against us, but against the LORD." {16:9} Then Moses said to Aaron, "Say to the entire Israelite community, 'Come before the LORD, for he has heard your grumbling.'" {16:10} As Aaron spoke to the whole Israelite community, they looked toward the wilderness, and there was the glory of the LORD appearing in the cloud. {16:11} The LORD said to Moses, {16:12} "I have heard the grumbling of the Israelites. Tell them, 'At twilight you will eat meat, and in the morning you will be filled with bread. Then you will know that I am the LORD your God.'" {16:13} That evening, quail came and covered the camp, and in the morning there was a layer of dew around the camp. {16:14} When the dew was gone, thin flakes like frost appeared on the ground. {16:15} When the Israelites saw it, they said to each other, "What is it?" (For they did not know what it was.) Moses said to them, "It is the bread the LORD has given you to eat. {16:16} This is what the LORD has commanded: 'Everyone is to gather as much as they need. Take an omer for each person you have in your tent.'" {16:17} The Israelites did as they were told; some gathered much, some little. {16:18} And when they measured it by the omer, the one who gathered much did not have too much, and the one who gathered little did not have too little. Everyone gathered just as much as they needed. {16:19} Then Moses said to them, "No one is to keep any of it until morning." {16:20} However, some of them paid no attention to Moses; they kept part of it until morning, but it was full of maggots and began to smell. So Moses was angry with them. {16:21} Each morning everyone gathered as much as they needed, and when the sun grew hot, it melted away. {16:22} On the sixth day, they gathered twice as much, two omers for each person, and all the leaders of the community came and reported this to Moses. {16:23} He said to them, "This is what the LORD commanded: 'Tomorrow will be a day of rest, a holy Sabbath to the LORD. Bake what you want to bake and boil what you want to boil. Save whatever is left and keep it until morning.'" {16:24} So they saved it until morning, as Moses commanded, and it did not stink or have any maggots in it. {16:25} "Eat it today," Moses said, "for today is a Sabbath to the LORD. You will not find any of it on the ground today. {16:26} Six days you are to gather it, but on the seventh day, the Sabbath, there will not be any." {16:27} Nevertheless, some of the people went out on the seventh day to gather it, but they found none. {16:28} Then the LORD said to Moses, "How long will you refuse to keep my commands and my instructions? {16:29} Bear in mind that the LORD has given you the Sabbath; that is why on the sixth day he gives you bread for two days. Everyone is to stay where they are on the seventh day; no one is to go out." {16:30} So the people rested on the seventh day. {16:31} The Israelites called the bread manna. It was like coriander seed, white, and the taste of it was like wafers made with honey. {16:32} Moses said, "This is what the LORD has commanded: 'Take an omer of manna and keep it for the generations to come so they can see the bread I gave you to eat in the wilderness when I brought you out of Egypt.'" {16:33} So Moses said to Aaron, "Take a jar and put an omer of manna in it. Then place it before the LORD to be kept for the generations to come." {16:34} As the LORD commanded Moses, Aaron put the manna with the tablets of the covenant law, so it might be preserved. {16:35} The Israelites ate manna for forty years until they came to a land that was settled; they ate manna until they reached the border of Canaan. {16:36} (An omer is one-tenth of an ephah.) {16:37} This manna served as a constant reminder of God's provision during their wilderness journey, a sign of His faithfulness to sustain them.

{17:1} The entire Israelite community traveled from the wilderness of Sin, following the LORD's instructions, and camped at Rephidim, but there was no water for the people to drink. {17:2} So the people argued with Moses, saying, "Give us water to drink." Moses replied, "Why are you arguing with me? Why are you testing the LORD?" {17:3} The people were thirsty and complained against Moses, saying, "Why did you bring us out of Egypt to kill us, our children, and our livestock with thirst?" {17:4} Moses cried out to the LORD, "What should I do with these people? They are almost ready to stone me." {17:5} The LORD said to Moses, "Walk ahead of the people. Take some of the elders of Israel with you, and take in your hand the staff you used to strike the Nile, and go. {17:6} I will stand there before you by the rock at Horeb. Strike the rock, and water will come out of it for the people to drink." So Moses did this in the sight of the elders of Israel. {17:7} He named the place Massah (Testing) and Meribah (Quarreling) because the Israelites argued and tested the LORD, saying, "Is the LORD among us or not?" {17:8} Then Amalek came and fought against Israel at Rephidim. {17:9} Moses said to Joshua, "Choose some men and go out to fight Amalek. Tomorrow I will stand on top of the hill with the staff of God in my hand." {17:10} So Joshua did as Moses told him and fought against Amalek, while Moses, Aaron, and Hur went up to the top of the hill. {17:11} When Moses held up his hands, Israel prevailed, but when he lowered his hands, Amalek prevailed. {17:12} When Moses' hands grew heavy, they took a stone and put it under him, and he sat on it. Aaron and Hur held up his hands, one on one side and the other on the other side, so his hands remained steady until sunset. {17:13} Joshua defeated Amalek and his people with the sword. {17:14} The LORD said to Moses, "Write this down as a memorial in a book and recite it to Joshua, because I will completely blot out the memory of Amalek from under heaven." {17:15} Moses built an altar and named it The LORD Is My Banner. {17:16} He said, "The LORD has sworn that the LORD will have war with Amalek from generation to generation."

{18:1} When Jethro, the priest of Midian and Moses' father-in-law, heard about all that God had done for Moses and for Israel, His people, and how the LORD had brought Israel out of Egypt, {18:2} Jethro took Zipporah, Moses' wife, whom he had sent back, {18:3} along with her two sons. The name of one was Gershom, for Moses said, "I have been an outsider in a foreign land," {18:4} and the name of the other was Eliezer, for he said, "The God of my father was my help and rescued me from Pharaoh's sword." {18:5} Jethro, Moses' father-in-law, came with his sons and wife to Moses in the wilderness, where he was camped at the mountain of God. {18:6} He said to Moses, "I, your father-in-law Jethro, have come to you with your wife and her two sons." {18:7} Moses went out to meet his father-in-law, bowed down, and kissed him. They asked each other how they were doing and went into the tent. {18:8} Moses told his father-in-law everything the LORD had done to Pharaoh and the Egyptians for Israel's sake, and all the hardships they had faced along the way, and how the LORD had delivered them. {18:9} Jethro rejoiced for all the goodness the LORD had shown to Israel, rescuing them from the Egyptians. {18:10} Jethro said, "Blessed be the LORD, who has rescued you from the Egyptians and Pharaoh, and has delivered the people from under the Egyptians' control." {18:11} Now I know that the LORD is greater than all other gods because He was victorious in the matters where they acted arrogantly. {18:12} Jethro, Moses' father-in-law, offered a burnt offering and sacrifices to God, and Aaron and all the elders of Israel came to eat bread with Moses' father-in-law before God. {18:13} The next day, Moses sat to judge the people, and they stood around him from morning until evening. {18:14} When Jethro saw what Moses was doing for the people, he asked, "What is this you are doing for the people? Why do you sit alone, while all the people stand around you from morning until evening?" {18:15} Moses answered his father-in-law, "Because the people come to me to seek God's guidance. {18:16} When they have a dispute, they come to me, and I decide between them and inform them of God's laws and instructions." {18:17} Jethro replied, "What you are doing is not good. {18:18} You will wear yourself out, and the people as well; this task is too heavy for you to handle alone." {18:19} Now listen to me; I will give you some advice, and God will be with you. You should represent the people before God and bring their cases to Him. {18:20} Teach them the statutes and laws, and show them how they should live and what they should do. {18:21} Furthermore, you should select capable men from all the people—men who fear God, who are trustworthy and hate dishonest gain—and appoint them as leaders over the people, to be rulers of thousands, hundreds, fifties, and tens. {18:22} Let them judge the people at all times; have them bring the difficult cases to you, but let them decide the smaller cases themselves. This will make it easier for you, and they will bear the burden with you. {18:23} If you do this and God so commands you, you will be able to endure, and all these people will return home in peace." {18:24} So Moses listened to his father-in-law and did everything he said. {18:25} Moses chose capable men from all Israel and made them leaders over the people, rulers of thousands, hundreds, fifties, and tens. {18:26} They judged the people at all times; the difficult cases they brought to Moses, but the smaller cases they decided themselves. {18:27} Then Moses let his father-in-law depart, and Jethro went back to his own land.

{19:1} In the third month after the children of Israel had left Egypt, they arrived in the wilderness of Sinai on the same day. {19:2} They had left Rephidim and come to the desert of Sinai, where they camped at the foot of the mountain. {19:3} Moses went up to God, and the LORD called to him from the mountain, saying, "This is what you should say to the descendants of Jacob and tell the people of Israel: {19:4} You have seen what I did to the Egyptians and how I carried you on eagles' wings and brought you to Myself. {19:5} Now, if you will truly obey My voice and keep My covenant, you will be My treasured possession among all people, for the whole earth is Mine. {19:6} You will be for Me a kingdom of priests and a holy nation. These are the words you should speak to the people of Israel." {19:7} Moses came and called the elders of the people and presented to them all the words the LORD had commanded him. {19:8} All the people answered together and said, "All that the LORD has spoken, we will do." Moses returned the words of the people to the LORD. {19:9} The LORD said to Moses, "I will come to you in a thick cloud so that the people may hear when I speak with you and always believe you." Moses reported the words of the people to the LORD. {19:10} The LORD said to Moses, "Go to the people and consecrate them today and tomorrow; have them wash their clothes, {19:11} and be ready for the third day, because on the third day the LORD will come down in the sight of all the people on Mount Sinai. {19:12} Set limits for the people around the mountain and tell them, 'Be careful not to go up the mountain or touch its edge. Anyone who touches the mountain shall be put to death. {19:13} No hand shall touch it; they shall be stoned or shot with arrows; whether animal or human, they shall not live.' When the trumpet sounds a long blast, they may approach the mountain." {19:14} So Moses went down to the people and consecrated them, and they washed their clothes. {19:15} He said to the people, "Be ready for the third day; do not approach your wives." {19:16} On the morning of the third day, there was thunder and lightning, and a thick cloud over the mountain, along with the loud blast of a trumpet, so that all the people in the camp trembled. {19:17} Moses led the people out of the camp to meet God, and they stood at the foot of the mountain. {19:18} Mount Sinai was completely enveloped in smoke because the LORD descended on it in fire; the smoke rose like the smoke from a furnace, and the whole mountain trembled violently. {19:19} As the trumpet sounded louder and louder, Moses spoke, and God answered him with thunder. {19:20} The LORD descended on Mount Sinai, at the top of the mountain, and called Moses to the top. So Moses went up. {19:21} The LORD said to Moses, "Go down and warn the people so they do not break through to see the LORD, and many of them perish. {19:22} Let the priests who approach the LORD also consecrate themselves, or the LORD will break out against them." {19:23} Moses said to the LORD, "The people cannot come up to Mount Sinai because You warned us, saying, 'Set limits around the mountain and consecrate it.'" {19:24} The LORD said, "Go down and bring Aaron up with you, but do not let the priests or the people break through to come up to the LORD, or He will break out against them." {19:25} So Moses went down to the people and told them. He emphasized the holiness of God's presence, urging the people to honor the boundaries set by the LORD, lest they face His wrath.

{20:1} And God spoke all these words, saying, {20:2} "I am the LORD your God, who brought you out of the land of Egypt, out of the house of slavery. {20:3} You shall have no other gods before Me. {20:4} You shall not make for yourself a graven image or any likeness of anything that is in heaven above, on the earth below, or in the water beneath the earth. {20:5} You shall not bow down to them or serve them, for I, the LORD your God, am a jealous God, visiting the iniquity (wrongdoing) of the fathers upon the children to the third and fourth generation of those who hate Me; {20:6} but showing mercy to thousands of those who love Me and keep My commandments. {20:7} You shall not take the name of the LORD your God in vain, for the LORD will not hold anyone guiltless who takes His name in vain. {20:8} Remember the Sabbath day to keep it holy. {20:9} Six days you shall labor and do all your work, {20:10} but the seventh day is a Sabbath to the LORD your God. On it, you shall not do any work, you, your son, your daughter, your male or female servant, your livestock, or any foreigner residing in your towns. {20:11} For in six days the LORD made heaven and earth, the sea, and everything in them, and rested on the seventh day. Therefore, the LORD blessed the Sabbath day and made it holy. {20:12} Honor your father and your mother, so that your days may be long in the land that the LORD your God is giving you. {20:13} You shall not kill. {20:14} You shall not commit adultery. {20:15} You shall not steal. {20:16} You shall not bear false witness against your neighbor. {20:17} You shall not covet your neighbor's house; you shall not covet your neighbor's wife, or his male or female servant, his ox, his donkey, or anything that belongs to your neighbor. {20:18} And all the people saw the thunder and lightning, the sound of the trumpet, and the mountain smoking. When the people saw it, they trembled and stood at a distance. {20:19} They said to Moses, "Speak to us, and we will listen, but do not let God speak to us, or we will die." {20:20} Moses said to the people, "Do not be afraid, for God has come to test you, so that the fear of Him may be before you, that you do not sin." {20:21} The people stood at a distance, while Moses approached the thick darkness where God was. {20:22} And the LORD said to Moses, "Thus you shall say to the children of Israel: 'You have seen that I have spoken with you from heaven. {20:23} You shall not make gods of silver alongside Me, nor shall you make for yourselves gods of gold. {20:24} You shall make an altar of earth for Me and sacrifice your burnt offerings and peace offerings, your sheep and your oxen. In every place where I record My name, I will come to you and bless you. {20:25} If you make an altar of stone for Me, do not build it with hewn (cut or shaped) stones, for if you use a tool on it, you have polluted it. {20:26} And do not go up to My altar by steps, so that your nakedness (exposure) is not uncovered."

{21:1} Now these are the laws that you shall set before them. {21:2} If you buy a Hebrew servant, he shall serve for six years, and in the seventh year, he shall go free without any payment. {21:3} If he came in alone, he shall leave alone; if he was married when he came in, then his wife shall go out with him. {21:4} If his master gave him a wife and she bore him sons or daughters, the wife and her children shall belong to her master, and he shall go out by himself. {21:5} But if the servant declares, "I love my master, my wife, and my children; I do not want to go free," {21:6} then his master shall bring him to the judges and take him to the door or the doorpost. His master shall pierce his ear with an awl (sharp tool), and he shall serve him forever. {21:7} If a man sells his daughter as a maidservant, she shall not go out as the male servants do. {21:8} If she does not please her master who has betrothed her to himself, he shall allow her to be redeemed (bought back); he has no power to sell her to a foreign nation, since he has dealt deceitfully with her. {21:9} If he has betrothed her to his son, he shall treat her as a daughter. {21:10} If he takes another wife, he shall not diminish her food, clothing, or marital rights. {21:11} If he does not provide these three things for her, she shall go out free without payment. {21:12} Anyone who strikes a person and causes their death shall surely be put to death. {21:13} But if a man did not plan to kill but God allowed it to happen, I will appoint a place to which he may flee. {21:14} However, if someone attacks their neighbor with the intent to kill, you shall take them from My altar to be put to death. {21:15} Anyone who strikes their father or mother shall surely be put to death. {21:16} Anyone who kidnaps a person and sells them, or is found in possession of them, shall surely be put to death. {21:17} Anyone who curses their father or mother shall surely be put to death. {21:18} If men quarrel and one strikes another with a stone or with their fist and does not die but is confined to bed, {21:19} if they get up and walk around with a staff, the one who struck them shall not be held liable; they shall only pay for the loss of time and ensure the injured party is fully healed. {21:20} If a man strikes his servant or maid with a rod and they die under his hand, he shall be surely punished. {21:21} However, if they survive for a day or two, he shall not be punished, for they are his property. {21:22} If men quarrel and hurt a pregnant woman so that her child is born prematurely but no further harm follows, he shall be surely punished according to the woman's husband's demands, and he shall pay as the judges determine. {21:23} But if there is further harm, then you shall give life for life, {21:24} eye for eye, tooth for tooth, hand for hand, foot for foot, {21:25} burn for burn, wound for wound, stripe for stripe. {21:26} If a man strikes the eye of his servant or maid and destroys it, he shall let them go free for the sake of their eye. {21:27} If he knocks out the tooth of his manservant or maidservant, he shall let them go free for the sake of their tooth. {21:28} If an ox gores a man or woman so that they die, the ox shall be surely stoned, and its flesh shall not be eaten; but the owner of the ox shall be acquitted. {21:29} However, if the ox had a history of goring and its owner had been warned but did not restrain it, and it kills a man or woman, the ox shall be stoned, and the owner shall also be put to death. {21:30} If a fine is imposed on him, he shall pay for the redemption of his life whatever is imposed. {21:31} Whether the ox gored a son or a daughter, the same judgment shall apply. {21:32} If the ox gores a servant or maidservant, the owner shall pay their master thirty shekels of silver, and the ox shall be stoned. {21:33} If a man opens a pit or digs a pit and does not cover it, and an ox or donkey falls in, {21:34} the owner of the pit shall make restitution and give money to the owner of the animal, and the dead animal shall be his. {21:35} If one man's ox injures another's so that it dies, they shall sell the live ox and divide the money, and they shall also divide the dead ox. {21:36} But if it is known that the ox had a history of goring and its owner did not keep it restrained, he shall surely pay ox for ox, and the dead animal shall be his own.

{22:1} If a man steals an ox or a sheep and kills it or sells it, he shall repay five oxen for each ox and four sheep for each sheep. {22:2} If a thief is caught breaking in and is struck so that he dies, no blood guilt shall be incurred. {22:3} If the sun has risen on him, there is blood guilt; he must make full restitution. If he has nothing, he shall be sold for his theft. {22:4} If the stolen item is found alive in his possession, whether it's an ox, donkey, or sheep, he shall repay double. {22:5} If a man allows his animal to graze in another person's field or vineyard and it eats from that field, he shall make restitution from the best of his own field and vineyard. {22:6} If a fire breaks out and spreads to thorns so that the stacks of grain or standing grain or field are burned, the person who started the fire shall make restitution. {22:7} If a man entrusts money or goods to his neighbor for safekeeping and they are stolen from the man's house, if the thief is found, he shall pay double. {22:8} If the thief is not found, then the owner of the house shall be brought before the judges to determine if he took his neighbor's goods. {22:9} For any type of trespass, whether it involves oxen, donkeys, sheep, clothing, or any lost item claimed by another, both parties shall come before the judges, and the one judged guilty shall pay double to their neighbor. {22:10} If a man gives his neighbor a donkey, ox, sheep, or any animal to keep and it dies, is hurt, or is driven away without anyone seeing it, {22:11} there shall be an oath before the LORD between them that he has not put his hand on his neighbor's property, and the owner shall accept this, and he shall not make it good. {22:12} If it is stolen from him, he shall make restitution to the owner. {22:13} If it is torn apart, he shall bring proof, and he shall not make good what was torn. {22:14} If a man borrows anything from his neighbor and it is hurt or dies while the owner is not present, he shall make good what was borrowed. {22:15} But if the owner is present, he shall not make good; if it was hired, it came for its hire. {22:16} If a man entices a virgin who is not engaged and sleeps with her, he must surely pay her father the bride price to make her his wife. {22:17} If her father completely refuses to give her to him, he must pay money according to the dowry for virgins. {22:18} You shall not allow a witch to live. {22:19} Anyone who has sexual relations with an animal shall surely be put to death. {22:20} Whoever sacrifices to any god other than the LORD shall be completely destroyed. {22:21} You shall not mistreat or oppress a stranger, for you were strangers in the land of Egypt. {22:22} You shall not afflict any widow or orphan. {22:23} If you afflict them in any way and they cry out to me, I will surely hear their cry; {22:24} and my anger will be hot, and I will kill you with the sword, and your wives will become widows and your children orphans. {22:25} If you lend money to any of my people who are poor, you shall not act like a moneylender, and you shall not charge them interest. {22:26} If you take your neighbor's cloak as collateral, you shall return it to him before sunset, {22:27} for it is his only covering; it is the cloak for his skin. What will he sleep in? If he cries out to me, I will hear, for I am gracious. {22:28} You shall not revile God, nor curse the ruler of your people. {22:29} You shall not delay to offer the first of your ripe fruits and of your liquors; you shall give your firstborn sons to me. {22:30} You shall do the same with your oxen and your sheep: for seven days it shall remain with its mother; on the eighth day, you shall give it to me. {22:31} You shall be holy people to me; you shall not eat any flesh torn by wild animals in the field; you shall throw it to the dogs.

{23:1} You must not spread a false report; do not join with the wicked to be an unjust witness. {23:2} You shall not follow the crowd in doing wrong; do not testify in a case to side with the majority to pervert justice. {23:3} You shall not show favoritism to a poor person in their dispute. {23:4} If you encounter your enemy's ox or donkey wandering away, you must return it to him. {23:5} If you see the donkey of someone who hates you lying under its load and you want to avoid helping, you must surely help with it. {23:6} You must not twist justice for the poor in their case. {23:7} Stay far away from false matters; do not kill the innocent and righteous, for I will not justify the wicked. {23:8} You shall take no bribe, for a bribe blinds the wise and twists the words of the righteous. {23:9} You shall not oppress a stranger, for you know the heart of a stranger, having been strangers in the land of Egypt. {23:10} For six years, you shall sow your land and gather its produce; {23:11} but in the seventh year, you shall let it rest and lie fallow so that the poor of your people may eat, and what they leave the beasts of the field may eat. You shall do the same with your vineyard and your olive grove. {23:12} Six days you shall work, and on the seventh day, you shall rest, so that your ox and donkey may have a break, and the son of your female servant and the stranger may be refreshed. {23:13} Be careful to do everything I have said to you, and do not mention the names of other gods; let them not be heard from your lips. {23:14} Three times a year you shall hold a festival for me. {23:15} You shall keep the Feast of Unleavened Bread: you shall eat unleavened bread for seven days, as I commanded you, at the time appointed in the month of Abib, for in that month you came out of Egypt; and none shall appear before me empty-handed. {23:16} Also, you shall keep the Feast of Harvest, the first fruits of your labors from what you sow in the field; and the Feast of Ingathering at the end of the year when you gather in your crops from the field. {23:17} Three times a year all your males shall appear before the Lord GOD. {23:18} You shall not offer the blood of my sacrifice with leavened bread; nor shall the fat of my feast remain until morning. {23:19} The best of the first fruits of your land you shall bring into the house of the LORD your God. You shall not boil a young goat in its mother's milk. {23:20} Behold, I send an angel before you to guard you on the way and bring you to the place I have prepared. {23:21} Pay attention to him and obey his voice; do not provoke him, for he will not pardon your transgressions, for my name is in him. {23:22} But if you truly obey his voice and do all that I say, then I will be an enemy to your enemies and an adversary to your adversaries. {23:23} For my angel will go before you and bring you into the land of the Amorites, Hittites, Perizzites, Canaanites, Hivites, and Jebusites, and I will cut them off. {23:24} You shall not bow down to their gods or serve them, nor do according to their works; but you shall utterly overthrow them and break their sacred pillars. {23:25} You shall serve the LORD your God, and he will bless your bread and your water, and I will take sickness away from your midst. {23:26} No one shall miscarry or be barren in your land; I will fulfill the number of your days. {23:27} I will send my terror ahead of you and throw into confusion all the people you encounter, and I will make all your enemies turn their backs to you. {23:28} I will send hornets ahead of you to drive out the Hivites, Canaanites, and Hittites before you. {23:29} I will not drive them out from before you in one year, lest the land become desolate and the beasts of the field multiply against you. {23:30} Little by little, I will drive them out from before you until you have increased and inherit the land. {23:31} I will set your borders from the Red Sea to the Sea of the Philistines and from the wilderness to the river, for I will deliver the inhabitants of the land into your hand, and you shall drive them out before you. {23:32} You shall make no covenant with them or with their gods. {23:33} They shall not dwell in your land, lest they make you sin against me, for if you serve their gods, it will surely be a snare to you.

{24:1} The LORD said to Moses, "Come up to the LORD, you, Aaron, Nadab, Abihu, and seventy of the elders of Israel; and worship from a distance." {24:2} Only Moses may come near the LORD; they must not approach, nor may the people go up with him. {24:3} So Moses went and told the people all the words of the LORD and all the laws; and all the people answered in unison, saying, "We will do everything the LORD has said." {24:4} Moses wrote down all the words of the LORD. He got up early the next morning, built an altar at the foot of the mountain, and set up twelve pillars for the twelve tribes of Israel. {24:5} He sent young men from the Israelites, who offered burnt offerings and sacrificed young bulls as peace offerings to the LORD. {24:6} Moses took half of the blood and put it in bowls, and the other half he sprinkled on the altar. {24:7} He took the Book of the Covenant and read it in the hearing of the people, and they said, "We will do everything the LORD has said; we will be obedient." {24:8} Then Moses sprinkled the blood on the people and said, "This is the blood of the covenant that the LORD has made with you in accordance with all these words." {24:9} Moses, Aaron, Nadab, Abihu, and the seventy elders of Israel went up {24:10} and saw the God of Israel. Under his feet was something like a pavement made of sapphire, as clear as the sky itself. {24:11} God did not raise his hand against the nobles of the Israelites; they saw God, and they ate and drank. {24:12} The LORD said to Moses, "Come up to me on the mountain and stay here, and I will give you the tablets of stone and the law and commandments that I have written, so you can teach them." {24:13} Moses set out with his assistant Joshua and went up the mountain of God. {24:14} He told the elders, "Stay here for us until we return to you. Aaron and Hur are here with you; anyone who has a dispute can go to them." {24:15} When Moses went up the mountain, a cloud covered it. {24:16} The glory of the LORD settled on Mount Sinai, and the cloud covered it for six days. On the seventh day, he called to Moses from within the cloud. {24:17} To the Israelites, the glory of the LORD looked like a consuming fire on top of the mountain. {24:18} Moses entered the cloud as he went up the mountain, and he was there for forty days and forty nights.

{25:1} The LORD spoke to Moses, saying, {25:2} "Tell the Israelites to bring me an offering; you are to receive my offering from everyone whose heart prompts them to give. {25:3} Here's what you should collect from them: gold, silver, and bronze, {25:4} blue, purple, and scarlet yarn, fine linen, and goat hair, {25:5} ram skins dyed red, and other types of leather, and acacia wood, {25:6} oil for the light, spices for the anointing oil, and for the sweet incense, {25:7} onyx stones, and stones to be set in the ephod and the breastplate. {25:8} Let them make a sanctuary for me, so that I may dwell among them. {25:9} Make it according to all that I show you, the pattern of the tabernacle and all its furnishings. {25:10} They are to make an ark of acacia wood, two and a half cubits long, a cubit and a half wide, and a cubit and a half high. {25:11} Overlay it with pure gold, inside and out, and put a gold molding around it. {25:12} Cast four gold rings for it and fasten them to its four feet, with two rings on one side and two rings on the other. {25:13} Make poles of acacia wood and overlay them with gold. {25:14} Put the poles into the rings on the sides of the ark to carry it. {25:15}

The poles must remain in the rings of the ark; they must not be removed. {25:16} Then put in the ark the tablets of the covenant that I will give you. {25:17} Make a mercy seat of pure gold; it is to be two and a half cubits long and a cubit and a half wide. {25:18} Make two cherubim out of gold, make them of hammered work, at the two ends of the mercy seat. {25:19} Make one cherub on one end and the other cherub on the other end. The cherubim are to be on the two ends of the mercy seat. {25:20} The cherubim are to have their wings spread upward, covering the mercy seat with their wings, and facing each other, with their faces looking toward the mercy seat. {25:21} Place the mercy seat on top of the ark and put in the ark the tablets of the covenant that I will give you. {25:22} There, above the mercy seat, between the two cherubim that are over the ark of the covenant, I will meet with you and give you all my commands for the Israelites. {25:23} Make a table of acacia wood; it is to be two cubits long, a cubit wide, and a cubit and a half high. {25:24} Overlay it with pure gold and make a gold molding around it. {25:25} Make a rim a handbreadth wide around it and put a gold molding on the rim. {25:26} Make four gold rings for the table and attach the rings to the four corners where the four legs are. {25:27} The rings are to be close to the rim to hold the poles used to carry the table. {25:28} Make the poles of acacia wood and overlay them with gold, so the table may be carried with them. {25:29} Make its plates and dishes, as well as its pitchers and bowls for pouring, of pure gold. {25:30} Put the bread of the Presence on the table before me at all times. {25:31} Make a lampstand of pure gold; make the lampstand of hammered work. Its base and shaft, its cups, its calyxes (cup-like structures), and its blossoms shall be of one piece. {25:32} Six branches are to extend from the sides of the lampstand—three on one side and three on the other. {25:33} Each branch shall have three cups shaped like almond blossoms, with a calyx and a blossom. {25:34} On the lampstand itself there are to be four cups shaped like almond blossoms, with their calyxes and blossoms. {25:35} There shall be a calyx under the first pair of branches, a calyx under the second pair, and a calyx under the third pair, for the six branches that extend from the lampstand. {25:36} Their calyxes and branches shall all be of one piece with the lampstand, hammered from pure gold. {25:37} Make its seven lamps and set them up so that they light the space in front of it. {25:38} Its wick trimmers and trays shall be of pure gold. {25:39} A talent (about 75 pounds) of pure gold is to be used for the lampstand and all these accessories. {25:40} See that you make them according to the pattern shown you on the mountain."

{26:1} You are to make the tabernacle with ten curtains of finely twisted linen, in blue, purple, and scarlet, with skillfully embroidered cherubim on them. {26:2} Each curtain is to be twenty-eight cubits long and four cubits wide, and all the curtains will have the same size. {26:3} Join five of the curtains together, and then join the other five together as well. {26:4} Make loops of blue yarn on the edge of the outer curtain in the first set and do the same on the edge of the outer curtain in the second set. {26:5} You will make fifty loops on the edge of one curtain and fifty loops on the edge of the curtain in the second set so that the loops connect with each other. {26:6} Make fifty clasps of gold to join the curtains together; this will make one tabernacle. {26:7} Then make curtains of goat hair as a covering for the tabernacle; you are to make eleven curtains. {26:8} Each curtain will be thirty cubits long and four cubits wide, and all eleven curtains will have the same dimensions. {26:9} Join five curtains together separately and six curtains separately, with the sixth curtain doubled over at the front of the tabernacle. {26:10} Make fifty loops on the edge of the outer curtain in the first set and fifty loops on the edge of the curtain in the second set. {26:11} Make fifty clasps of bronze and put them into the loops to join the tent together as one. {26:12} The leftover part of the tent curtains, the half curtain that remains, will hang over the back of the tabernacle. {26:13} There will be a cubit hanging on each side of what remains in the length of the tent curtains, to cover the sides of the tabernacle. {26:14} You are to make a covering for the tent of ram skins dyed red and a covering above that of other types of leather. {26:15} Construct the boards for the tabernacle from acacia wood, standing upright. {26:16} Each board will be ten cubits long and a cubit and a half wide. {26:17} Each board will have two tenons (projections) to fit into each other, and you will do this for all the boards of the tabernacle. {26:18} You are to make twenty boards for the south side of the tabernacle. {26:19} Under the twenty boards, you will make forty silver bases; two bases under each board for its two tenons. {26:20} For the north side of the tabernacle, you will make twenty boards {26:21} with forty silver bases—two bases under each board. {26:22} For the west side of the tabernacle, you will make six boards. {26:23} Make two boards for the corners of the tabernacle at the two ends. {26:24} These will be joined at the bottom and at the top with a single ring; this will apply to both corners. {26:25} There will be a total of eight boards and sixteen silver bases, with two bases under each board. {26:26} You will make crossbars of acacia wood—five for the boards on one side of the tabernacle, {26:27} five for the boards on the other side, and five for the boards on the west side of the tabernacle. {26:28} The middle bar will extend from end to end. {26:29} Overlay the boards with gold and make gold rings for the bars; overlay the bars with gold as well. {26:30} Set up the tabernacle according to the plan shown to you on the mountain. {26:31} You are to make a veil of blue, purple, and scarlet yarn, and finely twisted linen, with skillful work; it will have cherubim on it. {26:32} Hang it on four acacia wood pillars overlaid with gold, with gold hooks, standing on four silver bases. {26:33} Hang the veil under the clasps, and bring in the ark of the testimony behind the veil; the veil will separate the holy place from the Most Holy Place. {26:34} Place the mercy seat on the ark of the testimony in the Most Holy Place. {26:35} Set the table outside the veil and place the lampstand opposite the table on the south side of the tabernacle, while the table will be on the north side. {26:36} Make a curtain for the entrance of the tent, of blue, purple, and scarlet yarn, and finely twisted linen, crafted with needlework. {26:37} Make for the curtain five acacia wood pillars, overlay them with gold, with gold hooks, and cast five bronze bases for them.

{27:1} You are to make an altar from acacia wood, five cubits long and five cubits wide; the altar will be square, and its height will be three cubits. {27:2} You will make horns for it at the four corners; these horns will be part of it, and you will overlay the altar with bronze. {27:3} You will make pans to collect the ashes, shovels, basins, flesh hooks, and firepans; all these vessels will be made of bronze. {27:4} Create a grate of bronze mesh for it, and make four bronze rings at the four corners of the grate. {27:5} Place it underneath the altar so that the net is even with the middle of the altar. {27:6} You will make poles for the altar from acacia wood and overlay them with bronze. {27:7} The poles will be inserted into the rings, and they will be on the two sides of the altar to carry it. {27:8} Make the altar hollow with boards, just as you were shown on the mountain. {27:9} You will create the court of the tabernacle; on the south side, there will be hangings made of finely twisted linen, a hundred cubits long. {27:10} There will be twenty pillars and their twenty bronze bases; the hooks for the pillars and their connecting rods will be silver. {27:11} Similarly, for the north side, there will be hangings of a hundred cubits long, with twenty pillars and twenty bronze bases, and silver hooks and rods. {27:12} For the west side of the court, the hangings will be fifty cubits wide, with ten pillars and ten bases. {27:13} The east side of the court will also be fifty cubits wide. {27:14} The hangings on one side of the gate will be fifteen cubits long, with three pillars and three bases. {27:15} On the other side, there will also be fifteen cubits of hangings, with three pillars and three bases. {27:16} For the gate of the court, there will be a hanging of twenty cubits, made of blue, purple, and scarlet yarn, and finely twisted linen, crafted with needlework; it will have four pillars and four bases. {27:17} All the pillars around the court will have silver rods, silver hooks, and bronze bases. {27:18} The court will be a hundred cubits long and fifty cubits wide everywhere, with a height of five cubits of finely twisted linen, and bronze bases. {27:19} All the vessels used in the tabernacle and all the pins for it and for the court will be made of bronze. {27:20} You will command the Israelites to bring you pure olive oil, crushed (beaten) for the light, so that the lamp may burn continuously. {27:21} In the tabernacle of the congregation, outside the veil in front of the testimony, Aaron and his sons will tend it from evening to morning before the LORD; this will be a permanent statute for future generations for the children of Israel.

{28:1} You are to bring your brother Aaron and his sons from among the Israelites so that he can serve as my priest—Aaron, along with his sons Nadab, Abihu, Eleazar, and Ithamar. {28:2} You will make sacred garments for Aaron, your brother, to bring him honor and beauty. {28:3} Speak to all those who are wise-hearted, whom I have filled with the spirit of wisdom, to make Aaron's garments for his consecration, so he can serve as my priest. {28:4} These are the garments they will make: a breastplate, an ephod, a robe, a woven coat, a headdress, and a sash. They will create holy garments for Aaron and his sons, so they can minister to me as priests. {28:5} They will use gold, blue, purple, scarlet yarn, and finely twisted linen. {28:6} The ephod will be made of gold, blue, purple, scarlet yarn, and finely twisted linen, crafted skillfully. {28:7} It will have two shoulder pieces joined at the edges, and it will be securely fastened. {28:8} The intricately designed sash of the ephod will be made of the same materials: gold, blue, purple, scarlet yarn, and finely twisted linen. {28:9} You will take two onyx stones and engrave the names of the children of Israel on them. {28:10} Six names on one stone and six names on the other, according to their birth order. {28:11} Engrave the stones like the engravings of a seal and set them in gold settings. {28:12} Place the two stones on the shoulders of the ephod as a memorial for the children of Israel; Aaron will bear their names before the LORD on his shoulders as a reminder. {28:13} You will make gold settings; {28:14} and two pure gold chains, braided, to attach to the settings. {28:15} You will make the breastplate of judgment skillfully, following the design of the ephod, made of gold, blue, purple, scarlet yarn, and finely twisted linen. {28:16} It will be square and folded double, a span long and a span wide. {28:17} You will set four rows of stones in it: the first row will have a sardius, a topaz, and a carbuncle; this will be the first row. {28:18} The second row will have an emerald, a sapphire, and a diamond. {28:19} The third row will include a ligure, an agate, and an amethyst. {28:20} The fourth row will feature a beryl, an onyx, and a jasper; they will be set in gold settings. {28:21} The stones will bear the names of the children of Israel, twelve in total, each according to their name, engraved like a seal, representing the twelve tribes. {28:22} You will make chains of pure gold for the breastplate at its ends, braided together. {28:23} You will also make two rings of gold for the breastplate and place them at its two ends. {28:24} Attach the two braided chains of gold to the rings at the ends of the breastplate. {28:25} The other ends of the two braided chains will be fastened to the gold settings on the shoulders of the ephod. {28:26} You will make two rings of gold and place them on the two ends of the breastplate on its inner edge, next to the ephod. {28:27} Make two additional rings of gold for the two sides of the ephod, underneath, toward the front, opposite the other connections above the sash of the ephod. {28:28} They will tie the breastplate to the ephod using a blue cord, ensuring it is above the sash of the ephod so that the breastplate does not come loose from the ephod. {28:29} Aaron will bear the names of the children of Israel in the breastplate of judgment over his heart when he enters the holy place, as a continual reminder before the LORD. {28:30} You will place the Urim and Thummim in the breastplate of judgment; they will be over Aaron's heart when he goes in before the LORD, and Aaron will carry the judgments of the children of Israel on his heart before the LORD continually. {28:31} You will make the robe of the ephod entirely of blue. {28:32} There will be an opening in the top, in the middle; it will have a woven border around the opening, like a soldier's tunic, so it doesn't tear. {28:33} At the hem of the robe, you will make pomegranates of blue, purple, and scarlet yarn, all around the hem, with golden bells between them. {28:34} There will be a golden bell and a pomegranate, a golden bell and a pomegranate, around the hem of the robe. {28:35} This will be on Aaron when he ministers; the sound will be heard when he enters the holy place before the LORD and when he leaves, so he does not die. {28:36} You will make a plate of pure gold and engrave on it, like a seal, "HOLINESS TO THE LORD." {28:37} Place it on a blue cord, so it can be worn on the front of the headdress. {28:38} It will be on Aaron's forehead so that Aaron may bear the iniquity (sin) of the holy things that the Israelites consecrate in all their holy gifts; it will always be on his forehead so that they may be accepted before the LORD. {28:39} You will embroider the linen coat and make the headdress and the sash from finely twisted linen. {28:40} For Aaron's sons, you will make coats, sashes, and headdresses for glory and beauty. {28:41} You will put these on Aaron and his sons, anoint them, consecrate them, and set them apart to minister to me as priests. {28:42} You will make linen undergarments to cover their nakedness, reaching from the waist to the thighs. {28:43} These will be worn by Aaron and his sons when they enter the tabernacle or approach the altar to minister in the holy place, so they do not incur guilt and die; this will be a lasting ordinance for him and his descendants.

{29:1} Here's what you are to do to consecrate them for service as priests: take one young bull and two rams without blemish. {29:2} You will also need unleavened bread, cakes made without yeast mixed with oil, and unleavened wafers brushed with oil—make them from fine wheat flour. {29:3} Place all these in one basket and bring the basket along with the bull and the two rams. {29:4} Bring Aaron and his sons to the entrance of the Tabernacle and wash them with water. {29:5} You will dress Aaron in the coat, the robe of the ephod, the ephod itself, and the breastplate, fastening him with the intricate sash of the ephod. {29:6} Put the headdress on his head and place the holy crown on the headdress. {29:7} Then take the anointing oil and pour it over his head to anoint him. {29:8} Bring his sons and put coats on them. {29:9} Fasten sashes around Aaron and his sons, and place bonnets on them; this priesthood will be theirs as a lasting ordinance, and you shall consecrate Aaron and his sons. {29:10} You will bring a bull to the entrance of the Tabernacle, and Aaron and his sons will lay their hands on its head. {29:11} You will kill the bull before the LORD at the entrance of the Tabernacle. {29:12} Take some of the bull's blood and put it on the horns of the altar with your finger, and pour the rest of the blood at the base of the altar. {29:13} Take all the fat that covers the innards, the membrane over the liver, the two kidneys, and the fat on them, and burn them on the altar. {29:14} But burn the flesh, skin, and dung of the bull outside the camp; it is a sin offering. {29:15} You will also take one ram, and Aaron and his sons will lay their hands on its head. {29:16} You will kill the ram and sprinkle its blood around the altar. {29:17} Cut the ram into pieces, wash its innards and legs, and place them with the pieces and its head. {29:18} You will burn the whole ram on the altar; it is a burnt offering to the LORD, a pleasing aroma made by fire. {29:19} Take the second ram, and Aaron and his sons will lay their hands on its head. {29:20} You will kill the ram and put some of its blood on the tip of Aaron's right ear, the tips of his sons' right ears, the thumbs of their right hands, and the big toes of their right feet, sprinkling the blood around the altar. {29:21} Take some of the blood from the altar and the anointing oil, and sprinkle it on Aaron and his garments, and on his sons and their garments; he and his garments, along with his sons and their garments, will be consecrated. {29:22} Also, take the fat and the tail of the ram, the fat covering the innards, the membrane over the liver, the two kidneys, and the fat on them, and the right shoulder, since it is a ram of consecration. {29:23} Include one loaf of bread, one cake of oiled bread, and one wafer from the basket of unleavened bread before the LORD. {29:24} Put all of these into the hands of Aaron and his sons, and wave them as a wave offering before the LORD. {29:25} Then you will receive them from their hands and burn them on the altar as a burnt offering, a pleasing aroma made by fire to the LORD. {29:26} You will take the breast from the ram of Aaron's consecration and wave it as a wave offering before the LORD; this will be your share. {29:27} You will consecrate the breast of the wave offering and the shoulder of the heave offering, which is waved and raised, from the ram of consecration, both for Aaron and his sons. {29:28} This will be theirs as a lasting ordinance from the Israelites; it is a heave offering and will be given from the peace offerings made to the LORD. {29:29} Aaron's sacred garments will be passed down to his sons after him so they can be anointed and consecrated in them. {29:30} The son who succeeds him as priest will wear them for seven days when he enters the Tabernacle to minister in the holy place. {29:31} You will take the ram of consecration and boil its flesh in the holy place. {29:32} Aaron and his sons will eat the flesh of the ram and the bread in the basket at the entrance of the Tabernacle. {29:33} They will eat these things used for atonement to consecrate and sanctify them; a stranger may not eat them, for they are holy. {29:34} If any of the flesh from the consecration or the bread remains until morning, it must be burned with fire; it is not to be eaten, for it is holy. {29:35} You are to do everything I have commanded you for Aaron and his sons over the seven days of their consecration. {29:36} Each day you will offer a bull for a sin offering for atonement; cleanse the altar after making atonement for it and anoint it to sanctify it. {29:37} For seven days, you will make atonement for the altar and sanctify it, and it will be the most holy altar; whatever touches the altar will be holy. {29:38} This is what you will offer on the altar: two lambs a year old every day, continuously. {29:39} Offer one lamb in the morning and the other lamb in the evening. {29:40} With the first lamb, offer a tenth of an ephah of fine flour mixed with a fourth of a hin of beaten oil and a fourth of a hin of wine for a drink offering. {29:41} For the other lamb, do the same according to the grain and drink offerings in the evening, creating a pleasing aroma made by fire to the LORD. {29:42} This will be a continual burnt offering throughout your generations at the entrance of the Tabernacle before the LORD, where I will meet you to speak to you. {29:43} There I will meet with the Israelites, and the Tabernacle will be sanctified by my glory. {29:44} I will sanctify the Tabernacle and the altar, and I will also sanctify Aaron and his sons to serve me as priests. {29:45} I will dwell among the Israelites and be their God. {29:46} They will know that I am the LORD their God, who brought them out of the land of Egypt so that I may dwell among them; I am the LORD their God.

{30:1} You are to make an altar for burning incense; use acacia wood to make it. {30:2} It should be one cubit long and one cubit wide; it will be square and two cubits high, with horns on its corners made from the same material. {30:3} Overlay the top, sides, and horns with pure gold, and create a gold crown around it. {30:4} Make two golden rings for it, placed below the crown at the two corners on its sides; these will hold the poles for carrying it. {30:5} The poles should be made of acacia wood and overlaid with gold. {30:6} Place the altar in front of the veil that is before the Ark of the Testimony, in front of the mercy seat where I will meet with you. {30:7} Aaron shall burn fragrant incense on it every morning when he tends the lamps. {30:8} And when he lights the lamps in the evening, he shall also burn incense; this will be a regular incense offering before the LORD for generations to come. {30:9} Do not offer any unauthorized incense on it, nor burnt sacrifices or grain offerings; do not pour drink offerings on it. {30:10} Once a year, Aaron will make atonement on its horns with the blood of the sin offering; he will make atonement for it once a year for all generations; it is most holy to the LORD. {30:11} The LORD spoke to Moses, saying, {30:12} "When you take a census of the Israelites, each one must pay a ransom for himself to the LORD when you number them, so that no plague will come upon them. {30:13} Each person counted must give half a shekel, according to the sanctuary shekel (a shekel is twenty gerahs); this half shekel will be the offering to the LORD. {30:14} Everyone who is counted, twenty years old and over, must give an offering to the LORD. {30:15} The rich shall not give more, and the poor shall not give less than half a shekel as an offering to the LORD to make atonement for their lives. {30:16} You shall take the atonement money from the Israelites and use it for the service of the Tabernacle; it will be a memorial for the Israelites before the LORD, to make atonement for their lives. {30:17} The LORD spoke to Moses, saying, {30:18} "You are to make a bronze basin for washing, with a bronze stand, and place it between the Tabernacle and the altar, filling it with water. {30:19} Aaron and his sons shall wash their hands and feet from it. {30:20} Whenever they enter the Tabernacle, they must wash with water to avoid death, and when they approach the altar to offer a fire offering to the LORD, {30:21} they must wash their hands and feet so they will not die. This will be a lasting ordinance for them and their descendants." {30:22} Moreover, the LORD spoke to Moses, saying, {30:23} "Take for yourself the finest spices: five hundred shekels of pure myrrh, two hundred and fifty shekels of sweet cinnamon, and two hundred and fifty shekels of sweet calamus, {30:24} and five hundred shekels of cassia, according to the sanctuary shekel, and one hin of olive oil. {30:25} Make it into a sacred anointing oil, a perfumed blend made by a skilled perfumer; it will be a holy anointing oil. {30:26} You are to use it to anoint the Tabernacle of Meeting, the Ark of the Testimony, {30:27} the table and all its utensils, the lampstand and its utensils, the altar of incense, {30:28} the altar of burnt offering and all its utensils, and the basin and its stand. {30:29} You shall consecrate them, so they will be most holy; whatever touches them will be holy. {30:30} You shall anoint Aaron and his sons and consecrate them so they may serve me as priests. {30:31} Speak to the Israelites and say, 'This will be my holy anointing oil for generations to come. {30:32} Do not pour it on ordinary flesh, and do not make any other oil like it; it is holy, and it must be treated as holy. {30:33} Anyone who blends oil like it or puts it on a stranger shall be cut off from his people.' {30:34} The LORD said to Moses, "Take sweet spices: stacte, onycha, and galbanum; these sweet spices along with pure frankincense must be of equal weight. {30:35} Make it into a fragrant blend, the work of a perfumer, pure and holy. {30:36} You shall crush some of it into fine powder and put it before the Testimony in the Tabernacle of Meeting, where I will meet with you; it shall be most holy to you. {30:37} As for the perfume you make, do not make it for yourselves according to its formula; it will be holy to you for the LORD. {30:38} Anyone who makes anything like it to smell it will be cut off from his people."

{31:1} The LORD spoke to Moses, saying, {31:2} "Look, I have called by name Bezaleel, son of Uri, son of Hur, from the tribe of Judah. {31:3} I have filled him with the Spirit of God, with wisdom, understanding, knowledge, and all kinds of craftsmanship, {31:4} to design artistic works, to work with gold, silver, and bronze, {31:5} to cut stones for setting, and to carve wood, and to perform all kinds of craftsmanship. {31:6} Moreover, I have given him Aholiab, son of Ahisamach, from the tribe of Dan, and I have put wisdom in the hearts of all who are wise-hearted, so they may create all that I have commanded you; {31:7} the Tabernacle of Meeting, the Ark of the Testimony, the mercy seat on it, and all the furnishings of the Tabernacle, {31:8} the table and its furnishings, the pure lampstand and all its accessories, and the altar of incense, {31:9} the altar of burnt offering and all its furnishings, and the basin and its stand, {31:10} and the service garments, and the holy garments for Aaron the priest and the garments of his sons for ministry in the priest's office, {31:11} as well as the anointing oil and sweet incense for the holy place; they shall do everything according to all that I have commanded you." {31:12} The LORD spoke to Moses again, saying, {31:13} "Tell the Israelites, 'You must observe my Sabbaths, for it is a sign between me and you for all generations, so that you may know that I am the LORD who sanctifies you. {31:14} Keep the Sabbath because it is holy to you; anyone who desecrates it will surely be put to death. Anyone who does work on that day will be cut off from their people. {31:15} You may work for six days, but the seventh day is a Sabbath of rest, holy to the LORD. Anyone who works on the Sabbath will surely be put to death. {31:16} Therefore, the Israelites shall observe the Sabbath, celebrating it for generations as a lasting covenant. {31:17} It is a sign forever between me and the Israelites; for in six days the LORD made heaven and earth, and on the seventh day he rested and was refreshed.' {31:18} When He finished speaking with Moses on Mount Sinai, He gave him two stone tablets of the Testimony, written with the finger of God."

{32:1} When the people saw that Moses was taking a long time to come down from the mountain, they gathered around Aaron and said to him, "Come, make us gods to go before us, for as for this Moses, the man who brought us out of Egypt, we don't know what has happened to him." {32:2} Aaron said to them, "Take off the gold earrings from your wives, sons, and daughters, and bring them to me." {32:3} So all the people took off their gold earrings and brought them to Aaron. {32:4} He took what they gave him and made a mold of a calf. Then they said, "These are your gods, O Israel, who brought you up out of the land of Egypt!" {32:5} When Aaron saw this, he built an altar in front of the calf and made a proclamation: "Tomorrow there will be a feast to the LORD." {32:6} The next day, the people rose early, offered burnt offerings, and brought peace offerings. They sat down to eat and drink and then got up to play. {32:7} The LORD said to Moses, "Go down, because your people, whom you brought out of Egypt, have become corrupt. {32:8} They have turned away quickly from what I commanded them; they have made themselves a molten calf, worshipped it, and sacrificed to it, saying, 'These are your gods, O Israel, who brought you out of the land of Egypt.'" {32:9} The LORD said to Moses, "I have seen this people, and they are a stiff-necked (stubborn) people. {32:10} Now leave me alone so that my anger may burn against them and that I may destroy them. Then I will make you into a great nation." {32:11} But Moses sought the favor of the LORD his God and said, "LORD, why should your anger burn against your people, whom you brought out of Egypt with great power and a mighty hand? {32:12} Why should the Egyptians say, 'It was with evil intent that he brought them out, to kill them in the mountains and to wipe them off the face of the earth'? Turn from your fierce anger, relent (change your mind) and do not bring disaster on your people. {32:13} Remember your servants Abraham, Isaac, and Israel, to whom you swore by your own self: 'I will multiply your descendants as the stars in the sky and will give your descendants all this land I promised them, and it will be their inheritance forever.'" {32:14} So the LORD relented from the disaster he had threatened to bring on his people. {32:15} Moses turned and went down the mountain with the two tablets of the Testimony in his hands. They were inscribed on both sides, front and back. {32:16} The tablets were the work of God; the writing was the writing of God, engraved on the tablets. {32:17} When Joshua heard the noise of the people shouting, he said to Moses, "There is the sound of war in the camp." {32:18} Moses replied, "It is not the sound of victory; it is not the sound of defeat. It is the sound of singing that I hear." {32:19} When Moses approached the camp and saw the calf and the dancing, his anger burned, and he threw the tablets out of his hands, breaking them at the foot of the mountain. {32:20} He took the calf they had made, burned it in the fire, ground it to powder, scattered it on the water, and made the Israelites drink it. {32:21} He said to Aaron, "What did these people do to you that you led them into such great sin?" {32:22} "Do not be angry, my lord," Aaron answered. "You know how prone (inclined) these people are to evil. {32:23} They said to me, 'Make us gods to go before us. As for this fellow Moses, we don't know what has happened to him.' {32:24} So I told them, 'Whoever has any gold, take it off.' They gave me the gold, and I threw it into the fire, and out came this calf!" {32:25} Moses saw that the people were running wild (acting recklessly), for Aaron had let them get out of control, and so they became a laughingstock to their enemies. {32:26} So he stood at the entrance to the camp and said, "Whoever is for the LORD, come to me." And all the Levites rallied to him. {32:27} He said to them, "This is what the LORD, the God of Israel, says: 'Each man strap a sword to his side. Go back and forth through the camp from one end to the other, killing your brothers, friends, and neighbors.'" {32:28} The Levites did as Moses commanded, and that day about three thousand of the people died. {32:29} Then Moses said, "You have been set apart (consecrated) to the LORD today, for you were against your own sons and brothers, and he has blessed you this day." {32:30} The next day, Moses said to the people, "You have committed a great sin. But now I will go up to the LORD; perhaps I can make atonement for your sin." {32:31} So Moses went back to the LORD and said, "Oh, what a great sin these people have committed! They have made themselves gods of gold. {32:32} But now, please forgive their sin, but if not, then blot me out of the book you have written." {32:33} The LORD replied to Moses, "Whoever has sinned against me, I will blot out of my book. {32:34} Now go, lead the people to the place I spoke of, and my angel will go before you. However, when the time comes for me to punish, I will punish them for their sin." {32:35} And the LORD struck the people with a plague because of what they did with the calf Aaron had made.

{33:1} The LORD said to Moses, "Leave this place, you and the people you brought out of Egypt, and go to the land I promised to Abraham, Isaac, and Jacob, saying, 'I will give it to your descendants.' {33:2} I will send an angel ahead of you and drive out the Canaanites, Amorites, Hittites, Perizzites, Hivites, and Jebusites. {33:3} You will go to a land flowing with milk and honey, but I will not go with you, because you are a stiff-necked (stubborn) people, and I might destroy you on the way." {33:4} When the people heard these bad news, they mourned, and no one put on their ornaments. {33:5} The LORD had told Moses to say to the Israelites, "You are a stiff-necked people. If I were to go among you for even a moment, I might destroy you. So now take off your ornaments, and I will decide what to do with you." {33:6} So the Israelites stripped off their ornaments at Mount Horeb. {33:7} Moses took the tent and pitched it outside the camp, far away, and called it the Tabernacle of Meeting. Anyone who sought the LORD would go out to the Tabernacle of Meeting, which was outside the camp. {33:8} Whenever Moses went out to the Tabernacle, all the people rose and stood at the entrances of their tents, watching Moses until he entered the Tabernacle. {33:9} As Moses entered the Tabernacle, the pillar of cloud would descend and stand at the entrance, and the LORD would speak with Moses. {33:10} All the people saw the pillar of cloud standing at the entrance of the Tabernacle, and they all worshiped, each at the entrance to their tent. {33:11} The LORD spoke to Moses face to face, as a man speaks to his friend. Then Moses would return to the camp, but his young aide Joshua son of Nun did not leave the Tabernacle. {33:12} Moses said to the LORD, "You have been telling me, 'Lead these people,' but you have not let me know whom you will send with me. You said, 'I know you by name and you have found favor in my sight.' {33:13} If you are pleased with me, teach me your ways so I may know you and continue to find favor in your sight. Remember that this nation is your people." {33:14} The LORD replied, "My Presence will go with you, and I will give you rest." {33:15} Then Moses said to him, "If your Presence does not go with us, do not send us up from here. {33:16} How will anyone know that you are pleased with me and with your people unless you go with us? What else will distinguish me and your people from all the other people on the face of the earth?" {33:17} The LORD said to Moses, "I will do the very thing you have asked because I am pleased with you and I know you by name." {33:18} Then Moses said, "Now show me your glory." {33:19} The LORD said, "I will cause all my goodness to pass in front of you, and I will proclaim my name, the LORD, in your presence. I will have mercy on whom I will have mercy, and I will have compassion on whom I will have compassion." {33:20} But he said, "You cannot see my face, for no one may see me and live." {33:21} Then the LORD said, "There is a place near me where you may stand on a rock. {33:22} When my glory passes by, I will put you in a cleft (crack) in the rock and cover you with my hand until I have passed by. {33:23} Then I will remove my hand and you will see my back; but my face must not be seen."

{34:1} The LORD said to Moses, "Carve out two stone tablets like the first ones, and I will write on these tablets the words that were on the first ones, which you broke. {34:2} Be ready in the morning and come up to Mount Sinai. Present yourself to me at the top of the mountain. {34:3} No one else should come with you, and no one should be seen anywhere on the mountain. Even the flocks and herds must not graze near that mountain." {34:4} So Moses carved out two stone tablets like the first ones. Early in the morning, he went up Mount Sinai as the LORD had commanded him, carrying the two tablets of stone. {34:5} The LORD descended in the cloud and stood there with him and proclaimed his name, the LORD. {34:6} The LORD passed by in front of Moses, proclaiming, "The LORD, the LORD, the compassionate and gracious God, slow to anger, abounding in love and faithfulness, {34:7} maintaining love to thousands, and forgiving wickedness, rebellion, and sin. Yet he does not leave the guilty unpunished; he punishes the children and their children for the sin of the parents to the third and fourth generation." {34:8} Moses bowed to the ground at once and worshiped. {34:9} "If I have found favor in your eyes, Lord," he said, "then let the Lord go with us. This is a stiff-necked (stubborn) people; forgive our wickedness and sin, and take us as your inheritance." {34:10} The LORD replied, "I am making a covenant with you. Before all your people, I will do wonders never before done in any nation in all the world. The people you live among will see how awesome is the work that I, the LORD, will do for you. {34:11} Obey what I command you today. I will drive out before you the Amorites, Canaanites, Hittites, Perizzites, Hivites, and Jebusites. {34:12} Be careful not to make a treaty with those who live in the land where you are going, or they will be a snare (trap) among you. {34:13} Break down their altars, smash their sacred stones, and cut down their Asherah poles (wooden images). {34:14} Do not worship any other god, for the LORD, whose name is Jealous, is a jealous God. {34:15} Be careful not to make a treaty with those who live in the land; if you do, they will invite you to eat their sacrifices. {34:16} And when you choose some of their daughters as wives for your sons, and those daughters, in turn, lead your sons to worship their gods." {34:17} "Do not make any idols." {34:18} "Celebrate the Festival of Unleavened Bread. For seven days eat bread made without yeast, as I commanded you, at the appointed time in the month of Abib (March-April), for in that month you came out of Egypt. {34:19} The firstborn of every womb belongs to me, and all the firstborn males of your livestock, whether from herd or flock, are mine. {34:20} Redeem (buy back) the firstborn of a donkey with a lamb, but if you do not redeem it, break its neck. Redeem all your firstborn sons. No one is to appear before me empty-handed." {34:21} "Work for six days, but rest on the seventh day. Even during plowing time and harvest, you must rest." {34:22} "Celebrate the Festival of Weeks with the first fruits of the wheat harvest, and the Festival of Ingathering at the turn of the year." {34:23} "Three times a year, all your men must appear before the Sovereign LORD, the God of Israel. {34:24} I will drive out nations before you and enlarge your territory, and no one will covet your land when you go up three times each year to appear before the LORD your God." {34:25} "Do not offer the blood of a sacrifice to me along with anything made with yeast. The sacrifice of the Passover Festival must not be left until morning." {34:26} "Bring the best of the first fruits of your soil to the house of the LORD your God. Do not cook a young goat in its mother's milk." {34:27} The LORD said to Moses, "Write down these words, for in accordance with these words I have made a covenant with you and with Israel." {34:28} Moses was there with the LORD for forty days and forty nights. He did not eat bread or drink water, and he wrote on the tablets the words of the covenant—the Ten Commandments. {34:29} When Moses came down from Mount Sinai with the two tablets of the covenant in his hands, he was not aware that his face was radiant (shining) because he had spoken with the LORD. {34:30} When Aaron and all the Israelites saw Moses, his face was radiant, and they were afraid to come near him. {34:31} But Moses called to them; so Aaron and all the leaders of the community came back to him, and he spoke to them. {34:32} Afterward, all the Israelites came near him, and he gave them all the commands the LORD had given him on Mount Sinai. {34:33} When Moses finished speaking to them, he put a veil over his face. {34:34} But whenever he entered the LORD's presence to speak with him, he removed the veil until he came out. And when he came out and told the Israelites what he had been commanded, {34:35} they saw that his face was radiant. Then Moses would put the veil back over his face until he went in to speak with the LORD again.

{35:1} Moses gathered all the people of Israel and said to them, "These are the instructions the LORD has commanded you to follow. {35:2} For six days work may be done, but on the seventh day, you must observe a holy day, a Sabbath of rest to the LORD. Anyone who works on that day must be put to death. {35:3} Do not light a fire in any of your homes on the Sabbath." {35:4} Moses then told the whole congregation of Israel, "This is what the LORD has commanded: {35:5} Take an offering for the LORD from among you. Whoever has a willing heart should bring it as an offering to the LORD: gold, silver, and bronze, {35:6} blue, purple, and scarlet yarn, fine linen, goat hair, {35:7} ram skins dyed red, the hides of sea cows, and acacia wood, {35:8} oil for the light, spices for the anointing oil and for fragrant incense, {35:9} and onyx stones and other gems to be mounted on the ephod and the breastplate. {35:10} Every skilled person among you is to come and make everything the LORD has commanded: {35:11} the tabernacle and its tent, its covering, its hooks, its boards, its bars, its pillars, and its bases; {35:12} the ark and its poles, with the atonement cover and the curtain that shields it; {35:13} the table and its poles, all its articles, and the bread of the Presence; {35:14} the lampstand that is for light and its accessories, its lamps, and the oil for the light; {35:15} the altar of incense and its poles, the anointing oil, the fragrant incense, and the curtain for the entrance to the tabernacle; {35:16} the altar of burnt offering and its bronze grating, its poles, and all its utensils, the basin with its stand; {35:17} the hangings of the courtyard, its pillars and bases, and the curtain for the entrance to the courtyard; {35:18} the tent pegs for the tabernacle and for the courtyard, along with their ropes; {35:19} the garments for ministering in the holy place, and the sacred garments for Aaron the priest and his sons to serve as priests." {35:20} Then the whole congregation of the Israelites left Moses' presence. {35:21} Everyone who was willing and whose heart moved them came and brought an offering to the LORD for the work on the tent of meeting, for all its service, and for the sacred garments. {35:22} Both men and women came, all whose hearts were willing. They brought gold jewelry of all kinds: brooches, earrings, rings, and necklaces; they all presented their gold as a wave offering to the LORD. {35:23} Everyone who had blue, purple, or scarlet yarn, fine linen, goat hair, ram skins dyed red, or the hides of sea cows brought them. {35:24} Those who were willing brought silver or bronze as an offering to the LORD, and everyone who had acacia wood for any part of the work brought it. {35:25} Every skilled woman spun with her hands and brought what she had spun—blue, purple, or scarlet yarn and fine linen. {35:26} All the women who were willing and had the skill spun goat hair. {35:27} The leaders brought onyx stones and other gems to be mounted on the ephod and the breastplate; {35:28} they also brought spices and oil for the light, the anointing oil, and the fragrant incense. {35:29} All the Israelites brought their willing offerings to the LORD, every man and woman whose heart prompted them to bring for all the work the LORD had commanded through Moses. {35:30} Moses said to the Israelites, "The LORD has chosen Bezaleel son of Uri, the son of Hur, of the tribe of Judah, {35:31} and he has filled him with the Spirit of God, with wisdom, with understanding, with knowledge, and with all kinds of skills, {35:32} to make artistic designs for work in gold, silver, and bronze, {35:33} to cut and set stones, to work in wood, and to engage in all kinds of artistic craftsmanship. {35:34} And he has given both him and Oholiab son of Ahisamach, of the tribe of Dan, the ability to teach others. {35:35} He has filled them with skill to do all kinds of work as engravers, designers, embroiderers in blue, purple, and scarlet yarn, and fine linen, and as weavers—those skilled in all kinds of artistic work."

{36:1} Bezaleel, Aholiab, and every skilled craftsman in whom the LORD had placed wisdom and understanding, worked on the construction of the sanctuary, doing all the work that the LORD had commanded. {36:2} Moses called Bezaleel, Aholiab, and all the craftsmen who were gifted with wisdom from the LORD, and whose hearts were moved to come and help with the work. {36:3} They received from Moses all the offerings the Israelites had brought for the construction of the sanctuary. But the people continued to bring freewill offerings every morning. {36:4} All the skilled workers who were working on the sanctuary came from their tasks {36:5} and told Moses, "The people are bringing more than enough materials for the work the LORD has commanded us to do." {36:6} So Moses gave an order, and a message was sent throughout the camp: "No man or woman is to make anything else as an offering for the sanctuary." So the people were restrained from bringing more. {36:7} The materials they had were more than sufficient to complete all the work. {36:8} All the skilled workers among them made ten curtains of fine twisted linen, and blue, purple, and scarlet yarn, with cherubim (angelic figures) skillfully embroidered on them. {36:9} Each curtain was twenty-eight cubits long and four cubits wide; all the curtains were the same size. {36:10} They joined five of the curtains together, and the other five curtains were also joined together. {36:11} They made loops of blue material along the edge of the end curtain in one set, and the same was done on the edge of the end curtain in the other set. {36:12} They made fifty loops on one curtain and fifty loops on the edge of the curtain in the second set; the loops were opposite each other. {36:13} Then they made fifty gold clasps and used them to fasten the two sets of curtains together so that the tabernacle was one complete unit. {36:14} They made curtains of goat hair to be used as a tent covering over the tabernacle; they made eleven such curtains. {36:15} Each curtain was thirty cubits long and four cubits wide; the eleven curtains were all the same size. {36:16} They joined five of the curtains together into one set and the other six into another set. {36:17} Then they made fifty loops along the edge of the end curtain in one set and fifty loops along the edge of the end curtain in the other set. {36:18} They made fifty bronze clasps to join the tent together as a single unit. {36:19} They made a covering for the tent of ram skins dyed red, and over that a covering of durable leather. {36:20} For the framework of the tabernacle, they made upright frames of acacia wood (also called shittim wood). {36:21} Each frame was ten cubits long and a cubit and a half wide. {36:22} Each frame had two projections set parallel to each other; this was done for all the frames of the tabernacle. {36:23} They made twenty frames for the south side of the tabernacle, {36:24} and they made forty silver bases to go under them—two bases for each frame, one under each projection. {36:25} For the north side of the tabernacle, they made twenty frames {36:26} and forty silver bases—two bases for each frame. {36:27} They made six frames for the rear of the tabernacle, on the west side, {36:28} and two frames were made for the corners of the tabernacle at the rear. {36:29} At the two corners, the frames were doubled from the bottom all the way to the top and fitted into a single ring. The same was done at both corners. {36:30} So there were eight frames and sixteen silver bases—two under each frame. {36:31} They also made crossbars of acacia wood: five for the frames on one side of the tabernacle, {36:32} five for those on the other side, and five for the frames on the west, at the rear of the tabernacle. {36:33} They made the center crossbar so that it extended from end to end at the middle of the frames. {36:34} They overlaid the frames with gold and made gold rings to hold the crossbars. They also overlaid the crossbars with gold. {36:35} They made the curtain of blue, purple, and scarlet yarn and finely twisted linen, with cherubim skillfully embroidered on it. {36:36} They made four posts of acacia wood for it and overlaid them with gold. They also cast four silver bases for them. {36:37} For the entrance to the tent, they made a curtain of blue, purple, and scarlet yarn and finely twisted linen—the work of an embroiderer; {36:38} and they made five posts with hooks for them. They overlaid the tops of the posts and their bands with gold, and made their five bases of bronze.

{37:1} Bezaleel made the Ark out of acacia (shittim) wood. It was two and a half cubits long, one and a half cubits wide, and one and a half cubits high. {37:2} He covered it with pure gold inside and out and made a gold molding around it. {37:3} He cast four gold rings for it and attached them to its four corners, two rings on each side. {37:4} He made poles out of acacia wood and covered them with gold. {37:5} He inserted the poles into the rings on the sides of the Ark to carry it. {37:6} He made the atonement cover (mercy seat) out of pure gold, two and a half cubits long and one and a half cubits wide. {37:7} He made two cherubim (angels) out of hammered gold at the ends of the atonement cover, {37:8} one cherub on each end. He made them as one piece with the atonement cover. {37:9} The cherubim spread their wings upward, overshadowing the atonement cover, and faced each other, with their faces toward the cover. {37:10} He made the table out of acacia wood, two cubits long, one cubit wide, and one and a half cubits high. {37:11} He covered it with pure gold and made a gold molding around it. {37:12} He made a rim a handbreadth (a hand's width) wide and put a gold molding around the rim. {37:13} He cast four gold rings for the table and fastened them to the four corners where the four legs were. {37:14} The rings were attached near the rim to hold the poles used to carry the table. {37:15} He made the poles out of acacia wood and covered them with gold to carry the table. {37:16} He also made the plates, dishes, bowls, and pitchers used for pouring offerings, all out of pure gold. {37:17} He made the lampstand out of pure, hammered gold. Its base, shaft, branches, decorative cups, buds, and flowers were all made of one piece. {37:18} Six branches extended from the sides of the lampstand, three on one side and three on the other. {37:19} Each of the six branches had three decorative cups shaped like almond flowers, each with a bud and a flower. {37:20} The lampstand itself had four cups shaped like almond flowers, each with buds and flowers. {37:21} There was a bud under each pair of branches, three on one side and three on the other. {37:22} The buds and branches were all one piece with the lampstand, hammered out of pure gold. {37:23} He made its seven lamps, wick trimmers, and trays out of pure gold. {37:24} The lampstand and all its accessories were made from one talent (a unit of weight) of pure gold. {37:25} He made the incense altar out of acacia wood. It was square, one cubit long and one cubit wide, and two cubits high, with horns of one piece with it. {37:26} He covered the top, sides, and horns with pure gold and made a gold molding around it. {37:27} He made two gold rings below the molding on opposite sides to hold the poles used to carry it. {37:28} He made the poles out of acacia wood and covered them with gold. {37:29} He also made the sacred anointing oil and the pure, fragrant incense, the work of a skilled perfumer.

{38:1} He made the altar of burnt offering from acacia wood, measuring five cubits long, five cubits wide (making it square), and three cubits high. {38:2} He made horns on each of its four corners, all of one piece with the altar, and overlaid the entire altar with bronze. {38:3} He made all the utensils for the altar, including pots, shovels, basins, meat forks, and firepans, all out of bronze. {38:4} He made a bronze grating for the altar, a network under its ledge halfway up the altar. {38:5} He cast four bronze rings to hold the grating at the four corners. {38:6} He made poles of acacia wood and overlaid them with bronze. {38:7} He inserted the poles into the rings on the sides of the altar to carry it, and he made the altar hollow, using boards. {38:8} He made the bronze basin and its stand from the mirrors of the women who served at the entrance to the tent of meeting. {38:9} He made the courtyard: on the south side, the hangings of the courtyard were made of finely twisted linen, 100 cubits long. {38:10} There were 20 posts and 20 bronze bases, with silver hooks and bands on the posts. {38:11} The north side was also 100 cubits long, with 20 posts and 20 bronze bases, and silver hooks and bands on the posts. {38:12} The west side was 50 cubits long, with curtains, 10 posts, and 10 bases, and silver hooks and bands on the posts. {38:13} The east side, also 50 cubits long, {38:14} had curtains 15 cubits long on one side of the entrance, with three posts and three bases, {38:15} and curtains 15 cubits long on the other side, with three posts and three bases. {38:16} All the curtains around the courtyard were made of finely twisted linen. {38:17} The bases for the posts were bronze, their hooks and bands were silver, and their tops were overlaid with silver; all the posts of the courtyard had silver bands. {38:18} The curtain for the entrance to the courtyard was made of blue, purple, and scarlet yarn, and finely twisted linen, the work of an embroiderer. It was 20 cubits long and 5 cubits high, like the curtains of the courtyard. {38:19} It was supported by four posts and four bronze bases, with silver hooks, and the tops of the posts were overlaid with silver, with silver bands. {38:20} All the tent pegs of the tabernacle and the surrounding courtyard were bronze. {38:21} This is the inventory of the tabernacle, the tabernacle of the covenant law, which was recorded at Moses' command by the Levites under the direction of Ithamar, son of Aaron the priest. {38:22} Bezalel son of Uri, the son of Hur, from the tribe of Judah, made everything the Lord commanded Moses. {38:23} With him was Oholiab son of Ahisamak, from the tribe of Dan, who was a skilled craftsman and designer, and an embroiderer in blue, purple, and scarlet yarn, and fine linen. {38:24} The total amount of gold from the wave offering used for all the work on the sanctuary was 29 talents and 730 shekels, according to the sanctuary shekel. {38:25} The silver obtained from those who were counted in the census was 100 talents and 1,775 shekels, according to the sanctuary shekel. {38:26} A beka, or half a shekel, for each man counted in the census, from 20 years old and up, came to 603,550 men. {38:27} The 100 talents of silver were used to cast the bases for the sanctuary and the curtain—100 bases from the 100 talents, one talent for each base. {38:28} With the 1,775 shekels, he made hooks for the posts, overlaid their tops, and made bands for them. {38:29} The bronze from the wave offering was 70 talents and 2,400 shekels. {38:30} With it, he made the bases for the entrance to the tent of meeting, the bronze altar with its bronze grating and all its utensils, {38:31} the bases for the surrounding courtyard and for the entrance, and all the tent pegs for the tabernacle and the courtyard.

{39:1} They made the garments for ministry in the sanctuary from blue, purple, and scarlet yarn, as well as the holy garments for Aaron, as the LORD had commanded Moses. {39:2} They made the ephod from gold, blue, purple, and scarlet yarn, and finely twisted linen. {39:3} They hammered the gold into thin sheets and cut it into strands to work into the blue, purple, and scarlet yarn, and the fine linen, with skilled craftsmanship. {39:4} They made shoulder pieces for the ephod, which were joined at its two ends. {39:5} The finely woven waistband of the ephod was made in the same way, from gold, blue, purple, and scarlet yarn, and finely twisted linen, as the LORD commanded Moses. {39:6} They mounted the onyx stones in gold filigree settings and engraved them like a seal with the names of the sons of Israel. {39:7} Then they fastened them on the shoulder pieces of the ephod as memorial stones for the sons of Israel, as the LORD commanded Moses. {39:8} They made the breastplate with skilled craftsmanship like the ephod, out of gold, blue, purple, and scarlet yarn, and finely twisted linen. {39:9} It was square—a span long and a span wide—and folded double. {39:10} They mounted four rows of gemstones on it: the first row was a ruby, a topaz, and a beryl; {39:11} the second row was a turquoise, a sapphire, and an emerald; {39:12} the third row was a jacint, an agate, and an amethyst; {39:13} and the fourth row was a chrysolite, an onyx, and a jasper. They were mounted in gold filigree settings. {39:14} The stones corresponded to the names of the sons of Israel, twelve stones with twelve names, engraved like a seal, each with the name of one of the twelve tribes. {39:15} They made braided chains of pure gold for the breastplate, like cords. {39:16} They made two gold filigree settings and two gold rings, and fastened the rings to two corners of the breastplate. {39:17} They attached the two gold chains to the rings at the corners of the breastplate, {39:18} and the other ends of the chains to the filigree settings, which they fastened to the shoulder pieces of the ephod at the front. {39:19} They made two gold rings and attached them to the other two corners of the breastplate, on the inside edge next to the ephod. {39:20} They made two more gold rings and attached them to the bottom of the shoulder pieces on the front of the ephod, close to the seam just above the waistband. {39:21} They tied the rings of the breastplate to the rings of the ephod with a blue cord, so that the breastplate would rest securely above the waistband and not come loose from the ephod, as the LORD commanded Moses. {39:22} They made the robe of the ephod entirely of blue cloth, the work of a weaver. {39:23} With an opening in the center of the robe, like the opening of a collar, and a band around this opening so it would not tear. {39:24} They made pomegranates of blue, purple, and scarlet yarn, and finely twisted linen around the hem of the robe. {39:25} They also made bells of pure gold and placed them between the pomegranates around the hem of the robe, {39:26} alternating bells and pomegranates around the hem, for ministering, as the LORD commanded Moses. {39:27} For Aaron and his sons, they made tunics of fine linen, the work of a weaver, {39:28} and the turban of fine linen, the linen headbands, and the undergarments of finely twisted linen. {39:29} They also made the sash of finely twisted linen, blue, purple, and scarlet yarn—the work of an embroiderer, as the LORD commanded Moses. {39:30} They made the plate, the holy diadem, out of pure gold and engraved on it, like an inscription on a seal, "HOLINESS TO THE LORD." {39:31} They fastened a blue cord to it to attach it to the turban, as the LORD commanded Moses. {39:32} So all the work for the tabernacle, the tent of meeting, was completed. The Israelites did everything just as the LORD commanded Moses. {39:33} Then they brought the tabernacle to Moses: the tent and all its furnishings, its clasps, frames, crossbars, posts, and bases; {39:34} the covering of ram skins dyed red, the covering of hides of sea cows, and the shielding curtain; {39:35} the ark of the testimony with its poles and the atonement cover; {39:36} the table with all its articles and the bread of the Presence; {39:37} the pure gold lampstand with its row of lamps and all its accessories, and the oil for the light; {39:38} the gold altar, the anointing oil, the fragrant incense, and the curtain for the entrance to the tent; {39:39} the bronze altar with its bronze grating, its poles, and all its utensils; the basin with its stand; {39:40} the curtains of the courtyard with its posts and bases, and the curtain for the entrance to the courtyard; the ropes and tent pegs for the courtyard—all the equipment for the service of the tabernacle, the tent of meeting; {39:41} and the woven garments worn for ministering in the sanctuary, both the sacred garments for Aaron the priest and the garments for his sons when serving as priests. {39:42} The Israelites had done all the work just as the LORD commanded Moses. {39:43} Moses inspected the work and saw that they had done it just as the LORD had commanded. So Moses blessed them.

{40:1} The LORD spoke to Moses, saying, {40:2} "On the first day of the first month, you shall set up the tabernacle, the tent of meeting. {40:3} Place the ark of the testimony in it and shield the ark with the veil. {40:4} Bring in the table and arrange what belongs on it, then bring in the lampstand and light its lamps. {40:5} Set the gold altar of incense in front of the ark of the testimony, and hang the curtain at the entrance to the tabernacle. {40:6} Place the altar for burnt offerings in front of the entrance of the tabernacle, the tent of meeting. {40:7} Set the basin between the tent of meeting and the altar and put water in it. {40:8} Set up the courtyard around the tabernacle and altar, and hang the curtain at the entrance to the courtyard. {40:9} Take the anointing oil and anoint the tabernacle and everything in it; consecrate it and all its furnishings, and it will be holy. {40:10} Anoint the altar for burnt offerings and all its utensils; consecrate the altar, and it will be most holy. {40:11} Anoint the basin and its stand and consecrate them. {40:12} Then bring Aaron and his sons to the entrance of the tent of meeting and wash them with water. {40:13} Dress Aaron in the holy garments, anoint him, and consecrate him, so he may serve me as priest. {40:14} Bring his sons and clothe them with tunics. {40:15} Anoint them just as you anointed their father, so they may serve me as priests. Their anointing will be a lasting priesthood throughout their generations." {40:16} Moses did everything just as the LORD commanded him. {40:17} On the first day of the first month of the second year, the tabernacle was set up. {40:18} Moses set up the tabernacle, placing its bases, setting up its frames, inserting its crossbars, and setting up its posts. {40:19} Then he spread the tent over the tabernacle and put the covering over the tent, as the LORD commanded him. {40:20} He took the testimony and placed it inside the ark, attached the poles to the ark, and put the mercy seat on top of the ark. {40:21} He brought the ark into the tabernacle, hung the shielding veil, and shielded the ark of the testimony, as the LORD commanded him. {40:22} Moses placed the table in the tent of meeting on the north side of the tabernacle, outside the veil, {40:23} and set the bread in order on it before the LORD, as the LORD commanded him. {40:24} He placed the lampstand in the tent of meeting opposite the table, on the south side of the tabernacle, {40:25} and set up the lamps before the LORD, as the LORD commanded him. {40:26} Moses placed the gold altar in the tent of meeting, in front of the veil, {40:27} and burned fragrant incense on it, as the LORD commanded him. {40:28} Then he put up the curtain at the entrance to the tabernacle. {40:29} He set the altar of burnt offering at the entrance to the tabernacle, the tent of meeting, and offered on it burnt offerings and grain offerings, as the LORD commanded him. {40:30} He placed the basin between the tent of meeting and the altar, and put water in it for washing. {40:31} Moses, Aaron, and his sons washed their hands and feet with water from it. {40:32} Whenever they entered the tent of meeting or approached the altar, they washed, as the LORD commanded Moses. {40:33} Then Moses set up the courtyard around the tabernacle and altar and hung the curtain at the entrance to the courtyard. And so Moses finished the work. {40:34} Then the cloud covered the tent of meeting, and the glory of the LORD filled the tabernacle. {40:35} Moses could not enter the tent of meeting because the cloud had settled on it, and the glory of the LORD filled the tabernacle. {40:36} In all the travels of the Israelites, whenever the cloud lifted from above the tabernacle, they would set out. {40:37} But if the cloud did not lift, they did not set out until the day it lifted. {40:38} So the cloud of the LORD was over the tabernacle by day, and fire was in the cloud by night, in the sight of all the Israelites during all their travels.

The Third Book of Moses, called Leviticus

{1:1} The LORD called to Moses and spoke to him from the tent of meeting, saying, {1:2} "Speak to the people of Israel and say to them: If any of you brings an offering to the LORD, you should bring your offering from the herd or from the flock. {1:3} If your offering is a burnt sacrifice from the herd, you must offer a male without any defects. You should bring it willingly to the entrance of the tent of meeting before the LORD. {1:4} You must lay your hand on the head of the burnt offering, and it will be accepted on your behalf to make atonement for you. {1:5} You shall slaughter the bull before the LORD, and Aaron's sons, the priests, will take the blood and sprinkle it around the altar that is by the entrance of the tent of meeting. {1:6} You shall then skin the burnt offering and cut it into pieces. {1:7} Aaron's sons, the priests, will put fire on the altar and arrange the wood on the fire. {1:8} The priests, the sons of Aaron, will arrange the parts—the head and the fat—on the wood that is on the fire on the altar. {1:9} But you must wash the innards and the legs with water, and the priest will burn everything on the altar as a burnt sacrifice, an offering made by fire, with a pleasing aroma to the LORD. {1:10} If your offering is from the flock, either from sheep or goats, for a burnt sacrifice, you must bring a male without defects. {1:11} You shall kill it on the north side of the altar before the LORD, and Aaron's sons, the priests, will sprinkle its blood around the altar. {1:12} You must cut it into pieces, including the head and the fat, and the priest will arrange them on the wood that is on the fire on the altar. {1:13} You shall wash the innards and the legs with water, and the priest will bring everything and burn it on the altar; it is a burnt sacrifice, an offering made by fire, with a pleasing aroma to the LORD. {1:14} If your burnt sacrifice to the LORD is from birds, then you may bring turtledoves or young pigeons. {1:15} The priest will bring it to the altar, wring off its head, and burn it on the altar; the blood will be drained out at the side of the altar. {1:16} He shall remove the crop with its feathers and throw it beside the altar on the east side, where the ashes are. {1:17} He shall cut it open at the wings, but not divide it completely. The priest shall burn it on the altar, on the wood that is on the fire; it is a burnt sacrifice, an offering made by fire, with a pleasing aroma to the LORD.

{2:1} When anyone brings a grain offering to the LORD, it must be made of fine flour. He should pour oil on it and add frankincense. {2:2} He will bring it to Aaron's sons, the priests. The priest will take a handful of the flour, oil, and all the frankincense and burn it as a memorial offering on the altar; this will be a fire offering with a pleasing aroma to the LORD. {2:3} The rest of the grain offering will belong to Aaron and his sons; it is most holy from the offerings made by fire to the LORD. {2:4} If you bring a grain offering baked in the oven, it should consist of unleavened cakes made of fine flour mixed with oil or unleavened wafers anointed with oil. {2:5} If your grain offering is baked in a pan, it should be made of unleavened fine flour mixed with oil. {2:6} You shall cut it into pieces and pour oil on it; this is a grain offering. {2:7} If your grain offering is cooked in a frying pan, it should also be made of fine flour with oil. {2:8} You will bring the grain offering made from these ingredients to the LORD, and when presented to the priest, he will bring it to the altar. {2:9} The priest will take a portion of the grain offering as a memorial and burn it on the altar; it is a fire offering with a pleasing aroma to the LORD. {2:10} What remains of the grain offering will belong to Aaron and his sons; it is most holy from the offerings made by fire to the LORD. {2:11} No grain offering you bring to the LORD should contain leaven; you must not burn leaven or honey in any fire offering to the LORD. {2:12} As for the firstfruits offering, you shall present them to the LORD, but they must not be burned on the altar as a pleasing aroma. {2:13} Every grain offering must be seasoned with salt; do not leave out the salt of the covenant of your God from your grain offering. You should offer salt with all your offerings. {2:14} If you bring a grain offering of your firstfruits to the LORD, it should consist of green ears of corn that have been dried by fire, even corn beaten from full ears. {2:15} You should put oil on it and lay frankincense on it; this is a grain offering. {2:16} The priest will burn part of it as a memorial, including some of the beaten corn and part of the oil, along with all the frankincense; it is a fire offering to the LORD.

{3:1} If someone offers a peace offering sacrifice from the herd, whether male or female, it must be without blemish presented before the LORD. {3:2} He will lay his hand on the head of the offering and kill it at the entrance of the tabernacle; Aaron's sons, the priests, will sprinkle the blood around the altar. {3:3} He will present part of the peace offering as a fire offering to the LORD, including the fat that covers the internal organs and all the fat on the organs, {3:4} the two kidneys and the fat on them, which is near the flanks, and the membrane over the liver along with the kidneys, which he will remove. {3:5} Aaron's sons will burn this on the altar on top of the burnt sacrifice, which is on the wood that is burning; it is a fire offering with a pleasing aroma to the LORD. {3:6} If the peace offering is from the flock, whether male or female, it must also be without blemish. {3:7} If he offers a lamb, he will present it before the LORD. {3:8} He will lay his hand on its head and kill it in front of the tabernacle; Aaron's sons will sprinkle its blood around the altar. {3:9} He will present part of the peace offering as a fire offering to the LORD, including the fat and the entire tail, which he will remove near the backbone, along with the fat that covers the internal organs and all the fat on the organs, {3:10} the two kidneys and the fat on them near the flanks, and the membrane over the liver, which he will remove with the kidneys. {3:11} The priest will burn it on the altar; it is the food of the fire offering to the LORD. {3:12} If his offering is a goat, he will present it before the LORD. {3:13} He will lay his hand on its head and kill it at the entrance of the tabernacle; Aaron's sons will sprinkle its blood around the altar. {3:14} He will present part of it as a fire offering to the LORD, including the fat that covers the internal organs and all the fat on the organs, {3:15} the two kidneys and the fat on them near the flanks, and the membrane over the liver, which he will remove with the kidneys. {3:16} The priest will burn these on the altar; it is the food of the fire offering with a pleasing aroma. All the fat belongs to the LORD. {3:17} This is to be a lasting ordinance for your generations and throughout all your dwellings: you must not eat any fat or blood.

{4:1} The LORD spoke to Moses, saying, {4:2} "Tell the Israelites that if someone sins unintentionally against any of the LORD's commandments regarding things that should not be done, and does any of them: {4:3} If the anointed priest sins, bringing guilt upon the people, he must bring a young bull without blemish to the LORD as a sin offering for his sin. {4:4} He will bring the bull to the entrance of the tabernacle and lay his hand on its head, then kill it before the LORD. {4:5} The anointed priest will take some of the bull's blood and bring it to the tabernacle. {4:6} He will dip his finger in the blood and sprinkle it seven times before the LORD, in front of the curtain of the sanctuary. {4:7} He will put some of the blood on the horns of the altar of incense before the LORD, which is in the tabernacle, and pour all the rest of the blood at the base of the altar of burnt offering at the entrance of the tabernacle. {4:8} He will remove all the fat from the bull for the sin offering: the fat that covers the internal organs and all the fat on the organs, {4:9} the two kidneys and the fat near them by the flanks, and the membrane over the liver, which he will remove along with the kidneys. {4:10} This is done just as with the fat from the peace offerings; the priest will burn them on the altar of burnt offerings. {4:11} The skin of the bull, along with all its flesh, its head, legs, internal organs, and dung, {4:12} must be carried outside the camp to a clean place where the ashes are disposed of and burned on wood with fire; where the ashes are poured out, it must be burned. {4:13} If the entire congregation of Israel sins unintentionally and the matter is hidden from the assembly, and they commit something against the LORD's commandments that should not be done, they are guilty. {4:14} When the sin they have committed is made known, the congregation must offer a young bull for the sin and bring it before the tabernacle. {4:15} The elders of the congregation will lay their hands on the head of the bull before the LORD, and it will be killed before the LORD. {4:16} The anointed priest will take some of the bull's blood to the tabernacle. {4:17} He will dip his finger in the blood and sprinkle it seven times before the LORD, even before the curtain. {4:18} He will put some of the blood on the horns of the altar before the LORD, which is in the tabernacle, and pour all the blood at the base of the altar of burnt offering at the entrance of the tabernacle. {4:19} He will remove all the fat from it and burn it on the altar. {4:20} He will do with this bull as he did with the previous sin offering, and the priest will make atonement for them, and they will be forgiven. {4:21} He will carry the bull outside the camp and burn it just as he burned the first bull; it is a sin offering for the congregation. {4:22} When a ruler sins and does something unintentionally against the commandments of the LORD his God that should not be done, he is guilty. {4:23} If he realizes his sin, he must bring his offering: a male goat without blemish. {4:24} He will lay his hand on the goat's head and kill it in the same place where the burnt offerings are killed; it is a sin offering. {4:25} The priest will take some of the blood from the sin offering and put it on the horns of the altar of burnt offering, pouring out the rest of the blood at the base of the altar. {4:26} He will burn all its fat on the altar, just as with the fat from the peace offerings; the priest will make atonement for him concerning his sin, and it will be forgiven. {4:27} If any of the common people sins unintentionally against any of the LORD's commandments that should not be done and is guilty, {4:28} or if he realizes his sin, he must bring a female goat without blemish for the sin he has committed. {4:29} He will lay his hand on the head of the sin offering and kill it in the same place as the burnt offering. {4:30} The priest will take some of its blood with his finger and put it on the horns of the altar of burnt offering, pouring out all the blood at the base of the altar. {4:31} He will remove all the fat just as it is taken from the peace offerings, and the priest will burn it on the altar as a pleasing aroma to the LORD; the priest will make atonement for him, and it will be forgiven. {4:32} If he brings a lamb for a sin offering, it must be a female without blemish. {4:33} He will lay his hand on the head of the sin offering and kill it for a sin offering in the place where they kill the burnt offering. {4:34} The priest will take some of the blood of the sin offering with his finger and put it on the horns of the altar of burnt offering, pouring out all the blood at the base of the altar. {4:35} He will remove all the fat just as the fat of the lamb is taken from the peace offerings, and the priest will burn them on the altar according to the fire offerings to the LORD; the priest will make atonement for the sin he has committed, and it will be forgiven.

{5:1} If someone sins and hears a voice of swearing, and is a witness, whether he has seen or knows about it, if he does not speak up, he will be responsible for his guilt. {5:2} Or if someone touches any unclean thing, whether it's a dead body of an unclean animal, or the carcass of unclean cattle, or the dead body of unclean insects, and it is hidden from him, he will also be unclean and guilty. {5:3} If he touches a human uncleanness, whatever it is that makes a person unclean, and it is hidden from him, when he realizes it, he will be guilty. {5:4} If someone swears, intending to do evil or good, whatever he swears by, and it is hidden from him, when he realizes it, he will be guilty in any of these cases. {5:5} When he is guilty in any of these matters, he must confess that he has sinned. {5:6} He will bring his guilt offering to the LORD for his sin, a female from the flock, a lamb or a goat kid, as a sin offering; and the priest will make atonement for him regarding his sin. {5:7} If he cannot afford a lamb, he will bring two turtledoves or two young pigeons to the LORD; one for a sin offering and the other for a burnt offering. {5:8} He will bring them to the priest, who will first offer the one for the sin offering, wringing off its head from its neck without dividing it. {5:9} He will sprinkle some of the blood from the sin offering on the side of the altar, and the rest of the blood will be poured out at the base of the altar; it is a sin offering. {5:10} He will offer the second bird as a burnt offering, following the prescribed procedure, and the priest will make atonement for him for the sin he has committed, and it will be forgiven. {5:11} If he cannot bring two turtledoves or two young pigeons, he will bring a tenth of an ephah (a measure of grain) of fine flour for a sin offering; he must not put oil or frankincense on it, because it is a sin offering. {5:12} He will bring it to the priest, who will take a handful of it as a memorial portion and burn it on the altar, following the fire offerings to the LORD; it is a sin offering. {5:13} The priest will make atonement for him regarding the sin he has committed in one of these ways, and it will be forgiven; the remainder will belong to the priest as a grain offering. {5:14} The LORD spoke to Moses, saying, {5:15} "If someone commits a trespass and sins unintentionally regarding the holy things of the LORD, he must bring a ram without blemish from the flock, valued according to your estimation in shekels of silver, based on the sanctuary shekel, as a trespass offering to the LORD. {5:16} He will make restitution for the harm he has done to the holy thing, adding one-fifth of its value, and give it to the priest; the priest will make atonement for him with the ram of the trespass offering, and it will be forgiven. {5:17} If someone sins and does any of these things that are forbidden by the commandments of the LORD, even if he is unaware, he is guilty and will bear his iniquity. {5:18} He will bring a ram without blemish from the flock, valued according to your estimation, as a trespass offering to the priest; and the priest will make atonement for him concerning his unintentional sin, and it will be forgiven. {5:19} This is a trespass offering; he has certainly trespassed against the LORD.

{6:1} The LORD spoke to Moses, saying, {6:2} "If someone sins and commits a trespass against the LORD, lying to their neighbor about something entrusted to them, or in a matter of fellowship, or something taken by force, or deceiving their neighbor; {6:3} or if they find something lost and lie about it, swearing falsely; in any of these acts, a person commits sin: {6:4} then, because they have sinned and are guilty, they must restore what they took by force, or what they gained deceitfully, or what was entrusted to them, or the lost item they found, {6:5} or whatever they swore falsely about; they must return it in full and add a fifth of its value, giving it to the rightful owner on the day of their trespass offering. {6:6} They shall bring their trespass offering to the LORD, a ram without blemish from the flock, valued according to your estimation, as a trespass offering to the priest. {6:7} The priest will make atonement for them before the LORD, and it will be forgiven for anything they have done in trespassing. {6:8} The LORD spoke to Moses, saying, {6:9} "Command Aaron and his sons, saying, 'This is the law of the burnt offering: It is the burnt offering because it is consumed on the altar all night until morning, and the fire of the altar must always be kept burning. {6:10} The priest shall put on his linen garments, and his linen undergarments, and gather the ashes that the fire has consumed from the burnt offering on the altar, and place them beside the altar. {6:11} He shall take off his garments, put on other clothes, and carry the ashes outside the camp to a clean place. {6:12} The fire on the altar must be kept burning; it shall not be put out. The priest shall burn wood on it every morning, arrange the burnt offering on it, and burn the fat of the peace offerings on it. {6:13} The fire must always be kept burning on the altar; it shall never go out. {6:14} This is the law of the grain offering: Aaron's sons shall present it before the LORD at the altar. {6:15} The priest shall take a handful of the fine flour from the grain offering, along with the oil and all the frankincense, and burn it on the altar as a sweet aroma, a memorial portion to the LORD. {6:16} The remainder of it shall be eaten by Aaron and his sons; it shall be eaten with unleavened bread in a holy place, in the court of the tabernacle. {6:17} It shall not be baked with leaven; I have given it to them as their share of my offerings made by fire; it is most holy, just like the sin offering and the trespass offering. {6:18} All the males among Aaron's descendants may eat it; it is a permanent statute for your generations regarding the offerings made by fire to the LORD: anyone who touches them shall be holy. {6:19} The LORD spoke to Moses, saying, {6:20} "This is the offering of Aaron and his sons that they shall present to the LORD on the day he is anointed: a tenth of an ephah of fine flour as a perpetual grain offering, half in the morning and half at night. {6:21} It shall be made with oil in a pan; when it is baked, you shall bring it in, and the baked pieces of the grain offering shall be offered as a sweet aroma to the LORD. {6:22} The priest, who is anointed in his place, shall offer it; it is a permanent statute for the LORD; it shall be entirely burned. {6:23} Every grain offering for the priest shall be entirely burned; it shall not be eaten. {6:24} The LORD spoke to Moses, saying, {6:25} "Speak to Aaron and his sons, saying, 'This is the law of the sin offering: where the burnt offering is killed, the sin offering shall be killed before the LORD; it is most holy. {6:26} The priest who offers it for sin shall eat it; it shall be eaten in the holy place, in the court of the tabernacle. {6:27} Whatever touches its flesh shall be holy, and if any of its blood is sprinkled on a garment, you shall wash it in a holy place. {6:28} But if it is cooked in an earthen vessel, it shall be broken; and if it is cooked in a bronze pot, it shall be scoured and rinsed in water. {6:29} All the males among the priests shall eat it; it is most holy. {6:30} No sin offering, where any of the blood is brought into the tabernacle to make atonement in the holy place, shall be eaten; it shall be burned in the fire."

{7:1} Likewise, this is the law of the trespass offering: it is most holy. {7:2} It must be killed in the same place where they kill the burnt offering, and its blood shall be sprinkled around the altar. {7:3} All the fat must be offered, including the tail, the fat covering the inner organs, {7:4} the two kidneys and the fat on them by the flanks, and the membrane above the liver, along with the kidneys; {7:5} the priest shall burn them on the altar as a fire offering to the LORD: it is a trespass offering. {7:6} Every male among the priests shall eat it; it shall be eaten in a holy place: it is most holy. {7:7} Just as with the sin offering, so is the trespass offering: there is one law for both; the priest who makes atonement with it shall have it. {7:8} The priest who offers anyone's burnt offering shall keep the skin of the burnt offering he has offered for himself. {7:9} All the grain offerings baked in the oven, prepared in a frying pan, or cooked in a pot shall belong to the priest who offers them. {7:10} Every grain offering mixed with oil or dry shall be shared equally among all of Aaron's sons. {7:11} This is the law of the peace offerings that he shall offer to the LORD. {7:12} If he offers it for thanksgiving, he shall bring unleavened cakes mixed with oil, unleavened wafers anointed with oil, and fried cakes made with fine flour and oil, {7:13} along with leavened bread for the sacrifice of thanksgiving from his peace offerings. {7:14} From the whole offering, he shall present one part as a wave offering to the LORD, and it shall belong to the priest who sprinkles the blood of the peace offerings. {7:15} The meat from the sacrifice of his peace offerings for thanksgiving shall be eaten the same day it is offered; nothing of it shall be left until morning. {7:16} But if the offering is for a vow or a voluntary offering, it may be eaten the same day and the remainder can be eaten the next day; {7:17} however, anything left over on the third day must be burned in the fire. {7:18} If any of the flesh from the sacrifice of his peace offerings is eaten on the third day, it will not be accepted, nor will it be credited to the one who offered it; it shall be an abomination, and the person who eats it shall bear their guilt. {7:19} The flesh that touches anything unclean shall not be eaten; it must be burned with fire. Only clean flesh may be eaten. {7:20} But if someone eats the flesh of the peace offering that belongs to the LORD while they are unclean, that person shall be cut off from their people. {7:21} Furthermore, if someone touches any unclean thing, whether it's human uncleanness, an unclean animal, or any unclean object, and then eats the flesh of the peace offerings belonging to the LORD, that person shall be cut off from their people. {7:22} The LORD spoke to Moses, saying, {7:23} "Tell the Israelites that they must not eat any fat from oxen, sheep, or goats. {7:24} The fat from animals that die of themselves or are torn by other animals may be used for other purposes, but you must not eat it. {7:25} Anyone who eats the fat of an animal offered as a fire offering to the LORD shall be cut off from their people. {7:26} You must not eat any blood, whether from birds or animals, in any of your homes. {7:27} Anyone who eats any blood shall be cut off from their people." {7:28} The LORD spoke to Moses, saying, {7:29} "Tell the Israelites that anyone who offers a sacrifice of their peace offerings to the LORD must bring their offering to the LORD from the peace offerings. {7:30} Their own hands shall bring the fire offerings to the LORD, including the fat with the breast, so that the breast may be waved as a wave offering before the LORD. {7:31} The priest shall burn the fat on the altar, but the breast shall belong to Aaron and his sons. {7:32} You shall give the right shoulder to the priest as a heave offering from your peace offerings. {7:33} The priest's sons who offer the blood and the fat of the peace offerings shall receive the right shoulder as their share. {7:34} I have taken the wave breast and the heave shoulder from the Israelites' peace offerings and given them to Aaron the priest and his sons as a permanent statute throughout their generations. {7:35} This is the portion set aside for Aaron and his sons from the offerings made by fire to the LORD on the day they were anointed to serve as priests. {7:36} The LORD commanded that these gifts be given to them by the Israelites on the day he anointed them, as a permanent statute throughout their generations. {7:37} This is the law for the burnt offering, the grain offering, the sin offering, the trespass offering, the consecration offerings, and the peace offerings; {7:38} which the LORD commanded Moses on Mount Sinai when he commanded the Israelites to bring their offerings to the LORD in the wilderness of Sinai.

{8:1} The LORD spoke to Moses, saying, {8:2} "Take Aaron and his sons with him, along with the garments, the anointing oil, a bull for the sin offering, two rams, and a basket of unleavened bread. {8:3} Gather all the congregation together at the entrance of the tabernacle." {8:4} Moses did as the LORD commanded him, and the assembly gathered at the entrance of the tabernacle. {8:5} Moses said to the congregation, "This is what the LORD has commanded to be done." {8:6} Moses brought Aaron and his sons and washed them with water. {8:7} He put the tunic on Aaron, fastened the sash around him, clothed him with the robe, placed the ephod on him, and fastened the special sash of the ephod around him. {8:8} He placed the breastplate on him, adding the Urim and Thummim into the breastplate. {8:9} He set the turban on his head and placed the golden plate, the holy crown, on the front of the turban, as the LORD commanded Moses. {8:10} Moses took the anointing oil and anointed the tabernacle and everything in it, consecrating them. {8:11} He sprinkled some of the oil on the altar seven times, anointing the altar and all its utensils, including the basin and its stand, to consecrate them. {8:12} He poured some of the anointing oil on Aaron's head and anointed him to consecrate him. {8:13} Moses brought Aaron's sons, put tunics on them, fastened sashes around them, and placed turbans on them, as the LORD commanded Moses. {8:14} He brought the bull for the sin offering, and Aaron and his sons laid their hands on its head. {8:15} He killed it, and Moses took the blood, put it on the horns of the altar all around with his finger, purified the altar, and poured the blood at the base of the altar, consecrating it to make atonement for it. {8:16} He took all the fat from the inner organs, the membrane above the liver, the two kidneys and their fat, and Moses burned them on the altar. {8:17} But he burned the bull, its hide, flesh, and waste with fire outside the camp, as the LORD commanded Moses. {8:18} He brought the ram for the burnt offering, and Aaron and his sons laid their hands on its head. {8:19} He killed it, and Moses sprinkled the blood on the altar all around. {8:20} He cut the ram into pieces; Moses burned the head, pieces, and fat. {8:21} He washed the inner organs and legs in water, and Moses burned the whole ram on the altar: it was a burnt offering with a pleasing aroma, a fire offering to the LORD, as the LORD commanded Moses. {8:22} He brought the other ram, the ram of consecration, and Aaron and his sons laid their hands on its head. {8:23} He killed it, and Moses took some of its blood and put it on the tip of Aaron's right ear, the thumb of his right hand, and the big toe of his right foot. {8:24} He brought Aaron's sons and put some of the blood on the tips of their right ears, the thumbs of their right hands, and the big toes of their right feet; and Moses sprinkled the blood on the altar all around. {8:25} He took the fat, the tail, all the fat from the inner organs, the membrane above the liver, the two kidneys and their fat, and the right shoulder; {8:26} from the basket of unleavened bread that was before the LORD, he took one unleavened cake, one cake of oiled bread, and one wafer, and placed them on the fat and the right shoulder. {8:27} He put everything on Aaron's hands and his sons' hands and waved them as a wave offering before the LORD. {8:28} Moses took them from their hands and burned them on the altar on top of the burnt offering; they were consecrations with a pleasing aroma, a fire offering to the LORD. {8:29} Moses took the breast and waved it as a wave offering before the LORD, for it was Moses' share from the ram of consecration, as the LORD commanded Moses. {8:30} Moses took some of the anointing oil and some of the blood that was on the altar and sprinkled it on Aaron, his garments, his sons, and their garments with him, consecrating Aaron, his garments, his sons, and their garments. {8:31} Moses said to Aaron and his sons, "Boil the flesh at the entrance of the tabernacle and eat it with the bread in the basket of consecrations, as I commanded, saying, 'Aaron and his sons shall eat it.' {8:32} Whatever remains of the flesh and bread you shall burn with fire. {8:33} You shall not leave the entrance of the tabernacle for seven days, until your consecration is complete, because for seven days the LORD shall consecrate you. {8:34} What has been done today is what the LORD has commanded to atone for you. {8:35} Therefore, you shall remain at the entrance of the tabernacle day and night for seven days, and keep watch over the LORD's charge, so that you do not die, for this is what I have been commanded." {8:36} So Aaron and his sons did everything the LORD commanded through Moses.

{9:1} On the eighth day, Moses called Aaron, his sons, and the elders of Israel. {9:2} He said to Aaron, "Take a young calf for a sin offering and a ram for a burnt offering, both without blemish, and offer them before the LORD. {9:3} Speak to the children of Israel, saying, 'Take a goat kid for a sin offering, and a calf and a lamb, both a year old and without blemish, for a burnt offering. {9:4} Also take a bull and a ram for peace offerings to sacrifice before the LORD, and a grain offering mixed with oil, for today the LORD will appear to you.' {9:5} They brought what Moses commanded to the entrance of the tabernacle, and all the congregation gathered and stood before the LORD. {9:6} Moses said, "This is what the LORD commanded you to do, and the glory of the LORD will appear to you." {9:7} He told Aaron, "Go to the altar, offer your sin offering and your burnt offering, and make atonement for yourself and the people. Offer the people's offering and make atonement for them, as the LORD commanded." {9:8} So Aaron went to the altar and killed the calf for the sin offering, which was for himself. {9:9} Aaron's sons brought him the blood, and he dipped his finger in the blood, putting it on the horns of the altar and pouring the blood at the base of the altar. {9:10} But he burned the fat, kidneys, and the membrane above the liver of the sin offering on the altar, as the LORD commanded Moses. {9:11} He burned the flesh and hide with fire outside the camp. {9:12} He killed the burnt offering, and Aaron's sons brought him the blood, which he sprinkled all around the altar. {9:13} They presented the burnt offering to him, along with its pieces and the head, which he burned on the altar.

{9:14} He washed the inner organs and legs and burned them on the burnt offering on the altar. {9:15} Then he brought the people's offering, took the goat for the sin offering for the people, killed it, and offered it as a sin offering, just like the first. {9:16} He brought the burnt offering and offered it according to the prescribed manner. {9:17} He brought the grain offering, took a handful, and burned it on the altar beside the burnt sacrifice of the morning. {9:18} He also killed the bull and the ram for the peace offerings for the people; Aaron's sons presented him the blood, which he sprinkled on the altar all around. {9:19} They presented the fat of the bull and the ram—the tail, the fat covering the inner organs, the kidneys, and the membrane above the liver. {9:20} They placed the fat on the breasts, and he burned the fat on the altar. {9:21} Aaron waved the breasts and the right shoulder as a wave offering before the LORD, as Moses commanded. {9:22} Aaron lifted his hand toward the people and blessed them, then came down from offering the sin offering, the burnt offering, and the peace offerings. {9:23} Moses and Aaron went into the tabernacle and came out, blessing the people, and the glory of the LORD appeared to all the people. {9:24} Fire came out from before the LORD and consumed the burnt offering and the fat on the altar; when all the people saw it, they shouted and fell on their faces.

{10:1} Nadab and Abihu, the sons of Aaron, each took their own censer, put fire in it, added incense, and offered unauthorized fire before the LORD, which He had not commanded them. {10:2} Fire came out from the LORD and consumed them, and they died before the LORD. {10:3} Then Moses said to Aaron, "This is what the LORD meant when He said, 'I will be honored among those who come near Me, and I will be glorified before all the people.'" And Aaron remained silent. {10:4} Moses called Mishael and Elzaphan, the sons of Uzziel, Aaron's uncle, and said to them, "Come forward and carry your relatives away from the sanctuary, out of the camp." {10:5} So they approached and carried them in their coats out of the camp, as Moses had instructed. {10:6} Moses said to Aaron and to Eleazar and Ithamar, his remaining sons, "Do not uncover your heads or tear your clothes, or you will die, and the LORD's anger will come upon the whole community. Instead, let your relatives, the whole house of Israel, mourn for the fire the LORD has set ablaze. {10:7} You must not leave the entrance of the tabernacle, or you will die, because the LORD's anointing oil is upon you." And they did as Moses said. {10:8} Then the LORD spoke to Aaron, saying, {10:9} "You and your sons must not drink wine or strong drink when you go into the tabernacle, or you will die. This is to be a lasting ordinance for you throughout your generations. {10:10} This is so you can distinguish between the holy and the common, and between the unclean and the clean. {10:11} You are to teach the children of Israel all the decrees the LORD has given them through Moses." {10:12} Moses spoke to Aaron and to Eleazar and Ithamar, his remaining sons, saying, "Take the grain offering that remains from the offerings made by fire to the LORD and eat it without yeast beside the altar, for it is most holy. {10:13} You must eat it in the holy place because it is your share and that of your sons from the sacrifices made by fire to the LORD, as I have been commanded. {10:14} The wave breast and the heave shoulder you must eat in a clean place, you and your sons and daughters with you, for they are your share and that of your sons, given from the sacrifices of the peace offerings of the children of Israel. {10:15} The heave shoulder and the wave breast shall be brought with the offerings made by fire from the fat, to present them as a wave offering before the LORD; they will be yours and your sons' by a lasting ordinance, as the LORD has commanded." {10:16} Moses carefully looked for the goat of the sin offering, and it had been burned up. He was angry with Eleazar and Ithamar, the sons of Aaron who were still alive, saying, {10:17} "Why didn't you eat the sin offering in the holy place? It is most holy, and God has given it to you to carry the guilt of the congregation and to make atonement for them before the LORD. {10:18} The blood of it was not brought into the holy place; you should have eaten it in the holy place, as I commanded." {10:19} Aaron said to Moses, "Today they have offered their sin offering and their burnt offering before the LORD, and such things have happened to me. If I had eaten the sin offering today, would it have been acceptable in the LORD's sight?" {10:20} When Moses heard this, he was satisfied.

{11:1} The LORD spoke to Moses and Aaron, saying to them, {11:2} "Speak to the Israelites and tell them, 'These are the animals you may eat from all the animals on the earth. {11:3} You may eat any animal that has a divided hoof and chews the cud. {11:4} However, you must not eat those that chew the cud or have divided hooves, like the camel, because it chews the cud but does not have a divided hoof; it is unclean for you. {11:5} The hyrax (coney) is also unclean for you because it chews the cud but does not have a divided hoof. {11:6} The hare is unclean for you because it chews the cud but does not have a divided hoof. {11:7} The pig is unclean for you, though it has a divided hoof and is cloven-footed; it does not chew the cud. {11:8} You must not eat their flesh or touch their carcasses; they are unclean for you. {11:9} These are the animals you may eat from the waters: you may eat any that have fins and scales in the seas and rivers. {11:10} But anything in the seas and rivers that does not have fins and scales, whether it moves in the water or is a living creature, is an abomination to you. {11:11} They are indeed an abomination; you must not eat their flesh, and their carcasses are detestable to you. {11:12} Anything that does not have fins or scales in the waters is an abomination to you. {11:13} And these are the birds you must consider unclean and must not eat: the eagle, the vulture, and the osprey, {11:14} the kite, and every kind of raven, {11:15} the owl, the night hawk, the cuckoo, and the hawk of every kind, {11:16} the little owl, the cormorant, and the great owl, {11:17} the swan, the pelican, and the griffon vulture, {11:18} the stork, the heron of every kind, the hoopoe, and the bat. {11:19} All flying insects that walk on all fours are an abomination to you. {11:20} However, you may eat any flying insect that walks on all fours and has jointed legs for hopping on the ground; {11:21} you may eat the locusts of any kind, the bald locusts of any kind, the crickets of any kind, and the grasshoppers of any kind. {11:22} But all other flying insects that have four legs are an abomination to you. {11:23} You will be unclean because of these: whoever touches their carcasses will be unclean until evening. {11:24} Whoever carries any of their carcasses must wash their clothes and will be unclean until evening. {11:25} The carcasses of every animal that has a divided hoof and is not cloven-footed or does not chew the cud are unclean to you; anyone who touches them will be unclean. {11:26} And any animal that walks on paws among all kinds of animals that walk on all fours is unclean to you; whoever touches their carcass will be unclean until evening. {11:27} Anyone who carries their carcass must wash their clothes and will be unclean until evening; they are unclean to you. {11:28} These are also unclean to you among the creatures that crawl on the ground: the weasel, the mouse, and the tortoise of any kind, {11:29} the ferret, the chameleon, the lizard, the snail, and the mole. {11:30} These are unclean to you among all crawling creatures; anyone who touches them when they are dead will be unclean until evening. {11:31} Anything that falls on any of them when they are dead will be unclean; whether it is a wooden vessel, clothing, leather, or a sack, any vessel in which work is done must be put in water and will be unclean until evening; then it will be clean. {11:32} Every earthen vessel that has any of them fall into it will be unclean, and you must break it. {11:33} Any food that may be eaten on which such water comes will be unclean, and any drink that may be drunk in such a vessel will be unclean. {11:34} Anything that a part of their carcass falls upon will be unclean, whether it is an oven or a stove; they must be broken down, for they are unclean and will be unclean to you. {11:35} However, a spring or cistern that holds water will be clean, but anyone who touches their carcass will be unclean. {11:36} If a part of their carcass falls on sowing seeds that are to be sown, they will be clean. {11:37} But if water is put on the seed and any part of their carcass falls on it, it will be unclean for you. {11:38} If an animal you may eat dies, anyone who touches its carcass will be unclean until evening. {11:39} Anyone who eats of its carcass must wash their clothes and will be unclean until evening; anyone who carries its carcass must wash their clothes and will be unclean until evening. {11:40} Every crawling creature that crawls on the earth is an abomination; it must not be eaten. {11:41} Whatever crawls on its belly, or walks on all fours, or has many feet among all crawling creatures, you must not eat, for they are an abomination. {11:42} Do not make yourselves unclean with any crawling creature, and do not defile yourselves with them. {11:43} For I am the LORD your God; you must sanctify yourselves and be holy, because I am holy. Do not make yourselves unclean with any kind of crawling creature that crawls on the earth. {11:44} For I am the LORD who brought you up out of the land of Egypt to be your God; you must therefore be holy, because I am holy. {11:45} This is the law regarding animals, birds, and every living creature that moves in the waters, and every creature that crawls on the earth, {11:46} to distinguish between the unclean and the clean, and between the animals that may be eaten and those that may not be eaten.

{12:1} The LORD spoke to Moses, saying, {12:2} "Tell the Israelites that if a woman becomes pregnant and gives birth to a boy, she will be unclean for seven days, just like she is during her menstrual period (infirmity). {12:3} On the eighth day, the boy's foreskin must be circumcised. {12:4} Then she must continue in her purification for thirty-three days; she must not touch any holy thing or enter the sanctuary until her purification period is complete. {12:5} If she gives birth to a girl, she will be unclean for two weeks, as during her menstrual period, and she will continue in her purification for sixty-six days. {12:6} When her purification period is complete, whether for a son or a daughter, she must bring a year-old lamb for a burnt offering and a young pigeon or a turtle dove for a sin offering to the entrance of the Tabernacle, to the priest. {12:7} He will present them before the LORD and make atonement for her, and she will be cleansed from her blood flow. This is the law for a woman who gives birth to a male or female child. {12:8} If she cannot afford a lamb, she may bring two turtle doves or two young pigeons; one for the burnt offering and the other for a sin offering. The priest will make atonement for her, and she will be clean.

{13:1} The LORD spoke to Moses and Aaron, saying, {13:2} "When a man has a swelling, scab, or bright spot on his skin that looks like a leprosy plague, he must be brought to Aaron the priest or one of his sons, the priests. {13:3} The priest will examine the condition on the skin: if the hair in the affected area has turned white and the condition appears to be deeper than the skin, it is leprosy, and the priest will declare him unclean. {13:4} If the bright spot is white and does not appear deeper than the skin and the hair is not turned white, then the priest must isolate him for seven days. {13:5} On the seventh day, the priest will check him again; if the condition has not changed and has not spread, he will isolate him for another seven days. {13:6} On the following seventh day, if the condition looks darker and has not spread, the priest will declare him clean: it is just a scab, and he must wash his clothes and be clean. {13:7} But if the scab spreads after he has been declared clean, he must be examined by the priest again. {13:8} If the priest sees that the scab has spread, he will declare him unclean: it is leprosy. {13:9} When someone has a leprosy plague, they must be brought to the priest; {13:10} the priest will examine him: if the affected area is white and has turned the hair white, with raw flesh present, {13:11} it is old leprosy, and the priest will declare him unclean without isolating him, as he is unclean. {13:12} If the leprosy breaks out and covers the entire body from head to foot, wherever the priest looks, {13:13} he will examine it, and if it has covered all the skin and turned white, he will declare him clean, as he is completely white. {13:14} However, if raw flesh appears, he will be unclean. {13:15} The priest will see the raw flesh and declare him unclean, for raw flesh is unclean: it is leprosy. {13:16} If the raw flesh turns white again, he must come to the priest; {13:17} and if the priest sees that the plague has turned white, he will declare him clean. {13:18} If a boil appears on the skin and heals, {13:19} but a white or reddish spot appears where the boil was, shown to the priest; {13:20} if it is lower than the skin and the hair has turned white, the priest will declare him unclean, as it is a leprosy from the boil. {13:21} But if the priest examines it and sees no white hairs and it is not lower than the skin but somewhat dark, he will isolate him for seven days. {13:22} If it spreads, the priest will declare him unclean: it is a plague. {13:23} If the bright spot remains in place and does not spread, it is a burning boil, and the priest will declare him clean. {13:24} If there is any hot burn on the skin with a white or reddish spot, {13:25} the priest will examine it, and if the hair in the bright spot has turned white and it appears deeper than the skin, it is leprosy from the burn, and the priest will declare him unclean. {13:26} If the priest examines it and sees no white hair and it is not lower than the surrounding skin but somewhat dark, he will isolate him for seven days. {13:27} On the seventh day, the priest will look at it; if it has spread, he will declare him unclean: it is leprosy. {13:28} If the bright spot remains in place and does not spread, but is somewhat dark, it is an inflammation from the burn, and the priest will declare him clean. {13:29} If a man or woman has a plague on the head or beard, {13:30} the priest will examine it; if it is deeper than the skin and there is yellow thin hair, he will declare them unclean: it is a dry scale, a leprosy on the head or beard. {13:31} If the priest examines the scale and it is not deeper than the skin and there is no black hair, he will isolate the person with the scale for seven days. {13:32} On the seventh day, the priest will examine it; if the scale has not spread and there is no yellow hair, and it is not deeper than the skin, {13:33} the hair will be shaved but the scale will not be shaved; the priest will isolate him for another seven days. {13:34} On the seventh day, if the scale has not spread or is not deeper than the skin, the priest will declare him clean; he must wash his clothes and be clean. {13:35} But if the scale spreads after being declared clean, {13:36} the priest will examine him; if the scale has spread, he will not look for yellow hair, and he is unclean. {13:37} If the scale appears stable and black hair has grown in, the scale is healed, and he is clean; the priest will declare him clean. {13:38} If a man or woman has bright white spots on their skin, {13:39} the priest will examine them; if the bright spots are darkish white, it is just a freckled spot, and they are clean. {13:40} If a man's hair has fallen out and he is bald, he is clean. {13:41} If his hair has fallen out from the forehead towards his face, he is forehead bald, yet he is clean. {13:42} If there is a white reddish sore on the bald head or forehead, it is leprosy. {13:43} The priest will examine it; if the sore is white reddish on the bald head or forehead, like leprosy on the skin, {13:44} he is leprous and unclean; the priest will declare him utterly unclean as the plague is in his head. {13:45} The leper with the plague must tear his clothes, bare his head, cover his upper lip, and cry, "Unclean, unclean!" {13:46} As long as the plague is on him, he is defiled and unclean; he must live alone, outside the camp. {13:47} Any garment with leprosy, whether wool or linen, {13:48} in the weave or knit, or made of skin; if the plague is greenish or reddish, {13:49} it is leprosy and must be shown to the priest. {13:50} The priest will examine it and isolate the one who has the plague for seven days. {13:51} He will check it on the seventh day; if it has spread in the garment or skin, it is a fretting leprosy and is unclean. {13:52} The garment must be burned in fire, whether it is wool or linen or made of skin, as it is a fretting leprosy. {13:53} If the priest sees that the plague has not spread in the garment or skin, {13:54} he will command it to be washed and isolate it for another seven days. {13:55} After washing, if the plague has not changed color or spread, it is unclean and must be burned in the fire, as it is an internal decay, whether inside or outside. {13:56} If the priest sees that the plague is somewhat dark after washing, he will remove it from the garment or skin. {13:57} If it still appears in the garment or skin, it is a spreading plague, and that must be burned in fire. {13:58} If the garment, whether weave or knit, or any skin that has been washed, shows the plague has departed, it must be washed again and will be clean. {13:59} This is the law regarding the leprosy plague in woolen or linen garments, whether in the weave or knit, or any skin, to declare it clean or unclean.

{14:1} The LORD spoke to Moses, saying, {14:2} This is the law for a person with leprosy on the day they are cleansed: they must be brought to the priest. {14:3} The priest will go outside the camp and examine them; if the leprosy has healed, {14:4} the priest will command that two live, clean birds, cedar wood, scarlet yarn, and hyssop be brought for the person being cleansed. {14:5} The priest will then order one of the birds to be killed in an earthen vessel over running water. {14:6} For the living bird, he will take it along with the cedar wood, scarlet yarn, and hyssop, and dip them and the living bird in the blood of the killed bird over the running water. {14:7} He will sprinkle the person being cleansed from leprosy seven times, declare them clean, and release the living bird into an open field. {14:8} The person to be cleansed must wash their clothes, shave off all their hair, and wash themselves in water to become clean. After this, they may come into the camp, but they must remain outside their tent for seven days. {14:9} On the seventh day, they must shave all the hair off their head, beard, and eyebrows, washing their clothes and body in water to be clean. {14:10} On the eighth day, they must bring two unblemished male lambs, one unblemished female lamb from the first year, and three-tenths of a measure of fine flour mixed with oil for a grain offering, and one log of oil. {14:11} The priest who makes them clean will present them and the offerings before the LORD at the entrance of the tabernacle. {14:12} The priest will take one male lamb and offer it as a guilt offering, along with the log of oil, and wave them as a wave offering before the LORD. {14:13} He will slaughter the lamb in the same place where the sin offering and burnt offering are killed, in the holy place, for the guilt offering is as sacred as the sin offering. {14:14} The priest will take some of the blood from the guilt offering and put it on the right ear lobe, right thumb, and right big toe of the person being cleansed. {14:15} He will then take some of the log of oil and pour it into the palm of his left hand. {14:16} The priest will dip his right finger into the oil in his left hand and sprinkle some of the oil before the LORD seven times. {14:17} He will put some of the oil from his hand on the right ear lobe, right thumb, and right big toe of the person being cleansed, over the blood of the guilt offering. {14:18} The remainder of the oil in the priest's hand he will pour on the head of the person being cleansed to make atonement for them before the LORD. {14:19} The priest will offer the sin offering and make atonement for the person cleansed from their uncleanness, then he will slaughter the burnt offering. {14:20} The priest will offer the burnt offering and the grain offering on the altar, and he will make atonement for the person, and they will be clean. {14:21} If the person is poor and cannot afford so much, they may take one lamb for a guilt offering to be waved for atonement, and one-tenth of a measure of fine flour mixed with oil for a grain offering, and one log of oil; {14:22} and two turtledoves or two young pigeons, whichever they can afford, with one as a sin offering and the other as a burnt offering. {14:23} They must bring them on the eighth day for their cleansing to the priest at the entrance of the tabernacle before the LORD. {14:24} The priest will take the lamb of the guilt offering and the log of oil, and wave them as a wave offering before the LORD. {14:25} He will kill the lamb for the guilt offering, take some of the blood, and put it on the right ear lobe, right thumb, and right big toe of the person being cleansed. {14:26} The priest will pour some of the oil into the palm of his left hand. {14:27} He will sprinkle some of the oil with his right finger seven times before the LORD. {14:28} He will place the oil from his hand on the right ear lobe, right thumb, and right big toe of the person being cleansed, over the place of the blood from the guilt offering. {14:29} The rest of the oil in the priest's hand he will put on the head of the person being cleansed to make atonement for them before the LORD. {14:30} The person must offer one of the turtledoves or young pigeons they can afford; {14:31} one for a sin offering and the other for a burnt offering, along with the grain offering, and the priest will make atonement for the person being cleansed before the LORD. {14:32} This is the law for anyone with the plague of leprosy who cannot afford what is required for their cleansing. {14:33} The LORD spoke to Moses and Aaron, saying, {14:34} When you enter the land of Canaan, which I am giving you as a possession, and I put the plague of leprosy in a house in that land; {14:35} the owner of the house must come and tell the priest, "It seems to me there is a plague in my house." {14:36} The priest will command that the house be emptied before he goes in to examine the plague, so that everything inside does not become unclean; then he will go in to inspect the house. {14:37} He will examine the plague, and if the plague is on the walls of the house with hollow areas, greenish or reddish, which appear lower than the wall, {14:38} the priest will go outside the house to its entrance and shut up the house for seven days. {14:39} The priest will return on the seventh day and inspect it again; if the plague has spread on the walls, {14:40} the priest will command that the stones showing the plague be removed and thrown into an unclean place outside the city. {14:41} He will cause the house to be scraped all around and will pour the dust scraped off into an unclean place outside the city. {14:42} They will take other stones and replace the ones that were removed, and will use new mortar to plaster the house. {14:43} If the plague returns and breaks out in the house after the stones have been removed, the house has been scraped, and plastered; {14:44} the priest will come and examine it again, and if the plague has spread, it is a serious leprosy in the house; it is unclean. {14:45} The priest will tear down the house, including the stones, timber, and all the mortar, and carry them outside the city to an unclean place. {14:46} Anyone who goes into the house while it is shut up will be unclean until evening. {14:47} Anyone who sleeps in the house must wash their clothes, and anyone who eats in the house must wash their clothes. {14:48} If the priest comes in and inspects it, and the plague has not spread in the house after it was plastered, then the priest will declare the house clean because the plague is healed. {14:49} He will take two birds, cedar wood, scarlet yarn, and hyssop to cleanse the house; {14:50} he will kill one of the birds in an earthen vessel over running water. {14:51} He will take the cedar wood, hyssop, scarlet yarn, and the living bird, dip them in the blood of the slain bird and in the running water, and sprinkle the house seven times. {14:52} He will cleanse the house with the blood of the bird, the running water, the living bird, cedar wood, hyssop, and scarlet yarn; {14:53} then he will let the living bird go outside the city into open fields, making atonement for the house, and it will be clean. {14:54} This is the law for all kinds of leprosy and skin diseases, {14:55} and for the leprosy of garments and houses, {14:56} for eruptions, scabs, and bright spots; {14:57} to teach when something is unclean and when it is clean. This is the law of leprosy.

{15:1} The LORD spoke to Moses and Aaron, saying, {15:2} Tell the Israelites that when any man has a discharge from his body, he is unclean because of it. {15:3} This will be his uncleanness: whether his discharge is continuous or has stopped, he is still considered unclean. {15:4} Any bed he lies on while he has the discharge is unclean, and everything he sits on will also be unclean. {15:5} Anyone who touches his bed must wash their clothes, bathe in water, and will be unclean until evening. {15:6} Anyone who sits on something he has sat on must wash their clothes, bathe in water, and will be unclean until evening. {15:7} Anyone who touches the body of a man with a discharge must wash their clothes, bathe in water, and will be unclean until evening. {15:8} If the man with the discharge spits on someone who is clean, that person must wash their clothes, bathe in water, and will be unclean until evening. {15:9} Any saddle the man rides will be unclean. {15:10} Anyone who touches anything under him will be unclean until evening, and anyone carrying those things must wash their clothes, bathe in water, and will be unclean until evening. {15:11} If a man with a discharge touches someone who has not rinsed their hands in water, that person must wash their clothes, bathe in water, and will be unclean until evening. {15:12} Any clay vessel he touches will be broken, and any wooden vessel must be rinsed in water. {15:13} When the man with the discharge is cleansed, he will count seven days for his cleansing, wash his clothes, and bathe in running water to be clean. {15:14} On the eighth day, he must take two turtledoves or two young pigeons to the entrance of the tabernacle and give them to the priest. {15:15} The priest will offer one as a sin offering and the other as a burnt offering, making atonement for him before the LORD for his discharge. {15:16} If a man's semen leaves his body, he must wash his whole body in water and will be unclean until evening. {15:17} Any garment or leather where the semen is will be washed with water and will be unclean until evening. {15:18} The woman he lies with must also bathe in water and will be unclean until evening. {15:19} If a woman has a discharge of blood, she must be set apart for seven days; anyone who touches her will be unclean until evening. {15:20} Everything she lies on during her separation will be unclean, and everything she sits on will be unclean. {15:21} Anyone who touches her bed must wash their clothes, bathe in water, and will be unclean until evening. {15:22} Anyone who touches anything she sat on must wash their clothes, bathe in water, and will be unclean until evening. {15:23} If someone touches her bed or anything she sat on, they will be unclean until evening. {15:24} If a man lies with her while she has her period, he will be unclean for seven days, and the bed he lies on will be unclean. {15:25} If a woman has a discharge of blood for many days outside her regular period, or if it continues beyond that time, all the days of her discharge will be like the days of her separation; she will be unclean. {15:26} Any bed she lies on during her discharge will be treated like her bed during her separation, and anything she sits on will be unclean like the uncleanness of her separation. {15:27} Anyone who touches those things will be unclean, must wash their clothes, bathe in water, and will be unclean until evening. {15:28} But if she is cleansed of her discharge, she must count seven days, and afterward she will be clean. {15:29} On the eighth day, she must take two turtledoves or two young pigeons to the priest at the entrance of the tabernacle. {15:30} The priest will offer one for a sin offering and the other for a burnt offering, making atonement for her before the LORD for the discharge of her uncleanness. {15:31} This is how you will separate the Israelites from their uncleanness, so they do not die in their uncleanness by defiling my tabernacle that is among them. {15:32} This is the law for a man with a discharge, for him whose semen leaves his body, and for her who is menstruating, as well as for a man who lies with a woman who is unclean.

{16:1} The LORD spoke to Moses after the death of Aaron's two sons, who died after offering unauthorized fire before the LORD. {16:2} The LORD said to Moses, Tell your brother Aaron not to enter the holy place at any time he wants, beyond the curtain in front of the mercy seat on the ark, or he will die, because I will appear in the cloud over the mercy seat. {16:3} This is how Aaron is to enter the holy place: with a young bull for a sin offering and a ram for a burnt offering. {16:4} He must put on the holy linen tunic, linen undergarments, a linen sash, and a linen turban; these are holy garments. He must wash his body in water before putting them on. {16:5} He must take from the congregation of the Israelites two male goats for a sin offering and one ram for a burnt offering. {16:6} Aaron will offer his bull as a sin offering for himself and make atonement for himself and his household. {16:7} He will take the two goats and present them before the LORD at the entrance of the tabernacle. {16:8} Aaron will cast lots for the two goats: one lot for the LORD and the other lot for the scapegoat. {16:9} He will bring the goat chosen by lot for the LORD and offer it as a sin offering. {16:10} But the goat chosen for the scapegoat will be presented alive before the LORD to make atonement and then sent away into the wilderness. {16:11} Aaron will bring the bull for the sin offering, which is for himself, and make atonement for himself and his household, and he will kill the bull for the sin offering for himself. {16:12} He will take a censer full of burning coals from the altar before the LORD, and his hands full of finely ground sweet incense, and bring it inside the curtain. {16:13} He will put the incense on the fire before the LORD so that the smoke of the incense covers the mercy seat; otherwise, he will die. {16:14} He will take some of the bull's blood and sprinkle it with his finger on the mercy seat eastward; he will sprinkle the blood seven times in front of the mercy seat. {16:15} Then he will kill the goat for the sin offering for the people and bring its blood inside the curtain, doing with that blood as he did with the bull's blood, sprinkling it on the mercy seat and in front of it. {16:16} He will make atonement for the holy place because of the uncleanness of the Israelites and their transgressions in all their sins, and he will do the same for the tabernacle that remains among them in the midst of their uncleanness. {16:17} No one is to be in the tabernacle when he goes in to make atonement in the holy place until he comes out and has made atonement for himself, his household, and the entire community of Israel. {16:18} He will then go out to the altar that is before the LORD and make atonement for it, taking some of the bull's blood and some of the goat's blood and putting it on the horns of the altar all around. {16:19} He will sprinkle some of the blood on it with his finger seven times and cleanse it, setting it apart from the uncleanness of the Israelites. {16:20} When he has finished making atonement for the holy place, the tabernacle, and the altar, he will bring the live goat. {16:21} Aaron will lay both his hands on the head of the live goat and confess over it all the iniquities of the Israelites, all their transgressions and sins, putting them on the goat's head, and then send it away by the hand of a designated man into the wilderness. {16:22} The goat will carry on itself all their iniquities to a remote area; and the man will release it in the wilderness. {16:23} Aaron will then enter the tabernacle and take off the linen garments he put on when he entered the holy place, leaving them there. {16:24} He will wash his body with water in the holy place, put on his regular garments, come out, and offer his burnt offering and the burnt offering of the people, making atonement for himself and the people. {16:25} He will burn the fat of the sin offering on the altar. {16:26} The man who released the scapegoat must wash his clothes and bathe his body in water, and afterward he may come into the camp. {16:27} The bull for the sin offering and the goat for the sin offering, whose blood was brought into the holy place to make atonement, must be taken outside the camp and burned; their hides, flesh, and intestines must be burned in the fire. {16:28} The one who burns them must wash his clothes and bathe his body in water before coming into the camp. {16:29} This is to be a lasting ordinance for you: On the tenth day of the seventh month, you must deny yourselves (or, fast) and do no work at all, whether native-born or a foreigner residing among you. {16:30} Because on this day the priest will make atonement for you to cleanse you, so you will be clean from all your sins before the LORD. {16:31} It will be a day of sabbath rest for you, and you must deny yourselves; this is a lasting ordinance. {16:32} The priest who is anointed and ordained to serve as priest in his father's place will make atonement; he will put on the holy linen garments. {16:33} He will make atonement for the most holy place, the tabernacle, the altar, the priests, and all the people of the community. {16:34} This is to be a lasting ordinance for you to make atonement for the Israelites for all their sins once a year. And Aaron did as the LORD commanded Moses.

{17:1} The LORD spoke to Moses, saying, {17:2} Speak to Aaron, his sons, and all the Israelites, and tell them: This is what the LORD has commanded, saying, {17:3} Any man from the house of Israel who kills an ox, lamb, or goat in the camp, or outside the camp, {17:4} and does not bring it to the entrance of the tabernacle to offer it to the LORD before the LORD's tabernacle, that man will be held responsible for shedding blood; he has shed blood, and he will be cut off from his people. {17:5} This is so that the Israelites may bring their sacrifices, which they offer in the open field, to the LORD at the entrance of the tabernacle, to the priest, and offer them as peace offerings to the LORD. {17:6} The priest will sprinkle the blood on the LORD's altar at the entrance of the tabernacle and burn the fat as a pleasing aroma to the LORD. {17:7} They must no longer offer their sacrifices to demons (or, goat idols) they have chased after. This is to be a lasting ordinance for them throughout their generations. {17:8} You shall say to them, Any man from the house of Israel or any foreigner residing among you who offers a burnt offering or sacrifice {17:9} and does not bring it to the entrance of the tabernacle to offer it to the LORD will be cut off from his people. {17:10} Any man from the house of Israel or any foreigner residing among you who eats any kind of blood, I will set my face against that person and cut him off from his people. {17:11} For the life of a creature is in the blood, and I have given it to you to make atonement for your lives on the altar; it is the blood that makes atonement for one's life. {17:12} Therefore, I said to the Israelites, None of you may eat blood, nor may any foreigner residing among you eat blood. {17:13} Any Israelite or foreigner residing among you who hunts and kills any animal or bird that may be eaten must pour out the blood and cover it with dirt. {17:14} For the life of every creature is its blood; therefore, I said to the Israelites, You must not eat the blood of any creature because the life of every creature is its blood; anyone who eats it will be cut off. {17:15} Anyone who eats an animal that died of itself or was killed by wild beasts, whether a native or a foreigner, must wash his clothes and bathe himself in water, and he will be unclean until evening; then he will be clean. {17:16} But if he does not wash them or bathe his body, he will bear his guilt.

{18:1} The LORD spoke to Moses, saying, {18:2} Speak to the Israelites and tell them, I am the LORD your God. {18:3} You must not do as they do in Egypt, where you used to live, nor do as they do in Canaan, where I am bringing you; do not follow their customs. {18:4} You must follow my laws and keep my decrees; you must observe them. I am the LORD your God. {18:5} Keep my decrees and laws, for the person who obeys them will live by them. I am the LORD. {18:6} No one is to approach any close relative to have sexual relations; I am the LORD. {18:7} You must not uncover the nakedness of your father or mother; she is your mother; you must not uncover her nakedness. {18:8} You must not uncover the nakedness of your father's wife; that is your father's nakedness. {18:9} You must not uncover the nakedness of your sister, whether she is your father's daughter or your mother's daughter, born at home or abroad; you must not uncover their nakedness. {18:10} You must not uncover the nakedness of your granddaughter; their nakedness is your own. {18:11} You must not uncover the nakedness of your father's wife's daughter, born to your father; she is your sister; you must not uncover her nakedness. {18:12} You must not uncover the nakedness of your father's sister; she is your father's close relative. {18:13} You must not uncover the nakedness of your mother's sister; she is your mother's close relative.

{18:14} You must not uncover the nakedness of your father's brother; you must not approach his wife; she is your aunt. {18:15} You must not uncover the nakedness of your daughter-in-law; she is your son's wife; you must not uncover her nakedness. {18:16} You must not uncover the nakedness of your brother's wife; that is your brother's nakedness. {18:17} You must not uncover the nakedness of a woman and her daughter, nor take her granddaughter, either her son's daughter or her daughter's daughter, to uncover her nakedness; they are her close relatives; it is wickedness. {18:18} You must not marry a woman and her sister as rivals, while she is still alive, to uncover her nakedness. {18:19} You must not approach a woman to uncover her nakedness during her period of menstrual uncleanness. {18:20} You must not have sexual relations with your neighbor's wife and defile yourself with her. {18:21} You must not give any of your children to be sacrificed to Molech (a Canaanite god); you must not profane the name of your God; I am the LORD. {18:22} You must not lie with a man as one lies with a woman; that is an abomination. {18:23} You must not have sexual relations with any animal to defile yourself with it; a woman must not present herself to an animal to have sexual relations; that is perversion. {18:24} Do not defile yourselves in any of these ways, because that is how the nations that I am driving out before you became defiled. {18:25} The land is defiled; therefore, I am punishing it for its sin, and the land will vomit out its inhabitants. {18:26} But you must keep my decrees and laws and must not commit any of these detestable practices, neither the native-born nor any foreigner residing among you. {18:27} For all these things were done by the people who lived in the land before you, and the land became defiled. {18:28} And if you defile the land, it will vomit you out as it vomited out the nations that were before you. {18:29} Anyone who does any of these detestable things, such persons must be cut off from their people. {18:30} Keep my ordinances and do not commit any of these abominable customs that were practiced before you, and do not make yourselves unclean by them; I am the LORD your God.

{19:1} The LORD spoke to Moses, saying, {19:2} Speak to all the people of Israel and tell them, You shall be holy, because I, the LORD your God, am holy. {19:3} Each of you must respect your mother and father and observe my Sabbaths; I am the LORD your God. {19:4} Do not turn to idols or make molten (shaped by pouring molten material) gods for yourselves; I am the LORD your God. {19:5} If you offer a peace offering to the LORD, you may do so voluntarily. {19:6} It must be eaten the same day you offer it or the next day; anything left over by the third day must be burned. {19:7} If it is eaten on the third day, it is unclean and will not be accepted. {19:8} Anyone who eats it will be held responsible for profaning the holy offering of the LORD and will be cut off from their people. {19:9} When you harvest your land, do not harvest the corners of your field or gather the gleanings (leftovers) of your harvest. {19:10} Do not pick your vineyard clean or gather every grape; leave them for the poor and the stranger; I am the LORD your God. {19:11} You must not steal, lie, or deceive one another. {19:12} Do not swear falsely by my name or profane the name of your God; I am the LORD. {19:13} Do not defraud or rob your neighbor; do not hold back the wages of a hired worker until morning. {19:14} Do not curse the deaf or put a stumbling block in front of the blind; fear your God; I am the LORD. {19:15} Do not pervert justice; do not show favoritism to the poor or honor the rich, but judge your neighbor fairly. {19:16} Do not spread gossip among your people or stand idly by when your neighbor's life is at stake; I am the LORD. {19:17} Do not hate your brother in your heart; rebuke your neighbor frankly so you will not share in their guilt. {19:18} Do not seek revenge or bear a grudge against anyone among your people, but love your neighbor as yourself; I am the LORD. {19:19} Keep my decrees: do not mate different kinds of animals; do not plant your field with two kinds of seed; do not wear clothing woven of two kinds of material. {19:20} If a man has sexual relations with a female slave who is promised to another man and has not been redeemed or given her freedom, they must be punished, but they will not be put to death because she was not free. {19:21} He must bring a ram as a guilt offering to the LORD at the entrance to the tent of meeting. {19:22} The priest will make atonement for him with the ram before the LORD for the sin he has committed, and he will be forgiven. {19:23} When you enter the land and plant fruit trees, regard their fruit as forbidden for the first three years; do not eat it. {19:24} In the fourth year, all the fruit will be holy, an offering of praise to the LORD. {19:25} In the fifth year, you may eat the fruit, and it will yield even more for you; I am the LORD your God. {19:26} Do not eat any meat with blood still in it; do not practice divination (foretelling the future) or seek omens. {19:27} Do not cut the hair at the sides of your head or clip off the edges of your beard. {19:28} Do not cut your bodies for the dead or put tattoo marks on yourselves; I am the LORD. {19:29} Do not degrade your daughter by making her a prostitute, or the land will turn to prostitution and be filled with wickedness. {19:30} Keep my Sabbaths and revere my sanctuary; I am the LORD. {19:31} Do not turn to mediums or seek out spiritists, for you will be defiled by them; I am the LORD your God. {19:32} Stand up in the presence of the elderly and show respect for the aged; fear your God; I am the LORD. {19:33} When a foreigner resides among you in your land, do not mistreat them. {19:34} The foreigner residing among you must be treated as your native-born; love them as yourself, for you were foreigners in Egypt; I am the LORD your God. {19:35} Do not use dishonest standards when measuring length, weight, or quantity. {19:36} Use honest scales and honest weights; I am the LORD your God, who brought you out of Egypt. {19:37} Keep all my decrees and all my laws and follow them; I am the LORD.

{20:1} The LORD spoke to Moses, saying, {20:2} Again, you are to say to the people of Israel, Anyone from Israel or any foreigner living in Israel who gives any of their children to Molech must be put to death; the people of the land must stone them. {20:3} I will turn my face against that person and cut them off from their people because they have given their child to Molech, defiling my sanctuary and profaning my holy name. {20:4} If the people of the land ignore this man when he gives his child to Molech and do not kill him, {20:5} I will turn my face against that man and his family, and I will cut off everyone who follows him in their unfaithfulness to Molech from among their people. {20:6} I will set my face against anyone who consults spirits or wizards and goes after them; I will cut them off from among their people. {20:7} Consecrate yourselves and be holy, because I am the LORD your God. {20:8} Keep my decrees and follow them; I am the LORD who sanctifies (makes holy) you. {20:9} Anyone who curses their father or mother must be put to death; they have cursed their father or mother, and their blood will be on them. {20:10} If a man commits adultery with another man's wife, both the adulterer and the adulteress must be put to death. {20:11} If a man has sexual relations with his father's wife, he has uncovered his father's nakedness; both of them must be put to death; their blood is on them. {20:12} If a man sleeps with his daughter-in-law, both must be put to death; they have acted in a perverse way; their blood is on them. {20:13} If a man has sexual relations with another man as with a woman, both have committed an abomination; they must be put to death; their blood is on them. {20:14} If a man takes a wife and her mother, it is wickedness; both he and they must be burned with fire, so that there will be no wickedness among you. {20:15} If a man has sexual relations with a beast, he must be put to death, and you must kill the beast. {20:16} If a woman approaches any beast to have sexual relations, you must kill both the woman and the beast; they must be put to death; their blood is on them. {20:17} If a man takes his sister, his father's daughter, or his mother's daughter, and sees her nakedness, and she sees his nakedness, it is a disgrace; they must be cut off from their people, for he has uncovered his sister's nakedness; he will bear his guilt. {20:18} If a man has sexual relations with a woman during her period, he has exposed her source of blood, and she has exposed the source of her blood; both must be cut off from their people. {20:19} You must not uncover the nakedness of your aunt or uncle; for they are your close relatives; they will bear their guilt. {20:20} If a man sleeps with his uncle's wife, he has uncovered his uncle's nakedness; they will bear their sin and die childless. {20:21} If a man takes his brother's wife, it is a shameful thing; he has uncovered his brother's nakedness; they will die childless. {20:22} Therefore, you must keep all my decrees and laws and follow them, so the land where I am bringing you to live will not vomit you out. {20:23} Do not follow the practices of the nations I am driving out before you; they did all these things, and I abhorred (hated) them. {20:24} But I have said to you, You will inherit their land, and I will give it to you to possess, a land flowing with milk and honey; I am the LORD your God, who has separated you from the other peoples. {20:25} You must distinguish between clean and unclean animals and between unclean birds and clean; do not make yourselves unclean by any animal, bird, or creeping thing that I have separated from you as unclean. {20:26} You are to be holy to me, for I, the LORD, am holy and have set you apart from the nations to be mine. {20:27} A man or woman who has a familiar spirit or who is a wizard must be put to death; they must be stoned to death; their blood is on them.

{21:1} The LORD said to Moses, Speak to the priests, the sons of Aaron, and tell them that none of them should become defiled for the dead among their people. {21:2} They may become defiled only for their close relatives: their mother, father, son, daughter, or brother. {21:3} They may also become defiled for a virgin sister who is close to them and has had no husband. {21:4} However, they must not defile themselves as leaders among their people by doing so. {21:5} They must not shave their heads, trim the edges of their beards, or make cuts in their skin. {21:6} They must be holy to their God and not profane the name of their God, for they offer the fire offerings and the bread of their God; therefore, they must be holy. {21:7} They must not marry a woman who is a prostitute or has been profaned, nor take a divorced woman, for he is holy to his God. {21:8} You must consider him holy, as he offers the bread of your God; he must be holy to you, for I, the LORD, who sanctify you, am holy. {21:9} If a priest's daughter profanes herself by becoming a prostitute, she brings shame on her father; she must be burned with fire. {21:10} The high priest, who is among his brothers, on whose head the anointing oil has been poured and who is consecrated to wear the priestly garments, must not uncover his head or tear his clothes. {21:11} He must not go near any dead body or defile himself for his father or mother. {21:12} He must not leave the sanctuary or profane the sanctuary of his God, for the anointing oil of his God is on him; I am the LORD. {21:13} He must take a wife in her virginity. {21:14} He must not take a widow, a divorced woman, a profaned woman, or a prostitute; he must take a virgin from his own people as his wife. {21:15} He must not profane his offspring among his people, for I, the LORD, sanctify him. {21:16} The LORD spoke to Moses, saying, {21:17} Speak to Aaron, saying, Any descendant of yours in their generations who has any physical defect must not approach to offer the bread of his God. {21:18} No man who has a defect may approach: a blind man, a lame man, one with a flat nose, or any abnormality, {21:19} or a man with a broken foot or broken hand, {21:20} or a hunchback, or a dwarf, or someone with an eye defect, or who is scabby or has broken testicles. {21:21} No man from the line of Aaron the priest with any defect may approach to offer the offerings made by fire to the LORD; he has a defect and must not approach to offer the bread of his God. {21:22} He may eat the bread of his God, both of the most holy and of the holy. {21:23} However, he must not go near the veil or approach the altar because he has a defect; otherwise, he would profane my sanctuaries, for I, the LORD, sanctify them. {21:24} Moses told this to Aaron, his sons, and all the people of Israel.

{22:1} The LORD spoke to Moses, saying, {22:2} Speak to Aaron and his sons, telling them to separate themselves from the holy things of the Israelites and not to profane my holy name in the offerings they present to me; I am the LORD. {22:3} Say to them, Any one of your descendants throughout your generations who goes to the holy things, which the Israelites dedicate to the LORD, while having any uncleanness on them, that person shall be cut off from my presence; I am the LORD. {22:4} Any man of Aaron's descendants who is a leper or has a bodily discharge must not eat the holy things until he is clean. And whoever touches anything unclean due to a dead body or a man who has an emission, {22:5} or touches any creeping thing that could make him unclean, or touches any person who might make him unclean, whatever the source of uncleanness may be; {22:6} the person who has touched any of these will be unclean until evening and must not eat from the holy things unless he washes his body with water. {22:7} When the sun sets, he will be clean, and then he may eat from the holy things because it is his food. {22:8} He must not eat anything that has died naturally or has been torn by wild animals, as it would defile him; I am the LORD. {22:9} They must keep my ordinances, or they will bear the consequences and die if they profane them; I, the LORD, sanctify them. {22:10} No outsider may eat from the holy offerings; a hired servant or a temporary resident may not eat the holy offerings. {22:11} But if a priest buys a person with his own money, that person may eat from it, and those born in his house may eat from his food. {22:12} If a priest's daughter marries a stranger, she may not eat from the holy offerings. {22:13} However, if the priest's daughter is widowed or divorced and has no children and returns to her father's house as she did in her youth, she may eat from her father's food, but no outsider may eat from it. {22:14} If someone eats a holy offering accidentally, they must add a fifth of its value to it and give it to the priest along with the offering. {22:15} They must not profane the holy offerings of the Israelites, which they present to the LORD, {22:16} nor allow them to bear the consequences of guilt when they eat the holy offerings; for I, the LORD, sanctify them. {22:17} The LORD spoke to Moses, saying, {22:18} Speak to Aaron, his sons, and all the Israelites, telling them that anyone from the house of Israel or any foreigner living in Israel who wants to present their offering for any of their vows or for any of their freewill offerings to the LORD as a burnt offering {22:19} must present a male without blemish from the cattle, sheep, or goats. {22:20} But any offering that has a blemish shall not be accepted; it will not be acceptable to you. {22:21} Whoever offers a peace offering to the LORD to fulfill a vow or as a freewill offering from the cattle or sheep must offer a perfect animal; it must have no blemish. {22:22} You must not offer blind, broken, maimed, or having growths, scabby, or diseased animals to the LORD, nor make a fire offering of them on the altar to the LORD. {22:23} You may offer a bull or lamb that has some extra growth or lacks something as a freewill offering, but for a vow, it will not be accepted. {22:24} You must not offer anything that is bruised, crushed, broken, or cut; nor shall you make any offering of these in your land. {22:25} You must not accept such offerings from a foreigner because their corruption is in them, and blemishes are in them; they shall not be accepted for you. {22:26} The LORD spoke to Moses, saying, {22:27} When a bull, sheep, or goat is born, it must stay with its mother for seven days; from the eighth day onward, it will be acceptable as an offering made by fire to the LORD. {22:28} Whether cow or ewe, you must not kill both the mother and her young on the same day. {22:29} When you present a thanksgiving sacrifice to the LORD, offer it at your own will. {22:30} It must be eaten the same day; you must leave none of it until the next morning; I am the LORD. {22:31} Therefore, you must keep my commandments and follow them; I am the LORD. {22:32} You must not profane my holy name; I will be honored among the Israelites; I am the LORD who sanctifies you, {22:33} who brought you out of the land of Egypt to be your God; I am the LORD.

{23:1} The LORD spoke to Moses, saying, {23:2} Speak to the Israelites and tell them about the feasts of the LORD, which you are to proclaim as holy gatherings; these are my feasts. {23:3} Six days you shall work, but the seventh day is a day of rest, a holy gathering; you shall do no work on it; it is the Sabbath of the LORD in all your homes. {23:4} These are the feasts of the LORD, holy gatherings that you shall declare in their seasons. {23:5} On the fourteenth day of the first month, at twilight, is the LORD's Passover. {23:6} On the fifteenth day of the same month is the Feast of Unleavened Bread to the LORD; for seven days you must eat unleavened bread. {23:7} On the first day, you shall have a holy gathering; you shall do no work on that day. {23:8} You shall present an offering made by fire to the LORD for seven days; on the seventh day is a holy gathering; you shall do no work on that day. {23:9} The LORD spoke to Moses, saying, {23:10} Speak to the Israelites and tell them, When you enter the land I give you and reap its harvest, you shall bring a sheaf of the firstfruits of your harvest to the priest. {23:11} He shall wave the sheaf before the LORD to be accepted for you; on the day after the Sabbath, the priest shall wave it. {23:12} On that day when you wave the sheaf, you shall offer a one-year-old lamb without blemish as a burnt offering to the LORD. {23:13} The grain offering shall be two-tenths of an ephah (a measure of flour) mixed with oil, an offering made by fire to the LORD for a sweet aroma, and the drink offering shall be of wine, a fourth of a hin (a measure). {23:14} You shall eat neither bread, parched grain, nor fresh grain until that same day when you bring your offering to your God; this is to be a lasting statute for you throughout your generations in all your homes. {23:15} From the day after the Sabbath, from the day you bring the sheaf of the wave offering, you shall count seven Sabbaths; {23:16} until the day after the seventh Sabbath, you shall count fifty days and then present a new grain offering to the LORD. {23:17} From your homes, you shall bring two wave loaves of two-tenths of an ephah; they shall be made of fine flour and baked with leaven; they are the firstfruits to the LORD. {23:18} With the bread, you shall present seven one-year-old lambs without blemish, one young bull, and two rams; they shall be a burnt offering to the LORD, along with their grain and drink offerings, an offering made by fire with a sweet aroma to the LORD. {23:19} Then you shall sacrifice one goat for a sin offering and two lambs of the first year for a peace offering. {23:20} The priest shall wave them along with the bread of the firstfruits as a wave offering before the LORD with the two lambs; they shall be holy to the LORD for the priest. {23:21} On that same day, you shall proclaim it as a holy gathering; you shall do no work on that day; this is a lasting statute throughout your generations in all your homes. {23:22} When you reap the harvest of your land, do not completely harvest the corners of your field or gather the gleanings of your harvest; leave them for the poor and for the foreigner; I am the LORD your God. {23:23} The LORD spoke to Moses, saying, {23:24} Speak to the Israelites, saying, On the first day of the seventh month, you shall have a Sabbath, a memorial with trumpet blasts, a holy gathering. {23:25} You shall do no work on that day, but you shall present an offering made by fire to the LORD. {23:26} The LORD spoke to Moses, saying, {23:27} Also, on the tenth day of this seventh month, there shall be a Day of Atonement; it shall be a holy gathering for you; you shall afflict your souls and present an offering made by fire to the LORD. {23:28} You shall do no work on that day, for it is a Day of Atonement to make atonement for you before the LORD your God. {23:29} Any person who does not afflict themselves on that day shall be cut off from their people. {23:30} Any person who does any work on that day, I will destroy from among their people. {23:31} You shall do no work; this is a lasting statute throughout your generations in all your homes. {23:32} It shall be a Sabbath of rest for you, and you shall afflict your souls on the ninth day of the month at twilight; from twilight to twilight, you shall celebrate your Sabbath. {23:33} The LORD spoke to Moses, saying, {23:34} Speak to the Israelites, saying, On the fifteenth day of this seventh month, there shall be the Feast of Tabernacles for seven days to the LORD. {23:35} On the first day, there shall be a holy gathering; you shall do no work on that day. {23:36} For seven days, you shall present offerings made by fire to the LORD; on the eighth day, there shall be a holy gathering for you, and you shall present offerings made by fire to the LORD; it is a solemn assembly; you shall do no work on that day. {23:37} These are the feasts of the LORD that you shall proclaim as holy gatherings to present offerings made by fire to the LORD, including burnt offerings, grain offerings, sacrifices, and drink offerings, everything on its designated day. {23:38} In addition to the Sabbaths of the LORD, and your gifts, and all your vows, and all your freewill offerings, which you present to the LORD. {23:39} Also, on the fifteenth day of the seventh month, when you have gathered the fruit of the land, you shall celebrate a feast to the LORD for seven days; on the first day, there shall be a Sabbath, and on the eighth day, there shall be a Sabbath. {23:40} On the first day, you shall take the boughs of goodly trees, branches of palm trees, boughs of thick trees, and willows from the brook; you shall rejoice before the LORD your God for seven days. {23:41} You shall celebrate it as a feast to the LORD for seven days each year; this is a lasting statute for your generations; you shall celebrate it in the seventh month. {23:42} You shall live in booths for seven days; all Israelites born must live in booths, {23:43} so that your generations may know that I made the Israelites live in booths when I brought them out of the land of Egypt; I am the LORD your God. {23:44} Moses declared to the Israelites the feasts of the LORD.

{24:1} The LORD spoke to Moses, saying, {24:2} Command the Israelites to bring you pure olive oil, crushed for the light, so that the lamps may burn continually. {24:3} Outside the curtain of the testimony in the tabernacle, Aaron shall tend to it from evening until morning before the LORD continuously; this is to be a lasting statute for your generations. {24:4} He shall keep the lamps burning on the pure lampstand before the LORD at all times. {24:5} You shall take fine flour and bake twelve loaves of bread; each loaf shall consist of two-tenths of an ephah (a measure of flour). {24:6} You shall place them in two rows, six in each row, on the pure table before the LORD. {24:7} You shall put pure frankincense on each row, as a memorial for the bread, an offering made by fire to the LORD. {24:8} Every Sabbath, he shall arrange it before the LORD continuously, taken from the Israelites as an everlasting covenant. {24:9} It shall belong to Aaron and his sons; they shall eat it in a holy place, for it is most holy to him among the offerings of the LORD made by fire, by a perpetual statute. {24:10} Now, the son of an Israelite woman, whose father was Egyptian, went out among the Israelites, and this son of the Israelite woman and a man of Israel got into a fight in the camp. {24:11} The son of the Israelite woman blasphemed the name of the LORD and cursed. They brought him to Moses; (his mother's name was Shelomith, the daughter of Dibri, of the tribe of Dan). {24:12} They put him in custody until the mind of the LORD could be shown to them. {24:13} The LORD spoke to Moses, saying, {24:14} Bring out the one who has cursed outside the camp; let all who heard him lay their hands on his head, and let the entire congregation stone him. {24:15} You shall tell the Israelites, Anyone who curses their God shall bear their sin. {24:16} Anyone who blasphemes the name of the LORD shall surely be put to death; the entire congregation shall stone him, whether a foreigner or a native, when he blasphemes the name of the LORD, he shall be put to death. {24:17} Anyone who kills another person shall surely be put to death. {24:18} Anyone who kills an animal shall make restitution; life for life. {24:19} If someone causes a physical injury to their neighbor, what they have done shall be done to them; {24:20} fracture for fracture, eye for eye, tooth for tooth; as they have caused a physical injury to a person, so shall it be done to them. {24:21} Anyone who kills an animal shall restore it, and anyone who kills a person shall be put to death. {24:22} You shall have one standard of law, both for the foreigner and for your own countrymen; for I am the LORD your God. {24:23} Moses spoke to the Israelites that they should bring out the one who had cursed from the camp and stone him with stones. The Israelites did as the LORD commanded Moses.

{25:1} The LORD spoke to Moses on Mount Sinai, saying, {25:2} Speak to the Israelites and tell them that when you enter the land I am giving you, the land shall observe a Sabbath to the LORD. {25:3} For six years, you shall sow your fields and prune your vineyards, gathering their produce. {25:4} But in the seventh year, the land shall have a Sabbath of rest, a Sabbath for the LORD; you shall not sow your fields or prune your vineyards. {25:5} You shall not reap what grows of its own accord or gather the grapes of your unpruned vines, for it is a year of rest for the land. {25:6} The Sabbath of the land shall provide food for you, for your servants, for your maids, for your hired workers, and for the foreigners living among you, {25:7} as well as for your livestock and the wild animals in your land; all the increase shall be food for you. {25:8} You shall count seven Sabbaths of years, seven times seven years, so that the period of seven Sabbaths of years shall be forty-nine years. {25:9} Then you shall sound the trumpet of Jubilee on the tenth day of the seventh month; on the Day of Atonement, you shall sound it throughout your land. {25:10} You shall consecrate the fiftieth year and proclaim liberty throughout the land to all its inhabitants; it shall be a Jubilee for you, and each of you shall return to your own property, and each shall return to their own family. {25:11} The fiftieth year shall be a Jubilee for you; you shall not sow or reap what grows of itself, nor gather the grapes of your unpruned vines. {25:12} For it is a Jubilee; it shall be holy for you; you shall eat the produce from the field. {25:13} In this Jubilee year, you shall return to your own property. {25:14} If you sell anything to your neighbor or buy from your neighbor, you shall not wrong each other. {25:15} According to the number of years after the Jubilee, you shall buy from your neighbor, and according to the number of years of the crops, he shall sell to you. {25:16} The longer the time until the Jubilee, the higher the price you shall pay, and the shorter the time, the lower the price; for it is the number of crops that he is selling to you. {25:17} You shall not wrong one another, but you shall fear your God; for I am the LORD your God. {25:18} Therefore, you shall follow my statutes and keep my judgments and do them; and you shall live in safety in the land. {25:19} The land will yield its fruit, and you will eat your fill and live securely in it. {25:20} If you say, "What will we eat in the seventh year, if we do not sow or gather our crops?" {25:21} Then I will command my blessing on you in the sixth year, and it will produce a crop sufficient for three years. {25:22} You shall sow in the eighth year and eat from the old harvest until the ninth year, until the new harvest comes in, you shall eat from the old store. {25:23} The land shall not be sold permanently, for the land is mine; you are strangers and residents with me. {25:24} In all the land you hold, you must provide for the redemption of the land. {25:25} If your brother becomes poor and sells some of his property, his nearest relative may come to redeem what his brother has sold. {25:26} If a man has no one to redeem it, but is able to redeem it himself, {25:27} he shall calculate the years since the sale and repay the excess to the man to whom he sold it, so that he may return to his property. {25:28} But if he is not able to redeem it, then what was sold shall remain with the buyer until the Year of Jubilee; in the Jubilee, it shall be released, and he shall return to his property. {25:29} If a man sells a house in a walled city, he may redeem it within a year of its sale; for a full year he may redeem it. {25:30} If it is not redeemed within a year, the house in the walled city shall be permanently transferred to the buyer throughout their generations; it shall not be released in the Jubilee. {25:31} However, the houses of the villages that have no walls around them shall be treated as fields in the countryside; they may be redeemed, and they shall be released in the Jubilee. {25:32} Nevertheless, the cities of the Levites and the houses in the cities of their possession may be redeemed at any time. {25:33} If a man purchases a house from the Levites, then the house that was sold and the city of his possession shall be released in the Jubilee; for the houses in the cities of the Levites are their possession among the Israelites. {25:34} But the fields of the suburbs of their cities may not be sold, for they are their perpetual possession. {25:35} If your brother becomes poor and cannot maintain himself among you, you shall support him, whether he is a foreigner or a resident; that he may live among you. {25:36} Do not take interest from him or increase; but fear your God, that your brother may live among you. {25:37} You shall not lend him your money at interest, nor give him your food for profit. {25:38} I am the LORD your God, who brought you out of the land of Egypt, to give you the land of Canaan and to be your God. {25:39} If your brother becomes poor and sells himself to you, you shall not make him serve as a slave, {25:40} but he shall be like a hired worker or a temporary resident; he shall serve with you until the Year of Jubilee. {25:41} Then he and his children shall be released from you and shall return to their own family and to the possession of their ancestors. {25:42} For they are my servants, whom I brought out of the land of Egypt; they shall not be sold as slaves. {25:43} You shall not rule over them ruthlessly, but you shall fear your God. {25:44} As for your male and female slaves that you may have, they shall come from the nations around you; from them you may buy male and female slaves. {25:45} Furthermore, you may acquire the children of the foreigners who reside among you, and they shall be your property. {25:46} You shall leave them as an inheritance for your children after you to inherit as property; they shall be your slaves forever. But over your fellow Israelites, you shall not rule one over another ruthlessly. {25:47} If a foreigner or resident becomes wealthy among you and your brother becomes poor and sells himself to the foreigner or resident, {25:48} after he is sold, he may be redeemed; one of his brothers may redeem him, {25:49} or his uncle or his cousin may redeem him, or any one of his close relatives may redeem him, or if he is able, he may redeem himself. {25:50} He shall determine the period of his sale and the price of his redemption shall be based on the number of years from the year he was sold until the Year of Jubilee; the price shall be set according to the time of a hired worker. {25:51} If there are many years remaining, according to them, he shall refund the cost of his redemption from the price he was sold for. {25:52} If there are only a few years until the Year of Jubilee, he shall calculate and pay according to the years remaining for his redemption. {25:53} He shall be treated like a hired worker; the buyer shall not rule over him ruthlessly in your sight. {25:54} If he is not redeemed in these years, he shall go free in the Year of Jubilee, both he and his children with him. {25:55} For the Israelites are my servants; they are my servants whom I brought out of the land of Egypt; I am the LORD your God.

{26:1} You shall not make idols or carved images, nor shall you set up a standing image or erect any stone image in your land to bow down to, for I am the LORD your God. {26:2} You shall observe my Sabbaths and respect my sanctuary; I am the LORD. {26:3} If you follow my statutes and keep my commandments and do them, {26:4} then I will give you rain at the right time, and the land will yield its harvest, and the trees of the field will bear fruit. {26:5} Your threshing will last until the vintage, and the vintage will last until sowing time; you shall eat your bread to the full and live safely in your land. {26:6} I will grant peace in the land, and you shall lie down without fear; I will remove wild animals from the land, and the sword shall not pass through your territory. {26:7} You shall pursue your enemies, and they shall fall before you by the sword. {26:8} Five of you shall chase a hundred, and a hundred of you shall put ten thousand to flight; your enemies shall fall before you by the sword. {26:9} For I will look upon you favorably and make you fruitful and multiply you and establish my covenant with you. {26:10} You shall eat old stores and bring forth the old because of the new. {26:11} I will set my dwelling among you, and my soul shall not reject you. {26:12} I will walk among you, and I will be your God, and you shall be my people. {26:13} I am the LORD your God, who brought you out of the land of Egypt, so that you would not be slaves; I have broken the bars of your yoke and made you walk upright. {26:14} But if you do not listen to me and do not obey all these commandments, {26:15} and if you despise my statutes or your soul rejects my judgments so that you do not keep all my commandments but break my covenant, {26:16} then I will do this to you: I will bring terror, wasting disease, and fever that will consume your eyes and cause sorrow in your heart; you shall sow your seed in vain, for your enemies shall eat it. {26:17} I will set my face against you, and you shall be defeated by your enemies; those who hate you shall rule over you, and you shall flee when no one pursues you. {26:18} If you still do not listen to me, then I will punish you seven times more for your sins. {26:19} I will break the pride of your power, and I will make your skies like iron and your ground like bronze. {26:20} Your strength will be spent in vain, for your land will not yield its harvest, nor will the trees of the land bear their fruit. {26:21} If you walk contrary to me and do not listen to me, I will bring seven times more plagues upon you according to your sins. {26:22} I will also send wild animals among you, which will rob you of your children, destroy your livestock, and make you few in number; your roads shall be deserted. {26:23} If you will not be corrected by these things but continue to walk contrary to me, {26:24} then I will also walk contrary to you and punish you seven times for your sins. {26:25} I will bring a sword upon you to avenge the quarrel of my covenant; and when you gather in your cities, I will send the pestilence among you, and you shall be delivered into the hand of the enemy. {26:26} When I break the supply of your bread, ten women shall bake your bread in one oven, and they shall deliver your bread by weight; you shall eat but not be satisfied. {26:27} If you do not listen to me and walk contrary to me, {26:28} then I will walk contrary to you in fury, and I, even I, will punish you seven times for your sins. {26:29} You shall eat the flesh of your sons, and you shall eat the flesh of your daughters. {26:30} I will destroy your high places, cut down your images, and cast your carcasses upon the carcasses of your idols, and my soul shall reject you. {26:31} I will make your cities waste and bring your sanctuaries to desolation, and I will not smell the pleasing aroma of your offerings. {26:32} I will bring the land into desolation; your enemies who dwell there shall be astonished at it. {26:33} I will scatter you among the nations, and I will draw a sword after you; your land shall be desolate, and your cities waste. {26:34} Then the land shall enjoy its Sabbaths as long as it lies desolate and you are in your enemies' land; then the land shall rest and enjoy its Sabbaths. {26:35} As long as it lies desolate, it shall rest, because it did not rest during your Sabbaths while you lived on it. {26:36} To those who are left alive of you, I will bring faintness into their hearts in the lands of their enemies; the sound of a shaken leaf shall chase them, and they shall flee as if fleeing from a sword, and they shall fall when no one pursues them. {26:37} They shall fall one upon another as if before a sword when no one pursues; and you shall have no power to stand before your enemies. {26:38} You shall perish among the nations, and the land of your enemies shall consume you. {26:39} Those who are left of you shall waste away in their iniquity in the lands of your enemies; and also in the iniquities of their fathers, they shall waste away with them. {26:40} If they confess their iniquity and the iniquity of their fathers, with their trespass which they trespassed against me, and that they have walked contrary to me, {26:41} and that I also have walked contrary to them and brought them into the land of their enemies; if then their uncircumcised hearts are humbled and they accept the punishment for their iniquity, {26:42} then I will remember my covenant with Jacob, and my covenant with Isaac, and my covenant with Abraham, and I will remember the land. {26:43} The land shall be left desolate and shall enjoy its Sabbaths while it lies desolate without them; and they shall accept the punishment for their iniquity because they despised my judgments and their soul rejected my statutes. {26:44} Yet for all that, when they are in the land of their enemies, I will not cast them away, nor will I reject them, to destroy them completely and break my covenant with them; for I am the LORD their God. {26:45} But I will remember the covenant of their ancestors, whom I brought out of the land of Egypt in the sight of the nations, that I might be their God; I am the LORD. {26:46} These are the statutes, judgments, and laws which the LORD made between himself and the Israelites at Mount Sinai by the hand of Moses.

{27:1} The LORD spoke to Moses, saying, {27:2} "Speak to the children of Israel and tell them, when a man makes a special vow, the value of the person shall be determined by your estimate for the LORD. {27:3} Your estimate for a male from twenty to sixty years old shall be fifty shekels of silver, based on the sanctuary shekel. {27:4} If it is a female, your estimate shall be thirty shekels. {27:5} For a male from five to twenty years old, your estimate shall be twenty shekels, and for a female, ten shekels. {27:6} For a male from one month to five years old, your estimate shall be five shekels of silver, and for a female, three shekels of silver. {27:7} If a person is sixty years old or older, for a male, your estimate shall be fifteen shekels, and for a female, ten shekels. {27:8} If he is poorer than your estimate, he shall present himself before the priest, and the priest shall value him according to what he can afford. {27:9} If it is an animal that people bring as an offering to the LORD, everything anyone gives of such to the LORD shall be considered holy. {27:10} He shall not exchange it or change a good animal for a bad one or a bad one for a good one; if he does exchange one animal for another, both it and the exchange shall be holy. {27:11} If it is any unclean animal that cannot be offered as a sacrifice to the LORD, he shall present it before the priest. {27:12} The priest shall evaluate it, whether it is good or bad; as the priest assesses it, so shall it be. {27:13} If he chooses to redeem it, he shall add one-fifth to your estimate. {27:14} When a man dedicates his house as holy to the LORD, the priest shall evaluate it, whether it is good or bad; as the priest assesses it, so shall it stand. {27:15} If the one who dedicated it wishes to redeem his house, he shall add one-fifth of the money of your estimate to it, and it shall be his. {27:16} If a man dedicates a part of his field to the LORD, your estimate shall be based on its seed; a homer of barley seed shall be valued at fifty shekels of silver. {27:17} If he dedicates his field in the Year of Jubilee, your estimate shall remain as is. {27:18} If he dedicates his field after the Jubilee, the priest shall calculate its value based on the years that remain until the Jubilee, and it shall be reduced from your estimate. {27:19} If the one who dedicated the field wants to redeem it, he shall add one-fifth of the money of your estimate, and it shall be secure for him. {27:20} If he does not redeem the field, or if he sells it to another person, it shall not be redeemed anymore. {27:21} However, the field shall be holy to the LORD when it is released in the Jubilee, as a field devoted; its ownership shall belong to the priest. {27:22} If a man dedicates a field that he has bought, which is not part of his inherited land, {27:23} the priest shall calculate its worth based on your estimate until the Year of Jubilee; he shall give your estimate that day as a holy thing to the LORD. {27:24} In the Year of Jubilee, the field shall return to the owner from whom it was bought, to whom the land originally belonged. {27:25} All your estimates shall be based on the sanctuary shekel: twenty gerahs shall be the shekel. {27:26} Only the firstborn of the animals, which belong to the LORD, cannot be dedicated; whether it is an ox or a sheep, it is the LORD's. {27:27} If it is an unclean animal, he shall redeem it based on your estimate and add one-fifth of its value; if it is not redeemed, it shall be sold based on your estimate. {27:28} However, no devoted thing, whether man or beast or field, can be sold or redeemed; every devoted thing is most holy to the LORD. {27:29} No human devoted to the LORD can be redeemed; they shall surely be put to death. {27:30} All the tithe of the land, whether of the seed or of the fruit of the tree, belongs to the LORD; it is holy to the LORD. {27:31} If a man wants to redeem any of his tithes, he shall add one-fifth to it. {27:32} Regarding the tithe of the herd or flock, whatever passes under the rod, the tenth shall be holy to the LORD. {27:33} He shall not check whether it is good or bad, nor shall he change it; if he changes it, both the original and the change shall be holy; it shall not be redeemed. {27:34} These are the commandments that the LORD commanded Moses for the children of Israel at Mount Sinai.

The Fourth Book of Moses, called Numbers

{1:1} The LORD spoke to Moses in the wilderness of Sinai, in the meeting tent, on the first day of the second month, in the second year after they had come out of Egypt, saying, {1:2} "Take a census of the whole community of the Israelites, by their families and their ancestral houses, counting the names of every male, {1:3} from twenty years old and up, all who are able to fight in Israel. You and Aaron shall count them by their military units. {1:4} Each tribe will have one leader with you; he will be the head of his family. {1:5} Here are the names of the leaders: from the tribe of Reuben, Elizur son of Shedeur; {1:6} from Simeon, Shelumiel son of Zurishaddai; {1:7} from Judah, Nahshon son of Amminadab; {1:8} from Issachar, Nethaneel son of Zuar; {1:9} from Zebulun, Eliab son of Helon; {1:10} from the children of Joseph: from Ephraim, Elishama son of Ammihud; from Manasseh, Gamaliel son of Pedahzur; {1:11} from Benjamin, Abidan son of Gideoni; {1:12} from Dan, Ahiezer son of Ammishaddai; {1:13} from Asher, Pagiel son of Ocran; {1:14} from Gad, Eliasaph son of Deuel; {1:15} from Naphtali, Ahira son of Enan. {1:16} These were the respected leaders of the community, the heads of their ancestral tribes, leaders of thousands in Israel. {1:17} Moses and Aaron called these men by name {1:18} and gathered the entire community together on the first day of the second month. They declared their genealogies by families and ancestral houses, counting all the males from twenty years old and upward. {1:19} As the LORD commanded Moses, he counted them in the wilderness of Sinai. {1:20} The descendants of Reuben, Israel's firstborn, were counted by their generations, families, and ancestral houses, with every male from twenty years old and up, all able to fight in war. {1:21} The total number from the tribe of Reuben was forty-six thousand five hundred. {1:22} From the descendants of Simeon, by their generations, families, and ancestral houses, every male from twenty years old and up, all able to fight in war, {1:23} the total was fifty-nine thousand three hundred. {1:24} From the descendants of Gad, by their generations, families, and ancestral houses, every male from twenty years old and up, all able to fight in war, {1:25} the total was forty-five thousand six hundred fifty. {1:26} From the descendants of Judah, by their generations, families, and ancestral houses, every male from twenty years old and up, all able to fight in war, {1:27} the total was seventy-four thousand six hundred. {1:28} From the descendants of Issachar, by their generations, families, and ancestral houses, every male from twenty years old and up, all able to fight in war, {1:29} the total was fifty-four thousand four hundred. {1:30} From the descendants of Zebulun, by their generations, families, and ancestral houses, every male from twenty years old and up, all able to fight in war, {1:31} the total was fifty-seven thousand four hundred. {1:32} From the descendants of Joseph, namely from Ephraim, by their generations, families, and ancestral houses, every male from twenty years old and up, all able to fight in war, {1:33} the total was forty thousand five hundred. {1:34} From the descendants of Manasseh, by their generations, families, and ancestral houses, every male from twenty years old and up, all able to fight in war, {1:35} the total was thirty-two thousand two hundred. {1:36} From the descendants of Benjamin, by their generations, families, and ancestral houses, every male from twenty years old and up, all able to fight in war, {1:37} the total was thirty-five thousand four hundred. {1:38} From the descendants of Dan, by their generations, families, and ancestral houses, every male from twenty years old and up, all able to fight in war, {1:39} the total was sixty-two thousand seven hundred. {1:40} From the descendants of Asher, by their generations, families, and ancestral houses, every male from twenty years old and up, all able to fight in war, {1:41} the total was forty-one thousand five hundred. {1:42} From the descendants of Naphtali, by their generations, families, and ancestral houses, every male from twenty years old and up, all able to fight in war, {1:43} the total was fifty-three thousand four hundred.

{1:44} These are the totals of those counted by Moses and Aaron, along with the leaders of Israel, who numbered twelve men, one for each ancestral house. {1:45} All the Israelites counted, by their ancestral houses, from twenty years old and up, all able to fight in war, {1:46} totaled six hundred three thousand five hundred fifty. {1:47} But the Levites were not counted among them by their ancestral tribe. {1:48} For the LORD had told Moses, {1:49} "Do not count the tribe of Levi, nor include them in the census of the Israelites. {1:50} Instead, appoint the Levites to take care of the tabernacle of the testimony and all its furnishings, and they will be responsible for it. They will carry the tabernacle and all its equipment, and serve it, encamping around the tabernacle. {1:51} When the tabernacle is to be moved, the Levites will take it down; when it is time to set up the tabernacle, they will set it up. Anyone else who approaches shall be put to death. {1:52} The Israelites will camp, each by their own camp and each by their own standard, throughout their encampment. {1:53} But the Levites will camp around the tabernacle of testimony so that there will be no wrath on the community of the Israelites. The Levites will keep charge of the tabernacle of testimony. {1:54} The Israelites did everything the LORD commanded Moses; they followed all His instructions.

{2:1} The LORD spoke to Moses and Aaron, saying, {2:2} "Each man from the Israelites must camp by his own standard, with the emblem of his father's house; they will camp at a distance from the meeting tent. {2:3} On the east side, facing the sunrise, the camp of Judah will pitch its tents with their military units, led by Nahshon son of Amminadab. {2:4} His group, those counted, totaled seventy-four thousand six hundred. {2:5} Next to him will be the tribe of Issachar, led by Nethaneel son of Zuar. {2:6} His group, those counted, totaled fifty-four thousand four hundred. {2:7} Then comes the tribe of Zebulun, led by Eliab son of Helon. {2:8} His group, those counted, totaled fifty-seven thousand four hundred. {2:9} All those counted in the camp of Judah totaled one hundred eighty thousand six hundred. They will lead the way. {2:10} On the south side will be the camp of Reuben, with their military units, led by Elizur son of Shedeur. {2:11} His group, those counted, totaled forty-six thousand five hundred. {2:12} Next to him will be the tribe of Simeon, led by Shelumiel son of Zurishaddai. {2:13} His group, those counted, totaled fifty-nine thousand three hundred. {2:14} Then comes the tribe of Gad, led by Eliasaph son of Reuel. {2:15} His group, those counted, totaled forty-five thousand six hundred fifty. {2:16} All those counted in the camp of Reuben totaled one hundred fifty-one thousand four hundred fifty. They will march in the second position. {2:17} The tabernacle of the meeting will move forward with the Levites in the center of the camp; as they camp, so they will move, each man in his place by their standards. {2:18} On the west side will be the camp of Ephraim, with their military units, led by Elishama son of Ammihud. {2:19} His group, those counted, totaled forty thousand five hundred. {2:20} Next to him will be the tribe of Manasseh, led by Gamaliel son of Pedahzur. {2:21} His group, those counted, totaled thirty-two thousand two hundred. {2:22} Then comes the tribe of Benjamin, led by Abidan son of Gideoni. {2:23} His group, those counted, totaled thirty-five thousand four hundred. {2:24} All those counted in the camp of Ephraim totaled one hundred eight thousand one hundred. They will march in the third position. {2:25} The camp of Dan will be on the north side with their military units, led by Ahiezer son of Ammishaddai. {2:26} His group, those counted, totaled sixty-two thousand seven hundred. {2:27} Next to him will be the tribe of Asher, led by Pagiel son of Ocran. {2:28} His group, those counted, totaled forty-one thousand five hundred. {2:29} Then comes the tribe of Naphtali, led by Ahira son of Enan. {2:30} His group, those counted, totaled fifty-three thousand four hundred. {2:31} All those counted in the camp of Dan totaled one hundred fifty-seven thousand six hundred. They will march last with their standards. {2:32} These are the totals of the Israelites counted by their ancestral houses: all those counted in the camps totaled six hundred three thousand five hundred fifty. {2:33} But the Levites were not counted among the Israelites, as the LORD commanded Moses. {2:34} The Israelites did everything the LORD commanded Moses; they camped by their standards and set forward, each family according to their ancestral house.

{3:1} These are the generations of Aaron and Moses on the day the LORD spoke to Moses at Mount Sinai. {3:2} These are the names of Aaron's sons: Nadab the firstborn, Abihu, Eleazar, and Ithamar. {3:3} These are the names of the anointed priests that Aaron consecrated to serve in the priesthood. {3:4} Nadab and Abihu died before the LORD when they offered unauthorized fire before Him in the wilderness of Sinai; they had no children, and Eleazar and Ithamar served in the priest's office in the sight of their father Aaron. {3:5} The LORD spoke to Moses, saying, {3:6} "Bring the tribe of Levi near and present them to Aaron the priest so they can serve him. {3:7} They will take care of his responsibilities and those of the entire congregation in front of the tabernacle, performing the duties of the tabernacle. {3:8} They will manage all the furnishings of the tabernacle and the responsibilities of the Israelites in serving the tabernacle. {3:9} You will give the Levites to Aaron and his sons; they are entirely dedicated to him from the children of Israel. {3:10} You will appoint Aaron and his sons, and they will oversee the priest's office; anyone who comes near will be put to death. {3:11} The LORD spoke to Moses, saying, {3:12} "Look, I have taken the Levites from among the Israelites instead of all the firstborn that open the womb among the Israelites; therefore, the Levites will be Mine. {3:13} All the firstborn are Mine, for on the day I struck all the firstborn in the land of Egypt, I consecrated all the firstborn in Israel, both man and beast; they are Mine; I am the LORD." {3:14} The LORD spoke to Moses in the wilderness of Sinai, saying, {3:15} "Number the children of Levi by their families and ancestral houses; every male from one month old and upward shall be counted." {3:16} Moses numbered them according to the word of the LORD, as he was commanded. {3:17} These were the sons of Levi by name: Gershon, Kohath, and Merari. {3:18} These are the names of the sons of Gershon by their families: Libni and Shimei. {3:19} The sons of Kohath by their families: Amram, Izehar, Hebron, and Uzziel. {3:20} The sons of Merari by their families: Mahli and Mushi. These are the families of the Levites according to their ancestral houses. {3:21} From Gershon came the family of the Libnites and the family of the Shimites; these are the families of the Gershonites. {3:22} Those counted among them, all males from one month old and upward, totaled seven thousand five hundred. {3:23} The families of the Gershonites will camp behind the tabernacle to the west. {3:24} The leader of the house of the Gershonites will be Eliasaph son of Lael. {3:25} The responsibilities of the sons of Gershon in the tabernacle will include the tabernacle, the tent, its covering, and the curtain for the entrance to the tabernacle. {3:26} They will also handle the hangings of the courtyard and the curtain for the entrance to the courtyard by the tabernacle and the altar, along with all the cords needed for service. {3:27} From Kohath came the family of the Amramites, the family of the Izeharites, the family of the Hebronites, and the family of the Uzzielites; these are the families of the Kohathites. {3:28} The total number of males from one month old and upward was eight thousand six hundred, responsible for the care of the sanctuary. {3:29} The families of the Kohathites will camp on the south side of the tabernacle. {3:30} The leader of the house of the families of the Kohathites will be Elizaphan son of Uzziel. {3:31} Their responsibilities will include the ark, the table, the lampstand, the altars, and the sanctuary vessels used in their ministry, along with all the service associated with these items. {3:32} Eleazar son of Aaron the priest will be the chief over the Levites and oversee those who take care of the sanctuary. {3:33} From Merari came the family of the Mahlites and the family of the Mushites; these are the families of Merari. {3:34} Those counted among them, all males from one month old and upward, totaled six thousand two hundred. {3:35} The leader of the house of the families of Merari will be Zuriel son of Abihail; they will camp on the north side of the tabernacle. {3:36} Under the care of the sons of Merari will be the frames of the tabernacle, its bars, its pillars, its bases, and all its vessels, along with all that serves them, {3:37} and the pillars of the courtyard surrounding it, along with their bases, pegs, and cords. {3:38} Those who camp in front of the tabernacle, toward the east, will be Moses, Aaron, and his sons, responsible for the sanctuary duties for the Israelites; anyone who comes near will be put to death. {3:39} All the Levites counted by Moses and Aaron, at the command of the LORD, by their families, all males from one month old and upward, totaled twenty-two thousand. {3:40} The LORD said to Moses, "Number all the firstborn males of the Israelites from one month old and upward, and record their names. {3:41} You will take the Levites for Me (I am the LORD) instead of all the firstborn among the

Israelites, and the livestock of the Levites instead of all the firstborn among the cattle of the Israelites. {3:42} Moses numbered all the firstborn among the Israelites as the LORD commanded him. {3:43} The total number of firstborn males, recorded by name from one month old and upward, was twenty-two thousand two hundred seventy-three. {3:44} The LORD spoke to Moses, saying, {3:45} "Take the Levites instead of all the firstborn among the Israelites, and the livestock of the Levites instead of their livestock; the Levites will be Mine; I am the LORD. {3:46} For those who need to be redeemed from the two hundred seventy-three firstborn of the Israelites, who are more than the Levites, {3:47} you will take five shekels each, according to the sanctuary shekel (the shekel is twenty gerahs). {3:48} You will give the money for the extra number to Aaron and his sons. {3:49} Moses took the redemption money for those who were over and above those redeemed by the Levites. {3:50} From the firstborn of the Israelites, he took the money; one thousand three hundred sixty-five shekels, according to the sanctuary shekel. {3:51} Moses gave the redemption money to Aaron and his sons, as the LORD commanded Moses.

{4:1} The LORD spoke to Moses and Aaron, saying, {4:2} "Take a census of the sons of Kohath from among the sons of Levi, by their families and ancestral houses, {4:3} from thirty years old to fifty years old, all who are able to serve in the tabernacle of the congregation. {4:4} This will be the service of the sons of Kohath in the tabernacle regarding the most sacred items: {4:5} When the camp sets out, Aaron and his sons will come and take down the veil that covers the ark of the testimony; {4:6} they will cover it with the hides of sea cows (badgers' skins), and spread a blue cloth over it and insert its poles. {4:7} On the table of showbread, they will spread a blue cloth, place the dishes, spoons, bowls, and covers for the bread, and the continual bread will be there. {4:8} They will spread a scarlet cloth over them, cover that with a covering of badgers' skins, and insert its poles. {4:9} They will take a blue cloth and cover the lampstand and its lamps, tongs, snuffers, and all the oil vessels used in its service. {4:10} They will place all of this within a covering of badgers' skins and put it on a pole. {4:11} On the golden altar, they will spread a blue cloth, cover it with a covering of badgers' skins, and insert its poles. {4:12} They will take all the tools for ministry used in the sanctuary, put them in a blue cloth, cover them with a covering of badgers' skins, and place them on a pole. {4:13} They will remove the ashes from the altar and spread a purple cloth over it. {4:14} They will put all the vessels used for ministering at the altar on it, including the censers, fleshhooks, shovels, and basins, covering it with a covering of badgers' skins, and inserting its poles. {4:15} When Aaron and his sons have finished covering the sanctuary and all its vessels as the camp prepares to move, the sons of Kohath will come to carry them, but they must not touch any holy thing, or they will die. This is the responsibility of the sons of Kohath in the tabernacle of the congregation. {4:16} The office of Eleazar, son of Aaron the priest, includes the oil for the light, the sweet incense, the daily grain offering, the anointing oil, and oversight of the entire tabernacle and all its sacred vessels. {4:17} The LORD spoke to Moses and Aaron, saying, {4:18} "Do not cut off the tribe of the families of the Kohathites from among the Levites. {4:19} Instead, do this for them so they may live and not die when they approach the most sacred things: Aaron and his sons will go in and assign each of them their duties and loads. {4:20} But they must not go in to see when the holy things are being covered, or they will die." {4:21} The LORD spoke to Moses, saying, {4:22} "Also take a census of the sons of Gershon, by their families and ancestral houses; {4:23} from thirty years old to fifty years old, count all those able to perform the service in the tabernacle of the congregation. {4:24} This is the service of the families of the Gershonites: {4:25} they will carry the curtains of the tabernacle, the tabernacle of the congregation, its covering, the covering of badgers' skins above it, and the hanging for the entrance to the tabernacle. {4:26} They will also manage the hangings of the courtyard, the hanging for the entrance to the courtyard by the tabernacle and the altar, along with their cords and all the tools needed for their service. {4:27} All the service of the Gershonites will be assigned by Aaron and his sons, along with all their burdens. {4:28} This is the service of the families of the Gershonites in the tabernacle of the congregation, and their responsibility will be under the care of Ithamar, son of Aaron the priest. {4:29} For the sons of Merari, you will count them by their families and ancestral houses; {4:30} from thirty years old to fifty years old, count everyone who can serve in the tabernacle of the congregation. {4:31} This is their responsibility according to all their service in the tabernacle of the congregation: the boards of the tabernacle, its bars, pillars, and bases, {4:32} the pillars of the courtyard, their bases, pegs, cords, and all their tools and service items. You will list the instruments of their service by name. {4:33} This is the service of the families of the Merarites according to all their service in the tabernacle of the congregation, under the care of Ithamar, son of Aaron the priest. {4:34} Moses, Aaron, and the leaders of the congregation counted the sons of Kohath by their families and ancestral houses, {4:35} from thirty years old to fifty years old, all who were able to serve in the tabernacle of the congregation. {4:36} Those counted by their families were two thousand seven hundred fifty. {4:37} These are the numbers of the families of the Kohathites, all who could serve in the tabernacle of the congregation, which Moses and Aaron counted according to the command of the LORD. {4:38} Those counted among the sons of Gershon by their families and ancestral houses, {4:39} from thirty years old to fifty years old, all who were able to serve in the tabernacle of the congregation, {4:40} were two thousand six hundred thirty. {4:41} These are the numbers of the families of the sons of Gershon, all who could serve in the tabernacle of the congregation, whom Moses and Aaron counted according to the command of the LORD. {4:42} Those counted among the families of the sons of Merari by their families and ancestral houses, {4:43} from thirty years old to fifty years old, all who were able to serve in the tabernacle of the congregation, {4:44} were three thousand two hundred. {4:45} These are the numbers of the families of the sons of Merari, whom Moses and Aaron counted according to the command of the LORD. {4:46} All those counted among the Levites, whom Moses, Aaron, and the leaders of Israel counted by their families and ancestral houses, {4:47} from thirty years old to fifty years old, all who were able to perform the service of ministry and the burdens of the tabernacle of the congregation, {4:48} totaled eight thousand five hundred eighty. {4:49} According to the command of the LORD, they were counted by Moses, each according to his service and burden; this is how they were numbered as the LORD commanded Moses.

{5:1} The LORD spoke to Moses, saying, {5:2} "Command the children of Israel to expel from the camp every leper, anyone with an infection (issue), and anyone who is defiled by the dead. {5:3} Both men and women must be put outside the camp so they do not defile the camp where I dwell." {5:4} The children of Israel did as the LORD commanded Moses and expelled them from the camp. {5:5} The LORD spoke to Moses, saying, {5:6} "Speak to the children of Israel, and say to them: If a man or woman commits any sin that people commit, violating the LORD's command, and that person is guilty, {5:7} they must confess their sin and repay what they have taken or the value of what they have wrongfully acquired, adding one-fifth of it, and give it to the person they wronged. {5:8} If the person has no relative to whom they can make restitution, the repayment should be made to the LORD, specifically to the priest, in addition to the ram of atonement that will be offered to make atonement for them. {5:9} Every offering of the holy things brought by the children of Israel to the priest will belong to the priest. {5:10} Each person's holy gifts will be their own; whatever anyone gives to the priest will be his." {5:11} The LORD spoke to Moses, saying, {5:12} "Speak to the children of Israel, and say to them: If a man's wife goes astray and commits a trespass against him, {5:13} and a man has sexual relations with her secretly, and it remains hidden from her husband, and she is defiled, with no witnesses against her, and she is not caught in the act; {5:14} and if jealousy comes over her husband, and he becomes jealous of his wife, whether she is defiled or not: {5:15} Then the man must bring his wife to the priest and offer for her the tenth part of an ephah of barley flour; he must not pour oil on it or put frankincense on it, for it is a grain offering of jealousy, a memorial offering to bring iniquity to remembrance. {5:16} The priest shall bring her near and set her before the LORD. {5:17} The priest shall take holy water in an earthen vessel and put some dust from the tabernacle floor into the water. {5:18} The priest shall set the woman before the LORD, uncover her head, and place the memorial offering in her hands, which is the jealousy offering, while holding the bitter water that brings the curse. {5:19} The priest shall make her take an oath and say to her, 'If no man has had sexual relations with you, and if you have not gone aside to uncleanness with another man besides your husband, you will be free from this bitter water that brings the curse. {5:20} But if you have gone aside to another man and have been defiled, and if a man has had sexual relations with you beside your husband, {5:21} then the priest shall make you take an oath of cursing, and he shall say to you: "The LORD make you a curse and an oath among your people, when the LORD causes your thigh to waste away and your abdomen to swell; {5:22} and this water that brings the curse shall enter your body, causing your abdomen to swell and your thigh to waste away." And the woman shall say, 'Amen, amen.' {5:23} The priest shall write these curses in a book and then blot them out with the bitter water. {5:24} He shall make the woman drink the bitter water that brings the curse, and the water that brings the curse shall enter her and become bitter. {5:25} Then the priest shall take the jealousy offering from the woman's hand, wave it before the LORD, and offer it on the altar. {5:26} The priest shall take a handful of the offering, even its memorial portion, and burn it on the altar, and afterward, he shall make the woman drink the water. {5:27} When he has made her drink the water, if she has been defiled and has committed a trespass against her husband, the water that brings the curse will enter her and become bitter, causing her abdomen to swell and her thigh to waste away, and she will become a curse among her people. {5:28} But if the woman is not defiled and is clean, she will be free and will conceive. {5:29} This is the law concerning jealousy when a wife goes astray and is defiled; {5:30} or when a spirit of jealousy comes over a husband who is jealous of his wife, he shall bring the woman before the LORD, and the priest shall carry out all this law. {5:31} Then the man will be free from iniquity, and the woman will bear her iniquity."

{6:1} The LORD spoke to Moses, saying, {6:2} "Speak to the children of Israel and tell them that when either a man or a woman separates themselves to make a vow of a Nazarite, dedicating themselves to the LORD, {6:3} they must abstain from wine and strong drink, and must not drink vinegar made from wine or from strong drink. They should not drink any kind of liquor made from grapes, nor eat fresh or dried grapes. {6:4} Throughout the days of their separation, they must not eat anything made from the vine, from the seeds to the skins. {6:5} During the entire period of their vow, no razor should touch their head; as long as they are separated to the LORD, they must be holy and let their hair grow long. {6:6} Throughout the days they are dedicated to the LORD, they must not come near a dead body. {6:7} They must not make themselves unclean for their father, mother, brother, or sister when they die, because the consecration (dedication) of their God is upon their head. {6:8} For the entire duration of their separation, they are holy to the LORD. {6:9} If a person dies unexpectedly near them and they defile their consecrated head, they must shave their head on the day of their cleansing, which is the seventh day. {6:10} On the eighth day, they must bring two turtle doves or two young pigeons to the priest at the entrance of the tabernacle of the congregation. {6:11} The priest will offer one as a sin offering and the other as a burnt offering, making atonement for them because they sinned by being near the dead, and they will consecrate their head on that same day. {6:12} They must dedicate the days of their separation to the LORD and bring a year-old lamb for a guilt offering; however, the days that were before will be lost because their separation was defiled. {6:13} This is the law for the Nazarite when the days of their separation are completed: they must be brought to the entrance of the tabernacle of the congregation. {6:14} They must present their offerings to the LORD: one year-old male lamb without blemish for a burnt offering, one year-old female lamb without blemish for a sin offering, and one ram without blemish for peace offerings, {6:15} along with a basket of unleavened bread, cakes made of fine flour mixed with oil, and wafers of unleavened bread anointed with oil, plus their grain offering and drink offerings. {6:16} The priest will bring them before the LORD and present the sin offering and the burnt offering. {6:17} He will offer the ram as a peace offering to the LORD along with the basket of unleavened bread; the priest will also present the grain offering and the drink offering. {6:18} The Nazarite will shave their head at the entrance of the tabernacle of the congregation, take the hair from their head, and put it in the fire under the sacrifice of the peace offerings. {6:19} The priest will take the boiled shoulder of the ram, one unleavened cake from the basket, and one unleavened wafer, and will place them in the hands of the Nazarite after their hair has been shaved. {6:20} The priest will wave them as a wave offering before the LORD; this will be holy for the priest, along with the wave breast and heave shoulder, and afterward, the Nazarite may drink wine. {6:21} This is the law for the Nazarite who has made a vow and for their offerings to the LORD for their separation, in addition to what they can afford. According to the vow they made, they must do according to the law of their separation. {6:22} The LORD spoke to Moses, saying, {6:23} "Speak to Aaron and his sons, saying, 'This is how you are to bless the children of Israel: {6:24} The LORD bless you and keep you; {6:25} The LORD make His face shine upon you and be gracious to you; {6:26} The LORD turn His face toward you and give you peace.' {6:27} So they will put My name on the children of Israel, and I will bless them."

{7:1} On the day that Moses completed setting up the tabernacle, anointing and sanctifying it along with all its furnishings, including the altar and its vessels, {7:2} the leaders of Israel, heads of their families and tribes, brought their offerings. {7:3} They presented before the LORD six covered wagons and twelve oxen, a wagon for two leaders, with one ox for each wagon, and brought them to the tabernacle. {7:4} The LORD spoke to Moses, saying, {7:5} "Accept these from them so they can be used for the service of the tabernacle of the congregation; give them to the Levites, distributing them according to their duties." {7:6} So Moses took the wagons and the oxen and gave them to the Levites. {7:7} He gave two wagons and four oxen to the sons of Gershon, according to their service; {7:8} and he gave four wagons and eight oxen to the sons of Merari, according to their service, under the supervision of Ithamar, son of Aaron the priest. {7:9} But he gave none to the sons of Kohath, because their service involved carrying the holy items on their shoulders. {7:10} The leaders offered their gifts for the dedication of the altar on the day it was anointed, and each leader presented their offerings before the altar. {7:11} The LORD told Moses that each leader should offer their gifts on their designated day for the altar's dedication. {7:12} The first day, Nahshon son of Amminadab from the tribe of Judah offered, {7:13} bringing a silver charger weighing one hundred thirty shekels, a silver bowl weighing seventy shekels (according to the sanctuary's weight), both filled with fine flour mixed with oil for a grain offering; {7:14} one gold spoon weighing ten shekels, full of incense; {7:15} one young bull, one ram, and one lamb of the first year for a burnt offering; {7:16} one goat kid for a sin offering; {7:17} and for peace offerings, two oxen, five rams, five male goats, and five lambs of the first year. This was the offering of Nahshon son of Amminadab. {7:18} On the second day, Nethaneel son of Zuar, leader of Issachar, offered: {7:19} one silver charger weighing one hundred thirty shekels, one silver bowl weighing seventy shekels (according to the sanctuary's weight), both filled with fine flour mixed with oil for a grain offering; {7:20} one gold spoon weighing ten shekels, full of incense; {7:21} one young bull, one ram, and one lamb of the first year for a burnt offering; {7:22} one goat kid for a sin offering; {7:23} and for peace offerings, two oxen, five rams, five male goats, and five lambs of the first year. This was the offering of Nethaneel son of Zuar. {7:24} On the third day, Eliab son of Helon, leader of Zebulun, offered: {7:25} one silver charger weighing one hundred thirty shekels, one silver bowl weighing seventy shekels (according to the sanctuary's weight), both filled with fine flour mixed with oil for a grain offering; {7:26} one gold spoon weighing ten shekels, full of incense; {7:27} one young bull, one ram, and one lamb of the first year for a burnt offering; {7:28} one goat kid for a sin offering; {7:29} and for peace offerings, two oxen, five rams, five male goats, and five lambs of the first year. This was the offering of Eliab son of Helon. {7:30} On the fourth day, Elizur son of Shedeur, leader of Reuben, offered: {7:31} one silver charger weighing one hundred thirty shekels, one silver bowl weighing seventy shekels (according to the sanctuary's weight), both filled with fine flour mixed with oil for a grain offering; {7:32} one gold spoon weighing ten shekels, full of incense; {7:33} one young bull, one ram, and one lamb of the first year for a burnt offering; {7:34} one goat kid for a sin offering; {7:35} and for peace offerings, two oxen, five rams, five male goats, and five lambs of the first year. This was the offering of Elizur son of Shedeur. {7:36} On the fifth day, Shelumiel son of Zurishaddai, leader of Simeon, offered: {7:37} one silver charger weighing one hundred thirty shekels, one silver bowl weighing seventy shekels (according to the sanctuary's weight), both filled with fine flour mixed with oil for a grain offering; {7:38} one gold spoon weighing ten shekels, full of incense; {7:39} one young bull, one ram, and one lamb of the first year for a burnt offering; {7:40} one goat kid for a sin offering; {7:41} and for peace offerings, two oxen, five rams, five male goats, and five lambs of the first year. This was the offering of Shelumiel son of Zurishaddai. {7:42} On the sixth day, Eliasaph son of Deuel, leader of Gad, offered: {7:43} one silver charger weighing one hundred thirty shekels, one silver bowl weighing seventy shekels (according to the sanctuary's weight), both filled with fine flour mixed with oil for a grain offering; {7:44} one gold spoon weighing ten shekels, full of incense; {7:45} one young bull, one ram, and one lamb of the first year for a burnt offering; {7:46} one goat kid for a sin offering; {7:47} and for peace offerings, two oxen, five rams, five male goats, and five lambs of the first year. This was the offering of Eliasaph son of Deuel. {7:48} On the seventh day, Elishama son of Ammihud, leader of Ephraim, offered: {7:49} one silver charger weighing one hundred thirty shekels, one silver bowl weighing seventy shekels (according to the sanctuary's weight), both filled with fine flour mixed with oil for a grain offering; {7:50} one gold spoon weighing ten shekels, full of incense; {7:51} one young bull, one ram, and one lamb of the first year for a burnt offering; {7:52} one goat kid for a sin offering; {7:53} and for peace offerings, two oxen, five rams, five male goats, and five lambs of the first year. This was the offering of Elishama son of Ammihud. {7:54} On the eighth day, Gamaliel son of Pedahzur, leader of Manasseh, offered: {7:55} one silver charger weighing one hundred thirty shekels, one silver bowl weighing seventy shekels (according to the sanctuary's weight), both filled with fine flour mixed with oil for a grain offering; {7:56} one gold spoon weighing ten shekels, full of incense; {7:57} one young bull, one ram, and one lamb of the first year for a burnt offering; {7:58} one goat kid for a sin offering; {7:59} and for peace offerings, two oxen, five rams, five male goats, and five lambs of the first year. This was the offering of Gamaliel son of Pedahzur. {7:60} On the ninth day, Abidan son of Gideoni, leader of Benjamin, offered: {7:61} one silver charger weighing one hundred thirty shekels, one silver bowl weighing seventy shekels (according to the sanctuary's weight), both filled with fine flour mixed with oil for a grain offering; {7:62} one gold spoon weighing ten shekels, full of incense; {7:63} one young bull, one ram, and one lamb of the first year for a burnt offering; {7:64} one goat kid for a sin offering; {7:65} and for peace offerings, two oxen, five rams, five male goats, and five lambs of the first year. This was the offering of Abidan son of Gideoni. {7:66} On the tenth day, Ahiezer son of Ammishaddai, leader of Dan, offered: {7:67} one silver charger weighing one hundred thirty shekels, one silver bowl weighing seventy shekels (according to the sanctuary's weight), both filled with fine flour mixed with oil for a grain offering; {7:68} one gold spoon weighing ten shekels, full of incense; {7:69} one young bull, one ram, and one lamb of the first year for a burnt offering; {7:70} one goat kid for a sin offering; {7:71} and for peace offerings, two oxen, five rams, five male goats, and five lambs of the first year. This was the offering of Ahiezer son of Ammishaddai. {7:72} On the eleventh day, Pagiel son of Ocran, leader of Asher, offered: {7:73} one silver charger weighing one hundred thirty shekels, one silver bowl weighing seventy shekels (according to the sanctuary's weight), both filled with fine flour mixed with oil for a grain offering; {7:74} one gold spoon weighing ten shekels, full of incense; {7:75} one young bull, one ram, and one lamb of the first year for a burnt offering; {7:76} one goat kid for a sin offering; {7:77} and for peace offerings, two oxen, five rams, five male goats, and five lambs of the first year. This was the offering of Pagiel son of Ocran. {7:78} On the twelfth day, Ahira son of Enan, leader of Naphtali, offered: {7:79} one silver charger weighing one hundred thirty shekels, one silver bowl weighing seventy shekels (according to the sanctuary's weight), both filled with fine flour mixed with oil for a grain offering; {7:80} one gold spoon weighing ten shekels, full of incense; {7:81} one young bull, one ram, and one lamb of the first year for a burnt offering; {7:82} one goat kid for a sin offering; {7:83} and for peace offerings, two oxen, five rams, five male goats, and five lambs of the first year. This was the offering of Ahira son of Enan. {7:84} This was the dedication of the altar on the day it was anointed by the leaders of Israel: twelve silver chargers, twelve silver bowls, and twelve gold spoons. {7:85} Each silver charger weighed one hundred thirty shekels, each bowl seventy shekels; all the silver vessels weighed two thousand four hundred shekels (according to the sanctuary's weight). {7:86} The twelve gold spoons, filled with incense, weighed ten shekels each (according to the sanctuary's weight), totaling one hundred twenty shekels. {7:87} The total for the burnt offerings included twelve young bulls, twelve rams, and twelve lambs of the first year, with their grain offerings; and twelve goat kids for sin offerings. {7:88} The total for the peace offerings included twenty-four young bulls, sixty rams, sixty male goats, and sixty lambs of the first year. This was the dedication of the altar after it was anointed. {7:89} When Moses entered the tabernacle of the congregation to speak with the LORD, he heard the voice of someone speaking to him from the mercy seat on the ark of the testimony, between the two cherubim; and He spoke to him.

{8:1} The LORD spoke to Moses, saying, {8:2} "Tell Aaron that when he lights the lamps, the seven lamps should shine in front of the lampstand." {8:3} Aaron did as the LORD commanded and lit the lamps in front of the lampstand. {8:4} The lampstand was made of hammered gold, from its base to its flowers, crafted according to the pattern the LORD showed Moses. {8:5} The LORD spoke to Moses again, saying, {8:6} "Take the Levites from the Israelites and purify them. {8:7} Here's how you will purify them: Sprinkle them with the water of purification, have them shave their whole bodies, and wash their clothes to make themselves clean. {8:8} Then they must bring a young bull with a grain offering of fine flour mixed with oil, and another young bull for a sin offering. {8:9} You shall bring the Levites before the tabernacle of the congregation and gather all the Israelites together. {8:10} Present the Levites before the LORD, and the Israelites will lay their hands on the Levites. {8:11} Aaron will present the Levites before the LORD as an offering from the Israelites so they can perform the service of the LORD. {8:12} The Levites will lay their hands on the heads of the bulls, and you will offer one as a sin offering and the other as a burnt offering to the LORD to make atonement for the Levites. {8:13} You will set the Levites before Aaron and his sons and offer them to the LORD. {8:14} This will separate the Levites from the Israelites, and the Levites will belong to Me. {8:15} After this, the Levites may enter to perform the service of the tabernacle, and you will cleanse them and present them as an offering. {8:16} They are entirely dedicated to Me from among the Israelites; instead of every firstborn that opens the womb, I have taken them for Myself. {8:17} All the firstborn of the Israelites are Mine, both human and animal; on the day I struck down every firstborn in the land of Egypt, I consecrated them for Myself. {8:18} I have taken the Levites in place of all the firstborn of the Israelites. {8:19} I have given the Levites as a gift to Aaron and his sons from among the Israelites, to serve the Israelites in the tabernacle and to make atonement for them, so there will be no plague among the Israelites when they approach the sanctuary. {8:20} Moses, Aaron, and the entire Israelite community did everything the LORD commanded regarding the Levites. {8:21} The Levites were purified, they washed their clothes, and Aaron presented them as an offering before the LORD and made atonement for them to cleanse them. {8:22} After this, the Levites entered to perform their service in the tabernacle in front of Aaron and his sons, just as the LORD had commanded Moses. {8:23} The LORD spoke to Moses, saying, {8:24} "This is what applies to the Levites: they must be twenty-five years old or older to enter the service of the tabernacle. {8:25} At fifty years old, they will retire from the service and no longer work there, {8:26} but they can assist their fellow Levites in the tabernacle, keeping watch, but they will not perform any service. This is how you will handle the Levites and their duties."

{9:1} The LORD spoke to Moses in the wilderness of Sinai, in the first month of the second year after they left Egypt, saying, {9:2} "The Israelites must celebrate the Passover at its appointed time. {9:3} On the fourteenth day of this month, at dusk, you shall celebrate it, following all its rituals and ceremonies." {9:4} Moses instructed the Israelites to keep the Passover. {9:5} They celebrated the Passover on the fourteenth day of the first month at dusk in the wilderness of Sinai, doing everything the LORD commanded Moses. {9:6} Some men were unclean because they had come into contact with a dead body, and they couldn't celebrate the Passover that day. They approached Moses and Aaron, {9:7} saying, "We are unclean due to a dead body. Why are we excluded from presenting the LORD's offering at its appointed time among the Israelites?" {9:8} Moses replied, "Wait here, and I will find out what the LORD commands regarding you." {9:9} The LORD spoke to Moses, saying, {9:10} "Tell the Israelites that if any man or his descendants is unclean due to a dead body or is away on a journey, he must still celebrate the Passover for the LORD. {9:11} They shall celebrate it on the fourteenth day of the second month at dusk, and they shall eat it with unleavened bread and bitter herbs. {9:12} They must leave none of it until morning and must not break any of its bones; they should follow all the regulations of the Passover." {9:13} However, a man who is clean and not away on a journey but neglects to celebrate the Passover will be cut off from his people, as he did not present the LORD's offering at the appointed time and will bear his sin. {9:14} If a foreigner lives among you and wants to celebrate the Passover to the LORD, he must follow its regulations and rituals; you will have the same law for both the foreigner and the native-born. {9:15} On the day the tabernacle was set up, a cloud covered it, specifically the tent of the testimony, and at night there was an appearance of fire on the tabernacle until morning. {9:16} This was the case all the time: the cloud covered it by day, and there was fire at night. {9:17} Whenever the cloud lifted from the tabernacle, the Israelites would set out; and wherever the cloud settled, the Israelites would pitch their tents. {9:18} The Israelites traveled at the command of the LORD and pitched their tents at His command; they remained in their tents as long as the cloud stayed over the tabernacle. {9:19} If the cloud lingered over the tabernacle for many days, the Israelites followed the LORD's instructions and did not travel. {9:20} When the cloud was over the tabernacle for a few days, they would stay in their tents at the LORD's command and would travel when He commanded. {9:21} If the cloud remained from evening until morning, and then lifted in the morning, they would travel; whether it was by day or night when the cloud lifted, they would set out. {9:22} If the cloud stayed for two days, a month, or a year, the Israelites would remain in their tents and not travel; but when it lifted, they would journey. {9:23} They traveled and rested at the LORD's command, keeping His instructions as directed by Moses.

{10:1} The LORD spoke to Moses, saying, {10:2} "Make two silver trumpets from a single piece of metal; use them to call the assembly and signal the movement of the camps. {10:3} When you blow them, the entire assembly must gather at the entrance of the tabernacle. {10:4} If you blow just one trumpet, the leaders of the thousands of Israel will gather to you. {10:5} When you sound an alarm, the camps on the east side shall set out. {10:6} When you sound the alarm a second time, the camps on the south side shall move; you will blow alarms for their journeys. {10:7} But when gathering the congregation, you should blow without sounding an alarm. {10:8} The sons of Aaron, the priests, shall blow the trumpets; this will be a lasting ordinance for you throughout your generations. {10:9} If you go to war in your land against enemies who oppress you, blow the trumpets as an alarm, and you will be remembered before the LORD your God, and He will save you from your enemies. {10:10} Also, on your joyful days, solemn days, and the beginnings of your months, blow the trumpets over your burnt offerings and peace offerings; this will serve as a reminder before your God: I am the LORD your God. {10:11} On the twentieth day of the second month, in the second year, the cloud lifted from the tabernacle of the testimony. {10:12} The Israelites set out from the wilderness of Sinai, and the cloud rested in the wilderness of Paran. {10:13} They began their journey as the LORD commanded through Moses. {10:14} The first to set out was the standard of the camp of the children of Judah, led by Nahshon the son of Amminadab. {10:15} Nethaneel the son of Zuar led the tribe of Issachar. {10:16} Eliab the son of Helon led the tribe of Zebulun. {10:17} The tabernacle was taken down, and the sons of Gershon and Merari set out, carrying the tabernacle. {10:18} The standard of the camp of Reuben followed, led by Elizur the son of Shedeur. {10:19} Shelumiel the son of Zurishaddai led the tribe of Simeon. {10:20} Eliasaph the son of Deuel led the tribe of Gad. {10:21} The Kohathites set out, carrying the sanctuary, while the others set up the tabernacle as they arrived. {10:22} The standard of the camp of Ephraim followed, led by Elishama the son of Ammihud. {10:23} Gamaliel the son of Pedahzur led the tribe of Manasseh. {10:24} Abidan the son of Gideoni led the tribe of Benjamin. {10:25} The standard of the camp of Dan set out last, bringing up the rear of all the camps, led by Ahiezer the son of Ammishaddai. {10:26} Pagiel the son of Ocran led the tribe of Asher. {10:27} Ahira the son of Enan led the tribe of Naphtali. {10:28} This is how the Israelites journeyed according to their divisions as they set out. {10:29} Moses said to Hobab, the son of Raguel the Midianite, Moses' father-in-law, "We are traveling to the place the LORD promised to give us; come with us, and we will treat you well, for the LORD has spoken good concerning Israel." {10:30} Hobab replied, "I will not go; I will return to my own land and to my relatives." {10:31} Moses urged him, "Please don't leave us, because you know how we are to camp in the wilderness, and you can be our guide. {10:32} "If you come with us, whatever good the LORD does for us, we will do the same for you." {10:33} They traveled for three days from the mountain of the LORD, with the ark of the covenant going ahead to find a resting place for them. {10:34} The cloud of the LORD was over them by day as they left the camp. {10:35} When the ark set out, Moses said, "Rise up, LORD, and let Your enemies be scattered; let those who hate You flee before You." {10:36} When it came to rest, he said, "Return, O LORD, to the countless thousands of Israel."

{11:1} When the people complained, it displeased the LORD, and He heard it; His anger was kindled, and the fire of the LORD burned among them, consuming those in the outer parts of the camp. {11:2} The people cried out to Moses, and when Moses prayed to the LORD, the fire was extinguished. {11:3} He named the place Taberah because the fire of the LORD burned among them. {11:4} The mixed multitude that was with them began to crave food, and the Israelites also wept again, saying, "Who will give us meat to eat? {11:5} We remember the fish we ate in Egypt for free, along with cucumbers, melons, leeks, onions, and garlic. {11:6} But now our souls are dried up; we have nothing except this manna before our eyes." {11:7} The manna was like coriander seed, and its color was like that of bdellium (a fragrant resin). {11:8} The people went around, gathered it, ground it in mills or beat it in mortars, baked it in pans, and made cakes of it; its taste was like the taste of fresh oil. {11:9} When the dew fell on the camp at night, the manna fell with it. {11:10} Moses heard the people weeping in their families, every man at the door of his tent, and the LORD's anger grew greatly; Moses was also displeased. {11:11} Moses said to the LORD, "Why have You afflicted Your servant? Why haven't I found favor in Your sight that You lay the burden of this entire people on me? {11:12} Did I conceive this people? Did I give birth to them that You say to me, 'Carry them in your arms like a nursing father bears a child to the land You promised their ancestors'? {11:13} Where can I get meat to give to all this people? They keep crying to me, saying, 'Give us meat to eat.' {11:14} I can't bear this people alone; it's too heavy for me. {11:15} If You're going to deal with me like this, kill me now if I have found favor in Your sight; don't let me see my wretchedness." {11:16} The LORD said to Moses, "Gather for Me seventy elders of Israel, whom you know to be the elders of the people and their officers, and bring them to the tabernacle of the congregation so they can stand there with you. {11:17} I will come down and speak with you there; I will take some of the spirit that is upon you and put it on them, so they can share the burden of the people with you and not bear it alone. {11:18} Tell the people, 'Consecrate yourselves for tomorrow, and you will eat meat, for you have wept in the ears of the LORD, saying, "Who will give us meat to eat? It was good for us in Egypt." Therefore, the LORD will give you meat, and you will eat. {11:19} You will not eat for just one day, two days, five days, ten days, or twenty days, {11:20} but for a whole month until it comes out of your nostrils and becomes loathsome to you, because you have despised the LORD who is among you and have cried before Him, saying, "Why did we ever leave Egypt?" {11:21} Moses said, "The people I am with number six hundred thousand footmen, and You have said, 'I will give them meat to eat for a month.' {11:22} Should we slaughter all our flocks and herds to satisfy them? Should we gather all the fish in the sea for them?" {11:23} The LORD said to Moses, "Is the LORD's arm too short? You will see whether My word comes true for you or not." {11:24} Moses went out and told the people the words of the LORD. He gathered the seventy elders of the people and placed them around the tabernacle.

{11:25} The LORD came down in a cloud and spoke to him. He took some of the spirit that was upon Moses and gave it to the seventy elders. When the spirit rested upon them, they prophesied but did not continue. {11:26} Two men remained in the camp; their names were Eldad and Medad. The spirit rested upon them; they were among those listed but did not go to the tabernacle, and they prophesied in the camp. {11:27} A young man ran and told Moses, "Eldad and Medad are prophesying in the camp." {11:28} Joshua the son of Nun, Moses' assistant, said, "My lord Moses, stop them!" {11:29} But Moses replied, "Are you jealous for my sake? I wish that all the LORD's people were prophets and that the LORD would put His spirit upon them!" {11:30} Then Moses returned to the camp with the elders of Israel. {11:31} A wind from the LORD blew quails from the sea and let them fall near the camp, about a day's journey on this side and a day's journey on the other side, all around the camp, and about two cubits high on the ground. {11:32} The people worked all that day, night, and the next day, gathering quails; the least anyone gathered was ten homers (about 1,100 liters), and they spread them out around the camp. {11:33} While the meat was still between their teeth, before it was chewed, the LORD's anger was kindled against the people, and He struck them with a very severe plague. {11:34} He named the place Kibrothhattaavah because there they buried the people who craved meat. {11:35} The people journeyed from Kibrothhattaavah to Hazeroth and stayed at Hazeroth.

{12:1} Miriam and Aaron spoke against Moses because of the Cushite woman he had married; he had married a Cushite woman. {12:2} They said, "Has the LORD really spoken only through Moses? Hasn't He also spoken through us?" And the LORD heard it. {12:3} (Now Moses was very humble, more than anyone else on the face of the earth.) {12:4} Suddenly the LORD spoke to Moses, Aaron, and Miriam, saying, "Come out, you three, to the tabernacle of the congregation." So the three of them came out. {12:5} The LORD came down in a pillar of cloud, stood at the entrance of the tabernacle, and called Aaron and Miriam, and they both came forward. {12:6} He said, "Listen to My words: If there is a prophet among you, I, the LORD, will make Myself known to him in a vision and will speak to him in a dream. {12:7} My servant Moses is not like that; he is faithful in all My house. {12:8} With him, I will speak face to face, clearly, and not in riddles; he will see the form of the LORD. Why then were you not afraid to speak against My servant Moses?" {12:9} The LORD's anger was kindled against them, and He departed. {12:10} The cloud moved away from the tabernacle, and suddenly Miriam became leprous, as white as snow. Aaron looked at Miriam, and she was leprous. {12:11} Aaron said to Moses, "Oh, my lord, please don't hold this sin against us, for we have acted foolishly and have sinned. {12:12} Don't let her be like a stillborn child, whose flesh is half consumed when it comes out of its mother's womb." {12:13} Moses cried out to the LORD, saying, "Please heal her, O God." {12:14} The LORD said to Moses, "If her father had merely spit in her face, wouldn't she have to be ashamed for seven days? Let her be shut out from the camp for seven days, and afterward, she may be received back." {12:15} So Miriam was shut out from the camp for seven days, and the people did not move on until she was brought back in. {12:16} Afterward, the people moved from Hazeroth and camped in the wilderness of Paran.

{13:1} The LORD spoke to Moses, saying, {13:2} "Send men to explore the land of Canaan, which I am giving to the children of Israel. From each tribe of their fathers, send a man, each one a leader among them." {13:3} So, at the LORD's command, Moses sent them from the wilderness of Paran; all these men were heads of the children of Israel. {13:4} Here are their names: from the tribe of Reuben, Shammua the son of Zaccur. {13:5} From the tribe of Simeon, Shaphat the son of Hori. {13:6} From the tribe of Judah, Caleb the son of Jephunneh. {13:7} From the tribe of Issachar, Igal the son of Joseph. {13:8} From the tribe of Ephraim, Oshea the son of Nun. {13:9} From the tribe of Benjamin, Palti the son of Raphu. {13:10} From the tribe of Zebulun, Gaddiel the son of Sodi. {13:11} From the tribe of Joseph, specifically from the tribe of Manasseh, Gaddi the son of Susi. {13:12} From the tribe of Dan, Ammiel the son of Gemalli. {13:13} From the tribe of Asher, Sethur the son of Michael. {13:14} From the tribe of Naphtali, Nahbi the son of Vophsi. {13:15} From the tribe of Gad, Geuel the son of Machi. {13:16} These are the names of the men that Moses sent to scout the land. Moses called Oshea the son of Nun "Joshua." {13:17} Moses sent them to scout the land of Canaan and said, "Go up this way southward and into the mountain. {13:18} Look at the land: what it is, and the people living there—are they strong or weak, few or many? {13:19} What is the land like where they live—good or bad? What are the cities like—do they live in open camps or fortified cities? {13:20} Is the land rich or poor? Is there timber in it or not? Be of good courage, and bring back some of the fruit of the land." (It was the season for the first ripe grapes.) {13:21} So they went up and explored the land from the wilderness of Zin to Rehob, near Hamath. {13:22} They went up through the south and came to Hebron, where Ahiman, Sheshai, and Talmai, the descendants of Anak, lived. (Hebron had been built seven years before Zoan in Egypt.) {13:23} They came to the Valley of Eshcol and cut down a branch with a single cluster of grapes, which they carried on a pole between two men. They also brought pomegranates and figs. {13:24} That place was called the Valley of Eshcol because of the cluster of grapes that the children of Israel cut down there. {13:25} They returned from exploring the land after forty days. {13:26} They went to Moses, Aaron, and the whole Israelite community in the wilderness of Paran at Kadesh, and they reported to them and to the whole community, showing them the fruit of the land. {13:27} They told Moses, "We went to the land you sent us, and it truly flows with milk and honey; here is its fruit. {13:28} However, the people living there are strong, and the cities are fortified and very large. Moreover, we saw the descendants of Anak there. {13:29} The Amalekites live in the Negev; the Hittites, Jebusites, and Amorites live in the hill country, and the Canaanites live by the sea and along the Jordan." {13:30} Caleb silenced the people before Moses and said, "We should go up and take possession of the land, for we can certainly do it." {13:31} But the men who had gone up with him said, "We can't attack those people; they are stronger than we are." {13:32} And they spread a bad report about the land they had explored, saying, "The land we explored devours those living in it, and all the people we saw there are of great size. {13:33} We even saw giants there, the descendants of Anak. We felt like grasshoppers in our own eyes, and we looked the same to them."

{14:1} All the congregation raised their voices and cried, and the people wept that night. {14:2} All the children of Israel grumbled against Moses and Aaron, and the whole congregation said to them, "Would that we had died in the land of Egypt or in this wilderness! {14:3} Why has the LORD brought us to this land, to fall by the sword, so that our wives and children would be taken as plunder? Wouldn't it be better for us to return to Egypt?" {14:4} They said to one another, "Let's appoint a leader and go back to Egypt." {14:5} Then Moses and Aaron fell on their faces before the whole assembly of the children of Israel. {14:6} Joshua son of Nun and Caleb son of Jephunneh, who were among those who explored the land, tore their clothes {14:7} and spoke to all the people of Israel, saying, "The land we explored is an exceptionally good land. {14:8} If the LORD is pleased with us, He will bring us into this land and give it to us—a land flowing with milk and honey. {14:9} Only do not rebel against the LORD, and do not fear the people of the land, for they are our prey; their protection has departed from them, and the LORD is with us; do not fear them." {14:10} But the whole congregation threatened to stone them with stones. Then the glory of the LORD appeared at the tent of meeting before all the children of Israel. {14:11} The LORD said to Moses, "How long will this people provoke Me? How long will they refuse to believe in Me, despite all the signs I have performed among them? {14:12} I will strike them with a plague and disinherit them, and I will make you into a nation greater and mightier than they." {14:13} But Moses said to the LORD, "Then the Egyptians will hear about it, for You brought this people up by Your great power from among them. {14:14} They will tell the inhabitants of this land, for they have heard that You, LORD, are among this people, that You, LORD, are seen face to face, and that Your cloud stands over them, and that You go before them in a pillar of cloud by day and a pillar of fire by night. {14:15} Now if You kill all this people as one man, then the nations that have heard of Your fame will say, {14:16} 'The LORD was not able to bring this people into the land He swore to give them; therefore, He killed them in the wilderness.'" {14:17} Now please let the power of my Lord be great, as You have declared, saying, {14:18} "The LORD is slow to anger, abounding in love, forgiving iniquity and transgression, yet He does not leave the guilty unpunished; He visits the iniquity of the fathers on the children to the third and fourth generation." {14:19} Pardon the iniquity of this people, I ask, according to Your great mercy, just as You have forgiven this people from Egypt until now. {14:20} The LORD said, "I have pardoned according to your word; {14:21} but as truly as I live, all the earth will be filled with the glory of the LORD. {14:22} Because all those men who have seen My glory and the signs I performed in Egypt and in the wilderness, and have tested Me now these ten times and have not obeyed My voice, {14:23} surely they will not see the land I swore to give their fathers, nor will any of those who provoked Me see it. {14:24} But my servant Caleb, because he has a different spirit and has followed Me wholeheartedly, I will bring him into the land where he went, and his descendants will possess it. {14:25} (Now the Amalekites and Canaanites live in the valley.) Tomorrow, turn around and head back into the wilderness by the Red Sea." {14:26} The LORD spoke to Moses and Aaron, saying, {14:27} "How long will I endure this evil congregation that grumbles against Me? I have heard the complaints of the children of Israel, which they make against Me. {14:28} Say to them, 'As surely as I live,' says the LORD, 'I will do to you the very thing I heard you say: {14:29} Your bodies will fall in this wilderness, and all who were numbered among you, from twenty years old and upward, who have grumbled against Me, {14:30} will certainly not enter the land I swore to give you, except Caleb son of Jephunneh and Joshua son of Nun. {14:31} But your little ones, whom you said would become a prey, I will bring in, and they will know the land you have rejected. {14:32} But as for you, your bodies will fall in this wilderness. {14:33} Your children will wander in the wilderness for forty years and bear your iniquities until your bodies are wasted in the wilderness. {14:34} According to the number of days you explored the land—forty days—each day will count for a year, and you will suffer for your iniquities for forty years, and you will know My breach of promise. {14:35} I, the LORD, have spoken; I will certainly do this to all this evil congregation that has gathered against Me: in this wilderness they will be consumed, and there they will die." {14:36} The men whom Moses sent to explore the land, and who made the entire congregation grumble against him by spreading a bad report about the land, {14:37} those men who brought up the evil report about the land died of a plague before the LORD. {14:38} But Joshua son of Nun and Caleb son of Jephunneh, who were among the men who explored the land, survived. {14:39} When Moses reported these words to all the children of Israel, the people mourned greatly. {14:40} They got up early the next morning and went up to the top of the mountain, saying, "Here we are; we will go up to the place the LORD promised, for we have sinned." {14:41} But Moses said, "Why are you now disobeying the command of the LORD? It won't succeed. {14:42} Do not go up, for the LORD is not with you; you will be defeated by your enemies. {14:43} The Amalekites and Canaanites are there before you, and you will fall by the sword, because you have turned away from the LORD; the LORD will not be with you." {14:44} But they assumed they could go up to the hilltop, yet the ark of the covenant of the LORD and Moses did not leave the camp. {14:45} Then the Amalekites and Canaanites who lived in that hill country came down and attacked them and defeated them all the way to Hormah.

{15:1} The LORD spoke to Moses, saying, {15:2} "Speak to the children of Israel and tell them that when you enter the land I am giving you, {15:3} and make an offering by fire to the LORD, whether it's a burnt offering, a sacrifice for a vow, a freewill offering, or part of your solemn feasts, to create a pleasing aroma to the LORD from your herds or flocks: {15:4} the person offering the sacrifice must bring a grain offering of a tenth of an ephah (a measure of flour) mixed with a quarter of a hin (about a liter) of oil. {15:5} You must also prepare a quarter of a hin of wine as a drink offering with the burnt offering or sacrifice for one lamb. {15:6} If you prepare a ram, then for the grain offering, you should bring two-tenths of an ephah of flour mixed with a third of a hin of oil. {15:7} For the drink offering, offer a third of a hin of wine, creating a pleasing aroma to the LORD. {15:8} When you prepare a bull for a burnt offering, or for a vow or peace offering to the LORD, {15:9} you must bring with the bull a grain offering of three-tenths of an ephah of flour mixed with half a hin of oil. {15:10} And you should bring half a hin of wine for the drink offering, as an offering made by fire, creating a pleasing aroma to the LORD. {15:11} This is how it should be done for one bull, one ram, one lamb, or one goat kid. {15:12} According to the number of animals you prepare, so shall you do for each one. {15:13} Everyone born in the country must follow these instructions for offering an offering made by fire, creating a pleasing aroma to the LORD. {15:14} If a foreigner resides among you or anyone from your generations wants to offer an offering made by fire, creating a pleasing aroma to the LORD, they must do as you do. {15:15} There will be one law for you and for the foreigner who resides among you, a lasting ordinance for your generations: as you are, so shall the foreigner be before the LORD. {15:16} One law and one practice shall be for both you and the foreigner living among you. {15:17} The LORD spoke to Moses, saying, {15:18} "Speak to the children of Israel, and say to them, when you come into the land I am giving you, {15:19} then when you eat of the bread of the land, you shall offer a portion to the LORD. {15:20} You shall offer a cake from the first of your dough as a heave offering; as you do with the heave offering from the threshing floor, you shall offer it. {15:21} From the first of your dough, you shall give a heave offering to the LORD throughout your generations. {15:22} If you have erred and not observed all these commandments the LORD has given to Moses, {15:23} all that the LORD has commanded you through Moses from the day He commanded Moses and onward among your generations; {15:24} then if anything is done inadvertently without the knowledge of the congregation, the whole congregation must offer a young bull as a burnt offering, creating a pleasing aroma to the LORD, with its grain offering and drink offering according to the proper manner, and one goat kid for a sin offering. {15:25} The priest will make atonement for all the congregation of the children of Israel, and it will be forgiven them; for it was done in ignorance. They must bring their offering, a fire sacrifice to the LORD, and their sin offering before the LORD for their ignorance. {15:26} It shall be forgiven for all the congregation of the children of Israel and the foreigners living among them, since all the people were unaware. {15:27} If anyone sins unintentionally, they shall bring a year-old female goat for a sin offering. {15:28} The priest will make atonement for the person who sins unintentionally before the LORD, to make atonement for them, and it will be forgiven. {15:29} There will be one law for the person who sins unintentionally, both for the native-born among the children of Israel and for the foreigner who resides among them. {15:30} But the person who acts defiantly, whether native-born or foreigner, reproaches the LORD; that person will be cut off from among their people. {15:31} Because they have despised the word of the LORD and broken His commandment, that person shall be completely cut off; their guilt will remain on them. {15:32} While the children of Israel were in the wilderness, they found a man gathering sticks on the Sabbath day. {15:33} Those who found him gathering sticks brought him to Moses and Aaron and to the whole congregation. {15:34} They put him in custody, because it had not been declared what should be done to him. {15:35} The LORD said to Moses, "The man must surely be put to death; the whole congregation must stone him with stones outside the camp." {15:36} So the whole congregation took him outside the camp and stoned him with stones, and he died, as the LORD commanded Moses. {15:37} The LORD spoke to Moses, saying, {15:38} "Speak to the children of Israel and instruct them to make tassels on the corners of their garments throughout their generations, and to put a blue cord on the tassels. {15:39} It shall be a tassel for you to look at and remember all the commandments of the LORD and do them, and not follow after your own heart and your own eyes, which lead you to be unfaithful. {15:40} So you will remember and keep all My commandments and be holy to your God. {15:41} I am the LORD your God, who brought you out of the land of Egypt to be your God; I am the LORD your God."

{16:1} Now Korah, the son of Izhar, the son of Kohath, the son of Levi, along with Dathan and Abiram, the sons of Eliab, and On, the son of Peleth, from the tribe of Reuben, gathered some men together. {16:2} They confronted Moses with two hundred and fifty leaders from the assembly, renowned men in the congregation. {16:3} They came together against Moses and Aaron and said to them, "You take too much authority for yourselves, seeing that the whole congregation is holy, every one of them, and the LORD is among them. Why do you set yourselves above the congregation of the LORD?" {16:4} When Moses heard this, he fell on his face. {16:5} He spoke to Korah and all his followers, saying, "Tomorrow the LORD will show who belongs to Him and who is holy, and He will bring the one He chooses near to Him. {16:6} This is what you should do: Korah and all your followers, take censers; {16:7} put fire in them and place incense in them before the LORD tomorrow. The man whom the LORD chooses will be holy. You are taking too much upon yourselves, you sons of Levi." {16:8} Moses said to Korah, "Listen, you sons of Levi: {16:9} Is it not enough for you that the God of Israel has separated you from the congregation of Israel to bring you near to Himself to serve in the tabernacle of the LORD and to stand before the congregation to minister to them? {16:10} He has brought you and all your fellow Levites near to Him, and now you seek the priesthood as well? {16:11} This is why you and your followers have gathered against the LORD. What is Aaron that you complain about him?" {16:12} Moses sent for Dathan and Abiram, the sons of Eliab, but they replied, "We will not come up. {16:13} Is it not enough that you brought us up from a land flowing with milk and honey to kill us in the wilderness, unless you make yourself a prince over us? {16:14} Furthermore, you haven't brought us into a land flowing with milk and honey or given us any inheritance of fields and vineyards. Are you trying to blind these men? We will not come up." {16:15} Moses was very angry and said to the LORD, "Do not accept their offering. I have not taken a single donkey from them, nor have I harmed any of them." {16:16} Moses said to Korah, "You and all your followers should present yourselves before the LORD tomorrow, you and they and Aaron. {16:17} Each man must take his censer, put incense in it, and bring it before the LORD—two hundred and fifty censers in all. You and Aaron each must also have your own censer." {16:18} So every man took his censer, put fire in them, and laid incense on them. They stood at the entrance of the tabernacle with Moses and Aaron. {16:19} Korah gathered all the congregation against them at the entrance of the tabernacle, and the glory of the LORD appeared to all the congregation. {16:20} The LORD spoke to Moses and Aaron, saying, {16:21} "Separate yourselves from this congregation so that I may consume them in a moment." {16:22} They fell on their faces and said, "O God, God of the spirits of all flesh, will one man sin and be angry with the entire congregation?" {16:23} The LORD spoke to Moses, saying, {16:24} "Tell the congregation to get away from the tents of Korah, Dathan, and Abiram." {16:25} Moses stood up and went to Dathan and Abiram, and the elders of Israel followed him. {16:26} He said to the congregation, "Depart from the tents of these wicked men, and touch nothing of theirs, or you will be consumed in all their sins." {16:27} So they moved away from the tents of Korah, Dathan, and Abiram. Dathan and Abiram came out and stood at the entrance of their tents with their wives, children, and little ones. {16:28} Moses said, "By this you will know that the LORD has sent me to do all these works; I have not done them of my own accord. {16:29} If these men die a natural death or experience what usually happens to all men, then the LORD has not sent me. {16:30} But if the LORD performs a new thing and the ground opens its mouth and swallows them up with everything that belongs to them, and they go down alive into the pit, then you will know that these men have provoked the LORD." {16:31} As he finished speaking, the ground split open beneath them. {16:32} The earth opened its mouth and swallowed them up, their households, and everyone associated with Korah, along with all their possessions. {16:33} They and all that belonged to them went down alive into the pit, and the earth closed over them, and they perished from the congregation. {16:34} All Israel around them fled at their cries, saying, "The earth might swallow us too!" {16:35} Fire came out from the LORD and consumed the two hundred and fifty men who offered incense. {16:36} The LORD spoke to Moses, saying, {16:37} "Tell Eleazar, the son of Aaron the priest, to take the censers out of the fire and scatter the coals away, for they are holy. {16:38} The censers of these men who have sinned against their own souls must be made into broad plates for a covering of the altar, for they offered them before the LORD, and so they are holy; they will be a sign for the children of Israel." {16:39} Eleazar the priest took the bronze censers, which the burned men had offered, and made broad plates for a covering of the altar. {16:40} This will serve as a reminder to the children of Israel that no unauthorized person, not of Aaron's lineage, should come near to offer incense before the LORD, so they do not become like Korah and his followers, as the LORD commanded through Moses. {16:41} The next day, the entire congregation of the children of Israel complained against Moses and Aaron, saying, "You have killed the LORD's people." {16:42} When the congregation gathered against Moses and Aaron, they looked toward the tabernacle, and behold, the cloud covered it, and the glory of the LORD appeared. {16:43} Moses and Aaron came before the tabernacle. {16:44} The LORD spoke to Moses, saying, {16:45} "Get away from this congregation, so I may consume them in an instant." They fell on their faces. {16:46} Moses said to Aaron, "Take a censer, put fire from the altar in it, add incense, and go quickly to the congregation to make atonement for them, for the LORD's wrath has gone out, and the plague has begun." {16:47} Aaron did as Moses commanded, ran into the midst of the congregation, and saw that the plague had started among the people. He put incense on and made atonement for the people. {16:48} He stood between the dead and the living, and the plague was halted. {16:49} Fourteen thousand seven hundred died in the plague, besides those who died because of Korah. {16:50} Aaron returned to Moses at the entrance of the tabernacle, and the plague was stopped.

{17:1} The LORD spoke to Moses, saying, {17:2} "Speak to the children of Israel and take a rod from each of them, one for each family, with twelve rods representing the leaders from each tribe. Write each man's name on his rod. {17:3} Write Aaron's name on the rod of Levi, as it will represent the head of that family. {17:4} Place the rods in the tabernacle of meeting before the testimony, where I will meet with you. {17:5} The rod of the man I choose will blossom, and I will put an end to the complaints of the children of Israel against you." {17:6} Moses spoke to the children of Israel, and each of their leaders gave him a rod, totaling twelve rods, including Aaron's rod. {17:7} Moses placed the rods before the LORD in the tabernacle of testimony. {17:8} The next day, Moses entered the tabernacle of testimony and saw that Aaron's rod for the house of Levi had sprouted, produced buds, bloomed blossoms, and yielded almonds. {17:9} Moses brought all the rods out from before the LORD to the children of Israel, and they looked and took their rods. {17:10} The LORD said to Moses, "Bring Aaron's rod back before the testimony to be kept as a sign against the rebels, so their complaints do not lead to their deaths." {17:11} Moses did as the LORD commanded him. {17:12} The children of Israel said to Moses, "We are going to die; we are all perishing! {17:13} Anyone who gets too close to the tabernacle of the LORD will die. Are we going to be consumed with death?"

{18:1} The LORD said to Aaron, "You, your sons, and your father's household will bear the guilt associated with the sanctuary, and you and your sons will bear the guilt of your priesthood. {18:2} Bring your fellow Levites, the tribe of your father, to join you and assist you, but you and your sons will minister before the tabernacle of witness. {18:3} They will keep your responsibilities and the responsibilities of the entire tabernacle, but they must not go near the sanctuary or the altar, or both they and you will die. {18:4} They will be joined to you and keep the charge of the tabernacle of the congregation, as no outsider may approach you. {18:5} You must keep the responsibilities of the sanctuary and the altar, so that there is no more wrath upon the children of Israel. {18:6} I have taken your fellow Levites from among the children of Israel; they are a gift to you for the LORD, to serve at the tabernacle of the congregation. {18:7} Therefore, you and your sons will keep your priestly duties for everything at the altar and inside the veil; you will serve. I have given you this priestly office as a gift, and anyone who approaches will be put to death. {18:8} The LORD spoke to Aaron, saying, "I have given you the responsibility for my heave offerings and all the sacred things of the children of Israel; they are given to you because of your anointing, and to your sons by a lasting ordinance. {18:9} You will receive the most holy offerings, which are reserved from the fire: every offering, grain offering, sin offering, and guilt offering they present to me will be most holy for you and your sons. {18:10} You are to eat it in the most holy place; every male may eat it. It will be holy to you. {18:11} This is yours: the heave offering from their gifts, including all the wave offerings of the children of Israel. I have given them to you and your sons and daughters as a lasting statute; anyone who is clean in your household may eat of it. {18:12} You will receive the best of the oil, wine, and wheat; the firstfruits they present to the LORD are yours. {18:13} Whatever is first ripe in the land and brought to the LORD will be yours; anyone who is clean in your household may eat of it. {18:14} Everything devoted in Israel will be yours. {18:15} Everything that opens the womb among all flesh, which they bring to the LORD, whether of humans or animals, will be yours; however, you must redeem the firstborn of humans and the firstborn of unclean animals. {18:16} Those that are to be redeemed from a month old must be redeemed at your estimation for five shekels, according to the shekel of the sanctuary, which is twenty gerahs. {18:17} But the firstborn of a cow, sheep, or goat must not be redeemed; they are holy. You will sprinkle their blood on the altar and burn their fat as an offering by fire, a sweet aroma to the LORD. {18:18} Their flesh will be yours, just as the wave breast and the right shoulder are yours. {18:19} All the heave offerings of the holy things that the children of Israel offer to the LORD are given to you and your sons and daughters as a lasting statute; this is a covenant of salt forever before the LORD for you and your descendants. {18:20} The LORD spoke to Aaron, saying, "You will have no inheritance in their land, nor will you have any part among them; I am your portion and your inheritance among the children of Israel. {18:21} I have given the children of Levi all the tithes in Israel as their inheritance for the service they provide, even the service of the tabernacle of the congregation. {18:22} The children of Israel must not approach the tabernacle of the congregation, lest they bear sin and die. {18:23} The Levites will do the service of the tabernacle, and they will bear their iniquity; this will be a lasting statute throughout your generations, meaning they will have no inheritance among the children of Israel. {18:24} The tithes of the children of Israel, which they offer as a heave offering to the LORD, I have given to the Levites as their inheritance; therefore, I have said to them that they will have no inheritance among the children of Israel." {18:25} The LORD spoke to Moses, saying, {18:26} "Speak to the Levites and say to them: When you receive the tithes from the children of Israel, which I have given you for your inheritance, you must offer a heave offering of a tenth of those tithes to the LORD. {18:27} This heave offering will be counted to you as if it were from the grain of the threshing floor and the fullness of the winepress. {18:28} Likewise, you must offer a heave offering to the LORD from all your tithes that you receive from the children of Israel; you will give the LORD's heave offering to Aaron the priest. {18:29} From all your gifts, you must offer every heave offering of the LORD, the best and most holy part of it. {18:30} Therefore, you must say to them, 'When you have lifted the best part from it, it will be counted for the Levites as the increase from the threshing floor and the increase from the winepress. {18:31} You and your households may eat it anywhere, as it is your reward for your service in the tabernacle of the congregation. {18:32} You will not bear sin by reason of it when you have lifted the best part from it, nor shall you pollute the holy things of the children of Israel, or you will die.'"

{19:1} The LORD spoke to Moses and Aaron, saying, {19:2} "This is the ordinance of the law that the LORD has commanded: Speak to the children of Israel and have them bring you a red heifer without spot or blemish, on which no yoke has ever been placed. {19:3} You will give her to Eleazar the priest, who will take her outside the camp and have her killed in his presence. {19:4} Eleazar the priest will take some of her blood with his finger and sprinkle it directly before the tabernacle of the congregation seven times. {19:5} He will then burn the heifer in his sight, along with her skin, flesh, blood, and dung. {19:6} The priest will take cedar wood, hyssop, and scarlet and throw them into the fire while the heifer is burning. {19:7} After this, the priest must wash his clothes and bathe his body in water, and he will remain unclean until evening. {19:8} The person who burns her must also wash his clothes and bathe his body in water, and he will be unclean until evening. {19:9} A clean person will gather the ashes of the heifer and place them in a clean place outside the camp; these ashes will be kept for the congregation of the children of Israel as a water of separation, which is a purification for sin. {19:10} The person gathering the ashes must wash his clothes and will be unclean until evening; this will be a statute forever for the children of Israel and for any foreigner living among them. {19:11} Anyone who touches the dead body of a person will be unclean for seven days. {19:12} He must purify himself with the ashes on the third day, and on the seventh day he will be clean. But if he does not purify himself on the third day, he will not be clean on the seventh day. {19:13} Anyone who touches a dead body and does not purify himself defiles the tabernacle of the LORD; that person will be cut off from Israel, as the water of separation was not sprinkled on him, and he remains unclean. {19:14} This is the law regarding a person who dies in a tent: anyone who enters the tent and everything in it will be unclean for seven days. {19:15} Every open container without a cover will be unclean. {19:16} Anyone who touches someone slain with a sword in the open fields, or a dead body, or a bone, or a grave will be unclean for seven days. {19:17} For an unclean person, they will take some ashes from the burnt heifer for purification from sin and mix them with running water in a container. {19:18} A clean person will take hyssop, dip it in the water, and sprinkle it on the tent, the vessels, the people there, and anyone who has touched a bone, a slain person, a dead body, or a grave. {19:19} The clean person will sprinkle the unclean person on the third day and on the seventh day; on the seventh day, he will purify himself, wash his clothes, bathe in water, and be clean by evening. {19:20} If a person is unclean and does not purify himself, he will be cut off from the congregation because he has defiled the sanctuary of the LORD; the water of separation has not been sprinkled on him, and he is unclean. {19:21} This will be a lasting statute for them: whoever sprinkles the water of separation must wash his clothes, and anyone who touches the water of separation will be unclean until evening. {19:22} Anything the unclean person touches will be unclean, and anyone who touches it will be unclean until evening."

{20:1} The whole congregation of the children of Israel arrived in the desert of Zin during the first month, and they camped in Kadesh. Miriam died there and was buried there. {20:2} There was no water for the congregation, so they gathered against Moses and Aaron. {20:3} The people argued with Moses, saying, "If only we had died when our brothers died before the LORD! {20:4} Why have you brought the congregation of the LORD into this wilderness to die here, along with our livestock? {20:5} Why did you make us leave Egypt to bring us to this awful place? It has no grain, figs, vines, or pomegranates, and there's no water to drink." {20:6} Moses and Aaron went from the assembly to the entrance of the tabernacle and fell on their faces; the glory of the LORD appeared to them. {20:7} The LORD spoke to Moses, saying, {20:8} "Take the rod, gather the assembly, you and your brother Aaron, and speak to the rock before their eyes. It will provide water, and you will give the congregation and their livestock drink." {20:9} So Moses took the rod from before the LORD as he was commanded. {20:10} Moses and Aaron gathered the congregation in front of the rock, and he said to them, "Listen now, you rebels; must we get water for you from this rock?" {20:11} Then Moses raised his hand and struck the rock twice with his rod. Water gushed out abundantly, and the congregation and their livestock drank. {20:12} The LORD spoke to Moses and Aaron, saying, "Because you did not trust me enough to honor me in the sight of the children of Israel, you will not bring this congregation into the land I have given them." {20:13} This is the water of Meribah (which means "strife"), because the children of Israel argued with the LORD, and He was honored among them. {20:14} Moses sent messengers from Kadesh to the king of Edom, saying, "Your brother Israel says: You know all the hardships that have come upon us. {20:15} Our ancestors went down to Egypt, and we have been there a long time. The Egyptians oppressed us and our ancestors. {20:16} When we cried out to the LORD, He heard our cry, sent an angel, and brought us out of Egypt. Now we are in Kadesh, a city at the edge of your territory. {20:17} Please let us pass through your land. We won't go through the fields or vineyards, and we won't drink from your wells. We will stay on the king's highway and will not turn to the right or the left until we have passed through your borders." {20:18} But Edom replied, "You may not pass through my land, or I will come out against you with the sword." {20:19} The children of Israel said to him, "We will stay on the highway. If we drink your water, I will pay for it. I will only pass through on foot." {20:20} But Edom said, "You shall not go through." Then Edom came out against them with a large force and a strong army. {20:21} So Edom refused to let Israel pass through his territory, and Israel turned away from him. {20:22} The whole congregation of the children of Israel journeyed from Kadesh and came to Mount Hor. {20:23} The LORD spoke to Moses and Aaron at Mount Hor, near the border of Edom, saying, {20:24} "Aaron will be gathered to his people; he will not enter the land I have given to the children of Israel, because you rebelled against my command at the water of Meribah. {20:25} Take Aaron and his son Eleazar and bring them up Mount Hor. {20:26} Remove Aaron's garments and put them on Eleazar his son, and Aaron will be gathered to his people and die there." {20:27} Moses did as the LORD commanded, and they went up Mount Hor in the sight of all the congregation. {20:28} Moses stripped Aaron of his garments and put them on Eleazar his son; Aaron died there on top of the mountain, and Moses and Eleazar came down from the mountain. {20:29} When all the congregation saw that Aaron was dead, they mourned for him for thirty days, all the house of Israel.

{21:1} When King Arad the Canaanite, who lived in the south, heard that Israel was coming through the way of the spies, he fought against Israel and took some of them captive. {21:2} Israel made a vow to the LORD, saying, "If you will truly deliver this people into my hands, then I will completely destroy their cities." {21:3} The LORD listened to Israel's voice and delivered the Canaanites to them, and they completely destroyed them and their cities, naming the place Hormah. {21:4} They journeyed from Mount Hor along the way to the Red Sea to go around the land of Edom, and the people grew very discouraged because of the long journey. {21:5} The people spoke against God and against Moses, saying, "Why did you bring us out of Egypt to die in this wilderness? There is no bread or water, and we detest this miserable food." {21:6} The LORD sent fiery serpents among the people, and they bit them; many in Israel died. {21:7} Therefore, the people came to Moses and said, "We have sinned, for we have spoken against the LORD and against you; pray to the LORD that He will take away the serpents from us." And Moses prayed for the people. {21:8} The LORD told Moses, "Make a fiery serpent and put it on a pole. When anyone who is bitten looks at it, they will live." {21:9} So Moses made a bronze serpent and put it on a pole; when a serpent bit someone, if they looked at the bronze serpent, they lived. {21:10} The children of Israel moved on and camped at Oboth. {21:11} They journeyed from Oboth and camped at Ijeabarim in the wilderness east of Moab, toward the sunrise. {21:12} From there, they moved and camped in the Valley of Zared. {21:13} Then they moved and camped on the other side of Arnon, which is in the wilderness coming out of the borders of the Amorites, for Arnon is the border of Moab, between Moab and the Amorites. {21:14} Therefore, it is said in the Book of the Wars of the LORD, what He did at the Red Sea and in the streams of Arnon, {21:15} and at the stream that goes down to the dwelling of Ar, lying on the border of Moab. {21:16} From there, they went to Beer, which is the well where the LORD spoke to Moses, saying, "Gather the people together, and I will give them water." {21:17} Then Israel sang this song: "Spring up, O well; sing to it!" {21:18} The princes dug the well, the nobles of the people dug it, by the direction of the lawgiver with their staffs. From the wilderness, they went to Mattanah. {21:19} From Mattanah to Nahaliel, and from Nahaliel to Bamoth; {21:20} and from Bamoth in the valley, which is in the country of Moab, to the top of Pisgah, which overlooks Jeshimon. {21:21} Israel sent messengers to Sihon, king of the Amorites, saying, {21:22} "Let us pass through your land. We won't turn into fields or vineyards; we won't drink from your wells. We will go along the king's highway until we are past your borders." {21:23} But Sihon would not let Israel pass through his border. Instead, he gathered all his people and went out against Israel in the wilderness, and he came to Jahaz and fought against Israel. {21:24} Israel struck him with the sword and took possession of his land from Arnon to Jabbok, up to the children of Ammon, for the border of the children of Ammon was strong. {21:25} Israel captured all these cities and settled in all the cities of the Amorites, in Heshbon and its villages. {21:26} Heshbon was the city of Sihon, king of the Amorites, who had fought against the former king of Moab and taken all his land up to Arnon. {21:27} Therefore, those who speak in proverbs say, "Come to Heshbon; let the city of Sihon be rebuilt and restored." {21:28} For a fire has gone out from Heshbon, a flame from the city of Sihon, consuming Ar of Moab and the lords of the high places of Arnon. {21:29} Woe to you, Moab! You are undone, O people of Chemosh! He has given his sons who escaped and his daughters into captivity to Sihon, king of the Amorites. {21:30} We have shot at them; Heshbon has perished all the way to Dibon, and we have laid waste to Nophah, which reaches to Medeba. {21:31} Thus, Israel settled in the land of the Amorites. {21:32} Moses sent spies to Jaazer, and they took its villages and drove out the Amorites there. {21:33} They turned and went up the way to Bashan, and Og, the king of Bashan, came out against them with all his people to battle at Edrei. {21:34} The LORD said to Moses, "Do not be afraid of him, for I have delivered him into your hands, along with all his people and his land; you shall do to him as you did to Sihon, king of the Amorites, who lived at Heshbon." {21:35} So they struck him, his sons, and all his people until no one was left alive, and they took possession of his land.

{22:1} The children of Israel moved on and camped in the plains of Moab, on the east side of the Jordan River near Jericho. {22:2} Balak, the son of Zippor, saw all that Israel had done to the Amorites. {22:3} Moab was greatly afraid of the people because they were numerous, and Moab was distressed because of the children of Israel. {22:4} Moab said to the elders of Midian, "This horde will lick up everything around us, just like an ox licks up the grass in the field." Balak, the son of Zippor, was king of the Moabites at that time. {22:5} He sent messengers to Balaam, the son of Beor, at Pethor, which is near the river in the land of his people, to call him, saying, "Look, a people has come out of Egypt. They cover the face of the earth and are camping next to me. {22:6} Please come and curse this people for me, for they are too mighty for us. Perhaps I will be able to defeat them and drive them out of the land, for I know that whoever you bless is blessed, and whoever you curse is cursed." {22:7} The elders of Moab and Midian departed with the rewards of divination (foretelling the future) in their hands, and they came to Balaam and spoke to him the words of Balak. {22:8} Balaam said to them, "Stay here tonight, and I will bring you back a word, as the LORD speaks to me." So the princes of Moab stayed with Balaam. {22:9} God came to Balaam and asked, "Who are these men with you?" {22:10} Balaam replied, "Balak, the son of Zippor, king of Moab, has sent for me, saying, {22:11} 'Look, a people has come out of Egypt and covers the face of the earth. Come now, curse them for me; perhaps I will be able to overcome them and drive them out.'" {22:12} God said to Balaam, "You shall not go with them; you shall not curse the people, for they are blessed." {22:13} Balaam rose early in the morning and said to the princes of Balak, "Go back to your land, for the LORD has refused to let me go with you." {22:14} The princes of Moab returned to Balak and said, "Balaam refuses to come with us." {22:15} Balak sent more princes, more numerous and more honorable than the first. {22:16} They came to Balaam and said to him, "Thus says Balak, the son of Zippor: 'Do not let anything hinder you from coming to me. {22:17} For I will promote you to great honor and do whatever you say. Please come and curse this people for me.'" {22:18} Balaam answered and said to the servants of Balak, "If Balak were to give me his house full of silver and gold, I could not go beyond the word of the LORD my God to do less or more. {22:19} Now, please stay here tonight, that I may find out what more the LORD will say to me." {22:20} God came to Balaam that night and said, "If the men come to call you, rise and go with them; but only the word that I speak to you, that you shall do." {22:21} Balaam rose in the morning, saddled his donkey, and went with the princes of Moab. {22:22} But God's anger was kindled because he went, and the angel of the LORD stood in the way as an adversary against him. Now he was riding on his donkey, and his two servants were with him. {22:23} The donkey saw the angel of the LORD standing in the way with a drawn sword in his hand, and the donkey turned aside out of the way and went into the field. Balaam struck the donkey to turn her back to the way. {22:24} Then the angel of the LORD stood in a narrow path between the vineyards, with a wall on this side and a wall on that side. {22:25} When the donkey saw the angel of the LORD, she pressed herself against the wall, crushing Balaam's foot against the wall, and he struck her again. {22:26} The angel of the LORD went further and stood in a narrow place where there was no way to turn either to the right or to the left. {22:27} When the donkey saw the angel of the LORD, she fell down under Balaam. Balaam's anger was kindled, and he struck the donkey with a staff. {22:28} Then the LORD opened the mouth of the donkey, and she said to Balaam, "What have I done to you that you have struck me these three times?" {22:29} Balaam said to the donkey, "Because you have mocked me; I wish there were a sword in my hand, for now I would kill you." {22:30} The donkey said to Balaam, "Am I not your donkey, on which you have ridden all your life until this day? Have I ever treated you this way?" And he said, "No." {22:31} Then the LORD opened Balaam's eyes, and he saw the angel of the LORD standing in the way with his sword drawn in his hand, and he bowed his head and fell flat on his face. {22:32} The angel of the LORD said to him, "Why have you struck your donkey these three times? Behold, I have come out to withstand you because your way is perverse before me. {22:33} The donkey saw me and turned aside from me these three times. If she had not turned aside, surely I would have slain you and saved her alive." {22:34} Balaam said to the angel of the LORD, "I have sinned, for I did not know your stood in the way against me. Now therefore, if it displeases you, I will go back." {22:35} The angel of the LORD said to Balaam, "Go with the men, but only the word that I speak to you, that you shall speak." So Balaam went with the princes of Balak. {22:36} When Balak heard that Balaam was coming, he went out to meet him at a city of Moab on the border of Arnon, at the edge of the territory. {22:37} Balak said to Balaam, "Did I not earnestly send for you to call you? Why did you not come to me? Am I not able to promote you to honor?" {22:38} Balaam said to Balak, "Look, I have come to you. Have I any power at all to say anything? The word that God puts in my mouth, that I will speak." {22:39} Balaam went with Balak, and they came to Kirjathhuzoth. {22:40} Balak offered oxen and sheep and sent to Balaam and the princes who were with him. {22:41} The next morning, Balak took Balaam up to the high places of Baal, so that he could see the farthest part of the people.

{23:1} Balaam said to Balak, "Build me seven altars here, and prepare seven bulls and seven rams for me." {23:2} Balak did as Balaam had instructed, and Balak and Balaam offered a bull and a ram on each altar. {23:3} Balaam said to Balak, "Stand by your burnt offering, and I will go. Perhaps the LORD will come to meet me, and whatever He shows me, I will tell you." So he went to a high place. {23:4} God met Balaam and said, "I have prepared seven altars and offered a bull and a ram on each altar." {23:5} The LORD put a word in Balaam's mouth and said, "Return to Balak and say this." {23:6} Balaam returned to Balak, who was standing by his burnt sacrifice along with all the princes of Moab. {23:7} Balaam took up his parable and said, "Balak, king of Moab, has brought me from Aram, from the mountains of the east, saying, 'Come, curse Jacob for me, and come, defy Israel.' {23:8} How can I curse whom God has not cursed? How can I defy whom the LORD has not defied? {23:9} From the top of the rocks I see him; from the hills I behold him: look, the people will dwell alone and not be counted among the nations. {23:10} Who can count the dust of Jacob, or number the fourth part of Israel? Let me die the death of the righteous, and let my end be like his!" {23:11} Balak said to Balaam, "What have you done to me? I brought you to curse my enemies, and behold, you have blessed them altogether!" {23:12} Balaam answered, "Must I not take care to speak what the LORD has put in my mouth?" {23:13} Balak said to him, "Come with me to another place where you can see them. You will see only the farthest part of them and not all of them; curse them for me from there." {23:14} Balak brought him to the field of Zophim, to the top of Pisgah, and built seven altars and offered a bull and a ram on each altar. {23:15} He said to Balak, "Stand here by your burnt offering while I meet the LORD over there." {23:16} The LORD met Balaam and put a word in his mouth and said, "Go again to Balak and say this." {23:17} When Balaam came to him, behold, he stood by his burnt offering, and the princes of Moab were with him. Balak asked, "What has the LORD spoken?" {23:18} Balaam took up his parable and said, "Rise up, Balak, and listen; hear me, son of Zippor. {23:19} God is not a man that He should lie, nor the son of man that He should repent. Has He said, and will He not do it? Or has He spoken, and will He not make it good? {23:20} Look, I have received a command to bless; He has blessed, and I cannot change it. {23:21} He has not seen iniquity in Jacob, nor has He seen wickedness in Israel. The LORD his God is with him, and the shout of a king is among them. {23:22} God brought them out of Egypt; they have the strength of a wild ox. {23:23} Surely there is no enchantment against Jacob, nor any divination against Israel. According to this time it will be said of Jacob and Israel, 'What has God done!' {23:24} Look, the people rise up like a lion and lift themselves like a young lion; they do not lie down until they eat the prey and drink the blood of the slain." {23:25} Balak said to Balaam, "Do not curse them at all, nor bless them at all." {23:26} Balaam answered and said to Balak, "Did I not tell you, 'Whatever the LORD says, I must do'?" {23:27} Balak said to Balaam, "Come, I will take you to another place; perhaps it will please God that you may curse them for me from there." {23:28} Balak brought Balaam to the top of Peor, which overlooks Jeshimon. {23:29} Balaam said to Balak, "Build me seven altars here and prepare seven bulls and seven rams for me." {23:30} Balak did as Balaam said and offered a bull and a ram on each altar.

{24:1} When Balaam saw that it pleased the LORD to bless Israel, he did not, like before, seek enchantments; instead, he set his face toward the wilderness. {24:2} Balaam lifted his eyes and saw Israel camped in their tents by tribes, and the Spirit of God came upon him. {24:3} He took up his parable and said, "Balaam, son of Beor, has said, and the man whose eyes are open has said: {24:4} He has said, who heard the words of God and saw the vision of the Almighty while falling into a trance but having his eyes open: {24:5} How goodly are your tents, O Jacob, and your dwellings, O Israel! {24:6} They spread out like valleys, like gardens by the riverside, like trees of lign aloes planted by the LORD, and like cedar trees beside the waters. {24:7} He shall pour water from his buckets, and his seed will be in many waters; his king will be greater than Agag, and his kingdom will be exalted. {24:8} God brought him out of Egypt; he has the strength of a wild ox: he will devour his enemies and crush their bones, piercing them with his arrows. {24:9} He crouches, lies down like a lion, and like a great lion: who will stir him up? Blessed is he who blesses you, and cursed is he who curses you." {24:10} Balak's anger was kindled against Balaam; he clapped his hands together and said to Balaam, "I called you to curse my enemies, and behold, you have blessed them these three times! {24:11} Now, therefore, flee to your place; I thought to promote you to great honor, but the LORD has kept you from honor." {24:12} Balaam said to Balak, "Did I not also speak to your messengers whom you sent to me, saying, {24:13} 'If Balak gave me his house full of silver and gold, I cannot go beyond the command of the LORD, to do either good or bad on my own; I will speak only what the LORD says'? {24:14} Now, behold, I am going to my people; come, and I will inform you what this people will do to your people in the latter days." {24:15} He took up his parable and said, "Balaam, son of Beor, has said, and the man whose eyes are open has said: {24:16} He has said, who heard the words of God, knew the knowledge of the Most High, and saw the vision of the Almighty while falling into a trance but having his eyes open: {24:17} I see him, but not now; I behold him, but not near: a Star shall come out of Jacob, and a Scepter shall rise out of Israel and crush the corners of Moab, and destroy all the children of Sheth. {24:18} Edom shall be a possession; Seir shall also be a possession for his enemies, and Israel shall act valiantly. {24:19} A ruler will come out of Jacob, and will destroy those who remain in the city. {24:20} When he looked on Amalek, he took up his parable and said, "Amalek was the first of the nations, but his end will be that he perishes forever." {24:21} He looked on the Kenites, took up his parable, and said, "Strong is your dwelling place, and you put your nest in a rock. {24:22} Nevertheless, the Kenite shall be wasted until Asshur carries you away captive." {24:23} He took up his parable and said, "Alas! Who will live when God does this? {24:24} Ships shall come from the coast of Chittim and afflict Asshur and Eber, and he also shall perish forever." {24:25} Balaam rose up and went back to his place, and Balak also went his way.

{25:1} While the Israelites were staying in Shittim, the people began to engage in immoral behavior with the daughters of Moab. {25:2} The Moabites invited the Israelites to their sacrifices to their gods, and the people ate the food offered to these gods and worshipped them. {25:3} So, Israel joined itself to Baalpeor (a pagan god), and the LORD became angry with Israel. {25:4} The LORD told Moses, "Take the leaders of the people and hang them up before the LORD in the sun so that my anger may be turned away from Israel." {25:5} Then Moses told the judges of Israel, "Each of you must kill the men who have joined themselves to Baalpeor." {25:6} Just then, one of the Israelites came and brought a Midianite woman to his family in the sight of Moses and all the people of Israel, who were crying at the entrance to the Tabernacle (place of worship). {25:7} When Phinehas, the son of Eleazar and grandson of Aaron the priest, saw this, he got up from among the congregation, took a spear, {25:8} and followed the Israelite into the tent. There he thrust the spear through both the Israelite and the woman, killing them, and so the plague on the Israelites was stopped. {25:9} The number of people who died in the plague was twenty-four thousand. {25:10} Then the LORD spoke to Moses, saying, {25:11} "Phinehas, the son of Eleazar and grandson of Aaron the priest, has turned my anger away from the Israelites by being zealous for me, so that I did not destroy them in my jealousy." {25:12} Therefore, tell him that I give him my covenant of peace. {25:13} He and his descendants will have this covenant, an everlasting priesthood, because he was zealous for his God and made atonement (a way to make up for sins) for the Israelites. {25:14} The name of the Israelite man who was killed, along with the Midianite woman, was Zimri, the son of Salu, a leader from the Simeon tribe. {25:15} The name of the Midianite woman who was killed was Cozbi, the daughter of Zur, a leader of a people and a chief family in Midian. {25:16} Then the LORD spoke to Moses, saying, {25:17} "Attack the Midianites and destroy them, {25:18} for they have been troubling you with their deceitful ways, which led you into the worship of Peor and the sin with Cozbi, the daughter of a Midianite chief, who was killed during the plague for the sin of Peor."

{26:1} After the plague, the LORD spoke to Moses and Eleazar, the son of Aaron the priest, saying, {26:2} "Take a census of the entire congregation of the children of Israel, from twenty years old and upward, throughout their families, all those able to go to war in Israel." {26:3} Moses and Eleazar spoke with them in the plains of Moab by the Jordan near Jericho, saying, {26:4} "Take the census of the people, from twenty years old and upward, as the LORD commanded Moses regarding the children of Israel who went out of the land of Egypt." {26:5} Reuben, the eldest son of Israel: the children of Reuben were Hanoch, whose family is called the Hanochites; Pallu, whose family is called the Palluites; {26:6} Hezron, whose family is called the Hezronites; and Carmi, whose family is called the Carmites. {26:7} These are the families of the Reubenites, and those counted were forty-three thousand seven hundred and thirty. {26:8} The sons of Pallu were Eliab. {26:9} The sons of Eliab were Nemuel, Dathan, and Abiram. This is the Dathan and Abiram who were famous in the congregation for opposing Moses and Aaron alongside Korah when they rebelled against the LORD. {26:10} The earth opened its mouth and swallowed them, along with Korah, when that group died, and fire consumed two hundred and fifty men; they became a sign. {26:11} However, the children of Korah did not die. {26:12} The sons of Simeon by their families were: Nemuel, whose family is called the Nemuelites; Jamin, whose family is called the Jaminites; Jachin, whose family is called the Jachinites; {26:13} Zerah, whose family is called the Zarhites; and Shaul, whose family is called the Shaulites. {26:14} These are the families of the Simeonites, totaling twenty-two thousand two hundred. {26:15} The children of Gad by their families were: Zephon, whose family is called the Zephonites; Haggi, whose family is called the Haggites; Shuni, whose family is called the Shunites; {26:16} Ozni, whose family is called the Oznites; Eri, whose family is called the Erites; {26:17} Arod, whose family is called the Arodites; and Areli, whose family is called the Arelites. {26:18} These are the families of the children of Gad, and those counted were forty thousand five hundred. {26:19} The sons of Judah were Er and Onan, and both died in the land of Canaan. {26:20} The sons of Judah by their families were: Shelah, whose family is called the Shelanites; Pharez, whose family is called the Pharzites; and Zerah, whose family is called the Zarhites. {26:21} The sons of Pharez were: Hezron, whose family is called the Hezronites; and Hamul, whose family is called the Hamulites. {26:22} These are the families of Judah, and those counted were sixty-six thousand five hundred. {26:23} The sons of Issachar by their families were: Tola, whose family is called the Tolaites; Pua, whose family is called the Punites; {26:24} Jashub, whose family is called the Jashubites; and Shimron, whose family is called the Shimronites. {26:25} These are the families of Issachar, and those counted were sixty-four thousand three hundred. {26:26} The sons of Zebulun by their families were: Sered, whose family is called the Sardites; Elon, whose family is called the Elonites; and Jahleel, whose family is called the Jahleelites. {26:27} These are the families of the Zebulunites, and those counted were sixty thousand five hundred. {26:28} The sons of Joseph by their families were Manasseh and Ephraim. {26:29} The sons of Manasseh were Machir, whose family is called the Machirites, and Machir begot Gilead; from Gilead came the family of the Gileadites. {26:30} These are the sons of Gilead: Jeezer, whose family is called the Jeezerites; Helek, whose family is called the Helekites; {26:31} Asriel, whose family is called the Asrielites; Shechem, whose family is called the Shechemites; {26:32} Shemida, whose family is called the Shemidaites; and Hepher, whose family is called the Hepherites. {26:33} Zelophehad, the son of Hepher, had no sons but only daughters, and the names of Zelophehad's daughters were Mahlah, Noah, Hoglah, Milcah, and Tirzah. {26:34} These are the families of Manasseh, and those counted were fifty-two thousand seven hundred. {26:35} These are the sons of Ephraim by their families: Shuthelah, whose family is called the Shuthalhites; Becher, whose family is called the Bachrites; and Tahan, whose family is called the Tahanites. {26:36} The sons of Shuthelah were Eran, whose family is called the Eranites. {26:37} These are the families of the sons of Ephraim, and those counted were thirty-two thousand five hundred. These are the sons of Joseph by their families. {26:38} The sons of Benjamin by their families were: Bela, whose family is called the Belaites; Ashbel, whose family is called the Ashbelites; Ahiram, whose family is called the Ahiramites; {26:39} Shupham, whose family is called the Shuphamites; and Hupham, whose family is called the Huphamites. {26:40} The sons of Bela were Ard and Naaman; Ard's family is called the Ardites, and Naaman's family is called the Naamites. {26:41} These are the sons of Benjamin by their families, and those counted were forty-five thousand six hundred. {26:42} These are the sons of Dan by their families: Shuham, whose family is called the Shuhamites. These are the families of Dan. {26:43} All the families of the Shuhamites, and those counted, were sixty-four thousand four hundred. {26:44} The children of Asher by their families were: Jimna, whose family is called the Jimnites; Jesui, whose family is called the Jesuites; and Beriah, whose family is called the Beriites. {26:45} The sons of Beriah were Heber, whose family is called the Heberites; and Malchiel, whose family is called the Malchielites. {26:46} The name of Asher's daughter was Sarah. {26:47} These are the families of Asher, and those counted were fifty-three thousand four hundred. {26:48} The sons of Naphtali by their families were: Jahzeel, whose family is called the Jahzeelites; Guni, whose family is called the Gunites; {26:49} Jezer, whose family is called the Jezerites; and Shillem, whose family is called the Shillemites. {26:50} These are the families of Naphtali, and those counted were forty-five thousand four hundred. {26:51} The total number of the children of Israel was six hundred thousand one thousand seven hundred thirty. {26:52} The LORD spoke to Moses, saying, {26:53} "To these the land shall be divided for an inheritance according to the number of names. {26:54} To many you shall give a larger inheritance, and to few you shall give a smaller inheritance; each will receive an inheritance according to the number of those counted. {26:55} The land shall be divided by lot; according to the names of the tribes of their fathers, they shall inherit. {26:56} The possession will be divided between many and few according to the lot." {26:57} These are those numbered among the Levites by their families: Gershon, whose family is called the Gershonites; Kohath, whose family is called the Kohathites; and Merari, whose family is called the Merarites. {26:58} These are the families of the Levites: the Libnites, the Hebronites, the Mahlites, the Mushites, and the Korathites. Kohath fathered Amram. {26:59} The name of Amram's wife was Jochebed, the daughter of Levi, whom her mother bore to Levi in Egypt. She bore Amram Aaron, Moses, and their sister Miriam. {26:60} To Aaron were born Nadab, Abihu, Eleazar, and Ithamar. {26:61} Nadab and Abihu died when they offered unauthorized fire before the LORD. {26:62} Those counted among them were twenty-three thousand, all males a month old and upward, because they were not counted among the children of Israel, since no inheritance was given to them among the children of Israel. {26:63} These are those counted by Moses and Eleazar the priest, who counted the children of Israel in the plains of Moab by the Jordan near Jericho. {26:64} Among these, there was not one man counted whom Moses and Aaron the priest numbered when they counted the children of Israel in the wilderness of Sinai. {26:65} For the LORD had said of them, "They shall surely die in the wilderness." Not one of them was left, except Caleb, the son of Jephunneh, and Joshua, the son of Nun. {26:66} This fulfillment of God's judgment marked the end of an entire generation, with only Caleb and Joshua surviving to enter the promised land.

{27:1} Then the daughters of Zelophehad, the son of Hepher, from the family line of Gilead, who was the son of Machir, the son of Manasseh, of the families of Manasseh, the son of Joseph, came forward. Their names were Mahlah, Noah, Hoglah, Milcah, and Tirzah. {27:2} They stood before Moses, Eleazar the priest, the leaders, and all the congregation at the entrance of the tabernacle, saying, {27:3} "Our father died in the wilderness; he was not part of those who gathered against the LORD in the company of Korah. He died for his own sin and had no sons. {27:4} Why should our father's name be removed from his family because he had no son? Please give us a share of the inheritance among our father's relatives." {27:5} Moses brought their case before the LORD. {27:6} The LORD spoke to Moses, saying, {27:7} "The daughters of Zelophehad are right. You must certainly give them a share of the inheritance among their father's relatives, and their father's inheritance shall pass to them. {27:8} Tell the children of Israel this: If a man dies and has no son, his inheritance should pass to his daughter. {27:9} If he has no daughter, give his inheritance to his brothers. {27:10} If he has no brothers, give his inheritance to his father's brothers. {27:11} If his father has no brothers, give his inheritance to the nearest relative in his family, and he shall possess it. This will be a statute for the children of Israel, as the LORD commanded Moses." {27:12} The LORD then said to Moses, "Climb up this mountain, Abarim, and see the land I have given to the children of Israel. {27:13} After you have seen it, you too will be gathered to your people, as your brother Aaron was. {27:14} This is because you rebelled against my command in the wilderness of Zin, during the strife of the congregation, to honor me at the water before their eyes. This is the water of Meribah in Kadesh in the wilderness of Zin." {27:15} Moses spoke to the LORD, saying, {27:16} "Let the LORD, the God of the spirits of all flesh, appoint a man over the congregation, {27:17} who can go out before them and come in before them, and lead them out and bring them in, so the congregation of the LORD will not be like sheep without a shepherd." {27:18} The LORD said to Moses, "Take Joshua, the son of Nun, a man in whom is the Spirit, and lay your hands on him; {27:19} set him before Eleazar the priest and the whole congregation, and give him a charge in their sight. {27:20} Put some of your honor on him so that the whole congregation of the children of Israel may obey him. {27:21} He will stand before Eleazar the priest, who will inquire for him by the judgment of Urim before the LORD. At his command, they will go out, and at his command, they will come in, he and all the children of Israel with him." {27:22} Moses did as the LORD commanded him. He took Joshua, set him before Eleazar the priest and the whole congregation, {27:23} laid his hands on him, and gave him a charge, just as the LORD commanded through Moses.

{28:1} The LORD spoke to Moses, saying, {28:2} "Command the children of Israel to offer My offerings and My bread for the sacrifices made by fire, which are a pleasing aroma to Me, at their appointed times. {28:3} Say to them, 'This is the offering made by fire that you shall present to the LORD: two lambs, a year old and without blemish, shall be offered daily as a continual burnt offering. {28:4} You shall offer one lamb in the morning and the other lamb in the evening; {28:5} and you shall offer a tenth of an ephah of flour mixed with a fourth of a hin of beaten oil as a grain offering. {28:6} This is a continual burnt offering that was established at Mount Sinai as a pleasing aroma, a sacrifice made by fire to the LORD. {28:7} The drink offering for each lamb shall be a fourth of a hin of wine; in the holy place, you shall pour out strong wine as a drink offering to the LORD. {28:8} The other lamb you shall offer in the evening, along with the grain offering and the drink offering, just as you do in the morning. This will be a sacrifice made by fire, a pleasing aroma to the LORD. {28:9} On the Sabbath day, you shall offer two lambs, a year old and without blemish, along with two tenths of flour mixed with oil for a grain offering, and their drink offerings. {28:10} This is the burnt offering for every Sabbath, in addition to the continual burnt offering and its drink offering. {28:11} At the beginning of your months, you shall present a burnt offering to the LORD: two young bulls, one ram, and seven lambs, a year old and without blemish; {28:12} and for each bull, you shall offer three tenths of flour mixed with oil, and for the ram, two tenths of flour mixed with oil; {28:13} and you shall offer one tenth of flour mixed with oil for each lamb throughout the seven lambs. {28:14} Their drink offerings shall be half a hin of wine for each bull, a third of a hin for the ram, and a fourth of a hin for each lamb. This is the burnt offering for every month throughout the year. {28:15} You shall also offer one kid of the goats as a sin offering to the LORD, in addition to the continual burnt offering and its drink offering. {28:16} On the fourteenth day of the first month is the Passover of the LORD. {28:17} On the fifteenth day of this month, the feast begins; you shall eat unleavened bread for seven days. {28:18} The first day shall be a holy convocation; you shall not do any regular work. {28:19} Instead, you shall offer a burnt offering to the LORD: two young bulls, one ram, and seven lambs, a year old, without blemish; {28:20} and their grain offering shall be flour mixed with oil: three tenths for a bull and two tenths for a ram; {28:21} and you shall offer one tenth for each lamb throughout the seven lambs. {28:22} You shall also offer one goat for a sin offering to make atonement for you. {28:23} These offerings shall be in addition to the burnt offering in the morning, which is for the continual burnt offering. {28:24} You shall offer these daily for the seven days as a food offering made by fire, a pleasing aroma to the LORD, in addition to the continual burnt offering and its drink offering. {28:25} On the seventh day, you shall have a holy convocation; you shall not do any regular work. {28:26} Also, on the day of the firstfruits, when you present a new grain offering to the LORD after the weeks are complete, you shall have a holy convocation and do no regular work. {28:27} You shall present a burnt offering as a pleasing aroma to the LORD: two young bulls, one ram, and seven lambs, a year old; {28:28} and their grain offering shall be flour mixed with oil: three tenths for one bull, two tenths for one ram, {28:29} and one tenth for each lamb throughout the seven lambs; {28:30} and one kid of the goats to make atonement for you. {28:31} You shall offer these in addition to the continual burnt offering and its grain offering; they shall be without blemish, along with their drink offerings.

{29:1} On the first day of the seventh month, you shall have a holy convocation; you shall do no regular work, for it is a day of blowing trumpets for you. {29:2} You shall offer a burnt offering as a pleasing aroma to the LORD: one young bull, one ram, and seven lambs, a year old and without blemish. {29:3} Their grain offering shall be flour mixed with oil: three tenths for the bull, and two tenths for the ram. {29:4} You shall offer one tenth for each lamb throughout the seven lambs. {29:5} Also, you shall offer one goat as a sin offering to make atonement for you. {29:6} This is in addition to the monthly burnt offering, its grain offering, the daily burnt offering, its grain offering, and their drink offerings, according to their prescribed manner, as a pleasing aroma, a sacrifice made by fire to the LORD. {29:7} On the tenth day of this seventh month, you shall have a holy convocation; you shall humble yourselves and do no work. {29:8} You shall offer a burnt offering to the LORD as a pleasing aroma: one young bull, one ram, and seven lambs, a year old and without blemish. {29:9} Their grain offering shall be flour mixed with oil: three tenths for the bull, two tenths for the ram, {29:10} and one tenth for each lamb throughout the seven lambs. {29:11} You shall offer one goat as a sin offering, in addition to the sin offering for atonement, the continual burnt offering, its grain offering, and their drink offerings. {29:12} On the fifteenth day of the seventh month, you shall have a holy convocation; you shall do no regular work, and you shall celebrate a feast to the LORD for seven days. {29:13} You shall offer a burnt offering, a sacrifice made by fire, as a pleasing aroma to the LORD: thirteen young bulls, two rams, and fourteen lambs, a year old and without blemish. {29:14} Their grain offering shall be flour mixed with oil: three tenths for each of the thirteen bulls, two tenths for each of the two rams, {29:15} and one tenth for each of the fourteen lambs. {29:16} You shall also offer one goat as a sin offering, in addition to the continual burnt offering, its grain offering, and its drink offering. {29:17} On the second day, you shall offer twelve young bulls, two rams, and fourteen lambs, a year old and without blemish. {29:18} Their grain offerings and drink offerings for the bulls, for the rams, and for the lambs shall be according to their number, as prescribed. {29:19} You shall offer one goat as a sin offering, in addition to the continual burnt offering, its grain offering, and their drink offerings. {29:20} On the third day, you shall offer eleven young bulls, two rams, and fourteen lambs, a year old and without blemish. {29:21} Their grain offerings and drink offerings shall be according to their number, as prescribed. {29:22} You shall offer one goat as a sin offering, in addition to the continual burnt offering, its grain offering, and its drink offering. {29:23} On the fourth day, you shall offer ten young bulls, two rams, and fourteen lambs, a year old and without blemish. {29:24} Their grain offerings and drink offerings shall be according to their number, as prescribed. {29:25} You shall offer one goat as a sin offering, in addition to the continual burnt offering, its grain offering, and its drink offering. {29:26} On the fifth day, you shall offer nine young bulls, two rams, and fourteen lambs, a year old and without blemish. {29:27} Their grain offerings and drink offerings shall be according to their number, as prescribed. {29:28} You shall offer one goat as a sin offering, in addition to the continual burnt offering, its grain offering, and its drink offering. {29:29} On the sixth day, you shall offer eight young bulls, two rams, and fourteen lambs, a year old and without blemish. {29:30} Their grain offerings and drink offerings shall be according to their number, as prescribed. {29:31} You shall offer one goat as a sin offering, in addition to the continual burnt offering, its grain offering, and its drink offering. {29:32} On the seventh day, you shall offer seven young bulls, two rams, and fourteen lambs, a year old and without blemish. {29:33} Their grain offerings and drink offerings shall be according to their number, as prescribed. {29:34} You shall offer one goat as a sin offering, in addition to the continual burnt offering, its grain offering, and its drink offering. {29:35} On the eighth day, you shall have a solemn assembly; you shall do no regular work. {29:36} You shall offer a burnt offering, a sacrifice made by fire, as a pleasing aroma to the LORD: one bull, one ram, and seven lambs, a year old and without blemish. {29:37} Their grain offerings and drink offerings shall be according to their number, as prescribed. {29:38} You shall also offer one goat as a sin offering, in addition to the continual burnt offering, its grain offering, and its drink offering. {29:39} These offerings you shall present to the LORD during your appointed feasts, in addition to your vows and freewill offerings for your burnt offerings, grain offerings, drink offerings, and peace offerings. {29:40} Moses told the children of Israel everything that the LORD commanded him.

{30:1} Moses spoke to the leaders of the tribes of Israel, saying, "This is what the LORD has commanded. {30:2} If a man makes a vow to the LORD or swears an oath to bind himself, he must not break his word; he must do everything he has said. {30:3} If a woman makes a vow to the LORD while living in her father's house as a young woman, {30:4} and her father hears her vow and her bond (commitment) and says nothing, then all her vows will stand and every bond she has made will remain valid. {30:5} But if her father disallows her on the day he hears it, none of her vows or bonds will stand, and the LORD will forgive her because her father disallowed her. {30:6} If she is married when she makes a vow or speaks a commitment, {30:7} and her husband hears it and says nothing, then her vows will stand and her bonds will remain valid. {30:8} But if her husband disallows her on the day he hears it, he will cancel her vow and the commitment she made, and the LORD will forgive her. {30:9} Every vow made by a widow or a divorced woman will stand against her. {30:10} If she made a vow in her husband's house or made a commitment with an oath, {30:11} and her husband hears it and says nothing, then all her vows will stand and every bond she has made will remain valid. {30:12} But if her husband completely cancels them on the day he hears them, then whatever she has said regarding her vows or her commitments will not be valid; her husband has made them void, and the LORD will forgive her. {30:13} Every vow and every binding oath to afflict the soul can be established or canceled by her husband. {30:14} If her husband says nothing day after day, he confirms all her vows and all her bonds because he remained silent on the day he heard them. {30:15} But if he decides to cancel them after hearing them, he must bear her guilt. {30:16} These are the regulations that the LORD commanded Moses regarding a man and his wife, and a father and his daughter while she is still living in her father's house.

{31:1} The LORD spoke to Moses, saying, {31:2} "Avenge the Israelites against the Midianites. Afterward, you will be gathered to your people." {31:3} So Moses told the people, "Prepare for war. Send some of your men to fight against the Midianites and carry out the LORD's vengeance on them." {31:4} Send one thousand men from each tribe of Israel to fight in this war. {31:5} So, one thousand men from each tribe were chosen, making twelve thousand men armed for battle. {31:6} Moses sent them to fight, along with Phinehas, the son of Eleazar, the priest. Phinehas took the holy instruments and the trumpets for blowing, and went with them into battle. {31:7} They fought against the Midianites as the LORD commanded Moses, and they killed all the males. {31:8} They also killed the five kings of Midian—Evi, Rekem, Zur, Hur, and Reba—along with Balaam the son of Beor, whom they killed with the sword. {31:9} The Israelites took all the Midianite women and children captive, and they seized all their cattle, flocks, and possessions. {31:10} They burned down all the cities where the Midianites had lived, along with all their beautiful castles, setting them on fire. {31:11} They took all the spoil, both from the men and the animals. {31:12} The captives, the spoil, and all the plunder were brought to Moses, Eleazar the priest, and the congregation of Israel at the camp on the plains of Moab, near the Jordan River, across from Jericho. {31:13} Moses, Eleazar the priest, and all the leaders of the congregation went out to meet them outside the camp. {31:14} Moses was angry with the officers, the captains of thousands, and the captains of hundreds who had come back from the battle. {31:15} Moses said to them, "Have you spared all the women alive? {31:16} Look, these women were the ones who, through the advice of Balaam, caused the Israelites to sin against the LORD in the incident at Peor, which brought a plague upon the LORD's congregation." {31:17} "Now, kill every male child and every woman who has had sexual relations with a man. {31:18} But spare the young girls who have not had relations with men; keep them alive for yourselves." {31:19} "You must remain outside the camp for seven days. Anyone who has killed a person or touched a dead body must purify themselves and their captives on the third day and the seventh day. {31:20} You must purify all your clothing, everything made of animal skins, everything made of goat's hair, and all wooden items." {31:21} Eleazar the priest said to the men who had fought in the battle, "This is the law that the LORD has commanded Moses: {31:22} Only the gold, silver, bronze, iron, tin, and lead, {31:23} all things that can withstand fire, must be passed through the fire, and they will be clean. However, they must also be purified with the water of separation (a special water used for purification); anything that cannot withstand fire must be passed through water. {31:24} On the seventh day, wash your clothes, and you will be clean. After that, you may return to the camp." {31:25} The LORD spoke to Moses, saying, {31:26} "Take a census of the plunder that was taken, both from the people and the animals—both you and Eleazar the priest, along with the chief fathers of the congregation. {31:27} Divide the plunder into two parts: one part for the men who went to war, and the other for the whole congregation. {31:28} From the men who went to war, take a tribute to the LORD—one out of every five hundred persons, cattle, donkeys, and sheep. {31:29} Take this tribute from their half and give it to Eleazar the priest as a gift to the LORD. {31:30} From the Israelites' half, take one portion of every fifty—people, cattle, donkeys, and flocks—and give it to the Levites who care for the tabernacle of the LORD." {31:31} Moses and Eleazar the priest did exactly as the LORD commanded Moses. {31:32} The rest of the plunder taken by the soldiers consisted of 675,000 sheep, {31:33} 72,000 cattle, {31:34} 61,000 donkeys, {31:35} and 32,000 women who had not had relations with men. {31:36} The portion for those who went to war was 337,500 sheep, {31:37} and the LORD's share of the sheep was 675. {31:38} The cattle numbered 36,000, and the LORD's share of the cattle was 72. {31:39} The donkeys numbered 30,500, and the LORD's share of the donkeys was 61. {31:40} The total number of people was 16,000, and the LORD's share of the people was 32. {31:41} Moses gave the LORD's portion of the plunder to Eleazar the priest, as the LORD had commanded Moses. {31:42} From the Israelites' half, which Moses divided from the soldiers, {31:43} the portion belonging to the congregation was 330,500 sheep, {31:44} 36,000 cattle, {31:45} 30,500 donkeys, {31:46} and 16,000 persons. {31:47} From the Israelites' half, Moses took one portion of fifty—both from people and animals—and gave it to the Levites who cared for the tabernacle of the LORD, as the LORD commanded Moses. {31:48} The officers who were over the thousands of the army, the captains of thousands and hundreds, approached Moses. {31:49} They said to Moses, "Your servants have taken a census of the soldiers under our command, and not one man is missing. {31:50} So we have brought an offering to the LORD: each of us has contributed gold items—jewels, chains, bracelets, rings, earrings, and pendants—to make atonement for our souls before the LORD." {31:51} Moses and Eleazar the priest received the gold from them—all the crafted items. {31:52} The total amount of gold the captains of thousands and hundreds offered to the LORD was 16,750 shekels. {31:53} (For the soldiers had taken the plunder for themselves.) {31:54} Moses and Eleazar the priest brought the gold from the captains of thousands and hundreds into the tabernacle as a memorial for the Israelites before the LORD.

{32:1} The children of Reuben and the children of Gad had a very large number of cattle. When they saw the land of Jazer and the land of Gilead, they realized that it was a great place for livestock. {32:2} So, the children of Gad and Reuben came to speak with Moses, Eleazar the priest, and the leaders of the congregation, saying, {32:3} "Ataroth, Dibon, Jazer, Nimrah, Heshbon, Elealeh, Shebam, Nebo, and Beon— {32:4} the land the LORD defeated before the congregation of Israel is perfect for cattle, and we have cattle. {32:5} Therefore, if we have found favor in your sight, let this land be given to us as our possession, and do not bring us over the Jordan." {32:6} Moses replied to the children of Gad and Reuben, "Will your brothers go to war while you stay here? {32:7} Why do you discourage the hearts of the children of Israel from going into the land that the LORD has given them? {32:8} Your fathers did the same thing when I sent them from Kadeshbarnea to explore the land. {32:9} They went up to the Valley of Eshcol and saw the land, and they discouraged the hearts of the children of Israel so that they would not enter the land the LORD had given them. {32:10} The LORD became angry at that time and swore, saying, {32:11} "Surely none of the men who came up out of Egypt, from twenty years old and up, will see the land I swore to Abraham, Isaac, and Jacob, because they did not fully follow me. {32:12} Only Caleb, the son of Jephunneh the Kenezite, and Joshua, the son of Nun, because they fully followed the LORD." {32:13} The LORD's anger was kindled against Israel, and He made them wander in the wilderness for forty years until all that evil generation was consumed. {32:14} And now you have risen up in your fathers' place, a group of sinful men, to increase the LORD's fierce anger against Israel. {32:15} If you turn away from following Him, He will again leave them in the wilderness, and you will destroy this people." {32:16} They approached him and said, "We will build sheepfolds for our cattle and cities for our children. {32:17} But we will be ready and armed before the children of Israel until we have brought them to their place. Our little ones will stay in the fortified cities because of the inhabitants of the land. {32:18} We will not return to our homes until every Israelite has received their inheritance. {32:19} For we will not inherit with them across the Jordan or further, because our inheritance has fallen to us on this side of the Jordan, eastward." {32:20} Moses said to them, "If you do this, if you go armed before the LORD to battle, {32:21} and all of you cross over the Jordan before the LORD until He has driven out His enemies, {32:22} and the land is subdued before the LORD, then afterward you may return and be guiltless before the LORD and before Israel, and this land shall be your possession before the LORD. {32:23} But if you do not do so, you have sinned against the LORD, and be sure your sin will find you out. {32:24} Build cities for your little ones and folds for your sheep, and do what you have promised." {32:25} The children of Gad and Reuben replied to Moses, saying, "Your servants will do what you command. {32:26} Our little ones, wives, flocks, and all our cattle will stay in the cities of Gilead. {32:27} But your servants will cross over, every man armed for battle, as you have said." {32:28} So, Moses commanded Eleazar the priest, Joshua the son of Nun, and the leaders of the tribes of the children of Israel regarding them: {32:29} "If the children of Gad and Reuben cross over with you armed before the LORD, and the land is subdued before you, then you shall give them the land of Gilead as their possession. {32:30} But if they do not cross over with you armed, they shall have possessions among you in the land of Canaan." {32:31} The children of Gad and Reuben answered, "As the LORD has said to your servants, so we will do. {32:32} We will cross over armed before the LORD into the land of Canaan, so that our inheritance on this side of the Jordan may be ours." {32:33} Moses gave to them, to the children of Gad, the children of Reuben, and half the tribe of Manasseh, the son of Joseph, the kingdoms of Sihon, king of the Amorites, and Og, king of Bashan, the land, with its cities and surrounding country. {32:34} The children of Gad built Dibon, Ataroth, and Aroer, {32:35} Atroth, Shophan, Jaazer, and Jogbehah, {32:36} Bethnimrah and Bethharan, fortified cities, and folds for sheep. {32:37} The children of Reuben built Heshbon, Elealeh, and Kirjathaim, {32:38} Nebo, Baalmeon (renaming them), and Shibmah; they gave other names to the cities they built. {32:39} The children of Machir, the son of Manasseh, went to Gilead, took it, and dispossessed the Amorite who was in it. {32:40} Moses gave Gilead to Machir, the son of Manasseh, and he settled there. {32:41} Jair, the son of Manasseh, went and took the small towns and named them Havothjair. {32:42} Nobah went and took Kenath and its villages, naming it Nobah after himself.

{33:1} These are the journeys of the children of Israel, who left the land of Egypt with their armies under the leadership of Moses and Aaron. {33:2} Moses recorded their departures according to their journeys as commanded by the LORD, and these are their journeys as they left. {33:3} They left Rameses in the first month, on the fifteenth day; the day after Passover, the children of Israel went out boldly in front of all the Egyptians. {33:4} The Egyptians buried all their firstborn, whom the LORD had struck down among them; the LORD also executed judgments against their gods. {33:5} The children of Israel moved from Rameses and camped in Succoth. {33:6} They departed from Succoth and camped in Etham, at the edge of the wilderness. {33:7} They left Etham and turned back to Pihahiroth, which is in front of Baalzephon, and camped before Migdol. {33:8} They departed from Pihahiroth, passed through the midst of the sea into the wilderness, traveled three days in the wilderness of Etham, and camped at Marah. {33:9} They moved from Marah and came to Elim, where there were twelve fountains of water and seventy palm trees, and they camped there. {33:10} They left Elim and camped by the Red Sea. {33:11} They departed from the Red Sea and camped in the wilderness of Sin. {33:12} They took their journey from the wilderness of Sin and camped in Dophkah. {33:13} They left Dophkah and camped in Alush. {33:14} They moved from Alush and camped at Rephidim, where there was no water for the people to drink. {33:15} They departed from Rephidim and camped in the wilderness of Sinai. {33:16} They moved from the desert of Sinai and camped at Kibrothhattaavah. {33:17} They left Kibrothhattaavah and camped at Hazeroth. {33:18} They departed from Hazeroth and camped in Rithmah. {33:19} They left Rithmah and camped at Rimmonparez. {33:20} They departed from Rimmonparez and camped in Libnah. {33:21} They moved from Libnah and camped at Rissah. {33:22} They traveled from Rissah and camped in Kehelathah. {33:23} They went from Kehelathah and camped at Mount Shapher. {33:24} They departed from Mount Shapher and camped in Haradah. {33:25} They moved from Haradah and camped in Makheloth. {33:26} They departed from Makheloth and camped at Tahath. {33:27} They left Tahath and camped at Tarah. {33:28} They moved from Tarah and camped in Mithcah. {33:29} They went from Mithcah and camped in Hashmonah. {33:30} They departed from Hashmonah and camped at Moseroth. {33:31} They left Moseroth and camped in Benejaakan. {33:32} They moved from Benejaakan and camped at Horhagidgad. {33:33} They traveled from Horhagidgad and camped in Jotbathah. {33:34} They departed from Jotbathah and camped at Ebronah. {33:35} They left Ebronah and camped at Eziongaber. {33:36} They moved from Eziongaber and camped in the wilderness of Zin, which is Kadesh. {33:37} They departed from Kadesh and camped at Mount Hor, at the edge of the land of Edom. {33:38} Aaron the priest went up Mount Hor at the command of the LORD and died there, in the fortieth year after the children of Israel left the land of Egypt, on the first day of the fifth month. {33:39} Aaron was one hundred and twenty-three years old when he died on Mount Hor. {33:40} King Arad the Canaanite, who lived in the south of Canaan, heard about the coming of the children of Israel. {33:41} They departed from Mount Hor and camped in Zalmonah. {33:42} They moved from Zalmonah and camped in Punon. {33:43} They left Punon and camped in Oboth. {33:44} They departed from Oboth and camped in Ijeabarim, on the border of Moab. {33:45} They left

Iim and camped in Dibongad. {33:46} They moved from Dibongad and camped in Almondiblathaim. {33:47} They departed from Almondiblathaim and camped in the mountains of Abarim, in front of Nebo. {33:48} They left the mountains of Abarim and camped in the plains of Moab, by the Jordan near Jericho. {33:49} They camped by the Jordan, from Bethjesimoth to Abelshittim, in the plains of Moab. {33:50} The LORD spoke to Moses in the plains of Moab, by the Jordan near Jericho, saying, {33:51} "Speak to the children of Israel and say to them, 'When you have crossed the Jordan into the land of Canaan, {33:52} you shall drive out all the inhabitants of the land before you, destroy all their idols, and demolish all their high places. {33:53} You shall take possession of the land and dwell in it, for I have given you the land to possess. {33:54} You shall divide the land by lot for an inheritance among your families; to the larger groups, you shall give a larger inheritance, and to the smaller groups, a smaller inheritance. Each person's inheritance shall be where their lot falls; according to the tribes of your fathers, you shall inherit. {33:55} But if you do not drive out the inhabitants of the land before you, those whom you allow to remain will be like thorns in your sides and will vex you in the land where you dwell. {33:56} Moreover, I will do to you as I intended to do to them.'"

{34:1} The LORD spoke to Moses, saying, {34:2} "Command the children of Israel and tell them that when you enter the land of Canaan, this will be the land that you inherit, the land of Canaan with its borders. {34:3} Your southern boundary will start from the wilderness of Zin, along the border of Edom, and your southern border will be the edge of the Salt Sea to the east. {34:4} Your border will turn from the south to the ascent of Akrabbim, then go on to Zin; it will extend from the south to Kadeshbarnea, continuing on to Hazaraddar, and then to Azmon. {34:5} The border will make a loop from Azmon to the River of Egypt, with its exit at the sea. {34:6} For the western border, you will have the Great Sea as your boundary; this will be your western border. {34:7} Your northern border will be from the Great Sea, extending to Mount Hor. {34:8} From Mount Hor, you will mark your border to the entrance of Hamath, with the border extending to Zedad. {34:9} The border will continue to Ziphron, and its exit will be at Hazarenan; this will be your northern border. {34:10} You will mark your eastern border from Hazarenan to Shepham. {34:11} The border will go down from Shepham to Riblah, on the east side of Ain; it will descend and reach the eastern side of the Sea of Chinnereth. {34:12} The border will go down to the Jordan, with its exit at the Salt Sea; this will be your land with its surrounding borders. {34:13} Moses commanded the children of Israel, saying, "This is the land you will inherit by lot, which the LORD has commanded to give to the nine tribes and the half tribe. {34:14} For the tribe of the children of Reuben, according to their family, and the tribe of the children of Gad, according to their family, have received their inheritance, as well as half the tribe of Manasseh. {34:15} These two tribes and the half tribe have received their inheritance on this side of the Jordan near Jericho, to the east, toward the sunrise. {34:16} The LORD spoke to Moses, saying, {34:17} "These are the names of the men who will divide the land for you: Eleazar the priest and Joshua the son of Nun. {34:18} You shall take one leader from each tribe to divide the land by inheritance. {34:19} The names of the leaders are these: from the tribe of Judah, Caleb the son of Jephunneh; {34:20} from the tribe of Simeon, Shemuel the son of Ammihud; {34:21} from the tribe of Benjamin, Elidad the son of Chislon; {34:22} from the tribe of Dan, Bukki the son of Jogli; {34:23} from the tribe of Joseph, for the tribe of Manasseh, Hanniel the son of Ephod; {34:24} from the tribe of Ephraim, Kemuel the son of Shiphtan; {34:25} from the tribe of Zebulun, Elizaphan the son of Parnach; {34:26} from the tribe of Issachar, Paltiel the son of Azzan; {34:27} from the tribe of Asher, Ahihud the son of Shelomi; {34:28} and from the tribe of Naphtali, Pedahel the son of Ammihud. {34:29} These are the men whom the LORD has commanded to divide the inheritance to the children of Israel in the land of Canaan."

{35:1} The LORD spoke to Moses in the plains of Moab, by the Jordan near Jericho, saying, {35:2} "Command the children of Israel to give cities to the Levites from their inheritance, so they can live in them; you will also give the Levites suburbs around those cities. {35:3} They will have cities to live in, and the suburbs will be for their cattle, possessions, and all their animals. {35:4} The suburbs of the cities you give to the Levites will extend a thousand cubits from the city wall outward. {35:5} Measure from outside the city: two thousand cubits on the east side, two thousand on the south, two thousand on the west, and two thousand on the north; the city will be in the center. This will be the suburbs of the cities. {35:6} Among the cities you give to the Levites, there will be six cities of refuge for those who accidentally kill someone, so they can flee there; you will also add forty-two cities. {35:7} In total, the Levites will have forty-eight cities, along with their suburbs. {35:8} The cities you give will come from the land of the children of Israel; from those with many cities, you will give many, and from those with few, you will give few. Each person will give cities to the Levites based on their own inheritance. {35:9} The LORD spoke to Moses again, saying, {35:10} "Tell the children of Israel that when you cross the Jordan into the land of Canaan, {35:11} you will designate cities as cities of refuge, so that anyone who kills someone unintentionally can flee there. {35:12} These cities will provide refuge from the avenger of blood, so the manslayer does not die until he stands before the congregation for judgment. {35:13} You will have six cities set aside for refuge. {35:14} Three of these cities will be on this side of the Jordan, and three will be in the land of Canaan, serving as cities of refuge. {35:15} These six cities will be a refuge for both the children of Israel and for the foreigner or traveler among them, so that anyone who accidentally kills someone can flee there. {35:16} If someone kills another with an iron tool, making him die, he is a murderer; the murderer must be put to death. {35:17} If he kills with a stone that could kill, he is a murderer; the murderer must be put to death. {35:18} If he kills with a wooden weapon that could kill, he is a murderer; the murderer must be put to death. {35:19} The avenger of blood must kill the murderer when he encounters him. {35:20} If he acts out of hatred or throws something at someone lying in wait, and that person dies; {35:21} or if he strikes someone out of animosity and they die, the person who struck must be put to death, as he is a murderer; the avenger of blood will kill him when he encounters him. {35:22} But if he strikes someone suddenly without animosity, or throws something without intending harm, {35:23} or if he accidentally strikes someone with a stone without seeing him, and he dies, having had no previous conflict with him, {35:24} then the congregation will judge between the slayer and the avenger of blood based on these rules. {35:25} The congregation will protect the slayer from the avenger of blood and will restore him to the city of refuge he fled to, and he will remain there until the death of the high priest who was anointed with holy oil. {35:26} If the slayer ever leaves the borders of the city of refuge he fled to, {35:27} and the avenger of blood finds him outside the borders of that city and kills him, he will not be guilty of bloodshed, {35:28} because he should have remained in the city of refuge until the death of the high priest; after that, the slayer may return to his own land. {35:29} These rules will be a statute of judgment for you throughout your generations in all your dwellings. {35:30} Anyone who kills a person must be put to death based on the testimony of witnesses; but one witness alone cannot testify against anyone to put him to death. {35:31} You must not accept any payment for the life of a murderer who deserves death; he must surely be put to death. {35:32} You must not accept payment for someone who has fled to a city of refuge, allowing him to return to live in the land until the death of the priest. {35:33} Do not pollute the land you live in, for bloodshed defiles the land, and the land cannot be cleansed of bloodshed except by the blood of the one who shed it. {35:34} Therefore, do not defile the land where you live, for I dwell among the children of Israel; I am the LORD."

{36:1} The leaders of the families of the children of Gilead, the son of Machir, the son of Manasseh, from the families of the sons of Joseph, approached Moses and the leaders, the chief fathers of the children of Israel. {36:2} They said, "The LORD commanded my lord to allocate the land as an inheritance by lot to the children of Israel, and my lord was instructed by the LORD to give the inheritance of our brother Zelophehad to his daughters. {36:3} If they marry any of the sons from other tribes of the children of Israel, their inheritance will be taken from the inheritance of our fathers and added to the inheritance of the tribe they marry into; thus it will be taken from the lot of our inheritance. {36:4} When the Jubilee of the children of Israel occurs, their inheritance will be added to the inheritance of the tribe they belong to, and their inheritance will be removed from the inheritance of our father's tribe. {36:5} Moses commanded the children of Israel according to the word of the LORD, saying, "The tribe of the sons of Joseph has spoken rightly. {36:6} This is what the LORD commands regarding the daughters of Zelophehad: they may marry whomever they choose, but only within the family of their father's tribe. {36:7} This way, the inheritance of the children of Israel will not transfer from tribe to tribe, for each of the children of Israel will retain the inheritance of their father's tribe. {36:8} Any daughter who inherits land in any tribe of the children of Israel must marry someone from her father's family, so that every Israelite may enjoy the inheritance of their forefathers. {36:9} The inheritance must not shift from one tribe to another; every tribe of the children of Israel must keep its own inheritance. {36:10} Just as the LORD commanded Moses, the daughters of Zelophehad did as they were instructed. {36:11} Mahlah, Tirzah, Hoglah, Milcah, and Noah, the daughters of Zelophehad, married their father's brothers' sons. {36:12} They married into the families of the sons of Manasseh, the son of Joseph, and their inheritance remained within their father's tribe. {36:13} These are the commands and regulations that the LORD gave through Moses to the children of Israel in the plains of Moab, by the Jordan near Jericho.

The Fifth Book of Moses, called Deuteronomy

{1:1} These are the words that Moses spoke to all Israel on this side of the Jordan in the wilderness, in the plain opposite the Red Sea, between Paran, Tophel, Laban, Hazeroth, and Dizahab. {1:2} (It is an eleven-day journey from Horeb by the way of Mount Seir to Kadeshbarnea.) {1:3} In the fortieth year, in the eleventh month, on the first day of the month, Moses spoke to the children of Israel, sharing everything the LORD had commanded him. {1:4} This was after he had defeated Sihon, the king of the Amorites, who lived in Heshbon, and Og, the king of Bashan, who lived at Astaroth in Edrei. {1:5} On this side of the Jordan, in the land of Moab, Moses began to declare this law, saying, {1:6} "The LORD our God spoke to us at Horeb, saying, 'You have stayed long enough at this mountain. {1:7} Turn and take your journey to the mountain of the Amorites and all the surrounding places, in the plain, the hills, the valleys, the south, and by the seashore, to the land of the Canaanites and to Lebanon, to the great river, the Euphrates.' {1:8} Look, I have set the land before you: go in and take possession of the land that the LORD swore to your fathers, Abraham, Isaac, and Jacob, to give to them and their descendants after them. {1:9} At that time, I told you, 'I cannot carry you alone. {1:10} The LORD your God has multiplied you, and today you are as numerous as the stars in the sky. {1:11} (May the LORD, the God of your fathers, increase you a thousand times more than you are and bless you, as He has promised!) {1:12} How can I carry your burdens and struggles by myself? {1:13} Choose wise and understanding men known among your tribes, and I will appoint them as leaders over you.' {1:14} You answered me, 'What you have said is good for us to do.' {1:15} So I took the leaders of your tribes, wise and respected men, and appointed them as heads over you: captains over thousands, hundreds, fifties, tens, and officials among your tribes. {1:16} I instructed your judges at that time, saying, 'Hear the disputes among your people and judge fairly between a man and his brother, and the foreigner who lives with him. {1:17} Do not show favoritism in judgment; listen to the small as well as the great. Do not be afraid of anyone, for judgment belongs to God. If a case is too difficult for you, bring it to me, and I will hear it.' {1:18} I commanded you at that time all the things you should do. {1:19} When we left Horeb, we traveled through that great and terrible wilderness that you saw on the way to the mountain of the Amorites, as the LORD our God commanded us, and we arrived at Kadeshbarnea. {1:20} I said to you, 'You have come to the mountain of the Amorites, which the LORD our God is giving us. {1:21} Look, the LORD your God has set the land before you: go up and take possession of it, as the LORD, the God of your fathers, has said; do not be afraid or discouraged.' {1:22} Then each of you came to me and said, 'Let us send men ahead to scout the land and bring back word about how we should go up and the cities we will come to.' {1:23} This pleased me well; so I took twelve men from among you, one from each tribe. {1:24} They turned and went up into the hill country, arriving at the Valley of Eshcol, where they explored the land. {1:25} They took some of the fruit of the land in their hands and brought it back to us, reporting, 'It is a good land that the LORD our God is giving us.' {1:26} But you were unwilling to go up, and you rebelled against the command of the LORD your God. {1:27} You complained in your tents and said, 'The LORD hates us; He brought us out of Egypt to deliver us into the hands of the Amorites to destroy us.' {1:28} Where can we go? Our brothers have discouraged us, saying, 'The people are bigger and taller than we are; the cities are large and fortified to the heavens; and we have seen the descendants of the Anakim.' {1:29} I said to you, 'Do not be terrified or afraid of them. {1:30} The LORD your God, who goes before you, will fight for you, just as He did for you in Egypt before your very eyes. {1:31} And in the wilderness, you saw how the LORD your God carried you, just as a father carries his son, throughout your journey until you came to this place.' {1:32} Yet in this matter, you did not trust the LORD your God, {1:33} who went ahead of you on your journey to find you a place to camp, in fire by night and in a cloud by day, to show you the way to go. {1:34} The LORD heard what you said and was angry, and swore, saying, {1:35} 'Not one of this evil generation will see the good land I swore to give to your fathers, {1:36} except Caleb, the son of Jephunneh; he will see it, and I will give him and his descendants the land he walked on, because he fully followed the LORD.' {1:37} The LORD was also angry with me because of you, saying, 'You also will not enter there. {1:38} But Joshua, the son of Nun, who stands before you, will enter there; encourage him, for he will lead Israel to inherit it. {1:39} Furthermore, your little ones, whom you said would be taken captive, and your children who do not yet know good from evil, will enter there, and I will give it to them, and they will possess it. {1:40} As for you, turn around and head back into the wilderness along the route to the Red Sea.' {1:41} Then you answered me, 'We have sinned against the LORD; we will go up and fight, as the LORD our God commanded us.' When each of you had put on your weapons of war, you were ready to go up into the hill country. {1:42} But the LORD said to me, 'Tell them, "Do not go up or fight, for I am not among you; otherwise, you will be defeated by your enemies."' {1:43} I told you, but you would not listen; you rebelled against the command of the LORD and presumptuously went up into the hill country. {1:44} The Amorites who lived in that hill country came out against you and chased you like bees do, and they defeated you at Seir, all the way to Hormah. {1:45} You returned and wept before the LORD, but He would not listen to your voice or pay attention to you. {1:46} So you stayed at Kadesh for a long time, as long as you had been there.

{2:1} Then we turned and set out for the wilderness along the route to the Red Sea, as the LORD had instructed me. We circled Mount Seir for many days. {2:2} The LORD spoke to me, saying, {2:3} "You have circled this mountain long enough; now turn northward. {2:4} Command the people, saying, 'You are to pass through the territory of your relatives, the descendants of Esau, who live in Seir. They will be afraid of you, so be very careful. {2:5} Do not provoke them, for I will not give you any of their land, not even a foot of it, because I have given Mount Seir to Esau as a possession. {2:6} You may buy food from them for money so that you can eat, and you may buy water from them for money so that you can drink. {2:7} The LORD your God has blessed you in all the work of your hands. He knows your journey through this great wilderness; for forty years the LORD your God has been with you, and you have lacked nothing." {2:8} When we passed by our relatives, the descendants of Esau, who live in Seir, on the road from Elath and Eziongaber, we turned and went along the road to the wilderness of Moab. {2:9} The LORD said to me, "Do not harass the Moabites or start a fight with them, for I will not give you any of their land as a possession; I have given Ar to the descendants of Lot as a possession." {2:10} The Emims lived there in the past, a great and numerous people, tall like the Anakim; {2:11} they were also considered giants, as the Anakim were. The Moabites called them Emims. {2:12} The Horites lived in Seir before; but the descendants of Esau drove them out and settled in their place, as Israel did to the land that the LORD gave them as a possession. {2:13} Now rise up, I said, and cross the Zered Brook. So we crossed the Zered Brook. {2:14} The time from when we left

Kadeshbarnea until we crossed the Zered Brook was thirty-eight years, until the entire generation of the men of war had perished, just as the LORD had sworn to them. {2:15} The LORD's hand was against them to eliminate them from the camp until they were gone. {2:16} When all the men of war had died among the people, {2:17} the LORD spoke to me, saying, {2:18} "Today you are to cross the border of Moab at Ar. {2:19} When you approach the descendants of Ammon, do not harass them or provoke them, for I will not give you any of the land of the Ammonites as a possession; I have given it to the descendants of Lot as a possession." {2:20} (That land was also regarded as a land of giants; giants lived there in ancient times, and the Ammonites called them Zamzummims; {2:21} a great and numerous people, tall like the Anakim, but the LORD destroyed them before the Ammonites, who drove them out and settled in their place. {2:22} This is what He did to the descendants of Esau, who live in Seir, when He destroyed the Horites before them, allowing them to settle in their place until today. {2:23} The Avims, who lived in Hazerim as far as Azzah, were destroyed by the Caphtorim, who came from Caphtor, and they settled in their place.) {2:24} Get up, take your journey, and cross the Arnon River. Look, I have delivered Sihon the Amorite, king of Heshbon, and his land into your hands; begin to take possession and engage him in battle. {2:25} This day I will start to put the fear and dread of you upon the nations under all of heaven. They will hear reports of you and tremble in anguish because of you. {2:26} I sent messengers from the wilderness of Kedemoth to Sihon, king of Heshbon, with words of peace, saying, {2:27} "Let me pass through your land. I will go along the main road; I will not turn to the right or to the left. {2:28} You shall sell me food for money that I may eat, and give me water for money that I may drink; only let me pass through on foot, {2:29} just as the descendants of Esau who live in Seir and the Moabites who live in Ar did for me, until I cross the Jordan into the land that the LORD our God is giving us." {2:30} But Sihon, king of Heshbon, would not let us pass through, for the LORD your God hardened his spirit and made his heart obstinate in order to deliver him into your hands, as is evident today. {2:31} The LORD said to me, "Look, I have begun to deliver Sihon and his land into your hands; begin to possess it so you may inherit his land." {2:32} Then Sihon came out against us, he and all his people, to fight at Jahaz. {2:33} The LORD our God delivered him into our hands, and we defeated him, his sons, and all his people. {2:34} At that time, we captured all his cities and completely destroyed the men, women, and children of every city; we left no one alive. {2:35} We took only the livestock as plunder for ourselves, along with the spoil of the cities we captured. {2:36} From Aroer, by the bank of the Arnon River, and from the city by the river, as far as Gilead, not one city was too strong for us; the LORD our God delivered all to us. {2:37} But we did not approach the land of the Ammonites, nor any place along the Jabbok River, nor the cities in the mountains, nor anything that the LORD our God forbade us.

{3:1} Then we turned and went up the road to Bashan, and Og, the king of Bashan, came out against us, he and all his people, to fight at Edrei. {3:2} The LORD said to me, "Do not be afraid of him, for I will deliver him, all his people, and his land into your hands; you will do to him as you did to Sihon, king of the Amorites, who lived in Heshbon." {3:3} So the LORD our God delivered Og, the king of Bashan, and all his people into our hands, and we struck him down until no one was left alive. {3:4} At that time, we took all his cities; there wasn't a city we didn't capture from them—sixty cities, all the region of Argob, the kingdom of Og in Bashan. {3:5} All these cities were fortified with high walls, gates, and bars; besides, there were many unwalled towns. {3:6} We completely destroyed them, as we had done to Sihon, king of Heshbon, destroying every man, woman, and child in every city. {3:7} But we took the livestock and the spoil from the cities as plunder for ourselves. {3:8} At that time, we took from the two kings of the Amorites the land on this side of the Jordan, from the Arnon River to Mount Hermon; {3:9} (Mount Hermon is called Sirion by the Sidonians, and the Amorites call it Shenir.) {3:10} We took all the cities of the plain, all of Gilead, and all of Bashan, as far as Salchah and Edrei, cities of the kingdom of Og in Bashan. {3:11} For only Og, king of Bashan, remained of the remnant of the giants; indeed, his bed was made of iron. Is it not in Rabbath of the Ammonites? It was nine cubits long and four cubits wide, according to the cubit of a man. {3:12} This land, which we possessed at that time, from Aroer, by the Arnon River, and half of Mount Gilead, along with its cities, I gave to the Reubenites and Gadites. {3:13} The rest of Gilead and all of Bashan, which is the kingdom of Og, I gave to the half tribe of Manasseh; all the region of Argob, along with all of Bashan, which is known as the land of giants. {3:14} Jair, the son of Manasseh, took all the area of Argob, as far as the borders of Geshuri and Maachathi, and named them after himself, Bashanhavothjair, to this day. {3:15} I gave Gilead to Machir. {3:16} To the Reubenites and Gadites, I gave from Gilead to the Arnon River, half of the valley, and the border to the Jabbok River, which is the border of the Ammonites; {3:17} the plain, the Jordan River, and its banks, from Chinnereth to the Salt Sea, below Ashdothpisgah, eastward. {3:18} At that time, I commanded you, saying, "The LORD your God has given you this land to possess it. You shall pass over armed before your fellow Israelites, all who are fit for battle. {3:19} But your wives, children, and livestock (for I know you have a lot of livestock) shall stay in the cities I have given you, {3:20} until the LORD gives rest to your fellow Israelites, as He has given to you, and until they also possess the land that the LORD your God is giving them beyond the Jordan. Then each of you may return to your possession, which I have given you." {3:21} I commanded Joshua at that time, saying, "Your eyes have seen all that the LORD your God has done to these two kings; He will do the same to all the kingdoms you encounter. {3:22} Do not fear them, for the LORD your God will fight for you." {3:23} At that time, I pleaded with the LORD, saying, {3:24} "O Lord GOD, You have begun to show Your servant Your greatness and Your mighty hand; for what god is there in heaven or on earth that can do according to Your works and according to Your might? {3:25} I ask You, let me cross over and see the good land that is beyond the Jordan, that beautiful mountain, and Lebanon." {3:26} But the LORD was angry with me because of you, and He would not listen to me. The LORD said to me, "That is enough; do not speak to Me anymore about this matter. {3:27} Go up to the top of Mount Pisgah and look westward, northward, southward, and eastward; behold it with your eyes, for you shall not cross over this Jordan. {3:28} But charge Joshua, encourage him & strengthen him; for he shall go over before this people & he shall cause them to inherit the land that you will see." {3:29} So we stayed in the valley opposite Bethpeor.

{4:1} Now, listen, O Israel, to the statutes and judgments that I teach you, so that you may follow them and live, and go in to possess the land which the LORD God of your ancestors is giving you. {4:2} You must not add to the word I command you, nor take away from it, so that you can keep the commandments of the LORD your God which I command you. {4:3} Your eyes have seen what the LORD did because of Baalpeor; all the men who followed Baalpeor, the LORD your God destroyed from among you. {4:4} But you who held fast to the LORD your God are all alive today. {4:5} Behold, I have taught you statutes and judgments, just as the LORD my God commanded me, so that you may do so in the land you are about to possess. {4:6} Therefore, keep and do them; for this is your wisdom and understanding in the sight of the nations, who will hear of all these statutes and say, "Surely this great nation is a wise and understanding people." {4:7} For what nation is there so great that has God so near to them as the LORD our God is in all things we call upon Him for? {4:8} And what nation is there so great that has statutes and judgments so righteous as this law which I set before you today? {4:9} Only be careful and keep your soul diligently, lest you forget the things your eyes have seen and let them depart from your heart all the days of your life; teach them to your children and grandchildren. {4:10} Especially remember the day you stood before the LORD your God at Horeb, when the LORD said to me, "Gather the people together, and I will make them hear My words so they may learn to fear Me all the days they live on the earth, and that they may teach their children." {4:11} You came near and stood at the foot of the mountain, and the mountain burned with fire to the middle of heaven, with darkness, clouds, and thick darkness. {4:12} The LORD spoke to you from the midst of the fire; you heard the voice of the words but saw no form; only you heard a voice. {4:13} He declared to you His covenant, which He commanded you to perform, even the ten commandments; He wrote them on two tablets of stone. {4:14} The LORD commanded me at that time to teach you statutes and judgments so that you might do them in the land you are about to possess. {4:15} Therefore, take great care to yourselves, for you saw no form on the day the LORD spoke to you at Horeb from the midst of the fire. {4:16} Do not corrupt yourselves by making a graven image, the likeness of any figure, the likeness of male or female, {4:17} the likeness of any beast that is on the earth, the likeness of any winged bird that flies in the air, {4:18} the likeness of anything that creeps on the ground, or the likeness of any fish in the waters beneath the earth. {4:19} And do not lift your eyes to heaven, and when you see the sun, moon, and stars, all the host of heaven, be driven to worship and serve them, which the LORD your God has divided for all nations under the whole heaven. {4:20} But the LORD has taken you and brought you out of the iron furnace, out of Egypt, to be His people, as you are today. {4:21} Furthermore, the LORD was angry with me because of you and swore that I would not cross the Jordan or enter the good land the LORD your God is giving you for an inheritance. {4:22} But I must die in this land; I must not cross the Jordan. You shall cross over and possess that good land. {4:23} Take heed to yourselves, lest you forget the covenant of the LORD your God, which He made with you, and make for yourselves a graven image or any likeness of anything the LORD your God has forbidden you. {4:24} For the LORD your God is a consuming fire, a jealous God. {4:25} When you beget children and grandchildren and have remained long in the land, if you corrupt yourselves and make a graven image or any likeness of anything and do evil in the sight of the LORD your God, provoking Him to anger, {4:26} I call heaven and earth to witness against you today that you will soon utterly perish from the land you are entering to possess; you will not prolong your days upon it, but will be utterly destroyed. {4:27} The LORD will scatter you among the nations, and you will be left few in number among the peoples where the LORD will lead you. {4:28} There you will serve gods, the work of men's hands, wood and stone, which neither see, hear, eat, nor smell. {4:29} But if from there you seek the LORD your God, you will find Him, if you seek Him with all your heart and with all your soul. {4:30} When you are in tribulation and all these things come upon you, in the latter days, if you turn to the LORD your God and are obedient to His voice; {4:31} (for the LORD your God is a merciful God) He will not forsake you, destroy you, or forget the covenant of your ancestors which He swore to them. {4:32} For ask now about the former days that were before you, since the day God created man on the earth, and ask from one end of heaven to the other if there has been any such thing as this great thing or has been heard like it. {4:33} Did any people ever hear the voice of God speaking out of the midst of the fire, as you have heard, and live? {4:34} Or has God ever attempted to take a nation for Himself from the midst of another nation by trials, signs, wonders, war, a mighty hand, an outstretched arm, and great terrors, according to all that the LORD your God did for you in Egypt before your eyes? {4:35} To you it was shown, that you might know that the LORD is God; there is no other besides Him. {4:36} Out of heaven, He made you hear His voice so He could instruct you; and on earth, He showed you His great fire; you heard His words from the midst of the fire. {4:37} Because He loved your ancestors, He chose their descendants after them and brought you out of Egypt with His mighty power. {4:38} He drove out nations greater and mightier than you, to bring you in, to give you their land for an inheritance, as it is today. {4:39} Know therefore this day and consider it in your heart that the LORD is God in heaven above and on the earth below; there is no other. {4:40} Therefore, keep His statutes and commandments, which I command you today, so that it may go well with you and your children after you, and that you may prolong your days on the earth which the LORD your God is giving you forever. {4:41} Then Moses set apart three cities on this side of the Jordan toward the sunrise, {4:42} that the manslayer might flee there, who accidentally kills his neighbor without having hated him in the past; by fleeing to one of these cities, he might live: {4:43} namely, Bezer in the wilderness, in the plain country, for the Reubenites; Ramoth in Gilead, for the Gadites; and Golan in Bashan, for the Manassites. {4:44} This is the law which Moses set before the children of Israel: {4:45} these are the testimonies, statutes, and judgments which Moses spoke to the children of Israel after they came out of Egypt, {4:46} on this side of the Jordan, in the valley opposite Bethpeor, in the land of Sihon, king of the Amorites, who lived in Heshbon, whom Moses and the children of Israel struck down after they came out of Egypt. {4:47} They possessed his land and the land of Og, king of Bashan, two kings of the Amorites, which were on this side of the Jordan toward the sunrise; {4:48} from Aroer, which is by the bank of the Arnon River, as far as Mount Sion, which is Hermon, {4:49} and all the plain on this side of the Jordan eastward, as far as the sea of the plain, below the springs of Pisgah.

{5:1} And Moses called all Israel and said to them, "Listen, O Israel, to the statutes and judgments that I speak to you today, so that you may learn them, keep them, and do them. {5:2} The LORD our God made a covenant with us at Horeb. {5:3} The LORD did not make this covenant with our ancestors but with us, all of us who are here alive today. {5:4} The LORD spoke to you face to face at the mountain from the midst of the fire. {5:5} (I stood between the LORD and you at that time to declare to you the word of the LORD, for you were afraid because of the fire and did not go up the mountain.) He said, {5:6} "I am the LORD your God who brought you out of the land of Egypt, from the house of bondage. {5:7} You shall have no other gods before Me. {5:8} You shall not make for yourself any graven image or any likeness of anything that is in heaven above, on the earth below, or in the waters beneath the earth. {5:9} You shall not bow down to them or serve them, for I, the LORD your God, am a jealous God, punishing the iniquity of the fathers upon the children to the third and fourth generation of those who hate Me, {5:10} but showing mercy to thousands of those who love Me and keep My commandments. {5:11} You shall not take the name of the LORD your God in vain, for the LORD will not hold him guiltless who takes His name in vain. {5:12} Keep the Sabbath day to sanctify it, as the LORD your God has commanded you. {5:13} Six days you shall labor and do all your work, {5:14} but the seventh day is the Sabbath of the LORD your God; on it, you shall not do any work, you, your son, your daughter, your male servant, your female servant, your ox, your donkey, or any of your livestock, nor the stranger who is within your gates, so that your male and female servants may rest as you do. {5:15} Remember that you were a servant in the land of Egypt, and the LORD your God brought you out from there with a mighty hand and an outstretched arm; therefore, the LORD your God commanded you to keep the Sabbath day. {5:16} Honor your father and your mother, as the LORD your God has commanded you, so that your days may be prolonged and that it may go well with you in the land the LORD your God is giving you. {5:17} You shall not murder. {5:18} You shall not commit adultery. {5:19} You shall not steal. {5:20} You shall not bear false witness against your neighbor. {5:21} You shall not covet your neighbor's wife, nor desire your neighbor's house, field, male servant, female servant, ox, donkey, or anything that belongs to your neighbor. {5:22} These words the LORD spoke to all your assembly from the midst of the fire, the cloud, and the thick darkness with a loud voice; He added no more. He wrote them on two tablets of stone and gave them to me. {5:23} When you heard the voice from the midst of the darkness (for the mountain was burning with fire), all the heads of your tribes and your elders came near to me. {5:24} You said, "Behold, the LORD our God has shown us His glory and greatness, and we have heard His voice from the midst of the fire; we have seen today that God speaks with man, and he lives. {5:25} Now, why should we die? For this great fire will consume us; if we hear the voice of the LORD our God any more, we shall die. {5:26} For who is there of all flesh that has heard the voice of the living God speaking from the midst of the fire, as we have, and lived? {5:27} You go near and hear all that the LORD our God says; then speak to us all that the LORD our God tells you, and we will listen and do it." {5:28} The LORD heard the voice of your words when you spoke to me, and the LORD said to me, "I have heard the voice of the words of this people, which they have spoken to you; they have well said all that they have spoken. {5:29} Oh, that they had such a heart in them that they would fear Me and keep all My commandments always, so it might go well with them and their children forever! {5:30} Go and say to them, 'Return to your tents.' {5:31} But as for you, stand here by Me, and I will speak to you all the commandments, statutes, and judgments that you shall teach them, so they may do them in the land which I give them to possess. {5:32} You shall be careful to do as the LORD your God has commanded you; you shall not turn aside to the right or to the left. {5:33} You shall walk in all the ways which the LORD your God has commanded you, so that you may live & it may go well with you, that you may prolong your days in the land you shall possess.

{6:1} Now these are the commandments, statutes, and judgments that the LORD your God commanded you to teach so that you may follow them in the land you are about to possess. {6:2} This is so you may fear the LORD your God, to keep all His statutes and commandments that I command you, you, your son, and your grandson, all the days of your life, so that your days may be prolonged. {6:3} Therefore, listen, O Israel, and be careful to do it, so that it may go well with you and so that you may greatly increase, as the LORD God of your fathers has promised you, in a land flowing with milk and honey. {6:4} Hear, O Israel: The LORD our God is one LORD. {6:5} You shall love the LORD your God with all your heart, with all your soul, and with all your might. {6:6} And these words that I command you today shall be in your heart. {6:7} You shall teach them diligently to your children and talk about them when you sit in your house, when you walk along the way, when you lie down, and when you rise up. {6:8} You shall bind them as a sign on your hand, and they shall be as frontlets between your eyes. {6:9} You shall write them on the doorposts of your house and on your gates. {6:10} And when the LORD your God brings you into the land He swore to your fathers, to Abraham, Isaac, and Jacob, to give you great and good cities that you did not build, {6:11} and houses filled with all good things that you did not fill, and wells dug that you did not dig, vineyards and olive trees that you did not plant; when you have eaten and are full, {6:12} then beware lest you forget the LORD who brought you out of the land of Egypt, from the house of bondage. {6:13} You shall fear the LORD your God and serve Him, and you shall swear by His name. {6:14} You shall not go after other gods, the gods of the peoples around you, {6:15} (for the LORD your God is a jealous God among you) lest the anger of the LORD your God be kindled against you and destroy you from off the face of the earth. {6:16} You shall not tempt the LORD your God, as you tempted Him at Massah. {6:17} You shall diligently keep the commandments of the LORD your God, His testimonies, and His statutes that He has commanded you. {6:18} And you shall do what is right and good in the sight of the LORD so that it may go well with you, and you may go in and possess the good land that the LORD swore to your fathers, {6:19} to cast out all your enemies before you, as the LORD has spoken. {6:20} When your son asks you in the future, saying, "What do the testimonies, statutes, and judgments that the LORD our God has commanded mean?" {6:21} then you shall say to your son, "We were Pharaoh's bondmen in Egypt, and the LORD brought us out of Egypt with a mighty hand. {6:22} The LORD showed signs and wonders, great and terrible, upon Egypt, upon Pharaoh, and upon all his household before our eyes. {6:23} And He brought us out from there in order to bring us in, to give us the land that He swore to our fathers. {6:24} And the LORD commanded us to observe all these statutes, to fear the LORD our God, for our good always, so that He might preserve us alive, as it is today. {6:25} It will be our righteousness if we are careful to do all these commandments before the LORD our God, as He has commanded us.

{7:1} When the LORD your God brings you into the land you are going to possess and has cast out many nations before you, the Hittites, Girgashites, Amorites, Canaanites, Perizzites, Hivites, and Jebusites—seven nations greater and mightier than you— {7:2} and when the LORD your God delivers them to you, you shall defeat them and completely destroy them. You shall make no covenant with them and show them no mercy. {7:3} You shall not intermarry with them; you shall not give your daughter to their son, nor take their daughter for your son. {7:4} For they will turn your son away from following Me to serve other gods, and the anger of the LORD will be kindled against you, and He will destroy you suddenly. {7:5} Instead, you shall deal with them this way: destroy their altars, break down their images, cut down their groves, and burn their graven images with fire. {7:6} For you are a holy people to the LORD your God. The LORD your God has chosen you to be a special people for Himself, above all the peoples on the face of the earth. {7:7} The LORD did not set His love upon you or choose you because you were more in number than any people; you were the fewest of all peoples. {7:8} But because the LORD loved you and wanted to keep the oath He swore to your fathers, He brought you out with a mighty hand and redeemed you from the house of bondage, from the hand of Pharaoh, king of Egypt. {7:9} Know therefore that the LORD your God is God, the faithful God, who keeps covenant and mercy with those who love Him and keep His commandments to a thousand generations. {7:10} And He repays those who hate Him to their face, to destroy them. He will not be slow to repay those who hate Him. {7:11} Therefore, you shall keep the commandments, statutes, and judgments that I command you today to do them. {7:12} If you listen to these judgments and keep and do them, the LORD your God will keep the covenant and mercy He swore to your fathers. {7:13} He will love you, bless you, and multiply you. He will also bless the fruit of your womb, the fruit of your land, your grain, your wine, your oil, the increase of your cattle, and the flocks of your sheep in the land He swore to your fathers to give you. {7:14} You shall be blessed above all peoples; there will be no barren male or female among you or among your livestock. {7:15} And the LORD will take away from you all sickness and will not put any of the evil diseases of Egypt upon you, which you know, but will lay them on all who hate you. {7:16} You shall destroy all the peoples that the LORD your God delivers to you; you shall show them no pity, nor serve their gods, for that will be a snare to you. {7:17} If you say in your heart, "These nations are greater than I; how can I dispossess them?" {7:18} you shall not be afraid of them; but you shall remember well what the LORD your God did to Pharaoh and to all Egypt. {7:19} The great trials your eyes saw, the signs and wonders, the mighty hand, and the outstretched arm, by which the LORD your God brought you out—so will the LORD your God do to all the peoples of whom you are afraid. {7:20} Moreover, the LORD your God will send the hornet among them until those who are left and hide from you are destroyed. {7:21} You shall not be terrified by them, for the LORD your God is among you, a mighty God and terrible. {7:22} The LORD your God will drive out those nations before you little by little; you may not consume them all at once, lest the beasts of the field increase upon you. {7:23} But the LORD your God will deliver them to you and will destroy them with a mighty destruction until they are destroyed. {7:24} He will deliver their kings into your hand, and you shall destroy their name from under heaven; no one will be able to stand before you until you have destroyed them. {7:25} You shall burn with fire the graven images of their gods; you shall not covet the silver or gold that is on them or take it for yourselves, lest you be snared by it, for it is an abomination to the LORD your God. {7:26} You shall not bring an abomination into your house, lest you become a cursed thing like it; you shall utterly detest it and abhor it, for it is a cursed thing.

{8:1} All the commandments that I command you today, you shall observe and do, so that you may live, multiply, and go in and possess the land that the LORD swore to your fathers. {8:2} You shall remember all the ways that the LORD your God led you these forty years in the wilderness, to humble you, to test you, and to know what was in your heart, whether you would keep His commandments or not. {8:3} He humbled you and allowed you to hunger, and then fed you with manna, which you did not know, nor did your fathers know, so that He might make you understand that man does not live by bread alone, but by every word that comes from the mouth of the LORD. {8:4} Your clothes did not wear out on you, nor did your foot swell during these forty years. {8:5} You should also consider in your heart that, just as a man disciplines his son, so the LORD your God disciplines you. {8:6} Therefore, you shall keep the commandments of the LORD your God, walk in His ways, and fear Him. {8:7} For the LORD your God is bringing you into a good land, a land with brooks of water, springs, and depths that flow from valleys and hills; {8:8} a land of wheat and barley, of vines, fig trees, and pomegranates; a land of olive oil and honey; {8:9} a land where you will eat bread without scarcity; you will lack nothing in it; a land whose stones are iron, and from whose hills you can dig copper. {8:10} When you have eaten and are full, then you shall bless the LORD your God for the good land He has given you. {8:11} Beware that you do not forget the LORD your God by not keeping His commandments, judgments, and statutes, which I command you today. {8:12} Lest, when you have eaten and are full, and have built good houses and lived in them; {8:13} and when your herds and flocks multiply, and your silver and gold multiply, and all that you have multiplies; {8:14} then your heart will be lifted up, and you will forget the LORD your God, who brought you out of the land of Egypt, from the house of bondage. {8:15} He led you through that great and terrible wilderness, with fiery serpents, scorpions, and thirst, where there was no water; He brought you water from the rock of flint; {8:16}

He fed you in the wilderness with manna, which your fathers did not know, to humble you and test you, to do you good in the end. {8:17} And you might say in your heart, "My power and the might of my hand have gained me this wealth." {8:18} But you shall remember the LORD your God, for it is He who gives you the power to get wealth, that He may establish His covenant which He swore to your fathers, as it is this day. {8:19} If you forget the LORD your God and walk after other gods, serving and worshiping them, I testify against you today that you shall surely perish. {8:20} Like the nations that the LORD destroys before you, so shall you perish, because you would not be obedient to the voice of the LORD your God.

{9:1} Listen, O Israel: Today you are crossing over the Jordan to go in and take possession of nations that are greater and mightier than you, cities that are large and fortified up to the sky. {9:2} A great and tall people, the descendants of the Anakites, whom you know and have heard about, saying, "Who can stand against the children of Anak?" {9:3} Therefore, understand today that the LORD your God is the one who goes before you; like a consuming fire, He will destroy them and bring them down before you. You will drive them out and destroy them quickly, as the LORD has promised you. {9:4} Do not say in your heart, after the LORD your God has cast them out before you, "It is because of my righteousness that the LORD has brought me in to possess this land," but it is because of the wickedness of these nations that the LORD is driving them out before you. {9:5} It is not for your righteousness or the uprightness of your heart that you are going in to possess their land, but it is because of the wickedness of these nations that the LORD your God is driving them out before you, and to fulfill the promise He swore to your fathers, Abraham, Isaac, and Jacob. {9:6} So, understand that the LORD your God is not giving you this good land to possess because of your righteousness; you are a stiff-necked (stubborn) people. {9:7} Remember, and do not forget, how you provoked the LORD your God to anger in the wilderness. From the day you left Egypt until you arrived at this place, you have been rebellious against the LORD. {9:8} Even at Horeb, you provoked the LORD to anger, and He was ready to destroy you. {9:9} When I went up the mountain to receive the tablets of stone, the tablets of the covenant that the LORD made with you, I stayed on the mountain forty days and forty nights, without eating bread or drinking water. {9:10} The LORD gave me two tablets of stone, written with the finger of God, containing all the words that the LORD spoke to you on the mountain from the fire on the day of assembly. {9:11} At the end of forty days and forty nights, the LORD gave me the two tablets of stone, the tablets of the covenant. {9:12} The LORD said to me, "Get up, go down quickly from here, for your people whom you brought out of Egypt have corrupted themselves; they have quickly turned aside from the way I commanded them and made a molten image." {9:13} Furthermore, the LORD said to me, "I have seen this people, and indeed, they are a stiff-necked people. {9:14} Let Me alone so that I may destroy them and blot out their name from under heaven, and I will make you into a nation greater and mightier than they." {9:15} So I turned and came down from the mountain, and the mountain was burning with fire, and the two tablets of the covenant were in my hands. {9:16} I looked, and you had sinned against the LORD your God by making a molten calf; you had turned aside quickly from the way the LORD had commanded you. {9:17} I took the two tablets and threw them out of my hands and broke them before your eyes. {9:18} I fell down before the LORD as I did before, for forty days and forty nights; I did not eat bread or drink water because of all your sins that you committed, doing wickedly in the sight of the LORD to provoke Him to anger. {9:19} I was afraid of the anger and hot displeasure that the LORD had against you, ready to destroy you, but the LORD listened to me that time. {9:20} The LORD was very angry with Aaron, ready to destroy him, and I prayed for Aaron at that time. {9:21} I took your sin, the calf you had made, and burned it in the fire, and ground it very small until it was like dust, and I cast the dust into the brook that flows down from the mountain. {9:22} At Taberah, Massah, and Kibroth-hattaavah, you provoked the LORD to anger. {9:23} Likewise, when the LORD sent you from Kadesh-barnea, saying, "Go up and possess the land I have given you," you rebelled against the command of the LORD your God and did not believe Him or listen to His voice. {9:24} You have been rebellious against the LORD since the day I knew you. {9:25} Therefore, I fell down before the LORD for forty days and forty nights, as I did the first time, because the LORD said He would destroy you. {9:26} I prayed to the LORD and said, "O Lord GOD, do not destroy Your people and Your inheritance, whom You redeemed through Your greatness, whom You brought out of Egypt with a mighty hand. {9:27} Remember Your servants, Abraham, Isaac, and Jacob; do not look at the stubbornness of this people or their wickedness or their sin. {9:28} Lest the land from which You brought us out say, 'The LORD was not able to bring them into the land He promised them, and because He hated them, He brought them out to kill them in the wilderness.' {9:29} Yet they are Your people and Your inheritance, whom You brought out by Your mighty power and Your outstretched arm.

{10:1} At that time, the LORD said to me, "Cut two tablets of stone like the first ones, and come up to me on the mountain. Also, make an ark of wood." {10:2} I will write on the tablets the words that were on the first tablets that you broke, and you will put them in the ark. {10:3} So, I made an ark of acacia wood, cut two tablets of stone like the first ones, and went up the mountain with the two tablets in my hands. {10:4} He wrote on the tablets, just like the first writing, the Ten Commandments, which the LORD spoke to you on the mountain from the fire on the day of the assembly. The LORD gave them to me. {10:5} I turned and came down from the mountain, putting the tablets in the ark I had made, and they are there, as the LORD commanded me. {10:6} The Israelites traveled from Beeroth of the children of Jaakan to Mosera; there Aaron died and was buried, and his son Eleazar took over the priestly duties. {10:7} From there, they journeyed to Gudgodah, and from Gudgodah to Jotbath, a land of flowing rivers. {10:8} At that time, the LORD set apart the tribe of Levi to carry the ark of the covenant of the LORD, to stand before the LORD to serve Him, and to bless in His name, as it is today. {10:9} Therefore, Levi has no part or inheritance with his brothers; the LORD is his inheritance, as the LORD your God promised him. {10:10} I stayed on the mountain for forty days and forty nights, as I did the first time; the LORD listened to me that time as well, and He did not want to destroy you. {10:11} The LORD said to me, "Get up, take your journey before the people, so they may go in and possess the land I swore to give their fathers." {10:12} And now, Israel, what does the LORD your God require of you? To fear the LORD your God, to walk in all His ways, to love Him, and to serve the LORD your God with all your heart and soul, {10:13} and to keep the commandments and statutes of the LORD that I command you today for your good. {10:14} Look, the heavens, even the highest heavens, belong to the LORD your God, and the earth and everything in it. {10:15} The LORD was delighted in your ancestors to love them, and He chose their descendants after them, even you, above all people, as it is today. {10:16} Therefore, circumcise your hearts and stop being stubborn. {10:17} For the LORD your God is the God of gods and Lord of lords, a great, mighty, and awesome God who shows no favoritism and does not take bribes. {10:18} He defends the cause of the fatherless and the widow and loves the stranger, giving him food and clothing. {10:19} Therefore, love the stranger, for you were strangers in the land of Egypt. {10:20} You shall fear the LORD your God; serve Him, hold fast to Him, and swear by His name. {10:21} He is your praise, and He is your God, who has done for you these great and awesome things that your eyes have seen. {10:22} Your ancestors went down to Egypt with seventy people, and now the LORD your God has made you as numerous as the stars in the sky.

{11:1} Therefore, you shall love the LORD your God and keep His requirements, His statutes, His judgments, and His commandments always. {11:2} Know this day that I am not speaking to your children who have not known or seen the discipline of the LORD your God, His greatness, His mighty hand, and His outstretched arm, {11:3} and His miracles and acts that He did in Egypt against Pharaoh, the king of Egypt, and all his land; {11:4} and what He did to the army of Egypt, their horses, and their chariots—how He made the waters of the Red Sea overflow them as they pursued you, and how the LORD has destroyed them to this day; {11:5} and what He did to you in the wilderness until you arrived at this place; {11:6} and what He did to Dathan and

Abiram, the sons of Eliab, the son of Reuben—how the earth opened its mouth and swallowed them, their households, their tents, and all their possessions in the midst of all Israel. {11:7} But your own eyes have seen all the great acts of the LORD that He has done. {11:8} Therefore, you shall keep all the commandments I am giving you today so that you may be strong and go in and possess the land you are about to enter; {11:9} and so that you may prolong your days in the land that the LORD swore to give your ancestors and their descendants, a land flowing with milk and honey. {11:10} For the land you are entering to possess is not like the land of Egypt, from which you came, where you planted your seed and watered it by foot like a vegetable garden; {11:11} but the land you are going to possess is a land of hills and valleys, which drinks water from the rain of heaven. {11:12} It is a land that the LORD your God cares for; the eyes of the LORD your God are always on it, from the beginning of the year to the end of the year. {11:13} And it will come to pass, if you listen carefully to my commandments that I am giving you today, to love the LORD your God and serve Him with all your heart and soul, {11:14} then I will give you the rain for your land in its season—the early rain and the latter rain—so that you may gather in your grain, wine, and oil. {11:15} I will send grass in your fields for your cattle, so that you may eat and be full. {11:16} Be careful not to be deceived, and turn aside to serve other gods and worship them; {11:17} then the LORD's anger will be kindled against you, and He will shut up the heavens so that there will be no rain, and the land will not yield its produce, and you will perish quickly from the good land that the LORD is giving you. {11:18} Therefore, you shall lay up these words of mine in your heart and soul, and bind them as a sign on your hands, so that they may be as frontlets between your eyes. {11:19} You shall teach them to your children, speaking of them when you sit in your house, when you walk along the road, when you lie down, and when you rise up. {11:20} You shall write them on the doorposts of your house and on your gates, {11:21} so that your days may be multiplied, and the days of your children in the land that the LORD swore to give your ancestors, as long as the days of heaven are on the earth. {11:22} For if you carefully keep all these commandments that I am giving you to do, to love the LORD your God, to walk in all His ways, and to hold fast to Him, {11:23} then the LORD will drive out all these nations before you, and you will possess nations greater and mightier than yourselves. {11:24} Every place where you set your foot will be yours: from the wilderness and Lebanon, from the Euphrates River to the Mediterranean Sea, your territory will extend. {11:25} No one will be able to stand against you; for the LORD your God will lay the fear and dread of you on all the land you tread upon, as He has said to you. {11:26} Look, I am setting before you today a blessing and a curse; {11:27} a blessing if you obey the commandments of the LORD your God, which I am commanding you today; {11:28} and a curse if you do not obey the commandments of the LORD your God but turn aside from the way that I am commanding you today to follow other gods that you have not known. {11:29} When the LORD your God has brought you into the land you are going to possess, you shall proclaim the blessing from Mount Gerizim and the curse from Mount Ebal. {11:30} Are they not across the Jordan, toward the west, in the land of the Canaanites, who dwell in the Arabah, opposite Gilgal, beside the plains of Moreh? {11:31} For you are about to cross the Jordan to enter and possess the land that the LORD your God is giving you, and you shall possess it and dwell there. {11:32} You shall be careful to observe all the statutes and judgments that I set before you today.

{12:1} These are the laws and regulations that you shall follow in the land that the LORD God of your ancestors is giving you to possess for all the days you live on the earth. {12:2} You must completely destroy all the places where the nations you will drive out worshiped their gods—on the high mountains, on the hills, and under every leafy tree. {12:3} You shall demolish their altars, break their sacred pillars, and burn their groves (a type of tree or sacred site) with fire; you shall cut down the carved images of their gods and eliminate their names from that place. {12:4} You must not do this to the LORD your God. {12:5} Instead, seek the place that the LORD your God will choose from among all your tribes to put His name there, that is where you will go. {12:6} You shall bring your burnt offerings, sacrifices, tithes, and contributions to the place He chooses, including your vows and freewill offerings, as well as the firstborn of your herds and flocks. {12:7} There you shall eat before the LORD your God and rejoice in everything you put your hands to, you and your households, in which the LORD your God has blessed you. {12:8} You must not do what we do here today, with everyone doing what seems right in their own eyes. {12:9} For you have not yet come to the rest and inheritance that the LORD your God is giving you. {12:10} But when you cross the Jordan and live in the land that the LORD your God is giving you to inherit, and He gives you rest from all your enemies around you so that you can live in safety; {12:11} then there will be a place that the LORD your God will choose for His name to dwell. To that place, you will bring all that I command you: your burnt offerings, sacrifices, tithes, and any special vows you make to the LORD. {12:12} You will rejoice before the LORD your God, along with your sons, daughters, servants, and the Levite who lives within your gates, since he has no portion or inheritance with you. {12:13} Be careful not to offer your burnt offerings in any place you see; {12:14} but only in the place that the LORD will choose in one of your tribes will you offer your burnt offerings and do everything I command you. {12:15} However, you may slaughter and eat meat in all your towns, whatever your heart desires, according to the blessing the LORD your God has given you. Both the unclean and the clean may eat it, just like the deer and the gazelle. {12:16} Only you must not eat the blood; you shall pour it on the ground like water. {12:17} You may not eat in your towns the tithe of your grain, new wine, or oil, or the firstborn of your herds or flocks, or any of your vows, freewill offerings, or contributions. {12:18} Instead, you must eat them before the LORD your God at the place He will choose, you, your son, your daughter, your servant, your maidservant, and the Levite within your gates, and you shall rejoice before the LORD your God in all that you do. {12:19} Be careful not to neglect the Levite as long as you live in your land. {12:20} When the LORD your God enlarges your territory as He has promised you, and you say, "I will eat meat because you long to eat it," you may eat whatever your heart desires. {12:21} If the place the LORD your God has chosen to put His name is too far from you, then you may slaughter any of your herd or flock that the LORD has given you, as I have commanded you, and you may eat it in your towns, whatever your heart desires. {12:22} Just as the deer and the gazelle are eaten, so you may eat them; the unclean and the clean may eat them alike. {12:23} Only be sure not to eat the blood, for the blood is the life, and you must not eat the life with the flesh. {12:24} You must not eat it; instead, pour it out on the ground like water. {12:25} You must not eat it so that it may go well with you and your children after you when you do what is right in the sight of the LORD. {12:26} Only take your holy things and your vows and go to the place that the LORD will choose. {12:27} There you shall offer your burnt offerings, the flesh and the blood on the altar of the LORD your God; the blood of your sacrifices shall be poured out on the altar of the LORD your God, and you shall eat the flesh. {12:28} Be careful to observe all these words that I command you so that it may go well with you and your children after you forever when you do what is good and right in the sight of the LORD your God. {12:29} When the LORD your God has cut off the nations before you, wherever you go to possess them, and you take their place and dwell in their land, {12:30} be careful not to be ensnared by following them after they have been destroyed before you, and do not inquire about their gods, asking, "How did these nations serve their gods? I will do likewise." {12:31} You must not do this to the LORD your God, for every abomination that the LORD hates they have done to their gods; they even burned their sons and daughters in the fire to their gods. {12:32} Whatever I command you, be careful to do it; do not add to it or take away from it.

{13:1} If a prophet or a dreamer of dreams arises among you and gives you a sign or wonder, {13:2} and if the sign or wonder comes to pass, and they say to you, "Let us follow other gods," gods that you have not known, and let us serve them, {13:3} you must not listen to the words of that prophet or dreamer of dreams. The LORD your God is testing you to know whether you love Him with all your heart and with all your soul. {13:4} You shall follow the LORD your God, fear Him, keep His commandments, obey His voice, serve Him, and hold fast to Him. {13:5} But that prophet or dreamer of dreams must be put to death, because they have encouraged rebellion against the LORD your God, who brought you out of Egypt and redeemed you from the house of slavery.

They have tried to lead you away from the path the LORD your God has commanded you to walk. You must purge the evil from among you. {13:6} If your brother, the son of your mother, or your son or daughter, or the wife you cherish, or your closest friend secretly entices you, saying, "Let us go and serve other gods"—gods you or your ancestors have not known—{13:7} gods of the peoples around you, whether near or far, from one end of the earth to the other, {13:8} do not give in to them or listen to them. Do not show them pity or spare them, and do not protect them. {13:9} You must certainly put them to death. Your hand must be the first to strike them, and then the hands of all the people. {13:10} You shall stone them to death, because they sought to turn you away from the LORD your God, who brought you out of Egypt, out of the house of bondage (slavery). {13:11} Then all Israel will hear about it and be afraid, and no one will again commit such wickedness among you. {13:12} If you hear it said about one of the towns the LORD your God is giving you to live in, {13:13} that wicked men have arisen among you and led the people of their town astray, saying, "Let us go and serve other gods," gods you have not known, {13:14} then you must investigate, examine, and question thoroughly. If it is proven true that this detestable thing has been done among you, {13:15} you must completely destroy the inhabitants of that town, killing them with the sword, along with everything in it, even the cattle. {13:16} You must gather all the plunder into the middle of the town's public square and burn the entire town and all its plunder as a whole offering to the LORD your God. It must remain a heap of ruins forever, never to be rebuilt. {13:17} Nothing set apart for destruction shall remain in your hand, so that the LORD may turn from His fierce anger, show you mercy, have compassion on you, and multiply you as He promised your ancestors. {13:18} This will happen if you obey the LORD your God, keeping all His commandments that I am giving you today, and doing what is right in the eyes of the LORD your God.

{14:1} You are the children of the LORD your God; you must not cut yourselves or make bald spots on your heads for the dead. {14:2} For you are a holy people to the LORD your God, and the LORD has chosen you to be a special people for Himself, above all the nations on the earth. {14:3} You must not eat any detestable thing. {14:4} These are the animals you may eat: the ox, the sheep, and the goat, {14:5} the deer, the gazelle, the roe deer, the wild goat, the antelope, the wild ox, and the mountain goat. {14:6} Every animal that has split hooves completely and chews the cud among the animals is clean for you to eat. {14:7} However, you must not eat the following: the camel, the hare, and the rock badger; they chew the cud but do not have split hooves; they are unclean for you. {14:8} The pig is also unclean for you because it has split hooves but does not chew the cud; you must not eat its meat or touch its dead body. {14:9} These you may eat from the water: any that have fins and scales. {14:10} Anything that does not have fins and scales is unclean for you; you must not eat it. {14:11} You may eat all clean birds. {14:12} But these are the birds you must not eat: the eagle, the vulture, the osprey, {14:13} the kite, and any kind of raven, {14:14} the ostrich, the nighthawk, the seagull, and the hawk of any kind, {14:15} the little owl, the great owl, the horned owl, {14:16} the pelican, the carrion vulture, and the cormorant, {14:17} the stork, the heron of any kind, the hoopoe, and the bat. {14:18} Every flying insect that swarms is unclean for you; they must not be eaten. {14:19} But all clean flying insects you may eat. {14:20} You must not eat any animal that dies naturally; you may give it to the foreigner residing in your towns, so they may eat it, or you may sell it to a foreigner, for you are a holy people to the LORD your God. You must not cook a young goat in its mother's milk. {14:22} You must set aside a tenth of all the produce of your seed each year. {14:23} You must eat before the LORD your God in the place He will choose to establish His name, the tithe of your grain, new wine, and olive oil, and the firstborn of your herds and flocks, so that you may learn to revere the LORD your God always. {14:24} If the distance is too great for you to carry your tithe, or if the place the LORD your God will choose to put His name is too far away, when the LORD your God has blessed you, {14:25} then you may exchange your tithe for silver, and take the silver in your hand and go to the place the LORD your God will choose. {14:26} There you may spend the silver on anything you desire: cattle, sheep, wine, or other strong drink, or anything you wish; you and your household shall eat there in the presence of the LORD your God and rejoice. {14:27} Do not neglect the Levite residing in your towns, for he has no share or inheritance with you. {14:28} At the end of every three years, bring the entire tithe of your produce for that year and store it in your towns. {14:29} Then the Levite, because he has no share or inheritance with you, and the foreigner, the fatherless, and the widow who live in your towns may come and eat and be satisfied, and the LORD your God may bless you in all the work of your hands.

{15:1} At the end of every seven years, you must declare a release. {15:2} This is how the release works: Every creditor who has lent anything to his neighbor must forgive the debt; he must not demand it back from his neighbor or his brother, because it is called the LORD's release. {15:3} You may demand it back from a foreigner, but whatever is yours with your brother, you must release. {15:4} There should be no poor people among you, for the LORD will greatly bless you in the land that the LORD your God is giving you as an inheritance. {15:5} Only if you carefully listen to the voice of the LORD your God and observe all these commandments I am giving you today. {15:6} For the LORD your God will bless you as He promised you; you will lend to many nations but will not borrow, and you will rule over many nations, but they will not rule over you. {15:7} If there is a poor man among you, one of your brothers, in any of your towns in the land that the LORD your God is giving you, do not harden your heart or close your hand against your poor brother. {15:8} Instead, open your hand and lend him whatever he needs. {15:9} Be careful not to have a wicked thought in your heart, saying, "The seventh year, the year of release, is near," and then look at your poor brother with evil and give him nothing; he may cry out to the LORD against you, and it will be counted as sin for you. {15:10} You must give generously, and your heart should not be grieved when you give to him, because for this very thing the LORD your God will bless you in all your work and everything you put your hand to. {15:11} There will always be poor people in the land; therefore, I command you to open your hand wide to your brother, to the poor, and to the needy in your land. {15:12} If your brother, an Hebrew man or woman, is sold to you and serves you for six years, in the seventh year, you must let them go free. {15:13} When you send them out free, do not let them go empty-handed. {15:14} Provide for them generously from your flock, your threshing floor, and your winepress; give them what the LORD your God has blessed you with. {15:15} Remember that you were a slave in the land of Egypt, and the LORD your God redeemed you; that is why I command you today. {15:16} If they say to you, "I do not want to leave you because I love you and your household, and I am well off with you," {15:17} then take an awl and pierce their ear to the door, and they will become your servant for life. Do the same for your female servant. {15:18} It should not seem hard for you to send them away free, for they have served you six years and are worth double the wages of a hired servant; the LORD your God will bless you in all that you do. {15:19} You must set apart all the firstborn males of your herds and flocks for the LORD your God; do not work with the firstborn of your ox or shear the firstborn of your sheep. {15:20} Each year, you and your household must eat them in the presence of the LORD your God at the place He will choose. {15:21} If there is any blemish in the animal, such as being lame, blind, or having any serious defect, you must not sacrifice it to the LORD your God. {15:22} You may eat it within your own towns; the clean and the unclean alike may eat it, as they do with the deer or the gazelle. {15:23} But you must not eat the blood; pour it out on the ground like water.

{16:1} Observe the month of Abib and celebrate the Passover to the LORD your God, for in the month of Abib, the LORD your God brought you out of Egypt at night. {16:2} Therefore, you must sacrifice the Passover to the LORD your God from your flock and herd at the place the LORD will choose to place His name. {16:3} Do not eat any leavened bread with it; for seven days, you shall eat unleavened bread, the bread of affliction, because you left the land of Egypt in haste. This will help you remember the day you left Egypt all your life. {16:4} There should be no leavened bread seen in your territory for seven days, and nothing from the flesh you sacrificed on the first evening should remain until morning. {16:5} You cannot sacrifice the Passover within any of your towns that the LORD your God is giving you. {16:6} Instead, you must sacrifice the Passover at the place the LORD your God will choose, at sunset, during the season when you left Egypt. {16:7} You shall roast and eat it at the place the LORD your God will choose, and then you will return to your tents in the morning. {16:8} For six days, you shall eat unleavened bread, and on the seventh day, there shall be a solemn assembly to the LORD your God; do no work on that day. {16:9} Count seven weeks from the time you first put the sickle to the grain. {16:10} You shall celebrate the Feast of Weeks to the LORD your God with a freewill offering based on how the LORD has blessed you. {16:11} Rejoice before the LORD your God, you, your son, your daughter, your male and female servants, the Levite in your towns, the stranger, the fatherless, and the widow among you, at the place the LORD your God will choose. {16:12} Remember that you were a slave in Egypt, and carefully observe these statutes. {16:13} Celebrate the Feast of Tabernacles for seven days after you have gathered your harvest of grain and wine. {16:14} Rejoice in your feast, you, your son, your daughter, your male and female servants, the Levite, the stranger, the fatherless, and the widow within your towns. {16:15} For seven days, keep a solemn feast to the LORD your God at the place He will choose, because the LORD your God will bless you in all your harvest and in all the work of your hands, and you will surely rejoice. {16:16} Three times a year, all your males must appear before the LORD your God at the place He will choose: during the Feast of Unleavened Bread, the Feast of Weeks, and the Feast of Tabernacles, and they must not appear before the LORD empty-handed. {16:17} Each man must give as he is able, according to the blessing the LORD your God has given you. {16:18} Appoint judges and officials in all your towns that the LORD your God is giving you, throughout your tribes, and they shall judge the people with just judgment. {16:19} Do not distort justice, do not show favoritism, and do not accept bribes, for a bribe blinds the eyes of the wise and twists the words of the righteous. {16:20} Follow what is altogether just so that you may live and inherit the land the LORD your God is giving you. {16:21} Do not plant any tree near the altar of the LORD your God that you will make. {16:22} Do not set up any sacred pillar; the LORD your God hates such things.

{17:1} Do not sacrifice to the LORD your God any bull or sheep that has a defect or is unhealthy, for that is an abomination to the LORD your God. {17:2} If you find a man or woman among you, within any of your towns that the LORD your God is giving you, who has committed wickedness in the sight of the LORD by breaking His covenant, {17:3} and has gone and served other gods, worshiping either the sun, moon, or any of the stars, which I have not commanded, {17:4} and you hear about it and investigate carefully, and find that it is true, that such an abomination has been committed in Israel, {17:5} then you must bring that man or woman to your gates and stone them to death. {17:6} At the testimony of two or three witnesses, the one deserving death shall be put to death; but if there is only one witness, that person shall not be put to death. {17:7} The hands of the witnesses shall be the first to strike the blow against them, and then the hands of all the people. This is how you will remove the evil from among you. {17:8} If a case arises that is too difficult for you to judge, involving matters of blood, legal disputes, or physical injuries, that are controversial within your towns, then you shall go up to the place that the LORD your God will choose; {17:9} and you will go to the priests, the Levites, and the judge who is in those days, and ask them for a ruling. They will give you the sentence of judgment. {17:10} You must do according to the sentence they declare to you from that place which the LORD will choose, and you must be careful to do everything they instruct you. {17:11} You shall follow their instructions according to the law they teach you and the judgment they tell you; do not turn aside from the sentence they give you, either to the right or the left. {17:12} The person who acts presumptuously and does not listen to the priest who stands to minister before the LORD your God or to the judge shall die, and you must remove the evil from Israel. {17:13} All the people shall hear of it and fear, and they will no longer act presumptuously. {17:14} When you enter the land that the LORD your God is giving you, and you take possession of it and settle there, you may say, "I will set a king over me, like all the nations around me." {17:15} You must set as king over you the one whom the LORD your God chooses, from among your fellow Israelites; do not choose a foreigner who is not one of your own. {17:16} The king must not acquire many horses for himself or make the people return to Egypt to get more horses, because the LORD has said to you, "You shall not return that way again." {17:17} The king must not take many wives, or his heart will turn away; nor shall he accumulate large amounts of silver and gold for himself. {17:18} When he takes the throne of his kingdom, he must write for himself a copy of this law on a scroll taken from the priests, the Levites. {17:19} It shall be with him, and he shall read it all the days of his life, so he may learn to revere the LORD his God and follow carefully all the words of this law and these decrees. {17:20} His heart must not be lifted above his fellow Israelites, and he must not turn from the law to the right or to the left, so that he and his descendants may reign a long time over his kingdom in Israel.

{18:1} The priests, the Levites, and all the tribe of Levi will have no part or inheritance with Israel; they will eat the offerings made by fire to the LORD and their inheritance. {18:2} Therefore, they will have no inheritance among their fellow Israelites; the LORD is their inheritance, as He has said to them. {18:3} This is what the priests are entitled to from the people, from those who offer a sacrifice, whether it is an ox or a sheep; they shall give the priest the shoulder, the two cheeks, and the stomach. {18:4} You must also give him the first fruits of your grain, your wine, and your oil, as well as the first of the fleece from your sheep. {18:5} For the LORD your God has chosen him out of all your tribes to stand and minister in the name of the LORD, he and his sons forever. {18:6} If a Levite comes from any of your towns in Israel where he has been living and comes with all his heart to the place that the LORD will choose, {18:7} he shall minister in the name of the LORD his God, just like all his fellow Levites who stand there before the LORD. {18:8} They will have equal portions to eat, in addition to what comes from the sale of their family estate. {18:9} When you enter the land that the LORD your God is giving you, do not learn to imitate the detestable practices of those nations. {18:10} Do not let anyone be found among you who sacrifices their son or daughter in the fire, who practices divination, or is an astrologer, or a sorcerer, or a witch, {18:11} or a charmer, or a medium, or a wizard, or a necromancer. {18:12} For those who do these things are detestable to the LORD; and because of these detestable practices, the LORD your God will drive them out before you. {18:13} You must be blameless before the LORD your God. {18:14} The nations you will dispossess listen to those who practice divination and to sorcerers, but as for you, the LORD your God has not permitted you to do so. {18:15} The LORD your God will raise up for you a prophet like me from among your fellow Israelites; you must listen to him. {18:16} This is what you asked of the LORD your God at Horeb on the day of the assembly, saying, "Do not let me hear the voice of the LORD my God, nor let me see this great fire anymore, or I will die." {18:17} The LORD said to me, "What they say is good." {18:18} I will raise up for them a prophet like you from among their fellow Israelites, and I will put my words in his mouth; he will tell them everything I command him. {18:19} I myself will hold accountable anyone who does not listen to my words that the prophet speaks in my name. {18:20} But if a prophet presumes to speak in my name anything I have not commanded, or speaks in the name of other gods, that prophet must die. {18:21} If you say in your heart, "How will we know if a message has not been spoken by the LORD?" {18:22} When a prophet speaks in the name of the LORD, if the message does not come true or does not happen, that is a message the LORD has not spoken; the prophet has spoken presumptuously. Do not be afraid of him.

{19:1} When the LORD your God has destroyed the nations whose land He is giving you, and you take possession of their cities and houses, {19:2} you must set aside three cities in the middle of your land that the LORD your God is giving you to possess. {19:3} You shall prepare a road and divide the land the LORD your God is giving you into three parts so that anyone who kills can flee there. {19:4} This is the case of someone who can flee there and live: if someone accidentally kills their neighbor—someone they did not hate in the past— {19:5} like when a man goes into the woods with his neighbor to chop wood, and the axe head slips off the handle and strikes his neighbor, causing their death, that person may flee to one of those cities and live. {19:6} Otherwise, the blood avenger might pursue the killer with a hot heart and catch them, since the road is long, and kill them, even though they did not deserve death because they did not hate their neighbor previously. {19:7} Therefore, I command you to set aside three cities. {19:8} If the LORD your God enlarges your territory as He swore to your ancestors and gives you all the land He promised them, {19:9} and if you keep all these commandments that I command you today, to love the LORD your God and walk in His ways, then you shall add three more cities to these three. {19:10} This is to prevent innocent blood from being shed in your land that the LORD your God is giving you as an inheritance, so that blood will not be on you. {19:11} However, if someone hates their neighbor, lies in wait for them, rises up against them, and strikes them mortally so they die, and then flees to one of these cities, {19:12} the elders of their city shall send for them and deliver them into the hands of the blood avenger, so they may die. {19:13} You must not show pity; rather, you shall remove the guilt of innocent blood from Israel so that it may go well with you. {19:14} You shall not move your neighbor's boundary stone that has been set in your inheritance, which you will receive in the land the LORD your God is giving you to possess. {19:15} A single witness shall not rise up against a person for any wrongdoing or sin; the matter must be established by the testimony of two or three witnesses. {19:16} If a false witness rises up against someone to testify falsely, {19:17} then both parties involved in the dispute shall stand before the LORD, before the priests and judges who are in office at that time. {19:18} The judges shall carefully investigate; if the witness is found to be false and has given false testimony against their brother, {19:19} then you shall do to them as they intended to do to their brother. You must remove the evil from among you. {19:20} The rest shall hear and fear and never again commit such evil among you. {19:21} You must not show pity; life shall be for life, eye for eye, tooth for tooth, hand for hand, foot for foot.

{20:1} When you go out to battle against your enemies and see horses, chariots, and a people more numerous than you, do not be afraid of them, for the LORD your God is with you; He brought you up out of the land of Egypt. {20:2} As you approach the battle, the priest shall come forward and speak to the people, {20:3} saying, "Hear, O Israel! You are approaching this day to battle against your enemies. Let not your hearts faint; do not fear or tremble, nor be terrified because of them. {20:4} For the LORD your God goes with you to fight for you against your enemies, to save you." {20:5} The officers shall then speak to the people, asking, "What man has built a new house and has not dedicated it? Let him go home, lest he die in battle and someone else dedicate it. {20:6} And what man has planted a vineyard and has not yet eaten from it? Let him go home, lest he die in battle and someone else eat from it. {20:7} And what man is betrothed to a wife but has not taken her? Let him go home, lest he die in battle and someone else take her." {20:8} The officers will also ask, "What man is fearful and fainthearted? Let him go home, so that his brother's hearts do not faint as well." {20:9} After the officers finish speaking to the people, they shall appoint captains to lead the armies. {20:10} When you approach a city to fight against it, proclaim peace to it. {20:11} If it accepts your offer of peace and opens its gates to you, then all the people found there will become your subjects and serve you. {20:12} But if it refuses to make peace and chooses to make war against you, then you shall besiege it. {20:13} When the LORD your God delivers it into your hands, you shall kill every male with the sword. {20:14} However, you may take the women, children, livestock, and all the goods in the city as spoils for yourselves; you shall eat the spoils from your enemies, which the LORD your God has given you. {20:15} You shall do this to all the cities that are very far from you, which are not part of the cities of these nations. {20:16} But for the cities of the people that the LORD your God is giving you as an inheritance, you shall not leave anything alive that breathes. {20:17} You shall completely destroy them, including the Hittites, Amorites, Canaanites, Perizzites, Hivites, and Jebusites, as the LORD your God has commanded you, {20:18} so that they do not teach you to do all the abominations they have done for their gods, leading you to sin against the LORD your God. {20:19} When you besiege a city for a long time in order to capture it, do not destroy its trees by wielding an axe against them, for you may eat from them, and you must not cut them down (for the tree of the field is a person's life) to use in the siege. {20:20} Only destroy the trees you know are not fruit-bearing; cut them down and build siege works against the city that is making war with you until it is subdued.

{21:1} If a person is found murdered in the land that the LORD your God is giving you to possess, lying in the field, and it is not known who killed him, {21:2} then your elders and judges shall come forward and measure the distances to the nearby cities. {21:3} The city closest to the slain man shall have its elders take a heifer that has never been worked or yoked. {21:4} The elders of that city will bring the heifer down to a valley that is rough and uncultivated, and there they shall kill the heifer. {21:5} The priests, who are the sons of Levi, shall come near; they have been chosen by the LORD your God to minister and bless in His name, and by their word every dispute and injury shall be resolved. {21:6} All the elders of the city nearest to the slain man shall wash their hands over the heifer that was killed in the valley, {21:7} and they shall declare, "Our hands have not shed this blood, nor have our eyes seen it." {21:8} "Be merciful, O LORD, to Your people Israel, whom You have redeemed, and do not hold innocent blood against them." The blood will be forgiven them. {21:9} This will remove the guilt of innocent blood from among you when you do what is right in the sight of the LORD. {21:10} When you go out to battle against your enemies, and the LORD your God delivers them into your hands, and you take them captive, {21:11} and you see among the captives a beautiful woman and desire her as your wife, {21:12} then you shall bring her home to your house; she shall shave her head and trim her nails, {21:13} and remove the clothes of her captivity. She shall stay in your house and mourn for her father and mother for a full month. After that, you may go in to her, and she shall be your wife. {21:14} If you are not pleased with her, you shall let her go wherever she wants, but you must not sell her for money or treat her as merchandise because you have humbled her. {21:15} If a man has two wives, one loved and the other hated, and both have borne him children, and if the firstborn son is from the hated wife, {21:16} then when he divides his inheritance among his sons, he must not give the son of the loved wife the rights of the firstborn ahead of the son of the hated wife, who is the actual firstborn. {21:17} He must acknowledge the son of the hated wife as the firstborn by giving him a double portion of all he has, for he is the beginning of his strength; the rights of the firstborn belong to him. {21:18} If a man has a stubborn and rebellious son who will not obey his father or mother, and who, when they discipline him, will not listen to them, {21:19} then his parents shall take hold of him and bring him to the elders of the city at the gate of his home. {21:20} They shall say to the elders, "This son of ours is stubborn and rebellious; he will not obey our voice; he is a glutton and a drunkard." {21:21} Then all the men of the city shall stone him to death; thus, you will remove evil from among you, and all Israel shall hear and fear. {21:22} If a man has committed a crime deserving death and is executed, and you hang him on a tree, {21:23} his body must not remain on the tree overnight, but you must surely bury him that day, for anyone who is hanged is under God's curse; you must not defile the land that the LORD your God is giving you as an inheritance.

{22:1} You must not ignore your brother's ox or sheep if they go astray; you should definitely bring them back to your brother. {22:2} If your brother is not nearby, or if you don't know him, then you should take the animal to your own house, and it will stay with you until your brother comes looking for it, and you will return it to him. {22:3} You should do the same with his donkey, clothing, and anything else your brother has lost that you find; you cannot ignore it. {22:4} You must not see your brother's donkey or ox fall down on the road and ignore it; you must help him lift it up again. {22:5} A woman must not wear anything that pertains to a man, and a man must not wear a woman's garment, for anyone who does this is an abomination to the LORD your God. {22:6} If you happen upon a bird's nest on the way, whether in a tree or on the ground, with the mother bird sitting on the young or on the eggs, you must not take the mother with the young. {22:7} You must let the mother go and take the young for yourself so that it may go well with you, and you may prolong your days. {22:8} When you build a new house, you must make a railing for your roof so that you do not bring blood guilt upon your house if someone falls from it. {22:9} You must not plant your vineyard with different kinds of seeds, or else the fruit of your seeds and the fruit of your vineyard will be defiled. {22:10} You must not plow with an ox and a donkey together. {22:11} You must not wear garments made of two kinds of material, like wool and linen mixed together. {22:12} You must make tassels on the four corners of your clothing that you wear. {22:13} If a man marries a woman, has sexual relations with her, and then comes to hate her, {22:14} and falsely accuses her and slanders her by saying, "I married this woman, and found she was not a virgin," {22:15} then the father and mother of the young woman shall bring out the evidence of her virginity to the elders of the city at the gate. {22:16} The girl's father shall say to the elders, "I gave my daughter to this man as a wife, and he hates her. {22:17} He has accused her falsely, saying, 'I did not find your daughter a virgin,' but here are the signs of my daughter's virginity." They shall spread the cloth before the elders of the city. {22:18} The elders of the city shall take that man and punish him; {22:19} they shall fine him a hundred shekels of silver and give them to the girl's father because he has slandered a virgin of Israel, and she shall remain his wife; he may not divorce her all his days. {22:20} But if this charge is true and no evidence of her virginity is found, {22:21} they shall bring the girl to the door of her father's house, and the men of her city shall stone her to death because she has committed a disgraceful act in Israel by being promiscuous in her father's house; thus, you will remove the evil from among you. {22:22} If a man is found lying with a woman who is married to another man, both the man and the woman shall die; you must remove the evil from Israel. {22:23} If a virgin is engaged to a man and another man finds her in the city and lies with her, {22:24} you shall bring them both to the gate of that city and stone them to death; the young woman because she did not cry out for help in the city, and the man because he humiliated his neighbor's wife; thus, you will remove the evil from among you. {22:25} But if a man finds the engaged young woman in the field and forces her and lies with her, only the man who lay with her shall die. {22:26} You must do nothing to the young woman; there is no sin worthy of death for her, for just as a man rises against his neighbor and kills him, so is this matter. {22:27} For he found her in the field, and the engaged young woman cried out, but there was no one to save her. {22:28} If a man finds a virgin who is not engaged, takes hold of her, and lies with her, and they are discovered, {22:29} the man who lay with her shall pay the girl's father fifty shekels of silver, and she shall become his wife because he has humiliated her; he may not divorce her all his days. {22:30} A man must not take his father's wife or uncover his father's nakedness.

{23:1} No one who has been injured in the genitals or who has had their private parts cut off may enter the congregation of the LORD. {23:2} A person born out of wedlock (bastard) may not enter the congregation of the LORD; even to the tenth generation, they shall not be permitted to enter the congregation of the LORD. {23:3} An Ammonite or Moabite may not enter the congregation of the LORD; even to their tenth generation, they shall not enter the congregation of the LORD forever. {23:4} This is because they did not meet you with bread and water on your journey when you came out of Egypt, and because they hired Balaam, the son of Beor from Pethor in Mesopotamia, to curse you. {23:5} However, the LORD your God did not listen to Balaam; instead, the LORD your God turned the curse into a blessing for you because He loved you. {23:6} You must not seek their peace or prosperity for all time. {23:7} You must not despise an Edomite, for he is your brother; and you must not despise an Egyptian because you were once a stranger in his land. {23:8} The children born to them may enter the congregation of the LORD in the third generation. {23:9} When the army goes out to battle against your enemies, be sure to avoid any wicked thing. {23:10} If there is a man among you who is unclean due to nighttime impurity, he must go outside the camp and not come inside. {23:11} But at evening, he must wash with water; and when the sun sets, he may return to the camp. {23:12} You must also have a designated place outside the camp to go relieve yourself. {23:13} You should carry a tool with you; when you need to relieve yourself, you shall dig there and cover up what comes from you. {23:14} For the LORD your God walks in the midst of your camp to deliver you and to hand over your enemies to you; therefore, your camp must be holy, so that He does not see anything unclean among you and turn away from you. {23:15} You must not return a runaway slave to his master. {23:16} He shall live with you, wherever he chooses within your gates, in the place he likes best; you must not oppress him. {23:17} There shall be no prostitute among the daughters of Israel, nor shall there be any male shrine prostitute among the sons of Israel. {23:18} You must not bring the earnings of a prostitute or the price of a dog into the house of the LORD your God to fulfill any vow, for both of these are detestable to the LORD your God. {23:19} You must not lend to your brother with interest; whether it be money, food, or anything else lent at interest. {23:20} You may lend to a foreigner with interest, but to your brother, you must not lend with interest, so that the LORD your God may bless you in everything you put your hand to in the land you are entering to possess. {23:21} When you make a vow to the LORD your God, do not delay in fulfilling it, for the LORD your God will surely demand it of you, and it would be sin for you. {23:22} But if you choose not to vow, it is not a sin for you. {23:23} You must keep your word and fulfill what you promised, even a freewill offering, as you vowed to the LORD your God with your mouth. {23:24} When you enter your neighbor's vineyard, you may eat grapes to your fill, but you must not put any in your container. {23:25} When you go into your neighbor's grain field, you may pick the ears with your hand, but you must not use a sickle on your neighbor's grain.

{24:1} When a man marries a woman and later finds that she does not please him because he has discovered some uncleanness (something shameful) in her, he may write her a certificate of divorce, give it to her, and send her away from his house. {24:2} After she leaves his house, she is free to marry another man. {24:3} If her second husband dislikes her, writes her a certificate of divorce, and sends her away, or if he dies, {24:4} her first husband, who divorced her, cannot take her back as his wife after she has been with another man; this is considered an abomination before the LORD. You must not bring guilt upon the land that the LORD your God is giving you as an inheritance. {24:5} When a man takes a new wife, he should not go to war or be assigned any duties; he should be free at home for one year to make his wife happy. {24:6} No one shall take a lower or upper millstone as collateral, for doing so would endanger a man's life. {24:7} If a man is caught stealing one of his fellow Israelites and sells him or treats him as merchandise, that thief shall die; this will remove evil from among you. {24:8} Be careful about the disease of leprosy; observe it diligently and follow all the instructions given by the priests and Levites, just as I commanded them. {24:9} Remember what the LORD your God did to Miriam on the journey after you left Egypt. {24:10} When you lend something to your brother, do not enter his house to get his collateral. {24:11} Instead, stand outside, and let him bring the collateral to you. {24:12} If the man is poor, do not keep his collateral overnight. {24:13} You must return the collateral to him by sunset so that he can sleep in his own clothes and bless you; this will be counted as righteousness before the LORD your God. {24:14} Do not oppress a hired servant who is poor and needy, whether he is one of your fellow Israelites or a foreigner residing in your towns. {24:15} You must pay him his wages on the same day; do not let the sun set without paying him, for he is poor and relies on it. If he cries out to the LORD against you, it will be counted as sin for you. {24:16} Parents should not be put to death for the sins of their children, nor shall children be put to death for the sins of their parents; each person will die for their own sin. {24:17} Do not twist justice against a foreigner or an orphan, and do not take a widow's garment as collateral. {24:18} Remember that you were once a slave in Egypt, and the LORD your God redeemed you from there; that is why I command you to do these things. {24:19} When you harvest your field and forget a sheaf in the field, do not go back to get it; it should be left for the foreigner, the orphan, and the widow, so that the LORD your God may bless you in all the work of your hands. {24:20} When you harvest your olives, do not go over the branches a second time; leave them for the foreigner, the orphan, and the widow. {24:21} When you gather grapes from your vineyard, do not pick the vines clean; leave what is left for the foreigner, the orphan, and the widow. {24:22} And remember that you were a slave in Egypt; that is why I command you to do these things.

{25:1} If there is a dispute between two men and they come to court for judgment, the judges shall declare the righteous person justified and condemn the wicked one. {25:2} If the wicked person deserves to be punished, the judge shall have him lie down and be beaten publicly, according to the severity of his wrongdoing, up to a specific limit. {25:3} He may give him forty lashes, but not exceed that number; if he does, and beats him more than this, your brother will be dishonored in your eyes. {25:4} You must not muzzle an ox while it is treading out the grain. {25:5} If brothers live together and one of them dies without having a child, the widow of the deceased shall not marry outside the family; instead, her husband's brother shall go to her and marry her, fulfilling his duty as her brother-in-law. {25:6} The firstborn son she bears shall carry on the name of his deceased brother so that his name will not be wiped out from Israel. {25:7} If the man does not want to marry his brother's widow, she shall go to the elders at the city gate and say, "My brother-in-law refuses to raise up a name for his brother in Israel; he will not fulfill his duty as a brother-in-law." {25:8} The elders will then call him and talk to him, and if he insists that he does not want to marry her, {25:9} the brother's widow shall approach him in front of the elders, remove his sandal from his foot, spit in his face, and say, "This is how it will be done to the man who will not build up his brother's family." {25:10} From then on, he will be known in Israel as "the man whose sandal was removed." {25:11} If two men are fighting and the wife of one comes to rescue her husband from the one attacking him, and she reaches out and grabs him by his private parts, {25:12} you must cut off her hand; do not show pity. {25:13} You must not have differing weights in your bag, one heavy and one light. {25:14} You must not have differing measures in your house, one large and one small. {25:15} You must have honest and accurate weights and measures so that your days may be prolonged in the land that the LORD your God is giving you. {25:16} For all who do these things and act unjustly are an abomination to the LORD your God. {25:17} Remember what Amalek did to you on your way out of Egypt; {25:18} how he attacked you and struck down those who were lagging behind when you were tired and weary, and he did not fear God. {25:19} Therefore, when the LORD your God gives you rest from all your enemies surrounding you in the land He is giving you as an inheritance, you shall wipe out the memory of Amalek from under heaven; do not forget this.

{26:1} When you enter the land that the LORD your God is giving you as an inheritance and you take possession of it and settle there, {26:2} you shall take some of the first fruits of all the produce of the land that the LORD your God has given you, put it in a basket, and go to the place that the LORD your God will choose to place His name. {26:3} You shall go to the priest who is serving at that time and say to him, "I declare today to the LORD your God that I have come to the land the LORD swore to our ancestors to give us." {26:4} The priest will take the basket from your hand and set it down before the altar of the LORD your God. {26:5} Then you shall declare before the LORD your God, "My father was a wandering Aramean (Syrian); he went down to Egypt with a few people and lived there and became a great nation, mighty and numerous. {26:6} The Egyptians treated us badly, oppressed us, and imposed hard labor on us. {26:7} When we cried out to the LORD, the God of our ancestors, He heard our cry and saw our misery, toil, and oppression. {26:8} So the LORD brought us out of Egypt with a mighty hand, an outstretched arm, and with great terror, signs, and wonders. {26:9} He brought us to this place and gave us this land, a land flowing with milk and honey. {26:10} And now I bring the first fruits of the land that You, LORD, have given me." You shall set it before the LORD your God and worship before Him. {26:11} You shall rejoice in all the good things the LORD your God has given you, your household, the Levites, and the foreigners residing among you. {26:12} After you have finished paying all the tithes of your crops in the third year, the year of tithing, and have given it to the Levite, the foreigner, the orphan, and the widow so they may eat within your towns and be satisfied, {26:13} you shall say before the LORD your God, "I have removed the sacred portion from my house and given it to the Levite, the foreigner, the orphan, and the widow, in accordance with all Your commandments that You have given me; I have not transgressed any of Your commands or forgotten them. {26:14} I have not eaten any of the sacred portion while in mourning, nor have I removed any of it for an unclean use, nor have I offered any of it for the dead. I have obeyed the LORD my God and have done everything You commanded me." {26:15} Look down from Your holy dwelling place, from heaven, and bless Your people Israel and the land You have given us, as You promised our ancestors, a land flowing with milk and honey. {26:16} Today the LORD your God commands you to follow these decrees and laws; therefore, you shall be careful to follow them with all your heart and soul. {26:17} You have declared this day that the LORD is your God and that you will walk in His ways, obey His statutes, commands, and laws, and listen to His voice. {26:18} And the LORD has declared this day that you are His people, His treasured possession, as He promised you, and that you are to keep all His commands. {26:19} He will set you in praise, fame, and honor high above all the nations He has made, and you will be a holy people to the LORD your God, as He has spoken.

{27:1} Moses and the elders of Israel commanded the people, saying, "Keep all the commandments that I am giving you today. {27:2} When you cross over the Jordan into the land that the LORD your God is giving you, set up large stones and coat them with plaster. {27:3} You shall write all the words of this law on those stones after you have crossed over, so you may enter the land that the LORD your God is giving you, a land flowing with milk and honey, as the LORD, the God of your ancestors, has promised you. {27:4} So when you have crossed the Jordan, set up these stones that I am commanding you today on Mount Ebal, and coat them with plaster. {27:5} There you shall build an altar to the LORD your God, an altar made of stones; do not use any iron tools on them. {27:6} You must build the altar of the LORD your God using whole stones and offer burnt offerings on it to the LORD your God. {27:7} You shall also offer peace offerings, eat there, and rejoice before the LORD your God. {27:8} Write all the words of this law clearly on the stones. {27:9} Moses and the priests, the Levites, said to all Israel, "Be silent and listen, O Israel; today you have become the people of the LORD your God. {27:10} You shall therefore obey the voice of the LORD your God and follow His commandments and statutes that I am giving you today." {27:11} On that same day, Moses commanded the people, saying, {27:12} "These tribes shall stand on Mount Gerizim to bless the people when you cross over the Jordan: Simeon, Levi, Judah, Issachar, Joseph, and Benjamin. {27:13} And these tribes shall stand on Mount Ebal to pronounce curses: Reuben, Gad, Asher, Zebulun, Dan, and Naphtali. {27:14} The Levites shall speak and say to all the people of Israel in a loud voice, {27:15} 'Cursed is the man who makes a carved or cast idol, an abomination to the LORD, the work of a craftsman, and sets it up in secret.' And all the people shall respond, 'Amen.' {27:16} 'Cursed is he who dishonors his father or mother.' And all the people shall say, 'Amen.' {27:17} 'Cursed is he who moves his neighbor's boundary marker.' And all the people shall say, 'Amen.' {27:18} 'Cursed is he who leads the blind astray on the road.' And all the people shall say, 'Amen.' {27:19} 'Cursed is he who perverts the justice due to the foreigner, the orphan, and the widow.' And all the people shall say, 'Amen.' {27:20} 'Cursed is he who sleeps with his father's wife, for he dishonors his father.' And all the people shall say, 'Amen.' {27:21} 'Cursed is he who has sexual relations with any animal.' And all the people shall say, 'Amen.' {27:22} 'Cursed is he who sleeps with his sister, whether she is the daughter of his father or mother.' And all the people shall say, 'Amen.' {27:23} 'Cursed is he who sleeps with his mother-in-law.' And all the people shall say, 'Amen.' {27:24} 'Cursed is he who secretly attacks his neighbor.' And all the people shall say, 'Amen.' {27:25} 'Cursed is he who accepts a bribe to kill an innocent person.' And all the people shall say, 'Amen.' {27:26} 'Cursed is he who does not uphold the words of this law by doing them.' And all the people shall say, 'Amen.'

{28:1} If you listen carefully to the voice of the LORD your God and follow all His commandments that I am giving you today, then the LORD your God will elevate you above all the nations on the earth. {28:2} All these blessings will come upon you and overtake you if you listen to the voice of the LORD your God. {28:3} You will be blessed in the city and blessed in the field. {28:4} The fruit of your body, your crops, and the livestock—your cattle and sheep—will be blessed. {28:5} Your basket and your store will be blessed.

{28:6} You will be blessed when you come in and blessed when you go out. {28:7} The LORD will make your enemies who rise up against you be defeated before you; they will come at you one way and flee from you seven ways. {28:8} The LORD will command blessings upon you in your storehouses and in all that you put your hand to; He will bless you in the land that the LORD your God is giving you. {28:9} The LORD will establish you as His holy people, as He promised you, if you keep the commandments of the LORD your God and walk in His ways. {28:10} All the peoples of the earth will see that you are called by the name of the LORD, and they will fear you. {28:11} The LORD will make you abundantly prosperous in goods, in the fruit of your body, your livestock, and your crops, in the land that the LORD swore to your ancestors to give you. {28:12} The LORD will open His good treasure, the heavens, to give rain to your land in its season and to bless all the work of your hands; you will lend to many nations, but you will not borrow. {28:13} The LORD will make you the head and not the tail; you will be above only and not beneath, if you listen to the commandments of the LORD your God, which I am giving you today, and follow them. {28:14} Do not turn aside from any of the words I am commanding you today, to the right or to the left, to follow other gods and serve them. {28:15} However, if you do not listen to the voice of the LORD your God and do not follow all His commandments and statutes that I am giving you today, all these curses will come upon you and overtake you. {28:16} You will be cursed in the city and cursed in the field. {28:17} Your basket and your store will be cursed. {28:18} The fruit of your body, your crops, and the increase of your livestock will be cursed. {28:19} You will be cursed when you come in and cursed when you go out. {28:20} The LORD will send upon you cursing, confusion, and rebuke in all that you undertake until you are destroyed and perish quickly because of the wickedness of your actions in forsaking Him. {28:21} The LORD will make pestilence cling to you until He has consumed you from the land you are going to possess. {28:22} The LORD will strike you with wasting diseases, fever, inflammation, extreme heat, and plagues, and they will pursue you until you perish. {28:23} The sky over your head will be like bronze, and the ground beneath you will be like iron. {28:24} The LORD will make the rain on your land turn to dust and powder; it will come down on you from the sky until you are destroyed. {28:25} The LORD will cause you to be defeated before your enemies; you will go out against them one way and flee before them seven ways, and you will be a horror to all the kingdoms of the earth. {28:26} Your dead body will be food for all the birds of the air and the beasts of the earth, and no one will scare them away. {28:27} The LORD will strike you with the boils of Egypt, tumors, scabs, and itch that you cannot be healed from. {28:28} The LORD will strike you with madness, blindness, and confusion of mind. {28:29} You will grope at noon as the blind gropes in darkness and will not succeed in your ways; you will be continually oppressed and robbed, and no one will save you. {28:30} You will betroth a wife, but another man will sleep with her; you will build a house, but you will not live in it; you will plant a vineyard, but you will not gather its grapes. {28:31} Your ox will be slaughtered before your eyes, but you will not eat any of it; your donkey will be violently taken away from you, and it will not be restored to you; your sheep will be given to your enemies, and you will have no one to rescue them. {28:32} Your sons and daughters will be given to another people, and you will look at them all day long, but you will have no strength in your hand. {28:33} The fruit of your land and all your labor will be consumed by a nation you do not know, and you will be continually oppressed and crushed. {28:34} You will be driven mad by what your eyes will see. {28:35} The LORD will strike you on the knees and legs with a painful boil that cannot be healed, from the soles of your feet to the top of your head. {28:36} The LORD will bring you and your king, whom you set over you, to a nation you or your ancestors have not known, and there you will serve other gods of wood and stone. {28:37} You will become an astonishment, a proverb, and a byword among all the peoples where the LORD will drive you. {28:38} You will carry much seed into the field, but gather very little, for the locust will consume it. {28:39} You will plant vineyards and cultivate them, but will neither drink the wine nor gather the grapes, for worms will eat them. {28:40} You will have olive trees throughout your territory, but you will not anoint yourself with the oil, for your olives will drop off. {28:41} You will father sons and daughters, but you will not enjoy them, for they will go into captivity. {28:42} All your trees and the fruit of your land will be eaten by locusts. {28:43} The foreigner residing among you will rise higher and higher above you, while you sink lower and lower. {28:44} He will lend to you, but you will not lend to him; he will be the head, and you will be the tail. {28:45} Moreover, all these curses will come upon you and pursue you and overtake you until you are destroyed, because you did not listen to the voice of the LORD your God to keep His commandments and statutes that He commanded you. {28:46} They will be a sign and a wonder upon you and your descendants forever. {28:47} Because you did not serve the LORD your God with joy and gladness of heart, for the abundance of everything; {28:48} therefore you will serve your enemies whom the LORD will send against you, in hunger, thirst, nakedness, and lack of all things; He will put a yoke of iron on your neck until He has destroyed you. {28:49} The LORD will bring a nation against you from afar, from the end of the earth, swift as an eagle flies; a nation whose language you do not understand; {28:50} a fierce nation that will not respect the old or show favor to the young. {28:51} They will consume the fruit of your livestock and your crops until you are destroyed, and they will leave you neither grain, wine, oil, nor the increase of your cattle or flocks until they have destroyed you. {28:52} They will besiege you in all your towns until your high and fortified walls fall, the walls you trusted in throughout your land; and they will besiege you in all your towns throughout the land that the LORD your God has given you. {28:53} You will eat the fruit of your own body, the flesh of your sons and daughters, whom the LORD your God has given you, during the siege and in the distress that your enemies will inflict on you. {28:54} The most tender and delicate man among you will have an evil eye toward his brother, toward his wife, and toward the remaining children he has. {28:55} He will not give any of them the flesh of his children whom he will eat, because he has nothing left during the siege and in the distress that your enemies will inflict on you in all your towns. {28:56} The most tender and delicate woman among you, who would not venture to set her foot on the ground because of her delicateness, will have an evil eye toward her husband, her son, and her daughter, {28:57} and toward her newborn and her children; she will secretly eat them for lack of everything during the siege and the distress that your enemies will inflict on you in your towns. {28:58} If you do not carefully observe all the words of this law that are written in this book and fear this glorious and awesome name, THE LORD YOUR GOD, {28:59} then the LORD will bring upon you and your descendants extraordinary plagues, severe and lasting plagues, and chronic sicknesses. {28:60} He will bring upon you all the diseases of Egypt that you feared, and they will cling to you. {28:61} Also, every sickness and plague that is not written in this book of the law will come upon you until you are destroyed. {28:62} You will be left with few in number, whereas you were as numerous as the stars of heaven because you did not obey the voice of the LORD your God. {28:63} It will come to pass that as the LORD rejoiced over you to do good and multiply you, so the LORD will rejoice over you to destroy you and bring you to nothing; and you will be uprooted from the land you are going to possess. {28:64} The LORD will scatter you among all nations, from one end of the earth to the other; there you will serve other gods, which neither you nor your ancestors have known, gods of wood and stone. {28:65} Among those nations, you will find no peace, and your foot will find no rest; but the LORD will give you a trembling heart, failing eyes, and a sorrowful mind. {28:66} Your life will hang in doubt before you; you will fear night and day, and have no assurance of your life. {28:67} In the morning, you will wish it were evening, and in the evening you will wish it were morning, because of the fear that will fill your heart and the sight of what your eyes will see. {28:68} The LORD will bring you back to Egypt in ships, by the way He said you would never see again; there you will be sold to your enemies as male and female slaves, but no one will buy you.

{29:1} These are the words of the covenant that the LORD commanded Moses to establish with the Israelites in the land of Moab, in addition to the covenant He made with them at Horeb. {29:2} Moses called all Israel and said to them, "You have seen all that the LORD did before your eyes in Egypt, against Pharaoh, his servants, and all his land; {29:3} the great trials your eyes have witnessed, the signs, and those mighty miracles. {29:4} Yet the LORD has not given you a heart to understand, eyes to see, or ears to hear to this day. {29:5} I have led you for forty years in the wilderness; your clothes have not worn out on you, and your sandals have not worn off your feet. {29:6} You have not eaten bread or drunk wine or strong drink, so that you may know that I am the LORD your God. {29:7} When you arrived at this place, Sihon king of Heshbon and Og king of Bashan came out against us for battle, but we defeated them. {29:8} We took their land and gave it as an inheritance to the Reubenites, the Gadites, and the half-tribe of Manasseh. {29:9} Therefore, keep the words of this covenant and do them, so that you may prosper in all that you do. {29:10} Today, you stand before the LORD your God: your tribal leaders, elders, officers, and all the men of Israel, {29:11} your little ones, your wives, and the foreigners in your camp, from the woodcutter to the water-drawer. {29:12} You are to enter into covenant with the LORD your God and into His oath, which the LORD your God makes with you today, {29:13} so that He may establish you as His people and be your God, as He promised you and swore to your ancestors, to Abraham, Isaac, and Jacob. {29:14} This covenant and oath are not just with you today; {29:15} they are also for those standing here with us today before the LORD our God, and for those not here with us today. {29:16} For you know how we lived in Egypt and how we passed through the nations you encountered; {29:17} you have seen their detestable practices and their idols, made of wood, stone, silver, and gold. {29:18} Beware that there is not among you a man, woman, family, or tribe whose heart turns away from the LORD our God to serve the gods of those nations; beware that there is not a root among you bearing poisonous fruit. {29:19} It may happen that when he hears the words of this curse, he will bless himself in his heart, saying, 'I will have peace, though I follow the stubbornness of my heart,' adding drunkenness to thirst. {29:20} The LORD will not spare him, but His anger and jealousy will burn against that man, and all the curses written in this book will fall upon him, and the LORD will blot out his name from under heaven. {29:21} The LORD will set him apart for evil from all the tribes of Israel, according to all the curses of the covenant written in this book of the law. {29:22} The future generations of your children, who rise up after you, and the foreigners from distant lands will see the plagues of that land and the sicknesses the LORD has brought upon it; {29:23} they will see that the whole land is brimstone, salt, and burning, not sown or bearing, with no grass growing in it, like the destruction of Sodom and Gomorrah, Admah, and Zeboim, which the LORD overthrew in His anger and wrath. {29:24} All nations will ask, 'Why has the LORD done this to this land? What does the heat of this great anger mean?' {29:25} People will answer, 'It is because they have forsaken the covenant of the LORD God of their ancestors, which He made with them when He brought them out of Egypt. {29:26} They went and served other gods and worshiped them, gods they did not know and that He had not given to them. {29:27} The anger of the LORD was kindled against this land, bringing upon it all the curses written in this book. {29:28} The LORD uprooted them from their land in anger, wrath, and great indignation, and cast them into another land, as it is today. {29:29} The secret things belong to the LORD our God, but the revealed things belong to us and our children forever, so that we may follow all the words of this law.

{30:1} When all these things come upon you—the blessings and the curses I have set before you—and you reflect on them among all the nations where the LORD your God has driven you, {30:2} and you return to the LORD your God and obey His voice according to all that I command you today, you and your children, with all your heart and soul, {30:3} then the LORD your God will restore your fortunes and have compassion on you; He will gather you from all the nations where the LORD your God has scattered you. {30:4} Even if you are driven out to the farthest parts of heaven, the LORD your God will gather you from there and bring you back. {30:5} The LORD your God will bring you into the land your ancestors possessed, and you will possess it; He will do you good and increase your numbers even more than your ancestors. {30:6} The LORD your God will change your heart and the hearts of your descendants so that you will love the LORD your God with all your heart and soul, enabling you to live. {30:7} The LORD your God will put all these curses on your enemies, on those who hate and persecute you. {30:8} You will return and obey the voice of the LORD, doing all His commandments that I command you today. {30:9} The LORD your God will make you abundant in every work of your hands, in the fruit of your body, your livestock, and your land, for good; the LORD will again rejoice over you for good, as He rejoiced over your ancestors. {30:10} If you obey the voice of the LORD your God and keep His commandments and statutes written in this book of the law, and if you turn to the LORD your God with all your heart and soul. {30:11} For this commandment I give you today is not too difficult for you or beyond your reach. {30:12} It is not in heaven so that you have to ask, "Who will go up to heaven for us and bring it to us so we can hear it and do it?" {30:13} Nor is it across the sea, so that you have to ask, "Who will cross the sea for us and bring it to us so we can hear it and do it?" {30:14} But the word is very near you, in your mouth and in your heart, so you can do it. {30:15} Look, I have set before you today life and good, death and evil. {30:16} I command you today to love the LORD your God, walk in His ways, and keep His commandments, statutes, and judgments, so that you may live and multiply, and the LORD your God will bless you in the land you are entering to possess. {30:17} But if your heart turns away and you do not listen, but are drawn away to worship other gods and serve them, {30:18} I declare to you today that you will surely perish; you will not prolong your days in the land you are crossing the Jordan to enter and possess. {30:19} I call heaven and earth as witnesses against you today; I have set before you life and death, blessing and cursing; therefore choose life, so that you and your descendants may live, {30:20} loving the LORD your God, obeying His voice, and holding fast to Him, for He is your life and the length of your days, that you may dwell in the land the LORD swore to your ancestors, to Abraham, Isaac, and Jacob, to give them.

{31:1} Moses went and spoke these words to all Israel. {31:2} He said to them, "Today I am 120 years old; I can no longer go in and out. The LORD has told me, 'You shall not cross this Jordan.' {31:3} The LORD your God will cross over ahead of you; He will destroy these nations before you, and you will possess their land. Joshua will lead you across, as the LORD has said. {31:4} The LORD will do to them what He did to Sihon and Og, the kings of the Amorites, and to their land, which He destroyed. {31:5} The LORD will give them over to you, and you are to do to them according to all the commandments I have given you. {31:6} Be strong and courageous; do not be afraid or terrified because of them, for the LORD your God goes with you; He will never leave you nor forsake you." {31:7} Moses called Joshua and said to him in front of all Israel, "Be strong and courageous, for you must go with this people into the land that the LORD swore to their ancestors to give them, and you will help them take possession of it. {31:8} The LORD goes before you; He will be with you; He will never leave you nor forsake you. Do not be afraid; do not be discouraged." {31:9} Moses wrote this law and gave it to the priests, the descendants of Levi, who carry the ark of the covenant of the LORD, and to all the elders of Israel. {31:10} Moses commanded them, saying, "At the end of every seven years, during the Year of Release, at the Feast of Tabernacles, {31:11} when all Israel comes to appear before the LORD your God at the place He will choose, you shall read this law before them in their hearing. {31:12} Assemble the people—men, women, children, and the foreigners residing in your towns—so they can listen and learn to fear the LORD your God and follow carefully all the words of this law. {31:13} Their children, who do not know this law, must hear it and learn to fear the LORD your God as long as you live in the land you are crossing the Jordan to possess." {31:14} The LORD said to Moses, "The time has come for you to die. Call Joshua and present yourselves at the tent of meeting so I can commission him." So Moses and Joshua went and presented themselves at the tent of meeting. {31:15} The LORD appeared at the tent in a pillar of cloud, and the cloud stood over the entrance to the tent. {31:16} The LORD said to Moses, "You are going to rest with your ancestors, and this people will rise up and turn to the gods of the foreign nations in the land they are entering. They will forsake Me and break the covenant I made with them. {31:17} My anger will be aroused against them in that day; I will forsake them and hide My face from them, and they will be destroyed. Many disasters and difficulties will come upon them, and they will say in that day, 'Have not these disasters come upon us because our God is not with us?' {31:18} I will certainly hide My face in that day because of all their wickedness in turning to other gods. {31:19} Now write down this song and teach it to the Israelites and have them sing it, so that it may be a witness for Me against them. {31:20} When I bring them into the land I swore to their ancestors, a land flowing with milk and honey, and they eat their fill and thrive, they will turn to other gods and worship them, rejecting Me and breaking My covenant. {31:21} And when many disasters and difficulties come upon them, this song will testify against them as a witness, because it will not be forgotten by their descendants. I know what they are inclined to do, even now, before I bring them into the land I swore to give them." {31:22} So Moses wrote this song that day and taught it to the Israelites. {31:23} The LORD gave Joshua son of Nun a charge and said, "Be strong and courageous, for you will bring the Israelites into the land I swore to them, and I will be with you." {31:24} When Moses had finished writing down the words of this law in a book, {31:25} he gave this command to the Levites who carry the ark of the covenant of the LORD: {31:26} "Take this Book of the Law and place it beside the ark of the covenant of the LORD your God, so it may be there as a witness against you. {31:27} For I know how rebellious and stiff-necked you are. If you have been rebellious against the LORD while I am still alive with you, how much more will you be after my death! {31:28} Assemble all the elders of your tribes and your officials so I can speak these words in their hearing and call heaven and earth to testify against them. {31:29} For I know that after my death you are sure to become corrupt and turn from the way I have commanded you; in days to come disaster will overtake you because you will do evil in the sight of the LORD, provoking Him to anger through the work of your hands." {31:30} And Moses recited the words of this song from beginning to end in the hearing of the whole assembly of Israel.

{32:1} Listen, O heavens, and I will speak; hear, O earth, the words of my mouth. {32:2} My teaching will fall like rain, my words will flow like dew, like gentle rain on young plants, and like showers on the grass. {32:3} For I will proclaim the name of the LORD; praise the greatness of our God. {32:4} He is the Rock; His work is perfect, and all His ways are just. He is a faithful God who does no wrong, upright and just is He. {32:5} They have acted corruptly toward Him; their spot is not like that of His children; they are a perverse and crooked generation. {32:6} Is this how you repay the LORD, you foolish and unwise people? Is He not your Father, your Creator, who made you and established you? {32:7} Remember the days of old; consider the years of many generations. Ask your father, and he will tell you; your elders, and they will explain to you. {32:8} When the Most High gave nations their inheritance, when He divided the human race, He set the boundaries for the peoples according to the number of the children of Israel. {32:9} For the LORD's portion is His people; Jacob is His allotted inheritance. {32:10} He found him in a desert land, in a wasteland of howling wilderness; He shielded him and cared for him; He guarded him as the apple of His eye. {32:11} Like an eagle that stirs up its nest and hovers over its young, that spreads its wings to catch them and carries them aloft, {32:12} the LORD alone guided him; no foreign god was with him. {32:13} He made him ride on the heights of the land and fed him with the produce of the fields; He nourished him with honey from the rock and with oil from the flinty crag, {32:14} with curds from the herd and milk from the flock, with fattened lambs and goats, with the finest grains of wheat. You drank the foaming blood of the grape. {32:15} But Jeshurun grew fat and kicked; filled with food, they became heavy and sleek. They abandoned the God who made them and rejected the Rock, their Savior. {32:16} They made Him jealous with their foreign gods and angered Him with their detestable idols. {32:17} They sacrificed to demons, which are not God, to gods they had not known, to new gods that had just arrived, which their ancestors did not fear. {32:18} You deserted the Rock who fathered you; you forgot the God who gave you birth. {32:19} The LORD saw this and rejected them because He was angered by His sons and daughters. {32:20} He said, "I will hide My face from them; I will see what their end will be, for they are a perverse generation, children who are unfaithful. {32:21} They made Me jealous by what is no god and angered Me with their worthless idols; I will make them envious by those who are not a people; I will make them angry by a nation that has no understanding. {32:22} For a fire has been kindled in My anger and will burn to the depths of the grave; it will devour the earth and its harvests and set afire the foundations of the mountains. {32:23} I will heap calamities upon them and spend My arrows against them. {32:24} I will send wasting famine against them, consuming pestilence and deadly plague; I will send against them the teeth of beasts and the venom of snakes that glide in the dust. {32:25} In the street the sword will make them childless; in their homes, terror will reign. Young men and young women will perish, infants and gray-haired men. {32:26} I said I would scatter them and erase their name from humanity, {32:27} but I feared the hostile reaction of their enemies, lest the adversaries misunderstand and say, 'Our own hand has triumphed; the LORD has not done all this.' {32:28} They are a nation without sense; there is no discernment in them. {32:29} If only they were wise and would understand this and discern what their end will be! {32:30} How could one man chase a thousand, or two put ten thousand to flight unless their Rock had sold them, unless the LORD had given them up? {32:31} For their rock is not like our Rock, as even our enemies concede. {32:32} Their vine comes from the vine of Sodom and from the fields of Gomorrah; their grapes are filled with poison, and their clusters are bitter. {32:33} Their wine is the venom of serpents, the deadly poison of cobras. {32:34} Have I not kept this in reserve and sealed it in My vaults? {32:35} It is Mine to avenge; I will repay. In due time their foot will slip; their day of disaster is near and their doom rushes upon them." {32:36} The LORD will vindicate His people and relent concerning His servants when He sees their strength is gone and no one is left, slave or free. {32:37} He will say, "Now where are their gods, the rock they took refuge in, {32:38} the gods who ate the fat of their sacrifices and drank the wine of their drink offerings? Let them rise up to help you; let them give you shelter. {32:39} See now that I, even I, am He, and there is no god besides Me. I put to death and I bring to life, I have wounded and I will heal, and no one can deliver out of My hand. {32:40} I lift My hand to heaven and declare: As surely as I live forever, {32:41} when I sharpen My flashing sword and My hand grasps it in judgment, I will take vengeance on My adversaries and repay those who hate Me. {32:42} I will make My arrows drunk with blood, and My sword will devour flesh, the blood of the slain and the captives, the heads of the enemy leaders." {32:43} Rejoice, you nations, with His people, for He will avenge the blood of His servants; He will take vengeance on His enemies and make atonement for His land and people. {32:44} Moses came with Hoshea son of Nun and spoke all the words of this song in the hearing of the people. {32:45} When Moses finished reciting all these words to all Israel, {32:46} he said to them, "Take to heart all the words I have solemnly declared to you this day, so that you may command your children to obey carefully all the words of this law. {32:47} They are not just idle words for you—they are your life. By them you will live long in the land you are crossing the Jordan to possess." {32:48} That same day the LORD told Moses, {32:49} "Go up to this mountain in the Abarim mountain range, to Mount Nebo in Moab, across from Jericho, and view the land of Canaan, which I am giving to the Israelites as their own. {32:50} There on the mountain that you have climbed, you will die and be gathered to your people, just as your brother Aaron died on Mount Hor and was gathered to his people. {32:51} This is because both of you broke faith with Me in the presence of the Israelites at the waters of Meribah Kadesh in the Desert of Zin and because you did not uphold My holiness among the Israelites. {32:52} Therefore, you will see the land only from a distance; you will not enter the land I am giving to the people of Israel."

{33:1} This is the blessing that Moses, the man of God, gave to the children of Israel before his death. {33:2} He said, "The LORD came from Sinai and rose up from Seir; He shone forth from Mount Paran and came with thousands of holy ones. From His right hand, He gave a fiery law. {33:3} Yes, He loved His people; all His saints are in Your hand. They sat down at Your feet, and everyone will receive Your words. {33:4} Moses commanded us a law, the inheritance of the congregation of Jacob. {33:5} He was king in Jeshurun when the leaders of the people and the tribes of Israel gathered together. {33:6} Let Reuben live and not die, and let his men be many. {33:7} This is the blessing of Judah: "Hear, LORD, the voice of Judah, and bring him to his people. Let his hands be sufficient for him, and be a help against his enemies." {33:8} Of Levi, he said, "Let your Thummim and your Urim be with your faithful one, whom You tested at Massah and contended with at the waters of Meribah; {33:9} who said to his father and mother, 'I have not seen them,' nor did he acknowledge his brothers or know his own children, for they observed Your word and kept Your covenant. {33:10} They will teach Jacob Your judgments and Israel Your law; they will put incense before You and whole burnt offerings on Your altar. {33:11} Bless, LORD, his substance and accept the work of his hands. Strike down those who rise against him and those who hate him, so that they do not rise again." {33:12} Of Benjamin, he said, "The beloved of the LORD will dwell in safety by Him; the LORD will cover him all day long, and he will dwell between His shoulders." {33:13} Of Joseph, he said, "Blessed by the LORD is his land, with the best from heaven above, with the dew and the deep lying beneath, {33:14} with the precious fruits produced by the sun and the precious things produced by the moon, {33:15} with the chief things of the ancient mountains and the precious things of the everlasting hills, {33:16} with the precious things of the earth and its fullness, and with the good will of Him who dwelt in the bush. Let the blessing come upon the head of Joseph and upon the crown of the head of the one separated from his brothers. {33:17} His glory is like the firstborn of his bull; his horns are like the horns of a wild ox. With them, he will push the people to the ends of the earth; they are the ten thousands of Ephraim, and they are the thousands of Manasseh." {33:18} Of Zebulun, he said, "Rejoice, Zebulun, in your going out, and Issachar, in your tents. {33:19} They will call people to the mountain; there they will offer sacrifices of righteousness. They will partake of the abundance of the seas and the treasures hidden in the sand." {33:20} Of Gad, he said, "Blessed be he who enlarges Gad! He dwells like a lion, tearing the arm and the crown of the head. {33:21} He provided the first part for himself, because there the lawgiver's portion was reserved. He came with the heads of the people; he executed the justice of the LORD and His judgments with Israel." {33:22} Of Dan, he said, "Dan is a lion's cub; he shall leap from Bashan." {33:23} Of Naphtali, he said, "O Naphtali, satisfied with favor and full of the blessing of the LORD; possess the west and the south." {33:24} Of Asher, he said, "Let Asher be blessed with children; let him be acceptable to his brothers, and let him dip his foot in oil. {33:25} Your shoes shall be iron and brass, and as your days, so shall your strength be." {33:26} There is no one like the God of Jeshurun, who rides across the heavens to help you, and in His majesty on the clouds. {33:27} The eternal God is your refuge, and underneath are the everlasting arms. He will drive out your enemies before you, saying, "Destroy them!" {33:28} Israel will dwell in safety alone; the fountain of Jacob will be in a land of grain and wine; His heavens will drop down dew. {33:29} Happy are you, O Israel! Who is like you, a people saved by the LORD? He is your shield and your helper, and He is the sword of your triumph. Your enemies will cower before you, and you will tread on their high places.

{34:1} Moses went up from the plains of Moab to the mountain of Nebo, to the top of Pisgah, which is opposite Jericho. The LORD showed him all the land of Gilead, as far as Dan, {34:2} and all of Naphtali, the land of Ephraim and Manasseh, and all the land of Judah, as far as the Mediterranean Sea, {34:3} and the south, including the plain of the valley of Jericho, the city of palm trees, as far as Zoar. {34:4} The LORD said to him, "This is the land I promised to Abraham, Isaac, and Jacob, saying, 'I will give it to your descendants.' I have allowed you to see it with your eyes, but you will not cross over into it." {34:5} So Moses, the servant of the LORD, died there in the land of Moab, just as the LORD had said. {34:6} He was buried in a valley in the land of Moab, opposite Bethpeor, but no one knows his burial place to this day. {34:7} Moses was one hundred and twenty years old when he died; his eyesight was clear, and he was still strong. {34:8} The children of Israel mourned for Moses in the plains of Moab for thirty days, and the days of mourning for Moses came to an end. {34:9} Joshua, the son of Nun, was filled with the spirit of wisdom because Moses had laid his hands on him. The children of Israel listened to him and did what the LORD commanded Moses. {34:10} No prophet has arisen in Israel like Moses, whom the LORD knew face to face, {34:11} and who performed all the signs and wonders that the LORD sent him to do in the land of Egypt, to Pharaoh, to all his officials, and to all his land, {34:12} and with that mighty power and the great terror that Moses showed in the sight of all Israel.

The Book of Joshua

{1:1} After the death of Moses, the servant of the LORD, the LORD spoke to Joshua, the son of Nun, Moses' assistant, saying, {1:2} "Moses, my servant, is dead; now get up, cross this Jordan, you and all this people, to the land I am giving them, the children of Israel. {1:3} Every place where the sole of your foot treads, I have given to you, just as I promised Moses. {1:4} From the wilderness and Lebanon to the great river, the Euphrates, all the land of the Hittites, and the Great Sea toward the west, will be your territory. {1:5} No one will be able to stand against you all the days of your life. Just as I was with Moses, I will be with you; I will not fail you or abandon you. {1:6} Be strong and courageous, for you will divide this land as an inheritance for the people, which I promised to their ancestors. {1:7} Only be strong and very courageous; be sure to obey all the law that Moses, my servant, commanded you. Do not turn from it to the right or to the left, so you may be successful wherever you go. {1:8} This book of the law must not depart from your mouth; you must meditate on it day and night, so you may carefully follow everything written in it. Then you will be prosperous and successful. {1:9} Have I not commanded you? Be strong and courageous; do not be afraid or discouraged, for the LORD your God is with you wherever you go." {1:10} Then Joshua commanded the officers of the people, saying, {1:11} "Go through the camp and tell the people, 'Prepare your provisions, for in three days you will cross this Jordan to take possession of the land the LORD your God is giving you.'" {1:12} Joshua said to the Reubenites, the Gadites, and half the tribe of Manasseh, {1:13} "Remember what Moses, the servant of the LORD, commanded you: 'The LORD your God has given you rest and has granted you this land.' {1:14} Your wives, children, and livestock may stay in the land Moses gave you on this side of the Jordan, but you must cross over armed before your fellow Israelites and help them {1:15} until the LORD gives them rest, as he has done for you, and they possess the land the LORD your God is giving them. Then you may return to your own land and enjoy it, which Moses, the servant of the LORD, gave you on this side of the Jordan toward the east." {1:16} They answered Joshua, "Whatever you have commanded us, we will do, and wherever you send us, we will go. {1:17} Just as we fully obeyed Moses, we will obey you. May the LORD your God be with you as he was with Moses. {1:18} Anyone who rebels against your command and does not obey your words will be put to death. Only be strong and courageous."

{2:1} Joshua, the son of Nun, sent two men from Shittim to secretly spy on the land, saying, "Go and view the land, especially Jericho." They went and entered the house of a prostitute named Rahab and stayed there. {2:2} It was reported to the king of Jericho, "Look, men from the children of Israel have come here tonight to search out the land." {2:3} The king of Jericho sent a message to Rahab, saying, "Bring out the men who came to you and entered your house, because they have come to search the whole country." {2:4} But the woman took the two men and hid them; she said, "Yes, the men came to me, but I didn't know where they were from. {2:5} At dusk, when the gate was about to close, the men went out. I don't know where they went. Chase after them quickly, and you will catch up with them." {2:6} She had actually taken them up to the roof and hidden them among the stalks of flax she had laid out there. {2:7} The men pursued them toward the Jordan as far as the fords, and as soon as the pursuers had gone out, the gate was shut. {2:8} Before the spies lay down for the night, she came up to them on the roof {2:9} and said, "I know that the LORD has given you this land and that fear of you has fallen on us, and everyone in the land is terrified because of you. {2:10} We have heard how the LORD dried up the water of the Red Sea for you when you came out of Egypt, and what you did to the two kings of the Amorites, Sihon and Og, whom you completely destroyed. {2:11} When we heard these things, our hearts melted in fear, and no one had any courage left because of you, for the LORD your God is God in heaven above and on the earth below. {2:12} Now please swear to me by the LORD that you will show kindness to my family because I have shown kindness to you. Give me a true sign {2:13} that you will spare the lives of my father, mother, brothers, sisters, and all their belongings, and deliver us from death." {2:14} The men answered her, "Our lives for yours! If you don't tell what we are doing, we will treat you kindly and faithfully when the LORD gives us the land." {2:15} Then she let them down by a rope through the window, for her house was part of the city wall, and she lived in the wall. {2:16} She said to them, "Go to the hills so the pursuers won't find you. Hide there for three days until they return, and then you can go on your way." {2:17} The men said to her, "We will be free from this oath you made us swear. {2:18} When we enter the land, you must tie this scarlet cord in the window through which you let us down, and bring your family into your house. {2:19} If anyone goes out of the doors of your house into the street, their blood will be on their own heads, and we will be innocent; but if anyone is with you in the house and harm comes to them, their blood will be on our heads. {2:20} If you tell anyone about this, we will be free from the oath you made us swear." {2:21} She said, "Agreed! Let it be as you say." She sent them away, and they departed; she tied the scarlet cord in the window. {2:22} They went to the hills and stayed there for three days until the pursuers returned. They searched all along the road but did not find them. {2:23} Then the two men returned, descended from the hills, crossed over, and came to Joshua, son of Nun, and told him everything that had happened. {2:24} They said to Joshua, "The LORD has surely given the whole land into our hands; all the people are melting in fear because of us."

{3:1} Early in the morning, Joshua rose up, and he and all the children of Israel left Shittim and arrived at the Jordan River, where they camped before crossing over. {3:2} After three days, the officers went through the camp {3:3} and commanded the people, "When you see the ark of the covenant of the LORD your God, carried by the priests, the Levites, you are to move from your place and follow it. {3:4} There should be a distance of about two thousand cubits (approximately 3,000 feet) between you and the ark; do not come near it so that you may know the way to go, for you have not traveled this way before." {3:5} Joshua told the people, "Consecrate yourselves, for tomorrow the LORD will perform wonders among you." {3:6} He then spoke to the priests, saying, "Take up the ark of the covenant and lead the people." They picked up the ark and went ahead of the people. {3:7} The LORD said to Joshua, "Today I will begin to exalt you in the eyes of all Israel, so they may know that I am with you just as I was with Moses {3:8} Command the priests carrying the ark of the covenant: when you reach the edge of the Jordan River, stand still in the water." {3:9} Joshua said to the children of Israel, "Come here and listen to the words of the LORD your God. {3:10} This is how you will know that the living God is among you and that He will drive out the Canaanites, Hittites, Hivites, Perizzites, Girgashites, Amorites, and Jebusites before you. {3:11} Look, the ark of the covenant of the LORD of all the earth is going to cross the Jordan ahead of you. {3:12} Now choose twelve men from the tribes of Israel, one from each tribe. {3:13} As soon as the soles of the feet of the priests carrying the ark of the LORD, the LORD of all the earth, touch the water of the Jordan, the water will stop flowing and will be cut off upstream, and the water will stand in a heap." {3:14} When the people broke camp to cross the Jordan, and the priests carrying the ark went ahead of them, {3:15} as soon as the priests' feet touched the edge of the water (for the Jordan is overflowing its banks during the harvest), {3:16} the water upstream stood still and rose up in a heap very far away at a place called Adam, near Zaretan, while the water flowing down to the Sea of the Arabah (also known as the Dead Sea) was completely cut off. So the people crossed over opposite Jericho. {3:17} The priests carrying the ark of the covenant of the LORD stood firm on dry ground in the middle of the Jordan, and all the Israelites crossed on dry ground until the whole nation had completed the crossing.

{4:1} When all the people had completely crossed over the Jordan, the LORD spoke to Joshua, saying, {4:2} "Choose twelve men from the people, one from each tribe, {4:3} and command them, 'Take twelve stones from the middle of the Jordan, from the spot where the priests' feet stood firm. Carry them with you and place them in the lodging area where you will stay tonight.'" {4:4} So Joshua called the twelve men he had appointed from the children of Israel, one from each tribe. {4:5} He said to them, "Go ahead of the ark of the LORD your God into the middle of the Jordan and each of you take a stone on your shoulder, according to the number of the tribes of the children of Israel. {4:6} This will serve as a sign among you. In the future, when your children ask, 'What do these stones mean?' {4:7} you will tell them, 'The waters of the Jordan were cut off before the ark of the covenant of the LORD when it crossed the Jordan, and these stones will be a memorial for the children of Israel forever.'" {4:8} The children of Israel did as Joshua commanded; they took twelve stones from the middle of the Jordan, just as the LORD had instructed Joshua, and carried them to their lodging place, laying them down there. {4:9} Joshua set up twelve stones in the middle of the Jordan, at the spot where the priests who carried the ark of the covenant stood, and they are there to this day. {4:10} The priests who carried the ark stood in the middle of the Jordan until everything the LORD commanded Joshua was accomplished, just as Moses had instructed. Meanwhile, the people hurried and crossed over. {4:11} When all the people had completely crossed over, the ark of the LORD and the priests crossed over in the sight of the people. {4:12} The children of Reuben, the children of Gad, and half the tribe of Manasseh crossed over armed before the rest of the children of Israel, as Moses had instructed them. {4:13} About forty thousand prepared for battle crossed over before the LORD to the plains of Jericho. {4:14} On that day, the LORD exalted Joshua in the sight of all Israel, and they feared him just as they had feared Moses all his life. {4:15} The LORD spoke to Joshua, saying, {4:16} "Command the priests who carry the ark of the testimony to come up out of the Jordan." {4:17} Joshua then commanded the priests, "Come up out of the Jordan." {4:18} When the priests carrying the ark of the covenant of the LORD came up out of the Jordan and their feet touched dry ground, the waters of the Jordan returned to their place and overflowed its banks as before. {4:19} The people came up out of the Jordan on the tenth day of the first month and camped at Gilgal, on the eastern border of Jericho. {4:20} Joshua set up the twelve stones they had taken from the Jordan at Gilgal. {4:21} He spoke to the children of Israel, saying, "When your children ask their fathers in the future, 'What do these stones mean?' {4:22} you will tell your children, 'Israel crossed over this Jordan on dry land.' {4:23} For the LORD your God dried up the waters of the Jordan before you until you had crossed over, just as the LORD your God did to the Red Sea, drying it up until we crossed over. {4:24} This is so that all the people of the earth may know that the hand of the LORD is powerful, and so that you may fear the LORD your God forever."

{5:1} When all the kings of the Amorites, who lived on the western side of the Jordan, and all the kings of the Canaanites, who were by the sea, heard that the LORD had dried up the waters of the Jordan for the children of Israel until they had crossed over, their hearts melted, and they lost their spirit because of the children of Israel. {5:2} At that time, the LORD said to Joshua, "Make sharp knives and circumcise the children of Israel again." {5:3} So Joshua made sharp knives and circumcised the children of Israel at a place called the Hill of Foreskins. {5:4} The reason Joshua circumcised them was that all the men who had come out of Egypt, who were warriors, had died in the wilderness during their journey after leaving Egypt. {5:5} All the people who had come out were circumcised, but all the people born in the wilderness during their journey from Egypt had not been circumcised. {5:6} The children of Israel had wandered for forty years in the wilderness until all the men of war who came out of Egypt had died, because they did not obey the voice of the LORD. The LORD had sworn that He would not let them see the land He had promised to their fathers, a land flowing with milk and honey. {5:7} Joshua circumcised their children who had taken their place, for they were uncircumcised because they had not been circumcised during their journey. {5:8} After they had circumcised all the people, they stayed in their places in the camp until they had healed. {5:9} The LORD said to Joshua, "Today I have rolled away the reproach of Egypt from you." Therefore, the place was called Gilgal to this day. {5:10} The children of Israel camped at Gilgal and celebrated the Passover on the fourteenth day of the month in the evening on the plains of Jericho. {5:11} The next day after the Passover, they ate from the produce of the land, unleavened bread and roasted grain on that same day. {5:12} The manna stopped the day after they ate from the produce of the land; the children of Israel no longer had manna, but they ate the crops of the land of Canaan that year. {5:13} When Joshua was near Jericho, he looked up and saw a man standing in front of him with a drawn sword in his hand. Joshua approached him and asked, "Are you for us or for our enemies?" {5:14} He replied, "Neither! I have come as the commander of the army of the LORD." Joshua fell facedown to the ground in reverence and asked him, "What message does my lord have for his servant?" {5:15} The commander of the LORD's army said to Joshua, "Take off your sandals, for the place where you are standing is holy." And Joshua did so.

{6:1} Jericho was tightly shut up because of the children of Israel; no one went out and no one came in. {6:2} The LORD said to Joshua, "See, I have given you Jericho, its king, and its mighty warriors." {6:3} You and all your fighting men shall march around the city once each day for six days. {6:4} Have seven priests carry seven trumpets made from rams' horns in front of the ark. On the seventh day, march around the city seven times, and the priests will blow the trumpets. {6:5} When they make a long blast with the ram's horn and you hear the sound of the trumpet, all the people shall shout with a great shout, and the wall of the city will collapse, allowing everyone to go straight in. {6:6} So Joshua son of Nun called the priests and said to them, "Take up the ark of the covenant, and have seven priests carry seven trumpets in front of the ark of the LORD." {6:7} He told the people, "Advance and march around the city, with the armed men going ahead of the ark of the LORD." {6:8} When Joshua had spoken to the people, the seven priests carrying the seven trumpets went ahead of the LORD, blowing the trumpets, while the ark of the covenant of the LORD followed them. {6:9} The armed men marched in front of the priests who blew the trumpets, and the rear guard followed the ark, while the priests continued to blow the trumpets. {6:10} Joshua commanded the people, "Do not shout or make any noise with your voices, and do not let a word come out of your mouths until the day I tell you to shout; then shout." {6:11} The ark of the LORD marched around the city once and returned to the camp where they stayed overnight. {6:12} Joshua rose early the next morning, and the priests took up the ark of the LORD. {6:13} The seven priests carrying the seven trumpets went continuously before the ark of the LORD and blew the trumpets; the armed men went before them, and the rear guard followed the ark, with the priests blowing the trumpets. {6:14} On the second day, they marched around the city once and returned to the camp; they did this for six days. {6:15} On the seventh day, they got up at dawn and marched around the city seven times, following the same pattern as before. {6:16} At the seventh time, when the priests blew the trumpets, Joshua said to the people, "Shout, for the LORD has given you the city! {6:17} The city and everything in it is to be devoted to the LORD; only Rahab the prostitute and all who are with her in her house shall be spared, because she hid the messengers we sent. {6:18} But keep away from the devoted things, so you do not bring about your own destruction by taking any of them and causing the camp of Israel to be accursed and troubled. {6:19} All the silver and gold, and the bronze and iron vessels are sacred to the LORD and must go into His treasury." {6:20} When the people shouted and the priests blew the trumpets, and when the people heard the sound of the trumpet and shouted with a great shout, the wall fell flat, and the people went up into the city, each person going straight in and taking the city. {6:21} They completely destroyed everything in the city—men and women, young and old, cattle, sheep, and donkeys—using the sword. {6:22} Joshua said to the two men who had spied on the land, "Go to the prostitute's house and bring her out and all she has, as you promised her." {6:23} The young men who were spies went in and brought out Rahab, her father, her mother, her brothers, and all she had, and they brought out her entire family and placed them outside the camp of Israel. {6:24} They burned the city and everything in it, but they put the silver, gold, and the bronze and iron vessels into the treasury of the house of the LORD. {6:25} Joshua spared Rahab the prostitute, her father's household, and all she had; she lives among the Israelites to this day because she hid the messengers Joshua had sent to spy on Jericho. {6:26} At that time, Joshua pronounced a curse: "Cursed be anyone who rebuilds this city, Jericho; at the cost of his firstborn he will lay its foundations, and at the cost of his youngest son he will set up its gates." {6:27} So the LORD was with Joshua, and his fame spread throughout the land.

{7:1} But the Israelites violated the ban on certain things; Achan, son of Carmi, son of Zabdi, son of Zerah, from the tribe of Judah, took some of the banned items, and the LORD's anger burned against the Israelites. {7:2} Joshua sent men from Jericho to Ai, which is near Bethaven, east of Bethel, telling them, "Go up and scout the land." The men went up and scouted Ai. {7:3} They returned to Joshua and said, "Don't have all the people go up; about two or three thousand men are enough to attack Ai. Don't make all the people toil there, for they are few." {7:4} So about three thousand men went up, but they fled before the men of Ai. {7:5} The men of Ai killed about thirty-six of them; they chased them from the city gate to Shebarim and struck them down on the slope. The hearts of the people melted and became like water. {7:6} Joshua tore his clothes and fell facedown to the ground before the ark of the LORD until evening, along with the elders of Israel, who sprinkled dust on their heads. {7:7} Joshua said, "Alas, Lord GOD, why did You ever bring this people across the Jordan to deliver us into the hands of the Amorites and destroy us? If only we had been content to stay on the other side of the Jordan! {7:8} What can I say, Lord, now that Israel has turned its back to its enemies? {7:9} The Canaanites and all the inhabitants of the land will hear about this and surround us and eliminate our name from the earth. What will You do for Your great name?" {7:10} The LORD said to Joshua, "Stand up! Why are you lying on your face like this? {7:11} Israel has sinned; they have violated My covenant, which I commanded them. They have taken some of the banned items, stolen, and concealed them among their own belongings. {7:12} That's why the Israelites cannot stand against their enemies; they turn their backs because they are under a curse. I will no longer be with you unless you destroy the banned items from among you. {7:13} Get up, sanctify (set apart) the people, and tell them to sanctify themselves for tomorrow, for the LORD, the God of Israel, says there are banned items among you, Israel; you cannot stand against your enemies until you remove those banned items. {7:14} In the morning, present yourselves by your tribes, and the LORD will select a tribe; then the tribe the LORD chooses will come by clans, and the clan the LORD chooses will come by households, and the household the LORD chooses will come one by one. {7:15} Whoever is caught with the banned items shall be burned with fire, along with everything he has, for he has violated the covenant of the LORD and committed a shameful act in Israel." {7:16} So Joshua rose early in the morning and had Israel come forward by tribes, and the tribe of Judah was selected. {7:17} He brought the family of Judah forward, and took the family of the Zarhites; he brought the family of the Zarhites forward, man by man, and Zabdi was selected. {7:18} He brought his household forward, man by man, and Achan, son of Carmi, son of Zabdi, son of Zerah, from the tribe of Judah, was selected. {7:19} Joshua said to Achan, "My son, give glory to the LORD God of Israel, and make confession to Him. Tell me what you have done; don't hide it from me." {7:20} Achan replied to Joshua, "Indeed, I have sinned against the LORD God of Israel. Here's what I did: {7:21} When I saw among the spoils a beautiful Babylonian garment, two hundred shekels of silver, and a wedge of gold weighing fifty shekels, I coveted (desired) them and took them. They are hidden in the ground inside my tent, with the silver underneath." {7:22} Joshua sent messengers who ran to the tent and found the items hidden there, with the silver underneath. {7:23} They took the items from the tent and brought them to Joshua and all the Israelites, laying them out before the LORD. {7:24} Then Joshua, along with all Israel, took Achan son of Zerah, the silver, the garment, the wedge of gold, his sons, his daughters, his oxen, his donkeys, his sheep, and his tent and all that he had to the Valley of Achor. {7:25} Joshua said, "Why have you brought trouble on us? The LORD will bring trouble on you today." Then all Israel stoned him with stones and burned them with fire after stoning them. {7:26} They raised a large pile of stones over him, which remains to this day. Then the LORD turned from His fierce anger, and that place is called the Valley of Achor to this day.

{8:1} The LORD said to Joshua, "Do not be afraid or discouraged. Take all the soldiers with you and go up to Ai. Look, I have handed over to you the king of Ai, his people, his city, and his land. {8:2} You shall treat Ai and its king as you did Jericho and its king. However, you may take the plunder and livestock for yourselves. Set an ambush behind the city." {8:3} So Joshua and all his soldiers went up against Ai, choosing thirty thousand mighty warriors and sending them out at night. {8:4} He commanded them, "You will lie in ambush behind the city; don't go too far from it. Be ready! {8:5} I and all the people with me will approach the city.

When they come out to fight us, as they did before, we will flee from them. {8:6} They will come out after us until we have drawn them away from the city, thinking, 'They are fleeing from us as before,' and so we will run from them. {8:7} Then you will rise up from the ambush and seize the city, for the LORD your God will hand it over to you. {8:8} Once you have taken the city, set it on fire, as the LORD has commanded. I have given you this command." {8:9} Joshua sent them out, and they went to lie in ambush between Bethel and Ai, on the west side of Ai. Joshua stayed that night among the people. {8:10} Early the next morning, Joshua mustered the people and, along with the elders of Israel, went up to Ai. {8:11} All the soldiers went up and took their positions north of Ai, with a valley between them and the city. {8:12} Joshua took about five thousand men and set them in ambush between Bethel and Ai, on the west side of the city. {8:13} Once the people were in position, with the main force to the north and the ambushers on the west, Joshua went into the valley that night. {8:14} When the king of Ai saw this, he hurriedly rose early and assembled his men to fight Israel at a designated place before the plain, unaware that there were ambushers behind the city. {8:15} Joshua and all Israel acted like they were defeated and fled toward the wilderness. {8:16} All the men of Ai were called to pursue them, and they pursued Joshua, drawing away from the city. {8:17} Not a man was left in Ai or Bethel who did not go out after Israel; they left the city open and pursued Israel. {8:18} Then the LORD said to Joshua, "Stretch out the spear that is in your hand toward Ai, for I am giving it into your hand." Joshua stretched out his spear toward the city. {8:19} The ambushers quickly rose from their place and rushed in as soon as he stretched out his hand. They entered the city, took it, and set it on fire. {8:20} When the men of Ai looked behind them, they saw smoke rising from the city, and they had no strength to flee this way or that. The people who had fled to the wilderness turned back on their pursuers. {8:21} When Joshua and all Israel saw that the ambush had taken the city and the smoke was rising, they turned back and struck down the men of Ai. {8:22} The ambushers came out from the city against them, and they were in the midst of Israel, some on one side and some on the other, striking them down so that none remained or escaped. {8:23} They took the king of Ai alive and brought him to Joshua. {8:24} When Israel had finished killing all the inhabitants of Ai in the fields and in the wilderness where they had chased them, all the Israelites returned to Ai and struck it with the sword. {8:25} That day, twelve thousand men and women fell, all the men of Ai. {8:26} Joshua did not withdraw his hand that held the spear until he had completely destroyed all the inhabitants of Ai. {8:27} Only the livestock and the plunder of that city did Israel take for themselves, according to the LORD's command to Joshua. {8:28} Joshua burned Ai and made it a permanent heap of ruins, a desolation that remains to this day. {8:29} He hanged the king of Ai on a tree until evening. As soon as the sun went down, Joshua commanded that his body be taken down and thrown at the entrance of the city gate, raising a large heap of stones over it that remains to this day. {8:30} Then Joshua built an altar to the LORD God of Israel on Mount Ebal, {8:31} as Moses the servant of the LORD had commanded the Israelites, as written in the book of the law of Moses: an altar of whole stones, over which no iron tool had been used. They offered burnt offerings to the LORD and sacrificed fellowship offerings. {8:32} He wrote on the stones a copy of the law of Moses in the presence of the Israelites. {8:33} All Israel, including their elders, officers, and judges, stood on either side of the ark, before the priests who carried the ark of the covenant of the LORD, as well as the foreigners and those born among them; half stood in front of Mount Gerizim and half in front of Mount Ebal, just as Moses the servant of the LORD had commanded them to bless the people of Israel. {8:34} Afterward, he read all the words of the law, the blessings and curses, as written in the book of the law. {8:35} There was not a word of all that Moses had commanded that Joshua did not read to the entire assembly of Israel, including the women, children, and foreigners living among them.

{9:1} When all the kings on this side of the Jordan, in the hills, valleys, and along the coastline of the great sea opposite Lebanon—the Hittites, Amorites, Canaanites, Perizzites, Hivites, and Jebusites—heard about this, {9:2} they gathered together to fight against Joshua and Israel with one purpose. {9:3} When the inhabitants of Gibeon heard what Joshua had done to Jericho and Ai, {9:4} they acted cunningly, pretending to be ambassadors. They took old sacks for their donkeys, along with worn-out and torn wine bottles, {9:5} and wore old shoes and patched garments. All their bread was dry and moldy. {9:6} They went to Joshua at the camp in Gilgal and said to him and the Israelites, "We have come from a far country; make a treaty with us." {9:7} The men of Israel replied to the Hivites, "Perhaps you live among us; how can we make a treaty with you?" {9:8} They said to Joshua, "We are your servants." Joshua asked them, "Who are you? Where do you come from?" {9:9} They answered, "Your servants have come from a very distant country because of the reputation of the LORD your God. We have heard of His fame and all that He did in Egypt, {9:10} and all He did to the two kings of the Amorites beyond the Jordan, to Sihon king of Heshbon and Og king of Bashan, who was at Ashtaroth. {9:11} Our elders and all the inhabitants of our country told us, 'Take provisions for the journey and go to meet them. Say to them, "We are your servants; make a treaty with us."' {9:12} This bread was hot when we took it from our homes the day we left to come to you, but now it is dry and moldy. {9:13} These wine bottles were new when we filled them, but now they are torn; our garments and shoes are worn out from the long journey." {9:14} The men sampled their provisions but did not seek counsel from the LORD. {9:15} Joshua made peace with them and agreed to let them live, and the leaders of the congregation swore an oath to them. {9:16} Three days later, after making the treaty, they learned that these people were their neighbors and lived among them. {9:17} The Israelites traveled to their cities on the third day; these cities were Gibeon, Chephirah, Beeroth, and Kirjathjearim. {9:18} The Israelites did not attack them because the leaders had sworn an oath to them in the name of the LORD God of Israel. The whole congregation murmured against the leaders. {9:19} But all the leaders said to the congregation, "We have sworn an oath to them in the name of the LORD God of Israel; we cannot touch them now. {9:20} This is what we will do to them: we will let them live so that we will not incur wrath because of the oath we swore to them." {9:21} The leaders said to the people, "Let them live, but they will be woodcutters and water carriers for the entire congregation," as the leaders had promised them. {9:22} Joshua summoned them and said, "Why have you deceived us by saying, 'We are from a far country,' when you actually live among us? {9:23} Therefore, you are cursed, and you will never be free from being bondmen, woodcutters, and water carriers for the house of my God." {9:24} They answered Joshua, "We were clearly told that the LORD your God commanded His servant Moses to give you all the land and to destroy all the inhabitants before you. We were terrified for our lives because of you, so we did this. {9:25} Now we are in your hands; do to us whatever seems good and right to you." {9:26} So Joshua did this and did not allow the Israelites to kill them. {9:27} That day, Joshua made them woodcutters and water carriers for the congregation and for the altar of the LORD, serving to this day in the place the LORD would choose.

{10:1} When Adonizedek, king of Jerusalem, heard that Joshua had captured Ai and completely destroyed it, just as he had done with Jericho and its king, and how the inhabitants of Gibeon had made peace with Israel and were now among them, {10:2} he was greatly afraid because Gibeon was a large city, like one of the royal cities, and it was bigger than Ai, with all its men being strong warriors. {10:3} Therefore, Adonizedek sent messages to Hoham, king of Hebron, Piram, king of Jarmuth, Japhia, king of Lachish, and Debir, king of Eglon, saying, {10:4} "Come help me attack Gibeon, for it has made peace with Joshua and the Israelites." {10:5} So the five kings of the Amorites—king of Jerusalem, king of Hebron, king of Jarmuth, king of Lachish, and king of Eglon—gathered their armies and camped against Gibeon to wage war. {10:6} The men of Gibeon sent word to Joshua at the camp in Gilgal, saying, "Don't relax your hand from your servants; come quickly to save us, for all the kings of the Amorites in the mountains have gathered against us." {10:7} So Joshua went up from Gilgal with all the fighting men and the mighty warriors. {10:8} The LORD said to Joshua, "Do not be afraid of them, for I have delivered them into your hand; none of them will stand against you." {10:9} Joshua came upon them suddenly, marching up all night from Gilgal. {10:10} The LORD confused them before Israel, and they were struck down with a great slaughter at Gibeon, and the Israelites chased them along the road to Bethhoron, striking them down as far as Azekah and Makkedah. {10:11} As they fled down the slope to Bethhoron, the LORD hurled large hailstones down on them from heaven to Azekah, and more died from the hail than from the swords of the Israelites. {10:12} Then Joshua spoke to the LORD on the day the LORD delivered the Amorites before the Israelites, saying in front of all Israel, "Sun, stand still over Gibeon, and Moon, stop in the Valley of Ajalon." {10:13} The sun stood still, and the moon stopped until the nation avenged itself on its enemies. Is this not written in the Book of Jasher? So the sun stopped in the middle of the sky and did not hurry to go down for about a full day. {10:14} There has been no day like it before or since, when the LORD listened to a man; the LORD fought for Israel. {10:15} Then Joshua returned with all Israel to the camp at Gilgal. {10:16} Meanwhile, the five kings fled and hid in a cave at Makkedah. {10:17} It was reported to Joshua that the five kings were hidden in the cave at Makkedah. {10:18} Joshua said, "Roll large stones to cover the mouth of the cave and set men there to guard it. {10:19} Don't stop; pursue your enemies and attack the rear guard; don't let them enter their cities, for the LORD your God has delivered them into your hand." {10:20} When Joshua and the Israelites had finished striking down their very great number of enemies until they were destroyed, the survivors entered fortified cities. {10:21} All the people returned safely to Joshua at Makkedah; no one spoke a word against the Israelites. {10:22} Then Joshua said, "Open the mouth of the cave and bring those five kings out to me." {10:23} They did as he said and brought out the five kings: the king of Jerusalem, the king of Hebron, the king of Jarmuth, the king of Lachish, and the king of Eglon. {10:24} When they had brought the kings to Joshua, he called for all the men of Israel and said to the commanders of the soldiers, "Come forward and put your feet on the necks of these kings." They came forward and put their feet on their necks. {10:25} Joshua said to them, "Do not be afraid; do not be discouraged. Be strong and courageous, for this is what the LORD will do to all your enemies you fight." {10:26} Afterward, Joshua struck them down and killed them, hanging them on five trees, where they remained until evening. {10:27} At sunset, Joshua commanded that they be taken down from the trees, thrown into the cave where they had hidden, and great stones were placed at the mouth of the cave, which remain there to this day. {10:28} That day, Joshua captured Makkedah, struck it down with the sword, and completely destroyed its king and all the people in it, leaving no survivors, just as he had done to the king of Jericho. {10:29} Then Joshua and all Israel moved on from Makkedah to Libnah and fought against it. {10:30} The LORD also gave Libnah and its king into the hands of Israel, who struck it down with the sword, leaving no survivors, just as he had done to the king of Jericho. {10:31} Joshua and all Israel went from Libnah to Lachish, camped against it, and fought against it. {10:32} The LORD delivered Lachish into the hands of Israel, who captured it on the second day and struck it down with the sword, killing everyone in it, just as they had done to Libnah. {10:33} Then Horam, king of Gezer, came up to help Lachish, but Joshua struck him and his people down, leaving no survivors. {10:34} From Lachish, Joshua and all Israel moved to Eglon and camped against it, fighting it. {10:35} They captured it that day, struck it down with the sword, and destroyed everyone in it, just as they had done to Lachish. {10:36} Joshua went up from Eglon to Hebron, and they fought against it. {10:37} They captured it, struck it down with the sword, killing its king and all its cities and all the people in it, leaving no survivors, just as he had done to Eglon. {10:38} Joshua returned to Debir and fought against it. {10:39} He captured it, along with its king and all its cities, striking them down with the sword and completely destroying everyone in it, leaving no survivors. He treated Debir just as he had treated Hebron and Libnah and their kings. {10:40} Joshua struck down the whole region, including the hill country, the southern area, the valleys, and the springs, leaving no survivors, as the LORD God of Israel had commanded. {10:41} He defeated them from Kadeshbarnea to Gaza, and all the region of Goshen to Gibeon. {10:42} Joshua captured all these kings and their territories at one time, because the LORD God of Israel fought for Israel. {10:43} Then Joshua and all Israel returned to the camp at Gilgal.

{11:1} When Jabin, king of Hazor, heard about these events, he sent messages to Jobab, king of Madon, to the king of Shimron, and to the king of Achshaph, {11:2} and to the kings in the northern mountains and the plains south of Chinneroth, in the valley, and in the borders of Dor to the west, {11:3} as well as to the Canaanites in the east and west, the Amorites, the Hittites, the Perizzites, the Jebusites in the mountains, and the Hivites under Hermon in the land of Mizpeh. {11:4} They all came out with their armies, a great multitude as numerous as the sand on the seashore, with many horses and chariots. {11:5} When all these kings joined forces, they camped together at the waters of Merom to fight against Israel. {11:6} The LORD said to Joshua, "Don't be afraid of them; by this time tomorrow, I will hand them all over to you, slain. You are to hamstring their horses and burn their chariots." {11:7} So Joshua and all his fighting men attacked them suddenly by the waters of Merom, and they fell upon them. {11:8} The LORD gave them into the hands of Israel, who struck them down and chased them all the way to great Zidon, Misrephothmaim, and the valley of Mizpeh to the east, until none were left. {11:9} Joshua did as the LORD commanded; he hamstrung their horses and burned their chariots. {11:10} At that time, Joshua turned back and captured Hazor, killing its king with the sword, because Hazor had previously been the head of all those kingdoms. {11:11} They struck down everyone in it with the sword, completely destroying them; not one person was left alive, and he burned Hazor with fire. {11:12} Joshua took all the cities of those kings and struck them down with the sword, completely destroying them, as the LORD's servant Moses had commanded. {11:13} However, he burned none of the fortified cities except Hazor, which he did burn. {11:14} The Israelites took all the plunder from these cities, including the livestock, for themselves, but they struck down every person with the sword until none remained. {11:15} Just as the LORD commanded Moses, Moses commanded Joshua, and Joshua followed through, leaving nothing undone of all that the LORD commanded. {11:16} Joshua took all that land—the hills, the southern region, the land of Goshen, the valley, the plains, the mountains of Israel, and the valleys nearby; {11:17} from Mount Halak, which ascends to Seir, to Baalgad in the valley of Lebanon at the foot of Mount Hermon; he captured all their kings and struck them down. {11:18} Joshua fought against these kings for a long time. {11:19} No city made peace with the Israelites except the Hivites who lived in Gibeon; all others were taken in battle. {11:20} It was the LORD who hardened their hearts to come against Israel in battle, so He could utterly destroy them, showing them no mercy, as the LORD had commanded Moses. {11:21} At that time, Joshua cut off the Anakim from the mountains, from Hebron, Debir, Anab, and all the mountains of Judah and Israel; he completely destroyed them and their cities. {11:22} There were no Anakim left in the land of the Israelites, only in Gaza, Gath, and Ashdod did some remain. {11:23} So Joshua took the whole land, just as the LORD had said to Moses, and he gave it as an inheritance to Israel according to their tribal divisions. The land then rested from war.

{12:1} These are the kings of the land that the Israelites defeated and whose territory they took on the eastern side of the Jordan, from the Arnon River to Mount Hermon, and all the plains to the east: {12:2} Sihon, king of the Amorites, who lived in Heshbon and ruled from Aroer on the bank of the Arnon River, through the middle of the river and half of Gilead, up to the Jabbok River, which marks the border of the Ammonites; {12:3} and from the plains to the Sea of Chinneroth in the east, and to the Salt Sea in the east, along the road to Bethjeshimoth, and to the south, at the foot of Ashdothpisgah; {12:4} and the territory of Og, king of Bashan, who was one of the last of the giants, living at Ashtaroth and Edrei, {12:5} and reigned over Mount Hermon, Salcah, and all of Bashan, up to the border of the Geshurites and the Maachathites, and half of Gilead, which was the border of Sihon, king of Heshbon. {12:6} These were defeated by Moses, the servant of the LORD, and the Israelites, and Moses gave this land to the Reubenites, Gadites, and the half-tribe of Manasseh as their possession. {12:7} These are the kings of the region that Joshua and the Israelites defeated on the western side of the Jordan, from Baalgad in the Valley of Lebanon to Mount Halak, which leads up to Seir; this land was given to the tribes of Israel as their inheritance according to their divisions; {12:8} in the mountains, valleys, plains, springs, wilderness, and southern regions; the Hittites, Amorites, Canaanites, Perizzites, Hivites, and Jebusites: {12:9} the king of Jericho, one; the king of Ai, near Bethel, one; {12:10} the king of Jerusalem, one; the king of Hebron, one; {12:11} the king of Jarmuth, one; the king of Lachish, one; {12:12} the king of Eglon, one; the king of Gezer, one; {12:13} the king of Debir, one; the king of Geder, one;

{12:14} the king of Hormah, one; the king of Arad, one; {12:15} the king of Libnah, one; the king of Adullam, one; {12:16} the king of Makkedah, one; the king of Bethel, one; {12:17} the king of Tappuah, one; the king of Hepher, one; {12:18} the king of Aphek, one; the king of Lasharon, one; {12:19} the king of Madon, one; the king of Hazor, one; {12:20} the king of Shimronmeron, one; the king of Achshaph, one; {12:21} the king of Taanach, one; the king of Megiddo, one; {12:22} the king of Kedesh, one; the king of Jokneam of Carmel, one; {12:23} the king of Dor in the coastal region of Dor, one; the king of the nations in Gilgal, one; {12:24} and the king of Tirzah, one: in total, there were thirty-one kings.

{13:1} Joshua was now old and well advanced in years, and the LORD said to him, "You are old and well advanced in years, and there is still much land to be possessed." {13:2} This is the land that remains: all the borders of the Philistines and all Geshuri, {13:3} from Sihor, which is before Egypt, to the borders of Ekron to the north, which is considered part of the Canaanites; there are five lords of the Philistines: the Gazathites, Ashdothites, Eshkalonites, Gittites, and Ekronites, along with the Avites; {13:4} from the south, all the land of the Canaanites, and Mearah, which is beside the Sidonians, to Aphek, to the borders of the Amorites; {13:5} and the land of the Giblites, and all of Lebanon toward the east, from Baalgad under Mount Hermon to the entrance of Hamath. {13:6} I will drive out all the inhabitants of the hill country from Lebanon to Misrephothmaim, and all the Sidonians; you are to divide this land by lot among the Israelites as their inheritance, as I have commanded you. {13:7} Therefore, divide this land as an inheritance for the nine tribes and the half-tribe of Manasseh, {13:8} alongside the Reubenites and Gadites, who have received their inheritance that Moses gave them, beyond the Jordan to the east, just as Moses, the servant of the LORD, commanded; {13:9} from Aroer on the bank of the Arnon River, and the city in the middle of the river, and all the plain of Medeba to Dibon; {13:10} and all the cities of Sihon, king of the Amorites, who reigned in Heshbon, up to the border of the Ammonites; {13:11} and Gilead, and the border of the Geshurites and Maachathites, all of Mount Hermon, and all of Bashan to Salcah; {13:12} all the kingdom of Og in Bashan, who reigned in Ashtaroth and Edrei, and was one of the last of the giants; Moses defeated these and drove them out. {13:13} However, the Israelites did not expel the Geshurites or the Maachathites; instead, the Geshurites and Maachathites continue to live among the Israelites to this day. {13:14} Only to the tribe of Levi did Moses give no inheritance; the sacrifices made to the LORD God of Israel by fire are their inheritance, as He told them. {13:15} Moses gave the tribe of Reuben their inheritance according to their families. {13:16} Their territory was from Aroer on the bank of the Arnon River, and the city in the middle of the river, and all the plain by Medeba; {13:17} Heshbon, and all its cities in the plain; Dibon, Bamothbaal, and Bethbaalmeon, {13:18} Jahazah, Kedemoth, and Mephaath, {13:19} Kirjathaim, Sibmah, and Zarethshahar in the mountains of the valley, {13:20} Bethpeor, Ashdothpisgah, and Bethjeshimoth, {13:21} and all the cities of the plain, and all the kingdom of Sihon, king of the Amorites, who reigned in Heshbon; Moses defeated him along with the princes of Midian: Evi, Rekem, Zur, Hur, and Reba, who were dukes of Sihon, living in the region. {13:22} Balaam, the son of Beor, the soothsayer, was also killed by the Israelites among those they defeated. {13:23} The border of the Reubenites was the Jordan River and its border. This was the inheritance of the Reubenites by their families, including their cities and villages. {13:24} Moses also gave the tribe of Gad their inheritance, according to their families. {13:25} Their territory included Jazer, all the cities of Gilead, and half the land of the Ammonites, up to Aroer, which is before Rabbah; {13:26} and from Heshbon to Ramathmizpeh, and Betonim; from Mahanaim to the border of Debir; {13:27} and in the valley: Betharam, Bethnimrah, Succoth, and Zaphon, the remainder of the kingdom of Sihon, king of Heshbon, as well as the Jordan and its border, all the way to the edge of the Sea of Chinnereth on the other side of the Jordan to the east. {13:28} This is the inheritance of the Gadites by their families, including their cities and villages. {13:29} Moses also gave inheritance to the half-tribe of Manasseh; this was the possession of the half-tribe of Manasseh by their families. {13:30} Their territory was from Mahanaim, all of Bashan, the entire kingdom of Og, and all the towns of Jair in Bashan, which amounted to sixty cities; {13:31} and half of Gilead, along with Ashtaroth and Edrei, cities of the kingdom of Og in Bashan, belonged to the children of Machir, son of Manasseh, including half of Machir's descendants by their families. {13:32} These are the territories that Moses distributed as an inheritance in the plains of Moab, on the eastern side of the Jordan, near Jericho. {13:33} But to the tribe of Levi, Moses did not give any inheritance; the LORD God of Israel was their inheritance, as He told them.

{14:1} These are the areas that the Israelites inherited in the land of Canaan, which Eleazar the priest, Joshua son of Nun, and the heads of the families of the tribes of Israel distributed among them as their inheritance. {14:2} Their inheritance was determined by lot, as the LORD commanded through Moses, for the nine tribes and the half-tribe. {14:3} Moses had given the inheritance of two tribes and a half-tribe on the other side of the Jordan, but he gave no inheritance to the Levites among them. {14:4} The descendants of Joseph were two tribes, Manasseh and Ephraim; therefore, they did not give the Levites any land, except for cities to live in, along with pasturelands for their livestock and possessions. {14:5} As the LORD commanded Moses, the Israelites divided the land. {14:6} Then the children of Judah approached Joshua at Gilgal, and Caleb son of Jephunneh the Kenezite said to him, "You know what the LORD said to Moses, the man of God, about you and me in Kadeshbarnea. {14:7} I was forty years old when Moses, the servant of the LORD, sent me from Kadeshbarnea to explore the land, and I brought him back a report based on my conviction. {14:8} However, my fellow scouts made the hearts of the people melt with fear, but I fully followed the LORD my God. {14:9} On that day, Moses swore to me, 'The land you have walked on will be your inheritance and that of your descendants forever, because you have fully followed the LORD my God.' {14:10} And now, look, the LORD has kept me alive for these forty-five years since He spoke this word to Moses while the Israelites wandered in the wilderness; today, I am eighty-five years old. {14:11} I am just as strong today as I was the day Moses sent me; my strength is as it was then for battle, whether to go out or to come in. {14:12} So now, give me this mountain that the LORD spoke about that day; you heard then how the Anakims were there and that their cities were large and fortified. If the LORD is with me, I will drive them out, as the LORD said." {14:13} Joshua blessed Caleb and gave him Hebron as an inheritance. {14:14} Therefore, Hebron has belonged to Caleb son of Jephunneh the Kenezite ever since, because he fully followed the LORD God of Israel. {14:15} The former name of Hebron was Kirjatharba, named after Arba, who was a great man among the Anakims. The land had rest from war.

{15:1} This was the territory allocated to the tribe of Judah by their families; it extended to the border of Edom and the wilderness of Zin in the south. {15:2} Their southern border started from the shore of the Salt Sea, from the bay that faces south. {15:3} It went south to Maalehacrabbim, passed through Zin, and climbed up the southern side to Kadeshbarnea, continuing to Hezron, then up to Adar, and made a turn towards Karkaa. {15:4} From there, it went towards Azmon and reached the River of Egypt, with the coastline ending at the sea; this marked their southern border. {15:5} The eastern border was the Salt Sea up to the end of the Jordan River. The northern border began at the bay of the sea at the furthest point of the Jordan. {15:6} The border went up to Bethhogla and passed north of Betharabah, then up to the stone of Bohan, son of Reuben. {15:7} It moved north toward Debir from the valley of Achor, looking toward Gilgal, which is before the ascent to Adummim, located on the south side of the river. The border then continued towards the waters of Enshemesh, ending at Enrogel. {15:8} The border ascended by the valley of the son of Hinnom to the south side of the Jebusite, which is Jerusalem, and went up to the top of the mountain facing the valley of Hinnom to the west, at the end of the valley of the giants to the north. {15:9} The border extended from the top of the hill to the spring of the water of Nephtoah, and reached the cities on Mount Ephron, then continued to Baalah, which is Kirjathjearim. {15:10} The border turned from Baalah westward to Mount Seir, passing along the side of Mount Jearim, which is Chesalon, to the north, then down to Bethshemesh, and on to Timnah. {15:11} The border reached the side of Ekron to the north, extended to Shicron, then continued to Mount Baalah, and ended at Jabneel; the boundary of the territory was at the sea. {15:12} The western border ran along the Great Sea and its coastline. This is the territory of the tribe of Judah, according to their families. {15:13} Caleb son of Jephunneh received a portion among the children of Judah, as the LORD commanded Joshua, specifically the city of Arba, the father of Anak, which is Hebron. {15:14} Caleb drove out from there the three sons of Anak: Sheshai, Ahiman, and Talmai. {15:15} He then went up to the inhabitants of Debir, which was formerly known as Kirjathsepher. {15:16} Caleb announced, "Whoever attacks Kirjathsepher and captures it, I will give my daughter Achsah in marriage." {15:17} Othniel son of Kenaz, Caleb's brother, captured it, and Caleb gave him Achsah, his daughter, as his wife. {15:18} When she came to him, she urged him to ask her father for a field. She dismounted from her donkey, and Caleb asked her, "What do you want?" {15:19} She replied, "Give me a blessing; since you have given me a southern land, also give me springs of water." He gave her the upper springs and the lower springs. {15:20} This is the inheritance of the tribe of Judah according to their families. {15:21} The most distant cities of the tribe of Judah towards the Edom border in the south were Kabzeel, Eder, and Jagur, {15:22} along with Kinah, Dimonah, and Adadah, {15:23} and Kedesh, Hazor, and Ithnan, {15:24} as well as Ziph, Telem, and Bealoth, {15:25} plus Hazor, Hadattah, Kerioth, and Hezron, which is Hazor, {15:26} Amam, Shema, and Moladah, {15:27} Hazargaddah, Heshmon, and Bethpalet, {15:28} along with Hazarshual, Beersheba, and Bizjothjah, {15:29} and Baalah, Iim, and Azem, {15:30} plus Eltolad, Chesil, and Hormah, {15:31} Ziklag, Madmannah, and Sansannah, {15:32} and Lebaoth, Shilhim, Ain, and Rimmon; a total of twenty-nine cities with their villages. {15:33} In the valley, there were Eshtaol, Zoreah, and Ashnah, {15:34} Zanoah, Engannim, Tappuah, and Enam, {15:35} Jarmuth, Adullam, Socoh, and Azekah, {15:36} along with Sharaim, Adithaim, Gederah, and Gederothaim; fourteen cities with their villages. {15:37} Zenan, Hadashah, and Migdalgad, {15:38} Dilean, Mizpeh, and Joktheel, {15:39} Lachish, Bozkath, and Eglon, {15:40} Cabbon, Lahmam, and Kithlish, {15:41} Gederoth, Bethdagon, Naamah, and Makkedah; sixteen cities with their villages. {15:42} Libnah, Ether, and Ashan, {15:43} Jiphtah, Ashnah, and Nezib, {15:44} along with Keilah, Achzib, and Mareshah; nine cities with their villages. {15:45} Ekron, with its towns and villages; {15:46} from Ekron to the sea, all that lay near Ashdod, with their villages; {15:47} Ashdod with its towns and villages, Gaza with its towns and villages, extending to the River of Egypt, and the Great Sea and its border. {15:48} In the mountains were Shamir, Jattir, and Socoh, {15:49} Dannah, Kirjathsannah, which is Debir, {15:50} Anab, Eshtemoh, and Anim, {15:51} along with Goshen, Holon, and Giloh; eleven cities with their villages. {15:52} Arab, Dumah, and Eshean, {15:53} Janum, Bethtappuah, and Aphekah, {15:54} Humtah, and Kirjatharba, which is Hebron, and Zior; nine cities with their villages. {15:55} Maon, Carmel, Ziph, and Juttah, {15:56} along with Jezreel, Jokdeam, and Zanoah, {15:57} Cain, Gibeah, and Timnah; ten cities with their villages. {15:58} Halhul, Bethzur, and Gedor, {15:59} along with Maarath, Bethanoth, and Eltekon; six cities with their villages. {15:60} Kirjathbaal, which is Kirjathjearim, and Rabbah; two cities with their villages. {15:61} In the wilderness were Betharabah, Middin, and Secacah, {15:62} along with Nibshan, the city of Salt, and Engedi; six cities with their villages. {15:63} However, the Jebusites, the inhabitants of Jerusalem, could not be driven out by the children of Judah; the Jebusites continue to dwell with the children of Judah in Jerusalem to this day.

{16:1} The territory of the descendants of Joseph began at the Jordan River near Jericho, extending to the waters of Jericho in the east, and up into the wilderness that rises from Jericho all the way to Mount Bethel. {16:2} It continued from Bethel to Luz, then along the borders of Archi to Ataroth. {16:3} The border moved westward to the region of Japhleti, reaching the lower Bethhoron and Gezer, with the boundary ending at the sea. {16:4} Thus, the descendants of Joseph—Manasseh and Ephraim—received their inheritance. {16:5} The border for the tribe of Ephraim, according to their families, was as follows: the eastern boundary began at Atarothaddar and extended to the upper Bethhoron. {16:6} The border then went out toward the sea to Michmethah on the northern side, moving eastward to Taanathshiloh, passing it on the east side to Janohah. {16:7} From Janohah, the border went down to Ataroth and Naarath, reaching Jericho, and then it exited at the Jordan River. {16:8} The border extended westward from Tappuah to the Kanah River, ending at the sea. This constitutes the inheritance of the tribe of Ephraim by their families. {16:9} The cities set apart for the descendants of Ephraim were located within the inheritance of the descendants of Manasseh, including all the cities with their villages. {16:10} They did not drive out the Canaanites who lived in Gezer; thus, the Canaanites still dwell among the Ephraimites to this day and serve under tribute (taxes).

{17:1} There was also a territory allocated for the tribe of Manasseh, who was the firstborn of Joseph. Specifically, it was for Machir, the firstborn of Manasseh and the father of Gilead. Because Machir was a man of war, he received Gilead and Bashan. {17:2} Additionally, there was a territory for the rest of the descendants of Manasseh by their families, including the children of Abiezer, Helek, Asriel, Shechem, Hepher, and Shemida. These were the male descendants of Manasseh, the son of Joseph, by their families. {17:3} However, Zelophehad, the son of Hepher, the son of Gilead, the son of Machir, the son of Manasseh, had no sons—only daughters. The names of his daughters were Mahlah, Noah, Hoglah, Milcah, and Tirzah. {17:4} They approached Eleazar the priest, Joshua the son of Nun, and the leaders, saying, "The LORD commanded Moses to give us an inheritance among our brothers." So, according to the LORD's command, they received an inheritance among their father's relatives. {17:5} Thus, ten portions fell to Manasseh, in addition to the land of Gilead and Bashan, which were on the other side of the Jordan. {17:6} The daughters of Manasseh received an inheritance among his sons, and the rest of Manasseh's sons received the land of Gilead. {17:7} The territory of Manasseh extended from Asher to Michmethah, which lies before Shechem, and the border went along to the right toward the inhabitants of Entappuah. {17:8} Manasseh had the land of Tappuah, but Tappuah on Manasseh's border belonged to the descendants of Ephraim. {17:9} The border extended down to the Kanah River, south of the river; these cities of Ephraim are included among the cities of Manasseh. The territory of Manasseh was on the north side of the river, with the boundary ending at the sea. {17:10} To the south, it belonged to Ephraim, and to the north, it belonged to Manasseh, with the sea as its western border. They met in Asher to the north and in Issachar to the east. {17:11} Manasseh also held territories in Issachar and Asher, including Bethshean and its towns, Ibleam and its towns, and the inhabitants of Dor, Endor, Taanach, and Megiddo, totaling three regions. {17:12} However, the children of Manasseh could not drive out the inhabitants of those cities; the Canaanites continued to live in that land. {17:13} When the Israelites grew stronger, they forced the Canaanites to pay tribute, but they did not completely drive them out. {17:14} The descendants of Joseph spoke to Joshua, saying, "Why have you given us only one lot and one portion to inherit, since we are a great people, and the LORD has blessed us so far?" {17:15} Joshua replied, "If you are a great people, then go up to the forested area and clear land for yourselves in the territory of the Perizzites and the giants if the hill country of Ephraim is too small for you." {17:16} The descendants of Joseph said, "The hill country is not enough for us, and all the Canaanites living in the valley have iron chariots, both those in Bethshean and its towns, and those in the valley of Jezreel." {17:17} Joshua spoke to the house of Joseph, including Ephraim and Manasseh, saying, "You are a great people and have great power; you will not have just one lot. {17:18} The mountain will be yours; it is forested, and you will clear it. Its outskirts will be yours, and you will drive out the Canaanites, even though they have iron chariots and are strong."

{18:1} The entire congregation of the Israelites gathered at Shiloh and set up the tabernacle of meeting there, and the land was subdued before them. {18:2} However, seven tribes of Israel had not yet received their inheritance. {18:3} Joshua asked the Israelites, "How long will you hesitate to take possession of the land that the LORD, the God of your ancestors, has given you? {18:4} Choose three men from each tribe, and I will send them to explore the land. They will describe it according to the inheritance of their tribes and return to me. {18:5} They will divide it into seven parts: Judah will remain in their territory in the south, and the house of Joseph will remain in their territory in the north. {18:6} You must describe the land in seven parts and bring the description to me, so that I can cast lots for you here before the LORD our God. {18:7} The Levites, however, do not receive a portion among you, for the priesthood of the LORD is their inheritance. Gad, Reuben, and half the tribe of Manasseh have already received their inheritance beyond the Jordan to the east, which Moses the servant of the LORD gave them. {18:8} The men got up and went away, and Joshua instructed them to explore the land, saying, "Go, walk through the land, describe it, and return to me so I can cast lots for you before the LORD at Shiloh." {18:9} The men traveled throughout the land, describing it by cities in a book and returned to Joshua at the camp in Shiloh. {18:10} Joshua cast lots for them in Shiloh before the LORD, dividing the land among the Israelites according to their divisions. {18:11} The lot for the tribe of Benjamin came up according to their families, and their territory was between the children of Judah and the children of Joseph. {18:12} Their northern border began at the Jordan and extended to the side of Jericho, moving westward into the mountains; the boundary ended at the wilderness of Bethaven. {18:13} From there, the border went toward Luz, on the side of Luz, which is Bethel, southward, and it descended to Atarothadar, near the hill on the south side of lower Bethhoron. {18:14} The border was drawn from there, encircling the southern corner of the sea from the hill that lies before Bethhoron, and the boundary ended at Kirjathbaal, which is Kirjathjearim, a city of the children of Judah; this was the western boundary. {18:15} The southern boundary began at the end of Kirjathjearim, and the boundary extended west to the water source of Nephtoah. {18:16} The boundary then descended to the end of the mountain that lies before the valley of the son of Hinnom, which is in the valley of the giants to the north, and went down into the valley of Hinnom to the side of Jebusi on the south, and descended to Enrogel. {18:17} It went north to Enshemesh and toward Geliloth, which is across from the ascent of Adummim, and descended to the stone of Bohan, the son of Reuben. {18:18} The border continued along the north side opposite Arabah and went down to Arabah. {18:19} The border then ran northward beside Bethhoglah, and the boundary ended at the northern bay of the Salt Sea, at the southern end of the Jordan; this was the southern border. {18:20} The Jordan River formed the eastern border. This was the inheritance of the children of Benjamin, by their surrounding borders, according to their families. {18:21} The cities of the tribe of Benjamin by their families included Jericho, Bethhoglah, and the valley of Keziz, {18:22} as well as Betharabah, Zemaraim, and Bethel, {18:23} along with Avim, Parah, and Ophrah, {18:24} Chepharhaammonai, Ophni, and Gaba—twelve cities with their villages. {18:25} Other cities included Gibeon, Ramah, and Beeroth, {18:26} Mizpeh, Chephirah, and Mozah, {18:27} Rekem, Irpeel, and Taralah, {18:28} Zelah, Eleph, Jebusi (which is Jerusalem), Gibeath, and Kirjath—fourteen cities with their villages. This is the inheritance of the children of Benjamin according to their families.

{19:1} The second lot was drawn for the tribe of Simeon, according to their families, and their inheritance was within the territory of the children of Judah. {19:2} They received in their inheritance Beersheba (or Sheba), and Moladah, {19:3} along with Hazarshual, Balah, and Azem, {19:4} Eltolad, Bethul, and Hormah, {19:5} Ziklag, Bethmarcaboth, and Hazarsusah, {19:6} Bethlebaoth, and Sharuhen—thirteen cities and their villages. {19:7} They also had Ain, Remmon, Ether, and Ashan—four cities and their villages. {19:8} Additionally, all the villages around these cities as far as Baalathbeer and Ramath of the south completed the inheritance of the tribe of Simeon according to their families. {19:9} The inheritance of the children of Simeon came from the portion of the children of Judah, for Judah's territory was too large for them, so Simeon received their inheritance within it. {19:10} The third lot was for the children of Zebulun, according to their families, and their border extended to Sarid. {19:11} Their border went up toward the sea, including Maralah, reaching Dabbasheth and the river near Jokneam. {19:12} Then it turned from Sarid eastward toward the sunrise to the border of Chislothtabor, going out to Daberath, and up to Japhia, {19:13} passing eastward to Gittahhepher, Ittahkazin, and out to Remmonmethoar and Neah. {19:14} The border then encompassed Hannathon on the north side, with the boundary ending in the valley of Jiphthahel. {19:15} This included Kattath, Nahallal, Shimron, Idalah, and Bethlehem—twelve cities with their villages. {19:16} This is the inheritance of the children of Zebulun according to their families, including these cities and their villages. {19:17} The fourth lot was drawn for Issachar, for the children of Issachar according to their families. {19:18} Their border included Jezreel, Chesulloth, and Shunem, {19:19} Hapharaim, Shion, and Anaharath, {19:20} Rabbith, Kishion, and Abez, {19:21} Remeth, Engannim, Enhaddah, and Bethpazzez. {19:22} Their border reached Tabor, Shahazimah, and Bethshemesh, with the boundaries ending at the Jordan—sixteen cities with their villages. {19:23} This is the inheritance of the tribe of the children of Issachar according to their families, including the cities and their villages. {19:24} The fifth lot was for the tribe of Asher according to their families. {19:25} Their border included Helkath, Hali, Beten, and Achshaph, {19:26} Alammelech, Amad, and Misheal, reaching Carmel westward and Shihorlibnath. {19:27} It turned eastward to Bethdagon, extending to Zebulun and the valley of Jiphthahel on the north side of Bethemek, Neiel, and went out to Cabul on the left, {19:28} including Hebron, Rehob, Hammon, and Kanah, up to great Zidon. {19:29} The border then turned to Ramah and the strong city of Tyre, then turned to Hosah, with the boundary ending at the sea from the coast to Achzib. {19:30} Other cities included Ummah, Aphek, and Rehob—twenty-two cities with their villages. {19:31} This is the inheritance of the tribe of the children of Asher according to their families, including these cities and their villages. {19:32} The sixth lot was for the children of Naphtali, according to their families. {19:33} Their border extended from Heleph, Allon to Zaanannim, Adami, Nekeb, and Jabneel to Lakum, with the boundaries ending at the Jordan. {19:34} The border then turned westward to Aznothtabor, going out from there to Hukkok, reaching Zebulun on the south side, Asher on the west side, and Judah toward the Jordan in the east. {19:35} The fortified cities included Ziddim, Zer, Hammath, Rakkath, and Chinnereth, {19:36} along with Adamah, Ramah, and Hazor, {19:37} Kedesh, Edrei, and Enhazor, {19:38} Iron, Migdalel, Horem, Bethanath, and Bethshemesh—nineteen cities with their villages. {19:39} This is the inheritance of the tribe of the children of Naphtali according to their families, including the cities and their villages. {19:40} The seventh lot was drawn for the tribe of Dan according to their families. {19:41} Their border included Zorah, Eshtaol, and Irshemesh, {19:42} Shaalabbin, Ajalon, and Jethlah, {19:43} Elon, Thimnathah, and Ekron, {19:44} Eltekeh, Gibbethon, and Baalath, {19:45} Jehud, Beneberak, and Gathrimmon, {19:46} Mejarkon, Rakkon, with the border before Japho. {19:47} The territory of the children of Dan was too small for them, so they went up to fight against Leshem, captured it, killed its inhabitants, and settled there, naming it Dan after their father. {19:48} This is the inheritance of the tribe of the children of Dan according to their families, including these cities and their villages. {19:49} After completing the division of the land by its borders, the Israelites gave an inheritance to Joshua, the son of Nun, among them. {19:50} Following the command of the LORD, they gave him the city he requested, Timnathserah in the hill country of Ephraim, and he built the city and settled there. {19:51} These are the inheritances that Eleazar the priest, Joshua, the son of Nun, and the leaders of the tribes of Israel divided by lot at Shiloh before the LORD, at the entrance of the tabernacle of meeting. This concluded the division of the land.

{20:1} The LORD spoke to Joshua, saying, {20:2} "Tell the Israelites to designate cities of refuge, as I instructed you through Moses. {20:3} These cities are for anyone who kills a person accidentally and without intent to harm; they can flee there and find safety from the avenger of blood. {20:4} When someone flees to one of these cities, they should stand at the city gate and explain their case to the elders of that city. The elders will take them into the city and provide them a place to live among them. {20:5} If the avenger of blood pursues them, the city elders must not hand over the person who killed someone unintentionally, since they did so without malice and did not hate the victim beforehand. {20:6} They will stay in that city until they have a trial before the congregation and until the death of the high priest in office at that time; then the killer may return to their own city and home, to the place from which they fled. {20:7} They designated Kedesh in Galilee in the hill country of Naphtali, Shechem in the hill country of Ephraim, and Kirjatharba (which is Hebron) in the hill country of Judah. {20:8} On the east side of the Jordan River, near

Jericho, they appointed Bezer in the wilderness in the territory of Reuben, Ramoth in Gilead in the territory of Gad, and Golan in Bashan in the territory of Manasseh. {20:9} These cities were established for all the Israelites and for any foreigner living among them, so that anyone who accidentally kills a person can flee there and not die at the hands of the avenger of blood before standing trial before the congregation."

{21:1} The leaders of the Levite families approached Eleazar the priest, Joshua son of Nun, and the heads of the tribes of Israel; {21:2} and they spoke to them at Shiloh in the land of Canaan, saying, "The LORD commanded through Moses to give us cities to live in, along with the surrounding areas for our livestock." {21:3} So, the Israelites gave the Levites cities from their inheritance, as the LORD commanded through Moses, along with their surrounding areas. {21:4} The lot was drawn for the families of the Kohathites, and the children of Aaron the priest, who were Levites, received by lot from the tribes of Judah, Simeon, and Benjamin, a total of thirteen cities. {21:5} The remaining Kohathites received by lot from the families of the tribes of Ephraim, Dan, and the half-tribe of Manasseh, a total of ten cities. {21:6} The children of Gershon received by lot from the families of the tribes of Issachar, Asher, Naphtali, and the half-tribe of Manasseh in Bashan, a total of thirteen cities. {21:7} The children of Merari received by their families from the tribes of Reuben, Gad, and Zebulun, a total of twelve cities. {21:8} The Israelites gave these cities with their surrounding areas to the Levites by lot, as the LORD commanded through Moses. {21:9} They gave cities from the tribe of Judah and from the tribe of Simeon, which are listed here by name, {21:10} which were given to the children of Aaron, from the families of the Kohathites, who belonged to the tribe of Levi, as theirs was the first lot. {21:11} They gave them the city of Arba, the father of Anak, which is Hebron, in the hill country of Judah, along with its surrounding areas. {21:12} However, the fields of the city and the villages were given to Caleb son of Jephunneh for his possession. {21:13} Thus, they gave to the children of Aaron the priest Hebron with its surrounding areas, to be a city of refuge for someone who accidentally killed someone; and Libnah with its surrounding areas, {21:14} and Jattir with its surrounding areas, and Eshtemoa with its surrounding areas, {21:15} and Holon with its surrounding areas, and Debir with its surrounding areas, {21:16} and Ain with its surrounding areas, and Juttah with its surrounding areas, and Bethshemesh with its surrounding areas; a total of nine cities from those two tribes. {21:17} From the tribe of Benjamin, they gave Gibeon with its surrounding areas, Geba with its surrounding areas, {21:18} Anathoth with its surrounding areas, and Almon with its surrounding areas; four cities in total. {21:19} All the cities of the children of Aaron, the priests, totaled thirteen cities with their surrounding areas. {21:20} The families of the children of Kohath, the Levites who remained, received their cities by lot from the tribe of Ephraim. {21:21} They were given Shechem with its surrounding areas in the hill country of Ephraim, to be a city of refuge for someone who accidentally killed someone; and Gezer with its surrounding areas, {21:22} and Kibzaim with its surrounding areas, and Bethhoron with its surrounding areas; four cities in total. {21:23} From the tribe of Dan, they gave Eltekeh with its surrounding areas, Gibbethon with its surrounding areas, {21:24} Aijalon with its surrounding areas, and Gathrimmon with its surrounding areas; four cities in total. {21:25} From the half-tribe of Manasseh, they gave Tanach with its surrounding areas, and Gathrimmon with its surrounding areas; two cities. {21:26} In total, there were ten cities with their surrounding areas for the families of the children of Kohath who remained. {21:27} To the children of Gershon, from the families of the Levites, from the other half-tribe of Manasseh, they gave Golan in Bashan with its surrounding areas, to be a city of refuge for someone who accidentally killed someone; and Beeshterah with its surrounding areas; two cities. {21:28} From the tribe of Issachar, they gave Kishon with its surrounding areas, Dabareh with its surrounding areas, {21:29} Jarmuth with its surrounding areas, and Engannim with its surrounding areas; four cities in total. {21:30} From the tribe of Asher, they gave Mishal with its surrounding areas, Abdon with its surrounding areas, {21:31} Helkath with its surrounding areas, and Rehob with its surrounding areas; four cities in total. {21:32} From the tribe of Naphtali, they gave Kedesh in Galilee with its surrounding areas, to be a city of refuge for someone who accidentally killed someone; and Hammothdor with its surrounding areas, and Kartan with its surrounding areas; three cities in total. {21:33} All the cities of the Gershonites according to their families totaled thirteen cities with their surrounding areas. {21:34} For the families of the children of Merari, the remaining Levites, from the tribe of Zebulun, they gave Jokneam with its surrounding areas, and Kartah with its surrounding areas, {21:35} Dimnah with its surrounding areas, and Nahalal with its surrounding areas; four cities in total. {21:36} From the tribe of Reuben, they gave Bezer with its surrounding areas, and Jahazah with its surrounding areas, {21:37} Kedemoth with its surrounding areas, and Mephaath with its surrounding areas; four cities in total. {21:38} From the tribe of Gad, they gave Ramoth in Gilead with its surrounding areas, to be a city of refuge for someone who accidentally killed someone; and Mahanaim with its surrounding areas, {21:39} Heshbon with its surrounding areas, and Jazer with its surrounding areas; four cities in total. {21:40} In total, all the cities for the children of Merari by their families, which were remaining of the Levites, were twelve cities by lot. {21:41} All the cities of the Levites within the possession of the children of Israel were forty-eight cities with their surrounding areas. {21:42} Each of these cities had its surrounding areas; thus, all these cities were accounted for. {21:43} The LORD gave Israel all the land He had promised to their ancestors, and they took possession of it and settled there. {21:44} The LORD gave them peace all around, just as He promised to their ancestors; not one of their enemies stood against them; the LORD delivered all their enemies into their hands. {21:45} Not one of the good things the LORD had promised to the house of Israel failed; everything came to pass.

{22:1} Then Joshua called the Reubenites, the Gadites, and the half-tribe of Manasseh, {22:2} and said to them, "You have kept all that Moses, the servant of the LORD, commanded you, and have obeyed my voice in everything I commanded you. {22:3} You have not abandoned your fellow Israelites these many days up to now but have kept the charge of the commandment of the LORD your God. {22:4} Now the LORD your God has given rest to your fellow Israelites, as He promised them; therefore, you may return to your tents and to the land of your possession, which Moses, the servant of the LORD, gave you on the other side of the Jordan. {22:5} But be very careful to follow the commandment and the law that Moses, the servant of the LORD, charged you: to love the LORD your God, to walk in all His ways, to keep His commandments, to hold fast to Him, and to serve Him with all your heart and with all your soul." {22:6} So Joshua blessed them and sent them away, and they returned to their tents. {22:7} Now to the half-tribe of Manasseh, Moses had given land in Bashan, but to the other half, Joshua gave land among their brothers on this side of the Jordan, westward. When Joshua sent them away to their tents, he blessed them, {22:8} and spoke to them, saying, "Return with great wealth to your tents, with a lot of livestock, silver, gold, bronze, iron, and a lot of clothing. Divide the spoils of your enemies with your brothers." {22:9} The children of Reuben, Gad, and the half-tribe of Manasseh returned and departed from the children of Israel at Shiloh in the land of Canaan to go to the country of Gilead, to the land they possessed according to the word of the LORD through Moses. {22:10} When they arrived at the borders of the Jordan in the land of Canaan, the children of Reuben, Gad, and the half-tribe of Manasseh built a large altar by the Jordan, visible from afar. {22:11} The children of Israel heard, "Look, the children of Reuben, Gad, and the half-tribe of Manasseh have built an altar across from the land of Canaan, at the border of the Jordan, at the crossing for the children of Israel." {22:12} When the Israelites heard of it, the entire congregation gathered at Shiloh to go to war against them. {22:13} The children of Israel sent Phinehas son of Eleazar the priest to the children of Reuben, Gad, and the half-tribe of Manasseh in the land of Gilead, {22:14} along with ten princes, one from each tribe of Israel, each one a head of their family among the thousands of Israel. {22:15} They went to the children of Reuben, Gad, and the half-tribe of Manasseh in Gilead and said to them, {22:16} "The whole congregation of the LORD says, 'What is this sin you have committed against the God of Israel, turning away from following the LORD today by building yourselves an altar, rebelling against the LORD? {22:17} Is the sin of Peor too small for us? We are not cleansed from it even today, although there was a plague among the congregation of the

LORD. {22:18} If you turn away today from following the LORD, tomorrow He will be angry with the whole congregation of Israel. {22:19} However, if your land is unclean, then cross over to the LORD's land where His tabernacle dwells, and take possession among us. But do not rebel against the LORD or against us by building an altar beside the altar of the LORD our God. {22:20} Did not Achan son of Zerah commit a sin regarding the accursed things, bringing wrath on all the congregation of Israel? That man did not perish alone for his iniquity." {22:21} Then the children of Reuben, Gad, and the half-tribe of Manasseh answered the heads of the thousands of Israel, {22:22} "The LORD God of gods knows, and Israel will know; if we have rebelled or transgressed against the LORD, do not save us this day. {22:23} If we have built an altar to turn away from following the LORD, or to offer burnt offerings or grain offerings, or to offer peace offerings, let the LORD Himself hold us accountable. {22:24} But we did it for fear that in the future your children might say to our children, 'What do you have to do with the LORD God of Israel? {22:25} For the LORD made the Jordan a boundary between us and you, children of Reuben and Gad; you have no share in the LORD,' so your children might make our children stop fearing the LORD. {22:26} Therefore, we said, 'Let us build an altar, not for burnt offerings or sacrifices, {22:27} but as a witness between us and you and our generations after us, that we may serve the LORD before Him with our burnt offerings, sacrifices, and peace offerings; so your children will not say to our children in the future, "You have no share in the LORD." {22:28} Therefore, when they say this to us or to future generations, we can say, "Look at the pattern of the altar of the LORD which our fathers made; it is not for burnt offerings or sacrifices, but it is a witness between us and you." {22:29} God forbid that we should rebel against the LORD and turn away from following Him today by building an altar for burnt offerings, grain offerings, or sacrifices beside the altar of the LORD our God that stands before His tabernacle." {22:30} When Phinehas the priest and the leaders of the congregation and the heads of the thousands of Israel who were with him heard the words that the children of Reuben, Gad, and Manasseh spoke, they were pleased. {22:31} Phinehas son of Eleazar the priest said to the children of Reuben, Gad, and Manasseh, "Today we know that the LORD is among us because you have not committed this sin against the LORD. Now you have saved the children of Israel from the hand of the LORD." {22:32} Phinehas son of Eleazar the priest and the leaders returned from the children of Reuben and Gad in the land of Gilead to the land of Canaan, to the children of Israel, and brought them word again. {22:33} The matter pleased the children of Israel, and they blessed God, and they did not intend to go to war against them to destroy the land where the children of Reuben and Gad lived. {22:34} The children of Reuben and Gad called the altar Ed, for it shall be a witness between us that the LORD is God.

{23:1} A long time later, after the LORD had given Israel rest from all their enemies around them, Joshua grew old and advanced in age. {23:2} So Joshua called for all Israel, along with their elders, leaders, judges, and officers, and said to them, "I am old and advanced in age. {23:3} You have seen all that the LORD your God has done to these nations because of you; the LORD your God is the one who fought for you. {23:4} Look, I have divided these remaining nations by lot to be an inheritance for your tribes, from the Jordan and all the nations I have cut off, all the way to the Great Sea to the west. {23:5} The LORD your God will drive them out before you and will push them out of your sight; you will possess their land, as the LORD your God has promised you. {23:6} Therefore, be very courageous to keep and do all that is written in the book of the law of Moses, and do not turn aside from it to the right or to the left. {23:7} Do not associate with these remaining nations among you; do not mention the names of their gods, do not swear by them, do not serve them, and do not bow down to them. {23:8} Instead, hold firmly to the LORD your God, as you have done to this day. {23:9} For the LORD has driven out great and strong nations before you, and as for you, no one has been able to stand against you to this day. {23:10} One of you will chase a thousand, for the LORD your God fights for you, as He promised. {23:11} Therefore, be very careful to love the LORD your God. {23:12} But if you turn back and cling to the remnant of these nations that remain among you, and make marriages with them, and go in to them and they to you, {23:13} know for certain that the LORD your God will no longer drive out any of these nations before you; they will become snares and traps for you, whips on your sides, and thorns in your eyes, until you perish from this good land which the LORD your God has given you. {23:14} And look, this day I am going the way of all the earth, and you know in your hearts and souls that not one thing has failed of all the good things the LORD your God spoke concerning you; everything has come to pass, and not one thing has failed. {23:15} Therefore, just as all the good things have come upon you, which the LORD your God promised you, so the LORD will bring upon you all the evil things until He has destroyed you from this good land which the LORD your God has given you. {23:16} When you have broken the covenant of the LORD your God, which He commanded you, and have gone and served other gods, and bowed down to them, then the LORD's anger will be kindled against you, and you will quickly perish from the good land He has given you.

{24:1} Joshua gathered all the tribes of Israel at Shechem and called for the elders, leaders, judges, and officers; they presented themselves before God. {24:2} Joshua said to all the people, "This is what the LORD God of Israel says: Your ancestors lived on the other side of the river long ago, including Terah, the father of Abraham and Nahor, and they served other gods. {24:3} But I took your ancestor Abraham from the other side of the river and led him throughout the land of Canaan, multiplied his descendants, and gave him Isaac. {24:4} To Isaac I gave Jacob and Esau; I gave Esau the hill country of Seir to possess, while Jacob and his children went down into Egypt. {24:5} I sent Moses and Aaron, and I plagued Egypt with the wonders I performed there; afterward, I brought you out. {24:6} I brought your ancestors out of Egypt; you came to the sea, and the Egyptians pursued your ancestors with chariots and horsemen to the Red Sea. {24:7} When they cried out to the LORD, He put darkness between you and the Egyptians and brought the sea upon them, covering them. You saw with your own eyes what I did in Egypt, and you lived in the wilderness for a long time. {24:8} I brought you into the land of the Amorites, who lived on the other side of the Jordan; they fought against you, but I gave them into your hands so you could possess their land, and I destroyed them before you. {24:9} Then Balak son of Zippor, king of Moab, arose to fight against Israel and sent for Balaam son of Beor to curse you. {24:10} But I refused to listen to Balaam, so he blessed you instead; I delivered you out of his hand. {24:11} You crossed the Jordan and came to Jericho, where the men of Jericho fought against you, along with the Amorites, Perizzites, Canaanites, Hittites, Girgashites, Hivites, and Jebusites; I gave them into your hands. {24:12} I sent the hornet ahead of you, which drove them out before you, including the two kings of the Amorites, but not with your sword or bow. {24:13} I gave you a land for which you did not labor, and cities you did not build, and you live in them; you eat from vineyards and olive groves you did not plant. {24:14} Now, fear the LORD and serve Him in sincerity and truth; put away the gods your ancestors served beyond the river and in Egypt, and serve the LORD. {24:15} If it seems evil to you to serve the LORD, choose for yourselves today whom you will serve, whether the gods your ancestors served beyond the river or the gods of the Amorites, in whose land you live. But as for me and my household, we will serve the LORD." {24:16} The people answered, "Far be it from us to forsake the LORD to serve other gods! {24:17} It was the LORD our God who brought us and our ancestors out of Egypt, from the house of bondage, who performed those great signs before our eyes and preserved us along all the way we went and among all the people through whom we passed. {24:18} The LORD drove out before us all the nations, including the Amorites who lived in the land; therefore, we will also serve the LORD, for He is our God." {24:19} Joshua said to the people, "You cannot serve the LORD, for He is a holy God; He is a jealous God. He will not forgive your transgressions or your sins. {24:20} If you forsake the LORD and serve foreign gods, He will turn and bring disaster upon you, and consume you after having done you good." {24:21} The people said to Joshua, "No! We will serve the LORD." {24:22} Joshua replied, "You are witnesses against yourselves that you have chosen the LORD to serve Him." And they said, "We are witnesses." {24:23} "Now then," he said, "put away the foreign gods that are among you and direct your hearts to the LORD, the God of Israel." {24:24} The people replied to Joshua, "We will serve the LORD our God and obey His voice." {24:25} So Joshua made a covenant with the people that day and set for them a statute and an ordinance at Shechem. {24:26} Joshua wrote these words in the Book of the Law of God and took a large stone and set it up there under the oak that was near the sanctuary of the LORD. {24:27} Joshua said to all the people, "Look, this stone will be a witness against us, for it has heard all the words of the LORD that He spoke to us. It will be a witness against you, so you do not deny your God." {24:28} Then Joshua dismissed the people, each to their own inheritance. {24:29} After these events, Joshua son of Nun, the servant of the LORD, died at the age of one hundred and ten. {24:30} They buried him in the territory of his inheritance at Timnathserah, in the hill country of Ephraim, north of the hill of Gaash. {24:31} Israel served the LORD throughout the lifetime of Joshua and the elders who outlived him and who had experienced all the works of the LORD that He had done for Israel. {24:32} The bones of Joseph, which the Israelites had brought up from Egypt, they buried at Shechem in the plot of ground Jacob had bought from the sons of Hamor, the father of Shechem, for a hundred pieces of silver; it became the inheritance of Joseph's descendants. {24:33} Eleazar son of Aaron died, and they buried him on a hill belonging to his son Phinehas, which was given to him in the hill country of Ephraim.

The Book of Judges

{1:1} After Joshua's death, the Israelites asked the LORD, "Who will go first to fight against the Canaanites?" {1:2} The LORD replied, "Judah will go; I have delivered the land into his hands." {1:3} Judah then said to his brother Simeon, "Come with me to my territory so we can fight the Canaanites, and I will help you with yours." So Simeon joined him. {1:4} Judah went up, and the LORD delivered the Canaanites and Perizzites into their hands; they killed ten thousand of them at Bezek. {1:5} They found Adonibezek in Bezek and fought against him, defeating the Canaanites and Perizzites. {1:6} Adonibezek fled, but they pursued him, caught him, and cut off his thumbs and big toes. {1:7} Adonibezek said, "Seventy kings, with their thumbs and big toes cut off, used to gather scraps under my table; God has repaid me for what I did." They brought him to Jerusalem, where he died. {1:8} The people of Judah fought against Jerusalem, captured it, killed its inhabitants, and set the city on fire. {1:9} After that, the people of Judah went to fight the Canaanites living in the mountains, the south, and the valleys. {1:10} Judah attacked the Canaanites in Hebron (formerly called Kirjatharba), killing Sheshai, Ahiman, and Talmai. {1:11} From there, he went against the inhabitants of Debir (previously called Kirjathsepher). {1:12} Caleb said, "Whoever attacks and captures Kirjathsepher, I will give my daughter Achsah in marriage." {1:13} Othniel, the son of Kenaz and Caleb's younger brother, captured it, and Caleb gave him his daughter Achsah as a wife. {1:14} When she came to him, she urged him to ask her father for a field; she got down from her donkey, and Caleb asked her, "What do you want?" {1:15} She said, "Give me a blessing; you have given me land in the Negev; now give me also springs of water." Caleb gave her the upper and lower springs. {1:16} The Kenites, Moses' father-in-law, went up from the City of Palms with the people of Judah into the wilderness of Judah, south of Arad, and settled among them. {1:17} Judah and Simeon fought against the Canaanites in Zephath and completely destroyed it, calling the city Hormah. {1:18} Judah also captured Gaza, Askelon, and Ekron along with their territories. {1:19} The LORD was with Judah; he drove out the inhabitants of the hill country but could not drive out those in the valley because they had iron chariots. {1:20} Caleb was given Hebron, as Moses had said, and he drove out the three sons of Anak from there. {1:21} However, the tribe of Benjamin did not drive out the Jebusites who lived in Jerusalem, and they continue to live there alongside the Benjaminites. {1:22} The house of Joseph also went up against Bethel, and the LORD was with them. {1:23} The house of Joseph sent spies to scout Bethel (formerly known as Luz). {1:24} The spies saw a man coming out of the city and said to him, "Show us how to enter the city, and we will spare your life." {1:25} He showed them the entrance, and they killed everyone in the city but let the man and his family go free. {1:26} The man went to the land of the Hittites and built a city, naming it Luz, which it is still called today. {1:27} Neither did Manasseh drive out the inhabitants of Bethshean and its towns, nor Taanach and its towns, nor the inhabitants of Dor and its towns, nor those of Ibleam and its towns, nor Megiddo and its towns; the Canaanites remained in that land. {1:28} When Israel became strong, they put the Canaanites to forced labor but did not completely drive them out. {1:29} Ephraim did not drive out the Canaanites living in Gezer; instead, the Canaanites lived among them. {1:30} Zebulun did not drive out the inhabitants of Kitron or Nahalol; the Canaanites lived among them and became their laborers. {1:31} Asher did not drive out the inhabitants of Accho, Zidon, Ahlab, Achzib, Helbah, Aphik, or Rehob; {1:32} the people of Asher lived among the Canaanites in the land and did not drive them out. {1:33} Naphtali did not drive out the inhabitants of Bethshemesh or Bethanath; instead, he lived among the Canaanites, who became laborers for them. {1:34} The Amorites forced the people of Dan into the mountains, refusing to let them come down into the valley. {1:35} The Amorites continued to live in Mount Heres, Aijalon, and Shaalbim, but the house of Joseph was strong enough to make them laborers. {1:36} The territory of the Amorites extended from the ascent of Akrabbim, from the rock, and upward.

{2:1} An angel of the LORD came up from Gilgal to Bochim and said, "I brought you out of Egypt and into the land I promised your ancestors. I will never break my covenant with you. {2:2} You must not make any agreements with the inhabitants of this land; you must tear down their altars. But you have not obeyed my voice. Why have you done this? {2:3} Therefore, I will not drive them out from before you; they will be like thorns in your sides, and their gods will trap you." {2:4} When the angel of the LORD spoke these words to all the Israelites, the people raised their voices and wept. {2:5} They named that place Bochim and offered sacrifices to the LORD there. {2:6} After Joshua dismissed the people, each Israelite went to their inheritance to take possession of the land. {2:7} The people served the LORD throughout Joshua's lifetime and during the lifetimes of the elders who outlived him, those who had seen all the great works the LORD had done for Israel. {2:8} Joshua, the son of Nun, the servant of the LORD, died at the age of one hundred and ten. {2:9} They buried him at the border of his inheritance in Timnathheres, in the hill country of Ephraim, north of Mount Gaash. {2:10} That entire generation was gathered to their ancestors, and another generation arose after them that did not know the LORD or the works He had done for Israel. {2:11} The Israelites did evil in the sight of the LORD and served the Baals. {2:12} They abandoned the LORD, the God of their ancestors who had brought them out of Egypt, and followed other gods, the gods of the peoples around them. They bowed down to these gods and provoked the LORD to anger. {2:13} They forsook the LORD and served Baal and Ashtaroth. {2:14} The LORD's anger burned against Israel, and He gave them into the hands of raiders who plundered them. He sold them to their enemies all around, and they could no longer stand against their enemies. {2:15} Wherever they went, the hand of the LORD was against them for harm, as the LORD had said and sworn to them, and they were greatly distressed. {2:16} Nevertheless, the LORD raised up judges who delivered them from the hands of their plunderers. {2:17} Yet they did not listen to their judges but went after other gods and bowed down to them. They quickly turned away from the path their ancestors had walked, obeying the LORD's commands; they did not do so. {2:18} When the LORD raised up judges for them, He was with the judge and delivered them from their enemies as long as the judge lived. The LORD was moved to pity when they groaned under those who oppressed and afflicted them. {2:19} But when the judge died, they returned to corrupt themselves more than their ancestors, serving other gods and bowing down to them. They did not cease from their evil practices or stubborn ways. {2:20} The LORD's anger burned against Israel, and He said, "Because this people has violated my covenant that I commanded their ancestors and has not listened to my voice, {2:21} I will no longer drive out any of the nations Joshua left when he died. {2:22} I will use them to test Israel and see whether they will keep the way of the LORD and walk in it, as their ancestors did." {2:23} Therefore, the LORD left those nations in place without driving them out quickly, nor did He deliver them into the hands of Joshua.

{3:1} These are the nations that the LORD left to test Israel, specifically those who had not experienced the wars in Canaan. {3:2} This was so that the generations of the Israelites would know and learn about war, at least those who had previously known nothing about it. {3:3} The nations included five lords of the Philistines, all the Canaanites, the Sidonians, and the Hivites who lived in Mount Lebanon, from Mount Baalhermon to the entrance of Hamath. {3:4} They were meant to test Israel to see if they would follow the LORD's commandments, which He had given to their ancestors through Moses. {3:5} The Israelites lived among the Canaanites, Hittites, Amorites, Perizzites, Hivites, and Jebusites. {3:6} They took their daughters as wives and gave their own daughters to their sons, serving their gods. {3:7} The Israelites did evil in the sight of the LORD, forgetting their God and serving the Baals and Asherah poles (groves). {3:8} As a result, the LORD's anger burned against Israel, and He sold them into the hands of Chushanrishathaim, the king of Mesopotamia, and the Israelites served him for eight years. {3:9} When the Israelites cried out to the LORD, He raised up a deliverer for them, Othniel, the son of Kenaz, Caleb's younger brother. {3:10} The Spirit of the LORD came upon him, and he judged Israel; he went to war, and the LORD delivered Chushanrishathaim into his hands, and he was victorious over him. {3:11} The land had peace for forty years, until Othniel, the son of Kenaz, died. {3:12} The Israelites did evil again in the sight of the LORD, and the LORD strengthened Eglon, the king of Moab, against them because they had done evil. {3:13} He allied with the Ammonites and Amalekites, attacked Israel, and captured the city of palm trees. {3:14} The Israelites served Eglon, the king of Moab, for eighteen years. {3:15} When the Israelites cried out to the LORD, He raised up a deliverer for them, Ehud, the son of Gera, a left-handed Benjamite. By him, the Israelites sent a tribute to Eglon, the king of Moab. {3:16} Ehud made a double-edged dagger about a foot long and strapped it to his right thigh under his clothing. {3:17} He brought the tribute to Eglon, who was a very fat man. {3:18} After he finished presenting the tribute, he sent away the people who had carried it. {3:19} But he turned back from the quarries near Gilgal and said, "I have a secret message for you, O king." The king said, "Keep quiet," and all his attendants left. {3:20} Ehud approached him while he was sitting in his private summer chamber and said, "I have a message from God for you." The king got up from his seat. {3:21} Ehud reached with his left hand, took the dagger from his right thigh, and plunged it into the king's belly. {3:22} The blade went in after the handle, and the fat closed around it, making it impossible for him to pull the dagger out. Waste came out. {3:23} Then Ehud went out through the porch, shut the doors of the chamber behind him, and locked them. {3:24} When the servants arrived and saw that the doors were locked, they said, "Surely he is relieving himself in his private chamber." {3:25} They waited until they were embarrassed, but when he did not open the doors, they took the key, opened them, and found their lord fallen dead on the floor. {3:26} Meanwhile, Ehud had escaped while they were waiting and passed beyond the quarries, reaching Seirath. {3:27} When he arrived, he blew a trumpet in the hill country of Ephraim, and the Israelites went down with him from the hills, with him leading them. {3:28} He said to them, "Follow me, for the LORD has given your enemies, the Moabites, into your hands." They followed him, capturing the fords of the Jordan River toward Moab, preventing anyone from crossing. {3:29} At that time, they killed about ten thousand Moabite men, all vigorous and capable warriors; not a single one escaped. {3:30} Thus, Moab was subdued that day under Israel's control, and the land had peace for eighty years. {3:31} After him came Shamgar, the son of Anath, who killed six hundred Philistines with an ox goad and also delivered Israel.

{4:1} The Israelites again did evil in the sight of the LORD after Ehud died. {4:2} So the LORD sold them into the hands of Jabin, the king of Canaan, who reigned in Hazor. His army commander was Sisera, who lived in Harosheth of the Gentiles. {4:3} The Israelites cried out to the LORD because he had nine hundred iron chariots and had harshly oppressed them for twenty years. {4:4} At that time, Deborah, a prophetess and the wife of Lapidoth, was judging Israel. {4:5} She held court under the palm tree of Deborah between Ramah and Bethel in the hill country of Ephraim, and the Israelites came to her for judgment. {4:6} She sent for Barak, the son of Abinoam, from Kedesh in Naphtali and told him, "Hasn't the LORD God of Israel commanded you to go and take with you ten thousand men from the tribes of Naphtali and Zebulun to Mount Tabor? {4:7} I will lure Sisera, the commander of Jabin's army, with his chariots and troops to the Kishon River and give him into your hands." {4:8} Barak replied, "If you go with me, I will go; but if you don't go with me, I won't go." {4:9} She said, "Certainly, I will go with you. However, because of the way you are going, you will receive no glory. The LORD will hand Sisera over to a woman." Deborah then went with Barak to Kedesh. {4:10} Barak called Zebulun and Naphtali to Kedesh, and he went up with ten thousand men following him, while Deborah went with him. {4:11} Now Heber the Kenite, a descendant of Hobab, Moses' father-in-law, had separated from the Kenites and pitched his tent near the great tree in Zaanaim, close to Kedesh. {4:12} They informed Sisera that Barak, the son of Abinoam, had gone up to Mount Tabor. {4:13} Sisera gathered all his chariots, nine hundred iron chariots, and his troops from Harosheth of the Gentiles to the Kishon River. {4:14} Deborah said to Barak, "Get ready! This is the day the LORD has given Sisera into your hands. Isn't the LORD going ahead of you?" So Barak went down from Mount Tabor, followed by ten thousand men. {4:15} The LORD confused Sisera and all his chariots and troops before Barak's sword, so Sisera abandoned his chariot and fled on foot. {4:16} Barak pursued the chariots and army all the way to Harosheth of the Gentiles, and all Sisera's troops fell by the sword; not a single man was left. {4:17} Meanwhile, Sisera fled to the tent of Jael, the wife of Heber the Kenite, because there was peace between Jabin, the king of Hazor, and the house of Heber the Kenite. {4:18} Jael went out to meet Sisera and said to him, "Come, my lord, come in here. Don't be afraid." So he entered her tent, and she covered him with a blanket. {4:19} He said to her, "I'm thirsty. Please give me some water." She opened a container of milk, gave him a drink, and covered him up. {4:20} "Stand at the entrance of the tent," he said. "If anyone asks you, 'Is there a man here?' say, 'No.'" {4:21} But Jael, Heber's wife, took a tent peg and a hammer, went quietly to him while he lay fast asleep, and drove the peg through his temple into the ground, and he died. {4:22} Just then, Barak came by in pursuit of Sisera, and Jael went out to meet him. "Come," she said, "I will show you the man you are looking for." So he went into her tent, and there was Sisera lying dead with the tent peg in his temple. {4:23} On that day, God subdued Jabin, the king of Canaan, before the Israelites. {4:24} The Israelites pressed harder and harder against Jabin, the king of Canaan, until they destroyed him.

{5:1} On that day, Deborah and Barak, the son of Abinoam, sang this song: {5:2} "Praise the LORD for avenging Israel, when the people willingly offered themselves." {5:3} "Listen, O kings; pay attention, O princes! I will sing to the LORD; I will praise the LORD, the God of Israel." {5:4} "LORD, when you went out from Seir, when you marched from the field of Edom, the earth trembled, and the heavens poured rain; the clouds dropped water." {5:5} "The mountains shook before the LORD, even Sinai, before the LORD, the God of Israel." {5:6} "In the days of Shamgar, the son of Anath, and in the days of Jael, the roads were abandoned, and travelers took winding paths." {5:7} "The villagers ceased to exist; they ceased until I, Deborah, arose; I became a mother in Israel." {5:8} "They chose new gods; then there was war at the gates. Was a shield or spear seen among forty thousand in Israel?" {5:9} "My heart is with the leaders of Israel who willingly offered themselves among the people. Praise the LORD!" {5:10} "Speak, you who ride on white donkeys, you who sit in judgment and walk along the road." {5:11} "Let those who are rescued from the noise of the archers at the water's edge recount the righteous acts of the LORD, the righteous acts toward the villagers in Israel. Then the people of the LORD will go down to the gates." {5:12} "Awake, awake, Deborah! Wake up and sing! Arise, Barak, and lead your captives away, son of Abinoam." {5:13} "Then the remnant came down to the nobles among the people; the LORD made me like a mighty leader." {5:14} "From Ephraim came a root against Amalek; after you, Benjamin, with your people; from Machir came governors, and from Zebulun those who handle the pen." {5:15} "The leaders of Issachar were with Deborah; yes, Issachar was with Barak; he was sent on foot into the valley. Reuben's divisions had great thoughts of heart." {5:16} "Why do you stay among the sheepfolds, to hear the bleating of the flocks? For Reuben's divisions had great searchings of heart." {5:17} "Gilead stayed beyond the Jordan; and why did

Dan remain in the ships? Asher stayed on the coast and remained in his harbors." {5:18} "Zebulun and Naphtali risked their lives to the death on the heights of the field." {5:19} "The kings came and fought; the kings of Canaan fought at Taanach by the waters of Megiddo, but they took no plunder." {5:20} "They fought from the heavens; the stars in their courses fought against Sisera." {5:21} "The river Kishon swept them away, that ancient river, the river Kishon. My soul, you have trodden down strength!" {5:22} "Then the hooves of the horses were broken by the galloping of the mighty." {5:23} "Curse Meroz," said the angel of the LORD, "curse its inhabitants bitterly, because they did not come to help the LORD against the mighty." {5:24} "Blessed above women shall Jael, the wife of Heber the Kenite, be; blessed shall she be above women in the tent." {5:25} "He asked for water, and she gave him milk; she brought him yogurt in a noble dish." {5:26} "She took a tent peg in her left hand and a hammer in her right, and with the hammer she struck Sisera, smashing his head, piercing and striking through his temples." {5:27} "At her feet he bowed, fell, and lay down; at her feet he bowed, fell; where he bowed, there he fell dead." {5:28} "The mother of Sisera looked out from a window and cried through the lattice, 'Why is his chariot so long in coming? Why do the wheels of his chariots delay?'" {5:29} "Her wise ladies answered her; yes, she returned to herself." {5:30} "Have they not sped? Have they not divided the spoils? To each man a girl or two; for Sisera, plunder of colorful garments, plunder of embroidered garments on both sides, suitable for the necks of those who take the spoil?" {5:31} "So let all your enemies perish, O LORD, but let those who love Him be like the sun when it rises in its strength." And the land had rest for forty years.

{6:1} The children of Israel did evil in the sight of the LORD, and He handed them over to Midian for seven years. {6:2} The Midianites were powerful against Israel, and because of them, the Israelites made dens in the mountains, caves, and strongholds. {6:3} Whenever Israel planted crops, the Midianites, along with the Amalekites and people from the east, came up against them. {6:4} They camped against them and destroyed the produce of the land, as far as Gaza, leaving no sustenance for Israel—neither sheep, oxen, nor donkeys. {6:5} They came with their cattle and tents, like swarms of locusts; they were so numerous that neither they nor their camels could be counted, and they entered the land to destroy it. {6:6} Israel was greatly impoverished because of the Midianites, and the children of Israel cried out to the LORD. {6:7} When they cried out to the LORD because of the Midianites, {6:8} He sent them a prophet who said, "This is what the LORD, the God of Israel, says: I brought you up from Egypt and out of the house of bondage; {6:9} I delivered you from the Egyptians and from all who oppressed you. I drove them out before you and gave you their land. {6:10} I said to you, 'I am the LORD your God; do not fear the gods of the Amorites in whose land you live,' but you did not obey my voice." {6:11} Then an angel of the LORD came and sat under an oak tree in Ophrah, which belonged to Joash the Abiezrite. His son Gideon was threshing wheat in the winepress to hide it from the Midianites. {6:12} The angel of the LORD appeared to him and said, "The LORD is with you, mighty warrior." {6:13} Gideon replied, "Pardon me, my lord, but if the LORD is with us, why has all this happened to us? Where are all His wonders that our ancestors told us about, saying, 'Didn't the LORD bring us up from Egypt?' But now the LORD has abandoned us and given us into the hands of the Midianites." {6:14} The LORD turned to him and said, "Go in the strength you have and save Israel out of Midian's hand. Am I not sending you?" {6:15} "Pardon me, my lord," Gideon said, "but how can I save Israel? My clan is the weakest in Manasseh, and I am the least in my family." {6:16} The LORD answered, "I will be with you, and you will strike down all the Midianites, leaving none alive." {6:17} Gideon replied, "If I have found favor in your eyes, give me a sign that it is really you talking to me. {6:18} Please do not go away until I come back and bring my offering and set it before you." "I will wait until you return," He said. {6:19} Gideon went inside, prepared a young goat, and made unleavened bread from an ephah of flour. He put the meat in a basket and the broth in a pot, and he brought them out to Him under the oak and presented them. {6:20} The angel of God said to him, "Take the meat and the unleavened bread, lay them on this rock, and pour out the broth." Gideon did so. {6:21} Then the angel of the LORD touched the meat and the unleavened bread with the tip of the staff that was in his hand; fire flared from the rock, consuming the meat and the unleavened bread. The angel of the LORD then disappeared. {6:22} When Gideon realized that it was the angel of the LORD, he exclaimed, "Alas, Sovereign LORD! I have seen the angel of the LORD face to face!" {6:23} But the LORD said to him, "Peace! Do not be afraid. You are not going to die." {6:24} So Gideon built an altar to the LORD there and called it The LORD Is Peace. To this day it stands in Ophrah of the Abiezrites. {6:25} That same night, the LORD said to him, "Take the second bull from your father's herd, the one seven years old. Tear down your father's altar to Baal and cut down the Asherah pole beside it. {6:26} Then build a proper altar to the LORD your God on the top of this height, using the wood of the Asherah pole that you cut down. Offer the second bull as a burnt offering." {6:27} So Gideon took ten of his servants and did as the LORD told him. But because he was afraid of his family and the townspeople, he did it at night rather than in the daytime. {6:28} In the morning, when the people of the town got up, there was Baal's altar, demolished, with the Asherah pole beside it cut down, and the second bull sacrificed on the newly built altar. {6:29} They asked each other, "Who did this?" When they carefully investigated, they were told, "Gideon son of Joash did it." {6:30} The townspeople said to Joash, "Bring out your son. He must die because he has broken down Baal's altar and cut down the Asherah pole." {6:31} But Joash replied to the hostile crowd around him, "Are you going to plead Baal's cause? Are you trying to save him? Whoever fights for him shall be put to death by morning. If Baal really is a god, he can defend himself when someone breaks down his altar." {6:32} So that day, they called Gideon Jerub-Baal, saying, "Let Baal contend with him, because he broke down Baal's altar." {6:33} Now all the Midianites, Amalekites, and the people of the east joined forces and crossed over the Jordan and camped in the Valley of Jezreel. {6:34} Then the Spirit of the LORD came on Gideon, and he blew a trumpet, summoning the Abiezrites to follow him. {6:35} He sent messengers throughout Manasseh, calling them to arms, and also sent messengers to Asher, Zebulun, and Naphtali, and they came up to meet them. {6:36} Gideon said to God, "If you will save Israel by my hand as you have promised, {6:37} look, I will place a wool fleece on the threshing floor. If there is dew only on the fleece and all the ground is dry, then I will know that you will save Israel by my hand, as you said." {6:38} And that is exactly what happened. Gideon rose early the next day; he squeezed the fleece and wrung out the dew—a bowl full of water. {6:39} Then Gideon said to God, "Do not be angry with me. Let me ask just once more: allow me to test with the fleece, but this time make the fleece dry and let there be dew on the ground." {6:40} That night God did so. Only the fleece was dry; all the ground was covered with dew.

{7:1} Then Jerubbaal, who is Gideon, and all the people with him got up early and camped beside the well of Harod, while the Midianite army was to the north, by the hill of Moreh in the valley. {7:2} The LORD said to Gideon, "You have too many people with you for me to deliver Midian into their hands, or else Israel will boast against me, saying, 'My own strength has saved me.' {7:3} Now, announce to the people, 'Anyone who is afraid or fearful may leave and go home.'" So twenty-two thousand men left, and ten thousand remained. {7:4} The LORD said to Gideon, "There are still too many. Take them down to the water, and I will test them for you there. If I say, 'This one shall go with you,' he shall go; but if I say, 'This one shall not go with you,' he shall not go." {7:5} So Gideon took the men down to the water, and the LORD told him, "Separate those who lap water with their tongues like a dog from those who kneel down to drink." {7:6} The number of those who lapped with their hands to their mouths was three hundred men, but all the rest knelt down to drink. {7:7} The LORD said to Gideon, "With the three hundred men who lapped, I will save you and give the Midianites into your hands. Let all the others go home." {7:8} So the men took provisions and their trumpets, and Gideon sent the rest of the Israelites home, but kept the three hundred. The Midianite camp was below him in the valley. {7:9} That night, the LORD said to him, "Get up and go down against the camp, for I have delivered it into your hands. {7:10} If you are afraid to go down, take your servant Phurah with you. {7:11} Listen to what they are saying; afterward you will be encouraged to go down against the camp." So he went down with his servant to the outposts of the camp. {7:12} The Midianites, Amalekites, and all the people from the east were camped in the valley like swarms of locusts; their camels were as numerous as the sand on the seashore. {7:13} Gideon arrived just as a man was telling his friend about a dream. He said, "I had a dream: A round loaf of barley bread came tumbling into the Midianite camp. It struck the tent with such force that the tent overturned and collapsed." {7:14} His friend responded, "This can be nothing other than the sword of Gideon son of Joash, a man of Israel. God has given the Midianites and the whole camp into his hands." {7:15} When Gideon heard the dream and its interpretation, he worshiped God. He returned to the camp of Israel and called out, "Get up! The LORD has given the Midianite camp into your hands." {7:16} Dividing the three hundred men into three companies, he placed trumpets and empty jars in the hands of all of them, along with torches inside the jars. {7:17} "Watch me," he told them. "Follow my lead. When I get to the edge of the camp, do exactly as I do. {7:18} When I and all who are with me blow our trumpets, then you blow yours all around the camp and shout, 'For the LORD and for Gideon!'" {7:19} Gideon and the hundred men with him reached the edge of the camp at the beginning of the middle watch, just after they had changed the guard. They blew their trumpets and broke the jars that were in their hands. {7:20} The three companies blew their trumpets and smashed the jars, grasping the torches in their left hands and holding in their right hands the trumpets they were to blow. They shouted, "A sword for the LORD and for Gideon!" {7:21} Each man stood in his place around the camp, and all the Midianites ran, crying out as they fled. {7:22} When the three hundred trumpets sounded, the LORD caused the men throughout the camp to turn on each other with their swords, and the Midianites fled to Beth Shittah, toward Zererath, and as far as the border of Abel Meholah near Tabbath. {7:23} The men of Israel from Naphtali, Asher, and all Manasseh were called out, and they pursued the Midianites. {7:24} Gideon sent messengers throughout the hill country of Ephraim, saying, "Come down against the Midianites and seize the waters of Beth Barah and the Jordan River." So all the men of Ephraim gathered together and took the waters of Beth Barah and the Jordan. {7:25} They captured two Midianite leaders, Oreb and Zeeb. They killed Oreb at the rock of Oreb and Zeeb at the winepress of Zeeb. They pursued the Midianites and brought the heads of Oreb and Zeeb to Gideon, who was by the Jordan.

{8:1} The men of Ephraim came to Gideon and said, "Why did you treat us this way? Why didn't you call us when you went to fight the Midianites?" They argued with him fiercely. {8:2} But he replied, "What have I done compared to you? Isn't the leftover grapes of Ephraim better than the whole harvest of Abiezer? {8:3} God has delivered the princes of Midian, Oreb and Zeeb, into your hands. What was I able to do compared to you?" When he said this, their anger toward him subsided. {8:4} Gideon and his 300 men, exhausted but still in pursuit, crossed over the Jordan. {8:5} He said to the men of Succoth, "Please give loaves of bread to the men following me; they are weary, and I am pursuing Zebah and Zalmunna, kings of Midian." {8:6} But the leaders of Succoth replied, "Are Zebah and Zalmunna already in your hands? Why should we give bread to your army?" {8:7} Gideon responded, "When the LORD has delivered Zebah and Zalmunna into my hand, I will tear your flesh with thorns and briers from the desert." {8:8} From there, he went to Penuel and made the same request, but the men of Penuel answered as the men of Succoth had. {8:9} So he told them, "When I return in peace, I will tear down this tower." {8:10} Meanwhile, Zebah and Zalmunna were in Karkor with about 15,000 men, all that were left of the army of the eastern people; 120,000 had already fallen in battle. {8:11} Gideon took the route of those living in tents east of Nobah and Jogbehah and attacked the unsuspecting army. {8:12} Zebah and Zalmunna fled, but Gideon pursued and captured them, defeating their entire army. {8:13} After the battle, Gideon, the son of Joash, returned by the way of the Heres Pass before sunrise. {8:14} He captured a young man from Succoth and questioned him. The young man wrote down for him the names of the 77 elders and leaders of Succoth. {8:15} Then Gideon went to the men of Succoth and said, "Here are Zebah and Zalmunna, about whom you taunted me, saying, 'Are they in your hands now, that we should give bread to your men?'" {8:16} He took the elders of the city and punished them with thorns and briers from the desert. {8:17} He also tore down the tower of Penuel and killed the men of the city. {8:18} Then Gideon asked Zebah and Zalmunna, "What kind of men did you kill at Tabor?" They replied, "They were like you, each one looked like a son of a king." {8:19} Gideon said, "Those were my brothers, the sons of my mother. As surely as the LORD lives, if you had spared them, I would not kill you now." {8:20} He said to Jether, his firstborn, "Get up and kill them." But the boy was too afraid to draw his sword, as he was still young. {8:21} Zebah and Zalmunna said, "Come, do it yourself. As the man is, so is his strength." So Gideon got up and killed Zebah and Zalmunna and took the ornaments off their camels' necks. {8:22} Then the Israelites said to Gideon, "Rule over us—you, your son, and your grandson—because you have saved us from Midian." {8:23} But Gideon told them, "I will not rule over you, nor will my son. The LORD will rule over you." {8:24} He added, "But I do have one request: that each of you give me an earring from your share of the plunder." (The Midianites, who were Ishmaelites, wore gold earrings.) {8:25} They said, "We'll gladly give them." So they spread out a garment, and each man threw an earring from his plunder onto it. {8:26} The total weight of the gold earrings was 1,700 shekels (about 43 pounds), not counting the ornaments, pendants, purple garments worn by the kings of Midian, or the chains on their camels' necks. {8:27} Gideon made the gold into an ephod (a ceremonial garment), which he placed in Ophrah, his hometown. All Israel prostituted themselves by worshiping it there, and it became a trap to Gideon and his family. {8:28} So Midian was subdued before the Israelites and did not raise its head again. During Gideon's lifetime, the land had peace for 40 years. {8:29} Jerubbaal (Gideon), the son of Joash, went back to live in his own house. {8:30} He had 70 sons by many wives. {8:31} His concubine, who lived in Shechem, also bore him a son, whom he named Abimelech. {8:32} Gideon, the son of Joash, died at a good old age and was buried in the tomb of his father Joash in Ophrah of the Abiezrites. {8:33} No sooner had Gideon died than the Israelites again prostituted themselves to the Baals (false gods). They set up Baal-Berith as their god. {8:34} The Israelites did not remember the LORD their God, who had rescued them from the hands of all their enemies on every side. {8:35} They also failed to show kindness to the family of Jerubbaal (that is, Gideon), despite all the good he had done for Israel.

{9:1} Abimelech, the son of Jerubbaal, went to Shechem to his mother's relatives and spoke to them and the whole family of his mother's father, saying, {9:2} "Please speak in the ears of all the men of Shechem and ask them, 'Which is better for you: to have all seventy sons of Jerubbaal rule over you, or just one? Remember, I am your own flesh and blood.'" {9:3} So his mother's relatives spoke on his behalf to all the men of Shechem, and their hearts were inclined to follow Abimelech, for they said, "He is our brother." {9:4} They gave him seventy pieces of silver from the temple of Baalberith, which Abimelech used to hire reckless and worthless men to follow him. {9:5} He went to his father's house at Ophrah and killed his brothers, the seventy sons of Jerubbaal, on one stone. But Jotham, the youngest son of Jerubbaal, survived because he hid. {9:6} Then all the men of Shechem and the house of Millo gathered and made Abimelech king by the oak pillar in Shechem. {9:7} When Jotham was told, he went and stood on Mount Gerizim, raised his voice, and shouted, "Listen to me, men of Shechem, so that God may listen to you! {9:8} Once the trees set out to anoint a king over them. They said to the olive tree, 'Reign over us.' {9:9} But the olive tree replied, 'Should I give up my oil, by which both gods and humans are honored, to hold sway over the trees?' {9:10} Then the trees said to the fig tree, 'Come and reign over us.' {9:11} But the fig tree said, 'Should I give up my sweetness and my good fruit to hold sway over the trees?' {9:12} Then the trees said to the vine, 'Come and reign over us.' {9:13} But the vine answered, 'Should I give up my wine, which cheers both gods and humans, to hold sway over the trees?' {9:14} Finally, all the trees said to the bramble (a thorny shrub), 'Come and reign over us.' {9:15} The bramble said, 'If you truly want to anoint me king, come and take shelter in my shade; but if not, let fire come out of the bramble and consume the cedars of Lebanon.' {9:16} Now, if you have acted honorably and sincerely in making Abimelech king, and if you have treated Jerubbaal and his family well, as he deserved— {9:17} because my father fought for you, risked his life, and delivered you from the hand of Midian— {9:18} but today you have risen against my father's family, killed his seventy sons on one stone, and made Abimelech, the son of his maidservant, king over the men of Shechem because he is your relative— {9:19} if you have acted honorably and sincerely toward Jerubbaal and his family today, then rejoice in Abimelech, and let him rejoice in you. {9:20} But if not, let fire come out from Abimelech and consume the men of Shechem and the house of Millo, and let fire come out from the men of Shechem and the house of Millo and consume Abimelech." {9:21} Then Jotham fled, escaping to Beer, where he lived in fear of his brother Abimelech. {9:22} Abimelech ruled over Israel for three years. {9:23} Then God sent an evil spirit between Abimelech and the men of Shechem, and they dealt treacherously with Abimelech, {9:24} so that the violence done to Jerubbaal's seventy sons might be avenged, and their blood might fall on Abimelech, their brother, who killed them, and on the men of Shechem who helped him kill his brothers. {9:25} The men of Shechem set ambushes in the hills, and they robbed all who passed by; this was reported to Abimelech. {9:26} Then Gaal, the son of Ebed, moved into Shechem with his brothers, and the men of Shechem put their trust in him. {9:27} They went out into the fields, gathered the grapes from their vineyards, trod them, held a festival, and went into the temple of their god, where they ate, drank, and cursed Abimelech. {9:28} Gaal, the son of Ebed, said, "Who is Abimelech, and who is Shechem, that we should serve him? Isn't he the son of Jerubbaal, and isn't Zebul his officer? Serve the descendants of Hamor, Shechem's founder! Why should we serve him? {9:29} If only these people were under my command! I would get rid of Abimelech." Then he said to Abimelech, "Call out your army and come out!" {9:30} When Zebul, the ruler of the city, heard what Gaal, the son of Ebed, said, he was furious. {9:31} He sent messengers secretly to Abimelech, saying, "Gaal, the son of Ebed, and his brothers have come to Shechem and are stirring up the city against you. {9:32} Now, come by night with your men and lie in wait in the fields. {9:33} In the morning, at sunrise, attack the city, and when Gaal and his men come out against you, do whatever your hand finds to do." {9:34} So Abimelech and all his men set out by night and took up positions near Shechem in four companies. {9:35} When Gaal, the son of Ebed, went out and stood at the entrance of the city gate, Abimelech and his men rose from their hiding places. {9:36} Gaal saw them and said to Zebul, "Look, people are coming down from the tops of the mountains!" But Zebul replied, "You mistake the shadows of the mountains for men." {9:37} Gaal spoke again, "Look, people are coming down from the center of the land, and another company is coming from the direction of the Diviners' Oak." {9:38} Then Zebul said to him, "Where is your big talk now, you who said, 'Who is Abimelech that we should serve him?' Aren't these the men you ridiculed? Go out now and fight them!" {9:39} So Gaal went out, leading the men of Shechem, and fought Abimelech. {9:40} Abimelech chased him, and many were wounded and fell as they fled, all the way to the entrance of the gate. {9:41} Abimelech stayed in Arumah, and Zebul drove Gaal and his brothers out of Shechem. {9:42} The next day, the people of Shechem went out to the fields, and this was reported to Abimelech. {9:43} So he took his men, divided them into three companies, and set an ambush in the fields. When he saw the people coming out of the city, he attacked them. {9:44} Abimelech and his company rushed forward and took up positions at the entrance of the city gate, while the other two companies attacked those in the fields and struck them down. {9:45} Abimelech fought against the city all that day. He captured it, killed its people, destroyed the city, and scattered salt over it. {9:46} When the leaders of the tower of Shechem heard about this, they went into the stronghold of the temple of El-Berith. {9:47} Abimelech was told that all the leaders of the tower of Shechem had gathered there. {9:48} So he and all his men went up Mount Zalmon. He took an ax, cut a branch from the trees, lifted it to his shoulder, and said to his men, "Quick, do what you have seen me do!" {9:49} Each of his men cut down a branch, followed Abimelech, and piled them against the stronghold. Then they set the stronghold on fire, and about a thousand men and women died inside the tower of Shechem. {9:50} Next, Abimelech went to Thebez, besieged it, and captured it. {9:51} Inside the city was a strong tower, and all the men and women, along with the leaders of the city, fled to it. They locked themselves in and climbed to the roof of the tower. {9:52} Abimelech came to the tower and attacked it. As he approached the entrance to set it on fire, {9:53} a woman dropped an upper millstone on his head, cracking his skull. {9:54} He quickly called to his young armor-bearer and said, "Draw your sword and kill me, so they won't say a woman killed him." So his servant ran him through, and he died. {9:55} When the Israelites saw that Abimelech was dead, they went home. {9:56} In this way, God repaid Abimelech for the evil he had done to his father by killing his seventy brothers. {9:57} Likewise, God brought all the wickedness of the men of Shechem back upon their own heads, and the curse of Jotham, the son of Jerubbaal, came upon them.

{10:1} After Abimelech, Tola, the son of Puah and grandson of Dodo, a man from the tribe of Issachar, arose to defend Israel. He lived in Shamir in the hill country of Ephraim. {10:2} Tola judged Israel for twenty-three years and then died, being buried in Shamir. {10:3} After him, Jair, a Gileadite, arose and judged Israel for twenty-two years. {10:4} He had thirty sons who rode on thirty donkeys, and they controlled thirty cities in Gilead, which are still called Havoth-Jair today. {10:5} Jair died and was buried in Camon. {10:6} Once again, the Israelites did evil in the sight of the LORD. They served the Baals, Ashtaroth, and the gods of Syria, Sidon, Moab, Ammon, and the Philistines, forsaking the LORD and not serving Him. {10:7} The anger of the LORD burned against Israel, and He sold them into the hands of the Philistines and the Ammonites. {10:8} That year, they oppressed and distressed the Israelites for eighteen years, especially those on the east side of the Jordan in the land of the Amorites, which is in Gilead. {10:9} The Ammonites also crossed the Jordan to fight against Judah, Benjamin, and the house of Ephraim, putting Israel in great distress. {10:10} The Israelites cried out to the LORD, saying, "We have sinned against You, for we have forsaken our God and served the Baals." {10:11} The LORD replied to the Israelites, "Didn't I rescue you from the Egyptians, the Amorites, the Ammonites, and the Philistines? {10:12} The Sidonians, Amalekites, and Maonites also oppressed you, and you cried out to me, and I delivered you from their hands. {10:13} Yet you have forsaken me and served other gods; therefore, I will no longer deliver you. {10:14} Go cry out to the gods you have chosen; let them save you in your time of trouble." {10:15} The Israelites said to the LORD, "We have sinned; do to us whatever seems good to You; just deliver us today, we pray." {10:16} They put away their foreign gods and served the LORD, and His soul was grieved by the misery of Israel. {10:17} The Ammonites gathered together and camped in Gilead, while the Israelites assembled and camped at Mizpeh. {10:18} The people and leaders of Gilead said to one another, "Who will be the man to lead the fight against the Ammonites? He will be head over all the inhabitants of Gilead."

{11:1} Jephthah, the Gileadite, was a mighty warrior and the son of a prostitute; Gilead was his father. {11:2} Gilead's wife bore him sons, but when they grew up, they drove Jephthah away, saying, "You will not inherit anything in our father's house, for you are the son of a strange woman." {11:3} Jephthah fled from his brothers and settled in the land of Tob, where he attracted a group of reckless men who joined him. {11:4} Eventually, the Ammonites went to war against Israel. {11:5} When the Ammonites made war against Israel, the elders of Gilead went to bring Jephthah back from Tob. {11:6} They said to him, "Come be our commander so we can fight the Ammonites." {11:7} Jephthah responded, "Didn't you hate me and expel me from my father's house? Why are you coming to me now that you're in trouble?" {11:8} The elders of Gilead replied, "We've turned to you now because we need you to go with us and fight the Ammonites, and be our leader over all the inhabitants of Gilead." {11:9} Jephthah said to the elders, "If you bring me back to fight the Ammonites and the LORD gives them to me, will I be your leader?" {11:10} The elders of Gilead assured Jephthah, "The LORD is our witness; we will do as you say." {11:11} So Jephthah went with the elders of Gilead, and the people made him their leader and commander. He spoke all his words before the LORD at Mizpeh. {11:12} Jephthah sent messengers to the king of the Ammonites, asking, "What do you want with me that you've come to fight in my land?" {11:13} The king of the Ammonites replied to Jephthah's messengers, "Israel took my land when they came out of Egypt, from Arnon to Jabbok and to the Jordan. Now, restore those lands peacefully." {11:14} Jephthah sent messengers back to the king of the Ammonites, {11:15} saying, "Jephthah says Israel did not take the land of Moab or the land of the Ammonites. {11:16} When Israel came from Egypt, they walked through the wilderness to the Red Sea and reached Kadesh. {11:17} Israel sent messengers to the king of Edom, asking to pass through his land, but he refused. They also asked the king of Moab, who also denied them, so Israel remained at Kadesh. {11:18} They then traveled through the wilderness, circled the land of Edom and Moab, and camped on the east side of Moab, not crossing into Moab since Arnon was its border. {11:19} Israel sent messengers to Sihon, king of the Amorites, asking to pass through his land. {11:20} But Sihon did not trust Israel and gathered his people to fight at Jahaz. {11:21} The LORD God of Israel gave Sihon and his people into Israel's hands, and Israel defeated them, taking possession of the land of the Amorites. {11:22} They took all the territory from Arnon to Jabbok and from the wilderness to the Jordan. {11:23} So now, since the LORD God of Israel has dispossessed the Amorites for His people, should you take it? {11:24} Aren't you going to claim what Chemosh, your god, gives you? Whatever the LORD our God drives out before us, we will possess. {11:25} And are you any better than Balak, son of Zippor, king of Moab? Did he ever argue or fight against Israel {11:26} while Israel lived in Heshbon and its towns, and in Aroer and its towns, along the Arnon for three hundred years? Why didn't you recover them during that time? {11:27} So I haven't sinned against you, but you are wrong to make war against me. The LORD will judge between the Israelites and the Ammonites today." {11:28} However, the king of the Ammonites ignored the message Jephthah sent him. {11:29} Then the Spirit of the LORD came upon Jephthah, and he passed through Gilead and Manasseh, and crossed over Mizpeh of Gilead to the Ammonites. {11:30} Jephthah made a vow to the LORD, saying, "If you give the Ammonites into my hands, {11:31} whatever comes out of the doors of my house to meet me when I return in peace will be the LORD's, and I will offer it as a burnt offering." {11:32} Jephthah crossed over to fight the Ammonites, and the LORD delivered them into his hands. {11:33} He struck them from Aroer to Minnith, a total of twenty cities, and he caused a great slaughter in the plain of vineyards. Thus, the Ammonites were subdued before the Israelites. {11:34} When Jephthah returned home to Mizpeh, his daughter came out to meet him with tambourines and dancing; she was his only child, and he had no other son or daughter. {11:35} When he saw her, he tore his clothes and exclaimed, "Oh no, my daughter! You have brought me low, and you are one of those who bring me trouble. I have made a vow to the LORD, and I cannot take it back." {11:36} She said to him, "My father, if you have made a vow to the LORD, do to me as you promised, since the LORD has avenged you against your enemies, the Ammonites." {11:37} Then she said to her father, "Let this be done for me: allow me two months to roam the mountains and weep for my virginity, I and my friends." {11:38} He said, "Go." He sent her away for two months, and she went with her friends to weep for her virginity on the mountains. {11:39} After two months, she returned to her father, who did to her as he had vowed; she remained a virgin. This became a custom in Israel, {11:40} that the young women of Israel would go yearly to lament the daughter of Jephthah the Gileadite for four days each year.

{12:1} The men of Ephraim gathered together and went north to confront Jephthah. They asked, "Why did you go to fight the Ammonites without calling us to join you? We will burn down your house with fire." {12:2} Jephthah replied, "My people and I were in a great struggle with the Ammonites, and when I called you for help, you did not rescue me from their hands. {12:3} When I saw that you weren't coming to help, I risked my life and went to fight the Ammonites, and the LORD gave them into my hands. So why are you coming to fight me now?" {12:4} Then Jephthah gathered all the men of Gilead and fought against Ephraim. The men of Gilead defeated Ephraim because they said, "You Gileadites are fugitives from Ephraim, living among both Ephraim and Manasseh." {12:5} The Gileadites seized control of the fords (river crossings) of the Jordan before the Ephraimites could escape. When an Ephraimite fugitive came and said, "Let me cross," the men of Gilead would ask him, "Are you an Ephraimite?" If he said, "No," {12:6} they would tell him to say "Shibboleth." But if he said "Sibboleth" (because he couldn't pronounce it correctly), they would seize him and kill him at the Jordan crossings. At that time, forty-two thousand Ephraimites were killed. {12:7} Jephthah judged Israel for six years. Then Jephthah the Gileadite died and was buried in one of the cities of Gilead. {12:8} After him, Ibzan of Bethlehem judged Israel. {12:9} He had thirty sons and thirty daughters. He sent his daughters to marry outside his clan and brought in thirty daughters from outside for his sons. He judged Israel for seven years. {12:10} Ibzan died and was buried in Bethlehem. {12:11} After him, Elon the Zebulunite judged Israel, and he judged Israel for ten years. {12:12} Then Elon the Zebulunite died and was buried in Aijalon, in the land of Zebulun. {12:13} After him, Abdon the son of Hillel, a Pirathonite, judged Israel. {12:14} He had forty sons and thirty grandsons, who rode on seventy young donkeys. He judged Israel for eight years. {12:15} Then Abdon the son of Hillel the Pirathonite died and was buried in Pirathon, in the land of Ephraim, in the hill country of the Amalekites.

{13:1} The Israelites did evil again in the eyes of the LORD, and as a result, the LORD handed them over to the Philistines for forty years. {13:2} There was a man from Zorah, from the family of the Danites, named Manoah. His wife was unable to have children. {13:3} The angel of the LORD appeared to her and said, "You are barren and haven't had any children, but you will conceive and give birth to a son. {13:4} Be careful now; do not drink wine or strong drink, and don't eat anything unclean. {13:5} You will conceive and give birth to a son, and no razor shall touch his head because the child will be a Nazarite (a person dedicated to God) from the womb. He will begin to rescue Israel from the Philistines." {13:6} The woman ran to her husband and said, "A man of God came to me. His appearance was like that of an angel of God, very frightening. I didn't ask him where he was from, and he didn't tell me his name. {13:7} But he said to me, 'You will conceive and bear a son, so don't drink wine or strong drink, and don't eat anything unclean, for the child will be a Nazarite to God from the womb until his death.'" {13:8} Manoah prayed to the LORD, saying, "O my Lord, please let the man of God whom you sent come again to teach us what we should do for the child who will be born." {13:9} God listened to Manoah, and the angel of God returned to the woman while she was in the field; her husband Manoah was not with her. {13:10} The woman hurried to tell her husband, "The man who appeared to me the other day has come back!" {13:11} Manoah got up and followed his wife, and when he found the man, he asked, "Are you the one who spoke to my wife?" The angel replied, "I am." {13:12} Manoah said, "Now let your words come true. How should we raise the child?" {13:13} The angel of the LORD told Manoah, "Everything I said to your wife must be observed. {13:14} She must not eat anything from the vine, drink wine or strong drink, or eat anything unclean. She should follow all my instructions." {13:15} Manoah said to the angel of the LORD, "Please stay with us until we prepare a young goat for you." {13:16} The angel of the LORD replied, "Even if you detain me, I won't eat your food, but if you want to offer a burnt offering, it must be to the LORD." Manoah did not realize he was an angel of the LORD. {13:17} Manoah asked, "What is your name? When your words come true, we want to honor you." {13:18} The angel of the LORD said, "Why do you ask for my name? It is beyond understanding." {13:19} Manoah took a young goat and a grain offering and offered it on a rock to the LORD, and the angel performed a miraculous act while Manoah and his wife watched. {13:20} As the flame rose toward heaven from the altar, the angel of the LORD ascended in the flame, and Manoah and his wife fell on their faces to the ground. {13:21} The angel of the LORD did not appear again to Manoah and his wife, and then Manoah realized he was an angel of the LORD. {13:22} Manoah said to his wife, "We will surely die because we have seen God!" {13:23} But his wife replied, "If the LORD wanted to kill us, He wouldn't have accepted our burnt offering and grain offering or shown us all these things or told us such things at this time." {13:24} The woman gave birth to a son and named him Samson. The child grew, and the LORD blessed him. {13:25} The Spirit of the LORD began to stir him at times in the camp of Dan, between Zorah and Eshtaol.

{14:1} Samson went down to Timnah and saw a woman there who was one of the Philistines. {14:2} He returned and told his father and mother, "I found a woman in Timnah from the Philistines. Get her for me as my wife." {14:3} His father and mother replied, "Isn't there a woman among your own relatives or among all our people that you want to marry a Philistine who is uncircumcised?" But Samson insisted, "Get her for me; she looks good to me." {14:4} His parents didn't realize this was from the

LORD, who was looking for a reason to confront the Philistines, since they were ruling over Israel at that time. {14:5} Samson and his parents went down to Timnah, and while they were in the vineyards, a young lion roared at him. {14:6} The Spirit of the LORD came powerfully upon him, and he tore the lion apart as easily as one would tear a young goat, but he didn't tell his parents what he had done. {14:7} Then he went down and talked to the woman, and she pleased him. {14:8} Later, when he returned to marry her, he turned aside to see the lion's carcass, and there was a swarm of bees and honey in it. {14:9} He scooped some honey into his hands and ate it while walking. He also gave some to his father and mother, but he didn't tell them it came from the lion's carcass. {14:10} His father went down to see the woman, and Samson prepared a feast, as was the custom for young men. {14:11} When the Philistines saw him, they brought thirty companions to be with him. {14:12} Samson said to them, "I will give you a riddle. If you can solve it within the seven days of the feast, I will give you thirty linen garments and thirty sets of clothes. {14:13} But if you cannot solve it, then you must give me thirty linen garments and thirty sets of clothes." They agreed, "Tell us your riddle so we can hear it." {14:14} He said, "Out of the eater came something to eat, and out of the strong came something sweet." They couldn't figure out the riddle in three days. {14:15} On the seventh day, they said to Samson's wife, "Get your husband to explain the riddle to us, or we will burn you and your father's house. Did you invite us here just to take what we have?" {14:16} Samson's wife cried before him, saying, "You hate me and don't love me! You posed a riddle to my people but didn't tell me the answer." He replied, "I haven't even told my father or mother, so why should I tell you?" {14:17} She cried for the whole seven days of the feast, and finally, on the seventh day, he told her because she pressed him so hard. She then told the riddle to her people. {14:18} The men of the city said to him just before sunset on the seventh day, "What is sweeter than honey? What is stronger than a lion?" He answered, "If you hadn't plowed with my heifer, you wouldn't have solved my riddle." {14:19} Then the Spirit of the LORD came upon him, and he went down to Ashkelon, killed thirty men, took their belongings, and gave the changes of clothes to those who had solved the riddle. His anger flared up, and went back to his father's house. {14:20} Samson's wife was given to his companion, who had been his friend.

{15:1} After some time, during the wheat harvest, Samson went to visit his wife, bringing a young goat as a gift. He said, "I will go to my wife's room," but her father wouldn't let him go in. {15:2} Her father said, "I thought you hated her, so I gave her to your companion. Isn't her younger sister more attractive? Please take her instead." {15:3} Samson replied, "This time I will be blameless in doing harm to the Philistines." {15:4} So Samson caught three hundred foxes, tied their tails together in pairs, and fastened a torch to every pair of tails. {15:5} He lit the torches and let the foxes loose in the standing grain of the Philistines, burning the grain, including the stacked grain, vineyards, and olive groves. {15:6} The Philistines asked, "Who did this?" They were told, "Samson, the son-in-law of the Timnite, because his father-in-law gave his wife to his companion." So the Philistines went up and burned her and her father to death. {15:7} Samson said to them, "Since you've done this, I won't stop until I get my revenge on you." {15:8} He attacked them viciously, slaughtering many of them, and then went to live in a cave in the rock of Etam. {15:9} The Philistines went up and camped in Judah, spreading out near Lehi. {15:10} The people of Judah asked, "Why have you come against us?" They replied, "We've come to capture Samson, to do to him as he did to us." {15:11} Three thousand men from Judah went to the cave in the rock of Etam and said to Samson, "Don't you realize the Philistines are rulers over us? What have you done to us?" He answered, "I only did to them what they did to me." {15:12} They said, "We've come to tie you up and hand you over to the Philistines." Samson said, "Swear to me that you won't kill me yourselves." {15:13} They assured him, "We will only tie you up and hand you over to them; we won't kill you." So they bound him with two new ropes and led him up from the rock. {15:14} As he approached Lehi, the Philistines came toward him shouting. The Spirit of the Lord came powerfully upon him. The ropes on his arms became like charred flax, and the bindings dropped from his hands. {15:15} Finding a fresh jawbone of a donkey, he grabbed it and struck down a thousand men. {15:16} Then Samson said, "With the jawbone of a donkey, I've made heaps upon heaps; with the jawbone of a donkey, I've killed a thousand men." {15:17} When he finished speaking, he threw away the jawbone and named the place Ramath Lehi (which means "Jawbone Hill"). {15:18} Because he was very thirsty, he called out to the Lord, "You have given your servant this great victory. Must I now die of thirst and fall into the hands of the uncircumcised?" {15:19} Then God opened up a hollow place in Lehi, and water came out of it. When Samson drank, his strength returned, and he revived. So the place was called En Hakkore (which means "Caller's Spring"), and it is still in Lehi to this day. {15:20} Samson led Israel for twenty years in the days of the Philistines.

{16:1} Samson went to Gaza, where he saw a prostitute and spent the night with her. {16:2} The people of Gaza were told, "Samson has come here!" So they surrounded the place and waited for him all night at the city gate. They stayed quiet, thinking, "At dawn, we'll kill him." {16:3} But Samson lay there only until midnight. Then he got up, took hold of the doors of the city gate together with the two posts, lifted them, and carried them on his shoulders to the top of the hill that faces Hebron. {16:4} Some time later, he fell in love with a woman in the Valley of Sorek, whose name was Delilah. {16:5} The rulers of the Philistines went to her and said, "Trick him into telling you the secret of his great strength and how we can overpower him, so we may tie him up and subdue him. Each of us will give you eleven hundred pieces of silver." {16:6} So Delilah said to Samson, "Please tell me the secret of your great strength and how you can be tied up and subdued." {16:7} Samson answered her, "If anyone ties me with seven fresh bowstrings that have not been dried, I'll become as weak as any other man." {16:8} Then the rulers of the Philistines brought her seven fresh bowstrings, and she tied him with them. {16:9} With men hidden in the room, she called out, "Samson, the Philistines are upon you!" But he snapped the bowstrings as easily as a piece of string snaps when it touches a flame. So the secret of his strength was not discovered. {16:10} Then Delilah said to Samson, "You've made a fool of me; you lied to me. Now tell me how you can be tied." {16:11} He said, "If anyone ties me securely with new ropes that have never been used, I'll become as weak as any other man." {16:12} So Delilah took new ropes and tied him with them. Then, with men hidden in the room, she called out, "Samson, the Philistines are upon you!" But he snapped the ropes off his arms like they were threads. {16:13} Delilah then said to Samson, "Until now, you've been making a fool of me and lying to me. Tell me how you can be tied." He replied, "If you weave the seven braids of my head into the fabric on the loom and tighten it with the pin, I'll become as weak as any other man." {16:14} So while he was sleeping, Delilah took the seven braids of his hair, wove them into the fabric, and tightened it with the pin. Again she called to him, "Samson, the Philistines are upon you!" He awoke from his sleep and pulled out the pin and the loom with the fabric. {16:15} Then she said to him, "How can you say, 'I love you,' when you won't confide in me? This is the third time you have made a fool of me and haven't told me the secret of your great strength." {16:16} With such nagging, she prodded him day after day until he was sick to death of it. {16:17} So he told her everything: "No razor has ever been used on my head," he said, "because I have been a Nazarite (one set apart for God) dedicated to God from my mother's womb. If my head were shaved, my strength would leave me, and I would become as weak as any other man." {16:18} When Delilah saw that he had told her everything, she sent word to the rulers of the Philistines, "Come back once more; he has told me everything." So the rulers of the Philistines returned with the silver in their hands. {16:19} After putting him to sleep on her lap, she called for someone to shave off the seven braids of his hair, and so she began to subdue him, and his strength left him. {16:20} Then she called, "Samson, the Philistines are upon you!" He awoke from his sleep and thought, "I'll go out as before and shake myself free." But he did not know that the LORD had left him. {16:21} The Philistines seized him, gouged out his eyes, and took him down to Gaza. Binding him with bronze shackles, they set him to grinding grain in the prison. {16:22} But the hair on his head began to grow again after it had been shaved. {16:23} The rulers of the Philistines assembled to offer a great sacrifice to Dagon, their god, and to celebrate, saying, "Our god has delivered Samson, our enemy, into our hands." {16:24} When the people saw him, they praised their god, saying, "Our god has delivered our enemy into our hands, the one who laid waste to our land and multiplied our dead." {16:25} While they were in high spirits, they shouted, "Bring out Samson to entertain us." So they called Samson out of the prison, and he performed for them. When they stood him among the pillars, {16:26} Samson said to the servant who held his hand, "Put me where I can feel the pillars that support the temple, so that I may lean against them." {16:27} Now the temple was crowded with men and women; all the rulers of the Philistines were there, and on the roof were about three thousand men and women watching Samson perform. {16:28} Then Samson prayed to the LORD, "Sovereign LORD, remember me. Please, God, strengthen me just once more, and let me with one blow get revenge on the Philistines for my two eyes." {16:29} Then Samson reached toward the two central pillars on which the temple stood. Bracing himself against them, his right hand on the one and his left hand on the other, {16:30} Samson said, "Let me die with the Philistines!" Then he pushed with all his might, and the temple fell on the rulers and all the people in it. Thus he killed many more when he died than while he lived. {16:31} Then his brothers and his father's whole family went down to get him. They brought him back and buried him between Zorah and Eshtaol in the tomb of Manoah his father. He had led Israel for twenty years.

{17:1} There was a man from the hill country of Ephraim named Micah. {17:2} He said to his mother, "The eleven hundred shekels of silver that were stolen from you, which you cursed and mentioned to me, I have it with me; I took it." His mother said, "Blessed be you by the LORD, my son." {17:3} After he returned the eleven hundred shekels of silver to her, she said, "I had dedicated that silver to the LORD for my son to make a carved image and a metal image, so now I will give it back to you." {17:4} But he returned the money to her, and she took two hundred shekels of silver and gave them to a silversmith, who made a carved image and a metal image. These were in Micah's house. {17:5} Micah had a shrine with gods, made an ephod (a priestly garment), and teraphim (household gods), and he appointed one of his sons as a priest. {17:6} In those days, there was no king in Israel, so everyone did what they thought was right. {17:7} A young man from Bethlehem in Judah, from the family of Judah, was a Levite, and he stayed there for a while. {17:8} He left Bethlehem in Judah to find a place to live and came to the hill country of Ephraim, to Micah's house, on his journey. {17:9} Micah asked him, "Where are you from?" The young man replied, "I'm a Levite from Bethlehem in Judah, and I'm looking for a place to stay." {17:10} Micah said, "Stay with me, be a father and a priest to me, and I will give you ten shekels of silver a year, a suit of clothes, and your food." So the Levite agreed to stay. {17:11} The Levite was happy to live with Micah, and the young man was like a son to him. {17:12} Micah consecrated the Levite, and the young man became his priest and served in Micah's house. {17:13} Then Micah said, "Now I know that the LORD will bless me, since I have a Levite as my priest."

{18:1} In those days, there was no king in Israel, and the tribe of Dan was looking for a territory to settle in, as they had not received their full inheritance among the tribes of Israel. {18:2} The Danites sent five brave men from their clan, from Zorah and Eshtaol, to scout the land. They told them, "Go and explore the land." When they reached the hill country of Ephraim, they stayed at Micah's house. {18:3} While they were at Micah's house, they recognized the voice of the young Levite and asked him, "Who brought you here? What are you doing in this place, and what do you have?" {18:4} He replied, "Micah has hired me, and I am his priest." {18:5} They said, "Please ask God whether our journey will be successful." {18:6} The priest answered, "Go in peace; the LORD is with you on your journey." {18:7} The five men left and went to Laish, where they found the people living securely, like the Zidonians, quiet and untroubled. There was no ruler in the land to shame them for anything, and they were far from the Zidonians and had no dealings with anyone. {18:8} They returned to their fellow Danites in Zorah and Eshtaol, and their brethren asked them what they had discovered. {18:9} They replied, "Get ready to go up against them; we've seen that the land is very good. Don't hesitate to act and take possession of it." {18:10} When you go, you will find a people living securely in a spacious land; God has given it to you, a place where there is no shortage of anything. {18:11} So from Zorah and Eshtaol, six hundred armed men from the Danite clan set out. {18:12} They camped at Kirjath-jearim in Judah, and that place has been called Mahaneh-dan (Dan's camp) to this day; it's behind Kirjath-jearim. {18:13} From there, they moved on to the hill country of Ephraim and came to Micah's house. {18:14} The five men who had scouted Laish said to their companions, "Did you know there are idols, an ephod, and teraphim (household gods) in Micah's house? Consider what you should do." {18:15} They turned towards Micah's house and greeted the young Levite. {18:16} The six hundred armed men from Dan stood at the entrance of the gate. {18:17} The five men went inside, took the carved image, the ephod, the teraphim, and the molten image, while the priest stood at the gate with the armed men. {18:18} They entered Micah's house and took the carved image, the ephod, and the teraphim. The priest asked them, "What are you doing?" {18:19} They answered, "Be quiet, put your hand over your mouth, and come with us. Be a father and a priest to us. Is it better for you to be a priest for one man's house or for a tribe and family in Israel?" {18:20} The priest was pleased and took the ephod, the teraphim, and the carved image, and went along with the people. {18:21} They turned and left, placing their children, livestock, and belongings in front of them. {18:22} When they were a good distance from Micah's house, the nearby townspeople gathered and caught up with the Danites. {18:23} They called out to the Danites, who turned around and asked Micah, "What's wrong? Why have you gathered such a large group?" {18:24} Micah replied, "You've taken my gods that I made and my priest, and you've gone away. What do I have left? Why are you asking me what's wrong?" {18:25} The Danites warned him, "Don't let your voice be heard among us, or angry men will attack you, and you'll lose your life and the lives of your family." {18:26} The Danites continued on their way, and when Micah saw they were too strong for him, he returned home. {18:27} They took the idols Micah had made and his priest, and went to Laish, a peaceful and secure people, and they attacked and burned the city. {18:28} There was no one to save them because they were far from Zidon and had no dealings with anyone; it was in the valley near Beth-rehob. They built a city and settled there. {18:29} They named the city Dan after their ancestor Dan, who was born to Israel, though the city had originally been called Laish. {18:30} The Danites set up the carved image for themselves, and Jonathan, the son of Gershom, the son of Manasseh, and his descendants became priests for the tribe of Dan until the land was taken captive. {18:31} They maintained Micah's carved image as long as the house of God was in Shiloh.

{19:1} In those days, when there was no king in Israel, there was a Levite living on the side of Mount Ephraim who took a concubine from Bethlehem in Judah. {19:2} His concubine was unfaithful to him and left for her father's house in Bethlehem, where she stayed for four months. {19:3} Her husband got up and went after her to speak kindly to her and bring her back, taking his servant and a couple of donkeys with him. She brought him into her father's house, and when her father saw him, he was glad to meet him. {19:4} Her father retained him, and he stayed with him for three days, during which they ate and drank together. {19:5} On the fourth day, they got up early to leave, but the girl's father said to his son-in-law, "Have something to eat to strengthen yourself before you go." {19:6} They sat down to eat and drink together, and the girl's father said, "Please, be happy and stay the night." {19:7} When the man got up to leave, his father-in-law urged him to stay, so he lodged there again. {19:8} On the fifth day, he got up to depart, but the father said, "Please, take some time to relax." They stayed until the afternoon and ate together. {19:9} When the man rose to leave, he, his concubine, and his servant were told by the father-in-law, "Look, the day is almost over. Stay the night here, and tomorrow you can start your journey home." {19:10} But the man refused to stay that night; he got up and left, arriving near Jebus (Jerusalem), with his concubine and two donkeys. {19:11} As they were near Jebus, it was getting late, and the servant said to his master, "Let's stop and stay in this city of the Jebusites." {19:12} But his master replied, "We won't stay in a city that isn't of Israel; we will go on to Gibeah." {19:13} He then said to his servant, "Let's go to one of these places and stay overnight, either in Gibeah or Ramah." {19:14} They continued on their journey, and as the sun set, they arrived at Gibeah, which belongs to the tribe of

Benjamin. {19:15} They turned in there to lodge, but when he entered the city, no one offered to take them in for the night. {19:16} Just then, an old man came in from the field as the sun was setting. He was from the hill country of Ephraim and was living in Gibeah, but the men of that city were Benjamites. {19:17} When the old man saw the traveler in the street, he asked, "Where are you going? Where did you come from?" {19:18} The Levite answered, "We're passing from Bethlehem in Judah to the side of Mount Ephraim, where I am from. I went to Bethlehem but am now on my way to the house of the LORD, and there's no one to take me in." {19:19} He continued, "We have straw and feed for our donkeys, and bread and wine for me, your servant, and for the young man with us. We lack nothing." {19:20} The old man said, "Peace be with you; just let me take care of your needs. Please don't stay in the street." {19:21} So he brought them into his house, fed the donkeys, washed their feet, and they ate and drank together. {19:22} While they were enjoying themselves, some wicked men from the city, sons of Belial (worthless men), surrounded the house, beating on the door and demanding the old man, "Bring out the man who came to your house so we can know him." {19:23} The master of the house went out to them and said, "Please, my brothers, don't act so wickedly. This man has come into my house; don't do this disgraceful thing." {19:24} He offered, "Here's my virgin daughter and his concubine. Let me bring them out, and you can humiliate them and do what you like, but don't do anything to this man." {19:25} But the men refused to listen to him, so the Levite took his concubine and brought her outside to them. They abused her all night and let her go at dawn. {19:26} At dawn, the woman fell at the door of the man's house where her master was until it was light. {19:27} When her master got up in the morning and opened the door to leave, he found her lying at the door with her hands on the threshold. {19:28} He said to her, "Get up; let's go." But there was no answer. He lifted her onto a donkey and set out for his home. {19:29} When he got home, he took a knife, cut his concubine into twelve pieces, and sent her throughout all the territories of Israel. {19:30} Everyone who saw it said, "Such a thing has never been seen since the Israelites came out of Egypt. Think about it; discuss it, and let us know what to do."

{20:1} Then all the Israelites from Dan to Beersheba, including the land of Gilead, came together as one assembly before the LORD at Mizpah. {20:2} The leaders of all the tribes of Israel took their places in the assembly of God's people—four hundred thousand soldiers armed with swords. {20:3} (The Benjamites heard that the Israelites had gone up to Mizpah.) The Israelites asked, "Tell us, how did this evil thing happen?" {20:4} The Levite, the husband of the murdered woman, answered, "My concubine and I came to Gibeah, a town that belongs to Benjamin, to spend the night. {20:5} The men of Gibeah surrounded the house and attacked me at night. They intended to kill me, but instead they violated my concubine, and she died. {20:6} So I took my concubine, cut her into pieces, and sent her throughout Israel's inheritance, because they committed an outrageous and wicked act in Israel. {20:7} Now, all you Israelites, speak up and give your advice and decision." {20:8} All the people rose up together and said, "None of us will go home. No one will return to his house. {20:9} Here's what we'll do to Gibeah: We'll cast lots to decide how to attack it. {20:10} We'll take ten men out of every hundred from all the tribes of Israel, and a hundred out of a thousand, and a thousand out of ten thousand, to supply provisions for the army. When the army arrives at Gibeah in Benjamin, they will punish them for the wickedness they committed in Israel." {20:11} So all the men of Israel gathered together and united as one against the city. {20:12} The tribes of Israel sent men throughout the tribe of Benjamin, saying, "What is this wickedness that has been done among you? {20:13} Now, surrender the wicked men of Gibeah so that we may put them to death and purge the evil from Israel." But the Benjamites would not listen to their fellow Israelites. {20:14} Instead, they gathered from their cities and came to Gibeah to fight against the Israelites. {20:15} That day, the Benjamites mustered twenty-six thousand men armed with swords, besides the seven hundred able men of Gibeah. {20:16} Among all these soldiers were seven hundred left-handed men, each of whom could sling a stone at a hair and not miss. {20:17} The Israelites, excluding Benjamin, mustered four hundred thousand men armed with swords, all experienced warriors. {20:18} The Israelites went up to Bethel and inquired of God. They asked, "Who of us is to go up first to fight against the Benjamites?" The LORD replied, "Judah shall go first." {20:19} The next morning the Israelites got up and pitched camp near Gibeah. {20:20} The Israelites went out to fight the Benjamites and took up battle positions against them at Gibeah. {20:21} The Benjamites came out of Gibeah and cut down twenty-two thousand Israelites on the battlefield that day. {20:22} But the Israelites encouraged each other and again took up their positions where they had stationed themselves the first day. {20:23} (The Israelites went up and wept before the LORD until evening, and they asked the LORD, "Shall we go up again to fight against the Benjamites, our fellow Israelites?" The LORD answered, "Go up against them.") {20:24} Then the Israelites drew near to Benjamin the second day. {20:25} This time, the Benjamites came out from Gibeah to oppose them and again cut down eighteen thousand Israelites, all of whom drew the sword. {20:26} Then all the Israelites, the whole army, went up to Bethel, and there they sat weeping before the LORD. They fasted that day until evening and presented burnt offerings and fellowship offerings to the LORD. {20:27} And the Israelites inquired of the LORD. (In those days the ark of the covenant of God was there, {20:28} with Phinehas son of Eleazar, the son of Aaron, ministering before it.) They asked, "Shall we go up again to fight against the Benjamites, our fellow Israelites, or not?" The LORD responded, "Go, for tomorrow I will give them into your hands." {20:29} Then Israel set an ambush around Gibeah. {20:30} They went up against the Benjamites on the third day and took their positions against Gibeah as they had done before. {20:31} The Benjamites came out to meet them and were drawn away from the city. They began to inflict casualties on the Israelites as before, on the roads, one of which leads to Bethel and the other to Gibeah, and in the open fields, about thirty Israelites fell. {20:32} The Benjamites thought, "We are defeating them as before." But the Israelites said, "Let's retreat and draw them away from the city to the roads." {20:33} All the men of Israel moved from their places and took up positions at Baal Tamar, and the Israelite ambush charged out of its place west of Gibeah. {20:34} Then ten thousand of Israel's finest men attacked Gibeah. The fighting was so heavy that the Benjamites did not realize how disaster was closing in on them. {20:35} The LORD defeated Benjamin before Israel, and on that day the Israelites struck down twenty-five thousand one hundred Benjamites, all armed with swords. {20:36} Then the Benjamites saw that they were beaten. Now the men of Israel had given way before Benjamin, because they relied on the ambush they had set near Gibeah. {20:37} Those in the ambush made a sudden dash into Gibeah, spread out, and put the whole city to the sword. {20:38} The Israelites had arranged with the ambush that a great cloud of smoke should rise from the city as a signal. {20:39} When the Israelites counterattacked, the Benjamites had already begun to inflict casualties on about thirty of them, thinking, "Surely they are defeated as in the first battle." {20:40} But when the signal, a column of smoke, began to rise from the city, the Benjamites turned and saw the whole city going up in smoke. {20:41} Then the Israelites counterattacked, and the Benjamites were terrified, because they realized that disaster had come on them. {20:42} So they fled before the Israelites in the direction of the wilderness, but they could not escape the battle. And the Israelites who came out of the towns cut them down there. {20:43} They surrounded the Benjamites, chased them, and easily overran them in the vicinity of Gibeah toward the east. {20:44} Eighteen thousand Benjamites fell, all of them valiant fighters. {20:45} As they turned and fled toward the wilderness to the rock of Rimmon, the Israelites cut down five thousand men along the roads. They kept pressing after the Benjamites as far as Gidom and struck down two thousand more. {20:46} On that day twenty-five thousand Benjamites who drew the sword fell, all of them valiant fighters. {20:47} But six hundred men turned and fled into the wilderness to the rock of Rimmon, where they stayed for four months. {20:48} The men of Israel went back to Benjamin and put all the towns to the sword, including the animals and everything else they found. All the towns they came across, they set on fire.

{21:1} The men of Israel had sworn at Mizpeh that no one among them would give his daughter to a Benjaminite as a wife. {21:2} The people went to the house of God and stayed there until evening, lifting their voices and weeping bitterly. {21:3} They said, "O LORD God of Israel, why has this happened in Israel, making one tribe lacking today?" {21:4} The next day, the people rose early, built an altar, and offered burnt and peace offerings. {21:5} The Israelites asked, "Who among all the tribes of Israel did not come up to the LORD at Mizpeh?" They had made a serious oath against anyone who did not join them, saying he must be put to death. {21:6} The Israelites felt remorse for their brother Benjamin, saying, "Today, one tribe has been cut off from Israel." {21:7} They wondered how they would provide wives for those who remained since they had sworn by the LORD not to give their daughters to them. {21:8} They asked, "Which tribe of Israel did not come to Mizpeh?" They discovered that no one from Jabeshgilead had joined the assembly. {21:9} The people were counted, and it was found that none of the inhabitants of Jabeshgilead were there. {21:10} The congregation sent twelve thousand of the bravest men with orders to go and kill the inhabitants of Jabeshgilead, including women and children. {21:11} They were commanded to destroy every male and every woman who had been with a man. {21:12} They found four hundred young virgins among the inhabitants of Jabeshgilead who had never been with a man, and they brought them to the camp at Shiloh in Canaan. {21:13} The whole congregation sent messengers to the Benjaminites who were at the rock of Rimmon, calling them to peace. {21:14} The Benjaminites returned at that time, and they gave them the wives they had saved from Jabeshgilead, but it was still not enough for them. {21:15} The people felt sorry for Benjamin because the LORD had caused a divide among the tribes of Israel. {21:16} Then the elders of the congregation said, "How can we provide wives for those who remain, since the women of Benjamin have been destroyed?" {21:17} They concluded that there needed to be an inheritance for the survivors of Benjamin, so that a tribe would not be wiped out from Israel. {21:18} However, they could not give their daughters as wives because the Israelites had sworn an oath saying, "Cursed is anyone who gives a wife to Benjamin." {21:19} Then they said, "Look, there is an annual festival of the LORD at Shiloh, located north of Bethel, east of the road that goes from Bethel to Shechem, and south of Lebonah." {21:20} So they instructed the Benjaminites, saying, "Go and hide in the vineyards; {21:21} and watch. If the daughters of Shiloh come out to dance, then you can come out of the vineyards and each man can catch a wife from the daughters of Shiloh and return to the land of Benjamin. {21:22} If their fathers or brothers come to complain, we will say to them, 'Be kind to them for our sake, because we did not provide enough wives for them during the war; you will not be guilty for not giving them wives this time.'" {21:23} The Benjaminites did as instructed and took wives for themselves from among those who danced, and they returned to their land, rebuilt their cities, and settled there. {21:24} The Israelites then departed, each man to his tribe and family, and they returned to their own inheritances. {21:25} In those days, there was no king in Israel; everyone did what was right in their own eyes.

The Book of Ruth

{1:1} During the time when judges ruled Israel, there was a famine in the land. A man from Bethlehem in Judah, along with his wife and two sons, went to live temporarily in the country of Moab. {1:2} The man's name was Elimelech, his wife's name was Naomi, and their two sons were named Mahlon and Chilion. They were Ephrathites from Bethlehem in Judah, and they settled in Moab. {1:3} Elimelech, Naomi's husband, died, leaving her and her two sons. {1:4} The sons married Moabite women; one was named Orpah and the other Ruth, and they lived there for about ten years. {1:5} Mahlon and Chilion also died, leaving Naomi without her two sons and her husband. {1:6} Then Naomi decided to return from Moab, having heard that the LORD had visited His people and provided food for them. {1:7} So she set out from the place where she was, with her two daughters-in-law, to return to the land of Judah. {1:8} Naomi said to her daughters-in-law, "Go back, each of you, to your mother's house. May the LORD show you kindness, as you have shown to the dead and to me. {1:9} May the LORD grant that you find rest, each in the home of your husband." She kissed them, and they wept aloud. {1:10} They said to her, "No, we will go back with you to your people." {1:11} But Naomi replied, "Return home, my daughters. Why would you come with me? Am I going to have any more sons, who could become your husbands? {1:12} Return home, my daughters; I am too old to have another husband. Even if I thought there was still hope for me, and I had a husband tonight and gave birth to sons, {1:13} would you wait until they grew up? Would you remain unmarried for them? No, my daughters; it is more bitter for me than for you, because the LORD's hand has turned against me." {1:14} At this, they wept again. Orpah kissed her mother-in-law goodbye, but Ruth clung to her. {1:15} Naomi said, "Look, your sister-in-law is going back to her people and her gods. You should go back with her." {1:16} But Ruth replied, "Don't urge me to leave you or to turn back from you. Where you go, I will go, and where you stay, I will stay. Your people will be my people, and your God my God. {1:17} Where you die, I will die, and there I will be buried. May the LORD deal with me, be it ever so severely, if even death separates you and me." {1:18} When Naomi realized that Ruth was determined to go with her, she stopped urging her. {1:19} So the two women went on until they came to Bethlehem. When they arrived in Bethlehem, the whole town was stirred because of them, and the women exclaimed, "Is this Naomi?" {1:20} "Don't call me Naomi," she told them. "Call me Mara (bitter), because the Almighty has made my life very bitter. {1:21} I went away full, but the LORD has brought me back empty. Why call me Naomi, since the LORD has afflicted me and the Almighty has brought misfortune upon me?" {1:22} So Naomi returned from Moab, accompanied by Ruth the Moabitess, her daughter-in-law, and they arrived in Bethlehem at the beginning of the barley harvest.

{2:1} Naomi had a relative on her husband's side, a wealthy and influential man from the family of Elimelech, named Boaz. {2:2} Ruth the Moabitess said to Naomi, "Let me go to the fields and pick up the leftover grain behind anyone whose eyes I find favor in." Naomi replied, "Go ahead, my daughter." {2:3} So Ruth went out, entered a field, and began to glean behind the harvesters. It just so happened that she was working in a field belonging to Boaz, who was a relative of Elimelech. {2:4} Boaz arrived from Bethlehem and greeted the harvesters, saying, "The LORD be with you!" They answered, "The LORD bless you!" {2:5} Boaz asked his foreman, "Who is that young woman?" {2:6} The foreman replied, "She is the Moabitess who came back with Naomi from Moab. {2:7} She said, 'Please let me glean and gather among the sheaves behind the harvesters.' She has been in the field all day, except for a short rest in the house." {2:8} Boaz said to Ruth, "Listen, my daughter. Don't go and glean in another field. Stay here with my female workers. {2:9} Watch the field they are harvesting and follow along after the women. I have told the men not to lay a hand on you, and whenever you are thirsty, go and get a drink from the water jars the men have filled." {2:10} Ruth fell on her face, bowing down to the ground and asked him, "Why have I found such favor in your eyes that you notice me—a foreigner?" {2:11} Boaz replied, "I have been told all about what you have done for your mother-in-law since the death of your husband, how you left your father and mother and your homeland to live with a people you did not know before. {2:12} May the LORD repay you for what you have done. May you be richly rewarded by the LORD, the God of Israel, under whose wings you have come to take refuge." {2:13} Ruth said, "May I continue to find favor in your eyes, my lord. You have put me at ease by speaking kindly to me, though I do not have the standing of one of your female servants." {2:14} At mealtime, Boaz said to her, "Come over here. Have some bread and dip it in the wine vinegar." She sat down with the harvesters, and he offered her some roasted grain. She ate all she wanted and had some leftover. {2:15} As she got up to glean, Boaz instructed his men, "Let her gather among the sheaves and don't reprimand her. {2:16} Even pull out some stalks for her from the bundles and leave them for her to glean. Don't rebuke her." {2:17} So Ruth gleaned in the field until evening. Then she threshed the barley she had gathered, and it amounted to about an ephah (a unit of measurement). {2:18} She carried it back to town, and her mother-in-law saw how much she had gleaned. Ruth also brought out and gave her what she had left over after she had eaten enough. {2:19} Her mother-in-law asked, "Where did you glean today? Where did you work? Blessed be the man who took notice of you!" Then Ruth told her mother-in-law about the one at whose place she had been working. "The name of the man I worked with today is Boaz," she said. {2:20} Naomi said to her daughter-in-law, "The LORD bless him! He has not stopped showing his kindness to the living and the dead." She added, "That man is our close relative; he is one of our guardian-redeemers." {2:21} Then Ruth the Moabitess said, "He even said to me, 'Stay with my workers until they finish harvesting all my grain.'" {2:22} Naomi said to Ruth, "It will be good for you, my daughter, to go with the young women who work for him, because in someone else's field you might be harmed." {2:23} So Ruth stayed close to the women of Boaz to glean until the barley and wheat harvests were finished, and she lived with her mother-in-law.

{3:1} Naomi, her mother-in-law, said to her, "My daughter, shouldn't I try to find a secure home for you so that you will be well taken care of? {3:2} Isn't Boaz, with whom you have been working, a relative of ours? Tonight, he will be winnowing barley at the threshing floor. {3:3} So wash and perfume yourself, and put on your best clothes. Then go down to the threshing floor, but don't let him know you're there until he has finished eating and drinking. {3:4} When he lies down, note the place where he is lying. Then go in and uncover his feet and lie down. He will tell you what to do." {3:5} Ruth replied, "I will do everything you say." {3:6} So she went down to the threshing floor and did everything her mother-in-law told her to do. {3:7} When Boaz had finished eating and drinking, and was in good spirits, he went over to lie down at the far end of the grain pile. Ruth approached quietly, uncovered his feet, and lay down. {3:8} At midnight, Boaz was startled and turned over, and there was a woman lying at his feet. {3:9} He asked, "Who are you?" She replied, "I am Ruth, your servant. Spread the corner of your garment over me, since you are a guardian-redeemer." {3:10} "The LORD bless you, my daughter," he said. "This kindness is greater than that which you showed earlier; you have not run after the younger men, whether rich or poor. {3:11} And now, my daughter, don't be afraid. I will do for you all you ask. All the people of my town know that you are a woman of noble character. {3:12} It is true that I am a guardian-redeemer of our family, but there is a guardian-redeemer nearer than I. {3:13} Stay here for the night, and in the morning, if he wants to redeem you, good; let him redeem you. But if he is not willing, as surely as the LORD lives, I will do it for you. Lie here until morning." {3:14} So she lay at his feet until morning, but got up before anyone could be recognized. He said, "No one must know that a woman came to the threshing floor." {3:15} He also said, "Bring me the shawl you are wearing and hold it out." When she did so, he poured six measures of barley into it and placed it on her. Then he went back to town. {3:16} When Ruth came to her mother-in-law, Naomi asked, "How did it go, my daughter?" Ruth told her everything Boaz had done for her. {3:17} She said, "He gave me these six measures of barley, saying, 'Don't go back to your mother-in-law empty-handed.'" {3:18} Then Naomi said, "Wait, my daughter, until you find out what happens. For the man will not rest until the matter is settled today."

{4:1} Boaz went up to the city gate and sat down there. Just then, the relative Boaz had mentioned came by, and Boaz said, "Come over here, friend & sit down." So he went over and sat down. {4:2} Boaz then took ten men from the elders of the city and said, "Sit here." They sat down. {4:3} He said to the relative, "Naomi, who has returned from Moab, is selling a piece of land that belonged to our brother Elimelech. {4:4} I thought I should let you know and suggest that you buy it in the presence of those seated here and the elders of my people. If you want to redeem it, do so. But if you don't, let me know, because I am next in line to redeem it." The relative replied, "I will redeem it." {4:5} Then Boaz said, "On the day you buy the land from Naomi, you also acquire Ruth the Moabitess, the widow of the deceased, in order to maintain the name of the dead with his property." {4:6} The relative answered, "I can't redeem it myself, or I might endanger my own inheritance. You redeem it; I cannot do it." {4:7} (Now in earlier times in Israel, for the redemption and transfer of property, one party removed his sandal and gave it to the other. This was the method of legalizing transactions in Israel.) {4:8} So the relative said to Boaz, "Buy it yourself." And he removed his sandal. {4:9} Boaz announced to the elders and all the people, "You are witnesses today that I have bought from Naomi all the property of Elimelech, Chilion, and Mahlon. {4:10} I have also acquired Ruth the Moabitess, Mahlon's widow, as my wife, to maintain the name of the deceased with his property so that his name will not disappear from among his relatives or from the gate of his hometown. You are witnesses today." {4:11} The people at the gate and the elders replied, "We are witnesses. May the LORD make the woman who is coming into your home like Rachel and Leah, who together built up the house of Israel. May you have standing in Ephrathah and be famous in Bethlehem. {4:12} Through the offspring the LORD gives you by this young woman, may your family be like that of Perez, whom Tamar bore to Judah." {4:13} So Boaz took Ruth, and she became his wife. When he made love to her, the LORD enabled her to conceive, and she gave birth to a son. {4:14} The women said to Naomi, "Praise be to the LORD, who this day has not left you without a guardian-redeemer. May he become famous throughout Israel! {4:15} He will renew your life and sustain you in your old age, for your daughter-in-law, who loves you and who is better to you than seven sons, has given him birth." {4:16} Then Naomi took the child in her arms and cared for him. {4:17} The women living there said, "Naomi has a son!" And they named him Obed. He was the father of Jesse, the father of David. {4:18} This is the family line of Perez: Perez was the father of Hezron, {4:19} Hezron the father of Ram, Ram the father of Amminadab, {4:20} Amminadab the father of Nahshon, Nahshon the father of Salmon, {4:21} Salmon the father of Boaz, Boaz the father of Obed, {4:22} Obed the father of Jesse, and Jesse the father of David.

The First Book of Samuel

{1:1} There was a man from Ramathaimzophim in the hill country of Ephraim, named Elkanah, the son of Jeroham, the son of Elihu, the son of Tohu, the son of Zuph, an Ephrathite. {1:2} He had two wives: one was named Hannah and the other Peninnah. Peninnah had children, but Hannah did not. {1:3} Every year, this man went from his city to worship and sacrifice to the LORD of hosts at Shiloh, where the two sons of Eli, Hophni and Phinehas, were priests of the LORD. {1:4} When the time came for Elkanah to offer his sacrifice, he would give portions to Peninnah, his wife, and to all her sons and daughters. {1:5} But to Hannah, he gave a double portion because he loved her, even though the LORD had closed her womb. {1:6} Her rival provoked her severely to irritate her, because the LORD had closed her womb. {1:7} This happened year after year. Whenever Hannah went up to the house of the LORD, Peninnah would provoke her, and Hannah would weep and refuse to eat. {1:8} Elkanah her husband would ask her, "Hannah, why are you weeping? Why aren't you eating? Why are you so downhearted? Don't I mean more to you than ten sons?" {1:9} After they had eaten and drunk in Shiloh, Hannah stood up. Eli the priest was sitting on a chair near the doorpost of the LORD's temple. {1:10} In her deep anguish, Hannah prayed to the LORD, weeping bitterly. {1:11} She made a vow, saying, "LORD of hosts, if you will look on the affliction of your servant and remember me and not forget your servant, but give her a son, then I will give him to the LORD all the days of his life, and no razor shall ever be used on his head." {1:12} As she continued praying before the LORD, Eli observed her mouth. {1:13} Hannah was praying in her heart, and her lips were moving, but her voice was not heard. Therefore, Eli thought she was drunk. {1:14} Eli said to her, "How long will you remain drunk? Put away your wine!" {1:15} Hannah answered, "No, my lord. I am a woman who is deeply troubled. I have not been drinking wine or strong drink; I was pouring out my soul to the LORD. {1:16} Do not take your servant for a wicked woman; I have been praying here out of my great anguish and grief." {1:17} Eli answered, "Go in peace, and may the God of Israel grant you what you have asked of him." {1:18} Hannah said, "May your servant find favor in your eyes." Then she went her way and ate something, and her face was no longer downcast. {1:19} Early the next morning, they rose and worshiped before the LORD and then went back to their home in Ramah. Elkanah knew Hannah, his wife, and the LORD remembered her. {1:20} So in the course of time, Hannah became pregnant and gave birth to a son. She named him Samuel, saying, "Because I asked the LORD for him." {1:21} Elkanah and his family went up to offer the annual sacrifice to the LORD and to fulfill his vow. {1:22} But Hannah did not go up. She told her husband, "After the boy is weaned, I will take him to appear before the LORD and to stay there forever." {1:23} Elkanah her husband replied, "Do what seems best to you. Stay here until you have weaned him; only may the LORD make good his word." So the woman stayed home and nursed her son until she had weaned him. {1:24} After he was weaned, she took the boy with her, along with three bulls, an ephah of flour, and a skin of wine, and brought him to the house of the LORD at Shiloh. The boy was very young. {1:25} When they had slaughtered the bull, they brought the boy to Eli. {1:26} And she said to him, "Pardon me, my lord. As surely as you live, I am the woman who stood here beside you praying to the LORD. {1:27} I prayed for this child, and the LORD has granted me what I asked of him. {1:28} So now I give him to the LORD. For his whole life he will be given over to the LORD." And he worshiped the LORD there.

{2:1} Hannah prayed and said, "My heart rejoices in the LORD; my strength is lifted up in the LORD. My mouth is wide open against my enemies because I celebrate in your salvation. {2:2} There is no one as holy as the LORD; there is no one besides you; there is no rock like our God. {2:3} Don't talk so arrogantly; let no pride come from your mouth, for the LORD is a God of knowledge, and he weighs actions. {2:4} The bows of mighty men are broken, but those who stumble are strengthened. {2:5} Those who were full have now hired themselves out for bread, while the hungry have ceased to hunger; the barren has given birth to seven, but she who has many children is now weak. {2:6} The LORD kills and makes alive; he brings down to the grave and raises up. {2:7} The LORD makes poor and makes rich; he humbles and exalts. {2:8} He lifts the poor from the dust and the beggar from the dunghill (a place of refuse) to set them among princes and to give them an inheritance of glory, for the pillars of the earth are the LORD's, and he has set the world on them. {2:9} He protects the feet of his saints, but the wicked will be silenced in darkness, for no man will prevail by strength. {2:10} The adversaries of the LORD will be shattered; he will thunder from heaven against them. The LORD will judge the ends of the earth and give strength to his king, exalting the strength of his anointed one. {2:11} Elkanah went home to Ramah, and the child ministered to the LORD before Eli the priest. {2:12} Now Eli's sons were corrupt; they did not know the LORD. {2:13} The priests' custom with the people was that when anyone offered a sacrifice, the priest's servant would come with a three-pronged fork while the meat was boiling; {2:14} he would strike it into the pot, and whatever the fork brought up, the priest would take for himself. They did this in Shiloh to all the Israelites who came there. {2:15} Before they burned the fat, the priest's servant would come and say to the man who was sacrificing, "Give me meat to roast for the priest; he won't take boiled meat from you, but only raw." {2:16} If the man said, "Let the fat be burned first, and then you can take as much as you want," the servant would answer, "No, you must give it to me now, or I will take it by force." {2:17} This sin of the young men was very great before the LORD, for men despised the offerings of the LORD. {2:18} But Samuel ministered before the LORD, wearing a linen ephod as a child. {2:19} Each year, his mother made him a small robe and brought it to him when she came with her husband for the yearly sacrifice. {2:20} Eli blessed Elkanah and his wife, saying, "May the LORD give you children from this woman for the loan you have given to the LORD." Then they returned home. {2:21} The LORD visited Hannah, and she conceived and bore three sons and two daughters, while the child Samuel grew before the LORD. {2:22} Eli was very old and heard all that his sons were doing to all Israel, how they lay with the women who served at the entrance to the tabernacle. {2:23} He said to them, "Why are you doing these things? I hear about your evil deeds from all the people. {2:24} No, my sons, this is a bad report I hear; you are causing the LORD's people to sin. {2:25} If one man sins against another, the judge will judge him, but if a man sins against the LORD, who can intercede for him?" But they did not listen to their father, for the LORD intended to kill them. {2:26} Meanwhile, the child Samuel grew in stature and favor with the LORD and with people. {2:27} A man of God came to Eli and said, "This is what the LORD says: Did I not reveal myself to your ancestor's house when they were in Egypt under Pharaoh? {2:28} Did I not choose your ancestor from all the tribes of Israel to be my priest, to offer sacrifices on my altar, to burn incense, and to wear an ephod before me? Did I not give your ancestor's house all the offerings made by fire from the Israelites? {2:29} Why do you scorn my sacrifice and offerings that I commanded in my dwelling? Why do you honor your sons more than me by fattening yourselves with the choice parts of every offering made by my people Israel? {2:30} Therefore, the LORD God of Israel says: I promised that your house and your father's house would minister before me forever. But now the LORD says: Be it far from me; those who honor me I will honor, but those who despise me will be treated with contempt. {2:31} The time is coming when I will cut off your strength and the strength of your father's house, and there will not be an old man in your house. {2:32} You will see distress in my dwelling, despite all the good I do for Israel, and there will not be an old man in your house forever. {2:33} Any man of yours whom I do not cut off from my altar will be left to die in the flower of his age, and all the increase of your family will die. {2:34} This will be a sign to you: Your two sons, Hophni and Phinehas, will die on the same day. {2:35} I will raise up a faithful priest who will do according to my heart and mind. I will build him a sure house, and he will serve before my anointed one forever. {2:36} Everyone left in your family will come and bow down to him for a piece of silver and a crust of bread, and will say, "Please put me in one of the priest's offices so I can have something to eat."

{3:1} The child Samuel served the LORD under Eli. The word of the LORD was rare in those days; there were not many visions. {3:2} One night, Eli, whose eyes were becoming so dim that he could barely see, was lying down in his usual place. {3:3} The lamp of God had not yet gone out, and Samuel was lying down in the temple of the LORD, where the ark of God was. {3:4} Then the LORD called Samuel, and he answered, "Here I am." {3:5} He ran to Eli and said, "Here I am; you called me." But Eli said, "I did not call you; go back and lie down." So he went back and lay down. {3:6} The LORD called Samuel again. Samuel got up and went to Eli and said, "Here I am; you called me." But Eli answered, "My son, I did not call you; go back and lie down." {3:7} Samuel did not yet know the LORD, and the word of the LORD had not yet been revealed to him. {3:8} The LORD called Samuel a third time. Samuel got up and went to Eli and said, "Here I am; you called me." Then Eli realized that the LORD was calling the boy. {3:9} So Eli told Samuel, "Go back and lie down. If he calls you, say, 'Speak, LORD, for your servant is listening.'" So Samuel went back and lay down in his place. {3:10} The LORD came and stood there, calling as before, "Samuel! Samuel!" And Samuel said, "Speak, for your servant is listening." {3:11} The LORD said to Samuel, "See, I am about to do something in Israel that will make the ears of everyone who hears it tingle. {3:12} At that time, I will carry out against Eli everything I spoke against his family, from beginning to end. {3:13} I told him that I would judge his family forever because of the wickedness he knew about; his sons made themselves vile, and he did not restrain them. {3:14} Therefore, I swore to the house of Eli that the wickedness of Eli's family would not be atoned for by sacrifice or offering forever." {3:15} Samuel lay down until morning and then opened the doors of the house of the LORD. He was afraid to tell Eli the vision. {3:16} But Eli called Samuel and said, "Samuel, my son." Samuel answered, "Here I am." {3:17} Eli asked, "What did the LORD say to you? Do not hide it from me. May God deal with you, be it ever so severely, if you hide from me anything he told you." {3:18} So Samuel told him everything, hiding nothing from him. Then Eli said, "He is the LORD; let him do what is good in his eyes." {3:19} The LORD was with Samuel as he grew up, and he let none of Samuel's words fall to the ground. {3:20} And all Israel from Dan to Beersheba recognized that Samuel was attested as a prophet of the LORD. {3:21} The LORD continued to appear at Shiloh, and there he revealed himself to Samuel through his word.

{4:1} The word of Samuel came to all Israel. Now Israel went out to battle against the Philistines and camped at Ebenezer, while the Philistines camped at Aphek. {4:2} The Philistines arranged themselves against Israel, and when the battle began, Israel was defeated by the Philistines, losing about four thousand men in the field. {4:3} When the people returned to the camp, the elders of Israel asked, "Why has the LORD defeated us today before the Philistines? Let us bring the ark of the covenant of the LORD from Shiloh so that it may come among us and save us from our enemies." {4:4} So the people sent to Shiloh to bring the ark of the covenant of the LORD of hosts, who is enthroned between the cherubim. Eli's two sons, Hophni and Phinehas, were there with the ark of the covenant of God. {4:5} When the ark of the covenant of the LORD entered the camp, all Israel shouted so loudly that the ground shook. {4:6} When the Philistines heard the noise of the shout, they asked, "What does this loud shouting in the camp of the Hebrews mean?" They understood that the ark of the LORD had come into the camp. {4:7} The Philistines were afraid and said, "God has come into the camp. Woe to us! We have never seen anything like this before." {4:8} They said, "Woe to us! Who will rescue us from the hands of these mighty gods? These are the gods who struck the Egyptians with all the plagues in the wilderness." {4:9} Be strong and act like men, O Philistines, so that you do not become slaves to the Hebrews, as they have been to you. Act like men and fight! {4:10} So the Philistines fought, and Israel was defeated, and each man fled to his tent. There was a great slaughter; thirty thousand Israelite foot soldiers fell. {4:11} The ark of God was captured, and Eli's two sons, Hophni and Phinehas, were killed. {4:12} A man from the tribe of Benjamin ran from the battle line and went to Shiloh that same day, with his clothes torn and dust on his head. {4:13} When he arrived, Eli was sitting on a seat by the road watching, because his heart trembled for the ark of God. When the man entered the city and told what had happened, the whole city cried out. {4:14} Eli heard the noise of the crying and asked, "What is this uproar?" The man hurried to tell Eli. {4:15} Eli was ninety-eight years old, and his eyes were so dim that he could not see. {4:16} The man said to Eli, "I am the one who escaped from the battle. I fled from the army today." Eli asked, "What happened, my son?" {4:17} The messenger answered, "Israel has fled before the Philistines, and there has been a great slaughter among the people. Your two sons, Hophni and Phinehas, are dead, and the ark of God has been captured." {4:18} When he mentioned the ark of God, Eli fell backward off his seat by the gate, broke his neck, and died, for he was an old man and heavy. He had judged Israel for forty years. {4:19} Eli's daughter-in-law, the wife of Phinehas, was pregnant and near the time of delivery. When she heard the news that the ark of God was taken and that her father-in-law and her husband were dead, she went into labor and gave birth, for her pains came upon her. {4:20} As she was dying, the women who stood by her said, "Don't be afraid; you have given birth to a son." But she did not respond or pay attention. {4:21} She named the child Ichabod, saying, "The glory has departed from Israel," because the ark of God had been taken and because of her father-in-law and her husband. {4:22} She said, "The glory has departed from Israel, for the ark of God has been taken."

{5:1} The Philistines took the ark of God and brought it from Ebenezer to Ashdod. {5:2} They brought the ark into the house of Dagon and set it beside Dagon. {5:3} When the people of Ashdod rose early the next morning, they found Dagon fallen on his face to the ground before the ark of the LORD. They took Dagon and set him back in his place. {5:4} The next morning, when they rose again, they saw Dagon fallen on his face to the ground before the ark of the LORD; his head and hands had been cut off and were lying on the threshold; only the stump of Dagon remained. {5:5} That is why neither the priests of Dagon nor anyone who enters Dagon's house step on the threshold in Ashdod to this day. {5:6} The hand of the LORD was heavy upon the people of Ashdod, and he destroyed them and afflicted them with tumors (or "emerods"), both Ashdod and its territories. {5:7} When the men of Ashdod saw what was happening, they said, "The ark of the God of Israel cannot stay with us, for his hand is heavy upon us and upon Dagon our god." {5:8} So they gathered all the lords of the Philistines together and asked, "What should we do with the ark of the God of Israel?" They replied, "Let the ark of the God of Israel be moved to Gath." So they moved the ark of the God of Israel there. {5:9} After they had moved it, the hand of the LORD was against the city, causing a great panic, and he struck the men of the city, both young and old, with tumors. {5:10} So they sent the ark of God to Ekron. As the ark of God entered Ekron, the Ekronites cried out, "They have brought the ark of the God of Israel to us to kill us and our people!" {5:11} So they gathered all the lords of the Philistines and said, "Send the ark of the God of Israel away; let it go back to its own place so it does not kill us and our people, for there was a deadly panic throughout the city. The hand of God was very heavy there." {5:12} The men who did not die were afflicted with tumors, and the cry of the city went up to heaven.

{6:1} The ark of the LORD was in the territory of the Philistines for seven months. {6:2} The Philistines summoned their priests and diviners, asking, "What should we do with the ark of the LORD? Tell us how we should send it back to its place." {6:3} They answered, "If you send away the ark of the God of Israel, don't send it back empty; make sure to include a guilt offering. Then you will be healed, and you will know why his hand hasn't been removed from you." {6:4} They asked, "What should the guilt offering be?" They replied, "Five golden tumors (or "emerods") and five golden mice, according to the number of the Philistine lords, because the same plague has afflicted all of you and your lords." {6:5} Therefore, make images of your tumors and images of your mice that have ravaged the land, and give glory to the God of Israel. Maybe he will lighten his hand on you, your gods, and your land. {6:6} Why do you harden your hearts, like the Egyptians and Pharaoh did? When he dealt wondrously with them, didn't they let the people go? {6:7} Now make a new cart and take two milk cows that have never been yoked. Tie the cows to the cart and take their calves back home. {6:8} Put the ark of the LORD on the cart and place the gold items, which you are returning as a guilt offering, in a box beside it. Then send it on its way. {6:9} Watch to see if it goes up by the road to its own territory to Bethshemesh. If it does, he has done this great evil to us; but if not, we will know that it wasn't his hand that struck us; it was just a coincidence. {6:10} The men did as instructed; they took two milk cows, tied them to the cart, and kept their calves at home. {6:11} They placed the ark of the LORD on the cart along with the box containing the golden mice and images of their tumors. {6:12} The cows went straight to the road to Bethshemesh, lowing as they went, without turning to the right or left, while the Philistine lords followed them to the border of Bethshemesh. {6:13} The people of Bethshemesh were harvesting their wheat in the valley, and when they looked up, they saw the ark and rejoiced to see it. {6:14} The cart came to the field of Joshua, a Bethshemite, and stopped there by a large stone. They split the cart's wood and offered the cows as a burnt offering to the LORD. {6:15} The Levites took down the ark of the LORD and the box that was with it, containing the gold items, and placed them on the large stone. The men of Bethshemesh offered burnt offerings and made sacrifices to the LORD that day. {6:16} When the five Philistine lords saw it, they returned to Ekron that same day. {6:17} These are the golden tumors the Philistines returned as a guilt offering to the LORD: one for Ashdod, one for Gaza, one for Askelon, one for Gath, and one for Ekron. {6:18} The golden mice were based on the number of all the cities of the Philistines belonging to the five lords, both fortified cities and country villages, even up to the large stone of Abel, where they set the ark of the LORD. That stone remains in the field of Joshua, the Bethshemite, to this day. {6:19} The LORD struck down the men of Bethshemesh because they looked into the ark of the LORD. He struck down fifty thousand and seventy men, and the people mourned because the LORD had inflicted a great slaughter upon them. {6:20} The men of Bethshemesh asked, "Who is able to stand before this holy LORD God? To whom should the ark go from here?" {6:21} They sent messengers to the people of Kirjathjearim, saying, "The Philistines have brought back the ark of the LORD; come and take it up to you."

{7:1} The men of Kirjathjearim came and took the ark of the LORD, bringing it to the house of Abinadab on the hill, and they consecrated his son Eleazar to guard the ark of the LORD. {7:2} While the ark remained in Kirjathjearim, a long time passed; it was twenty years, and all the people of Israel mourned and sought the LORD. {7:3} Samuel spoke to all the house of Israel, saying, "If you are returning to the LORD with all your hearts, then put away the foreign gods and the Ashtaroth from among you, and prepare your hearts for the LORD, and serve him only. He will deliver you from the Philistines." {7:4} So the Israelites put away the Baals and the Ashtaroth and served the LORD only. {7:5} Samuel said, "Gather all Israel at Mizpeh, and I will pray to the LORD for you." {7:6} They gathered at Mizpeh, drew water, poured it out before the LORD, fasted that day, and confessed, "We have sinned against the LORD." Samuel judged the Israelites at Mizpeh. {7:7} When the Philistines heard that the Israelites had gathered at Mizpeh, the lords of the Philistines went up against Israel. When the Israelites heard of it, they were afraid of the Philistines. {7:8} They said to Samuel, "Do not stop crying out to the LORD our God for us, that he may save us from the hand of the Philistines." {7:9} Samuel took a suckling lamb and offered it as a whole burnt offering to the LORD. He cried out to the LORD on behalf of Israel, and the LORD answered him. {7:10} As Samuel was offering the burnt offering, the Philistines approached to battle against Israel, but the LORD thundered with a loud thunder that day against the Philistines and confused them, so they were defeated before Israel. {7:11} The men of Israel emerged from Mizpeh and pursued the Philistines, striking them down until they reached Bethcar. {7:12} Then Samuel took a stone and set it up between Mizpeh and Shen, and named it Ebenezer, saying, "Thus far the LORD has helped us." {7:13} So the Philistines were subdued and did not enter Israel's territory again, and the hand of the LORD was against the Philistines all the days of Samuel. {7:14} The towns the Philistines had taken from Israel were restored to Israel, from Ekron to Gath, and the territories were delivered from the hands of the Philistines. There was peace between Israel and the Amorites. {7:15} Samuel judged Israel all the days of his life. {7:16} He went from year to year on a circuit to Bethel, Gilgal, and Mizpeh, judging Israel in all those places. {7:17} His return was to Ramah, for that was where his home was; there he judged Israel and built an altar to the LORD.

{8:1} When Samuel grew old, he appointed his sons as judges over Israel. {8:2} His firstborn son was named Joel, and his second was Abiah; they served as judges in Beersheba. {8:3} However, his sons did not follow his ways; they turned aside for dishonest gain, accepted bribes, and distorted justice. {8:4} Then all the elders of Israel gathered together and came to Samuel at Ramah, {8:5} saying, "You are old, and your sons do not walk in your ways. Now appoint a king to lead us, just like all the other nations." {8:6} This request displeased Samuel, so he prayed to the LORD. {8:7} The LORD told Samuel, "Listen to all that the people are saying to you. It is not you they have rejected, but they have rejected me as their king. {8:8} They have done this since the day I brought them out of Egypt to this day, forsaking me and serving other gods. Now they are doing the same to you. {8:9} Now listen to their voice, but solemnly warn them and let them know what the king who will reign over them will be like." {8:10} So Samuel told all the words of the LORD to the people who were asking him for a king. {8:11} He said, "This is what the king who will reign over you will be like: he will take your sons and make them serve with his chariots and horses, and they will run in front of his chariots. {8:12} He will appoint commanders over thousands and fifties, and make them plow his ground and reap his harvest, and produce weapons of war and equipment for his chariots. {8:13} He will take your daughters to be perfumers, cooks, and bakers. {8:14} He will take the best of your fields, vineyards, and olive groves and give them to his servants. {8:15} He will take a tenth of your grain and your vineyards and give it to his officers and servants. {8:16} He will take your male and female servants, your best young men, and your donkeys, and put them to his work. {8:17} He will take a tenth of your sheep, and you yourselves will become his servants. {8:18} When that day comes, you will cry out for relief from the king you have chosen, but the LORD will not answer you in that day." {8:19} But the people refused to listen to Samuel; they said, "No! We want a king over us. {8:20} Then we will be like all the other nations, with a king to lead us and to go out before us and fight our battles." {8:21} Samuel listened to all the people and reported it to the LORD. {8:22} The LORD said to Samuel, "Listen to their voice and give them a king." So Samuel said to the Israelites, "Each of you go back to your own city."

{9:1} There was a man from Benjamin named Kish, the son of Abiel, the son of Zeror, the son of Bechorath, the son of Aphiah, a Benjamite, who was a mighty man of wealth. {9:2} He had a son named Saul, a handsome young man; there was no one among the Israelites more handsome than he was. He was a head taller than any of the others. {9:3} Now the donkeys of Kish, Saul's father, had gone missing. Kish said to his son Saul, "Take one of the servants with you and go look for the donkeys." {9:4} They went through the hill country of Ephraim and the land of Shalisha, but they did not find them. They passed through the land of Shalim but were not there, and they went through the land of the Benjamites, but they did not find them. {9:5} When they arrived in the land of Zuph, Saul said to his servant, "Let's go back, or my father will stop worrying about the donkeys and start worrying about us." {9:6} The servant replied, "Look! In this city there is a man of God. He is highly respected, and everything he says comes true. Let's go there; perhaps he will tell us what way to take." {9:7} Saul said to his servant, "But if we go, what can we give the man? The bread in our bags is gone, and we have no gift to take to the man of God. What do we have?" {9:8} The servant answered Saul again, "Look! I have a quarter of a shekel of silver. I can give that to the man of God to tell us which way to go." {9:9} (In Israel, when someone went to inquire of God, they used to say, "Come, let's go to the seer." The prophet of today was previously called a seer.) {9:10} Saul said to his servant, "Good idea! Let's go." So they went to the city where the man of God was. {9:11} As they were going up the hill to the city, they met some young women coming out to draw water. They asked them, "Is the seer here?" {9:12} "Yes," they answered, "he is ahead of you. Hurry! He has just come to the city today because the people are having a sacrifice at the high place. {9:13} As soon as you enter the city, you will find him before he goes up to the high place to eat, for the people will not eat until he arrives, because he must bless the sacrifice. Afterwards, those who are invited will eat. So now go up; you should find him about this time." {9:14} They went up into the city, and just as they entered it, there was Samuel coming out toward them to go up to the high place. {9:15} Now the LORD had revealed to Samuel the day before Saul arrived, {9:16} saying, "Tomorrow about this time I will send you a man from the land of Benjamin, and you are to anoint him ruler over my people Israel. He will deliver my people from the hand of the Philistines, for I have looked upon my people, for their cry has reached me." {9:17} When Samuel saw Saul, the LORD said to him, "This is the man I spoke to you about; he will govern my people." {9:18} Saul approached Samuel at the gate and asked, "Would you please tell me where the seer's house is?" {9:19} "I am the seer," Samuel replied. "Go up ahead of me to the high place, for today you will eat with me, and in the morning I will send you on your way and tell you everything that is in your heart. {9:20} As for the donkeys you lost three days ago, don't worry about them; they have been found. And to whom is all the desire of Israel? Is it not to you and your father's family?" {9:21} Saul answered, "But I'm a Benjamite, from the smallest tribe in Israel, and my family is the least of all the families of that tribe. Why do you say such a thing to me?" {9:22} Samuel took Saul and his servant and brought them into the hall and made them sit in the place of honor among those who were invited, about thirty in number. {9:23} Samuel said to the cook, "Bring the piece of meat I gave you, the one I told you to keep aside." {9:24} So the cook took up the thigh and what was on it and set it before Saul. Samuel said, "Here is what was left! Set it before you and eat, because it has been kept for you since I said, 'I have invited the people.'" So Saul ate with Samuel that day. {9:25} After they came down from the high place into the city, Samuel talked with Saul on the roof. {9:26} They got up early, and at dawn, Samuel called to Saul on the roof, "Get up, so I can send you on your way." Saul got up, and both he and Samuel went outside. {9:27} As they were going down to the edge of the city, Samuel said to Saul, "Tell the servant to go on ahead of us" (and he went on), "but you stay here a while, so I can tell you what God has said."

{10:1} Then Samuel took a flask of oil, poured it on Saul's head, kissed him, and said, "Is it not because the LORD has anointed you as leader over His people?" {10:2} When you leave me today, you will meet two men near Rachel's tomb in the territory of Benjamin at Zelzah. They will say to you, "The donkeys you went to find have been found, and your father has stopped worrying about the donkeys and is now worried about you, saying, 'What should I do for my son?'" {10:3} Then you will go on from there and come to the plain of Tabor, where you will meet three men going up to God at Bethel. One will be carrying three young goats, another three loaves of bread, and another a bottle of wine. {10:4} They will greet you and offer you two loaves of bread, which you should accept from them. {10:5} After that, you will come to the hill of God, where there is a Philistine garrison. When you arrive in the city, you will meet a group of prophets coming down from the high place, with musical instruments like a lyre, a tambourine, a flute, and a harp. They will be prophesying. {10:6} The Spirit of the LORD will come upon you, and you will prophesy with them, and you will be changed into a different person. {10:7} When these signs happen, do whatever your hand finds to do, for God is with you. {10:8} Go down ahead of me to Gilgal. I will come to you to offer burnt offerings and peace offerings. You must wait seven days until I come to you and tell you what to do. {10:9} As Saul turned to leave Samuel, God changed his heart, and all those signs happened that day. {10:10} When they arrived at the hill, a group of prophets met him, and the Spirit of God came upon him, and he prophesied among them. {10:11} When those who knew him previously saw him prophesying with the prophets, they asked each other, "What has happened to the son of Kish? Is Saul also among the prophets?" {10:12} A man from that area answered, "Who is their father?" This became a saying: "Is Saul also among the prophets?" {10:13} After he finished prophesying, he went to the high place. {10:14} Saul's uncle asked him and his servant, "Where did you go?" Saul replied, "To look for the donkeys. When we saw they weren't there, we went to Samuel." {10:15} Saul's uncle said, "Tell me what Samuel said to you." {10:16} Saul answered, "He told us that the donkeys were found. But about the matter of the kingdom, which Samuel spoke of, he did not tell me." {10:17} Samuel summoned the people to the LORD at Mizpah {10:18} and said to the Israelites, "This is what the LORD, the God of Israel, says: 'I brought Israel up out of Egypt and rescued you from the power of the Egyptians and from the power of all the kingdoms that oppressed you.' {10:19} But today you have rejected your God, who saves you from all your troubles and calamities. You have said, 'No! We want a king over us.' Present yourselves before the LORD by your tribes and clans." {10:20} When Samuel brought all the tribes of Israel near, the tribe of Benjamin was chosen. {10:21} When he brought the tribe of Benjamin near by its clans, the clan of Matri was chosen, and Saul, son of Kish, was chosen. But when they looked for him, he could not be found. {10:22} So they asked the LORD if the man had come there yet, and the LORD said, "He is hiding among the supplies." {10:23} They ran and brought him out, and when he stood among the people, he was a head taller than anyone else. {10:24} Samuel said to all the people, "Do you see the man the LORD has chosen? There is no one like him among all the people!" And the people shouted, "Long live the king!" {10:25} Samuel explained to the people the regulations of the kingdom and wrote them down on a scroll, which he placed before the LORD. Then he sent everyone home. {10:26} Saul also went home to Gibeah, accompanied by a group of men whose hearts God had touched. {10:27} But some troublemakers said, "How can this man save us?" They despised him and brought him no gifts, but Saul kept silent.

{11:1} Then Nahash the Ammonite came and camped against Jabesh Gilead, and all the men of Jabesh said to Nahash, "Make a treaty with us, and we will serve you." {11:2} Nahash the Ammonite replied, "I will make a treaty with you on one condition: that I gouge out the right eye of every one of you and so bring disgrace on all Israel." {11:3} The elders of Jabesh said to him, "Give us seven days to send messengers throughout Israel. If no one comes to rescue us, we will surrender to you." {11:4} When the messengers came to Gibeah of Saul and reported these terms to the people, they all wept aloud. {11:5} Just then Saul was returning from the fields behind his oxen, and he asked, "What is wrong with the people? Why are they weeping?" They told him what the men of Jabesh had said. {11:6} When Saul heard their words, the Spirit of God came upon him in power, and he burned with anger. {11:7} He took a pair of oxen, cut them into pieces, and sent the pieces by messenger throughout Israel, proclaiming, "This is what will be done to the oxen of anyone who does not follow Saul and Samuel." Then the terror of the LORD fell on the people, and they came out together as one. {11:8} When Saul mustered them at Bezek, the Israelites numbered three hundred thousand and the men of Judah thirty thousand. {11:9} They told the messengers who had come, "Say to the men of Jabesh Gilead, 'Tomorrow you will be rescued; when the sun is hot, you will be delivered.'" When the messengers went back and reported this to the men of Jabesh, they were elated. {11:10} They said to the Ammonites, "Tomorrow we will surrender to you, and you can do to us whatever you like." {11:11} The next day Saul separated his men into three divisions; during the last watch of the night they broke into the camp of the Ammonites and slaughtered them until the heat of the day. Those who survived were scattered, and no two of them were left together. {11:12} The people then said to Samuel, "Who was it that asked, 'Shall Saul reign over us?' Turn these men over to us so we can put them to death." {11:13} But Saul said, "No one will be put to death today, for this day the LORD has rescued Israel." {11:14} Then Samuel said to the people, "Come, let's go to Gilgal and renew the kingship there." {11:15} So all the people went to Gilgal and made Saul king in the presence of the LORD. There they sacrificed fellowship offerings to the LORD, and Saul and all the Israelites held a great celebration.

{12:1} Samuel said to all Israel, "I have listened to your voice in everything you said and have made a king over you. {12:2} Now look, the king is walking before you; I am old and gray, and my sons are with you. I have been leading you since my childhood until this day. {12:3} Here I am; testify against me before the LORD and His anointed: Whose ox have I taken? Whose donkey have I taken? Have I defrauded anyone? Have I oppressed anyone? Have I taken a bribe to close my eyes to injustice? If I have, I will make it right." {12:4} They replied, "You have not defrauded us or oppressed us. You have not taken anything from anyone's hand." {12:5} Samuel said to them, "The LORD is witness against you, and His anointed is witness today that you have found nothing in my hand." And they said, "He is witness." {12:6} Samuel continued, "It is the LORD who appointed Moses and Aaron and brought your ancestors up out of Egypt. {12:7} Now stand here, so I can reason with you before the LORD about all the righteous acts He has done for you and your ancestors. {12:8} When Jacob entered Egypt, your ancestors cried out to the LORD, and the LORD sent Moses and Aaron, who brought your ancestors out of Egypt and settled them in this place. {12:9} But they forgot the LORD their God, so He sold them into the hands of Sisera, the commander of the army of Hazor, and into the hands of the Philistines, and the king of Moab, who fought against them. {12:10} They cried out to the LORD and said, 'We have sinned; we have forsaken the LORD and served the Baals and Ashtaroth. Now deliver us from the hands of our enemies, and we will serve You.' {12:11} The LORD sent Jerubbaal, Bedan, Jephthah, and Samuel to rescue you from the hands of your enemies on every side, and you lived in safety. {12:12} But when you saw that Nahash, the king of the Ammonites, was coming against you, you said to me, 'No! We want a king to rule over us,' even though the LORD your God was your king. {12:13} Now here is the king you have chosen, the one you asked for! The LORD has set a king over you. {12:14} If you fear the LORD and serve Him and listen to His voice and do not rebel against the command of the LORD, then both you and your king who reigns over you will follow the LORD your God. {12:15} But if you do not listen to the LORD and rebel against His commands, His hand will be against you, as it was against your ancestors. {12:16} Now stand still and see this great thing the LORD is about to do in your sight. {12:17} Is it not the wheat harvest today? I will call on the LORD, and He will send thunder and rain. Then you will realize how wicked you have been in asking for a king." {12:18} So Samuel called on the LORD, and that same day the LORD sent thunder and rain, and all the people feared the LORD and Samuel greatly. {12:19} The people said to Samuel, "Pray to the LORD your God for your servants, so we will not die! We have added to all our sins the evil of asking for a king." {12:20} Samuel replied, "Don't be afraid. You have done all this evil, yet do not turn away from the LORD, but serve Him with all your heart. {12:21} Do not turn away after useless idols; they can do you no good nor rescue you because they are useless. {12:22} For the LORD will not forsake His people for His great name's sake, because it has pleased the LORD to make you His people. {12:23} As for me, far be it from me to sin against the LORD by failing to pray for you. I will teach you the way that is good and right. {12:24} But be sure to fear the LORD and serve Him faithfully with all your heart; consider what great things He has done for you. {12:25} Yet if you persist in doing evil, both you and your king will be swept away."

{13:1} Saul was thirty years old when he became king, and he reigned over Israel for forty-two years. {13:2} Saul chose three thousand men from Israel; two thousand were with him at Michmash and in the hill country of Bethel, and a thousand were with Jonathan at Gibeah in Benjamin. The rest of the men he sent back to their homes. {13:3} Jonathan attacked the Philistine outpost at Geba, and the Philistines heard about it. Then Saul blew the trumpet throughout the land and said, "Let the Hebrews hear!"

{13:4} So all Israel heard the news: "Saul has attacked the Philistine outpost at Geba, and now Israel has become a stench to the Philistines." And the people were summoned to join Saul at Gilgal. {13:5} The Philistines assembled to fight Israel, with three thousand chariots, six thousand horsemen, and soldiers as numerous as the sand on the seashore. They went up and camped at Michmash, east of Bethaven. {13:6} When the Israelites saw that their situation was critical and that their army was hard pressed, they hid in caves and thickets, among the rocks, and in pits. {13:7} Some Hebrews even crossed the Jordan to the land of Gad and Gilead. Saul remained at Gilgal, and all the people followed him, trembling. {13:8} He waited seven days, the time set by Samuel; but Samuel did not come to Gilgal, and Saul's men began to scatter. {13:9} So he said, "Bring me the burnt offering and the fellowship offerings." And Saul offered up the burnt offering. {13:10} Just as he finished making the offering, Samuel arrived, and Saul went out to greet him. {13:11} "What have you done?" asked Samuel. Saul replied, "When I saw that the men were scattering and that you did not come at the set time, and that the Philistines were assembling at Michmash, {13:12} I thought, 'Now the Philistines will come down against me at Gilgal, and I have not sought the LORD's favor.' So I felt compelled to offer the burnt offering." {13:13} "You have done a foolish thing," Samuel said. "You have not kept the command the LORD your God gave you; if you had, He would have established your kingdom over Israel for all time. {13:14} But now your kingdom will not endure; the LORD has sought out a man after His own heart and appointed him ruler of His people, because you have not kept the LORD's command." {13:15} Then Samuel left Gilgal and went up to Gibeah in Benjamin, and Saul counted the men who were with him; they numbered about six hundred. {13:16} Saul and his son Jonathan and the men with them were staying in Gibeah, while the Philistines camped at Michmash. {13:17} Raiding parties went out from the Philistine camp in three detachments: one turned toward Ophrah in the region of Shual, {13:18} another toward Beth Horon, and the third toward the border that overlooks the valley of Zeboim, facing the wilderness. {13:19} Not a blacksmith could be found in the whole land of Israel, because the Philistines had said, "Otherwise, the Hebrews will make swords or spears!" {13:20} So all Israel went down to the Philistines to have their plowshares, mattocks, axes, and sickles sharpened. {13:21} The price was two-thirds of a shekel for sharpening plowshares and mattocks, and a third of a shekel for sharpening forks and axes and for turning the goats. {13:22} So on the day of the battle, not a soldier with Saul and Jonathan had a sword or spear in his hand; only Saul and his son Jonathan had them. {13:23} Now a detachment of the Philistines had gone out to the pass at Michmash.

{14:1} One day, Jonathan, the son of Saul, said to his armor-bearer, "Come, let's go over to the Philistine garrison on the other side." But he didn't tell his father. {14:2} Saul was staying at the outskirts of Gibeah under a pomegranate tree in Migron, with about six hundred men with him. {14:3} Ahiah, the son of Ahitub and brother of Ichabod, the son of Phinehas, the son of Eli, was the priest of the LORD in Shiloh, and he was wearing an ephod. The people didn't know that Jonathan had left. {14:4} Between the passes where Jonathan planned to go over to the Philistine garrison, there were sharp rocks on both sides: one was named Bozez and the other Seneh. {14:5} The front of one faced north toward Michmash, and the other faced south toward Gibeah. {14:6} Jonathan said to his armor-bearer, "Come, let's go over to the garrison of these uncircumcised men; maybe the LORD will act on our behalf, for nothing can hinder the LORD from saving, whether by many or by few." {14:7} His armor-bearer said to him, "Do what you have in mind; I'm with you, heart and soul." {14:8} Jonathan said, "We will go over to them and let them see us. {14:9} If they say to us, 'Wait until we come to you,' we will stay where we are and not go up to them. {14:10} But if they say, 'Come up to us,' we will go up, because that will be our sign that the LORD has given them into our hands." {14:11} So both of them let the Philistine garrison see them, and the Philistines said, "Look! The Hebrews are coming out of the holes where they have been hiding!" {14:12} The men of the garrison shouted to Jonathan and his armor-bearer, "Come up to us, and we'll show you something." Jonathan said to his armor-bearer, "Climb up after me; the LORD has given them into the hand of Israel." {14:13} Jonathan climbed up using his hands and feet, with his armor-bearer following him. They fell before Jonathan, and his armor-bearer killed those who followed. {14:14} In that first attack, Jonathan and his armor-bearer killed about twenty men in an area that a yoke of oxen could plow in half an acre. {14:15} There was panic in the Philistine camp, in the field, and among all the people; even the garrison and raiders trembled, and the earth shook— it was a great panic. {14:16} The watchmen of Saul in Gibeah of Benjamin saw the army melting away and they were beating each other down. {14:17} Saul said to the men with him, "Count and see who has left us." When they counted, they saw that Jonathan and his armor-bearer were missing. {14:18} Saul said to Ahiah, "Bring the ark of God." (At that time, the ark was with the Israelites.) {14:19} While Saul was talking to the priest, the noise in the Philistine camp grew louder, so Saul said to the priest, "Withdraw your hand." {14:20} Saul and all his men assembled and went to the battle. There they saw that every man's sword was turned against his fellow, and there was confusion in the camp. {14:21} The Hebrews who had been with the Philistines before now turned to be with the Israelites who were with Saul and Jonathan. {14:22} Likewise, all the Israelites who had hidden in the hills of Ephraim heard that the Philistines were on the run, and they joined the fight. {14:23} So the LORD saved Israel that day, and the battle moved on to Bethaven. {14:24} The men of Israel were distressed that day, because Saul had made an oath, saying, "Cursed be anyone who eats food before evening; I want to be avenged on my enemies." So no one ate anything. {14:25} When they entered the woods, they found honey on the ground. {14:26} When the men entered the woods, they saw the honey oozing, but no one put their hand to their mouths, because they feared the oath. {14:27} But Jonathan had not heard his father charge the people with the oath, so he dipped the end of his staff into the honeycomb and ate some. His eyes brightened. {14:28} Then someone told him, "Your father strictly charged the people with an oath, saying, 'Cursed be anyone who eats food today,' and the people are weak." {14:29} Jonathan replied, "My father has made trouble for the land. Look how my eyes have brightened because I tasted a little of this honey. {14:30} How much better it would have been if the people had eaten freely from the plunder they took from their enemies! Would there not have been even greater slaughter among the Philistines?" {14:31} They struck down the Philistines that day from Michmash to Aijalon, and the people were very weak. {14:32} They rushed on the plunder, taking sheep, oxen, and calves, and slaughtered them on the ground. The people ate them with the blood still in them. {14:33} Then someone told Saul, "Look, the people are sinning against the LORD by eating meat with the blood still in it." Saul said, "You have broken faith; roll a large stone over here." {14:34} And Saul said, "Disperse yourselves among the people and tell them, 'Bring me every man's ox and sheep, and slaughter them here. Do not sin against the LORD by eating meat with the blood still in it.'" So that night, everyone brought their ox with them and slaughtered it there. {14:35} Saul built an altar to the LORD; this was the first altar he built to the LORD. {14:36} Saul said, "Let's go down after the Philistines by night and plunder them until dawn; let's not leave a single man alive." They answered, "Do whatever seems good to you." But the priest said, "Let's approach God." {14:37} Saul asked God, "Shall I go down after the Philistines? Will you give them into Israel's hand?" But God did not answer him that day. {14:38} Saul said, "Come here, all you leaders of the people, and let's find out what sin has been committed today. {14:39} As surely as the LORD lives, who saves Israel, even if it is my son Jonathan, he must die!" But no one in the crowd answered. {14:40} Then he said to all Israel, "You stand on one side, and I and Jonathan will stand on the other side." The people said to Saul, "Do what seems good to you." {14:41} Therefore, Saul said to the LORD, God of Israel, "Show us the right lot." Jonathan and Saul were chosen, but the people were cleared. {14:42} Saul said, "Cast lots between me and Jonathan." Jonathan was chosen. {14:43} Saul said to Jonathan, "Tell me what you have done." Jonathan told him, "I just tasted a little honey with the end of my rod, and now I must die!" {14:44} Saul replied, "May God deal with me, be it ever so severely, if you do not die, Jonathan." {14:45} But the people said to Saul, "Should Jonathan die, who has brought about this great deliverance in Israel? Never! As surely as the LORD lives, not a hair on his head will fall to the ground, for he did this today with God's help." So the people rescued Jonathan, and he was not put to death. {14:46} Then Saul stopped pursuing the Philistines, and they returned to their own territory. {14:47} So Saul took charge of the kingdom of Israel, and he fought against all his enemies on every side, against Moab, the Ammonites, Edom, the kings of Zobah, and the Philistines; wherever he turned, he inflicted punishment. {14:48} He gathered an army and defeated the Amalekites, delivering Israel from the hands of those who plundered them. {14:49} Saul's sons were Jonathan, Ishui, and Melchishua; his two daughters were Merab, the older one, and Michal, the younger one. {14:50} Saul's wife was Ahinoam, daughter of Ahimaaz, and the commander of his army was Abner, son of Ner, Saul's uncle. {14:51} Kish was Saul's father, and Ner, the father of Abner, was the son of Abiel. {14:52} There was fierce war against the Philistines all the days of Saul. Whenever he saw a strong or brave man, he took him into his service.

{15:1} Samuel said to Saul, "The LORD sent me to anoint you as king over His people, Israel. Now listen to the words of the LORD. {15:2} This is what the LORD of hosts says: 'I remember what Amalek did to Israel, how they ambushed them on their way out of Egypt. {15:3} Now go and attack the Amalekites and completely destroy everything they have. Do not spare them. Kill both men and women, children and infants, oxen and sheep, camels and donkeys.'" {15:4} Saul gathered the people and counted them at Telaim—two hundred thousand foot soldiers and ten thousand men from Judah. {15:5} Saul went to the city of Amalek and set an ambush in the valley. {15:6} He said to the Kenites, "Go, depart from the Amalekites, or I will destroy you with them, for you showed kindness to the Israelites when they came up from Egypt." So the Kenites left the Amalekites. {15:7} Saul attacked the Amalekites from Havilah all the way to Shur, near the border of Egypt. {15:8} He captured Agag, the king of the Amalekites, alive but completely destroyed all the people with the sword. {15:9} However, Saul and the people spared Agag and kept the best of the sheep, oxen, fatlings (well-fed animals), and lambs—everything that was good. They were unwilling to completely destroy them, but everything worthless or of poor quality they destroyed. {15:10} Then the word of the LORD came to Samuel, saying, {15:11} "I regret that I made Saul king, for he has turned away from following Me and has not carried out My commands." Samuel was deeply troubled, and he cried out to the LORD all night. {15:12} Early in the morning, Samuel went to meet Saul, but someone told him, "Saul went to Carmel. He has set up a monument for himself, and then he has gone down to Gilgal." {15:13} When Samuel reached him, Saul said, "The LORD bless you! I have carried out the LORD's instructions." {15:14} But Samuel replied, "Then what is this bleating of sheep and lowing of oxen that I hear?" {15:15} Saul answered, "The soldiers brought them from the Amalekites; they spared the best of the sheep and oxen to sacrifice to the LORD your God, but we completely destroyed the rest." {15:16} Samuel said to Saul, "Stop! Let me tell you what the LORD said to me last night." Saul said, "Tell me." {15:17} Samuel continued, "Though you were once small in your own eyes, did you not become the head of the tribes of Israel? The LORD anointed you king over Israel. {15:18} And He sent you on a mission, saying, 'Go and completely destroy the wicked Amalekites; wage war against them until they are wiped out.' {15:19} Why did you not obey the LORD? Why did you rush upon the plunder and do evil in the LORD's sight?" {15:20} Saul replied, "But I did obey the LORD! I went on the mission the LORD assigned me. I completely destroyed the Amalekites and brought back Agag, their king. {15:21} The soldiers took sheep and oxen from the plunder—the best of what was devoted to God—in order to sacrifice them to the LORD your God at Gilgal." {15:22} But Samuel said, "Does the LORD delight in burnt offerings and sacrifices as much as in obeying the LORD? To obey is better than sacrifice, and to listen is better than the fat of rams. {15:23} Rebellion is like the sin of divination (witchcraft), and arrogance like the evil of idolatry. Because you have rejected the word of the LORD, He has rejected you as king." {15:24} Then Saul said to Samuel, "I have sinned. I violated the LORD's command and your instructions. I was afraid of the people, so I gave in to them. {15:25} Now I beg you, forgive my sin and come back with me, so that I may worship the LORD." {15:26} But Samuel said to Saul, "I will not go back with you. You have rejected the word of the LORD, and the LORD has rejected you as king over Israel." {15:27} As Samuel turned to leave, Saul grabbed the edge of his robe, and it tore. {15:28} Samuel said to him, "The LORD has torn the kingdom of Israel from you today and has given it to one of your neighbors, someone better than you. {15:29} The Glory of Israel does not lie or change His mind; for He is not a human, that He should change His mind." {15:30} Saul replied, "I have sinned. But please honor me before the elders of my people and before Israel; come back with me, so that I may worship the LORD your God." {15:31} So Samuel went back with Saul, and Saul worshiped the LORD. {15:32} Then Samuel said, "Bring me Agag, king of the Amalekites." Agag came to him confidently, thinking, "Surely the bitterness of death is past." {15:33} But Samuel said, "As your sword has made women childless, so will your mother be childless among women." And Samuel put Agag to death before the LORD at Gilgal. {15:34} Then Samuel left for Ramah, but Saul went up to his home in Gibeah of Saul. {15:35} Until the day he died, Samuel did not go to see Saul again, though he mourned for him. And the LORD regretted that He had made Saul king over Israel.

{16:1} The LORD said to Samuel, "How long will you mourn for Saul, since I have rejected him as king over Israel? Fill your horn with oil and go; I am sending you to Jesse from Bethlehem, for I have chosen a king from his sons." {16:2} Samuel replied, "How can I go? If Saul hears about it, he will kill me." The LORD said, "Take a heifer with you and say, 'I have come to sacrifice to the LORD.' {16:3} Invite Jesse to the sacrifice, and I will show you what to do. You are to anoint the one I indicate to you." {16:4} Samuel did what the LORD said and went to Bethlehem. The elders of the town trembled when they met him and asked, "Do you come in peace?" {16:5} He replied, "Yes, in peace. I have come to sacrifice to the LORD. Consecrate yourselves and come to the sacrifice with me." He consecrated Jesse and his sons and invited them to the sacrifice. {16:6} When they arrived, Samuel saw Eliab and thought, "Surely the LORD's anointed stands here before the LORD." {16:7} But the LORD said to Samuel, "Do not consider his appearance or his height, for I have rejected him. The LORD does not look at the things people look at; people look at the outward appearance, but the LORD looks at the heart." {16:8} Then Jesse called Abinadab and had him pass before Samuel, who said, "The LORD has not chosen this one either." {16:9} Jesse then had Shammah pass by, but Samuel said, "Nor has the LORD chosen this one." {16:10} Jesse had seven of his sons pass before Samuel, but Samuel said to him, "The LORD has not chosen any of these." {16:11} So he asked Jesse, "Are these all the sons you have?" "There is still the youngest," Jesse answered, "but he is tending the sheep." Samuel said, "Send for him; we will not sit down until he arrives." {16:12} So he sent for him and had him brought in. He was glowing with health and had a fine appearance and handsome features. Then the LORD said, "Rise and anoint him; this is the one." {16:13} So Samuel took the horn of oil and anointed him in the presence of his brothers, and from that day on, the Spirit of the LORD came powerfully upon David. Samuel then went to Ramah. {16:14} Now the Spirit of the LORD had departed from Saul, and an evil spirit from the LORD tormented him. {16:15} Saul's attendants said to him, "See, an evil spirit from God is tormenting you. {16:16} Let our lord command his servants here to search for someone who can play the lyre (a musical instrument). He will play when the evil spirit from God comes on you, and you will feel better." {16:17} So Saul said to his attendants, "Find someone who plays well and bring him to me." {16:18} One of the servants answered, "I have seen a son of Jesse from Bethlehem who knows how to play the lyre. He is a brave man and a warrior. He speaks well and is a fine-looking man, and the LORD is with him." {16:19} Then Saul sent messengers to Jesse and said, "Send me your son David, who is with the sheep." {16:20} Jesse took a donkey loaded with bread, a skin of wine, and a young goat and sent them with his son David to Saul. {16:21} David came to Saul and entered his service. Saul liked him very much, and David became one of his armor-bearers. {16:22} Then Saul sent word to Jesse, saying, "Allow David to remain in my service, for I am pleased with him." {16:23} Whenever the spirit from God came on Saul, David would take his lyre and play. Then relief would come to Saul; he would feel better, and the evil spirit would leave him.

{17:1} The Philistines gathered their forces for war and assembled at Shochoh in Judah. They pitched their camp between Shochoh and Azekah, in Ephesdammim. {17:2} Saul and the Israelites assembled and camped in the valley of Elah and drew up their battle line to meet the Philistines. {17:3} The Philistines occupied one hill and the Israelites another, with the valley between them. {17:4} A champion named Goliath, who was from Gath, came out of the Philistine camp. He was over nine feet tall. {17:5} He had a bronze helmet on his head and wore a coat of scale armor (a type of armor made of overlapping plates) that weighed about 125 pounds. {17:6} On his legs, he wore bronze greaves (shin guards), and a bronze javelin was slung on his back. {17:7} His spear shaft was like a weaver's beam, and its iron point weighed about 15 pounds. His shield-bearer went ahead of him. {17:8} Goliath stood and shouted to the ranks of Israel, "Why do you come out and line up for battle? Am I not a Philistine, and are you not the servants of Saul? Choose a man and have him come down to me. {17:9} If he is able to fight and kill me, we will become your subjects; but if I overcome him and kill him, you will become our subjects and serve us." {17:10} Then the Philistine said, "This day I defy the armies of Israel! Give me a man and let us fight each other." {17:11} On hearing the Philistine's words, Saul and all the Israelites were dismayed and terrified. {17:12} Now David was the son of an Ephrathite named Jesse, who was from Bethlehem in Judah. Jesse had eight sons, and in Saul's time, he was very old. {17:13} Jesse's three oldest sons had followed Saul to the war. The firstborn was Eliab; the second was Abinadab; and the third was Shammah. {17:14} David was the youngest. The three oldest followed Saul, {17:15} but David went back and forth from Saul to tend his father's sheep at Bethlehem. {17:16} For forty days the Philistine came forward every morning and evening and took his stand. {17:17} Now Jesse said to his son David, "Take this ephah (a measurement) of roasted grain and these ten loaves of bread for your brothers and hurry to their camp. {17:18} Take along these ten cheeses to the commander of their unit. See how your brothers are and bring back some assurance from them." {17:19} They are with Saul and all the men of Israel in the valley of Elah, fighting against the Philistines. {17:20} Early in the morning, David left the flock with a keeper, loaded up and set out, as Jesse had directed. He reached the camp as the army was going out to its battle positions, shouting the war cry. {17:21} Israel and the Philistines were drawing up their lines facing each other. {17:22} David left his things with the keeper of supplies, ran to the battle lines and greeted his brothers. {17:23} As he was talking with them, Goliath, the Philistine champion from Gath, stepped out from his lines and shouted his usual defiance, and David heard it. {17:24} Whenever the Israelites saw the man, they all fled from him in great fear. {17:25} Now the Israelites had been saying, "Do you see how this man keeps coming out? He comes out to defy Israel. The king will give great wealth to the man who kills him. He will also give him his daughter in marriage and exempt his family from taxes in Israel." {17:26} David asked the men standing near him, "What will be done for the man who kills this Philistine and removes this disgrace from Israel? Who is this uncircumcised Philistine that he should defy the armies of the living God?" {17:27} They repeated to him what they had been saying and told him, "This is what will be done for the man who kills him." {17:28} When Eliab, David's oldest brother, heard him speaking with the men, he burned with anger at him and asked, "Why have you come down here? And with whom did you leave those few sheep in the wilderness? I know how conceited you are and how wicked your heart is; you came down only to watch the battle." {17:29} "Now what have I done?" said David. "Can't I even speak?" {17:30} He then turned away to someone else and brought up the same matter, and the men answered him as before. {17:31} What David said was overheard and reported to Saul, and Saul sent for him. {17:32} David said to Saul, "Let no one lose heart on account of this Philistine; your servant will go and fight him." {17:33} Saul replied, "You are not able to go out against this Philistine and fight him; you are only a young man, and he has

{18:1} After David finished speaking to Saul, the soul of Jonathan was bonded with David's soul, and Jonathan loved him as he loved himself. {18:2} From that day on, Saul kept David with him and did not let him return to his father's house. {18:3} Jonathan and David made a covenant because Jonathan loved David as his own soul. {18:4} Jonathan took off his robe and gave it to David, along with his garments, sword, bow, and belt. {18:5} David went out wherever Saul sent him and acted wisely. Saul put him in charge of the men of war, and he was well-received by all the people and by Saul's servants. {18:6} When David returned from defeating the Philistine, the women came out from all the cities of Israel, singing and dancing to meet King Saul, with tambourines, joy, and musical instruments. {18:7} The women sang to one another as they played, "Saul has slain his thousands, and David his tens of thousands." {18:8} Saul became very angry, and this saying upset him; he said, "They have credited David with tens of thousands, but me with only thousands. What more can he get but the kingdom?" {18:9} From that day on, Saul eyed David with suspicion. {18:10} The next day, an evil spirit from God came upon Saul, and he prophesied in his house while David played the harp as usual. Saul had a javelin in his hand. {18:11} Saul threw the javelin, thinking, "I will pin David to the wall." But David eluded him twice. {18:12} Saul was afraid of David because the LORD was with David and had departed from Saul. {18:13} So Saul removed David from his presence and made him a commander of a thousand. David led the troops in and out before the people. {18:14} David behaved wisely in all his ways, and the LORD was with him. {18:15} When Saul saw how wisely David acted, he was afraid of him. {18:16} But all Israel and Judah loved David because he led them in and out. {18:17} Saul said to David, "Here is my older daughter Merab. I will give her to you as a wife; only be brave and fight the LORD's battles." Saul thought, "Let me not be the one to kill him; let the Philistines do it." {18:18} David replied to Saul, "Who am I, and what is my family or my father's clan in Israel that I should become the king's son-in-law?" {18:19} But when the time came for Merab to be given to David, she was instead given to Adriel of Meholah as his wife. {18:20} Now Michal, Saul's daughter, loved David, and they told Saul about it, and this pleased him. {18:21} Saul said, "I will give her to him; she will be a trap for him, and the hand of the Philistines will be against him." So he told David, "You will be my son-in-law today." {18:22} Saul instructed his servants to speak with David privately and say, "The king is pleased with you, and all his servants love you; become the king's son-in-law." {18:23} Saul's servants conveyed these words to David, and David replied, "Do you think it is a trivial matter to become the king's son-in-law? I am a poor man and of low status." {18:24} The servants reported what David said to Saul. {18:25} Saul then said, "Tell David, 'The king wants no dowry except for a hundred Philistine foreskins as revenge on his enemies.'" Saul was hoping to have David killed by the Philistines. {18:26} When the servants told David this, it pleased him to become the king's son-in-law. The time had not yet expired. {18:27} David rose up, went out with his men, and killed two hundred Philistines; he brought their foreskins back and presented them to the king to become the king's son-in-law. So Saul gave him Michal, his daughter, as a wife. {18:28} Saul realized that the LORD was with David and that Michal loved him. {18:29} Saul became even more afraid of David and became his continual enemy. {18:30} Then the leaders of the Philistines went out to battle, and as often as they did, David behaved more wisely than all of Saul's servants, so his name became highly regarded.

{19:1} Saul spoke to Jonathan, his son, and to all his servants, saying that they should kill David. {19:2} But Jonathan, Saul's son, greatly loved David, so he warned David, "My father is trying to kill you. Be careful until morning; hide in a secret place. {19:3} I will go out and talk to my father about you; I'll let you know what I find out." {19:4} Jonathan spoke well of David to his father Saul, saying, "Don't sin against your servant David; he hasn't sinned against you, and his deeds have been very good to you. {19:5} He risked his life to kill the Philistine, and the LORD brought about a great victory for all Israel. You saw it and rejoiced. Why would you want to kill an innocent man for no reason?" {19:6} Saul listened to Jonathan and swore, "As the LORD lives, David will not be killed." {19:7} Jonathan called David and told him everything. Then he brought David to Saul, and David was in Saul's presence as before. {19:8} Once again, there was war, and David went out, fought the Philistines, and inflicted a great defeat on them, causing them to flee. {19:9} The evil spirit from the LORD came upon Saul as he sat in his house with a javelin in his hand, while David played the harp. {19:10} Saul tried to pin David to the wall with the javelin, but David escaped, and the javelin stuck in the wall. David fled and escaped that night. {19:11} Saul sent messengers to David's house to watch for him and kill him in the morning, but Michal, David's wife, warned him, "If you don't escape tonight, you will be killed tomorrow." {19:12} So she let David down through a window, and he fled and escaped. {19:13} Michal took an idol, laid it in the bed, put a goat's hair pillow at its head, and covered it with a blanket. {19:14} When Saul sent messengers to capture David, she said, "He is sick." {19:15} Saul sent the messengers back to see David, saying, "Bring him up to me in his bed so I can kill him." {19:16} When the messengers entered, they found the idol in the bed with the goat's hair pillow. {19:17} Saul asked Michal, "Why have you deceived me like this and let my enemy escape?" Michal answered, "He said to me, 'Let me go! Why should I kill you?'" {19:18} David fled and escaped, and went to Samuel at Ramah and told him everything Saul had done to him. Then he and Samuel went and stayed at Naioth. {19:19} It was reported to Saul that David was at Naioth in Ramah. {19:20} So Saul sent messengers to capture David, but when they saw the prophets prophesying and Samuel standing there as their leader, the Spirit of God came upon Saul's messengers, and they prophesied too. {19:21} Saul was informed, so he sent more messengers, and they prophesied likewise. Saul sent messengers a third time, and they also prophesied. {19:22} Finally, Saul himself went to Ramah and came to a large well in Sechu. He asked, "Where are Samuel and David?" Someone answered, "They are at Naioth in Ramah." {19:23} So he went to Naioth in Ramah, and the Spirit of God came upon him, and he prophesied until he arrived at Naioth in Ramah. {19:24} He stripped off his clothes and prophesied before Samuel in the same way, lying down naked all that day and night. That's why people say, "Is Saul also among the prophets?"

{20:1} David fled from Naioth in Ramah and went to Jonathan. He asked, "What have I done? What is my wrongdoing? What is my sin against your father that he seeks to kill me?" {20:2} Jonathan replied, "God forbid! You won't die. My father won't do anything, great or small, without telling me. Why would he hide this from me? It's not true." {20:3} David swore again, saying, "Your father knows I have found favor in your eyes, and he says, 'Don't let Jonathan know this, or he will be upset.' But as the LORD lives, there's only a step between me and death." {20:4} Jonathan said to David, "Whatever you want, I'll do for you." {20:5} David replied, "Tomorrow is the new moon, and I must sit with the king for the meal. Please let me go and hide in the field until the evening of the third day." {20:6} If your father misses me at all, say, 'David earnestly asked for my permission to go to Bethlehem, his hometown, for a yearly sacrifice for the family.' {20:7} If he says, 'That's fine,' then your servant will be safe. But if he is very angry, then you can be sure he intends harm." {20:8} "Therefore, be kind to your servant, for you brought me into a covenant with the LORD. If I have done anything wrong, kill me yourself. Why should you take me to your father?" {20:9} Jonathan said, "Far from it! If I knew that my father intended to harm you, wouldn't I tell you?" {20:10} David asked Jonathan, "Who will tell me? What if your father responds harshly?" {20:11} Jonathan suggested, "Come, let's go into the field." They went into the field together. {20:12} Jonathan said, "O LORD God of Israel, if I learn anything from my father about tomorrow or the third day, and if there's good toward David and I don't tell you, {20:13} may the LORD do so and more to Jonathan! But if my father intends to harm you, I'll let you know and send you away in peace. The LORD be with you, as He has been with my father." {20:14} "And while I live, show me the kindness of the LORD, so I don't die. {20:15} Don't ever cut off your kindness from my family, not even when the LORD has eliminated all David's enemies from the earth." {20:16} So Jonathan made a covenant with David's family, saying, "Let the LORD hold David's enemies accountable." {20:17} Jonathan made David swear again because he loved him like his own soul. {20:18} Then Jonathan said, "Tomorrow is the new moon, and you'll be missed because your seat will be empty. {20:19} When you've stayed three days, hurry back to the place where you hid when this matter arose, and stay by the stone Ezel. {20:20} "I will shoot three arrows to the side of it as if I'm aiming at a target. {20:21} Then I'll send a boy to find the arrows. If I say, 'The arrows are on this side of you, bring them back,' then come, for there's peace for you. {20:22} But if I say, 'The arrows are beyond you,' then go, for the LORD has sent you away." {20:23} "As for the matter we discussed, may the LORD be between you and me forever." {20:24} So David hid in the field, and when the new moon came, the king sat down to eat. {20:25} The king sat in his usual place by the wall, and Jonathan stood up. Abner sat beside Saul, but David's place was empty. {20:26} Saul didn't say anything that day, thinking, "Something must have happened to him; he must be unclean." {20:27} On the next day, the second of the month, David's seat was still empty, and Saul asked Jonathan, "Why hasn't the son of Jesse been here, neither yesterday nor today?" {20:28} Jonathan answered, "David asked for my permission to go to Bethlehem. {20:29} He said, 'Please let me go, for our family has a sacrifice in the city, and my brother commanded me to be there. If I have found favor in your eyes, let me go see my brothers.' That's why he isn't here at the king's table." {20:30} Saul's anger flared at Jonathan, and he said, "You son of a rebellious woman! Don't I know you've chosen the son of Jesse to your own shame and to the shame of your mother? {20:31} As long as the son of Jesse is alive, you won't be established in your kingdom. Send for him; he must die!" {20:32} Jonathan replied to Saul, "Why should he be killed? What has he done?" {20:33} Saul threw a javelin at Jonathan to kill him, and Jonathan realized that his father was determined to kill David. {20:34} So Jonathan stood up from the table in a rage and didn't eat on the second day of the month, grieving for David because his father had brought shame on him. {20:35} The next morning, Jonathan went out to the field at the appointed time with a boy. {20:36} He said to the boy, "Run and find the arrows I shoot." As the boy ran, Jonathan shot an arrow beyond him. {20:37} When the boy reached the spot where Jonathan shot, Jonathan called out, "Isn't the arrow beyond you?" {20:38} He called out, "Hurry! Don't stop!" The boy gathered up the arrows and returned to his master. {20:39} The boy knew nothing; only Jonathan and David knew the plan. {20:40} Jonathan gave his equipment to the boy and said, "Take these to the city." {20:41} After the boy left, David came out from hiding, fell to the ground, and bowed three times. They kissed and wept until David wept more. {20:42} Jonathan said to David, "Go in peace, since we have both sworn in the name of the LORD, saying, 'The LORD be between us and our descendants forever.'" David left, and Jonathan returned to the city.

{21:1} David went to Nob to see Ahimelech the priest. Ahimelech was afraid to meet David and asked, "Why are you alone? Why is no one with you?" {21:2} David answered, "The king has commanded me on a secret mission and told me not to let anyone know about it. I have directed my men to a certain place." {21:3} "Now, what do you have on hand? Give me five loaves of bread or whatever you have." {21:4} The priest replied, "I don't have any ordinary bread, but I do have holy bread, if the young men have kept themselves from women." {21:5} David assured him, "Of course, women have been off-limits to us for three days since I came out, and the young men's vessels are holy, so the bread is common, even though it was sanctified today." {21:6} So the priest gave him the holy bread, because there was no other bread except the showbread that was removed from before the LORD to put hot bread in its place. {21:7} A certain servant of Saul was there that day, detained before the LORD. His name was Doeg, an Edomite, the chief herdsman belonging to Saul. {21:8} David asked Ahimelech, "Do you have a spear or sword here? I didn't bring my weapons because the king's business was urgent." {21:9} The priest said, "The sword of Goliath the Philistine, whom you killed in the valley of Elah, is here, wrapped in a cloth behind the ephod. If you want it, take it; there's no other here." David replied, "There's none like it; give it to me." {21:10} David then arose and fled that day for fear of Saul, going to Achish, the king of Gath. {21:11} The servants of Achish said to him, "Isn't this David, the king of the land? Didn't they sing of him in dances, saying, 'Saul has slain his thousands, and David his ten thousands?'" {21:12} David kept these words in his heart and was very afraid of Achish, the king of Gath. {21:13} So he changed his behavior before them and pretended to be insane. He scribbled on the doors of the gate and let his saliva run down his beard. {21:14} Achish said to his servants, "You see, the man is insane! Why have you brought him to me? {21:15} Do I need madmen that you have brought this fellow to act insane in my presence? Should this man come into my house?"

{22:1} David left and escaped to the cave of Adullam. When his brothers and all his father's household heard of it, they went down to him there. {22:2} Everyone who was in distress, in debt, or discontented gathered to him, and he became their leader. About four hundred men were with him. {22:3} From there, David went to Mizpeh in Moab and asked the king of Moab, "Please let my father and mother stay with you until I learn what God will do for me." {22:4} He left them with the king of Moab, and they stayed there as long as David was in the stronghold. {22:5} But the prophet Gad said to David, "Do not stay in the stronghold. Go into the land of Judah." So David left and went to the forest of Hareth. {22:6} When Saul heard that David and his men had been discovered—Saul was sitting under a tree in Gibeah with his spear in his hand and his servants around him—{22:7} he said to them, "Listen, men of Benjamin! Will the son of Jesse give all of you fields and vineyards? Will he make you all commanders of thousands and hundreds? {22:8} Is that why you have all conspired against me? No one informs me that my own son has made a covenant with the son of Jesse. None of you cares about me or tells me that my son has stirred up my servant to lie in wait for me, as he is doing today." {22:9} Then Doeg the Edomite, who was in charge of Saul's servants, said, "I saw the son of Jesse come to Nob, to Ahimelech son of Ahitub. {22:10} Ahimelech inquired of the LORD for him, gave him provisions, and also gave him the sword of Goliath the Philistine." {22:11} Then the king summoned Ahimelech the priest, son of Ahitub, and all the priests of his family from Nob, and they all came to the king. {22:12} Saul said, "Listen now, son of Ahitub." Ahimelech replied, "Here I am, my lord." {22:13} Saul said to him, "Why have you conspired against me, you and the son of Jesse, by giving him bread and a sword and inquiring of God for him, so that he has rebelled against me and lies in wait for me today?" {22:14} Ahimelech answered the king, "Who among all your servants is as loyal as David, the king's son-in-law, captain of your bodyguard, and highly respected in your household? {22:15} Was this the first time I inquired of God for him? Of course not! Let not the king accuse your servant or anyone in my father's family, for your servant knew nothing of all this, large or small." {22:16} But the king said, "You will surely die, Ahimelech, you and your whole family." {22:17} Then the king ordered the guards at his side, "Turn and kill the priests of the LORD because they are on David's side. They knew he was fleeing, but they did not inform me." But the king's servants refused to raise a hand to strike the priests of the LORD. {22:18} So the king ordered Doeg, "You turn and strike down the priests." Doeg the Edomite turned and killed eighty-five men who wore the linen ephod. {22:19} He also put Nob, the city of the priests, to the sword—men and women, children and infants, cattle, donkeys, and sheep. {22:20} But one of the sons of Ahimelech, son of Ahitub, named Abiathar, escaped and fled to join David. {22:21} Abiathar told David that Saul had killed the LORD's priests. {22:22} Then David said to Abiathar, "That day, when Doeg the Edomite was there, I knew he would surely tell Saul. I am responsible for the deaths of your entire family. {22:23} Stay with me and do not be afraid. The one who seeks my life seeks your life, but you will be safe with me."

{23:1} Then David was told, "The Philistines are fighting against Keilah and robbing the threshing floors." {23:2} So David asked the LORD, "Should I go and attack these Philistines?" The LORD answered him, "Go and attack the Philistines and save Keilah." {23:3} But David's men said to him, "We are afraid here in Judah; how much more if we go to Keilah against the Philistine armies!" {23:4} Once again, David inquired of the LORD, and the LORD answered him, "Go down to Keilah, for I will give the Philistines into your hand." {23:5} So David and his men went to Keilah, fought the Philistines, carried off their livestock, and inflicted heavy losses on them. So David saved the people of Keilah. {23:6} Now Abiathar son of Ahimelech had brought the ephod down with him when he fled to David at Keilah. {23:7} Saul was told that David had gone to Keilah, and he said, "God has delivered him into my hands, for David has trapped himself by entering a town with gates and bars." {23:8} And Saul called up all his forces for battle, to go down to Keilah to besiege David and his men. {23:9} When David learned that Saul was plotting against him, he said to Abiathar the priest, "Bring the ephod." {23:10} David said, "O LORD, God of Israel, your servant has heard that Saul plans to come to Keilah and destroy the town on my account. {23:11} Will the citizens of Keilah hand me over to him? Will Saul come down as your servant has heard? O LORD, God of Israel, tell your servant." And the LORD said, "He will come down." {23:12} Again David asked, "Will the citizens of Keilah surrender me and my men to Saul?" And the LORD said, "They will." {23:13} So David and his men, about six hundred in number, left Keilah and kept moving from place to place. When Saul was told that David had escaped from Keilah, he did not go there. {23:14} David stayed in the wilderness strongholds and in the hills of the Desert of Ziph. Day after day Saul searched for him, but God did not give David into his hands. {23:15} While David was at Horesh in the Desert of Ziph, he learned that Saul had come out to take his life. {23:16} And Saul's son Jonathan went to David at Horesh and helped him find strength in God. {23:17} "Don't be afraid," Jonathan said. "My father Saul will not lay a hand on you. You will be king over Israel, and I will be second to you. Even my father Saul knows this." {23:18} The two of them made a covenant before the LORD. Then Jonathan went home, but David remained at Horesh. {23:19} The Ziphites went up to Saul at Gibeah and said, "Isn't David hiding among us in the strongholds at Horesh, on the hill of Hachilah, south of Jeshimon? {23:20} Now, O king, come down whenever it pleases you to do so, and we will be responsible for giving him into your hands." {23:21} Saul replied, "The LORD bless you for your concern for me. {23:22} Go and make sure once again; find out where David usually goes and who has seen him there. They tell me he is very crafty. {23:23} Find out about all the hiding places he uses and come back to me with definite information. Then I will go with you, and if he is in the area, I will track him down among all the clans of Judah." {23:24} So they set out and went to Ziph ahead of Saul. Now David and his men were in the Desert of Maon, in the Arabah south of Jeshimon. {23:25} Saul and his men began the search, and when David was told about it, he went down to the rock and stayed in the Desert of Maon. When Saul heard this, he pursued David there. {23:26} Saul was going along one side of the mountain, and David and his men were on the other side, hurrying to get away from Saul. But as Saul and his forces were closing in on David and his men to capture them, {23:27} a messenger came to Saul, saying, "Come quickly! The Philistines are raiding the land." {23:28} Then Saul broke off his pursuit of David and went to meet the Philistines. That is why they call this place Selahammahlekoth (Rock of Escape). {23:29} And David went up from there and lived in the strongholds of En Gedi.

{24:1} When Saul returned from pursuing the Philistines, he was informed that David was in the wilderness of Engedi. {24:2} Saul then chose three thousand of the best men from all of Israel and set out to find David and his men in the rocky areas where wild goats lived. {24:3} Along the way, he came to some sheep pens and found a cave, where he went in to relieve himself. David and his men were hiding at the back of the cave. {24:4} David's men said to him, "Today is the day the LORD spoke to you, saying, 'I will deliver your enemy into your hands; do whatever seems good to you.'" David quietly cut off a corner of Saul's robe. {24:5} But afterward, David's conscience bothered him for cutting off the corner of Saul's robe. {24:6} He said to his men, "The LORD forbid that I should do this to my master, the LORD's anointed, by attacking him, since he is the anointed of the LORD." {24:7} With these words, David persuaded his men and did not allow them to attack Saul. Saul then left the cave and went on his way. {24:8} Afterward, David also got up, went out of the cave, and called after Saul, "My lord the king!" When Saul turned around, David bowed down with his face to the ground. {24:9} David asked Saul, "Why do you listen to people who say, 'David intends to harm you'? {24:10} This day you have seen with your own eyes how the LORD delivered you into my hands in the cave. Some urged me to kill you, but I spared you because I said, 'I will not raise my hand against my lord, for he is the LORD's anointed.' {24:11} My father, look at this piece of your robe in my hand! I cut off the corner of your robe but did not kill you. Know and understand that I have not done any wrong or rebellion against you, and you are hunting me down to take my life. {24:12} May the LORD judge between us. May the LORD avenge me against you, but I will not lay a hand on you. {24:13} As the old saying goes, 'Wickedness comes from the wicked,' but my hand will not be against you. {24:14} After whom has the king of Israel come out? After whom are you pursuing? A dead dog? A flea? {24:15} May the LORD be our judge and decide between us. He will see my cause and deliver me from your hand." {24:16} When David finished saying this, Saul recognized his voice and wept, saying, "Is that your voice, David my son?" {24:17} And he said to David, "You are more righteous than I, for you have treated me well, while I have treated you badly. {24:18} You have shown today how you have dealt well with me. When the LORD put me in your hands, you did not kill me. {24:19} If a man finds his enemy, will he let him go unharmed? May the LORD reward you for the good you have done to me today. {24:20}

And now, I know that you will surely be king, and that the kingdom of Israel will be established in your hands. {24:21} Swear to me, therefore, by the LORD that you will not cut off my descendants after me or wipe out my name from my father's family." {24:22} David swore to Saul. Then Saul went home, but David and his men went up to their stronghold.

{25:1} Samuel died, and all Israel gathered to mourn him and buried him at his home in Ramah. Then David went down to the wilderness of Paran. {25:2} There was a wealthy man in Maon who had property in Carmel. He had three thousand sheep and a thousand goats and was shearing his sheep in Carmel. {25:3} The man's name was Nabal, and his wife's name was Abigail. She was intelligent and beautiful, but Nabal was harsh and mean. He was from the Calebite clan. {25:4} David heard that Nabal was shearing his sheep. {25:5} So David sent ten young men and instructed them, "Go to Carmel, greet Nabal in my name, {25:6} and say to him, 'Long life to you! Peace be to you, to your household, and to all that you have!' {25:7} I hear that you are shearing sheep. When your shepherds were with us, we did them no harm, and nothing was missing during the time they were at Carmel. {25:8} Ask your young men, and they will tell you. Therefore, let my men find favor in your eyes, for we come at a festive time. Please give your servants and your son David whatever you can spare." {25:9} When David's young men arrived, they gave Nabal the message in David's name. Then they waited. {25:10} But Nabal answered David's servants, "Who is David? Who is the son of Jesse? There are many servants these days who run away from their masters. {25:11} Should I take my bread, my water, and the meat I have slaughtered for my shearers and give it to men coming from who knows where?" {25:12} David's men turned around and went back. When they arrived, they reported every word. {25:13} David said to his men, "Put on your swords!" So they did. David strapped on his sword as well, and about four hundred men followed him, while two hundred stayed behind with the supplies. {25:14} One of the young men told Abigail, Nabal's wife, "David sent messengers from the wilderness to greet our master, but he hurled insults at them. {25:15} Yet the men treated us very well. We were not harmed, and nothing was missing while we were with them in the fields. {25:16} They were a wall around us both day and night the whole time we were herding our sheep near them. {25:17} Now think it over and see what you can do, because disaster is hanging over our master and his whole household. He is such a wicked man that no one can talk to him." {25:18} Abigail acted quickly. She took two hundred loaves of bread, two skins of wine, five dressed sheep, five measures of roasted grain, a hundred cakes of raisins, and two hundred cakes of figs and loaded them on donkeys. {25:19} Then she told her servants, "Go on ahead; I'll follow you." But she did not tell her husband Nabal. {25:20} As she came riding her donkey into a mountain ravine, she saw David and his men coming toward her, and she met them. {25:21} David had just said, "It has been useless— all my watching over this fellow's property in the wilderness so that nothing of his was missing. He has paid me back evil for good. {25:22} May God deal with David, be it ever so severely, if by morning I leave alive one male of all who belong to him!" {25:23} When Abigail saw David, she quickly got off her donkey and bowed down before David with her face to the ground. {25:24} She fell at his feet and said, "Pardon your servant, my lord, and let me speak to you; hear what your servant has to say. {25:25} Please pay no attention to that wicked man Nabal. He is just like his name—his name means fool, and folly goes with him. But as for me, your servant, I did not see the men my lord sent. {25:26} And now, my lord, as surely as the LORD lives and as you live, since the LORD has kept you from bloodshed and from avenging yourself with your own hands, may your enemies and all who are intent on harming my lord be like Nabal. {25:27} And let this gift, which your servant has brought to my lord, be given to the men who follow you. {25:28} Please forgive your servant's offense, for the LORD will certainly make a lasting dynasty for my lord, because you fight the LORD's battles, and no wrongdoing of yours will be found as long as you live. {25:29} Even though someone is pursuing you to take your life, the life of my lord will be bound securely in the bundle of the living with the LORD your God, but the lives of your enemies he will hurl away as from the pocket of a sling. {25:30} When the LORD has fulfilled for my lord every good thing he promised concerning him and has appointed him ruler over Israel, {25:31} my lord will not have on his conscience the staggering burden of needless bloodshed or of having avenged himself. And when the LORD has dealt well with my lord, remember your servant." {25:32} David said to Abigail, "Praise be to the LORD, the God of Israel, who has sent you today to meet me. {25:33} May you be blessed for your good judgment and for keeping me from bloodshed this day and from avenging myself with my own hands. {25:34} Otherwise, as surely as the LORD, the God of Israel lives, who has kept me from harming you, if you had not come quickly to meet me, not one male belonging to Nabal would have been left by daybreak." {25:35} Then David accepted from her hand what she had brought him and said, "Go home in peace. I have heard your words and granted your request." {25:36} When Abigail went to Nabal, he was in the house holding a banquet like that of a king. He was in high spirits and very drunk, so she told him nothing until daybreak. {25:37} Then in the morning, when Nabal was sober, his wife told him all these things, and his heart failed him and he became like a stone. {25:38} About ten days later, the LORD struck Nabal and he died. {25:39} When David heard that Nabal was dead, he said, "Praise be to the LORD, who has upheld my cause against Nabal for treating me with contempt and has kept his servant from wrongdoing. The LORD has brought Nabal's wrongdoing down on his own head." Then David sent word to Abigail asking her to become his wife. {25:40} His servants went to Abigail in Carmel and said to her, "David has sent us to you to take you to him as his wife." {25:41} She bowed down with her face to the ground and said, "Here is your servant, ready to serve and wash the feet of my lord's servants." {25:42} Abigail quickly got on her donkey and, attended by her five female servants, went with David's messengers and became his wife. {25:43} David had also taken Ahinoam from Jezreel, and both of them were his wives. {25:44} But Saul had given David's wife Michal to Paltiel son of Laish, who was from Gallim.

{26:1} The Ziphites came to Saul at Gibeah and said, "Isn't David hiding on the hill of Hachilah, which is opposite Jeshimon?" {26:2} So Saul got up and went down to the wilderness of Ziph, taking three thousand of Israel's best men to look for David in the wilderness. {26:3} Saul camped on the hill of Hachilah, which is opposite Jeshimon, along the way. But David stayed in the wilderness and saw that Saul had come after him there. {26:4} David sent out spies and confirmed that Saul had indeed come. {26:5} David went to the place where Saul was camped and saw where Saul lay, with Abner son of Ner, the commander of his army. Saul was lying inside the camp, and the troops were all around him. {26:6} David asked Ahimelech the Hittite and Abishai son of Zeruiah, Joab's brother, "Who will go down with me to Saul in the camp?" Abishai answered, "I will go with you." {26:7} So David and Abishai went to the army at night. There was Saul lying asleep inside the camp, with his spear stuck in the ground near his head. Abner and the troops were lying around him. {26:8} Abishai said to David, "Today God has delivered your enemy into your hands. Let me pin him to the ground with one thrust of the spear; I won't have to strike him twice." {26:9} But David said to Abishai, "Don't destroy him! Who can lay a hand on the LORD's anointed and be guiltless?" {26:10} David said, "As surely as the LORD lives, the LORD will strike him down; either his time will come and he will die, or he will go into battle and perish. {26:11} The LORD forbid that I should lay a hand on the LORD's anointed! Now take the spear that is near his head and the jug of water, and let's go." {26:12} So David took the spear and the jug of water from Saul's head, and they got away without anyone seeing or knowing it; all the soldiers were asleep because a deep sleep from the LORD had fallen on them. {26:13} Then David crossed over to the other side and stood on the top of a hill some distance away. {26:14} He called out to the army and to Abner son of Ner, "Aren't you going to answer me, Abner?" Abner replied, "Who are you that calls to the king?" {26:15} David said, "You are a great man, aren't you, Abner? Who is like you in Israel? Why didn't you guard your lord the king? Someone came to destroy your lord the king. {26:16} What you have done is not good. As surely as the LORD lives, you deserve to die because you did not guard your master, the LORD's anointed. Look around you! Where is the king's spear and the jug of water that was near his head?" {26:17} Saul recognized David's voice and asked, "Is that your voice, David my son?" David replied, "Yes, it is my voice, my lord, O king." {26:18} And he said, "Why is my lord pursuing his servant? What have I done? What wrong have I done? {26:19} Now please listen to your servant's words. If the LORD has stirred you up against me, may he accept an offering. But if it is human beings who have done it, may they be cursed before the LORD because they have driven me today from my share in the LORD's inheritance, saying, 'Go, serve other gods.' {26:20} Don't let my blood fall to the ground far from the presence of the LORD! The king of Israel has come out to look for a flea, like someone hunting a partridge in the mountains." {26:21} Then Saul said, "I have sinned. Come back, David my son, because I will not harm you again. You have been a valuable person in my eyes today. I have acted foolishly and made a terrible mistake." {26:22} David replied, "Here is the king's spear! Let one of the young men come and get it. {26:23} The LORD rewards everyone for their righteousness and faithfulness. The LORD delivered you into my hands today, but I did not lay a hand on the LORD's anointed. {26:24} Just as you valued my life today, may the LORD value my life and rescue me from all trouble." {26:25} Saul said to David, "May you be blessed, my son David! You will do great things and surely prevail." So David went on his way, and Saul returned home.

{27:1} But David thought to himself, "One of these days I will be killed by Saul. There's nothing better for me than to escape to the land of the Philistines. Then Saul will give up searching for me in Israel and I will escape from his hand." {27:2} So David and his six hundred men went to Achish son of Maoch, king of Gath. {27:3} David and his men settled in Gath with Achish, each man with his family. David had two wives with him: Ahinoam of Jezreel and Abigail, Nabal's widow from Carmel. {27:4} When Saul was told that David had fled to Gath, he no longer searched for him. {27:5} David said to Achish, "If I have found favor in your eyes, let me have a place in one of the country towns so I can settle there. Why should your servant live in the royal city with you?" {27:6} So Achish gave him Ziklag, and that's why Ziklag has belonged to the kings of Judah to this day. {27:7} David lived in the Philistine territory for a year and four months. {27:8} Now David and his men went up and raided the Geshurites, the Gezrites, and the Amalekites; these were people who lived in the land, going as far as Shur and the land of Egypt. {27:9} David attacked the land and did not leave a man or woman alive, taking sheep, cattle, donkeys, camels, and clothes. Then he returned to Achish. {27:10} Achish asked, "Where did you raid today?" David replied, "Against the Negev of Judah, the Negev of the Jerahmeelites, and the Negev of the Kenites." {27:11} David did not leave a man or woman alive to bring to Gath, for he thought, "They might inform on us and say, 'This is what David did.'" And such was his practice as long as he lived in the Philistine territory. {27:12} Achish trusted David, thinking, "He has become an utter stench to his people Israel; he will be my servant for life."

{28:1} In those days, the Philistines gathered their armies for war to fight against Israel. Achish said to David, "You can be sure that you and your men will go out with me to battle." {28:2} David replied to Achish, "You will know what your servant can do." Achish said to David, "Then I will make you my bodyguard for life." {28:3} Now Samuel was dead, and all Israel mourned for him and buried him in Ramah, his own city. Saul had expelled those who had familiar spirits and the wizards from the land. {28:4} The Philistines assembled and camped at Shunem, while Saul gathered all Israel and set up camp at Gilboa. {28:5} When Saul saw the Philistine army, he was afraid and his heart trembled greatly. {28:6} He inquired of the LORD, but the LORD did not answer him, neither through dreams, Urim, nor by prophets. {28:7} So Saul said to his servants, "Find me a woman who has a familiar spirit so I can go to her and ask her." His servants replied, "There's a woman at Endor who has a familiar spirit." {28:8} Saul disguised himself, put on different clothes, and went to the woman at night with two men. He said, "Please consult your spirit for me and bring up the person I name to you." {28:9} The woman said to him, "You know what Saul has done. He has cut off those who have familiar spirits and wizards from the land. Why are you trying to trap me and cause my death?" {28:10} Saul swore to her by the LORD, "As the LORD lives, you will not be punished for this." {28:11} Then the woman asked, "Whom shall I bring up for you?" He replied, "Bring up Samuel." {28:12} When the woman saw Samuel, she screamed at the top of her voice and said to Saul, "Why have you deceived me? You are Saul!" {28:13} The king said to her, "Don't be afraid. What do you see?" The woman said to Saul, "I see gods (or spirits) ascending from the earth." {28:14} He asked, "What does he look like?" She replied, "An old man is coming up, and he is wearing a robe." Saul realized it was Samuel, and he bowed down with his face to the ground. {28:15} Samuel asked Saul, "Why have you disturbed me by bringing me up?" Saul answered, "I'm in great distress, for the Philistines are waging war against me, and God has turned away from me and no longer answers me—neither through prophets nor dreams. So I've called you to tell me what I should do." {28:16} Samuel said, "Why do you ask me, since the LORD has turned away from you and become your enemy? {28:17} The LORD has done to you what he spoke through me: he has torn the kingdom from your hand and given it to your neighbor, David. {28:18} Because you did not obey the LORD and did not carry out his fierce anger against Amalek, the LORD has done this to you today. {28:19} Furthermore, the LORD will hand Israel over to the Philistines, and tomorrow you and your sons will be with me. The LORD will also hand the army of Israel over to the Philistines." {28:20} Immediately, Saul fell to the ground, terrified by Samuel's words, and there was no strength left in him, for he had eaten nothing all day and night. {28:21} The woman came to Saul and saw that he was greatly shaken. She said, "Your servant has obeyed you. I took my life in my hands and listened to what you said. {28:22} Now please listen to me and let me give you something to eat so you may have strength when you go on your way." {28:23} But he refused, saying, "I won't eat." His servants and the woman urged him, and he listened to them. He got up from the ground and sat on the bed. {28:24} The woman had a fat calf at home, so she hurried, killed it, took flour, and made unleavened bread. {28:25} She brought it to Saul and his servants, and they ate. Then they rose and left that night.

{29:1} The Philistines assembled all their armies at Aphek, and the Israelites camped by a spring in Jezreel. {29:2} The lords of the Philistines marched by hundreds and thousands, but David and his men followed behind with Achish. {29:3} The commanders of the Philistines asked, "What are these Hebrews doing here?" Achish replied to the Philistine leaders, "Isn't this David, the servant of Saul king of Israel? He has been with me for quite a while, and I have found no fault in him since he defected to me." {29:4} The Philistine commanders were angry with Achish and said, "Send this man back so he can return to the place you assigned him. He must not go with us into battle, or he will turn against us during the fight. How could he regain his master's favor? Wouldn't it be with the heads of our men? {29:5} Isn't this the David they sang about in their dances, saying, 'Saul has slain his thousands, and David his tens of thousands'?" {29:6} Achish called David and said to him, "As surely as the LORD lives, you have been reliable, and I would be pleased to have you serve in my army. I haven't found anything wrong with you from the day you came to me until now. But the lords don't approve of you. {29:7} So return home and go in peace. Don't do anything to upset the lords of the Philistines." {29:8} David asked Achish, "What have I done? What have you found against me since I came to you to this day? Why can't I fight against the enemies of my lord the king?" {29:9} Achish answered, "I know you are as good as an angel of God, but the Philistine commanders have said you must not go with us into battle. {29:10} Therefore, get up early in the morning with the servants of your lord who have come with you. As soon as it is light, leave." {29:11} So David and his men got up early in the morning to return to the land of the Philistines, while the Philistines went up to Jezreel.

{30:1} When David and his men returned to Ziklag on the third day, they discovered that the Amalekites had invaded the Negev and Ziklag, attacking it and burning it down. {30:2} They had taken the women captive, but did not kill anyone, either great or small; they carried them away and continued on their journey. {30:3} David and his men arrived at the city and found it burned to the ground, with their wives, sons, and daughters taken captive. {30:4} David and the people with him cried loudly until they had no strength left to weep. {30:5} David's two wives were among those captured: Ahinoam from Jezreel and Abigail, the widow of Nabal from Carmel. {30:6} David was greatly distressed because the people talked about stoning him, as they were all bitter over the loss of their sons and daughters. But David found strength in the LORD his God. {30:7} David said to Abiathar the priest, son of Ahimelech, "Bring me the ephod." Abiathar brought it to David. {30:8} David inquired of the LORD, "Should I pursue this raiding party? Will I catch them?" The LORD answered him, "Pursue them; you will certainly overtake them and succeed in rescuing everyone." {30:9} So David went, along with the six hundred men who were with him, and they came to the brook Besor, where some of them stayed behind. {30:10} David continued the pursuit with four hundred men, while two hundred stayed behind because they were too exhausted to cross the brook. {30:11} They found an Egyptian in the field and brought him to David. They gave him bread, and he ate; they provided him water to drink. {30:12} They also gave him a piece of fig cake and two clusters of raisins. After eating, he regained his strength, for he had not eaten bread or drunk water for three days and nights. {30:13} David asked him, "Who do you belong to, and where are you from?" He replied, "I am a young Egyptian, a servant of an Amalekite. My master left me behind because I got sick three days ago. {30:14} We raided the Negev of the Cherethites and the territory belonging to Judah, and we burned Ziklag." {30:15} David asked, "Can you lead me to this raiding party?" The young man said, "Swear to me by God that you won't kill me or hand me over to my master, and I will take you down to them." {30:16} When he had brought David down, they were spread out all over the countryside, eating and drinking and celebrating because of the great amount of plunder they had taken from the land of the Philistines and from Judah. {30:17} David attacked them from dusk until the evening of the next day, and none of them escaped except four hundred young men who rode off on camels. {30:18} David recovered everything the Amalekites had taken, including his two wives. {30:19} Nothing was missing, whether small or great, sons or daughters, or anything else that had been taken; David recovered it all. {30:20} He took all the flocks and herds, which were driven ahead of the other livestock, and said, "This is David's plunder." {30:21} When David returned to the two hundred men who had been too exhausted to follow him and had stayed by the brook Besor, they went out to meet David and the people with him. When David approached them, he greeted them. {30:22} But all the wicked men and troublemakers among David's followers said, "Since they didn't go with us, we won't share with them any of the plunder we recovered, except for their wives and children; let them take them and go." {30:23} David replied, "You must not do that, my brothers, with what the LORD has given us. He has protected us and delivered into our hands the raiding party that came against us. {30:24} Who will listen to what you say? The share of the man who stayed with the supplies is to be the same as that of him who went down to the battle. All will share alike." {30:25} From that day forward, David made this a statute and an ordinance for Israel. {30:26} When David arrived in Ziklag, he sent some of the plunder to the elders of Judah, his friends, saying, "Here is a gift for you from the plunder of the LORD's enemies." {30:27} He sent it to those in Bethel, and to those in south Ramoth, and to those in Jattir, {30:28} and to those in Aroer, and to those in Siphmoth, and to those in Eshtemoa, {30:29} and to those in Rachal, and to the cities of the Jerahmeelites, and to the cities of the Kenites, {30:30} and to those in Hormah, and to those in Chorashan, and to those in Athach, {30:31} and to those in Hebron, and to all the places where David and his men had roamed.

{31:1} The Philistines fought against Israel, and the men of Israel fled before them, falling slain on Mount Gilboa. {31:2} The Philistines pressed hard after Saul and his sons, killing Jonathan, Abinadab, and Malchishua, the sons of Saul. {31:3} The battle pressed heavily on Saul, and the archers found him and wounded him severely. {31:4} Saul said to his armor-bearer, "Draw your sword and run me through, or these uncircumcised will come and abuse me." But his armor-bearer was terrified and refused to do it. So Saul took his own sword and fell on it. {31:5} When his armor-bearer saw that Saul was dead, he too fell on his sword and died with him. {31:6} So Saul, his three sons, his armor-bearer, and all his men died together that day. {31:7} When the Israelites on the other side of the valley and those across the Jordan saw that their army had fled and that Saul and his sons were dead, they abandoned their towns and fled, and the Philistines came and occupied them. {31:8} The next day, when the Philistines came to strip the dead, they found Saul and his three sons fallen on Mount Gilboa. {31:9} They cut off Saul's head, stripped off his armor, and sent messengers throughout the land of the Philistines to proclaim the news in the temple of their idols and to the people. {31:10} They put Saul's armor in the temple of Ashtaroth and fastened his body to the wall of Beth-shan. {31:11} When the inhabitants of Jabesh-gilead heard what the Philistines had done to Saul, {31:12} all the valiant men arose and traveled all night to take the bodies of Saul and his sons from the wall of Beth-shan. They went to Jabesh, burned them there, {31:13} and took their bones and buried them under a tree in Jabesh. They fasted seven days.

The Second Book of Samuel

{1:1} After Saul's death, David returned from defeating the Amalekites and stayed in Ziklag for two days. {1:2} On the third day, a man arrived from Saul's camp with his clothes torn and dirt on his head, a sign of mourning. He came to David and bowed down before him. {1:3} David asked him, "Where do you come from?" The man replied, "I have escaped from the Israelite camp." {1:4} David asked, "What happened? Tell me." The man answered, "The army has fled from the battle, and many have died, including Saul and his son Jonathan." {1:5} David asked the young man, "How do you know that Saul and Jonathan are dead?" {1:6} The man explained, "I happened to be on Mount Gilboa and saw Saul leaning on his spear, with chariots and horsemen closing in on him. {1:7} He looked behind him, saw me, and called out to me. I said, 'Here I am.' {1:8} He asked me who I was, and I told him I was an Amalekite. {1:9} Then he said, 'Come over here and kill me, for I am in agony, and my life is still in me.' {1:10} So I went over and killed him, because I knew he couldn't survive after he had fallen. I took his crown and bracelet and brought them here to my lord." {1:11} David and all the men with him tore their clothes in grief, {1:12} and they mourned, wept, and fasted until evening for Saul, Jonathan, and the people of Israel who had died in battle. {1:13} David asked the young man, "Where are you from?" The man replied, "I am an Amalekite, the son of a foreigner." {1:14} David said, "Weren't you afraid to lift your hand to kill the LORD's anointed?" {1:15} David called one of his men and said, "Strike him down!" The man struck the Amalekite, and he died. {1:16} David said, "Your blood is on your own head. Your own mouth testified against you when you said you killed the LORD's anointed." {1:17} Then David sang a lament for Saul and Jonathan, {1:18} and he ordered that the people of Judah be taught the "Song of the Bow," which is recorded in the Book of Jasher (a lost book of songs and records). {1:19} David sang, "The glory of Israel lies slain on your heights. How the mighty have fallen! {1:20} Don't announce it in Gath, don't proclaim it in the streets of Ashkelon, or the daughters of the Philistines will rejoice, and the daughters of the uncircumcised (non-Israelites) will celebrate. {1:21} O mountains of Gilboa, may you have neither dew nor rain, nor fields that yield offerings, for the shield of the mighty was dishonored there—the shield of Saul, no longer anointed with oil. {1:22} From the blood of the slain, from the flesh of the mighty, Jonathan's bow did not turn back, and Saul's sword did not return empty. {1:23} Saul and Jonathan—beloved and pleasant in life, inseparable in death—were swifter than eagles, stronger than lions. {1:24} Daughters of Israel, weep for Saul, who clothed you in scarlet and fine clothing, who adorned your garments with gold. {1:25} How the mighty have fallen in battle! Jonathan lies slain on your heights. {1:26} I grieve for you, my brother Jonathan; you were very dear to me. Your love for me was wonderful, surpassing the love of women. {1:27} How the mighty have fallen, and the weapons of war have perished!"

{2:1} After this, David asked the LORD, "Shall I go up to any of the cities of Judah?" The LORD replied, "Go up." David asked, "Where shall I go?" And the LORD said, "To Hebron." {2:2} So David went to Hebron with his two wives, Ahinoam of Jezreel and Abigail, the widow of Nabal of Carmel. {2:3} David also took his men and their families, and they settled in the towns of Hebron. {2:4} Then the men of Judah came and anointed David as king over the tribe of Judah. They told David that the men of Jabesh-gilead had buried

Saul. {2:5} So David sent messengers to the men of Jabesh-gilead and said, "May the LORD bless you for showing this kindness to your lord Saul by burying him. {2:6} May the LORD now show you kindness and faithfulness, and I too will repay you for this noble deed. {2:7} Now, be strong and brave, for your master Saul is dead, and the house of Judah has anointed me as king over them." {2:8} However, Abner, son of Ner, the commander of Saul's army, took Saul's son Ish-bosheth and brought him to Mahanaim, {2:9} where he made him king over Gilead, the Ashurites, Jezreel, Ephraim, Benjamin, and all Israel. {2:10} Ish-bosheth, Saul's son, was forty years old when he began to reign over Israel, and he ruled for two years. But the house of Judah followed David. {2:11} David was king in Hebron over the tribe of Judah for seven years and six months. {2:12} Abner, son of Ner, and the servants of Ish-bosheth went from Mahanaim to Gibeon. {2:13} Joab, son of Zeruiah, and David's men also went to meet them at the pool of Gibeon. The two groups sat down on opposite sides of the pool. {2:14} Abner said to Joab, "Let the young men get up and fight." Joab replied, "Let them fight." {2:15} So twelve men from each side got up and fought, and each man grabbed his opponent by the head and stabbed him with his sword, so they all fell together. The place was called Helkath-hazzurim (field of sword edges) near Gibeon. {2:17} A fierce battle followed, and Abner and the men of Israel were defeated by David's forces. {2:18} The three sons of Zeruiah were there: Joab, Abishai, and Asahel. Asahel was as fast as a wild gazelle. {2:19} He chased Abner, refusing to turn aside. {2:20} Abner looked back and asked, "Is that you, Asahel?" Asahel replied, "Yes, it is." {2:21} Abner said, "Turn aside and fight one of the young men and take his armor." But Asahel refused to turn away. {2:22} Abner warned him again, "Turn aside, or I'll have to kill you! How could I face your brother Joab?" {2:23} But Asahel refused, so Abner thrust the back end of his spear into Asahel's stomach, and the spear came out through his back. He fell there and died on the spot. Everyone who came to the place where Asahel died stood still. {2:24} Joab and Abishai continued to pursue Abner, and as the sun was setting, they reached the hill of Ammah near Giah, on the road to the wilderness of Gibeon. {2:25} The men of Benjamin rallied around Abner and took their stand on a hilltop. {2:26} Abner called out to Joab, "Must the sword devour forever? Don't you realize this will end in bitterness? How long before you order your men to stop pursuing their fellow Israelites?" {2:27} Joab answered, "As surely as God lives, if you hadn't spoken, my men would have continued the pursuit until morning." {2:28} So Joab blew the trumpet, and his men stopped pursuing Israel and ceased fighting. {2:29} Abner and his men marched all night through the valley, crossed the Jordan, and went to Mahanaim. {2:30} When Joab gathered his men, he found that nineteen of David's men were missing, including Asahel. {2:31} But David's men had killed three hundred sixty of Abner's men from the tribe of Benjamin. {2:32} Asahel was taken and buried in his father's tomb at Bethlehem. Then Joab and his men marched all night and reached Hebron by dawn.

{3:1} There was a long war between the house of Saul and the house of David, but David grew stronger and stronger, while the house of Saul grew weaker and weaker. {3:2} Sons were born to David in Hebron: the firstborn was Amnon, son of Ahinoam the Jezreelitess; {3:3} the second was Chileab, son of Abigail, the widow of Nabal the Carmelite; the third was Absalom, son of Maacah, daughter of Talmai, king of Geshur; {3:4} the fourth was Adonijah, son of Haggith; the fifth was Shephatiah, son of Abital; {3:5} and the sixth was Ithream, son of Eglah, David's wife. These were born to David in Hebron. {3:6} During the war between the house of Saul and the house of David, Abner grew strong within Saul's household. {3:7} Now Saul had a concubine named Rizpah, daughter of Aiah, and Ishbosheth (Saul's son) accused Abner, saying, "Why have you slept with my father's concubine?" {3:8} Abner became very angry because of this accusation and said, "Am I a dog's head loyal to Judah? This very day I have shown kindness to the house of Saul, your father, his family, and friends, and have not handed you over to David, and yet you accuse me concerning this woman! {3:9} May God deal with me, be it ever so severely, if I do not do for David what the Lord promised him: {3:10} to transfer the kingdom from Saul's house and establish David's throne over Israel and Judah, from Dan to Beersheba." {3:11} Ishbosheth could not say a word to Abner because he was afraid of him. {3:12} Then Abner sent messengers to David, saying, "Whose land is this? Make a covenant with me, and I will help bring all Israel to you." {3:13} David replied, "Good, I will make a covenant with you, but there is one condition: You must bring Saul's daughter Michal when you come to see me." {3:14} Then David sent messengers to Ishbosheth, Saul's son, demanding, "Give me my wife Michal, whom I betrothed for the price of one hundred Philistine foreskins." {3:15} So Ishbosheth took Michal from her husband, Paltiel, son of Laish. {3:16} Her husband followed her, weeping behind her all the way to Bahurim. Then Abner said to him, "Go back," and he went back. {3:17} Abner spoke to the elders of Israel, saying, "For some time you have wanted David to be your king. {3:18} Now do it! For the Lord has promised David, 'By my servant David I will rescue my people Israel from the hand of the Philistines and all their enemies.'" {3:19} Abner also spoke to the Benjamites, and then he went to Hebron to tell David everything Israel and Benjamin were willing to do. {3:20} When Abner came to David at Hebron with twenty men, David prepared a feast for Abner and his men. {3:21} Then Abner said to David, "Let me go at once and assemble all Israel for my lord the king, so they may make a covenant with you and you may rule over all that your heart desires." So David sent Abner away, and he went in peace. {3:22} Just then David's men and Joab returned from a raid, bringing a great deal of plunder with them. But Abner was no longer with David in Hebron, as he had been sent away in peace. {3:23} When Joab and all the soldiers with him arrived, they were told that Abner had been with the king and that David had sent him away in peace. {3:24} So Joab went to the king and said, "What have you done? Abner came to you. Why did you let him go? Now he's gone! {3:25} You know Abner, son of Ner, he came to deceive you, to find out about your movements and everything you are doing." {3:26} Joab then left David and sent messengers after Abner, and they brought him back from the well of Sirah, though David did not know about it. {3:27} When Abner returned to Hebron, Joab took him aside into the gateway, as though to speak with him privately. There Joab stabbed him in the stomach, killing him in revenge for the blood of his brother Asahel. {3:28} Later, when David heard about this, he said, "I and my kingdom are forever innocent before the Lord concerning the blood of Abner, son of Ner. {3:29} May Joab and his entire family be held guilty! May his descendants always suffer from a discharge, leprosy, those who lean on a crutch, those who die by the sword, and those who lack food." {3:30} Joab and his brother Abishai killed Abner because he had killed their brother Asahel in the battle at Gibeon. {3:31} Then David said to Joab and all the people with him, "Tear your clothes and put on sackcloth and mourn for Abner." King David himself followed the bier. {3:32} They buried Abner in Hebron, and the king wept aloud at Abner's tomb. All the people wept also. {3:33} The king sang this lament for Abner: "Should Abner have died as the lawless die? {3:34} Your hands were not bound, your feet were not fettered. You fell as one falls before the wicked." And all the people wept over him again. {3:35} Then they all came to urge David to eat something while it was still day, but David took an oath, saying, "May God deal with me, be it ever so severely, if I taste bread or anything else before the sun sets." {3:36} All the people took note and were pleased; indeed, everything the king did pleased them. {3:37} So on that day all the people and all Israel knew that the king had no part in the murder of Abner, son of Ner. {3:38} Then the king said to his men, "Do you not realize that a commander and a great man has fallen in Israel today? {3:39} And today, though I am the anointed king, I am weak, and these sons of Zeruiah are too violent for me. May the Lord repay the evildoer according to his evil deeds."

{4:1} When Ishbosheth, Saul's son, heard that Abner had died in Hebron, he lost courage, and all Israel became alarmed. {4:2} Now Saul's son had two men who were leaders of raiding bands. One was named Baanah and the other Rechab, sons of Rimmon the Beerothite from the tribe of Benjamin (Beeroth is considered part of Benjamin, {4:3} because the people of Beeroth fled to Gittaim and have lived there as foreigners to this day). {4:4} Jonathan, Saul's son, had a son who was lame in both feet. He was five years old when the news about Saul and Jonathan came from Jezreel. His nurse picked him up and fled, but as she hurried to leave, he fell and became disabled. His name was Mephibosheth. {4:5} Now Rechab and Baanah, the sons of Rimmon the Beerothite, set out for the house of Ishbosheth, and they arrived there in the heat of the day, while he was taking his midday rest. {4:6} They went into the inner part of the house as if to get some wheat, and they stabbed him in the stomach. Then Rechab and his brother Baanah slipped away. {4:7} They had gone into the house while he was lying on the bed in his bedroom; after they stabbed and killed him, they cut off his head. Taking it with them, they traveled all night by way of the Arabah. {4:8} They brought the head of Ishbosheth to David at Hebron and said to the king, "Here is the head of Ishbosheth, son of Saul, your enemy, who tried to kill you. This day the Lord has avenged my lord the king against Saul and his offspring." {4:9} David answered Rechab and his brother Baanah, the sons of Rimmon the Beerothite, "As surely as the Lord lives, who has delivered me out of every trouble, {4:10} when someone told me, 'Saul is dead,' thinking he was bringing good news, I seized him and killed him in Ziklag, that was the reward I gave him for his news! {4:11} How much more—when wicked men have killed an innocent man in his own house and on his own bed—should I not now demand his blood from your hand and rid the earth of you!" {4:12} So David gave an order to his men, and they killed them. They cut off their hands and feet and hung the bodies by the pool in Hebron.

{5:1} All the tribes of Israel came to David at Hebron and said, "Look, we are your flesh and blood. {5:2} In the past, when Saul was king, you were the one who led Israel in and out. The LORD said to you, 'You will shepherd my people Israel and be their ruler.'" {5:3} So all the elders of Israel came to King David at Hebron, and David made a covenant with them before the LORD. They anointed David as king over Israel. {5:4} David was thirty years old when he began to reign, and he reigned for forty years. {5:5} In Hebron, he ruled over Judah for seven years and six months, and in Jerusalem, he reigned for thirty-three years over all Israel and Judah. {5:6} The king and his men went to Jerusalem to confront the Jebusites, the inhabitants of the land, who said to David, "You will not enter here; even the blind and the lame can defend this place," thinking David could never get in. {5:7} However, David captured the stronghold of Zion, which is now known as the City of David. {5:8} On that day, David declared, "Whoever climbs up to the water shaft and attacks the Jebusites—those blind and lame whom I hate—will be chief and commander." Therefore, they said, "The blind and the lame will not enter the palace." {5:9} David lived in the stronghold and called it the City of David. He built up the area around it, from Millo inward. {5:10} David became more powerful, and the LORD God Almighty was with him. {5:11} Hiram, king of Tyre, sent messengers to David along with cedar trees, carpenters, and stonemasons to build him a palace. {5:12} David realized that the LORD had established him as king over Israel and had elevated his kingdom for the sake of His people. {5:13} After coming from Hebron to Jerusalem, David took more concubines and wives, and more sons and daughters were born to him. {5:14} These are the names of the children born to him in Jerusalem: Shammua, Shobab, Nathan, Solomon, {5:15} Ibhar, Elishua, Nepheg, Japhia, {5:16} Elishama, Eliada, and Eliphalet. {5:17} When the Philistines heard that David had been anointed king over Israel, they went to find him. David learned of this and went down to the stronghold. {5:18} The Philistines spread out in the Valley of Rephaim. {5:19} David asked the LORD, "Should I go up against the Philistines? Will you deliver them into my hands?" The LORD replied, "Go up, for I will certainly deliver the Philistines into your hands." {5:20} David went to Baal-perazim and defeated them there, saying, "The LORD has broken through my enemies like a flood." Therefore, he named that place Baal-perazim. {5:21} The Philistines left their idols there, and David and his men burned them. {5:22} The Philistines came up again and spread out in the Valley of Rephaim. {5:23} When David asked the LORD again, He said, "Don't go straight up; instead, circle around behind them and attack them near the mulberry trees. {5:24} When you hear the sound of marching in the tops of the mulberry trees, act quickly, for then the LORD will have gone out ahead of you to strike the Philistine army." {5:25} David did as the LORD commanded and struck down the Philistines from Geba to Gazer.

{6:1} David gathered all the choice men of Israel, about thirty thousand. {6:2} He and all his men set out from Baale of Judah to bring up the Ark of God, which is called by the name of the LORD Almighty, who is enthroned between the cherubim. {6:3} They placed the Ark of God on a new cart and brought it from Abinadab's house, which was in Gibeah. Uzzah and Ahio, Abinadab's sons, drove the new cart. {6:4} They carried the Ark out of Abinadab's house and Ahio walked in front of it. {6:5} David and all Israel played music before the LORD with all kinds of instruments made of wood, including harps, lyres, tambourines, rattles, and cymbals. {6:6} When they reached the threshing floor of Nacon, Uzzah reached out and took hold of the Ark because the oxen stumbled. {6:7} The LORD's anger burned against Uzzah, and God struck him down for his irreverence, and he died there beside the Ark of God. {6:8} David was angry because the LORD's wrath had broken out against Uzzah, and to this day, that place is called Perez-uzzah. {6:9} David was afraid of the LORD that day and asked, "How can the Ark of the LORD ever come to me?" {6:10} He decided not to take the Ark of the LORD to the City of David but instead took it to the house of Obed-Edom the Gittite. {6:11} The Ark of the LORD remained in the house of Obed-Edom for three months, and the LORD blessed him and his entire household. {6:12} David was told, "The LORD has blessed the house of Obed-Edom and everything he has because of the Ark of God." So David went to bring up the Ark of God from Obed-Edom's house to the City of David with rejoicing. {6:13} When those carrying the Ark of the LORD had taken six steps, David sacrificed a bull and a fattened calf. {6:14} Wearing a linen ephod, David danced before the LORD with all his might. {6:15} While he and the entire house of Israel brought up the Ark of the LORD with shouts and the sound of trumpets, {6:16} Michal, Saul's daughter, watched from a window. When she saw King David leaping and dancing before the LORD, she despised him in her heart. {6:17} They brought the Ark of the LORD and set it in its place inside the tent David had pitched for it. David offered burnt offerings and fellowship offerings before the LORD. {6:18} After David had finished offering the burnt offerings and fellowship offerings, he blessed the people in the name of the LORD Almighty. {6:19} He then distributed a cake of bread, a piece of meat, and a cake of raisins to each person in the whole crowd of Israelites, both men and women. Then everyone went home. {6:20} When David returned home to bless his household, Michal came out to meet him and said, "How the king of Israel has distinguished himself today, going around half-naked in full view of the servant girls of his subjects, like a vulgar person!" {6:21} David replied to Michal, "It was before the LORD, who chose me rather than your father or anyone from his house when He appointed me ruler over the LORD's people Israel. Therefore, I will celebrate before the LORD. {6:22} I will become even more undignified than this, and I will be humiliated in my own eyes. But by these servant girls you mentioned, I will be held in honor." {6:23} And Michal, Saul's daughter, had no children to the day of her death.

{7:1} After the king had settled into his house and the LORD had given him rest from all his enemies around him, {7:2} he said to Nathan the prophet, "Look, I live in a house made of cedar, but the Ark of God is housed in a tent." {7:3} Nathan replied to the king, "Go and do whatever you have in mind, for the LORD is with you." {7:4} That night, the word of the LORD came to Nathan, saying, {7:5} "Go and tell my servant David, 'This is what the LORD says: Are you the one to build me a house to dwell in? {7:6} I have not dwelt in a house since the day I brought the Israelites up from Egypt to this very day. I have been moving around in a tent and a tabernacle. {7:7} Wherever I have moved with all the Israelites, did I ever say to any of their rulers whom I commanded to shepherd my people Israel, "Why haven't you built me a house of cedar?" {7:8} Now, tell my servant David, 'This is what the LORD Almighty says: I took you from the pasture and from following the sheep to be ruler over my people Israel. {7:9} I have been with you wherever you have gone, and I have cut off all your enemies from before you. Now, I will make your name great, like the names of the greatest men on earth. {7:10} I will provide a place for my people Israel and will plant them so they can have a home of their own and no longer be disturbed. Wicked people will not oppress them anymore, as they did in the past, {7:11} ever since I appointed leaders over my people Israel. I will give you rest from all your enemies. The LORD also declares to you that he will make a house for you. {7:12} When your days are over and you rest with your ancestors, I will raise up your offspring to succeed you, your own flesh and blood, and I will establish his kingdom. {7:13} He will build a house for my name, and I will establish the throne of his kingdom forever. {7:14} I will be his father, and he will be my son. When he does wrong, I will punish him with a rod wielded by men, with floggings inflicted by human hands. {7:15} But my love will never be taken away from him, as I took it away from Saul, whom I removed before you. {7:16} Your house and your kingdom will endure forever before me; your throne will be established forever.'" {7:17} Nathan reported all these words and this vision to David. {7:18} Then King David went in and sat before the LORD, and he said, "Who am I, Sovereign LORD, and what is my family that you have brought me this far? {7:19} And as if this were not enough in your sight, Sovereign LORD, you have also spoken about the future of my family. Is this your usual way of dealing with people, Sovereign LORD? {7:20} What more can David say to you? For you know your servant, Sovereign LORD. {7:21} For the sake of your word and according to your will, you have done this great thing and made it known to your servant. {7:22} How great you are, Sovereign LORD! There is no one like you, and there is no God but you, as we have heard with our own ears. {7:23} And who is like your people Israel—the one nation on earth that God went out to redeem as a people for himself, and to make a name for himself, and to perform great and awesome wonders by driving out nations and their gods from before your people, whom you redeemed from Egypt? {7:24} You have established your people Israel as your very own forever, and you, LORD, have become their God. {7:25} And now, LORD God, keep forever the promise you have made concerning your servant and his house. Do as you promised, {7:26} so that your name will be great forever. Then people will say, 'The LORD Almighty is God over Israel!' And the house of your servant David will be established before you. {7:27} LORD Almighty, God of Israel, you have revealed this to your servant, saying, 'I will build you a house.' So your servant has found courage to pray this prayer to you. {7:28} Sovereign LORD, you are God! Your covenant is trustworthy, and you have promised these good things to your servant. {7:29} Now be pleased to bless the house of your servant, that it may continue forever in your sight; for you, Sovereign LORD, have spoken, and with your blessing, the house of your servant will be blessed forever."

{8:1} After this, David defeated the Philistines and subdued them, and he took Methegammah from the Philistines. {8:2} He also struck down Moab and measured them with a line, making them lie down on the ground. He measured two lines to put them to death and one full line to keep alive. The Moabites became David's subjects and brought him tribute. {8:3} David also defeated Hadadezer, son of Rehob, king of Zobah, as he went to restore his control along the Euphrates River. {8:4} David captured a thousand chariots, seven hundred horsemen, and twenty thousand foot soldiers. He hamstrung (cut the tendons of) all but a hundred of the chariot horses. {8:5} When the Arameans (Syrians) from Damascus came to help Hadadezer, David struck down twenty-two thousand of them. {8:6} He put garrisons in the Aramean (Syrian) capital of Damascus, and the Arameans became subjects to David and brought him tribute. The LORD gave David victory wherever he went. {8:7} David took the gold shields that belonged to the officers of Hadadezer and brought them to Jerusalem. {8:8} From Tebah and Berothai, towns that belonged to Hadadezer, David took a great quantity of bronze. {8:9} When Toi, king of Hamath, heard that David had defeated the entire army of Hadadezer, {8:10} he sent his son Joram to King David to greet him and congratulate him for fighting against Hadadezer and defeating him. (Hadadezer had been at war with Toi.) Joram brought with him articles of silver, gold, and bronze. {8:11} King David dedicated these articles to the LORD, along with the silver and gold he had dedicated from all the nations he had subdued— {8:12} from Edom, Moab, the Ammonites, the Philistines, and Amalek, and the plunder from Hadadezer son of Rehob, king of Zobah. {8:13} David became famous after he returned from striking down eighteen thousand Edomites in the Valley of Salt. {8:14} He put garrisons throughout Edom, and all the Edomites became David's subjects. The LORD gave David victory wherever he went. {8:15} David reigned over all Israel, doing what was just and right for all his people. {8:16} Joab son of Zeruiah was over the army; Jehoshaphat son of Ahilud was recorder; {8:17} Zadok son of Ahitub and Ahimelech son of Abiathar were priests; Seraiah was secretary; {8:18} Benaiah son of Jehoiada was in charge of the Kerethites and Pelethites; and David's sons were chief officials.

{9:1} David asked, "Is there anyone left from the house of Saul to whom I can show kindness for Jonathan's sake?" {9:2} There was a servant of Saul's household named Ziba. When they summoned him to David, the king asked him, "Are you Ziba?" He replied, "Yes, your servant." {9:3} The king then asked, "Is there no one left from the house of Saul to whom I can show the kindness of God?" Ziba answered the king, "Jonathan has a son who is lame in both feet." {9:4} The king asked, "Where is he?" Ziba replied, "He is at the house of Machir son of Ammiel in Lodebar." {9:5} So King David sent for him and brought him from the house of Machir son of Ammiel in Lodebar. {9:6} When Mephibosheth, the son of Jonathan and grandson of Saul, came to David, he fell on his face in reverence. David said, "Mephibosheth!" He replied, "Your servant is here!" {9:7} David said, "Don't be afraid, for I will surely show you kindness for the sake of your father Jonathan. I will restore to you all the land that belonged to your grandfather Saul, and you will always eat at my table." {9:8} Mephibosheth bowed down and said, "What is your servant that you should notice a dead dog like me?" {9:9} The king called Ziba, Saul's servant, and said to him, "I have given your master's grandson everything that belonged to Saul and his family. {9:10} You and your sons and your servants are to farm the land for him and bring in the crops so that your master's grandson may be provided for. And Mephibosheth, your master's grandson, will always eat at my table." Ziba had fifteen sons and twenty servants. {9:11} Then Ziba said to the king, "Your servant will do whatever my lord the king commands." And as for Mephibosheth, the king said, "He will eat at my table like one of the king's sons." {9:12} Mephibosheth had a young son named Micha, and all the servants in Ziba's household were servants of Mephibosheth. {9:13} So Mephibosheth lived in Jerusalem because he always ate at the king's table; he was lame in both feet.

{10:1} Some time later, the king of the Ammonites died, and his son Hanun succeeded him as king. {10:2} David said, "I will show kindness to Hanun son of Nahash, just as his father showed kindness to me." So David sent his servants to console him concerning his father. When David's servants came to the Ammonite territory, {10:3} the Ammonite leaders said to Hanun, "Do you think David is honoring your father by sending envoys to you? Hasn't David sent his servants to you to explore the city and spy it out and overthrow it?" {10:4} So Hanun seized David's envoys, shaved off half of each man's beard, cut their garments in the middle up to their hips, and sent them away. {10:5} When David was told about this, he sent messengers to meet the men, for they were greatly humiliated. The king said, "Stay at Jericho until your beards have grown, and then come back." {10:6} When the Ammonites realized that they had become a stench to David, they hired the Arameans (Syrians) of Beth-Rehob and the Arameans of Zobah—twenty thousand foot soldiers—as well as the king of Maacah with a thousand men and the men of Ishtob, twelve thousand men in all. {10:7} David heard about it and sent Joab out with the entire army of fighting men. {10:8} The Ammonites came out and drew up their battle lines at the entrance of their city gate, while the Arameans of Zobah and Rehob and the men of Ishtob and Maacah were in the open country. {10:9} Joab saw that there were battle lines in front of him and behind him, so he selected some of the best troops in Israel and deployed them against the Arameans. {10:10} He put the rest of the men under the command of his brother Abishai and deployed them against the Ammonites. {10:11} Joab said, "If the Arameans are too strong for me, then you come to my rescue; but if the Ammonites are too strong for you, I will come to rescue you. {10:12} Be strong, and let us fight bravely for our people and the cities of our God. The LORD will do what is good in his sight." {10:13} Then Joab and the troops with him advanced to fight the Arameans, and they fled before him. {10:14} When the Ammonites saw that the Arameans were fleeing, they fled before Abishai and went inside the city. So Joab returned to Jerusalem. {10:15} After the Arameans saw that they had been routed by Israel, they regrouped. {10:16} Hadadezer sent and had the Arameans brought from beyond the Euphrates River; they went to Helam, with Shobach the commander of Hadadezer's army leading them. {10:17} When David was told of this, he gathered all Israel and crossed the Jordan. He went to Helam, where the Arameans drew up their battle lines to meet David and fought against him. {10:18} But they fled before Israel, and David killed seven hundred of their charioteers and forty thousand of their foot soldiers. He also killed Shobach the commander of their army. {10:19} When all the kings who were vassals of Hadadezer saw that they had been defeated by Israel, they made peace with Israel and became subject to them. So the Arameans were afraid to help the Ammonites anymore.

{11:1} After a year had passed, at the time when kings typically go to war, David sent Joab and his servants with him, along with all of Israel. They destroyed the Ammonites and besieged Rabbah, but David stayed in Jerusalem. {11:2} One evening, David got up from his bed and walked on the roof of the palace. From the roof, he saw a woman bathing, and she was very beautiful. {11:3} David sent someone to find out about her. The messenger said, "Isn't this Bathsheba, the daughter of Eliam, and the wife of Uriah the Hittite?" {11:4} David sent messengers to get her, and she came to him, and he slept with her. She had just completed her purification after her period, and then she went back home. {11:5} The woman became pregnant and sent word to David, saying, "I'm pregnant." {11:6} David sent a message to Joab to bring Uriah the Hittite to him. Joab sent Uriah to David. {11:7} When Uriah arrived, David asked him how Joab was, how the soldiers were, and how the war was going. {11:8} David told Uriah, "Go home and wash your feet." Uriah left the king's palace, and a gift of food from the king was sent after him. {11:9} However, Uriah slept at the entrance of the king's palace with all the servants and did not go down to his house. {11:10} David was informed that Uriah did not go home, so he asked Uriah, "Haven't you just come from a journey? Why didn't you go home?" {11:11} Uriah replied, "The Ark and Israel and Judah are staying in tents, and my lord Joab and his men are camped in the open fields. How could I go home to eat and drink and sleep with my wife? As surely as you live and as your soul lives, I will not do this!" {11:12} David said to Uriah, "Stay here today, and tomorrow I will send you back." So Uriah stayed in Jerusalem that day and the next. {11:13} David invited him to eat and drink with him, and David got him drunk. But in the evening, Uriah went out to sleep on his bed with the king's servants and did not go home. {11:14} In the morning, David wrote a letter to Joab and sent it with Uriah. {11:15} In the letter, he wrote, "Put Uriah in the front lines where the fighting is fiercest. Then withdraw from him so he will be struck down and die." {11:16} So while Joab was besieging the city, he assigned Uriah to a place where he knew the strongest defenders were. {11:17} When the men of the city came out and fought against Joab, some of David's men fell; Uriah the Hittite also died. {11:18} Joab sent word to David about everything that had happened in the battle. {11:19} He instructed the messenger, "When you have finished reporting all the news to the king, {11:20} if his anger rises and he asks you, 'Why did you get so close to the city to fight? Didn't you know they would shoot from the wall? {11:21} Who killed Abimelech son of Jerub-Besheth? Didn't a woman drop an upper millstone on him from the wall so that he died at Thebez? Why did you get so close to the wall?' then tell him, 'Your servant Uriah the Hittite is dead also.'" {11:22} The messenger set out and when he arrived, he told David everything Joab had sent him to say. {11:23} The messenger said to David, "The men overpowered us and came out against us in the field, but we drove them back to the entrance of the city. {11:24} Then the archers shot at your servants from the wall, and some of the king's servants are dead, and your servant Uriah the Hittite is dead too." {11:25} David told the messenger, "Say this to Joab: 'Don't let this upset you; the sword devours one as well as another. Press the attack against the city and destroy it. Encourage Joab!'" {11:26} When Uriah's wife heard that her husband was dead, she mourned for him. {11:27} After the time of mourning was over, David sent for her and brought her to his house, and she became his wife and bore him a son. However, what David had done displeased the LORD.

{12:1} The LORD sent Nathan to David. When he arrived, he said, "There were two men in a certain city: one rich and the other poor. {12:2} The rich man had a very large number of sheep and cattle, {12:3} but the poor man had nothing except one little ewe lamb he had bought. He raised it and it grew up with him and his children. It shared his food, drank from his cup, and even slept in his arms. It was like a daughter to him. {12:4} Now a traveler came to the rich man, but the rich man refrained from taking one of his own sheep or cattle to prepare a meal for the traveler who had come to him. Instead, he took the poor man's lamb and prepared it for the one who had come to him." {12:5} David burned with anger against the man and said to Nathan, "As surely as the LORD lives, the man who did this deserves to die! {12:6} He must pay for that lamb four times over because he did such a thing and had no pity." {12:7} Then Nathan said to David, "You are the man! This is what the LORD, the God of Israel, says: 'I anointed you king over Israel, and I delivered you from the hand of Saul. {12:8} I gave you your master's house and your master's wives into your arms. I gave you all Israel and Judah. And if all this had been too little, I would have given you even more. {12:9} Why did you despise the word of the LORD by doing what is evil in his eyes? You killed Uriah the Hittite with the sword and took his wife to be your own, and you killed him with the sword of the Ammonites. {12:10} Now, therefore, the sword will never depart from your house because you despised me and took the wife of Uriah the Hittite to be your own. {12:11} This is what the LORD says: 'Out of your own household I am going to bring calamity upon you. Before your very eyes, I will take your wives and give them to one who is close to you, and he will lie with your wives in broad daylight. {12:12} You did this in secret, but I will do this thing in broad daylight before all Israel.'" {12:13} Then David said to Nathan, "I have sinned against the LORD." Nathan replied, "The LORD has taken away your sin. You are not going to die. {12:14} But because by doing this you have made the enemies of the LORD show utter contempt, the son born to you will die." {12:15} After Nathan had gone home, the LORD struck the child that Uriah's wife bore to David, and he became ill. {12:16} David pleaded with God for the child. He fasted and spent the nights lying on the ground. {12:17} The elders of his household stood beside him to get him up from the ground, but he refused and would not eat any food with them. {12:18} On the seventh day, the child died. David's attendants were afraid to tell him that the child was dead, for they thought, "While the child was still alive, we spoke to him, but he wouldn't listen to us. How can we tell him the child is dead? He may do something desperate." {12:19} David noticed that his attendants were whispering among themselves, and he realized the child was dead. So he asked them, "Is the child dead?" "Yes," they replied, "he is dead." {12:20} Then David got up from the ground. After he had washed, put on lotions, and changed his clothes, he went into the house of the LORD and worshiped. Then he went to his own house and at his request, they served him food, and he ate. {12:21} His attendants asked him, "Why are you acting this way? While the child was alive, you fasted and wept, but now that the child is dead, you get up and eat!" {12:22} He answered, "While the child was still alive, I fasted and wept. I thought, 'Who knows? The LORD may be gracious to me and let the child live.' {12:23} But now that he is dead, why should I go on fasting? Can I bring him back again? I will go to him, but he will not return to me." {12:24} Then David comforted his wife Bathsheba, and he went to her and made love to her. She gave birth to a son and named him Solomon. The LORD loved him; {12:25} and because the LORD loved him, he sent word through Nathan the prophet to name him Jedidiah. {12:26} Meanwhile, Joab fought against Rabbah of the Ammonites and captured the royal city. {12:27} Joab sent messengers to David, saying, "I have fought against Rabbah and taken its water supply. {12:28} Now gather the rest of the troops and besiege the city and capture it, or I will take the city, and it will be named after me." {12:29} So David gathered all the troops and went to Rabbah and attacked it and captured it. {12:30} He took the crown from the head of their king. Its weight was a talent of gold, and it was set with gems. It was placed on David's head. He took a great quantity of plunder from the city. {12:31} He brought out the people there and put them to work with saws, with iron picks, and with axes. He made them pass through the brick kilns. This is what he did to all the Ammonite towns. Then David and his entire army returned to Jerusalem.

{13:1} After this, Absalom, David's son, had a beautiful sister named Tamar, and Amnon, David's son, fell in love with her. {13:2} Amnon was so obsessed with his sister Tamar that he became ill because she was a virgin, and he thought it impossible to do anything to her. {13:3} But Amnon had a friend named Jonadab, the son of David's brother Shimeah, and Jonadab was a very clever man. {13:4} He asked Amnon, "Why do you, the king's son, look so miserable day after day? Won't you tell me?" Amnon replied, "I am in love with Tamar, my brother Absalom's sister." {13:5} Jonadab said, "Lie down on your bed and pretend to be ill. When your father comes to see you, say to him, 'Please let my sister Tamar come and give me something to eat. Let her prepare the food in my sight so I may eat from her hand.'" {13:6} So Amnon lay down and pretended to be sick. When the king came to see him, Amnon said, "Please let my sister Tamar come and make a couple of cakes in my sight so I can eat from her hand." {13:7} David sent word to Tamar at her home, saying, "Go to your brother Amnon's house and prepare some food for him." {13:8} So Tamar went to her brother Amnon's house, where he was lying down. She took dough, kneaded it, made the cakes in her sight, and baked them. {13:9} Then she took the pan and served him the cakes, but he refused to eat. Amnon said, "Send everyone out of here." So everyone left. {13:10} Then Amnon said to Tamar, "Bring the food into my bedroom so I may eat from your hand." Tamar took the cakes she had made and brought them to Amnon in his bedroom. {13:11} But when she brought them to him to eat, he grabbed her and said, "Come to bed with me, my sister." {13:12} "No, my brother!" she said to him. "Don't force me! Such a thing should not be done in Israel. Don't do this wicked thing. {13:13} What about me? Where could I go to get rid of my disgrace? And you would be like one of the wicked fools in Israel. Please, speak to the king; he will not refuse to give me to you." {13:14} But Amnon refused to listen to her, and since he was stronger than she was, he raped her. {13:15} Then Amnon hated her with intense hatred. In fact, he hated her more than he had loved her. Amnon said to her, "Get up and leave!" {13:16} She said to him, "No! Sending me away now would be a greater wrong than what you've already done to me." But he refused to listen to her. {13:17} He called his personal servant and said, "Get this woman out of here and bolt the door after her." {13:18} So his servant put her out and bolted the door behind her. She was wearing an ornate robe, for this was how the virgin daughters of the king dressed. {13:19} Tamar put ashes on her head and tore the ornate robe she was wearing. She put her hands on her head and went away, weeping aloud as she went. {13:20} Her brother Absalom said to her, "Has Amnon, your brother, been with you? Be quiet for now, my sister; he is your brother. Don't take this thing to heart." And Tamar lived in her brother Absalom's house, desolate. {13:21} When King David heard all this, he was furious. {13:22} And Absalom never spoke a word to Amnon, either good or bad; he hated Amnon because he had disgraced his sister Tamar. {13:23} Two years later, when Absalom's sheepshearers were at Baal Hazor near Ephraim, he invited all the king's sons to come there. {13:24} Absalom went to the king and said, "Your servant has sheepshearers. Will the king and his attendants please join me?" {13:25} The king replied, "No, my son. All of us should not go; we would only be a burden to you." Although Absalom urged him, he refused to go but gave him his blessing. {13:26} Then Absalom said, "If not, please let my brother Amnon come with us." The king asked, "Why should he go with you?" {13:27} But Absalom pressed him, so he sent with him Amnon and the rest of the king's sons. {13:28} Absalom ordered his men, "Listen! When Amnon is in high spirits from drinking wine and I say to you, 'Strike Amnon down,' then kill him. Don't be afraid. Have I not given you this order? Be strong and brave." {13:29} So Absalom's men did to Amnon what Absalom had ordered. Then all the king's sons got up, mounted their mules, and fled. {13:30} While they were on their way, the report came to David: "Absalom has struck down all the king's sons; not one of them is left." {13:31} The king stood up, tore his clothes, and lay down on the ground; and all his attendants stood by with their clothes torn. {13:32} But Jonadab, the son of David's brother Shimeah, said, "My lord should not think that they killed all the princes; only Amnon is dead. This has been Absalom's plan ever since the day Amnon raped his sister Tamar. {13:33} My lord the king should not be concerned about the report that all the king's sons are dead. Only Amnon is dead." {13:34} Meanwhile, Absalom had fled. Now the man standing watch looked up and saw many people on the road west of him, coming down the side of the hill. {13:35} Jonadab said to the king, "See, the king's sons have come; it has happened just as your servant said." {13:36} As he finished speaking, the king's sons came in, wailing loudly. The king, too, and all his attendants wept very bitterly. {13:37} Absalom fled and went to Talmai, son of Ammihud, the king of Geshur. But King David mourned many days for his son. {13:38} After Absalom fled and went to Geshur, he stayed there three years. {13:39} And King David longed to go to Absalom, for he was consoled concerning Amnon's death.

{14:1} Now, Joab, the son of Zeruiah, noticed that the king's heart was inclined towards Absalom. {14:2} So, Joab sent for a wise woman from Tekoah and told her, "Please pretend to be a mourner. Dress in mourning clothes, don't put any oil on yourself, and act like a woman who has been mourning a long time for the dead." {14:3} Then, go to the king and speak to him this way." And Joab gave her the words to say. {14:4} When the woman from Tekoah came to the king, she bowed down with her face to the ground and said, "Help, O king." {14:5} The king asked her, "What is troubling you?" And she answered, "I am a widow; my husband is dead. {14:6} I had two sons, and they fought together in a field. There was no one to separate them, and one of them struck the other and killed him. {14:7} Now, the whole family has risen up against me and demands that I give them the one who killed his brother, so they can execute him. They also want to destroy the heir, leaving my husband's name and property without a trace on earth." {14:8} The king told her, "Go back to your home, and I will take care of the matter." {14:9} The woman from Tekoah responded, "My lord, king, let the guilt be on me and my father's house, but let the king and his throne be guiltless." {14:10} The king said, "Whoever says anything to you, bring him to me, and he will never trouble you again." {14:11} Then she said, "Please, let the king remember the Lord your God so that the avengers of blood don't keep killing, lest they destroy my son." The king replied, "As the Lord lives, not a hair of your son will fall to the ground." {14:12} The woman said, "Please let your servant speak one more word to my lord the king." And he said, "Speak." {14:13} She said, "Why then have you thought such a thing against the people of God? For in this matter, the king is acting as one who is guilty, because the king does not bring back his banished son. {14:14} We must all die, and we are like water spilled on the ground, which cannot be gathered up again. Yet God does not take away life, but devises ways so that his banished ones are not expelled from Him." {14:15} "Now I have come to speak to my lord the king because the people have made me afraid. I said, 'I will speak to the king; perhaps he will fulfill the request of his servant.' {14:16} For the king will listen, and deliver his servant from the man who would destroy me and my son from the inheritance of God." {14:17} The woman continued, "Then your servant said, 'Let the word of my lord the king bring peace, for as an angel of God, my lord the king has the ability to discern good from evil. May the Lord your God be with you.'" {14:18} Then the king answered, "Don't hide anything from me that I ask you." And the woman said, "Let my lord the king speak." {14:19} The king asked, "Isn't Joab behind all this?" And the woman replied, "As surely as you live, my lord the king, nothing can turn to the right or left from all that my lord the king has spoken. It was your servant Joab who told me to say these things and put all these words in the mouth of your servant." {14:20} "Joab did this to change the course of events. My lord is wise, like an angel of God, knowing everything that happens in the land." {14:21} The king then told Joab, "Alright, I have agreed to this. Go, bring back Absalom." {14:22} Joab fell to the ground, bowed down, and thanked the king. He said, "Today your servant knows that I have found favor in your sight, my lord, O king, because you have granted the request of your servant." {14:23} So, Joab went to Geshur and brought Absalom back to Jerusalem. {14:24} The king said, "Let him go to his own house and not see my face." So Absalom returned to his house and did not see the king's face. {14:25} In all of Israel, no one was praised as much as Absalom for his beauty. From the soles of his feet to the top of his head, there was no blemish on him. {14:26} When he cut his hair (which he did at the end of every year because his hair was heavy on him), he weighed it, and it weighed two hundred shekels according to the king's weight. {14:27} Absalom had three sons and one daughter. His daughter's name was Tamar, and she was a beautiful woman. {14:28} Absalom lived in Jerusalem for two full years but never saw the king's face. {14:29} So Absalom sent for Joab, intending for him to take a message to the king, but Joab refused to come. When he sent again the second time, Joab still refused to come. {14:30} Then Absalom said to his servants, "Look, Joab's field is near mine, and he has barley there. Go and set it on fire." So Absalom's servants set the field on fire. {14:31} Joab got up, came to Absalom's house, and said, "Why have your servants set my field on fire?" {14:32} Absalom replied, "I sent for you, saying, 'Come here so I can send you to the king to ask why I was brought back from Geshur. It would have been better for me to remain there.' Now let me see the king's face, and if there's any sin in me, let him kill me." {14:33} So Joab went to the king, told him what Absalom had said, and when king called for Absalom, he came and bowed down with his face to the ground before the king, and the king kissed Absalom.

{15:1} After this, Absalom got himself chariots and horses, and appointed fifty men to run ahead of him. {15:2} Absalom got up early and stood by the gate. Whenever someone with a dispute came to the king for judgment, Absalom would call out to him, asking, "Which city are you from?" The man would reply, "Your servant is from one of the tribes of Israel." {15:3} Absalom would then say, "Your case is good and right, but there's no one appointed by the king to hear you." {15:4} He would add, "If only I were made judge in the land! Everyone with a complaint could come to me, and I would give them justice!" {15:5} Whenever someone approached to bow to him, he would extend his hand, take hold of him, and kiss him. {15:6} This is how Absalom treated all the people of Israel who came to the king for judgment, and so he won the hearts of the men of Israel. {15:7} After four years, Absalom said to the king, "Please let me go to Hebron to fulfill a vow I made to the LORD. {15:8} I made this vow while I was in Geshur, Syria, saying, 'If the LORD brings me back to Jerusalem, I will serve Him.'" {15:9} The king replied, "Go in peace." So Absalom went to Hebron. {15:10} However, he sent spies throughout all the tribes of Israel, instructing them, "As soon as you hear the sound of the trumpet, say, 'Absalom reigns in Hebron!'" {15:11} With Absalom went two hundred men from Jerusalem who had been invited and were unaware of what was happening. {15:12} Absalom also sent for Ahithophel the Gilonite, David's counselor, from his city, Giloh, while he offered sacrifices. The conspiracy grew stronger, and the people continued to rally around Absalom. {15:13} A messenger came to David, saying, "The hearts of the men of Israel are with Absalom." {15:14} David said to all his servants in Jerusalem, "Get up and let us flee, or else we won't escape from Absalom. Hurry to depart, or he will catch us unexpectedly and bring disaster upon us, striking the city with the sword." {15:15} The king's servants replied, "We are ready to do whatever our lord the king commands." {15:16} The king left, along with all his household, and he left ten concubines to take care of the palace. {15:17} The king and all his followers went out and stopped at a spot far away. {15:18} All his servants passed on beside him, including the Cherethites, Pelethites, and six hundred Gittites from Gath, who passed on ahead of the king. {15:19} The king asked Ittai the Gittite, "Why are you going with us? Go back and stay with the king, for you are a foreigner and an exile. {15:20} You only arrived yesterday. Should I make you wander around with us today? Return and take your brothers with you. May kindness and truth be with you." {15:21} Ittai answered the king, "As the LORD lives, and as you live, wherever you go, whether in life or death, I will be there with you." {15:22} David said to Ittai, "Go ahead and cross over." So Ittai the Gittite crossed over, along with all his men and their families. {15:23} The whole country wept loudly as all the people passed over. The king also crossed the Kidron Valley, and the people went toward the wilderness. {15:24} Zadok and all the Levites were with him, carrying the ark of the covenant of God. They set down the ark, and Abiathar went up until all the people had left the city. {15:25} The king said to Zadok, "Take the ark of God back into the city. If I find favor in the LORD's eyes, He will bring me back and show me both it and His dwelling place. {15:26} But if He says, 'I have no pleasure in you,' here I am; let Him do to me whatever seems good to Him." {15:27} The king also said to Zadok the priest, "Are you not a seer? Go back to the city in peace, along with your two sons, Ahimaaz and Jonathan, son of Abiathar. {15:28} I will wait in the wilderness until I receive word from you." {15:29} So Zadok and Abiathar took the ark of God back to Jerusalem and stayed there. {15:30} David went up the Mount of Olives, weeping as he went. His head was covered, and he walked barefoot. All the people with him also covered their heads and wept as they went up. {15:31} Someone told David, "Ahithophel is among the conspirators with Absalom." David prayed, "LORD, please turn Ahithophel's counsel into foolishness." {15:32} When David reached the top of the mount, where he worshiped God, Hushai the Archite met him with his coat torn and dust on his head. {15:33} David said to him, "If you go with me, you will be a burden to me. {15:34} But if you return to the city and say to Absalom, 'I will be your servant, O king; as I was your father's servant before, so I will now be your servant,' you can help me defeat Ahithophel's counsel. {15:35} Don't you have Zadok and Abiathar the priests with you? Whenever you hear anything from the king's house, tell it to Zadok and Abiathar the priests. {15:36} They have their two sons with them, Ahimaaz, son of Zadok, and Jonathan, son of Abiathar. You can send them to me with any news you hear." {15:37} So Hushai, David's friend, returned to the city, and Absalom entered Jerusalem.

{16:1} When David had just passed the top of the hill, Ziba, the servant of Mephibosheth, met him with two donkeys saddled and carrying two hundred loaves of bread, a hundred bunches of raisins, a hundred summer fruits, and a bottle of wine. {16:2} The king asked Ziba, "What do you mean by these?" Ziba replied, "The donkeys are for the king's household to ride on, and the bread and summer fruit are for the young men to eat; the wine is for anyone who is faint in the wilderness." {16:3} The king asked, "Where is your master's son?" Ziba answered, "He's staying in Jerusalem, saying, 'Today the house of Israel will restore to me my father's kingdom.'" {16:4} The king said to Ziba, "Everything that belonged to Mephibosheth is now yours." Ziba said, "I humbly ask that I may find favor in your sight, my lord, O king." {16:5} When King David came to Bahurim, a man from the family of Saul, named Shimei son of Gera, came out, cursing as he approached. {16:6} He threw stones at David and at all the king's officials, and all the mighty men were on his right and left. {16:7} Shimei shouted as he cursed, "Get out, get out, you bloody man, you worthless man! {16:8} The LORD has repaid you for all the blood of Saul's house, in whose place you have reigned; the LORD has given the kingdom into the hands of your son Absalom. You are in trouble because you are a bloody man!" {16:9} Abishai, son of Zeruiah, asked the king, "Why should this dead dog curse my lord the king? Let me go over and cut off his head!" {16:10} The king replied, "What does this have to do with you, sons of Zeruiah? Let him curse, for the LORD has told him to. Who can ask, 'Why are you doing this?' {16:11} David said to Abishai and all his servants, "My own son is trying to kill me; how much more can this Benjamite do it? Leave him alone and let him curse, for the LORD has commanded him. {16:12} Perhaps the LORD will see my affliction and repay me with good for his cursing today." {16:13} As David and his men walked along the road, Shimei followed along the hillside, cursing and throwing stones at them and kicking up dust. {16:14} The king and all the people with him grew weary and refreshed themselves there. {16:15} Absalom and all the men of Israel came to Jerusalem, and Ahithophel was with him. {16:16} When Hushai the Archite, David's friend, came to Absalom, he said, "Long live the king! Long live the king!" {16:17} Absalom asked Hushai, "Is this your loyalty to your friend? Why didn't you go with your friend?" {16:18} Hushai replied to Absalom, "No, but whom the LORD and this people choose, along with all the men of Israel, that's who I will serve, and I will remain with him. {16:19} And who should I serve? Shouldn't I serve in the presence of his son? As I have served your father, so I will serve you." {16:20} Absalom then said to Ahithophel, "Give us your advice on what we should do." {16:21} Ahithophel advised Absalom, "Go in and sleep with your father's concubines, whom he left to take care of the house. Then all Israel will hear that you have made yourself a stench to your father, and the hands of everyone with you will be strengthened." {16:22} So they pitched a tent for Absalom on the roof, and he went in to his father's concubines in the sight of all Israel. {16:23} The advice of Ahithophel, which he gave in those days, was like asking God for guidance; it was regarded as if it were the very word of God, whether it was for David or for Absalom.

{17:1} Ahithophel said to Absalom, "Let me choose twelve thousand men, and I will go after David tonight. {17:2} I'll catch him when he's tired and weak, and make him afraid. All the people with him will scatter, and I will only kill the king. {17:3} Then I'll bring back everyone else to you. The man you seek will be as if all the people returned, so the entire nation will be at peace." {17:4} This advice pleased Absalom and all the elders of Israel. {17:5} Then Absalom said, "Call Hushai the Archite as well, and let's hear what he has to say." {17:6} When Hushai came to Absalom, Absalom said to him, "Ahithophel has given this advice. Should we follow it, or do you have something different to suggest?" {17:7} Hushai replied, "The advice that Ahithophel gave is not good at this moment. {17:8} You know your father and his men. They are mighty warriors, and they are angry, like a bear robbed of her cubs in the field. Your father is a skilled fighter and will not be resting with the people. {17:9} He is hiding in a pit or somewhere else. If we attack and some of his men are killed, those who hear about it will say there's been a slaughter among those following Absalom. {17:10} Even the bravest men will be terrified, because everyone knows your father is a mighty man, and those with him are brave warriors. {17:11} So, I suggest gathering all of Israel to you, from Dan to Beersheba, in such great numbers that it's like sand on the seashore. Then, you should go into battle yourself. {17:12} We will surprise him wherever he is found, and we will fall on him like dew on the ground. None of his men will escape. {17:13} If he hides in a city, we will bring ropes and pull the city into the river, until there is not even a small stone left." {17:14} Absalom and all the men of Israel agreed, saying, "Hushai's advice is better than Ahithophel's." The Lord had determined to defeat Ahithophel's good advice, so that evil could come upon Absalom. {17:15} Then Hushai told Zadok and Abiathar the priests, "This is what Ahithophel advised Absalom, and this is what I advised. {17:16} Now, send word quickly to David, telling him not to spend the night in the wilderness, but to cross the Jordan River quickly, or he and his people will be destroyed." {17:17} Jonathan and Ahimaaz stayed at Enrogel, where they couldn't be seen entering the city. A servant girl went and told them, and they went to tell David. {17:18} But a boy saw them, and told Absalom. They quickly left and went to the house of a man in Bahurim who had a well in his courtyard, where they hid. {17:19} The woman covered the well with a cloth and spread grain on top of it, so no one knew they were hiding there. {17:20} When Absalom's men came to ask the woman where Ahimaaz and Jonathan were, she replied, "They've crossed the water." When they couldn't find them, they returned to Jerusalem. {17:21} After they left, Jonathan and Ahimaaz climbed out of the well and went to tell David. They warned him, "Get up and cross the Jordan River quickly, because Ahithophel has given advice against you." {17:22} So David and all his people crossed the Jordan by morning, and by the time the sun rose, none of them were left behind. {17:23} When Ahithophel saw that his advice had not been followed, he saddled his donkey and went home. He put his house in order, then hanged himself and died. He was buried in his father's tomb. {17:24} Then David arrived at Mahanaim, and Absalom crossed the Jordan with all the men of Israel. {17:25} Absalom made Amasa the commander of his army, replacing Joab. Amasa was the son of Ithra, an Israelite, who had married Abigail, the sister of Zeruiah, Joab's mother. {17:26} So Israel and Absalom set up camp in the land of Gilead. {17:27} When David came to Mahanaim, Shobi, the son of Nahash from Rabbah of the Ammonites, Machir, the son of Ammiel from Lodebar, and Barzillai, the Gileadite from Rogelim, {17:28} brought beds, basins, pottery, wheat, barley, flour, roasted grain, beans, lentils, roasted seeds, {17:29} honey, butter, sheep, and cheese for David and his people to eat, because they were hungry, tired, and thirsty in the wilderness.

{18:1} David counted the men who were with him and appointed captains over thousands and hundreds. {18:2} He sent a third of the troops under Joab's command, another third under Abishai, the son of Zeruiah (Joab's brother), and the last third under Ittai the Gittite. The king said to the people, "I will also go out with you." {18:3} But the people replied, "You must not go with us, because if we flee, they won't care about us. Even if half of us die, they won't care, but you are worth ten thousand of us. It's better for you to stay and support us from the city." {18:4} The king agreed, saying, "I'll do what you think is best." Then he stood by the gate, and all the people passed out by hundreds and thousands. {18:5} The king gave Joab, Abishai, and Ittai orders, saying, "Be gentle with the young man, Absalom, for my sake." The people heard this command regarding Absalom. {18:6} The battle took place in the forest of Ephraim, {18:7} where the Israelites were defeated by David's men. There was a great slaughter that day, with twenty thousand men killed. {18:8} The battle was spread across the whole area, and the forest claimed more lives than the sword that day. {18:9} Absalom came upon David's servants. He was riding on a mule, and the mule went under the thick branches of a large oak. His head got caught in the tree, and he was left hanging between heaven and earth, while the mule he was riding ran off. {18:10} A man saw it and reported to Joab, saying, "I saw Absalom hanging in an oak." {18:11} Joab asked the man, "You saw him? Why didn't you kill him right there? I would have given you ten shekels of silver and a belt." {18:12} The man replied, "Even if I received a thousand shekels of silver, I wouldn't have harmed the king's son. We all heard the king tell you, Abishai, and Ittai to beware not to harm Absalom. {18:13} If I had done that, it would have been treason against my own life. There's nothing hidden from the king, and you would have turned against me." {18:14} Joab said, "I can't waste time with you." He took three spears, thrust them into Absalom's heart while he was still alive in the oak, {18:15} and ten of Joab's men surrounded Absalom and killed him. {18:16} Joab blew a trumpet, and the troops stopped pursuing Israel, for Joab had held them back. {18:17} They took Absalom's body and threw it into a large pit in the forest, then piled a great heap of stones over it. All Israel fled, each to his tent. {18:18} While alive, Absalom had built a pillar for himself in the King's Valley, because he had no son to keep his name alive. He called the pillar after his own name, and it's still called "Absalom's Place" to this day. {18:19} Ahimaaz, the son of Zadok, said, "Let me run and bring the king news that the Lord has delivered him from his enemies." {18:20} Joab told him, "You won't carry the news today, but later you can. Today, you have no news, because the king's son is dead." {18:21} Joab told Cushi, "Go tell the king what you have seen." Cushi bowed to Joab and ran. {18:22} Ahimaaz begged Joab, "Let me also run after Cushi." Joab asked, "Why do you want to run? You have no news to bring." {18:23} Ahimaaz replied, "Let me run." Joab said, "Run." So Ahimaaz ran by way of the plain and outran Cushi. {18:24} David was sitting between the two gates, and the watchman went up to the roof above the gate to the wall. He lifted up his eyes, and saw a man running by himself. {18:25} The watchman called out and told the king. The king said, "If he's alone, he must have news to tell." The man came closer, running toward them. {18:26} Then the watchman saw another man running, and he called to the porter (the gatekeeper), saying, "Look, another man is running alone." The king replied, "He must also be bringing news." {18:27} The watchman said, "It seems to me that the running of the first man is like that of Ahimaaz, the son of Zadok." The king said, "He is a good man, and he brings good news." {18:28} Ahimaaz called out and said to the king, "All is well." He fell down on his face before the king, and said, "Praise be to the Lord your God, who has delivered the men who rebelled against my lord the king." {18:29} The king asked, "Is the young man Absalom safe?" Ahimaaz replied, "When Joab sent me and your servant, I saw a great commotion, but I didn't know what it was." {18:30} The king told him, "Turn aside and stand here." So he stepped aside and stood still. {18:31} Just then, Cushi came. Cushi said, "Good news, my lord the king! The Lord has avenged you today on all those who rose up against you." {18:32} The king asked Cushi, "Is the young man Absalom safe?" Cushi answered, "May the enemies of my lord the king, and all who rise up against you to harm you, be like that young man." {18:33} The king was deeply moved. He went up to the chamber over the gate and wept. As he walked, he said, "Oh, my son Absalom, my son, my son Absalom! I wish I had died instead of you, Absalom, my son, my son!"

{19:1} Joab was told, "Look, the king is weeping and mourning for Absalom." {19:2} That day, the victory turned into mourning for all the people, as they heard how the king was grieved for his son. {19:3} The people sneaked back into the city that day, like those who are ashamed and try to escape after a battle. {19:4} The king covered his face and cried out loudly, "O my son Absalom, O Absalom, my son, my son!" {19:5} Joab went into the king's house and said, "You have shamed your servants today, the ones who saved your life, and the lives of your sons and daughters, and your wives and concubines. {19:6} You love your enemies and hate your friends. You've made it clear today that you don't care about princes or servants; if Absalom were alive and all of us were dead, you'd be pleased." {19:7} "So get up, go out, and speak kindly to your servants. I swear by the LORD, if you don't go out, not one of them will stay with you tonight, and that will be worse for you than all the evil you've faced from your youth until now." {19:8} Then the king got up and sat at the gate. The people were told, "Look, the king is sitting at the gate." All the people came before the king, as Israel had fled, each man to his tent. {19:9} The people argued throughout the tribes of Israel, saying, "The king saved us from our enemies and delivered us from the Philistines, yet now he has fled the land because of Absalom." {19:10} "Absalom, whom we anointed over us, is dead in battle. So why aren't you saying anything about bringing the king back?" {19:11} King David sent a message to Zadok and Abiathar the priests, saying, "Speak to the elders of Judah: why are you the last to bring the king back to his house? All of Israel has spoken to the king, even to his house." {19:12} "You are my brothers, my own flesh and blood; why then are you the last to bring back the king?" {19:13} "And say to Amasa, 'Aren't you my own flesh and blood? May God do so to me, and more, if you aren't captain of the army before me continually in place of Joab.'" {19:14} Amasa won over the hearts of all the men of Judah, like one man, so they sent this message to the king: "Return, you and all your servants." {19:15} So the king returned and came to the Jordan. Judah went to Gilgal to meet the king and bring him across the Jordan. {19:16} Shimei son of Gera, a Benjaminite from Bahurim, hurried down with the men of Judah to meet King David. {19:17} He had a thousand men of Benjamin with him, and Ziba, the servant of Saul's household, with his fifteen sons and twenty servants, went ahead of the king across the Jordan. {19:18} They used a ferry boat to carry the king's household and whatever he wanted to do. Shimei son of Gera fell down before the king as he crossed the Jordan, {19:19} and said, "Let not my lord hold me guilty or remember what I did wrong on the day my lord the king left Jerusalem. Please don't take it to heart. {19:20} Your servant knows I have sinned, and I have come today as the first of all the house of Joseph to meet my lord the king." {19:21} But Abishai son of Zeruiah said, "Shouldn't Shimei be put to death for this, since he cursed the LORD's anointed?" {19:22} David replied, "What do I have to do with you, sons of Zeruiah? Should anyone be put to death today in Israel? Don't I know that I am king over Israel today?" {19:23} So the king said to Shimei, "You won't die." And the king swore to him. {19:24} Mephibosheth son of Saul came down to meet the king. He had not taken care of his feet, trimmed his beard, or washed his clothes since the day the king left until the day he returned safely. {19:25} When he came to Jerusalem to meet the king, the king asked him, "Why didn't you go with me, Mephibosheth?" {19:26} He replied, "My lord, O king, my servant deceived me. Your servant said, 'I will saddle a donkey for myself so I can ride it and go with the king,' because your servant is lame. {19:27} He has slandered your servant to my lord the king. But my lord the king is like an angel of God; so do what is good in your eyes. {19:28} All my father's house deserved death before my lord the king, but you set your servant among those who eat at your own table. So what right do I have to cry out anymore to the king?" {19:29} The king said to him, "Why keep talking about your matters? I have decided that you and Ziba will divide the land." {19:30} Mephibosheth said to the king, "Let him take it all, since my lord the king has returned safely to his own house." {19:31} Barzillai the Gileadite came down from Rogelim to accompany the king across the Jordan. {19:32} Barzillai was very old, eighty years old, and he had provided for the king while he stayed at Mahanaim, for he was a very great man. {19:33} The king said to Barzillai, "Come with me, and I will provide for you in Jerusalem." {19:34} Barzillai replied to the king, "How long do I have to live, that I should go up with the king to Jerusalem? {19:35} I am eighty years old today. Can I discern between good and evil? Can your servant taste what I eat or drink? Can I still hear the voice of singing men and singing women? Why then should your servant be a burden to my lord the king? {19:36} Your servant will go a little way over the Jordan with the king. Why should the king reward me with such a reward? {19:37} Please let your servant return so I can die in my own city and be buried by my father and mother. But look, let your servant Chimham go over with my lord the king, and do for him whatever seems good to you." {19:38} The king answered, "Chimham will go over with me, and I will do for him what seems good to you, and whatever you require of me, I will do for you." {19:39} All the people crossed the Jordan, and when the king had crossed, he kissed Barzillai and blessed him, and he returned to his own home. {19:40} The king went on to Gilgal, and Chimham went with him. All the people of Judah escorted the king, and also half the people of Israel. {19:41} Then all the men of Israel came to the king and said to him, "Why have our brothers, the men of Judah, stolen you away and brought the king, his household, and all David's men across the Jordan?" {19:42} The men of Judah replied to the men of Israel, "The king is closely related to us; why then are you angry about this? Have we eaten any of the king's cost, or has he given us any gift?" {19:43} The men of Israel answered the men of Judah, "We have ten shares in the king, and we have more right in David than you do. Why then did you despise us? We were not consulted first in bringing back our king." And the words of the men of Judah were harsher than those of the men of Israel.

{20:1} A man of Belial (worthless man) named Sheba son of Bichri, a Benjaminite, happened to be there. He blew a trumpet and said, "We have no share in David, nor do we have an inheritance in the son of Jesse; every man to his tents, O Israel!" {20:2} So every man of Israel deserted David and followed Sheba son of Bichri. But the men of Judah stayed with their king, from the Jordan to Jerusalem. {20:3} When David came to his house in Jerusalem, he took the ten concubines he had left to take care of the house, put them in confinement, and provided for them, but he did not have sexual relations with them. They were kept in confinement until the day they died, living as widows. {20:4} The king said to Amasa, "Gather the men of Judah for me within three days, and be here yourself." {20:5} Amasa went to gather the men of Judah, but he took longer than the time he had set. {20:6} David said to Abishai, "Now Sheba son of Bichri will do us more harm than Absalom did. Take your lord's servants and pursue him, so he doesn't get into fortified cities and escape us." {20:7} Joab's men went out with the Cherethites, the Pelethites, and all the mighty men to pursue Sheba son of Bichri. {20:8} When they were at the great stone in Gibeon, Amasa went ahead of them. Joab's garment was on him, and he had a sword fastened to his side in a sheath. As he went along, it fell out. {20:9} Joab said to Amasa, "Are you well, my brother?" Joab took Amasa by the beard with his right hand to kiss him. {20:10} But Amasa didn't notice the sword in Joab's hand. Joab struck him in the stomach, spilling his insides onto the ground, and did not strike him again. Amasa died. Joab and Abishai his brother pursued after Sheba son of Bichri. {20:11} One of Joab's men stood by him and said, "Whoever is for Joab and whoever is for David, follow Joab." {20:12} Amasa lay in his blood in the middle of the road. When the man saw that everyone stood still, he removed Amasa from the road into a field and covered him with a cloth, since everyone who came by him paused. {20:13} When Amasa was removed from the road, all the people went after Joab to pursue Sheba son of Bichri. {20:14} Sheba went through all the tribes of Israel to Abel, to Bethmaachah, and all the Berites gathered together and followed him. {20:15} They besieged him in Abel of Bethmaachah and built a mound against the city. All the people with Joab were battering the wall to bring it down. {20:16} A wise woman from the city cried out, "Listen! Come near me, I pray you, to speak with you." When Joab came near her, she said, "Are you Joab?" He replied, "I am." {20:17} She said, "Listen to the words of your servant." He answered, "I am listening." {20:18} She said, "In old times, they used to say, 'Ask counsel at Abel,' and that settled the matter. {20:19} I am one of those who are peaceable and faithful in Israel; you seek to destroy a city that is a mother in Israel. Why would you swallow up the LORD's inheritance?" {20:20} Joab answered, "Far be it, far be it from me to destroy or swallow up. {20:21} That's not the case; a man from the hill country of Ephraim, Sheba son of Bichri by name, has lifted his hand against the king, against David. Deliver him only, and I will withdraw from the city." The woman said to Joab, "His head will be thrown to you over the wall." {20:22} Then the woman went to all the people and told them her wisdom. They cut off Sheba son of Bichri's head and threw it to Joab. He blew the trumpet, and they all left the city, each to his tent. Joab returned to Jerusalem to the king. {20:23} Joab was in command of all the army of Israel; Benaiah son of Jehoiada was over the Cherethites and the Pelethites. {20:24} Adoram was over the forced labor; Jehoshaphat son of Ahilud was the recorder; {20:25} Sheva was the scribe; Zadok and Abiathar were the priests; {20:26} and Ira the Jairite was chief ruler under David.

{21:1} During David's reign, there was a famine that lasted three years, and David sought the LORD's guidance. The LORD said it was because of Saul and his bloody household, as he killed the Gibeonites. {21:2} So the king summoned the Gibeonites, explaining that they were not Israelites but remnants of the Amorites, and that the Israelites had sworn an oath to them. Saul, in his zeal for

Israel and Judah, sought to kill them. {21:3} David asked the Gibeonites, "What can I do for you? How can I make atonement so you will bless the LORD's inheritance?" {21:4} The Gibeonites replied, "We don't want silver or gold from Saul or his household, nor do you need to kill anyone in Israel for us." David asked, "What do you want me to do?" {21:5} They answered the king, "The man who destroyed us and plotted against us to wipe us out from Israel's territory— {21:6} let seven of his sons be handed over to us, and we will hang them before the LORD in Gibeah, the city Saul chose." The king agreed to this. {21:7} However, the king spared Mephibosheth, the son of Jonathan, Saul's son, because of the oath made between David and Jonathan. {21:8} David took the two sons of Rizpah, daughter of Aiah, whom she bore to Saul, named Armoni and Mephibosheth, along with the five sons of Michal, Saul's daughter, whom she raised for Adriel, son of Barzillai the Meholathite. {21:9} He handed them over to the Gibeonites, who hanged them on a hill before the LORD. All seven were put to death during the barley harvest. {21:10} Rizpah, daughter of Aiah, took sackcloth and spread it on a rock, guarding the bodies from birds by day and beasts by night from the beginning of harvest until rain fell on them. {21:11} David was informed of what Rizpah had done. {21:12} He then went and retrieved the bones of Saul and Jonathan from the men of Jabesh-gilead, who had stolen them from the public square of Bethshan, where the Philistines had hung them after killing Saul at Gilboa. {21:13} David brought the bones of Saul and Jonathan, along with the bones of those hanged. {21:14} They buried Saul and Jonathan in the land of Benjamin, in Zelah, in the tomb of Kish, Saul's father, and they did everything the king commanded. After that, God was moved to respond to the land. {21:15} The Philistines waged war against Israel again, and David went down with his men to fight the Philistines, but David grew faint. {21:16} Ishbibenob, a descendant of the giants, had a spear weighing three hundred shekels of bronze, and he thought he could kill David. {21:17} But Abishai, son of Zeruiah, came to David's aid and killed the Philistine. David's men vowed to him, saying, "You shall not go out to battle with us anymore, lest you extinguish the light of Israel." {21:18} After this, there was another battle with the Philistines at Gob, where Sibbechai the Hushathite killed Saph, one of the giants. {21:19} Another battle took place in Gob, where Elhanan, son of Jaare-oregim from Bethlehem, killed Goliath's brother, who had a spear like a weaver's beam. {21:20} There was yet another battle in Gath with a giant who had six fingers on each hand and six toes on each foot, twenty-four in total. He was also a descendant of the giants. {21:21} When he challenged Israel, Jonathan, son of Shimea, David's brother, killed him. {21:22} These four were born to the giants in Gath and fell by the hand of David and his servants.

{22:1} David sang to the LORD the words of this song on the day the LORD rescued him from his enemies and from Saul. {22:2} He said, "The LORD is my rock, my fortress, and my deliverer. {22:3} My God, my rock in whom I take refuge, my shield, and the horn of my salvation, my stronghold and my savior— you save me from violence. {22:4} I will call upon the LORD, who is worthy to be praised, and I shall be saved from my enemies. {22:5} The waves of death surrounded me, and the torrents of ungodly men terrified me; {22:6} the cords of hell entangled me; the snares of death confronted me. {22:7} In my distress, I called upon the LORD; I cried to my God. He heard my voice from His temple, and my cry entered His ears. {22:8} The earth shook and trembled; the foundations of heaven shook because He was angry. {22:9} Smoke went up from His nostrils, and devouring fire from His mouth; coals were kindled by it. {22:10} He bent the heavens and came down; thick darkness was under His feet. {22:11} He rode on a cherub and flew; He was seen on the wings of the wind. {22:12} He made darkness His canopy, thick clouds of the skies. {22:13} Through the brightness before Him, coals of fire were kindled. {22:14} The LORD thundered from heaven; the Most High uttered His voice. {22:15} He sent arrows and scattered them; lightning and confused them. {22:16} The channels of the sea appeared, and the foundations of the world were uncovered at the rebuke of the LORD, at the blast of the breath of His nostrils. {22:17} He reached down from on high and took me; He drew me out of many waters. {22:18} He rescued me from my strong enemy and from those who hated me, for they were too strong for me. {22:19} They confronted me in the day of my calamity, but the LORD was my support. {22:20} He brought me out to a broad place; He delivered me because He delighted in me. {22:21} The LORD rewarded me according to my righteousness; according to the cleanness of my hands, He recompensed me. {22:22} For I have kept the ways of the LORD and have not wickedly departed from my God. {22:23} All His judgments were before me; as for His statutes, I did not depart from them. {22:24} I was also blameless before Him, and I kept myself from my iniquity. {22:25} Therefore, the LORD has recompensed me according to my righteousness; according to my cleanness in His sight. {22:26} With the merciful, You show Yourself merciful; with the upright, You show Yourself upright. {22:27} With the pure, You show Yourself pure; but with the devious, You show Yourself shrewd. {22:28} You save the afflicted people, but Your eyes are on the haughty to bring them down. {22:29} For You are my lamp, O LORD; the LORD will lighten my darkness. {22:30} By You, I can run against a troop; by my God, I can leap over a wall. {22:31} As for God, His way is perfect; the word of the LORD is tested; He is a shield for all who take refuge in Him. {22:32} For who is God, except the LORD? Who is a rock, except our God? {22:33} God is my strength and power; He makes my way perfect. {22:34} He makes my feet like those of a deer and sets me on high places. {22:35} He trains my hands for battle; my arms can bend a bow of bronze. {22:36} You have also given me the shield of Your salvation; Your gentleness has made me great. {22:37} You have enlarged my steps under me, so my feet did not slip. {22:38} I pursued my enemies and destroyed them, and did not turn back until I had consumed them. {22:39} I have consumed them and wounded them, so they could not rise; they have fallen under my feet. {22:40} For You have equipped me with strength for battle; those who rose against me, You have subdued under me. {22:41} You have also given me the necks of my enemies, that I might destroy those who hate me. {22:42} They looked, but there was no one to save; even to the LORD, but He did not answer them. {22:43} Then I beat them as fine dust of the earth; I stamped them like mud in the streets and spread them out. {22:44} You also delivered me from the strife of my people; You kept me to be the head of the nations; a people I did not know shall serve me. {22:45} Foreigners will submit to me; as soon as they hear, they will obey me. {22:46} Foreigners will disappear, and they will tremble from their strongholds. {22:47} The LORD lives! Blessed be my rock; exalted be the God of my salvation. {22:48} It is God who takes vengeance for me and brings down the people under me, {22:49} who brings me out from my enemies; you have lifted me high above those who rise against me; you have delivered me from the violent man. {22:50} Therefore, I will give thanks to you, O LORD, among the nations, and I will sing praises to your name. {22:51} He is the stronghold of salvation for his king and shows mercy to his anointed one, to David and his descendants forever.

{23:1} These are the final words of David. David, the son of Jesse, spoke; he was the man lifted up high, the anointed one of the God of Jacob, and the sweet psalmist of Israel. {23:2} The Spirit of the LORD spoke through me, and His word was on my tongue. {23:3} The God of Israel said, the Rock of Israel spoke to me: "The ruler over people must be just, ruling with the fear of God." {23:4} He will be like the light of the morning when the sun rises, a morning without clouds; like fresh grass growing after rain. {23:5} Even though my house isn't what it should be with God, He has made an everlasting covenant with me, arranged in all things and secure; this is my salvation and my desire, even if He doesn't make it grow. {23:6} But the wicked will be like thorns, thrown away, because they cannot be handled. {23:7} Anyone who touches them must be armed with iron and the staff of a spear; they will be completely burned with fire in that place. {23:8} Here are the names of the mighty men who served David: The Tachmonite who sat in the seat, chief among the captains, was Adino the Eznite; he raised his spear against eight hundred men and killed them all at once. {23:9} Next was Eleazar, son of Dodo the Ahohite, one of the three mighty men with David, who fought against the Philistines when they gathered to battle, and the men of Israel had fled. {23:10} He rose up and struck down the Philistines until his hand grew tired, and his hand stuck to the sword; the LORD gave a great victory that day, and the people returned only to collect the spoils. {23:11} After him was Shammah, son of Agee the Hararite. The Philistines gathered in a troop where there was a field of lentils, and the people fled from them. {23:12} But he stood in the middle of the field, defended it, and killed the Philistines;

the LORD granted a great victory. {23:13} Three of the thirty chiefs came down to David during the harvest at the cave of Adullam, while the Philistine troop was in the valley of Rephaim. {23:14} David was in a stronghold, and the Philistine garrison was in Bethlehem. {23:15} David longed for water and said, "Oh, that someone would give me a drink from the well of Bethlehem, near the gate!" {23:16} So the three mighty men broke through the Philistine camp, drew water from the well of Bethlehem, and brought it back to David; but he refused to drink it and poured it out to the LORD. {23:17} He said, "Far be it from me, O LORD, that I should do this; isn't this the blood of the men who risked their lives?" So he would not drink it. These are the deeds of the three mighty men. {23:18} Abishai, brother of Joab, son of Zeruiah, was the chief of the three; he raised his spear against three hundred men and killed them, earning a name among the three. {23:19} Was he not the most honored of the three? So he was their captain, but he did not reach the status of the first three. {23:20} Benaiah, son of Jehoiada, from Kabzeel, who performed many great acts, killed two lion-like men from Moab; he also went down and killed a lion in a pit during snow. {23:21} He killed a tall Egyptian who had a spear; Benaiah went down to him with a staff, took the spear from the Egyptian's hand, and killed him with his own spear. {23:22} These are the deeds of Benaiah, son of Jehoiada; he was renowned among the three mighty men. {23:23} He was more honorable than the thirty, but did not attain to the first three; David appointed him over his bodyguard. {23:24} Asahel, brother of Joab, was one of the thirty; Elhanan, son of Dodo, from Bethlehem, {23:25} Shammah the Harodite, Elika the Harodite, {23:26} Helez the Paltite, Ira, son of Ikkesh the Tekoite, {23:27} Abiezer the Anethothite, Mebunnai the Hushathite, {23:28} Zalmon the Ahohite, Maharai the Netophathite, {23:29} Heleb, son of Baanah, a Netophathite, Ittai, son of Ribai, from Gibeah, of Benjamin, {23:30} Benaiah the Pirathonite, Hiddai from the brooks of Gaash, {23:31} Abialbon the Arbathite, Azmaveth the Barhumite, {23:32} Eliahba the Shaalbonite, of the sons of Jashen, Jonathan, {23:33} Shammah the Hararite, Ahiam, son of Sharar the Hararite, {23:34} Eliphelet, son of Ahasbai, from Maachah, Eliam, son of Ahithophel the Gilonite, {23:35} Hezrai the Carmelite, Paarai the Arbite, {23:36} Igal, son of Nathan from Zobah, Bani the Gadite, {23:37} Zelek the Ammonite, Naharai the Beerothite, armor-bearer to Joab, son of Zeruiah, {23:38} Ira the Ithrite, Gareb the Ithrite, {23:39} Uriah the Hittite; thirty-seven in all.

{24:1} Again the anger of the LORD burned against Israel, and He incited David against them to say, "Go, count Israel and Judah." {24:2} The king said to Joab, the captain of the army with him, "Go now through all the tribes of Israel, from Dan to Beersheba, and count the people so I can know how many there are." {24:3} Joab said to the king, "May the LORD your God multiply the people a hundredfold, and may the eyes of my lord the king see it; but why does my lord delight in this?" {24:4} Nevertheless, the king's order prevailed over Joab and the captains. So Joab and the captains went out from the king's presence to count the people of Israel. {24:5} They crossed the Jordan and camped at Aroer, on the right side of the city in the middle of the valley of Gad, and went toward Jazer. {24:6} Then they came to Gilead and the land of Tahtimhodshi; they went to Danjaan and near Zidon, {24:7} to the fortified cities of Tyre, and to all the cities of the Hivites and Canaanites; they went south to Judah, even to Beersheba. {24:8} When they had gone through all the land, they came to Jerusalem at the end of nine months and twenty days. {24:9} Joab reported the total to the king; there were in Israel eight hundred thousand valiant men who drew the sword, and the men of Judah were five hundred thousand. {24:10} David's heart troubled him after he counted the people. He said to the LORD, "I have sinned greatly in what I have done; please take away the guilt of your servant, for I have acted very foolishly." {24:11} In the morning, the word of the LORD came to the prophet Gad, David's seer, saying, {24:12} "Go and tell David, 'The LORD says: I offer you three options; choose one of them for me to do to you.'" {24:13} Gad went to David and told him, "Shall there be seven years of famine in your land? Or will you flee for three months before your enemies while they pursue you? Or shall there be three days of plague in your land? Consider and tell me what answer I should return to Him who sent me." {24:14} David said to Gad, "I am in deep distress; let us fall into the hand of the LORD, for His mercies are great, but do not let me fall into the hand of man." {24:15} So the LORD sent a plague on Israel from the morning until the appointed time; seventy thousand men died from Dan to Beersheba. {24:16} When the angel stretched out his hand to destroy Jerusalem, the LORD relented concerning the disaster and said to the angel who was destroying the people, "Enough! Withdraw your hand." The angel of the LORD was at the threshing floor of Araunah the Jebusite. {24:17} David spoke to the LORD when he saw the angel striking down the people and said, "I have sinned; I have done wrong. But these sheep, what have they done? Let Your hand be against me and my father's house." {24:18} On that day Gad came to David and said, "Go up and build an altar to the LORD on the threshing floor of Araunah the Jebusite." {24:19} David followed Gad's instructions and went up as the LORD commanded. {24:20} Araunah looked and saw the king and his servants coming toward him; he went out and bowed facedown before the king. {24:21} Araunah asked, "Why has my lord the king come to his servant?" David replied, "To buy your threshing floor so I can build an altar to the LORD, that the plague may be halted." {24:22} Araunah said to David, "Let my lord the king take whatever he wishes and offer it up; here are oxen for the burnt offering, and you can use the threshing implements and oxen for wood." {24:23} Araunah gave everything as a king to David and said, "May the LORD your God accept you." {24:24} But David replied, "No, I will buy it at full price; I will not offer to the LORD my God burnt offerings that cost me nothing." So David bought the threshing floor and the oxen for fifty shekels of silver. {24:25} David built an altar to the LORD there and offered burnt offerings and peace offerings. The LORD answered his prayer for the land, and the plague was halted in Israel.

The First Book of Kings

{1:1} King David was now old and advanced in years; even when they covered him with blankets, he could not get warm. {1:2} So his servants said to him, "Let us find a young virgin for our lord the king. She should attend to the king and lie in his arms so that our lord the king may feel warm." {1:3} They searched for a beautiful young woman throughout all the territories of Israel and found Abishag, a Shunammite, and brought her to the king. {1:4} The young woman was very beautiful and cared for the king, but the king did not have sexual relations with her. {1:5} Then Adonijah, the son of Haggith, exalted himself, saying, "I will be king." He prepared chariots, horsemen, and fifty men to run before him. {1:6} His father had never upset him by asking, "Why have you done that?" He was also a very handsome man, and his mother had given birth to him after Absalom. {1:7} Adonijah conferred with Joab, the son of Zeruiah, and Abiathar the priest, and they supported him. {1:8} But Zadok the priest, Benaiah, the son of Jehoiada, Nathan the prophet, Shimei, Rei, and the mighty men who belonged to David were not with Adonijah. {1:9} Adonijah sacrificed sheep, oxen, and fattened cattle near the stone of Zoheleth, which is by Enrogel, and called all his brothers, the king's sons, and all the men of Judah who were servants of the king. {1:10} But Nathan the prophet, Benaiah, the mighty men, and Solomon, his brother, he did not invite. {1:11} Therefore, Nathan spoke to Bathsheba, the mother of Solomon, saying, "Have you not heard that Adonijah, the son of Haggith, has become king, and our lord David does not know it? {1:12} Now, therefore, come, let me give you some advice so you can save your own life and the life of your son Solomon. {1:13} Go to King David and say to him, 'Did you not, my lord, O king, swear to your servant, saying, "Solomon your son shall reign after me, and he shall sit on my throne"? Why then is Adonijah king?' {1:14} While you are still talking to the king, I will come in after you and confirm your words." {1:15} Bathsheba went into the king's chamber; the king was very old, and Abishag the Shunammite was attending him. {1:16} Bathsheba bowed down and showed respect to the king. The king asked, "What do you want?" {1:17} She said to him, "My lord, you swore by the LORD your God to your servant, saying, 'Solomon your son shall reign after me, and he shall sit on my throne.' {1:18} Now, behold, Adonijah is king, and you, my lord the king, do not know it. {1:19} He has sacrificed oxen, fattened cattle, and sheep in abundance, and he has called all the king's sons, Abiathar the priest, and Joab, the captain of the army, but he has not called Solomon, your servant. {1:20} And now, my lord the king, the eyes of all Israel are upon you to tell them who shall sit on the throne of my lord the king after him. {1:21} Otherwise, when my lord the king sleeps with his ancestors, my son Solomon and I will be regarded as offenders." {1:22} Just then, while she was still talking to the king, Nathan the prophet also came in. {1:23} They told the king, "Nathan the prophet is here." When he came in before the king, he bowed with his face to the ground. {1:24} Nathan said, "My lord, O king, have you said, 'Adonijah shall reign after me, and he shall sit on my throne'? {1:25} For he has gone down today and has sacrificed oxen, fattened cattle, and sheep in abundance, and he has called all the king's sons, the captains of the army, and Abiathar the priest; and they are eating and drinking before him, saying, 'Long live King Adonijah!' {1:26} But me, your servant, Zadok the priest, Benaiah, the son of Jehoiada, and your servant Solomon, he has not called. {1:27} Is this thing done by my lord the king, and you have not told your servant who should sit on the throne of my lord the king after him?" {1:28} Then King David answered, "Call me Bathsheba." She came into the king's presence and stood before him. {1:29} The king swore, saying, "As the LORD lives, who has rescued my soul from every distress, {1:30} even as I swore to you by the LORD God of Israel, saying, 'Solomon your son shall reign after me, and he shall sit on my throne in my place,' I will do this today." {1:31} Then Bathsheba bowed down with her face to the ground and honored the king, saying, "May my lord King David live forever!" {1:32} King David said, "Call me Zadok the priest, Nathan the prophet, and Benaiah, the son of Jehoiada." They came before the king. {1:33} The king said to them, "Take your lord's servants with you and have Solomon my son ride on my own mule and take him down to Gihon. {1:34} Let Zadok the priest and Nathan the prophet anoint him there king over Israel. Blow the trumpet and say, 'Long live King Solomon!' {1:35} Then you shall come up after him, so that he may come and sit on my throne, for he shall be king in my place; I have appointed him as ruler over Israel and Judah." {1:36} Benaiah, the son of Jehoiada, answered the king, "Amen! May the LORD God of my lord the king say so too. {1:37} As the LORD has been with my lord the king, may he be with Solomon and make his throne even greater than the throne of my lord King David." {1:38} So Zadok the priest, Nathan the prophet, Benaiah, the son of Jehoiada, the Cherethites, and the Pelethites went down and had Solomon ride on King David's mule, and they brought him to Gihon. {1:39} Zadok the priest took a horn of oil from the tabernacle and anointed Solomon. They blew the trumpet, and all the people said, "Long live King Solomon!" {1:40} All the people followed him, and the people played flutes and rejoiced with great joy, so that the ground shook with their sound. {1:41} Adonijah and all the guests who were with him heard it as they finished eating. When Joab heard the sound of the trumpet, he said, "Why is this noise of the city in an uproar?" {1:42} While he was still speaking, Jonathan, the son of Abiathar the priest, came. Adonijah said to him, "Come in; for you are a brave man and bring good news." {1:43} Jonathan answered Adonijah, "No! Our lord King David has made Solomon king. {1:44} The king has sent with him Zadok the priest, Nathan the prophet, Benaiah, the son of Jehoiada, the Cherethites, and the Pelethites, and they have had him ride on the king's mule. {1:45} Zadok the priest and Nathan the prophet have anointed him king at Gihon, and they have come up from there rejoicing, so that the city is in an uproar. This is the noise you heard. {1:46} Also, Solomon sits on the throne of the kingdom. {1:47} Moreover, the king's servants have come to bless our lord King David, saying, 'May God make the name of Solomon better than your name and make his throne greater than your throne.' And the king bowed himself on the bed. {1:48} The king also said, 'Blessed be the LORD God of Israel, who has given someone to sit on my throne today; my own eyes have seen it.' {1:49} All the guests who were with Adonijah were afraid, and they rose up and each went their own way. {1:50} Adonijah feared because of Solomon, and he arose, went, and took hold of the horns of the altar. {1:51} It was reported to Solomon, saying, "Adonijah fears King Solomon, for he has taken hold of the horns of the altar, saying, 'Let King Solomon swear to me today that he will not kill his servant with the sword.' {1:52} Solomon said, 'If he shows himself to be a worthy man, not a hair of his head shall fall to the ground; but if wickedness is found in him, he shall die.' {1:53} So King Solomon sent, and they brought him down from the altar. He came and bowed down to King Solomon, and Solomon said to him, 'Go to your house.'"

{2:1} As the days of David were nearing the time for his death, he gave his son Solomon a final charge, saying, {2:2} "I am about to go the way of all the earth. Be strong, therefore, and show yourself to be a man. {2:3} And observe the commands of the LORD your God, walking in His ways, keeping His statutes, His commandments, His judgments, and His testimonies, as it is written in the Law of Moses, so that you may prosper in all you do and wherever you go. {2:4} The LORD will fulfill His promise to me, saying, 'If your descendants are careful to live in the way I have taught them, walking in truth with all their heart and soul, there will never fail to be a man on the throne of Israel.' {2:5} You also know what Joab, the son of Zeruiah, did to me, what he did to the two captains of the armies of Israel—Abner, the son of Ner, and Amasa, the son of Jether. He killed them, shedding innocent blood during a time of peace, putting the blood of war on his belt and his shoes. {2:6} Therefore, act according to your wisdom, and do not let his gray head go down to the grave in peace. {2:7} But show kindness to the sons of Barzillai the Gileadite, and let them eat at your table, for they helped me when I fled from your brother Absalom. {2:8} And remember Shimei, the son of Gera, a Benjaminite from Bahurim, who cursed me with a terrible curse the day I went to Mahanaim. He came to meet me at the Jordan River, and I swore to him by the LORD, saying, 'I will not put you to death with the sword.' {2:9} Now, therefore, do not let him go unpunished. You are a wise man and know what to do to him. But make sure his gray head is brought down to the grave with blood." {2:10} So David died and was buried in the city of David. {2:11} David reigned over Israel for forty years—seven years in Hebron and thirty-three years in Jerusalem. {2:12} Then Solomon sat on the throne of his father David, and his kingdom was firmly established. {2:13} Adonijah, the son of Haggith, came to Bathsheba, Solomon's mother. She asked, "Do you come in peace?" He replied, "Yes, in peace." {2:14} He added, "I have something to say to you." She said, "Speak." {2:15} He said, "You know that the kingdom was mine and that all Israel had set their hearts on me to be king. But the kingdom has now turned and belongs to my brother, for it was his from the LORD. {2:16} Now, I have one request of you. Do not deny me." She said, "Speak." {2:17} He asked her to speak to King Solomon for him, saying, "He will not refuse you. Ask him to give me Abishag, the Shunammite, as my wife." {2:18} Bathsheba said, "All right, I will speak to the king on your behalf." {2:19} Bathsheba went to King Solomon to speak to him on behalf of Adonijah. The king rose to meet her, bowed down to her, and had a seat set for her on his right hand. {2:20} Then she said, "I have one small request. Please do not refuse me." The king answered her, "Ask, my mother, for I will not refuse you." {2:21} She said, "Let Abishag, the Shunammite, be given to Adonijah your brother as his wife." {2:22} King Solomon replied, "Why do you ask for Abishag for Adonijah? Ask for the kingdom for him as well, since he is my older brother, and for Abiathar the priest and Joab, the son of Zeruiah." {2:23} Then Solomon swore by the LORD, saying, "May God do so to me, and more, if Adonijah does not deserve to die for this request." {2:24} "Now, as the LORD lives, who has established me and set me on the throne of David my father, and who has made a house for me, as He promised, Adonijah will be put to death today." {2:25} So King Solomon sent Benaiah, the son of Jehoiada, and he struck Adonijah down, and he died. {2:26} To Abiathar the priest, Solomon said, "Go to your fields at Anathoth. You deserve to die, but I will not put you to death now, because you carried the Ark of the LORD God before my father David and because you suffered everything my father went through." {2:27} So Solomon expelled Abiathar from serving as priest to the LORD, fulfilling the word of the LORD spoken concerning the house of Eli in Shiloh. {2:28} When Joab heard about this, he also sided with Adonijah. Joab, however, had not sided with Absalom, and he fled to the tabernacle of the LORD, taking hold of the horns of the altar. {2:29} It was told King Solomon that Joab had fled to the tabernacle and was by the altar. Solomon sent Benaiah, the son of Jehoiada, saying, "Go, strike him down." {2:30} Benaiah went to the tabernacle and said to Joab, "The king says, 'Come out.'" But Joab answered, "No, I will die here." So Benaiah returned with the king's message. {2:31} The king replied, "Do as he has said, and strike him down. Bury him so you can remove the guilt of innocent blood that Joab shed from me and my father's house." {2:32} The LORD will repay Joab's blood on his own head, because he killed two men more righteous and better than he, Abner, the son of Ner, and Amasa, the son of Jether, whom Joab killed without my father's knowledge. {2:33} Their blood will return upon Joab and his descendants forever, but there will be peace for David, his descendants, and his house, and his throne, forever from the LORD. {2:34} So Benaiah went and struck Joab down, and Joab was buried in his own house in the wilderness. {2:35} Then Solomon appointed Benaiah, the son of Jehoiada, in Joab's place as commander of the army, and Zadok the priest in place of Abiathar. {2:36} The king then summoned Shimei and said, "Build yourself a house in Jerusalem and stay there. Do not leave the city for any reason. {2:37} On the day you leave and cross the Kidron Valley, you will surely die. Your blood will be on your own head." {2:38} Shimei replied to the king, "The word is good, as you have said, so will your servant do." So Shimei lived in Jerusalem for a long time. {2:39} But after three years, two of Shimei's servants ran away to King Achish of Gath. When Shimei was told that his servants were in Gath, {2:40} he saddled his donkey and went to Gath to search for them. He found them and brought them back to Jerusalem. {2:41} Solomon was told that Shimei had left Jerusalem and gone to Gath, and had returned. {2:42} So the king sent for Shimei and asked him, "Did I not make you swear by the LORD and warn you, saying, 'On the day you leave and go anywhere, you will surely die'? And you said, 'The word I have heard is good.' {2:43} Why then have you not kept the oath of the LORD and obeyed the command I gave you?" {2:44} The king said to Shimei, "You know in your heart all the wicked things you did to my father David. The LORD will return your wickedness on your own head. {2:45} But King Solomon will be blessed, and the throne of David will be established before the LORD forever." {2:46} Then the king commanded Benaiah, the son of Jehoiada, to go and strike Shimei down, and he died. So the kingdom was firmly established in Solomon's hands.

{3:1} Solomon formed an alliance with Pharaoh, the king of Egypt, by marrying Pharaoh's daughter and brought her to the City of David, until he finished building his own palace, the temple of the LORD, and the wall around Jerusalem. {3:2} The people continued to sacrifice at high places because there was no temple built in the name of the LORD until that time. {3:3} Solomon loved the LORD, following the statutes of his father David, but he also sacrificed and burned incense at high places. {3:4} The king went to Gibeon to offer sacrifices there, for that was the most important high place, and Solomon offered a thousand burnt offerings on that altar. {3:5} At Gibeon, the LORD appeared to Solomon in a dream at night and said, "Ask for whatever you want me to give you." {3:6} Solomon replied, "You have shown great kindness to your servant David my father, because he walked before you in faithfulness, righteousness, and integrity of heart; and you have continued this great kindness by giving him a son to sit on his throne this day. {3:7} Now, LORD my God, you have made me king in place of my father David, but I am just a child; I do not know how to carry out my duties. {3:8} Your servant is here among your chosen people, a great nation, too numerous to count or number. {3:9} So give your servant a discerning heart to govern your people and to distinguish between right and wrong, for who is able to govern this great people of yours?" {3:10} This request pleased the LORD, that Solomon had asked for this. {3:11} So God said to him, "Since you have asked for this and not for long life, wealth, or the death of your enemies, but for wisdom to discern judgment, {3:12} I will do what you have asked. I will give you a wise and discerning heart, so that there will never be anyone like you, nor will there ever be. {3:13} I will also give you what you have not asked for, both wealth and honor, so that in your lifetime you will have no equal among kings. {3:14} And if you walk in my ways and keep my statutes and commands, as David your father did, I will give you a long life." {3:15} Solomon awoke, and it had been a dream. He returned to Jerusalem, stood before the ark of the covenant of the LORD, and offered burnt offerings and fellowship offerings, and gave a feast for all his servants. {3:16} Then two women who were prostitutes came to the king and stood before him. {3:17} One woman said, "My lord, this woman and I live in the same house, and I gave birth to a child while she was there with me. {3:18} Three days after my child was born, this woman also gave birth. We were alone; there was no one in the house but the two of us. {3:19} During the night, this woman's baby died because she lay on him. {3:20} She got up in the middle of the night and took my son from my side while I was asleep. She put him in her arms and laid her dead baby in my arms. {3:21} When I woke up in the morning to nurse my son, I saw that he was dead. But when I looked closer, I realized it wasn't the son I had borne." {3:22} The other woman said, "No! The living one is my son; the dead one is yours." The first one insisted, "No! The dead one is yours; the living one is my son." They argued before the king. {3:23} The king said, "One says, 'My son is alive, and your son is dead,' while the other says, 'No! Your son is dead, and my son is alive.'" {3:24} Then the king said, "Bring me a sword." So they brought a sword for the king. {3:25} He then ordered, "Cut the living child in two and give half to one and half to the other." {3:26} The woman who was the child's mother was deeply moved out of love for her son and cried out, "Please, my lord, give her the living baby! Don't kill him!" But the other said, "Neither I nor you shall have him. Cut him in two!" {3:27} Then the king gave his ruling: "Give the living baby to the first woman. Do not kill him; she is his mother." {3:28} When all Israel heard the verdict the king had given, they held the king in awe because they saw that he had wisdom from God to administer justice.

{4:1} King Solomon ruled over all Israel. {4:2} These were his officials: Azariah, son of Zadok the priest, {4:3} Elihoreph and Ahiah, the sons of Shisha, who were scribes; Jehoshaphat, son of Ahilud, was the recorder. {4:4} Benaiah, son of Jehoiada, was in charge of the army, while Zadok and Abiathar served as priests. {4:5} Azariah, son of Nathan, was over the officers, and Zabud, son of Nathan, was the chief officer and the king's friend. {4:6} Ahishar was in charge of the palace, and Adoniram, son of Abda, managed the tribute. {4:7} Solomon had twelve officers over all Israel who provided food for the king and his household; each one was responsible for supplying food for one month of the year. {4:8} Here are their names: the son of Hur in the hill country of Ephraim; {4:9} the son of Dekar in Makaz, Shaalbim, Bethshemesh, and Elonbethhanan; {4:10} the son of Hesed in Aruboth, which included Sochoh and all the land of Hepher; {4:11} the son of Abinadab in all the region of Dor, who had Taphath, the daughter of Solomon, as his wife; {4:12} Baana, son of Ahilud, who managed Taanach, Megiddo, and all Bethshean, near Zartanah below Jezreel, from Bethshean to Abelmeholah, all the way to the area beyond Jokneam; {4:13} the son of Geber in Ramothgilead, overseeing the towns of Jair, son of Manasseh, in Gilead, as well as the region of Argob in Bashan, which had sixty large fortified cities with walls and bronze bars; {4:14} Ahinadab, son of Iddo, managed Mahanaim; {4:15} Ahimaaz was in Naphtali and also married Basmath, the daughter of Solomon; {4:16} Baanah, son of Hushai, was in Asher and Aloth; {4:17} Jehoshaphat, son of Paruah, served in Issachar; {4:18} Shimei, son of Elah, managed Benjamin; {4:19} Geber, son of Uri, was in Gilead, overseeing the territories of Sihon, king of the Amorites, and Og, king of Bashan; he was the only officer in that area. {4:20} Judah and Israel were as numerous as the sand by the sea, enjoying food and drink and celebrating. {4:21} Solomon ruled over all kingdoms from the Euphrates River to the land of the Philistines and to the border of Egypt; they brought him tribute and served him all the days of his life. {4:22} Solomon's provisions for one day included thirty measures of fine flour and sixty measures of meal, {4:23} ten fat oxen, twenty pasture-fed oxen, and a hundred sheep, in addition to deer, gazelles, roebucks, and fatted birds. {4:24} He had dominion over all the territory west of the Euphrates River, from Tiphsah to Azzah, over all the kings in that region, and he enjoyed peace on all sides. {4:25} Judah and Israel lived in safety, each person under their vine and fig tree, from Dan to Beersheba, throughout Solomon's reign. {4:26} Solomon had forty thousand stalls for his chariots and twelve thousand horsemen. {4:27} These officials provided food for King Solomon and all who came to his table, ensuring that everyone had enough. {4:28} They also brought barley and straw for the horses and the other animals to the designated place, each according to their responsibility. {4:29} God gave Solomon immense wisdom and understanding, as well as a vast heart, like the sand on the seashore. {4:30} Solomon's wisdom was greater than all the wisdom of the people from the East and all the wisdom of Egypt. {4:31} He was wiser than anyone else, including Ethan the Ezrahite, Heman, Chalcol, and Darda, the sons of Mahol; his fame spread to all the surrounding nations. {4:32} He spoke three thousand proverbs and wrote a thousand and five songs. {4:33} He spoke about trees, from the cedar of Lebanon to the hyssop that grows out of walls; he also spoke about animals, birds, reptiles, and fish. {4:34} People from all nations came to hear the wisdom of Solomon, sent by all the kings of the earth who had heard of his wisdom.

{5:1} King Hiram of Tyre sent his servants to Solomon because he had heard that Solomon had been anointed king in place of his father, and Hiram had always been a friend of David. {5:2} Solomon sent a message to Hiram, saying, {5:3} "You know that my father David could not build a house for the name of the LORD his God because he was surrounded by wars until the LORD put them under his control. {5:4} But now the LORD my God has given me peace on every side, so that there are no adversaries or evil occurrences. {5:5} Behold, I intend to build a house for the name of the LORD my God, as the LORD spoke to my father David, saying, 'Your son, whom I will place on your throne in your place, will build a house for my name.' {5:6} Therefore, command that they cut down cedar trees for me from Lebanon, and my servants will work alongside your servants. I will pay your servants whatever you specify, for you know that no one among us has the skill to cut timber like the Sidonians." {5:7} When Hiram heard Solomon's words, he greatly rejoiced and said, "Blessed be the LORD today, who has given David a wise son to rule over this great people." {5:8} Hiram sent a message to Solomon, saying, "I have considered your request and will fulfill all your needs regarding cedar and fir timber. {5:9} My servants will bring them down from Lebanon to the sea, and I will transport them by sea in rafts to the place you designate. I will ensure they are unloaded there, and you will provide for my household in return." {5:10} So Hiram provided Solomon with cedar and fir trees as he desired. {5:11} In exchange, Solomon gave Hiram twenty thousand measures of wheat for food for his household, and twenty measures of pure oil; this was Solomon's annual gift to Hiram. {5:12} The LORD gave Solomon wisdom, as He had promised, and there was peace between Hiram and Solomon; they made a treaty together. {5:13} King Solomon raised a labor force from all Israel, totaling thirty thousand men. {5:14} He sent them to Lebanon in shifts of ten thousand each month; they would spend one month in Lebanon and two months at home. Adoniram was in charge of the labor force. {5:15} Solomon had seventy thousand men to carry burdens and eighty thousand stonecutters in the mountains, {5:16} in addition to three thousand three hundred chief officers who supervised the workers. {5:17} The king commanded that they bring great stones, expensive stones, and stones that were cut to lay the foundation of the house. {5:18} Solomon's builders and Hiram's builders, along with stonecutters, prepared timber and stones to build the house.

{6:1} In the four hundred and eightieth year after the Israelites came out of Egypt, in the fourth year of Solomon's reign over Israel, during the month of Zif (the second month), he began to build the house of the LORD. {6:2} The house that King Solomon built for the LORD was sixty cubits long, twenty cubits wide, and thirty cubits high. {6:3} The porch in front of the temple was twenty cubits long, matching the width of the house, and ten cubits wide in front of the house. {6:4} For the house, he made narrow windows. {6:5} He built chambers around the walls of the house, both for the temple and for the most holy place. {6:6} The lowest chamber was five cubits wide, the middle chamber six cubits wide, and the third chamber seven cubits wide, with narrowing ledges in the wall of the house so that the beams would not be fixed in the walls. {6:7} While the house was being built, it was constructed of prepared stone, so there was no sound of hammer, axe, or any tool of iron heard in the house. {6:8} The door for the middle chamber was on the right side of the house; they went up winding stairs to the middle chamber and from the middle chamber to the third. {6:9} So he built the house and finished it, covering it with beams and boards of cedar. {6:10} He also built chambers around all the house, five cubits high, resting on the house with cedar timber. {6:11} Then the word of the LORD came to Solomon, saying, {6:12} "Concerning this house you are building, if you walk in my statutes, execute my judgments, and keep all my commandments, then I will fulfill my promise to you, which I spoke to your father David: {6:13} I will dwell among the Israelites and will not forsake my people Israel." {6:14} So Solomon built the house and finished it. {6:15} He lined the inside walls of the house with cedar boards and covered the floor with fir planks. {6:16} He built the walls on both sides of the house with cedar boards, even for the most holy place. {6:17} The temple in front of it was forty cubits long. {6:18} Inside, the cedar was carved with ornamental designs of buds and open flowers, and all was cedar; no stone was visible. {6:19} He prepared the most holy place inside the house to house the ark of the covenant of the LORD. {6:20} The most holy place was twenty cubits long, twenty cubits wide, and twenty cubits high, and he overlaid it with pure gold, covering the altar of cedar as well. {6:21} Solomon overlaid the inside of the house with pure gold, making a gold chain partition before the most holy place, which he also covered with gold. {6:22} He overlaid the whole house with gold, finishing all of it, including the altar near the most holy place. {6:23} In the most holy place, he made two cherubim of olive wood, each ten cubits high. {6:24} One wing of each cherub was five cubits long, and the other wing was also five cubits long, making the total wingspan of each cherub ten cubits. {6:25} The other cherub was also ten cubits high; both cherubim were of the same size and shape. {6:26} The height of each cherub was ten cubits. {6:27} He placed the cherubim inside the inner room, stretching their wings so that one touched one wall and the other touched the opposite wall, with their wings meeting in the middle of the room. {6:28} He overlaid the cherubim with gold. {6:29} He carved figures of cherubim, palm trees, and open flowers on all the walls of the house, inside and out. {6:30} The floor of the house was also overlaid with gold, inside and out. {6:31} For the entrance to the most holy place, he made doors of olive wood, with the lintel and side posts being one-fifth the thickness of the wall. {6:32} The two doors of the most holy place were also made of olive wood, carved with figures of cherubim, palm trees, and open flowers, and overlaid with gold, spreading gold over the cherubim and palm trees. {6:33} He also made posts of olive wood for the entrance of the temple, one-fourth the thickness of the wall. {6:34} The two doors of the temple were made of fir tree; the two leaves of one door folded, and the two leaves of the other door also folded. {6:35} He carved cherubim, palm trees, and open flowers on them and covered them with gold that was fitted to the carvings. {6:36} He built the inner court with three rows of hewn stone and a row of cedar beams. {6:37} The foundation of the house of the LORD was laid in the fourth year during the month of Zif. {6:38} In the eleventh year, during the month of Bul (the eighth month), the house was completed in all its parts and according to all its specifications. It took Solomon seven years to build it.

{7:1} Solomon built his own house for thirteen years and completed it. {7:2} He also built the House of the Forest of Lebanon, which was a hundred cubits long, fifty cubits wide, and thirty cubits high, supported by four rows of cedar pillars with cedar beams on top. {7:3} The roof was covered with cedar above the beams, which rested on forty-five pillars, arranged in fifteen rows. {7:4} There were windows in three rows, allowing light to shine through in three ranks. {7:5} All the doors and posts were square, with the windows also allowing light in three ranks. {7:6} He created a porch of pillars that was fifty cubits long and thirty cubits wide, with additional pillars and a thick beam in front. {7:7} Then he made a porch for the throne where he would judge, called the Porch of Judgment, covered with cedar from one side of the floor to the other. {7:8} His house had another courtyard within the porch, built similarly. Solomon also made a house for Pharaoh's daughter, whom he had married, similar to the porch. {7:9} All these were built with costly stones, precisely cut, and sawed inside and out, from the foundation up to the coping, including the exterior facing the great court. {7:10} The foundation consisted of expensive stones, large stones measuring ten cubits and eight cubits. {7:11} Above were costly stones, also measured and cut, along with cedar. {7:12} The great court surrounding it had three rows of hewn stones and a row of cedar beams, both for the inner court of the house of the LORD and for the porch of the house. {7:13} King Solomon sent for Hiram from Tyre. {7:14} Hiram was a widow's son from the tribe of Naphtali; his father was a skilled worker in bronze from Tyre. He was filled with wisdom, understanding, and skill in all kinds of bronze work. He came to King Solomon and performed all his tasks. {7:15} He cast two bronze pillars, each eighteen cubits high, with a circumference of twelve cubits. {7:16} He made two capitals (decorative tops) of molten bronze to place on top of the pillars; each capital was five cubits high. {7:17} He created decorative nets and wreaths for the capitals, seven for each capital. {7:18} He built the pillars and two rows around each net, covering the capitals with pomegranates, and did the same for the other capital. {7:19} The capitals on top of the pillars were crafted with lily designs in the porch, standing four cubits high. {7:20} The capitals on the two pillars also had pomegranates above, over against the belly (middle) that was by the net; there were two hundred pomegranates arranged in rows around each capital. {7:21} He set up the pillars in the porch of the temple: he positioned the right pillar and named it Jachin, and he set up the left pillar and named it Boaz. {7:22} The capitals had lily work on top; thus, the work on the pillars was completed. {7:23} He made a molten sea, measuring ten cubits from brim to brim, completely round and five cubits high, with a circumference of thirty cubits. {7:24} Around the brim there were decorative knobs, ten for every cubit, arranged in two rows when it was cast. {7:25} It stood on twelve oxen, three facing north, three facing west, three facing south, and three facing east, with the sea resting above them and their backs turned inward. {7:26} The sea was a handbreadth thick, and its brim was shaped like the brim of a cup, adorned with lily designs; it held two thousand baths (a measure of liquid). {7:27} He made ten bronze bases, each four cubits long, four cubits wide, and three cubits high. {7:28} The bases were constructed with borders, and the borders were between the ledges. {7:29} The borders had lions, oxen, and cherubim on them, with a base above and thin work underneath the lions and oxen. {7:30} Each base had four bronze wheels and bronze plates, with undersetters (supports) at the four corners of each base; the undersetters were part of the base itself. {7:31} The mouth of the basin inside the capital was a cubit wide, while the mouth itself was round, measuring a cubit and a half, with engravings on the mouth that were square rather than round. {7:32} Four wheels were under the borders, and the axletrees (axles) of the wheels were attached to the base, with a wheel height of a cubit and a half. {7:33} The wheels were designed like chariot wheels, with molten axletrees, hubs, felloes, and spokes. {7:34} There were four undersetters at the four corners of each base, which were part of the base itself. {7:35} At the top of each base was a circular rim half a cubit high, and the ledges and borders on top were of the same material. {7:36} On the plates of the ledges and borders, he engraved cherubim, lions, and palm trees in proportion, with additional decorations around them. {7:37} In this manner, he made all ten bases, ensuring they were identical in casting, measure, and size. {7:38} He then made ten bronze lavers, each capable of holding forty baths; each laver measured four cubits, and one was placed on each of the ten bases. {7:39} He positioned five bases on the right side of the house and five on the left side, setting the sea on the right side of the house, facing east toward the south. {7:40} Hiram made the lavers, shovels, and basins, completing all the work he had done for King Solomon in the house of the LORD: {7:41} the two pillars, the two capitals on top of the pillars, the two networks covering the capitals, {7:42} and four hundred pomegranates for the two networks, with two rows of pomegranates on each network to cover the capitals on the pillars; {7:43} the ten bases and the ten lavers on the bases; {7:44} the sea and the twelve oxen under the sea; {7:45} the pots, shovels, and basins. All these vessels that Hiram made for King Solomon in the house of the LORD were made of bright bronze. {7:46} The king cast them in the plain of Jordan, in the clay ground between Succoth and Zarthan. {7:47} Solomon left all the vessels unweighed because they were too numerous to count; the weight of the bronze was never determined. {7:48} Solomon made all the vessels for the house of the LORD: the altar of gold, the table of gold for the showbread, {7:49} and the pure gold lampstands, five on the right side and five on the left before the most holy place, along with the flowers, lamps, and tongs of gold, {7:50} the bowls, snuffers, basins, spoons, and censers of pure gold; and the hinges of gold for the doors of the inner house, the most holy place, and for the doors of the temple. {7:51} Thus, all the work that King Solomon did for the house of the LORD was completed. Solomon brought in the items that his father David had dedicated, including the silver, gold, and vessels, and placed them among the treasures of the house of the LORD.

{8:1} Then Solomon gathered the elders of Israel, along with the leaders of the tribes and the heads of the families of Israel, to meet with him in Jerusalem so they could bring the Ark of the Covenant of the LORD from the City of David, which is Zion. {8:2} All the men of Israel came together to King Solomon at the feast during the month of Ethanim, which is the seventh month. {8:3} The elders of Israel arrived, and the priests lifted the Ark. {8:4} They brought the Ark of the LORD, the Tabernacle of the congregation, and all the holy items that were in the Tabernacle; the priests and the Levites carried them all up. {8:5} King Solomon and the whole assembly of Israel, who had gathered around him, were in front of the Ark, offering so many sheep and oxen for sacrifices that they could not be counted. {8:6} The priests brought the Ark of the Covenant of the LORD to its place, inside the innermost room of the temple, the Most Holy Place, beneath the wings of the cherubim. {8:7} The cherubim spread their two wings over the Ark and the poles, covering the Ark and its poles from above. {8:8} They pulled out the poles so that the ends were visible in the holy place in front of the innermost room, but they could not be seen outside; they remain there to this day. {8:9} There was nothing in the Ark except for the two stone tablets that Moses placed there at Horeb, when the LORD made a covenant with the Israelites after they came out of Egypt. {8:10} When the priests came out of the holy place, a cloud filled the house of the LORD, {8:11} so the priests could not continue their service because of the cloud; the glory of the LORD had filled the house. {8:12} Then Solomon said, "The LORD said he would dwell in thick darkness. {8:13} I have indeed built you a magnificent temple, a dwelling place for you to live in forever." {8:14} The king turned to face all the assembly of Israel and blessed them (all the people stood). {8:15} He said, "Praise be to the LORD, the God of Israel, who spoke to my father David and fulfilled his promise with his own hand, saying, {8:16} 'Since the day I brought my people Israel out of Egypt, I have not chosen a city among any of the tribes of Israel to have a temple built for my Name, but I chose David to rule my people.' {8:17} David, my father, had it in his heart to build a temple for the Name of the LORD, the God of Israel. {8:18} But the LORD said to David, 'You did well to have this in your heart. {8:19} Nevertheless, you will not build the temple; your son, who will come from your own body, will build the temple for my Name.' {8:20} The LORD has kept his promise to me; I have risen in place of my father David and sit on the throne of Israel, as the LORD promised, and I have built a temple for the Name of the LORD, the God of Israel. {8:21} I have provided a place there for the Ark, which contains the covenant of the LORD that he made with our ancestors when he brought them out of Egypt." {8:22} Solomon stood before the altar of the LORD in front of all the people of Israel and spread his hands toward heaven. {8:23} He said, "LORD, God of Israel, there is no God like you in heaven above or on earth below. You keep your covenant and show mercy to your servants who walk before you with all their hearts. {8:24} You have kept your promise to your servant David, my father; you spoke with your mouth and fulfilled it with your hand, as it is today. {8:25} Now, LORD, God of Israel, keep your promise to your servant David, my father, saying, 'You will never fail to have a man sit before me on the throne of Israel, provided your descendants pay attention to how they live and walk before me faithfully, as you have done.' {8:26} And now, God of Israel, let your word that you promised your servant David be confirmed. {8:27} But will God really dwell on earth? The heavens, even the highest heavens, cannot contain you; how much less this temple I have built! {8:28} Yet, LORD my God, give attention to your servant's prayer and his plea for mercy. Hear the cry and the prayer that your servant is praying in your presence today. {8:29} May your eyes be open toward this temple night and day, this place of which you said, 'My Name shall be there,' so that you will hear the prayer your servant prays toward this place. {8:30} Hear the supplication of your servant and of your people Israel when they pray toward this place. Hear from heaven, your dwelling place, and when you hear, forgive. {8:31} If anyone wrongs a neighbor and is required to take an oath and comes to this altar to swear an oath, {8:32} then hear from heaven and act. Judge between your servants, condemning the guilty and bringing down on their heads what they have done; vindicating the innocent by treating them in accordance with their innocence. {8:33} When your people Israel are defeated by an enemy because they have sinned against you, and when they turn back to you and confess your Name, praying and making supplication to you in this temple, {8:34} then hear from heaven and forgive the sin of your people Israel and bring them back to the land you gave to their ancestors. {8:35} When the heavens are shut up and there is no rain because your people have sinned against you, and when they pray toward this place and confess your Name and turn from their sin because you have afflicted them, {8:36} then hear from heaven and forgive the sin of your servants and of your people Israel. Teach them the good way to live and send rain on your land that you gave your people as an inheritance. {8:37} If there is famine in the land, if there is pestilence, blight, mildew, locusts, or if there is an enemy besieging them in their cities, whatever disaster or disease may come, {8:38} and if a prayer or plea is made by anyone among your people Israel, being aware of their own afflictions and spreading out their hands toward this temple, {8:39} then hear from heaven, your dwelling place, and forgive and act. Deal with everyone according to their ways, since you alone know every human heart. {8:40} So that they will fear you all the days they live in the land you gave to our ancestors. {8:41} As for the foreigner who does not belong to your people Israel but has come from a distant land because of your Name— {8:42} for they will hear of your great Name and your mighty hand and your outstretched arm—when they come and pray toward this temple, {8:43} then hear from heaven, your dwelling place, and do whatever the foreigner asks of you, so that all the peoples of the earth may know your Name and fear you, as do your own people Israel, and may know that this house I have built bears your Name. {8:44} When your people go to war against their enemies, wherever you send them, and when they pray to the LORD toward the city you have chosen and the temple I have built for your Name, {8:45} then hear their prayer and their plea from heaven and uphold their cause. {8:46} When they sin against you—for there is no one who does not sin—and you become angry with them and give them over to the enemy, who takes them captive to his own land, far or near, {8:47} and if they have a change of heart in the land where they are held captive and repent and plead with you in the land of their captors and say, 'We have sinned; we have done wrong and acted wickedly,' {8:48} and if they turn back to you with all their heart and soul in the land of their enemies who took them captive, and pray to you toward their own land, which you gave to their ancestors, the city you have chosen, and the temple I have built for your Name; {8:49} then hear their prayer and their plea from heaven, your dwelling place, and uphold their cause. {8:50} Forgive your people who have sinned against you; forgive all their offenses they have committed against you, and grant them compassion in the presence of their captors, so that they will have compassion on them; {8:51} for they are your people and your inheritance, whom you brought out of Egypt, out of the iron-smelting furnace. {8:52} May your eyes be open to your servant's plea and to the plea of your people Israel, and may you listen to them whenever they call to you. {8:53} For you, LORD, separated them from all the nations of the earth to be your own inheritance, as you declared through your servant Moses when you brought our ancestors out of Egypt." {8:54} When Solomon had finished praying all these prayers and supplications to the LORD, he rose from kneeling before the altar of the LORD, having his hands spread out toward heaven. {8:55} He stood and blessed the whole assembly of Israel in a loud voice, saying, {8:56} "Praise be to the LORD, who has given rest to his people Israel just as he promised. Not one word has failed of all the good promises he gave through his servant Moses. {8:57} May the LORD our God be with us as he was with our ancestors. May he never leave us nor forsake us. {8:58} May he turn our hearts to him, to walk in obedience to him and to keep his commands, decrees, and laws he gave our ancestors. {8:59} And may these words of mine, which I have prayed before the LORD, be near to the LORD our God day and night, that he may uphold the cause of his servant and the cause of his people Israel according to each day's need. {8:60} So that all the peoples of the earth may know that the LORD is God, and that there is no other. {8:61} And may your hearts be fully committed to the LORD our God, to live by his decrees and obey his commands, as at this time." {8:62} Then the king and all Israel with him offered sacrifices before the LORD. {8:63} Solomon offered a fellowship offering to the LORD, twenty-two thousand oxen and one hundred twenty thousand sheep. So the king and all the Israelites dedicated the temple of the LORD. {8:64} On that same day, the king consecrated the middle of the courtyard in front of the temple of the LORD, and there he offered burnt offerings, grain offerings, and the fat of the fellowship offerings, because the bronze altar before the LORD was too small to hold the burnt offerings and grain offerings and the fat of the fellowship offerings. {8:65} So Solomon held a festival at that time, and all Israel with him, a great assembly from the entrance of Hamath to the Wadi of Egypt, before the LORD our God, for seven days and seven days, fourteen days in total. {8:66} On the eighth day, he sent the people away, and they blessed the king and went home, joyful and glad in heart for all the good things the LORD had done for David his servant and for his people Israel.

{9:1} When Solomon finished building the temple of the LORD, the royal palace, and everything he desired to accomplish, {9:2} the LORD appeared to Solomon a second time, just as He had at Gibeon. {9:3} The LORD said to him, "I have heard your prayer and supplication that you made before me. I have consecrated this house you built to put my Name there forever; my eyes and my heart will be there perpetually. {9:4} If you walk before me as your father David walked, with integrity of heart and uprightness, doing everything I commanded you and keeping my statutes and judgments, {9:5} then I will establish your throne over Israel forever, as I promised your father David, saying, 'You will never lack a man on the throne of Israel.' {9:6} But if you or your children turn away from following me and do not keep my commandments and statutes that I set before you, but go and serve other gods and worship them, {9:7} then I will cut off Israel from the land I have given them, and this house, which I consecrated for my Name, I will cast out of my sight. Israel will become a proverb and a byword among all peoples. {9:8} And though this house is so high, everyone passing by will be astonished and hiss, saying, 'Why has the LORD done this to this land and this house?' {9:9} They will answer, 'Because they forsook the LORD their God, who brought their ancestors up out of Egypt, and they embraced other gods and worshiped them, and served them. That is why the LORD brought all this disaster upon them.' {9:10} At the end of twenty years, when Solomon had built the two houses, the temple of the LORD and the royal palace, {9:11} (Hiram king of Tyre had supplied Solomon with cedar and cypress timber, and gold in great quantity, according to his desire) Solomon gave Hiram twenty cities in the land of Galilee. {9:12} Hiram went out from Tyre to see the cities Solomon had given him, but they did not please him. {9:13} He asked, "What cities are these you have given me, my brother?" And he called them the land of Cabul to this day. {9:14} Hiram then sent the king 120 talents of gold. {9:15} This is the reason for the forced labor that King Solomon conscripted: to build the temple of the LORD, his own palace, the Millo, the wall of Jerusalem, and Hazor, Megiddo, and Gezer. {9:16} Pharaoh king of Egypt had come up and captured Gezer, burning it down, killing its Canaanite inhabitants, and giving it as a gift to his daughter, Solomon's wife. {9:17} Solomon rebuilt Gezer, and also Beth-horon the lower, {9:18} Baalath, and Tadmor in the wilderness, in the land, {9:19} as well as all the storage cities Solomon had, cities for his chariots, and cities for his horsemen, and whatever he desired to build in Jerusalem, Lebanon, and throughout all his dominion. {9:20} All the people who were left of the Amorites, Hittites, Perizzites, Hivites, and Jebusites—those who were not Israelites— {9:21} their descendants who remained in the land, whom the Israelites were unable to completely destroy, Solomon conscripted as forced laborers to this day. {9:22} But he did not conscript any of the Israelites; they were men of war, his officials, captains, and commanders of his chariots and horsemen. {9:23} These were the chief officers over Solomon's work, numbering 550, who supervised the people doing the work. {9:24} Pharaoh's daughter came up from the City of David to her house Solomon had built for her; then he built the Millo. {9:25} Three times a year Solomon offered burnt offerings and fellowship offerings on the altar he built for the LORD, burning incense before the LORD. So he finished the temple. {9:26} King Solomon also built a fleet of ships at Ezion-geber, which is near Eloth, on the shore of the Red Sea in the land of Edom. {9:27} Hiram sent his servants, experienced sailors, with the servants of Solomon. {9:28} They went to Ophir and brought back 420 talents of gold to King Solomon.

{10:1} When the queen of Sheba heard about Solomon's fame regarding the name of the LORD, she came to test him with difficult questions. {10:2} She arrived in Jerusalem with a large entourage, including camels carrying spices, a lot of gold, and precious stones. When she came to Solomon, she spoke to him about everything that was on her mind. {10:3} Solomon answered all her questions; there was nothing hidden from the king that he did not explain to her. {10:4} After the queen of Sheba saw all of Solomon's wisdom, the palace he had built, {10:5} the food on his table, the seating of his officials, the attendance of his servants, their robes, his cupbearers, and the way he went up to the temple of the LORD, she was left breathless. {10:6} She said to the king, "The report I heard in my own country about your achievements and wisdom is true! {10:7} I did not believe what they said until I came and saw it with my own eyes. Indeed, the half was not told to me; your wisdom and prosperity far exceed the fame I heard. {10:8} Your men must be happy, and these servants who continually stand before you and hear your wisdom are fortunate. {10:9} Praise be to the LORD your God, who has delighted in you and placed you on the throne of Israel! Because the LORD loves Israel forever, He has made you king to maintain justice and righteousness." {10:10} She gave the king 120 talents of gold, a large quantity of spices, and precious stones. Never again did such a quantity of spices come as those the queen of Sheba gave to King Solomon. {10:11} Hiram's navy brought gold from Ophir, along with a great quantity of almug trees and precious stones. {10:12} The king made pillars of the almug trees for the temple of the LORD and for the royal palace, as well as harps and lyres for the singers. Such almug trees have never been seen before or since. {10:13} King Solomon gave the queen of Sheba everything she desired, as well as gifts from his royal bounty. Then she returned to her own country with her servants. {10:14} The total amount of gold that came to Solomon in one year was 666 talents, {10:15} not counting what he received from merchants, spice traders, and all the kings of Arabia, as well as the governors of the region. {10:16} King Solomon made 200 large gold shields; each shield required 600 shekels of gold. {10:17} He also made 300 smaller gold shields; each of these shields required 3 pounds of gold. The king placed them in the House of the Forest of Lebanon. {10:18} Additionally, the king made a great throne of ivory and overlaid it with the best gold. {10:19} The throne had six steps, with a rounded back; there were armrests on either side of the seat, and two lions stood beside the armrests. {10:20} Twelve lions stood on each side of the six steps. No kingdom had anything like it. {10:21} All King Solomon's drinking vessels were made of gold, and all the vessels in the House of the Forest of Lebanon were pure gold. Silver was not valued in Solomon's days. {10:22} The king had a fleet of ships at sea in the port of Tarshish, along with Hiram's fleet. Once every three years, the Tarshish fleet returned, bringing gold, silver, ivory, apes, and peacocks. {10:23} King Solomon became richer and wiser than all the kings of the earth. {10:24} People from all nations sought his wisdom, which God had placed in his heart. {10:25} They brought him gifts: silver and gold vessels, clothing, armor, spices, horses, and mules, year by year. {10:26} Solomon gathered chariots and horsemen; he had 1,400 chariots and 12,000 horsemen, which he stationed in the chariot cities and with the king in Jerusalem. {10:27} The king made silver as common in Jerusalem as stones and made cedar as abundant as sycamore trees in the foothills. {10:28} Solomon imported horses from Egypt and linen yarn; the king's merchants purchased the linen yarn at a set price. {10:29} A chariot imported from Egypt cost 600 shekels of silver, and a horse cost 150 shekels. They exported them to all the kings of the Hittites and the kings of Syria.

{11:1} King Solomon loved many foreign women, including Pharaoh's daughter, women from Moab, Ammon, Edom, Sidon, and Hittite nations. {11:2} The LORD had warned the Israelites not to intermarry with these nations, saying they would turn their hearts to their gods. Solomon held fast to these women in love. {11:3} He had 700 wives, who were princesses, and 300 concubines, and his wives led his heart astray. {11:4} As Solomon grew old, his wives turned his heart to other gods, and his heart was not fully devoted to the LORD his God, as his father David's had been. {11:5} Solomon followed Ashtoreth, the goddess of the Sidonians, and Milcom, the detestable god of the Ammonites. {11:6} Solomon did what was evil in the eyes of the LORD; he did not follow the LORD completely, as his father David had. {11:7} He built high places for Chemosh, the detestable god of Moab, on the hill east of Jerusalem, and for Molech, the detestable god of the Ammonites. {11:8} He did the same for all his foreign wives, who burned incense and offered sacrifices to their gods. {11:9} The LORD became angry with Solomon because his heart had turned away from the LORD, the God of Israel, who had appeared to him twice. {11:10} God had warned him not to follow other gods, but Solomon did not keep the command. {11:11} Therefore, the LORD said to Solomon, "Since you have done this and have not kept my covenant and my decrees that I commanded you, I will surely tear the kingdom away from you and give it to your servant. {11:12} Yet, for the sake of your father David, I will not do it during your lifetime; I will tear it out of the hand of your son. {11:13} Nevertheless, I will not take the whole kingdom; I will give one tribe to your son for the sake of my servant David and for the sake of Jerusalem, which I have chosen." {11:14} The LORD raised up against Solomon an adversary, Hadad the Edomite, who was of royal descent in Edom. {11:15} When David was in Edom, Joab, the commander of the army, went to bury the dead and struck down every male in Edom. {11:16} Joab and all Israel stayed there for six months until he had destroyed all the men in Edom. {11:17} Hadad fled to Egypt with some Edomite servants of his father. Hadad was still a young child at that time. {11:18} They set out from Midian and went to Paran, where they took some men with them and went to Egypt, to Pharaoh, king of Egypt. Pharaoh gave Hadad a house, provided him with food, and gave him land. {11:19} Hadad gained great favor in Pharaoh's sight, so Pharaoh gave him his wife's sister, the sister of Queen Tahpenes. {11:20} The sister of Tahpenes bore him a son named Genubath, whom Tahpenes weaned in Pharaoh's palace; Genubath lived there among Pharaoh's children. {11:21} When Hadad heard in Egypt that David had died and that Joab was also dead, he said to Pharaoh, "Let me go back to my own country." {11:22} Pharaoh asked him, "What have you lacked here that you want to go back to your own country?" Hadad replied, "Nothing, but please let me go." {11:23} God stirred up another adversary against Solomon, Rezon son of Eliadah, who had fled from his master, Hadadezer king of Zobah. {11:24} Rezon gathered men around him and became their leader after David had killed the Zobahites. He went to Damascus and settled there, becoming king of Damascus. {11:25} He was an adversary of Israel throughout Solomon's reign, in addition to the trouble caused by Hadad; he loathed Israel and ruled over Syria. {11:26} Jeroboam son of Nebat, an Ephrathite from Zereda, a servant of Solomon, rebelled against the king. {11:27} This was the reason he rebelled: Solomon had built Millo and repaired the gaps in the City of David his father. {11:28} Jeroboam was a man of standing, and when Solomon saw how industrious he was, he put him in charge of the labor force of the house of Joseph. {11:29} About that time, Jeroboam was leaving Jerusalem when the prophet Ahijah the Shilonite met him on the road. Ahijah was wearing a new cloak, and the two of them were alone in a field. {11:30} Ahijah took hold of the new cloak he was wearing and tore it into twelve pieces. {11:31} Then he said to Jeroboam, "Take ten pieces for yourself, for this is what the LORD, the God of Israel, says: 'I am going to tear the kingdom out of Solomon's hand and give you ten tribes. {11:32} But for the sake of my servant David and the city of Jerusalem, which I have chosen, he will have one tribe.' {11:33} This is because they have forsaken me and worshiped Ashtoreth, the goddess of the Sidonians, Chemosh, the god of the Moabites, and Milcom, the god of the Ammonites. They have not walked in my ways, doing what is right in my eyes and keeping my decrees and laws, as David did. {11:34} I will not take the whole kingdom from him; I will let him rule all his days for the sake of my servant David, whom I chose and who kept my commands and decrees. {11:35} But I will take the kingdom from his son and give you ten tribes. {11:36} I will give one tribe to his son so that David my servant will always have a lamp before me in Jerusalem, the city I chose to put my name there. {11:37} I will take you, and you will rule over all your heart desires; you will be king over Israel. {11:38} If you listen to what I command you and walk in my ways, doing what is right in my eyes by keeping my decrees and commands, as David my servant did, I will be with you and will build you a lasting dynasty, as I built for David, and give Israel to you. {11:39} I will afflict the descendants of David because of this, but not forever." {11:40} Solomon tried to kill Jeroboam, but Jeroboam fled to Egypt, to Shishak, and stayed there until Solomon died. {11:41} The rest of Solomon's acts, including all he did and his wisdom, are they not written in the Book of the Acts of Solomon? {11:42} Solomon reigned in Jerusalem over all Israel for 40 years. {11:43} Then Solomon rested with his ancestors and was buried in the City of David. His son Rehoboam succeeded him as king.

{12:1} Rehoboam went to Shechem, for all Israel had gathered there to make him king. {12:2} When Jeroboam son of Nebat, who was in Egypt (having fled from King Solomon), heard about it, {12:3} he was summoned, and he and all the congregation of Israel spoke to Rehoboam, saying, {12:4} "Your father made our yoke heavy; now lighten the harsh service and heavy yoke he put on us, and we will serve you." {12:5} Rehoboam replied, "Go away for three days and come back to me." So the people left. {12:6} King Rehoboam consulted the elders who had served his father Solomon during his lifetime, asking, "How do you advise me to answer these people?" {12:7} They answered, "If you will be a servant to these people today and serve them, and give them a favorable answer, they will always be your servants." {12:8} But he rejected the advice of the elders and consulted the young men who had grown up with him and were serving him. {12:9} He asked them, "What do you advise that we say to these people who said to me, 'Lighten the yoke your father put on us'?" {12:10} The young men replied, "Tell the people who have said to you, 'Your father made our yoke heavy, but make it lighter for us,' say to them, 'My little finger is thicker than my father's waist. {12:11} My father laid a heavy yoke on you; I will make it even heavier. My father beat you with whips, but I will beat you with scorpions.'" {12:12} So Jeroboam and all the people returned to Rehoboam on the third day, as the king had directed. {12:13} The king answered them harshly, rejecting the advice of the elders. {12:14} He told them what the young men had advised: "My father made your yoke heavy, and I will make it heavier; my father beat you with whips, but I will beat you with scorpions." {12:15} The king did not listen to the people, for this turn of events was from the LORD to fulfill his word that the LORD had spoken through Ahijah the Shilonite to Jeroboam son of Nebat. {12:16} When all Israel saw that the king refused to listen to them, they answered the king, "What share do we have in David? We have no inheritance in the son of Jesse! To your tents, Israel! Look after your own house, David!" So the Israelites went home. {12:17} But as for the Israelites living in the towns of Judah, Rehoboam ruled over them. {12:18} King Rehoboam sent out Adoram, who was in charge of forced labor, but all Israel stoned him to death. King Rehoboam managed to get into his chariot and escape to Jerusalem. {12:19} So Israel has been in rebellion against the house of David to this day. {12:20} When all Israel heard that Jeroboam had returned, they sent for him and made him king over all Israel; only the tribe of Judah remained loyal to the house of David. {12:21} When Rehoboam arrived in Jerusalem, he mustered the whole house of Judah and the tribe of Benjamin—180,000 able young men—to go to war against Israel and regain the kingdom for Rehoboam son of Solomon. {12:22} But God's word came to Shemaiah the man of God: {12:23} "Say to Rehoboam son of Solomon, king of Judah, and to all the Israelites in Judah and Benjamin, {12:24} 'This is what the LORD says: Do not go up to fight against your fellow Israelites. Go home, every one of you, for this is my doing.'" So they obeyed the word of the LORD and went home, as the LORD had instructed. {12:25} Jeroboam built up Shechem in the hill country of Ephraim and lived there. From there he went out and built Penuel. {12:26} Jeroboam thought to himself, "The kingdom will now likely revert to the house of David. {12:27} If these people go up to offer sacrifices at the temple of the LORD in Jerusalem, they will again give their allegiance to their lord, Rehoboam king of Judah. They will kill me and return to King Rehoboam." {12:28} After seeking advice, the king made two golden calves. He said to the people, "It is too much for you to go up to Jerusalem. Here are your gods, Israel, who brought you up out of Egypt." {12:29} One he set up in Bethel, and the other in Dan. {12:30} This became a sin; the people came to worship the one at Bethel and went as far as Dan to worship the other. {12:31} Jeroboam built shrines on high places and appointed priests from all sorts of people, even though they were not Levites. {12:32} Jeroboam instituted a festival on the fifteenth day of the eighth month, like the festival held in Judah, and offered sacrifices on the altar. He did this in Bethel, sacrificing to the calves he had made, and he placed in Bethel the priests of the high places he had made. {12:33} On the fifteenth day of the eighth month, the day he had devised from his own heart, Jeroboam offered sacrifices on the altar he had built in Bethel. He instituted a festival for the Israelites and went up to the altar to burn incense.

{13:1} A man of God from Judah came to Bethel by the word of the LORD, and Jeroboam was standing by the altar to burn incense. {13:2} He shouted against the altar by the word of the LORD, saying, "O altar, altar! This is what the LORD says: A child will be born to the house of David, named Josiah. He will sacrifice the priests of the high places who burn incense on you, and human bones will be burned on you." {13:3} That day, he gave a sign, saying, "This is the sign that the LORD has declared: The altar will be torn apart, and the ashes on it will be poured out." {13:4} When King Jeroboam heard the man of God crying against the altar in Bethel, he pointed at him and said, "Seize him!" But his hand, which he stretched out toward the man of God, shriveled up, and he could not pull it back. {13:5} The altar was also torn apart, and the ashes spilled out, just as the man of God had predicted by the word of the LORD. {13:6} The king said to the man of God, "Intercede with the LORD your God and pray for me so my hand may be restored." The man of God prayed to the LORD, and the king's hand was restored to him and became as it was before. {13:7} The king then said to the man of God, "Come home with me, and refresh yourself, and I will give you a reward." {13:8} But the man of God replied, "Even if you gave me half your kingdom, I would not go with you or eat bread or drink water in this place, {13:9} for the LORD commanded me, 'Eat no bread or drink water, and do not return by the way you came.'" {13:10} So he took another route and did not return the way he had come to Bethel. {13:11} There was an old prophet living in Bethel, and his sons came and told him everything the man of God had done that day in Bethel, including the words he had spoken to the king. {13:12} The old prophet asked, "Which way did he go?" His sons had seen which way the man of God from Judah had gone. {13:13} So he said to his sons, "Saddle the donkey for me." They saddled it, and he rode off to find the man of God. {13:14} He found him sitting under an oak tree and asked, "Are you the man of God who came from Judah?" The man of God replied, "I am." {13:15} The old prophet said, "Come home with me and eat bread." {13:16} The man of God said, "I cannot return with you or go in with you. I cannot eat bread or drink water with you in this place, {13:17} because the LORD said to me, 'Do not eat bread or drink water there, and do not return by the way you came.'" {13:18} The old prophet said, "I am also a prophet like you, and an angel spoke to me by the word of the LORD, saying, 'Bring him back with you to your house so he may eat bread and drink water.'" But he was lying. {13:19} So the man of God went back with him and ate bread in his house and drank water. {13:20} While they were sitting at the table, the word of the LORD came to the old prophet who had brought him back. {13:21} He cried out to the man of God from Judah, "This is what the LORD says: Because you have disobeyed the LORD and have not kept the command the LORD your God gave you, {13:22} but have come back and eaten bread and drunk water in the place where he told you not to eat or drink, your body will not be buried in the tomb of your ancestors." {13:23} After the man of God had eaten and drunk, the old prophet saddled his donkey for him. {13:24} When the man of God had left, a lion met him on the road and killed him. His body lay on the road, with the donkey standing beside it and the lion also standing by the body. {13:25} People passed by and saw the body lying in the road and the lion standing beside it. They went and reported this in the city where the old prophet lived. {13:26} When the old prophet heard the news, he said, "It is the man of God who disobeyed the word of the LORD. The LORD has delivered him to the lion, which has mauled him and killed him, as the LORD spoke to him." {13:27} He said to his sons, "Saddle the donkey for me." They did so, {13:28} and he went and found the body lying in the road, with the donkey and the lion standing beside it. The lion had not eaten the body or attacked the donkey. {13:29} The prophet picked up the body of the man of God and laid it on the donkey and brought it back. The old prophet came to the city to mourn and bury him. {13:30} He laid the body in his own grave and mourned over him, saying, "Alas, my brother!" {13:31} After burying him, he said to his sons, "When I die, bury me in the grave where the man of God is buried; lay my bones beside his bones, {13:32} for the message he proclaimed by the word of the LORD against the altar in Bethel and against all the shrines on the high places in the towns of Samaria will certainly come to pass." {13:33} After this event, Jeroboam did not turn away from his evil ways but appointed priests from the lowest of the people for the high places. Anyone who wanted to become a priest he consecrated, and he became one of the priests of the high places. {13:34} This became sin to the house of Jeroboam, leading to its destruction and removal from the earth. {13:35} Despite the warning, Jeroboam's persistence in idolatry and corruption sealed the fate of his dynasty, fulfilling the prophecy of judgment.

{14:1} At that time, Abijah, the son of Jeroboam, fell sick. {14:2} Jeroboam said to his wife, "Get up, please, and disguise yourself so that no one will recognize you as my wife. Go to Shiloh; there you will find Ahijah the prophet, who told me I would be king over this people. {14:3} Take with you ten loaves of bread, some cakes, and a jar of honey, and go to him. He will tell you what will happen to the child." {14:4} Jeroboam's wife did as he instructed. She arose, went to Shiloh, and entered the house of Ahijah. However, Ahijah couldn't see because his eyesight had worsened due to old age. {14:5} The LORD said to Ahijah, "Look, Jeroboam's wife is coming to ask you about her son, for he is sick. This is what you are to say to her: she will pretend to be someone else." {14:6} When Ahijah heard her footsteps as she entered the door, he said, "Come in, wife of Jeroboam. Why are you pretending to be someone else? I have been sent to you with heavy news? {14:7} Go back and tell Jeroboam, 'This is what the LORD God of Israel says: I raised you up from among the people and made you ruler over my people Israel. {14:8} I tore the kingdom away from the house of David and gave it to you, yet you have not been like my servant David, who kept my commandments and followed me with all his heart, doing what was right in my eyes. {14:9} You have done more evil than all who came before you; you have made for yourself other gods and molten images to provoke me to anger, casting me behind your back. {14:10} Therefore, I will bring disaster upon the house of Jeroboam and will cut off every male in his family, both slave and free, in Israel. I will take away the remnant of the house of Jeroboam as one removes dung until it is all gone. {14:11} Those who die in the city will be eaten by dogs, and those who die in the fields will be eaten by birds, for the LORD has declared it. {14:12} So get up and return to your home. When you step into the city, the child will die. {14:13} All Israel will mourn for him and bury him; he is the only one from Jeroboam who will be buried, because he has something good found in him toward the LORD God of Israel in the house of Jeroboam. {14:14} Furthermore, the LORD will raise up a king over Israel who will cut off the house of Jeroboam that very day. {14:15} For the LORD will strike Israel, like a reed shaken in water, and he will uproot Israel from this good land he gave their ancestors and scatter them beyond the river, because they have made sacred groves, provoking the LORD to anger. {14:16} He will give Israel up because of the sins of Jeroboam, who sinned and made Israel sin." {14:17} Jeroboam's wife got up and left, returning to Tirzah. As she reached the threshold of the door, the child died. {14:18} They buried him, and all Israel mourned for him, as the LORD had spoken through his servant Ahijah the prophet. {14:19} The rest of the acts of Jeroboam, including his wars and reign, are written in the book of the chronicles of the kings of Israel. {14:20} Jeroboam reigned for twenty-two years and then died, and his son Nadab became king in his place. {14:21} Rehoboam, the son of Solomon, reigned in Judah. Rehoboam was forty-one years old when he began to reign, and he reigned for seventeen years in Jerusalem, the city the LORD chose from all the tribes of Israel to put his name there. His mother's name was Naamah, an Ammonite. {14:22} Judah did evil in the sight of the LORD and provoked him to jealousy with their sins, which were worse than what their ancestors had done. {14:23} They also built high places, set up sacred stones, and planted groves on every high hill and under every green tree. {14:24} There were also male cult prostitutes in the land, following the detestable practices of the nations that the LORD had driven out before the Israelites. {14:25} In the fifth year of King Rehoboam, Shishak, king of Egypt, attacked Jerusalem. {14:26} He took away the treasures of the house of the LORD and the treasures of the king's palace; he carried everything off, including all the gold shields Solomon had made. {14:27} King Rehoboam made bronze shields to replace them and gave them to the commanders of the guard who protected the entrance to the royal palace. {14:28} Whenever the king went to the house of the LORD, the guards carried the shields and then returned them to the guardroom. {14:29} The rest of the acts of Rehoboam and all he did are written in the book of the chronicles of the kings of Judah. {14:30} There was war between Rehoboam and Jeroboam throughout their reigns. {14:31} Rehoboam died and was buried with his ancestors in the City of David. His mother's name was Naamah, an Ammonite, and his son Abijam succeeded him as king.

{15:1} In the eighteenth year of King Jeroboam, the son of Nebat, Abijam became king over Judah. {15:2} He reigned in Jerusalem for three years. His mother's name was Maachah, the daughter of Abishalom. {15:3} He followed all the sins of his father, which he committed before him, and his heart was not fully devoted to the LORD his God, as the heart of his father David had been. {15:4} Yet, for the sake of David, the LORD his God gave him a lamp in Jerusalem, to set up his son after him and to establish Jerusalem. {15:5} David did what was right in the eyes of the LORD and did not turn aside from anything he commanded him all the days of his life, except in the matter of Uriah the Hittite. {15:6} There was war between Rehoboam and Jeroboam throughout his life. {15:7} The rest of the acts of Abijam and all that he did are written in the book of the chronicles of the kings of Judah. There was also war between Abijam and Jeroboam. {15:8} Abijam died and was buried with his ancestors in the City of David. His son Asa became king in his place. {15:9} In the twentieth year of King Jeroboam of Israel, Asa began to reign over Judah. {15:10} He reigned in Jerusalem for forty-one years. His mother's name was Maachah, the daughter of Abishalom. {15:11} Asa did what was right in the eyes of the LORD, as his father David had done. {15:12} He removed the male cult prostitutes from the land and got rid of all the idols his ancestors had made. {15:13} He even removed his mother Maachah from being queen because she had made an idol in a grove; Asa destroyed her idol and burned it in the Kidron Valley. {15:14} However, the high places were not removed; nevertheless, Asa's heart was fully devoted to the LORD all his days. {15:15} He brought into the house of the LORD the items his father had dedicated and his own items, including silver, gold, and utensils. {15:16} There was war between Asa and Baasha, king of Israel, throughout their reigns. {15:17} Baasha, king of Israel, went up against Judah and built Ramah to prevent anyone from going in or out to King Asa of Judah. {15:18} Asa took all the silver and gold that were left in the treasures of the house of the LORD and the king's palace and handed them to his officials. He sent them to Benhadad, the son of Tabrimon, the son of Hezion, king of Syria, who was living in Damascus, saying, {15:19} "There is a treaty between me and you, and between my father and your father. I have sent you a gift of silver and gold; come and break your treaty with Baasha, king of Israel, so he will withdraw from me." {15:20} Benhadad agreed to King Asa and sent the commanders of his armies against the cities of Israel, attacking Ijon, Dan, Abel-beth-maachah, and all of Naphtali's territory. {15:21} When Baasha heard about this, he stopped building Ramah and settled in Tirzah. {15:22} Then King Asa made a proclamation throughout all Judah; no one was exempted. They took away the stones and timber from Ramah, which Baasha had built, and King Asa built with them Geba of Benjamin and Mizpah. {15:23} The rest of the acts of Asa, his might, what he did, and the cities he built are written in the book of the chronicles of the kings of Judah. However, in his old age, he became diseased in his feet. {15:24} Asa died and was buried with his ancestors in the City of David, and his son Jehoshaphat became king in his place. {15:25} Nadab, the son of Jeroboam, began to reign over Israel in the second year of Asa, king of Judah, and reigned for two years. {15:26} He did evil in the sight of the LORD and followed the ways of his father and the sin he caused Israel to commit. {15:27} Baasha, the son of Ahijah from the tribe of Issachar, conspired against him and struck him down at Gibbethon, which belonged to the Philistines, while Nadab and all Israel were laying siege to Gibbethon. {15:28} In the third year of Asa, king of Judah, Baasha killed him and succeeded him as king. {15:29} When he became king, he killed all the house of Jeroboam; he did not leave a single male alive in Jeroboam's family, fulfilling the word of the LORD spoken through his servant Ahijah the Shilonite. {15:30} This was because of the sins of Jeroboam, which he had committed and caused Israel to commit, provoking the LORD God of Israel to anger. {15:31} The rest of the acts of Nadab and all that he did are written in the book of the chronicles of the kings of Israel. {15:32} There was war between Asa and Baasha, king of Israel, throughout their reigns. {15:33} In the third year of Asa, king of Judah, Baasha, the son of Ahijah, began to reign over all Israel in Tirzah, and he reigned for twenty-four years. {15:34} He did evil in the sight of the LORD and followed the ways of Jeroboam and the sin that caused Israel to sin.

{16:1} Then the word of the LORD came to Jehu, the son of Hanani, regarding Baasha, saying, {16:2} "Because I lifted you out of the dust and made you prince over my people Israel, yet you walked in the ways of Jeroboam and caused my people Israel to sin, provoking me to anger with their sins; {16:3} behold, I will remove the descendants of Baasha and his family, and I will make your house like the house of Jeroboam, the son of Nebat. {16:4} Those who die in the city of Baasha will be eaten by dogs, and those who die in the fields will be eaten by birds." {16:5} Now the rest of the acts of Baasha and all he did, and his might, are they not written in the book of the chronicles of the kings of Israel? {16:6} So Baasha died and was buried in Tirzah, and his son Elah became king in his place. {16:7} The word of the LORD also came through the prophet Jehu, the son of Hanani, against Baasha and his house for all the evil he did in the sight of the LORD, provoking him to anger with the work of his hands, being like the house of Jeroboam, and for killing him. {16:8} In the twenty-sixth year of Asa, king of Judah, Elah, the son of Baasha, began to reign over Israel in Tirzah for two years. {16:9} His servant Zimri, captain of half his chariots, conspired against him while he was in Tirzah, drinking heavily in the house of Arza, the steward of his house. {16:10} Zimri entered and struck him down, killing him in the twenty-seventh year of Asa, king of Judah, and reigned in his place. {16:11} As soon as he began to reign and sat on his throne, he killed all the descendants of Baasha; he did not leave a single male alive, neither his relatives nor his friends. {16:12} Thus, Zimri destroyed all the house of Baasha, fulfilling the word of the LORD that he spoke against Baasha through Jehu the prophet, {16:13} for all the sins of Baasha and the sins of his son Elah, by which they sinned and made Israel sin, provoking the LORD God of Israel to anger with their worthless acts. {16:14} Now the rest of the acts of Elah and all he did are they not written in the book of the chronicles of the kings of Israel? {16:15} In the twenty-seventh year of Asa, king of Judah, Zimri reigned for seven days in Tirzah. The people were encamped against Gibbethon, which belonged to the Philistines. {16:16} The troops in camp heard that Zimri had conspired and killed the king; so all Israel made Omri, the captain of the army, king over Israel that day in the camp. {16:17} Omri and all Israel went up from Gibbethon and besieged Tirzah. {16:18} When Zimri saw that the city was captured, he went into the palace and burned the king's house over himself, and died, {16:19} because of his sins that he committed, doing evil in the sight of the LORD, walking in the ways of Jeroboam and his sin that caused Israel to sin. {16:20} Now the rest of the acts of Zimri and the treachery he committed are they not written in the book of the chronicles of the kings of Israel? {16:21} Then the people of Israel were divided into two factions: half followed Tibni, the son of Ginath, wanting to make him king, while half followed Omri. {16:22} But the followers of Omri prevailed against those of Tibni, so Tibni died, and Omri became king. {16:23} In the thirty-first year of Asa, king of Judah, Omri began to reign over Israel for twelve years; six years he reigned in Tirzah. {16:24} He bought the hill of Samaria from Shemer for two talents of silver and built a city on the hill, naming the city Samaria after Shemer, the owner of the hill. {16:25} But Omri did evil in the eyes of the LORD and did worse than all who came before him. {16:26} He walked in all the ways of Jeroboam, the son of Nebat, and in his sin, which caused Israel to sin, provoking the LORD God of Israel to anger with their worthless acts. {16:27} Now the rest of the acts of Omri and all he did and his might are they not written in the book of the chronicles of the kings of Israel? {16:28} So Omri died and was buried in Samaria, and his son Ahab became king in his place. {16:29} In the thirty-eighth year of Asa, king of Judah, Ahab, the son of Omri, began to reign over Israel, and he reigned for twenty-two years in Samaria. {16:30} Ahab, the son of Omri, did evil in the sight of the LORD more than all who came before him. {16:31} As if it had been a trivial thing for him to walk in the sins of Jeroboam, the son of Nebat, he took as his wife Jezebel, the daughter of Ethbaal, king of the Sidonians, and began to serve Baal and worship him. {16:32} He built an altar for Baal in the house of Baal, which he built in Samaria. {16:33} Ahab also made an Asherah pole (a sacred tree or pole), and Ahab provoked the LORD God of Israel to anger more than all the kings of Israel who came before him. {16:34} In his days, Hiel of Bethel rebuilt Jericho; he laid its foundations at the cost of his firstborn son, Abiram, and set up its gates at the cost of his youngest son, Segub, fulfilling the word of the LORD spoken by Joshua, the son of Nun.

{17:1} Elijah the Tishbite, from the inhabitants of Gilead, said to Ahab, "As the LORD God of Israel lives, before whom I stand, there will be neither dew nor rain in these years except at my word." {17:2} Then the word of the LORD came to him, saying, {17:3} "Leave here, turn eastward, and hide by the brook Cherith, which is east of the Jordan. {17:4} You will drink from the brook, and I have commanded the ravens to feed you there." {17:5} So he went and did according to the word of the LORD; he stayed by the brook Cherith, east of the Jordan. {17:6} The ravens brought him bread and meat in the morning and bread and meat in the evening, and he drank from the brook. {17:7} After a while, the brook dried up because there had been no rain in the land. {17:8} Then the word of the LORD came to him, saying, {17:9} "Get up, go to Zarephath, which belongs to Sidon, and stay there; I have commanded a widow there to provide for you." {17:10} So he got up and went to Zarephath. When he arrived at the city gate, there was a widow gathering sticks. He called to her, "Please bring me a little water in a jar so I may drink." {17:11} As she was going to get it, he called to her again, "Please bring me a piece of bread." {17:12} She answered, "As the LORD your God lives, I don't have any baked bread; I only have a handful of flour in a jar and a little oil in a jug. I'm gathering a few sticks to take home and make a meal for myself and my son, that we may eat it and die." {17:13} Elijah said to her, "Don't be afraid; go home and do as you said. But first make a small cake of bread for me from what you have and bring it to me, and then make something for yourself and your son. {17:14} For this is what the LORD God of Israel says: 'The jar of flour will not be used up and the jug of oil will not run dry until the day the LORD sends rain on the land.'" {17:15} She went away and did as Elijah had told her. So there was food every day for Elijah and for the woman and her family. {17:16} The jar of flour was not used up, and the jug of oil did not run dry, in keeping with the word of the LORD spoken by Elijah. {17:17} Sometime later, the son of the woman who owned the house became ill. He grew worse and worse, and finally stopped breathing. {17:18} She said to Elijah, "What do you have against me, man of God? Did you come to remind me of my sin and kill my son?" {17:19} "Give me your son," Elijah replied. He took him from her arms, carried him to the upper room where he was staying, and laid him on his own bed. {17:20} Then he cried out to the LORD, "O LORD my God, have you brought tragedy upon this widow I am staying with by causing her son to die?" {17:21} He stretched himself out on the boy three times and cried out to the LORD, "O LORD my God, let this boy's life return to him!" {17:22} The LORD heard Elijah's cry, and the boy's life returned to him, and he lived. {17:23} Elijah picked up the child and brought him down from the room into the house. He gave him to his mother and said, "Look, your son is alive!" {17:24} Then the woman said to Elijah, "Now I know that you are a man of God and that the word of the LORD from your mouth is true."

{18:1} After many days, the word of the LORD came to Elijah in the third year, saying, "Go, present yourself to Ahab, and I will send rain on the earth." {18:2} So Elijah went to present himself to Ahab. Meanwhile, there was a severe famine in Samaria. {18:3} Ahab called Obadiah, who was in charge of his palace. (Obadiah greatly feared the LORD; {18:4} when Jezebel killed the LORD's prophets, Obadiah took a hundred prophets and hid them in two caves, fifty in each, and supplied them with bread and water.) {18:5} Ahab said to Obadiah, "Go throughout the land to all the springs and valleys; perhaps we can find some grass to keep the horses and mules alive, so we don't lose any of the animals." {18:6} So they divided the land to explore it; Ahab went one way and Obadiah went another. {18:7} While Obadiah was on his way, he met Elijah. Recognizing him, he fell on his face and asked, "Is it you, my lord Elijah?" {18:8} "Yes," he replied. "Go tell your master, 'Elijah is here.'" {18:9} Obadiah said, "What sin have I committed that you would hand your servant over to Ahab to be killed? {18:10} As the LORD your God lives, there is no nation or kingdom where my master hasn't sent to look for you. When they said, 'He is not here,' Ahab made them swear that they couldn't find you. {18:11} And now you say, 'Go tell your master, Elijah is here.' {18:12} As soon as I leave you, the Spirit of the LORD may carry you away to some unknown place. When I go and tell Ahab and he can't find you, he will kill me. I, your servant, have feared the LORD since my youth. {18:13} Was it not reported to my master what I did when Jezebel killed the LORD's prophets? I hid a hundred of the LORD's prophets, fifty in each cave, and supplied them with bread and water. {18:14} And now you say, 'Go tell your master, Elijah is here,' and he will kill me." {18:15} Elijah replied, "As the LORD of hosts lives, before whom I stand, I will surely present myself to him today." {18:16} So Obadiah went to meet Ahab and told him. Ahab went to meet Elijah. {18:17} When Ahab saw Elijah, he said, "Is it you, you who are bringing trouble to Israel?" {18:18} Elijah answered, "I have not brought trouble to Israel, but you and your father's house have. You have forsaken the LORD's commandments and followed Baal. {18:19} Now, therefore, send and gather all Israel at Mount Carmel, along with the 450 prophets of Baal and the 400 prophets of the Asherah who eat at Jezebel's table." {18:20} So Ahab sent word throughout all Israel and gathered the prophets to Mount Carmel. {18:21} Elijah approached all the people and said, "How long will you waver between two opinions? If the LORD is God, follow him; but if Baal is God, follow him." The people said nothing. {18:22} Then Elijah said, "I am the only remaining prophet of the LORD, but Baal's prophets total 450 men. {18:23} Bring us two bulls. Let them choose one bull for themselves, cut it into pieces, and lay it on the wood without setting fire to it. I will prepare the other bull and lay it on the wood without putting fire under it. {18:24} Then you call on the name of your gods, and I will call on the name of the LORD. The God who answers by fire—he is God." The people responded, "What you say is good." {18:25} Elijah said to the prophets of Baal, "Choose one of the bulls and prepare it first, since there are many of you. Call on the name of your god, but do not light the fire." {18:26} They took the bull given them and prepared it. They called on the name of Baal from morning until noon, shouting, "Baal, answer us!" But there was no response; no one answered. They danced around the altar they had made. {18:27} At noon, Elijah mocked them, saying, "Shout louder! Surely he is a god. Perhaps he is deep in thought, busy, or on a journey. Maybe he is sleeping and must be awakened." {18:28} So they shouted louder and cut themselves with knives and spears, as was their custom, until their blood flowed. {18:29} Midday passed, and they continued their frantic prophesying until the time for the evening sacrifice, but there was no response, no one answered, no one paid attention. {18:30} Then Elijah said to all the people, "Come here to me." They came to him, and he repaired the altar of the LORD that had been torn down. {18:31} Elijah took twelve stones, one for each of the tribes descended from Jacob, to whom the word of the LORD had come, saying, "Israel will be your name." {18:32} With the stones, he built an altar in the name of the LORD and dug a trench around it large enough to hold two measures of seed. {18:33} He arranged the wood, cut the bull into pieces, and laid it on the wood. Then he said, "Fill four jars with water and pour it on the offering and on the wood." {18:34} He said, "Do it again." And they did it again. "Do it a third time," he ordered. And they did it a third time. {18:35} The water ran down around the altar and even filled the trench. {18:36} At the time of the evening sacrifice, the prophet Elijah approached the altar and said, "LORD, God of Abraham, Isaac, and Israel, let it be known today that you are God in Israel and that I am your servant and have done all these things at your command. {18:37} Answer me, LORD, answer me, so these people will know that you, LORD, are God and that you are turning their hearts back again." {18:38} Then the fire of the LORD fell and consumed the burnt offering, the wood, the stones, and the soil, and licked up the water in the trench. {18:39} When all the people saw this, they fell prostrate and cried, "The LORD—he is God! The LORD—he is God!" {18:40} Elijah commanded them, "Seize the prophets of Baal. Don't let anyone get away!" They seized them, and Elijah brought them down to the Kishon Valley and slaughtered them there. {18:41} Elijah said to Ahab, "Go, eat and drink, for there is a sound of a heavy rain." {18:42} So Ahab went off to eat and drink, but Elijah climbed to the top of Mount Carmel, bent down to the ground, and put his face between his knees. {18:43} "Go and look toward the sea," he told his servant. So he went up and looked, but said, "There is nothing." Elijah said, "Go back." He said this seven times. {18:44} The seventh time the servant reported, "A cloud as small as a man's hand is rising from the sea." So Elijah said, "Go and tell Ahab, 'Hitch up your chariot and go down before the rain stops you.'" {18:45} Meanwhile, the sky grew black with clouds, the wind rose, and a heavy rain came on. Ahab rode off to Jezreel. {18:46} The hand of the LORD came on Elijah and, tucking his cloak into his belt, he ran ahead of Ahab all the way to the entrance of Jezreel.

{19:1} Ahab told Jezebel everything Elijah had done, including how he had killed all the prophets with the sword. {19:2} Jezebel sent a messenger to Elijah, saying, "May the gods deal with me, be it ever so severely, if I do not make your life like that of one of them by this time tomorrow." {19:3} When Elijah saw that, he got up and ran for his life. He went to Beersheba in Judah and left his servant there. {19:4} He himself traveled a day's journey into the wilderness. He sat down under a juniper tree and prayed that he might die, saying, "I have had enough, LORD. Take my life; I am no better than my ancestors." {19:5} As he lay down and slept under the tree, an angel touched him and said, "Get up and eat." {19:6} He looked around, and there by his head was a loaf of bread baked over hot coals and a jar of water. He ate and drank and then lay down again. {19:7} The angel of the LORD came back a second time and touched him, saying, "Get up and eat, for the journey is too much for you." {19:8} So he got up, ate and drank, strengthened by that food. He traveled forty days and forty nights to Horeb, the mountain of God. {19:9} There he went into a cave and spent the night. The word of the LORD came to him, saying, "What are you doing here, Elijah?" {19:10} He replied, "I have been very zealous for the LORD God Almighty. The Israelites have rejected your covenant, torn down your altars, and put your prophets to death with the sword. I am the only one left, and now they are trying to kill me too." {19:11} The LORD said, "Go out and stand on the mountain in the presence of the LORD, for the LORD is about to pass by." Then a great and powerful wind tore the mountains apart and shattered the rocks before the LORD, but the LORD was not in the wind. After the wind, there was an earthquake, but the LORD was not in the earthquake. {19:12} After the earthquake came a fire, but the LORD was not in the fire. And after the fire came a gentle whisper. {19:13} When Elijah heard it, he pulled his cloak over his face and went out and stood at the mouth of the cave. Then a voice said to him, "What are you doing here, Elijah?" {19:14} He replied, "I have been very zealous for the LORD God Almighty. The Israelites have rejected your covenant, torn down your altars, and put your prophets to death with the sword. I am the only one left, and now they are trying to kill me too." {19:15} The LORD said to him, "Go back the way you came, and go to the desert of Damascus. When you get there, anoint Hazael king over Aram. {19:16} Also, anoint Jehu son of Nimshi king over Israel, and anoint Elisha son of Shaphat from Abel Meholah to succeed you as prophet. {19:17} Jehu will put to death any who escape the sword of Hazael, and Elisha will put to death any who escape the sword of Jehu. {19:18} Yet I reserve seven thousand in Israel—all whose knees have not bowed down to Baal and whose mouths have not kissed him." {19:19} So Elijah went from there and found Elisha son of Shaphat. He was plowing with twelve yoke of oxen, and he himself was driving the twelfth pair. Elijah went up to him and threw his cloak around him. {19:20} Elisha then left his oxen and ran after Elijah. "Let me kiss my father and mother goodbye," he said, "and then I will come with you." "Go back," Elijah replied. "What have I done to you?" {19:21} So Elisha left him and went back. He took his yoke of oxen and slaughtered them. He burned the plowing equipment to cook the meat and gave it to the people, and they ate. Then he set out to follow Elijah and became his servant.

{20:1} Benhadad, the king of Syria, gathered all his army together; there were thirty-two kings with him, along with horses and chariots. He went up and besieged Samaria and waged war against it. {20:2} He sent messengers to Ahab, king of Israel, in the city, saying, "This is what Benhadad says: {20:3} Your silver and gold are mine; your wives and children, the most beautiful, are also mine." {20:4} The king of Israel answered, "My lord, O king, I am yours, and everything I have is yours." {20:5} The messengers came back and said, "Benhadad says, 'Although I have already sent to you, saying you must deliver your silver, gold, wives, and children, {20:6} I will send my servants to you tomorrow at this time, and they will search your house and the houses of your servants. Whatever pleases you, they will take away.'" {20:7} Then the king of Israel called all the elders of the land and said, "Pay attention and see how this man seeks trouble. He has sent to me for my wives, children, silver, and gold, and I did not deny him." {20:8} All the elders and the people said to him, "Do not listen to him or agree." {20:9} So he told the messengers of Benhadad, "Tell my lord the king, 'I will do everything you asked me at first, but I cannot agree to this.'" The messengers departed and brought him back word. {20:10} Benhadad sent another message saying, "May the gods deal with me, be it ever so severely, if there is enough dust from Samaria to give to all the people who follow me." {20:11} The king of Israel replied, "Tell him, 'Let not the one who puts on his armor boast like the one who takes it off.'" {20:12} When Benhadad heard this message, he was drinking with the kings in the pavilions and said to his servants, "Prepare to attack!" So they prepared to attack the city. {20:13} A prophet came to Ahab, king of Israel, and said, "This is what the LORD says: 'Have you seen this great multitude? I will deliver it into your hands today, and you will know that I am the LORD.'" {20:14} Ahab asked, "By whom?" The prophet replied, "This is what the LORD says: 'By the young men of the rulers of the provinces.'" Ahab asked, "Who will start the battle?" The prophet answered, "You." {20:15} So Ahab counted the young men of the rulers of the provinces, and there were two hundred thirty-two. After them, he counted all the people of Israel, which totaled seven thousand. {20:16} They went out at noon, while Benhadad and the thirty-two kings who were helping him were drinking heavily in the pavilions. {20:17} The young men of the rulers of the provinces went out first. Benhadad sent out scouts and was told, "Some men have come out of Samaria." {20:18} He said, "If they have come out for peace, take them alive; if they have come out for war, take them alive." {20:19} So the young men of the rulers of the provinces went out of the city, along with the army following them. {20:20} They killed each of their opponents, and the Syrians fled; Israel pursued them, and Benhadad, king of Syria, escaped on a horse with some horsemen. {20:21} The king of Israel went out and struck down the horses and chariots, killing the Syrians with a great slaughter. {20:22} The prophet came to the king of Israel and said, "Go, strengthen yourself, and consider what you should do, for at the turn of the year the king of Syria will come against you." {20:23} The servants of the king of Syria said to him, "Their gods are gods of the hills; that is why they were stronger than we were. But if we fight them in the plains, we will be stronger than they." {20:24} "Do this: remove the kings, each from his position, and replace them with captains. {20:25} Then muster an army like the one you lost, horse for horse and chariot for chariot, and we will fight them in the plains, and we will surely be stronger than they." He listened to their advice and did so. {20:26} At the turn of the year, Benhadad mustered the Syrians and went up to Aphek to fight against Israel. {20:27} The Israelites were mustered and presented themselves against the Syrians, and the Israelites looked like two little flocks of goats, but the Syrians filled the countryside. {20:28} Then a man of God came to the king of Israel and said, "This is what the LORD says: 'Because the Syrians have said, "The LORD is God of the hills, but not God of the valleys," I will deliver this great multitude into your hands, and you will know that I am the LORD.'" {20:29} They pitched their tents opposite each other for seven days, and on the seventh day, the battle began. The Israelites killed one hundred thousand Syrian foot soldiers in a single day. {20:30} The rest fled to Aphek, into the city, and the wall fell on twenty-seven thousand of the men who remained. Benhadad fled and took refuge in the inner chamber of the city. {20:31} His servants said to him, "Look, we have heard that the kings of Israel are merciful. Let us wear sackcloth around our waists and ropes on our heads, and go out to the king of Israel; perhaps he will spare your life." {20:32} So they put on sackcloth around their waists and ropes on their heads and went to the king of Israel. They said, "Your servant Benhadad says, 'Please let me live.'" Ahab replied, "Is he still alive? He is my brother." {20:33} The men watched for a sign and quickly took it, saying, "Your brother Benhadad." Ahab said, "Go bring him here." When Benhadad came out to him, Ahab had him come up into his chariot. {20:34} Benhadad said to him, "The cities my father took from your father, I will restore, and you may set up streets for yourself in Damascus, as my father did in Samaria." Ahab said, "I will send you away with this treaty." So he made a treaty with him and sent him away. {20:35} A certain man of the sons of the prophets said to his companion by the word of the LORD, "Strike me, please." But the man refused to strike him. {20:36} Then he said, "Because you have not obeyed the voice of the LORD, as soon as you leave me, a lion will kill you." When he left, a lion found him and killed him. {20:37} The prophet found another man and said, "Strike me, please." The man struck him, inflicting a wound. {20:38} The prophet went away and waited for the king on the road, disguising himself with a bandage over his eyes. {20:39} As the king passed by, he cried out to him: "Your servant went out into the midst of the battle. A man turned aside and brought a man to me, saying, 'Guard this man. If he is missing, your life will be for his life, or you must pay a talent of silver.' {20:40} While your servant was busy here and there, he was gone." The king of Israel said to him, "So shall your punishment be; you yourself have decided it." {20:41} The prophet quickly removed the bandage from his eyes, and the king of Israel recognized him as one of the prophets. {20:42} He said to him, "This is what the LORD says: 'Because you let a man escape whom I had destined for destruction, your life will be for his life, and your people for his people.'" {20:43} The king of Israel went home heavy-hearted and angry, and he came to Samaria.

{21:1} After these events, Naboth the Jezreelite had a vineyard in Jezreel, right next to the palace of Ahab, king of Samaria. {21:2} Ahab spoke to Naboth, saying, "Give me your vineyard so I can have it for a herb garden, since it's close to my house. I will give you a better vineyard in exchange, or if you prefer, I'll pay you its value in money." {21:3} Naboth replied to Ahab, "The LORD forbid that I should give you the inheritance of my ancestors." {21:4} Ahab went home upset and angry because of what Naboth had said; he had told him, "I will not give you my inheritance." He lay down on his bed, turned away his face, and refused to eat. {21:5} But his wife Jezebel came to him and asked, "Why are you so sad that you aren't eating?" {21:6} He answered, "I spoke to Naboth and said, 'Give me your vineyard for money, or I will give you another vineyard in exchange.' But he said, 'I will not give you my vineyard.'" {21:7} Jezebel, his wife, said to him, "Are you the king of Israel? Get up, eat, and cheer up! I will get you Naboth's vineyard." {21:8} So she wrote letters in Ahab's name, sealed them with his seal, and sent them to the elders and nobles who lived in Naboth's city. {21:9} In the letters, she wrote, "Proclaim a fast and seat Naboth in a prominent place among the people. {21:10} Then have two worthless men sit opposite him and testify against him, saying, 'You have blasphemed God and the king.' Then take him out and stone him to death." {21:11} The men of the city, including the elders and nobles who lived there, did as Jezebel instructed in the letters she sent. {21:12} They proclaimed a fast and seated Naboth in a prominent place among the people. {21:13} Then two worthless men came in and sat opposite him. The worthless men testified against Naboth in front of the people, saying, "Naboth has blasphemed God and the king." So they took him outside the city and stoned him to death. {21:14} They sent word to Jezebel, saying, "Naboth has been stoned and is dead." {21:15} When Jezebel heard that Naboth had been stoned and was dead, she said to Ahab, "Get up, take possession of the vineyard of Naboth the Jezreelite, which he refused to sell you for money; for Naboth is dead." {21:16} As soon as Ahab heard that Naboth was dead, he got up to go down to Naboth's vineyard to take possession of it. {21:17} Then the word of the LORD came to Elijah the Tishbite, saying, {21:18} "Go down to meet Ahab, king of Israel, who is in Samaria; he is in Naboth's vineyard where he has gone to take possession. {21:19} Speak to him and say, 'This is what the LORD says: Have you murdered and taken possession? This is what the LORD says: In the place where dogs licked up Naboth's blood, dogs will lick up your blood too.'" {21:20} Ahab said to Elijah, "Have you found me, my enemy?" Elijah answered, "I have found you because you have sold yourself to do evil in the sight of the LORD. {21:21} I will bring disaster upon you and will cut off your descendants. I will eliminate every male in your family, whether slave or free, in Israel. {21:22} I will make your house like the house of Jeroboam son of Nebat and like the house of Baasha son of Ahijah, because you have provoked me to anger and caused Israel to sin." {21:23} The LORD also spoke concerning Jezebel, saying, "Dogs will eat Jezebel by the wall of Jezreel. {21:24} Those who die in Ahab's city will be eaten by dogs, and those who die in the field will be eaten by birds." {21:25} There was no one like Ahab who sold himself to do evil in the sight of the LORD; his wife Jezebel stirred him up. {21:26} He acted very wickedly in following idols, just as the Amorites did, whom the LORD drove out before the Israelites. {21:27} When Ahab heard these words, he tore his clothes, put on sackcloth, and fasted. He lay in sackcloth and went around dejectedly. {21:28} Then the word of the LORD came to Elijah the Tishbite, saying, {21:29} "Do you see how Ahab has humbled himself before me? Because he has humbled himself, I will not bring disaster during his lifetime, but I will bring it on his house in the days of his son." {21:30} Ahab's moment of repentance delayed the judgment, yet the consequences of his sins would still be felt by future generations.

{22:1} They continued for three years without any war between Syria and Israel. {22:2} In the third year, Jehoshaphat, the king of Judah, visited the king of Israel. {22:3} The king of Israel said to his servants, "Do you know that Ramoth in Gilead belongs to us? Why are we sitting here and not taking it from the king of Syria?" {22:4} He asked Jehoshaphat, "Will you go with me to battle at Ramothgilead?" Jehoshaphat replied to the king of Israel, "I am as you are; my people are your people, and my horses are your horses." {22:5} Jehoshaphat then said to the king of Israel, "Please seek the word of the LORD today." {22:6} The king of Israel gathered about four hundred prophets and asked them, "Should I go to war against Ramothgilead or not?" They replied, "Go up, for the LORD will hand it over to the king." {22:7} Jehoshaphat asked, "Is there not a prophet of the LORD here that we might ask?" {22:8} The king of Israel said to Jehoshaphat, "There is one man, Micaiah son of Imlah, by whom we can inquire of the LORD, but I hate him because he never prophesies anything good about me, only bad." Jehoshaphat said, "Don't say that." {22:9} Then the king of Israel called an officer and said, "Quickly bring Micaiah son of Imlah." {22:10} The king of Israel and Jehoshaphat, king of Judah, sat on their thrones, dressed in their royal robes, at the entrance of the gate of Samaria, and all the prophets were prophesying before them. {22:11} Zedekiah son of Chenaanah made iron horns and declared, "This is what the LORD says: With these horns, you will push the Syrians until they are destroyed." {22:12} All the other prophets said the same, insisting, "Go up to Ramothgilead and be victorious, for the LORD will deliver it into the king's hands." {22:13} The messenger who went to summon Micaiah said to him, "Look, the prophets are all speaking good things to the king. Please make your word like theirs and speak favorably." {22:14} Micaiah replied, "As surely as the LORD lives, I will say only what the LORD tells me." {22:15} When he arrived, the king asked him, "Micaiah, should we go to battle at Ramothgilead or not?" Micaiah answered, "Go and succeed, for the LORD will hand it over to you." {22:16} The king said, "How many times must I make you swear to tell me nothing but the truth in the name of the LORD?" {22:17} Micaiah responded, "I saw all Israel scattered on the hills like sheep without a shepherd. The LORD said, 'These people have no master; let each return home in peace.'" {22:18} The king of Israel turned to Jehoshaphat and said, "Didn't I tell you that he would not prophesy anything good about me, only bad?" {22:19} Micaiah continued, "Therefore, hear the word of the LORD: I saw the LORD sitting on His throne, with all the heavenly host standing beside Him on His right and left. {22:20} The LORD asked, 'Who will entice Ahab into going up to fall at Ramothgilead?' One suggested this and another that. {22:21} Finally, a spirit came forward and stood before the LORD, saying, 'I will entice him.' {22:22} The LORD asked, 'How will you do that?' The spirit answered, 'I will go out and be a lying spirit in the mouths of all his prophets.' The LORD said, 'You will entice him and succeed; go out and do it.' {22:23} So now the LORD has put a lying spirit in the mouths of all these prophets of yours, and the LORD has decreed disaster for you." {22:24} Zedekiah son of Chenaanah approached and slapped Micaiah on the cheek, saying, "Which way did the Spirit of the LORD go when He left me to speak to you?" {22:25} Micaiah replied, "You will find out on the day you go to hide in an inner room." {22:26} The king of Israel then ordered, "Take Micaiah and return him to Amon, the governor of the city, and to Joash, the king's son. {22:27} Say to them, 'This is what the king says: Put this man in prison and feed him only bread and water until I return safely.'" {22:28} Micaiah declared, "If you return safely, then the LORD has not spoken through me." And he added, "Listen, everyone!" {22:29} So the king of Israel and Jehoshaphat went up to Ramothgilead. {22:30} The king of Israel said to Jehoshaphat, "I will disguise myself and go into battle, but you wear your royal robes." So the king of Israel disguised himself and went into battle. {22:31} The king of Syria had ordered his thirty-two captains of chariots not to fight anyone small or great, but only the king of Israel. {22:32} When the captains of the chariots saw Jehoshaphat, they said, "Surely this is the king of Israel." So they turned to attack him, but Jehoshaphat cried out. {22:33} When the captains saw that he was not the king of Israel, they turned back from pursuing him. {22:34} But someone drew his bow at random and struck the king of Israel between the joints of his armor. He said to his chariot driver, "Turn around and take me out of the battle, for I am wounded." {22:35} The battle raged that day, and the king was propped up in his chariot facing the Syrians. He died in the evening, and blood from his wound flowed into the chariot. {22:36} A herald went out throughout the army, saying, "Every man to his city, every man to his own country!" {22:37} So the king died and was brought to Samaria, where he was buried. {22:38} They washed the chariot in the pool of Samaria, and dogs licked up his blood, as the LORD had declared. {22:39} The rest of the acts of Ahab, including everything he did, the ivory palace he built, and all the cities he built, are they not recorded in the book of the chronicles of the kings of Israel? {22:40} Ahab died and was buried with his ancestors, and his son Ahaziah reigned in his place. {22:41} Jehoshaphat son of Asa began to reign over Judah in the fourth year of Ahab, king of Israel. {22:42} Jehoshaphat was thirty-five years old when he became king, and he reigned for twenty-five years in Jerusalem. His mother was Azubah, daughter of Shilhi. {22:43} He walked in all the ways of his father Asa and did not turn aside from them, doing what was right in the eyes of the LORD; however, the high places were not removed, and the people still offered sacrifices and burned incense there. {22:44} Jehoshaphat made peace with the king of Israel. {22:45} The rest of Jehoshaphat's acts, his might, and how he waged war, are they not written in the book of the chronicles of the kings of Judah? {22:46} He removed the remnants of the male shrine prostitutes that remained in the days of his father Asa. {22:47} At that time, there was no king in Edom; a deputy ruled. {22:48} Jehoshaphat built ships to go to Ophir for gold, but they never sailed because the ships were wrecked at Eziongeber. {22:49} Ahaziah son of Ahab said to Jehoshaphat, "Let my servants join your servants on the ships." But Jehoshaphat refused. {22:50} Jehoshaphat rested with his ancestors and was buried in the City of David. His son Jehoram succeeded him. {22:51} Ahaziah son of Ahab began to reign over Israel in Samaria in the seventeenth year of Jehoshaphat, king of Judah, and he reigned for two years over Israel. {22:52} He did evil in the sight of the LORD, following the ways of his father, his mother, and Jeroboam son of Nebat, who caused Israel to sin. {22:53} He served Baal and worshiped him, provoking the LORD God of Israel to anger, just as his father had done.

The Second Book of Kings

{1:1} After the death of Ahab, Moab rebelled against Israel. {1:2} Ahaziah fell through a lattice in his upper room in Samaria and was injured. He sent messengers to ask, "Go and inquire of Baalzebub, the god of Ekron, whether I will recover from this illness." {1:3} But the angel of the LORD told Elijah the Tishbite, "Get up and meet the king's messengers. Ask them, 'Is it because there is no God in Israel that you are going to inquire of Baalzebub, the god of Ekron?' {1:4} Therefore, this is what the LORD says: You will not come down from the bed you are lying on; you will certainly die." Then Elijah left. {1:5} When the messengers returned to the king, he asked them, "Why have you returned?" {1:6} They replied, "A man came to meet us and said, 'Go back to the king who sent you and tell him: This is what the LORD says: Is it because there is no God in Israel that you send to inquire of Baalzebub, the god of Ekron? You will not come down from the bed you are lying on; you will surely die.'" {1:7} The king asked, "What kind of man was he who came to meet you and told you this?" {1:8} They answered, "He had a garment made of hair and wore a leather belt." The king said, "That was Elijah the Tishbite." {1:9} So the king sent a captain with fifty men to Elijah. When they found him sitting on a hill, the captain said, "Man of God, the king has said, 'Come down!'" {1:10} Elijah answered, "If I am a man of God, may fire come down from heaven and consume you and your fifty men." Fire came down from heaven and consumed them. {1:11} The king sent another captain with fifty men. The captain said, "Man of God, this is what the king says: Come down at once!" {1:12} Elijah replied, "If I am a man of God, let fire come down from heaven and consume you and your fifty men." Again, fire from heaven consumed them. {1:13} The king sent a third captain with fifty men. This captain fell on his knees before Elijah and begged, "Man of God, please let my life and the lives of these fifty men be precious to you. {1:14} Fire has fallen from heaven and consumed the first two captains and their men; please let my life be spared." {1:15} The angel of the LORD said to Elijah, "Go down with him; don't be afraid." So Elijah got up and went down with him to the king. {1:16} Elijah told the king, "This is what the LORD says: Because you have sent messengers to inquire of Baalzebub, the god of Ekron, instead of seeking the LORD God of Israel, you will not leave the bed you are lying on; you will surely die." {1:17} So Ahaziah died, just as the LORD had said through Elijah. Jehoram became king in his place during the second year of Jehoram son of Jehoshaphat, king of Judah, because Ahaziah had no son. {1:18} The rest of the acts of Ahaziah are recorded in the book of the chronicles of the kings of Israel.

{2:1} When the LORD was about to take Elijah up to heaven in a whirlwind, Elijah and Elisha were on their way from Gilgal. {2:2} Elijah said to Elisha, "Stay here; the LORD has sent me to Bethel." But Elisha replied, "As surely as the LORD lives and as you live, I will not leave you." So they went down to Bethel. {2:3} The prophets in Bethel came to Elisha and asked, "Do you know that the LORD is going to take your master from you today?" "Yes, I know," he replied. "Be quiet." {2:4} Elijah said to him, "Stay here, Elisha; the LORD has sent me to Jericho." "As surely as the LORD lives and as you live, I will not leave you," Elisha said. So they went to Jericho. {2:5} The prophets in Jericho approached Elisha and asked, "Do you know that the LORD is going to take your master from you today?" "Yes, I know," he replied. "Be quiet." {2:6} Then Elijah said, "Stay here; the LORD has sent me to the Jordan." "As surely as the LORD lives and as you live, I will not leave you," Elisha said. So the two of them walked on. {2:7} Fifty men from the company of the prophets went and stood at a distance, facing the place where Elijah and Elisha had stopped by the Jordan. {2:8} Elijah took his cloak, rolled it up, and struck the water with it. The water divided, and the two of them crossed over on dry ground. {2:9} When they had crossed, Elijah said to Elisha, "Tell me, what can I do for you before I am taken from you?" "Let me inherit a double portion of your spirit," Elisha replied. {2:10} "You have asked a difficult thing," Elijah said. "Yet if you see me when I am taken from you, it will be yours; otherwise, it will not." {2:11} As they were walking along and talking together, suddenly a chariot of fire and horses of fire appeared and separated the two of them, and Elijah went up to heaven in a whirlwind. {2:12} Elisha saw this and cried out, "My father! My father! The chariots and horsemen of Israel!" And Elisha saw him no more. He then took hold of his own clothes and tore them apart. {2:13} He picked up Elijah's cloak that had fallen from him and went back and stood on the bank of the Jordan. {2:14} He took the cloak that had fallen from Elijah and struck the water with it. "Where now is the LORD God of Elijah?" he asked. When he struck the water, it divided to the right and to the left, and he crossed over. {2:15} The company of the prophets from Jericho who were watching said, "The spirit of Elijah is resting on Elisha." They went to meet him and bowed to the ground before him. {2:16} "Look," they said, "we have fifty able men; let them go and look for your master. Perhaps the Spirit of the LORD has picked him up and set him down on some mountain or in some valley." "No," Elisha replied, "do not send them." {2:17} But they urged him until he was too ashamed to refuse. So he said, "Send them." And they sent fifty men who searched for three days but did not find him. {2:18} When they returned to Elisha, who was staying in Jericho, he said, "Did I not tell you not to go?" {2:19} The people of the city said to Elisha, "Look, our lord, this town is well situated, as you can see, but the water is bad and the land is unproductive." {2:20} "Bring me a new bowl and put salt in it," he said. So they brought it to him. {2:21} Then he went out to the spring and threw the salt into it, saying, "This is what the LORD says: I have healed this water. Never again will it cause death or make the land unproductive." {2:22} And the water has remained pure to this day, according to the word Elisha had spoken. {2:23} From there, Elisha went up to Bethel. As he was walking along the road, some boys came out of the town and jeered at him. "Get out of here, baldy! Get out of here, baldy!" they said. {2:24} He turned around, looked at them, and called down a curse in the name of the LORD. Then two bears came out of the woods and mauled forty-two of the boys. {2:25} And he went on to Mount Carmel and then returned to Samaria.

{3:1} Jehoram, the son of Ahab, began to rule over Israel in Samaria during the eighteenth year of Jehoshaphat, king of Judah, and he reigned for twelve years. {3:2} He did evil in the sight of the LORD, but not as badly as his father and mother did; he removed the idol of Baal that his father had made. {3:3} However, he continued in the sins of Jeroboam, the son of Nebat, which led Israel to sin, and he did not turn away from them. {3:4} Meanwhile, Mesha, the king of Moab, was a sheep breeder and used to send the king of Israel one hundred thousand lambs and one hundred thousand rams, with their wool. {3:5} But when Ahab died, the king of Moab rebelled against the king of Israel. {3:6} So King Jehoram set out from Samaria and took a census of all Israel. {3:7} He then sent a message to Jehoshaphat, the king of Judah, saying, "The king of Moab has rebelled against me. Will you join me in battle against Moab?" Jehoshaphat replied, "I will go with you. I am as you are; my people are your people, and my horses are your horses." {3:8} Jehoram asked, "Which route shall we take?" Jehoshaphat answered, "The route through the wilderness of Edom." {3:9} So the king of Israel, along with the king of Judah and the king of Edom, set out on a seven-day journey, but there was no water for the troops or for the animals with them. {3:10} The king of Israel exclaimed, "Oh no! The LORD has brought these three kings together to hand them over to Moab!" {3:11} Jehoshaphat then asked, "Is there no prophet of the LORD here so that we can inquire of the LORD through him?" One of the king of Israel's officers answered, "Elisha, the son of Shaphat, is here; he used to pour water on the hands of Elijah." {3:12} Jehoshaphat said, "The word of the LORD is with him." So the king of Israel, Jehoshaphat, and the king of Edom went down to him. {3:13} Elisha said to the king of Israel, "What do you want from me? Go to the prophets of your father and mother!" The king of Israel replied, "No, for the LORD has called these three kings together to hand them over to Moab." {3:14} Elisha said, "As surely as the LORD Almighty lives, whom I serve, if I did not respect the presence of Jehoshaphat, the king of Judah, I would not even look at you or acknowledge you. {3:15} Now bring me a musician." And when the musician played, the hand of the LORD came upon Elisha. {3:16} He said, "This is what the LORD says: Make this valley full of ditches. {3:17} For the LORD says, 'You will not see wind or rain, yet this valley will be filled with water, and you, your cattle, and your animals will drink.' {3:18} This is an easy thing in the sight of the LORD; he will also deliver Moab into your hands. {3:19} You will strike down every fortified city and every important city; you will cut down every good tree, stop up all the wells, and ruin every good piece of land with stones." {3:20} The next morning, at the time of the offering, water suddenly came from the direction of Edom, and the land was filled with water. {3:21} When all the Moabites heard that the kings had come to fight against them, they gathered everyone who could wield a sword and stood at the border. {3:22} They got up early in the morning, and when the sun shone on the water, the Moabites saw the water across the valley looking as red as blood. {3:23} They said, "Look, the kings must have fought and killed each other! Now, Moab, to the plunder!" {3:24} When they arrived at the Israelite camp, the Israelites rose up and struck down the Moabites, who fled before them, but the Israelites continued to attack the Moabites in their own country. {3:25} They tore down the cities, and in every good piece of land, each person threw in stones and filled it. They stopped up all the wells of water and cut down all the good trees, leaving only the stones of Kirharaseth. The slingers surrounded it and attacked it. {3:26} When the king of Moab saw that the battle was going badly for him, he took seven hundred swordsmen to break through to the king of Edom, but they failed. {3:27} So he took his eldest son, who would have succeeded him as king, and offered him as a burnt offering on the city wall. This caused great anger against Israel, and they withdrew and returned to their own land.

{4:1} A certain woman from the wives of the sons of the prophets cried out to Elisha, "Your servant, my husband, is dead, and you know that he feared the LORD. Now the creditor is coming to take my two sons as his slaves." {4:2} Elisha asked her, "What can I do for you? Tell me, what do you have in your house?" She replied, "Your servant has nothing there at all except a small jar of oil." {4:3} He said, "Go and ask all your neighbors for empty jars. Don't ask for just a few. {4:4} Then go inside and shut the door behind you and your sons. Pour oil into all the jars, and as each is filled, put it to one side." {4:5} She left him and shut the door behind her and her sons. They brought the jars to her, and she kept pouring. {4:6} When all the jars were full, she said to her son, "Bring me another jar." He replied, "There is not a jar left." Then the oil stopped flowing. {4:7} She went and told the man of God, and he said, "Go, sell the oil and pay your debts, and you and your sons can live on what is left." {4:8} One day, Elisha went to Shunem, and a prominent woman there urged him to eat some food. So whenever he passed by, he stopped there to eat. {4:9} She said to her husband, "I know that this man who often passes by is a holy man of God. {4:10} Let us make a small room on the roof and put in it a bed, a table, a chair, and a lamp for him. Then when he comes to us, he can stay there." {4:11} One day when he came, he went into the room and lay down there. {4:12} He said to his servant Gehazi, "Call this Shunammite." So he called her, and she stood before him. {4:13} Elisha said to Gehazi, "Tell her, 'You have gone to all this trouble for us. What can we do for you? Can we speak on your behalf to the king or the commander of the army?'" She replied, "I have a home among my own people." {4:14} "What can we do for her?" Elisha asked. Gehazi said, "She has no son, and her husband is old." {4:15} Elisha said, "Call her." So Gehazi called her, and she stood in the doorway. {4:16} Elisha said, "About this time next year, you will hold a son in your arms." "No, my lord," she objected. "Don't mislead your servant, O man of God!" {4:17} But the woman became pregnant, and the next year about that same time she gave birth to a son, just as Elisha had told her. {4:18} The child grew, and one day he went out to his father, who was with the reapers. {4:19} He said to his father, "My head! My head!" His father told a servant, "Carry him to his mother." {4:20} After the servant had lifted him up and had brought him to his mother, the boy sat on her lap until noon, and then he died. {4:21} She went up and laid him on the bed of the man of God, then shut the door and went out. {4:22} She called her husband and said, "Send me one of the servants and a donkey so I can go to the man of God quickly and return." {4:23} "Why go to him today?" he asked. "It's not the New Moon or the Sabbath." "It's all right," she said. {4:24} She saddled the donkey and said to her servant, "Lead on; don't slow down for me unless I tell you." {4:25} So she set out and came to the man of God at Mount Carmel. When he saw her in the distance, he said to Gehazi, "Look, there's the Shunammite! {4:26} Run to meet her and ask her, 'Are you all right? Is your husband all right? Is your child all right?'" "Everything is all right," she said. {4:27} When she reached the man of God at the mountain, she took hold of his feet. Gehazi came over to push her away, but the man of God said, "Leave her alone. She is in bitter distress, and the LORD has hidden it from me; he did not tell me why." {4:28} "Did I ask you for a son, my lord? Didn't I tell you, 'Don't raise my hopes'?" {4:29} Elisha said to Gehazi, "Tuck your cloak into your belt, take my staff in your hand, and run. If you meet anyone, do not greet him; and if anyone greets you, do not answer. Lay my staff on the boy's face." {4:30} The child's mother said, "As surely as the LORD lives and as you live, I will not leave you." So he got up and followed her. {4:31} Gehazi went ahead and laid the staff on the boy's face, but there was no sound or response. So Gehazi went back to meet Elisha and told him, "The boy has not awakened." {4:32} When Elisha reached the house, there was the boy lying dead on his bed. {4:33} He went in, shut the door, and prayed to the LORD. {4:34} Then he got on the bed and lay on the boy, mouth to mouth, eyes to eyes, hands to hands. As he stretched himself out on him, the boy's body grew warm. {4:35} Elisha turned away and walked back and forth in the room, then got on the bed and stretched out on him once more. The boy sneezed seven times and opened his eyes. {4:36} Elisha summoned Gehazi and said, "Call the Shunammite." He did, and when she came in, he said, "Take your son!" {4:37} She came in, fell at his feet, and bowed to the ground. Then she took her son and went out. {4:38} Elisha returned to Gilgal, and there was a famine in the land. While the sons of the prophets were meeting with him, he said to his servant, "Put on the large pot and cook some stew for these men." {4:39} One of them went out into the field to gather herbs and found a wild vine. He gathered some of its gourds and came back, shredded them into the pot, though they did not realize they were poisonous. {4:40} The stew was served to the men, but as they ate it, they cried out, "Man of God, there is death in the pot!" And they could not eat it. {4:41} Elisha said, "Get some flour." He threw it into the pot and said, "Serve it to the people to eat." And there was nothing harmful in the pot. {4:42} A man came from Baalshalisha, bringing the man of God twenty loaves of barley bread and some ears of grain in his sack. Elisha said, "Give it to the people to eat." {4:43} "How can I set this before a hundred men?" his servant asked. But Elisha answered, "Give it to the people to eat, for this is what the LORD says: 'They will eat and have some left over.'" {4:44} So he set it before them, and they ate and had some left over, according to the word of the LORD.

{5:1} Naaman, the commander of the army of the king of Syria, was highly regarded by his master and was a great man because the LORD had given victory to Syria through him; he was also a mighty warrior, but he had leprosy. {5:2} The Syrians had gone out in bands and brought back a captive from the land of Israel—a young girl who served Naaman's wife. {5:3} She said to her mistress, "If only my master were with the prophet in Samaria! He would cure him of his leprosy." {5:4} Someone went in and told Naaman, "The girl from Israel said this." {5:5} Naaman went to the king of Syria and said, "I need to send a letter to the king of Israel." The king said, "Go ahead." Naaman took with him ten talents of silver, six thousand pieces of gold, and ten changes of clothes. {5:6} He brought the letter to the king of Israel, which said, "When this letter arrives, I'm sending my servant Naaman to you so that you may cure him of his leprosy." {5:7} When the king of Israel read the letter, he tore his clothes and said, "Am I God, to kill and make alive, that this man sends someone to me to be cured of leprosy? This is just a pretext to find a reason to fight me!" {5:8} When Elisha, the man of God, heard that the king of Israel had torn his clothes, he sent a message to the king: "Why have you torn your clothes? Let him come to me, and he will know that there is a prophet in Israel." {5:9} So Naaman came with his horses and chariot and stopped at the entrance to Elisha's house. {5:10} Elisha sent a messenger to say, "Go wash in the Jordan seven times, and your skin will be restored, and you will be cleansed." {5:11} Naaman was angry and went away. He said, "I thought he would surely come out to me, stand and call on the name of the LORD his God, wave his hand over the spot, and cure me of my leprosy. {5:12} Are not the rivers of Damascus, Abana and Pharpar, better than all the waters of Israel? Couldn't I wash in them and be cleansed?" So he turned and went away in a rage. {5:13} His servants went to him and said, "My father, if the prophet had told you to do something great, wouldn't you have done it? How much more then, when he tells you, 'Wash and be cleansed'?" {5:14} So he went down and dipped himself in the Jordan seven times, as the man of God had told him. His skin was restored and became clean like that of a young boy. {5:15} Naaman returned to the man of God, he and all his attendants. He stood before Elisha and said, "Now I know that there is no God in all the world except in Israel. Please accept a gift from your servant." {5:16} Elisha said, "As surely as the LORD lives, whom I serve, I will not accept a thing." And even though Naaman urged him, he refused. {5:17} Naaman said, "If you won't take anything, please let me, your servant, be given as much earth as a pair of mules can carry. For your servant will never again make burnt offerings and sacrifices to any other god but the LORD. {5:18} But may the LORD forgive your servant for this one thing: When my master enters the temple of Rimmon to bow down there, and he leans on my arm, and I bow there too—when I bow down in the temple of Rimmon, may the LORD forgive your servant in this matter." {5:19} Elisha said, "Go in peace." So Naaman left him a short distance away. {5:20} But Gehazi, the servant of Elisha, the man of God, said to himself, "My master was too easy on Naaman, this Syrian, by not accepting from him what he brought. As surely as the LORD lives, I will run after him and get something from him." {5:21} So Gehazi hurried after Naaman. When Naaman saw him running after him, he got down from his chariot to meet him and asked, "Is everything all right?" {5:22} "Everything is all right," Gehazi answered. "My master sent me to say, 'Two young men from the company of the prophets have just come to me from the hill country of Ephraim. Please give them a talent of silver and two sets of clothing.'" {5:23} "By all means, take two talents," said Naaman. He urged Gehazi to accept them and tied up the two talents of silver in two bags, along with two sets of clothing. He gave them to two of his servants, and they carried them ahead of Gehazi. {5:24} When Gehazi came to the hill, he took the things from the servants and put them away in the house. He sent the men away, and they left. {5:25} When he went in and stood before his master, Elisha asked him, "Where have you been,

Gehazi?" "Your servant didn't go anywhere," Gehazi answered. {5:26} But Elisha said to him, "Was not my spirit with you when the man got down from his chariot to meet you? Is this the time to take money or to accept clothes, olive groves, vineyards, flocks, or herds, or male and female servants? {5:27} Naaman's leprosy will cling to you and to your descendants forever." Gehazi went out from Elisha's presence and his skin was leprous—it had become as white as snow.

{6:1} The company of the prophets said to Elisha, "Look, the place where we meet with you is too small for us. {6:2} Let us go to the Jordan, where each of us can get a pole and let us build a place there for us to meet." Elisha said, "Go." {6:3} Then one said, "Please come with your servants." "I will," Elisha replied. {6:4} And he went with them. They went to the Jordan and began to cut down trees. {6:5} As one of them was cutting down a tree, the iron axe head fell into the water. "Oh no, my lord!" he cried out. "It was borrowed!" {6:6} The man of God asked, "Where did it fall?" When he showed him the place, Elisha cut a stick and threw it there, and the iron floated. {6:7} "Lift it out," he said. Then the man reached out his hand and took it. {6:8} Now the king of Aram was at war with Israel. After conferring with his officers, he said, "I will set up my camp in such and such a place." {6:9} The man of God sent word to the king of Israel: "Beware of passing that place, because the Arameans are going down there." {6:10} So the king of Israel checked on the place indicated by the man of God. Time and again Elisha warned the king, so that he was on his guard in such places. {6:11} This enraged the king of Aram. He summoned his officers and demanded of them, "Tell me, which of us is on the side of the king of Israel?" {6:12} "None of us, my lord the king," said one of his officers, "but Elisha, the prophet in Israel, tells the king of Israel the very words you speak in your bedroom." {6:13} "Go, find out where he is," the king ordered, "so I can send men and capture him." The report came back: "He is in Dothan." {6:14} Then he sent horses and chariots and a strong force there. They went by night and surrounded the city. {6:15} When the servant of the man of God got up and went out early the next morning, an army with horses and chariots had surrounded the city. "Oh no, my lord! What shall we do?" the servant asked. {6:16} "Don't be afraid," the prophet answered. "Those who are with us are more than those who are with them." {6:17} And Elisha prayed, "Open his eyes, LORD, so that he may see." Then the LORD opened the servant's eyes, and he looked and saw the hills full of horses and chariots of fire all around Elisha. {6:18} As the enemy came down toward him, Elisha prayed to the LORD, "Strike this army with blindness." So he struck them with blindness, as Elisha had asked. {6:19} Elisha told them, "This is not the road, and this is not the city. Follow me, and I will lead you to the man you are looking for." And he led them to Samaria.{6:20} When they arrived in Samaria, Elisha prayed, "LORD, open the eyes of these men so they can see." The LORD opened their eyes, and they saw that they were in the middle of Samaria. {6:21} The king of Israel saw them and asked Elisha, "My father, should I strike them down? Should I strike them down?" {6:22} Elisha replied, "You should not strike them. Would you strike down those you've taken captive with your sword and bow? Set food and water before them so they can eat and drink, and then go back to their master." {6:23} He prepared a great feast for them, and after they ate and drank, he sent them away, and they returned to their master. As a result, the raiding parties from Syria no longer entered the land of Israel. {6:24} After this, Ben-Hadad, king of Syria, gathered his entire army and besieged Samaria. {6:25} There was a severe famine in Samaria, so much so that an ass's head was sold for eighty pieces of silver, and a quarter of a cab (about a liter) of dove's dung was sold for five pieces of silver. {6:26} As the king of Israel was walking along the wall, a woman shouted to him, "Help me, my lord, O king!" {6:27} He replied, "If the LORD doesn't help you, how can I help you? From the granary or from the winepress?" {6:28} The king asked her, "What's wrong?" She answered, "This woman said to me, 'Give me your son so we can eat him today, and we'll eat my son tomorrow.' {6:29} So we boiled my son and ate him. The next day, I told her, 'Give me your son so we can eat him,' but she has hidden her son." {6:30} When the king heard the woman's words, he tore his clothes. As he walked along the wall, the people looked, and he had sackcloth (a rough material often worn as a sign of mourning) on his body. {6:31} Then he said, "May God do so to me and more if Elisha, son of Shaphat, is still alive by the end of today." {6:32} Elisha was sitting in his house with the elders when the king sent a messenger ahead. Before the messenger arrived, Elisha said to the elders, "Do you see how this son of a murderer has sent someone to take my head? When the messenger arrives, shut the door and hold it shut; his master's footsteps are right behind him." {6:33} While he was still talking to them, the messenger came down to him and said, "This disaster is from the LORD; why should I wait for the LORD any longer?"

{7:1} Elisha said, "Listen to the word of the LORD: Tomorrow at this time, a measure of fine flour will be sold for a shekel, and two measures of barley for a shekel at the gate of Samaria." {7:2} An officer on whom the king leaned responded to the man of God, saying, "Even if the LORD opened the windows of heaven, could this really happen?" Elisha replied, "You will see it with your own eyes, but you won't eat any of it." {7:3} Four leprous men were sitting at the entrance of the gate, and they said to each other, "Why are we sitting here until we die? {7:4} If we enter the city, the famine is there, and we will die. If we stay here, we will die too. So let's go to the camp of the Syrians; if they spare us, we'll live, and if they kill us, we will die." {7:5} They got up at twilight to go to the camp of the Syrians, and when they reached the edge of the camp, there was no one there. {7:6} The LORD had caused the Syrians to hear the sound of chariots and horses, a great army. They said to each other, "The king of Israel has hired the kings of the Hittites and Egyptians to attack us." {7:7} So they got up and fled in the twilight, abandoning their tents, horses, and donkeys, and they ran for their lives. {7:8} When the lepers reached the edge of the camp, they entered one of the tents, ate and drank, and carried away silver, gold, and clothes, hiding them. Then they entered another tent and did the same. {7:9} They said to each other, "We're not doing right. This is a day of good news, and we're keeping silent. If we wait until morning light, we will be punished. Let's go and tell the king's household." {7:10} So they went and called to the gatekeeper of the city, telling him, "We went to the camp of the Syrians, and there was no one there, not a single person; only horses and donkeys tied up, and the tents were intact." {7:11} The gatekeeper called the porters, and they reported it to the king's household. {7:12} The king got up at night and said to his servants, "I will tell you what the Syrians are doing. They know we're hungry, so they have left the camp to hide in the fields, thinking that when we come out of the city, they will catch us alive and enter the city." {7:13} One of his servants suggested, "Let's take five of the horses left in the city (they're just like the entire Israelite army that is left: they're as good as all the Israelites who have already perished) and send them to see." {7:14} So they took two chariot horses, and the king sent them to follow the Syrian army, saying, "Go and see." {7:15} They went as far as the Jordan and found the whole road strewn with garments and equipment that the Syrians had thrown away in their haste. The messengers returned and reported to the king. {7:16} Then the people went out and plundered the tents of the Syrians. A measure of fine flour was sold for a shekel, and two measures of barley for a shekel, just as the LORD had said. {7:17} The king had put the officer in charge of the gate, but the people trampled him in the gate, and he died, as the man of God had foretold when the king came down to him. {7:18} It happened just as Elisha had predicted to the king: "Two measures of barley for a shekel, and a measure of fine flour for a shekel will happen tomorrow at the gate of Samaria." {7:19} That officer had responded to the man of God, "Even if the LORD opened the windows of heaven, could such a thing happen?" Elisha said, "You will see it with your own eyes, but you will not eat any of it." {7:20} And so it happened to him: the people trampled him in the gate, and he died.

{8:1} Elisha spoke to the woman whose son he had brought back to life, saying, "Get up, you and your household, and go wherever you can, for the LORD has called for a famine, and it will last seven years." {8:2} The woman got up and did as the man of God said; she went with her household and lived in the land of the Philistines for seven years. {8:3} At the end of the seven years, the woman returned from the land of the Philistines and went to cry out to the king for her house and land. {8:4} The king was talking with Gehazi, the servant of the man of God, saying, "Tell me about all the great things Elisha has done." {8:5} While Gehazi was telling the king how Elisha had restored a dead body to life, the woman whose son he had brought back to life came to the king for her house and land. Gehazi said, "This is the woman, and this is her son whom Elisha restored to life." {8:6} When the king asked the woman, she told him. The king appointed an official to restore everything that belonged to her, along with all the produce from her land since the day she left until now. {8:7} Elisha went to Damascus, and Ben-Hadad, the king of Syria, was ill. It was reported to him, "The man of God has come here." {8:8} The king said to Hazael, "Take a gift and go meet the man of God. Ask him if I will recover from this illness." {8:9} So Hazael went to meet him, taking along a gift of every good thing from Damascus—forty camels' loads—and he stood before Elisha and said, "Your son Ben-Hadad, king of Syria, has sent me to ask if he will recover from this illness." {8:10} Elisha replied, "Go tell him you will certainly recover; however, the LORD has shown me that he will surely die." {8:11} Elisha stared at Hazael until he felt ashamed, and then the man of God wept. {8:12} Hazael asked, "Why are you weeping, my lord?" Elisha answered, "Because I know the harm you will do to the Israelites: You will burn their strongholds, kill their young men with the sword, dash their little children, and rip open their pregnant women." {8:13} Hazael said, "What? Is your servant a mere dog that he could do such a thing?" Elisha replied, "The LORD has shown me that you will be king over Syria." {8:14} Hazael left Elisha and went to his master, who asked, "What did Elisha say to you?" Hazael answered, "He told me you would recover." {8:15} But the next day, Hazael took a thick cloth, dipped it in water, and spread it over the king's face, killing him. Hazael then became king in his place. {8:16} In the fifth year of Joram son of Ahab, king of Israel, Jehoshaphat was king of Judah, and Jehoram, son of Jehoshaphat, became king of Judah. {8:17} He was thirty-two years old when he became king, and he reigned for eight years in Jerusalem. {8:18} He followed the ways of the kings of Israel, as the house of Ahab had done, because he married Ahab's daughter, and he did evil in the sight of the LORD. {8:19} Yet the LORD did not destroy Judah for the sake of His servant David, since He had promised to give him a lamp and his descendants forever. {8:20} During his reign, Edom revolted against Judah and set up their own king. {8:21} So Joram went to Zair with all his chariots and attacked the Edomites who had surrounded him, but his troops fled to their tents. {8:22} Edom has been in revolt against Judah to this day. Libnah revolted at the same time. {8:23} The rest of Joram's acts are recorded in the book of the chronicles of the kings of Judah. {8:24} Joram rested with his ancestors and was buried with them in the City of David. His son Ahaziah succeeded him as king. {8:25} In the twelfth year of Joram son of Ahab, king of Israel, Ahaziah, son of Jehoram, became king of Judah. {8:26} Ahaziah was twenty-two years old when he began to reign, and he ruled for one year in Jerusalem. His mother was Athaliah, the daughter of Omri, king of Israel. {8:27} He followed the ways of the house of Ahab and did evil in the sight of the LORD, like the house of Ahab, for he was related by marriage to Ahab's family. {8:28} He went with Joram, son of Ahab, to war against Hazael, king of Syria, at Ramoth-Gilead, and the Syrians wounded Joram. {8:29} King Joram went back to Jezreel to recover from the wounds he had received in Ramoth, while Ahaziah, son of Jehoram, king of Judah, went down to see Joram, son of Ahab, in Jezreel because he was ill.

{9:1} Elisha the prophet called one of the young prophets and said to him, "Tuck in your cloak, take this flask of oil in your hand, and go to Ramoth-Gilead. {9:2} When you arrive, look for Jehu son of Jehoshaphat, son of Nimshi. Go in, get him up from among his brothers, and take him to an inner room. {9:3} Then take the flask of oil, pour it on his head, and say, 'This is what the LORD says: I have anointed you king over Israel.' After that, open the door and run away; don't wait." {9:4} So the young prophet went to Ramoth-Gilead. {9:5} When he arrived, he found the captains of the army sitting there, and he said, "I have a message for you, captain." Jehu asked, "For which of us?" He replied, "For you, captain." {9:6} Jehu got up and went into the house, and the young prophet poured the oil on his head and said to him, "This is what the LORD God of Israel says: I have anointed you king over the people of the LORD, over Israel. {9:7} You are to destroy the house of Ahab your master so that I can avenge the blood of my prophets and the blood of all the LORD's servants that Jezebel has shed. {9:8} The whole house of Ahab will perish, and I will cut off from Ahab every last male in Israel, whether slave or free. {9:9} I will make the house of Ahab like the house of Jeroboam son of Nebat and like the house of Baasha son of Ahijah. {9:10} As for Jezebel, dogs will eat her by the wall of Jezreel, and no one will bury her." Then he opened the door and fled. {9:11} When Jehu came out to his fellow officers, one of them asked, "Is everything alright? Why did this madman come to you?" Jehu replied, "You know the man and what he said." {9:12} They said, "That's not true! Tell us!" Jehu said, "He told me that the LORD has anointed me king over Israel." {9:13} They hurried and took their cloaks and spread them under Jehu on the bare steps. Then they blew the trumpet and shouted, "Jehu is king!" {9:14} Jehu son of Jehoshaphat, son of Nimshi, conspired against Joram. (Now Joram had been defending Ramoth-Gilead, he and all Israel, against Hazael king of Syria. {9:15} But King Joram had returned to Jezreel to recover from the wounds the Syrians had inflicted on him in battle.) Jehu said, "If you are with me, don't let anyone escape the city to go tell it in Jezreel." {9:16} Jehu got into his chariot and went to Jezreel, where Joram was lying down. Ahaziah king of Judah had gone down to see Joram. {9:17} A lookout standing on the tower in Jezreel saw Jehu's troops approaching and shouted, "I see a company!" Joram ordered, "Get a horseman and send him to meet them. Ask if everything is alright." {9:18} The horseman rode out to meet Jehu and said, "This is what the king says: Is everything alright?" Jehu replied, "What do you have to do with peace? Fall in behind me." The lookout reported, "The messenger has reached them, but he isn't coming back." {9:19} Joram sent out a second horseman, who came to them and said, "This is what the king says: Is everything alright?" Jehu answered, "What do you have to do with peace? Fall in behind me." {9:20} The lookout said, "He has reached them, but he isn't coming back. The driving is like that of Jehu son of Nimshi; he drives like a madman." {9:21} Joram said, "Get my chariot ready." His chariot was made ready, and Joram king of Israel and Ahaziah king of Judah rode out, each in his chariot, to meet Jehu. They met him at the plot of land belonging to Naboth the Jezreelite. {9:22} When Joram saw Jehu, he asked, "Is it peace, Jehu?" Jehu replied, "How can there be peace as long as your mother Jezebel's immoralities and witchcrafts are so many?" {9:23} Joram turned around and fled, calling out to Ahaziah, "Treachery, Ahaziah!" {9:24} Then Jehu drew his bow and shot Joram between the shoulders. The arrow pierced his heart, and he slumped down in his chariot. {9:25} Jehu said to Bidkar his officer, "Take him up and throw him on the plot of land belonging to Naboth the Jezreelite. Remember when you and I were riding together after Ahab his father? The LORD spoke this prophecy against him: {9:26} 'Yesterday I saw the blood of Naboth and the blood of his sons,' says the LORD, 'and I will repay you on this plot of land,' says the LORD. Now take him and throw him on that plot, as the LORD said." {9:27} When Ahaziah king of Judah saw what happened, he fled along the road to Beth Haggan. Jehu chased him, shouting, "Kill him too!" They wounded him in his chariot on the way up to Gur, which is near Ibleam. Ahaziah fled to Megiddo and died there. {9:28} His servants took him by chariot to Jerusalem and buried him with his ancestors in the city of David. {9:29} In the eleventh year of Joram son of Ahab, Ahaziah began to reign over Judah. {9:30} When Jehu arrived in Jezreel, Jezebel heard about it. She painted her eyes, arranged her hair, and looked out the window. {9:31} As Jehu entered the gate, she asked, "Have you come in peace, you Zimri, you murderer of your master?" {9:32} Jehu looked up at the window and called out, "Who is on my side? Who?" Two or three eunuchs looked down at him. {9:33} He said, "Throw her down!" So they threw her down, and some of her blood spattered the wall and the horses as they trampled her underfoot. {9:34} Jehu went in and ate and drank. "Take care of that cursed woman," he said, "and bury her, for she was a king's daughter." {9:35} But when they went to bury her, they found no more of her than the skull, the feet, and the palms of her hands. {9:36} They went back and told Jehu, who said, "This is the word of the LORD that he spoke through his servant Elijah the Tishbite: 'In the plot of land at Jezreel, dogs will eat Jezebel's flesh. {9:37} As for Jezebel's body, it will be like refuse on the ground in the plot at Jezreel, so that no one will be able to say, "This is Jezebel."

{10:1} Ahab had seventy sons in Samaria. Jehu wrote letters and sent them to Samaria, to the rulers of Jezreel, the elders, and those who raised Ahab's children, saying, {10:2} "As soon as this letter reaches you, since your master's sons are with you, and you have chariots, horses, a fortified city, and armor, {10:3} select the best and most suitable of your master's sons, set him on his father's throne, and fight for your master's house." {10:4} But they were very afraid and said, "Look, two kings couldn't stand against him, so how can we?" {10:5} So the one in charge of the house, the one in charge of the city, the elders, and those who raised the children sent a message to Jehu, saying, "We are your servants and will do whatever you ask. We won't appoint anyone as king. Do whatever you think is best." {10:6} Jehu wrote them a second letter, saying, "If you are loyal to me and willing to obey my orders, then take the heads of your master's sons and come to me in Jezreel by this time tomorrow." Now, the seventy sons of the king were with the city's leaders who raised them. {10:7} When the letter arrived, they took the king's sons, killed all seventy of them, put their heads in baskets, and sent them to Jehu in Jezreel. {10:8} A messenger came and told Jehu, "They have brought the heads of the king's sons." And he said, "Place them in two heaps at the entrance of the city gate until morning." {10:9} In the morning, he went out and said to all the people, "You are innocent. I conspired against my master and killed him, but who killed all these? {10:10} Know this: nothing the LORD spoke concerning Ahab's house will fail. The LORD has done what He said through His servant Elijah." {10:11} So Jehu killed everyone who remained of Ahab's family in Jezreel, including all his great men, relatives, and priests, leaving no one alive. {10:12} Then Jehu set out for Samaria. On the way, at Beth Eked of the Shepherds, {10:13} he met some relatives of Ahaziah, king of Judah, and asked, "Who are you?" They answered, "We are the relatives of Ahaziah, and we're going to visit the sons of the king and the sons of the queen mother." {10:14} Jehu ordered, "Take them alive!" So they took them alive and killed them at the well of Beth Eked, forty-two men in total, leaving none alive. {10:15} After leaving there, Jehu met Jehonadab, son of Rechab, who was coming to meet him. Jehu greeted him and asked, "Is your heart right, as my heart is with yours?" Jehonadab replied, "It is." "If it is," said Jehu, "give me your hand." So Jehonadab gave him his hand, and Jehu helped him into the chariot. {10:16} Jehu said, "Come with me and see my zeal for the LORD." So Jehonadab rode with him in the chariot. {10:17} When Jehu arrived in Samaria, he killed everyone who remained of Ahab's family there, destroying them completely, as the LORD had told Elijah. {10:18} Jehu gathered all the people and said to them, "Ahab served Baal a little, but Jehu will serve him much. {10:19} So call all the prophets of Baal, all his servants, and all his priests. Let no one be missing, for I am going to offer a great sacrifice to Baal. Anyone who fails to come will not live." But Jehu was deceiving them in order to destroy the worshippers of Baal. {10:20} Then Jehu ordered, "Proclaim a solemn assembly for Baal." So they proclaimed it. {10:21} Jehu sent word throughout Israel, and all the worshippers of Baal came. Not one stayed behind. They crowded into the temple of Baal until it was full from one end to the other. {10:22} Jehu said to the keeper of the wardrobe, "Bring out robes for all the worshippers of Baal." So he brought out robes for them. {10:23} Then Jehu and Jehonadab, son of Rechab, went into the temple of Baal. Jehu said to the worshippers of Baal, "Make sure no servants of the LORD are here with you—only the worshippers of Baal." {10:24} So they went in to offer sacrifices and burnt offerings. Now Jehu had stationed eighty men outside with this warning: "If any of the men I am handing over to you escape, your life will be taken in place of theirs." {10:25} As soon as Jehu finished offering the burnt offering, he ordered the guards and officers, "Go in and kill them all. Let no one escape." So they killed them with the sword and threw their bodies out. Then the guards and officers went into the inner room of the temple of Baal. {10:26} They brought out the sacred pillars (idols) of the temple of Baal and burned them. {10:27} They smashed the sacred pillar of Baal and demolished the temple of Baal, turning it into a public toilet, which it remains to this day. {10:28} So Jehu destroyed Baal worship in Israel. {10:29} However, Jehu did not turn away from the sins that Jeroboam, son of Nebat, had caused Israel to commit—the worship of the golden calves in Bethel and Dan. {10:30} The LORD said to Jehu, "Because you have done well in carrying out what is right in My eyes and have done to Ahab's family all that was in My heart, your descendants will sit on the throne of Israel to the fourth generation." {10:31} But Jehu was not careful to follow the law of the LORD, the God of Israel, with all his heart. He did not turn away from the sins of Jeroboam, which had led Israel into sin. {10:32} In those days, the LORD began to reduce the size of Israel. Hazael (king of Aram) defeated them throughout the territory of Israel, {10:33} from the Jordan eastward—through the entire land of Gilead, including the Gadites, Reubenites, and Manassites—from Aroer by the Arnon Valley through Gilead and Bashan. {10:34} The rest of the events of Jehu's reign, all his accomplishments, and all his power, are written in the book of the chronicles of the kings of Israel. {10:35} Jehu rested with his ancestors and was buried in Samaria. His son Jehoahaz succeeded him as king. {10:36} Jehu reigned over Israel in Samaria for twenty-eight years.

{11:1} When Athaliah, the mother of Ahaziah, saw that her son was dead, she rose up and killed all the royal family. {11:2} But Jehosheba, the daughter of King Joram and sister of Ahaziah, took Joash, the son of Ahaziah, and hid him away from the other princes who were being killed. She hid him and his nurse in a bedroom, so Athaliah wouldn't kill him. {11:3} Joash stayed hidden in the Lord's temple for six years, while Athaliah ruled the land. {11:4} In the seventh year, Jehoiada the priest summoned the commanders of hundreds, the captains, and the guards, brought them into the Lord's house, made a covenant with them, and had them swear an oath in the temple. He then showed them the king's son. {11:5} He gave them orders, saying, "This is what you must do: A third of you who come on duty on the Sabbath shall guard the royal palace. {11:6} Another third shall station themselves at the Sur Gate, and the final third at the gate behind the guards. You will take turns keeping watch over the temple to prevent any break-ins. {11:7} Two groups, those who are going off duty on the Sabbath, shall guard the temple for the king. {11:8} Surround the king with weapons in hand, and anyone who tries to approach must be killed. Stay with the king, whether he goes out or comes in." {11:9} The commanders of hundreds did everything as Jehoiada the priest commanded. They each took their men, those coming on duty on the Sabbath and those going off duty, and reported to Jehoiada. {11:10} The priest gave the commanders King David's spears and shields, which were stored in the temple of the Lord. {11:11} The guards, each armed with their weapons, took up positions from the right to the left side of the temple, near the altar and the temple itself, surrounding the king. {11:12} Then Jehoiada brought out the king's son, put the crown on him, presented him with the royal scroll, and anointed him. They proclaimed him king, clapped their hands, and shouted, "Long live the king!" {11:13} When Athaliah heard the noise of the guards and the people, she went to the temple of the Lord, where the crowd was. {11:14} She saw the king standing by the pillar as was the custom, with the leaders and trumpeters by him, and all the people of the land rejoicing and blowing trumpets. Athaliah tore her clothes and shouted, "Treason! Treason!" {11:15} But Jehoiada the priest ordered the commanders of hundreds, the officers of the army, to take her outside the temple and kill anyone who followed her, for he said, "Do not put her to death in the Lord's temple." {11:16} So they seized her and killed her at the entrance to the king's palace, where the horses enter. {11:17} Jehoiada then made a covenant between the Lord, the king, and the people that they would be the Lord's people, and also between the king and the people. {11:18} All the people went to the temple of Baal, tore it down, smashed the altars and idols, and killed Mattan, the priest of Baal, in front of the altars. Then Jehoiada the priest placed guards over the Lord's temple. {11:19} Jehoiada took the commanders of hundreds, the captains, the guards, and all the people of the land, and they escorted the king from the Lord's temple to the palace, entering through the guards' gate. And the king sat on the royal throne. {11:20} So all the people of the land rejoiced, and the city remained peaceful, for Athaliah had been killed by the sword at the king's palace. {11:21} Joash (also called Jehoash) was seven years old when he became king.

{12:1} In the seventh year of Jehu's reign, Jehoash (Joash) became king, and he reigned in Jerusalem for forty years. His mother's name was Zibiah, from Beersheba. {12:2} Jehoash did what was right in the sight of the Lord all the days when Jehoiada the priest instructed him. {12:3} However, the high places (places of worship outside the main temple) were not removed, and the people still sacrificed and burned incense there. {12:4} Jehoash said to the priests, "Collect all the money that is dedicated to the temple of the

Lord—whether it comes from those who are registered, from voluntary contributions, or any other source. {12:5} Each priest is to collect from his acquaintances, and they are to use the funds to repair any damage to the temple." {12:6} But by the twenty-third year of King Jehoash's reign, the priests still hadn't repaired the temple. {12:7} So King Jehoash summoned Jehoiada and the other priests and asked, "Why haven't you repaired the temple? Don't take any more money from your acquaintances; instead, hand it over for the temple repairs." {12:8} The priests agreed to no longer collect money from the people and to stop being responsible for the temple repairs. {12:9} Then Jehoiada the priest took a chest, bored a hole in its lid, and placed it beside the altar on the right side as one entered the temple. The priests who guarded the entrance put into the chest all the money brought to the temple. {12:10} When they saw that there was a lot of money in the chest, the king's scribe and the high priest would come and count the money that was brought into the Lord's temple and tie it up in bags. {12:11} They would give the money to the supervisors of the temple work, who used it to pay the carpenters, builders, {12:12} masons, and stonecutters, and to buy timber and cut stone to repair the damages to the Lord's temple. {12:13} However, none of the money brought into the Lord's temple was used to make silver bowls, snuffers, basins, trumpets, or any other gold or silver items for the temple. {12:14} It was all given to the workmen, and they used it to repair the temple. {12:15} They did not ask for an accounting from those to whom they gave the money to pay the workers, because they acted with integrity. {12:16} The money from guilt offerings and sin offerings was not brought into the Lord's temple; it belonged to the priests. {12:17} At that time, Hazael, king of Syria, went up and attacked Gath, and after capturing it, he planned to attack Jerusalem. {12:18} But Jehoash, king of Judah, took all the sacred objects that had been dedicated by his ancestors—Jehoshaphat, Jehoram, and Ahaziah, the previous kings of Judah—as well as his own sacred objects, and all the gold found in the treasuries of the Lord's temple and the royal palace, and sent it to Hazael, king of Syria. So Hazael withdrew from Jerusalem. {12:19} The rest of the acts of Jehoash and all he did are recorded in the book of the chronicles of the kings of Judah. {12:20} But his servants conspired against him and killed him at Beth Millo, on the road down to Silla. {12:21} Jozachar, son of Shimeath, and Jehozabad, son of Shomer, his servants, struck him down, and he died. He was buried with his ancestors in the City of David, and his son Amaziah succeeded him as king.

{13:1} In the twenty-third year of Joash, the son of Ahaziah, king of Judah, Jehoahaz, the son of Jehu, began to reign over Israel in Samaria, and he reigned for seventeen years. {13:2} He did evil in the sight of the LORD, following the sins of Jeroboam, the son of Nebat, which led Israel to sin; he did not turn away from them. {13:3} The anger of the LORD was kindled against Israel, and He delivered them into the hands of Hazael, king of Syria, and into the hands of Benhadad, the son of Hazael, throughout their days. {13:4} Jehoahaz pleaded with the LORD, and the LORD listened to him because He saw the oppression of Israel, as the king of Syria was oppressing them. {13:5} (The LORD provided a savior for Israel so they could escape the hands of the Syrians, and the children of Israel lived in their tents as they had before. {13:6} Yet they did not turn away from the sins of the house of Jeroboam, which made Israel sin, and the Asherah pole remained in Samaria.) {13:7} Jehoahaz was left with only fifty horsemen, ten chariots, and ten thousand foot soldiers; for the king of Syria had destroyed them and made them as dust in the threshing. {13:8} The rest of the acts of Jehoahaz, all that he did, and his strength, are they not written in the book of the chronicles of the kings of Israel? {13:9} Jehoahaz died and was buried in Samaria, and his son Joash reigned in his place. {13:10} In the thirty-seventh year of Joash, king of Judah, Jehoash, the son of Jehoahaz, began to reign over Israel in Samaria and reigned for sixteen years. {13:11} He also did evil in the sight of the LORD; he did not turn away from the sins of Jeroboam, the son of Nebat, who made Israel sin; he walked in those ways. {13:12} The rest of the acts of Joash, all he did, and his strength in fighting against Amaziah, king of Judah, are they not written in the book of the chronicles of the kings of Israel? {13:13} Joash died and was buried with his ancestors, and Jeroboam sat on his throne; Joash was buried in Samaria with the kings of Israel. {13:14} Now Elisha had fallen sick with the illness from which he would die. King Joash of Israel went down to him, wept over him, and said, "O my father, my father, the chariot of Israel and its horsemen!" {13:15} Elisha said to him, "Take a bow and some arrows." So he took a bow and arrows. {13:16} Elisha then said to the king of Israel, "Put your hand on the bow." He put his hand on it, and Elisha put his hands on the king's hands. {13:17} Elisha said, "Open the window toward the east." He opened it, and Elisha said, "Shoot!" He shot, and Elisha said, "This is the arrow of the LORD's deliverance, the arrow of deliverance from Syria; you will strike the Syrians at Aphek until you have destroyed them." {13:18} Elisha said, "Take the arrows." He took them, and Elisha said to the king of Israel, "Strike the ground." He struck it three times and stopped. {13:19} The man of God was angry with him and said, "You should have struck five or six times; then you would have struck Syria until you had destroyed it. Now you will only strike Syria three times." {13:20} Elisha died and was buried. At the beginning of the year, bands of Moabites invaded the land. {13:21} As they were burying a man, they saw a band of men; so they threw the man into Elisha's tomb. When the man touched the bones of Elisha, he revived and stood on his feet. {13:22} But Hazael, king of Syria, oppressed Israel all the days of Jehoahaz. {13:23} The LORD was gracious to them, had compassion on them, and paid attention to them because of His covenant with Abraham, Isaac, and Jacob, and He would not destroy them or cast them from His presence yet. {13:24} So Hazael, king of Syria, died, and his son Benhadad reigned in his place. {13:25} Jehoash, the son of Jehoahaz, recovered the cities that Benhadad, the son of Hazael, had taken from Jehoahaz, his father, by war. Three times Joash defeated him and recovered the cities of Israel.

{14:1} In the second year of Joash, the son of Jehoahaz, king of Israel, Amaziah, the son of Joash, king of Judah, began to reign. {14:2} He was twenty-five years old when he began to reign, and he reigned for twenty-nine years in Jerusalem. His mother's name was Jehoaddan from Jerusalem. {14:3} He did what was right in the sight of the LORD, but not like his father David; he did according to all things as Joash, his father, had done. {14:4} However, the high places were not taken away; the people still sacrificed and burned incense on those high places. {14:5} As soon as the kingdom was firmly established in his hand, he killed his servants who had murdered his father, the king. {14:6} But he did not kill the children of the murderers, following what is written in the book of the law of Moses, where the LORD commanded, "Fathers shall not be put to death for their children, nor shall children be put to death for their fathers; each person shall be put to death for their own sin." {14:7} He struck down ten thousand Edomites in the Valley of Salt and took Selah by war, naming it Joktheel, and it remains that way to this day. {14:8} Then Amaziah sent messengers to Jehoash, the son of Jehoahaz, the son of Jehu, king of Israel, saying, "Come, let us meet face to face." {14:9} King Jehoash of Israel sent a reply to Amaziah, king of Judah, saying, "The thistle in Lebanon sent a message to the cedar in Lebanon: 'Give your daughter to my son in marriage.' But a wild beast passed by and trampled the thistle down. {14:10} You have indeed defeated Edom, and your heart has lifted you up. Take pride in this, but stay at home. Why should you stir up trouble that could lead to your downfall and that of Judah?" {14:11} But Amaziah would not listen. So King Jehoash of Israel went up; he and Amaziah, king of Judah, met face to face at Bethshemesh, which belongs to Judah. {14:12} Judah was defeated by Israel, and they fled, each to their tents. {14:13} King Jehoash of Israel captured Amaziah, the son of Joash, the son of Ahaziah, at Bethshemesh and went to Jerusalem. He broke down the wall of Jerusalem from the Gate of Ephraim to the Corner Gate, a distance of four hundred cubits. {14:14} He took all the gold and silver, all the vessels found in the house of the LORD and in the treasures of the king's palace, and hostages, and returned to Samaria. {14:15} The rest of the acts of Jehoash, all he did, and his strength, how he fought with Amaziah, king of Judah, are they not written in the book of the chronicles of the kings of Israel? {14:16} Jehoash died and was buried with his ancestors in Samaria, and his son Jeroboam reigned in his place. {14:17} Amaziah, the son of Joash, king of Judah, lived fifteen years after the death of Joash, son of Jehoahaz, king of Israel. {14:18} The rest of the acts of Amaziah are they not written in the book of the chronicles of the kings of Judah? {14:19} A conspiracy was formed against him in Jerusalem, and he fled to Lachish; but they sent men after him to Lachish and killed him there. {14:20} They brought him back on horses, and he was buried in Jerusalem with his ancestors in the city of David. {14:21} All the people of Judah took Azariah, who was sixteen years old, and made him king in place of his father Amaziah. {14:22} He built Elath and restored it to Judah after the king rested with his ancestors. {14:23} In the fifteenth year of Amaziah, the son of Joash, king of Judah, Jeroboam, the son of Joash, king of Israel, began to reign in Samaria and reigned for forty-one years. {14:24} He did evil in the sight of the LORD; he did not turn away from the sins of Jeroboam, the son of Nebat, who made Israel sin. {14:25} He restored the borders of Israel from the entrance of Hamath to Sea of the Arabah, according to the word of the LORD God of Israel, which He spoke through His servant Jonah, the son of Amittai, the prophet from Gath-hepher. {14:26} The LORD saw how bitterly Israel was suffering; there was no one left, no one to help them. {14:27} The LORD had not said He would erase the name of Israel from under heaven, but He saved them by the hand of Jeroboam, the son of Joash. {14:28} The rest of the acts of Jeroboam, all he did, and his strength, how he fought, and how he recovered Damascus and Hamath, which belonged to Judah, for Israel, are they not written in the book of the chronicles of the kings of Israel? {14:29} Jeroboam died and was buried with the kings of Israel, and his son Zachariah reigned in his place.

{15:1} In the twenty-seventh year of Jeroboam, king of Israel, Azariah, son of Amaziah, began to reign as king of Judah. {15:2} He was sixteen years old when he started his reign, and he ruled for fifty-two years in Jerusalem. His mother's name was Jecholiah from Jerusalem. {15:3} He did what was right in the sight of the LORD, following the example of his father Amaziah. {15:4} However, the high places were not removed; the people continued to sacrifice and burn incense on those high places. {15:5} The LORD struck the king, so he became a leper (a person with a skin disease) until the day he died and lived in a separate house. His son Jotham was in charge of the palace, judging the people of the land. {15:6} The rest of the acts of Azariah and all he did are recorded in the book of the chronicles of the kings of Judah. {15:7} Azariah died and was buried with his ancestors in the city of David; his son Jotham succeeded him as king. {15:8} In the thirty-eighth year of Azariah, Zachariah, son of Jeroboam, reigned over Israel in Samaria for six months. {15:9} He did evil in the sight of the LORD, just like his fathers had done; he did not turn away from the sins of Jeroboam, son of Nebat, who led Israel to sin. {15:10} Shallum, son of Jabesh, conspired against him, struck him down before the people, killed him, and took his place as king. {15:11} The rest of the acts of Zachariah are written in the book of the chronicles of the kings of Israel. {15:12} This was the word of the LORD that He spoke to Jehu, saying, "Your sons will sit on the throne of Israel to the fourth generation." And that came true. {15:13} Shallum, son of Jabesh, began to reign in the thirty-ninth year of Uzziah, king of Judah; he reigned for a full month in Samaria. {15:14} Menahem, son of Gadi, came up from Tirzah, attacked Shallum in Samaria, killed him, and took his place as king. {15:15} The rest of the acts of Shallum and his conspiracy are recorded in the book of the chronicles of the kings of Israel. {15:16} Menahem attacked Tiphsah and all the people there, including the territories around it, because they did not open their gates to him. He devastated it and ripped open all the pregnant women. {15:17} In the thirty-ninth year of Azariah, Menahem, son of Gadi, began to reign over Israel and ruled for ten years in Samaria. {15:18} He did what was evil in the sight of the LORD and never turned away from the sins of Jeroboam, son of Nebat, who made Israel sin. {15:19} King Pul of Assyria came against the land, and Menahem paid him a thousand talents of silver to ensure his support and keep his kingdom secure. {15:20} Menahem collected this money from Israel, demanding fifty shekels of silver from each wealthy man to give to the king of Assyria. So, the king of Assyria withdrew and did not stay in the land. {15:21} The rest of the acts of Menahem and all he did are written in the book of the chronicles of the kings of Israel. {15:22} Menahem died and was buried with his ancestors, and his son Pekahiah succeeded him as king. {15:23} In the fiftieth year of Azariah, king of Judah, Pekahiah, son of Menahem, began to reign over Israel in Samaria and ruled for two years. {15:24} He did what was evil in the sight of the LORD, never turning away from the sins of Jeroboam, son of Nebat, who made Israel sin. {15:25} Pekah, son of Remaliah, a captain of his, conspired against him, struck him down in Samaria, in the palace, with Argob and Arieh, and with him were fifty men from Gilead; he killed him and took his place as king. {15:26} The rest of the acts of Pekahiah and all he did are written in the book of the chronicles of the kings of Israel. {15:27} In the fifty-second year of Azariah, Pekah, son of Remaliah, began to reign over Israel in Samaria and ruled for twenty years. {15:28} He did what was evil in the sight of the LORD, never turning away from the sins of Jeroboam, son of Nebat, who made Israel sin. {15:29} During Pekah's reign, Tiglath-pileser, king of Assyria, came and captured Ijon, Abel-beth-maachah, Janoah, Kedesh, Hazor, Gilead, and Galilee, along with all the land of Naphtali, and carried the people away to Assyria. {15:30} Hoshea, son of Elah, conspired against Pekah, struck him down, killed him, and took his place as king in the twentieth year of Jotham, son of Uzziah. {15:31} The rest of the acts of Pekah and all he did are written in the book of the chronicles of the kings of Israel. {15:32} In the second year of Pekah, son of Remaliah, king of Israel, Jotham, son of Uzziah, began to reign as king of Judah. {15:33} He was twenty-five years old when he began to reign, and he ruled for sixteen years in Jerusalem. His mother's name was Jerusha, daughter of Zadok. {15:34} He did what was right in the sight of the LORD, following the example of his father Uzziah. {15:35} However, the high places were not removed; the people still sacrificed and burned incense on those high places. He built the upper gate of the house of the LORD. {15:36} The rest of the acts of Jotham and all he did are written in the book of the chronicles of the kings of Judah. {15:37} In those days, the LORD began to send against Judah Rezin, king of Syria, and Pekah, son of Remaliah. {15:38} Jotham died and was buried with his ancestors in the city of David; his son Ahaz succeeded him as king.

{16:1} In the seventeenth year of Pekah, son of Remaliah, Ahaz, son of Jotham, king of Judah, began to reign. {16:2} Ahaz was twenty years old when he began his reign, and he ruled for sixteen years in Jerusalem. He did not do what was right in the sight of the LORD, his God, like his ancestor David. {16:3} Instead, he followed the ways of the kings of Israel and even made his son pass through the fire (a practice involving child sacrifice), imitating the detestable practices of the nations the LORD had driven out before the Israelites. {16:4} He sacrificed and burned incense on the high places, on the hills, and under every green tree. {16:5} Then Rezin, king of Syria, and Pekah, son of Remaliah, king of Israel, came up to Jerusalem to wage war; they besieged Ahaz but could not conquer him. {16:6} At that time, Rezin, king of Syria, recovered Elath for Syria, driving the Jews out of Elath; the Syrians settled there to this day. {16:7} Ahaz sent messengers to Tiglath-pileser, king of Assyria, saying, "I am your servant and your son; come up and save me from the hand of the king of Syria and the king of Israel, who are rising against me." {16:8} Ahaz took the silver and gold found in the house of the LORD and in the treasures of the king's palace and sent it as a gift to the king of Assyria. {16:9} The king of Assyria listened to him; he went up against Damascus, captured it, and carried the people away to Kir, killing Rezin. {16:10} King Ahaz went to Damascus to meet Tiglath-pileser, king of Assyria, and saw an altar there. He sent to Urijah the priest the design of the altar and the pattern of its construction. {16:11} Urijah the priest built an altar according to all that King Ahaz had sent from Damascus, so it was ready before King Ahaz returned from Damascus. {16:12} When the king returned from Damascus, he saw the altar; he approached it and offered sacrifices on it. {16:13} He burned his burnt offering and grain offering, poured out his drink offering, and sprinkled the blood of his peace offerings on the altar. {16:14} He brought the bronze altar that was before the LORD from the front of the house, between the altar and the house of the LORD, and placed it on the north side of the altar. {16:15} King Ahaz commanded Urijah the priest, saying, "On the great altar, burn the morning burnt offering, the evening grain offering, the king's burnt offering, the grain offering of all the people of the land, and their drink offerings; sprinkle all the blood from the burnt offerings and sacrifices on it. The bronze altar will be for me to consult." {16:16} Urijah the priest did everything King Ahaz commanded. {16:17} King Ahaz cut off the borders of the bases, removed the basin from them, took down the sea from the bronze oxen that were under it, and placed it on a stone pavement. {16:18} He turned away the covered area for the Sabbath that had been built in the house and the king's entry from the house of the LORD because of the king of Assyria.

{16:19} The rest of the acts of Ahaz are written in the book of the chronicles of the kings of Judah. {16:20} Ahaz died and was buried with his ancestors in the city of David, and his son Hezekiah succeeded him as king.

{17:1} In the twelfth year of Ahaz, king of Judah, Hoshea, son of Elah, began to reign in Samaria over Israel for nine years. {17:2} He did what was evil in the sight of the LORD, but not as the kings of Israel who ruled before him. {17:3} Shalmaneser, king of Assyria, came against him; and Hoshea became his servant and gave him gifts. {17:4} The king of Assyria discovered that Hoshea had conspired against him, for he had sent messengers to So, king of Egypt, and had not brought gifts to the king of Assyria as he had done year after year. Therefore, the king of Assyria shut him up and imprisoned him. {17:5} Then the king of Assyria invaded the whole land, went up to Samaria, and besieged it for three years. {17:6} In the ninth year of Hoshea, the king of Assyria took Samaria and carried Israel away to Assyria, placing them in Halah, Habor by the river of Gozan, and in the cities of the Medes. {17:7} This happened because the people of Israel had sinned against the LORD their God, who had brought them up from the land of Egypt, out from under the hand of Pharaoh, king of Egypt, and had feared other gods. {17:8} They walked in the statutes of the nations whom the LORD had cast out before the children of Israel and of the kings of Israel that they had made. {17:9} The children of Israel did secretly things that were not right against the LORD their God; they built high places in all their cities, from the watchtower to the fortified city. {17:10} They set up images and groves (sacred trees) on every high hill and under every green tree. {17:11} There they burned incense in all the high places, just like the nations whom the LORD had carried away before them, and did wicked things to provoke the LORD to anger. {17:12} They served idols, of which the LORD had said to them, "You shall not do this." {17:13} Yet the LORD testified against Israel and Judah by all the prophets and seers, saying, "Turn from your evil ways and keep my commandments and statutes according to all the law which I commanded your fathers and sent to you by my servants the prophets." {17:14} But they would not listen, and they hardened their necks like their fathers who did not believe in the LORD their God. {17:15} They rejected his statutes, his covenant that he made with their fathers, and his testimonies which he testified against them; they followed emptiness, became empty themselves, and went after the nations around them, concerning whom the LORD had charged them not to do like them. {17:16} They left all the commandments of the LORD their God, made molten images, two calves, made a grove, and worshipped all the host of heaven and served Baal. {17:17} They caused their sons and daughters to pass through the fire (a practice involving child sacrifice), used divination and enchantments, and sold themselves to do evil in the sight of the LORD to provoke him to anger. {17:18} Therefore, the LORD was very angry with Israel and removed them from his sight; none remained but the tribe of Judah only. {17:19} Judah did not keep the commandments of the LORD their God but walked in the statutes of Israel which they made. {17:20} The LORD rejected all the descendants of Israel, afflicted them, and delivered them into the hands of spoilers until he had cast them out of his sight. {17:21} For he tore Israel from the house of David, and they made Jeroboam, son of Nebat, king. Jeroboam drove Israel away from following the LORD and made them commit a great sin. {17:22} The children of Israel walked in all the sins of Jeroboam that he did; they did not depart from them. {17:23} Until the LORD removed Israel from his sight, as he had said through all his servants the prophets. So Israel was carried away from their own land to Assyria to this day. {17:24} The king of Assyria brought people from Babylon, Cuthah, Ava, Hamath, and Sepharvaim, and placed them in the cities of Samaria instead of the children of Israel. They took possession of Samaria and dwelt in its cities. {17:25} It was so that at the beginning of their dwelling there, they did not fear the LORD; therefore, the LORD sent lions among them, which killed some of them. {17:26} So they spoke to the king of Assyria, saying, "The nations whom you have removed and placed in the cities of Samaria do not know the manner of the God of the land; therefore, he has sent lions among them, and they are killing them because they do not know the manner of the God of the land." {17:27} Then the king of Assyria commanded, "Carry one of the priests you brought from there, and let him go and dwell there and teach them the manner of the God of the land." {17:28} So one of the priests whom they had carried away from Samaria came and dwelt in Bethel and taught them how they should fear the LORD. {17:29} However, every nation made gods of their own and put them in the houses of the high places which the Samaritans had made, every nation in their cities where they dwelt. {17:30} The men of Babylon made Succothbenoth, the men of Cuth made Nergal, the men of Hamath made Ashima, {17:31} and the Avites made Nibhaz and Tartak; the Sepharvites burned their children in fire to Adrammelech and Anammelech, the gods of Sepharvaim. {17:32} So they feared the LORD and made from among the lowest of them priests of the high places, who sacrificed for them in the houses of the high places. {17:33} They feared the LORD and served their own gods, following the customs of the nations from which they had been carried away. {17:34} To this day, they continue in their former practices; they do not fear the LORD, nor do they follow his statutes or ordinances or the law and commandment which the LORD commanded the children of Jacob, whom he named Israel. {17:35} The LORD had made a covenant with them, charging them, "You shall not fear other gods, nor bow yourselves to them, nor serve them, nor sacrifice to them. {17:36} But the LORD, who brought you up out of the land of Egypt with great power and an outstretched arm, him you shall fear, him you shall worship, and to him you shall make sacrifices. {17:37} And the statutes, ordinances, law, and commandment which he wrote for you shall observe to do forever; you shall not fear other gods. {17:38} And the covenant that I have made with you shall not be forgotten, nor shall you fear other gods. {17:39} But the LORD your God you shall fear, and he shall deliver you out of the hand of all your enemies. {17:40} However, they did not listen but continued in their former practices. {17:41} So these nations feared the LORD and served their graven images, both their children and their children's children; as their fathers did, so they do to this day.

{18:1} In the third year of Hoshea, son of Elah, king of Israel, Hezekiah, the son of Ahaz, became king of Judah. {18:2} He was twenty-five years old when he started to reign, and he ruled for twenty-nine years in Jerusalem. His mother's name was Abi, daughter of Zachariah. {18:3} He did what was right in the eyes of the Lord, just as David, his ancestor, had done. {18:4} He removed the high places (sites of unauthorized worship), smashed the sacred stones, cut down the Asherah poles (symbols of a pagan goddess), and broke into pieces the bronze serpent that Moses had made, for the Israelites had been burning incense to it. He called it Nehushtan (a mere piece of bronze). {18:5} He trusted in the Lord, the God of Israel, so that there was no one like him among all the kings of Judah, either before or after him. {18:6} He remained faithful to the Lord and did not turn from following Him, keeping all the commands the Lord had given to Moses. {18:7} And the Lord was with him; he was successful in everything he undertook. He rebelled against the king of Assyria and did not serve him. {18:8} He defeated the Philistines as far as Gaza and its surrounding territories, from watchtower to fortified city. {18:9} In the fourth year of King Hezekiah, which was the seventh year of Hoshea son of Elah, king of Israel, Shalmaneser, king of Assyria, marched against Samaria and besieged it. {18:10} After three years, Samaria was captured. This happened in the sixth year of Hezekiah, which was the ninth year of Hoshea, king of Israel. {18:11} The king of Assyria deported the Israelites to Assyria and settled them in Halah, on the Habor River in Gozan, and in the cities of the Medes. {18:12} This happened because they did not obey the voice of the Lord their God and violated His covenant—all that Moses, the servant of the Lord, had commanded. They neither listened to Him nor obeyed. {18:13} In the fourteenth year of King Hezekiah's reign, Sennacherib, king of Assyria, attacked all the fortified cities of Judah and captured them. {18:14} So Hezekiah, king of Judah, sent this message to the king of Assyria at Lachish: "I have done wrong; withdraw from me, and I will pay whatever you demand." The king of Assyria required Hezekiah to pay three hundred talents of silver and thirty talents of gold. {18:15} Hezekiah gave him all the silver that was found in the temple of the Lord and in the treasuries of the royal palace. {18:16} At that time, Hezekiah stripped the gold from the doors of the temple of the Lord and the doorposts he had overlaid with gold and gave it to the king of Assyria. {18:17} The king of Assyria sent his commanding officers—Tartan, Rabsaris, and Rabshakeh—from

Lachish to King Hezekiah in Jerusalem with a large army. They came up and stopped at the aqueduct of the Upper Pool, on the road to the Washerman's Field. {18:18} They called for the king, and Eliakim son of Hilkiah, the palace administrator, Shebna the scribe, and Joah son of Asaph, the recorder, went out to meet them. {18:19} Rabshakeh said to them, "Tell Hezekiah: 'This is what the great king, the king of Assyria, says: What is this confidence that you rely on? {18:20} You say (but they are just empty words), 'I have the strategy and strength for war.' Now, who are you depending on that you rebel against me? {18:21} Look, you are relying on Egypt, that splintered reed of a staff, which pierces the hand of anyone who leans on it. Such is Pharaoh, king of Egypt, to all who depend on him. {18:22} But if you say to me, 'We trust in the Lord our God,' isn't He the one whose high places and altars Hezekiah has removed, saying to Judah and Jerusalem, 'You must worship before this altar in Jerusalem'? {18:23} Come now, make a bargain with my master, the king of Assyria: I'll give you two thousand horses—if you can put riders on them! {18:24} How can you repulse one officer of the least of my master's officials, even though you are relying on Egypt for chariots and horsemen? {18:25} Furthermore, have I come to attack and destroy this place without the Lord's approval? The Lord Himself told me to march against this land and destroy it.'" {18:26} Then Eliakim son of Hilkiah, and Shebna, and Joah said to Rabshakeh, "Please speak to your servants in Aramaic, since we understand it. Don't speak to us in Hebrew in the hearing of the people on the wall." {18:27} But Rabshakeh replied, "Has my master sent me only to your master and to you to say these things, and not to the people sitting on the wall—who, like you, will have to eat their own excrement and drink their own urine?" {18:28} Then Rabshakeh stood and called out in a loud voice in Hebrew: "Hear the word of the great king, the king of Assyria! {18:29} This is what the king says: Do not let Hezekiah deceive you. He cannot deliver you from my hand! {18:30} Don't let Hezekiah persuade you to trust in the Lord by saying, 'The Lord will surely deliver us; this city will not be handed over to the king of Assyria.' {18:31} Do not listen to Hezekiah. This is what the king of Assyria says: 'Make peace with me and come out to me. Then each of you will eat from your own vine and fig tree and drink water from your own cistern, {18:32} until I come and take you to a land like your own—a land of grain and new wine, a land of bread and vineyards, a land of olive trees and honey. Choose life and not death! Don't listen to Hezekiah, for he is misleading you when he says, "The Lord will deliver us." {18:33} Has the god of any nation ever delivered his land from the hand of the king of Assyria? {18:34} Where are the gods of Hamath and Arpad? Where are the gods of Sepharvaim, Hena, and Ivvah? Have they rescued Samaria from my hand? {18:35} Who among all the gods of these lands have delivered their country from my hand, that the Lord should deliver Jerusalem from my hand?'" {18:36} But the people remained silent and said nothing in reply, because the king had commanded, "Do not answer him." {18:37} Then Eliakim son of Hilkiah, the palace administrator, Shebna the scribe, and Joah son of Asaph, the recorder, went to Hezekiah with their clothes torn and told him what Rabshakeh had said.

{19:1} When King Hezekiah heard this, he tore his clothes, put on sackcloth, and went into the house of the LORD. {19:2} He sent Eliakim, the palace administrator, Shebna the scribe, and the elders of the priests, all dressed in sackcloth, to Isaiah the prophet, the son of Amoz. {19:3} They told him, "This is what Hezekiah says: Today is a day of trouble, rebuke, and blasphemy, for the children are at the point of birth, but there is no strength to deliver them." {19:4} Perhaps the LORD your God will hear all the words of Rabshakeh, whom the king of Assyria has sent to insult the living God. He may rebuke the words that the LORD your God has heard; therefore, lift up your prayer for the remnant that is left." {19:5} So the servants of King Hezekiah went to Isaiah. {19:6} Isaiah said to them, "Tell your master this: 'The LORD says: Do not be afraid of the words you have heard from the king of Assyria's servants who have insulted me. {19:7} I will send a spirit upon him, and he will hear a rumor and return to his own land, and I will cause him to fall by the sword in his own land.'" {19:8} Rabshakeh returned and found the king of Assyria fighting against Libnah, for he had heard that the king had left Lachish. {19:9} When he heard that Tirhakah, king of Ethiopia, had come out to fight against him, he sent messengers again to Hezekiah, saying, {19:10} "Say to Hezekiah king of Judah: Don't let your God, whom you trust, deceive you by saying, 'Jerusalem will not be handed over to the king of Assyria.' {19:11} You have heard what the kings of Assyria have done to all the countries, destroying them completely. Will you be delivered? {19:12} Have the gods of the nations delivered those that my ancestors have destroyed, like Gozan, Haran, Rezeph, and the people of Eden in Telassar? {19:13} Where is the king of Hamath, the king of Arpad, the king of the city of Sepharvaim, Hena, and Ivah?" {19:14} Hezekiah received the letter from the messengers and read it. Then he went up to the house of the LORD and spread it out before the LORD. {19:15} Hezekiah prayed before the LORD, saying, "O LORD God of Israel, you who are enthroned between the cherubim, you alone are God over all the kingdoms of the earth. You made heaven and earth. {19:16} LORD, bend down your ear and hear. Open your eyes, LORD, and see. Hear the words of Sennacherib, who has sent them to insult the living God. {19:17} Truly, LORD, the kings of Assyria have destroyed the nations and their lands, {19:18} and have thrown their gods into the fire, for they were not gods but the work of men's hands, made of wood and stone. That is why they have destroyed them. {19:19} Now, O LORD our God, I ask you, save us from his hand, so that all the kingdoms of the earth may know that you alone, LORD, are God." {19:20} Then Isaiah son of Amoz sent a message to Hezekiah: "This is what the LORD, the God of Israel, says: I have heard your prayer concerning Sennacherib king of Assyria. {19:21} This is the word the LORD has spoken against him: The virgin daughter of Zion despises you and mocks you; the daughter of Jerusalem shakes her head at you. {19:22} Whom have you insulted and blasphemed? Against whom have you raised your voice and lifted your eyes in pride? Against the Holy One of Israel! {19:23} By your messengers, you have insulted the Lord. You have said, 'With my many chariots, I have ascended the heights of the mountains, the slopes of Lebanon; I will cut down its tallest cedars, the best of its junipers; I will go to its most distant heights, its thickest forests. {19:24} I have dug wells and drunk foreign waters, and with the soles of my feet, I have dried up all the streams of Egypt.' {19:25} Have you not heard? Long ago I ordained it. In days of old, I planned it; now I have brought it to pass that you have turned fortified cities into piles of stone. {19:26} Their people, drained of power, are dismayed and put to shame; they are like grass in the field, like tender green shoots, like grass on the rooftops that withers before it grows up. {19:27} But I know where you are and when you come and go and how you rage against me. {19:28} Because you rage against me and your insolence has reached my ears, I will put my hook in your nose and my bit in your mouth, and I will make you return by the way you came." {19:29} This will be the sign for you: This year you will eat what grows by itself, and the next year what springs up from that. But in the third year, sow and reap, plant vineyards and eat their fruit. {19:30} The remnant that has escaped of the house of Judah will again take root downward and bear fruit upward. {19:31} For out of Jerusalem will come a remnant, and out of Mount Zion a band of survivors. The zeal of the LORD Almighty will accomplish this. {19:32} Therefore this is what the LORD says concerning the king of Assyria: He will not enter this city or shoot an arrow here; he will not come before it with shield or build a siege ramp against it. {19:33} By the way that he came, he will return; he will not enter this city, declares the LORD. {19:34} I will defend this city and save it for my sake and for the sake of my servant David." {19:35} That night the angel of the LORD went out and put to death a hundred eighty-five thousand in the Assyrian camp. When the people got up the next morning, there were all the dead bodies! {19:36} So Sennacherib king of Assyria broke camp and withdrew. He returned to Nineveh and stayed there. {19:37} One day, while he was worshipping in the temple of his god Nisroch, his sons Adrammelech and Sharezer killed him with the sword, and they escaped to the land of Ararat. Esarhaddon his son succeeded him as king.

{20:1} At that time, Hezekiah was gravely ill. The prophet Isaiah son of Amoz came to him and said, "This is what the LORD says: Set your house in order, for you are going to die; you will not recover." {20:2} Hezekiah turned his face to the wall and prayed to the LORD, saying, {20:3} "Please, LORD, remember how I have walked before you in truth and with a sincere heart, and have done what is good in your sight." Hezekiah wept bitterly. {20:4} Before Isaiah had left the middle court, the word of the LORD came to him, saying, {20:5} "Go back and tell Hezekiah, the leader of my people, 'This is what the LORD, the God of your ancestor David, says: I have heard your prayer and seen your tears. I will heal you. On the third day, you will go up to the house of the LORD. {20:6} I will add fifteen years to your life, and I will deliver you and this city from the hand of the king of Assyria. I will defend this city for my own sake and for the sake of my servant David.'" {20:7} Isaiah said, "Take a lump of figs." They took the figs and applied them to the boil, and Hezekiah recovered. {20:8} Hezekiah asked Isaiah, "What will be the sign that the LORD will heal me and that I will go up to the house of the LORD on the third day?" {20:9} Isaiah replied, "This is the sign from the LORD that he will do what he has promised: Should the shadow go forward ten degrees or back ten degrees?" {20:10} Hezekiah answered, "It's an easy thing for the shadow to go down ten degrees; rather, let it go back ten degrees." {20:11} Then Isaiah the prophet cried out to the LORD, and the LORD made the shadow go back ten degrees on the dial of Ahaz. {20:12} At that time, Berodachbaladan, son of Baladan, king of Babylon, sent letters and a gift to Hezekiah because he had heard that Hezekiah was sick. {20:13} Hezekiah welcomed them and showed them everything in his treasure house—his silver, gold, spices, fine oil, and all his armory; there was nothing in his palace or in all his kingdom that Hezekiah did not show them. {20:14} Then Isaiah the prophet went to King Hezekiah and asked him, "What did these men say, and where did they come from?" Hezekiah replied, "They came from a distant country, from Babylon." {20:15} Isaiah asked, "What did they see in your house?" Hezekiah answered, "They saw everything in my house; there is nothing among my treasures that I did not show them." {20:16} Isaiah then said to Hezekiah, "Hear the word of the LORD. {20:17} The time will come when everything in your palace and all your ancestors have stored up will be carried off to Babylon; nothing will be left," says the LORD. {20:18} "And some of your descendants, your own flesh and blood, will be taken away and will become eunuchs in the palace of the king of Babylon." {20:19} Hezekiah said to Isaiah, "The word of the LORD you have spoken is good." He thought, "Will there not be peace and security in my lifetime?" {20:20} The rest of the acts of Hezekiah, including his might and how he made a pool and a tunnel to bring water into the city, are they not written in the book of the chronicles of the kings of Judah? {20:21} Hezekiah rested with his ancestors, and his son Manasseh succeeded him as king.

{21:1} Manasseh was twelve years old when he began to reign, and he ruled for fifty-five years in Jerusalem. His mother's name was Hephzibah. {21:2} He did what was evil in the sight of the LORD, following the detestable practices of the nations that the LORD had driven out before the Israelites. {21:3} He rebuilt the high places that his father Hezekiah had destroyed; he set up altars for Baal, made an Asherah pole (a type of idol), and worshiped all the starry hosts, serving them. {21:4} He built altars in the house of the LORD, of which the LORD had said, "In Jerusalem I will put my name." {21:5} He built altars for all the starry hosts in both courts of the house of the LORD. {21:6} He sacrificed his son in the fire, practiced divination, engaged in witchcraft, and consulted mediums and spiritists. He committed many terrible sins in the sight of the LORD, provoking him to anger. {21:7} He put a carved idol of the Asherah pole he had made in the house of the LORD, of which the LORD had said to David and his son Solomon, "In this house and in Jerusalem, which I have chosen from all the tribes of Israel, I will put my name forever. {21:8} I will never again remove the feet of Israel from the land I gave their ancestors, as long as they are careful to do everything I commanded them, and to observe the entire Law that my servant Moses gave them." {21:9} But they did not listen, and Manasseh led them to do even more evil than the nations the LORD had destroyed before the Israelites. {21:10} The LORD spoke through his servants the prophets, saying, {21:11} "Because Manasseh king of Judah has committed these detestable acts and has done wickedly more than the Amorites who were before him, and has led Judah into sin with his idols, {21:12} therefore this is what the LORD, the God of Israel, says: I am bringing such disaster on Jerusalem and Judah that the ears of everyone who hears of it will tingle. {21:13} I will measure Jerusalem by the same standard used for Samaria and by the same plumb line used for the house of Ahab, and I will wipe out Jerusalem as one wipes a dish, wiping it and turning it upside down. {21:14} I will forsake the remnant of my inheritance and give them into the hands of their enemies; they will become plunder and spoil to all their enemies, {21:15} because they have done evil in my sight and have provoked me to anger since the day their ancestors came out of Egypt until now." {21:16} Moreover, Manasseh shed so much innocent blood that he filled Jerusalem from one end to another, besides the sin he caused Judah to commit, doing what was evil in the sight of the LORD. {21:17} The rest of the acts of Manasseh, including everything he did and the sins he committed, are they not written in the book of the chronicles of the kings of Judah? {21:18} Manasseh rested with his ancestors and was buried in the garden of his own house, in the garden of Uzza; his son Amon succeeded him as king. {21:19} Amon was twenty-two years old when he became king, and he ruled for two years in Jerusalem. His mother's name was Meshullemeth, the daughter of Haruz of Jotbah. {21:20} He did what was evil in the sight of the LORD, just as his father Manasseh had done. {21:21} He followed all the ways of his father, serving the idols his father served and worshiping them. {21:22} He forsook the LORD, the God of his ancestors, and did not walk in the way of the LORD. {21:23} His servants conspired against him and killed the king in his own palace. {21:24} Then the people of the land killed all the conspirators against King Amon, and they made his son Josiah king in his place. {21:25} The rest of the acts of Amon are they not written in the book of the chronicles of the kings of Judah? {21:26} He was buried in his tomb in the garden of Uzza, and his son Josiah succeeded him as king.

{22:1} Josiah was eight years old when he began to reign, and he ruled for thirty-one years in Jerusalem. His mother's name was Jedidah, the daughter of Adaiah of Boscath. {22:2} He did what was right in the sight of the LORD, walking in all the ways of his ancestor David, not turning aside to the right or to the left. {22:3} In the eighteenth year of King Josiah, he sent Shaphan son of Azaliah, the son of Meshullam, the scribe, to the house of the LORD, saying, {22:4} "Go up to Hilkiah the high priest and have him count the silver that has been brought into the house of the LORD, which the doorkeepers have collected from the people. {22:5} Let them give it to the men appointed to supervise the work on the house of the LORD, and let them use it to repair the damages to the house, {22:6} to carpenters, builders, and masons, and to buy timber and dressed stone to repair the house." {22:7} However, they did not require an accounting from those to whom they gave the money, because they acted faithfully. {22:8} Hilkiah the high priest said to Shaphan the scribe, "I have found the Book of the Law in the house of the LORD." He gave it to Shaphan, who read it. {22:9} Shaphan the scribe went to the king and reported to him: "Your officials have paid out the money that was found in the house and have entrusted it to the workers and supervisors at the house of the LORD." {22:10} Then Shaphan the scribe informed the king, "Hilkiah the priest has given me a book." And Shaphan read it before the king. {22:11} When the king heard the words of the Book of the Law, he tore his robes. {22:12} He gave these orders to Hilkiah the priest, Ahikam son of Shaphan, Achbor son of Micaiah, Shaphan the scribe, and Asaiah the king's attendant: {22:13} "Go and inquire of the LORD for me and for the people and for all Judah about what is written in this book that has been found. Great is the LORD's anger that burns against us because those who have gone before us have not obeyed the words of this book; they have not acted in accordance with all that is written there concerning us." {22:14} Hilkiah the priest, Ahikam, Achbor, Shaphan, and Asaiah went to speak to the prophetess Huldah, who was the wife of Shallum son of Tikvah, the son of Harhas, the keeper of the wardrobe. (She lived in Jerusalem in the Second Quarter.) They said to her, {22:15} "This is what the LORD, the God of Israel, says: Tell the man who sent you to me, {22:16} 'This is what the LORD says: I am going to bring disaster on this place and its people, all the words of the book the king of Judah has read. {22:17} Because they have forsaken me and burned incense to other gods and provoked me to anger by all the idols their hands have made, my anger will burn against this place and will not be quenched.' {22:18} Tell the king of Judah who sent you to inquire of the LORD: 'This is what the LORD, the God of Israel, says concerning the words you heard: {22:19} Because your heart was responsive and you humbled yourself before the LORD when you heard what I had spoken against this place and its people, that they would become a curse and be laid waste, and because you tore your robes and wept in my presence, I have heard you,' declares the

LORD. {22:20} Therefore I will gather you to your ancestors, and you will be buried in peace. Your eyes will not see all the disaster I am going to bring on this place.'" So they took her answer back to the king.

{23:1} The king sent for all the elders of Judah and Jerusalem to gather around him. {23:2} He went up to the house of the LORD, accompanied by all the men of Judah, the inhabitants of Jerusalem, the priests, the prophets, and all the people, both small and great. He read to them all the words of the book of the covenant that had been found in the house of the LORD. {23:3} The king stood by a pillar and made a covenant before the LORD to follow Him, keeping His commandments, testimonies, and statutes with all his heart and soul, agreeing to carry out the words of the covenant written in the book. All the people pledged to this covenant. {23:4} The king commanded Hilkiah the high priest, the priests of the second order, and the keepers of the door to bring out of the temple of the LORD all the vessels made for Baal, the grove, and all the host of heaven. He burned them outside Jerusalem in the fields of Kidron and carried their ashes to Bethel. {23:5} He removed the idolatrous priests whom the kings of Judah had appointed to burn incense in the high places throughout Judah and around Jerusalem, those who burned incense to Baal, the sun, the moon, the planets, and all the host of heaven. {23:6} He brought out the grove from the house of the LORD to the brook Kidron, burned it there, ground it to powder, and scattered its ashes on the graves of the people. {23:7} He tore down the houses of the sodomites that were near the house of the LORD, where the women wove hangings for the grove. {23:8} He brought all the priests from the cities of Judah and desecrated the high places where they had burned incense, from Geba to Beersheba, tearing down the high places by the gate of Joshua, the governor of the city, which were on the left side as one entered the city. {23:9} However, the priests of the high places did not come up to the altar of the LORD in Jerusalem, but they ate unleavened bread among their fellow priests. {23:10} He desecrated Topheth, in the valley of the children of Hinnom, so that no one could make their son or daughter pass through the fire to Molech. {23:11} He removed the horses that the kings of Judah had given to the sun, by the entrance of the house of the LORD, near the chamber of Nathanmelech the chamberlain in the suburbs, and burned the chariots dedicated to the sun. {23:12} The altars on the roof of Ahaz's upper chamber, which the kings of Judah had made, and the altars Manasseh had made in the two courts of the house of the LORD, he smashed and cast their dust into the brook Kidron. {23:13} The high places that were before Jerusalem, on the right side of the Mount of Corruption, which King Solomon had built for Ashtoreth, the abomination of the Sidonians, and for Chemosh, the abomination of the Moabites, and for Milcom, the abomination of the Ammonites, he desecrated. {23:14} He smashed the images, cut down the groves, and filled their places with human bones. {23:15} He also broke down the altar at Bethel, and the high place Jeroboam son of Nebat had made, which caused Israel to sin. He burned the high place, crushed it to powder, and burned the grove. {23:16} As Josiah turned around, he noticed the tombs there on the mountain and sent for the bones to be taken out of the tombs. He burned them on the altar, polluting it, fulfilling the word of the LORD proclaimed by the man of God. {23:17} He asked, "What is that monument I see?" The men of the city told him, "It is the tomb of the man of God who came from Judah and proclaimed the things you have done against the altar at Bethel." {23:18} He said, "Leave it alone; don't move his bones." So they let his bones be, along with the bones of the prophet from Samaria. {23:19} Josiah removed all the houses of the high places in the cities of Samaria, which the kings of Israel had made to provoke the LORD to anger, and treated them according to all he had done in Bethel. {23:20} He killed all the priests of the high places who were on the altars, burned human bones on them, and returned to Jerusalem. {23:21} The king commanded all the people, saying, "Celebrate the Passover to the LORD your God, as it is written in the book of this covenant." {23:22} No Passover had been held like this since the days of the judges who ruled Israel, nor throughout all the days of the kings of Israel or the kings of Judah. {23:23} But in the eighteenth year of King Josiah, this Passover was celebrated to the LORD in Jerusalem. {23:24} Josiah also removed the workers with familiar spirits, the wizards, the images, the idols, and all the abominations found in the land of Judah and Jerusalem, to fulfill the words of the law found in the book that Hilkiah the priest discovered in the house of the LORD. {23:25} There had been no king like him before, who turned to the LORD with all his heart, soul, and might, following all the law of Moses; nor did any arise after him like him. {23:26} Yet the LORD did not turn away from the fierceness of His great wrath, which had been kindled against Judah because of all the provocations that Manasseh had caused. {23:27} The LORD said, "I will remove Judah from my sight, as I have removed Israel, and I will cast off this city Jerusalem, which I have chosen, and the house of which I said, 'My name shall be there.'" {23:28} Now the rest of the acts of Josiah and all he did, are they not written in the book of the chronicles of the kings of Judah? {23:29} In his days, Pharaoh Nechoh king of Egypt went up against the king of Assyria at the Euphrates River. King Josiah went to confront him, but he was killed at Megiddo when he encountered him. {23:30} His servants carried him dead in a chariot from Megiddo to Jerusalem and buried him in his own tomb. The people of the land took Jehoahaz, the son of Josiah, anointed him, and made him king in his father's place. {23:31} Jehoahaz was twenty-three years old when he began to reign, and he ruled for three months in Jerusalem. His mother's name was Hamutal, the daughter of Jeremiah of Libnah. {23:32} He did what was evil in the sight of the LORD, just like his ancestors. {23:33} Pharaoh Nechoh imprisoned him at Riblah in the land of Hamath, preventing him from ruling in Jerusalem, and imposed a tribute on the land of a hundred talents of silver and a talent of gold. {23:34} Pharaoh Nechoh made Eliakim, the son of Josiah, king in place of his father, changing his name to Jehoiakim, and took Jehoahaz away to Egypt, where he died. {23:35} Jehoiakim gave the silver and gold to Pharaoh, but he taxed the land to raise the money according to Pharaoh's command, collecting silver and gold from the people of the land based on their assessment to give to Pharaoh Nechoh. {23:36} Jehoiakim was twenty-five years old when he began to reign, and he ruled for eleven years in Jerusalem. His mother's name was Zebudah, the daughter of Pedaiah of Rumah. {23:37} He did what was evil in the sight of the LORD, just like his ancestors did.

{24:1} In his days, Nebuchadnezzar king of Babylon invaded, and Jehoiakim became his servant for three years. Then he turned and rebelled against him. {24:2} The LORD sent against him groups of Chaldeans, Syrians, Moabites, and Ammonites, sending them against Judah to destroy it, as the LORD had said through His prophets. {24:3} This happened at the command of the LORD, to remove them from His sight because of the sins of Manasseh, according to all he had done. {24:4} It was also due to the innocent blood he shed, for he filled Jerusalem with innocent blood, which the LORD would not pardon. {24:5} Now the rest of the acts of Jehoiakim and all he did are they not written in the book of the chronicles of the kings of Judah? {24:6} So Jehoiakim died, and his son Jehoiachin became king in his place. {24:7} The king of Egypt did not come out of his land anymore, for the king of Babylon had taken everything that belonged to the king of Egypt, from the river of Egypt to the river Euphrates. {24:8} Jehoiachin was eighteen years old when he began to reign, and he ruled in Jerusalem for three months. His mother's name was Nehushta, the daughter of Elnathan of Jerusalem. {24:9} He did what was evil in the sight of the LORD, according to all that his father had done. {24:10} At that time, the servants of Nebuchadnezzar king of Babylon came against Jerusalem, and the city was besieged. {24:11} Nebuchadnezzar king of Babylon came against the city, and his servants besieged it. {24:12} Jehoiachin, the king of Judah, went out to the king of Babylon, along with his mother, servants, princes, and officers, and the king of Babylon captured him in the eighth year of his reign. {24:13} He carried out all the treasures of the house of the LORD and the treasures of the king's house, and cut in pieces all the gold vessels that Solomon king of Israel had made in the temple of the LORD, as the LORD had said. {24:14} He carried away all Jerusalem, all the princes, and all the mighty warriors, taking ten thousand captives, along with all the craftsmen and smiths. None remained except for the poorest of the land. {24:15} He took Jehoiachin to Babylon, along with the king's mother, wives, officers, and the mighty of the land, all of whom he brought into captivity from Jerusalem to Babylon. {24:16} He also took seven thousand men of valor, a thousand craftsmen and smiths, all who were strong and skilled for war; the king of Babylon brought them captive to Babylon. {24:17} The king of Babylon made Mattaniah, his father's brother, king in his place, changing his name to Zedekiah. {24:18} Zedekiah was twenty-one years old when he began to reign, and he ruled for eleven years in Jerusalem. His mother's name was Hamutal, the daughter of Jeremiah of Libnah. {24:19} He did what was evil in the sight of the LORD, just as Jehoiakim had done. {24:20} Because of the anger of the LORD, this came to pass in Jerusalem and Judah until He had cast them out from His presence; Zedekiah rebelled against the king of Babylon.

{25:1} In the ninth year of Zedekiah's reign, on the tenth month and the tenth day, Nebuchadnezzar king of Babylon and his entire army came against Jerusalem and set up camp around it, building siege works against it. {25:2} The city was under siege until the eleventh year of King Zedekiah. {25:3} On the ninth day of the fourth month, famine struck the city, and there was no food for the people. {25:4} The city was breached, and all the soldiers fled by night through the gate between the two walls near the king's garden (the Chaldeans were surrounding the city), and the king went toward the plain. {25:5} The Chaldean army pursued him and caught up with him in the plains of Jericho; all his soldiers scattered from him. {25:6} They captured the king and brought him to Nebuchadnezzar at Riblah, where he was judged. {25:7} They killed Zedekiah's sons before his eyes, then blinded him and bound him with bronze chains, taking him to Babylon. {25:8} In the fifth month, on the seventh day, in the nineteenth year of King Nebuchadnezzar, Nebuzaradan, the captain of the guard and a servant of the king of Babylon, came to Jerusalem. {25:9} He burned down the house of the LORD, the king's house, all the houses of Jerusalem, and every significant man's house was burned to the ground. {25:10} The entire Chaldean army with the captain of the guard broke down the walls of Jerusalem all around. {25:11} The captain of the guard took the remaining people in the city, the fugitives who had surrendered to the king of Babylon, and the rest of the populace. {25:12} However, he left some of the poor of the land to be vine dressers and farmers. {25:13} The Chaldeans broke the bronze pillars, the bases, and the bronze sea that were in the house of the LORD, taking the bronze to Babylon. {25:14} They also took the pots, shovels, snuffers, spoons, and all the bronze vessels used in ministry. {25:15} They took away the firepans and bowls made of gold and silver. {25:16} The two pillars, the one sea, and the bases that Solomon had made for the house of the LORD were so heavy that their weight was unmeasurable. {25:17} One pillar was eighteen cubits tall, with a bronze capital three cubits high, adorned with decorative work and pomegranates all around, and the second pillar was similar with the same design. {25:18} The captain of the guard took Seraiah the chief priest, Zephaniah the second priest, and the three keepers of the door. {25:19} He also took an officer in charge of the soldiers, five of the king's advisors found in the city, the principal scribe who mustered the people, and sixty others from the land. {25:20} Nebuzaradan, the captain of the guard, took them and brought them to the king of Babylon at Riblah. {25:21} The king of Babylon struck them down and executed them at Riblah in the land of Hamath. Thus, Judah was taken away from its land. {25:22} As for the people remaining in Judah, whom Nebuchadnezzar had left, he appointed Gedaliah, the son of Ahikam, the son of Shaphan, as their governor. {25:23} When all the army commanders and their men heard that the king of Babylon had made Gedaliah governor, they came to Gedaliah at Mizpah, including Ishmael the son of Nethaniah, Johanan the son of Careah, Seraiah the son of Tanhumeth the Netophathite, and Jaazaniah the son of a Maachathite, along with their men. {25:24} Gedaliah assured them and said, "Do not be afraid to serve the Chaldeans. Stay in the land and serve the king of Babylon, and it will go well with you." {25:25} However, in the seventh month, Ishmael the son of Nethaniah, of the royal family, came with ten men and killed Gedaliah, as well as the Jews and Chaldeans who were with him at Mizpah. {25:26} Then all the people, from the least to the greatest, and the army commanders, got up and went to Egypt, fearing the Chaldeans. {25:27} In the thirty-seventh year of the captivity of Jehoiachin king of Judah, in the twelfth month, on the twenty-seventh day, Evilmerodach king of Babylon, in the year he began to reign, lifted up the head of Jehoiachin from prison. {25:28} He spoke kindly to him and set his throne above the thrones of the kings with him in Babylon. {25:29} He changed Jehoiachin's prison garments, and Jehoiachin ate bread continually in the king's presence for the rest of his life. {25:30} His daily allowance was provided by the king, a regular provision for each day throughout his life.

The First Book of Chronicles

{1:1} Adam, Sheth, and Enosh, {1:2} Kenan, Mahalaleel, and Jered, {1:3} Henoch, Methuselah, and Lamech, {1:4} Noah, Shem, Ham, and Japheth. {1:5} The sons of Japheth are Gomer, Magog, Madai, Javan, Tubal, Meshech, and Tiras. {1:6} The sons of Gomer are Ashchenaz, Riphath, and Togarmah. {1:7} The sons of Javan are Elishah, Tarshish, Kittim, and Dodanim. {1:8} The sons of Ham are Cush, Mizraim, Put, and Canaan. {1:9} The sons of Cush are Seba, Havilah, Sabta, Raamah, and Sabtecha. The sons of Raamah are Sheba and Dedan. {1:10} Cush became the father of Nimrod; he was a mighty warrior on the earth. {1:11} Mizraim became the father of Ludim, Anamim, Lehabim, and Naphtuhim, {1:12} and Pathrusim, Casluhim (from whom came the Philistines), and Caphthorim. {1:13} Canaan became the father of Zidon, his firstborn, and Heth, {1:14} the Jebusite, the Amorite, and the Girgashite, {1:15} the Hivite, the Arkite, and the Sinite, {1:16} the Arvadite, the Zemarite, and the Hamathite. {1:17} The sons of Shem are Elam, Asshur, Arphaxad, Lud, Aram, Uz, Hul, Gether, and Meshech. {1:18} Arphaxad became the father of Shelah, and Shelah became the father of Eber. {1:19} Eber had two sons: the name of one was Peleg, because in his days the earth was divided; his brother was named Joktan. {1:20} Joktan became the father of Almodad, Sheleph, Hazarmaveth, and Jerah, {1:21} Hadoram, Uzal, and Diklah, {1:22} Ebal, Abimael, and Sheba, {1:23} Ophir, Havilah, and Jobab. All these were the sons of Joktan. {1:24} Shem, Arphaxad, Shelah, {1:25} Eber, Peleg, Reu, {1:26} Serug, Nahor, Terah, {1:27} Abram, who is also called Abraham. {1:28} The sons of Abraham are Isaac and Ishmael. {1:29} Here are their descendants: the firstborn of Ishmael was Nebaioth; then Kedar, Adbeel, Mibsam, {1:30} Mishma, Dumah, Massa, Hadad, and Tema, {1:31} Jetur, Naphish, and Kedemah. These are the sons of Ishmael. {1:32} Now the sons of Keturah, Abraham's concubine, are Zimran, Jokshan, Medan, Midian, Ishbak, and Shuah. The sons of Jokshan are Sheba and Dedan. {1:33} The sons of Midian are Ephah, Epher, Henoch, Abida, and Eldaah. All these are the sons of Keturah. {1:34} Abraham became the father of Isaac. The sons of Isaac are Esau and Israel. {1:35} The sons of Esau are Eliphaz, Reuel, Jeush, Jaalam, and Korah. {1:36} The sons of Eliphaz are Teman, Omar, Zephi, Gatam, Kenaz, Timna, and Amalek. {1:37} The sons of Reuel are Nahath, Zerah, Shammah, and Mizzah. {1:38} The sons of Seir are Lotan, Shobal, Zibeon, Anah, Dishon, Ezer, and Dishan. {1:39} The sons of Lotan are Hori and Homam; Timna was Lotan's sister. {1:40} The sons of Shobal are Alian, Manahath, Ebal, Shephi, and Onam. The sons of Zibeon are Aiah and Anah. {1:41} The sons of Anah are Dishon. The sons of Dishon are Amram, Eshban, Ithran, and Cheran. {1:42} The sons of Ezer are Bilhan, Zavan, and Jakan. The sons of Dishan are Uz and Aran. {1:43} These are the kings who reigned in the land of Edom before any king ruled over the children of Israel: Bela, the son of Beor; the name of his city was Dinhabah. {1:44} When Bela died, Jobab, the son of Zerah from Bozrah, reigned in his place. {1:45} When Jobab died, Husham from the land of the Temanites reigned in his place. {1:46} When Husham died, Hadad, the son of Bedad, who defeated Midian in the field of Moab, reigned in his place; the name of his city was Avith. {1:47} When Hadad died, Samlah from Masrekah reigned in his place. {1:48} When Samlah died, Shaul from Rehoboth by the river reigned in his place. {1:49} When Shaul died, Baalhanan, the son of Achbor, reigned in his place. {1:50} When Baalhanan died, Hadad reigned in his place; the name of his city was Pai, and his wife's name was Mehetabel, the daughter of Matred, the daughter of Mezahab. {1:51} Hadad also died. The dukes of Edom are: Duke Timnah, Duke Aliah, Duke Jetheth, {1:52} Duke Aholibamah, Duke Elah, Duke Pinon, {1:53} Duke Kenaz, Duke Teman, Duke Mibzar, {1:54} Duke Magdiel, and Duke Iram. These are the dukes of Edom.

{2:1} These are the sons of Israel: Reuben, Simeon, Levi, Judah, Issachar, and Zebulun, {2:2} Dan, Joseph, and Benjamin, Naphtali, Gad, and Asher. {2:3} The sons of Judah are Er, Onan, and Shelah; these three were born to him by the daughter of Shua, the Canaanite woman. Er, the firstborn of Judah, was wicked in the sight of the LORD, so the LORD killed him. {2:4} Tamar, his daughter-in-law, bore him Pharez and Zerah. All the sons of Judah were five. {2:5} The sons of Pharez are Hezron and Hamul. {2:6} The sons of Zerah are Zimri, Ethan, Heman, Calcol, and Dara; there are five of them in total. {2:7} The sons of Carmi are Achar, the troubler of Israel, who committed a sin involving the accursed thing. {2:8} The son of Ethan is Azariah. {2:9} The sons born to Hezron are Jerahmeel, Ram, and Chelubai. {2:10} Ram became the father of Amminadab; Amminadab became the father of Nahshon, the prince of the children of Judah; {2:11} Nahshon became the father of Salma, and Salma became the father of Boaz, {2:12} Boaz became the father of Obed, and Obed became the father of Jesse, {2:13} and Jesse became the father of his firstborn Eliab, Abinadab the second, Shimma the third, {2:14} Nethaneel the fourth, Raddai the fifth, {2:15} Ozem the sixth, and David the seventh. {2:16} His sisters were Zeruiah and Abigail. The sons of Zeruiah are Abishai, Joab, and Asahel, three in total. {2:17} Abigail bore Amasa; the father of Amasa was Jether the Ishmaelite. {2:18} Caleb, the son of Hezron, had children with Azubah, his wife, and with Jerioth; her sons are Jesher, Shobab, and Ardon. {2:19} After Azubah died, Caleb took Ephrath as his wife, and she bore him Hur. {2:20} Hur became the father of Uri, and Uri became the father of Bezaleel. {2:21} Later, Hezron married the daughter of Machir, the father of Gilead; he married her when he was sixty years old, and she bore him Segub. {2:22} Segub became the father of Jair, who had twenty-three cities in the land of Gilead. {2:23} He took Geshur and Aram, along with the towns of Jair, and also Kenath and its towns, totaling sixty cities. All these belonged to the sons of Machir, the father of Gilead. {2:24} After Hezron died in Calebephratah, Abiah, Hezron's wife, bore him Ashur, the father of Tekoa. {2:25} The sons of Jerahmeel, Hezron's firstborn, are Ram, the firstborn, and Bunah, Oren, Ozem, and Ahijah. {2:26} Jerahmeel had another wife named Atarah; she was the mother of Onam. {2:27} The sons of Ram, Jerahmeel's firstborn, are Maaz, Jamin, and Eker. {2:28} The sons of Onam are Shammai and Jada. The sons of Shammai are Nadab and Abishur. {2:29} The name of Abishur's wife was Abihail, and she bore him Ahban and Molid. {2:30} The sons of Nadab are Seled and Appaim; Seled died without children. {2:31} The sons of Appaim are Ishi, and the sons of Ishi are Sheshan. The children of Sheshan are Ahlai. {2:32} The sons of Jada, the brother of Shammai, are Jether and Jonathan; Jether died without children. {2:33} The sons of Jonathan are Peleth and Zaza. These are the sons of Jerahmeel. {2:34} Now Sheshan had no sons, only daughters. Sheshan had an Egyptian servant named Jarha. {2:35} Sheshan gave his daughter to Jarha, his servant, as a wife, and she bore him Attai. {2:36} Attai became the father of Nathan, and Nathan became the father of Zabad, {2:37} Zabad became the father of Ephlal, and Ephlal became the father of Obed, {2:38} Obed became the father of Jehu, and Jehu became the father of Azariah, {2:39} Azariah became the father of Helez, and Helez became the father of Eleasah, {2:40} Eleasah became the father of Sisamai, and Sisamai became the father of Shallum, {2:41} Shallum became the father of Jekamiah, and Jekamiah became the father of Elishama. {2:42} The sons of Caleb, the brother of Jerahmeel, are Mesha, his firstborn, who was the father of Ziph; and the sons of Mareshah, the father of Hebron. {2:43} The sons of Hebron are Korah, Tappuah, Rekem, and Shema. {2:44} Shema became the father of Raham, the father of Jorkoam; Rekem became the father of Shammai. {2:45} The son of Shammai is Maon; Maon is the father of Bethzur. {2:46} Ephah, Caleb's concubine, bore Haran, Moza, and Gazez; Haran became the father of Gazez. {2:47} The sons of Jahdai are Regem, Jotham, Geshan, Pelet, Ephah, and Shaaph. {2:48} Maachah, Caleb's concubine, bore Sheber and Tirhanah. {2:49} She also bore Shaaph, the father of Madmannah, Sheva, the father of Machbenah, and the father of Gibea; Caleb's daughter was Achsah. {2:50} These are the sons of Caleb, the son of Hur, the firstborn of Ephratah; Shobal is the father of Kirjathjearim, {2:51} Salma is the father of Bethlehem, and Hareph is the father of Bethgader. {2:52} Shobal, the father of Kirjathjearim, had sons: Haroeh and half of the Manahethites. {2:53} The families of Kirjathjearim are the Ithrites, Puhites, Shumathites, and Mishraites; from them came the Zareathites and Eshtaulites. {2:54} The sons of Salma are Bethlehem, the Netophathites, Ataroth, the house of Joab, and half of the Manahethites, and the Zorites. {2:55} The families of the scribes who lived at Jabez are the Tirathites, Shimeathites, and Suchathites. These are the Kenites who descended from Hemath, the father of the house of Rechab.

{3:1} These are the sons of David, born to him in Hebron: the firstborn Amnon, by Ahinoam the Jezreelitess; the second, Daniel, by Abigail the Carmelitess. {3:2} The third was Absalom, the son of Maachah, the daughter of Talmai, king of Geshur; the fourth was Adonijah, the son of Haggith. {3:3} The fifth was Shephatiah, by Abital; the sixth was Ithream, by Eglah, his wife. {3:4} These six were born to him in Hebron, where he reigned for seven years and six months; and in Jerusalem, he reigned for thirty-three years. {3:5} Born to him in Jerusalem were Shimea, Shobab, Nathan, and Solomon, four, by Bathshua, the daughter of Ammiel. {3:6} He also had Ibhar, Elishama, and Eliphelet, {3:7} and Nogah, Nepheg, and Japhia, {3:8} and Elishama, Eliada, and Eliphelet, nine in total. {3:9} These were all the sons of David, besides the sons of his concubines and Tamar, their sister. {3:10} Solomon's son was Rehoboam; his son was Abia; Asa was his son; Jehoshaphat was his son; {3:11} Joram was his son; Ahaziah was his son; Joash was his son; {3:12} Amaziah was his son; Azariah was his son; Jotham was his son; {3:13} Ahaz was his son; Hezekiah was his son; Manasseh was his son; {3:14} Amon was his son; Josiah was his son. {3:15} The sons of Josiah were the firstborn Johanan, the second Jehoiakim, the third Zedekiah, and the fourth Shallum. {3:16} The sons of Jehoiakim were Jeconiah, his son, and Zedekiah, his son. {3:17} The sons of Jeconiah were Assir, Salathiel, his son, {3:18} Malchiram, Pedaiah, Shenazar, Jecamiah, Hoshama, and Nedabiah. {3:19} The sons of Pedaiah were Zerubbabel and Shimei; the sons of Zerubbabel were Meshullam, Hananiah, and their sister Shelomith. {3:20} Also included are Hashubah, Ohel, Berechiah, Hasadiah, and Jushabhesed, five in total. {3:21} The sons of Hananiah were Pelatiah and Jesaiah; the sons of Rephaiah, Arnan, Obadiah, and Shechaniah. {3:22} The sons of Shechaniah were Shemaiah; the sons of Shemaiah were Hattush, Igeal, Bariah, Neariah, and Shaphat, six in total. {3:23} The sons of Neariah were Elioenai, Hezekiah, and Azrikam, three. {3:24} The sons of Elioenai were Hodaiah, Eliashib, Pelaiah, Akkub, Johanan, Dalaiah, and Anani, seven.

{4:1} The sons of Judah were Pharez, Hezron, Carmi, Hur, and Shobal. {4:2} Reaiah, the son of Shobal, had a son named Jahath; Jahath had sons named Ahumai and Lahad. These are the families of the Zorathites. {4:3} From the father of Etam came Jezreel, Ishma, and Idbash; their sister was named Hazelelponi. {4:4} Penuel was the father of Gedor, and Ezer was the father of Hushah. These are the sons of Hur, the firstborn of Ephratah, who was the father of Bethlehem. {4:5} Ashur, the father of Tekoa, had two wives, Helah and Naarah. {4:6} Naarah bore him Ahuzam, Hepher, Temeni, and Haahashtari. These were the sons of Naarah. {4:7} The sons of Helah were Zereth, Jezoar, and Ethnan. {4:8} Coz had three sons: Anub, Zobebah, and the families of Aharhel, the son of Harum. {4:9} Jabez was more honorable than his brothers; his mother named him Jabez, saying, "I bore him with sorrow." {4:10} Jabez prayed to the God of Israel, saying, "Oh, that you would bless me indeed, enlarge my territory, and let your hand be with me, and keep me from evil so that it does not grieve me!" And God granted him what he requested. {4:11} Chelub, the brother of Shuah, had a son named Mehir, who was the father of Eshton. {4:12} Eshton became the father of Bethrapha, Paseah, and Tehinnah, the father of Irnahash. These are the men of Rechah. {4:13} The sons of Kenaz were Othniel and Seraiah; the sons of Othniel were Hathath. {4:14} Meonothai had a son named Ophrah; Seraiah was the father of Joab, the father of the valley of Charashim, because they were craftsmen. {4:15} The sons of Caleb, the son of Jephunneh, were Iru, Elah, and Naam; the sons of Elah included Kenaz. {4:16} The sons of Jehaleleel were Ziph, Ziphah, Tiria, and Asareel. {4:17} The sons of Ezra were Jether, Mered, Epher, and Jalon; he had a daughter named Miriam, and also Shammai, and Ishbah, the father of Eshtemoa. {4:18} His wife Jehudijah bore Jered, the father of Gedor, Heber, the father of Socho, and Jekuthiel, the father of Zanoah. These are the sons of Bithiah, the daughter of

Pharaoh, whom Mered married. {4:19} The sons of his wife Hodiah, the sister of Naham, were the father of Keilah the Garmite and Eshtemoa the Maachathite. {4:20} The sons of Shimon were Amnon, Rinnah, Benhanan, and Tilon. The sons of Ishi were Zoheth and Benzoheth. {4:21} The sons of Shelah, the son of Judah, were Er, the father of Lecah, Laadah, the father of Mareshah, and the families of the house of those who worked with fine linen from the house of Ashbea. {4:22} Jokim was also included, along with the men of Chozeba, Joash, and Saraph, who ruled in Moab, and Jashubilehem. These are ancient records. {4:23} These were the potters and those who lived among the plants and hedges; they worked for the king. {4:24} The sons of Simeon were Nemuel, Jamin, Jarib, Zerah, and Shaul; {4:25} Shallum was his son, Mibsam was his son, and Mishma was his son. {4:26} The sons of Mishma were Hamuel, Zacchur, and Shimei. {4:27} Shimei had sixteen sons and six daughters, but his brothers did not have many children, and their families did not multiply like those of Judah. {4:28} They lived in Beersheba, Moladah, and Hazarshual, {4:29} and at Bilhah, Ezem, and Tolad, {4:30} and at Bethuel, Hormah, and Ziklag, {4:31} and at Bethmarcaboth, Hazarsusim, Bethbirei, and Shaaraim. These were their cities until the reign of David. {4:32} Their villages included Etam, Ain, Rimmon, Tochen, and Ashan, five cities in total. {4:33} All their surrounding villages extended to Baal. These were their habitations and their genealogy. {4:34} Meshobab, Jamlech, and Joshah, the son of Amaziah, {4:35} and Joel, Jehu, the son of Josibiah, the son of Seraiah, the son of Asiel, {4:36} and Elioenai, Jaakobah, Jeshohaiah, Asaiah, Adiel, Jesimiel, and Benaiah, {4:37} and Ziza, the son of Shiphi, the son of Allon, the son of Jedaiah, the son of Shimri, the son of Shemaiah; {4:38} these names were the princes in their families, and the house of their fathers grew greatly. {4:39} They went to the entrance of Gedor, to the east side of the valley, to seek pasture for their flocks. {4:40} They found good pasture, with plenty of space, and the land was peaceful because people of Ham had lived there a long time. {4:41} Those recorded by name came during the days of Hezekiah, king of Judah, and attacked their tents, destroying all the dwellings they found there, and they settled there because there was pasture for their flocks. {4:42} Some of the sons of Simeon, five hundred men, went to Mount Seir, with captains Pelatiah, Neariah, Rephaiah, and Uzziel, the sons of Ishi. {4:43} They defeated the remaining Amalekites who had escaped and lived there until this day.

{5:1} The sons of Reuben, the firstborn of Israel (for he was the firstborn; but since he defiled his father's bed, his birthright was given to the sons of Joseph, the son of Israel, and the genealogy is not to be counted according to the birthright), {5:2} for Judah prevailed over his brothers, and from him came the chief ruler; but the birthright was Joseph's. {5:3} The sons of Reuben, the firstborn of Israel, were Hanoch, Pallu, Hezron, and Carmi. {5:4} The sons of Joel were Shemaiah, his son; Gog, his son; Shimei, his son; {5:5} Micah, his son; Reaia, his son; and Baal, his son. {5:6} Beerah, his son, was carried away captive by Tilgath-pilneser, king of Assyria; he was a prince of the Reubenites. {5:7} His brothers by their families, when their genealogies were counted, included Jeiel and Zechariah as the chiefs, {5:8} and Bela, the son of Azaz, the son of Shema, the son of Joel, who lived in Aroer, extending to Nebo and Baalmeon. {5:9} Eastward, he inhabited the region from the entrance of the wilderness to the Euphrates River because their cattle had multiplied in the land of Gilead. {5:10} In the days of Saul, they fought against the Hagarites, who fell by their hands, and they lived in their tents throughout all the eastern land of Gilead. {5:11} The children of Gad lived opposite them, in the land of Bashan, extending to Salchah. {5:12} The chiefs included Joel, Shapham, Jaanai, and Shaphat in Bashan. {5:13} Their brothers from the house of their fathers were Michael, Meshullam, Sheba, Jorai, Jachan, Zia, and Heber—seven in total. {5:14} These are the children of Abihail, the son of Huri, the son of Jaroah, the son of Gilead, the son of Michael, the son of Jeshishai, the son of Jahdo, the son of Buz; {5:15} Ahi, the son of Abdiel, the son of Guni, was the chief of the house of their fathers. {5:16} They lived in Gilead, in Bashan, in their towns, and in all the suburbs of Sharon, on their borders. {5:17} All these were recorded by genealogies in the days of Jotham, king of Judah, and in the days of Jeroboam, king of Israel. {5:18} The sons of Reuben, the Gadites, and half the tribe of Manasseh, all valiant men, skilled in battle and able to carry shields and swords, and to shoot bows, numbered forty-four thousand seven hundred and sixty who went out to war. {5:19} They made war against the Hagarites, Jetur, Nephish, and Nodab. {5:20} They were helped against them, and the Hagarites were delivered into their hands; they cried to God in battle, and He was receptive to them because they trusted in Him. {5:21} They took their cattle: fifty thousand camels, two hundred fifty thousand sheep, two thousand donkeys, and one hundred thousand men. {5:22} Many were slain because the battle was God's, and they lived in their place until the captivity. {5:23} The children of the half tribe of Manasseh lived in the land; they increased from Bashan to Baal-hermon, Senir, and Mount Hermon. {5:24} The heads of the house of their fathers included Epher, Ishi, Eliel, Azriel, Jeremiah, Hodaviah, and Jahdiel—mighty men of valor, famous men, and heads of their families. {5:25} They transgressed against the God of their fathers and worshiped the gods of the peoples of the land, whom God destroyed before them. {5:26} The God of Israel stirred up the spirit of Pul, king of Assyria, and the spirit of Tilgath-pilneser, king of Assyria, and he carried them away, including the Reubenites, the Gadites, and the half tribe of Manasseh, and brought them to Halah, Habor, Hara, and the river Gozan, where they remain to this day.

{6:1} The sons of Levi were Gershon, Kohath, and Merari. {6:2} The sons of Kohath were Amram, Izhar, Hebron, and Uzziel. {6:3} The children of Amram were Aaron, Moses, and Miriam. The sons of Aaron included Nadab, Abihu, Eleazar, and Ithamar. {6:4} Eleazar became the father of Phinehas, {6:5} Phinehas became the father of Abishua, {6:6} Abishua became the father of Bukki, and Bukki became the father of Uzzi. {6:7} Uzzi became the father of Zerahiah, and Zerahiah became the father of Meraioth. {6:8} Meraioth became the father of Amariah, and Amariah became the father of Ahitub. {6:9} Ahitub became the father of Zadok, and Zadok became the father of Ahimaaz. {6:10} Ahimaaz became the father of Azariah, and Azariah became the father of Johanan. {6:11} Johanan became the father of Azariah (it was he who served as priest in the temple that Solomon built in Jerusalem). {6:12} Azariah became the father of Amariah, and Amariah became the father of Ahitub. {6:13} Ahitub became the father of Zadok, and Zadok became the father of Shallum. {6:14} Shallum became the father of Hilkiah, and Hilkiah became the father of Azariah. {6:15} Azariah became the father of Seraiah, and Seraiah became the father of Jehozadak. {6:16} Jehozadak went into captivity when the LORD carried away Judah and Jerusalem through Nebuchadnezzar. {6:17} The sons of Levi were Gershom, Kohath, and Merari. {6:18} The names of the sons of Gershom were Libni and Shimei. {6:19} The sons of Kohath were Amram, Izhar, Hebron, and Uzziel. {6:20} The sons of Merari were Mahli and Mushi. These are the families of the Levites according to their fathers. {6:21} The family of Gershom included Libni, his son; Jahath, his son; Zimmah, his son; {6:22} Joah, his son; Iddo, his son; Zerah, his son; and Jeaterai, his son. {6:23} The sons of Kohath were Amminadab, his son; Korah, his son; Assir, his son; {6:24} Elkanah, his son; Ebiasaph, his son; and Assir, his son; {6:25} Tahath, his son; Uriel, his son; Uzziah, his son; and Shaul, his son. {6:26} The sons of Elkanah were Amasai and Ahimoth. {6:27} The sons of Elkanah included Zophai, his son; Nahath, his son; {6:28} Eliab, his son; Jeroham, his son; and Elkanah, his son. {6:29} The sons of Samuel were Vashni, the firstborn, and Abiah. {6:30} The sons of Merari included Mahli, Libni, his son; Shimei, his son; Uzza, his son; {6:31} Shimea, his son; Haggiah, his son; and Asaiah, his son. {6:32} These were the ones David appointed for the service of song in the house of the LORD after the ark had found rest. {6:33} They ministered before the dwelling place of the tabernacle of the congregation with singing until Solomon built the house of the LORD in Jerusalem, and then they performed their duties according to their order. {6:34} These are the ones who served with their children. Among the sons of the Kohathites was Heman, a singer, the son of Joel, the son of Shemuel; {6:35} the son of Elkanah, the son of Jeroham, the son of Eliel, the son of Toah; {6:36} the son of Zuph, the son of Elkanah, the son of Mahath, the son of Amasai; {6:37} the son of Elkanah, the son of Joel, the son of Azariah, the son of Zephaniah; {6:38} the son of Tahath, the son of Assir, the son of Ebiasaph, the son of Korah; {6:39} the son of Izhar, the son of Kohath, the son of Levi, the son of Israel. {6:40} His brother Asaph stood on his right hand; he was Asaph, the son of Berachiah, the son of Shimea; {6:41} the son of Michael, the son of

Baaseiah, the son of Malchiah; {6:42} the son of Ethni, the son of Zerah, the son of Adaiah; {6:43} the son of Ethan, the son of Zimmah, the son of Shimei; {6:44} the son of Jahath, the son of Gershom, the son of Levi. {6:45} Their brothers, the sons of Merari, stood on the left side: Ethan, the son of Kishi, the son of Abdi, the son of Malluch; {6:46} the son of Hashabiah, the son of Amaziah, the son of Hilkiah; {6:47} the son of Amzi, the son of Bani, the son of Shamer; {6:48} the son of Mahli, the son of Mushi, the son of Merari, the son of Levi. {6:49} Their brothers, the Levites, were assigned to all kinds of service in the tabernacle of the house of God. {6:50} However, Aaron and his sons offered sacrifices on the altar of burnt offerings and on the altar of incense, and were designated for all the work of the Most Holy Place, making atonement for Israel according to all that Moses, the servant of God, had commanded. {6:51} The sons of Aaron were Eleazar, his son; Phinehas, his son; Abishua, his son; {6:52} Bukki, his son; Uzzi, his son; Zerahiah, his son; {6:53} Meraioth, his son; Amariah, his son; Ahitub, his son; {6:54} Zadok, his son; and Ahimaaz, his son. {6:55} Now these are their dwelling places throughout their regions, among the sons of Aaron, from the families of the Kohathites, for theirs was the lot. {6:56} They were given Hebron in the land of Judah, along with the surrounding suburbs. {6:57} But the fields of the city and the villages were given to Caleb, the son of Jephunneh. {6:58} To the sons of Aaron, they gave the cities of Judah, namely Hebron, the city of refuge; Libnah with its suburbs; Jattir; and Eshtemoa with its suburbs; {6:59} and Hilen with its suburbs; Debir with its suburbs; {6:60} Ashan with its suburbs; and Beth-shemesh with its suburbs. {6:61} From the tribe of Benjamin, they received Geba with its suburbs; Alemeth with its suburbs; and Anathoth with its suburbs. In total, they received thirteen cities among their families. {6:62} The remaining sons of Kohath, from that family of the tribe, received ten cities from the half tribe of Manasseh by lot. {6:63} The sons of Gershom received thirteen cities from the tribe of Issachar, Asher, Naphtali, and the half tribe of Manasseh in Bashan, according to their families. {6:64} The sons of Merari received twelve cities by lot from the tribes of Reuben, Gad, and Zebulun. {6:65} The children of Israel gave these cities to the Levites with their suburbs. {6:66} They distributed cities by lot from the tribe of Judah, Simeon, and Benjamin, which are named after them. {6:67} The remaining families of the sons of Kohath received cities on their borders from the tribe of Ephraim. {6:68} They were given cities of refuge, such as Shechem in Mount Ephraim with its suburbs; they also received Gezer with its suburbs; {6:69} Jokmeam with its suburbs; and Beth-horon with its suburbs; {6:70} Aijalon with its suburbs; and Gath-rimmon with its suburbs. {6:71} From the half tribe of Manasseh, they received Aner with its suburbs and Bileam with its suburbs for the family of the remnant of the sons of Kohath. {6:72} The sons of Gershom received Golan in Bashan with its suburbs and Ashtaroth with its suburbs from the family of the half tribe of Manasseh. {6:73} From the tribe of Issachar, they received Kedesh with its suburbs; Daberath with its suburbs; {6:74} Ramoth with its suburbs; and Anem with its suburbs. {6:75} From the tribe of Asher, they received Mashal with its suburbs; Abdon with its suburbs; {6:76} Hukok with its suburbs; and Rehob with its suburbs. {6:77} From the tribe of Naphtali, they received Kedesh in Galilee with its suburbs; Hammon with its suburbs; and Kirjathaim with its suburbs. {6:78} The rest of the children of Merari received Rimmon with its suburbs and Tabor with its suburbs from the tribe of Zebulun. {6:79} On the other side of the Jordan near Jericho, on the east side of the Jordan, they were given Bezer in the wilderness with its suburbs; Jahzah with its suburbs; {6:80} Kedemoth with its suburbs; and Mephaath with its suburbs from the tribe of Reuben. {6:81} From the tribe of Gad, they received Ramoth in Gilead with its suburbs and Mahanaim with its suburbs; {6:82} Heshbon with its suburbs; and Jazer with its suburbs.

{7:1} The sons of Issachar were Tola, Puah, Jashub, and Shimron, four in total. {7:2} The sons of Tola were Uzzi, Rephaiah, Jeriel, Jahmai, Jibsam, and Shemuel, the heads of their father's household. They were valiant men of strength in their generations, and their number during the days of David was twenty-two thousand six hundred. {7:3} The sons of Uzzi were Izrahiah, and the sons of Izrahiah were Michael, Obadiah, Joel, and Ishiah, five in total, all of them chief men. {7:4} With them, by their generations and according to their families, were bands of soldiers for war, totaling thirty-six thousand men, for they had many wives and sons. {7:5} Among all the families of Issachar, their brothers were also valiant men, making a total of eighty-seven thousand according to their genealogies. {7:6} The sons of Benjamin were Bela, Becher, and Jediael, three in total. {7:7} The sons of Bela were Ezbon, Uzzi, Uzziel, Jerimoth, and Iri, five; these were the heads of their father's household, mighty men of valor, counted in their genealogies at twenty-two thousand thirty-four. {7:8} The sons of Becher were Zemira, Joash, Eliezer, Elioenai, Omri, Jerimoth, Abiah, Anathoth, and Alameth. All these are the sons of Becher. {7:9} Their number, according to their genealogies by generations, the heads of their fathers' households, mighty men of valor, was twenty thousand two hundred. {7:10} The sons of Jediael were Bilhan, and the sons of Bilhan were Jeush, Benjamin, Ehud, Chenaanah, Zethan, Tharshish, and Ahishahar. {7:11} All these were the sons of Jediael, the heads of their fathers' households, mighty men of valor, totaling seventeen thousand two hundred soldiers fit for battle. {7:12} Shuppim and Huppim were the children of Ir, and Hushim were the sons of Aher. {7:13} The sons of Naphtali were Jahziel, Guni, Jezer, and Shallum, the sons of Bilhah. {7:14} The sons of Manasseh were Ashriel, whom she bore; his concubine, the Aramean woman, bore Machir, the father of Gilead. {7:15} Machir took to wife the sister of Huppim and Shuppim, whose sister's name was Maachah. The name of the second was Zelophehad, and Zelophehad had daughters. {7:16} Maachah, the wife of Machir, bore a son, and she named him Peresh; his brother was named Sheresh, and his sons were Ulam and Rakem. {7:17} The sons of Ulam were Bedan. These were the sons of Gilead, the son of Machir, the son of Manasseh. {7:18} His sister Hammoleketh bore Ishod, Abiezer, and Mahalah. {7:19} The sons of Shemida were Ahian, Shechem, Likhi, and Aniam. {7:20} The sons of Ephraim were Shuthelah, Bered his son, Tahath his son, Eladah his son, and Tahath his son, {7:21} Zabad his son, Shuthelah his son, Ezer, and Elead. The men of Gath born in that land killed them because they went down to take their cattle. {7:22} Ephraim their father mourned many days, and his brothers came to comfort him. {7:23} When he went in to his wife, she conceived and bore a son, and he named him Beriah because it went badly for his house. {7:24} His daughter was Sherah, who built the lower and upper Beth-horon and Uzzensherah. {7:25} Rephah was his son, as well as Resheph, Telah his son, and Tahan his son. {7:26} Laadan his son, Ammihud his son, and Elishama his son, {7:27} Non his son, and Jehoshua his son. {7:28} Their possessions and habitations included Bethel and its towns, eastward Naaran, and westward Gezer with its towns; Shechem and its towns, extending to Gaza and its towns. {7:29} By the borders of the children of Manasseh were Beth-shean and its towns, Taanach and its towns, Megiddo and its towns, and Dor and its towns. In these, the children of Joseph, the son of Israel, lived. {7:30} The sons of Asher were Imnah, Isuah, Ishuai, Beriah, and their sister Serah. {7:31} The sons of Beriah were Heber and Malchiel, who is the father of Birzavith. {7:32} Heber became the father of Japhlet, Shomer, Hotham, and Shua their sister. {7:33} The sons of Japhlet were Pasach, Bimhal, and Ashvath. These are the children of Japhlet. {7:34} The sons of Shamer were Ahi, Rohgah, Jehubbah, and Aram. {7:35} The sons of his brother Helem were Zophah, Imna, Shelesh, and Amal. {7:36} The sons of Zophah were Suah, Harnepher, Shual, Beri, Imrah, {7:37} Bezer, Hod, Shamma, Shilshah, Ithran, and Beera. {7:38} The sons of Jether were Jephunneh, Pispah, and Ara. {7:39} The sons of Ulla were Arah, Haniel, and Rezia. {7:40} All these were the children of Asher, heads of their father's households, choice and mighty men of valor, chiefs among the princes. The total number of those able for war and battle was twenty-six thousand men.

{8:1} Benjamin became the father of Bela, his firstborn, Ashbel the second, and Aharah the third, {8:2} Nohah the fourth, and Rapha the fifth. {8:3} The sons of Bela were Addar, Gera, and Abihud, {8:4} Abishua, Naaman, and Ahoah, {8:5} Gera, Shephuphan, and Huram. {8:6} These are the sons of Ehud; they were the heads of the families of the inhabitants of Geba, and they moved them to Manahath. {8:7} Naaman, Ahiah, and Gera moved them and became the father of Uzza and Ahihud. {8:8} Shaharaim had children in the land of Moab after he sent them away; his wives were Hushim and Baara. {8:9} He had children by his wife Hodesh: Jobab, Zibia, Mesha, and Malcham, {8:10} Jeuz, Shachia, and Mirma. These were his sons, the heads of their families. {8:11} By Hushim, he became the father of Abitub and Elpaal. {8:12} The sons of Elpaal were Eber, Misham, and Shamed, who built Ono and

Lod with their towns. {8:13} Beriah and Shema were heads of the families of the inhabitants of Aijalon, who drove out the inhabitants of Gath. {8:14} Ahio, Shashak, and Jeremoth, {8:15} Zebadiah, Arad, and Ader, {8:16} Michael, Ispah, and Joha, the sons of Beriah; {8:17} Zebadiah, Meshullam, Hezeki, and Heber, {8:18} Ishmerai, Jezliah, and Jobab, the sons of Elpaal; {8:19} Jakim, Zichri, and Zabdi, {8:20} Elienai, Zilthai, and Eliel, {8:21} Adaiah, Beraiah, and Shimrath, the sons of Shimhi; {8:22} Ishpan, Heber, and Eliel, {8:23} Abdon, Zichri, and Hanan, {8:24} Hananiah, Elam, and Antothijah, {8:25} Iphedeiah and Penuel, the sons of Shashak; {8:26} Shamsherai, Shehariah, and Athaliah, {8:27} Jaresiah, Eliah, and Zichri, the sons of Jeroham. {8:28} These were heads of their families by their generations, chief men. They dwelt in Jerusalem. {8:29} In Gibeon lived the father of Gibeon, whose wife's name was Maachah. {8:30} His firstborn son was Abdon, and his other sons were Zur, Kish, Baal, Nadab, {8:31} Gedor, Ahio, and Zacher. {8:32} Mikloth became the father of Shimeah. These also lived with their brothers in Jerusalem, across from them. {8:33} Ner became the father of Kish, Kish became the father of Saul, and Saul became the father of Jonathan, Malchishua, Abinadab, and Eshbaal. {8:34} Jonathan's son was Meribbaal; Meribbaal became the father of Micah. {8:35} The sons of Micah were Pithon, Melech, Tarea, and Ahaz. {8:36} Ahaz became the father of Jehoadah; Jehoadah became the father of Alemeth, Azmaveth, and Zimri; Zimri became the father of Moza, {8:37} Moza became the father of Binea. Rapha was his son, Eleasah his son, and Azel his son. {8:38} Azel had six sons, whose names were Azrikam, Bocheru, Ishmael, Sheariah, Obadiah, and Hanan. All these were the sons of Azel. {8:39} The sons of his brother Eshek were Ulam his firstborn, Jehush the second, and Eliphelet the third. {8:40} The sons of Ulam were mighty men of valor, archers, and they had many sons and grandsons, totaling one hundred fifty. All these were the sons of Benjamin.

{9:1} All of Israel was counted by genealogies, and they were recorded in the book of the kings of Israel and Judah, who were taken to Babylon because of their sins. {9:2} The first inhabitants who lived in their possessions in their cities were the Israelites, the priests, Levites, and Nethinims (temple servants). {9:3} In Jerusalem lived some of the children of Judah, Benjamin, Ephraim, and Manasseh; {9:4} Uthai, the son of Ammihud, the son of Omri, the son of Imri, the son of Bani, from the children of Pharez, the son of Judah. {9:5} And from the Shilonites; Asaiah the firstborn, and his sons. {9:6} The sons of Zerah were Jeuel and his brothers, totaling six hundred ninety. {9:7} The sons of Benjamin were Sallu, the son of Meshullam, the son of Hodaviah, the son of Hasenuah, {9:8} Ibneiah, the son of Jeroham, Elah, the son of Uzzi, the son of Michri, and Meshullam, the son of Shephathiah, the son of Reuel, the son of Ibnijah; {9:9} and their brothers, according to their generations, totaled nine hundred fifty-six. All these men were chiefs of their families. {9:10} The priests included Jedaiah, Jehoiarib, and Jachin, {9:11} Azariah, the son of Hilkiah, the son of Meshullam, the son of Zadok, the son of Meraioth, the son of Ahitub, the ruler of the house of God; {9:12} Adaiah, the son of Jeroham, the son of Pashur, the son of Malchijah, and Maasiai, the son of Adiel, the son of Jahzerah, the son of Meshullam, the son of Meshillemith, the son of Immer; {9:13} and their brothers, the heads of their families, totaled one thousand seven hundred sixty; they were very capable men for the work of the service of the house of God. {9:14} The Levites included Shemaiah, the son of Hasshub, the son of Azrikam, the son of Hashabiah, from the sons of Merari; {9:15} Bakbakkar, Heresh, Galal, and Mattaniah, the son of Micah, the son of Zichri, the son of Asaph; {9:16} Obadiah, the son of Shemaiah, the son of Galal, the son of Jeduthun, and Berechiah, the son of Asa, the son of Elkanah, who lived in the villages of the Netophathites. {9:17} The porters were Shallum, Akkub, Talmon, Ahiman, and their brothers; Shallum was the chief. {9:18} They had been stationed at the king's gate eastward and served as porters in the groups of the children of Levi. {9:19} Shallum, the son of Kore, the son of Ebiasaph, the son of Korah, and his brothers, from the house of his father, the Korahites, were responsible for the service, keeping the gates of the tabernacle; their fathers had been responsible for the LORD's host and were keepers of the entry. {9:20} Phinehas, the son of Eleazar, had been the ruler over them in the past, and the LORD was with him. {9:21} Zechariah, the son of Meshelemiah, was the porter at the door of the tabernacle of the congregation. {9:22} All those chosen to be porters at the gates totaled two hundred twelve. They were recorded by their genealogy in their villages, whom David and Samuel the seer had appointed to their office. {9:23} So they and their children were responsible for the gates of the house of the LORD, which is the house of the tabernacle, by wards. {9:24} The porters were positioned in four quarters, toward the east, west, north, and south. {9:25} Their brothers who lived in their villages came to join them after seven days periodically. {9:26} These Levites, the four chief porters, were assigned to their office and were in charge of the chambers and treasuries of the house of God. {9:27} They stayed around the house of God because their duty was to guard it, and the opening of it every morning was their responsibility. {9:28} Some of them were in charge of the ministering vessels, ensuring they were brought in and out as needed. {9:29} Others were appointed to oversee the vessels, all the instruments of the sanctuary, and the fine flour, wine, oil, frankincense, and spices. {9:30} Some of the sons of the priests prepared the spice ointments. {9:31} Mattithiah, one of the Levites, who was the firstborn of Shallum the Korahite, was in charge of the items made in the pans. {9:32} Other brothers from the sons of the Kohathites were in charge of the showbread, preparing it every Sabbath. {9:33} These are the singers, the heads of the families of the Levites, who remained in the chambers and were free; they worked day and night. {9:34} These chief families of the Levites were leaders throughout their generations and lived in Jerusalem. {9:35} In Gibeon lived the father of Gibeon, Jehiel, whose wife's name was Maachah. {9:36} His firstborn son was Abdon, and then Zur, Kish, Baal, Ner, and Nadab, {9:37} Gedor, Ahio, Zechariah, and Mikloth. {9:38} Mikloth became the father of Shimeam. They also lived with their brothers in Jerusalem, opposite their brothers. {9:39} Ner became the father of Kish; Kish became the father of Saul; Saul became the father of Jonathan, Malchishua, Abinadab, and Eshbaal. {9:40} Jonathan's son was Meribbaal, and Meribbaal became the father of Micah. {9:41} The sons of Micah were Pithon, Melech, Tahrea, and Ahaz. {9:42} Ahaz became the father of Jarah; Jarah became the father of Alemeth, Azmaveth, and Zimri; Zimri became the father of Moza; {9:43} Moza became the father of Binea; Rephaiah was his son, Eleasah his son, and Azel his son. {9:44} Azel had six sons, whose names were Azrikam, Bocheru, Ishmael, Sheariah, Obadiah, and Hanan; these were the sons of Azel.

{10:1} The Philistines fought against Israel, and the Israelites fled from them, falling dead on Mount Gilboa. {10:2} The Philistines pursued Saul and his sons, killing Jonathan, Abinadab, and Malchishua, the sons of Saul. {10:3} The battle raged hard against Saul, and the archers struck him, wounding him severely. {10:4} Saul then told his armor-bearer, "Draw your sword and kill me, so these uncircumcised (a term used for non-Israelites) people don't come and torture me." But his armor-bearer was too afraid and refused, so Saul took his own sword and fell on it. {10:5} When the armor-bearer saw that Saul was dead, he also fell on his sword and died. {10:6} So Saul, his three sons, and all his household died together. {10:7} When the Israelites in the valley saw that their army had fled and that Saul and his sons were dead, they abandoned their towns and fled. The Philistines then moved in and occupied these towns. {10:8} The next day, when the Philistines came to strip the dead bodies, they found Saul and his sons lying on Mount Gilboa. {10:9} They stripped Saul, took his head and his armor, and sent messengers throughout the land of the Philistines to proclaim the news to their idols (false gods) and their people. {10:10} They placed his armor in the temple of their gods and fastened his head in the temple of Dagon (a Philistine god). {10:11} When the people of Jabesh Gilead heard what the Philistines had done to Saul, {10:12} all their valiant men went and recovered the bodies of Saul and his sons. They brought them to Jabesh, buried their bones under the oak tree in Jabesh, and fasted for seven days. {10:13} Saul died because of his unfaithfulness to the LORD, failing to obey the LORD's commands, and because he sought guidance from a medium (one who communicates with spirits), {10:14} rather than seeking guidance from the LORD. Therefore, the LORD put him to death and gave the kingdom to David, the son of Jesse.

{11:1} All Israel gathered around David at Hebron, saying, "We are your relatives, your own flesh and blood." {11:2} In the past, when Saul was king, you were the one who led Israel in and out. The LORD your God said to you, "You will shepherd my people Israel, and you will be their ruler." {11:3} So all the elders of Israel came to King David at Hebron, and David made a covenant with them before the LORD, and they anointed him king over Israel, following the word of the LORD spoken through Samuel. {11:4} David and all Israel went to Jerusalem, also known as Jebus, where the Jebusites lived. {11:5} The Jebusites told David, "You can't come here." Nevertheless, David captured the fortress of Zion, which is the City of David. {11:6} David said, "Whoever attacks the Jebusites first will be chief and commander." So Joab, the son of Zeruiah, went up first and became chief. {11:7} David then lived in the fortress, and that's why it's called the City of David. {11:8} He built the city around it, starting from Millo, and Joab restored the rest of the city. {11:9} David became more powerful because the LORD Almighty was with him. {11:10} These are the chief mighty men who supported David in his kingdom, along with all Israel, to make him king as the LORD had said concerning Israel. {11:11} Here's the list of David's mighty men: Jashobeam, a Hachmonite, was the chief of the captains; he killed three hundred men with his spear at one time. {11:12} Next was Eleazar, the son of Dodo, the Ahohite, one of the three mightiest warriors. {11:13} He was with David at Pasdammim when the Philistines gathered for battle in a field of barley, and the troops fled from the Philistines. {11:14} They took their stand in the middle of that field, defended it, and killed the Philistines, and the LORD brought about a great victory. {11:15} Three of the thirty captains went down to David at the cave of Adullam, while the Philistine camp was in the valley of Rephaim. {11:16} At that time, David was in the stronghold, and the Philistine garrison was at Bethlehem. {11:17} David longed for water and said, "If only someone would bring me a drink from the well at Bethlehem, near the gate!" {11:18} So the three broke through the Philistine camp, drew water from the well of Bethlehem by the gate, and brought it back to David. But David refused to drink it; instead, he poured it out to the LORD, {11:19} saying, "My God forbid that I should do this! Should I drink the blood of these men who risked their lives to bring it?" So he would not drink it. These were the exploits of the three mightiest men. {11:20} Abishai, the brother of Joab, was chief of the three; he raised his spear against three hundred men and killed them, gaining a name among the three. {11:21} Of the three, he was more honored than the others, becoming their captain, but he didn't reach the level of the first three. {11:22} Benaiah, the son of Jehoiada, a valiant man from Kabzeel, performed great deeds; he killed two lionlike men of Moab and also went down into a pit on a snowy day and killed a lion. {11:23} He killed an Egyptian who was five cubits tall; the Egyptian had a spear like a weaver's beam, but Benaiah went down to him with a club, took the spear from the Egyptian's hand, and killed him with his own spear. {11:24} Benaiah, the son of Jehoiada, earned a reputation among the three mightiest men. {11:25} He was honored among the thirty, but he didn't reach the first three; David put him in charge of his guard. {11:26} The valiant men of the armies included Asahel, the brother of Joab, Elhanan, the son of Dodo from Bethlehem, {11:27} Shammoth the Harorite, Helez the Pelonite, {11:28} Ira, the son of Ikkesh the Tekoite, Abiezer the Antothite, {11:29} Sibbecai the Hushathite, Ilai the Ahohite, {11:30} Maharai the Netophathite, Heled, the son of Baanah, the Netophathite, {11:31} Ithai, the son of Ribai from Gibeah, who belonged to the tribe of Benjamin, Benaiah the Pirathonite, {11:32} Hurai of the brooks of Gaash, Abiel the Arbathite, {11:33} Azmaveth the Baharumite, Eliahba the Shaalbonite, {11:34} the sons of Hashem the Gizonite, Jonathan, the son of Shage the Hararite, {11:35} Ahiam, the son of Sacar the Hararite, Eliphal, the son of Ur, {11:36} Hepher the Mecherathite, Ahijah the Pelonite, {11:37} Hezro the Carmelite, Naarai, the son of Ezbai, {11:38} Joel, the brother of Nathan, Mibhar, the son of Haggeri, {11:39} Zelek the Ammonite, Naharai the Berothite, Joab's armor-bearer, {11:40} Ira the Ithrite, Gareb the Ithrite, {11:41} Uriah the Hittite, Zabad, the son of Ahlai, {11:42} Adina, the son of Shiza, a captain of the Reubenites, along with thirty men, {11:43} Hanan, the son of Maachah, and Joshaphat the Mithnite, {11:44} Uzzia the Ashterathite, Shama and Jehiel, the sons of Hothan the Aroerite, {11:45} Jediael, the son of Shimri, and Joha, his brother, the Tizite, {11:46} Eliel the Mahavite, Jeribai, and Joshaviah, the sons of Elnaam, and Ithmah the Moabite, {11:47} Eliel, Obed, and Jasiel the Mesobaite.

{12:1} These are the men who came to David at Ziklag while he was staying there because of Saul, the son of Kish; they were among the mighty men who helped in the battle. {12:2} They were armed with bows and could use both their right and left hands for throwing stones and shooting arrows, including the men from Saul's family in Benjamin. {12:3} The chief among them was Ahiezer, then Joash, the sons of Shemaah from Gibeah; also Jeziel and Pelet, the sons of Azmaveth; and Berachah and Jehu the Antothite, {12:4} along with Ismaiah the Gibeonite, a mighty man among the thirty, who was in charge of them; and Jeremiah, Jahaziel, Johanan, and Josabad the Gederathite, {12:5} plus Eluzai, Jerimoth, Bealiah, Shemariah, and Shephatiah the Haruphite. {12:6} Elkanah, Jesiah, Azareel, Joezer, and Jashobeam were from the Korahite family, {12:7} and Joelah and Zebadiah were the sons of Jeroham of Gedor. {12:8} Among the Gadites, some separated themselves to David in the wilderness; they were mighty warriors, skilled in battle, able to handle shields and bucklers (large shields), with faces like lions and as swift as gazelles on the mountains. {12:9} Ezer was the first, Obadiah the second, Eliab the third, {12:10} Mishmannah the fourth, Jeremiah the fifth, {12:11} Attai the sixth, Eliel the seventh, {12:12} Johanan the eighth, Elzabad the ninth, {12:13} Jeremiah the tenth, and Machbanai the eleventh. {12:14} These were the leaders of the sons of Gad; one of the smallest groups had over a hundred men, while the largest had over a thousand. {12:15} They crossed the Jordan in the first month when it overflowed its banks and drove out all those in the valleys to the east and west. {12:16} Some from the tribes of Benjamin and Judah came to David at the stronghold. {12:17} David went out to meet them and asked, "If you have come to me in peace to help me, my heart will be with you; but if you have come to betray me to my enemies, knowing that I have done no wrong, may the God of our ancestors see it and judge you." {12:18} Then the Spirit came upon Amasai, chief of the captains, and he said, "We are yours, David, and we are on your side, son of Jesse! Peace, peace to you and to your helpers, for your God helps you." David welcomed them and made them captains of his troops. {12:19} Some men from Manasseh joined David when he went to battle against Saul with the Philistines, but they did not help him because the Philistine leaders sent him away, saying, "He will fall back to his master Saul, putting our heads in jeopardy." {12:20} As David went to Ziklag, men from Manasseh joined him: Adnah, Jozabad, Jediael, Michael, Jozabad, Elihu, and Zilthai, who were captains of thousands from Manasseh. {12:21} They helped David against raiding parties, for they were all mighty warriors and leaders in the army. {12:22} Day by day, more men came to help David until his army became as great as the army of God. {12:23} Here are the numbers of the armed bands that came to David at Hebron to turn Saul's kingdom over to him, according to the word of the LORD. {12:24} The men of Judah who carried shields and spears numbered six thousand eight hundred, ready for battle. {12:25} The men of Simeon, who were mighty warriors, numbered seven thousand one hundred. {12:26} The men of Levi numbered four thousand six hundred. {12:27} Jehoiada was the leader of the Aaronites, along with three thousand seven hundred men; {12:28} and Zadok, a brave young man, with twenty-two captains from his family. {12:29} The men of Benjamin, the relatives of Saul, numbered three thousand, for most of them had remained loyal to Saul's house. {12:30} The men of Ephraim numbered twenty thousand eight hundred, mighty warriors known throughout their families. {12:31} The half-tribe of Manasseh had eighteen thousand men specifically named to come and make David king. {12:32} The men of Issachar understood the times and knew what Israel should do; the heads of them were two hundred, and all their relatives were at their command. {12:33} The men of Zebulun, who were experienced in battle and could keep formation, numbered fifty thousand, and they were not double-minded. {12:34} The men of Naphtali included a thousand captains and thirty-seven thousand armed with shields and spears. {12:35} The men of Dan, experienced in battle, numbered twenty-eight thousand six hundred. {12:36} The men of Asher, who were experienced in battle, numbered forty thousand. {12:37} On the other side of the Jordan, the Reubenites, Gadites, and half-tribe of Manasseh, armed with all kinds of weapons for battle, numbered one hundred twenty thousand. {12:38} All these men of war, who could keep formation, came with a sincere heart to Hebron to make David king over all Israel; and all the rest of Israel were united in heart to make

David king. {12:39} They stayed with David for three days, eating and drinking, for their relatives had prepared provisions for them. {12:40} Additionally, those near them, including those from Issachar, Zebulun & Naphtali, brought food on donkeys, camels, mules & oxen, along with meat, meal, cakes of figs, raisins, wine, oil, oxen & sheep in abundance, for there was great joy in Israel.

{13:1} David consulted with the captains of thousands and hundreds, as well as with every leader. {13:2} David said to the entire congregation of Israel, "If it seems good to you and is from the LORD our God, let us send word to our relatives everywhere who are left in all the land of Israel, and also to the priests and Levites in their cities and areas, so they can gather with us. {13:3} Let's bring back the ark of our God, for we did not seek it during the days of Saul." {13:4} The whole congregation agreed to do this, for it seemed right to all the people. {13:5} So David gathered all of Israel, from Shihor in Egypt to the entrance of Hamath, to bring the ark of God from Kiriath-jearim. {13:6} David and all Israel went to Baalah, which is Kiriath-jearim, belonging to Judah, to bring up the ark of God, the LORD, who is enthroned between the cherubim (angelic beings), whose name is called upon it. {13:7} They carried the ark of God on a new cart from the house of Abinadab, with Uzza and Ahio driving the cart. {13:8} David and all Israel played music before God with all their might, singing and using harps, psalteries (stringed instruments), timbrels (hand-held drums), cymbals, and trumpets. {13:9} When they reached the threshing floor of Chidon, Uzza reached out his hand to steady the ark because the oxen stumbled. {13:10} The LORD's anger burned against Uzza, and He struck him because he put his hand on the ark; and he died there before God. {13:11} David was upset because the LORD had broken out against Uzza; so that place was called Perez-uzza (meaning "the breach of Uzza") to this day. {13:12} David was afraid of God that day and said, "How can I bring the ark of God home to me?" {13:13} So David did not take the ark home to the City of David, but instead carried it aside to the house of Obed-edom the Gittite. {13:14} The ark of God remained with the family of Obed-edom in his house for three months, and the LORD blessed Obed-edom and all that he had.

{14:1} King Hiram of Tyre sent messengers to David along with cedar timber, masons, and carpenters to build him a house. {14:2} David realized that the LORD had established him as king over Israel, for his kingdom was exalted because of his people Israel. {14:3} David took more wives in Jerusalem and had more sons and daughters. {14:4} These are the names of his children born in Jerusalem: Shammua, Shobab, Nathan, and Solomon, {14:5} as well as Ibhar, Elishua, and Elpalet, {14:6} Nogah, Nepheg, and Japhia, {14:7} Elishama, Beeliada, and Eliphalet. {14:8} When the Philistines heard that David had been anointed king over all Israel, they went up to search for David. David heard about it and went out to confront them. {14:9} The Philistines came and spread out in the valley of Rephaim. {14:10} David inquired of God, saying, "Shall I go up against the Philistines? Will You hand them over to me?" The LORD answered him, "Go up, for I will hand them over to you." {14:11} So they went up to Baal-perazim, and David struck them there. Then David said, "God has burst through my enemies like a flood," so they named that place Baal-perazim (meaning "the Lord of Breakthroughs"). {14:12} When the Philistines left their gods there, David commanded that they be burned. {14:13} The Philistines again spread out in the valley. {14:14} Therefore, David inquired of God again, and God said to him, "Don't go up after them; instead, turn away from them and come upon them opposite the mulberry trees. {14:15} When you hear a sound of marching in the tops of the mulberry trees, then you shall go out to battle, for God has gone out before you to strike down the Philistine army." {14:16} David did as God commanded him, and they struck down the Philistine army from Gibeon to Gazer. {14:17} David's fame spread throughout all the lands, and the LORD caused all nations to fear him.

{15:1} David built houses in the city of David and prepared a place for the ark of God, pitching a tent for it. {15:2} David said, "Only the Levites should carry the ark of God, for the LORD has chosen them to carry the ark and to serve Him forever." {15:3} So David gathered all Israel to Jerusalem to bring up the ark of the LORD to the place he had prepared for it. {15:4} He assembled the descendants of Aaron and the Levites: {15:5} from the sons of Kohath, Uriel the chief and his brothers, one hundred and twenty; {15:6} from the sons of Merari, Asaiah the chief and his brothers, two hundred and twenty; {15:7} from the sons of Gershom, Joel the chief and his brothers, one hundred and thirty; {15:8} from the sons of Elizaphan, Shemaiah the chief and his brothers, two hundred; {15:9} from the sons of Hebron, Eliel the chief and his brothers, eighty; {15:10} from the sons of Uzziel, Amminadab the chief and his brothers, one hundred and twelve. {15:11} David called for the priests Zadok and Abiathar, and for the Levites Uriel, Asaiah, Joel, Shemaiah, Eliel, and Amminadab, {15:12} and said to them, "You are the heads of the Levites; sanctify yourselves, both you and your brothers, so that you may bring up the ark of the LORD God of Israel to the place I have prepared for it. {15:13} Because you did not do it the first time, the LORD our God broke out against us, because we did not seek Him according to the prescribed order." {15:14} So the priests and the Levites sanctified themselves to bring up the ark of the LORD God of Israel. {15:15} The Levites carried the ark of God on their shoulders with the poles, as Moses had commanded according to the word of the LORD. {15:16} David instructed the chief of the Levites to appoint their brothers as singers with musical instruments, psalteries, harps, and cymbals, to raise their voices in joy. {15:17} The Levites appointed Heman the son of Joel, and his brothers Asaph the son of Berechiah, and from the sons of Merari their brothers, Ethan the son of Kushaiah; {15:18} and with them their brothers of the second degree: Zechariah, Ben, Jaaziel, Shemiramoth, Jehiel, Unni, Eliab, Benaiah, Maaseiah, Mattithiah, Elipheleh, Mikneiah, Obededom, and Jeiel, the porters. {15:19} The singers Heman, Asaph, and Ethan were appointed to sound the cymbals of brass; {15:20} and Zechariah, Aziel, Shemiramoth, Jehiel, Unni, Eliab, Maaseiah, and Benaiah played the psalteries on Alamoth; {15:21} and Mattithiah, Elipheleh, Mikneiah, Obededom, Jeiel, and Azaziah played the harps on the Sheminith to excel. {15:22} Chenaniah, the chief of the Levites, was responsible for the music because he was skillful. {15:23} Berechiah and Elkanah were doorkeepers for the ark. {15:24} Shebaniah, Jehoshaphat, Nethaneel, Amasai, Zechariah, Benaiah, and Eliezer, the priests, blew the trumpets before the ark of God, and Obededom and Jehiah were doorkeepers for the ark. {15:25} David, the elders of Israel, and the captains over thousands went to bring up the ark of the covenant of the LORD from the house of Obededom with joy. {15:26} When God helped the Levites who carried the ark of the covenant of the LORD, they offered seven bullocks and seven rams. {15:27} David was dressed in a robe of fine linen, as were all the Levites who carried the ark, the singers, and Chenaniah, the master of the song with the singers; David also wore a linen ephod. {15:28} Thus, all Israel brought up the ark of the covenant of the LORD with shouts, and with the sound of the cornet, trumpets, and cymbals, making noise with psalteries and harps. {15:29} As the ark of the covenant of the LORD entered the city of David, Michal, the daughter of Saul, looked out from a window and saw King David dancing and playing; she despised him in her heart.

{16:1} They brought the ark of God and set it in the tent that David had pitched for it. They offered burnt sacrifices and peace offerings before God. {16:2} When David finished offering the burnt and peace offerings, he blessed the people in the name of the LORD. {16:3} He distributed to every Israelite, both men and women, a loaf of bread, a piece of meat, and a jug of wine. {16:4} David appointed some of the Levites to minister before the ark of the LORD, to record, thank, and praise the LORD God of Israel: {16:5} Asaph the chief, with Zechariah, Jeiel, Shemiramoth, Jehiel, Mattithiah, Eliab, Benaiah, and Obededom, along with Jeiel playing the psalteries and harps; Asaph played the cymbals. {16:6} Benaiah and Jahaziel the priests blew trumpets continually before the ark of the covenant of God. {16:7} On that day, David delivered the first psalm of thanks to the LORD into the hands of Asaph and his brothers. {16:8} "Give thanks to the LORD, call upon His name, and make His deeds known among the people. {16:9} Sing to Him, sing psalms to Him, and talk about all His wonderful works. {16:10} Glory in His holy name; let the hearts of those who seek the LORD rejoice. {16:11} Seek the LORD and His strength; seek His face continually. {16:12} Remember His marvelous works that

He has done, His wonders, and the judgments of His mouth; {16:13} you descendants of Israel His servant, children of Jacob, His chosen ones. {16:14} He is the LORD our God; His judgments are in all the earth. {16:15} Always remember His covenant, the word He commanded for a thousand generations; {16:16} the covenant He made with Abraham and His oath to Isaac; {16:17} He confirmed it to Jacob as a law and to Israel as an everlasting covenant, {16:18} saying, "To you I will give the land of Canaan, the lot of your inheritance." {16:19} When you were few in number, strangers in it, {16:20} and when they went from nation to nation, from one kingdom to another, {16:21} He allowed no one to oppress them; indeed, He reproved kings for their sakes, {16:22} saying, "Do not touch My anointed ones, and do My prophets no harm." {16:23} Sing to the LORD, all the earth; proclaim His salvation day by day. {16:24} Declare His glory among the nations, His marvelous works among all peoples. {16:25} For great is the LORD, and greatly to be praised; He is to be feared above all gods. {16:26} For all the gods of the nations are idols, but the LORD made the heavens. {16:27} Glory and honor are in His presence; strength and joy are in His place. {16:28} Give to the LORD, you families of nations; give to the LORD glory and strength. {16:29} Give to the LORD the glory due to His name; bring an offering and come before Him; worship the LORD in the beauty of holiness. {16:30} Tremble before Him, all the earth; the world is firmly established; it cannot be moved. {16:31} Let the heavens be glad and the earth rejoice; let the nations say, "The LORD reigns!" {16:32} Let the sea roar and all its fullness; let the fields rejoice and everything in them. {16:33} Then the trees of the forest will sing for joy at the presence of the LORD, for He comes to judge the earth. {16:34} Give thanks to the LORD, for He is good; His mercy endures forever. {16:35} And say, "Save us, O God of our salvation; gather us together and deliver us from the nations, that we may give thanks to Your holy name and glory in Your praise." {16:36} Blessed be the LORD God of Israel forever and ever. All the people said, "Amen," and praised the LORD. {16:37} So David left Asaph and his brothers there to minister before the ark of the covenant of the LORD continually, as required each day. {16:38} Obededom and sixty-eight of his brothers were there, along with Obededom the son of Jeduthun and Hosah as porters. {16:39} Zadok the priest and his fellow priests were before the tabernacle of the LORD at the high place in Gibeon, {16:40} to offer burnt offerings to the LORD on the altar of burnt offerings continually, morning and evening, and to do everything written in the law of the LORD that He commanded Israel. {16:41} Heman and Jeduthun and the rest chosen by name were there to give thanks to the LORD, for His mercy endures forever. {16:42} Heman and Jeduthun were with trumpets and cymbals for those who made music, along with the instruments of God. The sons of Jeduthun were porters. {16:43} All the people departed, each to their own house, and David returned to bless his household.

{17:1} One day, as David was sitting in his house, he said to Nathan the prophet, "Look, I live in a house made of cedar, but the ark of the covenant of the LORD is under curtains." {17:2} Nathan replied to David, "Do whatever you have in mind, for God is with you." {17:3} That same night, the word of God came to Nathan, saying, {17:4} "Go and tell My servant David: This is what the LORD says: You are not to build Me a house to dwell in. {17:5} I have not dwelt in a house since the day I brought Israel up to this day. I have gone from tent to tent, and from one dwelling to another. {17:6} Wherever I have moved with all Israel, did I ever say a word to any of the judges of Israel, whom I commanded to shepherd My people, asking, 'Why have you not built Me a house of cedar?' {17:7} Now, therefore, tell My servant David: This is what the LORD of hosts says: I took you from the pasture, from following the sheep, to be ruler over My people Israel. {17:8} I have been with you wherever you have gone, and I have cut off all your enemies from before you. I will make your name like the names of the greatest men on earth. {17:9} I will also provide a place for My people Israel and will plant them so that they will dwell in their own place and not be disturbed anymore. Wicked people will not oppress them as they did at the beginning, {17:10} and during the time I appointed judges over My people Israel. I will also subdue all your enemies. Furthermore, the LORD declares that He will build you a house. {17:11} When your days are over and you go to be with your ancestors, I will raise up your offspring to succeed you, one of your own sons, and I will establish his kingdom. {17:12} He will build a house for Me, and I will establish his throne forever. {17:13} I will be his father, and he will be My son. I will never take My love away from him, as I took it away from your predecessor. {17:14} I will set him over My house and My kingdom forever, and his throne will be established forever." {17:15} Nathan reported to David all the words of this entire revelation. {17:16} Then King David went in and sat before the LORD and said, "Who am I, O LORD God, and what is my family that You have brought me this far? {17:17} And as if this were not enough in Your sight, O God, You have also spoken about the future of my family and regarded me as a man of high rank, O LORD God. {17:18} What more can David say to You for honoring Your servant? For You know Your servant. {17:19} O LORD, for the sake of Your servant and according to Your will, You have done this great thing and revealed all these great promises. {17:20} O LORD, there is no one like You, and there is no God but You, as we have heard with our own ears. {17:21} And who is like Your people Israel, the one nation on earth that God went out to redeem as His people, to make a name for Yourself by performing great and awesome wonders, by driving out nations before Your people whom You redeemed from Egypt? {17:22} You made Your people Israel Your very own forever, and You, LORD, became their God. {17:23} Now, LORD, let the promise You have made concerning Your servant and his family be established forever. Do as You have promised, {17:24} so that Your name will be magnified forever, saying, 'The LORD of hosts is the God of Israel, even a God to Israel.' Let the house of Your servant David be established before You. {17:25} For You, my God, have revealed to Your servant that You will build him a house. That is why Your servant has found the courage to pray before You. {17:26} And now, LORD, You are God and have promised this good thing to Your servant. {17:27} Now please let it be established that You bless the house of Your servant, so that it may stand before You forever, for You, O LORD, have blessed it, and it will be blessed forever."

{18:1} After this, David attacked the Philistines, defeated them, and took Gath and its towns from the Philistines. {18:2} He also struck down the Moabites, who then became David's subjects and brought him gifts. {18:3} David defeated Hadadezer, king of Zobah, as he went to establish his rule by the Euphrates River. {18:4} David took from him a thousand chariots, seven thousand horsemen, and twenty thousand foot soldiers. He also hamstrung all the chariot horses, but kept a hundred chariots. {18:5} When the Syrians from Damascus came to help Hadadezer, king of Zobah, David killed twenty-two thousand of them. {18:6} David set up garrisons in Syria of Damascus, and the Syrians became David's subjects and brought him gifts. The LORD preserved David wherever he went. {18:7} David took the gold shields that belonged to Hadadezer's servants and brought them to Jerusalem. {18:8} He also brought back a large amount of bronze from Tibhath and Chun, cities of Hadadezer. This bronze was used by Solomon to make the bronze sea, the pillars, and various bronze utensils. {18:9} When Tou, king of Hamath, heard how David had defeated all the forces of Hadadezer, {18:10} he sent his son Hadoram to King David to ask about his well-being and congratulate him for fighting against Hadadezer and defeating him, since Hadadezer had been at war with Tou. Hadoram brought all kinds of gold, silver, and bronze vessels. {18:11} King David dedicated these to the LORD, along with the silver and gold he had taken from all these nations: from Edom, Moab, the Ammonites, the Philistines, and the Amalekites. {18:12} Abishai, the son of Zeruiah, killed eighteen thousand Edomites in the Valley of Salt. {18:13} He established garrisons in Edom, and all the Edomites became David's subjects. The LORD preserved David wherever he went. {18:14} David reigned all Israel, administering justice and righteousness to all his people. {18:15} Joab, the son of Zeruiah, was the commander of the army, and Jehoshaphat, the son of Ahilud, was the recorder. {18:16} Zadok, the son of Ahitub, and Abimelech, the son of Abiathar, were the priests, and Shavsha was the scribe. {18:17} Benaiah, the son of Jehoiada, was in charge of Cherethites and Pelethites, and the sons of David were the king's chief advisors.

{19:1} After this, Nahash, the king of the Ammonites, died, and his son became king in his place. {19:2} David said, "I will show kindness to Hanun, the son of Nahash, because his father was kind to me." So David sent messengers to comfort him about his father. David's servants went to the land of the Ammonites to comfort Hanun. {19:3} However, the princes of the Ammonites said to Hanun, "Do you think David is honoring your father by sending you comforters? Aren't his servants here to spy on you and overthrow you?" {19:4} So Hanun took David's servants, shaved off their beards, cut their garments up to their buttocks, and sent them away. {19:5} When some people told David how his men had been treated, he sent someone to meet them because they were very ashamed. The king said, "Stay in Jericho until your beards have grown back, then return." {19:6} When the Ammonites realized they had made themselves repugnant to David, Hanun and the Ammonites sent a thousand talents of silver to hire chariots and horsemen from Mesopotamia, Syria of Maachah, and Zobah. {19:7} They hired thirty-two thousand chariots, and the king of Maachah and his people came and camped near Medeba. The Ammonites gathered from their cities and prepared for battle. {19:8} When David heard about it, he sent Joab and all the mighty men to fight. {19:9} The Ammonites came out and arranged their forces at the city gate, while the kings who had come were by themselves in the field. {19:10} When Joab saw that the battle was set against him from the front and the back, he selected the best of Israel and arranged them to face the Syrians. {19:11} The rest of the troops he placed under the command of his brother Abishai, who arranged them to face the Ammonites. {19:12} Joab said, "If the Syrians are too strong for me, you come to my rescue; but if the Ammonites are too strong for you, I will come to your rescue. {19:13} Be strong, and let us fight bravely for our people and the cities of our God. May the LORD do what is good in his sight." {19:14} So Joab and the troops with him advanced against the Syrians, and they fled before him. {19:15} When the Ammonites saw that the Syrians had fled, they also fled before Abishai and retreated into the city. Then Joab returned to Jerusalem. {19:16} When the Syrians saw they were losing to Israel, they sent messengers and brought out the Syrians beyond the river, with Shophach, the commander of Hadarezer's army, leading them. {19:17} David was informed and gathered all Israel, crossed the Jordan, and set up his forces against them. When David arranged his troops against the Syrians, they fought against him. {19:18} But the Syrians fled before Israel, and David killed seven thousand of the Syrians who fought in chariots and forty thousand foot soldiers, and he killed Shophach, the commander of the army. {19:19} When Hadarezer's servants saw they were losing to Israel, they made peace with David and became his subjects; the Syrians would no longer help the Ammonites.

{20:1} After a year had passed, at the time when kings go out to battle, Joab led the army and devastated the land of the Ammonites, then besieged Rabbah. However, David stayed in Jerusalem. Joab attacked and destroyed Rabbah. {20:2} David took the crown from the head of their king, which weighed a talent of gold and had precious stones in it, and it was placed on David's head. He also took a great amount of spoils from the city. {20:3} He brought out the people in it and used saws, iron harrows, and axes on them. That was how David dealt with all the cities of the Ammonites. Then David and all the people returned to Jerusalem. {20:4} After this, there was a war at Gezer with the Philistines. During this time, Sibbechai the Hushathite killed Sippai, one of the descendants of the giants, and they were subdued. {20:5} There was another battle with the Philistines, and Elhanan, the son of Jair, killed Lahmi, the brother of Goliath the Gittite, whose spear was like a weaver's beam. {20:6} Again, there was a war at Gath, where there was a giant with a great stature, who had twenty-four fingers and toes—six on each hand and six on each foot. He was also a descendant of the giants. {20:7} When he taunted Israel, Jonathan, the son of Shimea, David's brother, killed him. {20:8} These were the descendants of the giants in Gath, and they fell by the hand of David and his servants.

{21:1} Satan rose up against Israel and incited David to take a census of Israel. {21:2} David said to Joab and the leaders of the people, "Go and count the Israelites from Beersheba to Dan, and report back to me so I can know the total." {21:3} Joab replied, "May the LORD make his people a hundred times more than they are! But, my lord the king, why do you want this? Aren't they all your servants? Why put Israel in a position to sin?" {21:4} Nevertheless, the king's order was stronger than Joab's objections, so Joab left and traveled through all Israel before returning to Jerusalem. {21:5} Joab reported to David the total number of the fighting men: there were one million one hundred thousand in Israel and four hundred seventy thousand in Judah. {21:6} But he did not include the tribes of Levi and Benjamin in the count, because he found the king's command to be repugnant. {21:7} God was displeased with what David had done, so he punished Israel. {21:8} David said to God, "I have sinned greatly in what I have done. Please remove the guilt of your servant, for I have acted very foolishly." {21:9} The LORD spoke to Gad, David's seer, saying, {21:10} "Go and tell David, 'The LORD says: I am offering you three options. Choose one of them for me to carry out against you.'" {21:11} So Gad went to David and said, "The LORD says: Choose one of these options: {21:12} three years of famine, or three months of being swept away before your enemies while they pursue you, or three days of the sword of the LORD—pestilence in the land, with the angel of the LORD destroying throughout all the territory of Israel. Decide what answer I should give him who sent me." {21:13} David said to Gad, "I am in a terrible situation. Let me fall into the hands of the LORD, for his mercy is very great; but do not let me fall into the hands of men." {21:14} So the LORD sent a plague on Israel, and seventy thousand men of Israel fell dead. {21:15} God sent an angel to Jerusalem to destroy it, but as the angel was about to destroy the city, the LORD saw it and was grieved at the calamity and said to the angel who was destroying the people, "Enough! Withdraw your hand." The angel of the LORD was then standing at the threshing floor of Ornan the Jebusite. {21:16} David looked up and saw the angel of the LORD standing between heaven and earth, with a drawn sword in his hand extended over Jerusalem. David and the elders, dressed in sackcloth, fell facedown. {21:17} David said to God, "Was it not I who ordered the counting of the people? I am the one who has sinned and done wrong. But these sheep, what have they done? O LORD my God, let your hand fall on me and my family, but do not let this plague remain on your people." {21:18} Then the angel of the LORD told Gad to instruct David to go up and build an altar to the LORD on the threshing floor of Ornan the Jebusite. {21:19} So David went up at Gad's word, which he had spoken in the name of the LORD. {21:20} Ornan turned and saw the angel; his four sons who were with him hid themselves. Now Ornan was threshing wheat. {21:21} As David approached Ornan, Ornan saw him and went out from the threshing floor, bowing to David with his face to the ground. {21:22} David said to Ornan, "Sell me the site of this threshing floor so I can build an altar to the LORD. I will pay the full price so that the plague will be stopped from the people." {21:23} Ornan said to David, "Take it! Let my lord the king do whatever seems good to him. Look, I give you the oxen for burnt offerings, and the threshing sledges for wood, and the wheat for the grain offering; I give it all." {21:24} But King David replied to Ornan, "No, I insist on paying the full price. I will not take for the LORD what is yours or sacrifice a burnt offering that costs me nothing." {21:25} So David paid Ornan six hundred shekels of gold for the site. {21:26} David built an altar to the LORD there and offered burnt offerings and fellowship offerings. He called on the LORD, and the LORD answered him with fire from heaven on the altar of burnt offering. {21:27} The LORD commanded the angel, and he put his sword back into its sheath. {21:28} At that time, when David saw that the LORD had answered him at the threshing floor of Ornan the Jebusite, he sacrificed there. {21:29} The tabernacle of the LORD, which Moses had made in the wilderness, and the altar of burnt offering were at that time on the high place at Gibeon. {21:30} But David could not go before it to inquire of God because he was afraid of the sword of the angel of the LORD.

{22:1} David said, "This is the house of the LORD God, and this is the altar for burnt offerings for Israel." {22:2} David commanded that the foreigners living in Israel be gathered, and he appointed masons to cut stones for building the house of God. {22:3} He prepared an abundance of iron for the nails of the gates and for the joints, and he had more brass than could be weighed; {22:4} he also had plenty of cedar wood, as the Sidonians and Tyrians had brought much cedar to David. {22:5} David said, "My son Solomon is young and inexperienced, and the house that is to be built for the LORD must be exceptionally magnificent, renowned and glorious throughout all countries. I will make extensive preparations for it." So David made lavish preparations before his death.

{22:6} He then called for his son Solomon and charged him to build a house for the LORD God of Israel. {22:7} David said to Solomon, "My son, I had it in my heart to build a house for the name of the LORD my God, {22:8} but the word of the LORD came to me, saying, 'You have shed much blood and fought great battles; you shall not build a house for my name, because you have spilled so much blood on the earth in my sight. {22:9} However, a son will be born to you who will be a man of peace. I will give him peace from all his enemies around him, for his name will be Solomon, and I will grant peace and quietness to Israel during his reign. {22:10} He will build a house for my name, and he will be my son, and I will be his father. I will establish the throne of his kingdom over Israel forever. {22:11} Now, my son, may the LORD be with you; may you succeed and build the house of the LORD your God, as he has said you would. {22:12} May the LORD grant you wisdom and understanding, and give you charge over Israel, so that you may keep the law of the LORD your God. {22:13} Then you will prosper if you pay attention to fulfill the statutes and judgments that the LORD charged Moses with regarding Israel. Be strong and courageous; do not be afraid or discouraged. {22:14} Look, in my trouble I have prepared for the house of the LORD one hundred thousand talents of gold and one million talents of silver, along with an abundance of brass and iron that cannot be weighed. I have also prepared timber and stone, and you may add to that. {22:15} Moreover, there are plenty of workers with you: stone cutters and craftsmen for every kind of work. {22:16} The gold, silver, brass, and iron are in great quantity. So arise and get to work, and may the LORD be with you." {22:17} David also commanded all the leaders of Israel to assist his son Solomon, saying, {22:18} "Is not the LORD your God with you? Has he not given you rest on every side? For he has handed over the inhabitants of the land to me, and the land is subdued before the LORD and before his people. {22:19} Now set your heart and soul to seek the LORD your God; arise and build the sanctuary of the LORD God, to bring the ark of the covenant of the LORD & holy vessels of God into the house that is to be built for the name of the LORD."

{23:1} When David was old and had lived a full life, he made his son Solomon king over Israel. {23:2} He gathered all the leaders of Israel, along with the priests and Levites. {23:3} The Levites were counted from the age of thirty and older, and their total number was thirty-eight thousand men. {23:4} Among them, twenty-four thousand were assigned to oversee the work on the house of the LORD, six thousand were officers and judges, {23:5} four thousand were gatekeepers, and four thousand praised the LORD with the instruments that David made for praising him. {23:6} David divided them into groups among the sons of Levi: Gershon, Kohath, and Merari. {23:7} From the Gershonites, there were Laadan and Shimei. {23:8} The sons of Laadan included the chief, Jehiel, along with Zetham and Joel, three in total. {23:9} The sons of Shimei were Shelomith, Haziel, and Haran, three. These were the heads of the families of Laadan. {23:10} The sons of Shimei were Jahath, Zina, Jeush, and Beriah. These four were the sons of Shimei. {23:11} Jahath was the chief, and Zizah was the second; but Jeush and Beriah had few sons, so they were counted as one family. {23:12} The sons of Kohath were Amram, Izhar, Hebron, and Uzziel, four in total. {23:13} The sons of Amram were Aaron and Moses. Aaron was set apart to sanctify the most holy things, along with his sons, forever, to burn incense before the LORD, to minister to him, and to bless in his name forever. {23:14} As for Moses, the man of God, his sons were included among the tribe of Levi. {23:15} The sons of Moses were Gershom and Eliezer. {23:16} Shebuel was the chief among the sons of Gershom. {23:17} The sons of Eliezer included Rehabiah as the chief. Eliezer had no other sons, but the sons of Rehabiah were numerous. {23:18} The chief among the sons of Izhar was Shelomith. {23:19} The sons of Hebron were Jeriah the first, Amariah the second, Jahaziel the third, and Jekameam the fourth. {23:20} The sons of Uzziel were Michah the first and Jesiah the second. {23:21} The sons of Merari were Mahli and Mushi. The sons of Mahli were Eleazar and Kish. {23:22} Eleazar died and had no sons, only daughters; and their brothers, the sons of Kish, took them as wives. {23:23} The sons of Mushi were Mahli, Eder, and Jeremoth, three in total. {23:24} These were the sons of Levi, categorized by their family heads, counted by the number of names, who did the work for the service of the house of the LORD, from the age of twenty years and older. {23:25} For David said, "The LORD God of Israel has given rest to his people, so they may dwell in Jerusalem forever. {23:26} And to the Levites, they will no longer carry the tabernacle or its vessels for service." {23:27} By David's last instructions, the Levites were counted from twenty years old and above. {23:28} Their duty was to assist the sons of Aaron in the service of the house of the LORD, in the courts, in the chambers, in purifying all holy things, and in the work of the service of God; {23:29} both for the showbread, fine flour for grain offerings, unleavened cakes, and anything baked in a pan or fried, and for all measures and sizes; {23:30} and to stand every morning to give thanks and praise the LORD, and likewise in the evening; {23:31} and to offer all burnt offerings to the LORD on the sabbaths, new moons, and set feasts, according to the prescribed order, continually before the LORD; {23:32} and to keep charge of the tabernacle of meeting, the holy place, and the duties of the sons of Aaron, their brothers, in the service of the house of the LORD.

{24:1} These are the divisions of the sons of Aaron: the sons of Aaron were Nadab, Abihu, Eleazar, and Ithamar. {24:2} Nadab and Abihu died before their father and had no children, so Eleazar and Ithamar served as priests. {24:3} David assigned their duties, with Zadok from the line of Eleazar and Ahimelech from the line of Ithamar, according to their responsibilities in service. {24:4} There were more leaders among the sons of Eleazar than among the sons of Ithamar, so they were divided accordingly. Among the sons of Eleazar, there were sixteen leaders of their families, while there were eight among the sons of Ithamar. {24:5} They were assigned by lot, with one group being Eleazar's and another being Ithamar's; the governors of the sanctuary and the house of God were from both lines. {24:6} Shemaiah, the son of Nethaneel the scribe, one of the Levites, recorded them before the king, the leaders, Zadok the priest, Ahimelech the son of Abiathar, and the heads of the priestly and Levitical families: one principal household was chosen for Eleazar and one for Ithamar. {24:7} The first lot was for Jehoiarib, the second for Jedaiah, {24:8} the third for Harim, the fourth for Seorim, {24:9} the fifth for Malchijah, the sixth for Mijamin, {24:10} the seventh for Hakkoz, the eighth for Abijah, {24:11} the ninth for Jeshua, the tenth for Shecaniah, {24:12} the eleventh for Eliashib, the twelfth for Jakim, {24:13} the thirteenth for Huppah, the fourteenth for Jeshebeab, {24:14} the fifteenth for Bilgah, the sixteenth for Immer, {24:15} the seventeenth for Hezir, the eighteenth for Aphses, {24:16} the nineteenth for Pethahiah, the twentieth for Jehezekel, {24:17} the twenty-first for Jachin, the twenty-second for Gamul, {24:18} the twenty-third for Delaiah, and the twenty-fourth for Maaziah. {24:19} These were the assignments for their service in the house of the LORD, according to their divisions, under their father Aaron, as the LORD God of Israel had commanded him. {24:20} The rest of the sons of Levi were these: from the sons of Amram, Shubael; from the sons of Shubael, Jehdeiah. {24:21} Regarding Rehabiah, the first was Isshiah. {24:22} From the Izharites, Shelomoth; from the sons of Shelomoth, Jahath. {24:23} The sons of Hebron were Jeriah the first, Amariah the second, Jahaziel the third, and Jekameam the fourth. {24:24} From the sons of Uzziel, Michah; from the sons of Michah, Shamir. {24:25} The brother of Michah was Isshiah; from the sons of Isshiah, Zechariah. {24:26} The sons of Merari were Mahli and Mushi; from the sons of Jaaziah, Beno. {24:27} The sons of Merari from Jaaziah were Beno, Shoham, Zaccur, and Ibri. {24:28} Mahli had a son named Eleazar, who had no sons. {24:29} Regarding Kish, the son of Kish was Jerahmeel. {24:30} The sons of Mushi were Mahli, Eder, and Jerimoth. These were the sons of the Levites by their families. {24:31} They also cast lots alongside their brothers, the sons of Aaron, in the presence of King David, Zadok, Ahimelech, and the leaders of the priestly and Levitical families, with the principal fathers standing against their younger brothers.

{25:1} David and the captains of the army set apart the sons of Asaph, Heman, and Jeduthun for the service of prophesying with harps, psalteries, and cymbals. The number of those who worked in this service was as follows: {25:2} Among the sons of Asaph were Zaccur, Joseph, Nethaniah, and Asarelah, under the leadership of Asaph, who prophesied according to the king's instructions. {25:3} From Jeduthun's line, there were Gedaliah, Zeri, Jeshaiah, Hashabiah, and Mattithiah, making six, who served under their father Jeduthun, prophesying with a harp to give thanks and praise to the LORD. {25:4} The sons of Heman included Bukkiah, Mattaniah, Uzziel, Shebuel, Jerimoth, Hananiah, Hanani, Eliathah, Giddalti, Romamtiezer, Joshbekashah, Mallothi, Hothir, and Mahazioth. {25:5} All these were the sons of Heman, the king's seer, who lifted up the horn in the words of God. God gave Heman fourteen sons and three daughters. {25:6} All of these were under their father for singing in the house of the LORD, using cymbals, psalteries, and harps for the service of God, according to the king's orders to Asaph, Jeduthun, and Heman. {25:7} The total number of those, along with their brothers who were skilled in the songs of the LORD, was two hundred eighty-eight. {25:8} They cast lots, ward by ward, both small and great, teacher and student alike. {25:9} The first lot was for Joseph of Asaph; the second for Gedaliah, who had twelve with his brothers and sons. {25:10} The third lot was for Zaccur, who also had twelve with his sons and brothers. {25:11} The fourth lot was for Izri, who had twelve with his sons and brothers. {25:12} The fifth was for Nethaniah, who had twelve with his sons and brothers. {25:13} The sixth lot went to Bukkiah, who had twelve with his sons and brothers. {25:14} The seventh was for Jesharelah, who had twelve with his sons and brothers. {25:15} The eighth was for Jeshaiah, who had twelve with his sons and brothers. {25:16} The ninth lot was for Mattaniah, who had twelve with his sons and brothers. {25:17} The tenth was for Shimei, who had twelve with his sons and brothers. {25:18} The eleventh went to Azareel, who had twelve with his sons and brothers. {25:19} The twelfth was for Hashabiah, who had twelve with his sons and brothers. {25:20} The thirteenth lot was for Shubael, who had twelve with his sons and brothers. {25:21} The fourteenth was for Mattithiah, who had twelve with his sons and brothers. {25:22} The fifteenth lot was for Jeremoth, who had twelve with his sons and brothers. {25:23} The sixteenth was for Hananiah, who had twelve with his sons and brothers. {25:24} The seventeenth was for Joshbekashah, who had twelve with his sons and brothers. {25:25} The eighteenth was for Hanani, who had twelve with his sons and brothers. {25:26} The nineteenth was for Mallothi, who had twelve with his sons and brothers. {25:27} The twentieth was for Eliathah, who had twelve with his sons and brothers. {25:28} The twenty-first was for Hothir, who had twelve with his sons and brothers. {25:29} The twenty-second was for Giddalti, who had twelve with his sons and brothers. {25:30} The twenty-third was for Mahazioth, who had twelve with his sons and brothers. {25:31} The twenty-fourth was for Romamtiezer, who had twelve with his sons and brothers.

{26:1} Regarding the divisions of the gatekeepers: Meshelemiah, the son of Kore from the Korhite clan, was among the sons of Asaph. {26:2} Meshelemiah's sons included Zechariah the firstborn, Jediael the second, Zebadiah the third, Jathniel the fourth, {26:3} Elam the fifth, Jehohanan the sixth, and Elioenai the seventh. {26:4} The sons of Obededom were Shemaiah the firstborn, Jehozabad the second, Joah the third, Sacar the fourth, and Nethaneel the fifth. {26:5} Ammiel was the sixth, Issachar the seventh, and Peulthai the eighth; God blessed him. {26:6} Shemaiah also had sons who became leaders in their father's household because they were strong men of valor. {26:7} The sons of Shemaiah included Othni, Rephael, Obed, and Elzabad, whose brothers were strong men: Elihu and Semachiah. {26:8} All these sons of Obededom and their families were skilled in strength for service, totaling sixty-two. {26:9} Meshelemiah had sons and brothers who were strong men, totaling eighteen. {26:10} Hosah, from the Merari clan, had sons too: Simri was the chief (though not the firstborn, his father made him chief); {26:11} Hilkiah was the second, Tebaliah the third, and Zechariah the fourth. All the sons and brothers of Hosah totaled thirteen. {26:12} These divisions of the gatekeepers were among the chief men, set to serve in the house of the LORD, {26:13} and they cast lots, both small and great, according to their families, for every gate. {26:14} The lot for the east gate fell to Shelemiah, and for his son Zechariah, a wise counselor, the lot came out for the north gate. {26:15} The lot for Obededom was for the south, and for his sons, the house of Asuppim. {26:16} The lot for Shuppim and Hosah came forth for the west, along with the gate Shallecheth, by the causeway of the going up, ward against ward. {26:17} Eastward, there were six Levites; northward, four daily; southward, four daily; and toward Asuppim, two and two. {26:18} At Parbar westward, there were four at the causeway and two at Parbar. {26:19} These are the divisions of the gatekeepers among the sons of Kore and Merari. {26:20} Among the Levites, Ahijah was in charge of the treasures of the house of God and the treasures of the dedicated things. {26:21} Concerning the sons of Laadan, the chief fathers of the Gershonite Laadan were Jehieli. {26:22} The sons of Jehieli were Zetham and his brother Joel, who were in charge of the treasures of the house of the LORD. {26:23} Among the Amramites, Izharites, Hebronites, and Uzzielites: {26:24} Shebuel, the son of Gershom, the son of Moses, was ruler of the treasures. {26:25} His brothers by Eliezer were Rehabiah, Jeshaiah, Joram, Zichri, and Shelomith. {26:26} Shelomith and his brothers oversaw all the treasures of the dedicated things, which King David, the chief fathers, captains over thousands and hundreds, and captains of the army had dedicated. {26:27} They dedicated spoils won in battles to maintain the house of the LORD. {26:28} All that Samuel the seer, Saul the son of Kish, Abner the son of Ner, and Joab the son of Zeruiah had dedicated was also under the supervision of Shelomith and his brothers. {26:29} Of the Izharites, Chenaniah and his sons were responsible for the outward business over Israel, including officers and judges. {26:30} Among the Hebronites, Hashabiah and his brothers, valiant men numbering one thousand seven hundred, served as officers for the people of Israel west of the Jordan in all matters of the LORD and for the king's service. {26:31} Among the Hebronites, Jerijah was the chief according to his family line. In the fortieth year of David's reign, they were sought out, and found among them mighty men of valor at Jazer of Gilead. {26:32} His brothers, valiant men, numbered two thousand seven hundred chief fathers, whom King David appointed as rulers over the Reubenites, Gadites, and half the tribe of Manasseh for every matter concerning God and the affairs of the king.

{27:1} The children of Israel were counted, including the chief fathers, captains of thousands and hundreds, and their officers who served the king in various capacities, totaling twenty-four thousand for each monthly rotation throughout the year. {27:2} Jashobeam, the son of Zabdiel, was over the first course for the first month, which included twenty-four thousand men. {27:3} The chief captain for the first month was from the family of Perez. {27:4} The captain for the second month was Dodai the Ahohite, and Mikloth was the ruler over his course, which also had twenty-four thousand men. {27:5} The third captain for the third month was Benaiah, the son of Jehoiada, a chief priest, and his course consisted of twenty-four thousand men. {27:6} This is the same Benaiah who was renowned among the thirty elite warriors and even above them; his son Ammizabad was with him in his course. {27:7} Asahel, the brother of Joab, was the fourth captain for the fourth month, followed by his son Zebadiah; his course also had twenty-four thousand men. {27:8} The fifth captain for the fifth month was Shamhuth the Izrahite, and his course included twenty-four thousand men. {27:9} The sixth captain for the sixth month was Ira, the son of Ikkesh the Tekoite, with twenty-four thousand men in his course. {27:10} Helez the Pelonite, from the tribe of Ephraim, was the seventh captain for the seventh month, with twenty-four thousand men in his course. {27:11} The eighth captain for the eighth month was Sibbecai the Hushathite, from the Zarhites, and his course also had twenty-four thousand men. {27:12} The ninth captain for the ninth month was Abiezer the Anetothite, from the tribe of Benjamin, with twenty-four thousand men in his course. {27:13} The tenth captain for the tenth month was Maharai the Netophathite, from the Zarhites, and he had twenty-four thousand men in his course. {27:14} The eleventh captain for the eleventh month was Benaiah the Pirathonite, from the tribe of Ephraim, with twenty-four thousand men in his course. {27:15} The twelfth captain for the twelfth month was Heldai the Netophathite, of Othniel, and his course also had twenty-four thousand men. {27:16} Over the tribes of Israel: Eliezer, the son of Zichri, was the ruler of the Reubenites; Shephatiah, the son of Maachah, was over the Simeonites; {27:17} Hashabiah, the son of Kemuel, was over the Levites; Zadok was over the Aaronites; {27:18} Elihu, one of David's brothers, was over Judah; Omri, the son of Michael, was over Issachar; {27:19} Ishmaiah, the son of Obadiah, was over Zebulun; Jerimoth, the son of Azriel, was over Naphtali; {27:20} Hoshea, the son of Azaziah, was over Ephraim; Joel, the son of Pedaiah, was over half the tribe of Manasseh; {27:21} Iddo, the son of Zechariah, was over the other half of Manasseh in Gilead; Jaasiel, the son of Abner, was over Benjamin; {27:22} Azareel, the son of Jeroham, was over Dan. These were the leaders of the tribes of Israel. {27:23} David did not take a census of those twenty years old and younger because the LORD had promised to multiply Israel like the stars in the sky. {27:24} Joab, the son of Zeruiah, started to count them but did not finish, as God's wrath came upon Israel for this; thus, the number was not recorded in the annals of King David. {27:25} Azmaveth, the son of Adiel, was in charge of the king's treasures, while Jehonathan, the son of Uzziah, oversaw the storehouses in the fields, cities, villages, and castles. {27:26} Ezri, the son of Chelub, was in charge of those working the fields. {27:27} Shimei the Ramathite managed the vineyards, while Zabdi the Shiphmite oversaw the produce for the wine cellars. {27:28} Baalhanan the Gederite was responsible for the olive and sycamore trees in the lowlands, and Joash oversaw the oil cellars. {27:29} Shitrai the Sharonite was in charge of the herds that grazed in Sharon, and Shaphat, the son of Adlai, managed the herds in the valleys. {27:30} Obil the Ishmaelite was in charge of the camels, and Jehdeiah the Meronothite was over the donkeys. {27:31} Jaziz the Hagerite managed the flocks. All these were the overseers of King David's property. {27:32} Jonathan, David's uncle, was a counselor, a wise man, and a scribe, while Jehiel, the son of Hachmoni, was with the king's sons. {27:33} Ahithophel was the king's counselor, and Hushai the Archite was the king's companion. {27:34} Following Ahithophel was Jehoiada, the son of Benaiah, and Abiathar; Joab was the commander of the king's army.

{28:1} David gathered all the leaders of Israel, including the leaders of the tribes, captains of the divisions that served the king, captains over thousands and hundreds, stewards responsible for all the king's possessions and those of his sons, as well as officers, mighty men, and all the brave warriors, to Jerusalem. {28:2} King David stood up and said, "Listen to me, my brothers and my people. I had it in my heart to build a resting place for the ark of the covenant of the LORD and for the footstool of our God, and I had made preparations for the building. {28:3} But God said to me, 'You shall not build a house for my name because you have been a warrior and have shed blood.' {28:4} Nevertheless, the LORD God of Israel chose me from all my father's house to be king over Israel forever. He chose Judah to be the ruler, and from the house of Judah, He chose my father's house, and among my father's sons, He favored me to be king over all Israel. {28:5} Of all my sons (for the LORD has given me many sons), He has chosen my son Solomon to sit on the throne of the kingdom of the LORD over Israel. {28:6} He told me, 'Your son Solomon will build my house and my courts, for I have chosen him to be my son, and I will be his father. {28:7} I will establish his kingdom forever if he remains steadfast in keeping my commandments and my judgments, as he does today. {28:8} Therefore, in the sight of all Israel, the assembly of the LORD, and in the hearing of our God, observe and seek all the commandments of the LORD your God, so that you may possess this good land and leave it for an inheritance to your children forever. {28:9} And you, Solomon my son, acknowledge the God of your father and serve Him with a whole heart and a willing mind, for the LORD searches all hearts and understands every thought. If you seek Him, He will be found by you; but if you forsake Him, He will reject you forever. {28:10} Take heed now, for the LORD has chosen you to build a house for the sanctuary. Be strong and do it. {28:11} Then David gave his son Solomon the blueprint for the temple, including the layout of the porch, the houses, the storerooms, the upper chambers, the inner rooms, and the place of the mercy seat. {28:12} He also provided the plans for all that he had received by the Spirit concerning the courts of the house of the LORD and all the surrounding chambers, the storerooms of the house of God, and the storerooms for the dedicated gifts. {28:13} He provided instructions for the divisions of the priests and the Levites, the work of serving in the house of the LORD, and for all the vessels used in that service. {28:14} He gave gold by weight for the gold items needed for service, silver by weight for the silver items, ensuring every instrument was accounted for. {28:15} He specified the weight for the gold candlesticks and their lamps, and the weight for the silver candlesticks and lamps according to their use. {28:16} He also gave weight for the gold tables for the showbread, as well as silver tables. {28:17} He provided pure gold for the flesh hooks, bowls, and cups, and for each gold basin, he gave gold by weight, along with silver basins by weight. {28:18} He specified refined gold for the altar of incense and gold for the design of the chariot of the cherubim, which spread their wings and covered the ark of the covenant of the LORD. {28:19} David said, "All of this, the LORD made me understand in writing by His hand upon me, even all the details of this plan." {28:20} David then said to his son Solomon, "Be strong and courageous, and do it. Do not be afraid or dismayed, for the LORD God, my God, will be with you; He will not fail you or forsake you until you have finished all the work for the service of the house of the LORD. {28:21} Moreover, the divisions of the priests and Levites will be with you for all the service of the house of God, and every skilled man willing to work will be at your command, as will the princes and all the people."

{29:1} King David said to the entire assembly, "Solomon my son, whom God has chosen alone, is young and inexperienced, and the task is great because the palace is not for a human being but for the LORD God. {29:2} I have prepared with all my strength for the house of my God the gold for items made of gold, the silver for items made of silver, the bronze for items made of bronze, the iron for items made of iron, the wood for items made of wood, onyx stones, and stones for setting, glittering stones, various colors, precious stones, and abundant marble. {29:3} Moreover, because I have devoted myself to the house of my God, I have given from my personal wealth of gold and silver to the house of my God, in addition to all that I have already prepared for the holy house. {29:4} I have given three thousand talents of gold from the gold of Ophir and seven thousand talents of refined silver to cover the walls of the houses. {29:5} The gold for items of gold, the silver for items of silver, and for all kinds of work to be done by skilled craftsmen. So who is willing to dedicate their service to the LORD today? {29:6} Then the leaders of the tribes of Israel, the captains of thousands and hundreds, and the overseers of the king's work offered willingly. {29:7} They gave for the service of the house of God five thousand talents of gold and ten thousand darics, ten thousand talents of silver, eighteen thousand talents of bronze, and one hundred thousand talents of iron. {29:8} Those who had precious stones gave them to the treasury of the house of the LORD, through Jehiel the Gershonite. {29:9} The people rejoiced because they had offered willingly, with a perfect heart, to the LORD; King David also rejoiced greatly. {29:10} Therefore, David blessed the LORD before all the assembly and said, "Blessed are you, LORD God of Israel, our father, forever and ever. {29:11} Yours, O LORD, is the greatness, the power, the glory, the victory, and the majesty, for everything in heaven and earth belongs to you; yours is the kingdom, O LORD, and you are exalted as head over all. {29:12} Both riches and honor come from you; you rule over all, and in your hand are power and might; it is in your hand to make great and to give strength to all. {29:13} Now, our God, we thank you and praise your glorious name. {29:14} But who am I, and what is my people, that we should be able to offer so willingly in this manner? For everything comes from you, and we have given you only what comes from your hand. {29:15} For we are strangers and temporary residents before you, just like our ancestors; our days on earth are like a shadow, and there is no permanence. {29:16} O LORD our God, all this abundance that we have prepared to build you a house for your holy name comes from your hand, and it all belongs to you. {29:17} I know, my God, that you test the heart and take pleasure in integrity. As for me, in the uprightness of my heart, I have willingly offered all these things; and now I have seen with joy your people who are present here offering willingly to you. {29:18} O LORD God of Abraham, Isaac, and Israel, our ancestors, keep this forever in the thoughts and intentions of your people and prepare their hearts for you. {29:19} Give my son Solomon a perfect heart to keep your commandments, your testimonies, and your statutes, and to do all these things and to build the palace for which I have made provision. {29:20} David said to all the assembly, "Now bless the LORD your God." So all the assembly blessed the LORD God of their ancestors, bowed their heads, and worshipped the LORD and the king. {29:21} The next day, they sacrificed offerings to the LORD and presented burnt offerings, a thousand bulls, a thousand rams, and a thousand lambs, with their drink offerings and sacrifices in abundance for all Israel. {29:22} They ate and drank before the LORD with great joy that day. They made Solomon, the son of David, king for the second time and anointed him to be the chief governor, and Zadok as priest. {29:23} Then Solomon sat on the throne of the LORD as king in place of his father David, and he prospered; all Israel obeyed him. {29:24} All the leaders, mighty men, and all the sons of King David submitted to King Solomon. {29:25} The LORD greatly exalted Solomon in the sight of all Israel and bestowed royal majesty upon him such as had not been seen in any king before him in Israel. {29:26} Thus, David the son of Jesse reigned over all Israel. {29:27} He reigned for forty years; seven years in Hebron and thirty-three years in Jerusalem. {29:28} He died at a good old age, full of days, wealth, and honor; and his son Solomon succeeded him. {29:29} The acts of King David, both the beginning and the end, are recorded in the book of Samuel the seer, the book of Nathan the prophet, and the book of Gad the seer, {29:30} with all his reign and power, and the events that happened to him, to Israel, and to all the kingdoms of the countries.

The Second Book of Chronicles

{1:1} Solomon, the son of David, was strengthened in his kingdom, and the LORD his God was with him and greatly magnified him. {1:2} Then Solomon spoke to all Israel, to the captains of thousands and hundreds, to the judges, and to every governor in all Israel, and to the heads of the families. {1:3} So Solomon and the entire assembly went to the high place at Gibeon because there was the tabernacle of the congregation of God, which Moses, the servant of the LORD, had made in the wilderness. {1:4} But David had brought the ark of God from Kirjath-jearim to the place he had prepared for it, where he pitched a tent for it in Jerusalem. {1:5} Moreover, he placed the bronze altar that Bezaleel, the son of Uri, the son of Hur, had made before the tabernacle of the LORD, and Solomon and the congregation sought the LORD there. {1:6} Solomon went up to the bronze altar before the LORD at the tabernacle of the congregation and offered a thousand burnt offerings on it. {1:7} That night, God appeared to Solomon and said, "Ask what I shall give you." {1:8} Solomon replied, "You have shown great mercy to my father David and have made me king in his place. {1:9} Now, O LORD God, let your promise to my father David be established, for you have made me king over a people as numerous as the dust of the earth. {1:10} Give me wisdom and knowledge so that I may lead this people, for who can judge this great people of yours?" {1:11} God said to Solomon, "Since this was in your heart and you did not ask for riches, wealth, or honor, nor for the life of your enemies, or long life, but have asked for wisdom and knowledge for yourself to judge my people, over whom I have made you king, {1:12} wisdom and knowledge are granted to you. I will also give you riches, wealth, and honor, such as no king before you had and no king after you will have." {1:13} Then Solomon returned from the high place at Gibeon to Jerusalem, from before the tabernacle of the congregation, and reigned over Israel. {1:14} Solomon gathered chariots and horsemen; he had fourteen hundred chariots and twelve thousand horsemen, which he stationed in the chariot cities and with the king in Jerusalem. {1:15} The king made silver and gold in Jerusalem as abundant as stones, and cedar trees as plentiful as sycamore trees in the lowlands. {1:16} Solomon imported horses from Egypt, and linen yarn; the king's merchants received the linen yarn at a price. {1:17} They brought up a chariot from Egypt for six hundred shekels of silver and a horse for one hundred and fifty shekels; they also exported horses for all the kings of the Hittites and the kings of Syria by their means.

{2:1} Solomon decided to build a house for the name of the LORD and a house for his kingdom. {2:2} He assigned seventy thousand men to carry loads, eighty thousand to cut stone in the mountains, and three thousand six hundred to supervise them. {2:3} Solomon sent a message to Huram, the king of Tyre, saying, "Just as you dealt with my father David by sending him cedar trees to build a house to live in, do the same for me. {2:4} I am building a house for the name of the LORD my God, to dedicate it to Him, to burn sweet incense before Him, to provide the continual bread, and to offer burnt offerings morning and evening, on the sabbaths, on the new moons, and on the solemn feasts of the LORD our God. This is a lasting ordinance for Israel. {2:5} The house I build will be great because our God is greater than all gods. {2:6} But who is able to build a house for Him, since even the heavens and the highest heavens cannot contain Him? Who am I, then, that I should build a house for Him, except to offer sacrifices before Him? {2:7} Send me, therefore, a skilled man who can work with gold, silver, bronze, iron, purple, crimson, and blue, and who can engrave (carve designs) skillfully alongside the skilled men I have in Judah and Jerusalem, whom my father David provided. {2:8} Also, send me cedar, fir, and algum trees from Lebanon, for I know that your servants are skilled in cutting timber in Lebanon; my servants will work alongside yours {2:9} to prepare an abundant supply of timber, for the house I am about to build will be magnificent. {2:10} I will give your servants, the woodcutters, twenty thousand measures of beaten wheat, twenty thousand measures of barley, twenty thousand baths of wine, and twenty thousand baths of oil. {2:11} Then Huram, the king of Tyre, replied in writing to Solomon, "Because the LORD loves His people, He has made you king over them. {2:12} Huram also said, 'Blessed be the LORD God of Israel, who made heaven and earth, for He has given David the king a wise son, endowed with prudence and understanding, to build a house for the LORD and a house for his kingdom.' {2:13} Now I have sent a skilled man, endowed with understanding, from Huram my father, {2:14} the son of a woman from the tribe of Dan; his father was a man of Tyre, skilled in working with gold, silver, bronze, iron, stone, and timber, as well as in purple, blue, fine linen, and crimson; he can engrave any design and is capable of finding out every creative idea that may be presented to him, along with your skilled workers and the skilled workers of my lord David your father. {2:15} Now, regarding the wheat, barley, oil, and wine that my lord mentioned, let him send them to his servants. {2:16} We will cut as much wood from Lebanon as you need and bring it to you by sea in rafts to Joppa; you can then transport it up to Jerusalem. {2:17} Solomon counted all the foreigners in the land of Israel, just as David his father had counted them; and they found one hundred fifty-three thousand six hundred. {2:18} He assigned seventy thousand of them to be carriers of burdens, eighty thousand to be stone cutters in the mountains, and three thousand six hundred supervisors to manage the work.

{3:1} Solomon began to build the house of the LORD in Jerusalem on Mount Moriah, where the LORD had appeared to David his father, at the site that David had prepared on the threshing floor of Ornan the Jebusite. {3:2} He started construction on the second day of the second month in the fourth year of his reign. {3:3} These are the measurements Solomon was given for building the house of God: the length was sixty cubits and the width was twenty cubits. {3:4} The porch in front of the house was the same width as the house, twenty cubits long, and one hundred twenty cubits high; he overlaid it inside with pure gold. {3:5} The larger room was paneled with fir trees, which he covered with fine gold and decorated with palm trees and chains. {3:6} He adorned the house with precious stones for beauty, and the gold he used was from Parvaim. {3:7} He overlaid the house, including the beams, posts, walls, and doors, with gold, and engraved cherubim on the walls. {3:8} He made the most holy place, which was also twenty cubits long and twenty cubits wide, and he covered it with fine gold, amounting to six hundred talents. {3:9} The weight of the nails was fifty shekels of gold, and he overlaid the upper chambers with gold. {3:10} In the most holy place, he made two cherubim out of carved work and overlaid them with gold. {3:11} The wings of the cherubim were twenty cubits long: one wing of one cherub was five cubits, reaching to the wall of the house, and the other wing was five cubits, reaching to the wing of the other cherub. {3:12} One wing of the other cherub was five cubits, reaching to the wall of the house, and the other wing was five cubits, joining to the wing of the other cherub. {3:13} The wings of these cherubim spread out twenty cubits, and they stood on their feet, facing inward. {3:14} He made the veil of blue, purple, crimson, and fine linen, and embroidered cherubim on it. {3:15} He also made two pillars in front of the house, each thirty-five cubits high, and the capital (top part) on each was five cubits high. {3:16} He made chains for the tops of the pillars and placed one hundred pomegranates on the chains. {3:17} He raised up the pillars in front of the temple, one on the right and the other on the left, naming the one on the right Jachin and the one on the left Boaz.

{4:1} Solomon made a bronze altar that was twenty cubits long, twenty cubits wide, and ten cubits high. {4:2} He also created a molten sea that was ten cubits from brim to brim, circular in shape, and five cubits high; it was surrounded by a line that measured thirty cubits. {4:3} Under it were the likenesses of oxen, encircling it: ten in a cubit, forming two rows of oxen when it was cast. {4:4} It rested on twelve oxen—three facing north, three west, three south, and three east; the sea was set above them, with their hindquarters turned inward. {4:5} The thickness of the sea was a handbreadth, and the rim resembled the design of a cup with lily flowers; it could hold three thousand baths. {4:6} He also made ten lavers, placing five on the right and five on the left for washing; the offerings for burnt sacrifices were washed in them, but the sea was for the priests to wash in. {4:7} He created ten golden lampstands according to their design, placing five on the right side and five on the left in the temple. {4:8} He made ten tables, placing five on the right and five on the left, and he made one hundred basins of gold. {4:9} Furthermore, he constructed the court of the priests and the great court, adding doors for the court, which he overlaid with bronze. {4:10} He positioned the sea on the right side at the east end, facing south. {4:11} Huram made the pots, shovels, and basins, completing the work for King Solomon for the house of God. {4:12} This included the two pillars, the capitals on top of the pillars, and the two wreaths to cover the capitals. {4:13} He added four hundred pomegranates on the two wreaths—two rows of pomegranates on each wreath, covering the capitals. {4:14} He also made bases and lavers placed on the bases, {4:15} along with one sea and twelve oxen underneath it. {4:16} Huram made the pots, shovels, fleshhooks, and all the instruments for King Solomon's house of the LORD from bright brass. {4:17} The king cast them in the Jordan plain, in the clay ground between Succoth and Zeredathah. {4:18} Solomon made all these items in great abundance, so much so that the weight of the brass could not be determined. {4:19} He also made all the vessels for the house of God, including the golden altar and the tables for the showbread. {4:20} Additionally, he crafted the lampstands with their lamps, to burn in front of the oracle, all made of pure gold {4:21} The flowers, lamps, and tongs were made of gold, and all were made from perfect gold. {4:22} The snuffers, basins, spoons, and censers were made of pure gold, and the entrance to the house, the inner doors of the most holy place, and the doors of the temple were also made of gold.

{5:1} All the work that Solomon did for the house of the LORD was completed. Solomon brought in all the things that David, his father, had dedicated, including silver, gold, and all the instruments, and placed them among the treasures of the house of God. {5:2} Solomon then gathered the elders of Israel, the heads of the tribes, and the leaders of the families of Israel to Jerusalem to bring up the ark of the covenant of the LORD from the city of David, which is Zion. {5:3} All the men of Israel gathered to the king for the feast in the seventh month. {5:4} The elders of Israel came, and the Levites carried the ark. {5:5} They brought up the ark, the tabernacle of meeting, and all the holy vessels in the tabernacle, which the priests and Levites carried. {5:6} King Solomon and the entire congregation of Israel that had assembled before the ark sacrificed sheep and oxen in such great numbers that they couldn't be counted. {5:7} The priests brought the ark of the covenant of the LORD to its place, into the inner sanctuary of the house, the most holy place, beneath the wings of the cherubim. {5:8} The cherubim spread their wings over the place of the ark, covering the ark and its poles above. {5:9} They pulled out the poles of the ark so that the ends could be seen from the ark in front of the inner sanctuary, but they weren't visible outside. And they remain that way to this day. {5:10} The ark contained only the two stone tablets that Moses placed there at Horeb when the LORD made a covenant with the children of Israel after they came out of Egypt. {5:11} When the priests came out of the holy place—(all the priests present had consecrated themselves and were not waiting according to their divisions)— {5:12} the Levites, who were the singers, including all of Asaph, Heman, and Jeduthun, along with their sons and brothers, dressed in white linen, with cymbals, psalteries, and harps, stood at the east end of the altar. Alongside them were one hundred and twenty priests sounding trumpets. {5:13} When the trumpeters and singers joined together to make one sound, praising and thanking the LORD, and when they lifted their voices with the trumpets, cymbals, and musical instruments, praising the LORD, saying, "For he is good; his mercy endures forever," the house was filled with a cloud, the house of the LORD. {5:14} The priests could not stand to minister because of cloud, for glory of the LORD had filled house of God.

{6:1} Then Solomon said, "The LORD has declared that He would dwell in thick darkness. {6:2} But I have built a house for Your habitation, a place for You to dwell forever." {6:3} The king turned his face and blessed the whole congregation of Israel, and all the congregation of Israel stood. {6:4} He said, "Blessed be the LORD God of Israel, who has fulfilled with His hands what He spoke with His mouth to my father David, saying, {6:5} 'Since the day I brought My people out of the land of Egypt, I chose no city among all the tribes of Israel to build a house, that My name might be there; nor did I choose any man to be a ruler over My people Israel. {6:6} But I have chosen Jerusalem, that My name might be there, and I have chosen David to be over My people Israel.' {6:7} Now it was in the heart of my father David to build a house for the name of the LORD God of Israel. {6:8} But the LORD said to my father David, 'Because it was in your heart to build a house for My name, you did well that it was in your heart. {6:9} Nevertheless, you shall not build the house; your son, who will come from your body, he shall build the house for My name.' {6:10} The LORD has fulfilled His word that He spoke, for I have risen up in the place of my father David, and I am seated on the throne of Israel, as the LORD promised, and have built the house for the name of the LORD God of Israel. {6:11} In it, I have placed the ark, which contains the covenant of the LORD that He made with the children of Israel. {6:12} Solomon stood before the altar of the LORD in the presence of all the congregation of Israel and spread out his hands. {6:13} For Solomon had made a bronze platform, five cubits long, five cubits wide, and three cubits high, and had set it in the midst of the court. On it, he stood, knelt down before all the congregation of Israel, and spread out his hands toward heaven. {6:14} He said, "O LORD God of Israel, there is no God like You in heaven or on earth; You keep covenant and show mercy to Your servants who walk before You with all their hearts. {6:15} You have kept Your promise to Your servant David, my father; You spoke with Your mouth, and with Your hand, You have fulfilled it this day. {6:16} Now, O LORD God of Israel, keep Your promise to Your servant David, my father, saying, 'You shall not fail to have a man in My sight to sit on the throne of Israel, provided your children take heed to their way to walk in My law, as you have walked before Me.' {6:17} Now, O LORD God of Israel, let Your word be confirmed, which You have spoken to Your servant David. {6:18} But will God really dwell with men on the earth? Behold, heaven and the highest heaven cannot contain You; how much less this house that I have built! {6:19} Yet regard the prayer of Your servant and his supplication, O LORD my God, to listen to the cry and the prayer which Your servant prays before You. {6:20} Let Your eyes be open toward this house day and night, toward the place where You said You would put Your name, to listen to the prayer that Your servant prays toward this place. {6:21} Listen to the supplications of Your servant and of Your people Israel, when they pray toward this place; hear from Your dwelling place in heaven, and when You hear, forgive. {6:22} If a man sins against his neighbor and is made to take an oath, and comes before Your altar in this house, {6:23} then hear from heaven and act; judge Your servants by repaying the wicked, bringing his way upon his own head, and justifying the righteous by giving him according to his righteousness. {6:24} If Your people Israel are defeated before the enemy because they have sinned against You, and return and confess Your name, and pray and make supplication before You in this house, {6:25} then hear from heaven, and forgive the sin of Your people Israel, and bring them back to the land which You gave to them and to their fathers. {6:26} When the heavens are shut up and there is no rain because they have sinned against You; if they pray toward this place and confess Your name, and turn from their sin when You afflict them; {6:27} then hear from heaven and forgive the sin of Your servants and of Your people Israel, when You teach them the good way in which they should walk, and send rain on Your land which You have given to Your people as an inheritance. {6:28} If there is famine in the land, if there is pestilence, if there are blight or mildew, locusts, or caterpillars; if their enemies besiege them in the cities of their land; whatever plague or sickness there is, {6:29} then whatever prayer or supplication is made by any man or by all Your people Israel, when each one knows his own plague and his own grief, and spreads out his hands in this house; {6:30} then hear from heaven, Your dwelling place, and forgive, and render to every man according to all his ways, whose heart You know; for You alone know the hearts of the children of men. {6:31} That they may fear You, to walk in Your ways, as long as they live in the land which You gave to our fathers. {6:32} Moreover, concerning the foreigner who is not of Your people Israel but has come from a far country for Your great name's sake and Your mighty hand and Your outstretched arm; if he comes and prays in this house, {6:33} then hear from heaven, from Your dwelling place, and do according to all that the foreigner calls to You for; that all peoples of the earth may know Your name and fear You, as does Your people Israel, and may know that this house which I have built is called by Your name. {6:34} If Your people go out to battle against their enemies by the way that You send them, and they pray to You toward this city which You have chosen and the house which I have built for Your name, {6:35} then hear from heaven their prayer and supplication, and maintain their cause. {6:36} If they sin against You—for there is no one who does not sin—and You become angry with them and deliver them to the enemy, and they are carried away captive to a land far off or near; {6:37} yet if they return to their hearts in the land where they were taken captive and turn and pray to You in the land of their captivity, saying, 'We have sinned, we have done wrong, and have acted wickedly'; {6:38} if they return to You with all their heart and with all their soul in the land of their captivity, where they were taken captive, and pray toward their land, which You gave to their fathers, and toward the city which You have chosen, and toward the house which I have built for Your name; {6:39} then hear from heaven, from Your dwelling place, their prayer and supplications, and maintain their cause, and forgive Your people who have sinned against You. {6:40} Now, my God, I beseech You, let Your eyes be open and Your ears attentive to the prayer made in this place. {6:41} Now arise, O LORD God, to Your resting place, You and the ark of Your strength. Let Your priests, O LORD God, be clothed with salvation, and let Your saints rejoice in goodness. {6:42} O LORD God, do not turn away the face of Your anointed; remember the mercies of David, Your servant.

{7:1} When Solomon finished praying, fire came down from heaven and consumed the burnt offering and the sacrifices; the glory of the LORD filled the house. {7:2} The priests could not enter the house of the LORD because the glory of the LORD had filled the LORD's house. {7:3} When all the children of Israel saw how the fire came down and the glory of the LORD on the house, they bowed with their faces to the ground on the pavement, worshipped, and praised the LORD, saying, "For He is good; His mercy endures forever." {7:4} Then the king and all the people offered sacrifices before the LORD. {7:5} King Solomon offered a sacrifice of twenty-two thousand oxen and one hundred twenty thousand sheep; so the king and all the people dedicated the house of God. {7:6} The priests performed their duties, and the Levites played the musical instruments of the LORD that King David had made to praise the LORD, because His mercy endures forever, as David praised through their ministry. The priests sounded trumpets before them, and all Israel stood. {7:7} Furthermore, Solomon consecrated the middle of the court in front of the house of the LORD, where he offered burnt offerings and the fat from peace offerings, because the bronze altar that Solomon made could not hold the burnt offerings, the grain offerings, and the fat. {7:8} At that time, Solomon celebrated the feast for seven days, and all Israel was with him, a very great congregation, from the entrance of Hamath to the river of Egypt. {7:9} On the eighth day, they held a solemn assembly; they kept the dedication of the altar for seven days and the feast for seven days. {7:10} On the twenty-third day of the seventh month, he sent the people away to their tents, glad and joyful in heart for the goodness that the LORD had shown to David, to Solomon, and to His people Israel. {7:11} Thus, Solomon finished the house of the LORD and the king's house; everything that came into Solomon's heart to make in the house of the LORD and in his own house he successfully accomplished. {7:12} The LORD appeared to Solomon at night and said to him, "I have heard your prayer and have chosen this place for Myself as a house of sacrifice. {7:13} If I shut up heaven so there is no rain, or if I command locusts to devour the land, or if I send pestilence among My people; {7:14} if My people, who are called by My name, humble themselves, pray, seek My face, and turn from their wicked ways, then I will hear from heaven, forgive their sin, and heal their land. {7:15} Now My eyes will be open, and My ears attentive to the prayer made in this place. {7:16} For now I have chosen and consecrated this house, that My name may be there forever; My eyes and My heart will be there perpetually. {7:17} As for you, if you walk before Me as your father David walked, and do according to all that I have commanded you, and observe My statutes and My judgments; {7:18} then I will establish the throne of your kingdom, as I covenanted with David your father, saying, 'You shall not lack a man to rule in Israel.' {7:19} But if you turn away and forsake My statutes and My commandments, which I have set before you, and go and serve other gods and worship them; {7:20} then I will uproot them from My land which I have given them, and this house, which I have consecrated for My name, I will cast out of My sight and make it a proverb and a byword among all nations. {7:21} This house, which is high, will become an astonishment to everyone passing by; they will ask, 'Why has the LORD done this to this land and this house?' {7:22} It will be answered, 'Because they forsook the LORD God of their fathers, who brought them out of the land of Egypt, and held on to other gods, worshipped and served them; therefore He has brought all this evil upon them.'

{8:1} At the end of twenty years during which Solomon built the house of the LORD and his own house, {8:2} he built the cities that Huram had restored to him and settled the children of Israel there. {8:3} Solomon went to Hamathzobah and conquered it. {8:4} He built Tadmor in the wilderness and all the store cities he constructed in Hamath. {8:5} He also built Upper and Lower Bethhoron, fortified cities with walls, gates, and bars; {8:6} and Baalath, along with all the store cities he had, the chariot cities, and the cities for horsemen, as well as everything else he desired to build in Jerusalem, Lebanon, and throughout his entire dominion. {8:7} As for the people who were left of the Hittites, Amorites, Perizzites, Hivites, and Jebusites, who were not of Israel, {8:8} Solomon made their children, who remained in the land after them and whom the children of Israel did not consume, pay tribute until this day. {8:9} Solomon did not make servants from the children of Israel for his work; they were his men of war, chief captains, and captains of his chariots and horsemen. {8:10} These were the chief officers of King Solomon, two hundred fifty in total, who ruled over the people. {8:11} Solomon brought the daughter of Pharaoh from the City of David to the house he built for her, saying, "My wife shall not dwell in the house of David, king of Israel, because the places are holy where the ark of the LORD has come." {8:12} Solomon offered burnt offerings to the LORD on the altar he had built before the porch, {8:13} following a specific schedule every day, according to the commandment of Moses, on the Sabbaths, new moons, and solemn feasts, three times a year: during the Feast of Unleavened Bread, the Feast of Weeks, and the Feast of Tabernacles. {8:14} He appointed the courses of the priests for their service and the Levites for their duties, to praise and minister before the priests as required daily; the porters also followed their courses at every gate, as David, the man of God, had commanded. {8:15} They did not depart from the commandment of the king regarding the priests and Levites, or concerning any matter, including the treasures. {8:16} All the work of Solomon was prepared from the day the foundation of the house of the LORD was laid until it was finished; thus, the house of the LORD was perfected. {8:17} Solomon then went to Eziongeber and Eloth, by the seaside in the land of Edom. {8:18} Huram sent him ships and servants skilled in the sea, who went with Solomon's servants to Ophir, and took from there four hundred fifty talents of gold, which they brought to King Solomon.

{9:1} When the queen of Sheba heard about Solomon's fame, she came to test him with hard questions in Jerusalem, bringing a very large company, camels carrying spices, a lot of gold, and precious stones. When she arrived, she talked with Solomon about everything that was on her mind. {9:2} Solomon answered all her questions; nothing was hidden from him that he did not explain. {9:3} After the queen of Sheba saw Solomon's wisdom and the house he had built, {9:4} as well as the food on his table, the seating of his servants, the attendance of his ministers, their clothing, his cupbearers, and their clothing, and the way he ascended to the house of the LORD, she was left breathless. {9:5} She said to the king, "The report I heard in my own land about your actions and wisdom was true! {9:6} However, I did not believe their words until I came and saw with my own eyes. Indeed, the half of your greatness was not told to me; you surpass the fame I heard. {9:7} Happy are your men, and happy are your servants, who stand continually before you and hear your wisdom. {9:8} Blessed be the LORD your God, who delighted in you and set you on His throne to be king for the LORD your God! Because your God loved Israel and established them forever, He made you king over them to ensure judgment and justice." {9:9} She gave the king one hundred twenty talents of gold, a great abundance of spices, and precious stones. There were no spices like those that the queen of Sheba gave to King Solomon. {9:10} Huram's servants and Solomon's servants brought gold from Ophir and also algum trees and precious stones. {9:11} The king made terraces from the algum trees for the house of the LORD and for the king's palace, as well as harps and lyres for singers. Such things had never been seen in the land of Judah before. {9:12} King Solomon gave the queen of Sheba everything she desired, whatever she asked for, besides what she had brought to the king. Then she turned and returned to her own land with her servants. {9:13} The weight of gold that came to Solomon in one year was six hundred sixty-six talents of gold, {9:14} besides what the merchants and traders brought. All the kings of Arabia and governors of the country brought gold and silver to Solomon. {9:15} King Solomon made two hundred gold targets; each target required six hundred shekels of gold. {9:16} He also made three hundred gold shields; each shield required three hundred shekels of gold. The king placed them in the House of the Forest of Lebanon. {9:17} Additionally, the king made a great throne of ivory and overlaid it with pure gold. {9:18} There were six steps leading up to the throne, with a golden footstool attached to it. There were armrests on each side of the throne, and two lions stood by the armrests. {9:19} Twelve lions stood on each side of the six steps. Nothing like this had been made in any kingdom. {9:20} All the drinking vessels of King Solomon were made of gold, and all the vessels in the House of the Forest of Lebanon were pure gold; silver was not valued at all during Solomon's reign. {9:21} The king's ships went to Tarshish with Huram's servants; every three years, the Tarshish ships brought back gold, silver, ivory, apes, and peacocks. {9:22} King Solomon surpassed all the kings of the earth in riches and wisdom. {9:23} All the kings of the earth sought Solomon's presence to hear the wisdom that God had placed in his heart. {9:24} Each king brought gifts, including silver and gold vessels, clothing, harnesses, spices, horses, and mules, a regular yearly tribute. {9:25} Solomon had four thousand stalls for horses and chariots and twelve thousand horsemen, whom he stationed in the chariot cities and with the king in Jerusalem. {9:26} He ruled over all the kings from the Euphrates River to the land of the Philistines and the border of Egypt. {9:27} The king made silver in Jerusalem as common as stones, and he made cedar trees as abundant as sycamore trees in the lowlands. {9:28} They brought horses for Solomon from Egypt and from all the lands. {9:29} Now, the rest of Solomon's acts, both the first and the last, are they not written in the book of Nathan the prophet, in the prophecy of Ahijah the Shilonite, and in the visions of Iddo the seer concerning Jeroboam son of Nebat? {9:30} Solomon reigned in Jerusalem over all Israel for forty years. {9:31} Solomon passed away and was buried in the City of David, his father; and his son Rehoboam reigned in his place.

{10:1} Rehoboam went to Shechem, for all Israel had gathered there to make him king. {10:2} When Jeroboam son of Nebat, who had fled to Egypt from King Solomon, heard about this, he returned from Egypt. {10:3} They sent for him, and Jeroboam and all Israel spoke to Rehoboam, saying, {10:4} "Your father made our yoke hard; now lighten the harsh servitude he imposed on us, and we will serve you." {10:5} He replied, "Come back to me in three days." So the people left. {10:6} King Rehoboam consulted the elders who had served his father Solomon during his lifetime. He asked, "What advice do you give me in response to this people?" {10:7} They advised him, "If you are kind to this people and speak good words to them, they will be your servants forever." {10:8} But he rejected the advice of the elders and instead consulted the young men who had grown up with him and were now serving him. {10:9} He asked them, "What do you suggest we say to these people who want me to lighten the yoke my father imposed on them?" {10:10} The young men replied, "Tell the people who said to you, 'Your father made our yoke heavy; lighten it for us,' that you will make it even heavier. Say to them, 'My little finger is thicker than my father's waist. {10:11} My father laid a heavy yoke on you, but I will make it even heavier; my father used whips on you, but I will use scorpions.'" {10:12} So Jeroboam and all the people returned to Rehoboam on the third day, as the king had instructed. {10:13} The king answered them harshly and rejected the advice of the elders. {10:14} He spoke to them according to the advice of the young men, saying, "My father made your yoke heavy, but I will add to it; my father chastised you with whips, but I will chastise you with scorpions." {10:15} The king did not listen to the people, for this turn of events was from God, so that the LORD might fulfill His word spoken through Ahijah the Shilonite to Jeroboam son of Nebat. {10:16} When all Israel saw that the king refused to listen to them, they answered the king, "What share do we have in David? We have no inheritance in the son of Jesse. Everyone to your tents, Israel! Look after your own house, David!" So all Israel went to their tents. {10:17} But Rehoboam reigned over the people of Judah. {10:18} King Rehoboam sent Hadoram, who was in charge of the forced labor, but the Israelites stoned him to death. King Rehoboam quickly jumped into his chariot and fled to Jerusalem. {10:19} Israel has been in rebellion against the house of David to this day.

{11:1} When Rehoboam arrived in Jerusalem, he gathered 180,000 chosen warriors from the tribes of Judah and Benjamin to fight against Israel in an attempt to restore the kingdom to himself. {11:2} However, the word of the LORD came to Shemaiah, the man of God, saying, {11:3} "Speak to Rehoboam son of Solomon, king of Judah, and to all Israel in Judah and Benjamin, saying, {11:4} 'This is what the LORD says: You shall not go up or fight against your brothers. Each of you must return home, for this situation is from Me.'" They obeyed the LORD's words and did not march against Jeroboam. {11:5} Rehoboam stayed in Jerusalem and built fortified cities in Judah. {11:6} He built Bethlehem, Etam, and Tekoa, {11:7} Bethzur, Shoco, and Adullam, {11:8} Gath, Mareshah, and Ziph, {11:9} Adoraim, Lachish, and Azekah, {11:10} Zorah, Aijalon, and Hebron, which were fortified cities in Judah and Benjamin. {11:11} He strengthened the fortifications, appointed captains, and stored food, oil, and wine in them. {11:12} In every city, he placed shields and spears and made them very strong, having the support of Judah and Benjamin. {11:13} The priests and Levites from all Israel came to him from their territories. {11:14} The Levites left their towns and property to join Judah and Jerusalem because Jeroboam and his sons had rejected them from serving as priests of the LORD. {11:15} He appointed priests for the high places, for the idols, and for the calves he had made. {11:16} Those from all the tribes of Israel who set their hearts to seek the LORD God of Israel came to Jerusalem to sacrifice to the LORD, the God of their ancestors. {11:17} This strengthened the kingdom of Judah and made Rehoboam son of Solomon strong for three years, as they followed the ways of David and Solomon during that time. {11:18} Rehoboam took Mahalath, the daughter of Jerimoth son of David, as his wife, and Abihail, the daughter of Eliab son of Jesse; {11:19} she bore him children: Jeush, Shamariah, and Zaham. {11:20} After her, he married Maachah, the daughter of Absalom, who bore him Abijah, Attai, Ziza, and Shelomith. {11:21} Rehoboam loved Maachah, the daughter of Absalom, more than all his wives and concubines; (he had eighteen wives and sixty concubines, and he fathered twenty-eight sons and sixty daughters.) {11:22} Rehoboam made Abijah son of Maachah the chief, to be ruler among his brothers, thinking of making him king. {11:23} He acted wisely and distributed his children throughout all the territories of Judah and Benjamin, in every fortified city, providing them with abundant provisions. He desired many wives.

{12:1} When Rehoboam had established his kingdom and strengthened his rule, he forsook the law of the LORD, and all Israel followed him. {12:2} In the fifth year of King Rehoboam's reign, Shishak, king of Egypt, came up against Jerusalem because they had sinned against the LORD. {12:3} He had 1,200 chariots and 60,000 horsemen, and the people who came with him from Egypt were countless, including the Lubims, the Sukkiims, and the Ethiopians. {12:4} He captured the fortified cities belonging to Judah and advanced to Jerusalem. {12:5} Then the prophet Shemaiah came to Rehoboam and the princes of Judah, who had gathered in Jerusalem because of Shishak, and said to them, "This is what the LORD says: You have forsaken Me, and so I have also abandoned you to Shishak." {12:6} The princes of Israel and the king humbled themselves and said, "The LORD is righteous." {12:7} When the LORD saw that they had humbled themselves, the word of the LORD came to Shemaiah, saying, "They have humbled themselves; therefore I will not destroy them, but I will grant them some deliverance. My wrath will not be poured out on Jerusalem through Shishak." {12:8} Nevertheless, they will become his servants so that they may learn the difference between serving Me and serving the kingdoms of the countries. {12:9} So Shishak, king of Egypt, attacked Jerusalem and took away the treasures of the house of the LORD and the treasures of the king's palace; he took everything, including the gold shields that Solomon had made. {12:10} In their place, King Rehoboam made bronze shields and entrusted them to the chief of the guard, who kept watch at the entrance of the king's palace. {12:11} Whenever the king entered the house of the LORD, the guards would bring them out and return them to the guard chamber. {12:12} When he humbled himself, the LORD's anger turned away from him so that He did not completely destroy him, and things went well in Judah. {12:13} King Rehoboam strengthened his position in Jerusalem and reigned; he was 41 years old when he began to reign and ruled for 17 years in Jerusalem, the city the LORD had chosen from all the tribes of Israel to put His name there. His mother's name was Naamah, an Ammonite. {12:14} He did evil because he did not prepare his heart to seek the LORD. {12:15} The acts of Rehoboam, from beginning to end, are written in the book of Shemaiah the prophet and in the visions of Iddo the seer regarding genealogies. There were continual wars between Rehoboam and Jeroboam. {12:16} Rehoboam passed away and was buried in the city of David, and his son Abijah reigned in his place.

{13:1} In the eighteenth year of King Jeroboam's reign, Abijah began to reign over Judah. {13:2} He ruled for three years in Jerusalem. His mother's name was Michaiah, the daughter of Uriel from Gibeah. There was war between Abijah and Jeroboam. {13:3} Abijah prepared for battle with an army of 400,000 brave warriors, while Jeroboam gathered an army of 800,000 mighty men of valor against him. {13:4} Abijah stood on Mount Zemaraim, which is in the hill country of Ephraim, and said, "Listen to me, Jeroboam and all Israel; {13:5} do you not know that the LORD God of Israel gave the kingdom of Israel to David and his descendants forever, through a covenant of salt? {13:6} Yet Jeroboam, the son of Nebat, a servant of Solomon, has risen up and rebelled against his lord. {13:7} A group of worthless men has gathered around him, the sons of Belial, and has strengthened themselves against Rehoboam, the son of Solomon, when he was young and tenderhearted and unable to resist them. {13:8} And now you think you can withstand the kingdom of the LORD in the hands of the sons of David. You are a great multitude, and you have golden calves that Jeroboam made as your gods. {13:9} Have you not driven out the priests of the LORD, the sons of Aaron, and the Levites, and made your own priests like the nations of other lands? Anyone who comes to consecrate himself with a young bull and seven rams can become a priest of those who are no gods. {13:10} But we have not forsaken the LORD; the priests who minister before the LORD are the sons of Aaron, and the Levites attend to their duties. {13:11} They burn sacrifices to the LORD every morning and evening and offer sweet incense. They also set the showbread in order on the pure table and light the gold lampstand with its lamps to burn every evening. We keep the charge of the LORD our God, but you have forsaken Him. {13:12} And behold, God Himself is with us as our captain, and His priests with sounding trumpets to call you to battle. O children of Israel, do not fight against the LORD God of your fathers, for you will not succeed." {13:13} But Jeroboam had set an ambush behind them, so they were surrounded by Judah. {13:14} When Judah looked back, they saw the battle was in front and behind them; they cried out to the LORD, and the priests sounded the trumpets. {13:15} Then the men of Judah shouted, and as they shouted, God struck down Jeroboam and all Israel before Abijah and Judah. {13:16} The children of Israel fled before Judah, and God delivered them into their hands. {13:17} Abijah and his people inflicted a great slaughter, and 500,000 chosen men of Israel fell slain. {13:18} Thus, the children of Israel were subdued at that time, and the children of Judah prevailed because they relied on the LORD God of their fathers. {13:19} Abijah pursued Jeroboam and captured cities from him, including Bethel with its villages, Jeshanah with its villages, and Ephrain with its villages. {13:20} Jeroboam did not recover strength again during Abijah's reign, and the LORD struck him, and he died. {13:21} Meanwhile, Abijah grew strong, married 14 wives, and fathered 22 sons and 16 daughters. {13:22} The rest of the acts of Abijah, his ways, and his sayings are recorded in the story of the prophet Iddo.

{14:1} Abijah passed away and was buried in the city of David, and his son Asa took over as king. During Asa's reign, the land was peaceful for ten years. {14:2} Asa did what was good and right in the eyes of the LORD his God. {14:3} He removed the altars of foreign gods, the high places, broke down the images, and cut down the groves. {14:4} He commanded Judah to seek the LORD God of their ancestors and to follow His laws and commandments. {14:5} Asa also removed the high places and the images from all the cities of Judah, and the kingdom was quiet during his reign. {14:6} He built fortified cities in Judah because the land was at rest, and he had no wars during those years, as the LORD had given him peace. {14:7} So he said to Judah, "Let us build these cities and surround them with walls, towers, gates, and bars, while the land is still available to us. Since we have sought the LORD our God, He has given us peace on every side." So they built and prospered. {14:8} Asa had an army of 300,000 men from Judah who carried shields and spears, and 280,000 from Benjamin who carried shields and drew bows; all these were mighty men of valor. {14:9} Then Zerah the Ethiopian came out against them with an army of a million men and 300 chariots, and approached Mareshah. {14:10} Asa went out to face him, and they arranged their battle in the valley of Zephathah at Mareshah. {14:11} Asa cried out to the LORD his God and said, "LORD, it's nothing for You to help, whether with many or with those who have no power. Help us, O LORD our God; we rely on You, and in Your name, we go against this multitude. O LORD, You are our God; do not let mere men prevail against You." {14:12} The LORD struck down the Ethiopians before Asa and Judah, and the Ethiopians fled. {14:13} Asa and the people with him pursued them as far as Gerar, and the Ethiopians were defeated, unable to recover, for they were destroyed before the LORD and His army; they took a great amount of plunder. {14:14} They also attacked all the cities around Gerar, for the fear of the LORD fell upon them, and they plundered all those cities because there was a lot of spoil in them. {14:15} They also struck the tents of the cattle and took many sheep and camels, and then returned to Jerusalem.

{15:1} The Spirit of God came upon Azariah, the son of Oded. {15:2} He went out to meet Asa and said, "Listen to me, Asa, and all Judah and Benjamin: The LORD is with you as long as you are with Him. If you seek Him, He will be found by you, but if you forsake Him, He will forsake you. {15:3} For a long time, Israel has been without the true God, without a teaching priest, and without the law. {15:4} But when they turned to the LORD God of Israel in their trouble and sought Him, He was found by them. {15:5} In those times, there was no peace for those who went out or came in, but great disturbances were upon all the inhabitants of the countries. {15:6} Nation was destroyed by nation, and city by city, for God troubled them with every kind of adversity. {15:7} So be strong and do not let your hands be weak, for your work will be rewarded. {15:8} When Asa heard these words and the prophecy of Oded the prophet, he took courage and removed the detestable idols from all the land of Judah and Benjamin, as well as from the cities he had captured in the hill country of Ephraim. He renewed the altar of the LORD that stood before the porch of the LORD. {15:9} He gathered all Judah and Benjamin, along with the foreigners living among them from Ephraim, Manasseh, and Simeon, for many had defected to him from Israel when they saw that the LORD his God was with him. {15:10} They gathered together at Jerusalem in the third month of the fifteenth year of Asa's reign. {15:11} At that time, they offered to the LORD 700 oxen and 7,000 sheep from the plunder they had brought. {15:12} They entered into a covenant to seek the LORD God of their ancestors with all their heart and soul. {15:13} Anyone who did not seek the LORD God of Israel was to be put to death, whether small or great, man or woman. {15:14} They took an oath to the LORD with loud voices, shouting, and with trumpets and cornets. {15:15} All Judah rejoiced at the oath because they had sworn with all their hearts and sought Him with their entire desire, and He was found by them, giving them rest all around. {15:16} Asa also removed Maachah, the mother of King Asa, from her position as queen because she had made an idol in a grove. Asa cut down her idol, crushed it, and burned it in the Kidron Valley. {15:17} However, the high places were not removed from Israel, but Asa's heart was fully committed all his days. {15:18} He brought into the house of God the dedicated items his father had set aside, as well as what he himself had dedicated: silver, gold, and utensils. {15:19} There was no more war until the thirty-fifth year of Asa's reign.

{16:1} In the thirty-sixth year of Asa's reign, Baasha, king of Israel, came up against Judah and built Ramah to prevent anyone from going in or out to Asa, king of Judah. {16:2} Asa took silver and gold from the treasures of the house of the LORD and the king's palace and sent it to Benhadad, king of Syria, who lived in Damascus, saying, {16:3} "There is an agreement between you and me, as there was between my father and your father. Look, I am sending you silver and gold; go, break your alliance with Baasha, king of Israel, so that he will withdraw from me." {16:4} Benhadad agreed to King Asa's request and sent the commanders of his armies against the cities of Israel. They attacked Ijon, Dan, Abelmaim, and all the storage cities of Naphtali. {16:5} When Baasha heard this, he stopped building Ramah and ceased his work. {16:6} Then King Asa gathered all of Judah, and they took the stones and timber Baasha had used to build Ramah and built Geba and Mizpah with them. {16:7} At that time, Hanani the seer came to Asa, king of Judah, and said, "Because you have relied on the king of Syria and not on the LORD your God, the army of the king of Syria has escaped from your hand. {16:8} Were not the Ethiopians and the Lubims a vast army with many chariots and horsemen? Yet, because you relied on the LORD, He delivered them into your hand. {16:9} For the eyes of the LORD roam throughout the earth to strengthen those whose hearts are fully committed to Him. You have acted foolishly in this; from now on, you will have wars." {16:10} Asa was angry with the seer and put him in prison because he was furious with him over this matter. At the same time, Asa oppressed some of the people. {16:11} The acts of Asa, from beginning to end, are written in the book of the kings of Judah and Israel. {16:12} In the thirty-ninth year of his reign, Asa became ill in his feet, and his condition was severe; yet even in his illness, he did not seek help from the LORD but turned to physicians. {16:13} Asa rested with his ancestors and died in the forty-first year of his reign. {16:14} They buried him in his own tombs that he had made in the city of David, and laid him on a bed filled with sweet spices and various kinds of perfumes prepared by the perfumers' art, and they made a very great fire in his honor.

{17:1} Jehoshaphat, his son, succeeded him as king and strengthened himself against Israel. {17:2} He stationed troops in all the fortified cities of Judah and set up garrisons throughout the land of Judah and in the cities of Ephraim that his father Asa had captured. {17:3} The LORD was with Jehoshaphat because he followed the earlier ways of his father David and did not seek the Baals. {17:4} Instead, he sought the LORD God of his father, followed His commandments, and did not act like the people of Israel. {17:5} Therefore, the LORD established his kingdom firmly; and all Judah brought gifts to Jehoshaphat, and he became wealthy and respected. {17:6} His heart was devoted to the ways of the LORD, and he removed the high places and Asherah poles from Judah. {17:7} In the third year of his reign, he sent his officials, including Benhail, Obadiah, Zechariah, Nethaneel, and Michaiah, to teach in the cities of Judah. {17:8} He also sent Levites: Shemaiah, Nethaniah, Zebadiah, Asahel, Shemiramoth, Jehonathan, Adonijah, Tobijah, and Tobadonijah, along with priests Elishama and Jehoram. {17:9} They taught in Judah, carrying the Book of the Law of the LORD with them, and went from city to city teaching the people. {17:10} The fear of the LORD fell upon all the kingdoms surrounding Judah, and they did not wage war against Jehoshaphat. {17:11} Some of the Philistines brought Jehoshaphat gifts and tribute silver, and the Arabs brought him flocks, 7,700 rams and 7,700 male goats. {17:12} Jehoshaphat became very powerful; he built castles and store cities in Judah. {17:13} He had much business in the cities of Judah, and there were mighty warriors in Jerusalem. {17:14} These are the numbers of them according to their ancestral houses: from Judah, the commanders of thousands: Adnah the chief, with 300,000 mighty warriors. {17:15} Next to him was Jehohanan the captain, with 280,000. {17:16} Next was Amasiah, son of Zichri, who willingly offered himself to the LORD, with 200,000 mighty warriors. {17:17} From Benjamin, Eliada, a mighty warrior, with 200,000 armed men carrying bows and shields. {17:18} Next to him was Jehozabad, with 180,000 ready for battle. {17:19} These men served the king, besides those the king had stationed in the fortified cities throughout all Judah.

{18:1} Jehoshaphat had great wealth and honor and made an alliance with Ahab. {18:2} After some years, he went down to Ahab in Samaria, where Ahab prepared a feast of sheep and oxen in abundance for him and for the people who were with him, and he urged Jehoshaphat to go with him to Ramothgilead. {18:3} Ahab, king of Israel, asked Jehoshaphat, king of Judah, "Will you go with me to Ramothgilead?" Jehoshaphat replied, "I am as you are, and my people are as your people; we will be with you in battle." {18:4} Jehoshaphat then said to the king of Israel, "Please inquire of the LORD today." {18:5} So, the king of Israel gathered 400 prophets and asked them, "Shall we go to Ramothgilead to fight, or should I refrain?" They answered, "Go up, for God will deliver it into the king's hands." {18:6} But Jehoshaphat asked, "Is there not a prophet of the LORD here, that we may inquire of him?" {18:7} The king of Israel replied to Jehoshaphat, "There is still one man through whom we can inquire of the LORD, but I hate him because he never prophesies anything good about me; he always prophesies evil. His name is Micaiah son of Imla." Jehoshaphat said, "Let the king not say that." {18:8} So the king of Israel called for one of his officials and said, "Quickly bring Micaiah son of Imla." {18:9} The king of Israel and Jehoshaphat, king of Judah, sat on their thrones, dressed in their robes, at the threshing floor at the entrance of the gate of Samaria; and all the prophets were prophesying before them. {18:10} Zedekiah son of Chenaanah had made iron horns and declared, "This is what the LORD says: 'With these you will push back the Arameans until they are destroyed.'" {18:11} All the prophets prophesied the same, saying, "Go up to Ramothgilead and succeed, for the LORD will deliver it into the king's hands." {18:12} The messenger who had gone to summon Micaiah said to him, "Look, the words of the prophets are unanimous in favor of the king; let your word be like theirs and speak favorably." {18:13} Micaiah replied, "As surely as the LORD lives, I will speak only what my God tells me." {18:14} When he arrived before the king, the king asked him, "Micaiah, shall we go to Ramothgilead to fight, or should I refrain?" He answered, "Go up and succeed, for they will be delivered into your hands." {18:15} The king said to him, "How many times must I make you swear to tell me nothing but the truth in the name of the LORD?" {18:16} Then Micaiah said, "I saw all Israel scattered on the hills like sheep without a shepherd, and the LORD said, 'These people have no master. Let each one go home in peace.'" {18:17} The king of Israel turned to Jehoshaphat and said, "Didn't I tell you that he never prophesies anything good about me, but only bad?" {18:18} Micaiah continued, "Therefore hear the word of the LORD: I saw the LORD sitting on His throne with all the heavenly host standing beside Him on His right and on His left. {18:19} The LORD said, 'Who will entice Ahab, king of Israel, into going up and falling at Ramothgilead?' Some said one thing and others said another. {18:20} Finally, a spirit came forward, stood before the LORD, and said, 'I will entice him.' The LORD asked, 'How?' {18:21} The spirit answered, 'I will go out and be a lying spirit in the mouths of all his prophets.' 'You will succeed in enticing him,' said the LORD. 'Go and do it.' {18:22} So now the LORD has put a lying spirit in the mouths of these prophets of yours. The LORD has decreed disaster against you." {18:23} Then Zedekiah son of Chenaanah went up and slapped Micaiah on the cheek and asked, "Which way did the Spirit of the LORD go when he went from me to speak to you?" {18:24} Micaiah replied, "You will find out on the day you go to hide in an inner room." {18:25} The king of Israel then ordered, "Take Micaiah and send him back to Amon the governor of the city and to Joash the king's son {18:26} and say, 'This is what the king says: Put this man in prison and feed him with the bread of affliction and the water of affliction until I return safely.'" {18:27} Micaiah said, "If you ever return safely, the LORD has not spoken through me." And he added, "Mark my words, all you people!" {18:28} So the king of Israel and Jehoshaphat, king of Judah, went up to Ramothgilead. {18:29} The king of Israel said to Jehoshaphat, "I will disguise myself and go into battle, but you wear your royal robes." So the king of Israel disguised himself, and they went into battle. {18:30} Now the king of Aram had ordered his chariot commanders, "Fight only against the king of Israel, and don't worry about the others." {18:31} When the chariot commanders saw Jehoshaphat, they said, "Surely this is the king of Israel." So they turned to attack him, but Jehoshaphat cried out, and the LORD helped him; God diverted them away from him. {18:32} When the chariot commanders realized he was not the king of Israel, they turned back from pursuing him. {18:33} But someone drew his bow at random and struck the king of Israel between the joints of his armor. He said to his chariot driver, "Get me out of the fighting; I'm badly wounded!" {18:34} The battle raged that day, and the king of Israel propped himself up in his chariot facing the Arameans until evening. At sunset, he died.

{19:1} Jehoshaphat, the king of Judah, returned home peacefully to Jerusalem. {19:2} Jehu, the son of Hanani the seer, went out to meet him and said to king Jehoshaphat, "Should you help the wicked and love those who hate the LORD? Because of this, the LORD's wrath is upon you." {19:3} Nevertheless, good things are found in you, for you have removed the groves (sacred trees or places of worship) from the land and have prepared your heart to seek God. {19:4} Jehoshaphat stayed in Jerusalem and went out again among the people from Beersheba to Mount Ephraim, bringing them back to the LORD, the God of their ancestors. {19:5} He appointed judges throughout all the fortified cities of Judah, city by city, {19:6} and said to the judges, "Consider carefully what you do, for you are not judging for man but for the LORD, who is with you when you pass judgment. {19:7} Now let the fear of the LORD be upon you; be careful and act accordingly, for there is no injustice with the LORD our God, nor favoritism, nor taking bribes." {19:8} In Jerusalem, Jehoshaphat appointed some of the Levites, priests, and heads of Israel's families for the judgment of the LORD and for settling disputes when they returned to Jerusalem. {19:9} He instructed them, saying, "You must serve in the fear of the LORD, with faithfulness and with a whole heart. {19:10} Any case that comes to you from your fellow Israelites in their cities, whether it involves bloodshed, laws, commands, statutes, or judgments, you must warn them not to sin against the LORD so that His wrath does not come upon you and your fellow Israelites. This is how you should act, and you will not sin." {19:11} Furthermore, Amariah the chief priest is over you in all matters related to the LORD, and Zebadiah son of Ishmael, the ruler of the house of Judah, is in charge of all the king's matters. The Levites will serve as officials before you. Act courageously, and the LORD will be with those who do good.

{20:1} After this, the children of Moab, the children of Ammon, and some others joined them to fight against Jehoshaphat. {20:2} Some messengers came to Jehoshaphat, saying, "A great multitude is coming against you from beyond the sea, from Syria; they are in Hazazontamar, which is Engedi." {20:3} Jehoshaphat was afraid and set himself to seek the LORD, proclaiming a fast throughout all Judah. {20:4} Judah gathered together to ask for help from the LORD; they came from all the cities of Judah to seek Him. {20:5} Jehoshaphat stood in the assembly of Judah and Jerusalem in the house of the LORD, before the new court, {20:6} and said, "O LORD God of our ancestors, are You not God in heaven? Do You not rule over all the kingdoms of the nations? In Your hand are power and might, so that no one can withstand You? {20:7} Are You not our God, who drove out the inhabitants of this land before Your people Israel and gave it forever to the descendants of Abraham, Your friend? {20:8} They settled there and built You a sanctuary for Your name, saying, {20:9} 'If disaster comes upon us, whether by sword, judgment, plague, or famine, and we stand before this house and before You (for Your name is in this house) and cry out to You in our distress, then You will hear and help.' {20:10} Now, see how the children of Ammon and Moab and Mount Seir, whom You would not allow Israel to invade when they came from Egypt, have turned against us to cast us out of Your possession that You have given us. {20:11} O our God, will You not judge them? For we have no power against this great multitude coming against us; we do not know what to do, but our eyes are on You." {20:12} All Judah stood before the LORD with their little ones, their wives, and their children. {20:13} Then the Spirit of the LORD came upon Jahaziel son of Zechariah, the son of Benaiah, the son of Jeiel, the son of Mattaniah, a Levite from the sons of Asaph, in the midst of the congregation; {20:14} and he said, "Listen, all Judah and you inhabitants of Jerusalem, and you, king Jehoshaphat: Thus says the LORD to you, 'Do not be afraid or dismayed because of this great multitude, for the battle is not yours, but God's. {20:16} Tomorrow, go down against them; they will come up by the ascent of Ziz, and you will find them at the end of the brook before the wilderness of Jeruel. {20:17} You will not need to fight in this battle; take your positions, stand firm, and see the salvation of the LORD on your behalf, O Judah and Jerusalem. Do not be afraid or dismayed; tomorrow, go out against them, for the LORD will be with you.'" {20:18} Jehoshaphat bowed his head with his face to the ground, and all Judah and the inhabitants of Jerusalem fell before the LORD, worshiping Him. {20:19} The Levites from the Kohathites and Korahites stood up to praise the LORD God of Israel with a loud voice. {20:20} Early the next morning, they went out into the wilderness of Tekoa. As they set out, Jehoshaphat stood and said, "Listen to me, O Judah and inhabitants of Jerusalem; believe in the LORD your God, and you will be established; believe His prophets, and you will succeed." {20:21} After consulting the people, he appointed singers to the LORD to praise the beauty of holiness as they went out ahead of the army, saying, "Give thanks to the LORD, for His mercy endures forever." {20:22} As they began to sing and praise, the LORD set ambushes against the children of Ammon, Moab, and Mount Seir, who had come against Judah, and they were defeated. {20:23} For the children of Ammon and Moab turned against the inhabitants of Mount Seir, destroying them completely; and when they had finished with the inhabitants of Seir, they helped destroy one another. {20:24} When Judah came to the watchtower in the wilderness and looked toward the multitude, they saw only dead bodies lying on the ground; no one had escaped. {20:25} When Jehoshaphat and his people went to take the spoil, they found an abundance of goods, precious jewels, and more than they could carry; it took them three days to gather the spoil because it was so much. {20:26} On the fourth day, they assembled in the Valley of Berachah (which means "blessing") to bless the LORD; therefore, that place has been called the Valley of Berachah to this day. {20:27} Then every man of Judah and Jerusalem, with Jehoshaphat at their head, returned to Jerusalem with joy, for the LORD had made them rejoice over their enemies. {20:28} They came to Jerusalem with harps, lyres, and trumpets to the house of the LORD. {20:29} The fear of God came upon all the kingdoms of the countries when they heard that the LORD had fought against the enemies of Israel. {20:30} So the realm of Jehoshaphat was quiet, for his God gave him rest all around. {20:31} Jehoshaphat reigned over Judah; he was thirty-five years old when he began to reign and reigned for twenty-five years in Jerusalem. His mother's name was Azubah, the daughter of Shilhi. {20:32} He followed the ways of his father Asa and did not turn aside from it, doing what was right in the sight of the LORD. {20:33} However, the high places were not taken away, for the people had not yet prepared their hearts to seek the God of their ancestors. {20:34} Now the rest of the acts of Jehoshaphat, from beginning to end, are written in the book of Jehu son of Hanani, which is mentioned in the book of the kings of Israel. {20:35} After this, Jehoshaphat king of Judah allied himself with Ahaziah king of Israel, who acted very wickedly. {20:36} He joined him in making ships to go to Tarshish, and they made the ships in Eziongeber. {20:37} Then Eliezer son of Dodavah of Mareshah prophesied against Jehoshaphat, saying, "Because you have allied yourself with Ahaziah, the LORD has destroyed your works." The ships were wrecked, so they were unable to go to Tarshish.

{21:1} Jehoshaphat rested with his ancestors and was buried with them in the City of David. His son Jehoram succeeded him as king. {21:2} Jehoram had brothers, the sons of Jehoshaphat: Azariah, Jehiel, Zechariah, Azariah, Michael, and Shephatiah. All these were the sons of Jehoshaphat king of Israel. {21:3} Their father gave them generous gifts of silver, gold, and precious items, along with fortified cities in Judah, but he gave the kingdom to Jehoram because he was the firstborn. {21:4} When Jehoram became king, he strengthened his position and killed all his brothers with the sword, along with some of the princes of Israel. {21:5} Jehoram was thirty-two years old when he began to reign, and he reigned for eight years in Jerusalem. {21:6} He followed the ways of the kings of Israel, like the house of Ahab, because he married Ahab's daughter; he did evil in the sight of the LORD. {21:7} However, the LORD did not destroy the house of David because of the covenant He had made with David and His promise to give a light to David and his descendants forever. {21:8} During his reign, the Edomites revolted from under Judah's control and appointed their own king. {21:9} Jehoram went out with his officers and all his chariots; he attacked the Edomites by night, surrounding them and their chariot commanders. {21:10} The Edomites have been in revolt against Judah to this day. At the same time, Libnah also revolted against him because he had forsaken the LORD God of his ancestors. {21:11} He built high places in the mountains of Judah and caused the inhabitants of Jerusalem to engage in idolatry, compelling Judah to do the same. {21:12} A letter came to him from the prophet Elijah, saying, "Thus says the LORD God of your father David: Because you have not walked in the ways of your father Jehoshaphat or Asa king of Judah, {21:13} but have walked in the ways of the kings of Israel, causing Judah and the inhabitants of Jerusalem to engage in idolatry like the idolatry of the house of Ahab, and you have killed your brothers from your father's house who were better than you, {21:14} behold, the LORD will strike your people, your children, your wives, and all your goods with a great plague. {21:15} You will suffer from a severe disease of your bowels until your bowels fall out due to the sickness day by day." {21:16} Moreover, the LORD stirred up against Jehoram the spirit of the Philistines and the Arabs near the Ethiopians; {21:17} they came against Judah, broke into it, and carried away everything found in the king's palace, including his sons and wives, leaving him with only his youngest son Jehoahaz. {21:18} After all this, the LORD afflicted him in his bowels with an incurable disease. {21:19} Eventually, after two years, his bowels fell out due to his sickness, and he died from severe illnesses. His people did not honor him with a funeral like those of his ancestors. {21:20} He was thirty-two years old when he began to reign, and he reigned in Jerusalem for eight years, departing without being desired. He was buried in the City of David, but not in the tombs of the kings.

{22:1} The inhabitants of Jerusalem made Ahaziah, his youngest son, king in his place, because the group of men who had come with the Arabs to the camp had killed all the older brothers. So Ahaziah, the son of Jehoram king of Judah, reigned. {22:2} Ahaziah was forty-two years old when he began to reign, and he reigned for one year in Jerusalem. His mother's name was Athaliah, the daughter of Omri. {22:3} He followed the ways of the house of Ahab because his mother was his advisor in doing wickedly. {22:4} Therefore, he did evil in the sight of the LORD like the house of Ahab, for they were his advisors after the death of his father, leading him to destruction. {22:5} He also followed their advice and went to war with Jehoram, the son of Ahab, king of Israel, against Hazael, king of Syria, at Ramoth-gilead; and the Syrians wounded Joram. {22:6} He returned to be healed in Jezreel because of the wounds he received at Ramah during his battle with Hazael, king of Syria. Azariah, the son of Jehoram king of Judah, went down to see Jehoram, the son of Ahab, in Jezreel because he was sick. {22:7} Ahaziah's destruction was from God when he went to Joram; for when he arrived, he went out with Jehoram against Jehu, the son of Nimshi, whom the LORD had anointed to destroy the house of Ahab. {22:8} As Jehu was carrying out judgment on the house of Ahab, he found the princes of Judah and the sons of Ahaziah's brothers who served him, and he killed them. {22:9} He searched for Ahaziah and captured him (for he was hiding in Samaria) and brought him to Jehu; they killed him and buried him because, they said, he was the son of Jehoshaphat, who sought the LORD with all his heart. So the house of Ahaziah had no power to maintain the kingdom. {22:10} When Athaliah, the mother of Ahaziah, saw that her son was dead, she arose and destroyed all the royal family of the house of Judah. {22:11} However, Jehoshabeath, the daughter of the king, took Joash, the son of Ahaziah, and hid him from among the king's sons who were killed. She placed him and his nurse in a bedroom. Jehoshabeath, the daughter of king Jehoram and the wife of Jehoiada the priest (for she was the sister of Ahaziah), hid him from Athaliah so that she would not kill him. {22:12} Joash was hidden with them in the house of God for six years while Athaliah reigned over the land.

{23:1} In the seventh year, Jehoiada strengthened himself and took the captains of hundreds—Azariah, the son of Jeroham, Ishmael, the son of Jehohanan, Azariah, the son of Obed, Maaseiah, the son of Adaiah, and Elishaphat, the son of Zichri—into a covenant with him. {23:2} They went throughout Judah, gathering the Levites from all the cities of Judah and the leaders of the families of Israel, and they came to Jerusalem. {23:3} The whole congregation made a covenant with the king in the house of God. He said to them, "Look, the king's son shall reign, as the LORD has spoken regarding the sons of David. {23:4} Here's what you shall do: A third of you, entering on the Sabbath, of the priests and Levites, shall be porters of the doors; {23:5} another third shall be at the king's house, and a third at the gate of the foundation; and all the people shall be in the courts of the house of the LORD. {23:6} But let none enter the house of the LORD except the priests and those Levites who minister; they may go in because they are holy, but all the people shall keep watch for the LORD. {23:7} The Levites shall surround the king, each man with his weapon in hand; and anyone else who enters the house shall be put to death. You shall be with the king when he enters and when he leaves." {23:8} So the Levites and all Judah did according to everything that Jehoiada the priest commanded, taking each man his group for the Sabbath, and those who were to go out on the Sabbath, for Jehoiada the priest did not dismiss the courses. {23:9} Moreover, Jehoiada the priest gave to the captains of hundreds spears, bucklers, and shields that had belonged to King David, which were in the house of God. {23:10} He arranged all the people, each man having his weapon in hand, from the right side of the temple to the left side of the temple, by the altar and the temple, surrounding the king. {23:11} Then they brought out the king's son, placed the crown on him, and gave him the testimony, making him king. Jehoiada and his sons anointed him and said, "Long live the king!" {23:12} When Athaliah heard the noise of the people running and praising the king, she came to the people in the house of the LORD. {23:13} She looked, and behold, the king stood at his pillar at the entrance, with the princes and the trumpeters by the king. All the people of the land rejoiced and sounded trumpets, and the singers with musical instruments taught to sing praises. Then Athaliah tore her clothes and shouted, "Treason! Treason!" {23:14} Jehoiada the priest brought out the captains of hundreds who were in charge of the army and said to them, "Take her outside the ranges, and whoever follows her, let him be killed with the sword." For the priest said, "Do not kill her in the house of the LORD." {23:15} So they seized her, and when she reached the entrance of the horse gate by the king's house, they killed her there. {23:16} Jehoiada made a covenant between himself, all the people, and the king that they would be the LORD's people. {23:17} Then all the people went to the house of Baal, tore it down, broke its altars and images into pieces, and killed Mattan, the priest of Baal, before the altars. {23:18} Jehoiada appointed the offices of the house of the LORD by the hand of the priests, the Levites, whom David had distributed in the house of the LORD to offer burnt offerings to the LORD, as it is written in the law of Moses, with rejoicing and singing, as David had ordained. {23:19} He set the porters at the gates of the house of the LORD, so that none who were unclean in any way should enter. {23:20} He took the captains of hundreds, the nobles, the governors of the people, and all the people of the land, and brought the king down from the house of the LORD. They came through the high gate into the king's house and placed the king upon the throne of the kingdom. {23:21} All the people of the land rejoiced, and the city was quiet after they had slain Athaliah with the sword.

{24:1} Joash was seven years old when he began to reign, and he reigned for forty years in Jerusalem. His mother's name was Zibiah of Beersheba. {24:2} Joash did what was right in the sight of the LORD all the days of Jehoiada the priest. {24:3} Jehoiada took for him two wives, and he had sons and daughters. {24:4} After this, Joash decided to repair the house of the LORD. {24:5} He gathered the priests and the Levites and said to them, "Go out to the cities of Judah and collect money from all Israel to repair the house of your God from year to year, and make sure you hurry the matter." However, the Levites did not hurry it. {24:6} The king called for Jehoiada the chief and said to him, "Why haven't you asked the Levites to bring in the collection from Judah and Jerusalem according to the commandment of Moses, the servant of the LORD, and the congregation of Israel for the tabernacle of witness?" {24:7} For the sons of Athaliah, that wicked woman, had broken up the house of God, and they had given all the dedicated things of the house of the LORD to Baalim (gods). {24:8} At the king's command, they made a chest and set it outside at the gate of the house of the LORD. {24:9} They made a proclamation throughout Judah and Jerusalem to bring in to the LORD the collection that Moses, the servant of God, laid upon Israel in the wilderness. {24:10} All the princes and the people rejoiced, bringing in and casting into the chest until they finished. {24:11} When the chest was brought to the king's office by the Levites and they saw there was much money, the king's scribe and the high priest's officer came, emptied the chest, and took it back to its place. They did this day by day and gathered money in abundance. {24:12} The king and Jehoiada gave it to those doing the work for the service of the house of the LORD, hiring masons and carpenters to repair the house of the LORD, and also those who worked with iron and brass to mend the house of the LORD. {24:13} The workers worked, and the work was completed by them, restoring the house of God to its original state and strengthening it. {24:14} When they finished, they brought the rest of the money before the king and Jehoiada, from which they made vessels for the house of the LORD—vessels for ministering and offerings, and spoons, as well as vessels of gold and silver. They offered burnt offerings in the house of the LORD continually all the days of Jehoiada. {24:15} Jehoiada grew old and was full of days when he died; he was one hundred thirty years old at his death. {24:16} They buried him in the city of David among the kings, because he had done good in Israel, both toward God and His house. {24:17} After the death of Jehoiada, the princes of Judah came and paid respect to the king. Then the king listened to them. {24:18} They abandoned the house of the LORD, the God of their fathers, and served groves and idols, and wrath came upon Judah and Jerusalem for this trespass. {24:19} Yet he sent prophets to bring them back to the LORD, and they testified against them, but they would not listen. {24:20} The Spirit of God came upon Zechariah, the son of Jehoiada the priest, who stood above the people and said to them, "Thus says God, why do you transgress the commandments of the LORD so that you cannot prosper? Because you have forsaken the LORD, He has also forsaken you." {24:21} They conspired against him and stoned him with stones at the command of the king in the court of the house of the LORD. {24:22} Joash the king did not remember the kindness which Jehoiada his father had shown him but killed his son. When he died, he said, "The LORD look upon it and require it." {24:23} At the end of the year, the army of Syria came up against him and destroyed all the princes of the people, sending all their spoils to the king of Damascus. {24:24} Although the army of the Syrians came with a small company of men, the LORD delivered a very great host into their hand because they had forsaken the LORD God of their fathers. So they executed judgment against Joash. {24:25} When they had departed from him (for they left him with great diseases), his own servants conspired against him for the blood of the sons of Jehoiada the priest and killed him on his bed. He died and was buried in the city of David, but they did not bury him in the tombs of the kings. {24:26} Those who conspired against him were Zabad, the son of Shimeath, an Ammonite woman, and Jehozabad, the son of Shimrith, a Moabite woman. {24:27} Now concerning his sons and the greatness of the burdens laid upon him and the repairing of the house of God, they are written in the story of the book of the kings. Amaziah, his son, reigned in his place.

{25:1} Amaziah was twenty-five years old when he began to reign, and he reigned for twenty-nine years in Jerusalem. His mother's name was Jehoaddan of Jerusalem. {25:2} He did what was right in the sight of the LORD, but not with a perfect heart. {25:3} When his kingdom was firmly established, he killed the servants who had murdered his father, the king. {25:4} However, he did not kill their children, but followed what is written in the law in the book of Moses, where the LORD commanded that fathers shall not die for their children, nor shall children die for their fathers; each person shall die for their own sin. {25:5} Amaziah gathered Judah together and appointed captains over thousands and hundreds according to their families throughout all Judah and Benjamin. He counted them from twenty years old and above and found three hundred thousand choice men able to go to war, capable of handling spear and shield. {25:6} He also hired a hundred thousand mighty men of valor from Israel for a hundred talents of silver. {25:7} But a man of God came to him, saying, "O king, do not let the army of Israel go with you, for the LORD is not with Israel, especially with the children of Ephraim." {25:8} "If you do go, be strong for battle; God will make you fall before the enemy, for God has the power to help or to throw down." {25:9} Amaziah said to the man of God, "But what will we do about the hundred talents I have given to the army of Israel?" The man of God answered, "The LORD is able to give you much more than this." {25:10} So Amaziah dismissed the troops that had come to him from Ephraim, sending them home. Their anger against Judah was greatly kindled, and they returned home in great anger. {25:11} Amaziah then strengthened himself and led his people to the Valley of Salt, where he struck down ten thousand of the children of Seir. {25:12} The children of Judah took another ten thousand alive and brought them to the top of a rock, where they threw them down, breaking them into pieces. {25:13} The soldiers that Amaziah had sent back, who were not allowed to go into battle, attacked the cities of Judah, from Samaria to Bethhoron, killing three thousand of them and taking much spoil. {25:14} After Amaziah returned from slaughtering the Edomites, he brought back the gods of the children of Seir, set them up as his gods, bowed down to them, and burned incense to them. {25:15} Therefore, the anger of the LORD was kindled against Amaziah, and He sent a prophet who said, "Why have you sought the gods of a people that could not even deliver their own people from your hand?" {25:16} While he was talking with him, the king said, "Are you made of the king's counsel? Stop; why should you be struck?" Then the prophet stopped and said, "I know that God has determined to destroy you because you have done this and have not listened to my counsel." {25:17} Then King Amaziah of Judah consulted and sent a message to Joash, the son of Jehoahaz, the son of Jehu, king of Israel, saying, "Come, let us face each other." {25:18} Joash, king of Israel, replied to Amaziah, king of Judah, "The thistle that was in Lebanon sent a message to the cedar in Lebanon, saying, 'Give your daughter to my son as a wife.' But a wild beast that passed by trampled down the thistle." {25:19} "You say, 'Look, you have defeated the Edomites,' and your heart has lifted you up to boast; stay home now; why should you meddle to your own harm and fall, you and Judah with you?" {25:20} Amaziah would not listen, for it came from God that He might deliver them into the hand of their enemies because they sought after the gods of Edom. {25:21} So Joash, king of Israel, went up, and they met each other face to face, both he and Amaziah, king of Judah, at Bethshemesh, which belongs to Judah. {25:22} Judah was defeated before Israel, and every man fled to his tent. {25:23} Joash, king of Israel, captured Amaziah, king of Judah, the son of Joash, the son of Jehoahaz, at Bethshemesh, and brought him to Jerusalem. He broke down the wall of Jerusalem from the gate of Ephraim to the corner gate, a distance of four hundred cubits. {25:24} He took all the gold and silver, and all the vessels found in the house of God with Obededom, and the treasures of the king's house, and the hostages, and returned to Samaria. {25:25} Amaziah, the son of Joash, king of Judah, lived for fifteen years after the death of Joash, son of Jehoahaz, king of Israel. {25:26} Now the rest of the acts of Amaziah, from first to last, are they not written in the book of the kings of Judah and Israel? {25:27} After Amaziah turned away from following the LORD, they conspired against him in Jerusalem, and he fled to Lachish. They sent men after him to Lachish and killed him there. {25:28} They brought him back on horses and buried him with his fathers in the city of Judah.

{26:1} Then all the people of Judah took Uzziah, who was sixteen years old, and made him king in place of his father Amaziah. {26:2} He built Eloth and restored it to Judah after the king died. {26:3} Uzziah was sixteen years old when he began to reign, and he reigned for fifty-two years in Jerusalem. His mother's name was Jecoliah of Jerusalem. {26:4} He did what was right in the sight of the LORD, following all that his father Amaziah had done. {26:5} He sought God during the days of Zechariah, who had understanding of the visions of God; and as long as he sought the LORD, God made him prosper. {26:6} He went out and fought against the Philistines, broke down the walls of Gath, Jabneh, and Ashdod, and built cities around Ashdod and among the Philistines. {26:7} God helped him against the Philistines and the Arabians who lived in Gurbaal, as well as the Mehunims. {26:8} The Ammonites brought gifts to Uzziah, and his fame spread even to the entrance of Egypt, for he had become very powerful. {26:9} Uzziah built towers in Jerusalem at the corner gate, valley gate, and turning of the wall, fortifying them. {26:10} He also built towers in the desert and dug many wells, for he had much cattle in the low country and plains. He had farmers and vine dressers in the mountains and in Carmel because he loved agriculture. {26:11} Uzziah had an army of fighting men who went out to war in groups, counted by Jeiel the scribe and Maaseiah the ruler, under Hananiah, one of the king's captains. {26:12} The total number of chiefs among the mighty men of valor was two thousand six hundred. {26:13} Under their command was an army of three hundred thousand seven thousand five hundred, equipped for battle to help the king against the enemy. {26:14} Uzziah provided them with shields, spears, helmets, body armor, bows, and slings to throw stones. {26:15} He also made engines in Jerusalem, invented by skilled men, to be on the towers and walls to shoot arrows and large stones. His fame spread far because he was marvelously helped until he became strong. {26:16} But when he became strong, his heart was lifted up to his destruction; he transgressed against the LORD his God and entered the temple of the LORD to burn incense on the altar of incense. {26:17} Azariah the priest went in after him, accompanied by eighty brave priests of the LORD. {26:18} They confronted King Uzziah and said, "It is not for you, Uzziah, to burn incense to the LORD, but for the priests, the sons of Aaron, who are consecrated to burn incense. Get out of the sanctuary, for you have trespassed, and it will not be honored by the LORD God." {26:19} Uzziah was angry, holding a censer in his hand to burn incense. While he was angry with the priests, leprosy broke out on his forehead in front of the priests in the house of the LORD, beside the incense altar. {26:20} Azariah the chief priest and all the priests looked at him, and behold, he was leprous on his forehead. They rushed him out, and he himself hurried to leave because the LORD had struck him. {26:21} King Uzziah was a leper until the day of his death and lived in a separate house, being a leper; he was cut off from the house of the LORD. His son Jotham was in charge of the king's house, judging the people of the land. {26:22} The rest of the acts of Uzziah, from first to last, are written by Isaiah the prophet, the son of Amoz. {26:23} So Uzziah slept with his fathers, and they buried him with his fathers in the field of burial that belonged to the kings, for they said, "He is a leper." Jotham, his son, reigned in his place.

{27:1} Jotham was twenty-five years old when he began to reign, and he reigned for sixteen years in Jerusalem. His mother's name was Jerushah, the daughter of Zadok. {27:2} He did what was right in the sight of the LORD, following all that his father Uzziah had done; however, he did not enter the temple of the LORD, and the people continued to act corruptly. {27:3} He built the high gate of the house of the LORD and made significant improvements on the wall of Ophel. {27:4} He also built cities in the mountains of Judah and constructed castles and towers in the forests. {27:5} He fought against the king of the Ammonites and was victorious. That same year, the Ammonites gave him one hundred talents of silver, ten thousand measures of wheat, and ten thousand measures of barley. The Ammonites paid him this tribute both the second and third years as well. {27:6} Thus, Jotham became powerful because he prepared his ways before the LORD his God. {27:7} Now the rest of the acts of Jotham, along with all his wars and his ways, are written in the book of the kings of Israel and Judah. {27:8} He was twenty-five years old when he began to reign and ruled for sixteen years in Jerusalem. {27:9} Jotham slept with his ancestors, and they buried him in the city of David; his son Ahaz reigned in his place.

{28:1} Ahaz was twenty years old when he began to reign, and he ruled for sixteen years in Jerusalem. However, he did not do what was right in the sight of the LORD, like his father David. {28:2} Instead, he followed the ways of the kings of Israel and made molten images for Baalim (false gods). {28:3} He burned incense in the Valley of the Son of Hinnom and even sacrificed his children in the fire, following the detestable practices of the nations that the LORD had driven out before the Israelites. {28:4} He also sacrificed and burned incense on the high places, in the hills, and under every green tree. {28:5} Therefore, the LORD his God delivered him into the hands of the king of Syria, who struck him and carried away a large number of captives to Damascus. He was also delivered into the hands of the king of Israel, who inflicted a great slaughter on him. {28:6} Pekah, the son of Remaliah, killed one hundred and twenty thousand valiant men in Judah in one day because they had forsaken the LORD God of their ancestors. {28:7} Zichri, a mighty man of Ephraim, killed Maaseiah, the king's son, and Azrikam, the governor of the palace, and Elkanah, who was next to the king. {28:8} The Israelites took captive two hundred thousand of their fellow countrymen, including women, sons, and daughters, and they took a large amount of spoil and brought it to Samaria. {28:9} But a prophet of the LORD named Oded went out to meet the army coming to Samaria and said to them, "Look, because the LORD God of your ancestors was angry with Judah, He has delivered them into your hands, and you have killed them in a rage that has reached up to heaven. {28:10} Now you plan to make the people of Judah and Jerusalem your bondmen and bondwomen, but are there not sins with you against the LORD your God? {28:11} So listen to me and return the captives you have taken from your brothers, for the fierce wrath of the LORD is upon you." {28:12} Then some of the leaders of the children of Ephraim—Azariah, the son of Johanan, Berechiah, the son of Meshillemoth, Jehizkiah, the son of Shallum, and Amasa, the son of Hadlai—stood up against those who had come from the war {28:13} and said to them, "You must not bring the captives here, for we have already offended the LORD, and you intend to add to our sins and guilt. Our guilt is great, and there is fierce wrath against Israel." {28:14} So the armed men left the captives and the spoil before the princes and all the assembly. {28:15} Then the men mentioned by name rose up, took the captives, clothed those who were naked among them, and provided them with clothes, sandals, food, and drink. They anointed the injured and carried the weak on donkeys, bringing them to Jericho, the city of palm trees, to their brothers, and then they returned to Samaria. {28:16} At that time, King Ahaz sent a message to the kings of Assyria to help him. {28:17} For the Edomites had again come and attacked Judah, taking captives. {28:18} The Philistines also invaded the cities in the low country and in the south of Judah, capturing Bethshemesh, Ajalon, Gederoth, Shocho and its villages, and Timnah and its villages, as well as Gimzo and its villages; and they settled there. {28:19} The LORD brought Judah low because of Ahaz, king of Israel, for he made Judah unfaithful and greatly transgressed against the LORD. {28:20} King Tilgath-Pilneser of Assyria came to him but distressed him instead of strengthening him. {28:21} Ahaz took some of the items from the house of the LORD, from the king's house, and from the princes, and gave them to the king of Assyria, but he did not help him. {28:22} In his time of distress, Ahaz became even more unfaithful to the LORD; this is that King Ahaz. {28:23} He sacrificed to the gods of Damascus, who had defeated him, saying, "Because the gods of the kings of Syria help them, I will sacrifice to them so that they may help me." But they were the ruin of him and all Israel. {28:24} Ahaz gathered together the utensils of the house of God, cut them in pieces, shut the doors of the house of the LORD, and made altars in every corner of Jerusalem. {28:25} In every city of Judah, he made high places to burn incense to other gods, provoking the LORD God of his ancestors to anger. {28:26} Now the rest of his acts, along with all his ways, first and last, are written in the book of the kings of Judah and Israel. {28:27} Ahaz slept with his ancestors and was buried in the city, in Jerusalem, but they did not bring him into the tombs of the kings of Israel; his son Hezekiah reigned in his place.

{29:1} Hezekiah began to reign when he was twenty-five years old and ruled for twenty-nine years in Jerusalem. His mother's name was Abijah, the daughter of Zechariah. {29:2} He did what was right in the sight of the LORD, following the example of his father David. {29:3} In the first year of his reign, in the first month, he opened the doors of the house of the LORD and repaired them. {29:4} He brought in the priests and the Levites and gathered them in the east square. {29:5} He said to them, "Listen to me,

Levites! Consecrate yourselves and sanctify the house of the LORD God of your ancestors. Remove all the filth from the holy place. {29:6} Our ancestors have been unfaithful and done evil in the eyes of the LORD our God. They have forsaken Him and turned their faces away from the LORD's dwelling place, turning their backs on Him. {29:7} They shut the doors of the portico, extinguished the lamps, and did not burn incense or offer burnt offerings in the holy place to the God of Israel. {29:8} Therefore, the wrath of the LORD was upon Judah and Jerusalem, and He has delivered them to trouble, to astonishment, and to ridicule, as you see with your own eyes. {29:9} Our ancestors fell by the sword, and our sons, daughters, and wives are in captivity because of this. {29:10} Now I intend to make a covenant with the LORD God of Israel, so that His fierce anger may turn away from us. {29:11} My sons, do not be negligent, for the LORD has chosen you to stand before Him, to serve Him, and to minister to Him by burning incense." {29:12} Then the Levites arose: Mahath, the son of Amasai, and Joel, the son of Azariah, from the Kohathites; and from the Merarites, Kish, the son of Abdi, and Azariah, the son of Jehalelel; and from the Gershonites, Joah, the son of Zimmah, and Eden, the son of Joah. {29:13} From the sons of Elizaphan: Shimri and Jeiel; and from the sons of Asaph: Zechariah and Mattaniah; {29:14} and from the sons of Heman: Jehiel and Shimei; and from the sons of Jeduthun: Shemaiah and Uzziel. {29:15} They gathered their fellow Levites, consecrated themselves, and came, according to the king's command and the words of the LORD, to cleanse the house of the LORD. {29:16} The priests went into the inner part of the house of the LORD to cleanse it and brought out all the uncleanness they found in the temple of the LORD into the courtyard. The Levites took it to carry it out to the brook Kidron. {29:17} They began to sanctify on the first day of the first month, and on the eighth day of the month, they came to the portico of the LORD. They sanctified the house of the LORD in eight days, and on the sixteenth day of the first month, they finished. {29:18} They went to King Hezekiah and said, "We have cleansed the entire house of the LORD, the altar of burnt offering, and all its utensils, and the table for the showbread with all its utensils." {29:19} Moreover, all the utensils that King Ahaz discarded in his unfaithfulness have been prepared and consecrated, and they are before the altar of the LORD. {29:20} King Hezekiah rose early, gathered the rulers of the city, and went up to the house of the LORD. {29:21} They brought seven bulls, seven rams, seven lambs, and seven male goats for a sin offering for the kingdom, the sanctuary, and Judah. He commanded the priests, the sons of Aaron, to offer them on the altar of the LORD. {29:22} So they killed the bulls, and the priests received the blood and sprinkled it on the altar. When they killed the rams, they sprinkled the blood on the altar, and they also killed the lambs and sprinkled the blood on the altar. {29:23} They brought forth the male goats for the sin offering before the king and the congregation, and they laid their hands on them. {29:24} The priests killed them and made reconciliation with their blood on the altar to atone for all Israel, for the king commanded that the burnt offering and the sin offering be made for all Israel. {29:25} He appointed the Levites in the house of the LORD with cymbals, lyres, and harps, according to the command of David, Gad the king's seer, and Nathan the prophet, for this was the command of the LORD through His prophets. {29:26} The Levites stood with the instruments of David, and the priests with the trumpets. {29:27} Hezekiah commanded them to offer the burnt offering on the altar. When the burnt offering began, the song of the LORD began with the trumpets and the instruments ordained by David, king of Israel. {29:28} The whole congregation worshiped, and the singers sang, and the trumpeters sounded, and this continued until the burnt offering was finished. {29:29} When they finished offering, the king and all who were present bowed down and worshiped. {29:30} Moreover, King Hezekiah and the princes commanded the Levites to sing praises to the LORD with the words of David and Asaph the seer. They sang praises with gladness, bowing their heads and worshiping. {29:31} Then Hezekiah said, "Now that you have consecrated yourselves to the LORD, come near and bring sacrifices and thank offerings to the house of the LORD." The congregation brought sacrifices and thank offerings, and those with willing hearts brought burnt offerings. {29:32} The number of burnt offerings the congregation brought was seventy bulls, one hundred rams, and two hundred lambs, all for burnt offerings to the LORD. {29:33} The consecrated things included six hundred oxen and three thousand sheep. {29:34} But the priests were too few to skin all the burnt offerings, so their fellow Levites helped them until the work was finished and the other priests had consecrated themselves, for the Levites were more upright in heart to consecrate themselves than the priests. {29:35} The burnt offerings were abundant, along with the fat of the peace offerings and the drink offerings for every burnt offering. So the service of the house of the LORD was established. {29:36} Hezekiah and all the people rejoiced because God had prepared the people, for the thing was done suddenly.

{30:1} Hezekiah sent messages to all Israel and Judah and also wrote letters to Ephraim and Manasseh, inviting them to come to the house of the LORD in Jerusalem to celebrate the Passover to the LORD God of Israel. {30:2} The king had consulted with his officials and all the congregation in Jerusalem to keep the Passover in the second month. {30:3} They couldn't keep it at the appointed time because the priests had not consecrated themselves sufficiently, nor had the people gathered in Jerusalem. {30:4} This proposal pleased the king and all the congregation. {30:5} So they established a decree to announce throughout all Israel, from Beersheba to Dan, that they should come to celebrate the Passover to the LORD God of Israel in Jerusalem, for they had not done it in a long time as prescribed. {30:6} The couriers went with letters from the king and his officials throughout Israel and Judah, following the king's command, saying, "Children of Israel, return to the LORD God of Abraham, Isaac, and Israel, and He will return to the remnant of you who have escaped from the hand of the kings of Assyria. {30:7} Do not be like your ancestors and your brothers who were unfaithful to the LORD God of their ancestors, leading to their destruction, as you can see. {30:8} Do not be stubborn like your ancestors were, but yield yourselves to the LORD, enter His sanctuary, which He has consecrated forever, and serve the LORD your God so that His fierce anger may turn away from you. {30:9} If you return to the LORD, your brothers and children will find compassion from those who have taken them captive, and they will return to this land, for the LORD your God is gracious and merciful and will not turn away His face from you if you return to Him." {30:10} The couriers passed from city to city throughout the land of Ephraim and Manasseh, even to Zebulun, but they were laughed at and mocked. {30:11} Nevertheless, some from Asher, Manasseh, and Zebulun humbled themselves and went to Jerusalem. {30:12} Also, in Judah, the hand of God was upon them, giving them one heart to follow the command of the king and his officials according to the word of the LORD. {30:13} A great crowd assembled in Jerusalem to celebrate the Feast of Unleavened Bread in the second month. {30:14} They got up and removed the altars in Jerusalem and took away all the incense altars and threw them into the Kidron Valley. {30:15} Then they killed the Passover lamb on the fourteenth day of the second month. The priests and Levites felt ashamed, consecrated themselves, and brought in the burnt offerings to the house of the LORD. {30:16} They stood in their designated places according to the law of Moses, the man of God. The priests sprinkled the blood they received from the Levites. {30:17} Since many in the congregation had not consecrated themselves, the Levites were responsible for killing the Passover lambs for everyone who was not clean to consecrate them to the LORD. {30:18} A large number of the people, including many from Ephraim, Manasseh, Issachar, and Zebulun, had not cleansed themselves, yet they ate the Passover differently than prescribed. But Hezekiah prayed for them, saying, "May the good LORD pardon everyone {30:19} who prepares his heart to seek God, the LORD God of his ancestors, even if he is not cleansed according to the purification rules of the sanctuary." {30:20} The LORD listened to Hezekiah and healed the people. {30:21} The Israelites present in Jerusalem celebrated the Feast of Unleavened Bread for seven days with great joy, and the Levites and priests praised the LORD day by day, singing with loud instruments to the LORD. {30:22} Hezekiah spoke encouragingly to all the Levites who taught the good knowledge of the LORD. They ate throughout the feast for seven days, offering peace offerings and making confession to the LORD God of their ancestors. {30:23} The whole assembly decided to celebrate for another seven days, and they kept it with joy. {30:24} King Hezekiah of Judah gave the congregation a thousand bulls and seven thousand sheep; and the officials gave the congregation a thousand bulls and ten thousand sheep, and a great number of priests consecrated themselves. {30:25} All the congregation of Judah, along with the priests and Levites, and all who came from Israel and the foreigners dwelling in Judah rejoiced. {30:26} There was great joy in Jerusalem, for since the time of Solomon, son of David, king of Israel, there had been nothing like this in Jerusalem. {30:27} The priests and Levites stood and blessed the people, and their voices were heard; their prayer reached His holy dwelling place in heaven.

{31:1} After all this was completed, all Israel that was present went out to the cities of Judah, broke the idols into pieces, cut down the groves (trees used for pagan worship), and demolished the high places and altars throughout Judah and Benjamin, as well as in Ephraim and Manasseh, until they had completely destroyed them all. Then all the Israelites returned, each to his own possession, in their own cities. {31:2} Hezekiah appointed the divisions of the priests and the Levites according to their orders, assigning each man to his service, including the priests and Levites for burnt offerings and peace offerings, to minister, give thanks, and praise in the gates of the LORD's tents. {31:3} He also set aside a portion of his own possessions for the burnt offerings, specifically for the morning and evening sacrifices, and for the burnt offerings on the Sabbaths, new moons, and appointed feasts, as instructed in the law of the LORD. {31:4} Furthermore, he commanded the people living in Jerusalem to provide for the priests and Levites so they could be encouraged in following the law of the LORD. {31:5} As soon as the command was made known, the Israelites brought in abundant firstfruits of grain, wine, oil, honey, and all the produce of the fields; they also brought in a tithe of everything abundantly. {31:6} The people of Israel and Judah who lived in the cities of Judah brought in the tithe of oxen and sheep, as well as the tithe of sacred offerings consecrated to the LORD their God, and laid them in piles. {31:7} In the third month, they began laying the foundations of these piles and completed them in the seventh month. {31:8} When Hezekiah and the officials came and saw the piles, they blessed the LORD and His people Israel. {31:9} Then Hezekiah asked the priests and Levites about the piles. {31:10} Azariah, the chief priest of the house of Zadok, answered him, saying, "Since the people began bringing their offerings to the house of the LORD, we have had enough to eat and plenty left over, for the LORD has blessed His people, and what remains is this great amount." {31:11} Hezekiah then commanded that storerooms be prepared in the house of the LORD, and they were prepared. {31:12} The offerings, tithes, and consecrated things were brought in faithfully, with Cononiah the Levite in charge, and his brother Shimei next to him. {31:13} Jehiel, Azaziah, Nahath, Asahel, Jerimoth, Jozabad, Eliel, Ismachiah, Mahath, and Benaiah were overseers under the supervision of Cononiah and his brother Shimei, following the command of King Hezekiah and Azariah, the ruler of the house of God. {31:14} Kore, the son of Imnah the Levite, who served as gatekeeper at the east, was in charge of distributing the freewill offerings to God and the most holy things. {31:15} Next to him were Eden, Miniamin, Jeshua, Shemaiah, Amariah, and Shecaniah, in the cities of the priests, fulfilling their duties to provide for their brethren in their divisions, both for the great and the small. {31:16} They also maintained a genealogy of males from three years old and up, to ensure everyone who entered the house of the LORD received their daily portion for their service according to their divisions; {31:17} this included the genealogies of the priests according to their family houses and the Levites from twenty years old and up, based on their divisions. {31:18} They also kept track of all their little ones, wives, sons, and daughters throughout the congregation, as they had sanctified themselves in holiness for their assigned tasks. {31:19} Among the sons of Aaron, the priests who lived in the fields of their cities, the men named specifically were to distribute portions to all the males among the priests and all those listed by genealogy among the Levites. {31:20} Hezekiah did this throughout all Judah, and he did what was good, right, and true before the LORD his God. {31:21} In every work he began in the service of the house of God, and in the law and commandments to seek his God, he did it wholeheartedly and prospered.

{32:1} After these events and the establishment of Hezekiah's reforms, Sennacherib, the king of Assyria, came and entered Judah, laying siege to the fortified cities, intending to capture them for himself. {32:2} When Hezekiah saw that Sennacherib had arrived and was planning to attack Jerusalem, {32:3} he consulted with his officials and mighty men to stop up the water sources outside the city, and they helped him. {32:4} A large group of people gathered to stop all the springs and the brook that flowed through the land, saying, "Why should the kings of Assyria come and find plenty of water?" {32:5} He also strengthened himself by repairing all the broken walls, building towers, adding another wall outside, and restoring Millo (a structure in the city of David). He made plenty of weapons, including darts and shields. {32:6} He appointed military commanders over the people, gathering them in the street at the city gate, and spoke encouragingly to them, saying, {32:7} "Be strong and courageous; don't be afraid or discouraged because of the king of Assyria or his vast army. There are more with us than with him. {32:8} He has only human strength, but we have the LORD our God to help us and fight our battles." The people relied on the words of Hezekiah, king of Judah. {32:9} After this, Sennacherib, king of Assyria, sent his servants to Jerusalem (while he himself was besieging Lachish with his full force), to Hezekiah, king of Judah, and to all Judah in Jerusalem, saying, {32:10} "This is what Sennacherib, king of Assyria, says: On what are you basing your confidence that you remain besieged in Jerusalem? {32:11} Is Hezekiah misleading you to surrender and die of hunger and thirst by claiming, 'The LORD our God will deliver us from the hand of the king of Assyria'? {32:12} Didn't Hezekiah remove his high places and altars, and tell Judah and Jerusalem, 'You must worship before one altar and burn incense on it'? {32:13} Don't you know what I and my ancestors have done to all the peoples of other lands? Were the gods of those nations able to save their lands from my hand? {32:14} Which of the gods of those nations that my fathers utterly destroyed could rescue their people from my hand? So how can your God deliver you from my hand? {32:15} Therefore, don't let Hezekiah deceive you or persuade you like this, and don't believe him; for no god of any nation or kingdom has been able to deliver his people from my hand or the hand of my ancestors. How much less will your God deliver you from my hand?" {32:16} His servants also spoke more against the LORD God and against His servant Hezekiah. {32:17} He wrote letters to ridicule the LORD God of Israel, saying, "Just as the gods of the nations of other lands have not delivered their people from my hand, so the God of Hezekiah will not deliver His people from my hand." {32:18} They shouted loudly in Hebrew to the people of Jerusalem on the wall, trying to frighten and confuse them so they could capture the city. {32:19} They spoke against the God of Jerusalem, as if He were one of the gods made by human hands. {32:20} For this reason, King Hezekiah and the prophet Isaiah, son of Amoz, prayed and cried out to heaven. {32:21} The LORD sent an angel, who wiped out all the fighting men, leaders, and commanders in the Assyrian camp. So Sennacherib returned home in disgrace. When he entered the temple of his god, his own sons killed him with the sword. {32:22} Thus, the LORD saved Hezekiah and the inhabitants of Jerusalem from Sennacherib, king of Assyria, and from all others, and He guided them on every side. {32:23} Many brought gifts to the LORD in Jerusalem and valuable presents for Hezekiah, king of Judah, so that he was highly regarded by all nations from that time on. {32:24} During those days, Hezekiah became ill to the point of death and prayed to the LORD, who spoke to him and gave him a sign. {32:25} However, Hezekiah did not respond according to the kindness shown to him, for his heart was proud; therefore, the LORD's anger was against him and against Judah and Jerusalem. {32:26} Yet, Hezekiah humbled himself, along with the inhabitants of Jerusalem, so that the LORD's anger did not come upon them during Hezekiah's days. {32:27} Hezekiah had immense wealth and honor; he made treasuries for silver, gold, precious stones, spices, shields, and all kinds of valuable items. {32:28} He also built storehouses for grain, wine, and oil, and stables for all kinds of livestock, and pens for flocks. {32:29} Moreover, he provided cities and vast herds and flocks, for God had given him great wealth. {32:30} This same Hezekiah stopped the upper water source of Gihon and brought it directly down to the west side of the city of David. Hezekiah prospered in all his works. {32:31} However, regarding the ambassadors from the princes of Babylon who sent to ask about the miraculous sign that had occurred in the land, God left him to test him, so that He might know everything that was in his heart. {32:32} Now the rest of Hezekiah's acts and his goodness are recorded in the vision of Isaiah, the prophet, son of Amoz, and in the book of the kings of Judah and Israel. {32:33} Hezekiah died and was buried in the tombs of the kings in City of David, and all Judah and the inhabitants of Jerusalem honored him at his death. His son Manasseh succeeded him as king.

{33:1} Manasseh was twelve years old when he began to reign, and he reigned for fifty-five years in Jerusalem. {33:2} However, he did what was evil in the sight of the LORD, following the detestable practices of the nations that the LORD had driven out before the Israelites. {33:3} He rebuilt the high places that his father Hezekiah had destroyed, erected altars for the Baals, made groves (sacred groves), and worshipped all the starry hosts, serving them. {33:4} He also built altars in the house of the LORD, of which the LORD had said, "In Jerusalem, my name will be forever." {33:5} He built altars for all the starry hosts in the two courtyards of the house of the LORD. {33:6} He made his children pass through the fire in the Valley of the Son of Hinnom, practiced divination, used enchantments, engaged in witchcraft, consulted spirits, and dealt with wizards, committing many evil acts that angered the LORD. {33:7} He placed a carved idol, the image he had made, in the house of God, of which God had said to David and Solomon, "In this house, and in Jerusalem, which I have chosen above all the tribes of Israel, I will put my name forever. {33:8} I will never again remove the feet of Israel from the land I assigned to your ancestors, as long as they are careful to do everything I commanded them, according to the whole Law, the statutes, and the ordinances given through Moses." {33:9} So, Manasseh led Judah and the inhabitants of Jerusalem astray, causing them to do worse than the nations whom the LORD had destroyed before the Israelites. {33:10} The LORD spoke to Manasseh and his people, but they would not listen. {33:11} Therefore, the LORD brought against them the commanders of the army of the king of Assyria, who captured Manasseh when he was in distress, bound him with chains, and took him to Babylon. {33:12} While in captivity, he sought the LORD his God and humbled himself greatly before the God of his ancestors. {33:13} He prayed to Him, and God was moved by his plea and listened to his supplication, bringing him back to Jerusalem and to his kingdom. Then Manasseh realized that the LORD was God. {33:14} After this, he built a wall outside the City of David, on the west side of Gihon, in the valley, up to the Fish Gate, surrounding Ophel, raising it to a great height, and appointed military leaders in all the fortified cities of Judah. {33:15} He removed the foreign gods and the idol from the house of the LORD, along with all the altars he had built on the mountain of the house of the LORD and in Jerusalem, and threw them out of the city. {33:16} He restored the altar of the LORD and sacrificed peace offerings and thank offerings on it, commanding Judah to serve the LORD, the God of Israel. {33:17} Nevertheless, the people still sacrificed at the high places, but only to the LORD their God. {33:18} The rest of Manasseh's acts, his prayer to his God, and the words of the seers who spoke to him in the name of the LORD God of Israel are written in the Book of the Kings of Israel. {33:19} His prayer and how God was moved by it, along with all his sins, his unfaithfulness, and the places where he built high places and set up groves and carved images before he humbled himself, are recorded among the sayings of the seers. {33:20} So Manasseh died and was buried in his own house, and his son Amon succeeded him as king. {33:21} Amon was twenty-two years old when he began to reign, and he reigned for two years in Jerusalem. {33:22} He did what was evil in the sight of the LORD, just as his father Manasseh had done. Amon sacrificed to all the carved images that his father had made and served them. {33:23} He did not humble himself before the LORD, as Manasseh had humbled himself; instead, Amon became even more unfaithful. {33:24} His officials conspired against him and killed him in his own house. {33:25} But the people of the land killed all those who had conspired against King Amon, and the people made Josiah, his son, king in his place.

{34:1} Josiah was eight years old when he began to reign, and he reigned for thirty-one years in Jerusalem. {34:2} He did what was right in the sight of the LORD and followed the ways of his father David, not turning to the right or to the left. {34:3} In the eighth year of his reign, while he was still young, he began to seek the God of David his father. In the twelfth year, he started to cleanse Judah and Jerusalem of the high places, groves (sacred groves), carved images, and molten images. {34:4} He demolished the altars of the Baals in his presence, cut down the high places, and smashed the groves, carved images, and molten images into dust, spreading the dust over the graves of those who had sacrificed to them. {34:5} He burned the bones of the priests on their altars, purifying Judah and Jerusalem. {34:6} He did the same in the cities of Manasseh, Ephraim, and Simeon, even as far as Naphtali, using axes (tools) all around. {34:7} After breaking down the altars and groves, grinding the carved images to powder, and cutting down all the idols throughout Israel, he returned to Jerusalem. {34:8} In the eighteenth year of his reign, after purging the land and the temple, he sent Shaphan son of Azaliah, Maaseiah the governor of the city, and Joah son of Joahaz the recorder to repair the house of the LORD his God. {34:9} When they arrived at Hilkiah the high priest, they gave him the money brought into the house of God, which the Levites who kept the doors had collected from the people of Manasseh, Ephraim, and all the remnant of Israel, as well as from all Judah and Benjamin; and they returned to Jerusalem. {34:10} They handed it over to the workmen overseeing the house of the LORD, who used it to pay the workers repairing and restoring the temple. {34:11} They also gave it to the artisans and builders to buy hewn stone and timber for supports, and to restore the structures that the kings of Judah had destroyed. {34:12} The men did their work faithfully, with overseers Jahath and Obadiah, the Levites from the Merari clan, and Zechariah and Meshullam from the Kohathite clan supervising; along with other Levites skilled in music. {34:13} They also oversaw the bearers of burdens and managed all the workers in various services, including scribes, officers, and porters from among the Levites. {34:14} While they were taking out the money brought into the house of the LORD, Hilkiah the priest found a book of the Law of the LORD given through Moses. {34:15} Hilkiah said to Shaphan the scribe, "I have found the book of the Law in the house of the LORD," and he gave the book to Shaphan. {34:16} Shaphan took the book to the king and reported back to him, saying, "All that was committed to your servants, they are doing." {34:17} They have gathered the money found in the house of the LORD and given it to the overseers and the workers. {34:18} Then Shaphan the scribe told the king, "Hilkiah the priest has given me a book." Shaphan read it before the king. {34:19} When the king heard the words of the Law, he tore his robes in grief. {34:20} The king commanded Hilkiah, Ahikam son of Shaphan, Abdon son of Micah, Shaphan the scribe, and Asaiah a servant of the king, saying, {34:21} "Go, inquire of the LORD for me and for those who are left in Israel and Judah about the words of this book that has been found; for great is the LORD's anger that is poured out on us because our ancestors have not kept the word of the LORD by doing everything written in this book." {34:22} Hilkiah and the king's appointed officials went to Huldah the prophetess, wife of Shallum son of Tikvath, son of Hasrah, the keeper of the wardrobe; (she lived in Jerusalem in the Second District) and they spoke to her about this matter. {34:23} She said to them, "This is what the LORD God of Israel says: Tell the man who sent you to me, {34:24} 'This is what the LORD says: I am going to bring disaster on this place and its inhabitants, all the curses written in the book that has been read before the king of Judah. {34:25} Because they have forsaken me and burned incense to other gods, provoking me to anger with all the works of their hands, my wrath will be poured out on this place and will not be quenched.' {34:26} As for the king of Judah who sent you to inquire of the LORD, tell him, 'This is what the LORD God of Israel says concerning the words you have heard: {34:27} Because your heart was tender and you humbled yourself before God when you heard his words against this place and its inhabitants, and because you humbled yourself before me and tore your robes and wept before me, I have heard you,' declares the LORD. {34:28} 'I will gather you to your ancestors, and you will be buried in peace; your eyes will not see all the disaster I am going to bring on this place and its inhabitants.'" So they took the answer back to the king. {34:29} Then the king summoned all the elders of Judah and Jerusalem. {34:30} The king went up to the house of the LORD, and with him all the men of Judah and the inhabitants of Jerusalem, the priests, the Levites, and all the people, great and small; he read in their hearing all the words of the Book of the Covenant found in the house of the LORD. {34:31} The king stood in his place and made a covenant before the LORD to follow the LORD and keep his commandments, statutes, and decrees with all his heart and soul, to fulfill the words of the covenant written in this book. {34:32} He made all who were present in Jerusalem and Benjamin pledge themselves to it. The people of Jerusalem did according to the covenant of God, the God of their ancestors. {34:33} Josiah removed all the detestable idols from all the territories belonging to the Israelites and made all who were present in Israel serve the LORD their God. Throughout his lifetime, they did not turn away from following the LORD, the God of their ancestors.

{35:1} Josiah kept a Passover festival for the LORD in Jerusalem, and they sacrificed the Passover lambs on the fourteenth day of the first month. {35:2} He assigned the priests to their duties and encouraged them in the service of the house of the LORD. {35:3} He instructed the Levites, who taught all Israel and were dedicated to the LORD, to place the holy ark in the temple that Solomon, son of David, king of Israel, had built, saying it should no longer be a burden on their shoulders; they were to serve the LORD their God and His people Israel. {35:4} They were to prepare themselves by the houses of their ancestors, according to the divisions set out by David king of Israel and his son Solomon. {35:5} They were to stand in the holy place according to the divisions of the families of their fellow Israelites, and according to the divisions of the Levites. {35:6} So they were to sacrifice the Passover lambs, sanctify themselves, and prepare their fellow Israelites to follow the instructions given by the LORD through Moses. {35:7} Josiah provided for the people from his own flocks, giving them lambs and kids (young goats) for the Passover offerings, a total of thirty thousand lambs and three thousand bullocks (young cattle); these were from the king's own livestock. {35:8} His officials also generously gave to the people, the priests, and the Levites. Hilkiah, Zechariah, and Jehiel, rulers of the house of God, contributed two thousand six hundred small cattle and three hundred oxen for the Passover offerings. {35:9} Conaniah, Shemaiah, Nethaneel, and his brothers, as well as Hashabiah, Jeiel, and Jozabad, chief Levites, gave five thousand small cattle and five hundred oxen for the Passover offerings. {35:10} The service was set up, with the priests taking their positions and the Levites in their divisions, following the king's command. {35:11} They sacrificed the Passover lambs, the priests sprinkled the blood from their hands, and the Levites skinned the animals. {35:12} They removed the burnt offerings to give them according to the family divisions of the people, as prescribed in the book of Moses. They did the same with the oxen. {35:13} They roasted the Passover lambs over the fire according to the regulations, while the other holy offerings were boiled in pots, cauldrons, and pans, and quickly divided among all the people. {35:14} Afterward, they prepared food for themselves and for the priests, because the priests, the sons of Aaron, were busy with the burnt offerings and the fat until night. So the Levites prepared for themselves and for the priests, the sons of Aaron. {35:15} The singers, descendants of Asaph, were in their places as commanded by David, Asaph, Heman, and Jeduthun, the king's seer. The gatekeepers stood at every gate so that they would not depart from their duties, while their fellow Levites prepared for them. {35:16} All the service of the LORD was prepared that day to keep the Passover and offer burnt offerings on the altar of the LORD, following the command of King Josiah. {35:17} The Israelites present celebrated the Passover at that time, along with the Feast of Unleavened Bread for seven days. {35:18} No Passover like this had been kept in Israel since the days of the prophet Samuel; none of the kings of Israel had kept such a Passover as Josiah did, along with the priests, Levites, all Judah and Israel present, and the inhabitants of Jerusalem. {35:19} This Passover was celebrated in the eighteenth year of Josiah's reign. {35:20} After all this, when Josiah had restored the temple, King Necho of Egypt marched to fight against Carchemish by the Euphrates River, and Josiah went out to confront him. {35:21} But Necho sent messengers to him, saying, "What do I have to do with you, king of Judah? I am not here against you today but against the house that I am at war with, for God has commanded me to hurry. Stay out of my way, or He will destroy you." {35:22} However, Josiah refused to turn back and disguised himself in order to fight him. He did not heed Necho's warning from God and engaged in battle in the Valley of Megiddo. {35:23} The archers shot King Josiah, and he said to his servants, "Take me away; I am badly wounded." {35:24} His servants took him out of the chariot and placed him in the second chariot he had. They brought him to Jerusalem, where he died and was buried in one of the tombs of his ancestors. All Judah and Jerusalem mourned for Josiah. {35:25} Jeremiah lamented for Josiah, and all the singers and singing women spoke of him in their lamentations to this day, making it a custom in Israel; and they are recorded in the lamentations. {35:26} The rest of the acts of Josiah, and his goodness as recorded in the Law of the LORD, {35:27} and his deeds, both the earliest and the latest, are written in the book of the kings of Israel and Judah.

{36:1} Then the people of the land took Jehoahaz, the son of Josiah, and made him king in his father's place in Jerusalem. {36:2} Jehoahaz was twenty-three years old when he began to reign, and he reigned for three months in Jerusalem. {36:3} The king of Egypt removed him from power in Jerusalem and imposed a fine of a hundred talents of silver and a talent of gold on the land. {36:4} The king of Egypt made Eliakim, his brother, king over Judah and Jerusalem, and changed his name to Jehoiakim. Necho took Jehoahaz, his brother, and carried him off to Egypt. {36:5} Jehoiakim was twenty-five years old when he began to reign, and he reigned for eleven years in Jerusalem, doing what was evil in the sight of the LORD his God. {36:6} King Nebuchadnezzar of Babylon came against him, bound him in chains, and took him to Babylon. {36:7} Nebuchadnezzar also carried away the articles from the house of the LORD to Babylon and placed them in his temple there. {36:8} The rest of the acts of Jehoiakim, along with his abominations and everything found in him, are written in the book of the kings of Israel and Judah. Jehoiachin, his son, succeeded him as king. {36:9} Jehoiachin was eight years old when he began to reign, and he reigned for three months and ten days in Jerusalem, doing what was evil in the sight of the LORD. {36:10} When the year was over, King Nebuchadnezzar sent for him, brought him to Babylon with the valuable articles from the house of the LORD, and made Zedekiah, his brother, king over Judah and Jerusalem. {36:11} Zedekiah was twenty-one years old when he began to reign, and he reigned for eleven years in Jerusalem. {36:12} He also did what was evil in the sight of the LORD his God and did not humble himself before Jeremiah the prophet, who spoke from the mouth of the LORD. {36:13} He rebelled against King Nebuchadnezzar, who had made him swear an oath by God, but Zedekiah stiffened his neck and hardened his heart against turning to the LORD, the God of Israel. {36:14} Furthermore, all the chief priests and the people committed many sins, following the abominations of the nations, and defiled the house of the LORD, which He had consecrated in Jerusalem. {36:15} The LORD God of their ancestors sent messengers to them repeatedly, because He had compassion on His people and His dwelling place. {36:16} But they mocked the messengers of God, despised His words, and mistreated His prophets until the LORD's anger arose against His people, and there was no remedy. {36:17} Therefore, He brought upon them the king of the Chaldeans, who killed their young men with the sword in the house of their sanctuary, showing no compassion for young or old, and handed them all over to him. {36:18} He took all the articles from the house of God, both great and small, and the treasures of the house of the LORD, and the treasures of the king and his officials; all of these he brought to Babylon. {36:19} They burned the house of God, broke down the wall of Jerusalem, burned all the palaces with fire, and destroyed all the valuable articles. {36:20} Those who escaped the sword were taken to Babylon, where they became servants to him and his sons until the reign of the kingdom of Persia. {36:21} This was to fulfill the word of the LORD spoken by the mouth of Jeremiah until the land had enjoyed its Sabbaths; as long as it lay desolate, it kept the Sabbath to fulfill seventy years. {36:22} Now in the first year of Cyrus king of Persia, to fulfill the word of the LORD spoken by Jeremiah, the LORD stirred up the spirit of Cyrus king of Persia, who made a proclamation throughout his entire kingdom and also put it in writing, saying, {36:23} "Thus says Cyrus king of Persia: The LORD, the God of heaven, has given me all the kingdoms of the earth and has appointed me to build a temple for Him in Jerusalem, which is in Judah. Who among you of all His people? May the LORD his God be with him, and let him go up."

The Book of Ezra

{1:1} In the first year of Cyrus, king of Persia, to fulfill the word of the LORD spoken by Jeremiah, the LORD stirred up the spirit of Cyrus, king of Persia, so that he made a proclamation throughout his entire kingdom and put it in writing, saying, {1:2} "Thus says Cyrus, king of Persia: The LORD God of heaven has given me all the kingdoms of the earth, and He has appointed me to build a temple for Him in Jerusalem, which is in Judah. {1:3} Who among you of all His people? May his God be with him, and let him go up to Jerusalem, which is in Judah, to build the house of the LORD God of Israel (He is the God) that is in Jerusalem. {1:4} And whoever remains in any place where he dwells, let the people of that place help him with silver, gold, goods, and livestock, in addition to the freewill offerings for the house of God in Jerusalem. {1:5} Then the leaders of the families of Judah and Benjamin, along with the priests and Levites, rose up, along with everyone whose spirit God had stirred, to go up and rebuild the house of the LORD in Jerusalem. {1:6} All those around them supported their efforts with silver vessels, gold, goods, and livestock, as well as precious items, besides all that was willingly offered. {1:7} Cyrus, the king, also brought out the vessels of the house of the LORD, which Nebuchadnezzar had taken from Jerusalem and placed in the house of his gods. {1:8} Cyrus, king of Persia, brought these out by the hand of Mithredath the treasurer and counted them for Sheshbazzar, the prince of Judah. {1:9} This is their count: thirty gold basins, one thousand silver basins, and twenty-nine knives, {1:10} thirty gold bowls, four hundred ten silver bowls of a second kind, and one thousand other vessels. {1:11} All the vessels of gold and silver totaled five thousand four hundred. Sheshbazzar brought all these with him when the exiles returned from Babylon to Jerusalem.

{2:1} These are the people of the province who returned from captivity, those whom Nebuchadnezzar, king of Babylon, had carried away to Babylon and who came back to Jerusalem and Judah, each to his own city; {2:2} They came with Zerubbabel: Jeshua, Nehemiah, Seraiah, Reelaiah, Mordecai, Bilshan, Mispar, Bigvai, Rehum, and Baanah. The number of the men of Israel is as follows: {2:3} The descendants of Parosh, two thousand one hundred seventy-two. {2:4} The descendants of Shephatiah, three hundred seventy-two. {2:5} The descendants of Arah, seven hundred seventy-five. {2:6} The descendants of Pahathmoab, of the descendants of Jeshua and Joab, two thousand eight hundred twelve. {2:7} The descendants of Elam, one thousand two hundred fifty-four. {2:8} The descendants of Zattu, nine hundred forty-five. {2:9} The descendants of Zaccai, seven hundred sixty. {2:10} The descendants of Bani, six hundred forty-two. {2:11} The descendants of Bebai, six hundred twenty-three. {2:12} The descendants of Azgad, one thousand two hundred twenty-two. {2:13} The descendants of Adonikam, six hundred sixty-six. {2:14} The descendants of Bigvai, two thousand fifty-six. {2:15} The descendants of Adin, four hundred fifty-four. {2:16} The descendants of Ater of Hezekiah, ninety-eight. {2:17} The descendants of Bezai, three hundred twenty-three. {2:18} The descendants of Jorah, one hundred twelve. {2:19} The descendants of Hashum, two hundred twenty-three. {2:20} The descendants of Gibbar, ninety-five. {2:21} The descendants of Bethlehem, one hundred twenty-three. {2:22} The men of Netophah, fifty-six. {2:23} The men of Anathoth, one hundred twenty-eight. {2:24} The descendants of Azmaveth, forty-two. {2:25} The descendants of Kirjatharim, Chephirah, and Beeroth, seven hundred forty-three. {2:26} The descendants of Ramah and Gaba, six hundred twenty-one. {2:27} The men of Michmas, one hundred twenty-two. {2:28} The men of Bethel and Ai, two hundred twenty-three. {2:29} The descendants of Nebo, fifty-two. {2:30} The descendants of Magbish, one hundred fifty-six. {2:31} The descendants of the other Elam, one thousand two hundred fifty-four. {2:32} The descendants of Harim, three hundred twenty. {2:33} The descendants of Lod, Hadid, and Ono, seven hundred twenty-five. {2:34} The descendants of Jericho, three hundred forty-five. {2:35} The descendants of Senaah, three thousand six hundred thirty. {2:36} The priests: the descendants of Jedaiah, of the house of Jeshua, nine hundred seventy-three. {2:37} The descendants of Immer, one thousand fifty-two. {2:38} The descendants of Pashur, one thousand two hundred forty-seven. {2:39} The descendants of Harim, one thousand seventeen. {2:40} The Levites: the descendants of Jeshua and Kadmiel, of the descendants of Hodaviah, seventy-four. {2:41} The singers: the descendants of Asaph, one hundred twenty-eight. {2:42} The gatekeepers: the descendants of Shallum, the descendants of Ater, the descendants of Talmon, the descendants of Akkub, the descendants of Hatita, and the descendants of Shobai, a total of one hundred thirty-nine. {2:43} The Nethinims: the descendants of Ziha, the descendants of Hasupha, and the descendants of Tabbaoth, {2:44} the descendants of Keros, the descendants of Siaha, and the descendants of Padon, {2:45} the descendants of Lebanah, the descendants of Hagabah, and the descendants of Akkub, {2:46} the descendants of Hagab, the descendants of Shalmai, and the descendants of Hanan, {2:47} the descendants of Giddel, the descendants of Gahar, and the descendants of Reaiah, {2:48} the descendants of Rezin, the descendants of Nekoda, and the descendants of Gazzam, {2:49} the descendants of Uzza, the descendants of Paseah, and the descendants of Besai, {2:50} the descendants of Asnah, the descendants of Mehunim, and the descendants of Nephusim, {2:51} the descendants of Bakbuk, the descendants of Hakupha, and the descendants of Harhur, {2:52} the descendants of Bazluth, the descendants of Mehida, and the descendants of Harsha, {2:53} the descendants of Barkos, the descendants of Sisera, and the descendants of Thamah, {2:54} the descendants of Neziah and the descendants of Hatipha. {2:55} The descendants of Solomon's servants: the descendants of Sotai, the descendants of Sophereth, and the descendants of Peruda, {2:56} the descendants of Jaalah, the descendants of Darkon, and the descendants of Giddel, {2:57} the descendants of Shephatiah, the descendants of Hattil, the descendants of Pochereth of Zebaim, and the descendants of Ami. {2:58} All the Nethinims and the descendants of Solomon's servants numbered three hundred ninety-two. {2:59} These were the ones who returned from Telmelah, Telharsa, Cherub, Addan, and Immer, but they could not prove their ancestral houses or their lineage, whether they were of Israel: {2:60} the descendants of Delaiah, the descendants of Tobiah, and the descendants of Nekoda, six hundred fifty-two. {2:61} Of the descendants of the priests: the descendants of Habaiah, the descendants of Koz, and the descendants of Barzillai, who took a wife from the daughters of Barzillai the Gileadite and was named after their name. {2:62} These sought their genealogical records, but they were not found; therefore, they were considered unclean and excluded from the priesthood. {2:63} The governor told them that they should not eat of the most holy things until a priest with Urim and Thummim stood up. {2:64} The entire assembly together was forty-two thousand three hundred sixty, {2:65} besides their male and female servants, totaling seven thousand three hundred thirty-seven; among them were two hundred singing men and singing women. {2:66} Their horses numbered seven hundred thirty-six; their mules, two hundred forty-five; {2:67} their camels, four hundred thirty-five; their donkeys, six thousand seven hundred twenty. {2:68} Some of the leaders, when they arrived at the house of the LORD in Jerusalem, offered freely for the house of God to establish it in its place. {2:69} They gave according to their ability to the treasury for the work, totaling sixty-one thousand drams of gold, five thousand pounds of silver, and one hundred priestly garments. {2:70} So the priests, the Levites, some of the people, the singers, the gatekeepers, and the Nethinims settled in their cities, with all of Israel in their cities.

{3:1} When the seventh month arrived and the Israelites were in their cities, the people gathered as one to Jerusalem. {3:2} Jeshua son of Jozadak and his fellow priests, along with Zerubbabel son of Shealtiel and his brothers, stood up and built the altar of the God of Israel to offer burnt offerings on it, as prescribed in the law of Moses, the man of God. {3:3} They set the altar on its bases, fearing the surrounding peoples, and offered burnt offerings to the LORD, morning and evening. {3:4} They also celebrated the Feast of Tabernacles, as written, and offered daily burnt offerings in number, according to the custom for each day; {3:5} and afterward, they offered the continual burnt offering for the new moons and all the appointed feasts of the LORD that were consecrated, along with anyone who willingly offered a freewill offering to the LORD. {3:6} They began offering burnt offerings to the LORD from the first day of the seventh month, but the foundation of the temple of the LORD had not yet been laid. {3:7} They also gave money to the masons and carpenters and provided food, drink, and oil to the people of Sidon and Tyre to bring cedar logs from Lebanon to the coast at Joppa, as Cyrus king of Persia had authorized. {3:8} In the second year after their arrival at the house of God in Jerusalem, in the second month, Zerubbabel son of Shealtiel, Jeshua son of Jozadak, and the rest of their fellow priests and Levites, along with everyone who had returned from captivity, appointed the Levites who were twenty years old and older to oversee the work on the house of the LORD. {3:9} Jeshua, along with his sons and brothers, Kadmiel and his sons, and the descendants of Judah, stood together to supervise the workers in the house of God, along with the descendants of Henadad and their brothers the Levites. {3:10} When the builders laid the foundation of the temple of the LORD, they dressed the priests in their robes with trumpets and the Levites, the sons of Asaph, with cymbals to praise the LORD, according to the instructions of David king of Israel. {3:11} They sang together in praise and thanks to the LORD, saying, "He is good; his love endures forever toward Israel." And all the people gave a great shout of praise to the LORD when the foundation of the house of the LORD was laid. {3:12} But many of the priests, Levites, and older leaders who had seen the first temple wept loudly when they saw the foundation of this temple being laid, while many shouted for joy. {3:13} The people could not distinguish the sound of the joyful shouting from the sound of their weeping, for the people shouted so loudly that the noise was heard far away.

{4:1} When the adversaries of Judah and Benjamin heard that the exiles were building the temple of the LORD God of Israel, {4:2} they approached Zerubbabel and the leaders and said, "Let us join you in building, for we seek your God just as you do, and we have been sacrificing to him since the days of Esarhaddon king of Assyria, who brought us here." {4:3} But Zerubbabel, Jeshua, and the other leaders of Israel replied, "You have no part with us in building a house for our God; we alone will build for the LORD God of Israel, as King Cyrus of Persia has commanded us." {4:4} Then the people of the land discouraged the people of Judah and made them afraid to build. {4:5} They hired advisors against them to frustrate their plans during the entire reign of Cyrus king of Persia, and continued until the reign of Darius king of Persia. {4:6} In the reign of Ahasuerus, at the beginning of his reign, they wrote an accusation against the inhabitants of Judah and Jerusalem. {4:7} In the days of Artaxerxes, Bishlam, Mithredath, Tabeel, and their associates wrote a letter to Artaxerxes king of Persia; it was written in Aramaic and translated into Aramaic. {4:8} Rehum the chancellor and Shimshai the scribe wrote a letter against Jerusalem to King Artaxerxes, saying: {4:9} "Rehum the chancellor, Shimshai the scribe, and their companions—the Dinaites, the Apharsathchites, the Tarpelites, the Apharsites, the Archevites, the Babylonians, the Susanchites, the Dehavites, and the Elamites— {4:10} and the rest of the nations whom the great and noble Asnappar brought over and settled in the cities of Samaria and the region beyond the River. {4:11} This is a copy of the letter they sent to him: To King Artaxerxes, from your servants who are on this side of the River. {4:12} Let it be known to the king that the Jews who came up from you to us have gone to Jerusalem and are rebuilding that rebellious and wicked city. They are restoring the walls and repairing the foundations. {4:13} Be aware, O king, that if this city is rebuilt and its walls are restored, they will no longer pay taxes, tribute, or customs, and that will damage the royal revenues. {4:14} Since we are under the king's authority and it is not right for us to witness the king's dishonor, we are sending this report to inform the king. {4:15} We suggest that a search be made in the annals of your predecessors; you will find that this city has a long history of rebellion against kings and has been a threat to the provinces; that is why it was destroyed. {4:16} We inform the king that if this city is rebuilt and its walls restored, he will have no share in this region beyond the River." {4:17} The king sent an answer to Rehum the chancellor, Shimshai the scribe, and their companions dwelling in Samaria and the region beyond the River: "Greetings. {4:18} The letter you sent has been read before me. {4:19} I ordered a search, and it has been found that this city has a long history of rebellion against kings, and that it has been a center for insurrection. {4:20} Mighty kings have ruled over Jerusalem and have exercised authority over the region beyond the River, and taxes, tribute, and customs were paid to them. {4:21} Now issue an order for these men to stop work, and this city must not be rebuilt until I give further orders. {4:22} Be very careful not to neglect this matter. Why should damage increase to the detriment of the kings?" {4:23} As soon as the copy of King Artaxerxes' letter was read to Rehum, Shimshai the scribe, and their companions, they hurried to Jerusalem and forced the Jews to stop working. {4:24} So the work on the house of God in Jerusalem came to a halt, and it remained stopped until the second year of the reign of Darius king of Persia.

{5:1} Then the prophets Haggai and Zechariah, son of Iddo, prophesied to the Jews in Judah and Jerusalem in the name of the God of Israel. {5:2} Zerubbabel son of Shealtiel and Jeshua son of Jozadak rose up and began to build the house of God in Jerusalem, and the prophets of God were with them, helping them. {5:3} At that time, Tatnai, the governor of the region beyond the River, and Shetharboznai, along with their companions, came to them and asked, "Who commanded you to build this house and to restore this wall?" {5:4} We responded by asking them, "What are the names of the men who are building this structure?" {5:5} But the eye of their God was on the elders of the Jews, and they could not stop them until the matter was brought to Darius; then they sent a letter regarding this issue. {5:6} This is a copy of the letter that Tatnai, governor of the region beyond the River, and Shetharboznai, along with their companions the Apharsachites, sent to King Darius: {5:7} They sent a letter to him that said: "To King Darius, greetings. {5:8} Let it be known to the king that we went to the province of Judea to the house of the great God, which is being built with large stones, and timber is being laid in the walls; this work is progressing quickly and is thriving in their hands. {5:9} We asked the elders, 'Who commanded you to build this house and to restore these walls?' {5:10} We also asked for their names to inform you so we could write down the names of the leaders." {5:11} They replied, "We are the servants of the God of heaven and earth, and we are rebuilding the house that was built many years ago by a great king of Israel. {5:12} But after our ancestors provoked the God of heaven to anger, he gave them into the hand of Nebuchadnezzar king of Babylon, the Chaldean, who destroyed this house and carried the people away to Babylon. {5:13} However, in the first year of Cyrus king of Babylon, King Cyrus issued a decree to rebuild this house of God. {5:14} He also took the gold and silver vessels from the house of God, which Nebuchadnezzar had taken from the temple in Jerusalem and brought to the temple in Babylon, and gave them to a man named Sheshbazzar, whom he had appointed governor. {5:15} Cyrus said to him, 'Take these vessels, go, carry them to the temple in Jerusalem, and let the house of God be rebuilt in its place.' {5:16} Then Sheshbazzar came and laid the foundation of the house of God in Jerusalem; it has been under construction since then, but it is not yet finished. {5:17} Now, if it seems good to the king, let a search be made in the king's treasury in Babylon to see if a decree was issued by King Cyrus to build this house of God in Jerusalem, and let the king send us his decision concerning this matter."

{6:1} Then King Darius made a decree, and a search was conducted in the house of the archives, where the treasures were kept in Babylon. {6:2} They found at Achmetha, in the palace in the province of the Medes, a scroll, and it contained a record that read: {6:3} "In the first year of King Cyrus, he made a decree concerning the house of God in Jerusalem: Let the house be built, the place where sacrifices are offered, and let its foundations be firmly laid, with a height of sixty cubits and a width of sixty cubits; {6:4} with three rows of large stones and one row of new timber, and let the expenses be paid from the king's treasury. {6:5} Also, let the gold and silver vessels of the house of God, which Nebuchadnezzar took from the temple in Jerusalem and brought to Babylon, be returned and brought back to the temple in Jerusalem, each to its place, to be placed in the house of God. {6:6} Now, therefore, Tatnai, governor of the region beyond the River, Shetharboznai, and your companions the Apharsachites, who are beyond the River, stay away from there. {6:7} Leave the work of this house of God alone; let the governor of the Jews and the elders of the Jews rebuild this house of God on its site. {6:8} Furthermore, I decree that you shall provide for the elders of these Jews building the house of God from the king's resources, including the tribute from beyond the River, so that they are not hindered. {6:9} Whatever they need—young bulls, rams, and lambs for burnt offerings to the God of heaven, as well as wheat, salt, wine, and oil, according to the orders of the priests in Jerusalem—let it be given to them day by day without fail. {6:10} This is so they can offer pleasing sacrifices to the God of heaven and pray for the life of the king and his sons. {6:11} Also, I have issued a decree that anyone who alters this word should have timber pulled down from their house, be impaled on it, and their house made into a garbage dump. {6:12} And may the God who has caused his name to dwell there destroy any king or people who attempts to change or destroy this house of God in Jerusalem. I, Darius, have issued this decree; let it be carried out swiftly." {6:13} Then Tatnai, governor of the region beyond the River, Shetharboznai, and their companions did as King Darius had ordered, quickly. {6:14} The elders of the Jews built and prospered through the prophesying of Haggai the prophet and Zechariah son of Iddo. They built and completed it according to the command of the God of Israel and in accordance with the command of Cyrus, Darius, and Artaxerxes, king of Persia. {6:15} The house was finished on the third day of the month Adar in the sixth year of King Darius's reign. {6:16} The Israelites, the priests, the Levites, and the rest of the exiles celebrated the dedication of this house of God with joy. {6:17} At the dedication of this house of God, they offered one hundred bulls, two hundred rams, and four hundred lambs; and for a sin offering for all Israel, twelve male goats, one for each of the tribes of Israel. {6:18} They appointed the priests to their divisions and the Levites to their courses for the service of God in Jerusalem, as it is written in the book of Moses. {6:19} The exiles kept the Passover on the fourteenth day of the first month. {6:20} The priests and Levites purified themselves, and all of them were clean; they slaughtered the Passover lamb for all the exiles and for their fellow priests and for themselves. {6:21} The Israelites who had returned from exile and all those who had separated themselves from the impurity of the nations of the land to seek the LORD God of Israel ate the Passover. {6:22} They celebrated the Feast of Unleavened Bread for seven days with joy, for the LORD had made them joyful and turned the heart of the king of Assyria toward them to strengthen their hands in the work of the house of God, the God of Israel.

{7:1} After these events, during the reign of Artaxerxes, king of Persia, Ezra, son of Seraiah, son of Azariah, son of Hilkiah, {7:2} son of Shallum, son of Zadok, son of Ahitub, {7:3} son of Amariah, son of Azariah, son of Meraioth, {7:4} son of Zerahiah, son of Uzzi, son of Bukki, {7:5} son of Abishua, son of Phinehas, son of Eleazar, son of Aaron, the chief priest, {7:6} this Ezra went up from Babylon. He was a skilled scribe in the law of Moses, which the LORD God of Israel had given, and the king granted him everything he requested, due to the good hand of his God upon him. {7:7} Some of the Israelites, including priests, Levites, singers, gatekeepers, and temple servants, went up to Jerusalem in the seventh year of King Artaxerxes. {7:8} Ezra arrived in Jerusalem in the fifth month of the seventh year of the king. {7:9} He began his journey from Babylon on the first day of the first month and arrived in Jerusalem on the first day of the fifth month, thanks to the good hand of his God upon him. {7:10} Ezra had prepared his heart to seek the law of the LORD, to obey it, and to teach its statutes and judgments to Israel. {7:11} This is a copy of the letter that King Artaxerxes gave to Ezra the priest, the scribe, a scribe well-versed in the words of the commandments of the LORD and his statutes to Israel. {7:12} Artaxerxes, king of kings, sends greetings to Ezra the priest, a scribe of the law of the God of heaven, perfect peace, and at such a time. {7:13} I issue a decree that all Israelites, including priests and Levites, in my kingdom who are willing to go to Jerusalem with you may do so. {7:14} Since you are sent by the king and his seven counselors to inquire about Judah and Jerusalem according to the law of your God, which is in your hand; {7:15} and to carry silver and gold that the king and his counselors have freely offered to the God of Israel, whose dwelling is in Jerusalem, {7:16} and all the silver and gold you can find in the province of Babylon, along with the freewill offerings of the people and priests who willingly give for the house of their God in Jerusalem: {7:17} use this money to buy quickly bullocks, rams, and lambs, along with their grain offerings and drink offerings, and offer them on the altar of the house of your God in Jerusalem. {7:18} Do whatever seems good to you and your brothers with the rest of the silver and gold, following the will of your God. {7:19} Deliver the vessels given to you for the service of the house of your God before the God of Jerusalem. {7:20} And whatever else is needed for the house of your God, which you may need to provide, you may draw from the king's treasury. {7:21} I, King Artaxerxes, decree to all treasurers beyond the River that whatever Ezra, the priest and scribe of the law of the God of heaven, requests from you must be provided without delay: {7:22} up to one hundred talents of silver, one hundred measures of wheat, one hundred baths of wine, one hundred baths of oil, and salt without limit. {7:23} Whatever is commanded by the God of heaven, let it be diligently done for the house of the God of heaven; for why should there be wrath against the kingdom of the king and his sons? {7:24} Also, we inform you that it shall not be lawful to impose tax, tribute, or customs on any priests, Levites, singers, gatekeepers, temple servants, or ministers of this house of God. {7:25} And you, Ezra, according to the wisdom of your God that is in your hand, appoint magistrates and judges who may judge all the people beyond the River, all those who know the laws of your God; and teach those who do not know them. {7:26} Anyone who does not obey the law of your God and the law of the king must be punished swiftly, whether by death, banishment, confiscation of goods, or imprisonment. {7:27} Blessed be the LORD God of our ancestors, who has put this into the king's heart to beautify the house of the LORD in Jerusalem {7:28} and has shown me kindness before the king, his counselors, and all the king's mighty princes. I was strengthened as the hand of the LORD my God was upon me, and I gathered leading men from Israel to go up with me.

{8:1} These are the heads of their families, and this is the genealogy of those who came up with me from Babylon during the reign of King Artaxerxes. {8:2} From the descendants of Phinehas: Gershom; from the descendants of Ithamar: Daniel; from the descendants of David: Hattush. {8:3} From the descendants of Shecaniah, from the descendants of Parosh: Zechariah, and with him were recorded one hundred and fifty males by genealogy. {8:4} From the descendants of Pahath-Moab: Elihoenai, the son of Zerahiah, and with him two hundred males. {8:5} From the descendants of Shecaniah: the son of Jahaziel, and with him three hundred males. {8:6} From the descendants of Adin: Ebed, the son of Jonathan, and with him fifty males. {8:7} From the descendants of Elam: Jeshaiah, the son of Athaliah, and with him seventy males. {8:8} From the descendants of Shephatiah: Zebadiah, the son of Michael, and with him eighty males. {8:9} From the descendants of Joab: Obadiah, the son of Jehiel, and with him two hundred and eighteen males. {8:10} From the descendants of Shelomith: the son of Josiphiah, and with him one hundred and sixty males. {8:11} From the descendants of Bebai: Zechariah, the son of Bebai, and with him twenty-eight males. {8:12} From the descendants of Azgad: Johanan, the son of Hakkatan, and with him one hundred and ten males. {8:13} From the last of the descendants of Adonikam, these were their names: Eliphelet, Jeiel, and Shemaiah, and with them sixty males. {8:14} From the descendants of Bigvai: Uthai and Zabbud, and with them seventy males. {8:15} I gathered them by the river that flows toward Ahava, where we camped for three days. I reviewed the people and the priests, but I found no descendants of Levi among them. {8:16} So I sent for Eliezer, Ariel, Shemaiah, Elnathan, Jarib, another Elnathan, Nathan, Zechariah, and Meshullam, who were leaders; and also for Joiarib and yet another Elnathan, who were men of insight. {8:17} I sent them with instructions to Iddo, the leader at the place called Casiphia. I told them what to say to Iddo and his fellow servants, the Nethinims (temple servants), asking them to send us ministers for the house of our God. {8:18} Because the gracious hand of our God was upon us, they brought us a man of understanding, Sherebiah, a descendant of Mahli, who was a descendant of Levi, son of Israel, and Sherebiah came with his sons and brothers, a total of eighteen men. {8:19} Also, Hashabiah and with him Jeshaiah, from the descendants of Merari, and his brothers and their sons, totaling twenty men. {8:20} Additionally, two hundred and twenty Nethinims, whom David and the officials had appointed to assist the Levites in their service, were also brought. All of them were recorded by name. {8:21} Then, at the river of Ahava, I proclaimed a fast, so we could humble ourselves before our God and seek a safe journey for us, our children, and all our possessions. {8:22} I was embarrassed to ask the king for soldiers and horsemen to protect us from enemies along the way, because we had already told the king, "The hand of our God is upon all who seek Him for good, but His wrath is against all who forsake Him." {8:23} So we fasted and prayed earnestly to our God for this, and He answered our prayer. {8:24} Then I selected twelve of the chief priests, Sherebiah, Hashabiah, and ten of their brothers with them, {8:25} and I weighed out to them the silver, the gold, and the vessels, which had been offered for the house of our God by the king, his advisors, his officers, and all the Israelites who were present. {8:26} I weighed out into their hands six hundred and fifty talents of silver, silver vessels worth one hundred talents, and one hundred talents of gold. {8:27} There were also twenty gold bowls worth a thousand darics (Persian coins), and two vessels of fine polished bronze, as precious as gold. {8:28} I told them, "You are holy to the LORD, and these vessels are holy, as well. The silver and gold are a freewill offering to the LORD, the God of your ancestors. {8:29} Guard them carefully until you weigh them out in the presence of the chief priests, the Levites, and the family leaders of Israel in the chambers of the house of the LORD in Jerusalem." {8:30} So the priests and Levites took the silver, the gold, and the vessels, in order to bring them to the house of our God in Jerusalem. {8:31} On the twelfth day of the first month, we left the river of Ahava to go to Jerusalem. The hand of our God was upon us, and He protected us from enemies and ambushes along the way. {8:32} We arrived in Jerusalem and rested there for three days. {8:33} On the fourth day, the silver, the gold, and the vessels were weighed in the house of our God by Meremoth, son of Uriah the priest, along with Eleazar, son of Phinehas, and with them were Jozabad, son of Jeshua, and Noadiah, son of Binnui, who were Levites. {8:34} Everything was counted and weighed, and the total weight was recorded at that time. {8:35} Then the Israelites who had returned from captivity offered burnt offerings to the God of Israel: twelve bulls for all Israel, ninety-six rams, seventy-seven lambs, and twelve male goats as a sin offering. All of these were burnt offerings to the LORD. {8:36} Finally, they delivered the king's orders to the royal officials and the governors of the province Beyond the River, and they supported the people and the house of God.

{9:1} After these things were completed, the leaders came to me and said, "The people of Israel, including the priests and the Levites, have not separated themselves from the surrounding nations and their detestable practices, which are like those of the Canaanites, Hittites, Perizzites, Jebusites, Ammonites, Moabites, Egyptians, and Amorites. {9:2} For they have taken daughters from these nations as wives for themselves and their sons, so the holy seed (the people set apart by God) has mingled with the people of these lands. Worse still, the leaders and officials have been the foremost in this unfaithfulness." {9:3} When I heard this, I tore my garment and my cloak, pulled hair from my head and beard, and sat down in utter shock. {9:4} Then all who trembled at the words of the God of Israel, because of the unfaithfulness of the exiles, gathered around me as I sat there appalled until the evening sacrifice. {9:5} At the time of the evening sacrifice, I rose from my state of grief, with my garment and cloak still torn, and I knelt down, spreading out my hands to the LORD my God, {9:6} and I said, "O my God, I am too ashamed and embarrassed to lift my face to you, my God, because our sins are higher than our heads, and our guilt has reached the heavens. {9:7} From the days of our ancestors until now, we have been deeply guilty, and because of our sins, we, along with our kings and priests, have been handed over to foreign kings to face the sword, captivity, plunder, and humiliation, as is the case today. {9:8} But now, for a brief moment, the LORD our God has shown us grace by leaving us a remnant and giving us a secure foothold in His holy place, so that our God may give light to our eyes and a small measure of relief in our slavery. {9:9} Though we are slaves, our God has not abandoned us in our bondage. He has shown us kindness in the sight of the kings of Persia by granting us new life to rebuild the house of our God, restore its ruins, and give us a protective wall in Judah and Jerusalem. {9:10} But now, our God, what can we say after this? We have forsaken your commands {9:11} which you gave through your servants the prophets, saying, 'The land you are entering to take possession of is defiled by the corruption of its peoples and their abominable practices, which have polluted it from one end to the other with their uncleanness. {9:12} Therefore, do not give your daughters in marriage to their sons or take their daughters for your sons. Never seek peace or prosperity from these peoples, so that you may be strong, eat the good things of the land, and leave it as an inheritance for your children forever.' {9:13} Even after all that has happened to us because of our evil deeds and our great guilt, seeing that you, our God, have punished us less than our sins deserved and have given us this deliverance, {9:14} should we once again break your commands and intermarry with these peoples who commit such detestable practices? Would you not become so angry with us that you would destroy us, leaving no remnant or survivor? {9:15} O LORD, God of Israel, you are righteous, for we are left with a remnant that has escaped, as it is today. Here we stand before you in our guilt, and because of it, none of us can stand in your presence."

{10:1} As Ezra prayed and confessed, weeping and prostrating himself before the house of God, a large assembly of Israelites—men, women, and children—gathered around him, weeping bitterly. {10:2} Then Shechaniah, the son of Jehiel, from the descendants of Elam, spoke to Ezra, saying, "We have sinned against our God by marrying foreign women from the peoples of the land, but there is still hope for Israel regarding this matter. {10:3} So now, let us make a covenant with our God to send away all these wives and their children, following the counsel of my lord and of those who fear the commandments of our God. Let this be done in accordance with the Law. {10:4} Arise, for this is your responsibility, and we are with you. Be strong and act." {10:5} So Ezra stood up and made the leading priests, Levites, and all Israel swear to do as had been proposed, and they took the oath. {10:6} Then Ezra left the house of God and went to the room of Johanan, the son of Eliashib, where he stayed without eating bread or drinking water, for he mourned over the unfaithfulness of the exiles. {10:7} A proclamation was then issued throughout Judah and Jerusalem to all the exiles, calling them to gather in Jerusalem. {10:8} Anyone who failed to appear within three days, according to the decision of the leaders and elders, would forfeit all their property and be expelled from the assembly of the exiles. {10:9} Within three days, all the men of Judah and Benjamin had gathered in Jerusalem. It was the ninth month, on the twentieth day, and all the people sat in the open square before the house of God, trembling because of the seriousness of the situation and because of the heavy rain. {10:10} Ezra the priest stood up and said to them, "You have been unfaithful by marrying foreign women, adding to the guilt of Israel. {10:11} Now, make your confession to the LORD, the God of your ancestors, and do His will. Separate yourselves from the people of the land and from these foreign wives." {10:12} The whole assembly responded with a loud voice, "You are right! We must do as you say. {10:13} But there are many people here, and it is the rainy season, so we cannot stand outside. Besides, this is not something that can be settled in a day or two, because we have sinned greatly in this matter. {10:14} Let our leaders represent the whole assembly. Let those in our cities who have married foreign wives come at appointed times, along with the elders and judges of each city, until the fierce anger of our God concerning this matter is turned away from us." {10:15} Only Jonathan, the son of Asahel, and Jahaziah, the son of Tikvah, opposed this, and they were supported by Meshullam and Shabbethai the Levite. {10:16} So the exiles did as proposed. Ezra the priest selected men who were family heads, one from each family division, and all of them were designated by name. On the first day of the tenth month, they sat down to investigate the cases, {10:17} and by the first day of the first month, they had finished dealing with all the men who had married foreign wives. {10:18} Among the descendants of the priests, the following were found to have married foreign women: from the descendants of Jeshua, son of Jozadak, and his brothers, Maaseiah, Eliezer, Jarib, and Gedaliah. {10:19} They all pledged to send their wives away, and for their guilt, they offered a ram from the flock as a guilt offering. {10:20} From the descendants of Immer: Hanani and Zebadiah. {10:21} From the descendants of Harim: Maaseiah, Elijah, Shemaiah, Jehiel, and Uzziah. {10:22} From the descendants of Pashur: Elioenai, Maaseiah, Ishmael, Nethaneel, Jozabad, and Elasah. {10:23} Among the Levites: Jozabad, Shimei, Kelaiah (also known as Kelita), Pethahiah, Judah, and Eliezer. {10:24} From the singers: Eliashib. From the gatekeepers: Shallum, Telem, and Uri. {10:25} From the other Israelites: from the descendants of Parosh: Ramiah, Jeziah, Malchiah, Miamin, Eleazar, Malchijah, and

Benaiah. {10:26} From the descendants of Elam: Mattaniah, Zechariah, Jehiel, Abdi, Jeremoth, and Elijah. {10:27} From the descendants of Zattu: Elioenai, Eliashib, Mattaniah, Jeremoth, Zabad, and Aziza. {10:28} From the descendants of Bebai: Jehohanan, Hananiah, Zabbai, and Athlai. {10:29} From the descendants of Bani: Meshullam, Malluch, Adaiah, Jashub, Sheal, and Ramoth. {10:30} From the descendants of Pahath-Moab: Adna, Chelal, Benaiah, Maaseiah, Mattaniah, Bezaleel, Binnui, and Manasseh. {10:31} From the descendants of Harim: Eliezer, Ishijah, Malchiah, Shemaiah, Shemaiah, Shimeon, {10:32} Benjamin, Malluch, and Shemariah. {10:33} From the descendants of Hashum: Mattenai, Mattattah, Zabad, Eliphelet, Jeremai, Manasseh, and Shimei. {10:34} From the descendants of Bani: Maadai, Amram, Uel, {10:35} Benaiah, Bedeiah, Cheluh, {10:36} Vaniah, Meremoth, Eliashib, {10:37} Mattaniah, Mattenai, and Jaasau. {10:38} From the descendants of Binnui: Shimei, {10:39} Shelemiah, Nathan, Adaiah, {10:40} Machnadebai, Shashai, Sharai, {10:41} Azareel, Shelemiah, Shemariah, {10:42} Shallum, Amariah, and Joseph. {10:43} From the descendants of Nebo: Jeiel, Mattithiah, Zabad, Zebina, Jaddai, Joel, and Benaiah. {10:44} All these men had married foreign women, and some of them had children by these wives.

The Book of Nehemiah

{1:1} The words of Nehemiah, son of Hachaliah. In the month of Chisleu, in the twentieth year, while I was in the palace at Shushan, {1:2} Hanani, one of my brothers, arrived with some men from Judah. I asked them about the Jews who had survived and about Jerusalem. {1:3} They told me that those who survived the exile are in great trouble and shame; the wall of Jerusalem is broken down, and its gates have been burned with fire. {1:4} When I heard this, I sat down and wept; I mourned for several days, fasting and praying before the God of heaven. {1:5} I prayed, "Lord God of heaven, great and awesome God, who keeps covenant and mercy for those who love Him and obey His commandments: {1:6} please let Your ear be attentive and Your eyes open to hear the prayer of Your servant, which I pray before You day and night for the people of Israel, confessing the sins of the Israelites, including my own and my family's sins. {1:7} We have acted very wickedly against You and have not kept the commandments, the statutes, or the judgments that You gave to Your servant Moses. {1:8} Remember the instruction You gave to Your servant Moses, saying, 'If you are unfaithful, I will scatter you among the nations. {1:9} But if you return to Me and obey My commandments, then even if your exiled people are at the ends of the earth, I will gather them from there and bring them to the place I have chosen as a dwelling for My name.' {1:10} They are Your servants and Your people, whom You redeemed by Your great power and strong hand. {1:11} Lord, please let Your ear be attentive to the prayer of Your servant and to the prayers of Your servants who delight in revering Your name. Give Your servant success today and grant him favor in the presence of this man." I was the king's cupbearer.

{2:1} In the month of Nisan, in the twentieth year of King Artaxerxes, when wine was before him, I took the wine and gave it to the king. I had never been sad in his presence before. {2:2} So the king asked me, "Why is your face sad? You aren't sick; this must be sadness of heart." I was very much afraid {2:3} and said to the king, "May the king live forever! Why shouldn't my face be sad when the city where my ancestors are buried lies in ruins and its gates have been destroyed by fire?" {2:4} The king asked me, "What do you want?" So I prayed to the God of heaven {2:5} and answered the king, "If it pleases the king and if your servant has found favor in your sight, please send me to Judah, to the city of my ancestors' tombs, so I can rebuild it." {2:6} The king, with the queen sitting beside him, asked, "How long will your journey take, and when will you return?" It pleased the king to send me, and I set a time. {2:7} I also said to the king, "If it pleases the king, let letters be given to me for the governors of the province west of the Euphrates River so they will provide me safe passage until I arrive in Judah. {2:8} And a letter to Asaph, the keeper of the king's forest, instructing him to give me timber to make beams for the gates of the citadel by the temple and for the wall of the city, and for the house I will occupy." The king granted my requests because the gracious hand of my God was on me. {2:9} I went to the governors of the province west of the Euphrates and gave them the king's letters. The king had also sent army officers and cavalry with me. {2:10} When Sanballat the Horonite and Tobiah the Ammonite official heard about this, they were very displeased that someone had come to promote the welfare of the Israelites. {2:11} I arrived in Jerusalem and was there for three days. {2:12} Then I set out during the night with a few others. I had not told anyone what my God had put in my heart to do for Jerusalem. There were no mounts with me except the one I was riding. {2:13} By night, I went through the Valley Gate toward the Jackal Well and the Dung Gate, examining the walls of Jerusalem, which had been broken down, and its gates that had been destroyed by fire. {2:14} Then I moved on toward the Fountain Gate and the King's Pool, but there was not enough room for my mount to get through. {2:15} So I went up the valley by night, examining the wall. Finally, I turned back and entered through the Valley Gate. {2:16} The officials did not know where I had gone or what I was doing, because as yet I had said nothing to the Jews or the priests or the nobles or the officials or any others who would be doing the work. {2:17} Then I said to them, "You see the trouble we are in: Jerusalem lies in ruins, and its gates have been burned with fire. Come, let us rebuild the wall of Jerusalem, and we will no longer be in disgrace." {2:18} I also told them about the gracious hand of my God on me and what the king had said to me. They replied, "Let us start rebuilding." So they began this good work. {2:19} But when Sanballat the Horonite, Tobiah the Ammonite servant, and Geshem the Arab heard about it, they mocked and ridiculed us. "What is this you are doing? Are you rebelling against the king?" they asked. {2:20} I answered them by saying, "The God of heaven will give us success. We His servants will start rebuilding, but as for you, you have no share in Jerusalem or any claim or historic right to it."

{3:1} Eliashib the high priest and his fellow priests began rebuilding the Sheep Gate; they dedicated it and set up its doors, dedicating it all the way to the Tower of Meah and the Tower of Hananeel. {3:2} Next to them, the men from Jericho built. Next to them was Zaccur, son of Imri. {3:3} The sons of Hassenaah rebuilt the Fish Gate; they laid its beams and set up its doors, locks, and bars. {3:4} Next to them, Meremoth, son of Urijah, son of Koz, repaired the wall. Next to him was Meshullam, son of Berechiah, son of Meshezabeel. Next to him was Zadok, son of Baana. {3:5} The Tekoites made repairs next to them, but their nobles did not put their shoulders to the work of their Lord. {3:6} Jehoiada, son of Paseah, and Meshullam, son of Besodeiah, repaired the Old Gate; they laid its beams and set up its doors, locks, and bars. {3:7} Next to them, Melatiah the Gibeonite and Jadon the Meronothite, along with the men of Gibeon and Mizpah, worked as far as the governor's throne on the west side of the river. {3:8} Uzziel, son of Harhaiah, a goldsmith, repaired next to him. Also, Hananiah, son of one of the apothecaries, worked alongside him, and they fortified Jerusalem to the Broad Wall. {3:9} Rephaiah, son of Hur, ruler of half of Jerusalem, repaired next to them. {3:10} Jedaiah, son of Harumaph, repaired across from his house, and Hattush, son of Hashabniah, worked next to him. {3:11} Malchijah, son of Harim, and Hashub, son of Pahathmoab, repaired another section and the Tower of the Furnaces. {3:12} Shallum, son of Halohesh, ruler of half of Jerusalem, and his daughters repaired next to him. {3:13} The Valley Gate was repaired by Hanun and the inhabitants of Zanoah; they built it, set up its doors, locks, and bars, and built a thousand cubits of the wall to the Dung Gate. {3:14} Malchiah, son of Rechab, ruler of part of Bethhaccerem, repaired the Dung Gate; he built it, set up its doors, locks, and bars. {3:15} Shallun, son of Colhozeh, ruler of part of Mizpah, repaired the Fountain Gate; he built it, covered it, and set up its doors, locks, and bars, along with the wall of the Pool of Siloah by the king's garden and the stairs that go down from the City of David. {3:16} Nehemiah, son of Azbuk, ruler of half of Bethzur, repaired next to him, up to the tombs of David and the pool that was made, and to the house of the mighty. {3:17} The Levites repaired after him; Rehum, son of Bani, worked next to him, and Hashabiah, ruler of half of Keilah, repaired in his section. {3:18} Their brothers, Bavai, son of Henadad, ruler of half of Keilah, repaired after him. {3:19} Ezer, son of Jeshua, ruler of Mizpah, repaired another section across from the ascent to the armory at the bend in the wall. {3:20}

Baruch, son of Zabbai, diligently repaired the section from the bend in the wall to the door of the house of Eliashib the high priest. {3:21} Meremoth, son of Urijah, son of Koz, repaired another section from the door of the house of Eliashib to the end of his house. {3:22} The priests, the men of the plain, repaired after him. {3:23} Benjamin and Hashub repaired across from their houses. Azariah, son of Maaseiah, son of Ananiah, repaired next to his house. {3:24} Binnui, son of Henadad, repaired another section from the house of Azariah to the bend in the wall, even to the corner. {3:25} Palal, son of Uzai, repaired opposite the bend in the wall and the tower that projects from the king's high house, near the court of the prison. Pedaiah, son of Parosh, worked after him. {3:26} The Nethinims lived in Ophel, across from the Water Gate to the east, and the tower that projects. {3:27} The Tekoites repaired another section, across from the great tower that projects to the wall of Ophel. {3:28} The priests repaired each section opposite their own houses, starting from above the Horse Gate. {3:29} Zadok, son of Immer, repaired next to his house, and Shemaiah, son of Shechaniah, keeper of the East Gate, worked after him. {3:30} Hananiah, son of Shelemiah, and Hanun, the sixth son of Zalaph, repaired another section. Meshullam, son of Berechiah, worked across from his room. {3:31} Malchiah, son of the goldsmith, repaired up to the place of the Nethinims and merchants, across from the Miphkad Gate and the ascent of the corner. {3:32} Between the ascent of the corner and the Sheep Gate, the goldsmiths and merchants made repairs.

{4:1} When Sanballat heard that we were rebuilding the wall, he was very angry and mocked the Jews. {4:2} He spoke before his brothers and the army of Samaria, saying, "What are these weak Jews doing? Will they restore their city? Will they offer sacrifices? Will they finish it in a day? Can they bring the stones back to life from the heaps of burned rubble?" {4:3} Tobiah the Ammonite was beside him, saying, "Whatever they build, even a fox would break down their stone wall." {4:4} Hear, O our God, for we are despised; turn their insults back on their own heads and give them up to be plundered in a land of captivity. {4:5} Do not cover up their guilt or let their sin be erased from Your sight, for they have provoked You to anger before the builders. {4:6} So we rebuilt the wall, and it was joined together to half its height, for the people worked with all their heart. {4:7} When Sanballat, Tobiah, the Arabs, the Ammonites, and the Ashdodites heard that the repairs to Jerusalem's walls had gone ahead and that the gaps were being closed, they were very angry. {4:8} They all plotted together to come and fight against Jerusalem and to stir up trouble against it. {4:9} But we prayed to our God and posted a guard day and night to meet this threat. {4:10} Judah said, "The strength of the laborers is giving out, and there is so much rubble that we cannot rebuild the wall." {4:11} Our enemies said, "Before they know it or see us, we will be right there among them and will kill them and put an end to the work." {4:12} Then the Jews living near them came and told us ten times, "Wherever you turn, they will attack us." {4:13} So I stationed some of the people behind the lowest points of the wall at the exposed places, posting them by families with their swords, spears, and bows. {4:14} After I looked things over, I stood up and said to the nobles, the officials, and the rest of the people, "Don't be afraid of them. Remember the Lord, who is great and awesome, and fight for your families, your sons and daughters, your wives and homes." {4:15} When our enemies heard that we were aware of their plot and that God had frustrated it, we all returned to the wall, each to our own work. {4:16} From that day on, half of my men did the work while the other half were equipped with spears, shields, bows, and armor. The officers posted themselves behind all the people of Judah. {4:17} Those who built the wall and those who carried burdens did their work with one hand and held a weapon in the other. {4:18} Each of the builders wore his sword at his side as he worked. The man who sounded the trumpet stayed with me. {4:19} I said to the nobles, the officials, and the rest of the people, "The work is extensive and spread out, and we are widely separated from each other along the wall. {4:20} Wherever you hear the sound of the trumpet, join us there. Our God will fight for us!" {4:21} So we continued to work, with half the men holding spears from dawn till the stars came out. {4:22} At that time I also said to the people, "Have every man and his helper stay inside Jerusalem at night so they can serve us as guards by night and work by day." {4:23} Neither I nor my brothers nor my men nor the guards with me took off our clothes; each had his weapon even when he went for water.

{5:1} There was a loud outcry from the people and their wives against their fellow Jews. {5:2} Some were saying, "We, our sons, and our daughters are numerous; we need grain so we can eat and stay alive." {5:3} Others said, "We've mortgaged our fields, vineyards, and houses to buy grain because of the famine." {5:4} Some also mentioned, "We've borrowed money to pay the king's tax, putting our fields and vineyards at risk." {5:5} Yet now our flesh is the same as our brothers', our children are like theirs, and we are forced to sell our sons and daughters as slaves. Some of our daughters are already in bondage, and we can't redeem them because other men own our fields and vineyards. {5:6} I was very angry when I heard their outcry and these complaints. {5:7} After thinking it over, I rebuked the nobles and officials, saying, "You are charging interest to your fellow Jews." So I called a large assembly against them. {5:8} I told them, "We've redeemed our Jewish brothers who were sold to the Gentiles; now, will you sell your own brothers? Or should they be sold to us?" They were silent and had no answer. {5:9} I also said, "What you are doing is not good. Shouldn't you walk in the fear of our God to avoid the reproach of our Gentile enemies?" {5:10} I, along with my brothers and my servants, have been charging them money and grain. I urge you, let's stop this interest. {5:11} Give back to them today their fields, vineyards, olive groves, and houses, along with the interest you've charged on money, grain, wine, and oil. {5:12} They replied, "We will give it back and demand nothing more from them; we will do as you say." Then I summoned the priests and made them swear to do as they had promised. {5:13} I shook out the fold of my robe and said, "So may God shake out every man from his house and from his work if he does not keep this promise. May he be shaken out and emptied." All the assembly said, "Amen," and praised the Lord. The people did as they had promised. {5:14} From the time I was appointed governor in Judah, from the twentieth year to the thirty-second year of King Artaxerxes, for twelve years, neither I nor my brothers ate the governor's provisions. {5:15} But former governors had burdened the people, taking food and wine from them, plus forty shekels of silver; even their servants ruled over the people. But I did not do so because of the fear of God. {5:16} I also continued the work on this wall and did not buy any land. All my servants were gathered there for the work. {5:17} At my table were one hundred and fifty Jews and officials, besides those who came to us from the surrounding nations. {5:18} The provisions prepared for me each day included one ox, six choice sheep, and some fowl, along with an abundance of wine every ten days. Yet I did not demand the governor's provisions because the people were already suffering. {5:19} Remember me with favor, my God, for all I have done for this people.

{6:1} When Sanballat, Tobiah, Geshem the Arab, and the rest of our enemies heard that I had rebuilt the wall and there were no more gaps (though at that time I had not yet set the doors in the gates), {6:2} Sanballat and Geshem sent me a message saying, "Come, let's meet together in one of the villages on the plain of Ono." But they intended to harm me. {6:3} I sent messengers to them, saying, "I am carrying on a great project and cannot go down. Why should the work stop while I leave it to go down to you?" {6:4} They sent me the same message four times, and I answered them the same way each time. {6:5} Then Sanballat sent his servant to me a fifth time with an open letter in his hand, {6:6} in which it was written: "It is reported among the Gentiles, and Geshem says it is true, that you and the Jews are planning to rebel, and that is why you are building the wall. According to these reports, you are going to become their king. {6:7} You have also appointed prophets to proclaim about you in Jerusalem, saying, 'There is a king in Judah!' Now this report will get back to the king. So come, let's meet together." {6:8} I sent him this reply: "Nothing like what you are saying is happening; you are just making it up out of your head." {6:9} They were all trying to frighten us, thinking, "Their hands will get too weak for the work, and it won't be completed." But I prayed, "Now strengthen my hands." {6:10} I went to the house of Shemaiah, son of Delaiah, the son of Mehetabeel, who was shut in at his home. He said, "Let's meet in the house of God, inside the temple, and close the temple doors because they are coming to kill you; they will come in the night."

{6:11} I said, "Should a man like me run away? Or should someone like me go into the temple to save his life? I will not go in!" {6:12} I realized that God had not sent him, but that he had prophesied against me because Tobiah and Sanballat had hired him. {6:13} He was hired to intimidate me so that I would commit a sin by doing this and then they would give me a bad name to discredit me. {6:14} My God, remember Tobiah and Sanballat for what they have done, and also the prophetess Noadiah and the rest of the prophets who have been trying to intimidate me. {6:15} So the wall was completed on the twenty-fifth day of the month Elul, in fifty-two days. {6:16} When all our enemies heard about this, and all the surrounding nations saw it, they lost their confidence because they realized that this work had been done with the help of our God. {6:17} During those days, the nobles of Judah were sending many letters to Tobiah, and replies from Tobiah kept coming to them. {6:18} Many in Judah were under oath to him, since he was the son-in-law of Shechaniah, son of Arah, and his son Johanan had married the daughter of Meshullam, son of Berechiah. {6:19} Moreover, they kept reporting to me his good deeds and telling him what I said, and Tobiah sent letters to intimidate me.

{7:1} When the wall was built and the doors were set up, I appointed the gatekeepers, singers, and Levites. {7:2} I put my brother Hanani and Hananiah, the ruler of the palace, in charge of Jerusalem because he was a trustworthy man who feared God more than most. {7:3} I instructed them, "Don't let the gates of Jerusalem be opened until the sun is hot. While the gatekeepers are on duty, let them shut and lock the doors. Appoint guards from the inhabitants of Jerusalem—each one at their post, in front of their own house." {7:4} The city was large and impressive, but the people in it were few, and the houses had not yet been built. {7:5} My God put it in my heart to gather the nobles, officials, and the people so they could be counted by genealogy. I found a register of those who had returned first and found it written: {7:6} These are the people of the province who returned from captivity—those whom King Nebuchadnezzar of Babylon had taken away and who returned to Jerusalem and Judah, each to their own city. {7:7} They came with Zerubbabel, Jeshua, Nehemiah, Azariah, Raamiah, Nahamani, Mordecai, Bilshan, Mispereth, Bigvai, Nehum, and Baanah. The number of the men of Israel was: {7:8} The children of Parosh: two thousand one hundred seventy-two. {7:9} The children of Shephatiah: three hundred seventy-two. {7:10} The children of Arah: six hundred fifty-two. {7:11} The children of Pahathmoab, of the children of Jeshua and Joab: two thousand eight hundred eighteen. {7:12} The children of Elam: one thousand two hundred fifty-four. {7:13} The children of Zattu: eight hundred forty-five. {7:14} The children of Zaccai: seven hundred sixty. {7:15} The children of Binnui: six hundred forty-eight. {7:16} The children of Bebai: six hundred twenty-eight. {7:17} The children of Azgad: two thousand three hundred twenty-two. {7:18} The children of Adonikam: six hundred sixty-seven. {7:19} The children of Bigvai: two thousand sixty-seven. {7:20} The children of Adin: six hundred fifty-five. {7:21} The children of Ater of Hezekiah: ninety-eight. {7:22} The children of Hashum: three hundred twenty-eight. {7:23} The children of Bezai: three hundred twenty-four. {7:24} The children of Hariph: one hundred twelve. {7:25} The children of Gibeon: ninety-five. {7:26} The men of Bethlehem and Netophah: one hundred eighty-eight. {7:27} The men of Anathoth: one hundred twenty-eight. {7:28} The men of Bethazmaveth: forty-two. {7:29} The men of Kirjathjearim, Chephirah, and Beeroth: seven hundred forty-three. {7:30} The men of Ramah and Geba: six hundred twenty-one. {7:31} The men of Michmas: one hundred twenty-two. {7:32} The men of Bethel and Ai: one hundred twenty-three. {7:33} The men of the other Nebo: fifty-two. {7:34} The children of the other Elam: one thousand two hundred fifty-four. {7:35} The children of Harim: three hundred twenty. {7:36} The children of Jericho: three hundred forty-five. {7:37} The children of Lod, Hadid, and Ono: seven hundred twenty-one. {7:38} The children of Senaah: three thousand nine hundred thirty. {7:39} The priests: the children of Jedaiah, of the house of Jeshua: nine hundred seventy-three. {7:40} The children of Immer: one thousand fifty-two. {7:41} The children of Pashur: one thousand two hundred forty-seven. {7:42} The children of Harim: one thousand seventeen. {7:43} The Levites: the children of Jeshua, of Kadmiel, and the children of Hodevah: seventy-four. {7:44} The singers: the children of Asaph: one hundred forty-eight. {7:45} The gatekeepers: the children of Shallum, the children of Ater, the children of Talmon, the children of Akkub, the children of Hatita, and the children of Shobai: one hundred thirty-eight. {7:46} The Nethinims: the children of Ziha, the children of Hashupha, the children of Tabbaoth, {7:47} the children of Keros, the children of Sia, the children of Padon, {7:48} the children of Lebana, the children of Hagaba, the children of Shalmai, {7:49} the children of Hanan, the children of Giddel, the children of Gahar, {7:50} the children of Reaiah, the children of Rezin, and the children of Nekoda, {7:51} the children of Gazzam, the children of Uzza, and the children of Phaseah, {7:52} the children of Besai, the children of Meunim, and the children of Nephishesim, {7:53} the children of Bakbuk, the children of Hakupha, and the children of Harhur, {7:54} the children of Bazlith, the children of Mehida, and the children of Harsha, {7:55} the children of Barkos, the children of Sisera, and the children of Tamah, {7:56} the children of Neziah and the children of Hatipha. {7:57} The children of Solomon's servants: the children of Sotai, the children of Sophereth, and the children of Perida, {7:58} the children of Jaala, the children of Darkon, and the children of Giddel, {7:59} the children of Shephatiah, the children of Hattil, the children of Pochereth of Zebaim, and the children of Amon. {7:60} All the Nethinims and the children of Solomon's servants numbered three hundred ninety-two. {7:61} These also came up from Telmelah, Telharesha, Cherub, Addon, and Immer, but they could not prove their families or their lineage to show they were from Israel. {7:62} The children of Delaiah, the children of Tobiah, and the children of Nekoda: six hundred forty-two. {7:63} Among the priests: the children of Habaiah, the children of Koz, and the children of Barzillai, who had married a daughter of Barzillai the Gileadite and was called by their name. {7:64} These sought their family records among those registered by genealogy, but they could not be found; therefore, they were considered unclean and excluded from the priesthood. {7:65} The governor told them they should not eat any of the most sacred foods until there was a priest to consult with the Urim and Thummim (objects used for divination). {7:66} The whole assembly together numbered forty-two thousand three hundred sixty, {7:67} excluding their male and female servants, who numbered seven thousand three hundred thirty-seven. They also had two hundred forty-five singing men and women. {7:68} Their horses numbered seven hundred thirty-six, their mules two hundred forty-five, {7:69} their camels four hundred thirty-five, and their donkeys six thousand seven hundred twenty. {7:70} Some of the leaders gave to the work. The governor contributed one thousand drams of gold, fifty basins, and five hundred thirty priestly garments. {7:71} Some of the leaders gave twenty thousand drams of gold and two thousand two hundred pounds of silver for the work. {7:72} The rest of the people gave twenty thousand drams of gold, two thousand pounds of silver, and sixty-seven priestly garments. {7:73} So the priests, Levites, gatekeepers, singers, and some of the people, along with the Nethinims, all of Israel, settled in their towns. When the seventh month arrived, the Israelites were in their towns.

{8:1} On the first day of the seventh month, all the people gathered together as one in the street by the Water Gate and asked Ezra the scribe to bring out the Book of the Law of Moses that the Lord had commanded for Israel. {8:2} Ezra the priest brought the law before the assembly, including men and women and all who could understand. {8:3} He read it aloud from morning until midday in front of the men, women, and those who could understand, and all the people listened attentively to the Book of the Law. {8:4} Ezra stood on a wooden platform they had made for the occasion, and beside him were Mattithiah, Shema, Anaiah, Urijah, Hilkiah, and Maaseiah on his right, and Pedaiah, Mishael, Malchiah, Hashum, Hashbadana, Zechariah, and Meshullam on his left. {8:5} Ezra opened the book in front of everyone, and when he did, all the people stood up. {8:6} Ezra blessed the Lord, the great God, and all the people responded, "Amen, Amen," lifting their hands, bowing their heads, and worshiping the Lord with their faces to the ground. {8:7} The Levites, Jeshua, Bani, Sherebiah, Jamin, Akkub, Shabbethai, Hodijah, Maaseiah, Kelita, Azariah, Jozabad, Hanan, and Pelaiah helped the people understand the law while the people remained in their places. {8:8} They read from the Book of the Law of God clearly, giving the meaning so that the people could understand what was being read. {8:9}

Nehemiah (the governor), Ezra the priest and scribe, and the Levites who taught the people said to all of them, "This day is holy to the Lord your God; do not mourn or weep," for all the people were weeping as they heard the words of the law. {8:10} Then he said to them, "Go and enjoy choice food and sweet drinks, and send some to those who have nothing prepared. This day is holy to our Lord. Do not grieve, for the joy of the Lord is your strength." {8:11} The Levites calmed all the people, saying, "Be still, for this is a holy day; do not grieve." {8:12} Then all the people went away to eat and drink, to send portions, and to celebrate with great joy because they now understood the words that had been made known to them. {8:13} On the second day, the heads of the families, along with the priests and Levites, gathered around Ezra the scribe to gain insight into the words of the law. {8:14} They discovered written in the law that the Lord had commanded through Moses that the Israelites should live in booths during the festival of the seventh month. {8:15} They were to proclaim this in all their cities and in Jerusalem: "Go out to the hill country and bring back branches from olive trees, wild olive trees, myrtle trees, palm trees, and other leafy trees to make booths," as it is written. {8:16} So the people went out and brought back branches and made booths on their rooftops, in their courtyards, and in the courts of the house of God, and in the square by the Water Gate and the one by the Gate of Ephraim. {8:17} The whole assembly that had returned from exile built booths and sat under them. Since the days of Joshua son of Nun until that day, the Israelites had not celebrated like this, and their joy was very great. {8:18} Day after day, from the first day to the last, Ezra read from the Book of the Law of God. They celebrated the festival for seven days, and on the eighth day, there was a solemn assembly, in accordance with the regulation.

{9:1} On the twenty-fourth day of the same month, the Israelites gathered together, fasting and wearing sackcloth, and had dust on their heads. {9:2} Those of Israelite descent separated themselves from all foreigners and stood in their places and confessed their sins and the iniquities of their ancestors. {9:3} They stood where they were and read from the Book of the Law of the Lord their God for a quarter of the day, and spent another quarter in confession and in worshiping the Lord their God. {9:4} The Levites—Jeshua, Bani, Kadmiel, Shebaniah, Bunni, Sherebiah, Bani, and Chenani—stood on the stairs and cried out with a loud voice to the Lord their God. {9:5} The Levites said, "Stand up and praise the Lord your God, who is from everlasting to everlasting. Blessed be your glorious name, and may it be exalted above all blessing and praise." {9:6} You alone are the Lord. You made the heavens, even the highest heavens, and all their starry host, the earth and all that is on it, the seas and all that is in them. You give life to everything, and the multitudes of heaven worship you. {9:7} You are the Lord God, who chose Abram and brought him out of Ur of the Chaldeans and named him Abraham. {9:8} You found his heart faithful to you and made a covenant with him to give him the land of the Canaanites, Hittites, Amorites, Perizzites, Jebusites, and Girgashites; you have kept your promise because you are righteous. {9:9} You saw the suffering of our ancestors in Egypt; you heard their cry at the Red Sea. {9:10} You sent signs and wonders against Pharaoh, against all his officials and all the people of his land, for you knew how arrogantly they treated them. You made a name for yourself, which remains to this day. {9:11} You divided the sea before them so that they passed through it on dry ground, but you hurled their pursuers into the depths like a stone into mighty waters. {9:12} By day you led them with a pillar of cloud, and by night with a pillar of fire to give them light on the way they were to take. {9:13} You came down on Mount Sinai; you spoke to them from heaven. You gave them regulations and laws that are just and right, and decrees and commands that are good. {9:14} You made known to them your holy Sabbath and gave them commands, decrees, and laws through your servant Moses. {9:15} In their hunger you gave them bread from heaven and brought them water from the rock; you told them to go in and take possession of the land you had sworn to give them. {9:16} But they, our ancestors, became arrogant and stiff-necked, and they did not obey your commands. {9:17} They refused to listen and failed to remember the miracles you performed among them. They became stiff-necked and in their rebellion appointed a leader in order to return to their slavery. But you are a forgiving God, gracious and compassionate, slow to anger and abounding in love. Therefore you did not desert them. {9:18} Even when they cast for themselves an image of a calf and said, "These are your gods who brought you up out of Egypt," they committed terrible blasphemies. {9:19} Because of your great compassion, you did not abandon them in the wilderness. The pillar of cloud did not leave them by day to guide them on their path, nor the pillar of fire by night to shine on the way they were to take. {9:20} You gave your good Spirit to instruct them. You did not withhold your manna from their mouths, and you gave them water for their thirst. {9:21} For forty years you sustained them in the wilderness; they lacked nothing; their clothes did not wear out, and their feet did not swell. {9:22} You gave them kingdoms and nations, allotting them to them as their borders; they took over the country of Sihon and the country of the king of Heshbon and the country of Og king of Bashan. {9:23} Their children you multiplied like the stars in the sky and brought them into the land you told their ancestors to enter and possess. {9:24} So their children went in and took possession of the land. You subdued before them the Canaanites who lived in the land; you gave them into their hands, along with their kings and the peoples of the land, to deal with them as they pleased. {9:25} They captured fortified cities and fertile land; they took possession of houses filled with all kinds of good things, wells already dug, vineyards, olive groves, and fruit trees in abundance. They ate to the full and were well-nourished; they reveled in your great goodness. {9:26} But they were disobedient and rebelled against you; they turned their backs on your law. They killed your prophets who had admonished them to turn back to you; they committed terrible blasphemies. {9:27} So you delivered them into the hands of their enemies, who oppressed them. But when they were oppressed, they cried out to you. From heaven, you heard them, and in your great compassion, you gave them deliverers, who rescued them from the hand of their enemies. {9:28} But as soon as they were at rest, they again did what was evil in your sight. Then you abandoned them to the hand of their enemies so they ruled over them. When they cried out to you again, you heard from heaven, and in your compassion you delivered them time after time. {9:29} You warned them to return to your law, but they became arrogant and did not obey your commands. They sinned against your ordinances, of which you said, "The person who obeys them will live by them." They turned a stubborn shoulder and became stiff-necked and refused to listen. {9:30} For many years you were patient with them. You warned them through your Spirit in your prophets, but they paid no attention. So you gave them into the hands of the neighboring peoples. {9:31} But in your great mercy, you did not put an end to them or abandon them, for you are a gracious and merciful God. {9:32} Now therefore, our God, the great, mighty, and awesome God, who keeps his covenant of love, do not let all this hardship seem insignificant in your eyes—the hardship that has come upon us, on our kings and leaders, on our priests and prophets, and on our ancestors, and all your people from the time of the kings of Assyria until today. {9:33} In all that has happened to us, you have remained righteous; you have acted faithfully, while we acted wickedly. {9:34} Our kings, our leaders, our priests, and our ancestors did not follow your law; they did not pay attention to your commands or the statutes you warned them to keep. {9:35} Even while they were in their own kingdom, enjoying your great goodness to them in the spacious and fertile land you gave them, they did not serve you or turn from their wicked ways. {9:36} Here we are, slaves today, in the land you gave our ancestors so they could eat its fruit and other good things. Here we are, slaves in it. {9:37} The abundant harvest goes to the kings you have placed over us because of our sins; they rule over our bodies and our livestock as they please. We are in great distress. {9:38} In view of all this, we are making a binding agreement, putting it in writing, and our leaders, Levites, and priests are affixing their seals to it.

{10:1} Now the names of those who sealed the agreement were Nehemiah the governor, the son of Hachaliah, and Zidkijah. {10:2} Seraiah, Azariah, and Jeremiah. {10:3} Pashur, Amariah, and Malchijah. {10:4} Hattush, Shebaniah, and Malluch. {10:5} Harim, Meremoth, and Obadiah. {10:6} Daniel, Ginnethon, and Baruch. {10:7} Meshullam, Abijah, and Mijamin. {10:8} Maaziah, Bilgai, and Shemaiah: these were the priests. {10:9} And the Levites included Jeshua the son of Azaniah, Binnui from the family of Henadad, and Kadmiel; {10:10} along with their relatives: Shebaniah, Hodijah, Kelita, Pelaiah, and Hanan. {10:11} Micha, Rehob, and Hashabiah. {10:12} Zaccur, Sherebiah, and Shebaniah. {10:13} Hodijah, Bani, and Beninu. {10:14} The leaders of the people included Parosh, Pahathmoab, Elam, Zatthu, and Bani. {10:15} Bunni, Azgad, and Bebai. {10:16} Adonijah, Bigvai, and Adin. {10:17} Ater, Hizkijah, and Azzur. {10:18} Hodijah, Hashum, and Bezai. {10:19} Hariph, Anathoth, and Nebai. {10:20} Magpiash, Meshullam, and Hezir. {10:21} Meshezabeel, Zadok, and Jaddua. {10:22} Pelatiah, Hanan, and Anaiah. {10:23} Hoshea, Hananiah, and Hashub. {10:24} Hallohesh, Pileha, and Shobek. {10:25} Rehum, Hashabnah, and Maaseiah. {10:26} And Ahijah, Hanan, and Anan. {10:27} Malluch, Harim, and Baanah. {10:28} The rest of the people, including the priests, Levites, gatekeepers, singers, and temple servants, along with all those who separated themselves from the surrounding nations to follow the law of God, their wives, sons, and daughters—all who could understand— {10:29} joined their leaders and took an oath to follow God's law, which was given through Moses, His servant, to obey all the commands of the LORD our God, including His regulations and decrees. {10:30} They agreed not to give their daughters in marriage to the people of the land, nor to take their daughters for their sons. {10:31} If the people of the land brought goods or food to sell on the Sabbath, they agreed not to buy from them on the Sabbath or on any holy day; and they would let the land rest in the seventh year and cancel every debt. {10:32} They also established rules for themselves, agreeing to contribute annually one-third of a shekel for the service of the house of our God; {10:33} this included offerings for the showbread, the daily grain offerings, the daily burnt offerings, the offerings for the Sabbaths, the new moons, the appointed feasts, and the sin offerings to make atonement for Israel, and for all the work of the house of our God. {10:34} They cast lots among the priests, Levites, and the people to determine the wood offering, bringing it to the house of our God at designated times each year to burn on the altar of the LORD our God, as it is written in the law. {10:35} They also committed to bring the firstfruits of their ground and the firstfruits of all their trees to the house of the LORD each year. {10:36} This included the firstborn of their sons and livestock, as required by the law, to bring to the house of our God for the priests who serve there. {10:37} They would bring the firstfruits of their dough and offerings, along with the produce of all kinds of trees, wine, and oil, to the priests at the chambers of the house of our God, and the tithes of their ground to the Levites so that the Levites might receive the tithes in all the cities where they worked. {10:38} The priest, a descendant of Aaron, was to be with the Levites when they received the tithes; the Levites would then bring up a tenth of the tithes to the house of our God, to the chambers of the treasury. {10:39} For the Israelites and the Levites were to bring the offerings of grain, new wine, and oil to the chambers where the sacred utensils were, along with the priests who minister there, gatekeepers, and the singers; and they promised not to neglect the house of our God.

{11:1} The leaders of the people settled in Jerusalem, and the rest of the people cast lots to bring one out of ten to live in Jerusalem, the holy city, while the other nine remained in their own towns. {11:2} The people blessed all those who volunteered to live in Jerusalem. {11:3} These are the leaders of the province who lived in Jerusalem, while the people of Judah settled in their own towns, including Israel, the priests, Levites, temple servants, and the descendants of Solomon's servants. {11:4} Some of the descendants of Judah and Benjamin settled in Jerusalem. From Judah: Athaiah, the son of Uzziah, the son of Zechariah, the son of Amariah, the son of Shephatiah, the son of Mahalaleel, from the family of Perez; {11:5} and Maaseiah, the son of Baruch, the son of Colhozeh, the son of Hazaiah, the son of Adaiah, the son of Joiarib, the son of Zechariah, the son of Shiloni. {11:6} The descendants of Perez who lived in Jerusalem numbered 468 valiant men. {11:7} These are the descendants of Benjamin: Sallu, the son of Meshullam, the son of Joed, the son of Pedaiah, the son of Kolaiah, the son of Maaseiah, the son of Ithiel, the son of Jesaiah. {11:8} And Gabbai and Sallai numbered 928. {11:9} Joel, the son of Zichri, was their supervisor, and Judah, the son of Senuah, was second in command of the city. {11:10} Among the priests were Jedaiah, the son of Joiarib, and Jachin. {11:11} Seraiah, the son of Hilkiah, the son of Meshullam, the son of Zadok, the son of Meraioth, the son of Ahitub, was the leader of the house of God. {11:12} Their fellow priests who worked in the house numbered 822, and Adaiah, the son of Jeroham, the son of Pelaliah, the son of Amzi, the son of Zechariah, the son of Pashur, the son of Malchiah, {11:13} and his fellow chiefs of families numbered 242, while Amashai, the son of Azareel, the son of Ahasai, the son of Meshillemoth, the son of Immer, {11:14} and their fellow mighty men numbered 128, with Zabdiel, the son of one of the great men, as their supervisor. {11:15} Among the Levites were Shemaiah, the son of Hashub, the son of Azrikam, the son of Hashabiah, the son of Bunni; {11:16} and Shabbethai and Jozabad, who were in charge of the external work of the house of God. {11:17} Mattaniah, the son of Micha, the son of Zabdi, the son of Asaph, was the leader in starting the thanksgiving in prayer; Bakbukiah was second among his brothers, and Abda, the son of Shammua, the son of Galal, the son of Jeduthun. {11:18} All the Levites in the holy city numbered 284. {11:19} The gatekeepers, Akkub, Talmon, and their relatives, totaled 172. {11:20} The remaining Israelites, priests, and Levites lived in all the towns of Judah, each on their own land. {11:21} The temple servants lived in Ophel, and Ziha and Gispa were in charge of them. {11:22} The supervisor of the Levites in Jerusalem was Uzzi, the son of Bani, the son of Hashabiah, the son of Mattaniah, the son of Micha. The singers were in charge of the work of the house of God. {11:23} It was the king's command that a certain portion should be allotted for the singers, each day. {11:24} Pethahiah, the son of Meshezabeel, from the descendants of Zerah, the son of Judah, was the king's representative in all matters concerning the people. {11:25} In the villages and their fields, some of the descendants of Judah lived at Kirjatharba and its villages, at Dibon and its villages, and at Jekabzeel and its villages, {11:26} at Jeshua, at Moladah, and at Bethphelet, {11:27} at Hazarshual, at Beersheba, and in its villages, {11:28} at Ziklag, at Mekonah, and in its villages, {11:29} at Enrimmon, at Zareah, and at Jarmuth, {11:30} at Zanoah, Adullam, and in their villages, at Lachish and its fields, at Azekah and in its villages. They settled from Beersheba to the Valley of Hinnom. {11:31} The descendants of Benjamin from Geba settled in Michmash, Aija, Bethel, and its villages, {11:32} and at Anathoth, Nob, Ananiah, {11:33} Hazor, Ramah, Gittaim, {11:34} Hadid, Zeboim, Neballat, {11:35} Lod, and Ono, the valley of craftsmen. {11:36} The Levites had divisions in Judah and Benjamin.

{12:1} These are the priests and Levites who went up with Zerubbabel, the son of Shealtiel, and Jeshua: Seraiah, Jeremiah, Ezra, {12:2} Amariah, Malluch, Hattush, {12:3} Shechaniah, Rehum, Meremoth, {12:4} Iddo, Ginnetho, Abijah, {12:5} Miamin, Maadiah, Bilgah, {12:6} Shemaiah, Joiarib, Jedaiah, {12:7} Sallu, Amok, Hilkiah, and Jedaiah. These were the leaders of the priests and their relatives during Jeshua's time. {12:8} The Levites included Jeshua, Binnui, Kadmiel, Sherebiah, Judah, and Mattaniah, who was in charge of the thanksgiving, along with his brothers. {12:9} Bakbukiah and Unni, their brothers, were assigned to the watches opposite them. {12:10} Jeshua was the father of Joiakim, Joiakim was the father of Eliashib, and Eliashib was the father of Joiada, {12:11} and Joiada was the father of Jonathan, and Jonathan was the father of Jaddua. {12:12} During Joiakim's time, the priests, who were the leaders of the families, included: Seraiah, Meraiah; Jeremiah, Hananiah; {12:13} Ezra, Meshullam; Amariah, Jehohanan; {12:14} Melicu, Jonathan; Shebaniah, Joseph; {12:15} Harim, Adna; Meraioth, Helkai; {12:16} Iddo, Zechariah; Ginnethon, Meshullam; {12:17} Abijah, Zichri; Miniamin, Moadiah, Piltai; {12:18} Bilgah, Shammua; Shemaiah, Jehonathan; {12:19} Joiarib, Mattenai; Jedaiah, Uzzi; {12:20} Sallai, Kallai; Amok, Eber; {12:21} Hilkiah, Hashabiah; Jedaiah, Nethaneel. {12:22} The Levites during the days of Eliashib, Joiada, Johanan, and Jaddua were recorded as the leaders of the families, along with the priests, until the reign of Darius the Persian. {12:23} The descendants of Levi, the leaders of the families, were documented in the book of chronicles until the days of Johanan, the son of Eliashib. {12:24} The leaders of the Levites were Hashabiah, Sherebiah, and Jeshua, the son of Kadmiel, along with their brothers, who were positioned to praise and give thanks according to the command of David, the man of God, ward by ward. {12:25} Mattaniah, Bakbukiah, Obadiah, Meshullam, Talmon, and Akkub were the gatekeepers at the thresholds of the gates. {12:26} These were in the days of Joiakim, the son of Jeshua, the son of Jozadak, during the time of Nehemiah the governor and Ezra the priest and scribe. {12:27} At the dedication of the wall of Jerusalem, they sought out the Levites from all their locations to bring them to Jerusalem to celebrate the dedication with joy, thanksgivings, singing, cymbals, psalteries, and harps. {12:28} The sons of the singers gathered from the surrounding area and the villages of Netophathi; {12:29} also from the house of Gilgal and from the fields of Geba and Azmaveth, as the singers had built villages around Jerusalem. {12:30} The priests and Levites purified themselves, and they purified the people, the gates, and the wall. {12:31} Then I brought the leaders of Judah onto the wall and appointed two large groups of people to give thanks; one group went to the right toward the Dung Gate, {12:32} and following them were Hoshaiah and half of the leaders of Judah, {12:33} along with Azariah, Ezra, and Meshullam, {12:34} Judah, Benjamin, Shemaiah, and Jeremiah, {12:35} and some of the priests' sons with trumpets, namely Zechariah, the son of Jonathan, the son of Shemaiah, the son of Mattaniah, the son of Michaiah, the son of Zaccur, the son of Asaph; {12:36} and his brothers, Shemaiah, Azarael, Milalai, Gilalai, Maai, Nethaneel, and Judah, Hanani, with the musical instruments of David, the man of God, with Ezra the scribe leading them. {12:37} At the Fountain Gate, which was opposite them, they went up by the steps of the City of David, at the ascent of the wall, above the house of David, even to the Water Gate eastward. {12:38} The other group of those who gave thanks went in the opposite direction, and I followed them with half of the people on the wall, from beyond the Tower of the Furnaces to the Broad Wall; {12:39} and from above the Gate of Ephraim, the Old Gate, the Fish Gate, the Tower of Hananeel, and the Tower of Meah, all the way to the Sheep Gate, where they stopped at the Prison Gate. {12:40} So the two groups of those who gave thanks stood in the house of God, and I, along with half of the leaders with me, {12:41} and the priests: Eliakim, Maaseiah, Miniamin, Michaiah, Elioenai, Zechariah, and Hananiah, with trumpets; {12:42} and Maaseiah, Shemaiah, Eleazar, Uzzi, Jehohanan, Malchijah, Elam, and Ezer. The singers sang loudly, led by Jezrahiah, their overseer. {12:43} On that day, they offered great sacrifices and rejoiced, for God had made them rejoice with great joy; the wives and children also rejoiced, so that the joy of Jerusalem could be heard from far away. {12:44} At that time, some were appointed over the storerooms for the treasures, offerings, firstfruits, and tithes, to gather the portions of the law for the priests and Levites from the fields of the cities, for Judah rejoiced for the priests and Levites who served. {12:45} Both the singers and the gatekeepers maintained their duties for their God and the purification, following the commands of David and his son Solomon. {12:46} For in the days of David and Asaph, there were leaders of the singers and songs of praise and thanksgiving to God. {12:47} And all Israel, in the days of Zerubbabel and Nehemiah, provided for the singers and the gatekeepers, giving them their portions every day; they set aside holy things for the Levites, and the Levites set them apart for the descendants of Aaron.

{13:1} On that day, they read from the book of Moses in the presence of the people, and it was found written that the Ammonite and the Moabite should never enter the congregation of God; {13:2} because they did not meet the Israelites with bread and water, but hired Balaam to curse them. However, our God turned the curse into a blessing. {13:3} When they heard the law, they separated from Israel all the mixed multitude. {13:4} Before this, Eliashib the priest, who oversaw the storeroom of the house of our God, was allied with Tobiah. {13:5} He had prepared for Tobiah a large room where the offerings, incense, and the vessels, along with the tithes of the grain, new wine, and oil—things that were supposed to be given to the Levites, singers, and gatekeepers—were previously stored. {13:6} But during all this time, I was not in Jerusalem; in the thirty-second year of King Artaxerxes of Babylon, I went to the king and later obtained leave from him. {13:7} When I arrived in Jerusalem, I learned about the wrong Eliashib had done for Tobiah by providing him a room in the courts of the house of God. {13:8} This distressed me greatly, so I threw out all of Tobiah's belongings from the room. {13:9} Then I commanded that the rooms be purified, and I brought back the vessels of the house of God, along with the grain offerings and incense. {13:10} I noticed that the portions for the Levites had not been provided, so the Levites and singers who did the work had fled to their fields. {13:11} I contended with the officials and asked, "Why is the house of God forsaken?" I gathered them and set them in their places. {13:12} Then all of Judah brought in the tithes of the grain, new wine, and oil to the storerooms. {13:13} I appointed treasurers over the storerooms: Shelemiah the priest, Zadok the scribe, and Pedaiah from the Levites; Hanan, the son of Zaccur, the son of Mattaniah, was next to them, for they were considered trustworthy, and their role was to distribute to their brothers. {13:14} Remember me, O my God, for this, and do not forget the good deeds I have done for the house of my God and its services. {13:15} In those days, I saw people in Judah treading wine presses on the Sabbath, bringing in sheaves, and loading donkeys with wine, grapes, figs, and all kinds of goods to bring into Jerusalem on the Sabbath. I protested against them on the day they sold food. {13:16} There were also Tyrians living there who brought fish and various goods and sold them on the Sabbath to the people of Judah and in Jerusalem. {13:17} I contended with the nobles of Judah and said to them, "What is this evil you are doing? Why are you profaning the Sabbath? {13:18} Didn't your ancestors do this, and didn't our God bring all this disaster upon us and this city? Yet you bring even more wrath upon Israel by profaning the Sabbath." {13:19} When the gates of Jerusalem began to darken before the Sabbath, I ordered that the gates be shut and commanded that they not be opened until after the Sabbath. Some of my servants were stationed at the gates to ensure that no load would be brought in on the Sabbath. {13:20} As a result, the merchants and sellers of all kinds of goods camped outside Jerusalem once or twice. {13:21} I testified against them and said, "Why are you camping around the wall? If you do this again, I will lay hands on you." From that time on, they did not come back on the Sabbath. {13:22} I commanded the Levites to purify themselves and to come and guard the gates to sanctify the Sabbath. Remember me, O my God, for this also, and spare me according to the greatness of your mercy. {13:23} At that time, I also saw Jews who had married women from Ashdod, Ammon, and Moab. {13:24} Their children spoke half in the language of Ashdod and could not speak the language of the Jews, but spoke according to the language of each people. {13:25} I contended with them, cursed them, struck some of them, pulled out their hair, and made them swear by God, saying, "You shall not give your daughters to their sons or take their daughters for your sons or for yourselves." {13:26} Did not Solomon, king of Israel, sin because of these things? Among many nations, there was no king like him; he was beloved by his God, and God made him king over all Israel. Nevertheless, even he was led into sin by foreign women. {13:27} Should we then listen to you and do all this great evil, transgressing against our God by marrying foreign wives? {13:28} One of the sons of Joiada, the son of Eliashib the high priest, was a son-in-law of Sanballat the Horonite; therefore, I drove him away from me. {13:29} Remember them, O my God, because they have defiled the priesthood and the covenant of the priesthood and of the Levites. {13:30} So I purified them from everything foreign and appointed duties for the priests and Levites, assigning each to his task; {13:31} and for the wood offering at the appointed times and for the firstfruits. Remember me, O my God, for good.

The Book of Esther

{1:1} It happened during the days of Ahasuerus, who ruled over one hundred twenty-seven provinces, from India to Ethiopia. {1:2} In those days, when King Ahasuerus was sitting on his throne in the palace at Shushan, {1:3} in the third year of his reign, he held a feast for all his officials and servants, including the powerful nobles and leaders of the provinces who were there with him. {1:4} He displayed the riches of his glorious kingdom and the splendor of his majesty for many days—one hundred eighty days in total. {1:5} After these days, the king hosted a feast for all the people present in Shushan, both great and small, for seven days in the court of the garden of the king's palace. {1:6} The garden was decorated with white, green, and blue curtains fastened with fine linen and purple cords to silver rings and marble pillars; the beds were made of gold and silver, set on a pavement of red, blue, white, and black marble. {1:7} They served drinks in gold vessels of various designs, and royal wine was offered in abundance, in keeping with the king's generosity. {1:8} The drinking was done according to custom; no one was forced to drink, for the king had instructed all the officials to allow each person to drink as they pleased. {1:9} Queen Vashti also held a feast for the women in the royal palace belonging to King Ahasuerus. {1:10} On the seventh day, when the king was feeling cheerful from the wine, he commanded his seven eunuchs—Mehuman, Biztha, Harbona, Bigtha, Abagtha, Zethar, and Carcas—who served him in his presence, {1:11} to bring Queen Vashti before him, wearing her royal crown, so he could show off her beauty to the people and nobles, for she was very attractive. {1:12} But Queen Vashti refused to come at the king's command brought by the eunuchs, which made the king very angry. {1:13} He then asked the wise men who understood the times, for it was the king's practice to consult those knowledgeable in law and judgment. {1:14} The closest of these were Carshena, Shethar, Admatha, Tarshish, Meres, Marsena, and Memucan, the seven princes of Persia and Media who had access to the king and sat at the king's side. {1:15} He asked them, "What should we do to Queen Vashti according to the law, since she did not obey King Ahasuerus' command brought by the eunuchs?" {1:16} Memucan replied to the king and the princes, "Queen Vashti has not wronged the king only, but also all the princes and all the people in all the provinces of King Ahasuerus. {1:17} This deed will be made known to all women, and they will treat their husbands with contempt when they hear that the king commanded Vashti to be brought before him, but she did not come. {1:18} This very day, the noble women of Persia and Media will say the same thing to all the king's officials, leading to much contempt and anger. {1:19} If it pleases the king, let a royal decree be issued and let it be written in the laws of the Persians and Medes, which cannot be revoked, that Vashti may never again appear before King Ahasuerus, and let the king give her royal position to someone better than she. {1:20} When the king's decree is published throughout his vast empire, all wives will honor their husbands, both great and small." {1:21} The king and the princes liked this advice, so the king acted according to Memucan's suggestion. {1:22} He sent letters to all the provinces, to each province in its own script and to each people in their own language, declaring that every man should be the ruler in his own home and that this should be proclaimed in the language of each people.

{2:1} After these events, when King Ahasuerus' anger had calmed down, he remembered Vashti and what she had done and the decree issued against her. {2:2} Then the king's servants, who attended him, said, "Let beautiful young virgins be sought for the king. {2:3} Let the king appoint officials in every province of his kingdom to gather all the beautiful young virgins to Shushan the palace, to the harem under the custody of Hege, the king's eunuch, who is in charge of the women, and let them be given the required beauty treatments. {2:4} The girl who pleases the king should be queen in place of Vashti." This proposal pleased the king, and he agreed. {2:5} Now in Shushan the palace lived a Jew named Mordecai, son of Jair, son of Shimei, son of Kish, a Benjaminite. {2:6} He had been taken captive from Jerusalem with those exiled with Jeconiah, king of Judah, whom Nebuchadnezzar, king of Babylon, had carried away. {2:7} Mordecai had brought up Hadassah, also known as Esther, his uncle's daughter, for she had no father or mother; the girl was beautiful and lovely. When her father and mother died, Mordecai adopted her as his own daughter. {2:8} When the king's command and decree were announced, many young women were gathered to Shushan the palace, and Esther was taken to the king's palace, to the custody of Hege, the keeper of the women. {2:9} The young woman pleased him and won his favor, and he quickly provided her with her beauty treatments and special food, and assigned her seven maids from the king's palace, moving her and her maids to the best place in the harem. {2:10} Esther had not revealed her ethnicity or family background, because Mordecai had instructed her not to do so. {2:11} Every day, Mordecai walked back and forth near the courtyard of the harem to find out how Esther was and what was happening to her. {2:12} When it was time for each young woman to go in to King Ahasuerus after being prepared for twelve months, following the regulations for women—six months with oil of myrrh and six months with perfumes and other beauty treatments—{2:13} each girl was allowed to take with her whatever she wanted from the harem to the king's palace. {2:14} In the evening she would go in, and in the morning she would return to another part of the harem, to the custody of Shaashgaz, the king's eunuch in charge of the concubines; she would not go in to the king again unless he was pleased with her and summoned her by name. {2:15} When it was Esther's turn to go in to King Ahasuerus, she asked for nothing except what Hege, the king's eunuch, who was in charge of the women, suggested. Esther won the favor of everyone who saw her. {2:16} So Esther was taken to King Ahasuerus in his royal palace in the tenth month, which is the month Tebeth, in the seventh year of his reign. {2:17} The king loved Esther more than all the other women, and she found grace and favor in his sight more than all the virgins, so he placed the royal crown on her head and made her queen instead of Vashti. {2:18} Then the king gave a great feast for all his officials and servants, which was called Esther's feast. He also proclaimed a holiday for the provinces and gave gifts according to the generosity of the king. {2:19} When the virgins were gathered a second time, Mordecai was sitting at the king's gate. {2:20} Esther still had not revealed her family background or her people, as Mordecai had instructed her; she continued to follow his instructions just as when she was brought up by him. {2:21} During those days while Mordecai was sitting at the king's gate, two of the king's eunuchs, Bigthan and Teresh, who guarded the entrance, became angry and plotted to assassinate King Ahasuerus. {2:22} Mordecai learned of the plot and informed Queen Esther, who in turn reported it to the king, giving credit to Mordecai. {2:23} When the matter was investigated and found to be true, both men were hanged on a gallows, and it was recorded in the royal diary in the presence of the king.

{3:1} After these events, King Ahasuerus promoted Haman, the son of Hammedatha the Agagite, and elevated him, placing him above all the other officials. {3:2} All the king's servants at the king's gate bowed down and honored Haman, as the king had commanded. But Mordecai did not bow down or show him respect. {3:3} The king's servants at the gate asked Mordecai, "Why are you disobeying the king's command?" {3:4} When they spoke to him every day and he didn't listen, they informed Haman to see if Mordecai's behavior would continue since he had told them he was a Jew. {3:5} When Haman saw that Mordecai did not bow down or show him respect, he became furious. {3:6} However, he decided not to just punish Mordecai alone, for they had shown him Mordecai's people; so Haman sought to destroy all the Jews throughout the kingdom of Ahasuerus, including Mordecai's people. {3:7} In the first month, the month of Nisan, in the twelfth year of King Ahasuerus, they cast lots (Pur) before Haman day after day, and month after month, until the twelfth month, which is the month of Adar. {3:8} Haman then said to King Ahasuerus, "There is a certain people scattered and separated among the people in all the provinces of your kingdom; their customs are different from everyone else's, and they do not obey the king's laws. It is not in your best interest to tolerate them. {3:9} If it pleases the king, let an order be issued to destroy them, and I will pay ten thousand talents of silver to the officials who are in charge of this matter, to put it into the king's treasury." {3:10} The king took his ring from his hand and gave it to Haman, the son of Hammedatha the Agagite, the enemy of the Jews. {3:11} The king said to Haman, "The silver is yours, and the people are also yours to do with as you see fit." {3:12} So the king's scribes were summoned on the thirteenth day of the first month, and everything Haman commanded was written down for the king's lieutenants, governors of each province, and the rulers of every people, in their own languages, in the name of King Ahasuerus, and sealed with the king's ring. {3:13} Letters were sent by couriers to all the king's provinces, instructing them to destroy, kill, and eliminate all Jews, young and old, including women and children, in one day, on the thirteenth day of the twelfth month, which is the month of Adar, and to take their possessions as plunder. {3:14} A copy of the decree was published in every province so that all the people would be ready for that day. {3:15} The couriers sped out, urged on by the king's command, and the decree was given in Shushan the palace. Meanwhile, the king and Haman sat down to drink, but the city of Shushan was bewildered.

{4:1} When Mordecai learned of all that had been done, he tore his clothes, put on sackcloth and ashes, and went out into the city, crying loudly and bitterly. {4:2} He even came to the king's gate, for no one was allowed to enter the king's gate wearing sackcloth.

{4:3} In every province where the king's command and decree arrived, there was great mourning among the Jews, with fasting, weeping, and wailing; many lay in sackcloth and ashes. {4:4} Esther's maids and eunuchs came and told her about it, and the queen was deeply distressed. She sent clothes to Mordecai to cover his sackcloth, but he would not accept them. {4:5} Then Esther called for Hatach, one of the king's eunuchs appointed to attend her, and ordered him to find out what was troubling Mordecai and why. {4:6} Hatach went out to Mordecai in the city square in front of the king's gate. {4:7} Mordecai told him everything that had happened to him, including the amount of money Haman had promised to pay into the king's treasury for the destruction of the Jews. {4:8} He also gave Hatach a copy of the decree issued in Shushan to destroy the Jews, so he could show it to Esther and explain it to her, and urge her to go to the king to plead for her people. {4:9} Hatach returned and told Esther what Mordecai had said. {4:10} Then Esther spoke to Hatach and instructed him to tell Mordecai, {4:11} "All the king's servants and the people of the king's provinces know that anyone, whether man or woman, who approaches the king in the inner court without being summoned is subject to death, unless the king extends the golden scepter to them, allowing them to live. But I have not been summoned to see the king for thirty days." {4:12} When Mordecai was informed of Esther's words, {4:13} he sent back this answer: "Do not think that because you are in the king's palace you will escape any more than all the other Jews. {4:14} If you remain silent at this time, relief and deliverance for the Jews will arise from another place, but you and your father's family will perish. And who knows but that you have come to your royal position for such a time as this?" {4:15} Then Esther sent this reply to Mordecai: {4:16} "Go, gather all the Jews in Shushan and fast for me; do not eat or drink for three days, night or day. My maids and I will fast as well. After that, I will go to the king, even though it is against the law, and if I perish, I perish." {4:17} So Mordecai went away and did everything Esther had instructed him to do.

{5:1} On the third day, Esther dressed in her royal robes and stood in the inner court of the king's palace, across from the king's house, while the king sat on his royal throne at the entrance. {5:2} When the king saw Queen Esther standing in the court, she found favor in his sight, and he extended the golden scepter that was in his hand. Esther approached and touched the tip of the scepter. {5:3} The king asked her, "What do you want, Queen Esther? What is your request? It will be granted, even up to half the kingdom." {5:4} Esther replied, "If it pleases the king, let him and Haman come today to the banquet I have prepared for them." {5:5} The king ordered, "Quickly bring Haman so that he may do as Esther has requested." So the king and Haman went to the banquet Esther had prepared. {5:6} While they were drinking wine, the king asked Esther again, "What is your petition? It will be granted. What is your request? Even up to half the kingdom, it will be done." {5:7} Esther answered, "My petition and request is this: {5:8} If I have found favor in the king's eyes, and if it pleases the king to grant my petition and fulfill my request, let the king and Haman come to the banquet I will prepare for them tomorrow, and I will answer the king's question." {5:9} That day, Haman left feeling happy and in high spirits, but when he saw Mordecai at the king's gate, not standing or showing fear, he was filled with rage against Mordecai. {5:10} Yet Haman controlled himself and went home, where he called for his friends and his wife, Zeresh. {5:11} Haman told them about his great wealth, his many children, and how the king had honored him, promoting him above all the other officials. {5:12} Haman added, "Moreover, no one but me was invited to come with the king to the banquet she prepared, and tomorrow I am also invited to it." {5:13} But all this means nothing to me as long as I see Mordecai the Jew sitting at the king's gate. {5:14} Zeresh and all his friends advised him, "Have a gallows built, seventy-five feet high, and in the morning ask the king to hang Mordecai on it. Then go joyfully with the king to the banquet." This pleased Haman, and he had the gallows made.

{6:1} That night, the king could not sleep, so he ordered the book of records to be brought and read to him. {6:2} It was found written that Mordecai had reported the plot of Bigthana and Teresh, two of the king's officials who guarded the door and had tried to assassinate King Ahasuerus. {6:3} The king asked, "What honor has been given to Mordecai for this?" His attendants answered, "Nothing has been done for him." {6:4} The king then asked, "Who is in the court?" Now Haman had just entered the outer court to speak to the king about hanging Mordecai on the gallows he had prepared. {6:5} The attendants said, "Haman is standing in the court." The king said, "Let him come in." {6:6} So Haman came in, and the king asked him, "What should be done for the man the king wishes to honor?" Haman thought to himself, "Who could the king want to honor more than me?" {6:7} Haman replied, "For the man the king wishes to honor, {6:8} let royal robes be brought that the king has worn, and let the king's horse, which he has ridden, be brought, along with the royal crown on its head. {6:9} Let these robes and the horse be entrusted to one of the king's most noble officials to dress the man the king wishes to honor, and let him lead the man on horseback through the city streets, proclaiming, 'This is what is done for the man the king wishes to honor!'" {6:10} The king said to Haman, "Hurry! Take the robes and the horse as you have said, and do this for Mordecai the Jew who sits at the king's gate. Do not neglect anything you have suggested." {6:11} So Haman took the robes and the horse, dressed Mordecai, and led him on horseback through the city streets, proclaiming, "This is what is done for the man the king wishes to honor!" {6:12} Afterward, Mordecai returned to the king's gate, but Haman rushed home, mourning and with his head covered. {6:13} Haman told Zeresh and his friends everything that had happened to him. His wise men and Zeresh replied, "Since Mordecai is of Jewish descent and you have begun to fall before him, you will surely come to ruin." {6:14} While they were still talking with him, the king's eunuchs arrived and hurried to bring Haman to the banquet Esther had prepared.

{7:1} So the king and Haman came to dine with Queen Esther. {7:2} On the second day of the banquet, the king again asked Esther, "What is your petition, Queen Esther? It will be granted. What is your request? Even up to half the kingdom, it will be done." {7:3} Esther replied, "If I have found favor in your sight, O king, and if it pleases you, grant me my life at my request and my people at my petition. {7:4} For we are sold, I and my people, to be destroyed, killed, and wiped out. If we had merely been sold as slaves, I would have remained silent, as the enemy could not compensate for the king's loss." {7:5} The king Ahasuerus asked Esther, "Who is he, and where is he, who dares to do this?" {7:6} Esther said, "The adversary and enemy is this wicked Haman." Then Haman was terrified before the king and queen. {7:7} The king, rising in anger from the banquet, went into the palace garden, while Haman stood up to plead for his life to Esther, realizing that the king had decided to harm him. {7:8} When the king returned from the garden to the banquet hall, he found Haman falling on the couch where Esther was. The king said, "Will he even assault the queen while I am in the house?" As soon as the king spoke, they covered Haman's face. {7:9} Harbonah, one of the king's eunuchs, said, "Look, the gallows Haman built for Mordecai, who spoke up for the king, stands at Haman's house, seventy-five feet high." The king said, "Hang him on it." {7:10} So they hanged Haman on the gallows he had prepared for Mordecai, and the king's anger was appeased.

{8:1} That same day, King Ahasuerus gave Haman's estate to Queen Esther. Then Mordecai was brought before the king, for Esther had revealed his relationship to her. {8:2} The king removed his ring from Haman and gave it to Mordecai. Esther appointed Mordecai to oversee Haman's estate. {8:3} Esther again spoke to the king, falling at his feet and weeping, begging him to revoke Haman the Agagite's evil plan against the Jews. {8:4} The king extended the golden scepter toward Esther, and she rose and stood before him. {8:5} She said, "If it pleases the king, and if I have found favor in his sight, and if the matter seems right to the king, and I am pleasing in his eyes, let a decree be written to revoke the letters Haman wrote to destroy the Jews in all the king's provinces. {8:6} For how can I bear to see the calamity that would come upon my people? How can I endure to see the destruction of my relatives?" {8:7} King Ahasuerus said to Esther and Mordecai, "I have given Esther Haman's estate, and he has been hanged because he intended to harm the Jews. {8:8} Write a decree for the Jews as you see fit, in the king's name, and seal it with the king's ring, for whatever is written in the king's name and sealed with his ring cannot be revoked." {8:9} The king's scribes were summoned on the twenty-third day of the third month, Sivan, and everything Mordecai instructed was written to the Jews and the governors of the provinces from India to Ethiopia, a total of one hundred twenty-seven provinces, each in their own script and language. {8:10} Mordecai wrote in the name of King Ahasuerus, sealed it with the king's ring, and sent letters by mounted couriers and riders on mules, camels, and young dromedaries. {8:11} The king granted the Jews in every city the right to assemble and defend their lives, to destroy, kill, and annihilate any armed force that might attack them, including women and children, and to plunder their possessions. {8:12} This would take place on the thirteenth day of the twelfth month, Adar. {8:13} A copy of the decree was sent out as a command in every province, making it known that the Jews should be ready to take revenge on their enemies. {8:14} The couriers rode out quickly, urged on by the king's command, and the decree was issued at the palace in Shushan. {8:15} Mordecai left the king's presence wearing royal garments of blue and white, with a large crown of gold and a fine linen and purple robe. The city of Shushan celebrated and rejoiced. {8:16} The Jews had light, joy, gladness, and honor. {8:17} In every province and city, wherever the king's decree reached, the Jews celebrated with joy and gladness, feasting and having a good day. Many of the people of other nationalities became Jews because fear of the Jews had seized them.

{9:1} On the thirteenth day of the twelfth month, Adar, when the king's command and decree were about to be executed, the enemies of the Jews hoped to overpower them. However, the situation turned, and the Jews gained power over those who hated them. {9:2} The Jews gathered in their cities throughout the provinces of King Ahasuerus to defend themselves against those who sought to harm them, and no one could withstand them, for fear of them fell upon all people. {9:3} All the rulers of the provinces, the officials, and the king's officers supported the Jews because the fear of Mordecai had gripped them. {9:4} Mordecai was prominent in the king's palace, and his fame spread throughout the provinces; he became more and more powerful. {9:5} The Jews struck down all their enemies with swords, killing and destroying them, and did as they pleased to those who hated them. {9:6} In Shushan the palace, the Jews killed five hundred men. {9:7} Among those slain were Parshandatha, Dalphon, Aspatha, {9:8} Poratha, Adalia, Aridatha, {9:9} Parmashta, Arisai, Aridai, and Vajezatha, {9:10} the ten sons of Haman, the enemy of the Jews. However, they did not take any of the spoils. {9:11} On that day, the number of those killed in Shushan was reported to the king. {9:12} The king said to Queen Esther, "The Jews have killed five hundred men in Shushan and the ten sons of Haman. What have they done in the rest of the king's provinces? What is your petition? It will be granted. What is your request?" {9:13} Esther replied, "If it pleases the king, let the Jews in Shushan be allowed to do tomorrow what they did today, and let Haman's ten sons be hanged on the gallows." {9:14} The king commanded that it be done, and the decree was issued in Shushan; they hanged Haman's ten sons. {9:15} The Jews in Shushan gathered again on the fourteenth day of Adar and killed three hundred men, but they did not take any of the spoils. {9:16} The other Jews in the king's provinces gathered and defended their lives, resting from their enemies, and killed seventy-five thousand of their foes, but they did not take any of the spoils. {9:17} This happened on the thirteenth day of Adar, and they rested on the fourteenth, making it a day of feasting and joy. {9:18} The Jews in Shushan assembled on the thirteenth and fourteenth days, and on the fifteenth day they rested and celebrated with feasting and joy. {9:19} Therefore, the Jews in the unwalled towns observed the fourteenth day of Adar as a day of joy and feasting, sending portions to one another. {9:20} Mordecai recorded these events and sent letters to all the Jews in all the provinces of King Ahasuerus, both near and far, {9:21} establishing that they should observe the fourteenth and fifteenth days of Adar each year, {9:22} as the days when the Jews rested from their enemies and the month that was transformed from sorrow to joy and mourning to celebration, encouraging feasting and joy, sending portions to one another and gifts to the poor. {9:23} The Jews agreed to continue as they had begun, following what Mordecai had written to them; {9:24} because Haman, the Agagite, had plotted to destroy the Jews and had cast lots (Pur) to annihilate them. {9:25} But when Esther approached the king, he ordered by letter that Haman's wicked plot against the Jews return upon his own head, and that he and his sons be hanged on the gallows. {9:26} Therefore, these days were called Purim after the name of Pur. Thus, they agreed to observe all the details of this letter and what they had experienced regarding this matter. {9:27} The Jews committed themselves, their descendants, and all who joined them to ensure they would celebrate these two days according to their writing and their appointed time every year. {9:28} These days should be remembered and observed in every generation, family, province, and city, ensuring that the days of Purim should never cease among the Jews, nor should their memory perish from their descendants. {9:29} Then Queen Esther, daughter of Abihail, and Mordecai the Jew wrote with full authority to confirm this second letter of Purim. {9:30} They sent letters to all the Jews in the one hundred twenty-seven provinces of King Ahasuerus with words of peace and truth, {9:31} to establish these days of Purim at their appointed times, as Mordecai the Jew and Queen Esther had instructed them, as they had established for themselves and their descendants, including the matters of fasting and their lament. {9:32} The decree of Esther confirmed these matters of Purim, and it was recorded in the book.

{10:1} King Ahasuerus imposed a tribute on the land and the coastal islands. {10:2} All his mighty acts and the account of Mordecai's greatness, which the king promoted, are recorded in the chronicles of the kings of Media and Persia. {10:3} For Mordecai the Jew was second in rank to King Ahasuerus, great among the Jews, and well-liked by many of his fellow Jews, seeking the welfare of his people and speaking peace to all his descendants.

The Book of Job

{1:1} There was a man in the land of Uz named Job; he was blameless and upright, fearing God and turning away from evil. {1:2} He had seven sons and three daughters. {1:3} His wealth included seven thousand sheep, three thousand camels, five hundred yoke of oxen, five hundred female donkeys, and a very large household, making him the greatest man in the East. {1:4} His sons would take turns holding feasts in their homes and invite their three sisters to eat and drink with them. {1:5} After the feasting days were over, Job would send and sanctify his children. He would rise early in the morning and offer burnt offerings for each of them, saying, "Perhaps my sons have sinned and cursed God in their hearts." This was Job's regular practice. {1:6} One day, the angels came to present themselves before the LORD, and Satan also appeared among them. {1:7} The LORD asked Satan, "Where have you come from?" Satan answered, "From roaming throughout the earth, going back and forth on it." {1:8} The LORD said to Satan, "Have you considered my servant Job? There is no one like him; he is blameless and upright, a man who fears God and shuns evil." {1:9} Satan replied, "Does Job fear God for nothing? {1:10} Have you not put a hedge around him and his household and everything he has? You have blessed the work of his hands, so that his flocks and herds are spread throughout the land. {1:11} But stretch out your hand and strike everything he has, and he will surely curse you to your face." {1:12} The LORD said to Satan, "Very well, everything he has is in your power, but on the man himself do not lay a finger." So Satan went out from the presence of the LORD. {1:13} One day, when Job's sons and daughters were feasting and drinking wine at their oldest brother's house, {1:14} a messenger came to Job and said, "The oxen were plowing and the donkeys were grazing nearby, {1:15} when the Sabeans attacked and carried them off; they killed the servants with the sword, and I am the only one who has escaped to tell you." {1:16} While he was still speaking, another messenger arrived and said, "The fire of God fell from the sky and burned up the sheep and the servants; I am the only one who has escaped to tell you." {1:17} While he was still speaking, another messenger came and said, "The Chaldeans formed three raiding parties and swept down on your camels and carried them off; they killed the servants with the sword, and I am the only one who has escaped to tell you." {1:18} While he was still speaking, yet another messenger came and said, "Your sons and daughters were feasting and drinking wine at their oldest brother's house, {1:19} when suddenly a mighty wind swept in from the desert and struck the four corners of the house. It collapsed on them, and they are dead; I am the only one who has escaped to tell you." {1:20} At this, Job got up, tore his robe, shaved his head, and fell to the ground in worship. {1:21} He said, "Naked I came from my mother's womb, and naked I shall return. The LORD gave, and the LORD has taken away; blessed be the name of the LORD." {1:22} In all this, Job did not sin nor blame God.

{2:1} Again, there was a day when the angels came to present themselves before the LORD, and Satan also came among them to present himself before the LORD. {2:2} The LORD asked Satan, "Where have you come from?" Satan answered, "From roaming throughout the earth, going back and forth on it." {2:3} The LORD said to Satan, "Have you considered my servant Job? There is no one like him; he is blameless and upright, a man who fears God and shuns evil. And he still maintains his integrity, though you incited me against him to ruin him without reason." {2:4} Skin for skin, Satan replied, "A man will give all he has for his own life. {2:5} But stretch out your hand and strike his flesh and bones, and he will surely curse you to your face." {2:6} The LORD said to Satan, "Very well, he is in your hands; but you must spare his life." {2:7} So Satan went out from the presence of the LORD and afflicted Job with painful sores from the soles of his feet to the crown of his head. {2:8} Then Job took a piece of broken pottery and scraped himself with it as he sat among the ashes. {2:9} His wife said to him, "Are you still holding on to your integrity? Curse God and die!" {2:10} He replied, "You are talking like a foolish woman. Shall we accept good from God and not trouble?" In all this, Job did not sin in what he said. {2:11} When Job's three friends, Eliphaz the Temanite, Bildad the Shuhite, and Zophar the Naamathite, heard about all the troubles that had come upon him, they met together and decided to go and sympathize with him and comfort him. {2:12} When they saw him from a distance, they could hardly recognize him; they began to weep aloud, and they tore their robes and sprinkled dust on their heads. {2:13} Then they sat on the ground with him for seven days and seven nights. No one said a word to him, because they saw how great his suffering was.

{3:1} After this, Job opened his mouth and cursed the day of his birth. {3:2} He said, {3:3} "May the day I was born perish, and the night it was announced, 'A boy is conceived.' {3:4} May that day be darkness; may God above not care about it, nor let any light shine on it. {3:5} May darkness and the shadow of death claim it; may a cloud settle over it; may the blackness of the day overwhelm it. {3:6} As for that night, may darkness seize it; may it not be included among the days of the year or listed in the months. {3:7} Let that night be desolate; let no joyful voice be heard in it. {3:8} Let those who curse that day curse it, those who are ready to rouse Leviathan (a mythical sea creature). {3:9} May its twilight stars be dark; may it look for light but find none; may it never see the dawn. {3:10} Because it did not shut the doors of my mother's womb or hide sorrow from my eyes. {3:11} Why didn't I die at birth? Why didn't I perish as I came from the womb? {3:12} Why were there knees to receive me, and breasts that I might nurse? {3:13} For now, I would be lying still and quiet; I would be at rest, {3:14} with kings and counselors of the earth who built for themselves places now in ruins, {3:15} or with princes who had gold, who filled their houses with silver. {3:16} Or like a stillborn child, I would not have been, like infants who never saw the light. {3:17} There the wicked cease from turmoil, and there the weary are at rest. {3:18} Captives are at ease together; they do not hear the slave driver's shout. {3:19} The small and great are there, and the servant is free from his master. {3:20} Why is light given to those in misery and life to the bitter of soul, {3:21} to those who long for death that does not come, who search for it more than for hidden treasures, {3:22} who rejoice exceedingly and are glad when they find the grave? {3:23} Why is light given to a man whose path is hidden, whom God has hedged in? {3:24} For my groans come before I eat; my cries pour out like water. {3:25} What I feared has come upon me; what I dreaded has happened to me. {3:26} I have no peace, no quietness; I have no rest, but only turmoil.

{4:1} Then Eliphaz the Temanite replied, {4:2} "If we attempt to speak to you, will you be offended? But who can keep from talking? {4:3} Look, you have instructed many; you have strengthened weak hands. {4:4} Your words have supported those who stumbled; you have strengthened faltering knees. {4:5} But now trouble has come to you, and you are discouraged; it strikes you, and you are dismayed. {4:6} Is not your fear of God your confidence, and the integrity of your ways your hope? {4:7} Consider now: who, being innocent, has ever perished? Where were the upright ever destroyed? {4:8} As I have observed, those who plow iniquity and sow trouble reap it. {4:9} At the breath of God they perish; at the blast of his anger they are no more. {4:10} The lion may roar and the fierce lion growl, yet the teeth of the young lions are broken. {4:11} The lion dies for lack of prey, and the cubs of the lioness are scattered. {4:12} Now a word was secretly brought to me; my ears caught a whisper of it. {4:13} Amid disquieting visions in the night, when deep sleep falls on men, {4:14} fear and trembling seized me and made my bones shake. {4:15} A spirit glided past my face, and the hair on my body stood on end. {4:16} It stopped, but I could not tell what it was; an image was before my eyes, and there was silence; then I heard a voice say, {4:17} 'Can a mortal be more righteous than God? Can a mere human be more pure than his Maker? {4:18} If God places no trust in his angels, if he charges his angels with error, {4:19} how much more does he dwell in houses of clay, whose foundations are in the dust, crushed like a moth? {4:20} They are destroyed from morning till evening; they perish forever, with no one regarding it. {4:21} Does not their splendor (excellence) fade away? They die without wisdom."

{5:1} Call now, if there's anyone who will answer you; to which of the holy ones will you turn? {5:2} For anger kills the foolish, and jealousy destroys the simple. {5:3} I have seen the foolish taking root, but suddenly I cursed their dwelling. {5:4} Their children are far from safety; they are crushed at the city gate, and no one can rescue them. {5:5} The hungry consume their harvest, taking it even from among the thorns, and robbers swallow up their wealth. {5:6} Although trouble doesn't come from the dust, nor does distress spring from the ground, {5:7} yet humans are born for trouble, as surely as sparks fly upward. {5:8} I would seek God and present my case to Him. {5:9} He performs wonders that cannot be fathomed, miracles that cannot be counted. {5:10} He gives rain to the earth and sends water on the fields. {5:11} He lifts the humble to safety and restores those who mourn. {5:12} He frustrates the plans of the crafty, so their hands cannot achieve success. {5:13} He catches the wise in their own cleverness; the schemes of the crafty are brought to a swift end. {5:14} They encounter darkness in broad daylight and grope at noon as if it were night. {5:15} But He saves the needy from the sword, from the mouth of the mighty, and from the hand of the oppressor. {5:16} So the needy have hope, and injustice shuts its mouth. {5:17} Behold, happy is the one whom God corrects; do not despise the discipline of the Almighty. {5:18} For He wounds but also binds up; He injures but His hands heal. {5:19} He will deliver you from six troubles; in seven, no harm will touch you. {5:20} In famine, He will rescue you from death; in battle, from the power of the sword. {5:21} You will be protected from the lash of the tongue, and you will not fear destruction when it comes. {5:22} You will laugh at destruction and famine, and you will not fear the beasts of the earth. {5:23} For you will be in covenant with the stones of the field, and the wild animals will be at peace with you. {5:24} You will know that your tent is secure; you will visit your property and find nothing missing. {5:25} You will know that your offspring will be many, and your descendants like the grass of the earth. {5:26} You will come to your grave in a full age, like a sheaf gathered in season. {5:27} We have examined this, and it is true. Hear it and know for your own good.

{6:1} But Job answered, {6:2} "Oh, that my grief could be weighed and my calamity laid on the scales! {6:3} For it would surely be heavier than the sand of the sea; that's why my words have been swallowed up. {6:4} For the arrows of the Almighty are within me;

their poison drains my spirit; the terrors of God are arrayed against me. {6:5} Does a wild donkey bray when it has grass? Does an ox bellow over its fodder? {6:6} Is tasteless food eaten without salt? Is there any flavor in the white of an egg? {6:7} The things my soul refuses to touch are my sorrowful food. {6:8} Oh, that I might have my request, and that God would grant me what I long for! {6:9} Even that it would please God to crush me; let loose His hand and cut me off! {6:10} Then I would still have comfort; I would harden myself in sorrow; let Him not spare, for I have not concealed the words of the Holy One. {6:11} What strength do I have, that I should hope? What is my end, that I should prolong my life? {6:12} Is my strength like that of stones? Is my flesh bronze? {6:13} Is there any help in me, and is wisdom completely driven from me? {6:14} A friend should show kindness to a friend, but my friends have forsaken the fear of the Almighty. {6:15} My brothers are like a brook, like the streams of the brook that vanish; {6:16} they are darkened by the ice, and the snow is hidden. {6:17} When it gets warm, they disappear; when it's hot, they are consumed from their place. {6:18} The paths of their way turn aside; they go nowhere and perish. {6:19} The caravans of Tema look; the travelers of Sheba hope for them. {6:20} They are disappointed because they had hoped; they came there, and were ashamed. {6:21} For now you are nothing; you see my plight and are afraid. {6:22} Did I say, "Bring something to me"? Or, "Give a reward for me from your wealth"? {6:23} Or, "Rescue me from the hand of the enemy"? Or, "Redeem me from the hand of the mighty"? {6:24} Teach me, and I will be quiet; help me understand where I have erred. {6:25} How powerful are right words! But what does your arguing prove? {6:26} Do you think you can reprove words, and the speeches of one who is desperate, which are like wind? {6:27} Yes, you overwhelm the fatherless and dig a pit for your friend. {6:28} Now, therefore, be content; look at me; for it's clear to you if I lie. {6:29} Return, I ask you, let it not be wrong; yes, return again; my righteousness is in it. {6:30} Is there any injustice on my tongue? Cannot my taste discern the bitter?

{7:1} Is there not an appointed time for humans on earth? Are not their days like those of a hired worker? {7:2} Like a servant who longs for the shade, and a hired worker who looks for his wages, {7:3} so I have been given months of futility, and wearisome nights are assigned to me. {7:4} When I lie down, I ask, "When will I get up?" and the night drags on. I toss and turn until dawn. {7:5} My flesh is covered with worms and dust; my skin is broken and festering. {7:6} My days pass faster than a weaver's shuttle; they are spent without hope. {7:7} Remember that my life is a breath; my eyes will never see happiness again. {7:8} The eye of the one who sees me will see me no more; your eyes are upon me, and I am gone. {7:9} Like a cloud that fades and disappears, so the one who goes down to the grave will not return. {7:10} He will never come back to his house; his place will no longer recognize him. {7:11} Therefore, I will not hold back my mouth; I will speak in the anguish of my spirit; I will complain in the bitterness of my soul. {7:12} Am I a sea or a monster that you set a guard over me? {7:13} When I say, "My bed will comfort me, my couch will ease my complaint," {7:14} then you frighten me with dreams and terrify me with visions. {7:15} So that my soul chooses strangling and death rather than my life. {7:16} I loathe it; I would not live forever. Leave me alone, for my days are nothing. {7:17} What is humanity that you make so much of them, that you pay attention to them? {7:18} That you examine them every morning and test them every moment? {7:19} How long will you not look away from me or let me alone until I swallow my spit? {7:20} I have sinned; what can I do to you, O Preserver of humanity? Why have you made me your target, so that I am a burden to myself? {7:21} And why do you not pardon my transgression and take away my iniquity? For now I will sleep in the dust, and you will seek me, but I will be gone.

{8:1} Then Bildad the Shuhite answered and said, {8:2} "How long will you speak these things? How long will your words be like a strong wind? {8:3} Does God pervert justice? Does the Almighty distort what is right? {8:4} If your children have sinned against Him, and He has thrown them away for their transgression, {8:5} if you would seek God earnestly and plead with the Almighty, {8:6} if you were pure and upright, surely now He would awaken for you and restore your rightful habitation. {8:7} Though your beginning was small, your latter end would greatly increase. {8:8} For inquire, please, of the former generations and consider what their ancestors have found; {8:9} (for we are only of yesterday and know nothing, because our days on earth are a shadow). {8:10} Will they not teach you and tell you and utter words from their hearts? {8:11} Can the rush grow without mire? Can the reed grow without water? {8:12} While it is still green and not cut down, it withers before any other plant. {8:13} So are the paths of all who forget God; the hope of the hypocrite will perish. {8:14} His hope will be cut off, and his trust is like a spider's web. {8:15} He leans on his house, but it will not stand; he holds it fast, but it will not endure. {8:16} He is green before the sun, and his branch spreads out in his garden. {8:17} His roots are wrapped around a pile of stones. {8:18} If he is destroyed from his place, it will deny him, saying, "I have not seen you." {8:19} Behold, this is the joy of his way, and out of the earth others will grow. {8:20} Behold, God will not cast away a perfect man, nor will He help evildoers. {8:21} Until He fills your mouth with laughter and your lips with rejoicing. {8:22} Those who hate you will be clothed with shame, and the dwelling place of the wicked will come to nothing.

{9:1} Then Job answered and said, {9:2} "I know it is true, but how can a person be just before God? {9:3} If he wanted to argue with Him, he couldn't answer Him even once in a thousand times. {9:4} God is wise in heart and powerful in strength. Who has ever hardened himself against Him and prospered? {9:5} He removes mountains without anyone knowing; He overturns them in His anger. {9:6} He shakes the earth out of its place, and its foundations tremble. {9:7} He commands the sun not to rise and seals off the stars. {9:8} He alone stretches out the heavens and walks on the waves of the sea. {9:9} He made the constellations like Arcturus, Orion, and Pleiades, and the southern chambers. {9:10} He does great things beyond understanding, wonders without number. {9:11} If He passes by me, I do not see Him; if He goes by, I do not perceive Him. {9:12} If He takes something away, who can stop Him? Who can say to Him, "What are You doing?" {9:13} If God does not withdraw His anger, the proud helpers bow beneath Him. {9:14} How then can I answer Him or choose my words to argue with Him? {9:15} Even if I were innocent, I wouldn't answer Him; I would only plead with my Judge. {9:16} If I called and He answered me, I wouldn't believe that He listened to my voice. {9:17} For He crushes me with a storm and increases my wounds without cause. {9:18} He will not let me breathe but fills me with bitterness. {9:19} If I speak of strength, He is strong; and if of justice, who will set a time for me to plead? {9:20} If I justify myself, my own mouth will condemn me; if I say I am perfect, it will prove me perverse. {9:21} Although I were perfect, I wouldn't know my own soul; I would despise my life. {9:22} This is why I say, "He destroys both the perfect and the wicked." {9:23} If a scourge kills suddenly, He laughs at the plight of the innocent. {9:24} The earth is given into the hands of the wicked; He covers the faces of its judges. If not, then where is He, and who is He? {9:25} My days are swifter than a courier; they flee away without seeing any good. {9:26} They pass like swift ships, like the eagle that hastens to catch its prey. {9:27} If I say, "I will forget my complaint, I will put away my sadness and be cheerful," {9:28} I am afraid of all my pains; I know that You will not hold me innocent. {9:29} If I am wicked, why should I toil in vain? {9:30} If I wash myself with snow water and cleanse my hands with soap, {9:31} yet You will plunge me into the ditch, and my own clothes will despise me. {9:32} For He is not a mere man like me that I should answer Him, that we should come together in judgment. {9:33} There is no mediator between us to lay his hand on both of us. {9:34} Let Him take His rod away from me, and do not let His fear terrify me. {9:35} Then I would speak without fear of Him, but it is not so with me.

{10:1} My soul is weary of my life; I will leave my complaint to myself; I will speak in the bitterness of my soul. {10:2} I will say to God, "Do not condemn me; show me why You contend with me. {10:3} Is it good for You to oppress, to despise the work of Your hands, and shine on the counsel of the wicked? {10:4} Do You have eyes of flesh? Do You see as a human sees? {10:5} Are Your days like the days of a mortal? Are Your years like human years, {10:6} that You inquire about my iniquity and search for my sin? {10:7} You know that I am not wicked, and no one can rescue me from Your hand. {10:8} Your hands shaped and formed me, yet You destroy me. {10:9} Remember, I beseech You, that You made me like clay; will You bring me back to dust? {10:10} Did You not pour me out like milk and curdle me like cheese? {10:11} You clothed me with skin and flesh, and knit me together with bones and sinews. {10:12} You granted me life and favor, and Your care has preserved my spirit. {10:13} These things You have hidden in Your heart; I know this is with You. {10:14} If I sin, You mark me and will not acquit me of my iniquity. {10:15} If I am wicked, woe to me; and if I am righteous, I will not lift up my head. I am full of shame; therefore, see my affliction. {10:16} It increases; You hunt me like a fierce lion and show Your power against me. {10:17} You renew Your witnesses against me and increase Your anger toward me; changes and warfare are against me. {10:18} Why then did You bring me out of the womb? I wish I had died, and no eye had seen me! {10:19} I should have been carried straight from the womb to the grave. {10:20} Are not my days few? Stop then and leave me alone, so I can take comfort a little, {10:21} before I go to the land of darkness and the shadow of death, {10:22} a land of darkness, as dark as darkness itself, and of the shadow of death, where order is absent, and light is like darkness."

{11:1} Then Zophar the Naamathite answered and said, {11:2} "Shouldn't all these many words be answered? Should a man full of talk be justified? {11:3} Should your lies make people silent? When you mock, should no one be ashamed? {11:4} For you have said, 'My doctrine is pure, and I am clean in Your eyes.' {11:5} But oh, that God would speak and open His lips against you; {11:6} and that He would show you the secrets of wisdom, that they are double what you think! Know therefore that God demands less of you than what your iniquity deserves. {11:7} Can you, by searching, find out God? Can you find the Almighty to perfection? {11:8} It is as high as heaven—what can you do? Deeper than hell—what can you know? {11:9} Its measure is longer than the earth and broader than the sea. {11:10} If He cuts off, shuts up, or gathers, who can stop Him? {11:11} For He knows worthless men; He sees wickedness too—will He not consider it? {11:12} A worthless man would be wise, even though a man is born like a wild donkey's colt. {11:13} If you prepare your heart and reach out your hands toward Him; {11:14} if iniquity is in your hand, put it far away, and don't let wickedness dwell in your tents. {11:15} Then you will lift up your face without spot; you will stand firm and not fear, {11:16} because you will forget your misery and remember it like waters that have passed away. {11:17} Your age will be clearer than noon; you will shine like the morning. {11:18} You will feel secure, because there is hope; you will dig around you and take your rest in safety. {11:19} You will lie down, and no one will make you afraid; many will seek your favor. {11:20} But the eyes of the wicked will fail, and they will not escape, and their hope will be like giving up the ghost.

{12:1} And Job answered and said, {12:2} "No doubt you are the people, and wisdom will die with you. {12:3} But I have understanding as well as you; I am not inferior to you. Who doesn't know these things? {12:4} I am like one who is mocked by his neighbor, who calls upon God, and He answers him; the just and upright man is laughed at. {12:5} The one who is about to slip is like a lamp that is despised by the comfortable. {12:6} The tents of robbers prosper, and those who provoke God are secure; God brings them abundance. {12:7} But ask the animals, and they will teach you; the birds of the air will tell you. {12:8} Or speak to the earth, and it will teach you; the fish of the sea will declare it to you. {12:9} Who doesn't know that the hand of the LORD has done this? {12:10} In His hand is the soul of every living thing and the breath of all mankind. {12:11} Does not the ear test words as the mouth tastes food? {12:12} Wisdom is with the aged, and understanding comes with length of days. {12:13} With Him is wisdom and strength; He has counsel and understanding. {12:14} Behold, He breaks down, and it cannot be rebuilt; He shuts up a man, and there is no opening. {12:15} Behold, He withholds the waters, and they dry up; He sends them out, and they overturn the earth. {12:16} With Him is strength and wisdom; the deceived and the deceiver are His. {12:17} He leads counselors away spoiled and makes judges foolish. {12:18} He loosens the bonds of kings and binds their waist with a belt. {12:19} He leads princes away spoiled and overturns the mighty. {12:20} He removes the speech of the trustworthy and takes away the understanding of the aged. {12:21} He pours contempt on princes and weakens the strength of the mighty. {12:22} He uncovers deep things out of darkness and brings to light the shadow of death. {12:23} He increases nations and destroys them; He enlarges nations and constricts them again. {12:24} He takes away the heart of the chief people of the earth and causes them to wander in a wilderness where there is no way. {12:25} They grope in the dark without light, and He makes them stagger like a drunk man."

{13:1} Look, my eye has seen all this; my ear has heard and understood it. {13:2} What you know, I also know; I am not inferior to you. {13:3} Surely I would speak to the Almighty, and I desire to reason with God. {13:4} But you are forgers of lies; you are all worthless physicians. {13:5} Oh, that you would all hold your peace! That would be your wisdom. {13:6} Listen to my reasoning and hear the pleadings of my lips. {13:7} Will you speak wickedly for God and talk deceitfully for Him? {13:8} Will you accept His person? Will you contend for God? {13:9} Is it good for Him to search you out? Or do you mock Him like one man mocks another? {13:10} He will surely reprove you if you secretly accept persons. {13:11} Shouldn't His majesty make you afraid, and His dread fall upon you? {13:12} Your memories are like ashes, your bodies like clay. {13:13} Hold your peace; let me speak, and let whatever will happen come upon me. {13:14} Why should I take my flesh in my teeth and put my life in my hand? {13:15} Even if He kills me, I will trust in Him; I will maintain my own ways before Him. {13:16} He also will be my salvation, for no hypocrite can come before Him. {13:17} Listen carefully to my speech and my declaration with your ears. {13:18} Behold, I have ordered my cause; I know that I will be justified. {13:19} Who is he that will plead with me? If I hold my tongue, I will give up the ghost. {13:20} Only do not do two things to me: then I will not hide from you. {13:21} Withdraw Your hand far from me, and do not let Your dread make me afraid. {13:22} Then call, and I will answer, or let me speak, and You answer me. {13:23} How many are my iniquities and sins? Make me know my transgression and my sin. {13:24} Why do You hide Your face and consider me Your enemy? {13:25} Will You break a leaf that is driven to and fro? Will You pursue dry stubble? {13:26} For You write bitter things against me and make me inherit the iniquities of my youth. {13:27} You put my feet in the stocks and closely watch all my paths; You set a limit on the heels of my feet. {13:28} And He, like a rotten thing, consumes, like a garment that is moth-eaten.

{14:1} Man who is born of a woman is of few days and full of trouble. {14:2} He comes forth like a flower and is cut down; he flees like a shadow and does not continue. {14:3} And do You open Your eyes upon such a one and bring me into judgment with You? {14:4} Who can bring a clean thing out of an unclean? Not one. {14:5} Since his days are determined, the number of his months are with You; You have appointed his limits that he cannot pass. {14:6} Turn from him, that he may rest, until he accomplishes, like a hireling, his day. {14:7} For there is hope for a tree if it is cut down, that it will sprout again and its tender branch will not cease. {14:8} Though its root grows old in the earth, and its stump dies in the ground, {14:9} yet at the scent of water, it will bud and bring forth boughs like a plant. {14:10} But man dies and wastes away; yes, man gives up the ghost—where is he? {14:11} As the waters fail from the sea and the flood decays and dries up, {14:12} so man lies down and does not rise. Until the heavens are no more, they will not awake nor be raised from their sleep. {14:13} Oh, that You would hide me in the grave, that You would keep me secret until Your wrath is past, that You would appoint me a set time and remember me! {14:14} If a man dies, shall he live again? All the days of my appointed time will I wait until my change comes. {14:15} You shall call, and I will answer; You will desire the work of Your hands. {14:16} For now You number my steps; do You not watch over my sin? {14:17} My transgression is sealed up in a bag; You sew up my iniquity. {14:18} And surely, the mountain falling comes to nothing, and the rock is removed from its place. {14:19} The waters wear away the stones; You wash away the things which grow out of the dust of the earth and destroy the hope of man. {14:20} You prevail forever against him, and he passes; You change his countenance and send him away. {14:21} His sons come to honor, and he does not know it; they are brought low, but he perceives it not. {14:22} But his flesh upon him will have pain, and his soul within him will mourn.

{15:1} Then Eliphaz the Temanite answered and said, {15:2} Should a wise man speak empty knowledge and fill his belly with the east wind? {15:3} Should he argue with useless talk or with words that do no good? {15:4} Indeed, you cast off fear and restrain prayer before God. {15:5} For your mouth utters iniquity, and you choose the tongue of the crafty. {15:6} Your own mouth condemns you, not I; your own lips testify against you. {15:7} Are you the first man ever born? Were you made before the hills? {15:8} Have you heard the secret of God, and do you keep wisdom to yourself? {15:9} What do you know that we do not know? What do you understand that is not in us? {15:10} Among us are both gray-haired and very old men, much older than your father. {15:11} Are the consolations of God too small for you? Is there any secret thing with you? {15:12} Why does your heart carry you away, and what do your eyes waver at, {15:13} that you turn your spirit against God and let such words come out of your mouth? {15:14} What is man that he should be clean? And he who is born of a woman, that he should be righteous? {15:15} Look, He does not trust His saints; yes, the heavens are not clean in His sight. {15:16} How much more abominable and filthy is man, who drinks iniquity like water? {15:17} I will show you; listen to me, and what I have seen I will declare; {15:18} what wise men have told from their fathers and have not hidden. {15:19} To whom alone the earth was given, and no stranger passed among them. {15:20} The wicked man suffers pain all his days, and the number of years is hidden from the oppressor. {15:21} A dreadful sound is in his ears; in prosperity, the destroyer comes upon him. {15:22} He does not believe he will return from darkness; he is awaited by the sword. {15:23} He wanders for bread, saying, "Where is it?" He knows that the day of darkness is ready at hand. {15:24} Trouble and anguish will make him afraid; they will prevail against him like a king ready for battle. {15:25} For he stretches out his hand against God and strengthens himself against the Almighty. {15:26} He runs against Him, even on his neck, upon the thick shields. {15:27} Because he covers his face with fat and makes fat deposits on his flanks. {15:28} He dwells in desolate cities, in houses that no one inhabits, which are ready to become heaps. {15:29} He will not be rich, nor will his substance continue; he will not prolong his perfection upon the earth. {15:30} He will not depart from darkness; the flame will dry up his branches, and by the breath of His mouth, he will perish. {15:31} Let not him who is deceived trust in emptiness; for emptiness will be his reward. {15:32} It will be completed before his time, and his branch will not be green. {15:33} He will shake off his unripe grapes like a vine and cast off his blossoms like an olive tree. {15:34} For the congregation of hypocrites will be desolate, and fire will consume the tents of bribery. {15:35} They conceive mischief and give birth to emptiness; their womb prepares deceit.

{16:1} Then Job answered and said, {16:2} I have heard many such things; you are all miserable comforters. {16:3} Shall empty words have an end? Or what emboldens you that you answer? {16:4} I also could speak as you do; if your soul were in my place, I could heap up words against you and shake my head at you. {16:5} But I would strengthen you with my mouth, and the movement of my lips would ease your grief. {16:6} Though I speak, my grief is not eased; and if I hold back, what do I gain? {16:7} But now He has made me weary; you have made all my company desolate. {16:8} You have filled me with wrinkles, which is a witness against me; and my leanness rising up in me bears witness to my face. {16:9} He tears me in His wrath, who hates me; He gnashes upon me with His teeth; my enemy sharpens his eyes upon me. {16:10} They gape at me with their mouths; they strike me on the cheek in reproach; they gather themselves together against me. {16:11} God has delivered me to the ungodly and turned me over to the hands of the wicked. {16:12} I was at ease, but He has broken me apart; He has taken me by the neck and shaken me to pieces and set me up as His target. {16:13} His archers surround me; He cleaves my reins asunder and does not spare; He pours out my gall on the ground. {16:14} He breaks me with breach upon breach; He runs upon me like a giant. {16:15} I have sewn sackcloth upon my skin and defiled my horn in the dust. {16:16} My face is foul with weeping, and on my eyelids is the shadow of death; {16:17} not for any injustice in my hands; also, my prayer is pure. {16:18} O earth, do not cover my blood, and let my cry have no place. {16:19} Also now, look, my witness is in heaven, and my record is on high. {16:20} My friends scorn me; but my eye pours out tears to God. {16:21} Oh, that someone might plead for a man with God, as a man pleads for his neighbor! {16:22} When a few years have come, I will go the way from which I will not return.

{17:1} My breath is foul, my days are finished, and the grave is ready for me. {17:2} Are there not mockers with me? Does my eye not continue to be provoked by them? {17:3} Lay down a pledge for me; who will be my guarantor? {17:4} For You have hidden their hearts from understanding; therefore, You will not exalt them. {17:5} He who speaks flattery to his friends, even the eyes of his children will fail. {17:6} He has made me a byword among the people; I was once like a tambourine. {17:7} My eye is dim because of sorrow, and all my limbs are like a shadow. {17:8} Upright men will be astonished at this, and the innocent will stir himself against the hypocrite. {17:9} The righteous will hold on to their way, and he who has clean hands will grow stronger and stronger. {17:10} But as for you all, come back and talk to me now; I cannot find one wise man among you. {17:11} My days are gone, my plans are shattered, even the thoughts of my heart. {17:12} They change night into day; the light is short because of darkness. {17:13} If I wait, the grave is my home; I have made my bed in darkness. {17:14} I have said to corruption, "You are my father," and to the worm, "You are my mother and sister." {17:15} And where is my hope? Who will see my hope? {17:16} They will go down to the gates of the pit, when we rest together in the dust.

{18:1} Then Bildad the Shuhite answered and said, {18:2} How long before you put an end to words? Mark, and then we will speak. {18:3} Why are we considered as cattle and viewed as worthless in your sight? {18:4} He tears himself in his anger; will the earth be forsaken for you? Will the rock be moved from its place? {18:5} Yes, the light of the wicked will be extinguished, and the spark of their fire will not shine. {18:6} The light will be dark in his tent, and his lamp will go out with him. {18:7} The steps of his strength will be straitened, and his own counsel will throw him down. {18:8} For he is caught in a net by his own feet, and he walks on a snare. {18:9} The trap will take him by the heel, and the robber will prevail against him. {18:10} A snare is laid for him on the ground, and a trap is set for him on the way. {18:11} Terrors will make him afraid on every side and drive him to his feet. {18:12} His strength will be starved, and destruction will be ready at his side. {18:13} It will consume the strength of his skin; even the firstborn of death will consume his strength. {18:14} His confidence will be rooted out of his tent, and it will lead him to the king of terrors. {18:15} It will dwell in his tent because it is not his; sulfur will be scattered upon his habitation. {18:16} His roots will dry up beneath, and his branch will be cut off above. {18:17} His memory will perish from the earth, and he will have no name in the street. {18:18} He will be driven from light into darkness and chased out of the world. {18:19} He will have neither son nor nephew among his people, nor any remaining in his dwellings. {18:20} Those who come after him will be astonished at his day, as those who went before were terrified. {18:21} Surely such is the dwelling of the wicked, and this is the place of one who does not know God.

{19:1} Then Job answered and said, {19:2} How long will you torment my soul and crush me with words? {19:3} These ten times you have reproached me; you are not ashamed to treat me like this. {19:4} Even if I have erred, my error is with me. {19:5} If you want to exalt yourselves against me and plead my shame, {19:6} know that God has overthrown me and surrounded me with His net. {19:7} Behold, I cry out for help, but I am not heard; I shout loudly, but there is no justice. {19:8} He has blocked my path so I cannot pass, and has set darkness in my ways. {19:9} He has stripped me of my glory and taken the crown from my head. {19:10} He has destroyed me on every side, and I am gone; my hope has been pulled up like a tree. {19:11} He has also kindled His wrath against me; He counts me as one of His enemies. {19:12} His troops come together and raise their way against me, encamping around my tent. {19:13} He has put my brothers far from me, and my acquaintances have completely turned away from me. {19:14} My relatives have failed me, and my close friends have forgotten me. {19:15} Those who live in my house, even my maids, consider me a stranger; I am an alien in their eyes. {19:16} I called my servant, but he did not answer; I pleaded with him with my mouth. {19:17} My breath is strange to my wife, even though I plead for the sake of my own children. {19:18} Yes, young children despise me; I rise, and they speak against me. {19:19} All my closest friends abhor me; those I loved have turned against me. {19:20} My bones cling to my skin and flesh, and I have escaped with only the skin of my teeth. {19:21} Have pity on me, have pity on me, O my friends, for the hand of God has touched me. {19:22} Why do you persecute me as God does, and are not satisfied with my flesh? {19:23} Oh, that my words were written down! Oh, that they were inscribed in a book! {19:24} That they were engraved with an iron pen and lead in the rock forever! {19:25} For I know that my Redeemer lives, and He will stand at the last day upon the earth. {19:26} And though worms destroy this body, yet in my flesh I will see God. {19:27} I will see Him for myself, and my eyes will behold Him, and not another; though my heart is consumed within me. {19:28} But you should say, "Why do we persecute him, since the root of the matter is found in me?" {19:29} Fear the sword, for wrath brings the punishment of the sword, so that you may know there is judgment.

{20:1} Then Zophar the Naamathite answered and said, {20:2} Therefore, my thoughts compel me to answer, and for this, I hurry. {20:3} I have heard the rebuke of my shame, and the spirit of my understanding causes me to answer. {20:4} Do you not know this from old, since man was placed on earth, {20:5} that the triumph of the wicked is short, and the joy of the hypocrite lasts only for a moment? {20:6} Though his pride mounts to the heavens and his head reaches the clouds, {20:7} yet he will perish forever like his own dung; those who have seen him will say, "Where is he?" {20:8} He will fly away like a dream and will not be found; he will be chased away like a vision of the night. {20:9} The eye that saw him will see him no more; his place will no longer behold him. {20:10} His children will seek to please the poor, and his hands will restore their wealth. {20:11} His bones are full of the sin of his youth, which will lie down with him in the dust. {20:12} Though wickedness is sweet in his mouth, though he hides it under his tongue, {20:13} though he spares it and does not forsake it, but keeps it in his mouth, {20:14} yet his food in his belly will turn sour; it will be the venom of cobras within him. {20:15} He has swallowed riches, and he will vomit them up again; God will cast them out of his belly. {20:16} He will suck the poison of cobras; the viper's tongue will kill him. {20:17} He will not see the rivers, the streams, the brooks of honey and butter. {20:18} What he labored for he will restore, and he will not enjoy it; according to his substance, his restitution will be, and he will not rejoice in it. {20:19} Because he has oppressed and forsaken the poor, and has violently taken away a house which he did not build, {20:20} surely he will not find quietness in his belly; he will not save any of what he desired. {20:21} None of his food will be left; therefore, no one will look for his goods. {20:22} In the fullness of his sufficiency, he will be in distress; every hand of the wicked will come upon him. {20:23} When he is about to fill his belly, God will cast the fury of His wrath upon him and will rain it upon him while he is eating. {20:24} He will flee from the iron weapon, and the steel bow will pierce him. {20:25} It is drawn, and comes out of his body; yes, the glittering sword comes out of his gall; terrors are upon him. {20:26} All darkness will be hidden in his secret places; a fire not blown will consume him; it will go badly for him who is left in his tent. {20:27} The heavens will reveal his iniquity, and the earth will rise up against him. {20:28} The increase of his house will depart, and his goods will flow away in the day of His wrath. {20:29} This is the portion of a wicked man from God, and the heritage appointed to him by God.

{21:1} But Job answered and said, {21:2} Listen carefully to my words, and let this be your comfort. {21:3} Allow me to speak; after I have spoken, you can mock. {21:4} Is my complaint against a human? If so, why should my spirit not be troubled? {21:5} Pay attention to me and be amazed; put your hand over your mouth. {21:6} Even when I remember, I am afraid, and trembling grips my flesh. {21:7} Why do the wicked live, grow old, and become powerful? {21:8} Their children are established in their sight, and their offspring are before their eyes. {21:9} Their houses are safe from fear, and the rod of God is not upon them. {21:10} Their bulls breed without fail; their cows calve without losing their young. {21:11} They send their little ones out like a flock, and their children dance. {21:12} They take the tambourine and harp and rejoice at the sound of music. {21:13} They spend their days in wealth and go down to the grave in a moment. {21:14} Therefore, they say to God, "Leave us; we do not desire the knowledge of Your ways. {21:15} What is the Almighty that we should serve Him? What benefit do we get if we pray to Him?" {21:16} Look, their prosperity is not in their hands; the plans of the wicked are far from me. {21:17} How often is the lamp of the wicked extinguished! How often does their destruction come upon them! God distributes sorrows in His anger. {21:18} They are like stubble before the wind and like chaff that the storm blows away. {21:19} God stores up their iniquity for their children; He rewards them, and they will know it. {21:20} Their eyes will see their destruction, and they will drink the wrath of the Almighty. {21:21} For what pleasure does he have in his house after him when the number of his months is cut off? {21:22} Can anyone teach God knowledge, since He judges those who are high? {21:23} One dies in full strength, completely at ease and quiet. {21:24} His body is full of milk, and his bones are well-nourished. {21:25} Another dies in bitterness of soul, never enjoying anything good. {21:26} They both lie down alike in the dust, and worms cover them. {21:27} Behold, I know your thoughts and the schemes you wrongly imagine against me. {21:28} For you say, "Where is the house of the noble? Where are the homes of the wicked?" {21:29} Have you not asked those who travel the road? Do you not know their signs, {21:30} that the wicked are reserved for the day of destruction? They will be brought forth on the day of wrath. {21:31} Who can declare his way to his face? Who can repay him for what he has done? {21:32} Yet he will be brought to the grave and remain in the tomb. {21:33} The clods of the valley will be sweet to him, and every man will follow him, as countless have done before him. {21:34} How then can you comfort me in vain, seeing that your answers contain falsehood?

{22:1} Then Eliphaz the Temanite answered and said, {22:2} Can a person be of any benefit to God? Can a wise person benefit himself? {22:3} Does the Almighty take pleasure in your righteousness? Is it a gain to Him that you make your ways perfect? {22:4} Will He correct you for fear of you? Will He enter into judgment with you? {22:5} Is not your wickedness great? Are not your sins infinite? {22:6} For you have taken a pledge from your brother without cause and stripped the naked of their clothing. {22:7} You have not given water to the weary to drink, and you have withheld bread from the hungry. {22:8} But the mighty man has the earth, and the honorable man dwells in it. {22:9} You have sent widows away empty, and you have broken the arms of the fatherless. {22:10} Therefore, snares surround you, and sudden fear troubles you; {22:11} or darkness, so you cannot see; and the flood of waters covers you. {22:12} Is not God in the heights of heaven? Look at the height of the stars, how high they are! {22:13} And you say, "How does God know? Can He judge through the dark clouds?" {22:14} Thick clouds are a covering for Him, so He cannot see; He walks in the circuit of heaven. {22:15} Have you marked the old way that wicked men have walked? {22:16} They were cut down before their time, whose foundation was swept away by a flood. {22:17} They said to God, "Leave us; what can the Almighty do for us?" {22:18} Yet He filled their houses with good things, but the plans of the wicked are far from me. {22:19} The righteous see it and are glad; the innocent laugh at them. {22:20} Our substance is not cut down; the fire consumes only the remnant of them. {22:21} Now become acquainted with Him, and be at peace; good will come to you. {22:22} Receive, I pray, the law from His mouth, and lay up His words in your heart. {22:23} If you return to the Almighty, you will be restored; remove iniquity far from your tent. {22:24} Then you will lay up gold like dust and the gold of Ophir like the stones of the brooks. {22:25} Yes, the Almighty will be your defense, and you will have plenty of silver. {22:26} For then you will delight in the Almighty and lift up your face to God. {22:27} You will make your prayer to Him, and He will hear you; you will fulfill your vows. {22:28} You will also declare a thing, and it will be established for you, and light will shine on your ways. {22:29} When people are cast down, then you will say, "There is lifting up," and He will save the humble person. {22:30} He will deliver the innocent, and it will be delivered by the purity of your hands.

{23:1} Then Job answered and said, {23:2} My complaint is still bitter today; my suffering is heavier than my groaning. {23:3} Oh, that I knew where I might find Him! I would go to His seat! {23:4} I would present my case before Him and fill my mouth with arguments. {23:5} I would know the words He would answer me and understand what He would say to me. {23:6} Will He contend with me in His great power? No; He would strengthen me instead. {23:7} There the righteous might argue with Him, and I would be delivered forever from my judge. {23:8} Look, I go forward, but He is not there; backward, but I cannot perceive Him. {23:9} On the left, where He is working, I cannot see Him; He hides Himself on the right, and I cannot find Him. {23:10} But He knows the way that I take; when He has tested me, I will come forth like gold. {23:11} My feet have held His steps; I have kept His way and not turned aside. {23:12} I have not departed from the command of His lips; I have treasured the words of His mouth more than my necessary food. {23:13} But He is of one mind, and who can change Him? What He desires, He does. {23:14} For He fulfills what is appointed for me, and many such things are with Him. {23:15} Therefore, I am troubled in His presence; when I consider, I am afraid of Him. {23:16} For God has made my heart soft, and the Almighty troubles me. {23:17} Because I was not cut off before the darkness, nor has He covered the darkness from my face.

{24:1} Why, seeing that times are not hidden from the Almighty, do those who know Him not see His days? {24:2} Some remove landmarks; they violently take away flocks and feed on them. {24:3} They drive away the donkey of the fatherless and take the widow's ox as a pledge. {24:4} They push the needy out of the way; the poor of the earth hide together. {24:5} Look, like wild donkeys in the desert, they go out to their work, rising early to find prey; the wilderness provides food for them and their children. {24:6} They harvest their grain in the fields and gather the grapes of the wicked. {24:7} They cause the naked to lodge without clothing, leaving them without covering in the cold. {24:8} They are soaked by the mountain showers and embrace the rock for lack of shelter. {24:9} They pluck the fatherless from the breast and take a pledge from the poor. {24:10} They make him go naked without clothing and take away the sheaf from the hungry. {24:11} They produce oil within their walls and tread their winepresses, yet suffer thirst. {24:12} Men groan from the city, and the soul of the wounded cries out; yet God does not charge them with folly. {24:13} They are among those who rebel against the light; they do not know its ways nor abide in its paths. {24:14} The murderer rises with the light to kill the poor and needy, and at night, he is like a thief. {24:15} The eye of the adulterer waits for twilight, saying, "No eye will see me," and disguises his face. {24:16} In the dark, they dig through houses they have marked for themselves in the daytime; they do not know the light. {24:17} For morning is to them like the shadow of death; if someone knows them, they are in the terrors of the shadow of death. {24:18} They are swift as waters; their portion is cursed in the earth; they do not see the path of the vineyards. {24:19} Drought and heat consume the snow waters; so does the grave those who have sinned. {24:20} The womb will forget him; the worm will sweetly feed on him; he will no longer be remembered, and wickedness will be broken like a tree. {24:21} He treats the barren woman cruelly and does not do good to the widow. {24:22} He also draws in the mighty with his power; he rises up, and no one is sure of life. {24:23} Though it is given to him to be safe, on what he rests, yet his eyes are upon their ways. {24:24} They are exalted for a little while, but they are gone and brought low; they are taken out of the way like all others and cut off like the tops of the ears of corn. {24:25} And if this is not so now, who will prove me a liar and make my speech worthless?

{25:1} Then Bildad the Shuhite answered and said, {25:2} Dominion and fear are with Him; He makes peace in His high places. {25:3} Is there any number to His armies? And upon whom does His light not shine? {25:4} How then can a man be justified with God? Or how can someone born of a woman be clean? {25:5} Even the moon does not shine, and the stars are not pure in His sight. {25:6} How much less man, who is a worm, and the son of man, who is also a worm?

{26:1} But Job answered and said, {26:2} How have you helped him who has no power? How have you saved the arm that has no strength? {26:3} How have you given counsel to one without wisdom? And how have you declared the truth so abundantly? {26:4} To whom have you spoken these words? And whose spirit came from you? {26:5} The dead tremble under the waters and their inhabitants. {26:6} Hell is naked before Him, and destruction has no covering. {26:7} He stretches out the north over empty space and hangs the earth on nothing. {26:8} He binds up the waters in His thick clouds, and the clouds do not burst under them. {26:9} He holds back the face of His throne and spreads His cloud over it. {26:10} He has set boundaries for the waters until day and night come to an end. {26:11} The pillars of heaven tremble and are amazed at His rebuke. {26:12} He divides the sea with His power, and by His understanding, He strikes down the proud. {26:13} By His Spirit, He adorns the heavens; His hand has formed the crooked serpent. {26:14} Look, these are only parts of His ways; how small a whisper do we hear of Him! But the thunder of His power, who can understand?

{27:1} Moreover, Job continued his discourse and said, {27:2} As God lives, who has taken away my judgment, and the Almighty, who has troubled my soul; {27:3} while my breath is in me, and the spirit of God is in my nostrils; {27:4} my lips will not speak wickedness, nor will my tongue utter deceit. {27:5} God forbid that I should justify you; until I die, I will not remove my integrity from me. {27:6} I hold fast to my righteousness and will not let it go; my heart will not reproach me as long as I live. {27:7} Let my enemy be like the wicked, and he who rises up against me like the unrighteous. {27:8} For what is the hope of the hypocrite, even if he gains, when God takes away his soul? {27:9} Will God hear his cry when trouble comes upon him? {27:10} Will he delight himself in the Almighty? Will he always call upon God? {27:11} I will teach you by the hand of God; I will not conceal what is with the Almighty. {27:12} Behold, all of you have seen it; why then do you continue to be so vain? {27:13} This is the portion of a wicked man with God and the heritage of oppressors, which they shall receive from the Almighty. {27:14} If his children are multiplied, it is for the sword, and his offspring shall not be satisfied with bread. {27:15} Those who remain of him shall be buried in death, and his widows shall not weep. {27:16} Though he heaps up silver like dust and prepares clothing as plentiful as clay; {27:17} he may prepare it, but the just will wear it, and the innocent will divide the silver. {27:18} He builds his house like a moth's nest and like a booth that a keeper makes. {27:19} The rich man lies down, but he will not be gathered; he opens his eyes, and he is not. {27:20} Terrors take hold of him like waters; a tempest sweeps him away in the night. {27:21} The east wind carries him away, and he departs; as a storm hurls him out of his place. {27:22} For God shall cast upon him and not spare; he would eagerly flee from His hand. {27:23} Men shall clap their hands at him and hiss him out of his place.

{28:1} Surely there is a vein for silver and a place for gold where it is refined. {28:2} Iron is taken out of the earth, and brass is smelted from stone. {28:3} He sets an end to darkness and searches out all perfection; the stones of darkness and the shadow of death. {28:4} The flood breaks out from the inhabitant; even the waters forgotten by the foot are dried up, they are gone away from men. {28:5} As for the earth, out of it comes bread, and underneath it is turned up as if it were fire. {28:6} The stones of it are the place of sapphires, and it has dust of gold. {28:7} There is a path which no bird knows, and the vulture's eye has not seen. {28:8} The lion's whelps have not trodden it, nor has the fierce lion passed by it. {28:9} He puts forth his hand upon the rock; he overturns the mountains by their roots. {28:10} He cuts out rivers among the rocks, and his eye sees every precious thing. {28:11} He binds the floods from overflowing, and that which is hidden he brings forth to light. {28:12} But where shall wisdom be found? And where is the place of understanding? {28:13} Man does not know its price; it cannot be found in the land of the living. {28:14} The deep says, "It is not in me," and the sea says, "It is not with me." {28:15} It cannot be obtained for gold, nor shall silver be weighed for its price. {28:16} It cannot be valued with the gold of Ophir, with the precious onyx, or the sapphire. {28:17} Gold and crystal cannot equal it, nor can its exchange be for jewels of fine gold. {28:18} No mention shall be made of coral or pearls, for the price of wisdom is above rubies. {28:19} The topaz of Ethiopia cannot equal it, nor can it be valued with pure gold. {28:20} From where then does wisdom come? And where is the place of understanding? {28:21} Seeing it is hidden from the eyes of all living and kept close from the birds of the air. {28:22} Destruction and death say, "We have heard its fame with our ears." {28:23} God understands the way to it, and He knows its place. {28:24} For He looks to the ends of the earth and sees under the whole heaven; {28:25} to make the weight for the winds, and He measures the waters by measure. {28:26} When He made a decree for the rain and a way for the lightning of the thunder; {28:27} then He saw it and declared it; He prepared it, and searched it out. {28:28} And to man He said, "Behold, the fear of the Lord, that is wisdom; and to depart from evil is understanding."

{29:1} Moreover, Job continued his discourse and said, {29:2} Oh, that I were as I was in the months past, in the days when God protected me; {29:3} when His light shone upon my head, and by His light I walked through darkness; {29:4} as I was in the days of my youth, when the secret of God was upon my tent; {29:5} when the Almighty was still with me, when my children were around me; {29:6} when I washed my steps with butter, and the rock poured out rivers of oil for me; {29:7} when I went out to the city gate, and prepared my seat in the street! {29:8} The young men saw me and hid themselves, and the aged stood up and respected me. {29:9} The princes stopped talking and laid their hand over their mouth. {29:10} The nobles held their peace, and their tongues stuck to the roof of their mouths. {29:11} When the ear heard me, it blessed me; and when the eye saw me, it gave testimony to me, {29:12} because I delivered the poor who cried, and the fatherless, and those who had no one to help them. {29:13} The blessing of him who was ready to perish came upon me, and I made the widow's heart sing for joy. {29:14} I put on righteousness, and it clothed me; my judgment was like a robe and a crown. {29:15} I was eyes to the blind and feet to the lame. {29:16} I was a father to the poor, and I searched out matters I didn't know. {29:17} I broke the jaws of the wicked and took the prey from their teeth. {29:18} Then I said, "I shall die in my nest, and I shall multiply my days like the sand." {29:19} My roots were spread out by the waters, and the dew lay all night upon my branch. {29:20} My glory was fresh in me, and my bow was renewed in my hand. {29:21} Men listened to me and waited, and kept silent at my counsel. {29:22} After my words, they did not speak again, and my speech dropped upon them. {29:23} They waited for me like for rain, and they opened their mouths wide like for the spring rain. {29:24} If I laughed at them, they did not believe it, and they did not cast down the light of my face. {29:25} I chose their way, and I sat as chief, and dwelt like a king in the army, as one who comforts mourners.

{30:1} But now those younger than I mock me, whose fathers I would have disdained to set with my dogs. {30:2} What profit is the strength of their hands to me, since their old age is gone? {30:3} They are solitary because of want and famine; they fled into the wilderness, desolate and waste. {30:4} They cut up mallows by the bushes and juniper roots for their food. {30:5} They were driven away from among men (they cried after them as after a thief); {30:6} to dwell in the cliffs of the valleys, in caves of the earth and in the rocks. {30:7} Among the bushes, they brayed; under the thorns, they gathered together. {30:8} They were children of fools, yes, children of base men; they were worse than the earth. {30:9} And now I am their song; yes, I am their byword. {30:10} They abhor me; they flee far from me and do not hesitate to spit in my face. {30:11} Because God has loosened my cord and afflicted me, they have let loose the bridle before me. {30:12} On my right hand rise the youth; they push my feet away and raise up against me the ways of their destruction. {30:13} They ruin my path; they advance my calamity; they have no helper. {30:14} They come upon me like a wide breaking of waters; in desolation, they roll themselves upon me. {30:15} Terrors are turned upon me; they pursue my soul like the wind, and my welfare passes away like a cloud. {30:16} And now my soul is poured out within me; the days of affliction have seized me. {30:17} My bones are pierced in the night season, and my sinews have no rest. {30:18} By the great force of my disease, my garment is changed; it binds me like the collar of my coat. {30:19} He has cast me into the mire, and I have become like dust and ashes. {30:20} I cry out to You, but You do not hear me; I stand up, but You do not regard me. {30:21} You have become cruel to me; with Your strong hand, You oppose Yourself against me. {30:22} You lift me up to the wind; You cause me to ride upon it, and You dissolve my substance. {30:23} For I know that You will bring me to death, and to the house appointed for all living. {30:24} Yet, He will not stretch out His hand to the grave, though they cry out in destruction. {30:25} Did I not weep for him who was in trouble? Was my soul not grieved for the poor? {30:26} When I looked for good, then evil came to me; and when I waited for light, there came darkness. {30:27} My insides boiled and rested not; the days of affliction confronted me. {30:28} I went mourning without the sun; I stood up and cried in the congregation. {30:29} I am a brother to jackals and a companion to owls. {30:30} My skin is black upon me, and my bones are burned with heat. {30:31} My harp is turned to mourning, and my flute into the voice of those who weep.

{31:1} I made a covenant with my eyes; why then should I think about a young woman? {31:2} For what portion does God have from above? What inheritance does the Almighty have from on high? {31:3} Is not destruction the fate of the wicked? Is there not a strange punishment for those who do wrong? {31:4} Does He not see my ways and count all my steps? {31:5} If I have walked in vanity, or if my foot has rushed toward deceit; {31:6} let me be weighed in an even balance, so that God may know my integrity. {31:7} If my steps have turned away from the path, if my heart has followed my eyes, and if any stain has clung to my hands; {31:8} then let me sow, and let another eat; let my offspring be uprooted. {31:9} If my heart has been deceived by a woman, or if I have lurked at my neighbor's door; {31:10} then let my wife grind for another, and let others bow down upon her. {31:11} For this is a heinous crime; yes, it is an iniquity (wrongdoing) to be punished by the judges. {31:12} For it is a fire that consumes to destruction and would root out all my harvest. {31:13} If I have despised the cause of my servant or maidservant when they contended with me; {31:14} what then shall I do when God rises up? When He visits, what shall I answer Him? {31:15} Did not He who made me in the womb make them? Did not one fashion us in the womb? {31:16} If I have withheld anything from the poor, or caused the eyes of the widow to fail; {31:17} or if I have eaten my morsel alone, and the fatherless has not eaten from it; {31:18} (for from my youth, he was raised with me, as with a father, and I have guided her from my mother's womb); {31:19} if I have seen any perish for lack of clothing, or any poor without covering; {31:20} if his loins have not blessed me, and if he was not warmed with the fleece of my sheep; {31:21} if I have lifted my hand against the fatherless when I saw my help at the gate; {31:22} then let my arm fall from my shoulder blade, and let my arm be broken from the bone. {31:23} For destruction from God was a terror to me, and because of His greatness, I could not endure. {31:24} If I have made gold my hope, or said to fine gold, "You are my confidence"; {31:25} if I rejoiced because my wealth was great and because my hand had gained much; {31:26} if I beheld the sun when it shined, or the moon walking in brightness; {31:27} and my heart has been secretly enticed, or my mouth has kissed my hand; {31:28} this also would be iniquity to be punished by the judge, for I would have denied the God who is above. {31:29} If I rejoiced at the destruction of someone who hated me, or lifted myself up when evil found him; {31:30} neither have I allowed my mouth to sin by wishing a curse upon his soul. {31:31} If the men of my household did not say, "Oh, that we had some of his flesh! We cannot be satisfied."

{31:32} The stranger did not lodge in the street; I opened my doors to the traveler. {31:33} If I covered my transgressions like Adam, by hiding my iniquity in my bosom; {31:34} did I fear a great multitude, or did the contempt of families terrify me, that I kept silent and did not go out of the door? {31:35} Oh, that someone would hear me! Behold, my desire is that the Almighty would answer me, and that my adversary had written a book. {31:36} Surely I would take it upon my shoulder and bind it like a crown to me. {31:37} I would declare to Him the number of my steps; I would approach Him like a prince. {31:38} If my land cries out against me, or if its furrows complain; {31:39} if I have eaten its fruits without paying, or if I have caused its owners to lose their lives; {31:40} let thorns grow instead of wheat, and foul weeds instead of barley. The words of Job are ended.

{32:1} So these three men stopped answering Job, because he was righteous in his own eyes. {32:2} Then the anger of Elihu, son of Barachel the Buzite, of the family of Ram, was kindled against Job because he justified himself rather than God. {32:3} His anger was also kindled against Job's three friends because they had found no answer and yet had condemned Job. {32:4} Now Elihu had waited until Job had spoken because they were older than he. {32:5} When Elihu saw that there was no answer in the mouths of these three men, his anger was kindled. {32:6} And Elihu, son of Barachel the Buzite, answered and said, "I am young, and you are very old; therefore I was afraid and did not show you my opinion. {32:7} I said, 'Days should speak, and many years should teach wisdom.' {32:8} But there is a spirit in man, and the inspiration of the Almighty gives them understanding. {32:9} Great men are not always wise; neither do the aged understand judgment. {32:10} Therefore I said, 'Listen to me; I will also show my opinion.' {32:11} Behold, I waited for your words; I listened to your reasons while you searched out what to say. {32:12} Yes, I paid attention to you, and behold, there was none of you that convinced Job or that answered his words: {32:13} lest you should say, 'We have found wisdom; God has thrown him down, not man.' {32:14} Now he has not directed his words against me, nor will I answer him with your speeches. {32:15} They were amazed; they answered no more; they stopped speaking. {32:16} When I had waited (for they spoke not, but stood still and answered no more); {32:17} I said, 'I will answer also my part; I will show my opinion. {32:18} For I am full of matter; the spirit within me constrains me. {32:19} Behold, my belly is like wine that has no vent; it is ready to burst like new bottles. {32:20} I will speak so that I may be refreshed; I will open my lips and answer. {32:21} Let me not, I pray, accept any man's person, nor let me give flattering titles to any man. {32:22} For I do not know how to give flattering titles; in doing so, my Maker would soon take me away.

{33:1} Therefore, Job, I ask you to listen to my words and pay attention to all my thoughts. {33:2} Look, now I have opened my mouth; my tongue has spoken. {33:3} My words will come from the sincerity of my heart; my lips will express knowledge clearly. {33:4} The Spirit of God made me, and the breath of the Almighty gave me life. {33:5} If you can answer me, arrange your words before me and stand up. {33:6} Look, I am here in God's place, formed from clay just like you. {33:7} My terror will not frighten you, and my hand will not weigh heavily on you. {33:8} Surely you have spoken in my hearing, and I have heard your words, saying, {33:9} "I am clean without transgression; I am innocent; there is no wrongdoing in me." {33:10} Look, He finds reasons to oppose me; He considers me His enemy. {33:11} He puts my feet in the stocks and watches all my paths. {33:12} Look, in this you are not right; I will answer you: God is greater than man. {33:13} Why do you contend with Him? He does not need to explain any of His actions. {33:14} For God speaks once, yes, even twice, yet man does not perceive it. {33:15} In a dream, in a vision of the night, when deep sleep falls upon men and slumbering on the bed; {33:16} then He opens the ears of men and seals their instruction, {33:17} so that He may turn man from his purpose and hide pride from man. {33:18} He keeps back his soul from the pit and his life from perishing by the sword. {33:19} He is also chastened with pain upon his bed, and the multitude of his bones with strong pain. {33:20} So that his life hates bread, and his soul finds no appetite for delicacies. {33:21} His flesh wastes away so that it cannot be seen, and his bones, which were not seen, stick out. {33:22} Yes, his soul draws near to the grave, and his life to the destroyers. {33:23} If there is a messenger with him, an interpreter, one among a thousand, to show man his uprightness; {33:24} then He is gracious to him and says, "Deliver him from going down to the pit; I have found a ransom." {33:25} His flesh will be fresher than a child's; he will return to the days of his youth. {33:26} He will pray to God, and He will be favorable to him; he will see His face with joy, for He will render to man his righteousness. {33:27} He looks at men, and if any say, "I have sinned and perverted what was right, and it did not benefit me"; {33:28} He will deliver his soul from going into the pit, and his life will see the light. {33:29} Look, all these things God works with man often, {33:30} to bring back his soul from the pit, to be enlightened with the light of the living. {33:31} Pay attention, O Job, listen to me: hold your peace, and I will speak. {33:32} If you have anything to say, answer me; speak, for I want to justify you. {33:33} If not, listen to me: hold your peace, and I will teach you wisdom.

{34:1} Furthermore, Elihu answered and said, {34:2} "Listen to my words, O wise men; give ear to me, you who have knowledge. {34:3} For the ear tests words as the mouth tastes food. {34:4} Let us choose what is right for ourselves; let us know among ourselves what is good. {34:5} For Job has said, 'I am righteous, and God has taken away my judgment.' {34:6} Should I lie against my right? My wound is incurable without transgression. {34:7} What man is like Job, who drinks in scorn like water? {34:8} Who goes in the company of workers of wrongdoing and walks with wicked men? {34:9} For he has said, 'It profits a man nothing that he should delight himself in God.' {34:10} Therefore, listen to me, you men of understanding: far be it from God to do wickedness, and from the Almighty to commit wrongdoing. {34:11} For He will repay a man according to his work and cause every man to find according to his ways. {34:12} Yes, surely God will not do wickedly, nor will the Almighty pervert justice. {34:13} Who has given Him authority over the earth? Who has arranged the whole world? {34:14} If He set His heart on man, if He gathered to Himself His spirit and breath; {34:15} all flesh would perish together, and man would return to dust. {34:16} If you have understanding, hear this: listen to my words. {34:17} Should even the one who hates justice govern? Will you condemn the One who is most just? {34:18} Is it right to say to a king, 'You are wicked'? And to princes, 'You are ungodly'? {34:19} How much less to Him who does not show favoritism to princes and does not regard the rich more than the poor, for they all are the work of His hands. {34:20} In a moment they will die, and the people will be troubled at midnight and pass away; the mighty will be taken away without hand. {34:21} For His eyes are upon the ways of man, and He sees all his goings. {34:22} There is no darkness, nor shadow of death, where the workers of iniquity may hide themselves. {34:23} For He will not lay upon man more than right; that he should enter into judgment with God. {34:24} He will break in pieces mighty men without number and set others in their place. {34:25} Therefore He knows their works and overturns them in the night so that they are destroyed. {34:26} He strikes them as wicked men in the sight of others; {34:27} because they turned back from Him and would not consider any of His ways; {34:28} so that the cry of the poor comes to Him, and He hears the cry of the afflicted. {34:29} When He gives quietness, who can make trouble? And when He hides His face, who can see Him? Whether it is done against a nation or just against an individual: {34:30} that the hypocrite does not reign, lest the people be ensnared. {34:31} Surely it is appropriate to say to God, 'I have borne chastisement; I will not offend anymore. {34:32} Teach me what I do not see; if I have done wrongdoing, I will do no more.' {34:33} Should it be according to your mind? He will repay it, whether you refuse or choose; and not I: therefore speak what you know. {34:34} Let men of understanding tell me, and let a wise man listen to me. {34:35} Job has spoken without knowledge, and his words were without wisdom. {34:36} My desire is that Job may be tested to the end because of his responses for wicked men. {34:37} For he adds rebellion to his sin; he claps his hands among us and multiplies his words against God.

{35:1} Elihu spoke further and said, {35:2} "Do you think this is right, that you said, 'My righteousness is greater than God's'? {35:3} For you said, 'What advantage is it to you? What profit will I have if I am cleansed from my sin?' {35:4} I will answer you and your companions. {35:5} Look to the heavens and see; behold the clouds that are higher than you. {35:6} If you sin, what do you do to Him? If your transgressions increase, what do you do to Him? {35:7} If you are righteous, what do you give Him? What does He receive from your hand? {35:8} Your wickedness may hurt a fellow man; your righteousness may benefit a human being. {35:9} Because of the multitude of oppressions, they cause the oppressed to cry out; they cry out because of the power of the mighty. {35:10} But no one asks, 'Where is God my Maker, who gives songs in the night; {35:11} who teaches us more than the animals of the earth and makes us wiser than the birds of the sky?' {35:12} They cry out, but no one answers, because of the pride of evil people. {35:13} Surely God will not hear empty words, nor will the Almighty regard them. {35:14} Even though you say you will not see Him, judgment is before Him; therefore, trust in Him. {35:15} But now, because it is not so, He has visited in His anger, yet He does not know it in great extremity. {35:16} Therefore, Job opens his mouth in vain; he multiplies words without knowledge.

{36:1} Elihu also continued and said, {36:2} "Allow me a little time, and I will show you that I still have something to say on God's behalf. {36:3} I will gather my knowledge from far away and attribute righteousness to my Maker. {36:4} For truly, my words will not be false; He who is perfect in knowledge is with you. {36:5} Look, God is mighty and does not despise anyone; He is mighty in strength and wisdom. {36:6} He does not preserve the life of the wicked but gives justice to the poor. {36:7} He does not take His eyes away from the righteous; He places them with kings on thrones; yes, He establishes them forever, and they are exalted. {36:8} If they are bound in chains and held in cords of affliction, {36:9} then He shows them their work and their transgressions that have exceeded. {36:10} He also opens their ear to discipline and commands that they turn from wrongdoing. {36:11} If they obey and serve Him, they will spend their days in prosperity and their years in pleasure. {36:12} But if they do not obey, they will perish by the sword and die without knowledge. {36:13} But the hypocrites in heart store up anger; they do not cry out when He binds them. {36:14} They die in youth, and their lives are among the unclean. {36:15} He delivers the poor in their affliction and opens their ears in oppression. {36:16} He would have removed you from distress into a wide place where there is no trouble, and what should be set on your table would be full of abundance. {36:17} But you have fulfilled the judgment of the wicked; judgment and justice lay hold on you. {36:18} Because there is wrath, beware that He does not take you away with His stroke; then no great ransom can deliver you. {36:19} Will He value your riches? No, not gold, nor all the power you have. {36:20} Do not long for the night when people are cut off in their place. {36:21} Take heed; do not regard wrongdoing, for you have chosen this rather than affliction. {36:22} Look, God is exalted by His power; who teaches like Him? {36:23} Who has prescribed His way? Who can say, 'You have done wrong'? {36:24} Remember to magnify His work, which men can see. {36:25} Every man may see it; man can behold it from afar. {36:26} Look, God is great, and we do not know Him; nor can the number of His years be explored. {36:27} For He makes small the drops of water; they pour down rain according to its vapor. {36:28} Which the clouds drop and distill abundantly upon man. {36:29} Can anyone understand the spreadings of the clouds or the noise of His dwelling? {36:30} Look, He spreads His light upon it and covers the depths of the sea. {36:31} For by them He judges the people; He gives food in abundance. {36:32} With clouds, He covers the light and commands it not to shine through the cloud that comes between. {36:33} The noise thereof shows concerning it; the cattle also regarding the vapor.

{37:1} At this, my heart trembles and is moved from its place. {37:2} Listen closely to the sound of His voice, the noise that comes from His mouth. {37:3} He directs it under the whole heaven, and His lightning to the ends of the earth. {37:4} After it, a voice roars; He thunders with the voice of His majesty; and He will not hold back when His voice is heard. {37:5} God thunders marvelously with His voice; He does great things that we cannot comprehend. {37:6} For He says to the snow, 'Fall on the earth'; and to the small rain and the heavy rain of His strength. {37:7} He seals up the hand of every person so that all may know His work. {37:8} Then the animals go into their dens and remain in their places. {37:9} From the south comes the storm, and cold from the north. {37:10} By the breath of God, frost is given; the expanse of the waters is restrained. {37:11} Also, by watering, He tires out the thick clouds; He scatters His bright clouds. {37:12} They are turned around by His plans, to do whatever He commands them on the face of the earth. {37:13} He causes it to happen, whether for correction, for His land, or for mercy. {37:14} Listen to this, Job: stand still and consider the wonderful works of God. {37:15} Do you know when God set them in place and caused the light of His clouds to shine? {37:16} Do you know the balancing of the clouds, the wonderful works of Him who is perfect in knowledge? {37:17} How your clothes become warm when He quiets the earth by the south wind? {37:18} Have you spread out the sky with Him, strong like a polished mirror? {37:19} Teach us what we should say to Him; we cannot order our speech because of the darkness. {37:20} Should it be told to Him that I speak? If a man speaks, he will surely be swallowed up. {37:21} And now, men do not see the bright light that is in the clouds; but the wind passes and clears them. {37:22} Fair weather comes out of the north; with God is awesome majesty. {37:23} Concerning the Almighty, we cannot find Him out; He is excellent in power, in judgment, and in great justice; He will not oppress. {37:24} Therefore, people fear Him; He does not regard any who are wise in heart.

{38:1} Then the LORD answered Job out of the storm and said, {38:2} "Who is this that darkens counsel with words without knowledge? {38:3} Brace yourself like a man; I will demand of you, and you answer Me. {38:4} Where were you when I laid the foundations of the earth? Declare, if you have understanding. {38:5} Who has laid its measurements, if you know? Who has stretched the line upon it? {38:6} On what were its foundations set? Who laid its cornerstone, {38:7} when the morning stars sang together and all the sons of God shouted for joy? {38:8} Or who shut up the sea behind doors when it burst forth, as if it had come from the womb? {38:9} When I made the clouds its garment and thick darkness a swaddling band for it, {38:10} and broke up for it My decreed place, and set bars and doors, {38:11} and said, 'Thus far you may come, but no further; here shall your proud waves stop'? {38:12} Have you ever commanded the morning since your days began and caused the dawn to know its place, {38:13} that it might take hold of the ends of the earth and shake the wicked out of it? {38:14} It is changed like clay under a seal; they stand like a garment. {38:15} From the wicked, their light is withheld, and the high arm is broken. {38:16} Have you entered the springs of the sea? Have you walked in the depths of the ocean? {38:17} Have the gates of death been opened to you? Have you seen the doors of the shadow of death? {38:18} Have you comprehended the breadth of the earth? Declare if you know it all. {38:19} Where is the way where light dwells? And as for darkness, where is its place, {38:20} that you may take it to its territory and that you may know the paths to its house? {38:21} Do you know it, because you were born then? Or because the number of your days is great? {38:22} Have you entered the storehouses of the snow? Have you seen the storehouses of the hail, {38:23} which I have reserved for the time of trouble, for the day of battle and war? {38:24} By what way is the light divided, scattering the east wind upon the earth? {38:25} Who has divided a watercourse for the overflowing of waters, or a path for the lightning of thunder, {38:26} to cause it to rain on the earth where no person is, in the wilderness where there is no one; {38:27} to satisfy the desolate and waste ground and to cause the bud of the tender herb to spring forth? {38:28} Does the rain have a father? Who has begotten the drops of dew? {38:29} From whose womb did the ice come? And the hoary frost of heaven, who has gendered it? {38:30} The waters are hidden as with a stone, and the surface of the deep is frozen. {38:31} Can you bind the sweet influences of the Pleiades or loose the cords of Orion? {38:32} Can you bring forth Mazzaroth in its season? Or can you guide Arcturus with his sons? {38:33} Do you know the ordinances of heaven? Can you set their rule over the earth? {38:34} Can you lift up your voice to the clouds, that an abundance of waters may cover you? {38:35} Can you send forth lightning that they may go and say to you, 'Here we are'? {38:36} Who has put wisdom in the inward parts? Who has given understanding to the heart? {38:37} Who can number the clouds by wisdom? Who can empty the bottles of heaven, {38:38} when the dust hardens into a mass and the clods stick together? {38:39} Will you hunt for prey for the lion or fill the appetite of the young lions, {38:40} when they crouch in their dens and lie in wait in their lairs? {38:41} Who provides for the raven its food when its young ones cry out to God, wandering for lack of food?

{39:1} Do you know the time when the wild goats of the rock give birth? Can you observe when the deer calve? {39:2} Can you count the months they fulfill? Do you know the time they give birth? {39:3} They bow down, bring forth their young, and cast out their pains. {39:4} Their young ones thrive; they grow up with grain; they go out and do not return to them. {39:5} Who has set the wild donkey free? Who has loosed its bonds? {39:6} I have made the wilderness its home and the barren land its dwelling. {39:7} It scorns the crowd of the city; it does not heed the shouts of the driver. {39:8} The mountains are its pasture, and it searches for every green thing. {39:9} Will the unicorn (mythical creature) be willing to serve you or stay by your feeding trough? {39:10} Can you tie up the unicorn with a rope in the furrow? Will it plow the valleys for you? {39:11} Will you trust it because its strength is great? Will you leave your work to it? {39:12} Will you believe that it will bring home your harvest and gather it into your barn? {39:13} Did you give beautiful wings to the peacocks or wings and feathers to the ostrich? {39:14} She leaves her eggs on the ground and warms them in the dust, {39:15} forgetting that a foot may crush them or that a wild animal may break them. {39:16} She is hardened against her young ones as if they were not hers; her labor is in vain without fear; {39:17} because God has deprived her of wisdom and has not given her understanding. {39:18} When she lifts herself up on high, she scorns the horse and its rider. {39:19} Have you given the horse strength? Have you clothed its neck with thunder? {39:20} Can you make it afraid like a grasshopper? Its proud snorting is frightening. {39:21} It paws in the valley and rejoices in its strength; it goes to meet the armed men. {39:22} It mocks fear and is not afraid; it does not turn back from the sword. {39:23} The quiver rattles against it, the glittering spear and shield. {39:24} It swallows the ground with fierceness and rage; it does not believe that the sound of the trumpet is real. {39:25} It shouts among the trumpets, 'Ha, ha!' It smells battle from afar, the thunder of the captains, and the shouting. {39:26} Does the hawk fly by your wisdom and stretch its wings toward the south? {39:27} Does the eagle soar at your command and make its nest on high? {39:28} It dwells and rests on the rock, on the crag of the rock, and in the stronghold. {39:29} From there, it seeks its prey, and its eyes look far away. {39:30} Its young ones also drink blood, and where the slain are, there it is.

{40:1} Moreover, the LORD answered Job and said, {40:2} "Can the one who argues with the Almighty instruct Him? The one who accuses God, let him answer." {40:3} Then Job answered the LORD and said, {40:4} "I am unworthy; what should I say to You? I will put my hand over my mouth. {40:5} I have spoken once, but I will not answer; yes, twice, but I will proceed no further." {40:6} Then the LORD spoke to Job out of the whirlwind and said, {40:7} "Brace yourself like a man; I will demand of you, and you answer Me. {40:8} Will you annul My judgment? Will you condemn Me so that you can be righteous? {40:9} Do you have an arm like God? Can you thunder with a voice like His? {40:10} Dress yourself now with majesty and splendor; array yourself with glory and beauty. {40:11} Unleash the fury of your wrath, and look at everyone who is proud and bring them low. {40:12} Look at all who are proud and humble them; tread down the wicked in their place. {40:13} Hide them in the dust together; bind their faces in secret. {40:14} Then I will also confess to you that your own right hand can save you. {40:15} Look now at behemoth (a large creature), which I made along with you; it eats grass like an ox. {40:16} Look, its strength is in its loins, and its power is in the muscles of its belly. {40:17} It moves its tail like a cedar; the sinews of its thighs are wrapped together. {40:18} Its bones are like strong pieces of bronze; its limbs are like bars of iron. {40:19} It is the chief of the works of God; He who made it can make His sword approach it. {40:20} Surely the mountains bring it food, where all the beasts of the field play. {40:21} It lies under the shady trees, in the hiding place of the reeds and marshes. {40:22} The shady trees cover it with their shadow; the willows by the brook surround it. {40:23} Look, it drinks up a river and is not in haste; it trusts that it can draw the Jordan into its mouth. {40:24} It sees it with its eyes; its nose pierces through snares.

{41:1} Can you draw out Leviathan (a large sea creature) with a hook? Can you catch his tongue with a cord that you lower? {41:2} Can you put a hook in his nose? Can you pierce his jaw with a thorn? {41:3} Will he make many supplications to you? Will he speak soft words to you? {41:4} Will he make a covenant with you? Will you take him as a servant forever? {41:5} Will you play with him like a bird? Will you bind him for your maidens? {41:6} Will your companions feast on him? Will they divide him among the merchants? {41:7} Can you fill his skin with barbed irons? Can you pierce his head with fish spears? {41:8} Lay your hand on him; remember the battle and do no more. {41:9} Behold, hope in him is in vain; will not one be cast down even at the sight of him? {41:10} No one is so fierce that dares to stir him up; who then is able to stand before Me? {41:11} Who has challenged Me that I should repay him? Everything under heaven is Mine. {41:12} I will not conceal his parts, his power, or his majestic form. {41:13} Who can uncover the surface of his garment? Who can approach him with a double bridle? {41:14} Who can open the doors of his face? His teeth are fearsome all around. {41:15} His scales are his pride, tightly sealed. {41:16} They are so close together that no air can come between them. {41:17} They stick together and cannot be separated. {41:18} His snorting gives off light; his eyes are like the eyelids of the morning. {41:19} From his mouth come burning torches, and sparks of fire leap out. {41:20} Smoke billows from his nostrils, like a boiling pot or cauldron. {41:21} His breath sets coals ablaze, and a flame goes out of his mouth. {41:22} Strength resides in his neck, and joy turns to fear before him. {41:23} His flesh is tightly joined; it is firm and cannot be moved. {41:24} His heart is as hard as stone, yes, as hard as a lower millstone. {41:25} When he raises himself up, the mighty are afraid; they purify themselves because of his crushing. {41:26} The sword that reaches him cannot prevail; neither the spear, the dart, nor the armor. {41:27} He regards iron as straw and bronze as rotten wood. {41:28} The arrow cannot make him flee; sling stones are like chaff to him. {41:29} Darts are counted as chaff; he laughs at the shaking of a spear. {41:30} Sharp stones are under him; he spreads sharp points over the mud. {41:31} He makes the deep boil like a pot; he makes the sea like a pot of ointment. {41:32} He leaves a shining path behind him; one would think the deep is white with age. {41:33} On earth, there is nothing like him, made without fear. {41:34} He looks at all high things; he is king over all the children of pride.

{42:1} Then Job answered the LORD and said, {42:2} "I know that You can do everything, and that no thought can be withheld from You. {42:3} Who is he that hides counsel without knowledge? Therefore, I have uttered what I did not understand, things too wonderful for me, which I did not know. {42:4} Listen, I plead with You, and I will speak; I will ask You, and You declare to me. {42:5} I have heard of You by the hearing of the ear, but now my eye sees You. {42:6} Therefore, I despise myself and repent in dust and ashes." {42:7} After the LORD had spoken these words to Job, He said to Eliphaz the Temanite, "My anger is kindled against you and against your two friends, for you have not spoken of Me what is right, as My servant Job has. {42:8} Therefore, take for yourselves seven bulls and seven rams, and go to My servant Job and offer up a burnt offering for yourselves; and My servant Job shall pray for you, for I will accept him, lest I deal with you according to your folly, because you have not spoken of Me what is right, like My servant Job." {42:9} So Eliphaz the Temanite, Bildad the Shuhite, and Zophar the Naamathite went and did as the LORD commanded them; the LORD also accepted Job. {42:10} And the LORD restored Job's fortunes when he prayed for his friends, and the LORD gave Job twice as much as he had before. {42:11} Then all his brothers, sisters, and acquaintances came to eat bread with him in his house; they bemoaned him and comforted him for all the evil that the LORD had brought upon him. Each one also gave him a piece of money and an earring of gold. {42:12} So the LORD blessed the latter part of Job's life more than the beginning; he had fourteen thousand sheep, six thousand camels, a thousand yoke of oxen, and a thousand female donkeys. {42:13} He also had seven sons and three daughters. {42:14} He named the first Jemima, the second Kezia, and the third Kerenhappuch. {42:15} In all the land, no women were found as beautiful as Job's daughters, and their father gave them an inheritance among their brothers. {42:16} After this, Job lived a hundred and forty years and saw his children and their children to the fourth generation. {42:17} So Job died, old and full of days.

The Book of Psalms

{1:1} Blessed is the person who does not follow the advice of the wicked, nor stand in the path of sinners, nor sit with those who mock. {1:2} Instead, his joy is in the law of the LORD, and he reflects on it day and night. {1:3} He will be like a tree planted by streams of water, bearing fruit in its season; its leaves will not wither, and everything he does will succeed. {1:4} The wicked are not like this; they are like chaff that the wind blows away. {1:5} Therefore, the wicked will not stand in judgment, nor will sinners be part of the congregation of the righteous. {1:6} For the LORD knows the way of the righteous, but the way of the wicked will perish.

{2:1} Why do the nations rage, and the people plot in vain? {2:2} The kings of the earth take their stand, and the rulers gather together against the LORD and his anointed, saying, {2:3} "Let's break their chains and throw off their shackles." {2:4} The One who sits in heaven laughs; the LORD scoffs at them. {2:5} He will speak to them in his anger and terrify them in his wrath. {2:6} Yet I have installed my king on Zion, my holy mountain. {2:7} I will proclaim the LORD's decree: He said to me, "You are my Son; today I have become your Father. {2:8} Ask me, and I will make the nations your inheritance, the ends of the earth your possession. {2:9} You will break them with an iron scepter; you will dash them to pieces like pottery." {2:10} Therefore, you kings, be wise; be warned, you rulers of the earth. {2:11} Serve the LORD with fear and celebrate his rule with trembling. {2:12} Kiss the Son, or he will be angry, and your way will lead to destruction, for his wrath can flare up in a moment. Blessed are all who take refuge in him.

{3:1} LORD, how many are my foes! How many rise up against me! {3:2} Many are saying of me, "God will not deliver him." Selah. {3:3} But you, LORD, are a shield around me, my glory, the One who lifts my head high. {3:4} I call out to the LORD, and he answers me from his holy mountain. Selah. {3:5} I lie down and sleep; I wake again because the LORD sustains me. {3:6} I will not fear though tens of thousands assail me on every side. {3:7} Arise, LORD! Deliver me, my God! Strike all my enemies on the jaw; break the teeth of the wicked. {3:8} Salvation belongs to the LORD; may your blessing be on your people. Selah.

{4:1} Answer me when I call to you, my righteous God. Give me relief from my distress; have mercy on me and hear my prayer. {4:2} How long, you people, will you turn my glory into shame? How long will you love delusions and seek false gods? Selah. {4:3} Know that the LORD has set apart his faithful servant for himself; the LORD hears when I call to him. {4:4} Tremble and do not sin; when you are on your beds, search your hearts and be silent. Selah. {4:5} Offer the sacrifices of the righteous and trust in the LORD. {4:6} Many, LORD, are asking, "Who will bring us prosperity?" Let the light of your face shine on us. {4:7} Fill my heart with joy when their grain and new wine abound. {4:8} In peace I will lie down and sleep, for you alone, LORD, make me dwell in safety.

{5:1} Listen to my words, LORD, consider my lament. {5:2} Hear my cry for help, my King and my God, for to you I pray. {5:3} In the morning, LORD, you hear my voice; in the morning I lay my requests before you and wait expectantly. {5:4} For you are not a God who takes pleasure in wickedness; with you, evil people are not welcome. {5:5} The arrogant cannot stand in your presence; you hate all who do wrong. {5:6} You destroy those who tell lies; the LORD abhors the violent and deceitful. {5:7} But I, by your great love, can come into your house; in reverence, I bow down toward your holy temple. {5:8} Lead me, LORD, in your righteousness because of my enemies—make your way straight before me. {5:9} Not a word from their mouth can be trusted; their hearts are full of malice. Their throats are open graves; with their tongues, they tell lies. {5:10} Declare them guilty, O God! Let their intrigues be their downfall. Banish them for their many sins, for they have rebelled against you. {5:11} But let all who take refuge in you be glad; let them ever sing for joy. Spread your protection over them, that those who love your name may rejoice in you. {5:12} Surely, LORD, you bless the righteous; you surround them with your favor as with a shield.

{6:1} O LORD, don't rebuke me in your anger or discipline me in your hot displeasure. {6:2} Have mercy on me, O LORD, for I am weak; O LORD, heal me, for my bones are troubled. {6:3} My soul is also deeply troubled; but you, O LORD, how long will this last? {6:4} Turn, O LORD, and rescue my soul; save me because of your mercy. {6:5} For in death, there is no remembrance of you; in the grave, who will give you thanks? {6:6} I am worn out from my groaning; all night long I make my bed swim; I soak my couch with my tears. {6:7} My eyes grow weak with sorrow; they fail because of all my enemies. {6:8} Depart from me, all you who do evil, for the LORD has heard the voice of my weeping. {6:9} The LORD has heard my cry for mercy; the LORD accepts my prayer. {6:10} May all my enemies be ashamed and dismayed; may they turn back in sudden disgrace.

{7:1} O LORD my God, I put my trust in you; save me from all those who persecute me, and deliver me. {7:2} Or they will tear my soul like a lion and rip it to pieces; there's no one to rescue me. {7:3} O LORD my God, if I have done this, if there is guilt on my hands; {7:4} if I have repaid my friend with evil or without cause have robbed my foe— {7:5} then let my enemy pursue me and overtake me; let him trample my life to the ground and make me sleep in the dust. Selah. {7:6} Arise, O LORD, in your anger; rise up against the rage of my enemies. Awake, my God, and decree justice. {7:7} Let the assembly of the peoples gather around you; rule over them from on high. {7:8} Let the LORD judge the peoples; judge me, O LORD, according to my righteousness, according to my integrity, O Most High. {7:9} Bring to an end the violence of the wicked and make the righteous secure, you, the righteous God who probes minds and hearts. {7:10} My shield is God Most High, who saves the upright in heart. {7:11} God is a righteous judge, a God who displays his wrath every day. {7:12} If he does not relent, he will sharpen his sword; he will bend and string his bow. {7:13} He has prepared his deadly weapons; he makes ready his flaming arrows. {7:14} Whoever is pregnant with evil conceives trouble and gives birth to disillusionment. {7:15} Whoever digs a hole and scoops it out falls into the pit they have made. {7:16} The trouble they cause recoils on them; their violence comes down on their own heads. {7:17} I will give thanks to the LORD because of his righteousness; I will sing the praises of the name of the LORD Most High.

{8:1} O LORD, our Lord, how majestic is your name in all the earth! You have set your glory in the heavens. {8:2} Through the praise of children and infants, you have established a stronghold against your enemies, to silence the foe and the avenger. {8:3} When I consider your heavens, the work of your fingers, the moon and the stars, which you have set in place, {8:4} what is mankind that you are mindful of them, human beings that you care for them? {8:5} You have made them a little lower than the angels and crowned them with glory and honor. {8:6} You made them rulers over the works of your hands; you put everything under their feet: {8:7} all flocks and herds, and the animals of the wild, {8:8} the birds in the sky, and the fish in the sea, all that swim the paths of the seas. {8:9} O LORD, our Lord, how majestic is your name in all the earth!

{9:1} I will give thanks to you, LORD, with all my heart; I will tell of all your wonderful deeds. {9:2} I will be glad and rejoice in you; I will sing the praises of your name, O Most High. {9:3} My enemies turn back; they stumble and perish before you. {9:4} For you have upheld my right and my cause, sitting enthroned as the righteous judge. {9:5} You have rebuked the nations and destroyed the wicked; you have blotted out their name forever and ever. {9:6} Endless ruin has overtaken my enemies, you have uprooted their cities; even the memory of them has perished. {9:7} The LORD reigns forever; he has established his throne for judgment. {9:8} He rules the world in righteousness and judges the peoples with equity. {9:9} The LORD is a refuge for the oppressed, a stronghold in times of trouble. {9:10} Those who know your name trust in you, for you, LORD, have never forsaken those who seek you. {9:11} Sing the praises of the LORD, enthroned in Zion; proclaim among the nations what he has done. {9:12} For he who avenges blood remembers; he does not ignore the cries of the afflicted. {9:13} Have mercy on me, LORD; see how my enemies persecute me! Snatch me from the jaws of death, {9:14} that I may declare your praises in the gates of the Daughter of Zion and there rejoice in your salvation. {9:15} The nations have fallen into the pit they have dug; their feet are caught in the net they have hidden. {9:16} The LORD is known by his acts of justice; the wicked are ensnared by the work of their hands. Higgaion. Selah. {9:17} The wicked go down to the realm of the dead, all the nations that forget God. {9:18} The needy will not always be forgotten, nor the hope of the afflicted ever perish. {9:19} Arise, LORD, do not let mortals prevail; let the nations be judged in your presence. {9:20} Strike them with terror, LORD; let the nations know they are only mortal. Selah.

{10:1} Why, LORD, do you stand far off? Why do you hide yourself in times of trouble? {10:2} In his arrogance, the wicked man hunts down the weak; let them be caught in the schemes they have devised. {10:3} For the wicked boast about their cravings; they bless the greedy and revile the LORD. {10:4} In his pride, the wicked man does not seek him; in all his thoughts, there is no room for God. {10:5} His ways are always prosperous; your laws are rejected by him; he sneers at all his enemies. {10:6} He says to himself, "Nothing will ever shake me. I'll never be in trouble." {10:7} His mouth is full of lies and threats; trouble and evil are under his tongue. {10:8} He lies in wait near the villages; from ambush, he murders the innocent. His eyes watch in secret for his victims; {10:9} like a lion in cover, he lies in wait. He lies in wait to catch the helpless; he catches the helpless and drags them into his net. {10:10} His victims are crushed, they collapse; they fall under his strength. {10:11} He says to himself, "God will never notice; he covers his face and never sees." {10:12} Arise, LORD! O God, lift up your hand! Do not forget the helpless. {10:13} Why does the wicked man revile God? Why does he say to himself, "He won't call me to account"? {10:14} But you, God, see the trouble of the afflicted; you consider their grief and take it in hand. The victims commit themselves to you; you are the helper of the fatherless. {10:15} Break the arm of the wicked and evil man; call him to account for his wickedness that would not otherwise be found out. {10:16} The LORD is King for ever and ever; the nations will perish from his land. {10:17} You, LORD, hear the desire of the afflicted; you encourage them, and you listen to their cry, {10:18} defending the fatherless and the oppressed, so that mere earthly mortals will never again strike terror.

{11:1} In the LORD I take refuge; how can you say to me, "Flee like a bird to your mountain"? {11:2} For look, the wicked bend their bows; they set their arrows on the strings to shoot secretly at the upright in heart. {11:3} If the foundations are destroyed, what can the righteous do? {11:4} The LORD is in his holy temple; the LORD's throne is in heaven. His eyes observe; his eyelids test the children of men. {11:5} The LORD tests the righteous, but he hates the wicked and those who love violence. {11:6} He will rain coals of fire and brimstone on the wicked and a horrible storm will be their lot. {11:7} For the LORD is righteous; he loves righteousness; the upright will see his face.

{12:1} Help, LORD, for the godly are no more; the faithful have vanished from among men. {12:2} Everyone lies to their neighbor; they speak with flattering lips and a double heart. {12:3} The LORD will silence all flattering lips and every proud tongue. {12:4} They say, "With our tongues we will prevail; our lips are our own; who can be our master?" {12:5} Because of the oppression of the poor and the groaning of the needy, I will now arise, says the LORD; I will protect them from those who malign them. {12:6} The words of the LORD are pure, like silver refined in a furnace, purified seven times. {12:7} You, LORD, will keep them safe; you will protect them from this generation forever. {12:8} The wicked roam freely when the vilest men are exalted.

{13:1} How long, LORD? Will you forget me forever? How long will you hide your face from me? {13:2} How long must I wrestle with my thoughts and day after day have sorrow in my heart? How long will my enemy triumph over me? {13:3} Look on me and answer, LORD my God; give light to my eyes, or I will sleep in death. {13:4} And my enemy will say, "I have overcome him," and my foes will rejoice when I fall. {13:5} But I trust in your unfailing love; my heart rejoices in your salvation. {13:6} I will sing the LORD's praise, for he has been good to me.

{14:1} The fool says in his heart, "There is no God." They are corrupt; their deeds are vile; there is no one who does good. {14:2} The LORD looks down from heaven on all mankind to see if there are any who understand, any who seek God. {14:3} All have turned away, all have become corrupt; there is no one who does good, not even one. {14:4} Do all these evildoers know nothing? They devour my people as though eating bread; they do not call on the LORD. {14:5} There they are, overwhelmed with dread, for God is present in the company of the righteous. {14:6} You evildoers frustrate the plans of the poor, but the LORD is their refuge. {14:7} Oh, that salvation for Israel would come out of Zion! When the LORD restores his people, let Jacob rejoice and Israel be glad.

{15:1} LORD, who may dwell in your sacred tent? Who may live on your holy mountain? {15:2} The one who walks blamelessly, who does what is righteous, who speaks the truth from their heart. {15:3} Whose tongue utters no slander, who does no wrong to a neighbor, and casts no slur on others. {15:4} Who despises a vile person but honors those who fear the LORD; who keeps an oath even when it hurts and does not change their mind. {15:5} Who lends money to the poor without interest; who does not accept a bribe against the innocent. Whoever does these things will never be shaken.

{16:1} Protect me, God, for I trust in you. {16:2} My soul says to the LORD, "You are my Lord; my goodness does not reach you. {16:3} It is for the saints who are in the land, the glorious ones in whom is all my delight." {16:4} Their sorrows will increase who chase after other gods; I will not pour out their drink offerings of blood or speak their names. {16:5} The LORD is my inheritance and my cup; you maintain my lot. {16:6} The boundary lines have fallen for me in pleasant places; indeed, I have a beautiful inheritance. {16:7} I will praise the LORD, who gives me counsel; even at night my heart instructs me. {16:8} I keep the LORD always before me; because he is at my right hand, I will not be shaken. {16:9} Therefore my heart is glad, and my soul rejoices; my body also rests in hope. {16:10} For you will not abandon my soul to the grave, nor will you let your Holy One see decay. {16:11} You make known to me the path of life; in your presence is fullness of joy; at your right hand are eternal pleasures.

{17:1} Hear my righteous plea, LORD; listen to my cry; hear my prayer from lips free of deceit. {17:2} Let my vindication come from you; may your eyes see what is right. {17:3} You have examined my heart and visited me at night; you have tested me and found nothing; I am determined that my mouth will not sin. {17:4} Concerning what others do, by the word of your lips I have kept myself from the ways of the violent. {17:5} My steps have held to your paths; my feet have not slipped. {17:6} I call on you, my God, for you will answer me; turn your ear to me and hear my prayer. {17:7} Show me your marvelous love, you who save by your right hand those who take refuge in you from their foes. {17:8} Keep me as the apple of your eye; hide me in the shadow of your wings {17:9} from the wicked who are out to destroy me, from my mortal enemies who surround me. {17:10} They close up their callous hearts, and their mouths speak with arrogance. {17:11} They have tracked me down; now they surround me, watching my every step, eager to take my life. {17:12} They are like a lion hungry for prey, like a fierce lion crouching in hiding. {17:13} Arise, LORD! Confront them; bring them down; rescue me from the wicked by your sword. {17:14} By your hand, save me from such people, LORD, from those of this world whose reward is in this life. May their bellies be filled with your treasure; may their children gorge themselves on it and may there be leftovers for their little ones. {17:15} As for me, I will be vindicated and will see your face; when I awake, I will be satisfied with seeing your likeness.

{18:1} I love you, LORD, my strength. {18:2} The LORD is my rock, my fortress, and my deliverer; my God is my rock, in whom I take refuge, my shield and the horn of my salvation, my stronghold. {18:3} I call to the LORD, who is worthy of praise, and I am saved from my enemies. {18:4} The cords of death entangled me; the torrents of destruction overwhelmed me. {18:5} The cords of the grave coiled around me; the snares of death confronted me. {18:6} In my distress, I called to the LORD; I cried to my God for help. From his temple he heard my voice; my cry came before him, into his ears. {18:7} The earth trembled and quaked, and the foundations of the mountains shook; they trembled because he was angry. {18:8} Smoke rose from his nostrils; consuming fire came from his mouth, burning coals blazed out of it. {18:9} He parted the heavens and came down; dark clouds were under his feet. {18:10} He mounted the cherubim and flew; he soared on the wings of the wind. {18:11} He made darkness his covering, his canopy around him—the dark rain clouds of the sky. {18:12} Out of the brightness of his presence clouds advanced, with hailstones and bolts of lightning. {18:13} The LORD thundered from heaven; the voice of the Most High resounded. {18:14} He shot his arrows and scattered the enemy, with great bolts of lightning he routed them. {18:15} The valleys of the sea were exposed and the foundations of the earth laid bare at your rebuke, LORD, at the blast of breath from your nostrils. {18:16} He reached down from on high and took hold of me; he drew me out of deep waters. {18:17} He rescued me from my powerful enemy, from my foes who were too strong for me. {18:18} They confronted me in the day of my disaster, but the LORD was my support. {18:19} He brought me out into a spacious place; he rescued me because he delighted in me. {18:20} The LORD has dealt with me according to my righteousness; according to the cleanness of my hands he has rewarded me. {18:21} For I have kept the ways of the LORD; I am not guilty of turning from my God. {18:22} All his laws are before me; I have not turned away from his decrees. {18:23} I have been blameless before him and have kept myself from sin. {18:24} The LORD has rewarded me according to my righteousness, according to the cleanness of my hands in his sight. {18:25} To the faithful, you show yourself faithful; to the blameless, you show yourself blameless; {18:26} to the pure, you show yourself pure; but to the crooked, you show yourself shrewd. {18:27} You save the humble but bring low those whose eyes are haughty. {18:28} You, LORD, keep my lamp burning; my God turns my darkness into light. {18:29} With your help, I can advance against a troop; with my God, I can scale a wall. {18:30} As for God, his way is perfect: the LORD's word is flawless; he shields all who take refuge in him. {18:31} For who is God besides the LORD? And who is the Rock except our God? {18:32} It is God who arms me with strength and keeps my way secure. {18:33} He makes my feet like the feet of a deer; he causes me to stand on the heights. {18:34} He trains my hands for battle; my arms can bend a bow of bronze. {18:35} You make your saving help my shield, and your right hand sustains me; your help has made me great. {18:36} You provide a broad path for my feet, so that my ankles do not give way. {18:37} I pursued my enemies and overtook them; I did not turn back till they were destroyed. {18:38} I crushed them so they could not rise; they fell beneath my feet. {18:39} You armed me with strength for battle; you humbled my adversaries before me. {18:40} You made my enemies turn their backs in flight, and I destroyed those who hated me. {18:41} They cried for help, but there was no one to save them—to the LORD, but he did not answer. {18:42} I ground them as fine as dust borne on the wind; I swept them away like mud in the streets. {18:43} You have delivered me from the attacks of the people; you have made me the head of nations. People I did not know now serve me. {18:44} Foreigners cower before me; as soon as they hear of me, they obey me. {18:45} They all lose heart; they come trembling from their strongholds. {18:46} The LORD lives! Praise be to my Rock! Exalted be God my Savior! {18:47} He is the God who avenges me, who subdues nations under me, {18:48} who saves me from my enemies. You exalted me above my foes; from a violent man you rescued me. {18:49} Therefore I will praise you, LORD, among the nations; I will sing the praises of your name. {18:50} He gives his king great victories; he shows unfailing love to his anointed, to David and to his descendants forever.

{19:1} The heavens declare the glory of God; the skies proclaim the work of his hands. {19:2} Day after day they pour forth speech; night after night they reveal knowledge. {19:3} They have no speech, they use no words; no sound is heard from them. {19:4} Yet their voice goes out into all the earth, their words to the ends of the world. In the heavens, God has pitched a tent for the sun, {19:5} which is like a bridegroom coming out of his chamber, like a champion rejoicing to run his course. {19:6} It rises at one end of the heavens and makes its circuit to the other; nothing is deprived of its warmth. {19:7} The law of the LORD is perfect, refreshing the soul. The statutes of the LORD are trustworthy, making wise the simple. {19:8} The precepts of the LORD are right, giving joy to the heart. The commands of the LORD are radiant, giving light to the eyes. {19:9} The fear of the LORD is pure, enduring forever. The decrees of the LORD are firm, and all of them are righteous. {19:10} They are more precious than gold, than much pure gold; they are sweeter than honey, than honey from the honeycomb. {19:11} By them your servant is warned; in keeping them there is great reward. {19:12} But who can discern their own errors? Forgive my hidden faults. {19:13} Keep your servant also from willful sins; may they not rule over me. Then I will be blameless, innocent of great transgression. {19:14} May these words of my mouth and this meditation of my heart be pleasing in your sight, LORD, my Rock and my Redeemer.

{20:1} May the LORD answer you when you are in distress; may the name of the God of Jacob protect you. {20:2} May he send you help from the sanctuary and grant you support from Zion. {20:3} May he remember all your sacrifices and accept your burnt offerings. {20:4} May he give you the desire of your heart and make all your plans succeed. {20:5} We will shout for joy when you are victorious and will lift up our banners in the name of our God. May the LORD grant all your requests. {20:6} Now I know that the LORD saves his anointed; he answers him from his holy heaven with the victorious power of his right hand. {20:7} Some trust in chariots and some in horses, but we trust in the name of the LORD our God. {20:8} They are brought to their knees and fall, but we rise up and stand firm. {20:9} LORD, give victory to the king! Answer us when we call!

{21:1} The king rejoices in your strength, LORD; how greatly he rejoices in your salvation! {21:2} You have given him his heart's desire and have not withheld the request of his lips. Selah. {21:3} For you meet him with blessings of goodness; you place a crown of pure gold on his head. {21:4} He asked you for life, and you gave it to him, length of days forever and ever. {21:5} His glory is great in your salvation; you have bestowed honor and majesty upon him. {21:6} For you have made him most blessed forever; you have made him exceedingly glad with your presence. {21:7} The king trusts in the LORD, and through the mercy of the Most High, he will not be shaken. {21:8} Your hand will find all your enemies; your right hand will find those who hate you. {21:9} You will make them like a fiery oven in the time of your anger; the LORD will swallow them up in his wrath, and fire will consume them. {21:10} You will destroy their offspring from the earth and their descendants from among the children of men. {21:11} For they intended evil against you; they devised a plot that they cannot carry out. {21:12} Therefore, you will make them turn their backs when you prepare your arrows against them. {21:13} Be exalted, LORD, in your strength; we will sing and praise your power.

{22:1} My God, my God, why have you forsaken me? Why are you so far from helping me and from the words of my cry? {22:2} O my God, I cry out to you by day, but you do not answer; by night, I am not silent. {22:3} Yet you are holy, enthroned on the praises of Israel. {22:4} Our ancestors trusted in you; they trusted, and you delivered them. {22:5} They cried out to you and were saved; they trusted in you and were not disappointed. {22:6} But I am a worm, not a man; I am a disgrace to humanity and despised by the people. {22:7} All who see me mock me; they hurl insults, shaking their heads, saying, {22:8} "He trusted in the LORD; let the LORD rescue him. Let the LORD deliver him, since he delights in him." {22:9} Yet you brought me out of the womb; you made me hope when I was on my mother's breasts. {22:10} I was cast upon you from birth; you have been my God since I was in my mother's womb. {22:11} Do not be far from me, for trouble is near, and there is no one to help. {22:12} Many bulls surround me; strong bulls of Bashan encircle me. {22:13} They open their mouths wide against me, like a roaring and ravenous lion. {22:14} I am poured out like water, and all my bones are out of joint; my heart is like wax; it has melted within me. {22:15} My strength is dried up like a potsherd (broken pottery), and my tongue sticks to the roof of my mouth; you lay me in the dust of death. {22:16} For dogs have surrounded me; a pack of villains encircles me; they pierce my hands and my feet. {22:17} I can count all my bones; they gaze and stare at me. {22:18} They divide my garments among them and cast lots for my clothing. {22:19} But you, LORD, do not be far from me; you are my strength; come quickly to help me. {22:20} Deliver my soul from the sword, my precious life from the power of the dogs. {22:21} Save me from the lion's mouth; you have heard me from the horns of the wild oxen. {22:22} I will declare your name to my people; in the assembly, I will praise you. {22:23} You who fear the LORD, praise him; all you descendants of Jacob, honor him; revere him, all you descendants of Israel. {22:24} For he has not despised or scorned the suffering of the afflicted one; he has not hidden his face from him but has listened to his cry for help. {22:25} I will praise you in the great assembly; I will fulfill my vows in the presence of those who fear you. {22:26} The poor will eat and be satisfied; those who seek the LORD will praise him; may your hearts live forever! {22:27} All the ends of the earth will remember and turn to the LORD, and all the families of the nations will bow down before him. {22:28} For dominion belongs to the LORD and he rules over the nations. {22:29} All the rich of the earth will feast and worship; all who go down to the dust will kneel before him; those who cannot keep themselves alive. {22:30} Posterity will serve him; future generations will be told about the Lord. {22:31} They will proclaim his righteousness, declaring to a people yet unborn: he has done it!

{23:1} The LORD is my shepherd; I lack nothing. {23:2} He makes me lie down in green pastures; he leads me beside quiet waters. {23:3} He refreshes my soul. He guides me along the right paths for his name's sake. {23:4} Even though I walk through the darkest valley, I will fear no evil, for you are with me; your rod and your staff, they comfort me. {23:5} You prepare a table before me in the presence of my enemies; you anoint my head with oil; my cup overflows. {23:6} Surely your goodness and love will follow me all the days of my life, and I will dwell in the house of the LORD forever.

{24:1} The earth is the LORD's, and everything in it, the world, and all who live in it; {24:2} for he founded it upon the seas and established it upon the waters. {24:3} Who may ascend the mountain of the LORD? Who may stand in his holy place? {24:4} The one who has clean hands and a pure heart, who does not trust in an idol or swear by a false god. {24:5} They will receive blessing from the LORD and vindication from God their Savior. {24:6} Such is the generation of those who seek him, who seek your face, God of Jacob. Selah. {24:7} Lift up your heads, you gates; be lifted up, you ancient doors, that the King of glory may come in. {24:8} Who is this King of glory? The LORD strong and mighty, the LORD mighty in battle. {24:9} Lift up your heads, you gates; lift them up, you ancient doors, that the King of glory may come in. {24:10} Who is he, this King of glory? The LORD Almighty—he is the King of glory. Selah.

{25:1} To you, LORD, I lift up my soul. {25:2} I trust in you, my God. Do not let me be put to shame, nor let my enemies triumph over me. {25:3} No one who hopes in you will ever be put to shame, but shame will come on those who are treacherous without cause. {25:4} Show me your ways, LORD, teach me your paths. {25:5} Guide me in your truth and teach me, for you are God my Savior, and my hope is in you all day long. {25:6} Remember, LORD, your great mercy and love, for they are from of old. {25:7} Do not remember the sins of my youth and my rebellious ways; according to your love, remember me, for you, LORD, are good. {25:8} Good and upright is the LORD; therefore, he instructs sinners in his ways. {25:9} He guides the humble in what is right and teaches them his way. {25:10} All the LORD's paths are mercy and faithfulness for those who keep his covenant and statutes. {25:11} For the sake of your name, LORD, forgive my iniquity, though it is great. {25:12} Who, then, are those who fear the LORD? He will instruct them in the ways they should choose. {25:13} They will spend their days in prosperity, and their descendants will inherit the land. {25:14} The LORD confides in those who fear him; he makes his covenant known to them. {25:15} My eyes are ever on the LORD, for only he will release my feet from the snare. {25:16} Turn to me and be gracious to me, for I am lonely and afflicted. {25:17} Relieve the troubles of my heart and free me from my anguish. {25:18} Look upon my affliction and my distress and take away all my sins. {25:19} See how numerous are my enemies and how fiercely they hate me! {25:20} Guard my life and rescue me; do not let me be put to shame, for I take refuge in you. {25:21} May integrity and uprightness protect me, because my hope, LORD, is in you. {25:22} Deliver Israel, O God, from all their troubles.

{26:1} Judge me, LORD, for I have walked in my integrity; I have trusted in the LORD, so I will not stumble. {26:2} Examine me, LORD, and test me; try my heart and my mind. {26:3} For your love is always before me, and I have walked in your truth. {26:4} I have not sat with deceitful people, nor will I associate with hypocrites. {26:5} I have hated the assembly of evildoers and will not sit with the wicked. {26:6} I will wash my hands in innocence; I will go around your altar, LORD, {26:7} proclaiming thanksgiving and telling of all your wonderful deeds. {26:8} LORD, I love the house where you live, the place where your glory dwells. {26:9} Do not gather my soul with sinners or my life with violent people, {26:10} in whose hands are wicked schemes, whose right hands are full of bribes. {26:11} But I will walk in my integrity; redeem me and be merciful to me. {26:12} My feet stand on level ground; in the great assembly, I will praise the LORD.

{27:1} The LORD is my light and my salvation; whom shall I fear? The LORD is the stronghold of my life; of whom shall I be afraid? {27:2} When the wicked advance against me to devour my flesh, it is my enemies and foes who will stumble and fall. {27:3} Though an army besiege me, my heart will not fear; though war break out against me, even then I will be confident. {27:4} One thing I ask from the LORD, this only do I seek: that I may dwell in the house of the LORD all the days of my life, to gaze on the beauty of the LORD and to seek him in his temple. {27:5} For in the day of trouble he will hide me in his shelter; he will hide me in the secret place of his tent and set me high upon a rock. {27:6} Then my head will be exalted above the enemies who surround me; at his sacred tent, I will sacrifice with shouts of joy; I will sing and make music to the LORD. {27:7} Hear my voice when I call, LORD; be merciful to me and answer me. {27:8} My heart says of you, "Seek his face!" Your face, LORD, I will seek. {27:9} Do not hide your face from me; do not turn your servant away in anger; you have been my helper; do not reject me or forsake me, God my Savior. {27:10} Though my father and mother forsake me, the LORD will receive me. {27:11} Teach me your way, LORD; lead me in a straight path because of my oppressors. {27:12} Do not hand me over to the desire of my foes, for false witnesses rise up against me, spouting malicious accusations. {27:13} I remain confident of this: I will see the goodness of the LORD in the land of the living. {27:14} Wait for the LORD; be strong and take heart and wait for the LORD.

{28:1} To you, LORD, I call; you are my rock; do not turn a deaf ear to me. For if you remain silent, I will be like those who go down to the pit. {28:2} Hear my cry for mercy as I call to you for help, as I lift up my hands toward your Most Holy Place. {28:3} Do not drag me away with the wicked, with those who are evil, who speak cordially with their neighbors but harbor malice in their hearts. {28:4} Repay them for their deeds and for their evil work; repay them for what their hands have done and bring back on them what they deserve. {28:5} Because they do not regard the works of the LORD or the deeds of his hands, he will tear them down and never build them up again. {28:6} Praise be to the LORD, for he has heard my cry for mercy. {28:7} The LORD is my strength and my shield; my heart trusts in him, and he helps me. My heart leaps for joy, and I will praise him in song. {28:8} The LORD is the strength of his people, a fortress of salvation for his anointed one. {28:9} Save your people and bless your inheritance; be their shepherd and carry them forever.

{29:1} Ascribe to the LORD, you heavenly beings; ascribe to the LORD glory and strength. {29:2} Ascribe to the LORD the glory due his name; worship the LORD in the splendor of his holiness. {29:3} The voice of the LORD is over the waters; the God of glory thunders, the LORD thunders over the mighty waters. {29:4} The voice of the LORD is powerful; the voice of the LORD is full of majesty. {29:5} The voice of the LORD breaks the cedars; the LORD breaks in pieces the cedars of Lebanon. {29:6} He makes Lebanon leap like a calf, Sirion like a young wild ox. {29:7} The voice of the LORD strikes with flashes of lightning. {29:8} The voice of the LORD shakes the desert; the LORD shakes the Desert of Kadesh. {29:9} The voice of the LORD twists the oaks and strips the forests bare. And in his temple, all cry, "Glory!" {29:10} The LORD sits enthroned over the flood; the LORD is enthroned as King forever. {29:11} The LORD gives strength to his people; the LORD blesses his people with peace.

{30:1} I will exalt you, LORD, for you lifted me out of the depths and did not let my enemies gloat over me. {30:2} LORD my God, I called to you for help, and you healed me. {30:3} You, LORD, brought me up from the grave; you spared me from going down to the pit. {30:4} Sing the praises of the LORD, you his faithful people; praise his holy name. {30:5} For his anger lasts only a moment, but his favor lasts a lifetime; weeping may stay for the night, but joy comes in the morning. {30:6} When I felt secure, I said, "I will never be shaken." {30:7} LORD, when you favored me, you made my royal mountain stand firm; but when you hid your face, I was dismayed. {30:8} To you, LORD, I called; to the Lord I cried for mercy. {30:9} "What is gained if I am silenced, if I go down to the pit? Will the dust praise you? Will it proclaim your faithfulness? {30:10} Hear, LORD, and be merciful to me; LORD, be my help." {30:11} You turned my wailing into dancing; you removed my sackcloth and clothed me with joy, {30:12} that my heart may sing your praises and not be silent. LORD my God, I will praise you forever.

{31:1} In you, LORD, I place my trust; let me never be ashamed; deliver me in your righteousness. {31:2} Turn your ear to me; rescue me quickly; be my strong rock, my fortress to save me. {31:3} For you are my rock and my fortress; lead me and guide me for your name's sake. {31:4} Pull me out of the net they have secretly laid for me; you are my strength. {31:5} Into your hands I commit my spirit; you have redeemed me, LORD, God of truth. {31:6} I have hated those who cling to worthless idols; but I trust in the LORD. {31:7} I will be glad and rejoice in your mercy, for you have seen my trouble; you know my soul in adversity. {31:8} And you have not given me over to the enemy; you have set my feet in a spacious place. {31:9} Have mercy on me, LORD, for I am in trouble; my eye is consumed with grief, my soul and my body. {31:10} My life is spent with grief, and my years with sighing; my strength fails because of my sin, and my bones are weakened. {31:11} I am a disgrace to all my enemies, especially to my neighbors; I am a fear to my acquaintances; those who see me flee from me. {31:12} I am forgotten like a dead man, out of mind; I am like a broken vessel. {31:13} For I have heard the slander of many; fear is on every side; they conspire against me and plot to take my life. {31:14} But I trust in you, LORD; I say, "You are my God." {31:15} My times are in your hands; deliver me from the hand of my enemies and from those who persecute me. {31:16} Make your face shine upon your servant; save me for your mercy's sake. {31:17} Let me not be ashamed, LORD, for I have called upon you; let the wicked be ashamed and silent in the grave. {31:18} Let lying lips be silenced, those who speak arrogantly and contemptuously against the righteous. {31:19} Oh, how great is your goodness, which you have stored up for those who fear you; which you bestow upon those who trust in you in the sight of all men! {31:20} You hide them in the secret of your presence from human pride; you keep them safe in your dwelling from the strife of tongues. {31:21} Blessed be the LORD, for he has shown me his wonderful love in a fortified city. {31:22} In my alarm, I said, "I am cut off from your sight"; yet you heard my cry for mercy when I called to you. {31:23} Love the LORD, all you his faithful people! The LORD protects the loyal, but fully repays the arrogant. {31:24} Be strong and take heart, all you who hope in the LORD.

{32:1} Blessed is the one whose transgression is forgiven, whose sin is covered. {32:2} Blessed is the one to whom the LORD does not impute sin, and in whose spirit is no deceit. {32:3} When I kept silent, my bones wasted away through my groaning all day long. {32:4} For day and night your hand was heavy on me; my strength was sapped as in the heat of summer. Selah. {32:5} I acknowledged my sin to you and did not hide my iniquity; I said, "I will confess my transgressions to the LORD." And you forgave the guilt of my sin. Selah. {32:6} Therefore let all the faithful pray to you while you may be found; surely the rising waters will not reach them. {32:7} You are my hiding place; you will protect me from trouble and surround me with songs of deliverance. Selah. {32:8} I will instruct you and teach you in the way you should go; I will counsel you with my loving eye on you. {32:9} Do not be like the horse or the mule, which have no understanding but must be controlled by bit and bridle, or they will not come to you. {32:10} Many are the woes of the wicked, but the LORD's unfailing love surrounds the one who trusts in him. {32:11} Rejoice in the LORD and be glad, you righteous; sing, all you who are upright in heart!

{33:1} Rejoice in the LORD, you righteous; it is fitting for the upright to praise him. {33:2} Praise the LORD with the harp; make music to him on the ten-stringed lyre. {33:3} Sing to him a new song; play skillfully, and shout for joy. {33:4} For the word of the LORD is right and true; he is faithful in all he does. {33:5} The LORD loves righteousness and justice; the earth is full of his unfailing love. {33:6} By the word of the LORD the heavens were made, their starry host by the breath of his mouth. {33:7} He gathers the waters of the sea into jars; he puts the deep into storehouses. {33:8} Let all the earth fear the LORD; let all the people of the world revere him. {33:9} For he spoke, and it came to be; he commanded, and it stood firm. {33:10} The LORD foils the plans of the nations; he thwarts the purposes of the peoples. {33:11} But the plans of the LORD stand firm forever, the purposes of his heart through all generations. {33:12} Blessed is the nation whose God is the LORD, the people he chose for his inheritance. {33:13} From heaven the LORD looks down and sees all mankind; {33:14} from his dwelling place he watches all who live on earth— {33:15} he who forms the hearts of all, who considers everything they do. {33:16} No king is saved by the size of his army; no warrior escapes by his great strength. {33:17} A horse is a vain hope for deliverance; despite all its great strength, it cannot save. {33:18} But the eye of the LORD is on those who fear him, on those whose hope is in his unfailing love, {33:19} to deliver them from death and keep them alive in famine. {33:20} We wait in hope for the LORD; he is our help and our shield. {33:21} In him our hearts rejoice, for we trust in his holy name. {33:22} May your unfailing love be with us, LORD, even as we put our hope in you.

{34:1} I will extol the LORD at all times; his praise will always be on my lips. {34:2} I will glory in the LORD; let the afflicted hear and rejoice. {34:3} Glorify the LORD with me; let us exalt his name together. {34:4} I sought the LORD, and he answered me; he delivered me from all my fears. {34:5} Those who look to him are radiant; their faces are never covered with shame. {34:6} This poor man called, and the LORD heard him; he saved him out of all his troubles. {34:7} The angel of the LORD encamps around those who fear him, and he delivers them. {34:8} Taste and see that the LORD is good; blessed is the one who takes refuge in him. {34:9} Fear the LORD, you his holy people, for those who fear him lack nothing. {34:10} The lions may grow weak and hungry, but those who seek the LORD lack no good thing. {34:11} Come, my children, listen to me; I will teach you the fear of the LORD. {34:12} Whoever of you loves life and desires to see many good days, {34:13} keep your tongue from evil and your lips from telling lies. {34:14} Turn from evil and do good; seek peace and pursue it. {34:15} The eyes of the LORD are on the righteous, and his ears are attentive to their cry; {34:16} the face of the LORD is against those who do evil, to blot out their name from the earth. {34:17} The righteous cry out, and the LORD hears them; he delivers them from all their troubles. {34:18} The LORD is close to the brokenhearted and saves those who are crushed in spirit. {34:19} The righteous person may have many troubles, but the LORD delivers him from them all; {34:20} he protects all his bones; not one of them will be broken. {34:21} Evil will slay the wicked, and those who hate the righteous will be condemned. {34:22} The LORD will rescue his servants; no one who takes refuge in him will be condemned.

{35:1} Contend, LORD, with those who contend with me; fight against those who fight against me. {35:2} Take up shield and armor; arise and come to my aid. {35:3} Brandish spear and javelin against those who pursue me. Say to my soul, "I am your salvation." {35:4} May those who seek my life be disgraced and put to shame; may those who plot my ruin be turned back in dismay. {35:5} May they be like chaff before the wind, with the angel of the LORD driving them away. {35:6} May their path be dark and slippery, with the angel of the LORD pursuing them. {35:7} Since they hide their net for me without cause and set their traps for my life— {35:8} let destruction overtake them by surprise; let the net they hid catch them; let them fall into their own destruction. {35:9} Then my soul will rejoice in the LORD and delight in his salvation. {35:10} My whole being will exclaim, "Who is like you, LORD? You rescue the poor from those too strong for them, the poor and needy from those who rob them." {35:11} Ruthless witnesses come forward; they question me on things I know nothing about. {35:12} They repay me evil for good and leave me like one bereaved. {35:13} Yet when they were ill, I put on sackcloth and humbled myself with fasting. When my prayers returned to me unanswered, {35:14} I went about mourning as though for my friend or brother. I bowed my head in grief as though weeping for my mother. {35:15} But when I stumbled, they gathered in glee; they gathered against me; they slandered me without ceasing. {35:16} Like the ungodly they maliciously mocked; they gnashed their teeth at me. {35:17} LORD, how long will you look on? Rescue me from their ravages, my precious life from these lions. {35:18} I will give you thanks in the great assembly; among the throngs I will praise you. {35:19} Do not let those who are my enemies without cause rejoice over me; do not let those who hate me without reason mock me. {35:20} They do not speak peace but devise false accusations against those who live quietly in the land. {35:21} They open their mouths wide against me and say, "Aha! Aha! We saw it with our own eyes." {35:22} You have seen this, LORD; do not be silent. Do not be far from me, LORD. {35:23} Awake, and rise to my defense! Contend for me, my God and my Lord. {35:24} Vindicate me, LORD, my God, in accordance with your righteousness; do not let them gloat over me. {35:25} Do not let them think, "Aha! Just what we wanted!" or say, "We have swallowed him up." {35:26} May all who gloat over my distress be put to shame and confusion; may those who exalt themselves over me be clothed with shame and disgrace. {35:27} May they shout for joy and be glad, who favor my righteous cause; may they always say, "The LORD be exalted, who delights in the well-being of his servant." {35:28} My tongue will proclaim your righteousness, your praises all day long.

{36:1} The wicked are confident in their hearts, saying there is no fear of God before their eyes. {36:2} They flatter themselves until their sin is exposed and becomes despicable. {36:3} Their words are filled with deceit and wickedness; they have stopped being wise and doing good. {36:4} They plot evil while lying in bed; they choose paths that are not good and do not hate evil. {36:5} Your mercy, LORD, reaches to the heavens, and your faithfulness stretches to the clouds. {36:6} Your righteousness is like the great mountains; your judgments are like the depths of the sea. O LORD, you preserve both people and animals. {36:7} How great is your lovingkindness, O God! Therefore, the children of men take refuge in the shadow of your wings. {36:8} They will be abundantly satisfied with the richness of your house, and you will make them drink from the river of your delights. {36:9} For with you is the fountain of life; in your light, we see light. {36:10} Continue your lovingkindness to those who know you and your righteousness to the upright in heart. {36:11} Let not the foot of pride come against me, nor let the hand of the wicked drive me away. {36:12} There the workers of iniquity have fallen; they are thrown down and cannot rise.

{37:1} Do not fret because of evildoers or be envious of those who do wrong. {37:2} For they will soon wither like grass and fade away like green herbs. {37:3} Trust in the LORD and do good; dwell in the land and enjoy safe pasture. {37:4} Take delight in the LORD, and he will give you the desires of your heart. {37:5} Commit your way to the LORD; trust in him, and he will act. {37:6} He will make your righteousness shine like the dawn, the justice of your cause like the noonday sun. {37:7} Be still before the LORD and wait patiently for him; do not fret when people succeed in their ways, when they carry out their wicked schemes. {37:8} Refrain from anger and turn from wrath; do not fret—it leads only to evil. {37:9} For those who do evil will be destroyed, but those who hope in the LORD will inherit the land. {37:10} A little while, and the wicked will be no more; though you look for them, they will not be found. {37:11} But the meek will inherit the land and enjoy peace and prosperity. {37:12} The wicked plot against the righteous and gnash their teeth at them; {37:13} but the LORD laughs at the wicked, for he knows their day is coming. {37:14} The wicked draw the sword and bend the bow to bring down the poor and needy, to slay those whose ways are upright. {37:15} Their swords will pierce their own hearts, and their bows will be broken. {37:16} Better the little that the righteous have than the wealth of many wicked. {37:17} For the power of the wicked will be broken, but the LORD upholds the righteous. {37:18} The LORD knows the days of the blameless, and their inheritance will last forever. {37:19} They will not be put to shame in times of trouble; they will have plenty in days of famine. {37:20} But the wicked will perish; the enemies of the LORD will be like the flowers of the field—they will vanish; into smoke, they will disappear. {37:21} The wicked borrow and do not repay, but the righteous give generously. {37:22} Those the LORD blesses will inherit the land, but those he curses will be destroyed. {37:23} The LORD makes firm the steps of the one who delights in him; {37:24} though they stumble, they will not fall, for the LORD upholds them with his hand. {37:25} I was young and now I am old, yet I have never seen the righteous forsaken or their children begging bread. {37:26} They are always generous and lend freely; their children will be a blessing. {37:27} Turn from evil and do good; then you will dwell in the land forever. {37:28} For the LORD loves the just and will not forsake his faithful ones. They will be protected forever, but the offspring of the wicked will be cut off. {37:29} The righteous will inherit the land and dwell in it forever. {37:30} The mouths of the righteous utter wisdom, and their tongues speak what is just. {37:31} The law of their God is in their hearts; their feet do not slip. {37:32} The wicked lie in wait for the righteous, intent on putting them to death; {37:33} but the LORD will not leave them in the power of the wicked or let them be condemned when brought to trial. {37:34} Wait for the LORD and keep his way; he will exalt you to inherit the land; when the wicked are destroyed, you will see it. {37:35} I have seen a wicked and ruthless man flourishing like a luxuriant native tree, {37:36} but he soon passed away and was no more; though I looked for him, he could not be found. {37:37} Consider the blameless, observe the upright; a future awaits those who seek peace. {37:38} But all sinners will be destroyed; there will be no future for the wicked. {37:39} The salvation of the righteous comes from the LORD; he is their stronghold in time of trouble. {37:40} The LORD helps them and delivers them; he delivers them from the wicked and saves them because they take refuge in him.

{38:1} O LORD, do not rebuke me in your anger or discipline me in your wrath. {38:2} Your arrows have pierced me, and your hand presses down on me. {38:3} Because of your wrath, there is no health in my body; there is no soundness in my bones because of my sin. {38:4} My guilt has overwhelmed me like a burden too heavy to bear. {38:5} My wounds fester and stink because of my foolishness. {38:6} I am worn out and crushed; I groan in anguish all day long. {38:7} My back is filled with searing pain; there is no health in my body. {38:8} I am feeble and crushed; I groan in anguish of heart. {38:9} My LORD, my every desire is before you; my sighing is not hidden from you. {38:10} My heart races, my strength fails me; even the light has gone from my eyes. {38:11} My friends and companions avoid me because of my wounds; my neighbors stay far away. {38:12} Those who seek my life set their traps; those who seek my harm speak of my ruin and plot deception all day long. {38:13} But I am like a deaf man, who does not hear, like a mute who cannot speak. {38:14} I have become like a man who does not hear and whose mouth cannot offer rebuttal. {38:15} I wait for you, LORD; you will answer, my God. {38:16} For I said, "Do not let them gloat or exalt themselves over me when my foot slips." {38:17} For I am about to fall, and my pain is always before me. {38:18} I confess my guilt; I am troubled by my sin. {38:19} My enemies are strong and numerous; those who hate me without reason are many. {38:20} Those who repay good with evil slander me when I pursue good. {38:21} Do not forsake me, LORD; do not be far from me, my God. {38:22} Come quickly to help me, my Lord and Savior.

{39:1} I said, "I will be careful about what I say; I will put a guard over my mouth while the wicked are in my presence." {39:2} I remained silent and held my peace, even when it was good, and my sorrow grew. {39:3} My heart was hot within me; while I meditated, the fire burned; then I spoke with my tongue: {39:4} "LORD, show me my end and the measure of my days; let me know how fleeting my life is. {39:5} You have made my days a mere handbreadth; my life is nothing in your sight; everyone is but a breath, even those in their best state. Selah. {39:6} Surely everyone goes around like a mere phantom; in vain they rush about, heaping up wealth without knowing who will get it. {39:7} And now, LORD, what do I look for? My hope is in you. {39:8} Save me from all my transgressions; do not make me the scorn of fools. {39:9} I was silent; I did not open my mouth because you are the one who has done this. {39:10} Remove your scourge from me; I am overcome by the blow of your hand. {39:11} When you rebuke and discipline anyone for sin, you consume their wealth like a moth; surely everyone is but a breath. Selah. {39:12} Hear my prayer, LORD; listen to my cry for help; do not be silent at my tears. I am a foreigner and a stranger as all my ancestors were. {39:13} Look away from me, that I may enjoy life again before I depart and am no more."

{40:1} I waited patiently for the LORD; he turned to me and heard my cry. {40:2} He lifted me out of the pit of despair, out of the mud and mire; he set my feet on a rock and gave me a firm place to stand. {40:3} He put a new song in my mouth, a hymn of praise to our God. Many will see and fear the LORD and put their trust in him. {40:4} Blessed is the one who trusts in the LORD, who does not look to the proud, to those who turn aside to false gods. {40:5} Many, LORD my God, are the wonders you have done; the things you planned for us no one can compare with you. Were I to speak and tell of your deeds, they would be too many to declare. {40:6} Sacrifice and offering you did not desire, but my ears you have opened; burnt offerings and sin offerings you did not require. {40:7} Then I said, "Here I am, I have come—it is written about me in the scroll. {40:8} I desire to do your will, my God; your law is within my heart." {40:9} I proclaim your saving acts in the great assembly; I do not seal my lips, LORD, as you know. {40:10} I do not hide your righteousness in my heart; I speak of your faithfulness and your saving help. I do not conceal your love and your truth from the great assembly. {40:11} Do not withhold your mercy from me, LORD; may your love and faithfulness always protect me. {40:12} For troubles without number surround me; my sins have overtaken me, and I cannot see. They are more than the hairs of my head, and my heart fails within me. {40:13} Be pleased to save me, LORD; come quickly, LORD, to help me. {40:14} May all who want to take my life be put to shame and confusion; may all who desire my ruin be turned back in disgrace. {40:15} May those who say to me, "Aha! Aha!" be appalled at their own shame. {40:16} But may all who seek you rejoice and be glad in you; may those who long for your saving help always say, "The LORD is great!" {40:17} Yet I am poor and needy; may the LORD think of me. You are my help and my deliverer; you are my God, do not delay.

{41:1} Blessed is the one who cares for the poor; the LORD will rescue him in times of trouble. {41:2} The LORD will protect him and keep him alive; he will be blessed on the earth, and you will not give him over to his enemies' desires. {41:3} The LORD will strengthen him on his sickbed; you will restore him to health. {41:4} I said, "LORD, be merciful to me; heal my soul, for I have sinned against you." {41:5} My enemies speak evil of me, asking, "When will he die, and his name disappear?" {41:6} If he visits me, he speaks insincerity; his heart gathers wickedness; when he leaves, he tells it. {41:7} All who hate me whisper together against me; they plot my harm. {41:8} "An evil disease clings to him; now that he is down, he will not get up again." {41:9} Even my close friend, whom I trusted, who shared my bread, has turned against me. {41:10} But you, O LORD, be merciful to me and raise me up, so I may repay them. {41:11} By this, I know you favor me, because my enemy does not triumph over me. {41:12} And as for me, you uphold me in my integrity and set me before your face forever. {41:13} Blessed be the LORD God of Israel from everlasting to everlasting. Amen and Amen.

{42:1} As the deer longs for streams of water, so my soul longs for you, O God. {42:2} My soul thirsts for God, for the living God; when shall I come and appear before God? {42:3} My tears have been my food day and night, while they continually ask me, "Where is your God?" {42:4} When I remember these things, I pour out my soul; for I used to go with the multitude to the house of God, with a voice of joy and praise, among those who celebrated. {42:5} Why are you cast down, O my soul? And why are you disturbed within me? Hope in God, for I shall yet praise him for the help of his presence. {42:6} O my God, my soul is downcast within me; therefore, I will remember you from the land of Jordan, from the heights of Hermon, from the hill Mizar. {42:7} Deep calls to deep at the sound of your waterfalls; all your waves and billows have swept over me. {42:8} Yet the LORD will command his lovingkindness in the daytime, and at night his song will be with me, a prayer to the God of my life. {42:9} I will say to God my rock, "Why have you forgotten me? Why must I go mourning because of the oppression of my enemy?" {42:10} As with a sword in my bones, my enemies reproach me, while they daily ask me, "Where is your God?" {42:11} Why are you cast down, O my soul? And why are you disturbed within me? Hope in God, for I shall yet praise him, who is the health of my countenance and my God.

{43:1} Judge me, O God, and plead my cause against an ungodly nation; deliver me from deceitful and unjust men. {43:2} For you are the God of my strength; why do you cast me off? Why must I go mourning because of the oppression of my enemy? {43:3} Send out your light and your truth; let them lead me; let them bring me to your holy hill and to your tabernacles. {43:4} Then I will go to the altar of God, to God my exceeding joy; I will praise you on the harp, O God my God. {43:5} Why are you cast down, O my soul? And why are you disturbed within me? Hope in God, for I shall yet praise him, who is the health of my countenance and my God.

{44:1} We have heard with our ears, O God; our ancestors have told us what you did in their days, in times of old. {44:2} How you drove out the nations with your hand and planted them; how you afflicted peoples and cast them out. {44:3} For they did not gain possession of the land by their own sword, nor did their own arm save them; but your right hand, your arm, and the light of your face, because you favored them. {44:4} You are my King, O God; command victories for Jacob. {44:5} Through you, we will push down our enemies; through your name, we will trample those who rise against us. {44:6} For I will not trust in my bow, nor shall my sword save me. {44:7} But you have saved us from our enemies and put them to shame who hated us. {44:8} In God, we boast all day long and praise your name forever. Selah. {44:9} But you have cast us off and put us to shame; you do not go forth with our armies. {44:10} You make us turn back from the enemy, and those who hate us spoil for themselves. {44:11} You have made us like sheep for slaughter; you have scattered us among the nations. {44:12} You sell your people for nothing and do not increase your wealth by their price. {44:13} You make us a reproach to our neighbors, a scorn and derision to those around us. {44:14} You make us a byword among the nations, a shaking of the head among the people. {44:15} My confusion is continually before me, and the shame of my face covers me, {44:16} because of the voice of him who reproaches and blasphemes; because of the enemy and avenger. {44:17} All this has come upon us; yet we have not forgotten you, nor have we been false to your covenant. {44:18} Our heart has not turned back, nor have our steps declined from your way. {44:19} Though you have crushed us in the place of jackals and covered us with the shadow of death. {44:20} If we have forgotten the name of our God or stretched out our hands to a strange god, {44:21} will not God search this out? For he knows the secrets of the heart. {44:22} Yes, for your sake we are killed all day long; we are counted as sheep for the slaughter. {44:23} Awake! Why are you sleeping, O Lord? Arise! Do not cast us off forever. {44:24} Why do you hide your face and forget our affliction and oppression? {44:25} For our soul is bowed down to the dust; our body clings to the earth. {44:26} Arise for our help and redeem us for your mercies' sake.

{45:1} My heart is stirred by a noble theme; I address my verses to the king; my tongue is the pen of a skilled writer. {45:2} You are the most excellent of men, and your lips have been anointed with grace; therefore, God has blessed you forever. {45:3} Gird your sword on your side, O mighty one; clothe yourself with splendor and majesty. {45:4} In your majesty, ride forth victoriously in the cause of truth, humility, and justice; let your right hand display awesome deeds. {45:5} Let your arrows pierce the hearts of the king's enemies; let the nations fall beneath you. {45:6} Your throne, O God, will last forever and ever; the scepter of justice will be the scepter of your kingdom. {45:7} You love righteousness and hate wickedness; therefore, God, your God, has set you above your companions by anointing you with the oil of joy. {45:8} All your robes are fragrant with myrrh, aloes, and cassia; from palaces adorned with ivory, the music of the strings makes you glad. {45:9} Daughters of kings are among your honored women; at your right hand is the royal bride in gold of Ophir. {45:10} Listen, O daughter, consider and give ear; forget your people and your father's house. {45:11} The king is enthralled by your beauty; honor him, for he is your lord. {45:12} The daughter of Tyre will come with a gift; the rich among the people will seek your favor. {45:13} All glorious is the princess within her chamber; her gown is interwoven with gold. {45:14} In embroidered garments, she will be led to the king; her virgin companions will follow her and be brought to you. {45:15} They will enter the king's palace with joy and gladness; they will enter in. {45:16} Instead of your fathers, you will have sons; you will make them princes throughout the land. {45:17} I will make your name to be remembered in all generations; therefore, the nations will praise you forever and ever.

{46:1} God is our refuge and strength, a very present help in trouble. {46:2} Therefore, we will not fear, even if the earth gives way and the mountains are thrown into the sea; {46:3} though its waters roar and foam, and the mountains quake with their surging. Selah. {46:4} There is a river whose streams make glad the city of God, the holy dwelling place of the Most High. {46:5} God is within her; she will not fall; God will help her at break of day. {46:6} Nations are in uproar, kingdoms fall; he lifts his voice, the earth melts. {46:7} The LORD Almighty is with us; the God of Jacob is our fortress. Selah. {46:8} Come and see what the LORD has done, the desolations he has brought on the earth. {46:9} He makes wars cease to the ends of the earth; he breaks the bow and shatters the spear; he burns the shields with fire. {46:10} Be still, and know that I am God; I will be exalted among the nations, I will be exalted in the earth. {46:11} The LORD Almighty is with us; the God of Jacob is our fortress. Selah.

{47:1} Clap your hands, all you nations; shout to God with cries of joy. {47:2} For the LORD Most High is awesome; he is the great King over all the earth. {47:3} He subdues nations under us, and peoples under our feet. {47:4} He chooses our inheritance for us, the pride of Jacob whom he loved. Selah. {47:5} God has ascended amid shouts of joy, the LORD amid the sounding of trumpets. {47:6} Sing praises to God, sing praises; sing praises to our King, sing praises. {47:7} For God is the King of all the earth; sing to him a psalm of praise. {47:8} God reigns over the nations; God is seated on his holy throne. {47:9} The nobles of the nations assemble as the people of the God of Abraham, for the kings of the earth belong to God; he is greatly exalted.

{48:1} Great is the LORD, and greatly to be praised in the city of our God, the holy mountain. {48:2} Beautiful in its loftiness, the joy of the whole earth, is Mount Zion, the city of the great King. {48:3} God is in her citadels; he has shown himself to be her fortress. {48:4} When the kings joined forces, when they advanced together, {48:5} they saw her and were astounded; they fled in terror. {48:6} Trembling seized them there, pain like that of a woman in labor. {48:7} You destroyed them like ships of Tarshish shattered by an east wind. {48:8} As we have heard, so we have seen in the city of the LORD Almighty, in the city of our God: God establishes her forever. Selah. {48:9} We meditate on your unfailing love, O God, in the midst of your temple. {48:10} Your praise, like your name, reaches to the ends of the earth; your right hand is filled with righteousness. {48:11} Let Mount Zion rejoice, let the daughters of Judah be glad because of your judgments. {48:12} Walk about Zion, go around her, count her towers, {48:13} consider well her ramparts, view her citadels, that you may tell of them to the next generation. {48:14} For this God is our God for ever and ever; he will be our guide even to the end.

{49:1} Hear this, all you peoples; listen, all who live in the world, {49:2} both low and high, rich and poor alike. {49:3} My mouth will speak words of wisdom; the meditation of my heart will give you understanding. {49:4} I will turn my ear to a proverb; with the harp, I will expound my riddle. {49:5} Why should I fear when evil days come, when wicked deceivers surround me? {49:6} Those who trust in their wealth and boast of their great riches? {49:7} No one can redeem the life of another or give to God a ransom for them; {49:8} the ransom for a life is costly, no payment is ever enough, {49:9} so that they should live on forever and not see decay. {49:10} For all can see that wise men die; the foolish and the senseless also perish and leave their wealth to others. {49:11} Their tombs will remain their houses forever, their dwellings for endless generations, though they had named lands after themselves. {49:12} People, despite their wealth, do not endure; they are like the beasts that perish. {49:13} This is the fate of those who trust in themselves, and of their followers who approve their sayings. Selah. {49:14} They are like sheep and are destined for the grave, and death will feed on them. The upright will prevail over them in the morning; their forms will decay in the grave, far from their princely mansions. {49:15} But God will redeem me from the realm of the dead; he will surely take me to himself. Selah. {49:16} Do not be overawed when others grow rich, when the splendor of their houses increases; {49:17} for they will take nothing with them when they die; their splendor will not descend with them. {49:18} Though while they live they count themselves blessed, and people praise you when you prosper, {49:19} they will join those who have gone before them, who will never see the light of life. {49:20} People who have wealth but lack understanding are like the beasts that perish.

{50:1} The Mighty One, God, the LORD, speaks and summons the earth from the rising of the sun to where it sets. {50:2} From Zion, perfect in beauty, God shines forth. {50:3} Our God comes and will not be silent; a fire devours before him, and around him a tempest rages. {50:4} He summons the heavens above and the earth, that he may judge his people. {50:5} "Gather to me this consecrated people, who made a covenant with me by sacrifice." {50:6} And the heavens proclaim his righteousness, for he is a God of justice. Selah. {50:7} "Listen, my people, and I will speak; I will testify against you, Israel: I am God, your God. {50:8} I bring no charges against you concerning your sacrifices or concerning your burnt offerings, which are ever before me. {50:9} I have no need of a bull from your stall or of goats from your pens, {50:10} for every animal of the forest is mine, and the cattle on a thousand hills. {50:11} I know every bird in the mountains, and the insects in the fields are mine. {50:12} If I were hungry, I would not tell you, for the world is mine, and all that is in it. {50:13} Do I eat the flesh of bulls or drink the blood of goats? {50:14} Sacrifice thank offerings to God, fulfill your vows to the Most High, {50:15} and call on me in the day of trouble; I will deliver you, and you will honor me." {50:16} But to the wicked, God says: "What right do you have to recite my laws or take my covenant on your lips? {50:17} You hate my instruction and cast my words behind you. {50:18} When you see a thief, you join with him; you throw in your lot with adulterers. {50:19} You use your mouth for evil and harness your tongue to deceit. {50:20} You sit and testify against your brother and slander your own mother's son. {50:21} These things you have done, and I kept silent; you thought I was entirely like you. But I will rebuke you and accuse you to your face. {50:22} Consider this, you who forget God, or I will tear you to pieces, with no one to rescue you. {50:23} Those who sacrifice thank offerings honor me, and to the blameless, I will show my salvation."

{51:1} Have mercy on me, O God, according to your steadfast love; in your great compassion, blot out my offenses. {51:2} Wash away all my iniquity and cleanse me from my sin. {51:3} For I know my transgressions, and my sin is always before me. {51:4} Against you, you only, have I sinned and done what is evil in your sight; so you are right in your verdict and justified when you judge. {51:5} Surely I was sinful at birth, sinful from the time my mother conceived me. {51:6} Yet you desired faithfulness even in the womb; you taught me wisdom in that secret place. {51:7} Cleanse me with hyssop, and I will be clean; wash me, and I will be whiter than snow. {51:8} Let me hear joy and gladness; let the bones you have crushed rejoice. {51:9} Hide your face from my sins and blot out all my iniquity. {51:10} Create in me a pure heart, O God, and renew a steadfast spirit within me. {51:11} Do not cast me from your presence or take your Holy Spirit from me. {51:12} Restore to me the joy of your salvation and grant me a willing spirit, to sustain me. {51:13} Then I will teach transgressors your ways, and sinners will turn back to you. {51:14} Deliver me from the guilt of bloodshed, O God, you who are God my Savior, and my tongue will sing of your righteousness. {51:15} Open my lips, Lord, and my mouth will declare your praise. {51:16} You do not delight in sacrifice, or I would bring it; you do not take pleasure in burnt offerings. {51:17} My sacrifice, O God, is a broken spirit; a broken and contrite heart you, God, will not despise. {51:18} May it please you to prosper Zion, to build up the walls of Jerusalem. {51:19} Then you will delight in the sacrifices of the righteous, in burnt offerings offered whole; then bulls will be offered on your altar.

{52:1} Why do you boast of evil, you mighty hero? God's faithfulness endures all day long. {52:2} Your tongue plots destruction; it is like a sharpened razor, you deceitful tongue. {52:3} You love evil rather than good, falsehood instead of speaking the truth. Selah. {52:4} You love every harmful word, you deceitful tongue! {52:5} Surely God will bring you down to everlasting ruin; he will snatch you up and pluck you from your tent; he will uproot you from the land of the living. Selah. {52:6} The righteous will see and fear; they will laugh at you, saying, {52:7} "Here now is the man who did not make God his stronghold but trusted in his great wealth and grew strong by destroying others." {52:8} But I am like an olive tree flourishing in the house of God; I trust in God's unfailing love for ever and ever. {52:9} I will praise you forever for what you have done; I will hope in your name, for your name is good, in the presence of your faithful people.

{53:1} The fool says in his heart, "There is no God." They are corrupt, and their deeds are vile; there is no one who does good. {53:2} God looks down from heaven on all mankind to see if there are any who understand, any who seek God. {53:3} Everyone has turned away, all have become corrupt; there is no one who does good, not even one. {53:4} Do the evildoers know nothing? They devour my people as though eating bread; they never call on God. {53:5} There they are, overwhelmed with dread, where there was nothing to dread. God scattered the bones of those who attacked you; you put them to shame, for God despised them. {53:6} Oh, that salvation for Israel would come out of Zion! When God restores his people, let Jacob rejoice and Israel be glad.

{54:1} Save me, O God, by your name; vindicate me by your might. {54:2} Hear my prayer, O God; listen to the words of my mouth. {54:3} Arrogant foes are attacking me; ruthless people are trying to kill me—people without regard for God. Selah. {54:4} Surely God is my help; the Lord is the one who sustains me. {54:5} Let evil recoil on those who slander me; in your faithfulness destroy them. {54:6} I will sacrifice a freewill offering to you; I will praise your name, Lord, for it is good. {54:7} You have delivered me from all my troubles, and my eyes have looked in triumph on my foes.

{55:1} Listen to my prayer, O God, do not ignore my plea; hear me and answer me. {55:2} My thoughts trouble me and I am distraught {55:3} because of what my enemy is saying, because of the threats of the wicked; for they bring down suffering on me and assail me in their anger. {55:4} My heart is in anguish within me; the terrors of death have fallen on me. {55:5} Fear and trembling have beset me; horror has overwhelmed me. {55:6} I said, "Oh, that I had the wings of a dove! I would fly away and be at rest. {55:7} I would flee far away and stay in the desert. Selah. {55:8} I would hurry to my place of shelter, far from the tempest and storm." {55:9} Lord, confuse the wicked; confound their speech, for I see violence and strife in the city. {55:10} Day and night they prowl about on its walls; malice and abuse are within it. {55:11} Destructive forces are at work in the city; threats and lies never leave its streets. {55:12} If an enemy were insulting me, I could endure it; if a foe were rising against me, I could hide. {55:13} But it is you, a man like myself, my companion, my close friend, {55:14} with whom I once enjoyed sweet fellowship at the house of God, as we walked about among the worshipers. {55:15} Let death take my enemies by surprise; let them go down alive to the grave, for evil finds lodging among them. {55:16} As for me, I call to God, and the Lord saves me. {55:17} Evening, morning, and noon I cry out in distress, and he hears my voice. {55:18} He rescues me unharmed from the battle waged against me, even though many oppose me. {55:19} God, who is enthroned from of old, who does not change—he will hear them and humble them, because they have no fear of God. {55:20} My companion attacks his friends; he violates his covenant. {55:21} His talk is smooth as butter, yet war is in his heart; his words are more soothing than oil, yet they are drawn swords. {55:22} Cast your cares on the Lord and he will sustain you; he will never let the righteous be shaken. {55:23} But you, God, will bring down the wicked into the pit of decay; the bloodthirsty and deceitful will not live out half their days. But I will trust in you.

{56:1} Be merciful to me, O God, for people are trying to swallow me up; they fight against me all day long. {56:2} My enemies continually want to swallow me up, for there are many who fight against me, O Most High. {56:3} Whenever I am afraid, I will trust in you. {56:4} In God, I will praise his word; in God, I have put my trust; I will not be afraid of what mere mortals can do to me. {56:5} Every day they twist my words; all their thoughts are against me for evil. {56:6} They gather together, they hide, they watch my steps, waiting to take my life. {56:7} Will they escape because of their wickedness? In your anger, O God, bring down the nations. {56:8} You keep track of my wanderings; put my tears in your bottle—are they not in your book? {56:9} When I cry out to you, my enemies will turn back; this I know, for God is for me. {56:10} In God, I will praise his word; in the Lord, I will praise his word. {56:11} In God, I have put my trust; I will not be afraid of what humans can do to me. {56:12} Your vows are upon me, O God; I will give you thanks. {56:13} For you have delivered my soul from death; will you not keep my feet from stumbling so that I may walk before God in the light of the living?

{57:1} Be merciful to me, O God; be merciful to me, for my soul trusts in you; I will take refuge in the shadow of your wings until these calamities have passed. {57:2} I will cry out to God Most High, to God who fulfills his purpose for me. {57:3} He will send from heaven and save me, rebuking those who would swallow me up. Selah. God will send forth his mercy and truth. {57:4} My soul is among lions; I lie among those who are set on fire—among men whose teeth are spears and arrows, whose tongues are sharp swords. {57:5} Be exalted, O God, above the heavens; let your glory be over all the earth. {57:6} They have prepared a net for my feet; my soul is bowed down; they have dug a pit in my path, but they have fallen into it themselves. Selah. {57:7} My heart is steadfast, O God, my heart is steadfast; I will sing and make music. {57:8} Awake, my soul; awake, harp and lyre! I will awaken the dawn. {57:9} I will praise you, Lord, among the nations; I will sing of you among the peoples. {57:10} For your love is great, reaching to the heavens; your truth reaches to the skies. {57:11} Be exalted, O God, above the heavens; let your glory be over all the earth.

{58:1} Do you indeed speak righteousness, you rulers? Do you judge people with equity? {58:2} No, in your hearts you devise injustice; your hands mete out violence on the earth. {58:3} Even from birth the wicked go astray; from the womb they are wayward, spreading lies. {58:4} Their venom is like the venom of a snake, like that of a cobra that has stopped its ears. {58:5} They will not heed the tune of the charmer, however skillful the enchanter may be. {58:6} Break the teeth in their mouths, O God; Lord, tear out the fangs of those lions. {58:7} Let them vanish like water that flows away; when they draw the bow, let their arrows be blunted. {58:8} Like a slug that melts away as it moves along, like a stillborn child that never sees the sun. {58:9} Before your pots can feel the heat of the thorns—whether they be green or dry—the wicked will be swept away. {58:10} The righteous will be glad when they are avenged, when they dip their feet in the blood of the wicked. {58:11} Then people will say, "Surely the righteous still are rewarded; surely there is a God who judges the earth."

{59:1} Deliver me from my enemies, O my God; protect me from those who rise up against me. {59:2} Deliver me from those who do evil, and save me from bloodthirsty men. {59:3} See, they lie in wait for my life; mighty men conspire against me, not for any offense or sin of mine, O Lord. {59:4} I have done no wrong, yet they are ready to attack me. Awake to help me, look at me! {59:5} You, Lord God Almighty, you who are the God of Israel, rouse yourself to punish all the nations; show no mercy to wicked traitors. Selah. {59:6} They return at evening, snarling like dogs and prowling about the city. {59:7} See what they spew from their mouths; the words of their lips are sharp swords, and they say, "Who hears us?" {59:8} But you, Lord, laugh at them; you scoff at all the nations. {59:9} You are my strength; I watch for you; you, God, are my fortress, {59:10} my God on whom I can rely. God will go before me and will let me gloat over those who slander me. {59:11} Do not slay them, or my people will forget; in your might, make them wander about and bring them down, O Lord, our shield. {59:12} Because of their sins, because of the words of their mouths, let them be caught in their pride; for the curses and lies they utter. {59:13} Consume them in your wrath, consume them till they are no more. Then it will be known to the world that God rules in Jacob to the ends of the earth. Selah. {59:14} Let them return at evening, snarling like dogs and prowling about the city. {59:15} They wander about for food and howl if not satisfied. {59:16} But I will sing of your strength; I will sing aloud of your mercy in the morning, for you are my fortress, my refuge in times of trouble. {59:17} You are my strength, I sing praises to you; you, God, are my fortress, my God on whom I can rely.

{60:1} You have rejected us, O God, and burst upon us; you have been angry—now restore us! {60:2} You have shaken the land and torn it open; mend its fractures, for it is quaking. {60:3} You have shown your people desperate times; you have given us wine that makes us stagger. {60:4} But for those who fear you, you have raised a banner to be unfurled against the bow. Selah. {60:5} Save us and help us with your right hand, that those you love may be delivered. {60:6} God has spoken from his sanctuary: "In triumph I will parcel out Shechem and measure off the Valley of Succoth. {60:7} Gilead is mine, and Manasseh is mine; Ephraim is my helmet, Judah is my scepter. {60:8} Moab is my washbasin, on Edom I toss my sandal; over Philistia I shout in triumph." {60:9} Who will bring me to the fortified city? Who will lead me to Edom? {60:10} Is it not you, God, you who have now rejected us and no longer go out with our armies? {60:11} Give us aid against the enemy, for human help is worthless. {60:12} With God we will gain the victory, and he will trample down our enemies.

{61:1} Hear my cry, O God; listen to my prayer. {61:2} From the ends of the earth I call to you when my heart is overwhelmed; lead me to the rock that is higher than I. {61:3} For you have been my shelter and a strong tower against my enemy. {61:4} I will dwell in your sanctuary forever; I will take refuge under the cover of your wings. Selah. {61:5} For you, O God, have heard my vows; you have given me the inheritance of those who fear your name. {61:6} You will prolong the king's life, and his years will last through many generations. {61:7} He will dwell before God forever; prepare mercy and truth that may protect him. {61:8} So I will sing praise to your name forever, that I may fulfill my vows each day.

{62:1} Truly, my soul waits for God; my salvation comes from him. {62:2} He alone is my rock and my salvation; he is my defense; I will not be shaken. {62:3} How long will you plot against a man? You will all be destroyed; you will be like a leaning wall or a collapsing fence. {62:4} They only consult to bring him down from his position; they delight in lies; they bless with their mouths but curse inwardly. Selah. {62:5} My soul, wait only upon God, for my hope is from him. {62:6} He alone is my rock and my salvation; he is my defense; I will not be moved. {62:7} In God is my salvation and my glory; the rock of my strength, my refuge, is in God. {62:8} Trust in him at all times, you people; pour out your hearts to him, for God is a refuge for us. Selah. {62:9} Surely, the lowborn are but a breath, and the highborn are a lie; if weighed on a balance, they are nothing. {62:10} Do not trust in oppression or take pride in robbery; if riches increase, do not set your heart on them. {62:11} God has spoken once; I have heard it twice: that power belongs to God. {62:12} And also to you, Lord, belongs mercy; for you repay everyone according to what they have done.

{63:1} O God, you are my God; earnestly I seek you; my soul thirsts for you; my body longs for you in a dry and weary land where there is no water. {63:2} I have seen you in the sanctuary and beheld your power and your glory. {63:3} Because your love is better than life, my lips will glorify you. {63:4} I will praise you as long as I live, and in your name, I will lift up my hands. {63:5} My soul will be satisfied as with the richest of foods; with singing lips, my mouth will praise you. {63:6} On my bed, I remember you; I think of you through the watches of the night. {63:7} Because you are my help, I sing in the shadow of your wings. {63:8} I cling to you; your right hand upholds me. {63:9} Those who seek my life will be destroyed; they will go down to the depths of the earth. {63:10} They will be given over to the sword and become food for jackals. {63:11} But the king will rejoice in God; all who swear by God will glory in him, while the mouths of liars will be silenced.

{64:1} Hear my voice, O God, as I pray; protect my life from the fear of the enemy. {64:2} Hide me from the conspiracy of the wicked, from the plots of evildoers. {64:3} They sharpen their tongues like swords and aim their words like deadly arrows. {64:4} They shoot from ambush at the innocent; they shoot suddenly and without fear. {64:5} They encourage each other in evil plans; they talk about hiding their snares; they say, "Who will see it?" {64:6} They search out injustices; they have done a diligent search; the inner thoughts and hearts of men are deep. {64:7} But God will shoot them with arrows; suddenly they will be wounded. {64:8} They will make their own tongues fall on themselves; all who see them will flee away. {64:9} All people will fear; they will proclaim the works of God and ponder what he has done. {64:10} The righteous will rejoice in the Lord and take refuge in him; all the upright in heart will glory in him.

{65:1} Praise awaits you, O God, in Zion; to you our vows will be fulfilled. {65:2} You who hear prayer, to you all people will come. {65:3} When we were overwhelmed by sins, you forgave our transgressions. {65:4} Blessed is the one you choose and bring near to dwell in your courts; we are filled with the good things of your house, of your holy temple. {65:5} You answer us with awesome and righteous deeds, God our Savior, the hope of all the ends of the earth and of the farthest seas. {65:6} Who formed the mountains by your power, having armed yourself with strength? {65:7} Who stilled the roaring of the seas, the roaring of their waves, and the turmoil of the nations? {65:8} The whole earth is filled with awe at your wonders; where morning dawns and evening fades, you call forth songs of joy. {65:9} You care for the land and water it; you enrich it abundantly. The streams of God are filled with water to provide the people with grain, for so you have ordained it. {65:10} You drench its furrows and level its ridges; you soften it with showers and bless its crops. {65:11} You crown the year with your bounty, and your carts overflow with abundance. {65:12} The grasslands of the wilderness overflow, and the hills are clothed with gladness. {65:13} The meadows are covered with flocks, and the valleys are mantled with grain; they shout for joy and sing.

{66:1} Shout for joy to God, all you lands! {66:2} Sing the glory of his name; make his praise glorious. {66:3} Say to God, "How awesome are your deeds! Your great power makes your enemies submit to you." {66:4} All the earth bows down to you; they sing praise to you; they sing praises to your name. Selah. {66:5} Come and see what God has done; he is awesome in his actions toward humanity. {66:6} He turned the sea into dry land; they passed through the waters on foot; there we rejoiced in him. {66:7} He rules forever by his power; his eyes watch the nations; let not the rebellious rise up against him. Selah. {66:8} Bless our God, you people, and let the sound of his praise be heard! {66:9} He has preserved our lives and kept our feet from slipping. {66:10} For you, O God, have tested us; you have refined us like silver. {66:11} You brought us into prison and laid burdens on our backs. {66:12} You let men ride over our heads; we went through fire and water, but you brought us to a place of abundance. {66:13} I will come into your house with burnt offerings; I will fulfill my vows to you, {66:14} vows my lips promised and my mouth spoke when I was in trouble. {66:15} I will offer you burnt sacrifices of fat animals, along with the incense of rams; I will offer bulls and goats. Selah. {66:16} Come and hear, all you who fear God; let me tell you what he has done for me. {66:17} I cried out to him with my mouth; his praise was on my tongue. {66:18} If I had cherished sin in my heart, the Lord would not have listened; {66:19} but God has surely listened and has heard my prayer. {66:20} Praise be to God, who has not rejected my prayer or withheld his love from me.

{67:1} May God be gracious to us and bless us; may he shine his face upon us. Selah. {67:2} So that your ways may be known on earth, your salvation among all nations. {67:3} Let the people praise you, O God; let all the people praise you. {67:4} Let the nations be glad and sing for joy, for you will judge the peoples with fairness and govern the nations on earth. Selah. {67:5} Let the people praise you, O God; let all the people praise you. {67:6} Then the land will yield its harvest, and God, our God, will bless us. {67:7} God will bless us, and all the ends of the earth will fear him.

{68:1} Let God arise; let his enemies be scattered; let those who hate him flee before him. {68:2} As smoke is blown away, so drive them away; as wax melts before the fire, let the wicked perish in the presence of God. {68:3} But let the righteous be glad; let them rejoice before God; yes, let them rejoice with all their might. {68:4} Sing to God, sing praises to his name; extol him who rides on the clouds; rejoice before him. {68:5} A father to the fatherless, a defender of widows, is God in his holy dwelling. {68:6} God sets the lonely in families; he leads out the prisoners with singing; but the rebellious live in a sun-scorched land. {68:7} O God, when you went out before your people, when you marched through the wilderness, Selah. {68:8} The earth shook, the heavens poured down rain, before God, the One of Sinai, before God, the God of Israel. {68:9} You gave abundant showers, O God; you refreshed your weary inheritance. {68:10} Your people settled in it, and from your bounty, God, you provided for the poor. {68:11} The Lord announced the word, and great was the company of those who proclaimed it. {68:12} Kings and their armies flee in haste; the women at home divide the plunder. {68:13} Even while you sleep among the sheep pens, the wings of my dove are sheathed with silver, its feathers with shining gold. {68:14} When the Almighty scattered the kings in the land, it was like snow falling on Mount Zalmon. {68:15} The mountain of God is like the mighty mountain, the mountain of Bashan. {68:16} Why do you look with envy, you high mountains, at the mountain God desired for his dwelling? The Lord will dwell there forever. {68:17} The chariots of God are tens of thousands and thousands of thousands; the Lord has come from Sinai into his sanctuary. {68:18} When you ascended on high, you took many captives; you received gifts from people, even from the rebellious—that you, Lord God, might dwell there. {68:19} Praise be to the Lord, to God our Savior, who daily bears our burdens. Selah. {68:20} Our God is a God who saves; from the Sovereign Lord comes escape from death. {68:21} Surely God will crush the heads of his enemies, the hairy crowns of those who go on in their sins. {68:22} The Lord says, "I will bring them from Bashan; I will bring them from the depths of the sea, {68:23} so that your feet may be dipped in the blood of your foes, and the tongues of your dogs in the blood." {68:24} They have seen your procession, God, the procession of my God and King into the sanctuary. {68:25} In front are the singers, after them the musicians; with them are the young women playing the tambourines. {68:26} Praise God in the great congregation; praise the Lord in the assembly of Israel. {68:27} There is the little tribe of Benjamin, leading them, the princes of Judah in their company, the princes of Zebulun and the princes of Naphtali. {68:28} Summon your power, God; show us your strength, our God, as you have done before. {68:29} Because of your temple at Jerusalem, kings will bring you gifts. {68:30} Rebuke the beast among the reeds, the herd of bulls among the calves of the nations. Scatter the nations that delight in war. {68:31} Envoys will come from Egypt; Cush will submit herself to God. {68:32} Sing to God, you kingdoms of the earth; sing praises to the Lord. Selah. {68:33} To him who rides across the highest heavens, the ancient heavens; who thunders with mighty voice. {68:34} Proclaim the power of God, whose majesty is over Israel, whose power is in the heavens. {68:35} You, God, are awesome in your sanctuary; the God of Israel gives power and strength to his people. Praise be to God!

{69:1} Save me, O God, for the waters have risen to my neck. {69:2} I sink in deep mud, where there is no foothold; I have come into deep waters, and the floods engulf me. {69:3} I am worn out calling for help; my throat is parched; my eyes fail, looking for my God. {69:4} Those who hate me without reason outnumber the hairs of my head; many are my enemies without cause, those who seek to destroy me. I am forced to restore what I did not steal. {69:5} You, God, know my folly; my guilt is not hidden from you. {69:6} Do not let those who hope in you be ashamed because of me, Lord God Almighty; do not let those who seek you be dishonored because of me, God of Israel. {69:7} For I endure scorn for your sake, and shame covers my face. {69:8} I am a stranger to my own family, an alien to my mother's children. {69:9} For zeal for your house consumes me, and the insults of those who insult you fall on me. {69:10} When I wept and fasted, I did it to my shame. {69:11} When I made sackcloth my clothing, people made jokes about me. {69:12} Those who sit at the gate mock me, and I am the song of the drunkards. {69:13} But I pray to you, Lord, in the time of your favor; in your great love, O God, answer me with your sure salvation. {69:14} Rescue me from the mire, do not let me sink; deliver me from those who hate me, from the deep waters. {69:15} Do not let the floodwaters engulf me or the depths swallow me up or the pit close its mouth over me. {69:16} Answer me, Lord, out of the goodness of your love; in your great mercy turn to me. {69:17} Do not hide your face from your servant; answer me quickly, for I am in trouble. {69:18} Come near and rescue me; deliver me because of my enemies. {69:19} You know how I am scorned, disgraced, and shamed; all my enemies are before you. {69:20} Scorn has broken my heart and has left me helpless; I looked for sympathy, but there was none; for comforters, but I found none. {69:21} They put gall in my food and gave me vinegar for my thirst. {69:22} May the table set before them become a snare; may it become retribution and a trap. {69:23} May their eyes be darkened so they cannot see; and make their backs tremble continually. {69:24} Pour out your wrath on them; let your fierce anger overtake them. {69:25} May their place be deserted; let there be no one to dwell in their tents. {69:26} For they persecute those you wound and talk about the pain of those you hurt. {69:27} Charge them with crime upon crime; do not let them share in your salvation. {69:28} May they be blotted out of the book of life and not be listed with the righteous. {69:29} But I am in pain and distress; may your salvation, God, protect me. {69:30} I will praise God's name in song and glorify him with thanksgiving. {69:31} This will please the Lord more than an ox, more than a bull with horns and hooves. {69:32} The poor will see and be glad; you who seek God, may your hearts live! {69:33} The Lord hears the needy and does not despise his captive people. {69:34} Let heaven and earth praise him, the seas and all that move in them. {69:35} For God will save Zion and rebuild the cities of Judah. Then people will settle there and possess it. {69:36} The children of his servants will inherit it, and those who love his name will dwell there.

{70:1} Hasten, O God, to save me; come quickly, Lord, to help me. {70:2} May those who seek my life be put to shame and confusion; may all who desire my ruin be turned back in disgrace. {70:3} May those who say to me, "Aha! Aha!" turn back because of their shame. {70:4} But may all who seek you rejoice and be glad in you; may those who long for your saving help always say, "Let God be exalted!" {70:5} Yet I am poor and needy; come quickly to me, O God. You are my help and my deliverer; Lord, do not delay.

{71:1} In you, O Lord, I put my trust; let me never be put to shame. {71:2} Deliver me in your righteousness and help me escape; turn your ear to me and save me. {71:3} Be my strong refuge, where I can always go; you have commanded me to be saved, for you are my rock and my fortress. {71:4} Deliver me, O my God, from the hand of the wicked, from the hand of the unrighteous and cruel person. {71:5} For you are my hope, Lord God; you have been my trust since I was young. {71:6} From birth I have relied on you; you brought me out of my mother's womb; I will continually praise you. {71:7} I am a wonder to many, but you are my strong refuge. {71:8} Let my mouth be filled with your praise and your glory all day long. {71:9} Do not cast me off in old age; do not forsake me when my strength fails. {71:10} For my enemies speak against me; those who lie in wait for my life conspire together, {71:11} saying, "God has forsaken him; pursue and seize him, for there is no one to deliver him." {71:12} O God, do not be far from me; come quickly to help me, my God. {71:13} Let those who are my adversaries be ashamed and consumed; let those who seek my hurt be covered with disgrace and dishonor. {71:14} But I will hope continually and praise you more and more. {71:15} My mouth will declare your righteousness and your salvation all day long, though I do not know their full number. {71:16} I will come in the strength of the Lord God; I will mention your righteousness, yours alone. {71:17} O God, you have taught me since my youth, and to this day I declare your marvelous deeds. {71:18} Even when I am old and gray, do not forsake me, God, until I have declared your power to the next generation and your might to all who are to come. {71:19} Your righteousness, O God, reaches to the heavens; you have done great things; O God, who is like you? {71:20} You who have shown me great troubles will revive me again; you will bring me up again from the depths of the earth. {71:21} You will increase my greatness and comfort me on every side. {71:22} I will also praise you with the harp for your faithfulness, O my God; I will sing praises to you with the lyre, O Holy One of Israel. {71:23} My lips will rejoice when I sing to you; my soul, which you have redeemed. {71:24} My tongue will tell of your righteousness all day long, for those who seek my hurt will be ashamed and disgraced.

{72:1} Give the king your judgments, O God, and your righteousness to the king's son. {72:2} He will judge your people with righteousness and your poor with justice. {72:3} The mountains will bring peace to the people, and the hills will provide righteousness. {72:4} He will judge the poor of the people, save the needy, and crush the oppressor. {72:5} They will fear you as long as the sun and moon endure, throughout all generations. {72:6} He will come down like rain on the mown grass, like showers that water the earth. {72:7} In his days, the righteous will flourish, and there will be an abundance of peace as long as the moon lasts. {72:8} He will have dominion from sea to sea and from the river to the ends of the earth. {72:9} Those who dwell in the wilderness will bow before him, and his enemies will lick the dust. {72:10} The kings of Tarshish and the islands will bring presents; the kings of Sheba and Seba will offer gifts. {72:11} Yes, all kings will bow down before him; all nations will serve him. {72:12} For he will deliver the needy when they cry, the poor also, and those who have no helper. {72:13} He will spare the poor and needy and save their lives. {72:14} He will redeem them from oppression and violence; their blood will be precious in his sight. {72:15} He will live, and gold from Sheba will be given to him; people will pray for him continually and praise him all day long. {72:16} There will be abundance of grain on the earth on the mountaintops; its fruit will sway like the trees of Lebanon; and those in the city will flourish like grass in the field. {72:17} His name will endure forever; his name will continue as long as the sun shines; all nations will be blessed in him; they will call him blessed. {72:18} Blessed be the Lord God, the God of Israel, who alone does wondrous things. {72:19} Blessed be his glorious name forever; may the whole earth be filled with his glory. Amen and Amen. {72:20} The prayers of David son of Jesse are ended.

{73:1} Truly, God is good to Israel, to those who are pure in heart. {73:2} But as for me, my feet had almost slipped; I nearly lost my foothold. {73:3} For I was envious of the arrogant when I saw the prosperity of the wicked. {73:4} They have no struggles; their bodies are healthy and strong. {73:5} They are free from common human burdens; they are not plagued by human ills. {73:6} Therefore pride is their necklace; they clothe themselves with violence. {73:7} From their callous hearts comes iniquity; their evil imaginations have no limits. {73:8} They scoff and speak with malice; they threaten oppression. {73:9} Their mouths lay claim to heaven, and their tongues take possession of the earth. {73:10} Therefore, their people turn to them and drink up waters in abundance. {73:11} They say, "How would God know? Does the Most High know anything?" {73:12} This is what the wicked are like—always free of care, they go on amassing wealth. {73:13} Surely, in vain I have kept my heart pure and washed my hands in innocence. {73:14} All day long I have been afflicted, and every morning brings new punishments. {73:15} If I had spoken out like that, I would have betrayed your children. {73:16} When I tried to understand all this, it troubled me deeply, {73:17} till I entered the sanctuary of God; then I understood their final destiny. {73:18} Surely you place them on slippery ground; you cast them down to ruin. {73:19} How suddenly are they destroyed, completely swept away by terrors! {73:20} They are like a dream when one awakes; when you arise, Lord, you will despise them as fantasies. {73:21} When my heart was grieved and my spirit embittered, {73:22} I was senseless and ignorant; I was a brute beast before you. {73:23} Yet I am always with you; you hold me by my right hand. {73:24} You guide me with your counsel, and afterward you will take me into glory. {73:25} Whom have I in heaven but you? And earth has nothing I desire besides you. {73:26} My flesh and my heart may fail, but God is the strength of my heart and my portion forever. {73:27} Those who are far from you will perish; you destroy all who are unfaithful to you. {73:28} But as for me, it is good to be near God; I have made the Sovereign Lord my refuge; I will tell of all your deeds.

{74:1} O God, why have you rejected us forever? Why does your anger smolder against the sheep of your pasture? {74:2} Remember the people you purchased of old, the tribe of your inheritance, whom you redeemed—Mount Zion, where you dwelt. {74:3} Turn your steps toward these everlasting ruins, all this destruction the enemy has brought on the sanctuary. {74:4} Your foes roared in the place where you met with us; they set up their standards as signs. {74:5} They behaved like men wielding axes to cut through a thicket of trees. {74:6} They smashed all the carved paneling with their axes and hatchets. {74:7} They burned your sanctuary to the ground; they defiled the dwelling place of your Name. {74:8} They said in their hearts, "We will crush them completely!" They burned every place where God was worshiped in the land. {74:9} We are given no signs from God; no prophets are left, and none of us knows how long this will last. {74:10} How long, O God, will the enemy mock you? Will the foe revile your name forever? {74:11} Why do you hold back your hand, your right hand? Take it from the folds of your garment and destroy them! {74:12} But God is my King from long ago; he brings salvation on the earth. {74:13} It was you who split open the sea by your power; you broke the heads of the monster in the waters. {74:14} It was you who crushed the heads of Leviathan and gave it as food to the creatures of the desert. {74:15} It was you who opened up springs and streams; you dried up the ever-flowing rivers. {74:16} The day is yours, and yours also the night; you established the sun and moon. {74:17} It was you who set all the boundaries of the earth; you made both summer and winter. {74:18} Remember how the enemy has mocked you, Lord, how foolish people have reviled your name. {74:19} Do not hand over the life of your dove to wild beasts; do not forget the lives of your afflicted people forever. {74:20} Have regard for your covenant, because haunts of violence fill the dark places of the land. {74:21} Do not let the oppressed retreat in disgrace; may the poor and needy praise your name. {74:22} Arise, O God, and defend your cause; remember how fools mock you all day long. {74:23} Do not ignore the clamor of your adversaries, the uproar of your enemies, which rises continually.

{75:1} We give thanks to you, O God; we give thanks, for your name is near; we recount your wonderful deeds. {75:2} You say, "I choose the appointed time; it is I who judge with equity." {75:3} When the earth and all its people quake, it is I who hold its pillars firm. Selah. {75:4} To the arrogant I say, "Do not be arrogant," and to the wicked, "Do not lift up your horns. {75:5} Do not lift your horn against heaven; do not speak so defiantly." {75:6} No one from the east or the west or from the desert can exalt themselves. {75:7} It is God who judges: he brings one down, he exalts another. {75:8} In the hand of the Lord is a cup full of foaming wine mixed with spices; he pours it out, and all the wicked of the earth drink it down to its very dregs. {75:9} As for me, I will declare this forever; I will sing praises to the God of Jacob. {75:10} I will cut off the horns of all the wicked, but the horns of the righteous will be lifted high.

{76:1} God is known in Judah; his name is great in Israel. {76:2} In Salem, he has his tabernacle, and his dwelling place is in Zion. {76:3} There he shattered the arrows, the shield, and the sword, and the battle. Selah. {76:4} You are more glorious and excellent than the mountains full of prey. {76:5} The stronghearted are spoiled; they lie in sleep, and none of the mighty men can lift a hand. {76:6} At your rebuke, O God of Jacob, both chariot and horse fall into a deep sleep. {76:7} You, even you, are to be feared; who can stand in your presence when you are angry? {76:8} You made your judgment heard from heaven; the earth feared and was still, {76:9} when God arose to judge and to save all the meek of the earth. Selah. {76:10} Surely the wrath of man will praise you; the remnant of wrath you will restrain. {76:11} Make a vow and pay it to the LORD your God; let all around him bring gifts to him who is to be feared. {76:12} He will cut off the spirit of princes; he is terrifying to the kings of the earth.

{77:1} I cried out to God with my voice; I cried out to God, and he listened to me. {77:2} In my day of trouble, I sought the Lord; at night my hands were stretched out without ceasing; my soul refused to be comforted. {77:3} I remembered God and was troubled; I complained, and my spirit was overwhelmed. Selah. {77:4} You kept my eyes from closing; I was so troubled that I could not speak. {77:5} I considered the days of old, the years of ancient times. {77:6} I remembered my song in the night; I communed with my heart, and my spirit searched diligently. {77:7} Will the Lord reject us forever? Will he never show us favor again? {77:8} Has his mercy completely vanished? Does his promise fail forever? {77:9} Has God forgotten to be gracious? Has he in anger withheld his compassion? Selah. {77:10} Then I said, "This is my affliction; but I will remember the years of the right hand of the Most High." {77:11} I will remember the works of the LORD; surely I will remember your wonders of old. {77:12} I will meditate on all your work and talk about your deeds. {77:13} Your way, O God, is in the sanctuary; who is so great a God as our God? {77:14} You are the God who performs wonders; you have declared your strength among the peoples. {77:15} You redeemed your people, the sons of Jacob and Joseph. Selah. {77:16} The waters saw you, O God; the waters saw you and were afraid; the depths also trembled. {77:17} The clouds poured down water; the skies thundered; your arrows flashed back and forth. {77:18} The voice of your thunder was in the heavens; the lightning lit up the world; the earth trembled and shook. {77:19} Your way was through the sea, your path through the mighty waters, and your footsteps were not known. {77:20} You led your people like a flock by the hand of Moses and Aaron.

{78:1} Give ear, O my people, to my teaching; listen to the words of my mouth. {78:2} I will open my mouth in a parable; I will utter dark sayings from old, {78:3} which we have heard and known, and our fathers have told us. {78:4} We will not hide them from our children, telling the coming generation the praises of the LORD, his strength, and the wonderful works he has done. {78:5} For he established a testimony in Jacob and appointed a law in Israel, which he commanded our fathers to make known to their children, {78:6} so that the coming generation might know them, even the children yet to be born, who will arise and tell them to their children, {78:7} that they might set their hope in God and not forget the works of God but keep his commandments, {78:8} and not be like their fathers, a stubborn and rebellious generation, a generation that did not set its heart aright and whose spirit was not steadfast with God. {78:9} The children of Ephraim, armed and carrying bows, turned back on the day of battle. {78:10} They did not keep the covenant of God and refused to walk in his law; {78:11} they forgot his works and the wonders he had shown them. {78:12} He did marvelous things in the sight of their fathers in the land of Egypt, in the region of Zoan. {78:13} He divided the sea and led them through; he made the waters stand like a heap. {78:14} In the daytime, he led them with a cloud, and all night with a light of fire. {78:15} He split the rocks in the wilderness and gave them drink as from the great depths. {78:16} He brought streams out of the rock and caused waters to flow like rivers. {78:17} Yet they continued to sin against him by provoking the Most High in the wilderness. {78:18} They tested God in their hearts by asking for food to satisfy their cravings. {78:19} They spoke against God; they said, "Can God prepare a table in the wilderness?" {78:20} Look, he struck the rock, and water gushed out, and streams overflowed; can he also give bread? Can he provide meat for his people? {78:21} Therefore, the LORD heard this and was angry; so a fire was kindled against Jacob, and anger also rose against Israel, {78:22} because they did not believe in God and did not trust in his salvation. {78:23} Yet he commanded the clouds above and opened the doors of heaven; {78:24} he rained down manna upon them to eat and gave them the grain of heaven. {78:25} Man ate the bread of angels; he sent them food to the full. {78:26} He caused an east wind to blow in the heavens, and by his power, he brought in the south wind. {78:27} He rained down flesh upon them like dust, and winged birds like the sand of the sea; {78:28} he made them fall in the midst of their camp, all around their dwellings. {78:29} So they ate and were well filled, for he gave them what they desired. {78:30} They were not estranged from their cravings; but while the food was still in their mouths, {78:31} the anger of God rose against them and killed the strongest of them and struck down the chosen men of Israel. {78:32} Despite all this, they kept on sinning and did not believe in his wondrous works. {78:33} So he ended their days in futility and their years in disaster. {78:34} When he killed them, they sought him; they repented and earnestly sought God. {78:35} They remembered that God was their rock, the Most High God their redeemer. {78:36} But they flattered him with their mouths; they lied to him with their tongues. {78:37} Their hearts were not right with him, and they were not steadfast in his covenant. {78:38} Yet he was merciful; he forgave their iniquities and did not destroy them; many times he turned his anger away and did not stir up all his wrath. {78:39} For he remembered that they were but flesh, a passing breeze that does not return. {78:40} How often they rebelled against him in the wilderness and grieved him in the desert! {78:41} Again and again they tested God and limited the Holy One of Israel. {78:42} They did not remember his power or the day when he redeemed them from the enemy, {78:43} when he performed his signs in Egypt and his wonders in the region of Zoan. {78:44} He turned their rivers into blood, and their streams they could not drink. {78:45} He sent swarms of flies among them, which devoured them, and frogs, which destroyed them. {78:46} He gave their crops to the caterpillar and their labor to the locust. {78:47} He destroyed their vines with hail and their sycamore trees with frost. {78:48} He gave over their cattle to the hail and their flocks to lightning. {78:49} He unleashed against them his fierce anger, his wrath, indignation, and trouble, sending angels of destruction among them. {78:50} He made a path for his anger; he did not spare them from death but gave their lives over to the plague. {78:51} He struck down all the firstborn in Egypt, the first fruits of manhood in the tents of Ham. {78:52} But he brought his people out like a flock; he led them like sheep through the wilderness. {78:53} He guided them safely, so they did not fear; but the sea overwhelmed their enemies. {78:54} He brought them to the border of his sanctuary, to the hill country his right hand had taken. {78:55} He drove out nations before them and allotted their lands to them as an inheritance; he settled the tribes of Israel in their tents. {78:56} Yet they tested and rebelled against the Most High God; they did not keep his testimonies. {78:57} They turned back and were unfaithful like their ancestors; they were as unreliable as a faulty bow. {78:58} They angered him with their high places; they aroused his jealousy with their idols. {78:59} When God heard this, he was furious and greatly abhorred Israel. {78:60} So he forsook the tabernacle at Shiloh, the tent he had set up among men; {78:61} he delivered his strength into captivity and his glory into the enemy's hands. {78:62} He gave his people over to the sword and was angry with his inheritance. {78:63} The fire consumed their young men, and their maidens had no wedding songs. {78:64} Their priests fell by the sword, and their widows could not weep. {78:65} Then the Lord awoke as from sleep, as a warrior wakes up from the stupor of wine. {78:66} He struck down his enemies from behind; he put them to perpetual shame. {78:67} He rejected the tent of Joseph and did not choose the tribe of Ephraim; {78:68} but he chose the tribe of Judah, Mount Zion, which he loved. {78:69} He built his sanctuary like the heights, like the earth he has established forever. {78:70} He chose David his servant and took him from the sheep pens; {78:71} from tending the sheep he brought him to be the shepherd of his people Jacob, of Israel his inheritance. {78:72} And David shepherded them with integrity of heart; with skillful hands, he guided them.

{79:1} O God, the nations have invaded your inheritance; they have defiled your holy temple; they have laid Jerusalem in ruins. {79:2} They have given the dead bodies of your servants to the birds of the air, the flesh of your saints to the beasts of the earth. {79:3} Their blood has been poured out like water all around Jerusalem, and there is no one to bury them. {79:4} We have become a reproach to our neighbors, a scorn and derision to those around us. {79:5} How long, LORD? Will you be angry forever? Will your jealousy burn like fire? {79:6} Pour out your wrath on the nations that do not acknowledge you, on the kingdoms that do not call on your name; {79:7} for they have devoured Jacob and laid waste his dwelling place. {79:8} Do not remember against us the sins of our forefathers; let your mercy come quickly to meet us, for we are brought very low. {79:9} Help us, O God of our salvation, for the glory of your name; deliver us and atone for our sins for your name's sake. {79:10} Why should the nations say, "Where is their God?" Let it be known among the nations, in our sight, by avenging the blood of your servants that has been shed. {79:11} Let the groans of the prisoners come before you; according to your great power, preserve those condemned to die. {79:12} Pay back our neighbors seven times for the scorn they have hurled at you, O Lord. {79:13} Then we, your people, the sheep of your pasture, will give you thanks forever; we will proclaim your praise to all generations.

{80:1} Give ear, O Shepherd of Israel, you who lead Joseph like a flock; you who sit enthroned between the cherubim, shine forth. {80:2} Before Ephraim, Benjamin, and Manasseh, stir up your might and come to save us. {80:3} Restore us, O God; make your face shine on us, that we may be saved. {80:4} O LORD God Almighty, how long will your anger smolder against the prayers of your people? {80:5} You have fed them with the bread of tears; you have made them drink tears by the bowlful. {80:6} You have made us an object of contention to our neighbors, and our enemies mock us. {80:7} Restore us, O God Almighty; make your face shine on us, that we may be saved. {80:8} You brought a vine out of Egypt; you drove out the nations and planted it. {80:9} You cleared the ground for it, and it took root and filled the land. {80:10} The mountains were covered with its shade, the mighty cedars with its branches. {80:11} It sent out its boughs to the sea, its shoots as far as the River. {80:12} Why have you broken down its walls so that all who pass by pick its grapes? {80:13} Boars from the forest ravage it, and insects from the fields feed on it. {80:14} Return to us, O God Almighty! Look down from heaven and see; take care of this vine, {80:15} the root your right hand has planted, the son you have raised up for yourself. {80:16} Your vine is cut down, it is burned with fire; at your rebuke, your people perish. {80:17} Let your hand rest on the man at your right hand, the son of man you have raised up for yourself. {80:18} Then we will not turn away from you; revive us, and we will call on your name. {80:19} Restore us, O LORD God Almighty; make your face shine on us, that we may be saved.

{81:1} Sing joyfully to God our strength; shout out to the God of Jacob. {81:2} Take a psalm and bring the tambourine, the pleasant harp, and the lyre. {81:3} Blow the trumpet at the new moon, at the appointed time, on our feast day. {81:4} This was a statute for Israel and a law from the God of Jacob. {81:5} He established it in Joseph as a testimony when he went through the land of Egypt; I heard a language I did not understand. {81:6} I removed the burden from his shoulder; his hands were freed from the pots. {81:7} You called out in trouble, and I delivered you; I answered you in the secret place of thunder; I tested you at the waters of Meribah. Selah. {81:8} Hear, O my people, and I will testify to you; O Israel, if you would listen to me. {81:9} There shall be no foreign god among you; you shall not worship any strange god. {81:10} I am the LORD your God, who brought you out of Egypt; open your mouth wide, and I will fill it. {81:11} But my people would not listen to my voice; Israel would not have me. {81:12} So I gave them up to their own desires; they followed their own plans. {81:13} Oh, that my people had listened to me, and Israel had walked in my ways! {81:14} I would have quickly subdued their enemies and turned my hand against their adversaries. {81:15} Those who hate the LORD would have submitted to him, and their time would have lasted forever. {81:16} He would have fed them with the finest wheat and satisfied them with honey from the rock.

{82:1} God stands in the assembly of the mighty; he judges among the gods. {82:2} How long will you judge unjustly and show favoritism to the wicked? Selah. {82:3} Defend the poor and fatherless; do justice for the afflicted and needy. {82:4} Deliver the poor and needy; rescue them from the hands of the wicked. {82:5} They do not know or understand; they walk in darkness; all the foundations of the earth are shaken. {82:6} I said, "You are gods, and you are all children of the Most High." {82:7} But you will die like mere mortals; you will fall like any prince. {82:8} Arise, O God, judge the earth, for you will inherit all nations.

{83:1} Do not remain silent, O God; do not hold your peace and do not be still, O God. {83:2} For behold, your enemies make a commotion; those who hate you have raised their heads. {83:3} They have taken crafty counsel against your people and plotted against your treasured ones. {83:4} They said, "Come, let us cut them off from being a nation; let the name of Israel be remembered no more." {83:5} For they have conspired together with one mind; they are united against you: {83:6} the tents of Edom and the Ishmaelites; Moab and the Hagrites; {83:7} Gebal, Ammon, and Amalek; the Philistines with the inhabitants of Tyre; {83:8} Assyria has also joined them; they have helped the children of Lot. Selah. {83:9} Do to them as you did to the Midianites; as to Sisera and Jabin at the river Kishon, {83:10} who perished at Endor and became like dung on the ground. {83:11} Make their nobles like Oreb and Zeeb; yes, all their leaders like Zebah and Zalmunna, {83:12} who said, "Let us take possession of the houses of God." {83:13} O my God, make them like whirling leaves, like chaff before the wind. {83:14} As fire consumes a forest, as the flame sets the mountains ablaze, {83:15} so pursue them with your storm and terrify them with your whirlwind. {83:16} Fill their faces with shame, so they may seek your name, O LORD. {83:17} Let them be confounded and troubled forever; let them be put to shame and perish, {83:18} that people may know that you, whose name alone is the LORD, are the Most High over all the earth.

{84:1} How lovely are your dwelling places, O LORD of hosts! {84:2} My soul longs, yes, even faints for the courts of the LORD; my heart and my flesh cry out for the living God. {84:3} Even the sparrow finds a home, and the swallow a nest for herself, where she may lay her young, near your altars, O LORD of hosts, my King and my God. {84:4} Blessed are those who dwell in your house; they will always be praising you. Selah. {84:5} Blessed is the man whose strength is in you, in whose heart are your ways. {84:6} As they pass through the Valley of Baca, they make it a spring; the rain also fills the pools. {84:7} They go from strength to strength; each one appears before God in Zion. {84:8} O LORD God of hosts, hear my prayer; give ear, O God of Jacob. Selah. {84:9} Behold, O God our shield; look upon the face of your anointed. {84:10} For a day in your courts is better than a thousand elsewhere; I would rather be a doorkeeper in the house of my God than dwell in the tents of the wicked. {84:11} For the LORD God is a sun and shield; the LORD will give grace and glory; no good thing will he withhold from those who walk uprightly. {84:12} O LORD of hosts, blessed is the man who trusts in you.

{85:1} LORD, you have been favorable to your land; you have restored the fortunes of Jacob. {85:2} You have forgiven the iniquity of your people; you have covered all their sin. Selah. {85:3} You have taken away all your wrath; you have turned from the fierceness of your anger. {85:4} Restore us, O God of our salvation, and cause your anger toward us to cease. {85:5} Will you be angry with us forever? Will you prolong your anger to all generations? {85:6} Will you not revive us again, that your people may rejoice in you? {85:7} Show us your mercy, O LORD, and grant us your salvation. {85:8} I will hear what God the LORD will speak; for he will speak peace to his people and to his saints, but let them not turn back to folly. {85:9} Surely his salvation is near to those who fear him, that glory may dwell in our land. {85:10} Mercy and truth have met together; righteousness and peace have kissed each other. {85:11} Truth springs up from the earth, and righteousness looks down from heaven. {85:12} Yes, the LORD will give what is good, and our land will yield its increase. {85:13} Righteousness will go before him and will set us in the path of his steps.

{86:1} Bow down your ear, O LORD, and hear me, for I am poor and in need. {86:2} Preserve my soul, for I am holy; save your servant who trusts in you, O my God. {86:3} Be merciful to me, O Lord, for I cry out to you daily. {86:4} Rejoice the soul of your servant, for to you, O Lord, I lift up my soul. {86:5} For you, Lord, are good and ready to forgive; you are abundant in mercy to all who call upon you. {86:6} Give ear, O LORD, to my prayer; listen to my pleas for help. {86:7} In the day of my trouble, I will call upon you, for you will answer me. {86:8} Among the gods, there is none like you, O Lord; nor are there any works like yours. {86:9} All nations you have made shall come and worship before you, O Lord, and glorify your name. {86:10} For you are great and do wondrous things; you alone are God. {86:11} Teach me your way, O LORD; I will walk in your truth; unite my heart to fear your name. {86:12} I will praise you, O Lord my God, with all my heart; I will glorify your name forever. {86:13} For great is your mercy toward me; you have delivered my soul from the depths of the grave. {86:14} O God, the proud rise against me, and violent men seek my life; they do not set you before them. {86:15} But you, O Lord, are a God full of compassion, gracious, patient, and abundant in mercy and truth. {86:16} Turn to me and have mercy on me; give your strength to your servant and save the son of your maidservant. {86:17} Show me a sign for good, that those who hate me may see it and be ashamed, because you, LORD, have helped me and comforted me.

{87:1} His foundation is in the holy mountains. {87:2} The LORD loves the gates of Zion more than all the dwellings of Jacob. {87:3} Glorious things are said of you, O city of God. Selah. {87:4} I will mention Rahab and Babylon to those who know me; behold Philistia and Tyre, with Ethiopia; this man was born there. {87:5} And of Zion, it will be said, "This one and that one was born in her," and the Most High himself shall establish her. {87:6} The LORD will count when he registers the people, "This man was born there." Selah. {87:7} Both the singers and the players on instruments will be there; all my springs are in you.

{88:1} O LORD God of my salvation, I have cried out to you day and night. {88:2} Let my prayer come before you; incline your ear to my cry. {88:3} For my soul is full of troubles, and my life draws near to the grave. {88:4} I am counted with those who go down to the pit; I am like a man with no strength. {88:5} Free among the dead, like the slain who lie in the grave, whom you remember no more; they are cut off from your hand. {88:6} You have laid me in the lowest pit, in darkness, in the depths. {88:7} Your wrath lies heavy upon me, and you have afflicted me with all your waves. Selah. {88:8} You have removed my friends far from me; you have made me an object of scorn to them; I am shut in and cannot escape. {88:9} My eyes are dim with grief; LORD, I have called daily upon you; I have stretched out my hands to you. {88:10} Will you show wonders to the dead? Will the dead arise and praise you? Selah. {88:11} Will your lovingkindness be declared in the grave, or your faithfulness in destruction? {88:12} Will your wonders be known in the dark, and your righteousness in the land of forgetfulness? {88:13} But to you, O LORD, I have cried, and in the morning my prayer comes before you. {88:14} LORD, why do you cast off my soul? Why do you hide your face from me? {88:15} I am afflicted and ready to die from my youth; I suffer your terrors and am distracted. {88:16} Your fierce wrath goes over me; your terrors have cut me off. {88:17} They surround me daily like water; they encircle me completely. {88:18} Lover and friend you have put far from me, and my acquaintances into darkness.

{89:1} I will sing of the mercies of the LORD forever; with my mouth, I will make your faithfulness known to all generations. {89:2} For I have said, "Mercy will be built up forever; your faithfulness you will establish in the very heavens." {89:3} I have made a covenant with my chosen one; I have sworn to David my servant, {89:4} "I will establish your seed forever, and build up your throne for all generations." Selah. {89:5} The heavens will praise your wonders, O LORD, your faithfulness also in the assembly of the saints. {89:6} For who in the heavens can be compared to the LORD? Who among the sons of the mighty can be likened to the LORD? {89:7} God is greatly feared in the assembly of the saints and is held in reverence by all who are around him. {89:8} O LORD God of hosts, who is a strong LORD like you? Or your faithfulness round about you? {89:9} You rule the raging of the sea; when its waves rise, you still them. {89:10} You have broken Rahab in pieces like one who is slain; you have scattered your enemies with your strong arm. {89:11} The heavens are yours; the earth is also yours; the world and everything in it, you have founded them. {89:12} You created the north and the south; Tabor and Hermon rejoice in your name. {89:13} You have a mighty arm; strong is your hand, and high is your right hand. {89:14} Justice and judgment are the foundation of your throne; mercy and truth go before your face. {89:15} Blessed are the people who know the joyful sound; they walk, O LORD, in the light of your countenance. {89:16} In your name, they rejoice all day; in your righteousness, they are exalted. {89:17} For you are the glory of their strength; and by your favor, our horn is exalted. {89:18} For the LORD is our defense; the Holy One of Israel is our king. {89:19} Then you spoke in vision to your holy one and said, "I have laid help upon one who is mighty; I have exalted one chosen from the people." {89:20} I have found David my servant; with my holy oil, I have anointed him. {89:21} With whom my hand will be established; my arm will also strengthen him. {89:22} The enemy will not outsmart him, nor will the wicked afflict him. {89:23} I will beat down his foes before him and plague those who hate him. {89:24} But my faithfulness and my mercy shall be with him; in my name, his horn will be exalted. {89:25} I will set his hand over the sea and his right hand over the rivers. {89:26} He shall cry to me, "You are my Father, my God, and the rock of my salvation." {89:27} I will make him my firstborn, higher than the kings of the earth. {89:28} My mercy I will keep for him forever, and my covenant shall stand firm with him. {89:29} His seed I will make endure forever, and his throne as the days of heaven. {89:30} If his children forsake my law and do not walk in my judgments; {89:31} if they break my statutes and do not keep my commandments; {89:32} then I will punish their transgression with the rod and their iniquity with stripes. {89:33} Nevertheless, I will not utterly take my lovingkindness from him, nor allow my faithfulness to fail. {89:34} I will not break my covenant, nor alter what has gone out of my lips. {89:35} Once I have sworn by my holiness that I will not lie to David. {89:36} His seed shall endure forever, and his throne as the sun before me. {89:37} It shall be established forever like the moon, and as a faithful witness in heaven. Selah. {89:38} But you have cast off and rejected; you have become angry with your anointed. {89:39} You have made void the covenant of your servant; you have profaned his crown by casting it to the ground. {89:40} You have broken down all his defenses; you have brought his strongholds to ruin. {89:41} All who pass by spoil him; he is a reproach to his neighbors. {89:42} You have lifted the right hand of his adversaries; you have made all his enemies rejoice. {89:43} You have turned the edge of his sword, and have not made him stand in battle. {89:44} You have made his glory cease, and cast his throne down to the ground. {89:45} You have shortened the days of his youth; you have covered him with shame. Selah. {89:46} How long, LORD? Will you hide yourself forever? Will your wrath burn like fire? {89:47} Remember how short my time is; why have you made all men in vain? {89:48} What man lives and shall not see death? Can he deliver his soul from the hand of the grave? Selah. {89:49} Lord, where are your former lovingkindnesses, which you swore to David in your truth? {89:50} Remember, Lord, the reproach of your servants; how I bear in my heart the reproach of all the mighty people; {89:51} with which your enemies have reproached, O LORD; with which they have reproached the footsteps of your anointed. {89:52} Blessed be the LORD forever. Amen, and Amen.

{90:1} Lord, you have been our dwelling place in all generations. {90:2} Before the mountains were brought forth, or before you formed the earth and the world, even from everlasting to everlasting, you are God. {90:3} You turn man to destruction and say, "Return, O children of men." {90:4} For a thousand years in your sight are like yesterday when it is past, and like a watch in the night. {90:5} You carry them away like a flood; they are like a sleep; in the morning, they are like grass which grows up. {90:6} In the morning, it flourishes and grows; in the evening, it is cut down and withers. {90:7} For we are consumed by your anger, and by your wrath, we are troubled. {90:8} You have set our iniquities before you, our secret sins in the light of your countenance. {90:9} For all our days pass away in your wrath; we spend our years as a tale that is told. {90:10} The days of our years are seventy, and if by reason of strength they are eighty years, yet their strength is labor and sorrow; for it is soon cut off, and we fly away. {90:11} Who knows the power of your anger? According to your fear, so is your wrath. {90:12} So teach us to number our days, that we may apply our hearts to wisdom. {90:13} Return, O LORD; how long? Let it repent you concerning your servants. {90:14} O satisfy us early with your mercy, that we may rejoice and be glad all our days. {90:15} Make us glad according to the days in which you have afflicted us, and the years in which we have seen evil. {90:16} Let your work appear to your servants, and your glory to their children. {90:17} And let the beauty of the LORD our God be upon us; establish the work of our hands upon us; yes, establish the work of our hands.

{91:1} Whoever dwells in the secret place of the Most High will abide under the shadow of the Almighty. {91:2} I will say of the LORD, "He is my refuge and my fortress, my God; in him will I trust." {91:3} Surely he will deliver you from the snare of the fowler (a trapper) and from the deadly pestilence. {91:4} He will cover you with his feathers, and under his wings, you will find refuge; his truth will be your shield and buckler. {91:5} You will not be afraid of the terror by night, nor of the arrow that flies by day, {91:6} nor of the pestilence that walks in darkness, nor of the destruction that wastes at noon. {91:7} A thousand may fall at your side, and ten thousand at your right hand; but it will not come near you. {91:8} Only with your eyes will you look and see the reward of the wicked. {91:9} Because you have made the LORD, who is my refuge, even the Most High, your dwelling place, {91:10} no evil shall befall you, nor shall any plague come near your home. {91:11} For he will give his angels charge over you to keep you in all your ways. {91:12} They will lift you up in their hands, lest you strike your foot against a stone. {91:13} You will tread upon the lion and the cobra; you will trample the young lion and the serpent underfoot. {91:14} Because he has set his love upon me, therefore I will deliver him; I will set him on high, because he has known my name. {91:15} He will call upon me, and I will answer him; I will be with him in trouble; I will deliver him and honor him. {91:16} With long life, I will satisfy him and show him my salvation.

{92:1} It is good to give thanks to the LORD and to sing praises to your name, O Most High; {92:2} to show forth your lovingkindness in the morning and your faithfulness every night, {92:3} upon an instrument of ten strings, upon the lute, and upon the harp with a solemn sound. {92:4} For you, LORD, have made me glad through your work; I will rejoice in the works of your hands. {92:5} O LORD, how great are your works! Your thoughts are very deep. {92:6} A senseless man does not know, nor does a fool understand this. {92:7} When the wicked spring up like grass, and all the workers of iniquity flourish, it is that they will be destroyed forever. {92:8} But you, LORD, are on high forevermore. {92:9} For behold, your enemies, O LORD, your enemies shall perish; all the workers of iniquity will be scattered. {92:10} But you will exalt my horn like that of a wild ox; I will be anointed with fresh oil. {92:11} My eye will see my desire on my enemies, and my ears will hear my desire of the wicked who rise up against me. {92:12} The righteous will flourish like the palm tree; they will grow like a cedar in Lebanon. {92:13} Those who are planted in the house of the LORD will flourish in the courts of our God. {92:14} They will still bear fruit in old age; they will be healthy and flourishing, {92:15} to show that the LORD is upright; he is my rock, and there is no unrighteousness in him.

{93:1} The LORD reigns; he is clothed with majesty; the LORD is clothed with strength, with which he has girded himself; the world is established, and it cannot be moved. {93:2} Your throne is established of old; you are from everlasting. {93:3} The floods have lifted up, O LORD; the floods have lifted up their voice; the floods lift up their waves. {93:4} The LORD on high is mightier than the noise of many waters, yes, than the mighty waves of the sea. {93:5} Your testimonies are very sure; holiness adorns your house, O LORD, forever.

{94:1} O LORD God, to whom vengeance belongs; O God, to whom vengeance belongs, show yourself. {94:2} Lift up yourself, you judge of the earth; render a reward to the proud. {94:3} LORD, how long shall the wicked, how long shall the wicked triumph? {94:4} How long shall they speak hard things, and all the workers of iniquity boast themselves? {94:5} They break in pieces your people, O LORD, and afflict your heritage. {94:6} They kill the widow and the stranger, and murder the fatherless. {94:7} Yet they say, "The LORD does not see, nor does the God of Jacob regard it." {94:8} Understand, you senseless among the people; and you fools, when will you be wise? {94:9} He who planted the ear, will he not hear? He who formed the eye, will he not see? {94:10} He who chastises the nations, will he not correct? He who teaches man knowledge, will he not know? {94:11} The LORD knows the thoughts of man, that they are vanity. {94:12} Blessed is the man whom you chasten, O LORD, and teach him out of your law; {94:13} that you may give him rest from the days of adversity until the pit is dug for the wicked. {94:14} For the LORD will not cast off his people, nor will he forsake his inheritance. {94:15} But judgment will return to righteousness, and all the upright in heart will follow it. {94:16} Who will rise up for me against the evildoers? Or who will stand up for me against the workers of iniquity? {94:17} Unless the LORD had been my help, my soul would have almost dwelt in silence. {94:18} When I said, "My foot slips," your mercy, O LORD, held me up. {94:19} In the multitude of my thoughts within me, your comforts delight my soul. {94:20} Shall the throne of iniquity have fellowship with you, which frames mischief by law? {94:21} They gather together against the soul of the righteous and condemn the innocent blood. {94:22} But the LORD is my defense; my God is the rock of my refuge. {94:23} And he will bring upon them their own iniquity and will cut them off in their own wickedness; yes, the LORD our God will cut them off.

{95:1} O come, let us sing to the LORD; let us make a joyful noise to the rock of our salvation. {95:2} Let us come before his presence with thanksgiving and make a joyful noise to him with psalms. {95:3} For the LORD is a great God and a great King above all gods. {95:4} In his hand are the deep places of the earth; the strength of the hills is his also. {95:5} The sea is his, for he made it; and his hands formed the dry land. {95:6} O come, let us worship and bow down; let us kneel before the LORD our Maker. {95:7} For he is our God, and we are the people of his pasture and the sheep of his hand. Today, if you will hear his voice, {95:8} do not harden your hearts, as in the provocation, and as in the day of temptation in the wilderness; {95:9} when your fathers tempted me, tested me, and saw my work. {95:10} For forty years I was grieved with that generation and said, "It is a people that err in their heart, and they have not known my ways." {95:11} To whom I swore in my wrath that they should not enter into my rest.

{96:1} Sing to the LORD a new song; sing to the LORD, all the earth. {96:2} Sing to the LORD, bless his name; proclaim his salvation day after day. {96:3} Declare his glory among the nations, his wonders among all people. {96:4} For the LORD is great and greatly to be praised; he is to be feared above all gods. {96:5} For all the gods of the nations are idols, but the LORD made the heavens. {96:6} Honor and majesty are before him; strength and beauty are in his sanctuary. {96:7} Give to the LORD, you families of nations, give to the LORD glory and strength. {96:8} Give to the LORD the glory due to his name; bring an offering and come into his courts. {96:9} Worship the LORD in the splendor of holiness; tremble before him, all the earth. {96:10} Say among the nations, "The LORD reigns!" The world is firmly established, it cannot be moved; he will judge the peoples righteously. {96:11} Let the heavens rejoice, and let the earth be glad; let the sea roar, and all that is in it. {96:12} Let the fields be joyful, and all that is in them; then all the trees of the forest will sing for joy {96:13} before the LORD, for he comes to judge the earth; he will judge the world with righteousness and the peoples with his truth.

{97:1} The LORD reigns; let the earth rejoice; let the multitude of islands be glad. {97:2} Clouds and darkness surround him; righteousness and justice are the foundation of his throne. {97:3} A fire goes before him and consumes his enemies all around. {97:4} His lightning lights up the world; the earth sees and trembles. {97:5} The mountains melt like wax at the presence of the LORD, at the presence of the Lord of the whole earth. {97:6} The heavens declare his righteousness, and all the peoples see his glory. {97:7} Let all those be ashamed who serve graven images, who boast of idols; worship him, all you gods. {97:8} Zion heard and was glad; and the daughters of Judah rejoiced because of your judgments, O LORD. {97:9} For you, LORD, are high above all the earth; you are exalted far above all gods. {97:10} You who love the LORD, hate evil; he preserves the souls of his saints; he delivers them from the hand of the wicked. {97:11} Light is sown for the righteous and gladness for the upright in heart. {97:12} Rejoice in the LORD, you righteous, and give thanks at the remembrance of his holiness.

{98:1} Sing to the LORD a new song, for he has done marvelous things; his right hand and his holy arm have gained him the victory. {98:2} The LORD has made known his salvation; his righteousness he has revealed in the sight of the nations. {98:3} He has remembered his mercy and his faithfulness to the house of Israel; all the ends of the earth have seen the salvation of our God. {98:4} Make a joyful noise to the LORD, all the earth; make a loud noise, rejoice, and sing praise. {98:5} Sing to the LORD with the harp, with the harp and the voice of a psalm. {98:6} With trumpets and the sound of the horn, make a joyful noise before the LORD, the King. {98:7} Let the sea roar, and all that fills it; the world and those who dwell in it. {98:8} Let the rivers clap their hands; let the hills be joyful together {98:9} before the LORD, for he comes to judge the earth; with righteousness he shall judge the world and the peoples with equity.

{99:1} The LORD reigns; let the people tremble; he sits between the cherubim; let the earth be moved. {99:2} The LORD is great in Zion; he is high above all the people. {99:3} Let them praise your great and awesome name; for it is holy. {99:4} The king's strength loves justice; you establish equity; you execute judgment and righteousness in Jacob. {99:5} Exalt the LORD our God, and worship at his footstool; for he is holy. {99:6} Moses and Aaron were among his priests, and Samuel was among those who called upon his name; they called upon the LORD, and he answered them. {99:7} He spoke to them in the cloudy pillar; they kept his testimonies and the ordinance he gave them. {99:8} You answered them, O LORD our God; you were a God who forgave them, though you took vengeance on their deeds. {99:9} Exalt the LORD our God and worship at his holy hill; for the LORD our God is holy.

{100:1} Make a joyful noise to the LORD, all you lands. {100:2} Serve the LORD with gladness; come before his presence with singing. {100:3} Know that the LORD, he is God; it is he who made us, and not we ourselves; we are his people and the sheep of his pasture. {100:4} Enter his gates with thanksgiving and his courts with praise; give thanks to him and bless his name. {100:5} For the LORD is good; his mercy is everlasting, and his truth endures to all generations.

{101:1} I will sing about mercy and justice; to you, O LORD, I will sing. {101:2} I will act wisely in a perfect way. When will you come to me? I will walk in my house with a pure heart. {101:3} I will not look at anything wicked; I hate the actions of those who stray; they will not cling to me. {101:4} A crooked heart will be far from me; I will not associate with anyone who is wicked. {101:5} Whoever secretly slanders their neighbor, I will cut off; I will not tolerate anyone with a haughty look and a proud heart. {101:6} My eyes will be on the faithful of the land, so they may dwell with me; whoever walks blamelessly will serve me. {101:7} No deceitful person will stay in my house; anyone who tells lies will not remain in my sight. {101:8} I will destroy all the wicked in the land early on, to remove all wrongdoers from the city of the LORD.

{102:1} Hear my prayer, O LORD; let my cry come to you. {102:2} Do not hide your face from me on the day of my trouble; turn your ear to me; answer me quickly when I call. {102:3} My days vanish like smoke, and my bones burn like a furnace. {102:4} My heart is broken and withered like grass; I forget to eat my food. {102:5} Because of my groaning, my bones stick to my skin. {102:6} I am like a pelican in the wilderness; I am like an owl in the desert. {102:7} I watch, and I am like a solitary sparrow on the roof. {102:8} My enemies reproach me all day long; those who rage against me swear against me. {102:9} I have eaten ashes like food and mixed my drink with tears, {102:10} because of your anger and your wrath; you have lifted me up and cast me down. {102:11} My days are like a fading shadow; I wither away like grass. {102:12} But you, O LORD, will endure forever; your remembrance is to all generations. {102:13} You will arise and have mercy on Zion, for it is time to favor her; the appointed time has come. {102:14} For your servants delight in her stones and take pleasure in her dust. {102:15} The nations will fear the name of the LORD, and all the kings of the earth will see your glory. {102:16} When the LORD rebuilds Zion, he will appear in his glory. {102:17} He will regard the prayer of the destitute and will not despise their prayer. {102:18} This will be written for the generation to come; and the people created will praise the LORD. {102:19} For he has looked down from the height of his sanctuary; from heaven, the LORD observes the earth; {102:20} to hear the groaning of the prisoner and to set free those condemned to death; {102:21} to declare the name of the LORD in Zion and his praise in Jerusalem, {102:22} when the peoples gather together and the kingdoms, to serve the LORD. {102:23} He weakened my strength along the way; he shortened my days. {102:24} I said, "O my God, do not take me away in the midst of my days; your years endure throughout all generations. {102:25} Long ago you laid the foundation of the earth, and the heavens are the work of your hands. {102:26} They will perish, but you will endure; yes, all of them will wear out like a garment; like clothing, you will change them, and they will be changed. {102:27} But you are the same, and your years will have no end. {102:28} The children of your servants will continue, and their descendants will be established before you.

{103:1} Bless the LORD, O my soul, and all that is within me, bless his holy name. {103:2} Bless the LORD, O my soul, and forget not all his benefits: {103:3} who forgives all your iniquities, who heals all your diseases; {103:4} who redeems your life from destruction and crowns you with lovingkindness and tender mercies; {103:5} who satisfies your mouth with good things so that your youth is renewed like the eagle's. {103:6} The LORD executes righteousness and justice for all who are oppressed. {103:7} He made known his ways to Moses, his acts to the children of Israel. {103:8} The LORD is merciful and gracious, slow to anger, and abounding in mercy. {103:9} He will not always chide, nor will he keep his anger forever. {103:10} He has not dealt with us according to our sins, nor rewarded us according to our iniquities. {103:11} For as the heavens are high above the earth, so great is his mercy toward those who fear him. {103:12} As far as the east is from the west, so far has he removed our transgressions from us. {103:13} As a father pities his children, so the LORD pities those who fear him. {103:14} For he knows our frame; he remembers that we are dust. {103:15} As for man, his days are like grass; as a flower of the field, so he flourishes. {103:16} For the wind passes over it, and it is gone, and its place knows it no more. {103:17} But the mercy of the LORD is from everlasting to everlasting on those who fear him, and his righteousness to children's children; {103:18} to those who keep his covenant and remember his commandments to do them. {103:19} The LORD has established his throne in the heavens, and his kingdom rules over all. {103:20} Bless the LORD, you his angels, who excel in strength and do his commandments, listening for the voice of his word. {103:21} Bless the LORD, all you his hosts, you ministers who do his pleasure. {103:22} Bless the LORD, all his works in all places of his dominion. Bless the LORD, O my soul.

{104:1} Bless the LORD, O my soul. O LORD my God, you are very great; you are clothed with splendor and majesty. {104:2} You wrap yourself in light as with a garment; you stretch out the heavens like a curtain. {104:3} You lay the beams of your chambers in the waters; you make the clouds your chariot; you walk on the wings of the wind; {104:4} you make your angels spirits and your ministers a flaming fire. {104:5} You established the foundations of the earth, so it will never move. {104:6} You covered it with the deep as with a garment; the waters stood above the mountains. {104:7} At your rebuke, they fled; at the sound of your thunder, they hurried away. {104:8} They go up by the mountains; they go down into the valleys to the place you have appointed for them. {104:9} You set a boundary that they may not pass over, so they do not cover the earth again. {104:10} You send the springs into the valleys, which run among the hills. {104:11} They give drink to every beast of the field; the wild donkeys quench their thirst. {104:12} By them, the birds of heaven have their nests, singing among the branches. {104:13} You water the hills from your chambers; the earth is satisfied with the fruit of your works. {104:14} You cause grass to grow for the cattle and plants for the service of man, so he may bring forth food from the earth; {104:15} and wine that gladdens the heart of man, and oil to make his face shine, and bread that strengthens man's heart. {104:16} The trees of the LORD are full of sap; the cedars of Lebanon that he has planted; {104:17} where the birds build their nests; as for the stork, the fir trees are her home. {104:18} The high hills are a refuge for the wild goats, and the rocks are a shelter for the conies. {104:19} He made the moon for seasons; the sun knows when to set. {104:20} You make darkness, and it is night, when all the beasts of the forest creep out. {104:21} The young lions roar for their prey and seek their food from God. {104:22} The sun rises, they gather together and lie down in their dens. {104:23} Man goes out to his work and to his labor until evening. {104:24} O LORD, how manifold are your works! In wisdom, you have made them all; the earth is full of your riches. {104:25} So is this great and wide sea, where there are creatures without number, both small and great beasts. {104:26} There go the ships, and there is that leviathan you made to play there. {104:27} These all wait for you, that you may give them their food in due season. {104:28} You give to them, they gather; you open your hand, and they are satisfied with good. {104:29} You hide your face; they are troubled; you take away their breath; they die and return to their dust. {104:30} You send forth your Spirit, and they are created; and you renew the face of the earth. {104:31} The glory of the LORD will endure forever; the LORD will rejoice in his works. {104:32} He looks at the earth, and it trembles; he touches the hills, and they smoke. {104:33} I will sing to the LORD as long as I live; I will sing praise to my God while I have my being. {104:34} May my meditation be pleasing to him; I will rejoice in the LORD. {104:35} Let sinners be consumed from the earth, and let the wicked be no more. Bless the LORD, O my soul. Praise the LORD.

{105:1} O give thanks to the LORD; call upon his name; make known his deeds among the people. {105:2} Sing to him; sing psalms to him; tell of all his wondrous works. {105:3} Glory in his holy name; let the hearts of those who seek the LORD rejoice. {105:4} Seek the LORD and his strength; seek his face continually. {105:5} Remember his marvelous works that he has done, his wonders, and the judgments of his mouth; {105:6} O offspring of Abraham his servant, you children of Jacob his chosen. {105:7} He is the LORD our God; his judgments are in all the earth. {105:8} He remembers his covenant forever, the word he commanded for a thousand generations. {105:9} The covenant he made with Abraham, and his oath to Isaac; {105:10} and confirmed it to Jacob as a decree, to Israel as an everlasting covenant, {105:11} saying, "To you I will give the land of Canaan, the portion of your inheritance." {105:12} When they were but a few in number, very few, and strangers in it. {105:13} When they went from one nation to another, from one kingdom to another people, {105:14} he allowed no one to oppress them; he reproved kings for their sake, {105:15} saying, "Do not touch my anointed ones, and do my prophets no harm." {105:16} He called down famine upon the land and broke the whole staff of bread. {105:17} He sent a man before them, Joseph, who was sold as a slave. {105:18} They hurt his feet with shackles; he was laid in irons, {105:19} until the time that his word came; the word of the LORD tested him. {105:20} The king sent and released him; the ruler of the people set him free. {105:21} He made him lord of his house and ruler over all his possessions, {105:22} to bind his princes at his pleasure and teach his senators wisdom. {105:23} Israel also came into Egypt; Jacob sojourned in the land of Ham. {105:24} He increased his people greatly and made them stronger than their enemies. {105:25} He turned their hearts to hate his people, to deal treacherously with his servants. {105:26} He sent Moses his servant, and Aaron whom he had chosen. {105:27} They performed his signs among them and wonders in the land of Ham. {105:28} He sent darkness and made it dark; they did not rebel against his word. {105:29} He turned their waters into blood and killed their fish. {105:30} Their land brought forth frogs in abundance, even in the chambers of their kings. {105:31} He spoke, and there came swarms of flies and gnats in all their borders. {105:32} He gave them hail for rain and flaming fire in their land. {105:33} He struck down their vines and fig trees and shattered the trees of their borders. {105:34} He spoke, and locusts came, and caterpillars without number, {105:35} and they ate up all the vegetation in their land and devoured the fruit of their ground. {105:36} He struck down all the firstborn in their land, the chief of all their strength. {105:37} He brought them out with silver and gold, and there was not one feeble person among their tribes. {105:38} Egypt was glad when they departed, for fear of them had fallen upon them. {105:39} He spread a cloud for a covering and fire to give light in the night. {105:40} The people asked, and he brought quails and satisfied them with the bread of heaven. {105:41} He opened the rock, and the waters gushed out; they ran in the dry places like a river. {105:42} For he remembered his holy promise and Abraham his servant. {105:43} He brought forth his people with joy and his chosen with gladness; {105:44} and gave them the lands of the nations, and they inherited the labor of the peoples, {105:45} so that they might observe his statutes and keep his laws. Praise the LORD!

{106:1} Praise the LORD! Give thanks to the LORD, for he is good; his mercy lasts forever. {106:2} Who can declare the mighty acts of the LORD? Who can proclaim all his praise? {106:3} Blessed are those who uphold justice, and those who do what is right at all times. {106:4} Remember me, O LORD, with the favor you show to your people; visit me with your salvation. {106:5} Let me see the prosperity of your chosen people, let me rejoice in the joy of your nation, let me glory in your inheritance. {106:6} We have sinned, just like our ancestors; we have committed wrongs and acted wickedly. {106:7} Our ancestors did not understand your wonders in Egypt; they forgot the multitude of your mercies and provoked you by the sea, at the Red Sea. {106:8} Yet he saved them for his name's sake, to make his mighty power known. {106:9} He rebuked the Red Sea, and it dried up; he led them through the depths as through a desert. {106:10} He saved them from the hand of their enemy and redeemed them from their foes. {106:11} The waters covered their enemies; not one of them was left. {106:12} Then they believed his words and sang his praises. {106:13} But soon they forgot his works; they did not wait for his counsel. {106:14} Instead, they craved intensely in the wilderness and tested God in the desert. {106:15} He granted their request but sent leanness into their souls. {106:16} They envied Moses in the camp and Aaron, the holy one of the LORD. {106:17} The earth opened up and swallowed Dathan, and covered the company of Abiram. {106:18} A fire blazed among their group; the flame consumed the wicked. {106:19} They made a calf at Horeb and worshiped a molten image. {106:20} They exchanged their glory for the likeness of an ox that eats grass. {106:21} They forgot God, their Savior, who had done great things in Egypt. {106:22} Wondrous works in the land of Ham and terrible deeds at the Red Sea. {106:23} Therefore, he said he would destroy them, had not Moses, his chosen one, stood before him to turn away his wrath, so he would not destroy them. {106:24} They despised the pleasant land; they did not believe his word. {106:25} They grumbled in their tents and did not listen to the voice of the LORD. {106:26} So he raised his hand against them, to overthrow them in the wilderness. {106:27} To overthrow their descendants among the nations and scatter them throughout the lands. {106:28} They joined themselves to Baal-peor and ate sacrifices offered to the dead. {106:29} They provoked him to anger with their deeds, and a plague broke out among them. {106:30} Then Phinehas stood up and intervened, and the plague was halted. {106:31} That act was credited to him as righteousness for all generations forever. {106:32} They angered him at the waters of Meribah, and it went badly for Moses because of them. {106:33} They provoked his spirit, and he spoke rashly with his lips. {106:34} They did not destroy the nations as the LORD commanded them. {106:35} Instead, they mingled with the heathen and adopted their practices. {106:36} They served their idols, which became a snare to them. {106:37} They even sacrificed their sons and daughters to demons. {106:38} They shed innocent blood, the blood of their sons and daughters, whom they sacrificed to the idols of Canaan; and the land was polluted with blood. {106:39} They defiled themselves by their actions and were unfaithful to their own inventions. {106:40} Therefore, the LORD's anger was kindled against his people, and he loathed his own inheritance. {106:41} He handed them over to the nations, and those who hated them ruled over them. {106:42} Their enemies oppressed them, and they fell under their power. {106:43} Many times he delivered them, but they rebelled against him and were brought low because of their wrongdoing. {106:44} Yet he looked upon their affliction when he heard their cry. {106:45} He remembered his covenant and relented according to the abundance of his mercies. {106:46} He made them objects of pity among all who held them captive. {106:47} Save us, O LORD our God, and gather us from among the nations, that we may give thanks to your holy name and triumph in your praise. {106:48} Blessed be the LORD God of Israel from everlasting to everlasting! Let all the people say, Amen! Praise the LORD!

{107:1} O give thanks to the LORD, for he is good; his mercy lasts forever. {107:2} Let the redeemed of the LORD say so, whom he has redeemed from the hand of the enemy. {107:3} He gathered them from the lands, from the east and the west, from the north and the south. {107:4} They wandered in the wilderness in a desolate way; they found no city to dwell in. {107:5} Hungry and thirsty, their souls fainted within them. {107:6} Then they cried out to the LORD in their trouble, and he delivered them from their distress. {107:7} He led them by the right way to a city where they could live. {107:8} Oh that men would praise the LORD for his goodness and for his wonderful works to the children of men! {107:9} For he satisfies the longing soul and fills the hungry soul with good things. {107:10} Those who sit in darkness and the shadow of death, bound in affliction and iron. {107:11} Because they rebelled against the words of God and rejected the counsel of the Most High. {107:12} So he brought down their hearts through hard labor; they fell down, and there was no one to help. {107:13} Then they cried out to the LORD in their trouble, and he saved them from their distress. {107:14} He brought them out of darkness and the shadow of death and broke their chains. {107:15} Oh that men would praise the LORD for his goodness and for his wonderful works to the children of men! {107:16} For he has broken the gates of bronze and cut the bars of iron in two. {107:17} Fools, because of their transgressions and iniquities, suffer affliction. {107:18} Their souls abhor all kinds of food, and they draw near to the gates of death. {107:19} Then they cry out to the LORD in their trouble, and he saves them from their distress. {107:20} He sent his word and healed them and delivered them from their destructions. {107:21} Oh that men would praise the LORD for his goodness and for his wonderful works to the children of men! {107:22} Let them offer the sacrifices of thanksgiving and declare his works with rejoicing. {107:23} Those who go down to the sea in ships, who conduct business in great waters. {107:24} They see the works of the LORD and his wonders in the deep. {107:25} For he commands and raises the stormy wind, which lifts up the waves. {107:26} They rise to the heavens and sink down to the depths; their souls melt because of trouble. {107:27} They reel and stagger like drunken men and are at their wits' end. {107:28} Then they cry out to the LORD in their trouble, and he brings them out of their distress. {107:29} He makes the storm calm, so that the waves are still. {107:30} Then they are glad because they are quiet; he brings them to their desired haven. {107:31} Oh that men would praise the LORD for his goodness and for his wonderful works to the children of men! {107:32} Let them exalt him in the congregation of the people and praise him in the assembly of the elders. {107:33} He turns rivers into a wilderness and water springs into dry ground. {107:34} A fruitful land into barrenness because of the wickedness of those who dwell there. {107:35} He turns the wilderness into a pool of water and dry ground into water springs. {107:36} There he makes the hungry dwell, so they may prepare a city for habitation. {107:37} They sow fields and plant vineyards, which yield fruit in abundance. {107:38} He blesses them, so they are multiplied greatly and does not let their cattle decrease. {107:39} Again, they are diminished and brought low through oppression, affliction, and sorrow. {107:40} He pours contempt upon princes and causes them to wander in the wilderness, where there is no way. {107:41} Yet he sets the poor on high from affliction and makes their families like a flock. {107:42} The righteous see it and rejoice, and all iniquity stops its mouth. {107:43} Whoever is wise and observes these things will understand the lovingkindness of the LORD.

{108:1} O God, my heart is steadfast; I will sing and give praise, even with my whole being. {108:2} Awake, harp and lyre; I will awaken the dawn. {108:3} I will praise you, O LORD, among the people; I will sing praises to you among the nations. {108:4} For your mercy is great above the heavens, and your truth reaches to the clouds. {108:5} Be exalted, O God, above the heavens, and your glory above all the earth. {108:6} That your beloved may be delivered; save with your right hand and answer me. {108:7} God has spoken in his holiness; I will rejoice, I will divide Shechem and measure out the valley of Succoth. {108:8} Gilead is mine; Manasseh is mine; Ephraim is the strength of my head; Judah is my lawgiver. {108:9} Moab is my washbasin; I will toss my sandal over Edom; over Philistia I will triumph. {108:10} Who will bring me into the fortified city? Who will lead me into Edom? {108:11} Will you not, O God, who has rejected us? Will you not go forth with our armies, O God? {108:12} Give us help from trouble, for vain is the help of man. {108:13} With God, we will do valiantly, for he is the one who will trample down our enemies.

{109:1} Do not keep silent, O God of my praise; {109:2} for the mouth of the wicked and the deceitful are open against me; they have spoken against me with a lying tongue. {109:3} They surround me with words of hatred and fight against me without cause. {109:4} In return for my love, they accuse me; but I give myself to prayer. {109:5} They have rewarded me evil for good, and hatred for my love. {109:6} Set a wicked person over him, and let Satan stand at his right hand. {109:7} When he is judged, let him be found guilty; let his prayer become sin. {109:8} Let his days be few; let another take his position. {109:9} Let his children be fatherless, and his wife a widow. {109:10} Let his children be wandering beggars; let them seek their bread from desolate places. {109:11} Let the extortioner seize all he has; let strangers plunder his labor. {109:12} Let there be no one to extend mercy to him; let none favor his fatherless children. {109:13} Let his descendants be cut off; let their name be erased from the next generation. {109:14} Let the iniquity of his parents be remembered by the LORD; let not the sin of his mother be blotted out. {109:15} Let them be before the LORD continually, so he may cut off their memory from the earth. {109:16} Because he did not remember to show mercy but persecuted the poor and needy, seeking to slay the brokenhearted. {109:17} As he loved cursing, let it come upon him; as he did not delight in blessing, let it be far from him. {109:18} As he clothed himself with cursing like a garment, let it come into his innermost being like water and like oil into his bones. {109:19} Let it be to him as a garment that covers him and as a belt with which he is girded continuously. {109:20} This is the reward for my adversaries from the LORD and for those who speak evil against my soul. {109:21} But do thou for me, O GOD the Lord, for your name's sake; because your mercy is good, deliver me. {109:22} For I am poor and needy, and my heart is wounded within me. {109:23} I am like a shadow that fades; I am tossed about like a locust. {109:24} My knees are weak from fasting; my flesh fails because of lack of nourishment. {109:25} I have become a disgrace to them; when they see me, they shake their heads. {109:26} Help me, O LORD my God; save me according to your mercy. {109:27} Let them know that this is your hand, that you, LORD, have done it. {109:28} Let them curse, but bless you; when they rise, let them be ashamed; but let your servant rejoice. {109:29} Let my adversaries be clothed with shame, and let them cover themselves with their own confusion as with a cloak. {109:30} I will greatly praise the LORD with my mouth; I will praise him among the multitude. {109:31} For he shall stand at the right hand of the poor to save him from those who condemn his soul.

{110:1} The LORD said to my Lord, "Sit at my right hand until I make your enemies your footstool." {110:2} The LORD will send the rod of your strength from Zion; rule in the midst of your enemies. {110:3} Your people will offer themselves willingly on the day of your power, in the beauty of holiness, from the womb of the morning; you have the dew of your youth. {110:4} The LORD has sworn and will not change his mind, "You are a priest forever after the order of Melchizedek." {110:5} The Lord at your right hand will strike through kings on the day of his wrath. {110:6} He will judge among the nations; he will fill the places with dead bodies; he will wound the heads over many countries. {110:7} He will drink from the brook by the way; therefore, he will lift up his head.

{111:1} Praise the LORD! I will praise the LORD with my whole heart in the assembly of the upright and in the congregation. {111:2} The works of the LORD are great; they are sought out by all who take pleasure in them. {111:3} His work is honorable and glorious, and his righteousness lasts forever. {111:4} He has made his wonderful works to be remembered; the LORD is gracious and full of compassion. {111:5} He provides food for those who fear him; he will always be mindful of his covenant. {111:6} He has shown his people the power of his works, giving them the heritage of the nations. {111:7} The works of his hands are truth and justice; all his commandments are trustworthy. {111:8} They stand firm forever and ever, done in truth and uprightness. {111:9} He sent redemption to his people; he has commanded his covenant forever; holy and awesome is his name. {111:10} The fear of the LORD is the beginning of wisdom; all who follow his commandments have good understanding; his praise endures forever.

{112:1} Praise the LORD! Blessed is the person who fears the LORD and greatly delights in his commandments. {112:2} Their offspring will be powerful on the earth; the generation of the upright will be blessed. {112:3} Wealth and riches will be in their house, and their righteousness will last forever. {112:4} Light shines in the darkness for the upright; they are gracious, compassionate, and righteous. {112:5} A good person shows favor & lends; they manage their affairs with discretion. {112:6} Surely they will never be shaken; the righteous will be remembered forever. {112:7} They will not be afraid of bad news; their heart is steadfast, trusting in the LORD. {112:8} Their heart is steady; they will not be afraid until they see their desire upon their enemies. {112:9} They have distributed freely; they have given to the poor; their righteousness endures forever; their horn will be exalted in honor. {112:10} The wicked will see it and be vexed; they will gnash their teeth & melt away; the desire of the wicked will perish.

{113:1} Praise the LORD! Praise, O you servants of the LORD; praise the name of the LORD. {113:2} Blessed be the name of the LORD from this time forth and forevermore. {113:3} From the rising of the sun to its setting, the name of the LORD is to be praised. {113:4} The LORD is high above all nations, and his glory is above the heavens. {113:5} Who is like the LORD our God, who dwells on high, {113:6} who humbles himself to behold the things that are in heaven and on the earth? {113:7} He raises the poor from the dust and lifts the needy from the ash heap; {113:8} that he may seat them with princes, even with the princes of his people. {113:9} He makes the barren woman keep house and be a joyful mother of children. Praise the LORD!

{114:1} When Israel went out of Egypt, the house of Jacob from a people of strange language, {114:2} Judah became his sanctuary, and Israel his dominion. {114:3} The sea saw it and fled; the Jordan was driven back. {114:4} The mountains skipped like rams, and the little hills like lambs. {114:5} What was wrong, O sea, that you fled? O Jordan, that you turned back? {114:6} O mountains, that you skipped like rams, and you little hills, like lambs? {114:7} Tremble, O earth, at the presence of the Lord, at the presence of the God of Jacob, {114:8} who turned the rock into a pool of water and the flint into a fountain of waters.

{115:1} Not to us, O LORD, not to us, but to your name give glory for your mercy and for the sake of your truth. {115:2} Why should the nations say, "Where is their God?" {115:3} Our God is in heaven; he does whatever he pleases. {115:4} Their idols are silver and gold, made by human hands. {115:5} They have mouths, but they do not speak; they have eyes, but they do not see. {115:6} They have ears, but they do not hear; they have noses, but they do not smell. {115:7} They have hands, but they do not feel; they have feet, but they do not walk; they do not make a sound with their throats. {115:8} Those who make them are like them; so is everyone who trusts in them. {115:9} O Israel, trust in the LORD; he is their help and their shield. {115:10} O house of Aaron, trust in the LORD; he is their help and their shield. {115:11} You who fear the LORD, trust in the LORD; he is their help and their shield. {115:12} The LORD has been mindful of us; he will bless us; he will bless the house of Israel; he will bless the house of Aaron. {115:13} He will bless those who fear the LORD, both small and great. {115:14} The LORD will increase you more and more, you and your children. {115:15} You are blessed by the LORD who made heaven and earth. {115:16} The heavens belong to the LORD, but he has given the earth to the children of men. {115:17} The dead do not praise the LORD, nor do any who go down into silence. {115:18} But we will bless the LORD from now on and forever. Praise the LORD!

{116:1} I love the LORD because he has heard my voice and my supplications. {116:2} Because he has inclined his ear to me, I will call on him as long as I live. {116:3} The cords of death surrounded me, and the pains of hell (or, grave) laid hold of me; I found trouble and sorrow. {116:4} Then I called on the name of the LORD: O LORD, I plead with you, deliver my soul. {116:5} The LORD is gracious and righteous; indeed, our God is merciful. {116:6} The LORD preserves the simple; I was brought low, and he helped me. {116:7} Return to your rest, O my soul, for the LORD has dealt bountifully with you. {116:8} For you have delivered my soul from death, my eyes from tears, and my feet from falling. {116:9} I will walk before the LORD in the land of the living. {116:10} I believed, therefore I have spoken; I was greatly afflicted. {116:11} I said in my haste, "All men are liars." {116:12} What shall I render to the LORD for all his benefits toward me? {116:13} I will take the cup of salvation and call on the name of the LORD. {116:14} I will fulfill my vows to the LORD now in the presence of all his people. {116:15} Precious in the sight of the LORD is the death of his saints. {116:16} O LORD, truly I am your servant; I am your servant, the son of your maidservant; you have loosed my bonds. {116:17} I will offer you the sacrifice of thanksgiving and will call on the name of the LORD. {116:18} I will fulfill my vows to the LORD now in the presence of all his people, {116:19} in the courts of the LORD's house, in your midst, O Jerusalem. Praise the LORD!

{117:1} O praise the LORD, all you nations; praise him, all you peoples. {117:2} For his merciful kindness is great toward us, and the truth of the LORD endures forever. Praise the LORD!

{118:1} O give thanks to the LORD, for he is good; his mercy endures forever. {118:2} Let Israel now say, "His mercy endures forever." {118:3} Let the house of Aaron now say, "His mercy endures forever." {118:4} Let those who fear the LORD say, "His mercy endures forever." {118:5} I called upon the LORD in my distress; the LORD answered me and set me in a wide place. {118:6} The LORD is on my side; I will not fear. What can man do to me? {118:7} The LORD is my helper; therefore, I will look in triumph at those who hate me. {118:8} It is better to trust in the LORD than to put confidence in man. {118:9} It is better to trust in the LORD than to put confidence in princes. {118:10} All nations surrounded me; but in the name of the LORD, I will destroy them. {118:11} They surrounded me, yes, they surrounded me; but in the name of the LORD, I will destroy them. {118:12} They surrounded me like bees; they were quenched like a fire of thorns; for in the name of the LORD, I will destroy them. {118:13} You pushed me hard, that I might fall, but the LORD helped me. {118:14} The LORD is my strength and song, and he has become my salvation. {118:15} The voice of rejoicing and salvation is in the tents of the righteous; the right hand of the LORD does valiantly. {118:16} The right hand of the LORD is exalted; the right hand of the LORD does valiantly. {118:17} I shall not die, but live, and declare the works of the LORD. {118:18} The LORD has chastened me severely, but he has not given me over to death. {118:19} Open to me the gates of righteousness; I will go through them and praise the LORD. {118:20} This is the gate of the LORD, through which the righteous shall enter. {118:21} I will praise you, for you have heard me and have become my salvation. {118:22} The stone that the builders rejected has become the cornerstone. {118:23} This is the LORD's doing; it is marvelous in our eyes. {118:24} This is the day that the LORD has made; we will rejoice and be glad in it. {118:25} Save now, I beseech you, O LORD; O LORD, I beseech you, send now prosperity. {118:26} Blessed is he who comes in the name of the LORD; we bless you from the house of the LORD. {118:27} God is the LORD, who has shown us light; bind the sacrifice with cords to the horns of the altar. {118:28} You are my God, and I will praise you; you are my God, I will exalt you. {118:29} O give thanks to the LORD, for he is good; for his mercy endures forever.

{119:1} Blessed are those who are pure in their actions and walk in the Lord's law. {119:2} Blessed are those who keep his commandments and seek him wholeheartedly. {119:3} They do no wrong; they walk in his ways. {119:4} You have commanded us to carefully follow your instructions. {119:5} Oh, that my actions were aligned with your laws! {119:6} Then I would not be ashamed when I look at all your commandments. {119:7} I will praise you with a sincere heart when I learn your righteous laws. {119:8} I will keep your instructions; do not completely forsake me. {119:9} {BETH} How can a young person keep their path clean? By paying attention to your word. {119:10} I have sought you with all my heart; do not let me stray from your commandments. {119:11} I have hidden your word in my heart so that I might not sin against you. {119:12} Blessed are you, Lord; teach me your instructions. {119:13} With my lips, I have declared all the judgments from your mouth. {119:14} I have rejoiced in following your testimonies as much as in all riches. {119:15} I will reflect on your precepts and focus on your ways. {119:16} I will delight in your statutes; I will not forget your word. {119:17} {GIMEL} Treat your servant well so that I may live and keep your word. {119:18} Open my eyes so that I may see the wonderful things in your law. {119:19} I am a stranger on earth; do not hide your commandments from me. {119:20} My soul longs for your judgments at all times. {119:21} You have rebuked the proud, those who stray from your commandments. {119:22} Take away my disgrace and contempt, for I have kept your testimonies. {119:23} Even princes have sat and spoken against me, but your servant meditates on your statutes. {119:24} Your testimonies are my delight and my counselors. {119:25} {DALETH} My soul clings to the dust; revive me according to your word. {119:26} I have declared my ways, and you have answered me; teach me your statutes. {119:27} Help me understand the way of your precepts so I can talk about your wonderful works. {119:28} My soul melts from heaviness; strengthen me according to your word. {119:29} Remove the path of lies from me, and grant me your law graciously. {119:30} I have chosen the way of truth; I have set your judgments before me. {119:31} I cling to your testimonies; Lord, do not put me to shame. {119:32} I will run the path of your commandments when you expand my understanding. {119:33} {HE} Teach me, Lord, the way of your statutes, and I will keep it until the end. {119:34} Give me understanding, and I will keep your law; I will observe it with my whole heart. {119:35} Lead me in the path of your commandments, for that is where I find joy. {119:36} Turn my heart toward your testimonies and not toward selfish gain. {119:37} Turn my eyes away from worthless things; revive me in your way. {119:38} Establish your word to your servant, who is devoted to your fear. {119:39} Turn away my disgrace that I dread, for your judgments are good. {119:40} See how I long for your precepts; revive me in your righteousness. {119:41} {VAU} May your mercies come to me, Lord, your salvation according to your word. {119:42} Then I will have an answer for those who insult me, for I trust in your word. {119:43} Do not take your truth out of my mouth, for I have hoped in your judgments. {119:44} I will keep your law continually forever and ever. {119:45} I will walk in freedom, for I seek your precepts. {119:46} I will speak of your testimonies before kings and will not be ashamed. {119:47} I will delight in your commandments, which I love. {119:48} I will lift my hands to your commandments, which I love; and I will meditate on your statutes. {119:49} {ZAIN} Remember your word to your servant, on which you have caused me to hope. {119:50} This is my comfort in my suffering: your word has revived me. {119:51} The proud have mocked me greatly, yet I have not turned away from your law. {119:52} I remember your ancient judgments, Lord, and I find comfort. {119:53} Fear has seized me because of the wicked who forsake your law. {119:54} Your statutes have been my songs during my pilgrimage. {119:55} I have remembered your name, Lord, in the night, and I have kept your law. {119:56} This has been my practice, for I have kept your precepts. {119:57} {CHETH} You are my portion, Lord; I have said that I will keep your words. {119:58} I sought your favor with all my heart; be merciful to me according to your word. {119:59} I thought about my ways and turned my feet toward your testimonies. {119:60} I hurried and did not delay to keep your commandments. {119:61} The ropes of the wicked have bound me, but I have not forgotten your law. {119:62} At midnight, I will rise to give thanks to you for your righteous judgments. {119:63} I am a companion of all who fear you and of those who keep your precepts. {119:64} The earth, Lord, is full of your mercy; teach me your statutes. {119:65} {TETH} You have dealt well with your servant, Lord, according to your word. {119:66}

Teach me good judgment and knowledge, for I have believed your commandments. {119:67} Before I was afflicted, I went astray, but now I keep your word. {119:68} You are good and do good; teach me your statutes. {119:69} The proud have spread lies against me, but I will keep your precepts with my whole heart. {119:70} Their hearts are as fat as grease, but I delight in your law. {119:71} It is good for me that I have been afflicted, so that I might learn your statutes. {119:72} The law from your mouth is better to me than thousands of gold and silver. {119:73} {JOD} Your hands have made and fashioned me; give me understanding, that I may learn your commandments. {119:74} Those who fear you will be glad when they see me, because I have hoped in your word. {119:75} I know, Lord, that your judgments are right, and that in faithfulness you have afflicted me. {119:76} Let your merciful kindness be my comfort, according to your word to your servant. {119:77} Let your tender mercies come to me, that I may live, for your law is my delight. {119:78} Let the proud be ashamed, for they have wronged me without cause, but I will meditate on your precepts. {119:79} Let those who fear you turn to me, and those who know your testimonies. {119:80} Let my heart be sound in your statutes, so that I am not ashamed. {119:81} {CAPH} My soul longs for your salvation; I hope in your word. {119:82} My eyes fail for your word, saying, "When will you comfort me?" {119:83} I have become like a wineskin in the smoke, yet I do not forget your statutes. {119:84} How many are the days of your servant? When will you bring justice against those who persecute me? {119:85} The proud have dug pits for me that are not according to your law. {119:86} All your commandments are trustworthy; they persecute me wrongfully; help me. {119:87} They almost consumed me on earth, but I did not forsake your precepts. {119:88} Revive me according to your lovingkindness, and I will keep the testimony of your mouth. {119:89} {LAMED} Forever, Lord, your word is established in heaven. {119:90} Your faithfulness extends to all generations; you have established the earth, and it stands firm. {119:91} They continue today according to your ordinances, for all are your servants. {119:92} If your law had not been my delight, I would have perished in my suffering. {119:93} I will never forget your precepts, for through them you have revived me. {119:94} I am yours; save me, for I have sought your precepts. {119:95} The wicked have waited to destroy me, but I will consider your testimonies. {119:96} I have seen the limit of all perfection, but your commandment is exceedingly broad. {119:97} {MEM} Oh, how I love your law! It is my meditation all day long. {119:98} Through your commandments, you have made me wiser than my enemies, for they are ever with me. {119:99} I have more understanding than all my teachers, for your testimonies are my meditation. {119:100} I understand more than the elders because I keep your precepts. {119:101} I have kept my feet from every evil way so that I may keep your word. {119:102} I have not departed from your judgments, for you have taught me. {119:103} How sweet are your words to my taste! They are sweeter than honey to my mouth. {119:104} Through your precepts, I gain understanding; therefore, I hate every false way. {119:105} {NUN} Your word is a lamp to my feet and a light to my path. {119:106} I have sworn, and I will fulfill it; I will keep your righteous judgments. {119:107} I am very afflicted; revive me, Lord, according to your word. {119:108} Accept, I pray, the freewill offerings of my mouth, Lord, and teach me your judgments. {119:109} My soul is always in my hand; yet I do not forget your law. {119:110} The wicked have set a trap for me; yet I have not strayed from your precepts. {119:111} Your testimonies have become my heritage forever, for they are the joy of my heart. {119:112} I have set my heart to obey your statutes forever, even to the end. {119:113} {SAMECH} I hate empty thoughts, but I love your law. {119:114} You are my hiding place and my shield; I hope in your word. {119:115} Depart from me, you evildoers, for I will keep the commandments of my God. {119:116} Support me according to your word, that I may live, and do not let me be ashamed of my hope. {119:117} Hold me up, and I shall be safe; I will have respect for your statutes continually. {119:118} You have put away all who stray from your statutes, for their deceit is falsehood. {119:119} You put away all the wicked of the earth like dross; therefore, I love your testimonies. {119:120} My flesh trembles in fear of you, and I am afraid of your judgments. {119:121} {AIN} I have done what is right and just; do not leave me to my oppressors. {119:122} Be a guarantor for your servant for good; do not let the proud oppress me. {119:123} My eyes fail for your salvation and for your righteous word. {119:124} Deal with your servant according to your mercy, and teach me your statutes. {119:125} I am your servant; give me understanding so that I may know your testimonies. {119:126} It is time for you, Lord, to act, for they have made your law void. {119:127} Therefore, I love your commandments more than gold, even fine gold. {119:128} Therefore, I consider all your precepts to be right, and I hate every false way. {119:129} {PE} Your testimonies are wonderful; therefore, my soul keeps them. {119:130} The entrance of your words brings light; it gives understanding to the simple. {119:131} I opened my mouth and panted; I longed for your commandments. {119:132} Look upon me and be merciful to me, as you have always done to those who love your name. {119:133} Order my steps in your word, and let no iniquity have power over me. {119:134} Deliver me from the oppression of man; then I will keep your precepts. {119:135} Make your face shine upon your servant and teach me your statutes. {119:136} Rivers of tears flow down my eyes because they do not keep your law. {119:137} {TZADDI} Righteous are you, Lord, and upright are your judgments. {119:138} Your testimonies, which you have commanded, are righteous and very faithful. {119:139} My zeal consumes me because my enemies forget your words. {119:140} Your word is very pure; therefore, your servant loves it. {119:141} I am small and despised, yet I do not forget your precepts. {119:142} Your righteousness is everlasting righteousness, and your law is the truth. {119:143} Trouble and anguish have taken hold of me, yet your commandments are my delights. {119:144} The righteousness of your testimonies is everlasting; give me understanding, and I shall live. {119:145} {KOPH} I cried with my whole heart; hear me, Lord; I will keep your statutes. {119:146} I cried to you; save me, and I will keep your testimonies. {119:147} I anticipated the dawn and cried; I hoped in your word. {119:148} My eyes prevented the night watches, so that I might meditate in your word. {119:149} Hear my voice according to your lovingkindness; Lord, revive me according to your judgment. {119:150} Those who pursue mischief come near; they are far from your law. {119:151} You are near, Lord, and all your commandments are truth. {119:152} Regarding your testimonies, I have known of old that you have founded them forever. {119:153} {RESH} Consider my affliction and deliver me, for I do not forget your law. {119:154} Plead my case and deliver me; revive me according to your word. {119:155} Salvation is far from the wicked, for they do not seek your statutes. {119:156} Great are your tender mercies, Lord; revive me according to your judgments. {119:157} Many are my persecutors and my enemies, yet I do not turn away from your testimonies. {119:158} I looked at the transgressors and was grieved because they do not keep your word. {119:159} Consider how I love your precepts; revive me, Lord, according to your lovingkindness. {119:160} Your word is true from the beginning, and every one of your righteous judgments endures forever. {119:161} {SCHIN} Princes have persecuted me without cause, but my heart stands in awe of your word. {119:162} I rejoice at your word as one who finds great treasure. {119:163} I hate and abhor falsehood, but I love your law. {119:164} Seven times a day I praise you for your righteous judgments. {119:165} Great peace have those who love your law; nothing will offend them. {119:166} Lord, I have hoped for your salvation and kept your commandments. {119:167} My soul has kept your testimonies; I love them exceedingly. {119:168} I have kept your precepts and your testimonies, for all my ways are before you. {119:169} {TAU} Let my cry come near before you, Lord; give me understanding according to your word. {119:170} Let my supplication come before you; deliver me according to your word. {119:171} My lips shall praise you when you teach me your statutes. {119:172} My tongue shall speak of your word, for all your commandments are righteousness. {119:173} Let your hand help me, for I have chosen your precepts. {119:174} I have longed for your salvation, Lord, and your law is my delight. {119:175} Let my soul live, and it shall praise you; let your judgments help me. {119:176} I have gone astray like a lost sheep; seek your servant, for I do not forget your commandments.

{120:1} In my distress, I cried out to the Lord, and he heard me. {120:2} Deliver my soul, O Lord, from lying lips and from a deceitful tongue. {120:3} What will be given to you, or what will be done to you, you false tongue? {120:4} Sharp arrows of the mighty, with coals of juniper. {120:5} Woe is me, that I live in Meshech and dwell in the tents of Kedar! {120:6} My soul has long dwelt with those who hate peace. {120:7} I am for peace, but when I speak, they are for war.

{121:1} I will lift up my eyes to the hills, from where my help comes. {121:2} My help comes from the Lord, who made heaven and earth. {121:3} He will not let your foot slip; he who keeps you will not slumber. {121:4} Behold, he who keeps Israel will neither slumber nor sleep. {121:5} The Lord is your keeper; the Lord is your shade at your right hand. {121:6} The sun will not harm you by day, nor the moon by night. {121:7} The Lord will keep you from all evil; he will keep your soul. {121:8} The Lord will keep your going out and your coming in from now on and forevermore.

{122:1} I was glad when they said to me, "Let us go into the house of the Lord." {122:2} Our feet stand within your gates, O Jerusalem. {122:3} Jerusalem is built like a city that is compact together. {122:4} To where the tribes go up, the tribes of the Lord, to give thanks to the name of the Lord. {122:5} For there are thrones of judgment, the thrones of the house of David. {122:6} Pray for the peace of Jerusalem; may those who love you prosper. {122:7} Peace be within your walls, and prosperity within your palaces. {122:8} For my brethren and companions' sake, I will now say, "Peace be within you." {122:9} Because of the house of the Lord our God, I will seek your good.

{123:1} To you I lift up my eyes, O you who dwell in the heavens. {123:2} Behold, as the eyes of servants look to the hand of their masters, and as the eyes of a maid to the hand of her mistress, so our eyes wait upon the Lord our God until he has mercy upon us. {123:3} Have mercy upon us, O Lord; have mercy upon us, for we are exceedingly filled with contempt. {123:4} Our soul is exceedingly filled with the scorn of those who are at ease and with the contempt of the proud.

{124:1} If it had not been the Lord who was on our side, now Israel may say; {124:2} If it had not been the Lord who was on our side when men rose up against us, {124:3} then they would have swallowed us alive when their anger was kindled against us. {124:4} Then the waters would have overwhelmed us; the stream would have gone over our soul. {124:5} Then the proud waters would have gone over our soul. {124:6} Blessed be the Lord, who has not given us as prey to their teeth. {124:7} Our soul has escaped like a bird from the snare of the fowlers; the snare is broken, and we have escaped. {124:8} Our help is in the name of the Lord, who made heaven and earth.

{125:1} Those who trust in the Lord are like Mount Zion, which cannot be moved but endures forever. {125:2} As the mountains surround Jerusalem, so the Lord surrounds his people from now on and forever. {125:3} For the rod of the wicked shall not rest upon the lot of the righteous, lest the righteous stretch out their hands to iniquity. {125:4} Do good, O Lord, to those who are good, and to those who are upright in their hearts. {125:5} As for those who turn aside to their crooked ways, the Lord shall lead them away with the workers of iniquity, but peace shall be upon Israel.

{126:1} When the Lord restored the fortunes of Zion, we were like those who dream. {126:2} Then our mouths were filled with laughter, and our tongues with singing; then they said among the nations, "The Lord has done great things for them." {126:3} The Lord has done great things for us; we are glad. {126:4} Restore our fortunes, O Lord, like the streams in the Negev. {126:5} Those who sow in tears will reap in joy. {126:6} He who goes out weeping, carrying precious seed, will surely return with rejoicing, bringing his sheaves with him.

{127:1} Unless the Lord builds the house, those who build it labor in vain; unless the Lord guards the city, the watchman stays awake in vain. {127:2} It is vain for you to rise up early, to stay up late, to eat the bread of sorrows; for he gives to his beloved sleep. {127:3} Behold, children are a heritage from the Lord; the fruit of the womb is his reward. {127:4} Like arrows in the hand of a mighty man, so are the children of one's youth. {127:5} Happy is the man who has a full quiver of them; they will not be ashamed but will speak with their enemies at the gate.

{128:1} Blessed is everyone who fears the Lord, who walks in his ways. {128:2} For you will eat the labor of your hands; happy will you be, and it will go well with you. {128:3} Your wife will be like a fruitful vine in the heart of your house; your children like olive plants around your table. {128:4} Behold, this is how the man will be blessed who fears the Lord. {128:5} The Lord will bless you from Zion; you will see the good of Jerusalem all the days of your life. {128:6} Yes, you will see your children's children, and peace upon Israel.

{129:1} Many times they have oppressed me from my youth, let Israel now say. {129:2} Many times they have oppressed me from my youth, yet they have not prevailed against me. {129:3} The plowers plowed on my back; they made their furrows long. {129:4} The Lord is righteous; he has cut the cords of the wicked. {129:5} Let them all be confounded and turned back who hate Zion. {129:6} Let them be like the grass on the rooftops, which withers before it grows up. {129:7} With which the mower does not fill his hand, nor the binder of sheaves his bosom. {129:8} Nor do those who pass by say, "The blessing of the Lord be upon you; we bless you in the name of the Lord."

{130:1} Out of the depths I have cried to you, O Lord. {130:2} Lord, hear my voice; let your ears be attentive to the voice of my supplications. {130:3} If you, Lord, should mark iniquities, O Lord, who could stand? {130:4} But there is forgiveness with you, that you may be feared. {130:5} I wait for the Lord; my soul waits, and in his word I hope. {130:6} My soul waits for the Lord more than those who watch for the morning; yes, more than those who watch for the morning. {130:7} Let Israel hope in the Lord, for with the Lord there is mercy, and with him is abundant redemption. {130:8} And he will redeem Israel from all his iniquities.

{131:1} Lord, my heart is not proud, nor are my eyes arrogant; I don't concern myself with great matters or things too difficult for me. {131:2} Surely I have calmed and quieted my soul, like a weaned child with its mother; my soul is like a weaned child within me. {131:3} Let Israel hope in the Lord from now and forever.

{132:1} A Song of Ascents. Lord, remember David and all his hardships. {132:2} How he swore to the Lord and made a vow to the Mighty One of Jacob: {132:3} "Surely I will not enter my house or go to my bed; {132:4} I will not allow sleep to my eyes or slumber to my eyelids, {132:5} until I find a place for the Lord, a dwelling for the Mighty One of Jacob." {132:6} We heard of it in Ephrathah; we found it in the fields of the wood. {132:7} We will go into his tabernacles; we will worship at his footstool. {132:8} Arise, O Lord, into your resting place, you and the ark of your strength. {132:9} Let your priests be clothed with righteousness, and let your saints shout for joy. {132:10} For your servant David's sake, do not turn away the face of your anointed. {132:11} The Lord has sworn in truth to David; he will not turn from it: "Of the fruit of your body I will set upon your throne." {132:12} If your children keep my covenant and my testimonies that I teach them, their children will also sit upon your throne forever. {132:13} For the Lord has chosen Zion; he has desired it for his habitation. {132:14} This is my resting place forever; here I will dwell, for I have desired it. {132:15} I will abundantly bless her provisions; I will satisfy her poor with bread. {132:16} I will also clothe her priests with salvation, and her saints shall shout aloud for joy. {132:17} There I will make the horn of David flourish; I have ordained a lamp for my anointed. {132:18} His enemies I will clothe with shame, but upon himself, his crown will flourish.

{133:1} Behold, how good and pleasant it is for brothers to dwell together in unity! {133:2} It is like the precious oil on the head, running down on the beard, even Aaron's beard, that flows down to the edges of his garments; {133:3} like the dew of Hermon, which descends upon the mountains of Zion; for there the Lord commanded the blessing, even life forevermore.

{134:1} Behold, bless the Lord, all you servants of the Lord who stand by night in the house of the Lord. {134:2} Lift up your hands in the sanctuary and bless the Lord. {134:3} The Lord who made heaven and earth bless you from Zion.

{135:1} Praise the Lord! Praise the name of the Lord; praise him, you servants of the Lord. {135:2} You who stand in the house of the Lord, in the courts of the house of our God, {135:3} praise the Lord, for the Lord is good; sing praises to his name, for it is pleasant. {135:4} For the Lord has chosen Jacob for himself, and Israel for his special treasure. {135:5} For I know that the Lord is great, and our Lord is above all gods. {135:6} Whatever the Lord pleases, he does in heaven and on earth, in the seas, and all deep places. {135:7} He causes the vapors to ascend from the ends of the earth; he makes lightning for the rain; he brings the wind out of his treasuries. {135:8} Who struck down the firstborn of Egypt, both man and beast? {135:9} Who sent signs and wonders into the midst of you, O Egypt, upon Pharaoh and all his servants? {135:10} Who struck down great nations and killed mighty kings: {135:11} Sihon king of the Amorites, Og king of Bashan, and all the kingdoms of Canaan? {135:12} And he gave their land as a heritage, a heritage to Israel his people. {135:13} Your name, O Lord, endures forever; your renown, O Lord, throughout all generations. {135:14} For the Lord will judge his people, and he will have compassion on his servants. {135:15} The idols of the nations are silver and gold, the work of human hands. {135:16} They have mouths, but they do not speak; they have eyes, but they do not see; {135:17} they have ears, but they do not hear; nor is there any breath in their mouths. {135:18} Those who make them are like them; so is everyone who trusts in them. {135:19} Bless the Lord, O house of Israel; bless the Lord, O house of Aaron; {135:20} bless the Lord, O house of Levi; you who fear the Lord, bless the Lord. {135:21} Blessed be the Lord from Zion, who dwells in Jerusalem. Praise the Lord!

{136:1} Give thanks to the Lord, for he is good; his mercy endures forever. {136:2} Give thanks to the God of gods; his mercy endures forever. {136:3} Give thanks to the Lord of lords; his mercy endures forever. {136:4} To him who alone performs great wonders; his mercy endures forever. {136:5} To him who by wisdom made the heavens; his mercy endures forever. {136:6} To him who stretched out the earth above the waters; his mercy endures forever. {136:7} To him who made great lights; his mercy endures forever. {136:8} the sun to rule by day; his mercy endures forever. {136:9} the moon and stars to rule by night; his mercy endures forever. {136:10} To him who struck down Egypt's firstborn; his mercy endures forever. {136:11} and brought Israel out from among them; his mercy endures forever. {136:12} with a strong hand and an outstretched arm; his mercy endures forever. {136:13} To him who divided the Red Sea in two; his mercy endures forever. {136:14} and made Israel pass through the midst of it; his mercy endures forever. {136:15} but overthrew Pharaoh and his army in the Red Sea; his mercy endures forever. {136:16} To him who led his people through the wilderness; his mercy endures forever. {136:17} To him who struck down great kings; his mercy endures forever. {136:18} and killed famous kings; his mercy endures forever. {136:19} Sihon, king of the Amorites; his mercy endures forever. {136:20} and Og, the king of Bashan; his mercy endures forever. {136:21} and gave their land as a heritage; his mercy endures forever. {136:22} even a heritage to Israel his servant; his mercy endures forever. {136:23} Who remembered us in our low state; his mercy endures forever. {136:24} and has redeemed us from our enemies; his mercy endures forever. {136:25} Who gives food to all flesh; his mercy endures forever. {136:26} Give thanks to the God of heaven; his mercy endures forever.

{137:1} By the rivers of Babylon, we sat and wept when we remembered Zion. {137:2} We hung our harps on the willows there. {137:3} For there our captors asked us for songs, and our tormentors demanded joy, saying, "Sing us one of the songs of Zion." {137:4} How can we sing the Lord's song in a foreign land? {137:5} If I forget you, O Jerusalem, let my right hand forget its skill. {137:6} If I do not remember you, let my tongue cling to the roof of my mouth; if I do not prefer Jerusalem above my highest joy. {137:7} Remember, O Lord, against the Edomites the day of Jerusalem, how they said, "Tear it down! Tear it down! To its foundations!" {137:8} O daughter of Babylon, doomed to destruction, happy is he who repays you for what you have done to us. {137:9} Happy is he who seizes your infants and dashes them against the rocks.

{138:1} I will praise you with my whole heart; before the gods I will sing your praise. {138:2} I will bow down toward your holy temple and praise your name for your love and your faithfulness; for you have exalted your name and your word above all things. {138:3} On the day I called, you answered me; you made me bold and gave me strength. {138:4} All the kings of the earth will praise you, O Lord, when they hear the words of your mouth. {138:5} Yes, they will sing of the ways of the Lord, for great is the glory of the Lord. {138:6} Though the Lord is on high, he looks upon the lowly, but the proud he knows from afar. {138:7} Though I walk in the midst of trouble, you preserve my life; you stretch out your hand against the anger of my foes, and your right hand saves me. {138:8} The Lord will fulfill his purpose for me; your love, O Lord, endures forever—do not abandon the works of your hands.

{139:1} O Lord, you have searched me and known me. {139:2} You know when I sit and when I rise; you perceive my thoughts from afar. {139:3} You discern my going out and my lying down; you are familiar with all my ways. {139:4} Before a word is on my tongue, you, Lord, know it completely. {139:5} You hem me in behind and before, and you lay your hand upon me. {139:6} Such knowledge is too wonderful for me, too lofty for me to attain. {139:7} Where can I go from your Spirit? Where can I flee from your presence? {139:8} If I go up to the heavens, you are there; if I make my bed in the depths, you are there. {139:9} If I rise on the wings of the dawn, if I settle on the far side of the sea, {139:10} even there your hand will guide me, your right hand will hold me fast. {139:11} If I say, "Surely the darkness will hide me and the light become night around me," {139:12} even the darkness will not be dark to you; the night will shine like the day, for darkness is as light to you. {139:13} For you created my inmost being; you knit me together in my mother's womb. {139:14} I praise you because I am fearfully and wonderfully made; your works are wonderful, I know that full well. {139:15} My frame was not hidden from you when I was made in the secret place, when I was woven together in the depths of the earth. {139:16} Your eyes saw my unformed body; all the days ordained for me were written in your book before one of them came to be. {139:17} How precious to me are your thoughts, O God! How vast is the sum of them! {139:18} If I were to count them, they would outnumber the grains of sand; when I awake, I am still with you. {139:19} If only you, God, would slay the wicked! Away from me, you who are bloodthirsty! {139:20} They speak of you with evil intent; your adversaries misuse your name. {139:21} Do I not hate those who hate you, Lord, and abhor those who are in rebellion against you? {139:22} I have nothing but hatred for them; I count them my enemies. {139:23} Search me, God, and know my heart; test me and know my anxious thoughts. {139:24} See if there is any offensive way in me, and lead me in the way everlasting.

{140:1} Deliver me, O Lord, from evil men; protect me from violent men, {140:2} who devise evil plans in their hearts and stir up war all day long. {140:3} They make their tongues sharp like snakes; the venom of vipers is on their lips. Selah. {140:4} Keep me, O Lord, from the hands of the wicked; protect me from violent men who plan to trip me up. {140:5} The proud have set a snare for me; they have spread out cords along my path; they have set traps for me. Selah. {140:6} I say to the Lord, "You are my God; hear, Lord, my cry for mercy." {140:7} Sovereign Lord, my strong deliverer, you shield my head in the day of battle. {140:8} Do not grant the wicked their desires, Lord; do not let their plans succeed, or they will become proud. Selah. {140:9} Let the heads of those who surround me be covered with the trouble their lips have caused. {140:10} Let burning coals fall on them; let them be thrown into the fire, into miry pits, never to rise. {140:11} Do not let a slanderer be established in the land; may evil hunt down the violent man relentlessly. {140:12} I know that the Lord secures justice for the poor and upholds the cause of the needy. {140:13} Surely the righteous will praise your name, and the upright will live in your presence.

{141:1} Lord, I cry out to you; hurry to me and listen to my voice when I call to you. {141:2} Let my prayer be presented before you like incense, and the lifting of my hands like the evening sacrifice. {141:3} Set a guard, O Lord, over my mouth; keep watch over the door of my lips. {141:4} Do not let my heart be drawn to any evil thing, to practice wicked deeds with those who do wrong; and do not let me eat their delicacies. {141:5} Let the righteous strike me; it will be a kindness. Let him rebuke me; it will be like a nourishing oil, which will not break my head; for my prayer will still be against their wickedness. {141:6} When their judges are thrown down the cliffs, they will hear my words, for they are sweet. {141:7} Our bones are scattered at the mouth of the grave, like when one cuts and splits wood on the ground. {141:8} But my eyes are on you, O God the Lord; in you I trust; do not leave my soul destitute. {141:9} Keep me from the snares they have laid for me and the traps set by evil workers. {141:10} Let the wicked fall into their own nets, while I escape.

{142:1} I cried out to the Lord with my voice; I made my supplication to the Lord with my voice. {142:2} I poured out my complaint before him; I showed him my trouble. {142:3} When my spirit was overwhelmed within me, you knew my path. In the way I walked, they had hidden a trap for me. {142:4} I looked to my right and saw that there was no one who recognized me; refuge failed me; no one cared for my soul. {142:5} I cried to you, O Lord; I said, "You are my refuge and my portion in the land of the living." {142:6} Listen to my cry, for I am very low; deliver me from my persecutors, for they are stronger than I. {142:7} Bring my soul out of prison, that I may praise your name; the righteous will gather around me, for you will deal bountifully with me.

{143:1} Hear my prayer, O Lord; listen to my supplications. In your faithfulness, answer me, and in your righteousness. {143:2} Do not bring your servant into judgment, for no one living is righteous before you. {143:3} The enemy has pursued my soul; he has crushed my life to the ground; he has made me dwell in darkness like those who have been long dead. {143:4} Therefore my spirit is overwhelmed within me; my heart is desolate. {143:5} I remember the days of old; I meditate on all your works; I ponder the work of your hands. {143:6} I reach out my hands to you; my soul thirsts for you like a parched land. Selah. {143:7} Answer me quickly, O Lord; my spirit fails. Do not hide your face from me, or I will be like those who go down to the pit. {143:8} Let me hear your lovingkindness in the morning, for I trust in you. Show me the way I should go, for I lift up my soul to you. {143:9} Deliver me, O Lord, from my enemies; I take refuge in you. {143:10} Teach me to do your will, for you are my God; your Spirit is good; lead me into the land of uprightness. {143:11} Revive me, O Lord, for your name's sake; for your righteousness, bring my soul out of trouble. {143:12} In your mercy, cut off my enemies and destroy all those who afflict my soul, for I am your servant.

{144:1} Blessed be the Lord my strength, who teaches my hands to make war and my fingers to fight. {144:2} He is my goodness and my fortress; my high tower and my deliverer; my shield and the one in whom I trust; who subdues my people under me. {144:3} Lord, what is mankind that you take notice of him? Or the son of man that you think of him? {144:4} Man is like a breath; his days are like a fleeting shadow. {144:5} Bow down your heavens, O Lord, and come down; touch the mountains so they smoke. {144:6} Send forth lightning and scatter them; shoot your arrows and destroy them. {144:7} Reach down your hand from on high; rescue me and deliver me from great waters, from the hand of strangers, {144:8} whose mouths speak vanity, and whose right hands are deceitful. {144:9} I will sing a new song to you, O God; on a harp of ten strings, I will sing praises to you. {144:10} It is he who gives salvation to kings, who delivers David his servant from the deadly sword. {144:11} Rescue me and deliver me from the hand of strangers, whose mouths speak vanity and whose right hands are deceitful. {144:12} May our sons be like plants grown up in their youth; may our daughters be like cornerstones, polished like a palace. {144:13} May our granaries be full, providing all kinds of produce; may our sheep bring forth thousands and ten thousands in our streets. {144:14} May our oxen be strong for labor; may there be no breaking in or going out; may there be no cry of distress in our streets. {144:15} Blessed is that people that is in such a state; yes, blessed is that people whose God is the Lord.

{145:1} I will exalt you, my God, the King; I will praise your name forever and ever. {145:2} Every day I will praise you; I will extol your name forever and ever. {145:3} Great is the Lord and greatly to be praised; his greatness is unsearchable. {145:4} One generation shall commend your works to another and shall declare your mighty acts. {145:5} I will meditate on the glorious splendor of your majesty and on your wondrous works. {145:6} People will speak of the might of your awesome deeds, and I will declare your greatness. {145:7} They will celebrate your abundant goodness and joyfully sing of your righteousness. {145:8} The Lord is gracious and full of compassion, slow to anger and great in mercy. {145:9} The Lord is good to all; his tender mercies are over all his works. {145:10} All your works shall praise you, O Lord, and your faithful people shall bless you. {145:11} They shall speak of the glory of your kingdom and talk of your power; {145:12} to make known to the children of men your mighty acts and the glorious majesty of your kingdom. {145:13} Your kingdom is an everlasting kingdom, and your dominion endures throughout all generations. {145:14} The Lord upholds all who fall and raises up all who are bowed down. {145:15} The eyes of all look to you, and you give them their food in due season. {145:16} You open your hand and satisfy the desire of every living thing. {145:17} The Lord is righteous in all his ways and holy in all his works. {145:18} The Lord is near to all who call on him, to all who call on him in truth. {145:19} He will fulfill the desire of those who fear him; he will also hear their cry and save them. {145:20} The Lord preserves all who love him, but all the wicked he will destroy. {145:21} My mouth will speak the praise of the Lord & let all flesh bless his holy name forever and ever.

{146:1} Praise the Lord! Praise the Lord, O my soul. {146:2} As long as I live, I will praise the Lord; I will sing praises to my God while I have breath. {146:3} Do not put your trust in princes or in mortal men, who cannot help you. {146:4} When their breath departs, they return to the earth; on that very day their plans perish. {146:5} Blessed is he who has the God of Jacob for his help, whose hope is in the Lord his God. {146:6} He made heaven and earth, the sea, and everything in them; he keeps truth forever. {146:7} He upholds justice for the oppressed; he provides food for the hungry. The Lord frees the prisoners. {146:8} The Lord opens the eyes of the blind; the Lord lifts up those who are bowed down; the Lord loves the righteous. {146:9} The Lord watches over the strangers; he supports the fatherless and the widow, but he turns the way of the wicked upside down. {146:10} The Lord will reign forever, your God, O Zion, for all generations. Praise the Lord!

{147:1} Praise the Lord, for it is good to sing praises to our God; it is pleasant, and praise is beautiful. {147:2} The Lord builds up Jerusalem; he gathers the outcasts of Israel. {147:3} He heals the brokenhearted and binds up their wounds. {147:4} He counts the number of the stars; he calls them all by name. {147:5} Great is our Lord, and mighty in power; his understanding is infinite. {147:6} The Lord lifts up the humble, but casts the wicked to the ground. {147:7} Sing to the Lord with thanksgiving; sing praise to our God with the harp. {147:8} He covers the heavens with clouds, prepares rain for the earth, and makes grass grow on the mountains. {147:9} He gives food to the animals and to the young ravens that cry. {147:10} He does not delight in the strength of the horse or take pleasure in the legs of a man. {147:11} The Lord takes pleasure in those who fear him, in those who hope in his mercy. {147:12}

Praise the Lord, O Jerusalem; praise your God, O Zion. {147:13} For he strengthens the bars of your gates; he blesses your children within you. {147:14} He makes peace within your borders and fills you with the finest of wheat. {147:15} He sends his command throughout the earth; his word runs swiftly. {147:16} He gives snow like wool; he scatters frost like ashes. {147:17} He hurls down his hail like pieces of ice; who can withstand his cold? {147:18} He sends out his word and melts them; he causes his wind to blow, and the waters flow. {147:19} He reveals his word to Jacob, his statutes and judgments to Israel. {147:20} He has not done this for any other nation; they do not know his judgments. Praise the Lord!

{148:1} Praise the Lord! Praise the Lord from the heavens; praise him in the heights. {148:2} Praise him, all his angels; praise him, all his heavenly hosts. {148:3} Praise him, sun and moon; praise him, all you shining stars. {148:4} Praise him, you highest heavens, and you waters above the heavens. {148:5} Let them praise the name of the Lord, for he commanded, and they were created. {148:6} He established them forever and ever; he issued a decree that will not pass away. {148:7} Praise the Lord from the earth, you sea creatures and all deeps; {148:8} fire and hail, snow and vapor, stormy winds that do his bidding; {148:9} mountains and all hills, fruit trees and all cedars; {148:10} wild animals and all cattle, creeping things and flying birds; {148:11} kings of the earth and all peoples, princes and all judges of the earth; {148:12} both young men and women, old men and children; {148:13} let them praise the name of the Lord, for his name alone is exalted; his glory is above the earth and the heavens. {148:14} He has raised up a horn for his people, the praise of all his saints, the people of Israel, a people close to him. Praise the Lord!

{149:1} Praise the Lord! Sing to the Lord a new song, and his praise in the assembly of the saints. {149:2} Let Israel rejoice in their Maker; let the children of Zion be joyful in their King. {149:3} Let them praise his name with dancing; let them sing praises to him with tambourines and harps. {149:4} For the Lord takes pleasure in his people; he beautifies the humble with salvation. {149:5} Let the saints rejoice in glory; let them sing aloud on their beds. {149:6} Let the high praises of God be in their mouths, and a two-edged sword in their hands, {149:7} to execute vengeance on the nations and punishments on the peoples; {149:8} to bind their kings with chains and their nobles with iron shackles; {149:9} to carry out the judgment written against them. This honor is for all his saints. Praise the Lord!

{150:1} Praise the Lord! Praise God in his sanctuary; praise him in the firmament of his power. {150:2} Praise him for his mighty acts; praise him according to his excellent greatness. {150:3} Praise him with the sound of the trumpet; praise him with the harp and lyre. {150:4} Praise him with tambourine and dance; praise him with strings and pipe. {150:5} Praise him with loud cymbals; praise him with clashing cymbals. {150:6} Let everything that has breath praise the Lord. Praise the Lord!

The Book of Proverbs

The Proverbs of Solomon

{1:1} These are the proverbs of Solomon, the son of David, king of Israel. {1:2} They are meant to help you know wisdom and instruction, to understand the words of insight. {1:3} They teach you to receive wisdom, justice, and fair judgment. {1:4} They give subtlety to the simple and knowledge and discretion to the young. {1:5} A wise person will listen and increase their learning, and a person of understanding will attain wise counsel. {1:6} They will understand a proverb and its interpretation, the words of the wise, and their deep sayings. {1:7} The fear of the Lord is the beginning of knowledge, but fools despise wisdom and instruction. {1:8} My son, listen to your father's instruction and do not forsake your mother's teaching. {1:9} They will be a garland of grace for your head and chains around your neck. {1:10} My son, if sinners entice you, do not consent. {1:11} If they say, "Come with us, let us lie in wait for blood; let us lurk secretly for the innocent without cause," {1:12} let us swallow them alive like the grave, whole like those who go down into the pit. {1:13} We will find all kinds of precious goods; we will fill our houses with spoil. {1:14} Throw in your lot with us; we will all share one purse. {1:15} My son, do not walk in the way with them; keep your foot from their path. {1:16} For their feet run to evil and they hurry to shed blood. {1:17} Surely it is in vain that a net is spread in the sight of any bird. {1:18} They lie in wait for their own blood; they lurk secretly for their own lives. {1:19} Such are the ways of everyone who is greedy for gain; it takes away the life of its owners. {1:20} Wisdom cries out in the streets; she raises her voice in the public squares. {1:21} She calls out at the corners of the streets and at the entrance of the city; she speaks her words, saying, {1:22} "How long, you simple ones, will you love simplicity? How long will scoffers delight in their scoffing, and fools hate knowledge? {1:23} Turn at my reproof; behold, I will pour out my spirit on you; I will make my words known to you. {1:24} Because I called, and you refused; I stretched out my hand, and no one paid attention; {1:25} but you have ignored all my counsel and would not accept my reproof. {1:26} I will also laugh at your calamity; I will mock when your terror comes, {1:27} when your terror comes like a storm and your destruction comes like a whirlwind, when distress and anguish come upon you. {1:28} Then they will call on me, but I will not answer; they will seek me diligently, but they will not find me. {1:29} Because they hated knowledge and did not choose the fear of the Lord, {1:30} they would not accept my counsel; they despised all my reproof. {1:31} Therefore, they will eat the fruit of their own way and be filled with their own devices. {1:32} For the turning away of the simple will slay them, and the complacency of fools will destroy them. {1:33} But whoever listens to me will dwell safely and will be at ease from fear of evil.

{2:1} My son, if you will accept my words and hide my commandments within you, {2:2} so that you incline your ear to wisdom and apply your heart to understanding, {2:3} yes, if you cry out for knowledge and lift your voice for understanding, {2:4} if you seek her as silver and search for her as for hidden treasures, {2:5} then you will understand the fear of the Lord and find the knowledge of God. {2:6} For the Lord gives wisdom; from his mouth comes knowledge and understanding. {2:7} He stores up sound wisdom for the upright; he is a shield to those who walk with integrity. {2:8} He guards the paths of justice and preserves the way of his saints. {2:9} Then you will understand righteousness, justice, and equity; indeed, every good path. {2:10} When wisdom enters your heart and knowledge is pleasant to your soul, {2:11} discretion will preserve you, and understanding will keep you, {2:12} to deliver you from the way of evil, from the man who speaks perverse things, {2:13} who leaves the paths of uprightness to walk in the ways of darkness, {2:14} who rejoices in doing evil and delights in the perversity of the wicked, {2:15} whose ways are crooked and who is devious in their paths; {2:16} to deliver you from the immoral woman, from the seductive words of the stranger, {2:17} who forsakes the companion of her youth and forgets the covenant of her God. {2:18} For her house leads down to death, and her paths to the dead. {2:19} None who go to her return again, nor do they regain the paths of life. {2:20} So you may walk in the way of good men and keep to the paths of the righteous. {2:21} For the upright will dwell in the land, and the blameless will remain in it. {2:22} But the wicked will be cut off from the earth, and the unfaithful will be uprooted from it.

{3:1} My son, do not forget my teaching; let your heart keep my commandments. {3:2} For they will add length of days, long life, and peace to you. {3:3} Do not let mercy and truth leave you; tie them around your neck; write them on the tablet of your heart. {3:4} Then you will find favor and good judgment in the sight of God and people. {3:5} Trust in the Lord with all your heart, and do not rely on your own understanding. {3:6} In all your ways acknowledge him, and he will make your paths straight. {3:7} Do not be wise in your own eyes; fear the Lord and turn away from evil. {3:8} This will bring health to your body and nourishment to your bones. {3:9} Honor the Lord with your wealth and with the first fruits of all your increase. {3:10} Then your barns will be filled with plenty, and your vats will overflow with new wine. {3:11} My son, do not despise the Lord's discipline or be weary of his correction. {3:12} For whom the Lord loves, he corrects, just as a father corrects the son he delights in. {3:13} Blessed is the man who finds wisdom, and the man who gains understanding. {3:14} For her profit is better than the profit of silver, and her gain is better than fine gold. {3:15} She is more precious than rubies; nothing you desire can compare with her. {3:16} Length of days is in her right hand; in her left hand are riches and honor. {3:17} Her ways are ways of pleasantness, and all her paths are peace. {3:18} She is a tree of life to those who lay hold of her; happy is everyone who retains her. {3:19} The Lord by wisdom founded the earth; by understanding, he established the heavens. {3:20} By his knowledge, the depths were broken up, and the clouds drop down the dew. {3:21} My son, do not let these depart from your sight; keep sound wisdom and discretion. {3:22} They will be life to your soul and grace to your neck. {3:23} Then you will walk safely in your way, and your foot will not stumble. {3:24} When you lie down, you will not be afraid; yes, you will lie down, and your sleep will be sweet. {3:25} Do not be afraid of sudden fear, nor of the desolation of the wicked when it comes. {3:26} For the Lord will be your confidence and will keep your foot from being caught. {3:27} Do not withhold good from those to whom it is due when it is in your power to do it. {3:28} Do not say to your neighbor, "Go, and come back tomorrow; I will give it," when you have it with you. {3:29} Do not devise evil against your neighbor, seeing he dwells securely beside you. {3:30} Do not strive with a man without cause, if he has done you no harm. {3:31} Do not envy the oppressor and choose none of his ways. {3:32} For the perverse is an abomination to the Lord, but his secret is with the righteous. {3:33} The curse of the Lord is in the house of the wicked, but he blesses the dwelling of the just. {3:34} Surely he scorns the scorners, but he gives grace to the humble. {3:35} The wise will inherit glory, but shame will be the promotion of fools.

{4:1} Listen, my children, to your father's instruction, and pay attention to know understanding. {4:2} For I give you good doctrine; do not forsake my law. {4:3} For I was my father's son, tender and the only beloved in the sight of my mother. {4:4} He taught me also and said to me, "Let your heart hold on to my words; keep my commandments and live." {4:5} Get wisdom, get understanding; do not forget it, and do not turn away from the words of my mouth. {4:6} Do not forsake her, and she will preserve you; love her, and she will keep you. {4:7} Wisdom is the principal thing; therefore, get wisdom, and with all your getting, get understanding. {4:8} Exalt her, and she will promote you; she will bring you honor when you embrace her. {4:9} She will give you a garland of grace for your head; she will deliver to you a crown of glory. {4:10} Listen, my son, and receive my sayings, and the years of your life will be many. {4:11} I have taught you in the way of wisdom; I have led you in the right paths. {4:12} When you walk, your steps will not be hampered; and when you run, you will not stumble. {4:13} Hold on to instruction; do not let her go; keep her, for she is your life. {4:14} Do not enter the path of the wicked, and do not go in the way of evil men. {4:15} Avoid it; do not pass by it; turn away from it and go on your way. {4:16} For they cannot sleep unless they have done mischief; their sleep is taken away unless they cause someone to fall. {4:17} For they eat the bread of wickedness and drink the wine of violence. {4:18} But the path of the righteous is like the shining light that shines more and more until the perfect day. {4:19} The way of the wicked is like darkness; they do not know at what they stumble. {4:20} My son, pay attention to my words; incline your ear to my sayings. {4:21} Do not let them depart from your eyes; keep them in the midst of your heart. {4:22} For they are life to those who find them and health to all their flesh. {4:23} Keep your heart with all diligence, for out of it spring the issues of life. {4:24} Put away from you a deceitful mouth, and put perverse lips far from you. {4:25} Let your eyes look straight ahead, and let your eyelids look right before you. {4:26} Ponder the path of your feet, and let all your ways be established. {4:27} Do not turn to the right or to the left; remove your foot from evil.

{5:1} My son, pay attention to my wisdom and listen closely to my understanding. {5:2} This way you can maintain discretion and keep knowledge close to your lips. {5:3} For the words of a strange woman drip like honey, and her mouth is smoother than oil. {5:4} But in the end, she is as bitter as wormwood and sharp as a double-edged sword. {5:5} Her feet go down to death; her steps lead straight to the grave. {5:6} She makes it hard to understand the path of life; her ways are unstable, and you cannot know them. {5:7} Listen to me now, my children, and do not stray from the words of my mouth. {5:8} Stay far away from her and do not go near the door of her house. {5:9} Otherwise, you will give your honor to others and your years to the cruel. {5:10} Strangers will be filled with your wealth, and your hard work will end up in the house of someone else. {5:11} Then you will mourn at the end when your body is consumed. {5:12} You will say, "How I hated instruction and my heart despised correction! {5:13} I did not obey the voice of my teachers or listen to those who instructed me!" {5:14} I was almost completely caught up in evil among the congregation and assembly. {5:15} Drink water from your own cistern and flowing water from your own well. {5:16} Let your springs flow out into the streets and your rivers of water in public places. {5:17} Let them be for you alone and not for strangers with you. {5:18} Let your fountain be blessed, and rejoice with the wife of your youth. {5:19} Let her be like a loving doe and a graceful deer; let her breasts satisfy you at all times, and may you always be captivated by her love. {5:20} And why, my son, would you be captivated by a strange woman and embrace the bosom of a stranger? {5:21} For the ways of a man are before the eyes of the Lord, and he considers all his paths. {5:22} His own iniquities will trap the wicked, and he will be held fast by the cords of his sins. {5:23} He will die without instruction, and in the greatness of his folly, he will go astray.

{6:1} My son, if you have become surety (a guarantor) for your friend, if you have shaken hands with a stranger, {6:2} you are snared by the words of your mouth; you are taken by the words of your mouth. {6:3} Do this now, my son, and free yourself when you have come into the hand of your friend; go, humble yourself, and ensure your friend. {6:4} Do not give sleep to your eyes or slumber to your eyelids. {6:5} Free yourself like a gazelle from the hand of the hunter and like a bird from the hand of the fowler. {6:6} Go to the ant, you sluggard; consider her ways and be wise. {6:7} She has no chief, overseer, or ruler, {6:8} yet she provides her food in the summer and gathers her provisions in the harvest. {6:9} How long will you sleep, O sluggard? When will you rise from your sleep? {6:10} A little sleep, a little slumber, a little folding of the hands to rest: {6:11} and poverty will come upon you like a traveler, and your need like an armed man. {6:12} A worthless person, a wicked man, goes about with a crooked mouth. {6:13} He winks with his eyes, signals with his feet, and teaches with his fingers. {6:14} Perversity is in his heart; he devises evil continually and sows discord. {6:15} Therefore, calamity will come upon him suddenly; in an instant he will be broken without remedy. {6:16} There are six things that the Lord hates, and seven that are an abomination to him: {6:17} a proud look, a lying tongue, and hands that shed innocent blood, {6:18} a heart that devises wicked imaginations, feet that are swift in running to mischief, {6:19} a false witness who speaks lies, and one who sows discord among brethren. {6:20} My son, keep your father's commandment and do not forsake the law of your mother. {6:21} Bind them continually on your heart and tie them around your neck. {6:22} When you go, they will lead you; when you sleep, they will keep you; and when you wake up, they will speak to you. {6:23} For the commandment is a lamp, and the law is light; and reproofs of instruction are the way of life, {6:24} to keep you from the evil woman, from the flattering tongue of a strange woman. {6:25} Do not lust after her beauty in your heart, nor let her captivate you with her eyelids. {6:26} For by means of a whorish woman, a man is brought to a piece of bread; and the adulteress hunts for the precious life. {6:27} Can a man take fire in his bosom and not be burned? {6:28} Can one walk on hot coals and his feet not be scorched? {6:29} So is he who goes in to his neighbor's wife; whoever touches her will not be innocent. {6:30} People do not despise a thief if he steals to satisfy his soul when he is hungry; {6:31} but if he is found, he shall restore sevenfold; he shall give all the substance of his house.

{6:32} But whoever commits adultery with a woman lacks understanding; he who does so destroys his own soul. {6:33} Wounds and dishonor will he get, and his reproach will not be wiped away. {6:34} For jealousy is the rage of a man; therefore, he will not spare in the day of vengeance. {6:35} He will not accept any ransom, nor will he be satisfied, though you give him many gifts.

{7:1} My son, keep my words and treasure my commandments with you. {7:2} Keep my commandments and live; make my law the apple of your eye. {7:3} Bind them on your fingers; write them on the tablet of your heart. {7:4} Say to wisdom, "You are my sister," and call understanding your close relative. {7:5} This way they can keep you safe from the strange woman, from the one who flatters with her words. {7:6} For from the window of my house, I looked through my lattice and {7:7} saw among the simple ones; I discerned among the youths a young man lacking sense. {7:8} He was passing through the street near her corner and headed toward her house, {7:9} in the twilight, in the evening, in the black and dark night. {7:10} And behold, a woman met him dressed like a prostitute and crafty in heart. {7:11} She is loud and rebellious; her feet do not stay at home. {7:12} Now she is outside, now in the streets, waiting at every corner. {7:13} So she caught him, kissed him, and with a bold face said to him, {7:14} "I have peace offerings with me; today I fulfilled my vows. {7:15} Therefore, I came out to meet you, seeking you eagerly, and I have found you. {7:16} I have decorated my bed with colored coverings, with fine linens from Egypt. {7:17} I have perfumed my bed with myrrh, aloes, and cinnamon. {7:18} Come, let us take our fill of love until morning; let us delight ourselves with love. {7:19} For my husband is not at home; he has gone on a long journey. {7:20} He took a bag of money with him and will come home at the appointed time." {7:21} With her persuasive speech, she led him astray; with the flattery of her lips, she seduced him. {7:22} He followed her immediately, like an ox going to the slaughter or like a fool going to the correction of a stock. {7:23} Until an arrow pierces his liver; as a bird rushes into a trap and does not know it will cost him his life. {7:24} Now listen to me, you children, and pay attention to the words of my mouth. {7:25} Do not let your heart stray to her ways; do not wander into her paths. {7:26} For she has cast down many wounded; indeed, many strong men have been slain by her. {7:27} Her house is the way to hell, descending to chambers of death.

{8:1} Does not wisdom call out? Does not understanding raise her voice? {8:2} She stands at the top of high places, along the way, at the crossroads. {8:3} She cries out at the gates, at the entry of the city, at the entrance of the doors. {8:4} To you, O men, I call; and my voice is to the sons of men. {8:5} O you simple ones, understand wisdom; and you fools, have an understanding heart. {8:6} Listen, for I will speak excellent things, and the opening of my lips will be right things. {8:7} For my mouth will speak truth; wickedness is an abomination to my lips. {8:8} All the words of my mouth are in righteousness; there is nothing twisted or perverse in them. {8:9} They are all plain to him who understands and right to those who find knowledge. {8:10} Receive my instruction, and not silver; and knowledge rather than choice gold. {8:11} For wisdom is better than rubies, and all the things you may desire cannot compare with her. {8:12} I, wisdom, dwell with prudence and find knowledge of witty inventions. {8:13} The fear of the Lord is to hate evil; pride, arrogance, the evil way, and the perverse mouth I hate. {8:14} Counsel is mine, and sound wisdom; I am understanding; I have strength. {8:15} By me kings reign, and rulers decree justice. {8:16} By me princes rule, and all judges of the earth. {8:17} I love those who love me, and those who seek me diligently will find me. {8:18} Riches and honor are with me; enduring wealth and righteousness. {8:19} My fruit is better than gold, even fine gold, and my revenue better than choice silver. {8:20} I walk in the way of righteousness, in the midst of the paths of justice, {8:21} that I may cause those who love me to inherit wealth, and I will fill their treasuries. {8:22} The Lord possessed me at the beginning of his way, before his works of old. {8:23} I have been established from everlasting, from the beginning, before the earth ever was. {8:24} When there were no depths, I was brought forth; when there were no springs abounding with water. {8:25} Before the mountains were settled, before the hills, I was brought forth; {8:26} while he had not yet made the earth or the fields, nor the highest part of the dust of the world. {8:27} When he prepared the heavens, I was there; when he drew a circle on the face of the deep, {8:28} when he established the clouds above, when he strengthened the fountains of the deep, {8:29} when he set a limit for the sea so that the waters would not pass his command, when he appointed the foundations of the earth, {8:30} then I was beside him as a master craftsman, and I was daily his delight, rejoicing always before him; {8:31} rejoicing in his inhabited world, and my delight was with the sons of men. {8:32} Now therefore, listen to me, you children, for blessed are those who keep my ways. {8:33} Hear instruction and be wise, and do not disregard it. {8:34} Blessed is the man who listens to me, watching daily at my gates, waiting at the posts of my doors. {8:35} For whoever finds me finds life and obtains favor from the Lord. {8:36} But he who sins against me wrongs his own soul; all those who hate me love death.

{9:1} Wisdom has built her house; she has hewn out her seven pillars. {9:2} She has prepared her meat; she has mixed her wine; she has also set her table. {9:3} She has sent out her maidens; she calls from the highest places in the city, {9:4} "Whoever is simple, let him turn in here!" To him who lacks understanding, she says, {9:5} "Come, eat of my bread, and drink of the wine I have mixed. {9:6} Leave your foolishness, and live; go in the way of understanding." {9:7} He who corrects a mocker brings shame upon himself; he who rebukes a wicked man gets himself a blot. {9:8} Do not correct a mocker, or he will hate you; rebuke a wise man, and he will love you. {9:9} Give instruction to a wise man, and he will be even wiser; teach a righteous man, and he will increase in learning. {9:10} The fear of the Lord is the beginning of wisdom, and the knowledge of the Holy One is understanding. {9:11} For through me, your days will be multiplied, and the years of your life will be increased. {9:12} If you are wise, you will benefit yourself; if you mock, you alone will suffer. {9:13} A foolish woman is loud; she is simple and knows nothing. {9:14} She sits at the door of her house, on a seat at the high places of the city, {9:15} to call out to those who pass by, who go straight on their way. {9:16} "Whoever is simple, let him turn in here!" And to him who lacks understanding, she says, {9:17} "Stolen waters are sweet, and bread eaten in secret is pleasant." {9:18} But he does not know that the dead are there; that her guests are in the depths of hell.

{10:1} The proverbs of Solomon: A wise son makes a glad father, but a foolish son is the sorrow of his mother. {10:2} Treasures gained by wickedness profit nothing, but righteousness delivers from death. {10:3} The Lord will not allow the soul of the righteous to go hungry, but he casts away the substance of the wicked. {10:4} He becomes poor who works with a lazy hand, but the hand of the diligent makes rich. {10:5} He who gathers in summer is a wise son, but he who sleeps in harvest is a son who brings shame. {10:6} Blessings are upon the head of the righteous, but violence covers the mouth of the wicked. {10:7} The memory of the righteous is blessed, but the name of the wicked will rot. {10:8} The wise in heart will receive commands, but a babbling fool will fall. {10:9} He who walks uprightly walks securely, but he who perverts his ways will be known. {10:10} He who winks with his eye causes sorrow, but a babbling fool will fall. {10:11} The mouth of the righteous is a fountain of life, but violence covers the mouth of the wicked. {10:12} Hatred stirs up strife, but love covers all sins. {10:13} In the lips of him who has understanding, wisdom is found, but a rod is for the back of him who lacks understanding. {10:14} Wise men store up knowledge, but the mouth of the foolish is near destruction. {10:15} The rich man's wealth is his strong city; the destruction of the poor is their poverty. {10:16} The labor of the righteous leads to life; the fruit of the wicked leads to sin. {10:17} He is on the path of life who keeps instruction, but he who refuses reproof goes astray. {10:18} He who hides hatred with lying lips is a fool, and he who utters slander is a fool. {10:19} In the multitude of words, sin is not lacking, but he who restrains his lips is wise. {10:20} The tongue of the righteous is like choice silver; the heart of the wicked is of little worth. {10:21} The lips of the righteous feed many, but fools die for lack of wisdom. {10:22} The blessing of the Lord makes one rich, and he adds no sorrow with it. {10:23} It is sport to a fool to do mischief, but a man of understanding has wisdom. {10:24} The fear of the wicked will come upon him, but the desire of the righteous will be granted. {10:25} When the whirlwind passes, the wicked is no more, but the righteous is an everlasting foundation. {10:26} Like vinegar to the teeth and smoke to the eyes, so is the lazy person to those who send him. {10:27} The fear of the Lord prolongs days, but the years of the wicked will be shortened. {10:28} The hope of the righteous brings joy, but the expectation of the wicked will perish. {10:29} The way of the Lord is strength to the upright, but destruction will come to the workers of iniquity. {10:30} The righteous will never be removed, but the wicked will not inhabit the earth. {10:31} The mouth of the righteous brings forth wisdom, but the perverse tongue will be cut out. {10:32} The lips of the righteous know what is acceptable, but the mouth of the wicked speaks perversion.

{11:1} A false balance is an abomination to the Lord, but a fair weight is his delight. {11:2} When pride comes, then comes shame, but with the humble is wisdom. {11:3} The integrity of the upright will guide them, but the perverse ways of the wicked will destroy them. {11:4} Riches do not profit in the day of wrath, but righteousness delivers from death. {11:5} The righteousness of the blameless will direct their path, but the wicked will fall by their own wickedness. {11:6} The righteousness of the upright will save them, but the wicked will be caught in their own wickedness. {11:7} When a wicked man dies, his expectation will perish, and the hope of unjust men will be gone. {11:8} The righteous are delivered from trouble, and the wicked take their place. {11:9} A hypocrite destroys his neighbor with his mouth, but through knowledge, the righteous are delivered. {11:10} When things go well for the righteous, the city rejoices, and when the wicked perish, there is shouting. {11:11} By the blessing of the upright, the city is lifted up, but it is overthrown by the words of the wicked. {11:12} He who lacks wisdom despises his neighbor, but a man of understanding holds his peace. {11:13} A gossip reveals secrets, but a trustworthy spirit conceals the matter. {11:14} Where there is no counsel, the people fall, but in the multitude of counselors, there is safety. {11:15} He who guarantees a loan for a stranger will suffer for it, but he who hates cosigning is secure. {11:16} A gracious woman retains honor, and strong men retain riches. {11:17} A merciful person does good to his own soul, but he who is cruel troubles his own flesh. {11:18} The wicked engage in deceitful work, but he who sows righteousness will have a sure reward. {11:19} Just as righteousness leads to life, so he who pursues evil pursues it to his own death. {11:20} Those with a crooked heart are an abomination to the Lord, but those who are upright in their ways are his delight. {11:21} Though they join hands, the wicked will not go unpunished, but the offspring of the righteous will be delivered. {11:22} Like a gold ring in a pig's snout is a beautiful woman who lacks discretion. {11:23} The desire of the righteous is only good, but the expectation of the wicked is wrath. {11:24} There are those who scatter and yet increase; and those who withhold more than is right, but it leads to poverty. {11:25} A generous soul will be made fat, and he who waters will also be watered himself. {11:26} He who withholds grain, the people will curse him, but blessings will be upon the head of him who sells it. {11:27} He who diligently seeks good will procure favor, but he who seeks mischief will find it. {11:28} He who trusts in his riches will fall, but the righteous will flourish like a branch. {11:29} He who troubles his own house will inherit the wind, and a fool will be a servant to the wise in heart. {11:30} The fruit of the righteous is a tree of life, and he who wins souls is wise. {11:31} Behold, the righteous will be rewarded on earth; much more the wicked and the sinner.

{12:1} Whoever loves instruction loves knowledge, but he who hates reproof is brutish (lacking intelligence). {12:2} A good man obtains favor from the Lord, but a man of wicked schemes he condemns. {12:3} A man will not be established by wickedness, but the root of the righteous will not be moved. {12:4} A virtuous woman is a crown to her husband, but she who causes shame is like rottenness in his bones. {12:5} The thoughts of the righteous are just, but the plans of the wicked are deceitful. {12:6} The words of the wicked lie in wait for blood, but the mouth of the upright delivers them. {12:7} The wicked are overthrown and are no more, but the house of the righteous will stand. {12:8} A man will be commended according to his wisdom, but he who has a perverse heart will be despised. {12:9} He who is despised and has a servant is better than he who honors himself but lacks bread. {12:10} A righteous man regards the life of his animal, but the tender mercies of the wicked are cruel. {12:11} He who works his land will be satisfied with bread, but he who follows vain pursuits lacks understanding. {12:12} The wicked desire the catch of evil men, but the root of the righteous yields fruit. {12:13} The wicked is ensnared by the transgression of his lips, but the righteous will come out of trouble. {12:14} A man will be satisfied with good by the fruit of his mouth, and the reward of a man's hands will be rendered to him. {12:15} The way of a fool is right in his own eyes, but he who listens to counsel is wise. {12:16} A fool's wrath is readily apparent, but a prudent man covers shame. {12:17} He who speaks truth shows forth righteousness, but a false witness speaks deceit. {12:18} There are those who speak like the piercings of a sword, but the tongue of the wise brings health. {12:19} The lip of truth will be established forever, but a lying tongue is only for a moment. {12:20} Deceit is in the heart of those who plot evil, but joy is found in those who counsel peace. {12:21} No harm will come to the righteous, but the wicked will be filled with trouble. {12:22} Lying lips are an abomination to the Lord, but those who deal truthfully are his delight. {12:23} A prudent man conceals knowledge, but the heart of fools proclaims foolishness. {12:24} The hand of the diligent will rule, but the lazy will be put to forced labor. {12:25} Heaviness in the heart of man makes it stoop, but a good word makes it glad. {12:26} The righteous is more excellent than his neighbor, but the way of the wicked leads them astray. {12:27} The lazy man does not roast what he took in hunting, but the wealth of a diligent man is precious. {12:28} In the way of righteousness is life, and in its pathway, there is no death.

{13:1} A wise son listens to his father's instruction, but a scoffer does not listen to rebuke. {13:2} A man will enjoy good things from the fruit of his words, but the soul of the wicked will consume violence. {13:3} He who guards his mouth guards his life, but he who opens his lips wide will face destruction. {13:4} The soul of the lazy desires but gets nothing, while the soul of the diligent will be richly satisfied. {13:5} A righteous man hates lies, but a wicked man is vile and will face shame. {13:6} Righteousness protects those who are upright in their ways, but wickedness destroys sinners. {13:7} There are those who make themselves rich yet have nothing, and those who make themselves poor yet have great wealth. {13:8} A man's riches can be a ransom for his life, but the poor does not hear rebuke. {13:9} The light of the righteous brings joy, but the lamp of the wicked will be snuffed out. {13:10} Only through pride comes conflict, but wisdom is with the well-advised. {13:11} Wealth gained through vanity will dwindle, but he who gathers through hard work will increase. {13:12} Hope deferred makes the heart sick, but when desires are fulfilled, it is like a tree of life. {13:13} Whoever despises the word will be destroyed, but he who fears the commandment will be rewarded. {13:14} The law of the wise is a fountain of life, keeping one away from the snares of death. {13:15} Good understanding brings favor, but the way of the transgressors is difficult. {13:16} Every prudent person acts with knowledge, but a fool openly displays his folly. {13:17} A wicked messenger will fall into trouble, but a faithful ambassador brings health. {13:18} Poverty and shame come to those who refuse instruction, but he who heeds correction will be honored. {13:19} The fulfillment of desires is sweet to the soul, but it is a detestable thing to fools to turn away from evil. {13:20} He who walks with wise men will be wise, but a companion of fools will be destroyed. {13:21} Evil chases sinners, but to the righteous, good will be repaid. {13:22} A good man leaves an inheritance for his grandchildren, and the wealth of the sinner is stored up for the just. {13:23} There is much food in the tillage of the poor, but there are those who perish for lack of judgment. {13:24} He who spares the rod hates his son, but he who loves him disciplines him promptly. {13:25} The righteous eat to satisfy their souls, but the belly of the wicked craves more.

{14:1} Every wise woman builds her house, but a foolish woman tears it down with her own hands. {14:2} He who walks uprightly fears the Lord, but he who is perverse in his ways despises him. {14:3} In the mouth of a fool is a rod of pride, but the lips of the wise will protect them. {14:4} Where there are no oxen, the manger is clean, but much increase comes from the strength of the ox. {14:5} A faithful witness will not lie, but a false witness speaks lies. {14:6} A scoffer seeks wisdom and finds it not, but knowledge is easy for him who understands. {14:7} Avoid the presence of a foolish man when you do not see knowledge in him. {14:8} The wisdom of the prudent is to understand his path, but the folly of fools is deception. {14:9} Fools mock at sin, but among the righteous, there is favor. {14:10} The heart knows its own bitterness; a stranger does not share in its joy. {14:11} The house of the wicked will be overthrown, but the dwelling of the upright will flourish. {14:12} There is a way that seems right to a man, but its end is the way of death. {14:13} Even in laughter, the heart may be sorrowful, and the end of that mirth is heaviness. {14:14} The backslider in heart will be filled with his own ways, but a good man will be satisfied with himself. {14:15} The simple believe every word, but the prudent consider their steps. {14:16} A wise man fears and turns away from evil, but a fool is reckless and confident. {14:17} He who is quick to anger acts foolishly, and a man of wicked schemes is despised. {14:18} The simple inherit folly, but the prudent are crowned with knowledge. {14:19} The evil bow before the good, and the wicked stand at the gates of the righteous. {14:20} The poor is hated even by his own neighbor, but the rich has many friends. {14:21} He who despises his neighbor sins, but he who has mercy on the poor is happy. {14:22} Do they not err who devise evil? But mercy and truth will be to those who plan good. {14:23} In all labor there is profit, but mere talk leads to poverty. {14:24} The crown of the wise is their riches, but the foolishness of fools is folly. {14:25} A true witness saves lives, but a deceitful witness speaks lies. {14:26} In the fear of the Lord is strong confidence, and his children will have a place of refuge. {14:27} The fear of the Lord is a fountain of life, keeping one away from the snares of death. {14:28} In the multitude of people is the king's honor, but in the lack of people is the destruction of the prince. {14:29} He who is slow to anger has great understanding, but he who is quick-tempered exalts folly. {14:30} A calm heart is the life of the flesh, but envy rots the bones. {14:31} He who oppresses the poor insults his Maker, but he who honors him has mercy on the poor. {14:32} The wicked are driven away in their wickedness, but the righteous have hope in their death. {14:33} Wisdom rests in the heart of those who have understanding, but what is in the midst of fools is made known. {14:34} Righteousness exalts a nation, but sin is a disgrace to any people. {14:35} The king's favor is toward a wise servant, but his wrath is against him who causes shame.

{15:1} A gentle answer turns away anger, but harsh words stir up wrath. {15:2} The wise use their words to share knowledge, but fools pour out foolishness from their mouths. {15:3} The Lord sees everything, both evil and good, in every place. {15:4} A wholesome tongue is like a tree of life, but a perverse tongue breaks the spirit. {15:5} A fool despises his father's instruction, but the one who listens to correction is wise. {15:6} In the home of the righteous, there is great treasure, but the earnings of the wicked lead to trouble. {15:7} The lips of the wise spread knowledge, but the heart of the foolish does not. {15:8} The sacrifice of the wicked is an abomination to the Lord, but the prayer of the upright pleases Him. {15:9} The way of the wicked is detestable to the Lord, but He loves those who pursue righteousness. {15:10} Discipline is hard for those who abandon the right path, and he who hates correction will die. {15:11} Hell and destruction are before the Lord; how much more so are the hearts of men? {15:12} A scoffer does not love anyone who corrects him and will not go to wise people. {15:13} A joyful heart brightens the face, but sorrow in the heart crushes the spirit. {15:14} The heart of a person with understanding seeks knowledge, but the mouth of fools feeds on foolishness. {15:15} All the days of the afflicted are bad, but a cheerful heart has a continuous feast. {15:16} Better is a little with the fear of the Lord than great wealth with trouble. {15:17} Better is a meal of vegetables with love than a fattened ox with hatred. {15:18} A hot-tempered person stirs up conflict, but one who is slow to anger calms strife. {15:19} The path of the lazy is like a thorny hedge, but the way of the righteous is smooth. {15:20} A wise son makes his father happy, but a foolish man despises his mother. {15:21} Folly is joy to those lacking wisdom, but a person of understanding walks uprightly. {15:22} Without counsel, plans fail, but in the abundance of counselors, they succeed. {15:23} A man has joy in the answer of his mouth; how good is a timely word! {15:24} The path of life leads the wise upward to avoid hell below. {15:25} The Lord will tear down the house of the proud, but He will secure the widow's territory. {15:26} The thoughts of the wicked are an abomination to the Lord, but the words of the pure are pleasing. {15:27} He who is greedy for gain troubles his own home, but he who hates bribes will live. {15:28} The heart of the righteous considers how to respond, but the mouth of the wicked pours out evil. {15:29} The Lord is far from the wicked, but He hears the prayer of the righteous. {15:30} The light of the eyes brings joy to the heart, and a good report nourishes the bones. {15:31} The ear that hears life-giving correction will stay among the wise. {15:32} He who refuses instruction despises his own soul, but he who listens to correction gains understanding. {15:33} The fear of the Lord is the beginning of wisdom, and humility comes before honor.

{16:1} The plans of a man's heart and the answer of his tongue come from the Lord. {16:2} Every man's ways seem right in his own eyes, but the Lord weighs the spirits. {16:3} Commit your works to the Lord, and your thoughts will be established. {16:4} The Lord has made everything for Himself, even the wicked for the day of disaster. {16:5} Everyone who is proud in heart is an abomination to the Lord; though they join forces, they will not go unpunished. {16:6} Through mercy and truth, guilt is atoned for, and by the fear of the Lord, men turn away from evil. {16:7} When a man's ways please the Lord, He makes even his enemies live in peace with him. {16:8} Better is a little with righteousness than great profits without justice. {16:9} A man's heart plans his way, but the Lord directs his steps. {16:10} A divine sentence is on the lips of a king; his mouth does not betray justice. {16:11} Honest scales and balances belong to the Lord; all the weights in the bag are His work. {16:12} It is an abomination for kings to commit wicked acts, for a throne is established by righteousness. {16:13} Righteous lips are the delight of kings, and they love him who speaks what is right. {16:14} The wrath of a king is like messengers of death, but a wise man will appease it. {16:15} In the king's favor is life; his goodwill is like a refreshing rain. {16:16} How much better is it to gain wisdom than gold! To gain understanding is better than silver! {16:17} The highway of the upright is to turn away from evil; he who keeps his way protects his life. {16:18} Pride goes before destruction, and a haughty spirit before a fall. {16:19} It is better to be of a humble spirit with the lowly than to share spoils with the proud. {16:20} He who handles a matter wisely will find good, and whoever trusts in the Lord will be happy. {16:21} The wise in heart will be called prudent, and sweetness of the lips increases learning. {16:22} Understanding is a source of life for those who possess it, but the instruction of fools is foolishness. {16:23} The heart of the wise teaches his mouth and adds learning to his lips. {16:24} Pleasant words are like a honeycomb, sweet to the soul and health to the bones. {16:25} There is a way that seems right to a man, but its end is the way of death. {16:26} He who labors labors for himself, for his mouth craves it from him. {16:27} An ungodly man digs up evil, and his lips are like a burning fire. {16:28} A perverse man sows strife, and a whisperer separates close friends. {16:29} A violent man entices his neighbor and leads him down a path that is not good. {16:30} He shuts his eyes to devise wicked schemes; moving his lips, he brings evil to pass. {16:31} Gray hair is a crown of glory if found in the way of righteousness. {16:32} He who is slow to anger is better than the mighty, and he who rules his spirit is greater than he who captures a city. {16:33} The lot is cast into the lap, but every decision is from the Lord.

{17:1} Better is a dry piece of bread with peace than a house full of sacrifices but full of conflict. {17:2} A wise servant will rule over a son who brings shame and will share in the inheritance with his brothers. {17:3} The refining pot is for silver, and the furnace is for gold, but the Lord tests hearts. {17:4} A wicked person listens to false lips, and a liar pays attention to a deceitful tongue. {17:5} Whoever mocks the poor insults his Maker, and those who rejoice at others' misfortunes will face punishment. {17:6} Grandchildren are the crown of old men, and the glory of children is their fathers. {17:7} Excellent speech is not fitting for a fool; much less are lying lips appropriate for a prince. {17:8} A gift is like a precious stone in the eyes of its possessor; wherever it turns, it brings success. {17:9} He who covers over an offense seeks love, but he who keeps bringing up a matter separates close friends. {17:10} A wise man learns more from a single correction than a fool does from a hundred lashes. {17:11} An evil person only seeks rebellion; therefore, a cruel messenger will be sent against him. {17:12} It's better to encounter a bear robbed of her cubs than to meet a fool in his folly. {17:13} Whoever repays good with evil will not have evil depart from his house. {17:14} The beginning of strife is like releasing water; so stop the conflict before it escalates. {17:15} The Lord finds both the justification of the wicked and the condemnation of the righteous to be an abomination. {17:16} Why would a fool have money in his hand to buy wisdom when he has no heart for it? {17:17} A friend loves at all times, and a brother is born for difficult times. {17:18} A man lacking understanding strikes hands and becomes surety (guarantees payment) in the presence of his friend. {17:19} He who loves transgression loves strife; and he who builds up his gate seeks destruction. {17:20} A perverse heart finds no good, and a deceitful tongue leads to trouble. {17:21} A father who raises a fool does so to his own sorrow; the father of a fool has no joy. {17:22} A cheerful heart is like good medicine, but a broken spirit dries up the bones. {17:23} A wicked man accepts a bribe to pervert the course of justice. {17:24} Wisdom is in front of those with understanding, but a fool's eyes roam to the ends of the earth. {17:25} A foolish son brings grief to his father and bitterness to his mother. {17:26} It's not good to punish the innocent or to strike princes for being just. {17:27} A person with knowledge uses few words, and a person of understanding has a calm spirit. {17:28} Even a fool is thought wise if he keeps quiet, and he who shuts his lips is considered intelligent.

{18:1} A man who isolates himself seeks his own desires and quarrels against all sound wisdom. {18:2} A fool takes no pleasure in understanding, but only in expressing his own opinions. {18:3} When the wicked come, contempt also comes, and with dishonor comes reproach. {18:4} The words of a man's mouth are like deep waters, and the fountain of wisdom is like a flowing stream. {18:5} It's not good to favor the wicked or to deny justice to the righteous. {18:6} A fool's lips lead to quarrels, and his mouth invites a beating. {18:7} A fool's mouth is his downfall, and his lips are a trap for his soul. {18:8} The words of a gossip are like wounds, and they penetrate to the innermost parts of the body. {18:9} He who is lazy in his work is a brother to the destroyer. {18:10} The name of the Lord is a strong tower; the righteous run to it and are safe. {18:11} A rich man's wealth is like a fortified city, and he sees it as a high wall. {18:12} Before destruction, a man's heart is haughty, but humility comes before honor. {18:13} Answering a matter before hearing it is foolish and brings shame. {18:14} The spirit of a man can sustain his sickness, but who can bear a wounded spirit? {18:15} The heart of the prudent acquires knowledge, and the ear of the wise seeks knowledge. {18:16} A man's gift makes room for him and brings him before great people. {18:17} The first one to plead his case seems right until his neighbor comes and examines him. {18:18} Casting lots causes contentions to cease and separates powerful adversaries. {18:19} An offended brother is harder to win than a strong city, and their disputes are like the bars of a castle. {18:20} A man's stomach will be satisfied with the fruit of his mouth; with the increase of his lips, he will be filled. {18:21} Life and death are in the power of the tongue, and those who love it will eat its fruit. {18:22} He who finds a wife finds a good thing and receives favor from the Lord. {18:23} The poor plead for mercy, but the rich answer harshly. {18:24} A man with many friends must be friendly, but a true friend is closer than a brother.

{19:1} Better is a poor person who walks in integrity than a fool with perverse speech. {19:2} It's not good for the soul to lack knowledge; and he who rushes in his actions sins. {19:3} A man's foolishness distorts his path, and his heart frets against the Lord. {19:4} Wealth brings many friends, but the poor are separated from their neighbors. {19:5} A false witness will not go unpunished, and whoever lies will not escape. {19:6} Many people seek the favor of a ruler, and everyone is a friend to those who give gifts. {19:7} All the brothers of a poor person hate him; how much more will his friends stay away? He pursues them with words, yet they don't help him. {19:8} He who gains wisdom loves his own soul; he who keeps understanding will find good. {19:9} A false witness will not go unpunished, and whoever speaks lies will perish. {19:10} Delight is not fitting for a fool, much less for a servant to rule over princes. {19:11} A man's discretion delays his anger, and it is his glory to overlook an offense. {19:12} The king's wrath is like the roar of a lion, but his favor is like dew on the grass. {19:13} A foolish son is a disaster for his father, and a contentious wife is like a dripping faucet. {19:14} A house and wealth are inherited from parents, but a wise wife is a gift from the Lord. {19:15} Laziness leads to deep sleep, and an idle person will go hungry. {19:16} He who keeps the commandment protects his own soul, but he who despises his ways will die. {19:17} Whoever is kind to the poor lends to the Lord, and what he has given will be repaid. {19:18} Discipline your son while there is hope, and don't be willing to let him die because of his cries. {19:19} A man with great anger will face punishment; if you rescue him, you may have to do it again. {19:20} Listen to advice and accept instruction so you can be wise in the end. {19:21} Many plans are in a man's heart, but the Lord's counsel will prevail. {19:22} A man's desire is his kindness, and a poor man is better than a liar. {19:23} The fear of the Lord leads to life; he who has it will be satisfied and will not experience evil. {19:24} A lazy person hides his hand in his pocket and won't even bring it to his mouth. {19:25} Strike a scoffer, and the simple will become wary; rebuke a wise person, and he will gain knowledge. {19:26} He who ruins his father and chases away his mother brings shame and disgrace. {19:27} Stop, my son, listening to instruction that leads away from the words of knowledge. {19:28} An ungodly witness mocks justice, and the mouth of the wicked consumes iniquity. {19:29} Judgments are prepared for scoffers, and beatings for the backs of fools.

{20:1} Wine is a mocker, and strong drink is raging; whoever is deceived by them is not wise. {20:2} The fear of a king is like the roar of a lion; whoever provokes him to anger sins against his own soul. {20:3} It is an honor for a man to avoid strife, but every fool will be meddling. {20:4} The lazy person will not plow because of the cold; therefore, he will beg during harvest and have nothing. {20:5} Counsel in a man's heart is like deep water, but a man of understanding will draw it out. {20:6} Most people will proclaim their own goodness, but a faithful man, who can find? {20:7} A righteous man walks in integrity; his children are blessed after him. {20:8} A king sitting on the throne of judgment scatters all evil with his eyes. {20:9} Who can say, "I have made my heart clean; I am pure from my sin"? {20:10} Different weights and measures are both an abomination to the Lord. {20:11} Even a child is known by his actions, whether his work is pure and right. {20:12} The hearing ear and the seeing eye, the Lord made both. {20:13} Don't love sleep, or you will come to poverty; open your eyes, and you will be satisfied with food. {20:14} "This is no good, this is no good," says the buyer, but when he leaves, he boasts. {20:15} There is gold and a multitude of rubies, but the lips of knowledge are a precious jewel. {20:16} Take the garment of someone who guarantees a loan for a stranger, and take a pledge from him for a strange woman. {20:17} Deceitful bread is sweet to a man, but later his mouth will be filled with gravel. {20:18} Every purpose is established by counsel; make war with good advice. {20:19} A gossip reveals secrets; therefore, don't associate with someone who flatters with their lips. {20:20} Whoever curses his father or mother, his lamp will be put out in deep darkness. {20:21} An inheritance gained quickly at the beginning will not be blessed in the end. {20:22} Don't say, "I will repay evil"; wait for the Lord, and he will save you. {20:23} Different weights are an abomination to the Lord; a false balance is not good. {20:24} A man's steps are directed by the Lord; how then can a man understand his own way? {20:25} It is a trap for a man to say something holy and then investigate it later. {20:26} A wise king scatters the wicked and drives the wheel over them. {20:27} The spirit of man is the lamp of the Lord, searching all the inward parts of the belly. {20:28} Mercy and truth preserve the king, and his throne is upheld by mercy. {20:29} The glory of young men is their strength, and the beauty of old men is the gray hair. {20:30} The bruises of a wound cleanse away evil, so do stripes cleanse the inward parts of the belly.

{21:1} The king's heart is in the hand of the Lord, like rivers of water; He directs it wherever He wants. {21:2} Every person thinks their own way is right, but the Lord weighs the hearts. {21:3} Doing justice and fairness is more acceptable to the Lord than sacrifices. {21:4} A haughty look, a proud heart, and the actions of the wicked are sin. {21:5} The plans of the diligent lead to abundance, but the hasty only lead to want. {21:6} Gaining treasures through a lying tongue is a fleeting vanity for those who seek death. {21:7} The violence of the wicked will destroy them because they refuse to do justice. {21:8} A person's ways are perverse and strange, but the work of the pure is right. {21:9} It is better to live in a small corner of the roof than with a quarrelsome woman in a large house. {21:10} The soul of the wicked craves evil; their neighbor finds no favor in their eyes. {21:11} When the scoffer is punished, the simple become wise; and when the wise are taught, they gain knowledge. {21:12} A righteous person considers the house of the wicked; God overthrows the wicked for their wickedness. {21:13} Whoever ignores the cry of the poor will also cry out but will not be heard. {21:14} A secret gift calms anger, and a bribe in the chest pacifies strong wrath. {21:15} It is a joy for the righteous to do justice, but destruction awaits those who do evil. {21:16} The person who wanders from the path of understanding will remain in the company of the dead. {21:17} He who loves pleasure will become poor; he who loves wine and oil will not be rich. {21:18} The wicked will be a ransom for the righteous, and the unfaithful for the upright. {21:19} It is better to live in the wilderness than with a quarrelsome and angry woman. {21:20} There is desirable treasure and oil in the home of the wise, but a foolish person spends it all. {21:21} Whoever pursues righteousness and mercy will find life, righteousness, and honor. {21:22} A wise person can conquer the city of the mighty and bring down the stronghold they trust in. {21:23} Whoever keeps his mouth and tongue keeps his soul from troubles. {21:24} The proud and haughty scoffer is his name; he acts with proud anger. {21:25} The desire of the lazy kills him because his hands refuse to work. {21:26} He covets greedily all day long, but the righteous give and don't hold back. {21:27} The sacrifice of the wicked is an abomination; how much more when he brings it with an evil mind! {21:28} A false witness will perish, but the person who listens speaks constantly. {21:29} A wicked person hardens his face, but the upright directs his path. {21:30} There is no wisdom, understanding, or counsel against the Lord. {21:31} The horse is prepared for the day of battle, but safety is from the Lord.

{22:1} A good name is to be chosen rather than great riches; favor is better than silver and gold. {22:2} The rich and the poor have this in common: the Lord is the maker of them all. {22:3} A prudent person sees danger and hides, but the simple go on and suffer for it. {22:4} Riches, honor, and life come from humility and the fear of the Lord. {22:5} Thorns and snares are in the path of the perverse; whoever keeps his soul stays far from them. {22:6} Train up a child in the way he should go; and when he is old, he will not depart from it. {22:7} The rich rule over the poor, and the borrower is a servant to the lender. {22:8} Whoever sows iniquity will reap vanity, and the rod of his anger will fail. {22:9} He who is generous will be blessed, for he gives his bread to the poor. {22:10} Drive out the scoffer, and strife will leave; contention and reproach will cease. {22:11} He who loves a pure heart and speaks with grace will have the king as his friend. {22:12} The eyes of the Lord preserve knowledge, but He overthrows the words of the unfaithful. {22:13} The lazy person says, "There is a lion outside; I will be killed in the streets." {22:14} The mouth of an immoral woman is a deep pit; whoever is abhorred by the Lord will fall into it. {22:15} Foolishness is bound up in the heart of a child, but the rod of correction will drive it far from him. {22:16} He who oppresses the poor to increase his wealth, and he who gives to the rich, will surely come to want. {22:17} Incline your ear and hear the words of the wise; apply your heart to my knowledge. {22:18} It will be pleasant if you keep them in your heart and ready on your lips. {22:19} So that your trust may be in the Lord, I have made known to you this day, even to you. {22:20} Have I not written to you excellent things in counsel and knowledge, {22:21} to make you know the certainty of the words of truth, so you can give a true answer to those who send you? {22:22} Do not rob the poor because he is poor, nor oppress the afflicted at the gate, {22:23} for the Lord will plead their cause and ruin the soul of those who ruin them. {22:24} Make no friendship with an angry man, and don't go with a furious man, {22:25} lest you learn his ways and get a snare to your soul. {22:26} Don't be one of those who strike hands or guarantee debts. {22:27} If you have nothing to pay, why should he take away your bed from under you? {22:28} Don't remove the ancient landmark your fathers have set. {22:29} Do you see a man diligent in his business? He will stand before kings; he will not stand before obscure men.

{23:1} When you sit down to eat with a ruler, pay close attention to what is before you. {23:2} If you are someone who loves food, put a knife to your throat. {23:3} Don't crave his delicacies, for they are deceptive food. {23:4} Don't work to become rich; stop trusting in your own understanding. {23:5} Will you set your eyes on what is not? Riches certainly make themselves wings; they fly away like an eagle in the sky. {23:6} Don't eat the bread of someone who has an evil eye, and don't desire their fine foods. {23:7} For as he thinks in his heart, so is he. He says to you, "Eat and drink," but his heart is not with you. {23:8} The food you've eaten you will spit out, and you will lose your pleasant words. {23:9} Don't speak to a fool, for he will despise the wisdom of your words. {23:10} Don't remove the ancient boundary markers, and don't enter the fields of the fatherless. {23:11} For their Redeemer is mighty; He will plead their cause against you. {23:12} Apply your heart to instruction, and your ears to the words of knowledge. {23:13} Do not withhold discipline from a child; if you strike him with the rod, he won't die. {23:14} You will strike him with the rod and save his soul from hell. {23:15} My son, if your heart is wise, my heart will rejoice too. {23:16} Yes, my innermost being will rejoice when your lips speak what is right. {23:17} Don't let your heart envy sinners, but be filled with the fear of the Lord all day long. {23:18} For surely there is a future, and your hope will not be cut off. {23:19} Listen, my son, and be wise; guide your heart in the right direction. {23:20} Don't be among heavy drinkers or gluttonous eaters. {23:21} For the drunkard and the glutton will come to poverty, and drowsiness will clothe a man in rags. {23:22} Listen to your father who gave you life, and don't despise your mother when she is old. {23:23} Buy the truth and don't sell it; also wisdom, discipline, and understanding. {23:24} The father of the righteous will greatly rejoice; whoever begets a wise child will have joy in him. {23:25} Your father and mother will be glad, and she who bore you will rejoice. {23:26} My son, give me your heart, and let your eyes observe my ways. {23:27} For a prostitute is a deep pit; a forbidden woman is a narrow well. {23:28} She lies in wait like a predator and increases the transgressors among men. {23:29} Who has sorrow? Who has strife? Who has arguments? Who has complaints? Who has wounds without cause? Who has red eyes? {23:30} Those who linger long over wine, who go to sample mixed wine. {23:31} Don't gaze at the wine when it is red, when it sparkles in the cup, when it goes down smoothly. {23:32} In the end, it bites like a snake and stings like a viper. {23:33} Your eyes will see strange things, and your heart will utter perverse things. {23:34} You will be like one who lies down in the middle of the sea or on top of a mast. {23:35} You will say, "They struck me, but I wasn't hurt; they beat me, but I didn't feel it. When will I wake up? I will seek it again."

{24:1} Don't be envious of evil people or desire to be with them. {24:2} For their hearts plot destruction, and their lips talk of trouble. {24:3} By wisdom, a house is built; by understanding, it is established. {24:4} By knowledge, its rooms are filled with all precious and pleasant riches. {24:5} A wise person is strong; a person of knowledge increases strength. {24:6} For by wise counsel you will wage war, and in the multitude of counselors there is safety. {24:7} Wisdom is too high for a fool; he doesn't open his mouth at the city gate. {24:8} Whoever plans to do evil will be called a schemer. {24:9} The thought of foolishness is sin, and the scoffer is detestable to others. {24:10} If you faint in the day of adversity, your strength is small. {24:11} Deliver those who are drawn toward death, and hold back those stumbling to the slaughter. {24:12} If you say, "We didn't know about this," does not He who weighs the heart consider it? Does not He who keeps your soul know it? Will He not repay each person according to their deeds? {24:13} My son, eat honey because it is good, and the honeycomb, which is sweet to your taste. {24:14} So will the knowledge of wisdom be to your soul; when you have found it, there will be a future, and your hope will not be cut off. {24:15} Don't lay in wait, wicked man, against the dwelling of the righteous; don't spoil his resting place. {24:16} For a righteous man falls seven times and rises again, but the wicked will stumble into trouble. {24:17} Don't rejoice when your enemy falls, and don't let your heart be glad when he stumbles. {24:18} Lest the Lord see it and be displeased, and turn His wrath away from him. {24:19} Don't fret because of evil people, and don't be envious of the wicked. {24:20} For there will be no reward for the evil person; the lamp of the wicked will be put out. {24:21} My son, fear the Lord and the king; don't meddle with those who are given to change. {24:22} For their calamity will rise suddenly, and who knows the ruin both will bring? {24:23} These also are sayings of the wise: It is not good to show favoritism in judgment. {24:24} Whoever says to the wicked, "You are righteous," will be cursed by the people and hated by nations. {24:25} But those who rebuke the wicked will have delight, and a good blessing will come upon them. {24:26} Every person will kiss the lips of one who gives a right answer. {24:27} Prepare your work outside, and make it fit for yourself in the field; afterward, build your house. {24:28} Don't be a false witness against your neighbor without cause, and don't deceive with your lips. {24:29} Don't say, "I will do to him as he has done to me; I will repay the man according to his deeds." {24:30} I passed by the field of the lazy and the vineyard of a man lacking sense. {24:31} And behold, it was all overgrown with thorns, and nettles had covered the ground, and its stone wall was broken down. {24:32} Then I saw and considered it well; I looked at it and received instruction. {24:33} A little sleep, a little slumber, a little folding of the hands to rest, {24:34} and poverty will come upon you like a bandit, and your need like an armed man.

{25:1} These are also proverbs of Solomon, which the men of Hezekiah, king of Judah, transcribed. {25:2} It is the glory of God to conceal something, but it is the honor of kings to investigate a matter. {25:3} The height of heaven and the depth of the earth, but the heart of kings is unsearchable. {25:4} Remove the impurities from silver, and a vessel will emerge for the silversmith. {25:5} Remove the wicked from before the king, and his throne will be established in righteousness. {25:6} Don't present yourself in the presence of the king, and don't take a place among great men. {25:7} It is better for it to be said to you, "Come up here," than for you to be put lower in the presence of the prince whom you have seen. {25:8} Don't rush to argue, lest you find yourself in a situation where you don't know what to do when your neighbor puts you to shame. {25:9} Discuss your case with your neighbor, and don't reveal a secret to someone else. {25:10} Otherwise, the one who hears it may shame you, and your infamy may not be removed. {25:11} A word spoken at the right time is like golden apples in silver settings. {25:12} Like an earring of gold and a beautiful ornament, so is a wise reprover to an obedient ear. {25:13} Like the cold of snow during harvest, so is a faithful messenger to those who send him; he refreshes the soul of his masters. {25:14} Whoever boasts about a false gift is like clouds and wind without rain. {25:15} A prince is persuaded by long patience, and a gentle tongue can break a bone. {25:16} Have you found honey? Eat only what you need, lest you eat too much and vomit. {25:17} Stay away from your neighbor's house, lest he grow weary of you and come to hate you. {25:18} A man who bears false witness against his neighbor is like a hammer, a sword, and a sharp arrow. {25:19} Trusting an unfaithful person in times of trouble is like a broken tooth and a foot out of joint. {25:20} Like taking away a garment in cold weather, and like vinegar on soda, is singing songs to a heavy heart. {25:21} If your enemy is hungry, give him bread to eat; and if he is thirsty, give him water to drink. {25:22} For you will heap burning coals on his head, and the Lord will reward you. {25:23} The north wind drives away rain; so an angry face drives away a backbiting tongue. {25:24} It is better to live in the corner of a roof than to share a house with a quarrelsome woman. {25:25} Like cold water to a thirsty soul, so is good news from a far country. {25:26} A righteous person falling before the wicked is like a troubled fountain and a corrupt spring. {25:27} It is not good to eat too much honey; so it is not good for people to seek their own glory. {25:28} A person who has no control over their own spirit is like a city that is broken down and without walls.

The Instructions of Solomon

{26:1} Like snow in summer and rain during harvest, honor is not fitting for a fool. {26:2} Like a bird that wanders and a swallow that flies, a curse without cause will not land. {26:3} A whip for the horse, a bridle for the donkey, and a rod for the fool's back. {26:4} Don't answer a fool according to his foolishness, lest you become like him. {26:5} Answer a fool according to his foolishness, lest he become wise in his own eyes. {26:6} Sending a message by the hand of a fool is like cutting off your own feet and drinking damage. {26:7} The legs of the lame are not equal; so is a parable in the mouth of fools. {26:8} Like binding a stone in a sling, so is giving honor to a fool. {26:9} Like a thorn going into the hand of a drunkard, so is a parable in the mouth of fools. {26:10} The great God who created everything rewards both the fool and the transgressor. {26:11} Like a dog returning to its vomit, so a fool returns to his folly. {26:12} Do you see a person wise in their own eyes? There is more hope for a fool than for them. {26:13} The lazy person says, "There's a lion in the road; a lion is in the streets!" {26:14} Like a door turning on its hinges, so the lazy person turns on their bed. {26:15} The lazy person hides their hand in their bosom; it troubles them to bring it back to their mouth. {26:16} The sluggard is wiser in their own eyes than seven people who can give a sensible answer. {26:17} Whoever passes by and meddles in a quarrel that isn't theirs is like one who grabs a dog by the ears. {26:18} Like a madman who throws firebrands, arrows, and death, {26:19} is a person who deceives their neighbor and says, "Am I not just joking?" {26:20} Where there is no wood, the fire goes out; so where there is no gossip, conflict ceases. {26:21} Like coals to burning coals, and wood to fire, so is a contentious person to stir up strife. {26:22} The words of a gossip are like wounds, and they go deep into the innermost parts of the belly. {26:23} Burning lips and a wicked heart are like a potsherd covered with silver dross. {26:24} Whoever hates disguises it with their lips, but harbors deceit within. {26:25} When they speak kindly, don't believe them; for there are seven abominations in their heart. {26:26} Whoever hides their hatred with deceit, their wickedness will be revealed before the whole congregation. {26:27} Whoever digs a pit will fall into it & whoever rolls a stone will have it roll back on them. {26:28} A lying tongue hates those it hurts & a flattering mouth works ruin.

{27:1} Don't boast about tomorrow, because you don't know what a day may bring. {27:2} Let someone else praise you, not your own mouth; a stranger, not your own lips. {27:3} A stone is heavy, and sand is weighty, but a fool's anger is heavier than both. {27:4} Anger is cruel, and wrath is outrageous; but who can stand against envy? {27:5} Open rebuke is better than secret love. {27:6} Faithful are the wounds of a friend; but the kisses of an enemy are deceitful. {27:7} A full person despises honeycomb, but to a hungry person, every bitter thing is sweet. {27:8} Like a bird that wanders from its nest, so is a person who strays from their place. {27:9} Ointment and perfume bring joy to the heart; so does the sweetness of a friend's advice. {27:10} Don't forsake your own friend or your father's friend; and don't go to your brother's house on the day of your calamity; better is a neighbor nearby than a brother far away. {27:11} My son, be wise and make my heart glad, so I can respond to anyone who criticizes me. {27:12} A sensible person foresees danger and hides, but the naive go on and suffer for it. {27:13} Take his garment when he is surety (guaranteeing something) for a stranger, and take a pledge from him for a strange woman. {27:14} Whoever blesses their friend with a loud voice early in the morning will be considered a curse. {27:15} A continuous dripping on a very rainy day and a quarrelsome woman are alike. {27:16} Whoever hides her hides the wind and the ointment of his right hand, which reveals itself. {27:17} Iron sharpens iron, and one person sharpens another's face. {27:18} Whoever tends a fig tree will eat its fruit; so whoever waits on their master will be honored. {27:19} As in water, a face reflects another face, so a person's heart reflects another's. {27:20} Hell and destruction are never satisfied; so the eyes of people are never satisfied. {27:21} Like the refining pot for silver and the furnace for gold, so is a person to their praise. {27:22} Even if you grind a fool in a mortar among wheat with a pestle, their foolishness will not depart from them. {27:23} Be diligent to know the condition of your flocks and pay attention to your herds. {27:24} For riches are not forever; does the crown endure to every generation? {27:25} The hay appears, the tender grass shows itself, and the herbs of the mountains are gathered. {27:26} The lambs are for your clothing, and the goats are the price of the field. {27:27} You will have enough goat's milk for your food, for your household, and for your maidens' upkeep.

{28:1} The wicked flee when no one pursues, but the righteous are as bold as lions. {28:2} When a land transgresses, it has many rulers; but by a wise and knowledgeable person, its state will be prolonged. {28:3} A poor person who oppresses the poor is like a rain that leaves no food. {28:4} Those who abandon the law praise the wicked; but those who keep the law contend against them. {28:5} Evil people do not understand justice, but those who seek the Lord understand everything. {28:6} Better is a poor person who walks in integrity than a rich person who is perverse in their ways. {28:7} Whoever keeps the law is a wise child, but whoever associates with riotous people brings shame to their father. {28:8} Whoever increases their wealth through usury (charging interest) and unjust gain gathers it for someone who will be kind to the poor. {28:9} Whoever turns their ear away from hearing the law, even their prayer will be an abomination. {28:10} Whoever causes the righteous to stray in an evil way will fall into their own pit, but the upright will possess good things. {28:11} The rich person is wise in their own eyes, but the poor who has understanding can search them out. {28:12} When the righteous rejoice, there is great glory; but when the wicked rise, a person is hidden. {28:13} Whoever conceals their sins will not prosper, but whoever confesses and forsakes them will find mercy. {28:14} Happy is the person who fears continually, but whoever hardens their heart will fall into trouble. {28:15} Like a roaring lion and a roaming bear, so is a wicked ruler over the poor people. {28:16} A ruler who lacks understanding is a great oppressor, but whoever hates greed will prolong their days. {28:17} A person who commits violence against anyone's blood will flee to the pit; let no one support them. {28:18} Whoever walks uprightly will be saved, but whoever is perverse in their ways will fall suddenly. {28:19} Whoever works their land will have plenty of food, but whoever chases after empty things will have enough poverty. {28:20} A faithful person will abound with blessings, but whoever rushes to be rich will not be innocent. {28:21} Showing favoritism is not good; for a piece of bread, that person will transgress. {28:22} Whoever rushes to be rich has an evil eye and does not consider that poverty will come upon them. {28:23} Whoever rebukes a person later will find more favor than the one who flatters with their words. {28:24} Whoever robs their father or mother and says it's not a crime is the companion of a destroyer. {28:25} A proud heart stirs up strife, but whoever puts their trust in the Lord will be enriched. {28:26} Whoever trusts in their own heart is a fool, but whoever walks wisely will be delivered. {28:27} Whoever gives to the poor will not lack, but whoever hides their eyes will receive many curses. {28:28} When the wicked rise, people hide themselves; but when they perish, the righteous increase.

{29:1} Whoever is often rebuked and hardens their neck will be suddenly destroyed, and that without remedy. {29:2} When the righteous are in authority, the people rejoice; but when the wicked rule, the people mourn. {29:3} Whoever loves wisdom makes their father rejoice, but whoever associates with prostitutes wastes their wealth. {29:4} The king establishes the land through justice, but whoever accepts bribes overthrows it. {29:5} A person who flatters their neighbor sets a trap for their feet. {29:6} In the transgression of an evil person, there is a snare, but the righteous sing and rejoice. {29:7} The righteous care about the cause of the poor, but the wicked do not even consider it. {29:8} Scornful people bring a city to ruin, but wise people turn away wrath. {29:9} If a wise person argues with a foolish person, whether they rage or laugh, there is no rest. {29:10} Bloodthirsty people hate the upright, but the just seek to save their lives. {29:11} A fool expresses all their thoughts, but a wise person keeps it in until later. {29:12} If a ruler listens to lies, all their servants will be wicked. {29:13} The poor and the deceitful meet together; the Lord gives light to both their eyes. {29:14} A king who judges the poor faithfully will have their throne established forever. {29:15} The rod and reproof give wisdom, but a child left to themselves brings shame to their mother. {29:16} When the wicked multiply, transgression increases, but the righteous will see their downfall. {29:17} Correct your son, and he will give you peace; yes, he will bring joy to your soul. {29:18} Where there is no vision, the people perish, but whoever keeps the law is happy. {29:19} A servant will not be corrected by words; for even if they understand, they will not respond. {29:20} Do you see someone hasty in their words? There is more hope for a fool than for them. {29:21} Whoever raises their servant from childhood will have them become like a son in the end. {29:22} An angry person stirs up strife, and a furious person is full of transgression. {29:23} A person's pride brings them low, but honor upholds the humble in spirit. {29:24} Whoever partners with a thief hates their own soul; they hear cursing but do not disclose it. {29:25} The fear of man is a snare, but whoever puts their trust in the Lord will be safe. {29:26} Many seek the ruler's favor, but each person's judgment comes from the Lord. {29:27} An unjust person is an abomination to the just, and whoever walks uprightly is an abomination to the wicked.

{30:1} The words of Agur, son of Jakeh, are a prophecy; the man spoke to Ithiel, to Ithiel and Ucal. {30:2} Surely I am more brutish than any person and do not have the understanding of a human. {30:3} I have neither learned wisdom nor have the knowledge of the holy. {30:4} Who has ascended into heaven or descended? Who has gathered the wind in their fists? Who has wrapped the waters in a garment? Who has established the ends of the earth? What is his name, and what is his son's name, if you can tell? {30:5} Every word of God is pure; He is a shield to those who put their trust in Him. {30:6} Do not add to His words, or He will rebuke you, and you will be found a liar. {30:7} Two things I ask of you; do not deny me these before I die: {30:8} Keep vanity and lies far from me; give me neither poverty nor riches; feed me with the food that is right for me. {30:9} Lest I be full and deny you, and say, "Who is the Lord?" or lest I be poor and steal, and take the name of my God in vain. {30:10} Do not accuse a servant before their master, lest they curse you, and you be found guilty. {30:11} There is a generation that curses their father and does not bless their mother. {30:12} There is a generation that is pure in their own eyes, yet is not cleansed from their filthiness. {30:13} There is a generation whose eyes are lofty, and whose eyelids are lifted up. {30:14} There is a generation whose teeth are like swords, and whose jaws are like knives, to devour the poor from the earth and the needy among people. {30:15} The leech has two daughters, crying, "Give, give." There are three things that are never satisfied, yes, four that never say, "It is enough": {30:16} The grave, the barren womb, the earth that is not filled with water, and the fire that says, "It is enough." {30:17} The eye that mocks at their father and despises to obey their mother, the ravens of the valley shall pick it out, and the young eagles shall eat it. {30:18} There are three things that are too wonderful for me; yes, four that I do not understand: {30:19} The way of an eagle in the air, the way of a serpent on a rock, the way of a ship in the sea, and the way of a man with a maid. {30:20} Such is the way of an adulterous woman; she eats and wipes her mouth and says, "I have done no wickedness." {30:21} For three things the earth is disquieted, and for four that it cannot bear: {30:22} For a servant when they reign, and a fool when they are full of food; {30:23} For an odious woman when she is married, and a handmaid who is heir to her mistress. {30:24} There are four things which are little upon the earth, but they are exceedingly wise: {30:25} The ants are a people not strong, yet they prepare their food in summer; {30:26} The conies are but a feeble folk, yet they make their homes in the rocks; {30:27} The locusts have no king, yet they all advance in ranks; {30:28} The spider holds on with its hands and is in kings' palaces. {30:29} There are three things that go well, yes, four that are lovely in their going: {30:30} A lion, the strongest among beasts, and does not turn back for any; {30:31} A greyhound, a male goat, and a king against whom there is no rising up. {30:32} If you have acted foolishly in exalting yourself, or if you have thought evil, put your hand on your mouth. {30:33} Surely churning milk brings forth butter, and wringing the nose brings forth blood; so the forcing of wrath brings forth strife.

{31:1} The words of King Lemuel, the prophecy that his mother taught him. {31:2} What, my son? And what, son of my womb? And what, son of my vows? {31:3} Do not give your strength to women, nor your ways to that which destroys kings. {31:4} It is not for kings, O Lemuel, it is not for kings to drink wine; nor for princes to drink strong drink. {31:5} Lest they drink and forget the law and pervert the judgment of any of the afflicted. {31:6} Give strong drink to those who are about to perish, and wine to those who are heavy of heart. {31:7} Let them drink and forget their poverty and remember their misery no more. {31:8} Open your mouth for those who cannot speak, in the cause of all who are appointed to destruction. {31:9} Open your mouth, judge righteously, and plead the cause of the poor and needy. {31:10} Who can find a virtuous woman? Her worth is far above rubies. {31:11} The heart of her husband safely trusts in her, so he will have no need for spoil. {31:12} She will do him good and not harm all the days of her life. {31:13} She seeks wool and flax and works willingly with her hands. {31:14} She is like the merchant ships; she brings her food from afar. {31:15} She rises while it is still night and provides food for her household and portions for her maidens. {31:16} She considers a field and buys it; with the fruit of her hands, she plants a vineyard. {31:17} She girds her loins with strength and strengthens her arms. {31:18} She perceives that her merchandise is good; her lamp does not go out at night. {31:19} She puts her hands to the spindle, and her hands hold the distaff. {31:20} She extends her hand to the poor; yes, she reaches out her hands to the needy. {31:21} She is not afraid of the snow for her household, for all her household are clothed in scarlet. {31:22} She makes herself coverings of tapestry; her clothing is silk and purple. {31:23} Her husband is known at the city gates when he sits among the elders of the land. {31:24} She makes fine linen and sells it; she delivers belts to the merchants. {31:25} Strength and honor are her clothing; she shall rejoice in the time to come. {31:26} She opens her mouth with wisdom, and on her tongue is the law of kindness. {31:27} She watches over the ways of her household and does not eat the bread of idleness. {31:28} Her children rise up and call her blessed; her husband also, and he praises her. {31:29} Many daughters have done virtuously, but you excel them all. {31:30} Charm is deceptive, and beauty is vain; but a woman who fears the Lord, she shall be praised. {31:31} Give her the fruit of her hands, and let her own works praise her in the gates.

The Book of Ecclesiastes

{1:1} These are the words of the Preacher, the son of David, king in Jerusalem. {1:2} "Everything is meaningless," says the Preacher. "Everything is meaningless." {1:3} What do people gain from all their hard work under the sun? {1:4} Generations come and go, but the earth remains forever. {1:5} The sun rises and sets, and hurries back to where it rises. {1:6} The wind blows south, then turns north; it whirls around continually and returns on its course. {1:7} All the rivers flow into the sea, yet the sea is never full; to the place where the rivers flow, they return again. {1:8} Everything is full of labor; people can't explain it. The eye is never satisfied with seeing, nor the ear filled with hearing. {1:9} What has been will be again; what has been done will be done again. There is nothing new under the sun. {1:10} Is there anything of which one can say, "Look, this is new"? It has already been here long ago, before our time. {1:11} No one remembers former generations, and even those yet to come will not be remembered by those who follow them. {1:12} I, the Preacher, was king over Israel in Jerusalem. {1:13} I set my heart to seek and explore by wisdom all that is done under heaven. This heavy burden God has given to humanity to keep them occupied. {1:14} I have seen all the things that are done under the sun; and behold, everything is meaningless and a chasing after the wind. {1:15} What is crooked cannot be straightened; what is lacking cannot be counted. {1:16} I said to myself, "Look, I have increased in wisdom more than anyone who has ruled over Jerusalem before me; my heart has had great experience in wisdom and knowledge." {1:17} I set my heart to know wisdom and to know madness and folly; I learned that this too is chasing after the wind. {1:18} For with much wisdom comes much grief, and the more knowledge increases, the more sorrow increases.

{2:1} I said to myself, "Come now, I will test you with pleasure; enjoy what is good." But I found that this too was meaningless. {2:2} Of laughter, I said, "It is madness," and of pleasure, "What does it accomplish?" {2:3} I explored with my heart how to cheer my body with wine while still guiding my heart with wisdom, and how to embrace folly, so that I might see what was good for people to do under heaven during the few days of their lives. {2:4} I undertook great projects: I built houses and planted vineyards for myself. {2:5} I made gardens and parks and planted all kinds of fruit trees in them. {2:6} I made reservoirs to water groves of flourishing trees. {2:7} I acquired male and female servants, and had servants born in my house. I also owned more livestock than anyone in Jerusalem before me. {2:8} I amassed silver and gold for myself, and the treasure of kings and provinces. I gathered male and female singers and a harem as well, the delights of a man's heart. {2:9} So I became greater than anyone in Jerusalem before me. In all this, my wisdom stayed with me. {2:10} I denied myself nothing my eyes desired; I refused my heart no pleasure. My heart took delight in all my labor, and this was the reward for all my toil. {2:11} Yet when I surveyed all that my hands had done and what I had toiled to achieve, everything was meaningless, a chasing after the wind; nothing was gained under the sun. {2:12} Then I turned to consider wisdom, madness, and folly, for what more can the king's successor do than what has already been done? {2:13} I saw that wisdom is better than folly, just as light is better than darkness. {2:14} The wise have their eyes in their heads, while the fool walks in darkness; but I came to realize that the same fate overtakes them both. {2:15} Then I said to myself, "The fate of the fool will overtake me too. What then do I gain by being wise?" I said to myself, "This too is meaningless." {2:16} For the wise, like the fool, will not be long remembered; the days have already come when both have been forgotten. Like the fool, the wise too must die! {2:17} So I hated life because the work that is done under the sun was grievous to me; all of it is meaningless, a chasing after the wind. {2:18} I hated all the things I had toiled for under the sun because I must leave them to the one who comes after me. {2:19} And who knows whether that person will be wise or foolish? Yet they will have control over all the fruit of my labor into which I have poured my effort and skill under the sun. This too is meaningless. {2:20} So my heart began to despair over all my toilsome labor under the sun. {2:21} For a person may labor with wisdom, knowledge, and skill, and then they must leave all they own to another who has not worked for it. This too is meaningless and a great misfortune. {2:22} What do people get for all their hard work and the stress of their hearts through which they labor under the sun? {2:23} All their days are filled with pain, and their work is a burden; even at night, their minds do not rest. This too is meaningless. {2:24} A person can do nothing better than to eat and drink and find satisfaction in their own toil. This too, I saw, is from the hand of God. {2:25} For who can eat or find enjoyment apart from God? {2:26} To the person who pleases God, He gives wisdom, knowledge, and happiness, but to the sinner, He gathers wealth to give to one who pleases God; this too is meaningless, a chasing after the wind.

{3:1} There is a time for everything, and a season for every activity under heaven: {3:2} a time to be born and a time to die, a time to plant and a time to uproot what is planted; {3:3} a time to kill and a time to heal, a time to tear down and a time to build; {3:4} a time to weep and a time to laugh, a time to mourn and a time to dance; {3:5} a time to scatter stones and a time to gather them, a time to embrace and a time to refrain from embracing; {3:6} a time to search and a time to give up, a time to keep and a time to throw away; {3:7} a time to tear and a time to mend, a time to be silent and a time to speak; {3:8} a time to love and a time to hate, a time for war and a time for peace. {3:9} What do workers gain from their toil? {3:10} I have seen the burden God has laid on the human race. {3:11} He has made everything beautiful in its time; He has also set eternity in the human heart, yet no one can fathom what God has done from beginning to end. {3:12} I know that there is nothing better for people than to be happy and to do good while they live. {3:13} That each of them may eat and drink, and find satisfaction in all their toil—this is the gift of God. {3:14} I know that everything God does will endure forever; nothing can be added to it and nothing taken from it. God does this so that people will fear Him. {3:15} Whatever is has already been, and what will be has been before; and God will call the past to account. {3:16} And I saw something else under the sun: in the place of judgment, wickedness was there, and in the place of justice, wickedness was there. {3:17} I said to myself, "God will bring into judgment both the righteous and the wicked, for there will be a time for every activity, a time for every deed." {3:18} I said to myself, "As for humans, God tests them so that they may see that they are like the animals." {3:19} Surely the fate of human beings is like that of the animals; the same fate awaits them both: as one dies, so dies the other. All have the same breath; humans have no advantage over animals. Everything is meaningless. {3:20} All go to the same place; all come from dust, and to dust all return. {3:21} Who knows if the human spirit rises upward and if the animal spirit goes down into the earth? {3:22} So I saw that there is nothing better for a person than to enjoy their work, because that is their lot. For who can bring them to see what will happen after them?

{4:1} Again, I looked and saw all the oppression that was taking place under the sun: I saw the tears of the oppressed, and they have no comforter; power was on the side of their oppressors, and they have no comforter. {4:2} And I declared that the dead, who had already died, are happier than the living, who are still alive. {4:3} But better than both is the one who has never been born, who has not seen the evil that is done under the sun. {4:4} And I saw that all labor and all achievement spring from one person's envy of another. This too is meaningless, a chasing after the wind. {4:5} Fools fold their hands and ruin themselves. {4:6} Better one handful with tranquility than two handfuls with toil and chasing after the wind. {4:7} Again, I saw something meaningless under the sun: {4:8} there was a man all alone; he had neither son nor brother. There was no end to all his toil, yet his eyes were not content with his wealth. "For whom am I toiling?" he asked. "And why am I depriving myself of enjoyment?" This too is meaningless—a miserable business! {4:9} Two are better than one because they have a good return for their labor. {4:10} If either of them falls down, one can help the other up. But pity anyone who falls and has no one to help them up. {4:11} Also, if two lie down together, they will keep warm. But how can one keep warm alone? {4:12} Though one may be overpowered, two can defend themselves. A cord of three strands is not quickly broken. {4:13} Better a poor but wise youth than an old but foolish king who no longer knows how to heed a warning. {4:14} The youth may have come from prison to the kingship, or he may have been born in poverty within his kingdom. {4:15} I saw that all who lived and walked under the sun followed the youth, the king's successor. {4:16} There is no end to all the people who were before them. Those who come later will not rejoice in him. This too is meaningless, a chasing after the wind.

{5:1} Guard your steps when you go to the house of God. Go near to listen rather than to offer the sacrifice of fools, for they do not realize they are doing wrong. {5:2} Do not be quick with your mouth and do not be hasty in your heart to utter anything before God. God is in heaven and you are on earth, so let your words be few. {5:3} A dream comes when there are many cares, and the fool's voice is known by the multitude of words. {5:4} When you make a vow to God, do not delay in fulfilling it; He has no pleasure in fools. Fulfill your vow. {5:5} It is better not to make a vow than to make one and not fulfill it. {5:6} Do not let your mouth lead you into sin, and do not protest to the temple messenger that your vow was a mistake. Why should God be angry at what you say and destroy the work of your hands? {5:7} Much dreaming and many words are meaningless. Therefore, fear God. {5:8} If you see the poor oppressed in a district and justice and rights denied, do not be surprised at such things; for one official is eyed by a higher one, and over them both are others higher still. {5:9} The increase of the land is for all; the king himself profits from the fields. {5:10} Whoever loves money never has enough; whoever loves wealth is never satisfied with their income. This too is meaningless. {5:11} As goods increase, so do those who consume them. And what benefit are they to the owners except to gaze at them? {5:12} The sleep of a laborer is sweet, whether they eat little or much, but as for the rich, their abundance permits them no sleep. {5:13} I have seen a grievous evil under the sun: wealth hoarded to the harm of its owners. {5:14} Or wealth lost through some misfortune, so that when they have a child there is nothing left for them. {5:15} Everyone comes naked from their mother's womb, and as everyone comes, so they depart. They take nothing from their toil that they can carry in their hands. {5:16} This too is a grievous evil: as everyone comes, so they depart. And what do they gain, since they toil for the wind? {5:17} All their days they eat in darkness, with great frustration, affliction, and anger. {5:18} This is what I have observed to be good: that it is appropriate for a person to eat, drink, and find satisfaction in their toilsome labor under the sun during the few days of life God has given them—for this is their lot. {5:19} Moreover, when God gives someone wealth and possessions, and the ability to enjoy them, to accept their lot and find joy in their toil—this is a gift of God. {5:20} They seldom reflect on the days of their life, because God keeps them occupied with gladness of heart.

{6:1} I have seen another evil under the sun, and it weighs heavily on mankind: {6:2} God gives some people wealth, possessions, and honor so that they lack nothing their hearts desire, but God does not grant them the ability to enjoy them, and strangers enjoy them instead. This is meaningless, a grievous evil. {6:3} A man may have a hundred children and live many years, yet no matter how long he lives, if he does not enjoy his prosperity and does not receive a proper burial, I say that a stillborn child is better off than he. {6:4} It comes without meaning, it departs in darkness, and in darkness its name is shrouded. {6:5} Though it never saw the sun or knew anything, it has more rest than that man. {6:6} Even if he lives a thousand years twice over but does not enjoy his prosperity, do not all go to the same place? {6:7} Everyone's toil is for their mouth, yet their appetite is never satisfied. {6:8} What advantage have the wise over the fools? What do the poor gain by knowing how to conduct themselves before others? {6:9} Better what the eye sees than the roving of the appetite. This too is meaningless, a chasing after the wind. {6:10} Whatever exists has already been named, and what humanity is has been known; no one can contend with one stronger than they. {6:11} The more the words, the less meaning, & how does that benefit anyone? {6:12} For who knows what is good for a person in life, during the few & meaningless days they pass through like a shadow? Who can tell them what will happen under sun after they are gone?

{7:1} A good name is better than fine perfume, and the day of death is better than the day of birth. {7:2} It is better to go to a house of mourning than to a house of feasting, for that is the end of everyone; the living should take this to heart. {7:3} Sorrow is better than laughter, for sadness can improve the heart. {7:4} The heart of the wise is in the house of mourning, but the heart of fools is in the house of pleasure. {7:5} It is better to heed the rebuke of the wise than to listen to the song of fools. {7:6} Like the crackling of thorns under a pot, so is the laughter of fools; this too is meaningless. {7:7} Surely oppression drives the wise to madness, and a bribe corrupts the heart. {7:8} The end of a matter is better than its beginning, and patience is better than pride. {7:9} Do not be quickly provoked in your spirit, for anger resides in the lap of fools. {7:10} Do not say, "Why were the old days better than these?" For it is not wise to ask such questions. {7:11} Wisdom, like an inheritance, is a good thing and benefits those who see the sun. {7:12} Wisdom is a shelter, as money is a shelter, but the advantage of knowledge is this: wisdom preserves those who have it. {7:13} Consider the work of God: who can straighten what He has made crooked? {7:14} In the day of prosperity, be joyful, but in the day of adversity, consider: God has made the one as well as the other, so no one can discover anything about their future. {7:15} In my meaningless days, I have seen a righteous person perish in their righteousness, and a wicked person live long in their wickedness. {7:16} Do not be overly righteous, neither be overwise—why destroy yourself? {7:17} Do not be overly wicked, and do not be a fool—why die before your time? {7:18} It is good to grasp the one and not let go of the other. Whoever fears God will avoid all extremes. {7:19} Wisdom makes one wise person more powerful than ten rulers in a city. {7:20} There is no one righteous on earth who does what is right and never sins. {7:21} Do not pay attention to every word people say, or you may hear your servant cursing you. {7:22} For you know in your heart that many times you yourself have cursed others. {7:23} All this I tested by wisdom and I said, "I am determined to be wise," but it was beyond me. {7:24} Whatever exists is far off and very deep; who can discover it? {7:25}

I turned my mind to understand, to investigate, and to search out wisdom and the scheme of things, and to understand the madness of wickedness and the folly of foolishness. {7:26} I found more bitter than death the woman whose heart is snares and nets, whose hands are chains. The one who pleases God will escape her, but the sinner will be trapped by her. {7:27} Look, says the Teacher, this is what I have discovered: adding one thing to another to discover the scheme of things. {7:28} While I was still searching but not finding, I found one upright man among a thousand, but not one upright woman among them all. {7:29} This only have I found: God created mankind upright, but they have gone in search of many schemes.

{8:1} Who is like the wise? Who knows the explanation of things? A person's wisdom brightens their face and changes its hard appearance. {8:2} I say: Keep the king's command for the sake of your oath to God. {8:3} Do not be in a hurry to leave the king's presence. Do not stand up for a bad cause, for he will do whatever he pleases. {8:4} Since a king's word is supreme, who can say to him, "What are you doing?" {8:5} Whoever obeys his command will come to no harm, and the wise heart will know the proper time and procedure. {8:6} For there is a proper time and procedure for every matter, though a person may be weighed down by misery. {8:7} Since no one knows the future, who can tell someone else what is to come? {8:8} As no one has power over the wind to contain it, so no one has power over the time of their death. As no one is discharged in time of war, so wickedness will not release those who practice it. {8:9} All this I saw as I applied my mind to everything done under the sun: there is a time when a man rules over another to his own hurt. {8:10} Then I saw the wicked buried—those who used to come and go from the holy place and receive praise in the city where they did this. This too is meaningless. {8:11} When the sentence for a crime is not quickly carried out, people's hearts are filled with schemes to do wrong. {8:12} Although a sinner does evil a hundred times and still lives a long time, I know that it will go better for those who fear God, who are reverent before Him. {8:13} Yet, it will not go well with the wicked, and they will not prolong their days, which are like a shadow because they do not fear God. {8:14} There is something else meaningless that occurs on earth: the righteous who get what the wicked deserve, and the wicked who get what the righteous deserve. This too, I say, is meaningless. {8:15} So I commend the enjoyment of life, because there is nothing better for a person under the sun than to eat and drink and be glad. Then joy will accompany them in their toil all the days of the life God has given them under the sun. {8:16} When I applied my mind to know wisdom and to observe the labor that is done on earth—people getting no sleep day or night—{8:17} then I saw all that God has done. No one can comprehend what goes on under the sun. Despite all their efforts to search it out, no one can discover its meaning. Even if the wise claim they know, they cannot really comprehend it.

{10:1} Dead flies make the ointment of the perfumer smell bad; similarly, a little foolishness can ruin a person's reputation for wisdom and honor. {10:2} A wise person's heart is on their right side, but a fool's heart is on their left. {10:3} Even when a fool walks along the road, their lack of wisdom is evident, and they openly declare themselves as fools. {10:4} If the spirit of the ruler rises against you, do not leave your position, for calmness can settle great offenses. {10:5} I have seen an evil under the sun, an error that comes from the ruler: {10:6} folly is exalted, while the rich sit in lowly places. {10:7} I have seen servants riding horses while princes walk like servants on the ground. {10:8} Whoever digs a pit will fall into it; if someone breaks through a fence, a snake will bite them. {10:9} Anyone who removes stones will be hurt by them, and whoever splits wood will be endangered. {10:10} If the axe is dull and they do not sharpen its edge, they will need to use more strength, but wisdom is useful to direct the effort. {10:11} Surely, a snake will bite without being charmed, and a babbler is no better. {10:12} The words of a wise person are gracious, but the lips of a fool will bring their own downfall. {10:13} The beginning of a fool's words is foolishness, and the end of their speech is wicked madness. {10:14} A fool is full of words: no one knows what will happen next, and who can tell what will come after them? {10:15} The work of fools wearies everyone, because they do not know how to find their way to the city. {10:16} Woe to you, O land, when your king is a child, and your princes feast in the morning! {10:17} Blessed are you, O land, when your king is of noble birth, and your princes eat at the proper time, for strength, and not for drunkenness! {10:18} Through much laziness, the building decays; and because of idleness, the house falls apart. {10:19} A feast is made for laughter, and wine brings joy, but money answers all things. {10:20} Do not curse the king, not even in your thoughts; and do not curse the rich in your bedroom, for a bird in the sky may carry your words, and a winged creature may report what you say.

{11:1} Throw your bread on the waters, for you will find it after many days. {11:2} Share with seven, or even eight, for you do not know what disaster may come on the earth. {11:3} When the clouds are full of rain, they pour it out on the earth; and if a tree falls to the south or the north, it will lie where it falls. {11:4} Those who watch the wind will never plant, and those who pay attention to the clouds will never harvest. {11:5} Just as you do not know the path of the spirit or how bones grow in the womb of a pregnant woman, you do not know the work of God who makes everything. {11:6} Sow your seed in the morning, and in the evening do not hold back your hand, for you do not know which will succeed, whether this one or that one, or if both will do equally well. {11:7} Truly, light is sweet, and it is pleasant for the eyes to see the sun. {11:8} But if a man lives many years and enjoys them all, he should remember that the days of darkness will be many; everything that comes is vanity (meaningless). {11:9} Rejoice, O young man, in your youth, and let your heart bring you joy in your youth; walk in the ways of your heart and in the sight of your eyes, but know that for all these things God will bring you to judgment. {11:10} Therefore, remove sorrow from your heart and put away evil from your body, for childhood and youth are meaningless.

{12:1} Remember your Creator in the days of your youth, before the days of trouble come and the years approach when you will say, "I have no pleasure in them." {12:2} Before the sun, light, moon, or stars grow dark, and the clouds return after the rain. {12:3} On the day when the keepers of the house tremble, and the strong men stoop, and the grinders cease because they are few, and those looking through the windows grow dim. {12:4} And the doors will be shut in the streets when the sound of grinding is low, and one rises at the sound of a bird, and all the music is brought low. {12:5} Also, when people are afraid of heights, and dangers are along the way, and the almond tree blossoms, and the grasshopper drags itself along, and desire fails, because people go to their eternal home, and mourners go about the streets. {12:6} Before the silver cord is severed, or the golden bowl is broken, or the pitcher is shattered at the spring, or the wheel is broken at the well. {12:7} Then the dust will return to the ground as it was, and the spirit will return to God who gave it. {12:8} Meaningless, meaningless, says the Teacher; everything is meaningless. {12:9} Besides this, the Teacher was wise; he taught the people knowledge, and he carefully considered and arranged many proverbs. {12:10} The Teacher sought to find just the right words, and what he wrote was upright and true. {12:11} The words of the wise are like goads (a type of stick), like nails firmly fixed by a master craftsman; they are given by one shepherd. {12:12} And further, my son, be warned: of making many books, there is no end, and much study wearies the body. {12:13} Now all has been heard; here is the conclusion of the matter: Fear God and keep His commandments, for this is the whole duty of mankind. {12:14} For God will bring every deed into judgment, including every hidden thing, whether it is good or evil.

The Song of Solomon

{1:1} This is the song of songs, which is Solomon's. {1:2} Let him kiss me with the kisses of his mouth, for your love is better than wine. {1:3} The fragrance of your good ointments is like a name that is well-known; therefore, the young women love you. {1:4} Draw me, and we will run after you. The king has brought me into his chambers. We will be happy and rejoice in you; we will remember your love more than wine. The upright love you. {1:5} I am dark but lovely, O daughters of Jerusalem, like the tents of Kedar and the curtains of Solomon. {1:6} Don't look at me because I am dark, for the sun has tanned me. My mother's sons were angry with me; they made me the keeper of the vineyards, but my own vineyard I have not kept. {1:7} Tell me, O you whom my soul loves, where you feed your flock, where you make it rest at noon. Why should I be like one who turns aside by the flocks of your companions? {1:8} If you do not know, O fairest among women, go follow in the footsteps of the flock and feed your young goats beside the shepherds' tents. {1:9} I have compared you, O my love, to a group of horses in Pharaoh's chariots. {1:10} Your cheeks are beautiful with jewelry, your neck with chains of gold. {1:11} We will make you ornaments of gold with silver studs. {1:12} While the king is at his table, my spikenard (a type of perfume) sends forth its fragrance. {1:13} A bundle of myrrh is my beloved to me; he will lie all night between my breasts. {1:14} My beloved is to me a cluster of henna flowers in the vineyards of Engedi. {1:15} Behold, you are beautiful, my love; behold, you are beautiful; you have the eyes of a dove. {1:16} Behold, you are beautiful, my beloved, and pleasant; also our bed is green. {1:17} The beams of our house are cedar, and our rafters are fir.

{2:1} I am the rose of Sharon and the lily of the valleys. {2:2} Like a lily among thorns, so is my love among the daughters. {2:3} Like an apple tree among the trees of the forest, so is my beloved among the sons. I sat in his shade with great delight, and his fruit was sweet to my taste. {2:4} He brought me to the banquet hall, and his banner over me was love. {2:5} Sustain me with refreshments, comfort me with apples, for I am lovesick. {2:6} His left hand is under my head, and his right hand embraces me. {2:7} I charge you, O daughters of Jerusalem, by the gazelles and by the does of the field, do not awaken or stir up love until it pleases. {2:8} The voice of my beloved! Look, he comes leaping upon the mountains, skipping over the hills. {2:9} My beloved is like a gazelle or a young stag; look, he stands behind our wall, looking through the windows, showing himself through the lattice. {2:10} My beloved spoke and said to me, "Rise up, my love, my fair one, and come away. {2:11} For behold, the winter is past; the rain is over and gone. {2:12} The flowers appear on the earth; the time for singing has come, and the voice of the turtle dove is heard in our land. {2:13} The fig tree puts forth its green figs, and the vines with tender grapes give off a pleasant smell. Arise, my love, my fair one, and come away. {2:14} O my dove, in the clefts of the rock, in the secret places of the steep, let me see your face, let me hear your voice; for your voice is sweet, and your face is lovely. {2:15} Catch the little foxes that spoil the vines, for our vines have tender grapes. {2:16} My beloved is mine, and I am his; he feeds among the lilies. {2:17} Until the day breaks and the shadows flee away, turn, my beloved, and be like a gazelle or a young stag on the mountains of Bether.

{3:1} By night on my bed, I searched for the one my soul loves. I searched for him, but I could not find him. {3:2} I will rise now and go about the city, in the streets and in the wide ways. I will seek the one my soul loves. I sought him, but I found him not. {3:3} The watchmen who go about the city found me. To them, I said, "Have you seen the one my soul loves?" {3:4} Just a little while after I passed them, I found the one my soul loves. I held him and would not let him go until I had brought him to my mother's house, to the room of her who conceived me. {3:5} I charge you, O daughters of Jerusalem, by the gazelles and the does of the field, do not stir up or awaken my love until he pleases. {3:6} Who is this coming out of the wilderness like pillars of smoke, perfumed with myrrh and frankincense, with all the spices of the merchant? {3:7} Behold his bed, which is Solomon's; sixty mighty men surround it, all valiant men of Israel. {3:8} They all hold swords, skilled in warfare; every man has his sword at his side because of fear in the night. {3:9} King Solomon made himself a chariot of the wood of Lebanon. {3:10} He made its pillars of silver, its bottom of gold, its covering of purple, the inside paved with love for the daughters of Jerusalem. {3:11} Go forth, O daughters of Zion, and behold King Solomon with the crown his mother crowned him on the day of his wedding, the day of the joy of his heart.

{4:1} Behold, you are beautiful, my love; behold, you are beautiful; you have the eyes of a dove behind your veil. Your hair is like a flock of goats that appear from Mount Gilead. {4:2} Your teeth are like a flock of sheep that have just been shorn, coming up from the washing, every one of which bears twins, and none is barren among them. {4:3} Your lips are like a thread of scarlet, and your speech is lovely; your temples are like a piece of a pomegranate behind your veil. {4:4} Your neck is like the tower of David, built for an armory, on which hang a thousand shields, all shields of mighty men. {4:5} Your two breasts are like two young deer that feed among the lilies. {4:6} Until the day breaks and the shadows flee away, I will go to the mountain of myrrh and the hill of frankincense. {4:7} You are all beautiful, my love; there is no spot in you. {4:8} Come with me from Lebanon, my bride; come with me from Lebanon. Look from the top of Amana, from the top of Shenir and Hermon, from the dens of lions, from the mountains of leopards. {4:9} You have captivated my heart, my sister, my bride; you have captivated my heart with one glance of your eyes, with one jewel of your necklace. {4:10} How delightful is your love, my sister, my bride! How much better is your love than wine! And the fragrance of your ointments is more than all spices! {4:11} Your lips, O my bride, drip like honeycomb; honey and milk are under your tongue, and the fragrance of your garments is like the smell of Lebanon. {4:12} A garden enclosed is my sister, my bride; a spring shut up, a fountain sealed. {4:13} Your plants are an orchard of pomegranates with pleasant fruits, henna with spikenard, {4:14} spikenard and saffron, calamus and cinnamon, with all the trees of frankincense, myrrh and aloes, with all the chief spices. {4:15} A fountain of gardens, a well of living waters, and streams from Lebanon. {4:16} Awake, O north wind; and come, O south; blow upon my garden that its spices may flow out. Let my beloved come into his garden and eat its pleasant fruits.

{5:1} I have come into my garden, my sister, my bride: I have gathered my myrrh and spices; I have eaten my honeycomb and honey; I have drunk my wine and milk. Eat, O friends; drink, yes, drink abundantly, O beloved. {5:2} I sleep, but my heart is awake. It is the voice of my beloved knocking, saying, "Open to me, my sister, my love, my dove, my undefiled; for my head is drenched with dew and my hair with the drops of the night." {5:3} I have taken off my coat; how can I put it on again? I have washed my feet; how can I soil them? {5:4} My beloved put his hand through the opening of the door, and my heart stirred for him. {5:5} I rose up to open to my beloved; my hands dripped with myrrh, and my fingers with sweet-smelling myrrh, upon the handles of the lock. {5:6} I opened to my beloved, but my beloved had turned away and was gone. My heart sank when he spoke. I sought him, but could not find him; I called him, but he did not answer. {5:7} The watchmen who went about the city found me; they struck me and wounded me; the guards of the walls took my veil from me. {5:8} I charge you, O daughters of Jerusalem, if you find my beloved, tell him that I am lovesick. {5:9} What is your beloved more than another beloved, O fairest among women? What is your beloved more than another beloved that you so charge us? {5:10} My beloved is radiant and ruddy, the chief among ten thousand. {5:11} His head is like the finest gold; his hair is wavy and black as a raven. {5:12} His eyes are like doves by the rivers of waters, washed with milk, and perfectly set. {5:13} His cheeks are like a bed of spices, as sweet flowers; his lips are like lilies, dripping sweet-smelling myrrh. {5:14} His hands are like gold rings set with beryl; his belly is bright ivory overlaid with sapphires. {5:15} His legs are like pillars of marble set on bases of fine gold; his countenance is like Lebanon, excellent as the cedars. {5:16} His mouth is most sweet; yes, he is altogether lovely. This is my beloved, and this is my friend, O daughters of Jerusalem.

{6:1} Where has your beloved gone, O fairest among women? Where has your beloved turned aside? That we may seek him with you. {6:2} My beloved has gone down to his garden, to the beds of spices, to feed in the gardens and gather lilies. {6:3} I am my beloved's, and my beloved is mine; he feeds among the lilies. {6:4} You are beautiful, O my love, like Tirzah, lovely as Jerusalem, awe-inspiring as an army with banners. {6:5} Turn away your eyes from me, for they have overcome me; your hair is like a flock of goats that appear from Gilead. {6:6} Your teeth are like a flock of sheep that have just been shorn, coming up from the washing, every one of which bears twins, and none is barren among them. {6:7} Your temples are like a piece of a pomegranate behind your veil. {6:8} There are sixty queens, eighty concubines, and countless virgins. {6:9} My dove, my undefiled, is but one; she is the only one of her mother, the chosen one of her who bore her. The daughters saw her and praised her; yes, the queens and concubines blessed her. {6:10} Who is she that looks forth like the morning, beautiful as the moon, bright as the sun, and awe-inspiring as an army with banners? {6:11} I went down to the garden of nuts to see the fruits of the valley and to see if the vine had flourished and if the pomegranates had budded. {6:12} Before I was aware, my soul had made me like the chariots of my noble people. {6:13} Return, return, O Shulamite; return, return, that we may look upon you. What will you see in the Shulamite? As it were the company of two armies.

{7:1} How beautiful are your feet in shoes, O daughter of a prince! The curves of your thighs are like jewels, the work of a skilled craftsman. {7:2} Your navel is like a round goblet that never lacks for liquor; your belly is like a heap of wheat surrounded by lilies. {7:3} Your two breasts are like two young fawns, twins that graze together. {7:4} Your neck is like a tower of ivory; your eyes are like the fish pools in Heshbon, near the gate of Bathrabbim; your nose is like the tower of Lebanon that looks toward Damascus. {7:5} Your head on you is like Mount Carmel, and your hair is like purple; the king is captivated by your tresses. {7:6} How beautiful and pleasant you are, O love, for delights! {7:7} Your stature is like a palm tree, and your breasts are like clusters of grapes. {7:8} I said, "I will climb the palm tree and take hold of its branches." Now also your breasts shall be like clusters of the vine, and the fragrance of your breath like apples. {7:9} And the roof of your mouth like the best wine for my beloved, flowing smoothly, causing the lips of those who are asleep to speak. {7:10} I am my beloved's, and his desire is for me. {7:11} Come, my beloved, let us go out to the fields; let us spend the night in the villages. {7:12} Let us rise early to the vineyards; let us see if the vines have budded, if the blossoms are open, and if the pomegranates are in bloom. There I will give you my love. {7:13} The mandrakes give off a fragrance, and at our gates are all kinds of pleasant fruits, both new and old, which I have stored up for you, O my beloved.

{8:1} Oh, that you were like my brother, who nursed at my mother's breasts! If I found you outside, I would kiss you, and no one would despise me. {8:2} I would lead you and bring you into my mother's house, and she would instruct me. I would have you drink spiced wine from the juice of my pomegranate. {8:3} His left hand would be under my head, and his right hand would embrace me. {8:4} I charge you, O daughters of Jerusalem, do not stir up or awaken my love until he pleases. {8:5} Who is this coming up from the wilderness, leaning on her beloved? I awakened you under the apple tree; there your mother bore you; there she who bore you was in labor. {8:6} Set me as a seal upon your heart, as a seal upon your arm, for love is as strong as death; jealousy is as fierce as the grave; its flames are fiery flames, a most intense flame. {8:7} Many waters cannot quench love, nor can the floods drown it. If a man would give all the substance of his house for love, it would be utterly despised. {8:8} We have a little sister, and she has no breasts. What shall we do for our sister on the day she is spoken for? {8:9} If she is a wall, we will build upon her a palace of silver; and if she is a door, we will enclose her with boards of cedar. {8:10} I am a wall, and my breasts are like towers. Thus I have become in his eyes like one who found favor. {8:11} Solomon had a vineyard at Baalhamon; he let out the vineyard to keepers; each was to bring a thousand pieces of silver for its fruit. {8:12} My vineyard, which is mine, is before me. You, O Solomon, may have a thousand, and those who keep the fruit, two hundred. {8:13} You who dwell in the gardens, the companions are listening for your voice; let me hear it. {8:14} Make haste, my beloved, and be like a gazelle or a young stag on the mountains of spices.

The Book of Isaiah

{1:1} This is the vision that Isaiah, the son of Amoz, had concerning Judah and Jerusalem during the reigns of Uzziah, Jotham, Ahaz, and Hezekiah, kings of Judah. {1:2} Listen, O heavens, and pay attention, O earth: the LORD has spoken. I raised and nurtured children, but they have rebelled against me. {1:3} Even the ox knows its owner, and the donkey recognizes its master's feeding trough; but Israel does not know, my people do not understand. {1:4} Ah, sinful nation! A people burdened with guilt, a brood of evildoers, children who are corrupt: they have forsaken the LORD and provoked the Holy One of Israel to anger; they have turned away. {1:5} Why should you be punished anymore? You just keep rebelling: the whole head is sick, and the whole heart is faint. {1:6} From the soles of your feet to your head, there is no health in you; only wounds, bruises, and festering sores that have not been treated or bandaged or soothed with ointment. {1:7} Your country is desolate; your cities are burned down. Strangers are devouring your land right in front of you, and it is as desolate as if overthrown by outsiders. {1:8} The daughter of Zion is left like a hut in a vineyard, like a shack in a cucumber garden, like a besieged city. {1:9} If the LORD of hosts had not left us a very small remnant, we would have been like Sodom, and we would have been like Gomorrah. {1:10} Listen to the word of the LORD, you rulers of Sodom; pay attention to the law of our God, you people of Gomorrah. {1:11} What good are all your sacrifices to me? says the LORD. I am fed up with the burnt offerings of rams and the fat of fattened animals; I do not delight in the blood of bulls, lambs, or goats. {1:12} When you come to appear before me, who asked you to trample through my courts? {1:13} Stop bringing worthless offerings; your incense is detestable to me. Your new moons and sabbaths, your special assemblies, I cannot stand; they are a burden to me, I am weary of bearing them. {1:14} When you spread out your hands in prayer, I will hide my eyes from you; even if you pray many prayers, I will not listen. Your hands are full of blood. {1:15} Wash and make yourselves clean. Take your evil deeds out of my sight; stop doing wrong. {1:16} Learn to do right; seek justice, encourage the oppressed, defend the fatherless, plead the case of the widow. {1:17} Come now, let us settle the matter, says the LORD. Though your sins are like scarlet, they shall be as white as snow; though they are red as crimson, they shall be like wool. {1:18} If you are willing and obedient, you will eat the good things of the land; {1:19} but if you resist and rebel, you will be devoured by the sword. For the mouth of the LORD has spoken. {1:20} How the faithful city has become a harlot! She was full of justice; righteousness used to dwell in her, but now murderers. {1:21} Your silver has become dross (worthless material), your wine is watered down. {1:22} Your rulers are rebellious and companions of thieves; they all love bribes and chase after gifts. They do not defend the fatherless; the case of the widow does not come before them. {1:23} Therefore the Lord, the LORD of hosts, the Mighty One of Israel, declares: Ah, I will rid myself of my adversaries and take revenge on my enemies. {1:24} I will turn my hand against you; I will thoroughly purge away your dross and remove all your impurities. {1:25} I will restore your leaders as in the days of old, your counselors as at the beginning. Afterward, you will be called the City of Righteousness, the Faithful City. {1:26} Zion will be redeemed by justice, her penitent (repentant) ones by righteousness. {1:27} But rebels and sinners will both be broken, and those who forsake the LORD will perish. {1:28} You will be ashamed of the oaks you have desired; you will be confounded by the gardens you have chosen. {1:29} You will be like an oak whose leaves wither, like a garden without water. {1:30} The strong will become like tow (fluff for burning), and the maker of them like a spark; both will burn together, {1:31} with no one to quench the fire.

{2:1} This is the word that Isaiah, the son of Amoz, saw concerning Judah and Jerusalem. {2:2} In the last days, the mountain of the LORD's temple will be established as the highest of the mountains; it will be exalted above the hills, and all nations will stream to it. {2:3} Many people will come and say, "Come, let us go up to the mountain of the LORD, to the temple of the God of Jacob. He will teach us his ways so that we may walk in his paths." The law will go out from Zion, the word of the LORD from Jerusalem. {2:4} He will judge between the nations and will settle disputes for many peoples. They will beat their swords into plowshares and their spears into pruning hooks. Nation will not take up sword against nation, nor will they train for war anymore. {2:5} Come, house of Jacob, let us walk in the light of the LORD. {2:6} You have abandoned your people, the descendants of Jacob, because they are full of superstitions from the east and they practice divination like the Philistines; they clasp hands with foreigners. {2:7} Their land is full of silver and gold; there is no end to their treasures. Their land is full of horses; there is no end to their chariots. {2:8} Their land is full of idols; they bow down to the work of their hands, to what their fingers have made. {2:9} So people will be brought low, and everyone humbled; do not forgive them. {2:10} Go into the rocks, hide in the ground from the fearful presence of the LORD and the splendor of his majesty. {2:11} The eyes of the arrogant will be humbled, and human pride brought low; the LORD alone will be exalted in that day. {2:12} The LORD Almighty has a day in store for all the proud and lofty, for all that is exalted, and they will be humbled. {2:13} It will be against all the cedars of Lebanon, tall and lofty, against all the oaks of Bashan, {2:14} against all the high mountains, and against all the lofty hills, {2:15} against every tower and fortified wall, {2:16} against all the ships of Tarshish and all the splendid vessels. {2:17} The arrogance of man will be brought low, and human pride humbled; the LORD alone will be exalted in that day. {2:18} The idols will totally disappear. {2:19} People will flee to caves in the rocks and to holes in the ground from the fearful presence of the LORD and the splendor of his majesty, when he rises to shake the earth. {2:20} In that day, people will throw away to the moles and bats their idols of silver and gold, the idols they made to worship. {2:21} They will flee to the cliffs of the rocks and to the overhanging crags from the fearful presence of the LORD and the splendor of his majesty, when he rises to shake the earth. {2:22} Stop trusting in mere humans, who have but a breath in their nostrils. Why hold them in esteem?

{3:1} Look, the Lord, the LORD of hosts, is removing from Jerusalem and Judah all support—both food and water. {3:2} He is taking away the mighty man, the warrior, the judge, the prophet, the wise person, and the elder. {3:3} He is removing the captain of fifty, the honorable man, the advisor, the skilled craftsman, and the eloquent speaker. {3:4} Instead, I will give children as their leaders, and infants will rule over them. {3:5} People will oppress one another, and neighbors will do the same. A child will act arrogantly toward an elder, and the dishonorable will challenge the honorable. {3:6} When a man grabs his brother from his father's house, saying, "You have clothing; be our leader, and take charge of this disaster," {3:7} in that day he will swear, saying, "I won't be a healer; I have no food or clothing in my house. Don't make me a leader of the people." {3:8} For Jerusalem has stumbled, and Judah has fallen, because their words and actions are against the LORD, provoking his glorious presence. {3:9} Their appearance testifies against them; they openly declare their sin like Sodom and do not hide it. Woe to their souls! They have brought trouble upon themselves. {3:10} Tell the righteous that it will be well with them, for they will enjoy the fruit of their deeds. {3:11} Woe to the wicked! It will go badly for them, for they will reap the consequences of their actions. {3:12} My people are oppressed by children, and women rule over them. O my people, those who guide you lead you astray and ruin the path you should follow. {3:13} The LORD stands up to plead and judges the people. {3:14} The LORD will bring judgment against the elders and leaders of his people: "You have destroyed the vineyard; the plunder from the poor is in your homes." {3:15} What do you mean by crushing my people and grinding the faces of the poor? says the Lord GOD of hosts. {3:16} Furthermore, the LORD says, "Because the daughters of Zion are proud, walking with outstretched necks and seductive eyes, strutting along as they go and jingling their anklets, {3:17} therefore the Lord will strike their heads with sores, and the LORD will expose their private parts." {3:18} In that day, the Lord will remove their fine jewelry, including the anklets, headbands, and moon-shaped ornaments, {3:19} the chains, bracelets, and veils, {3:20} the headdresses, leg ornaments, headbands, perfume bottles, and earrings, {3:21} the rings and nose rings, {3:22} the stylish clothes, capes, and shawls, and the mirrors, fine linen, hoods, and veils. {3:23} Instead of fragrance, there will be a stench; instead of a sash, a rope; instead of well-coiffed hair, baldness; instead of a rich robe, a garment of sackcloth; and branding instead of beauty. {3:24} Your men will fall by the sword, and your warriors will die in battle. {3:25} Her gates will lament and mourn, and she will sit desolate on the ground.

{4:1} In that day, seven women will grab hold of one man, saying, "We will provide our own food and wear our own clothes; just let us be called by your name to take away our disgrace." {4:2} In that day, the branch of the LORD will be beautiful and glorious, and the fruit of the land will be excellent and appealing for those who survive in Israel. {4:3} Those who are left in Zion and remain in Jerusalem will be called holy, everyone recorded among the living in Jerusalem. {4:4} When the LORD has washed away the filth of the daughters of Zion and cleansed the bloodstains of Jerusalem by the spirit of judgment and the spirit of fire, {4:5} the LORD will create a cloud and smoke over every dwelling on Mount Zion and over her assemblies, and there will be a shining flame by night; for over all the glory there will be a protective canopy. {4:6} There will be a shelter for shade during the day from the heat and a refuge from storm and rain.

{5:1} Now I will sing a song to my beloved about his vineyard. My beloved has a vineyard on a very fertile hill. {5:2} He fenced it in, cleared the stones, planted the best vines, built a tower in the middle, and made a winepress there. He expected it to produce good grapes, but it produced wild grapes instead. {5:3} And now, O inhabitants of Jerusalem and people of Judah, please judge between me and my vineyard. {5:4} What more could I have done for my vineyard that I haven't done? Why, when I expected it to produce good grapes, did it produce wild grapes? {5:5} Now I will tell you what I will do to my vineyard: I will remove its hedge, and it will be devoured; I will break down its wall, and it will be trampled. {5:6} I will make it a wasteland; it won't be pruned or cultivated, and instead, briers and thorns will grow. I will also command the clouds not to rain on it. {5:7} For the vineyard of the LORD of hosts is the house of Israel, and the men of Judah are his cherished plants. He looked for justice, but saw oppression; for righteousness, but heard cries of distress. {5:8} Woe to those who join house to house and field to field until there is no space left, so that they may be alone in the midst of the land! {5:9} In my ears, the LORD of hosts said, "Truly, many houses will be desolate, even large and beautiful ones, with no inhabitants." {5:10} Ten acres of vineyard will yield only one bath (about 6 gallons), and a homer (about 6 bushels) will yield only an ephah (about 3/5 of a bushel). {5:11} Woe to those who rise early in the morning to pursue strong drink and continue until night, until wine inflames them! {5:12} The harp, lyre, tambourine, and flute are in their feasts, but they do not regard the work of the LORD or consider what his hands have done. {5:13} Therefore, my people go into exile for lack of knowledge; their honored men are starving, and the multitude is parched with thirst. {5:14} Therefore, hell has enlarged itself and opened its mouth without limit; their glory, multitude, and joy will descend into it. {5:15} The common man will be humbled, and the mighty will be brought low; the eyes of the proud will be humbled. {5:16} But the LORD of hosts will be exalted in judgment, and the Holy God will be shown to be holy in righteousness. {5:17} Then the lambs will graze as they wish, and the desolate areas of the wealthy will be eaten by strangers. {5:18} Woe to those who draw iniquity with ropes of deceit and sin as if with a cart rope. {5:19} They say, "Let him hurry, let his work come quickly, so we may see it; let the counsel of the Holy One of Israel draw near and let it come, so we may know it!" {5:20} Woe to those who call evil good and good evil, who put darkness for light and light for darkness, who put bitter for sweet and sweet for bitter! {5:21} Woe to those who are wise in their own eyes and clever in their own sight! {5:22} Woe to those who are heroes at drinking wine and champions at mixing strong drinks, {5:23} who justify the wicked for a bribe and deprive the righteous of his right! {5:24} Therefore, as the fire consumes stubble and the flame devours chaff, so their root will become like rottenness, and their blossom will blow away like dust, because they have rejected the law of the LORD of hosts and despised the word of the Holy One of Israel. {5:25} Therefore, the anger of the LORD is kindled against his people; he stretched out his hand against them and struck them; the mountains trembled, and their corpses lay in the streets. For all this, his anger is not turned away, and his hand is still stretched out. {5:26} He will lift up a banner for the nations from afar and will whistle for them from the ends of the earth. Look, they will come swiftly! {5:27} None will be weary or stumble among them; none will slumber or sleep; nor will the belt of their loins be loose, nor the strap of their sandals be broken. {5:28} Their arrows are sharp, and all their bows are bent; the hooves of their horses are like flint, and their chariot wheels are like a whirlwind. {5:29} Their roaring will be like a lion; they will roar like young lions. Yes, they will roar and seize their prey and carry it away safely, and no one will rescue it. {5:30} In that day, they will roar against them like the roaring of the sea; if one looks to the land, there will be darkness and distress, and the light will be darkened in the heavens.

{6:1} In the year that King Uzziah died, I also saw the Lord sitting on a throne, high and exalted, and the train of his robe filled the temple. {6:2} Above him stood the seraphim (heavenly beings); each had six wings: with two wings they covered their faces, with two they covered their feet, and with two they flew. {6:3} They called to one another and said, "Holy, holy, holy is the LORD of hosts; the whole earth is full of his glory." {6:4} The doorposts shook at the sound of their voices, and the temple was filled with smoke. {6:5} Then I said, "Woe to me! I am ruined! For I am a man of unclean lips, and I live among a people of unclean lips, for my eyes have seen the King, the LORD of hosts." {6:6} Then one of the seraphim flew to me with a live coal in his hand, which he had taken from the altar with tongs. {6:7} He touched my mouth with it and said, "See, this has touched your lips; your iniquity is taken away, and your sin is purged." {6:8} I also heard the voice of the Lord saying, "Whom shall I send, and who will go for us?" Then I said, "Here am I; send me." {6:9} And he said, "Go, and tell this people: 'You hear indeed, but do not understand; you see indeed, but do not perceive.' {6:10} Make the heart of this people dull, and their ears heavy, and shut their eyes; otherwise they might see with their eyes, hear with their ears, understand with their hearts, and turn, and be healed." {6:11} Then I said, "Lord, how long?" And he answered, "Until cities are wasted without inhabitant, houses without people, and the land is utterly desolate, {6:12} and the LORD has removed people far away, and there is a great forsaking in the midst of the land. {6:13} But there will still be a tenth of it, and it will return and be consumed, like a oak tree, whose substance remains when its leaves fall. The holy seed will be its substance."

{7:1} In the days of Ahaz, the son of Jotham, the son of Uzziah, king of Judah, King Rezin of Syria and Pekah, the son of Remaliah, king of Israel, marched against Jerusalem but could not defeat it. {7:2} It was reported to the house of David that Syria had allied with Ephraim. This news caused Ahaz and his people to tremble like trees swaying in the wind. {7:3} Then the LORD said to Isaiah, "Go meet Ahaz, you and your son Shearjashub, at the end of the conduit of the upper pool on the road to the fuller's field. {7:4} Say to him, 'Be careful, stay calm; don't be afraid or lose heart because of the two smoldering stumps of firebrands—because of the fierce anger of Rezin and Syria and the son of Remaliah.' {7:5} Syria, Ephraim, and the son of Remaliah have plotted evil against you, saying, {7:6} 'Let us go up against Judah and cause panic; let us tear it apart and set up a puppet king, the son of Tabeal.' {7:7} Thus says the Lord GOD: 'It will not happen; it will not come to pass. {7:8} For the head of Syria is Damascus, and the head of Damascus is Rezin. Within sixty-five years, Ephraim will be shattered so that it will no longer be a people. {7:9} The head of Ephraim is Samaria, and the head of Samaria is Remaliah's son. If you do not stand firm in your faith, you will not stand at all.' {7:10} Moreover, the LORD spoke to Ahaz again, saying, {7:11} 'Ask for a sign from the LORD your God; ask it either in the depths or in the heights above.' {7:12} But Ahaz said, 'I will not ask; I will not put the LORD to the test.' {7:13} Then Isaiah said, 'Hear now, O house of David: Is it not enough to weary men? Will you weary my God also? {7:14} Therefore, the Lord himself will give you a sign: The virgin will conceive and give birth to a son and will call him Immanuel (meaning "God with us"). {7:15} He will eat curds and honey at the time he knows enough to reject the wrong and choose the right. {7:16} For before the child knows enough to reject the wrong and choose the right, the land you dread will be forsaken by both its kings. {7:17} The LORD will bring upon you, upon your people, and upon your father's house days of distress that have not come since the day Ephraim broke away from Judah—he will bring the king of Assyria. {7:18} In that day, the LORD will whistle for the flies at the farthest streams of the Nile and for the bees in the land of Assyria. {7:19} They will all come and settle in the desolate valleys, the crevices of the rocks, and on all the thornbushes and at all the watering holes. {7:20} In that day, the Lord will use a razor hired from beyond the Euphrates River—the king of Assyria—to shave your heads and the hair on your legs and to take off your beards. {7:21} In that day, a man will keep alive a young cow and two goats. {7:22} Because of the abundance of milk they give, he will eat curds, for everyone left in the land will eat curds and honey. {7:23} In that day, every place where there were a thousand vines worth a thousand shekels will become briers and thorns. {7:24} Men will come there with bows and arrows, for the whole land will be briers and thorns. {7:25} As for all the hills once cultivated with a hoe, there will be neither fear of briers & thorns, but it will be a place for oxen to graze and for sheep to trample.

{8:1} Moreover, the LORD said to me, "Take a large scroll and write on it in clear letters concerning Mahershalalhashbaz (meaning "Swift is the Spoil, Hasty is the Prey"). {8:2} I took faithful witnesses to record: Uriah the priest and Zechariah, the son of Jeberechiah. {8:3} I went to the prophetess, and she conceived and bore a son. The LORD said to me, "Call him Mahershalalhashbaz. {8:4} For before the child knows how to say 'My father' or 'My mother,' the wealth of Damascus and the plunder of Samaria will be carried off by the king of Assyria." {8:5} The LORD spoke to me again, saying, {8:6} "Since this people has rejected the gentle waters of Shiloah and rejoices in Rezin and Remaliah's son, {8:7} therefore, the Lord is bringing against them the mighty floodwaters of the Euphrates—the king of Assyria and all his glory. It will overflow all its channels and spill over all its banks. {8:8} It will sweep on into Judah; it will overflow and pass through; it will reach up to the neck; and the spread of its wings will fill the breadth of your land, O Immanuel." {8:9} Raise the war cry, you nations, and be shattered; listen, all you distant lands. Prepare for battle, and be shattered! Prepare for battle, and be shattered! {8:10} Devise your strategy, but it will be thwarted; propose your plan, but it will not stand, for God is with us. {8:11} The LORD spoke to me with his strong hand upon me, warning me not to follow the way of this people. {8:12} Do not call conspiracy everything this people calls a conspiracy; do not fear what they fear, and do not dread it. {8:13} The LORD Almighty is the one you are to regard as holy, he is the one you are to fear; he is the one you are to dread. {8:14} He will be a holy place; for both Israel's houses, he will be a stone that causes men to stumble and a rock that makes them fall; and for the people of Jerusalem, he will be a trap and a snare. {8:15} Many of them will stumble; they will fall and be broken; they will be snared and captured. {8:16} Bind up this testimony of warning and seal up God's instruction among my disciples. {8:17} I will wait for the LORD, who is hiding his face from the house of Jacob; I will put my trust in him. {8:18} Here am I, and the children the LORD has given me are signs and symbols in Israel from the LORD Almighty, who dwells on Mount Zion. {8:19} When someone tells you to consult mediums and spirits of the dead, should not a people inquire of their God? Why consult the dead on behalf of the living? {8:20} Consult God's instruction and the testimony of warning. If anyone does not speak according to this word, they have no light of dawn. {8:21} Distressed and hungry, they will roam through the land; when they are famished, they will become enraged and will curse their king and their God. They will look upward. {8:22} Then they will look toward the earth and see only distress and darkness, and fearful gloom; and they will be driven into utter darkness.

{9:1} Nevertheless, the gloom will not be as it was in the past when the LORD lightly afflicted the land of Zebulun and Naphtali, and later brought more serious affliction by the way of the sea, beyond the Jordan, in Galilee of the nations. {9:2} The people who walked in darkness have seen a great light; those who live in the land of deep darkness—light has shone on them. {9:3} You have enlarged the nation and increased their joy; they rejoice before you as people rejoice at harvest time, as warriors rejoice when dividing the spoils. {9:4} For you have broken the yoke that burdens them, the bar across their shoulders, and the rod of their oppressor, just as you did in the day of Midian. {9:5} Every warrior's boot used in battle and every garment rolled in blood will be destined for burning, will be fuel for the fire. {9:6} For to us a child is born, to us a son is given, and the government will be on his shoulders. He will be called Wonderful Counselor, Mighty God, Everlasting Father, Prince of Peace. {9:7} Of the greatness of his government and peace there will be no end. He will reign on David's throne and over his kingdom, establishing and upholding it with justice and righteousness from that time on and forever. The zeal of the LORD Almighty will accomplish this. {9:8} The Lord has sent a message against Jacob; it will fall on Israel. {9:9} All the people will know it—Ephraim and the inhabitants of Samaria—who say with pride and arrogance of heart, {9:10} "The bricks have fallen down, but we will rebuild with dressed stone; the sycamore trees have been felled, but we will replace them with cedars." {9:11} Therefore, the LORD will set up adversaries against them and join their enemies together; {9:12} the Syrians in the front and the Philistines in the rear; they will devour Israel with open mouths. Yet for all this, his anger is not turned away, his hand is still stretched out. {9:13} But the people have not returned to him who struck them, nor have they sought the LORD Almighty. {9:14} So the LORD will cut off from Israel both head and tail, both palm branch and reed in a single day. {9:15} The elders and dignitaries are the head; the prophets who teach lies are the tail. {9:16} Those who guide this people mislead them, and those who are guided are led astray. {9:17} Therefore, the Lord will take no pleasure in the young men, nor will he pity the fatherless and widows, for everyone is ungodly and wicked; every mouth speaks folly. Yet for all this, his anger is not turned away, his hand is still stretched out. {9:18} Wickedness burns like a fire; it consumes briers and thorns and sets the forest thickets ablaze, so that it rises like the smoke. {9:19} By the wrath of the LORD Almighty, the land will be scorched, and the people will be fuel for the fire; no one will spare his brother. {9:20} On the right they will devour, but still be hungry; they will eat on the left but not be satisfied. Each will feed on the flesh of his own arm. {9:21} Manasseh will feed on Ephraim, and Ephraim on Manasseh; together they will turn against Judah. Yet for all this, his anger is not turned away, his hand is still stretched out.

{10:1} Woe to those who make unjust laws, to those who issue oppressive decrees, {10:2} to deprive the poor of their rights and withhold justice from the oppressed of my people, making widows their prey and robbing the fatherless. {10:3} What will you do on the day of reckoning, when disaster comes from afar? To whom will you run for help? Where will you leave your riches? {10:4} Nothing will remain but to crouch among the prisoners or fall among the slain. Yet for all this, his anger is not turned away, his hand is still stretched out. {10:5} O Assyrian, the rod of my anger, the staff in their hand is my indignation. {10:6} I send him against a godless nation, I dispatch him against a people who anger me, to seize loot and snatch plunder, and to trample them down like mud in the streets. {10:7} But this is not what he intends, this is not what he has in mind; his purpose is to destroy and to cut off many nations. {10:8} For he says, "Are not my commanders all kings? {10:9} Is not Calno like Carchemish? Is not Hamath like Arpad? Is not Samaria like Damascus? {10:10} As my hand has found the kingdoms of the idols, whose images were greater than those of Jerusalem and Samaria— {10:11} shall I not deal with Jerusalem and her images as I dealt with Samaria and her idols?" {10:12} When the Lord has finished all his work against Mount Zion and Jerusalem, he will say, "I will punish the king of Assyria for the willful pride of his heart and the haughty look in his eyes." {10:13} For he says, "By the strength of my hand I have done this, and by my wisdom, because I have understanding. I removed the boundaries of nations, I plundered their treasures; like a mighty one, I subdued their kings. {10:14} As one reaches into a nest, so my hand reached for the wealth of the nations; as people gather abandoned eggs, so I gathered all the earth; no one flapped a wing or opened his mouth to chirp." {10:15} Does the axe raise itself above the person who swings it, or the saw boast against the one who uses it? As if a rod were to wield the person who lifts it up, or a staff to lift up the one who is not wood! {10:16} Therefore, the Lord, the LORD Almighty, will send a wasting disease upon his sturdy warriors; under his pomp, a fire will be kindled like a blazing flame. {10:17} The Light of Israel will become a fire, their Holy One a flame; in a single day it will burn and consume his thorns and his briers. {10:18} It will consume the glory of his forests and fertile fields, both soul and body; it will be like a standard-bearer fainting. {10:19} The rest of the trees in his forest will be so few that a child could write them down. {10:20} In that day the remnant of Israel, the survivors of the house of Jacob, will no longer rely on him who struck them but will truly rely on the LORD, the Holy One of Israel. {10:21} A remnant will return, a remnant of Jacob will return to the Mighty God. {10:22} Though your people be like the sand by the sea, Israel, only a remnant will return. Destruction has been decreed, overwhelming and righteous. {10:23} For the Lord GOD Almighty will carry out the destruction decreed upon the whole land. {10:24} Therefore, this is what the Lord GOD Almighty says: "My people who live in Zion, do not be afraid of the Assyrians, who beat you with a rod and lift up a club against you, as Egypt did. {10:25} Very soon my anger against you will end and my wrath will be directed to their destruction." {10:26} The LORD Almighty will lash out against them with a whip, as he did when he struck down Midian at the rock of Oreb, and he will raise his staff over the waters, as he did in Egypt. {10:27} In that day, their burden will be lifted from your shoulders, their yoke will be destroyed because of the anointing. {10:28} They have gone through Aiath; they have passed through Migron; they store their equipment at Michmash. {10:29} They have gone over the pass and said, "We will camp at Geba"; Ramah trembles; Gibeah of Saul has fled. {10:30} Cry out, O daughter of Gallim! Listen, O Laish! Poor Anathoth! {10:31} Madmenah is in flight; the people of Gebim take cover. {10:32} This day they will halt at Nob; they will shake their fists at the Mount of the Daughter of Zion, at the hill of Jerusalem. {10:33} See, the Lord, the LORD Almighty, will lop off the boughs with great power; the lofty trees will be felled, the tall ones will be brought low. {10:34} He will cut down the forest thickets with an axe, and Lebanon will fall before the Mighty One.

{11:1} A shoot will come up from the stump of Jesse; from his roots, a Branch will bear fruit. {11:2} The Spirit of the LORD will rest on him—the Spirit of wisdom and understanding, the Spirit of counsel and might, the Spirit of knowledge and the fear of the LORD. {11:3} He will delight in the fear of the LORD; he will not judge by what he sees with his eyes, or decide by what he hears with his ears. {11:4} But he will judge the needy with righteousness; he will give decisions for the poor of the earth. He will strike the earth with the rod of his mouth; with the breath of his lips, he will slay the wicked. {11:5} Righteousness will be his belt and faithfulness the sash around his waist. {11:6} The wolf will live with the lamb, the leopard will lie down with the goat, the calf and the lion will feed together, and a little child will lead them. {11:7} The cow will feed with the bear, their young will lie down together, and the lion will eat straw like the ox. {11:8} The infant will play near the cobra's den, and the toddler will put his hand into the viper's nest. {11:9} They will neither harm nor destroy on all my holy mountain, for the earth will be filled with the knowledge of the LORD as the waters cover the sea. {11:10} In that day, the root of Jesse will stand as a banner for the people; the nations will rally to him, and his resting place will be glorious. {11:11} In that day, the Lord will reach out his hand a second time to reclaim the remnant that is left of his people from Assyria, Egypt, Pathros, Cush, Elam, Shinar, Hamath, and the islands of the sea. {11:12} He will raise a banner for the nations and gather the exiles of Israel; he will assemble the scattered people of Judah from the four corners of the earth. {11:13} Ephraim's jealousy will vanish, and Judah's enemies will be cut off; Ephraim will not be jealous of Judah, nor Judah hostile toward Ephraim. {11:14} They will swoop down on the slopes of the Philistines to the west; together they will plunder the people to the east. They will lay hands on Edom and Moab, and the Ammonites will be subject to them. {11:15} The LORD will dry up the Gulf of the Egyptian Sea; with a scorching wind, he will sweep his hand over the Euphrates River, breaking it up into seven streams so that men can cross over dry-shod. {11:16} There will be a highway for the remnant of his people that is left from Assyria, as there was for Israel when they came up from the land of Egypt.

{12:1} In that day you will say: "I will praise you, LORD. Although you were angry with me, your anger has turned away, and you have comforted me." {12:2} Surely God is my salvation; I will trust and not be afraid. The LORD, the LORD himself, is my strength and my defense; he has become my salvation. {12:3} With joy you will draw water from the wells of salvation. {12:4} In that day you will say: "Give praise to the LORD, proclaim his name; make known among the nations what he has done, and proclaim that his name is exalted." {12:5} Sing to the LORD, for he has done glorious things; let this be known to all the world. {12:6} Shout aloud and sing for joy, people of Zion, for great is the Holy One of Israel among you.

{13:1} The burden (prophecy) concerning Babylon that Isaiah son of Amoz saw. {13:2} Raise a banner on a high mountain, shout to them, wave your hand so they may enter the gates of the nobles. {13:3} I have commanded my consecrated ones; I have also summoned my warriors who rejoice in my majesty. {13:4} The noise of a multitude in the mountains is like that of a great people; a tumultuous noise of kingdoms gathered together. The LORD of hosts is mustering the army for battle. {13:5} They come from a distant land, from the ends of the heavens—the LORD and the weapons of his fury—to destroy the whole land. {13:6} Wail, for the day of the LORD is near; it will come like destruction from the Almighty. {13:7} Therefore, all hands will go limp, and every heart will melt with fear. {13:8} Terror will seize them; they will be in pain like a woman in labor; they will look at each other in astonishment; their faces will be aflame. {13:9} See, the day of the LORD is coming, a cruel day with wrath and fierce anger, to make the land desolate and to destroy the sinners within it. {13:10} The stars of heaven and their constellations will not show their light; the sun will be dark when it rises, and the moon will not give its light. {13:11} I will punish the world for its evil, the wicked for their iniquity; I will put an end to the arrogance of the haughty and will humble the pride of the ruthless. {13:12} I will make people scarcer than pure gold, more rare than the gold of Ophir. {13:13} Therefore, I will shake the heavens, and the earth will tremble from its place at the wrath of the LORD of hosts in the day of his fierce anger. {13:14} It will be like a hunted gazelle, like sheep without a shepherd; each will return to their own people and flee to their own land. {13:15} Whoever is captured will be thrust through; whoever is caught will fall by the sword. {13:16} Their infants will be dashed to pieces before their eyes; their houses will be looted, and their wives raped. {13:17} See, I will stir up the Medes against them; they will not care about silver, and they will not delight in gold. {13:18} Their bows will strike down the young men; they will have no mercy on infants; their eyes will not spare children. {13:19} Babylon, the jewel of kingdoms, the glory of the Chaldeans, will be like Sodom and Gomorrah when God overthrew them. {13:20} It will never be inhabited or lived in through all generations; no Arabian will pitch his tent there, and no shepherds will rest their flocks there. {13:21} But desert creatures will lie there, and their houses will be full of howling creatures; there owls will dwell, and wild goats will dance. {13:22} The hyenas will howl in their strongholds, and jackals in their luxurious palaces. Her time is near, and her days will not be prolonged.

{14:1} The LORD will have compassion on Jacob; he will again choose Israel and will settle them in their own land. Strangers will join them and unite with the descendants of Jacob. {14:2} Nations will take them and bring them to their own place; the house of Israel will possess them as male and female servants in the land of the LORD. They will take captives whose captives they were and will rule over their oppressors. {14:3} On the day the LORD gives you rest from your sorrow and turmoil, and from the hard service you were forced to do, {14:4} you will take up this taunt against the king of Babylon: "How the oppressor has come to an end! How his fury has ended!" {14:5} The LORD has broken the rod of the wicked, the scepter of the rulers. {14:6} He who struck down peoples in anger with unceasing blows, he who ruled the nations in anger is persecuted and no one hinders him. {14:7} The whole earth is at rest and quiet; they break into singing. {14:8} Even the pine trees and the cedars of Lebanon rejoice over you, saying, "Since you have been laid low, no one comes to cut us down." {14:9} The realm of the dead below is all astir to meet you at your coming; it rouses the spirits of the departed to greet you—all those who were leaders in the world; it makes them rise from their thrones—all those who were kings over the nations. {14:10} They will all respond, saying to you, "You also have become weak, as we are; you have become like us." {14:11} All your pomp has been brought down to the grave, along with the noise of your harps; maggots are spread out beneath you, and worms cover you. {14:12} How you have fallen from heaven, O morning star, son of the dawn! You have been cast down to the earth, you who once laid low the nations! {14:13} You said in your heart, "I will ascend to the heavens; I will raise my throne above the stars of God; I will sit enthroned on the mount of assembly, on the utmost heights of the sacred mountain. {14:14} I will ascend above the tops of the clouds; I will make myself like the Most High." {14:15} But you are brought down to the realm of the dead, to the depths of the pit. {14:16} Those who see you will stare at you and ponder your fate: "Is this the man who shook the earth and made kingdoms tremble, {14:17} the man who made the world a wilderness, who overthrew its cities and would not let his captives go home?" {14:18} All the kings of the nations lie in state, each in his own tomb. {14:19} But you are cast out of your tomb like a rejected branch, like a garment trampled underfoot. {14:20} You will not join them in burial, for you have destroyed your land and killed your people. The offspring of the wicked will never be mentioned again. {14:21} Prepare a place for his children because of the sins of their fathers; they are not to rise to inherit the land or cover the earth with cities. {14:22} I will rise up against them, declares the LORD of hosts. I will wipe out Babylon's name and survivors, descendants and offspring, declares the LORD. {14:23} I will make it a place for owls and marshes; I will sweep it with the broom of destruction, declares the LORD of hosts. {14:24} The LORD of hosts has sworn, "Surely, as I have planned, so it will be, and as I have purposed, so it will stand: {14:25} I will crush the Assyrian in my land; on my mountains I will trample him down. His yoke will be taken from my people, and his burden removed from their shoulders." {14:26} This is the plan determined for the whole earth; this is the hand stretched out over all nations. {14:27} For the LORD of hosts has purposed, and who can thwart him? His hand is stretched out, and who can turn it back? {14:28} This prophecy came in the year King Ahaz died. {14:29} Do not rejoice, all you of Philistia, because the rod that struck you is broken; for out of the root of that snake will spring up a viper, and its fruit will be a darting, venomous serpent. {14:30} The poorest of the poor will find pasture, and the needy will lie down in safety. But I will kill your root with famine, and your survivors will be slain. {14:31} Wail, O gate; cry out, O city; melt in fear, O Philistia; for a smoke comes from the north, and there is not a straggler in its ranks. {14:32} What answer will be given to the envoys of that nation? The LORD has established Zion, and in her, the poor of his people will find refuge.

{15:1} This is the burden (prophecy) concerning Moab. In the night, Ar of Moab is laid waste and silenced; in the night, Kir of Moab is laid waste and silenced. {15:2} They have gone up to Bajith and Dibon, the high places, to weep. Moab will wail over Nebo and Medeba; every head will be shaved and every beard cut off. {15:3} In their streets, they will wear sackcloth; on the roofs of their houses and in their streets, everyone will howl, weeping profusely. {15:4} Heshbon and Elealeh will cry out; their voices will be heard as far as Jahaz. Therefore, the armed soldiers of Moab will cry out; their lives will be bitter for them. {15:5} My heart cries out for Moab; the refugees will flee to Zoar, like a three-year-old calf. They will ascend Luhith with weeping; on the road to Horonaim, they will raise a cry of destruction. {15:6} The waters of Nimrim will be desolate; the grass is withered, and there is no green thing left. {15:7} So the abundance they have gained and stored will be carried away to the brook of willows. {15:8} The cries of Moab are heard all around; their howling reaches Eglaim and Beerelim. {15:9} The waters of Dimon will be full of blood, for I will bring more upon Dimon—lions upon those who escape from Moab and upon the remnant of the land.

{16:1} Send a lamb to the ruler of the land from Sela to the wilderness, to the mount of the daughter of Zion. {16:2} For it will be that, like a bird that has been cast out of its nest, the daughters of Moab will be at the fords of Arnon. {16:3} Take counsel and execute justice; make your shadow like night in the daytime; hide the outcasts and do not betray those who wander. {16:4} Let my outcasts dwell with you, Moab; be a shelter for them from the oppressor, for the extortioner has ended, the spoiler ceases, and the oppressors are gone from the land. {16:5} In mercy, a throne will be established, and he will sit on it in truth, in the tent of David, judging and seeking justice and hastening righteousness. {16:6} We have heard of Moab's pride; he is very proud, even of his arrogance, pride, and anger; but his lies will not last. {16:7} Therefore, Moab will wail for Moab; everyone will wail. The foundations of Kirhareseth will mourn; surely, they are stricken. {16:8} The fields of Heshbon wither, and the vine of Sibmah. The rulers of the nations have broken down its choicest plants, reaching even to Jazer; they wander through the wilderness, and its branches are stretched out; they have gone over the sea. {16:9} Therefore, I will mourn with the weeping of Jazer for the vine of Sibmah; I will water you with my tears, O Heshbon and Elealeh, for the shout over your summer fruits and harvest has fallen. {16:10} Gladness is taken away, and joy is gone from the fertile fields; in the vineyards, there will be no singing or shouting; the winepresses will not tread out wine; I have made their vintage shouting cease. {16:11} Therefore, my heart will sound like a harp for Moab, and my inner being for Kirharesh. {16:12} When Moab is weary on the high place, he will come to his sanctuary to pray, but he will not prevail. {16:13} This is the message the LORD has spoken concerning Moab since then. {16:14} But now the LORD says, "Within three years, as a hired worker counts his years, the glory of Moab will be humiliated, along with all that great multitude; the remnant will be very small and weak."

{17:1} This is the burden (prophecy) concerning Damascus. Look, Damascus will no longer be a city; it will become a heap of ruins. {17:2} The cities of Aroer will be deserted; they will be places for flocks to lie down, and no one will make them afraid. {17:3} The fortress of Ephraim will cease, and the kingdom from Damascus, along with the remnant of Syria, will be like the glory of the children of Israel, says the LORD of hosts. {17:4} In that day, the glory of Jacob will fade, and the fatness of his flesh will become lean. {17:5} It will be like when the harvest worker gathers the grain, reaping the ears with his arm; it will be like someone gathering ears in the valley of Rephaim. {17:6} Yet, some grapes will be left, like the shaking of an olive tree—two or three berries at the top of the highest branch, four or five on the outermost fruitful branches, says the LORD God of Israel. {17:7} In that day, a man will look to his Maker, and his eyes will turn to the Holy One of Israel. {17:8} He will not look to the altars, the work of his hands, nor will he regard what his fingers have made, whether the groves or the images. {17:9} In that day, his strong cities will be like a forsaken bough, an uppermost branch left because of the children of Israel, leading to desolation. {17:10} Because you have forgotten the God of your salvation and have not remembered the rock of your strength, you will plant delightful plants and set them with foreign slips (grafts). {17:11} On the day you make your plants grow, and in the morning you make your seeds flourish, the harvest will turn into a heap in a day of grief and desperate sorrow. {17:12} Woe to the multitude of many people who make a noise like the roaring of the seas, and to the rushing nations that make a sound like the rushing of mighty waters! {17:13} The nations will rush like the rushing of many waters, but God will rebuke them, and they will flee far away, chased like chaff on the mountains before the wind, and like a rolling thing before the whirlwind. {17:14} And look, at evening, trouble; before morning, it is gone. This is the fate of those who plunder us and the lot of those who rob us.

{18:1} Woe to the land shadowed by wings, which is beyond the rivers of Ethiopia! {18:2} That sends ambassadors by sea, in vessels of papyrus (bulrushes) on the waters, saying, "Go, you swift messengers, to a nation scattered and peeled (exposed), to a people formidable from their beginning until now; a nation measured out and trodden down, whose land the rivers have spoiled!" {18:3} All you inhabitants of the world and dwellers on the earth, see when he lifts up a banner on the mountains; when he blows a trumpet, listen! {18:4} For so the LORD said to me, "I will take my rest, and I will consider in my dwelling place like the clear heat upon herbs, and like a cloud of dew in the heat of harvest." {18:5} Before the harvest, when the bud is perfect and the sour grape is ripening in the flower, he will cut off the sprigs with pruning hooks and take away and cut down the branches. {18:6} They will be left together for the birds of the mountains and the beasts of the earth; the birds will summer upon them, and all the beasts of the earth will winter upon them. {18:7} In that time, a gift will be brought to the LORD of hosts from a people scattered and peeled, from a people formidable from their beginning until now; a nation measured out and trodden underfoot, whose land the rivers have spoiled, to the place of the name of the LORD of hosts, the mount Zion.

{19:1} This is the burden (prophecy) concerning Egypt. Look, the LORD rides on a swift cloud and will come into Egypt; the idols of Egypt will tremble at His presence, and the heart of Egypt will melt within it. {19:2} I will stir up the Egyptians against one another; they will fight each other, brother against brother, neighbor against neighbor, city against city, and kingdom against kingdom. {19:3} The spirit of Egypt will fail in the midst of it, and I will destroy their plans. They will seek guidance from the idols, from the mediums (charmers), and from those who have familiar spirits (ghosts), and from the wizards. {19:4} I will hand the Egyptians over to a cruel lord, and a fierce king will rule over them, says the Lord, the LORD of hosts. {19:5} The waters will fail from the sea, and the river will dry up and waste away. {19:6} The rivers will turn away, and the canals will be emptied and dried up; the reeds and rushes will wither. {19:7} The paper reeds by the canals, at the mouth of the brooks, and everything sown by the brooks will wither, be driven away, and be no more. {19:8} The fishermen will mourn, and all who cast their lines into the brooks will lament; those who spread nets upon the waters will be weak and exhausted. {19:9} Moreover, those who work with fine flax and weave networks will be ashamed. {19:10} All who make sluices and ponds for fish will be broken in their efforts. {19:11} Surely, the princes of Zoan are foolish; the wise counselors of Pharaoh have become senseless. How can you say to Pharaoh, "I am the son of the wise, the son of ancient kings?" {19:12} Where are they? Where are your wise men? Let them tell you now and let them know what the LORD of hosts has planned for Egypt. {19:13} The princes of Zoan have become fools, and the princes of Noph are deceived; they have misled Egypt, even those who are its main support. {19:14} The LORD has mixed a spirit of confusion in the midst of it; they have caused Egypt to err in all its work, like a drunken man reeling in his vomit. {19:15} There will be no work for Egypt that the head or tail, branch or rush, can do. {19:16} In that day, Egypt will be like women; it will be afraid and fear because of the shaking of the hand of the LORD of hosts that He shakes over it. {19:17} The land of Judah will be a terror to Egypt; everyone who mentions it will be afraid, because of the plan of the LORD of hosts that He has determined against it. {19:18} In that day, five cities in the land of Egypt will speak the language of Canaan and swear allegiance to the LORD of hosts; one will be called the City of Destruction. {19:19} In that day, there will be an altar to the LORD in the midst of the land of Egypt, and a pillar at its border dedicated to the LORD. {19:20} It will be a sign and a witness to the LORD of hosts in the land of Egypt; they will cry out to the LORD because of their oppressors, and He will send them a Savior, a great one, who will deliver them. {19:21} The LORD will be known to Egypt, and the Egyptians will know the LORD in that day and will offer sacrifices and offerings; yes, they will make vows to the LORD and fulfill them. {19:22} The LORD will strike Egypt; He will strike and then heal it, and they will return to the LORD, and He will be entreated by them and will heal them. {19:23} In that day, there will be a highway from Egypt to Assyria, and the Assyrians will come into Egypt, and the Egyptians into Assyria; the Egyptians will serve with the Assyrians. {19:24} In that day, Israel will be the third with Egypt and Assyria, a blessing in the midst of the land. {19:25} The LORD of hosts will bless them, saying, "Blessed be Egypt, My people, and Assyria, the work of My hands, and Israel, My inheritance."

{20:1} In the year that Tartan came to Ashdod (when Sargon, the king of Assyria, sent him), and fought against Ashdod and took it, {20:2} at that time, the LORD spoke through Isaiah, the son of Amoz, saying, "Go and remove the sackcloth from your waist and take off your sandals from your feet." And he did so, walking naked and barefoot. {20:3} The LORD said, "Just as My servant Isaiah has walked naked and barefoot for three years as a sign and a wonder against Egypt and Ethiopia, {20:4} so the king of Assyria will lead away the Egyptians as prisoners, and the Ethiopians as captives, young and old, naked and barefoot, even exposing their buttocks, to the shame of Egypt. {20:5} They will be afraid and ashamed of Ethiopia, their expectation, and of Egypt, their glory. {20:6} And the inhabitants of this isle will say in that day, 'Look, such is our expectation, where we flee for help to be delivered from the king of Assyria; and how shall we escape?'"

{21:1} This is the burden (prophecy) concerning the desert of the sea. Like whirlwinds in the south pass through, so it comes from the desert, from a terrifying land. {21:2} A distressing vision has been revealed to me; the treacherous one is dealing treacherously, and the plunderer is plundering. Go up, O Elam; lay siege, O Media; I have put an end to all its sighing. {21:3} Therefore my loins are filled with pain; pangs have taken hold of me like the pains of a woman in labor. I was bowed down at the hearing of it; I was dismayed at the sight of it. {21:4} My heart pounded; fear overwhelmed me. The night that brought me pleasure has turned into fear. {21:5} Prepare the table, watch in the watchtower, eat, drink; arise, you princes, and anoint the shield. {21:6} For the Lord said to me, "Go, set a watchman, let him declare what he sees." {21:7} He saw a chariot with horsemen, a chariot of donkeys, and a chariot of camels; he listened diligently with great care. {21:8} And he cried, "A lion!" My lord, I stand continually on the watchtower during the day and am stationed all night. {21:9} Look, here comes a chariot of men with horsemen." And he answered, "Babylon has fallen, has fallen; and all the carved images of her gods have been shattered to the ground." {21:10} O my threshing and the grain of my floor, what I have heard from the LORD of hosts, the God of Israel, I have declared to you. {21:11} The burden concerning Dumah. He calls to me from Seir, "Watchman, what of the night? Watchman, what of the night?" {21:12} The watchman said, "The morning comes, and also the night. If you will inquire, inquire; return, come." {21:13} The burden concerning Arabia. In the forest of Arabia, you will lodge, O traveling companies of Dedanim. {21:14} The inhabitants of the land of Tema brought water to him who was thirsty; they offered him bread when he fled. {21:15} For they fled from the swords, from the drawn sword, and from the bent bow, and from the severity of war. {21:16} For the Lord said to me, "Within a year, like the years of a hired worker, all the glory of Kedar will fail. {21:17} The remaining archers, the mighty men of the children of Kedar, will be diminished, for the LORD God of Israel has spoken it."

{22:1} This is the burden concerning the valley of vision. What is the matter with you now that you have completely gone up to the rooftops? {22:2} You who are full of tumult, a noisy city, a joyous city; your slain men are not killed with the sword nor dead in battle. {22:3} All your rulers have fled together; they are bound by the archers. All who are found in you are bound together, having fled from afar. {22:4} Therefore I said, "Look away from me; I will weep bitterly; do not try to comfort me because of the destruction of the daughter of my people." {22:5} For it is a day of trouble, a day of trampling, and a day of confusion from the Lord GOD of hosts in the valley of vision, breaking down the walls and crying to the mountains. {22:6} Elam bore the quiver with chariots of men and horsemen; Kir uncovered the shield. {22:7} It will come to pass that your choicest valleys will be full of chariots, and the horsemen will set themselves in order at the gate. {22:8} He uncovered the covering of Judah, and on that day you looked to the armor of the house of the forest. {22:9} You have seen the breaches in the city of David, that they are many; and you gathered the waters of the lower pool. {22:10} You have numbered the houses of Jerusalem, and you have broken down houses to fortify the wall. {22:11} You made a ditch between the two walls for the water of the old pool; but you have not looked to the Maker of it, nor had respect for Him who fashioned it long ago. {22:12} In that day the Lord GOD of hosts called for weeping and mourning, for baldness and for wearing sackcloth. {22:13} But look, joy and gladness, killing oxen, and slaughtering sheep, eating meat, and drinking wine; "Let us eat and drink, for tomorrow we die!" {22:14} It was revealed in my ears by the LORD of hosts, "Surely this iniquity will not be atoned for you until you die," says the Lord GOD of hosts. {22:15} Thus says the Lord GOD of hosts, "Go, get to this steward, even to Shebna, who is over the house, and say, {22:16} What are you doing here, and whom do you have here that you have hewn out a tomb for yourself here, as one who hews out a tomb on high and carves a dwelling for himself in the rock? {22:17} Look, the LORD will carry you away with a mighty captivity and will surely cover you. {22:18} He will surely violently toss you like a ball into a large country; there you will die, and there the chariots of your glory will be the shame of your lord's house. {22:19} I will drive you from your position, and from your station he will pull you down. {22:20} In that day, I will call My servant Eliakim, the son of Hilkiah. {22:21} I will clothe him with your robe and strengthen him with your belt, and I will commit your government into his hand; and he will be a father to the inhabitants of Jerusalem and to the house of Judah. {22:22} I will place the key of the house of David on his shoulder; he will open, and no one will shut; and he will shut, and no one will open. {22:23} I will fasten him like a nail in a sure place, and he will be a glorious throne to his father's house. {22:24} They will hang on him all the glory of his father's house, the offspring and the issue, all vessels of small quantity, from the vessels of cups to all the vessels of flagons. {22:25} In that day, says the LORD of hosts, the nail that is fastened in a sure place will be removed, cut down, and fall; and the burden that was upon it will be cut off, for the LORD has spoken it.

{23:1} This is the burden (prophecy) concerning Tyre. Howl, you ships of Tarshish, for it is laid waste, so that there is no house or entrance; it has been revealed to them from the land of Chittim. {23:2} Be still, you inhabitants of the island, you whom the merchants of Zidon, who cross the sea, have enriched. {23:3} The harvest from the river, the revenue of the seed of Sihor, is from the great waters, and Tyre is a marketplace for nations. {23:4} Be ashamed, O Zidon, for the sea has spoken, even the strength of the sea, saying, "I do not labor or give birth, nor do I nourish young men or raise up virgins." {23:5} Like the news concerning Egypt, they will be greatly pained at the news of Tyre. {23:6} Cross over to Tarshish; howl, you inhabitants of the island. {23:7} Is this your joyful city, whose origins are ancient? Its own feet will carry it far away to dwell. {23:8} Who has taken this counsel against Tyre, the crowning city, whose merchants are princes and whose traders are the honorable of the earth? {23:9} The LORD of hosts has planned it to bring down the pride of all glory and to humiliate all the honorable of the earth. {23:10} Pass through your land like a river, O daughter of Tarshish; there is no more strength. {23:11} He stretched out His hand over the sea, He shook the kingdoms. The LORD has given a command against the merchant city to destroy its strongholds. {23:12} He said, "You will no longer rejoice, O oppressed virgin, daughter of Zidon; arise, cross over to Chittim; there also you will find no rest." {23:13} Behold the land of the Chaldeans; this people did not exist until the Assyrian founded it for those who dwell in the wilderness. They built its towers and raised its palaces, and He brought it to ruin. {23:14} Howl, you ships of Tarshish, for your strength is laid waste. {23:15} In that day, Tyre will be forgotten for seventy years, like the days of one king; after the end of seventy years, Tyre will sing like a harlot. {23:16} Take a harp, go around the city, you forgotten harlot; make sweet melodies, sing many songs, so you may be remembered. {23:17} After seventy years, the LORD will visit Tyre, and she will return to her trade and will engage in illicit relations with all the kingdoms of the world on the face of the earth. {23:18} Her merchandise and her earnings will be sacred to the LORD; it will not be stored up or laid away; her merchandise will be for those who dwell before the LORD, to eat sufficiently, and for durable clothing.

{24:1} Behold, the LORD makes the earth empty and makes it waste; He turns it upside down and scatters its inhabitants. {24:2} It will be, as with the people, so with the priest; as with the servant, so with his master; as with the maid, so with her mistress; as with the buyer, so with the seller; as with the lender, so with the borrower; as with the taker of interest, so with the giver of interest. {24:3} The land will be completely emptied and utterly ruined, for the LORD has spoken this word. {24:4} The earth mourns and fades away; the world languishes and fades away; the haughty people of the earth languish. {24:5} The earth is also defiled under its inhabitants because they have transgressed the laws, changed the ordinances, and broken the everlasting covenant. {24:6}

Therefore, the curse has devoured the earth, and those who dwell in it are desolate; therefore the inhabitants of the earth are burned, and few people are left. {24:7} The new wine mourns; the vine languishes; all the merry-hearted sigh. {24:8} The joy of tambourines ceases; the sound of those who rejoice ends; the joy of the harp ceases. {24:9} They will not drink wine with a song; strong drink will be bitter to those who drink it. {24:10} The city of confusion is broken down; every house is shut up, so no one can enter. {24:11} There is a cry for wine in the streets; all joy is darkened; the mirth of the land is gone. {24:12} In the city, desolation is left, and the gate is struck with destruction. {24:13} When it shall be like this in the midst of the land among the people, it will be like the shaking of an olive tree and the gleaning of grapes when the harvest is done. {24:14} They will lift up their voice; they will sing for the majesty of the LORD; they will cry out from the sea. {24:15} Therefore glorify the LORD in the fires, even the name of the LORD God of Israel in the islands of the sea. {24:16} From the farthest part of the earth, we have heard songs, even glory to the righteous. But I said, "Woe to me! Woe to me! My leanness! My leanness! The treacherous dealers have dealt treacherously; yes, the treacherous dealers have dealt very treacherously." {24:17} Fear, and the pit, and the snare are upon you, O inhabitant of the earth. {24:18} It will come to pass that he who flees from the noise of fear will fall into the pit, and he who comes up out of the pit will be caught in the snare; for the windows from on high are opened, and the foundations of the earth shake. {24:19} The earth is utterly broken down; the earth is clean dissolved; the earth moves exceedingly. {24:20} The earth will reel to and fro like a drunkard and will be removed like a hut; and the transgression of it will be heavy upon it; it will fall and not rise again. {24:21} In that day, the LORD will punish the host of the high ones that are on high and the kings of the earth upon the earth. {24:22} They will be gathered together as prisoners are gathered in the pit and will be shut up in the prison; after many days, they will be visited. {24:23} Then the moon will be confounded, and the sun ashamed when the LORD of hosts reigns in Mount Zion and in Jerusalem and before His elders gloriously.

{25:1} O LORD, You are my God; I will exalt You and praise Your name, for You have done wonderful things; Your plans from long ago are faithfulness and truth. {25:2} For You have made a city into a heap, a fortified city into a ruin; a palace of strangers will never be rebuilt. {25:3} Therefore, strong people will glorify You; the city of terrifying nations will fear You. {25:4} For You have been a strength to the poor, a strength to the needy in their distress, a refuge from the storm, a shadow from the heat when the blast of the terrible ones is like a storm against a wall. {25:5} You will bring down the noise of strangers like heat in a dry place; even the heat will be like the shadow of a cloud; the pride of the terrible ones will be brought low. {25:6} And in this mountain, the LORD of hosts will prepare a feast of rich food, a feast of well-aged wines, of rich food full of marrow, of well-aged wines refined. {25:7} And He will destroy on this mountain the covering cast over all people and the veil that is spread over all nations. {25:8} He will swallow up death in victory, and the Lord GOD will wipe away tears from all faces; He will remove the disgrace of His people from all the earth, for the LORD has spoken it. {25:9} And it will be said in that day, "Look, this is our God; we have waited for Him, and He will save us. This is the LORD; we have waited for Him; we will be glad and rejoice in His salvation." {25:10} For on this mountain, the hand of the LORD will rest, and Moab will be trampled under Him, like straw is trampled down for the dung heap. {25:11} And He will spread out His hands in the midst of them like a swimmer spreads out his hands to swim, and He will bring down their pride along with the spoils of their hands. {25:12} And the fortress of the high walls will be brought low, laid low, and brought to the ground, even to the dust.

{26:1} In that day, this song will be sung in the land of Judah: "We have a strong city; salvation will God appoint for walls and bulwarks." {26:2} Open the gates so that the righteous nation that keeps the truth may enter in. {26:3} You will keep him in perfect peace, whose mind is stayed on You, because he trusts in You. {26:4} Trust in the LORD forever, for in the LORD JEHOVAH is everlasting strength. {26:5} For He brings down those who dwell on high; the lofty city, He lays low; He lays it low, even to the ground; He brings it to the dust. {26:6} The foot will tread it down, even the feet of the poor and the steps of the needy. {26:7} The way of the just is uprightness; You, most upright, weigh the path of the just. {26:8} Yes, in the way of Your judgments, O LORD, we have waited for You; the desire of our soul is for Your name and for the remembrance of You. {26:9} With my soul, I have desired You in the night; yes, with my spirit within me, I will seek You early; for when Your judgments are in the earth, the inhabitants of the world will learn righteousness. {26:10} Let favor be shown to the wicked, yet he will not learn righteousness; in the land of uprightness, he will deal unjustly and will not see the majesty of the LORD. {26:11} LORD, when Your hand is lifted up, they will not see; but they will see and be ashamed for their envy of the people; yes, the fire of Your enemies will devour them. {26:12} LORD, You will ordain peace for us, for You have also worked all our works in us. {26:13} O LORD our God, other lords besides You have had dominion over us; but by You only will we mention Your name. {26:14} They are dead; they will not live; they are deceased; they will not rise. Therefore, You have visited and destroyed them and made all their memory to perish. {26:15} You have increased the nation, O LORD; You have increased the nation; You are glorified; You have removed it far to all the ends of the earth. {26:16} LORD, in trouble, they have visited You; they poured out a prayer when Your chastening was upon them. {26:17} Like a woman with child, who draws near the time of her delivery, is in pain and cries out in her pangs; so have we been in Your sight, O LORD. {26:18} We have been with child; we have been in pain; we have, as it were, brought forth wind; we have not accomplished any deliverance in the earth; neither have the inhabitants of the world fallen. {26:19} Your dead shall live; together with my dead body, they will arise. Awake and sing, you who dwell in the dust; for Your dew is like the dew of herbs, and the earth will cast out the dead. {26:20} Come, my people, enter into your chambers and shut your doors about you; hide yourself for a little moment until the indignation is past. {26:21} For behold, the LORD comes out of His place to punish the inhabitants of the earth for their iniquity; the earth will also disclose her blood and will no longer cover her slain.

{27:1} In that day, the LORD with His fierce, great, and powerful sword will punish Leviathan, the piercing serpent, even Leviathan, the crooked serpent; and He will slay the dragon in the sea. {27:2} In that day, sing to her, "A vineyard of red wine." {27:3} I, the LORD, keep it; I will water it every moment; I will keep it night and day, so that no one hurts it. {27:4} I have no fury in Me: who would set thorns and briers against Me in battle? I would go through them; I would burn them all together. {27:5} Or let him take hold of My strength, that he may make peace with Me, and he will make peace with Me. {27:6} He will cause those who come from Jacob to take root; Israel will blossom and bud and fill the world with fruit. {27:7} Has He struck him as He struck those who struck him? Or has he been slain according to the slaughter of those slain by him? {27:8} In measure, when it shoots forth, You will debate with it; He stays His rough wind in the day of the east wind. {27:9} By this, Jacob's iniquity will be purged, and this is the entire fruit to take away his sin; when He makes all the stones of the altar like chalkstones that are broken, the groves and images will not stand. {27:10} Yet the fortified city will be desolate, the habitation forsaken and left like a wilderness; there the calf will feed and lie down, consuming its branches. {27:11} When its boughs are withered, they will be broken off; the women will come and set them on fire; for it is a people of no understanding; therefore, He who made them will not have mercy on them, and He who formed them will show them no favor. {27:12} And in that day, the LORD will beat off from the channel of the river to the stream of Egypt, and you will be gathered one by one, O children of Israel. {27:13} And in that day, a great trumpet will be blown, and those who were ready to perish in the land of Assyria & the outcasts in land of Egypt will come and worship the LORD on the holy mountain at Jerusalem.

{28:1} Woe to the crown of pride, to the drunkards of Ephraim, whose glorious beauty is a fading flower that is on the head of the fat valleys of those overcome with wine! {28:2} Behold, the Lord has a mighty and strong one, like a tempest of hail and a destroying storm, like a flood of mighty waters overflowing, who will cast down to the earth with His hand. {28:3} The crown of pride, the drunkards of Ephraim, will be trampled underfoot. {28:4} And the glorious beauty that is on the head of the fat valley will be a fading flower and like the early fruit before summer; when he who looks upon it sees it, while it is still in his hand, he eats it up. {28:5} In that day, the LORD of hosts will be for a crown of glory and for a diadem of beauty to the remnant of His people, {28:6} and for a spirit of judgment to him who sits in judgment, and for strength to those who turn the battle to the gate. {28:7} But they also have erred through wine, and through strong drink, they have gone astray; the priest and the prophet have erred through strong drink; they are swallowed up by wine; they go astray through strong drink; they err in vision and stumble in judgment. {28:8} For all tables are full of vomit and filthiness, so that there is no place clean. {28:9} Whom will He teach knowledge? And whom will He make to understand doctrine? Those who are weaned from milk and drawn from the breasts. {28:10} For precept must be upon precept, precept upon precept; line upon line, line upon line; here a little, and there a little. {28:11} For with stammering lips and another tongue, He will speak to this people. {28:12} To whom He said, "This is the rest with which you may cause the weary to rest; this is the refreshing," yet they would not hear. {28:13} But the word of the LORD was to them precept upon precept, precept upon precept; line upon line, line upon line; here a little, and there a little, so they might go and fall backward and be broken, and snared, and taken. {28:14} Therefore, hear the word of the LORD, you scornful men who rule this people in Jerusalem. {28:15} Because you have said, "We have made a covenant with death, and with hell we are in agreement; when the overflowing scourge passes through, it will not come to us; for we have made lies our refuge, and under falsehood we have hidden ourselves." {28:16} Therefore, thus says the Lord GOD: "Behold, I lay in Zion a foundation, a stone, a tested stone, a precious cornerstone, a sure foundation; he who believes will not act hastily." {28:17} Judgment will I lay to the line, and righteousness to the plumb line; and hail will sweep away the refuge of lies, and the waters will overflow the hiding place. {28:18} And your covenant with death will be annulled, and your agreement with hell will not stand; when the overflowing scourge passes through, then you will be trampled down by it. {28:19} As often as it goes forth, it will take you; for morning by morning it will pass over, by day and by night; it will be a vexation only to understand the report. {28:20} For the bed is shorter than a man can stretch on it, and the covering is narrower than he can wrap himself in it. {28:21} For the LORD will rise up as in Mount Perazim; He will be angry as in the valley of Gibeon, to do His work, His strange work, and to bring to pass His act, His strange act. {28:22} Now therefore, do not be mockers, lest your bands be made strong; for I have heard from the Lord GOD of hosts a destruction, even determined upon the whole earth. {28:23} Give ear, and hear my voice; listen and hear my speech. {28:24} Does the plowman plow all day to sow? Does he open and break up the clods of his ground? {28:25} When he has made plain the face of it, does he not cast abroad the fitches, and scatter the cummin, and cast in the principal wheat and the appointed barley and the rye in their place? {28:26} For his God instructs him in discretion and teaches him. {28:27} For the fitches are not threshed with a threshing instrument, nor is a cartwheel turned about upon the cummin; but the fitches are beaten out with a staff, and the cummin with a rod. {28:28} Bread corn is bruised because he will not always be threshing it, nor break it with the wheel of his cart, nor bruise it with his horsemen. {28:29} This also comes forth from the LORD of hosts, who is wonderful in counsel and excellent in working.

{29:1} Woe to Ariel, to Ariel, the city where David lived! Year after year, let them keep offering sacrifices. {29:2} Yet I will bring distress upon Ariel, and there will be heaviness and sorrow; it will be to Me like Ariel. {29:3} I will surround you and lay siege against you with a mound, and I will raise forts against you. {29:4} You will be brought down, and you will speak from the ground, and your speech will be low from the dust; your voice will be like that of a spirit speaking from the ground, and your words will whisper from the dust. {29:5} Moreover, the multitude of your strangers will be like tiny dust, and the multitude of the terrible ones will be like chaff that blows away; it will happen suddenly. {29:6} You will be visited by the LORD of hosts with thunder, and with earthquake, and great noise, with storm and tempest, and the flame of consuming fire. {29:7} And the multitude of all the nations that fight against Ariel, all who fight against her and her defenses, and distress her, will be like a dream from a night vision. {29:8} It will be like a hungry man dreaming he is eating, but when he awakens, his soul is empty; or like a thirsty man dreaming he is drinking, but when he awakens, he is faint, and his soul still craves: so will be the multitude of all the nations that fight against Mount Zion. {29:9} Be stunned and wonder; cry out and cry: they are drunk, but not with wine; they stagger, but not from strong drink. {29:10} For the LORD has poured out upon you the spirit of deep sleep and has closed your eyes; the prophets and your rulers, the seers, He has covered. {29:11} And the vision of all is like the words of a sealed book, which men give to someone who knows how to read, saying, "Read this, please," and he says, "I cannot; for it is sealed." {29:12} And the book is given to one who is uneducated, saying, "Read this, please," and he says, "I am not educated." {29:13} Therefore, the Lord said, "Because this people draw near to Me with their mouths and honor Me with their lips, but have removed their hearts far from Me, and their fear toward Me is taught by the precepts of men: {29:14} Therefore, behold, I will do a marvelous work among this people, a marvelous work and a wonder; for the wisdom of their wise men will perish, and the understanding of their prudent men will be hidden." {29:15} Woe to those who seek to hide their plans from the LORD, whose works are in the dark, and who say, "Who sees us? Who knows us?" {29:16} Surely your turning of things upside down will be like the potter's clay; for will the work say of him who made it, "He did not make me"? Or will the thing formed say of him who formed it, "He has no understanding"? {29:17} Is it not yet a little while until Lebanon is turned into a fruitful field, and the fruitful field is esteemed as a forest? {29:18} And in that day, the deaf will hear the words of the book, and the eyes of the blind will see out of obscurity and darkness. {29:19} The meek will also increase their joy in the LORD, and the poor among men will rejoice in the Holy One of Israel. {29:20} For the terrible one will be brought to nothing, and the scorner will be consumed, and all who watch for iniquity will be cut off: {29:21} those who make a man an offender for a word, and lay a snare for him who reproves in the gate, and turn aside the just for a trivial matter. {29:22} Therefore thus says the LORD, who redeemed Abraham, concerning the house of Jacob: Jacob will not now be ashamed, nor will his face turn pale. {29:23} But when he sees his children, the work of My hands, in his midst, they will sanctify My name and sanctify the Holy One of Jacob, and will fear the God of Israel. {29:24} Those who erred in spirit will come to understanding, and those who murmured will learn doctrine.

{30:1} Woe to the rebellious children, says the LORD, who take counsel, but not from Me; who cover themselves with a covering, but not of My Spirit, that they may add sin to sin: {30:2} who walk down to Egypt and have not asked at My mouth, to strengthen themselves in the strength of Pharaoh and to trust in the shadow of Egypt! {30:3} Therefore, the strength of Pharaoh will be your shame, and the trust in the shadow of Egypt will bring you confusion. {30:4} For his princes were at Zoan, and his ambassadors came to Hanes. {30:5} They were all ashamed of a people that could not benefit them, nor be a help or profit, but a shame and also a reproach. {30:6} The burden of the beasts of the south: into the land of trouble and anguish, where the young and old lion, the viper and fiery flying serpent come; they will carry their riches upon the shoulders of young donkeys and their treasures upon the humps of camels to a people that will not profit them. {30:7} For the Egyptians will help in vain, and to no purpose; therefore, I have cried concerning this: "Their strength is to sit still." {30:8} Now go, write it before them on a tablet and note it in a book, that it may be for the time to come forever and ever: {30:9} that this is a rebellious people, lying children, children who will not hear the law of the LORD: {30:10} who say to the seers, "Do not see"; and to the prophets, "Do not prophesy to us right things; speak to us smooth things, prophesy deceits: {30:11} get out of the way, turn aside from the path, cause the Holy One of Israel to cease from before us." {30:12} Therefore, thus says the Holy One of Israel: "Because you despise this word and trust in oppression and perverseness, and stay thereon: {30:13} this iniquity will be to you like a breach ready to fall, swelling out in a high wall, whose breaking comes suddenly at an instant. {30:14} He will break it like the breaking of a potter's vessel that is broken in pieces; He will not spare, so that there will not be found in its bursting a shard to take fire from the hearth or to take water from the pit. {30:15} For thus says the Lord GOD, the Holy One of Israel: "In returning and rest you will be saved; in quietness and confidence will be your strength," but you would not. {30:16} But you said, "No; we will flee upon horses"; therefore, you will flee: and, "We will ride upon swift horses"; therefore, those who pursue you will be swift. {30:17} One thousand will flee at the rebuke of one; at the rebuke of five you will flee, until you are left as a beacon on top of a mountain and like a flag on a hill. {30:18} And therefore the LORD will wait, that He may be gracious to you; and therefore He will be exalted, that He may have mercy on you; for the LORD is a God of judgment; blessed are all who wait for Him. {30:19} For the people will dwell in Zion at Jerusalem; you will weep no more. He will be very gracious to you at the sound of your cry; when He hears it, He will answer you. {30:20} And though the Lord gives you the bread of adversity and the water of affliction, yet your teachers will no longer be hidden, but your eyes will see your teachers: {30:21} and your ears will hear a word behind you saying, "This is the way; walk in it," whenever you turn to the right or the left. {30:22} You will also defile the covering of your carved images of silver and the ornament of your molten images of gold; you will cast them away like a menstruous cloth; you will say to it, "Get away from here." {30:23} Then He will give the rain for your seed that you will sow in the ground; and the bread from the increase of the earth, and it will be rich and plentiful; in that day your cattle will graze in large pastures. {30:24} The oxen and the young donkeys that work the ground will eat clean fodder, which has been winnowed with the shovel and the fan. {30:25} And there will be on every high mountain and every high hill rivers and streams of water in the day of the great slaughter, when the towers fall. {30:26} Moreover, the light of the moon will be like the light of the sun, and the light of the sun will be sevenfold, like the light of seven days, in the day that the LORD binds up the breach of His people and heals the stroke of their wound. {30:27} Behold, the name of the LORD comes from far away, burning with His anger, and the burden of it is heavy; His lips are full of indignation, and His tongue is like a devouring fire: {30:28} and His breath, like an overflowing stream, will reach to the midst of the neck, to sift the nations with the sieve of vanity, and there will be a bridle in the jaws of the people, causing them to err. {30:29} You will have a song, like in the night when a holy festival is kept; and gladness of heart, like when one goes with a flute to come into the mountain of the LORD, to the Mighty One of Israel. {30:30} And the LORD will cause His glorious voice to be heard, and will show the lightning down of His arm, with the indignation of His anger, and with the flame of a devouring fire, with scattering, tempest, and hailstones. {30:31} For through the voice of the LORD the Assyrian will be beaten down, who struck with a rod. {30:32} And in every place where the grounded staff will pass, which the LORD will lay upon him, it will be with tambourines and harps; and in the battles of shaking He will fight with it. {30:33} For Tophet is ordained of old; yes, for the king it is prepared; He has made it deep and large; the pile of it is fire and much wood; the breath of the LORD, like a stream of brimstone, will kindle it.

{31:1} Woe to those who go down to Egypt for help, who rely on horses and trust in chariots because they are many, and in horsemen because they are very strong; but they do not look to the Holy One of Israel, nor seek the LORD! {31:2} Yet He is also wise and will bring disaster; He will not take back His words but will rise against the house of evildoers and against the help of those who commit iniquity. {31:3} Now the Egyptians are just men, not God; and their horses are flesh, not spirit. When the LORD stretches out His hand, both the helper and the helped will fall, and they will all fail together. {31:4} For thus the LORD has spoken to me: like a lion and a young lion roaring over its prey, when a multitude of shepherds is called against it, it will not be afraid of their voices nor will it lower itself because of their noise; so the LORD of hosts will come down to fight for Mount Zion and its hill. {31:5} Like birds flying, so the LORD of hosts will defend Jerusalem; defending, He will deliver it; and passing over, He will preserve it. {31:6} Turn to Him from whom the children of Israel have deeply revolted. {31:7} For in that day, every man will cast away his silver and gold idols, which your own hands have made for sin. {31:8} Then the Assyrian will fall by a sword, not of a mighty man; and the sword, not of a common man, will devour him; but he will flee from the sword, and his young men will be dismayed. {31:9} He will retreat to his stronghold in fear, and his princes will be afraid of the standard, says the LORD, whose fire is in Zion and His furnace in Jerusalem.

{32:1} Behold, a king will reign in righteousness, and princes will rule with justice. {32:2} A man will be like a hiding place from the wind and a shelter from the tempest; like rivers of water in a dry place, like the shadow of a great rock in a weary land. {32:3} The eyes of those who see will not be dim, and the ears of those who hear will listen. {32:4} The heart of the rash will understand knowledge, and the tongues of the stammerers will speak plainly. {32:5} The vile person will no longer be called generous, nor will the miser be considered bountiful. {32:6} For the vile person will speak wickedness, and his heart will work iniquity, practicing hypocrisy and speaking error against the LORD, emptying the soul of the hungry and causing the thirsty to fail. {32:7} The instruments of the miser are evil; he devises wicked plans to destroy the poor with lying words, even when the needy speak rightly. {32:8} But the generous man devises generous things, and by his generosity he will stand. {32:9} Rise up, you women who are at ease; hear my voice, you careless daughters; give ear to my speech. {32:10} In many days and years you will be troubled, you careless women; for the harvest will fail, and the gathering will not come. {32:11} Tremble, you women who are at ease; be troubled, you careless ones; strip yourselves and make yourselves bare, and put sackcloth on your loins. {32:12} They will lament for the breasts, for the pleasant fields, for the fruitful vine. {32:13} Thorns and briers will come up in the land of My people; yes, upon all the houses of joy in the joyous city. {32:14} Because the palaces will be forsaken, the multitude of the city will be left; the forts and towers will become dens forever, a joy for wild donkeys, a pasture for flocks. {32:15} Until the Spirit is poured out upon us from on high, and the wilderness becomes a fruitful field, and the fruitful field is counted as a forest. {32:16} Then judgment will dwell in the wilderness, and righteousness will remain in the fruitful field. {32:17} And the work of righteousness will be peace, and the effect of righteousness, quietness and assurance forever. {32:18} My people will dwell in a peaceful habitation, in secure dwellings, and in quiet resting places; {32:19} when it hails, coming down on the forest, and the city will be laid low. {32:20} Blessed are you who sow beside all waters, who send out the feet of the ox and the donkey.

{33:1} Woe to you who plunder without being plundered, and deal treacherously without being dealt with treacherously! When you stop plundering, you will be plundered; when you end your treachery, they will be treacherous toward you. {33:2} O LORD, be gracious to us; we have waited for You. Be their strength every morning, our salvation in times of trouble. {33:3} At the noise of the tumult, the people fled; at Your rising, the nations were scattered. {33:4} Your plunder will be gathered like the gathering of locusts; like the rushing of locusts, they will run over them. {33:5} The LORD is exalted, for He dwells on high; He has filled Zion with justice and righteousness. {33:6} Wisdom and knowledge will be the stability of your times, and the strength of salvation; the fear of the LORD is His treasure. {33:7} Behold, their brave ones cry out; the ambassadors of peace weep bitterly. {33:8} The highways lie waste; the traveler ceases; he has broken the covenant and despised the cities, regarding no one. {33:9} The earth mourns and languishes; Lebanon is ashamed and cut down; Sharon is like a wilderness, and Bashan and Carmel shake off their fruits. {33:10} Now I will rise, says the LORD; now I will be exalted; now I will lift Myself up. {33:11} You will conceive chaff and bring forth stubble; your breath, like fire, will consume you. {33:12} The people will be like the burning of lime; like thorns cut up, they will be burned in the fire. {33:13} Hear, you who are far off, what I have done; and you who are near, acknowledge My might. {33:14} The sinners in Zion are afraid; trembling has seized the hypocrites. Who among us can dwell with the devouring fire? Who among us can dwell with everlasting burnings? {33:15} He who walks righteously and speaks uprightly; he who despises the gain of oppression, shakes his hands from holding bribes, stops his ears from hearing of bloodshed, and shuts his eyes from seeing evil— {33:16} he will dwell on high; his refuge will be the munitions of rocks; bread will be given to him; his waters will be sure. {33:17} Your eyes will see the king in his beauty; they will behold the land that is very far off. {33:18} Your heart will meditate terror. Where is the scribe? Where is the receiver? Where is he who counted the towers? {33:19} You will not see a fierce people, a people with a deeper language than you can perceive, of a stammering tongue that you cannot understand. {33:20} Look upon Zion, the city of our solemnities; your eyes will see Jerusalem, a quiet habitation, a tabernacle that will not be taken down; none of its stakes will ever be removed, nor will any of its cords be broken. {33:21} But there the glorious LORD will be for us a place of broad rivers and streams; where no galley with oars will pass, nor gallant ship sail by. {33:22} For the LORD is our judge, the LORD is our lawgiver, the LORD is our king; He will save us. {33:23} Your tackle is loosed; they could not strengthen their mast; they could not spread the sail; then the prey of a great spoil will be divided; the lame will take the prey. {33:24} And the inhabitants will not say, "I am sick"; the people who dwell there will be forgiven their iniquity.

{34:1} Come near, you nations, to hear; and listen, you people; let the earth hear and all that is in it, the world and all that comes from it. {34:2} For the LORD's indignation is upon all nations, and His fury upon all their armies; He has utterly destroyed them; He has delivered them to the slaughter. {34:3} Their slain will be cast out, and their stench will rise from their carcasses; and the mountains will melt with their blood. {34:4} All the host of heaven will be dissolved, and the heavens will be rolled up like a scroll; and all their host will fall down, like leaves falling from the vine and like figs from the fig tree. {34:5} For My sword will be bathed in heaven; behold, it will come down upon Idumea and upon the people of My curse, for judgment. {34:6} The sword of the LORD is filled with blood; it is made fat with fatness, and with the blood of lambs and goats, with the fat of the kidneys of rams; for the LORD has a sacrifice in Bozrah and a great slaughter in the land of Idumea. {34:7} And the unicorns will come down with them, and the bulls with the bullocks; their land will be soaked with blood, and their dust made fat with fatness. {34:8} For it is the day of the LORD's vengeance and the year of recompense for the controversy of Zion. {34:9} The streams will be turned into pitch, and the dust into brimstone, and the land will become burning pitch. {34:10} It will not be quenched night or day; its smoke will rise forever; from generation to generation, it will lie waste; none will pass through it forever and ever. {34:11} But the cormorant and the bittern will possess it; the owl and the raven will dwell in it; He will stretch out over it the line of confusion and the stones of emptiness. {34:12} They will call its nobles to the kingdom, but none will be there; and all its princes will be nothing. {34:13} Thorns will come up in its palaces, nettles and brambles in its fortresses; and it will be a habitation of jackals and a court for owls. {34:14} The wild beasts of the desert will meet with the wild beasts of the island; and the satyr will call to his fellow; the screech owl will rest there and find for herself a place of rest. {34:15} There the great owl will make her nest, lay eggs, hatch, and gather under her shadow; there the vultures will be gathered, each with her mate. {34:16} Seek from the book of the LORD and read; not one of these will fail; none will lack her mate; for My mouth has commanded, and His Spirit has gathered them. {34:17} He has cast the lot for them, and His hand has divided it for them by line; they will possess it forever; from generation to generation they will dwell there.

{35:1} The wilderness and the lonely places will be glad for them; the desert will rejoice and blossom like a rose. {35:2} It will bloom abundantly and rejoice with joy and singing; the glory of Lebanon will be given to it, the majesty of Carmel and Sharon; they will see the glory of the LORD and the majesty of our God. {35:3} Strengthen the weak hands and steady the feeble knees. {35:4} Say to those with fearful hearts, "Be strong, do not fear; behold, your God will come with vengeance, even God with recompense; He will come and save you." {35:5} Then the eyes of the blind will be opened, and the ears of the deaf will be unstopped. {35:6} Then the lame will leap like a deer, and the tongue of the mute will sing; for in the wilderness, waters will break out, and streams will flow in the desert. {35:7} The parched ground will become a pool, and the thirsty land springs of water; in the habitation of jackals, where they lay, there will be grass with reeds and rushes. {35:8} And there will be a highway, and a way, and it will be called the Way of Holiness; the unclean will not pass over it, but it will be for those; even if fools walk there, they will not go astray. {35:9} No lion will be there, nor will any ravenous beast go up on it; it will not be found there, but the redeemed will walk there. {35:10} And the ransomed of the LORD will return and come to Zion with songs and everlasting joy upon their heads; they will obtain joy and gladness, and sorrow and sighing will flee away.

{36:1} Now it came to pass in the fourteenth year of King Hezekiah that Sennacherib, king of Assyria, came against all the fortified cities of Judah and took them. {36:2} And the king of Assyria sent Rabshakeh from Lachish to Jerusalem to King Hezekiah with a great army. He stood by the conduit of the upper pool on the highway of the fuller's field. {36:3} Then Eliakim, the son of Hilkiah, who was over the household, Shebna the scribe, and Joah, the son of Asaph, the recorder, came out to him. {36:4} And Rabshakeh said to them, "Say now to Hezekiah, 'Thus says the great king, the king of Assyria: What confidence is this in which you trust? {36:5} I say, you speak empty words; I have counsel and strength for war. Now, on whom do you rely that you rebel against me? {36:6} Look, you trust in the staff of this broken reed, Egypt; if a man leans on it, it will pierce his hand. So is Pharaoh, king of Egypt, to all who trust in him. {36:7} But if you say to me, 'We trust in the LORD our God,' is it not He whose high places and altars Hezekiah has taken away, saying to Judah and Jerusalem, 'You shall worship before this altar'? {36:8} Now therefore, give pledges to my master, the king of Assyria, and I will give you two thousand horses if you are able to put riders on them. {36:9} How then will you turn away the face of one captain of the least of my master's servants and put your trust in Egypt for chariots and horsemen? {36:10} And am I now come up without the LORD against this land to destroy it? The LORD said to me, 'Go up against this land and destroy it.' {36:11} Then Eliakim, Shebna, and Joah said to Rabshakeh, "Speak, we pray you, to your servants in the Syrian language, for we understand it; and do not speak to us in the Jews' language, in the hearing of the people who are on the wall." {36:12} But Rabshakeh said, "Has my master sent me to your master and to you to speak these words? Has he not sent me to the men who sit on the wall, that they may eat their own dung and drink their own urine with you?" {36:13} Then Rabshakeh stood and cried with a loud voice in the Jews' language, saying, "Hear the words of the great king, the king of Assyria! {36:14} Thus says the king: 'Let not Hezekiah deceive you, for he will not be able to deliver you. {36:15} Nor let Hezekiah make you trust in the LORD, saying, "The LORD will surely deliver us; this city will not be given into the hand of the king of Assyria." {36:16} Do not listen to Hezekiah; for thus says the king of Assyria: "Make a bargain with me by a present and come out to me; and eat every one of his vine and every one of his fig tree, and drink every one the waters of his own cistern; {36:17} until I come and take you away to a land like your own land, a land of corn and wine, a land of bread and vineyards." {36:18} Beware lest Hezekiah persuade you, saying, "The LORD will deliver us." Has any of the gods of the nations delivered his land out of the hand of the king of Assyria? {36:19} Where are the gods of Hamath and Arphad? Where are the gods of Sepharvaim? And have they delivered Samaria out of my hand? {36:20} Who among all the gods of these lands has delivered their land out of my hand, that the LORD should deliver Jerusalem out of my hand?" {36:21} But they held their peace and answered him not a word, for the king's command was, "Do not answer him." {36:22} Then Eliakim, the son of Hilkiah, who was over the household, Shebna the scribe, and Joah, the son of Asaph, the recorder, came to Hezekiah with their clothes torn and told him the words of Rabshakeh.

{37:1} When King Hezekiah heard this, he tore his clothes, put on sackcloth, and went into the house of the LORD. {37:2} He sent Eliakim, who was in charge of the household, Shebna the scribe, and the elders of the priests, all dressed in sackcloth, to Isaiah the prophet, the son of Amoz. {37:3} They said to him, "This is what Hezekiah says: 'Today is a day of trouble, rebuke, and blasphemy; the children have come to the point of birth, but there is no strength to deliver them.' {37:4} It may be that the LORD your God will hear the words of Rabshakeh, whom the king of Assyria has sent to defy the living God, and will reprove the words that the LORD your God has heard. Therefore, lift up your prayer for the remnant that is left." {37:5} So the servants of King Hezekiah came to Isaiah. {37:6} Isaiah said to them, "Say to your master, 'Thus says the LORD: Do not be afraid of the words you have heard from the servants of the king of Assyria, who have blasphemed Me. {37:7} Look, I will send a spirit upon him, and he will hear a rumor and return to his own land; and I will cause him to fall by the sword in his own land.'" {37:8} So Rabshakeh returned and found the king of Assyria fighting against Libnah, for he had heard that he had departed from Lachish. {37:9} He heard that Tirhakah, king of Ethiopia, had come out to fight against him. When he heard this, he sent messengers to Hezekiah, saying, {37:10} "Say to Hezekiah, king of Judah: 'Let not your God in whom you trust deceive you, saying, "Jerusalem will not be given into the hand of the king of Assyria." {37:11} Look, you have heard what the kings of Assyria have done to all the lands, destroying them utterly; and will you be delivered? {37:12} Have the gods of the nations delivered those whom my fathers have destroyed, such as Gozan, Haran, Rezeph, and the children of Eden in Telassar? {37:13} Where is the king of Hamath, the king of Arphad, and the king of the city of Sepharvaim, Hena, and Ivah?" {37:14} Hezekiah received the letter from the messengers and read it; then he went up to the house of the LORD and spread it before the LORD. {37:15} Hezekiah prayed to the LORD, saying, {37:16} "O LORD of hosts, God of Israel, who dwells between the cherubim, You alone are God of all the kingdoms of the earth; You have made heaven and earth. {37:17} Incline Your ear, O LORD, and hear; open Your eyes, O LORD, and see; hear all the words of Sennacherib, who has sent to defy the living God. {37:18} Truly, O LORD, the kings of Assyria have laid waste all the nations and their lands, {37:19} and have cast their gods into the fire; for they were no gods, but the work of men's hands, wood and stone. Therefore, they have destroyed them. {37:20} Now, therefore, O LORD our God, save us from his hand, that all the kingdoms of the earth may know that You are the LORD, You alone." {37:21} Then Isaiah, son of Amoz, sent to Hezekiah, saying, "Thus says the LORD God of Israel: Because you have prayed to Me against Sennacherib, king of Assyria, {37:22} this is the word the LORD has spoken concerning him: 'The virgin, the daughter of Zion, has despised you and laughed you to scorn; the daughter of Jerusalem has shaken her head at you. {37:23} Whom have you reproached and blasphemed? Against whom have you exalted your voice and lifted up your eyes on high? Against the Holy One of Israel! {37:24} By your servants you have reproached the LORD, and have said, "By the multitude of my chariots I have come up to the height of the mountains, to the sides of Lebanon; I will cut down its tall cedars and the best fir trees; I will enter the height of its border, and the forest of its Carmel." {37:25} I have dug wells and drunk water, and with the sole of my feet I have dried up all the rivers of besieged places. {37:26} Have you not heard long ago how I have done it, and of ancient times that I formed it? Now I have brought it to pass that you should lay waste fortified cities into ruinous heaps. {37:27} Therefore, their inhabitants were of little power; they were dismayed and confounded; they were like the grass of the field and the green herb, like the grass on the rooftops, and like corn blasted before it is grown. {37:28} But I know your dwelling place, your going out, and your coming in, and your rage against Me. {37:29} Because your rage against Me and your tumult have come up into My ears, I will put My hook in your nose and My bridle in your lips, and I will turn you back by the way by which you came.' {37:30} And this shall be a sign to you: You shall eat this year what grows of itself, in the second year what springs from that; and in the third year sow and reap, plant vineyards, and eat the fruit of them. {37:31} And the remnant that has escaped of the house of Judah shall again take root downward and bear fruit upward. {37:32} For out of Jerusalem shall go forth a remnant, and those who escape from Mount Zion: the zeal of the LORD of hosts will do this. {37:33} Therefore, thus says the LORD concerning the king of Assyria: He shall not come into this city, nor shoot an arrow there, nor come before it with shields, nor cast a bank against it. {37:34} By the way that he came, by the same he shall return, and shall not come into this city, says the LORD. {37:35} For I will defend this city to save it for My own sake and for My servant David's sake." {37:36} Then the angel of the LORD went forth and struck down in the camp of the Assyrians a hundred and eighty-five thousand; when they arose early in the morning, behold, they were all dead bodies. {37:37} So Sennacherib, king of Assyria, departed and went back home and dwelt at Nineveh. {37:38} It came to pass that as he was worshiping in the house of Nisroch, his god, Adrammelech and Sharezer, his sons, struck him down with the sword; and they escaped into the land of Armenia, and Esarhaddon, his son, reigned in his place.

{38:1} In those days, Hezekiah was sick to the point of death. Isaiah the prophet, the son of Amoz, came to him and said, "Thus says the LORD: Set your house in order, for you shall die and not live." {38:2} Then Hezekiah turned his face to the wall and prayed to the LORD, {38:3} saying, "Remember now, O LORD, I beg You, how I have walked before You in truth and with a perfect heart, and have done what is good in Your sight." And Hezekiah wept bitterly. {38:4} Then the word of the LORD came to Isaiah, saying, {38:5} "Go, and say to Hezekiah: 'Thus says the LORD, the God of David your father: I have heard your prayer, I have seen your tears; behold, I will add to your days fifteen years. {38:6} I will deliver you and this city from the hand of the king of Assyria, and I will defend this city. {38:7} This shall be a sign to you from the LORD that the LORD will do this thing that He has spoken: {38:8} Look, I will bring the shadow of the sundial of Ahaz back ten degrees." So the sun returned ten degrees on the sundial by which it had gone down. {38:9} This is the writing of Hezekiah, king of Judah, when he had been sick and had recovered from his sickness: {38:10} "I said, 'In the prime of my life I shall go to the gates of the grave; I am deprived of the rest of my years. {38:11} I said, "I shall not see the LORD, the LORD in the land of the living; I shall look upon man no more among the inhabitants of the world. {38:12} My age is departed, and is removed from me like a shepherd's tent; I have cut off like a weaver my life; He will cut me off with pining sickness; from day to night You will make an end of me.' {38:13} I counted until morning, like a lion, so will He break all my bones; from day to night You will make an end of me. {38:14} Like a crane or a swallow, I chattered; I mourned like a dove; my eyes fail from looking upward; O LORD, I am oppressed; undertake for me. {38:15} What shall I say? He has both spoken to me and Himself has done it; I shall walk softly all my years in the bitterness of my soul. {38:16} O Lord, by these things men live, and in all these things is the life of my spirit; so will You recover me and make me live. {38:17} Look, for peace I had great bitterness; but You, in love for my soul, have delivered it from the pit of corruption; for You have cast all my sins behind Your back. {38:18} For the grave cannot praise You; death cannot celebrate You; those who go down into the pit cannot hope for Your truth. {38:19} The living, the living, he shall praise You, as I do this day; the father shall make known Your truth to the children. {38:20} The LORD was ready to save me; therefore, we will sing my songs with stringed instruments all the days of our life in the house of the LORD. {38:21} For Isaiah had said, "Let them take a lump of figs and lay it as a plaster on the boil, and he shall recover." {38:22} Hezekiah also said, "What is the sign that I shall go up to the house of the LORD?"

{39:1} At that time, Merodachbaladan, the son of Baladan, king of Babylon, sent letters and a gift to Hezekiah because he had heard that he had been sick and had recovered. {39:2} Hezekiah was pleased with them and showed them the treasures of his house: the silver, gold, spices, precious ointments, all his armor, and everything in his treasures; there was nothing in his house or in all his realm that Hezekiah did not show them. {39:3} Then Isaiah the prophet came to King Hezekiah and asked him, "What did these men say, and where did they come from?" Hezekiah replied, "They have come from a distant country to me, from Babylon." {39:4} Isaiah asked, "What have they seen in your house?" Hezekiah answered, "They have seen everything in my house; there is nothing among my treasures that I have not shown them." {39:5} Then Isaiah said to Hezekiah, "Hear the word of the LORD of hosts: {39:6} Behold, the days are coming when all that is in your house and what your ancestors have stored up until this day will be carried to Babylon; nothing will be left, says the LORD. {39:7} And some of your descendants who come from you, whom you will father, will be taken away; they will be eunuchs in the palace of the king of Babylon." {39:8} Then Hezekiah said to Isaiah, "The word of the LORD you have spoken is good." He added, "For there will be peace and truth in my days."

{40:1} "Comfort, comfort my people," says your God. {40:2} "Speak kindly to Jerusalem and proclaim to her that her warfare is ended, that her sin is forgiven; for she has received from the LORD's hand double for all her sins." {40:3} A voice cries out: "Prepare the way of the LORD; make straight in the desert a highway for our God. {40:4} Every valley shall be lifted up, and every mountain and hill made low; the uneven ground shall become level, and the rough places a plain. {40:5} And the glory of the LORD shall be revealed, and all flesh shall see it together, for the mouth of the LORD has spoken." {40:6} A voice said, "Cry out." And I said, "What shall I cry?" "All flesh is grass, and all its beauty is like the flower of the field. {40:7} The grass withers, the flower fades when the breath of the LORD blows upon it; surely the people are grass. {40:8} The grass withers, the flower fades, but the word of our God will stand forever." {40:9} O Zion, you who bring good news, go up to a high mountain; O Jerusalem, you who bring good news, lift up your voice with strength; lift it up, fear not; say to the cities of Judah, "Behold your God!" {40:10} Behold, the Lord GOD comes with might, and His arm rules for Him; behold, His reward is with Him, and His work is before Him. {40:11} He will tend His flock like a shepherd; He will gather the lambs in His arms, and carry them in His bosom and gently lead those that are with young. {40:12} Who has measured the waters in the hollow of His hand and marked off the heavens with a span, enclosed the dust of the earth in a measure, and weighed the mountains in scales and the hills in a balance? {40:13} Who has directed the Spirit of the LORD, or as His counselor has taught Him? {40:14} Whom did He consult to enlighten Him, and who taught Him the path of justice and taught Him knowledge, and showed Him the way of understanding? {40:15} Behold, the nations are like a drop from a bucket, and are counted as the small dust of the balance; behold, He takes up the isles like fine dust. {40:16} Lebanon would not suffice for fuel, nor are its beasts enough for a burnt offering. {40:17} All nations before Him are as nothing, and they are counted by Him less than nothing and emptiness. {40:18} To whom then will you liken God? Or what likeness will you compare with Him? {40:19} The craftsman casts an idol, and the goldsmith overlays it with gold and casts silver chains. {40:20} He who is too impoverished for an offering chooses wood that will not rot; he seeks out a skillful craftsman to set up an idol that will not move. {40:21} Have you not known? Have you not heard? Has it not been told to you from the beginning? Have you not understood from the foundations of the earth? {40:22} It is He who sits above the circle of the earth, and its inhabitants are like grasshoppers; who stretches out the heavens like a curtain, and spreads them like a tent to dwell in; {40:23} who brings princes to nothing and makes the rulers of the earth as emptiness. {40:24} Scarcely are they planted, scarcely sown, scarcely has their stem taken root in the earth, when He blows on them and they wither, and the tempest carries them off like stubble. {40:25} To whom then will you compare me, or who is my equal? says the Holy One. {40:26} Lift up your eyes on high and see: who created these? He who brings out their host by number, calling them all by name; by the greatness of His might and because He is strong in power, not one is missing. {40:27} Why do you say, O Jacob, and speak, O Israel, "My way is hidden from the LORD, and my right is disregarded by my God"? {40:28} Have you not known? Have you not heard? The everlasting God, the LORD, the Creator of the ends of the earth, does not grow faint or weary; His understanding is unsearchable. {40:29} He gives power to the faint, and to him who has no might, He increases strength. {40:30} Even youths shall faint and be weary, and young men shall fall exhausted; {40:31} but they who wait for the LORD shall renew their strength; they shall mount up with wings like eagles; they shall run & not be weary; they shall walk and not faint.

{41:1} "Be silent before me, O islands; let the people renew their strength. Let them come near and speak; let us come together for judgment. {41:2} Who raised up the righteous man from the east, called him to his feet, gave nations into his hands, and made him ruler over kings? He made them like dust for his sword and like chaff for his bow. {41:3} He pursued them and passed safely, even on a path he had never traveled. {41:4} Who has accomplished this, calling forth the generations from the beginning? I, the LORD, am the first, and I am also the last. {41:5} The islands saw it and feared; the ends of the earth were afraid, drawing near and coming together. {41:6} They helped one another, each encouraged their neighbor, saying, "Be strong!" {41:7} The carpenter encouraged the goldsmith, and the one who smooths with the hammer supported him who struck the anvil, saying, "It is ready for soldering." He fastened it with nails so it wouldn't be moved. {41:8} But you, Israel, are my servant, Jacob whom I have chosen, the descendants of Abraham my friend. {41:9} I took you from the ends of the earth and called you from its farthest corners, saying, "You are my servant; I have chosen you and not rejected you." {41:10} Do not fear, for I am with you; do not be dismayed, for I am your God. I will strengthen you; yes, I will help you; I will uphold you with my righteous right hand. {41:11} Look, all who were angry with you will be ashamed and confounded; they will be as nothing, and those who contend with you will perish. {41:12} You will seek them and not find them; those who wage war against you will be like nothing at all. {41:13} For I, the LORD your God, hold your right hand, saying to you, "Do not fear; I will help you." {41:14} Do not fear, you worm Jacob, and you people of Israel; I will help you, says the LORD, and your Redeemer, the Holy One of Israel. {41:15} Look, I will make you a new sharp threshing instrument with teeth; you will thresh the mountains and crush them, and make the hills like chaff. {41:16} You will winnow them, and the wind will carry them away, and the whirlwind will scatter them; you will rejoice in the LORD and glory in the Holy One of Israel. {41:17} When the poor and needy seek water and there is none, and their tongues fail for thirst, I, the LORD, will hear them; I, the God of Israel, will not forsake them. {41:18} I will open rivers in high places and fountains in the midst of valleys; I will make the wilderness a pool of water, and the dry land springs of water. {41:19} I will plant in the wilderness the cedar, the acacia, the myrtle, and the olive tree; I will set in the desert the fir tree, the pine, and the box tree together, {41:20} so that they may see, know, consider, and understand together that the hand of the LORD has done this, and the Holy One of Israel has created it. {41:21} Present your case, says the LORD; bring forth your strong reasons, says the King of Jacob. {41:22} Let them bring them forth and show us what will happen; let them show the former things, what they were, so we may consider them and know their latter end; or declare to us things to come. {41:23} Show us things that are to come hereafter, so we may know that you are gods; do good or do evil, that we may be dismayed and see it together. {41:24} Look, you are nothing, and your work is worthless; he who chooses you is an abomination. {41:25} I have raised one up from the north, and he will come; from the rising of the sun he will call on my name. He will come against princes as if they were mortar, and as a potter treads clay. {41:26} Who has declared this from the beginning, that we may know? And before time, that we may say, "He is righteous"? There is none who shows, there is none who declares, there is none who hears your words. {41:27} The first shall say to Zion, "Look, here they are"; and I will give to Jerusalem one who brings good tidings. {41:28} I looked, and there was no man; even among them, there was no counselor, that when I asked them, could answer a word. {41:29} Look, they are all vanity; their works are nothing; their molten images are wind and confusion.

{42:1} "Look at my servant, whom I uphold; my chosen one, in whom my soul delights. I have put my Spirit upon him; he will bring forth justice to the nations. {42:2} He will not shout or raise his voice, nor make it heard in the street. {42:3} A bruised reed he will not break, and a faintly burning wick he will not quench; he will bring forth justice in truth. {42:4} He will not falter or be discouraged until he has established justice on the earth; and the islands will wait for his law. {42:5} Thus says God the LORD, who created the heavens and stretched them out, who spread out the earth and what comes from it, who gives breath to the people on it and spirit to those who walk in it: {42:6} I, the LORD, have called you in righteousness, and will take you by the hand and keep you; I will give you as a covenant for the people, a light for the nations, {42:7} to open blind eyes, to bring out prisoners from the dungeon, and those who sit in darkness from the prison house. {42:8} I am the LORD; that is my name; my glory I will not give to another, nor my praise to carved idols. {42:9} Look, the former things have come to pass, and new things I now declare; before they spring forth I tell you of them. {42:10} Sing to the LORD a new song, and his praise from the end of the earth, you who go down to the sea and all that is in it, the coasts and their inhabitants. {42:11} Let the wilderness and its cities lift up their voice, the villages that Kedar inhabits; let the inhabitants of the rock sing, let them shout from the mountaintops. {42:12} Let them give glory to the LORD and declare his praise in the islands. {42:13} The LORD shall go forth like a mighty warrior; he will stir up his zeal like a man of war; he will cry out, yes, he will shout; he will prevail against his enemies. {42:14} I have long time held my peace; I have been still and restrained myself; now I will cry out like a woman in labor; I will destroy and devour at once. {42:15} I will make waste mountains and hills and dry up all their vegetation; I will turn rivers into islands, and dry up the pools. {42:16} I will lead the blind by a way they did not know; I will guide them in paths they have not known; I will make darkness light before them, and crooked places straight. These things I will do for them, and not forsake them. {42:17} They shall be turned back; they shall be greatly ashamed, those who trust in carved images, who say to the molten images, "You are our gods." {42:18} Hear, you deaf; and look, you blind, that you may see. {42:19} Who is blind but my servant? Or deaf as my messenger that I sent? Who is blind as he who is perfect, and blind as the LORD's servant? {42:20} Seeing many things, but you do not observe; opening the ears, but he does not hear. {42:21} The LORD is pleased for his righteousness' sake; he will magnify the law and make it honorable. {42:22} But this is a people robbed and spoiled; they are all snared in holes, and hidden in prison houses; they are for prey, and no one delivers; for spoil, and no one says, "Restore." {42:23} Who among you will listen to this? Who will hear and heed for the time to come? {42:24} Who gave Jacob for spoil and Israel to the robbers? Was it not the LORD, against whom we have sinned? For they would not walk in his ways, nor were they obedient to his law. {42:25} Therefore he poured out on him the fury of his anger and the strength of battle; and it set him on fire round about, yet he did not know; and it burned him, yet he did not lay it to heart.

{43:1} But now, says the LORD who created you, Jacob, and formed you, Israel, do not fear; for I have redeemed you, I have called you by name; you are mine. {43:2} When you pass through the waters, I will be with you; and when you go through the rivers, they will not overwhelm you; when you walk through fire, you will not be burned; the flames will not set you ablaze. {43:3} For I am the LORD your God, the Holy One of Israel, your Savior; I gave Egypt as your ransom, Cush and Seba in exchange for you. {43:4} Since you are precious in my sight, and honored, and I love you, I will give people in exchange for you, and nations for your life. {43:5} Do not fear, for I am with you; I will bring your descendants from the east, and gather you from the west; {43:6} I will say to the north, "Give them up!" and to the south, "Do not hold them back!" Bring my sons from afar and my daughters from the ends of the earth; {43:7} everyone who is called by my name, whom I created for my glory, whom I formed and made. {43:8} Bring out the blind people who have eyes and the deaf who have ears. {43:9} Let all the nations gather together, and let the people assemble; who among them can declare this and show us the former things? Let them bring their witnesses so they may be justified, or let them hear and say, "It is true." {43:10} You are my witnesses, says the LORD, and my servant whom I have chosen, so that you may know and believe me and understand that I am he; before me no god was formed, nor will there be any after me. {43:11} I, even I, am the LORD, and apart from me there is no Savior. {43:12} I have revealed and saved and proclaimed—I am not some foreign god among you; you are my witnesses, says the LORD, that I am God. {43:13} Yes, from ancient days I am he; no one can deliver out of my hand. When I act, who can reverse it? {43:14} This is what the LORD says, your Redeemer, the Holy One of Israel: For your sake I will send to Babylon and bring down as fugitives all the Babylonians, in the ships in which they took pride. {43:15} I am the LORD, your Holy One, the Creator of Israel, your King. {43:16} This is what the LORD says—he who made a way through the sea, a path through the mighty waters, {43:17} who drew out the chariots and horses, the army and reinforcements together, and they lay there, never to rise again, extinguished, snuffed out like a wick. {43:18} Forget the former things; do not dwell on the past. {43:19} See, I am doing a new thing! Now it springs up; do you not perceive it? I am making a way in the wilderness and streams in the wasteland. {43:20} The wild animals honor me, the jackals and the owls, because I provide water in the wilderness and streams in the wasteland, to give drink to my people, my chosen, {43:21} the people I formed for myself that they may proclaim my praise. {43:22} Yet you have not called on me, Jacob; you have not wearied yourselves for me, Israel. {43:23} You have not brought me sheep for burnt offerings, nor honored me with your sacrifices. I have not burdened you with grain offerings nor wearied you with demands for incense. {43:24} You have not bought me fragrant calamus (a type of plant) with money, nor have you filled me with the fat of your sacrifices. But you have burdened me with your sins and wearied me with your offenses. {43:25} I, even I, am he who blots out your transgressions for my own sake, and remembers your sins no more. {43:26} Review the past for me, let us argue the matter together; state your case so that you can be proved right. {43:27} Your first father (ancestor) sinned; those I sent to teach you rebelled against me. {43:28} So I disgraced the dignitaries of your temple; I consigned Jacob to destruction and Israel to scorn.

{44:1} Yet hear me now, Jacob my servant, Israel whom I have chosen: {44:2} This is what the LORD says—he who made you, who formed you in the womb, and who will help you: Do not be afraid, Jacob, my servant; Jeshurun (a poetic name for Israel) whom I have chosen. {44:3} For I will pour water on the thirsty land and streams on the dry ground; I will pour out my Spirit on your offspring and my blessing on your descendants. {44:4} They will spring up like grass in a meadow, like poplar trees by flowing streams. {44:5} One will say, "I belong to the LORD"; another will call himself by the name of Jacob; still another will write on his hand, "The LORD's," and will take the name Israel. {44:6} This is what the LORD says—Israel's King and Redeemer, the LORD Almighty: I am the first and I am the last; apart from me there is no God. {44:7} Who then is like me? Let him proclaim it. Let him declare and lay out before me what has happened since I established my ancient people, and what is yet to come—yes, let them foretell what will come. {44:8} Do not tremble; do not be afraid. Did I not proclaim this and foretell it long ago? You are my witnesses. Is there any God besides me? No, there is no other Rock; I know not one. {44:9} All who make idols are nothing, and the things they treasure are worthless. Those who would speak up for them are blind; they are ignorant, to their own shame. {44:10} Who shapes a god and casts an idol, which can profit nothing? {44:11} People who do that will be put to shame; such craftsmen are only human beings. Let them all come together and take their stand; they will be brought down to terror and shame. {44:12} The blacksmith takes a tool and works with it in the coals; he shapes an idol with hammers and forges it with the might of his arm. He gets hungry and loses his strength; he drinks no water and grows tired. {44:13} The carpenter measures with a line and makes an outline with a marker; he shapes it with chisels and marks it with compasses. He shapes it like a human being, like a beautiful person, to dwell in a shrine. {44:14} He cuts down cedars, or perhaps takes a cypress or oak. He lets it grow among the trees of the forest, or plants a pine, and the rain makes it grow. {44:15} It is used as fuel for burning; some of it he takes and warms himself; he kindles a fire and bakes bread; but he also fashions a god and worships it; he makes an idol and bows down to it. {44:16} Half of the wood he burns in the fire; over it he prepares his meal; he roasts his meat and eats his fill. He also warms himself and says, "Ah! I am warm; I see the fire." {44:17} From the rest he makes a god, his idol; he bows down to it and worships it; he prays to it and says, "Save me; you are my god." {44:18} They know nothing; they understand nothing; their eyes are plastered over so they cannot see, and their minds closed so they cannot understand. {44:19} No one stops to think; no one has the knowledge or understanding to say, "Half of it I used for fuel; I even baked bread over its coals, I roasted meat and I ate. Shall I make a detestable thing from what is left? Shall I bow down to a block of wood?" {44:20} Such a person feeds on ashes; a deluded heart misleads him; he cannot save himself, or say, "Is not this thing in my right hand a lie?" {44:21} Remember these things, Jacob, for you are my servant; Israel, I have made you; you are my servant; I will not forget you, Israel. {44:22} I have swept away your offenses like a cloud, your sins like the morning mist. Return to me, for I have redeemed you. {44:23} Sing for joy, you heavens, for the LORD has done this; shout, you earth below. Burst into song, you mountains, you forests, and all your trees, for the LORD has redeemed Jacob; he displays his glory in Israel. {44:24} This is what the LORD says—your Redeemer, who formed you in the womb: I am the LORD, who has made all things, who alone stretched out the heavens, who spread out the earth by myself; {44:25} who foils the signs of false prophets and makes fools of diviners, who overthrows the learning of the wise and turns it into nonsense, {44:26} who carries out the words of his servants and fulfills the predictions of his messengers; who says of Jerusalem, "It will be inhabited," of the towns of Judah, "They will be rebuilt," and of their ruins, "I will restore them." {44:27} Who says to the watery deep, "Be dry, and I will dry up your streams," {44:28} who says of Cyrus, "He is my shepherd and will accomplish all that I please; he will say of Jerusalem, 'Let it be rebuilt,' and of the temple, 'Let its foundations be laid.'"

{45:1} This is what the LORD says to his anointed, to Cyrus, whose right hand I have grasped to subdue nations before him; I will loosen the belts of kings and open the double doors before him, so that the gates will not be shut. {45:2} I will go before you and make the crooked paths straight; I will shatter the bronze gates and cut through the iron bars. {45:3} I will give you treasures hidden in darkness and riches stored in secret places, so that you may know that I, the LORD, who calls you by your name, am the God of Israel. {45:4} For the sake of my servant Jacob and Israel my chosen, I have called you by your name; I have given you a title, though you do not know me. {45:5} I am the LORD, and there is no other; there is no God besides me. I equipped you, though you do not know me. {45:6} So that from the east to the west, people may know that there is no one besides me. I am the LORD, and there is no other. {45:7} I create the light and make darkness; I bring peace and create disaster. I, the LORD, do all these things. {45:8} Let the heavens rain down righteousness; let the skies pour down salvation; let the earth open wide and let righteousness blossom; I, the LORD, have created it. {45:9} Woe to anyone who argues with their Maker! To the clay pot among the pots of the earth, does the clay say to the potter, "What are you making?" or "Your work has no hands?" {45:10} Woe to anyone who asks their father, "What are you begetting?" or to a woman, "What are you giving birth to?" {45:11} This is what the LORD, the Holy One of Israel, and your Maker says: Ask me about things to come concerning my children, and command me regarding the work of my hands. {45:12} I made the earth and created mankind on it; with my own hands I stretched out the heavens and commanded all their starry host. {45:13} I raised him up in righteousness, and I will make all his paths straight; he will rebuild my city and set my exiles free, not for a price or reward, says the LORD Almighty. {45:14} This is what the LORD says: The wealth of Egypt and the merchandise of Cush and the Sabeans (people from a region in Africa), tall men will come to you and be yours; they will come over in chains and bow down before you, saying, "Surely God is with you, and there is no other; there is no other God." {45:15} Truly, you are a God who hides himself, O God of Israel, the Savior. {45:16} All of them will be put to shame; those who make idols will be disgraced together. {45:17} But Israel will be saved by the LORD with an everlasting salvation; you will never be put to shame or disgraced, to ages everlasting. {45:18} For this is what the LORD says—he who created the heavens, who formed the earth and made it, who established it and did not create it to be empty, but formed it to be inhabited: I am the LORD, and there is no other. {45:19} I have not spoken in secret, from somewhere in a land of darkness; I did not say to the descendants of Jacob, "Seek me in vain." I, the LORD, speak the truth; I declare what is right. {45:20} Gather together and come; assemble, you fugitives from the nations. Ignorant are those who carry about idols of wood and pray to gods that cannot save. {45:21} Declare this, present it; let them take counsel together. Who foretold this long ago? Who declared it from the past? Was it not I, the LORD? There is no other God besides me, a righteous God and Savior; there is none but me. {45:22} Turn to me and be saved, all you ends of the earth; for I am God, and there is no other. {45:23} I have sworn by myself; the word has gone out of my mouth in righteousness and will not return: To me every knee will bow, every tongue will swear. {45:24} They will say of me, "In the LORD alone are righteousness and strength." All who have raged against him will come to him and be put to shame. {45:25} In the LORD all the descendants of Israel will be justified and will glory.

{46:1} Bel bows down, Nebo stoops; their idols are borne by beasts and cattle; the heavy load they are carrying is a burden for the weary animals. {46:2} They stoop and bow down together; they cannot rescue the burden; they themselves go off into captivity. {46:3} Listen to me, you descendants of Jacob, all the remnant of the house of Israel, whom I have upheld since your birth and have carried since you were born. {46:4} Even to your old age I am he; and when your hair is gray I will carry you; I have made you, and I will bear you; I will carry and will save you. {46:5} To whom will you compare me or count me equal? To whom will you liken me, that we may be compared? {46:6} Some pour out gold from their bags and weigh out silver on the scales; they hire a goldsmith to make it into a god, and they bow down and worship it. {46:7} They lift it to their shoulders and carry it; they set it in its place, and there it stands; from that spot it cannot move. Even though someone cries out to it, it cannot answer; it cannot save them from their troubles. {46:8} Remember this, and keep it in mind; take it to heart, you rebels. {46:9} Remember the former things, those of long ago; I am God, and there is no other; I am God, and there is none like me. {46:10} I make known the end from the beginning, from ancient times, what is still to come. I say, "My purpose will stand & I will do all that I please." {46:11} From the east I summon a bird of prey; from a far-off land, a man to fulfill my purpose. What I have said, that I will bring about; what I have planned, that I will do. {46:12} Listen to me, you stubborn-hearted, you who are now far from my righteousness. {46:13} I am bringing my righteousness near, it is not far away; and my salvation will not be delayed. I will grant salvation to Zion, my splendor to Israel.

{47:1} Come down and sit in the dust, O virgin daughter of Babylon; sit on the ground, for there is no throne, O daughter of the Chaldeans; you will no longer be called delicate and pampered. {47:2} Take the millstones and grind flour; uncover your hair, bare your legs, uncover your thighs, and cross the rivers. {47:3} Your nakedness will be exposed, and your shame will be seen; I will take vengeance, and I will not meet you as a man. {47:4} Our Redeemer—the LORD of hosts—is his name, the Holy One of Israel. {47:5} Sit in silence and go into darkness, O daughter of the Chaldeans; you will no longer be called the Lady of Kingdoms. {47:6} I was angry with my people; I defiled my inheritance and gave them into your hands. You showed them no mercy; you laid a heavy yoke on the aged. {47:7} You said, "I will be a lady forever," but you did not take these things to heart or remember the outcome. {47:8} Therefore, hear this, you who are given to pleasure, who live carelessly, who say in your heart, "I am, and there is no one else; I will never be a widow or suffer the loss of children." {47:9} But both of these things will come upon you in a moment, in one day: the loss of children and widowhood. They will come upon you completely because of your many sorceries and your great abundance of enchantments. {47:10} You have trusted in your wickedness and said, "No one sees me." Your wisdom and knowledge have led you astray, and you said in your heart, "I am, and there is no one else." {47:11} Therefore, disaster will come upon you, and you will not know where it comes from; calamity will fall upon you, and you will not be able to ward it off. Desolation will come upon you suddenly, and you will not know it. {47:12} Stand now with your enchantments and your many sorceries that you have labored at since your youth; perhaps you will be able to benefit; perhaps you will prevail. {47:13} You are wearied by the multitude of your counselors. Let the astrologers, stargazers, and monthly prognosticators stand up and save you from what will come upon you. {47:14} Behold, they will be like stubble; the fire will consume them; they will not be able to save themselves from the flames; there will not be a coal to warm them or a fire to sit by. {47:15} This is what they will be to you, with whom you have labored, even your merchants from your youth; they will wander, each to their own quarter; none will save you.

{48:1} Listen to this, O house of Jacob, called by the name of Israel and who came from the waters of Judah, who swear by the name of the LORD and mention the God of Israel, but not in truth or righteousness. {48:2} For they call themselves from the holy city and rely on the God of Israel; the LORD of hosts is his name. {48:3} I declared the former things from the beginning; they came out of my mouth, and I proclaimed them; I acted quickly, and they came to pass. {48:4} Because I knew that you are obstinate; your neck is an iron sinew, and your brow is bronze. {48:5} I declared it to you from the beginning; before it came to pass, I showed it to you so you wouldn't say, "My idol did this, and my graven image and my molten image commanded this." {48:6} You have heard and seen all this; will you not declare it? I have shown you new things, hidden things you did not know. {48:7} They are created now, not long ago; before today you have not heard of them, so you cannot say, "I knew them." {48:8} Yes, you have not heard; you have not known; your ear has not been opened from the past, for I knew that you would be very treacherous and were called a rebel from birth. {48:9} For my name's sake, I will delay my anger, and for my praise, I will restrain it for you so that I do not cut you off. {48:10} Behold, I have refined you, but not like silver; I have chosen you in the furnace of affliction. {48:11} For my own sake, for my own sake, I will do this; how can I allow my name to be dishonored? I will not give my glory to another. {48:12} Listen to me, O Jacob and Israel, my called; I am he; I am the first, and I am also the last. {48:13} My hand laid the foundation of the earth, and my right hand spread out the heavens; when I call to them, they stand up together. {48:14} All of you assemble and hear; which of them has declared these things? The LORD has loved him; he will carry out his purpose against Babylon, and his arm will be against the Chaldeans. {48:15} I, even I, have spoken; yes, I have called him; I have brought him, and he will succeed in his mission. {48:16} Come near to me and listen; I have not spoken in secret from the beginning; from the time it was, I am there. And now the Lord GOD and his Spirit have sent me. {48:17} This is what the LORD, your Redeemer, the Holy One of Israel, says: I am the LORD your God, who teaches you to benefit, who guides you in the way you should go. {48:18} If only you had listened to my commands! Then your peace would have been like a river, and your righteousness like the waves of the sea. {48:19} Your descendants would have been like the sand, and your offspring like its grains; their name would never be cut off or destroyed from my presence. {48:20} Go out from Babylon, flee from the Chaldeans; with a song of joy, declare this, and shout it to the ends of the earth; say, "The LORD has redeemed his servant Jacob." {48:21} They did not thirst when he led them through the deserts; he made water flow from the rock for them; he split the rock, and the water gushed out. {48:22} There is no peace, says the LORD, for the wicked.

{49:1} Listen, O islands, to me; and pay attention, you distant people; the LORD has called me from the womb; he mentioned my name while I was still in my mother's belly. {49:2} He has made my mouth like a sharp sword; in the shadow of his hand, he has hidden me and made me a polished arrow; in his quiver, he has hidden me. {49:3} He said to me, "You are my servant, O Israel, in whom I will be glorified." {49:4} Then I said, "I have labored in vain; I have spent my strength for nothing and in vain; yet surely my judgment is with the LORD, and my work is with my God." {49:5} And now, says the LORD who formed me from the womb to be his servant, to bring Jacob back to him, even though Israel is not gathered, I will be glorious in the eyes of the LORD, and my God will be my strength. {49:6} He said, "It is not enough for you to be my servant to raise up the tribes of Jacob and restore the preserved of Israel; I will also make you a light for the Gentiles so you can bring my salvation to the ends of the earth." {49:7} Thus says the LORD, the Redeemer of Israel and his Holy One, to him whom man despises, whom the nation abhors, to a servant of rulers: kings will see you and arise, princes will also worship, because of the LORD who is faithful, the Holy One of Israel, who has chosen you. {49:8} Thus says the LORD, "In an acceptable time, I have heard you, and in a day of salvation, I have helped you; I will preserve you and give you as a covenant to the people, to establish the earth and to restore the desolate heritages." {49:9} You will say to the prisoners, "Go forth"; to those in darkness, "Show yourselves." They will graze along the roads, and their pastures will be on all the high hills. {49:10} They will not hunger or thirst; neither will the heat nor the sun strike them; for he who has mercy on them will lead them, and he will guide them to springs of water. {49:11} I will make all my mountains a road, and my highways will be raised up. {49:12} Behold, these will come from far away; and, lo, these will come from the north and the west; and these from the land of Sinim (possibly referring to China). {49:13} Sing, O heavens, and be joyful, O earth; break forth into singing, O mountains, for the LORD has comforted his people and will have mercy on his afflicted. {49:14} But Zion said, "The LORD has forsaken me, and my Lord has forgotten me." {49:15} Can a woman forget her nursing child, so as not to have compassion on the child she bore? Yes, they may forget, yet I will not forget you. {49:16} Behold, I have engraved you on the palms of my hands; your walls are continually before me. {49:17} Your children will hurry back, and those who destroyed you and laid you waste will depart from you. {49:18} Lift up your eyes all around and see: they all gather and come to you. As I live, says the LORD, you will surely put them on like ornaments and bind them on like a bride. {49:19} For your waste and desolate places and the land of your destruction will be too narrow because of the inhabitants, and those who swallowed you up will be far away. {49:20} The children you lost will say again in your ears, "This place is too small for me; give me more space so I can dwell." {49:21} Then you will say in your heart, "Who has given me these, since I have lost my children and am desolate, a captive, and wandering to and fro? Who has raised these?" Behold, I was left alone; where have these come from? {49:22} Thus says the Lord GOD: "Behold, I will lift my hand to the Gentiles and set up my standard for the people; they will bring your sons in their arms & your daughters will be carried on their shoulders. {49:23} Kings will be your nursing fathers, and their queens your nursing mothers; they will bow down to you with their faces to the ground and lick the dust off your feet; then you will know that I am the LORD, for they will not be ashamed who wait for me. {49:24} Will the prey be taken from the mighty, or the lawful captive delivered? {49:25} But thus says the LORD: "Even the captives of the mighty will be taken away, and the prey of the terrible will be delivered; for I will contend with him who contends with you, and I will save your children. {49:26} I will feed those who oppress you with their own flesh, and they will be drunk with their own blood, as with sweet wine; and all flesh will know that I, the LORD, am your Savior and your Redeemer, the Mighty One of Jacob.

{50:1} Thus says the LORD: "Where is the bill of your mother's divorce, whom I put away? Or which of my creditors is it to whom I sold you? Behold, for your iniquities, you sold yourselves, and for your transgressions, your mother was put away. {50:2} Why, when I came, was there no one? When I called, was there no one to answer? Is my hand shortened that it cannot redeem? Or do I lack the power to deliver? Behold, at my rebuke, I dry up the sea; I make rivers a wilderness; their fish stink because there is no water, and die of thirst. {50:3} I clothe the heavens with darkness and make sackcloth their covering. {50:4} The Lord GOD has given me the tongue of the learned, that I should know how to speak a word in season to him who is weary; he awakens me morning by morning; he awakens my ear to hear as the learned. {50:5} The Lord GOD has opened my ear, and I was not rebellious; I did not turn away. {50:6} I gave my back to those who struck me and my cheeks to those who plucked out my beard; I did not hide my face from shame and spitting. {50:7} For the Lord GOD will help me; therefore, I will not be disgraced; therefore, I have set my face like flint, and I know I will not be ashamed. {50:8} He is near who justifies me; who will contend with me? Let us stand together; who is my adversary? Let him come near to me. {50:9} Behold, the Lord GOD will help me; who is he that will condemn me? Look, they will all wear out like a garment; the moth will eat them up. {50:10} Who among you fears the LORD and obeys the voice of his servant, who walks in darkness and has no light? Let him trust in the name of the LORD and rely on his God. {50:11} Behold, all you who kindle a fire and surround yourselves with sparks: walk in the light of your fire and in the sparks you have kindled. This will you have from my hand; you will lie down in sorrow.

{51:1} Listen to me, you who pursue righteousness, you who seek the LORD: look to the rock from which you were hewn and to the quarry from which you were dug. {51:2} Look to Abraham your father and to Sarah who bore you; for I called him alone, blessed him, and increased him. {51:3} For the LORD will comfort Zion; he will comfort all her desolate places and make her wilderness like Eden and her desert like the garden of the LORD; joy and gladness will be found in her, along with thanksgiving and the sound of music. {51:4} Listen to me, my people; pay attention, O my nation: a law will go forth from me, and I will establish my judgment as a light for the people. {51:5} My righteousness is near; my salvation has gone forth, and my arms will judge the people; the islands will wait for me, and on my arm they will trust. {51:6} Lift up your eyes to the heavens and look at the earth beneath; for the heavens will vanish like smoke, and the earth will wear out like a garment, and those who dwell in it will die likewise; but my salvation will be forever, and my righteousness will not be abolished. {51:7} Listen to me, you who know righteousness, you people in whose hearts is my law; do not fear the reproach of men, nor be afraid of their insults. {51:8} For the moth will eat them up like a garment, and the worm will consume them like wool; but my righteousness will be forever, and my salvation from generation to generation. {51:9} Awake, awake, put on strength, O arm of the LORD; awaken as in ancient days, in generations of old. Are you not the one who cut Rahab and wounded the dragon? {51:10} Are you not the one who dried up the sea, the waters of the great deep, and made a path through the depths of the sea for the ransomed to cross? {51:11} Therefore, the redeemed of the LORD will return and come to Zion with singing; everlasting joy will be upon their heads; they will obtain gladness and joy, and sorrow and mourning will flee away. {51:12} I, even I, am he who comforts you; who are you that you should be afraid of a man who will die, and of the son of man who is like grass? {51:13} And you forget the LORD your Maker, who stretched out the heavens and laid the foundations of the earth; and you have feared continually every day because of the fury of the oppressor, as if he were ready to destroy? And where is the fury of the oppressor? {51:14} The captive exile hastens to be loosed, so he will not die in the pit, nor will his bread fail. {51:15} But I am the LORD your God, who divided the sea, whose waves roared; the LORD of hosts is his name. {51:16} I have put my words in your mouth and covered you in the shadow of my hand, that I may plant the heavens, lay the foundations of the earth, and say to Zion, "You are my people." {51:17} Awake, awake, stand up, O Jerusalem, you who have drunk from the hand of the LORD the cup of his fury; you have drunk the dregs of the cup of trembling and drained it dry. {51:18} There is no one to guide her among all the sons she has borne; nor is there anyone who takes her by the hand among all the sons she has raised. {51:19} These two things have come upon you; who will mourn for you? Desolation and destruction, famine and the sword: by whom will I comfort you? {51:20} Your sons have fainted; they lie at the head of all the streets like a wild bull in a net; they are full of the fury of the LORD, the rebuke of your God. {51:21} Therefore, hear this, you afflicted, and drunk, but not with wine: {51:22} Thus says your Lord, the LORD, and your God who pleads the cause of his people: "Behold, I have taken from your hand the cup of trembling, even the dregs of the cup of my fury; you will no longer drink it again. {51:23} But I will put it into the hand of those who afflict you, who said to your soul, 'Bow down, so we may cross over'; and you laid your body like the ground and like the street for them to cross."

{52:1} Awake, awake; put on your strength, O Zion; put on your beautiful garments, O Jerusalem, the holy city; for from now on, the uncircumcised and the unclean will no longer enter you. {52:2} Shake off the dust; arise and sit down, O Jerusalem; free yourself from the chains around your neck, O captive daughter of Zion. {52:3} For thus says the LORD: "You have sold yourselves for nothing, and you will be redeemed without money." {52:4} For thus says the Lord GOD: "My people went down to Egypt to stay there for a while, and the Assyrian oppressed them without cause. {52:5} Now, therefore, what do I have here, says the LORD, that my people is taken away for nothing? Those who rule over them make them groan, says the LORD; my name is blasphemed continually every day. {52:6} Therefore my people will know my name; therefore they will know on that day that I am he who speaks: behold, it is I. {52:7} How beautiful on the mountains are the feet of those who bring good news, who publish peace, who bring good tidings of good, who publish salvation and say to Zion, "Your God reigns!" {52:8} Your watchmen will lift up their voices; together they will sing; for they will see eye to eye when the LORD brings back Zion. {52:9} Break forth into joy, sing together, you waste places of Jerusalem; for the LORD has comforted his people; he has redeemed Jerusalem. {52:10} The LORD has bared his holy arm in the sight of all the nations; and all the ends of the earth will see the salvation of our God. {52:11} Depart, depart; go out from there; touch no unclean thing; go out from the midst of her; be clean, you who bear the vessels of the LORD. {52:12} For you will not go out in haste, nor go by flight; for the LORD will go before you, and the God of Israel will be your rear guard. {52:13} Behold, my servant will deal wisely; he will be exalted and lifted up, and be very high. {52:14} Just as many were astonished at you, his appearance was marred more than any man, and his form more than the sons of men; {52:15} so he will sprinkle many nations; kings will shut their mouths at him; for what had not been told them they will see, and what they had not heard they will consider.

{53:1} Who has believed our report? And to whom has the arm of the LORD been revealed? {53:2} For he grew up before him like a tender plant and like a root out of dry ground; he had no form or majesty; when we see him, there is no beauty that we should desire him. {53:3} He is despised and rejected by men; a man of sorrows and familiar with grief; we hid our faces from him; he was despised, and we did not esteem him. {53:4} Surely he has borne our griefs and carried our sorrows; yet we considered him stricken, smitten by God, and afflicted. {53:5} But he was wounded for our transgressions; he was crushed for our iniquities; the punishment that brought us peace was upon him, and by his stripes, we are healed. {53:6} All we like sheep have gone astray; we have turned everyone to his own way; and the LORD has laid on him the iniquity of us all. {53:7} He was oppressed and afflicted, yet he did not open his mouth; he was led like a lamb to the slaughter, and like a sheep before its shearers is silent, so he did not open his mouth. {53:8} He was taken from prison and from judgment; and who can speak of his descendants? For he was cut off from the land of the living; he was stricken for the transgression of my people. {53:9} He made his grave with the wicked and with the rich in his death, because he had done no violence, nor was there any deceit in his mouth. {53:10} Yet it pleased the LORD to crush him; he has put him to grief; when you make his soul an offering for sin, he will see his offspring, he will prolong his days, and the will of the LORD will prosper in his hand. {53:11} He will see the fruit of the anguish of his soul and be satisfied; by his knowledge, my righteous servant will justify many; for he will bear their iniquities. {53:12} Therefore I will divide him a portion with the great, and he will divide the spoils with the strong; because he poured out his soul unto death and was numbered with the transgressors; he bore the sin of many and made intercession for the transgressors.

{54:1} Sing, O barren one, you who did not bear; break forth into singing and cry aloud, you who have not been in labor; for more are the children of the desolate than the children of the married woman, says the LORD. {54:2} Enlarge the place of your tent, and let them stretch out the curtains of your dwellings; do not spare; lengthen your cords and strengthen your stakes; {54:3} for you will break forth on the right and on the left; your descendants will inherit the nations and make the desolate cities inhabited. {54:4} Do not fear, for you will not be ashamed; do not be confounded, for you will not be put to shame; for you will forget the shame of your youth, and you will not remember the reproach of your widowhood anymore. {54:5} For your Maker is your husband; the LORD of hosts is his name; and your Redeemer is the Holy One of Israel; he is called the God of the whole earth. {54:6} For the LORD has called you as a woman forsaken and grieved in spirit, and as a wife of youth when you were refused, says your God. {54:7} For a brief moment, I forsook you, but with great mercies, I will gather you. {54:8} In a moment of anger, I hid my face from you, but with everlasting kindness, I will have mercy on you, says the LORD your Redeemer. {54:9} For this is like the waters of Noah to me; for as I swore that the waters of Noah would no longer cover the earth, so I have sworn that I will not be angry with you or rebuke you. {54:10} For the mountains may depart, and the hills be removed, but my kindness will not depart from you, nor will my covenant of peace be removed, says the LORD who has mercy on you. {54:11} O you afflicted one, tossed by the storm and not comforted, behold, I will lay your stones with beautiful colors and lay your foundations with sapphires. {54:12} I will make your windows of agates and your gates of carbuncles, and all your borders of pleasant stones. {54:13} All your children will be taught by the LORD, and great will be the peace of your children. {54:14} In righteousness, you will be established; you will be far from oppression, for you will not fear; and from terror, for it will not come near you. {54:15} Behold, they will surely gather, but not by me; whoever gathers against you will fall for your sake. {54:16} Behold, I have created the smith who blows the coals in the fire and creates a weapon for his work; and I have created the destroyer to ruin. {54:17} No weapon formed against you shall prosper, and every tongue that rises against you in judgment, you shall condemn. This is the heritage of the servants of the LORD, and their righteousness is from me, says the LORD.

{55:1} Ho! Everyone who is thirsty, come to the waters; and you who have no money, come, buy and eat; yes, come, buy wine and milk without money and without cost. {55:2} Why do you spend money for what is not bread, and your labor for what does not satisfy? Listen carefully to me, and eat what is good, and let your soul delight itself in abundance. {55:3} Incline your ear and come to me; hear, and your soul shall live; I will make an everlasting covenant with you, even the sure mercies of David. {55:4} Behold, I have given him as a witness to the people, a leader and commander for the people. {55:5} Behold, you will call a nation that you do not know, and nations that did not know you will run to you because of the LORD your God and for the Holy One of Israel; for he has glorified you. {55:6} Seek the LORD while he may be found; call upon him while he is near. {55:7} Let the wicked forsake his way and the unrighteous man his thoughts; let him return to the LORD, and he will have mercy on him; and to our God, for he will abundantly pardon. {55:8} For my thoughts are not your thoughts, nor are your ways my ways, says the LORD. {55:9} For as the heavens are higher than the earth, so are my ways higher than your ways, and my thoughts than your thoughts. {55:10} For as the rain comes down and the snow from heaven, and does not return there but waters the earth and makes it bring forth and bud, that it may give seed to the sower and bread to the eater, {55:11} so shall my word that goes forth from my mouth; it shall not return to me void, but it shall accomplish what I please, and it shall prosper in the thing for which I sent it. {55:12} For you shall go out with joy and be led forth with peace; the mountains and the hills shall break forth before you into singing, and all the trees of the field shall clap their hands. {55:13} Instead of the thornbush, the fir tree shall come up, and instead of the brier, the myrtle tree; and it shall be to the LORD for a name, for an everlasting sign that shall not be cut off.

{56:1} Thus says the LORD: Keep justice and do righteousness, for my salvation is near to come, and my righteousness will be revealed. {56:2} Blessed is the man who does this, and the son of man who lays hold of it; who keeps the Sabbath from polluting it and keeps his hand from doing any evil. {56:3} Let not the foreigner who has joined himself to the LORD say, "The LORD has utterly separated me from his people"; nor let the eunuch say, "I am a dry tree." {56:4} For thus says the LORD to the eunuchs who keep my Sabbaths, choose the things that please me, and hold fast to my covenant: {56:5} To them, I will give in my house and within my walls a place and a name better than that of sons and daughters; I will give them an everlasting name that will not be cut off. {56:6} Also, the sons of the foreigner who join themselves to the LORD, to serve him and to love the name of the LORD, to be his servants, everyone who keeps the Sabbath from polluting it and takes hold of my covenant; {56:7} I will bring them to my holy mountain and make them joyful in my house of prayer; their burnt offerings and sacrifices will be accepted on my altar; for my house shall be called a house of prayer for all nations. {56:8} The Lord GOD, who gathers the outcasts of Israel, says, "Yet I will gather others to him besides those who are gathered to him." {56:9} All you beasts of the field, come to devour, yes, all you beasts in the forest. {56:10} His watchmen are blind; they are all ignorant; they are all dumb dogs; they cannot bark; they lie down, loving to slumber. {56:11} Yes, they are greedy dogs which can never have enough; and they are shepherds who cannot understand; they all look to their own way, everyone for his own gain, from his own quarter. {56:12} "Come," they say, "I will fetch wine, and we will fill ourselves with strong drink; and tomorrow will be as this day, and even more abundant."

{57:1} The righteous perish, and no one takes it to heart; merciful people are taken away, and no one considers that the righteous are taken away from the coming evil. {57:2} He will enter into peace; they will rest in their beds, each one walking in his integrity. {57:3} But draw near here, you sons of the sorceress, the offspring of the adulterer and the prostitute. {57:4} Against whom do you make fun? Against whom do you stick out your tongue? Are you not children of transgression, a seed of falsehood? {57:5} You inflame yourselves with idols under every green tree, sacrificing children in the valleys under the cliffs of the rocks. {57:6} Among the smooth stones of the stream is your portion; they are your lot. You have poured out a drink offering to them and offered a grain offering. Should I take comfort in these? {57:7} On a lofty and high mountain, you set your bed; even there you went up to offer sacrifice. {57:8} Behind the doors and the doorposts, you set up your memorial; for you have uncovered yourself to another than me and gone up; you have enlarged your bed and made a covenant with them; you loved their bed where you saw it. {57:9} You went to the king with ointment and increased your perfumes; you sent your messengers far away and debased yourself even to the grave. {57:10} You are wearied in the greatness of your ways; yet you did not say, "There is no hope." You have found the life of your hand; therefore, you were not grieved. {57:11} And of whom have you been afraid or feared, that you lied and did not remember me nor laid it to heart? Have I not held my peace even of old, and you do not fear me? {57:12} I will declare your righteousness and your works, for they will not profit you. {57:13} When you cry out, let your companions deliver you; but the wind will carry them all away; vanity will take them. But he who puts his trust in me will possess the land and inherit my holy mountain. {57:14} And he will say, "Lift up, lift up, prepare the way, take the stumbling block out of the way of my people." {57:15} For thus says the high and exalted One who inhabits eternity, whose name is Holy: I dwell in the high and holy place, with him who is of a contrite (feeling remorse or regret) and humble spirit, to revive the spirit of the humble and to revive the heart of the contrite ones. {57:16} For I will not contend forever, nor will I be always angry; for the spirit would fail before me, and the souls which I have made. {57:17} For the iniquity (wickedness) of his covetousness, I was angry and struck him; I hid my face and was angry, and he went on stubbornly in the way of his heart. {57:18} I have seen his ways, and will heal him; I will lead him also and restore comforts to him and to his mourners. {57:19} I create the fruit of the lips; Peace, peace to him who is far off and to him who is near, says the LORD; and I will heal him. {57:20} But the wicked are like the troubled sea, when it cannot rest, whose waters cast up mire and dirt. {57:21} There is no peace, says my God, for the wicked.

{58:1} Cry aloud, spare not, lift up your voice like a trumpet, and show my people their transgression and the house of Jacob their sins. {58:2} Yet they seek me daily and delight to know my ways, as a nation that did righteousness and did not forsake the ordinance of their God; they ask of me the ordinances of justice; they delight in approaching God. {58:3} Why have we fasted, they say, and you do not see? Why have we afflicted our souls, and you take no notice? Behold, on the day of your fast, you find pleasure and exact all your labors. {58:4} Behold, you fast for strife and debate, and to strike with the fist of wickedness; you shall not fast as you do this day, to make your voice heard on high. {58:5} Is this the fast that I have chosen? A day for a man to afflict his soul? Is it to bow down his head like a bulrush (a type of plant) and to spread sackcloth and ashes under him? Will you call this a fast and an acceptable day to the LORD? {58:6} Is not this the fast that I have chosen? To loose the bands of wickedness, to undo the heavy burdens, and to let the oppressed go free, and that you break every yoke? {58:7} Is it not to share your bread with the hungry and to bring the poor who are cast out to your house? When you see the naked, cover him, and do not hide yourself from your own flesh? {58:8} Then your light will break forth like the morning, and your health will spring forth speedily; and your righteousness will go before you; the glory of the LORD will be your rear guard. {58:9} Then you will call, and the LORD will answer; you will cry, and he will say, "Here I am." If you take away the yoke from your midst, the pointing of the finger, and speaking vanity; {58:10} and if you extend your soul to the hungry and satisfy the afflicted soul, then your light will rise in darkness, and your darkness will be as the noonday. {58:11} And the LORD will guide you continually and satisfy your soul in drought and strengthen your bones; and you shall be like a watered garden and like a spring of water whose waters do not fail. {58:12} And those from among you shall build the old waste places; you shall raise up the foundations of many generations; and you shall be called the repairer of the breach (a break in something), the restorer of paths to dwell in. {58:13} If you turn away your foot from the Sabbath, from doing your pleasure on my holy day, and call the Sabbath a delight, the holy of the LORD, honorable; and honor him, not doing your own ways, nor finding your own pleasure, nor speaking your own words; {58:14} then you shall delight yourself in the LORD, and I will cause you to ride on the high places of the earth and feed you with the heritage of Jacob your father; for the mouth of the LORD has spoken it.

{59:1} Behold, the LORD's hand is not shortened that it cannot save, nor is his ear heavy that it cannot hear. {59:2} But your iniquities (wicked actions) have separated you from your God, and your sins have hidden his face from you, so that he will not hear. {59:3} For your hands are stained with blood, and your fingers with iniquity; your lips have spoken lies, and your tongue has muttered perverseness (wrongness). {59:4} No one calls for justice, nor does anyone plead for truth; they trust in emptiness and speak lies; they conceive mischief and bring forth iniquity. {59:5} They hatch the eggs of poisonous snakes and weave spider's webs; he who eats their eggs dies, and what is crushed breaks out into a viper. {59:6} Their webs will not become clothing, nor will they cover themselves with their works; their works are works of iniquity, and violence is in their hands. {59:7} Their feet run to evil, and they hurry to shed innocent blood; their thoughts are thoughts of iniquity; wasting and destruction are in their paths. {59:8} They do not know the way of peace, and there is no justice in their goings; they have made their paths crooked; whoever goes in them will not know peace. {59:9} Therefore, judgment is far from us, nor does justice overtake us; we wait for light, but behold, darkness; for brightness, but we walk in gloom. {59:10} We grope for the wall like the blind, and we grope as if we had no eyes; we stumble at noon as in the night; we are in desolate places like dead men. {59:11} We roar like bears, and mourn like doves; we look for judgment, but there is none; for salvation, but it is far from us. {59:12} For our transgressions are multiplied before you, and our sins testify against us; for our transgressions are with us, and we know our iniquities. {59:13} In transgressing and lying against the LORD, and turning away from our God, speaking oppression and rebellion, conceiving and uttering from the heart words of falsehood. {59:14} And judgment has turned back, and justice stands far away; for truth has fallen in the street, and fairness cannot enter. {59:15} Yes, truth fails; and he who departs from evil makes himself a prey; and the LORD saw it and was displeased that there was no judgment. {59:16} And he saw that there was no man, and wondered that there was no intercessor (someone who intervenes); therefore, his arm brought salvation to him, and his righteousness sustained him. {59:17} For he put on righteousness like a breastplate, and a helmet of salvation on his head; he put on garments of vengeance for clothing and was clothed with zeal (passion) like a cloak. {59:18} According to their deeds, he will repay, fury to his adversaries, recompense (payment) to his enemies; to the coastlands, he will repay recompense. {59:19} So they shall fear the name of the LORD from the west, and his glory from the rising of the sun. When the enemy comes in like a flood, the Spirit of the LORD will lift up a standard against him. {59:20} And the Redeemer will come to Zion, and to those who turn from transgression in Jacob, says the LORD. {59:21} As for me, this is my covenant with them, says the LORD; My Spirit that is upon you and my words which I have put in your mouth shall not depart from your mouth, nor from the mouth of your descendants, nor from the mouth of your descendants' descendants, says the LORD, from now on and forever.

{60:1} Arise, shine, for your light has come, and the glory of the LORD has risen upon you. {60:2} For behold, darkness shall cover the earth, and thick darkness the people; but the LORD will arise upon you, and his glory will be seen upon you. {60:3} And the Gentiles (non-Jews) shall come to your light, and kings to the brightness of your rising. {60:4} Lift up your eyes all around and see; they all gather together, they come to you; your sons shall come from afar, and your daughters shall be nursed at your side. {60:5} Then you shall see and flow together, and your heart shall fear and be enlarged; because the abundance of the sea shall be converted to you, the wealth of the Gentiles shall come to you. {60:6} The multitude of camels shall cover you, the dromedaries (camels) of Midian and Ephah; all those from Sheba shall come; they shall bring gold and incense and proclaim the praises of the LORD. {60:7} All the flocks of Kedar shall be gathered to you, the rams of Nebaioth shall minister to you; they shall come up with acceptance on my altar, and I will glorify the house of my glory. {60:8} Who are these who fly like a cloud, and like doves to their windows? {60:9} Surely the islands shall wait for me, and the ships of Tarshish first, to bring your sons from afar, their silver and gold with them, to the name of the LORD your God, and to the Holy One of Israel, because he has glorified you. {60:10} And the sons of foreigners shall build up your walls, and their kings shall minister to you; for in my wrath, I struck you, but in my favor, I have had mercy on you. {60:11} Therefore, your gates shall be open continually; they shall not be shut day or night; so that men may bring to you the wealth of the Gentiles, and their kings may be brought. {60:12} For the nation and kingdom that will not serve you shall perish; yes, those nations shall be utterly wasted. {60:13} The glory of Lebanon shall come to you, the fir tree, the pine tree, and the box tree together, to beautify the place of my sanctuary; and I will make the place of my feet glorious. {60:14} The sons of those who afflicted you shall come bowing to you, and all those who despised you shall bow down at your feet; and they shall call you, The city of the LORD, The Zion of the Holy One of Israel. {60:15} Whereas you have been forsaken and hated, so that no one passed through you, I will make you an everlasting excellence, a joy of many generations. {60:16} You shall also suck the milk of the Gentiles and suck the breast of kings; and you shall know that I, the LORD, am your Savior and your Redeemer, the Mighty One of Jacob. {60:17} Instead of bronze, I will bring gold, and instead of iron, I will bring silver, and instead of wood, bronze, and instead of stones, iron; I will also make your officers peace, and your exactors (tax collectors) righteousness. {60:18} Violence shall no more be heard in your land, wasting or destruction within your borders; but you shall call your walls Salvation and your gates Praise. {60:19} The sun shall no longer be your light by day, nor for brightness shall the moon give light to you; but the LORD will be your everlasting light, and your God your glory. {60:20} Your sun shall no longer go down, nor shall your moon withdraw itself; for the LORD will be your everlasting light, and the days of your mourning shall be ended. {60:21} Your people shall all be righteous; they shall inherit the land forever, the branch of my planting, the work of my hands, that I may be glorified. {60:22} A little one shall become a thousand, and a small one a strong nation; I, the LORD, will hasten it in its time.

{61:1} The Spirit of the Lord GOD is upon me; because the LORD has anointed me to bring good news to the humble; he has sent me to heal the brokenhearted, to proclaim freedom to the captives, and the opening of the prison to those who are bound. {61:2} To proclaim the year of the LORD's favor and the day of vengeance of our God; to comfort all who mourn. {61:3} To provide for those who mourn in Zion, to give them beauty instead of ashes, the oil of joy instead of mourning, and a garment of praise instead of a spirit of despair; that they might be called oaks of righteousness, the planting of the LORD, that he might be glorified. {61:4} They shall rebuild the ancient ruins, they shall raise up the former devastations, and they shall repair the ruined cities, the devastations of many generations. {61:5} Strangers shall stand and shepherd your flocks, and the children of foreigners shall be your farmers and vinedressers. {61:6} But you shall be called the priests of the LORD; people shall call you the ministers of our God; you shall eat the riches of the Gentiles, and in their glory, you shall boast. {61:7} Instead of your shame, you shall have double; and instead of humiliation, they shall rejoice in their portion; therefore, in their land, they shall possess double; everlasting joy shall be theirs. {61:8} For I, the LORD, love justice; I hate robbery and wrongs; I will direct their work in truth, and I will make an everlasting covenant with them. {61:9} Their descendants shall be known among the Gentiles, and their offspring among the peoples; all who see them shall acknowledge that they are the seed which the LORD has blessed. {61:10} I will greatly rejoice in the

LORD; my soul shall be joyful in my God; for he has clothed me with the garments of salvation, he has covered me with the robe of righteousness, like a bridegroom adorned with a crown, and like a bride who decorates herself with jewels. {61:11} For as the earth brings forth its bud, and as the garden causes what is sown in it to spring forth, so the Lord GOD will cause righteousness and praise to spring forth before all the nations.

{62:1} For Zion's sake, I will not be silent, and for Jerusalem's sake, I will not rest, until her righteousness shines like brightness, and her salvation like a lamp that burns. {62:2} And the Gentiles shall see your righteousness, and all kings your glory; and you shall be called by a new name, which the mouth of the LORD will give you. {62:3} You shall also be a crown of glory in the hand of the LORD, and a royal diadem in the hand of your God. {62:4} You shall no longer be called Forsaken, nor shall your land be called Desolate; but you shall be called Hephzibah, and your land Beulah (married); for the LORD delights in you, and your land shall be married. {62:5} For as a young man marries a virgin, so shall your sons marry you; and as the bridegroom rejoices over the bride, so shall your God rejoice over you. {62:6} I have set watchmen on your walls, O Jerusalem, who shall never be silent day or night; you who mention the LORD, give him no rest. {62:7} And give him no rest until he establishes, and until he makes Jerusalem a praise in the earth. {62:8} The LORD has sworn by his right hand, and by the arm of his strength, Surely I will no longer give your grain as food to your enemies; and the children of foreigners shall not drink your wine for which you have labored. {62:9} But those who have gathered it shall eat it and praise the LORD; and those who have brought it together shall drink it in the courts of my holiness. {62:10} Go through, go through the gates; prepare the way for the people; build up, build up the highway; gather out the stones; lift up a standard for the people. {62:11} Behold, the LORD has proclaimed to the end of the world, Say to the daughter of Zion, Behold, your salvation comes; behold, his reward is with him, and his work before him. {62:12} And they shall call them, The holy people, The redeemed of the LORD; and you shall be called, Sought out, A city not forsaken.

{63:1} Who is this coming from Edom, with stained clothes from Bozrah? This one is glorious in his apparel, traveling in the greatness of his strength? It is I, speaking in righteousness, mighty to save. {63:2} Why are your garments red, and your clothes like someone who treads in the winepress? {63:3} I have trodden the winepress alone; and no one was with me. I trampled them in my anger and crushed them in my fury; their blood splattered on my garments, and I stained all my clothes. {63:4} For the day of vengeance is in my heart, and the year of my redeemed has come. {63:5} I looked, and there was no one to help; I wondered that no one upheld me. Therefore, my own arm brought salvation to me, and my fury upheld me. {63:6} I will trample down the people in my anger, and make them drunk in my fury, and I will bring down their strength to the ground. {63:7} I will mention the lovingkindnesses of the LORD and the praises of the LORD, according to all that the LORD has done for us, and the great goodness toward the house of Israel, which he has shown them according to his mercies and the abundance of his lovingkindnesses. {63:8} For he said, Surely they are my people, children who will not lie; so he became their Savior. {63:9} In all their afflictions, he was afflicted, and the angel of his presence saved them; in his love and in his compassion, he redeemed them; he carried them and bore them all the days of old. {63:10} But they rebelled and grieved his holy Spirit; therefore, he became their enemy and fought against them. {63:11} Then he remembered the days of old, Moses and his people, saying, Where is he who brought them up out of the sea with the shepherd of his flock? Where is he who put his holy Spirit within him? {63:12} Who led them by the right hand of Moses with his glorious arm, dividing the waters before them, to make himself an everlasting name? {63:13} Who led them through the depths like a horse in the wilderness, so they would not stumble? {63:14} As a beast goes down into the valley, the Spirit of the LORD caused him to rest; so you led your people, to make for yourself a glorious name. {63:15} Look down from heaven, and behold from your holy and glorious dwelling place; where is your zeal and your strength, the yearning of your heart and your mercies toward me? Are they restrained? {63:16} Surely you are our Father, though Abraham does not know us, and Israel does not acknowledge us; you, O LORD, are our Father, our Redeemer; your name is from everlasting. {63:17} O LORD, why have you made us stray from your ways and hardened our hearts so we do not fear you? Return for the sake of your servants, the tribes of your inheritance. {63:18} Your holy people have possessed it but a little while; our adversaries have trampled down your sanctuary. {63:19} We are yours; you never ruled over them; they were not called by your name.

{64:1} Oh, that you would tear open the heavens and come down, that the mountains might flow down at your presence, {64:2} as when the fire causes the waters to boil, to make your name known to your adversaries, that the nations may tremble at your presence! {64:3} When you did awesome things we did not expect, you came down; the mountains flowed down at your presence. {64:4} For since the beginning of the world, men have not heard, nor perceived by the ear, neither has the eye seen, O God, besides you, what you have prepared for those who wait for you. {64:5} You meet him who rejoices and works righteousness, those who remember you in your ways; behold, you are angry, for we have sinned; in them, we continue, and we shall be saved. {64:6} But we are all like an unclean thing, and all our righteousnesses are like filthy rags; we all fade like a leaf, and our iniquities, like the wind, have taken us away. {64:7} And there is no one who calls upon your name, who stirs himself up to take hold of you; for you have hidden your face from us, and have consumed us because of our iniquities. {64:8} But now, O LORD, you are our Father; we are the clay, and you our potter; and we are all the work of your hand. {64:9} Do not be very angry, O LORD, neither remember iniquity forever; behold, see, we beseech you, we are all your people. {64:10} Your holy cities are a wilderness, Zion is a wilderness, Jerusalem is a desolation. {64:11} Our holy and beautiful house, where our fathers praised you, is burned with fire, and all our pleasant things are laid waste. {64:12} Will you restrain yourself because of these things, O LORD? Will you be silent and afflict us very much?

{65:1} I am sought by those who did not ask for me; I am found by those who did not seek me. I said, "Here I am, here I am," to a nation that was not called by my name. {65:2} I have held out my hands all day to a rebellious people who walk in ways that are not good, following their own thoughts; {65:3} a people who provoke me to anger continually to my face, who sacrifice in gardens and burn incense on brick altars; {65:4} who sit among the graves and spend the night in the monuments, who eat pork and have unclean food in their vessels; {65:5} who say, "Stay away; do not come near me, for I am holier than you." These are smoke in my nostrils, a fire that burns all day. {65:6} Behold, it is written before me: I will not remain silent but will repay them, even repay them to their own bosom. {65:7} Your iniquities and the iniquities of your fathers together, says the LORD, who burned incense on the mountains and blasphemed me on the hills; therefore, I will measure their former deeds into their bosom. {65:8} Thus says the LORD, "As new wine is found in a cluster, and someone says, 'Do not destroy it, for there is a blessing in it,' so will I do for my servants' sake, so that I will not destroy them all. {65:9} I will bring forth a remnant from Jacob, and from Judah, an inheritor of my mountains. My chosen ones will inherit it, and my servants will dwell there. {65:10} Sharon will become a pasture for flocks, and the Valley of Achor a resting place for herds, for my people who have sought me. {65:11} But you are those who forsake the LORD, who forget my holy mountain, who prepare a table for Fortune and offer drink to Destiny. {65:12} Therefore, I will number you for the sword, and you will all bow down to the slaughter; because when I called, you did not answer; when I spoke, you did not listen; but you did evil before my eyes and chose what I did not delight in. {65:13} Therefore, says the Lord GOD, "Behold, my servants will eat, but you will be hungry; behold, my servants will drink, but you will be thirsty; behold, my servants will rejoice, but you will be ashamed. {65:14} Behold, my servants will sing for joy of heart, but you will cry out in sorrow and howl for anguish of spirit. {65:15} And you will leave your name as a curse to my chosen ones, for the Lord GOD will slay you and call his servants by another name.

{65:16} He who blesses himself on the earth will bless himself in the God of truth, and he who swears on the earth will swear by the God of truth, because former troubles are forgotten and hidden from my eyes. {65:17} For behold, I create new heavens and a new earth, and the former will not be remembered or come to mind. {65:18} But be glad and rejoice forever in what I create, for behold, I create Jerusalem as a rejoicing and her people as a joy. {65:19} And I will rejoice in Jerusalem and be glad in my people; the sound of weeping will no longer be heard in her, nor the sound of crying. {65:20} There will no longer be an infant who lives but a few days, nor an old man who does not live out his days; for the child will die at a hundred years old, but the sinner, being a hundred years old, will be accursed. {65:21} They will build houses and inhabit them; they will plant vineyards and eat their fruit. {65:22} They will not build and another inhabit; they will not plant and another eat, for the days of my people will be like the days of a tree, and my chosen ones will long enjoy the work of their hands. {65:23} They will not labor in vain or bear children for trouble, for they are the offspring of the blessed of the LORD, and their descendants with them. {65:24} And it will come to pass that before they call, I will answer; while they are still speaking, I will hear. {65:25} The wolf and the lamb will feed together, and the lion will eat straw like the ox; and dust will be the serpent's food. They will not hurt or destroy in all my holy mountain, says the LORD.

{66:1} Thus says the LORD, "Heaven is my throne, and the earth is my footstool. Where is the house that you will build for me? Where is the place of my rest? {66:2} For all those things my hand has made, and all those things exist, says the LORD. But to this one I will look, even to him who is poor and of a contrite spirit, and trembles at my word. {66:3} He who kills an ox is as if he slays a man; he who sacrifices a lamb is as if he cuts off a dog's neck; he who offers a grain offering is as if he offers swine's blood; he who burns incense is as if he blesses an idol. Yes, they have chosen their own ways, and their souls delight in their abominations. {66:4} I will choose their delusions and bring their fears upon them, because when I called, no one answered; when I spoke, they did not hear. They did evil before my eyes and chose what I did not delight in. {66:5} Hear the word of the LORD, you who tremble at his word: Your brothers who hated you, who cast you out for my name's sake, said, 'Let the LORD be glorified,' but he will appear to your joy, and they will be ashamed. {66:6} A noise from the city, a voice from the temple, a voice of the LORD that recompenses his enemies. {66:7} Before she gave birth, she delivered; before her pain came, she gave birth to a male child. {66:8} Who has heard such a thing? Who has seen such things? Shall the earth be made to give birth in one day? Or shall a nation be born at once? For as soon as Zion travailed, she brought forth her children. {66:9} Shall I bring to the point of birth and not cause to bring forth? says the LORD. Shall I cause to bring forth and shut the womb? says your God. {66:10} Rejoice with Jerusalem and be glad for her, all you who love her; rejoice with her in joy, all you who mourn for her, {66:11} that you may nurse and be satisfied with the breasts of her consolations; that you may drink deeply and delight in the abundance of her glory. {66:12} For thus says the LORD: Behold, I will extend peace to her like a river and the glory of the Gentiles like a flowing stream. Then you shall nurse, you will be carried on her sides and be dandled on her knees. {66:13} As one whom his mother comforts, so will I comfort you; and you will be comforted in Jerusalem. {66:14} When you see this, your heart will rejoice, and your bones will flourish like an herb; and the hand of the LORD will be known toward his servants, and his indignation toward his enemies. {66:15} For behold, the LORD will come with fire and with his chariots like a whirlwind, to render his anger with fury and his rebuke with flames of fire. {66:16} For by fire and by his sword the LORD will plead with all flesh, and the slain of the LORD will be many. {66:17} Those who sanctify themselves and purify themselves in the gardens behind one tree in the midst, eating swine's flesh, and the abomination, and the mouse, will be consumed together, says the LORD. {66:18} For I know their works and their thoughts: it will come to pass that I will gather all nations and tongues, and they shall come and see my glory. {66:19} I will set a sign among them, and I will send those who escape of them to the nations, to Tarshish, Pul, and Lud, who draw the bow, to Tubal and Javan, to the distant islands that have not heard my fame nor seen my glory; and they shall declare my glory among the Gentiles. {66:20} They will bring all your brothers as an offering to the LORD out of all nations, on horses, in chariots, in litters, and on mules, and on swift beasts, to my holy mountain, Jerusalem, says the LORD, as the children of Israel bring an offering in a clean vessel to the house of the LORD. {66:21} I will also take some of them for priests and for Levites, says the LORD. {66:22} For as the new heavens and the new earth that I will make will remain before me, says the LORD, so will your descendants and your name remain. {66:23} It will come to pass that from one new moon to another, and from one Sabbath to another, all flesh will come to worship before me, says the LORD. {66:24} They will go out and look upon the corpses of the men who have transgressed against me, for their worm will not die, and their fire will not be quenched; they will be an abhorrence to all flesh.

The Book of Jeremiah

{1:1} The words of Jeremiah, the son of Hilkiah, one of the priests in Anathoth in the land of Benjamin: {1:2} The word of the LORD came to him during the days of Josiah, the son of Amon, king of Judah, in the thirteenth year of his reign. {1:3} It also came in the days of Jehoiakim, the son of Josiah, king of Judah, until the end of the eleventh year of Zedekiah, the son of Josiah, king of Judah, when Jerusalem was taken captive in the fifth month. {1:4} Then the word of the LORD came to me, saying, {1:5} "Before I formed you in the womb, I knew you; before you were born, I set you apart and appointed you as a prophet to the nations." {1:6} I said, "Ah, Lord GOD! I cannot speak because I am just a child." {1:7} But the LORD said to me, "Do not say, 'I am a child,' for you must go to everyone I send you to and say whatever I command you. {1:8} Do not be afraid of them, for I am with you and will rescue you," declares the LORD. {1:9} Then the LORD reached out his hand and touched my mouth and said to me, "See, I have put my words in your mouth. {1:10} Today I appoint you over nations and kingdoms to uproot and tear down, to destroy and overthrow, to build and to plant." {1:11} The word of the LORD came to me again, saying, "Jeremiah, what do you see?" I answered, "I see a branch of an almond tree." {1:12} The LORD said to me, "You have seen correctly, for I am watching to see that my word is fulfilled." {1:13} The word of the LORD came to me a second time, asking, "What do you see?" I replied, "I see a boiling pot, tilting away from the north." {1:14} The LORD said to me, "From the north, disaster will be poured out on all who live in the land. {1:15} I am about to summon all the peoples of the northern kingdoms," declares the LORD. "They will come and set their thrones in the entrance of the gates of Jerusalem; they will come against all its surrounding walls and against all the towns of Judah. {1:16} I will pronounce my judgments on my people because of their wickedness in forsaking me, in burning incense to other gods and in worshiping what their hands have made. {1:17} Get yourself ready! Stand up and say to them whatever I command you. Do not be terrified by them, or I will terrify you before them. {1:18} Today I have made you a fortified city, an iron pillar, and a bronze wall to stand against the whole land—against the kings of Judah, its officials, its priests, and the people of the land. {1:19} They will fight against you but will not overcome you, for I am with you and will rescue you," declares the LORD.

{2:1} The word of the LORD came to me: {2:2} "Go and proclaim in the hearing of Jerusalem: 'This is what the LORD says: I remember the devotion of your youth, how as a bride you loved me and followed me through the wilderness, through a land not sown. {2:3} Israel was holy to the LORD, the firstfruits of his harvest; all who devoured her were held guilty, and disaster overtook them,'" declares the LORD. {2:4} Hear the word of the LORD, you descendants of Jacob, all you clans of Israel. {2:5} This is what the LORD says: "What fault did your ancestors find in me that led them to stray so far from me? They followed worthless idols and became worthless themselves. {2:6} They did not ask, 'Where is the LORD who brought us up out of Egypt and led us through the barren wilderness, through a land of deserts and ravines, a land of drought and utter darkness, a land where no one travels and no one lives?' {2:7} I brought you into a fertile land to eat its fruit and rich produce. But you came and defiled my land and made my inheritance detestable. {2:8} The priests did not ask, 'Where is the LORD?' Those who deal with the law did not know me; the leaders rebelled against me. The prophets prophesied by Baal, following worthless idols. {2:9} Therefore I bring charges against you again," declares the LORD, "and I will bring charges against your children's children. {2:10} Cross over to the coasts of Cyprus and look, send to Kedar and observe closely; see if there has ever been anything like this: {2:11} Has a nation ever changed its gods? (Yet they are not gods at all.) But my people have exchanged their glorious God for worthless idols. {2:12} Be appalled at this, you heavens, and shudder with great horror," declares the LORD. {2:13} "My people have committed two sins: They have forsaken me, the spring of living water, and have dug their own cisterns, broken cisterns that cannot hold water. {2:14} Is Israel a servant, a slave by birth? Why then has he become plundered? {2:15} Lions have roared; they have growled at him. They have laid waste his land; his towns are burned and deserted. {2:16} Also, the men of Noph and Tahpanhes have cracked your skull. {2:17} Have you not brought this on yourselves by forsaking the LORD your God when he led you in the way? {2:18} Now why go to Egypt to drink water from the Nile? And why go to Assyria to drink water from the Euphrates? {2:19} Your wickedness will punish you; your backsliding will rebuke you. Consider then and realize how evil and bitter it is for you when you forsake the LORD your God and have no awe of me," declares the Lord, the LORD Almighty. {2:20} Long ago I broke your yoke and tore off your bonds, but you said, 'I will not serve you!' Indeed, on every high hill and under every spreading tree you lay down as a prostitute. {2:21} I had planted you like a choice vine of sound and reliable stock. How then did you turn against me into a corrupt, wild vine? {2:22} Although you wash yourself with soda and use an abundance of soap, the stain of your guilt is still before me," declares the Sovereign LORD. {2:23} How can you say, 'I am not defiled; I have not run after the Baals'? Look at the conduct of your actions in the valley; consider what you have done. You are a swift she-camel running here and there, {2:24} a wild donkey accustomed to the desert, sniffing the wind in her craving—who can restrain her? Any males that pursue her need not tire themselves; at mating time they will find her. {2:25} Do not run until your feet are bare and your throat is dry. But you said, 'It's no use! I love foreign gods, and I must go after them.' {2:26} As a thief is disgraced when he is caught, so the people of Israel are disgraced; they, their kings and their officials, their priests and their prophets, {2:27} they say to wood, 'You are my father,' and to stone, 'You gave me birth.' They have turned their backs to me and not their faces; yet when they are in trouble, they say, 'Come and save us!' {2:28} Where then are the gods you made for yourselves? Let them come if they can save you when you are in trouble! For you, Judah, have as many gods as you have towns. {2:29} Why do you bring charges against me? You have all rebelled against me," declares the LORD. {2:30} "In vain I punished your people; they did not respond to correction. Your sword has devoured your prophets like a ravenous lion. {2:31} You of this generation, consider the word of the LORD: Have I been a desert to Israel or a land of great darkness? Why do my people say, 'We are free to roam; we will come to you no more'? {2:32} Does a young woman forget her jewelry, a bride her wedding ornaments? Yet my people have forgotten me, days without number. {2:33} How skilled you are at pursuing love! Even the worst of women could learn from your ways. {2:34} Your skirts are stained with the blood of the innocent and the poor; I have not found it by stealth, but from your own actions. {2:35} Yet you say, 'I am innocent; he is not angry with me.' But I will pass judgment on you because you say, 'I have not sinned.' {2:36} Why do you go about so much, changing your ways? You will be disappointed by Egypt just as you were by Assyria. {2:37} You will also leave that place with your hands on your head, for the LORD has rejected those you trust; you will not be successful with them."

{3:1} They say, "If a man divorces his wife and she goes away from him and becomes another man's wife, can he return to her again? Wouldn't that land be greatly polluted? Yet you have acted like a prostitute with many lovers; but you can still return to me," declares the LORD. {3:2} Lift your eyes to the high places and see where you have not been unfaithful. You sit by the roadsides like an Arabian in the wilderness; you have polluted the land with your whoredoms and wickedness. {3:3} Therefore, the showers have been withheld, and there has been no late rain; you have a prostitute's forehead and refuse to feel ashamed. {3:4} Will you not call out to me from now on, "My Father, you are my guide from my youth"? {3:5} Will he hold onto his anger forever? Will he keep it to the end? Look, you have spoken and done evil things as you could. {3:6} The LORD said to me during the reign of King Josiah, "Have you seen what backsliding Israel has done? She has gone up to every high mountain and under every green tree, and there she has acted like a prostitute. {3:7} I said after she had done all these things, 'Return to me.' But she did not return. And her treacherous sister Judah saw it. {3:8} I saw that for all the reasons backsliding Israel committed adultery, I had put her away and given her a certificate of divorce; yet her treacherous sister Judah did not fear but went and acted like a prostitute as well. {3:9} And because of her casualness in her whoredom, she defiled the land and committed adultery with stones and wooden idols. {3:10} Yet for all this, her treacherous sister Judah has not turned to me with her whole heart, but only insincerely," says the LORD. {3:11} The LORD said to me, "Backsliding Israel has justified herself more than treacherous Judah. {3:12} Go and proclaim these words to the north, and say, 'Return, backsliding Israel,' says the LORD; 'I will not let my anger fall upon you, for I am merciful,' says the LORD, 'and I will not stay angry forever. {3:13} Just acknowledge your iniquity, that you have rebelled against the LORD your God, and have scattered your ways to strangers under every green tree, and you have not obeyed my voice,' says the LORD. {3:14} "Turn, O backsliding children," says the LORD, "for I am married to you; I will take you from one city and two from a family, and I will bring you to Zion. {3:15} I will give you shepherds after my own heart, who will feed you with knowledge and understanding. {3:16} And it will come to pass when you have multiplied and increased in the land, in those days," says the LORD, "they will no longer say, 'The ark of the covenant of the LORD'; it will not come to mind, nor will they remember it, nor will they visit it, nor will it be made again. {3:17} At that time, Jerusalem will be called the throne of the LORD, and all nations will gather there to the name of the LORD, to Jerusalem. They will no longer walk after the stubbornness of their evil hearts. {3:18} In those days, the house of Judah will walk with the house of Israel, and they will come together from the land of the north to the land I have given as an inheritance to your ancestors. {3:19} But I said, "How can I put you among the children and give you a pleasant land, a goodly heritage of the hosts of nations?" I said, "You will call me, 'My Father,' and you will not turn away from me. {3:20} Surely, like a wife who acts treacherously against her husband, so have you dealt treacherously with me, O house of Israel," says the LORD. {3:21} A voice is heard on the high places, weeping and supplications of the children of Israel, for they have perverted their way and forgotten the LORD their God. {3:22} "Return, you backsliding children, and I will heal your backslidings." Behold, we come to you, for you are the LORD our God. {3:23} Truly, salvation is not hoped for from the hills or from the multitude of mountains; truly, salvation for Israel comes from the LORD our God. {3:24} Shame has consumed the labor of our ancestors from our youth, their flocks and herds, their sons and daughters. {3:25} We lie in shame and confusion, having sinned against the LORD our God, we and our ancestors, from our youth to this day, and have not obeyed His voice.

{4:1} "If you will return, O Israel," says the LORD, "return to me; and if you will put away your abominations out of my sight, then you will not be removed. {4:2} And you shall swear, 'As the LORD lives,' in truth, in justice, and in righteousness; and the nations shall bless themselves in him, and in him they shall glory. {4:3} For thus says the LORD to the men of Judah and Jerusalem, 'Break up your unplowed ground and do not sow among thorns. {4:4} Circumcise yourselves to the LORD, and remove the foreskins of your hearts, you men of Judah and inhabitants of Jerusalem, or my fury will come forth like fire and burn with no one to quench it because of the evil of your deeds.' {4:5} Declare in Judah and proclaim in Jerusalem; say, "Blow the trumpet in the land; cry out, 'Gather together!' and say, 'Assemble yourselves, and let us go into the fortified cities.' {4:6} Set up a banner toward Zion; seek refuge; do not delay, for I will bring disaster from the north and a great destruction. {4:7} A lion has come up from his thicket, and a destroyer of nations is on his way; he has gone forth from his place to make your land desolate, and your cities shall be laid waste without inhabitants. {4:8} For this, put on sackcloth, lament, and howl, for the fierce anger of the LORD has not turned back from us. {4:9} And it will come to pass on that day," says the LORD, "that the heart of the king will perish, and the hearts of the princes; the priests will be astonished, and the prophets will wonder. {4:10} Then I said, "Ah, Lord GOD! Surely you have greatly deceived this people and Jerusalem, saying, 'You shall have peace,' whereas the sword reaches to the soul." {4:11} At that time, it will be said to this people and to Jerusalem, "A dry wind comes from the high places in the wilderness toward the daughter of my people, not to fan nor to cleanse. {4:12} Even a full wind will come from those places; now also, I will give sentence against them. {4:13} Behold, he shall come up like clouds, and his chariots will be like a whirlwind; his horses are swifter than eagles. Woe to us, for we are ruined! {4:14} O Jerusalem, wash your heart from wickedness so that you may be saved. How long will your vain thoughts lodge within you? {4:15} For a voice declares from Dan and publishes affliction from Mount Ephraim. {4:16} Make mention to the nations; behold, publish against Jerusalem, that watchmen come from a far country and give out their voice against the cities of Judah. {4:17} They are like keepers of a field around her, because she has been rebellious against me," says the LORD. {4:18} Your ways and your deeds have brought these things upon you; this is your wickedness, for it is bitter, it reaches to your heart. {4:19} My heart, my heart! I am pained at my very core; my heart makes a noise within me; I cannot hold my peace, because you have heard, O my soul, the sound of the trumpet, the alarm of war. {4:20} Destruction upon destruction is cried out; for the whole land is ruined; my tents are suddenly ruined, and my curtains in a moment. {4:21} How long will I see the banner and hear the sound of the trumpet? {4:22} For my people are foolish; they do not know me; they are senseless children, and they have no understanding; they are wise to do evil, but they have no knowledge to do good. {4:23} I looked at the earth, and behold, it was without form and void; and at the heavens, and they had no light. {4:24} I looked at the mountains, and behold, they trembled, and all the hills moved lightly. {4:25} I looked, and behold, there was no man, and all the birds of the heavens had fled. {4:26} I looked, and behold, the fruitful place was a wilderness, and all its cities were broken down at the presence of the LORD and by his fierce anger. {4:27} For thus says the LORD, "The whole land shall be desolate; yet I will not make a full end. {4:28} For this the earth shall mourn, and the heavens above be black, because I have spoken it; I have purposed it and will not repent; I will not turn back from it. {4:29} The whole city shall flee from the noise of the horsemen and archers; they shall go into thickets and climb up upon the rocks; every city shall be forsaken, and no man will dwell therein. {4:30} And when you are ruined, what will you do? Though you dress yourself in crimson, though you adorn yourself with ornaments of gold, though you paint your face in vain, your lovers will despise you; they will seek your life. {4:31} For I have heard a voice like that of a woman in labor and the anguish of one giving birth to her first child, the voice of the daughter of Zion, who laments and spreads her hands, saying, "Woe is me now! For my soul is weary because of murderers."

{5:1} Go through the streets of Jerusalem and look around. Search the wide places to see if you can find a single man who executes judgment and seeks the truth; if you do, I will forgive the city. {5:2} Even though they say, "As the LORD lives," they swear falsely. {5:3} O LORD, aren't your eyes set on the truth? You have struck them, but they haven't grieved; you have consumed them, but they refuse to accept correction. They have hardened their faces like rock and refuse to return. {5:4} So I thought, "Surely they are poor; they are foolish, for they do not know the way of the LORD or the judgment of their God." {5:5} I will go to the great men and speak to them, for they know the way of the LORD and the judgment of their God; but they have broken the yoke and torn off the bonds. {5:6} Therefore, a lion from the forest will kill them, and a wolf of the evenings will destroy them. A leopard will watch over their cities; anyone who goes out will be torn to pieces, because their transgressions are many and their backslidings have increased. {5:7} How can I forgive you for this? Your children have forsaken me and sworn by what are no gods. When I fed them to the full, they committed adultery and gathered by troops in the houses of prostitutes. {5:8} They were like well-fed horses in the morning; each one neighing after his neighbor's wife. {5:9} Should I not punish these things? says the LORD. Should my soul not be avenged on such a nation as this? {5:10} Go up on her walls and destroy, but don't make a full end. Remove her battlements, for they are not the LORD's. {5:11} For the house of Israel and the house of Judah have dealt very treacherously against me, says the LORD. {5:12} They have denied the LORD, saying, "He will not bring evil upon us; we won't see sword or famine." {5:13} And the prophets will become wind, and the word is not in them; it will happen to them as they say. {5:14} Therefore, thus says the LORD God of hosts, "Because you speak this word, behold, I will make my words in your mouth fire, and this people wood, and it will consume them." {5:15} Look, I will bring a nation against you from far away, O house of Israel, says the LORD. It is a mighty nation, an ancient nation, a nation whose language you do not know and cannot understand. {5:16} Their quiver is like an open grave; they are all mighty men. {5:17} They will eat your harvest and your bread, which your sons and daughters should eat. They will eat your flocks and herds; they will eat your vines and fig trees. They will impoverish your fortified cities, where you trusted, with the sword. {5:18} Nevertheless, in those days, says the LORD, I will not make a full end of you. {5:19} And it will come to pass, when you ask, "Why does the LORD our God do all these things to us?" you will answer them, "Just as you have forsaken me and served strange gods in your land, so you will serve strangers in a land that is not yours." {5:20} Declare this in the house of Jacob, and publish it in Judah, saying, {5:21} "Hear this, O foolish people, and without understanding, who have eyes but do not see, and ears but do not hear." {5:22} Do you not fear me? says the LORD. Will you not tremble at my presence, who set the sand as the boundary of the sea by a perpetual decree, which it cannot pass? Though the waves toss themselves, they cannot prevail; though they roar, they cannot pass over it. {5:23} But this people has a rebellious and revolting heart; they have revolted and gone. {5:24} They do not say in their hearts, "Let us now fear the LORD our God, who gives rain, both the former and the latter, in its season; he reserves for us the appointed weeks of harvest." {5:25} Your iniquities have turned away these blessings, and your sins have withheld good things from you. {5:26} For among my people are found wicked men; they lie in wait like those who set snares. They set traps to catch men. {5:27} Like a cage full of birds, so their houses are full of deceit; therefore they have become great and grown rich. {5:28} They have become fat; they shine. Yes, they surpass the deeds of the wicked; they do not judge fairly in the case of the fatherless, yet they prosper. They do not judge the rights of the needy. {5:29} Should I not punish these things? says the LORD. Should my soul not be avenged on such a nation as this? {5:30} A horrible and wonderful thing is happening in the land; {5:31} the prophets prophesy falsely, and the priests rule by their means. My people love to have it so; what will you do in the end?

{6:1} O children of Benjamin, gather yourselves to flee out of the midst of Jerusalem, and blow the trumpet in Tekoa, and set up a signal fire in Bethhaccerem, for evil is appearing from the north and great destruction. {6:2} I have likened the daughter of Zion to a beautiful and delicate woman. {6:3} The shepherds with their flocks will come to her; they will pitch their tents around her and feed each in his place. {6:4} Prepare for war against her; arise and let us go up at noon. Woe to us! For the day is fading, and the shadows of evening are stretching out. {6:5} Arise and let us go by night and destroy her palaces. {6:6} For thus says the LORD of hosts, "Cut down trees and build a mound against Jerusalem; this is the city to be punished; she is wholly oppression in the midst of her. {6:7} Like a fountain that pours out its waters, so she pours out her wickedness; violence and plunder are heard in her; I see continual grief and wounds. {6:8} Be instructed, O Jerusalem, or my soul will depart from you; lest I make you desolate, a land not inhabited. {6:9} Thus says the LORD of hosts, "They will thoroughly glean the remnant of Israel like a vine; turn back your hand like a grape gatherer into the baskets." {6:10} To whom shall I speak and give warning so they may hear? Look, their ears are uncircumcised (not open), and they cannot listen. Behold, the word of the LORD is a reproach to them; they take no delight in it. {6:11} Therefore, I am full of the fury of the LORD; I am weary of holding it in. I will pour it out on the children abroad and on the assembly of young men; for even the husband and wife will be taken, the aged and the one full of days. {6:12} Their houses will be turned over to others, along with their fields and wives, for I will stretch out my hand against the inhabitants of the land, says the LORD. {6:13} For from the least to the greatest, everyone is given to covetousness; from the prophet to the priest, everyone deals falsely. {6:14} They have healed the hurt of the daughter of my people slightly, saying, "Peace, peace," when there is no peace. {6:15} Were they ashamed when they committed abominations? No, they were not at all ashamed; they could not blush. Therefore, they will fall among those who fall; at the time I visit them, they will be cast down, says the LORD. {6:16} Thus says the LORD, "Stand in the ways and see, and ask for the old paths, where the good way is, and walk in it, and you will find rest for your souls." But they said, "We will not walk in it." {6:17} I also set watchmen over you, saying, "Listen to the sound of the trumpet." But they said, "We will not listen." {6:18} Therefore, hear, you nations, and know, O congregation, what is among them. {6:19} Hear, O earth: behold, I will bring evil upon this people, the fruit of their thoughts, because they have not heeded my words nor my law but have rejected it. {6:20} To what purpose does incense from Sheba come to me, and sweet cane from a far country? Your burnt offerings are not acceptable, nor are your sacrifices sweet to me. {6:21} Therefore, thus says the LORD, "Behold, I will lay stumbling blocks before this people, and both fathers and sons shall stumble over them; neighbors and friends shall perish." {6:22} Thus says the LORD, "Behold, a people comes from the north country, and a great nation will be raised from the ends of the earth. {6:23} They will take hold of bow and spear; they are cruel and have no mercy; their voice roars like the sea, and they ride on horses, arranged like men for war against you, O daughter of Zion. {6:24} We have heard the news; our hands grow weak; anguish has taken hold of us, and pain, like that of a woman in labor. {6:25} Do not go out into the field or walk by the way, for the sword of the enemy and fear are on every side. {6:26} O daughter of my people, dress yourself in sackcloth and roll in ashes; mourn like for an only son, most bitter lamentation, for the destroyer will suddenly come upon us. {6:27} I have set you as a tower and fortress among my people, that you may know and test their way. {6:28} They are all grievous rebels, walking with slanderers; they are brass and iron; they are all corrupt. {6:29} The bellows are burned; the lead is consumed by the fire; the founder melts in vain; for the wicked are not removed. {6:30} Reprobate (worthless) silver will be called them because the LORD has rejected them.

{7:1} The word that came to Jeremiah from the LORD was this: {7:2} "Stand at the gate of the LORD's house and proclaim this word: Hear the word of the LORD, all you people of Judah who enter through these gates to worship the LORD. {7:3} Thus says the LORD of hosts, the God of Israel: Change your ways and your actions, and I will let you live in this place. {7:4} Don't trust in deceptive words that say, 'The temple of the LORD, the temple of the LORD, the temple of the LORD!' {7:5} If you truly change your ways and actions; if you honestly judge between one person and another; {7:6} if you do not oppress the foreigner, the fatherless, and the widow, and do not shed innocent blood in this place, and do not follow other gods to your own harm, {7:7} then I will let you live in this place, in the land I gave to your ancestors, forever and ever. {7:8} But look, you trust in deceptive words that are worthless. {7:9} Will you steal, murder, commit adultery, swear falsely, burn incense to Baal, and follow other gods you do not know, {7:10} and then come and stand before me in this house that bears my name, and say, 'We are safe!'—safe to do all these detestable things? {7:11} Has this house, which bears my name, become a den of robbers in your eyes? Look, I have seen it, says the LORD. {7:12} Go now to my place in Shiloh, where I first made my name dwell, and see what I did to it because of the wickedness of my people Israel. {7:13} Now, because you have done all these things, says the LORD, and I spoke to you, rising up early and speaking, but you did not listen; I called you, but you did not answer. {7:14} Therefore, I will do to this house that bears my name, the one you trust in, and to the place I gave you and your ancestors, what I did to Shiloh. {7:15} I will cast you out of my sight as I did all your relatives, the whole family of Ephraim. {7:16} So do not pray for this people, nor offer any plea or petition for them; do not intercede with me, for I will not listen to you. {7:17} Do you not see what they are doing in the towns of Judah and in the streets of Jerusalem? {7:18} The children gather wood, the fathers light the fire, and the women knead the dough to make cakes for the queen of heaven and to pour out drink offerings to other gods, provoking me to anger. {7:19} But am I the one they are provoking? declares the LORD. Are they not rather harming themselves, to their own shame? {7:20} Therefore, this is what the Sovereign LORD says: My anger and my wrath will be poured out on this place, on humans and animals, on the trees of the field and on the crops of your land, and it will burn and not be quenched. {7:21} This is what the LORD Almighty, the God of Israel, says: Add your burnt offerings to your other sacrifices and eat the meat yourselves! {7:22} For when I brought your ancestors out of Egypt and spoke to them, I did not just give them commands about burnt offerings and sacrifices, {7:23} but I gave them this command: Obey me, and I will be your God, and you will be my people. Walk in obedience to all I command you, that it may go well with you. {7:24} But they did not listen or pay attention; they followed the stubborn inclinations of their evil hearts; they went backward and not forward. {7:25} From the time your ancestors left Egypt until now, day after day, again and again, I sent you my servants the prophets. {7:26} But they did not listen to me or pay attention. They were stiff-necked (stubborn) and did more evil than their ancestors. {7:27} You are to tell them all this, but they will not listen; you are to call to them, but they will not answer. {7:28} Say to them, 'This is the nation that has not obeyed the LORD its God or responded to correction. Truth has perished; it has vanished from their lips.' {7:29} Cut off your hair, Jerusalem, and throw it away; take up a lament on the barren heights, for the LORD has rejected and forsaken this generation that is under his wrath. {7:30} The people of Judah have done evil in my sight, declares the LORD; they have set up their detestable idols in the house that bears my name and have defiled it. {7:31} They have built the high places of Tophet in the Valley of Ben Hinnom to burn their sons and daughters in the fire, something I did not command, nor did it enter my mind. {7:32} So beware, the days are coming, declares the LORD, when it will no longer be called Tophet or the Valley of Ben Hinnom, but the Valley of Slaughter, for they will bury the dead in Tophet until there is no more room. {7:33} Then the carcasses of this people will become food for the birds and the wild animals, and there will be no one to frighten them away. {7:34} I will bring to an end the sounds of joy and gladness and the voices of bride & bridegroom in the towns of Judah & the streets of Jerusalem, for the land will become desolate."

{8:1} At that time, declares the LORD, the bones of the kings of Judah, the bones of its officials, the bones of the priests, the bones of the prophets, and the bones of the people of Jerusalem will be removed from their graves. {8:2} They will be exposed to the sun, the moon, and all the stars of the heavens, which they have loved and served and followed and sought and worshiped. They will not be gathered up or buried; they will be like dung on the ground. {8:3} Death will be chosen rather than life by all the remnant of those who remain from this evil family, those who remain in all the places where I have driven them, declares the LORD Almighty. {8:4} Say to them, 'This is what the LORD says: When people fall down, do they not get up? When someone turns away, does he not return? {8:5} Why then has this people of Jerusalem turned away in a persistent rebellion? They hold fast to deceit; they refuse to return. {8:6} I have listened attentively, but they do not say what is right. No one repents of their wickedness, saying, "What have I done?" Everyone turns to their own course, like a horse charging into battle. {8:7} Even the stork in the sky knows her appointed seasons, and the dove, the swift, and the thrush observe the time of their migration, but my people do not know the requirements of the LORD. {8:8} How can you say, "We are wise, for we have the law of the LORD"? When actually the scribes have handled it falsely. {8:9} The wise will be put to shame; they will be dismayed and trapped; since they have rejected the word of the LORD, what kind of wisdom do they have? {8:10} Therefore I will give their wives to other men and their fields to new owners. From the least to the greatest, all are greedy for gain; prophets and priests alike, all practice deceit. {8:11} They dress the wound of my people as though it were not serious. "Peace, peace," they say, when there is no peace. {8:12} Are they ashamed of their detestable conduct? No, they have no shame at all; they do not even know how to blush. So they will fall among the fallen; they will be brought down when I punish them, says the LORD. {8:13} I will take away their harvest, declares the LORD; there will be no grapes on the vine, no figs on the fig tree, and the leaves will wither. What I have given them will be taken from them. {8:14} Why are we sitting here?

Gather together; let us flee to the fortified cities and die there! For the LORD our God has doomed us to perish and given us poison (gall) to drink because we have sinned against him. {8:15} We hoped for peace, but no good has come; for a time of healing, but there is only terror. {8:16} The snorting of the enemy's horses is heard from Dan; at the sound of the neighing of their stallions, the whole land trembles. They have come to devour the land and everything in it, the city and all who live there. {8:17} I will send venomous snakes among you, vipers that cannot be charmed, and they will bite you, declares the LORD. {8:18} O my comforter in sorrow, my heart is faint within me. {8:19} Listen to the cry of my people from a land far away: "Is the LORD not in Zion? Is her King no longer there?" Why have they aroused my anger with their images, with their worthless foreign idols? {8:20} The harvest is past, the summer has ended, and we are not saved. {8:21} Since my people are crushed, I am crushed; I mourn, and horror grips me. {8:22} Is there no balm in Gilead? Is there no physician there? Why then is there no healing for the wound of my people?

{9:1} Oh, that my head were a fountain of water, and my eyes a well of tears, so I could weep day and night for the slain of my people! {9:2} If only I had a place in the wilderness where travelers could stay; I would leave my people and go away from them, for they are all unfaithful, a group of treacherous people. {9:3} They use their tongues like bows to shoot lies; they are not brave for the truth on the earth. They go from bad to worse, and they don't know me, says the LORD. {9:4} Each one should be careful of his neighbor, and don't trust any brother; for every brother will utterly deceive, and every neighbor will slander. {9:5} They deceive each other and don't speak the truth; they have trained their tongues to lie, and they work hard to commit wrongdoing. {9:6} Your home is full of deceit; through deceit, they refuse to know me, says the LORD. {9:7} Therefore, the LORD Almighty says: Look, I will melt them down and test them; how else can I help my people? {9:8} Their tongues are like arrows shot out; they speak deceit. One speaks peaceably to his neighbor with his mouth, but in his heart, he is waiting to trap him. {9:9} Shouldn't I punish them for these things? says the LORD. Shouldn't my soul be avenged on such a nation as this? {9:10} I will take up a lament for the mountains and a mourning for the pastures of the wilderness, because they are burned up, so that no one can pass through them; neither can anyone hear the voices of the cattle. The birds of the sky and the animals have fled; they are gone. {9:11} I will make Jerusalem a pile of ruins, a den of jackals, and I will make the cities of Judah desolate, with no inhabitants. {9:12} Who is the wise person who can understand this? Who has the mouth of the LORD spoken to, so that he can declare it? Why is the land perishing and burned up like a wilderness where no one passes through? {9:13} The LORD says it's because they have forsaken my law that I set before them, and they haven't obeyed my voice or walked in it; {9:14} but they have followed the stubbornness of their hearts and the worship of Baal, which their ancestors taught them. {9:15} Therefore, the LORD Almighty, the God of Israel, says: Look, I will feed this people with wormwood and give them poison to drink. {9:16} I will scatter them among the nations, whom neither they nor their ancestors have known, and I will send a sword after them until I have consumed them. {9:17} The LORD Almighty says: Consider and call for the mourning women to come; send for the skilled women to come. {9:18} Let them hurry and take up a wailing for us, so our eyes may run down with tears and our eyelids gush with water. {9:19} A voice of wailing is heard from Zion: "How are we ruined! We are greatly ashamed because we have forsaken the land; our homes have been torn down." {9:20} Yet hear the word of the LORD, you women, and let your ears receive the word from his mouth. Teach your daughters to wail, and each neighbor to lament. {9:21} Death has climbed in through our windows and entered our palaces to cut off the children from the streets and the young men from the public squares. {9:22} Say this: The bodies of people will fall like dung on the open field and like sheaves after the harvest, and no one will gather them. {9:23} The LORD says: Let not the wise person boast in his wisdom, nor the mighty person boast in his strength, nor the rich person boast in his riches. {9:24} But let the one who boasts boast in this: that he understands and knows me, that I am the LORD who exercises lovingkindness, justice, and righteousness on the earth, for in these things I delight, says the LORD. {9:25} Look, the days are coming, says the LORD, when I will punish all those who are circumcised along with the uncircumcised; {9:26} Egypt, Judah, Edom, the children of Ammon, Moab, and all who live in the farthest corners of the wilderness, for all these nations are uncircumcised, and all the house of Israel is uncircumcised in heart.

{10:1} Listen to the word that the LORD speaks to you, house of Israel. {10:2} The LORD says: Don't learn the ways of the nations or be alarmed by signs in the heavens, as the nations are alarmed by them. {10:3} The practices of the people are worthless; one cuts a tree from the forest, the work of a craftsman with an axe. {10:4} They adorn it with silver and gold; they fasten it with nails and hammers so it won't fall over. {10:5} They are upright like a palm tree, but they cannot speak. They must be carried because they cannot walk. Don't be afraid of them, for they can do no harm, nor is it in them to do good. {10:6} There is no one like you, O LORD; you are great, and your name is mighty. {10:7} Who would not fear you, King of nations? For it is your due. Among all the wise men of the nations and in all their kingdoms, there is none like you. {10:8} They are all senseless and foolish; the teachings they follow are worthless. {10:9} Silver is brought from Tarshish, and gold from Uphaz, the work of craftsmen and metalworkers. Blue and purple are their garments; they are all the work of skilled craftsmen. {10:10} But the LORD is the true God; he is the living God and an everlasting King. At his wrath, the earth trembles, and the nations cannot withstand his anger. {10:11} Say to them: The gods who did not make the heavens and the earth will perish from the earth and under the heavens. {10:12} He made the earth by his power, established the world by his wisdom, and stretched out the heavens by his understanding. {10:13} When he speaks, there is a roar of waters in the heavens; he causes vapors to rise from the ends of the earth; he makes lightning with rain and brings the wind from his storehouses. {10:14} Every person is stupid in his knowledge; every goldsmith is put to shame by his idols. His molten image is a lie, and there is no breath in them. {10:15} They are worthless and the work of delusion; in the time of their punishment, they will perish. {10:16} The portion of Jacob is not like them; he is the Creator of all things, and Israel is the tribe of his inheritance. The LORD Almighty is his name. {10:17} Gather your belongings from the land, you who live in the fortress. {10:18} For the LORD says: Look, I will throw out the inhabitants of the land at this time and will distress them, so they will know it's true. {10:19} Woe is me for my injury! My wound is grievous; but I said, "This is truly a grief, and I must bear it." {10:20} My tent is ruined, and all my ropes are broken; my children have gone away from me, and they are no more. There is no one to stretch out my tent anymore or set up my curtains. {10:21} For the shepherds have become stupid and haven't sought the LORD; therefore, they will not prosper, and all their flocks will be scattered. {10:22} Look, the noise of the report is coming, and a great commotion from the north is making the cities of Judah desolate, a den of jackals. {10:23} O LORD, I know that the way of man is not in himself; it is not in man who walks to direct his steps. {10:24} O LORD, correct me, but with justice; not in your anger, or you will bring me to nothing. {10:25} Pour out your wrath on the nations that do not know you and on the families that do not call on your name, for they have consumed Jacob and devoured him, and made his home desolate.

{11:1} The word that came to Jeremiah from the LORD was this: {11:2} Listen to the words of this covenant and speak to the men of Judah and the inhabitants of Jerusalem; {11:3} and say to them, This is what the LORD, the God of Israel, says: Cursed is the person who does not obey the words of this covenant, {11:4} which I commanded your ancestors when I brought them out of the land of Egypt, from the iron furnace. I said, Obey my voice and do all that I command you, and you will be my people, and I will be your God. {11:5} This way, I can fulfill the oath I swore to your ancestors to give them a land flowing with milk and honey, as it is today. Then I answered, So be it, O LORD. {11:6} The LORD said to me, Proclaim all these words in the cities of Judah and in the streets of Jerusalem, saying, Listen to the words of this covenant and do them. {11:7} For I earnestly warned your ancestors the day I brought them out of Egypt, even to this day, rising early and warning them, saying, Obey my voice. {11:8} Yet they did not obey or listen; each one walked in the stubbornness of their evil heart. Therefore, I will bring upon them all the words of this covenant, which I commanded them to do, but they did not do them. {11:9} The LORD said to me, A conspiracy is found among the men of Judah and the inhabitants of Jerusalem. {11:10} They have turned back to the sins of their ancestors, who refused to listen to my words, and they went after other gods to serve them. The house of Israel and the house of Judah have broken my covenant that I made with their ancestors. {11:11} Therefore, the LORD says: Look, I will bring disaster upon them from which they will not be able to escape; and even if they cry out to me, I will not listen. {11:12} Then the cities of Judah and the inhabitants of Jerusalem will go and cry out to the gods they offer incense to, but they will not save them at all in their time of trouble. {11:13} For according to the number of your cities, O Judah, are your gods; and according to the number of the streets of Jerusalem, you have set up altars to that shameful thing, altars to burn incense to Baal. {11:14} Therefore, do not pray for this people, nor lift up a cry or prayer for them, for I will not hear them when they cry out to me in their time of trouble. {11:15} What does my beloved have to do in my house, since she has committed many sins and the holy food has departed from you? When you do evil, you rejoice. {11:16} The LORD called you a green olive tree, beautiful and with good fruit; but with the noise of a great tumult, he has kindled fire upon it, and its branches are broken. {11:17} For the LORD of hosts, who planted you, has pronounced disaster against you for the evil of the house of Israel and the house of Judah, which they have done to provoke me to anger by offering incense to Baal. {11:18} The LORD has given me knowledge of it, and I know it; then you showed me their deeds. {11:19} But I was like a lamb or an ox being led to slaughter, and I did not know that they had devised plans against me, saying, Let us destroy the tree with its fruit and cut him off from the land of the living, so that his name will no longer be remembered. {11:20} But, O LORD of hosts, who judges righteously and tests the heart and mind, let me see your vengeance upon them, for I have revealed my cause to you. {11:21} Therefore, the LORD says concerning the men of Anathoth who seek your life, saying, Do not prophesy in the name of the LORD, or you will die by our hands: {11:22} therefore, the LORD of hosts says: Look, I will punish them; the young men will die by the sword, and their sons and daughters will die by famine. {11:23} There will be no survivors among them, for I will bring disaster upon the men of Anathoth in the year of their punishment.

{12:1} You are righteous, O LORD, when I bring my case before you; yet I would like to talk to you about your judgments: Why does the way of the wicked prosper? Why are all those who deal so treacherously happy? {12:2} You have planted them; they have taken root; they grow, they produce fruit. You are near in their mouths but far from their hearts. {12:3} But you, O LORD, know me; you have seen me and tested my heart toward you. Pull them out like sheep for the slaughter and prepare them for the day of slaughter. {12:4} How long will the land mourn and the grass of every field wither, because of the wickedness of those who live there? The animals and the birds are consumed because they said, He will not see our end. {12:5} If you have run with footmen and they have tired you, how can you contend with horses? If in a peaceful land where you trusted, they have worn you out, how will you manage in the swelling of the Jordan? {12:6} For even your brothers, the members of your own family, have dealt treacherously with you; they have called out a multitude after you. Do not believe them, even though they speak kindly to you. {12:7} I have forsaken my house; I have left my inheritance; I have given the dearly beloved of my soul into the hands of her enemies. {12:8} My inheritance has become to me like a lion in the forest; it cries out against me; therefore, I hate it. {12:9} My inheritance has become to me like a speckled bird; the birds around are against her. Come, gather all the beasts of the field; come to devour. {12:10} Many shepherds have destroyed my vineyard; they have trampled my portion underfoot; they have made my pleasant portion a desolate wilderness. {12:11} They have made it desolate, and being desolate, it mourns for me; the whole land is made desolate because no one takes it to heart. {12:12} The destroyers have come upon all the high places in the wilderness; the sword of the LORD will devour from one end of the land to the other; no one will have peace. {12:13} They have sown wheat but will reap thorns; they have worked hard but will not benefit; they will be ashamed of their harvests because of the fierce anger of the LORD. {12:14} This is what the LORD says against all my evil neighbors who touch the inheritance I gave my people Israel: Look, I will uproot them from their land and uproot the house of Judah from among them. {12:15} And after I uproot them, I will have compassion on them and bring them back, each person to his inheritance and each person to his land. {12:16} And it will come to pass that if they will diligently learn the ways of my people and swear by my name, As the LORD lives, just as they taught my people to swear by Baal, then they will be built up in the midst of my people. {12:17} But if they do not obey, I will completely uproot and destroy that nation, says the LORD.

{13:1} The LORD said to me, Go and get a linen belt and put it around your waist, but do not put it in water. {13:2} So I got a belt as the LORD instructed and put it around my waist. {13:3} Then the word of the LORD came to me a second time, saying, {13:4} Take the belt you have, which is around your waist, and go to the Euphrates River. Hide it there in a crevice of a rock. {13:5} So I went and hid it by the Euphrates, as the LORD commanded me. {13:6} After many days, the LORD said to me, Arise, go to the Euphrates and take the belt from there, which I commanded you to hide. {13:7} I went to the Euphrates, dug, and took the belt from the place where I had hidden it. Behold, the belt was ruined; it was good for nothing. {13:8} Then the word of the LORD came to me, saying, {13:9} This is what the LORD says: I will ruin the pride of Judah and the great pride of Jerusalem. {13:10} This evil people, who refuse to listen to my words and follow the stubbornness of their hearts, and go after other gods to serve and worship them, will be like this belt, which is good for nothing. {13:11} Just as a belt clings to a person's waist, I made the whole house of Israel and the whole house of Judah cling to me, says the LORD, so that they would be my people, for my name, for praise, and for glory; but they would not listen. {13:12} Therefore, you will speak this word to them: This is what the LORD, the God of Israel, says: Every jug will be filled with wine. And they will say to you, Don't we already know that every jug will be filled with wine? {13:13} Then you will say to them, This is what the LORD says: Look, I will fill all the inhabitants of this land, including the kings who sit on David's throne, the priests, the prophets, and all the inhabitants of Jerusalem, with drunkenness. {13:14} I will smash them against one another, parents and children together, says the LORD. I will not show pity, nor spare, nor have mercy, but will destroy them. {13:15} Listen and pay attention; do not be proud, for the LORD has spoken. {13:16} Give glory to the LORD your God before he brings darkness, and before your feet stumble on the dark mountains; and while you look for light, he will turn it into deep darkness. {13:17} But if you will not listen, my soul will weep in secret for your pride; my eyes will weep bitterly and run down with tears because the LORD's flock is taken captive. {13:18} Say to the king and the queen, Humble yourselves and sit down, for your crowns will come down, even the crown of your glory. {13:19} The cities of the south will be shut up, and no one will open them; Judah will be entirely taken captive. {13:20} Lift up your eyes and see those who come from the north: Where is the flock that was given to you, your beautiful flock? {13:21} What will you say when he punishes you? For you have taught them to be captains, and they are your leaders. Will not pains seize you like those of a woman in labor? {13:22} And if you say in your heart, Why have these things happened to me? It is because of the greatness of your iniquity that your skirts are uncovered and your heels are bare. {13:23} Can an Ethiopian change his skin, or a leopard change its spots? Then you also can do good, who are accustomed to doing evil. {13:24} Therefore, I will scatter them like chaff that passes away in the wind of the wilderness. {13:25} This is your lot, the portion I have measured out for you, says the LORD, because you have forgotten me and trusted in falsehood. {13:26} Therefore, I will expose your skirts to your face, so that your shame may appear. {13:27} I have seen your adulteries & your lustful neighing, the lewdness of your whoredom & your abominations in the hills and fields. Woe to you, O Jerusalem! Will you not be made clean? When will you be made clean?

{14:1} The word of the LORD that came to Jeremiah concerning the drought. {14:2} Judah mourns, and her gates languish; they are darkened to the ground, and the cry of Jerusalem has gone up. {14:3} Their nobles have sent their servants for water; they went to the cisterns but found no water. They returned with their vessels empty; they were ashamed and dismayed, and they covered their heads. {14:4} Because the ground is cracked, for there has been no rain in the land, the farmers are ashamed; they cover their heads. {14:5} Even the doe in the field gives birth and abandons her young because there is no grass. {14:6} Wild donkeys stand on the barren heights; they pant like jackals; their eyes fail because there is no grass. {14:7} O LORD, though our iniquities testify against us, act for your name's sake; for our backslidings are many; we have sinned against you. {14:8} O hope of Israel, its savior in time of trouble, why should you be like a stranger in the land and like a traveler who turns aside to stay for a night? {14:9} Why should you be like a man confused, like a mighty man who cannot save? Yet you, O LORD, are in our midst, and we are called by your name; do not leave us. {14:10} Thus says the LORD to this people: They have loved to wander; they have not restrained their feet, so the LORD does not accept them; he will now remember their iniquity and visit their sins. {14:11} Then the LORD said to me, Do not pray for this people for their good. {14:12} When they fast, I will not hear their cry; and when they offer burnt offerings and grain offerings, I will not accept them; but I will consume them by the sword, famine, and pestilence. {14:13} Then I said, Ah, Lord GOD! The prophets say to them, You will not see the sword, nor will you have famine; but I will give you assured peace in this place. {14:14} Then the LORD said to me, The prophets prophesy lies in my name; I did not send them, nor did I command them, nor did I speak to them. They prophesy to you a false vision, divination, and the deceit of their own hearts. {14:15} Therefore, this is what the LORD says concerning the prophets who prophesy in my name, yet I did not send them, and they say, Sword and famine will not be in this land; by sword and famine those prophets will be consumed. {14:16} The people to whom they prophesy will be thrown out into the streets of Jerusalem because of famine and sword; and there will be no one to bury them, neither their wives, nor their sons, nor their daughters, for I will pour out their wickedness upon them. {14:17} Therefore, you will say this word to them: Let my eyes run down with tears night and day; let them not cease, for the virgin daughter of my people is broken with a great breach, with a very grievous blow. {14:18} If I go out into the field, look, those slain by the sword! And if I enter the city, look, those sick from famine! Both the prophet and the priest go about in a land they do not know. {14:19} Have you utterly rejected Judah? Has your soul loathed Zion? Why have you struck us so that there is no healing for us? We looked for peace, but there was no good; and for a time of healing, but behold, trouble! {14:20} We acknowledge, O LORD, our wickedness and the iniquity of our ancestors; for we have sinned against you. {14:21} Do not reject us, for your name's sake; do not disgrace the throne of your glory; remember, do not break your covenant with us. {14:22} Are there any among the idols of the nations that can cause rain? Or can the heavens give showers? Are you not he, O LORD our God? Therefore, we will wait for you, for you have made all these things.

{15:1} The LORD said to me, Even if Moses and Samuel stood before me, my mind would not be directed toward this people. Cast them out of my sight and let them go. {15:2} If they ask you, Where shall we go? tell them, This is what the LORD says: Those destined for death will die; those destined for the sword will be killed; those destined for famine will starve; and those destined for captivity will be taken captive. {15:3} I will appoint four kinds of destruction for them, says the LORD: the sword to kill, dogs to tear, birds of the air, and wild animals to devour and destroy. {15:4} I will make them a desolation in all the kingdoms of the earth, because of Manasseh, the son of Hezekiah, king of Judah, for what he did in Jerusalem. {15:5} Who will have pity on you, O Jerusalem? Who will mourn for you? Who will go aside to ask how you are doing? {15:6} You have forsaken me, says the LORD; you have turned away from me. Therefore, I will stretch out my hand against you and destroy you; I am tired of repenting. {15:7} I will winnow them like chaff at the gates of the land; I will take away their children and destroy my people because they do not turn from their ways. {15:8} Their widows will increase more than the sand of the seas. I have brought upon them a destroyer at noonday; I have caused him to fall suddenly upon the city, bringing terror. {15:9} She who has borne seven children will languish; she will give up her life. Her sun has set while it is still day; she will be ashamed and humiliated. The remnant will I deliver to the sword before their enemies, says the LORD. {15:10} Woe to me, my mother, that you bore me a man of strife and contention for the whole earth! I have neither lent money at interest, nor have I borrowed money; yet all of them curse me. {15:11} The LORD said, Surely it will be well with your remnant; I will make the enemy treat you well in the time of evil and in the time of trouble. {15:12} Can iron break northern iron and bronze? {15:13} I will give your wealth and treasures as plunder without cost, for all your sins, even in all your borders. {15:14} I will make you pass with your enemies into a land you do not know, for a fire is kindled in my anger, which will burn upon you. {15:15} O LORD, you know: remember me, and visit me, and take vengeance on my persecutors; do not take me away in your long-suffering. Know that for your sake I have suffered disgrace. {15:16} Your words were found, and I ate them; your word was the joy and rejoicing of my heart, for I am called by your name, O LORD God of hosts. {15:17} I did not sit in the assembly of the mockers, nor did I rejoice; I sat alone because of your hand, for you have filled me with indignation. {15:18} Why is my pain perpetual and my wound incurable, which refuses to be healed? Will you be altogether like a liar to me, like waters that fail? {15:19} Therefore, this is what the LORD says: If you return, I will bring you back, and you will stand before me. If you take the precious from the worthless, you will be like my mouth. Let them return to you, but you must not return to them. {15:20} I will make you a fortified wall to this people, and they will fight against you, but they will not prevail against you; for I am with you to save you and deliver you, says the LORD. {15:21} I will rescue you from the hand of the wicked and redeem you from the grasp of the terrible.

{16:1} The word of the LORD also came to me, saying, {16:2} You shall not take a wife, nor shall you have sons or daughters in this place. {16:3} For this is what the LORD says about the sons and daughters born in this place, and about their mothers who bore them, and about their fathers who fathered them in this land: {16:4} They will die of terrible deaths; they will not be lamented; they will not be buried, but will be like dung on the face of the earth. They will be consumed by the sword and by famine, and their corpses will be food for the birds of the air and the beasts of the earth. {16:5} For this is what the LORD says: Do not enter the house of mourning, nor go to lament or grieve for them, for I have taken my peace from this people, says the LORD, even lovingkindness and mercy. {16:6} Both great and small will die in this land; they will not be buried, nor will people lament for them, nor cut themselves, nor shave their heads for them. {16:7} Nor will people tear themselves in mourning to comfort them for the dead; nor will anyone give them the cup of consolation to drink for their father or mother. {16:8} You shall not go into the house of feasting to sit with them, to eat and drink. {16:9} For this is what the LORD of hosts, the God of Israel, says: Behold, I will cause to cease in this place, before your eyes and in your days, the sound of joy, the sound of gladness, the voice of the bridegroom, and the voice of the bride. {16:10} When you tell this people all these words, they will ask you, Why has the LORD pronounced all this great evil against us? What is our iniquity? What is our sin that we have committed against the LORD our God? {16:11} Then you shall say to them, Because your ancestors have forsaken me, says the LORD, and have walked after other gods, and have served them and worshipped them, and have forsaken me and not kept my law; {16:12} and you have done worse than your fathers, for each of you follows the stubbornness of your evil heart, so that you do not listen to me. {16:13} Therefore, I will cast you out of this land into a land you do not know, neither you nor your fathers; and there you will serve other gods day and night, where I will not show you favor. {16:14} Therefore, behold, the days are coming, says the LORD, when it will no longer be said, The LORD lives, who brought the children of Israel up out of the land of Egypt; {16:15} but, The LORD lives, who brought up the children of Israel from the land of the north and from all the lands where I had driven them; and I will bring them back into their land that I gave to their fathers. {16:16} Behold, I will send for many fishermen, says the LORD, and they will fish for them; and after that, I will send for many hunters, and they will hunt them from every mountain, and from every hill, and out of the holes of the rocks. {16:17} For my eyes are upon all their ways; they are not hidden from my face, nor is their iniquity hidden from my eyes. {16:18} First, I will repay them for their iniquity and their sin double; because they have defiled my land, they have filled my inheritance with the corpses of their detestable and abominable things. {16:19} O LORD, my strength, my fortress, and my refuge in the day of trouble, the nations will come to you from the ends of the earth and will say, Surely our ancestors inherited lies, worthless things, and things that do not profit. {16:20} Can a man make gods for himself, and they are not gods? {16:21} Therefore, behold, I will once again make them know; I will make them know my power and my might; and they will know that my name is The LORD.

{17:1} The sin of Judah is inscribed with an iron pen, and with a diamond point; it is engraved on the tablet of their hearts and on the corners of your altars. {17:2} While their children remember their altars and their sacred groves near the green trees on the high hills. {17:3} O my mountain in the field, I will give your wealth and all your treasures as plunder, and your high places for sin throughout all your borders. {17:4} You yourself will lose the inheritance I gave you; and I will make you serve your enemies in a land you do not know, for you have kindled a fire in my anger that will burn forever. {17:5} Thus says the LORD: Cursed is the person who trusts in man, who relies on human strength, and whose heart departs from the LORD. {17:6} They will be like a shrub in the desert and will not see when good comes; they will live in parched places in the wilderness, in a salt land that is uninhabited. {17:7} Blessed is the person who trusts in the LORD, whose hope is the LORD. {17:8} They will be like a tree planted by the waters, spreading out its roots by the river; they will not fear when heat comes, but their leaves will be green; they will not be anxious in the year of drought and will not cease to bear fruit. {17:9} The heart is deceitful above all things and desperately wicked; who can know it? {17:10} I, the LORD, search the heart; I test the mind, to give each person according to their ways, according to the fruit of their deeds. {17:11} Like a partridge sitting on eggs it did not lay, so is the one who gains riches unjustly; in the midst of their days, they will lose them, and at the end, they will be fools. {17:12} A glorious high throne from the beginning is the place of our sanctuary. {17:13} O LORD, the hope of Israel, all who forsake you will be ashamed, and those who depart from me will be written in the dust, because they have forsaken the LORD, the fountain of living waters. {17:14} Heal me, O LORD, and I will be healed; save me, and I will be saved, for you are my praise. {17:15} Behold, they say to me, Where is the word of the LORD? Let it come now. {17:16} As for me, I have not hurried to be a pastor to follow you, nor have I desired the woeful day; you know that what came from my lips was right before you. {17:17} Do not be a terror to me; you are my hope in the day of evil. {17:18} Let those who persecute me be ashamed, but do not let me be ashamed; let them be dismayed, but do not let me be dismayed; bring upon them the day of evil and destroy them with double destruction. {17:19} Thus said the LORD to me: Go and stand at the gate of the people's children, by which the kings of Judah come in and go out, and at all the gates of Jerusalem; {17:20} and say to them, Hear the word of the LORD, you kings of Judah, and all Judah, and all the inhabitants of Jerusalem who enter by these gates: {17:21} Thus says the LORD: Take heed to yourselves and do not carry any burden on the Sabbath day, nor bring it in through the gates of Jerusalem; {17:22} nor carry a burden out of your houses on the Sabbath day; do no work, but keep the Sabbath day holy, as I commanded your ancestors. {17:23} Yet they did not obey or incline their ear, but made their neck stiff so that they would not hear or receive instruction. {17:24} It shall come to pass that if you listen carefully to me, says the LORD, and bring in no burden through the gates of this city on the Sabbath day, but keep the Sabbath day holy by doing no work on it; {17:25} then kings and princes will enter through the gates of this city, sitting on the throne of David, riding in chariots and on horses, they and their princes, the men of Judah and the inhabitants of Jerusalem; and this city will remain forever. {17:26} They will come from the cities of Judah, from the places around Jerusalem, from the land of Benjamin, from the lowland, from the mountains, and from the south, bringing burnt offerings, sacrifices, grain offerings, and incense, and bringing thank offerings to the house of the LORD. {17:27} But if you will not listen to me to keep the Sabbath day holy, and not to carry a burden, even entering through the gates of Jerusalem on the Sabbath day; then I will kindle a fire in its gates, and it will consume the palaces of Jerusalem, and it will not be quenched.

{18:1} The word that came to Jeremiah from the LORD, saying, {18:2} Arise and go down to the potter's house, and there I will have you hear my words. {18:3} So I went down to the potter's house, and there he was making something on the wheels. {18:4} And the vessel he made of clay was marred in the hand of the potter; so he made it again into another vessel, as it seemed good to the potter to make. {18:5} Then the word of the LORD came to me, saying, {18:6} O house of Israel, cannot I do with you as this potter? says the LORD. Behold, as the clay is in the potter's hand, so are you in my hand, O house of Israel. {18:7} At any moment I may speak concerning a nation or a kingdom, to pluck up, pull down, and destroy it; {18:8} if that nation, against which I have pronounced, turns from their evil, I will repent of the evil I thought to do to them. {18:9} And at any moment I may speak concerning a nation or a kingdom, to build and to plant it; {18:10} if it does evil in my sight, not obeying my voice, then I will repent of the good with which I said I would benefit them. {18:11} Now therefore, go and speak to the men of Judah and to the inhabitants of Jerusalem, saying, Thus says the LORD: Behold, I am framing evil against you and devising a plan against you; return now everyone from their evil way and make your ways and your doings good. {18:12} But they said, There is no hope; we will walk after our own plans, and everyone will do the imagination of their evil heart. {18:13} Therefore, thus says the LORD: Ask now among the nations, who has heard such things? The virgin of Israel has done a very horrible thing. {18:14} Will a man leave the snow of Lebanon, which comes from the rock of the field? Or will cold flowing waters from another place be forsaken? {18:15} Because my people have forgotten me, they have burned incense to worthless things, and they have caused them to stumble in their ways, from the ancient paths, to walk in paths that are not well-trodden; {18:16} to make their land desolate, a perpetual hissing; everyone who passes by will be astonished and shake their head. {18:17} I will scatter them as with an east wind before the enemy; I will show them my back, not my face, in the day of their calamity. {18:18} Then they said, Come, and let us devise plans against Jeremiah; for the law will not perish from the priest, nor counsel from the wise, nor the word from the prophet. Come, let us strike him with our tongues and let us not pay attention to any of his words. {18:19} Give heed to me, O LORD, and listen to the voice of those who contend with me. {18:20} Shall evil be repaid for good? For they have dug a pit for my soul. Remember that I stood before you to speak good for them and to turn away your wrath from them. {18:21} Therefore, deliver up their children to famine, and pour out their blood by the force of the sword; let their wives be bereaved of children and become widows; and let their men be put to death; let their young men be slain by the sword in battle. {18:22} Let a cry be heard from their houses when you bring a troop suddenly upon them; for they have dug a pit to take me and hidden snares for my feet. {18:23} Yet, LORD, you know all their counsel against me to slay me; do not forgive their iniquity or blot out their sin from your sight, but let them be overthrown before you; deal with them in your anger.

{19:1} Thus says the LORD: Go and get a potter's earthen jar, and take some of the elders of the people and of the priests; {19:2} and go out to the valley of the son of Hinnom, which is near the entrance of the east gate, and proclaim there the words that I will tell you. {19:3} And say, Hear the word of the LORD, O kings of Judah and inhabitants of Jerusalem; thus says the LORD of hosts, the God of Israel: Behold, I will bring disaster upon this place; whoever hears of it will tingle with shock. {19:4} Because they have forsaken me and have made this place foreign, and have burned incense in it to other gods that neither they nor their ancestors nor the kings of Judah have known, and have filled this place with the blood of innocents; {19:5} they have built the high places of Baal to burn their sons in fire as burnt offerings to Baal, something I did not command, nor did I ever speak of, nor did it ever enter my mind. {19:6} Therefore, behold, the days are coming, says the LORD, when this place will no longer be called Tophet, or the valley of the son of Hinnom, but the valley of slaughter. {19:7} I will nullify the plans of Judah and Jerusalem in this place, and I will cause them to fall by the sword before their enemies and by the hands of those who seek their lives; their bodies will become food for the birds of the air and for the beasts of the earth. {19:8} I will make this city a desolation and an object of hissing; everyone who passes by will be astonished and hiss because of all its plagues. {19:9} I will cause them to eat the flesh of their sons and the flesh of their daughters, and they will eat one another's flesh in the siege and the distress that their enemies and those who seek their lives will bring upon them. {19:10} Then you shall break the jar in the sight of the men who go with you, {19:11} and you shall say to them, Thus says the LORD of hosts: Just as I will break this people and this city, like one breaks a potter's vessel that cannot be made whole again; and they shall bury them in Tophet until there is no more room to bury. {19:12} Thus will I do to this place, says the LORD, and to its inhabitants; I will make this city like Tophet. {19:13} The houses of Jerusalem and the houses of the kings of Judah will be defiled like the place of Tophet, because of all the houses where they have burned incense to all the host of heaven and have poured out drink offerings to other gods. {19:14} Then Jeremiah came from Tophet, where the LORD had sent him to prophesy, and he stood in the court of the LORD's house and said to all the people, {19:15} Thus says the LORD of hosts, the God of Israel: Behold, I will bring upon this city and all its towns all the disaster that I have pronounced against it, because they have hardened their necks so that they would not hear my words.

{20:1} Now Pashur the son of Immer, the priest, who was also chief governor in the house of the LORD, heard that Jeremiah was prophesying these things. {20:2} Then Pashur struck Jeremiah the prophet and put him in stocks at the upper gate of Benjamin, which was by the house of the LORD. {20:3} The next day, when Pashur released Jeremiah from the stocks, Jeremiah said to him, The LORD has not called your name Pashur, but Magormissabib (meaning "terror on every side"). {20:4} For thus says the LORD: Behold, I will make you a terror to yourself and to all your friends; they will fall by the sword of their enemies, and you will see it with your own eyes; and I will give all Judah into the hand of the king of Babylon, and he shall carry them captive to Babylon and slay them with the sword. {20:5} Moreover, I will deliver all the strength of this city, all its labor, all its precious things, and all the treasures of the kings of Judah into the hand of their enemies, who shall plunder them, take them, and carry them to Babylon. {20:6} And you, Pashur, and all who live in your house will go into captivity; you will come to Babylon, and there you will die and be buried there, you and all your friends to whom you have prophesied lies. {20:7} O LORD, you have deceived me, and I was deceived; you are stronger than I, and you have prevailed; I am in derision daily; everyone mocks me. {20:8} For since I spoke, I cried out, I shouted violence and ruin; because the word of the LORD has become a reproach to me and a derision daily. {20:9} Then I said, I will not mention him, nor speak any more in his name. But his word was in my heart like a burning fire shut up in my bones; I was weary of holding it back, and I could not. {20:10} For I heard the defaming of many; fear is on every side. They say, Report, and we will report it. All my acquaintances watched for my stumbling, saying, Perhaps he will be deceived, and we can prevail against him and take our revenge on him. {20:11} But the LORD is with me like a mighty warrior; therefore my persecutors will stumble, and they will not prevail; they will be greatly ashamed, for they will not succeed; their everlasting shame will never be forgotten. {20:12} But, O LORD of hosts, who tests the righteous and sees the heart and mind, let me see your vengeance on them, for to you I have committed my cause. {20:13} Sing to the LORD; praise the LORD, for he has delivered the soul of the poor from the hand of evildoers. {20:14} Cursed be the day I was born; let not the day my mother bore me be blessed. {20:15} Cursed be the man who brought the news to my father, saying, A male child has been born to you, making him very glad. {20:16} Let that man be like the cities which the LORD overthrew and did not repent; and let him hear the cry in the morning and the shout at noon. {20:17} Because he did not kill me in the womb; that my mother might have been my grave, and her womb always great with me. {20:18} Why did I come forth from the womb to see labor and sorrow, that my days should be consumed with shame?

{21:1} The word that came to Jeremiah from the LORD when King Zedekiah sent Pashur the son of Melchiah and Zephaniah the son of Maaseiah the priest to him, saying, {21:2} "Please inquire of the LORD for us, for Nebuchadnezzar king of Babylon is making war against us; perhaps the LORD will act according to all his wonderful works so that he will withdraw from us." {21:3} Then Jeremiah said to them, "You shall say to Zedekiah: {21:4} Thus says the LORD God of Israel: Behold, I will turn back the weapons of war that are in your hands, with which you fight against the king of Babylon and the Chaldeans who are besieging you outside the walls; and I will gather them in the midst of this city. {21:5} I myself will fight against you with an outstretched hand and a strong arm, in anger, in fury, and in great wrath. {21:6} I will strike the inhabitants of this city, both man and beast; they shall die from a great pestilence. {21:7} And afterward, says the LORD, I will deliver King Zedekiah of Judah and his servants and the people who are left in this city from the pestilence, the sword, and famine into the hand of Nebuchadnezzar king of Babylon, and into the hands of their enemies who seek their lives; he will strike them down with the sword; he will not spare them, nor have pity, nor show mercy. {21:8} And to this people you shall say, Thus says the LORD: Behold, I set before you the way of life and the way of death. {21:9} He who stays in this city shall die by the sword, famine, and pestilence; but he who goes out and surrenders to the Chaldeans who are besieging you shall live, and his life shall be like a prize to him. {21:10} For I have set my face against this city for evil, not for good, says the LORD; it shall be given into the hand of the king of Babylon, and he shall burn it with fire. {21:11} And concerning the house of the king of Judah, say, Hear the word of the LORD: {21:12} O house of David, thus says the LORD: Administer justice in the morning, and rescue the one who has been robbed out of the hand of the oppressor, lest my fury go forth like fire, and burn so that no one can quench it because of the evil of your deeds. {21:13} Behold, I am against you, O inhabitant of the valley and rock of the plain, says the LORD; who say, "Who shall come down against us? Or who shall enter our dwellings?" {21:14} But I will punish you according to the fruit of your deeds, says the LORD; I will kindle a fire in your forest, and it will consume all around it.

{22:1} Thus says the LORD: Go down to the house of the king of Judah and speak there this word, {22:2} and say, Hear the word of the LORD, O king of Judah, who sits on the throne of David, you, your servants, and your people who enter through these gates: {22:3} Thus says the LORD: Execute judgment and righteousness, and deliver the spoiled out of the hand of the oppressor; do no wrong, do no violence to the stranger, the fatherless, or the widow, nor shed innocent blood in this place. {22:4} For if you indeed do this, then kings sitting on the throne of David will enter through the gates of this house, riding in chariots and on horses, he and his servants and his people. {22:5} But if you will not heed these words, I swear by myself, says the LORD, that this house shall become a desolation. {22:6} For thus says the LORD concerning the house of the king of Judah: You are like Gilead to me, like the summit of Lebanon; yet surely I will make you a wilderness, and cities that are not inhabited. {22:7} I will prepare destroyers against you, everyone with his weapons, and they will cut down your choice cedars and throw them into the fire. {22:8} And many nations will pass by this city, and they will say to one another, Why has the LORD done this to this great city? {22:9} Then they will answer, Because they have forsaken the covenant of the LORD their God and worshiped other gods and served them. {22:10} Do not weep for the dead, nor bemoan him; weep rather for him who goes away, for he shall return no more, nor see his native country. {22:11} For thus says the LORD concerning Shallum the son of Josiah, king of Judah, who reigned instead of his father Josiah and went forth from this place: He shall not return there anymore. {22:12} But he shall die in the place where they have led him captive, and he shall see this land no more. {22:13} Woe to him who builds his house by unrighteousness and his chambers by wrong; who uses his neighbor's service without wages and gives him nothing for his work; {22:14} who says, I will build myself a large house with spacious chambers, and who cuts out windows for it, and it is paneled with cedar and painted in vermilion. {22:15} Will you reign because you enclose yourself with cedar? Did not your father eat and drink and execute judgment and justice, and then it went well with him? {22:16} He judged the cause of the poor and needy; then it was well with him. Was this not to know me? says the LORD. {22:17} But your eyes and your heart are only for your covetousness, for shedding innocent blood, and for oppression and violence, to do it. {22:18} Therefore thus says the LORD concerning Jehoiakim the son of Josiah, king of Judah: They shall not lament for him, saying, Ah my brother! or, Ah sister! They shall not lament for him, saying, Ah lord! or, Ah his glory! {22:19} He shall be buried with the burial of a donkey, dragged and cast beyond the gates of Jerusalem. {22:20} Go up to Lebanon and cry out; lift up your voice in Bashan, and cry from the passages, for all your lovers are destroyed. {22:21} I spoke to you in your prosperity, but you said, I will not hear. This has been your manner from your youth; you have not obeyed my voice. {22:22} The wind shall consume all your shepherds, and your lovers shall go into captivity; then you shall be ashamed and confounded for all your wickedness. {22:23} O inhabitant of Lebanon, who makes your nest in the cedars, how gracious will you be when pangs come upon you, like the pain of a woman in labor! {22:24} As I live, says the LORD, though Coniah (also known as Jeconiah) the son of Jehoiakim, king of Judah, were the signet on my right hand, yet I would pluck you off; {22:25} and I will give you into the hand of those who seek your life and into the hand of those whose face you dread, even into the hand of Nebuchadnezzar king of Babylon and into the hands of the Chaldeans. {22:26} I will cast you out and your mother who bore you into another country where you were not born; and there you shall die. {22:27} But to the land to which they desire to return, they shall not return. {22:28} Is this man Coniah a despised broken idol? Is he a vessel in which there is no pleasure? Why then are they cast out, he and his descendants, and thrown into a land they do not know? {22:29} O earth, earth, earth, hear the word of the LORD. {22:30} Thus says the LORD: Write this man down as childless, a man who shall not prosper in his days; for no man of his descendants shall prosper, sitting on the throne of David and ruling any longer in Judah.

{23:1} Woe to the shepherds who destroy and scatter the sheep of my pasture, says the LORD. {23:2} Therefore, thus says the LORD God of Israel against the shepherds who feed my people: You have scattered my flock, driven them away, and have not taken care of them. Behold, I will visit you for the evil of your actions, says the LORD. {23:3} I will gather the remnant of my flock from all the countries where I have driven them and will bring them back to their folds, and they shall be fruitful and multiply. {23:4} I will set up shepherds over them who will feed them, and they shall fear no more, nor be dismayed, nor shall they lack anything, says the LORD. {23:5} Behold, the days are coming, says the LORD, when I will raise up for David a righteous Branch, and a King shall reign and prosper, executing judgment and justice on the earth. {23:6} In his days Judah will be saved, and Israel will dwell securely; and this is the name by which he shall be called: THE LORD OUR RIGHTEOUSNESS. {23:7} Therefore, behold, the days are coming, says the LORD, when they shall no longer say, "The LORD lives, who brought up the children of Israel out of the land of Egypt." {23:8} But they shall say, "The LORD lives, who brought up and led the descendants of the house of Israel from the north country and from all the countries where I had driven them; and they shall dwell in their own land." {23:9} My heart is broken within me because of the prophets; all my bones shake; I am like a drunken man, like a man overcome by wine, because of the LORD and because of the words of his holiness. {23:10} For the land is full of adulterers; because of swearing the land mourns; the pleasant places of the wilderness are dried up, and their course is evil, and their strength is not right. {23:11} Both the prophet and the priest are profane; indeed, in my house I have found their wickedness, says the LORD. {23:12} Therefore, their way shall be to them like slippery paths in the darkness; they shall be driven on and fall in them; for I will bring disaster upon them in the year of their punishment, says the LORD. {23:13} I have seen folly in the prophets of Samaria; they prophesied in Baal and led my people Israel astray. {23:14} And in the prophets of Jerusalem I have seen a horrible thing: they commit adultery and walk in lies; they strengthen the hands of evildoers so that none turns from his wickedness; they are all like Sodom to me, and its inhabitants like Gomorrah. {23:15} Therefore, thus says the LORD of hosts concerning the prophets: Behold, I will feed them with wormwood (bitter substance) and make them drink the water of gall (poison); for from the prophets of Jerusalem, wickedness has gone forth into all the land. {23:16} Thus says the LORD of hosts: Do not listen to the words of the prophets who prophesy to you; they make you vain; they speak a vision of their own heart, not from the mouth of the LORD. {23:17} They still say to those who despise me, "The LORD has said, You shall have peace," and they say to everyone who walks after the imagination of his own heart, "No evil shall come upon you." {23:18} For who has stood in the counsel of the LORD and has perceived and heard his word? Who has marked his word and heard it? {23:19} Behold, a whirlwind of the LORD has gone forth in fury, even a grievous whirlwind; it shall fall heavily upon the head of the wicked. {23:20} The anger of the LORD shall not return until he has executed and performed the thoughts of his heart; in the latter days you shall understand it perfectly. {23:21} I have not sent these prophets, yet they ran; I have not spoken to them, yet they prophesied. {23:22} But if they had stood in my counsel and caused my people to hear my words, then they would have turned them from their evil way and from the evil of their actions. {23:23} Am I a God near at hand, says the LORD, and not a God far off? {23:24} Can anyone hide himself in secret places that I shall not see him, says the LORD? Do I not fill heaven and earth? says the LORD. {23:25} I have heard what the prophets said, who prophesy lies in my name, saying, "I have dreamed, I have dreamed." {23:26} How long shall this be in the hearts of the prophets who prophesy lies? Yes, they are prophets of the deceit of their own hearts; {23:27} who think to make my people forget my name by their dreams, which they tell each man to his neighbor, as their fathers have forgotten my name for Baal. {23:28} Let the prophet who has a dream tell his dream, and he who has my word speak my word faithfully. What is the chaff to the wheat? says the LORD. {23:29} Is not my word like fire, says the LORD, and like a hammer that breaks the rock in pieces? {23:30} Therefore, behold, I am against the prophets, says the LORD, who steal my words, each from his neighbor. {23:31} Behold, I am against the prophets, says the LORD, who use their tongues and say, "He says." {23:32} Behold, I am against those who prophesy false dreams, says the LORD, and tell them, causing my people to err by their lies and their lightness; yet I did not send them or command them; therefore, they shall not profit this people at all, says the LORD. {23:33} And when this people, or the prophet, or a priest shall ask you, saying, "What is the burden of the LORD?" you shall then say to them, "What burden? I will forsake you, says the LORD." {23:34} And as for the prophet, the priest, and the people who say, "The burden of the LORD," I will punish that man and his house. {23:35} Thus you shall say to each neighbor and each brother, "What has the LORD answered?" and "What has the LORD spoken?" {23:36} And the burden of the LORD you shall mention no more; for every man's word shall be his burden; for you have perverted the words of the living God, the LORD of hosts our God. {23:37} Thus you shall say to the prophet, "What has the LORD answered you?" and "What has the LORD spoken?" {23:38} But since you say, "The burden of the LORD," therefore, thus says the LORD: Because you say this word, "The burden of the LORD," and I have sent to you saying, "You shall not say, 'The burden of the LORD,'" {23:39} therefore, behold, I, even I, will utterly forget you, and I will forsake you and the city that I gave you and your ancestors, and cast you out of my presence. {23:40} And I will bring upon you an everlasting disgrace and a perpetual shame that shall not be forgotten.

{24:1} The LORD showed me, and behold, two baskets of figs were set before the temple of the LORD, after Nebuchadnezzar king of Babylon had carried away captive Jeconiah the son of Jehoiakim, king of Judah, and the princes of Judah, along with the carpenters and smiths, from Jerusalem and brought them to Babylon. {24:2} One basket had very good figs, like the figs that are first ripe; and the other basket had very bad figs that could not be eaten, they were so bad. {24:3} Then the LORD said to me, "What do you see, Jeremiah?" And I said, "Figs; the good figs are very good, and the bad figs are very bad, they cannot be eaten, they are so bad." {24:4} Again, the word of the LORD came to me, saying, {24:5} Thus says the LORD, the God of Israel: Like these good figs, so will I acknowledge those who are carried away captive of Judah, whom I have sent out of this place into the land of the Chaldeans for their good. {24:6} For I will set my eyes upon them for good, and I will bring them back to this land; I will build them up and not tear them down; I will plant them and not uproot them. {24:7} I will give them a heart to know me, that I am the LORD; and they shall be my people, and I will be their God; for they shall return to me with their whole heart. {24:8} And as for the bad figs that cannot be eaten, they are so bad, surely, thus says the LORD: So will I give Zedekiah king of Judah, his princes, and the remnant of Jerusalem that remain in this land, and those who dwell in the land of Egypt: {24:9} And I will deliver them to be scattered among all the kingdoms of the earth for their harm, to be a reproach and a proverb, a taunt and a curse, in all the places where I shall drive them. {24:10} And I will send the sword, famine, and pestilence among them until they are consumed from off the land that I gave to them and to their ancestors.

{25:1} The word that came to Jeremiah concerning all the people of Judah in the fourth year of Jehoiakim son of Josiah, king of Judah, which was also the first year of Nebuchadnezzar, king of Babylon; {25:2} Jeremiah the prophet spoke to all the people of Judah and to all the inhabitants of Jerusalem, saying, {25:3} From the thirteenth year of Josiah son of Amon, king of Judah, until this day, which is the twenty-third year, the word of the LORD has come to me, and I have spoken to you, rising early and speaking; but you have not listened. {25:4} The LORD has sent to you all his servants the prophets, rising early and sending them; but you have not listened or inclined your ear to hear. {25:5} They said, "Turn now, everyone from your evil ways and from the evil of your actions, and dwell in the land that the LORD has given to you and your ancestors forever and ever; {25:6} and do not go after other gods to serve and worship them, and do not provoke me to anger with the works of your hands; then I will do you no harm." {25:7} Yet you have not listened to me, says the LORD, so you provoke me to anger with the works of your hands to your own detriment. {25:8} Therefore, thus says the LORD of hosts: Because you have not heard my words, {25:9} behold, I will send and take all the families of the north, says the LORD, along with Nebuchadnezzar, king of Babylon, my servant, and will bring them against this land, its inhabitants, and all the surrounding nations, and will utterly destroy them, making them an astonishment, a hissing, and perpetual desolations. {25:10} Moreover, I will take away the sound of joy and gladness, the voice of the bridegroom and the bride, the sound of the millstones, and the light of the candle. {25:11} This whole land will become a desolation and an astonishment; and these nations will serve the king of Babylon for seventy years. {25:12} And it will come to pass, when seventy years are completed, that I will punish the king of Babylon and that nation, says the LORD, for their wrongdoing, and the land of the Chaldeans, and will make it a perpetual desolation. {25:13} I will bring upon that land all my words that I have pronounced against it, even all that is written in this book, which Jeremiah has prophesied against all the nations. {25:14} For many nations and great kings will make them their servants; I will repay them according to their deeds and the works of their own hands. {25:15} For thus says the LORD God of Israel to me: Take this wine cup of fury from my hand, and cause all the nations to whom I send you to drink it. {25:16} They will drink, stagger, and go mad because of the sword that I will send among them. {25:17} Then I took the cup from the LORD's hand and made all the nations drink it, to whom the LORD had sent me: {25:18} including Jerusalem and the cities of Judah, its kings and princes, to make them a desolation, an astonishment, a hissing, and a curse, as it is this day; {25:19} Pharaoh, king of Egypt, his servants, his princes, and all his people; {25:20} and all the mixed people, all the kings of the land of Uz, all the kings of the land of the Philistines, Ashkelon, Azzah, Ekron, and the remnant of Ashdod, {25:21} Edom, Moab, and the children of Ammon; {25:22} all the kings of Tyre, all the kings of Sidon, the kings of the isles across the sea, {25:23} Dedan, Tema, Buz, and all who are in the farthest corners, {25:24} all the kings of Arabia, and all the kings of the mixed people who dwell in the desert, {25:25} all the kings of Zimri, all the kings of Elam, all the kings of the Medes, {25:26} and all the kings of the north, far and near, one with another, and all the kingdoms of the world that are upon the face of the earth; and the king of Sheshach will drink after them. {25:27} Therefore you shall say to them, thus says the LORD of hosts, the God of Israel: Drink, be drunk, vomit, fall, and rise no more because of the sword that I will send among you. {25:28} And if they refuse to take the cup from your hand to drink, then you shall say to them, thus says the LORD of hosts: You shall certainly drink. {25:29} For behold, I begin to bring evil upon the city that is called by my name; and should you be utterly unpunished? You shall not be unpunished, for I will call for a sword upon all the inhabitants of the earth, says the LORD of hosts. {25:30} Therefore prophesy against them all these words, and say to them, The LORD will roar from on high and utter his voice from his holy dwelling; he will roar mightily against his dwelling; he will give a shout, as those who tread grapes, against all the inhabitants of the earth. {25:31} A noise will reach the ends of the earth, for the LORD has a controversy with the nations; he will plead with all flesh; he will give the wicked to the sword, says the LORD. {25:32} Thus says the LORD of hosts: Behold, evil will go forth from nation to nation, and a great whirlwind will be raised up from the coasts of the earth. {25:33} The slain of the LORD will be at that day from one end of the earth to the other; they will not be lamented, gathered, or buried; they will be like dung upon the ground. {25:34} Howl, you shepherds, and cry; roll in the ashes, you leaders of the flock; for the days of your slaughter and dispersion are accomplished, and you will fall like a precious vessel. {25:35} The shepherds will have no way to flee, nor the leaders of the flock to escape. {25:36} A voice of the cry of the shepherds and howling of the leaders of the flock will be heard, for the LORD has destroyed their pasture. {25:37} The peaceful dwellings are cut down because of the fierce anger of the LORD. {25:38} He has forsaken his hiding place, like a lion; for their land is desolate because of the fierceness of the oppressor and his fierce anger.

{26:1} In the beginning of the reign of Jehoiakim son of Josiah, king of Judah, this word came from the LORD, saying, {26:2} thus says the LORD: Stand in the court of the LORD's house and speak to all the cities of Judah that come to worship in the LORD's house all the words that I command you to speak to them; do not diminish a word. {26:3} Perhaps they will listen and turn each from their evil ways, that I may repent of the evil I plan to do to them because of their wickedness. {26:4} And you shall say to them, thus says the LORD: If you will not listen to me, to walk in my law, which I have set before you, {26:5} and to heed the words of my servants the prophets, whom I sent to you, rising up early and sending them, but you have not listened; {26:6} then I will make this house like Shiloh and make this city a curse to all the nations of the earth. {26:7} So the priests, the prophets, and all the people heard Jeremiah speaking these words in the house of the LORD. {26:8} Now it came to pass, when Jeremiah had finished speaking all that the LORD had commanded him to say to all the people, that the priests and the prophets and all the people seized him, saying, "You shall surely die." {26:9} Why have you prophesied in the name of the LORD, saying, "This house will be like Shiloh, and this city will be desolate without inhabitants"? And all the people were gathered against Jeremiah in the house of the LORD. {26:10} When the princes of Judah heard these things, they came up from the king's house to the house of the LORD and sat down in the entry of the new gate of the LORD's house. {26:11} Then the priests and the prophets spoke to the princes and all the people, saying, "This man is worthy to die, for he has prophesied against this city, as you have heard with your own ears." {26:12} Then Jeremiah spoke to all the princes and all the people, saying, "The LORD sent me to prophesy against this house and against this city all the words that you have heard. {26:13} Therefore now amend your ways and your actions, and obey the voice of the LORD your God; and the LORD will relent concerning the evil he has pronounced against you. {26:14} As for me, behold, I am in your hand; do with me as seems good and right to you. {26:15} But know for certain that if you put me to death, you will surely bring innocent blood upon yourselves and upon this city and its inhabitants; for I have truly been sent to you by the LORD to speak all these words in your ears." {26:16} Then the princes and all the people said to the priests and the prophets, "This man is not worthy to die; for he has spoken to us in the name of the LORD our God." {26:17} Then some of the elders of the land rose up and spoke to all the assembly of the people, saying, {26:18} "Micah the Morasthite prophesied in the days of Hezekiah, king of Judah, and spoke to all the people of Judah, saying, thus says the LORD of hosts: 'Zion will be plowed like a field, and Jerusalem will become heaps, and the mountain of the house like the high places of a forest.' {26:19} Did Hezekiah, king of Judah, and all Judah put him to death? Did he not fear the LORD and beseech the LORD, and the LORD relented concerning the evil he had pronounced against them? So we might bring great evil upon ourselves." {26:20} And there was also a man who prophesied in the name of the LORD, Urijah son of Shemaiah of Kirjathjearim, who prophesied against this city and against this land according to all the words of Jeremiah. {26:21} When Jehoiakim the king, with all his mighty men and all the princes, heard his words, the king sought to put him to death; but when Urijah heard it, he was afraid, and fled to Egypt. {26:22} Jehoiakim the king sent men to Egypt, namely, Elnathan son of Achbor and certain men with him into Egypt. {26:23} They brought Urijah out of Egypt and brought him to Jehoiakim the king, who killed him with the sword and cast his dead body into the graves of the common people. {26:24} Nevertheless, the hand of Ahikam son of Shaphan was with Jeremiah, so they did not give him into the hand of the people to put him to death.

{27:1} In the beginning of the reign of Jehoiakim son of Josiah, king of Judah, the word came to Jeremiah from the LORD, saying, {27:2} Thus says the LORD to me: Make bonds and yokes and put them on your neck, {27:3} and send them to the king of Edom, the king of Moab, the king of the Ammonites, the king of Tyre, and the king of Sidon, by the hand of the messengers who come to Jerusalem to Zedekiah king of Judah; {27:4} and command them to say to their masters: Thus says the LORD of hosts, the God of Israel: Thus you shall say to your masters: {27:5} I have made the earth, the man and the beast that are upon the ground, by my great power and by my outstretched arm, and have given it to whomever it seemed good to me. {27:6} And now I have given all these lands into the hand of Nebuchadnezzar, king of Babylon, my servant; and the beasts of the field have I given him also to serve him. {27:7} All nations shall serve him, his son, and his grandson, until the time comes for his land; and then many nations and great kings will serve themselves from him. {27:8} It will come to pass that the nation and kingdom which will not serve Nebuchadnezzar, king of Babylon, and will not put their neck under the yoke of the king of Babylon, that nation will I punish, says the LORD, with the sword, with famine, and with pestilence, until I have consumed them by his hand. {27:9} Therefore do not listen to your prophets, diviners, dreamers, enchanters, or sorcerers, who say to you, "You shall not serve the king of Babylon." {27:10} For they prophesy a lie to you, to remove you far from your land; and that I should drive you out, and you should perish. {27:11} But the nations that bring their neck under the yoke of the king of Babylon and serve him, I will let remain still in their own land, says the LORD; and they shall cultivate it and dwell there. {27:12} I also spoke to Zedekiah king of Judah according to all these words, saying, Bring your necks under the yoke of the king of Babylon and serve him and his people, and live. {27:13} Why will you die, you and your people, by the sword, famine, and pestilence, as the LORD has spoken against the nation that will not serve the king of Babylon? {27:14} Therefore do not listen to the words of the prophets who say to you, "You shall not serve the king of Babylon," for they prophesy a lie to you. {27:15} For I have not sent them, says the LORD, yet they prophesy a lie in my name; that I might drive you out and that you might perish, you and the prophets that prophesy to you. {27:16} I also spoke to the priests and all this people, saying, Thus says the LORD: Do not listen to the words of your prophets who prophesy to you, saying, "The vessels of the LORD's house will soon be brought back from Babylon," for they prophesy a lie to you. {27:17} Do not listen to them; serve the king of Babylon and live; why should this city be laid waste? {27:18} But if they are prophets, and if the word of the LORD is with them, let them now make intercession to the LORD of hosts that the vessels which are left in the house of the LORD, in the house of the king of Judah, and in Jerusalem, do not go to Babylon. {27:19} For thus says the LORD of hosts concerning the pillars, concerning the sea, concerning the bases, and concerning the residue of the vessels that remain in this city, {27:20} which Nebuchadnezzar king of Babylon did not take when he carried away captive Jeconiah son of Jehoiakim king of Judah from Jerusalem to Babylon, and all the nobles of Judah and Jerusalem; {27:21} yes, thus says the LORD of hosts, the God of Israel, concerning the vessels that remain in the house of the LORD, and in the house of the king of Judah and of Jerusalem; {27:22} They shall be carried to Babylon, and there they shall be until the day that I visit them, says the LORD; then I will bring them up and restore them to this place.

{28:1} And it came to pass the same year, in the beginning of the reign of Zedekiah king of Judah, in the fourth year, and in the fifth month, that Hananiah son of Azur the prophet, who was from Gibeon, spoke to me in the house of the LORD, in the presence of the priests and all the people, saying, {28:2} Thus speaks the LORD of hosts, the God of Israel, saying, I have broken the yoke of the king of Babylon. {28:3} Within two full years I will bring back to this place all the vessels of the LORD's house that Nebuchadnezzar king of Babylon took away from this place and carried to Babylon; {28:4} and I will bring back to this place Jeconiah son of Jehoiakim king of Judah, with all the captives of Judah who went to Babylon, says the LORD, for I will break the yoke of the king of Babylon. {28:5} Then the prophet Jeremiah said to the prophet Hananiah in the presence of the priests and all the people who stood in the house of the LORD, {28:6} "Amen! The LORD do so! The LORD perform your words which you have prophesied, to bring back the vessels of the LORD's house and all that was carried away captive from Babylon to this place." {28:7} Nevertheless, hear now this word that I speak in your ears and in the ears of all the people; {28:8} the prophets who were before me and before you prophesied against many countries and great kingdoms, of war, evil, and pestilence. {28:9} The prophet who prophesies of peace, when the word of the prophet comes to pass, then the prophet will be known to have been truly sent by the LORD. {28:10} Then Hananiah the prophet took the yoke from off the neck of the prophet Jeremiah and broke it. {28:11} And Hananiah spoke in the presence of all the people, saying, Thus says the LORD: Even so will I break the yoke of Nebuchadnezzar king of Babylon from the neck of all nations within two full years. And the prophet Jeremiah went his way. {28:12} Then the word of the LORD came to Jeremiah after Hananiah the prophet had broken the yoke from off the neck of the prophet Jeremiah, saying, {28:13} Go and tell Hananiah, saying, Thus says the LORD: You have broken the yokes of wood; but you shall make for them yokes of iron. {28:14} For thus says the LORD of hosts, the God of Israel: I have put a yoke of iron upon the neck of all these nations, that they may serve Nebuchadnezzar king of Babylon; and they shall serve him, and I have given him the beasts of the field also. {28:15} Then Jeremiah said to Hananiah the prophet, Hear now, Hananiah; the LORD has not sent you, but you make this people trust in a lie. {28:16} Therefore thus says the LORD: Behold, I will cast you from off the face of the earth; this year you shall die, because you have taught rebellion against the LORD. {28:17} So Hananiah the prophet died the same year in the seventh month.

{29:1} Now these are the words of the letter that Jeremiah the prophet sent from Jerusalem to the remaining elders who were taken captive, as well as to the priests, prophets, and all the people whom Nebuchadnezzar had carried away from Jerusalem to Babylon; {29:2} after Jeconiah the king, the queen, the eunuchs, the leaders of Judah and Jerusalem, and the carpenters and blacksmiths had departed from Jerusalem. {29:3} By the hand of Elasah son of Shaphan and Gemariah son of Hilkiah, whom Zedekiah king of Judah sent to Babylon to Nebuchadnezzar king of Babylon, saying, {29:4} Thus says the LORD of hosts, the God of Israel, to all who are carried away captives, whom I caused to be carried away from Jerusalem to Babylon: {29:5} Build houses and live in them; plant gardens and eat their produce. {29:6} Take wives and have sons and daughters; take wives for your sons and give your daughters in marriage so they may bear sons and daughters; that you may be increased there and not diminished. {29:7} Seek the peace of the city where I have caused you to be carried away captives, and pray to the LORD for it, for in its peace you will have peace. {29:8} For thus says the LORD of hosts, the God of Israel: Let not your prophets and diviners who are among you deceive you, nor listen to your dreams which you cause to be dreamed. {29:9} For they prophesy falsely to you in my name; I have not sent them, says the LORD. {29:10} For thus says the LORD: After seventy years are completed in Babylon, I will visit you and fulfill my good promise to you by bringing you back to this place. {29:11} For I know the thoughts I think toward you, says the LORD, thoughts of peace and not of evil, to give you a future and a hope. {29:12} Then you will call upon me, and you will go and pray to me, and I will listen to you. {29:13} You will seek me and find me when you search for me with all your heart. {29:14} I will be found by you, says the LORD, and I will restore your fortunes and gather you from all the nations and from all the places where I have driven you, says the LORD, and I will bring you back to the place from which I sent you into exile. {29:15} Because you have said, "The LORD has raised up prophets for us in Babylon," {29:16} know that thus says the LORD concerning the king who sits on David's throne, and concerning all the people who dwell in this city, your brothers who did not go out with you into exile: {29:17} Thus says the LORD of hosts: Behold, I will send on them the sword, famine, and pestilence, and will make them like bad figs that cannot be eaten, they are so bad. {29:18} I will pursue them with the sword, famine, and pestilence, and I will deliver them to be a horror and a curse, an object of scorn, and a reproach among all the nations where I have driven them. {29:19} Because they have not listened to my words, says the LORD, which I sent to them by my servants the prophets, rising up early and sending them; but you would not listen, says the LORD. {29:20} Therefore hear the word of the LORD, all you of the captivity whom I have sent from Jerusalem to Babylon: {29:21} Thus says the LORD of hosts, the God of Israel, concerning Ahab son of Kolaiah and Zedekiah son of Maaseiah, who prophesy a lie to you in my name: Behold, I will deliver them into the hand of Nebuchadnezzar king of Babylon, and he shall slay them before your eyes. {29:22} And of them shall be taken up a curse by all the exiles of Judah who are in Babylon, saying, "The LORD make you like Zedekiah and Ahab, whom the king of Babylon roasted in the fire." {29:23} Because they have committed abomination in Israel, have committed adultery with their neighbors' wives, and have spoken lying words in my name, which I have not commanded them; I know and am a witness, says the LORD. {29:24} Thus you shall also speak to Shemaiah the Nehelamite, saying, {29:25} Thus says the LORD of hosts, the God of Israel: Because you have sent letters in your name to all the people in Jerusalem, and to Zephaniah son of Maaseiah the priest, and to all the priests, saying, {29:26} "The LORD has made you priest instead of Jehoiada the priest, to be officers in the house of the LORD for every man who is mad and makes himself a prophet, that you should put him in prison and in stocks," {29:27} now why have you not rebuked Jeremiah of Anathoth, who makes himself a prophet to you? {29:28} For he sent us in Babylon, saying, "This captivity is long; build houses and live in them; plant gardens and eat their produce." {29:29} And Zephaniah the priest read this letter in the hearing of Jeremiah the prophet. {29:30} Then the word of the LORD came to Jeremiah, saying, {29:31} Send to all those in captivity, saying, Thus says the LORD concerning Shemaiah the Nehelamite: Because Shemaiah has prophesied to you and I did not send him, and he caused you to trust in a lie, {29:32} therefore thus says the LORD: Behold, I will punish Shemaiah the Nehelamite and his descendants; he shall not have a man to dwell among this people, nor shall he see the good that I will do for my people, says the LORD, because he has taught rebellion against the LORD.

{30:1} The word that came to Jeremiah from the LORD, saying, {30:2} Thus says the LORD God of Israel: Write down all the words that I have spoken to you in a book. {30:3} For behold, the days are coming, says the LORD, when I will bring back the captives of my people Israel and Judah, says the LORD, and I will cause them to return to the land that I gave to their fathers, and they shall possess it. {30:4} And these are the words that the LORD spoke concerning Israel and Judah. {30:5} For thus says the LORD: We have heard a voice of trembling, of fear, and not of peace. {30:6} Ask now, and see if a man gives birth; why do I see every man with his hands on his stomach like a woman in labor, and all faces turned pale? {30:7} Alas! for that day is great, so that none is like it; it is the time of Jacob's trouble, but he shall be saved out of it. {30:8} For it shall come to pass in that day, says the LORD of hosts, that I will break the yoke from your neck and will burst your bonds, and foreigners shall no longer serve themselves from him. {30:9} But they shall serve the LORD their God and David their king, whom I will raise up for them. {30:10} Therefore do not fear, O my servant Jacob, says the LORD; do not be dismayed, O Israel; for behold, I will save you from afar and your descendants from the land of their captivity; Jacob shall return and be at rest and in peace, and no one shall make him afraid. {30:11} For I am with you, says the LORD, to save you; though I make a full end of all nations where I have scattered you, yet I will not make a full end of you; but I will correct you in measure and will not leave you unpunished. {30:12} For thus says the LORD: Your injury is incurable and your wound is severe. {30:13} There is no one to plead your cause, that you may be bound up; you have no healing medicines. {30:14} All your lovers have forgotten you; they do not seek you; for I have wounded you with the wound of an enemy, with the chastisement of a cruel one, for the multitude of your iniquity; because your sins have increased. {30:15} Why do you cry for your affliction? Your sorrow is incurable for the multitude of your iniquity; because your sins have increased, I have done these things to you. {30:16} Therefore all who devour you shall be devoured, and all your adversaries, every one of them, shall go into captivity; those who plunder you shall be a plunder, and all who prey upon you I will give as prey. {30:17} For I will restore health to you, and I will heal your wounds, says the LORD, because they called you an Outcast, saying, "This is Zion, whom no one seeks." {30:18} Thus says the LORD: Behold, I will bring back the captives of Jacob's tents and have mercy on his dwelling places; the city shall be rebuilt on its own mound, and the palace shall remain as it was. {30:19} Out of them shall come thanksgiving and the voice of those who make merry; and I will multiply them, and they shall not be few; I will also glorify them, and they shall not be small. {30:20} Their children shall be as before, and their congregation shall be established before me, and I will punish all who oppress them. {30:21} Their leaders shall come from among themselves, and their governor shall come from their midst; I will cause him to approach me; for who is this who has engaged his heart to approach me? says the LORD. {30:22} You shall be my people, and I will be your God. {30:23} Behold, the whirlwind of the LORD goes forth with fury, a continuing whirlwind; it shall fall with pain upon the head of the wicked. {30:24} The fierce anger of the LORD shall not return until he has done it and until he has fulfilled the intents of his heart; in the latter days you shall consider it.

{31:1} At that time, says the LORD, I will be the God of all the families of Israel, and they will be my people. {31:2} Thus says the LORD: The people who survived the sword found grace in the wilderness; even Israel, when I went to give him rest. {31:3} The LORD has appeared to me of old, saying, Yes, I have loved you with an everlasting love; therefore, I have drawn you with lovingkindness. {31:4} I will rebuild you, O virgin of Israel; you will again be adorned with tambourines and go out dancing with those who make merry. {31:5} You will yet plant vineyards on the mountains of Samaria; the planters will plant and eat their fruit. {31:6} For there will be a day when the watchmen on the mountains of Ephraim will call out, "Arise, let us go up to Zion, to the LORD our God." {31:7} For thus says the LORD: Sing with joy for Jacob, and shout among the chief of the nations; proclaim and praise, saying, "O LORD, save your people, the remnant of Israel." {31:8} Behold, I will bring them from the north country and gather them from the ends of the earth, including the blind and the lame, the pregnant woman and the one in labor together; a great company will return here. {31:9} They will come with weeping, and with supplications I will lead them; I will guide them by rivers of water in a straight path where they will not stumble; for I am a father to Israel, and Ephraim is my firstborn. {31:10} Hear the word of the LORD, O nations, and declare it in the distant islands, saying, "He who scattered Israel will gather him and keep him as a shepherd does his flock." {31:11} For the LORD has redeemed Jacob and ransomed him from the hand of someone stronger than he. {31:12} Therefore, they will come and sing on the heights of Zion, and they will flow together to the goodness of the LORD, for grain, wine, oil, and for the young of the flock and herd; their souls will be like a well-watered garden, and they will no longer sorrow. {31:13} Then the virgin will rejoice in the dance, both young men and old together; for I will turn their mourning into joy, and I will comfort them and make them rejoice from their sorrow. {31:14} I will satisfy the priests with abundance, and my people will be satisfied with my goodness, says the LORD. {31:15} Thus says the LORD: A voice was heard in Ramah, lamentation, and bitter weeping; Rachel weeping for her children refused to be comforted for her children because they were no more. {31:16} Thus says the LORD: Refrain from weeping and your eyes from tears; for your work will be rewarded, says the LORD; and they will come back from the land of the enemy. {31:17} There is hope for your future, says the LORD, that your children will come back to their own border. {31:18} I have surely heard Ephraim bemoaning himself: "You have chastised me, and I was chastised like a calf unaccustomed to the yoke; turn me, and I shall be turned, for you are the LORD my God." {31:19} Surely after I was turned, I repented; and after I was instructed, I struck my thigh; I was ashamed and even confounded because I bore the reproach of my youth. {31:20} Is Ephraim my dear son? Is he a pleasant child? For since I spoke against him, I remember him still; therefore, my heart is troubled for him; I will surely have mercy upon him, says the LORD. {31:21} Set up road signs, make high piles of stones; set your heart toward the highway, the way you went; return, O virgin of Israel, return to your cities. {31:22} How long will you wander, O backsliding daughter? For the LORD has created a new thing in the earth: A woman will encompass a man. {31:23} Thus says the LORD of hosts, the God of Israel: They will use this saying in the land of Judah and in its cities when I bring back their captives: "The LORD bless you, O habitation of justice, and mountain of holiness." {31:24} And there will dwell in Judah itself, and in all its cities, farmers and those who go out with flocks. {31:25} For I have satisfied the weary soul, and I have replenished every sorrowful soul. {31:26} Upon this I awoke and saw; my sleep was sweet to me. {31:27} Behold, the days are coming, says the LORD, that I will sow the house of Israel and the house of Judah with the seed of man and the seed of beasts. {31:28} And it will come to pass that just as I have watched over them to uproot, tear down, destroy, and afflict, so I will watch over them to build and plant, says the LORD. {31:29} In those days they shall no longer say, "The fathers have eaten sour grapes, and the children's teeth are set on edge." {31:30} But each one shall die for his own iniquity; every man who eats sour grapes, his teeth will be set on edge. {31:31} Behold, the days are coming, says the LORD, when I will make a new covenant with the house of Israel and the house of Judah. {31:32} Not like the covenant I made with their fathers when I took them by the hand to bring them out of the land of Egypt; which covenant they broke, although I was a husband to them, says the LORD. {31:33} But this shall be the covenant that I will make with the house of Israel: After those days, says the LORD, I will put my law in their minds and write it on their hearts; and I will be their God, and they shall be my people. {31:34} They will no longer teach each man his neighbor, and every man his brother, saying, "Know the LORD," for they shall all know me, from the least to the greatest, says the LORD; for I will forgive their iniquity and remember their sin no more. {31:35} Thus says the LORD, who gives the sun for light by day, and the ordinances of the moon and stars for light by night, who divides the sea when its waves roar; the LORD of hosts is his name: {31:36} If those ordinances depart from before me, says the LORD, then the seed of Israel will cease from being a nation before me forever. {31:37} Thus says the LORD: If heaven above can be measured, and the foundations of the earth searched out beneath, I will also cast off all the seed of Israel for all they have done, says the LORD. {31:38} Behold, the days are coming, says the LORD, when the city shall be built to the LORD from the tower of Hananel to the corner gate. {31:39} The measuring line will yet go forth over against it on the hill Gareb and will compass about to Goath. {31:40} And the whole valley of the dead bodies, of the ashes, and all the fields to the brook of Kidron, to the corner of the horse gate toward the east, shall be holy to the LORD; it shall not be uprooted nor thrown down any more forever.

{32:1} The word that came to Jeremiah from the LORD in the tenth year of Zedekiah king of Judah, which was the eighteenth year of Nebuchadnezzar. {32:2} For then the army of Babylon besieged Jerusalem, and Jeremiah the prophet was shut up in the court of the prison, which was in the king of Judah's house. {32:3} For Zedekiah king of Judah had shut him up, saying, "Why do you prophesy and say, 'Thus says the LORD: Behold, I will give this city into the hand of the king of Babylon, and he shall take it; {32:4} and Zedekiah king of Judah will not escape from the hand of the Chaldeans, but will surely be delivered into the hand of the king of Babylon, and will speak with him face to face, and his eyes will see his eyes; {32:5} and he will lead Zedekiah to Babylon, and there he will be until I visit him, says the LORD; though you fight against the Chaldeans, you will not prosper.'" {32:6} And Jeremiah said, The word of the LORD came to me, saying, {32:7} "Behold, Hanameel the son of Shallum your uncle will come to you, saying, 'Buy my field that is in Anathoth, for you have the right of redemption to buy it.'" {32:8} So Hanameel my uncle's son came to me in the court of the prison according to the word of the LORD, and said to me, "Buy my field in Anathoth, which is in the territory of Benjamin; for the right of inheritance is yours, and the redemption is yours; buy it for yourself." Then I knew that this was the word of the LORD. {32:9} I bought the field of Hanameel my uncle's son, that was in Anathoth, and weighed him the money, even seventeen shekels of silver. {32:10} I signed the deed, sealed it, took witnesses, and weighed the money in the balances. {32:11} So I took the deed of purchase, both that which was sealed according to the law and custom, and that which was open. {32:12} I gave the deed of purchase to Baruch the son of Neriah, the son of Maaseiah, in the presence of Hanameel my uncle's son, and in the presence of the witnesses who subscribed the deed before all the Jews who sat in the court of the prison. {32:13} I charged Baruch before them, saying, {32:14} "Thus says the LORD of hosts, the God of Israel: Take these evidences, both this deed of purchase, which is sealed, and this deed which is open, and put them in an earthen vessel, that they may continue many days. {32:15} For thus says the LORD of hosts, the God of Israel: Houses and fields and vineyards will again be possessed in this land." {32:16} Now when I had delivered the deed of purchase to Baruch the son of Neriah, I prayed to the LORD, saying, {32:17} "Ah, Lord GOD! Behold, you have made the heavens and the earth by your great power and outstretched arm; there is nothing too hard for you. {32:18} You show lovingkindness to thousands, and recompense the iniquity of the fathers into the bosom of their children after them; the Great, the Mighty God, the LORD of hosts is his name, {32:19} great in counsel and mighty in work; for your eyes are open upon all the ways of the sons of men, to give everyone according to his ways and according to the fruit of his doings. {32:20} You have set signs and wonders in the land of Egypt, even to this day, and in Israel and among other men; and have made yourself a name, as at this day; {32:21} and have brought your people Israel out of the land of Egypt with signs, wonders, a strong hand, an outstretched arm, and great terror; {32:22} and have given them this land, which you swore to their fathers to give them, a land flowing with milk and honey. {32:23} They came in and possessed it; but they did not obey your voice or walk in your law; they have done nothing of all that you commanded them to do; therefore you have caused all this evil to come upon them. {32:24} Behold, the siege ramps have come to the city to take it; and the city is given into the hand of the Chaldeans who fight against it because of the sword, famine, and pestilence; and what you have spoken has come to pass; and behold, you see it. {32:25} And you have said to me, "O Lord GOD, buy the field for money, and take witnesses; for the city is given into the hand of the Chaldeans." {32:26} Then came the word of the LORD to Jeremiah, saying, {32:27} "Behold, I am the LORD, the God of all flesh; is there anything too hard for me? {32:28} Therefore, thus says the LORD: Behold, I will give this city into the hand of the Chaldeans and into the hand of Nebuchadnezzar king of Babylon, and he will take it. {32:29} The Chaldeans who fight against this city will come and set fire to it and burn it with the houses on whose roofs they have offered incense to Baal and poured out drink offerings to other gods to provoke me to anger. {32:30} For the children of Israel and the children of Judah have done only evil before me from their youth; the children of Israel have provoked me to anger with the work of their hands, says the LORD. {32:31} For this city has been to me a provocation of my anger and my fury from the day it was built until this day; that I should remove it from before my face, {32:32} because of all the evil of the children of Israel and the children of Judah, which they have done to provoke me to anger; they, their kings, their princes, their priests, and their prophets, and the men of Judah, and the inhabitants of Jerusalem. {32:33} They have turned their back to me, and not their face; though I taught them, rising up early and teaching them, yet they have not listened to receive instruction. {32:34} But they have set their abominations in the house which is called by my name, to defile it. {32:35} And they built the high places of Baal, which are in the valley of the son of Hinnom, to cause their sons and daughters to pass through the fire to Molech; which I did not command them, nor did it come into my mind that they should do this abomination to cause Judah to sin. {32:36} Now therefore thus says the LORD, the God of Israel, concerning this city, of which you say, "It shall be delivered into the hand of the king of Babylon by the sword, by famine, and by pestilence." {32:37} Behold, I will gather them out of all countries where I have driven them in my anger, fury, and great wrath; and I will bring them back to this place and cause them to dwell safely. {32:38} They will be my people, and I will be their God. {32:39} I will give them one heart and one way, that they may fear me forever, for their good and for the good of their children after them. {32:40} I will make an everlasting covenant with them, that I will not turn away from them to do them good; but I will put my fear in their hearts so that they will not depart from me. {32:41} Yes, I will rejoice over them to do them good, and I will plant them in this land assuredly with my whole heart and soul. {32:42} For thus says the LORD: Just as I have brought all this great evil upon this people, so I will bring upon them all the good that I have promised them. {32:43} And fields will be bought in this land, of which you say, "It is desolate without man or beast; it is given into the hand of the Chaldeans." {32:44} Men will buy fields for money, subscribe deeds, seal them, and take witnesses in the land of Benjamin, in the places around Jerusalem, in the cities of Judah, and in the cities of the mountains, and in the cities of the valley, and in the cities of the south; for I will cause their captivity to return, says the LORD.

{33:1} The word of the LORD came to Jeremiah a second time while he was still confined in the prison courtyard, saying, {33:2} "Thus says the LORD, the Creator, the one who formed it to establish it; the LORD is his name. {33:3} Call to me, and I will answer you, and show you great and mighty things that you do not know. {33:4} For thus says the LORD, the God of Israel, regarding the houses of this city and the houses of the kings of Judah, which are broken down by the siege mounds and the sword; {33:5} they come to fight against the Chaldeans, but it is to fill them with the dead bodies of men whom I have killed in my anger and fury, for whose wickedness I have hidden my face from this city. {33:6} Behold, I will bring health and healing to it, and I will heal them and reveal to them an abundance of peace and truth. {33:7} I will restore the fortunes of Judah and Israel and rebuild them as they were at first. {33:8} I will cleanse them from all their wrongdoing by which they have sinned against me, and I will forgive all their iniquities by which they have sinned and transgressed against me. {33:9} This will be to me a name of joy, a praise, and an honor before all the nations of the earth, which will hear about all the good I do for them, and they will fear and tremble for all the goodness and prosperity I bring to it. {33:10} Thus says the LORD: Again, there will be heard in this place, which you say is desolate, without man and beast, even in the cities of Judah and the streets of Jerusalem that are desolate, without man, inhabitant, or beast, {33:11} the sound of joy and gladness, the voices of the bridegroom and the bride, and the voices of those who will say, "Praise the LORD of hosts, for the LORD is good; his mercy endures forever," and of those who will bring the sacrifice of praise into the house of the LORD. For I will restore the fortunes of the land as they were at first, says the LORD. {33:12} Thus says the LORD of hosts: Again in this place, which is desolate, without man and beast, and in all its cities, there will be a habitation of shepherds causing their flocks to lie down. {33:13} In the cities of the mountains, in the cities of the valley, in the cities of the south, in the land of Benjamin, around Jerusalem, and in the cities of Judah, flocks will again pass under the hands of the shepherd, says the LORD. {33:14} Behold, the days are coming, says the LORD, when I will fulfill the good promise I made to the house of Israel and the house of Judah. {33:15} In those days and at that time, I will cause a righteous Branch to grow up for David; he will execute judgment and righteousness in the land. {33:16} In those days, Judah will be saved, and Jerusalem will dwell safely. This is the name by which she will be called: The LORD our righteousness. {33:17} For thus says the LORD: David shall never lack a man to sit on the throne of the house of Israel; {33:18} neither shall the priests, the Levites, lack a man before me to offer burnt offerings, to kindle grain offerings, and to sacrifice continually. {33:19} The word of the LORD came to Jeremiah, saying, {33:20} "Thus says the LORD: If you can break my covenant of day and my covenant of night, so that there will not be day and night in their season, {33:21} then my covenant with David my servant can also be broken, so that he will not have a son to reign on his throne; and with the Levites, the priests, my ministers. {33:22} As the host of heaven cannot be numbered, nor the sand of the sea measured, so will I multiply the descendants of David my servant and the Levites who minister to me." {33:23} Moreover, the word of the LORD came to Jeremiah, saying, {33:24} "Do you not consider what this people have spoken, saying, 'The two families which the LORD has chosen, he has cast them off'? They have despised my people, so that they should no longer be a nation before them. {33:25} Thus says the LORD: If my covenant is not with day and night, and if I have not appointed the ordinances of heaven and earth, {33:26} then I will cast away the descendants of Jacob and David my servant, so that I will not take any of his descendants to be rulers over the descendants of Abraham, Isaac, and Jacob; for I will restore their fortunes and have mercy on them."

{34:1} The word that came to Jeremiah from the LORD when Nebuchadnezzar king of Babylon, all his army, and all the kingdoms of the earth under his dominion, and all the people fought against Jerusalem and all its cities, saying, {34:2} "Thus says the LORD, the God of Israel: Go and speak to Zedekiah king of Judah, and tell him, 'Thus says the LORD: Behold, I will give this city into the hand of the king of Babylon, and he will burn it with fire. {34:3} You shall not escape from his hand, but you will surely be captured and delivered into his hand; your eyes will see the eyes of the king of Babylon, and he will speak with you face to face, and you will go to Babylon.' {34:4} Yet hear the word of the LORD, O Zedekiah king of Judah: Thus says the LORD concerning you: You shall not die by the sword, {34:5} but you shall die in peace, and with the burnings of your fathers, the former kings who were before you, they shall burn spices for you, and they will lament for you, saying, 'Ah, lord!' for I have pronounced the word, says the LORD." {34:6} Then Jeremiah the prophet spoke all these words to Zedekiah king of Judah in Jerusalem, {34:7} when the king of Babylon's army was fighting against Jerusalem and against all the cities of Judah that remained, against Lachish and against Azekah, for these fortified cities were the only ones left in the land. {34:8} This is the word that came to Jeremiah from the LORD after King Zedekiah had made a covenant with all the people who were in Jerusalem to proclaim liberty to them; {34:9} that every man should let his Hebrew manservant and every man his Hebrew maidservant go free, so that none should serve themselves of a Jew, his brother. {34:10} Now when all the princes and all the people who had entered into the covenant heard that everyone should let his manservant and maidservant go free, they obeyed and let them go. {34:11} But afterward they turned and brought back the servants and maidservants whom they had let go free, and brought them back into subjection as servants and handmaids. {34:12} Therefore, the word of the LORD came to Jeremiah, saying, {34:13} "Thus says the LORD, the God of Israel: I made a covenant with your fathers when I brought them out of the land of Egypt, out of the house of bondage, saying, {34:14} 'At the end of seven years, let every man his Hebrew brother, who has been sold to you, go free. When he has served you six years, you shall let him go free from you.' But your fathers did not listen to me or incline their ear. {34:15} And you now have turned and done what is right in my sight, by proclaiming liberty to everyone to his neighbor, and you made a covenant before me in the house that is called by my name. {34:16} But you turned and profaned my name, and caused every man his servant and every man his maidservant, whom you had set at liberty, to return, and brought them back into subjection as servants and handmaids. {34:17} Therefore, thus says the LORD: You have not listened to me in proclaiming liberty, every one to his brother and neighbor; behold, I proclaim a liberty for you, says the LORD, to the sword, to pestilence, and to famine, and I will make you to be removed into all the kingdoms of the earth. {34:18} And I will give the men who have transgressed my covenant, who have not fulfilled the words of the covenant they made before me when they cut the calf in two and passed between the parts of it, {34:19} the princes of Judah, the princes of Jerusalem, the eunuchs, the priests, and all the people of the land who passed between the parts of the calf. {34:20} I will give them into the hand of their enemies and into the hand of those who seek their lives; their dead bodies shall be food for the birds of the air and the beasts of the earth. {34:21} And Zedekiah king of Judah and his princes I will give into the hand of their enemies and into the hand of those who seek their lives, and into the hand of the army of the king of Babylon, which has gone up from you. {34:22} Behold, I will command, says the LORD, and cause them to return to this city; they shall fight against it, take it, and burn it with fire; and I will make the cities of Judah a desolation without inhabitant."

{35:1} The word of the LORD came to Jeremiah during the reign of Jehoiakim, son of Josiah, king of Judah, saying, {35:2} "Go to the house of the Rechabites, speak to them, and bring them to the house of the LORD, into one of the chambers, and offer them wine to drink." {35:3} So I took Jaazaniah, son of Jeremiah, son of Habaziniah, along with his brothers and all his sons, and the entire house of the Rechabites; {35:4} and I brought them into the house of the LORD, into the chamber of the sons of Hanan, son of Igdaliah, a man of God, which was near the chamber of the princes, above the chamber of Maaseiah, son of Shallum, the keeper of the door. {35:5} I set pots full of wine and cups before the sons of the Rechabites and said to them, "Drink wine." {35:6} But they answered, "We will drink no wine, for Jonadab, son of Rechab, our father, commanded us, saying, 'You shall drink no wine, neither you nor your sons, forever. {35:7} You shall not build houses, sow seeds, plant vineyards, or have any; but all your days you shall live in tents, so that you may live many days in the land where you are strangers.' {35:8} We have obeyed the voice of Jonadab, son of Rechab, our father, in everything he charged us: we drink no wine all our days, we, our wives, our sons, or our daughters; {35:9} nor do we build houses to dwell in; we have no vineyard, field, or seed. {35:10} We have dwelt in tents and have obeyed and done according to all that Jonadab, our father, commanded us. {35:11} But when Nebuchadnezzar, king of Babylon, came up into the land, we said, 'Come, let us go to Jerusalem for fear of the army of the Chaldeans and the army of the Syrians.' So we dwell in Jerusalem." {35:12} Then the word of the LORD came to Jeremiah, saying, {35:13} "Thus says the LORD of hosts, the God of Israel: Go and tell the men of Judah and the inhabitants of Jerusalem, 'Will you not receive instruction to heed my words?' says the LORD. {35:14} The words of Jonadab, son of Rechab, that he commanded his sons not to drink wine are followed; to this day they drink none and obey their father's command. Yet I have spoken to you, rising early and speaking, but you have not listened to me. {35:15} I have also sent all my servants the prophets, rising up early and sending them, saying, 'Return now, every man from his evil way, and amend your doings, and do not follow other gods to serve them, and you shall dwell in the land which I have given to you and your fathers.' But you have not inclined your ear or listened to me. {35:16} Because the sons of Jonadab, son of Rechab, have performed their father's command, but this people has not listened to me. {35:17} Therefore, thus says the LORD God of hosts, the God of Israel: Behold, I will bring upon Judah and all the inhabitants of Jerusalem all the evil that I have pronounced against them, because I have spoken to them, but they have not heard; I have called to them, but they have not answered. {35:18} And Jeremiah said to the house of the Rechabites, "Thus says the LORD of hosts, the God of Israel: Because you have obeyed the commandment of Jonadab your father, kept all his precepts, and done according to all that he commanded you, {35:19} therefore, thus says the LORD of hosts, the God of Israel: Jonadab, son of Rechab, shall not lack a man to stand before me forever."

{36:1} It came to pass in the fourth year of Jehoiakim, son of Josiah, king of Judah, that this word came to Jeremiah from the LORD, saying, {36:2} "Take a scroll and write in it all the words that I have spoken to you against Israel, Judah, and all the nations, from the day I spoke to you, from the days of Josiah until this day. {36:3} Perhaps the house of Judah will hear all the evil which I plan to bring upon them, that they may return every man from his evil way; then I may forgive their iniquity and their sin." {36:4} So Jeremiah called Baruch, son of Neriah, and Baruch wrote from the mouth of Jeremiah all the words of the LORD that he had spoken to him on a scroll. {36:5} Jeremiah commanded Baruch, saying, "I am shut up; I cannot go into the house of the LORD. {36:6} Therefore, go, and read from the scroll which you have written from my mouth in the ears of the people in the house of the LORD on the day of fasting; and also read them in the ears of all Judah who come from their cities. {36:7} It may be they will present their supplication before the LORD and will return every one from his evil way; for great is the anger and fury that the LORD has pronounced against this people." {36:8} Baruch, son of Neriah, did according to all that Jeremiah the prophet commanded him, reading in the book the words of the LORD in the house of the LORD. {36:9} Now it came to pass in the fifth year of Jehoiakim, son of Josiah, king of Judah, in the ninth month, that they proclaimed a fast before the LORD to all the people in Jerusalem and to all the people that came from the cities of Judah to Jerusalem. {36:10} Then Baruch read in the book the words of Jeremiah in the house of the LORD, in the chamber of Gemariah, son of Shaphan the scribe, in the higher court, at the entry of the new gate of the house of the LORD, in the ears of all the people. {36:11} When Michaiah, son of Gemariah, son of Shaphan, heard all the words of the LORD from the book, {36:12} he went down to the king's house, into the scribe's chamber, and lo, all the princes were sitting there: Elishama the scribe, Delaiah, son of Shemaiah, Elnathan, son of Achbor, Gemariah, son of Shaphan, Zedekiah, son of Hananiah, and all the princes. {36:13} Then Michaiah declared to them all the words he had heard when Baruch read the book in the ears of the people. {36:14} Therefore all the princes sent Jehudi, son of Nethaniah, son of Shelemiah, son of Cushi, to Baruch, saying, "Take in your hand the scroll in which you have read in the ears of the people, and come." So Baruch, son of Neriah, took the scroll in his hand and came to them. {36:15} They said to him, "Sit down now and read it in our ears." So Baruch read it in their ears. {36:16} Now it came to pass, when they had heard all the words, they were afraid, both one and another, and said to Baruch, "We will surely tell the king of all these words." {36:17} They asked Baruch, saying, "Tell us now, how did you write all these words at his mouth?" {36:18} Then Baruch answered them, "He pronounced all these words to me with his mouth, and I wrote them with ink in the book." {36:19} Then the princes said to Baruch, "Go, hide yourself, you and Jeremiah; and let no man know where you are." {36:20} They went into the king, into the court, but they laid up the scroll in the chamber of Elishama, the scribe, and told all the words in the ears of the king. {36:21} So the king sent Jehudi to get the scroll; and he took it out of the chamber of Elishama, the scribe. Jehudi read it in the ears of the king and in the ears of all the princes who stood beside the king. {36:22} Now the king sat in the winter house in the ninth month, and there was a fire on the hearth burning before him. {36:23} It came to pass that when Jehudi had read three or four columns, he cut it with a penknife and threw it into the fire that was on the hearth until the entire scroll was consumed in the fire that was on the hearth. {36:24} Yet they were not afraid, nor did they tear their garments, neither the king nor any of his servants who heard all these words. {36:25} Nevertheless, Elnathan, Delaiah, and Gemariah had made intercession to the king that he would not burn the scroll, but he would not listen to them. {36:26} But the king commanded Jerahmeel, son of Hammelech, Seraiah, son of Azriel, and Shelemiah, son of Abdeel, to take Baruch, the scribe, and Jeremiah, the prophet; but the LORD hid them. {36:27} Then the word of the LORD came to Jeremiah after the king had burned the scroll and the words which Baruch wrote at the mouth of Jeremiah, saying, {36:28} "Take another scroll and write in it all the former words that were in the first scroll, which Jehoiakim, king of Judah, has burned. {36:29} And you shall say to Jehoiakim, king of Judah, 'Thus says the LORD: You have burned this scroll, saying, "Why have you written in it, saying, the king of Babylon shall certainly come and destroy this land and cause man and beast to cease from there?" {36:30} Therefore, thus says the LORD concerning Jehoiakim, king of Judah: He shall have no one to sit upon the throne of David, and his dead body shall be cast out in the day to the heat and in the night to the frost. {36:31} I will punish him and his seed and his servants for their iniquity; and I will bring upon them and upon the inhabitants of Jerusalem and upon the men of Judah all the evil that I have pronounced against them; but they did not listen." {36:32} Then Jeremiah took another scroll and gave it to Baruch, the scribe, son of Neriah, who wrote in it from the mouth of Jeremiah all the words of the book which Jehoiakim, king of Judah, had burned in the fire; and many similar words were added to them.

{37:1} King Zedekiah, son of Josiah, reigned in place of Coniah, son of Jehoiakim, whom Nebuchadnezzar, king of Babylon, made king over Judah. {37:2} But neither he nor his officials nor the people of the land listened to the words of the LORD that He spoke through the prophet Jeremiah. {37:3} So King Zedekiah sent Jehucal, son of Shelemiah, and Zephaniah, son of Maaseiah the priest, to the prophet Jeremiah, saying, "Pray now to the LORD our God for us." {37:4} Jeremiah came and went among the people, for they had not imprisoned him. {37:5} Then Pharaoh's army came out of Egypt, and when the Chaldeans besieging Jerusalem heard news of them, they withdrew from Jerusalem. {37:6} Then the word of the LORD came to the prophet Jeremiah, saying, {37:7} "Thus says the LORD, the God of Israel: Tell the king of Judah who sent you to inquire of me, 'Behold, Pharaoh's army that has come out to help you will return to Egypt, their own land. {37:8} The Chaldeans will return and fight against this city, capture it, and burn it with fire. {37:9} Thus says the LORD: Don't deceive yourselves, saying, "The Chaldeans will surely leave us," for they will not leave. {37:10} Even if you defeated the entire Chaldean army that fights against you and only wounded men were left, they would rise up in their tents and burn this city with fire.' {37:11} It happened that when the Chaldean army withdrew from Jerusalem because of Pharaoh's army, {37:12} Jeremiah went out from Jerusalem to go into the land of Benjamin to separate himself from the people. {37:13} When he was at the Benjamin Gate, a captain of the guard named Irijah, son of Shelemiah, son of Hananiah, took Jeremiah the prophet, saying, "You are defecting to the Chaldeans!" {37:14} Jeremiah replied, "That's false; I'm not defecting to the Chaldeans." But Irijah did not listen to him, so he took Jeremiah and brought him to the officials. {37:15} The officials were angry with Jeremiah, beat him, and put him in prison in the house of Jonathan the scribe, which had been made into a prison. {37:16} When Jeremiah had been put into the dungeon and remained there many days, {37:17} King Zedekiah sent for him and had him brought to his house, asking him privately, "Is there any word from the LORD?" Jeremiah replied, "Yes, you will be handed over to the king of Babylon." {37:18} Moreover, Jeremiah said to King Zedekiah, "What have I done wrong against you, your officials, or this people that you have put me in prison? {37:19} Where are now your prophets who prophesied to you, saying, 'The king of Babylon will not come against you or against this land'? {37:20} Therefore, I ask you, my lord the king, let my plea be accepted before you; don't send me back to the house of Jonathan the scribe, or I will die there." {37:21} So King Zedekiah commanded that Jeremiah be kept in the court of the prison and that he be given a daily portion of bread from the bakers' street until all the bread in the city was gone. Thus Jeremiah remained in the court of the prison.

{38:1} Then Shephatiah, son of Mattan, Gedaliah, son of Pashur, Jucal, son of Shelemiah, and Pashur, son of Malchiah, heard the words that Jeremiah had spoken to all the people, saying, {38:2} "Thus says the LORD: Those who remain in this city will die by the sword, famine, and pestilence; but whoever goes out to the Chaldeans will live; he will have his life as a prize and will live." {38:3} "Thus says the LORD: This city will surely be given into the hand of the army of the king of Babylon." {38:4} Therefore, the officials said to the king, "We request that this man be put to death, for he is weakening the hands of the soldiers left in this city and the hands of all the people by speaking such words to them; he seeks not the welfare of this people, but their harm." {38:5} King Zedekiah said, "He is in your hands; the king cannot do anything against you." {38:6} So they took Jeremiah and cast him into the dungeon of Malchiah, son of Hammelech, in the court of the prison, and they lowered him with ropes. There was no water in the dungeon, only mud, and Jeremiah sank in the mud. {38:7} When Ebedmelech the Ethiopian, one of the eunuchs in the king's house, heard that they had put Jeremiah in the dungeon, while the king was sitting at the Benjamin Gate, {38:8} Ebedmelech went from the king's house and spoke to the king, saying, {38:9} "My lord the king, these men have acted wickedly in all they have done to Jeremiah the prophet, whom they have cast into the dungeon; he is likely to die from hunger in that place, for there is no more bread in the city." {38:10} Then the king commanded Ebedmelech the Ethiopian, saying, "Take thirty men with you and lift Jeremiah the prophet out of the dungeon before he dies." {38:11} So Ebedmelech took the men with him and went into the king's house under the treasury and took old rags and worn-out clothes and let them down by ropes into the dungeon to Jeremiah. {38:12} Ebedmelech the Ethiopian said to Jeremiah, "Put these old rags and worn-out clothes under your arms, under the ropes." Jeremiah did so. {38:13} They drew up Jeremiah with the ropes and took him out of the dungeon, and Jeremiah remained in the court of the prison. {38:14} Then King Zedekiah sent for Jeremiah the prophet to come to him at the third entry of the house of the LORD, and the king said to Jeremiah, "I will ask you something; hide nothing from me." {38:15} Jeremiah said to Zedekiah, "If I tell you, will you not put me to death? And if I give you advice, you will not listen to me?" {38:16} So King Zedekiah swore secretly to Jeremiah, saying, "As the LORD lives, who made our souls, I will not put you to death, nor will I give you into the hand of these men who seek your life." {38:17} Then Jeremiah said to Zedekiah, "Thus says the LORD of hosts, the God of Israel: If you surrender to the princes of the king of Babylon, your soul will live, and this city will not be burned with fire; you and your house will live. {38:18} But if you do not surrender to the princes of the king of Babylon, this city will be given into the hand of the Chaldeans, and they will burn it with fire, and you will not escape out of their hand." {38:19} Zedekiah said to Jeremiah, "I am afraid of the Jews who have defected to the Chaldeans, lest they deliver me into their hands and mock me." {38:20} But Jeremiah said, "They will not deliver you. Obey the voice of the LORD, which I speak to you, so it will be well with you, and your soul will live. {38:21} But if you refuse to surrender, this is the word that the LORD has shown me: {38:22} Behold, all the women who are left in the king of Judah's house will be brought out to the princes of the king of Babylon, and those women will say, 'Your friends have prevailed against you; your feet are sunk in the mud, and they are turning back.' {38:23} They will bring out all your wives and children to the Chaldeans, and you will not escape from their hand, but will be captured by the king of Babylon, and this city will be burned with fire." {38:24} Then Zedekiah said to Jeremiah, "Let no one know of these words, or you will die. {38:25} But if the officials hear that I have talked with you and come to you and say, 'Tell us what you said to the king; don't hide it from us, and we will not put you to death,' {38:26} then you shall say to them, 'I presented my plea before the king not to return to the house of Jonathan to die there.'" {38:27} All the officials came to Jeremiah and asked him, and he told them according to all the words the king had commanded. So they left off speaking with him, for the matter was not known. {38:28} Jeremiah remained in the court of the prison until the day Jerusalem was taken, and he was there when Jerusalem was taken.

{39:1} In the ninth year of King Zedekiah of Judah, in the tenth month, Nebuchadnezzar, king of Babylon, and all his army came against Jerusalem and besieged it. {39:2} In the eleventh year of Zedekiah, on the fourth month, the ninth day of the month, the city was breached. {39:3} All the officials of the king of Babylon came in and sat in the Middle Gate, including Nergalsharezer, Samgarnebo, Sarsechim, Rabsaris, Nergalsharezer, Rabmag, and all the other officials of the king of Babylon. {39:4} When Zedekiah, king of Judah, saw them and all the soldiers, he fled and went out of the city by night through the king's garden and by the gate between the two walls, and he went out toward the plain. {39:5} But the Chaldean army pursued them and caught up with Zedekiah in the plains of Jericho. When they captured him, they brought him to Nebuchadnezzar, king of Babylon, at Riblah in the land of Hamath, where he gave judgment against him. {39:6} The king of Babylon executed Zedekiah's sons in Riblah before his eyes, and he also killed all the nobles of Judah. {39:7} Moreover, he blinded Zedekiah, bound him with chains, and took him to Babylon. {39:8} The Chaldeans burned the king's palace and the houses of the people and broke down the walls of Jerusalem. {39:9} Then Nebuzaradan, the captain of the guard, carried away to Babylon the remnant of the people who remained in the city, along with those who had defected to him, and the rest of the people who remained. {39:10} But Nebuzaradan left some of the poor of the land, those who had nothing, and gave them vineyards and fields at that time. {39:11} Now Nebuchadnezzar, king of Babylon, gave orders concerning Jeremiah to Nebuzaradan, the captain of the guard, saying, {39:12} "Take him and look after him; do him no harm, but do for him whatever he says." {39:13} So Nebuzaradan, the captain of the guard, sent for Jeremiah and Nebushasban, Rabsaris, Nergalsharezer, Rabmag, and all the princes of the king of Babylon. {39:14} They sent for Jeremiah, took him out of the court of the prison, and committed him to Gedaliah, son of Ahikam, son of Shaphan, to carry him home; so he dwelt among the people. {39:15} Now the word of the LORD came to Jeremiah while he was still shut up in the court of the prison, saying, {39:16} "Go and speak to Ebedmelech the Ethiopian, saying, 'Thus says the LORD of hosts, the God of Israel: I am bringing my words upon this city for evil, not for good, and they will be accomplished in that day before you. {39:17} But I will deliver you on that day, says the

LORD, and you shall not be given into the hand of those you fear. {39:18} For I will surely deliver you, and you shall not fall by the sword, but your life shall be a prize for you, because you have put your trust in me, says the LORD."

{40:1} The word that came to Jeremiah from the LORD, after Nebuzaradan, the captain of the guard, had let him go from Ramah, when he had taken him bound in chains among all those carried away captive from Jerusalem and Judah to Babylon. {40:2} The captain of the guard took Jeremiah and said to him, "The LORD your God has pronounced this disaster upon this place. {40:3} Now the LORD has brought it and done as He said, because you have sinned against the LORD and have not obeyed His voice; therefore, this has come upon you. {40:4} And now, behold, I am releasing you today from the chains that were on your hands. If it seems good to you to come with me to Babylon, come, and I will look after you; but if it seems bad to you to come with me to Babylon, you can stay. Behold, all the land is before you; go wherever it seems good and right for you to go." {40:5} While he was not yet gone back, he said, "Go back also to Gedaliah, son of Ahikam, son of Shaphan, whom the king of Babylon has made governor over the cities of Judah, and dwell with him among the people, or go wherever it seems convenient for you to go." So the captain of the guard gave him provisions and a reward and let him go. {40:6} Then Jeremiah went to Gedaliah, son of Ahikam, at Mizpah and dwelt with him among the people who were left in the land. {40:7} When all the captains of the forces in the fields heard that the king of Babylon had made Gedaliah, son of Ahikam, governor in the land, and had committed to him men, women, children, and the poor of the land who had not been carried away captive to Babylon, {40:8} they came to Gedaliah at Mizpah, including Ishmael, son of Nethaniah, Johanan and Jonathan, the sons of Kareah, Seraiah, son of Tanhumeth, the sons of Ephai the Netophathite, and Jezaniah, son of a Maachathite, along with their men. {40:9} Gedaliah, son of Ahikam, son of Shaphan, swore to them and their men, saying, "Don't be afraid to serve the Chaldeans; dwell in the land and serve the king of Babylon, and it will be well with you. {40:10} As for me, behold, I will dwell at Mizpah to serve the Chaldeans who come to us; but you gather wine, summer fruits, and oil, and put them in your vessels and dwell in the cities that you have taken." {40:11} Likewise, when all the Jews who were in Moab, among the Ammonites, in Edom, and in all the countries heard that the king of Babylon had left a remnant of Judah and had set over them Gedaliah, son of Ahikam, son of Shaphan, {40:12} all the Jews returned from all the places where they had been driven and came to the land of Judah, to Gedaliah at Mizpah, and gathered a great quantity of wine and summer fruits. {40:13} Moreover, Johanan, son of Kareah, and all the captains of the forces that were in the fields, came to Gedaliah at Mizpah, {40:14} and said to him, "Do you certainly know that Baalis, king of the Ammonites, has sent Ishmael, son of Nethaniah, to kill you?" But Gedaliah, son of Ahikam, did not believe them. {40:15} Then Johanan, son of Kareah, spoke to Gedaliah in Mizpah secretly, saying, "Let me go, please, and I will kill Ishmael, son of Nethaniah, and no one will know it. Why should he kill you so that all the Jews gathered to you would be scattered, and the remnant in Judah perish?" {40:16} But Gedaliah, son of Ahikam, said to Johanan, son of Kareah, "You shall not do this thing, for you are speaking falsely about Ishmael."

{41:1} In the seventh month, Ishmael son of Nethaniah, the son of Elishama, who was of royal lineage, came with ten men to Gedaliah son of Ahikam at Mizpah. While they were eating together in Mizpah, {41:2} Ishmael and the ten men with him got up and killed Gedaliah son of Ahikam, the son of Shaphan, with a sword, the one whom the king of Babylon had appointed as governor over the land. {41:3} Ishmael also killed all the Jews who were with Gedaliah at Mizpah, as well as the Chaldean soldiers present there. {41:4} The day after Gedaliah was murdered, before anyone knew what had happened, {41:5} eighty men came from Shechem, Shiloh, and Samaria. They had shaved their beards, torn their clothes, and cut themselves (signs of mourning), and they carried grain offerings and incense to bring to the house of the Lord. {41:6} Ishmael went out from Mizpah to meet them, weeping as he went. When he met them, he said, "Come to Gedaliah son of Ahikam." {41:7} But when they entered the city, Ishmael and his men killed them and threw their bodies into a pit. {41:8} However, ten of the men pleaded with Ishmael, saying, "Don't kill us, for we have hidden treasures of wheat, barley, oil, and honey in the fields." So Ishmael spared their lives and did not kill them along with their companions. {41:9} The pit where Ishmael threw the bodies of those he had killed was the same one King Asa had made to protect against Baasha, the king of Israel. Ishmael filled it with the bodies of the slain. {41:10} Then Ishmael took captive the rest of the people in Mizpah, including the king's daughters, and everyone else whom Nebuzaradan, the captain of the guard, had entrusted to Gedaliah. He carried them away and set out to go to the land of the Ammonites. {41:11} When Johanan son of Kareah and all the army officers with him heard about the crimes Ishmael had committed, {41:12} they gathered their men and pursued him. They found him by the large pool of water at Gibeon. {41:13} When the people Ishmael had taken captive saw Johanan and his men, they were overjoyed. {41:14} All the captives turned and went to Johanan son of Kareah. {41:15} But Ishmael and eight of his men escaped from Johanan and fled to the land of the Ammonites. {41:16} Then Johanan and the army officers with him gathered all the people they had rescued from Ishmael, including the soldiers, women, children, and eunuchs, and brought them back from Gibeon. {41:17} They went and stayed at the lodging place of Chimham near Bethlehem, intending to go to Egypt {41:18} because they were afraid of the Chaldeans. They feared retaliation since Ishmael had killed Gedaliah, whom the king of Babylon had appointed as governor.

{42:1} Then all the army officers, along with Johanan son of Kareah, Jezaniah son of Hoshaiah, and all the people, from the least to the greatest, approached {42:2} Jeremiah the prophet and said, "Please, hear our request. Pray to the Lord your God for us, for we are only a few now, though once we were many, as you can see. {42:3} Ask the Lord your God to show us the way we should go and what we should do." {42:4} Jeremiah responded, "I have heard you. I will pray to the Lord your God as you've asked, and I will tell you whatever He says. I will not withhold anything from you." {42:5} They replied to Jeremiah, "May the Lord be a true and faithful witness against us if we do not act in accordance with everything the Lord your God sends through you to us. {42:6} Whether it is favorable or unfavorable, we will obey the Lord our God, to whom we are sending you, so that things will go well for us." {42:7} Ten days later, the word of the Lord came to Jeremiah. {42:8} He summoned Johanan, the army officers, and all the people, from the least to the greatest, {42:9} and said to them, "This is what the Lord, the God of Israel, says: You asked me to present your petition to Him, and {42:10} if you stay in this land, I will build you up and not tear you down. I will plant you and not uproot you, for I am sorry for the disaster I have brought upon you. {42:11} Do not be afraid of the king of Babylon, whom you fear. Do not fear him, declares the Lord, for I am with you to save you and deliver you from his power. {42:12} I will show you compassion so that he will have mercy on you and allow you to return to your land. {42:13} But if you say, 'We will not stay in this land,' and do not obey the Lord your God, {42:14} and instead say, 'No, we will go to Egypt where we will not face war, hear the sound of the trumpet, or suffer hunger,' {42:15} then listen to what the Lord says: If you are determined to go to Egypt and settle there, {42:16} then the sword you fear will overtake you, and the famine you dread will follow you to Egypt, and there you will die. {42:17} All who decide to go to Egypt to live will die by the sword, famine, or plague. None will survive or escape the disaster I will bring upon them. {42:18} This is what the Lord Almighty, the God of Israel, says: Just as my anger and wrath were poured out on the people of Jerusalem, so will my fury be poured out on you when you go to Egypt. You will become an object of cursing and horror, condemnation, and reproach, and you will never see this place again." {42:19} The Lord has spoken concerning you, remnant of Judah. Do not go to Egypt. Be sure of this: I have warned you today. {42:20} You were not sincere when you sent me to the Lord your God, saying, "Pray for us to the Lord our God, and tell us everything He says, and we will do it." {42:21} I have told you today, but you have not obeyed the Lord your God in anything He sent me to tell you. {42:22} So now, be certain of this: You will die by the sword, famine, and plague in the place where you desire to go and settle."

{43:1} When Jeremiah finished speaking all the words the LORD their God had sent him to convey to the people, {43:2} Azariah, son of Hoshaiah, Johanan, son of Kareah, and all the proud men spoke to Jeremiah, saying, "You are speaking falsely. The LORD our God has not sent you to tell us not to go to Egypt and live there. {43:3} Instead, Baruch, son of Neriah, is inciting you against us to deliver us into the hands of the Chaldeans so they can kill us and carry us away to Babylon." {43:4} So Johanan, son of Kareah, all the captains of the forces, and all the people did not obey the voice of the LORD to remain in the land of Judah. {43:5} Instead, Johanan, son of Kareah, and all the captains took all the remnant of Judah who had returned from all the nations where they had been driven, to live in the land of Judah. {43:6} This included men, women, children, the king's daughters, and everyone Nebuzaradan, the captain of the guard, had left with Gedaliah, son of Ahikam, son of Shaphan, as well as Jeremiah the prophet and Baruch, son of Neriah. {43:7} They entered the land of Egypt, for they did not obey the voice of the LORD, and they went as far as Tahpanhes. {43:8} Then the word of the LORD came to Jeremiah in Tahpanhes, saying, {43:9} "Take large stones in your hand and hide them in the clay at the brick kiln at the entrance of Pharaoh's house in Tahpanhes, in front of the men of Judah. {43:10} Say to them, 'Thus says the LORD of hosts, the God of Israel: Look, I will send and take Nebuchadnezzar, king of Babylon, my servant, and set his throne on these stones that I have hidden; he will spread his royal canopy over them. {43:11} When he comes, he will strike the land of Egypt and deliver those destined for death to death, those destined for captivity to captivity, and those destined for the sword to the sword. {43:12} I will set fire to the houses of the gods of Egypt, and he will burn them and take them captive; he will wrap himself in the land of Egypt as a shepherd puts on his garment and will leave there in peace. {43:13} He will break the images of Bethshemesh, in the land of Egypt, and burn the houses of the gods of the Egyptians with fire."

{44:1} The word that came to Jeremiah concerning all the Jews who dwell in the land of Egypt, at Migdol, Tahpanhes, Noph, and in the region of Pathros, saying, {44:2} "Thus says the LORD of hosts, the God of Israel: You have seen all the evil I have brought upon Jerusalem and all the cities of Judah; today they are desolate, and no one lives there, {44:3} because of their wickedness, which provoked me to anger as they burned incense and served other gods they did not know, neither you nor your fathers. {44:4} Yet I sent all my servants the prophets to you, rising early and sending them, saying, 'Oh, do not do this abominable thing that I hate.' {44:5} But they did not listen or incline their ear to turn from their wickedness and stop burning incense to other gods. {44:6} Therefore my fury and anger were poured out and kindled in the cities of Judah and in the streets of Jerusalem; they are wasted and desolate, as it is today. {44:7} Therefore, thus says the LORD, the God of hosts, the God of Israel: Why are you committing this great evil against your own souls by cutting off from you man and woman, child and infant, from Judah, leaving none to remain? {44:8} You provoke me to wrath with the works of your hands, burning incense to other gods in the land of Egypt, where you have gone to live, thus cutting yourselves off and becoming a curse and a reproach among all the nations of the earth. {44:9} Have you forgotten the wickedness of your fathers, the wickedness of the kings of Judah, the wickedness of their wives, and your own wickedness, and the wickedness of your wives, committed in the land of Judah and the streets of Jerusalem? {44:10} They are not humbled to this day, nor have they feared, nor walked in my law or in my statutes that I set before you and your fathers. {44:11} Therefore, thus says the LORD of hosts, the God of Israel: Look, I will set my face against you for evil and cut off all Judah. {44:12} I will take the remnant of Judah who have set their faces to go into Egypt to live there; they will all be consumed and fall in the land of Egypt; they will be consumed by the sword and famine; they will die, from the least to the greatest, by the sword and famine, and they will be a curse, an astonishment, a desolation, and a reproach. {44:13} I will punish those living in the land of Egypt, as I have punished Jerusalem, with sword, famine, and pestilence. {44:14} So none of the remnant of Judah who have gone into the land of Egypt to live there will escape or remain to return to the land of Judah, to which they long to return; none will return except those who escape." {44:15} Then all the men who knew their wives had burned incense to other gods, along with a great multitude of women and all the people dwelling in the land of Egypt in Pathros, answered Jeremiah, saying, {44:16} "As for the word you have spoken to us in the name of the LORD, we will not listen to you. {44:17} Instead, we will do everything that comes from our own mouths: we will burn incense to the queen of heaven and pour out drink offerings to her, just as we and our fathers, our kings, and our princes did in the cities of Judah and the streets of Jerusalem; for then we had plenty of food, were well off, and saw no evil. {44:18} But since we stopped burning incense to the queen of heaven and pouring out drink offerings to her, we have lacked everything and have been consumed by the sword and famine. {44:19} When we burned incense to the queen of heaven and poured out drink offerings to her, did we make cakes to worship her and pour out drink offerings to her without our men?" {44:20} Then Jeremiah said to all the people, to the men and women, and to all the people who had given him that answer, {44:21} "The incense you burned in the cities of Judah and the streets of Jerusalem, you, your fathers, your kings, and your princes, did not the LORD remember them? Did they not come to His mind? {44:22} The LORD could no longer bear it because of the evil of your doings and the abominations you committed; therefore your land has become a desolation, an astonishment, and a curse, without inhabitants, as it is today. {44:23} Because you have burned incense and sinned against the LORD, and have not obeyed the voice of the LORD, nor walked in His law, nor in His statutes, nor in His testimonies, this evil has happened to you, as it is today. {44:24} Moreover, Jeremiah said to all the people, including all the women, "Hear the word of the LORD, all Judah who dwell in the land of Egypt: {44:25} Thus says the LORD of hosts, the God of Israel: You and your wives have both spoken with your mouths and fulfilled with your hands, saying, 'We will surely perform our vows to burn incense to the queen of heaven and pour out drink offerings to her.' You will surely fulfill your vows and perform your vows." {44:26} Therefore, hear the word of the LORD, all Judah who dwell in the land of Egypt: Look, I have sworn by my great name, says the LORD, that my name will no longer be mentioned by any man of Judah in all the land of Egypt, saying, 'As surely as the Lord GOD lives.' {44:27} Look, I will watch over them for evil and not for good; all the men of Judah in the land of Egypt will be consumed by sword and famine until there is an end to them. {44:28} Yet a small number who escape the sword will return from the land of Egypt to the land of Judah, and all the remnant of Judah who have gone into Egypt to live there will know whose words will stand, mine or theirs. {44:29} This will be a sign to you, says the LORD, that I will punish you in this place so you may know that my words will surely stand against you for evil: {44:30} Thus says the LORD: Look, I will give Pharaoh Hophra, king of Egypt, into the hands of his enemies and those seeking his life, just as I gave Zedekiah, king of Judah, into the hands of Nebuchadnezzar, king of Babylon, his enemy who sought his life.

{45:1} This is the word that Jeremiah the prophet spoke to Baruch, son of Neriah, when Baruch had written these words in a book at Jeremiah's command, in the fourth year of Jehoiakim, son of Josiah, king of Judah, saying, {45:2} "Thus says the LORD, the God of Israel, to you, O Baruch: {45:3} You said, 'Woe is me now! For the LORD has added grief to my sorrow; I am faint from my sighing, and I find no rest.' {45:4} Say this to him: 'The LORD says: Look, I will break down what I have built, and uproot what I have planted, even this whole land.' {45:5} Are you seeking great things for yourself? Don't seek them, for look, I will bring disaster upon all flesh, says the LORD; but I will spare your life wherever you go."

{46:1} The word of the LORD that came to Jeremiah the prophet concerning the nations; {46:2} concerning Egypt, against the army of Pharaoh Necho, king of Egypt, which was by the river Euphrates in Carchemish, which Nebuchadnezzar, king of Babylon, defeated in the fourth year of Jehoiakim, son of Josiah, king of Judah. {46:3} Prepare your shields and bucklers, and get ready for battle. {46:4} Harness the horses; mount up, you horsemen, and stand ready with your helmets; polish your spears, and put on your armor. {46:5} Why do I see them dismayed and turning back? Their mighty ones are beaten down, and they flee without looking back, for fear surrounds them, says the LORD. {46:6} Let not the swift flee, nor the strong escape; they will stumble and fall toward the north by the river Euphrates. {46:7} Who is this rising like a flood, whose waters are like rivers? {46:8} Egypt rises like a flood, and its waters are like rivers; it says, 'I will go up and cover the earth; I will destroy the city and its inhabitants.' {46:9} Come forth, you horses; rage, you chariots; let the mighty men come out, the Ethiopians and the Libyans who handle the shield, and the Lydians who draw the bow. {46:10} For this is the day of the Lord GOD of hosts, a day of vengeance to avenge Himself on His adversaries; the sword will devour and be filled with their blood, for the Lord GOD of hosts has a sacrifice in the north country by the river Euphrates. {46:11} Go up to Gilead and take balm, O virgin daughter of Egypt; in vain will you use many medicines, for you will not be healed. {46:12} The nations have heard of your shame, and your cry has filled the land; for the mighty man has stumbled against the mighty, and they have both fallen together. {46:13} This is the word that the LORD spoke to Jeremiah the prophet regarding how Nebuchadnezzar, king of Babylon, would come and strike the land of Egypt. {46:14} Declare in Egypt, and publish in Migdol, and publish in Noph and in Tahpanhes: say, 'Stand firm and prepare yourself, for the sword will devour you all around.' {46:15} Why are your valiant men swept away? They did not stand, for the LORD drove them away. {46:16} He made many fall; one fell upon another. They said, 'Arise, and let us go back to our own people and to the land of our birth, away from the oppressing sword.' {46:17} They cried there, 'Pharaoh, king of Egypt, is but a noise; he has passed the appointed time.' {46:18} As I live, says the King, whose name is the LORD of hosts, surely as Tabor is among the mountains, and as Carmel is by the sea, so he will come. {46:19} O daughter dwelling in Egypt, prepare yourself to go into captivity, for Noph will be waste and desolate without an inhabitant. {46:20} Egypt is like a very beautiful cow, but destruction comes; it comes out of the north. {46:21} Her hired men are in the midst of her like fatted calves; they too have turned back and fled together; they did not stand, for the day of their calamity has come upon them, the time of their punishment. {46:22} The sound of their advance will be like a serpent; for they will march with an army and come against her with axes like woodcutters. {46:23} They will cut down her forest, says the LORD, though it cannot be measured, for they are more numerous than locusts and are without number. {46:24} The daughter of Egypt will be ashamed; she will be delivered into the hand of the people from the north. {46:25} The LORD of hosts, the God of Israel, says: Look, I will punish the multitude of No, and Pharaoh, and Egypt, along with their gods and their kings; even Pharaoh and all who trust in him. {46:26} I will deliver them into the hands of those who seek their lives, and into the hands of Nebuchadnezzar, king of Babylon, and his servants; and afterward, the land will be inhabited as in days of old, says the LORD. {46:27} But do not fear, O my servant Jacob, and do not be dismayed, O Israel; for look, I will save you from afar and your descendants from the land of their captivity; Jacob will return and be at rest and at ease, and no one will make him afraid. {46:28} Do not fear, O Jacob my servant, says the LORD; for I am with you. I will completely destroy all the nations where I have driven you, but I will not completely destroy you; I will correct you in measure, yet I will not leave you unpunished.

{47:1} This is the word of the LORD that came to Jeremiah the prophet concerning the Philistines, before Pharaoh struck Gaza. {47:2} The LORD says: Look, waters are rising from the north and will become an overflowing flood, covering the land and everything in it—the city and its inhabitants. Then the people will cry out, and all the residents of the land will wail. {47:3} At the sound of the pounding hooves of his strong horses, the rush of his chariots, and the rumbling of their wheels, fathers will not look back at their children because their hands will be weak. {47:4} This is because the day is coming to destroy all the Philistines and cut off every helper remaining from Tyre and Sidon; the LORD will plunder the Philistines, the remnant from the island of Caphtor. {47:5} Baldness has come upon Gaza; Ashkelon is cut off with the remnants of their valley. How long will you continue to harm yourself? {47:6} O sword of the LORD, how long will you remain quiet? Sheathe yourself, rest, and be still. {47:7} How can you be still, when the LORD has given you a command against Ashkelon and against the seashore? There He has appointed you.

{48:1} Concerning Moab, the LORD of hosts, the God of Israel, says: Woe to Nebo! It is ruined; Kiriathaim is ashamed and taken; Misgab is dismayed and broken. {48:2} There will be no more praise for Moab; in Heshbon they have devised evil against it, saying, 'Come, let us cut it off from being a nation.' Also you, O Madmen, will be cut down; the sword will pursue you. {48:3} A voice of crying will come from Horonaim, of devastation and great destruction. {48:4} Moab is destroyed; its little ones make a cry heard. {48:5} As Luhith rises, there will be continual weeping; as Horonaim descends, the enemies will hear a cry of destruction. {48:6} Flee, save your lives, and be like the heath (a type of shrub) in the wilderness. {48:7} Because you have trusted in your works and treasures, you will be captured; Chemosh will go into captivity along with his priests and princes. {48:8} The destroyer will come upon every city, and no city will escape; the valley will perish, and the plain will be destroyed, as the LORD has spoken. {48:9} Give wings to Moab so it can flee and get away, for its cities will be desolate, with no one living in them. {48:10} Cursed is he who does the work of the LORD deceitfully, and cursed is he who keeps his sword back from bloodshed. {48:11} Moab has been at ease from its youth; it has settled on its dregs and has not been emptied from vessel to vessel or gone into captivity. Therefore, its taste remains in it, and its scent is unchanged. {48:12} Therefore, look, the days are coming, says the LORD, when I will send wanderers to him who will cause him to wander and empty his vessels and break their jars. {48:13} Moab will be ashamed of Chemosh, as the house of Israel was ashamed of Bethel, their confidence. {48:14} How can you say, 'We are mighty and strong men for battle'? {48:15} Moab is spoiled and has left its cities; its chosen young men have gone down to the slaughter, says the King, whose name is the LORD of hosts. {48:16} The calamity of Moab is near, and its affliction is fast approaching. {48:17} All of you surrounding it, mourn for it; and all of you who know its name, say, 'How is the strong staff broken, the beautiful rod?' {48:18} O daughter who dwells in Dibon, come down from your glory and sit in thirst, for the destroyer of Moab will come upon you, and he will destroy your strongholds. {48:19} O inhabitant of Aroer, stand by the way and watch; ask him who flees and her who escapes, and say, 'What has happened?' {48:20} Moab is confounded; it is broken down. Howl and cry; announce it in Arnon that Moab is spoiled. {48:21} Judgment has come upon the plain country—upon Holon, Jahazah, and Mephaath, {48:22} upon Dibon, Nebo, and Beth-diblathaim, {48:23} upon Kiriathaim, Beth-gamul, and Beth-meon, {48:24} upon Kerioth, Bozrah, and all the cities of the land of Moab, both far and near. {48:25} The horn of Moab is cut off, and its arm is broken, says the LORD. {48:26} Make him drunk, for he has magnified himself against the LORD; Moab will wallow in its vomit and become a laughingstock. {48:27} For was not Israel a laughingstock to you? Was he found among thieves? For whenever you spoke of him, you rejoiced. {48:28} O you who dwell in Moab, leave the cities and dwell in the rocks, be like the dove that makes her nest in the sides of the cave. {48:29} We have heard of the pride of Moab (he is very proud), of his haughtiness and arrogance, and the pride of his heart. {48:30} I know his wrath, says the LORD, but it will not be so; his lies will not prevail. {48:31} Therefore, I will howl for Moab; I will cry out for all Moab; my heart will mourn for the men of Kirheres. {48:32} O vine of Sibmah, I will weep for you with the weeping of Jazer; your plants have gone over the sea, reaching to the sea of Jazer; the destroyer has fallen upon your summer fruits and your harvest. {48:33} Joy and gladness have been taken from the fertile field and from the land of Moab; I have caused wine to fail from the winepresses; no one will tread with shouting; their shouting will not be heard. {48:34} From the cry of Heshbon even to Elealeh and Jahaz, they have raised their voices; from Zoar even to Horonaim, like a three-year-old heifer; for the waters of Nimrim will be desolate. {48:35} Moreover, I will cause to cease in Moab, says the LORD, him who offers sacrifices on the high places and him who burns incense to his gods. {48:36} Therefore, my heart will sound like pipes for Moab, and my heart will sound like pipes for the men of Kirheres because the riches they have gained are gone. {48:37} Every head will be bald, and every beard clipped; on all hands will be cuts, and on the loins, sackcloth. {48:38} There will be lamentation everywhere on the rooftops of Moab and in its streets, for I have broken Moab like a vessel of no worth, says the LORD. {48:39} They will howl, saying, 'How is it broken down! How has Moab turned its back in shame!' Moab will become a laughingstock and a terror to all around it. {48:40} For thus says the LORD: Behold, he will fly like an eagle and spread his wings over Moab. {48:41} Kerioth is captured, and the strongholds are surprised; the hearts of the mighty men in Moab that day will be like a woman in labor. {48:42} Moab will be destroyed from being a people because he has magnified himself against the LORD. {48:43} Fear, the pit, and the snare will be upon you, O inhabitant of Moab, says the LORD. {48:44} He who flees from fear will fall into the pit; and he who escapes from the pit will be caught in the snare, for I will bring upon it, even upon Moab, the year of their punishment, says the LORD. {48:45} Those who fled will stand under the shadow of Heshbon because of the pressure; but a fire will come forth from Heshbon and a flame from within Sihon, which will devour the corner of Moab and the crown of the head of the tumultuous ones. {48:46} Woe to you, O Moab! The people of Chemosh perish, for your sons are taken captive, and your daughters are captives. {48:47} Yet I will bring back the captives of Moab in the latter days, says the LORD. This is the judgment concerning Moab.

{49:1} Concerning the Ammonites, the LORD says: Does Israel have no sons? Does he have no heir? Why then does their king inherit Gad, and why do his people live in its cities? {49:2} Therefore, the days are coming, says the LORD, when I will sound an alarm of war in Rabbah of the Ammonites; it will become a desolate heap, and its daughters will be burned with fire. Then Israel will inherit those who were once his heirs, says the LORD. {49:3} Howl, O Heshbon, for Ai is ruined; cry out, daughters of Rabbah, put on sackcloth, mourn, and run back and forth by the hedges, for their king will go into captivity, along with his priests and princes. {49:4} Why do you boast in the valleys, your fertile valley, O rebellious daughter? You trust in your treasures, saying, Who will come against me? {49:5} Look, I will bring fear upon you, says the Lord GOD of hosts, from all those around you; you will be driven out, each one straight ahead, and no one will gather up those who wander. {49:6} And afterward, I will restore the captives of the children of Ammon, says the LORD. {49:7} Concerning Edom, the LORD of hosts says: Is there no wisdom left in Teman? Has counsel perished from the wise? Is their wisdom gone? {49:8} Flee, turn back, and dwell deep, O inhabitants of Dedan, for I will bring the disaster of Esau upon him, the time I will visit him. {49:9} If grape harvesters come to you, would they not leave some grapes behind? If thieves come by night, they will destroy only until they have enough. {49:10} But I have made Esau bare; I have uncovered his secret places, and he will not be able to hide. His offspring, his brothers, and his neighbors are destroyed, and he is no more. {49:11} Leave your fatherless children; I will keep them alive, and let your widows trust in me. {49:12} For thus says the LORD: Behold, those whose judgment was not to drink from the cup have certainly drunk from it; and are you the one who will go unpunished? You will not go unpunished, but you will surely drink from it. {49:13} For I have sworn by myself, says the LORD, that Bozrah will become a desolation, a disgrace, a waste, and a curse; and all its cities will be permanent wastes. {49:14} I have heard a report from the LORD, and a messenger is sent to the nations, saying, Gather together, and come against her, and prepare for battle. {49:15} For look, I will make you small among the nations and despised among men. {49:16} Your terrifying power has deceived you, and the pride of your heart, O you who dwell in the clefts of the rock and hold the height of the hill; even if you make your nest as high as the eagle, I will bring you down, says the LORD. {49:17} Edom will also become a desolation; everyone who passes by will be astonished and will hiss at all its disasters. {49:18} Just like the overthrow of Sodom and Gomorrah and their neighboring cities, says the LORD, no man will live there, nor will any son of man dwell in it. {49:19} Behold, he will come up like a lion from the rising of the Jordan against the stronghold; but I will suddenly make him run away from her. Who is the chosen man I may appoint over her? Who is like me? Who can appoint me a time? Who is that shepherd that will stand before me? {49:20} Therefore, hear the counsel of the LORD, which he has taken against Edom, and his plans against the inhabitants of Teman. Surely the least of the flock will drag them out; surely he will make their dwellings desolate along with them. {49:21} The earth trembles at the noise of their fall; the sound of it reaches the Red Sea. {49:22} Behold, he will come up and fly like an eagle, spreading his wings over Bozrah, and on that day the hearts of the mighty men of Edom will be like the heart of a woman in labor. {49:23} Concerning Damascus: Hamath and Arpad are confused; they have heard bad news; they are fainthearted; there is sorrow on the sea; it cannot be calm. {49:24} Damascus has grown weak and is turning to flee; fear has seized her; anguish and sorrows have taken hold of her like a woman in labor. {49:25} How has the city of praise not been abandoned, the city of my joy! {49:26} Therefore, her young men will fall in her streets, and all her warriors will be cut off in that day, says the LORD of hosts. {49:27} I will set fire to the wall of Damascus, and it will consume the palaces of Benhadad. {49:28} Concerning Kedar and the kingdoms of Hazor, which Nebuchadnezzar king of Babylon will strike, the LORD says: Rise, go up to Kedar, and plunder the men of the east. {49:29} Their tents and flocks will be taken away; they will take their curtains, all their utensils, and their camels; and they will cry out, Fear is on every side! {49:30} Flee, get far away, dwell deep, O inhabitants of Hazor, says the LORD, for Nebuchadnezzar king of Babylon has taken counsel against you and has devised a plan against you. {49:31} Arise, go against the complacent nation, says the LORD, which dwells without care, with neither gates nor bars, and which lives alone. {49:32} Their camels will be a plunder, and the multitude of their cattle a spoil; I will scatter to all winds those in the farthest corners, and I will bring their calamity from every side, says the LORD. {49:33} Hazor will become a dwelling for jackals and a desolation forever; no man will live there, nor will any son of man dwell in it. {49:34} The word of the LORD that came to Jeremiah the prophet against Elam at the beginning of the reign of Zedekiah king of Judah, saying, {49:35} Thus says the LORD of hosts: Behold, I will break the bow of Elam, the chief of their strength. {49:36} I will bring the four winds from the four corners of heaven upon Elam, and I will scatter them in all those winds; and there will be no nation where the outcasts of Elam will not go. {49:37} For I will cause Elam to be terrified before their enemies and before those who seek their lives; I will bring disaster upon them, even my fierce anger, says the LORD, and I will send the sword after them until I have consumed them. {49:38} I will set my throne in Elam and destroy the king and the princes from there, says the LORD. {49:39} But it will come to pass in the latter days that I will restore the captives of Elam, says the LORD.

{50:1} The word that the LORD spoke against Babylon and against the land of the Chaldeans through Jeremiah the prophet. {50:2} Declare among the nations and publish it; set up a banner, publish, and do not conceal: say, Babylon has been captured, Bel is confounded, Merodach is shattered; her idols are dismayed, and her images are broken. {50:3} For a nation comes from the north against her, which will make her land desolate, and none will dwell in it; they will remove, they will depart, both man and beast. {50:4} In those days, and at that time, says the LORD, the children of Israel will come, they and the children of Judah together, going and weeping; they will seek the LORD their God. {50:5} They will ask for the way to Zion, with their faces toward it, saying, Come, let us join ourselves to the LORD in an everlasting covenant that will not be forgotten. {50:6} My people have been lost sheep; their shepherds have caused them to stray; they have turned them away on the mountains; they have gone from mountain to hill; they have forgotten their resting place. {50:7} All who found them have devoured them, and their adversaries said, We are not guilty, because they have sinned against the LORD, the dwelling place of justice, even the LORD, the hope of their ancestors. {50:8} Depart from the midst of Babylon, and go out of the land of the Chaldeans, and be like the goats before the flocks. {50:9} For, look, I will raise and cause to come up against Babylon an assembly of great nations from the north; and they will set themselves against her; from there she will be taken; their arrows will be like those of a skilled archer; none will return in vain. {50:10} Chaldea will be plundered; all who plunder her will be satisfied, says the LORD. {50:11} Because you were glad, because you rejoiced, O you destroyers of my heritage, because you have grown fat like a well-fed heifer and bellow like bulls; {50:12} your mother will be greatly ashamed; she who bore you will be humiliated: behold, the least of the nations will become a wilderness, a dry land, and a desert. {50:13} Because of the wrath of the LORD, it will not be inhabited, but will be completely desolate; all who go by Babylon will be astonished and hiss at all her disasters. {50:14} Surround Babylon, all you who bend the bow; shoot at her, spare no arrows; for she has sinned against the LORD. {50:15} Shout against her all around; she has given her hand; her foundations have fallen; her walls are thrown down; for it is the vengeance of the LORD: take vengeance upon her, as she has done, do to her. {50:16} Cut off the sower from Babylon, and the one who wields the sickle in the time of harvest; for fear of the oppressing sword they will turn to their own people, and each will flee to his own land. {50:17} Israel is a scattered sheep; lions have driven them away: first, the king of Assyria has devoured them; and last, Nebuchadnezzar king of Babylon has broken their bones. {50:18} Therefore, thus says the LORD of hosts, the God of Israel: Behold, I will punish the king of Babylon and his land, just as I punished the king of Assyria. {50:19} I will bring Israel back to his home, and he will graze on Carmel and Bashan, and his soul will be satisfied on Mount Ephraim and Gilead. {50:20} In those days, and at that time, says the LORD, the iniquity of Israel will be sought, and there will be none; and the sins of Judah, and they will not be found; for I will pardon those I reserve. {50:21} Go up against the land of Merathaim and against the inhabitants of Pekod; waste and utterly destroy them, says the LORD, and do according to all that I have commanded you. {50:22} A sound of battle is in the land, and of great destruction. {50:23} How has the hammer of the whole earth been cut down and broken! How has Babylon become a desolation among the nations! {50:24} I have laid a trap for you, and you are also caught, O Babylon, and you were unaware; you are found and caught because you have fought against the LORD. {50:25} The LORD has opened his armory and brought forth the weapons of his anger; for this is the work of the Lord GOD of hosts in the land of the Chaldeans. {50:26} Come against her from the farthest border, open her storehouses; cast her up like heaps, and destroy her completely; let nothing of her remain. {50:27} Kill all her bulls; let them go down to the slaughter; woe to them! For their day has come, the time of their punishment. {50:28} The voice of those who flee and escape from the land of Babylon will declare in Zion the vengeance of the LORD our God, the vengeance for his temple. {50:29} Call together the archers against Babylon; all you who bend the bow, camp around her, let none escape: repay her according to her deeds; according to all that she has done, do to her; for she has been proud against the LORD, against the Holy One of Israel. {50:30} Therefore, her young men will fall in the streets, and all her warriors will be cut off in that day, says the LORD. {50:31} Behold, I am against you, O most proud, says the Lord GOD of hosts; for your day has come, the time I will visit you. {50:32} The proud will stumble and fall, and no one will lift him up; I will kindle a fire in his cities, and it will devour everything around him. {50:33} Thus says the LORD of hosts: The children of Israel and the children of Judah were oppressed together; all who took them captive held them fast; they refused to let them go. {50:34} Their Redeemer is strong; the LORD of hosts is his name: he will thoroughly plead their case, so that he may give rest to the land and disturb the inhabitants of Babylon. {50:35} A sword is upon the Chaldeans, says the LORD, and upon the inhabitants of Babylon, and upon her princes, and upon her wise men. {50:36} A sword is upon the liars; and they will go mad; a sword is upon her mighty men; and they will be terrified. {50:37} A sword is upon their horses, and upon their chariots, and upon all the mixed peoples who are in her midst; they will become like women; a sword is upon her treasures; and they will be robbed. {50:38} A drought is upon her waters; they will be dried up; for it is the land of graven images, and they are mad about their idols. {50:39} Therefore, the wild beasts of the desert and the wild beasts of the islands will dwell there, and owls will live there; it will never be inhabited again, nor will it be lived in from generation to generation. {50:40} Just as God overthrew Sodom and Gomorrah and the neighboring cities, says the LORD, so no man will live there, nor will any son of man dwell in it. {50:41} Behold, a people will come from the north, and a great nation, and many kings will be raised up from the ends of the earth. {50:42} They will hold the bow and the lance; they are cruel and will show no mercy; their voice will roar like the sea, and they will ride on horses, each one arranged for battle against you, O daughter of Babylon. {50:43} The king of Babylon has heard their report, and his hands grew weak; anguish took hold of him, and he experienced pains like a woman in labor. {50:44} Behold, he will come up like a lion from the rising of the Jordan against the stronghold, but I will make them run away from her suddenly. Who is the chosen man I may appoint over her? Who is like me? Who will appoint me a time? Who is that shepherd that will stand before me? {50:45} Therefore, hear the counsel of the LORD, which he has taken against Babylon, and his purposes against the land of the Chaldeans: Surely the least of the flock will drag them out; surely he will make their dwellings desolate with them. {50:46} At the noise of Babylon's capture, the earth trembles, and the cry is heard among the nations.

{51:1} The LORD says: Look, I will raise up against Babylon and those living among them who oppose me, a destructive wind. {51:2} I will send fanners to Babylon, who will fan her and empty her land; in the day of trouble, they will be surrounding her. {51:3} Against those who shoot, let the archer draw his bow, and against those who are equipped for battle, do not spare the young men; completely destroy all her forces. {51:4} The slain will fall in the land of the Chaldeans, and those pierced will lie in her streets. {51:5} For Israel has not been forsaken, nor has Judah been abandoned by his God, the LORD of hosts; even though their land was filled with sin against the Holy One of Israel. {51:6} Escape from Babylon, and save yourselves! Don't be cut off in her sins, for this is the time of the LORD's vengeance; He will repay her. {51:7} Babylon has been a golden cup in the LORD's hand, making all the earth drunk; the nations have drunk her wine, so the nations are mad. {51:8} Babylon has suddenly fallen and been destroyed; wail for her! Take balm for her pain; perhaps she can be healed. {51:9} We would have healed Babylon, but she cannot be healed; forsake her, and let each person return to his own country, for her judgment has reached up to heaven, and is lifted up even to the skies. {51:10} The LORD has brought forth our righteousness; come, let us declare in Zion the work of the LORD our God. {51:11} Make the arrows bright; gather the shields, for the LORD has raised up the spirit of the kings of the Medes; his plan is against Babylon to destroy it, because it is the vengeance of the LORD, the vengeance for His temple. {51:12} Set up a banner on the walls of Babylon; make the guards strong, set up watchmen, prepare ambushes; for the LORD has both devised and carried out what He has spoken against the inhabitants of Babylon. {51:13} You who dwell by many waters, rich in treasures, your end has come, and the measure of your greed is full. {51:14} The LORD of hosts has sworn by Himself, saying, Surely I will fill you with men, like locusts, and they will raise a shout against you. {51:15} He has made the earth by His power, established the world by His wisdom, and stretched out the heavens by His understanding. {51:16} When He speaks, there is a multitude of waters in the heavens; He causes the vapors to rise from the ends of the earth; He makes lightning with rain, and brings forth the wind from His treasures. {51:17} Every person is brutish in his knowledge; every craftsman is confounded by the carved image; for his molten image is falsehood, and there is no breath in them. {51:18} They are vanity, the work of errors; in the time of their punishment, they will perish. {51:19} The portion of Jacob is not like them; for He is the former of all things; and Israel is the rod of His inheritance; the LORD of hosts is His name. {51:20} You are my battle axe and weapons of war; with you I will break nations in pieces, and with you I will destroy kingdoms. {51:21} With you, I will break in pieces the horse and its rider; and with you, I will break in pieces the chariot and its driver. {51:22} With you, I will also break in pieces man and woman; and with you, I will break in pieces the old and the young; and with you, I will break in pieces the young man and the maid. {51:23} I will also break in pieces with you the shepherd and his flock; and with you, I will break in pieces the farmer and his oxen; and with you, I will break in pieces captains and rulers. {51:24} I will repay Babylon and all the inhabitants of Chaldea for all the evil they have done in Zion in your sight, says the LORD. {51:25} Behold, I am against you, O destroying mountain, says the LORD, which destroys all the earth; I will stretch out my hand upon you, and roll you down from the rocks, and make you a burnt mountain. {51:26} They will not take from you a stone for a corner or a stone for foundations; but you shall be desolate forever, says the LORD. {51:27} Set up a standard in the land, blow the trumpet among the nations, prepare the nations against her, call together against her the kingdoms of Ararat, Minni, and Ashchenaz; appoint a captain against her; let the horses come up like swarming locusts. {51:28} Prepare the nations with the kings of the Medes, their captains, and all their rulers, and all the land of their dominion. {51:29} The land will tremble and be in pain; for every purpose of the LORD will be fulfilled against Babylon, to make the land of Babylon a desolation without an inhabitant. {51:30} The mighty men of Babylon have given up fighting; they have remained in their strongholds; their strength has failed; they have become like women; they have burned her dwelling places; her gates are broken. {51:31} One messenger will run to meet another, and one messenger will meet another, to show the king of Babylon that his city has been taken at one end, {51:32} and that the passages are stopped, and the reeds they have burned with fire, and the men of war are terrified. {51:33} For thus says the LORD of hosts, the God of Israel: The daughter of Babylon is like a threshing floor; it is time to thresh her; yet a little while, and the time of her harvest will come. {51:34} Nebuchadnezzar king of Babylon has devoured me; he has crushed me; he has made me an empty vessel; he has swallowed me like a dragon; he has filled his belly with my delicacies; he has cast me out. {51:35} The violence done to me and to my flesh will be upon Babylon, will the inhabitant of Zion say; and my blood upon the inhabitants of Chaldea, will Jerusalem say. {51:36} Therefore, thus says the LORD: Behold, I will plead your cause and take vengeance for you; and I will dry up her sea and make her springs dry. {51:37} And Babylon will become heaps, a dwelling place for dragons, an astonishment, and a hissing, without an inhabitant. {51:38} They will roar together like lions; they will growl like lion cubs. {51:39} In their heat I will make their feasts, and I will make them drunk, so they may rejoice, and sleep a perpetual sleep, and not wake, says the LORD. {51:40} I will bring them down like lambs to the slaughter, like rams with goats. {51:41} How is Sheshach taken! and how is the praise of the whole earth surprised! how has Babylon become an astonishment among the nations! {51:42} The sea has come up upon Babylon; she is covered with the multitude of her waves. {51:43} Her cities are a desolation, a dry land, and a wilderness, a land where no man dwells, nor does any son of man pass by. {51:44} I will punish Bel in Babylon, and I will bring forth out of his mouth what he has swallowed; and the nations will not flow together to him anymore; yes, the wall of Babylon will fall. {51:45} My people, go out from the midst of her, and save yourselves, every man from the fierce anger of the LORD. {51:46} And lest your hearts faint, and you fear for the rumor that shall be heard in the land; a rumor will come both this year, and after that in another year, there will be violence in the land, ruler against ruler. {51:47} Therefore, behold, the days come, says the LORD, that I will judge the carved images of Babylon; and her whole land will be confounded, and all her slain will fall in the midst of her. {51:48} Then the heaven and the earth, and all that is in them, will sing for Babylon; for the spoilers will come upon her from the north, says the LORD. {51:49} As Babylon has caused the slain of Israel to fall, so at Babylon will fall the slain of all the earth. {51:50} You who have escaped the sword, go away, stand not still; remember the LORD from afar, and let Jerusalem come to your mind. {51:51} We are confounded because we have heard reproach; shame has covered our faces; for strangers have come into the sanctuaries of the LORD's house. {51:52} Therefore, behold, the days come, says the LORD, that I will judge her carved images; and throughout her land, the wounded will groan. {51:53} Though Babylon should ascend to heaven, and though she should fortify the height of her strength, yet from me, spoilers will come upon her, says the LORD. {51:54} A sound of a cry comes from Babylon, and great destruction from the land of the Chaldeans. {51:55} Because the LORD has spoiled Babylon and destroyed her great voice; when her waves roar like great waters, a noise of their voice is uttered. {51:56} Because the spoiler has come upon her, even upon Babylon, and her mighty men are taken, every one of their bows is broken; for the LORD God of recompenses will surely repay. {51:57} I will make her princes drunk, her wise men, her captains, her rulers, and her mighty men; and they will sleep a perpetual sleep, and not wake, says the King, whose name is the LORD of hosts. {51:58} Thus says the LORD of hosts: The broad walls of Babylon will be utterly broken, and her high gates will be burned with fire; and the people will labor in vain, and the folk in the fire, and they will be weary. {51:59} The word which Jeremiah the prophet commanded Seraiah son of Neriah, son of Maaseiah, when he went with Zedekiah king of Judah into Babylon in the fourth year of his reign. And this Seraiah was a quiet prince. {51:60} So Jeremiah wrote in a book all the evil that would come upon Babylon, even all these words that are written against Babylon. {51:61} And Jeremiah said to Seraiah, When you come to Babylon and see and read all these words, {51:62} then you shall say, O LORD, you have spoken against this place, to cut it off, so that none shall remain in it, neither man nor beast, but that it shall be desolate forever. {51:63} And it shall be, when you have finished reading this book, that you shall bind a stone to it and cast it into the midst of Euphrates. {51:64} And you shall say, Thus shall Babylon sink, and shall not rise from the evil that I will bring upon her; and they shall be weary. Thus far are the words of Jeremiah.

{52:1} Zedekiah was twenty-one years old when he began to reign, and he reigned eleven years in Jerusalem. His mother's name was Hamutal, the daughter of Jeremiah of Libnah. {52:2} He did evil in the sight of the LORD, according to all that Jehoiakim had done. {52:3} Because of the LORD's anger, it came to pass in Jerusalem and Judah, until He had cast them out from His presence, that Zedekiah rebelled against the king of Babylon. {52:4} And it came to pass in the ninth year of his reign, in the tenth month, on the tenth day of the month, that Nebuchadnezzar king of Babylon came, he and all his army, against Jerusalem, and pitched against it, and built forts around it. {52:5} So the city was besieged until the eleventh year of king Zedekiah. {52:6} In the fourth month, on the ninth day of the month, the famine was severe in the city, so that there was no bread for the people of the land. {52:7} Then the city was broken up, and all the men of war fled, and went forth out of the city by night by the way of the gate between the two walls, which was by the king's garden; (now the Chaldeans were around the city;) and they went by the way of the plain. {52:8} But the army of the Chaldeans pursued after the king, and overtook Zedekiah in the plains of Jericho; and all his army was scattered from him. {52:9} Then they took the king and carried him up to the king of Babylon to Riblah in the land of Hamath; where he pronounced judgment upon him. {52:10} The king of Babylon killed Zedekiah's sons before his eyes; he also killed all the princes of Judah in Riblah. {52:11} Then he put out Zedekiah's eyes; and the king of Babylon bound him in chains and carried him to Babylon, where he was imprisoned until the day of his death. {52:12} Now in the fifth month, on the tenth day of the month, in the nineteenth year of Nebuchadnezzar king of Babylon, Nebuzaradan, captain of the guard, who served the king of Babylon, came to Jerusalem, {52:13} and burned the house of the LORD, the king's house, and all the houses of Jerusalem, and all the houses of the great men he burned with fire. {52:14} And all the army of the Chaldeans, that were with the captain of the guard, broke down all the walls of Jerusalem round about. {52:15} Then Nebuzaradan the captain of the guard carried away captive certain of the poor of the people, and the residue of the people that remained in the city, and those that fell away to the king of Babylon, and the rest of the multitude. {52:16} But Nebuzaradan the captain of the guard left certain of the poor of the land to be vinedressers and farmers. {52:17} Also, the pillars of bronze that were in the house of the LORD, and the bases, and the bronze sea that was in the house of the LORD, the Chaldeans broke and carried all the bronze to Babylon. {52:18} They also took away the caldrons, shovels, snuffers, bowls, and spoons, and all the vessels of bronze used in the service. {52:19} They took away the basins, firepans, bowls, caldrons, candlesticks, spoons, and cups; everything that was of gold in gold, and everything that was of silver in silver, the captain of the guard took away. {52:20} The two pillars, one sea, and twelve bronze bulls that were under the bases, which King Solomon had made in the house of the LORD: the bronze of all these vessels was beyond weight. {52:21} As for the pillars, the height of one pillar was eighteen cubits; a fillet of twelve cubits surrounded it; and its thickness was four fingers; it was hollow. {52:22} A chapiter of bronze was on it; the height of one chapiter was five cubits, with network and pomegranates upon the chapiters all around, all of bronze. The second pillar and the pomegranates were similar. {52:23} There were ninety-six pomegranates on a side; and all the pomegranates upon the network were a hundred all around. {52:24} The captain of the guard took Seraiah the chief priest, and Zephaniah the second priest, and the three keepers of the door. {52:25} He also took out of the city an eunuch, who had charge of the men of war; and seven men near the king's person who were found in the city; and the principal scribe of the host, who mustered the people of the land; and sixty men of the people of the land, who were found in the city. {52:26} So Nebuzaradan the captain of the guard took them and brought them to the king of Babylon to Riblah. {52:27} The king of Babylon killed them and put them to death in Riblah in the land of Hamath. Thus Judah was carried away captive out of its own land. {52:28} This is the people whom Nebuchadnezzar carried away captive: in the seventh year, three thousand and twenty-three Jews; {52:29} in the eighteenth year of Nebuchadnezzar, he carried away captive from Jerusalem eight hundred thirty-two persons; {52:30} in the twenty-third year of Nebuchadnezzar, Nebuzaradan the captain of the guard carried away captive of the Jews seven hundred forty-five persons: all the persons were four thousand six hundred. {52:31} It came to pass in the thirty-seventh year of the captivity of Jehoiachin king of Judah, in the twelfth month, on the twenty-fifth day of the month, that Evilmerodach king of Babylon in the first year of his reign lifted up the head of Jehoiachin king of Judah and brought him out of prison, {52:32} and spoke kindly to him, and set his throne above the thrones of the kings that were with him in Babylon, {52:33} and changed his prison garments; and he continually ate bread before him all the days of his life. {52:34} For his diet, there was a continual allowance given him by the king of Babylon, every day a portion until the day of his death, all the days of his life.

The Book of Lamentations

{1:1} How lonely the city sits now that was once full of people! She has become like a widow; she who was great among the nations and a princess among the provinces is now a tribute payer! {1:2} She weeps bitterly in the night, and her tears are on her cheeks. Among all her lovers, there is no one to comfort her; all her friends have betrayed her and have become her enemies. {1:3} Judah has gone into captivity due to affliction and hard labor; she lives among the nations and finds no rest. All her persecutors have caught up with her in the narrow places. {1:4} The roads to Zion mourn, for no one comes to the solemn feasts; all her gates are desolate. Her priests sigh, her young women are suffering, and she is in deep sorrow. {1:5} Her enemies are the leaders; her foes are prospering, for the LORD has afflicted her because of her many transgressions. Her children have gone into captivity in front of the enemy. {1:6} From the daughter of Zion, all her splendor is gone; her leaders have become like deer that find no pasture, and they have lost their strength before the pursuer. {1:7} Jerusalem remembers, in her days of affliction and misery, all her pleasant things that she had in the days of old when her people fell into the hands of the enemy, and no one helped her. Her adversaries saw her and mocked her festivals. {1:8} Jerusalem has sinned greatly; therefore she has become an outcast. All who honored her now despise her because they have seen her shame. Yes, she sighs and turns away. {1:9} Her filthiness is in her skirts; she does not remember her final end. Therefore, she has come down strangely; she has no comforter. O LORD, look at my suffering, for the enemy has magnified himself. {1:10} The adversary has stretched out his hand over all her pleasant things, for she has seen that the nations entered her sanctuary, whom You commanded should not enter Your congregation. {1:11} All her people sigh; they seek bread. They have traded their pleasant things for food to revive their souls. Look, O LORD, and consider, for I have become worthless. {1:12} Is it nothing to you, all you who pass by? Look and see if there is any sorrow like my sorrow, which has come upon me, with which the LORD has afflicted me in the day of His fierce anger. {1:13} From above, He has sent fire into my bones, and it prevails against them. He has spread a net for my feet; He has turned me back. He has made me desolate and weak all day long. {1:14} The yoke of my transgressions is bound by His hand; they are wrapped around my neck. He has made my strength fail; the LORD has delivered me into their hands, from which I cannot rise. {1:15} The LORD has trampled all my mighty men in my midst; He has called a meeting against me to crush my young men. The LORD has trampled the virgin daughter of Judah like a winepress. {1:16} For these things, I weep; my eyes, my eyes pour down with water because the comforter who should relieve my soul is far from me. My children are desolate because the enemy has prevailed. {1:17} Zion stretches out her hands, but there is no one to comfort her. The LORD has commanded concerning Jacob that his adversaries should surround him. Jerusalem is like a woman in her period among them. {1:18} The LORD is righteous, for I have rebelled against His command. Hear, I pray you, all people, and see my sorrow. My young women and my young men have gone into captivity. {1:19} I called for my lovers, but they deceived me. My priests and my elders have died in the city while they sought food to relieve their souls. {1:20} Look, O LORD, for I am in distress. My insides are troubled; my heart is turned within me because I have greatly rebelled. Outside, the sword takes away; at home, it is like death. {1:21} They have heard that I sigh; there is no one to comfort me. All my enemies have heard of my trouble; they are glad that You have done it. You will bring the day You have called, and they will be like me. {1:22} Let all their wickedness come before You; and do to them as You have done to me for all my transgressions, for my sighs are many, and my heart is weak.

{2:1} How has the Lord covered the daughter of Zion with a cloud in His anger and cast down from heaven to earth the beauty of Israel, forgetting His footstool in the day of His anger? {2:2} The Lord has consumed all the dwellings of Jacob and has not shown pity. He has thrown down in His wrath the strongholds of the daughter of Judah; He has brought them down to the ground and defiled the kingdom and its princes. {2:3} He has cut off all the strength of Israel in His fierce anger. He has withdrawn His right hand from before the enemy and burned against Jacob like a raging fire that devours all around. {2:4} He has bent His bow like an enemy; He stands with His right hand like an adversary and has slain all that was beautiful in the tabernacle of the daughter of Zion. He has poured out His fury like fire. {2:5} The Lord was like an enemy; He has consumed Israel, swallowed up all her palaces, destroyed her strongholds, and increased mourning and lamentation in the daughter of Judah. {2:6} He has violently taken away His dwelling place, as if it were a garden; He has destroyed His meeting places. The LORD has caused the solemn feasts and sabbaths to be forgotten in Zion and has despised the king and the priest in the fury of His anger. {2:7} The Lord has cast off His altar; He has loathed His sanctuary. He has given up the walls of her palaces into the hands of the enemy; they make noise in the house of the LORD like on the day of a solemn feast. {2:8} The LORD has decided to destroy the wall of the daughter of Zion; He has measured it, and He has not withdrawn His hand from destroying it. Therefore, He made the rampart and the wall mourn; they have both faded away. {2:9} Her gates have sunk into the ground; He has destroyed and broken her bars. Her king and her princes are among the nations; the law is no more, and her prophets find no vision from the LORD. {2:10} The elders of the daughter of Zion sit on the ground in silence; they have thrown dust on their heads and dressed themselves in sackcloth. The young women of Jerusalem have bowed their heads to the ground. {2:11} My eyes fail with tears; my insides are troubled; my liver is poured out on the ground because of the destruction of the daughter of my people. The children and the infants faint in the streets of the city. {2:12} They say to their mothers, "Where is grain and wine?" as they faint like the wounded in the streets of the city when their souls are poured out into their mothers' arms. {2:13} What can I take to witness for you? What can I compare you to, O daughter of Jerusalem? What can I liken you to that I may comfort you, O virgin daughter of Zion? For your wound is great like the sea; who can heal you? {2:14} Your prophets have seen false and foolish things for you; they have not discovered your iniquity to turn away your captivity but have seen for you false burdens and causes of exile. {2:15} All who pass by clap their hands at you; they hiss and shake their heads at the daughter of Jerusalem, saying, "Is this the city that people call The perfection of beauty, The joy of the whole earth?" {2:16} All your enemies have opened their mouths against you; they hiss and grind their teeth, saying, "We have swallowed her up. Certainly, this is the day we hoped for; we have found it; we have seen it." {2:17} The LORD has done what He planned; He has fulfilled His word that He commanded in days of old. He has thrown down and has not shown pity; He has caused your enemies to rejoice over you and has raised the strength of your adversaries. {2:18} Their hearts cry out to the Lord, "O wall of the daughter of Zion, let your tears flow down like a river day and night; give yourself no rest; let not the apple of your eye cease." {2:19} Arise, cry out in the night; at the beginning of the watches, pour out your heart like water before the face of the Lord. Lift up your hands toward Him for the life of your young children who faint for hunger in the streets. {2:20} Look, O LORD, and consider to whom You have done this. Should women eat their own fruit, the children they have nursed? Should the priest and the prophet be killed in the sanctuary of the Lord? {2:21} The young and the old lie on the ground in the streets; my young women and young men have fallen by the sword; You have slain them in the day of Your anger; You have killed, and have not shown pity. {2:22} You have called my terrors around me like on a solemn day, so that in the day of the LORD'S anger, none escaped or remained. Those I have swaddled and raised have been consumed by my enemy.

{3:1} I am the man who has seen affliction by the rod of His wrath. {3:2} He has led me and brought me into darkness, not into light. {3:3} Surely He is against me; He turns His hand against me all day long. {3:4} He has made my flesh and my skin grow old; He has broken my bones. {3:5} He has built a siege against me and surrounded me with bitterness and hardship. {3:6} He has placed me in dark places, like those long dead. {3:7} He has surrounded me so I cannot escape; He has made my chains heavy. {3:8} Even when I cry and shout, He shuts out my prayer. {3:9} He has enclosed my paths with hewn stone and made my ways crooked. {3:10} He is like a bear lying in wait for me, like a lion in secret places. {3:11} He has turned aside my paths and torn me to pieces; He has made me desolate. {3:12} He has bent His bow and set me as a target for His arrows. {3:13} He has caused the arrows from His quiver to pierce my heart. {3:14} I have become a joke to all my people, their song all day long. {3:15} He has filled me with bitterness; He has made me drunk with wormwood (bitter herb). {3:16} He has also broken my teeth with gravel; He has covered me with ashes. {3:17} You have removed my soul far from peace; I have forgotten what happiness is. {3:18} I said, "My strength and my hope have perished from the LORD." {3:19} Remembering my affliction and my misery, the wormwood and the bitterness. {3:20} My soul still remembers them and is humbled within me. {3:21} This I call to mind, and therefore I have hope. {3:22} It is because of the LORD's mercies that we are not consumed, for His compassions never fail. {3:23} They are new every morning; great is Your faithfulness. {3:24} The LORD is my portion, says my soul; therefore, I will hope in Him. {3:25} The LORD is good to those who wait for Him, to the soul that seeks Him. {3:26} It is good for a man to hope and quietly wait for the salvation of the LORD. {3:27} It is good for a man to bear the yoke in his youth. {3:28} Let him sit alone and keep silent because he has laid it on him. {3:29} Let him put his mouth in the dust; perhaps there is hope. {3:30} Let him offer his cheek to the one who strikes him; let him be filled with disgrace. {3:31} For the Lord will not reject forever. {3:32} Though He causes grief, yet He will show compassion according to the multitude of His mercies. {3:33} For He does not afflict willingly or grieve the children of men. {3:34} To crush underfoot all the prisoners of the earth, {3:35} to deny a man justice in the presence of the Most High, {3:36} to subvert a man in his cause, the Lord does not approve. {3:37} Who can speak and have it happen if the Lord has not commanded it? {3:38} Is it not from the mouth of the Most High that both good and evil come? {3:39} Why should a living man complain, a man for the punishment of his sins? {3:40} Let us search and examine our ways and turn back to the LORD. {3:41} Let us lift our hearts and hands to God in heaven. {3:42} We have transgressed and rebelled; You have not pardoned. {3:43} You have covered Yourself with anger and persecuted us; You have slain; You have not shown pity. {3:44} You have covered Yourself with a cloud so that our prayers do not pass through. {3:45} You have made us like refuse and scum in the midst of the people. {3:46} All our enemies open their mouths against us. {3:47} Fear and a snare have come upon us, desolation and destruction. {3:48} My eyes overflow with rivers of water for the destruction of the daughter of my people. {3:49} My eyes flow down and do not cease, without any interruption, {3:50} until the LORD looks down and sees from heaven. {3:51} My eye affects my heart because of all the daughters of my city. {3:52} My enemies pursued me like a bird without cause. {3:53} They cut off my life in the dungeon and threw a stone on me. {3:54} Waters flowed over my head; then I said, "I am cut off." {3:55} I called upon Your name, O LORD, from the depths of the dungeon. {3:56} You have heard my voice; do not hide Your ear from my breathing, my cry. {3:57} You drew near on the day I called upon You; You said, "Do not fear." {3:58} O Lord, You have pleaded the case of my soul; You have redeemed my life. {3:59} O LORD, You have seen my wrong; judge my cause. {3:60} You have seen all their vengeance and all their plans against me. {3:61} You have heard their reproach, O LORD, and all their plans against me; {3:62} the lips of those who rise up against me, and their scheming all day long. {3:63} Look at their sitting down and rising up; I am their song. {3:64} Render to them a reward, O LORD, according to the work of their hands. {3:65} Give them sorrow of heart; Your curse upon them. {3:66} Pursue and destroy them in anger from under the heavens of the LORD.

{4:1} How the gold has lost its luster! How the finest gold has changed! The stones of the sanctuary are scattered in the streets. {4:2} The precious sons of Zion, valued like fine gold, how are they regarded as clay pots, the work of a potter's hands! {4:3} Even the sea monsters nurse their young; the daughter of my people has become cruel, like ostriches in the wilderness. {4:4} The tongue of the infant sticks to the roof of his mouth with thirst; the little children ask for bread, and no one breaks it for them. {4:5} Those who once ate delicately are now desolate in the streets; those raised in luxury embrace garbage heaps. {4:6} The punishment for the iniquity of my people is greater than the punishment of Sodom, which was destroyed in an instant, with no one to help her. {4:7} Her Nazarites were purer than snow, whiter than milk; they were more ruddy in body than rubies; their appearance was like sapphires. {4:8} Their appearance is darker than coal; they are not recognized in the streets; their skin clings to their bones; it has withered and become like a stick. {4:9} Those killed by the sword are better off than those who die of hunger; the latter waste away, stricken by the lack of food. {4:10} The compassionate women have cooked their own children; they were their food during the destruction of my people. {4:11} The LORD has fulfilled His anger; He has poured out His fierce wrath and kindled a fire in Zion, consuming its foundations. {4:12} The kings of the earth and all the inhabitants of the world would not have believed that the enemy would enter the gates of Jerusalem. {4:13} This happened because of the sins of her prophets and the iniquities of her priests, who shed the blood of the innocent in her midst. {4:14} They wandered like blind men in the streets; they were soiled with blood, making it impossible for anyone to touch their garments. {4:15} They cried out to each other, "Stay away; it's unclean! Stay away, don't touch!" As they fled and wandered, they said among the nations, "They will never return here." {4:16} The LORD's anger has scattered them; He will no longer regard them; they did not honor the priests or show favor to the elders. {4:17} As for us, our eyes are still failing in vain hope; we have watched for a nation that could not save us. {4:18} They hunt our steps, so we cannot walk in our streets; our end is near; our days are numbered; our end has come. {4:19} Our persecutors are swifter than eagles in the sky; they pursued us over the mountains and laid in wait for us in the wilderness. {4:20} The breath of our nostrils, the LORD's anointed, was captured in their traps; we said, "Under his shadow, we will live among the nations." {4:21} Rejoice and be glad, O daughter of Edom, living in the land of Uz; the cup will pass to you as well; you will become drunk and expose yourself. {4:22} The punishment for your iniquity is complete, O daughter of Zion; He will no longer send you into captivity; He will punish your iniquity, O daughter of Edom; He will uncover your sins.

{5:1} Remember, O LORD, what has happened to us; consider and look at our disgrace. {5:2} Our inheritance has been given to strangers, our homes to foreigners. {5:3} We are orphans and fatherless; our mothers are like widows. {5:4} We have to pay for our water; our wood is sold to us. {5:5} Our necks are under oppression; we toil without rest. {5:6} We have made agreements with the Egyptians and the Assyrians to get food. {5:7} Our ancestors sinned, and they are gone; we bear their iniquities. {5:8} Servants have taken control over us; there is no one to rescue us from their grasp. {5:9} We obtain our bread at the cost of our lives because of the threats in the wilderness. {5:10} Our skin has become as dark as an oven due to the severe famine. {5:11} They have violated the women in Zion and the young women in the cities of Judah. {5:12} Princes are hanged by their hands; the elders are not honored. {5:13} They took the young men to do the grinding, and the children fell beneath the load of wood. {5:14} The elders have stopped gathering at the gates, and the young men no longer play music. {5:15} The joy of our hearts has ceased; our dances have turned into mourning. {5:16} The crown has fallen from our heads; woe to us, for we have sinned! {5:17} Because of this, our hearts are faint; our eyes are dim from these troubles. {5:18} Because of the desolation of Mount Zion, foxes roam over it. {5:19} You, O LORD, remain forever; Your throne endures from generation to generation. {5:20} Why do You forget us forever and forsake us for so long? {5:21} Restore us to Yourself, O LORD, and we will be restored; renew our days as in the past. {5:22} But You have completely rejected us; You are very angry with us.

The Book of Ezekiel

{1:1} In the thirtieth year, on the fifth day of the fourth month, while I was among the captives by the Chebar River, the heavens opened up, and I saw visions of God. {1:2} This happened on the fifth day of the month, in the fifth year of King Jehoiachin's captivity. {1:3} The word of the LORD came specifically to Ezekiel the priest, the son of Buzi, in the land of the Chaldeans by the Chebar River; the hand of the LORD was upon him. {1:4} I looked, and there was a whirlwind coming from the north, a great cloud with fire swirling within it, and brightness surrounded it, with a color like amber coming from the fire. {1:5} From the midst of this, I saw the likeness of four living creatures, which looked like humans. {1:6} Each had four faces and four wings. {1:7} Their legs were straight, and their feet resembled the feet of a calf, shining like polished bronze. {1:8} They had human hands under their wings on all four sides, and each of them had their own faces and wings. {1:9} Their wings were connected to each other; they didn't turn when they moved but went straight forward. {1:10} As for their faces, each had the face of a human, the face of a lion on the right, the face of an ox on the left, and the face of an eagle. {1:11} This is how their faces appeared; their wings were stretched upward; two wings of each creature were joined together, and two covered their bodies. {1:12} They moved straight ahead; wherever the spirit wanted to go, they went without turning. {1:13} The living creatures looked like burning coals of fire or lamps; they moved back and forth among them, and the fire was bright, with lightning flashing out of the fire. {1:14} The creatures dashed back and forth like lightning. {1:15} As I watched the living creatures, I noticed a wheel on the ground beside them, with four faces. {1:16} The wheels looked like a beryl (a type of gemstone), and all four looked alike; their appearance and movement was like a wheel inside another wheel. {1:17} When they moved, they moved on their four sides, and they didn't turn as they went. {1:18} Their rims were terrifying and were full of eyes all around. {1:19} When the living creatures moved, the wheels moved with them; when the creatures rose from the ground, the wheels also rose. {1:20} Wherever the spirit wanted to go, they went; the wheels rose next to them because the spirit of the living creatures was in the wheels. {1:21} When the creatures moved, the wheels moved, and when they stood still, the wheels stood still; when they rose from the ground, the wheels rose alongside them, for the spirit of the living creatures was in the wheels. {1:22} Above the heads of the living creatures was something like a firmament (an expanse), shining like crystal, stretched over them. {1:23} Under the firmament, their wings were straight, one toward another; each creature had two wings covering one side and two covering the other side of their bodies. {1:24} When they moved, I heard the noise of their wings, like the sound of rushing waters, like the voice of the Almighty, like the noise of an army; when they stood still, they lowered their wings. {1:25} There was a voice from above the firmament that was over their heads when they stood and let down their wings. {1:26} Above the firmament was the likeness of a throne, looking like sapphire; on the throne was the likeness of a man. {1:27} I saw something that looked like amber, with fire all around it from the waist up, and from the waist down, it looked like fire, and there was brightness all around. {1:28} The appearance of brightness around it was like a rainbow in the clouds on a rainy day; this was the likeness of the glory of the LORD. When I saw it, I fell on my face and heard a voice speaking.

{2:1} He said to me, "Son of man, stand up, and I will speak to you." {2:2} The spirit entered me when he spoke, and set me on my feet, so I could hear him. {2:3} He said, "Son of man, I am sending you to the people of Israel, to a rebellious nation that has rebelled against me; they and their ancestors have turned against me up to this very day. {2:4} They are stubborn and hard-hearted. I am sending you to them, and you will say to them, 'This is what the Lord GOD says.' {2:5} They will know that a prophet has been among them, whether they listen or not, because they are a rebellious house. {2:6} But you, son of man, do not be afraid of them or their words, even if they are thorns and thistles around you, and you live among scorpions. Don't be afraid of what they say or how they look, for they are a rebellious house. {2:7} You must speak my words to them, whether they listen or not, for they are most rebellious. {2:8} But you, son of man, listen to what I say to you; do not be rebellious like that rebellious house. Open your mouth and eat what I give you." {2:9} When I looked, I saw a hand stretched out to me, and in it was a scroll. {2:10} He spread it before me, and it was written on both sides; it contained lamentations, mourning, and woe.

{3:1} He said to me, "Son of man, eat what you find; eat this scroll and then go speak to the house of Israel." {3:2} So I opened my mouth, and he made me eat the scroll. {3:3} He said, "Son of man, fill your stomach and your insides with this scroll I give you." I ate it, and it was as sweet as honey in my mouth. {3:4} Then he said, "Go to the house of Israel and speak my words to them. {3:5} You are not sent to a people with a strange language and difficult speech, but to the house of Israel. {3:6} Not to many people with a strange language and difficult speech that you cannot understand. If I had sent you to them, they would have listened to you. {3:7} But the house of Israel will not listen to you, because they will not listen to me; all the house of Israel is stubborn and hard-hearted. {3:8} Look, I have made your face strong against their faces, and your forehead strong against their foreheads. {3:9} I have made your forehead harder than flint; do not be afraid of them or discouraged by their looks, though they are a rebellious house. {3:10} Moreover, he said to me, "Son of man, receive all my words in your heart and listen carefully. {3:11} Go to the exiles, to the children of your people, and speak to them, and tell them, 'This is what the Lord GOD says,' whether they listen or not." {3:12} Then the spirit lifted me up, and I heard behind me the sound of a great rushing, saying, "Blessed be the glory of the LORD from his place." {3:13} I also heard the noise of the wings of the living creatures touching each other, and the noise of the wheels beside them, and the sound of a great rushing. {3:14} So the spirit lifted me up and took me away, and I went in bitterness and the heat of my spirit, but the hand of the LORD was strong upon me. {3:15} I came to the exiles at Telabib, who lived by the Chebar River, and I sat where they sat and remained there stunned for seven days. {3:16} At the end of seven days, the word of the LORD came to me, saying, {3:17} "Son of man, I have made you a watchman for the house of Israel; therefore, listen to the word I speak and warn them from me. {3:18} When I say to the wicked, 'You will surely die,' and you do not warn them or speak to them to turn from their wicked ways to save their lives, that wicked person will die for their sin, but I will hold you responsible for their blood. {3:19} However, if you warn the wicked and they do not turn from their wickedness or their evil ways, they will die for their sin, but you have saved yourself. {3:20} Again, if a righteous person turns from their righteousness and commits sin, and I put a stumbling block before them, they will die; since you did not warn them, they will die in their sin, and their righteous acts will not be remembered, but I will hold you responsible for their blood. {3:21} Yet if you warn the righteous person not to sin and they do not sin, they will surely live because they were warned; and you will have saved yourself. {3:22} The hand of the LORD was upon me, and he said, "Get up, go out to the plain, and I will speak to you there." {3:23} So I got up and went out to the plain, and there was the glory of the LORD standing there, as I had seen by the Chebar River, and I fell on my face. {3:24} Then the spirit entered me and set me on my feet, and he spoke to me, saying, "Go, shut yourself inside your house. {3:25} But you, son of man, know this: they will put ropes on you and bind you so you cannot go out among them. {3:26} I will make your tongue stick to the roof of your mouth so that you will be mute and not be a reprover to them, for they are a rebellious house. {3:27} But when I speak to you, I will open your mouth, and you will say to them, 'This is what the Lord GOD says.' Let the one who hears listen, and let the one who refuses to listen refuse, for they are a rebellious house.

{4:1} "You, son of man, take a brick and lay it before you; draw the city of Jerusalem on it. {4:2} Lay siege against it, build a fort around it, and cast a mound against it; set a camp against it and place battering rams around it. {4:3} Take an iron pan and set it as an iron wall between you and the city; set your face against it, and it will be under siege, and you will lay siege against it. This will be a sign to the house of Israel. {4:4} Lie on your left side and bear the iniquity of the house of Israel on it; according to the number of the days you lie on it, you will bear their iniquity. {4:5} I have laid upon you the years of their iniquity, 390 days; you will bear the iniquity of the house of Israel. {4:6} When you have finished, lie on your right side for 40 days; I have appointed you each day for a year. {4:7} Therefore, set your face toward the siege of Jerusalem, and bare your arm and prophesy against it. {4:8} I will put ropes on you, and you will not turn from one side to another until you have completed the days of your siege. {4:9} Take wheat, barley, beans, lentils, millet, and spelt (a type of grain) and put them in one container; make bread from them for the number of days you lie on your side, eating it for 390 days. {4:10} Your food will be weighed out to you: twenty shekels a day; you will eat it at fixed times. {4:11} You will drink water by measure, one-sixth of a hin (about a liter); you will drink it at fixed times. {4:12} You will eat it like barley cakes, baking it in their sight over human dung. {4:13} The LORD said, "This is how the people of Israel will eat their unclean food among the nations where I will drive them." {4:14} Then I said, "Ah, Lord GOD! Look, I have never been defiled; from my youth until now, I have never eaten anything that died of itself or was torn by wild animals; nor has any unclean meat ever entered my mouth." {4:15} He said to me, "Very well, I have given you cow dung instead of human dung, and you will prepare your bread with it." {4:16} Moreover, he said to me, "Son of man, I will break the supply of bread in Jerusalem; they will eat bread by weight and in fear, and they will drink water by measure and in dismay. {4:17} They will lack bread and water and be appalled with one another and waste away because of their iniquity."

{5:1} "And you, son of man, take a sharp knife, a barber's razor, and shave your head and beard. Then take scales to weigh the hair and divide it. {5:2} A third of it you shall burn in the fire in the middle of the city when the days of the siege are over; another third you will strike with a knife around it, and a third you will scatter in the wind. I will draw a sword after them. {5:3} You shall also take a few of them and bind them in your clothes. {5:4} Then take some of those and throw them into the fire and burn them, for a fire will come out of it into all the house of Israel. {5:5} This is what the Lord GOD says: This is Jerusalem. I have set her in the middle of the nations and surrounding countries. {5:6} She has changed my laws into wickedness more than the nations, and my statutes more than the countries around her; for they have rejected my laws and my statutes; they have not followed them. {5:7} Therefore, this is what the Lord GOD says: Because you have multiplied more than the nations around you and have not followed my statutes or kept my judgments, nor have you done according to the judgments of the nations around you, {5:8} therefore, this is what the Lord GOD says: Look, I, even I, am against you, and I will execute judgments among you in the sight of the nations. {5:9} I will do things in you that I have not done before, and will not do again, because of all your detestable things. {5:10} Therefore, parents will eat their children in your midst, and children will eat their parents; I will execute judgments in you, and I will scatter the whole remnant of you into all the winds. {5:11} As I live, says the Lord GOD, surely because you have defiled my sanctuary with all your detestable things and abominations, I will also reduce you; my eye will not spare you, nor will I have any pity. {5:12} A third of you will die by plague, and another third will be consumed by famine in your midst, and another third will fall by the sword around you. I will scatter the last third into all the winds and will draw a sword after them. {5:13} This is how my anger will be satisfied, and I will cause my fury to rest upon them, and they will know that I, the LORD, have spoken it in my zeal when I accomplish my fury upon them. {5:14} Moreover, I will make you a wasteland and a reproach among the nations around you in the sight of all who pass by. {5:15} It will be a reproach and a taunt, a lesson and a shock to the nations around you when I execute judgments among you in anger and fury and furious rebukes. I, the LORD, have spoken it. {5:16} When I send upon them the evil arrows of famine, which will be for their destruction, I will increase the famine on you and break your supply of bread. {5:17} I will send famine and wild beasts against you, and they will deprive you; pestilence and blood will pass through you, and I will bring the sword upon you. I, the LORD, have spoken it.

{6:1} The word of the LORD came to me, saying, {6:2} "Son of man, set your face toward the mountains of Israel and prophesy against them. {6:3} Say, 'You mountains of Israel, hear the word of the Lord GOD. This is what the Lord GOD says to the mountains, hills, rivers, and valleys: Look, I will bring a sword against you, and I will destroy your high places. {6:4} Your altars will be desolate, and your images will be broken. I will throw down the slain before your idols. {6:5} I will lay the dead bodies of the people of Israel before their idols and scatter your bones around your altars. {6:6} In all your dwelling places, the cities will be laid waste, and the high places will be desolate, so that your altars may be laid waste and made desolate, and your idols may be broken and cease, and your images may be cut down, and your works may be abolished. {6:7} The slain will fall among you, and you will know that I am the LORD. {6:8} Yet I will leave a remnant so that some of you will escape the sword among the nations when you are scattered throughout the countries. {6:9} Those who escape will remember me among the nations where they were taken captive, because I am crushed by their unfaithful hearts that have turned away from me, and by their eyes that lust after their idols. They will loathe themselves for the evils they have committed in all their detestable acts. {6:10} They will know that I am the LORD, and that I have not spoken in vain about bringing this disaster upon them. {6:11} This is what the Lord GOD says: Strike your hands and stomp your feet and say, 'Alas for all the detestable abominations of the house of Israel! They will fall by the sword, famine, and pestilence.' {6:12} Those who are far away will die of plague, and those who are near will fall by the sword, and those who remain and are besieged will die by famine. Thus, I will accomplish my fury upon them. {6:13} Then you will know that I am the LORD when their slain are among their idols around their altars, on every high hill, on all the mountaintops, and under every green tree and thick oak, where they offered sweet aroma to all their idols. {6:14} So I will stretch out my hand against them and make the land more desolate than the wilderness toward Diblath in all their places of habitation. Then they will know that I am the LORD."

{7:1} The word of the LORD came to me, saying, {7:2} "Also, son of man, this is what the Lord GOD says to the land of Israel: The end, the end has come upon the four corners of the land. {7:3} Now the end has come upon you; I will send my anger upon you and judge you according to your ways, and I will repay you for all your detestable acts. {7:4} My eye will not spare you, nor will I have pity. I will repay you according to your ways, and your detestable acts will be in your midst; then you will know that I am the LORD. {7:5} This is what the Lord GOD says: An evil, a terrible evil, has come. {7:6} The end has come; the end has come. It watches for you; look, it has come. {7:7} The morning has come upon you, O you who dwell in the land; the time has come, the day of trouble is near, and not the joyful sounds of mountains. {7:8} Now I will shortly pour out my fury upon you and accomplish my anger against you. I will judge you according to your ways and repay you for all your detestable acts. {7:9} My eye will not spare, nor will I have pity. I will repay you according to your ways and the detestable acts in your midst; then you will know that I am the LORD who strikes. {7:10} Behold, the day has come; it has arrived. The morning has gone forth; the rod has blossomed, pride has budded. {7:11} Violence has risen up into a rod of wickedness: none of them will remain, neither their multitude nor any of theirs; there will be no mourning for them. {7:12} The time has come; the day is near. Let not the buyer rejoice, nor the seller mourn, for wrath is upon all the multitude. {7:13} The seller will not return to what was sold, even while they are still alive, for the vision is concerning the whole multitude, which will not return; nor will anyone strengthen themselves in the iniquity of their lives. {7:14} They have blown the trumpet to prepare everyone, but no one goes to battle, for my wrath is upon all the multitude. {7:15} The sword is outside, and pestilence and famine are inside. Those in the field will die by the sword, and those in the city will be devoured by famine and pestilence. {7:16} But those who escape will flee to the mountains like doves from the valleys, all of them mourning for their iniquity. {7:17} All hands will be weak, and all knees will be as weak as water. {7:18} They will put on sackcloth, and terror will cover them; shame will be on all faces, and baldness on all heads. {7:19} They will throw their silver into the streets, and their gold will be discarded; their silver and gold will not be able to save them in the day of the LORD's wrath. They will not satisfy their souls or fill their stomachs, for it has become a stumbling block because of their iniquity. {7:20} As for the beauty of their ornaments, they set it in majesty, but they made the images of their detestable things within it; therefore, I have set it far from them. {7:21} I will give it into the hands of strangers as plunder, and to the wicked of the earth as spoil, and they will defile it. {7:22} I will also turn my face from them, and they will pollute my secret place, for robbers will enter it and defile it. {7:23} Make a chain, for the land is full of bloody crimes, and the city is full of violence. {7:24} Therefore, I will bring the worst of the nations, and they will take possession of their houses. I will also put an end to the pride of the strong, and their holy places will be defiled. {7:25} Destruction comes, and they will seek peace, but there will be none. {7:26} Disaster will come upon disaster, and rumor upon rumor; then they will seek a vision from the prophet, but the law will perish from the priest, and counsel from the elders. {7:27} The king will mourn, and the prince will be clothed in despair, and the hands of the people of the land will tremble. I will deal with them according to their ways and judge them according to their deeds; and they will know that I am the LORD.

{8:1} In the sixth year, in the sixth month, on the fifth day of the month, as I sat in my house, and the elders of Judah sat before me, the hand of the Lord GOD fell upon me there. {8:2} Then I looked, and behold, a likeness like the appearance of fire: from his waist down was fire, and from his waist up was the appearance of brightness, like amber. {8:3} He stretched out the form of a hand and took me by a lock of my hair; the Spirit lifted me up between earth and heaven and brought me in the visions of God to Jerusalem, to the entrance of the inner gate that faces north, where the seat of the image of jealousy, which provokes jealousy, was located. {8:4} And behold, the glory of the God of Israel was there, according to the vision I had seen in the plain. {8:5} Then he said to me, "Son of man, lift up your eyes toward the north." So I lifted my eyes toward the north, and behold, northward at the gate of the altar was this image of jealousy at the entrance. {8:6} He said to me, "Son of man, do you see what they are doing? The great detestable acts the house of Israel is committing here that I should go far away from my sanctuary? But turn again, and you will see greater abominations." {8:7} He brought me to the door of the court, and when I looked, behold, there was a hole in the wall. {8:8} Then he said to me, "Son of man, dig now in the wall." When I had dug in the wall, behold, there was a door. {8:9} He said to me, "Go in and see the wicked abominations they are doing here." {8:10} So I went in and saw; behold, every form of creeping things, and detestable beasts, and all the idols of the house of Israel were portrayed all around on the wall. {8:11} And there stood before them seventy men of the elders of the house of Israel, and in their midst stood Jaazaniah the son of Shaphan, with every man having his censer in his hand; and a thick cloud of incense went up. {8:12} Then he said to me, "Son of man, have you seen what the elders of the house of Israel do in the dark, every man in the chambers of his imagery? For they say, 'The LORD does not see us; the LORD has forsaken the earth.'" {8:13} He said also to me, "Turn again, and you will see greater detestable acts that they are doing." {8:14} Then he brought me to the door of the gate of the LORD'S house, which faces north; and behold, there sat women weeping for Tammuz. {8:15} Then he said to me, "Have you seen this, O son of man? Turn again, and you will see greater abominations than these." {8:16} He brought me into the inner court of the LORD'S house, and behold, at the door of the temple of the LORD, between the porch and the altar, were about twenty-five men with their backs toward the temple of the LORD and their faces toward the east; and they worshiped the sun toward the east. {8:17} Then he said to me, "Have you seen this, O son of man? Is it a trivial thing for the house of Judah to commit the abominations they commit here? For they have filled the land with violence and have returned to provoke me to anger; and indeed, they put the branch to their nose. {8:18} Therefore, I will deal in fury; my eye will not spare, nor will I have pity; and though they cry out in my ears with a loud voice, I will not hear them."

{9:1} He cried out in my ears with a loud voice, saying, "Let those who have charge over the city come near, each man with his destructive weapon in his hand." {9:2} And behold, six men came from the direction of the higher gate, which faces north, each holding a weapon of destruction. One man among them was clothed in linen, carrying a writer's inkhorn by his side, and they came and stood beside the bronze altar. {9:3} Then the glory of the God of Israel rose from above the cherubim, where it had been, and moved to the threshold of the house. He called to the man clothed in linen, who had the writer's inkhorn by his side, {9:4} and the LORD said to him, "Go through the middle of the city, through the midst of Jerusalem, and put a mark on the foreheads of the men who sigh and cry over all the abominations being committed within it." {9:5} To the others, He said in my hearing, "Follow him through the city and strike; do not let your eyes show mercy, nor spare anyone. {9:6} Kill utterly the old and young, both maids and children, as well as women. But do not come near anyone on whom is the mark, and start at my sanctuary." So they began with the elders (ancient men) who were before the temple. {9:7} And He said to them, "Defile the temple and fill its courts with the dead. Go out and slay them." So they went out and struck down the people in the city. {9:8} As they were killing, and I was left alone, I fell on my face and cried out, "Ah, Lord GOD! Will you destroy the entire remnant of Israel in pouring out Your fury on Jerusalem?" {9:9} Then He said to me, "The sin (iniquity) of the house of Israel and Judah is exceedingly great. The land is full of bloodshed, and the city is filled with injustice (perverseness). For they say, 'The LORD has forsaken the land, and the LORD does not see.' {9:10} As for me, my eye will not show mercy, nor will I have pity. I will repay them according to their deeds." {9:11} And behold, the man clothed in linen, who had the inkhorn by his side, returned and reported, "I have done as You commanded me."

{10:1} Then I looked, and in the sky (firmament) above the heads of the cherubim, there appeared something like a sapphire stone, resembling a throne in appearance. {10:2} And He spoke to the man clothed in linen and said, "Go between the wheels beneath the cherubim, fill your hands with burning coals from among the cherubim, and scatter them over the city." And he went in before my eyes. {10:3} The cherubim were standing on the right side of the house when the man went in, and a cloud filled the inner court. {10:4} Then the glory of the LORD rose up from above the cherubim and stood over the threshold of the house, and the house was filled with the cloud, while the court was filled with the brightness of the LORD's glory. {10:5} The sound of the wings of the cherubim was heard as far as the outer court, like the voice of Almighty God when He speaks. {10:6} When He had commanded the man clothed in linen to take fire from between the wheels, from between the cherubim, the man went in and stood beside the wheels. {10:7} Then one of the cherubim stretched out his hand from between the cherubim to the fire that was between them. He took some of it and placed it into the hands of the man clothed in linen, who then went out. {10:8} Under the wings of the cherubim, there appeared something resembling a human hand. {10:9} As I looked, I saw four wheels beside the cherubim, one wheel beside each cherub, and the appearance of the wheels was like the color of beryl (a precious stone). {10:10} As for their appearance, the four wheels all looked alike, as though one wheel were within another. {10:11} When they moved, they went in any of the four directions they faced, without turning as they moved. They followed in the direction that their head faced, without turning aside. {10:12} Their entire bodies, including their backs, hands, wings, and wheels, were covered with eyes all around, even the wheels themselves. {10:13} I heard the wheels being called "the whirling wheels" (O wheel) in my hearing. {10:14} Each of the cherubim had four faces: one had the face of a cherub, the second had the face of a man, the third had the face of a lion, and the fourth had the face of an eagle. {10:15} Then the cherubim rose up. These were the living creatures I had seen by the river Chebar. {10:16} When the cherubim moved, the wheels moved beside them, and when the cherubim lifted their wings to rise from the earth, the wheels stayed beside them. {10:17} When they stood still, the wheels stood still; when they rose up, the wheels rose with them, for the spirit of the living creatures was in the wheels. {10:18} Then the glory of the LORD departed from the threshold of the temple and stood above the cherubim. {10:19} The cherubim lifted up their wings and rose from the earth before my eyes. As they went out, the wheels went with them. They stopped at the entrance of the east gate of the LORD's house, and the glory of the God of Israel was above them. {10:20} These were the living creatures I had seen beneath the God of Israel by the river Chebar, and I recognized that they were cherubim. {10:21} Each had four faces and four wings, and under their wings was the form of human hands. {10:22} Their faces looked just like the faces I had seen by the river Chebar. Each creature moved straight ahead.

{11:1} The spirit lifted me up and brought me to the east gate of the LORD's house, which faces east. There, at the entrance of the gate, were twenty-five men; among them I saw Jaazaniah son of Azur and Pelatiah son of Benaiah, leaders of the people. {11:2} Then he said to me, "Son of man, these are the men who plot evil and give wicked counsel in this city. {11:3} They say, 'It is not near; let us build houses; this city is the pot, and we are the meat.' {11:4} Therefore, prophesy against them; prophesy, O son of man." {11:5} The Spirit of the LORD fell upon me and said to me, "Speak! This is what the LORD says: I know the thoughts that come into your minds, every one of them. {11:6} You have multiplied your slain in this city and filled its streets with the dead. {11:7} Therefore, this is what the Lord GOD says: Your slain whom you have laid in its midst are the meat, and this city is the pot; but I will bring you out of the midst of it. {11:8} You have feared the sword, and I will bring a sword upon you, says the Lord GOD. {11:9} I will bring you out of the midst of it and deliver you into the hands of strangers; I will execute judgments among you. {11:10} You shall fall by the sword; I will judge you at the border of Israel, and you will know that I am the LORD. {11:11} This city will not be your pot, nor will you be the meat in its midst; I will judge you at the border of Israel. {11:12} You will know that I am the LORD, for you have not walked in my statutes or followed my judgments but have acted according to the customs of the nations around you. {11:13} It happened that when I prophesied, Pelatiah son of Benaiah died. Then I fell face down and cried out loudly, "Ah, Lord GOD! Will you completely destroy the remnant of Israel?" {11:14} Again, the word of the LORD came to me, saying, {11:15} "Son of man, your relatives, your fellow exiles, and all the house of Israel, are those to whom the inhabitants of Jerusalem have said, 'Get away from the LORD; this land has been given to us as a possession.' {11:16} Therefore say, 'This is what the Lord GOD says: Although I have scattered them among the nations and dispersed them among the countries, yet I will be to them a little sanctuary in the countries where they go.' {11:17} Therefore say, 'This is what the Lord GOD says: I will gather you from the people and assemble you out of the countries where you have been scattered and give you the land of Israel.' {11:18} They will go there and remove all its detestable things and all its abominations from it. {11:19} I will give them one heart and put a new spirit within them; I will remove the heart of stone from their flesh and give them a heart of flesh, {11:20} so that they may walk in my statutes, keep my ordinances, and obey them. They will be my people, and I will be their God. {11:21} But as for those whose hearts are devoted to their detestable things and abominations, I will repay their actions on their own heads, says the Lord GOD." {11:22} Then the cherubim lifted their wings, and the wheels beside them, and the glory of the God of Israel was above them. {11:23} The glory of the LORD went up from the midst of the city and stood on the mountain east of the city. {11:24} Afterwards, the Spirit took me up and brought me in a vision by the Spirit of God to Chaldea (Babylon) to the exiles. So the vision I had seen went up from me. {11:25} Then I spoke to the exiles all the things that the LORD had shown me.

{12:1} The word of the LORD also came to me, saying, {12:2} "Son of man, you dwell in the midst of a rebellious house, who have eyes to see but do not see; ears to hear but do not hear, for they are a rebellious house. {12:3} Therefore, son of man, prepare supplies for exile and remove by day in their sight; you shall remove from your place to another place in their sight. Perhaps they will consider, though they are a rebellious house. {12:4} You shall bring out your supplies by day in their sight, as supplies for exile; and in the evening you shall go out in their sight, as those who go into captivity. {12:5} Dig through the wall in their sight and carry your belongings out through it. {12:6} In their sight, you shall bear it on your shoulder and carry it out in the twilight; you shall cover your face so that you cannot see the ground, for I have made you a sign to the house of Israel. {12:7} So I did as I was commanded: I brought out my supplies by day, as supplies for captivity, and in the evening I dug through the wall with my hand; I brought it out in the twilight and bore it on my shoulder in their sight. {12:8} In the morning, the word of the LORD came to me, saying, {12:9} "Son of man, has not the house of Israel, that rebellious house, asked you, 'What are you doing?' {12:10} Say to them, 'This is what the Lord GOD says: This burden concerns the prince in Jerusalem and all the house of Israel among them.' {12:11} Say, 'I am your sign: just as I have done, it will be done to them; they shall go into exile.' {12:12} The prince among them shall bear on his shoulder in the twilight and go out; they shall dig through the wall to carry their belongings out, and he shall cover his face so that he cannot see the ground with his eyes. {12:13} I will spread my net over him, and he shall be caught in my snare; I will bring him to Babylon, to the land of the Chaldeans, yet he will not see it, though he will die there. {12:14} I will scatter toward every wind all who are around him to help him and all his troops; I will draw out the sword after them. {12:15} They will know that I am the LORD when I scatter them among the nations and disperse them in the countries. {12:16} But I will leave a few of them from the sword, famine, and pestilence, so they may declare all their abominations among the nations where they go, and they will know that I am the LORD." {12:17} Moreover, the word of the LORD came to me, saying, {12:18} "Son of man, eat your bread with trembling and drink your water with anxiety; {12:19} and say to the people of the land, 'This is what the Lord GOD says to the inhabitants of Jerusalem and the land of Israel: They shall eat their bread with anxiety and drink their water with astonishment, because her land will be desolate from all that is in it, because of the violence of all who dwell there.' {12:20} The inhabited cities shall be laid waste, and the land shall be desolate; then you will know that I am the LORD." {12:21} The word of the LORD came to me, saying, {12:22} "Son of man, what is that proverb you have in the land of Israel, saying, 'The days are prolonged, and every vision fails'? {12:23} Tell them, 'This is what the Lord GOD says: I will make this proverb cease; they will no longer use it as a proverb in Israel. Say to them, "The days are at hand, and the fulfillment of every vision is near." {12:24} For there shall be no more false visions or flattering divination in the house of Israel. {12:25} For I am the LORD; I will speak, and the word I speak will come to pass; it will no longer be delayed, for in your days, O rebellious house, I will say the word and perform it, says the Lord GOD.' {12:26} Again, the word of the LORD came to me, saying, {12:27} "Son of man, the house of Israel says, 'The vision he sees is for many days from now, and he prophesies of times far off.' {12:28} Therefore say to them, 'This is what the Lord GOD says: None of my words will be delayed any longer; the word which I have spoken shall be done, says the Lord GOD.'"

{13:1} The word of the LORD came to me, saying, {13:2} "Son of man, prophesy against the prophets of Israel who prophesy, and say to them, those who prophesy out of their own hearts, 'Listen to the word of the LORD.' {13:3} This is what the Lord GOD says: Woe to the foolish prophets who follow their own spirits and have seen nothing! {13:4} O Israel, your prophets are like foxes in the deserts. {13:5} You have not gone up into the gaps, nor built up the wall for the house of Israel to stand firm in battle on the day of the LORD. {13:6} They have seen false visions and lying divinations, saying, 'The LORD says,' when the LORD has not sent them; and they have made others hope that they would confirm the word. {13:7} Have you not seen a false vision, and have you not spoken a lying divination, while you say, 'The LORD says it,' even though I have not spoken? {13:8} Therefore, this is what the Lord GOD says: Because you have spoken falsehoods and seen lies, behold, I am against you, says the Lord GOD. {13:9} My hand will be against the prophets who see false visions and who divine lies; they shall not be in the assembly of my people, nor will they be written in the records of the house of Israel, nor will they enter the land of Israel; and you will know that I am the Lord GOD. {13:10} Because they have led my people astray, saying, 'Peace,' when there was no peace; and when one builds a wall, they cover it with untempered mortar (mortar that is not strong enough): {13:11} Say to those who plaster it with untempered mortar that it will fall; there will be a pouring rain, and you, O great hailstones, will fall; and a stormy wind will tear it down. {13:12} When the wall falls, will it not be said to you, 'Where is the plaster you used to cover it?' {13:13} Therefore, this is what the Lord GOD says: I will tear it down with a stormy wind in my fury; and there will be a pouring rain in my anger, and great hailstones in my fury to destroy it. {13:14} I will break down the wall that you have covered with untempered mortar and bring it down to the ground, so that its foundation will be revealed, and it will fall, and you will be consumed in the midst of it; and you will know that I am the LORD. {13:15} I will accomplish my wrath upon the wall and upon those who covered it with untempered mortar, and I will say to you, 'The wall is no more, nor are those who covered it.' {13:16} Specifically, the prophets of Israel who prophesy concerning Jerusalem and see visions of peace for her, when there is no peace, says the Lord GOD. {13:17} Likewise, son of man, set your face against the daughters of your people who prophesy out of their own hearts; prophesy against them, {13:18} and say, 'This is what the Lord GOD says: Woe to the women who sew magic charms on all their wrists and make veils for heads of every height to hunt souls! Will you hunt the souls of my people and save the souls of those who come to you? {13:19} Will you pollute me among my people for handfuls of barley and pieces of bread, killing the souls that should not die and saving the souls that should not live, by your lies to my people who listen to your lies? {13:20} Therefore, this is what the Lord GOD says: Behold, I am against your magic charms, with which you hunt souls to make them fly; I will tear them from your arms and let the souls go, even the souls you hunt to make them fly. {13:21} I will tear your veils, and deliver my people out of your hands; they will no longer be in your hands to be hunted, and you will know that I am the LORD. {13:22} Because with lies you have made the heart of the righteous sad, whom I have not made sad; and you have strengthened the hands of the wicked, so he does not turn from his wicked way by promising him life. {13:23} Therefore, you will see no false visions nor flattering divinations; for I will deliver my people out of your hands, and you will know that I am the LORD.

{14:1} Then some of the elders of Israel came to me and sat before me. {14:2} The word of the LORD came to me, saying, {14:3} "Son of man, these men have set up their idols in their hearts and put the stumbling block of their iniquity before their faces; should I be consulted by them at all? {14:4} Therefore speak to them and say to them, 'This is what the Lord GOD says: Every man of the house of Israel who sets up his idols in his heart and puts the stumbling block of his iniquity before his face, and comes to a prophet; I, the LORD, will answer him that comes according to the multitude of his idols. {14:5} I will take the house of Israel in their own hearts, because they are all estranged from me through their idols. {14:6} Therefore say to the house of Israel, 'This is what the Lord GOD says: Repent and turn away from your idols; turn your faces away from all your abominations.' {14:7} For every one of the house of Israel or of the strangers who dwell in Israel, who separates himself from me and sets up his idols in his heart, and puts the stumbling block of his iniquity before his face, and comes to a prophet to inquire of him concerning me; I, the LORD, will answer him by myself. {14:8} I will set my face against that man and make him a sign and a proverb; I will cut him off from the midst of my people; and you will know that I am the LORD. {14:9} And if the prophet is deceived when he speaks a word, I, the LORD, have deceived that prophet; and I will stretch out my hand against him and destroy him from the midst of my people Israel. {14:10} They will bear the punishment of their iniquity; the punishment of the prophet shall be the same as the punishment of him who seeks him. {14:11} This way, the house of Israel may no longer stray from me, nor be polluted with all their transgressions; but they may be my people, and I may be their God, says the Lord GOD. {14:12} The word of the LORD came to me again, saying, {14:13} "Son of man, when the land sins against me by acting unfaithfully, I will stretch out my hand against it, break its supply of bread, send famine upon it, and cut off man and beast from it. {14:14} Even if these three men, Noah, Daniel, and Job, were in it, they would deliver only their own souls by their righteousness, says the Lord GOD. {14:15} If I bring harmful animals through the land and they spoil it, so that it becomes desolate and no one can pass through because of the animals, {14:16} even if these three men were in it, as I live, says the Lord GOD, they will deliver neither sons nor daughters; they will only deliver their own souls, but the land will be desolate. {14:17} Or if I bring a sword upon that land and say, 'Sword, go through the land,' so that I cut off man and beast from it; {14:18} even if these three men were in it, as I live, says the Lord GOD, they will deliver neither sons nor daughters; they will only deliver themselves. {14:19} Or if I send a plague upon that land and pour out my fury upon it in blood, cutting off man and beast from it; {14:20} even if Noah, Daniel, and Job were in it, as I live, says the Lord GOD, they will deliver neither son nor daughter; they will only deliver their own souls by their righteousness. {14:21} For this is what the Lord GOD says: How much more when I send my four dreadful judgments upon Jerusalem: the sword, famine, harmful animals, and pestilence, to cut off from it man and beast? {14:22} Yet, behold, a remnant will be left that will be brought forth, both sons and daughters; behold, they will come out to you, and you will see their ways and their deeds, and you will be comforted concerning the evil that I have brought upon Jerusalem, concerning all that I have brought upon it. {14:23} They will comfort you when you see their ways and their deeds, and you will know that I have not acted without cause in all that I have done to it, says the Lord GOD."

{15:1} The word of the LORD came to me, saying, {15:2} "Son of man, what is the vine tree compared to any other tree, or to a branch among the trees of the forest? {15:3} Can wood be taken from it to do any work? Can someone take a pin from it to hang something on? {15:4} Look, it is thrown into the fire for fuel; the fire consumes both ends and the middle. Is it good for any work? {15:5} When it was whole, it was good for no work; how much less will it be useful after the fire has consumed it and it is burned? {15:6} Therefore, this is what the Lord GOD says: As the vine tree among the trees of the forest, which I have given to the fire for fuel, so will I give the inhabitants of Jerusalem. {15:7} I will set my face against them; they will escape one fire, and another fire will consume them. You will know that I am the LORD when I set my face against them. {15:8} I will make the land desolate because they have sinned, says the Lord GOD.

{16:1} Again the word of the LORD came to me, saying, {16:2} "Son of man, let Jerusalem know her abominations. {16:3} Say, 'This is what the Lord GOD says to Jerusalem: Your birth and origin are from the land of Canaan; your father was an Amorite, and your mother was a Hittite. {16:4} And regarding your birth, on the day you were born, your navel was not cut, you were not washed in water to make you clean, you were not salted at all, nor swaddled. {16:5} No one had compassion on you to do any of these things for you; you were thrown out into an open field, loathed on the day you were born. {16:6} When I passed by and saw you polluted in your own blood, I said to you, 'Live!' Yes, I said to you, 'Live!' {16:7} I made you grow like the bud of the field; you increased and grew great, coming to excellent beauty: your breasts were fashioned and your hair grew, while you were naked and bare. {16:8} When I passed by and looked upon you, behold, it was the time for love; I spread my skirt over you and covered your nakedness. Yes, I made a covenant with you, says the Lord GOD, and you became mine. {16:9} Then I washed you with water; I thoroughly washed away your blood from you and anointed you with oil. {16:10} I clothed you with embroidered garments and shod you with badger skin; I wrapped you in fine linen and covered you with silk. {16:11} I adorned you with ornaments, putting bracelets on your hands and a chain around your neck. {16:12} I placed a jewel on your forehead, earrings in your ears, and a beautiful crown on your head. {16:13} Thus you were adorned with gold and silver; your clothes were of fine linen, silk, and embroidered work; you ate fine flour, honey, and oil; you were exceedingly beautiful and prospered into a kingdom. {16:14} Your renown spread among the nations for your beauty; it was perfect through my splendor which I had bestowed upon you, says the Lord GOD. {16:15} But you trusted in your own beauty and played the harlot because of your renown, pouring out your fornications on everyone who passed by. {16:16} You took your garments and decked your high places with many colors, playing the harlot on them; such things should not come, nor should it be so. {16:17} You also took the beautiful jewels of my gold and silver, which I had given you, and made images of men, committing fornication with them. {16:18} You took your embroidered garments and covered them; you set my oil and my incense before them. {16:19} My food, which I gave you, the fine flour, oil, and honey, with which I fed you, you set it before them as a pleasing aroma; thus it was, says the Lord GOD. {16:20} Moreover, you took your sons and daughters, whom you bore to me, and sacrificed them to be devoured. Is this not a small matter of your harlotries, {16:21} that you have slain my children and delivered them to pass through the fire for them? {16:22} In all your abominations and your harlotries, you did not remember the days of your youth, when you were naked and bare, polluted in your blood. {16:23} After all your wickedness, woe, woe to you! says the Lord GOD. {16:24} You also built an eminent place and made a high place in every street. {16:25} You built your high places at every head of the way and made your beauty to be loathed; you opened your feet to everyone who passed by and multiplied your harlotries. {16:26} You committed fornication with the Egyptians, your neighbors, great of flesh; you increased your harlotries to provoke me to anger. {16:27} Therefore, I have stretched out my hand against you and diminished your ordinary food, and delivered you to the will of those who hate you, the daughters of the Philistines, who are ashamed of your lewd way. {16:28} You played the harlot with the Assyrians because you were unsatisfied; yes, you played the harlot with them, and yet you were not satisfied. {16:29} You multiplied your fornications in the land of Canaan to Chaldea; yet you were not satisfied with this. {16:30} How weak is your heart, says the Lord GOD, seeing you do all these things, the work of an imperious harlot. {16:31} In that you build your eminent place at the head of every way and make your high place in every street; you have not been like a harlot, since you scorn hire. {16:32} But as a wife who commits adultery, taking strangers instead of her husband! {16:33} They give gifts to all harlots; but you give your gifts to all your lovers and hire them to come to you on every side for your harlotry. {16:34} The opposite is true of you compared to other women in your harlotries, since none follows you to commit harlotries; in that you give a reward and no reward is given to you, therefore you are contrary. {16:35} Therefore, O harlot, hear the word of the LORD: {16:36} Thus says the Lord GOD: Because your filthiness was poured out and your nakedness uncovered through your harlotries with your lovers and with all the idols of your abominations, and by the blood of your children, which you gave to them; {16:37} behold, I will gather all your lovers, with whom you took pleasure, and all whom you loved and hated; I will gather them around you and expose your nakedness to them, that they may see all your nakedness. {16:38} I will judge you as women who break wedlock and shed blood are judged; I will give you blood in fury and jealousy. {16:39} I will also give you into their hand, and they shall tear down your eminent place and break down your high places; they shall strip you of your clothes, take your fair jewels, and leave you naked and bare. {16:40} They shall bring up a company against you, and they shall stone you with stones and thrust you through with their swords. {16:41} They shall burn down your houses with fire and execute judgments upon you in the sight of many women; I will cause you to cease from playing the harlot, and you will no longer give hire. {16:42} So I will make my fury toward you rest, and my jealousy shall depart from you; I will be quiet and will no longer be angry. {16:43} Because you have not remembered the days of your youth but have angered me in all these things; therefore, I will also recompense your ways upon your head, says the Lord GOD, and you will not commit this lewdness above all your abominations. {16:44} Behold, everyone who uses proverbs will use this proverb against you, saying, 'Like mother, like daughter.' {16:45} You are your mother's daughter, who loathed her husband and her children; you are the sister of your sisters, who loathed their husbands and children; your mother was a Hittite, and your father an Amorite. {16:46} Your older sister is Samaria, she and her daughters who dwell at your left hand; your younger sister, who dwells at your right hand, is Sodom and her daughters. {16:47} Yet you have not walked in their ways nor done their abominations; but as if that were a very little thing, you were corrupted more than they in all your ways. {16:48} As I live, says the Lord GOD, Sodom your sister has not done, she nor her daughters, as you have done, you and your daughters.{16:49} Look, this was the sin of your sister Sodom: she was proud, had plenty of food, and was idle, and she did not help the poor and needy. {16:50} They were arrogant and committed terrible acts before me; therefore, I removed them as I saw fit. {16:51} Samaria hasn't committed half as many sins as you have; you have multiplied your offenses more than they have, and you have justified your sisters in all the wickedness you have done. {16:52} You who have judged your sisters must bear your own shame for your sins, which are more horrible than theirs. They are more righteous than you; yes, be ashamed and bear your disgrace because you have justified your sisters. {16:53} When I bring back the captives of Sodom and her daughters and the captives of Samaria and her daughters, then I will bring back your captives in the midst of them. {16:54} You will bear your own shame and be embarrassed by all you have done, as you are a comfort to them. {16:55} When your sisters, Sodom and her daughters, return to their former state, and Samaria and her daughters return to theirs, then you and your daughters will return to your former state. {16:56} For your sister Sodom was not even mentioned by you on the day of your pride. {16:57} Before your wickedness was revealed, at the time you mocked the daughters of Syria and all those around her, the daughters of the Philistines who despise you. {16:58} You have borne your lewdness and your abominations, says the LORD. {16:59} For thus says the Lord GOD: I will treat you as you have treated others, for you have broken the covenant. {16:60} Nevertheless, I will remember my covenant with you from your youth and establish an everlasting covenant with you. {16:61} Then you will remember your ways and be ashamed when you receive your sisters, both your older and your younger; I will give them to you as daughters, but not based on your covenant. {16:62} I will establish my covenant with you, and you will know that I am the LORD. {16:63} You will remember and be ashamed, and never open your mouth again because of your shame when I am at peace with you for all you have done, says the Lord GOD.

{17:1} The word of the LORD came to me again, saying, {17:2} Son of man, tell a riddle and speak a parable to the house of Israel. {17:3} Say, thus says the Lord GOD: A great eagle with large wings, long feathers, and many colors came to Lebanon and took the top branch of a cedar tree. {17:4} He broke off the top of its young twigs and carried it to a land of trade; he set it in a city of merchants. {17:5} He also took some of the seed from the land and planted it in a fertile field; he put it by abundant waters and made it like a willow tree. {17:6} It grew and became a low vine whose branches turned toward him, and its roots were under him; so it became a vine and produced branches and shoots. {17:7} There was also another great eagle with large wings and many feathers, and behold, this vine bent its roots toward him and shot forth its branches toward him so he might water it in the furrows of its planting. {17:8} It was planted in good soil by abundant waters so it could produce branches and bear fruit, making it a good vine. {17:9} Say, thus says the Lord GOD: Will it thrive? Will he not pull up its roots and cut off its fruit so it withers? It will wither in all the leaves of its spring, even without much power or many people to pull it up by its roots. {17:10} Yes, look, being planted, will it thrive? Will it not utterly wither when the east wind touches it? It will wither in the furrows where it grew. {17:11} Moreover, the word of the LORD came to me, saying, {17:12} Say to the rebellious house, Do you not understand what these things mean? Tell them, Behold, the king of Babylon has come to Jerusalem, taken its king and its princes, and led them to Babylon. {17:13} He has taken some of the royal family and made a covenant with him, swearing an oath; he has also taken the mighty of the land. {17:14} This was so the kingdom would be humble and not lift itself up, but that it might stand by keeping his covenant. {17:15} But he rebelled against him by sending his envoys to Egypt to get horses and many people. Will he prosper? Will he escape who does such things? Will he break the covenant and be delivered? {17:16} As I live, says the Lord GOD, surely in the place where the king dwells who made him king, whose oath he despised and whose covenant he broke, he will die in Babylon. {17:17} Neither shall Pharaoh with his mighty army and great company help him in battle by building up ramps and fortifications to cut off many. {17:18} Since he despised the oath by breaking the covenant, after giving his hand and doing all these things, he will not escape. {17:19} Therefore, thus says the Lord GOD: As I live, surely my oath that he has despised and my covenant that he has broken will be brought back upon his own head. {17:20} I will spread my net over him, and he will be caught in my snare, and I will bring him to Babylon and plead with him there for the trespass he has committed against me. {17:21} All his fugitives and his bands will fall by the sword, and those who remain will be scattered in all directions, and you will know that I, the LORD, have spoken it. {17:22} Thus says the Lord GOD: I will take from the highest branch of the high cedar and set it; I will crop off a tender one from the top of its young twigs and plant it on a high mountain. {17:23} In the mountain of the height of Israel, I will plant it; it will bring forth boughs, bear fruit, and become a good cedar; and under it, every bird will nest, and in the shadow of its branches, they will dwell. {17:24} All the trees of the field will know that I, the LORD, have brought down the high tree, exalted the low tree, dried up the green tree, and made the dry tree flourish; I, the LORD, have spoken and done it.

{18:1} The word of the LORD came to me again, saying, {18:2} What do you mean by using this proverb about the land of Israel: The fathers have eaten sour grapes, and the children's teeth are set on edge? {18:3} As I live, says the Lord GOD, you will not have the opportunity to use this proverb in Israel anymore. {18:4} Look, all souls are mine; as the soul of the father, so also the soul of the son is mine: the soul that sins will die. {18:5} But if a man is righteous and does what is lawful and right, {18:6} and does not eat on the mountains, does not look at the idols of the house of Israel, does not defile his neighbor's wife, and does not approach a menstruating woman, {18:7} and does not oppress anyone, but returns what he has pledged to the debtor, does not take by violence, gives his food to the hungry, and covers the naked with a garment; {18:8} he who does not lend with interest or take a profit, who withdraws his hand from wrongdoing, and executes true judgment between man and man, {18:9} who walks in my statutes and keeps my judgments to deal truly; he is righteous; he will surely live, says the Lord GOD. {18:10} If he has a son who is a robber, a murderer, and does any of these things, {18:11} and does not do any of those duties, but has eaten on the mountains and defiled his neighbor's wife, {18:12} has oppressed the poor and needy, has taken by violence, has not restored the pledge, and has looked at the idols, has committed abominations, {18:13} has lent with interest and taken profits: will he then live? He will not live; he has done all these abominations; he will surely die; his blood will be upon him. {18:14} Now, look, if he has a son who sees all his father's sins that he has done, and considers, and does not do like them, {18:15} who has not eaten on the mountains, has not looked at the idols of the house of Israel, has not defiled his neighbor's wife, {18:16} has not oppressed anyone, has not withheld the pledge, has not taken by violence, but has given his food to the hungry, and covered the naked with a garment, {18:17} who has withdrawn his hand from the poor, who has not taken interest or profit, who has executed my judgments, and has walked in my statutes; he will not die for his father's iniquity; he will surely live. {18:18} As for his father, because he cruelly oppressed and took from his brother by violence and did what is not good among his people, he will die in his iniquity. {18:19} Yet you say, Why? Does not the son bear the iniquity of the father? When the son has done what is lawful and right and has kept all my statutes and done them, he will surely live. {18:20} The soul that sins will die. The son will not bear the iniquity of the father, nor will the father bear the iniquity of the son: the righteousness of the righteous will be upon him, and the wickedness of the wicked will be upon him. {18:21} But if the wicked turns from all his sins that he has committed and keeps all my statutes, and does what is lawful and right, he will surely live; he will not die. {18:22} All his transgressions that he has committed will not be remembered against him; in his righteousness that he has done, he will live. {18:23} Do I have any pleasure at all that the wicked should die? says the Lord GOD. Should he not turn from his ways and live? {18:24} But when the righteous turns away from his righteousness and commits iniquity, and does according to all the abominations that the wicked man does, will he live? All his righteousness that he has done will not be mentioned; in his trespass that he has trespassed and in his sin that he has sinned, he will die in them. {18:25} Yet you say, The way of the Lord is not fair. Now listen, O house of Israel; Is not my way fair? Are not your ways unfair? {18:26} When a righteous man turns away from his righteousness and commits iniquity, he will die for his iniquity. {18:27} Again, when the wicked man turns away from his wickedness that he has committed and does what is lawful and right, he will save his life. {18:28} Because he considers and turns away from all his transgressions that he has committed, he will surely live; he will not die. {18:29} Yet the house of Israel says, The way of the Lord is not fair. O house of Israel, are not my ways fair? Are not your ways unfair? {18:30} Therefore, I will judge you, O house of Israel, each one according to his ways, says the Lord GOD. Repent, and turn from all your transgressions, so iniquity will not be your ruin. {18:31} Cast away from you all your transgressions, by which you have sinned; and make yourselves a new heart and a new spirit; for why should you die, O house of Israel? {18:32} For I have no pleasure in the death of anyone who dies, says the Lord GOD; therefore, turn and live.

{19:1} Moreover, take up a lament for the leaders of Israel, {19:2} and say, What is your mother? A lioness; she lay down among lions, and she raised her cubs among young lions. {19:3} She brought up one of her cubs, and it grew into a young lion that learned to hunt and devoured people. {19:4} The nations heard about him; he was caught in their trap, and they brought him in chains to the land of Egypt. {19:5} When she saw that she had waited and her hope was lost, she took another of her cubs and made him a young lion. {19:6} He roamed among the lions, became a young lion, learned to catch prey, and devoured people. {19:7} He knew their ruined palaces and laid waste to their cities; the land was desolate because of the noise of his roaring. {19:8} Then nations surrounded him from all sides and spread their net over him; he was caught in their trap. {19:9} They put him in a cage in chains and brought him to the king of Babylon, where he was imprisoned so that his voice would no longer be heard on the mountains of Israel. {19:10} Your mother is like a vine in your blood, planted by the waters; she was fruitful and full of branches because of the many waters. {19:11} She had strong branches for the rulers, and her height was exalted among the thick branches; she appeared in her height with the multitude of her branches. {19:12} But she was uprooted in anger, cast down to the ground, and the east wind dried up her fruit; her strong branches were broken and withered; fire consumed them. {19:13} Now she is planted in the wilderness, in a dry and thirsty land. {19:14} A fire has gone out of a branch that devoured her fruit, so that she has no strong branch left to rule. This is a lament, and it shall be for lamentation.

{20:1} It came to pass in the seventh year, in the fifth month, on the tenth day of the month, that certain elders of Israel came to inquire of the LORD and sat before me. {20:2} Then the word of the LORD came to me, saying, {20:3} Son of man, speak to the elders of Israel and say to them, Thus says the Lord GOD: Are you coming to inquire of me? As I live, says the Lord GOD, I will not be inquired of by you. {20:4} Will you judge them, son of man? Will you judge them? Cause them to know the abominations of their fathers: {20:5} and say to them, Thus says the Lord GOD: On the day I chose Israel and lifted my hand to the descendants of Jacob, making myself known to them in the land of Egypt, when I lifted my hand to them, saying, I am the LORD your God; {20:6} on the day I lifted my hand to bring them out of the land of Egypt into a land I had inspected for them, flowing with milk and honey, which is the glory of all lands: {20:7} then I said to them, Cast away every man the abominations of your eyes, and do not defile yourselves with the idols of Egypt; I am the LORD your God. {20:8} But they rebelled against me and did not listen; they did not cast away the abominations of their eyes or forsake the idols of Egypt. Then I said, I will pour out my fury on them to accomplish my anger against them in the midst of the land of Egypt. {20:9} But I worked for my name's sake, so it would not be polluted before the nations among whom they were, in whose sight I made myself known to them by bringing them out of the land of Egypt. {20:10} Therefore, I led them out of Egypt and brought them into the wilderness. {20:11} I gave them my statutes and showed them my judgments, which if a man follows, he will live in them. {20:12} I also gave them my sabbaths as a sign between me and them, so they would know that I am the LORD who sanctifies them. {20:13} But the house of Israel rebelled against me in the wilderness; they did not walk in my statutes and despised my judgments, which if a man does, he will live in them. They greatly polluted my sabbaths. Then I said, I would pour out my fury on them in the wilderness to consume them. {20:14} But I worked for my name's sake, so it would not be polluted before the nations in whose sight I brought them out. {20:15} Yet I lifted my hand to them in the wilderness, that I would not bring them into the land I had given them, flowing with milk and honey, which is the glory of all lands; {20:16} because they despised my judgments and did not walk in my statutes but polluted my sabbaths; their hearts went after their idols. {20:17} Nevertheless, my eye spared them from destroying them; I did not make an end of them in the wilderness. {20:18} But I said to their children in the wilderness, Do not walk in the statutes of your fathers, nor observe their judgments, nor defile yourselves with their idols. {20:19} I am the LORD your God; walk in my statutes, keep my judgments, and do them; {20:20} and hallow my sabbaths; they shall be a sign between me and you, so you may know that I am the LORD your God. {20:21} Yet the children rebelled against me; they did not walk in my statutes or keep my judgments, which if a man does, he will live in them. They polluted my sabbaths. Then I said, I would pour out my fury on them to accomplish my anger against them in the wilderness. {20:22} Nevertheless, I withdrew my hand and worked for my name's sake, so it would not be polluted in the sight of the nations, in whose sight I brought them forth. {20:23} I lifted my hand to them also in the wilderness, that I would scatter them among the nations and disperse them through the countries; {20:24} because they did not execute my judgments, despised my statutes, and polluted my sabbaths; their eyes were set on their fathers' idols. {20:25} Therefore, I gave them statutes that were not good and judgments by which they could not live; {20:26} and I polluted them in their own gifts, as they caused to pass through the fire all that opened the womb, so that I might make them desolate, to the end that they might know that I am the LORD. {20:27} Therefore, son of man, speak to the house of Israel and say to them, Thus says the Lord GOD: Yet in this your fathers have blasphemed me by committing a trespass against me. {20:28} For when I brought them into the land, which I lifted my hand to give them, they saw every high hill and all the thick trees and offered sacrifices there, presenting their offerings, making sweet aromas, and pouring out drink offerings. {20:29} Then I said to them, What is the high place where you go? Its name is called Bamah to this day. {20:30} Therefore, say to the house of Israel, Thus says the Lord GOD: Are you polluted after the manner of your fathers? Do you commit whoredom after their abominations? {20:31} For when you offer your gifts and make your sons pass through the fire, you pollute yourselves with your idols even to this day. Shall I be inquired of by you, O house of Israel? As I live, says the Lord GOD, I will not be inquired of by you. {20:32} And what comes into your mind shall not be at all, that you say, We will be like the nations, like the families of the countries, to serve wood and stone. {20:33} As I live, says the Lord GOD, surely with a mighty hand, with an outstretched arm, and with fury poured out, I will rule over you. {20:34} I will bring you out from the peoples and gather you out of the countries where you are scattered, with a mighty hand, an outstretched arm, and fury poured out. {20:35} I will bring you into the wilderness of the peoples and there I will plead with you face to face. {20:36} Just as I pleaded with your fathers in the wilderness of the land of Egypt, so will I plead with you, says the Lord GOD. {20:37} I will cause you to pass under the rod and bring you into the bond of the covenant; {20:38} and I will purge out the rebels and those who transgress against me. I will bring them out of the country where they dwell, and they shall not enter into the land of Israel; and you will know that I am the LORD. {20:39} As for you, O house of Israel, thus says the Lord GOD: Go, serve your idols, every one of you, and hereafter, if you will not listen to me, do not pollute my holy name anymore with your gifts and idols. {20:40} For on my holy mountain, on the mountain of the height of Israel, says the Lord GOD, there shall all the house of Israel, all of them in the land, serve me; there I will accept them and require your offerings and the firstfruits of your oblations with all your holy things. {20:41} I will accept you with your sweet aroma when I bring you out from the peoples and gather you out of the countries where you have been scattered, and I will be sanctified in you before the nations. {20:42} You will know that I am the LORD when I bring you into the land of Israel, into the country I lifted my hand to give to your fathers. {20:43} There you will remember your ways and all your doings in which you have been defiled, and you will loathe yourselves in your own sight for all the evils you have committed. {20:44} You will know that I am the LORD when I have worked with you for my name's sake, not according to your wicked ways or your corrupt deeds, O house of Israel, says the Lord GOD. {20:45} Moreover, the word of the LORD came to me, saying, {20:46} Son of man, set your face toward the south, and drop your word toward the south; prophesy against the forest of the south field; {20:47} and say to the forest of the south, Hear the word of the LORD: Thus says the Lord GOD: Behold, I will kindle a fire in you, and it will devour every green tree and every dry tree. The flaming flame shall not be quenched, and all faces from the south to the north shall be burned in it. {20:48} All flesh shall see that I the LORD have kindled it; it shall not be quenched. {20:49} Then I said, Ah Lord GOD! They say of me, Does he not speak in parables?

{21:1} The word of the LORD came to me, saying, {21:2} Son of man, set your face toward Jerusalem, speak against the holy places, and prophesy against the land of Israel, {21:3} and say to the land of Israel, Thus says the LORD: Look, I am against you, and I will unsheathe my sword to cut off both the righteous and the wicked from you. {21:4} Since I will cut off both the righteous and the wicked, my sword will go out against all flesh from the south to the north. {21:5} So all people will know that I the LORD have unsheathed my sword; it will not return anymore. {21:6} Therefore, sigh, son of man, with a broken heart, and sigh bitterly in front of them. {21:7} When they ask you, Why are you sighing? you will answer, Because of the news that is coming. Every heart will melt, hands will grow weak, spirits will faint, and knees will be weak as water. Look, it is coming and will happen, says the Lord GOD. {21:8} Again, the word of the LORD came to me, saying, {21:9} Son of man, prophesy and say, Thus says the LORD: A sword! A sword is sharpened and polished! {21:10} It is sharpened for a great slaughter; it is polished to shine. Should we then rejoice? It despises the scepter of my son, as every tree. {21:11} He has given it to be polished so it can be handled; this sword is sharpened and polished to be put into the hands of the slayer. {21:12} Cry and wail, son of man, for it will be upon my people, upon all the leaders of Israel. Terror because of the sword will be upon my people; therefore, strike your thigh in anguish. {21:13} Because it is a test, and what if the sword despises even the scepter? It will be no more, says the Lord GOD. {21:14} Therefore, son of man, prophesy, and strike your hands together; let the sword be doubled for the third time, the sword of the slain. It is the sword of the great leaders that are slain, which goes into their inner chambers. {21:15} I have set the point of the sword against all their gates, so their hearts may faint, and their ruins may be multiplied. Ah! It is made bright, it is wrapped up for the slaughter. {21:16} Go one way or the other, either to the right or the left, wherever your face is set. {21:17} I will also strike my hands together, and my fury will rest. I the LORD have said it. {21:18} The word of the LORD came to me again, saying, {21:19} Also, son of man, appoint two ways for the sword of the king of Babylon to come. Both shall come from one land; choose a place at the head of the way to the city. {21:20} Designate a way for the sword to come to Rabbah of the Ammonites and to Judah in Jerusalem, the fortified city. {21:21} For the king of Babylon stands at the fork in the road, at the head of the two ways, to use divination. He shakes his arrows, consults images, and examines the liver. {21:22} On his right is the divination for Jerusalem, to appoint captains, to open the mouth for slaughter, to shout with a loud voice, to set up battering rams against the gates, to cast a mound, and to build a fort. {21:23} But this will be like a false divination in their sight to those who have sworn oaths. He will call to mind their wickedness, so they may be taken. {21:24} Therefore, thus says the Lord GOD: Because you have made your wickedness known and your sins are revealed in all your actions, since I say you will be remembered, you will be taken by force. {21:25} And you, profane, wicked prince of Israel, your day has come, the day when iniquity will end. {21:26} Thus says the Lord GOD: Remove the crown, and take off the diadem; it will not be the same. Exalt the low, and humble the high. {21:27} I will overturn, overturn, overturn it; it will be no more until he comes whose right it is; I will give it to him. {21:28} And you, son of man, prophesy and say, Thus says the Lord GOD concerning the Ammonites and their reproach. Say, The sword! The sword is drawn for slaughter, polished to consume because it shines. {21:29} While they see a false vision for you, while they divine a lie for you, to bring you upon the necks of the slain, of the wicked, whose day has come, when their iniquity will end. {21:30} Should I cause it to return to its sheath? I will judge you in the place where you were created, in the land of your birth. {21:31} I will pour out my fury upon you, I will blow against you in the fire of my wrath, and deliver you into the hands of cruel men skilled in destruction. {21:32} You will be fuel for the fire; your blood will be in the midst of the land; you will no longer be remembered, for I the LORD have spoken it.

{22:1} Moreover, the word of the LORD came to me, saying, {22:2} Now, son of man, will you judge the bloody city? Yes, you shall show her all her abominations. {22:3} Then say, Thus says the Lord GOD: The city sheds blood in the midst of it, so its time may come, and it makes idols to defile itself. {22:4} You are guilty for the blood you have shed and have defiled yourself with the idols you have made. You have caused your days to draw near and have reached your years; therefore, I have made you a reproach to the nations and a mockery to all countries. {22:5} Those near and those far from you will mock you, you who are infamous and much vexed. {22:6} Look, the leaders of Israel are all in you, eager to shed blood. {22:7} In you, they have disregarded father and mother; in your midst, they have oppressed the stranger; they have mistreated the fatherless and the widow. {22:8} You have despised my holy things and profaned my sabbaths. {22:9} There are men in you who carry tales to shed blood; in you, they feast on the mountains; in the midst of you, they commit lewd acts. {22:10} In you, they have exposed their fathers' nakedness; in you, they have humiliated the one set apart for impurity. {22:11} One has committed an abomination with his neighbor's wife; another has lewdly defiled his daughter-in-law; another has humiliated his sister, his father's daughter. {22:12} In you, they have taken bribes to shed blood; you have taken interest and gain, and have greedily extorted your neighbors, and have forgotten me, says the Lord GOD. {22:13} Look, therefore, I have struck my hand at your dishonest gain and the blood that has been in your midst. {22:14} Can your heart endure, or can your hands be strong, in the days when I deal with you? I the LORD have spoken it, and will do it. {22:15} I will scatter you among the nations and disperse you in the countries, and will cleanse your filthiness from you. {22:16} You will take your inheritance in yourself in the sight of the nations, and you will know that I am the LORD. {22:17} The word of the LORD came to me, saying, {22:18} Son of man, the house of Israel has become dross to me. All are brass, tin, iron, and lead in the midst of the furnace; they are even the dross of silver. {22:19} Therefore, thus says the Lord GOD: Because you have all become dross, behold, I will gather you into the midst of Jerusalem. {22:20} As they gather silver, brass, iron, lead, and tin into the furnace to blow the fire upon it to melt it, so will I gather you in my anger and my fury, and I will leave you there to melt. {22:21} Yes, I will gather you and blow upon you in the fire of my wrath, and you will be melted in the midst of it. {22:22} As silver is melted in the furnace, so will you be melted in the midst of it, and you will know that I the LORD have poured out my fury upon you. {22:23} The word of the LORD came to me, saying, {22:24} Son of man, say to her, You are the land that is not cleansed, nor rained upon in the day of indignation. {22:25} There is a conspiracy of her prophets in the midst of her, like a roaring lion tearing its prey. They have devoured souls; they have taken treasures and precious things; they have made many widows in the midst of her. {22:26} Her priests have violated my law and profaned my holy things; they have not distinguished between the holy and the profane, nor have they shown the difference between the clean and the unclean, and they have hidden their eyes from my sabbaths, and I am profaned among them. {22:27} Her leaders in the midst of her are like wolves tearing their prey, shedding blood, and destroying lives for dishonest gain. {22:28} And her prophets have plastered them with untempered mortar, seeing false visions, and divining lies for them, saying, Thus says the Lord GOD, when the LORD has not spoken. {22:29} The people of the land have practiced oppression and robbery, and have mistreated the poor and needy; yes, they have wrongfully oppressed the stranger. {22:30} And I searched for a man among them who would build up the wall and stand in the gap before me for the land, so I would not destroy it; but I found no one. {22:31} Therefore, I have poured out my indignation upon them; I have consumed them with the fire of my wrath; their own ways have been recompensed upon their heads, says the Lord GOD.

{23:1} The word of the Lord came to me again, saying, {23:2} "Son of man, there were two women, daughters of the same mother. {23:3} They were unfaithful in Egypt; they were unfaithful in their youth. There their breasts were fondled, and their virginity was violated. {23:4} The elder one was named Aholah, and her sister was Aholibah. They became mine, and they bore sons and daughters. Aholah represents Samaria, and Aholibah represents Jerusalem. {23:5} Aholah was unfaithful to me and lusted after her lovers, the Assyrians, her neighbors, {23:6} who were dressed in blue, leaders and commanders, all of them handsome young men, horsemen riding on horses. {23:7} She gave herself to them, all the elite of Assyria, and defiled herself with all the idols she lusted after. {23:8} She did not abandon the unfaithfulness she had learned in Egypt, where men had slept with her in her youth, fondled her breasts, and poured out their lust upon her. {23:9} Therefore, I handed her over to her lovers, the Assyrians she lusted after. {23:10} They stripped her naked, took her sons and daughters, and killed her with the sword. She became a byword among women, and they carried out judgment upon her. {23:11} Her sister Aholibah saw this, yet she was more corrupt in her lust than her sister, and in her unfaithfulness she was worse than Aholah. {23:12} She too lusted after the Assyrians, leaders and commanders, handsomely dressed horsemen, all of them desirable young men. {23:13} I saw that she too had defiled herself, both sisters followed the same path. {23:14} But Aholibah went further, for she saw men portrayed on the wall, images of Babylonians painted in bright red, {23:15} with belts around their waists and flowing turbans on their heads. All of them looked like Babylonian officers, born in Chaldea. {23:16} As soon as she saw them, she lusted after them and sent messengers to them in Babylon. {23:17} Then the Babylonians came to her bed of love, and in their lust they defiled her. After she was defiled by them, she turned away from them in disgust. {23:18} When she exposed her unfaithfulness and revealed her nakedness, I turned away from her in disgust, just as I had turned away from her sister. {23:19} Yet she multiplied her acts of unfaithfulness, remembering the days of her youth when she prostituted herself in Egypt. {23:20} She lusted after her lovers, whose genitals were like those of donkeys and whose emission was like that of horses. {23:21} So you longed for the lewdness of your youth, when in Egypt your breasts were fondled and your virgin bosom was caressed. {23:22} Therefore, Aholibah, this is what the Lord God says: I will stir up your lovers against you, those you turned away from in disgust, and I will bring them against you on every side—{23:23} the Babylonians and all the Chaldeans, the men of Pekod, Shoa, and Koa, and all the Assyrians with them—handsome young men, leaders and commanders, officers and men of renown, all riding on horses. {23:24} They will come against you with weapons, chariots, and wagons, with a host of people. They will surround you with shields, helmets, and armor. I will give them authority to judge you, and they will judge you according to their laws. {23:25} I will direct my jealousy against you, and they will deal with you in fury. They will cut off your nose and ears, and those who remain will fall by the sword. They will take your sons and daughters, and those who survive will be consumed by fire. {23:26} They will also strip you of your clothes and take your fine jewelry. {23:27} So I will put an end to your lewdness and your prostitution brought from Egypt. You will no longer look to them or remember Egypt anymore. {23:28} For this is what the Lord God says: I will deliver you into the hands of those you hate, into the hands of those you turned away from in disgust. {23:29} They will deal with you in hatred, take away everything you have worked for, and leave you naked and bare. The shame of your prostitution will be exposed. Your lewdness and promiscuity {23:30} have brought this upon you because you lusted after the nations and defiled yourself with their idols. {23:31} You have followed the path of your sister, so I will put her cup into your hand. {23:32} This is what the Lord God says: You will drink from your sister's cup, a cup large and deep. It will bring scorn and derision, for it holds much. {23:33} You will be filled with drunkenness and sorrow, the cup of ruin and desolation, the cup of your sister Samaria. {23:34} You will drink it and drain it dry; you will break its pieces and tear your breasts, for I have spoken, declares the Lord God. {23:35} Therefore, this is what the Lord God says: Because you have forgotten me and cast me behind your back, you must bear the consequences of your lewdness and prostitution." {23:36} The Lord said to me, "Son of man, will you judge Aholah and Aholibah? Confront them with their detestable practices, {23:37} for they have committed adultery and blood is on their hands. They committed adultery with their idols; they even sacrificed their children, whom they bore to me, as food for these idols. {23:38} They have also done this to me: On the same day they defiled my sanctuary and profaned my Sabbaths. {23:39} On the very day they sacrificed their children to their idols, they entered my sanctuary and desecrated it. That is what they did in my house. {23:40} They even sent messengers for men to come from far away, and when they arrived, you bathed yourself, painted your eyes, and adorned yourself with jewelry. {23:41} You sat on an elegant couch, with a table spread before it, on which you had placed my incense and my oil. {23:42} The sound of a carefree crowd was around her; Sabeans from the desert were brought in, and they put bracelets on her arms and beautiful crowns on her head. {23:43} Then I said about the one worn out by adultery, 'Now let them use her as a prostitute, for that is what she is.' {23:44} And they went to her, as men go to a prostitute. So they went in to Aholah and Aholibah, the lewd women. {23:45} But righteous men will judge them as adulteresses and murderers, for they are adulteresses, and blood is on their hands. {23:46} This is what the Lord God says: I will bring a mob against them, and they will be stoned and cut down with their swords. {23:47} They will kill their sons and daughters and burn down their houses. {23:48} So I will put an end to lewdness in the land, that all women may take warning and not imitate your lewdness. {23:49} You will suffer the penalty for your lewdness and bear the consequences of your sins of idolatry. Then you will know that I am the Lord God."

{24:1} In the ninth year, in the tenth month, on the tenth day, the word of the Lord came to me: {24:2} "Son of man, record this date, this very day, because the king of Babylon has laid siege to Jerusalem this very day. {24:3} Tell this rebellious people a parable and say to them: 'This is what the Lord God says: Put a pot on the fire; put it on and pour water into it. {24:4} Put into it the pieces of meat, all the choice pieces—the leg and the shoulder. Fill it with the best of the bones; {24:5} take the choicest of the flock. Pile wood beneath it for the bones; bring it to a boil and cook the bones in it.' {24:6} For this is what the Lord God says: Woe to the city of bloodshed, to the pot now encrusted, whose deposit will not go away! Take the meat out piece by piece in whatever order it comes. {24:7} For the blood she shed is in her midst: She poured it on the bare rock; she did not pour it on the ground, where the dust would cover it. {24:8} To stir up wrath and take vengeance, I put her blood on the bare rock, so it would not be covered. {24:9} Therefore, this is what the Lord God says: Woe to the city of bloodshed! I too will pile the wood high.{24:10} Pile on the wood, light the fire, cook the meat, and season it well, and let the bones be burned. {24:11} Then set the empty pot on the coals so it can heat up and its bronze will glow; let the impurities within it melt away and be consumed. {24:12} But the city has exhausted itself with deceit, and its great impurities have not gone out of it; therefore, its scum will remain in the fire. {24:13} In your uncleanness is lewdness, and even though I tried to cleanse you, you would not be purified. You will not be cleaned anymore until I unleash my wrath upon you. {24:14} I, the LORD, have spoken; it will happen, and I will act. I will not hold back, show pity, or change my mind. You will be judged according to your conduct and actions, declares the Sovereign LORD. {24:15} Again, the word of the LORD came to me, saying, {24:16} Son of man, I am about to take away from you the delight of your eyes with a single blow, but you must not mourn, cry, or shed any tears. {24:17} Groan silently, but do not weep or mourn for the dead. Keep your head covered and your sandals on your feet. Do not cover your lips (a sign of mourning), and do not eat the customary food of mourners. {24:18} So I spoke to the people in the morning, and that evening my wife died. The next morning I did as I had been commanded. {24:19} The people asked me, "Will you not tell us what these things mean for us, why you are acting like this?" {24:20} So I said to them, The word of the LORD came to me, saying, {24:21} Tell the house of Israel, 'This is what the Sovereign LORD says: I am about to desecrate my sanctuary—the stronghold in which you take pride, the delight of your eyes, and the object of your affection. And your sons and daughters whom you left behind will fall by the sword. {24:22} And you will do as I have done: You will not cover your lips or eat the bread of mourners. {24:23} You will keep your turbans on your heads and your sandals on your feet. You will not mourn or weep but will waste away because of your sins and groan among yourselves. {24:24} Ezekiel will be a sign to you; you will do just as he has done. When this happens, you will know that I am the Sovereign LORD.' {24:25} And you, son of man, on the day I take away their stronghold, their joy and glory, the delight of their eyes, their hearts' desire, along with their sons and daughters— {24:26} on that day a fugitive will come to you & report the news. {24:27} On that day your mouth will be opened to the one who has escaped, and you will speak & no longer be silent. You will be a sign to them, and they will know that I am the LORD.

{25:1} The word of the LORD came to me again, saying, {25:2} "Son of man, turn your face toward the Ammonites and prophesy against them; {25:3} and say to the Ammonites, 'Hear the word of the Lord GOD: This is what the Lord GOD says: Because you said, "Aha!" against my sanctuary when it was profaned, and against the land of Israel when it was desolate, and against the house of Judah when they went into captivity; {25:4} behold, I will deliver you to the people of the east as a possession. They will set up their palaces in you and make their homes in you; they will eat your fruit and drink your milk. {25:5} I will make Rabbah a pasture for camels and the Ammonites a resting place for flocks; then you will know that I am the LORD. {25:6} For this is what the Lord GOD says: Because you clapped your hands, stomped your feet, and rejoiced with a spiteful heart against the land of Israel, {25:7} behold, I will stretch out my hand against you, and I will give you as plunder to the nations. I will cut you off from the people and cause you to perish from the countries; I will destroy you, and you will know that I am the LORD. {25:8} This is what the Lord GOD says: Because Moab and Seir say, "Look, the house of Judah is like all the other nations," {25:9} therefore, behold, I will open up the side of Moab from the cities, from its cities at the border, the glory of the country—Bethjeshimoth, Baalmeon, and Kiriathaim— {25:10} to the people of the east along with the Ammonites, and I will give them possession so that the Ammonites may not be remembered among the nations. {25:11} I will execute judgments upon Moab, and they will know that I am the LORD. {25:12} This is what the Lord GOD says: Because Edom has acted against the house of Judah by taking vengeance and has greatly offended and sought revenge against them; {25:13} therefore, this is what the Lord GOD says: I will stretch out my hand against Edom, and I will cut off both man & beast from it; I will make it desolate from Teman, and those of Dedan will fall by the sword. {25:14} I will lay my vengeance upon Edom by the hand of my people Israel; they will carry out my anger and fury against Edom, and they will know my vengeance, says the Lord GOD. {25:15} This is what the Lord GOD says: Because the Philistines have acted out of revenge & taken vengeance with a spiteful heart to destroy for old hatred; {25:16} therefore, this is what the Lord says: Behold, I will stretch out my hand against the Philistines, and I will cut off the Cherethites and destroy the remnant of the seacoast. {25:17} I will execute great vengeance upon them with furious rebukes, and they will know that I am the LORD when I lay my vengeance upon them.

{26:1} In the eleventh year, on the first day of the month, the word of the LORD came to me, saying, {26:2} "Son of man, because Tyrus has said against Jerusalem, 'Aha! She is broken, who was the gates of the people; she has turned to me; I shall be replenished now that she is laid waste,' {26:3} therefore, this is what the Lord GOD says: Behold, I am against you, O Tyrus, and I will bring many nations against you, like the waves of the sea. {26:4} They will destroy the walls of Tyrus and break down her towers; I will scrape her dust from her and make her like the top of a rock. {26:5} It will be a place for spreading nets in the midst of the sea; for I have spoken it, says the Lord GOD, and it will become plunder for the nations. {26:6} Her daughters in the field will be slain by the sword, and they will know that I am the LORD. {26:7} For this is what the Lord GOD says: Behold, I will bring upon Tyrus Nebuchadnezzar, king of Babylon, a king of kings from the north, with horses, chariots, horsemen, and a vast army. {26:8} He will slay your daughters in the field; he will make a fort against you, cast a mound against you, and raise a shield against you. {26:9} He will set up siege engines against your walls, and with his axes he will break down your towers. {26:10} Because of the abundance of his horses, their dust will cover you; your walls will shake at the noise of the horsemen, the wheels, and the chariots when he enters your gates like a man entering a city that has been breached. {26:11} With the hooves of his horses he will trample all your streets; he will slay your people by the sword, and your strongholds will fall to the ground. {26:12} They will make a spoil of your riches and prey on your merchandise; they will break down your walls, destroy your pleasant houses, and throw your stones, timber, and dust into the water. {26:13} I will cause the noise of your songs to cease, and the sound of your harps will no longer be heard. {26:14} I will make you like the top of a rock; you will become a place to spread nets upon; you will never be rebuilt, for I the LORD have spoken it, says the Lord GOD. {26:15} This is what the Lord GOD says to Tyrus: Will not the islands shake at the sound of your fall, when the wounded cry and the slaughter is made among you? {26:16} Then all the princes of the sea will come down from their thrones, lay aside their robes, and put off their embroidered garments; they will clothe themselves with trembling and sit on the ground, trembling at every moment, astonished at you. {26:17} They will take up a lament for you and say to you, 'How have you been destroyed, you renowned city inhabited by seafaring men, strong at sea, you and your inhabitants who caused terror among those who haunt it?' {26:18} Now the islands will tremble on the day of your fall; yes, the islands in the sea will be troubled at your departure. {26:19} For this is what the Lord GOD says: When I make you a desolate city, like the cities that are not inhabited; when I bring up the deep upon you, and great waters cover you; {26:20} when I bring you down with those who go down to the pit, with people of old, and set you in the low parts of the earth, in places desolate of old, with those who go down to the pit so that you will not be inhabited; and I will set glory in the land of the living; {26:21} I will make you a terror, and you will be no more; though you will be sought for, you will never be found again, says the Lord GOD.

{27:1} The word of the LORD came to me again, saying, {27:2} "Now, son of man, take up a lament for Tyrus; {27:3} and say to Tyrus, 'O you who are located at the entrance of the sea, a merchant for the people of many islands, this is what the Lord GOD says: O Tyrus, you have said, "I am perfect in beauty." {27:4} Your borders are in the midst of the seas, and your builders have perfected your beauty. {27:5} They made all your ship boards from fir trees of Senir; they took cedars from Lebanon to make masts for you. {27:6} They used the oaks of Bashan for your oars; the company of the Ashurites made your benches from ivory, brought from the islands of Chittim. {27:7} Fine linen with embroidered work from Egypt was what you spread for your sail; blue and purple from the islands of Elishah covered you. {27:8} The inhabitants of Zidon and Arvad were your sailors; your wise men, O Tyrus, were your pilots. {27:9} The elders of Gebal and their wise men were your caulkers; all the ships of the sea and their sailors were in you to conduct your trade. {27:10} The men of Persia, Lud, and Phut were in your army, your warriors; they hung shields and helmets on you and made your beauty perfect. {27:11} The men of Arvad were on your walls all around, and the Gammadims were in your towers; they hung their shields on your walls all around and made your beauty perfect. {27:12} Tarshish was your merchant because of the abundance of all kinds of riches; they traded silver, iron, tin, and lead at your fairs. {27:13} Javan, Tubal, and Meshech were your merchants; they traded human lives and bronze vessels in your markets. {27:14} The house of Togarmah traded in your fairs with horses, horsemen, and mules. {27:15} The men of Dedan were your merchants; many islands were the merchandise of your hand; they brought you gifts of ivory and ebony. {27:16} Syria was your merchant because of the many goods you produced; they traded in your fairs with emeralds, purple, embroidered work, fine linen, coral, and agate. {27:17} Judah and the land of Israel were your merchants; they traded in your market wheat from Minnith, Pannag, honey, oil, and balm. {27:18} Damascus was your merchant because of the abundance of your goods; they traded wine from Helbon and white wool. {27:19} Dan and Javan traveled back and forth in your fairs; bright iron, cassia, and calamus were in your market. {27:20} Dedan was your merchant in fine clothes for chariots. {27:21} Arabia and all the princes of Kedar traded with you in lambs, rams, and goats; these were your merchants. {27:22} The merchants of Sheba and Raamah were your merchants; they traded with you in the finest spices, precious stones, and gold. {27:23} Haran, Canneh, and Eden, the merchants of Sheba, Asshur, and Chilmad were your merchants. {27:24} These were your merchants in all sorts of things: blue clothes, embroidered work, chests of rich apparel bound with cords and made of cedar, among your merchandise. {27:25} The ships of Tarshish sang of you in your market; you were filled and made very glorious in the midst of the seas. {27:26} Your rowers brought you into deep waters; the east wind has broken you in the midst of the seas. {27:27} Your riches, your fairs, your merchandise, your sailors, and your pilots, your caulkers, and all who trade your merchandise, and all your warriors in you, and all your crew in the midst of you, will fall into the sea on the day of your ruin. {27:28} The coasts will shake at the sound of your sailors' cries. {27:29} All who handle the oar, the sailors, and all the pilots of the sea will come down from their ships; they will stand on the land; {27:30} and they will raise their voices against you, crying bitterly, and will throw dust on their heads, and roll in ashes. {27:31} They will make themselves completely bald for you, and put on sackcloth, and will weep for you with bitterness of heart and deep mourning. {27:32} In their mourning, they will take up a lament for you, saying, 'What city is like Tyrus, like the destroyed city in the midst of the sea?' {27:33} When your goods went out to the seas, you enriched many people; you enriched the kings of the earth with the multitude of your riches and merchandise. {27:34} Now you are broken by the seas in the depths of the waters; your merchandise and all your crew will fall in the midst of you. {27:35} All the inhabitants of the islands will be astonished at you, and their kings will be filled with fear; they will be troubled in their faces. {27:36} The merchants among the people will hiss at you; you will be a terror and will never exist again.'"

{28:1} The word of the LORD came to me again, saying, {28:2} "Son of man, say to the prince of Tyrus, 'This is what the Lord GOD says: Because your heart is lifted up, and you have said, "I am a God; I sit in the seat of God in the midst of the seas," yet you are a man and not a God, though you set your heart like the heart of God. {28:3} Behold, you are wiser than Daniel; there is no secret that they can hide from you. {28:4} With your wisdom and understanding, you have gained wealth and accumulated gold and silver in your treasures. {28:5} By your great wisdom and through your trade, you have increased your wealth, and your heart is lifted up because of your riches. {28:6} Therefore, this is what the Lord GOD says: Because you have set your heart like the heart of God, {28:7} behold, I will bring strangers against you, the most ruthless of the nations; they will draw their swords against the beauty of your wisdom and will defile your splendor. {28:8} They will bring you down to the pit, and you will die the deaths of those who are slain in the midst of the seas. {28:9} Will you still say before the one who slays you, "I am a God"? You will be a man and not a God, in the hands of the one who slays you. {28:10} You will die the deaths of the uncircumcised by the hands of strangers; for I have spoken it, says the Lord GOD. {28:11} Moreover, the word of the LORD came to me, saying, {28:12} "Son of man, take up a lament for the king of Tyrus, and say to him, 'This is what the Lord GOD says: You were the seal of perfection, full of wisdom and perfect in beauty. {28:13} You were in Eden, the garden of God; every precious stone was your covering: sardius, topaz, and diamond, beryl, onyx, and jasper, sapphire, emerald, and carbuncle; the workmanship of your tambourines and pipes was prepared for you on the day you were created. {28:14} You were the anointed cherub who covers; I established you; you were on the holy mountain of God; you walked among the fiery stones. {28:15} You were perfect in your ways from the day you were created, until iniquity was found in you. {28:16} Through the abundance of your trade, you filled your midst with violence, and you sinned; therefore, I will cast you as a profane thing out of the mountain of God, and I will destroy you, O covering cherub, from the midst of the fiery stones. {28:17} Your heart was lifted up because of your beauty; you corrupted your wisdom for the sake of your splendor. I will cast you to the ground; I will lay you before kings, that they may see you. {28:18} You defiled your sanctuaries by the multitude of your iniquities, by the iniquity of your trade; therefore, I will bring forth a fire from your midst, and it will devour you, and I will bring you to ashes on the earth in the sight of all who see you. {28:19} All who know you among the people will be astonished at you; you will be a terror, and you will never exist again." {28:20} Again, the word of the LORD came to me, saying, {28:21} "Son of man, set your face against Zidon and prophesy against it, {28:22} and say, 'This is what the Lord GOD says: Behold, I am against you, O Zidon, and I will be glorified in your midst; and they will know that I am the LORD when I execute judgments in you and am sanctified in you. {28:23} For I will send a plague upon you, and blood will be in your streets; and the wounded will fall in your midst, by the sword upon every side; and they will know that I am the LORD. {28:24} And there shall be no more a pricking brier to the house of Israel, nor any grieving thorn of all that are round about them, who despised them; and they shall know that I am the Lord GOD. {28:25} Thus says the Lord GOD: When I gather the house of Israel from the people among whom they are scattered, and shall be sanctified in them in the sight of the nations, then they will dwell in their own land, which I gave to my servant Jacob. {28:26} And they will dwell safely there, and build houses and plant vineyards; yes, they will dwell with confidence when I execute judgments upon all those who despise them around them; and they will know that I am the LORD their God."

{29:1} In the tenth year, on the tenth month, on the twelfth day, the word of the LORD came to me, saying, {29:2} "Son of man, set your face against Pharaoh, king of Egypt, and prophesy against him and all of Egypt. {29:3} Say, 'This is what the Lord GOD says: Behold, I am against you, Pharaoh, king of Egypt, the great dragon lying in the midst of his rivers, who says, "My river is my own; I made it for myself." {29:4} But I will put hooks in your jaws and make the fish of your rivers stick to your scales; I will bring you up out of the rivers, and all the fish will stick to your scales. {29:5} I will leave you thrown into the wilderness, you and all the fish of your rivers; you will fall in the open fields and will not be gathered or collected. I have given you as food to the beasts of the field and the birds of the air. {29:6} Then all the inhabitants of Egypt will know that I am the LORD because they have been a broken reed to the house of Israel. {29:7} When they took hold of you, you broke and caused all their shoulders to dislocate; when they leaned on you, you broke and made their backs stand still. {29:8} Therefore, this is what the Lord GOD says: Behold, I will bring a sword against you and cut off man and beast from you. {29:9} The land of Egypt will become desolate and waste; then they will know that I am the LORD because they have said, "The river is mine, and I made it." {29:10} Behold, I am against you and your rivers, and I will make the land of Egypt utterly desolate, from the tower of Syene to the border of Ethiopia. {29:11} No foot of man or beast will pass through it; it will not be inhabited for forty years. {29:12} I will make the land of Egypt desolate among desolate countries, and her cities among the cities laid waste will be desolate for forty years; I will scatter the Egyptians among the nations and disperse them throughout the countries. {29:13} Yet, this is what the Lord GOD says: At the end of forty years, I will gather the Egyptians from the nations where they were scattered. {29:14} I will bring back the captives of Egypt and cause them to return to the land of Pathros, their homeland; they will be a lowly kingdom. {29:15} It will be the lowest of the kingdoms; it will no longer lift itself up above the nations, for I will diminish them so they will no longer rule over the nations. {29:16} It will no longer be a source of confidence for the house of Israel, bringing to mind their iniquity when they look after them; but they will know that I am the Lord GOD. {29:17} In the twenty-seventh year, on the first month, on the first day, the word of the LORD came to me, saying, {29:18} "Son of man, Nebuchadnezzar, king of Babylon, made his army serve a great service against Tyrus; every head was made bald, and every shoulder was scraped, yet he received no wages, nor did his army, for the service they rendered against Tyrus. {29:19} Therefore, this is what the Lord GOD says: Behold, I will give the land of Egypt to Nebuchadnezzar, king of Babylon; he will take her multitude, her spoil, and her prey; it will be the wages for his army. {29:20} I have given him the land of Egypt for his labor against it because they worked for me, says the Lord GOD. {29:21} In that day, I will cause the horn of the house of Israel to bud, and I will give you an opening of the mouth in their midst; they will know that I am the LORD.

{30:1} The word of the LORD came to me again, saying, {30:2} "Son of man, prophesy and say, 'Thus says the Lord GOD: Woe to the day! {30:3} For the day is near, even the day of the LORD; it is a cloudy day, a time for the nations. {30:4} A sword will come upon Egypt, and great pain will be in Ethiopia when the slain fall in Egypt, and they will take away her multitude, and her foundations will be broken down. {30:5} Ethiopia, Libya, Lydia, and all the mingled people, and Chub, along with the men of the land who are in league, will fall with them by the sword. {30:6} Thus says the LORD: Those who support Egypt will fall, and the pride of her power will come down; from the tower of Syene, they will fall by the sword, says the Lord GOD. {30:7} They will be desolate among desolate countries, and her cities will be among the cities that are laid waste. {30:8} They will know that I am the LORD when I set a fire in Egypt, and all her helpers will be destroyed. {30:9} In that day, messengers will go out from me in ships to frighten the careless Ethiopians, and great pain will come upon them, as in the day of Egypt; for it is coming. {30:10} Thus says the Lord GOD: I will also cause the multitude of Egypt to cease by the hand of Nebuchadnezzar, king of Babylon. {30:11} He and his people, the fiercest of nations, will come to destroy the land; they will draw their swords against Egypt and fill the land with the slain. {30:12} I will make the rivers dry and sell the land into the hands of the wicked; I will make the land waste, and all that is in it, by the hand of strangers; I, the LORD, have spoken it. {30:13} Thus says the Lord GOD: I will also destroy the idols and cause their images to cease out of Noph; there will no longer be a prince in the land of Egypt, and I will put fear in the land of Egypt. {30:14} I will make Pathros desolate and set fire in Zoan, and I will execute judgments in No. {30:15} I will pour my fury upon Sin, the strength of Egypt; I will cut off the multitude of No. {30:16} I will set fire in Egypt; Sin will have great pain, and No will be torn apart, and Noph will suffer daily distress. {30:17} The young men of Aven and Pibeseth will fall by the sword, and these cities will go into captivity. {30:18} At Tehaphnehes, the day will be darkened when I break the yokes of Egypt; the pride of her strength will cease; a cloud will cover her, and her daughters will go into captivity. {30:19} Thus will I execute judgments in Egypt, and they will know that I am the LORD. {30:20} In the eleventh year, on the first month, on the seventh day, the word of the LORD came to me, saying, {30:21} "Son of man, I have broken the arm of Pharaoh, king of Egypt; it will not be bound up to heal it or to put a roller to make it strong enough to hold a sword. {30:22} Therefore, this is what the Lord GOD says: Behold, I am against Pharaoh, king of Egypt, and I will break his arms, both the strong and the broken, and I will cause the sword to fall out of his hand. {30:23} I will scatter the Egyptians among the nations and disperse them throughout the countries. {30:24} I will strengthen the arms of the king of Babylon and put my sword in his hand; but I will break Pharaoh's arms, and he will groan like a man fatally wounded. {30:25} I will strengthen the arms of the king of Babylon, while the arms of Pharaoh will fall; and they will know that I am the LORD when I put my sword in the hand of the king of Babylon and he stretches it out over the land of Egypt. {30:26} I will scatter the Egyptians among the nations and disperse them among the countries; and they will know that I am the LORD."

{31:1} In the eleventh year, on the third month, on the first day, the word of the LORD came to me, saying, {31:2} "Son of man, speak to Pharaoh, king of Egypt, and to his multitude; whom are you like in your greatness? {31:3} Consider this: the Assyrian was a cedar in Lebanon, with beautiful branches, a shadowy canopy, and of great height; his top was among the thick branches. {31:4} The waters made him great; the deep waters lifted him up high with rivers surrounding his plants, and sent out little rivers to all the trees of the field. {31:5} His height was exalted above all the trees of the field; his branches were multiplied, and they grew long because of the abundance of water when he sprouted. {31:6} All the birds of the sky made their nests in his branches, and under his branches, all the beasts of the field gave birth; under his shadow lived all the great nations. {31:7} Thus, he was beautiful in his greatness, in the length of his branches, because his roots were by great waters. {31:8} The cedars in God's garden could not hide him; the fir trees were not like his branches, and the chestnut trees were not like his boughs; no tree in God's garden was as beautiful as he. {31:9} I made him beautiful by the multitude of his branches, so that all the trees of Eden in God's garden envied him. {31:10} Therefore, this is what the Lord GOD says: Because you have lifted yourself up in height, and your top has shot up among the thick branches, and your heart is lifted up in your height, {31:11} I have delivered you into the hand of the mighty one of the nations; he will surely deal with you: I have cast you out for your wickedness. {31:12} Strangers, the most fearsome of nations, have cut you down and left you; on the mountains and in all the valleys, your branches have fallen, and your boughs are broken by all the rivers of the land; all the people of the earth have gone down from your shadow and left you. {31:13} On your ruin will all the birds of the sky remain, and all the beasts of the field will be upon your branches. {31:14} So that none of all the trees by the waters will exalt themselves for their height, nor shoot up their tops among the thick boughs; all those that drink water will be delivered to death, to the depths of the earth, among the children of men, with those who go down to the pit. {31:15} This is what the Lord GOD says: On the day he went down to the grave, I caused a mourning; I covered the deep waters for him, restrained the floods, and the great waters were stopped; Lebanon mourned for him, and all the trees of the field fainted for him. {31:16} I made the nations tremble at the sound of his fall when I cast him down to the grave with those who descend into the pit; all the trees of Eden, the best and choicest of Lebanon, all that drink water, will be comforted in the depths of the earth. {31:17} They also went down to the grave with him, with those slain by the sword; and those who were his strength, who dwelt under his shadow among the nations. {31:18} To whom are you thus like in glory and greatness among the trees of Eden? Yet you will be brought down with the trees of Eden to the depths of the earth; you will lie among the uncircumcised (not circumcised) with those slain by the sword. This is Pharaoh and all his multitude, says the Lord GOD.

{32:1} In the twelfth year, on the twelfth month, on the first day, the word of the LORD came to me, saying, {32:2} "Son of man, take up a lament (a passionate expression of grief) for Pharaoh, king of Egypt, and say to him, 'You are like a young lion among the nations, and like a whale in the seas; you came forth with your rivers and troubled the waters with your feet, and fouled their rivers. {32:3} This is what the Lord GOD says: I will spread my net over you with a company of many people; they will bring you up in my net. {32:4} Then I will leave you on the land; I will cast you forth upon the open field, and I will cause all the birds of the sky to remain upon you, and I will fill the beasts of the whole earth with you. {32:5} I will lay your flesh upon the mountains, and fill the valleys with your height. {32:6} I will also water the land where you swim with your blood, even to the mountains; the rivers will be full of you. {32:7} And when I put you out, I will cover the heavens and darken their stars; I will cover the sun with a cloud, and the moon will not give her light. {32:8} All the bright lights of heaven will be dark over you, and darkness will be upon your land, says the Lord GOD. {32:9} I will also disturb the hearts of many people when I bring your destruction among the nations, into the countries you have not known. {32:10} Yes, I will make many people amazed at you, and their kings will be horrified because of you when I brandish my sword before them; they will tremble at every moment, each man for his own life, on the day of your fall. {32:11} For this is what the Lord GOD says: The sword of the king of Babylon will come against you. {32:12} By the swords of the mighty, I will cause your multitude to fall, the most fearsome of the nations, all of them; they will spoil the splendor of Egypt, and all its multitude will be destroyed. {32:13} I will also destroy all the beasts beside the great waters; neither will the foot of man trouble them any more, nor the hooves of beasts trouble them. {32:14} Then I will make their waters deep, and cause their rivers to run like oil, says the Lord GOD. {32:15} When I make the land of Egypt desolate, and the country becomes destitute of all it was full of, when I strike all who dwell therein, then they will know that I am the LORD. {32:16} This is the lamentation with which they will lament her: the daughters of the nations will lament her; they will lament for her, for Egypt and all her multitude, says the Lord GOD. {32:17} It also came to pass in the twelfth year, on the fifteenth day of the month, that the word of the LORD came to me, saying, {32:18} "Son of man, wail for the multitude of Egypt, and cast them down, even her and the daughters of the famous nations, to the depths of the earth, with those who go down into the pit. {32:19} Whom do you surpass in beauty? Go down and lie with the uncircumcised. {32:20} They will fall in the midst of those slain by the sword; she is delivered to the sword; draw her and all her multitudes. {32:21} The strong among the mighty will speak to him out of the midst of hell with those who helped him: they have gone down; they lie uncircumcised, slain by the sword. {32:22} Assyria is there with all her company; their graves are around her; all of them are slain, fallen by the sword. {32:23} Their graves are set in the sides of the pit, and her company is round about her grave; all of them are slain, fallen by the sword, which caused terror in the land of the living. {32:24} There is Elam and all her multitude round about her grave; all of them are slain, fallen by the sword, who have gone down uncircumcised to the depths of the earth, causing terror in the land of the living; yet they have borne their shame with those who go down to the pit. {32:25} They have set her a bed in the midst of the slain with all her multitude; her graves are around her, all of them uncircumcised, slain by the sword; though they caused terror in the land of the living, they have borne their shame with those who go down to the pit; he is placed among the slain. {32:26} There is Meshech, Tubal, and all her multitude; their graves are around her, all of them uncircumcised, slain by the sword, though they caused their terror in the land of the living. {32:27} They will not lie with the mighty who have fallen among the uncircumcised, who have gone down to hell with their weapons of war; they have laid their swords under their heads, but their iniquities will be upon their bones, though they were the terror of the mighty in the land of the living. {32:28} Yes, you will be broken in the midst of the uncircumcised and will lie with those slain by the sword. {32:29} There is Edom, her kings and all her princes, who with their might are laid with those slain by the sword; they will lie with the uncircumcised and with those who go down to the pit. {32:30} There are the princes of the north, all of them, and all the Zidonians, who have gone down with the slain; with their terror, they are ashamed of their might, and they lie uncircumcised with those slain by the sword, and bear their shame with those who go down to the pit. {32:31} Pharaoh will see them and will be comforted over all his multitude, even Pharaoh and all his army slain by the sword, says the Lord GOD. {32:32} For I have caused my terror in the land of the living; and he will be laid among the uncircumcised with those slain by the sword, even Pharaoh and all his multitude, says the Lord GOD.

{33:1} Again, the word of the LORD came to me, saying, {33:2} "Son of man, speak to the people of your land and say to them, 'When I bring a sword (a threat of war or destruction) upon a land, if the people take a man from among them and appoint him as their watchman, {33:3} if he sees the sword coming upon the land and blows the trumpet to warn the people, {33:4} then whoever hears the sound of the trumpet and does not take warning—if the sword comes and takes him away, his blood will be on his own head. {33:5} He heard the sound of the trumpet and did not take warning; his blood will be on him. But whoever takes warning will save their life. {33:6} But if the watchman sees the sword coming and does not blow the trumpet, and the people are not warned, and the sword comes and takes someone away, that person will be taken away in their sin, but I will hold the watchman accountable for their blood. {33:7} So, son of man, I have made you a watchman for the house of Israel; therefore, you will hear the word from my mouth and warn them from me. {33:8} When I say to the wicked, 'You will surely die,' and you do not speak to warn the wicked to turn from their ways, that wicked person will die in their sin, but I will hold you accountable for their blood. {33:9} However, if you warn the wicked to turn from their ways and they do not turn, they will die in their sin, but you will have saved your own life. {33:10} Therefore, son of man, say to the house of Israel: 'You say, "Our sins and transgressions weigh upon us, and we waste away because of them. How can we live?"' {33:11} Say to them, 'As I live, declares the Lord GOD, I have no pleasure in the death of the wicked, but rather that the wicked turn from their ways and live. Turn, turn from your evil ways! Why will you die, O house of Israel?' {33:12} Therefore, son of man, say to your people: 'The righteousness of the righteous will not save them when they sin, nor will the wickedness of the wicked cause them to stumble when they turn from their wickedness; nor will the righteous be able to live by their righteousness on the day they sin. {33:13} If I say to the righteous that they will surely live, but they trust in their own righteousness and commit sin, none of their righteous deeds will be remembered, and they will die for their sin. {33:14} Again, if I say to the wicked, "You will surely die," and they turn from their sin and do what is lawful and right, {33:15} if the wicked returns what they took in pledge, gives back what they robbed, walks in the statutes of life without committing iniquity, they will surely live; they will not die. {33:16} None of the sins they committed will be remembered against them; they have done what is lawful and right; they will surely live. {33:17} Yet your people say, "The way of the LORD is not fair," but it is their way that is not fair. {33:18} When the righteous turn from their righteousness and commit sin, they will die because of it. {33:19} But if the wicked turn from their wickedness and do what is lawful and right, they will live because of it. {33:20} Yet you say, "The way of the LORD is not fair." O house of Israel, I will judge each of you according to your own ways.' {33:21} In the twelfth year of our exile, in the tenth month, on the fifth day of the month, a man who had escaped from Jerusalem came to me and said, 'The city has been taken.' {33:22} Now the hand of the LORD was upon me in the evening before the escaped man came to me, and he opened my mouth until he came to me in the morning; my mouth was opened, and I was no longer mute. {33:23} Then the word of the LORD came to me, saying, {33:24} "Son of man, those who live in the ruins of the land of Israel say, 'Abraham was one man, and he inherited the land; but we are many, and the land is given to us as our inheritance.' {33:25} Therefore, say to them, 'Thus says the Lord GOD: You eat meat with the blood still in it, lift your eyes to your idols, and shed blood. Do you think you will possess the land? {33:26} You rely on your sword, commit abominations, and defile your neighbor's wife. Do you think you will possess the land? {33:27} Say this to them: 'Thus says the Lord GOD: As I live, surely those in the ruins will fall by the sword, and I will give those in the open fields to the beasts to be devoured, and those in strongholds and caves will die of pestilence. {33:28} For I will make the land desolate, and the pride of her strength will cease; the mountains of Israel will be desolate, so that no one will pass through. {33:29} Then they will know that I am the LORD when I make the land desolate because of all the detestable things they have done.' {33:30} And as for you, son of man, your people are still talking against you by the walls and in the doors of the houses, saying to one another, 'Come, hear what the word is that comes from the LORD.' {33:31} They come to you as my people come, and they sit before you as my people, and they hear your words, but they do not act on them; for with their mouths they express much love, but their hearts pursue their own gain. {33:32} Indeed, you are like a very lovely song to them, one who has a beautiful voice and plays well on an instrument; they hear your words, but they do not do them. {33:33} And when what you have prophesied comes to pass—look, it will come—then they will know that a prophet has been among them."

{34:1} And the word of the LORD came to me, saying, {34:2} "Son of man, prophesy against the shepherds of Israel; prophesy and say to them, 'Thus says the Lord GOD: Woe to the shepherds of Israel who feed themselves! Should not the shepherds feed the flock? {34:3} You eat the fat, clothe yourselves with the wool, and kill those that are fed, but you do not feed the flock. {34:4} You have not strengthened the diseased, healed the sick, bound up the broken, brought back those driven away, or sought the lost; instead, you have ruled them with force and cruelty. {34:5} So they were scattered because there was no shepherd, and they became food for all the beasts of the field when they were scattered. {34:6} My sheep wandered over the mountains and every high hill; yes, my flock was scattered across the face of the earth, and no one searched or sought for them. {34:7} Therefore, you shepherds, hear the word of the LORD: {34:8} As I live, says the Lord GOD, surely because my flock has become prey and food for every beast of the field because there was no shepherd, and my shepherds did not search for my flock, but fed themselves instead of feeding my flock, {34:9} therefore, O shepherds, hear the word of the LORD. {34:10} Thus says the Lord GOD: Behold, I am against the shepherds, and I will hold them accountable for my flock and cause them to cease from feeding the flock; they will no longer feed themselves, for I will rescue my flock from their mouths so that they will not be food for them. {34:11} For thus says the Lord GOD: Behold, I, even I, will search for my sheep and seek them out. {34:12} As a shepherd seeks out his flock on the day he is among his scattered sheep, so I will seek out my sheep and rescue them from all the places where they have been scattered on a cloudy and dark day. {34:13} I will bring them out from the peoples, gather them from the countries, and bring them to their own land; I will feed them on the mountains of Israel, by the rivers, and in all the inhabited places of the country. {34:14} I will feed them in good pastures, and they will lie down on the high mountains of Israel; there they will lie in good fold and feed on fat pastures. {34:15} I will tend my flock and cause them to lie down, says the Lord GOD. {34:16} I will seek what was lost, bring back what was driven away, bind up what was broken, and strengthen what was sick; but I will destroy the fat and the strong; I will feed them with justice. {34:17} As for you, my flock, thus says the Lord GOD: Behold, I will judge between cattle and cattle, between rams and goats. {34:18} Is it a small thing for you to have eaten up the good pasture, but you must trample down the rest with your feet? And to have drunk of the deep waters, but you foul the rest with your feet? {34:19} My flock eats what you have trampled, and they drink what you have fouled with your feet. {34:20} Therefore, thus says the Lord GOD to them: Behold, I will judge between the fat cattle and the lean cattle. {34:21} Because you have pushed with side and shoulder and butted all the weak with your horns until you have scattered them abroad, {34:22} therefore I will save my flock, and they will no longer be a prey; I will judge between cattle and cattle. {34:23} I will set up one shepherd over them, and he will feed them, even my servant David; he will feed them and be their shepherd. {34:24} And I the LORD will be their God, and my servant David will be a prince among them; I the LORD have spoken it. {34:25} I will make a covenant of peace with them, and cause the evil beasts to cease from the land; they will dwell safely in the wilderness and sleep in the woods. {34:26} I will make them and the places around my hill a blessing; I will cause showers of blessing to come down in their season. {34:27} The trees of the field will yield their fruit, and the earth will yield her increase, and they will be safe in their land; they will know that I am the LORD when I break the bands of their yoke and deliver them from the hand of those who enslaved them. {34:28} They will no longer be prey for the nations, nor will the beasts of the land devour them; they will dwell safely, and no one will make them afraid. {34:29} I will raise up for them a renowned plant, and they will no longer suffer hunger in the land, nor bear the shame of the nations anymore. {34:30} Thus they will know that I the LORD their God am with them, and that they, even the house of Israel, are my people, says the Lord GOD. {34:31} And you, my flock, the flock of my pasture, are men, and I am your God, says the Lord GOD.

{35:1} The word of the LORD came to me, saying, {35:2} "Son of man, set your face against Mount Seir and prophesy against it, {35:3} and say to it, 'Thus says the Lord GOD: Behold, Mount Seir, I am against you. I will stretch out my hand against you and make you a desolate wasteland. {35:4} I will lay waste your cities, and you will be desolate. Then you will know that I am the LORD. {35:5} Because you have had a perpetual hatred and have shed the blood of the children of Israel with the sword during their calamity, at the time when their iniquity came to an end, {35:6} therefore, as I live, says the Lord GOD, I will prepare you for bloodshed, and blood will pursue you. Since you have not hated bloodshed, blood will pursue you. {35:7} Thus I will make Mount Seir a desolate wasteland and cut off from it those who pass through and those who return. {35:8} I will fill your mountains with slain men; in your hills, valleys, and rivers, those slain by the sword will fall. {35:9} I will make you a perpetual desolation, and your cities will not return; then you will know that I am the LORD. {35:10} Because you have said, 'These two nations and these two countries will be mine, and we will possess them,' even though the LORD was there, {35:11} therefore, as I live, says the Lord GOD, I will act according to your anger and your envy, which you have shown out of your hatred against them, and I will make myself known among them when I judge you. {35:12} You will know that I am the LORD and that I have heard all your blasphemies spoken against the mountains of Israel, saying, 'They are desolate; they have been given to us to consume.' {35:13} You have boasted against me with your mouth and multiplied your words against me; I have heard them. {35:14} Thus says the Lord GOD: When the whole earth rejoices, I will make you desolate. {35:15} Just as you rejoiced at the inheritance of the house of Israel because it was desolate, so I will do to you: you will be desolate, O Mount Seir, and all Idumea; all of it, and they shall know that I am the LORD."

{36:1} Also, son of man, prophesy to the mountains of Israel and say, "You mountains of Israel, hear the word of the LORD: {36:2} Thus says the Lord GOD: Because the enemy has said against you, 'Aha! Even the ancient high places are ours in possession,' {36:3} therefore prophesy and say, 'Thus says the Lord GOD: Because they have made you desolate and swallowed you up on every side, so that you have become a possession to the remnant of the heathen (nations), and you have been made a mockery by the people, {36:4} therefore, you mountains of Israel, hear the word of the Lord GOD: Thus says the Lord GOD to the mountains, hills, rivers, valleys, desolate wastes, and forsaken cities, which have become prey and derision to the remaining heathen around you: {36:5} Therefore, thus says the Lord GOD: Surely in my jealous anger, I have spoken against the remnant of the heathen and against all Idumea, who have taken my land as their possession with joy and despiteful minds, seeking to cast it out for a prey. {36:6} Prophesy therefore concerning the land of Israel and say to the mountains, hills, rivers, and valleys: Thus says the Lord GOD: Behold, I have spoken in my jealousy and fury, because you have borne the shame of the heathen. {36:7} Therefore, thus says the Lord GOD: I have lifted my hand, and surely the heathen around you will bear their shame. {36:8} But you, O mountains of Israel, will shoot forth your branches and yield your fruit to my people Israel, for they are about to come. {36:9} For, behold, I am for you; I will turn to you, and you will be tilled and sown. {36:10} I will multiply men upon you, all the house of Israel, even all of it; and the cities will be inhabited, and the desolate places will be rebuilt. {36:11} I will multiply both man and beast upon you, and they will increase and produce fruit. I will settle you according to your old ways and will do better for you than at your beginnings; then you will know that I am the LORD. {36:12} Yes, I will cause men to walk upon you, even my people Israel; they will possess you, and you will be their inheritance; you will no longer bereave them of children. {36:13} Thus says the Lord GOD: Because they say to you, 'You land devours men and bereaves your nations,' {36:14} therefore, you will no longer devour men or bereave your nations anymore, says the Lord GOD. {36:15} Neither will I let men hear in you the shame of the heathen anymore; you will no longer bear the reproach of the people, nor cause your nations to fall, says the Lord GOD. {36:16} Moreover, the word of the LORD came to me, saying, {36:17} "Son of man, when the house of Israel lived in their own land, they defiled it by their ways and deeds; their ways were before me like the uncleanness of a woman in her menstrual period. {36:18} Therefore, I poured out my fury upon them for the blood they shed on the land and for the idols with which they polluted it. {36:19} I scattered them among the nations, and they were dispersed through the countries; according to their ways and deeds, I judged them. {36:20} And when they entered the nations where they went, they profaned my holy name, saying to them, 'These are the people of the LORD, and they have come out of his land.' {36:21} But I had pity for my holy name, which the house of Israel had profaned among the nations where they went. {36:22} Therefore, say to the house of Israel: Thus says the Lord GOD: I do not do this for your sake, O house of Israel, but for my holy name's sake, which you have profaned among the nations where you went. {36:23} I will sanctify my great name, which has been profaned among the nations, and which you have profaned in their midst; then the nations will know that I am the LORD, says the Lord GOD, when I am sanctified in you before their eyes. {36:24} For I will take you from among the nations, gather you from all countries, and bring you into your own land. {36:25} Then I will sprinkle clean water on you, and you will be clean from all your filthiness and from all your idols; I will cleanse you. {36:26} I will give you a new heart and put a new spirit within you; I will take away the stony heart from your flesh and give you a heart of flesh. {36:27} I will put my Spirit within you and cause you to walk in my statutes; you will keep my judgments and do them. {36:28} You will dwell in the land that I gave to your fathers; you will be my people, and I will be your God. {36:29} I will also save you from all your uncleanness; I will call for the grain and increase it, and I will not bring famine upon you. {36:30} I will multiply the fruit of the tree and the increase of the field, so you will no longer suffer the shame of famine among the nations. {36:31} Then you will remember your evil ways and your deeds that were not good, and you will loathe yourselves for your iniquities and your abominations. {36:32} Not for your sake do I do this, says the Lord GOD; be ashamed and confounded for your own ways, O house of Israel. {36:33} Thus says the Lord GOD: On the day when I cleanse you from all your iniquities, I will also cause you to dwell in the cities, and the desolate places will be rebuilt. {36:34} The desolate land will be cultivated, which has lain desolate in the sight of all who pass by. {36:35} They will say, 'This land that was desolate has become like the Garden of Eden, and the wasted, desolate, and ruined cities are now fenced and inhabited.' {36:36} Then the nations that are left around you will know that I, the LORD, have rebuilt the ruined places and planted what was desolate. I, the LORD, have spoken it, and I will do it. {36:37} Thus says the Lord GOD: I will yet be inquired of by the house of Israel to do it for them; I will increase them with men like a flock. {36:38} Like the holy flock, like the flock of Jerusalem during her solemn feasts, so the wasted cities will be filled with flocks of men, and they will know that I am the LORD."

{37:1} The hand of the LORD was upon me, and He carried me out in the Spirit of the LORD and set me down in the middle of a valley that was full of bones. {37:2} He made me walk around them, and I saw that there were very many in the open valley, and they were very dry. {37:3} Then He asked me, "Son of man, can these bones live?" I answered, "O Lord GOD, You know." {37:4} Again, He said to me, "Prophesy to these bones and say to them, 'O dry bones, hear the word of the LORD.' {37:5} This is what the Lord GOD says to these bones: 'Look, I will cause breath to enter you, and you will live. {37:6} I will put sinews (tendons) on you, bring up flesh upon you, cover you with skin, and put breath in you, and you will live; then you will know that I am the LORD.' {37:7} So I prophesied as I was commanded; and as I prophesied, there was a noise, and behold, a shaking, and the bones came together, bone to its bone. {37:8} When I looked, the sinews and flesh appeared on them, and skin covered them, but there was no breath in them. {37:9} Then He said to me, "Prophesy to the wind; prophesy, son of man, and say to the wind, 'This is what the Lord GOD says: Come from the four winds, O breath, and breathe on these slain so they may live.'" {37:10} So I prophesied as He commanded me, and the breath entered them, and they lived and stood up on their feet, a vast army. {37:11} Then He said to me, "Son of man, these bones are the whole house of Israel. They say, 'Our bones are dried up, and our hope is lost; we are cut off for our parts.' {37:12} Therefore prophesy and say to them, 'This is what the Lord GOD says: Look, O My people, I will open your graves and bring you up out of your graves and bring you into the land of Israel. {37:13} You will know that I am the LORD when I have opened your graves, O My people, and brought you up from your graves. {37:14} I will put My Spirit in you, and you will live, and I will place you in your own land; then you will know that I, the LORD, have spoken it and performed it, says the LORD.' {37:15} The word of the LORD came again to me, saying, {37:16} "Moreover, son of man, take one stick and write on it, 'For Judah and for the children of Israel his companions.' Then take another stick and write on it, 'For Joseph, the stick of Ephraim, and for all the house of Israel his companions.' {37:17} Join them one to another into one stick, and they shall become one in your hand. {37:18} When the children of your people speak to you, saying, 'Will you not show us what you mean by these?' {37:19} Say to them, 'This is what the Lord GOD says: Look, I will take the stick of Joseph, which is in the hand of Ephraim and the tribes of Israel, and I will join it with the stick of Judah, and they will become one stick in My hand.' {37:20} The sticks on which you write shall be in your hand before their eyes. {37:21} Say to them, 'This is what the Lord GOD says: Look, I will take the children of Israel from among the nations where they have gone, gather them from every side, and bring them into their own land. {37:22} I will make them one nation in the land upon the mountains of Israel, and one king shall be king over them all; they shall no longer be two nations, nor shall they ever be divided into two kingdoms again. {37:23} They will no longer defile themselves with their idols or with their detestable things or any of their transgressions; but I will save them from all their dwelling places where they have sinned, and I will cleanse them. They shall be My people, and I will be their God. {37:24} My servant David will be king over them, and they will all have one shepherd; they will walk in My judgments, observe My statutes, and do them. {37:25} They shall dwell in the land that I have given to Jacob My servant, where your fathers lived; they shall dwell there, they and their children and their children's children forever, and My servant David shall be their prince forever. {37:26} Moreover, I will make a covenant of peace with them; it will be an everlasting covenant with them. I will place them and multiply them, and I will set My sanctuary in their midst forevermore.

{37:27} My tabernacle will also be with them; yes, I will be their God, and they will be My people. {37:28} The nations will know that I, the LORD, sanctify Israel when My sanctuary is in their midst forevermore.

{38:1} And the word of the LORD came to me, saying, {38:2} "Son of man, set your face against Gog, the land of Magog, the chief prince of Meshech and Tubal, and prophesy against him, {38:3} and say, 'This is what the Lord GOD says: Look, I am against you, O Gog, the chief prince of Meshech and Tubal. {38:4} I will turn you back, put hooks in your jaws, and bring you out, along with your entire army, horses and horsemen, all of them fully armed, even a great company with shields and weapons, all of them handling swords. {38:5} Persia, Ethiopia, and Libya will be with them; all of them with shields and helmets. {38:6} Gomer and all its troops; the house of Togarmah from the far north and all its troops; and many people with you. {38:7} Prepare yourself and get ready, you and all your company that have assembled against you, and be a guard for them. {38:8} After many days, you will be visited; in the latter years, you will come into the land that has been brought back from the sword and gathered from many peoples, against the mountains of Israel, which have been always waste, but now is brought forth out of the nations, and they shall dwell safely, all of them. {38:9} You will rise up and come like a storm; you will be like a cloud covering the land, you and all your troops and many peoples with you. {38:10} This is what the Lord GOD says: At that time, evil thoughts will come to your mind, {38:11} and you will say, 'I will go up against the land of unwalled villages; I will go to those at rest, who dwell safely, all of them living without walls, bars, or gates, {38:12} to take spoil and prey, to turn your hand against the desolate places that are now inhabited, and upon the people gathered from the nations who have acquired cattle and goods, dwelling in the midst of the land.' {38:13} Sheba and Dedan and the merchants of Tarshish with all the young lions will say to you, 'Have you come to take spoil? Have you gathered your troops to take prey? To carry away silver and gold, to take cattle and goods, a great spoil?' {38:14} Therefore, son of man, prophesy and say to Gog, 'This is what the Lord GOD says: On the day when My people of Israel dwell safely, will you not know it? {38:15} You will come from your place in the far north, you and many peoples with you, all of them riding on horses, a great company and a mighty army. {38:16} You will come up against My people Israel like a cloud covering the land; it will be in the latter days, and I will bring you against My land, so that the nations may know Me when I am sanctified in you, O Gog, before their eyes. {38:17} This is what the Lord GOD says: Are you the one I spoke about in ancient times through My servants the prophets of Israel, who prophesied many years ago that I would bring you against them? {38:18} It will come to pass that when Gog comes against the land of Israel, says the Lord GOD, My fury will rise in My face. {38:19} For in My jealousy and in the fire of My wrath, I have spoken: Surely in that day, there will be a great shaking in the land of Israel. {38:20} The fish of the sea, the birds of the air, the beasts of the field, and all creeping things that crawl on the earth, and all the men on the face of the earth will shake at My presence, and the mountains will be thrown down, the steep places will fall, and every wall will fall to the ground. {38:21} I will call for a sword against him throughout all My mountains, says the Lord GOD; every man's sword will be against his brother. {38:22} I will judge him with pestilence and blood; I will rain down overflowing rain, great hailstones, fire, and brimstone upon him and his troops and the many people with him. {38:23} Thus, I will magnify and sanctify Myself, and I will be known in the eyes of many nations; then they will know that I am the LORD.

{39:1} Therefore, son of man, prophesy against Gog and say, "This is what the Lord GOD says: Behold, I am against you, O Gog, the chief prince of Meshech and Tubal. {39:2} I will turn you back, leaving only a sixth of your forces, and I will bring you down from the northern regions to the mountains of Israel. {39:3} I will strike your bow from your left hand and make your arrows fall from your right hand. {39:4} You will fall on the mountains of Israel, you and all your troops, and the people with you; I will give you to the birds of prey and the beasts of the field to be devoured. {39:5} You will fall in the open field, for I have spoken, says the Lord GOD. {39:6} I will send fire upon Magog and on those who live in security in the coastlands, and they will know that I am the LORD. {39:7} I will make My holy name known among My people Israel, and I will no longer let them profane My holy name; then the nations will know that I am the LORD, the Holy One in Israel. {39:8} Behold, it has come, and it is done, says the Lord GOD; this is the day I have spoken about. {39:9} The inhabitants of the cities of Israel will go out and burn the weapons—both shields and bucklers, bows and arrows, and staves and spears—and they will burn them for seven years. {39:10} They will not need to gather wood from the fields or cut down trees from the forests, for they will burn the weapons with fire; they will plunder those who plundered them and loot those who looted them, says the Lord GOD. {39:11} On that day, I will give Gog a burial place in Israel, the Valley of the Travelers, east of the sea; it will stop the noses of travelers, and they will bury Gog and all his multitude there. They will call it the Valley of Hamongog. {39:12} The house of Israel will spend seven months burying them to cleanse the land. {39:13} Yes, all the people of the land will bury them, and it will be a renown for them on the day I am glorified, says the Lord GOD. {39:14} They will assign men of continual employment, passing through the land to bury with the travelers those who remain on the earth, to cleanse it; after the seven months, they will search. {39:15} Whenever a traveler sees a man's bone, he will set up a marker until the buriers have buried it in the Valley of Hamongog. {39:16} The name of the city will be Hamonah. Thus they will cleanse the land. {39:17} And you, son of man, this is what the Lord GOD says: Speak to every bird and every beast of the field, 'Assemble yourselves and come; gather around for My sacrifice that I am preparing for you, a great sacrifice on the mountains of Israel, so you may eat flesh and drink blood. {39:18} You will eat the flesh of mighty men and drink the blood of the princes of the earth, of rams, lambs, goats, and bulls, all of them fatlings from Bashan. {39:19} You will be filled at My table with horses and chariots, with mighty men and all men of war, says the Lord GOD. {39:20} I will set My glory among the nations, and all nations will see My judgment that I have executed and My hand that I have laid upon them. {39:21} So the house of Israel will know that I am the LORD their God from that day onward. {39:22} The nations will also know that the house of Israel went into captivity for their iniquity, because they trespassed against Me; therefore, I hid My face from them and gave them into the hands of their enemies, so they fell by the sword. {39:23} According to their uncleanness and their transgressions, I dealt with them and hid My face from them. {39:24} Therefore, this is what the Lord GOD says: Now I will restore the fortunes of Jacob and have mercy on the whole house of Israel, and I will be zealous for My holy name. {39:25} After they have borne their shame and all their sins against Me, when they dwelt safely in their land with no one to make them afraid. {39:26} When I have restored them from the nations and gathered them from their enemies' lands, and am sanctified in them in the sight of many nations; {39:27} then they will know that I am the LORD their God, who caused them to be led into captivity among the nations, but I have gathered them to their own land and left none of them there anymore. {39:28} I will no longer hide My face from them, for I have poured out My Spirit upon the house of Israel, says the Lord GOD.

{40:1} In the twenty-fifth year of our captivity, at the beginning of the year, on the tenth day of the month, in the fourteenth year after the city was struck, on that very day, the hand of the LORD was upon me, and He brought me there. {40:2} In visions of God, He brought me to the land of Israel and set me on a very high mountain, and there was something like a city on the south. {40:3} He brought me there, and behold, there was a man whose appearance was like bronze, with a linen cord and a measuring reed in his hand; and he stood at the gate. {40:4} The man said to me, "Son of man, look with your eyes and hear with your ears, and set your heart upon all that I will show you; for I am bringing you here to show you, declare to the house of Israel all that you see." {40:5} And behold, there was a wall on the outside of the house all around, and the man had a measuring reed in his hand that was six cubits long, each cubit and a handbreadth (about 1.5 inches longer than a cubit). He measured the width of the building, one reed, and the height, one reed. {40:6} Then he went to the gate facing east and went up the stairs; he measured the threshold of the gate, which was one reed wide, and the other threshold of the gate, which was also one reed wide. {40:7} Each little chamber was one reed long and one reed wide; between the little chambers, there were five cubits; the threshold of the gate by the porch inside was one reed. {40:8} He also measured the porch of the gate inside, one reed. {40:9} Then he measured the porch of the gate, eight cubits wide, and the posts were two cubits wide; the porch of the gate was inward. {40:10} The little chambers of the gate eastward were three on this side and three on that side; the three were of one measure, and the posts had one measure on both sides. {40:11} He measured the width of the entrance of the gate, ten cubits, and the length of the gate, thirteen cubits. {40:12} The space before the little chambers was one cubit on this side and one cubit on that side; the little chambers were six cubits on each side. {40:13} He measured the gate from the roof of one little chamber to the roof of another; the width was twenty-five cubits, door against door. {40:14} He also made posts sixty cubits high, reaching to the post of the outer court surrounding the gate. {40:15} From the front of the gate of the entrance to the front of the porch of the inner gate was fifty cubits. {40:16} There were narrow windows to the little chambers and to their posts around the gate, and also to the arches; windows were all around inward, and palm trees were on each post. {40:17} Then he brought me into the outer court, and lo, there were chambers and a pavement made for the court all around; thirty chambers were on the pavement. {40:18} The pavement by the side of the gates opposite the length of the gates was the lower pavement. {40:19} Then he measured the width from the front of the lower gate to the front of the inner court without, one hundred cubits eastward and northward. {40:20} He measured the gate of the outer court that looked toward the north, including its length and width. {40:21} The little chambers were three on each side; the posts and arches were measured the same as the first gate; the length was fifty cubits and the width was twenty-five cubits. {40:22} Their windows, arches, and palm trees were the same as those of the gate facing east; they went up to it by seven steps, and the arches were before them. {40:23} The gate of the inner court was opposite the gate toward the north and the east; he measured from gate to gate one hundred cubits. {40:24} After that, he brought me toward the south, and behold, a gate toward the south; he measured its posts and arches according to these measurements. {40:25} There were windows in it and in the arches all around, its length was fifty cubits, and its width was twenty-five cubits. {40:26} There were seven steps to go up to it, and the arches were before them; and there were palm trees, one on this side and another on that side on the posts. {40:27} There was a gate in the inner court toward the south; he measured from gate to gate toward the south one hundred cubits. {40:28} He brought me to the inner court by the south gate, and he measured the south gate according to these measurements; {40:29} the little chambers, posts, and arches were according to these measurements; there were windows in it and in the arches all around; it was fifty cubits long and twenty-five cubits wide. {40:30} The arches all around were twenty-five cubits long and five cubits wide. {40:31} The arches were toward the outer court, and palm trees were on the posts on both sides; the steps leading up to it had eight steps. {40:32} He brought me into the inner court toward the east; he measured the gate according to these measurements. {40:33} The little chambers, posts, and arches were according to these measurements; there were windows in it and in the arches all around; it was fifty cubits long and twenty-five cubits wide. {40:34} The arches were toward the outer court, and palm trees were on the posts on both sides; the steps leading up to it had eight steps. {40:35} He brought me to the north gate and measured it according to these measurements; {40:36} the little chambers, posts, arches, and windows all around were fifty cubits long and twenty-five cubits wide. {40:37} The posts were toward the outer court, and palm trees were on the posts on both sides; the steps leading up to it had eight steps. {40:38} The chambers and entries were by the posts of the gates where they washed the burnt offerings. {40:39} In the porch of the gate were two tables on each side, to slay the burnt offerings, sin offerings, and trespass offerings. {40:40} On the outer side, as one goes up to the entry of the north gate, were two tables; and on the other side, at the porch of the gate, were two tables. {40:41} There were four tables on one side and four tables on the other side, by the sides of the gate; eight tables on which they slaughtered their sacrifices. {40:42} The four tables were made of hewn stone, each one and a half cubits long, one and a half cubits wide, and one cubit high; they also laid the instruments for slaughtering the burnt offerings and sacrifices on them. {40:43} There were hooks, an handbreadth wide, fastened all around, and upon the tables was the flesh of the offerings. {40:44} Outside the inner gate were the chambers of the singers in the inner court, at the side of the north gate, facing south; one at the side of the east gate facing north. {40:45} He said to me, "This chamber, whose view is toward the south, is for the priests who keep charge of the house. {40:46} The chamber whose view is toward the north is for the priests who keep charge of the altar; these are the sons of Zadok among the sons of Levi who draw near to the LORD to minister to Him. {40:47} He measured the court, one hundred cubits long and one hundred cubits wide, a square; and the altar that was before the house. {40:48} He brought me to the porch of the house and measured each post of the porch; it was five cubits on this side and five cubits on that side; the width of the gate was three cubits on this side and three cubits on that side. {40:49} The length of the porch was twenty cubits and the width eleven cubits; he brought me by the steps that led up to it, and there were pillars by the posts, one on this side and another on that side.

{41:1} Afterward, he brought me to the temple and measured the posts; they were six cubits wide on one side and six cubits wide on the other side, which was the width of the tabernacle. {41:2} The width of the door was ten cubits, with five cubits on each side; he measured the length at forty cubits and the width at twenty cubits. {41:3} Then he went inside and measured the post of the door, which was two cubits, and the door itself, which was six cubits wide; the width of the door was seven cubits. {41:4} He measured the length at twenty cubits and the width at twenty cubits in front of the temple, and he said to me, "This is the most holy place." {41:5} After measuring the wall of the house, it was six cubits thick, and the width of each side chamber was four cubits all around the house. {41:6} The side chambers were three stories high and thirty in total; they entered into the wall of the house for support but did not hold onto the wall itself. {41:7} There was an expansion and a spiral going upward to the side chambers, as the structure rose; therefore, the width of the house increased from the lowest to the highest chamber. {41:8} I also saw the height of the house around; the foundations of the side chambers were a full reed, which is six large cubits. {41:9} The thickness of the wall for the side chamber outside was five cubits, leaving space for the side chambers inside. {41:10} Between the chambers, there was a width of twenty cubits all around the house. {41:11} The doors of the side chambers faced the space left over, with one door facing north and another facing south; the space left was five cubits all around. {41:12} The building that was in front of the separate place toward the west was seventy cubits wide, with walls five cubits thick all around, and its length was ninety cubits. {41:13} He measured the house, which was one hundred cubits long; the separate place and the building, including the walls, were also one hundred cubits long. {41:14} The width of the front of the house and the separate place toward the east was one hundred cubits. {41:15} He measured the length of the building opposite the separate place behind it, along with the galleries on both sides, which were one hundred cubits long, including the inner temple and the porches of the court. {41:16} The doorposts, narrow windows, and galleries around on their three stories, facing the door, were paneled with wood all the way from the ground up to the windows, and the windows were covered. {41:17} Above the door, and within and around the entire wall, both inside and outside, were measured. {41:18} It was adorned with cherubim and palm trees, so that there was a palm tree between each cherub; every cherub had two faces. {41:19} The face of a man was toward the palm tree on one side, and the face of a young lion was toward the palm tree on the other side; this design was all around the house. {41:20} From the ground up to above the door, there were cherubim and palm trees carved into the wall of the temple. {41:21} The posts of the temple were squared, and the face of the sanctuary had the same appearance as the other. {41:22} The wooden altar was three cubits high and two cubits long; the corners, length, and walls were made of wood; he said to me, "This is the table that is before the LORD." {41:23} The temple and the sanctuary had two doors. {41:24} Each door had two leaves; two turning leaves for one door and two for the other door. {41:25} They were decorated with cherubim and palm trees, similar to the walls; thick planks were placed on the outer surface of the porch.

{41:26} There were narrow windows and palm trees on both sides of the porch and on the side chambers of the house, along with thick planks.

{42:1} Then he brought me outside to the outer court, going north, and he brought me to the chamber opposite the separate place, which was in front of the building toward the north. {42:2} The north door measured one hundred cubits long and fifty cubits wide. {42:3} Across from the twenty cubits of the inner court and opposite the pavement of the outer court, there was a gallery facing another gallery in three stories. {42:4} In front of the chambers was a walkway ten cubits wide inward, with a one-cubit space, and their doors faced north. {42:5} The upper chambers were shorter because the galleries were higher than those of the lower and middle buildings. {42:6} They were in three stories but lacked pillars like the pillars of the courts; thus, the structure was narrower than the lowest and middle stories. {42:7} The outer wall facing the chambers toward the outer court was fifty cubits long. {42:8} The length of the chambers in the outer court was fifty cubits, and before the temple, it was one hundred cubits long. {42:9} From under these chambers was an entrance on the east side, as one enters from the outer court. {42:10} The chambers were within the thickness of the wall of the court facing east, opposite the separate place and the building. {42:11} The entrance to them resembled the appearance of the chambers facing north; they were the same length and width, and all their exits were according to their designs and doors. {42:12} There was a door at the head of the way, directly before the wall toward the east, as one enters them from the south. {42:13} He said to me, "The north and south chambers, which are before the separate place, are holy chambers where the priests who approach the LORD shall eat the most holy things; they will store the most holy items, along with the grain offering, sin offering, and guilt offering, for this place is holy." {42:14} When the priests enter, they shall not leave the holy place to go into the outer court, but they will lay aside the garments they wore while ministering, for they are holy, and they will put on other garments to approach those things meant for the people. {42:15} After he finished measuring the inner house, he brought me out toward the east gate and measured it all around. {42:16} He measured the east side with the measuring rod, five hundred rods all around. {42:17} He measured the north side, five hundred rods all around. {42:18} He measured the south side, five hundred rods with the measuring rod. {42:19} Then he turned to the west side and measured five hundred rods with the measuring rod. {42:20} He measured it on all four sides; it had a wall all around, five hundred rods long and five hundred wide, creating a separation between the sanctuary and the profane place.

{43:1} Afterward, he brought me to the gate that faces east. {43:2} And behold, the glory of the God of Israel came from the east, and his voice was like the sound of many waters; the earth shone with his glory. {43:3} It matched the vision I had when I came to destroy the city; the visions were like those I saw by the river Chebar, and I fell on my face. {43:4} The glory of the LORD entered the house through the east gate. {43:5} Then the spirit lifted me up and brought me into the inner court; behold, the glory of the LORD filled the house. {43:6} I heard him speaking to me from within the house, and the man stood beside me. {43:7} He said to me, "Son of man, this is the place of my throne and the place for the soles of my feet, where I will dwell among the children of Israel forever. My holy name will no longer be defiled by the Israelites or their kings through their idolatry or by the remains of their kings in their high places. {43:8} They have defiled my holy name by placing their threshold next to my thresholds and their posts next to my posts, with a wall between me and them; they have committed abominations, which is why I consumed them in my anger. {43:9} Now let them remove their idolatry and the remains of their kings far from me, and I will dwell among them forever. {43:10} Son of man, show the house to the house of Israel so they may be ashamed of their iniquities and let them measure the design. {43:11} If they are ashamed of all they have done, show them the layout of the house, its design, its entrances and exits, and all its regulations and laws; write it down in their sight so they can follow the entire design and all its regulations and do them. {43:12} This is the law of the house: the entire area on top of the mountain will be most holy. Behold, this is the law of the house. {43:13} These are the measurements of the altar according to the cubits: a cubit is a cubit and a handbreadth; the base will be one cubit high, and the width will be one cubit, with a border around it measuring a span; this will be the elevated part of the altar. {43:14} From the ground to the lower ledge will be two cubits high and one cubit wide; from the lower ledge to the higher ledge will be four cubits high and one cubit wide. {43:15} The altar will be four cubits high, and from the altar upward, there will be four horns. {43:16} The altar will measure twelve cubits long and twelve cubits wide, square in shape. {43:17} The ledge will measure fourteen cubits long and fourteen cubits wide on all sides; the border will be half a cubit wide, and the base will be one cubit around it, and its stairs will face east. {43:18} He said to me, "Son of man, this is what the Lord GOD says: these are the regulations for the altar on the day they will construct it to offer burnt offerings and sprinkle blood on it. {43:19} You will give to the priests, the Levites from the line of Zadok, who approach me to minister, a young bull for a sin offering. {43:20} You will take some of its blood and put it on the four horns of the altar, on the four corners of the ledge, and on the border all around; this will cleanse and purify it. {43:21} You will take the bull for the sin offering and burn it in the designated area of the house, outside the sanctuary. {43:22} On the second day, you will offer a flawless goat for a sin offering, and they will cleanse the altar as they did with the bull. {43:23} When you finish cleansing it, you will offer a young bull without blemish and a ram from the flock without blemish. {43:24} You will present them before the LORD, and the priests will sprinkle salt on them and offer them up as burnt offerings to the LORD. {43:25} For seven days, you will prepare a goat for a sin offering every day; they will also prepare a young bull and a ram from the flock without blemish. {43:26} For seven days, they will cleanse the altar and purify it, and they will consecrate themselves. {43:27} After these days are completed, on the eighth day and onward, the priests will present your burnt offerings and peace offerings on the altar, and I will accept you, says the Lord GOD.

{44:1} Then he brought me back to the outer gate of the sanctuary that faces east, and it was shut. {44:2} Then the LORD said to me, "This gate shall be shut; it will not be opened, and no man shall enter through it. Because the LORD, the God of Israel, has entered through it, therefore it shall remain shut. {44:3} This gate is for the prince; he will sit in it to eat bread before the LORD; he will enter by the way of the porch of that gate and will go out the same way." {44:4} Then he brought me through the north gate in front of the house, and I looked; behold, the glory of the LORD filled the house of the LORD, and I fell on my face. {44:5} The LORD said to me, "Son of man, pay close attention and listen carefully to all I say to you concerning all the ordinances of the house of the LORD and all its laws; pay attention to how the house is entered and how the sanctuary exits. {44:6} You will say to the rebellious house of Israel, 'Thus says the Lord GOD: O house of Israel, you have had enough of all your abominations. {44:7} You have brought strangers, uncircumcised in heart and flesh, into my sanctuary, to pollute it, even my house, by offering my bread, the fat, and the blood, and breaking my covenant because of your abominations. {44:8} You have not kept charge of my holy things, but you have appointed keepers of my charge in my sanctuary for yourselves. {44:9} Thus says the Lord GOD: No stranger, uncircumcised in heart or flesh, shall enter my sanctuary, including any stranger among the children of Israel. {44:10} The Levites who went far from me when Israel strayed after their idols will bear their iniquity. {44:11} Yet they will be ministers in my sanctuary, responsible for the gates of the house and ministering to the house; they will slay the burnt offerings and sacrifices for the people and will stand before them to minister to them. {44:12} Because they ministered to them before their idols and caused the house of Israel to fall into sin, I lifted my hand against them, says the Lord GOD, and they will bear their iniquity. {44:13} They will not come near me to serve as priests or approach any of my holy things, in the most holy place; instead, they will bear their shame and the abominations they committed. {44:14} However, I will make them keepers of charge of the house for all the services and everything done there. {44:15} The priests, the Levites, the sons of Zadok, who kept charge of my sanctuary when the children of

Israel went astray, they will come near to minister to me and stand before me to offer me the fat and the blood, says the Lord GOD. {44:16} They will enter my sanctuary and come near my table to minister to me and keep my charge. {44:17} When they enter the gates of the inner court, they will wear linen garments; they must not wear wool while ministering in the gates of the inner court and within. {44:18} They will have linen turbans on their heads and linen trousers on their bodies; they must not wear anything that causes sweat. {44:19} When they go out to the outer court, to the people, they will take off the garments they ministered in, lay them in the holy chambers, and put on other garments; they must not sanctify the people with their garments. {44:20} They must not shave their heads or let their hair grow long; they will only trim their hair. {44:21} No priest shall drink wine when they enter the inner court. {44:22} They must not marry a widow or a divorced woman; they may only take maidens from the house of Israel or a widow who was previously married to a priest. {44:23} They will teach my people the difference between the holy and the profane and help them discern between the clean and the unclean. {44:24} In controversies, they shall stand in judgment and judge according to my judgments; they will keep my laws and statutes in all my assemblies and keep my Sabbaths holy. {44:25} They will not come near any dead person to defile themselves, except for their father, mother, son, daughter, brother, or unmarried sister; they may defile themselves. {44:26} After being cleansed, they will wait seven days. {44:27} On the day they go into the sanctuary to minister in the inner court, they will offer their sin offering, says the Lord GOD. {44:28} It will be their inheritance: I am their inheritance; you shall not give them any possession in Israel; I am their possession. {44:29} They will eat the grain offerings, sin offerings, and guilt offerings; everything dedicated in Israel will belong to them. {44:30} The first of all the firstfruits and every offering of any sort will be for the priests; you shall also give the priest the first of your dough so that a blessing may rest in your house. {44:31} The priests shall not eat anything that dies of itself or is torn by beasts, whether fowl or animal.

{45:1} When you divide the land as an inheritance, you shall offer a special portion to the LORD; this holy area will measure twenty-five thousand cubits in length and ten thousand cubits in width, making it holy throughout its borders. {45:2} Of this area, there will be a section for the sanctuary measuring five hundred cubits in length and five hundred cubits in width, square all around, with fifty cubits set aside for its suburbs. {45:3} Measure out twenty-five thousand cubits in length and ten thousand in width, and within this area will be the sanctuary and the Most Holy Place. {45:4} The holy portion of the land will belong to the priests who minister in the sanctuary and come near to serve the LORD; it will be a place for their houses and a holy place for the sanctuary. {45:5} The twenty-five thousand cubits in length and ten thousand in width will also be for the Levites, who serve in the house, as a possession for twenty chambers. {45:6} You shall designate a city possession measuring five thousand cubits wide and twenty-five thousand cubits long, adjacent to the holy portion; this will be for the entire house of Israel. {45:7} A portion will also be for the prince, on both sides of the holy portion and the city possession, extending from the western border to the eastern border, aligning with one of the portions. {45:8} In this land, the prince will have his possession in Israel, and my princes will no longer oppress my people; the remainder of the land will be given to the house of Israel according to their tribes. {45:9} Thus says the Lord GOD: Enough, O princes of Israel; remove violence and exploitation, and practice justice and righteousness; stop your exactions from my people, says the Lord GOD. {45:10} You shall use just weights and measures; a just ephah and a just bath shall be your standard. {45:11} The ephah and the bath shall have the same measure, with the bath containing one-tenth of a homer, and the ephah also one-tenth of a homer; these will be based on the homer measurement. {45:12} The shekel will be twenty gerahs; your maneh will consist of twenty shekels, or twenty-five shekels, or fifteen shekels. {45:13} This is the offering you shall present: one-sixth of an ephah from a homer of wheat and one-sixth of an ephah from a homer of barley. {45:14} Regarding the oil, you shall offer one-tenth of a bath from a cor, which is ten baths, since ten baths equal one homer. {45:15} Also, you will provide one lamb from the flock, two hundred from the best pastures of Israel, for a grain offering, a burnt offering, and peace offerings to make atonement for them, says the Lord GOD. {45:16} All the people of the land shall provide this offering for the prince in Israel. {45:17} It will be the prince's responsibility to provide burnt offerings, grain offerings, and drink offerings during the feasts, new moons, and sabbaths, as well as in all solemn assemblies of the house of Israel; he shall prepare the sin offering, the grain offering, the burnt offering, and the peace offerings to make atonement for the house of Israel. {45:18} Thus says the Lord GOD: On the first day of the first month, you shall take a young bull without blemish and cleanse the sanctuary. {45:19} The priest will take some of the blood from the sin offering and put it on the doorposts of the house, on the four corners of the altar, and on the posts of the inner court gate. {45:20} You shall do this on the seventh day of the month for everyone who has erred and for those who are simple-minded; this will reconcile the house. {45:21} On the fourteenth day of the first month, you shall celebrate the Passover, a feast lasting seven days; unleavened bread will be eaten. {45:22} On that day, the prince will prepare for himself and for all the people of the land a bull for a sin offering. {45:23} Throughout the seven days of the feast, he will prepare a daily burnt offering for the LORD: seven bulls and seven rams without blemish each day, along with a goat for a sin offering each day. {45:24} He shall prepare a grain offering of one ephah for a bull and one ephah for a ram, along with one hin of oil for each ephah. {45:25} In the seventh month, on the fifteenth day, he shall do the same during the seven-day feast, following the guidelines for the sin offering, the burnt offering, the grain offering, and the oil.

{46:1} Thus says the Lord GOD: The inner court gate that faces east shall remain shut for six days of work; but on the sabbath and on the new moon, it shall be opened. {46:2} The prince shall enter through the porch of that gate and stand by the gatepost; the priests shall prepare his burnt and peace offerings, and he shall worship at the threshold of the gate; then he shall leave, but the gate shall not be shut until evening. {46:3} Likewise, the people of the land shall worship at the gate's entrance before the LORD on the sabbaths and new moons. {46:4} The burnt offering that the prince presents to the LORD on the sabbath day shall be six lambs without blemish and a ram without blemish. {46:5} The grain offering shall be one ephah for a ram and as much as he can provide for the lambs, along with one hin of oil for each ephah. {46:6} On the day of the new moon, he shall offer a young bull without blemish, along with six lambs and a ram, all without blemish. {46:7} He shall prepare a grain offering: one ephah for a bull and one ephah for a ram, and for the lambs as much as he can provide, along with one hin of oil for each ephah. {46:8} When the prince enters, he shall go in through the porch of that gate and leave the same way. {46:9} When the people come to worship the LORD during the solemn feasts, those entering through the north gate shall exit through the south gate, and those entering through the south gate shall exit through the north gate; they shall not return the same way they came in, but shall go out opposite. {46:10} The prince shall go in with them when they enter and go out with them when they leave. {46:11} During the feasts and solemnities, the grain offering shall be one ephah for a bull, one ephah for a ram, and for the lambs as much as he can provide, along with one hin of oil for each ephah. {46:12} When the prince offers a voluntary burnt offering or peace offering to the LORD, the gate facing east shall be opened for him, and he shall prepare his offerings as he did on the sabbath; then he shall leave, and the gate shall be shut after he exits. {46:13} You shall prepare a daily burnt offering for the LORD: one lamb of the first year without blemish, prepared every morning. {46:14} You shall prepare a grain offering for it every morning: one-sixth of an ephah and one-third of a hin of oil to mix with the fine flour; this is a perpetual grain offering to the LORD. {46:15} Thus, they shall prepare the lamb, the grain offering, and the oil every morning for a continual burnt offering. {46:16} Thus says the Lord GOD: If the prince gifts any of his sons, the inheritance will belong to his sons; it will be their possession by inheritance. {46:17} But if he gives a gift of his inheritance to one of his servants, it shall remain with that servant until the year of jubilee; then it shall return to the prince, but his inheritance will remain with his sons. {46:18} Moreover, the prince shall not take from the people's inheritance through oppression, forcing them out of their possessions; he shall give his sons their inheritance from his own possessions, so that my people will not be scattered from their inheritance. {46:19} After he brought me through the entrance beside the gate into the holy chambers of the priests, which face north, I saw a place on both sides to the west. {46:20} Then he said to me, "This is where the priests shall boil the guilt and sin offerings, and where they shall bake the grain offerings; they must not carry them out into the outer court to sanctify the people." {46:21} He then brought me into the outer court and led me around the corners of the court; I saw that in every corner there was a court. {46:22} In each of the four corners of the court, there were courts measuring forty cubits long and thirty cubits wide; these four corners had the same dimensions. {46:23} There was a row of buildings all around them, with boiling places under the rows surrounding them. {46:24} Then he said to me, "These are the cooking places for the ministers of the house, where they will boil the sacrifices of the people."

{47:1} Then he brought me back to the entrance of the temple, and I saw water flowing out from beneath the threshold of the temple toward the east (for the temple faced east). The water was flowing down from the south side of the temple, from the south side of the altar. {47:2} He led me out through the north gate and around to the outer gate that faces east, and I saw water flowing from the south side. {47:3} The man went eastward with a measuring line in his hand. He measured off a thousand cubits (about 1,500 feet) and led me through water that was ankle-deep. {47:4} He measured another thousand cubits and led me through water that was knee-deep. Again, he measured a thousand cubits and brought me through water that was up to my waist. {47:5} He measured another thousand cubits, but now it was a river that I could not cross because the water had risen and was deep enough to swim in, too deep to walk through. {47:6} He asked me, "Son of man, do you see this?" Then he led me back to the bank of the river. {47:7} When I returned, I saw many trees on both sides of the riverbank. {47:8} He said to me, "This water flows toward the eastern region, down into the desert, and enters the Dead Sea. When it flows into the sea, the salty water there becomes fresh. {47:9} Wherever the river flows, every living creature that moves will thrive. There will be a great abundance of fish because this water flows there and makes the saltwater fresh. So everything will live where the river flows. {47:10} Fishermen will stand along the shore; from En Gedi to En Eglaim, there will be places for spreading nets. The fish will be of many kinds, like the fish of the Mediterranean Sea, in great numbers. {47:11} But the swamps and marshes will not be purified; they will be left for salt. {47:12} Fruit trees of all kinds will grow on both banks of the river. Their leaves will not wither, nor will their fruit fail. They will bear new fruit every month because the water from the sanctuary flows to them. Their fruit will serve for food and their leaves for healing." {47:13} This is what the Sovereign LORD says: "These are the boundaries of the land you are to divide among the twelve tribes of Israel, with Joseph receiving two portions. {47:14} You are to divide it equally, as I swore to give it to your ancestors. This land will become your inheritance. {47:15} The northern boundary will extend from the Mediterranean Sea by the way of Hethlon toward Lebo-Hamath, to Zedad, {47:16} Berothah, Sibraim (which is between the borders of Damascus and Hamath), and Hazer-Hatticon, which is on the border of Hauran. {47:17} The boundary will extend from the Mediterranean Sea to Hazar-Enan, along the northern border of Damascus, with the border of Hamath to the north. This will be the northern boundary. {47:18} On the east side, the boundary will run between Hauran and Damascus, along the Jordan between Gilead and the land of Israel, to the eastern sea as far as Tamar. This will be the eastern boundary. {47:19} On the south side, the boundary will extend from Tamar to the waters of Meribah Kadesh, along the Wadi of Egypt to the Mediterranean Sea. This will be the southern boundary. {47:20} On the west side, the boundary will be the Mediterranean Sea, from the southern boundary to a point opposite Lebo-Hamath. This will be the western boundary. {47:21} You are to distribute this land among yourselves according to the tribes of Israel. {47:22} You are to allot it as an inheritance for yourselves and for the foreigners residing among you who have children. You are to consider them as native-born Israelites; they are to be allotted an inheritance among the tribes of Israel. {47:23} In whatever tribe a foreigner resides, there you are to give them their inheritance, declares the Sovereign LORD."

{48:1} "These are the tribes, listed by name: At the northern frontier, Dan will have one portion; it will extend eastward to westward. {48:2} Asher will have one portion; it will border Dan from east to west. {48:3} Naphtali will have one portion; it will border Asher from east to west. {48:4} Manasseh will have one portion; it will border Naphtali from east to west. {48:5} Ephraim will have one portion; it will border Manasseh from east to west. {48:6} Reuben will have one portion; it will border Ephraim from east to west. {48:7} Judah will have one portion; it will border Reuben from east to west. {48:8} Bordering Judah from east to west will be the portion you are to present as a special gift. It will be 25,000 cubits (about 8 miles) wide, and its length will be equal to the portions of the tribes, from east to west, with the sanctuary in the center. {48:9} The special portion you will offer to the LORD will be 25,000 cubits long and 10,000 cubits wide. {48:10} This will be the holy portion for the priests: It will be 25,000 cubits long on the north, 10,000 cubits wide on the west, 10,000 cubits wide on the east, and 25,000 cubits long on the south. The sanctuary of the LORD will be in the center of it. {48:11} It will be for the priests, the consecrated ones of the family of Zadok, who kept my charge and did not go astray like the Levites when the Israelites went astray. {48:12} It will be a special gift to them from the land, a most holy portion adjacent to the land of the Levites. {48:13} Alongside the territory of the priests, the Levites will have an allotment 25,000 cubits long and 10,000 cubits wide. The total length will be 25,000 cubits and the width 10,000 cubits. {48:14} They must not sell or exchange any of it; this is a special portion, holy to the LORD. {48:15} The remaining area, 5,000 cubits wide and 25,000 cubits long, will be for common use by the city, for houses and for pastureland. The city will be in the center of it. {48:16} These will be its measurements: The north side will be 4,500 cubits, the south side 4,500 cubits, the east side 4,500 cubits, and the west side 4,500 cubits. {48:17} The pasturelands for the city will extend 250 cubits to the north, 250 cubits to the south, 250 cubits to the east, and 250 cubits to the west. {48:18} The rest of the length, alongside the holy portion, will be 10,000 cubits eastward and 10,000 cubits westward. Its produce will provide food for the workers of the city. {48:19} The city workers from all the tribes of Israel will cultivate it. {48:20} The entire portion will be a square: 25,000 cubits by 25,000 cubits. You are to set aside the holy portion, along with the city property. {48:21} The remainder of the land will belong to the prince. It will border the holy portion and the city property, extending westward to the Mediterranean Sea and eastward to the Jordan River, alongside the allotments of the tribes. The prince's land will be next to the holy portion, with the sanctuary at its center. {48:22} So the land of the Levites and the city property, which are in the middle of the land belonging to the prince, will be between Judah's territory and Benjamin's territory. {48:23} As for the rest of the tribes, Benjamin will have one portion; it will extend from the east side to the west side. {48:24} Simeon will have one portion; it will border Benjamin from east to west. {48:25} Issachar will have one portion; it will border Simeon from east to west. {48:26} Zebulun will have one portion; it will border Issachar from east to west. {48:27} Gad will have one portion; it will border Zebulun from east to west. {48:28} The southern boundary of Gad will extend from Tamar to the waters of Meribah Kadesh, then along the Wadi of Egypt to the Mediterranean Sea. {48:29} This is the land you are to allot as an inheritance to the tribes of Israel, and these will be their portions, declares the Sovereign LORD. {48:30} These will be the exits of the city: Beginning on the north side, which is 4,500 cubits long, {48:31} the city will have three gates: the gate of Reuben, the gate of Judah, and the gate of Levi. {48:32} On the east side, which is 4,500 cubits long, there will be three gates: the gate of Joseph, the gate of Benjamin, and the gate of Dan. {48:33} On the south side, which is 4,500 cubits long, there will be three gates: the gate of Simeon, the gate of Issachar, and the gate of Zebulun. {48:34} On the west side, which is 4,500 cubits long, there will be three gates: the gate of Gad, the gate of Asher, and the gate of Naphtali. {48:35} The distance all around the city will be 18,000 cubits (about 6 miles). And the name of the city from that time on will be: The LORD is there.

The Book of Daniel

{1:1} In the third year of King Jehoiakim's reign in Judah, Nebuchadnezzar, the king of Babylon, came to Jerusalem and laid siege to it. {1:2} The Lord allowed Jehoiakim, the king of Judah, to be defeated, and part of the sacred items from the temple of God were taken. Nebuchadnezzar brought these items to the land of Shinar (Babylon) to the house of his god and placed them in the treasury of that god. {1:3} The king ordered Ashpenaz, the chief of his eunuchs, to bring some of the Israelites, including members of the royal family and nobility; {1:4} young men without any physical defects, handsome, skilled in all wisdom, knowledgeable, well-versed in science, and capable of serving in the king's palace. They were to be taught the language and literature of the Chaldeans (Babylonians). {1:5} The king assigned them daily rations of his own food and the wine he drank, nourishing them for three years, after which they were to serve him. {1:6} Among these young men were Daniel, Hananiah, Mishael, and Azariah from Judah. {1:7} The chief of the eunuchs gave them Babylonian names: Daniel became Belteshazzar, Hananiah became Shadrach, Mishael became Meshach, and Azariah became Abednego. {1:8} But Daniel made up his mind not to defile himself with the king's food or wine, so he asked the chief of the eunuchs if he could avoid defiling himself. {1:9} God caused the chief of the eunuchs to favor Daniel and show him kindness. {1:10} The chief of the eunuchs replied to Daniel, "I'm afraid of my lord the king, who has appointed your food and drink. Why should he see you looking worse than the other young men your age? Then he would endanger my life." {1:11} Daniel then spoke to Melzar, the steward appointed by the chief of the eunuchs to take care of him, Hananiah, Mishael, and Azariah, {1:12} and said, "Please test your servants for ten days. Let us be given vegetables to eat and water to drink. {1:13} Then compare our appearance with the young men who eat the king's food and see how we look. Deal with your servants according to what you see." {1:14} So he agreed to this and tested them for ten days. {1:15} At the end of the ten days, they looked healthier and better nourished than all the young men who ate the king's food. {1:16} So Melzar took away their portion of food and wine and gave them vegetables instead. {1:17} God gave these four young men knowledge and understanding in every kind of literature and wisdom; and Daniel had insight into all visions and dreams. {1:18} At the end of the training period the king had specified, the chief of the eunuchs brought them in before Nebuchadnezzar. {1:19} The king talked with them, and among them all, none was found like Daniel, Hananiah, Mishael, and Azariah. Therefore, they entered the king's service. {1:20} In every matter of wisdom and understanding that the king asked them about, he found them ten times better than all the magicians and enchanters in his entire kingdom. {1:21} Daniel remained there until the first year of King Cyrus.

{2:1} In the second year of Nebuchadnezzar's reign, he had dreams that troubled him, making it impossible for him to sleep. {2:2} So the king commanded the magicians, enchanters, sorcerers, and Chaldeans to come and tell him what he had dreamed. They came and stood before the king. {2:3} The king said to them, "I have had a dream that troubles me, and I want to know what it means." {2:4} The Chaldeans spoke to the king in Aramaic, "O king, live forever! Tell your servants the dream, and we will interpret it." {2:5} The king replied, "I'm not sure about this. If you do not tell me what I dreamed and its interpretation, you will be cut into pieces, and your houses will be made into piles of rubble. {2:6} But if you tell me the dream and its interpretation, I will reward you with gifts, great honor, and promotion. So tell me the dream and its interpretation." {2:7} They answered again, "Let the king tell his servants the dream, and we will interpret it." {2:8} The king said, "I know you're trying to buy time because you see that I have decided something. {2:9} If you do not tell me the dream, there is only one penalty for you. You have conspired to tell me misleading and false things, hoping the situation will change. So tell me the dream, and I will know you can give me its interpretation." {2:10} The Chaldeans replied, "There is no man on earth who can do what you're asking. No king, lord, or ruler has ever asked such a thing of any magician, enchanter, or Chaldean. {2:11} What you ask is too difficult; no one can reveal it to the king except the gods, and they do not live among humans." {2:12} This made the king so angry and furious that he ordered the execution of all the wise men of Babylon. {2:13} So the order was issued to put the wise men to death, and they looked for Daniel and his friends to kill them. {2:14} When Daniel spoke with Arioch, the commander of the king's guard who had gone out to execute the wise men of Babylon, he asked, "Why did the king issue such a harsh decree?" Arioch explained the situation to Daniel. {2:15} Daniel went in and asked the king to give him some time, and he would tell him the interpretation. {2:16} Then Daniel returned to his house and informed his friends Hananiah, Mishael, and Azariah about the matter. {2:17} He urged them to pray for mercy from the God of heaven concerning this mystery so they would not be executed with the rest of the wise men. {2:18} The mystery was revealed to Daniel in a night vision, and he praised the God of heaven. {2:19} Daniel said, "Praise be to the name of God forever and ever; wisdom and power belong to him. {2:20} He changes times and seasons; he deposes kings and raises up others. He gives wisdom to the wise and knowledge to the discerning. {2:21} He reveals deep and hidden things; he knows what lies in darkness, and light dwells with him. {2:22} I thank and praise you, O God of my ancestors: you have given me wisdom and power, and you have made known to me what we asked of you. You have made known to us the king's matter." {2:23} Therefore, Daniel went to Arioch, whom the king had appointed to execute the wise men of Babylon. He said, "Don't destroy the wise men of Babylon. Take me to the king, and I will interpret his dream for him." {2:24} Arioch took Daniel to the king quickly and said, "I have found a man from the captives of Judah who can tell the king what his dream means." {2:25} The king asked Daniel, who was named Belteshazzar, "Are you able to tell me what I saw in my dream and its interpretation?" {2:26} Daniel replied, "No wise man, enchanter, magician, or diviner can explain to the king the mystery he has asked about. {2:27} But there is a God in heaven who reveals mysteries, and he has shown King Nebuchadnezzar what will happen in the days to come. Your dream and the visions that passed through your mind as you lay on your bed are these: {2:28} As you, O king, were lying there, your thoughts turned to what will happen in the future. The revealer of mysteries has shown you what is to come. {2:29} As for me, this mystery has been revealed to me not because I have greater wisdom than any other living person, but so that you may know the interpretation and understand what went through your mind. {2:30} You looked, O king, and there before you stood a large statue—an enormous, dazzling statue, awesome in appearance. {2:31} The head of the statue was made of pure gold, its chest and arms of silver, its belly and thighs of bronze, {2:32} its legs of iron, its feet partly of iron and partly of baked clay. {2:33} While you were watching, a rock was cut out, but not by human hands. It struck the statue on its feet of iron and clay and smashed them. {2:34} Then the iron, clay, bronze, silver, and gold were broken to pieces at the same time and became like chaff on a threshing floor in the summer. The wind swept them away without leaving a trace, but the rock that struck the statue became a huge mountain and filled the whole earth. {2:35} This was the dream, and now we will interpret it for the king. {2:36} You, O king, are the king of kings. The God of heaven has given you dominion and power and might and glory; {2:37} In your hand, he has placed all mankind and the beasts of the field and the birds in the sky. Wherever they live, he has made you ruler over them all. You are that head of gold. {2:38} After you, another kingdom will arise, inferior to yours. Next, a third kingdom, one of bronze, will rule over the whole earth. {2:39} Finally, there will be a fourth kingdom, strong as iron, for iron breaks and smashes everything. As iron breaks things to pieces, so it will crush and break all the others. {2:40} Just as you saw that the feet and toes were partly of baked clay and partly of iron, so this will be a divided kingdom; yet it will have some of the strength of iron in it, even as you saw iron mixed with clay. {2:41} As the toes were partly iron and partly clay, so this kingdom will be partly strong and partly brittle. {2:42} And just as you saw iron mixed with baked clay, so the people will be a mixture and will not remain united, any more than iron mixes with clay. {2:43} In the time of those kings, the God of heaven will set up a kingdom that will never be destroyed, nor will it be left to another people. It will crush all those kingdoms and bring them to an end, but it will itself endure forever. {2:44} This is the meaning of the rock cut out of the mountain, but not by human hands—it smashed the iron, the bronze, the clay, the silver, and the gold. The great God has shown the king what will take place in the future. The dream is true, and its interpretation is trustworthy." {2:45} Then King Nebuchadnezzar fell prostrate before Daniel and paid him honor and ordered that an offering and incense be presented to him. {2:46} The king said to Daniel, "Surely your God is the God of gods and the Lord of kings and a revealer of mysteries, for you were able to reveal this mystery." {2:47} The king placed Daniel in a high position and lavished many gifts on him. He made him ruler over the entire province of Babylon and placed him in charge of all its wise men. {2:48} Moreover, at Daniel's request, the king appointed Shadrach, Meshach, and Abednego administrators over the province of Babylon, while Daniel himself remained at the royal court.

{3:1} King Nebuchadnezzar made a huge golden statue, 90 feet tall and 9 feet wide, and set it up on the plain of Dura in Babylon. {3:2} He then sent for the rulers, governors, captains, judges, treasurers, counselors, and officials from all the provinces to come to the dedication of the statue he had set up. {3:3} So all these leaders gathered for the dedication and stood before the statue. {3:4} Then a herald shouted, "You are commanded, O peoples, nations, and languages, {3:5} that when you hear the sound of the horn, flute, harp, lyre, and all kinds of music, you must fall down and worship the golden statue that King Nebuchadnezzar has set up. {3:6} Anyone who does not fall down and worship will be thrown into a blazing furnace." {3:7} Therefore, when all the people heard the music, they fell down and worshipped the golden statue. {3:8} At that time, some Chaldeans came forward and accused the Jews. {3:9} They said to King Nebuchadnezzar, "O king, live forever! {3:10} You have made a decree that everyone who hears the music must fall down and worship the golden statue. {3:11} Anyone who does not worship will be thrown into a blazing furnace. {3:12} There are some Jews whom you appointed over the province of Babylon—Shadrach, Meshach, and Abednego. They pay no attention to you, O king; they do not serve your gods or worship the golden statue." {3:13} Nebuchadnezzar was furious and commanded that Shadrach, Meshach, and Abednego be brought before him. {3:14} He asked them, "Is it true, Shadrach, Meshach, and Abednego, that you do not serve my gods or worship the golden statue I have set up? {3:15} Now, if you are ready to hear the music and fall down and worship the statue, that's good. But if you don't, you will be thrown into the blazing furnace. Who is the god that can rescue you from my power?" {3:16} Shadrach, Meshach, and Abednego replied, "O Nebuchadnezzar, we do not need to defend ourselves before you. {3:17} If we are thrown into the blazing furnace, the God we serve is able to save us, and he will rescue us from your hand, O king. {3:18} But even if he does not, we want you to know that we will not serve your gods or worship the golden statue." {3:19} Nebuchadnezzar was furious, and his face became distorted with anger at Shadrach, Meshach, and Abednego. He ordered the furnace to be heated seven times hotter than usual. {3:20} He commanded the strongest soldiers to bind them and throw them into the blazing furnace. {3:21} So they were bound and thrown into the furnace, fully clothed. {3:22} The king's command was urgent, and the furnace was extremely hot; the flames killed the soldiers who took them up. {3:23} The three men fell into the blazing furnace, still tied up. {3:24} Then Nebuchadnezzar leaped to his feet in amazement and asked his advisors, "Didn't we throw three men into the fire?" They replied, "Yes, O king." {3:25} He said, "Look! I see four men walking around in the fire, unbound and unharmed, and the fourth looks like a divine being." {3:26} Nebuchadnezzar approached the opening of the furnace and shouted, "Shadrach, Meshach, and Abednego, servants of the Most High God, come out!" So they came out of the fire. {3:27} The governors, officials, and king's counselors gathered and saw that the fire had not harmed their bodies; not a hair on their heads was singed, their clothes were unaffected, and there was no smell of fire on them. {3:28} Nebuchadnezzar said, "Praise be to the God of Shadrach, Meshach, and Abednego, who sent his angel and rescued his servants! They trusted in him and defied the king's command and were willing to give up their lives rather than serve or worship any god except their own. {3:29} Therefore, I decree that the people of any nation or language who say anything against the God of Shadrach, Meshach, and Abednego will be cut into pieces, and their homes will be turned into piles of rubble, for no other god can save this way." {3:30} Then the king promoted Shadrach, Meshach, and Abednego in the province of Babylon.

{4:1} King Nebuchadnezzar sent a message to all peoples, nations, and languages on earth: "Peace be multiplied to you! {4:2} I want to share the miraculous signs and wonders that the Most High God has done for me. {4:3} How great are his signs! How mighty are his wonders! His kingdom is everlasting, and his dominion is from generation to generation. {4:4} I, Nebuchadnezzar, was at home in my palace, enjoying prosperity. {4:5} But I had a dream that frightened me, and the visions I saw while lying in bed disturbed me. {4:6} So I issued a decree to bring all the wise men of Babylon before me to interpret the dream. {4:7} The magicians, astrologers, Chaldeans, and diviners came in, and I told them the dream, but they couldn't interpret it for me. {4:8} Finally, Daniel came in, whose name is Belteshazzar (after my god), and in him is the spirit of the holy gods. I told him the dream, {4:9} saying, "Belteshazzar, master of the magicians, I know that the spirit of the holy gods is in you, and no mystery is too difficult for you. Tell me the visions of my dream." {4:10} Here are the visions I saw while lying in bed: I saw a huge tree in the middle of the earth, and it was very tall. {4:11} The tree grew large and strong, reaching to the sky and visible to the ends of the earth. {4:12} Its leaves were beautiful, its fruit abundant, and it provided food for all. The animals found shade under it, and the birds nested in its branches; all creatures were fed from it. {4:13} While I was watching in my vision, a holy one came down from heaven. {4:14} He shouted, "Cut down the tree and trim off its branches, strip its leaves, and scatter its fruit! Let the animals flee from under it, and the birds from its branches. {4:15} But leave the stump and roots in the ground, surrounded by a band of iron and bronze, in the grass of the field. Let him be drenched with the dew of heaven and eat grass like the animals for seven years. {4:16} Let his mind be changed from that of a man and let him be given the mind of an animal until seven times pass by for him. {4:17} This is the decree of the watchers, the sentence of the holy ones, so that the living may know that the Most High rules the kingdom of men and gives it to whomever he wishes and sets over it the lowliest of men. {4:18} This is the dream I, King Nebuchadnezzar, had. Now, Belteshazzar, explain its meaning, because none of the wise men can do so, but you can, for the spirit of the holy gods is in you." {4:19} Then Daniel, whose name was Belteshazzar, was perplexed for a time, and his thoughts terrified him. The king said, "Belteshazzar, don't let the dream or its meaning trouble you." Belteshazzar answered, "My lord, if only the dream applied to your enemies and its meaning to your adversaries! {4:20} The tree you saw, which grew and became strong, reaching to the sky and visible to all the earth, {4:21} with beautiful leaves and abundant fruit, providing food for all, under which the animals lived and in whose branches the birds nested— {4:22} that tree is you, O king! You have grown and become strong; your greatness has grown until it reaches the sky, and your dominion extends to the ends of the earth. {4:23} The king saw a holy one coming down from heaven saying, 'Cut down the tree and destroy it, but leave the stump and roots in the ground,' until seven times pass over him. {4:24} This is the interpretation, O king, and this is the decree of the Most High that has come upon my lord the king: {4:25} You will be driven away from people and live with the animals; you will eat grass like an ox and be drenched with the dew of heaven. Seven times will pass over you until you acknowledge that the Most High rules over the kingdom of men and gives it to whomever he wishes. {4:26} As for the stump left in the tree roots, your kingdom will be restored to you when you acknowledge that Heaven rules. {4:27} Therefore, O king, be pleased to accept my advice: renounce your sins by doing what is right and your wickedness by being kind to the oppressed. It may be that your prosperity will continue." {4:28} All this happened to King Nebuchadnezzar. {4:29} Twelve months later, as the king was walking on the roof of the royal palace in Babylon, {4:30} he said, "Isn't this the great Babylon I have built as a royal residence, by my mighty power and for the glory of my majesty?" {4:31} The words were still on his lips when a voice came from heaven: "This is what is decreed for you, King Nebuchadnezzar: Your royal authority has been taken from you. {4:32} You will be driven away from people and will live with the animals; you will eat grass like an ox. Seven times will pass over you until you acknowledge that the Most High rules the kingdom of men and gives it to whomever he wishes." {4:33} Immediately, what had been said about Nebuchadnezzar was fulfilled: he was driven away from people and ate grass like an ox; his body was drenched with the dew of heaven until his hair grew like the feathers of an eagle and his nails like the claws of a bird. {4:34} At the end of that time, I, Nebuchadnezzar, raised my eyes toward heaven, and my sanity was restored. I praised the Most High; I honored and glorified him who lives forever. His dominion is an everlasting dominion, and his kingdom endures from generation to generation. {4:35} All the peoples of the earth are regarded as nothing. He does as he pleases with the powers of heaven and the peoples of the earth. No one can hold back his hand or say to him, "What have you done?" {4:36} At the same time that my sanity was restored, my honor and splendor returned to me for the glory of my kingdom. My advisors and nobles sought me out, and I was restored to my throne and became even greater than before. {4:37} Now I, Nebuchadnezzar, praise and exalt and glorify the King of heaven, because everything he does is right, and all his ways are just. Those who walk in pride he is able to humble.

{5:1} King Belshazzar gave a great feast for a thousand of his lords and drank wine in front of them. {5:2} While he tasted the wine, he ordered the golden and silver vessels that his father Nebuchadnezzar had taken from the temple in Jerusalem to be brought in, so that he, his nobles, his wives, and his concubines could drink from them. {5:3} They brought in the golden vessels taken from the temple of God in Jerusalem, and the king and his nobles, wives, and concubines drank from them. {5:4} They drank wine and praised the gods of gold, silver, bronze, iron, wood, and stone. {5:5} At that moment, fingers of a human hand appeared and wrote on the plaster of the wall in the king's palace, near the lampstand. The king saw the hand that wrote. {5:6} Then the king's face turned pale, and he was so frightened that his knees knocked together. {5:7} The king shouted for the astrologers, Chaldeans, and diviners. He said to the wise men of Babylon, "Whoever can read this writing and tell me what it means will be clothed in purple, have a gold chain around his neck, and be the third ruler in the kingdom." {5:8} All the king's wise men came in, but they could not read the writing or tell the king what it meant. {5:9} King Belshazzar became greatly troubled, and his face turned pale, and his nobles were confused. {5:10} The queen, hearing the king and his nobles talking, came into the banquet hall and said, "O king, live forever! Don't let your thoughts trouble you, or your face be pale. {5:11} There is a man in your kingdom who has the spirit of the holy gods in him. In the days of your father, he had light and understanding and wisdom like that of the gods. King Nebuchadnezzar, your father, made him chief of the magicians, astrologers, Chaldeans, and diviners. {5:12} He has an extraordinary spirit, knowledge, and understanding, able to interpret dreams, explain riddles, and solve problems. Call for Daniel, whom the king named Belteshazzar, and he will tell you what it means." {5:13} Daniel was brought in before the king, who asked him, "Are you that Daniel from the Jewish exile whom my father brought from Judah? {5:14} I have heard that the spirit of the gods is in you, and that you have insight, intelligence, and extraordinary wisdom. {5:15} The wise men and astrologers were brought before me to read this writing and tell me what it means, but they could not explain it. {5:16} I have heard that you can interpret dreams and solve problems. If you can read this writing and tell me what it means, you will be clothed in purple, wear a gold chain around your neck, and be the third ruler in the kingdom." {5:17} Daniel answered the king, "You may keep your gifts for yourself and give your rewards to someone else. But I will read the writing for the king and tell him what it means. {5:18} O king, the Most High God gave your father Nebuchadnezzar sovereignty, greatness, glory, and honor. {5:19} Because of the greatness he gave him, all peoples, nations, and men of every language dreaded and feared him. He killed whom he wished, spared whom he wished, honored whom he wished, and humbled whom he wished. {5:20} But when his heart became arrogant and hardened with pride, he was deposed from his royal throne and stripped of his glory. {5:21} He was driven away from people and given the mind of an animal; he lived with the wild donkeys and ate grass like an ox. His body was drenched with the dew of heaven until he acknowledged that the Most High God rules the kingdom of men and gives it to anyone he wishes. {5:22} But you, his son Belshazzar, have not humbled yourself, even though you knew all this. {5:23} Instead, you have set yourself up against the Lord of heaven. You brought the vessels from his temple, and you and your nobles, wives, and concubines drank wine from them. You praised the gods of silver, gold, bronze, iron, wood, and stone, which cannot see, hear, or understand. But you did not honor the God who holds in his hand your life and all your ways. {5:24} Therefore, he sent the hand that wrote the inscription. {5:25} This is the inscription that was written: MENE, MENE, TEKEL, UPHARSIN. {5:26} This is what these words mean: MENE: God has numbered your kingdom and brought it to an end. {5:27} TEKEL: You have been weighed on the scales and found wanting. {5:28} PERES: Your kingdom is divided and given to the Medes and Persians." {5:29} Belshazzar gave the command, and Daniel was clothed in purple, with a gold chain around his neck, and proclaimed the third ruler in the kingdom. {5:30} That very night, Belshazzar, king of the Chaldeans, was slain. {5:31} And Darius the Mede took over the kingdom at the age of sixty-two.

{6:1} It pleased Darius to appoint 120 satraps (governors) to rule throughout the kingdom. {6:2} Over them, he placed three administrators, one of whom was Daniel, so that the satraps might give an account to them and the king would not suffer loss. {6:3} Now Daniel so distinguished himself among the administrators and the satraps by his exceptional qualities that the king planned to set him over the entire kingdom. {6:4} At this, the administrators and satraps tried to find grounds for charges against Daniel in his conduct of government affairs, but they were unable to do so. They could find no corruption in him because he was trustworthy and neither corrupt nor negligent. {6:5} Finally, these men said, "We will never find any basis for charges against this Daniel unless it has something to do with the law of his God." {6:6} So the administrators and satraps went as a group to the king and said: "May King Darius live forever! {6:7} The royal administrators, prefects, satraps, advisers, and governors have all agreed that the king should issue an edict and enforce the decree that anyone who prays to any god or human during the next thirty days, except to you, O king, shall be thrown into the lions' den. {6:8} Now, O king, issue the decree and put it in writing so that it cannot be altered, in accordance with the laws of the Medes and Persians, which cannot be repealed." {6:9} So King Darius put the decree in writing. {6:10} Now when Daniel learned that the decree had been published, he went home to his upstairs room where the windows opened toward Jerusalem. Three times a day he got down on his knees and prayed, giving thanks to his God, just as he had done before. {6:11} Then these men went as a group and found Daniel praying and asking God for help. {6:12} They went to the king and spoke to him about his royal decree: "Did you not publish a decree that during the next thirty days anyone who prays to any god or human except to you, O king, would be thrown into the lions' den?" The king answered, "The decree stands in accordance with the laws of the Medes and Persians, which cannot be repealed." {6:13} Then they said to the king, "Daniel, who is one of the exiles from Judah, pays no attention to you, O king, or to the decree you put in writing. He still prays three times a day." {6:14} When the king heard this, he was greatly distressed; he was determined to rescue Daniel and made every effort until sundown to save him. {6:15} Then the men went as a group to King Darius and said to him: "Remember, O king, that according to the law of the Medes and Persians no decree or edict that the king issues can be changed." {6:16} So the king gave the order, and they brought Daniel and threw him into the lions' den. The king said to Daniel, "May your God, whom you serve continually, rescue you!" {6:17} A stone was brought and placed over the mouth of the den, and the king sealed it with his own signet ring and with the rings of his nobles, so that Daniel's situation might not be changed. {6:18} Then the king returned to his palace and spent the night without eating and without any entertainment being brought to him. He could not sleep. {6:19} At the first light of dawn, the king got up and hurried to the lions' den. {6:20} When he came near the den, he called out to Daniel in an anguished voice, "Daniel, servant of the living God, has your God, whom you serve continually, been able to rescue you from the lions?" {6:21} Daniel answered, "O king, live forever! {6:22} My God sent his angel, and he shut the mouths of the lions. They have not hurt me, because I was found innocent in his sight. Nor have I ever done any wrong before you, O king." {6:23} The king was overjoyed and gave orders to lift Daniel out of the den. When Daniel was lifted from the den, no wound was found on him because he had trusted in his God. {6:24} At the king's command, the men who had falsely accused Daniel were brought in and thrown into the lions' den, along with their wives and children. Before they reached the floor of the den, the lions overpowered them and crushed all their bones. {6:25} Then King Darius wrote to all the nations and peoples of every language in all the earth: "May you prosper greatly! {6:26} I issue a decree that in every part of my kingdom people must fear and reverence the God of Daniel. For he is the living God and he endures forever; his kingdom will not be destroyed, and his dominion will never end. {6:27} He rescues and saves; he performs signs and wonders in the heavens and on the earth. He has rescued Daniel from the power of the lions." {6:28} So Daniel prospered during the reign of Darius and the reign of Cyrus the Persian.

{7:1} In the first year of King Belshazzar of Babylon, Daniel had a dream and visions in his mind while lying in bed; he wrote down the dream, summarizing the events. {7:2} Daniel said, "In my night vision, I saw the four winds of heaven stirring up the great sea. {7:3} Four great beasts came up out of the sea, each different from the others. {7:4} The first was like a lion but had eagle's wings; I watched until the wings were plucked off, and it was lifted from the ground and made to stand like a man, and a man's heart was given to it. {7:5} Then I saw another beast, a second one like a bear, raised up on one side, with three ribs in its mouth between its teeth. They said to it, 'Get up, eat your fill of flesh.' {7:6} After this, I looked, and there was another beast, like a leopard, which had four wings of a bird on its back and four heads; it was given authority. {7:7} After this, in my night visions, I saw a fourth beast, terrifying and powerful, with huge iron teeth. It crushed and devoured its victims and trampled underfoot whatever was left; it was different from all the beasts that had come before it, and it had ten horns. {7:8} I was considering the horns when another horn, a little one, came up among them, and three of the first horns were uprooted before it. This horn had eyes like a man and a mouth that spoke boastfully. {7:9} I watched until thrones were set in place, and the Ancient of Days took his seat. His clothing was white as snow, and the hair of his head was like pure wool. His throne was fiery flames, and its wheels were burning fire. {7:10} A river of fire flowed out from before him. Thousands upon thousands attended him; ten thousand times ten thousand stood before him. The court was seated, and the books were opened. {7:11} I continued to watch because of the boastful words of the horn. I watched until the beast was slain, its body destroyed, and thrown into the fire. {7:12} As for the other beasts, their dominion was taken away, but their lives were prolonged for a season and a time. {7:13} In my night visions, I saw one like a Son of Man coming with the clouds of heaven. He approached the Ancient of Days and was led into his presence. {7:14} He was given authority, glory, and sovereign power; all peoples, nations, and languages worshiped him. His dominion is an everlasting dominion that will not pass away, and his kingdom is one that will never be destroyed. {7:15} I, Daniel, was troubled in spirit, and the visions that passed through my mind disturbed me. {7:16} I approached one of those standing there and asked him the meaning of all this. So he told me and gave me the interpretation of these things. {7:17} These four great beasts are four kings that will rise from the earth. {7:18} But the holy people of the Most High will receive the kingdom and will possess it forever—yes, forever and ever. {7:19} Then I wanted to know the meaning of the fourth beast, which was different from all the others, exceedingly terrifying, with iron teeth and bronze claws; it devoured, crushed, and trampled underfoot whatever was left. {7:20} I also wanted to know about the ten horns on its head and about the other horn that came up, before which three of them fell, the horn that looked more imposing than the others and had eyes and a mouth that spoke boastfully. {7:21} As I watched, this horn waged war against the holy people and was defeating them. {7:22} Until the Ancient of Days came and judgment was given in favor of the holy people of the Most High; the time came when they possessed the kingdom. {7:23} He gave me this explanation: "The fourth beast is a fourth kingdom that will appear on earth; it will be different from all the other kingdoms and will devour the whole earth, trampling it down and crushing it. {7:24} The ten horns are ten kings who will arise from this kingdom. Another king will arise after them; he will be different from the earlier ones and will subdue three kings. {7:25} He will speak against the Most High and oppress his holy people and try to change the set times and the laws. The holy people will be delivered into his hands for a time, times, and half a time. {7:26} But the court will sit, and his power will be taken away and completely destroyed forever. {7:27} Then the sovereignty, power, and greatness of all the kingdoms under heaven will be handed over to the holy people of the Most High. His kingdom will be an everlasting kingdom, and all rulers will worship and obey him." {7:28} This is the end of the matter. As for me, Daniel, my thoughts were greatly troubling me, and my face turned pale; but I kept the matter to myself.

{8:1} In the third year of King Belshazzar's reign, a vision appeared to me, Daniel, after the one that had already appeared to me. {8:2} In this vision, I was in the citadel of Susa in the province of Elam, by the Ulai River. {8:3} I looked up, and there before me was a ram with two horns, standing by the river. The two horns were long, but one was longer than the other, and the longer one came up last. {8:4} I watched the ram as it charged westward, northward, and southward. No beast could stand against it, and none could rescue from its power; it did as it pleased and became great. {8:5} As I was thinking about this, a goat with a prominent horn between its eyes came from the west, crossing the whole earth without touching the ground. {8:6} It came toward the ram that had two horns and charged at it in great rage. {8:7} I saw it attack the ram, striking it and breaking its two horns. The ram was powerless to stand against it; the goat knocked it to the ground and trampled on it, and none could rescue the ram from its power. {8:8} The goat became very great, but at the height of its power, the large horn was broken off, and in its place, four prominent horns grew up toward the four winds of heaven. {8:9} Out of one of them came a little horn that grew exceedingly great toward the south and the east and toward the beautiful land. {8:10} It grew until it reached the host of heaven and threw some of the starry host down to the earth and trampled on them. {8:11} It set itself up to be as great as the Commander of the host; it took away the daily sacrifice from him and desecrated his sanctuary. {8:12} Because of rebellion, the host of the saints and the daily sacrifice were given over to it. It prospered in everything it did, and truth was thrown to the ground. {8:13} Then I heard a holy one speaking, and another holy one said to him, "How long will it take for the vision to be fulfilled—the vision concerning the daily sacrifice, the rebellion that causes desolation, and the surrender of the sanctuary and of the host that will be trampled underfoot?" {8:14} He said to me, "It will take 2,300 evenings and mornings; then the sanctuary will be reconsecrated." {8:15} While I, Daniel, was watching the vision and trying to understand it, there before me stood one who looked like a man. {8:16} And I heard a man's voice calling from the Ulai River, "Gabriel, tell this man the meaning of the vision." {8:17} As he came near the place where I was standing, I was terrified and fell prostrate. "Son of man," he said to me, "understand that the vision concerns the time of the end." {8:18} While he was speaking to me, I was in a deep sleep, with my face to the ground. Then he touched me and raised me to my feet. {8:19} He said: "I am going to tell you what will happen later in the time of wrath, because the vision concerns the appointed time of the end. {8:20} The ram you saw with the two horns stands for the kings of Media and Persia. {8:21} The shaggy goat is the king of Greece, and the large horn between its eyes is the first king. {8:22} The four horns that replaced the one that was broken off represent four kingdoms that will emerge from his nation but will not have the same power. {8:23} In the latter part of their reign, when rebels have become completely wicked, a fierce-looking king, a master of intrigue, will arise. {8:24} His power will be great, but not by his own power; he will cause astounding devastation and will succeed in whatever he does. He will destroy those who are mighty, the holy people. {8:25} He will cause deceit to prosper, and he will consider himself superior. When they feel secure, he will destroy many and take his stand against the Prince of princes. Yet he will be destroyed, but not by human power. {8:26} The vision of the evenings and mornings that has been given you is true, but seal up the vision, for it concerns the distant future." {8:27} I, Daniel, was worn out. I lay exhausted for several days; then I got up and went about the king's business. I was appalled by the vision; it was beyond understanding.

{9:1} In the first year of Darius, son of Ahasuerus, from the Medes, who became king over the Chaldeans, {9:2} in the first year of his reign, I, Daniel, understood from the scriptures the number of years that, according to the word of the LORD given to the prophet Jeremiah, must pass before the desolation of Jerusalem would be completed: seventy years. {9:3} So I turned to the Lord God and sought him with prayer and pleading, with fasting, sackcloth, and ashes. {9:4} I prayed to the LORD my God and confessed, saying, "O Lord, the great and awesome God, who keeps his covenant and shows steadfast love to those who love him and keep his commandments, {9:5} we have sinned and done wrong; we have acted wickedly and rebelled, turning away from your commands and laws. {9:6} We have not listened to your servants, the prophets, who spoke in your name to our kings, our princes, our ancestors, and all the people of the land. {9:7} O Lord, you are righteous, but this day we are covered with shame—the people of Judah, the inhabitants of Jerusalem, and all Israel, both near and far, in all the countries where you have scattered us because of our unfaithfulness to you. {9:8} O Lord, shame belongs to us, to our kings, our princes, and our ancestors, because we have sinned against you. {9:9} The Lord our God is merciful and forgiving, even though we have rebelled against him; {9:10} we have not obeyed the voice of the LORD our God by following his laws that he set before us through his servants, the prophets. {9:11} All Israel has rejected your law and turned away, refusing to listen; so the curses and oaths written in the Law of Moses, the servant of God, have been poured out on us because we have sinned against him. {9:12} He has confirmed his words spoken against us and against our rulers by bringing upon us a great disaster; under the whole heaven, nothing has ever been done like what has been done to Jerusalem. {9:13} As it is written in the Law of Moses, all this disaster has come upon us, yet we did not make our prayer before the LORD our God to turn from our iniquities and understand your truth. {9:14} Therefore the LORD kept the disaster in mind and brought it upon us; for the LORD our God is righteous in all his actions, but we have not obeyed his voice. {9:15} Now, O Lord our God, who brought your people out of Egypt with a mighty hand and made a name for yourself that endures to this day; we have sinned, we have done wrong. {9:16} O Lord, in keeping with all your righteous acts, I ask you to turn away your anger and your fury from your city Jerusalem, your holy mountain; because of our sins and the iniquities of our ancestors, Jerusalem and your people have become a reproach to all those around us. {9:17} Now, our God, hear the prayers and petitions of your servant; for your sake, Lord, look with favor on your desolate sanctuary. {9:18} O my God, incline your ear and hear; open your eyes and see the desolation of the city that bears your name. We do not make requests of you because we are righteous, but because of your great mercy. {9:19} Lord, listen! Lord, forgive! Lord, hear and act! For your sake, my God, do not delay, because your city and your people bear your Name. {9:20} While I was speaking and praying, confessing my sin and the sin of my people Israel and making my request to the LORD my God for the holy mountain of my God, {9:21} while I was still in prayer, Gabriel, the man I had seen in the earlier vision, came to me in swift flight about the time of the evening sacrifice. {9:22} He instructed me and said to me, "Daniel, I have now come to give you insight and understanding. {9:23} As soon as you began to pray, a word went out, which I have come to tell you, for you are highly esteemed; therefore, consider the word and understand the vision. {9:24} Seventy weeks are decreed for your people and your holy city to finish transgression, to put an end to sin, to atone for wickedness, to bring in everlasting righteousness, to seal up vision and prophecy, and to anoint the Most Holy Place. {9:25} Know and understand this: From the issuing of the decree to restore and rebuild Jerusalem until the Anointed One, the ruler, comes, there will be seven sevens and sixty-two sevens. It will be rebuilt with streets and a trench, but in times of trouble. {9:26} After the sixty-two sevens, the Anointed One will be put to death and will have nothing. The people of the ruler who will come will destroy the city and the sanctuary. The end will come like a flood: War will continue until the end, and desolations have been decreed. {9:27} He will confirm a covenant with many for one week. In the middle of that week, he will put an end to sacrifice and offering. And at the temple, he will set up an abomination that causes desolation, until the end that is decreed is poured out on the desolator.

{10:1} In the third year of King Cyrus of Persia, a revelation was given to Daniel (also called Belteshazzar). Its message was true and concerned a great conflict; he understood the vision. {10:2} At that time, I, Daniel, mourned for three weeks. {10:3} I ate no choice food; no meat or wine touched my lips, and I used no lotions at all until the three weeks were over. {10:4} On the twenty-fourth day of the first month, as I was standing by the great river, the Tigris, {10:5} I looked up and there before me was a man dressed in linen, with a belt of fine gold from Uphaz around his waist. {10:6} His body was like topaz, his face like lightning, his eyes like flaming torches, his arms and legs like the gleam of burnished bronze, and his voice like the sound of a multitude. {10:7} I, Daniel, was the only one who saw the vision; those who were with me did not see it, but such terror overwhelmed them that they fled and hid themselves. {10:8} So I was left alone, gazing at this great vision; I had no strength left, my face turned deathly pale, and I was helpless. {10:9} Then I heard him speaking, and as I listened to him, I fell into a deep sleep, my face to the ground. {10:10} A hand touched me and set me trembling on my hands and knees. {10:11} He said, "Daniel, you are highly esteemed. Consider carefully the words I am about to speak to you and stand up, for I have now been sent to you." And when he said this, I stood up trembling. {10:12} Then he continued, "Do not be afraid, Daniel. Since the first day that you set your mind to gain understanding and to humble yourself before your God, your words were heard, and I have come in response to them. {10:13} But the prince of the Persian kingdom resisted me twenty-one days. Then Michael, one of the chief princes, came to help me because I was detained there with the king of Persia. {10:14} Now I have come to explain to you what will happen to your people in the future, for the vision concerns a time yet to come." {10:15} While he was saying this to me, I bowed with my face toward the ground and was speechless. {10:16} Then one who looked like a man touched my lips, and I opened my mouth and began to speak. I said to the one standing before me, "I am overwhelmed with anguish because of the vision, my Lord, and I feel weak. {10:17} How can I, your servant, talk with you, my Lord? My strength is gone, and I can hardly breathe." {10:18} Again the one who looked like a man touched me and gave me strength. {10:19} "Do not be afraid, you who are highly esteemed," he said. "Peace! Be strong now; be strong." When he spoke to me, I was strengthened and said, "Speak, my Lord, since you have given me strength." {10:20} So he said, "Do you know why I have come to you? Soon I will return to fight against the prince of Persia, and when I go, the prince of Greece will come; {10:21} but first, I will tell you what is written in the Book of Truth. No one supports me against them except Michael, your prince."

{11:1} In the first year of Darius the Mede, I stood to support and strengthen him. {11:2} Now I will reveal the truth: there will be three more kings in Persia, and the fourth will be much richer than all of them. Through his wealth, he will stir up everyone against Greece. {11:3} A powerful king will arise who will rule with great authority and act according to his own will. {11:4} But when he rises, his kingdom will be broken and divided in all directions; it will not go to his descendants or follow the greatness he had, as it will be taken away and given to others. {11:5} The king of the south will be strong, and one of his officials will be even stronger and have great authority. {11:6} In the end, they will join forces; the king's daughter from the south will go to the king of the north to make a deal. However, she will not maintain her power, nor will he or his strength endure; she will be given up, along with those who brought her and those who supported her at that time. {11:7} But from her roots, a branch will rise to take his place, coming with an army to attack the fortress of the king of the north, and he will prevail. {11:8} He will also carry captives and their gods into Egypt, along with their princes and valuable treasures of silver and gold; he will last longer than the king of the north. {11:9} Then the king of the south will come into his kingdom but will return to his own land. {11:10} His sons will be stirred up and gather a large army; one of them will come and overflow and invade, then return and be stirred up against his fortress. {11:11} The king of the south will become furious and go out to fight the king of the north; he will set forth a great multitude, but the multitude will be given into his hand. {11:12} After defeating the multitude, his heart will be lifted up, and he will cast down many thousands, but he will not be strengthened by it. {11:13} The king of the north will return with an even larger army after some years, bringing great wealth. {11:14} During those times, many will rise against the king of the south; even the robbers of your people will attempt to fulfill the vision, but they will fall. {11:15} The king of the north will come and build a siege ramp and take the strongest cities; the southern forces will not be able to withstand him, nor will his chosen people have any strength. {11:16} Whoever comes against him will act according to his own will, and no one will stand before him. He will stand in the glorious land, which he will consume. {11:17} He will also set his sights on entering with the full strength of his kingdom, bringing upright individuals with him; he will give the daughter of women (a woman of high status) to corrupt her, but she will not support him or be loyal to him. {11:18} After this, he will turn his attention to the islands, taking many, but a prince will cause his disgrace to cease, turning the reproach back on him. {11:19} Then he will turn toward the fortresses of his own land, but he will stumble and fall, and will not be found. {11:20} A tax raiser will take his place in the glory of the kingdom, but within a few days he will be destroyed, neither in anger nor in battle. {11:21} In his place, a contemptible person will arise; they will not honor him with the kingdom, but he will come in peacefully and obtain the kingdom through flattery. {11:22} With a flood of forces, they will be swept away before him, including the prince of the covenant. {11:23} After forming an alliance with him, he will act deceitfully; he will rise and become strong with a small group of people. {11:24} He will enter peacefully into the richest parts of the province and do what his forefathers never did; he will distribute plunder, spoil, and riches among them, and he will plot against strongholds for a time. {11:25} He will gather his strength and courage to fight against the king of the south with a great army, and the king of the south will mobilize a very large and mighty army for battle, but he will not stand, for they will devise schemes against him. {11:26} Those who eat from his provisions will destroy him, and his army will overflow, and many will fall slain. {11:27} Both kings will have hearts intent on evil, and they will speak lies at the same table, but it will not succeed, for the end is still yet to come. {11:28} He will return to his land with great wealth, and his heart will be set against the holy covenant, and he will act against it and then return to his own land. {11:29} At the appointed time, he will return and head toward the south, but it will not be like the first or the last time. {11:30} For ships from the coastlands will come against him, causing him to be troubled, and he will return with anger against the holy covenant, and he will act deceitfully toward those who abandon the holy covenant. {11:31} Forces will rise up on his behalf, and they will pollute the sanctuary and take away the daily sacrifice, and they will set up the abomination that causes desolation. {11:32} He will corrupt those who act wickedly against the covenant with flattery, but those who know their God will be strong and carry out great exploits. {11:33} Those who have insight among the people will instruct many, but they will fall by the sword, fire, captivity, and plunder for many days. {11:34} When they fall, they will receive a little help, but many will join them with flattery. {11:35} Some of the wise will fall to test them and purify them, and make them white until the time of the end, for it is still for the appointed time. {11:36} The king will do as he pleases, exalting and magnifying himself above every god and speaking marvelous things against the God of gods, and he will succeed until the anger is fulfilled; what has been determined will be done. {11:37} He will not regard the God of his fathers, nor the desire of women, nor pay attention to any god, but he will magnify himself above all. {11:38} In his place, he will honor the god of fortresses, and a god his forefathers did not know he will honor with gold, silver, precious stones, and pleasant things. {11:39} He will act against the strongest fortresses with a foreign god, whom he will acknowledge and increase with glory, and he will cause them to rule over many and divide the land for profit. {11:40} At the end of time, the king of the south will push against him, and the king of the north will come against him like a whirlwind with chariots, horsemen, and many ships, and he will enter the countries, overflow, and pass through. {11:41} He will enter the glorious land, and many nations will fall, but Edom, Moab, and the prominent people of Ammon will escape from his grasp. {11:42} He will stretch out his hand against other countries, and Egypt will not escape. {11:43} He will gain power over the treasures of gold and silver and all the precious things of Egypt; the Libyans and the Ethiopians will follow him. {11:44} But reports from the east and the north will trouble him; therefore, he will go out in great fury to destroy and annihilate many. {11:45} He will pitch his royal tents between the seas at the glorious holy mountain, but he will come to his end, and no one will help him.

{12:1} At that time, Michael will stand up, the great prince who stands for the children of your people; there will be a time of trouble unlike any that has occurred since nations began until that time. But at that time, your people will be delivered, everyone whose name is found written in the book. {12:2} Many of those who sleep in the dust of the earth will awake, some to everlasting life, and others to shame and everlasting contempt. {12:3} Those who are wise will shine like the brightness of the heavens, and those who lead many to righteousness will shine like the stars for ever and ever. {12:4} But you, Daniel, close up these words and seal the book until the time of the end; many will run to and fro, and knowledge will increase. {12:5} Then I, Daniel, looked, and there were two others standing, one on either bank of the river. {12:6} One of them asked the man dressed in linen who was above the waters of the river, "How long will it be until the end of these wonders?" {12:7} The man dressed in linen, who was above the waters of the river, raised his right hand and his left hand toward heaven and swore by him who lives forever that it would be for a time, times, and half a time; when the power of the holy people has been scattered, all these things will be completed. {12:8} I heard, but I did not understand; so I asked, "My Lord, what will be the outcome of these things?" {12:9} He replied, "Go your way, Daniel, for the words are sealed until the time of the end. {12:10} Many will be purified, made spotless and refined, but the wicked will continue to be wicked; none of the wicked will understand, but the wise will understand. {12:11} From the time that the daily sacrifice is taken away and the abomination that causes desolation is set up, there will be 1,290 days. {12:12} Blessed is the one who waits for and reaches the 1,335 days. {12:13} As for you, go your way till the end; you will rest, and then at the end of the days you will rise to receive your allotted inheritance.

The Book of Hosea

{1:1} The word of the LORD came to Hosea, son of Beeri, during the reigns of Uzziah, Jotham, Ahaz, and Hezekiah, kings of Judah, and Jeroboam, son of Joash, king of Israel. {1:2} This is the beginning of the LORD's message through Hosea. The LORD said to Hosea, "Go, marry a promiscuous woman and have children with her, for the land is guilty of great unfaithfulness, turning away from the LORD." {1:3} So he went and married Gomer, the daughter of Diblaim, and she became pregnant and bore him a son. {1:4} Then the LORD said to him, "Name him Jezreel, because in a little while, I will punish the house of Jehu for the massacre at Jezreel and put an end to the kingdom of Israel. {1:5} On that day, I will break Israel's bow in the Valley of Jezreel." {1:6} Gomer conceived again and gave birth to a daughter. The LORD said to Hosea, "Name her Loruhamah (meaning 'not loved'), for I will no longer show love to Israel, that I should forgive them. {1:7} But I will show love to the house of Judah; I will save them not by bow, sword, or battle, or by horses or horsemen." {1:8} After she had weaned Loruhamah, Gomer had another son. {1:9} Then God said, "Name him Loammi (meaning 'not my people'), for you are not my people, and I am not your God." {1:10} Yet the Israelites will be like the sand of the sea, which cannot be measured or counted. In the place where it was said to them, "You are not my people," they will be called "children of the living God." {1:11} The people of Judah and the people of Israel will come together; they will appoint one leader and will come up out of the land, for great will be the day of Jezreel.

{2:1} Say to your brothers, "My people," and to your sisters, "My loved one." {2:2} Plead with your mother, plead, for she is not my wife and I am not her husband. Let her remove her promiscuity from her face and her adultery from between her breasts, {2:3} or I will strip her naked and make her like a desert, like a dry land, and I will kill her with thirst. {2:4} I will not show love to her children, because they are children of promiscuity. {2:5} Their mother has been unfaithful and has conceived them in shame. She said, "I will go after my lovers, who give me my food and water, my wool and linen, my olive oil and drink." {2:6} Therefore, I will block her path with thornbushes; I will wall her in so she cannot find her way. {2:7} She will chase after her lovers but not catch them; she will look for them but not find them. Then she will say, "I will go back to my husband, for I was better off then than I am now." {2:8} She has not acknowledged that I was the one who gave her the grain, the new wine, and the oil, who lavished on her the silver and gold, which they used for Baal. {2:9} Therefore, I will take away my grain when it ripens and my new wine when it is ready. I will recover my wool and linen, intended to cover her nakedness. {2:10} Now I will expose her lewdness in the sight of her lovers; no one will be able to rescue her out of my hand. {2:11} I will put an end to all her celebrations, her yearly festivals, her New Moons, her Sabbath days—all her appointed festivals. {2:12} I will destroy her vines and fig trees, which she said were her pay from her lovers. I will make them a thicket, and the wild animals will devour them. {2:13} I will punish her for the days she burned incense to the Baals; she decked herself with rings and jewelry and went after her lovers, but forgot me, declares the LORD. {2:14} Therefore, I am now going to allure her; I will lead her into the wilderness and speak tenderly to her. {2:15} There I will give her back her vineyards and make the Valley of Achor a door of hope. There she will respond as in the days of her youth, as in the day she came up out of Egypt. {2:16} In that day, declares the LORD, you will call me "my husband"; you will no longer call me "my master." {2:17} I will remove the names of the Baals from her lips; no longer will their names be invoked. {2:18} In that day, I will make a covenant for them with the beasts of the field and the birds in the sky and the creatures that move along the ground. Bow and sword and battle I will abolish from the land, so that all may lie down in safety. {2:19} I will betroth you to me forever; I will betroth you in righteousness and justice, in love and compassion. {2:20} I will betroth you in faithfulness, and you will acknowledge the LORD. {2:21} In that day, I will respond, declares the LORD; I will respond to the heavens, and they will respond to the earth. {2:22} And the earth will respond to the grain, the new wine, and the olive oil, and they will respond to Jezreel. {2:23} I will plant her for myself in the land; I will show love to those I called "not my loved one." I will say to those called "not my people," "You are my people"; and they will say, "You are my God."

{3:1} The LORD said to me, "Go again and love a woman who is loved by another man and is unfaithful, just as the LORD loves the Israelites, though they turn to other gods and love their wine." {3:2} So I bought her for fifteen shekels of silver and a homer and a half of barley. {3:3} Then I told her, "You must live with me for many days; you must not be a prostitute or be with any man, and I will behave the same way toward you." {3:4} For the Israelites will live many days without a king or prince, without sacrifices, sacred stones, and without idols. {3:5} Afterward, the Israelites will return and seek the LORD their God and David their king. They will come trembling to the LORD and to his blessings in the last days.

{4:1} Hear the word of the LORD, you Israelites, for the LORD has a case against the inhabitants of the land because there is no truth, no mercy, and no knowledge of God in the land. {4:2} There is swearing, lying, murder, stealing, and adultery; they break all bounds, and bloodshed follows bloodshed. {4:3} Therefore, the land will mourn, and everyone living in it will waste away, along with the wild animals and the birds in the sky; even the fish in the sea will be swept away. {4:4} Yet let no one bring a case or argue; for your people are like those who bring charges against a priest. {4:5} You will stumble by day, and the prophet will stumble with you by night; I will destroy your mother. {4:6} My people are destroyed from lack of knowledge. Because you have rejected knowledge, I will also reject you as my priests; because you have ignored the law of your God, I will also ignore your children. {4:7} The more priests there were, the more they sinned against me; they exchanged their glorious God for something disgraceful. {4:8} They feed on the sins of my people and relish their wickedness. {4:9} Like people, like priests; I will punish both of them for their wicked ways and repay them for their deeds. {4:10} They will eat but not have enough; they will engage in prostitution but not flourish, because they have deserted the LORD. {4:11} Prostitution, wine, and new wine take away their understanding. {4:12} My people consult a wooden idol, and a diviner's rod speaks to them; a spirit of unfaithfulness leads them astray; they are unfaithful to their God. {4:13} They offer sacrifices on the mountaintops and burn incense on the hills, under oak, poplar, and terebinth, where the shade is pleasant. Therefore, your daughters turn to prostitution and your daughters-in-law commit adultery. {4:14} I will not hold your daughters accountable when they turn to prostitution or your daughters-in-law when they commit adultery, because the men themselves consort with prostitutes and sacrifice with shrine prostitutes. A people without understanding will come to ruin. {4:15} Though you, Israel, are unfaithful, do not let Judah become guilty. Do not go to Gilgal; do not go up to Bethaven (meaning 'house of evil'), and do not swear, "As surely as the LORD lives." {4:16} The Israelites are stubborn, like a stubborn calf; now the LORD will feed them like a lamb in a broad pasture. {4:17} Ephraim is joined to idols; let him alone. {4:18} Their alcohol is bitter; they continually engage in unfaithfulness. Their rulers dearly love shameful things. {4:19} The wind has wrapped them in its wings, and they will be ashamed because of their sacrifices.

{5:1} Hear this, you priests; listen, house of Israel; pay attention, house of the king; judgment is coming for you because you have been a trap at Mizpah and a net spread out on Tabor. {5:2} The rebels are deep in slaughter, even though I have been warning them all. {5:3} I know Ephraim, and Israel is not hidden from me; for now, Ephraim, you are unfaithful, and Israel is defiled. {5:4} They will not adjust their actions to return to their God, for the spirit of unfaithfulness is in them, and they do not know the LORD. {5:5} The pride of Israel testifies against them; therefore, Israel and Ephraim will stumble in their sin; Judah will stumble with them. {5:6} They will go with their flocks and herds to seek the LORD, but they will not find him; he has withdrawn from them. {5:7} They have acted treacherously against the LORD; they have given birth to illegitimate children; now a month will devour them with their possessions. {5:8} Blow the horn in Gibeah, and the trumpet in Ramah; cry out at Bethaven, follow after you, Benjamin. {5:9} Ephraim will be desolate on the day of rebuke; among the tribes of Israel, I have revealed what is certain. {5:10} The princes of Judah are like those who remove landmarks; therefore, I will pour out my wrath on them like water. {5:11} Ephraim is oppressed and crushed in judgment because he willingly followed the commandments. {5:12} Therefore, I will be to Ephraim like a moth and to the house of Judah like rottenness. {5:13} When Ephraim saw his sickness and Judah saw his wound, Ephraim went to the Assyrian and sent to King Jareb; yet he could not heal you or cure your wound. {5:14} For I will be like a lion to Ephraim, like a young lion to the house of Judah; I, even I, will tear and go away; I will take away, and no one will rescue him. {5:15} I will go back to my place until they acknowledge their guilt and seek my face; in their distress, they will seek me early.

{6:1} Come, let us return to the LORD, for he has torn us, and he will heal us; he has struck us down, and he will bandage us. {6:2} After two days, he will revive us; on the third day, he will raise us up, and we will live in his presence. {6:3} Then we will know if we pursue to know the LORD; his coming is as certain as the morning; he will come to us like the rain, like the spring rain that waters the earth. {6:4} O Ephraim, what shall I do to you? O Judah, what shall I do to you? Your goodness is like a morning cloud; it disappears like the early dew. {6:5} Therefore, I have cut them down through the prophets; I have killed them with the words of my mouth; and your judgments are like the light that shines forth. {6:6} For I desire mercy, not sacrifice; and the knowledge of God more than burnt offerings. {6:7} But they, like humans, have broken the covenant; there they have acted treacherously against me. {6:8} Gilead is a city of evildoers, stained with blood. {6:9} Just as a band of robbers waits for a person, so the company of priests murder on way by consent; they commit immoral acts. {6:10} I have seen something horrible in the house of Israel: unfaithfulness of Ephraim; Israel is defiled. {6:11} Also, O Judah, he has set a harvest for you when I restore the fortunes of my people.

{7:1} When I wanted to heal Israel, the sin of Ephraim was revealed, and the wickedness of Samaria; for they commit falsehood, and thieves break in, and a gang of robbers plunders outside. {7:2} They do not consider in their hearts that I remember all their wickedness; now their own actions surround them; they are before my face. {7:3} They make the king happy with their wickedness, and the princes with their lies. {7:4} They are all unfaithful, like an oven heated by the baker, who stops raising the dough after kneading it until it is leavened. {7:5} On the day of our king, the princes have made him sick with bottles of wine; he stretches out his hand with scoffers. {7:6} For they have prepared their hearts like an oven while they lie in wait; their baker sleeps all night; in the morning, it burns like a raging fire. {7:7} They are all hot like an oven and have consumed their judges; all their kings have fallen; there is none among them who calls out to me. {7:8} Ephraim has mixed himself among the people; Ephraim is like an unturned cake. {7:9} Strangers have consumed his strength, and he does not know it; gray hairs are appearing here and there on him, yet he does not realize it. {7:10} And the pride of Israel testifies against him; they do not return to the LORD their God, nor seek him despite all this. {7:11} Ephraim is like a foolish dove without sense; they call to Egypt, they go to Assyria. {7:12} When they go, I will spread my net over them; I will bring them down like the birds of the air; I will punish them, as their congregation has heard. {7:13} Woe to them! For they have fled from me; destruction is theirs! Because they have transgressed against me; although I have redeemed them, they have spoken lies against me. {7:14} They have not cried out to me from their hearts, when they wail on their beds; they gather together for grain and wine, and they rebel against me. {7:15} Although I have bound and strengthened their arms, they still plot evil against me. {7:16} They return, but not to the Most High; they are like a deceitful bow; their princes will fall by the sword because of their angry words; this will be their ridicule in the land of Egypt.

{8:1} Set the trumpet to your mouth. He will come like an eagle against the house of the LORD because they have violated my covenant and rebelled against my law. {8:2} Israel will cry out to me, "My God, we know you." {8:3} Israel has rejected what is good; the enemy will pursue him. {8:4} They have set up kings, but not by me; they have appointed princes, and I did not know it; from their silver and gold, they have made idols, so they may be cut off. {8:5} Your calf, O Samaria, has cast you off; my anger is stirred against them; how long will it be before they attain innocence? {8:6} For it was made by a craftsman; therefore, it is not God; but the calf of Samaria will be shattered into pieces. {8:7} They have sown the wind, and they will reap the whirlwind; it has no stalk; the bud will produce no grain; even if it does, strangers will swallow it up. {8:8} Israel is swallowed up; now they will be among the nations like a vessel with no pleasure. {8:9} For they have gone up to Assyria, like a wild donkey alone by itself; Ephraim has hired lovers. {8:10} Yes, even though they have hired among the nations, now I will gather them, and they will grieve a little for the burden of the king of princes. {8:11} Because Ephraim has made many altars to sin, altars will be to him for sin. {8:12} I have written to him the great things of my law, but they were considered a strange thing. {8:13} They sacrifice flesh for the sacrifices of my offerings, and eat it; but the LORD does not accept them; now he will remember their sin and visit their iniquities: they will return to Egypt. {8:14} For Israel has forgotten his Maker and built temples; and Judah has multiplied fortified cities; but I will send fire upon his cities, and it will consume their palaces.

{9:1} Do not rejoice, O Israel, like other people do, for you have been unfaithful to your God, and you have loved rewards at every threshing floor. {9:2} The threshing floor and the winepress will not feed them, and the new wine will fail. {9:3} They will not dwell in the LORD's land; Ephraim will return to Egypt, and they will eat unclean food in Assyria. {9:4} They will not offer wine offerings to the LORD, nor will they be pleasing to him; their sacrifices will be like the bread of mourners; all who eat it will be defiled, for their bread for their soul will not come into the house of the LORD. {9:5} What will you do on the day of solemn assembly, and on the day of the feast of the LORD? {9:6} For behold, they are gone because of destruction; Egypt will gather them, Memphis will bury them; the pleasant places for their silver will be overgrown with nettles; thorns will be in their tents. {9:7} The days of punishment have come; the days of recompense have arrived; Israel will know it: the prophet is a fool, the spiritual man is mad, because of your great iniquity and deep hatred. {9:8} The watchman of Ephraim was with my God, but the prophet is a trapper in all his ways, and there is hatred in the house of his God. {9:9} They have deeply corrupted themselves, like in the days of Gibeah; therefore, he will remember their iniquity and visit their sins. {9:10} I found Israel like grapes in the wilderness; I saw your ancestors like the first ripe figs on the fig tree; but they went to Baalpeor and dedicated themselves to that shame; their abominations were as they desired. {9:11} As for Ephraim, their glory will fly away like a bird, from birth, from the womb, and from conception. {9:12} Though they raise their children, I will bereave them, so that not a single man will be left; yes, woe to them when I depart from them! {9:13} Ephraim, as I saw Tyre, is planted in a pleasant place; but Ephraim will bring forth his children to the murderer. {9:14} Give them, O LORD; what will you give? Give them a womb that miscarries and dry breasts. {9:15} All their wickedness is in Gilgal; I hated them there; because of the wickedness of their actions, I will drive them out of my house; I will love them no more; all their princes are rebellious. {9:16} Ephraim is struck down; their root is dried up; they will bear no fruit; even if they give birth, I will kill even the beloved fruit of their womb. {9:17} My God will cast them away because they did not listen to him, and they will be wanderers among the nations.

{10:1} Israel is like a vine that produces nothing; he brings forth fruit only for himself; as his fruit has multiplied, he has increased the altars; according to the goodness of his land, they have made beautiful images. {10:2} Their hearts are divided; now they will be found guilty; he will tear down their altars and destroy their images. {10:3} For now they will say, "We have no king," because we did not fear the LORD; what then can a king do for us? {10:4} They have spoken empty words, swearing falsely in making a covenant; thus, judgment springs up like poison in the furrows of the field. {10:5} The inhabitants of Samaria will fear because of the calves of Bethaven; the people there will mourn over it, and the priests who rejoiced over it will be filled with shame, because its glory has departed. {10:6} It will also be carried to Assyria as a gift to king Jareb; Ephraim will receive shame, and Israel will be ashamed of his own counsel. {10:7} As for Samaria, her king is cut off like foam on the water. {10:8} The high places of Aven, the sin of Israel, will be destroyed; thornbushes and thistles will grow on their altars; and they will say to the mountains, "Cover us," and to the hills, "Fall on us." {10:9} O Israel, you have sinned since the days of Gibeah; there they stood; the battle against the children of iniquity did not overtake them. {10:10} It is my desire to punish them; and the people will be gathered against them when they bind themselves in their two furrows. {10:11} Ephraim is like a trained heifer that loves to tread out the grain; but I passed over her beautiful neck; I will make Ephraim ride; Judah will plow, and Jacob will break the clods. {10:12} Sow for yourselves righteousness, reap mercy; break up your unplowed ground, for it is time to seek the LORD until he comes and rains righteousness on you. {10:13} You have plowed wickedness, you have reaped iniquity; you have eaten the fruit of lies, because you trusted in your way and in the multitude of your mighty men. {10:14} Therefore, a tumult will arise among your people, and all your strongholds will be plundered, as Shalman plundered Betharbel in the day of battle; a mother was dashed in pieces upon her children. {10:15} So will Bethel do to you because of your great wickedness; in the morning, the king of Israel will be utterly cut off.

{11:1} When Israel was a child, I loved him and called my son out of Egypt. {11:2} But as they called them, they went away from me; they sacrificed to Baal and burned incense to carved images. {11:3} I taught Ephraim to walk, taking them by their arms, but they did not realize that I healed them. {11:4} I drew them with human cords, with bands of love; I was like one who lifts the yoke from their jaws and provides food for them. {11:5} They will not return to the land of Egypt, but the Assyrian will be their king because they refused to return. {11:6} The sword will rest on their cities, consuming their branches and devouring them because of their own plans. {11:7} My people are bent on turning away from me; although they called to the Most High, no one would exalt him. {11:8} How can I give you up, Ephraim? How can I hand you over, Israel? How can I make you like Admah? How can I treat you like Zeboim? My heart is changed within me; my compassion is stirred. {11:9} I will not unleash the full force of my anger; I will not return to destroy Ephraim, for I am God, not man; the Holy One among you; I will not come in wrath. {11:10} They will follow the LORD; he will roar like a lion; when he roars, his children will tremble from the west. {11:11} They will tremble like birds from Egypt and like doves from the land of Assyria, and I will place them in their homes, says the LORD. {11:12} Ephraim surrounds me with lies, and the house of Israel with deceit; but Judah still rules with God and is faithful to the saints.

{12:1} Ephraim feeds on the wind and pursues the east wind; he daily increases lies and destruction, and they make a covenant with the Assyrians, while oil is sent to Egypt. {12:2} The LORD also has a dispute with Judah and will punish Jacob according to his ways; according to his deeds, he will repay him. {12:3} In the womb, he took his brother by the heel, and in his strength, he struggled with God. {12:4} Yes, he struggled with an angel and prevailed; he wept and pleaded with him; he found him at Bethel and there he spoke with us. {12:5} The LORD God of hosts, the LORD is his name. {12:6} Therefore, return to your God; maintain love and justice, and wait for your God continually. {12:7} He is a merchant; the balances of deceit are in his hand; he loves to oppress. {12:8} Ephraim says, "I have become rich; I have found wealth; in all my labors, they will find no sin in me." {12:9} I am the LORD your God from the land of Egypt; I will again make you dwell in tents as in the days of the festival. {12:10} I spoke to you by the prophets; I multiplied visions and used parables through the ministry of the prophets. {12:11} Is there iniquity in Gilead? Surely they are worthless; they sacrifice bulls in Gilgal; their altars are like piles of stones in the furrows of the fields. {12:12} Jacob fled to the country of Syria, and Israel served for a wife, and for a wife, he kept sheep. {12:13} By a prophet, the LORD brought Israel out of Egypt, and by a prophet, he was preserved. {12:14} Ephraim provoked him to anger most bitterly; therefore, his blood guilt will remain upon him, and his Lord will hold him accountable for his reproach.

{13:1} When Ephraim spoke, he trembled and lifted himself up in Israel, but when he sinned against Baal, he died. {13:2} Now they keep sinning more and more, making molten images of their silver and idols according to their own understanding, all made by craftsmen; they say to those who sacrifice, "Let the men kiss the calves." {13:3} Therefore, they will be like the morning cloud, like the early dew that disappears, like chaff driven away by the wind, and like smoke from a chimney. {13:4} Yet I am the LORD your God from the land of Egypt, and you shall know no god but me; there is no savior besides me. {13:5} I knew you in the wilderness, in the land of great drought. {13:6} As they were filled according to their pasture, their hearts became proud, and they forgot me. {13:7} Therefore, I will be like a lion to them; like a leopard, I will watch them on the path. {13:8} I will meet them like a bear bereaved of her cubs, and I will tear open their hearts; I will devour them like a lion; the wild beast will tear them apart. {13:9} O Israel, you have destroyed yourself, but in me is your help. {13:10} I will be your king; where is any other that can save you in all your cities? And your judges, of whom you said, "Give me a king and princes"? {13:11} I gave you a king in my anger and took him away in my wrath. {13:12} The iniquity of Ephraim is wrapped up; his sin is hidden. {13:13} The pains of a woman in labor will come upon him; he is an unwise son, for he should not stay long in the place of childbirth. {13:14} I will ransom them from the power of the grave; I will redeem them from death: O death, I will be your plagues; O grave, I will be your destruction; repentance will be hidden from my eyes. {13:15} Though he be fruitful among his brothers, an east wind will come; the wind of the LORD will rise from the wilderness, and his spring will become dry, and his fountain will dry up; he will spoil the treasures of all pleasant vessels. {13:16} Samaria will become desolate because she has rebelled against her God; they will fall by the sword; their infants will be dashed to pieces, and pregnant women will be ripped open.

{14:1} O Israel, return to the LORD your God, for you have stumbled because of your iniquity. {14:2} Take words with you and return to the LORD; say to him, "Take away all iniquity and receive us graciously; then we will offer the calves of our lips." {14:3} Assyria will not save us; we will not ride on horses; we will no longer say to the work of our hands, "You are our gods," for in you the fatherless finds mercy. {14:4} I will heal their backsliding; I will love them freely, for my anger is turned away from him. {14:5} I will be like the dew to Israel; he will blossom like the lily and take root like the cedars of Lebanon. {14:6} His branches will spread, and his beauty will be like the olive tree, and his fragrance like Lebanon. {14:7} Those who dwell in his shade will return; they will revive like the grain and grow like the vine; their scent will be like the wine of Lebanon. {14:8} Ephraim will say, "What do I have to do anymore with idols?" I have heard him and observed him; I am like a green fir tree; from me comes your fruit. {14:9} Who is wise? Let him understand these things. Who is prudent? Let him know them, for the ways of the LORD are right, and the righteous walk in them, but transgressors will stumble in them.

The Book of Amos

{1:1} These are the words of Amos, a shepherd from Tekoa, which he received concerning Israel during the days of Uzziah, king of Judah, and Jeroboam, son of Joash, king of Israel, two years before the earthquake. {1:2} He said, "The LORD will roar from Zion and speak from Jerusalem; the pastures of the shepherds will mourn, and the top of Mount Carmel will wither." {1:3} Thus says the LORD: "For three sins of Damascus, and for four, I will not hold back my punishment, because they have threshed Gilead with iron sledges. {1:4} I will send fire upon the house of Hazael, which will consume the palaces of Benhadad. {1:5} I will break the gate of Damascus and cut off the inhabitants from the plain of Aven, and the ruler from the house of Eden; the people of Syria will go into captivity to Kir," says the LORD. {1:6} Thus says the LORD: "For three sins of Gaza, and for four, I will not hold back my punishment, because they took entire communities captive to deliver them up to Edom. {1:7} I will send fire on the wall of Gaza, which will consume its palaces. {1:8} I will cut off the inhabitants from Ashdod and the ruler from Ashkelon, and I will turn my hand against Ekron; the remnant of the Philistines will perish," says the Lord GOD. {1:9} Thus says the LORD: "For three sins of Tyre, and for four, I will not hold back my punishment, because they delivered entire communities to Edom and did not remember the brotherly covenant. {1:10} I will send fire upon the wall of Tyre, which will consume its palaces. {1:11} Thus says the LORD: "For three sins of Edom, and for four, I will not hold back my punishment, because he pursued his brother with the sword, showing no pity; his anger tore perpetually, and he kept his wrath forever. {1:12} I will send fire upon Teman, which will consume the palaces of Bozrah. {1:13} Thus says the LORD: "For three sins of the children of Ammon, and for four, I will not hold back my punishment, because they ripped open the pregnant women of Gilead to enlarge their territory. {1:14} I will kindle a fire in the wall of Rabbah, which will consume its palaces, with shouting on the day of battle and with a storm on the day of the whirlwind. {1:15} Their king will go into captivity, he and his princes together," says the LORD.

{2:1} Thus says the LORD: "For three sins of Moab, and for four, I will not hold back my punishment, because he burned the bones of the king of Edom to lime. {2:2} I will send fire upon Moab, which will consume the palaces of Kerioth, and Moab will die in turmoil, with shouting and the sound of the trumpet. {2:3} I will cut off the judge from among them and slay all their princes with him," says the LORD. {2:4} Thus says the LORD: "For three sins of Judah, and for four, I will not hold back my punishment, because they have despised the law of the LORD and not kept his commandments; their lies have led them astray, following the ways their ancestors walked. {2:5} I will send fire upon Judah, which will consume the palaces of Jerusalem. {2:6} Thus says the LORD: "For three sins of Israel, and for four, I will not hold back my punishment, because they sold the righteous for silver and the poor for a pair of sandals. {2:7} They trample on the heads of the poor and push the meek aside; a man and his father go into the same girl, profaning my holy name. {2:8} They lie down on clothes taken as security by every altar and drink the wine of the condemned in the house of their god. {2:9} Yet I destroyed the Amorite before them, whose height was like the cedars and who was as strong as oaks; I destroyed his fruit from above and his roots from below. {2:10} I also brought you up from the land of Egypt and led you forty years through the wilderness to possess the land of the Amorite. {2:11} I raised up prophets from among your sons and Nazarites from among your young men. Is this not true, O Israelites?" says the LORD. {2:12} But you made the Nazarites drink wine and told the prophets, "Do not prophesy." {2:13} Behold, I am pressed down beneath you, as a cart is pressed down when it is full of sheaves. {2:14} Therefore, the swift will perish, and the strong will not muster their strength; the mighty will not save themselves. {2:15} The archer will not stand his ground; the fleet-footed soldier will not escape, nor will he who rides a horse save himself. {2:16} The bravest among the warriors will flee away naked in that day," says the LORD.

{3:1} Listen to this word that the LORD has spoken against you, O people of Israel, against the whole family I brought up from Egypt, saying, {3:2} "You alone have I known among all the families of the earth; therefore, I will punish you for all your sins." {3:3} Do two walk together unless they agree? {3:4} Does a lion roar in the forest when it has no prey? Does a young lion let out a cry from its den if it has caught nothing? {3:5} Can a bird fall into a trap on the ground where there is no bait? Does anyone pick up a trap from the ground and find nothing at all? {3:6} If a trumpet is blown in the city, will the people not be afraid? If there is disaster in a city, has the LORD not done it? {3:7} Surely the Lord GOD does nothing without revealing his plan to his servants the prophets. {3:8} The lion has roared—who will not fear? The Lord GOD has spoken—who can but prophesy? {3:9} Proclaim this in the palaces of Ashdod and in the palaces of Egypt: "Assemble on the mountains of Samaria and see the great turmoil within, and the oppression among the people." {3:10} For they do not know how to do right, says the LORD, those who store up violence and robbery in their palaces. {3:11} Therefore, the Lord GOD says: "An enemy will surround the land, and he will bring down your strength, and your palaces will be looted." {3:12} Thus says the LORD: "As a shepherd rescues from the lion's mouth only two legs or a piece of an ear, so will the Israelites be rescued, those who dwell in Samaria, in the corner of a bed, and in Damascus on a couch." {3:13} Hear and testify against the house of Jacob, says the Lord GOD, the God of hosts, {3:14} "On the day I punish Israel for its sins, I will also punish the altars of Bethel; the horns of the altar will be cut off and fall to the ground. {3:15} I will destroy the winter and summer houses; the houses adorned with ivory will be destroyed, and the mansions will end," says the LORD.

{4:1} Hear this word, you cows of Bashan, who are on the mountain of Samaria, who oppress the poor and crush the needy, who say to their masters, "Bring us drinks." {4:2} The Lord GOD has sworn by his holiness that the days will come upon you when he will take you away with hooks, and your descendants with fishhooks. {4:3} You will go out through the breaches, every cow in front of her; and you will be thrown into the palace, says the LORD. {4:4} Come to Bethel and sin; at Gilgal, sin even more; bring your sacrifices every morning, and your tithes every three years. {4:5} Offer a sacrifice of thanksgiving with leaven and proclaim your freewill offerings; this pleases you, O people of Israel, says the Lord GOD. {4:6} I also gave you clean teeth in all your cities and lack of bread in all your places; yet you have not returned to me, says the LORD. {4:7} I withheld rain from you when there were still three months until harvest; I caused it to rain on one city, but withheld it from another city; one field received rain, and the field that did not receive rain withered. {4:8} So two or three cities wandered to one city to drink water, but they were not satisfied; yet you have not returned to me, says the LORD. {4:9} I struck you with blight and mildew; when your gardens and vineyards and fig trees and olive trees increased, the locust devoured them; yet you have not returned to me, says the LORD. {4:10} I sent plagues among you like those of Egypt; I killed your young men with the sword and took away your horses; I made the stench of your camps rise to your nostrils; yet you have not returned to me, says the LORD. {4:11} I overthrew some of you as God overthrew Sodom and Gomorrah; you were like a burning stick snatched from the fire; yet you have not returned to me, says the LORD. {4:12} Therefore, this is what I will do to you, O Israel; because I will do this to you, prepare to meet your God, O Israel. {4:13} For, behold, he who forms the mountains, creates the wind, and reveals his thoughts to man, who turns dawn to darkness and treads on the high places of the earth—The LORD, the God of hosts, is his name.

{5:1} Listen to this word that I have against you, a lament for the house of Israel. {5:2} The young woman of Israel has fallen; she will not rise again; she is forsaken in her land, and no one can lift her up. {5:3} For this is what the Lord GOD says: "The city that went out with a thousand will only return with a hundred, and the one that went out with a hundred will only return with ten to the house of Israel." {5:4} For this is what the LORD says to the house of Israel: "Seek me and live. {5:5} Do not seek Bethel, do not enter Gilgal, and do not go to Beersheba; for Gilgal will go into captivity, and Bethel will become nothing." {5:6} Seek the LORD and live, or he will break out like fire in the house of Joseph, and it will devour everything, and no one will be able to quench it in Bethel. {5:7} You who turn justice into bitterness and cast righteousness aside in the earth, {5:8} seek him who made the Pleiades and Orion, who turns darkness into morning and darkens the day into night; who calls for the waters of the sea and pours them out on the surface of the earth—the LORD is his name— {5:9} who strengthens the plundered against the strong, so that the plundered will come against the fortress. {5:10} They hate the one who reproves in the gate, and they despise the one who speaks honestly. {5:11} Therefore, since you trample on the poor and take grain from them, you have built houses of hewn stone, but you will not live in them; you have planted beautiful vineyards, but you will not drink their wine. {5:12} For I know your many sins and your mighty transgressions: you oppress the righteous, take bribes, and deny justice to the poor at the gate. {5:13} Therefore the prudent remain silent in such times, for it is an evil time. {5:14} Seek good, not evil, so that you may live, and the LORD God of hosts will be with you, as you have said. {5:15} Hate evil, love good, and establish justice in the gate; perhaps the LORD God of hosts will be gracious to the remnant of Joseph. {5:16} Therefore, the LORD, the God of hosts, says: "There will be wailing in all the streets, and they will say in all the highways, 'Alas! Alas!' They will call the farmer to mourning and those skilled in lamentation to wailing. {5:17} In all vineyards there will be wailing, for I will pass through you," says the LORD. {5:18} Woe to you who long for the day of the LORD! What will it be for you? The day of the LORD will be darkness, not light. {5:19} It will be as if a man fled from a lion and met a bear; or went into the house and leaned against the wall, and a snake bit him. {5:20} Will not the day of the LORD be darkness, not light—pitch dark, without any brightness? {5:21} I hate, I despise your festivals, and I take no delight in your solemn assemblies. {5:22} Even if you bring me burnt offerings and grain offerings, I will not accept them; I will not regard the peace offerings of your fat animals. {5:23} Take away from me the noise of your songs; I will not listen to the melody of your harps. {5:24} But let justice roll on like a river, righteousness like a never-failing stream! {5:25} Did you bring me sacrifices and offerings in the wilderness for forty years, O house of Israel? {5:26} You have lifted up the shrine of your king, the pedestal of your idols, the star of your god that you made for yourselves. {5:27} Therefore I'll send you into exile beyond Damascus," says the LORD, whose name is God of hosts.

{6:1} Woe to those who are at ease in Zion, and to those who feel secure on the mountain of Samaria, the notable people of the nations, to whom the house of Israel comes! {6:2} Go to Calneh and see; from there go to great Hamath and then down to Gath of the Philistines. Are they better than these kingdoms? Is their land larger than your land? {6:3} You who put off the evil day and bring near the seat of violence; {6:4} who lie on beds of ivory, stretch out on your couches, eat lambs from the flock and calves from the stall; {6:5} who sing idle songs to the sound of the harp and invent their own musical instruments like David; {6:6} who drink wine from bowls and anoint themselves with the finest oils; but they are not grieved over the ruin of Joseph. {6:7} Therefore, they will now go into exile with the first to go into exile, and the revelry of those who stretched themselves out will cease. {6:8} The Lord GOD has sworn by himself, says the LORD God of hosts: "I despise the pride of Jacob, and hate his palaces; therefore, I will hand over the city and everything in it. {6:9} And if ten men remain in one house, they will die. {6:10} And when a relative takes his body to burn it, he will ask the one next to him, 'Is there anyone else with you?' and the other will reply, 'No.' Then he will say, 'Be quiet; we must not mention the name of the LORD.' {6:11} For behold, the LORD commands, and he will strike the great house with breaches and the little house with clefts. {6:12} Do horses run on rocks? Does one plow there with oxen? For you have turned justice into poison and the fruit of righteousness into bitterness. {6:13} You who rejoice in what is worthless, who say, 'Have we not taken for ourselves horns by our own strength?' {6:14} But behold, I will raise up a nation against you, O house of Israel, says the LORD God of hosts; and they will afflict you from the entrance of Hamath to the river of the wilderness.

{7:1} Thus the Lord GOD showed me: he formed grasshoppers at the beginning of the new growth, right after the king's harvest. {7:2} And when they finished eating the grass of the land, I said, "O Lord GOD, forgive, I beg you: by whom shall Jacob rise? For he is small." {7:3} The LORD relented regarding this: "It will not happen," says the LORD. {7:4} Then the Lord GOD showed me again: the Lord GOD called to contend with fire, and it consumed the great deep and devoured part of the land. {7:5} I said, "O Lord GOD, stop, I beg you: by whom shall Jacob rise? For he is small." {7:6} The LORD relented regarding this: "This also will not happen," says the Lord GOD. {7:7} Then he showed me: the Lord stood on a wall made with a plumb line, with a plumb line in his hand. {7:8} The LORD said to me, "Amos, what do you see?" I answered, "A plumb line." The LORD said, "Look, I will set a plumb line among my people Israel; I will no longer overlook them. {7:9} The high places of Isaac will be desolate, and the sanctuaries of Israel will be laid waste; I will rise against the house of Jeroboam with the sword." {7:10} Then Amaziah, the priest of Bethel, sent to Jeroboam king of Israel, saying, "Amos has conspired against you in the midst of the house of Israel; the land cannot bear all his words. {7:11} For this is what Amos says: 'Jeroboam will die by the sword, and Israel will surely go into exile from its own land.'" {7:12} Amaziah also said to Amos, "You seer, go, flee to the land of Judah, and there eat bread and prophesy there. {7:13} But do not prophesy anymore at Bethel, for it is the king's sanctuary and the royal court." {7:14} Amos answered Amaziah, "I was no prophet, nor was I a prophet's son; I was a shepherd and a gatherer of sycamore fruit. {7:15} But the LORD took me as I followed the flock, and the LORD said to me, 'Go, prophesy to my people Israel.' {7:16} Now therefore hear the word of the LORD: You say, 'Do not prophesy against Israel, and do not drop your words against the house of Isaac.' {7:17} Therefore, this is what the LORD says: 'Your wife will become a prostitute in the city, and your sons and daughters will fall by the sword; your land will be divided up, and you will die in a defiled land; and Israel will surely go into exile from its land.'"

{8:1} Thus the Lord GOD showed me: a basket of summer fruit. {8:2} He said, "Amos, what do you see?" I said, "A basket of summer fruit." Then the LORD said to me, "The end has come upon my people Israel; I will not overlook them anymore. {8:3} The songs of the temple will become howls in that day," says the Lord GOD: "There will be many dead bodies in every place; they will be thrown out in silence." {8:4} Hear this, you who swallow up the needy and make the poor of the land fail, {8:5} saying, "When will the new moon be over so we can sell grain? When will the Sabbath be gone so we can set forth wheat, making the ephah small and the shekel great, and falsifying the balances by deceit?" {8:6} So we can buy the poor for silver and the needy for a pair of shoes; yes, even sell the refuse of the wheat? {8:7} The LORD has sworn by the pride of Jacob: "Surely I will never forget any of their deeds. {8:8} Will not the land tremble for this, and will everyone mourn who dwells therein? It will rise up like a flood and be cast out and drowned like the flood of Egypt. {8:9} And it will come to pass in that day," says the Lord GOD, "that I will make the sun go down at noon, and I will darken the earth in broad daylight. {8:10} I will turn your feasts into mourning, and all your songs into lamentation; I will put sackcloth on all loins and baldness on every head; I will make it like the mourning for an only son, and its end will be like a bitter day. {8:11} Behold, the days are coming," says the Lord GOD, "that I will send a famine in the land, not a famine of bread or a thirst for water, but of hearing the words of the LORD. {8:12} They will wander from sea to sea and from the north to the east; they will run to and fro to seek the word of the LORD, but they will not find it. {8:13} In that day, the lovely virgins and young men will faint from thirst. {8:14} Those who swear by the sin of Samaria, and say, 'Your god, O Dan, lives,' and 'The manner of Beersheba lives,' they will fall and never rise again."

{9:1} I saw the Lord standing by the altar, and He said, "Strike the top of the pillars so that the doorposts shake, and shatter them on the heads of everyone. Those who are left, I will kill with the sword; no one who runs away will escape, and no one who tries to flee will be saved. {9:2} Even if they dig down to the depths of the grave (hell), my hand will grab them; and if they climb up to the heavens, I will bring them down from there. {9:3} If they hide at the top of Mount Carmel, I will search for them and take them out. If they hide from my sight at the bottom of the sea, I will command the serpent to bite them. {9:4} Even if they are taken into exile by their enemies, I will command the sword to kill them there. I will keep my eyes on them to bring harm, not good. {9:5} The Lord, the God of hosts, touches the land, and it melts, and everyone who lives there mourns. The land rises like the Nile and sinks like the river of Egypt. {9:6} He builds his upper rooms in the heavens and establishes his foundation on the earth. He calls for the waters of the sea and pours them out on the land. The LORD is His name. {9:7} "Are you Israelites not the same to me as the Ethiopians?" declares the LORD. "Did I not bring Israel out of Egypt, the Philistines from Caphtor, and the Syrians from Kir? {9:8} Look, the eyes of the Lord GOD are on this sinful kingdom, and I will destroy it from the face of the earth. However, I will not completely wipe out the house of Jacob," declares the LORD. {9:9} "For I will give the command, and I will sift the people of Israel among the nations like grain is sifted in a sieve, yet not even the smallest kernel will fall to the ground. {9:10} All the sinners among my people, those who say, 'Disaster will not overtake or catch us,' will die by the sword. {9:11} On that day, I will rebuild the fallen shelter of David. I will repair its broken walls and restore its ruins, and I will rebuild it as it used to be, {9:12} so that they may take possession of the remnant of Edom and all the nations that bear my name," declares the LORD, who will do these things. {9:13} "The days are coming," says the LORD, "when the plowman will overtake the reaper, and the one who treads grapes will catch up with the one who sows seed. The mountains will drip with sweet wine, and all the hills will flow with it. {9:14} I will bring my people Israel back from captivity. They will rebuild the ruined cities and live in them. They will plant vineyards and drink their wine; they will make gardens and eat their fruit. {9:15} I will plant them in their land, and they will never again be uprooted from the land I have given them," says the LORD your God.

The Book of Micah

{1:1} The word of the LORD came to Micah the Morasthite during the reigns of Jotham, Ahaz, and Hezekiah, kings of Judah, concerning Samaria and Jerusalem. {1:2} Listen, all you people; pay attention, O earth, and everything in it: let the Lord GOD be a witness against you, the Lord from his holy temple. {1:3} For behold, the LORD is coming out of his place; he will come down and tread on the high places of the earth. {1:4} The mountains will melt beneath him, and the valleys will split apart like wax before the fire and like waters poured down a steep slope. {1:5} All this is because of Jacob's transgression and the sins of the house of Israel. What is Jacob's transgression? Is it not Samaria? And what are the high places of Judah? Are they not Jerusalem? {1:6} Therefore, I will make Samaria a heap of rubble in the field, like a vineyard; I will pour her stones into the valley and expose her foundations. {1:7} All her idols will be shattered, and all her earnings will be burned in the fire; I will make her desolate because she collected them like a prostitute, and they will return to the hire of a prostitute. {1:8} Therefore, I will mourn and wail; I will go stripped and naked; I will make a mourning like the dragons and lament like the owls. {1:9} For her wound is incurable; it has come to Judah; it has reached the gate of my people, even to Jerusalem. {1:10} Don't declare it in Gath; don't weep at all; roll in the dust in the house of Aphrah. {1:11} Leave, you inhabitants of Saphir, with your shame exposed; the inhabitants of Zaanan did not come out in the mourning of Bethezel; they will receive their standing from you. {1:12} For the inhabitants of Maroth eagerly waited for good, but evil came down from the LORD to the gate of Jerusalem. {1:13} O inhabitant of Lachish, tie the chariot to the swift horse; she is the beginning of sin for the daughter of Zion, for the transgressions of Israel were found in you. {1:14} Therefore, you will give gifts to Moreshethgath; the houses of Achzib will deceive the kings of Israel. {1:15} Yet I will bring an heir to you, O inhabitant of Mareshah; he will come to Adullam, the glory of Israel. {1:16} Make yourself bald and shave your head for your delicate children; enlarge your baldness like the eagle, for they have gone into captivity from you.

{2:1} Woe to those who plot iniquity and work evil on their beds! When morning comes, they practice it because they have the power to do so. {2:2} They covet fields and take them by violence; they seize houses and take them away; they oppress a man and his home, even a man and his inheritance. {2:3} Therefore, the LORD says: Behold, against this family I am devising a disaster from which you will not remove your necks; you will not walk proudly, for this time is evil. {2:4} In that day, one will take up a proverb against you and lament with a bitter lamentation, saying, "We are utterly ruined; he has changed the inheritance of my people; how has he taken it from me! He has divided our fields." {2:5} Therefore, you will have no one to cast a lot in the assembly of the LORD. {2:6} They say, "Do not prophesy to us," to those who prophesy; they shall not prophesy to them, so they will not be ashamed. {2:7} O you who are called the house of Jacob, is the spirit of the LORD restricted? Are these his doings? Don't my words do good to those who walk uprightly? {2:8} Recently, my people have risen up as an enemy; you strip off the robe from those who pass by securely like men returning from war. {2:9} You have driven the women of my people from their pleasant homes; you have taken away my glory from their children forever. {2:10} Arise and depart, for this is not your resting place because it is polluted; it will destroy you with a grievous destruction. {2:11} If a man lies and says, "I will prophesy to you about wine and strong drink," he will be the prophet of this people. {2:12} I will surely assemble all of you, O Jacob; I will gather the remnant of Israel; I will put them together like sheep in a pen, like a flock in its pasture; they will make a great noise because of the multitude of men. {2:13} The one who breaks open the way will go up before them; they will break through and pass the gate and go out by it; their king will go before them, and the LORD will be at the head of them.

{3:1} Then I said, "Listen, please, you leaders of Jacob and you rulers of the house of Israel; isn't it your responsibility to understand justice? {3:2} You hate what is good and love what is evil; you strip the skin off my people and tear the flesh from their bones. {3:3} You eat the flesh of my people and strip their skin off them; you break their bones and chop them into pieces like meat in a pot or flesh in a cauldron. {3:4} Then they will cry out to the LORD, but he won't answer them; he will even hide his face from them at that time, as they have behaved badly in their actions. {3:5} This is what the LORD says about the prophets who mislead my people; they bite with their teeth and cry, 'Peace,' but they prepare for war against anyone who doesn't put food in their mouths. {3:6} Therefore, it will be night for you; you will have no vision; it will be dark for you; you will not be able to prophesy; the sun will set on the prophets, and the day will be dark for them. {3:7} Then the seers will be ashamed, and the diviners will be embarrassed; they will all cover their mouths because there is no answer from God. {3:8} But truly, I am filled with power by the Spirit of the LORD, and with justice and strength, to declare to Jacob his transgression and to Israel his sin. {3:9} Listen to this, you leaders of the house of Jacob and rulers of the house of Israel, who hate justice and twist all that is right. {3:10} They build Zion with blood and Jerusalem with wrongdoing. {3:11} Its leaders judge for a bribe, its priests teach for a fee, and its prophets tell fortunes for money; yet they lean on the LORD and say, 'Is not the LORD among us? No disaster will come upon us.' {3:12} Therefore, for your sake, Zion will be plowed like a field, Jerusalem will become a heap of rubble, and mountain of the house will be like high places of a forest.

{4:1} But in the last days, it will come to pass that the mountain of the house of the LORD will be established at the highest point of the mountains and will be exalted above the hills, and people will stream to it. {4:2} Many nations will come and say, "Come, let us go up to the mountain of the LORD, to the house of the God of Jacob; he will teach us his ways, and we will walk in his paths," for the law will go out from Zion, and the word of the LORD from Jerusalem. {4:3} He will judge between many peoples and will settle disputes for strong nations far and wide; they will beat their swords into plowshares and their spears into pruning hooks; nation will not take up sword against nation, nor will they train for war anymore. {4:4} Everyone will sit under their own vine and under their own fig tree, and no one will make them afraid, for the mouth of the LORD Almighty has spoken. {4:5} All nations will walk in the name of their gods; we will walk in the name of the LORD our God forever and ever. {4:6} In that day, says the LORD, I will gather the lame, I will assemble the exiles and those I have afflicted; {4:7} I will make the lame my remnant, those driven away a strong nation; and the LORD will reign over them on Mount Zion from that time on and forever. {4:8} As for you, O watchtower of the flock, O stronghold of the daughter of Zion, the former dominion will be restored to you; kingship will come to the daughter of Jerusalem. {4:9} Now why do you cry out loud? Is there no king in you? Has your counselor perished? Pain has seized you like that of a woman in labor. {4:10} Writhe in agony, O daughter of Zion, like a woman in labor, for now you must leave the city and dwell in the open country; you will go to Babylon. There you will be rescued; there the LORD will redeem you from the hand of your enemies. {4:11} Now many nations are gathered against you, saying, "Let her be defiled," and "Let our eyes gloat over Zion." {4:12} But they do not know the thoughts of the LORD; they do not understand his plan, for he will gather them like sheaves to the threshing floor. {4:13} Rise and thresh, O daughter of Zion, for I will make your horn iron and your hooves bronze; you will crush many nations and dedicate their plunder to the LORD, their wealth to the Lord of the whole earth.

{5:1} Now gather yourself together, O daughter of troops; he has laid siege against us. They will strike the judge of Israel on the face with a rod. {5:2} But you, Bethlehem Ephrathah, though you are small among the thousands of Judah, out of you will come for me one who will be ruler in Israel, whose origins are from ancient times, from everlasting. {5:3} Therefore, he will give them up until the time she who is in labor gives birth; then the remnant of his brothers will return to the children of Israel. {5:4} He will stand and shepherd his flock in the strength of the LORD, in the majesty of the name of the LORD his God, and they will live securely, for then he will be great to the ends of the earth. {5:5} And this man will be our peace when the Assyrian invades our land; when he tramples in our palaces, we will raise up against him seven shepherds and eight leaders. {5:6} They will devastate the land of Assyria with the sword, and the land of Nimrod at its entrances; he will deliver us from the Assyrian when he invades our land and when he treads within our borders. {5:7} The remnant of Jacob will be among many peoples like dew from the LORD, like showers on the grass, which do not wait for anyone or depend on humans. {5:8} The remnant of Jacob will be like a lion among the animals of the forest, like a young lion among flocks of sheep; when it goes through, it will trample and tear to pieces, and no one can rescue. {5:9} Your hand will be lifted up against your enemies, and all your foes will be cut off. {5:10} In that day, says the LORD, I will destroy your horses from among you and tear down your chariots. {5:11} I will destroy the cities of your land and throw down all your strongholds. {5:12} I will eliminate witchcraft from your hands, and you will no longer have fortune-tellers. {5:13} I will cut off your carved images and your sacred pillars from among you; you will no longer worship the work of your hands. {5:14} I will uproot your Asherah poles from among you; thus I will destroy your cities. {5:15} I will execute vengeance in anger and wrath upon the nations that have not heard.

{6:1} Listen now to what the LORD says: Arise, plead your case before the mountains, and let the hills hear your voice. {6:2} Hear, you mountains, the LORD's case, and you strong foundations of the earth; for the LORD has a case against his people, and he will contend with Israel. {6:3} My people, what have I done to you? How have I burdened you? Answer me. {6:4} For I brought you up from the land of Egypt and redeemed you from the house of slavery; I sent before you Moses, Aaron, and Miriam. {6:5} My people, remember what Balak king of Moab plotted and what Balaam son of Beor answered him from Shittim to Gilgal; that you may know the righteous acts of the LORD. {6:6} With what shall I come before the LORD and bow down before the exalted God? Shall I come before him with burnt offerings, with calves a year old? {6:7} Will the LORD be pleased with thousands of rams, with ten thousand rivers of oil? Shall I offer my firstborn for my transgression, the fruit of my body for the sin of my soul? {6:8} He has shown you, O man, what is good. And what does the LORD require of you? To act justly, to love mercy, and to walk humbly with your God. {6:9} The voice of the LORD calls to the city, and the one who has wisdom will heed your name; listen to the rod and the one who appointed it. {6:10} Are there still treasures of wickedness in the house of the wicked, and the scant measure that is detestable? {6:11} Should I regard them as pure with the wicked scales and with a bag of deceitful weights? {6:12} For the rich men in it are full of violence, and its inhabitants have spoken lies; their tongues are deceitful in their mouths. {6:13} Therefore, I will make you sick, striking you down, desolating you because of your sins. {6:14} You will eat but not be satisfied; your stomach will be empty. You will hold on, but will not escape; and what you rescue I will give to the sword. {6:15} You will sow but not reap; you will tread olives but not anoint yourselves with oil; you will press grapes but not drink the wine. {6:16} For you have kept the statutes of Omri and all the works of the house of Ahab, and you walk in their counsel; therefore, I will make you a desolation, and the inhabitants will be a hissing; you will bear the reproach of my people.

{7:1} Woe is me! I feel like someone gathering summer fruits, like those who pick the leftover grapes from the harvest; there's no cluster to eat, and my soul longs for the first ripe fruit. {7:2} The good person has perished from the earth, and there is no one upright among men; they all lie in wait for blood, hunting every man his brother with a net. {7:3} They are eager to do evil with both hands; the ruler asks for a bribe, the judge seeks a reward, and the great man expresses his wicked desires, wrapping them up together. {7:4} The best among them is like a thorn bush; the most upright is sharper than a thorn hedge; the day of your watchmen and your visitation is coming; now they will be in confusion. {7:5} Do not trust in a friend; do not put confidence in a guide; guard the doors of your mouth from her who lies in your bosom. {7:6} For a son dishonors his father, a daughter rises against her mother, a daughter-in-law against her mother-in-law; a man's enemies are the men of his own household. {7:7} Therefore, I will look to the LORD; I will wait for the God of my salvation; my God will hear me. {7:8} Do not rejoice over me, my enemy; when I fall, I will arise; when I sit in darkness, the LORD will be a light for me. {7:9} I will bear the indignation of the LORD because I have sinned against him until he pleads my cause and executes judgment for me; he will bring me into the light, and I will see his righteousness. {7:10} Then my enemy will see it, and shame will cover her who said to me, "Where is the LORD your God?" My eyes will see her, and she will be trampled down like the mud of the streets. {7:11} On the day your walls are to be rebuilt, that decree will be far removed. {7:12} On that day, he will come to you from Assyria, from the fortified cities, from the fortress to the river, from sea to sea, and from mountain to mountain. {7:13} Nevertheless, the land will be desolate because of those who dwell therein, for the fruit of their actions. {7:14} Shepherd your people with your staff, the flock of your heritage, who dwell alone in the woods, in the midst of Carmel; let them graze in Bashan and Gilead, as in the days of old. {7:15} As in the days you came out of the land of Egypt, I will show him marvelous things. {7:16} The nations will see and be ashamed of all their might; they will lay their hands on their mouths, their ears will be deaf. {7:17} They will lick the dust like a serpent; they will crawl out of their holes like worms of the earth; they will be afraid of the LORD our God and fear because of you. {7:18} Who is a God like you, who pardons iniquity & passes over the transgression of the remnant of his heritage? He does not retain his anger forever because he delights in mercy. {7:19} He will have compassion on us again; he will subdue our iniquities; you will cast all their sins into the depths of sea. {7:20} You will be faithful to Jacob & show mercy to Abraham, which you have sworn to our ancestors from days of old.

The Book of Joel

{1:1} The word of the LORD came to Joel, the son of Pethuel. {1:2} Listen to this, you elders, and pay attention, all you inhabitants of the land. Has anything like this happened in your lifetime or in the days of your ancestors? {1:3} Tell your children about it, and let your children tell their children, and their children another generation. {1:4} What the locust has left, the grasshopper has eaten; what the grasshopper has left, the blight has eaten; and what the blight has left, the caterpillar has eaten. {1:5} Wake up, you drunkards, and weep; and wail, all you wine drinkers, because of the new wine, for it has been taken from your lips. {1:6} For a powerful nation has invaded my land, strong and without number; its teeth are like the teeth of a lion, and it has the fangs of a fierce lion. {1:7} It has laid waste my vine and ruined my fig tree; it has stripped off the bark and thrown it away; the branches are made white. {1:8} Mourn like a young woman dressed in sackcloth for the husband of her youth. {1:9} The grain offering and the drink offering are cut off from the house of the LORD; the priests, who are the LORD's ministers, mourn. {1:10} The fields are ruined, and the land mourns; for the grain is destroyed, the new wine is dried up, and the oil fails. {1:11} Be ashamed, you farmers; wail, you vine growers, for the wheat and barley, because the harvest of the field has perished. {1:12} The vine has dried up, and the fig tree is withered; the pomegranate tree, the palm tree, and the apple tree, all the trees of the field are dried up; for joy has withered away from the children of men. {1:13} Put on sackcloth and mourn, you priests; wail, you ministers of the altar; come, spend the night in sackcloth, you ministers of my God, for the grain offering and the drink offering are withheld from the house of your God. {1:14} Declare a holy fast, call a solemn assembly, gather the elders and all the inhabitants of the land into the house of the LORD your God, and cry out to the LORD. {1:15} Alas for the day! For the day of the LORD is near, and it will come as destruction from the Almighty. {1:16} Is not the food cut off before our eyes, joy and gladness from the house of our God? {1:17} The seeds are shriveled under the clods; the granaries are empty, and the barns are in ruins, for the grain has withered. {1:18} How the animals groan! The herds of cattle are confused because they have no pasture; even the flocks of sheep are suffering. {1:19} To you, LORD, I cry out, for fire has devoured the pastures in the wilderness, and flames have burned up all the trees of the field. {1:20} The animals of the field also cry out to you; for the streams of water are dried up, and fire has devoured the pastures in the wilderness.

{2:1} Blow the trumpet in Zion and sound an alarm on my holy mountain; let all the inhabitants of the land tremble, for the day of the LORD is coming, it is near! {2:2} It will be a day of darkness and gloom, a day of clouds and thick darkness, like the morning spread over the mountains. A great and powerful people will come; there has never been anything like it before, and there will never be anything like it again for many generations. {2:3} A fire devours in front of them, and behind them a flame burns. The land is like the Garden of Eden in front of them, but behind them it is a desolate wilderness; nothing will escape them. {2:4} Their appearance is like that of horses, and like war horses they run. {2:5} They leap over the mountains like the sound of chariots, like the noise of a flame of fire that consumes the stubble, like a strong people arranged for battle. {2:6} At their presence, people will be in anguish; all faces will turn pale. {2:7} They will run like mighty men; they will scale the wall like soldiers; each will march in his own path, and they will not break ranks. {2:8} No one will push another; they will all walk in their own path, and when they fall upon the sword, they will not be hurt. {2:9} They will run to and fro in the city; they will run on the wall, climb into the houses, and enter through the windows like a thief. {2:10} The earth will quake before them; the heavens will tremble; the sun and the moon will be dark, and the stars will lose their brightness. {2:11} The LORD will utter his voice before his army, for his camp is very great; he is strong who carries out his word. The day of the LORD is great and very terrible; who can endure it? {2:12} Therefore, says the LORD, return to me with all your heart, with fasting, weeping, and mourning. {2:13} Rend your hearts and not your garments; return to the LORD your God, for he is gracious and merciful, slow to anger, and abounding in steadfast love, and he relents from sending calamity. {2:14} Who knows? He may turn and relent and leave behind a blessing—grain offerings and drink offerings for the LORD your God. {2:15} Blow the trumpet in Zion, declare a holy fast, call a solemn assembly. {2:16} Gather the people, sanctify the congregation, assemble the elders, gather the children and those nursing at the breast; let the bridegroom leave his room and the bride her chamber. {2:17} Let the priests, the ministers of the LORD, weep between the porch and the altar, and let them say, "Spare your people, LORD, and do not make your inheritance an object of scorn, a byword among the nations. Why should they say among the peoples, 'Where is their God?'" {2:18} Then the LORD will be jealous for his land and take pity on his people. {2:19} Yes, the LORD will reply, "I am sending you grain, new wine, and olive oil, and you will be satisfied; never again will I make you an object of scorn among the nations. {2:20} I will drive the northern army far from you, pushing it into a barren and desolate land, with its front facing the eastern sea and its back toward the western sea. Its stench will rise; its foul odor will come up because it has done great things." {2:21} Do not fear, land; be glad and rejoice, for the LORD has done great things. {2:22} Do not be afraid, you wild animals, for the grasslands in the wilderness are becoming green; the trees are bearing their fruit; the fig tree and the vine yield their riches. {2:23} Be glad, people of Zion, rejoice in the LORD your God, for he has given you the autumn rains in righteousness; he sends you abundant showers, both autumn and spring rains, as before. {2:24} The threshing floors will be filled with grain; the vats will overflow with new wine and oil. {2:25} I will repay you for the years the locusts have eaten—the great locust and the young locust, the other locusts and the locust swarm—my great army that I sent among you. {2:26} You will have plenty to eat, until you are full, and you will praise the name of the LORD your God, who has worked wonders for you; never again will my people be ashamed. {2:27} Then you will know that I am in Israel, that I am the LORD your God, and that there is no other; never again will my people be ashamed. {2:28} And afterward, I will pour out my Spirit on all people. Your sons and daughters will prophesy, your old men will dream dreams, your young men will see visions. {2:29} Even on my servants, both men and women, I will pour out my Spirit in those days. {2:30} I will show wonders in the heavens and on the earth, blood and fire and billows of smoke. {2:31} The sun will be turned to darkness and the moon to blood before the coming of the great and dreadful day of the LORD. {2:32} And everyone who calls on the name of the LORD will be saved; for on Mount Zion and in Jerusalem there will be deliverance, as the LORD has said, among the survivors whom the LORD calls.

{3:1} For behold, in those days, and at that time, when I restore the fortunes of Judah and Jerusalem, {3:2} I will gather all nations and bring them down to the Valley of Jehoshaphat. There I will put them on trial for my people and my heritage Israel, whom they scattered among the nations and divided up my land. {3:3} They cast lots for my people and traded boys for prostitutes; they sold girls for wine that they might drink. {3:4} What do you have against me, Tyre and Sidon, and all you regions of Philistia? Are you paying me back for something I did? If you are, I will swiftly bring down on your own heads what you have done. {3:5} For you took my silver and gold and carried off my finest treasures to your temples. {3:6} You sold the people of Judah and Jerusalem to the Greeks, that you might send them far from their homeland. {3:7} See, I am going to rouse them out of the place to which you sold them, and I will return on your own head what you have done. {3:8} I will sell your sons and daughters to the people of Judah, and they will sell them to the Sabeans, a nation far away. The LORD has spoken. {3:9} Proclaim this among the nations: Prepare for war! Rouse the warriors! Let all the soldiers draw near and attack. {3:10} Beat your plowshares into swords and your pruning hooks into spears. Let the weakling say, "I am strong!" {3:11} Come quickly, all you nations from every side, and assemble there. Bring down your warriors, LORD! {3:12} Let the nations be roused and come up to the Valley of Jehoshaphat, for there I will sit to judge all the nations on every side. {3:13} Swing the sickle, for the harvest is ripe. Come, trample the grapes, for the winepress is full and the vats overflow—so great is their wickedness! {3:14} Multitudes, multitudes in the valley of decision! For the day of the LORD is near in the valley of decision. {3:15} The sun and moon will be darkened, and the stars no longer shine. {3:16} The LORD will roar from Zion and thunder from Jerusalem; the earth and the heavens will tremble. But the LORD will be a refuge for his people, a stronghold for the people of Israel. {3:17} Then you will know that I, the LORD your God, dwell in Zion, my holy hill. Jerusalem will be holy; never again will foreigners invade her. {3:18} In that day, the mountains will drip new wine, and the hills will flow with milk; all the ravines of Judah will run with water. A fountain will flow out of the LORD's house and will water the valley of acacias. {3:19} Egypt will be desolate, Edom a desert waste, because of the violence done to the people of Judah, in whose land they shed innocent blood. {3:20} But Judah will be inhabited forever, and Jerusalem through all generations. {3:21} Their blood guilt, which I have not pardoned, I will pardon. The LORD dwells in Zion.

The Book of Obadiah

{1:1} This is the vision of Obadiah. The Lord GOD has spoken concerning Edom: We have heard a message from the LORD, and a messenger has been sent among the nations. "Rise up, and let us attack her in battle!" {1:2} Look, I have made you small among the nations; you are greatly despised. {1:3} The pride of your heart has deceived you, you who live in the clefts of the rock and make your home high up, saying to yourself, "Who can bring me down to the ground?" {1:4} Even if you soar like the eagle and set your nest among the stars, I will bring you down, says the LORD. {1:5} If thieves came to you, if robbers came by night—would they not steal only what they wanted? If grape pickers came to you, would they not leave some grapes? {1:6} How are the things of Esau searched out! How are his hidden treasures sought after! {1:7} All your allies have brought you to the border; the men at peace with you have deceived you and have prevailed against you. Those who eat your bread have laid a trap for you; there is no understanding in them. {1:8} Will I not, on that day, says the LORD, destroy the wise men out of Edom and the understanding out of the mountains of Esau? {1:9} Your warriors, O Teman, will be terrified, and everyone on the mountains of Esau will be cut down in slaughter. {1:10} Because of your violence against your brother Jacob, shame will cover you, and you will be cut off forever. {1:11} On the day you stood aloof while strangers carried off his wealth and foreigners entered his gates and cast lots for Jerusalem, you were like one of them. {1:12} But you should not have gloated over your brother on the day of his misfortune; you should not have rejoiced over the people of Judah in the day of their destruction; you should not have spoken arrogantly in the day of their distress. {1:13} You should not have entered the gate of my people on the day of their calamity; you should not have looked on their misfortune in the day of their calamity, nor laid hands on their possessions in the day of their calamity. {1:14} You should not have stood at the crossroads to cut down those who escaped; you should not have handed over those who remained in the day of distress. {1:15} The day of the LORD is near for all nations; as you have done, it will be done to you; your deeds will return upon your own head. {1:16} Just as you drank on my holy mountain, all the nations will drink continually; they will drink and swallow down, and they will be as though they had never been. {1:17} But on Mount Zion there will be deliverance; it will be holy, and the house of Jacob will possess their possessions. {1:18} The house of Jacob will be a fire, the house of Joseph a flame, and the house of Esau will be like stubble; they will set them on fire and consume them, and there will be no survivors from the house of Esau, for the LORD has spoken. {1:19} Those from the Negev will possess the mountains of Esau, and those from the foothills will possess the land of the Philistines. They will possess the fields of Ephraim & the fields of Samaria, and Benjamin will possess Gilead. {1:20} The exiles of this host of the Israelites will possess Canaan as far as Zarephath; the exiles from Jerusalem, who are in Sepharad, will possess the cities of the Negev. {1:21} Deliverers will go up on Mount Zion to govern the mountains of Esau & kingdom will be the LORD's.

The Book of Jonah

{1:1} Now the word of the LORD came to Jonah, the son of Amittai, saying, {1:2} "Get up, go to Nineveh, that great city, and cry out against it, for their wickedness has come up before me." {1:3} But Jonah got up to flee to Tarshish from the presence of the LORD. He went down to Joppa and found a ship going to Tarshish; so he paid the fare and went down into it to travel with them to Tarshish, away from the presence of the LORD. {1:4} But the LORD sent a great wind into the sea, and there was a mighty storm, so that the ship was about to break apart. {1:5} The sailors were afraid, and each cried out to his god. They threw the cargo that was in the ship into the sea to lighten the load. But Jonah had gone below deck, where he lay down and fell asleep. {1:6} The captain went to him and said, "What do you mean, sleeper? Get up and call on your God! Perhaps your God will pay attention to us so that we do not perish." {1:7} Each sailor said to his companion, "Come, let us cast lots to find out who is responsible for this trouble." So they cast lots, and the lot fell on Jonah. {1:8} They asked him, "Tell us, who is responsible for making this trouble for us? What is your occupation? Where do you come from? What is your country? From what people are you?" {1:9} He answered, "I am a Hebrew, and I fear the LORD, the God of heaven, who made the sea and the dry land." {1:10} This terrified them, and they asked, "What have you done?" They knew he was running away from the LORD because he had already told them. {1:11} They said to him, "What should we do to you to make the sea calm for us?" The sea was getting rougher. {1:12} He replied, "Pick me up and throw me into the sea; it will become calm for you. I know that it is my fault that this great storm has come upon you." {1:13} Instead, the men rowed hard to get back to land, but they could not, for the sea grew even wilder against them. {1:14} Then they cried out to the LORD, "Please, LORD, do not let us die for taking this man's life, and do not hold us accountable for innocent blood, for you, LORD, have done as you pleased." {1:15} So they took Jonah and threw him overboard, and the raging sea grew calm. {1:16} At this, the men greatly feared the LORD, and they offered a sacrifice to the LORD and made vows. {1:17} Now the LORD had prepared a great fish to swallow Jonah, and Jonah was in the belly of the fish for three days and three nights.

{2:1} Then Jonah prayed to the LORD his God from the belly of the fish, {2:2} and he said, "I cried out to the LORD because of my affliction, and he answered me. From the belly of the grave (hell) I cried for help, and you heard my voice. {2:3} You cast me into the deep, into the heart of the seas, and the currents surrounded me; all your waves and billows swept over me. {2:4} I said, 'I have been banished from your sight, yet I will look again toward your holy temple.' {2:5} The waters engulfed me, threatening my life; the deep surrounded me; seaweed was wrapped around my head. {2:6} To the roots of the mountains I sank down; the earth beneath barred me in forever. But you, LORD my God, brought my life up from the pit. {2:7} When my life was ebbing away, I remembered the LORD, and my prayer rose to you, to your holy temple. {2:8} Those who cling to worthless idols forfeit the grace that could be theirs. {2:9} But I, with shouts of grateful praise, will sacrifice to you. What I have vowed, I will make good. Salvation comes from the LORD." {2:10} And the LORD commanded the fish, and it vomited Jonah onto dry land.

{3:1} Then the word of the LORD came to Jonah a second time, saying, {3:2} "Get up, go to Nineveh, that great city, and deliver the message I give you." {3:3} So Jonah got up and went to Nineveh, following the word of the LORD. Now Nineveh was an incredibly large city, taking three days to cross. {3:4} Jonah began to enter the city, and after walking for a day, he cried out, "In forty days, Nineveh will be overthrown!" {3:5} The people of Nineveh believed God and declared a fast; they dressed in sackcloth from the greatest to the least. {3:6} When the news reached the king of Nineveh, he rose from his throne, removed his royal robe, covered himself with sackcloth, and sat in ashes. {3:7} He issued a proclamation throughout Nineveh by the decree of the king and his nobles: "Let neither people nor animals, herds nor flocks, taste anything; do not let them eat or drink water. {3:8} But let both people and animals be covered with sackcloth and let them cry out to God urgently. Let everyone turn from their evil ways and from the violence they have committed. {3:9} Who knows? God may yet relent and with compassion turn from his fierce anger so that we will not perish." {3:10} When God saw what they did and how they turned from their evil ways, he had compassion and did not bring upon them the destruction he had threatened.

{4:1} But Jonah was greatly displeased and became very angry. {4:2} He prayed to the LORD, saying, "LORD, isn't this what I said when I was still at home? That's why I tried to flee to Tarshish. I knew that you are a gracious and compassionate God, slow to anger and abounding in love, a God who relents from sending calamity. {4:3} Now, LORD, take my life away, for it is better for me to die than to live." {4:4} But the LORD replied, "Is it right for you to be angry?" {4:5} Jonah went out of the city and sat down east of it. There he made a shelter and sat in its shade to see what would happen to the city. {4:6} Then the LORD God provided a plant and made it grow up over Jonah to give shade for his head to ease his discomfort. Jonah was very happy about the plant. {4:7} But at dawn the next day, God provided a worm that chewed the plant so that it withered. {4:8} When the sun rose, God provided a scorching east wind, and the sun blazed on Jonah's head so that he grew faint. He wished to die and said, "It would be better for me to die than to live." {4:9} But God said to Jonah, "Is it right for you to be angry about the plant?" "It is," he said. "And I'm so angry I wish I were dead." {4:10} But the LORD said, "You have been concerned about this plant, though you did not tend it or make it grow. It sprang up overnight and died overnight. {4:11} And should I not have concern for the great city of Nineveh, in which there are more than one hundred twenty thousand people who cannot tell their right hand from their left, and also many animals?"

The Book of Nahum

{1:1} This is the burden against Nineveh. The book of the vision of Nahum, who was from Elkosh. {1:2} God is jealous and the LORD takes vengeance; the LORD takes vengeance and is furious; the LORD will take revenge on his enemies and reserves his wrath for his foes. {1:3} The LORD is slow to anger but great in power and will not leave the guilty unpunished. The LORD has his way in the whirlwind and the storm, and the clouds are the dust beneath his feet. {1:4} He rebukes the sea and makes it dry; he dries up all the rivers. Bashan and Carmel wither, and the blossoms of Lebanon fade. {1:5} The mountains quake before him, and the hills melt. The earth burns in his presence; the world and all who live in it are laid waste. {1:6} Who can stand before his anger? Who can endure his fierce wrath? His fury is poured out like fire, and the rocks are shattered before him. {1:7} The LORD is good, a refuge in times of trouble. He knows those who take refuge in him. {1:8} But with an overwhelming flood, he will make a complete end of Nineveh, and darkness will pursue his enemies. {1:9} What are you plotting against the LORD? He will make a complete end; trouble will not rise up a second time. {1:10} They are like tangled thorns and drunkards who are consumed like dry stubble. {1:11} From you, a wicked counselor has come forth, imagining evil against the LORD. {1:12} The LORD says, "Even though they are powerful and numerous, they will be cut down when I pass through. Though I have afflicted you, I will afflict you no more." {1:13} Now I will break their yoke from your neck and tear your shackles apart. {1:14} The LORD has commanded concerning you: "No one from your family line will be left. I will destroy the idols and images from the temple of your gods. I will prepare your grave, for you are vile." {1:15} Look! On the mountains, the feet of one who brings good news, who proclaims peace! O Judah, celebrate your festivals and fulfill your vows, for the wicked will never invade you again; they will be completely destroyed.

{2:1} An attacker advances against you, Nineveh! Guard the fortress, watch the road, brace yourselves, and strengthen your power! {2:2} The LORD has restored the splendor of Jacob like the splendor of Israel, for the plunderers have plundered them and ruined their vine branches. {2:3} The shields of the soldiers are red; the warriors are clad in scarlet. The chariots are flashing with fire on the day they prepare; the juniper trees shake with fear. {2:4} The chariots race through the streets; they rush back and forth in the squares. They look like torches; they dash about like lightning. {2:5} He calls his officers; they stumble as they go; they hurry to the wall and the shield is put in place. {2:6} The river gates are thrown open and the palace collapses. {2:7} It is decreed that Huzzab will be led away captive; her female servants will moan like doves, beating their breasts. {2:8} Nineveh is like a pool of water from the days of old, but they flee away. "Stop! Stop!" they cry, but no one turns back. {2:9} Plunder the silver! Plunder the gold! The supply is endless, the wealth from all its treasures. {2:10} She is desolate, empty, and wasted; hearts melt and knees tremble; anguish is in every face, and their faces grow pale. {2:11} Where now is the lions' den, the place where they fed their cubs, where the lion and lioness went, and the lion's whelps had no fear? {2:12} The lion killed enough prey for his cubs and strangled the kill for his lionesses. He filled his dens with the prey and his lairs with the remains. {2:13} "I am against you," declares the LORD Almighty. "I will burn your chariots in smoke, and the sword will devour your young lions. I will cut off your prey from the earth, and the voices of your messengers will no longer be heard."

{3:1} Woe to the bloody city! It is full of lies and robbery; the victims never leave. {3:2} There's the sound of whips, the rattling of wheels, the prancing of horses, and the clattering of chariots. {3:3} The horsemen raise both their shining swords and gleaming spears, and there is a multitude of slain, with countless corpses piled up; they stumble over the dead bodies. {3:4} This is because of the many adulteries of the beautiful prostitute, the mistress of sorcery, who sells nations through her sexual immorality and families through her witchcraft. {3:5} Look! I am against you, declares the LORD Almighty; I will lift your skirts and expose you to the nations, showing your nakedness to the kingdoms and your shame to the world. {3:6} I will pour out disgusting filth upon you, making you vile, and I will make you a spectacle for all to see. {3:7} All who look at you will flee from you and say, "Nineveh is destroyed! Who will mourn for her? Where can I find anyone to comfort you?" {3:8} Are you better than Thebes (or No), that city by the rivers, surrounded by water, whose defenses were the sea and whose wall was from the sea? {3:9} Ethiopia and Egypt were her strength, and they were without limits; Put and Lubim were her allies. {3:10} Yet she was carried away and went into captivity. Her children were dashed to pieces at every street corner, and they cast lots for her respected leaders, binding all her great men in chains. {3:11} You too will be drunk; you will hide, and you will seek strength because of your enemies. {3:12} Your strongholds will be like fig trees with ripe figs; if shaken, they will fall into the mouth of the eater. {3:13} Look! Your people are women in your midst; the gates of your land will be wide open to your enemies, and fire will consume your bars. {3:14} Gather water for the siege; strengthen your strongholds. Go into the clay, and prepare the mortar; make the brick kiln strong. {3:15} There the fire will consume you; the sword will cut you off, and it will eat you up like a locust. Make yourself numerous like the locusts; make yourself numerous like the grasshoppers. {3:16} You have increased your merchants more than the stars of heaven; the locust spoils and then flies away. {3:17} Your guards are like locusts, and your leaders are like great grasshoppers that camp in the hedges on a cold day, but when the sun rises, they flee away, and no one knows where they are. {3:18} Your shepherds are asleep, O king of Assyria; your nobles lie in the dust. Your people are scattered on the mountains, with no one to gather them. {3:19} There is no healing for your wound; your injury is severe. All who hear the news about you will clap their hands over you, for who has not experienced your continual wickedness?

The Book of Habakkuk

{1:1} This is the message that Habakkuk the prophet received. {1:2} O LORD, how long must I cry for help, but you do not listen? I cry out to you about violence, but you do not save! {1:3} Why do you show me wrongdoing and make me see trouble? Destruction and violence are before me; there is strife and conflict. {1:4} Therefore, the law is paralyzed, and justice never prevails. The wicked surround the righteous; so justice is perverted. {1:5} Look among the nations and watch—be utterly amazed! For I am going to do something in your days that you would not believe, even if you were told. {1:6} I am raising up the Babylonians (Chaldeans), that fierce and impetuous nation, who sweep across the whole earth to seize dwelling places that are not their own. {1:7} They are a feared and dreaded people; they are a law to themselves and promote their own honor. {1:8} Their horses are swifter than leopards, fiercer than wolves at dusk. Their riders come from far away; they fly like an eagle swooping down to eat. {1:9} They all come intent on violence; their faces are set like the east wind. They gather captives like sand. {1:10} They mock kings and scoff at rulers. They laugh at all fortified cities; they build earthen ramps and capture them. {1:11} Then they change their minds and charge ahead. They are guilty; their own strength is their god. {1:12} Are you not from everlasting, O LORD my God, my Holy One? We will not die. O LORD, you have appointed them for judgment; O Rock, you have established them to punish. {1:13} Your eyes are too pure to look on evil; you cannot tolerate wrong. Why then do you tolerate the treacherous? Why are you silent while the wicked swallow up those more righteous than themselves? {1:14} You have made people like the fish in the sea, like the sea creatures that have no ruler. {1:15} The wicked foe pulls all of them up with hooks; he catches them in his net and gathers them in his dragnet. So he rejoices and is glad. {1:16} Therefore, he sacrifices to his net and burns incense to his dragnet, for by his net he lives in luxury and enjoys the choicest food. {1:17} Is he to keep on emptying his net, destroying nations without mercy?

{2:1} I will stand at my watch and station myself on the ramparts; I will look to see what he will say to me and what answer I am to give to this complaint. {2:2} Then the LORD replied: "Write down the revelation and make it plain on tablets so that a herald may run with it. {2:3} For the revelation awaits an appointed time; it speaks of the end and will not prove false. Though it linger, wait for it; it will certainly come and will not delay. {2:4} See, the enemy is puffed up; his desires are not upright—but the righteous person will live by his faithfulness. {2:5} Indeed, wine betrays him; he is arrogant and never at rest. Because he is as greedy as the grave and like death is never satisfied, he gathers to himself all the nations and takes captive all the peoples. {2:6} Will not all of them taunt him with ridicule and scorn, saying, "Woe to him who piles up stolen goods and makes himself wealthy by extortion!" {2:7} How long will this go on? Will your creditors not suddenly arise? Will they not wake up and make you tremble? {2:8} Because you have plundered many nations, the peoples who are left will plunder you. For you have shed human blood; you have destroyed lands and cities and everyone in them. {2:9} Woe to him who builds his house by unjust gain, setting his nest on high to escape the clutches of ruin! {2:10} You have plotted the ruin of many peoples, shaming your own house and forfeiting your life. {2:11} The stones of the wall will cry out, and the beams of the woodwork will echo it. {2:12} Woe to him who builds a city with bloodshed and establishes a town by injustice! {2:13} Has not the LORD Almighty determined that the people's labor is only fuel for the fire, that the nations exhaust themselves for nothing? {2:14} For the earth will be filled with the knowledge of the glory of the LORD as the waters cover the sea. {2:15} Woe to him who gives drink to his neighbors, pouring it from the wineskin till they are drunk, so he can gaze on their naked bodies. {2:16} You will be filled with shame instead of glory. Now it is your turn! Drink and let your nakedness be exposed! The cup from the LORD's right hand is coming around to you, and disgrace will cover your glory. {2:17} The violence you have done to Lebanon will overwhelm you, and your destruction of animals will terrify you. For you have shed human blood; you have destroyed lands and cities and everyone in them. {2:18} Of what value is an idol carved by a craftsman? Or an image that teaches lies? For the one who makes it trusts in his own creation; he makes idols that cannot speak. {2:19} Woe to him who says to wood, "Come to life!" Or to lifeless stone, "Wake up!" Can it give guidance? It is covered with gold and silver; there is no breath in it. {2:20} The LORD is in his holy temple; let all the earth be silent before him.

{3:1} A prayer of Habakkuk the prophet, sung to a lively tune. {3:2} O LORD, I have heard your message, and I am afraid. O LORD, revive your work in our time; in our time, make it known. In your anger, remember mercy. {3:3} God came from Teman, the Holy One from Mount Paran. Selah. His glory covered the heavens, and the earth was full of his praise. {3:4} His brightness was like the sunlight; he had rays coming from his hand, where his power was hidden. {3:5} Before him went pestilence, and burning coals followed at his feet. {3:6} He stood and measured the earth; he looked and shook the nations. The ancient mountains crumbled, and the everlasting hills bowed down. His ways are eternal. {3:7} I saw the tents of Cushan in distress; the curtains of the land of Midian trembled. {3:8} Was the LORD angry with the rivers? Was your wrath against the rivers? Was your anger against the sea, when you rode on your horses and your chariots of salvation? {3:9} Your bow was made bare, according to the oaths of the tribes. Selah. You split the earth with rivers. {3:10} The mountains saw you and trembled; the rushing waters swept by. The deep gave forth its voice and lifted its hands high. {3:11} The sun and moon stood still in their place; at the flash of your arrows, they fled, at the brightness of your shining spear. {3:12} You marched through the land in anger; you trampled the nations in fury. {3:13} You went out to save your people, to save your anointed one. You crushed the leader of the wicked and exposed the foundation to the neck. Selah. {3:14} You struck the leaders of the villages with his own weapons; they came like a whirlwind to scatter me, their joy was to secretly devour the poor. {3:15} You walked through the sea with your horses, through the great waters. {3:16} When I heard this, my stomach trembled; my lips quivered at your voice. Decay entered my bones, and I trembled in fear, so I could be calm in the day of trouble. When he comes up to invade the people, he will invade them with his troops. {3:17} Though the fig tree does not blossom, and there are no grapes on the vines; though the olive crop fails and the fields produce no food; though there are no sheep in the pen and no cattle in the stalls, {3:18} yet I will rejoice in the LORD; I will be joyful in God my Savior. {3:19} The Sovereign LORD is my strength; he makes my feet like the feet of a deer; he enables me to tread on the heights. For the director of music on my stringed instruments.

The Book of Zephaniah

{1:1} The word of the LORD that came to Zephaniah, the son of Cushi, the son of Gedaliah, the son of Amariah, the son of Hizkiah, during the days of Josiah, the son of Amon, king of Judah. {1:2} I will completely remove everything from the land, says the LORD. {1:3} I will remove both humans and animals; I will take away the birds in the sky and the fish in the sea, and I will remove the stumbling blocks with the wicked. I will cut off humanity from the land, says the LORD. {1:4} I will also reach out my hand against Judah and all the inhabitants of Jerusalem; I will remove the remnant of Baal from this place and the names of the priests of the idols. {1:5} I will remove those who worship the host of heaven on their rooftops and those who swear by the LORD and also swear by their idols. {1:6} I will remove those who have turned back from the LORD and those who have not sought the LORD or inquired of him. {1:7} Be silent in the presence of the Lord GOD, for the day of the LORD is near. The LORD has prepared a sacrifice; he has invited his guests. {1:8} On the day of the LORD's sacrifice, I will punish the officials, the king's children, and all those dressed in foreign attire. {1:9} On that same day, I will punish those who leap over the threshold, filling their masters' houses with violence and deceit. {1:10} On that day, says the LORD, there will be a cry from the Fish Gate, a wailing from the Second District, and a great crash from the hills. {1:11} Wail, you inhabitants of Maktesh, for all the merchants will be destroyed; all who carry silver will be cut off. {1:12} At that time, I will search Jerusalem with lamps and punish those who are complacent, saying in their hearts, "The LORD will do nothing, good or bad." {1:13} Therefore their goods will become plunder, and their houses will be desolate. They will build houses but not live in them; they will plant vineyards but not drink the wine. {1:14} The great day of the LORD is near, it is near and coming quickly. The cry on the day of the LORD will be bitter; even the mighty will cry out. {1:15} That day will be a day of wrath, a day of trouble and distress, a day of devastation and desolation, a day of darkness and gloom, a day of clouds and thick darkness, {1:16} a day of trumpet blasts and alarm against fortified cities and against high towers. {1:17} I will bring distress on people, and they will walk like blind men because they have sinned against the LORD. Their blood will be poured out like dust and their flesh like dung. {1:18} Neither their silver nor gold will be able to save them in the day of the LORD's wrath; the whole land will be consumed by the fire of his jealousy, for he will make a swift end of all who live in the land. His anger will not be quenched, and no one will escape the judgment that falls upon the earth.

{2:1} Gather together, gather, O nation without shame; {2:2} before the decree takes effect, before the day passes like chaff, before the fierce anger of the LORD comes upon you, before the day of the LORD's anger comes upon you. {2:3} Seek the LORD, all you humble of the earth, you who have obeyed his commands; seek righteousness, seek humility. Perhaps you will be hidden on the day of the LORD's anger. {2:4} For Gaza will be abandoned, and Ashkelon will be desolate. They will drive out Ashdod at midday, and Ekron will be uprooted. {2:5} Woe to you who live by the sea, you nation of the Cherethites! The word of the LORD is against you, O Canaan, land of the Philistines. I will destroy you so that no one is left. {2:6} The coast will become pasture land with shelters for shepherds and folds for flocks. {2:7} The coast will belong to the remnant of the house of Judah; they will graze there. In the houses of Ashkelon, they will lie down in the evening, for the LORD their God will visit them and restore their fortunes. {2:8} I have heard the taunts of Moab and the insults of the Ammonites, who have taunted my people and boasted against their territory. {2:9} Therefore, as I live, says the LORD of Hosts, the God of Israel, surely Moab will be like Sodom and the Ammonites like Gomorrah—a land of weeds and salt pits, a perpetual desolation. The remnant of my people will plunder them, and the survivors of my nation will possess them. {2:10} This is what they will get for their pride, because they have taunted and boasted against the people of the LORD of Hosts. {2:11} The LORD will be terrifying to them; he will starve all the gods of the earth, and people will worship him, each from their own place, including all the coastlands of the nations. {2:12} You too, O Ethiopians, will be slain by my sword. {2:13} He will stretch out his hand against the north and destroy Assyria, making Nineveh a desolation, dry like a wilderness. {2:14} Flocks and herds will lie down in the midst of her; all the animals of the nations will rest there. The cormorant and the bittern will nest on her ledges; their voices will sing from the windows; desolation will be on the thresholds, for he will uncover the cedar work. {2:15} This is the city that lived in safety, that said to herself, "I am, and there is none beside me." How has she become a desolation, a place for wild animals to lie down! Everyone who passes by her hisses and shakes their fists. Her once-glorious streets are now silent, and her people are scattered, a haunting reminder of pride before ruin.

{3:1} Woe to her who is filthy and corrupt, the city that oppresses! {3:2} She did not listen to the voice; she did not accept correction; she did not trust in the LORD; she did not draw near to her God. {3:3} Her leaders are like roaring lions; her judges are like evening wolves, who leave nothing for the morning. {3:4} Her prophets are reckless and deceitful; her priests have polluted the sanctuary and violated the law. {3:5} The just LORD is in her midst; he does not commit injustice. Every morning he brings his judgment to light; he does not fail, but the unjust know no shame. {3:6} I have cut off the nations; their towers are in ruins. I made their streets desolate, so no one passes through; their cities are destroyed, with no one left, no inhabitant. {3:7} I thought, "Surely you will fear me; you will receive instruction," so your dwelling would not be cut off, despite my punishments. But they rose early and corrupted all their actions. {3:8} Therefore, wait for me, says the LORD, until the day I rise to take action; my plan is to gather the nations and assemble the kingdoms to pour out my indignation, my fierce anger, for the whole earth will be consumed by the fire of my jealousy. {3:9} For then I will restore to the people a pure language, so they may all call upon the name of the LORD and serve him with one purpose. {3:10} From beyond the rivers of Ethiopia, my worshipers, even the daughters of my scattered people, will bring me offerings. {3:11} On that day, you will not be ashamed of your actions in which you have sinned against me, for then I will remove from your midst those who rejoice in your pride, and you will no longer be haughty because of my holy mountain. {3:12} I will leave in your midst a humble and afflicted people, and they will trust in the name of the LORD. {3:13} The remnant of Israel will not commit injustice or speak lies; no deceitful tongue will be found in their mouths, for they will graze and lie down, with no one to frighten them. {3:14} Sing, O daughter of Zion; shout, O Israel; be glad and rejoice with all your heart, O daughter of Jerusalem. {3:15} The LORD has taken away your judgments; he has expelled your enemy. The king of Israel, the LORD, is in your midst; you will see no more evil. {3:16} On that day, it will be said to Jerusalem, "Do not fear," and to Zion, "Do not let your hands hang limp." {3:17} The LORD your God is in your midst, a mighty Savior. He will take delight in you with gladness; he will quiet you by his love; he will rejoice over you with singing. {3:18} I will gather those who are sorrowful for the appointed feast, those who have borne its burden. {3:19} Behold, at that time I will remove all that afflict you; I will save the lame and gather those who were driven away; I will give them praise and fame in every land where they have been put to shame. {3:20} At that time, I will bring you back, even at the time I gather you, for I will make you a name and a praise among all the peoples of the earth when I restore your fortunes before your eyes, says the LORD. You will no longer be ashamed, but your prosperity and glory will testify to My faithfulness and power.

The Book of Haggai

{1:1} In the second year of King Darius, on the first day of the sixth month, the word of the LORD came through the prophet Haggai to Zerubbabel son of Shealtiel, the governor of Judah, and to Joshua son of Josedech, the high priest, saying, {1:2} "Thus says the LORD of hosts: This people says, 'The time has not yet come to rebuild the LORD's house.' {1:3} Then the word of the LORD came through Haggai the prophet, saying, {1:4} "Is it a time for you to dwell in your paneled houses while this house lies in ruins? {1:5} Now therefore, says the LORD of hosts, consider your ways. {1:6} You have sown much, but harvested little; you eat, but are never satisfied; you drink, but you are not filled; you clothe yourselves, but no one is warm; and whoever earns wages earns them to put into a bag with holes. {1:7} Thus says the LORD of hosts: Consider your ways. {1:8} Go up to the mountains, bring wood, and build the house; I will take pleasure in it and be glorified, says the LORD. {1:9} You looked for much, but it came to little; and when you brought it home, I blew it away. Why? says the LORD of hosts. Because my house lies in ruins while each of you runs to his own house. {1:10} Therefore, the heavens above you have withheld the dew, and the earth has withheld its produce. {1:11} I called for a drought on the land, the mountains, the grain, the new wine, the oil, and everything the ground produces, as well as on people and livestock and all the labor of your hands. {1:12} Then Zerubbabel son of Shealtiel, and Joshua son of Josedech, the high priest, along with all the remnant of the people, obeyed the voice of the LORD their God and the words of the prophet Haggai, as the LORD their God had sent him, and the people feared the LORD. {1:13} Then Haggai, the LORD's messenger, spoke the LORD's message to the people, saying, "I am with you, says the LORD." {1:14} And the LORD stirred up the spirit of Zerubbabel son of Shealtiel, governor of Judah, and the spirit of Joshua son of Josedech, the high priest, and the spirit of all the remnant of the people; they came and began to work on the house of the LORD of hosts, their God, {1:15} on the twenty-fourth day of the sixth month, in the second year of King Darius.

{2:1} In the seventh month, on the twenty-first day of the month, the word of the LORD came through the prophet Haggai, saying, {2:2} "Speak now to Zerubbabel son of Shealtiel, governor of Judah, to Joshua son of Josedech, the high priest, and to the remnant of the people, saying, {2:3} 'Who among you is left that saw this house in its former glory? How does it look to you now? Does it not seem to you like nothing in comparison? {2:4} Yet now be strong, O Zerubbabel, says the LORD; be strong, O Joshua son of Josedech, the high priest; be strong, all you people of the land, says the LORD, and work, for I am with you, says the LORD of hosts. {2:5} According to the covenant I made with you when you came out of Egypt, my Spirit remains among you; do not fear. {2:6} For thus says the LORD of hosts: In a little while, I will shake the heavens, the earth, the sea, and the dry land; {2:7} and I will shake all nations, and the desire of all nations shall come; and I will fill this house with glory, says the LORD of hosts. {2:8} The silver is mine, and the gold is mine, says the LORD of hosts. {2:9} The glory of this latter house will be greater than the former, says the LORD of hosts; and in this place, I will give peace, says the LORD of hosts. {2:10} On the twenty-fourth day of the ninth month, in the second year of Darius, the word of the LORD came through Haggai the prophet, saying, {2:11} "Thus says the LORD of hosts: Ask the priests for a ruling, saying, {2:12} 'If someone carries holy meat in the fold of his garment and touches bread, stew, wine, oil, or any other food, will it become holy?'" The priests answered and said, "No." {2:13} Then Haggai said, "If someone who is unclean because of a dead body touches any of these, will it be unclean?" The priests answered, "It will be unclean." {2:14} Then Haggai replied, "So it is with this people and this nation before me, says the LORD; so is every work of their hands; and what they offer there is unclean. {2:15} Now, please consider from this day and upward, from before a stone was laid upon a stone in the temple of the LORD: {2:16} since those days, when one came to a heap of twenty measures, there were only ten; when one came to the winepress to draw fifty vessels from the press, there were only twenty. {2:17} I struck you with blight, mildew, and hail in all the work of your hands; yet you did not turn to me, says the LORD. {2:18} Consider now from this day and upward, from the twenty-fourth day of the ninth month, from the day the foundation of the LORD's temple was laid, consider it. {2:19} Is the seed yet in the barn? As yet the vine, the fig tree, the pomegranate, and the olive tree have not borne fruit. From this day on, I will bless you." {2:20} Again the word of the LORD came to Haggai on the twenty-fourth day of the month, saying, {2:21} "Speak to Zerubbabel, governor of Judah, saying, 'I will shake the heavens and the earth; {2:22} I will overthrow the thrones of kingdoms and destroy the strength of the kingdoms of the nations; I will overthrow the chariots and those who ride in them; the horses and their riders will fall, each by the sword of his brother. {2:23} On that day, says the LORD of hosts, I will take you, O Zerubbabel my servant, son of Shealtiel, says the LORD, and I will make you like a signet ring, for I have chosen you, says the LORD of hosts."

The Book of Zechariah

{1:1} In the eighth month of the second year of Darius, the word of the LORD came to Zechariah, son of Berechiah, son of Iddo, the prophet, saying, {1:2} "The LORD has been very angry with your ancestors. {1:3} Therefore, say to them, 'Thus says the LORD of hosts: Return to me, says the LORD of hosts, and I will return to you, says the LORD of hosts.' {1:4} Don't be like your ancestors, to whom the former prophets cried, saying, 'Thus says the LORD of hosts: Turn from your evil ways and from your evil deeds.' But they did not listen or pay attention to me, says the LORD. {1:5} Where are your ancestors now? And the prophets, do they live forever? {1:6} But my words and my decrees, which I commanded my servants the prophets, did they not take hold of your ancestors? And they returned and said, 'Just as the LORD of hosts intended to do to us according to our ways and deeds, so he has dealt with us.' {1:7} On the twenty-fourth day of the eleventh month, which is the month of Shebat, in the second year of Darius, the word of the LORD came to Zechariah, son of Berechiah, son of Iddo, the prophet, saying, {1:8} "I had a vision at night, and behold, a man riding a red horse stood among the myrtle trees in a ravine; behind him were red, speckled, and white horses. {1:9} I asked, 'O my lord, what are these?' And the angel who talked with me said, 'I will show you what they are.' {1:10} And the man standing among the myrtle trees answered and said, 'These are they whom the LORD has sent to patrol the earth.' {1:11} And they answered the angel of the LORD who stood among the myrtle trees, saying, 'We have patrolled the earth, and behold, all the earth is at rest and quiet.' {1:12} Then the angel of the LORD said, 'O LORD of hosts, how long will you not have mercy on Jerusalem and the cities of Judah, against which you have been angry these seventy years?' {1:13} And the LORD answered the angel who talked with me with good and comforting words. {1:14} So the angel who spoke with me said, 'Proclaim, saying, Thus says the LORD of hosts: I am jealous for Jerusalem and for Zion with great jealousy. {1:15} And I am very angry with the nations that are at ease; for I was only a little angry, and they helped forward the affliction.' {1:16} Therefore, thus says the LORD: I have returned to Jerusalem with mercy; my house will be built in it, says the LORD of hosts, and a measuring line will be stretched over Jerusalem. {1:17} Proclaim further, saying, Thus says the LORD of hosts: My cities will overflow with prosperity, and the LORD will again comfort Zion and choose Jerusalem. {1:18} Then I looked up my eyes and saw four horns. {1:19} I asked the angel who talked with me, 'What are these?' He answered me, 'These are the horns that have scattered Judah, Israel, and Jerusalem.' {1:20} And the LORD showed me four craftsmen. {1:21} I asked, "What are these coming to do?" He replied, "These are the horns that scattered Judah, leaving it helpless. Now they have come to terrify and defeat the nations that opposed Judah."

{2:1} I lifted my eyes again and looked, and behold, a man with a measuring line in his hand. {2:2} I asked, 'Where are you going?' He said to me, 'To measure Jerusalem, to see how wide and how long it is.' {2:3} And behold, the angel who talked with me went out, and another angel came to meet him, {2:4} and said to him, 'Run, tell this young man, Jerusalem will be inhabited as towns without walls because of the multitude of people and livestock in it. {2:5} For I, says the LORD, will be a wall of fire around her, and I will be the glory in her midst.' {2:6} "Come, come! Flee from the land of the north, says the LORD, for I have spread you abroad as the four winds of heaven, says the LORD. {2:7} Deliver yourself, O Zion, you who dwell with the daughter of Babylon. {2:8} For thus says the LORD of hosts: After glory, he sent me to the nations that plundered you; for he who touches you touches the apple of his eye. {2:9} For behold, I will shake my hand over them, and they will become plunder for their servants; and you will know that the LORD of hosts has sent me. {2:10} Sing and rejoice, O daughter of Zion, for behold, I come and will dwell in your midst, says the LORD. {2:11} Many nations will join the LORD in that day and will become my people, and I will dwell in your midst, and you will know that the LORD of hosts has sent me to you. {2:12} And the LORD will inherit Judah as his portion in the holy land and will again choose Jerusalem. {2:13} Be silent, all flesh, before the LORD, for he has roused himself from his holy habitation."

{3:1} He showed me Joshua the high priest standing before the angel of the LORD, and Satan standing at his right hand to oppose him. {3:2} And the LORD said to Satan, "The LORD rebuke you, O Satan; the LORD who has chosen Jerusalem rebuke you! Is this not a brand plucked from the fire?" {3:3} Now Joshua was dressed in filthy clothes as he stood before the angel. {3:4} The angel spoke to those standing before him, saying, "Take off his filthy clothes." And to Joshua he said, "Look, I have taken away your iniquity and will dress you in splendid robes." {3:5} I said, "Let them put a clean turban on his head." So they put a clean turban on his head and clothed him while the angel of the LORD stood by. {3:6} The angel of the LORD solemnly assured Joshua, saying, {3:7} "Thus says the LORD of hosts: If you will walk in my ways and keep my charge, then you shall also judge my house and keep my courts, and I will give you places to walk among those standing here. {3:8} Hear now, O Joshua the high priest, you and your companions who sit before you, for they are a sign: behold, I will bring forth my servant the BRANCH. {3:9} For behold, the stone that I have set before Joshua; on that one stone are seven eyes. Behold, I will engrave its inscription, says the LORD of hosts, and I will remove the iniquity of that land in one day. {3:10} In that day, says the LORD of hosts, everyone will invite his neighbor to sit under his vine and under his fig tree."

{4:1} The angel who talked with me came again and woke me up, as a man wakes from sleep, {4:2} and said to me, "What do you see?" I replied, "I have looked, and behold, a lampstand all of gold, with a bowl on top of it, and seven lamps on it, and seven pipes to the seven lamps which are on top of it. {4:3} And two olive trees are by it, one on the right side of the bowl and the other on the left side." {4:4} So I answered and spoke to the angel who talked with me, saying, "What are these, my lord?" {4:5} The angel who talked with me answered and said, "Do you not know what these are?" I said, "No, my lord." {4:6} Then he answered and said to me, "This is the word of the LORD to Zerubbabel: Not by might, nor by power, but by my Spirit, says the LORD of hosts. {4:7} Who are you, O great mountain? Before Zerubbabel you shall become a plain, and he shall bring forth the capstone with shouts of 'Grace, grace to it!' {4:8} Moreover, the word of the LORD came to me, saying, {4:9} 'The hands of Zerubbabel have laid the foundation of this house; his hands shall also finish it; then you will know that the LORD of hosts has sent me to you. {4:10} For who has despised the day of small things? For these seven rejoice when they see the plumb line in the hand of Zerubbabel; they are the eyes of the LORD, which scan to and fro throughout the whole earth.' {4:11} Then I asked the angel, "What are these two olive trees on the right side of the lampstand and on its left?" {4:12} And I answered again, "What are these two olive branches that empty the golden oil out of themselves through the two golden pipes?" {4:13} He answered me and said, "Do you not know what these are?" I said, "No, my lord." {4:14} Then he said, "These are the two anointed ones who stand by the Lord of the whole earth."

{5:1} Then I turned and lifted my eyes, and looked, and behold, a flying scroll. {5:2} He said to me, "What do you see?" I answered, "I see a flying scroll; its length is twenty cubits and its width is ten cubits." {5:3} He said to me, "This is the curse that goes out over the face of the whole earth: for everyone who steals will be cut off as on this side, and everyone who swears falsely will be cut off as on that side." {5:4} I will bring it forth, says the LORD of hosts, and it shall enter the house of the thief and the house of him who swears falsely by my name; it will remain in the midst of his house and consume it, along with its timbers and stones. {5:5} Then the angel who talked with me went out and said, "Lift your eyes now and see what this is that is going out." {5:6} I said, "What is it?" He said, "This is an ephah that is going out." He said further, "This is their appearance throughout the earth." {5:7} And behold, a talent of lead was lifted, and this is a woman sitting in the midst of the ephah. {5:8} He said, "This is wickedness." And he threw her into the midst of the ephah and cast the lead weight upon its opening. {5:9} Then I lifted my eyes and looked, and behold, there came out two women, and the wind was in their wings; for they had wings like the wings of a stork, and they lifted up the ephah between the earth and the heavens. {5:10} I said to the angel who talked with me, "Where are these carrying the ephah?" {5:11} He said to me, "To build a house for it in the land of Shinar; it shall be established and set there upon its own base."

{6:1} I turned and lifted my eyes and looked, and behold, there came four chariots coming out from between two mountains, and the mountains were mountains of bronze. {6:2} In the first chariot were red horses; in the second chariot were black horses; {6:3} in the third chariot were white horses; and in the fourth chariot were dappled and bay horses. {6:4} I asked the angel who talked with me, "What are these, my lord?" {6:5} The angel answered and said to me, "These are the four spirits of heaven, who go out from standing before the Lord of all the earth. {6:6} The black horses go toward the north country, and the white ones go after them, while the dappled go toward the south country. {6:7} The bay horses went out, seeking to walk to and fro through the earth. He said, "Go, walk to and fro through the earth." So they walked to and fro through the earth. {6:8} Then he called to me and spoke to me, saying, "Behold, those who go toward the north country have given rest to my Spirit in the north country." {6:9} The word of the LORD came to me, saying, {6:10} "Take from among the exiles, from Heldai, Tobijah, and Jedaiah, who have come from Babylon, and go the same day to the house of Josiah, the son of Zephaniah. {6:11} Take silver and gold, and make crowns, and set them on the head of Joshua, the son of Josedech, the high priest. {6:12} Speak to him, saying, 'Thus says the LORD of hosts: Behold, the man whose name is The BRANCH; he shall grow up out of his place and build the temple of the LORD. {6:13} It is he who shall build the temple of the LORD and bear the glory, and shall sit and rule on his throne, and he shall be a priest on his throne; the counsel of peace shall be between them both. {6:14} The crowns shall be for Helem, Tobijah, Jedaiah & Hen, the son of Zephaniah, as a memorial in the temple of the LORD. {6:15} And those who are far off shall come and build the temple of the LORD, & you shall know that the LORD of hosts has sent me to you. This shall come to pass if you diligently obey the voice of the LORD your God."

{7:1} In the fourth year of King Darius, the word of the LORD came to Zechariah on the fourth day of the ninth month, which is Chisleu. {7:2} They sent Sherezer and Regemmelech, along with their men, to pray before the LORD at the house of God. {7:3} They asked the priests at the house of the LORD of hosts and the prophets, "Should I weep in the fifth month, separating myself as I have done for so many years?" {7:4} Then the word of the LORD of hosts came to me, saying, {7:5} "Speak to all the people of the land and to the priests, saying, 'When you fasted and mourned in the fifth and seventh months for these seventy years, did you really fast for me, to me? {7:6} And when you ate and drank, did you not do so for yourselves?' {7:7} Should you not listen to the words which the LORD has proclaimed through the former prophets when Jerusalem was inhabited and prosperous, along with the cities around her, when men inhabited the Negev and the plain?" {7:8} The word of the LORD came to Zechariah, saying, {7:9} "Thus says the LORD of hosts: 'Execute true judgment, show mercy and compassion to one another. {7:10} Do not oppress the widow, the fatherless, the stranger, or the poor; and let none of you devise evil against your brother in your heart.' {7:11} But they refused to listen, they shrugged their shoulders, and stopped their ears so they would not hear. {7:12} They made their hearts as hard as flint, so they could not hear the law and the words which the LORD of hosts had sent by His Spirit through the former prophets; therefore, great wrath came from the LORD of hosts. {7:13} So it has come to pass that as He cried out and they would not listen, so they cried out and I would not listen, says the LORD of hosts. {7:14} I scattered them with a whirlwind among nations they did not know. The land became desolate, with no one passing through or returning, for they made the pleasant land desolate."

{8:1} Again, the word of the LORD of hosts came to me, saying, {8:2} "Thus says the LORD of hosts: 'I am jealous for Zion with great jealousy, and I am jealous for her with great fury. {8:3} Thus says the LORD: 'I have returned to Zion and will dwell in the midst of Jerusalem, and Jerusalem shall be called the City of Truth, and the mountain of the LORD of hosts, the holy mountain.' {8:4} Thus says the LORD of hosts: 'Old men and old women shall sit in the streets of Jerusalem, each with their staff in hand because of great age. {8:5} The streets of the city shall be full of boys and girls playing in the streets.' {8:6} Thus says the LORD of hosts: 'If it is marvelous in the eyes of the remnant of this people in these days, should it also be marvelous in my eyes?' says the LORD of hosts. {8:7} Thus says the LORD of hosts: 'Behold, I will save my people from the east country and from the west country; {8:8} and I will bring them, and they shall dwell in the midst of Jerusalem, and they shall be my people, and I will be their God, in truth and righteousness.' {8:9} Thus says the LORD of hosts: 'Let your hands be strong, you who hear in these days these words from the mouth of the prophets who spoke when the foundation of the house of the LORD of hosts was laid for the temple to be built. {8:10} Before these days there was no hire for man, nor any hire for beast; there was no peace for him who went out or came in because of the affliction, for I set all men against one another. {8:11} But now I will not be to the remnant of this people as in the former days,' says the LORD of hosts. {8:12} For the seed shall be prosperous; the vine shall yield its fruit, the ground shall give its increase, and the heavens shall give their dew; and I will cause the remnant of this people to possess all these things. {8:13} And it shall come to pass that as you were a curse among the nations, O house of Judah and house of Israel, so will I save you, and you shall be a blessing. Do not fear, but let your hands be strong. {8:14} For thus says the LORD of hosts: 'As I thought to punish you when your fathers provoked me to wrath,' says the LORD of hosts, 'and I did not relent, {8:15} so again have I thought in these days to do good to Jerusalem and to the house of Judah. Do not fear.' {8:16} These are the things you shall do: Speak each man the truth to his neighbor; execute the judgment of truth and peace in your gates. {8:17} And let none of you think evil in your hearts against your neighbor, and do not love false oaths, for all these are things that I hate,' says the LORD." {8:18} The word of the LORD of hosts came to me, saying, {8:19} "Thus says the LORD of hosts: 'The fast of the fourth month, the fast of the fifth, the fast of the seventh, and the fast of the tenth shall be joy and gladness and cheerful feasts for the house of Judah; therefore, love truth and peace.' {8:20} Thus says the LORD of hosts: 'It shall yet come to pass that people and the inhabitants of many cities shall come; {8:21} and the inhabitants of one city shall go to another, saying, 'Let us go quickly to pray before the LORD and seek the LORD of hosts; I will go also.' {8:22} Yes, many peoples and strong nations shall come to seek the LORD of hosts in Jerusalem and to pray before the LORD. {8:23} Thus says the LORD of hosts: 'In those days, ten men from all languages of the nations shall take hold of the skirt of a Jew, saying, 'We will go with you, for we have heard that God is with you.'"

{9:1} The burden of the word of the LORD is against the land of Hadrach, and Damascus will find rest in it; when the eyes of all people, as well as all the tribes of Israel, are turned toward the LORD. {9:2} Hamath will also border it; Tyre and Sidon, though they are very wise. {9:3} Tyre built herself a stronghold, heaping up silver like dust and fine gold like the mud in the streets. {9:4} Look, the Lord will cast her out; He will strike her power in the sea, and she shall be consumed by fire. {9:5} Ashkelon will see this and fear; Gaza will also see it and be very sorrowful, and Ekron, for her expectation will be ashamed; the king will perish from Gaza, and Ashkelon will be uninhabited. {9:6} A worthless person will dwell in Ashdod, and I will remove the pride of the Philistines. {9:7} I will remove the blood from his mouth and his abominations from between his teeth; but he who remains will be for our God, and he will be like a governor in Judah, and Ekron will be like a Jebusite. {9:8} I will encamp around my house because of the army, because of him who passes by, and because of him who returns; and no oppressor shall pass through them anymore, for I have seen with my own eyes. {9:9} Rejoice greatly, O daughter of Zion; shout, O daughter of Jerusalem: look, your King is coming to you; He is righteous and has salvation; He is humble and riding on a donkey, on a colt, the foal of a donkey. {9:10} I will cut off the chariot from Ephraim and the horse from Jerusalem, and the battle bow will be cut off; and He will speak peace to the nations, and His dominion will be from sea to sea, and from the river to the ends of the earth. {9:11} As for you, by the blood of your covenant I have sent your prisoners out of the pit where there is no water. {9:12} Return to the stronghold, you prisoners of hope; today I declare that I will restore double to you. {9:13} When I have bent Judah for me, filled the bow with Ephraim, and raised up your sons, O Zion, against your sons, O Greece, and made you like the sword of a mighty man. {9:14} The LORD will be seen over them, and His arrow will go forth like lightning; the Lord God will sound the trumpet and go with the whirlwinds from the south. {9:15} The LORD of hosts will protect them; they will devour and subdue with sling stones; they will drink and make noise like wine; they will be filled like bowls, like the corners of the altar. {9:16} The LORD their God will save them that day as the flock of His people; for they will be like the jewels in a crown, lifted up as a banner in His land. {9:17} For how great is His goodness, and how great is His beauty! Grain will make the young men cheerful, and new wine the young women.

{10:1} Ask the LORD for rain in the time of the latter rain; the LORD will make bright clouds and give them showers of rain, to everyone grass in the field. {10:2} For the idols have spoken emptiness, and the diviners have seen lies and told false dreams; they comfort in vain; therefore, they went their way like a flock, troubled because there was no shepherd. {10:3} My anger was kindled against the shepherds, and I punished the goats; for the LORD of hosts has visited His flock, the house of Judah, and has made them like His goodly horse in battle. {10:4} From him came the cornerstone, from him the peg, from him the battle bow, and from him every oppressor together. {10:5} They will be like mighty men who trample their enemies in the mire of the streets in battle; they will fight because the LORD is with them, and the riders on horses will be confounded. {10:6} I will strengthen the house of Judah, and I will save the house of Joseph, and I will bring them back because I have mercy on them; they will be as though I had not cast them off, for I am the LORD their God, and I will hear them. {10:7} Those of Ephraim will be like mighty men, and their hearts will rejoice as with wine; yes, their children will see it and be glad; their hearts will rejoice in the LORD. {10:8} I will whistle for them and gather them, for I have redeemed them, and they will increase as they once increased. {10:9} I will sow them among the nations, and they will remember me in far countries; they will live with their children and return. {10:10} I will bring them back from the land of Egypt and gather them from Assyria; I will bring them into the land of Gilead and Lebanon, and there will be no room found for them. {10:11} He will pass through the sea of troubles and strike the waves in the sea; all the depths of the river will dry up; the pride of Assyria will be brought down, and the scepter of Egypt will depart. {10:12} I will strengthen them in the LORD, and they will walk up and down in His name, says the LORD.

{11:1} Open your doors, O Lebanon, so that fire may consume your cedars. {11:2} Howl, O fir tree, for the cedar has fallen; because the mighty have been ruined: howl, O oaks of Bashan, for the forest of the vintage has come down. {11:3} There is a voice of the howling of the shepherds, for their glory has been spoiled; a voice of young lions roaring, for the pride of Jordan is ruined. {11:4} Thus says the LORD my God: Feed the flock destined for slaughter; {11:5} whose owners kill them and feel no guilt; and those who sell them say, "Blessed be the LORD, for I am rich," yet their own shepherds show them no compassion. {11:6} For I will no longer have pity on the inhabitants of the land, says the LORD; indeed, I will deliver everyone into the hand of his neighbor and into the hand of his king; and they shall strike the land, and I will not deliver them from their hand. {11:7} I will feed the flock destined for slaughter, even you, O poor of the flock. I took for myself two staffs; one I called Beauty and the other I called Bands, and I fed the flock. {11:8} I cut off three shepherds in one month; my soul loathed them, and their souls also abhorred me. {11:9} Then I said, "I will not feed you; let the dying die, and let those who are to be cut off be cut off; and let the rest eat one another's flesh." {11:10} I took my staff, Beauty, and broke it in pieces to break my covenant that I had made with all the people. {11:11} It was broken that day; so the poor of the flock who waited for me knew that it was the word of the LORD. {11:12} I said to them, "If it seems good to you, give me my price; but if not, don't." So they weighed for my price thirty pieces of silver. {11:13} The LORD said to me, "Throw it to the potter; a goodly price at which I was valued by them." So I took the thirty pieces of silver and threw them to the potter in the house of the LORD. {11:14} Then I broke my other staff, Bands, to break the brotherhood between Judah and Israel. {11:15} The LORD said to me, "Take for yourself yet the instruments of a foolish shepherd. {11:16} For behold, I will raise up a shepherd in the land who will not visit those who are cut off, nor seek the young, nor heal what is broken, nor feed what stands still; but he will eat the flesh of the fat and tear their claws in pieces. {11:17} Woe to the idle shepherd who leaves the flock! The sword shall be upon his arm and upon his right eye; his arm shall be completely dried up, and his right eye shall be utterly darkened.

{12:1} The burden of the word of the LORD concerning Israel, says the LORD, who stretches out the heavens, lays the foundation of the earth, and forms the spirit of man within him. {12:2} Look, I will make Jerusalem a cup of trembling for all the surrounding people when they lay siege against Judah and Jerusalem. {12:3} In that day I will make Jerusalem a heavy stone for all people; all who try to lift it will be severely injured, though all the nations of the earth gather against it. {12:4} In that day, says the LORD, I will strike every horse with panic and its rider with madness; I will open my eyes upon the house of Judah and strike every horse of the nations with blindness. {12:5} The governors of Judah will say in their hearts, "The inhabitants of Jerusalem are my strength in the LORD of hosts, their God." {12:6} In that day I will make the governors of Judah like a firepot among the wood, and like a torch of fire among the sheaves; and they will devour all the surrounding people on the right and on the left, and Jerusalem will again be inhabited in her own place, even in Jerusalem. {12:7} The LORD will also save the tents of Judah first, so that the glory of the house of David and the glory of the inhabitants of Jerusalem do not magnify themselves against Judah. {12:8} In that day the LORD will defend the inhabitants of Jerusalem; the feeble among them will be like David, and the house of David will be like God, like the angel of the LORD before them. {12:9} It will come to pass in that day that I will seek to destroy all the nations that come against Jerusalem. {12:10} I will pour out on the house of David and the inhabitants of Jerusalem the spirit of grace and supplication; they will look upon me whom they have pierced and mourn for him as one mourns for an only son, and they will be in bitterness for him like one who is in bitterness for his firstborn. {12:11} In that day there will be a great mourning in Jerusalem, like the mourning of Hadadrimmon in the valley of Megiddon. {12:12} The land will mourn, every family by itself; the family of the house of David by itself, and their wives by themselves; the family of the house of Nathan by itself, and their wives by themselves; {12:13} the family of the house of Levi by itself, and their wives by themselves; the family of Shimei by itself, and their wives by themselves; {12:14} all the families that remain, every family by itself, and their wives by themselves.

{13:1} In that day, a fountain will be opened for the house of David and the inhabitants of Jerusalem for sin and for impurity. {13:2} And it will come to pass in that day, says the LORD of hosts, that I will remove the names of the idols from the land, and they will no longer be remembered; I will also cause the prophets and the unclean spirit to depart from the land. {13:3} It will come to pass that when someone prophesies, his father and mother who gave him life will say to him, "You shall not live, for you speak lies in the name of the LORD." And his father and mother who gave him life will stab him when he prophesies. {13:4} In that day, the prophets will be ashamed of their visions when they prophesy; they will no longer wear rough clothing to deceive. {13:5} Instead, he will say, "I am no prophet; I am a farmer, for a man taught me to keep cattle from my youth." {13:6} Someone will ask him, "What are these wounds on your hands?" Then he will answer, "These are the wounds I received in the house of my friends." {13:7} Awake, O sword, against my shepherd and against the man who is my companion, says the LORD of hosts; strike the shepherd, and the sheep will be scattered, and I will turn my hand against the little ones. {13:8} It will come to pass that in all the land, says the LORD, two-thirds of the people will be cut off and die, but one-third will be left. {13:9} I will bring the third part through the fire and refine them like silver is refined and test them like gold is tested; they will call on my name, and I will hear them; I will say, "They are my people," and they will say, "The LORD is my God."

{14:1} Behold, the day of the LORD is coming, and your spoil will be divided in your midst. {14:2} For I will gather all nations against Jerusalem to battle; the city will be taken, the houses will be looted, and the women will be violated; half of the city will go into captivity, but the rest of the people will not be cut off from the city. {14:3} Then the LORD will go out and fight against those nations as when he fought on the day of battle. {14:4} His feet will stand on that day on the Mount of Olives, which is before Jerusalem on the east, and the Mount of Olives will split in two from east to west, forming a very large valley; half of the mountain will move north, and half south. {14:5} You will flee to the valley of the mountains, for the valley of the mountains will reach to Azal; yes, you will flee, just as you fled from the earthquake in the days of Uzziah king of Judah. The LORD my God will come, and all the saints with you. {14:6} On that day, the light will not be clear or dark; {14:7} it will be a unique day known to the LORD, neither day nor night, but it will come to pass that at evening time, it will be light. {14:8} On that day, living waters will flow out from Jerusalem, half of them toward the eastern sea and half toward the western sea; in summer and winter, it will happen. {14:9} The LORD will be king over all the earth; in that day there will be one LORD, and his name will be one. {14:10} The whole land will be turned into a plain from Geba to Rimmon, south of Jerusalem; it will be lifted up and inhabited in its place, from Benjamin's gate to the site of the first gate, to the corner gate, and from the tower of Hananeel to the king's winepresses. {14:11} People will dwell in it, and there will be no more destruction; Jerusalem will be safely inhabited. {14:12} This will be the plague with which the LORD will strike all the people who fought against Jerusalem; their flesh will rot while they stand on their feet, their eyes will rot in their sockets, and their tongues will rot in their mouths. {14:13} It will come to pass on that day that there will be a great panic from the LORD among them; they will lay hold of one another's hand, and their hands will rise against their neighbors. {14:14} Judah will also fight at Jerusalem; the wealth of all the surrounding nations will be gathered together, gold, silver, and clothing, in great abundance. {14:15} This will be the plague on the horses, mules, camels, donkeys, and all the beasts in those camps. {14:16} It will come to pass that everyone who is left of all the nations that came against Jerusalem will go up year after year to worship the King, the LORD of hosts, and to celebrate the Feast of Tabernacles. {14:17} It will be that whoever does not go up from all the families of the earth to Jerusalem to worship the King, the LORD of hosts, will receive no rain. {14:18} If the family of Egypt does not go up and come, they will have no rain; this will be the plague with which the LORD will strike the nations that do not come up to celebrate the Feast of Tabernacles. {14:19} This will be the punishment of Egypt and the punishment of all nations that do not go up to celebrate the Feast of Tabernacles. {14:20} On that day, there will be inscribed on the bells of the horses, "HOLINESS TO THE LORD"; and the pots in the house of the LORD will be like the bowls before the altar. {14:21} Yes, every pot in Jerusalem and in Judah will be holy to the LORD of hosts, and all who sacrifice will come and take from them and cook in them. On that day, there will be no more Canaanite in the house of the LORD of hosts.

The Book of Malachi

{1:1} This is the burden of the word of the LORD to Israel through Malachi. {1:2} I have loved you, says the LORD. Yet you ask, "How have you loved us?" Was not Esau Jacob's brother? says the LORD; yet I loved Jacob, {1:3} and I hated Esau, and made his mountains and his heritage a wasteland for the wild animals of the desert. {1:4} While Edom says, "We are poor, but we will rebuild the ruins," the LORD of hosts says, "They will build, but I will tear down; they will be called the territory of wickedness and the people against whom the LORD has everlasting anger." {1:5} Your eyes will see this, and you will say, "The LORD is great even beyond the borders of Israel." {1:6} A son honors his father, and a servant honors his master. If I am a father, where is my honor? And if I am a master, where is my respect? says the LORD of hosts to you, O priests, who despise my name. Yet you ask, "How have we despised your name?" {1:7} You offer polluted bread on my altar, and you ask, "How have we polluted you?" By saying, "The table of the LORD is contemptible." {1:8} And if you offer the blind for sacrifice, is that not wrong? And if you offer the lame and sick, is that not wrong? Present it now to your governor; will he be pleased with you or accept your offering? says the LORD of hosts. {1:9} Now, I pray you, plead with God to be gracious to us; this has come from your actions: will he regard your offerings? says the LORD of hosts. {1:10} Is there anyone among you who would shut the doors for nothing? You do not kindle fire on my altar for nothing. I have no pleasure in you, says the LORD of hosts, and I will not accept an offering from you. {1:11} From the rising of the sun to its setting, my name will be great among the Gentiles; in every place, incense will be offered to my name, and a pure offering; my name will be great among the nations, says the LORD of hosts. {1:12} But you have profaned it by saying, "The table of the LORD is polluted, and the fruit of it, its food, is contemptible." {1:13} You said, "What a weariness this is!" and you snorted at it, says the LORD of hosts; you brought what was torn, lame, and sick, and you offered that as your sacrifice. Should I accept this from your hands? says the LORD. {1:14} Cursed be the deceiver who has a male in his flock and vows to offer it, but sacrifices a blemished animal to the LORD; for I am a great King, says the LORD of hosts, and my name is feared among the nations.

{2:1} And now, O priests, this command is for you. {2:2} If you will not listen, and if you do not take it to heart to give glory to my name, says the LORD of hosts, I will send a curse upon you, and I will curse your blessings; yes, I have already cursed them because you do not take it to heart. {2:3} Behold, I will corrupt your descendants and cover you with dung, even the dung from your festivals; and one will take you away with it. {2:4} You will know that I have sent this command to you, so that my covenant with Levi may continue, says the LORD of hosts. {2:5} My covenant was with him, of life and peace; I gave these to him out of reverence for me, and he was afraid before my name. {2:6} True instruction was in his mouth, and no wrongdoing was found on his lips; he walked with me in peace and uprightness and turned many away from sin. {2:7} For the lips of a priest should preserve knowledge, and people should seek instruction from his mouth, for he is the messenger of the LORD of hosts. {2:8} But you have turned away from the path; you have caused many to stumble by your teaching; you have corrupted the covenant of Levi, says the LORD of hosts. {2:9} Therefore, I have made you despised and lowly before all people because you have not kept my ways but have shown favoritism in your teaching. {2:10} Do we not all have one Father? Did not one God create us? Why then do we betray each other by profaning the covenant of our ancestors? {2:11} Judah has been unfaithful, and an abomination has been committed in Israel and in Jerusalem; for Judah has profaned the sanctuary of the LORD, which he loves, and has married the daughter of a foreign god. {2:12} The LORD will cut off the man who does this, whether master or scholar, from the tents of Jacob, and those who bring offerings to the LORD of hosts. {2:13} And this is what you do: you cover the altar of the LORD with tears, weeping, and crying out, so that he no longer pays attention to the offering or accepts it with pleasure from your hands. {2:14} Yet you ask, "Why?" Because the LORD has been a witness between you and the wife of your youth, against whom you have been unfaithful, though she is your companion and the wife of your covenant. {2:15} Did he not make them one? With a portion of the Spirit in their union? And why one? Because he sought godly offspring. Therefore, guard yourselves in your spirit, and do not be unfaithful to the wife of your youth. {2:16} For the LORD, the God of Israel, says that he hates divorce, and the one who covers his garment with violence, says the LORD of hosts. Therefore, guard yourselves in your spirit and do not be unfaithful. {2:17} You have wearied the LORD with your words. Yet you ask, "How have we wearied him?" When you say, "Everyone who does evil is good in the sight of the LORD, and he delights in them," or "Where is the God of justice?"

{3:1} Look, I will send my messenger, and he will prepare the way before me. The Lord, whom you seek, will suddenly come to his temple, the messenger of the covenant you desire; look, he will come, says the LORD of hosts. {3:2} But who can endure the day of his coming? Who can stand when he appears? For he is like a refiner's fire and like the soap used by launderers. {3:3} He will sit as a refiner and purifier of silver; he will purify the sons of Levi and refine them like gold and silver, so they may offer to the LORD an offering in righteousness. {3:4} Then the offerings of Judah and Jerusalem will be pleasing to the LORD, as in the days of old and in former years. {3:5} I will come near to you for judgment; I will be a swift witness against sorcerers, adulterers, liars, and those who cheat workers out of their wages, oppress widows and orphans, and deny justice to immigrants. They do not fear me, says the LORD of hosts. {3:6} For I am the LORD; I do not change. That's why you descendants of Jacob are not destroyed. {3:7} Ever since the days of your ancestors, you have turned away from my laws and have not kept them. Return to me, and I will return to you, says the LORD of hosts. But you ask, "How can we return?" {3:8} Can a man rob God? Yet you rob me. But you ask, "How have we robbed you?" In tithes and offerings. {3:9} You are under a curse, your whole nation, because you are robbing me. {3:10} Bring the whole tithe into the storehouse, that there may be food in my house. Test me in this, says the LORD of hosts, and see if I will not open the windows of heaven and pour out a blessing so great that you will not have enough room for it. {3:11} I will prevent pests from devouring your crops, and the vines in your fields will not drop their fruit before it is ripe, says the LORD of hosts. {3:12} Then all nations will call you blessed, for you will be a delightful land, says the LORD of hosts. {3:13} Your words have been harsh against me, says the LORD. Yet you ask, "What have we said against you?" {3:14} You have said, "It is useless to serve God. What do we gain by keeping his requirements and going about like mourners before the LORD of hosts? {3:15} So now we call the arrogant blessed. Not only are the evildoers prosperous, but they put God to the test and get away with it." {3:16} Then those who feared the LORD talked with each other, and the LORD listened and heard. A scroll of remembrance was written in his presence for those who feared the LORD and honored his name. {3:17} "They will be mine," says the LORD of hosts, "in that day when I make up my treasured possession; I will spare them, as a father spares his own son who serves him. {3:18} And you will again see the distinction between the righteous and the wicked, between those who serve God and those who do not."

{4:1} For surely the day is coming that will burn like a furnace; all the arrogant and every evildoer will be stubble, and that day will set them on fire, says the LORD of hosts, leaving them neither root nor branch. {4:2} But for you who fear my name, the Sun of Righteousness will rise with healing in its wings; and you will go out and leap like calves released from the stall. {4:3} You will trample down the wicked, for they will be ashes under the soles of your feet on the day when I act, says the LORD of hosts. {4:4} Remember the law of my servant Moses, the decrees and laws I gave him at Horeb for all Israel. {4:5} Look, I will send you the prophet Elijah before that great and dreadful day of the LORD comes. {4:6} He will turn the hearts of the parents to their children, and the hearts of the children to their parents, or else I will come and strike the land with total destruction.

~ THE NEW ~
TESTAMENT

The Gospel of Matthew

{1:1} This is the record of the ancestry of Jesus Christ, the son of David, the son of Abraham. {1:2} Abraham was the father of Isaac, Isaac was the father of Jacob, and Jacob was the father of Judah and his brothers. {1:3} Judah was the father of Perez and Zerah by Tamar; Perez was the father of Hezron, and Hezron was the father of Ram. {1:4} Ram was the father of Amminadab; Amminadab was the father of Nahshon, and Nahshon was the father of Salmon. {1:5} Salmon was the father of Boaz by Rahab; Boaz was the father of Obed by Ruth, and Obed was the father of Jesse. {1:6} Jesse was the father of King David; King David was the father of Solomon by her who had been the wife of Uriah. {1:7} Solomon was the father of Rehoboam; Rehoboam was the father of Abijah, and Abijah was the father of Asa. {1:8} Asa was the father of Jehoshaphat; Jehoshaphat was the father of Joram, and Joram was the father of Uzziah. {1:9} Uzziah was the father of Jotham; Jotham was the father of Ahaz, and Ahaz was the father of Hezekiah. {1:10} Hezekiah was the father of Manasseh; Manasseh was the father of Amon, and Amon was the father of Josiah. {1:11} Josiah was the father of Jeconiah and his brothers at the time they were taken to Babylon. {1:12} After they were brought to Babylon, Jeconiah was the father of Shealtiel, and Shealtiel was the father of Zerubbabel. {1:13} Zerubbabel was the father of Abiud; Abiud was the father of Eliakim, and Eliakim was the father of Azor. {1:14} Azor was the father of Zadok; Zadok was the father of Achim, and Achim was the father of Elihud. {1:15} Elihud was the father of Eleazar; Eleazar was the father of Matthan, and Matthan was the father of Jacob. {1:16} Jacob was the father of Joseph, the husband of Mary, of whom was born Jesus, who is called Christ. {1:17} So all the generations from Abraham to David are fourteen generations; from David until the exile to Babylon are fourteen generations; and from the exile to Babylon to Christ are fourteen generations. {1:18} Now the birth of Jesus Christ happened this way: When his mother Mary was engaged to Joseph, before they came together, she was found to be pregnant by the Holy Spirit. {1:19} Because Joseph her husband was a righteous man and did not want to expose her to public disgrace, he had in mind to divorce her quietly. {1:20} But while he was considering these things, an angel of the Lord appeared to him in a dream, saying, "Joseph, son of David, do not be afraid to take Mary as your wife, for what is conceived in her is from the Holy Spirit. {1:21} She will give birth to a son, and you are to give him the name Jesus because he will save his people from their sins." {1:22} All this took place to fulfill what the Lord had said through the prophet: {1:23} "The virgin will conceive and give birth to a son, and they will call him Immanuel," which means "God with us." {1:24} When Joseph woke up, he did what the angel of the Lord had commanded him and took Mary as his wife. {1:25} He did not have relations with her until she gave birth to her firstborn son; and he named him Jesus.

{2:1} After Jesus was born in Bethlehem in Judea during the time of King Herod, wise men from the east came to Jerusalem. {2:2} They asked, "Where is the one who has been born king of the Jews? We saw his star when it rose and have come to worship him." {2:3} When King Herod heard this, he was disturbed, and all Jerusalem with him. {2:4} He called together all the chief priests and teachers of the law and asked them where the Messiah was to be born. {2:5} "In Bethlehem in Judea," they replied, "for this is what the prophet has written: {2:6} 'But you, Bethlehem, in the land of Judah, are by no means least among the rulers of Judah; for out of you will come a ruler who will shepherd my people Israel.'" {2:7} Then Herod secretly called the wise men and found out from them the exact time the star had appeared. {2:8} He sent them to Bethlehem and said, "Go and search carefully for the child. As soon as you find him, report to me, so that I too may go and worship him." {2:9} After they had heard the king, they went on their way, and the star they had seen when it rose went ahead of them until it stopped over the place where the child was. {2:10} When they saw the star, they were overjoyed. {2:11} On coming to the house, they saw the child with his mother Mary, and they bowed down and worshiped him. Then they opened their treasures and presented him with gifts of gold, frankincense, and myrrh. {2:12} And having been warned in a dream not to go back to Herod, they returned to their country by another route. {2:13} When they had gone, an angel of the Lord appeared to Joseph in a dream. "Get up," he said, "take the child and his mother and escape to Egypt. Stay there until I tell you, for Herod is going to search for the child to kill him." {2:14} So he got up, took the child and his mother during the night, and left for Egypt. {2:15} Where he stayed until the death of Herod. And so was fulfilled what the Lord had said through the prophet: "Out of Egypt I called my son." {2:16} When Herod realized that he had been outwitted by the Magi, he was furious, and he gave orders to kill all the boys in Bethlehem and its vicinity who were two years old and under, in accordance with the time he had learned from the Magi. {2:17} Then what was said through the prophet Jeremiah was fulfilled: {2:18} "A voice is heard in Ramah, weeping and great mourning, Rachel weeping for her children and refusing to be comforted, because they are no more." {2:19} After Herod died, an angel of the Lord appeared in a dream to Joseph in Egypt. {2:20} "Get up," he said, "take the child and his mother and go to the land of Israel, for those who were trying to take the child's life are dead." {2:21} So he got up, took the child and his mother and went to the land of Israel. {2:22} But when he heard that Archelaus was reigning in Judea in place of his father Herod, he was afraid to go there. Having been warned in a dream, he withdrew to the district of Galilee, {2:23} and he went and lived in a town called Nazareth. So was fulfilled what was said through the prophets: "He will be called a Nazarene."

{3:1} In those days, John the Baptist appeared, preaching in the wilderness of Judea {3:2} and saying, "Repent, for the kingdom of heaven has come near." {3:3} This is the one spoken of by the prophet Isaiah, saying, "A voice of one calling in the wilderness, 'Prepare the way for the Lord, make his paths straight.'" {3:4} John wore clothes made of camel's hair and had a leather belt around his waist; his diet consisted of locusts and wild honey. {3:5} People from Jerusalem, all of Judea, and the whole region around the Jordan went out to him {3:6} and were baptized by him in the Jordan River, confessing their sins. {3:7} But when he saw many of the Pharisees and Sadducees coming to where he was baptizing, he said to them, "You brood of vipers! Who warned you to flee from the coming wrath? {3:8} Produce fruit in keeping with repentance. {3:9} And do not think you can say to yourselves, 'We have Abraham as our father.' I tell you that out of these stones God can raise up children for Abraham. {3:10} The ax has been laid to the root of the trees, and every tree that does not produce good fruit will be cut down and thrown into the fire. {3:11} I baptize you with water for repentance, but after me comes one who is more powerful than I, whose sandals I am not worthy to carry. He will baptize you with the Holy Spirit and fire. {3:12} His winnowing fork is in his hand, and he will clear his threshing floor, gathering his wheat into the barn and burning up the chaff with unquenchable fire." {3:13} Then Jesus came from Galilee to the Jordan to be baptized by John. {3:14} But John tried to deter him, saying, "I need to be baptized by you, and do you come to me?" {3:15} Jesus replied, "Let it be so now; it is proper for us to do this to fulfill all righteousness." Then John consented. {3:16} As soon as Jesus was baptized, he went up out of the water. At that moment heaven was opened, and he saw the Spirit of God descending like a dove and alighting on him. {3:17} And a voice from heaven said, "This is my Son, whom I love; with him I am well pleased."

{4:1} Then Jesus was led by the Spirit into the wilderness to be tempted by the devil. {4:2} After fasting forty days and forty nights, he was hungry. {4:3} The tempter came to him and said, "If you are the Son of God, tell these stones to become bread." {4:4} Jesus answered, "It is written: 'Man shall not live on bread alone, but on every word that comes from the mouth of God.'" {4:5} Then the devil took him to the holy city and had him stand on the highest point of the temple. {4:6} "If you are the Son of God," he said, "throw yourself down, for it is written: 'He will command his angels concerning you, and they will lift you up in their hands, so that you will not strike your foot against a stone.'" {4:7} Jesus answered him, "It is also written: 'Do not put the Lord your God to the test.'" {4:8} Again, the devil took him to a very high mountain and showed him all the kingdoms of the world and their splendor. {4:9} "All this I will give you," he said, "if you will bow down and worship me." {4:10} Jesus said to him, "Away from me, Satan! For it is written: 'Worship the Lord your God, and serve him only.'" {4:11} Then the devil left him, and angels came and attended him. {4:12} When Jesus heard that John had been put in prison, he withdrew to Galilee. {4:13} Leaving Nazareth, he went and lived in Capernaum, which is by the lake in the area of Zebulun and Naphtali. {4:14} To fulfill what was said through the prophet Isaiah: {4:15} "Land of Zebulun and land of Naphtali, the way of the sea, beyond the Jordan, Galilee of the Gentiles— {4:16} the people living in darkness have seen a great light; on those living in the land of the shadow of death a light has dawned." {4:17} From that time on, Jesus began to preach, "Repent, for the kingdom of heaven has come near." {4:18} As Jesus was walking beside the Sea of Galilee, he saw two brothers, Simon called Peter and his brother Andrew. They were casting a net into the lake, for they were fishermen. {4:19} "Come, follow me," Jesus said, "and I will send you out to fish for people." {4:20} At once they left their nets and followed him. {4:21} Going on from there, he saw two other brothers, James son of Zebedee and his brother John. They were in a boat with their father Zebedee, preparing their nets. Jesus called them, {4:22} and immediately they left the boat and their father and followed him. {4:23} Jesus went throughout Galilee, teaching in their synagogues, proclaiming the good news of the kingdom, and healing every disease and sickness among the people. {4:24} News about him spread all over Syria, and people brought to him all who were ill with various diseases, those suffering severe pain, the demon-possessed, those having seizures, and the paralyzed; and he healed them. {4:25} Large crowds from Galilee, the Decapolis, Jerusalem, Judea, and the region across the Jordan followed him.

{5:1} Seeing the crowds, Jesus went up on a mountainside and sat down. His disciples came to him, {5:2} and he began to teach them, saying: {5:3} "Blessed are the poor in spirit, for theirs is the kingdom of heaven. {5:4} Blessed are those who mourn, for they will be comforted. {5:5} Blessed are the meek, for they will inherit the earth. {5:6} Blessed are those who hunger and thirst for righteousness, for they will be filled. {5:7} Blessed are the merciful, for they will be shown mercy. {5:8} Blessed are the pure in heart, for they will see God. {5:9} Blessed are the peacemakers, for they will be called children of God. {5:10} Blessed are those who are persecuted because of righteousness, for theirs is the kingdom of heaven. {5:11} Blessed are you when people insult you, persecute you, and falsely say all kinds of evil against you because of me. {5:12} Rejoice and be glad, because great is your reward in heaven, for in the same way they persecuted the prophets who were before you. {5:13} You are the salt of the earth, but if the salt loses its flavor, how can it be made salty again? It is no longer good for anything except to be thrown out and trampled underfoot. {5:14} You are the light of the world. A town built on a hill cannot be hidden. {5:15} Neither do people light a lamp and put it under a bowl. Instead, they put it on its stand, and it gives light to everyone in the house. {5:16} In the same way, let your light shine before others, that they may see your good deeds and glorify your Father in heaven. {5:17} Do not think that I have come to abolish the Law or the Prophets; I have not come to abolish them but to fulfill them. {5:18} For truly I tell you, until heaven and earth disappear, not the smallest letter, not the least stroke of a pen, will by any means disappear from the Law until everything is accomplished. {5:19} Therefore anyone who sets aside one of the least of these commands and teaches others accordingly will be called least in the kingdom of heaven, but whoever practices and teaches these commands will be called great in the kingdom of heaven. {5:20} For I tell you that unless your righteousness surpasses that of the Pharisees and the teachers of the law, you will certainly not enter the kingdom of heaven. {5:21} You have heard that it was said to the people long ago, 'You shall not murder, and anyone who murders will be subject to judgment.' {5:22} But I tell you that anyone who is angry with a brother or sister will be subject to judgment. Again, anyone who says to a brother or sister, 'Raca' (meaning empty-headed), is answerable to the court; and anyone who says, 'You fool!' will be in danger of the fire of hell. {5:23} Therefore, if you are offering your gift at the altar and there remember that your brother or sister has something against you, {5:24} leave your gift there in front of the altar. First, go and be reconciled to them; then come and offer your gift. {5:25} Settle matters quickly with your adversary who is taking you to court. Do it while you are still together on the way, or your adversary may hand you over to the judge, and the judge may hand you over to the officer, and you may be thrown into prison. {5:26} Truly I tell you, you will not get out until you have paid the last penny. {5:27} You have heard that it was said, 'You shall not commit adultery.' {5:28} But I tell you that anyone who looks at a woman lustfully has already committed adultery with her in his heart. {5:29} If your right eye causes you to stumble, gouge it out and throw it away. It is better for you to lose one part of your body than for your whole body to be thrown into hell. {5:30} And if your right hand causes you to stumble, cut it off and throw it away. It is better for you to lose one part of your body than for your whole body to go into hell. {5:31} It has been said, 'Anyone who divorces his wife must give her a certificate of divorce.' {5:32} But I tell you that anyone who divorces his wife, except for sexual immorality, makes her the victim of adultery, and anyone who marries a divorced woman commits adultery. {5:33} Again, you have heard that it was said to the people long ago, 'Do not break your oath, but fulfill to the Lord the vows you have made.' {5:34} But I tell you, do not swear an oath at all: either by heaven, for it is God's throne; {5:35} or by the earth, for it is his footstool; or by Jerusalem, for it is the city of the great King. {5:36} And do not swear by your head, for you cannot make even one hair white or black. {5:37} All you need to say is simply 'Yes' or 'No'; anything beyond this comes from the evil one. {5:38} You have heard that it was said, 'Eye for eye, and tooth for tooth.' {5:39} But I tell you, do not resist an evil person. If anyone slaps you on the right cheek, turn to them the other cheek also. {5:40} And if anyone wants to sue you and take your shirt, hand over your coat as well. {5:41} If anyone forces you to go one mile, go with them two miles. {5:42} Give to the one who asks you, and do not turn away from the one who wants to borrow from you. {5:43} You have heard that it was said, 'Love your neighbor and hate your enemy.' {5:44} But I tell you, love your enemies and pray for those who persecute you, {5:45} that you may be children of your Father in heaven. He causes his sun to rise on the evil and the good, and sends rain on the righteous and the unrighteous. {5:46} If you love those who love you, what reward will you get? Are not even the tax collectors doing that? {5:47} And if you greet only your own people, what are you doing more than others? Do not even pagans do that? {5:48} Be perfect, therefore, as your heavenly Father is perfect.

{6:1} Be careful not to practice your righteousness in front of others to be seen by them. If you do, you will have no reward from your Father in heaven. {6:2} So when you give to the needy, do not announce it with trumpets, as the hypocrites do in the synagogues and on the streets, to be honored by others. Truly I tell you, they have received their reward in full. {6:3} But when you give to the needy, do not let your left hand know what your right hand is doing, {6:4} so that your giving may be in secret. Then your Father, who sees what is done in secret, will reward you. {6:5} And when you pray, do not be like the hypocrites, for they love to pray standing in the synagogues and on the street corners to be seen by others. Truly I tell you, they have received their reward in full. {6:6} But when you pray, go into your room, close the door and pray to your Father, who is unseen. Then your Father, who sees what is done in secret, will reward you. {6:7} And when you pray, do not keep on babbling like pagans, for they think they will be heard because of their many words. {6:8} Do not be like them, for your Father knows what you need before you ask him. {6:9} This, then, is how you should pray: Our Father in heaven, hallowed be your name, {6:10} your kingdom come, your will be done, on earth as it is in heaven. {6:11} Give us today our daily bread. {6:12} And forgive us our debts, as we also have forgiven our debtors. {6:13} And lead us not into temptation, but deliver us from the evil one. For yours is the kingdom and the power and the glory forever. Amen. {6:14} For if you forgive other people when they sin against you, your heavenly Father will also forgive you. {6:15} But if you do not forgive others their sins, your Father will not forgive your sins. {6:16} When you fast, do not look somber as the hypocrites do, for they disfigure their faces to show others they are fasting. Truly I tell you, they have received their reward in full. {6:17} But when you fast, anoint your head and wash your face, {6:18} so that it will not be obvious to others that you are fasting, but only to your Father, who is unseen; and your Father, who sees what is done in secret, will reward you. {6:19} Do not store up for yourselves treasures on earth, where moths and vermin destroy, and where thieves break in and steal. {6:20} But store up for yourselves treasures in heaven, where moths and vermin do not destroy, and where thieves do not break in and steal. {6:21} For where your treasure is, there your heart will be also. {6:22} The eye is the lamp of the body. If your eyes are healthy, your whole body will be full of light. {6:23} But if your eyes are unhealthy, your whole body will be full of darkness. If then the light within you is darkness, how great is that darkness! {6:24} No one can serve two masters. Either you will hate the one and love the other, or you will be devoted to the one and despise the other. You cannot serve both God and money. {6:25} Therefore I tell you, do not worry about your life, what you will eat or drink; or about your body, what you will wear. Is not life more than food, and the body more than clothes? {6:26} Look at the birds of the air; they do not sow or reap or store away in barns, and yet your heavenly Father feeds them. Are you not much more valuable than they? {6:27} Can any one of you by worrying add a single hour to your life? {6:28} And why do you worry about clothes? See how the flowers of the field grow. They do not labor or spin. {6:29} Yet I tell you that not even Solomon in all his splendor was dressed like one of these. {6:30} If that is how God clothes the grass of the field, which is here today and tomorrow is thrown into the fire, will he not much more clothe you—you of little faith? {6:31} So do not worry, saying, 'What shall we eat?' or 'What shall we drink?' or 'What shall we wear?' {6:32} For the pagans run after all these things, and your heavenly Father knows that you need them. {6:33} But seek first his kingdom and his righteousness, and all these things will be given to you as well. {6:34} Therefore do not worry about tomorrow, for tomorrow will worry about itself. Each day has enough trouble of its own.

{7:1} "Do not judge, or you too will be judged. {7:2} For in the same way you judge others, you will be judged, and with the measure you use, it will be measured to you. {7:3} Why do you look at the speck of sawdust in your brother's eye and pay no attention to the plank in your own eye? {7:4} How can you say to your brother, 'Let me take the speck out of your eye,' when all the time there is a plank in your own eye? {7:5} You hypocrite, first take the plank out of your own eye, and then you will see clearly to remove the speck from your brother's eye. {7:6} Do not give dogs what is sacred; do not throw your pearls to pigs. If you do, they may trample them under their feet and turn and tear you to pieces. {7:7} Ask, and it will be given to you; seek, and you will find; knock, and the door will be opened to you. {7:8} For everyone who asks receives; the one who seeks finds; and to the one who knocks, the door will be opened. {7:9} Which of you, if your son asks for bread, will give him a stone? {7:10} Or if he asks for a fish, will give him a snake? {7:11} If you, then, though you are evil, know how to give good gifts to your children, how much more will your Father in heaven give good gifts to those who ask him! {7:12} So in everything, do to others what you would have them do to you, for this sums up the Law and the Prophets. {7:13} Enter through the narrow gate. For wide is the gate and broad is the road that leads to destruction, and many enter through it. {7:14} But small is the gate and narrow the road that leads to life, and only a few find it. {7:15} Watch out for false prophets. They come to you in sheep's clothing, but inwardly they are ferocious wolves. {7:16} By their fruit you will recognize them. Do people pick grapes from thornbushes, or figs from thistles? {7:17} Likewise, every good tree bears good fruit, but a bad tree bears bad fruit. {7:18} A good tree cannot bear bad fruit, and a bad tree cannot bear good fruit. {7:19} Every tree that does not bear good fruit is cut down and thrown into the fire. {7:20} Thus, by their fruit you will recognize them. {7:21} Not everyone who says to me, 'Lord, Lord,' will enter the kingdom of heaven, but only the one who does the will of my Father who is in heaven. {7:22} Many will say to me on that day, 'Lord, Lord, did we not prophesy in your name, and in your name drive out demons and in your name perform many miracles?' {7:23} Then I will tell them plainly, 'I never knew you. Away from me, you evildoers!' {7:24} Therefore everyone who hears these words of mine and puts them into practice is like a wise man who built his house on the rock. {7:25} The rain came down, the streams rose, and the winds blew and beat against that house; yet it did not fall, because it had its foundation on the rock. {7:26} But everyone who hears these words of mine and does not put them into practice is like a foolish man who built his house on sand. {7:27} The rain came down, the streams rose, and the winds blew and beat against that house, and it fell with a great crash." {7:28} When Jesus had finished saying these things, the crowds were amazed at his teaching, {7:29} because he taught as one who had authority, and not as their teachers of the law.

{8:1} When he came down from the mountainside, large crowds followed him. {8:2} A man with leprosy came and knelt before him and said, "Lord, if you are willing, you can make me clean." {8:3} Jesus reached out his hand and touched the man. "I am willing," he said. "Be clean!" Immediately he was cleansed of his leprosy. {8:4} Then Jesus said to him, "See that you don't tell anyone. But go, show yourself to the priest and offer the gift Moses commanded as a testimony to them." {8:5} When Jesus had entered Capernaum, a centurion came to him, asking for help. {8:6} "Lord," he said, "my servant lies at home paralyzed, suffering terribly." {8:7} Jesus said to him, "Shall I come and heal him?" {8:8} The centurion replied, "Lord, I do not deserve to have you come under my roof. But just say the word, and my servant will be healed. {8:9} For I myself am a man under authority, with soldiers under me. I tell this one, 'Go,' and he goes; and that one, 'Come,' and he comes. I say to my servant, 'Do this,' and he does it." {8:10} When Jesus heard this, he was amazed and said to those following him, "Truly I tell you, I have not found anyone in Israel with such great faith. {8:11} I say to you that many will come from the east and the west, and will take their places at the feast with Abraham, Isaac, and Jacob in the kingdom of heaven. {8:12} But the subjects of the kingdom will be thrown outside, into the darkness, where there will be weeping and gnashing of teeth." {8:13} Then Jesus said to the centurion, "Go! Let it be done just as you believed it would." And his servant was healed at that moment. {8:14} When Jesus came into Peter's house, he saw Peter's mother-in-law lying in bed with a fever. {8:15} He touched her hand and the fever left her, and she got up and began to wait on him. {8:16} When evening came, many who were demon-possessed were brought to him, and he drove out the spirits with a word and healed all the sick. {8:17} This was to fulfill what was spoken through the prophet Isaiah: "He took up our infirmities and bore our diseases." {8:18} When Jesus saw the crowd around him, he gave orders to cross to the other side of the lake. {8:19} Then a teacher of the law came to him and said, "Teacher, I will follow you wherever you go." {8:20} Jesus replied, "Foxes have dens and birds have nests, but the Son of Man has no place to lay his head." {8:21} Another disciple said to him, "Lord, first let me go and bury my father." {8:22} But Jesus told him, "Follow me, and let the dead bury their own dead." {8:23} Then he got into the boat and his disciples followed him. {8:24} Suddenly a furious storm came up on the lake, so that the waves swept over the boat. But Jesus was sleeping. {8:25} The disciples went and woke him, saying, "Lord, save us! We're going to drown!" {8:26} He replied, "You of little faith, why are you so afraid?" Then he got up and rebuked the winds and the waves, and it was completely calm. {8:27} The men were amazed and asked, "What kind of man is this? Even the winds and the waves obey him!" {8:28} When he arrived at the other side in the region of the Gadarenes, two demon-possessed men coming from the tombs met him. They were so violent that no one could pass that way. {8:29} "What do you want with us, Son of God?" they shouted. "Have you come here to torture us before the appointed time?" {8:30} Some distance from them a large herd of pigs was feeding. {8:31} The demons begged Jesus, "If you drive us out, send us into the herd of pigs." {8:32} He said to them, "Go!" So they came out and went into the pigs, and the whole herd rushed down the steep bank into the lake and died in the water. {8:33} Those tending the pigs ran off, went into the town and reported all this, including what had happened to the demon-possessed men. {8:34} Then the whole town went out to meet Jesus. And when they saw him, they pleaded with him to leave their region.

{9:1} After getting into a boat, he crossed over and came to his own city. {9:2} They brought him a man who was paralyzed, lying on a bed. When Jesus saw their faith, he said to the paralyzed man, "Take heart, son; your sins are forgiven." {9:3} Some of the scribes thought to themselves, "This man is blaspheming." {9:4} Jesus knew their thoughts and asked, "Why do you think evil in your hearts? {9:5} Which is easier to say: 'Your sins are forgiven' or 'Get up and walk'? {9:6} But to show you that the Son of Man has authority on earth to forgive sins," he said to the paralyzed man, "Get up, take your bed, and go home." {9:7} The man got up and went home. {9:8} When the crowd saw it, they were amazed and praised God for giving such authority to men. {9:9} As Jesus went on from there, he saw a man named Matthew sitting at the tax collector's booth. He said to him, "Follow me." And Matthew got up and followed him. {9:10} While Jesus was at the table in Matthew's house, many tax collectors and sinners came and ate with him and his disciples. {9:11} When the Pharisees saw this, they asked his disciples, "Why does your teacher eat with tax collectors and sinners?" {9:12} On hearing this, Jesus said, "It is not the healthy who need a doctor, but the sick. {9:13} Go and learn what this means: 'I desire mercy, not sacrifice,' for I have not come to call the righteous, but sinners." {9:14} Then John's disciples came to him and asked, "How is it that we and the Pharisees fast often, but your disciples do not fast?" {9:15} Jesus answered, "How can the guests of the bridegroom mourn while he is with them? The time will come when the bridegroom will be taken from them; then they will fast." {9:16} No one sews a patch of unshrunk cloth on an old garment, for the patch will pull away from the garment, making the tear worse. {9:17} Neither do people pour new wine into old wineskins. If they do, the skins will burst; the wine will run out and the wineskins will be ruined. No, they pour new wine into new wineskins, and both are preserved. {9:18} While he was saying this, a ruler came and knelt before him, saying, "My daughter has just died. But come and put your hand on her, and she will live." {9:19} Jesus got up and followed him, and so did his disciples. {9:20} Just then, a woman who had been subject to bleeding for twelve years came up behind him and touched the edge of his cloak. {9:21} She said to herself, "If I only touch his cloak, I will be healed." {9:22} Jesus turned and saw her. "Take heart, daughter," he said, "your faith has healed you." And the woman was healed at that moment. {9:23} When Jesus entered the ruler's house and saw the flute players and the noisy crowd, {9:24} he said, "Go away. The girl is not dead but asleep." But they laughed at him. {9:25} After the crowd had been put outside, he went in and took the girl by the hand, and she got up. {9:26} News of this spread throughout that region. {9:27} As Jesus went on from there, two blind men followed him, calling out, "Have mercy on us, Son of David!" {9:28} When he had gone indoors, the blind men came to him, and he asked them, "Do you believe that I am able to do this?" "Yes, Lord," they replied. {9:29} Then he touched their eyes and said, "According to your faith let it be done to you"; {9:30} and their sight was restored. Jesus warned them sternly, "See that no one knows about this." {9:31} But they went out and spread the news about him all over that region. {9:32} While they were going out, a man who was demon-possessed and could not talk was brought to Jesus. {9:33} And when the demon was driven out, the man who had been mute spoke. The crowd was amazed and said, "Nothing like this has ever been seen in Israel." {9:34} But the Pharisees said, "It is by the prince of demons that he drives out demons." {9:35} Jesus went through all the towns and villages, teaching in their synagogues, proclaiming the good news of the kingdom, and healing every disease and sickness. {9:36} When he saw the crowds, he had compassion on them, because they were harassed and helpless, like sheep without a shepherd. {9:37} Then he said to his disciples, "The harvest is plentiful but the workers are few. {9:38} Ask the Lord of the harvest, therefore, to send out workers into his harvest field."

{10:1} Jesus called his twelve disciples to him and gave them authority to drive out impure spirits and to heal every disease and sickness. {10:2} These are the names of the twelve apostles: first, Simon (who is called Peter) and his brother Andrew; James son of Zebedee, and his brother John; {10:3} Philip and Bartholomew; Thomas and Matthew the tax collector; James son of Alphaeus, and Thaddaeus; {10:4} Simon the Zealot and Judas Iscariot, who betrayed him. {10:5} These twelve Jesus sent out, instructing them: "Do not go among the Gentiles or enter a Samaritan town. {10:6} Go rather to the lost sheep of Israel. {10:7} As you go, proclaim this message: 'The kingdom of heaven has come near.' {10:8} Heal the sick, raise the dead, cleanse those who have leprosy, drive out demons. Freely you have received; freely give. {10:9} Do not get any gold or silver or copper to take with you in your belts— {10:10} no bag for the journey, or extra shirt, or sandals, or a staff, for the worker is worth his keep. {10:11} Whatever town or village you enter, search there for some worthy person and stay at that house until you leave. {10:12} As you enter the home, give it your greeting. {10:13} If the home is deserving, let your peace rest on it; if it is not, let your peace return to you. {10:14} If anyone will not welcome you or listen to your words, leave that home or town and shake the dust off your feet. {10:15} Truly I tell you, it will be more bearable for Sodom and Gomorrah on the day of judgment than for that town. {10:16} I am sending you out like sheep among wolves. Therefore be as shrewd as snakes and as innocent as doves. {10:17} Be on your guard; you will be handed over to the local councils and be flogged in the synagogues. {10:18} On my account you will be brought before governors and kings as witnesses to them and to the Gentiles. {10:19} But when they arrest you, do not worry about what to say or how to say it. At that time you will be given what to say, {10:20} for it will not be you speaking, but the Spirit of your Father speaking through you. {10:21} Brother will betray brother to death, and a father his child; children will rebel against their parents and have them put to death. {10:22} You will be hated by everyone because of me, but the one who stands firm to the end will be saved. {10:23} When you are persecuted in one place, flee to another. Truly I tell you, you will not finish going through the towns of Israel before the Son of Man comes. {10:24} The student is not above the teacher, nor a servant above his master. {10:25} It is enough for students to be like their teachers, and servants like their masters. If the head of the household has been called Beelzebul, how much more the members of his household! {10:26} So do not be afraid of them, for there is nothing concealed that will not be disclosed, or hidden that will not be made known. {10:27} What I tell you in the dark, speak in the daylight; what is whispered in your ear, proclaim from the roofs. {10:28} Do not be afraid of those who kill the body but cannot kill the soul. Rather, be afraid of the One who can destroy both soul and body in hell. {10:29} Are not two sparrows sold for a penny? Yet not one of them will fall to the ground outside your Father's care. {10:30} And even the very hairs of your head are all numbered. {10:31} So don't be afraid; you are worth more than many sparrows. {10:32} Whoever acknowledges me before others, I will also acknowledge before my Father in heaven. {10:33} But whoever disowns me before others, I will disown before my Father in heaven. {10:34} Do not suppose that I have come to bring peace to the earth. I did not come to bring peace, but a sword. {10:35} For I have come to turn 'a man against his father, a daughter against her mother, a daughter-in-law against her mother-in-law— {10:36} a man's enemies will be the members of his own household.' {10:37} Anyone who loves their father or mother more than me is not worthy of me; anyone who loves their son or daughter more than me is not worthy of me. {10:38} Whoever does not take up their cross and follow me is not worthy of me. {10:39} Whoever finds their life will lose it, and whoever loses their life for my sake will find it. {10:40} Anyone who welcomes you welcomes me, and anyone who welcomes me welcomes the one who sent me. {10:41} Whoever welcomes a prophet as a prophet will receive a prophet's reward, and whoever welcomes a righteous person as a righteous person will receive a righteous person's reward. {10:42} And if anyone gives even a cup of cold water to one of these little ones because they are my disciple, truly I tell you, that person will certainly not lose their reward.

{11:1} After Jesus finished instructing his twelve disciples, he went on from there to teach and preach in their towns. {11:2} When John heard in prison about the deeds of Christ, he sent two of his disciples {11:3} to ask him, "Are you the one who is to come, or should we expect someone else?" {11:4} Jesus replied, "Go back and report to John what you hear and see: {11:5} The blind receive sight, the lame walk, those with leprosy are cleansed, the deaf hear, the dead are raised, and the good news is proclaimed to the poor. {11:6} Blessed is anyone who does not stumble on account of me." {11:7} As they were leaving, Jesus began to speak to the crowd about John: "What did you go out into the wilderness to see? A reed swayed by the wind? {11:8} What did you go out to see? A man dressed in fine clothes? No, those who wear fine clothes are in king's palaces. {11:9} So what did you go out to see? A prophet? Yes, I tell you, and more than a prophet. {11:10} This is the one about whom it is written: 'I will send my messenger ahead of you, who will prepare your way before you.' {11:11} Truly I tell you, among those born of women there has not risen anyone greater than

John the Baptist; yet whoever is least in the kingdom of heaven is greater than he. {11:12} From the days of John the Baptist until now, the kingdom of heaven has been subjected to violence, and violent people have been raiding it. {11:13} For all the Prophets and the Law prophesied until John. {11:14} And if you are willing to accept it, he is the Elijah who was to come. {11:15} Whoever has ears, let them hear. {11:16} To what can I compare this generation? They are like children sitting in the marketplaces and calling out to others, {11:17} 'We played the flute for you, and you did not dance; we sang a dirge, and you did not mourn.' {11:18} For John came neither eating nor drinking, and they say, 'He has a demon.' {11:19} The Son of Man came eating and drinking, and they say, 'Here is a glutton and a drunkard, a friend of tax collectors and sinners.' But wisdom is proved right by her deeds." {11:20} Then Jesus began to denounce the towns in which most of his miracles had been performed, because they did not repent. {11:21} "Woe to you, Chorazin! Woe to you, Bethsaida! For if the miracles that were performed in you had been performed in Tyre and Sidon, they would have repented long ago in sackcloth and ashes. {11:22} But I tell you, it will be more bearable for Tyre and Sidon on the day of judgment than for you. {11:23} And you, Capernaum, will you be lifted to the heavens? No, you will go down to Hades. For if the miracles that were performed in you had been performed in Sodom, it would have remained to this day. {11:24} But I tell you that it will be more bearable for Sodom on the day of judgment than for you." {11:25} At that time Jesus said, "I praise you, Father, Lord of heaven and earth, because you have hidden these things from the wise and learned, and revealed them to little children. {11:26} Yes, Father, for this is what you were pleased to do. {11:27} All things have been committed to me by my Father. No one knows the Son except the Father, and no one knows the Father except the Son and those to whom the Son chooses to reveal him. {11:28} Come to me, all you who are weary and burdened, and I will give you rest. {11:29} Take my yoke upon you and learn from me, for I am gentle and humble in heart, and you will find rest for your souls. {11:30} For my yoke is easy and my burden is light."

{12:1} At that time Jesus went through the grain fields on the Sabbath, and his disciples were hungry and began to pick some heads of grain and eat them. {12:2} When the Pharisees saw this, they said to him, "Look! Your disciples are doing what is unlawful on the Sabbath." {12:3} He answered, "Haven't you read what David did when he and his companions were hungry? {12:4} He entered the house of God and he and his companions ate the consecrated bread, which was not lawful for them to do, but only for the priests. {12:5} Or haven't you read in the Law that the priests on Sabbath duty in the temple desecrate the Sabbath and yet are innocent? {12:6} I tell you that something greater than the temple is here. {12:7} If you had known what these words mean, 'I desire mercy, not sacrifice,' you would not have condemned the innocent. {12:8} For the Son of Man is Lord of the Sabbath." {12:9} Going on from that place, he went into their synagogue, {12:10} and a man with a shriveled hand was there. Looking for a reason to accuse Jesus, they asked him, "Is it lawful to heal on the Sabbath?" {12:11} He said to them, "If any of you has a sheep and it falls into a pit on the Sabbath, will you not take hold of it and lift it out? {12:12} How much more valuable is a person than a sheep! Therefore it is lawful to do good on the Sabbath." {12:13} Then he said to the man, "Stretch out your hand." So he stretched it out, and it was completely restored, just as sound as the other. {12:14} But the Pharisees went out and plotted how they might kill Jesus. {12:15} Aware of this, Jesus withdrew from that place. Many followed him, and he healed all their sick, {12:16} warning them not to tell others about him. {12:17} This was to fulfill what was spoken through the prophet Isaiah: {12:18} "Here is my servant whom I have chosen, the one I love, in whom I delight; I will put my Spirit on him, and he will proclaim justice to the nations. {12:19} He will not quarrel or cry out; no one will hear his voice in the streets. {12:20} A bruised reed he will not break, and a smoldering wick he will not snuff out, till he has brought justice through to victory. {12:21} In his name the nations will put their hope." {12:22} Then they brought him a demon-possessed man who was blind and mute, and Jesus healed him, so that he could both talk and see. {12:23} All the people were astonished and said, "Could this be the Son of David?" {12:24} But when the Pharisees heard this, they said, "It is only by Beelzebul, the prince of demons, that this fellow drives out demons." {12:25} Jesus knew their thoughts and said to them, "Every kingdom divided against itself will be ruined, and every city or household divided against itself will not stand. {12:26} If Satan drives out Satan, he is divided against himself. How then can his kingdom stand? {12:27} And if I drive out demons by Beelzebul, by whom do your people drive them out? So then, they will be your judges. {12:28} But if it is by the Spirit of God that I drive out demons, then the kingdom of God has come upon you. {12:29} Or again, how can anyone enter a strong man's house and carry off his possessions unless he first ties up the strong man? Then he can plunder his house. {12:30} Whoever is not with me is against me, and whoever does not gather with me scatters. {12:31} And so I tell you, every kind of sin and slander can be forgiven, but blasphemy against the Spirit will not be forgiven. {12:32} Anyone who speaks a word against the Son of Man will be forgiven, but anyone who speaks against the Holy Spirit will not be forgiven, either in this age or in the age to come. {12:33} Make a tree good and its fruit will be good, or make a tree bad and its fruit will be bad, for a tree is recognized by its fruit. {12:34} You brood of vipers, how can you who are evil say anything good? For the mouth speaks what the heart is full of. {12:35} A good man brings good things out of the good stored up in him, and an evil man brings evil things out of the evil stored up in him. {12:36} But I tell you that everyone will have to give account on the day of judgment for every empty word they have spoken. {12:37} For by your words you will be acquitted, and by your words you will be condemned." {12:38} Then some of the Pharisees and teachers of the law said to him, "Teacher, we want to see a sign from you." {12:39} He answered, "A wicked and adulterous generation asks for a sign! But none will be given it except the sign of the prophet Jonah. {12:40} For as Jonah was three days and three nights in the belly of a huge fish, so the Son of Man will be three days and three nights in the heart of the earth. {12:41} The men of Nineveh will stand up at the judgment with this generation and condemn it; for they repented at the preaching of Jonah, and now something greater than Jonah is here. {12:42} The Queen of the South will rise at the judgment with this generation and condemn it; for she came from the ends of the earth to listen to Solomon's wisdom, and now something greater than Solomon is here. {12:43} When an impure spirit comes out of a person, it goes through arid places seeking rest and does not find it. {12:44} Then it says, 'I will return to the house I left.' When it arrives, it finds the house unoccupied, swept clean and put in order. {12:45} Then it goes and takes with it seven other spirits more wicked than itself, and they go in and live there. And the final condition of that person is worse than the first. That is how it will be with this wicked generation." {12:46} While Jesus was still talking to the crowd, his mother and brothers stood outside, wanting to speak to him. {12:47} Someone told him, "Your mother and brothers are standing outside, wanting to speak to you." {12:48} He replied to him, "Who is my mother, and who are my brothers?" {12:49} Pointing to his disciples, he said, "Here are my mother and my brothers. {12:50} For whoever does the will of my Father in heaven is my family."

{13:1} That same day, Jesus left the house and sat by the seaside. {13:2} Large crowds gathered around him, so he got into a boat and sat down, while the whole crowd stood on the shore. {13:3} He spoke many things to them in parables, saying, "A farmer went out to sow his seeds. {13:4} As he sowed, some seeds fell along the path, and the birds came and ate them up. {13:5} Some fell on rocky ground, where there wasn't much soil. They sprang up quickly because the soil was shallow. {13:6} But when the sun rose, they were scorched, and because they had no roots, they withered away. {13:7} Other seeds fell among thorns, which grew up and choked the plants. {13:8} But some seeds fell on good soil and produced a crop—some a hundred times what was sown, some sixty, and some thirty. {13:9} Whoever has ears, let them hear." {13:10} The disciples came to him and asked, "Why do you speak to the people in parables?" {13:11} He replied, "Because the knowledge of the secrets of the kingdom of heaven has been given to you, but not to them. {13:12} Whoever has will be given more, and they will have an abundance. Whoever does not have, even what they have will be taken from them. {13:13} This is why I speak to them in parables: Though seeing, they do not see; though hearing, they do not hear or understand. {13:14} In them is fulfilled the prophecy of Isaiah: 'You will be ever hearing but never understanding; you will be ever seeing but never perceiving.' {13:15} For this people's heart has become calloused; they hardly hear with their ears, and they have closed their eyes. Otherwise, they might see with their eyes, hear with their ears, understand with their hearts, and turn, and I would heal them. {13:16} But blessed are your eyes because they see, and your ears because they hear. {13:17} For truly I tell you, many prophets and righteous people longed to see what you see but did not see it, and to hear what you hear but did not hear it. {13:18} Listen then to the parable of the sower. {13:19} When anyone hears the message about the kingdom and does not understand it, the evil one comes and snatches away what was sown in their heart. This is the seed sown along the path. {13:20} The seed falling on rocky ground refers to someone who hears the word and at once receives it with joy. {13:21} But since they have no root, they last only a short time. When trouble or persecution comes because of the word, they quickly fall away. {13:22} The seed falling among the thorns refers to someone who hears the word, but the worries of this life and the deceitfulness of wealth choke the word, making it unfruitful. {13:23} But the seed falling on good soil refers to someone who hears the word and understands it. This is the one who produces a crop, yielding a hundred, sixty, or thirty times what was sown." {13:24} Jesus told them another parable: "The kingdom of heaven is like a man who sowed good seeds in his field. {13:25} But while everyone was sleeping, his enemy came and sowed weeds among the wheat, and went away. {13:26} When the wheat sprouted and formed heads, then the weeds also appeared. {13:27} The owner's servants came to him and said, 'Sir, didn't you sow good seed in your field? Where then did the weeds come from?' {13:28} 'An enemy did this,' he replied. The servants asked him, 'Do you want us to go and pull them up?' {13:29} 'No,' he answered, 'because while you are pulling the weeds, you may root up the wheat with them. {13:30} Let both grow together until the harvest. At that time, I will tell the harvesters: First collect the weeds and tie them in bundles to be burned; then gather the wheat and bring it into my barn.'" {13:31} He told them another parable: "The kingdom of heaven is like a mustard seed, which a man took and planted in his field. {13:32} Though it is the smallest of all seeds, yet when it grows, it is the largest of garden plants and becomes a tree, so that the birds come and perch in its branches." {13:33} He told them still another parable: "The kingdom of heaven is like yeast that a woman took and mixed into about sixty pounds of flour until it worked all through the dough." {13:34} Jesus spoke all these things to the crowd in parables; he did not say anything to them without using a parable. {13:35} So was fulfilled what was spoken through the prophet: "I will open my mouth in parables, I will utter things hidden since the creation of the world." {13:36} Then he left the crowd and went into the house. His disciples came to him and said, "Explain to us the parable of the weeds in the field." {13:37} He answered, "The one who sowed the good seed is the Son of Man. {13:38} The field is the world, and the good seed stands for the people of the kingdom. The weeds are the people of the evil one, {13:39} and the enemy who sows them is the devil. The harvest is the end of the age, and the harvesters are angels. {13:40} As the weeds are pulled up and burned in the fire, so it will be at the end of the age. {13:41} The Son of Man will send out his angels, and they will weed out of his kingdom everything that causes sin and all who do evil. {13:42} They will throw them into the blazing furnace, where there will be weeping and gnashing of teeth. {13:43} Then the righteous will shine like the sun in the kingdom of their Father. Whoever has ears, let them hear." {13:44} "The kingdom of heaven is like treasure hidden in a field. When a man found it, he hid it again, and then in his joy went and sold all he had and bought that field." {13:45} "Again, the kingdom of heaven is like a merchant looking for fine pearls. {13:46} When he found one of great value, he went away and sold everything he had and bought it." {13:47} "Once again, the kingdom of heaven is like a net that was let down into the lake and caught all kinds of fish. {13:48} When it was full, the fishermen pulled it ashore. Then they sat down and collected the good fish in baskets, but threw the bad away. {13:49} This is how it will be at the end of the age. The angels will come and separate the wicked from the righteous {13:50} and throw them into the blazing furnace, where there will be weeping and gnashing of teeth." {13:51} "Have you understood all these things?" Jesus asked. "Yes," they replied. {13:52} He said to them, "Therefore every teacher of the law who has become a disciple in the kingdom of heaven is like the owner of a house who brings out of his storeroom new treasures as well as old." {13:53} When Jesus had finished these parables, he moved on from there. {13:54} Coming to his hometown, he began teaching the people in their synagogue, and they were amazed. "Where did this man get this wisdom and these miraculous powers?" they asked. {13:55} "Isn't this the carpenter's son? Isn't his mother's name Mary? And aren't his brothers James, Joseph, Simon, and Judas? {13:56} Aren't all his sisters with us? Where then did this man get all these things?" {13:57} And they took offense at him. But Jesus said to them, "A prophet is not without honor except in his own town and in his own home." {13:58} And he did not do many miracles there because of their lack of faith.

{14:1} At that time, Herod the tetrarch heard the reports about Jesus, {14:2} and he said to his attendants, "This is John the Baptist; he has risen from the dead! That is why miraculous powers are at work in him." {14:3} (For Herod had arrested John and bound him and put him in prison because of Herodias, his brother Philip's wife. {14:4} For John had been saying to him, "It is not lawful for you to have her.") {14:5} Herod wanted to kill John, but he was afraid of the people, because they considered John a prophet. {14:6} On Herod's birthday, the daughter of Herodias danced for the guests and pleased Herod. {14:7} So he promised with an oath to give her whatever she asked. {14:8} Prompted by her mother, she said, "Give me here on a platter the head of John the Baptist." {14:9} The king was distressed, but because of his oaths and his dinner guests, he ordered that her request be granted {14:10} and had John beheaded in the prison. {14:11} His head was brought in on a platter and given to the girl, who carried it to her mother. {14:12} John's disciples came and took his body and buried it. Then they went and told Jesus. {14:13} When Jesus heard what had happened, he withdrew by boat privately to a solitary place. Hearing of this, the crowds followed him on foot from the towns. {14:14} When Jesus landed and saw a large crowd, he had compassion on them and healed their sick. {14:15} As evening approached, the disciples came to him and said, "This is a remote place, and it's already getting late. Send the crowds away so they can go to the villages and buy themselves some food." {14:16} Jesus replied, "They do not need to go away. You give them something to eat." {14:17} "We have here only five loaves of bread and two fish," they answered. {14:18} "Bring them here to me," he said. {14:19} And he directed the people to sit down on the grass. Taking the five loaves and the two fish and looking up to heaven, he gave thanks and broke the loaves. Then he gave them to the disciples, and the disciples gave them to the people. {14:20} They all ate and were satisfied, and the disciples picked up twelve basketfuls of broken pieces that were left over. {14:21} The number of those who ate was about five thousand men, besides women and children. {14:22} Immediately, Jesus made the disciples get into the boat and go on ahead of him to the other side, while he dismissed the crowd. {14:23} After he had dismissed them, he went up on a mountainside by himself to pray. Later that night, he was there alone, {14:24} and the boat was already a considerable distance from land, buffeted by the waves because the wind was against it. {14:25} Shortly before dawn, Jesus went out to them, walking on the lake. {14:26} When the disciples saw him walking on the lake, they were terrified. "It's a ghost!" they said, and cried out in fear. {14:27} But Jesus immediately said to them: "Take courage! It is I. Don't be afraid." {14:28} "Lord, if it's you," Peter replied, "tell me to come to you on the water." {14:29} "Come," he said. Then Peter got down out of the boat, walked on the water, and came toward Jesus. {14:30} But when he saw the wind, he was afraid and, beginning to sink, cried out, "Lord, save me!" {14:31} Immediately, Jesus reached out his hand and caught him. "You of little faith," he said, "why did you doubt?" {14:32} And when they climbed into the boat, the wind died down. {14:33} Then those who were in the boat worshiped him, saying, "Truly you are the Son of God." {14:34} When they had crossed over, they landed at Gennesaret. {14:35} And when the men of that place recognized Jesus, they sent word to all the surrounding country. People brought all their sick to him {14:36} and begged him to let the sick just touch the edge of his cloak, and all who touched it were healed.

{15:1} Then the scribes and Pharisees from Jerusalem came to Jesus and said, {15:2} "Why do your disciples break the tradition of the elders? They don't wash their hands before they eat!" {15:3} He replied, "And why do you break God's command for the sake of your tradition? {15:4} For God commanded, 'Honor your father and mother,' and 'Anyone who curses their father or mother is to be put to death.' {15:5} But you say that if anyone declares what they might have given to their parents as a gift, {15:6} then they are not required to honor their father or mother. In this way, you have nullified (made ineffective) the word of God for the sake of your tradition. {15:7} You hypocrites! Isaiah was right when he prophesied about you, saying, {15:8} 'These people honor me with their lips, but their hearts are far from me. {15:9} They worship me in vain; they teach as doctrines the commandments of men.' {15:10} Jesus called the crowd and said, "Listen and understand: {15:11} It's not what goes into the mouth that defiles (makes unclean) a person, but what comes out of the mouth that defiles them." {15:12} Then the disciples came to him and said, "Do you know that the Pharisees were offended when they heard this?" {15:13} He replied, "Every plant my heavenly Father has not planted will be pulled up by the roots. {15:14} Leave them alone; they are blind guides. If the blind lead the blind, both will fall into a pit." {15:15} Peter responded, "Explain this parable to us." {15:16} Jesus said, "Are you still so dull (slow to understand)? {15:17} Don't you see that whatever enters the mouth goes into the stomach and then out of the body? {15:18} But the things that come out of a person's mouth come from the heart, and these defile them. {15:19} For out of the heart come evil thoughts, murder, adultery, sexual immorality, theft, false testimony, slander (making false statements): {15:20} these are what defile a person; but eating with unwashed hands does not defile them." {15:21} Jesus then left and went to the region of Tyre and Sidon. {15:22} A Canaanite woman from that vicinity came to him, crying out, "Lord, Son of David, have mercy on me! My daughter is suffering terribly from demon possession." {15:23} Jesus did not answer a word. So his disciples came to him and urged him, "Send her away, for she keeps crying out after us." {15:24} He answered, "I was sent only to the lost sheep of Israel." {15:25} The woman came and knelt before him. "Lord, help me!" she said. {15:26} He replied, "It is not right to take the children's bread and toss it to the dogs." {15:27} "Yes, it is, Lord," she said, "even the dogs eat the crumbs that fall from their masters' table." {15:28} Then Jesus said, "Woman, you have great faith! Your request is granted." And her daughter was healed at that moment. {15:29} Jesus left there and went along the Sea of Galilee. He went up on a mountainside and sat down. {15:30} Great crowds came to him, bringing the lame, blind, crippled, mute, and many others, and laid them at his feet; and he healed them. {15:31} The people were amazed when they saw the mute speaking, the crippled made well, the lame walking, and the blind seeing; and they praised the God of Israel. {15:32} Jesus called his disciples to him and said, "I have compassion for these people; they have already been with me three days and have nothing to eat. I do not want to send them away hungry, or they may collapse on the way." {15:33} His disciples answered, "Where could we get enough bread in this remote place to feed such a crowd?" {15:34} "How many loaves do you have?" Jesus asked. "Seven," they replied, "and a few small fish." {15:35} He told the crowd to sit down on the ground. {15:36} Then he took the seven loaves and the fish, and gave thanks, broke them, and gave them to the disciples, and they in turn to the people. {15:37} They all ate and were satisfied, and the disciples picked up seven baskets of leftover pieces. {15:38} The number of those who ate was four thousand men, besides women and children. {15:39} After Jesus had sent the crowd away, he got into the boat and went to the vicinity of Magdala.

{16:1} The Pharisees and Sadducees came to Jesus and tested him by asking him to show them a sign from heaven. {16:2} He replied, "When evening comes, you say, 'It will be fair weather, for the sky is red,' {16:3} and in the morning, 'Today it will be stormy, for the sky is red and overcast (cloudy).' You know how to interpret the appearance of the sky, but you cannot interpret the signs of the times. {16:4} A wicked and adulterous generation asks for a sign, but none will be given it except the sign of the prophet Jonah." Jesus then left them and went away. {16:5} When they went across the lake, the disciples forgot to take bread. {16:6} "Be careful," Jesus said to them. "Watch out for the yeast of the Pharisees and Sadducees." {16:7} They discussed this among themselves and said, "It is because we didn't bring any bread." {16:8} Aware of their discussion, Jesus asked, "You of little faith, why are you talking among yourselves about having no bread? {16:9} Do you still not understand? Don't you remember the five loaves for the five thousand and how many basketfuls you gathered? {16:10} Or the seven loaves for the four thousand and how many basketfuls you gathered? {16:11} How is it you don't understand that I was not talking to you about bread? But be on your guard against the yeast of the Pharisees and Sadducees." {16:12} Then they understood that he was not telling them to guard against the yeast used in bread, but against the teaching of the Pharisees and Sadducees. {16:13} When Jesus came to the region of Caesarea Philippi, he asked his disciples, "Who do people say the Son of Man is?" {16:14} They replied, "Some say John the Baptist; others say Elijah; and still others, Jeremiah or one of the prophets." {16:15} "But what about you?" he asked. "Who do you say I am?" {16:16} Simon Peter replied, "You are the Messiah, the Son of the living God." {16:17} Jesus replied, "Blessed are you, Simon son of Jonah, for this was not revealed to you by flesh and blood, but by my Father in heaven. {16:18} And I tell you that you are Peter, and on this rock I will build my church, and the gates of hell will not overcome it. {16:19} I will give you the keys of the kingdom of heaven; whatever you bind on earth will be bound in heaven, and whatever you loose on earth will be loosed in heaven." {16:20} Then he ordered his disciples not to tell anyone that he was the Messiah. {16:21} From that time on, Jesus began to explain to his disciples that he must go to Jerusalem and suffer many things at the hands of the elders, the chief priests, and the teachers of the law, and that he must be killed and on the third day be raised to life. {16:22} Peter took him aside and began to rebuke him. "Never, Lord!" he said. "This shall never happen to you!" {16:23} Jesus turned and said to Peter, "Get behind me, Satan! You are a stumbling block to me; you do not have in mind the concerns of God, but merely human concerns." {16:24} Then Jesus said to his disciples, "Whoever wants to be my disciple must deny themselves and take up their cross and follow me. {16:25} For whoever wants to save their life will lose it, but whoever loses their life for me will find it. {16:26} What good will it be for someone to gain the whole world, yet forfeit their soul? Or what can anyone give in exchange for their soul? {16:27} For the Son of Man is going to come in his Father's glory with his angels, and then he will reward each person according to what they have done. {16:28} Truly I tell you, some who are standing here will not taste death before they see the Son of Man coming in his kingdom.

{17:1} Six days later, Jesus took Peter, James, and his brother John and led them up a high mountain by themselves. {17:2} There, he was transformed before them; his face shone like the sun, and his clothes became as white as light. {17:3} Suddenly, Moses and Elijah appeared and were talking with him. {17:4} Peter said to Jesus, "Lord, it's good for us to be here. If you want, I can set up three shelters: one for you, one for Moses, and one for Elijah." {17:5} While he was still speaking, a bright cloud overshadowed them, and a voice from the cloud said, "This is my beloved Son, whom I love; listen to him." {17:6} When the disciples heard this, they fell facedown and were terrified. {17:7} But Jesus came and touched them, saying, "Get up; don't be afraid." {17:8} When they looked up, they saw no one except Jesus. {17:9} As they were coming down the mountain, Jesus instructed them, "Don't tell anyone about this vision until the Son of Man has been raised from the dead." {17:10} The disciples asked him, "Why then do the scribes say that Elijah must come first?" {17:11} Jesus replied, "Elijah does come, and he will restore all things. {17:12} But I tell you, Elijah has already come, and they didn't recognize him but did to him whatever they wanted. In the same way, the Son of Man is going to suffer at their hands." {17:13} Then the disciples understood that he was talking about John the Baptist. {17:14} When they returned to the crowd, a man approached Jesus and knelt before him. {17:15} "Lord, have mercy on my son," he said. "He is suffering terribly. He often falls into the fire or into the water. {17:16} I brought him to your disciples, but they could not heal him." {17:17} Jesus replied, "You unbelieving and perverse generation, how long shall I stay with you? How long shall I put up with you? Bring the boy here to me." {17:18} Jesus rebuked the demon, and it came out of the boy, and he was healed at that moment. {17:19} Then the disciples came to Jesus privately and asked, "Why couldn't we drive it out?" {17:20} He replied, "Because you have so little faith. Truly I tell you, if you have faith as small as a mustard seed, you can say to this mountain, 'Move from here to there,' and it will move. Nothing will be impossible for you." {17:21} However, this kind does not go out except by prayer and fasting. {17:22} While they were in

Galilee, Jesus said to them, "The Son of Man is going to be delivered into the hands of men. {17:23} They will kill him, and on the third day, he will be raised to life." And the disciples were filled with grief. {17:24} After they arrived in Capernaum, the collectors of the temple tax came to Peter and asked, "Doesn't your teacher pay the temple tax?" {17:25} "Yes, he does," he replied. When Peter came into the house, Jesus was the first to speak. "What do you think, Simon?" he asked. "From whom do the kings of the earth collect duty and taxes—from their own children or from others?" {17:26} "From others," Peter answered. "Then the children are exempt," Jesus said. {17:27} "But so that we may not cause offense, go to the lake and throw out your line. Take the first fish you catch; open its mouth and you will find a four-drachma coin. Take it and give it to them for my tax and yours."

{18:1} At that time, the disciples came to Jesus and asked, "Who then is the greatest in the kingdom of heaven?" {18:2} He called a little child to him and placed the child among them. {18:3} "Truly I tell you," he said, "unless you change and become like little children, you will never enter the kingdom of heaven. {18:4} Therefore, whoever takes the lowly position of this child is the greatest in the kingdom of heaven. {18:5} And whoever welcomes one such child in my name welcomes me. {18:6} If anyone causes one of these little ones—those who believe in me—to stumble, it would be better for them to have a large millstone (a heavy stone used for grinding) hung around their neck and to be drowned in the depths of the sea. {18:7} Woe to the world because of the things that cause people to stumble! Such things must come, but woe to the person who brings them about! {18:8} If your hand or your foot causes you to stumble, cut it off and throw it away. It is better for you to enter life maimed or crippled than to have two hands or two feet and be thrown into eternal fire. {18:9} And if your eye causes you to stumble, gouge it out and throw it away. It is better for you to enter life with one eye than to have two eyes and be thrown into the fire of hell. {18:10} See that you do not despise one of these little ones. For I tell you that their angels in heaven always see the face of my Father in heaven. {18:11} For the Son of Man came to save the lost. {18:12} What do you think? If a man owns a hundred sheep and one of them wanders away, will he not leave the ninety-nine on the hills and go to look for the one that wandered off? {18:13} And if he finds it, truly I tell you, he is happier about that one sheep than about the ninety-nine that did not wander off. {18:14} In the same way, your Father in heaven is not willing that any of these little ones should perish. {18:15} If your brother or sister sins, go and point out their fault, just between the two of you. If they listen to you, you have won them over. {18:16} But if they will not listen, take one or two others along, so that "every matter may be established by the testimony of two or three witnesses." {18:17} If they still refuse to listen, tell it to the church; and if they refuse to listen even to the church, treat them as you would a pagan or a tax collector. {18:18} Truly I tell you, whatever you bind on earth will be bound in heaven, and whatever you loose on earth will be loosed in heaven. {18:19} Again, truly I tell you that if two of you on earth agree about anything they ask for, it will be done for them by my Father in heaven. {18:20} For where two or three gather in my name, there am I with them. {18:21} Then Peter came to Jesus and asked, "Lord, how many times shall I forgive my brother or sister who sins against me? Up to seven times?" {18:22} Jesus answered, "I tell you, not seven times, but seventy-seven times. {18:23} Therefore, the kingdom of heaven is like a king who wanted to settle accounts with his servants. {18:24} As he began the settlement, a man who owed him ten thousand bags of gold was brought to him. {18:25} Since he was not able to pay, the master ordered that he and his wife and children and all that he had be sold to repay the debt. {18:26} At this, the servant fell on his knees before him. "Be patient with me," he begged, "and I will pay back everything." {18:27} The servant's master took pity on him, canceled the debt and let him go. {18:28} But when that servant went out, he found one of his fellow servants who owed him a hundred silver coins. He grabbed him and began to choke him. "Pay back what you owe me!" he demanded. {18:29} His fellow servant fell to his knees and begged him, "Be patient with me, and I will pay it back." {18:30} But he refused. Instead, he went off and had the man thrown into prison until he could pay the debt. {18:31} When the other servants saw what had happened, they were outraged and went and told their master everything that had happened. {18:32} Then the master called the servant in. "You wicked servant," he said, "I canceled all that debt of yours because you begged me to. {18:33} Shouldn't you have had mercy on your fellow servant just as I had on you?" {18:34} In anger, his master handed him over to the jailers to be tortured until he should pay back all he owed. {18:35} This is how my heavenly Father will treat each of you unless you forgive your brother or sister from your heart.

{19:1} After Jesus finished these sayings, he left Galilee and went to the regions of Judea beyond the Jordan. {19:2} Large crowds followed him, and he healed them there. {19:3} The Pharisees approached him, trying to test him, and asked, "Is it lawful for a man to divorce his wife for any reason?" {19:4} He answered, "Haven't you read that at the beginning the Creator made them male and female? {19:5} And he said, 'For this reason, a man will leave his father and mother and be united to his wife, and the two will become one flesh.' {19:6} So they are no longer two, but one flesh. Therefore, what God has joined together, let no one separate." {19:7} They asked him, "Why then did Moses command that a man give his wife a certificate of divorce and send her away?" {19:8} Jesus replied, "Moses permitted you to divorce your wives because your hearts were hard, but it wasn't this way from the beginning. {19:9} I tell you that anyone who divorces his wife, except for sexual immorality, and marries another woman commits adultery; and anyone who marries a divorced woman commits adultery." {19:10} The disciples said to him, "If this is the situation between a husband and wife, it is better not to marry." {19:11} Jesus replied, "Not everyone can accept this teaching, but only those to whom it has been given. {19:12} For there are eunuchs who were born that way, and there are eunuchs who have been made eunuchs by others, and there are those who choose to live like eunuchs for the sake of the kingdom of heaven. The one who can accept this should accept it." {19:13} Then people brought little children to Jesus for him to place his hands on them and pray for them, but the disciples rebuked them. {19:14} Jesus said, "Let the little children come to me and do not hinder them, for the kingdom of heaven belongs to such as these." {19:15} And he placed his hands on them and went on from there. {19:16} Just then a man came up to Jesus and asked, "Teacher, what good thing must I do to get eternal life?" {19:17} "Why do you ask me about what is good?" Jesus replied. "There is only one who is good. If you want to enter life, keep the commandments." {19:18} "Which ones?" he asked. Jesus replied, "You shall not murder, you shall not commit adultery, you shall not steal, you shall not give false testimony, {19:19} honor your father and mother, and love your neighbor as yourself." {19:20} "All these I have kept," the young man said. "What do I still lack?" {19:21} Jesus answered, "If you want to be perfect, go, sell your possessions and give to the poor, and you will have treasure in heaven. Then come, follow me." {19:22} When the young man heard this, he went away sad because he had great wealth. {19:23} Then Jesus said to his disciples, "Truly I tell you, it is hard for someone who is rich to enter the kingdom of heaven. {19:24} Again I tell you, it is easier for a camel to go through the eye of a needle than for someone who is rich to enter the kingdom of God." {19:25} When the disciples heard this, they were greatly astonished and asked, "Who then can be saved?" {19:26} Jesus looked at them and said, "With man this is impossible, but with God all things are possible." {19:27} Peter answered him, "We have left everything to follow you. What then will there be for us?" {19:28} Jesus said to them, "Truly I tell you, at the renewal of all things, when the Son of Man sits on his glorious throne, you who have followed me will also sit on twelve thrones, judging the twelve tribes of Israel. {19:29} And everyone who has left houses or brothers or sisters or father or mother or wife or children or fields for my sake will receive a hundred times as much and will inherit eternal life. {19:30} But many who are first will be last, and many who are last will be first.

{20:1} For the kingdom of heaven is like a landowner who went out early in the morning to hire workers for his vineyard. {20:2} He agreed to pay them a denarius (a day's wage) for the day and sent them into his vineyard. {20:3} About nine in the morning, he went out and saw others standing in the marketplace doing nothing. {20:4} He told them, 'You also go and work in my vineyard, and I will pay you whatever is right.' So they went. {20:5} He went out again about noon and about three in the afternoon and did the same thing. {20:6} And about five in the afternoon he went out and found still others standing around. He asked them, 'Why have you been standing here all day long doing nothing?' {20:7} 'Because no one has hired us,' they answered. He said to them, 'You also go and work in my vineyard.' {20:8} When evening came, the owner of the vineyard said to his foreman, 'Call the workers and pay them their wages, beginning with the last ones hired and going on to the first.' {20:9} The workers who were hired about five in the afternoon came and each received a denarius. {20:10} So when those came who were hired first, they expected to receive more, but each one of them also received a denarius. {20:11} When they received it, they began to grumble against the landowner. {20:12} 'These who were hired last worked only one hour,' they said, 'and you have made them equal to us who have borne the burden of the work and the heat of the day.' {20:13} But he answered one of them, 'I am not being unfair to you, friend. Didn't you agree to work for a denarius? {20:14} Take your pay and go. I want to give the one who was hired last the same as I gave you. {20:15} Don't I have the right to do what I want with my own money? Or are you envious because I am generous?' {20:16} So the last will be first, and the first will be last. For many are invited, but few are chosen." {20:17} Now Jesus was going up to Jerusalem. On the way, he took the twelve disciples aside and said to them, {20:18} "We are going up to Jerusalem, and the Son of Man will be delivered over to the chief priests and the teachers of the law. They will condemn him to death {20:19} and will hand him over to the Gentiles to be mocked, flogged, and crucified. On the third day, he will be raised to life!" {20:20} Then the mother of Zebedee's sons came to Jesus with her sons and kneeling down asked a favor of him. {20:21} "What is it you want?" he asked. She said, "Grant that one of these two sons of mine may sit at your right and the other at your left in your kingdom." {20:22} Jesus replied, "You don't know what you are asking. Can you drink the cup I am going to drink?" "We can," they answered. {20:23} Jesus said to them, "You will indeed drink from my cup, but to sit at my right or left is not for me to grant. These places belong to those for whom they have been prepared by my Father." {20:24} When the ten heard about this, they were indignant with the two brothers. {20:25} Jesus called them together and said, "You know that the rulers of the Gentiles lord it over them, and their high officials exercise authority over them. {20:26} Not so with you. Instead, whoever wants to become great among you must be your servant, {20:27} and whoever wants to be first must be your slave— {20:28} just as the Son of Man did not come to be served, but to serve and to give his life as a ransom for many." {20:29} As Jesus and his disciples were leaving Jericho, a large crowd followed him. {20:30} Two blind men were sitting by the roadside, and when they heard that Jesus was going by, they shouted, "Lord, Son of David, have mercy on us!" {20:31} The crowd rebuked them and told them to be quiet, but they shouted all the louder, "Lord, Son of David, have mercy on us!" {20:32} Jesus stopped & called them. "What do you want me to do for you?" he asked. {20:33} "Lord," they answered, "we want our sight." {20:34} Jesus had compassion & touched their eyes. Immediately they received their sight & followed him.

{21:1} As they got close to Jerusalem and reached Bethphage on the Mount of Olives, Jesus sent two of his disciples, {21:2} saying to them, "Go to the village ahead of you. You'll immediately find a donkey tied there with her colt. Untie them and bring them to me. {21:3} If anyone asks you anything, say that the Lord needs them, and they'll send them right away." {21:4} This happened to fulfill what was spoken by the prophet, saying, {21:5} "Say to the daughter of Zion, 'Look, your King is coming to you, humble and riding on a donkey, on a colt, the foal of a donkey.'" {21:6} The disciples went and did as Jesus instructed. {21:7} They brought the donkey and the colt, placed their clothes on them, and Jesus sat on them. {21:8} A large crowd spread their cloaks on the road; others cut branches from the trees and spread them on the road. {21:9} The crowds that went ahead of him and those that followed shouted, "Hosanna to the Son of David! Blessed is he who comes in the name of the Lord! Hosanna in the highest!" {21:10} When Jesus entered Jerusalem, the whole city was stirred and asked, "Who is this?" {21:11} The crowds answered, "This is Jesus, the prophet from Nazareth in Galilee." {21:12} Jesus entered the temple and drove out all who were buying and selling there. He overturned the tables of the money changers and the benches of those selling doves, {21:13} and said to them, "It is written: 'My house will be called a house of prayer,' but you are making it a den of robbers." {21:14} The blind and the lame came to him at the temple, and he healed them. {21:15} But when the chief priests and the teachers of the law saw the wonderful things he did and the children shouting in the temple, "Hosanna to the Son of David," they were indignant. {21:16} "Do you hear what these children are saying?" they asked him. "Yes," replied Jesus, "have you never read, 'From the lips of children and infants you, Lord, have called forth your praise'?" {21:17} He left them and went out of the city to Bethany, where he spent the night. {21:18} In the morning, as he was on his way back to the city, he was hungry. {21:19} Seeing a fig tree by the road, he went up to it but found nothing on it except leaves. Then he said to it, "May you never bear fruit again!" Immediately, the fig tree withered. {21:20} When the disciples saw this, they were amazed. "How did the fig tree wither so quickly?" they asked. {21:21} Jesus replied, "Truly I tell you, if you have faith and do not doubt, not only can you do what was done to the fig tree, but also you can say to this mountain, 'Go, throw yourself into the sea,' and it will be done. {21:22} And whatever you ask in prayer, believing, you will receive." {21:23} Jesus entered the temple courts, and while he was teaching, the chief priests and the elders of the people came to him. "By what authority are you doing these things?" they asked. "And who gave you this authority?" {21:24} Jesus replied, "I will ask you one question. If you answer me, I will tell you by what authority I am doing these things. {21:25} John's baptism—where did it come from? Was it from heaven, or of human origin?" They discussed it among themselves and said, "If we say, 'From heaven,' he will ask, 'Then why didn't you believe him?' {21:26} But if we say, 'Of human origin'—we're afraid of the people, for they all hold that John was a prophet." {21:27} So they answered Jesus, "We don't know." Then he said, "Neither will I tell you by what authority I am doing these things." {21:28} "What do you think? There was a man who had two sons. He went to the first and said, 'Son, go and work in the vineyard today.' {21:29} 'I will not,' he answered, but later he changed his mind and went. {21:30} Then the father went to the other son and said the same thing. He answered, 'I will, sir,' but he did not go. {21:31} Which of the two did what his father wanted?" "The first," they answered. Jesus said to them, "Truly I tell you, the tax collectors and the prostitutes are entering the kingdom of God ahead of you. {21:32} For John came to you to show you the way of righteousness, and you did not believe him, but the tax collectors and the prostitutes did. And even after you saw this, you did not repent and believe him." {21:33} Listen to another parable: There was a landowner who planted a vineyard. He put a wall around it, dug a winepress in it, and built a watchtower. Then he rented the vineyard to some farmers and went away. {21:34} When the harvest time approached, he sent his servants to the tenants to collect his fruit. {21:35} The tenants seized his servants; they beat one, killed another, and stoned a third. {21:36} Then he sent other servants to them, more than the first time, and the tenants treated them the same way. {21:37} Last of all, he sent his son to them. 'They will respect my son,' he said. {21:38} But when the tenants saw the son, they said to each other, 'This is the heir. Come, let's kill him and take his inheritance.' {21:39} So they took him and threw him out of the vineyard and killed him. {21:40} Therefore, when the owner of the vineyard comes, what will he do to those tenants?" {21:41} "He will bring those wretches to a wretched end," they replied, "and he will rent the vineyard to other tenants who will give him his share of the crop at harvest time." {21:42} Jesus said to them, "Have you never read in the Scriptures: 'The stone the builders rejected has become the cornerstone; the Lord has done this, and it is marvelous in our eyes'? {21:43} Therefore I tell you that the kingdom of God will be taken away from you and given to a people who will produce its fruit. {21:44} Anyone who falls on this stone will be broken to pieces; anyone on whom it falls will be crushed." {21:45} When the chief priests and the Pharisees heard Jesus' parables, they knew he was talking about them. {21:46} They looked for a way to arrest him, but they were afraid of the crowd because the people held that he was a prophet.

{22:1} Jesus spoke to them again in parables, saying: {22:2} "The kingdom of heaven is like a king who prepared a wedding banquet for his son. {22:3} He sent his servants to those who had been invited to the banquet to tell them to come, but they refused to come. {22:4} Then he sent more servants and said, 'Tell those who have been invited that I have prepared my dinner. My oxen and fattened cattle have been killed, and everything is ready. Come to the wedding banquet.' {22:5} But they paid no attention and went off—one to his field, another to his business. {22:6} The rest seized his servants, mistreated them, and killed them. {22:7} The king was enraged. He sent his army and destroyed those murderers and burned their city. {22:8} Then he said to his servants, 'The wedding banquet is ready, but those I invited did not deserve to come. {22:9} Go to the street corners and invite to the banquet anyone you find.' {22:10} So the servants went out into the streets and gathered all the people they could find, both good and bad, and the wedding hall was filled with guests. {22:11} But when the king came in to see the guests, he noticed a man there who was not wearing wedding clothes. {22:12} 'Friend,' he asked, 'how did you get in here without wedding clothes?' The man was speechless. {22:13} Then the king told the attendants, 'Tie him hand and foot, and throw him outside, into the darkness, where there will be weeping and gnashing of teeth.' {22:14} For many are invited, but few are chosen." {22:15} Then the Pharisees went out and laid plans to trap him in his words. {22:16} They sent their disciples to him along with the Herodians. "Teacher," they said, "we know you are a man of integrity and that you teach the way of God in accordance with the truth. You aren't swayed by others because you pay no attention to who they are. {22:17} Tell us then, what is your opinion? Is it right to pay the imperial tax to Caesar, or not?" {22:18} But Jesus, knowing their evil intent, said, "You hypocrites, why are you trying to trap me? {22:19} Show me the coin used for paying the tax." They brought him a denarius, {22:20} and he asked them, "Whose image is this? And whose inscription?" {22:21} "Caesar's," they replied. Then he said to them, "So give back to Caesar what is Caesar's, and to God what is God's." {22:22} When they heard this, they were amazed. So they left him and went away. {22:23} That same day, the Sadducees, who say there is no resurrection, came to him with a question. {22:24} "Teacher," they said, "Moses told us that if a man dies without having children, his brother must marry the widow and raise up offspring for him. {22:25} Now there were seven brothers among us. The first one married and died, and since he had no children, he left his wife to his brother. {22:26} The same thing happened to the second and third brother, right on down to the seventh. {22:27} Finally, the woman died. {22:28} Now then, at the resurrection, whose wife will she be of the seven, since all of them were married to her?" {22:29} Jesus replied, "You are in error because you do not know the Scriptures or the power of God. {22:30} At the resurrection, people will neither marry nor be given in marriage; they will be like the angels in heaven. {22:31} But about the resurrection of the dead—have you not read what God said to you, {22:32} 'I am the God of Abraham, the God of Isaac, and the God of Jacob'? He is not the God of the dead but of the living." {22:33} When the crowds heard this, they were astonished at his teaching. {22:34} Hearing that Jesus had silenced the Sadducees, the Pharisees gathered together. {22:35} One of them, an expert in the law, tested him with this question: {22:36} "Teacher, which is the greatest commandment in the Law?" {22:37} Jesus replied: "Love the Lord your God with all your heart and with all your soul and with all your mind. {22:38} This is the first and greatest commandment. {22:39} And the second is like it: 'Love your neighbor as yourself.' {22:40} All the Law and the Prophets hang on these two commandments." {22:41} While the Pharisees were gathered together, Jesus asked them, {22:42} "What do you think about the Messiah? Whose son is he?" "The Son of David," they replied. {22:43} He said to them, "How is it then that David, speaking by the Spirit, calls him 'Lord'? For he says, {22:44} 'The Lord said to my Lord: Sit at my right hand until I put your enemies under your feet'? {22:45} If then David calls him 'Lord,' how can he be his son?" {22:46} No one could say a word in reply, and from that day on no one dared to ask him any more questions.

{23:1} Then Jesus spoke to the crowd and his disciples, {23:2} saying, "The scribes and the Pharisees sit in Moses' seat. {23:3} So you must do everything they tell you, but do not follow their example. They say one thing but do another. {23:4} They impose heavy burdens on people but won't lift a finger to help. {23:5} Everything they do is for show: they make their prayer boxes (phylacteries) large and wear long tassels on their robes. {23:6} They love the best seats at feasts and the most important places in the synagogues, {23:7} and they love to be greeted in the marketplace and to be called 'Rabbi' by others. {23:8} But you are not to be called 'Rabbi,' for you have one Teacher, and you are all brothers. {23:9} And do not call anyone on earth 'father,' for you have one Father, who is in heaven. {23:10} Nor are you to be called instructors, for you have one Instructor, the Messiah. {23:11} The greatest among you will be your servant. {23:12} For those who exalt themselves will be humbled, and those who humble themselves will be exalted. {23:13} Woe to you, scribes and Pharisees, hypocrites! You shut the kingdom of heaven in people's faces. You do not enter yourselves, and you do not let those enter who are trying to. {23:14} Woe to you, scribes and Pharisees, hypocrites! You devour widows' houses and, for a show, make lengthy prayers. Because of this, you will be punished more severely. {23:15} Woe to you, scribes and Pharisees, hypocrites! You go to great lengths to make a single convert, and when you do, you make them twice as much a child of hell as you are. {23:16} Woe to you, blind guides! You say, 'If anyone swears by the temple, it means nothing, but if anyone swears by the gold of the temple, they are bound by their oath.' {23:17} You blind fools! Which is greater: the gold, or the temple that makes the gold sacred? {23:18} You also say, 'If anyone swears by the altar, it means nothing, but if anyone swears by the gift on the altar, they are bound by their oath.' {23:19} You blind men! Which is greater: the gift, or the altar that makes the gift sacred? {23:20} Therefore, anyone who swears by the altar swears by it and everything on it. {23:21} And anyone who swears by the temple swears by it and by the one who dwells in it. {23:22} And anyone who swears by heaven swears by God's throne and by the one who sits on it. {23:23} Woe to you, scribes and Pharisees, hypocrites! You give a tenth of your spices—mint, dill, and cumin—but you neglect the more important matters of the law—justice, mercy, and faithfulness. You should have practiced the latter, without neglecting the former. {23:24} You blind guides! You strain out a gnat but swallow a camel. {23:25} Woe to you, scribes and Pharisees, hypocrites! You clean the outside of the cup and dish, but inside they are full of greed and self-indulgence. {23:26} Blind Pharisee! First clean the inside of the cup and dish, and then the outside will also be clean. {23:27} Woe to you, scribes and Pharisees, hypocrites! You are like whitewashed tombs, which look beautiful on the outside but on the inside are full of the bones of the dead and everything unclean. {23:28} In the same way, on the outside you appear to people as righteous but on the inside you are full of hypocrisy and wickedness. {23:29} Woe to you, scribes and Pharisees, hypocrites! You build tombs for the prophets and decorate the graves of the righteous, {23:30} and you say, 'If we had lived in the days of our ancestors, we would not have taken part with them in shedding the blood of the prophets.' {23:31} So you testify against yourselves that you are the descendants of those who murdered the prophets. {23:32} Go ahead, then, and complete what your ancestors started! {23:33} You snakes! You brood of vipers! How will you escape being condemned to hell? {23:34} Therefore I am sending you prophets and sages and teachers. Some of them you will kill and crucify; others you will flog in your synagogues and pursue from town to town. {23:35} And so upon you will come all the righteous blood that has been shed on earth, from the blood of righteous Abel to the blood of Zechariah son of Barachiah, whom you murdered between the temple and the altar. {23:36} Truly I tell you, all this will come upon this generation. {23:37} Jerusalem, you who kill the prophets and stone those sent to you, how often I have longed to gather your children together, as a hen gathers her chicks under her wings, and you were not willing! {23:38} Look, your house is left to you desolate. {23:39} For I tell you, you will not see me again until you say, 'Blessed is he who comes in the Lord's name.'"

{24:1} Jesus left the temple and was walking away when his disciples came up to him to call his attention to its buildings. {24:2} "Do you see all these things?" he asked. "Truly I tell you, not one stone here will be left on another; every one will be thrown down." {24:3} As Jesus was sitting on the Mount of Olives, the disciples came to him privately. "Tell us," they said, "when will this happen, and what will be the sign of your coming and of the end of the age?" {24:4} Jesus answered: "Watch out that no one deceives you. {24:5} For many will come in my name, claiming, 'I am the Messiah,' and will deceive many. {24:6} You will hear of wars and rumors of wars, but see to it that you are not alarmed. Such things must happen, but the end is still to come. {24:7} Nation will rise against nation, and kingdom against kingdom. There will be famines and earthquakes in various places. {24:8} All these are the beginning of birth pains. {24:9} Then you will be handed over to be persecuted and put to death, and you will be hated by all nations because of me. {24:10} At that time many will turn away from the faith and will betray and hate each other, {24:11} and many false prophets will appear and deceive many people. {24:12} Because of the increase of wickedness, the love of most will grow cold, {24:13} but the one who stands firm to the end will be saved. {24:14} And this gospel of the kingdom will be preached in the whole world as a testimony to all nations, and then the end will come. {24:15} So when you see standing in the holy place 'the abomination that causes desolation,' spoken of through the prophet Daniel (let the reader understand), {24:16} then let those who are in Judea flee to the mountains. {24:17} Let no one on the housetop go down to take anything out of the house. {24:18} Let no one in the field go back to get their cloak. {24:19} How dreadful it will be in those days for pregnant women and nursing mothers! {24:20} Pray that your flight will not take place in winter or on the Sabbath. {24:21} For then there will be great distress, unequaled from the beginning of the world until now, and never to be equaled again. {24:22} If those days had not been cut short, no one would survive, but for the sake of the elect those days will be shortened. {24:23} At that time if anyone says to you, 'Look, here is the Messiah!' or 'There he is!' do not believe it. {24:24} For false messiahs and false prophets will appear and perform great signs and wonders to deceive, if possible, even the elect. {24:25} See, I have told you ahead of time. {24:26} So if anyone tells you, 'There he is, out in the wilderness,' do not go out; or 'Here he is, in the inner rooms,' do not believe it. {24:27} For as lightning that comes from the east is visible even in the west, so will be the coming of the Son of Man. {24:28} Wherever there is a carcass, there the vultures will gather. {24:29} Immediately after the distress of those days 'the sun will be darkened, and the moon will not give its light; the stars will fall from the sky, and the heavenly bodies will be shaken.' {24:30} Then will appear the sign of the Son of Man in heaven, and all the peoples of the earth will mourn. They will see the Son of Man coming on the clouds of heaven with power and great glory. {24:31} And he will send his angels with a loud trumpet call, and they will gather his elect from the four winds, from one end of the heavens to the other. {24:32} Now learn this lesson from the fig tree: As soon as its twigs get tender and its leaves come out, you know that summer is near. {24:33} Even so, when you see all these things, you know that it is near, right at the door. {24:34} Truly I tell you, this generation will certainly not pass away until all these things have happened. {24:35} Heaven and earth will pass away, but my words will never pass away. {24:36} But about that day or hour no one knows, not even the angels in heaven, nor the Son, but only the Father. {24:37} As it was in the days of Noah, so it will be at the coming of the Son of Man. {24:38} For in the days before the flood, people were eating and drinking, marrying and giving in marriage, up to the day Noah entered the ark; {24:39} and they knew nothing about what would happen until the flood came and took them all away. That is how it will be at the coming of the Son of Man. {24:40} Two men will be in the field; one will be taken and the other left. {24:41} Two women will be grinding with a hand mill; one will be taken and the other left. {24:42} Therefore keep watch, because you do not know on what day your Lord will come. {24:43} But understand this: If the owner of the house had known at what time of night the thief was coming, he would have kept watch and would not have let his house be broken into. {24:44} So you also must be ready, because the Son of Man will come at an hour when you do not expect him. {24:45} Who then is the faithful and wise servant, whom the master has put in charge of the servants in his household to give them their food at the proper time? {24:46} It will be good for that servant whose master finds him doing so when he returns. {24:47} Truly I tell you, he will put him in charge of all his possessions. {24:48} But suppose that servant is wicked and says to himself, 'My master is staying away a long time,' {24:49} and he then begins to beat his fellow servants and to eat and drink with drunkards. {24:50} The master of that servant will come on a day when he does not expect him and at an hour he is not aware of. {24:51} He will cut him to pieces and assign him a place with the hypocrites, where there will be weeping and gnashing of teeth.

{25:1} At that time, the kingdom of heaven will be compared to ten young women who took their lamps and went out to meet the bridegroom. {25:2} Five of them were wise, and five were foolish. {25:3} The foolish ones took their lamps but did not take any extra oil with them. {25:4} The wise ones, however, took oil in jars along with their lamps. {25:5} As the bridegroom delayed, they all became drowsy and fell asleep. {25:6} At midnight, a shout rang out: "Here's the bridegroom! Come out to meet him!" {25:7} Then all the young women woke up and prepared their lamps. {25:8} The foolish ones said to the wise, "Give us some of your oil; our lamps are going out." {25:9} "No," they replied, "there may not be enough for both us and you. Instead, go to those who sell oil and buy some for yourselves." {25:10} While they were on their way to buy the oil, the bridegroom arrived. The ones who were ready went in with him to the wedding banquet. Then the door was shut. {25:11} Later, the other young women came and said, "Lord, Lord, open the door for us!" {25:12} But he replied, "Truly I tell you, I don't know you." {25:13} Therefore, keep watch, because you do not know the day or the hour when the Son of Man will come. {25:14} Again, the kingdom of heaven is like a man going on a journey who called his servants and entrusted his wealth to them. {25:15} To one, he gave five bags of gold, to another two bags, and to another one bag, each according to his ability. Then he went on his journey. {25:16} The man who had received five bags went at once and put his money to work and gained five more bags. {25:17} So also, the one with two bags gained two more. {25:18} But the man who had received one bag went off, dug a hole in the ground, and hid his master's money. {25:19} After a long time, the master of those servants returned and settled accounts with them. {25:20} The man who had received five bags brought the other five. "Master," he said, "you entrusted me with five bags of gold. See, I have gained five more." {25:21} His master replied, "Well done, good and faithful servant! You have been faithful with a few things; I will put you in charge of many things. Come and share in your master's happiness!" {25:22} The man with two bags of gold also came. "Master," he said, "you entrusted me with two bags of gold. See, I have gained two more." {25:23} His master replied, "Well done, good and faithful servant! You have been faithful with a few things; I will put you in charge of many things. Come and share in your master's happiness!" {25:24} Then the man who had received one bag came. "Master," he said, "I knew that you are a hard man, harvesting where you have not sown and gathering where you have not scattered seed. {25:25} So I was afraid and went out and hid your gold in the ground. See, here is what belongs to you." {25:26} His master replied, "You wicked and lazy servant! So you knew that I harvest where I have not sown and gather where I have not scattered seed? {25:27} Well then, you should have put my money on deposit with the bankers, so that when I returned, I would have received it back with interest. {25:28} Take the bag of gold from him and give it to the one who has ten bags. {25:29} For whoever has will be given more, and they will have an abundance. Whoever does not have, even what they have will be taken from them. {25:30} And throw that worthless servant outside, into the darkness, where there will be weeping and gnashing of teeth. {25:31} When the Son of Man comes in his glory, and all the angels with him, he will sit on his glorious throne. {25:32} All the nations will be gathered before him, and he will separate the people one from another as a shepherd separates the sheep from the goats. {25:33} He will put the sheep on his right and the goats on his left. {25:34} Then the King will say to those on his right, "Come, you who are blessed by my Father; take your inheritance, the kingdom prepared for you since the creation of the world. {25:35} For I was hungry and you gave me something to eat; I was thirsty and you gave me something to drink; I was a stranger and you invited me in; {25:36} I needed clothes and you clothed me; I was sick and you looked after me; I was in prison and you came to visit me." {25:37} Then the righteous will answer him, "Lord, when did we see you hungry and feed you, or thirsty and give you something to drink? {25:38} When did we see you a stranger and invite you in, or needing clothes and clothe you? {25:39} When did we see you sick or in prison and go to visit you?" {25:40} The King will reply, "Truly I tell you, whatever you did for one of the least of these brothers and sisters of mine, you did for me." {25:41} Then he will say to those on his left, "Depart from me, you who are cursed, into the eternal fire prepared for the devil and his angels. {25:42} For I was hungry and you gave me nothing to eat; I was thirsty and you gave me nothing to drink; {25:43} I was a stranger and you did not invite me in; I needed clothes and you did not clothe me; I was sick and in prison and you did not look after me." {25:44} They also will answer, "Lord, when did we see you hungry or thirsty or a stranger or needing clothes or sick or in prison and did not help you?" {25:45} He will reply, "Truly I tell you, whatever you did not do for one of the least of these, you did not do for me." {25:46} Then they will go away to eternal punishment, but the righteous to eternal life.

{26:1} When Jesus had finished saying all these things, he said to his disciples, {26:2} "You know that the Passover is two days away—and the Son of Man will be handed over to be crucified." {26:3} Then the chief priests and the elders of the people assembled in the palace of the high priest, whose name was Caiaphas, {26:4} and they schemed to arrest Jesus secretly and kill him. {26:5} "But not during the festival," they said, "or there may be a riot among the people." {26:6} While Jesus was in Bethany, in the home of Simon the Leper, {26:7} a woman came to him with an alabaster jar of very expensive perfume, which she poured on his head as he was reclining at the table. {26:8} When the disciples saw this, they were indignant. "Why this waste?" they asked. {26:9} "This perfume could have been sold at a high price and the money given to the poor." {26:10} Aware of this, Jesus said to them, "Why are you bothering this woman? She has done a beautiful thing for me. {26:11} The poor you will always have with you, but you will not always have me. {26:12} When she poured this perfume on my body, she did it to prepare me for burial. {26:13} Truly I tell you, wherever this gospel is preached throughout the world, what she has done will also be told, in memory of her." {26:14} Then one of the Twelve—the one called Judas Iscariot—went to the chief priests {26:15} and asked, "What are you willing to give me if I deliver him over to you?" So they counted out for him thirty pieces of silver. {26:16} From then on, Judas watched for an opportunity to hand him over. {26:17} On the first day of the Festival of Unleavened Bread, the disciples came to Jesus and asked, "Where do you want us to prepare for you to eat the Passover?" {26:18} He replied, "Go into the city to a certain man and tell him, 'The Teacher says: My appointed time is near. I am going to celebrate the Passover at your house with my disciples.'" {26:19} The disciples did as Jesus had directed them and prepared the Passover. {26:20} When evening came, Jesus was reclining at the table with the Twelve. {26:21} And while they were eating, he said, "Truly I tell you, one of you will betray me." {26:22} They were very sad and began to say to him one after the other, "Surely you don't mean me, Lord?" {26:23} Jesus replied, "The one who dips his hand into the bowl with me is the one who will betray me. {26:24} The Son of Man will go just as it is written about him. But woe to that man who betrays the Son of Man! It would be better for him if he had not been born." {26:25} Judas, who betrayed him, asked, "Rabbi, is it me?" Jesus replied, "You have said so." {26:26} While they were eating, Jesus took bread, blessed it, broke it, and gave it to his disciples, saying, "Take, eat; this is my body." {26:27} Then he took a cup, gave thanks, and gave it to them, saying, "Drink from it, all of you. {26:28} This is my blood of the new covenant, which is poured out for many for the forgiveness of sins. {26:29} I tell you, I will not drink from this fruit of the vine from now on until that day when I drink it new with you in my Father's kingdom." {26:30} After they had sung a hymn, they went out to the Mount of Olives. {26:31} Then Jesus said to them, "You will all fall away because of me this night, for it is written, 'I will strike the shepherd, and the sheep of the flock will be scattered.' {26:32} But after I am raised, I will go ahead of you into Galilee." {26:33} Peter replied, "Even if all fall away on account of you, I never will." {26:34} Jesus answered, "Truly I tell you, this very night, before the rooster crows, you will disown me three times." {26:35} Peter declared, "Even if I have to die with you, I will never disown you." And all the disciples said the same. {26:36} Then Jesus went with them to a place called Gethsemane and said to his disciples, "Sit here while I go over there and pray." {26:37} He took Peter and the two sons of Zebedee along with him, and he began to be sorrowful and troubled. {26:38} Then he said to them, "My soul is overwhelmed with sorrow to the point of death. Stay here and keep watch with me." {26:39} Going a little farther, he fell with his face to the ground and prayed, "My Father, if it is possible, may this cup be taken from me. Yet not as I will, but as you will." {26:40} Then he returned to his disciples and found them sleeping. "Couldn't you men keep watch with me for one hour?" he asked Peter. {26:41} "Watch and pray so that you will not fall into temptation. The spirit is willing, but the flesh is weak." {26:42} He went away a second time and prayed, "My Father, if it is not possible for this cup to be taken away unless I drink it, may your will be done." {26:43} When he came back, he found them sleeping again, because their eyes were heavy. {26:44} So he left them and went away once more and prayed the third time, saying the same thing. {26:45} Then he returned to his disciples and said to them, "Are you still sleeping and resting? Look, the hour has come, and the Son of Man is delivered into the hands of sinners. {26:46} Rise, let us go! Here comes my betrayer!" {26:47} While he was still speaking, Judas, one of the Twelve, arrived. With him was a large crowd armed with swords and clubs, sent from the chief priests and the elders of the people. {26:48} Now the betrayer had arranged a signal with them: "The one I kiss is the man; arrest him." {26:49} Going at once to Jesus, Judas said, "Greetings, Rabbi!" and kissed him. {26:50} Jesus replied, "Friend, do what you came for." Then the men stepped forward, seized Jesus, and arrested him. {26:51} With that, one of those who were with Jesus reached for his sword, drew it out, and struck the servant of the high priest, cutting off his ear. {26:52} "Put your sword back in its place," Jesus said to him, "for all who draw the sword will die by the sword. {26:53} Do you think I cannot call on my Father, and he will at once put at my disposal more than twelve legions of angels? {26:54} But how then would the Scriptures be fulfilled that say it must happen in this way?" {26:55} In that hour, Jesus said to the crowd, "Am I leading a rebellion, that you have come out with swords and clubs to capture me? Every day I sat in the temple courts teaching, and you did not arrest me. {26:56} But this has all taken place that the writings of the prophets might be fulfilled." Then all the disciples deserted him and fled. {26:57} Those who had arrested Jesus took him to Caiaphas, the high priest, where the teachers of the law and the elders had assembled. {26:58} But Peter followed him at a distance, right up to the courtyard of the high priest. He entered and sat down with the guards to see the outcome. {26:59} The chief priests and the whole Sanhedrin were looking for false evidence against Jesus so they could put him to death. {26:60} But they did not find any, though many false witnesses came forward. Finally, two came forward {26:61} and declared, "This fellow said, 'I am able to destroy the temple of God and rebuild it in three days.'" {26:62} Then the high priest stood up and said to Jesus, "Are you not going to answer? What is this testimony these men are bringing against you?" {26:63} But Jesus remained silent. The high priest said to him, "I charge you under oath by the living God: Tell us if you are the Messiah, the Son of God." {26:64} "You have said so," Jesus replied. "But I say to all of you: From now on you will see the Son of Man sitting at the right hand of the Mighty One and coming on the clouds of heaven." {26:65} Then the high priest tore his clothes and said, "He has spoken blasphemy! Why do we need any more witnesses? Look, now you have heard the blasphemy. {26:66} What do you think?" "He is worthy of death," they answered. {26:67} Then they spit in his face and struck him with their fists. Others slapped him {26:68} and said, "Prophesy to us, Messiah. Who hit you?" {26:69} Now Peter was sitting out in the courtyard, and a servant girl came to him. "You also were with Jesus of Galilee," she said. {26:70} But he denied it before them all. "I don't know what you're talking about," he said. {26:71} Then he went out to the entryway, where another servant girl saw him and said to those there, "This fellow was with Jesus of Nazareth." {26:72} He denied it again, with an oath: "I don't know the man!" {26:73} After a little while, those standing there went up to Peter and said, "Surely you are one of them; your accent gives you away." {26:74} Then he began to call down curses, and he swore to them, "I don't know the man!" Immediately, a rooster crowed. {26:75} Then Peter remembered the word Jesus had spoken: "Before rooster crows, you will disown me three times." And he went outside & wept bitterly.

{27:1} When morning came, all the chief priests and elders of the people met to discuss how to put Jesus to death. {27:2} After binding him, they led him away and handed him over to Pontius Pilate, the governor. {27:3} Then Judas, who had betrayed him, saw that Jesus was condemned, felt remorse, and returned the thirty pieces of silver to the chief priests and elders, {27:4} saying, "I have sinned by betraying innocent blood." They replied, "What is that to us? That's your problem." {27:5} So he threw down the silver in the temple, left, and hanged himself. {27:6} The chief priests picked up the pieces of silver and said, "It's not lawful to put this in the treasury because it's blood money." {27:7} They decided to use it to buy the potter's field to bury strangers in. {27:8} That's why the field has been called the Field of Blood to this day. {27:9} Then what was spoken by the prophet Jeremiah was fulfilled: "And they took the thirty pieces of silver, the price of the one valued by the children of Israel; {27:10} and gave them for the potter's field, as the Lord commanded me." {27:11} Jesus stood before the governor, and the governor asked him, "Are you the King of the Jews?" Jesus replied, "You say so." {27:12} When he was accused by the chief priests and elders, he said nothing. {27:13} Then Pilate asked him, "Don't you hear how many charges they are bringing against you?" {27:14} But Jesus didn't reply, even to a single charge, which amazed the governor. {27:15} Now it was the governor's custom at the festival to release a prisoner chosen by the crowd. {27:16} At that time, they had a notorious prisoner named Barabbas. {27:17} So when the crowd had gathered, Pilate asked them, "Which one do you want me to release: Barabbas or Jesus who is called the Messiah?" {27:18} For he knew it was out of envy that they had handed Jesus over to him. {27:19} While Pilate was sitting on the judge's seat, his wife sent him this message: "Don't have anything to do with that innocent man, for I have suffered a great deal today in a dream because of him." {27:20} But the chief priests and elders persuaded the crowd to ask for Barabbas and to have Jesus executed. {27:21} "Which of the two do you want me to release to you?" Pilate asked. "Barabbas," they answered. {27:22} "What shall I do, then, with Jesus who is called the Messiah?" Pilate asked. "Crucify him!" they all answered. {27:23} "Why? What crime has he committed?" Pilate asked. But they shouted all the louder, "Crucify him!" {27:24} When Pilate saw that he was getting nowhere but instead an uproar was starting, he took water and washed his hands in front of the crowd. "I am innocent of this man's blood," he said. "It's your responsibility!" {27:25} All the people answered, "His blood is on us and on our children!" {27:26} Then he released Barabbas to them, but he had Jesus flogged and handed him over to be crucified. {27:27} Then the governor's soldiers took Jesus into the Praetorium and gathered the whole company of soldiers around him. {27:28} They stripped him and put a scarlet robe on him, {27:29} and then twisted together a crown of thorns and set it on his head. They put a staff in his right hand. Then they knelt in front of him and mocked him, saying, "Hail, King of the Jews!" {27:30} They spit on him, took the staff, and struck him on the head again and again. {27:31} After they had mocked him, they took off the robe and put his own clothes on him. Then they led him away to crucify him. {27:32} As they were going out, they met a man from Cyrene named Simon, and they forced him to carry the cross. {27:33} They came to a place called Golgotha (which means the place of the skull). {27:34} There they offered Jesus wine to drink mixed with gall, but after tasting it, he refused to drink it. {27:35} When they had crucified him, they divided up his clothes by casting lots, and sitting down, they kept watch over him there. {27:36} Above his head, they placed the written charge against him: "This is Jesus, the King of the Jews." {27:37} Two rebels were crucified with him, one on his right and one on his left. {27:38} Those who passed by hurled insults at him, shaking their heads {27:39} and saying, "You who are going to destroy the temple and build it in three days, save yourself! Come down from the cross, if you are the Son of God!" {27:40} In the same way, the chief priests, the teachers of the law, and the elders mocked him. {27:41} "He saved others," they said, "but he can't save himself! He's the King of Israel! Let him come down now from the cross, and we will believe in him. {27:43} He trusts in God. Let God rescue him now if he wants him, for he said, 'I am the Son of God.'" {27:44} In the same way, the rebels who were crucified with him also heaped insults on him. {27:45} From the sixth hour until the ninth hour, darkness came over all the land. {27:46} About the ninth hour, Jesus cried out in a loud voice, "Eli, Eli, lema sabachthani?" which means, "My God, my God, why have you forsaken me?" {27:47} When some of those standing there heard this, they said, "He's calling Elijah." {27:48} Immediately one of them ran and got a sponge. He filled it with vinegar, put it on a stick, and offered it to Jesus to drink. {27:49} The rest said, "Now leave him alone. Let's see if Elijah comes to save him." {27:50} And when Jesus had cried out again in a loud voice, he gave up his spirit. {27:51} At that moment, the curtain of the temple was torn in two from top to bottom. The earth shook, the rocks split {27:52} and the tombs broke open. The bodies of many holy people who had died were raised to life. {27:53} They came out of the tombs after Jesus' resurrection and went into the holy city and appeared to many people. {27:54} When the centurion and those with him who were guarding Jesus saw the earthquake and all that had happened, they were terrified, and exclaimed, "Surely he was the Son of God!" {27:55} Many women were there watching from a distance. They had followed Jesus from Galilee to care for his needs. {27:56} Among them were Mary Magdalene, Mary the mother of James and Joseph, and the mother of Zebedee's sons. {27:57} As evening approached, there came a rich man from Arimathea named Joseph, who had himself become a disciple of Jesus. {27:58} Going to Pilate, he asked for Jesus' body, and Pilate ordered that it be given to him. {27:59} Joseph took the body, wrapped it in a clean linen cloth, {27:60} and placed it in his own new tomb that he had cut out of the rock. He rolled a big stone in front of the entrance to the tomb and went away. {27:61} Mary Magdalene and the other Mary were sitting there opposite the tomb. {27:62} The next day, the one after Preparation Day, the chief priests and the Pharisees went to Pilate. {27:63} "Sir," they said, "we remember that while he was still alive that deceiver said, 'After three days I will rise again.' {27:64} So give the order for the tomb to be made secure until the third day. Otherwise, his disciples may come and steal the body and tell the people that he has been raised from the dead. This last deception will be worse than the first." {27:65} "Take a guard," Pilate answered. "Go, make the tomb as secure as you know how." {27:66} So they went and made the tomb secure by sealing the stone and posting the guard.

{28:1} After the Sabbath, at dawn on the first day of the week, Mary Magdalene and the other Mary went to look at the tomb. {28:2} There was a violent earthquake, for an angel of the Lord came down from heaven and, going to the tomb, rolled back the stone and sat on it. {28:3} His appearance was like lightning, and his clothes were white as snow. {28:4} The guards were so afraid of him that they shook and became like dead men. {28:5} The angel said to the women, "Do not be afraid, for I know that you are looking for Jesus, who was crucified. {28:6} He is not here; he has risen, just as he said. Come and see the place where he lay. {28:7} Then go quickly and tell his disciples: 'He has risen from the dead and is going ahead of you into Galilee. There you will see him.' Now I have told you." {28:8} So the women hurried away from the tomb, afraid yet filled with joy, and ran to tell his disciples. {28:9} Suddenly Jesus met them. "Greetings," he said. They came to him, clasped his feet and worshiped him. {28:10} Then Jesus said to them, "Do not be afraid. Go and tell my brothers to go to Galilee; there they will see me." {28:11} While the women were on their way, some of the guards went into the city and reported to the chief priests everything that had happened. {28:12} When the chief priests had met with the elders and devised a plan, they gave the soldiers a large sum of money {28:13} telling them, "You are to say, 'His disciples came during the night and stole him away while we were asleep.' {28:14} If this report gets to the governor, we will satisfy him and keep you out of trouble." {28:15} So the soldiers took the money and did as they were instructed. And this story has been widely circulated among the Jews to this very day. {28:16} Then the eleven disciples went to Galilee, to the mountain where Jesus had told them to go. {28:17} When they saw him, they worshiped him; but some doubted. {28:18} Then Jesus came to them and said, "All authority in heaven and on earth has been given to me. {28:19} Therefore go & make disciples of all nations, baptizing them in name of the Father, and of the Son, and of the Holy Spirit, {28:20} and teaching them to obey everything I have commanded you. And surely I am with you always, to the very end of the age."

The Gospel of Mark

{1:1} The beginning of the good news about Jesus Christ, the Son of God. {1:2} As it is written in the prophets, "I will send my messenger ahead of you, who will prepare your way." {1:3} "A voice of one calling in the wilderness, 'Prepare the way for the Lord, make straight paths for him.'" {1:4} So John the Baptist appeared in the wilderness, preaching a baptism of repentance for the forgiveness of sins. {1:5} The whole Judean countryside and all the people of Jerusalem went out to him. Confessing their sins, they were baptized by him in the Jordan River. {1:6} John wore clothes made of camel's hair, with a leather belt around his waist, and he ate locusts and wild honey. {1:7} He preached, "After me comes one more powerful than I, the straps of whose sandals I am not worthy to stoop down and untie. {1:8} I baptize you with water, but he will baptize you with the Holy Spirit." {1:9} At that time, Jesus came from Nazareth in Galilee and was baptized by John in the Jordan. {1:10} As Jesus was coming up out of the water, he saw heaven being torn open and the Spirit descending on him like a dove. {1:11} And a voice came from heaven: "You are my Son, whom I love; with you I am well pleased." {1:12} At once the Spirit sent him out into the wilderness, {1:13} and he was in the wilderness for forty days, being tempted by Satan. He was with the wild animals, and angels attended him. {1:14} After John was put in prison, Jesus went into Galilee, proclaiming the good news of God. {1:15} "The time has come," he said. "The kingdom of God has come near. Repent and believe the good news!" {1:16} As Jesus walked beside the Sea of Galilee, he saw Simon and his brother Andrew casting a net into the lake, for they were fishermen. {1:17} "Come, follow me," Jesus said, "and I will send you out to fish for people." {1:18} At once they left their nets and followed him. {1:19} When he had gone a little farther, he saw James son of Zebedee and his brother John in a boat preparing their nets. {1:20} Without delay, he called them, and they left their father Zebedee in the boat with the hired men and followed him. {1:21} They went to Capernaum, and when the Sabbath came, Jesus went into the synagogue and began to teach. {1:22} The people were amazed at his teaching because he taught them as one who had authority, not as the teachers of the law. {1:23} Just then a man in their synagogue who was possessed by an impure spirit cried out, {1:24} "What do you want with us, Jesus of Nazareth? Have you come to destroy us? I know who you are—the Holy One of God!" {1:25} "Be quiet!" said Jesus sternly. "Come out of him!" {1:26} The impure spirit shook the man violently and came out of him with a shriek. {1:27} The people were all so amazed that they asked each other, "What is this? A new teaching—and with authority! He even gives orders to impure spirits and they obey him." {1:28} News about him spread quickly over the whole region of Galilee. {1:29} As soon as they left the synagogue, they went with James and John to the home of Simon and Andrew. {1:30} Simon's mother-in-law was in bed with a fever, and they immediately told Jesus about her. {1:31} So he went to her, took her hand and helped her up. The fever left her, and she began to wait on them. {1:32} That evening after sunset, the people brought to Jesus all the sick and demon-possessed. {1:33} The whole town gathered at the door, {1:34} and Jesus healed many who had various diseases. He also drove out many demons, but he would not let the demons speak because they knew who he was. {1:35} Very early in the morning, while it was still dark, Jesus got up, left the house, and went off to a solitary place, where he prayed. {1:36} Simon and his companions went to look for him, {1:37} and when they found him, they exclaimed: "Everyone is looking for you!" {1:38} Jesus replied, "Let us go somewhere else—to the nearby villages—so I can preach there also. That is why I have come." {1:39} So he traveled throughout Galilee, preaching in their synagogues and driving out demons. {1:40} A man with leprosy came to him and begged him on his knees, "If you are willing, you can make me clean." {1:41} Jesus was indignant (or compassionate); he reached out his hand and touched the man. "I am willing," he said. "Be clean!" Immediately, the leprosy left him and he was cleansed. {1:42} Jesus sent him away at once with a strong warning: {1:43} "See that you don't tell this to anyone. But go, show yourself to the priest and offer the sacrifices that Moses commanded for your cleansing, as a testimony to them." {1:44} Instead he went out and began to talk freely, spreading the news. As a result, Jesus could no longer enter a town openly but stayed outside in lonely places. Yet the people still came to him from everywhere.

{2:1} A few days later, Jesus entered Capernaum again, and news spread that he was at home. {2:2} So many gathered that there was no room left, not even outside the door, and he preached the word to them. {2:3} Some people came bringing a paralyzed man, carried by four of them. {2:4} Since they could not get him to Jesus because of the crowd, they made an opening in the roof above Jesus by digging through it and then lowered the mat the paralyzed man was lying on. {2:5} When Jesus saw their faith, he said to the paralyzed man, "Son, your sins are forgiven." {2:6} Now some teachers of the law were sitting there, thinking to themselves, {2:7} "Why does this fellow talk like that? He's blaspheming! Who can forgive sins but God alone?" {2:8} Immediately Jesus knew in his spirit that this was what they were thinking in their hearts, and he said to them, "Why are you thinking these things? {2:9} Which is easier: to say to this paralyzed man, 'Your sins are forgiven,' or to say, 'Get up, take your mat and walk'? {2:10} But I want you to know that the Son of Man has authority on earth to forgive sins." So he said to the man, {2:11} "I tell you, get up, take your mat and go home." {2:12} He got up, took his mat and walked out in full view of them all. This amazed everyone and they praised God, saying, "We have never seen anything like this!" {2:13} Once again Jesus went out beside the lake. A large crowd came to him, and he began to teach them. {2:14} As he walked along, he saw Levi son of Alphaeus sitting at the tax collector's booth. "Follow me," Jesus told him, and Levi got up and followed him. {2:15} While Jesus was having dinner at Levi's house, many tax collectors and sinners were eating with him and his disciples, for there were many who followed him. {2:16} When the teachers of the law who were Pharisees saw him eating with the sinners and tax collectors, they asked his disciples, "Why does he eat with tax collectors and sinners?" {2:17} On hearing this, Jesus said to them, "It is not the healthy who need a doctor, but the sick. I have not come to call the righteous, but sinners." {2:18} Now John's disciples and the Pharisees were fasting. Some people came and asked Jesus, "How is it that John's disciples and the disciples of the Pharisees are fasting, but yours are not?" {2:19} Jesus answered, "How can the guests of the bridegroom fast while he is with them? They cannot, so long as they have him with them. {2:20} But the time will come when the bridegroom will be taken from them, and on that day they will fast." {2:21} No one sews a patch of unshrunk cloth on an old garment. Otherwise, the new piece will pull away from the old, making the tear worse. {2:22} And no one pours new wine into old wineskins. Otherwise, the wine will burst the skins; and both the wine and the wineskins will be ruined. No, they pour new wine into new wineskins. {2:23} One Sabbath Jesus was going through the grainfields, and his disciples began to pick some heads of grain. {2:24} The Pharisees said to him, "Look! Why are they doing what is unlawful on the Sabbath?" {2:25} He answered, "Have you never read what David did when he and his companions were hungry and in need? {2:26} In the days of Abiathar the high priest, he entered the house of God and ate the consecrated bread, which is lawful only for priests to eat. And he also gave some to his companions." {2:27} Then he said to them, "The Sabbath was made for man, not man for the Sabbath. {2:28} So the Son of Man is Lord even of the Sabbath."

{3:1} Another time Jesus went into the synagogue, and a man with a shriveled hand was there. {3:2} Some of them were looking for a reason to accuse Jesus, so they watched him closely to see if he would heal him on the Sabbath. {3:3} Jesus said to the man with the shriveled hand, "Stand up in front of everyone." {3:4} Then Jesus asked them, "Which is lawful on the Sabbath: to do good or to do evil, to save life or to kill?" But they remained silent. {3:5} He looked around at them in anger and, deeply distressed at their stubborn hearts, said to the man, "Stretch out your hand." He stretched it out, and his hand was completely restored. {3:6} Then the Pharisees went out and began to plot with the Herodians how they might kill Jesus. {3:7} Jesus withdrew with his disciples to the lake, and a large crowd from Galilee followed. {3:8} When they heard about all he was doing, many people came to him from Judea, {3:9} Jerusalem, Idumea, and the regions across the Jordan and around Tyre and Sidon. {3:10} Because he had healed many, those with diseases were pushing forward to touch him. {3:11} Whenever the impure spirits saw him, they fell down before him and cried out, "You are the Son of God." {3:12} But he gave them strict orders not to tell others about him. {3:13} Jesus went up on a mountainside and called to him those he wanted, and they came to him. {3:14} He appointed twelve that they might be with him and that he might send them out to preach {3:15} and to have authority to drive out demons. {3:16} These are the twelve he appointed: Simon (to whom he gave the name Peter), {3:17} James son of Zebedee and his brother John (to them he gave the name

Boanerges, which means "sons of thunder"), {3:18} Andrew, Philip, Bartholomew, Matthew, Thomas, James son of Alphaeus, Thaddaeus, and Simon the Zealot. {3:19} Judas Iscariot, who betrayed him, was one of the twelve. {3:20} Then Jesus entered a house, and again a crowd gathered, so that he and his disciples were not even able to eat. {3:21} When his family heard about this, they went to take charge of him, for they said, "He is out of his mind." {3:22} And the teachers of the law who came down from Jerusalem said, "He is possessed by Beelzebul! By the prince of demons he is driving out demons." {3:23} So Jesus called them over to him and began to speak to them in parables: "How can Satan drive out Satan? {3:24} If a kingdom is divided against itself, that kingdom cannot stand. {3:25} If a house is divided against itself, that house cannot stand. {3:26} And if Satan opposes himself and is divided, he cannot stand; his end has come. {3:27} In fact, no one can enter a strong man's house without first tying him up. Then he can plunder the strong man's house. {3:28} Truly I tell you, people can be forgiven all their sins and every slander they utter, {3:29} but whoever blasphemes against the Holy Spirit will never be forgiven; they are guilty of an eternal sin." {3:30} He said this because they were saying, "He has an impure spirit." {3:31} Then Jesus' mother and brothers arrived. Standing outside, they sent someone in to call him. {3:32} A crowd was sitting around him, and they told him, "Your mother and brothers are outside looking for you." {3:33} "Who are my mother and my brothers?" he asked. {3:34} Then he looked at those seated in a circle around him and said, "Here are my mother and my brothers! {3:35} Whoever does God's will is my brother and sister and mother."

{4:1} Again Jesus began to teach by the lake, and a large crowd gathered around him, so he got into a boat and sat in it while the people were along the shore. {4:2} He taught them many things in parables, saying, {4:3} "Listen! A farmer went out to sow seed. {4:4} As he was scattering the seed, some fell along the path, and the birds came and ate it up. {4:5} Some fell on rocky places, where it didn't have much soil. It sprang up quickly because the soil was shallow. {4:6} But when the sun came up, the plants were scorched, and they withered because they had no root. {4:7} Other seed fell among thorns, which grew up and choked the plants, so they did not bear grain. {4:8} Still, other seed fell on good soil. It came up, grew and produced a crop, multiplying thirty, sixty, or even a hundred times." {4:9} Then Jesus said, "Whoever has ears to hear, let them hear." {4:10} When he was alone, the Twelve and others around him asked him about the parables. {4:11} He told them, "The secret of the kingdom of God has been given to you. But to those on the outside, everything is said in parables, {4:12} so that they may be ever seeing but never perceiving, and ever hearing but never understanding; otherwise, they might turn and be forgiven." {4:13} Then Jesus said to them, "Don't you understand this parable? How then will you understand any parable? {4:14} The farmer sows the word. {4:15} Some people are like seed along the path, where the word is sown. As soon as they hear it, Satan comes and takes away the word that was sown in them. {4:16} Others, like seed sown on rocky places, hear the word and at once receive it with joy. {4:17} But since they have no root, they last only a short time. When trouble or persecution comes because of the word, they quickly fall away. {4:18} Still others, like seed sown among thorns, hear the word; {4:19} but the worries of this life, the deceitfulness of wealth, and the desires for other things come in and choke the word, making it unfruitful. {4:20} Others, like seed sown on good soil, hear the word, accept it, and produce a crop—some thirty, some sixty, some a hundred times what was sown." {4:21} He said to them, "Do you bring in a lamp to put it under a bowl or a bed? Instead, don't you put it on its stand? {4:22} For whatever is hidden is meant to be disclosed, and whatever is concealed is meant to be brought out into the open. {4:23} If anyone has ears to hear, let them hear." {4:24} "Consider carefully what you hear," he continued. "With the measure you use, it will be measured to you—and even more. {4:25} Whoever has will be given more; whoever does not have, even what they think they have will be taken from them." {4:26} He also said, "This is what the kingdom of God is like. A man scatters seed on the ground. {4:27} Night and day, whether he sleeps or gets up, the seed sprouts and grows, though he does not know how. {4:28} All by itself the soil produces grain—first the stalk, then the head, then the full kernel in the head. {4:29} As soon as the grain is ripe, he puts the sickle to it, because the harvest has come." {4:30} Again he said, "What shall we say the kingdom of God is like, or what parable shall we use to describe it? {4:31} It is like a mustard seed, which is the smallest seed you plant in the ground. {4:32} Yet when planted, it grows and becomes the largest of all garden plants, with such big branches that the birds can perch in its shade." {4:33} With many similar parables, Jesus spoke the word to them, as much as they could understand. {4:34} He did not say anything to them without using a parable. But when he was alone with his own disciples, he explained everything. {4:35} That day when evening came, he said to his disciples, "Let's go over to the other side." {4:36} Leaving the crowd behind, they took him along, just as he was, in the boat. There were also other boats with him. {4:37} A furious storm came up, and the waves broke over the boat, so that it was nearly swamped. {4:38} Jesus was in the stern, sleeping on a cushion. The disciples woke him and said to him, "Teacher, don't you care if we drown?" {4:39} He got up, rebuked the wind and said to the waves, "Quiet! Be still!" Then the wind died down and it was completely calm. {4:40} He said to his disciples, "Why are you so afraid? Do you still have no faith?" {4:41} They were terrified and asked each other, "Who is this? Even the wind and the waves obey him!"

{5:1} They went across the lake to the region of the Gerasenes. {5:2} When Jesus got out of the boat, a man with an unclean spirit came from the tombs to meet him. {5:3} This man lived in the tombs, and no one could bind him, not even with chains. {5:4} For he had often been chained hand and foot, but he tore the chains apart and broke the irons on his feet. No one was strong enough to subdue him. {5:5} Night and day among the tombs and in the hills, he would cry out and cut himself with stones. {5:6} When he saw Jesus from a distance, he ran and fell on his knees in front of him. {5:7} He shouted at the top of his voice, "What do you want with me, Jesus, Son of the Most High God? In God's name, don't torture me!" {5:8} For Jesus had said to him, "Come out of this man, you unclean spirit!" {5:9} Then Jesus asked him, "What is your name?" "My name is Legion," he replied, "for we are many." {5:10} And he begged Jesus again and again not to send them out of the area. {5:11} A large herd of pigs was feeding on the nearby hillside. {5:12} The demons begged Jesus, "Send us among the pigs; allow us to go into them." {5:13} He gave them permission, and the unclean spirits came out and went into the pigs. The herd, about two thousand in number, rushed down the steep bank into the lake and were drowned. {5:14} Those tending the pigs ran off and reported this in the town and countryside, and the people went out to see what had happened. {5:15} When they came to Jesus, they saw the man who had been possessed by the legion of demons sitting there, dressed and in his right mind; and they were afraid. {5:16} Those who had seen it told the people what had happened to the demon-possessed man—and about the pigs as well. {5:17} Then the people began to plead with Jesus to leave their region. {5:18} As Jesus was getting into the boat, the man who had been demon-possessed begged to go with him. {5:19} Jesus did not let him, but said, "Go home to your own people and tell them how much the Lord has done for you, and how he has had mercy on you." {5:20} So the man went away and began to tell in the Decapolis (a group of ten cities) how much Jesus had done for him, and all the people were amazed. {5:21} When Jesus had again crossed over by boat to the other side of the lake, a large crowd gathered around him while he was by the lake. {5:22} Then one of the synagogue leaders, named Jairus, came, and when he saw Jesus, he fell at his feet. {5:23} He pleaded earnestly with him, "My little daughter is dying. Please come and put your hands on her so she will be healed and live." {5:24} So Jesus went with him. A large crowd followed and pressed around him. {5:25} And a woman was there who had been subject to bleeding for twelve years. {5:26} She had suffered a great deal under the care of many doctors and had spent all she had, yet instead of getting better, she grew worse. {5:27} When she heard about Jesus, she came up behind him in the crowd and touched his cloak, {5:28} because she thought, "If I just touch his clothes, I will be healed." {5:29} Immediately her bleeding stopped, and she felt in her body that she was freed from her suffering. {5:30} At once, Jesus realized that power had gone out from him. He turned around in the crowd and asked, "Who touched my clothes?" {5:31} "You see the people crowding against you," his disciples answered, "and yet you can ask, 'Who touched me?'" {5:32} But Jesus kept looking around to see who had done it. {5:33} Then the woman, knowing what had happened to her, came and fell at his feet and, trembling with fear, told him the whole truth. {5:34} He said to her, "Daughter, your faith has healed you. Go in peace and be freed from your suffering." {5:35} While Jesus was still speaking, some people came from the house of Jairus, the synagogue leader. "Your daughter is dead," they said. "Why bother the teacher anymore?" {5:36} Overhearing what they said, Jesus told him, "Don't be afraid; just believe." {5:37} He did not let anyone follow him except Peter, James, and John, the brother of James. {5:38} When they came to the home of the synagogue leader, Jesus saw a commotion, with people crying and wailing loudly. {5:39} He went in and said to them, "Why all this commotion and wailing? The child is not dead but asleep." {5:40} But they laughed at him. After he put them all out, he took the child's father and mother and the disciples who were with him and went in where the child was. {5:41} He took her by the hand and said to her, "Talitha koum!" (which means "Little girl, I say to you, get up!"). {5:42} Immediately the girl stood up and began to walk around (she was twelve years old). At this they were completely astonished. {5:43} He gave them strict orders not to let anyone know about this and told them to give her something to eat.

{6:1} Jesus left there and went to his hometown, accompanied by his disciples. {6:2} When the Sabbath came, he began to teach in the synagogue, and many who heard him were amazed. They asked, "Where did this man get these things? What wisdom is this that has been given to him, that he even performs such miracles?" {6:3} "Isn't this the carpenter, the son of Mary, and the brother of James, Joses, Judas, and Simon? Aren't his sisters here with us?" And they took offense at him. {6:4} Jesus said to them, "A prophet is not without honor except in his own town, among his relatives, and in his own home." {6:5} He could not do any miracles there, except lay his hands on a few sick people and heal them. {6:6} He was amazed at their lack of faith. Then he went around teaching from village to village. {6:7} Calling the Twelve to him, he began to send them out two by two and gave them authority over unclean spirits. {6:8} These were his instructions: "Take nothing for the journey except a staff—no bread, no bag, no money in your belts. {6:9} Wear sandals, but not an extra tunic. {6:10} Whenever you enter a house, stay there until you leave that town. {6:11} And if any place will not welcome you or listen to you, leave that place and shake the dust off your feet as a testimony against them. Truly I tell you, it will be more bearable for Sodom and Gomorrah on the Day of Judgment than for that town." {6:12} They went out and preached that people should repent. {6:13} They drove out many demons and anointed many sick people with oil and healed them. {6:14} King Herod heard about this, for Jesus' name had become well known. Some were saying, "John the Baptist has been raised from the dead, and that is why miraculous powers are at work in him." {6:15} Others said, "He is Elijah." Still others claimed, "He is a prophet, like one of the prophets." {6:16} But when Herod heard this, he said, "John, whom I beheaded, has been raised from the dead!" {6:17} For Herod himself had given orders to have John arrested, and he had him bound and put in prison. He did this because of Herodias, his brother Philip's wife, whom he had married. {6:18} For John had been saying to Herod, "It is not lawful for you to have your brother's wife." {6:19} So Herodias nursed a grudge against John and wanted to kill him, but she was not able to, {6:20} because Herod feared John and protected him, knowing him to be a righteous and holy man. When Herod heard John, he was greatly puzzled; yet he liked to listen to him. {6:21} Finally, the opportune time came. On his birthday, Herod gave a banquet for his high officials and military commanders and the leading men of Galilee. {6:22} When the daughter of Herodias came in and danced, she pleased Herod and his dinner guests. The king said to the girl, "Ask me for anything you want, and I'll give it to you." {6:23} And he promised her with an oath, "Whatever you ask, I will give you, up to half my kingdom." {6:24} She went out and said to her mother, "What shall I ask for?" "The head of John the Baptist," she answered. {6:25} At once, the girl hurried in to the king with the request: "I want you to give me right now the head of John the Baptist on a platter." {6:26} The king was greatly distressed, but because of his oaths and his dinner guests, he did not want to refuse her. {6:27} So he immediately sent an executioner with orders to bring John's head. The man went, beheaded John in the prison, {6:28} and brought back his head on a platter. He presented it to the girl, and she gave it to her mother. {6:29} On hearing this, John's disciples came and took his body and laid it in a tomb. {6:30} The apostles gathered around Jesus and reported to him all they had done and taught. {6:31} Then, because so many people were coming and going that they did not even have a chance to eat, he said to them, "Come with me by yourselves to a quiet place and get some rest." {6:32} So they went away by themselves in a boat to a solitary place. {6:33} But many who saw them leaving recognized them and ran on foot from all the towns and got there ahead of them. {6:34} When Jesus landed and saw a large crowd, he had compassion on them, because they were like sheep without a shepherd. So he began teaching them many things. {6:35} By this time it was late in the day, so his disciples came to him. "This is a remote place," they said, "and it's already very late. {6:36} Send the people away so that they can go to the surrounding countryside and villages and buy themselves something to eat." {6:37} But he answered, "You give them something to eat." They said to him, "That would take more than half a year's wages! Are we to go and spend that much on bread and give it to them to eat?" {6:38} "How many loaves do you have?" he asked. "Go and see." When they found out, they said, "Five—and two fish." {6:39} Then Jesus directed them to have all the people sit down in groups on the green grass. {6:40} So they sat down in groups of hundreds and fifties. {6:41} Taking the five loaves and the two fish and looking up to heaven, he gave thanks and broke the loaves. Then he gave them to his disciples to distribute to the people. He also divided the two fish among them all. {6:42} They all ate and were satisfied, {6:43} and the disciples picked up twelve basketfuls of broken pieces of bread and fish. {6:44} The number of the men who had eaten was five thousand. {6:45} Immediately, Jesus made his disciples get into the boat and go on ahead of him to Bethsaida, while he dismissed the crowd. {6:46} After leaving them, he went up on a mountainside to pray. {6:47} Later that night, the boat was in the middle of the lake, and he was alone on land. {6:48} He saw the disciples straining at the oars because the wind was against them. Shortly before dawn, he went out to them, walking on the lake. He was about to pass by them, {6:49} but when they saw him walking on the lake, they thought he was a ghost. They cried out, {6:50} because they all saw him and were terrified. Immediately, he spoke to them and said, "Take courage! It is I. Don't be afraid." {6:51} Then he climbed into the boat with them, and the wind died down. They were completely amazed, {6:52} for they had not understood about the loaves; their hearts were hardened. {6:53} When they had crossed over, they landed at Gennesaret and anchored there. {6:54} As soon as they got out of the boat, people recognized Jesus. {6:55} They ran throughout that whole region and carried the sick on mats to wherever they heard he was. {6:56} And wherever he went—into villages, towns, or countryside—they placed the sick in the marketplaces. They begged him to let them touch even the edge of his cloak, and all who touched it were healed.

{7:1} The Pharisees and some of the scribes who had come from Jerusalem gathered around Jesus. {7:2} They noticed that some of his disciples were eating bread with defiled, that is, unwashed hands, and they criticized them. {7:3} The Pharisees and all the Jews, unless they wash their hands often, do not eat, holding to the tradition of the elders. {7:4} When they come from the marketplace, they do not eat unless they wash first. They also follow many other traditions, such as the washing of cups, pots, copper vessels, and tables. {7:5} So the Pharisees and scribes asked Jesus, "Why don't your disciples live according to the tradition of the elders instead of eating bread with unwashed hands?" {7:6} He replied, "Isaiah was right when he prophesied about you hypocrites; as it is written: 'These people honor me with their lips, but their hearts are far from me. {7:7} They worship me in vain; their teachings are merely human rules.' {7:8} You have let go of the commands of God and are holding on to human traditions, such as the washing of pots and cups. You do many things like that." {7:9} He continued, "You have a fine way of rejecting the commands of God in order to keep your own tradition! {7:10} For Moses said, 'Honor your father and mother,' and 'Anyone who curses their father or mother is to be put to death.' {7:11} But you say that if anyone declares that what might have been used to help their father or mother is Corban (which means devoted to God), then they no longer let them do anything for their father or mother. {7:12}

Thus you nullify the word of God by your tradition that you have handed down. And you do many things like that." {7:13} Again Jesus called the crowd to him and said, "Listen to me, everyone, and understand this: {7:14} Nothing outside a person can defile them by going into them. Rather, it is what comes out of a person that defiles them." {7:15} If anyone has ears to hear, let them hear. {7:16} After he had left the crowd and entered the house, his disciples asked him about this parable. {7:17} "Are you so dull?" he asked. "Don't you see that nothing that enters a person from the outside can defile them? {7:18} For it doesn't go into their heart but into their stomach, and then out of the body." (In saying this, Jesus declared all foods clean.) {7:19} He went on: "What comes out of a person is what defiles them. {7:20} For it is from within, out of a person's heart, that evil thoughts come—sexual immorality, theft, murder, {7:21} adultery, greed, malice, deceit, lewdness, envy, slander, arrogance, and folly. {7:22} All these evils come from inside and defile a person." {7:23} Jesus left that place and went to the region of Tyre. He entered a house and did not want anyone to know it; yet he could not keep his presence secret. {7:24} In fact, as soon as she heard about him, a woman whose little daughter was possessed by an impure spirit came and fell at his feet. {7:25} The woman was a Greek, born in Syrian Phoenicia. She begged Jesus to drive the demon out of her daughter. {7:26} "First let the children eat all they want," he told her, "for it is not right to take the children's bread and toss it to the dogs." {7:27} "Lord," she replied, "even the dogs under the table eat the children's crumbs." {7:28} Then he told her, "For such a reply, you may go; the demon has left your daughter." {7:29} She went home and found her child lying on the bed, and the demon gone. {7:30} Then Jesus left the vicinity of Tyre and went through Sidon, down to the Sea of Galilee and into the region of the Decapolis. {7:31} There some people brought to him a man who was deaf and could hardly talk, and they begged Jesus to place his hand on him. {7:32} After he took him aside, away from the crowd, Jesus put his fingers in the man's ears. Then he spit and touched the man's tongue. {7:33} He looked up to heaven and with a deep sigh said to him, "Ephphatha!" (which means "Be opened!"). {7:34} At this, the man's ears were opened, his tongue was loosened, and he began to speak plainly. {7:35} Jesus commanded them not to tell anyone. But the more he did so, the more they kept talking about it. {7:36} People were overwhelmed with amazement. "He has done everything well," they said. "He even makes deaf hear & mute speak."

{8:1} During those days another large crowd gathered. Since they had nothing to eat, Jesus called his disciples to him and said, {8:2} "I have compassion for these people; they have already been with me three days and have nothing to eat. {8:3} If I send them home hungry, they will collapse on the way, because some of them have come a long distance." {8:4} His disciples answered, "But where in this remote place can anyone get enough bread to feed them?" {8:5} "How many loaves do you have?" Jesus asked. "Seven," they replied. {8:6} He told the crowd to sit down on the ground. When he had taken the seven loaves and given thanks, he broke them and gave them to his disciples to distribute to the people, and they did so. {8:7} They had a few small fish as well; he gave thanks for them also and told the disciples to distribute them. {8:8} The people ate and were satisfied. Afterward, the disciples picked up seven basketfuls of broken pieces that were left over. {8:9} About four thousand were present. After he had sent them away, {8:10} he got into the boat with his disciples and went to the region of Dalmanutha. {8:11} The Pharisees came and began to question Jesus. To test him, they asked for a sign from heaven. {8:12} He sighed deeply and said, "Why does this generation ask for a sign? Truly I tell you, no sign will be given to it." {8:13} Then he left them, got back into the boat and crossed to the other side. {8:14} The disciples had forgotten to bring bread, except for one loaf they had with them in the boat. {8:15} "Be careful," Jesus warned them. "Watch out for the yeast of the Pharisees and that of Herod." {8:16} They discussed this with one another and said, "It is because we have no bread." {8:17} Aware of their discussion, Jesus asked them: "Why are you talking about having no bread? Do you still not see or understand? Are your hearts hardened? {8:18} Do you have eyes but fail to see, and ears but fail to hear? And don't you remember? {8:19} When I broke the five loaves for the five thousand, how many basketfuls of pieces did you pick up?" "Twelve," they replied. {8:20} "And when I broke the seven loaves for the four thousand, how many basketfuls of pieces did you pick up?" They answered, "Seven." {8:21} He said to them, "Do you still not understand?" {8:22} They came to Bethsaida, and some people brought a blind man and begged Jesus to touch him. {8:23} He took the blind man by the hand and led him outside the village. When he had spat on the man's eyes and put his hands on him, Jesus asked, "Do you see anything?" {8:24} He looked up and said, "I see people; they look like trees walking around." {8:25} Once more, Jesus put his hands on the man's eyes. Then his eyes were opened, his sight was restored, and he saw everything clearly. {8:26} Jesus sent him home, saying, "Don't go into the village." {8:27} Jesus and his disciples went on to the villages around Caesarea Philippi. On the way, he asked them, "Who do people say I am?" {8:28} They replied, "Some say John the Baptist; others say Elijah; and still others, one of the prophets." {8:29} "But what about you?" he asked. "Who do you say I am?" Peter answered, "You are the Messiah." {8:30} Jesus warned them not to tell anyone about him. {8:31} He then began to teach them that the Son of Man must suffer many things and be rejected by the elders, the chief priests, and the teachers of the law, and that he must be killed and after three days rise again. {8:32} He spoke plainly about this, and Peter took him aside and began to rebuke him. {8:33} But when Jesus turned and looked at his disciples, he rebuked Peter. "Get behind me, Satan!" he said. "You do not have in mind the concerns of God, but merely human concerns." {8:34} Then he called the crowd to him along with his disciples and said: "Whoever wants to be my disciple must deny themselves and take up their cross and follow me. {8:35} For whoever wants to save their life will lose it, but whoever loses their life for me and for the gospel will save it. {8:36} What good is it for someone to gain the whole world, yet forfeit their soul? {8:37} Or what can anyone give in exchange for their soul? {8:38} If anyone is ashamed of me and my words in this adulterous and sinful generation, the Son of Man will be ashamed of them when he comes in his Father's glory with the holy angels."

{9:1} Jesus said to them, "Truly I tell you, some of those standing here will not taste death before they see the kingdom of God come with power." {9:2} After six days, Jesus took Peter, James, and John and led them up a high mountain, where they were alone. He was transfigured before them. {9:3} His clothes became dazzling white, whiter than anyone on earth could bleach them. {9:4} Elijah and Moses appeared and were talking with Jesus. {9:5} Peter said to Jesus, "Rabbi, it's good for us to be here. Let's put up three shelters—one for you, one for Moses, and one for Elijah." {9:6} He didn't know what to say, because they were so frightened. {9:7} Then a cloud appeared and covered them, and a voice came from the cloud: "This is my Son, whom I love. Listen to him!" {9:8} Suddenly, when they looked around, they no longer saw anyone with them except Jesus. {9:9} As they were coming down the mountain, Jesus gave them orders not to tell anyone what they had seen until the Son of Man had risen from the dead. {9:10} They kept the matter to themselves, discussing what "rising from the dead" meant. {9:11} They asked him, "Why do the teachers of the law say that Elijah must come first?" {9:12} Jesus replied, "To be sure, Elijah does come first, and restores all things. Why then is it written that the Son of Man must suffer much and be rejected? {9:13} But I tell you, Elijah has already come, and they have done to him everything they wished, just as it is written about him." {9:14} When they came to the other disciples, they saw a large crowd around them and the teachers of the law arguing with them. {9:15} As soon as all the people saw Jesus, they were overwhelmed with wonder and ran to greet him. {9:16} "What are you arguing with them about?" he asked. {9:17} A man in the crowd answered, "Teacher, I brought you my son, who is possessed by a spirit that has robbed him of speech. {9:18} Whenever it seizes him, it throws him to the ground. He foams at the mouth, gnashes his teeth, and becomes rigid. I asked your disciples to drive out the spirit, but they could not." {9:19} "You unbelieving generation," Jesus replied. "How long shall I stay with you? How long shall I put up with you? Bring the boy to me." {9:20} So they brought him. When the spirit saw Jesus, it immediately threw the boy into a convulsion. He fell to the ground and rolled around, foaming at the mouth. {9:21} Jesus asked the boy's father, "How long has he been like this?" "From childhood," he answered. {9:22} "It has often thrown him into fire or water to kill him. But if you can do anything, take pity on us and help us." {9:23} "If you can?" said Jesus. "Everything is possible for one who believes." {9:24}

Immediately the boy's father exclaimed, "I do believe; help me overcome my unbelief!" {9:25} When Jesus saw that a crowd was running to the scene, he rebuked the impure spirit. "You deaf and mute spirit," he said, "I command you, come out of him and never enter him again." {9:26} The spirit shrieked, convulsed him violently, and came out. The boy looked so much like a corpse that many said, "He's dead." {9:27} But Jesus took him by the hand and lifted him to his feet, and he stood up. {9:28} After Jesus had gone indoors, his disciples asked him privately, "Why couldn't we drive it out?" {9:29} He replied, "This kind can come out only by prayer and fasting." {9:30} They left that place and passed through Galilee. Jesus did not want anyone to know where they were, {9:31} because he was teaching his disciples. He said to them, "The Son of Man is going to be delivered into the hands of men. They will kill him, and after three days he will rise." {9:32} But they did not understand what he meant and were afraid to ask him about it. {9:33} They came to Capernaum. When he was in the house, he asked them, "What were you arguing about on the road?" {9:34} But they kept quiet because on the way they had argued about who was the greatest. {9:35} Sitting down, Jesus called the Twelve and said, "Anyone who wants to be first must be the very last, and the servant of all." {9:36} He took a little child whom he placed among them. Taking the child in his arms, he said to them, {9:37} "Whoever welcomes one of these little children in my name welcomes me; and whoever welcomes me does not welcome me but the one who sent me." {9:38} "Teacher," said John, "we saw someone driving out demons in your name and we told him to stop, because he was not one of us." {9:39} "Do not stop him," Jesus said. "No one who does a miracle in my name can in the next moment say anything bad about me, {9:40} for whoever is not against us is for us. {9:41} Truly I tell you, anyone who gives you a cup of water in my name because you belong to the Messiah will certainly not lose their reward. {9:42} If anyone causes one of these little ones—those who believe in me—to stumble, it would be better for them if a large millstone were hung around their neck and they were thrown into the sea. {9:43} If your hand causes you to stumble, cut it off. It is better for you to enter life maimed than with two hands to go into hell, where the fire never goes out. {9:44} (This verse is not included in some manuscripts.) {9:45} And if your foot causes you to stumble, cut it off. It is better for you to enter life crippled than to have two feet and be thrown into hell. {9:46} (This verse is not included in some manuscripts.) {9:47} And if your eye causes you to stumble, pluck it out. It is better for you to enter the kingdom of God with one eye than to have two eyes and be thrown into hell, {9:48} where "the worms that eat them do not die, and the fire is not quenched." {9:49} Everyone will be salted with fire. {9:50} Salt is good, but if it loses its saltiness, how can you make it salty again? Have salt among yourselves, and be at peace with each other.

{10:1} Jesus then left that place and went into the region of Judea and across the Jordan. Again crowds of people came to him, and as was his custom, he taught them. {10:2} Some Pharisees came and tested him by asking, "Is it lawful for a man to divorce his wife?" {10:3} "What did Moses command you?" he replied. {10:4} They said, "Moses permitted a man to write a certificate of divorce and send her away." {10:5} "It was because your hearts were hard that Moses wrote you this law," Jesus replied. {10:6} "But at the beginning of creation God 'made them male and female.' {10:7} For this reason, a man will leave his father and mother {10:8} and be united to his wife, and the two will become one flesh.' So they are no longer two, but one flesh. {10:9} Therefore what God has joined together, let no one separate." {10:10} When they were in the house again, the disciples asked Jesus about this. {10:11} He answered, "Anyone who divorces his wife and marries another woman commits adultery against her. {10:12} And if she divorces her husband and marries another man, she commits adultery." {10:13} People were bringing little children to Jesus for him to place his hands on them, but the disciples rebuked them. {10:14} When Jesus saw this, he was indignant. He said to them, "Let the little children come to me and do not hinder them, for the kingdom of God belongs to such as these. {10:15} Truly I tell you, anyone who will not receive the kingdom of God like a little child will never enter it." {10:16} And he took the children in his arms, placed his hands on them, and blessed them. {10:17} As Jesus started on his way, a man ran up to him and fell on his knees before him. "Good teacher," he asked, "what must I do to inherit eternal life?" {10:18} "Why do you call me good?" Jesus answered. "No one is good—except God alone. {10:19} You know the commandments: 'You shall not murder, you shall not commit adultery, you shall not steal, you shall not give false testimony, you shall not defraud, honor your father and mother.'" {10:20} "Teacher," he declared, "all these I have kept since I was a boy." {10:21} Jesus looked at him and loved him. "One thing you lack," he said. "Go, sell everything you have and give to the poor, and you will have treasure in heaven. Then come, follow me." {10:22} At this the man's face fell. He went away sad because he had great wealth. {10:23} Jesus looked around and said to his disciples, "How hard it is for the rich to enter the kingdom of God!" {10:24} The disciples were amazed at his words. But Jesus said again, "Children, how hard it is to enter the kingdom of God! {10:25} It is easier for a camel to go through the eye of a needle than for someone who is rich to enter the kingdom of God." {10:26} The disciples were even more amazed and said to each other, "Who then can be saved?" {10:27} Jesus looked at them and said, "With man this is impossible, but not with God; all things are possible with God." {10:28} Then Peter spoke up, "We have left everything to follow you!" {10:29} "Truly I tell you," Jesus replied, "no one who has left home or brothers or sisters or mother or father or children or fields for me and the gospel {10:30} will fail to receive a hundred times as much in this present age—homes, brothers, sisters, mothers, children and fields—along with persecutions—and in the age to come eternal life. {10:31} But many who are first will be last, and the last first." {10:32} They were on their way up to Jerusalem, with Jesus leading the way, and the disciples were astonished, while those who followed were afraid. Again he took the Twelve aside and told them what was going to happen to him. {10:33} "We are going up to Jerusalem," he said, "and the Son of Man will be delivered over to the chief priests and the teachers of the law. They will condemn him to death and will hand him over to the Gentiles, {10:34} who will mock him and spit on him, flog him and kill him. Three days later he will rise." {10:35} Then James and John, the sons of Zebedee, came to him. "Teacher," they said, "we want you to do for us whatever we ask." {10:36} "What do you want me to do for you?" he asked. {10:37} They replied, "Let one of us sit at your right and the other at your left in your glory." {10:38} "You don't know what you are asking," Jesus said. "Can you drink the cup I drink or be baptized with the baptism I am baptized with?" {10:39} "We can," they answered. Jesus said to them, "You will drink the cup I drink and be baptized with the baptism I am baptized with, {10:40} but to sit at my right or left is not for me to grant. These places belong to those for whom they have been prepared." {10:41} When the ten heard about this, they became indignant with James and John. {10:42} Jesus called them together and said, "You know that those who are regarded as rulers of the Gentiles lord it over them, and their high officials exercise authority over them. {10:43} Not so with you. Instead, whoever wants to become great among you must be your servant, {10:44} and whoever wants to be first must be slave of all. {10:45} For even the Son of Man did not come to be served, but to serve, and to give his life as a ransom for many." {10:46} Then they came to Jericho. As Jesus and his disciples, together with a large crowd, were leaving the city, a blind man, Bartimaeus (which means "son of Timaeus"), was sitting by the roadside begging. {10:47} When he heard that it was Jesus of Nazareth, he began to shout, "Jesus, Son of David, have mercy on me!" {10:48} Many rebuked him and told him to be quiet, but he shouted all the more, "Son of David, have mercy on me!" {10:49} Jesus stopped and said, "Call him." So they called to the blind man, "Cheer up! On your feet! He's calling you." {10:50} Throwing his cloak aside, he jumped to his feet and came to Jesus. {10:51} "What do you want me to do for you?" Jesus asked him. The blind man said, "Rabbi, I want to see." {10:52} "Go," said Jesus, "your faith has healed you." Immediately he received his sight and followed Jesus along the road.

{11:1} As they approached Jerusalem, near Bethphage and Bethany at the Mount of Olives, Jesus sent two of his disciples ahead. {11:2} He told them, "Go to the village ahead of you. As soon as you enter, you'll find a colt tied there, one that no one has ever ridden. Untie it and bring it here. {11:3} If anyone asks you, 'Why are you doing this?' say that the Lord needs it, and he will send it back shortly." {11:4} They went and found the colt tied at a doorway on the street, and they untied it. {11:5} Some people standing there asked, "What are you doing, untying that colt?" {11:6} They answered as Jesus had told them, and the people let them go. {11:7} They brought the colt to Jesus and threw their cloaks over it, and he sat on it. {11:8} Many people spread their cloaks on the road, while others spread branches they had cut in the fields. {11:9} Those who went ahead and those who followed shouted, "Hosanna! Blessed is he who comes in the name of the Lord! {11:10} Blessed is the coming kingdom of our father David! Hosanna in the highest heaven!" {11:11} Jesus entered Jerusalem and went into the temple courts. He looked around at everything, but since it was already late, he went out to Bethany with the Twelve. {11:12} The next day, as they were leaving Bethany, Jesus was hungry. {11:13} Seeing in the distance a fig tree in leaf, he went to find out if it had any fruit. When he reached it, he found nothing but leaves, because it was not the season for figs. {11:14} Then he said to the tree, "May no one ever eat fruit from you again." And his disciples heard him say it. {11:15} On reaching Jerusalem, Jesus entered the temple and began driving out those who were buying and selling there. He overturned the tables of the money changers and the benches of those selling doves, {11:16} and would not allow anyone to carry merchandise through the temple courts. {11:17} And as he taught them, he said, "Is it not written: 'My house will be called a house of prayer for all nations'? But you have made it a den of robbers.'" {11:18} The chief priests and the teachers of the law heard this and began looking for a way to kill him, for they feared him, because the whole crowd was amazed at his teaching. {11:19} When evening came, Jesus and his disciples went out of the city. {11:20} In the morning, as they went along, they saw the fig tree withered from the roots. {11:21} Peter remembered and said to Jesus, "Rabbi, look! The fig tree you cursed has withered!" {11:22} "Have faith in God," Jesus answered. {11:23} "Truly I tell you, if anyone says to this mountain, 'Go, throw yourself into the sea,' and does not doubt in their heart but believes that what they say will happen, it will be done for them. {11:24} Therefore I tell you, whatever you ask for in prayer, believe that you have received it, and it will be yours. {11:25} And when you stand praying, if you hold anything against anyone, forgive them, so that your Father in heaven may forgive you your sins." {11:26} (This verse is not included in some manuscripts.) {11:27} They arrived again in Jerusalem, and while Jesus was walking in the temple courts, the chief priests, the teachers of the law, and the elders came to him. {11:28} "By what authority are you doing these things?" they asked. "Who gave you the authority to do this?" {11:29} Jesus replied, "I will ask you one question. Answer me, and I will tell you by what authority I am doing these things. {11:30} John's baptism—was it from heaven, or of human origin? Tell me!" {11:31} They discussed it among themselves and said, "If we say, 'From heaven,' he will ask, 'Then why didn't you believe him?' {11:32} But if we say, 'Of human origin'..." (They feared the people, for everyone held that John really was a prophet.) {11:33} So they answered Jesus, "We don't know." Jesus said, "Neither will I tell you by what authority I am doing these things."

{12:1} Then Jesus began to speak to them in parables: "A man planted a vineyard. He put a wall around it, dug a pit for the winepress, and built a watchtower. Then he rented the vineyard to some farmers and went away on a journey. {12:2} At harvest time, he sent a servant to the tenants to collect from them some of the fruit of the vineyard. {12:3} But they seized him, beat him, and sent him away empty-handed. {12:4} Then he sent another servant to them; they struck this man on the head and treated him shamefully. {12:5} He sent still another, and that one they killed. He sent many others; some of them they beat, others they killed. {12:6} He had one left to send, a son whom he loved. He sent him last of all, saying, 'They will respect my son.' {12:7} But the tenants said to one another, 'This is the heir. Come, let's kill him, and the inheritance will be ours.' {12:8} So they took him and killed him, and threw him out of the vineyard. {12:9} What then will the owner of the vineyard do? He will come and kill those tenants and give the vineyard to others. {12:10} Haven't you read this passage of Scripture: 'The stone the builders rejected has become the cornerstone; {12:11} the Lord has done this, and it is marvelous in our eyes'?" {12:12} Then the chief priests, the teachers of the law, and the elders looked for a way to arrest him because they knew he had spoken the parable against them. But they were afraid of the crowd, so they left him and went away. {12:13} Later they sent some of the Pharisees and Herodians to Jesus to catch him in his words. {12:14} "Teacher," they said, "we know you are a man of integrity. You aren't swayed by others because you pay no attention to who they are, but you teach the way of God in accordance with the truth. Is it right to pay the imperial tax to Caesar or not? {12:15} Should we pay or shouldn't we?" But Jesus knew their hypocrisy. "Why are you trying to trap me?" he asked. "Bring me a denarius (a coin), and let me look at it." {12:16} They brought the coin, and he asked them, "Whose image is this? And whose inscription?" "Caesar's," they replied. {12:17} Jesus said to them, "Give back to Caesar what is Caesar's and to God what is God's." And they were amazed at him. {12:18} Then the Sadducees, who say there is no resurrection, came to him with a question. {12:19} "Teacher," they said, "Moses wrote for us that if a man's brother dies and leaves a wife but no children, the man must marry the widow and raise up offspring for his brother. {12:20} Now there were seven brothers. The first one married and died without leaving any children. {12:21} The second one married the widow, but he also died, leaving no child. It was the same with the third. {12:22} In fact, none of the seven left any children. Last of all, the woman died too. {12:23} At the resurrection, whose wife will she be, since the seven were married to her?" {12:24} Jesus replied, "Are you not in error because you do not know the Scriptures or the power of God? {12:25} When the dead rise, they will neither marry nor be given in marriage; they will be like the angels in heaven. {12:26} Now about the dead rising: have you not read in the Book of Moses, in the account of the bush, how God said to him, 'I am the God of Abraham, the God of Isaac, and the God of Jacob'? {12:27} He is not the God of the dead, but of the living. You are badly mistaken!" {12:28} One of the teachers of the law came and heard them debating. Noticing that Jesus had given them a good answer, he asked him, "Of all the commandments, which is the most important?" {12:29} "The most important one," answered Jesus, "is this: 'Hear, O Israel: The Lord our God, the Lord is one. {12:30} Love the Lord your God with all your heart and with all your soul and with all your mind and with all your strength.' {12:31} The second is this: 'Love your neighbor as yourself.' There is no commandment greater than these." {12:32} "Well said, teacher," the man replied. "You are right in saying that God is one and there is no other but him. {12:33} To love him with all your heart, with all your understanding, with all your strength, and to love your neighbor as yourself is more important than all burnt offerings and sacrifices." {12:34} When Jesus saw that he had answered wisely, he said to him, "You are not far from the kingdom of God." And from then on, no one dared ask him any more questions. {12:35} While Jesus was teaching in the temple courts, he asked, "Why do the teachers of the law say that the Messiah is the son of David? {12:36} David himself, speaking by the Holy Spirit, declared: 'The Lord said to my Lord: Sit at my right hand until I put your enemies under your feet.' {12:37} David himself calls him 'Lord.' How then can he be his son?" The large crowd listened to him with delight. {12:38} As he taught, Jesus said, "Watch out for the teachers of the law. They like to walk around in flowing robes and be greeted with respect in the marketplaces, {12:39} and have the most important seats in the synagogues and the places of honor at banquets. {12:40} They devour widows' houses and for a show make lengthy prayers. These men will be punished most severely." {12:41} Jesus sat down opposite the place where the offerings were put and watched the crowd putting money into the temple treasury. Many rich people threw in large amounts. {12:42} But a poor widow came and put in two very small copper coins, worth only a few cents. {12:43} Calling his disciples to him, Jesus said, "Truly I tell you, this poor widow has put more into the treasury than all the others. {12:44} They all gave out of their wealth, but she, out of her poverty, put in everything—all she had to live on."

{13:1} As Jesus was leaving the temple, one of his disciples said to him, "Look, Teacher! What massive stones! What impressive buildings!" {13:2} Jesus replied, "Do you see these great buildings? Not one stone will be left on another; every one will be thrown down." {13:3} As Jesus sat on the Mount of Olives, opposite the temple, Peter, James, John, and Andrew asked him privately, {13:4} "Tell us, when will these things happen? And what will be the sign that they are about to be fulfilled?" {13:5} Jesus said to them, "Watch out that no one deceives you. {13:6} Many will come in my name, claiming, 'I am he,' and will deceive many. {13:7} When you hear of wars and rumors of wars, don't be alarmed. Such things must happen, but the end is still to come. {13:8} Nation will rise against nation, and kingdom against kingdom. There will be earthquakes in various places, and famines. These are the beginning of birth pains. {13:9} You must be on your guard; you will be handed over to the local councils and flogged in the synagogues. On account of me, you will stand before governors and kings as witnesses to them. {13:10} And the gospel must first be preached to all nations. {13:11} Whenever you are arrested and brought to trial, do not worry beforehand about what to say. Just say whatever is given you at the time, for it is not you speaking, but the Holy Spirit. {13:12} Brother will betray brother to death, and a father his child. Children will rebel against their parents and have them put to death. {13:13} Everyone will hate you because of me, but the one who stands firm to the end will be saved. {13:14} When you see the 'abomination that causes desolation' standing where it does not belong—let the reader understand—then let those who are in Judea flee to the mountains. {13:15} Let no one on the housetop go down or enter the house to take anything out. {13:16} Let no one in the field go back to get their cloak. {13:17} How dreadful it will be in those days for pregnant women and nursing mothers! {13:18} Pray that this will not take place in winter, {13:19} because those will be days of distress unequaled from the beginning when God created the world until now—and never to be equaled again. {13:20} If the Lord had not cut short those days, no one would survive, but for the sake of the elect, whom he has chosen, he has shortened them. {13:21} At that time if anyone says to you, 'Look, here is the Messiah!' or, 'Look, there he is!' do not believe it. {13:22} For false messiahs and false prophets will appear and perform signs and wonders to deceive, if possible, even the elect. {13:23} So be on your guard; I have told you everything in advance. {13:24} But in those days, following that distress, the sun will be darkened, and the moon will not give its light; {13:25} the stars will fall from the sky, and the heavenly bodies will be shaken. {13:26} At that time, people will see the Son of Man coming in clouds with great power and glory. {13:27} And he will send his angels and gather his elect from the four winds, from the ends of the earth to the ends of the heavens. {13:28} Now learn this lesson from the fig tree: As soon as its twigs get tender and its leaves come out, you know that summer is near. {13:29} Even so, when you see these things happening, you know that it is near, right at the door. {13:30} Truly I tell you, this generation will certainly not pass away until all these things have happened. {13:31} Heaven and earth will pass away, but my words will never pass away. {13:32} But about that day or hour, no one knows, not even the angels in heaven, nor the Son, but only the Father. {13:33} Be on guard! Be alert! You do not know when that time will come. {13:34} It's like a man going away: he leaves his house and puts his servants in charge, each with their assigned task, and tells the one at the door to keep watch. {13:35} Therefore keep watch because you do not know when the owner of the house will come back—whether in evening, or at midnight, or when the rooster crows, or at dawn. {13:36} If he comes suddenly, don't let him find you sleeping. {13:37} What I say to you, I say to everyone: Watch!"

{14:1} Now the Passover and the Festival of Unleavened Bread were only two days away, and the chief priests and the teachers of the law were scheming to arrest Jesus secretly and kill him. {14:2} "But not during the festival," they said, "or the people may riot." {14:3} While he was in Bethany, reclining at the table in the home of Simon the leper, a woman came with an alabaster jar of very expensive perfume made of pure nard. She broke the jar and poured the perfume on his head. {14:4} Some of those present were saying indignantly to one another, "Why this waste? {14:5} It could have been sold for more than a year's wages and the money given to the poor." And they rebuked her harshly. {14:6} "Leave her alone," said Jesus. "Why are you bothering her? She has done a beautiful thing for me. {14:7} The poor you will always have with you, and you can help them anytime you want. But you will not always have me. {14:8} She did what she could. She poured perfume on my body beforehand to prepare for my burial. {14:9} Truly I tell you, wherever the gospel is preached throughout the world, what she has done will also be told in memory of her." {14:10} Then Judas Iscariot, one of the Twelve, went to the chief priests to betray Jesus to them. {14:11} They were delighted to hear this and promised to give him money. So he watched for an opportunity to hand him over. {14:12} On the first day of the Festival of Unleavened Bread, when it was customary to sacrifice the Passover lamb, Jesus' disciples asked him, "Where do you want us to go and make preparations for you to eat the Passover?" {14:13} He sent two of his disciples, telling them, "Go into the city, and a man carrying a jar of water will meet you. Follow him. {14:14} Say to the owner of the house he enters, 'The Teacher asks: Where is my guest room, where I may eat the Passover with my disciples?' {14:15} He will show you a large upper room, furnished and ready. Make preparations for us there." {14:16} The disciples left, went into the city, and found things just as Jesus had told them. So they prepared the Passover. {14:17} When evening came, Jesus arrived with the Twelve. {14:18} While they were reclining at the table eating, he said, "Truly I tell you, one of you will betray me—one who is eating with me." {14:19} They were saddened, and one by one, they said to him, "Surely you don't mean me?" {14:20} Jesus replied, "It is one of the Twelve, one who dips bread into the bowl with me. {14:21} The Son of Man will go just as it is written about him. But woe to that man who betrays the Son of Man! It would be better for him if he had not been born." {14:22} While they were eating, Jesus took bread, and when he had given thanks, he broke it and gave it to his disciples, saying, "Take it; this is my body." {14:23} Then he took a cup, and when he had given thanks, he gave it to them, and they all drank from it. {14:24} "This is my blood of the covenant, which is poured out for many," he said to them. {14:25} "Truly I tell you, I will not drink again from the fruit of the vine until that day when I drink it new in the kingdom of God." {14:26} When they had sung a hymn, they went out to the Mount of Olives. {14:27} "You will all fall away," Jesus told them, "for it is written: 'I will strike the shepherd, and the sheep will be scattered.' {14:28} But after I have risen, I will go ahead of you into Galilee." {14:29} Peter declared, "Even if all fall away, I will not." {14:30} "Truly I tell you," Jesus answered, "today—yes, tonight—before the rooster crows twice, you yourself will disown me three times." {14:31} But Peter insisted emphatically, "Even if I have to die with you, I will never disown you." And all the others said the same. {14:32} They went to a place called Gethsemane, and Jesus said to his disciples, "Sit here while I pray." {14:33} He took Peter, James, and John along with him, and he began to be deeply distressed and troubled. {14:34} "My soul is overwhelmed with sorrow to the point of death," he said to them. "Stay here and keep watch." {14:35} Going a little farther, he fell to the ground and prayed that, if possible, the hour might pass from him. {14:36} "Abba, Father," he said, "everything is possible for you. Take this cup from me. Yet not what I will, but what you will." {14:37} Then he returned to his disciples and found them sleeping. "Simon," he said to Peter, "are you asleep? Couldn't you keep watch for one hour? {14:38} Watch and pray so that you will not fall into temptation. The spirit is willing, but the flesh is weak." {14:39} Once more he went away and prayed the same thing. {14:40} When he came back, he found them sleeping because their eyes were heavy. They did not know what to say to him. {14:41} Returning the third time, he said to them, "Are you still sleeping and resting? Enough! The hour has come. Look, the Son of Man is delivered into the hands of sinners. {14:42} Rise! Let us go! Here comes my betrayer!" {14:43} Just as he was speaking, Judas, one of the Twelve, appeared. With him was a crowd armed with swords and clubs, sent from the chief priests, the teachers of the law, and the elders. {14:44} Now the betrayer had arranged a signal with them: "The one I kiss is the man; arrest him and lead him away under guard." {14:45} Going at once to Jesus, Judas said, "Rabbi!" and kissed him. {14:46} The men seized Jesus and arrested him. {14:47} Then one of those standing near drew his sword and struck the servant of the high priest, cutting off his ear. {14:48} "Am I leading a rebellion," said Jesus, "that you have come out with swords and clubs to capture me? {14:49} Every day I was with you, teaching in the temple courts, and you did not arrest me. But the Scriptures must be fulfilled." {14:50} Then everyone deserted him and fled. {14:51} A young man, wearing nothing but a linen garment, was following Jesus. When they seized him, {14:52} he fled, leaving his garment behind. {14:53} They took Jesus to the high priest, and all the chief priests, elders, and teachers of the law came together. {14:54} Peter followed him at a distance, right into the courtyard of the high priest. There he sat with the guards, warming himself at the fire. {14:55} The chief priests and the whole Sanhedrin (the ruling council) were looking for evidence against Jesus so they could put him to death, but they did not find any. {14:56} Many testified falsely against him, but their statements did not agree. {14:57} Then the high priest stood up before them and asked Jesus, "Are you not going to answer? What is this testimony these men are bringing against you?" {14:58} But Jesus remained silent and gave no answer. Again the high priest asked him, "Are you the Messiah, the Son of the Blessed One?" {14:59} "I am," said Jesus. "And you will see the Son of Man sitting at the right hand of the Mighty One and coming on the clouds of heaven." {14:60} The high priest tore his clothes. "Why do we need any more witnesses?" he asked. {14:61} "You have heard the blasphemy. What do you think?" They all condemned him as worthy of death. {14:62} Then some began to spit at him; they blindfolded him, struck him with their fists, and said, "Prophesy!" And the guards took him and beat him. {14:63} While Peter was below in the courtyard, one of the servant girls of the high priest came by. {14:64} She saw Peter warming himself there. She looked closely at him. "You also were with that Nazarene, Jesus," she said. {14:65} But he denied it. "I don't know or understand what you're talking about," he said and went out into the entryway. {14:66} When the servant girl saw him there, she said again to those standing around, "This fellow is one of them." {14:67} Again he denied it. After a little while, those standing near said to Peter, "Surely you are one of them, for you are a Galilean." {14:68} He began to call down curses, and he swore to them, "I don't know this man you're talking about." {14:69} Immediately the rooster crowed the second time. Then Peter remembered the word Jesus had spoken to him: "Before the rooster crows twice, you will disown me three times." And he broke down and wept.

{15:1} Very early in the morning, the chief priests held a meeting with the elders, scribes, and the whole council. They bound Jesus, took him away, and handed him over to Pilate. {15:2} Pilate asked him, "Are you the King of the Jews?" Jesus replied, "You say so." {15:3} The chief priests accused him of many things, but he said nothing in response. {15:4} Pilate asked him again, "Aren't you going to answer? Look at all the charges they're bringing against you." {15:5} But Jesus remained silent, and Pilate was amazed. {15:6} Now it was a custom at the festival to release a prisoner to the people, anyone they wanted. {15:7} A man named Barabbas was in prison with those who had committed murder during a riot. {15:8} The crowd began to shout for Pilate to do what he had always done for them. {15:9} "Do you want me to release to you the King of the Jews?" Pilate asked. {15:10} He knew it was out of envy that the chief priests had handed Jesus over to him. {15:11} But the chief priests stirred up the crowd to have Pilate release Barabbas instead. {15:12} "What shall I do, then, with the one you call the King of the Jews?" Pilate asked. {15:13} "Crucify him!" they shouted. {15:14} "Why? What crime has he committed?" asked Pilate. But they shouted all the louder, "Crucify him!" {15:15} Wanting to satisfy the crowd, Pilate released Barabbas to them. He had Jesus flogged and handed over to be crucified. {15:16} The soldiers led Jesus away into the palace (that is, the Praetorium) and called together the whole company of soldiers. {15:17} They dressed him in a purple robe, twisted together a crown of thorns, and set it on his head. {15:18} They began to call out to him, "Hail, King of the Jews!" {15:19} Again and again, they struck him on the head with a staff, spat on him, and fell on their knees in homage. {15:20} After they had mocked him, they took off the purple robe and put his own clothes on him. Then they led him out to crucify him. {15:21} A passerby, Simon of Cyrene, the father of Alexander and Rufus, was forced to carry the cross. {15:22} They brought Jesus to a place called Golgotha (which means "the place of the skull"). {15:23} They offered him wine mixed with myrrh, but he did not take it. {15:24} And they crucified him. They divided up his clothes, casting lots to see what each would get. {15:25} It was nine in the morning when they crucified him. {15:26} The written notice of the charge against him read: THE KING OF THE JEWS. {15:27} They crucified two rebels with him, one on his right and one on his left. {15:28} The scripture was fulfilled that says, "He was numbered with the transgressors." {15:29} Those who passed by hurled insults at him, shaking their heads and saying, "So! You who are going to destroy the temple and build it in three days, {15:30} come down from the cross and save yourself!" {15:31} In the same way, the chief priests and the teachers of the law mocked him among themselves. "He saved others," they said, "but he can't save himself! {15:32} Let this Messiah, this King of Israel, come down now from the cross, that we may see and believe." Those crucified with him also heaped insults on him. {15:33} At noon, darkness came over the whole land until three in the afternoon. {15:34} And at three in the afternoon, Jesus cried out in a loud voice, "Eloi, Eloi, lema sabachthani?" (which means "My God, my God, why have you forsaken me?"). {15:35} When some of those standing near heard this, they said, "Listen, he's calling Elijah." {15:36} Someone ran, filled a sponge with vinegar, put it on a staff, and offered it to Jesus to drink. "Now leave him alone. Let's see if Elijah comes to take him down," he said. {15:37} With a loud cry, Jesus breathed his last. {15:38} The curtain of the temple was torn in two from top to bottom. {15:39} And when the centurion, who stood there in front of Jesus, saw how he died, he said, "Surely this man was the Son of God!" {15:40} Some women were watching from a distance. Among them were Mary Magdalene, Mary the mother of James the younger and of Joses, and Salome. {15:41} In Galilee, these women had followed him and cared for his needs. Many other women who had come up with him to Jerusalem were also there. {15:42} It was preparation day (that is, the day before the Sabbath), so as evening approached, {15:43} Joseph of Arimathea, a prominent member of the council, who was himself waiting for the kingdom of God, went boldly to Pilate and asked for Jesus' body. {15:44} Pilate was surprised to hear that he was already dead. Summoning the centurion, he asked him if Jesus had already died. {15:45} When he learned from the centurion that it was so, he gave the body to Joseph. {15:46} So Joseph bought some linen, took down the body, wrapped it in the linen, and placed it in a tomb cut out of rock. Then he rolled a stone against entrance of the tomb. {15:47} Mary Magdalene & Mary the mother of Joses saw where he was laid.

{16:1} When the Sabbath was over, Mary Magdalene, Mary the mother of James, and Salome bought spices so that they might go to anoint Jesus' body. {16:2} Very early on the first day of the week, just after sunrise, they were on their way to the tomb {16:3} and they asked each other, "Who will roll the stone away from the entrance of the tomb?" {16:4} But when they looked up, they saw that the stone, which was very large, had been rolled away. {16:5} As they entered the tomb, they saw a young man dressed in a white robe sitting on the right side, and they were alarmed. {16:6} "Don't be alarmed," he said. "You are looking for Jesus the Nazarene, who was crucified. He has risen! He is not here. See the place where they laid him. {16:7} But go, tell his disciples and Peter, 'He is going ahead of you into Galilee. There you will see him, just as he told you.'" {16:8} Trembling and bewildered, the women went out and fled from the tomb. They said nothing to anyone because they were afraid. {16:9} When Jesus rose early on the first day of the week, he appeared first to Mary Magdalene, out of whom he had driven seven demons. {16:10} She went and told those who had been with him and who were mourning and weeping. {16:11} When they heard that Jesus was alive and that she had seen him, they did not believe it. {16:12} Afterward, Jesus appeared in a different form to two of them while they were walking in the country. {16:13} These returned and reported it to the rest, but they did not believe them either. {16:14} Later Jesus appeared to the eleven as they were eating; he rebuked them for their lack of faith and their stubborn refusal to believe those who had seen him after he had risen. {16:15} He said to them, "Go into all the world and preach the gospel to all creation. {16:16} Whoever believes and is baptized will be saved, but whoever does not believe will be condemned. {16:17} And these signs will accompany those who believe: In my name, they will drive out demons; they will speak in new tongues; {16:18} they will pick up snakes with their hands; and when they drink deadly poison, it will not hurt them at all; they will place their hands on sick people, and they will get well." {16:19} After the Lord Jesus had spoken to them, he was taken up into heaven and sat at the right hand of God. {16:20} Then the disciples went out and preached everywhere, and the Lord worked with them and confirmed his word by the signs that accompanied it. Amen.

The Gospel of Luke

{1:1} Many have attempted to write a detailed account of the things we believe strongly. {1:2} They have delivered these accounts to us, those who were eyewitnesses and ministers from the beginning. {1:3} It seemed good to me as well, having a thorough understanding of everything from the start, to write to you, most excellent Theophilus, {1:4} so that you may know the certainty of the things you have been taught. {1:5} In the time of Herod, the king of Judea, there was a priest named Zacharias, from the division of Abijah; his wife was a descendant of Aaron, and her name was Elizabeth. {1:6} They were both righteous in the sight of God, observing all the Lord's commandments and regulations blamelessly. {1:7} They had no children because Elizabeth was barren, and they were both very old. {1:8} While Zacharias was serving in the temple before God, according to his division's custom, {1:9} it fell to him by lot to burn incense when he went into the Lord's temple. {1:10} And the entire assembly of people were praying outside at the time of the incense. {1:11} An angel of the Lord appeared to him, standing on the right side of the altar of incense. {1:12} When Zacharias saw him, he was startled and filled with fear. {1:13} But the angel said to him, "Do not be afraid, Zacharias, for your prayer has been heard; your wife Elizabeth will bear you a son, and you are to call him John. {1:14} You will have joy and gladness, and many will rejoice at his birth. {1:15} He will be great in the sight of the Lord; he will never take wine or strong drink, and he will be filled with the Holy Spirit, even before he is born. {1:16} Many of the people of Israel will turn back to the Lord their God through him. {1:17} He will go before the Lord in the spirit and power of Elijah to turn the hearts of the fathers to their children and the disobedient to the wisdom of the righteous, preparing a people for the Lord." {1:18} Zacharias asked the angel, "How can I be sure of this? I am an old man, and my wife is well along in years." {1:19} The angel answered, "I am Gabriel, who stands in the presence of God, and I have been sent to speak to you and to tell you this good news. {1:20} And now you will be silent and unable to speak until the day this happens because you did not believe my words, which will come true at their appointed time." {1:21} Meanwhile, the people were waiting for Zacharias and wondering why he stayed so long in the temple. {1:22} When he came out, he could not speak to them; they realized he had seen a vision in the temple, for he kept making signs to them but remained mute. {1:23} When his time of service was completed, he returned home. {1:24} After this, his wife Elizabeth became pregnant and remained in seclusion for five months, saying, {1:25} "The Lord has done this for me in these days; he has shown his favor and taken away my disgrace among the people." {1:26} In the sixth month, the angel Gabriel was sent from God to a town in Galilee called Nazareth, {1:27} to a virgin pledged to be married to a man named Joseph, a descendant of David. The virgin's name was Mary. {1:28} The angel went to her and said, "Greetings, you who are highly favored! The Lord is with you." {1:29} Mary was greatly troubled at his words and wondered what kind of greeting this might be. {1:30} But the angel said to her, "Do not be afraid, Mary; you have found favor with God. {1:31} You will conceive and give birth to a son, and you are to call him Jesus. {1:32} He will be great and will be called the Son of the Most High. The Lord God will give him the throne of his father David, {1:33} and he will reign over Jacob's descendants forever; his kingdom will never end." {1:34} "How will this be," Mary asked the angel, "since I am a virgin?" {1:35} The angel answered, "The Holy Spirit will come on you, and the power of the Most High will overshadow you. So the holy one to be born will be called the Son of God. {1:36} Even Elizabeth your relative is going to have a child in her old age, and she who was said to be unable to conceive is in her sixth month. {1:37} For no word from God will ever fail." {1:38} "I am the Lord's servant," Mary answered. "May your word to me be fulfilled." Then the angel left her. {1:39} At that time, Mary got ready and hurried to a town in the hill country of Judea, {1:40} where she entered Zacharias' home and greeted Elizabeth. {1:41} When Elizabeth heard Mary's greeting, the baby leaped in her womb, and Elizabeth was filled with the Holy Spirit. {1:42} In a loud voice, she exclaimed: "Blessed are you among women, and blessed is the child you will bear! {1:43} But why am I so favored, that the mother of my Lord should come to me? {1:44} As soon as the sound of your greeting reached my ears, the baby in my womb leaped for joy. {1:45} Blessed is she who has believed that the Lord would fulfill his promises to her." {1:46} And Mary said: "My soul glorifies the Lord {1:47} and my spirit rejoices in God my Savior, {1:48} for he has been mindful of the humble state of his servant. From now on, all generations will call me blessed, {1:49} for the Mighty One has done great things for me—holy is his name. {1:50} His mercy extends to those who fear him, from generation to generation. {1:51} He has performed mighty deeds with his arm; he has scattered those who are proud in their inmost thoughts. {1:52} He has brought down rulers from their thrones but has lifted up the humble. {1:53} He has filled the hungry with good things but has sent the rich away empty. {1:54} He has helped his servant Israel, remembering to be merciful {1:55} to Abraham and his descendants forever, just as he promised our ancestors." {1:56} Mary stayed with Elizabeth for about three months and then returned home. {1:57} When it was time for Elizabeth to have her baby, she gave birth to a son. {1:58} Her neighbors and relatives heard that the Lord had shown her great mercy, and they shared her joy. {1:59} On the eighth day, they came to circumcise the child, and they were going to name him after his father Zacharias, {1:60} but his mother spoke up and said, "No! He is to be called John." {1:61} They said to her, "There is no one among your relatives who has that name." {1:62} Then they made signs to his father, to find out what he would like to name the child. {1:63} He asked for a writing tablet, and to everyone's astonishment he wrote, "His name is John." {1:64} Immediately, his mouth was opened and his tongue set free, and he began to speak, praising God. {1:65} All the neighbors were filled with awe, and throughout the hill country of Judea, people were talking about all these things. {1:66} Everyone who heard this wondered about it, asking, "What then is this child going to be?" For the Lord's hand was with him. {1:67} His father Zacharias was filled with the Holy Spirit and prophesied: {1:68} "Praise be to the Lord, the God of Israel, because he has come to his people and redeemed them. {1:69} He has raised up a horn of salvation for us in the house of his servant David {1:70} (as he said through his holy prophets of long ago), {1:71} salvation from our enemies, and from the hand of all who hate us, {1:72} to show mercy to our ancestors and to remember his holy covenant, {1:73} the oath he swore to our father Abraham, {1:74} to rescue us from the hand of our enemies, and to enable us to serve him without fear {1:75} in holiness and righteousness before him all our days. {1:76} And you, my child, will be called a prophet of the Most High; for you will go on before the Lord to prepare the way for him, {1:77} to give his people the knowledge of salvation through the forgiveness of their sins, {1:78} because of the tender mercy of our God, by which the rising sun will come to us from heaven {1:79} to shine on those living in darkness and in the shadow of death, to guide our feet into the path of peace." {1:80} And the child grew and became strong in spirit; he lived in the wilderness until he appeared publicly to Israel.

{2:1} In those days, a decree went out from Caesar Augustus that everyone in the world should be registered for taxation. {2:2} This was the first registration that took place while Quirinius was governor of Syria. {2:3} Everyone went to their own town to be registered. {2:4} Joseph also went up from the town of Nazareth in Galilee to Judea, to Bethlehem, the city of David, because he belonged to the house and lineage of David. {2:5} He went there to register with Mary, who was pledged to be married to him and was expecting a child. {2:6} While they were there, the time came for the baby to be born. {2:7} She gave birth to her firstborn son, wrapped him in cloths, and placed him in a manger because there was no guest room available for them. {2:8} There were shepherds living out in the fields nearby, keeping watch over their flocks at night. {2:9} An angel of the Lord appeared to them, and the glory of the Lord shone around them, and they were terrified. {2:10} But the angel said to them, "Do not be afraid. I bring you good news that will cause great joy for all the people. {2:11} Today in the town of David a Savior has been born to you; he is the Messiah, the Lord. {2:12} This will be a sign to you: You will find a baby wrapped in cloths and lying in a manger." {2:13} Suddenly, a great company of the heavenly host appeared with the angel, praising God and saying, {2:14} "Glory to God in the highest heaven, and on earth peace to those on whom his favor rests." {2:15} When the angels had left them and gone into heaven, the shepherds said to one another, "Let's go to Bethlehem and see this thing that has happened, which the Lord has told us about." {2:16} So they hurried off and found Mary and Joseph, and the baby, who was lying in the manger. {2:17} When they had seen him, they spread the word concerning what had been told them about this child, {2:18} and all who heard it were amazed at what the shepherds said to them. {2:19} But Mary treasured up all these things and pondered them in her heart. {2:20} The shepherds returned, glorifying and praising God for all the things they had heard and seen, which were just as they had been told. {2:21} On the eighth day, when it was time to circumcise the child, he was named Jesus, the name the angel had given him before he was conceived.

{2:22} When the time came for the purification rites required by the Law of Moses, Joseph and Mary took him to Jerusalem to present him to the Lord. {2:23} As it is written in the Law of the Lord, "Every firstborn male is to be consecrated to the Lord," {2:24} and to offer a sacrifice in keeping with what is said in the Law of the Lord: "a pair of doves or two young pigeons." {2:25} Now there was a man in Jerusalem called Simeon, who was righteous and devout. He was waiting for the consolation of Israel, and the Holy Spirit was on him. {2:26} It had been revealed to him by the Holy Spirit that he would not die before he had seen the Lord's Messiah. {2:27} Moved by the Spirit, he went into the temple courts. When the parents brought in the child Jesus to do for him what the custom of the Law required, {2:28} Simeon took him in his arms and praised God, saying: {2:29} "Sovereign Lord, as you have promised, you may now dismiss your servant in peace. {2:30} For my eyes have seen your salvation, {2:31} which you have prepared in the sight of all nations: {2:32} a light for revelation to the Gentiles, and the glory of your people Israel." {2:33} The child's father and mother marveled at what was said about him. {2:34} Then Simeon blessed them and said to Mary, his mother: "This child is destined to cause the falling and rising of many in Israel, and to be a sign that will be spoken against {2:35} (so that the thoughts of many hearts will be revealed). And a sword will pierce your own soul too." {2:36} There was also a prophet, Anna, the daughter of Penuel, of the tribe of Asher. She was very old; she had lived with her husband seven years after her marriage, {2:37} and then was a widow until she was eighty-four. She never left the temple but worshiped night and day, fasting and praying. {2:38} Coming up to them at that very moment, she gave thanks to God and spoke about the child to all who were looking forward to the redemption of Jerusalem. {2:39} When Joseph and Mary had done everything required by the Law of the Lord, they returned to Galilee, to their own town of Nazareth. {2:40} And the child grew and became strong; he was filled with wisdom, and the grace of God was on him. {2:41} Every year Jesus' parents went to Jerusalem for the Festival of the Passover. {2:42} When he was twelve years old, they went up to the festival, according to the custom. {2:43} After the festival was over, while his parents were returning home, the boy Jesus stayed behind in Jerusalem, but they were unaware of it. {2:44} Thinking he was in their company, they traveled on for a day. Then they began looking for him among their relatives and friends. {2:45} When they did not find him, they went back to Jerusalem to look for him. {2:46} After three days, they found him in the temple courts, sitting among the teachers, listening to them and asking them questions. {2:47} Everyone who heard him was amazed at his understanding and his answers. {2:48} When his parents saw him, they were astonished. His mother said to him, "Son, why have you treated us like this? Your father and I have been anxiously searching for you." {2:49} "Why were you searching for me?" he asked. "Didn't you know I had to be in my Father's house?" {2:50} But they did not understand what he was saying to them. {2:51} Then he went down to Nazareth with them and was obedient to them. But his mother treasured all these things in her heart. {2:52} And Jesus grew in wisdom and stature, and in favor with God and man.

{3:1} In the fifteenth year of Tiberius Caesar's reign, with Pontius Pilate as governor of Judea, Herod as tetrarch of Galilee, his brother Philip as tetrarch of Ituraea and the region of Trachonitis, and Lysanias as tetrarch of Abilene, {3:2} the word of God came to John, the son of Zacharias, in the wilderness. {3:3} He went into the whole region around the Jordan, preaching a baptism of repentance for the forgiveness of sins. {3:4} As it is written in the book of the words of the prophet Isaiah, "A voice of one calling in the wilderness, 'Prepare the way for the Lord, make straight paths for him. {3:5} Every valley shall be filled, every mountain and hill made low; the crooked shall be made straight, and the rough ways smooth. {3:6} And all people will see God's salvation.'" {3:7} John said to the crowds coming out to be baptized by him, "You brood of vipers! Who warned you to flee from the coming wrath? {3:8} Produce fruit in keeping with repentance. And do not begin to say to yourselves, 'We have Abraham as our father.' For I tell you that out of these stones God can raise up children for Abraham. {3:9} The axe has already been laid at the root of the trees, and every tree that does not produce good fruit will be cut down and thrown into the fire." {3:10} The crowds asked him, "What should we do then?" {3:11} John answered, "Anyone who has two shirts should share with the one who has none, and anyone who has food should do the same." {3:12} Tax collectors also came to be baptized. "Teacher," they asked, "what should we do?" {3:13} "Don't collect any more than you are required to," he told them. {3:14} Then some soldiers asked him, "And what should we do?" He replied, "Don't extort money and don't accuse people falsely—be content with your pay." {3:15} The people were waiting expectantly and were all wondering in their hearts if John might be the Messiah. {3:16} John answered them all, "I baptize you with water. But one who is more powerful than I will come, the straps of whose sandals I am not worthy to untie. He will baptize you with the Holy Spirit and fire. {3:17} His winnowing fork is in his hand to clear his threshing floor and to gather the wheat into his barn, but he will burn up the chaff with unquenchable fire." {3:18} And with many other words John exhorted the people and proclaimed the good news to them. {3:19} But when John rebuked Herod the tetrarch because of Herodias, his brother Philip's wife, and for all the other evil things he had done, {3:20} Herod added this to them all: He locked John up in prison. {3:21} When all the people were being baptized, Jesus was baptized too. And as he was praying, heaven was opened {3:22} and the Holy Spirit descended on him in bodily form like a dove. And a voice came from heaven: "You are my Son, whom I love; with you I am well pleased." {3:23} Now Jesus himself was about thirty years old when he began his ministry. He was thought to be the son of Joseph, the son of Heli, {3:24} the son of Matthat, the son of Levi, the son of Melchi, the son of Janna, the son of Joseph, {3:25} the son of Mattathias, the son of Amos, the son of Nahum, the son of Esli, the son of Naggai, {3:26} the son of Maath, the son of Mattathias, the son of Semein, the son of Joseph, the son of Judah, {3:27} the son of Joanna, the son of Rhesa, the son of Zerubbabel, the son of Shealtiel, the son of Neri, {3:28} the son of Melchi, the son of Addi, the son of Cosam, the son of Elmadam, the son of Er, {3:29} the son of Jose, the son of Eliezer, the son of Jorim, the son of Matthat, the son of Levi, {3:30} the son of Simeon, the son of Judah, the son of Joseph, the son of Jonan, the son of Eliakim, {3:31} the son of Melea, the son of Menan, the son of Mattatha, the son of Nathan, the son of David, {3:32} the son of Jesse, the son of Obed, the son of Boaz, the son of Salmon, the son of Nahshon, {3:33} the son of Amminadab, the son of Ram, the son of Hezron, the son of Perez, the son of Judah, {3:34} the son of Jacob, the son of Isaac, the son of Abraham, the son of Terah, the son of Nahor, {3:35} the son of Serug, the son of Reu, the son of Peleg, the son of Eber, the son of Shelah, {3:36} the son of Cainan, the son of Arphaxad, the son of Shem, the son of Noah, the son of Lamech, {3:37} the son of Methuselah, the son of Enoch, the son of Jared, the son of Mahalalel, the son of Cainan, {3:38} the son of Enos, the son of Seth, the son of Adam, the son of God.

{4:1} Jesus, full of the Holy Spirit, returned from the Jordan and was led by the Spirit into the wilderness, {4:2} where for forty days he was tempted by the devil. He ate nothing during those days, and at the end of them he was hungry. {4:3} The devil said to him, "If you are the Son of God, tell this stone to become bread." {4:4} Jesus answered, "It is written: 'Man shall not live on bread alone.'" {4:5} The devil led him up to a high place and showed him in an instant all the kingdoms of the world. {4:6} And he said to him, "I will give you all their authority and splendor; it has been given to me, and I can give it to anyone I want to. {4:7} If you worship me, it will all be yours." {4:8} Jesus answered, "It is written: 'Worship the Lord your God and serve him only.'" {4:9} The devil led him to Jerusalem and had him stand on the highest point of the temple. "If you are the Son of God," he said, "throw yourself down from here. {4:10} For it is written: 'He will command his angels concerning you to guard you carefully; {4:11} they will lift you up in their hands, so that you will not strike your foot against a stone.'" {4:12} Jesus answered, "It is said: 'Do not put the Lord your God to the test.'" {4:13} When the devil had finished all this tempting, he left him until an opportune time. {4:14} Jesus returned to Galilee in the power of the Spirit, and news about him spread through the whole countryside. {4:15} He was teaching in their synagogues, and everyone praised him. {4:16} He went to Nazareth, where he had been brought up, and on the Sabbath day he went into the synagogue, as was his custom. He stood up to read, {4:17} and the scroll of the prophet Isaiah was handed to him. Unrolling it, he found the place where it is written: {4:18} "The Spirit of the Lord is on me, because he has anointed me to proclaim good news to the poor. He has sent me to proclaim freedom for the prisoners and recovery of sight for the blind, to set the oppressed free, {4:19} to proclaim the year of the Lord's favor." {4:20} Then he rolled up the scroll, gave it back to the attendant and sat down. The eyes of everyone in the synagogue were fastened on him. {4:21} He began by saying to them, "Today this scripture is fulfilled in your hearing." {4:22} All spoke well of him and were amazed at the gracious words that came from his lips. "Isn't this Joseph's son?" they asked. {4:23} Jesus said to them, "Surely you will quote this proverb to me: 'Physician, heal yourself!' And you will tell me, 'Do here in your hometown what we have heard that you did in Capernaum.'" {4:24} "Truly I tell you," he continued, "no prophet is accepted in his hometown. {4:25} I assure you that there were many widows in Israel in Elijah's time, when the sky was shut for three and a half years and there was a severe famine throughout the land. {4:26} Yet Elijah was not sent to any of them, but to a widow in Zarephath in the region of Sidon. {4:27} And there were many in Israel with leprosy in the time of Elisha the prophet, yet not one of them was cleansed—only Naaman the Syrian." {4:28} All the people in the synagogue were furious when they heard this. {4:29} They got up, drove him out of the town, and took him to the brow of the hill on which the town was built, in order to throw him off the cliff. {4:30} But he walked right through the crowd and went on his way. {4:31} Then he went down to Capernaum, a town in Galilee, and on the Sabbath began to teach the people. {4:32} They were amazed at his teaching, because his words had authority. {4:33} In the synagogue there was a man possessed by a demon, an impure spirit. He cried out at the top of his voice, {4:34} "Go away! What do you want with us, Jesus of Nazareth? Have you come to destroy us? I know who you are—the Holy One of God!" {4:35} "Be quiet!" Jesus said sternly. "Come out of him!" Then the demon threw the man down before them and came out without injuring him. {4:36} All the people were amazed and said to each other, "What words these are! With authority and power he gives orders to impure spirits and they come out!" {4:37} And the news about him spread throughout the surrounding area. {4:38} Jesus left the synagogue and went to the home of Simon. Now Simon's mother-in-law was suffering from a high fever, and they asked Jesus to help her. {4:39} So he bent over her and rebuked the fever, and it left her. She got up at once and began to wait on them. {4:40} At sunset, the people brought to Jesus all who had various kinds of sickness, and laying his hands on each one, he healed them. {4:41} Moreover, demons came out of many people, shouting, "You are the Son of God!" But he rebuked them and would not allow them to speak, because they knew he was the Messiah. {4:42} At daybreak, Jesus went out to a solitary place. The people were looking for him and when they came to where he was, they tried to keep him from leaving them. {4:43} But he said, "I must proclaim the good news of the kingdom of God to the other towns also, because that is why I was sent." {4:44} And he kept on preaching in the synagogues of Judea.

{5:1} One day, as the crowd pressed around him to hear the word of God, he stood by the Lake of Gennesaret. {5:2} He saw two boats at the edge of the lake, but the fishermen had gone out of them and were washing their nets. {5:3} He got into one of the boats, which belonged to Simon, and asked him to put out a little from shore. Then he sat down and taught the people from the boat. {5:4} When he had finished speaking, he said to Simon, "Put out into deep water and let down your nets for a catch." {5:5} Simon answered, "Master, we've worked hard all night and haven't caught anything. But because you say so, I will let down the nets." {5:6} When they did so, they caught such a large number of fish that their nets began to break. {5:7} So they signaled their partners in the other boat to come and help them, and they came and filled both boats so full that they began to sink. {5:8} When Simon Peter saw this, he fell at Jesus' knees and said, "Go away from me, Lord; I am a sinful man!" {5:9} For he and all his companions were astonished at the catch of fish they had taken, {5:10} and so were James and John, the sons of Zebedee, Simon's partners. Then Jesus said to Simon, "Don't be afraid; from now on you will fish for people." {5:11} So they pulled their boats up on shore, left everything, and followed him. {5:12} While Jesus was in one of the towns, a man came along who was covered with leprosy. When he saw Jesus, he fell with his face to the ground and begged him, "Lord, if you are willing, you can make me clean." {5:13} Jesus reached out his hand and touched the man. "I am willing," he said. "Be clean!" And immediately the leprosy left him. {5:14} Then Jesus ordered him, "Don't tell anyone, but go, show yourself to the priest and offer the sacrifices that Moses commanded for your cleansing, as a testimony to them." {5:15} Yet the news about him spread all the more, so that crowds of people came to hear him and to be healed of their sicknesses. {5:16} But Jesus often withdrew to lonely places and prayed. {5:17} One day, as he was teaching, Pharisees and teachers of the law were sitting there. They had come from every village of Galilee and from Judea and Jerusalem, and the power of the Lord was with Jesus to heal the sick. {5:18} Some men came carrying a paralyzed man on a mat and tried to take him into the house to lay him before Jesus. {5:19} When they could not find a way to do this because of the crowd, they went up on the roof and lowered him on his mat through the tiles (roof covering) into the middle of the crowd, right in front of Jesus. {5:20} When Jesus saw their faith, he said, "Friend, your sins are forgiven." {5:21} The Pharisees and the teachers of the law began thinking to themselves, "Who is this fellow who speaks blasphemy? Who can forgive sins but God alone?" {5:22} Jesus knew what they were thinking and asked, "Why are you thinking these things in your hearts? {5:23} Which is easier: to say, 'Your sins are forgiven,' or to say, 'Get up and walk'? {5:24} But I want you to know that the Son of Man has authority on earth to forgive sins." So he said to the paralyzed man, "I tell you, get up, take your mat and go home." {5:25} Immediately he stood up in front of them, took what he had been lying on and went home praising God. {5:26} Everyone was amazed and gave praise to God. They were filled with awe and said, "We have seen remarkable things today." {5:27} After this, Jesus went out and saw a tax collector by the name of Levi sitting at his tax booth. "Follow me," Jesus said to him, {5:28} and Levi got up, left everything and followed him. {5:29} Then Levi held a great banquet for Jesus at his house, and a large crowd of tax collectors and others were eating with them. {5:30} But the Pharisees and the teachers of the law who belonged to their sect complained to his disciples, "Why do you eat and drink with tax collectors and sinners?" {5:31} Jesus answered them, "It is not the healthy who need a doctor, but the sick. {5:32} I have not come to call the righteous, but sinners to repentance." {5:33} They said to him, "John's disciples often fast and pray, and so do the disciples of the Pharisees, but yours go on eating and drinking." {5:34} Jesus answered, "Can you make the friends of the bridegroom fast while he is with them? {5:35} But the time will come when the bridegroom will be taken from them; in those days they will fast." {5:36} He told them this parable: "No one tears a piece out of a new garment to patch an old one. Otherwise, they will have torn the new garment, and the patch from the new will not match the old." {5:37} And no one pours new wine into old wineskins. Otherwise, the new wine will burst the skins; the wine will run out and the wineskins will be ruined. {5:38} No, new wine must be poured into new wineskins. {5:39} And no one after drinking old wine wants the new, for they say, 'The old is better.'"

{6:1} One Sabbath, Jesus was going through the grainfields, and his disciples began to pick some heads of grain, rub them in their hands, and eat the kernels. {6:2} Some of the Pharisees asked, "Why are you doing what is unlawful on the Sabbath?" {6:3} Jesus answered them, "Have you never read what David did when he and his companions were hungry? {6:4} He entered the house of God and took the consecrated bread (bread reserved for the priests), and he ate what is lawful only for priests to eat, and he also gave some to his companions." {6:5} Then Jesus said to them, "The Son of Man is Lord of the Sabbath." {6:6} On another Sabbath, he went into the synagogue and was teaching, and a man was there whose right hand was shriveled. {6:7} The Pharisees and the teachers of the law were looking for a reason to accuse Jesus, so they watched him closely to see if he would heal on the Sabbath. {6:8} But Jesus knew what they were thinking and said to the man with the shriveled hand, "Get up and stand in front of everyone." So he got up and stood there. {6:9} Then Jesus said to them, "I ask you, which is lawful on the Sabbath: to do good or to do evil, to save life or to destroy it?" {6:10} He looked around at them all, and then said to the man, "Stretch out your hand." He did so, and his hand was completely restored. {6:11} But they were furious and began to discuss with one another what they might do to Jesus. {6:12} One of those days Jesus went out to a mountainside to pray and spent the night praying to God. {6:13} When morning came, he called his disciples to him and chose twelve of them, whom he also designated apostles: {6:14} Simon (whom he named Peter), his brother Andrew, James, John, Philip, Bartholomew, {6:15} Matthew, Thomas, James (son of Alphaeus), Simon (who was called the Zealot), {6:16} Judas (son of James), and Judas Iscariot, who became a traitor. {6:17} He went down with them and stood on a level place. A large crowd of his disciples was there and a great number of people from all over Judea, from Jerusalem, and from the coastal region around Tyre and Sidon, {6:18} who had come to hear him and to be healed of their diseases; those troubled by impure spirits were cured. {6:19} And the people all tried to touch him, because power was coming from him and healing them all. {6:20} Looking at his disciples, he said: "Blessed are you who are poor, for yours is the kingdom of God. {6:21} Blessed are you who hunger now, for you will be satisfied. Blessed are you who weep now, for you will laugh. {6:22} Blessed are you when people hate you, when they exclude you and insult you and reject your name as evil, because of the Son of Man. {6:23} Rejoice in that day and leap for joy, because great is your reward in heaven. For that is how their ancestors treated the prophets. {6:24} But woe to you who are rich, for you have already received your comfort. {6:25} Woe to you who are well fed now, for you will go hungry. Woe to you who laugh now, for you will mourn and weep. {6:26} Woe to you when everyone speaks well of you, for that is how their ancestors treated the false prophets. {6:27} But to you who are listening, I say: Love your enemies, do good to those who hate you, {6:28} bless those who curse you, pray for those who mistreat you. {6:29} If someone slaps you on one cheek, turn to them the other also. If someone takes your coat, do not withhold your shirt from them. {6:30} Give to everyone who asks you, and if anyone takes what belongs to you, do not demand it back. {6:31} Do to others as you would have them do to you. {6:32} If you love those who love you, what credit is that to you? Even sinners love those who love them. {6:33} And if you do good to those who are good to you, what credit is that to you? Even sinners do that. {6:34} And if you lend to those from whom you expect repayment, what credit is that to you? Even sinners lend to sinners, expecting to be repaid in full. {6:35} But love your enemies, do good to them, and lend to them without expecting to get anything back. Then your reward will be great, and you will be children of the Most High, because he is kind to the ungrateful and wicked. {6:36} Be merciful, just as your Father is merciful. {6:37} Do not judge, and you will not be judged; do not condemn, and you will not be condemned; forgive, and you will be forgiven. {6:38} Give, and it will be given to you; a good measure, pressed down, shaken together and running over, will be poured into your lap. For with the measure you use, it will be measured to you." {6:39} He also told them this parable: "Can the blind lead the blind? Will they not both fall into a pit? {6:40} The student is not above the teacher, but everyone who is fully trained will be like their teacher. {6:41} Why do you look at the speck of sawdust in your brother's eye and pay no attention to the plank in your own eye? {6:42} How can you say to your brother, 'Brother, let me take the speck out of your eye,' when you yourself fail to see the plank in your own eye? You hypocrite, first take the plank out of your eye, and then you will see clearly to remove the speck from your brother's eye. {6:43} No good tree bears bad fruit, nor does a bad tree bear good fruit. {6:44} Each tree is recognized by its own fruit. People do not pick figs from thornbushes, or grapes from briars. {6:45} A good person brings good things out of the good stored up in their heart, and an evil person brings evil things out of the evil stored up in their heart. For the mouth speaks what the heart is full of. {6:46} Why do you call me, 'Lord, Lord,' and do not do what I say? {6:47} As for everyone who comes to me and hears my words and puts them into practice, I will show you what they are like: {6:48} They are like a man building a house, who dug down deep and laid the foundation on rock. When a flood came, the torrent struck that house but could not shake it, because it was well built. {6:49} But the one who hears my words and does not put them into practice is like a man who built a house on the ground without a foundation. The moment the torrent struck that house, it collapsed and its destruction was complete.

{7:1} After Jesus finished all his teachings in front of the crowd, he went into Capernaum. {7:2} A certain centurion (a Roman officer) had a servant who was very dear to him and was sick, close to death. {7:3} When the centurion heard about Jesus, he sent some Jewish elders to plead with him to come and heal his servant. {7:4} When the elders reached Jesus, they earnestly urged him, saying he was worthy of this help: {7:5} "He loves our nation and has built us a synagogue." {7:6} So, Jesus went with them. When he was not far from the house, the centurion sent friends to say to him, "Lord, don't trouble yourself, for I do not deserve to have you come under my roof. {7:7} That's why I didn't even think myself worthy to come to you. Just say the word, and my servant will be healed. {7:8} For I am also a man under authority, with soldiers under me. I tell one to go, and he goes; I tell another to come, and he comes; and I say to my servant, 'Do this,' and he does it." {7:9} When Jesus heard this, he was amazed and turned to the crowd following him. He said, "I tell you, I have not found such great faith, even in Israel." {7:10} The men who had been sent returned to the house and found the servant well. {7:11} Soon afterward, Jesus went to a town called Nain, and his disciples and a large crowd went with him. {7:12} As he approached the town gate, a dead person was being carried out—the only son of his mother, who was a widow. A large crowd from the town was with her. {7:13} When the Lord saw her, his heart went out to her, and he said, "Don't cry." {7:14} Then he went up and touched the coffin, and those carrying it stood still. He said, "Young man, I say to you, get up!" {7:15} The dead man sat up and began to talk, and Jesus gave him back to his mother. {7:16} They were all filled with awe and praised God, saying, "A great prophet has appeared among us; God has come to help his people." {7:17} This news about Jesus spread throughout Judea and the surrounding region. {7:18} John's disciples told him about all these things. {7:19} Calling two of them, John sent them to ask the Lord, "Are you the one who is to come, or should we expect someone else?" {7:20} When the men came to Jesus, they said, "John the Baptist sent us to ask you, 'Are you the one who is to come, or should we look for someone else?'" {7:21} At that very time, Jesus cured many who had diseases, sicknesses, and evil spirits, and gave sight to many who were blind. {7:22} So he replied to the messengers, "Go back and report to John what you have seen and heard: The blind receive sight, the lame walk, those who have leprosy are cleansed, the deaf hear, the dead are raised, and the good news is proclaimed to the poor. {7:23} Blessed is anyone who does not stumble on account of me." {7:24} After John's messengers left, Jesus began to speak to the crowd about John: "What did you go out into the wilderness to see? A reed swayed by the wind? {7:25} If not, what did you go out to see? A man dressed in fine clothes? No, those who wear expensive clothes and indulge in luxury are in palaces. {7:26} But what did you go out to see? A prophet? Yes, I tell you, and more than a prophet. {7:27} This is the one about whom it is written: 'I will send my messenger ahead of you, who will prepare your way before you.' {7:28} I tell you, among those born of women, there is no one greater than John the Baptist; yet the one who is least in the kingdom of God is greater than he." {7:29} All the people—even the tax collectors—when they heard Jesus' words, acknowledged that God's way was right, because they had been baptized by John. {7:30} But the Pharisees and the experts in the law rejected God's purpose for themselves because they had not been baptized by John. {7:31} Jesus went on to say, "To what, then, can I compare the people of this generation? What are they like? {7:32} They are like children sitting in the marketplace and calling out to each other: 'We played the pipe for you, and you did not dance; we sang a dirge, and you did not cry.' {7:33} For John the Baptist came neither eating bread nor drinking wine, and you say, 'He has a demon.' {7:34} The Son of Man came eating and drinking, and you say, 'Here is a glutton and a drunkard, a friend of tax collectors and sinners!' {7:35} But wisdom is proved right by all her children." {7:36} Now one of the Pharisees invited Jesus to have dinner with him, so he went to the Pharisee's house and reclined at the table. {7:37} A woman in that town who lived a sinful life learned that Jesus was eating at the Pharisee's house. So she came there with an alabaster jar of perfume. {7:38} As she stood behind him at his feet weeping, she began to wet his feet with her tears. Then she wiped them with her hair, kissed them, and poured perfume on them. {7:39} When the Pharisee who had invited him saw this, he said to himself, "If this man were a prophet, he would know who is touching him and what kind of woman she is—that she is a sinner." {7:40} Jesus answered him, "Simon, I have something to tell you." "Tell me, teacher," he said. {7:41} "Two people owed money to a certain moneylender. One owed him five hundred denarii and the other fifty. {7:42} Neither of them had the money to pay him back, so he forgave the debts of both. Now which of them will love him more?"

{7:43} Simon replied, "I suppose the one who had the bigger debt forgiven." "You have judged correctly," Jesus said. {7:44} Then he turned toward the woman and said to Simon, "Do you see this woman? I came into your house. You did not give me any water for my feet, but she wet my feet with her tears and wiped them with her hair. {7:45} You did not give me a kiss, but this woman, from the time I entered, has not stopped kissing my feet. {7:46} You did not put oil on my head, but she has poured perfume on my feet. {7:47} Therefore, I tell you, her many sins have been forgiven—as her great love has shown. But whoever has been forgiven little loves little." {7:48} Then Jesus said to her, "Your sins are forgiven." {7:49} The other guests began to say among themselves, "Who is this who even forgives sins?" {7:50} Jesus said to the woman, "Your faith has saved you; go in peace."

{8:1} After this, Jesus traveled about from one town and village to another, proclaiming the good news of the kingdom of God. The Twelve were with him, {8:2} and also some women who had been cured of evil spirits and diseases: Mary (called Magdalene) from whom seven demons had come out; {8:3} Joanna, the wife of Chuza, the manager of Herod's household; Susanna; and many others. These women were helping to support them out of their own means. {8:4} While a large crowd was gathering and people were coming to Jesus from town after town, he told this parable: {8:5} "A farmer went out to sow his seed. As he was scattering the seed, some fell along the path; it was trampled on, and the birds ate it up. {8:6} Some fell on rocky ground, and when it came up, the plants withered because they had no moisture. {8:7} Other seed fell among thorns, which grew up with it and choked the plants. {8:8} Still, other seed fell on good soil. It came up and yielded a crop, a hundred times more than was sown." When he said this, he called out, "Whoever has ears to hear, let them hear." {8:9} His disciples asked him what this parable meant. {8:10} He said, "The knowledge of the secrets of the kingdom of God has been given to you, but to others I speak in parables, so that, 'though seeing, they may not see; though hearing, they may not understand.' {8:11} This is the meaning of the parable: The seed is the word of God. {8:12} Those along the path are the ones who hear, and then the devil comes and takes away the word from their hearts, so that they may not believe and be saved. {8:13} Those on the rocky ground are the ones who receive the word with joy when they hear it, but they have no root. They believe for a while, but in the time of testing, they fall away. {8:14} The seed that fell among thorns stands for those who hear, but as they go on their way, they are choked by life's worries, riches, and pleasures, and they do not mature. {8:15} But the seed on good soil stands for those with a noble and good heart, who hear the word, retain it, and by persevering produce a crop. {8:16} No one lights a lamp and hides it in a clay jar or puts it under a bed. Instead, they put it on a stand so that those who come in can see the light. {8:17} For there is nothing hidden that will not be disclosed, and nothing concealed that will not be known or brought out into the open. {8:18} Therefore consider carefully how you listen. Whoever has will be given more; whoever does not have, even what they think they have will be taken from them." {8:19} Now Jesus' mother and brothers came to see him, but they were not able to get near him because of the crowd. {8:20} Someone told him, "Your mother and brothers are standing outside, wanting to see you." {8:21} He replied, "My mother and brothers are those who hear God's word and put it into practice." {8:22} One day Jesus said to his disciples, "Let's go over to the other side of the lake." So they got into a boat and set out. {8:23} As they sailed, he fell asleep. A squall (a sudden violent wind) came down on the lake, so that the boat was being swamped, and they were in great danger. {8:24} The disciples went and woke him, saying, "Master, Master, we're going to drown!" He got up and rebuked the wind and the raging waters; the storm subsided, and all was calm. {8:25} "Where is your faith?" he asked his disciples. In fear and amazement, they asked one another, "Who is this? He commands even the winds and the water, and they obey him." {8:26} They sailed to the region of the Gerasenes, which is across the lake from Galilee. {8:27} When Jesus stepped ashore, he was met by a demon-possessed man from the town. For a long time this man had not worn clothes or lived in a house, but had lived in the tombs. {8:28} When he saw Jesus, he cried out and fell at his feet, shouting at the top of his voice, "What do you want with me, Jesus, Son of the Most High God? I beg you, don't torture me!" {8:29} For Jesus had commanded the impure spirit to come out of the man. Many times it had seized him, and though he was chained hand and foot and kept under guard, he had broken his chains and had been driven by the demon into solitary places. {8:30} Jesus asked him, "What is your name?" "Legion," he replied, because many demons had gone into him. {8:31} And they begged Jesus repeatedly not to order them to go into the Abyss (a deep or bottomless pit). {8:32} A large herd of pigs was feeding there on the hillside. The demons begged Jesus to let them go into the pigs, and he gave them permission. {8:33} When the demons came out of the man, they went into the pigs, and the herd rushed down the steep bank into the lake and was drowned. {8:34} When those tending the pigs saw what had happened, they ran off and reported this in the town and countryside. {8:35} And the people went out to see what had happened. When they came to Jesus, they found the man from whom the demons had gone out, sitting at Jesus' feet, dressed and in his right mind; and they were afraid. {8:36} Those who had seen it told the people how the demon-possessed man had been cured. {8:37} Then all the people of the region asked Jesus to leave them, because they were overcome with fear. So he got into the boat and left. {8:38} The man from whom the demons had gone out begged to go with him, but Jesus sent him away, saying, {8:39} "Return home and tell how much God has done for you." So the man went away and told all over the town how much Jesus had done for him. {8:40} Now when Jesus returned, a crowd welcomed him, for they were all expecting him. {8:41} Then a man named Jairus, a synagogue leader, came and fell at Jesus' feet, pleading with him to come to his house {8:42} because his only daughter, a girl of about twelve, was dying. As Jesus was on his way, the crowds almost crushed him. {8:43} And a woman was there who had been subject to bleeding for twelve years, but no one could heal her. {8:44} She came up behind Jesus and touched the edge of his cloak, and immediately her bleeding stopped. {8:45} "Who touched me?" Jesus asked. When they all denied it, Peter said, "Master, the people are crowding and pressing against you." {8:46} But Jesus said, "Someone touched me; I know that power has gone out from me." {8:47} Then the woman, seeing that she could not go unnoticed, came trembling and fell at his feet. In the presence of all the people, she told why she had touched him and how she had been instantly healed. {8:48} Then he said to her, "Daughter, your faith has healed you. Go in peace." {8:49} While Jesus was still speaking, someone came from the house of Jairus, the synagogue leader. "Your daughter is dead," he said. "Don't bother the teacher anymore." {8:50} Hearing this, Jesus said to Jairus, "Don't be afraid; just believe, and she will be healed." {8:51} When he arrived at the house of Jairus, he did not let anyone go in with him except Peter, John, and James, and the child's father and mother. {8:52} Meanwhile, all the people were wailing and mourning for her. "Stop wailing," Jesus said. "She is not dead but asleep." {8:53} They laughed at him, knowing that she was dead. {8:54} But he took her by the hand and said, "My child, get up!" {8:55} Her spirit returned, and at once she stood up. Then Jesus told them to give her something to eat. {8:56} Her parents were astonished, but he ordered them not to tell anyone what had happened.

{9:1} Then Jesus called his twelve disciples together and gave them power and authority over all demons and to heal diseases. {9:2} He sent them to proclaim the kingdom of God and to heal the sick. {9:3} He told them, "Take nothing for your journey—no staff, no bag, no bread, no money, and do not take two coats." {9:4} "Whatever house you enter, stay there until you leave that town. {9:5} If people do not welcome you, shake the dust off your feet when you leave that town as a testimony against them." {9:6} So they set out and went from village to village, preaching the gospel and healing everywhere. {9:7} Now Herod the tetrarch heard about all that was happening, and he was perplexed because some were saying that John had been raised from the dead; {9:8} others said that Elijah had appeared, and still others claimed that one of the old prophets had risen. {9:9} Herod said, "I beheaded John. Who then is this I hear such things about?" And he wanted to see Jesus. {9:10} When the apostles returned, they reported to Jesus what they had done. Then he took them with him and withdrew by themselves to a town called Bethsaida. {9:11} But the crowds learned about it and followed him. He welcomed them and spoke to them about the kingdom of God and healed those who needed healing. {9:12} As the day was drawing to a close, the Twelve came to him and said, "Send the crowd away so they can go to the surrounding villages and countryside and find food and lodging, because we are in a remote place." {9:13} He replied, "You give them something to eat." They answered, "We only have five loaves of bread and two fish, unless we go and buy food for all this crowd." {9:14} (There were about five thousand men.) He said to his disciples, "Have them sit down in groups of about fifty each." {9:15} The disciples did so, and everyone sat down. {9:16} Taking the five loaves and two fish, and looking up to heaven, he gave thanks and broke them. Then he gave them to the disciples to distribute to the people. {9:17} They all ate and were satisfied, and the disciples picked up twelve basketfuls of broken pieces that were left over. {9:18} Once when Jesus was praying in private and his disciples were with him, he asked them, "Who do the crowds say I am?" {9:19} They replied, "Some say John the Baptist; others say Elijah; and still others, that one of the prophets of long ago has come back to life." {9:20} "But what about you?" he asked. "Who do you say I am?" Peter answered, "God's Messiah." {9:21} Jesus strictly warned them not to tell this to anyone. {9:22} He said, "The Son of Man must suffer many things and be rejected by the elders, the chief priests, and the teachers of the law, and he must be killed and on the third day be raised to life." {9:23} Then he said to them all, "Whoever wants to be my disciple must deny themselves and take up their cross daily and follow me. {9:24} For whoever wants to save their life will lose it, but whoever loses their life for me will save it. {9:25} What good is it for someone to gain the whole world, and yet lose or forfeit their very self? {9:26} Whoever is ashamed of me and my words, the Son of Man will be ashamed of them when he comes in his glory and in the glory of the Father and of the holy angels. {9:27} Truly I tell you, some who are standing here will not taste death before they see the kingdom of God." {9:28} About eight days after Jesus said this, he took Peter, John, and James with him and went up onto a mountain to pray. {9:29} As he was praying, the appearance of his face changed, and his clothes became as bright as a flash of lightning. {9:30} Two men, Moses and Elijah, appeared in glorious splendor, talking with Jesus. {9:31} They spoke about his departure, which he was about to bring to fulfillment at Jerusalem. {9:32} Peter and his companions were very sleepy, but when they became fully awake, they saw his glory and the two men standing with him. {9:33} As the men were leaving Jesus, Peter said to him, "Master, it is good for us to be here. Let's put up three shelters—one for you, one for Moses, and one for Elijah." (He did not know what he was saying.) {9:34} While he was speaking, a cloud appeared and enveloped them, and they were afraid as they entered the cloud. {9:35} A voice came from the cloud, saying, "This is my Son, whom I have chosen; listen to him." {9:36} When the voice had spoken, they found that Jesus was alone. The disciples kept this to themselves and did not tell anyone at that time what they had seen. {9:37} The next day, when they came down from the mountain, a large crowd met him. {9:38} A man in the crowd called out, "Teacher, I beg you to look at my son, for he is my only child. {9:39} An evil spirit seizes him and suddenly screams. It throws him into convulsions (fits) so that he foams at the mouth. It scarcely ever leaves him and is destroying him. {9:40} I begged your disciples to drive out the spirit, but they could not." {9:41} "You unbelieving and perverse generation," Jesus replied, "how long shall I stay with you and put up with you? Bring your son here." {9:42} Even while the boy was coming, the demon threw him to the ground in a convulsion. But Jesus rebuked the evil spirit, healed the boy, and gave him back to his father. {9:43} And they were all amazed at the greatness of God. While everyone was marveling at all that Jesus did, he said to his disciples, {9:44} "Listen carefully to what I am about to tell you: The Son of Man is going to be delivered into the hands of men." {9:45} But they did not understand what this meant. It was hidden from them, so they did not grasp it, and they were afraid to ask him about it. {9:46} An argument started among the disciples as to which of them would be the greatest. {9:47} Jesus, knowing their thoughts, took a little child and had him stand beside him. {9:48} Then he said to them, "Whoever welcomes this little child in my name welcomes me; and whoever welcomes me welcomes the one who sent me. For it is the one who is least among you all who is the greatest." {9:49} "Master," said John, "we saw someone driving out demons in your name and we tried to stop him because he is not one of us." {9:50} "Do not stop him," Jesus said, "for whoever is not against you is for you." {9:51} As the time approached for him to be taken up to heaven, Jesus resolutely set out for Jerusalem. {9:52} He sent messengers on ahead, who went into a Samaritan village to get things ready for him; {9:53} but the people there did not welcome him because he was heading for Jerusalem. {9:54} When the disciples James and John saw this, they asked, "Lord, do you want us to call down fire from heaven to destroy them?" {9:55} But Jesus turned and rebuked them. {9:56} Then he and his disciples went to another village. {9:57} As they were walking along the road, a man said to him, "I will follow you wherever you go." {9:58} Jesus replied, "Foxes have dens and birds have nests, but the Son of Man has no place to lay his head." {9:59} He said to another man, "Follow me." But he replied, "Lord, first let me go and bury my father." {9:60} Jesus said to him, "Let the dead bury their own dead, but you go and proclaim the kingdom of God." {9:61} Still another said, "I will follow you, Lord; but first let me go back and say goodbye to my family." {9:62} Jesus replied, "No one who puts a hand to the plow and looks back is fit for service in the kingdom of God."

{10:1} After this, the Lord appointed seventy others and sent them out in pairs ahead of him to every town and place he was about to go. {10:2} He told them, "The harvest is plentiful, but the workers are few. Ask the Lord of the harvest to send out workers into his harvest field. {10:3} Go! I am sending you out like lambs among wolves. {10:4} Do not take a purse or bag or sandals; and do not greet anyone on the road. {10:5} When you enter a house, first say, 'Peace to this house.' {10:6} If a person of peace is there, your peace will rest on them; if not, it will return to you. {10:7} Stay in that house, eating and drinking whatever they give you, for the worker deserves his wages. Do not move around from house to house. {10:8} When you enter a town and are welcomed, eat what is offered to you. {10:9} Heal the sick who are there and tell them, 'The kingdom of God has come near to you.' {10:10} But when you enter a town and are not welcomed, go into its streets and say, {10:11} 'Even the dust of your town that sticks to our feet we wipe off as a warning to you. Yet be sure of this: The kingdom of God has come near.' {10:12} I tell you, it will be more bearable on that day for Sodom than for that town. {10:13} Woe to you, Chorazin! Woe to you, Bethsaida! For if the miracles that were performed in you had been done in Tyre and Sidon, they would have repented long ago, sitting in sackcloth and ashes. {10:14} But it will be more bearable for Tyre and Sidon at the judgment than for you. {10:15} And you, Capernaum, will you be lifted to the heavens? No, you will go down to Hades. {10:16} Whoever listens to you listens to me; whoever rejects you rejects me; but whoever rejects me rejects the one who sent me." {10:17} The seventy returned with joy and said, "Lord, even the demons submit to us in your name." {10:18} He replied, "I saw Satan fall like lightning from heaven. {10:19} I have given you authority to trample on snakes and scorpions and to overcome all the power of the enemy; nothing will harm you. {10:20} However, do not rejoice that the spirits submit to you, but rejoice that your names are written in heaven." {10:21} At that time Jesus, full of joy through the Holy Spirit, said, "I praise you, Father, Lord of heaven and earth, because you have hidden these things from the wise and learned and revealed them to little children. Yes, Father, for this is what you were pleased to do. {10:22} All things have been committed to me by my Father. No one knows who the Son is except the Father, and no one knows who the Father is except the Son and those to whom the Son chooses to reveal him." {10:23} Then he turned to his disciples and said privately, "Blessed are the eyes that see what you see. {10:24} For I tell you that many prophets and kings wanted to see what you see but did not see it, and to hear what you hear but did not hear it." {10:25} On one occasion, an expert in the law stood up to test Jesus. "Teacher," he asked, "what must I do to inherit eternal life?" {10:26} "What is written in the Law?" he replied. "How do you read it?" {10:27} He answered, "Love the Lord your God with all your heart and with all your soul and with all your strength and with all your mind; and love your neighbor as yourself." {10:28} "You have answered correctly," Jesus replied. "Do this and you will live." {10:29} But he wanted to justify himself, so he asked Jesus, "And who is my neighbor?" {10:30} In reply, Jesus said: "A man was going down from Jerusalem to Jericho when he was attacked by robbers. They stripped him of his clothes, beat him and went away, leaving him half dead. {10:31} A priest happened to be going down the same road, and when he saw the man, he passed by on the other side. {10:32} So too, a Levite, when he came to the place and saw him, passed by on the other side. {10:33} But a Samaritan, as he traveled, came where the man was; and when he saw him, he took pity on him. {10:34} He went to him and bandaged his wounds, pouring on oil and wine. Then he put the man on his own donkey, took him to an inn and took care of him. {10:35} The next day he took out two denarii (coins) and gave them to the innkeeper. 'Look after him,' he said, 'and when I return, I will reimburse you for any extra expense you may have.' {10:36} Which of these three do you think was a neighbor to the man who fell into the hands of robbers?" {10:37} The expert in the law replied, "The one who had mercy on him." Jesus told him, "Go and do likewise." {10:38} As Jesus and his disciples were on their way, he came to a village where a woman named Martha opened her home to him. {10:39} She had a sister called Mary, who sat at the Lord's feet listening to what he said. {10:40} But Martha was distracted by all the preparations that had to be made. She came to him and asked, "Lord, don't you care that my sister has left me to do the work by myself? Tell her to help me!" {10:41} "Martha, Martha," the Lord answered, "you are worried and upset about many things, {10:42} but few things are needed—or indeed only one. Mary has chosen what is better, and it will not be taken away from her."

{11:1} One day, while Jesus was praying in a certain place, when he finished, one of his disciples said to him, "Lord, teach us to pray, just as John taught his disciples." {11:2} He said to them, "When you pray, say: Our Father in heaven, may your name be honored. May your kingdom come. May your will be done on earth as it is in heaven. {11:3} Give us our daily bread each day. {11:4} And forgive us our sins, for we also forgive everyone who is indebted to us. And lead us not into temptation but deliver us from evil." {11:5} Then he said to them, "Suppose one of you has a friend, and goes to him at midnight and says, 'Friend, lend me three loaves of bread; {11:6} because a friend of mine has come to me from a journey, and I have nothing to set before him.' {11:7} And the one inside answers, 'Don't bother me. The door is already locked, and my children are with me in bed. I can't get up and give you anything.' {11:8} I tell you, even though he will not get up and give him anything because he is his friend, yet because of the man's boldness, he will get up and give him as much as he needs. {11:9} So I say to you, Ask, and it will be given to you; seek, and you will find; knock, and the door will be opened to you. {11:10} For everyone who asks receives; he who seeks finds; and to him who knocks, the door will be opened. {11:11} Which of you, if your son asks for bread, will give him a stone? Or if he asks for a fish, will give him a snake? {11:12} Or if he asks for an egg, will give him a scorpion? {11:13} If you then, though you are evil, know how to give good gifts to your children, how much more will your Father in heaven give the Holy Spirit to those who ask him?" {11:14} Jesus was driving out a demon that was mute. When the demon left, the man who had been mute spoke, and the crowd was amazed. {11:15} But some of them said, "By Beelzebub, the prince of demons, he is driving out demons." {11:16} Others tested him by asking for a sign from heaven. {11:17} Jesus knew their thoughts and said to them, "Every kingdom divided against itself will be ruined, and a house divided against itself will fall. {11:18} If Satan is divided against himself, how can his kingdom stand? I say this because you claim that I drive out demons by Beelzebub. {11:19} Now if I drive out demons by Beelzebub, by whom do your followers drive them out? So then, they will be your judges. {11:20} But if I drive out demons by the finger of God, then the kingdom of God has come upon you. {11:21} When a strong man, fully armed, guards his own house, his possessions are safe. {11:22} But when someone stronger attacks and overpowers him, he takes away the armor in which the man trusted and divides up the spoils. {11:23} Whoever is not with me is against me, and whoever does not gather with me scatters. {11:24} When an impure spirit comes out of a person, it goes through arid places seeking rest and does not find it. Then it says, 'I will return to the house I left.' {11:25} When it arrives, it finds the house swept clean and put in order. {11:26} Then it goes and takes seven other spirits more wicked than itself, and they go in and live there. And the final condition of that person is worse than the first." {11:27} As Jesus was saying these things, a woman in the crowd called out, "Blessed is the mother who gave you birth and nursed you." {11:28} He replied, "Blessed rather are those who hear the word of God and obey it." {11:29} As the crowds increased, Jesus said, "This is a wicked generation. It asks for a sign, but none will be given it except the sign of Jonah. {11:30} For as Jonah was a sign to the Ninevites, so also will the Son of Man be a sign to this generation. {11:31} The Queen of the South will rise at the judgment with the people of this generation and condemn them; for she came from the ends of the earth to listen to Solomon's wisdom, and now something greater than Solomon is here. {11:32} The people of Nineveh will stand up at the judgment with this generation and condemn it; for they repented at the preaching of Jonah, and now something greater than Jonah is here. {11:33} No one lights a lamp and puts it in a place where it will be hidden, or under a bowl. Instead, they put it on its stand, so that those who come in may see the light. {11:34} Your eye is the lamp of your body. When your eyes are healthy, your whole body is full of light; but when they are unhealthy, your body also is full of darkness. {11:35} See to it, then, that the light within you is not darkness. {11:36} Therefore, if your whole body is full of light and no part of it dark, it will be just as full of light as when the lamp shines its light on you." {11:37} When Jesus had finished speaking, a Pharisee invited him to eat with him; so he went in and reclined at the table. {11:38} But the Pharisee was surprised when he noticed that Jesus did not first wash before the meal. {11:39} Then the Lord said to him, "Now then, you Pharisees clean the outside of the cup and dish, but inside you are full of greed and wickedness. {11:40} You foolish people! Did not the one who made the outside make the inside also? {11:41} But now as for what is inside you—be generous to the poor, and everything will be clean for you. {11:42} Woe to you, Pharisees, because you give God a tenth of your mint, rue, and all other kinds of garden herbs, but you neglect justice and the love of God. You should have practiced the latter without leaving the former undone. {11:43} Woe to you, Pharisees! Because you love the most important seats in the synagogues and greetings in the marketplaces. {11:44} Woe to you, teachers of the law and Pharisees, you hypocrites! You are like unmarked graves, which people walk over without knowing it." {11:45} One of the experts in the law answered him, "Teacher, when you say these things, you insult us also." {11:46} Jesus replied, "And you experts in the law, woe to you, because you load people down with burdens they can hardly carry, and you yourselves will not lift one finger to help them. {11:47} Woe to you! Because you build tombs for the prophets, and it was your ancestors who killed them. {11:48} So you testify that you approve of what your ancestors did; they killed the prophets, and you build their tombs. {11:49} Because of this, God in his wisdom said, 'I will send them prophets and apostles, some of whom they will kill and others they will persecute.' {11:50} Therefore this generation will be held responsible for the blood of all the prophets that has been shed since the beginning of the world, {11:51} from the blood of Abel to the blood of Zechariah, who was killed between the altar and the sanctuary. Yes, I tell you, this generation will be held responsible for it all. {11:52} Woe to you, experts in the law, because you have taken away the key to knowledge. You yourselves have not entered, and you have hindered those who were entering." {11:53} When Jesus went outside, the Pharisees and the teachers of the law began to oppose him fiercely and to besiege him with questions, {11:54} waiting to catch him in something he might say.

{12:1} Meanwhile, when a crowd of many thousands had gathered, so that they were trampling on one another, Jesus began to speak first to his disciples, saying: "Be on your guard against the yeast of the Pharisees, which is hypocrisy. {12:2} There is nothing concealed that will not be disclosed, or hidden that will not be made known. {12:3} What you have said in the dark will be heard in the daylight, and what you have whispered in the ear in the inner rooms will be proclaimed from the roofs. {12:4} I tell you, my friends, do not be afraid of those who kill the body and after that can do no more. {12:5} But I will show you whom you should fear: Fear him who, after your body has been killed, has authority to throw you into hell. Yes, I tell you, fear him. {12:6} Are not five sparrows sold for two pennies? Yet not one of them is forgotten by God. {12:7} Indeed, the very hairs of your head are all numbered. Don't be afraid; you are worth more than many sparrows. {12:8} I tell you, whoever publicly acknowledges me before others, the Son of Man will also acknowledge before the angels of God. {12:9} But whoever disowns me before others will be disowned before the angels of God. {12:10} And everyone who speaks a word against the Son of Man will be forgiven, but anyone who blasphemes against the Holy Spirit will not be forgiven. {12:11} When you are brought before synagogues, rulers, and authorities, do not worry about how you will defend yourselves or what you will say, {12:12} for the Holy Spirit will teach you at that time what you should say." {12:13} Someone in the crowd said to him, "Teacher, tell my brother to divide the inheritance with me." {12:14} Jesus replied, "Man, who appointed me a judge or an arbiter between you?" {12:15} Then he said to them, "Watch out! Be on your guard against all kinds of greed; life does not consist in an abundance of possessions." {12:16} And he told them this parable: "The ground of a certain rich man yielded an abundant harvest. {12:17} He thought to himself, 'What shall I do? I have no place to store my crops.' {12:18} Then he said, 'This is what I'll do: I will tear down my barns and build bigger ones, and there I will store my surplus grain. {12:19} And I'll say to myself, "You have plenty of grain laid up for many years. Take life easy; eat, drink and be merry." {12:20} But God said to him, 'You fool! This very night your life will be demanded from you. Then who will get what you have prepared for yourself?' {12:21} This is how it will be with whoever stores up things for themselves but is not rich toward God." {12:22} Then Jesus said to his disciples: "Therefore I tell you, do not worry about your life, what you will eat; or about your body, what you will wear. {12:23} Life is more than food, and the body more than clothes. {12:24} Consider the ravens: They do not sow or reap, they have no storeroom or barn; yet God feeds them. And how much more valuable you are than birds! {12:25} Who of you by worrying can add a single hour to your life? {12:26} Since you cannot do this very little thing, why do you worry about the rest? {12:27} Consider how the wild flowers grow. They do not labor or spin. Yet I tell you, not even Solomon in all his splendor was dressed like one of these. {12:28} If that is how God clothes the grass of the field, which is here today and tomorrow is thrown into the fire, how much more will he clothe you—you of little faith! {12:29} And do not set your heart on what you will eat or drink; do not worry about it. {12:30} For the pagan world runs after all such things, and your Father knows that you need them. {12:31} But seek his kingdom, and these things will be given to you as well. {12:32} Do not be afraid, little flock, for your Father has been pleased to give you the kingdom. {12:33} Sell your possessions and give to the poor. Provide purses for yourselves that will not wear out, a treasure in heaven that will never fail, where no thief comes near and no moth destroys. {12:34} For where your treasure is, there your heart will be also. {12:35} Be dressed ready for service and keep your lamps burning, {12:36} like servants waiting for their master to return from a wedding banquet, so that when he comes and knocks they can immediately open the door for him. {12:37} It will be good for those servants whose master finds them watching when he comes. Truly I tell you, he will dress himself to serve; will have them recline at the table and will come and wait on them. {12:38} It will be good for those servants whose master finds them ready, even if he comes in the middle of the night or toward daybreak. {12:39} But understand this: If the owner of the house had known at what hour the thief was coming, he would not have let his house be broken into. {12:40} You also must be ready, because the Son of Man will come at an hour when you do not expect him." {12:41} Peter asked, "Lord, are you telling this parable to us, or to everyone?" {12:42} The Lord answered, "Who then is the faithful and wise manager, whom the master puts in charge of his servants to give them their food allowance at the proper time? {12:43} It will be good for that servant whom the master finds doing so when he returns. {12:44} Truly I tell you, he will put him in charge of all his possessions. {12:45} But suppose the servant says to himself, 'My master is taking a long time in coming,' and he then begins to beat the other servants, both men and women, and to eat and drink and get drunk. {12:46} The master of that servant will come on a day when he does not expect him and at an hour he is not aware of. He will cut him to pieces and assign him a place with the unbelievers. {12:47} The servant who knows the master's will and does not get ready or does not do what the master wants will be beaten with many blows. {12:48} But the one who does not know and does things deserving punishment will be beaten with few blows. From everyone who has been given much, much will be demanded; and from the one who has been entrusted with much, much more will be asked. {12:49} I have come to bring fire on the earth, and how I wish it were already kindled! {12:50} But I have a baptism to undergo, and what constraint I am under until it is completed! {12:51} Do you think I came to bring peace on earth? No, I tell you, but division. {12:52} From now on there will be five in one family divided against each other, three against two and two against three. {12:53} They will be divided, father against son and son against father, mother against daughter and daughter against mother, mother-in-law against daughter-in-law and daughter-in-law against mother-in-law." {12:54} He said to the crowd: "When you see a cloud rising in the west, immediately you say, 'It's going to rain,' and it does. {12:55} And when the south wind blows, you say, 'It's going to be hot,' and it is. {12:56} Hypocrites! You know how to interpret the appearance of the earth and the sky. How is it that you don't know how to interpret this present time? {12:57} Why don't you judge for yourselves what is right? {12:58} As you are going with your adversary to the magistrate, try hard to be reconciled on the way, or your adversary may drag you off to the judge, and the judge turn you over to the officer, and the officer throw you into prison. {12:59} I tell you, you will not get out until you have paid the last penny."

{13:1} At that time, some people told Jesus about the Galileans whose blood Pilate had mixed with their sacrifices. {13:2} Jesus answered them, "Do you think these Galileans were worse sinners than all the other Galileans because they suffered this? {13:3} No, I tell you; unless you repent, you too will all perish. {13:4} Or those eighteen people who were killed when the tower in Siloam fell on them—do you think they were more guilty than all the others living in Jerusalem? {13:5} No, I tell you; unless you repent, you too will all perish." {13:6} Then he told this parable: "A man had a fig tree planted in his vineyard, and he went looking for fruit on it but found none. {13:7} So he said to the gardener, 'For three years now, I've been coming to look for fruit on this fig tree and haven't found any. Cut it down! Why should it use up the soil?' {13:8} The gardener replied, 'Sir, leave it alone for one more year, and I'll dig around it and fertilize it. {13:9} If it bears fruit next year, fine! If not, then cut it down.'" {13:10} On a Sabbath, Jesus was teaching in one of the synagogues. {13:11} A woman was there who had been crippled by a spirit for eighteen years. She was bent over and could not straighten up at all. {13:12} When Jesus saw her, he called her forward and said, "Woman, you are set free from your infirmity." {13:13} Then he put his hands on her, and immediately she straightened up and praised God. {13:14} Indignant because Jesus had healed on the Sabbath, the synagogue leader said to the people, "There are six days for work. So come and be healed on those days, not on the Sabbath." {13:15} The Lord answered him, "You hypocrite! Doesn't each of you on the Sabbath untie your ox or donkey from the stall and lead it out to give it water? {13:16} Then should not this woman, a daughter of Abraham whom Satan has kept bound for eighteen long years, be set free on the Sabbath day from what bound her?" {13:17} When he said this, all his opponents were humiliated, but the people were delighted with all the wonderful things he was doing. {13:18} Then Jesus asked, "What is the kingdom of God like? To what shall I compare it? {13:19} It is like a mustard seed that a man took and planted in his garden. It grew and became a tree, and the birds perched in its branches." {13:20} Again he asked, "What shall I compare the kingdom of God to? {13:21} It is like yeast that a woman took and mixed into about sixty pounds (27 kg) of flour until it worked all through the dough." {13:22} Then Jesus went through the towns and villages, teaching as he made his way to Jerusalem. {13:23} Someone asked him, "Lord, are only a few people going to be saved?" He said to them, {13:24} "Make every effort to enter through the narrow door, because many, I tell you, will try to enter and will not be able to. {13:25} Once the owner of the house gets up and closes the door, you will stand outside knocking and pleading, 'Sir, open the door for us.' But he will answer, 'I don't know you or where you come from.' {13:26} Then you will say, 'We ate and drank with you, and you taught in our streets.' {13:27} But he will reply, 'I don't know you or where you come from. Away from me, all you evildoers!' {13:28} There will be weeping there, and gnashing of teeth, when you see Abraham, Isaac, and Jacob and all the prophets in the kingdom of God, but you yourselves thrown out. {13:29} People will come from the east and the west, the north and the south, and will take their places at the feast in the kingdom of God. {13:30} Indeed, there are those who are last who will be first, and first who will be last." {13:31} At that time some Pharisees came to Jesus and said to him, "Leave this place and go somewhere else. Herod wants to kill you." {13:32} He replied, "Go tell that fox, 'I will keep on driving out demons and healing people today and tomorrow, and on the third day I will reach my goal.' {13:33} In any case,

I must press on today and tomorrow and the next day—for surely no prophet can die outside Jerusalem! {13:34} Jerusalem, Jerusalem, you who kill the prophets and stone those sent to you, how often I have longed to gather your children together, as a hen gathers her chicks under her wings, and you were not willing! {13:35} Look, your house is left to you desolate. I tell you, you will not see me again until you say, 'Blessed is he who comes in the name of the Lord.'"

{14:1} One Sabbath, when Jesus went to eat in the house of a prominent Pharisee, he was being carefully watched. {14:2} There in front of him was a man suffering from abnormal swelling of his body. {14:3} Jesus asked the Pharisees and experts in the law, "Is it lawful to heal on the Sabbath or not?" {14:4} They remained silent. So he took hold of the man and healed him and sent him on his way. {14:5} Then he asked them, "If one of you has a child or an ox that falls into a well on the Sabbath day, will you not immediately pull it out?" {14:6} And they had no reply. {14:7} When he noticed how the guests picked the places of honor at the table, he told them this parable: {14:8} "When someone invites you to a wedding feast, do not take the place of honor, for a more distinguished person than you may have been invited. {14:9} If so, the host who invited both of you will come and say to you, 'Give this person your seat.' Then, humiliated, you will have to take the least important place. {14:10} But when you are invited, take the lowest place, so that when your host comes, he will say to you, 'Friend, move up to a better place.' Then you will be honored in the presence of all the other guests. {14:11} For all those who exalt themselves will be humbled, and those who humble themselves will be exalted." {14:12} Then Jesus said to his host, "When you give a luncheon or dinner, do not invite your friends, your brothers or sisters, your relatives, or your rich neighbors; if you do, they may invite you back and so you will be repaid. {14:13} But when you give a banquet, invite the poor, the crippled, the lame, the blind, {14:14} and you will be blessed. Although they cannot repay you, you will be repaid at the resurrection of the righteous." {14:15} When one of those at the table with him heard this, he said to Jesus, "Blessed is the one who will eat at the feast in the kingdom of God." {14:16} Jesus replied: "A certain man was preparing a great banquet and invited many guests. {14:17} At the time of the banquet he sent his servant to tell those who had been invited, 'Come, for everything is now ready.' {14:18} But they all alike began to make excuses. The first said, 'I have just bought a field, and I must go and see it. Please excuse me.' {14:19} Another said, 'I have just bought five yoke of oxen, and I'm on my way to try them out. Please excuse me.' {14:20} Still another said, 'I just got married, so I can't come.' {14:21} The servant came back and reported this to his master. Then the owner of the house became angry and ordered his servant, 'Go out quickly into the streets and alleys of the town and bring in the poor, the crippled, the blind, and the lame.' {14:22} 'Sir,' the servant said, 'what you ordered has been done, but there is still room.' {14:23} Then the master told his servant, 'Go out to the roads and country lanes and compel them to come in, so that my house will be full. {14:24} I tell you, not one of those who were invited will get a taste of my banquet.'" {14:25} Large crowds were traveling with Jesus, and turning to them he said: {14:26} "If anyone comes to me and does not hate father and mother, wife and children, brothers and sisters—yes, even their own life—such a person cannot be my disciple. {14:27} And whoever does not carry their cross and follow me cannot be my disciple. {14:28} Suppose one of you wants to build a tower. Won't you first sit down and estimate the cost to see if you have enough money to complete it? {14:29} For if you lay the foundation and are not able to finish it, everyone who sees it will ridicule you, {14:30} saying, 'This person began to build and wasn't able to finish.' {14:31} Or what king goes to war against another king without first sitting down to consider whether he is able with ten thousand men to oppose the one coming against him with twenty thousand? {14:32} If he is not able, he will send a delegation while the other is still a long way off and will ask for terms of peace. {14:33} In the same way, those of you who do not give up everything you have cannot be my disciples. {14:34} Salt is good, but if it loses its saltiness, how can it be made salty again? {14:35} It is fit neither for the soil nor for the manure pile; it is thrown out. Whoever has ears to hear, let them hear."

{15:1} Tax collectors and sinners were gathering around Jesus to hear him. {15:2} But the Pharisees and teachers of the law muttered, "This man welcomes sinners and eats with them." {15:3} Then Jesus told them this parable: {15:4} "Suppose one of you has a hundred sheep and loses one of them. Doesn't he leave the ninety-nine in the open country and go after the lost sheep until he finds it? {15:5} And when he finds it, he joyfully puts it on his shoulders {15:6} and goes home. Then he calls his friends and neighbors together and says, 'Rejoice with me; I have found my lost sheep.' {15:7} I tell you that in the same way, there will be more rejoicing in heaven over one sinner who repents than over ninety-nine righteous people who do not need to repent. {15:8} Or suppose a woman has ten silver coins and loses one. Doesn't she light a lamp, sweep the house, and search carefully until she finds it? {15:9} And when she finds it, she calls her friends and neighbors together and says, 'Rejoice with me; I have found my lost coin.' {15:10} In the same way, I tell you, there is rejoicing in the presence of the angels of God over one sinner who repents." {15:11} Jesus continued: "There was a man who had two sons. {15:12} The younger one said to his father, 'Father, give me my share of the estate.' So he divided his property between them. {15:13} Not long after that, the younger son got together all he had, set off for a distant country, and there squandered his wealth in wild living. {15:14} After he had spent everything, there was a severe famine in that whole country, and he began to be in need. {15:15} So he went and hired himself out to a citizen of that country, who sent him to his fields to feed pigs. {15:16} He longed to fill his stomach with the pods that the pigs were eating, but no one gave him anything. {15:17} When he came to his senses, he said, 'How many of my father's hired servants have food to spare, and here I am starving to death! {15:18} I will set out and go back to my father and say to him: Father, I have sinned against heaven and against you. {15:19} I am no longer worthy to be called your son; make me like one of your hired servants.' {15:20} So he got up and went to his father. But while he was still a long way off, his father saw him and was filled with compassion for him; he ran to his son, threw his arms around him and kissed him. {15:21} The son said to him, 'Father, I have sinned against heaven and in your sight. I am no longer worthy to be called your son.' {15:22} But the father said to his servants, 'Quick! Bring the best robe and put it on him. Put a ring on his finger and sandals on his feet. {15:23} Bring the fattened calf and kill it. Let's have a feast and celebrate. {15:24} For this son of mine was dead and is alive again; he was lost and is found.' So they began to celebrate. {15:25} Meanwhile, the older son was in the field. When he came near the house, he heard music and dancing. {15:26} So he called one of the servants and asked him what was going on. {15:27} 'Your brother has come,' he replied, 'and your father has killed the fattened calf because he has him back safe and sound.' {15:28} The older brother became angry and refused to go in. So his father went out and pleaded with him. {15:29} But he answered his father, 'Look! All these years I've been slaving for you and never disobeyed your orders. Yet you never gave me even a young goat so I could celebrate with my friends. {15:30} But when this son of yours who has squandered your property with prostitutes comes home, you kill the fattened calf for him!' {15:31} 'My son,' the father said, 'you are always with me, and everything I have is yours. {15:32} But we had to celebrate and be glad because this brother of yours was dead and is alive again; he was lost and is found.'"

{16:1} Jesus told his disciples: "There was a rich man whose manager was accused of wasting his possessions. {16:2} So he called him in and asked him, 'What is this I hear about you? Give an account of your management, because you cannot be manager any longer.' {16:3} The manager said to himself, 'What shall I do now? My master is taking away my job. I'm not strong enough to dig, and I'm ashamed to beg. {16:4} I know what I'll do so that when I lose my job here, people will welcome me into their houses.' {16:5} So he called in each one of his master's debtors. He asked the first, 'How much do you owe my master?' {16:6} 'Nine hundred gallons of olive oil,' he replied. 'Take your bill,' he said. 'Sit down quickly and make it four hundred and fifty.' {16:7} Then he asked the second, 'And how much do you owe?' 'A thousand bushels of wheat,' he replied. 'Take your bill and make it eight hundred.' {16:8} The master commended the dishonest manager because he had acted shrewdly; for the people of this world are more shrewd in dealing with their own kind than are the people of the light. {16:9} I tell you, use worldly wealth to gain friends for yourselves, so that when it is gone, you will be welcomed into eternal dwellings. {16:10} Whoever can be trusted with very little can also be trusted with much, and whoever is dishonest with very little will also be dishonest with much. {16:11} So if you have not been trustworthy in handling worldly wealth, who will trust you with true riches? {16:12} And if you have not been trustworthy with someone else's property, who will give you property of your own? {16:13} No one can serve two masters. Either you will hate the one and love the other, or you will be devoted to the one and despise the other. You cannot serve both God and money." {16:14} The Pharisees, who loved money, heard all this and were sneering at Jesus. {16:15} He said to them, "You are the ones who justify yourselves in the eyes of others, but God knows your hearts. What people value highly is detestable in God's sight. {16:16} The Law and the Prophets were proclaimed until John. Since that time, the good news of the kingdom of God is being preached, and everyone is forcing their way into it. {16:17} It is easier for heaven and earth to disappear than for the least stroke of a pen to drop out of the Law. {16:18} Anyone who divorces his wife and marries another woman commits adultery, and the man who marries a divorced woman commits adultery. {16:19} There was a rich man who was dressed in purple and fine linen and lived in luxury every day. {16:20} At his gate was laid a beggar named Lazarus, covered with sores {16:21} and longing to eat what fell from the rich man's table. Even the dogs came and licked his sores. {16:22} The time came when the beggar died and the angels carried him to Abraham's side. The rich man also died and was buried. {16:23} In Hades, where he was in torment, he looked up and saw Abraham far away, with Lazarus by his side. {16:24} So he called to him, 'Father Abraham, have pity on me and send Lazarus to dip the tip of his finger in water and cool my tongue, because I am in agony in this fire.' {16:25} But Abraham replied, 'Son, remember that in your lifetime you received your good things, while Lazarus received bad things, but now he is comforted here and you are in agony. {16:26} And besides all this, between us and you a great chasm has been set in place, so that those who want to go from here to you cannot, nor can anyone cross over from there to us.' {16:27} He answered, 'Then I beg you, father, send Lazarus to my family, {16:28} for I have five brothers. Let him warn them, so they will not also come to this place of torment.' {16:29} Abraham replied, 'They have Moses and the Prophets; let them listen to them.' {16:30} 'No, father Abraham,' he said, 'but if someone from the dead goes to them, they will repent.' {16:31} He said to him, 'If they do not listen to Moses and the Prophets, they will not be convinced even if someone rises from the dead.'"

{17:1} Jesus said to his disciples, "It is inevitable that offenses will come, but woe to the person through whom they come! {17:2} It would be better for that person to have a large millstone hung around their neck and be thrown into the sea than to cause one of these little ones to stumble. {17:3} Watch yourselves. If your brother sins against you, rebuke him; and if he repents, forgive him. {17:4} If he sins against you seven times in a day and comes back to you seven times saying, 'I repent,' you must forgive him." {17:5} The apostles said to the Lord, "Increase our faith!" {17:6} He replied, "If you had faith as small as a mustard seed, you could say to this mulberry tree, 'Be uprooted and planted in the sea,' and it would obey you. {17:7} Suppose one of you has a servant plowing or looking after sheep. Would you say to the servant when he comes in from the field, 'Come along now and sit down to eat'? {17:8} Wouldn't you rather say, 'Prepare my supper, get yourself ready, and wait on me while I eat and drink; after that you may eat and drink'? {17:9} Would he thank the servant because he did what he was told? {17:10} So you also, when you have done everything you were told to do, should say, 'We are unworthy servants; we have only done our duty.' {17:11} Now on his way to Jerusalem, Jesus traveled along the border between Samaria and Galilee. {17:12} As he was going into a village, ten men who had leprosy met him. They stood at a distance {17:13} and called out in a loud voice, "Jesus, Master, have pity on us!" {17:14} When he saw them, he said, "Go, show yourselves to the priests." And as they went, they were cleansed. {17:15} One of them, when he saw he was healed, came back, praising God in a loud voice. {17:16} He threw himself at Jesus' feet and thanked him—and he was a Samaritan. {17:17} Jesus asked, "Were not all ten cleansed? Where are the other nine? {17:18} Has no one returned to give praise to God except this foreigner?" {17:19} Then he said to him, "Rise and go; your faith has made you well." {17:20} Once, on being asked by the Pharisees when the kingdom of God would come, Jesus replied, "The kingdom of God does not come with your careful observation, {17:21} nor will people say, 'Here it is,' or 'There it is,' because the kingdom of God is within you." {17:22} Then he said to his disciples, "The time will come when you will long to see one of the days of the Son of Man, but you will not see it. {17:23} People will tell you, 'There he is!' or 'Here he is!' Do not go running off after them. {17:24} For the Son of Man in his day will be like the lightning that flashes and lights up the sky from one end to the other. {17:25} But first he must suffer many things and be rejected by this generation. {17:26} Just as it was in the days of Noah, so also will it be in the days of the Son of Man. {17:27} People were eating, drinking, marrying, and being given in marriage up to the day Noah entered the ark. Then the flood came and destroyed them all. {17:28} It was the same in the days of Lot. People were eating and drinking, buying and selling, planting and building. {17:29} But the day Lot left Sodom, fire and sulfur rained down from heaven and destroyed them all. {17:30} It will be just like this on the day the Son of Man is revealed. {17:31} On that day no one who is on the roof of his house should go down to take anything out of the house, and no one in the field should go back for anything. {17:32} Remember Lot's wife! {17:33} Whoever tries to keep their life will lose it, and whoever loses their life will preserve it. {17:34} I tell you, on that night two people will be in one bed; one will be taken and the other left. {17:35} Two women will be grinding grain together; one will be taken and the other left. {17:36} Two men will be in the field; one will be taken and the other left." {17:37} "Where, Lord?" they asked. He replied, "Where there is a dead body, there the vultures will gather."

{18:1} Then Jesus told his disciples a parable to show them that they should always pray and not give up. {18:2} He said: "In a certain town there was a judge who neither feared God nor cared what people thought. {18:3} And there was a widow in that town who kept coming to him with the plea, 'Grant me justice against my adversary.' {18:4} For some time he refused. But finally he said to himself, 'Even though I don't fear God or care what people think, {18:5} yet because this widow keeps bothering me, I will see that she gets justice, so that she won't eventually come and attack me!'" {18:6} And the Lord said, "Listen to what the unjust judge says. {18:7} And will not God bring about justice for his chosen ones, who cry out to him day and night? Will he keep putting them off? {18:8} I tell you, he will see that they get justice, and quickly. However, when the Son of Man comes, will he find faith on the earth?" {18:9} To some who were confident of their own righteousness and looked down on everyone else, Jesus told this parable: {18:10} "Two men went up to the temple to pray, one a Pharisee and the other a tax collector. {18:11} The Pharisee stood by himself and prayed: 'God, I thank you that I am not like other people—robbers, evildoers, adulterers—or even like this tax collector. {18:12} I fast twice a week and give a tenth of all I get.' {18:13} But the tax collector stood at a distance. He would not even look up to heaven, but beat his breast and said, 'God, have mercy on me, a sinner.' {18:14} I tell you that this man, rather than the other, went home justified before God. For all those who exalt themselves will be humbled, and those who humble themselves will be exalted." {18:15} People were also bringing babies to Jesus for him to place his hands on them. When the disciples saw this, they rebuked them. {18:16} But Jesus called the children to him and said, "Let the little children come to me, and do not hinder them, for the kingdom of God belongs to such as these. {18:17} Truly I tell you, anyone who will not receive the kingdom of God like a little child will never enter it." {18:18} A certain ruler asked him, "Good teacher, what must I do to inherit eternal life?" {18:19} "Why do you call me good?" Jesus answered. "No one is good—except God alone. {18:20} You know the commandments: 'You shall not commit adultery,' 'You shall not murder,' 'You shall not steal,' 'You shall not give false testimony,' 'Honor your father and mother.'" {18:21} "All these I have kept since I was a boy," he said. {18:22} When Jesus heard this, he said to him, "You still lack one thing: sell everything you have and give to the poor, and you will have treasure in heaven. Then come, follow me." {18:23} When he heard this, he became very sad because he was very wealthy. {18:24} Jesus looked at him and said, "How hard it is for the rich to enter the kingdom of God! {18:25} Indeed, it is easier for a camel to go through the eye of a needle than for someone who is rich to enter the kingdom of God." {18:26} Those who heard this asked, "Who then can be saved?" {18:27} Jesus replied, "What is impossible with man is possible with God." {18:28} Peter said to him, "We have left all we had to follow you!" {18:29} "Truly I tell you," Jesus said to them, "no one who has left home or wife or brothers or sisters or parents or children for the sake of the kingdom of God {18:30} will fail to receive many times as much in this age and in the age to come eternal life." {18:31} Jesus took the Twelve aside and told them, "We are going up to Jerusalem, and everything that is written by the prophets about the Son of Man will be fulfilled. {18:32} He will be delivered over to the Gentiles. They will mock him, insult him and spit on him; {18:33} they will flog him and kill him. On the third day he will rise again." {18:34} The disciples did not understand any of this. Its meaning was hidden from them, and they did not know what he was talking about. {18:35} As Jesus approached Jericho, a blind man was sitting by the roadside begging. {18:36} When he heard the crowd going by, he asked what was happening. {18:37} They told him, "Jesus of Nazareth is passing by." {18:38} He called out, "Jesus, Son of David, have mercy on me!" {18:39} Those who led the way rebuked him and told him to be quiet, but he shouted all the more, "Son of David, have mercy on me!" {18:40} Jesus stopped and ordered the man to be brought to him. When he came near, Jesus asked him, {18:41} "What do you want me to do for you?" "Lord, I want to see," he replied. {18:42} Jesus said to him, "Receive your sight; your faith has healed you." {18:43} Immediately he received his sight and followed Jesus, praising God. When all the people saw it, they also praised God.

{19:1} Jesus entered and passed through Jericho. {19:2} There was a man named Zacchaeus, who was the chief tax collector and was wealthy. {19:3} He wanted to see who Jesus was, but he couldn't because he was short. {19:4} So he ran ahead and climbed a sycamore tree to see him, since Jesus was going to pass that way. {19:5} When Jesus reached the spot, he looked up and said to him, "Zacchaeus, come down immediately. I must stay at your house today." {19:6} So he came down at once and welcomed him gladly. {19:7} All the people saw this and began to mutter, "He has gone to be the guest of a sinner." {19:8} But Zacchaeus stood up and said to the Lord, "Look, Lord! Here and now I give half of my possessions to the poor, and if I have cheated anyone out of anything, I will pay back four times the amount." {19:9} Jesus said to him, "Today salvation has come to this house, because this man, too, is a son of Abraham. {19:10} For the Son of Man came to seek and to save the lost." {19:11} While they were listening to this, he went on to tell them a parable because he was near Jerusalem and the people thought that the kingdom of God was going to appear at once. {19:12} He said: "A nobleman went to a distant country to have himself appointed king and then return. {19:13} He called ten of his servants and gave them ten minas (a type of currency). 'Put this money to work,' he said, 'until I come back.' {19:14} But his subjects hated him and sent a delegation after him to say, 'We don't want this man to be our king.' {19:15} He was made king, however, and returned home. Then he sent for the servants to whom he had given the money in order to find out what they had gained with it. {19:16} The first one came and said, 'Sir, your mina has earned ten more.' {19:17} 'Well done, good servant!' his master replied. 'Because you have been trustworthy in a very small matter, take charge of ten cities.' {19:18} The second came and said, 'Sir, your mina has earned five more.' {19:19} His master answered, 'You take charge of five cities.' {19:20} Then another servant came and said, 'Sir, here is your mina; I have kept it laid away in a piece of cloth. {19:21} I was afraid of you because you are a hard man. You take out what you did not put in and reap what you did not sow.' {19:22} His master replied, 'I will judge you by your own words, you wicked servant! You knew, did you, that I am a hard man, taking out what I did not put in and reaping what I did not sow? {19:23} Why then didn't you put my money on deposit, so that when I came back I could have collected it with interest?' {19:24} Then he said to those standing by, 'Take his mina away from him and give it to the one who has ten minas.' {19:25} 'Sir,' they said, 'he already has ten!' {19:26} He replied, 'I tell you that to everyone who has, more will be given, but as for the one who has nothing, even what they think they have will be taken away. {19:27} But those enemies of mine who did not want me to be king over them—bring them here and kill them in front of me.' {19:28} After Jesus had said this, he went on ahead, going up to Jerusalem. {19:29} As he approached Bethphage and Bethany at the hill called the Mount of Olives, he sent two of his disciples, {19:30} saying to them, "Go to the village ahead of you. There, as you enter, you will find a colt tied there, which no one has ever ridden. Untie it and bring it here. {19:31} If anyone asks you, 'Why are you untying it?' say, 'The Lord needs it.'" {19:32} Those who were sent ahead went and found it just as he had told them. {19:33} As they were untying the colt, its owners asked them, "Why are you untying the colt?" {19:34} They replied, "The Lord needs it." {19:35} They brought it to Jesus, threw their cloaks on the colt and put Jesus on it. {19:36} As he went along, people spread their cloaks on the road. {19:37} When he came near the place where the road goes down the Mount of Olives, the whole crowd of disciples began joyfully to praise God in loud voices for all the miracles they had seen: {19:38} "Blessed is the king who comes in the name of the Lord! Peace in heaven and glory in the highest!" {19:39} Some of the Pharisees in the crowd said to Jesus, "Teacher, rebuke your disciples!" {19:40} "I tell you," he replied, "if they keep quiet, the stones will cry out." {19:41} As he approached Jerusalem and saw the city, he wept over it {19:42} and said, "If you, even you, had only known on this day what would bring you peace—but now it is hidden from your eyes. {19:43} The days will come upon you when your enemies will build an embankment against you and encircle you and hem you in on every side. {19:44} They will dash you to the ground, you and the children within your walls. They will not leave one stone on another because you did not recognize the time of God's coming to you." {19:45} Then he entered the temple area and began driving out those who were selling. {19:46} "It is written," he said to them, "'My house will be a house of prayer,' but you have made it 'a den of robbers.'" {19:47} Every day he was teaching at the temple; but the chief priests, the teachers of the law and the leaders among the people were trying to kill him. {19:48} Yet they could not find any way to do it, because all the people hung on his words.

{20:1} One day as Jesus was teaching the people in the temple courts and proclaiming the good news, the chief priests and the teachers of the law, along with the elders, came up to him. {20:2} "Tell us by what authority you are doing these things," they said. "Who gave you this authority?" {20:3} He replied, "I will also ask you a question. Tell me, {20:4} John's baptism—was it from heaven, or of human origin?" {20:5} They discussed it among themselves and said, "If we say, 'From heaven,' he will ask, 'Why didn't you believe him?' {20:6} But if we say, 'Of human origin,' all the people will stone us, because they are persuaded that John was a prophet." {20:7} So they answered, "We don't know where it was from." {20:8} Jesus said, "Neither will I tell you by what authority I am doing these things." {20:9} He went on to tell the people this parable: "A man planted a vineyard, rented it to some farmers and went away for a long time. {20:10} At harvest time he sent a servant to the tenants so they would give him some of the fruit of the vineyard. But the tenants beat him and sent him away empty-handed. {20:11} He sent another servant, but that one also they beat and treated shamefully and sent away empty-handed. {20:12} He sent still a third, and they wounded him and threw him out. {20:13} Then the owner of the vineyard said, 'What shall I do? I will send my son, whom I love; perhaps they will respect him.' {20:14} But when the tenants saw him, they talked the matter over. "This is the heir," they said. "Let's kill him and the inheritance will be ours." {20:15} So they threw him out of the vineyard and killed him. "What then will the owner of the vineyard do to them? {20:16} He will come and kill those tenants and give the vineyard to others." When the people heard this, they said, "God forbid!" {20:17} Jesus looked directly at them and asked, "Then what is the meaning of that which is written: 'The stone the builders rejected has become the cornerstone'? {20:18} Everyone who falls on that stone will be broken to pieces; anyone on whom it falls will be crushed." {20:19} The teachers of the law and the chief priests looked for a way to arrest him immediately, because they knew he had spoken this parable against them. But they were afraid of the people. {20:20} Keeping a close watch on him, they sent spies who pretended to be honest. They hoped to catch Jesus in something he said so that they might hand him over to the power and authority of the governor. {20:21} So the spies questioned him: "Teacher, we know that you speak and teach what is right and that you do not show favoritism but teach the way of God in accordance with the truth. {20:22} Is it right for us to pay taxes to Caesar or not?" {20:23} He saw through their duplicity and said to them, "Show me a denarius. Whose image and inscription are on it?" {20:24} "Caesar's," they replied. He said to them, "Then give back to Caesar what is Caesar's, and to God what is God's." {20:25} They were unable to trap him in what he had said there in public. And astonished by his answer, they became silent. {20:26} Some of the Sadducees, who say there is no resurrection, came to Jesus with a question. {20:27} They said, "Teacher, Moses wrote for us that if a man's brother dies and leaves a wife but no children, the man must marry the widow and raise up offspring for his brother. {20:28} Now there were seven brothers. The first one married a woman and died childless. {20:29} The second and then the third married her, and in the same way the seven died, leaving no children. {20:30} Finally, the woman died too. {20:31} Now then, at the resurrection whose wife will she be, since the seven were married to her?" {20:32} Jesus replied, "The people of this age marry and are given in marriage. {20:33} But those who are considered worthy of taking part in that age and in the resurrection from the dead will neither marry nor be given in marriage. {20:34} They can no longer die; for they are like the angels. They are God's children, since they are children of the resurrection. {20:35} But about the resurrection of the dead—have you not read what Moses said in the account of the burning bush? He calls the Lord the God of Abraham, the God of Isaac, and the God of Jacob. {20:36} He is not the God of the dead, but of the living, for to him all are alive." {20:37} Some of the teachers of the law responded, "Well said, teacher!" {20:38} And no one dared to ask him any more questions. {20:39} He said to them, "How is it that they say the Messiah is the son of David? {20:40} David himself declares in the Book of Psalms: 'The Lord said to my Lord: "Sit at my right hand until I make your enemies a footstool for your feet."' {20:41} David calls him 'Lord.' How then can he be his son?" {20:42} While all the people were listening, Jesus said to his disciples, {20:43} "Beware of the teachers of the law. They like to walk around in flowing robes and love to be greeted with respect in the marketplaces {20:44} and have the most important seats in the synagogues and the places of honor at banquets. They devour widows' houses and for a show make lengthy prayers. These men will be punished most severely."

{21:1} Jesus looked up and saw the rich putting their gifts into the treasury. {21:2} He also saw a poor widow putting in two small coins. {21:3} He said, "Truly I tell you, this poor widow has put in more than all of them. {21:4} They all gave out of their wealth, but she, out of her poverty, gave all she had to live on." {21:5} Some were talking about the temple, how it was decorated with beautiful stones and gifts. But Jesus said, {21:6} "As for what you see here, the time will come when not one stone will be left on another; every one of them will be thrown down." {21:7} They asked him, "Teacher, when will these things happen? What will be the sign that they are about to take place?" {21:8} He replied, "Watch out that you are not deceived. For many will come in my name claiming, 'I am he,' and 'The time is near.' Do not follow them. {21:9} When you hear of wars and uprisings, do not be frightened. These things must happen first, but the end will not come right away." {21:10} Then he said to them: "Nation will rise against nation, and kingdom against kingdom. {21:11} There will be great earthquakes, famines, and pestilences in various places, and fearful events and great signs from heaven. {21:12} But before all this, they will lay hands on you and persecute you; they will deliver you to synagogues and prisons, and you will be brought before kings and governors all on account of my name. {21:13} This will result in you being witnesses to them. {21:14} But make up your mind not to worry beforehand how you will defend yourselves. {21:15} For I will give you words and wisdom that none of your adversaries will be able to resist or contradict. {21:16} You will be betrayed even by parents, siblings, relatives, and friends, and they will put some of you to death. {21:17} Everyone will hate you because of me. {21:18} Yet not a hair of your head will perish. {21:19} Stand firm, and you will win life. {21:20} When you see Jerusalem being surrounded by armies, you will know that its desolation is near. {21:21} Let those who are in Judea flee to the mountains; let those in the city get out, and let those in the country not enter the city. {21:22} For this is the time of punishment in fulfillment of all that has been written. {21:23} How dreadful it will be in those days for pregnant women and nursing mothers! There will be great distress in the land and wrath against this people. {21:24} They will fall by the sword and will be taken as prisoners to all nations; Jerusalem will be trampled on by the Gentiles until the times of the Gentiles are fulfilled. {21:25} There will be signs in the sun, moon, and stars. On the earth, nations will be in anguish and perplexity at the roaring and tossing of the sea. {21:26} People will faint from terror, apprehensive of what is coming on the world, for the heavenly bodies will be shaken. {21:27} At that time they will see the Son of Man coming in a cloud with power and great glory. {21:28} When these things begin to take place, stand up and lift up your heads, because your redemption is drawing near." {21:29} He told them this parable: "Look at the fig tree and all the trees. {21:30} When they sprout leaves, you can see for yourselves and know that summer is near. {21:31} Even so, when you see these things happening, you know that the kingdom of God is near. {21:32} Truly I tell you, this generation will certainly not pass away until all these things have happened. {21:33} Heaven and earth will pass away, but my words will never pass away. {21:34} Be careful, or your hearts will be weighed down with carousing, drunkenness, and the anxieties of life, and that day will close on you suddenly like a trap. {21:35} For it will come on all those who live on the face of the whole earth. {21:36} Be always on the watch, and pray that you may be able to escape all that is about to happen, and that you may be able to stand before the Son of Man." {21:37} Each day Jesus was teaching at the temple, and each evening he went out to spend the night on the hill called the Mount of Olives. {21:38} And all the people came early in the morning to hear him at the temple.

{22:1} Now the Festival of Unleavened Bread, called the Passover, was approaching, {22:2} and the chief priests and the teachers of the law were looking for some way to get rid of Jesus, for they were afraid of the people. {22:3} Then Satan entered Judas, called Iscariot, one of the Twelve. {22:4} And Judas went to the chief priests and the officers of the temple guard and discussed with them how he might betray Jesus. {22:5} They were delighted and agreed to give him money. {22:6} He consented and watched for an opportunity to hand Jesus over to them when no crowd was present. {22:7} Then came the Day of Unleavened Bread on which the Passover lamb had to be sacrificed. {22:8} Jesus sent Peter and John, saying, "Go and make preparations for us to eat the Passover." {22:9} "Where do you want us to prepare for it?" they asked. {22:10} He replied, "As you enter the city, a man carrying a jar of water will meet you. Follow him to the house that he enters. {22:11} Say to the owner of the house, 'The Teacher asks: Where is the guest room, where I may eat the Passover with my disciples?' {22:12} He will show you a large upper room, all furnished. Make preparations there." {22:13} They left and found things just as Jesus had told them. So they prepared the Passover. {22:14} When the hour came, Jesus and his apostles reclined at the table. {22:15} And he said to them, "I have eagerly desired to eat this Passover with you before I suffer. {22:16} For I tell you, I will not eat it again until it finds fulfillment in the kingdom of God." {22:17} After taking the cup, he gave thanks and said, "Take this and divide it among you. {22:18} For I tell you, I will not drink again from the fruit of the vine until the kingdom of God comes." {22:19} And he took bread, gave thanks, broke it and gave it to them, saying, "This is my body given for you; do this in remembrance of me." {22:20} In the same way, after the supper he took the cup, saying, "This cup is the new covenant in my blood, which is poured out for you. {22:21} But the hand of him who is going to betray me is with mine on the table. {22:22} The Son of Man will go as it has been decreed. Woe to that man who betrays him!" {22:23} They began to question among themselves which of them it might be who would do this. {22:24} Also a dispute arose among them as to which of them was considered to be the greatest. {22:25} Jesus said to them, "The kings of the Gentiles lord it over them; and those who exercise authority over them call themselves Benefactors. {22:26} But you are not to be like that. Instead, the greatest among you should be like the youngest, and the one who rules like the one who serves. {22:27} For who is greater, the one who is at the table or the one who serves? Is it not the one who is at the table? But I am among you as one who serves. {22:28} You are those who have stood by me in my trials. {22:29} And I confer on you a kingdom, just as my Father conferred one on me, {22:30} so that you may eat and drink at my table in my kingdom and sit on thrones, judging the twelve tribes of Israel." {22:31} Simon, Simon, Satan has asked to sift all of you as wheat. {22:32} But I have prayed for you, Simon, that your faith may not fail. And when you have turned back, strengthen your brothers." {22:33} But he replied, "Lord, I am ready to go with you to prison and to death." {22:34} Jesus answered, "I tell you, Peter, before the rooster crows today, you will deny three times that you know me." {22:35} Then Jesus asked them, "When I sent you without purse, bag, or sandals, did you lack anything?" "Nothing," they answered. {22:36} He said to them, "But now if you have a purse, take it, and also a bag; and if you don't have a sword, sell your cloak and buy one. {22:37} It is written: 'And he was numbered with the transgressors'; and I tell you that this must be fulfilled in me. Yes, what is written about me is reaching its fulfillment." {22:38} The disciples said, "See, Lord, here are two swords." "That's enough!" he replied. {22:39} Jesus went out as usual to the Mount of Olives, and his disciples followed him. {22:40} On reaching the place, he said to them, "Pray that you will not fall into temptation." {22:41} He withdrew about a stone's throw beyond them, knelt down and prayed, {22:42} "Father, if you are willing, take this cup from me; yet not my will, but yours be done." {22:43} An angel from heaven appeared to him and strengthened him. {22:44} And being in anguish, he prayed more earnestly, and his sweat was like drops of blood falling to the ground. {22:45} When he rose from prayer and went back to the disciples, he found them asleep, exhausted from sorrow. {22:46} "Why are you sleeping?" he asked them. "Get up and pray so that you will not fall into temptation." {22:47} While he was still speaking, a crowd came up, and the man who was called Judas, one of the Twelve, was leading them. He approached Jesus to kiss him. {22:48} But Jesus asked him, "Judas, are you betraying the Son of Man with a kiss?" {22:49} When Jesus' followers saw what was going to happen, they said, "Lord, should we strike with our swords?" {22:50} And one of them struck the servant of the high priest, cutting off his right ear. {22:51} But Jesus answered, "No more of this!" And he touched the man's ear and healed him. {22:52} Then Jesus said to the chief priests, the officers of the temple guard, and the elders who had come for him, "Am I leading a rebellion, that you have come with swords and clubs? {22:53} Every day I was with you in the temple courts, and you did not lay a hand on me. But this is your hour—when darkness reigns." {22:54} Then seizing him, they led him away and took him into the house of the high priest. Peter followed at a distance. {22:55} And when some there had kindled a fire in the middle of the courtyard and had sat down together, Peter sat down with them. {22:56} A servant girl saw him seated there in the firelight. She looked closely at him. "This man was with him," she said. {22:57} But he denied it. "Woman, I don't know him," he said. {22:58} A little later someone else saw him and said, "You also are one of them." "Man, I am not!" Peter replied. {22:59} About an hour later another asserted, "Certainly this fellow was with him, for he is a Galilean." {22:60} Peter replied, "Man, I don't know what you're talking about!" Just as he was speaking, the rooster crowed. {22:61} The Lord turned and looked straight at Peter. Then Peter remembered the word the Lord had spoken to him: "Before the rooster crows today, you will disown me three times." {22:62} And he went outside and wept bitterly. {22:63} The men who were guarding Jesus began mocking and beating him. {22:64} They blindfolded him and demanded, "Prophesy! Who hit you?" {22:65} And they said many other insulting things to him. {22:66} At daybreak, the council of the elders of the people, both the chief priests and the teachers of the law, met together, and Jesus was led before them. {22:67} "If you are the Messiah," they said, "tell us." Jesus answered, "If I tell you, you will not believe me. {22:68} And if I asked you, you would not answer. {22:69} But from now on, the Son of Man will be seated at the right hand of the mighty God." {22:70} They all asked, "Are you then the Son of God?" He replied, "You say that I am." {22:71} Then they said, "Why do we need any more testimony? We have heard it from his own lips."

{23:1} Then the entire crowd stood up and brought him to Pilate. {23:2} They began to accuse him, saying, "We found this man misleading our nation, forbidding us to pay taxes to Caesar, and claiming that he himself is the Messiah, a King." {23:3} Pilate asked him, "Are you the King of the Jews?" He answered, "You say so." {23:4} Pilate then said to the chief priests and the crowd, "I find no reason to charge this man." {23:5} But they insisted more strongly, saying, "He stirs up the people, teaching throughout all of Judea, starting in Galilee and coming here." {23:6} When Pilate heard this, he asked if the man was a Galilean. {23:7} As soon as he realized that Jesus was under Herod's authority, he sent him to Herod, who was also in Jerusalem at that time. {23:8} When Herod saw Jesus, he was very glad, for he had wanted to see him for a long time because he had heard many things about him and hoped to see him perform a miracle. {23:9} He questioned Jesus at length, but Jesus gave him no answer. {23:10} The chief priests and the teachers of the law stood there, vehemently accusing him. {23:11} Herod and his soldiers treated him with contempt, mocking him, and then dressed him in a splendid robe before sending him back to Pilate. {23:12} That day, Pilate and Herod became friends; before this, they had been enemies. {23:13} Pilate called together the chief priests, the rulers, and the people, {23:14} and said to them, "You brought me this man as one who was misleading the people. I have examined him in your presence and found no basis for your charges against him. {23:15} Neither did Herod, for I sent you to him. He has done nothing deserving death. {23:16} Therefore, I will have him punished and then release him." {23:17} (It was customary for him to release one prisoner to them at the Festival.) {23:18} But they shouted together, "Away with this man! Release Barabbas to us!" {23:19} Barabbas had been imprisoned for an insurrection (a violent uprising) in the city and for murder. {23:20} Pilate, wanting to release Jesus, spoke to them again. {23:21} But they shouted, "Crucify him! Crucify him!" {23:22} For the third time, he spoke to them, "Why? What wrong has he done? I have found no grounds for the death penalty. Therefore, I will have him punished and let him go." {23:23} But they kept shouting loudly, demanding that he be crucified, and their voices, along with those of the chief priests, prevailed. {23:24} Pilate decided to grant their demand. {23:25} He released the man who had been imprisoned for insurrection and murder, the one they asked for, but he handed Jesus over to their will. {23:26} As they led Jesus away, they seized a man named Simon, who was from Cyrene (a city in North Africa), and put the cross on him to carry behind Jesus. {23:27} A large number of people followed him, including women who mourned and wailed for him. {23:28} Jesus turned to them and said, "Daughters of Jerusalem, do not weep for me; weep for yourselves and for your children. {23:29} For the time will come when they will say, 'Blessed are the barren, the wombs that never bore, and the breasts that never nursed.' {23:30} Then they will say to the mountains, 'Fall on us!' and to the hills, 'Cover us!' {23:31} For if people do these things when the tree is green, what will happen when it is dry?" {23:32} Two other men, both criminals, were also led out with him to be executed. {23:33} When they came to the place called the Skull (or Golgotha), they crucified him there, along with the criminals—one on his right, the other on his left. {23:34} Jesus said, "Father, forgive them, for they do not know what they are doing." And they divided his clothes by casting lots. {23:35} The people stood watching, and the rulers even sneered at him. They said, "He saved others; let him save himself if he is God's Messiah, the Chosen One." {23:36} The soldiers also came up and mocked him. They offered him vinegar {23:37} and said, "If you are the King of the Jews, save yourself." {23:38} There was a written notice above him that read: THIS IS THE KING OF THE JEWS. {23:39} One of the criminals who hung there hurled insults at him, saying, "Aren't you the Messiah? Save yourself and us!" {23:40} But the other criminal rebuked him. "Don't you fear God," he said, "since you are under the same sentence? {23:41} We are punished justly, for we are getting what our deeds deserve. But this man has done nothing wrong." {23:42} Then he said, "Jesus, remember me when you come into your kingdom." {23:43} Jesus answered him, "Truly I tell you, today you will be with me in paradise." {23:44} It was now about noon, and darkness came over the whole land until three in the afternoon, {23:45} for the sun stopped shining. And the curtain of the temple was torn in two. {23:46} Jesus called out with a loud voice, "Father, into your hands I commit my spirit." When he had said this, he breathed his last. {23:47} The centurion, seeing what had happened, praised God and said, "Surely this was a righteous man." {23:48} When all the people who had gathered to witness this saw what took place, they beat their breasts and went away. {23:49} But all those who knew Jesus stood at a distance, watching these things. {23:50} Now there was a man named Joseph, a member of the Council, a good and upright man, {23:51} who had not consented to their decision and action. He came from the Judean town of Arimathea and was waiting for the kingdom of God. {23:52} Going to Pilate, he asked for Jesus' body. {23:53} Then he took it down, wrapped it in linen, and placed it in a tomb cut in the rock, one in which no one had yet been laid. {23:54} It was Preparation Day, and the Sabbath was about to begin. {23:55} The women who had come with Jesus from Galilee followed Joseph and saw the tomb and how his body was laid in it. {23:56} Then they went home and prepared spices and perfumes. But they rested on the Sabbath in obedience to the commandment.

{24:1} On the first day of the week, very early in the morning, the women went to the tomb, bringing the spices they had prepared, along with some others. {24:2} They found the stone rolled away from the tomb. {24:3} When they entered, they did not find the body of the Lord Jesus. {24:4} While they were wondering about this, suddenly two men in shining clothes stood beside them. {24:5} The women were terrified and bowed down with their faces to the ground. The men said to them, "Why do you look for the living among the dead? {24:6} He is not here; he has risen! Remember how he told you while he was still in Galilee, {24:7} that the Son of Man must be delivered into the hands of sinful men, be crucified, and rise on the third day." {24:8} Then they remembered his words, {24:9} and returned from the tomb and told all these things to the eleven disciples and to all the others. {24:10} It was Mary Magdalene, Joanna, Mary the mother of James, and the other women with them who told this to the apostles. {24:11} But the apostles didn't believe the women because their words seemed like nonsense. {24:12} However, Peter got up and ran to the tomb. Bending down, he saw the strips of linen lying by themselves, and he went away, wondering to himself what had happened. {24:13} Now that same day, two of them were going to a village called Emmaus, about seven miles from Jerusalem. {24:14} They were talking with each other about everything that had happened. {24:15} As they talked and discussed these things, Jesus himself came up and walked along with them; {24:16} but they were kept from recognizing him. {24:17} He asked them, "What are you discussing together as you walk along?" They stood still, their faces downcast. {24:18} One of them, named Cleopas, asked him, "Are you the only one visiting Jerusalem who does not know the things that have happened there in these days?" {24:19} "What things?" he asked. "About Jesus of Nazareth," they replied. "He was a prophet, powerful in word and deed before God and all the people. {24:20} The chief priests and our rulers handed him over to be sentenced to death, and they crucified him. {24:21} But we had hoped that he was the one who was going to redeem Israel. And what is more, it is the third day since all this took place. {24:22} In addition, some of our women amazed us. They went to the tomb early this morning {24:23} but didn't find his body. They came and told us that they had seen a vision of angels who said he was alive. {24:24} Then some of our companions went to the tomb and found it just as the women had said, but they did not see Jesus." {24:25} He said to them, "How foolish you are, and how slow to believe all that the prophets have spoken! {24:26} Did not the Messiah have to suffer these things and then enter his glory?" {24:27} And beginning with Moses and all the Prophets, he explained to them what was said in all the Scriptures concerning himself. {24:28} As they approached the village to which they were going, Jesus continued on as if he were going farther. {24:29} But they urged him strongly, "Stay with us, for it is nearly evening; the day is almost over." So he went in to stay with them. {24:30} When he was at the table with them, he took bread, gave thanks, broke it, and began to give it to them. {24:31} Then their eyes were opened and they recognized him, and he disappeared from their sight. {24:32} They asked each other, "Were not our hearts burning within us while he talked with us on the road and opened the Scriptures to us?" {24:33} They got up and returned at once to Jerusalem. There they found the Eleven and those with them, assembled together {24:34} and saying, "It is true! The Lord has risen and has appeared to Simon." {24:35} Then the two told what had happened on the way and how Jesus was recognized by them when he broke the bread. {24:36} While they were still talking about this, Jesus himself stood among them and said to them, "Peace be with you." {24:37} They were startled and frightened, thinking they saw a ghost. {24:38} He said to them, "Why are you troubled, and why do doubts rise in your minds? {24:39} Look at my hands and my feet. It is I myself! Touch me and see; a ghost does not have flesh and bones, as you see I have." {24:40} When he had said this, he showed them his hands and feet. {24:41} And while they still did not believe it because of joy and amazement, he asked them, "Do you have anything here to eat?" {24:42} They gave him a piece of broiled fish, {24:43} and he took it and ate it in their presence. {24:44} He said to them, "This is what I told you while I was still with you: Everything must be fulfilled that is written about me in the Law of Moses, the Prophets, and the Psalms." {24:45} Then he opened their minds so they could understand the Scriptures. {24:46} He told them, "This is what is written: The Messiah will suffer and rise from the dead on the third day, {24:47} and repentance for the forgiveness of sins will be preached in his name to all nations, beginning at Jerusalem. {24:48} You are witnesses of these things. {24:49} I am going to send you what my Father has promised; but stay in the city until you have been clothed with power from on high." {24:50} When he had led them out to the vicinity of Bethany, he lifted up his hands and blessed them. {24:51} While he was blessing them, he left them and was taken up into heaven. {24:52} Then they worshiped him and returned to Jerusalem with great joy. {24:53} And they stayed continually at the temple, praising God. Amen.

The Gospel of John

{1:1} In the beginning was the Word, and the Word was with God, and the Word was God. {1:2} He was there in the beginning with God. {1:3} Everything was made through him; nothing was made without him. {1:4} In him was life, and that life was the light of humanity. {1:5} The light shines in the darkness, and the darkness has not overcome it. {1:6} There was a man sent from God, whose name was John. {1:7} He came to be a witness, to testify about the Light so that everyone might believe through him. {1:8} He was not that Light, but came to bear witness to that Light. {1:9} That was the true Light, which gives light to everyone coming into the world. {1:10} He was in the world, and though the world was made through him, the world did not recognize him. {1:11} He came to his own, and his own people did not accept him. {1:12} But to all who did receive him, he gave the right to become children of God, to those who believe in his name. {1:13} They were born not of blood, nor of human desire, nor of human will, but of God. {1:14} The Word became flesh and lived among us, and we saw his glory, the glory of the only Son from the Father, full of grace and truth. {1:15} John testified about him and cried out, saying, "This is the one I spoke about: He who comes after me is greater than me, because he existed before me." {1:16} From his fullness, we have all received grace upon grace. {1:17} For the law was given through Moses; grace and truth came through Jesus Christ. {1:18} No one has ever seen God; the one and only Son, who is in close relationship with the Father, has made him known. {1:19} This is John's testimony when the Jewish leaders sent priests and Levites from Jerusalem to ask him, "Who are you?" {1:20} He confessed and did not deny it, but confessed, "I am not the Messiah." {1:21} They asked him, "Then who are you? Are you Elijah?" He said, "I am not." "Are you the Prophet?" He answered, "No." {1:22} Then they said to him, "Who are you? We need to give an answer to those who sent us. What do you say about yourself?" {1:23} He said, "I am the voice of one calling in the wilderness, 'Make straight the way for the Lord,' as said the prophet Isaiah." {1:24} Now those who had been sent were from the Pharisees. {1:25} They questioned him, "Why then are you baptizing if you are not the Messiah, nor Elijah, nor the Prophet?" {1:26} John answered them, "I baptize with water, but among you stands one you do not know. {1:27} He is the one who comes after me, whose sandals I am not worthy to untie." {1:28} These things happened in Bethany on the other side of the Jordan, where John was baptizing. {1:29} The next day, John saw Jesus coming toward him and said, "Look, the Lamb of God, who takes away the sin of the world! {1:30} This is the one I meant when I said, "A man who comes after me has surpassed me because he was before me." {1:31} I myself did not know him, but the reason I came baptizing with water was that he might be revealed to Israel. {1:32} Then John testified, "I saw the Spirit descending from heaven like a dove and remaining on him.

{1:33} I myself did not know him, but the one who sent me to baptize with water told me, 'The man on whom you see the Spirit descend and remain is the one who will baptize with the Holy Spirit.' {1:34} I have seen and I testify that this is the Son of God." {1:35} The next day John was there again with two of his disciples. {1:36} When he saw Jesus passing by, he said, "Look, the Lamb of God!" {1:37} When the two disciples heard him say this, they followed Jesus. {1:38} Turning around, Jesus saw them following and asked, "What do you want?" They said, "Rabbi" (which means Teacher), "where are you staying?" {1:39} "Come and see," he replied. So they went and saw where he was staying and spent that day with him. It was about four in the afternoon. {1:40} Andrew, Simon Peter's brother, was one of the two who heard what John had said and who had followed Jesus. {1:41} The first thing Andrew did was to find his brother Simon and tell him, "We have found the Messiah" (that is, the Christ). {1:42} And he brought him to Jesus. Jesus looked at him and said, "You are Simon son of John. You will be called Cephas" (which is translated as Peter). {1:43} The next day Jesus decided to leave for Galilee. Finding Philip, he said to him, "Follow me." {1:44} Philip, like Andrew and Peter, was from the town of Bethsaida. {1:45} Philip found Nathanael and told him, "We have found the one Moses wrote about in the Law, and about whom the prophets also wrote—Jesus of Nazareth, the son of Joseph." {1:46} "Nazareth! Can anything good come from there?" Nathanael asked. "Come and see," said Philip. {1:47} When Jesus saw Nathanael approaching, he said of him, "Here truly is an Israelite in whom there is no deceit." {1:48} "How do you know me?" Nathanael asked. Jesus answered, "I saw you while you were still under the fig tree before Philip called you." {1:49} Then Nathanael declared, "Rabbi, you are the Son of God; you are the King of Israel." {1:50} Jesus said, "You believe because I told you I saw you under the fig tree. You will see greater things than that." {1:51} He then added, "Very truly I tell you, you will see heaven open and the angels of God ascending and descending on the Son of Man."

{2:1} On the third day, a wedding took place at Cana in Galilee. Jesus' mother was there, {2:2} and Jesus and his disciples had also been invited to the wedding. {2:3} When the wine was gone, Jesus' mother said to him, "They have no more wine." {2:4} "Woman, why do you involve me?" Jesus replied. "My hour has not yet come." {2:5} His mother said to the servants, "Do whatever he tells you." {2:6} Nearby stood six stone water jars, the kind used by the Jews for ceremonial washing, each holding from twenty to thirty gallons. {2:7} Jesus said to the servants, "Fill the jars with water." So they filled them to the brim. {2:8} Then he told them, "Now draw some out and take it to the master of the banquet." They did so, {2:9} and the master of the banquet tasted the water that had been turned into wine. He did not realize where it had come from, though the servants who had drawn the water knew. Then he called the bridegroom aside {2:10} and said, "Everyone brings out the choice wine first and then the cheaper wine after the guests have had too much to drink; but you have saved the best till now." {2:11} What Jesus did here in Cana of Galilee was the first of the signs through which he revealed his glory; and his disciples believed in him. {2:12} After this he went down to Capernaum with his mother and brothers and his disciples. There they stayed for a few days. {2:13} When it was almost time for the Jewish Passover, Jesus went up to Jerusalem. {2:14} In the temple courts he found people selling cattle, sheep, and doves, and others sitting at tables exchanging money. {2:15} So he made a whip out of cords and drove all from the temple courts, both sheep and cattle; he scattered the coins of the money changers and overturned their tables. {2:16} To those who sold doves he said, "Get these out of here! Stop turning my Father's house into a market!" {2:17} His disciples remembered that it is written: "Zeal for your house will consume me." {2:18} The Jews then responded to him, "What sign can you show us to prove your authority to do all this?" {2:19} Jesus answered them, "Destroy this temple, and I will raise it again in three days." {2:20} They replied, "It has taken forty-six years to build this temple, and you are going to raise it in three days?" {2:21} But the temple he had spoken of was his body. {2:22} After he was raised from the dead, his disciples recalled what he had said; then they believed the scripture and the words that Jesus had spoken. {2:23} Now while he was in Jerusalem at the Passover Festival, many people saw the signs he was performing and believed in his name. {2:24} But Jesus would not entrust himself to them, for he knew all people. {2:25} He did not need any testimony about mankind, for he knew what was in each person.

{3:1} There was a man from the Pharisees named Nicodemus, a leader of the Jews. {3:2} He came to Jesus at night and said to him, "Rabbi, we know you are a teacher who has come from God, for no one could perform the signs you do unless God is with him." {3:3} Jesus replied, "Very truly I tell you, no one can see the kingdom of God unless they are born again." {3:4} Nicodemus asked, "How can someone be born when they are old? Can they enter a second time into their mother's womb and be born?" {3:5} Jesus answered, "Very truly I tell you, no one can enter the kingdom of God unless they are born of water and the Spirit. {3:6} Flesh gives birth to flesh, but the Spirit gives birth to spirit. {3:7} You should not be surprised at my saying, 'You must be born again.' {3:8} The wind blows where it pleases. You hear its sound, but you cannot tell where it comes from or where it is going. So it is with everyone born of the Spirit." {3:9} Nicodemus asked, "How can this be?" {3:10} Jesus replied, "You are Israel's teacher, and do you not understand these things? {3:11} Very truly I tell you, we speak of what we know, and we testify to what we have seen, but still, you people do not accept our testimony. {3:12} I have spoken to you of earthly things and you do not believe; how then will you believe if I speak of heavenly things? {3:13} No one has ever gone into heaven except the one who came from heaven—the Son of Man. {3:14} Just as Moses lifted up the snake in the wilderness, so the Son of Man must be lifted up, {3:15} that everyone who believes may have eternal life in him. {3:16} For God so loved the world that he gave his one and only Son, that whoever believes in him shall not perish but have eternal life. {3:17} For God did not send his Son into the world to condemn the world, but to save the world through him. {3:18} Whoever believes in him is not condemned, but whoever does not believe stands condemned already because they have not believed in the name of God's one and only Son. {3:19} This is the verdict: Light has come into the world, but people loved darkness instead of light because their deeds were evil. {3:20} Everyone who does evil hates the light and will not come into the light for fear that their deeds will be exposed. {3:21} But whoever lives by the truth comes into the light, so that it may be seen plainly that what they have done has been done in the sight of God. {3:22} After this, Jesus and his disciples went out into the Judean countryside, where he spent some time with them, and baptized. {3:23} Now John also was baptizing at Aenon near Salim, because there was plenty of water, and people were coming and being baptized. {3:24} (This was before John was put in prison.) {3:25} An argument developed between some of John's disciples and a certain Jew over the matter of ceremonial washing. {3:26} They came to John and said to him, "Rabbi, that man who was with you on the other side of the Jordan—the one you testified about—look, he is baptizing, and everyone is going to him." {3:27} To this John replied, "A person can receive only what is given them from heaven. {3:28} You yourselves can testify that I said, 'I am not the Messiah but am sent ahead of him.' {3:29} The bride belongs to the bridegroom. The friend who attends the bridegroom waits and listens for him and is full of joy when he hears the bridegroom's voice. That joy is mine, and it is now complete. {3:30} He must become greater; I must become less." {3:31} The one who comes from above is above all; the one who is from the earth belongs to the earth and speaks as one from the earth. The one who comes from heaven is above all. {3:32} He testifies to what he has seen and heard, but no one accepts his testimony. {3:33} Whoever has accepted it has certified that God is truthful. {3:34} For the one whom God has sent speaks the words of God, for God gives the Spirit without limit. {3:35} The Father loves the Son and has placed everything in his hands. {3:36} Whoever believes in the Son has eternal life, but whoever rejects the Son will not see life, for God's wrath remains on them.

{4:1} Now Jesus learned that the Pharisees had heard that he was gaining and baptizing more disciples than John— {4:2} although in fact it was not Jesus who baptized, but his disciples. {4:3} So he left Judea and went back once more to Galilee. {4:4} Now he had to go through Samaria. {4:5} So he came to a town in Samaria called Sychar, near the plot of ground Jacob had given to his son Joseph. {4:6} Jacob's well was there, and Jesus, tired as he was from the journey, sat down by the well. It was about noon. {4:7} When a Samaritan woman came to draw water, Jesus said to her, "Will you give me a drink?" {4:8} (His disciples had gone into the town to buy food.) {4:9} The Samaritan woman said to him, "You are a Jew and I am a Samaritan woman. How can you ask me for a drink?" (For Jews do not associate with Samaritans.) {4:10} Jesus answered her, "If you knew the gift of God and who it is that asks you for a drink, you would have asked him and he would have given you living water." {4:11} "Sir," the woman said, "you have nothing to draw with and the well is deep. Where can you get this living water? {4:12} Are you greater than our father Jacob, who gave us the well and drank from it himself, as did also his sons and his livestock?" {4:13} Jesus answered, "Everyone who drinks this water will be thirsty again, {4:14} but whoever drinks the water I give them will never thirst. Indeed, the water I give them will become in them a spring of water welling up to eternal life." {4:15} The woman said to him, "Sir, give me this water so that I won't get thirsty and have to keep coming here to draw water." {4:16} He told her, "Go, call your husband and come back." {4:17} "I have no husband," she replied. Jesus said to her, "You are right when you say you have no husband. {4:18} The fact is, you have had five husbands, and the man you now have is not your husband. What you have just said is quite true." {4:19} "Sir," the woman said, "I can see that you are a prophet. {4:20} Our ancestors worshiped on this mountain, but you Jews claim that the place where we must worship is in Jerusalem." {4:21} "Woman," Jesus replied, "believe me, a time is coming when you will worship the Father neither on this mountain nor in Jerusalem. {4:22} You Samaritans worship what you do not know; we worship what we do know, for salvation is from the Jews. {4:23} Yet a time is coming and has now come when the true worshipers will worship the Father in the Spirit and in truth, for they are the kind of worshipers the Father seeks. {4:24} God is spirit, and his worshipers must worship in the Spirit and in truth." {4:25} The woman said, "I know that Messiah" (called Christ) "is coming. When he comes, he will explain everything to us." {4:26} Then Jesus declared, "I, the one speaking to you—I am he." {4:27} Just then his disciples returned and were surprised to find him talking with a woman, but no one asked, "What do you want?" or "Why are you talking with her?" {4:28} Then, leaving her water jar, the woman went back to the town and said to the people, {4:29} "Come, see a man who told me everything I ever did. Could this be the Messiah?" {4:30} They came out of the town and made their way toward him. {4:31} Meanwhile, his disciples urged him, "Rabbi, eat something." {4:32} But he said to them, "I have food to eat that you know nothing about." {4:33} Then his disciples said to each other, "Could someone have brought him food?" {4:34} "My food," said Jesus, "is to do the will of him who sent me and to finish his work. {4:35} Don't you have a saying, 'It's still four months until harvest'? I tell you, open your eyes and look at the fields! They are ripe for harvest. {4:36} Even now the one who reaps draws a wage and harvests a crop for eternal life, so that the sower and the reaper may be glad together. {4:37} Thus the saying 'One sows and another reaps' is true. {4:38} I sent you to reap what you have not worked for. Others have done the hard work, and you have reaped the benefits of their labor." {4:39} Many of the Samaritans from that town believed in him because of the woman's testimony, "He told me everything I ever did." {4:40} So when the Samaritans came to him, they urged him to stay with them, and he stayed two days. {4:41} And because of his words, many more became believers. {4:42} They said to the woman, "We no longer believe just because of what you said; now we have heard for ourselves, and we know that this man really is the Savior of the world." {4:43} After the two days, he left for Galilee. {4:44} (Now Jesus himself had pointed out that a prophet has no honor in his own country.) {4:45} When he arrived in Galilee, the Galileans welcomed him. They had seen all that he had done in Jerusalem at the Passover Festival, for they also had been there. {4:46} He went again to Cana in Galilee, where he had turned the water into wine. And there was a certain royal official whose son lay sick at Capernaum. {4:47} When this man heard that Jesus had arrived in Galilee from Judea, he went to him and begged him to come and heal his son, who was close to death. {4:48} "Unless you people see signs and wonders," Jesus told him, "you will never believe." {4:49} The royal official said, "Sir, come down before my child dies." {4:50} "Go," Jesus replied, "your son will live." The man took Jesus at his word and departed. {4:51} While he was still on his way, his servants met him with the news that his boy was living. {4:52} When he inquired as to the time when his son got better, they said to him, "Yesterday at one in the afternoon the fever left him." {4:53} Then the father realized that this was the exact time at which Jesus had said to him, "Your son will live." So he and his whole household believed. {4:54} This was the second sign Jesus performed after coming from Judea to Galilee.

{5:1} After this, there was a Jewish festival, and Jesus went up to Jerusalem. {5:2} In Jerusalem, near the Sheep Gate, there is a pool called Bethesda, which has five covered porches. {5:3} A large number of disabled people—blind, lame, and paralyzed—lay waiting for the water to be stirred. {5:4} An angel would come down at certain times to stir the water; the first one to enter the water after it was stirred would be healed of whatever disease they had. {5:5} One man was there who had been sick for thirty-eight years. {5:6} When Jesus saw him lying there and knew he had been in that condition for a long time, he asked him, "Do you want to get well?" {5:7} The sick man replied, "Sir, I have no one to help me into the pool when the water is stirred; while I am trying to get in, someone else goes down ahead of me." {5:8} Jesus said to him, "Get up! Pick up your mat and walk." {5:9} At once, the man was cured; he picked up his mat and walked. This happened on the Sabbath. {5:10} So the Jewish leaders said to the man who had been healed, "It is the Sabbath; the law forbids you to carry your mat." {5:11} But he replied, "The man who made me well said to me, 'Pick up your mat and walk.'" {5:12} They asked him, "Who is this fellow who told you to pick it up and walk?" {5:13} The man who was healed had no idea who it was, for Jesus had slipped away into the crowd that was there. {5:14} Later, Jesus found him at the temple and said to him, "See, you are well again. Stop sinning or something worse may happen to you." {5:15} The man went away and told the Jewish leaders that it was Jesus who had made him well. {5:16} So, the Jewish leaders began to persecute Jesus because he was doing these things on the Sabbath. {5:17} In response, Jesus said to them, "My Father is working until now, and I am working." {5:18} For this reason, they tried all the more to kill him; not only was he breaking the Sabbath, but he was even calling God his own Father, making himself equal with God. {5:19} Jesus gave them this answer: "Very truly I tell you, the Son can do nothing by himself; he can do only what he sees his Father doing, because whatever the Father does the Son also does. {5:20} For the Father loves the Son and shows him all he does. Yes, and he will show him even greater works than these, so that you will be amazed. {5:21} For just as the Father raises the dead and gives them life, even so, the Son gives life to whom he is pleased to give it. {5:22} Moreover, the Father judges no one, but has entrusted all judgment to the Son, {5:23} that all may honor the Son just as they honor the Father. Whoever does not honor the Son does not honor the Father who sent him. {5:24} Very truly I tell you, whoever hears my word and believes him who sent me has eternal life and will not be judged but has crossed over from death to life. {5:25} Very truly I tell you, a time is coming and has now come when the dead will hear the voice of the Son of God and those who hear will live. {5:26} For as the Father has life in himself, so he has granted the Son also to have life in himself. {5:27} And he has given him authority to judge because he is the Son of Man. {5:28} Do not be amazed at this, for a time is coming when all who are in their graves will hear his voice {5:29} and come out—those who have done what is good will rise to live, and those who have done what is evil will rise to be condemned. {5:30} By myself, I can do nothing; I judge only as I hear, and my judgment is just, for I seek not to please myself but him who sent me. {5:31} If I testify about myself, my testimony is not true. {5:32} There is another who testifies in my favor, and I know that his testimony about me is true. {5:33} You have sent to John and he has testified to the truth. {5:34} Not that I accept human testimony; but I mention it that you may be saved. {5:35} John was a lamp that burned and gave light, and you chose for a time to enjoy his light. {5:36} I have testimony weightier than that of John. For the works that the Father has given me to finish—the very works that I am doing—testify that the Father has sent me. {5:37} And the Father who sent me has himself testified concerning me. You have never heard his voice or seen his form, {5:38} nor does his word dwell in you, for you do not believe the one he sent. {5:39} You study the Scriptures diligently because you think that in them you have eternal life. These are the very Scriptures that testify about me, {5:40} yet you refuse to come to me to have life. {5:41} I do not accept glory from human beings, {5:42} but I know you. I know that you do not have the love of God in your hearts. {5:43} I have come in my Father's name, and you do not accept me; but if someone else comes in his own name, you will accept him. {5:44} How can you believe since you accept glory from one another but do not seek the glory that comes from the only God? {5:45} But do not think I will accuse you before the Father. Your accuser is Moses, on whom your hopes are set. {5:46} If you believed Moses, you would believe me, for he wrote about me. {5:47} But since you do not believe what he wrote, how are you going to believe what I say?

{6:1} After this, Jesus went across the Sea of Galilee (that is, the Sea of Tiberias). {6:2} A large crowd followed him because they saw the signs he had performed by healing the sick. {6:3} Then Jesus went up on a mountainside and sat down with his disciples. {6:4} The Jewish Passover Festival was near. {6:5} When Jesus looked up and saw a great crowd coming toward him, he said to Philip, "Where shall we buy bread for these people to eat?" {6:6} He asked this only to test him, for he already had in mind what he was going to do. {6:7} Philip answered him, "It would take more than half a year's wages to buy enough bread for each one to have a bite!" {6:8} Another of his disciples, Andrew, Simon Peter's brother, spoke up, {6:9} "Here is a boy with five small barley loaves and two small fish, but how far will they go among so many?" {6:10} Jesus said, "Have the people sit down." There was plenty of grass in that place, and they sat down (about five thousand men were there). {6:11} Jesus then took the loaves, gave thanks, and distributed to those who were seated as much as they wanted. He did the same with the fish. {6:12} When they had all had enough to eat, he said to his disciples, "Gather the pieces that are left over. Let nothing be wasted." {6:13} So they gathered them and filled twelve baskets with the pieces of the five barley loaves left over by those who had eaten. {6:14} After the people saw the sign Jesus performed, they began to say, "Surely this is the Prophet who is to come into the world." {6:15} Jesus, knowing that they intended to come and make him king by force, withdrew again to a mountain by himself. {6:16} When evening came, his disciples went down to the lake, {6:17} got into a boat and set off across the lake for Capernaum. By now it was dark, and Jesus had not yet joined them. {6:18} A strong wind was blowing, and the waters grew rough. {6:19} When they had rowed about three or four miles, they saw Jesus approaching the boat, walking on the water; and they were frightened. {6:20} But he said to them, "It is I; don't be afraid." {6:21} Then they were willing to take him into the boat, and immediately the boat reached the shore where they were heading. {6:22} The next day the crowd that had stayed on the opposite shore of the lake realized that only one boat had been there, and that Jesus had not entered it with his disciples, but that they had gone away alone. {6:23} Then some boats from Tiberias landed near the place where the people had eaten the bread after the Lord had given thanks. {6:24} Once the crowd realized that neither Jesus nor his disciples were there, they got into the boats and went to Capernaum in search of Jesus. {6:25} When they found him on the other side of the lake, they asked him, "Rabbi, when did you get here?" {6:26} Jesus answered, "Very truly I tell you, you are looking for me, not because you saw the signs I performed but because you ate the loaves and had your fill. {6:27} Do not work for food that spoils, but for food that endures to eternal life, which the Son of Man will give you. For on him God the Father has placed his seal of approval." {6:28} Then they asked him, "What must we do to do the works God requires?" {6:29} Jesus answered, "The work of God is this: to believe in the one he has sent." {6:30} So they asked him, "What sign then will you give that we may see it and believe you? What will you do? {6:31} Our ancestors ate the manna in the wilderness; as it is written: 'He gave them bread from heaven to eat.'" {6:32} Jesus said to them, "Very truly I tell you, it is not Moses who has given you the bread from heaven, but it is my Father who gives you the true bread from heaven. {6:33} For the bread of God is the bread that comes down from heaven and gives life to the world." {6:34} "Sir," they said, "always give us this bread." {6:35} Then Jesus declared, "I am the bread of life. Whoever comes to me will never go hungry, and whoever believes in me will never be thirsty. {6:36} But as I told you, you have seen me and still you do not believe. {6:37} All those the Father gives me will come to me, and whoever comes to me I will never drive away. {6:38} For I have come down from heaven not to do my will but to do the will of him who sent me. {6:39} And this is the will of him who sent me, that I shall lose none of those he has given me, but raise them up at the last day. {6:40} For my Father's will is that everyone who looks to the Son and believes in him shall have eternal life, and I will raise them up at the last day." {6:41} At this, the Jews there began to grumble about him because he said, "I am the bread that came down from heaven." {6:42} They said, "Is this not Jesus, the son of Joseph, whose father and mother we know? How can he now say, 'I came down from heaven'?" {6:43} "Stop grumbling among yourselves," Jesus answered. {6:44} "No one can come to me unless the Father who sent me draws them, and I will raise them up at the last day. {6:45} It is written in the Prophets: 'They will all be taught by God.' Everyone who has heard the Father and learned from him comes to me. {6:46} No one has seen the Father except the one who is from God; only he has seen the Father. {6:47} Very truly I tell you, the one who believes has eternal life. {6:48} I am the bread of life. {6:49} Your ancestors ate the manna in the wilderness, yet they died. {6:50} But here is the bread that comes down from heaven, which anyone may eat and not die. {6:51} I am the living bread that came down from heaven. Whoever eats this bread will live forever. This bread is my flesh, which I will give for the life of the world." {6:52} Then the Jews began to argue sharply among themselves, "How can this man give us his flesh to eat?" {6:53} Jesus said to them, "Very truly I tell you, unless you eat the flesh of the Son of Man and drink his blood, you have no life in you. {6:54} Whoever eats my flesh and drinks my blood has eternal life, and I will raise them up at the last day. {6:55} For my flesh is real food, and my blood is real drink. {6:56} Whoever eats my flesh and drinks my blood remains in me, and I in them. {6:57} Just as the living Father sent me and I live because of the Father, so the one who feeds on me will live because of me. {6:58} This is the bread that came down from heaven. Your ancestors ate manna and died, but whoever feeds on this bread will live forever." {6:59} He said this while teaching in the synagogue in Capernaum. {6:60} On hearing it, many of his disciples said, "This is a hard teaching. Who can accept it?" {6:61} Aware that his disciples were grumbling about this, Jesus said to them, "Does this offend you? {6:62} Then what if you see the Son of Man ascend to where he was before? {6:63} The Spirit gives life; the flesh counts for nothing. The words I have spoken to you—they are full of the Spirit and life. {6:64} Yet there are some of you who do not believe." For Jesus had known from the beginning which of them did not believe and who would betray him. {6:65} He went on to say, "This is why I told you that no one can come to me unless the Father has enabled them." {6:66} From this time many of his disciples turned back and no longer followed him. {6:67} "You do not want to leave too, do you?" Jesus asked the Twelve. {6:68} Simon Peter answered him, "Lord, to whom shall we go? You have the words of eternal life. {6:69} We have come to believe and to know that you are the Holy One of God." {6:70} Then Jesus replied, "Have I not chosen you, the Twelve? Yet one of you is a devil!" {6:71} He meant Judas, the son of Simon Iscariot, who, though one of the Twelve, was later to betray him.

{7:1} After this, Jesus walked in Galilee because he didn't want to walk in Judea, since the Jews were trying to kill him. {7:2} The Jewish Feast of Tabernacles was approaching. {7:3} So his brothers said to him, "Leave here and go to Judea so that your disciples can see the works you do. {7:4} No one who wants to be known publicly acts in secret. If you're doing these things, show yourself to the world." {7:5} For even his brothers did not believe in him. {7:6} Jesus told them, "My time has not yet come, but your time is always ready. {7:7} The world cannot hate you, but it hates me because I testify that its works are evil. {7:8} You go up to the feast. I am not going up to this feast yet, because my time has not fully come." {7:9} After saying this, he stayed in Galilee. {7:10} However, when his brothers had gone up, he also went up to the feast, not publicly but in secret. {7:11} The Jews were looking for him at the feast and asking, "Where is he?" {7:12} There was much debate among the people about him; some said, "He is a good man," while others said, "No, he deceives the people." {7:13} However, no one spoke openly about him for fear of the Jews. {7:14} About halfway through the feast, Jesus went up to the temple and began teaching. {7:15} The Jews were amazed and said, "How does this man know so much when he has never been educated?" {7:16} Jesus answered them, "My teaching is not my own, but it comes from the one who sent me. {7:17} If anyone wants to do God's will, they will know whether my teaching is from God or whether I speak on my own. {7:18} Those who speak for themselves seek their own glory, but the one who seeks the glory of the one who sent him is true, and there is no unrighteousness in him. {7:19} Didn't Moses give you the Law? Yet none of you keeps the Law. Why are you trying to kill me?" {7:20} The crowd replied, "You have a demon! Who is trying to kill you?" {7:21} Jesus answered, "I performed one miracle, and you are all amazed. {7:22} Yet because Moses gave you circumcision (not that it came from Moses, but from the fathers), you circumcise a boy on the Sabbath. {7:23} If a boy can be circumcised on the Sabbath so that the Law of Moses is not broken, why are you angry with me for making a whole man well on the Sabbath? {7:24} Stop judging by mere appearances, but instead judge correctly." {7:25} Some of the people of Jerusalem asked, "Isn't this the man they are trying to kill? {7:26} Here he is, speaking publicly, and they are saying nothing to him. Do the rulers know that this is truly the Christ? {7:27} But we know where this man is from; when the Christ comes, no one will know where he is from." {7:28} Then Jesus, still teaching in the temple, cried out, "You know me, and you know where I am from. I am not here on my own authority, but he who sent me is true, and you do not know him. {7:29} I know him because I am from him, and he sent me." {7:30} At this, they tried to seize him, but no one laid a hand on him because his hour had not yet come. {7:31} Many in the crowd believed in him and said, "When the Christ comes, will he do more signs than this man?" {7:32} The Pharisees heard the crowd whispering such things about him, and the chief priests and Pharisees sent officers to arrest him. {7:33} Jesus said, "I will be with you a little longer, and then I am going to the one who sent me. {7:34} You will look for me, but you will not find me; and where I am, you cannot come." {7:35} The Jews said to one another, "Where will he go that we will not find him? Will he go among the Greeks and teach the Greeks? {7:36} What did he mean when he said, 'You will look for me, but you will not find me; and where I am, you cannot come'?" {7:37} On the last and greatest day of the feast, Jesus stood and said in a loud voice, "If anyone is thirsty, let them come to me and drink. {7:38} Whoever believes in me, as Scripture has said, rivers of living water will flow from within them." {7:39} By this he meant the Spirit, whom those who believed in him were later to receive; up to that time, the Spirit had not been given, since Jesus had not yet been glorified. {7:40} On hearing his words, some of the people said, "Surely this man is the Prophet." {7:41} Others said, "He is the Christ." Still, others asked, "How can the Christ come from Galilee? {7:42} Doesn't Scripture say that the Christ will come from David's descendants and from Bethlehem, the town where David lived?" {7:43} So the people were divided because of Jesus. {7:44} Some wanted to seize him, but no one laid a hand on him. {7:45} Finally, the officers went back to the chief priests and Pharisees, who asked them, "Why didn't you bring him in?" {7:46} "No one ever spoke the way this man does," the officers replied. {7:47} "You mean he has deceived you also?" the Pharisees retorted. {7:48} "Have any of the rulers or any of the Pharisees believed in him? {7:49} No! But this mob that knows nothing of the law—there is a curse on them." {7:50} Nicodemus, who had gone to Jesus earlier and who was one of their own number, asked, {7:51} "Does our law condemn a man without first hearing him to find out what he has been doing?" {7:52} They replied, "Are you from Galilee too? Look into it, and you will find that a prophet does not come out of Galilee." {7:53} Then they all went home.

{8:1} But Jesus went to the Mount of Olives. {8:2} At dawn he appeared again in the temple courts, where all the people gathered around him, and he sat down to teach them. {8:3} The teachers of the law and the Pharisees brought in a woman caught in adultery; they made her stand before the group {8:4} and said to Jesus, "Teacher, this woman was caught in the act of adultery. {8:5} In the Law, Moses commanded us to stone such women. Now what do you say?" {8:6} They were using this question as a trap (temptation) in order to have a basis for accusing him. But Jesus bent down and started to write on the ground with his finger. {8:7} When they kept on questioning him, he straightened up and said to them, "Let any one of you who is without sin be the first to throw a stone at her." {8:8} Again he stooped down and wrote on the ground. {8:9} At this, those who heard began to go away one at a time, the older ones first, until only Jesus was left, with the woman still standing there. {8:10} Jesus straightened up and asked her, "Woman, where are they? Has no one condemned you?" {8:11} "No one, sir," she said. "Then neither do I condemn you," Jesus declared. "Go now and leave your life of sin." {8:12} When Jesus spoke again to the people, he said, "I am the light of the world. Whoever follows me will never walk in darkness, but will have the light of life." {8:13} The Pharisees challenged him, "Here you are, appearing as your own witness; your testimony is not valid." {8:14} Jesus answered, "Even if I testify on my own behalf, my testimony is valid, for I know where I came from and where I am going. But you have no idea where I come from or where I am going. {8:15} You judge by human standards; I pass judgment on no one. {8:16} But if I do judge, my decisions are true, because I am not alone. I stand with the Father, who sent me. {8:17} In your own Law, it is written that the testimony of two witnesses is true. {8:18} I am one who testifies for myself; my other witness is the Father, who sent me." {8:19} Then they asked him, "Where is your father?" "You do not know me or my Father," Jesus replied. "If you knew me, you would know my Father also." {8:20} He spoke these words while teaching in the temple courts near the place where the offerings were put. Yet no one seized him, because his hour had not yet come. {8:21} Once more Jesus said to them, "I am going away, and you will look for me, and you will die in your sin. Where I go, you cannot come." {8:22} This made the Jews ask, "Will he kill himself? Is that why he says, 'Where I go, you cannot come'?" {8:23} But he continued, "You are from below; I am from above. You are of this world; I am not of this world. {8:24} I told you that you would die in your sins; if you do not believe that I am he, you will indeed die in your sins." {8:25} "Who are you?" they asked. "Just what I have been telling you from the beginning," Jesus replied. {8:26} "I have much to say in judgment of you. But he who sent me is trustworthy, and what I have heard from him I tell the world." {8:27} They did not understand that he was telling them about his Father. {8:28} So Jesus said, "When you have lifted up the Son of Man, then you will know that I am he and that I do nothing on my own but speak just what the Father has taught me. {8:29} The one who sent me is with me; he has not left me alone, for I always do what pleases him." {8:30} Even as he spoke, many believed in him. {8:31} To the Jews who had believed him, Jesus said, "If you hold to my teaching, you are really my disciples. {8:32} Then you will know the truth, and the truth will set you free." {8:33} They answered him, "We are Abraham's descendants and have never been slaves of anyone. How can you say that we shall be set free?" {8:34} Jesus replied, "Very truly I tell you, everyone who sins is a slave to sin. {8:35} Now a slave has no permanent place in the family, but a son belongs to it forever. {8:36} So if the Son sets you free, you will be free indeed. {8:37} I know that you are Abraham's descendants. Yet you are looking for a way to kill me, because you have no room for my word. {8:38} I am telling you what I have seen in the Father's presence, and you are doing what you have heard from your father." {8:39} "Abraham is our father," they answered. "If you were Abraham's children," said Jesus, "then you would do what Abraham did. {8:40} As it is, you are looking for a way to kill me, a man who has told you the truth that I heard from God. Abraham did not do such things. {8:41} You are doing the works of your own father." "We are not illegitimate children," they protested. "The only Father we have is God himself." {8:42} Jesus said to them, "If God were your Father, you would love me, for I have come here from God. I have not come on my own; God sent me. {8:43} Why is my language not clear to you? Because you are unable to hear what I say. {8:44} You belong to your father, the devil, and you want to carry out your father's desires. He was a murderer from the beginning, not holding to the truth, for there is no truth in him. When he lies, he speaks his native language, for he is a liar and the father of lies. {8:45} Yet because I tell the truth, you do not believe me! {8:46} Can any of you prove me guilty of sin? If I am telling the truth, why don't you believe me? {8:47} Whoever belongs to God hears what God says; the reason you do not hear is that you do not belong to God." {8:48} The Jews answered him, "Aren't we right in saying that you are a Samaritan and demon-possessed?" {8:49} "I am not possessed by a demon," said Jesus, "but I honor my Father and you dishonor me. {8:50} I am not seeking glory for myself; but there is one who seeks it, and he is the judge. {8:51} Very truly I tell you, whoever obeys my word will never see death." {8:52} At this they exclaimed, "Now we know that you are demon-possessed! Abraham died, and so did the prophets, yet you say that whoever obeys your word will never taste death. {8:53} Are you greater than our father Abraham? He died, and so did the prophets. Who do you think you are?" {8:54} Jesus replied, "If I glorify myself, my glory means nothing. My Father, whom you claim as your God, is the one who glorifies me. {8:55} Though you do not know him, I know him. If I said I did not, I would be a liar like you, but I do know him and keep his word. {8:56} Your father Abraham rejoiced at the thought of seeing my day; he saw it & was glad." {8:57} "You are not yet 50 years old," they said to him, "and you've seen Abraham!" {8:58} "Very truly I tell you," Jesus answered, "before Abraham was born, I am!" {8:59} At this, they picked up stones to stone him, but Jesus hid himself, slipping away from temple grounds.

{9:1} As Jesus was walking along, he saw a man who had been blind from birth. {9:2} His disciples asked him, "Rabbi, who sinned, this man or his parents, that he was born blind?" {9:3} Jesus answered, "Neither this man nor his parents sinned. This happened so that the works of God might be displayed in him. {9:4} I must work the works of him who sent me while it is day; night is coming when no one can work. {9:5} While I am in the world, I am the light of the world." {9:6} After saying this, he spat on the ground, made some mud with the saliva, and put it on the man's eyes. {9:7} He told him, "Go, wash in the Pool of Siloam" (which means Sent). So the man went and washed, and came home seeing. {9:8} His neighbors and those who had seen him begging asked, "Isn't this the same man who used to sit and beg?" {9:9} Some said, "This is him," while others said, "No, he only looks like him." But the man said, "I am the one." {9:10} They asked him, "How were your eyes opened?" {9:11} He replied, "The man they call Jesus made some mud, put it on my eyes, told me to go to Siloam and wash. I went and washed, and then I could see." {9:12} "Where is this man?" they asked him. "I don't know," he said. {9:13} They brought to the Pharisees the man who had been blind. {9:14} Now the day on which Jesus had made the mud and opened the man's eyes was a Sabbath. {9:15} Therefore, the Pharisees asked him how he had received his sight. "He put mud on my eyes," the man replied. "I washed, and now I see." {9:16} Some of the Pharisees said, "This man is not from God, for he does not keep the Sabbath." But others asked, "How can a sinner perform such signs?" So they were divided. {9:17} Then they turned again to the blind man. "What have you to say about him? It was your eyes he opened." "He is a prophet," the man replied. {9:18} They still did not believe that he had been blind and had received his sight until they sent for his parents. {9:19} "Is this your son?" they asked. "Is this the one you say was born blind? How is it that now he can see?" {9:20} "We know he is our son," the parents answered, "and that he was born blind. {9:21} But how he can see now, or who opened his eyes, we don't know. He is of age; ask him. He will speak for himself." {9:22} His parents said this because they were afraid of the Jewish leaders, who had already decided that anyone who acknowledged that Jesus was the Messiah would be put out of the synagogue. {9:23} That's why his parents said, "He is of age; ask him." {9:24} A second time they summoned the man who had been blind. "Give glory to God by telling the truth," they said. "We know this man is a sinner." {9:25} He replied, "Whether he is a sinner or not, I don't know. One thing I do know: I was blind, but now I see!" {9:26} Then they asked him, "What did he do to you? How did he open your eyes?" {9:27} He answered, "I have told you already, and you did not listen. Why do you want to hear it again? Do you want to become his disciples too?" {9:28} Then they hurled insults at him and said, "You are this fellow's disciple! We are disciples of Moses! {9:29} We know that God spoke to Moses, but as for this fellow, we don't even know where he comes from." {9:30} The man answered, "Now that is remarkable! You don't know where he comes from, yet he opened my eyes. {9:31} We know that God does not listen to sinners. He listens to the godly person who does his will. {9:32} Nobody has ever heard of opening the eyes of a man born blind. {9:33} If this man were not from God, he could do nothing." {9:34} To this they replied, "You were steeped in sin at birth; how dare you lecture us!" And they threw him out. {9:35} Jesus heard that they had thrown him out, and when he found him, he said, "Do you believe in the Son of Man?" {9:36} "Who is he, sir?" the man asked. "Tell me so that I may believe in him." {9:37} Jesus said, "You have now seen him; in fact, he is the one speaking with you." {9:38} Then the man said, "Lord, I believe," and he worshiped him. {9:39} Jesus said, "For judgment I have come into this world, so that the blind will see and those who see will become blind." {9:40} Some Pharisees who were with him heard him say this and asked, "What? Are we blind too?" {9:41} Jesus said, "If you were blind, you would not be guilty of sin; but now that you claim you can see, your guilt remains."

{10:1} "Very truly I tell you, anyone who does not enter the sheep pen by the gate, but climbs in by some other way, is a thief and a robber. {10:2} The one who enters by the gate is the shepherd of the sheep. {10:3} The gatekeeper opens the gate for him, and the sheep listen to his voice. He calls his own sheep by name and leads them out. {10:4} When he has brought out all his own, he goes on ahead of them, and his sheep follow him because they know his voice. {10:5} But they will never follow a stranger; in fact, they will run away from him because they do not recognize a stranger's voice." {10:6} Jesus used this figure of speech, but the Pharisees did not understand what he was telling them. {10:7} Therefore Jesus said again, "Very truly I tell you, I am the gate for the sheep. {10:8} All who have come before me are thieves and robbers, but the sheep have not listened to them. {10:9} I am the gate; whoever enters through me will be saved. They will come in and go out, and find pasture. {10:10} The thief comes only to steal and kill and destroy; I have come that they may have life, and have it to the full. {10:11} I am the good shepherd. The good shepherd lays down his life for the sheep. {10:12} The hired hand is not the shepherd who owns the sheep. So when he sees the wolf coming, he abandons the sheep and runs away. Then the wolf attacks the flock and scatters it. {10:13} The man runs away because he is a hired hand and cares nothing for the sheep. {10:14} I am the good shepherd; I know my sheep and my sheep know me— {10:15} just as the Father knows me and I know the Father—and I lay down my life for the sheep. {10:16} I have other sheep that are not of this pen. I must bring them also. They too will listen to my voice, and there shall be one flock and one shepherd. {10:17} The reason my Father loves me is that I lay down my life—only to take it up again. {10:18} No one takes it from me, but I lay it down of my own accord. I have authority to lay it down and authority to take it up again. This command I received from my Father." {10:19} The Jews who heard these words were again divided. {10:20} Many of them said, "He is demon-possessed and raving mad. Why listen to him?" {10:21} But others said, "These are not the sayings of a man possessed by a demon. Can a demon open the eyes of the blind?" {10:22} Then came the Festival of Dedication at Jerusalem. It was winter, {10:23} and Jesus was in the temple courts walking in Solomon's Colonnade. {10:24} The Jews who were there gathered around him, saying, "How long will you keep us in suspense? If you are the Messiah, tell us plainly." {10:25} Jesus answered, "I did tell you, but you do not believe. The works I do in my Father's name testify about me, {10:26} but you do not believe because you are not my sheep. {10:27} My sheep hear my voice, and I know them, and they follow me. {10:28} I give them eternal life, and they will never perish; no one will snatch them out of my hand. {10:29} My Father, who has given them to me, is greater than all; no one can snatch them out of my Father's hand. {10:30} I and the Father are one." {10:31} Again his Jewish opponents picked up stones to stone him. {10:32} But Jesus said to them, "I have shown you many good works from the Father. For which of these do you stone me?" {10:33} "We are not stoning you for any good work," they replied, "but for blasphemy, because you, a mere man, claim to be God." {10:34} Jesus answered them, "Is it not written in your Law, 'I have said you are "gods"'? {10:35} If he called them 'gods,' to whom the word of God came—and Scripture cannot be set aside— {10:36} what about the one whom the Father set apart as his very own and sent into the world? Why then do you accuse me of blasphemy because I said, 'I am God's Son'? {10:37} Do not believe me unless I do the works of my Father. {10:38} But if I do them, even though you do not believe me, believe the works, that you may know and understand that the Father is in me, and I in the Father." {10:39} Again they tried to seize him, but he escaped their grasp. {10:40} Then Jesus went back across the Jordan to the place where John had been baptizing in the early days. There he stayed, {10:41} and many people came to him. They said, "Though John never performed a sign, all that John said about this man was true." {10:42} And in that place, many believed in Jesus.

{11:1} A man named Lazarus was sick; he lived in Bethany, the village of Mary and her sister Martha. {11:2} This is the same Mary who anointed the Lord with perfume and wiped his feet with her hair; her brother Lazarus was sick. {11:3} So his sisters sent a message to Jesus, saying, "Lord, the one you love is sick." {11:4} When Jesus heard this, he said, "This sickness will not end in death;

it is for God's glory so that the Son of God may be glorified through it." {11:5} Jesus loved Martha and her sister and Lazarus. {11:6} Yet, when he heard that Lazarus was sick, he stayed where he was for two more days. {11:7} Then he said to his disciples, "Let's go back to Judea." {11:8} The disciples replied, "Rabbi, the Jews just tried to stone you, and you're going back there?" {11:9} Jesus answered, "Are there not twelve hours of daylight? Anyone who walks in the daytime will not stumble, for they see by this world's light. {11:10} It is when a person walks at night that they stumble, for they have no light." {11:11} After he said this, he told them, "Our friend Lazarus has fallen asleep, but I am going there to wake him up." {11:12} His disciples replied, "Lord, if he sleeps, he will get better." {11:13} Jesus had been speaking of his death, but his disciples thought he meant natural sleep. {11:14} So he told them plainly, "Lazarus is dead, {11:15} and for your sake, I am glad I was not there, so that you may believe. But let us go to him." {11:16} Then Thomas (called Didymus) said to the rest of the disciples, "Let us also go, that we may die with him." {11:17} On his arrival, Jesus found that Lazarus had already been in the tomb for four days. {11:18} Bethany was near Jerusalem, about two miles away. {11:19} Many Jews had come to Martha and Mary to comfort them in the loss of their brother. {11:20} When Martha heard that Jesus was coming, she went out to meet him, but Mary stayed at home. {11:21} "Lord," Martha said to Jesus, "if you had been here, my brother would not have died. {11:22} But I know that even now God will give you whatever you ask." {11:23} Jesus said to her, "Your brother will rise again." {11:24} Martha answered, "I know he will rise again in the resurrection at the last day." {11:25} Jesus said to her, "I am the resurrection and the life. The one who believes in me will live, even though they die; {11:26} and whoever lives by believing in me will never die. Do you believe this?" {11:27} "Yes, Lord," she replied, "I believe that you are the Messiah, the Son of God, who is to come into the world." {11:28} After she said this, she went back and called her sister Mary aside. "The Teacher is here," she said, "and is asking for you." {11:29} When Mary heard this, she got up quickly and went to him. {11:30} Now Jesus had not yet entered the village, but was still at the place where Martha had met him. {11:31} When the Jews who had been with Mary in the house, comforting her, noticed how quickly she got up and went out, they followed her, supposing she was going to the tomb to mourn there. {11:32} When Mary reached the place where Jesus was and saw him, she fell at his feet and said, "Lord, if you had been here, my brother would not have died." {11:33} When Jesus saw her weeping, and the Jews who had come along with her also weeping, he was deeply moved in spirit and troubled. {11:34} "Where have you laid him?" he asked. "Come and see, Lord," they replied. {11:35} Jesus wept. {11:36} Then the Jews said, "See how he loved him!" {11:37} But some of them said, "Could not he who opened the eyes of the blind man have kept this man from dying?" {11:38} Jesus, once more deeply moved, came to the tomb. It was a cave with a stone laid across the entrance. {11:39} "Take away the stone," he said. "But, Lord," said Martha, the sister of the dead man, "by this time there is a bad odor, for he has been there four days." {11:40} Then Jesus said, "Did I not tell you that if you believe, you will see the glory of God?" {11:41} So they took away the stone. Then Jesus looked up and said, "Father, I thank you that you have heard me. {11:42} I knew that you always hear me, but I said this for the benefit of the people standing here, that they may believe that you sent me." {11:43} When he had said this, Jesus called out in a loud voice, "Lazarus, come out!" {11:44} The dead man came out, his hands and feet wrapped with strips of linen, and a cloth around his face. Jesus said to them, "Take off the grave clothes and let him go." {11:45} Therefore many of the Jews who had come to visit Mary, and had seen what Jesus did, believed in him. {11:46} But some of them went to the Pharisees and told them what Jesus had done. {11:47} Then the chief priests and the Pharisees called a meeting of the Sanhedrin. "What are we accomplishing?" they asked. "Here is this man performing many signs. {11:48} If we let him go on like this, everyone will believe in him, and then the Romans will come and take away both our temple and our nation." {11:49} Then one of them, named Caiaphas, who was high priest that year, spoke up. "You know nothing at all! {11:50} You do not realize that it is better for you that one man die for the people than that the whole nation perish." {11:51} He did not say this on his own, but as high priest that year he prophesied that Jesus would die for the Jewish nation, {11:52} and not only for that nation but also for the scattered children of God, to bring them together. {11:53} So from that day on they plotted to take his life. {11:54} Therefore Jesus no longer moved about publicly among the people of Judea. Instead, he withdrew to a region near the wilderness, to a village called Ephraim, where he stayed with his disciples. {11:55} When it was almost time for the Jewish Passover, many went up from the country to Jerusalem for their ceremonial cleansing before the Passover. {11:56} They kept looking for Jesus, and as they stood in the temple courts, they asked one another, "What do you think? Isn't he coming to the festival at all?" {11:57} But the chief priests and the Pharisees had given orders that anyone who found out where Jesus was should report it so that they might arrest him.

{12:1} Six days before the Passover, Jesus came to Bethany, where Lazarus lived, whom he had raised from the dead. {12:2} Here a dinner was given in Jesus' honor. Martha served, while Lazarus was among those reclining at the table with him. {12:3} Then Mary took about a pint of pure nard (a type of perfume), an expensive perfume; she poured it on Jesus' feet and wiped his feet with her hair. The house was filled with the fragrance of the perfume. {12:4} But one of his disciples, Judas Iscariot, who was later to betray him, objected, {12:5} "Why wasn't this perfume sold and the money given to the poor? It was worth a year's wages." {12:6} He did not say this because he cared about the poor but because he was a thief; as keeper of the money bag, he used to help himself to what was put into it. {12:7} "Leave her alone," Jesus replied. "It was intended that she should save this perfume for the day of my burial. {12:8} You will always have the poor among you, but you will not always have me." {12:9} Meanwhile, a large crowd of Jews found out that Jesus was there and came, not only because of him but also to see Lazarus, whom he had raised from the dead. {12:10} So the chief priests made plans to kill Lazarus as well, {12:11} for on account of him many of the Jews were going over to Jesus and believing in him. {12:12} The next day, the great crowd that had come for the festival heard that Jesus was on his way to Jerusalem. {12:13} They took palm branches and went out to meet him, shouting, "Hosanna! Blessed is he who comes in the name of the Lord! Blessed is the king of Israel!" {12:14} Jesus found a young donkey and sat on it, as it is written: {12:15} "Do not be afraid, Daughter Zion; see, your king is coming, seated on a donkey's colt." {12:16} At first, his disciples did not understand all this. Only after Jesus was glorified did they realize that these things had been written about him and that they had done these things to him. {12:17} Now the crowd that was with him when he called Lazarus from the tomb and raised him from the dead continued to spread the word. {12:18} Many people, because they had heard that he had performed this sign, went out to meet him. {12:19} So the Pharisees said to one another, "See, this is getting us nowhere. Look how the whole world has gone after him!" {12:20} Now there were some Greeks among those who went up to worship at the festival. {12:21} They came to Philip, who was from Bethsaida in Galilee, with a request. "Sir," they said, "we would like to see Jesus." {12:22} Philip went to tell Andrew; Andrew and Philip in turn told Jesus. {12:23} Jesus replied, "The hour has come for the Son of Man to be glorified. {12:24} Very truly I tell you, unless a kernel of wheat falls to the ground and dies, it remains only a single seed. But if it dies, it produces many seeds. {12:25} Anyone who loves their life will lose it, while anyone who hates their life in this world will keep it for eternal life. {12:26} Whoever serves me must follow me; and where I am, my servant also will be. My Father will honor the one who serves me. {12:27} Now my soul is troubled, and what shall I say? 'Father, save me from this hour'? No, it was for this very reason I came to this hour. {12:28} Father, glorify your name!" Then a voice came from heaven, "I have glorified it, and will glorify it again." {12:29} The crowd that was there and heard it said it had thundered; others said an angel had spoken to him. {12:30} Jesus said, "This voice was for your benefit, not mine. {12:31} Now is the time for judgment on this world; now the prince of this world will be driven out. {12:32} And I, when I am lifted up from the earth, will draw all people to myself." {12:33} He said this to show the kind of death he was going to die. {12:34} The crowd spoke up, "We have heard from the Law that the Messiah will remain forever, so how can you say, 'The Son of Man must be lifted up'? Who is this Son of Man?" {12:35} Then Jesus told them, "You are going to have the light just a little while longer. Walk while you have the light, before darkness overtakes you. Whoever walks in the dark does not know where they are going. {12:36} Believe in the light while you have the light, so that you may become children of light." When he had finished speaking, Jesus left and hid himself from them. {12:37} Even after Jesus had performed so many signs in their presence, they still would not believe in him. {12:38} This was to fulfill the word of Isaiah the prophet: "Lord, who has believed our message and to whom has the arm of the Lord been revealed?" {12:39} For this reason they could not believe, because, as Isaiah says elsewhere: {12:40} "He has blinded their eyes and hardened their hearts, so they can neither see with their eyes, nor understand with their hearts, nor turn—and I would heal them." {12:41} Isaiah said this because he saw Jesus' glory and spoke about him. {12:42} Yet at the same time many even among the leaders believed in him, but because of the Pharisees they would not openly acknowledge their faith for fear they would be put out of the synagogue; {12:43} for they loved human praise more than praise from God. {12:44} Then Jesus cried out, "Whoever believes in me does not believe in me only, but in the one who sent me. {12:45} The one who looks at me is seeing the one who sent me. {12:46} I have come into the world as a light, so that no one who believes in me should stay in darkness. {12:47} If anyone hears my words but does not keep them, I do not judge that person. For I did not come to judge the world, but to save the world. {12:48} There is a judge for the one who rejects me and does not accept my words; the very words I have spoken will condemn them at the last day. {12:49} For I did not speak on my own, but the Father who sent me commanded me to say all that I have spoken. {12:50} I know that his command leads to eternal life. So whatever I say is just what the Father has told me to say."

{13:1} Before the Passover festival, Jesus knew that his time had come to leave this world and go to the Father. Having loved his own who were in the world, he loved them to the very end. {13:2} The meal was in progress, and the devil had already prompted Judas Iscariot, the son of Simon, to betray Jesus. {13:3} Jesus knew that the Father had put all things under his power, that he had come from God and was returning to God. {13:4} So he got up from the meal, took off his outer clothing, and wrapped a towel around his waist. {13:5} After that, he poured water into a basin and began to wash his disciples' feet, drying them with the towel he had wrapped around himself. {13:6} He came to Simon Peter, who said to him, "Lord, are you going to wash my feet?" {13:7} Jesus replied, "You do not realize now what I am doing, but later you will understand." {13:8} "No," said Peter, "you shall never wash my feet." Jesus answered, "Unless I wash you, you have no part with me." {13:9} "Then, Lord," Simon Peter replied, "not just my feet but my hands and my head as well!" {13:10} Jesus answered, "Those who have had a bath need only to wash their feet; their whole body is clean. And you are clean, though not every one of you." {13:11} For he knew who was going to betray him, and that was why he said not everyone was clean. {13:12} When he had finished washing their feet, he put on his clothes and returned to his place. "Do you understand what I have done for you?" he asked them. {13:13} "You call me 'Teacher' and 'Lord,' and rightly so, for that is what I am. {13:14} Now that I, your Lord and Teacher, have washed your feet, you also should wash one another's feet. {13:15} I have set you an example that you should do as I have done for you. {13:16} Very truly I tell you, no servant is greater than his master, nor is a messenger greater than the one who sent him. {13:17} Now that you know these things, you will be blessed if you do them. {13:18} I am not referring to all of you; I know those I have chosen. But this is to fulfill this scripture: 'He who shares my bread has turned against me.' {13:19} I am telling you now before it happens, so that when it does happen you will believe that I am who I am. {13:20} Very truly I tell you, whoever accepts anyone I send accepts me; and whoever accepts me accepts the one who sent me." {13:21} After he had said this, Jesus was troubled in spirit and testified, "Very truly I tell you, one of you is going to betray me." {13:22} His disciples stared at one another, at a loss to know which of them he meant. {13:23} One of them, the disciple whom Jesus loved, was reclining next to him. {13:24} Simon Peter motioned to this disciple and said, "Ask him which one he means." {13:25} Leaning back against Jesus, he asked him, "Lord, who is it?" {13:26} Jesus answered, "It is the one to whom I will give this piece of bread when I have dipped it in the dish." Then, dipping the piece of bread, he gave it to Judas, the son of Simon Iscariot. {13:27} As soon as Judas took the bread, Satan entered into him. So Jesus told him, "What you are about to do, do quickly." {13:28} But no one at the meal understood why Jesus said this to him. {13:29} Since Judas had charge of the money, some thought Jesus was telling him to buy what was needed for the festival or to give something to the poor. {13:30} As soon as Judas had taken the bread, he went out. And it was night. {13:31} When he was gone, Jesus said, "Now the Son of Man is glorified and God is glorified in him. {13:32} If God is glorified in him, God will glorify the Son in himself and will glorify him at once. {13:33} My children, I will be with you only a little longer. You will look for me, and just as I told the Jews, so I tell you now: Where I am going, you cannot come. {13:34} A new command I give you: Love one another. As I have loved you, so you must love one another. {13:35} By this everyone will know that you are my disciples if you love one another." {13:36} Simon Peter asked him, "Lord, where are you going?" Jesus replied, "Where I am going, you cannot follow now, but you will follow later." {13:37} Peter asked, "Lord, why can't I follow you now? I will lay down my life for you." {13:38} Then Jesus answered, "Will you really lay down your life for me? Very truly I tell you, before the rooster crows, you will disown me three times."

{14:1} "Do not let your hearts be troubled. You believe in God; believe also in me. {14:2} My Father's house has many rooms; if that were not so, would I have told you that I am going there to prepare a place for you? {14:3} And if I go and prepare a place for you, I will come back and take you to be with me that you also may be where I am. {14:4} You know the way to the place where I am going." {14:5} Thomas said to him, "Lord, we don't know where you are going, so how can we know the way?" {14:6} Jesus answered, "I am the way and the truth and the life. No one comes to the Father except through me. {14:7} If you really know me, you will know my Father as well. From now on, you do know him and have seen him." {14:8} Philip said, "Lord, show us the Father and that will be enough for us." {14:9} Jesus answered, "Don't you know me, Philip, even after I have been among you such a long time? Anyone who has seen me has seen the Father. How can you say, 'Show us the Father'? {14:10} Don't you believe that I am in the Father, and that the Father is in me? The words I say to you I do not speak on my own authority. Rather, it is the Father, living in me, who is doing his work. {14:11} Believe me when I say that I am in the Father and the Father is in me; or at least believe on the evidence of the works themselves. {14:12} Very truly I tell you, whoever believes in me will do the works I have been doing, and they will do even greater things than these, because I am going to the Father. {14:13} And I will do whatever you ask in my name, so that the Father may be glorified in the Son. {14:14} You may ask me for anything in my name, and I will do it. {14:15} If you love me, keep my commands. {14:16} And I will ask the Father, and he will give you another advocate (comforter), to help you and be with you forever— {14:17} the Spirit of truth. The world cannot accept him because it neither sees him nor knows him. But you know him, for he lives with you and will be in you. {14:18} I will not leave you as orphans; I will come to you. {14:19} Before long, the world will not see me anymore, but you will see me. Because I live, you also will live. {14:20} On that day, you will realize that I am in my Father, and you are in me, and I am in you. {14:21} Whoever has my commands and keeps them is the one who loves me. The one who loves me will be loved by my Father, and I too will love them and show myself to them." {14:22} Then Judas (not Judas Iscariot) said, "But, Lord, why do you intend to show yourself to us and not to the world?" {14:23} Jesus replied, "Anyone who loves me will obey my teaching. My Father will love them, and we will come to them and make our home with them. {14:24} Anyone who does not love me will not obey my teaching. These words you hear are not my own; they belong to the Father who sent me. {14:25} All this I have spoken while still with you. {14:26} But the Advocate, the Holy Spirit, whom the Father will send in my name, will teach you all things and will remind you of everything I have said to you. {14:27} Peace I leave with you; my peace I give you. I do not give to you as the world gives.{14:27} Peace I leave with you; my peace I give you. I do not give to you as the world gives. Do not let your hearts be troubled and do not be afraid. {14:28} You heard me say, 'I am going away and I will come back to you.' If you loved me, you would be glad that I am going to the Father, for the Father is greater than I. {14:29} I have told you now before it happens, so that when it does happen, you will believe. {14:30} I will not say much more to you, for the prince of this world is coming. He has no hold over me. {14:31} But he comes so that the world may learn that I love the Father and do exactly what my Father has commanded me. Come now; let us leave.

{15:1} I am the true vine, and my Father is the gardener. {15:2} He cuts off every branch in me that bears no fruit, while every branch that does bear fruit he prunes so that it will be even more fruitful. {15:3} You are already clean because of the word I have spoken to you. {15:4} Remain in me, and I will remain in you. No branch can bear fruit by itself; it must remain in the vine. Neither can you bear fruit unless you remain in me. {15:5} I am the vine; you are the branches. If you remain in me and I in you, you will bear much fruit; apart from me you can do nothing. {15:6} If you do not remain in me, you are like a branch that is thrown away and withers; such branches are picked up, thrown into the fire, and burned. {15:7} If you remain in me and my words remain in you, ask whatever you wish, and it will be done for you. {15:8} This is to my Father's glory, that you bear much fruit, showing yourselves to be my disciples. {15:9} As the Father has loved me, so have I loved you. Now remain in my love. {15:10} If you keep my commands, you will remain in my love, just as I have kept my Father's commands and remain in his love. {15:11} I have told you this so that my joy may be in you and that your joy may be complete. {15:12} My command is this: Love each other as I have loved you. {15:13} Greater love has no one than this: to lay down one's life for one's friends. {15:14} You are my friends if you do what I command. {15:15} I no longer call you servants, because a servant does not know his master's business. Instead, I have called you friends, for everything that I learned from my Father I have made known to you. {15:16} You did not choose me, but I chose you and appointed you so that you might go and bear fruit—fruit that will last—and so that whatever you ask in my name the Father will give you. {15:17} This is my command: Love each other. {15:18} If the world hates you, keep in mind that it hated me first. {15:19} If you belonged to the world, it would love you as its own. As it is, you do not belong to the world, but I have chosen you out of the world. That is why the world hates you. {15:20} Remember what I told you: A servant is not greater than his master. If they persecuted me, they will persecute you also. If they obeyed my teaching, they will obey yours also. {15:21} They will treat you this way because of my name, for they do not know the one who sent me. {15:22} If I had not come and spoken to them, they would not be guilty of sin; but now they have no excuse for their sin. {15:23} Whoever hates me hates my Father as well. {15:24} If I had not done among them the works no one else did, they would not be guilty of sin. As it is, they have seen and hated both me and my Father. {15:25} But this is to fulfill what is written in their Law: 'They hated me without reason.' {15:26} When the Advocate (Comforter) comes, whom I will send to you from the Father—the Spirit of truth who goes out from the Father—he will testify about me. {15:27} And you also must testify, for you have been with me from the beginning.

{16:1} All this I have told you so that you will not fall away. {16:2} They will put you out of the synagogue; in fact, the time is coming when anyone who kills you will think they are offering a service to God. {16:3} They will do such things because they have not known the Father or me. {16:4} I have told you this so that when their time comes you will remember that I warned you about them. I did not tell you this from the beginning because I was with you. {16:5} Now I am going to him who sent me, and none of you asks me, 'Where are you going?' {16:6} Rather, you are filled with grief because I have said these things. {16:7} But very truly I tell you, it is for your good that I am going away. Unless I go away, the Advocate will not come to you; but if I go, I will send him to you. {16:8} When he comes, he will prove the world to be in the wrong about sin and righteousness and judgment: {16:9} about sin, because people do not believe in me; {16:10} about righteousness, because I am going to the Father, where you can see me no longer; {16:11} and about judgment, because the prince of this world now stands condemned. {16:12} I have much more to say to you, more than you can now bear. {16:13} But when he, the Spirit of truth, comes, he will guide you into all the truth. He will not speak on his own; he will speak only what he hears, and he will tell you what is yet to come. {16:14} He will glorify me because it is from me that he will receive what he will make known to you. {16:15} All that belongs to the Father is mine. That is why I said the Spirit will receive from me what he will make known to you. {16:16} In a little while, you will see me no more, and then after a little while, you will see me." {16:17} Some of his disciples said to one another, "What does he mean by saying, 'In a little while you will see me no more, and then after a little while you will see me,' and 'Because I am going to the Father'?" {16:18} They kept asking, "What does he mean by 'a little while'? We don't understand what he is saying." {16:19} Jesus saw that they wanted to ask him about this, so he said to them, "Are you asking one another what I meant when I said, 'In a little while you will see me no more, and then after a little while you will see me'? {16:20} Very truly I tell you, you will weep and mourn while the world rejoices. You will grieve, but your grief will turn to joy. {16:21} A woman giving birth to a child has pain because her time has come; but when her baby is born, she forgets the anguish because of her joy that a child is born into the world. {16:22} So with you: Now is your time of grief, but I will see you again and you will rejoice, and no one will take away your joy. {16:23} In that day you will no longer ask me anything. Very truly I tell you, my Father will give you whatever you ask in my name. {16:24} Until now you have not asked for anything in my name. Ask and you will receive, and your joy will be complete. {16:25} Though I have been speaking figuratively, a time is coming when I will no longer use this kind of language but will tell you plainly about my Father. {16:26} In that day you will ask in my name. I am not saying that I will ask the Father on your behalf. {16:27} No, the Father himself loves you because you have loved me and have believed that I came from God. {16:28} I came from the Father and entered the world; now I am leaving the world and going back to the Father." {16:29} Then Jesus' disciples said, "Now you are speaking clearly and without figures of speech. {16:30} Now we can see that you know all things and that you do not even need to have anyone ask you questions. This makes us believe that you came from God." {16:31} Jesus replied, "Do you now believe? {16:32} A time is coming and in fact has come when you will be scattered, each to your own home. You will leave me all alone. Yet I am not alone, for my Father is with me. {16:33} I have told you these things so that in me you may have peace. In this world you will have trouble. But take heart! I have overcome the world."

{17:1} After saying these things, Jesus looked up to heaven and said, "Father, the hour has come; glorify your Son so that your Son may glorify you. {17:2} For you have given him authority over all people so that he may give eternal life to all those you have given him. {17:3} Now this is eternal life: that they know you, the only true God, and Jesus Christ, whom you have sent. {17:4} I have brought you glory on earth by finishing the work you gave me to do. {17:5} And now, Father, glorify me in your presence with the glory I had with you before the world began. {17:6} I have revealed your name to those you gave me out of the world. They were yours; you gave them to me, and they have obeyed your word. {17:7} Now they know that everything you have given me comes from you. {17:8} For I gave them the words you gave me, and they accepted them. They knew with certainty that I came from you, and they believed that you sent me. {17:9} I pray for them. I am not praying for the world, but for those you have given me, for they are yours. {17:10} All I have is yours, and all you have is mine, and I am glorified in them. {17:11} I will remain in the world no longer, but they are still in the world, and I am coming to you. Holy Father, protect them by the power of your name, the name you gave me, so that they may be one as we are one. {17:12} While I was with them, I protected them and kept them safe by that name you gave me. None has been lost except the one doomed to destruction, so that Scripture would be fulfilled. {17:13} I am coming to you now, but I say these things while I am still in the world so that they may have the full measure of my joy within them. {17:14} I have given them your word, and the world has hated them, for they are not of the world any more than I am of the world. {17:15} My prayer is not that you take them out of the world but that you protect them from the evil one. {17:16} They are not of the world, even as I am not of it. {17:17} Sanctify them by the truth; your word is truth. {17:18} As you sent me into the world, I have sent them into the world. {17:19} For them I sanctify myself, that they too may be truly sanctified. {17:20} My prayer is not for them alone. I pray also for those who will believe in me through their message. {17:21} That all of them may be one, Father, just as you are in me and I am in you. May they also be in us so that the world may believe that you have sent me. {17:22} I have given them the glory that you gave me, that they may be one as we are one. {17:23} I in them and you in me, so that they may be brought to complete unity. Then the world will know that you sent me and have loved them even as you have loved me. {17:24} Father, I want those you have given me to be with me where I am, and to see my glory, the glory you have given me because you loved me before the creation of the world. {17:25} Righteous Father, though the world does not know you, I know you, and they know that you have sent me. {17:26} I have made you known to them, and will continue to make you known in order that the love you have for me may be in them and that I myself may be in them.

{18:1} When he had finished praying, Jesus left with his disciples and crossed the Kidron Valley. On the other side, there was a garden, and he and his disciples went into it. {18:2} Now Judas, who betrayed him, knew the place because Jesus had often met there with his disciples. {18:3} So Judas came to the garden, guiding a detachment of soldiers and some officials from the chief priests and the Pharisees. They were carrying torches, lanterns, and weapons. {18:4} Jesus, knowing all that was going to happen to him, went out and asked them, "Who is it you want?" {18:5} "Jesus of Nazareth," they replied. "I am he," Jesus said. (And Judas, the traitor, was standing there with them.) {18:6} When Jesus said, "I am he," they drew back and fell to the ground. {18:7} Again he asked them, "Who is it you want?" "Jesus of Nazareth," they said. {18:8} "I told you that I am he," Jesus said. "If you are looking for me, then let these men go." {18:9} This happened so that the words he had spoken would be fulfilled: "I have not lost one of those you gave me." {18:10} Then Simon Peter, who had a sword, drew it and struck the high priest's servant, cutting off his right ear. The servant's name was Malchus. {18:11} Jesus commanded Peter, "Put your sword away! Shall I not drink the cup the Father has given me?" {18:12} Then the detachment of soldiers with its commander and the Jewish officials arrested Jesus. They bound him {18:13} and brought him first to Annas, who was the father-in-law of Caiaphas, the high priest that year. {18:14} Caiaphas was the one who had advised the Jewish leaders that it would be good if one man died for the people. {18:15} Simon Peter and another disciple were following Jesus. Because this disciple was known to the high priest, he went with Jesus into the high priest's courtyard, {18:16} but Peter had to wait outside at the door. The other disciple, who was known to the high priest, came back, spoke to the servant girl on duty there, and brought Peter in. {18:17} "You aren't one of this man's disciples too, are you?" she asked Peter. He replied, "I am not." {18:18} It was cold, and the servants and officials stood around a fire they had made to keep warm. Peter also was standing with them, warming himself. {18:19} Meanwhile, the high priest questioned Jesus about his disciples and his teaching. {18:20} "I have spoken openly to the world," Jesus replied. "I always taught in synagogues or at the temple, where all the Jews come together. I said nothing in secret. {18:21} Why question me? Ask those who heard me. Surely they know what I said." {18:22} When Jesus said this, one of the officials nearby slapped him in the face. "Is this the way you answer the high priest?" he demanded. {18:23} "If I said something wrong," Jesus replied, "testify as to what is wrong. But if I spoke the truth, why did you strike me?" {18:24} Then Annas sent him bound to Caiaphas the high priest. {18:25} As Simon Peter stood warming himself, he was asked, "You aren't one of his disciples too, are you?" He denied it, saying, "I am not." {18:26} One of the high priest's servants, a relative of the man whose ear Peter had cut off, challenged him, "Didn't I see you with him in the garden?" {18:27} Again Peter denied it, and at that moment a rooster began to crow. {18:28} Then the Jewish leaders took Jesus from Caiaphas to the palace of the Roman governor. By now it was early morning, and to avoid ceremonial uncleanness, they did not enter the palace because they wanted to be able to eat the Passover. {18:29} So Pilate came out to them and asked, "What charges are you bringing against this man?" {18:30} "If he were not a criminal," they replied, "we would not have handed him over to you." {18:31} Pilate said, "Take him yourselves and judge him by your own law." "But we have no right to execute anyone," they objected. {18:32} This took place to fulfill what Jesus had said about the kind of death he was going to die. {18:33} Pilate then went back inside the palace, summoned Jesus and asked him, "Are you the king of the Jews?" {18:34} "Is that your own idea," Jesus asked, "or did others talk to you about me?" {18:35} "Am I a Jew?" Pilate replied. "Your own people and chief priests handed you over to me. What is it you have done?" {18:36} Jesus said, "My kingdom is not of this world. If it were, my servants would fight to prevent my arrest by the Jewish leaders. But now my kingdom is from another place." {18:37} "You are a king, then!" said Pilate. Jesus answered, "You say that I am a king. In fact, the reason I was born and came into the world is to testify to the truth. Everyone on side of truth listens to me." {18:38} "What is truth?" retorted Pilate. With this, he went out again to Jews, gathered around him and said, "I find no basis for a charge against him. {18:39} But it is your custom for me to release to you one prisoner at the time of the Passover. Do you want me to release 'the king of the Jews'?" {18:40} They shouted back, "Not him! Give us Barabbas!"

{19:1} Then Pilate took Jesus and had him whipped. {19:2} The soldiers wove a crown of thorns and put it on his head, and they dressed him in a purple robe. {19:3} They shouted, "Hail, King of the Jews!" and struck him with their hands. {19:4} Pilate went out again and said to them, "Look, I'm bringing him out to you to let you know that I find no basis for a charge against him." {19:5} When Jesus came out, wearing the crown of thorns and the purple robe, Pilate said to them, "Here is the man!" {19:6} When the chief priests and the guards saw him, they shouted, "Crucify him! Crucify him!" Pilate told them, "You take him and crucify him. I find no fault in him." {19:7} The Jews responded, "We have a law, and according to that law, he must die because he claimed to be the Son of God." {19:8} When Pilate heard this, he was even more afraid. {19:9} He went back into the palace and asked Jesus, "Where are you from?" But Jesus gave him no answer. {19:10} "Don't you realize I have power to either free you or crucify you?" Pilate said. {19:11} Jesus replied, "You would have no power over me if it were not given to you from above; therefore, the one who handed me over to you is guilty of a greater sin." {19:12} From then on, Pilate tried to set Jesus free, but the Jews kept shouting, "If you let this man go, you are no friend of Caesar. Anyone who claims to be a king opposes Caesar." {19:13} When Pilate heard this, he brought Jesus out and sat down on the judge's seat at a place known as the Stone Pavement (which in Aramaic is Gabbatha). {19:14} It was the day of Preparation for the Passover, about noon. "Here is your king!" Pilate said to the Jews. {19:15} "Take him away! Take him away! Crucify him!" they shouted. "Shall I crucify your king?" Pilate asked. "We have no king but Caesar," the chief priests answered. {19:16} Finally, Pilate handed him over to them to be crucified. They took Jesus away. {19:17} Carrying his own cross, Jesus went out to the place of the Skull (which is called Golgotha in Hebrew). {19:18} Here they crucified him, and with him two others—one on each side and Jesus in the middle. {19:19} Pilate had a sign prepared and fastened to the cross. It read: JESUS OF NAZARETH, THE KING OF THE JEWS. {19:20} Many of the Jews read this sign, for the place where Jesus was crucified was near the city, and it was written in Hebrew, Latin, and Greek. {19:21} The chief priests protested to Pilate, "Do not write, 'The King of the Jews,' but that this man claimed to be the King of the Jews." {19:22} Pilate answered, "What I have written, I have written." {19:23} When the soldiers crucified Jesus, they took his clothes, dividing them into four shares, one for each of them, with the undergarment remaining. This garment was seamless, woven in one piece from top to bottom. {19:24} They said to one another, "Let's not tear it, but cast lots to see who will get it." This happened that the scripture might be fulfilled that said, "They divided my garments among them and cast lots for my clothing." So this is what the soldiers did. {19:25} Near the cross of Jesus stood his mother, his mother's sister, Mary the wife of Clopas, and Mary Magdalene. {19:26} When Jesus saw his mother there, and the disciple whom he loved standing nearby, he said to her, "Woman, here is your son!" {19:27} And to the disciple, "Here is your mother!" From that time on, this disciple took her into his home. {19:28} Later, knowing that everything had now been finished, and so that Scripture would be fulfilled, Jesus said, "I am thirsty." {19:29} A jar of wine vinegar was there, so they soaked a sponge in it, put the sponge on a stalk of the hyssop plant, and lifted it to Jesus' lips. {19:30} When he had received the drink, Jesus said, "It is finished." With that, he bowed his head and gave up his spirit. {19:31} Now it was the day of Preparation, and the Jewish leaders did not want the bodies left on the crosses during the Sabbath. (That Sabbath was a special day.) They asked Pilate to have the legs broken and the bodies taken down. {19:32} So the soldiers came and broke the legs of the first man who had been crucified with Jesus, and those of the other. {19:33} But when they came to Jesus and found that he was already dead, they did not break his legs. {19:34} Instead, one of the soldiers pierced Jesus' side with a spear, bringing a sudden flow of blood and water. {19:35} The man who saw it has given testimony, and his testimony is true. He knows that he tells the truth, and he testifies so that you also may believe. {19:36} These things happened so that the scripture would be fulfilled: "Not one of his bones will be broken," {19:37} and, as another scripture says, "They will look on the one they have pierced." {19:38} Later, Joseph of Arimathea asked Pilate for the body of Jesus. Now Joseph was a disciple of Jesus, but secretly because he feared the Jewish leaders. With Pilate's permission, he came and took the body away. {19:39} He was accompanied by Nicodemus, the man who earlier had visited Jesus at night. Nicodemus brought a mixture of myrrh and aloes, about seventy-five pounds. {19:40} Taking Jesus' body, the two of them wrapped it, with the spices, in strips of linen. This was in accordance with Jewish burial customs. {19:41} At the place where Jesus was crucified, there was a garden, and in the garden a new tomb, in which no one had ever been laid. {19:42} Because it was the Jewish day of Preparation and since the tomb was nearby, they laid Jesus there.

{20:1} Early on the first day of the week, while it was still dark, Mary Magdalene went to the tomb and saw that the stone had been removed from the entrance. {20:2} So she came running to Simon Peter and the other disciple, the one Jesus loved, and said, "They have taken the Lord out of the tomb, and we don't know where they have put him!" {20:3} So Peter and the other disciple started for the tomb. {20:4} Both were running, but the other disciple outran Peter and reached the tomb first. {20:5} He bent over and looked in at the strips of linen lying there but did not go in. {20:6} Then Simon Peter came along behind him and went straight into the tomb. He saw the strips of linen lying there, {20:7} as well as the cloth that had been wrapped around Jesus' head. The cloth was still lying in its place, separate from the linen. {20:8} Finally, the other disciple, who had reached the tomb first, also went inside. He saw and believed. {20:9} They still did not understand from Scripture that Jesus had to rise from the dead. {20:10} Then the disciples went back to where they were staying. {20:11} But Mary stood outside the tomb crying. As she wept, she bent over to look into the tomb {20:12} and saw two angels in white, seated where Jesus' body had been, one at the head and the other at the foot. {20:13} They asked her, "Woman, why are you crying?" "They have taken my Lord away," she said, "and I don't know where they have put him." {20:14} At this, she turned around and saw Jesus standing there, but she did not realize that it was Jesus. {20:15} He asked her, "Woman, why are you crying? Who are you looking for?" Thinking he was the gardener, she said, "Sir, if you have carried him away, tell me where you have put him, and I will get him." {20:16} Jesus said to her, "Mary." She turned toward him and cried out in Aramaic, "Rabboni!" (which means "Teacher"). {20:17} Jesus said, "Do not hold on to me, for I have not yet ascended to the Father. Go instead to my brothers and tell them, 'I am ascending to my Father and your Father, to my God and your God.'" {20:18} Mary Magdalene went to the disciples with the news: "I have seen the Lord!" And she told them that he had said these things to her. {20:19} On the evening of that first day of the week, when the disciples were together, with the doors locked for fear of the Jewish leaders, Jesus came and stood among them and said, "Peace be with you!" {20:20} After he said this, he showed them his hands and side. The disciples were overjoyed when they saw the Lord. {20:21} Again Jesus said, "Peace be with you! As the Father has sent me, I am sending you." {20:22} And with that, he breathed on them and said, "Receive the Holy Spirit. {20:23} If you forgive anyone's sins, their sins are forgiven; if you do not forgive them, they are not forgiven." {20:24} Now Thomas (also known as Didymus), one of the Twelve, was not with the disciples when Jesus came. {20:25} So the other disciples told him, "We have seen the Lord!" But he said to them, "Unless I see the nail marks in his hands and put my finger where the nails were, and put my hand into his side, I will not believe." {20:26} A week later, his disciples were in the house again, and Thomas was with them. Though the doors were locked, Jesus came and stood among them and said, "Peace be with you!" {20:27} Then he said to Thomas, "Put your finger here; see my hands. Reach out your hand and put it into my side. Stop doubting and believe." {20:28} Thomas said to him, "My Lord and my God!" {20:29} Then Jesus told him, "Because you have seen me, you have believed; blessed are those who have not seen and yet have believed." {20:30} Jesus performed many other signs in the presence of his disciples, which are not recorded in this book. {20:31} But these are written that you may believe that Jesus is the Messiah, the Son of God, and that by believing you may have life in his name.

{21:1} After these things, Jesus showed himself again to the disciples at the Sea of Tiberias. This is how it happened. {21:2} Together were Simon Peter, Thomas (also called Didymus), Nathanael from Cana in Galilee, the sons of Zebedee, and two other disciples. {21:3} Simon Peter said to them, "I'm going fishing." They replied, "We'll go with you." So they went out and got into the boat, but that night they caught nothing. {21:4} Early in the morning, Jesus stood on the shore, but the disciples didn't realize it was him. {21:5} He called out to them, "Friends, haven't you any fish?" "No," they answered. {21:6} He said, "Throw your net on the right side of the boat and you will find some." When they did, they were unable to haul the net in because of the large number of fish. {21:7} Then the disciple whom Jesus loved said to Peter, "It is the Lord!" As soon as Simon Peter heard him say it was the Lord, he wrapped his outer garment around him (for he had taken it off) and jumped into the water. {21:8} The other disciples followed in the boat, towing the net full of fish, for they were not far from shore—about a hundred yards. {21:9} When they landed, they saw a fire of burning coals there with fish on it and some bread. {21:10} Jesus said to them, "Bring some of the fish you have just caught." {21:11} So Simon Peter climbed back into the boat and dragged the net ashore. It was full of large fish, one hundred fifty-three, but even with so many, the net was not torn. {21:12} Jesus said to them, "Come and have breakfast." None of the disciples dared ask him, "Who are you?" They knew it was the Lord. {21:13} Jesus came, took the bread and gave it to them, and he did the same with the fish. {21:14} This was now the third time Jesus appeared to his disciples after he was raised from the dead. {21:15} When they had finished eating, Jesus said to Simon Peter, "Simon son of John, do you love me more than these?" "Yes, Lord," he said, "you know that I love you." Jesus said, "Feed my lambs." {21:16} Again Jesus said, "Simon son of John, do you love me?" "Yes, Lord," he said, "you know that I love you." Jesus said, "Take care of my sheep." {21:17} The third time he said to him, "Simon son of John, do you love me?" Peter was hurt because Jesus asked him the third time, "Do you love me?" He said, "Lord, you know all things; you know that I love you." Jesus said, "Feed my sheep. {21:18} Very truly I tell you, when you were younger you dressed yourself and went where you wanted; but when you are old you will stretch out your hands, and someone else will dress you and lead you where you do not want to go." {21:19} Jesus said this to indicate the kind of death by which Peter would glorify God. Then he said to him, "Follow me!" {21:20} Peter turned and saw that the disciple whom Jesus loved was following them. This was the one who had leaned back against Jesus at the supper and had said, "Lord, who is going to betray you?" {21:21} When Peter saw him, he asked, "Lord, what about him?" {21:22} Jesus answered, "If I want him to remain alive until I return, what is that to you? You must follow me." {21:23} Because of this, the rumor spread among the believers that this disciple would not die. But Jesus did not say that he would not die; he only said, "If I want him to remain alive until I return, what is that to you?" {21:24} This is the disciple who testifies to these things and who wrote them down. We know that his testimony is true. {21:25} Jesus did many other things as well. If every one of them were written down, I suppose that even the whole world would not have room for the books that would be written. Amen.

{1:1} I previously wrote about everything that Jesus began to do and teach, O Theophilus, {1:2} until the day he was taken up after giving commands to the apostles he had chosen through the Holy Spirit. {1:3} To them, he also presented himself alive after his suffering, showing them many convincing proofs over the course of forty days and speaking about the kingdom of God. {1:4} While he was together with them, he instructed them not to leave Jerusalem but to wait for the promise of the Father, which he said they had heard from him. {1:5} John truly baptized with water, but they would soon be baptized with the Holy Spirit. {1:6} When they gathered together, they asked him, "Lord, are you at this time going to restore the kingdom to Israel?" {1:7} He replied, "It is not for you to know the times or dates that the Father has set by his own authority. {1:8} But you will receive power when the Holy Spirit comes on you; and you will be my witnesses in Jerusalem, and in all Judea and Samaria, and to the ends of the earth." {1:9} After he said this, they watched as he was taken up, and a cloud hid him from their sight. {1:10} They were looking intently up into the sky as he went, when suddenly two men dressed in white stood beside them. {1:11} They said, "Men of Galilee, why do you stand here looking into the sky? This same Jesus, who has been taken from you into heaven, will come back in the same way you have seen him go into heaven." {1:12} Then they returned to Jerusalem from the hill called the Mount of Olives, which is a Sabbath day's walk from the city. {1:13} When they arrived, they went upstairs to the room where they were staying. Those present were Peter, James, John, Andrew, Philip, Thomas, Bartholomew, Matthew, James (the son of Alphaeus), Simon the Zealot, and Judas (the son of James). {1:14} They all joined together constantly in prayer, along with the women and Mary the mother of Jesus, and with his brothers. {1:15} In those days, Peter stood up among the believers (a group numbering about one hundred and twenty) {1:16} and said, "Brothers and sisters, the Scripture had to be fulfilled in which the Holy Spirit spoke long ago through David concerning Judas, who served as a guide for those who arrested Jesus. {1:17} He was one of our number and shared in our ministry." {1:18} (With the payment he received for his wickedness, Judas bought a field; there he fell headlong, his body burst open and all his intestines spilled out. {1:19} Everyone in Jerusalem heard about this, so they called that field in their language Aceldama, that is, Field of Blood.) {1:20} For, said Peter, "It is written in the Book of Psalms: 'May his place be deserted; let there be no one to dwell in it,' and, 'May another take his place of leadership.' {1:21} Therefore it is necessary to choose one of the men who have been with us the whole time the Lord Jesus was living among us, {1:22} beginning from John's baptism to the time when Jesus was taken up from us. For one of these must become a witness with us of his resurrection." {1:23} So they nominated two men: Joseph called Barsabbas (also known as Justus) and Matthias. {1:24} Then they prayed, "Lord, you know everyone's heart. Show us which of these two you have chosen {1:25} to take over this apostolic ministry, which Judas left to go where he belongs." {1:26} Then they cast lots, and the lot fell to Matthias; so he was added to the eleven apostles.

{2:1} When the day of Pentecost came, they were all together in one place. {2:2} Suddenly a sound like the blowing of a violent wind came from heaven and filled the whole house where they were sitting. {2:3} They saw what seemed to be tongues of fire that separated and came to rest on each of them. {2:4} All of them were filled with the Holy Spirit and began to speak in other languages as the Spirit enabled them. {2:5} Now there were staying in Jerusalem God-fearing Jews from every nation under heaven. {2:6} When they heard this sound, a crowd came together in bewilderment, because each one heard their own language being spoken. {2:7} Utterly amazed, they asked: "Aren't all these who are speaking Galileans? {2:8} Then how is it that each of us hears them in our native language? {2:9} Parthians, Medes and Elamites; residents of Mesopotamia, Judea and Cappadocia, Pontus and Asia, {2:10} Phrygia and Pamphylia, Egypt and the parts of Libya near Cyrene; visitors from Rome {2:11} (both Jews and converts to Judaism); Cretans and Arabs—we hear them declaring the wonders of God in our own tongues!" {2:12} Amazed and perplexed, they asked one another, "What does this mean?" {2:13} Some, however, made fun of them and said, "They have had too much wine." {2:14} Then Peter stood up with the Eleven, raised his voice and addressed the crowd: "Fellow Jews and all of you who live in Jerusalem, let me explain this to you; listen carefully to what I say. {2:15} These people are not drunk, as you suppose. It's only nine in the morning! {2:16} No, this is what was spoken by the prophet Joel: {2:17} 'In the last days, God says, I will pour out my Spirit on all people. Your sons and daughters will prophesy, your young men will see visions, your old men will dream dreams. {2:18} Even on my servants, both men and women, I will pour out my Spirit in those days, and they will prophesy. {2:19} I will show wonders in the heavens above and signs on the earth below, blood and fire and billows of smoke. {2:20} The sun will be turned to darkness and the moon to blood before the coming of the great and glorious day of the Lord. {2:21} And everyone who calls on the name of the Lord will be saved.' {2:22} Fellow Israelites, listen to this: Jesus of Nazareth was a man accredited by God to you by miracles, wonders, and signs, which God did among you through him, as you yourselves know. {2:23} This man was handed over to you by God's deliberate plan and foreknowledge; and you, with the help of wicked men, put him to death by nailing him to the cross. {2:24} But God raised him from the dead, freeing him from the agony of death, because it was impossible for death to keep its hold on him. {2:25} David said about him: 'I saw the Lord always before me. Because he is at my right hand, I will not be shaken. {2:26} Therefore my heart is glad and my tongue rejoices; my body also will rest in hope, {2:27} because you will not abandon me to the realm of the dead, you will not let your holy one see decay. {2:28} You have made known to me the paths of life; you will fill me with joy in your presence.' {2:29} Fellow Israelites, I can tell you confidently that the patriarch David died and was buried, and his tomb is here to this day. {2:30} But he was a prophet and knew that God had promised him on oath that he would place one of his descendants on his throne. {2:31} Seeing what was to come, he spoke of the resurrection of the Messiah, that he was not abandoned to the realm of the dead, nor did his body see decay. {2:32} God has raised this Jesus to life, and we are all witnesses of it. {2:33} Exalted to the right hand of God, he has received from the Father the promised Holy Spirit and has poured out what you now see and hear. {2:34} For David did not ascend to heaven, and yet he said, 'The Lord said to my Lord: Sit at my right hand {2:35} until I make your enemies a footstool for your feet.' {2:36} Therefore let all Israel be assured of this: God has made this Jesus, whom you crucified, both Lord and Messiah." {2:37} When the people heard this, they were cut to the heart and said to Peter and the other apostles, "Brothers, what shall we do?" {2:38} Peter replied, "Repent and be baptized, every one of you, in the name of Jesus Christ for the forgiveness of your sins, and you will receive the gift of the Holy Spirit. {2:39} The promise is for you and your children and for all who are far off—for all whom the Lord our God will call." {2:40} With many other words, he warned them; and he pleaded with them, "Save yourselves from this corrupt generation." {2:41} Those who gladly accepted his message were baptized, and about three thousand people were added to their number that day. {2:42} They remained committed to the apostles' teaching and fellowship, to the breaking of bread, and to prayer. {2:43} A sense of awe came upon everyone, and many wonders and signs were performed by the apostles. {2:44} All the believers were united and shared everything in common; {2:45} they sold their property and possessions and distributed the proceeds to anyone who had need. {2:46} Every day they continued to meet together in the temple courts. They broke bread in their homes and ate together with glad and sincere hearts, {2:47} praising God and enjoying the favor of all the people. And the Lord added to their number daily those who were being saved.

{3:1} One day, Peter and John went together to the temple at the time of prayer, which was around three o'clock in the afternoon. {3:2} There was a man who had been lame from birth, and he was carried every day to the Beautiful Gate of the temple to beg for money from those entering the temple. {3:3} When he saw Peter and John about to go into the temple, he asked them for money. {3:4} Peter looked straight at him, as did John, and said, "Look at us." {3:5} The man gave them his attention, expecting to receive something from them. {3:6} Then Peter said, "I don't have any silver or gold, but what I do have I give you: in the name of Jesus

Christ of Nazareth, get up and walk." {3:7} Taking him by the right hand, Peter helped him up, and instantly the man's feet and ankles became strong. {3:8} He jumped up, stood on his feet, walked, and went with them into the temple, walking, jumping, and praising God. {3:9} Everyone saw him walking and praising God. {3:10} They recognized him as the same man who used to sit begging at the Beautiful Gate of the temple, and they were filled with wonder and amazement at what had happened to him. {3:11} While the healed man held on to Peter and John, all the people rushed to them in the Solomon's Colonnade, amazed. {3:12} When Peter saw this, he said to the people, "Men of Israel, why are you amazed at this? Why do you stare at us as if we had made this man walk by our own power or piety? {3:13} The God of Abraham, Isaac, and Jacob, the God of our fathers, has glorified His servant Jesus, whom you handed over and denied before Pilate, even though he wanted to let him go. {3:14} You denied the Holy and Righteous One and asked that a murderer be released to you. {3:15} You killed the author of life, but God raised Him from the dead; we are witnesses of this. {3:16} It is Jesus' name and faith in His name that has made this man strong, whom you see and know; it is Jesus who has given him this complete healing in your presence. {3:17} Now, brothers, I know that you acted in ignorance, as did your leaders. {3:18} But this is how God fulfilled what He had foretold through all the prophets, saying that His Christ would suffer. {3:19} Repent, then, and turn to God, so that your sins may be wiped out, that times of refreshing may come from the Lord. {3:20} He will send Jesus, who has been appointed for you. {3:21} Heaven must receive Him until the time comes for God to restore everything, as He promised long ago through His holy prophets. {3:22} For Moses said, 'The Lord your God will raise up for you a prophet like me from among your own people; you must listen to everything he tells you.' {3:23} Anyone who does not listen to him will be completely cut off from their people. {3:24} Indeed, all the prophets from Samuel on, as many as have spoken, have foretold these days. {3:25} And you are heirs of the prophets and of the covenant God made with your fathers. He said to Abraham, 'Through your offspring all peoples on earth will be blessed.' {3:26} When God raised up His servant, He sent Him first to you to bless you by turning each of you from your wicked ways.

{4:1} While Peter and John were speaking to the people, the priests, the captain of the temple, and the Sadducees came up to them. {4:2} They were greatly disturbed because the apostles were teaching the people and proclaiming in Jesus the resurrection of the dead. {4:3} They seized Peter and John and, because it was evening, they put them in jail until the next day. {4:4} But many who heard the message believed; so the number of men who believed grew to about five thousand. {4:5} The next day, the rulers, elders, and teachers of the law met in Jerusalem. {4:6} Annas the high priest was there, and so were Caiaphas, John, Alexander, and others of the high priest's family. {4:7} They had Peter and John brought before them and began to question them, "By what power or what name did you do this?" {4:8} Then Peter, filled with the Holy Spirit, said to them, "Rulers and elders of the people! {4:9} If we are being called to account today for an act of kindness shown to a cripple and are asked how he was healed, {4:10} then know this, you and all the people of Israel: It is by the name of Jesus Christ of Nazareth, whom you crucified but whom God raised from the dead, that this man stands before you healed. {4:11} Jesus is 'the stone you builders rejected, which has become the cornerstone.' {4:12} Salvation is found in no one else, for there is no other name under heaven given to mankind by which we must be saved." {4:13} When they saw the courage of Peter and John and realized that they were unschooled, ordinary men, they were astonished and took note that these men had been with Jesus. {4:14} But since they could see the man who had been healed standing there with them, there was nothing they could say. {4:15} So they ordered them to withdraw from the Sanhedrin and then conferred together. {4:16} "What are we going to do with these men?" they asked. "Everyone living in Jerusalem knows they have performed a notable sign, and we cannot deny it. {4:17} But to stop this thing from spreading any further among the people, we must warn them to speak no longer to anyone in this name." {4:18} Then they called them in again and commanded them not to speak or teach at all in the name of Jesus. {4:19} But Peter and John replied, "Which is right in God's eyes: to listen to you, or to Him? You be the judges! {4:20} As for us, we cannot help speaking about what we have seen and heard." {4:21} After further threats, they let them go. They could not decide how to punish them, because all the people were praising God for what had happened. {4:22} For the man who was miraculously healed was over forty years old. {4:23} On their release, Peter and John went back to their own people and reported all that the chief priests and elders had said to them. {4:24} When they heard this, they raised their voices together in prayer to God. "Sovereign Lord," they said, "You made the heavens and the earth, the sea, and everything in them. {4:25} You spoke by the Holy Spirit through the mouth of Your servant, our father David: 'Why do the nations rage and the peoples plot in vain? {4:26} The kings of the earth rise up and the rulers band together against the Lord and against His anointed one.' {4:27} Indeed Herod and Pontius Pilate met together with the Gentiles and the people of Israel in this city to conspire against Your holy servant Jesus, whom You anointed. {4:28} They did what Your power and will had decided beforehand should happen. {4:29} Now, Lord, consider their threats and enable Your servants to speak Your word with great boldness. {4:30} Stretch out Your hand to heal and perform signs and wonders through the name of Your holy servant Jesus." {4:31} After they prayed, the place where they were meeting was shaken, and they were all filled with the Holy Spirit and spoke the word of God boldly. {4:32} All the believers were one in heart and mind. No one claimed that any of their possessions was their own, but they shared everything they had. {4:33} With great power, the apostles continued to testify to the resurrection of the Lord Jesus, and God's grace was so powerfully at work in them all. {4:34} There were no needy persons among them. For from time to time, those who owned land or houses sold them, brought the money from the sales {4:35} and put it at the apostles' feet, and it was distributed to anyone who had need. {4:36} Joseph, a Levite from Cyprus, whom the apostles called Barnabas (which means "son of encouragement"), {4:37} sold a field he owned and brought the money and put it at the apostles' feet.

{5:1} But there was a man named Ananias, with his wife Sapphira, who sold a piece of property. {5:2} They kept back part of the money for themselves, with his wife's knowledge, and brought the rest and laid it at the apostles' feet. {5:3} Peter said, "Ananias, why has Satan filled your heart to lie to the Holy Spirit and keep back part of the money from the sale of the land? {5:4} Before it was sold, wasn't it yours? And after it was sold, wasn't the money at your disposal? Why have you thought of doing this? You have not lied just to human beings but to God." {5:5} When Ananias heard this, he fell down and died, and great fear seized all who heard what had happened. {5:6} Some young men came forward, wrapped up his body, carried him out, and buried him. {5:7} About three hours later, his wife came in, not knowing what had happened. {5:8} Peter asked her, "Tell me, is this the price you and Ananias got for the land?" "Yes," she said, "that is the price." {5:9} Peter said to her, "How could you conspire to test the Spirit of the Lord? Look! The feet of the men who buried your husband are at the door, and they will carry you out also." {5:10} At that moment, she fell down at his feet and died. The young men came in, found her dead, and, carrying her out, buried her beside her husband. {5:11} Great fear seized the whole church and all who heard about these events. {5:12} The apostles performed many signs and wonders among the people, and all the believers were together in Solomon's Colonnade. {5:13} No one else dared join them, but people held them in high regard. {5:14} Nevertheless, more and more men and women believed in the Lord and were added to their number. {5:15} As a result, people brought the sick into the streets and laid them on beds and mats so that at least Peter's shadow might fall on some of them as he passed by. {5:16} Crowds gathered also from the towns around Jerusalem, bringing their sick and those tormented by impure spirits, and all of them were healed. {5:17} Then the high priest and all his associates, who were members of the party of the Sadducees, were filled with jealousy. {5:18} They arrested the apostles and put them in the public jail. {5:19} But during the night, an angel of the Lord opened the doors of the jail and brought them out. {5:20} "Go, stand in the temple courts," he said, "and tell the people all about this new life." {5:21} At daybreak, they entered the temple courts as they had been told and began to teach the people. When the high priest and his associates arrived, they called together the Sanhedrin—the full assembly of the elders of Israel—and sent to the jail for the apostles. {5:22} But on arriving at the jail, the officers did not find them there. So they went back and reported, {5:23} "We found the jail securely locked, with the guards standing at the doors; but when we opened them, we found no one inside." {5:24} On hearing this report, the captain of the temple guard and the chief priests were at a loss, wondering what this might lead to. {5:25} Then someone came and said, "Look! The men you put in jail are standing in the temple courts teaching the people." {5:26} At that, the captain went with his officers and brought the apostles. They did not use force, because they feared that the people would stone them. {5:27} The apostles were brought in and made to appear before the Sanhedrin to be questioned by the high priest. {5:28} "We gave you strict orders not to teach in this name," he said. "Yet you have filled Jerusalem with your teaching and are determined to make us guilty of this man's blood." {5:29} Peter and the other apostles replied, "We must obey God rather than human beings! {5:30} The God of our ancestors raised Jesus from the dead—whom you killed by hanging him on a cross. {5:31} God exalted him to his own right hand as Prince and Savior that he might bring Israel to repentance and forgive their sins. {5:32} We are witnesses of these things, and so is the Holy Spirit, whom God has given to those who obey him." {5:33} When they heard this, they were furious and wanted to put them to death. {5:34} But a Pharisee named Gamaliel, a teacher of the law who was honored by all the people, stood up in the Sanhedrin and ordered that the men be put outside for a little while. {5:35} Then he addressed the Sanhedrin: "Men of Israel, consider carefully what you intend to do to these men. {5:36} Some time ago Theudas appeared, claiming to be somebody, and about four hundred men rallied to him. He was killed, and all his followers were dispersed and it all came to nothing. {5:37} After him, Judas the Galilean appeared in the days of the census and led a band of people in revolt. He too was killed, and all his followers were scattered. {5:38} Therefore, in the present case I advise you: leave these men alone! Let them go! For if their purpose or activity is of human origin, it will fail; {5:39} but if it is from God, you will not be able to stop these men; you will only find yourselves fighting against God." {5:40} His speech persuaded them. They called the apostles in and had them flogged (whipped). Then they ordered them not to speak in the name of Jesus and let them go. {5:41} The apostles left the Sanhedrin, rejoicing because they had been counted worthy of suffering disgrace for the Name. {5:42} Day after day, in the temple courts and from house to house, they never stopped teaching and proclaiming the good news that Jesus is the Messiah.

{6:1} In those days when the number of disciples was increasing, the Hellenistic Jews (Greek-speaking Jews) among them complained against the Hebraic Jews because their widows were being overlooked in the daily distribution of food. {6:2} So the Twelve gathered all the disciples together and said, "It would not be right for us to neglect the ministry of the word of God in order to wait on tables. {6:3} Brothers and sisters, choose seven men from among you who are known to be full of the Spirit and wisdom. We will turn this responsibility over to them {6:4} and will give our attention to prayer and the ministry of the word." {6:5} This proposal pleased the whole group. They chose Stephen, a man full of faith and of the Holy Spirit; also Philip, Prochorus, Nicanor, Timon, Parmenas, and Nicholas from Antioch, a convert to Judaism. {6:6} They presented these men to the apostles, who prayed and laid their hands on them. {6:7} So the word of God spread. The number of disciples in Jerusalem increased rapidly, and a large number of priests became obedient to the faith. {6:8} Now Stephen, a man full of God's grace and power, performed great wonders and signs among the people. {6:9} Opposition arose, however, from members of the Synagogue of the Freedmen (as it was called)—Jews of Cyrene and Alexandria, as well as the provinces of Cilicia and Asia—who began to argue with Stephen. {6:10} But they could not stand up against the wisdom the Spirit gave him as he spoke. {6:11} Then they secretly persuaded some men to say, "We have heard Stephen speak blasphemous words against Moses and against God." {6:12} So they stirred up the people and the elders and the teachers of the law. They seized Stephen and brought him before the Sanhedrin. {6:13} They produced false witnesses, who testified, "This fellow never stops speaking against this holy place and against the law; {6:14} for we have heard him say that this Jesus of Nazareth will destroy this place and change the customs Moses handed down to us." {6:15} All who were sitting in the Sanhedrin looked intently at Stephen, and they saw that his face was like the face of an angel.

{7:1} The high priest asked, "Is this true?" {7:2} Stephen replied, "Brothers and fathers, listen to me! The God of glory appeared to our ancestor Abraham while he was still in Mesopotamia, before he lived in Harran. {7:3} God said to him, 'Leave your country and your people and go to the land I will show you.' {7:4} So he left the land of the Chaldeans and settled in Harran. After the death of his father, God sent him to this land where you are now living. {7:5} He gave him no inheritance here, not even a foot of ground, but God promised him that he and his descendants would possess the land, even though at that time Abraham had no child. {7:6} God spoke to him and said that his descendants would be strangers in a foreign land and would be enslaved and mistreated for four hundred years. {7:7} But I will punish the nation they serve as slaves, God said, and afterward they will come out and worship me in this place. {7:8} Then God gave Abraham the covenant of circumcision. Abraham became the father of Isaac and circumcised him on the eighth day. Isaac became the father of Jacob, and Jacob became the father of the twelve patriarchs. {7:9} Because the patriarchs were jealous of Joseph, they sold him into Egypt. But God was with him {7:10} and rescued him from all his troubles. He gave Joseph wisdom and enabled him to gain the favor of Pharaoh, king of Egypt, who made him ruler over Egypt and all his palace. {7:11} Then a famine struck all Egypt and Canaan, bringing great suffering, and our ancestors could not find food. {7:12} When Jacob heard that there was grain in Egypt, he sent our ancestors there the first time. {7:13} On the second visit, Joseph revealed his identity to his brothers, and they became known to Pharaoh. {7:14} Joseph sent for his father Jacob and his whole family, seventy-five in all. {7:15} Then Jacob went down to Egypt, where he and our ancestors died. {7:16} Their bodies were taken to Shechem and buried in the tomb that Abraham had bought for a sum of money from the sons of Hamor at Shechem. {7:17} As the time drew near for God to fulfill his promise to Abraham, the number of our people in Egypt greatly increased. {7:18} Then a new king, to whom Joseph meant nothing, came to power in Egypt. {7:19} He dealt treacherously with our people and oppressed our ancestors by forcing them to throw out their newborn babies so they would die. {7:20} At that time, Moses was born, and he was no ordinary child. For three months he was cared for by his family. {7:21} When he was placed outside, Pharaoh's daughter took him and brought him up as her own son. {7:22} Moses was educated in all the wisdom of the Egyptians and was powerful in speech and action. {7:23} When Moses was forty years old, he decided to visit his own people, the Israelites. {7:24} He saw one of them being mistreated by an Egyptian, so he went to his defense and avenged him by killing the Egyptian. {7:25} Moses thought that his own people would realize that God was using him to rescue them, but they did not. {7:26} The next day, Moses came upon two Israelites who were fighting. He tried to reconcile them by saying, "Men, you are brothers; why do you want to hurt each other?" {7:27} But the man who was mistreating the other pushed Moses aside and said, "Who made you ruler and judge over us? {7:28} Are you thinking of killing me as you killed the Egyptian yesterday?" {7:29} When Moses heard this, he fled to Midian, where he settled as a foreigner and had two sons. {7:30} After forty years had passed, an angel appeared to him in the flames of a burning bush in the desert near Mount Sinai. {7:31} When he saw this, he was amazed at the sight. As he went over to get a closer look, he heard the Lord's voice: {7:32} "I am the God of your fathers, the God of Abraham, the God of Isaac, and the God of Jacob." Moses trembled with fear and did not dare to look. {7:33} Then the Lord said to him, "Take off your sandals, for the place where you are standing is holy ground. {7:34} I have indeed seen the oppression of my people in Egypt. I have heard their groaning and have come down to set them free. Now come, I will send you back to Egypt." {7:35} This is the same Moses whom they had rejected with the words, "Who made you ruler and judge?" He was sent to be their ruler and deliverer by God himself, through the angel who appeared to him in the bush. {7:36} He led them out of Egypt and performed wonders and signs in Egypt, at the Red Sea, and for forty years in the wilderness. {7:37} This is that Moses who told the Israelites, "God will raise up for you a prophet like me from your own people."

{7:38} He was in the assembly in the wilderness, with the angel who spoke to him on Mount Sinai and with our ancestors; and he received living words to pass on to us. {7:39} But our ancestors refused to obey him. Instead, they rejected him and in their hearts turned back to Egypt. {7:40} They told Aaron, "Make us gods who will go before us. As for this fellow Moses who led us out of Egypt—we don't know what has happened to him!" {7:41} That was the time they made an idol in the form of a calf. They brought sacrifices to it and reveled in what their own hands had made. {7:42} But God turned away from them and gave them over to the worship of the sun, moon, and stars. This agrees with what is written in the book of the prophets: "Did you bring me sacrifices and offerings forty years in the wilderness, people of Israel? {7:43} You have taken up the tabernacle of Moloch and the star of your god Rephan, the idols you made to worship. Therefore I will send you into exile beyond Babylon." {7:44} Our ancestors had the tabernacle of the covenant law with them in the wilderness. It had been made as God directed Moses, according to the pattern he had seen. {7:45} After receiving the tabernacle, our ancestors under Joshua brought it with them when they took the land from the nations God drove out before them. It remained in the land until the time of David, {7:46} who enjoyed God's favor and asked that he might provide a dwelling place for the God of Jacob. {7:47} But it was Solomon who built a house for him. {7:48} However, the Most High does not live in houses made by human hands, as the prophet says: {7:49} "Heaven is my throne, and the earth is my footstool. What kind of house will you build for me? says the Lord. Or where will my resting place be? {7:50} Has not my hand made all these things?" {7:51} You stiff-necked people, with uncircumcised hearts and ears! You are just like your ancestors: you always resist the Holy Spirit! {7:52} Was there ever a prophet your ancestors did not persecute? They even killed those who predicted the coming of the Righteous One, and now you have betrayed and murdered him— {7:53} you who have received the law that was given through angels but have not obeyed it." {7:54} When the members of the Sanhedrin heard this, they were furious and gnashed their teeth at him. {7:55} But Stephen, full of the Holy Spirit, looked up to heaven and saw the glory of God, and Jesus standing at the right hand of God. {7:56} "Look!" he said. "I see heaven open and the Son of Man standing at the right hand of God." {7:57} At this, they covered their ears and yelled at the top of their voices. They all rushed at him, {7:58} dragged him out of the city and began to stone him. Meanwhile, the witnesses laid their coats at the feet of a young man named Saul. {7:59} While they were stoning him, Stephen prayed, "Lord Jesus, receive my spirit." {7:60} Then he fell on his knees and cried out, "Lord, do not hold this sin against them." When he had said this, he fell asleep.

{8:1} Saul was in agreement with Stephen's death. At that time, a great persecution broke out against the church in Jerusalem, causing all the believers to scatter throughout Judea and Samaria, except for the apostles. {8:2} Devout men buried Stephen and mourned deeply for him. {8:3} Meanwhile, Saul was wreaking havoc on the church, going from house to house, dragging men and women off to prison. {8:4} Those who had been scattered preached the word wherever they went. {8:5} Philip went down to the city of Samaria and proclaimed Christ there. {8:6} The crowds listened intently to Philip, as they saw and heard the miracles he performed. {8:7} Unclean spirits came out of many possessed people, shrieking loudly, and many paralyzed or lame people were healed. {8:8} There was great joy in that city. {8:9} However, there was a man named Simon who had previously practiced sorcery in that city and amazed the people of Samaria, claiming to be someone great. {8:10} All the people, from the least to the greatest, paid attention to him, saying, "This man is the great power of God." {8:11} They followed him because he had amazed them for a long time with his magic. {8:12} But when they believed Philip's message about the kingdom of God and the name of Jesus Christ, they were baptized, both men and women. {8:13} Even Simon himself believed and was baptized. He stayed close to Philip and was astonished by the great signs and miracles he saw. {8:14} When the apostles in Jerusalem heard that Samaria had accepted the word of God, they sent Peter and John to them. {8:15} They arrived and prayed for the new believers that they might receive the Holy Spirit, {8:16} because the Holy Spirit had not yet come upon any of them; they had simply been baptized in the name of the Lord Jesus. {8:17} Then they laid their hands on them, and they received the Holy Spirit. {8:18} When Simon saw that the Spirit was given at the apostles' hands, he offered them money, {8:19} saying, "Give me this power too, so that everyone on whom I lay my hands may receive the Holy Spirit." {8:20} Peter answered, "May your money perish with you, because you thought you could buy the gift of God with money! {8:21} You have no part or share in this ministry, because your heart is not right before God. {8:22} Repent of this wickedness and pray to the Lord in the hope that he may forgive you for having such a thought in your heart. {8:23} For I see that you are full of bitterness and captive to sin." {8:24} Simon answered, "Pray to the Lord for me so that nothing you have said will happen to me." {8:25} After they had further proclaimed the word of the Lord and testified about Jesus, they returned to Jerusalem, preaching the gospel in many Samaritan villages. {8:26} An angel of the Lord said to Philip, "Go south to the road—the desert road—that goes down from Jerusalem to Gaza." {8:27} So he started out, and on his way he met an Ethiopian eunuch, an important official in charge of the treasury of the Kandake (queen of the Ethiopians). This man had gone to Jerusalem to worship {8:28} and was on his way home, sitting in his chariot reading the book of Isaiah the prophet. {8:29} The Spirit told Philip, "Go to that chariot and stay near it." {8:30} Philip ran up to the chariot and heard the man reading Isaiah the prophet. "Do you understand what you are reading?" Philip asked. {8:31} "How can I," he said, "unless someone explains it to me?" So he invited Philip to come up and sit with him. {8:32} The eunuch was reading this passage of Scripture: "He was led like a sheep to the slaughter, and as a lamb before its shearer is silent, so he did not open his mouth. {8:33} In his humiliation he was deprived of justice. Who can speak of his descendants? For his life was taken from the earth." {8:34} The eunuch asked Philip, "Tell me, please, who is the prophet talking about, himself or someone else?" {8:35} Then Philip began with that very passage of Scripture and told him the good news about Jesus. {8:36} As they traveled along the road, they came to some water, and the eunuch said, "Look, here is water. What can stand in the way of my being baptized?" {8:37} Philip said, "If you believe with all your heart, you may." The eunuch answered, "I believe that Jesus Christ is the Son of God." {8:38} He ordered the chariot to stop, then both Philip and the eunuch went down into the water and Philip baptized him. {8:39} When they came up out of the water, the Spirit of the Lord suddenly took Philip away, and the eunuch did not see him again, but went on his way rejoicing. {8:40} Philip, however, appeared at Azotus and traveled about, preaching the gospel in all the towns until he reached Caesarea.

{9:1} Meanwhile, Saul was still breathing out murderous threats against the Lord's disciples. He went to the high priest {9:2} and asked him for letters to the synagogues in Damascus, so that if he found any there who belonged to the Way (the followers of Jesus), whether men or women, he might take them as prisoners to Jerusalem. {9:3} As he neared Damascus on his journey, suddenly a light from heaven flashed around him. {9:4} He fell to the ground and heard a voice say to him, "Saul, Saul, why are you persecuting me?" {9:5} "Who are you, Lord?" Saul asked. "I am Jesus, whom you are persecuting," he replied. "Now get up and go into the city, and you will be told what you must do." {9:6} The men traveling with Saul stood there speechless; they heard the sound but did not see anyone. {9:7} Saul got up from the ground, but when he opened his eyes he could see nothing; so they led him by the hand into Damascus. {9:8} For three days he was blind and did not eat or drink anything. {9:9} In Damascus there was a disciple named Ananias. The Lord called to him in a vision, "Ananias!" "Yes, Lord," he answered. {9:10} The Lord told him, "Go to the house of Judas on Straight Street and ask for a man from Tarsus named Saul, for he is praying. {9:11} In a vision he has seen a man named Ananias come and place his hands on him to restore his sight." {9:12} "Lord," Ananias answered, "I have heard many reports about this man and all the harm he has done to your holy people in Jerusalem. {9:13} And he has come here with authority from the chief priests to arrest all who call on your name." {9:14} But the Lord said to Ananias, "Go! This man is my chosen instrument to proclaim my name to the Gentiles and their kings and to the people of Israel. {9:15} I will show him how much he must suffer for my name." {9:16} Then Ananias went to the house and entered it. Placing his hands on Saul, he said, "Brother Saul, the Lord—Jesus, who appeared to you on the road as you were coming here—has sent me so that you may see again and be filled with the Holy Spirit." {9:17} Immediately, something like scales fell from Saul's eyes, and he could see again. He got up and was baptized. {9:18} After taking some food, he regained his strength. Saul spent several days with the disciples in Damascus. {9:19} At once he began to preach in the synagogues that Jesus is the Son of God. {9:20} All those who heard him were astonished and asked, "Isn't he the man who raised havoc in Jerusalem among those who call on this name? And hasn't he come here to take them as prisoners to the chief priests?" {9:21} Yet Saul grew more and more powerful and baffled the Jews living in Damascus by proving that Jesus is the Messiah. {9:22} After many days had gone by, there was a conspiracy among the Jews to kill him, {9:23} but Saul learned of their plan. Day and night they kept close watch on the city gates in order to kill him. {9:24} But his followers took him by night and lowered him in a basket through an opening in the wall. {9:25} When he came to Jerusalem, he tried to join the disciples, but they were all afraid of him, not believing that he really was a disciple. {9:26} But Barnabas took him and brought him to the apostles. He told them how Saul on his journey had seen the Lord and that the Lord had spoken to him, and how in Damascus he had preached fearlessly in the name of Jesus. {9:27} So Saul stayed with them and moved about freely in Jerusalem, speaking boldly in the name of the Lord. {9:28} He talked and debated with the Hellenistic Jews, but they tried to kill him. {9:29} When the believers learned of this, they took him down to Caesarea and sent him off to Tarsus. {9:30} Then the church throughout Judea, Galilee, and Samaria enjoyed a time of peace and was strengthened; living in the fear of the Lord and encouraged by the Holy Spirit, it increased in numbers. {9:31} As Peter traveled around the country, he went to visit the Lord's people who lived in Lydda. {9:32} There he found a man named Aeneas who was paralyzed and had been bedridden for eight years. {9:33} "Aeneas," Peter said to him, "Jesus Christ heals you. Get up and roll up your mat." Immediately Aeneas got up. {9:34} All those who lived in Lydda and Sharon saw him and turned to the Lord. {9:35} In Joppa there was a disciple named Tabitha (which, when translated, is Dorcas); she was always doing good and helping the poor. {9:36} About that time she became sick and died, and her body was washed and placed in an upstairs room. {9:37} Lydda was near Joppa; so when the disciples heard that Peter was in Lydda, they sent two men to him and urged him, "Please come at once!" {9:38} Peter went with them, and when he arrived he was taken upstairs to the room. All the widows stood around him, crying and showing him the robes and other clothing that Dorcas had made while she was still with them. {9:39} Peter sent them all out of the room; then he got down on his knees and prayed. Turning toward the dead woman, he said, "Tabitha, get up." She opened her eyes and, seeing Peter, she sat up. {9:40} He took her by the hand and helped her to her feet. Then he called for the believers, especially the widows, and presented her to them alive. {9:41} This became known all over Joppa, and many people believed in the Lord. {9:42} Peter stayed in Joppa for some time with a tanner named Simon.

{10:1} There was a man in Caesarea named Cornelius, a centurion of a group called the Italian Regiment. {10:2} He was a devout man who feared God, along with his entire household. He gave generously to those in need and prayed to God regularly. {10:3} About three o'clock one afternoon, he had a vision in which he clearly saw an angel of God coming to him and saying, "Cornelius." {10:4} Cornelius stared at him in fear and asked, "What is it, Lord?" The angel answered, "Your prayers and gifts to the poor have come up as a memorial before God. {10:5} Now send men to Joppa to bring back a man named Simon, who is called Peter. {10:6} He is staying with Simon the tanner, whose house is by the sea. He will tell you what you need to do." {10:7} When the angel who spoke to him had left, Cornelius called two of his servants and a devout soldier who was one of his attendants. {10:8} He told them everything that had happened and sent them to Joppa. {10:9} The next day, as they were on their journey and approaching the city, Peter went up on the roof to pray at about noon. {10:10} He became hungry and wanted something to eat; and while the meal was being prepared, he fell into a trance. {10:11} He saw heaven opened and something like a large sheet being let down to earth by its four corners. {10:12} It contained all kinds of four-footed animals, as well as reptiles and birds. {10:13} Then a voice told him, "Get up, Peter. Kill and eat." {10:14} Peter replied, "Surely not, Lord! I have never eaten anything impure or unclean." {10:15} The voice spoke to him a second time, "Do not call anything impure that God has made clean." {10:16} This happened three times, and then the sheet was taken back to heaven. {10:17} While Peter was wondering about the meaning of the vision, the men sent by Cornelius found out where Simon's house was and stopped at the gate. {10:18} They called out, asking if Simon, who was known as Peter, was staying there. {10:19} While Peter was still thinking about the vision, the Spirit said to him, "Simon, three men are looking for you. {10:20} So get up and go downstairs. Do not hesitate to go with them, for I have sent them." {10:21} Peter went down and said to the men, "I'm the one you're looking for. Why have you come?" {10:22} The men replied, "We have come from Cornelius the centurion. He is a righteous and God-fearing man, respected by all the Jewish people. A holy angel told him to ask you to come to his house so he could hear what you have to say." {10:23} Then Peter invited the men into the house to be his guests. The next day Peter started out with them, and some of the believers from Joppa went along. {10:24} The following day he arrived in Caesarea. Cornelius was expecting them and had called together his relatives and close friends. {10:25} As Peter entered the house, Cornelius met him and fell at his feet in reverence. {10:26} But Peter made him get up. "Stand up," he said, "I am only a man myself." {10:27} While talking with him, Peter went inside and found a large gathering of people. {10:28} He said to them: "You are well aware that it is against our law for a Jew to associate with or visit a Gentile. But God has shown me that I should not call anyone impure or unclean. {10:29} So when I was sent for, I came without raising any objection. May I ask why you sent for me?" {10:30} Cornelius answered: "Four days ago I was in my house praying at this hour, and suddenly a man in shining clothes stood before me {10:31} and said, 'Cornelius, God has heard your prayer and remembered your gifts to the poor. {10:32} Send to Joppa for Simon, who is called Peter. He is a guest in the home of Simon the tanner, who lives by the sea.' {10:33} So I sent for you immediately, and it was good of you to come. Now we are all here in the presence of God to listen to everything the Lord has commanded you to tell us." {10:34} Then Peter began to speak: "I now realize how true it is that God does not show favoritism {10:35} but accepts from every nation the one who fears him and does what is right. {10:36} You know the message God sent to the people of Israel, announcing the good news of peace through Jesus Christ, who is Lord of all. {10:37} You know what has happened throughout the province of Judea, beginning in Galilee after the baptism that John preached— {10:38} how God anointed Jesus of Nazareth with the Holy Spirit and power, and how he went around doing good and healing all who were under the power of the devil because God was with him. {10:39} We are witnesses of everything he did in the country of the Jews and in Jerusalem. They killed him by hanging him on a cross, {10:40} but God raised him from the dead on the third day and caused him to be seen. {10:41} He was not seen by all the people, but by witnesses whom God had already chosen—by us who ate and drank with him after he rose from the dead. {10:42} He commanded us to preach to the people and to testify that he is the one whom God appointed as judge of the living and the dead. {10:43} All the prophets testify about him that everyone who believes in him receives forgiveness of sins through his name." {10:44} While Peter was still speaking these words, the Holy Spirit came on all who heard the message. {10:45} The circumcised believers who had come with Peter were astonished that the gift of the Holy Spirit had been poured out even on Gentiles. {10:46} For they heard them speaking in tongues and praising God. Then Peter said, {10:47} "Surely no one can stand in the way of their being baptized with water. They have received the Holy Spirit just as we have." {10:48} So he ordered that they be baptized in the name of Jesus Christ. Then they asked Peter to stay with them for a few days.

{11:1} The apostles and believers throughout Judea heard that the Gentiles also had received the word of God. {11:2} So when Peter went up to Jerusalem, the circumcised believers criticized him {11:3} and said, "You went into the house of uncircumcised men and ate with them." {11:4} Starting from the beginning, Peter told them the whole story: {11:5} "I was in the city of Joppa praying, and in a trance I saw a vision. I saw something like a large sheet being let down from heaven by its four corners and it came down to where I was. {11:6} I looked into it and saw four-footed animals of the earth, wild beasts, reptiles, and birds. {11:7} Then I heard a voice telling me, 'Get up, Peter. Kill and eat.' {11:8} I replied, 'Surely not, Lord! Nothing impure or unclean has ever entered my mouth.' {11:9} The voice spoke from heaven a second time, 'Do not call anything impure that God has made clean.' {11:10} This happened three times, and then it was all pulled up to heaven again. {11:11} Right then, three men who had been sent to me from Caesarea stopped at the house where I was staying. {11:12} The Spirit told me to have no hesitation about going with them. These six brothers also went with me, and we entered the man's house. {11:13} He told us how he had seen an angel appear in his house and say, 'Send to Joppa for Simon, who is called Peter. {11:14} He will bring you a message through which you and all your household will be saved.' {11:15} As I began to speak, the Holy Spirit came on them as he had come on us at the beginning. {11:16} Then I remembered what the Lord had said: 'John baptized with water, but you will be baptized with the Holy Spirit.' {11:17} So if God gave them the same gift as he gave us, who believed in the Lord Jesus Christ, who was I to think that I could stand in God's way?" {11:18} When they heard this, they had no further objections and praised God, saying, "So then, even to Gentiles God has granted repentance that leads to life." {11:19} Now those who had been scattered by the persecution that broke out when Stephen was killed traveled as far as Phoenicia, Cyprus, and Antioch, spreading the word only among Jews. {11:20} Some of them, however, men from Cyprus and Cyrene, went to Antioch and began to speak to Greeks also, telling them the good news about the Lord Jesus. {11:21} The Lord's hand was with them, and a great number of people believed and turned to the Lord. {11:22} News of this reached the church in Jerusalem, and they sent Barnabas to Antioch. {11:23} When he arrived and saw what the grace of God had done, he was glad and encouraged them all to remain true to the Lord with all their hearts. {11:24} He was a good man, full of the Holy Spirit and faith, and a great number of people were brought to the Lord. {11:25} Then Barnabas went to Tarsus to look for Saul, {11:26} and when he found him, he brought him to Antioch. So for a whole year Barnabas and Saul met with the church and taught great numbers of people. The disciples were called Christians first at Antioch. {11:27} During this time some prophets came down from Jerusalem to Antioch. {11:28} One of them, named Agabus, stood up and through the Spirit predicted that a severe famine would spread over the entire Roman world. This happened during the reign of Claudius. {11:29} The disciples, as each one was able, decided to provide help for the brothers and sisters living in Judea. {11:30} This they did, sending their gift to the elders by Barnabas and Saul.

{12:1} About that time, King Herod began to persecute some members of the church. {12:2} He killed James, the brother of John, with the sword. {12:3} When he saw that this pleased the Jews, he decided to seize Peter as well. (This was during the Days of Unleavened Bread.) {12:4} After arresting him, he put Peter in prison, handing him over to four squads of soldiers to guard him, intending to bring him out to the people after the Passover. {12:5} So Peter was kept in prison, but the church was earnestly praying to God for him. {12:6} The night before Herod was to bring him to trial, Peter was sleeping between two soldiers, bound with two chains, with sentries standing guard at the entrance. {12:7} Suddenly, an angel of the Lord appeared, and a light shone in the cell. The angel struck Peter on the side and woke him up, saying, "Get up quickly!" And the chains fell off his wrists. {12:8} The angel said to him, "Put on your clothes and sandals." Peter did so. "Wrap your cloak around you and follow me," the angel told him. {12:9} Peter followed him out of the prison, but he had no idea that what the angel was doing was really happening; he thought he was seeing a vision. {12:10} They passed the first and second guards and came to the iron gate leading to the city. It opened for them by itself, and they went through it. When they had walked the length of one street, suddenly the angel left him. {12:11} Then Peter came to himself and said, "Now I know without a doubt that the Lord has sent his angel and rescued me from Herod's clutches and from everything the Jewish people were anticipating." {12:12} When this had dawned on him, he went to the house of Mary the mother of John (also called Mark), where many people had gathered and were praying. {12:13} Peter knocked at the outer entrance, and a servant named Rhoda came to answer the door. {12:14} When she recognized Peter's voice, she was so overjoyed that she ran back without opening it and exclaimed, "Peter is at the door!" {12:15} "You're out of your mind," they told her. When she kept insisting that it was so, they said, "It must be his angel." {12:16} But Peter kept knocking, and when they opened the door and saw him, they were astonished. {12:17} Peter motioned with his hand for them to be quiet and described how the Lord had brought him out of prison. "Tell James and the other brothers and sisters about this," he said, and then he left for another place. {12:18} In the morning, there was no small commotion among the soldiers as to what had become of Peter. {12:19} After Herod had a thorough search made and didn't find him, he cross-examined the guards and ordered that they be executed. Then he went down from Judea to Caesarea and stayed there. {12:20} He had been quarreling with the people of Tyre and Sidon; they now joined together and sought an audience with him. After securing the support of Blastus, a trusted personal servant of the king, they asked for peace because they depended on the king's country for their food supply. {12:21} On the appointed day, Herod, wearing his royal robes, sat on his throne and delivered a public address to the people. {12:22} They shouted, "This is the voice of a god, not of a man!" {12:23} Immediately, because Herod did not give praise to God, an angel of the Lord struck him down, and he was eaten by worms and died. {12:24} But the word of God continued to spread and flourish. {12:25} When Barnabas and Saul had finished their mission in Jerusalem, they returned, taking with them John, also called Mark.

{13:1} In the church at Antioch, there were prophets and teachers: Barnabas, Simeon (called Niger), Lucius of Cyrene, Manaen (who had been brought up with Herod the tetrarch), and Saul. {13:2} While they were worshiping the Lord and fasting, the Holy Spirit said, "Set apart for me Barnabas and Saul for the work to which I have called them." {13:3} So after they had fasted and prayed, they placed their hands on them and sent them off. {13:4} The two of them, sent on their way by the Holy Spirit, went down to Seleucia and sailed from there to Cyprus. {13:5} When they arrived at Salamis, they proclaimed the word of God in the Jewish synagogues. John was with them as their helper. {13:6} They traveled through the whole island until they came to Paphos, where they met a Jewish sorcerer and false prophet named Bar-Jesus, {13:7} who was an attendant of the proconsul, Sergius Paulus. The proconsul, an intelligent man, sent for Barnabas and Saul because he wanted to hear the word of God. {13:8} But Elymas the sorcerer (for that is what his name means) opposed them and tried to turn the proconsul from the faith. {13:9} Then Saul, who was also called Paul, filled with the Holy Spirit, looked straight at Elymas {13:10} and said, "You are a child of the devil and an enemy of everything that is right! You are full of all kinds of deceit and trickery. Will you never stop perverting the right ways of the Lord? {13:11} Now the hand of the Lord is against you. You are going to be blind for a time, not even able to see the light of the sun." Immediately mist and darkness came over him, and he groped about, seeking someone to lead him by the hand. {13:12} When the proconsul saw what had happened, he believed, for he was amazed at the teaching about the Lord. {13:13} From Paphos, Paul and his companions sailed to Perga in Pamphylia, where John left them to return to Jerusalem. {13:14} From Perga they went on to Antioch in Pisidia. On the Sabbath they entered the synagogue and sat down. {13:15} After the reading from the Law and the Prophets, the leaders of the synagogue sent word to them, saying, "Brothers, if you have a word of exhortation (encouragement) for the people, please speak." {13:16} Standing up, Paul motioned with his hand and said: "Fellow Israelites and you Gentiles who worship God, listen to me! {13:17} The God of the people of Israel chose our ancestors; he made the people prosper during their stay in Egypt; with mighty power he led them out of that country; {13:18} for about forty years he endured their conduct in the wilderness; {13:19} and he overthrew seven nations in Canaan, giving their land to his people as their inheritance. {13:20} All this took about 450 years. After this, God gave them judges until the time of Samuel the prophet. {13:21} Then the people asked for a king, and he gave them Saul son of Kish, of the tribe of Benjamin, who ruled forty years. {13:22} After removing Saul, he made David their king. God testified concerning him: 'I have found David son of Jesse, a man after my own heart; he will do everything I want him to do.'

{13:23} "From this man's descendants God has brought to Israel the Savior Jesus, as he promised. {13:24} Before the coming of Jesus, John preached repentance and baptism to all the people of Israel. {13:25} As John was completing his work, he said: 'Who do you suppose I am? I am not the one you are looking for. But there is one coming after me whose sandals I am not worthy to untie.' {13:26} Fellow children of Abraham, and you God-fearing Gentiles, it is to us that this message of salvation has been sent. {13:27} The people of Jerusalem and their rulers did not recognize Jesus, yet in condemning him they fulfilled the words of the prophets that are read every Sabbath. {13:28} Though they found no proper ground for a death sentence, they asked Pilate to have him executed. {13:29} When they had carried out all that was written about him, they took him down from the cross and laid him in a tomb. {13:30} But God raised him from the dead, {13:31} and for many days he was seen by those who had traveled with him from Galilee to Jerusalem. They are now his witnesses to our people. {13:32} "We tell you the good news: What God promised our ancestors {13:33} he has fulfilled for us, their children, by raising up Jesus. As it is written in the second Psalm: 'You are my son; today I have become your father.' {13:34} God raised him from the dead so that he will never be subject to decay. As God said, 'I will give you the holy and sure blessings promised to David.' {13:35} So it is also stated elsewhere: 'You will not let your Holy One see decay.' {13:36} Now when David had served God's purpose in his own generation, he fell asleep; he was buried with his ancestors and his body decayed. {13:37} But the one whom God raised from the dead did not see decay. {13:38} "Therefore, my friends, I want you to know that through Jesus the forgiveness of sins is proclaimed to you. {13:39} Through him everyone who believes is set free from every sin, a justification (being made right) you were not able to obtain under the law of Moses. {13:40} Take care that what the prophets have said does not happen to you: {13:41} 'Look, you scoffers, wonder and perish, for I am going to do something in your days that you would never believe, even if someone told you.'" {13:42} As Paul and Barnabas were leaving the synagogue, the people invited them to speak further about these things on the next Sabbath. {13:43} When the congregation was dismissed, many of the Jews and devout converts to Judaism followed Paul and Barnabas, who talked with them and urged them to continue in the grace of God. {13:44} On the next Sabbath almost the whole city gathered to hear the word of the Lord. {13:45} When the Jews saw the crowds, they were filled with jealousy; they began to contradict what Paul was saying and heaped abuse on him. {13:46} Then Paul and Barnabas answered them boldly: "We had to speak the word of God to you first. Since you reject it and do not consider yourselves worthy of eternal life, we now turn to the Gentiles. {13:47} For this is what the Lord has commanded us: 'I have made you a light for the Gentiles, that you may bring salvation to the ends of the earth.'" {13:48} When the Gentiles heard this, they were glad and honored the word of the Lord; and all who were appointed for eternal life believed. {13:49} The word of the Lord spread through the whole region. {13:50} But the Jewish leaders incited the God-fearing women of high standing and the leading men of the city. They stirred up persecution against Paul and Barnabas and expelled them from their region. {13:51} So they shook the dust off their feet as a warning to them and went to Iconium. {13:52} And the disciples were filled with joy and with the Holy Spirit.

{14:1} In Iconium, Paul and Barnabas entered the Jewish synagogue and spoke in such a way that a large number of both Jews and Greeks believed. {14:2} However, the unbelieving Jews stirred up the Gentiles and poisoned their minds against the brothers. {14:3} So they stayed there for a long time, speaking boldly for the Lord, who testified to the message of his grace by enabling them to perform signs and wonders. {14:4} The city was divided: some sided with the Jews, while others sided with the apostles. {14:5} When an attempt was made by both Gentiles and Jews, along with their rulers, to mistreat and stone them, {14:6} they became aware of it and fled to the cities of Lystra and Derbe in Lycaonia, and the surrounding region. {14:7} There, they continued to preach the gospel. {14:8} In Lystra, a man who was crippled in his feet and had never walked sat there. {14:9} He listened to Paul as he spoke, and Paul, seeing that he had faith to be healed, {14:10} called out in a loud voice, "Stand up on your feet!" The man leaped up and began to walk. {14:11} When the crowd saw what Paul had done, they shouted in the Lycaonian language, "The gods have come down to us in human form!" {14:12} They called Barnabas Zeus and Paul Hermes, because he was the chief speaker. {14:13} The priest of Zeus, whose temple was just outside the city, brought bulls and wreaths to the gates and wanted to offer sacrifices with the crowds. {14:14} When the apostles, Barnabas and Paul, heard of this, they tore their clothes and rushed into the crowd, shouting, {14:15} "Friends, why are you doing this? We too are only human, like you. We are bringing you good news, telling you to turn from these worthless things to the living God, who made the heavens, the earth, the sea, and everything in them. {14:16} In the past, he let all nations go their own way. {14:17} Yet he has not left himself without testimony: he has shown kindness by giving you rain from heaven and crops in their seasons; he provides you with plenty of food and fills your hearts with joy." {14:18} Even with these words, they had difficulty keeping the crowd from sacrificing to them. {14:19} Then some Jews came from Antioch and Iconium and won the crowd over. They stoned Paul and dragged him out of the city, thinking he was dead. {14:20} But after the disciples had gathered around him, he got up and went back into the city. The next day, he and Barnabas left for Derbe. {14:21} They preached the gospel in that city and won a large number of disciples. Then they returned to Lystra, Iconium, and Antioch, {14:22} strengthening the disciples and encouraging them to remain true to the faith, saying, "We must go through many hardships to enter the kingdom of God." {14:23} Paul and Barnabas appointed elders for them in each church and, with prayer and fasting, committed them to the Lord, in whom they had put their trust. {14:24} After going through Pisidia, they came into Pamphylia. {14:25} When they had preached the word in Perga, they went down to Attalia. {14:26} From there, they sailed back to Antioch, where they had been committed to the grace of God for the work they had now completed. {14:27} On arriving there, they gathered the church together and reported all that God had done through them and how he had opened the door of faith to the Gentiles. {14:28} And they stayed there a long time with the disciples.

{15:1} Certain individuals came down from Judea to teach the believers, "Unless you are circumcised according to the custom taught by Moses, you cannot be saved." {15:2} This brought Paul and Barnabas into sharp dispute and debate with them. So they were appointed to go up to Jerusalem to see the apostles and elders about this question. {15:3} The church sent them on their way, and as they traveled through Phoenicia and Samaria, they told how the Gentiles had been converted. This news made all the believers very glad. {15:4} When they came to Jerusalem, they were welcomed by the church and the apostles and elders, to whom they reported everything God had done through them. {15:5} Then some of the believers who belonged to the party of the Pharisees stood up and said, "The Gentiles must be circumcised and required to keep the law of Moses." {15:6} The apostles and elders met to consider this question. {15:7} After much discussion, Peter got up and addressed them: "Brothers, you know that some time ago God made a choice among you that the Gentiles might hear from my lips the message of the gospel and believe. {15:8} God, who knows the heart, showed that he accepted them by giving the Holy Spirit to them, just as he did to us. {15:9} He did not discriminate between us and them, for he purified their hearts by faith. {15:10} Now then, why do you try to test God by putting on the necks of the Gentiles a yoke that neither we nor our ancestors have been able to bear? {15:11} No! We believe it is through the grace of our Lord Jesus that we are saved, just as they are." {15:12} The whole assembly became silent as they listened to Barnabas and Paul telling about the signs and wonders God had done among the Gentiles through them. {15:13} When they finished, James spoke up. "Brothers, listen to me. {15:14} Simon has described to us how God first intervened to choose a people for his name from the Gentiles. {15:15} The words of the prophets are in agreement with this, as it is written: {15:16} 'After this, I will return and rebuild David's fallen tent. Its ruins I will rebuild, and I will restore it, {15:17} that the rest of mankind may seek the Lord, and all the Gentiles who bear my name, says the Lord, who does these things.' {15:18} Things known from long ago. {15:19} It is my judgment, therefore, that we should not make it difficult for the Gentiles who are turning to God. {15:20} Instead, we should write to them, telling them to abstain from food polluted by idols, from sexual immorality, from the meat of strangled animals, and from blood. {15:21} For the law of Moses has been preached in every city from the earliest times and is read in the synagogues on every Sabbath." {15:22} Then the apostles and elders, with the whole church, decided to choose some of their own men and send them to Antioch with Paul and Barnabas. They chose Judas (called Barsabbas) and Silas, men who were leaders among the believers. {15:23} They wrote a letter to the Gentile believers in Antioch, Syria, and Cilicia. It said: {15:24} "We have heard that some went out from us without our authorization and disturbed you, troubling your minds by what they said. {15:25} So we all agreed to choose some men and send them to you with our dear friends Barnabas and Paul, {15:26} men who have risked their lives for the name of our Lord Jesus Christ. {15:27} Therefore, we are sending Judas and Silas to confirm by word of mouth what we are writing. {15:28} It seemed good to the Holy Spirit and to us not to burden you with anything beyond the following requirements: {15:29} You are to abstain from food sacrificed to idols, from blood, from the meat of strangled animals, and from sexual immorality. You will do well to avoid these things. Farewell." {15:30} The men were sent off and went down to Antioch, where they gathered the church together and delivered the letter. {15:31} The people read it and were glad for its encouraging message. {15:32} Judas and Silas, who themselves were prophets, said much to encourage and strengthen the believers. {15:33} After spending some time there, they were sent off in peace by the believers to those who had sent them. {15:34} (Silas decided to stay there.) {15:35} But Paul and Barnabas remained in Antioch, where they and many others taught and proclaimed the word of the Lord. {15:36} Some time later, Paul said to Barnabas, "Let us go back and visit the believers in all the towns where we preached the word of the Lord and see how they are doing." {15:37} Barnabas wanted to take John, also called Mark, with them. {15:38} But Paul did not think it wise to take him, because he had deserted them in Pamphylia and had not continued with them in the work. {15:39} They had such a sharp disagreement that they parted company. Barnabas took Mark and sailed for Cyprus, {15:40} but Paul chose Silas and left, commended by the believers to the grace of the Lord. {15:41} He went through Syria and Cilicia, strengthening the churches.

{16:1} Paul came to Derbe and Lystra, where he met a disciple named Timothy, the son of a Jewish woman who was a believer, his father was Greek. {16:2} Timothy was well spoken of by the brothers in Lystra and Iconium. {16:3} Paul wanted Timothy to accompany him, so he circumcised him because of the Jews in that area, as they all knew his father was Greek. {16:4} As they traveled through the cities, they delivered the decrees established by the apostles and elders in Jerusalem for them to follow. {16:5} The churches were strengthened in faith and grew in number daily. {16:6} They traveled through Phrygia and the region of Galatia, but the Holy Spirit forbade them to preach the word in Asia. {16:7} When they came to Mysia, they tried to enter Bithynia, but the Spirit did not allow them. {16:8} So they passed by Mysia and went down to Troas. {16:9} During the night, Paul had a vision of a man from Macedonia, who was pleading with him, "Come over to Macedonia and help us." {16:10} After Paul had seen the vision, we immediately sought to go to Macedonia, convinced that God had called us to preach the gospel there. {16:11} So, setting sail from Troas, we went directly to Samothrace and the following day to Neapolis. {16:12} From there, we traveled to Philippi, a leading city in that part of Macedonia, which is also a Roman colony. We stayed in that city for several days. {16:13} On the Sabbath, we went outside the city gate to the river, where we expected to find a place of prayer. We sat down and began to speak to the women who had gathered there. {16:14} One of those listening was a woman named Lydia, a dealer in purple cloth from the city of Thyatira, who worshiped God. The Lord opened her heart to respond to Paul's message. {16:15} When she and the members of her household were baptized, she invited us to her home, saying, "If you consider me a believer in the Lord, come and stay at my house." And she persuaded us. {16:16} As we were going to the place of prayer, we were met by a slave girl who had a spirit that enabled her to predict the future. She earned a great deal of money for her owners by fortune-telling. {16:17} She followed Paul and us, shouting, "These men are servants of the Most High God, who are telling you the way to be saved." {16:18} She kept this up for many days. Finally, Paul became so annoyed that he turned around and said to the spirit, "In the name of Jesus Christ, I command you to come out of her!" At that moment, the spirit left her. {16:19} When her owners realized that their hope of making money was gone, they seized Paul and Silas and dragged them into the marketplace to face the authorities. {16:20} They brought them before the magistrates and said, "These men are Jews and are throwing our city into an uproar {16:21} by advocating customs unlawful for us Romans to accept or practice." {16:22} The crowd joined in the attack against Paul and Silas, and the magistrates ordered them to be stripped and beaten. {16:23} After they had been severely flogged, they were thrown into prison, and the jailer was commanded to guard them carefully. {16:24} Upon receiving such orders, he put them in the inner cell and fastened their feet in the stocks. {16:25} About midnight, Paul and Silas were praying and singing hymns to God, and the other prisoners were listening to them. {16:26} Suddenly, there was a violent earthquake that shook the foundations of the prison. All at once, the prison doors flew open and everyone's chains came loose. {16:27} The jailer woke up, and when he saw the prison doors open, he drew his sword and was about to kill himself because he thought the prisoners had escaped. {16:28} But Paul shouted, "Don't harm yourself! We are all here!" {16:29} The jailer called for lights, rushed in and fell trembling before Paul and Silas. {16:30} He then brought them out and asked, "Sirs, what must I do to be saved?" {16:31} They replied, "Believe in the Lord Jesus, and you will be saved—you and your household." {16:32} Then they spoke the word of the Lord to him and to all the others in his house. {16:33} At that hour of the night, the jailer took them and washed their wounds; then immediately he and all his household were baptized. {16:34} The jailer brought them into his house and set a meal before them; he was filled with joy because he had come to believe in God—he and his whole household. {16:35} When it was daylight, the magistrates sent their officers to the jailer with the order: "Release those men." {16:36} The jailer told Paul, "The magistrates have ordered that you and Silas be released. Now you can leave. Go in peace." {16:37} But Paul said to the officers, "They beat us publicly without a trial, even though we are Roman citizens, and threw us into prison. And now do they want to get rid of us quietly? No! Let them come themselves and escort us out." {16:38} The officers reported this to the magistrates, and when they heard that Paul and Silas were Roman citizens, they were alarmed. {16:39} They came to appease them and escorted them from the prison, requesting them to leave the city. {16:40} After Paul and Silas came out of the prison, they went to Lydia's house, where they met with the brothers and encouraged them. Then they left.

{17:1} When they had traveled through Amphipolis and Apollonia, they came to Thessalonica, where there was a Jewish synagogue. {17:2} As was his custom, Paul went into the synagogue, and on three Sabbath days he reasoned with them from the Scriptures, {17:3} explaining and proving that the Messiah had to suffer and rise from the dead. "This Jesus I am proclaiming to you is the Messiah," he said. {17:4} Some of the Jews were persuaded and joined Paul and Silas, as did a large number of God-fearing Greeks and quite a few prominent women. {17:5} But other Jews were jealous; so they rounded up some bad characters from the marketplace, formed a mob and started a riot in the city. They rushed to Jason's house in search of Paul and Silas in order to bring them out to the crowd. {17:6} But when they did not find them, they dragged Jason and some other believers before the city officials, shouting, "These men who have caused trouble all over the world have now come here, {17:7} and Jason has welcomed them into his house. They are all defying Caesar's decrees, saying that there is another king, one called Jesus." {17:8} When they heard this, the crowd and the city officials were thrown into turmoil. {17:9} They made Jason and the others post bond and let them go. {17:10} As soon as it was night, the believers sent Paul and Silas away to Berea. On arriving there, they went to the Jewish synagogue. {17:11} Now the Bereans were of more noble character than the Thessalonians, for they received the message with great eagerness and examined the Scriptures every day to see if what Paul said was true. {17:12} As a result, many of them believed, as did also a number of prominent Greek women and many Greek men. {17:13} But when the Jews in Thessalonica learned that Paul was preaching the word of God at Berea, they went there too, agitating the crowds and stirring them up. {17:14} The believers immediately sent Paul to the coast, but Silas and Timothy stayed at Berea. {17:15} Those who accompanied Paul brought him to

Athens and went to get Silas and Timothy, urging them to join him as soon as possible. {17:16} While Paul was waiting for them in Athens, he was greatly distressed to see that the city was full of idols. {17:17} So he reasoned in the synagogue with both Jews and God-fearing Greeks, as well as in the marketplace day by day with those who happened to be there. {17:18} A group of Epicurean and Stoic philosophers began to debate with him. Some of them asked, "What is this babbler trying to say?" Others remarked, "He seems to be advocating foreign gods." They said this because Paul was preaching the good news about Jesus and the resurrection. {17:19} Then they took him and brought him to a meeting of the Areopagus, where they said to him, "May we know what this new teaching is that you are presenting? {17:20} You are bringing some strange ideas to our ears, and we would like to know what they mean." {17:21} (All the Athenians and the foreigners who lived there spent their time doing nothing but talking about and listening to the latest ideas.) {17:22} Paul then stood up in the meeting of the Areopagus and said: "People of Athens! I see that in every way you are very religious. {17:23} For as I walked around and looked carefully at your objects of worship, I even found an altar with this inscription: TO AN UNKNOWN GOD. So you are ignorant of the very thing you worship—and this is what I am going to proclaim to you. {17:24} The God who made the world and everything in it is the Lord of heaven and earth and does not live in temples built by human hands. {17:25} And he is not served by human hands, as if he needed anything. Rather, he himself gives everyone life and breath and everything else. {17:26} From one man he made all the nations, that they should inhabit the whole earth; and he marked out their appointed times in history and the boundaries of their lands. {17:27} God did this so they would seek him and perhaps reach out for him and find him, though he is not far from any one of us. {17:28} 'For in him we live and move and have our being.' As some of your own poets have said, 'We are his offspring.' {17:29} Therefore since we are God's offspring, we should not think that the divine being is like gold or silver or stone—an image made by human design and skill. {17:30} In the past God overlooked such ignorance, but now he commands all people everywhere to repent. {17:31} For he has set a day when he will judge the world with justice by the man he has appointed. He has given proof of this to everyone by raising him from the dead." {17:32} When they heard about the resurrection of the dead, some of them sneered, but others said, "We want to hear you again on this subject." {17:33} At that, Paul left the Council. {17:34} Some of the people became followers of Paul and believed. Among them was Dionysius, a member of the Areopagus, also a woman named Damaris, and a number of others.

{18:1} After these events, Paul left Athens and went to Corinth. {18:2} There he found a Jew named Aquila, originally from Pontus, who had recently come from Italy with his wife Priscilla, because Claudius had ordered all Jews to leave Rome. {18:3} Because they shared the same trade, Paul stayed with them and worked, as they were all tentmakers. {18:4} Every Sabbath, he reasoned in the synagogue, persuading both Jews and Greeks. {18:5} When Silas and Timothy arrived from Macedonia, Paul was moved in his spirit and testified to the Jews that Jesus was the Messiah. {18:6} When they opposed him and insulted him, he shook out his clothes and said to them, "Your blood is on your own heads; I am innocent. From now on, I will go to the Gentiles." {18:7} He then left and went to the house of a man named Justus, a worshiper of God, whose house was next to the synagogue. {18:8} Crispus, the synagogue leader, believed in the Lord, along with his entire household; many of the Corinthians who heard Paul believed and were baptized. {18:9} One night, the Lord spoke to Paul in a vision: "Do not be afraid; keep speaking and do not be silent. {18:10} For I am with you, and no one will attack you to harm you, because I have many people in this city." {18:11} So Paul stayed there for a year and a half, teaching the word of God among them. {18:12} While Gallio was proconsul of Achaia, the Jews united in opposition to Paul and brought him to the judgment seat, {18:13} accusing him, "This man persuades people to worship God in ways that are against the law." {18:14} Just as Paul was about to speak, Gallio said to the Jews, "If this were a matter of wrongdoing or serious crime, it would be reasonable for me to listen to you. {18:15} But if it concerns questions about words and names and your own law, settle it yourselves; I will not be a judge of such matters." {18:16} And he drove them off. {18:17} Then the crowd seized Sosthenes, the synagogue leader, and beat him in front of the judgment seat. Gallio showed no concern whatever. {18:18} Paul stayed in Corinth for a while longer, then said goodbye to the believers and sailed for Syria, accompanied by Priscilla and Aquila. He had his hair cut off at Cenchrea because of a vow he had taken. {18:19} They arrived in Ephesus, where he left them, but he himself went into the synagogue and reasoned with the Jews. {18:20} When they asked him to stay longer, he declined, {18:21} but said farewell, "I must keep this coming feast in Jerusalem, and I will return to you if God wills." Then he set sail from Ephesus. {18:22} After landing at Caesarea, he went up to greet the church and then went down to Antioch. {18:23} After spending some time there, he set out from there and traveled through Galatia and Phrygia, strengthening all the disciples. {18:24} Meanwhile, a Jew named Apollos, a native of Alexandria, came to Ephesus. He was an eloquent man, well-versed in the Scriptures. {18:25} He had been instructed in the way of the Lord and spoke with great fervor, teaching accurately about Jesus, though he only knew John's baptism. {18:26} He began to speak boldly in the synagogue. When Aquila and Priscilla heard him, they invited him to their home and explained to him the way of God more adequately. {18:27} When he decided to go to Achaia, the brothers wrote to the disciples there, urging them to welcome him. When he arrived, he was a great help to those who, by grace, had believed. {18:28} For he vigorously refuted his Jewish opponents in public debate, proving from the Scriptures that Jesus was the Messiah.

{19:1} While Apollos was at Corinth, Paul traveled through the interior regions and came to Ephesus. There he found some disciples {19:2} and asked them, "Did you receive the Holy Spirit when you believed?" They answered, "No, we have not even heard that there is a Holy Spirit." {19:3} So Paul asked, "Then what baptism did you receive?" "John's baptism," they replied. {19:4} Paul said, "John's baptism was a baptism of repentance. He told the people to believe in the one coming after him, that is, in Jesus." {19:5} On hearing this, they were baptized in the name of the Lord Jesus. {19:6} When Paul placed his hands on them, the Holy Spirit came on them, and they spoke in tongues and prophesied. {19:7} There were about twelve men in all. {19:8} Paul entered the synagogue and spoke boldly there for three months, arguing persuasively about the kingdom of God. {19:9} But some of them became obstinate; they refused to believe and publicly maligned the Way. So Paul left them. He took the disciples with him and had discussions daily in the lecture hall of Tyrannus. {19:10} This went on for two years, so that all the Jews and Greeks who lived in the province of Asia heard the word of the Lord. {19:11} God did extraordinary miracles through Paul, {19:12} so that even handkerchiefs and aprons that had touched him were taken to the sick, and their illnesses were cured and evil spirits left them. {19:13} Some Jews who went around driving out evil spirits tried to invoke the name of the Lord Jesus over those who were demon-possessed. They would say, "In the name of the Jesus whom Paul preaches, I command you to come out." {19:14} Seven sons of Sceva, a Jewish chief priest, were doing this. {19:15} One day the evil spirit answered them, "Jesus I know, and Paul I know about, but who are you?" {19:16} Then the man who had the evil spirit jumped on them and overpowered them all; he gave them such a beating that they ran out of the house naked and bleeding. {19:17} When this became known to the Jews and Greeks living in Ephesus, they were all seized with fear, and the name of the Lord Jesus was held in high honor. {19:18} Many of those who believed now came and openly confessed what they had done. {19:19} A number who had practiced sorcery brought their scrolls together and burned them publicly. When they calculated the value of the scrolls, the total came to fifty thousand drachmas (a silver coin). {19:20} In this way, the word of the Lord spread widely and grew in power. {19:21} After all this had happened, Paul decided to go to Jerusalem, passing through Macedonia and Achaia. "After I have been there," he said, "I must visit Rome also." {19:22} He sent two of his helpers, Timothy and Erastus, to Macedonia, while he stayed in the province of Asia a little longer. {19:23} About that time, there arose a great disturbance about the Way. {19:24} A silversmith named Demetrius, who made silver shrines of Artemis (the Greek goddess), brought in a lot of business for the craftsmen there. {19:25} He called them together along with the workers in related trades and said, "You know, my friends, that we receive a good income from this business. {19:26} And you see and hear how this fellow Paul has convinced and led astray a large number of people here in Ephesus and in practically the whole province of Asia. He says that gods made by human hands are no gods at all. {19:27} There is danger not only that our trade will lose its good name, but also that the temple of the great goddess Artemis will be discredited, and the goddess herself, who is worshiped throughout the province of Asia and the world, will be robbed of her divine majesty." {19:28} When they heard this, they were furious and began shouting, "Great is Artemis of the Ephesians!" {19:29} Soon the whole city was in an uproar. The people seized Gaius and Aristarchus, Paul's traveling companions from Macedonia, and rushed as one man into the theater. {19:30} Paul wanted to appear before the crowd, but the disciples would not let him. {19:31} Even some of the officials of the province, friends of Paul, sent him a message begging him not to venture into the theater. {19:32} The assembly was in confusion; some were shouting one thing, some another. Most of the people did not even know why they were there. {19:33} The Jews pushed Alexander to the front, and he motioned for silence in order to make a defense before the people. {19:34} But when they realized he was a Jew, they all shouted in unison for about two hours: "Great is Artemis of the Ephesians!" {19:35} The city clerk quieted the crowd and said: "Fellow Ephesians, doesn't all the world know that the city of Ephesus is the guardian of the temple of the great Artemis and of her image, which fell from heaven? {19:36} Therefore, since these facts are undeniable, you ought to calm down and not do anything rash. {19:37} You have brought these men here, though they have neither robbed temples nor blasphemed our goddess. {19:38} If then, Demetrius and his fellow craftsmen have a grievance against anybody, the courts are open and there are proconsuls. They can press charges. {19:39} If there is anything further you want to bring up, it must be settled in a legal assembly. {19:40} As it is, we are in danger of being charged with rioting because of what happened today. In that case, we would not be able to account for this commotion." {19:41} After he had said this, he dismissed the assembly.

{20:1} After the uproar had ceased, Paul called the disciples to him, embraced them, and departed to go to Macedonia. {20:2} When he had traveled through those parts and encouraged them greatly, he came into Greece, {20:3} where he stayed for three months. When the Jews plotted against him as he was about to sail to Syria, he decided to return through Macedonia. {20:4} He was accompanied into Asia by Sopater from Berea, Aristarchus and Secundus from Thessalonica, Gaius from Derbe, Timothy, and Tychicus and Trophimus from Asia. {20:5} These men went ahead and waited for us at Troas. {20:6} We sailed from Philippi after the Days of Unleavened Bread and joined them at Troas after five days, where we stayed for seven days. {20:7} On the first day of the week, when we gathered to break bread, Paul spoke to them, planning to leave the next day, and continued his message until midnight. {20:8} There were many lamps in the upstairs room where we were gathered. {20:9} A young man named Eutychus was sitting in a window, and as Paul talked on and on, he fell into a deep sleep. He fell from the third floor and was picked up dead. {20:10} Paul went down, threw himself on the young man, and embraced him, saying, "Don't be alarmed, his life is in him." {20:11} Then he went upstairs again, broke bread, ate, and talked with them a long time until daylight, and he departed. {20:12} The people took the young man home alive and were greatly comforted. {20:13} We went ahead to the ship and sailed for Assos, where we were to take Paul on board, for he had arranged it that way, intending to go there by foot. {20:14} When he met us at Assos, we took him aboard and went to Mitylene. {20:15} We sailed from there and arrived the next day opposite Chios. The following day we reached Samos and stayed at Trogyllium. The next day we came to Miletus. {20:16} Paul had decided to sail past Ephesus to avoid spending time in Asia, for he was eager to be in Jerusalem by Pentecost, if possible. {20:17} From Miletus, he sent to Ephesus and called for the elders of the church. {20:18} When they arrived, he said to them, "You know how I lived the whole time I was with you, from the first day I came to Asia, {20:19} serving the Lord with all humility, with tears and trials that happened because of the plots of the Jews. {20:20} I did not hesitate to preach anything that would be helpful to you but have taught you publicly and from house to house, {20:21} testifying to both Jews and Greeks about repentance toward God and faith in our Lord Jesus Christ. {20:22} And now, compelled by the Spirit, I am going to Jerusalem, not knowing what will happen to me there. {20:23} I only know that in every city the Holy Spirit warns me that prison and hardships are facing me. {20:24} However, I consider my life worth nothing to me; my only aim is to finish the race and complete the task the Lord Jesus has given me—the task of testifying to the good news of God's grace. {20:25} Now I know that none of you among whom I have gone about preaching the kingdom will ever see me again. {20:26} Therefore, I declare to you today that I am innocent of the blood of any of you. {20:27} For I have not hesitated to proclaim to you the whole will of God. {20:28} Keep watch over yourselves and all the flock of which the Holy Spirit has made you overseers. Be shepherds of the church of God, which he bought with his own blood. {20:29} I know that after I leave, savage wolves will come in among you and will not spare the flock. {20:30} Even from your own number, men will arise and distort the truth in order to draw away disciples after them. {20:31} So be on your guard! Remember that for three years I never stopped warning each of you night and day with tears. {20:32} Now I commit you to God and to the word of his grace, which can build you up and give you an inheritance among all those who are sanctified. {20:33} I have not coveted anyone's silver or gold or clothing. {20:34} You yourselves know that these hands of mine have supplied my own needs and the needs of my companions. {20:35} In everything I did, I showed you that by this kind of hard work we must help the weak, remembering the words the Lord Jesus himself said: 'It is more blessed to give than to receive.'" {20:36} When Paul had finished speaking, he knelt down with all of them and prayed. {20:37} They all wept as they embraced him and kissed him. {20:38} What grieved them most was his statement that they would never see his face again. Then they accompanied him to the ship.

{21:1} After we had torn ourselves away from them, we put out to sea and sailed straight to Cos, and the next day to Rhodes, and from there to Patara. {21:2} Finding a ship crossing over to Phoenicia, we went aboard and set sail. {21:3} After sighting Cyprus and leaving it on our left, we sailed on to Syria and landed at Tyre, where the ship was to unload its cargo. {21:4} We found some disciples there and stayed with them for seven days. Through the Spirit, they urged Paul not to go to Jerusalem. {21:5} When it was time to leave, we departed and were accompanied out of the city by all the disciples, including their wives and children. We knelt on the beach and prayed. {21:6} After saying goodbye to each other, we went aboard the ship, and they returned home. {21:7} We continued our voyage from Tyre and landed at Ptolemais, where we greeted the brothers and stayed with them for a day. {21:8} Leaving the next day, we reached Caesarea and stayed at the house of Philip the evangelist, one of the Seven. {21:9} He had four unmarried daughters who prophesied. {21:10} After we had been there a number of days, a prophet named Agabus came down from Judea. {21:11} Coming over to us, he took Paul's belt, tied his own hands and feet with it, and said, "The Holy Spirit says, 'In this way the Jewish leaders in Jerusalem will bind the owner of this belt and will hand him over to the Gentiles.'" {21:12} When we heard this, we and the people there pleaded with Paul not to go up to Jerusalem. {21:13} Then Paul answered, "Why are you weeping and breaking my heart? I am ready not only to be bound but also to die in Jerusalem for the name of the Lord Jesus." {21:14} When he would not be dissuaded, we gave up and said, "The Lord's will be done." {21:15} After this, we started on our way up to Jerusalem. {21:16} Some of the disciples from Caesarea accompanied us and brought us to the home of Mnason, a Cypriot, one of the early disciples, where we were to stay. {21:17} When we arrived at Jerusalem, the brothers and sisters received us warmly. {21:18} The next day, Paul and the rest of us went to see James, and all the elders were present. {21:19} Paul greeted them and reported in detail what God had done among the Gentiles through his ministry. {21:20} When they heard this, they praised God. Then they said to Paul: "You see, brother, how many thousands of Jews have believed, and all of them are zealous for the law. {21:21} They have been informed that you teach all the Jews living among the Gentiles to turn away from Moses, telling them not to circumcise their children or live according to our customs. {21:22} What shall we do? They will certainly hear that you have come. {21:23} So do what we tell you. There are four men with us who have made a vow. {21:24} Take these men, join in their purification rites, and pay their expenses so that they can have their heads shaved. Then everyone will know there is no truth in these reports about you, but that you yourself are living in obedience to the law. {21:25} As for the Gentile believers, we have written to them our decision that they should abstain from food sacrificed to idols, from blood, from the meat of strangled animals, and from sexual immorality." {21:26} The next day Paul took the men and purified himself along with them. Then he went into the temple to give notice of the date when the days of purification would end and the offering would be made for each of them. {21:27} When the seven days were nearly over, some Jews from the province of Asia saw Paul at the temple. They stirred up the whole crowd and seized him, {21:28} shouting, "Fellow Israelites, help us! This is the man who teaches everyone everywhere against our people and our law and this place. And besides, he has brought Greeks into the temple and defiled this holy place." {21:29} (They had previously seen Trophimus the Ephesian in the city with Paul and assumed that Paul had brought him into the temple.) {21:30} The whole city was aroused, and the people came running from all directions. Seizing Paul, they dragged him from the temple, and immediately the gates were shut. {21:31} While they were trying to kill him, news reached the commander of the Roman troops that the whole city of Jerusalem was in an uproar. {21:32} He at once took some officers and soldiers and ran down to the crowd. When the rioters saw the commander and his soldiers, they stopped beating Paul. {21:33} The commander came up and arrested him and ordered him to be bound with two chains. Then he asked who he was and what he had done. {21:34} Some in the crowd shouted one thing and some another, and since the commander could not get at the truth because of the uproar, he ordered that Paul be taken into the barracks. {21:35} When Paul reached the steps, the violence of the mob was so great that he had to be carried by the soldiers. {21:36} The crowd that followed kept shouting, "Get rid of him!" {21:37} As the soldiers were about to take Paul into the barracks, he asked the commander, "May I say something to you?" "Do you speak Greek?" he replied. {21:38} "Aren't you the Egyptian who started a revolt and led four thousand terrorists out into the wilderness some time ago?" {21:39} Paul answered, "I am a Jew, from Tarsus in Cilicia, a citizen of no ordinary city. Please let me speak to the people." {21:40} Having received the commander's permission, Paul stood on the steps and motioned to the crowd. When they were all silent, he said to them in Aramaic: "Brothers and fathers, listen now to my defense."

{22:1} "Brothers and fathers, listen now to my defense." {22:2} When they heard him speak in Hebrew, they became even quieter. He said, {22:3} "I am a Jew, born in Tarsus, a city in Cilicia, but brought up in this city at the feet of Gamaliel, educated in the strictest way of our law, and I was zealous for God, just as all of you are today. {22:4} I persecuted this way to the death, imprisoning and delivering both men and women. {22:5} The high priest and all the council can testify about me. I received letters from them to the brothers and went to Damascus to bring those who were there bound to Jerusalem for punishment. {22:6} As I was on my way and nearing Damascus around noon, a bright light from heaven suddenly shone around me. {22:7} I fell to the ground and heard a voice saying to me, 'Saul, Saul, why are you persecuting me?' {22:8} I asked, 'Who are you, Lord?' He replied, 'I am Jesus of Nazareth, whom you are persecuting.' {22:9} Those who were with me saw the light but did not hear the voice of the one speaking to me. {22:10} I asked, 'What should I do, Lord?' The Lord said to me, 'Get up and go into Damascus, and there you will be told all that you are appointed to do.' {22:11} Since I could not see because of the brightness of that light, I was led by the hand of those with me into Damascus. {22:12} A man named Ananias, a devout observer of the law and well spoken of by all the Jews living there, {22:13} came to me and said, 'Brother Saul, regain your sight!' In that very hour, I looked up at him. {22:14} He said, 'The God of our ancestors has chosen you to know his will, to see the Righteous One, and to hear the voice from his mouth. {22:15} For you will be his witness to all people of what you have seen and heard. {22:16} And now, why do you wait? Get up, be baptized, and wash away your sins, calling on his name.' {22:17} When I returned to Jerusalem and was praying in the temple, I fell into a trance. {22:18} I saw him saying to me, 'Hurry, get out of Jerusalem quickly, because they will not accept your testimony about me.' {22:19} I replied, 'Lord, they know I imprisoned and beat those who believed in you in every synagogue. {22:20} And when the blood of your witness Stephen was shed, I stood there giving my approval and guarding the clothes of those who were killing him.' {22:21} He said to me, 'Go, for I will send you far away to the Gentiles.' {22:22} The crowd listened to him until he said this. Then they raised their voices and shouted, 'Rid the earth of him! He is not fit to live!' {22:23} As they were shouting and throwing off their cloaks and tossing dust into the air, {22:24} the commander ordered Paul to be taken into the barracks. He instructed that he be examined by flogging to find out why they were shouting against him like this. {22:25} As they stretched him out to flog him, Paul said to the centurion standing there, 'Is it legal for you to flog a Roman citizen who hasn't even been found guilty?' {22:26} When the centurion heard this, he went to the commander and reported it. He said, 'What are you going to do? This man is a Roman citizen.' {22:27} The commander went to Paul and asked, 'Tell me, are you a Roman citizen?' 'Yes,' he answered. {22:28} The commander said, 'I had to pay a lot of money for my citizenship.' 'But I was born a citizen,' Paul replied. {22:29} Those who were about to interrogate him withdrew immediately. The commander himself was alarmed when he realized that he had put a Roman citizen in chains. {22:30} The next day, since the commander wanted to find out exactly why Paul was being accused by the Jews, he freed him from his bonds and ordered the chief priests and all the Sanhedrin to assemble. Then he brought Paul and had him stand before them.

{23:1} Paul looked straight at the Sanhedrin and said, "My brothers, I have fulfilled my duty to God in all good conscience to this day." {23:2} At this, the high priest Ananias ordered those standing near Paul to strike him on the mouth. {23:3} Then Paul said to him, "God will strike you, you whitewashed wall! You sit there to judge me according to the law, yet you yourself violate the law by commanding that I be struck!" {23:4} Those who were standing near said, "How dare you insult God's high priest?" {23:5} Paul replied, "Brothers, I did not realize that he was the high priest; for it is written: 'Do not speak evil about the ruler of your people.'" {23:6} Then Paul, knowing that some of them were Sadducees and the others Pharisees, called out in the Sanhedrin, "My brothers, I am a Pharisee, the son of a Pharisee. I stand on trial because of my hope in the resurrection of the dead." {23:7} When he said this, a dispute broke out between the Pharisees and the Sadducees, and the assembly was divided. {23:8} The Sadducees say that there is no resurrection, and that there are neither angels nor spirits, but the Pharisees believe all these things. {23:9} There was a great uproar, and some of the teachers of the law who were Pharisees stood up and argued vigorously, "We find nothing wrong with this man. What if a spirit or an angel has spoken to him?" {23:10} The dispute became so violent that the commander was afraid Paul would be torn to pieces by them. He ordered the soldiers to go down and take him away from them by force and bring him into the barracks. {23:11} The following night the Lord stood near Paul and said, "Take courage! As you have testified about me in Jerusalem, so you must also testify in Rome." {23:12} The next morning, some Jews formed a conspiracy and bound themselves with an oath not to eat or drink until they had killed Paul. {23:13} More than forty men were involved in this plot. {23:14} They went to the chief priests and the elders and said, "We have taken a solemn oath not to eat anything until we have killed Paul. {23:15} Now then, you and the Sanhedrin petition the commander to bring him before you on the pretext of wanting more accurate information about his case. We are ready to kill him before he gets here." {23:16} But when the son of Paul's sister heard of this plot, he went into the barracks and told Paul. {23:17} Paul called one of the centurions and said, "Take this young man to the commander; he has something to tell him." {23:18} So he took him to the commander. The centurion said, "Paul the prisoner sent for me and asked me to bring this young man to you because he has something to say to you." {23:19} The commander took the young man by the hand, drew him aside, and asked, "What is it you want to tell me?" {23:20} He said, "The Jews have agreed to ask you to bring Paul before the Sanhedrin tomorrow on the pretext of wanting more accurate information about him. {23:21} Don't give in to them, because more than forty of them are waiting in ambush for him. They have taken an oath not to eat or drink until they have killed him. They are ready now and waiting for your consent." {23:22} The commander dismissed the young man and cautioned him, "Don't tell anyone that you have reported this to me." {23:23} Then he called two of his centurions and ordered them, "Get ready a detachment of two hundred soldiers, seventy horsemen, and two hundred spearmen to go to Caesarea at nine tonight. {23:24} Provide horses for Paul so that he may be taken safely to Governor Felix." {23:25} He wrote a letter as follows: {23:26} "Claudius Lysias, to His Excellency, Governor Felix: Greetings. {23:27} This man was seized by the Jews and they were about to kill him, but I came with my troops and rescued him, for I had learned that he is a Roman citizen. {23:28} I wanted to know why they were accusing him, so I brought him to their Sanhedrin. {23:29} I found that the accusation had to do with questions about their law, but there was no charge against him that deserved death or imprisonment. {23:30} When I was informed of a plot to be carried out against the man, I sent him to you at once. I also told his accusers to present to you their case against him. Farewell." {23:31} The soldiers did as they were ordered: they took Paul during the night and brought him as far as Antipatris. {23:32} The next day they let the horsemen go on with him while they returned to the barracks. {23:33} When the horsemen arrived in Caesarea, they delivered the letter to the governor and presented Paul to him. {23:34} The governor read the letter and asked what province he was from. Learning that he was from Cilicia, {23:35} he said, "I will hear your case when your accusers get here." Then he ordered that Paul be kept under guard in Herod's palace.

{24:1} Five days later, the high priest Ananias went down with some elders and a lawyer named Tertullus to present their case against Paul to the governor. {24:2} When Paul was called in, Tertullus began his accusation, saying, "Your Excellency Felix, we enjoy great peace because of you, and your administration has brought many improvements to our nation. {24:3} We always and everywhere thank you for this, most noble Felix. {24:4} But I don't want to take up too much of your time, so I ask you to listen to us briefly. {24:5} We have found this man to be a troublemaker, stirring up riots among all the Jews throughout the world. He is a ringleader of the Nazarene sect. {24:6} He tried to desecrate the temple, and we seized him and intended to judge him according to our law. {24:7} But the commander Lysias intervened and took him from us with great force, {24:8} ordering his accusers to come before you so you can examine the case yourself. {24:9} The Jews joined in the accusation, asserting that these things were true. {24:10} Then Paul, who was given the opportunity to speak, replied, "Knowing that you have been a judge over this nation for many years, I gladly make my defense. {24:11} You can easily verify that it is no more than twelve days since I went up to Jerusalem to worship. {24:12} They did not find me arguing with anyone in the temple or stirring up a crowd in the synagogues or anywhere in the city. {24:13} And they cannot prove the charges they are making against me. {24:14} However, I admit that I follow the way they call a sect, worshiping the God of our ancestors, believing everything that is in the law and the prophets. {24:15} I have hope in God that there will be a resurrection of both the righteous and the unrighteous. {24:16} So I strive always to keep my conscience clear before God and man. {24:17} After several years, I came to bring gifts to my people and to present offerings. {24:18} While I was doing this, some Jews from Asia found me ceremonially clean in the temple and were not causing a disturbance. {24:19} They should be here before you to bring charges if they have anything against me. {24:20} Or these who are here should state what crime they found in me when I stood before the Sanhedrin, {24:21} unless it was this one thing I shouted as I stood among them: 'It is concerning the resurrection of the dead that I am on trial before you today.'" {24:22} Felix, who was well acquainted with the way, adjourned the hearing. He said, "When Lysias the commander comes, I will decide your case." {24:23} He ordered the centurion to keep Paul under guard but to give him some freedom and allow his friends to take care of his needs. {24:24} After some days, Felix came with his wife Drusilla, who was Jewish. He sent for Paul and listened to him as he spoke about faith in Christ. {24:25} As Paul discussed righteousness, self-control, and the coming judgment, Felix became afraid and said, "That's enough for now! You may leave. When I find it convenient, I will send for you." {24:26} At the same time, he was hoping that Paul would offer him a bribe, so he sent for him frequently and talked with him. {24:27} After two years had passed, Felix was succeeded by Porcius Festus. Because Felix wanted to grant a favor to the Jews, he left Paul in prison.

{25:1} Three days after Festus arrived in the province, he went up from Caesarea to Jerusalem. {25:2} There, the high priest and the leaders of the Jews brought charges against Paul and urged Festus {25:3} to have Paul transferred to Jerusalem, planning to ambush him and kill him on the way. {25:4} Festus answered, "Paul is being held at Caesarea, and I myself am going there soon. {25:5} Let some of your leaders go down with me and press charges against the man there if he has done anything wrong." {25:6} After spending eight or ten days with them, he went down to Caesarea. The next day, he took his seat on the tribunal and ordered Paul to be brought in. {25:7} When Paul arrived, the Jews who had come down from Jerusalem stood around him. They brought many serious accusations against him, but they could not prove them. {25:8} Paul denied the charges, saying, "I have done nothing wrong against the Jewish law or against the temple or against Caesar." {25:9} Festus, wanting to do the Jews a favor, asked Paul, "Are you willing to go up to Jerusalem and stand trial before me there on these charges?" {25:10} Paul answered, "I am now standing before Caesar's court, where I ought to be tried. I have not done any wrong to the Jews, as you yourself know very well. {25:11} If I am guilty of doing anything deserving death, I do not refuse to die. But if the charges brought against me by these men are not true, no one has the right to hand me over to them. I appeal to Caesar!" {25:12} After Festus had conferred with his council, he declared, "You have appealed to Caesar. To Caesar you will go!" {25:13} A few days later, King Agrippa and Bernice arrived at Caesarea to pay their respects to Festus. {25:14} Since they were spending many days there, Festus discussed Paul's case with the king. He said, "There is a man here whom Felix left as a prisoner. {25:15} When I went to Jerusalem, the chief priests and the elders of the Jews brought charges against him and asked that he be condemned. {25:16} I told them that it is not the Roman custom to hand over any man before the accused meets his accusers face to face and has the opportunity to defend himself against their charges. {25:17} When they came here, I did not delay the matter but sat on the tribunal the very next day and ordered the man to be brought in. {25:18} When his accusers got up to speak, they did not charge him with any of the crimes I had expected. {25:19} Instead, they had some points of dispute with him about their own religion and about a dead man named Jesus whom Paul claimed was alive. {25:20} Since I was at a loss how to investigate such matters, I asked if he would be willing to go to Jerusalem and stand trial there on these charges. {25:21} But when Paul made his appeal to be held over for the Emperor's decision, I ordered that he be held until I could send him to Caesar." {25:22} Then Agrippa said to Festus, "I would like to hear this man myself." He replied, "Tomorrow you will hear him." {25:23} The next day, Agrippa and Bernice came with great pomp and entered the audience hall with the high-ranking military officers and the prominent men of the city. At the command of Festus, Paul was brought in. {25:24} Festus said, "King Agrippa and all who are present with us, you see this man. The whole Jewish community has petitioned me about him in Jerusalem and here in Caesarea, shouting that he ought not to live any longer. {25:25} I found he had done nothing deserving of death, but because he made his appeal to the Emperor, I decided to send him to Rome. {25:26} But I have nothing definite to write to His Majesty about him. Therefore, I have brought him before all of you, and especially before you, King Agrippa, so that as you examine him, I might have something to write. {25:27} For I think it is unreasonable to send a prisoner without specifying the charges against him."

{26:1} Agrippa said to Paul, "You are allowed to speak for yourself." So Paul raised his hand and began to speak for himself. {26:2} "I feel fortunate, King Agrippa, to answer for myself today regarding all the accusations made against me by the Jews. {26:3} I especially appreciate that you are familiar with Jewish customs and questions, so I ask you to listen to me patiently. {26:4} All the Jews know my way of life from my youth, which began in my own nation in Jerusalem. {26:5} They can testify that I lived as a

Pharisee, following the strictest sect of our religion. {26:6} Now I stand here being judged for the hope of the promise God made to our ancestors. {26:7} Our twelve tribes hope to attain this promise by serving God day and night. It's for this hope that I am accused by the Jews. {26:8} Why is it considered incredible by any of you that God raises the dead? {26:9} I once thought it was my duty to oppose the name of Jesus of Nazareth. {26:10} I did this in Jerusalem, imprisoning many of the saints with authority from the chief priests, and I voted against them when they were put to death. {26:11} I frequently punished them in every synagogue and tried to force them to blaspheme; I was so enraged that I persecuted them even in foreign cities. {26:12} As I was on my way to Damascus with authority and a commission from the chief priests, {26:13} at midday, O king, I saw a light from heaven brighter than the sun, shining around me and those traveling with me. {26:14} We all fell to the ground, and I heard a voice speaking to me in Hebrew, saying, "Saul, Saul, why are you persecuting me? It's hard for you to kick against the goads (sharp points). {26:15} I asked, "Who are you, Lord?" And he replied, "I am Jesus, whom you are persecuting. {26:16} But rise and stand on your feet; I have appeared to you for this purpose, to appoint you as a minister and a witness of both the things you have seen and the things I will reveal to you. {26:17} I will rescue you from your own people and from the Gentiles, to whom I am sending you now. {26:18} Your mission is to open their eyes, turning them from darkness to light and from the power of Satan to God, so they may receive forgiveness for their sins and an inheritance among those who are sanctified by faith in me. {26:19} Therefore, King Agrippa, I was not disobedient to the heavenly vision. {26:20} Instead, I first proclaimed this message in Damascus, then in Jerusalem, throughout all Judea, and then to the Gentiles, urging them to repent and turn to God, performing deeds consistent with repentance. {26:21} For this reason, the Jews seized me in the temple and tried to kill me. {26:22} But God has helped me up to this day, and I stand here, testifying to both small and great, saying nothing except what the prophets and Moses said would happen: {26:23} that Christ would suffer, and that he would be the first to rise from the dead, and he would proclaim light to the people and to the Gentiles. {26:24} As Paul was making his defense, Festus shouted loudly, "You are out of your mind, Paul; too much learning is driving you insane!" {26:25} Paul replied, "I am not insane, most excellent Festus; I am speaking the words of truth and reason. {26:26} King Agrippa knows about these things; I am confident that none of these things are hidden from him, for they weren't done in secret. {26:27} King Agrippa, do you believe the prophets? I know you do." {26:28} Agrippa replied to Paul, "You almost persuade me to be a Christian." {26:29} Paul said, "I wish to God that not only you, but also all who hear me today, would become such as I am, except for these chains." {26:30} After he said this, the king stood up, along with the governor and Bernice, and they left the room. {26:31} When they had gone aside, they talked among themselves, saying, "This man has done nothing worthy of death or imprisonment." {26:32} Agrippa told Festus, "This man could have been released if he hadn't appealed to Caesar."

{27:1} When it was decided that we would sail to Italy, they handed Paul and some other prisoners over to a centurion named Julius from the Augustus Cohort. {27:2} We boarded a ship from Adramyttium and set sail to navigate along the coasts of Asia, accompanied by a Macedonian named Aristarchus from Thessalonica. {27:3} The next day we arrived at Sidon, and Julius treated Paul kindly, allowing him to go to his friends to be cared for. {27:4} After setting sail from there, we sailed under Cyprus because the winds were against us. {27:5} We traveled across the sea of Cilicia and Pamphylia and arrived at Myra, a city in Lycia. {27:6} There, the centurion found an Alexandrian ship sailing to Italy and put us on board. {27:7} After many days of slow sailing, and struggling to get past Cnidus, as the wind prevented us, we sailed under the island of Crete, near Salmone. {27:8} With difficulty, we reached a place called Fair Havens, near the city of Lasea. {27:9} After a considerable time had passed, and sailing had become dangerous because the Fast (Day of Atonement) had already gone by, Paul advised them, {27:10} saying, "Men, I perceive that this voyage will result in great damage and loss, not only of the cargo and the ship but also of our lives." {27:11} However, the centurion believed the captain and the owner of the ship more than what Paul said. {27:12} Since the harbor was unsuitable for wintering, most of the crew advised to set sail for Phoenix, a harbor of Crete that faces southwest and northwest, hoping to spend the winter there. {27:13} When a gentle south wind began to blow, they thought they had obtained what they wanted, so they weighed anchor and sailed close to Crete. {27:14} But soon, a tempestuous wind called Euroclydon arose against them. {27:15} The ship was caught in the storm and couldn't head into the wind, so we let it be driven along. {27:16} Running under the shelter of a small island called Clauda, we had to work hard to secure the lifeboat. {27:17} After they had taken it on board, they used cables to undergird the ship, fearing they would run aground on the sandbars; so they lowered the sail and were driven along. {27:18} The next day, being violently tossed by the storm, they began to lighten the ship; {27:19} and on the third day, they threw the ship's tackle overboard with their own hands. {27:20} When neither sun nor stars appeared for many days, and no small storm lay upon us, all hope of being saved was finally abandoned. {27:21} After they had gone without food for a long time, Paul stood up in their midst and said, "Men, you should have listened to me and not have set sail from Crete, thus sparing yourselves this damage and loss. {27:22} Now I urge you to take courage, for there will be no loss of life among you, but only of the ship. {27:23} For this very night an angel of God, to whom I belong and whom I serve, stood by me, {27:24} and said, 'Do not be afraid, Paul; you must stand before Caesar; and indeed, God has granted you all those who sail with you.' {27:25} Therefore, take courage, men, for I believe God that it will be just as he told me. {27:26} However, we must run aground on a certain island." {27:27} On the fourteenth night, as we were driven back and forth in the Adriatic Sea, about midnight the sailors sensed they were approaching land. {27:28} They took soundings and found it to be twenty fathoms; then, when they had gone a little further, they sounded again and found it to be fifteen fathoms. {27:29} Fearing we would run aground on the rocks, they cast four anchors from the stern and prayed for daybreak. {27:30} As the sailors were trying to escape from the ship, they let down the lifeboat into the sea, pretending they were going to put out anchors from the bow, {27:31} but Paul said to the centurion and the soldiers, "Unless these men stay in the ship, you cannot be saved." {27:32} The soldiers cut the ropes of the lifeboat and let it drop away. {27:33} As day was about to dawn, Paul urged them all to take food, saying, "Today is the fourteenth day you have waited and continued without food, eating nothing. {27:34} Therefore, I urge you to take some food, for this is for your safety; not a hair will fall from the head of any of you." {27:35} When he had said this, he took bread, gave thanks to God in front of them all, broke it, and began to eat. {27:36} All were encouraged and took food themselves. {27:37} In total, there were 276 people on the ship. {27:38} After they had eaten enough, they lightened the ship by throwing the wheat into the sea. {27:39} When daylight came, they did not recognize the land, but they saw a bay with a beach, where they planned, if possible, to run the ship aground. {27:40} They cut the anchors, left them in the sea, and at the same time untied the rudder ropes; then they hoisted the mainsail to the wind and made for the shore. {27:41} But they struck a reef where two seas met; the bow stuck fast and wouldn't move, but the stern was broken by the force of the waves. {27:42} The soldiers planned to kill the prisoners to prevent any of them from swimming away and escaping. {27:43} But the centurion, wanting to save Paul, prevented them from their intention and commanded that those who could swim should jump overboard first and get to land; {27:44} and the rest were to follow, some on planks & others on parts of the ship. So it was that they all escaped safely to land.

{28:1} After they had escaped, they realized the island was called Malta. {28:2} The locals showed us great kindness; they kindled a fire and welcomed us all because of the rain and the cold. {28:3} While Paul was gathering a bundle of sticks and laying them on the fire, a viper came out because of the heat and bit his hand. {28:4} When the locals saw the venomous snake hanging from his hand, they said to each other, "This man must be a murderer; though he escaped the sea, justice won't allow him to live." {28:5} Paul shook the snake off into the fire and suffered no harm. {28:6} They expected him to swell up or suddenly fall dead, but after waiting a long time and seeing nothing unusual happen to him, they changed their minds and said he was a god. {28:7} Nearby was the estate of a man named Publius, the chief official of the island. He welcomed us and entertained us for three days. {28:8} It happened that Publius's father was sick with a fever and dysentery; Paul went in to see him, prayed, laid his hands on him, and healed him. {28:9} After this, many others on the island who had diseases came and were healed. {28:10} They honored us in many ways, and when we were ready to sail, they supplied us with all the provisions we needed. {28:11} After three months, we set sail on an Alexandrian ship that had wintered on the island, marked with the figurehead of Castor and Pollux. {28:12} We arrived at Syracuse and stayed there for three days. {28:13} From there we sailed around and reached Rhegium; after one day, a south wind blew, and we arrived at Puteoli the next day. {28:14} There we found brothers who invited us to stay with them for seven days, and so we went toward Rome. {28:15} The brothers there had heard about us and came as far as the Forum of Appius and the Three Taverns to meet us. When Paul saw them, he thanked God and took courage. {28:16} When we got to Rome, the centurion delivered the prisoners to the captain of the guard, but Paul was allowed to live by himself with a soldier to guard him. {28:17} After three days, Paul called together the leaders of the Jews. When they had assembled, he said to them, "Brothers, although I have committed no crime against our people or the customs of our ancestors, I was arrested in Jerusalem and handed over to the Romans. {28:18} They examined me and wanted to release me because they found no basis for a death sentence against me. {28:19} But when the Jews objected, I was compelled to appeal to Caesar—not that I had any charge to bring against my own people. {28:20} This is why I have asked to see you and talk with you. It is because of the hope of Israel that I am bound with this chain." {28:21} They replied, "We have not received any letters from Judea concerning you, and none of the brothers who have come here has reported or said anything bad about you. {28:22} However, we want to hear what you think, for we know that people everywhere are talking against this sect." {28:23} They arranged to meet Paul on a certain day, and they came in large numbers to the place where he was staying. He witnessed to them from morning till evening, explaining about the kingdom of God and from the Law of Moses and the Prophets, he tried to persuade them about Jesus. {28:24} Some were convinced by what he said, but others would not believe. {28:25} They disagreed among themselves and began to leave after Paul made this final statement: "The Holy Spirit spoke the truth to your ancestors through the prophet Isaiah. {28:26} He said, 'Go to this people and say, "You will be ever hearing but never understanding; you will be ever seeing but never perceiving." {28:27} For this people's heart has become calloused; they hardly hear with their ears, and they have closed their eyes. Otherwise, they might see with their eyes, hear with their ears, understand with their hearts, and turn, and I would heal them.' {28:28} Therefore I want you to know that God's salvation has been sent to the Gentiles, and they will listen." {28:29} After he said this, the Jews left, arguing vigorously among themselves. {28:30} Paul stayed there for two whole years in his own rented house and welcomed all who came to see him. {28:31} He proclaimed the kingdom of God and taught about the Lord Jesus Christ—with all boldness and without hindrance.

The Epistle of Paul to the Romans

{1:1} Paul, a servant of Jesus Christ, called to be an apostle and set apart for the gospel of God, {1:2} which He promised beforehand through His prophets in the holy scriptures, {1:3} concerning His Son Jesus Christ our Lord, who was a descendant of David according to the flesh; {1:4} and who was declared to be the Son of God with power, according to the spirit of holiness, by His resurrection from the dead. {1:5} Through Him, we have received grace and apostleship to bring about the obedience of faith among all nations for His name; {1:6} among whom you also are called by Jesus Christ. {1:7} To all in Rome who are loved by God and called to be His holy people: Grace and peace to you from God our Father and the Lord Jesus Christ. {1:8} First, I thank my God through Jesus Christ for all of you, because your faith is being reported all over the world. {1:9} God, whom I serve in my spirit in preaching the gospel of His Son, is my witness that I constantly mention you in my prayers at all times; {1:10} and I pray that now at last by God's will, the way may be opened for me to come to you. {1:11} I long to see you so that I may impart to you some spiritual gift to make you strong— {1:12} that is, that you and I may be mutually encouraged by each other's faith. {1:13} I do not want you to be unaware, brothers and sisters, that I planned many times to come to you (but have been prevented from doing so until now) in order that I might have a harvest among you, just as I have had among the other Gentiles. {1:14} I am obligated both to Greeks and non-Greeks, both to the wise and the foolish. {1:15} That is why I am so eager to preach the gospel also to you who are in Rome. {1:16} For I am not ashamed of the gospel, because it is the power of God that brings salvation to everyone who believes: first to the Jew, then to the Gentile. {1:17} For in the gospel the righteousness of God is revealed—a righteousness that is by faith from first to last, just as it is written: "The righteous will live by faith." {1:18} The wrath of God is being revealed from heaven against all the godlessness and wickedness of people who suppress the truth by their wickedness, {1:19} since what may be known about God is plain to them, because God has made it plain to them. {1:20} For since the creation of the world, God's invisible qualities—His eternal power and divine nature—have been clearly seen, being understood from what has been made, so that people are without excuse. {1:21} For although they knew God, they neither glorified Him as God nor gave thanks to Him, but their thinking became futile and their foolish hearts were darkened. {1:22} Although they claimed to be wise, they became fools {1:23} and exchanged the glory of the immortal God for images made to look like a mortal human being and birds and animals and reptiles. {1:24} Therefore God gave them over in the sinful desires of their hearts to sexual impurity for the degrading of their bodies with one another. {1:25} They exchanged the truth about God for a lie, and worshiped and served created things rather than the Creator—who is forever praised. Amen. {1:26} Because of this, God gave them over to shameful lusts. Even their women exchanged natural sexual relations for unnatural ones. {1:27} In the same way, the men also abandoned natural relations with women and were inflamed with lust for one another. Men committed shameful acts with other men and received in themselves the due penalty for their error. {1:28} Furthermore, just as they did not think it worthwhile to retain the knowledge of God, so God gave them over to a depraved mind, so that they do what ought not to be done. {1:29} They have become filled with every kind of wickedness, evil, greed, and depravity. They are full of envy, murder, strife, deceit, and malice. They are gossips, {1:30} they are slanderers, God-haters, insolent, arrogant and boastful; they invent ways of doing evil; they disobey their parents; {1:31} they have no understanding, no fidelity, no love, no mercy. {1:32} Although they know God's righteous decree that those who do such things deserve death, they not only continue to do these very things but also approve of those who practice them.

{2:1} You, therefore, have no excuse, you who pass judgment on someone else, for at whatever point you judge another, you are condemning yourself, because you who pass judgment do the same things. {2:2} Now we know that God's judgment against those who do such things is based on truth. {2:3} So when you, a mere human being, pass judgment on them and yet do the same things, do you think you will escape God's judgment? {2:4} Or do you show contempt for the riches of His kindness, forbearance, and patience, not realizing that God's kindness is intended to lead you to repentance? {2:5} But because of your stubbornness and your unrepentant heart, you are storing up wrath against yourself for the day of God's wrath, when His righteous judgment will be revealed. {2:6} God "will repay each person according to what they have done." {2:7} To those who by persistence in doing good seek glory, honor, and immortality, He will give eternal life. {2:8} But for those who are self-seeking and who reject the truth and follow evil, there will be wrath and anger. {2:9} There will be trouble and distress for every human being who does evil: first for the Jew, then for the Gentile; {2:10} but glory, honor, and peace for everyone who does good: first for the Jew, then for the Gentile. {2:11} For God does not show favoritism. {2:12} All who sin apart from the law will also perish apart from the law, and all who sin under the law will be judged by the law; {2:13} for it is not those who hear the law who are righteous in God's sight, but it is those who obey the law who will be declared righteous. {2:14} (Indeed, when Gentiles, who do not have the law, do by nature things required by the law, they are a law for themselves, even though they do not have the law. {2:15} They show that the requirements of the law are written on their hearts, their consciences also bearing witness, and their thoughts sometimes accusing them and at other times defending them.) {2:16} This will take place on the day when God judges people's secrets through Jesus Christ, as my gospel declares. {2:17} Now you, if you call yourself a Jew; if you rely on the law and boast in God; {2:18} if you know His will and approve of what is superior because you are instructed by the law; {2:19} if you are convinced that you are a guide for the blind, a light for those who are in the dark, {2:20} an instructor of the foolish, a teacher of little children, because you have in the law the embodiment of knowledge and truth— {2:21} you, then, who teach others, do you not teach yourself? You who preach against stealing, do you steal? {2:22} You who say that people should not commit adultery, do you commit adultery? You who abhor idols, do you rob temples? {2:23} You who brag about the law, do you dishonor God by breaking the law? {2:24} As it is written: "God's name is blasphemed among the Gentiles because of you." {2:25} Circumcision has value if you observe the law, but if you break the law, you have become as though you had not been circumcised. {2:26} So then, if those who are not circumcised keep the law's requirements, will they not be regarded as though they were circumcised? {2:27} The one who is not circumcised physically and yet obeys the law will condemn you who, even though you have the written code and circumcision, are a lawbreaker. {2:28} A person is not a Jew who is one only outwardly, nor is circumcision merely outward and physical. {2:29} No, a person is a Jew who is one inwardly; and circumcision is circumcision of the heart, by the Spirit, not by the written code. Such a person's praise is not from other people, but from God.

{3:1} What advantage, then, is there in being a Jew? Or what is the benefit of circumcision? {3:2} Much in every way! Chiefly, because the oracles of God were entrusted to them. {3:3} What if some were unfaithful? Will their unfaithfulness nullify God's faithfulness? {3:4} Not at all! Let God be true, and every human being a liar, as it is written: "So that you may be proved right when you speak and prevail when you judge." {3:5} But if our unrighteousness brings out God's righteousness more clearly, what shall we say? That God is unjust in bringing His wrath on us? (I am using a human argument.) {3:6} Certainly not! If that were so, how could God judge the world? {3:7} Someone might argue, "If my falsehood enhances God's truthfulness and so increases His glory, why am I still condemned as a sinner?" {3:8} Why not say, "Let us do evil that good may result"? Their condemnation is just. {3:9} What shall we conclude then? Do we have any advantage? Not at all! For we have already made the charge that Jews and Gentiles alike are all under the power of sin. {3:10} As it is written: "There is no one righteous, not even one; {3:11} there is no one who understands; there is no one who seeks God. {3:12} All have turned away, they have together become worthless; there is no one who does good, not even one." {3:13} "Their throats are open graves; their tongues practice deceit." "The poison of vipers (snakes) is on their lips." {3:14} "Their mouths are full of cursing and bitterness." {3:15} "Their feet are swift to shed blood; {3:16} ruin and misery mark their ways, {3:17} and the way of peace they do not know." {3:18} "There is no fear of God before their eyes." {3:19} Now we know that whatever the law says, it says to those under the law, so that every mouth may be silenced and the whole world held accountable to God. {3:20} Therefore, no one will be declared righteous in God's sight by the works of the law; rather, through the law we become conscious of our sin. {3:21} But now apart from the law the righteousness of God has been made known, to which the Law and the Prophets testify. {3:22} This righteousness is given through faith in Jesus Christ to all who believe. There is no difference between Jew and Gentile, {3:23} for all have sinned and fall short of the glory of God, {3:24} and all are justified freely by His grace through the redemption that came by Christ Jesus. {3:25} God presented Christ as a sacrifice of atonement (reconciliation) through the shedding of His blood—to be received by faith. He did this to demonstrate His righteousness, because in His forbearance He had left the sins committed beforehand unpunished; {3:26} He did it to demonstrate His righteousness at the present time, so as to be just and the one who justifies those who have faith in Jesus. {3:27} Where, then, is boasting? It is excluded. Because of what law? The law that requires works? No, because of the law that requires faith. {3:28} For we maintain that a person is justified by faith apart from the works of the law. {3:29} Or is God the God of Jews only? Is He not the God of Gentiles too? Yes, of Gentiles too, {3:30} since there is only one God, who will justify the circumcised by faith and the uncircumcised through that same faith. {3:31} Do we, then, nullify the law by this faith? Not at all! Rather, we uphold the law.

{4:1} What then shall we say that Abraham, our forefather according to the flesh, discovered in this matter? {4:2} If, in fact, Abraham was justified by works, he had something to boast about—but not before God. {4:3} What does Scripture say? "Abraham believed God, and it was credited to him as righteousness." {4:4} Now to the one who works, wages are not credited as a gift but as an obligation. {4:5} However, to the one who does not work but trusts God who justifies the ungodly, their faith is credited as righteousness. {4:6} David says the same thing when he speaks of the blessedness of the one to whom God credits righteousness apart from the works: {4:7} "Blessed are those whose transgressions are forgiven, whose sins are covered. {4:8} Blessed is the one whose sin the Lord will never count against them." {4:9} Is this blessedness only for the circumcised, or also for the uncircumcised? We have been saying that Abraham's faith was credited to him as righteousness. {4:10} Under what circumstances was it credited? Was it after he was circumcised, or before? It was not after, but before! {4:11} And he received the sign of circumcision, a seal of the righteousness that he had by faith while he was still uncircumcised. So then, he is the father of all who believe but have not been circumcised, in order that righteousness might be credited to them. {4:12} And he is also the father of the circumcised who not only are circumcised but who also follow in the footsteps of the faith that our father Abraham had before he was circumcised. {4:13} It was not through the law that Abraham and his offspring received the promise that he would be heir of the world, but through the righteousness that comes by faith. {4:14} For if those who depend on the law are heirs, faith means nothing and the promise is worthless, {4:15} because the law brings wrath. And where there is no law, there is no transgression. {4:16} Therefore, the promise comes by faith, so that it may be by grace and may be guaranteed to all Abraham's offspring—not only to those who are of the law but also to those who have the faith of Abraham. He is the father of us all. {4:17} As it is written: "I have made you a father of many nations." He is our father in the sight of God, in whom he believed—the God who gives life to the dead and calls into being things that were not. {4:18} Against all hope, Abraham in hope believed and so became the father of many nations, just as it had been said to him: "So shall your offspring be." {4:19} Without weakening in his faith, he faced the fact that his body was as good as dead—since he was about a hundred years old—and that Sarah's womb was also dead. {4:20} Yet he did not waver through unbelief regarding the promise of God, but was strengthened in his faith and gave glory to God, {4:21} being fully persuaded that God had power to do what He had promised. {4:22} This is why "it was credited to him as righteousness." {4:23} The words "it was credited to him" were written not for him alone, {4:24} but also for us, to whom God will credit righteousness—for us who believe in Him who raised Jesus our Lord from the dead. {4:25} He was delivered over to death for our sins and was raised to life for our justification.

{5:1} Therefore, since we have been justified by faith, we have peace with God through our Lord Jesus Christ. {5:2} Through Him, we have gained access by faith into this grace in which we now stand, and we rejoice in the hope of the glory of God. {5:3} Not only that, but we also glory in our sufferings, because we know that suffering produces perseverance; {5:4} perseverance, character; and character, hope. {5:5} And hope does not put us to shame, because God's love has been poured out into our hearts through the Holy Spirit, who has been given to us. {5:6} You see, at just the right time, when we were still powerless, Christ died for the ungodly. {5:7} Very rarely will anyone die for a righteous person, though for a good person someone might possibly dare to die. {5:8} But God demonstrates His own love for us in this: While we were still sinners, Christ died for us. {5:9} Since we have now been justified by His blood, how much more shall we be saved from God's wrath through Him! {5:10} For if, while we were God's enemies, we were reconciled to Him through the death of His Son, how much more, having been reconciled, shall we be saved through His life! {5:11} Not only is this so, but we also boast in God through our Lord Jesus Christ, through whom we have now received reconciliation. {5:12} Therefore, just as sin entered the world through one man, and death through sin, in this way death came to all people, because all sinned— {5:13} to be sure, sin was in the world before the law was given, but sin is not charged against anyone's account where there is no law. {5:14} Nevertheless, death reigned from the time of Adam to the time of Moses, even over those who did not sin by breaking a command, as did Adam, who is a pattern of the one to come. {5:15} But the gift is not like the trespass. For if the many died by the trespass of the one man, how much more did God's grace and the gift that came by the grace of the one man, Jesus Christ, overflow to the many! {5:16} Nor can the gift of God be compared with the result of one man's sin: The judgment followed one sin and brought condemnation, but the gift followed many trespasses and brought justification. {5:17} For if, by the trespass of the one man, death reigned through that one man, how much more will those who receive God's abundant provision of grace and of the gift of righteousness reign in life through the one man, Jesus Christ! {5:18} Consequently, just as one trespass resulted in condemnation for all people, so also one righteous act resulted in justification and life for all people. {5:19} For just as through the disobedience of the one man the many were made sinners, so also through the obedience of the one man the many will be made righteous. {5:20} The law was brought in so that the trespass might increase. But where sin increased, grace increased all the more, {5:21} so that, just as sin reigned in death, so also grace might reign through righteousness to bring eternal life through Jesus Christ our Lord.

{6:1} What shall we say, then? Shall we go on sinning so that grace may increase? {6:2} By no means! We are those who have died to sin; how can we live in it any longer? {6:3} Or don't you know that all of us who were baptized into Christ Jesus were baptized into His death? {6:4} We were therefore buried with Him through baptism into death in order that, just as Christ was raised from the dead through the glory of the Father, we too may live a new life. {6:5} For if we have been united with Him in a death like His, we will certainly also be united with Him in a resurrection like His. {6:6} For we know that our old self was crucified with Him so that the body ruled by sin might be done away with, that we should no longer be slaves to sin— {6:7} because anyone who has died has been set free from sin. {6:8} Now if we died with Christ, we believe that we will also live with Him. {6:9} For we know that since Christ was raised from the dead, He cannot die again; death no longer has mastery over Him {6:10} The death He died, He died to sin once for all; but the life He lives, He lives to God. {6:11} In the same way, count yourselves dead to sin but alive to God in Christ Jesus. {6:12} Therefore do not let sin reign in your mortal body so that you obey its evil desires. {6:13} Do not offer any part of yourself to sin as an instrument of wickedness, but rather offer yourselves to God as those who have been brought from death to life; and offer every part of yourself to Him as an instrument of righteousness. {6:14} For sin shall no longer be your master, because you are not under the law, but under grace. {6:15} What then? Shall we sin because we are not under the law but under grace? By no means! {6:16} Don't you know that when you offer yourselves to someone as obedient slaves, you are slaves of the one you obey—whether you are slaves to sin, which leads to death, or to obedience, which leads to righteousness? {6:17} But thanks be to God that, though you used to be slaves to sin, you have come to obey from your heart the pattern of teaching that has now claimed your allegiance. {6:18} You have been set free from sin and have become slaves to righteousness. {6:19} I am using an example from everyday life because of your human limitations. Just as you used to offer yourselves as slaves to impurity and to ever-increasing wickedness, so now offer yourselves as slaves to righteousness leading to holiness. {6:20} When you were slaves to sin, you were free from the control of righteousness. {6:21} What benefit did you reap at that time from the things you are now ashamed of? Those things result in death! {6:22} But now that you have been set free from sin and have become slaves of God, the benefit you reap leads to holiness, and the result is eternal life. {6:23} For the wages of sin is death, but the gift of God is eternal life in Christ Jesus our Lord.

{7:1} Don't you know, brothers and sisters (for I am speaking to those who know the law), that the law has authority over someone as long as that person lives? {7:2} For example, a married woman is bound by law to her husband as long as he is alive; but if her husband dies, she is released from the law that binds her to him. {7:3} So then, if she marries another man while her husband is still alive, she is called an adulteress; but if her husband dies, she is free from that law and is not an adulteress even if she marries another man. {7:4} So, my brothers and sisters, you also died to the law through the body of Christ, that you might belong to another, to Him who was raised from the dead, in order that we might bear fruit for God. {7:5} For when we were in the realm of the flesh, the sinful passions aroused by the law were at work in us, so that we bore fruit for death. {7:6} But now, by dying to what once bound us, we have been released from the law so that we serve in the new way of the Spirit, and not in the old way of the written code. {7:7} What shall we say, then? Is the law sinful? Certainly not! I would not have known what sin was had it not been for the law; for I would not have known what coveting really was if the law had not said, "You shall not covet." {7:8} But sin, seizing the opportunity afforded by the commandment, produced in me every kind of coveting. For apart from the law, sin was dead. {7:9} Once I was alive apart from the law; but when the commandment came, sin sprang to life and I died. {7:10} I found that the very commandment that was intended to bring life actually brought death. {7:11} For sin, seizing the opportunity afforded by the commandment, deceived me, and through the commandment put me to death. {7:12} So the law is holy, and the commandment is holy, righteous, and good. {7:13} Did that which is good, then, become death to me? By no means! Nevertheless, in order that sin might be recognized as sin, it used what is good to bring about my death, so that through the commandment sin might become utterly sinful. {7:14} We know that the law is spiritual; but I am unspiritual, sold as a slave to sin. {7:15} I do not understand what I do. For what I want to do I do not do, but what I hate I do. {7:16} And if I do what I do not want to do, I agree that the law is good. {7:17} As it is, it is no longer I myself who do it, but it is sin living in me. {7:18} For I know that good itself does not dwell in me, that is, in my sinful nature. For I have the desire to do what is good, but I cannot carry it out. {7:19} For I do not do the good I want to do, but the evil I do not want to do—this I keep on doing. {7:20} Now if I do what I do not want to do, it is no longer I who do it, but it is sin living in me that does it. {7:21} So I find this law at work: although I want to do good, evil is right there with me. {7:22} For in my inner being I delight in God's law; {7:23} but I see another law at work in me, waging war against the law of my mind and making me a prisoner of the law of sin at work within me. {7:24} What a wretched man I am! Who will rescue me from this body that is subject to death? {7:25} Thanks be to God, who delivers me through Jesus Christ our Lord! So then, I myself in my mind am a slave to God's law, but in my sinful nature a slave to the law of sin.

{8:1} Therefore, there is now no condemnation for those who are in Christ Jesus, because through Christ Jesus the law of the Spirit who gives life has set you free from the law of sin and death. {8:2} For what the law was powerless to do because it was weakened by the flesh, God did by sending His own Son in the likeness of sinful flesh to be a sin offering. And so He condemned sin in the flesh, {8:3} in order that the righteous requirement of the law might be fully met in us, who do not live according to the flesh but according to the Spirit. {8:4} Those who live according to the flesh have their minds set on what the flesh desires; but those who live in accordance with the Spirit have their minds set on what the Spirit desires. {8:5} The mind governed by the flesh is death, but the mind governed by the Spirit is life and peace. {8:6} The mind governed by the flesh is hostile to God; it does not submit to God's law, nor can it do so. {8:7} Those who are in the realm of the flesh cannot please God. {8:8} You, however, are not in the realm of the flesh but are in the realm of the Spirit, if indeed the Spirit of God lives in you. And if anyone does not have the Spirit of Christ, they do not belong to Christ. {8:9} But if Christ is in you, then even though your body is subject to death because of sin, the Spirit gives life because of righteousness. {8:10} And if the Spirit of Him who raised Jesus from the dead is living in you, He who raised Christ from the dead will also give life to your mortal bodies because of His Spirit who lives in you. {8:11} Therefore, brothers and sisters, we have an obligation—but it is not to the flesh, to live according to it. {8:12} For if you live according to the flesh, you will die; but if by the Spirit you put to death the misdeeds of the body, you will live. {8:13} For those who are led by the Spirit of God are the children of God. {8:14} The Spirit you received does not make you slaves, so that you live in fear again; rather, the Spirit you received brought about your adoption to sonship. And by Him we cry, "Abba, Father." {8:15} The Spirit Himself testifies with our spirit that we are God's children. {8:16} Now if we are children, then we are heirs—heirs of God and co-heirs with Christ, if indeed we share in His sufferings in order that we may also share in His glory. {8:17} I consider that our present sufferings are not worth comparing with the glory that will be revealed in us. {8:18} For the creation waits in eager expectation for the children of God to be revealed. {8:19} For the creation was subjected to frustration, not by its own choice but by the will of the one who subjected it, in hope {8:20} that the creation itself will be liberated from its bondage to decay and brought into the freedom and glory of the children of God. {8:21} We know that the whole creation has been groaning as in the pains of childbirth right up to the present time. {8:22} Not only so, but we ourselves, who have the firstfruits of the Spirit, groan inwardly as we wait eagerly for our adoption to sonship, the redemption of our bodies. {8:23} For in this hope we were saved, but hope that is seen is no hope at all. Who hopes for what they already have? {8:24} But if we hope for what we do not yet have, we wait for it patiently. {8:25} In the same way, the Spirit helps us in our weakness. We do not know what we ought to pray for, but the Spirit Himself intercedes for us through wordless groans. {8:26} And He who searches our hearts knows the mind of the Spirit, because the Spirit intercedes for God's people in accordance with the will of God. {8:27} And we know that in all things God works for the good of those who love Him, who have been called according to His purpose. {8:28} For those God foreknew, He also predestined to be conformed to the image of His Son, that He might be the firstborn among many brothers and sisters. {8:29} And those He predestined, He also called; those He called, He also justified; those He justified, He also glorified. {8:30} What, then, shall we say in response to these things? If God is for us, who can be against us? {8:31} He who did not spare His own Son, but gave Him up for us all—how will He not also, along with Him, graciously give us all things? {8:32} Who will bring any charge against those whom God has chosen? It is God who justifies. {8:33} Who then is the one who condemns? No one. Christ Jesus who died—more than that, who was raised to life—is at the right hand of God and is also interceding for us. {8:34} Who shall separate us from the love of Christ? Shall trouble or hardship or persecution or famine or nakedness or danger or sword? {8:35} As it is written: "For Your sake we face death all day long; we are considered as sheep to be slaughtered." {8:36} No, in all these things we are more than conquerors through Him who loved us. {8:37} For I am convinced that neither death nor life, neither angels nor demons, neither the present nor the future, nor any powers, {8:38} neither height nor depth, nor anything else in all creation, will be able to separate us from the love of God that is in Christ Jesus our Lord.

{9:1} I am telling the truth in Christ; I am not lying, and my conscience confirms it through the Holy Spirit. {9:2} I have deep sorrow and unending anguish in my heart. {9:3} For I could wish that I myself were cursed and cut off from Christ for the sake of my people, those of my own race, {9:4} the Israelites. To them belong the adoption as children, the glory, the covenants, the giving of the law, the worship, and the promises; {9:5} theirs are the patriarchs, and from them is traced the human ancestry of the Messiah, who is God over all, forever praised! Amen. {9:6} It is not as though God's word had failed. For not all who are descended from Israel are Israel. {9:7} Nor because they are his descendants are they all Abraham's children. On the contrary, "It is through Isaac that your offspring will be reckoned." {9:8} In other words, it is not the children by physical descent who are God's children, but it is the children of the promise who are regarded as Abraham's offspring. {9:9} For this was how the promise was stated: "At the appointed time I will return, and Sarah will have a son." {9:10} Not only that, but Rebekah's children were conceived at the same time by our father Isaac. {9:11} Yet, before the twins were born or had done anything good or bad—in order that God's purpose in election might stand: {9:12} not by works but by Him who calls—she was told, "The older will serve the younger." {9:13} Just as it is written: "Jacob I loved, but Esau I hated." {9:14} What then shall we say? Is God unjust? Not at all! {9:15} For He says to Moses, "I will have mercy on whom I have mercy, and I will have compassion on whom I have compassion." {9:16} It does not, therefore, depend on human desire or effort, but on God's mercy. {9:17} For Scripture says to Pharaoh: "I raised you up for this very purpose, that I might display my power in you and that my name might be proclaimed in all the earth." {9:18} Therefore God has mercy on whom He wants to have mercy, and He hardens whom He wants to harden. {9:19} One of you will say to me: "Then why does God still blame us? For who is able to resist His will?" {9:20} But who are you, a human being, to talk back to God? "Shall what is formed say to the one who formed it, 'Why did you make me like this?'" {9:21} Does not the potter have the right to make out of the same lump of clay some pottery for special purposes and some for common use? {9:22} What if God, although choosing to show His wrath and make His power known, bore with great patience the objects of His wrath—prepared for destruction? {9:23} What if He did this to make the riches of His glory known to the objects of His mercy, whom He prepared in advance for glory— {9:24} even us, whom He also called, not only from the Jews but also from the Gentiles? {9:25} As He says in Hosea: "I will call them 'my people' who are not my people; and I will call her 'my loved one' who is not my loved one," {9:26} And, "In the very place where it was said to them, 'You are not my people,' there they will be called 'children of the living God.'" {9:27} Isaiah cries out concerning Israel: "Though the number of the Israelites be like the sand by the sea, only the remnant will be saved. {9:28} For the Lord will carry out His sentence on earth with speed and finality." {9:29} It is just as Isaiah said previously: "Unless the Lord Almighty had left us descendants, we would have become like Sodom, we would have been like Gomorrah." {9:30} What then shall we say? That the Gentiles, who did not pursue righteousness, have obtained it, a righteousness that is by faith; {9:31} but the people of Israel, who pursued the law as the way of righteousness, have not attained their goal. {9:32} Why not? Because they pursued it not by faith but as if it were by works. They stumbled over the stumbling stone; {9:33} as it is written: "See, I lay in Zion a stone that causes people to stumble and a rock that makes them fall, and the one who believes in Him will never be put to shame."

{10:1} Brothers and sisters, my heart's desire and prayer to God for the Israelites is that they may be saved. {10:2} For I can testify about them that they are zealous for God, but their zeal is not based on knowledge. {10:3} Since they did not know the righteousness of God and sought to establish their own, they did not submit to God's righteousness. {10:4} Christ is the culmination of the law so that there may be righteousness for everyone who believes. {10:5} Moses writes this about the righteousness that is by the law: "The person who does these things will live by them." {10:6} But the righteousness that is by faith says: "Do not say in your heart, 'Who will ascend into heaven?'" (that is, to bring Christ down) {10:7} "or 'Who will descend into the deep?'" (that is, to bring Christ up from the dead). {10:8} But what does it say? "The word is near you; it is in your mouth and in your heart," that is, the message concerning faith that we proclaim: {10:9} If you declare with your mouth, "Jesus is Lord," and believe in your heart that God raised Him from the dead, you will be saved. {10:10} For it is with your heart that you believe and are justified, and it is with your mouth that you profess your faith and are saved. {10:11} As Scripture says, "Anyone who believes in Him will never be put to shame." {10:12} For there is no difference between Jew and Gentile; the same Lord is Lord of all and richly blesses all who call on Him, {10:13} for "Everyone who calls on the name of the Lord will be saved." {10:14} How, then, can they call on the one they have not believed in? And how can they believe in the one of whom they have not heard? And how can they hear without someone preaching to them? {10:15} And how can anyone preach unless they are sent? As it is written: "How beautiful are the feet of those who bring good news!" {10:16} But not all the Israelites accepted the good news. For Isaiah says, "Lord, who has believed our message?" {10:17} Consequently, faith comes from hearing the message, and the message is heard through the word about Christ. {10:18} But I ask: Did they not hear? Of course they did: "Their voice has gone out into all the earth, their words to the ends of the world." {10:19} Again I ask: Did Israel not understand? First, Moses says, "I will make you envious by those who are not a nation; I will make you angry by a nation that has no understanding." {10:20} And Isaiah boldly says, "I was found by those who did not seek me; I revealed myself to those who did not ask for me." {10:21} But concerning Israel, he says, "All day long I have held out my hands to a disobedient and obstinate people."

{11:1} I ask, then, has God rejected His people? Not at all! I am an Israelite, a descendant of Abraham from the tribe of Benjamin. {11:2} God has not rejected His people whom He foreknew. Don't you know what the Scripture says about Elijah? How he appealed to God against Israel, saying, {11:3} "Lord, they have killed Your prophets and torn down Your altars; I am the only one left, and they are trying to kill me!" {11:4} And what was God's answer to him? "I have reserved for myself seven thousand who have not bowed the knee to Baal." {11:5} So too, at the present time there is a remnant chosen by grace. {11:6} And if by grace, then it cannot be based on works; if it were, grace would no longer be grace. But if it is by works, it is no longer grace; otherwise, work would no longer be work. {11:7} What then? Israel failed to obtain what it was seeking, but the elect did. The others were hardened, {11:8} as it is written: "God gave them a spirit of stupor, eyes so that they could not see and ears so that they could not hear, to this very day." {11:9} And David says, "May their table become a snare and a trap, a stumbling block and a retribution for them. {11:10} May their eyes be darkened so they cannot see, and their backs be bent forever." {11:11} Again I ask: Did they stumble so as to fall beyond recovery? Not at all! Rather, because of their transgression, salvation has come to the Gentiles to make Israel envious. {11:12} But if their transgression means riches for the world, and their loss means riches for the Gentiles, how much greater riches will their fullness bring! {11:13} I am talking to you Gentiles. Inasmuch as I am the apostle to the Gentiles, I take pride in my ministry {11:14} in the hope that I may somehow arouse my own people to envy and save some of them. {11:15} For if their rejection brought reconciliation to the world, what will their acceptance be but life from the dead? {11:16} If the part of the dough offered as firstfruits is holy, then the whole batch is holy; if the root is holy, so are the branches. {11:17} If some of the branches have been broken off, and you, though a wild olive shoot, have been grafted in among the others and now share in the nourishing sap from the olive root, {11:18} do not consider yourself to be superior to those branches. If you do, consider this: You do not support the root, but the root supports you. {11:19} You will say then, "Branches were broken off so that I could be grafted in." {11:20} Granted. But they were broken off because of unbelief, and you stand by faith. Do not be arrogant, but tremble. {11:21} For if God did not spare the natural branches, He will not spare you either. {11:22} Consider, therefore, the kindness and sternness of God: sternness to those who fell, but kindness to you, provided that you continue in His kindness. Otherwise, you also will be cut off. {11:23} And if they do not persist in unbelief, they will be grafted in, for God is able to graft them in again. {11:24} After all, if you were cut out of an olive tree that is wild by nature, and contrary to nature were grafted into a cultivated olive tree, how much more readily will these, the natural branches, be grafted into their own olive tree! {11:25} I do not want you to be ignorant of this mystery, brothers and sisters, so that you may not be conceited: Israel has experienced a hardening in part until the full number of the Gentiles has come in, {11:26} and in this way all Israel will be saved, as it is written: "The Deliverer will come from Zion; He will turn godlessness away from Jacob. {11:27} And this is my covenant with them when I take away their sins." {11:28} As far as the gospel is concerned, they are enemies for your sake; but as far as election is concerned, they are loved on account of the patriarchs, {11:29} for God's gifts and His call are irrevocable. {11:30} Just as you who were at one time disobedient to God have now received mercy as a result of their disobedience, {11:31} so they too have now become disobedient in order that they too may now receive mercy as a result of God's mercy to you. {11:32} For God has bound everyone over to disobedience so that He may have mercy on them all. {11:33} Oh, the depth of the riches of the wisdom and knowledge of God! How unsearchable His judgments, and His paths beyond tracing out! {11:34} Who has known the mind of the Lord? Or who has been His counselor? {11:35} Who has ever given to God, that God should repay them? {11:36} For from Him and through Him and for Him are all things. To Him be the glory forever! Amen.

{12:1} Therefore, I urge you, brothers and sisters, in view of God's mercy, to offer your bodies as a living sacrifice, holy and pleasing to God—this is your true and proper worship. {12:2} Do not conform to the pattern of this world, but be transformed by the renewing of your mind. Then you will be able to test and approve what God's will is—His good, pleasing and perfect will. {12:3} For by the grace given me, I say to every one of you: Do not think of yourself more highly than you ought, but rather think of yourself with sober judgment, in accordance with the faith God has distributed to each of you. {12:4} For just as each of us has one body with many members, and these members do not all have the same function, {12:5} so in Christ we, though many, form one body, and each member belongs to all the others. {12:6} We have different gifts, according to the grace given to each of us. If your gift is prophesying, then prophesy in accordance with your faith; {12:7} if it is serving, then serve; if it is teaching, then teach; {12:8} if it is to encourage, then give encouragement; if it is giving, then give generously; if it is to lead, do it diligently; if it is to show mercy, do it cheerfully. {12:9} Love must be sincere. Hate what is evil; cling to what is good. {12:10} Be devoted to one another in love. Honor one another above yourselves. {12:11} Never be lacking in zeal, but keep your spiritual fervor, serving the Lord. {12:12} Be joyful in hope, patient in affliction, faithful in prayer. {12:13} Share with the Lord's people who are in need. Practice hospitality. {12:14} Bless those who persecute you; bless and do not curse. {12:15} Rejoice with those who rejoice; mourn with those who mourn. {12:16} Live in harmony with one another. Do not be proud, but be willing to associate with people of low position. Do not be conceited. {12:17} Do not repay anyone evil for evil. Be careful to do what is right in the eyes of everyone. {12:18} If it is possible, as far as it depends on you, live at peace with everyone. {12:19} Do not take revenge, my dear friends, but leave room for God's wrath, for it is written: "It is mine to avenge; I will repay," says the Lord. {12:20} On the contrary: "If your enemy is hungry, feed him; if he is thirsty, give him something to drink. In doing this, you will heap burning coals on his head." {12:21} Do not be overcome by evil, but overcome evil with good.

{13:1} Let everyone be subject to the governing authorities, for there is no authority except that which God has established. The authorities that exist have been established by God. {13:2} Consequently, whoever rebels against the authority is rebelling against what God has instituted, and those who do so will bring judgment on themselves. {13:3} For rulers hold no terror for those who do right, but for those who do wrong. Do you want to be free from fear of the one in authority? Then do what is right, and you will be commended. {13:4} For the one in authority is God's servant for your good. But if you do wrong, be afraid, for rulers do not bear the sword for no reason. They are God's servants, agents of wrath to bring punishment on the wrongdoer. {13:5} Therefore, it is necessary to submit to the authorities, not only because of possible punishment but also as a matter of conscience. {13:6} This is also why you pay taxes, for the authorities are God's servants, who give their full time to governing. {13:7} Give to everyone what you owe them: If you owe taxes, pay taxes; if revenue, then revenue; if respect, then respect; if honor, then honor. {13:8} Let no debt remain outstanding, except the continuing debt to love one another, for whoever loves others has fulfilled the law. {13:9} The commandments, "You shall not commit adultery," "You shall not murder," "You shall not steal," "You shall not covet," and whatever other command there may be, are summed up in this one command: "Love your neighbor as yourself." {13:10} Love does no harm to a neighbor. Therefore, love is the fulfillment of the law. {13:11} And do this, understanding the present time: The hour has already come for you to wake up from your slumber, because our salvation is nearer now than when we first believed. {13:12} The night is nearly over; the day is almost here. So let us put aside the deeds of darkness and put on the armor of light. {13:13} Let us behave decently, as in the daytime, not in carousing and drunkenness, not in sexual immorality and debauchery, not in dissension and jealousy. {13:14} Rather, clothe yourselves with the Lord Jesus Christ, and do not think about how to gratify the desires of the flesh.

{14:1} Accept the one whose faith is weak, without quarreling over disputable matters. {14:2} One person's faith allows them to eat anything, but another, whose faith is weak, eats only vegetables. {14:3} The one who eats everything must not treat with contempt the one who does not, and the one who does not eat everything must not judge the one who does, for God has accepted them. {14:4} Who are you to judge someone else's servant? To their own master, servants stand or fall. And they will stand, for the Lord is able to make them stand. {14:5} One person considers one day more sacred than another; another considers every day alike. Each of them should be fully convinced in their own mind. {14:6} Whoever regards one day as special does so to the Lord. Whoever eats meat does so to the Lord, for they give thanks to God; and whoever abstains does so to the Lord and gives thanks to God. {14:7} For none of us lives for ourselves alone, and none of us dies for ourselves alone. {14:8} If we live, we live for the Lord; and if we die, we die for the Lord. So, whether we live or die, we belong to the Lord. {14:9} For this very reason, Christ died and returned to life so that He might be the Lord of both the dead and the living. {14:10} You, then, why do you judge your brother or sister? Or why do you treat them with contempt? For we will all stand before God's judgment seat. {14:11} It is written: "As surely as I live, says the Lord, every knee will bow before me; every tongue will acknowledge God." {14:12} So then, each of us will give an account of ourselves to God. {14:13} Therefore let us stop passing judgment on one another. Instead, make up your mind not to put any stumbling block or obstacle in the way of a brother or sister. {14:14} I am convinced, being fully persuaded in the Lord Jesus, that nothing is unclean in itself. But if anyone regards something as unclean, then for that person it is unclean. {14:15} If your brother or sister is distressed because of what you eat, you are no longer acting in love. Do not by your eating destroy someone for whom Christ died. {14:16} Therefore do not let what you know is good be spoken of as evil. {14:17} For the kingdom of God is not a matter of eating and drinking, but of righteousness, peace and joy in the Holy Spirit, {14:18} because anyone who serves Christ in this way is pleasing to God and receives human approval. {14:19} Let us therefore make every effort to do what leads to peace and to mutual edification. {14:20} Do not destroy the work of God for the sake of food. All food is clean, but it is wrong for a person to eat anything that causes someone else to stumble. {14:21} It is better not to eat meat or drink wine or to do anything else that will cause your brother or sister to fall. {14:22} So whatever you believe about these things, keep between yourself and God. Blessed is the one who does not condemn himself by what he approves. {14:23} But whoever has doubts is condemned if they eat, because their eating is not from faith; and everything that does not come from faith is sin.

{15:1} We who are strong ought to bear with the failings of the weak and not to please ourselves. {15:2} Each of us should please our neighbors for their good, to build them up. {15:3} For even Christ did not please Himself; as it is written, "The insults of those who insult you have fallen on me." {15:4} For everything that was written in the past was written to teach us, so that through the endurance taught in the Scriptures and the encouragement they provide, we might have hope. {15:5} May the God who gives endurance and encouragement give you the same attitude of mind toward each other that Christ Jesus had, {15:6} so that with one mind and one voice you may glorify the God and Father of our Lord Jesus Christ. {15:7} Accept one another, then, just as Christ accepted you, in order to bring praise to God. {15:8} For I tell you that Christ has become a servant of the Jews on behalf of God's truth, so that the promises made to the patriarchs might be confirmed {15:9} and, moreover, that the Gentiles might glorify God for His mercy. As it is written: "Therefore I will praise you among the Gentiles; I will sing the praises of your name." {15:10} Again, it says, "Rejoice, you Gentiles, with His people." {15:11} And again, "Praise the Lord, all you Gentiles; let all the peoples extol Him." {15:12} And again, Isaiah says, "The root of Jesse will spring up, one who will arise to rule over the nations; in Him the Gentiles will hope." {15:13} May the God of hope fill you with all joy and peace as you trust in Him, so that you may overflow with hope by the power of the Holy Spirit. {15:14} I myself am convinced, my brothers and sisters, that you yourselves are full of goodness, filled with knowledge and competent to instruct one another. {15:15} Yet I have written you quite boldly on some points to remind you of them again, because of the grace God gave me {15:16} to be a minister of Christ Jesus to the Gentiles. He gave me the priestly duty of proclaiming the gospel of God, so that the Gentiles might become an offering acceptable to God, sanctified by the Holy Spirit. {15:17} Therefore I glory in Christ Jesus in my service to God. {15:18} I will not venture to speak of anything except what Christ has accomplished through me in leading the Gentiles to obey God by what I have said and done— {15:19} by the power of signs and wonders, through the power of the Spirit of God. So from Jerusalem all the way around to Illyricum, I have fully proclaimed the gospel of Christ. {15:20} It has always been my ambition to preach the gospel where Christ was not known, so that I would not be building on someone else's foundation. {15:21} Rather, as it is written: "Those who were not told about Him will see, and those who have not heard will understand." {15:22} This is why I have often been hindered from coming to you. {15:23} But now that there is no more place for me to work in these regions, and since I have been longing for many years to see you, {15:24} I plan to do so when I go to Spain. I hope to see you while passing through and to have you assist me on my journey there, after I have enjoyed your company for a while. {15:25} Now, however, I am on my way to Jerusalem in the service of the Lord's people there. {15:26} For Macedonia and Achaia were pleased to make a contribution for the poor among the Lord's people in Jerusalem. {15:27} They were pleased to do it, and indeed they owe it to them. For if the Gentiles have shared in the Jews' spiritual blessings, they owe it to the Jews to share with them their material blessings. {15:28} So after I have completed this task and have made sure that they have received this contribution, I will go to Spain and visit you on the way. {15:29} I know that when I come to you, I will come in the full measure of the blessing of Christ. {15:30} I urge you, brothers and sisters, by our Lord Jesus Christ and by the love of the Spirit, to join me in my struggle by praying to God for me. {15:31} Pray that I may be kept safe from the unbelievers in Judea and that the contribution I take to Jerusalem may be acceptable to the Lord's people there, {15:32} so that I may come to you with joy, by God's will, and in your company be refreshed. {15:33} The God of peace be with you all. Amen.

{16:1} I commend to you our sister Phoebe, a deacon of the church in Cenchreae. {16:2} I ask you to receive her in the Lord in a way worthy of His people and to give her any help she may need from you, for she has been the benefactor of many people, including me. {16:3} Greet Priscilla and Aquila, my co-workers in Christ Jesus. {16:4} They risked their lives for me. Not only I but all the churches of the Gentiles are grateful to them. {16:5} Greet also the church that meets at their house. Greet my dear friend Epaenetus, who was the first convert to Christ in the province of Achaia. {16:6} Greet Mary, who worked very hard for you. {16:7} Greet Andronicus and Junia, my fellow Jews who have been in prison with me. They are outstanding among the apostles, and they were in Christ before I was. {16:8} Greet Ampliatus, my dear friend in the Lord. {16:9} Greet Urbanus, our co-worker in Christ, and my dear friend Stachys. {16:10} Greet Apelles, whose fidelity to Christ has stood the test. Greet those who belong to the household of Aristobulus. {16:11} Greet Herodion, my fellow Jew. Greet those in the household of Narcissus who are in the Lord. {16:12} Greet Tryphena and Tryphosa, those women who work hard in the Lord. Greet my dear friend Persis, another woman who has worked very hard in the Lord. {16:13} Greet Rufus, chosen in the Lord, and his mother, who has been a mother to me too. {16:14} Greet Asyncritus, Phlegon, Hermas, Patrobas, Hermes, and the other brothers and sisters with them. {16:15} Greet Philologus, Julia, Nereus, and his sister, and Olympas and all the Lord's people who are with them. {16:16} Greet one another with a holy kiss. All the churches of Christ send greetings. {16:17} I urge you, brothers and sisters, to watch out for those who cause divisions and put obstacles in your way that are contrary to the teaching you have learned. Keep away from them. {16:18} For such people are not serving our Lord Christ but their own appetites. By smooth talk and flattery, they deceive the minds of naive people. {16:19} Everyone has heard about your obedience, so I rejoice because of you; but I want you to be wise about what is good, and innocent about what is evil. {16:20} The God of peace will soon crush Satan under your feet. The grace of our Lord Jesus be with you. {16:21} Timothy, my co-worker, sends his greetings to you, as do Lucius, Jason, and Sosipater, my fellow Jews. {16:22} I, Tertius, who wrote down this letter, greet you in the Lord. {16:23} Gaius, whose hospitality I and the whole church here enjoy, sends you his greetings. Erastus, who is the city's director of public works, and our brother Quartus send you their greetings. {16:24} The grace of our Lord Jesus Christ be with you all. Amen. {16:25} Now to Him who is able to establish you in accordance with my gospel, the message I proclaim about Jesus Christ, in keeping with the revelation of the mystery hidden for long ages past, {16:26} but now revealed and made known through the prophetic writings by the command of the eternal God, so that all the Gentiles might come to the obedience that comes from faith— {16:27} to the only wise God be glory forever through Jesus Christ! Amen.

The First Epistle of Paul to the Corinthians

{1:1} Paul, called to be an apostle of Jesus Christ by the will of God, and our brother Sosthenes, {1:2} to the church of God in Corinth, to those who are sanctified in Christ Jesus and called to be holy, along with everyone everywhere who calls on the name of our Lord Jesus Christ, their Lord and ours: {1:3} Grace and peace to you from God our Father and the Lord Jesus Christ. {1:4} I always thank my God for you because of His grace given you in Christ Jesus. {1:5} For in Him, you have been enriched in every way—in all your speaking and in all your knowledge— {1:6} because our testimony about Christ was confirmed in you. {1:7} Therefore, you do not lack any spiritual gift as you eagerly wait for our Lord Jesus Christ to be revealed. {1:8} He will also keep you firm to the end so that you will be blameless on the day of our Lord Jesus Christ. {1:9} God is faithful, who has called you into fellowship with His Son, Jesus Christ our Lord. {1:10} I appeal to you, brothers and sisters, in the name of our Lord Jesus Christ, that all of you agree with one another in what you say and that there be no divisions among you, but that you be perfectly united in mind and thought. {1:11} My brothers and sisters, some from Chloe's household have informed me that there are quarrels among you. {1:12} What I mean is this: One of you says, "I follow Paul"; another, "I follow Apollos"; another, "I follow Cephas"; still another, "I follow Christ." {1:13} Is Christ divided? Was Paul crucified for you? Were you baptized in the name of Paul? {1:14} I thank God that I baptized none of you except Crispus and Gaius, {1:15} so no one can say that you were baptized in my name. {1:16} (Yes, I also baptized the household of Stephanas; beyond that, I don't remember if I baptized anyone else.) {1:17} For Christ did not send me to baptize, but to preach the gospel—not with wisdom and eloquence, so that the cross of Christ will not be emptied of its power. {1:18} For the message of the cross is foolishness to those who are perishing, but to us who are being saved it is the power of God. {1:19} For it is written: "I will destroy the wisdom of the wise; the intelligence of the intelligent I will frustrate." {1:20} Where is the wise person? Where is the teacher of the law? Where is the philosopher of this age? Has not God made foolish the wisdom of the world? {1:21} For since in the wisdom of God the world through its wisdom did not know Him, God was pleased through the foolishness of what was preached to save those who believe. {1:22} Jews demand signs and Greeks look for wisdom; {1:23} but we preach Christ crucified: a stumbling block to Jews and foolishness to Gentiles, {1:24} but to those whom God has called, both Jews and Greeks, Christ is the power of God and the wisdom of God. {1:25} For the foolishness of God is wiser than human wisdom, and the weakness of God is stronger than human strength. {1:26} Brothers and sisters, think of what you were when you were called. Not many of you were wise by human standards; not many were influential; not many were of noble birth. {1:27} But God chose the foolish things of the world to shame the wise; God chose the weak things of the world to shame the strong. {1:28} God chose the lowly things of this world and the despised things—and the things that are not—to nullify the things that are, {1:29} so that no one may boast before Him. {1:30} It is because of Him that you are in Christ Jesus, who has become for us wisdom from God—that is, our righteousness, holiness, and redemption. {1:31} Therefore, as it is written: "Let the one who boasts boast in the Lord."

{2:1} And so it was with me, brothers and sisters. When I came to you, I did not come with eloquence or human wisdom as I proclaimed to you the testimony about God. {2:2} For I resolved to know nothing while I was with you except Jesus Christ and Him crucified. {2:3} I came to you in weakness, with great fear and trembling. {2:4} My message and my preaching were not with wise and persuasive words, but with a demonstration of the Spirit's power, {2:5} so that your faith might not rest on human wisdom, but on God's power. {2:6} We do, however, speak a message of wisdom among the mature, but not the wisdom of this age or of the rulers of this age, who are coming to nothing. {2:7} No, we declare God's wisdom, a mystery that has been hidden and that God destined for our glory before time began. {2:8} None of the rulers of this age understood it, for if they had, they would not have crucified the Lord of glory. {2:9} However, as it is written: "What no eye has seen, what no ear has heard, and what no human mind has conceived—the things God has prepared for those who love Him." {2:10} These are the things God has revealed to us by His Spirit. The Spirit searches all things, even the deep things of God. {2:11} For who knows a person's thoughts except their own spirit within them? In the same way, no one knows the thoughts of God except the Spirit of God. {2:12} What we have received is not the spirit of the world, but the Spirit who is from God, so that we may understand what God has freely given us. {2:13} This is what we speak, not in words taught us by human wisdom but in words taught by the Spirit, explaining spiritual realities with Spirit-taught words. {2:14} The person without the Spirit does not accept the things that come from the Spirit of God but considers them foolishness, and cannot understand them because they are discerned only through the Spirit. {2:15} The person with the Spirit makes judgments about all things, but such a person is not subject to merely human judgments. {2:16} For, "Who has known the mind of the Lord so as to instruct Him?" But we have the mind of Christ.

{3:1} Brothers and sisters, I could not address you as spiritual people but as worldly—mere infants in Christ. {3:2} I gave you milk, not solid food, for you were not yet ready for it. Indeed, you are still not ready. {3:3} You are still worldly. For since there is jealousy and quarreling among you, are you not worldly? Are you not acting like mere humans? {3:4} For when one says, "I follow Paul," and another, "I follow Apollos," are you not mere humans? {3:5} What, after all, is Apollos? And what is Paul? Only servants, through whom you came to believe—as the Lord has assigned to each his task. {3:6} I planted the seed, Apollos watered it, but God has been making it grow. {3:7} So neither the one who plants nor the one who waters is anything, but only God, who makes things grow. {3:8} The one who plants and the one who waters have one purpose, and they will each be rewarded according to their own labor. {3:9} For we are co-workers in God's service; you are God's field, God's building. {3:10} By the grace God has given me, I laid a foundation as a wise builder, and someone else is building on it. But each one should build with care. {3:11} For no one can lay any foundation other than the one already laid, which is Jesus Christ. {3:12} If anyone builds on this foundation using gold, silver, costly stones, wood, hay, or straw, {3:13} their work will be shown for what it is, because the Day will bring it to light. It will be revealed with fire, and the fire will test the quality of each person's work. {3:14} If what has been built survives, the builder will receive a reward. {3:15} If it is burned up, the builder will suffer loss but yet will be saved—even though only as one escaping through the flames. {3:16} Don't you know that you yourselves are God's temple and that God's Spirit dwells in your midst? {3:17} If anyone destroys God's temple, God will destroy that person; for God's temple is sacred, and you together are that temple. {3:18} Do not deceive yourselves. If any of you think you are wise by the standards of this age, you should become "fools" so that you may become wise. {3:19} For the wisdom of this world is foolishness in God's sight. As it is written: "He catches the wise in their craftiness"; {3:20} and again, "The Lord knows that the thoughts of the wise are futile." {3:21} So then, no more boasting about human leaders! All things are yours, {3:22} whether Paul or Apollos or Cephas or the world or life or death or the present or the future—all are yours, {3:23} and you are of Christ, and Christ is of God.

{4:1} This, then, is how you ought to regard us: as servants of Christ and as those entrusted with the mysteries God has revealed. {4:2} Now it is required that those who have been given a trust must prove faithful. {4:3} I care very little if I am judged by you or by any human court; indeed, I do not even judge myself. {4:4} My conscience is clear, but that does not make me innocent. It is the Lord who judges me. {4:5} Therefore judge nothing before the appointed time; wait until the Lord comes. He will bring to light what is hidden in darkness and will expose the motives of the heart. At that time each will receive their praise from God. {4:6} Now, brothers and sisters, I have applied these things to myself and Apollos for your benefit, so that you may learn from us the meaning of the saying, "Do not go beyond what is written." Then you will not be puffed up in being a follower of one of us over against the other. {4:7} For who makes you different from anyone else? What do you have that you did not receive? And if you did receive it, why do you boast as though you did not? {4:8} Already you have all you want! Already you have become rich! You have begun to reign, and that without us! How I wish that you really had begun to reign so that we also might reign with you! {4:9} For it seems to me that God has put us apostles on display at the end of the procession, like those condemned to die in the arena. We have been made a spectacle to the whole universe, to angels as well as to human beings. {4:10} We are fools for Christ, but you are so wise in Christ! We are weak, but you are strong! You are honored, we are dishonored! {4:11} To this very hour we go hungry and thirsty, we are in rags, we are brutally treated, we are homeless. {4:12} We work hard with our own hands. When we are cursed, we bless; when we are persecuted, we endure it; {4:13} when we are slandered, we answer kindly. We have become the scum of the earth, the garbage of the world—right up to this moment. {4:14} I am not writing this to shame you, but to warn you as my dear children. {4:15} Even if you had ten thousand guardians in Christ, you do not have many fathers, for in Christ Jesus I became your father through the gospel. {4:16} Therefore I urge you to imitate me. {4:17} For this reason, I have sent to you Timothy, my son whom I love, who is faithful in the Lord. He will remind you of my way of life in Christ Jesus, which agrees with what I teach everywhere in every church. {4:18} Some of you have become arrogant, as if I were not coming to you. {4:19} But I will come to you very soon, if the Lord is willing, and then I will find out not only how these arrogant people are talking but what power they have. {4:20} For the kingdom of God is not a matter of talk but of power. {4:21} What do you prefer? Shall I come to you with a rod of discipline, or shall I come in love and with a gentle spirit?

{5:1} It is widely reported that there is sexual immorality among you, and such immorality as is not even tolerated among pagans—someone has his father's wife. {5:2} And you are proud! Shouldn't you rather have gone into mourning and put out of your fellowship the man who has been doing this? {5:3} For my part, even though I am not physically present, I am with you in spirit, and I have already passed judgment on the one who did this just as if I were present. {5:4} When you are assembled in the name of our Lord Jesus and I am with you in spirit, and the power of our Lord Jesus is present, {5:5} hand this man over to Satan for the destruction of the flesh, so that his spirit may be saved on the day of the Lord. {5:6} Your boasting is not good. Don't you know that a little yeast leavens the whole batch of dough? {5:7} Get rid of the old yeast so that you may be a new unleavened batch—as you really are. For Christ, our Passover lamb, has been sacrificed. {5:8} Therefore let us keep the Festival, not with the old yeast, the yeast of malice and wickedness, but with the unleavened bread of sincerity and truth. {5:9} I wrote to you in my letter not to associate with sexually immoral people. {5:10} Not at all meaning the people of this world who are immoral, or the greedy and swindlers, or idolaters. In that case, you would have to leave this world. {5:11} But now I am writing to you that you must not associate with anyone who claims to be a brother or sister but is sexually immoral or greedy, an idolater or slanderer, a drunkard or swindler. Do not even eat with such people. {5:12} What business is it of mine to judge those outside the church? Are you not to judge those inside? {5:13} God will judge those outside. Expel the wicked person from among you.

{6:1} If any of you has a dispute with another, do you dare to take it before the ungodly for judgment instead of before the Lord's people? {6:2} Or do you not know that the Lord's people will judge the world? And if you are to judge the world, are you not competent to judge trivial cases? {6:3} Do you not know that we will judge angels? How much more the things of this life! {6:4} Therefore, if you have disputes about such matters, do you ask for a ruling from those whose way of life is scorned in the church? {6:5} I say this to shame you. Is it possible that there is nobody among you wise enough to judge a dispute between believers? {6:6} But instead, one brother takes another to court—and this in front of unbelievers! {6:7} The very fact that you have lawsuits among you means you have been completely defeated already. Why not rather be wronged? Why not rather be cheated? {6:8} Instead, you yourselves cheat and do wrong, and you do this to your brothers and sisters. {6:9} Or do you not know that wrongdoers will not inherit the kingdom of God? Do not be deceived: Neither the sexually immoral nor idolaters nor adulterers nor men who have sex with men {6:10} nor thieves nor the greedy nor drunkards nor slanderers nor swindlers will inherit the kingdom of God. {6:11} And that is what some of you were. But you were washed, you were sanctified, you were justified in the name of the Lord Jesus Christ and by the Spirit of our God. {6:12} "I have the right to do anything," you say—but not everything is beneficial. "I have the right to do anything"—but I will not be mastered by anything. {6:13} You say, "Food for the stomach and the stomach for food," and God will destroy them both. The body, however, is not meant for sexual immorality but for the Lord, and the Lord for the body. {6:14} By his power, God raised the Lord from the dead, and he will raise us also. {6:15} Do you not know that your bodies are members of Christ himself? Shall I then take the members of Christ and unite them with a prostitute? Never! {6:16} Do you not know that he who unites himself with a prostitute is one with her in body? For it is said, "The two will become one flesh." {6:17} But whoever is united with the Lord is one with him in spirit. {6:18} Flee from sexual immorality! All other sins a person commits are outside the body, but whoever sins sexually, sins against their own body. {6:19} Do you not know that your bodies are temples of the Holy Spirit, who is in you, whom you have received from God? You are not your own; {6:20} you were bought at a price. Therefore honor God with your bodies.

{7:1} Now concerning the matters you wrote about: It is good for a man not to touch a woman. {7:2} However, to avoid sexual immorality, each man should have his own wife, and each woman should have her own husband. {7:3} The husband should fulfill his marital duty to his wife, and likewise the wife to her husband. {7:4} The wife does not have authority over her own body, but the husband does. In the same way, the husband does not have authority over his own body, but the wife does. {7:5} Do not deprive each other, except by mutual consent for a time, so that you may devote yourselves to prayer; then come together again so that Satan will not tempt you because of your lack of self-control. {7:6} I say this as a concession, not as a command. {7:7} I wish that all of you were as I am. But each of you has your own gift from God; one has this gift, another has that. {7:8} To the unmarried and the widows, I say: It is good for them to stay unmarried, as I do. {7:9} But if they cannot control themselves, they should marry, for it is better to marry than to burn with passion. {7:10} To the married, I give this command (not I, but the Lord): A wife must not separate from her husband. {7:11} But if she does, she must remain unmarried or be reconciled to her husband. And a husband must not divorce his wife. {7:12} To the rest, I say this (I, not the Lord): If any brother has a wife who is not a believer and she is willing to live with him, he must not divorce her. {7:13} And if a woman has a husband who is not a believer and he is willing to live with her, she must not divorce him. {7:14} For the unbelieving husband has been sanctified through his wife, and the unbelieving wife has been sanctified through her believing husband. Otherwise, your children would be unclean, but as it is, they are holy. {7:15} But if the unbeliever leaves, let it be so. The brother or sister is not bound in such circumstances; God has called us to live in peace. {7:16} How do you know, wife, whether you will save your husband? Or how do you know, husband, whether you will save your wife? {7:17} Nevertheless, each person should live as a believer in whatever situation the Lord has assigned to them, just as God has called them. This is the rule I lay down in all the churches. {7:18} Was a man already circumcised when he was called? He should not become uncircumcised. Was a man uncircumcised when he was called? He should not be circumcised. {7:19} Circumcision is nothing and uncircumcision is nothing. Keeping God's commands is what counts. {7:20} Each person should remain in the situation they were in when God called them. {7:21} Were you a slave when you were called? Don't let it trouble you; although if you can gain your freedom, do so. {7:22} For the one who was a slave when called to faith in the Lord is the Lord's freed person; similarly, the one who was free when called is Christ's slave. {7:23} You were bought at a price; do not become slaves of human beings. {7:24} Brothers and sisters, each person, as responsible to God, should remain in the situation they were in when God called them. {7:25} Now about virgins: I have no command from the Lord, but I give a judgment as one who by the Lord's mercy is trustworthy. {7:26} Because of the present crisis, I think that it is good for a man to remain as he is. {7:27} Are you pledged to a woman? Do not seek to be released. Are you free from such a commitment? Do not look for a wife. {7:28} But if you do marry, you have not sinned; and if a virgin marries, she has not sinned. But those who marry will face many troubles in this life, and I want to spare you this. {7:29} What I mean, brothers and sisters, is that the time is short. From now on, those who have wives should live as if they do not; {7:30} those who weep, as if they did not; those who rejoice, as if they did not; those who buy something, as if it were not theirs to keep; {7:31} those who use the things of the world, as if not engrossed in them. For this world in its present form is passing away. {7:32} I would like you to be free from concern. An unmarried man is concerned about the Lord's affairs—how he can please the Lord. {7:33} But a married man is concerned about the affairs of this world—how he can please his wife— {7:34} and his interests are divided. An unmarried woman or virgin is concerned about the Lord's affairs: her aim is to be devoted to the Lord in both body and spirit. But a married woman is concerned about the affairs of this world—how she can please her husband. {7:35} I am saying this for your own good, not to restrict you, but that you may live in a right way in undivided devotion to the Lord. {7:36} If anyone is worried that he might not be acting honorably toward the virgin he is engaged to, and if his passions are too strong and he feels he ought to marry, he should do as he wants. He is not sinning. They should get married. {7:37} But the man who has settled the matter in his own mind, who is under no compulsion but has control over his own will, and who has made up his mind not to marry the virgin, this man also does the right thing. {7:38} So then, he who marries the virgin does right, but he who does not marry her does even better. {7:39} A woman is bound to her husband as long as he is alive, but if her husband dies, she is free to marry anyone she wishes, but he must belong to the Lord. {7:40} In my judgment, she is happier if she stays as she is— and I think that I too have the Spirit of God.

{8:1} Now about food sacrificed to idols: We know that "We all possess knowledge." But knowledge puffs up while love builds up. {8:2} Those who think they know something do not yet know as they ought to know. {8:3} But whoever loves God is known by God. {8:4} So then, about eating food sacrificed to idols: We know that an idol is nothing at all in the world and that there is no God but one. {8:5} For even if there are so-called gods, whether in heaven or on earth (as indeed there are many "gods" and many "lords"), {8:6} yet for us there is but one God, the Father, from whom all things came and for whom we live; and there is but one Lord, Jesus Christ, through whom all things came and through whom we live. {8:7} But not everyone possesses this knowledge. Some people are still so accustomed to idols that when they eat sacrificial food they think of it as having been sacrificed to a god, and since their conscience is weak, it is defiled. {8:8} Food does not bring us near to God; we are no worse if we do not eat, and no better if we do. {8:9} Be careful, however, that the exercise of your rights does not become a stumbling block to the weak. {8:10} For if someone with a weak conscience sees you, with all your knowledge, eating in an idol's temple, won't that person be emboldened to eat what is sacrificed to idols? {8:11} So this weak brother or sister, for whom Christ died, is destroyed by your knowledge. {8:12} When you sin against them in this way and wound their weak conscience, you sin against Christ. {8:13} Therefore, if what I eat causes my brother or sister to fall into sin, I will never eat meat again, so that I will not cause them to fall.

{9:1} Am I not an apostle? Am I not free? Have I not seen Jesus Christ our Lord? Are you not my work in the Lord? {9:2} Even if I am not an apostle to others, surely I am to you, for you are the seal of my apostleship in the Lord. {9:3} This is my defense to those who examine me: {9:4} Do we not have the right to eat and drink? {9:5} Do we not have the right to take a believing wife along with us, as do the other apostles and the Lord's brothers and Cephas? {9:6} Or are Barnabas and I the only ones who do not have the right to not work for a living? {9:7} Who serves as a soldier at their own expense? Who plants a vineyard and does not eat its grapes? Who tends a flock and does not drink the milk? {9:8} Am I saying this merely on human authority? Doesn't the Law say the same thing? {9:9} For it is written in the Law of Moses, "Do not muzzle an ox while it is treading out the grain." Is it about oxen that God is concerned? {9:10} Surely he says this for us, doesn't he? Yes, this was written for us, because whoever plows and threshes should be able to do so in the hope of sharing in the harvest. {9:11} If we have sown spiritual seed among you, is it too much if we reap a material harvest from you? {9:12} If others have this right of support from you, shouldn't we have it all the more? But we did not use this right. On the contrary, we put up with anything rather than hinder the gospel of Christ. {9:13} Don't you know that those who serve in the temple get their food from the temple, and those who serve at the altar share in what is offered at the altar? {9:14} In the same way, the Lord has commanded that those who preach the gospel should receive their living from the gospel. {9:15} But I have not used any of these rights. And I am not writing this in the hope that you will do such things for me, for I would rather die than allow anyone to deprive me of this boast. {9:16} For when I preach the gospel, I cannot boast, since I am compelled to preach. Woe to me if I do not preach the gospel! {9:17} If I preach voluntarily, I have a reward; if not voluntarily, I am simply discharging the trust committed to me. {9:18} What then is my reward? Just this: that in preaching the gospel I may offer it free of charge, and so not make full use of my rights as a preacher of the gospel. {9:19} Though I am free and belong to no one, I have made myself a slave to everyone, to win as many as possible. {9:20} To the Jews, I became like a Jew, to win the Jews. To those under the law, I became like one under the law (though I myself am not under the law) so as to win those under the law. {9:21} To those not having the law, I became like one not having the law (though I am not free from God's law but am under Christ's law) so as to win those not having the law. {9:22} To the weak, I became weak, to win the weak. I have become all things to all people so that by all possible means I might save some. {9:23} I do all this for the sake of the gospel, that I may share in its blessings. {9:24} Do you not know that in a race all the runners run, but only one gets the prize? Run in such a way as to get the prize. {9:25} Everyone who competes in the games goes into strict training. They do it to get a crown that will not last, but we do it to get a crown that will last forever. {9:26} Therefore I do not run like someone running aimlessly; I do not fight like a boxer beating the air. {9:27} No, I strike a blow to my body and make it my slave so that after I have preached to others, I myself will not be disqualified for the prize.

{10:1} For I do not want you to be ignorant of the fact, brothers and sisters, that our ancestors were all under the cloud and that they all passed through the sea. {10:2} They were all baptized into Moses in the cloud and in the sea. {10:3} They all ate the same spiritual food {10:4} and drank the same spiritual drink; for they drank from the spiritual rock that accompanied them, and that rock was Christ. {10:5} Nevertheless, God was not pleased with most of them; their bodies were scattered in the wilderness. {10:6} Now these things occurred as examples to keep us from setting our hearts on evil things as they did. {10:7} Do not be idolaters, as some of them were; as it is written: "The people sat down to eat and drink and got up to indulge in revelry." {10:8} We should not commit sexual immorality, as some of them did—and in one day twenty-three thousand of them died. {10:9} We should not test Christ, as some of them did—and were killed by snakes. {10:10} And do not grumble, as some of them did—and were killed by the destroying angel. {10:11} These things happened to them as examples and were written down as warnings for us, on whom the culmination of the ages has come. {10:12} So, if you think you are standing firm, be careful that you don't fall! {10:13} No temptation has overtaken you except what is common to mankind. And God is faithful; he will not let you be tempted beyond what you can bear. But when you are tempted, he will also provide a way out so that you can endure it. {10:14} Therefore, my dear friends, flee from idolatry. {10:15} I speak to sensible people; judge for yourselves what I say. {10:16} Is not the cup of thanksgiving for which we give thanks a participation in the blood of Christ? And is not the bread that we break a participation in the body of Christ? {10:17} Because there is one loaf, we, who are many, are one body, for we all share the one loaf. {10:18} Consider the people of Israel: Do not those who eat the sacrifices participate in the altar? {10:19} Do I mean then that food sacrificed to an idol is anything, or that an idol is anything? {10:20} No, but the sacrifices of pagans are offered to demons, not to God, and I do not want you to be participants with demons. {10:21} You cannot drink the cup of the Lord and the cup of demons; you cannot have a part in both the Lord's table and the table of demons. {10:22} Are we trying to arouse the Lord's jealousy? Are we stronger than he? {10:23} "I have the right to do anything," you say, but not everything is beneficial. "I have the right to do anything," but not everything is constructive. {10:24} No one should seek their own good, but the good of others. {10:25} Eat anything sold in the meat market without raising questions of conscience, {10:26} for, "The earth is the Lord's, and everything in it." {10:27} If an unbeliever invites you to a meal and you want to go, eat whatever is put before you without raising questions of conscience. {10:28} But if someone says to you, "This has been offered in sacrifice," then do not eat it, both for the sake of the one who told you and for the sake of conscience. {10:29} I am referring to the other person's conscience, not yours. For why is my freedom being judged by another's conscience? {10:30} If I take part in the meal with thankfulness, why am I denounced because of something I thank God for? {10:31} So whether you eat or drink or whatever you do, do it all for the glory of God. {10:32} Do not cause anyone to stumble, whether Jews, Gentiles, or the church of God— {10:33} even as I try to please everyone in every way. For I am not seeking my own good but the good of many, so that they may be saved.

{11:1} Follow my example, as I follow the example of Christ. {11:2} I praise you for remembering me in everything and for holding to the traditions just as I passed them on to you. {11:3} But I want you to realize that the head of every man is Christ, the head of the woman is man, and the head of Christ is God. {11:4} Every man who prays or prophesies with his head covered dishonors his head. {11:5} But every woman who prays or prophesies with her head uncovered dishonors her head; it is the same as having her head shaved. {11:6} For if a woman's head is not covered, she might as well have her hair cut off; but if it is shameful for a woman to have her hair cut off or her head shaved, then she should cover her head. {11:7} A man ought not to cover his head, since he is the image and glory of God; but woman is the glory of man. {11:8} For man did not come from woman, but woman from man; {11:9} neither was man created for woman, but woman for man. {11:10} For this reason, and because of the angels, the woman ought to have a sign of authority on her head. {11:11} Nevertheless, in the Lord, woman is not independent of man, nor is man independent of woman. {11:12} For as woman came from man, so also man is born of woman. But everything comes from God. {11:13} Judge for yourselves: is it proper for a woman to pray to God with her head uncovered? {11:14} Does not the very nature of things teach you that if a man has long hair, it is a disgrace to him, {11:15} but that if a woman has long hair, it is her glory? For long hair is given to her as a covering. {11:16} If anyone wants to be contentious about this, we have no other practice—nor do the churches of God. {11:17} In the following directives, I have no praise for you, for your meetings do more harm than good. {11:18} In the first place, I hear that when you come together as a church, there are divisions among you, and to some extent, I believe it. {11:19} No doubt there have to be differences among you to show which of you have God's approval. {11:20} So then, when you come together, it is not the Lord's Supper you eat, {11:21} for when you are eating, some of you go ahead with your own private suppers. As a result, one person remains hungry and another gets drunk. {11:22} Don't you have homes to eat and drink in? Or do you despise the church of God by humiliating those who have nothing? What shall I say to you? Shall I praise you? Certainly not! {11:23} For I received from the Lord what I also passed on to you: The Lord Jesus, on the night he was betrayed, took bread, {11:24} and when he had given thanks, he broke it and said, "This is my body, which is for you; do this in remembrance of me." {11:25} In the same way, after supper, he took the cup, saying, "This cup is the new covenant in my blood; do this, whenever you drink it, in remembrance of me." {11:26} For whenever you eat this bread and drink this cup, you proclaim the Lord's death until he comes. {11:27} So then, whoever eats the bread or drinks the cup of the Lord in an unworthy manner will be guilty of sinning against the body and blood of the Lord. {11:28} Everyone ought to examine themselves before they eat of the bread and drink from the cup. {11:29} For those who eat and drink without discerning the body of Christ eat and drink judgment on themselves. {11:30} That is why many among you are weak and sick, and a number of you have fallen asleep. {11:31} But if we were more discerning with regard to ourselves, we would not come under such judgment. {11:32} Nevertheless, when we are judged in this way by the Lord, we are being disciplined so that we will not be finally condemned with the world. {11:33} So then, my brothers and sisters, when you gather to eat, you should all eat together. {11:34} Anyone who is hungry should eat something at home, so that when you meet together, it may not result in judgment. And when I come, I will give further directions.

{12:1} Now about the gifts of the Spirit, brothers and sisters, I do not want you to be uninformed. {12:2} You know that when you were pagans, somehow or other you were influenced and led astray to mute idols. {12:3} Therefore, I want you to know that no one who is speaking by the Spirit of God says, "Jesus be cursed," and no one can say, "Jesus is Lord," except by the Holy Spirit. {12:4} There are different kinds of gifts, but the same Spirit distributes them. {12:5} There are different kinds of service, but the same Lord. {12:6} There are different kinds of working, but in all of them and in everyone, it is the same God at work. {12:7} Now to each one the manifestation of the Spirit is given for the common good. {12:8} To one there is given through the Spirit a message of wisdom, to another a message of knowledge by means of the same Spirit, {12:9} to another faith by the same Spirit, to another gifts of healing by that one Spirit, {12:10} to another miraculous powers, to another prophecy, to another distinguishing between spirits, to another speaking in different kinds of tongues, and still another the interpretation of tongues. {12:11} All these are the work of one and the same Spirit, and he distributes them to each one, just as he determines. {12:12} Just as a body, though one, has many parts, but all its many parts form one body, so it is with Christ. {12:13} For we were all baptized by one Spirit so as to form one body—whether Jews or Gentiles, slave or free—and we were all given the one Spirit to drink. {12:14} Even so, the body is not made up of one part but of many. {12:15} Now if the foot should say, "Because I am not a hand, I do not belong to the body," it would not for that reason stop being part of the body. {12:16} And if the ear should say, "Because I am not an eye, I do not belong to the body," it would not for that reason stop being part of the body. {12:17} If the whole body were an eye, where would the sense of hearing be? If the whole body were an ear, where would the sense of smell be? {12:18} But in fact God has placed the parts in the body, every one of them, just as he wanted them to be. {12:19} If they were all one part, where would the body be? {12:20} As it is, there are many parts, but one body. {12:21} The eye cannot say to the hand, "I don't need you!" And the head cannot say to the feet, "I don't need you!" {12:22} On the contrary, those parts of the body that seem to be weaker are indispensable, {12:23} and the parts that we think are less honorable we treat with special honor. And the parts that are unpresentable are treated with special modesty, {12:24} while our presentable parts need no special treatment. But God has put the body together, giving greater honor to the parts that lacked it, {12:25} so that there should be no division in the body, but that its parts should have equal concern for each other. {12:26} If one part suffers, every part suffers with it; if one part is honored, every part rejoices with it. {12:27} Now you are the body of Christ, and each one of you is a part of it. {12:28} And God has placed in the church first of all apostles, second prophets, third teachers, then miracles, then gifts of healing, of helping, of guidance, and of different kinds of tongues. {12:29} Are all apostles? Are all prophets? Are all teachers? Do all work miracles? {12:30} Do all have gifts of healing? Do all speak in tongues? Do all interpret? {12:31} Now eagerly desire the greater gifts. And yet I will show you the most excellent way.

{13:1} If I speak in the languages of humans and of angels but do not have love, I am only a noisy gong or a clanging cymbal. {13:2} If I have the gift of prophecy and can fathom all mysteries and all knowledge, and if I have faith that can move mountains but do not have love, I am nothing. {13:3} If I give all I possess to the poor and give over my body to hardship that I may boast but do not have love, I gain nothing. {13:4} Love is patient, love is kind. It does not envy, it does not boast, it is not proud. {13:5} It does not dishonor others, it is not self-seeking, it is not easily angered, it keeps no record of wrongs. {13:6} Love does not delight in evil but rejoices with the truth. {13:7} It always protects, always trusts, always hopes, always perseveres. {13:8} Love never fails. But where there are prophecies, they will cease; where there are tongues, they will be stilled; where there is knowledge, it will pass away. {13:9} For we know in part and we prophesy in part, {13:10} but when completeness comes, what is in part disappears. {13:11} When I was a child, I talked like a child, I thought like a child, I reasoned like a child. When I became a man, I put the ways of childhood behind me. {13:12} For now we see only a reflection as in a mirror; then we shall see face to face. Now I know in part; then I shall know fully, even as I am fully known. {13:13} And now these three remain: faith, hope, and love. But the greatest of these is love.

{14:1} Follow the way of love and eagerly desire gifts of the Spirit, especially prophecy. {14:2} For anyone who speaks in a tongue does not speak to people but to God. Indeed, no one understands them; they utter mysteries by the Spirit. {14:3} But the one who prophesies speaks to people for their strengthening, encouraging, and comfort. {14:4} Anyone who speaks in a tongue edifies themselves, but the one who prophesies edifies the church. {14:5} I would like every one of you to speak in tongues, but I would rather have you prophesy. The one who prophesies is greater than the one who speaks in tongues, unless someone interprets, so that the church may be edified. {14:6} Now, brothers and sisters, if I come to you and speak in tongues, what good will I be to you unless I bring you some revelation or knowledge or prophecy or word of instruction? {14:7} Even in the case of lifeless things that make sounds, such as the flute or the harp, how will anyone know what tune is being played unless there is a distinction in the notes? {14:8} Again, if the trumpet does not sound a clear call, who will get ready for battle? {14:9} So it is with you. Unless you speak intelligible words with your tongue, how will anyone know what you are saying? You will just be speaking into the air. {14:10} Undoubtedly there are all sorts of languages in the world, yet none of them is without meaning. {14:11} If then I do not grasp the meaning of what someone is saying, I am a foreigner to the speaker, and the speaker is a foreigner to me. {14:12} So it is with you. Since you are eager for gifts of the Spirit, try to excel in those that build up the church. {14:13} For this reason, the one who speaks in a tongue should pray that they may interpret what they say. {14:14} For if I pray in a tongue, my spirit prays, but my mind is unfruitful. {14:15} So what shall I do? I will pray with my spirit, but I will also pray with my understanding. I will sing with my spirit, but I will also sing with my understanding. {14:16} Otherwise, when you are praising God in the Spirit, how can someone else, who is now put in the position of an inquirer, say "Amen" to your thanksgiving, since they do not know what you are saying? {14:17} You are giving thanks well enough, but no one else is edified. {14:18} I thank God that I speak in tongues more than all of you. {14:19} But in the church, I would rather speak five intelligible words to instruct others than ten thousand words in a tongue. {14:20} Brothers and sisters, stop thinking like children. In regard to evil, be infants, but in your thinking be adults. {14:21} In the Law it is written: "With other tongues and through the lips of foreigners I will speak to this people, but even then they will not listen to me," says the Lord. {14:22} Tongues, then, are a sign, not for believers but for unbelievers; prophecy, however, is not for unbelievers but for believers. {14:23} So if the whole church comes together and everyone speaks in tongues and inquirers or unbelievers come in, will they not say that you are out of your mind? {14:24} But if an unbeliever or an inquirer comes in while everyone is prophesying, they are convinced of sin and are brought under judgment by all, {14:25} as the secrets of their hearts are laid bare. So they will fall down and worship God, exclaiming, "God is really among you!" {14:26} What then shall we say, brothers and sisters? When you come together, each of you has a hymn, or a word of instruction, a revelation, a tongue, or an interpretation. Everything must be done so that the church may be built up. {14:27} If anyone speaks in a tongue, two—or at the most three—should speak, one at a time, and someone must interpret. {14:28} If there is no interpreter, the speaker should keep quiet in the church and speak to themselves and to God. {14:29} Two or three prophets should speak, and the others should weigh carefully what is said. {14:30} And if a revelation comes to someone who is sitting down, the first speaker should stop. {14:31} For you can all prophesy in turn so that everyone may be instructed and encouraged. {14:32} The spirits of prophets are subject to the control of prophets. {14:33} For God is not a God of disorder but of peace—as in all the congregations of the Lord's people. {14:34} Women should remain silent in the churches. They are not allowed to speak but must be in submission, as the law says. {14:35} If they want to inquire about something, they should ask their own husbands at home; for it is disgraceful for a woman to speak in the church. {14:36} Or did the word of God originate with you? Or are you the only people it has reached? {14:37} If anyone thinks they are a prophet or otherwise gifted by the Spirit, let them acknowledge that what I am writing to you is the Lord's command. {14:38} But if anyone ignores this, they will themselves be ignored. {14:39} Therefore, my brothers and sisters, be eager to prophesy, and do not forbid speaking in tongues. {14:40} But everything should be done in a fitting and orderly way.

{15:1} Now, brothers and sisters, I want to remind you of the gospel I preached to you, which you received and on which you have taken your stand. {15:2} By this gospel, you are saved, if you hold firmly to the word I preached to you. Otherwise, you have believed in vain. {15:3} For what I received I passed on to you as of first importance: that Christ died for our sins according to the Scriptures, {15:4} that he was buried, that he was raised on the third day according to the Scriptures, {15:5} and that he appeared to Cephas, and then to the Twelve. {15:6} After that, he appeared to more than five hundred of the brothers and sisters at the same time, most of whom are still living, though some have fallen asleep. {15:7} Then he appeared to James, then to all the apostles. {15:8} And last of all, he appeared to me also, as to one abnormally born. {15:9} For I am the least of the apostles and do not even deserve to be called an apostle, because I persecuted the church of God. {15:10} But by the grace of God, I am what I am, and his grace to me was not without effect. No, I worked harder than all of them—yet not I, but the grace of God that was with me. {15:11} Whether, then, it is I or they, this is what we preach, and this is what you believed. {15:12} But if it is preached that Christ has been raised from the dead, how can some of you say that there is no resurrection of the dead? {15:13} If there is no resurrection of the dead, then not even Christ has been raised. {15:14} And if Christ has not been raised, our preaching is useless and so is your faith. {15:15} More than that, we are then found to be false witnesses about God, for we have testified about God that he raised Christ from the dead. But he did not raise him if, in fact, the dead are not raised. {15:16} For if the dead are not raised, then Christ has not been raised either. {15:17} And if Christ has not been raised, your faith is futile; you are still in your sins. {15:18} Then those also who have fallen asleep in Christ are lost. {15:19} If only for this life we have hope in Christ, we are of all people most to be pitied. {15:20} But Christ has indeed been raised from the dead, the firstfruits of those who have fallen asleep. {15:21} For since death came through a man, the resurrection of the dead comes also through a man. {15:22} For as in Adam all die, so in Christ all will be made alive. {15:23} But each in turn: Christ, the firstfruits; then, when he comes, those who belong to him. {15:24} Then the end will come, when he hands over the kingdom to God the Father after he has destroyed all dominion, authority, and power. {15:25} For he must reign until he has put all his enemies under his feet. {15:26} The last enemy to be destroyed is death. {15:27} For he has put everything under his feet. Now when it says that everything has been put under him, it is clear that this does not include the one who put everything under him. {15:28} When he has done this, then the Son himself will be made subject to him who put everything under him, so that God may be all in all. {15:29} Now if there is no resurrection, what will those do who are baptized for the dead? If the dead are not raised at all, why are people baptized for them? {15:30} And as for us, why do we endanger ourselves every hour? {15:31} I face death every day—yes, just as surely as I boast about you in Christ Jesus our Lord. {15:32} If I fought wild beasts in Ephesus with no more than human hopes, what have I gained? If the dead are not raised, "Let us eat and drink, for tomorrow we die." {15:33} Do not be misled: "Bad company corrupts good character." {15:34} Come back to your senses as you ought, and stop sinning; for there are some who are ignorant of God. I say this to your shame. {15:35} But someone will ask, "How are the dead raised? With what kind of body will they come?" {15:36} How foolish! What you sow does not come to life unless it dies. {15:37} When you sow, you do not plant the body that will be, but just a seed, perhaps of wheat or of something else. {15:38} But God gives it a body as he has determined, and to each kind of seed he gives its own body. {15:39} Not all flesh is the same: People have one kind of flesh, animals have another, birds another, and fish another. {15:40} There are also heavenly bodies and there are earthly bodies; but the splendor of the heavenly bodies is one kind, and the splendor of the earthly bodies is another. {15:41} The sun has one kind of splendor, the moon another, and the stars another; and star differs from star in splendor. {15:42} So will it be with the resurrection of the dead. The body that is sown is perishable, it is raised imperishable; {15:43} it is sown in dishonor, it is raised in glory; it is sown in weakness, it is raised in power; {15:44} it is sown a natural body, it is raised a spiritual body. If there is a natural body, there is also a spiritual body. {15:45} So it is written: "The first man Adam became a living being"; the last Adam, a life-giving spirit. {15:46} The spiritual did not come first, but the natural, and after that the spiritual. {15:47} The first man was of the dust of the earth; the second man is of heaven. {15:48} As was the earthly man, so are those who are of the earth; and as is the heavenly man, so also are those who are of heaven. {15:49} And just as we have borne the image of the earthly man, we shall bear the image of the heavenly man. {15:50} I declare to you, brothers and sisters, that flesh and blood cannot inherit the kingdom of God, nor does the perishable inherit the imperishable. {15:51} Listen, I tell you a mystery: We will not all sleep, but we will all be changed— {15:52} in a flash, in the twinkling of an eye, at the last trumpet. For the trumpet will sound, the dead will be raised imperishable, and we will be changed. {15:53} For the perishable must clothe itself with the imperishable, and the mortal with immortality. {15:54} When the perishable has been clothed with the imperishable, and the mortal with immortality, then the saying that is written will come true: "Death has been swallowed up in victory." {15:55} Where, O death, is your victory? Where, O death, is your sting? {15:56} The sting of death is sin, and the power of sin is the law. {15:57} But thanks be to God! He gives us the victory through our Lord Jesus Christ. {15:58} Therefore, my dear brothers and sisters, stand firm. Let nothing move you. Always give yourselves fully to the work of the Lord, because you know that your labor in the Lord is not in vain.

{16:1} Now about the collection for the Lord's people: Do what I told the Galatian churches to do. {16:2} On the first day of every week, each one of you should set aside a sum of money in keeping with your income, so that when I come no collections will have to be made. {16:3} Then, when I arrive, I will give letters of introduction to the men you approve and send them with your gift to Jerusalem. {16:4} If it seems advisable for me to go also, they will accompany me. {16:5} After I go through Macedonia, I will come to you—for I will be going through Macedonia. {16:6} Perhaps I will stay with you a while, or even spend the winter, so that you can help me on my journey, wherever I go. {16:7} For I do not want to see you now and make only a passing visit; I hope to spend some time with you, if the Lord permits. {16:8} But I will stay on at Ephesus until Pentecost, {16:9} because a great door for effective work has opened to me, and there are many who oppose me. {16:10} When Timothy comes, see to it that he has nothing to fear while he is with you, for he is carrying on the work of the Lord, just as I am. {16:11} No one, then, should treat him with contempt. Send him on his way in peace, so that he may return to me. I am expecting him along with the brothers. {16:12} Now about our brother Apollos: I strongly urged him to go to you with the brothers. He was quite unwilling to go now, but he will go when he has the opportunity. {16:13} Be on your guard; stand firm in the faith; be courageous; be strong. {16:14} Do everything in love. {16:15} You know that the household of Stephanas were the first converts in Achaia, and they have devoted themselves to the service of the Lord's people. I urge you, brothers and sisters, {16:16} to submit to such people and to everyone who joins in the work and labors at it. {16:17} I was glad when Stephanas, Fortunatus, and Achaicus arrived, because they have supplied what was lacking from you. {16:18} For they refreshed my spirit and yours also. Such men deserve recognition. {16:19} The churches in the province of Asia send you greetings. Aquila and Priscilla greet you warmly in the Lord, and so does the church that meets at their house. {16:20} All the brothers and sisters here send you greetings. Greet one another with a holy kiss. {16:21} I, Paul, write this greeting in my own hand. {16:22} If anyone does not love the Lord, let that person be cursed! Come, Lord! {16:23} The grace of the Lord Jesus be with you. {16:24} My love to all of you in Christ Jesus. Amen.

The Second Epistle of Paul to the Corinthians

{1:1} Paul, an apostle of Jesus Christ by the will of God, and Timothy our brother, to the church of God in Corinth, along with all the saints in the region of Achaia: {1:2} Grace and peace to you from God our Father and the Lord Jesus Christ. {1:3} Praise be to God, the Father of our Lord Jesus Christ, the Father of compassion and the God of all comfort, {1:4} who comforts us in all our troubles, so that we can comfort those in any trouble, with the comfort we ourselves receive from God. {1:5} For just as the sufferings of Christ flow over into our lives, so also through Christ our comfort overflows. {1:6} If we are distressed, it is for your comfort and salvation, which is effective in enduring the same sufferings we suffer; if we are comforted, it is for your comfort and salvation. {1:7} And our hope for you is firm, because we know that just as you share in our sufferings, you also share in our comfort. {1:8} We do not want you to be uninformed, brothers and sisters, about the troubles we experienced in the province of Asia. We were under great pressure, far beyond our ability to endure, so that we despaired of life itself. {1:9} Indeed, we felt we had received the sentence of death. But this happened that we might not rely on ourselves but on God, who raises the dead. {1:10} He has delivered us from such a deadly peril, and he will deliver us again. On him we have set our hope that he will continue to deliver us, {1:11} as you help us by your prayers. Then many will give thanks on our behalf for the gracious favor granted us in answer to the prayers of many. {1:12} Now this is our boast: Our conscience testifies that we have conducted ourselves in the world, and especially in our relations with you, in the holiness and sincerity that are from God. We have done so, not according to worldly wisdom but according to God's grace. {1:13} For we do not write you anything you cannot read or understand. And I hope that, as you have understood us in part, you will come to understand fully that you can boast of us just as we will boast of you in the day of the Lord Jesus. {1:14} I was confident in this, that I intended to visit you first so that you might benefit twice. {1:15} I planned to visit you on my way to Macedonia and to come back to you from Macedonia and then to have you send me on my way to Judea. {1:16} When I planned this, did I do it lightly? Or do I make my plans in a worldly manner so that in the same breath I say "Yes, yes" and "No, no"? {1:17} But as surely as God is faithful, our message to you is not "Yes" and "No." {1:18} For the Son of God, Jesus Christ, who was preached among you by us—by me and Silas and Timothy—was not "Yes" and "No," but in him it has always been "Yes." {1:19} For no matter how many promises God has made, they are "Yes" in Christ. And so through him the "Amen" is spoken by us to the glory of God. {1:20} Now it is God who establishes us with you in Christ and anoints us, {1:21} set his seal of ownership on us, and put his Spirit in our hearts as a deposit, guaranteeing what is to come. {1:22} I call God as my witness—and I stake my life on it—that it was in order to spare you that I did not return to Corinth. {1:23} Not that we lord it over your faith, but we work with you for your joy, because it is by faith you stand.

{2:1} So I made up my mind that I would not make another painful visit to you. {2:2} For if I grieve you, who is left to make me glad but you whom I have grieved? {2:3} I wrote as I did, so that when I came I would not be distressed by those who should have made me rejoice. I had confidence in all of you, that you would all share my joy. {2:4} For I wrote to you out of great distress and anguish of heart and with many tears, not to grieve you but to let you know the depth of my love for you. {2:5} If anyone has caused grief, he has not so much grieved me as he has grieved all of you to some extent—not to put it too severely. {2:6} The punishment inflicted on him by the majority is sufficient. {2:7} Now instead, you ought to forgive and comfort him, so that he will not be overwhelmed by excessive sorrow. {2:8} I urge you, therefore, to reaffirm your love for him. {2:9} Another reason I wrote you was to see if you would stand the test and be obedient in everything. {2:10} If you forgive anyone, I also forgive them. And what I have forgiven, if there was anything to forgive, I have forgiven in the sight of Christ for your sake, {2:11} in order that Satan might not outwit us. For we are not unaware of his schemes. {2:12} Now when I went to Troas to preach the gospel of Christ and found that the Lord had opened a door for me, {2:13} I still had no peace of mind, because I did not find my brother Titus there. So I said goodbye to them and went on to Macedonia. {2:14} But thanks be to God, who always leads us as captives in Christ's triumphal procession and uses us to spread the aroma of the knowledge of him everywhere. {2:15} For we are to God the pleasing aroma of Christ among those who are being saved and those who are perishing. {2:16} To one we are an aroma that brings death; to the other, an aroma that brings life. And who is equal to such a task? {2:17} Unlike so many, we don't peddle word of God for profit. On contrary, in Christ we speak before God with sincerity, as those sent from God.

{3:1} Are we starting to commend ourselves again, or do we need, like some others, letters of recommendation to you or from you? {3:2} You yourselves are our letter, written on our hearts, known and read by everyone. {3:3} You show that you are a letter of Christ, delivered by us, not written with ink but with the Spirit of the living God; not on tablets of stone but on tablets of human hearts. {3:4} Such confidence we have through Christ before God. {3:5} Not that we are competent in ourselves to claim anything for ourselves, but our competence comes from God. {3:6} He has made us competent as ministers of a new covenant—not of the letter but of the Spirit; for the letter kills, but the Spirit gives life. {3:7} Now if the ministry that brought death, which was engraved in letters on stone, came with glory, so that the Israelites could not look steadily at the face of Moses because of its glory (fading though it was), {3:8} will not the ministry of the Spirit be even more glorious? {3:9} If the ministry that brought condemnation was glorious, how much more glorious is the ministry that brings righteousness! {3:10} For what was glorious has no glory now in comparison with the surpassing glory. {3:11} And if what was transitory came with glory, how much greater is the glory of that which lasts! {3:12} Therefore, since we have such a hope, we are very bold. {3:13} We are not like Moses, who would put a veil over his face to prevent the Israelites from seeing the end of what was passing away. {3:14} But their minds were made dull, for to this day the same veil remains when the old covenant is read; it has not been removed, because only in Christ is it taken away. {3:15} Even to this day when Moses is read, a veil covers their hearts. {3:16} But whenever anyone turns to the Lord, the veil is taken away. {3:17} Now the Lord is the Spirit, and where the Spirit is, there is freedom. {3:18} And we all, who with unveiled faces contemplate the Lord's glory, are being transformed into his image with ever-increasing glory, which comes from the Lord, who is the Spirit.

{4:1} Therefore, since through God's mercy we have this ministry, we do not lose heart. {4:2} Rather, we have renounced secret and shameful ways; we do not use deception, nor do we distort the word of God. On the contrary, by setting forth the truth plainly we commend ourselves to everyone's conscience in the sight of God. {4:3} And even if our gospel is veiled, it is veiled to those who are perishing. {4:4} The god of this age has blinded the minds of unbelievers, so they cannot see the light of the gospel that displays the glory of Christ, who is the image of God. {4:5} For what we preach is not ourselves, but Jesus Christ as Lord, and ourselves as your servants for Jesus' sake. {4:6} For God, who said, "Let light shine out of darkness," made his light shine in our hearts to give us the light of the knowledge of God's glory displayed in the face of Christ. {4:7} But we have this treasure in jars of clay (earthen vessels), to show that this all-surpassing power is from God and not from us. {4:8} We are hard pressed on every side, but not crushed; perplexed, but not in despair; {4:9} persecuted, but not abandoned; struck down, but not destroyed. {4:10} We always carry around in our body the death of Jesus, so that the life of Jesus may also be revealed in our body. {4:11} For we who are alive are always being given over to death for Jesus' sake, so that his life may also be revealed in our mortal body. {4:12} So then, death is at work in us, but life is at work in you. {4:13} It is written: "I believed; therefore I have spoken." Since we have that same spirit of faith, we also believe and therefore speak, {4:14} because we know that the one who raised the Lord Jesus from the dead will also raise us with Jesus and present us with you to himself. {4:15} All this is for your benefit, so that the grace that is reaching more and more people may cause thanksgiving to overflow to the glory of God. {4:16} Therefore we do not lose heart. Though outwardly we are wasting away, yet inwardly we are being renewed day by day. {4:17} For our light and momentary troubles are achieving for us an eternal glory that far outweighs them all. {4:18} So we fix our eyes not on what is seen, but on what is unseen, since what is seen is temporary, but what is unseen is eternal.

{5:1} For we know that if our earthly body, this tent, is destroyed, we have a building from God, an eternal house in heaven, not made by human hands. {5:2} Meanwhile, we groan, longing to be clothed with our heavenly dwelling, {5:3} because when we are clothed, we will not be found naked. {5:4} While we are in this tent, we groan and are burdened, not because we want to be unclothed but because we want to be clothed with life, so that mortality may be swallowed up by life. {5:5} Now the one who has fashioned us for this very purpose is God, who has given us the Spirit as a deposit (earnest). {5:6} Therefore, we are always confident, knowing that while we are at home in the body, we are away from the Lord. {5:7} For we live by faith, not by sight. {5:8} We are confident, I say, and would prefer to be away from the body and at home with the Lord. {5:9} So we make it our goal to please him, whether we are at home in the body or away from it. {5:10} For we must all appear before the judgment seat of Christ, so that each of us may receive what is due us for the things done while in the body, whether good or bad. {5:11} Since we know what it is to fear the Lord, we try to persuade others. What we are is plain to God, and I hope it is also plain to your conscience. {5:12} We are not trying to commend ourselves to you again, but are giving you an opportunity to take pride in us, so that you can answer those who take pride in what is seen rather than what is in the heart. {5:13} If we are out of our mind, as some say, it is for God; if we are in our right mind, it is for you. {5:14} For Christ's love compels us, because we are convinced that one died for all, and therefore all died. {5:15} And he died for all, that those who live should no longer live for themselves but for him who died for them and was raised again. {5:16} So from now on we regard no one from a worldly point of view. Though we once regarded Christ in this way, we do so no longer. {5:17} Therefore, if anyone is in Christ, the new creation has come: The old has gone, the new is here! {5:18} All this is from God, who reconciled us to himself through Christ and gave us the ministry of reconciliation. {5:19} That God was reconciling the world to himself in Christ, not counting people's sins against them. And he has committed to us the message of reconciliation. {5:20} We are therefore Christ's ambassadors, as though God were making his appeal through us. We implore you on Christ's behalf: Be reconciled to God. {5:21} God made him who had no sin to be sin for us, so that in him we might become the righteousness of God.

{6:1} As God's co-workers, we urge you not to receive God's grace in vain. {6:2} For he says, "In the time of my favor I heard you, and in the day of salvation I helped you." I tell you, now is the time of God's favor, now is the day of salvation. {6:3} We put no stumbling block in anyone's path, so that our ministry will not be discredited. {6:4} Rather, as servants of God we commend ourselves in every way: in great endurance; in troubles, hardships, and distresses; {6:5} in beatings, imprisonments, and riots; in hard work, sleepless nights, and hunger; {6:6} in purity, understanding, patience, and kindness; in the Holy Spirit and in sincere love; {6:7} in truthful speech and in the power of God; with weapons of righteousness in the right hand and in the left; {6:8} through glory and dishonor, bad report and good report; genuine, yet regarded as impostors; {6:9} known, yet regarded as unknown; dying, and yet we live on; beaten, and yet not killed; {6:10} sorrowful, yet always rejoicing; poor, yet making many rich; having nothing, and yet possessing everything. {6:11} We have spoken freely to you, Corinthians, and opened wide our hearts to you. {6:12} We are not withholding our affection from you, but you are withholding yours from us. {6:13} As a fair exchange—I speak as to my children—open wide your hearts also. {6:14} Do not be unequally yoked with unbelievers. For what do righteousness and wickedness have in common? Or what fellowship can light have with darkness? {6:15} What harmony is there between Christ and Belial (a term for evil)? What does a believer have in common with an unbeliever? {6:16} What agreement is there between the temple of God and idols? For we are the temple of the living God, as God has said: "I will live with them and walk among them, and I will be their God, and they will be my people." {6:17} Therefore come out from them and be separate, says the Lord. Touch no unclean thing, and I will receive you. {6:18} And I'll be a Father to you & you will be my sons and daughters, says the Lord Almighty.

{7:1} Therefore, beloved, since we have these promises, let us purify ourselves from everything that contaminates body and spirit, perfecting holiness out of reverence for God. {7:2} Make room in your hearts for us; we have wronged no one, we have corrupted no one, we have exploited no one. {7:3} I do not say this to condemn you; I have said before that you are in our hearts, so that we would live and die together. {7:4} I have great confidence in you; I take great pride in you. I am greatly encouraged; in all our troubles, my joy knows no bounds. {7:5} For when we came to Macedonia, we had no rest, but we were harassed at every turn—conflicts on the outside, fears within. {7:6} But God, who comforts the downcast, comforted us by the arrival of Titus; {7:7} and not only by his coming but also by the comfort you had given him. He told us about your longing for me, your deep sorrow, and your ardent concern for me, so that my joy was greater than ever. {7:8} Even if I caused you sorrow by my letter, I do not regret it. Though I did regret it, I see that my letter hurt you, but only for a little while. {7:9} Yet now I am happy, not because you were made sorry, but because your sorrow led you to repentance. For you became sorrowful as God intended and so were not harmed in any way by us. {7:10} Godly sorrow brings repentance that leads to salvation and leaves no regret, but worldly sorrow brings death. {7:11} See what this godly sorrow has produced in you: what earnestness, what eagerness to clear yourselves, what indignation, what alarm, what longing, what concern, what readiness to see justice done! At every point, you have proved yourselves to be innocent in this matter. {7:12} So even though I wrote to you, it was neither on account of the one who did the wrong nor on account of the injured party but rather that before God you could see for yourselves how devoted to us you are. {7:13} By all this we are encouraged. In addition to our own encouragement, we were especially delighted to see how happy Titus was, because his spirit has been refreshed by all of you. {7:14} I had boasted to him about you, and you have not embarrassed me. But just as everything we said to you was true, so our boasting about you to Titus has proved to be true as well. {7:15} And his affection for you is all the greater when he remembers that you were all obedient, receiving him with fear and trembling. {7:16} I am glad I can have complete confidence in you.

{8:1} And now, brothers and sisters, we want you to know about the grace that God has given the Macedonian churches. {8:2} In the midst of a very severe trial, their overflowing joy and their extreme poverty welled up in rich generosity. {8:3} For I testify that they gave as much as they were able, and even beyond their ability. Entirely on their own, {8:4} they urgently pleaded with us for the privilege of sharing in this service to the Lord's people. {8:5} And they exceeded our expectations: they gave themselves first of all to the Lord, and then by the will of God also to us. {8:6} So we urged Titus, just as he had earlier made a beginning, to bring also to completion this act of grace on your part. {8:7} But since you excel in everything—in faith, in speech, in knowledge, in complete earnestness, and in the love we have kindled in you—see that you also excel in this grace of giving. {8:8} I am not commanding you, but I want to test the sincerity of your love by comparing it with the earnestness of others. {8:9} For you know the grace of our Lord Jesus Christ, that though he was rich, yet for your sake he became poor, so that you through his poverty might become rich. {8:10} And here is my judgment about what is best for you in this matter: Last year you were the first not only to give but also to have the desire to do so. {8:11} Now finish the work, so that your eager willingness to do it may be matched by your completion of it, according to your means. {8:12} For if the willingness is there, the gift is acceptable according to what one has, not according to what one does not have. {8:13} Our desire is not that others might be relieved while you are hard pressed, but that there might be equality. {8:14} At the present time your plenty will supply what they need, so that in turn their plenty will supply what you need. The goal is equality, {8:15} as it is written: "The one who gathered much did not have too much, and the one who gathered little did not have too little." {8:16} Thanks be to God, who put into the heart of Titus the same concern I have for you. {8:17} For Titus not only welcomed our appeal, but he is coming to you with much enthusiasm and on his own initiative. {8:18} And we are sending along with him the brother who is praised by all the churches for his service to the gospel. {8:19} What is more, he was chosen by the churches to accompany us as we carry the offering, which we administer in order to honor the Lord himself and to show our eagerness to help. {8:20} We want to avoid any criticism of the way we administer this liberal gift. {8:21} For we are taking pains to do what is right, not only in the eyes of the Lord but also in the eyes of others. {8:22} In addition, we are sending with them our brother who has often proved to be diligent in many ways, and who is now even more diligent because of his great confidence in you. {8:23} If anyone asks about Titus, he is my partner and co-worker among you; if anyone asks about our brothers, they are representatives of the churches and an honor to Christ. {8:24} Therefore show these men the proof of your love and the reason for our pride in you, so that the churches can see it.

{9:1} Regarding the ministry to the saints, I don't need to write to you. {9:2} I know your eagerness to help, and I have been boasting about you to the Macedonians, telling them that Achaia was ready to give a year ago, and your enthusiasm has stirred up most of them. {9:3} But I have sent the brothers to make sure our boasting about you in this matter isn't empty; I want you to be ready, just as I said you would be. {9:4} For if the Macedonians come with me and find you unprepared, we—so that you won't be ashamed—would be embarrassed for having boasted about you. {9:5} Therefore, I thought it necessary to encourage the brothers to go ahead of you and arrange in advance the generous gift you had promised so that it would be ready as a gift, not as something you felt forced to give. {9:6} Remember, whoever sows sparingly will also reap sparingly, and whoever sows generously will also reap generously. {9:7} Each of you should give what you have decided in your heart to give, not reluctantly or under compulsion, for God loves a cheerful giver. {9:8} And God is able to bless you abundantly, so that in all things at all times, having all that you need, you will abound in every good work. {9:9} As it is written: "They have freely scattered their gifts to the poor; their righteousness endures forever." {9:10} Now he who supplies seed to the sower and bread for food will also supply and increase your store of seed and will enlarge the harvest of your righteousness. {9:11} You will be enriched in every way so that you can be generous on every occasion, and through us your generosity will result in thanksgiving to God. {9:12} This service that you perform is not only supplying the needs of the Lord's people but is also overflowing in many expressions of thanks to God. {9:13}

Because of the service by which you have proved yourselves, others will praise God for the obedience that accompanies your confession of the gospel of Christ and for your generosity in sharing with them and with everyone else. {9:14} And in their prayers for you, their hearts will go out to you because of the surpassing grace God has given you. {9:15} Thanks be to God for his indescribable gift!

{10:1} I, Paul, urge you by the meekness and gentleness of Christ. I who am timid when face to face with you, but bold toward you when away! {10:2} I beg you that when I come, I may not have to be as bold as I expect to be toward some people who think we live by the standards of this world. {10:3} For though we live in the world, we do not wage war as the world does. {10:4} The weapons we fight with are not the weapons of the world; on the contrary, they have divine power to demolish strongholds. {10:5} We demolish arguments and every pretension that sets itself up against the knowledge of God, and we take captive every thought to make it obedient to Christ. {10:6} And we will be ready to punish every act of disobedience, once your obedience is complete. {10:7} You are judging by appearances. If anyone is confident that they belong to Christ, they should consider again that we belong to Christ just as much as they do. {10:8} So even if I boast somewhat freely about the authority the Lord gave us for building you up rather than pulling you down, I will not be ashamed of it. {10:9} I do not want to seem to be trying to frighten you with my letters. {10:10} For some say, "His letters are weighty and forceful, but in person he is unimpressive and his speaking amounts to nothing." {10:11} Such people should realize that what we are in our letters when we are absent, we will be in our actions when we are present. {10:12} We do not dare to classify or compare ourselves with some who commend themselves. When they measure themselves by themselves and compare themselves with themselves, they are not wise. {10:13} We, however, will not boast beyond proper limits, but will confine our boasting to the field God has assigned to us, a field that reaches even to you. {10:14} We are not going too far in our boasting, as would be the case if we had not come to you, for we did get as far as you with the gospel of Christ. {10:15} Neither do we go beyond our limits by boasting of work done by others. Our hope is that as your faith continues to grow, our area of activity among you will greatly expand, {10:16} so that we can preach the gospel in the regions beyond you. For we do not want to boast about work already done in another's territory. {10:17} But, "Let the one who boasts boast in the Lord." {10:18} For it is not the one who commends himself who is approved, but the one whom the Lord commends.

{11:1} I wish you would put up with me a little in my foolishness; please bear with me. {11:2} I am jealous for you with a godly jealousy, for I have promised you to one husband, to present you as a pure virgin to Christ. {11:3} But I am afraid that just as the serpent deceived Eve by his cunning, your minds may be led astray from your sincere and pure devotion to Christ. {11:4} For if someone comes to you and preaches a different Jesus than the one we preached, or if you receive a different spirit from the one you received, or a different gospel from the one you accepted, you put up with it easily enough. {11:5} I do not think I am in the least inferior to those "super-apostles." {11:6} I may not be a polished speaker, but I do have knowledge; we have made this clear to you in every way. {11:7} Did I commit a sin by humbling myself so that you might be exalted, by preaching God's gospel free of charge? {11:8} I robbed other churches by receiving support from them so as to serve you. {11:9} And when I was with you and needed something, I was not a burden to anyone, for the brothers who came from Macedonia supplied what I needed. I have kept myself from being a burden to you in any way, and will continue to do so. {11:10} As surely as the truth of Christ is in me, nobody in the regions of Achaia will stop this boasting of mine. {11:11} Why? Because I do not love you? God knows I do. {11:12} And what I am doing, I will continue to do in order to cut the ground out from under those who want an opportunity to be regarded as equal with us in the things they boast about. {11:13} For such people are false apostles, deceitful workers, masquerading as apostles of Christ. {11:14} And no wonder, for Satan himself masquerades as an angel of light. {11:15} It is not surprising, then, if his servants also masquerade as servants of righteousness. Their end will be what their actions deserve. {11:16} I repeat: Let no one take me for a fool. But if you do, then accept me as a fool, so that I may do a little boasting. {11:17} In this self-confident boasting I am not talking as the Lord would, but as a fool. {11:18} Since many are boasting in the way the world does, I too will boast. {11:19} You gladly put up with fools since you are so wise! {11:20} In fact, you even put up with anyone who enslaves you or exploits you or takes advantage of you or puts on airs or slaps you in the face. {11:21} To my shame, I admit that we were too weak for that! What anyone else dares to boast about, I am speaking as a fool—I also dare to boast about. {11:22} Are they Hebrews? So am I. Are they Israelites? So am I. Are they Abraham's descendants? So am I. {11:23} Are they servants of Christ? (I am out of my mind to talk like this.) I am more. I have worked much harder, been in prison more frequently, been flogged more severely, and been exposed to death again and again. {11:24} Five times I received from the Jews the forty lashes minus one. {11:25} Three times I was beaten with rods, once I was pelted with stones, three times I was shipwrecked, I spent a night and a day in the open sea. {11:26} I have been constantly on the move; I have been in danger from rivers, in danger from bandits, in danger from my fellow Jews, in danger from Gentiles; in danger in the city, in danger in the country, in danger at sea; and in danger from false believers. {11:27} I have labored and toiled and have often gone without sleep; I have known hunger and thirst and have often gone without food; I have been cold and naked. {11:28} Besides everything else, I face daily the pressure of my concern for all the churches. {11:29} Who is weak, and I do not feel weak? Who is led into sin, and I do not inwardly burn? {11:30} If I must boast, I will boast of the things that show my weakness. {11:31} The God and Father of the Lord Jesus, who is to be praised forever, knows that I am not lying. {11:32} In Damascus, the governor under King Aretas had the city of the Damascenes guarded in order to arrest me. {11:33} But I was lowered in a basket through a window in the wall and slipped through his hands.

{12:1} It is not beneficial for me to boast; I will go on to visions and revelations from the Lord. {12:2} I know a man in Christ who fourteen years ago was caught up to the third heaven. Whether it was in the body or out of the body, I do not know—God knows. {12:3} And I know that this man—whether in the body or apart from the body I do not know, but God knows— {12:4} was caught up to paradise and heard inexpressible things, things that no one is permitted to tell. {12:5} I will boast about a man like that, but I will not boast about myself, except about my weaknesses. {12:6} Even if I should choose to boast, I would not be a fool because I would be speaking the truth. But I refrain, so no one will think more of me than is warranted by what I do or say. {12:7} Or because of these surpassingly great revelations, therefore, in order to keep me from becoming conceited, I was given a thorn in my flesh, a messenger of Satan, to torment me. {12:8} Three times I pleaded with the Lord to take it away from me. {12:9} But he said to me, "My grace is sufficient for you, for my power is made perfect in weakness." Therefore, I will boast all the more gladly about my weaknesses, so that Christ's power may rest on me. {12:10} That is why, for Christ's sake, I delight in weaknesses, in insults, in hardships, in persecutions, in difficulties. For when I am weak, then I am strong. {12:11} I have made a fool of myself, but you drove me to it. I ought to have been commended by you, for I am not in the least inferior to the "super-apostles," even though I am nothing. {12:12} The marks of a true apostle were signs, wonders, and miracles were done among you with great perseverance. {12:13} How were you inferior to the other churches, except that I was never a burden to you? Forgive me this wrong! {12:14} Now I am ready to visit you for the third time, and I will not be a burden to you, because what I want is not your possessions but you. After all, children should not have to save up for their parents, but parents for their children. {12:15} So I will very gladly spend for you everything I have and expend myself as well. If I love you more, will you love me less? {12:16} Be that as it may, I have not been a burden to you. Yet, crafty fellow that I am, I caught you by trickery. {12:17} Did I exploit you through any of the men I sent to you? {12:18} I urged Titus to go to you and I sent our brother with him. Titus did not exploit you, did he? Did we not act in the same spirit and follow the same course? {12:19} Have you been thinking all along that we have been defending ourselves to you? We have been speaking in the sight of God as those in Christ, and everything we do, dear friends, is for your strengthening. {12:20} For I am afraid that when I come I may not find you as I want you to be, and you may not find me as you want me to be. I fear that there may be discord, jealousy, fits of rage, selfish ambition, slander, gossip, arrogance, and disorder. {12:21} I am afraid that when I come again my God will humble me before you and I will be grieved over many who have sinned earlier and have not repented of the impurity, sexual sin, and debauchery they have practiced.

{13:1} This is the third time I am coming to you. Every matter must be established by the testimony of two or three witnesses. {13:2} I warned you before, and I now repeat it as if I were there with you the second time. While I'm absent, I write to those who have sinned earlier and to all the others that if I come again, I will not hold back. {13:3} Since you are looking for proof of Christ speaking in me, he is not weak in dealing with you, but is powerful among you. {13:4} For although he was crucified in weakness, he lives by the power of God. For we also are weak in him, but we will live with him by the power of God in our dealings with you. {13:5} Examine yourselves to see whether you are in the faith; test yourselves. Do you not realize that Christ Jesus is in you—unless, of course, you fail the test? {13:6} And I trust that you will discover that we have not failed the test. {13:7} Now I pray to God that you will not do anything wrong; not so that people will see that we have passed the test, but so that you will do what is right even though we may seem to have failed. {13:8} For we cannot do anything against the truth, but only for the truth. {13:9} We are glad whenever we are weak but you are strong; and our prayer is that you may be fully restored. {13:10} This is why I write these things when I am absent, so that when I come I may not have to be harsh in my use of authority—the authority the Lord gave me for building you up, not for tearing you down. {13:11} Finally, brothers and sisters, rejoice! Strive for full restoration, encourage one another, be of one mind, live in peace. And the God of love and peace will be with you. {13:12} Greet one another with a holy kiss. {13:13} All God's people here send their greetings. {13:14} May the grace of the Lord Jesus Christ, the love of God, and the fellowship of the Holy Spirit be with you all. Amen.

The Third Epistle of Paul to the Corinthians

{1:1} Stephanus and the elders—Daphnus, Eubulus, Theophilus, and Zenon—send greetings to Paul, their eternal brother, in the Lord. {1:2} Two men, Simon and Cleobius, have come to Corinth and are misleading many with corrupt teachings. {1:3} We ask that you examine and test these teachings, {1:4} for we have never heard such things from you or the other apostles. {1:5} All that we received from you and them we still hold firmly. {1:6} The Lord has shown us mercy by allowing us to receive these truths from you in person, {1:7} so if possible, please come to us or send a letter. {1:8} We trust, as revealed to Theonoe, that the Lord has delivered you from the hand of the lawless one. {1:9} These men are teaching dangerous ideas, including: {1:10} rejecting the prophets, {1:11} denying that God is almighty, {1:12} claiming there is no resurrection of the body, {1:13} asserting that humans were not created by God, {1:14} saying that Christ did not come in the flesh nor was born of Mary, {1:15} and declaring that the world was not created by God, but by angels. {1:16} Therefore, dear brother, we earnestly ask you to come to us so the church in Corinth may be strengthened and these men's errors revealed. Farewell always in the Lord.

{2:1} The deacons Threptus and Eutyches delivered this letter to Philippi, {2:2} where Paul, still in prison due to Stratonice, the wife of Apollophanes, received it. He momentarily forgot his chains but was deeply troubled, {2:3} exclaiming, "It would be better for me to depart and be with the Lord than to stay and hear such false teachings bringing calamity upon calamity." {2:4} Suffering under both his imprisonment and the spread of Satan's schemes, {2:5} Paul, in his distress, wrote a letter in reply.

{3:1} Paul, a prisoner of Jesus Christ, sends greetings to the brethren in Corinth. {3:2} Surrounded by many trials, I am not surprised that the evil one's teachings are spreading quickly. {3:3} But my Lord Jesus Christ will come swiftly to silence those who distort His words. {3:4} From the beginning, I shared with you what I received from the holy apostles who were always with Jesus Christ: {3:5} that our Lord was born of Mary, a descendant of David by the flesh, with the Holy Spirit sent from heaven by the Father through the angel Gabriel. {3:6} He came into this world to redeem all by His own body and raise us from the dead as He has shown us through His own resurrection. {3:7} Because we are made by His Father, {3:8} He sought us when we were lost, giving us new life through adoption. {3:9} God, who created heaven and earth, first sent the prophets to the Jews to call them away from sin. {3:10} His desire was to save Israel, so He gave the prophets a portion of Christ's Spirit and sent them to proclaim true worship. {3:11} But the enemy, seeking to be worshipped as God, opposed and killed them, enslaving all through evil desires. {3:12} Yet the just God did not abandon His creation but had compassion from heaven, {3:13} sending His Spirit into Mary in Galilee, {3:14} who believed fully and received the Holy Spirit, bringing Jesus into the world. {3:15} Through the very flesh in which evil first brought death, God would now show victory. {3:16} By His body, Jesus saved all humanity, restoring us to life, {3:17} so that His body might display true righteousness. {3:18} In Him, we find salvation if we believe. {3:19} Those who disagree are not children of righteousness but of wrath, rejecting God's wisdom by claiming heaven and earth were not made by Him. {3:20} They are indeed children of wrath, following the serpent's teachings. {3:21} Drive them out and avoid their doctrine. {3:22} For you are not children of disobedience but of the beloved church, {3:23} to whom the resurrection is proclaimed. {3:24} As for those who deny the resurrection of the body, they will face judgment instead of life, {3:25} for they do not believe in the One who rose from the dead. {3:26} They do not understand how seeds are planted and decay only to rise again, clothed by God's will. {3:27} The new growth is even greater than the seed sown. {3:28} If we must consider more noble examples than seeds, {3:29} remember Jonah, who tried to escape preaching in Nineveh and was swallowed by a sea creature. {3:30} After three days and nights, God heard his prayer and restored him without harm. {3:31} How much more will God raise you, who believe in Christ, just as He was raised. {3:32} Likewise, a man was raised from the dead when thrown on the prophet Elisha's bones. If he could be raised by touching the prophet's bones, {3:33} how much more will you, who have been united with the body of the Lord, be raised in the last day. {3:34} If you accept any other teaching, God will be a witness against you. {3:35} Let no one trouble me, for I bear these chains for Christ and His marks on my body as I strive for the resurrection. {3:36} Whoever follows the teachings of the prophets and the gospel will be rewarded by the Lord with eternal life at the resurrection. {3:37} But those who reject these truths will face fire, along with those who follow their path—people without God, {3:38} a generation of vipers. {3:39} Reject them with the Lord's strength, {3:40} and peace, grace, and love will be with you always.

The Epistle of Paul to the Galatians

{1:1} Paul, an apostle (not appointed by human beings or through any human agency, but by Jesus Christ and God the Father, who raised him from the dead), {1:2} and all the brothers and sisters with me, send this letter to the churches in Galatia. {1:3} Grace and peace to you from God the Father and our Lord Jesus Christ, {1:4} who gave himself for our sins to rescue us from this present evil age, according to the will of our God and Father. {1:5} To him be glory for ever and ever. Amen. {1:6} I am astonished that you are so quickly turning away from the one who called you to live in the grace of Christ and are turning to a different gospel— {1:7} which is really no gospel at all. Evidently, some people are throwing you into confusion and are trying to pervert the gospel of Christ. {1:8} But even if we or an angel from heaven should preach a gospel other than the one we preached to you, let them be under God's curse! {1:9} As we have already said, so now I say again: If anyone is preaching to you a gospel other than what you accepted, let them be under God's curse! {1:10} Am I now trying to win the approval of human beings, or of God? Or am I trying to please people? If I were still trying to please people, I would not be a servant of Christ. {1:11} I want you to know, brothers and sisters, that the gospel I preached is not of human origin. {1:12} I did not receive it from any man, nor was I taught it; rather, I received it by revelation from Jesus Christ. {1:13} For you have heard of my previous way of life in Judaism, how intensely I persecuted the church of God and tried to destroy it. {1:14} I was advancing in Judaism beyond many of my own age among my people and was extremely zealous for the traditions of my fathers. {1:15} But when God, who set me apart from my mother's womb and called me by his grace, was pleased {1:16} to reveal his Son in me so that I might preach him among the Gentiles, I did not consult any human being. {1:17} Nor did I go up to Jerusalem to see those who were apostles before I was, but I went into Arabia. Later I returned to Damascus. {1:18} Then, after three years, I went up to Jerusalem to get acquainted with Peter and stayed with him fifteen days. {1:19} I saw none of the other apostles—only James, the Lord's brother. {1:20} I assure you before God that what I am writing you is no lie. {1:21} Later I went to the regions of Syria and Cilicia. {1:22} I was personally unknown to the churches of Judea that are in Christ. {1:23} They only heard the report: "The man who formerly persecuted us is now preaching the faith he once tried to destroy." {1:24} And they praised God because of me.

{2:1} Fourteen years later I went up again to Jerusalem, this time with Barnabas, and I took Titus along also. {2:2} I went in response to a revelation and meeting privately with those esteemed as leaders, I presented to them the gospel that I preach among the Gentiles. I wanted to be sure I was not running and had not run my race in vain. {2:3} Yet not even Titus, who was with me, was compelled to be circumcised, even though he was a Greek. {2:4} This matter arose because some false believers had infiltrated our ranks to spy on the freedom we have in Christ Jesus and to make us slaves. {2:5} We did not give in to them for a moment, so that the truth of the gospel might be preserved for you. {2:6} As for those who were held in high esteem—whatever they were makes no difference to me; God does not show favoritism—they added nothing to my message. {2:7} On the contrary, they recognized that I had been entrusted with the task of preaching the gospel to the uncircumcised, just as Peter had been to the circumcised. {2:8} For God, who was at work in Peter as an apostle to the circumcised, was also at work in me as an apostle to the Gentiles. {2:9} James, Cephas (Peter), and John, those esteemed as pillars, gave me and Barnabas the right hand of fellowship when they recognized the grace given to me. They agreed that we should go to the Gentiles, and they to the circumcised. {2:10} All they asked was that we should continue to remember the poor, the very thing I had been eager to do all along. {2:11} When Peter came to Antioch, I opposed him to his face, because he stood condemned. {2:12} For before certain men came from James, he used to eat with the Gentiles. But when they arrived, he began to draw back and separate himself from the Gentiles because he was afraid of those who belonged to the circumcision group. {2:13} The other Jews joined him in his hypocrisy, so that by their hypocrisy even Barnabas was led astray. {2:14} When I saw that they were not acting in line with the truth of the gospel, I said to Peter in front of them all, "You are a Jew, yet you live like a Gentile and not like a Jew. How is it, then, that you force Gentiles to follow Jewish customs? {2:15} We who are Jews by birth and not sinful Gentiles {2:16} know that a person is not justified by the works of the law, but by faith in Jesus Christ. So we, too, have put our faith in Christ Jesus that we may be justified by faith in Christ and not by the works of the law, because by the works of the law no one will be justified. {2:17} But if, in seeking to be justified in Christ, we Jews find ourselves also among the sinners, doesn't that mean that Christ promotes sin? Absolutely not! {2:18} If I rebuild what I destroyed, then I really would be a lawbreaker. {2:19} For through the law I died to the law so that I might live for God. {2:20} I have been crucified with Christ and I no longer live, but Christ lives in me. The life I now live in the body, I live by faith in the Son of God, who loved me and gave himself for me. {2:21} I do not set aside the grace of God, for if righteousness could be gained through the law, Christ died for nothing!

{3:1} You foolish Galatians! Who has bewitched you? Before your very eyes, Jesus Christ was clearly portrayed as crucified. {3:2} I would like to learn just one thing from you: Did you receive the Spirit by the works of the law, or by believing what you heard? {3:3} Are you so foolish? After beginning by means of the Spirit, are you now trying to finish by means of the flesh? {3:4} Have you experienced so much in vain—if it really was in vain? {3:5} So again I ask: Does God give you his Spirit and work miracles among you by the works of the law, or by your believing what you heard? {3:6} So also Abraham "believed God, and it was credited to him as righteousness." {3:7} Understand, then, that those who have faith are children of Abraham. {3:8} Scripture foresaw that God would justify the Gentiles by faith and announced the gospel in advance to Abraham: "All nations will be blessed through you." {3:9} So those who rely on faith are blessed along with Abraham, the man of faith. {3:10} For all who rely on the works of the law are under a curse, as it is written: "Cursed is everyone who does not continue to do everything written in the Book of the Law." {3:11} Clearly no one who relies on the law is justified before God, because "the righteous will live by faith." {3:12} The law is not based on faith; on the contrary, it says, "The person who does these things will live by them." {3:13} Christ redeemed us from the curse of the law by becoming a curse for us, for it is written: "Cursed is everyone who is hung on a pole." {3:14} He redeemed us in order that the blessing given to Abraham might come to the Gentiles through Christ Jesus, so that by faith we might receive the promise of the Spirit. {3:15} Brothers and sisters, let me take an example from everyday life: Just as no one can set aside or add to a human covenant that has been duly established, {3:16} so it is in this case: The promises were spoken to Abraham and to his seed. Scripture does not say "and to seeds," meaning many people, but "and to your seed," meaning one person, who is Christ. {3:17} What I mean is this: The law, introduced 430 years later, does not set aside the covenant previously established by God and thus do away with the promise. {3:18} For if the inheritance depends on the law, then it no longer depends on the promise; but God in his grace gave it to Abraham through a promise. {3:19} Why, then, was the law given at all? It was added because of transgressions until the Seed to whom the promise referred had come. The law was given through angels and entrusted to a mediator. {3:20} A mediator, however, implies more than one party; but God is one. {3:21} Is the law, therefore, opposed to the promises of God? Absolutely not! For if a law had been given that could impart life, then righteousness would certainly have come by the law. {3:22} But Scripture has locked up everything under the control of sin, so that what was promised, being given through faith in Jesus Christ, might be given to those who believe. {3:23} Before the coming of this faith, we were held in custody under the law, locked up until the faith that was to come would be revealed. {3:24} So the law was our guardian until Christ came that we might be justified by faith. {3:25} Now that this faith has come, we are no longer under a guardian. {3:26} So in Christ Jesus you are all children of God through faith, {3:27} for all of you who were baptized into Christ have clothed yourselves with Christ. {3:28} There is neither Jew nor Gentile, neither slave nor free, nor is there male and female, for you are all one in Christ Jesus. {3:29} If you belong to Christ, then you are Abraham's seed, and heirs according to the promise.

{4:1} What I mean is that as long as an heir is underage, he is no different from a slave, although he owns the whole estate. {4:2} The heir is subject to guardians and trustees until the time set by his father. {4:3} So also, when we were underage, we were in slavery under the elemental spiritual forces of the world. {4:4} But when the set time had fully come, God sent his Son, born of a woman, born under the law, {4:5} to redeem those under the law, that we might receive adoption to sonship. {4:6} Because you are his sons, God sent the Spirit of his Son into our hearts, the Spirit who calls out, "Abba, Father." {4:7} So you are no longer a slave, but God's child; and since you are his child, God has made you also an heir. {4:8} Formerly, when you did not know God, you were slaves to those who by nature are not gods. {4:9} But now that you know God—or rather are known by God—how is it that you are turning back to those weak and miserable forces? Do you wish to be enslaved by them all over again? {4:10} You are observing special days and months and seasons and years! {4:11} I fear for you, that somehow I have wasted my efforts on you. {4:12} I plead with you, brothers and sisters, become like me, for I became like you. You did me no wrong. {4:13} As you know, it was because of an illness that I first preached the gospel to you. {4:14} And even though my illness was a trial to you, you did not treat me with contempt or scorn. Instead, you welcomed me as if I were an angel of God, as if I were Christ Jesus himself. {4:15} Where, then, is your blessing of me now? I can testify that, if you could have done so, you would have torn out your eyes and given them to me. {4:16} Have I now become your enemy by telling you the truth? {4:17} Those people are zealous to win you over, but for no good. What they want is to alienate you from us so that you may have zeal for them. {4:18} It is fine to be zealous, provided the purpose is good, and to be so always, not just when I am with you. {4:19} My dear children, for whom I am again in the pains of childbirth until Christ is formed in you, {4:20} how I wish I could be with you now and change my tone, because I am perplexed about you! {4:21} Tell me, you who want to be under the law, are you not aware of what the law says? {4:22} For it is written that Abraham had two sons, one by the slave woman and the other by the free woman. {4:23} His son by the slave woman was born according to the flesh, but his son by the free woman was born as the result of a divine promise. {4:24} These things are being taken figuratively: The women represent two covenants. One covenant is from Mount Sinai and bears children who are to be slaves: This is Hagar. {4:25} Now Hagar stands for Mount Sinai in Arabia and corresponds to the present city of Jerusalem, because she is in slavery with her children. {4:26} But the Jerusalem that is above is free, and she is our mother. {4:27} For it is written: "Be glad, barren woman, you who never bore a child; break forth and cry aloud, you who were never in labor; because more are the children of the desolate woman than of her who has a husband." {4:28} Now you, brothers and sisters, like Isaac, are children of promise. {4:29} At that time the son born according to the flesh persecuted the son born by the power of the Spirit. It is the same now. {4:30} But what does Scripture say? "Get rid of the slave woman and her son, for the slave woman's son will never share in the inheritance with the free woman's son." {4:31} Therefore, brothers and sisters, we are not children of the slave woman, but of the free woman.

{5:1} Stand firm, then, in the freedom Christ has given you, and do not let yourselves be burdened again by a yoke of slavery. {5:2} Mark my words! I, Paul, tell you that if you let yourselves be circumcised, Christ will be of no value to you at all. {5:3} Again I declare to every man who lets himself be circumcised that he is obligated to obey the whole law. {5:4} You who are trying to be justified by the law have been alienated from Christ; you have fallen away from grace. {5:5} For through the Spirit we eagerly await by faith the righteousness for which we hope. {5:6} For in Christ Jesus neither circumcision nor uncircumcision has any value. The only thing that counts is faith expressing itself through love. {5:7} You were running a good race. Who cut in on you to keep you from obeying the truth? {5:8} That kind of persuasion does not come from the one who calls you. {5:9} A little yeast works through the whole batch of dough. {5:10} I am confident in the Lord that you will take no other view. The one who is throwing you into confusion will pay the penalty, whoever they may be. {5:11} Brothers and sisters, if I am still preaching circumcision, why am I still being persecuted? In that case, the offense of the cross has been abolished. {5:12} As for those agitators, I wish they would go the whole way and emasculate themselves! {5:13} You, my brothers and sisters, were called to be free. But do not use your freedom to indulge the flesh; rather, serve one another humbly in love. {5:14} For the entire law is fulfilled in keeping this one command: "Love your neighbor as yourself." {5:15} If you bite and devour each other, watch out or you will be destroyed by each other. {5:16} So I say, walk by the Spirit, and you will not gratify the desires of the flesh. {5:17} For the flesh desires what is contrary to the Spirit, and the Spirit what is contrary to the flesh. They are in conflict with each other, so that you are not to do whatever you want. {5:18} But if you are led by the Spirit, you are not under the law. {5:19} The acts of the flesh are obvious: sexual immorality, impurity, and debauchery; {5:20} idolatry and witchcraft; hatred, discord, jealousy, fits of rage, selfish ambition, dissensions, factions and envy; {5:21} drunkenness, orgies, and the like. I warn you, as I did before, that those who live like this will not inherit the kingdom of God. {5:22} But the fruit of the Spirit is love, joy, peace, forbearance (patience), kindness, goodness, faithfulness, {5:23} gentleness and self-control. Against such things there is no law. {5:24} Those who belong to Christ Jesus have crucified the flesh with its passions and desires. {5:25} Since we live by the Spirit, let us keep in step with the Spirit. {5:26} Let us not become conceited, provoking and envying each other.

{6:1} Brothers and sisters, if someone is caught in a sin, you who live by the Spirit should restore that person gently. But watch yourselves, or you also may be tempted. {6:2} Carry each other's burdens, and in this way you will fulfill the law of Christ. {6:3} If anyone thinks they are something when they are not, they deceive themselves. {6:4} Each one should test their own actions. Then they can take pride in themselves alone, without comparing themselves to someone else, {6:5} for each one should carry their own load. {6:6} Nevertheless, the one who receives instruction in the word should share all good things with their instructor. {6:7} Do not be deceived: God cannot be mocked. A man reaps what he sows. {6:8} Whoever sows to please their flesh, from the flesh will reap destruction; whoever sows to please the Spirit, from the Spirit will reap eternal life. {6:9} Let us not become weary in doing good, for at the proper time we will reap a harvest if we do not give up. {6:10} Therefore, as we have opportunity, let us do good to all people, especially to those who belong to the family of believers. {6:11} See what large letters I use as I write to you with my own hand! {6:12} Those who want to impress people by means of the flesh are trying to compel you to be circumcised. The only reason they do this is to avoid being persecuted for the cross of Christ. {6:13} Not even those who are circumcised keep the law, yet they want you to be circumcised that they may boast about your circumcision in the flesh. {6:14} May I never boast except in the cross of our Lord Jesus Christ, through which the world has been crucified to me, and I to the world. {6:15} Neither circumcision nor uncircumcision means anything; what counts is the new creation. {6:16} Peace and mercy to all who follow this rule—to the Israel of God. {6:17} From now on, let no one cause me trouble, for I bear on my body the marks of Jesus. {6:18} The grace of our Lord Jesus Christ be with your spirit. Amen.

The Epistle of Paul to the Ephesians

{1:1} Paul, an apostle of Jesus Christ by the will of God, writes to the saints in Ephesus and to those who are faithful in Christ Jesus: {1:2} Grace and peace to you from God our Father and the Lord Jesus Christ. {1:3} Praise be to the God and Father of our Lord Jesus Christ, who has blessed us with every spiritual blessing in the heavenly realms in Christ. {1:4} For he chose us in him before the creation of the world to be holy and blameless in his sight. {1:5} In love, he predestined us for adoption to sonship through Jesus Christ, in accordance with his pleasure and will, {1:6} to the praise of his glorious grace, which he has freely given us in the One he loves. {1:7} In him, we have redemption through his blood, the forgiveness of sins, in accordance with the riches of God's grace {1:8} that he lavished on us. With all wisdom and understanding, {1:9} he made known to us the mystery of his will according to his good pleasure, which he purposed in Christ {1:10} to be put into effect when the times reach their fulfillment—to bring unity to all things in heaven and on earth under Christ. {1:11} In him, we were also chosen, having been predestined according to the plan of him who works out everything in conformity with the purpose of his will, {1:12} in order that we, who were the first to put our hope in Christ, might be for the praise of his glory. {1:13} And you also were included in Christ when you heard the message of truth, the gospel of your salvation. When you believed, you were marked in him with a seal, the promised Holy Spirit, {1:14} who is a deposit guaranteeing our inheritance until the redemption of those who are God's possession, to the praise of his glory. {1:15} For this reason, ever since I heard about your faith in the Lord Jesus and your love for all God's people, {1:16} I have not stopped giving thanks for you, remembering you in my prayers. {1:17} I keep asking that the God of our Lord Jesus Christ, the glorious Father, may give you the Spirit of wisdom and revelation, so that you may know him better. {1:18} I pray that the eyes of your heart may be enlightened in order that you may know the hope to which he has called you, the riches of his glorious inheritance in his holy people, {1:19} and his incomparably great power for us who believe. That power is the same as the mighty strength {1:20} he exerted when he raised Christ from the dead and seated him at his right hand in the heavenly realms, {1:21} far above all rule and authority, power and dominion, and every name that is invoked, not only in the present age but also in the one to come. {1:22} And God placed all things under his feet and appointed him to be head over everything for the church, {1:23} which is his body, the fullness of him who fills everything in every way.

{2:1} As for you, you were dead in your transgressions and sins, {2:2} in which you used to live when you followed the ways of this world and of the ruler of the kingdom of the air, the spirit who is now at work in those who are disobedient. {2:3} All of us also lived among them at one time, gratifying the cravings of our flesh and following its desires and thoughts. Like the rest, we were by nature deserving of wrath. {2:4} But because of his great love for us, God, who is rich in mercy, {2:5} made us alive with Christ even when we were dead in transgressions—it is by grace you have been saved. {2:6} And God raised us up with Christ and seated us with him in the heavenly realms in Christ Jesus, {2:7} in order that in the coming ages he might show the incomparable riches of his grace, expressed in his kindness to us in Christ Jesus. {2:8} For it is by grace you have been saved, through faith—and this is not from yourselves, it is the gift of God— {2:9} not by works, so that no one can boast. {2:10} For we are God's handiwork, created in Christ Jesus to do good works, which God prepared in advance for us to do. {2:11} Therefore, remember that formerly you who are Gentiles by birth and called "uncircumcised" by those who call themselves "the circumcision" (which is done in the body by human hands)— {2:12} remember that at that time you were separate from Christ, excluded from citizenship in Israel and foreigners to the covenants of the promise, without hope and without God in the world. {2:13} But now in Christ Jesus you who once were far away have been brought near by the blood of Christ. {2:14} For he himself is our peace, who has made the two groups one and has destroyed the barrier, the dividing wall of hostility, {2:15} by setting aside in his flesh the law with its commands and regulations. His purpose was to create in himself one new humanity out of the two, thus making peace, {2:16} and in one body to reconcile both of them to God through the cross, by which he put to death their hostility. {2:17} He came and preached peace to you who were far away and peace to those who were near. {2:18} For through him we both have access to the Father by one Spirit. {2:19} Consequently, you are no longer foreigners and strangers, but fellow citizens with God's people and also members of his household, {2:20} built on the foundation of the apostles and prophets, with Christ Jesus himself as the chief cornerstone. {2:21} In him, the whole building is joined together and rises to become a holy temple in the Lord. {2:22} And in him, you too are being built together to become a dwelling in which God lives by his Spirit.

{3:1} For this reason, I, Paul, a prisoner of Christ Jesus for the sake of you Gentiles, {3:2} if indeed you have heard about the administration of God's grace that was given to me for you. {3:3} That is, the mystery made known to me by revelation, as I have already written briefly. {3:4} In reading this, then, you will be able to understand my insight into the mystery of Christ, {3:5} which was not made known to people in other generations as it has now been revealed by the Spirit to God's holy apostles and prophets. {3:6} This mystery is that through the gospel, the Gentiles are heirs together with Israel, members together of one body, and sharers together in the promise in Christ Jesus. {3:7} I became a servant of this gospel by the gift of God's grace given me through the working of his power. {3:8} Although I am less than the least of all the Lord's people, this grace was given me: to preach to the Gentiles the boundless riches of Christ {3:9} and to make plain to everyone the administration of this mystery, which for ages past was kept hidden in God, who created all things. {3:10} His intent was that now, through the church, the manifold wisdom of God should be made known to the rulers and authorities in the heavenly realms, {3:11} according to his eternal purpose that he accomplished in Christ Jesus our Lord. {3:12} In him and through faith in him we may approach God with freedom and confidence. {3:13} I ask you, therefore, not to be discouraged because of my sufferings for you, which are your glory. {3:14} For this reason, I kneel before the Father, {3:15} from whom every family in heaven and on earth derives its name. {3:16} I pray that out of his glorious riches he may strengthen you with power through his Spirit in your inner being, {3:17} so that Christ may dwell in your hearts through faith. And I pray that you, being rooted and established in love, {3:18} may have power, together with all the Lord's holy people, to grasp how wide and long and high and deep is the love of Christ, {3:19} and to know this love that surpasses knowledge—that you may be filled to the measure of all the fullness of God. {3:20} Now to him who is able to do immeasurably more than all we ask or imagine, according to his power that is at work within us, {3:21} to him be glory in the church and in Christ Jesus throughout all generations, for ever and ever! Amen.

{4:1} As a prisoner for the Lord, then, I urge you to live a life worthy of the calling you have received. {4:2} Be completely humble and gentle; be patient, bearing with one another in love. {4:3} Make every effort to keep the unity of the Spirit through the bond of peace. {4:4} There is one body and one Spirit, just as you were called to one hope when you were called; {4:5} one Lord, one faith, one baptism; {4:6} one God and Father of all, who is over all and through all and in all. {4:7} But to each one of us grace has been given as Christ apportioned it. {4:8} This is why it says: "When he ascended on high, he took many captives and gave gifts to his people." {4:9} (What does "he ascended" mean except that he also descended to the lower, earthly regions? {4:10} He who descended is the very one who ascended higher than all the heavens, in order to fill the whole universe.) {4:11} So Christ himself gave the apostles, the prophets, the evangelists, the pastors and teachers, {4:12} to equip his people for works of service, so that the body of Christ may be built up {4:13} until we all reach unity in the faith and in the knowledge of the Son of God and become mature, attaining to the whole measure of the fullness of Christ. {4:14} Then we will no longer be infants, tossed back and forth by the waves, and blown here and there by every wind of teaching and by the cunning and craftiness of people in their deceitful scheming. {4:15} Instead, speaking the truth in love, we will grow to become in every respect the mature body of him who is the head, that is, Christ. {4:16} From him the whole body, joined and held together by every supporting ligament, grows and builds itself up in love, as each part does its work. {4:17} So I tell you this, and insist on it in the Lord, that you must no longer live as the Gentiles do, in the futility of their thinking. {4:18} They are darkened in their understanding and separated from the life of God because of the ignorance that is in them due to the hardening of their hearts. {4:19} Having lost all sensitivity, they have given themselves over to sensuality so as to indulge in every kind of impurity, and they are full of greed. {4:20} That, however, is not the way of life you learned {4:21} when you heard about Christ and were taught in him in accordance with the truth that is in Jesus. {4:22} You were taught, with regard to your former way of life, to put off your old self, which is being corrupted by its deceitful desires; {4:23} to be made new in the attitude of your minds; {4:24} and to put on the new self, created to be like God in true righteousness and holiness. {4:25} Therefore, each of you must put off falsehood and speak truthfully to your neighbor, for we are all members of one body. {4:26} "In your anger do not sin": Do not let the sun go down while you are still angry, {4:27} and do not give the devil a foothold. {4:28} Anyone who has been stealing must steal no longer, but must work, doing something useful with their own hands, that they may have something to share with those in need. {4:29} Do not let any unwholesome talk come out of your mouths, but only what is helpful for building others up according to their needs, that it may benefit those who listen. {4:30} And do not grieve the Holy Spirit of God, with whom you were sealed for the day of redemption. {4:31} Get rid of all bitterness, rage and anger, brawling and slander, along with every form of malice. {4:32} Be kind and compassionate to one another, forgiving each other, just as in Christ God forgave you.

{5:1} Therefore, be imitators of God, as beloved children; {5:2} and walk in love, just as Christ loved us and gave himself up for us as a fragrant offering and sacrifice to God. {5:3} But among you, there must not be even a hint of sexual immorality, or any kind of impurity, or greed, because these are improper for God's holy people. {5:4} Nor should there be obscenity, foolish talk, or coarse joking, which are out of place, but rather thanksgiving. {5:5} For of this you can be sure: No immoral, impure, or greedy person—such a person is an idolater—has any inheritance in the kingdom of Christ and of God. {5:6} Let no one deceive you with empty words, for because of such things God's wrath comes on those who are disobedient. {5:7} Therefore, do not be partners with them. {5:8} For you were once darkness, but now you are light in the Lord: live as children of light {5:9} (for the fruit of the light consists in all goodness, righteousness, and truth) {5:10} and find out what pleases the Lord. {5:11} Have nothing to do with the fruitless deeds of darkness, but rather expose them. {5:12} It is shameful even to mention what the disobedient do in secret. {5:13} But everything exposed by the light becomes visible—and everything that is illuminated becomes a light. {5:14} This is why it is said: "Wake up, sleeper, rise from the dead, and Christ will shine on you." {5:15} Be very careful, then, how you live—not as unwise but as wise, {5:16} making the most of every opportunity, because the days are evil. {5:17} Therefore do not be foolish, but understand what the Lord's will is. {5:18} Do not get drunk on wine, which leads to debauchery (excessive indulgence); instead, be filled with the Spirit, {5:19} speaking to one another with psalms, hymns, and songs from the Spirit. Sing and make music from your heart to the Lord, {5:20} always giving thanks to God the Father for everything, in the name of our Lord Jesus Christ. {5:21} Submit to one another out of reverence for Christ. {5:22} Wives, submit yourselves to your own husbands as you do to the Lord. {5:23} For the husband is the head of the wife as Christ is the head of the church, his body, of which he is the Savior. {5:24} Now as the church submits to Christ, so also wives should submit to their husbands in everything. {5:25} Husbands, love your wives, just as Christ loved the church and gave himself up for her {5:26} to make her holy, cleansing her by the washing with water through the word, {5:27} and to present her to himself as a radiant church, without stain or wrinkle or any other blemish, but holy and blameless. {5:28} In this same way, husbands ought to love their wives as their own bodies. He who loves his wife loves himself. {5:29} After all, no one ever hated their own body, but they feed and care for their body, just as Christ does the church— {5:30} for we are members of his body. {5:31} For this reason, a man will leave his father and mother and be united to his wife, and the two will become one flesh. {5:32} This is a profound mystery—but I am talking about Christ and the church. {5:33} However, each one of you also must love his wife as he loves himself, and the wife must respect her husband.

{6:1} Children, obey your parents in the Lord, for this is right. {6:2} "Honor your father and mother"—which is the first commandment with a promise— {6:3} so that it may go well with you and that you may enjoy long life on the earth. {6:4} Fathers, do not exasperate your children; instead, bring them up in the training and instruction of the Lord. {6:5} Slaves, obey your earthly masters with respect and fear, and with sincerity of heart, just as you would obey Christ. {6:6} Obey them not only to win their favor when their eye is on you, but as slaves of Christ, doing the will of God from your heart. {6:7} Serve wholeheartedly, as if you were serving the Lord, not people, {6:8} because you know that the Lord will reward each one for whatever good they do, whether they are slave or free. {6:9} And masters, treat your slaves in the same way. Do not threaten them, since you know that he who is both their Master and yours is in heaven, and there is no favoritism with him. {6:10} Finally, be strong in the Lord and in his mighty power. {6:11} Put on the full armor of God, so that you can take your stand against the devil's schemes. {6:12} For our struggle is not against flesh and blood, but against the rulers, against the authorities, against the powers of this dark world and against the spiritual forces of evil in the heavenly realms. {6:13} Therefore put on the full armor of God, so that when the day of evil comes, you may be able to stand your ground, and after you have done everything, to stand. {6:14} Stand firm then, with the belt of truth buckled around your waist, with the breastplate of righteousness in place, {6:15} and with your feet fitted with the readiness that comes from the gospel of peace. {6:16} In addition to all this, take up the shield of faith, with which you can extinguish all the flaming arrows of the evil one. {6:17} Take the helmet of salvation and the sword of the Spirit, which is the word of God. {6:18} And pray in the Spirit on all occasions with all kinds of prayers and requests. With this in mind, be alert and always keep on praying for all the Lord's people. {6:19} Pray also for me, that whenever I speak, words may be given me so that I will fearlessly make known the mystery of the gospel, {6:20} for which I am an ambassador in chains. Pray that I may declare it fearlessly, as I should. {6:21} Tychicus, the dear brother and faithful servant in the Lord, will tell you everything, so that you also may know how I am and what I am doing. {6:22} I am sending him to you for this very purpose, that you may know how we are, and that he may encourage you. {6:23} Peace to the brothers and sisters, and love with faith from God the Father and the Lord Jesus Christ. {6:24} Grace to all who love our Lord Jesus Christ with an undying love.

The Epistle of Paul to the Philippians

{1:1} Paul and Timothy, servants of Jesus Christ, to all the saints in Christ Jesus at Philippi, along with the bishops and deacons: {1:2} Grace and peace to you from God our Father and the Lord Jesus Christ. {1:3} I thank my God every time I remember you, {1:4} in all my prayers for all of you, I always pray with joy {1:5} because of your partnership in the gospel from the first day until now. {1:6} I am confident of this: that he who began a good work in you will carry it on to completion until the day of Christ Jesus. {1:7} It is right for me to feel this way about all of you, since I have you in my heart; for whether I am in chains or defending and confirming the gospel, all of you share in God's grace with me. {1:8} God can testify how I long for all of you with the affection of Christ Jesus. {1:9} And this is my prayer: that your love may abound more and more in knowledge and depth of insight, {1:10} so that you may be able to discern what is best and may be pure and blameless until the day of Christ, {1:11} filled with the fruit of righteousness that comes through Jesus Christ—to the glory and praise of God. {1:12} Now I want you to know, brothers and sisters, that what has happened to me has actually served to advance the gospel. {1:13} As a result, it has become clear throughout the whole palace guard and to everyone else that I am in chains for Christ. {1:14} And because of my chains, most of the brothers and sisters have become confident in the Lord and dare all the more to proclaim the gospel without fear. {1:15} It is true that some preach Christ out of envy and rivalry, but others out of goodwill. {1:16} The latter do so out of love, knowing that I am put here for the defense of the gospel. {1:17} The former preach Christ out of selfish ambition, not sincerely, supposing that they can stir up trouble for me while I am in chains. {1:18} But what does it matter? The important thing is that in every way, whether from false motives or true, Christ is preached. And because of this, I rejoice. Yes, and I will continue to rejoice, {1:19} for I know that through your prayers and God's provision of the Spirit of Jesus Christ, what has happened to me will turn out for my deliverance. {1:20} I eagerly expect and hope that I will in no way be ashamed, but will have sufficient courage so that now, as always, Christ will be exalted in my body, whether by life or by death. {1:21} For to me, to live is Christ and to die is gain. {1:22} If I am to go on living in the body, this will mean fruitful labor for me. Yet what shall I choose? I do not know! {1:23} I am torn between the two: I desire to depart and be with Christ, which is better by far; {1:24} but it is more necessary for you that I remain in the body. {1:25} Convinced of this, I know that I will remain, and I will continue with all of you for your progress and joy in the faith, {1:26} so that through my being with you again your joy in Christ Jesus will overflow on account of me. {1:27} Whatever happens, conduct yourselves in a manner worthy of the gospel of Christ. Then, whether I come and see you or only hear about you in my absence, I will know that you stand firm in the one Spirit, striving together as one for the faith of the gospel {1:28} without being frightened in any way by those who oppose you. This is a sign to them that they will be destroyed, but that you will be saved—and that by God. {1:29} For it has been granted to you on behalf of Christ not only to believe in him but also to suffer for him, {1:30} since you are going through the same struggle you saw I had, and now hear that I still have.

{2:1} Therefore, if you have any encouragement from being united with Christ, if any comfort from his love, if any common sharing in the Spirit, if any tenderness and compassion, {2:2} then make my joy complete by being like-minded, having the same love, being one in spirit and of one mind. {2:3} Do nothing out of selfish ambition or vain conceit. Rather, in humility value others above yourselves, {2:4} not looking to your own interests but each of you to the interests of the others. {2:5} In your relationships with one another, have the same mindset as Christ Jesus: {2:6} Who, being in very nature God, did not consider equality with God something to be used to his own advantage; {2:7} rather, he made himself nothing by taking the very nature of a servant, being made in human likeness. {2:8} And being found in appearance as a man, he humbled himself by becoming obedient to death—even death on a cross! {2:9} Therefore God exalted him to the highest place and gave him the name that is above every name, {2:10} that at the name of Jesus every knee should bow, in heaven and on earth and under the earth, {2:11} and every tongue acknowledge that Jesus Christ is Lord, to the glory of God the Father. {2:12} Therefore, my dear friends, as you have always obeyed—not only in my presence but now much more in my absence—continue to work out your salvation with fear and trembling, {2:13} for it is God who works in you to will and to act in order to fulfill his good purpose. {2:14} Do everything without grumbling or arguing, {2:15} so that you may become blameless and pure, children of God without fault in a warped and crooked generation, in which you shine like stars in the universe {2:16} as you hold firmly to the word of life. And then I will be able to boast on the day of Christ that I did not run or labor in vain. {2:17} But even if I am being poured out like a drink offering on the sacrifice and service coming from your faith, I am glad and rejoice with all of you. {2:18} So you too should be glad and rejoice with me. {2:19} I hope in the Lord Jesus to send Timothy to you soon, that I also may be cheered when I receive news about you. {2:20} I have no one else like him, who will show genuine concern for your welfare. {2:21} For everyone looks out for their own interests, not those of Jesus Christ. {2:22} But you know that Timothy has proved himself, because as a son with his father he has served with me in the work of the gospel. {2:23} I hope, therefore, to send him as soon as I see how things go with me. {2:24} And I am confident in the Lord that I myself will come soon. {2:25} But I think it necessary to send back to you Epaphroditus, my brother, co-worker and fellow soldier, who is also your messenger, whom you sent to take care of my needs. {2:26} For he longs for all of you and is distressed because you heard he was ill. {2:27} Indeed he was ill, and almost died. But God had mercy on him, and not only on him but also on me, to spare me sorrow upon sorrow. {2:28} Therefore I am all the more eager to send him, so that when you see him again you may be glad and I may have less anxiety. {2:29} So then, welcome him in the Lord with great joy, and honor people like him, {2:30} because he almost died for the work of Christ. He risked his life to make up for help you yourselves could not give me.

{3:1} Finally, my brothers and sisters, rejoice in the Lord. It's no trouble for me to write the same things to you again, and it is a safeguard for you. {3:2} Watch out for those dogs, those evildoers, those mutilators of the flesh. {3:3} For it is we who are the circumcision, we who serve God by his Spirit, who boast in Christ Jesus, and who put no confidence in the flesh. {3:4} Though I myself have reasons for such confidence. If someone else thinks they have reasons to put confidence in the flesh, I have more: {3:5} circumcised on the eighth day, of the people of Israel, of the tribe of Benjamin, a Hebrew of Hebrews; in regard to the law, a Pharisee; {3:6} as for zeal, persecuting the church; as for righteousness based on the law, faultless. {3:7} But whatever were gains to me, I now consider loss for the sake of Christ. {3:8} What is more, I consider everything a loss because of the surpassing worth of knowing Christ Jesus my Lord, for whose sake I have lost all things. I consider them garbage (or rubbish), that I may gain Christ {3:9} and be found in him, not having a righteousness of my own that comes from the law, but that which is through faith in Christ—the righteousness that comes from God on the basis of faith. {3:10} I want to know Christ—yes, to know the power of his resurrection and participation in his sufferings, becoming like him in his death, {3:11} and so, somehow, attaining to the resurrection from the dead. {3:12} Not that I have already obtained all this or have already arrived at my goal, but I press on to take hold of that for which Christ Jesus took hold of me. {3:13} Brothers and sisters, I do not consider myself yet to have taken hold of it. But one thing I do: Forgetting what is behind and straining toward what is ahead, {3:14} I press on toward the goal to win the prize for which God has called me heavenward in Christ Jesus. {3:15} All of us, then, who are mature should take such a view of things. And if on some point you think differently, that too God will make clear to you. {3:16} Only let us live up to what we have already attained. {3:17} Join together in following my example, brothers and sisters, and just as you have us as a model, keep your eyes on those who live as we do. {3:18} For, as I have often told you before and now tell you again even with tears, many live as enemies of the cross of Christ. {3:19} Their destiny is destruction, their god is their stomach, and their glory is in their shame. Their mind is set on earthly things. {3:20} But our citizenship is in heaven, and we eagerly await a Savior from there, the Lord Jesus Christ, {3:21} who, by the power that enables him to bring everything under his control, will transform our lowly bodies so that they will be like his glorious body.

{4:1} Therefore, my brothers and sisters, whom I love and long for, my joy and crown, stand firm in the Lord in this way, dear friends! {4:2} I plead with Euodia and I plead with Syntyche to be of the same mind in the Lord. {4:3} Yes, and I ask you, my true companion, help these women since they have contended at my side in the cause of the gospel, along with Clement and the rest of my co-workers, whose names are in the book of life. {4:4} Rejoice in the Lord always. I will say it again: Rejoice! {4:5} Let your gentleness be evident to all. The Lord is near. {4:6} Do not be anxious about anything, but in every situation, by prayer and petition, with thanksgiving, present your requests to God. {4:7} And the peace of God, which transcends all understanding, will guard your hearts and your minds in Christ Jesus. {4:8} Finally, brothers and sisters, whatever is true, whatever is noble, whatever is right, whatever is pure, whatever is lovely, whatever is admirable—if anything is excellent or praiseworthy—think about such things. {4:9} Whatever you have learned or received or heard from me, or seen in me—put it into practice. And the God of peace will be with you. {4:10} I rejoiced greatly in the Lord that at last you renewed your concern for me. Indeed, you were concerned, but you had no opportunity to show it. {4:11} I am not saying this because I am in need, for I have learned to be content whatever the circumstances. {4:12} I know what it is to be in need, and I know what it is to have plenty. I have learned the secret of being content in any and every situation, whether well fed or hungry, whether living in plenty or in want. {4:13} I can do all this through him who gives me strength. {4:14} Yet it was good of you to share in my troubles. {4:15} Moreover, as you Philippians know, in the early days of your acquaintance with the gospel, when I set out from Macedonia, not one church shared with me in the matter of giving and receiving, except you only; {4:16} for even when I was in Thessalonica, you sent me aid more than once when I was in need. {4:17} Not that I desire your gifts; what I desire is that more be credited to your account. {4:18} I have received full payment and have more than enough. I am amply supplied, now that I have received from Epaphroditus the gifts you sent. They are a fragrant offering, an acceptable sacrifice, pleasing to God. {4:19} And my God will meet all your needs according to the riches of his glory in Christ Jesus. {4:20} To our God and Father be glory for ever and ever. Amen. {4:21} Greet all God's people in Christ Jesus. The brothers and sisters who are with me send greetings. {4:22} All God's people here send you greetings, especially those who belong to Caesar's household. {4:23} The grace of the Lord Jesus Christ be with your spirit. Amen.

The Epistle of Paul to the Colossians

{1:1} Paul, an apostle of Jesus Christ by the will of God, and Timothy our brother, {1:2} to the saints and faithful brothers and sisters in Christ at Colossae: Grace and peace to you from God our Father and the Lord Jesus Christ. {1:3} We always thank God, the Father of our Lord Jesus Christ, when we pray for you, {1:4} because we have heard of your faith in Christ Jesus and of the love you have for all God's people, {1:5} the faith and love that spring from the hope stored up for you in heaven and about which you have already heard in the true message of the gospel {1:6} that has come to you. In the same way, the gospel is bearing fruit and growing throughout the whole world—just as it has been doing among you since the day you heard it and truly understood God's grace. {1:7} You learned it from Epaphras, our dear fellow servant, who is a faithful minister of Christ on our behalf, {1:8} and who also told us of your love in the Spirit. {1:9} For this reason, since the day we heard about you, we have not stopped praying for you. We continually ask God to fill you with the knowledge of his will through all the wisdom and understanding that the Spirit gives, {1:10} so that you may live a life worthy of the Lord and please him in every way: bearing fruit in every good work, growing in the knowledge of God, {1:11} being strengthened with all power according to his glorious might so that you may have great endurance and patience, {1:12} and giving joyful thanks to the Father, who has qualified you to share in the inheritance of his holy people in the kingdom of light. {1:13} For he has rescued us from the dominion of darkness and brought us into the kingdom of the Son he loves, {1:14} in whom we have redemption, the forgiveness of sins. {1:15} The Son is the image of the invisible God, the firstborn over all creation. {1:16} For in him all things were created: things in heaven and on earth, visible and invisible, whether thrones or powers or rulers or authorities; all things have been created through him and for him. {1:17} He is before all things, and in him all things hold together. {1:18} And he is the head of the body, the church; he is the beginning and the firstborn from among the dead, so that in everything he might have the supremacy. {1:19} For God was pleased to have all his fullness dwell in him, {1:20} and through him to reconcile to himself all things, whether things on earth or things in heaven, by making peace through his blood, shed on the cross. {1:21} Once you were alienated from God and were enemies in your minds because of your evil behavior. But now he has reconciled you by Christ's physical body through death to present you holy in his sight, without blemish and free from accusation— {1:23} if you continue in your faith, established and firm, and do not move from the hope held out in the gospel. This is the gospel that you heard and that has been proclaimed to every creature under heaven, and of which I, Paul, have become a servant. {1:24} Now I rejoice in what I am suffering for you, and I fill up in my flesh what is still lacking in regard to Christ's afflictions, for the sake of his body, which is the church. {1:25} I have become its servant by the commission God gave me to present to you the word of God in its fullness, {1:26} the mystery that has been kept hidden for ages and generations, but is now disclosed to the Lord's people. {1:27} To them God has chosen to make known among the Gentiles the glorious riches of this mystery, which is Christ in you, the hope of glory. {1:28} He is the one we proclaim, admonishing and teaching everyone with all wisdom, so we may present everyone fully mature in Christ. {1:29} To this end I strenuously contend with all energy Christ so powerfully works in me.

{2:1} I want you to know how hard I am contending for you and for those at Laodicea, and for all who have not met me personally. {2:2} My goal is that they may be encouraged in heart and united in love, so that they may have the full riches of complete understanding, in order that they may know the mystery of God, namely, Christ, {2:3} in whom are hidden all the treasures of wisdom and knowledge. {2:4} I tell you this so that no one may deceive you by fine-sounding arguments. {2:5} For though I am absent from you in body, I am present with you in spirit and delight to see how disciplined you are and how firm your faith in Christ is. {2:6} So then, just as you received Christ Jesus as Lord, continue to live your lives in him, {2:7} rooted and built up in him, strengthened in the faith as you were taught, and overflowing with thankfulness. {2:8} See to it that no one takes you captive through hollow and deceptive philosophy, which depends on human tradition and the elemental spiritual forces of this world rather than on Christ. {2:9} For in Christ all the fullness of the Deity lives in bodily form, {2:10} and in Christ you have been brought to fullness. He is the head over every power and authority. {2:11} In him you were also circumcised with a circumcision not performed by human hands. Your whole self ruled by the flesh was put off when you were circumcised by Christ, {2:12} having been buried with him in baptism, in which you were also raised with him through your faith in the working of God, who raised him from the dead. {2:13} When you were dead in your sins and in the uncircumcision of your flesh, God made you alive with Christ. He forgave us all our sins, {2:14} having canceled the charge of our legal indebtedness, which stood against us and condemned us; he has taken it away, nailing it to the cross. {2:15} And having disarmed the powers and authorities, he made a public spectacle of them, triumphing over them by the cross. {2:16} Therefore do not let anyone judge you by what you eat or drink, or with regard to a religious festival, a New Moon celebration or a Sabbath day. {2:17} These are a shadow of the things that were to come; the reality, however, is found in Christ. {2:18} Do not let anyone who delights in false humility and the worship of angels disqualify you. Such a person also goes into great detail about what they have seen; they are puffed up with idle notions by their unspiritual mind. {2:19} They have lost connection with the Head, from whom the whole body, supported and held together by its ligaments and sinews, grows as God causes it to grow. {2:20} Since you died with Christ to the elemental spiritual forces of this world, why, as though you still belonged to the world, do you submit to its rules: {2:21} "Do not handle! Do not taste! Do not touch!" {2:22} These rules, which have to do with things that are all destined to perish with use, are based on merely human commands and teachings. {2:23} Such regulations indeed have an appearance of wisdom, with their self-imposed worship, their false humility and their harsh treatment of the body, but they lack any value in restraining sensual indulgence.

{3:1} Since you have been raised with Christ, set your hearts on things above, where Christ is, seated at the right hand of God. {3:2} Set your minds on things above, not on earthly things. {3:3} For you died, and your life is now hidden with Christ in God. {3:4} When Christ, who is your life, appears, then you also will appear with him in glory. {3:5} Put to death, therefore, whatever belongs to your earthly nature: sexual immorality, impurity, lust, evil desires, and greed, which is idolatry. {3:6} Because of these, the wrath of God is coming on those who are disobedient. {3:7} You used to walk in these ways, in the life you once lived. {3:8} But now you must also rid yourselves of all such things as these: anger, rage, malice, slander, and filthy language from your lips. {3:9} Do not lie to each other, since you have taken off your old self with its practices {3:10} and have put on the new self, which is being renewed in knowledge in the image of its Creator. {3:11} Here there is no Gentile or Jew, neither circumcised nor uncircumcised, neither barbarian nor Scythian, neither slave nor free, but Christ is all, and is in all. {3:12} Therefore, as God's chosen people, holy and dearly loved, clothe yourselves with compassion, kindness, humility, gentleness, and patience. {3:13} Bear with each other and forgive one another if any of you has a grievance against someone. Forgive as the Lord forgave you. {3:14} And over all these virtues put on love, which binds them all together in perfect unity. {3:15} Let the peace of Christ rule in your hearts, since as members of one body you were called to peace. And be thankful. {3:16} Let the message of Christ dwell among you richly, as you teach and admonish one another with all wisdom through psalms, hymns, and songs from the Spirit, singing to God with gratitude in your hearts. {3:17} And whatever you do, whether in word or deed, do it all in the name of the Lord Jesus, giving thanks to God the Father through him. {3:18} Wives, submit yourselves to your husbands, as is fitting in the Lord. {3:19} Husbands, love your wives and do not be harsh with them. {3:20} Children, obey your parents in everything, for this pleases the Lord. {3:21} Fathers, do not embitter your children, or they will become discouraged. {3:22} Slaves, obey your earthly masters in everything; and do it not only when their eye is on you and to curry their favor, but with sincerity of heart and reverence for the Lord. {3:23}

Whatever you do, work at it with all your heart, as working for the Lord, not for human masters, {3:24} since you know that you will receive an inheritance from the Lord as a reward. It is the Lord Christ you are serving. {3:25} Anyone who does wrong will be repaid for their wrongs, and there is no favoritism.

{4:1} Masters, provide your slaves with what is right and fair, because you know that you also have a Master in heaven. {4:2} Devote yourselves to prayer, being watchful and thankful. {4:3} And pray for us, too, that God may open a door for our message, so that we may proclaim the mystery of Christ, for which I am in chains. {4:4} Pray that I may proclaim it clearly, as I should. {4:5} Be wise in the way you act toward outsiders; make the most of every opportunity. {4:6} Let your conversation be always full of grace, seasoned with salt, so that you may know how to answer everyone. {4:7} Tychicus will tell you all the news about me. He is a dear brother, a faithful minister, and fellow servant in the Lord. {4:8} I am sending him to you for the express purpose of telling you what is happening here and to encourage your hearts. {4:9} He is coming with Onesimus, our faithful and dear brother, who is one of you. They will tell you everything that is happening here. {4:10} My fellow prisoner Aristarchus sends you his greetings, as does Mark, the cousin of Barnabas (you have received instructions about him; if he comes to you, welcome him). {4:11} Jesus, who is called Justus, also sends greetings. These are the only Jews among my co-workers for the kingdom of God, and they have proved a comfort to me. {4:12} Epaphras, who is one of you and a servant of Christ Jesus, sends greetings. He is always wrestling in prayer for you, that you may stand firm in all the will of God, mature and fully assured. {4:13} I vouch for him that he is working hard for you and for those at Laodicea and Hierapolis. {4:14} Our dear friend Luke, the doctor, and Demas send greetings. {4:15} Give my greetings to the brothers and sisters at Laodicea, and to Nymphas and the church in her house. {4:16} After this letter has been read to you, see that it is also read in the church of the Laodiceans and that you in turn read the letter from Laodicea. {4:17} Tell Archippus: "See to it that you complete the ministry you have received in the Lord." {4:18} I, Paul, write this greeting in my own hand. Remember my chains. Grace be with you.

The First Epistle of Paul to the Thessalonians

{1:1} Paul, Silvanus, and Timothy, to the church of the Thessalonians in God the Father and the Lord Jesus Christ: Grace and peace to you from God our Father and the Lord Jesus Christ. {1:2} We always thank God for all of you and continually mention you in our prayers. {1:3} We remember before our God and Father your work produced by faith, your labor prompted by love, and your endurance inspired by hope in our Lord Jesus Christ. {1:4} For we know, brothers and sisters loved by God, that he has chosen you. {1:5} Our gospel came to you not simply with words but also with power, with the Holy Spirit, and deep conviction; you know how we lived among you for your sake. {1:6} You became imitators of us and of the Lord, for you welcomed the message in the midst of severe suffering, with the joy given by the Holy Spirit. {1:7} And so you became a model to all the believers in Macedonia and Achaia. {1:8} The Lord's message rang out from you not only in Macedonia and Achaia—your faith in God has become known everywhere. Therefore, we do not need to say anything about it. {1:9} For they themselves report what kind of reception you gave us. They tell how you turned to God from idols to serve the living and true God {1:10} and to wait for his Son from heaven, whom he raised from the dead—Jesus, who rescues us from the coming wrath.

{2:1} You know, brothers and sisters, that our visit to you was not without results. {2:2} We had previously suffered and been treated outrageously in Philippi, as you know, but with the help of our God we dared to tell you his gospel in the face of strong opposition. {2:3} For the appeal we make does not spring from error or impure motives, nor are we trying to trick you. {2:4} On the contrary, we speak as those approved by God to be entrusted with the gospel. We are not trying to please people but God, who tests our hearts. {2:5} You know we never used flattery, nor did we put on a mask to cover up greed—God is our witness. {2:6} We were not looking for praise from people, not from you or anyone else, even though as apostles of Christ we could have asserted our authority. {2:7} Instead, we were like young children among you. Just as a nursing mother cares for her children, {2:8} so we cared for you. Because we loved you so much, we were delighted to share with you not only the gospel of God but our lives as well, for you had become so dear to us. {2:9} Surely you remember, brothers and sisters, our toil and hardship; we worked night and day in order not to be a burden to anyone while we preached the gospel of God to you. {2:10} You are witnesses, and so is God, of how holy, righteous, and blameless we were among you who believed. {2:11} For you know that we dealt with each of you as a father deals with his own children, {2:12} encouraging, comforting, and urging you to live lives worthy of God, who calls you into his kingdom and glory. {2:13} And we also thank God continually because, when you received the word of God, which you heard from us, you accepted it not as a human word, but as it actually is, the word of God, which is indeed at work in you who believe. {2:14} For you, brothers and sisters, became imitators of God's churches in Judea, which are in Christ Jesus: you suffered from your own people the same things those churches suffered from the Jews, {2:15} who killed the Lord Jesus and the prophets and also drove us out. They displease God and are hostile to everyone {2:16} in their effort to keep us from speaking to the Gentiles so that they may be saved. In this way, they always heap up their sins to the limit. The wrath of God has come upon them at last. {2:17} But, brothers and sisters, when we were orphaned by being separated from you for a short time (in person, not in thought), out of our intense longing we made every effort to see you. {2:18} For we wanted to come to you—certainly I, Paul, did, again and again—but Satan blocked our way. {2:19} For what is our hope, our joy, or the crown in which we will glory in the presence of our Lord Jesus when he comes? Is it not you? {2:20} Indeed, you are our glory and joy.

{3:1} Therefore, when we could no longer stand it, we thought it best to be left alone in Athens. {3:2} We sent Timothy, our brother and God's minister, and our coworker in spreading the gospel of Christ, to strengthen and encourage you in your faith. {3:3} We didn't want anyone to be unsettled by these trials; you know quite well that we are destined for them. {3:4} In fact, when we were with you, we kept telling you that we would be persecuted, and it turned out that way, as you well know. {3:5} This is why, when I could stand it no longer, I sent to find out about your faith. I was afraid that in some way the tempter had tempted you and that our efforts might have been useless. {3:6} But Timothy has just now come to us from you and has brought good news about your faith and love. He told us that you always have pleasant memories of us and that you long to see us, just as we long to see you. {3:7} Therefore, brothers and sisters, in all our distress and persecution, we were encouraged about you because of your faith. {3:8} For now we really live, since you are standing firm in the Lord. {3:9} How can we thank God enough for you in return for all the joy we have in the presence of our God because of you? {3:10} Night and day we pray most earnestly that we may see you again and supply what is lacking in your faith. {3:11} Now may our God and Father himself and our Lord Jesus clear the way for us to come to you. {3:12} May the Lord make your love increase and overflow for each other and for everyone else, just as ours does for you. {3:13} May he strengthen your hearts so that you will be blameless and holy in the presence of our God and Father when our Lord Jesus comes with all his holy ones.

{4:1} As for other matters, brothers and sisters, we instructed you how to live in order to please God, as in fact you are living. Now we ask you and urge you in the Lord Jesus to do this more and more. {4:2} For you know what instructions we gave you by the authority of the Lord Jesus. {4:3} It is God's will that you should be sanctified: that you should avoid sexual immorality; {4:4} that each of you should learn to control your own body in a way that is holy and honorable, {4:5} not in passionate lust like the pagans, who do not know God; {4:6} and that in this matter no one should wrong or take advantage of a brother or sister. The Lord will punish all those who commit such sins, as we told you and warned you before. {4:7} For God did not call us to be impure, but to live a holy life. {4:8} Therefore, anyone who rejects this instruction does not reject a human being but God, the very God who gives you his Holy Spirit. {4:9} Now about your love for one another, we do not need to write to you, for you yourselves have been taught by God to love each other. {4:10} And in fact, you do love all of God's family throughout Macedonia. Yet we urge you, brothers and sisters, to do so more and more. {4:11} And to make it your ambition to lead a quiet life: you should mind your own business and work with your hands, just as we told you, {4:12} so that your daily life may win the respect of outsiders and so that you will not be dependent on anybody. {4:13} Brothers and sisters, we do not want you to be uninformed about those who sleep in death, so that you do not grieve like the rest of mankind, who have no hope. {4:14} For we believe that Jesus died and rose again, and so we believe that God will bring with Jesus those who have fallen asleep in him. {4:15} According to the Lord's word, we tell you that we who are still alive, who are left until the coming of the Lord, will certainly not precede those who have fallen asleep. {4:16} For the Lord himself will come down from heaven, with a loud command, with the voice of the archangel and with the trumpet call of God, and the dead in Christ will rise first. {4:17} After that, we who are still alive and are left will be caught up together with them in clouds to meet the Lord in air. And so we will be with the Lord forever. {4:18} Therefore encourage one another with these words.

{5:1} Now, brothers and sisters, about the times and dates, you don't need me to write to you. {5:2} For you know very well that the day of the Lord will come like a thief in the night. {5:3} While people are saying, "Peace and safety," destruction will come on them suddenly, like the pains of childbirth on a pregnant woman, and they will not escape. {5:4} But you, brothers and sisters, are not in darkness so that this day should surprise you like a thief. {5:5} You are all children of the light and children of the day. We do not belong to the night or to the darkness. {5:6} So then, let us not be like others, who are asleep, but let us be awake and sober. {5:7} For those who sleep, sleep at night, and those who get drunk, get drunk at night. {5:8} But since we belong to the day, let us be sober, putting on faith and love as a breastplate, and the hope of salvation as a helmet. {5:9} For God did not appoint us to suffer wrath but to receive salvation through our Lord Jesus Christ, {5:10} who died for us so that, whether we are awake or asleep, we may live together with him. {5:11} Therefore encourage one another and build each other up, just as in fact you are doing. {5:12} Now we ask you, brothers and sisters, to acknowledge those who work hard among you, who care for you in the Lord and who admonish you. {5:13} Hold them in the highest regard in love because of their work. Live in peace with each other. {5:14} And we urge you, brothers and sisters, warn those who are idle, encourage the disheartened, help the weak, be patient with everyone. {5:15} Make sure that nobody pays back wrong for wrong, but always strive to do what is good for each other and for everyone else. {5:16} Rejoice always. {5:17} Pray continually. {5:18} Give thanks in all circumstances; for this is God's will for you in Christ Jesus. {5:19} Do not quench the Spirit. {5:20} Do not treat prophecies with contempt. {5:21} Test all things; hold on to what is good. {5:22} Reject every kind of evil. {5:23} May God himself, the God of peace, sanctify you through and through. May your whole spirit, soul, and body be kept blameless at the coming of our Lord Jesus Christ. {5:24} The one who calls you is faithful, and he will do it. {5:25} Brothers and sisters, pray for us. {5:26} Greet all God's people with a holy kiss. {5:27} I charge you before the Lord to have this letter read to all the brothers and sisters. {5:28} The grace of our Lord Jesus Christ be with you. Amen.

The Second Epistle of Paul to the Thessalonians

{1:1} Paul, Silvanus, and Timothy, to the church of the Thessalonians in God our Father and the Lord Jesus Christ: {1:2} Grace and peace to you from God our Father and the Lord Jesus Christ. {1:3} We must always thank God for you, brothers and sisters, as it is right to do, because your faith is growing abundantly and the love of each one of you for one another is increasing. {1:4} Therefore, we boast about you among the churches of God for your perseverance and faith in all the persecutions and hardships you are enduring. {1:5} This is a clear sign of God's righteous judgment, so that you may be considered worthy of the kingdom of God for which you are suffering. {1:6} For it is just with God to repay those who trouble you with affliction; {1:7} and to give relief to you who are troubled, along with us, when the Lord Jesus is revealed from heaven with his mighty angels, {1:8} in blazing fire, inflicting vengeance on those who do not know God and on those who do not obey the gospel of our Lord Jesus Christ. {1:9} They will suffer the punishment of eternal destruction, away from the presence of the Lord and the glory of his might, {1:10} when he comes to be glorified in his saints and to be marveled at among all who have believed, because our testimony to you was believed on that day. {1:11} To this end, we always pray for you that our God may make you worthy of your calling and may fulfill by his power every good purpose of yours and every act prompted by your faith. {1:12} We pray this so that the name of our Lord Jesus may be glorified in you, and you in him, according to the grace of our God and the Lord Jesus Christ.

{2:1} Now, brothers and sisters, concerning the coming of our Lord Jesus Christ and our being gathered to him, {2:2} we ask you not to be easily unsettled or alarmed by the teaching allegedly from us, whether by a prophecy, by word of mouth, or by letter, asserting that the day of the Lord has already come. {2:3} Don't let anyone deceive you in any way, for that day will not come until the rebellion occurs and the man of lawlessness is revealed, the man doomed to destruction. {2:4} He will oppose and will exalt himself over everything that is called God or is worshiped, so that he sets himself up in God's temple, proclaiming himself to be God. {2:5} Don't you remember that when I was with you, I used to tell you these things? {2:6} And now you know what is holding him back so that he may be revealed at the proper time. {2:7} For the secret power of lawlessness is already at work, but the one who now holds it back will continue to do so till he is taken out of the way. {2:8} And then the lawless one will be revealed, whom the Lord Jesus will overthrow with the breath of his mouth and destroy by the splendor of his coming. {2:9} The coming of the lawless one will be in accordance with how Satan works. He will use all sorts of displays of power through signs and wonders that serve the lie, {2:10} and all the ways that wickedness deceives those who are perishing. They perish because they refused to love the truth and so be saved. {2:11} For this reason, God sends them a powerful delusion so that they will believe the lie {2:12} and so that all will be condemned who have not believed the truth but have delighted in wickedness. {2:13} But we ought always to thank God for you, brothers and sisters loved by the Lord, because God chose you as firstfruits to be saved through the sanctifying work of the Spirit and through belief in the truth. {2:14} He called you to this through our gospel, that you might share in the glory of our Lord Jesus Christ. {2:15} So then, brothers and sisters, stand firm and hold fast to the teachings we passed on to you, whether by word of mouth or by letter. {2:16} May our Lord Jesus Christ himself and God our Father, who loved us and by his grace gave us eternal encouragement and good hope, {2:17} encourage your hearts and strengthen you in every good deed and word.

{3:1} Finally, brothers and sisters, pray for us, that the message of the Lord may spread rapidly and be honored, just as it was with you. {3:2} And pray that we may be delivered from wicked and evil people, for not everyone has faith. {3:3} But the Lord is faithful, and he will strengthen you and protect you from the evil one. {3:4} We have confidence in the Lord that you are doing and will continue to do the things we command. {3:5} May the Lord direct your hearts into God's love and Christ's perseverance. {3:6} In the name of the Lord Jesus Christ, we command you, brothers and sisters, to keep away from every believer who is idle and disruptive and does not live according to the teaching you received from us. {3:7} For you yourselves know how you ought to follow our example. We were not idle when we were with you, {3:8} nor did we eat anyone's food without paying for it. On the contrary, we worked night and day, laboring and toiling so that we would not be a burden to any of you. {3:9} We did this not because we do not have the right to such help, but in order to offer ourselves as a model for you to imitate. {3:10} For even when we were with you, we gave you this rule: "The one who is unwilling to work shall not eat." {3:11} We hear that some among you are idle and disruptive. They are not busy; they are busybodies. {3:12} Such people we command and urge in the Lord Jesus Christ to settle down and earn the food they eat. {3:13} And as for you, brothers and sisters, never tire of doing what is good. {3:14} Take special note of anyone who does not obey our instruction in this letter. Do not associate with them in order that they may feel ashamed. {3:15} Yet do not regard them as an enemy, but warn them as you would a fellow believer. {3:16} Now may the Lord of peace himself give you peace at all times and in every way. The Lord be with all of you. {3:17} I, Paul, write this greeting in my own hand, which is the distinguishing mark in all my letters. This is how I write. {3:18} The grace of our Lord Jesus Christ be with you all. Amen.

The First Epistle of Paul to the Timothy

{1:1} Paul, an apostle of Jesus Christ by the command of God our Savior and the Lord Jesus Christ, our hope; {1:2} to Timothy, my true son in the faith: Grace, mercy, and peace from God our Father and Jesus Christ our Lord. {1:3} As I urged you to stay in Ephesus when I went to Macedonia, I want you to command certain people not to teach any different doctrine, {1:4} nor to devote themselves to myths and endless genealogies, which promote controversies rather than God's work—so just focus on that. {1:5} The goal of this command is love, which comes from a pure heart, a good conscience, and a sincere faith. {1:6} Some have deviated from these and turned to meaningless talk; {1:7} they want to be teachers of the law, but they do not understand what they are saying or the things they insist on. {1:8} We know that the law is good if one uses it properly; {1:9} we also know that the law is not made for the righteous but for the lawless and rebellious, the ungodly and sinful, the unholy and irreverent, for those who kill their fathers or mothers, for murderers, {1:10} for the sexually immoral, for those practicing homosexuality, for slave traders, liars, perjurers, and for whatever else is contrary to sound teaching {1:11} that conforms to the glorious gospel of the blessed God, which he entrusted to me. {1:12} I thank Christ Jesus our Lord, who has given me strength, that he considered me trustworthy, appointing me to his service. {1:13} Even though I was once a blasphemer and a persecutor and a violent man, I was shown mercy because I acted in ignorance and unbelief. {1:14} The grace of our Lord was poured out on me abundantly, along with the faith and love that are in Christ Jesus. {1:15} Here is a trustworthy saying that deserves full acceptance: Christ Jesus came into the world to save sinners, of whom I am the worst. {1:16} But for that very reason I was shown mercy so that in me, the worst of sinners, Christ Jesus might display his immense patience as an example for those who would believe in him and receive eternal life. {1:17} Now to the King eternal, immortal, invisible, the only God, be honor and glory for ever and ever. Amen. {1:18} Timothy, my son, I am giving you this command in keeping with the prophecies once made about you, so that by recalling them you may fight the battle well, {1:19} holding on to faith & a good conscience, which some have rejected and so have suffered shipwreck regarding their faith. {1:20} Among them are Hymenaeus & Alexander, whom I have handed over to Satan to be taught not to blaspheme.

{2:1} I urge, then, first of all, that petitions, prayers, intercession, and thanksgiving be made for all people; {2:2} for kings and all those in authority, that we may live peaceful and quiet lives in all godliness and holiness. {2:3} This is good, and pleases God our Savior, {2:4} who wants all people to be saved and to come to a knowledge of the truth. {2:5} For there is one God and one mediator between God and mankind, the man Christ Jesus, {2:6} who gave himself as a ransom for all people. This has now been witnessed to at the proper time. {2:7} And for this purpose, I was appointed a herald and an apostle (I am telling the truth, I am not lying), and a true and faithful teacher of the Gentiles. {2:8} Therefore, I want the men everywhere to pray, lifting up holy hands without anger or disputing. {2:9} I also want the women to dress modestly, with decency and propriety, adorning themselves, not with elaborate hairstyles or gold or pearls or expensive clothes, {2:10} but with good deeds, appropriate for women who profess to worship God. {2:11} A woman should learn in quietness and full submission. {2:12} I do not permit a woman to teach or to assume authority over a man; she must be quiet. {2:13} For Adam was formed first, then Eve. {2:14} And Adam was not the one deceived; it was the woman who was deceived and became a sinner. {2:15} But women will be saved through childbearing, if they continue in faith, love, and holiness with propriety.

{3:1} This is a trustworthy saying: If someone aspires to be a bishop, they desire a noble task. {3:2} Now a bishop must be above reproach, faithful to their spouse, self-controlled, respectable, hospitable, and able to teach; {3:3} not addicted to wine, not violent but gentle, not quarrelsome, and not a lover of money. {3:4} They must manage their own family well, with children who respect and obey them. {3:5} For if someone does not know how to manage their own household, how can they take care of God's church? {3:6} They should not be a recent convert, or they may become conceited and fall under the same judgment as the devil. {3:7} They must also have a good reputation with outsiders, so they will not fall into disgrace and into the devil's trap. {3:8} Deacons, likewise, must be worthy of respect, not double-tongued, not addicted to much wine, and not greedy for money; {3:9} they must hold the deep truths of the faith with a clear conscience. {3:10} They must first be tested; and then, if there is nothing against them, let them serve as deacons. {3:11} In the same way, their wives should be worthy of respect, not slanderers, but sober-minded and faithful in everything. {3:12} Deacons should be faithful to their spouse and manage their children and their own households well. {3:13} Those who have served well as deacons gain an excellent standing and great assurance in their faith in Christ Jesus. {3:14} Although I hope to come to you soon, I am writing these instructions to you {3:15} so that, if I am delayed, you will know how people ought to conduct themselves in God's household, which is the church of the living God, the pillar and foundation of the truth. {3:16} Beyond all question, the mystery of godliness is great: He appeared in the flesh, was vindicated by the Spirit, was seen by angels, was preached among the nations, was believed on in the world, and was taken up in glory.

{4:1} The Spirit clearly says that in later times some will abandon the faith and follow deceiving spirits and things taught by demons. {4:2} Such teachings come through hypocritical liars, whose consciences have been seared as with a hot iron. {4:3} They forbid people to marry and order them to abstain from certain foods, which God created to be received with thanksgiving by those who believe and who know the truth. {4:4} For everything God created is good, and nothing is to be rejected if it is received with thanksgiving, {4:5} because it is consecrated by the word of God and prayer. {4:6} If you point these things out to the brothers and sisters, you will be a good minister of Christ Jesus, nourished on the truths of the faith and of the good teaching that you have followed. {4:7} Have nothing to do with godless myths and old wives' tales; rather, train yourself to be godly. {4:8} For physical training is of some value, but godliness has value for all things, holding promise for both the present life and the life to come. {4:9} This is a trustworthy saying that deserves full acceptance. {4:10} This is why we labor and strive, because we have put our hope in the living God, who is the Savior of all people, and especially of those who believe. {4:11} Command and teach these things. {4:12} Don't let anyone look down on you because you are young, but set an example for the believers in speech, in conduct, in love, in faith, and in purity. {4:13} Until I come, devote yourself to the public reading of Scripture, to preaching, and to teaching. {4:14} Do not neglect your gift, which was given you through prophecy when the body of elders laid their hands on you. {4:15} Be diligent in these matters; give yourself wholly to them, so that everyone may see your progress. {4:16} Watch your life and doctrine closely. Persevere in them, because if you do, you will save both yourself and your hearers.

{5:1} Do not sharply rebuke an elder; instead, appeal to him as a father, and treat younger men as brothers. {5:2} Treat older women as mothers and younger women as sisters, with complete purity. {5:3} Honor widows who are truly in need. {5:4} However, if a widow has children or grandchildren, they should learn first to show godliness at home and repay their parents, for this pleases God. {5:5} A true widow, who is all alone, puts her hope in God and continues to pray night and day. {5:6} But the woman who indulges in pleasure is spiritually dead even while she lives. {5:7} Give these instructions so that no one will be open to blame. {5:8} Anyone who does not provide for their relatives, especially for their own household, has denied the faith and is worse than an unbeliever. {5:9} No widow should be enrolled in the church if she is under sixty years old and has been faithful to one husband, {5:10} and is well known for her good deeds, such as bringing up children, showing hospitality, washing the feet of the saints, helping those in trouble, and devoting herself to every good work. {5:11} Do not enroll younger widows, for when their sensual desires overcome their dedication to Christ, they will want to marry, {5:12} thus bringing judgment on themselves because they have disregarded their first pledge. {5:13} Besides, they get into the habit of being idle and going from house to house, and not only do they become idlers, but they also gossip and meddle in others' affairs, saying things they shouldn't. {5:14} So I counsel younger women to marry, have children, manage their households, and not give the enemy any opportunity for slander. {5:15} Some have already turned away to follow Satan. {5:16} If any believing woman has widows in her family, she should help them and not let the church be burdened, so it can help those widows who are truly in need. {5:17} The elders who direct the affairs of the church well are worthy of double honor, especially those who work hard at preaching and teaching. {5:18} For Scripture says, "Do not muzzle an ox while it is treading out the grain," and "The worker deserves his wages." {5:19} Do not entertain an accusation against an elder unless it is brought by two or three witnesses. {5:20} Those who sin are to be rebuked publicly, so that others may take warning. {5:21} I charge you in the sight of God and Christ Jesus and the elect angels to keep these instructions without partiality and to do nothing out of favoritism. {5:22} Do not be hasty in the laying on of hands, and do not share in the sins of others. Keep yourself pure. {5:23} Stop drinking only water and use a little wine because of your stomach and your frequent illnesses. {5:24} The sins of some are obvious, reaching the place of judgment ahead of them; the sins of others trail behind them. {5:25} In the same way, good deeds are obvious, and even those that are not obvious cannot remain hidden.

{6:1} All who are under the yoke of slavery should consider their masters worthy of full respect, so that God's name and our teaching will not be slandered. {6:2} Those who have believing masters should not show them disrespect because they are fellow believers. Instead, they should serve them even better because their masters are dear to them as fellow believers and are devoted to the welfare of their slaves. Teach these things and encourage them. {6:3} If anyone teaches otherwise and does not agree to the sound instruction of our Lord Jesus Christ and to godly teaching, {6:4} they are conceited and understand nothing. They have an unhealthy interest in controversies and quarrels about words that result in envy, strife, malicious talk, evil suspicions, {6:5} and constant friction between people of corrupt mind, who have been robbed of the truth and who think that godliness is a means to financial gain. Withdraw from such people. {6:6} But godliness with contentment is great gain. {6:7} For we brought nothing into the world, and we can take nothing out of it. {6:8} But if we have food and clothing, we will be content with that. {6:9} Those who want to get rich fall into temptation and a trap and into many foolish and harmful desires that plunge people into ruin and destruction. {6:10} For the love of money is the root of all kinds of evil. Some people, eager for money, have wandered from the faith and pierced themselves with many griefs. {6:11} But you, man of God, flee from all this, and pursue righteousness, godliness, faith, love, endurance, and gentleness. {6:12} Fight the good fight of the faith; take hold of the eternal life to which you were called when you made your good confession in the presence of many witnesses. {6:13} In the sight of God, who gives life to everything, and of Christ Jesus, who while testifying before Pontius Pilate made the good confession, I charge you {6:14} to keep this command without spot or blame until the appearing of our Lord Jesus Christ, {6:15} which God will bring about in his own time—God, the blessed and only Ruler, the King of kings and Lord of lords, {6:16} who alone is immortal and who lives in unapproachable light, whom no one has seen or can see. To him be honor and might forever. Amen. {6:17} Command those who are rich in this present world not to be arrogant nor to put their hope in wealth, which is so uncertain, but to put their hope in God, who richly provides us with everything for our enjoyment. {6:18} Command them to do good, to be rich in good deeds, and to be generous and willing to share. {6:19} In this way they will lay up treasure for themselves as a firm foundation for the coming age, so that they may take hold of the life that is truly life. {6:20} Timothy, guard what has been entrusted to your care. Turn away from godless chatter and the opposing ideas of what is falsely called knowledge, {6:21} which some have professed and in so doing have departed from the faith. Grace be with you all.

The Second Epistle of Paul to the Timothy

{1:1} Paul, an apostle of Jesus Christ by the will of God and according to the promise of life that is in Christ Jesus, {1:2} writes to Timothy, my dear son: Grace, mercy, and peace from God the Father and Christ Jesus our Lord. {1:3} I thank God, whom I serve with a clear conscience as my ancestors did, and I constantly remember you in my prayers day and night; {1:4} longing to see you, remembering your tears, so that I may be filled with joy; {1:5} recalling the sincere faith that you have, which first lived in your grandmother Lois and in your mother Eunice, and I am convinced now lives in you also. {1:6} Therefore, I remind you to fan into flame the gift of God, which is in you through the laying on of my hands. {1:7} For God did not give us a spirit of fear, but of power, love, and a sound mind. {1:8} So do not be ashamed of the testimony about our Lord or of me, His prisoner. Rather, join with me in suffering for the gospel, relying on the power of God; {1:9} He has saved us and called us to a holy life, not because of anything we have done but because of His own purpose and grace, which was given us in Christ Jesus before the beginning of time. {1:10} But it has now been revealed through the appearing of our Savior, Jesus Christ, who has destroyed death and has brought life and immortality to light through the gospel. {1:11} And of this gospel, I was appointed a preacher, an apostle, and a teacher. {1:12} That is why I am suffering as I am. Yet I am not ashamed, because I know whom I have believed, and I am convinced that He is able to guard what I have entrusted to Him until that day. {1:13} What you heard from me, keep as the pattern of sound teaching, with faith and love in Christ Jesus. {1:14} Guard the good deposit that was entrusted to you—guard it with the help of the Holy Spirit who lives in us. {1:15} You know that everyone in the province of Asia has deserted me, including Phygellus and Hermogenes. {1:16} May the Lord show mercy to the household of Onesiphorus, because he often refreshed me and was not ashamed of my chains. {1:17} On the contrary, when he was in Rome, he searched hard for me until he found me. {1:18} May the Lord grant that he will find mercy from the Lord on that day! You know very well in how many ways he helped me in Ephesus.

{2:1} You then, my son, be strong in the grace that is in Christ Jesus. {2:2} And the things you have heard me say in the presence of many witnesses, entrust to reliable people who will also be qualified to teach others. {2:3} Join with me in suffering, like a good soldier of Christ Jesus. {2:4} No one serving as a soldier gets entangled in civilian affairs, but rather tries to please his commanding officer. {2:5} Similarly, anyone who competes as an athlete does not receive the victor's crown except by competing according to the rules. {2:6} The hardworking farmer should be the first to receive a share of the crops. {2:7} Reflect on what I am saying, for the Lord will give you insight into all this. {2:8} Remember Jesus Christ, raised from the dead, descended from David. This is my gospel, {2:9} for which I am suffering even to the point of being chained like a criminal. But God's word is not chained. {2:10} Therefore I endure everything for the sake of the elect, that they too may obtain the salvation that is in Christ Jesus, with eternal glory. {2:11} Here is a trustworthy saying: If we died with Him, we will also live with Him; {2:12} if we endure, we will also reign with Him; if we disown Him, He will also disown us; {2:13} if we are faithless, He remains faithful, for He cannot disown Himself. {2:14} Keep reminding God's people of these things. Warn them before God against quarreling about words; it is of no value and only ruins those who listen. {2:15} Do your best to present yourself to God as one approved, a worker who does not need to be ashamed and who correctly handles the word of truth. {2:16} Avoid godless chatter, because those who indulge in it will become more and more ungodly. {2:17} Their teaching will spread like gangrene; among them are Hymenaeus and Philetus, {2:18} who have departed from the truth. They say that the resurrection has already taken place, and they destroy the faith of some. {2:19} Nevertheless, God's solid foundation stands firm, sealed with this inscription: "The Lord knows those who are His," and "Everyone who confesses the name of the Lord must turn away from wickedness." {2:20} In a large house, there are articles not only of gold and silver but also of wood and clay; some are for special purposes and some for common use. {2:21} Those who cleanse themselves from the latter will be instruments for special purposes, made holy, useful to the Master and prepared to do any good work. {2:22} Flee the evil desires of youth and pursue righteousness, faith, love, and peace, along with those who call on the Lord out of a pure heart. {2:23} Don't have anything to do with foolish and stupid arguments, because you know they produce quarrels. {2:24} And the Lord's servant must not be quarrelsome but must be kind to everyone, able to teach, not resentful. {2:25} Opponents must be gently instructed, in the hope that God will grant them repentance leading them to a knowledge of the truth, {2:26} and that they will come to their senses and escape from the trap of the devil, who has taken them captive to do his will.

{3:1} But know this: in the last days, difficult times will come. {3:2} People will be lovers of themselves, lovers of money, boastful, proud, abusive, disobedient to their parents, ungrateful, unholy, {3:3} without love, unforgiving, slanderous, without self-control, brutal, not lovers of the good, {3:4} treacherous, reckless, conceited, lovers of pleasure rather than lovers of God; {3:5} having a form of godliness but denying its power. Have nothing to do with such people. {3:6} They are the kind who worm their way into homes and gain control over gullible women, who are loaded down with sins and are swayed by all kinds of desires, {3:7} always learning but never able to come to a knowledge of the truth. {3:8} Just as Jannes and Jambres opposed Moses, so also these teachers oppose the truth. They are men of depraved minds, who, as far as the faith is concerned, are rejected. {3:9} But they will not get very far because, as in the case of those men, their folly will be clear to everyone. {3:10} You, however, know all about my teaching, my way of life, my purpose, faith, patience, love, endurance, {3:11} persecutions, sufferings—what kinds of things happened to me in Antioch, Iconium, and Lystra, the persecutions I endured. Yet the Lord rescued me from all of them. {3:12} In fact, everyone who wants to live a godly life in Christ Jesus will be persecuted. {3:13} While evildoers and impostors will go from bad to worse, deceiving and being deceived. {3:14} But as for you, continue in what you have learned and have become convinced of, because you know those from whom you learned it, {3:15} and how from infancy you have known the Holy Scriptures, which are able to make you wise for salvation through faith in Christ Jesus. {3:16} All Scripture is God-breathed and is useful for teaching, rebuking, correcting & training in righteousness, {3:17} so that servant of God may be thoroughly equipped for every good work.

{4:1} In the presence of God and of Christ Jesus, who will judge the living and the dead, and in view of His appearing and His kingdom, I give you this charge: {4:2} Preach the word; be prepared in season and out of season; correct, rebuke, and encourage—with great patience and careful instruction. {4:3} For the time will come when people will not put up with sound doctrine. Instead, to suit their own desires, they will gather around them a great number of teachers to say what their itching ears want to hear. {4:4} They will turn their ears away from the truth and turn aside to myths. {4:5} But you, keep your head in all situations, endure hardship, do the work of an evangelist, discharge all the duties of your ministry. {4:6} For I am already being poured out like a drink offering, and the time for my departure is near. {4:7} I have fought the good fight, I have finished the race, I have kept the faith. {4:8} Now there is in store for me the crown of righteousness, which the Lord, the righteous Judge, will award to me on that day—and not only to me, but also to all who have longed for His appearing. {4:9} Do your best to come to me quickly, {4:10} for Demas, because he loved this world, has deserted me and has gone to Thessalonica. Crescens has gone to Galatia, and Titus to Dalmatia. {4:11} Only Luke is with me. Get Mark and bring him with you, because he is helpful to me in my ministry. {4:12} I sent Tychicus to Ephesus. {4:13} When you come, bring the cloak that I left with Carpus at Troas, and my scrolls, especially the parchments. {4:14} Alexander the metalworker did me a great deal of harm. The Lord will repay him for what he has done. {4:15} You too should be on your guard against him, because he strongly opposed our message. {4:16} At my first defense, no one came to my support, but everyone deserted me. May it not be held against them. {4:17} But the Lord stood at my side and gave me strength, so that through me the message might be fully proclaimed and all the Gentiles might hear it. And I was delivered from the lion's mouth. {4:18} The Lord will rescue me from every evil attack and will bring me safely to His heavenly kingdom. To Him be glory for ever and ever. Amen. {4:19} Greet Priscilla and Aquila and the household of Onesiphorus. {4:20} Erastus stayed in Corinth, and I left Trophimus sick in Miletus. {4:21} Do your best to get here before winter. Eubulus greets you, and so do Pudens, Linus, Claudia, and all the brothers and sisters. {4:22} The Lord be with your spirit. Grace be with you all. Amen.

The Epistle of Paul to Titus

{1:1} Paul, a servant of God and an apostle of Jesus Christ, is writing to promote the faith of God's chosen ones and the acknowledgment of the truth that leads to godliness; {1:2} in hope of eternal life, which God, who cannot lie, promised before the world began. {1:3} At the right time, He revealed His word through preaching, which has been entrusted to me by the command of God our Savior; {1:4} to Titus, my true son in our common faith: Grace, mercy, and peace from God the Father and Christ Jesus our Savior. {1:5} I left you in Crete to put in order what was left unfinished and appoint elders in every town, as I directed you. {1:6} An elder must be blameless, the husband of one wife, a man whose children believe and are not open to the charge of being wild and disobedient. {1:7} Since an overseer manages God's household, he must be blameless—not overbearing, not quick-tempered, not given to drunkenness, not violent, not pursuing dishonest gain. {1:8} Rather, he must be hospitable, one who loves what is good, self-controlled, upright, holy, and disciplined. {1:9} He must hold firmly to the trustworthy message as it has been taught, so that he can encourage others by sound doctrine and refute those who oppose it. {1:10} For there are many rebellious people, mere talkers and deceivers, especially those of the circumcision group. {1:11} They must be silenced because they are disrupting whole households by teaching things they ought not to teach and that for the sake of dishonest gain. {1:12} One of their own prophets has said, "Cretans are always liars, evil brutes, lazy gluttons." {1:13} This saying is true. Therefore, rebuke them sharply, so they will be sound in the faith {1:14} and will pay no attention to Jewish myths or to the merely human commands of those who reject the truth. {1:15} To the pure, all things are pure, but to those who are corrupted and do not believe, nothing is pure. In fact, both their minds and consciences are corrupted. {1:16} They claim to know God, but by their actions, they deny Him. They are detestable, disobedient, and unfit for doing anything good.

{2:1} You, however, must teach what is appropriate to sound doctrine. {2:2} Teach the older men to be temperate, worthy of respect, self-controlled, and sound in faith, in love, and in endurance. {2:3} Likewise, teach the older women to be reverent in the way they live, not to be slanderers or addicted to much wine, but to teach what is good. {2:4} Then they can urge the younger women to love their husbands and children, {2:5} to be self-controlled and pure, to be busy at home, to be kind, and to be subject to their husbands, so that no one will malign the word of God. {2:6} Similarly, encourage the young men to be self-controlled. {2:7} In everything, set them an example by doing what is good. In your teaching, show integrity, seriousness, {2:8} and soundness of speech that cannot be condemned, so that those who oppose you may be ashamed because they have nothing bad to say about us. {2:9} Teach slaves to be subject to their masters in everything, to try to please them, not to talk back to them, {2:10} and not to steal from them, but to show that they can be fully trusted, so that in every way they will make the teaching about God our Savior attractive. {2:11} For the grace of God has appeared that offers salvation to all people. {2:12} It teaches us to say "No" to ungodliness and worldly passions and to live self-controlled, upright, and godly lives in this present age, {2:13} while we wait for the blessed hope—the appearing of the glory of our great God and Savior, Jesus Christ, {2:14} who gave Himself for us to redeem us from all wickedness and to purify for Himself a people that are His very own, eager to do what is good. {2:15} These, then, are the things you should teach. Encourage and rebuke with all authority. Do not let anyone despise you.

{3:1} Remind the people to be subject to rulers and authorities, to be obedient, to be ready to do whatever is good, {3:2} to slander no one, to be peaceable and considerate, and to show true humility toward all men. {3:3} At one time we too were foolish, disobedient, deceived, and enslaved by all kinds of passions and pleasures. We lived in malice and envy, being hated and hating one another. {3:4} But when the kindness and love of God our Savior appeared, {3:5} He saved us, not because of righteous things we had done, but because of His mercy. He saved us through the washing of rebirth and renewal by the Holy Spirit, {3:6} whom He poured out on us generously through Jesus Christ our Savior, {3:7} so that, having been justified by His grace, we might become heirs having the hope of eternal life. {3:8} This is a trustworthy saying, and I want you to stress these things, so that those who have trusted in God may be careful to devote themselves to doing what is good. These things are excellent and profitable for everyone. {3:9} But avoid foolish controversies and genealogies and arguments and quarrels about the law, because these are unprofitable and useless. {3:10} Warn a divisive person once, and then warn them a second time. After that, have nothing to do with them. {3:11} You may be sure that such people are warped and sinful; they are self-condemned. {3:12} As soon as I send Artemas or Tychicus to you, do your best to come to me at Nicopolis, because I have decided to winter there. {3:13} Do everything you can to help Zenas the lawyer and Apollos on their way and see that they have everything they need. {3:14} Our people must learn to devote themselves to doing what is good, in order that they may provide for the urgent needs and not live unproductive lives. {3:15} Everyone with me sends you greetings. Greet those who love us in the faith. Grace be with you all. Amen.

The Epistle of Paul to Philemon

{1:1} Paul, a prisoner of Christ Jesus, and Timothy, our brother, to Philemon, our dear friend and coworker, {1:2} and to Apphia, Archippus, and the church that meets in your home: {1:3} Grace and peace to you from God our Father and the Lord Jesus Christ. {1:4} I always thank my God when I remember you in my prayers, {1:5} hearing of your love and faith toward the Lord Jesus and all the saints. {1:6} I pray that your faith will be effective in sharing the good things you have in Christ Jesus. {1:7} Your love has brought great joy and encouragement to the hearts of the saints, because you have refreshed them, brother. {1:8} Though I could be very bold in Christ and order you to do what you ought to do, {1:9} I appeal to you instead on the basis of love. I, Paul, an old man and now also a prisoner for the sake of Christ Jesus, {1:10} appeal to you for my son Onesimus, who became my son while I was in chains. {1:11} He was once useless to you, but now he has become useful both to you and to me. {1:12} I am sending him back to you, and I would like you to receive him as you would receive me. {1:13} I would have liked to keep him with me so he could assist me in my chains for the gospel, {1:14} but I did not want to do anything without your consent, so that your kindness would not be by compulsion, but by your own free will. {1:15} Perhaps the reason he was separated from you for a little while was that you might have him back forever, {1:16} no longer as a slave, but better than a slave, as a dear brother in the Lord. He is very dear to me, but even more so to you, both as a fellow man and as a brother in Christ. {1:17} So if you consider me a partner in the faith, welcome him as you would welcome me. {1:18} If he has wronged you or owes you anything, charge it to me. {1:19} I, Paul, am writing this with my own hand: I will pay it back, though I don't want to mention that you owe me your very self. {1:20} Yes, brother, I wish to have some benefit from you in the Lord; refresh my heart in Christ. {1:21} Confident of your obedience, I am writing to you, knowing that you will do even more than I ask. {1:22} And one more thing: Prepare a guest room for me, because I hope to be restored to you through your prayers. {1:23} Epaphras, my fellow prisoner in Christ Jesus, sends greetings, {1:24} as do Mark, Aristarchus, Demas, and Luke, my fellow workers. {1:25} The grace of the Lord Jesus Christ be with your spirit. Amen.

The Epistle to the Hebrews

{1:1} God, who spoke at various times and in different ways to our ancestors through the prophets, {1:2} has in these last days spoken to us through his Son, whom he appointed heir of everything and through whom he also created the universe. {1:3} The Son is the radiance of God's glory and the exact representation of his being, sustaining all things by his powerful word. After he had provided purification for our sins, he sat down at the right hand of the Majesty in heaven. {1:4} So he became much superior to the angels as he has inherited a name that is more excellent than theirs. {1:5} For to which of the angels did God ever say, "You are my Son; today I have become your Father"? Or again, "I will be his Father, and he will be my Son"? {1:6} And again, when he brings his firstborn into the world, he says, "Let all God's angels worship him." {1:7} In speaking of the angels, he says, "He makes his angels spirits, and his ministers a flame of fire." {1:8} But about the Son, he says, "Your throne, O God, will last forever and ever; a scepter of justice will be the scepter of your kingdom." {1:9} You have loved righteousness and hated wickedness; therefore God, your God, has set you above your companions by anointing you with the oil of joy. {1:10} He also says, "In the beginning, Lord, you laid the foundations of the earth, and the heavens are the work of your hands. {1:11} They will perish, but you remain; they will all wear out like a garment. {1:12} You will roll them up like a robe; like a garment, they will be changed. But you remain the same, and your years will never end." {1:13} To which of the angels did he ever say, "Sit at my right hand until I make your enemies a footstool for your feet"? {1:14} Are not all angels ministering spirits sent to serve those who will inherit salvation?

{2:1} We must pay more careful attention, therefore, to what we have heard, so that we do not drift away. {2:2} For since the message spoken through angels was binding, and every violation and disobedience received its just punishment, {2:3} how shall we escape if we ignore so great a salvation? This salvation, which was first announced by the Lord, was confirmed to us by those who heard him. {2:4} God also testified to it by signs, wonders, and various miracles, and by gifts of the Holy Spirit distributed according to his will. {2:5} It is not to angels that he has subjected the world to come, about which we are speaking. {2:6} But there is a place where someone has testified: "What is mankind that you are mindful of them, a son of man that you care for him? {2:7} You made them a little lower than the angels; you crowned them with glory and honor and put everything under their feet." {2:8} In putting everything under them, God left nothing that is not subject to them. Yet at present we do not see everything subject to them. {2:9} But we do see Jesus, who was made a little lower than the angels for a short time, now crowned with glory and honor because he suffered death, so that by the grace of God he might taste death for everyone. {2:10} In bringing many sons and daughters to glory, it was fitting that God, for whom and through whom everything exists, should make the pioneer of their salvation perfect through what he suffered. {2:11} Both the one who makes people holy and those who are made holy are of the same family. So Jesus is not ashamed to call them brothers and sisters. {2:12} He says, "I will declare your name to my brothers and sisters; in the assembly, I will sing your praises." {2:13} And again, "I will put my trust in him." And again he says, "Here am I, and the children God has given me." {2:14} Since the children have flesh and blood, he too shared in their humanity so that by his death he might break the power of him who holds the power of death—that is, the devil— {2:15} and free those who all their lives were held in slavery by their fear of death. {2:16} For surely it is not angels he helps, but Abraham's descendants. {2:17} For this reason, he had to be made like them, fully human in every way, in order that he might become a merciful and faithful high priest in service to God and that he might make atonement for the sins of the people. {2:18} Because he himself suffered when he was tempted, he is able to help those who are being tempted.

{3:1} Therefore, holy brothers and sisters, who share in the heavenly calling, consider Jesus, the Apostle and High Priest of our faith; {3:2} he was faithful to the one who appointed him, just as Moses was faithful in all God's house. {3:3} Jesus has been found worthy of greater honor than Moses, just as the builder of a house has greater honor than the house itself. {3:4} For every house is built by someone, but God is the builder of everything. {3:5} Moses was faithful as a servant in all God's house, bearing witness to what would be spoken later; {3:6} but Christ is faithful as the Son over God's house. We are his house if we hold on to our courage and the hope in which we boast until the end. {3:7} So, as the Holy Spirit says: "Today, if you hear his voice, {3:8} do not harden your hearts as you did in the rebellion, during the time of testing in the wilderness, {3:9} where your ancestors tested and tried me, though for forty years they saw what I did. {3:10} That is why I was angry with that generation; I said, 'Their hearts are always going astray, and they have not known my ways.' {3:11} So I declared on oath in my anger, 'They shall never enter my rest.'" {3:12} See to it, brothers and sisters, that none of you has a sinful, unbelieving heart that turns away from the living God. {3:13} But encourage one another daily, as long as it is called "Today," so that none of you may be hardened by sin's deceitfulness. {3:14} We have come to share in Christ, if indeed we hold our original conviction firmly to the very end. {3:15} As has just been said: "Today, if you hear his voice, do not harden your hearts as you did in the rebellion." {3:16} Who were they who heard and rebelled? Were they not all those Moses led out of Egypt? {3:17} And with whom was God angry for 40 years? Was it not with those who sinned, whose bodies perished in the wilderness? {3:18} And to whom did God swear they wouldn't enter His rest, if not to the disobedient? {3:19} So we see that they were not able to enter because of their unbelief.

{4:1} Therefore, since the promise of entering his rest still stands, let us be careful that none of you be found to have fallen short of it. {4:2} For we also have had the gospel preached to us, just as they did; but the message they heard was of no value to them because they did not share the faith of those who obeyed. {4:3} Now we who have believed enter that rest, just as God has said: "So I declared on oath in my anger, they shall never enter my rest." And yet his works have been finished since the creation of the world. {4:4} For somewhere he has spoken about the seventh day in these words: "On the seventh day, God rested from all his works." {4:5} And again in the passage above he says, "They shall never enter my rest." {4:6} Therefore, since it still remains for some to enter that rest, and since those who formerly had the gospel preached to them did not go in because of their disobedience, {4:7} God again set a certain day, calling it "Today." This he did when a long time later he spoke through David, as in the passage already quoted: "Today, if you hear his voice, do not harden your hearts." {4:8} For if Joshua had given them rest, God would not have spoken later about another day. {4:9} There remains, then, a Sabbath-rest for the people of God; {4:10} for anyone who enters God's rest also rests from their works, just as God did from his. {4:11} Let us, therefore, make every effort to enter that rest, so that no one will perish by following their example of disobedience. {4:12} For the word of God is alive and active. Sharper than any double-edged sword, it penetrates even to dividing soul and spirit, joints and marrow; it judges the thoughts and attitudes of the heart. {4:13} Nothing in all creation is hidden from God's sight; everything is uncovered and laid bare before the eyes of him to whom we must give account. {4:14} Therefore, since we have a great high priest who has ascended into heaven, Jesus the Son of God, let us hold firmly to the faith we profess. {4:15} For we do not have a high priest who is unable to empathize with our weaknesses, but we have one who has been tempted in every way, just as we are—yet he did not sin. {4:16} Let us then approach God's throne of grace with confidence, so that we may receive mercy and find grace to help us in our time of need.

{5:1} Every high priest is chosen from among people and appointed to represent them in matters related to God, so he can offer gifts and sacrifices for sins. {5:2} He can deal gently with those who are ignorant and are going astray, since he himself is subject to weakness. {5:3} That is why he must offer sacrifices for his own sins as well as for the sins of the people. {5:4} No one takes this honor on themselves; they receive it when called by God, just as Aaron was. {5:5} In the same way, Christ did not glorify himself to become a high priest, but he was appointed by the one who said to him, "You are my Son; today I have become your Father." {5:6} And he says in another passage, "You are a priest forever, in the order of Melchizedek." {5:7} During his earthly life, Jesus offered up prayers and petitions with fervent cries and tears to the one who could save him from death, and he was heard because of his reverent submission. {5:8} Son though he was, he learned obedience from what he suffered; {5:9} and, once made perfect, he became the source of eternal salvation for all who obey him. {5:10} He was designated by God to be a high priest in the order of Melchizedek. {5:11} We have much to say about this, but it is hard to make it clear to you because you no longer try to understand. {5:12} In fact, though by this time you ought to be teachers, you need someone to teach you the elementary truths of God's word all over again. You need milk, not solid food! {5:13} Anyone who lives on milk, being still an infant, is not acquainted with the teaching about righteousness. {5:14} But solid food is for the mature, who have trained themselves to distinguish good from evil.

{6:1} Therefore, let us move beyond the elementary teachings about Christ and be taken forward to maturity, not laying again the foundation of repentance from acts that lead to death, and of faith in God, {6:2} instruction about cleansing rites (ceremonial washing), the laying on of hands, the resurrection of the dead, and eternal judgment. {6:3} And God permitting, we will do so. {6:4} It is impossible for those who have once been enlightened, who have tasted the heavenly gift, who have shared in the Holy Spirit, {6:5} who have tasted the goodness of the word of God and the powers of the coming age {6:6} and who have fallen away, to be brought back to repentance because, to their loss, they are crucifying the Son of God all over again and subjecting him to public disgrace. {6:7} Land that drinks in the rain often falling on it and that produces a crop useful to those for whom it is farmed receives the blessing of God. {6:8} But land that produces thorns and thistles is worthless and is in danger of being cursed; in the end, it will be burned. {6:9} Even though we speak like this, dear friends, we are convinced of better things in your case—the things that have to do with salvation. {6:10} God is not unjust; he will not forget your work and the love you have shown him as you have helped his people and continue to help them. {6:11} We want each of you to show this same diligence to the very end, so that what you hope for may be fully realized. {6:12} We do not want you to become lazy, but to imitate those who through faith and patience inherit what has been promised. {6:13} When God made his promise to Abraham, since there was no one greater for him to swear by, he swore by himself, {6:14} saying, "I will surely bless you and give you many descendants." {6:15} And so after waiting patiently, Abraham received what was promised. {6:16} People swear by someone greater than themselves, and the oath confirms what is said and puts an end to all argument. {6:17} Because God wanted to make the unchanging nature of his purpose very clear to the heirs of what was promised, he confirmed it with an oath. {6:18} God did this so that, by two unchangeable things in which it is impossible for God to lie, we who have fled to take hold of the hope set before us may be greatly encouraged. {6:19} We have this hope as an anchor for the soul, firm and secure. It enters the inner sanctuary behind the curtain, {6:20} where our forerunner, Jesus, has entered on our behalf. He has become a high priest forever, in the order of Melchizedek.

{7:1} This Melchizedek, king of Salem and priest of the Most High God, met Abraham as he was returning from defeating the kings and blessed him. {7:2} Abraham gave him a tenth of everything; first, his name means "king of righteousness," then also "king of Salem," which means "king of peace." {7:3} He has no father or mother, no genealogy (family line), and no beginning or end of life, resembling the Son of God; he remains a priest forever. {7:4} Consider how great he was; even Abraham, the patriarch, gave him a tenth of the spoils. {7:5} The descendants of Levi, who receive the priesthood, are commanded by the law to collect tithes from the people, including their fellow Israelites, even though they are descended from Abraham. {7:6} But Melchizedek, who does not share their ancestry, received tithes from Abraham and blessed him who had the promises. {7:7} And without a doubt, the lesser is blessed by the greater. {7:8} In the one case, tithes are received by mortal men; in the other case, by him who is testified to be alive. {7:9} One might even say that Levi, who collects the tithes, paid tithes through Abraham {7:10} because he was still in the body of his ancestor when Melchizedek met him. {7:11} If perfection could have been attained through the Levitical priesthood (for on the basis of it the law was given to the people), why was there still a need for another priest to come, one in the order of Melchizedek, not Aaron? {7:12} For when the priesthood is changed, the law must be changed as well. {7:13} The one about whom these things are said belongs to a different tribe, and no one from that tribe has ever served at the altar. {7:14} It is clear that our Lord descended from Judah, and in regard to that tribe, Moses said nothing about priests. {7:15} And what we have said is even more clear if another priest like Melchizedek appears, {7:16} one who has become a priest not on the basis of a regulation (law) as to his ancestry, but on the basis of the power of an indestructible life. {7:17} For it is declared: "You are a priest forever, in the order of Melchizedek." {7:18} The former regulation is set aside because it was weak and useless. {7:19} The law made nothing perfect, but a better hope is introduced, by which we draw near to God. {7:20} And it was not without an oath! Others became priests without any oath, {7:21} but he became a priest with an oath when God said to him, "The Lord has sworn and will not change his mind: You are a priest forever." {7:22} Because of this oath, Jesus has become the guarantor of a better covenant. {7:23} Now there have been many of those priests, since death prevented them from continuing in office; {7:24} but because Jesus lives forever, he has a permanent priesthood. {7:25} Therefore he is able to save completely those who come to God through him, because he always lives to intercede for them. {7:26} Such a high priest truly meets our need—one who is holy, blameless, set apart from sinners, exalted above the heavens. {7:27} Unlike the other high priests, he does not need to offer sacrifices day after day, first for his own sins, & then for sins of people. He sacrificed for their sins once for all when he offered himself. {7:28} For the law appoints as high priests men in all their weakness; but the oath, which came after the law, appointed the Son, who has been made perfect forever.

{8:1} Now the main point of what we are saying is this: We do have such a high priest, who sat down at the right hand of the throne of the Majesty in heaven, {8:2} and who serves in the sanctuary, the true tabernacle set up by the Lord, not by a mere human being. {8:3} Every high priest is appointed to offer both gifts and sacrifices; and so it was necessary for this one also to have something to offer. {8:4} If he were on earth, he would not be a priest, for there are already priests who offer the gifts prescribed by the law. {8:5} They serve at a sanctuary that is a copy and shadow of what is in heaven. This is why Moses was warned when he was about to build the tabernacle: "See to it that you make everything according to the pattern shown you on the mountain." {8:6} But in fact the ministry Jesus has received is superior to theirs as the covenant of which he is mediator is superior to the old one, since the new covenant is established on better promises. {8:7} For if there had been nothing wrong with that first covenant, no place would have been sought for another. {8:8} But God found fault with the people and said: "The days are coming, declares the Lord, when I will make a new covenant with the house of Israel and with the house of Judah. {8:9} It will not be like the covenant I made with their ancestors when I took them by the hand to lead them out of Egypt, because they did not remain faithful to my covenant, and I turned away from them, declares the Lord. {8:10} This is the covenant I will establish with the people of Israel after that time, declares the Lord. I will put my laws in their minds and write them on their hearts. I will be their God, and they will be my people. {8:11} No longer will they teach their neighbor, or say to one another, 'Know the Lord,' because they will all know me, from the least of them to the greatest. {8:12} For I will forgive their wickedness and will remember their sins no more." {8:13} By calling this covenant "new," he has made the first one obsolete; and what is obsolete and outdated will soon disappear.

{9:1} The first covenant had rules for worship and an earthly sanctuary. {9:2} A tabernacle was constructed; in the first part, known as the Holy Place, were the lampstand, the table, and the bread of the Presence. {9:3} Behind the second curtain was the part of the tabernacle called the Most Holy Place, {9:4} which contained the golden altar of incense and the Ark of the Covenant covered with gold. Inside the ark were the golden jar of manna, Aaron's rod that had budded, and the stone tablets of the covenant. {9:5} Above the ark were the cherubim of glory overshadowing the mercy seat. We cannot discuss these things in detail now. {9:6} When everything was prepared this way, the priests regularly entered the first part of the tabernacle to perform their duties. {9:7} But only the high priest entered the second part once a year, and he always brought blood, which he offered for himself and for the sins of the people. {9:8} The Holy Spirit indicated that the way into the Most Holy Place had not yet been disclosed as long as the first tabernacle was still standing. {9:9} This is an illustration for the present time, indicating that the gifts and sacrifices being offered were not able to cleanse the conscience of the worshiper. {9:10} They only deal with food and drink and various ceremonial washings—external regulations applying until the time of reform. {9:11} But when Christ came as high priest of the good things that are now already here, he went through the greater and more perfect tabernacle that is not made with human hands—that is to say, is not a part of this creation. {9:12} He did not enter by the blood of goats and calves; he entered the Most Holy Place once for all by his own blood, thus obtaining eternal redemption. {9:13} The blood of goats and bulls and the ashes of a heifer sprinkle those who are ceremonially unclean, sanctifying them so that they are outwardly clean. {9:14} How much more, then, will the blood of Christ, who through the eternal Spirit offered himself unblemished to God, cleanse our consciences from acts that lead to death, so that we may serve the living God! {9:15} For this reason, Christ is the mediator of a new covenant, that those who are called may receive the promised eternal inheritance now that he has died as a ransom to set them free from the sins committed under the first covenant. {9:16} In the case of a will, it is necessary to prove the death of the one who made it, {9:17} because a will is in force only when someone has died; it never takes effect while the one who made it is living. {9:18} This is why even the first covenant was not put into effect without blood. {9:19} When Moses had proclaimed every command of the law to all the people, he took the blood of calves and goats, along with water, scarlet wool, and branches of hyssop, and sprinkled the scroll and all the people. {9:20} He said, "This is the blood of the covenant that God has commanded you to keep." {9:21} In the same way, he sprinkled with the blood both the tabernacle and all the vessels used in its ministry. {9:22} In fact, the law requires that nearly everything be cleansed with blood, and without the shedding of blood there is no forgiveness. {9:23} It was necessary, then, for the copies of the heavenly things to be purified with these sacrifices, but the heavenly things themselves with better sacrifices than these. {9:24} For Christ did not enter a sanctuary made with human hands; that was only a copy of the true one. He entered heaven itself, now to appear for us in God's presence. {9:25} Nor did he enter heaven to offer himself again and again, the way the high priest enters the Most Holy Place every year with blood that is not his own. {9:26} Otherwise, Christ would have had to suffer many times since the creation of the world. But he has appeared once for all at the culmination of the ages to do away with sin by the sacrifice of himself. {9:27} Just as people are destined to die once, and after that to face judgment, {9:28} so Christ was sacrificed once to take away the sins of many; and he will appear a second time, not to bear sin, but to bring salvation to those who are waiting for him.

{10:1} The law is only a shadow of the good things that are coming—not the realities themselves. It can never make perfect those who draw near to worship, with the same sacrifices they offer repeatedly year after year. {10:2} Otherwise, would they not have stopped being offered? For the worshipers would have been cleansed once for all, and would no longer have felt guilty for their sins. {10:3} But those sacrifices are an annual reminder of sins. {10:4} It is impossible for the blood of bulls and goats to take away sins. {10:5} Therefore, when Christ came into the world, he said: "Sacrifice and offering you did not desire, but a body you prepared for me; {10:6} with burnt offerings and sin offerings you were not pleased. {10:7} Then I said, 'Here I am—it is written about me in the scroll—I have come to do your will, my God.'" {10:8} First he said, "Sacrifices and offerings, burnt offerings and sin offerings you did not desire, nor were you pleased with them" (though they were offered in accordance with the law). {10:9} Then he said, "Here I am, I have come to do your will." He sets aside the first to establish the second. {10:10} And by that will, we have been made holy through the sacrifice of the body of Jesus Christ once for all. {10:11} Day after day every priest stands and performs his religious duties; again and again he offers the same sacrifices, which can never take away sins. {10:12} But when this priest had offered for all time one sacrifice for sins, he sat down at the right hand of God, {10:13} and since that time he waits for his enemies to be made his footstool. {10:14} For by one sacrifice he has made perfect forever those who are being made holy. {10:15} The Holy Spirit also testifies to us about this. First he says: {10:16} "This is the covenant I will make with them after that time, says the Lord. I will put my laws in their hearts, and I will write them on their minds." {10:17} Then he adds: "Their sins and lawless acts I will remember no more." {10:18} And where there have been forgiven, there is no longer any sacrifice for sin. {10:19} Therefore, brothers and sisters, since we have confidence to enter the Most Holy Place by the blood of Jesus, {10:20} by a new and living way opened for us through the curtain, that is, his body, {10:21} and since we have a great priest over the house of God, {10:22} let us draw near to God with a sincere heart and with the full assurance that faith brings, having our hearts sprinkled to cleanse us from a guilty conscience and having our bodies washed with pure water. {10:23} Let us hold unswervingly to the hope we profess, for he who promised is faithful. {10:24} And let us consider how we may spur one another on toward love and good deeds, {10:25} not giving up meeting together, as some are in the habit of doing, but encouraging one another—and all the more as you see the Day approaching. {10:26} If we deliberately keep on sinning after we have received the knowledge of the truth, no sacrifice for sins is left, {10:27} but only a fearful expectation of judgment and of raging fire that will consume the enemies of God. {10:28} Anyone who rejected the law of Moses died without mercy on the testimony of two or three witnesses. {10:29} How much more severely do you think someone deserves to be punished who has trampled the Son of God underfoot, who has treated as an unholy thing the blood of the covenant that sanctified them, and who has insulted the Spirit of grace? {10:30} For we know him who said, "It is mine to avenge; I will repay," and again, "The Lord will judge his people." {10:31} It is a dreadful thing to fall into the hands of the living God. {10:32} Remember those earlier days after you had received the light, when you endured in a great conflict full of suffering. {10:33} Sometimes you were publicly exposed to insult and persecution; at other times you stood side by side with those who were so treated. {10:34} You suffered along with those in prison and joyfully accepted the confiscation of your property, because you knew that you yourselves had better and lasting possessions. {10:35} So do not throw away your confidence; it will be richly rewarded. {10:36} You need to persevere so that when you have done the will of God, you will receive what he has promised. {10:37} For, "In just a little while, he who is coming will come and will not delay." {10:38} And, "But my righteous one will live by faith. And I take no pleasure in the one who shrinks back." {10:39} But we do not belong to those who shrink back and are destroyed, but to those who have faith and are saved.

{11:1} Faith is the assurance of things hoped for, the conviction of things not seen. {11:2} For by it, the ancients gained approval. {11:3} By faith, we understand that the universe was formed by God's word, so that what is seen was made from things that are not visible. {11:4} By faith, Abel offered God a better sacrifice than Cain did, and through it, he was commended as righteous, God testifying about his gifts; and even though he is dead, he still speaks. {11:5} By faith, Enoch was taken away so that he did not see death; he was not found because God took him away. Before his removal, he had this testimony: he pleased God. {11:6} Without faith, it is impossible to please God, because anyone who comes to him must believe that he exists and that he rewards those who earnestly seek him. {11:7} By faith, Noah, warned about things not yet seen, built an ark to save his family. By his faith, he condemned the world and became heir of the righteousness that comes by faith. {11:8} By faith, Abraham obeyed when he was called to go to a place he would later receive as an inheritance; he went out, not knowing where he was going. {11:9} By faith, he lived in the promised land as a stranger, living in tents with Isaac and Jacob, who were heirs with him of the same promise. {11:10} For he was looking forward to the city with foundations, whose architect and builder is God. {11:11} By faith, even Sarah herself received the ability to conceive when she was past the age, because she considered him faithful who had promised. {11:12} So from this one man, and he as good as dead, came descendants as numerous as the stars in the sky and as countless as the sand on the seashore. {11:13} All these people died in faith, without receiving the promises, but they saw them from a distance and welcomed them, acknowledging that they were foreigners and strangers on the earth. {11:14} People who say such things show that they are seeking a homeland. {11:15} If they had been thinking of the country they had left, they would have had the opportunity to return. {11:16} Instead, they were longing for a better country—a heavenly one. Therefore, God is not ashamed to be called their God, for he has prepared a city for them. {11:17} By faith, Abraham, when tested, offered up Isaac. He who had received the promises was about to sacrifice his one and only son, {11:18} even though God had said to him, "It is through Isaac that your offspring will be reckoned." {11:19} Abraham reasoned that God could even raise the dead, and so in a manner of speaking, he did receive Isaac back from death. {11:20} By faith, Isaac blessed Jacob and Esau concerning things to come. {11:21} By faith, Jacob, when he was dying, blessed each of Joseph's sons and worshiped as he leaned on the top of his staff. {11:22} By faith, Joseph, when his end was near, spoke about the exodus of the Israelites from Egypt and gave instructions about his bones. {11:23} By faith, Moses' parents hid him for three months after he was born because they saw he was no ordinary child, and they were not afraid of the king's edict. {11:24} By faith, Moses, when he had grown up, refused to be known as the son of Pharaoh's daughter. {11:25} He chose to be mistreated along with the people of God rather than to enjoy the fleeting pleasures of sin. {11:26} He regarded disgrace for the sake of Christ as of greater value than the treasures of Egypt, because he was looking ahead to his reward. {11:27} By faith, he left Egypt, not fearing the king's anger; he persevered because he saw him who is invisible. {11:28} By faith, he kept the Passover and the application of blood, so that the destroyer of the firstborn would not touch the Israelites. {11:29} By faith, the people passed through the Red Sea as on dry land; but when the Egyptians tried to do so, they were drowned. {11:30} By faith, the walls of Jericho fell after the army had marched around them for seven days. {11:31} By faith, the prostitute Rahab, because she welcomed the spies, was not killed with those who were disobedient. {11:32} And what more shall I say? I do not have time to tell about Gideon, Barak, Samson, and Jephthah, about David and Samuel and the prophets, {11:33} who through faith conquered kingdoms, administered justice, and gained what was promised; who shut the mouths of lions, {11:34} quenched the fury of the flames, and escaped the edge of the sword; whose weakness was turned to strength; who became powerful in battle and routed foreign armies. {11:35} Women received back their dead, raised to life again. Others were tortured, refusing to be released so that they might gain an even better resurrection. {11:36} Some faced jeers and flogging, and even chains and imprisonment. {11:37} They were stoned; they were sawed in two; they were killed by the sword. They went about in sheepskins and goatskins, destitute, persecuted, and mistreated— {11:38} the world was not worthy of them. They wandered in deserts and mountains, living in caves and in holes in the ground. {11:39} These were all commended for their faith, yet none of them received what had been promised, {11:40} since God had planned something better for us so that only together with us would they be made perfect.

{12:1} Therefore, since we are surrounded by such a great cloud of witnesses, let us throw off everything that hinders and the sin that so easily entangles. Let us run with perseverance the race marked out for us, {12:2} fixing our eyes on Jesus, the pioneer and perfecter of faith. For the joy set before him, he endured the cross, scorning its shame, and sat down at the right hand of the throne of God. {12:3} Consider him who endured such opposition from sinners, so that you will not grow weary and lose heart. {12:4} In your struggle against sin, you have not yet resisted to the point of shedding your blood. {12:5} And have you completely forgotten this word of encouragement that addresses you as a father addresses his child? It says, "My son, do not make light of the Lord's discipline, and do not lose heart when he rebukes you, {12:6} because the Lord disciplines the one he loves, and he chastens everyone he accepts as his son." {12:7} Endure hardship as discipline; God is treating you as his children. For what children are not disciplined by their father? {12:8} If you are not disciplined—and everyone undergoes discipline—then you are not legitimate, not true sons and daughters at all. {12:9} Moreover, we have all had human fathers who disciplined us and we respected them for it. How much more should we submit to the Father of spirits and live? {12:10} They disciplined us for a little while as they thought best; but God disciplines us for our good, in order that we may share in his holiness. {12:11} No discipline seems pleasant at the time, but painful. Later on, however, it produces a harvest of righteousness and peace for those who have been trained by it {12:12} Therefore strengthen your feeble arms and weak knees. {12:13} Make level paths for your feet, so that the lame may not be disabled, but rather healed. {12:14} Make every effort to live in peace with everyone and to be holy; without holiness, no one will see the Lord. {12:15} See to it that no one falls short of the grace of God and that no bitter root grows up to cause trouble and defile many. {12:16} See that no one is sexually immoral or is godless like Esau, who sold his birthright for a single meal. {12:17} Afterward, as you know, when he wanted to inherit this blessing, he was rejected. He could bring about no change of mind, though he sought the blessing with tears. {12:18} You have not come to a mountain that can be touched and that is burning with fire; to darkness, gloom, and storm; {12:19} to a trumpet blast or to such a voice speaking words that those who heard it begged that no further word be spoken to them, {12:20} because they could not bear what was commanded: "If even an animal touches the mountain, it must be stoned." {12:21} The sight was so terrifying that Moses said, "I am trembling with fear." {12:22} But you have come to Mount Zion, to the city of the living God, the heavenly Jerusalem. You have come to thousands upon thousands of angels in joyful assembly, {12:23} to the church of the firstborn, whose names are written in heaven. You have come to God, the Judge of all, to the spirits of the righteous made perfect, {12:24} to Jesus, the mediator of a new covenant, and to the sprinkled blood that speaks a better word than the blood of Abel. {12:25} See to it that you do not refuse him who speaks. If they did not escape when they refused him who warned them on earth, how much less will we, if we turn away from him who warns us from heaven? {12:26} At that time his voice shook the earth, but now he has promised, "Once more I will shake not only the earth but also the heavens." {12:27} The words "once more" indicate the removing of what can be shaken—that is, created things—so that what cannot be shaken may remain. {12:28} Therefore, since we are receiving a kingdom that cannot be shaken, let us be thankful, and so worship God acceptably with reverence and awe, {12:29} for our God is a consuming fire.

{13:1} Let mutual love continue. {13:2} Do not forget to show hospitality to strangers, for by doing so, some people have entertained angels without knowing it. {13:3} Remember those in prison as if you were there with them, and those who are mistreated as if you were suffering with them. {13:4} Marriage should be honored by all, and the marriage bed kept pure, for God will judge the adulterer and all the sexually immoral. {13:5} Keep your lives free from the love of money and be content with what you have, because God has said, "Never will I leave you; never will I forsake you." {13:6} So we say with confidence, "The Lord is my helper; I will not be afraid. What can mere mortals do to me?" {13:7} Remember your leaders, who spoke the word of God to you. Consider the outcome of their way of life and imitate their faith. {13:8} Jesus Christ is the same yesterday, today, and forever. {13:9} Do not be carried away by all kinds of strange teachings. It is good for our hearts to be strengthened by grace, not by eating ceremonial foods, which are of no value to those who partake in them. {13:10} We have an altar from which those who serve at the tabernacle have no right to eat. {13:11} The high priest carries the blood of animals into the Most Holy Place as a sin offering, but their bodies are burned outside the camp. {13:12} And so Jesus also suffered outside the city gate to make the people holy through his own blood. {13:13} Let us then go to him outside the camp, bearing the disgrace he bore. {13:14} For here we do not have an enduring city, but we are looking for the city that is to come. {13:15} Through Jesus, therefore, let us continually offer to God a sacrifice of praise, the fruit of lips that openly profess his name. {13:16} And do not forget to do good and to share with others, for with such sacrifices God is pleased. {13:17} Have confidence in your leaders and submit to their authority, because they keep watch over you as those who must give an account. Do this so that their work will be a joy, not a burden, for that would be of no benefit to you. {13:18} Pray for us. We are sure that we have a clear conscience and desire to live honorably in every way. {13:19} I particularly urge you to pray so that I may be restored to you soon. {13:20} Now may the God of peace, who brought back from the dead our Lord Jesus, that great shepherd of the sheep, through the blood of the eternal covenant, {13:21} equip you with everything good for doing his will, and may he work in us what is pleasing to him, through Jesus Christ, to whom be glory for ever and ever. Amen. {13:22} I urge you, brothers and sisters, to bear with my word of exhortation, for in fact, I have written to you quite briefly. {13:23} I want you to know that our brother Timothy has been released. If he arrives soon, I will see you. {13:24} Greet all your leaders and all the Lord's people. Those from Italy send you their greetings. {13:25} Grace be with you all. Amen.

The Epistle of James

{1:1} James, a servant of God and of the Lord Jesus Christ, sends greetings to the twelve tribes scattered throughout the world. {1:2} My brothers and sisters, consider it pure joy whenever you face trials of many kinds, {1:3} because you know that the testing of your faith produces perseverance. {1:4} Let perseverance finish its work so that you may be mature and complete, lacking nothing. {1:5} If any of you lacks wisdom, you should ask God, who gives generously to all without finding fault, and it will be given to you. {1:6} But when you ask, you must believe and not doubt, because the one who doubts is like a wave of the sea, blown and tossed by the wind. {1:7} That person should not expect to receive anything from the Lord. {1:8} Such a person is double-minded and unstable in all they do. {1:9} Believers in humble circumstances ought to take pride in their high position. {1:10} But the rich should take pride in their humiliation, since they will pass away like a wildflower. {1:11} For the sun rises with scorching heat and withers the plant; its blossom falls and its beauty is destroyed. In the same way, the rich will fade away even while they go about their business. {1:12} Blessed is the one who perseveres under trial because, having stood the test, that person will receive the crown of life that the Lord has promised to those who love him. {1:13} When tempted, no one should say, "God is tempting me." For God cannot be tempted by evil, nor does he tempt anyone; {1:14} each person is tempted when they are dragged away by their own evil desire and enticed. {1:15} Then, after desire has conceived, it gives birth to sin; and sin, when it is full-grown, gives birth to death. {1:16} Don't be deceived, my dear brothers and sisters. {1:17} Every good and perfect gift is from above, coming down from the Father of the heavenly lights, who does not change like shifting shadows. {1:18} He chose to give us birth through the word of truth, that we might be a kind of firstfruits of all he created. {1:19} My dear brothers and sisters, take note of this:

Everyone should be quick to listen, slow to speak, and slow to become angry, {1:20} because human anger does not produce the righteousness that God desires. {1:21} Therefore, get rid of all moral filth and the evil that is so prevalent and humbly accept the word planted in you, which can save you. {1:22} Do not merely listen to the word, and so deceive yourselves. Do what it says. {1:23} Anyone who listens to the word but does not do what it says is like someone who looks at his face in a mirror {1:24} and, after looking at himself, goes away and immediately forgets what he looks like. {1:25} But whoever looks intently into the perfect law that gives freedom and continues in it—not forgetting what they have heard, but doing it—they will be blessed in what they do. {1:26} Those who consider themselves religious and yet do not keep a tight rein on their tongues deceive themselves, and their religion is worthless. {1:27} Religion that God our Father accepts as pure and faultless is this: to look after orphans and widows in their distress and to keep oneself from being polluted by the world.

{2:1} My brothers and sisters, believers in our glorious Lord Jesus Christ must not show favoritism. {2:2} Suppose a man comes into your meeting wearing a gold ring and fine clothes, and a poor man in filthy old clothes also comes in. {2:3} If you show special attention to the man wearing fine clothes and say, "Here's a good seat for you," but say to the poor man, "You stand there" or "Sit on the floor by my feet," {2:4} have you not discriminated among yourselves and become judges with evil thoughts? {2:5} Listen, my dear brothers and sisters: Has not God chosen those who are poor in the eyes of the world to be rich in faith and to inherit the kingdom he promised those who love him? {2:6} But you have dishonored the poor. Is it not the rich who are exploiting you? Are they not the ones who are dragging you into court? {2:7} Are they not the ones who are blaspheming the noble name of him to whom you belong? {2:8} If you really keep the royal law found in Scripture, "Love your neighbor as yourself," you are doing right. {2:9} But if you show favoritism, you sin and are convicted by the law as lawbreakers. {2:10} For whoever keeps the whole law and yet stumbles at just one point is guilty of breaking all of it. {2:11} For he who said, "You shall not commit adultery," also said, "You shall not murder." If you do not commit adultery but do commit murder, you have become a lawbreaker. {2:12} Speak and act as those who are going to be judged by the law that gives freedom, {2:13} because judgment without mercy will be shown to anyone who has not been merciful. Mercy triumphs over judgment. {2:14} What good is it, my brothers and sisters, if someone claims to have faith but has no deeds? Can such faith save them? {2:15} Suppose a brother or a sister is without clothes and daily food. {2:16} If one of you says to them, "Go in peace; keep warm and well fed," but does nothing about their physical needs, what good is it? {2:17} In the same way, faith by itself, if it is not accompanied by action, is dead. {2:18} But someone will say, "You have faith; I have deeds." Show me your faith without deeds, and I will show you my faith by my deeds. {2:19} You believe that there is one God. Good! Even the demons believe that—and shudder. {2:20} You foolish person, do you want evidence that faith without deeds is useless? {2:21} Was not our father Abraham considered righteous for what he did when he offered his son Isaac on the altar? {2:22} You see that his faith and his actions were working together, and his faith was made complete by what he did. {2:23} And the scripture was fulfilled that says, "Abraham believed God, and it was credited to him as righteousness," and he was called God's friend. {2:24} You see that a person is considered righteous by what they do and not by faith alone. {2:25} In the same way, was not even Rahab the prostitute considered righteous for what she did when she gave lodging to the spies and sent them off in a different direction? {2:26} As the body without the spirit is dead, so faith without deeds is dead.

{3:1} Not many of you should become teachers, my fellow believers, because you know that we who teach will be judged more strictly. {3:2} We all stumble in many ways. Anyone who is never at fault in what they say is perfect, able to keep their whole body in check. {3:3} When we put bits into the mouths of horses to make them obey us, we can turn the whole animal. {3:4} Or take ships as an example. Although they are so large and are driven by strong winds, they are steered by a very small rudder wherever the pilot wants to go. {3:5} Likewise, the tongue is a small part of the body, but it makes great boasts. Consider what a great forest is set on fire by a small spark! {3:6} The tongue also is a fire, a world of evil among the parts of the body. It corrupts the whole body, sets the whole course of one's life on fire, and is itself set on fire by hell. {3:7} All kinds of animals, birds, reptiles, and sea creatures are being tamed and have been tamed by mankind, {3:8} but no human being can tame the tongue. It is a restless evil, full of deadly poison. {3:9} With the tongue, we praise our Lord and Father, and with it, we curse human beings, who have been made in God's likeness. {3:10} Out of the same mouth come praise and cursing. My brothers and sisters, this should not be. {3:11} Can both fresh water and salt water flow from the same spring? {3:12} My brothers and sisters, can a fig tree bear olives, or a grapevine bear figs? Neither can a salt spring produce fresh water. {3:13} Who is wise and understanding among you? Let them show it by their good life, by deeds done in the humility that comes from wisdom. {3:14} But if you harbor bitter envy and selfish ambition in your hearts, do not boast about it or deny the truth. {3:15} Such "wisdom" does not come down from heaven but is earthly, unspiritual, and demonic. {3:16} For where you have envy and selfish ambition, there you find disorder and every evil practice. {3:17} But the wisdom that comes from heaven is first of all pure; then peace-loving, considerate, submissive, full of mercy and good fruit, impartial and sincere. {3:18} Peacemakers who sow in peace reap a harvest of righteousness.

{4:1} What causes fights and quarrels among you? Don't they come from your desires that battle within you? {4:2} You desire but do not have, so you kill. You covet but cannot get what you want, so you quarrel and fight. You do not have because you do not ask God. {4:3} When you ask, you do not receive, because you ask with wrong motives, that you may spend what you get on your pleasures. {4:4} You adulterous people! Don't you know that friendship with the world means enmity against God? Therefore, anyone who chooses to be a friend of the world becomes an enemy of God. {4:5} Or do you think Scripture says without reason that he jealously longs for the spirit he has caused to dwell in us? {4:6} But he gives us more grace. That is why Scripture says: "God opposes the proud but shows favor to the humble." {4:7} Submit yourselves, then, to God. Resist the devil, and he will flee from you. {4:8} Come near to God and he will come near to you. Wash your hands, you sinners, and purify your hearts, you double-minded. {4:9} Grieve, mourn, and wail. Change your laughter to mourning and your joy to gloom. {4:10} Humble yourselves before the Lord, and he will lift you up. {4:11} Brothers and sisters, do not slander one another. Anyone who speaks against a brother or sister or judges them speaks against the law and judges it. When you judge the law, you are not keeping it but sitting in judgment on it. {4:12} There is only one Lawgiver and Judge, the one who is able to save and destroy. But you—who are you to judge your neighbor? {4:13} Now listen, you who say, "Today or tomorrow we will go to this or that city, spend a year there, carry on business and make money." {4:14} Why, you do not even know what will happen tomorrow. What is your life? You are a mist that appears for a little while and then vanishes. {4:15} Instead, you ought to say, "If it is the Lord's will, we will live and do this or that." {4:16} As it is, you boast in your arrogant schemes. All such boasting is evil. {4:17} If anyone, then, knows the good they ought to do and doesn't do it, it is sin for them.

{5:1} Now listen, you rich people, weep and wail because of the misery that is coming on you. {5:2} Your wealth has rotted, and moths have eaten your clothes. {5:3} Your gold and silver are corroded, and their corrosion will testify against you and eat your flesh like fire. You have hoarded wealth in the last days. {5:4} Look! The wages you failed to pay the workers who mowed your fields are crying out against you. The cries of the harvesters have reached the ears of the Lord Almighty. {5:5} You have lived on earth in luxury and self-indulgence. You have fattened yourselves in the day of slaughter. {5:6} You have condemned and murdered the innocent one, who was not opposing you. {5:7} Be patient, then, brothers and sisters, until the Lord's coming. See how the farmer waits for the land to yield its valuable crop, patiently waiting for the autumn and spring rains. {5:8} You too, be patient and stand firm, because the Lord's coming is near. {5:9} Don't grumble against one another, brothers and sisters, or you will be judged. The Judge is standing at the door! {5:10} Brothers and sisters, as an example of patience in the face of suffering, take the prophets who spoke in the name of the Lord. {5:11} As you know, we count as blessed those who have persevered. You have heard of Job's perseverance and have seen what the Lord finally brought about. The Lord is full of compassion and mercy. {5:12} Above all, my brothers and sisters, do not swear—not by heaven or by earth or by anything else. All you need to say is a simple "Yes" or "No." Otherwise, you will be condemned. {5:13} Is anyone among you in trouble? Let them pray. Is anyone happy? Let them sing songs of praise. {5:14} Is anyone among you sick? Let them call the elders of the church to pray over them and anoint them with oil in the name of the Lord. {5:15} And the prayer offered in faith will make the sick person well; the Lord will raise them up. If they have sinned, they will be forgiven. {5:16} Therefore confess your sins to each other and pray for each other so that you may be healed. The prayer of a righteous person is powerful and effective. {5:17} Elijah was a human being, even as we are. He prayed earnestly that it would not rain, and it did not rain on the land for three and a half years. {5:18} Again he prayed, and the heavens gave rain, and the earth produced its crops. {5:19} My brothers and sisters, if one of you should wander from the truth and someone should bring that person back, {5:20} remember this: Whoever turns a sinner from the error of their way will save them from death and cover over a multitude of sins.

The First Epistle of Peter

{1:1} Peter, an apostle of Jesus Christ, to the strangers scattered throughout Pontus, Galatia, Cappadocia, Asia, and Bithynia, {1:2} chosen according to the foreknowledge of God the Father, through the sanctification of the Spirit, for obedience and the sprinkling of the blood of Jesus Christ: Grace and peace be multiplied to you. {1:3} Praise be to the God and Father of our Lord Jesus Christ! In his great mercy, he has given us new birth into a living hope through the resurrection of Jesus Christ from the dead, {1:4} and into an inheritance that can never perish, spoil, or fade—this inheritance is kept in heaven for you, {1:5} who through faith are shielded by God's power until the coming of the salvation that is ready to be revealed in the last time. {1:6} In this you greatly rejoice, though now for a little while you may have had to suffer grief in all kinds of trials. {1:7} These have come so that the proven genuineness of your faith—of greater worth than gold, which perishes even though refined by fire—may result in praise, glory, and honor when Jesus Christ is revealed. {1:8} Though you have not seen him, you love him; and even though you do not see him now, you believe in him and are filled with an inexpressible and glorious joy, {1:9} for you are receiving the end result of your faith, the salvation of your souls. {1:10} Concerning this salvation, the prophets, who spoke of the grace that was to come to you, searched intently and with the greatest care, {1:11} trying to find out the time and circumstances to which the Spirit of Christ in them was pointing when he predicted the sufferings of the Messiah and the glories that would follow. {1:12} It was revealed to them that they were not serving themselves but you, when they spoke of the things that have now been told you by those who have preached the gospel to you by the Holy Spirit sent from heaven. Even angels long to look into these things. {1:13} Therefore, with minds that are alert and fully sober, set your hope on the grace to be brought to you when Jesus Christ is revealed at his coming. {1:14} As obedient children, do not conform to the evil desires you had when you lived in ignorance. {1:15} But just as he who called you is holy, so be holy in all you do; {1:16} for it is written: "Be holy, because I am holy." {1:17} Since you call on a Father who judges each person's work impartially, live out your time as foreigners here in reverent fear. {1:18} For you know that it was not with perishable things such as silver or gold that you were redeemed from the empty way of life handed down to you from your ancestors, {1:19} but with the precious blood of Christ, a lamb without blemish or defect. {1:20} He was chosen before the creation of the world, but was revealed in these last times for your sake. {1:21} Through him you believe in God, who raised him from the dead and glorified him, and so your faith and hope are in God. {1:22} Now that you have purified yourselves by obeying the truth so that you have sincere love for each other, love one another deeply, from the heart. {1:23} For you have been born again, not of perishable seed, but of imperishable, through the living and enduring word of God. {1:24} For "All people are like grass, and all their glory is like the flowers of the field; the grass withers and the flowers fall, {1:25} but the word of the Lord endures forever." And this is the word that was preached to you.

{2:1} Therefore, rid yourselves of all malice and all deceit, hypocrisy, envy, and slander of every kind. {2:2} Like newborn babies, crave pure spiritual milk, so that by it you may grow up in your salvation, {2:3} now that you have tasted that the Lord is good. {2:4} As you come to him, the living Stone—rejected by humans but chosen by God and precious to him— {2:5} you also, like living stones, are being built into a spiritual house, to be a holy priesthood, offering spiritual sacrifices acceptable to God through Jesus Christ. {2:6} For in Scripture it says: "See, I lay a stone in Zion, a chosen and precious cornerstone, and the one who trusts in him will never be put to shame." {2:7} Now to you who believe, this stone is precious. But to those who do not believe, "The stone the builders rejected has become the cornerstone," {2:8} and, "A stone that causes people to stumble and a rock that makes them fall." They stumble because they disobey the message—which is also what they were destined for. {2:9} But you are a chosen people, a royal priesthood, a holy nation, God's special possession, that you may declare the praises of him who called you out of darkness into his wonderful light. {2:10} Once you were not a people, but now you are the people of God; once you had not received mercy, but now you have received mercy. {2:11} Dear friends, I urge you, as foreigners and exiles, to abstain from sinful desires, which wage war against your soul. {2:12} Live such good lives among the pagans that, though they accuse you of doing wrong, they may see your good deeds and glorify God on the day he visits us. {2:13} Submit yourselves for the Lord's sake to every human authority: whether to the emperor, as the supreme authority, {2:14} or to governors, who are sent by him to punish those who do wrong and to commend those who do right. {2:15} For it is God's will that by doing good you should silence the ignorant talk of foolish people. {2:16} Live as free people, but do not use your freedom as a cover-up for evil; live as God's slaves. {2:17} Show proper respect to everyone, love the family of believers, fear God, honor the emperor. {2:18} Slaves, in reverent fear of God submit yourselves to your masters, not only to those who are good and considerate, but also to those who are harsh. {2:19} For it is commendable if someone bears up under the pain of unjust suffering because they are conscious of God. {2:20} But how is it to your credit if you receive a beating for doing wrong and endure it? But if you suffer for doing good and you endure it, this is commendable before God. {2:21} To this you were called, because Christ suffered for you, leaving you an example, that you should follow in his steps. {2:22} "He committed no sin, and no deceit was found in his mouth." {2:23} When they hurled their insults at him, he did not retaliate; when he suffered, he made no threats. Instead, he entrusted himself to him who judges justly. {2:24} He himself bore our sins in his body on the cross, so that we might die to sins and live for righteousness; by his wounds you have been healed. {2:25} For you were like sheep going astray, but now you have returned to the Shepherd and Overseer of your souls.

{3:1} Likewise, you wives, be submissive to your own husbands so that if any of them do not believe the word, they may be won over without words by the behavior of their wives. {3:2} When they see the purity and reverence of your lives. {3:3} Your beauty should not come from outward adornment, such as elaborate hairstyles and the wearing of gold jewelry or fine clothes; {3:4} rather, it should be that of your inner self, the unfading beauty of a gentle and quiet spirit, which is of great worth in God's sight. {3:5} For this is how the holy women of the past who put their hope in God used to adorn themselves. They submitted to their own husbands, {3:6} like Sarah, who obeyed Abraham and called him her lord. You are her daughters if you do what is right and do not give way to fear. {3:7} In the same way, you husbands, be considerate as you live with your wives and treat them with respect as the weaker partner and as heirs with you of the gracious gift of life, so that nothing will hinder your prayers. {3:8} Finally, all of you, be like-minded, be sympathetic, love one another, be compassionate and humble. {3:9} Do not repay evil with evil or insult with insult. On the contrary, repay evil with blessing, because to this you were called so that you may inherit a blessing. {3:10} For, "Whoever would love life and see good days must keep their tongue from evil and their lips from deceitful speech. {3:11} They must turn from evil and do good; they must seek peace and pursue it. {3:12} For the eyes of the Lord are on the righteous and his ears are attentive to their prayer, but the face of the Lord is against those who do evil." {3:13} Who is going to harm you if you are eager to do good? {3:14} But even if you should suffer for what is right, you are blessed. Do not fear their threats; do not be frightened. {3:15} But in your hearts revere Christ as Lord. Always be prepared to give an answer to everyone who asks you to give the reason for the hope that you have. But do this with gentleness and respect, {3:16} keeping a clear conscience, so that those who speak maliciously against your good behavior in Christ may be ashamed of their slander. {3:17} For it is better, if it is God's will, to suffer for doing good than for doing evil. {3:18} For Christ also suffered once for sins, the righteous for the unrighteous, to bring you to God. He was put to death in the body but made alive in the Spirit. {3:19} After being made alive, he went and made proclamation to the imprisoned spirits— {3:20} to those who were disobedient long ago when God waited patiently in the days of Noah while the ark was being built. In it only a few people, eight in all, were saved through water, {3:21} and this water symbolizes baptism that now saves you also—not the removal of dirt from the body but the pledge of a clear conscience toward God. It saves you by the resurrection of Jesus Christ, {3:22} who has gone into heaven and is at God's right hand—with angels, authorities, and powers in submission to him.

{4:1} Therefore, since Christ suffered in his body, arm yourselves also with the same attitude, because whoever suffers in the body is done with sin. {4:2} As a result, they do not live the rest of their earthly lives for evil human desires, but rather for the will of God. {4:3} For you have spent enough time in the past doing what pagans choose to do—living in debauchery, lust, drunkenness, orgies, carousing, and detestable idolatry. {4:4} They are surprised that you do not join them in their reckless, wild living, and they heap abuse on you. {4:5} But they will have to give account to him who is ready to judge the living and the dead. {4:6} For this is the reason the gospel was preached even to those who are now dead, so that they might be judged according to human standards in regard to the body but live according to God in regard to the spirit. {4:7} The end of all things is near. Therefore be alert and of sober mind so that you may pray. {4:8} Above all, love each other deeply, because love covers over a multitude of sins. {4:9} Offer hospitality to one another without grumbling. {4:10} Each of you should use whatever gift you have received to serve others, as faithful stewards of God's grace in its various forms. {4:11} If anyone speaks, they should do so as one who speaks the very words of God; if anyone serves, they should do so with the strength God provides, so that in all things God may be praised through Jesus Christ. To him be the glory and the power forever and ever. Amen. {4:12} Dear friends, do not be surprised at the fiery ordeal that has come on you to test you, as though something strange were happening to you. {4:13} But rejoice inasmuch as you participate in the sufferings of Christ, so that you may be overjoyed when his glory is revealed. {4:14} If you are insulted because of the name of Christ, you are blessed, for the Spirit of glory and of God rests on you. {4:15} If you suffer, it should not be as a murderer or thief or any other kind of criminal, or even as a meddler. {4:16} However, if you suffer as a Christian, do not be ashamed, but praise God that you bear that name. {4:17} For it is time for judgment to begin with God's household; and if it begins with us, what will the outcome be for those who do not obey the gospel of God? {4:18} And, "If it is hard for the righteous to be saved, what will become of the ungodly and the sinner?" {4:19} So then, those who suffer according to God's will should commit themselves to their faithful Creator and continue to do good.

{5:1} To the elders among you, I appeal as a fellow elder, a witness of Christ's sufferings, and one who will share in the glory to be revealed: {5:2} Be shepherds of God's flock that is under your care, watching over them—not because you must, but because you are willing, as God wants you to be; not pursuing dishonest gain, but eager to serve; {5:3} not lording it over those entrusted to you, but being examples to the flock. {5:4} And when the Chief Shepherd appears, you will receive the crown of glory that will never fade away. {5:5} In the same way, you who are younger, submit yourselves to your elders. All of you, clothe yourselves with humility toward one another, because "God opposes the proud but shows favor to the humble." {5:6} Humble yourselves, therefore, under God's mighty hand, that he may lift you up in due time; {5:7} cast all your anxiety on him because he cares for you. {5:8} Be alert and of sober mind. Your enemy the devil prowls around like a roaring lion looking for someone to devour. {5:9} Resist him, standing firm in the faith, because you know that the family of believers throughout the world is undergoing the same kind of sufferings. {5:10} And the God of all grace, who called you to his eternal glory in Christ, after you have suffered a little while, will himself restore you and make you strong, firm, and steadfast. {5:11} To him be the power for ever and ever. Amen. {5:12} With the help of Silvanus, whom I regard as a faithful brother, I have written to you briefly, encouraging you and testifying that this is the true grace of God in which you stand. {5:13} She who is in Babylon, chosen together with you, sends you her greetings, and so does my son Mark. {5:14} Greet one another with a kiss of love. Peace to all of you who are in Christ. Amen.

The Second Epistle of Peter

{1:1} Simon Peter, a servant and apostle of Jesus Christ, to those who have obtained a faith as precious as ours through the righteousness of God and our Savior Jesus Christ: {1:2} May grace and peace be multiplied to you through the knowledge of God and of Jesus our Lord. {1:3} His divine power has given us everything we need for life and godliness through our knowledge of him who called us by his own glory and goodness. {1:4} Through these, he has given us very great and precious promises, so that through them you may participate in the divine nature, having escaped the corruption in the world caused by evil desires. {1:5} For this reason, make every effort to add to your faith goodness; and to goodness, knowledge; {1:6} and to knowledge, self-control; and to self-control, perseverance; and to perseverance, godliness; {1:7} and to godliness, mutual affection; and to mutual affection, love. {1:8} For if you possess these qualities in increasing measure, they will keep you from being ineffective and unproductive in your knowledge of our Lord Jesus Christ. {1:9} But whoever does not have them is nearsighted and blind, forgetting that they have been cleansed from their past sins. {1:10} Therefore, my brothers and sisters, make every effort to confirm your calling and election. If you do these things, you will never stumble, {1:11} and you will receive a rich welcome into the eternal kingdom of our Lord and Savior Jesus Christ. {1:12} So I will always remind you of these things, even though you know them and are firmly established in the truth you now have. {1:13} I think it is right to refresh your memory as long as I live in the tent of this body, {1:14} because I know that I will soon put it aside, as our Lord Jesus Christ has made clear to me. {1:15} And I will make every effort to see that after my departure you will always be able to remember these things. {1:16} For we did not follow cleverly devised stories when we told you about the coming of our Lord Jesus Christ in power, but we were eyewitnesses of his majesty. {1:17} He received honor and glory from God the Father when the voice came to him from the Majestic Glory, saying, "This is my Son, whom I love; with him, I am well pleased." {1:18} We ourselves heard this voice that came from heaven when we were with him on the sacred mountain. {1:19} We also have the prophetic message as something completely reliable, and you will do well to pay attention to it, as to a light shining in a dark place, until the day dawns and the morning star rises in your hearts. {1:20} Above all, you must understand that no prophecy of Scripture came about by the prophet's own interpretation of things. {1:21} For prophecy never had its origin in the human will, but prophets, though human, spoke from God as they were carried along by the Holy Spirit.

{2:1} But there were also false prophets among the people, just as there will be false teachers among you. They will secretly introduce destructive heresies, even denying the sovereign Lord who bought them, bringing swift destruction on themselves. {2:2} Many will follow their depraved conduct and will bring the way of truth into disrepute. {2:3} In their greed, these teachers will exploit you with fabricated stories. Their condemnation has long been hanging over them, and their destruction has not been sleeping. {2:4} For if God did not spare angels when they sinned, but sent them to hell, putting them in chains of darkness to be held for judgment; {2:5} if he did not spare the ancient world when he brought the flood on its ungodly people, but protected Noah, a preacher of righteousness, and seven others; {2:6} if he condemned the cities of Sodom and Gomorrah by burning them to ashes and made them an example of what is going to happen to the ungodly; {2:7} and if he rescued Lot, a righteous man, who was distressed by the depraved conduct of the lawless— {2:8} (for that righteous man, living among them day after day, was tormented in his righteous soul by the lawless deeds he saw and heard)— {2:9} if this is so, then the Lord knows how to rescue the godly from trials and to hold the unrighteous for punishment on the day of judgment. {2:10} This is especially true of those who follow the corrupt desire of the flesh and despise authority. Bold and arrogant, they are not afraid to heap abuse on celestial beings; {2:11} yet even angels, although they are stronger and more powerful, do not heap abuse on such beings when bringing judgment on them from the Lord. {2:12} These people blaspheme in matters they do not understand. They are like unreasoning animals, creatures of instinct, born only to be caught and destroyed, and like animals they too will perish. {2:13} They will be paid back with harm for the harm they have done. Their idea of pleasure is to carouse in broad daylight; they are blots and blemishes, reveling in their pleasure while they feast with you. {2:14} With eyes full of adultery, they never stop sinning; they seduce the unstable; they are experts in greed—an accursed brood! {2:15} They have left the straight way and wandered off to follow the way of Balaam son of Beor, who loved the wages of wickedness. {2:16} But he was rebuked for his wrongdoing by a donkey—an animal without speech—who spoke with a human voice and restrained the prophet's madness. {2:17} These people are springs without water and mists driven by a storm. Blackest darkness is reserved for them. {2:18} For they mouth empty, boastful words, and by appealing to the lustful desires of the flesh, they entice people who are just escaping from those who live in error. {2:19} They promise them freedom, while they themselves are slaves of depravity—for people are slaves to whatever has mastered them. {2:20} If they have escaped the corruption of the world by knowing our Lord and Savior Jesus Christ and are again entangled in it & are overcome, they are worse off at the end than they were at the beginning. {2:21} It would have been better for them not to have known the way of righteousness than to have known it and then to turn their backs on the sacred command that was passed on to them. {2:22} Of them, proverbs are true: "A dog returns to its vomit," & "A sow that is washed returns to her wallowing in the mud."

{3:1} Dear friends, this is now my second letter to you. I have written both of them as reminders to stimulate you to wholesome thinking. {3:2} I want you to recall the words spoken in the past by the holy prophets and the command given by our Lord and Savior through your apostles. {3:3} Above all, you must understand that in the last days scoffers will come, scoffing and following their own evil desires. {3:4} They will say, "Where is this 'coming' he promised? Ever since our ancestors died, everything goes on as it has since the beginning of creation." {3:5} But they deliberately forget that long ago by God's word the heavens came into being and the earth was formed out of water and by water. {3:6} By these waters also the world of that time was deluged and destroyed. {3:7} By the same word, the present heavens and earth are reserved for fire, being kept for the day of judgment and destruction of the ungodly. {3:8} But do not forget this one thing, dear friends: With the Lord a day is like a thousand years, and a thousand years are like a day. {3:9} The Lord is not slow in keeping his promise, as some understand slowness. Instead, he is patient with you, not wanting anyone to perish, but everyone to come to repentance. {3:10} But the day of the Lord will come like a thief. The heavens will disappear with a roar; the elements will be destroyed by fire, and the earth and everything done in it will be laid bare. {3:11} Since everything will be destroyed in this way, what kind of people ought you to be? You ought to live holy and godly lives {3:12} as you look forward to the day of God and speed its coming. That day will bring about the destruction of the heavens by fire, and the elements will melt in the heat. {3:13} But in keeping with his promise, we are looking forward to a new heaven and a new earth, where righteousness dwells. {3:14} So then, dear friends, since you are looking forward to this, make every effort to be found spotless, blameless, and at peace with him. {3:15} Bear in mind that our Lord's patience means salvation, just as our dear brother Paul also wrote you with the wisdom that God gave him. {3:16} He writes same way in all his letters, speaking in them of these matters. His letters contain some things that are hard to understand, which ignorant and unstable people distort, as they do the other Scriptures, to their own destruction. {3:17} Therefore, dear friends, since you already know this, be on your guard so that you may not be carried away by the error of the lawless and fall from your secure position. {3:18} But grow in the grace & knowledge of our Lord & Savior Jesus Christ. To him be glory both now & forever! Amen.

The First Epistle of John

{1:1} That which was from the beginning, which we have heard, which we have seen with our eyes, which we have looked at, and which our hands have touched, is concerning the Word of life; {1:2} for the life was revealed, and we have seen it and testify to it, and we proclaim to you the eternal life, which was with the Father and was revealed to us. {1:3} We proclaim to you what we have seen and heard, so that you may also have fellowship with us; and truly our fellowship is with the Father and with his Son Jesus Christ. {1:4} We write these things to you so that your joy may be complete. {1:5} This is the message we have heard from him and declare to you: God is light; in him, there is no darkness at all. {1:6} If we claim to have fellowship with him yet walk in darkness, we lie and do not live out the truth. {1:7} But if we walk in the light, as he is in the light, we have fellowship with one another, and the blood of Jesus Christ, his Son, cleanses us from all sin. {1:8} If we say we have no sin, we deceive ourselves, and the truth is not in us. {1:9} If we confess our sins, he is faithful and just to forgive us our sins and to cleanse us from all unrighteousness. {1:10} If we say we have not sinned, we make him out to be a liar, and his word is not in us.

{2:1} My dear children, I write this to you so that you will not sin. But if anyone does sin, we have an advocate with the Father—Jesus Christ, the Righteous One. {2:2} He is the atoning sacrifice for our sins, and not only for ours but also for the sins of the whole world. {2:3} We know that we have come to know him if we keep his commands. {2:4} Whoever says, "I know him," but does not do what he commands is a liar; the truth is not in that person. {2:5} But if anyone obeys his word, love for God is truly made complete in them. This is how we know we are in him: {2:6} whoever claims to live in him must live as Jesus did. {2:7} Dear friends, I am not writing you a new command but an old one, which you have had since the beginning. This old command is the message you have heard. {2:8} Yet I am writing you a new command; its truth is seen in him and in you, because the darkness is passing and the true light is already shining. {2:9} Anyone who claims to be in the light but hates a brother or sister is still in the darkness. {2:10} Anyone who loves their brother and sister lives in the light, and there is nothing in them to make them stumble. {2:11} But anyone who hates a brother or sister is in the darkness and walks around in the darkness; they do not know where they are going because the darkness has blinded them. {2:12} I am writing to you, dear children, because your sins have been forgiven on account of his name. {2:13} I am writing to you, fathers, because you know him who is from the beginning. I write to you, young people, because you have overcome the evil one. I write to you, dear children, because you know the Father. {2:14} I have written to you, fathers, because you know him who is from the beginning. I have written to you, young people, because you are strong, and the word of God lives in you, and you have overcome the evil one. {2:15} Do not love the world or anything in the world. If anyone loves the world, love for the Father is not in them. {2:16} For everything in the world—the lust of the flesh, the lust of the eyes, and the pride of life—comes not from the Father but from the world. {2:17} The world and its desires pass away, but whoever does the will of God lives forever. {2:18} Dear children, this is the last hour; and as you have heard that the antichrist (someone who opposes Christ) is coming, even now many antichrists have come. This is how we know it is the last hour. {2:19} They went out from us, but they did not really belong to us; for if they had belonged to us, they would have remained with us; but their going showed that none of them belonged to us. {2:20} But you have an anointing from the Holy One, and all of you know the truth. {2:21} I do not write to you because you do not know the truth, but because you do know it and because no lie comes from the truth. {2:22} Who is the liar? It is whoever denies that Jesus is the Christ. Such a person is the antichrist—denying the Father and the Son. {2:23} No one who denies the Son has the Father; whoever acknowledges the Son has the Father also. {2:24} As for you, see that what you have heard from the beginning remains in you. If it does, you will also remain in the Son and in the Father. {2:25} And this is what he promised us—eternal life. {2:26} I am writing these things to you about those who are trying to lead you astray. {2:27} As for you, the anointing you received from him remains in you, and you do not need anyone to teach you. But as his anointing teaches you about all things and as that anointing is real, not counterfeit—just as it has taught you, remain in him. {2:28} And now, dear children, continue in him, so that when he appears we may be confident and unashamed before him at his coming. {2:29} If you know that he is righteous, you know that everyone who does what is right has been born of him.

{3:1} See what great love the Father has lavished on us, that we should be called children of God! And that is what we are! The reason the world does not know us is that it did not know him. {3:2} Dear friends, now we are children of God, and what we will be has not yet been made known. But we know that when Christ appears, we shall be like him, for we shall see him as he is. {3:3} All who have this hope in him purify themselves, just as he is pure. {3:4} Everyone who sins breaks the law; in fact, sin is lawlessness. {3:5} But you know that he appeared so that he might take away our sins, and in him is no sin. {3:6} No one who lives in him keeps on sinning. No one who continues to sin has either seen him or known him. {3:7} Dear children, do not let anyone lead you astray. The one who does what is right is righteous, just as he is righteous. {3:8} The one who does what is sinful is of the devil, because the devil has been sinning from the beginning. The reason the Son of God appeared was to destroy the devil's work. {3:9} No one who is born of God will continue to sin, because God's seed remains in them; they cannot go on sinning because they have been born of God. {3:10} This is how we know who the children of God are and who the children of the devil are: Anyone who does not do what is right is not God's child, nor is anyone who does not love their brother and sister. {3:11} For this is the message you heard from the beginning: We should love one another. {3:12} Do not be like Cain, who belonged to the evil one and murdered his brother. And why did he murder him? Because his own actions were evil and his brother's were righteous. {3:13} Do not be surprised, my brothers and sisters, if the world hates you. {3:14} We know that we have passed from death to life because we love each other. Anyone who does not love remains in death. {3:15} Anyone who hates a brother or sister is a murderer, and you know that no murderer has eternal life residing in them. {3:16} This is how we know what love is: Jesus Christ laid down his life for us, and we ought to lay down our lives for our brothers and sisters. {3:17} If anyone has material possessions and sees a brother or sister in need but has no pity on them, how can the love of God be in that person? {3:18} Dear children, let us not love with words or speech but with actions and in truth. {3:19} This is how we know that we belong to the truth and how we set our hearts at rest in his presence: {3:20} if our hearts condemn us, we know that God is greater than our hearts, and he knows everything. {3:21} Dear friends, if our hearts do not condemn us, we have confidence before God {3:22} and receive from him anything we ask, because we keep his commands and do what pleases him. {3:23} And this is his command: to believe in the name of his Son, Jesus Christ, and to love one another as he commanded us. {3:24} The one who keeps God's commands lives in him, and he in them. And this is how we know that he lives in us: We know it by the Spirit he gave us.

{4:1} Dear friends, do not believe every spirit, but test the spirits to see whether they are from God, because many false prophets have gone out into the world. {4:2} This is how you can recognize the Spirit of God: Every spirit that acknowledges that Jesus Christ has come in the flesh is from God; {4:3} but every spirit that does not acknowledge Jesus is not from God. This is the spirit of the antichrist, which you have heard is coming and is already in the world. {4:4} You, dear children, are from God and have overcome them, because the one who is in you is greater than the one who is in the world. {4:5} They are from the world and therefore speak from the viewpoint of the world, and the world listens to them. {4:6} We are from God, and whoever knows God listens to us; but whoever is not from God does not listen to us. This is how we recognize the spirit of truth and the spirit of falsehood. {4:7} Dear friends, let us love one another, for love comes from God. Everyone who loves has been born of God and knows God. {4:8} Whoever does not love does not know God, because God is love. {4:9} This is how God showed his love among us: He sent his one and only Son into the world that we might live through him. {4:10} This is love: not that we loved God, but that he loved us and sent his Son as an atoning sacrifice for our sins. {4:11} Dear friends, since God so loved us, we also ought to love one another. {4:12} No one has ever seen God; but if we love one another, God lives in us and his love is made complete in us. {4:13} This is how we know that we live in him and he in us: He has given us of his Spirit. {4:14} And we have seen and testify that the Father has sent his Son to be the Savior of the world. {4:15} If anyone acknowledges that Jesus is the Son of God, God lives in them and they in God. {4:16} So we have come to know and to believe the love that God has for us. God is love. Whoever lives in love lives in God, and God in them. {4:17} This is how love is made complete among us so that we will have confidence on the day of judgment: In this world, we are like Jesus. {4:18} There is no fear in love. Perfect love drives out fear, because fear has to do with punishment. The one who fears is not made perfect in love. {4:19} We love because he first loved us. {4:20} Whoever claims to love God yet hates a brother or sister is a liar. For whoever does not love their brother and sister, whom they have seen, cannot love God, whom they have not seen. {4:21} And he has given us this command: Anyone who loves God must also love their brother and sister.

{5:1} Everyone who believes that Jesus is the Christ is born of God, and everyone who loves the father loves his child as well. {5:2} This is how we know that we love the children of God: by loving God and carrying out his commands. {5:3} In fact, this is love for God: to keep his commands. And his commands are not burdensome. {5:4} For everyone born of God overcomes the world. This is the victory that has overcome the world, even our faith. {5:5} Who is it that overcomes the world? Only the one who believes that Jesus is the Son of God. {5:6} This is the one who came by water and blood—Jesus Christ. He did not come by water only, but by water and blood. And it is the Spirit who testifies, because the Spirit is the truth. {5:7} For there are three that testify in heaven: the Father, the Word, and the Holy Spirit, and these three are one. {5:8} And there are three that testify on earth: the Spirit, the water, and the blood; and these three are in agreement. {5:9} We accept human testimony, but God's testimony is greater because it is the testimony of God, which he has given about his Son. {5:10} Whoever believes in the Son of God accepts this testimony. Whoever does not believe God has made him out to be a liar, because they have not believed the testimony God has given about his Son. {5:11} And this is the testimony: God has given us eternal life, and this life is in his Son. {5:12} Whoever has the Son has life; whoever does not have the Son of God does not have life. {5:13} I write these things to you who believe in the name of the Son of God so that you may know that you have eternal life. {5:14} This is the confidence we have in approaching God: that if we ask anything according to his will, he hears us. {5:15} And if we know that he hears us—whatever we ask—we know that we have what we asked of him. {5:16} If you see any brother or sister commit a sin that does not lead to death, you should pray and God will give them life. I refer to those whose sin does not lead to death. There is a sin that leads to death; I am not saying that you should pray about that. {5:17} All wrongdoing is sin, and there is sin that does not lead to death. {5:18} We know that anyone born of God does not continue to sin; the one who was born of God keeps them safe, and the evil one cannot harm them. {5:19} We know that we are children of God, and that the whole world is under the control of the evil one. {5:20} We also know that the Son of God has come and has given us understanding, so that we may know him who is true, and we are in him who is true, even in his Son Jesus Christ. He is the true God and eternal life. {5:21} Dear children, keep yourselves from idols. Amen.

The Second Epistle of John

{1:1} The elder to the chosen lady and her children, whom I love in the truth; and not only I, but also everyone who knows the truth, {1:2} because of the truth that lives in us and will be with us forever. {1:3} Grace, mercy, and peace be with you from God the Father and from the Lord Jesus Christ, the Son of the Father, in truth and love. {1:4} I was very happy to find some of your children walking in the truth, just as we received a command from the Father. {1:5} And now I ask you, lady, not as if I were writing you a new command, but the one we had from the beginning: that we love one another. {1:6} And this is love: that we walk according to his commands. This is the command you have heard from the beginning: that you should walk in it. {1:7} Many deceivers have gone out into the world who do not acknowledge that Jesus Christ came in the flesh. Such a person is a deceiver and an antichrist. {1:8} Watch yourselves so that you do not lose what we have worked for, but that you receive a full reward. {1:9} Anyone who runs ahead and does not continue in the teaching of Christ does not have God; whoever continues in the teaching has both the Father and the Son. {1:10} If anyone comes to you and does not bring this teaching, do not take them into your home or welcome them; {1:11} anyone who welcomes them shares in their wicked work. {1:12} Although I have much to write to you, I would rather not use paper and ink. Instead, I hope to visit you and talk with you face to face so that our joy may be complete. {1:13} The children of your chosen sister send their greetings. Amen.

The Third Epistle of John

{1:1} The elder to the beloved Gaius, whom I love in the truth. {1:2} Dear friend, I hope all is well with you and that you are in good health, just as your soul is doing well. {1:3} I was very happy when some of the brothers came and testified to the truth that is in you, just as you walk in the truth. {1:4} I have no greater joy than to hear that my children are walking in the truth. {1:5} Dear friend, you are doing a faithful job in everything you do for the brothers and for strangers. {1:6} They have testified about your love in front of the church. If you send them on their way in a manner worthy of God, you will do well, {1:7} because they went out for the sake of His name, taking nothing from the Gentiles. {1:8} Therefore, we ought to welcome such people so that we may be co-workers in the truth. {1:9} I wrote to the church, but Diotrephes, who loves to be the top dog among them, does not welcome us. {1:10} So if I come, I will remind him of his actions, spreading malicious nonsense about us; and not content with that, he refuses to welcome the brothers and stops those who want to do so, casting them out of the church. {1:11} Dear friend, do not imitate what is evil but what is good. Anyone who does good is from God; anyone who does evil has not seen God. {1:12} Demetrius has a good reputation with everyone, and even with the truth itself; we also speak well of him, and you know that our testimony is true. {1:13} I have many things to write, but I do not want to write them with ink and pen. {1:14} I hope to see you soon and talk face to face. Peace be with you. Our friends send their greetings. Greet the friends there by name.

The Epistle of Jude

{1:1} Jude, a servant of Jesus Christ and brother of James, to those who are sanctified by God the Father, preserved in Jesus Christ, and called: {1:2} Mercy, peace, and love be multiplied to you. {1:3} Dear friends, while I was eager to write to you about our common salvation, I found it necessary to urge you to contend earnestly for the faith that was once for all entrusted to the saints. {1:4} For certain individuals have secretly slipped in among you, who were long ago marked out for condemnation—ungodly people who pervert the grace of our God into a license for immorality and deny our only Master and Lord, Jesus Christ. {1:5} I want to remind you, though you already know this, that the Lord saved the people out of Egypt, but later destroyed those who did not believe. {1:6} And the angels who did not keep their proper positions but abandoned their own home, he has kept in darkness, bound with everlasting chains for judgment on the great Day. {1:7} In a similar way, Sodom and Gomorrah and the surrounding towns gave themselves up to sexual immorality and perversion; they serve as an example of those who suffer the punishment of eternal fire. {1:8} In the same way, these dreamers pollute their own bodies, reject authority, and slander celestial beings. {1:9} But the archangel Michael, when he disputed with the devil about the body of Moses, did not dare to bring a slanderous accusation against him but said, "The Lord rebuke you!" {1:10} Yet these people slander what they do not understand; they are like unreasoning animals, creatures of instinct, born only to be caught and destroyed, and like animals they too will perish. {1:11} Woe to them! They have taken the way of Cain; they have rushed for profit into Balaam's error; they have been destroyed in Korah's rebellion. {1:12} These people are blemishes at your love feasts, eating with you without the slightest qualm—shepherds who feed only themselves. They are clouds without rain, blown along by the wind; autumn trees, without fruit and uprooted—twice dead. {1:13} They are wild waves of the sea, foaming up their shame; wandering stars, for whom blackest darkness has been reserved forever. {1:14} Enoch, the seventh from Adam, prophesied about them: "See, the Lord is coming with thousands upon thousands of his holy ones {1:15} to judge everyone and to convict all of them of all the ungodly acts they have committed in their ungodliness, and of all the defiant words ungodly sinners have spoken against him." {1:16} These people are grumblers and faultfinders; they follow their own evil desires; they boast about themselves and flatter others for their own advantage. {1:17} But, dear friends, remember what the apostles of our Lord Jesus Christ foretold. {1:18} They said to you, "In the last times there will be scoffers who will follow their own ungodly desires." {1:19} These are the people who divide you, who follow mere natural instincts and do not have the Spirit. {1:20} But you, dear friends, by building yourselves up in your most holy faith and praying in the Holy Spirit, {1:21} keep yourselves in God's love as you wait for the mercy of our Lord Jesus Christ to bring you to eternal life. {1:22} Be merciful to those who doubt; {1:23} save others by snatching them from the fire and to others show mercy, mixed with fear—hating even the clothing stained by corrupted flesh. {1:24} To him who is able to keep you from stumbling and to present you before his glorious presence without fault and with great joy, {1:25} to the only God our Savior be glory, majesty, power, and authority, through Jesus Christ our Lord, before all ages, now and forevermore! Amen.

The Book of Revelation

{1:1} This is the Revelation of Jesus Christ, which God gave to him to show his servants what must soon take place. He sent it by his angel to his servant John, {1:2} who testified to everything he saw—that is, the word of God and the testimony of Jesus Christ. {1:3} Blessed is the one who reads aloud the words of this prophecy, and blessed are those who hear and take to heart what is written in it, because the time is near. {1:4} John to the seven churches in Asia: Grace and peace to you from him who is, who was, and who is to come, and from the seven spirits before his throne, {1:5} and from Jesus Christ, who is the faithful witness, the firstborn from the dead, and the ruler of the kings of the earth. To him who loves us and has freed us from our sins by his blood, {1:6} and has made us a kingdom and priests to serve his God and Father—to him be glory and power forever and ever! Amen. {1:7} Look, he is coming with the clouds, and every eye will see him, even those who pierced him; and all peoples on earth will mourn because of him. So shall it be! Amen. {1:8} I am the Alpha and the Omega, says the Lord God, who is, who was, and who is to come, the Almighty. {1:9} I, John, your brother and companion in the suffering and kingdom and patient endurance that are ours in Jesus, was on the island of Patmos because of the word of God and the testimony of Jesus. {1:10} On the Lord's Day, I was in the Spirit, and I heard behind me a loud voice like a trumpet, {1:11} which said: "Write on a scroll what you see and send it to the seven churches: to Ephesus, Smyrna, Pergamum, Thyatira, Sardis, Philadelphia, and Laodicea." {1:12} I turned around to see the voice that was speaking to me. And when I turned, I saw seven golden lampstands, {1:13} and among the lampstands was someone like a son of man, dressed in a robe reaching down to his feet and with a golden sash around his chest. {1:14} The hair on his head was white like wool, as white as snow, and his eyes were like blazing fire. {1:15} His feet were like bronze glowing in a furnace, and his voice was like the sound of rushing waters. {1:16} In his right hand, he held seven stars, and coming out of his mouth was a sharp double-edged sword. His face was like the sun shining in all its brilliance. {1:17} When I saw him, I fell at his feet as though dead. Then he placed his right hand on me and said: "Do not be afraid. I am the First and the Last. {1:18} I am the Living One; I was dead, and now look, I am alive forever and ever! And I hold the keys of death and Hades. {1:19} Write, therefore, what you have seen, what is now and what will take place later. {1:20} The mystery of the seven stars that you saw in my right hand and of the seven golden lampstands is this: The seven stars are the angels of the seven churches, and the seven lampstands are the seven churches.

{2:1} To the angel of the church in Ephesus write: These are the words of him who holds the seven stars in his right hand and walks among the seven golden lampstands: {2:2} I know your deeds, your hard work, and your perseverance. I know that you cannot tolerate wicked people, that you have tested those who claim to be apostles but are not, and have found them false. {2:3} You have persevered and have endured hardships for my name, and have not grown weary. {2:4} Yet I hold this against you: You have forsaken the love you had at first. {2:5} Consider how far you have fallen! Repent and do the things you did at first. If you do not repent, I will come to you and remove your lampstand from its place. {2:6} But you have this in your favor: You hate the practices of the Nicolaitans, which I also hate. {2:7} Whoever has ears, let them hear what the Spirit says to the churches. To the one who is victorious, I will give the right to eat from the tree of life, which is in the paradise of God. {2:8} To the angel of the church in Smyrna write: These are the words of him who is the First and the Last, who died and came to life again. {2:9} I know your afflictions and your poverty—yet you are rich! I know the slander of those who say they are Jews and are not, but are a synagogue of Satan. {2:10} Do not be afraid of what you are about to suffer. I tell you, the devil will put some of you in prison to test you, and you will suffer persecution for ten days. Be faithful, even to the point of death, and I will give you life as your victor's crown. {2:11} Whoever has ears, let them hear what the Spirit says to the churches. The one who is victorious will not be hurt at all by the second death. {2:12} To the angel of the church in Pergamum write: These are the words of him who has the sharp, double-edged sword. {2:13} I know where you live—where Satan has his throne. Yet you remain true to my name. You did not renounce your faith in me, not even in the days of Antipas, my faithful witness, who was put to death in your city—where Satan lives. {2:14} Nevertheless, I have a few things against you: There are some among you who hold to the teaching of Balaam, who taught Balak to entice the Israelites to sin by eating food sacrificed to idols and committing sexual immorality. {2:15} Likewise, you also have those who hold to the teaching of the Nicolaitans. {2:16} Repent therefore! Otherwise, I will soon come to you and will fight against them with the sword of my mouth. {2:17} Whoever has ears, let them hear what the Spirit says to the churches. To the one who is victorious, I will give some of the hidden manna. I will also give that person a white stone with a new name written on it, known only to the one who receives it. {2:18} To the angel of the church in Thyatira write: These are the words of the Son of God, whose eyes are like blazing fire and whose feet are like burnished bronze. {2:19} I know your deeds, your love and faith, your service and perseverance, and that you are now doing more than you did at first. {2:20} Nevertheless, I have this against you: You tolerate that woman Jezebel, who claims to be a prophet. By her teaching, she misleads my servants into sexual immorality and the eating of food sacrificed to idols. {2:21} I have given her time to repent of her immorality, but she is unwilling. {2:22} So I will cast her on a bed of suffering, and I will make those who commit adultery with her suffer intensely, unless they repent of her ways. {2:23} I will strike her children dead. Then all the churches will know that I am he who searches hearts and minds, and I will repay each of you according to your deeds. {2:24} Now I say to the rest of you in Thyatira, to you who do not hold to her teaching and have not learned Satan's so-called deep secrets: I will not impose any other burden on you, {2:25} except to hold on to what you have until I come. {2:26} To the one who is victorious and does my will to the end, I will give authority over the nations— {2:27} that one "will rule them with an iron scepter and will dash them to pieces like pottery," just as I have received authority from my Father. {2:28} I will also give that one the morning star. {2:29} Whoever has ears, let them hear what the Spirit says to the churches.

{3:1} To the angel of the church in Sardis write: These are the words of him who has the seven spirits of God and the seven stars. I know your deeds; you have a reputation of being alive, but you are dead. {3:2} Wake up! Strengthen what remains and is about to die, for I have found your deeds unfinished in the sight of my God. {3:3} Remember, therefore, what you have received and heard; hold it fast, and repent. If you do not wake up, I will come like a thief, and you will not know at what time I will come to you. {3:4} Yet you have a few people in Sardis who have not soiled their clothes. They will walk with me, dressed in white, for they are worthy. {3:5} The one who is victorious will, like them, be dressed in white. I will never blot out the name of that person from the book of life, but will acknowledge that name before my Father and his angels. {3:6} Whoever has ears, let them hear what the Spirit says to the churches. {3:7} To the angel of the church in Philadelphia write: These are the words of him who is holy and true, who holds the key of David. What he opens no one can shut, and what he shuts no one can open. {3:8} I know your deeds. See, I have placed before you an open door that no one can shut. I know that you have little strength, yet you have kept my word and have not denied my name. {3:9} I will make those who are of the synagogue of Satan, who claim to be Jews though they are not, but are liars, I will make them come and fall down at your feet and acknowledge that I have loved you. {3:10} Since you have kept my command to endure patiently, I will also keep you from the hour of trial that is going to come on the whole world to test the inhabitants of the earth. {3:11} I am coming soon. Hold on to what you have so that no one will take your crown. {3:12} The one who is victorious, I will make a pillar in the temple of my God. Never again will they leave it. I will write on them the name of my God and the name of the city of my God, the new Jerusalem, which is coming down out of heaven from my God; and I will also write on them my new name. {3:13} Whoever has ears, let them hear what the Spirit says to the churches. {3:14} To the angel of the church in Laodicea write: These are the words of the Amen, the faithful and true witness, the ruler of God's creation. {3:15} I know your deeds, that you are neither cold nor hot. I wish you were either one or the other! {3:16} So, because you are lukewarm—neither hot nor cold—I am about to spit you out of my mouth. {3:17} You say, 'I am rich; I have acquired wealth and do not need a thing.' But you do not realize that you are wretched, pitiful, poor, blind, and naked. {3:18} I counsel you to buy from me gold refined in the fire, so you can become rich; and white clothes to wear, so you can cover your shameful nakedness; and salve to put on your eyes, so you can see. {3:19} Those whom I love I rebuke and discipline. So be earnest and repent. {3:20} Here I am! I stand at the door and knock. If anyone hears my voice and opens the door, I will come in and eat with that person, and they with me. {3:21} To the one who is victorious, I will give the right to sit with me on my throne, just as I was victorious and sat down with my Father on his throne. {3:22} Whoever has ears, let them hear what the Spirit says to the churches.

{4:1} After this, I looked, and there before me was a door standing open in heaven. And the voice I had first heard speaking to me like a trumpet said, "Come up here, and I will show you what must take place after this." {4:2} At once I was in the Spirit, and there before me was a throne in heaven with someone sitting on it. {4:3} And the one who sat there had the appearance of jasper and ruby. A rainbow that shone like an emerald encircled the throne. {4:4} Surrounding the throne were twenty-four other thrones, and seated on them were twenty-four elders. They were dressed in white and had crowns of gold on their heads. {4:5} From the throne came flashes of lightning, rumblings, and peals of thunder. In front of the throne, seven lamps were blazing. These are the seven spirits of God. {4:6} Also in front of the throne there was what looked like a sea of glass, clear as crystal. In the center, around the throne, were four living creatures, and they were covered with eyes, in front and in back. {4:7} The first living creature was like a lion, the second was like an ox, the third had a face like a man, and the fourth was like a flying eagle. {4:8} Each of the four living creatures had six wings and was covered with eyes all around, even under its wings. Day and night they never stop saying: "Holy, holy, holy is the Lord God Almighty, who was, and is, and is to come." {4:9} Whenever the living creatures give glory, honor, and thanks to him who sits on the throne and who lives for ever and ever, {4:10} the twenty-four elders fall down before him who sits on the throne and worship him who lives for ever and ever. They lay their crowns before the throne and say: {4:11} "You are worthy, our Lord and God, to receive glory and honor and power, for you created all things, and by your will they were created and have their being."

{5:1} I saw in the right hand of him who sat on the throne a scroll written on both sides and sealed with seven seals. {5:2} I saw a mighty angel proclaiming in a loud voice, "Who is worthy to open the scroll and break its seals?" {5:3} But no one in heaven or on earth or under the earth could open the scroll or even look inside it. {5:4} I wept and wept because no one was found who was worthy to open the scroll or look inside. {5:5} Then one of the elders said to me, "Do not weep! See, the Lion of the tribe of Judah, the Root of David, has triumphed. He is able to open the scroll and its seven seals." {5:6} Then I saw a Lamb, looking as if it had been slain, standing at the center of the throne, encircled by the four living creatures and the elders. The Lamb had seven horns and seven eyes, which are the seven spirits of God sent out into all the earth. {5:7} He came and took the scroll from the right hand of him who sat on the throne. {5:8} And when he had taken it, the four living creatures and the twenty-four elders fell down before the Lamb. Each one had a harp and they were holding golden bowls full of incense, which are the prayers of God's people. {5:9} And they sang a new song, saying: "You are worthy to take the scroll and to open its seals because you were slain, and with your blood you purchased for God persons from every tribe and language and people and nation. {5:10} You have made them to be a kingdom and priests to serve our God, and they will reign on the earth." {5:11} Then I looked and heard the voice of many angels, numbering thousands upon thousands, and ten thousand times ten thousand. They encircled the throne and the living creatures and the elders. {5:12} In a loud voice they were saying: "Worthy is the Lamb who was slain, to receive power and wealth and wisdom and strength and honor and glory and praise!" {5:13} Then I heard every creature in heaven and on earth and under the earth and on the sea, and all that is in them, saying: "To him who sits on the throne and to the Lamb be praise and honor and glory and power, for ever and ever!" {5:14} The four living creatures said, "Amen," and the elders fell down and worshiped.

{6:1} I watched as the Lamb opened the first of the seven seals. Then I heard one of the four living creatures say in a voice like thunder, "Come!" {6:2} I looked, and there before me was a white horse! Its rider held a bow, and he was given a crown, and he rode out as a conqueror bent on conquest. {6:3} When the Lamb opened the second seal, I heard the second living creature say, "Come!" {6:4} Then another horse came out, a fiery red one. Its rider was given power to take peace from the earth and to make people kill each other. To him was given a large sword. {6:5} When the Lamb opened the third seal, I heard the third living creature say, "Come!" I looked, and there before me was a black horse! Its rider was holding a pair of scales in his hand. {6:6} Then I heard what sounded like a voice among the four living creatures, saying, "Two pounds of wheat for a day's wages, and six pounds of barley for a day's wages, and do not damage the oil and the wine!" {6:7} When the Lamb opened the fourth seal, I heard the voice of the fourth living creature say, "Come!" {6:8} I looked, and there before me was a pale horse! Its rider was named Death, and Hades was following close behind him. They were given power over a fourth of the earth to kill by sword, famine, and plague, and by the wild beasts of the earth. {6:9} When he opened the fifth seal, I saw under the altar the souls of those who had been slain because of the word of God and the testimony they had maintained. {6:10} They called out in a loud voice, "How long, Sovereign Lord, holy and true, until you judge the inhabitants of the earth and avenge our blood?" {6:11} Then each of them was given a white robe, and they were told to wait a little longer until the full number of their fellow servants, their brothers and sisters, were killed just as they had been. {6:12} I watched as he opened the sixth seal. There was a great earthquake. The sun turned black like sackcloth made of goat hair, the whole moon turned blood red, {6:13} and the stars in the sky fell to earth, as figs drop from a fig tree when shaken by a strong wind. {6:14} The heavens receded like a scroll being rolled up, and every mountain and island was removed from its place. {6:15} Then the kings of the earth, the princes, the generals, the rich, the mighty, and everyone else, both slave and free, hid in caves and among the rocks of the mountains. {6:16} They called to the mountains and the rocks, "Fall on us and hide us from the face of him who sits on the throne and from the wrath of the Lamb! {6:17} For the great day of their wrath has come, and who can withstand it?"

{7:1} After this, I saw four angels standing at the four corners of the earth, holding back the four winds so that no wind would blow on the earth, the sea, or any tree. {7:2} I saw another angel coming up from the east, holding the seal of the living God. He called out in a loud voice to the four angels who had been given power to harm the earth and the sea, {7:3} saying, "Do not harm the earth, the sea, or the trees until we have sealed the servants of our God on their foreheads." {7:4} I heard the number of those who were sealed: 144,000 from all the tribes of Israel. {7:5} From the tribe of Judah, 12,000 were sealed; from the tribe of Reuben, 12,000; from the tribe of Gad, 12,000. {7:6} From the tribe of Asher, 12,000; from the tribe of Naphtali, 12,000; from the tribe of Manasseh, 12,000. {7:7} From the tribe of Simeon, 12,000; from the tribe of Levi, 12,000; from the tribe of Issachar, 12,000. {7:8} From the tribe of Zebulun, 12,000; from the tribe of Joseph, 12,000; from the tribe of Benjamin, 12,000. {7:9} After this, I looked, and there was a great multitude that no one could count, from every nation, tribe, people, and language, standing before the throne and the Lamb, wearing white robes and holding palm branches in their hands. {7:10} They cried out in a loud voice, "Salvation belongs to our God, who sits on the throne, and to the Lamb!" {7:11} All the angels were standing around the throne, the elders, and the four living creatures. They fell on their faces before the throne and worshiped God, {7:12} saying, "Amen! Praise and glory and wisdom and thanks and honor and power and strength be to our God for ever and ever. Amen!" {7:13} One of the elders asked me, "These in white robes—who are they, and where did they come from?" {7:14} I answered, "Sir, you know." And he said, "These are they who have come out of the great tribulation; they have washed their robes and made them white in the blood of the Lamb. {7:15} Therefore, they are before the throne of God and serve him day and night in his temple; and he who sits on the throne will shelter them with his presence. {7:16} Never again will they hunger; never again will they thirst. The sun will not beat down on them, nor any scorching heat. {7:17} For the Lamb at the center of the throne will be their shepherd; he will lead them to springs of living water, and God will wipe away every tear from their eyes."

{8:1} When he opened the seventh seal, there was silence in heaven for about half an hour. {8:2} And I saw the seven angels who stand before God, and they were given seven trumpets. {8:3} Another angel came and stood at the altar with a golden censer, and he was given much incense to offer, along with the prayers of all God's people, on the golden altar in front of the throne. {8:4} The smoke of the incense, together with the prayers of God's people, went up before God from the angel's hand. {8:5} Then the angel took the censer, filled it with fire from the altar, and hurled it on the earth; and there came peals of thunder, rumblings, flashes of lightning, and an earthquake. {8:6} Then the seven angels who had the seven trumpets prepared to sound them. {8:7} The first angel sounded his trumpet, and there came hail and fire mixed with blood, and it was hurled down on the earth. A third of the earth was burned up, a third of the trees were burned up, and all the green grass was burned up. {8:8} The second angel sounded his trumpet, and something like a great mountain, burning with fire, was thrown into the sea. A third of the sea turned to blood, {8:9} a third of the living creatures in the sea died, and a third of the ships were destroyed. {8:10} The third angel sounded his trumpet, and a great star, blazing like a torch, fell from the sky on a third of the rivers and on the springs of water. {8:11} The name of the star is Wormwood (a plant known for its bitterness); a third of the waters turned bitter, and many people died from the waters that had become bitter. {8:12} The fourth angel sounded his trumpet, and a third of the sun was struck, a third of the moon, and a third of the stars, so that a third of them turned dark. A third of the day was without light, and also a third of the night. {8:13} As I watched, I heard an eagle flying in midair call out in a loud voice, "Woe! Woe! Woe to the inhabitants of the earth because of the trumpet blasts about to be sounded by the other three angels!"

{9:1} The fifth angel sounded his trumpet, and I saw a star that had fallen from heaven to the earth. The star was given the key to the abyss (bottomless pit). {9:2} He opened the abyss, and smoke rose from it like the smoke of a huge furnace, darkening the sun and the air. {9:3} Out of the smoke came locusts that went to the earth, and they were given power like the scorpions of the earth. {9:4} They were commanded not to harm the grass of the earth, any green plant, or any tree, but only those people who did not have the seal of God on their foreheads. {9:5} They were allowed to torment them for five months, but not to kill them. Their torment was like the sting of a scorpion when it strikes a person. {9:6} During those days, people will seek death but will not find it; they will long to die, but death will elude them. {9:7} The locusts looked like horses prepared for battle; they wore something like crowns of gold on their heads, and their faces resembled human faces. {9:8} Their hair was like women's hair, and their teeth were like lions' teeth. {9:9} They wore breastplates that looked like iron, and the sound of their wings was like the roar of many horses and chariots rushing into battle. {9:10} They had tails like scorpions with stingers in them, and they were given the power to torment people for five months. {9:11} They had a king over them, the angel of the abyss, whose name in Hebrew is Abaddon, and in Greek, it is Apollyon. {9:12} One woe is past; behold, two more woes are coming. {9:13} The sixth angel sounded his trumpet, and I heard a voice from the four horns of the golden altar before God, {9:14} telling the sixth angel who had the trumpet, "Release the four angels who are bound at the great river Euphrates." {9:15} The four angels were released, who had been prepared for that hour, day, month, and year, to kill a third of mankind. {9:16} The number of the mounted troops was two hundred million; I heard their number. {9:17} In my vision, I saw the horses and those who rode them. They wore breastplates that were fiery red, dark blue, and yellow, and the heads of the horses looked like the heads of lions. Fire, smoke, and sulfur (brimstone) came out of their mouths. {9:18} By these three plagues, a third of mankind was killed—by the fire, smoke, and sulfur that came out of their mouths. {9:19} Their power is in their mouths and in their tails, for their tails are like snakes with heads, and they use them to harm people. {9:20} The rest of mankind who were not killed by these plagues still did not repent of the works of their hands; they did not stop worshiping demons and idols of gold, silver, bronze, stone, and wood—idols that cannot see, hear, or walk. {9:21} Nor did they repent of their murders, their sorceries (magic), their sexual immorality, or their thefts.

{10:1} I saw another mighty angel coming down from heaven, wrapped in a cloud. A rainbow was on his head, his face was like the sun, and his feet were like fiery pillars. {10:2} He held a little open book in his hand, and he placed his right foot on the sea and his left foot on the land. {10:3} He cried out with a loud voice like a lion's roar, and when he cried out, seven thunders spoke their voices. {10:4} When the seven thunders spoke, I was about to write, but I heard a voice from heaven saying, "Seal up what the seven thunders said, and do not write it down." {10:5} The angel I saw standing on the sea and on the land raised his right hand to heaven {10:6} and swore by him who lives forever and ever, who created heaven, earth, and sea, and all that is in them, that there would be no more delay. {10:7} But in the days when the seventh angel is about to sound his trumpet, the mystery of God will be accomplished, just as he announced to his servants the prophets. {10:8} Then the voice I had heard from heaven spoke to me again, saying, "Go, take the little book that is open in the hand of the angel standing on the sea and the land." {10:9} So I went to the angel and asked him to give me the little book. He said to me, "Take it and eat it; it will turn your stomach sour, but in your mouth, it will be as sweet as honey." {10:10} I took the little book from the angel's hand and ate it. It was sweet in my mouth, but when I had eaten it, my stomach turned sour. {10:11} The angel said to me, "You must prophesy again about many peoples, nations, languages, and kings."

{11:1} I was given a measuring rod like a staff, and the angel stood saying, "Get up and measure the temple of God, the altar, and those who worship there." {11:2} But do not measure the outer court of the temple; leave that out, for it has been given to the Gentiles, and they will trample the holy city for forty-two months. {11:3} I will give power to my two witnesses, and they will prophesy for one thousand two hundred sixty days, dressed in sackcloth. {11:4} These are the two olive trees and the two lampstands that stand before the Lord of the earth. {11:5} If anyone tries to harm them, fire will come out of their mouths and consume their enemies; if anyone tries to harm them, they must be killed in this way. {11:6} They have the power to shut up the sky so that it does not rain during the days of their prophecy; they also have the power to turn waters into blood and to strike the earth with all kinds of plagues as often as they wish. {11:7} When they finish their testimony, the beast that comes up from the abyss will make war against them, conquer them, and kill them. {11:8} Their dead bodies will lie in the street of the great city, which is symbolically called Sodom and Egypt, where also their Lord was crucified. {11:9} People from various nations, tribes, languages, and cultures will look at their dead bodies for three and a half days and will not allow them to be buried. {11:10} Those who live on the earth will rejoice over them, celebrate, and send gifts to each other because these two prophets had tormented those who lived on the earth. {11:11} But after three and a half days, the breath of life from God entered them, and they stood on their feet, and great fear fell on those who saw them. {11:12} They heard a loud voice from heaven saying, "Come up here." And they ascended to heaven in a cloud, while their enemies looked on. {11:13} At that hour, there was a great earthquake, and a tenth of the city fell; seven thousand people were killed in the earthquake, and the rest were terrified and gave glory to the God of heaven. {11:14} The second woe has passed; look, the third woe is coming quickly. {11:15} The seventh angel sounded his trumpet, and loud voices in heaven said, "The kingdoms of this world have become the kingdoms of our Lord and of his Christ, and he will reign forever and ever." {11:16} The twenty-four elders who sat before God on their thrones fell on their faces and worshiped God, {11:17} saying, "We give you thanks, Lord God Almighty, who is, who was, and who is to come, because you have taken your great power and begun to reign. {11:18} The nations were angry, and your wrath has come, and the time for judging the dead, rewarding your servants the prophets and the saints, and those who fear your name, both small and great, and for destroying those who destroy the earth." {11:19} The temple of God in heaven was opened, and within his temple was seen the ark of his covenant, and there came flashes of lightning, rumblings, peals of thunder, an earthquake, and a severe hailstorm.

{12:1} A great sign appeared in heaven: a woman clothed with the sun, the moon at her feet, and a crown of twelve stars on her head. {12:2} She was pregnant and cried out in pain as she was about to give birth. {12:3} Another sign appeared in heaven: a huge red dragon with seven heads, ten horns, and seven crowns on his heads. {12:4} His tail swept a third of the stars out of the sky and hurled them to the earth. The dragon stood in front of the woman who was about to give birth so that he could devour her child as soon as it was born. {12:5} She gave birth to a son, who would rule all nations with an iron scepter. Her child was snatched up to God and to his throne. {12:6} The woman fled into the wilderness to a place prepared by God, where she would be taken care of for one thousand two hundred sixty days. {12:7} Then there was war in heaven; Michael and his angels fought against the dragon, and the dragon and his angels fought back, {12:8} but he was not strong enough, and they lost their place in heaven. {12:9} The great dragon was thrown down—that ancient serpent called the Devil, or Satan, who leads the whole world astray; he was hurled to the earth, and his angels with him. {12:10} Then I heard a loud voice in heaven say, "Now have come the salvation and the power and the kingdom of our God, and the authority of his Christ, for the accuser of our brothers and sisters, who accuses them before our God day and night, has been hurled down. {12:11} They triumphed over him by the blood of the Lamb and by the word of their testimony; they did not love their lives so much as to shrink from death. {12:12} Therefore rejoice, you heavens and you who dwell in them! But woe to the earth and the sea, because the devil has gone down to you! He is filled with fury because he knows that his time is short." {12:13} When the dragon saw that he had been hurled to the earth, he pursued the woman who had given birth to the male child. {12:14} The woman was given the two wings of a great eagle so that she might fly to the place prepared for her in the wilderness, where she would be taken care of for a time, times, and half a time, out of the serpent's reach {12:15} Then the serpent spewed water like a river out of his mouth to overtake the woman and sweep her away with the torrent. {12:16} But the earth helped the woman by opening its mouth and swallowing the river that the dragon had spewed out of his mouth. {12:17} The dragon was enraged at the woman and went off to wage war against the rest of her offspring—those who keep God's commands and hold fast their testimony about Jesus.

{13:1} I stood on the shore of the sea, and I saw a beast coming out of the sea. It had seven heads and ten horns, with ten crowns on its horns, and on each head a blasphemous name. {13:2} The beast I saw resembled a leopard, but had feet like those of a bear and a mouth like that of a lion. The dragon gave the beast his power, his throne, and great authority. {13:3} One of the heads of the beast seemed to have had a fatal wound, but the fatal wound had been healed. The whole world was filled with wonder and followed the beast. {13:4} People worshiped the dragon because he had given authority to the beast, and they asked, "Who is like the beast? Who can wage war against it?" {13:5} The beast was given a mouth to utter proud words and blasphemies and to exercise its authority for forty-two months. {13:6} It opened its mouth to blaspheme God and to slander his name and his dwelling place and those who live in heaven. {13:7} It was given power to wage war against God's holy people and to conquer them, and it was given authority over every tribe, people, language, and nation. {13:8} All inhabitants of the earth will worship the beast—all whose names have not been written in the Lamb's book of life, the Lamb who was slain from the creation of the world. {13:9} Whoever has ears, let them hear. {13:10} If anyone is to go into captivity, they will go into captivity; if anyone is to be killed with the sword, they will be killed with the sword. This calls for patient endurance and faithfulness on the part of God's people. {13:11} Then I saw a second beast, coming out of the earth. It had two horns like a lamb, but it spoke like a dragon. {13:12} It exercised all the authority of the first beast on its behalf and made the earth and its inhabitants worship the first beast, whose fatal wound had been healed. {13:13} And it performed great signs, even causing fire to come down from heaven to the earth in full view of the people. {13:14} Because of the signs it was given power to perform on behalf of the first beast, it deceived the inhabitants of the earth. It ordered them to set up an image in honor of the beast who was wounded by the sword and yet lived. {13:15} The second beast was given power to give breath to the image of the first beast so that the image could speak and cause all who refused to worship the image to be killed. {13:16} It also forced all people, great and small, rich and poor, free and slave, to receive a mark on their right hands or on their foreheads, {13:17} so that they could not buy or sell unless they had the mark, which is the name of the beast or the number of its name. {13:18} This calls for wisdom: let the one who has understanding calculate the number of the beast, for it is the number of a man; that number is six hundred sixty-six.

{14:1} Then I looked, and there was a Lamb standing on Mount Zion, and with him were one hundred forty-four thousand people who had his Father's name written on their foreheads. {14:2} I heard a voice from heaven that sounded like rushing waters and loud thunder, and I heard the sound of harpists playing their harps. {14:3} They sang a new song before the throne and before the four living creatures and the elders; no one could learn the song except the one hundred forty-four thousand who had been redeemed from the earth. {14:4} These are the ones who have not been defiled by women; they are virgins. They follow the Lamb wherever he goes. They were purchased from among humanity as the firstfruits to God and the Lamb. {14:5} No lie was found in their mouths; they are blameless before the throne of God. {14:6} Then I saw another angel flying in midair, and he had the eternal gospel to proclaim to those who live on the earth—to every nation, tribe, language, and people. {14:7} He said in a loud voice, "Fear God and give him glory, because the hour of his judgment has come; worship him who made the heavens, the earth, the sea, and the springs of water." {14:8} A second angel followed and said, "Fallen! Fallen is Babylon the Great, which made all the nations drink the maddening wine of her adulteries." {14:9} A third angel followed them and said in a loud voice, "If anyone worships the beast and its image and receives its mark on their forehead or hand, {14:10} they, too, will drink the wine of God's fury, which has been poured full strength into the cup of his wrath. They will be tormented with burning sulfur in the presence of the holy angels and of the Lamb. {14:11} And the smoke of their torment will rise forever and ever. There will be no rest day or night for those who worship the beast and its image, or for anyone who receives the mark of its name." {14:12} This calls for patient endurance on the part of the saints who keep God's commands and remain faithful to Jesus. {14:13} Then I heard a voice from heaven say, "Write this: Blessed are the dead who die in the Lord from now on." "Yes," says the Spirit, "they will rest from their labor, for their deeds will follow them." {14:14} I looked, and there before me was a white cloud, and seated on the cloud was one like a son of man, with a golden crown on his head and a sharp sickle in his hand. {14:15} Then another angel came out of the temple and called in a loud voice to him who was sitting on the cloud, "Take your sickle and reap, because the time to reap has come, for the harvest of the earth is ripe." {14:16} So he who was seated on the cloud swung his sickle over the earth, and the earth was harvested. {14:17} Another angel came out of the temple in heaven, and he too had a sharp sickle. {14:18} Still another angel, who had charge of the fire, came from the altar and called in a loud voice to him who had the sharp sickle, "Take your sharp sickle and gather the clusters of grapes from the earth's vine, because its grapes are ripe." {14:19} The angel swung his sickle on the earth, gathered its grapes, and threw them into the great winepress of God's wrath. {14:20} They were trampled in the winepress outside the city, and blood flowed out of the press, rising as high as the horses' bridles for a distance of one thousand six hundred stadia (about 200 miles).

{15:1} I saw in heaven another great and marvelous sign: seven angels with the seven last plagues—last because with them God's wrath is completed. {15:2} And I saw what looked like a sea of glass glowing with fire and standing beside the sea those who had been victorious over the beast and its image and over the number of its name. They held harps given them by God {15:3} and sang the song of God's servant Moses and of the Lamb: "Great and marvelous are your deeds, Lord God Almighty. Just and true are your ways, King of the nations. {15:4} Who will not fear you, Lord, and bring glory to your name? For you alone are holy. All nations will come and worship before you, for your righteous acts have been revealed." {15:5} After this, I looked, and I saw in heaven the temple—that is, the tabernacle of the covenant—and it was opened. {15:6} Out of the temple came the seven angels with the seven plagues. They were dressed in clean, shining linen and wore golden sashes around their chests. {15:7} Then one of the four living creatures gave to the seven angels seven golden bowls filled with the wrath of God, who lives forever and ever. {15:8} And the temple was filled with smoke from the glory of God and from his power, and no one could enter the temple until the seven plagues of the seven angels were completed.

{16:1} I heard a loud voice from the temple telling the seven angels, "Go and pour out the bowls of God's wrath on the earth." {16:2} The first angel went and poured out his bowl on the earth, and ugly and painful sores broke out on the people who had the mark of the beast and worshiped its image. {16:3} The second angel poured out his bowl on the sea, and it turned into the blood of a dead person, and every living thing in the sea died. {16:4} The third angel poured out his bowl on the rivers and springs, and they became blood. {16:5} I heard the angel in charge of the waters say, "You are just in these judgments, O Lord, you who are and who were; {16:6} for they have shed the blood of your holy people and your prophets, and you have given them blood to drink as they deserve." {16:7} And I heard another voice from the altar say, "Yes, Lord God Almighty, true and just are your judgments." {16:8} The fourth angel poured out his bowl on the sun, and it was allowed to scorch people with fire. {16:9} They were seared by the intense heat and cursed the name of God, who had control over these plagues, but they did not repent or give him glory. {16:10} The fifth angel poured out his bowl on the throne of the beast, and its kingdom was plunged into darkness; people gnawed their tongues in agony {16:11} and cursed the God of heaven because of their pains and sores, but they did not repent of their actions. {16:12} The sixth angel poured out his bowl on the great river Euphrates, and its water was dried up to prepare the way for the kings from the East. {16:13} Then I saw three impure spirits that looked like frogs; they came out of the mouth of the dragon, the beast, and the false prophet. {16:14} They are demonic spirits that perform signs, and they go out to the kings of the whole world to gather them for the battle on the great day of God Almighty. {16:15} "Look, I come like a thief! Blessed is the one who stays awake and remains clothed so as not to go naked and be shamefully exposed." {16:16} Then they gathered the kings together to the place that in Hebrew is called Armageddon. {16:17} The seventh angel poured out his bowl into the air, and out of the temple came a loud voice from the throne saying, "It is done!" {16:18} Then there came flashes of lightning, rumblings, peals of thunder, and a severe earthquake; no earthquake like it has ever occurred since mankind has been on the earth, so tremendous was the quake. {16:19} The great city split into three parts, and the cities of the nations collapsed; God remembered Babylon the Great and gave her the cup filled with the wine of the fury of his wrath. {16:20} Every island fled away, and the mountains could not be found. {16:21} Huge hailstones, each weighing about a hundred pounds, fell from the sky on people, and they cursed God on account of the plague of hail because the plague was so terrible.

{17:1} One of the seven angels who had the seven bowls came and said to me, "Come, I will show you the punishment of the great prostitute who sits by many waters. {17:2} With her the kings of the earth committed adultery, and the inhabitants of the earth were intoxicated with the wine of her adulteries." {17:3} Then the angel carried me away in the Spirit into a wilderness, and there I saw a woman sitting on a scarlet beast that was covered with blasphemous names and had seven heads and ten horns. {17:4} The woman was dressed in purple and scarlet, and was glittering with gold, precious stones, and pearls. She held a golden cup in her hand filled with abominable things and the filth of her adulteries. {17:5} The name written on her forehead was a mystery: "Babylon the Great, the Mother of Prostitutes and of the Abominations of the Earth." {17:6} I saw that the woman was drunk with the blood of God's holy people, the blood of those who bore testimony to Jesus. When I saw her, I was greatly astonished. {17:7} Then the angel said to me: "Why are you astonished? I will explain to you the mystery of the woman and of the beast she rides, which has the seven heads and ten horns. {17:8} The beast, which you saw, once was, now is not, and yet will come up out of the Abyss (bottomless pit) and go to its destruction. The inhabitants of the earth whose names have not been written in the book of life from the creation of the world will be astonished when they see the beast, because it once was, now is not, and yet will come. {17:9} This calls for a mind with wisdom: The seven heads are seven hills on which the woman sits. {17:10} They are also seven kings. Five have fallen, one is, and the other has not yet come; but when he does come, he must remain for only a little while. {17:11} The beast who once was, and now is not, is an eighth king. He belongs to the seven and is going to his destruction. {17:12} The ten horns you saw are ten kings who have not yet received a kingdom, but who for one hour will receive authority as kings along with the beast. {17:13} They have one purpose and will give their power and authority to the beast. {17:14} They will wage war against the Lamb, but the Lamb will triumph over them because he is Lord of lords and King of kings—and with him will be his called, chosen, and faithful followers. {17:15} Then the angel said to me, "The waters you saw, where the prostitute sits, are peoples, multitudes, nations, and languages. {17:16} The beast and the ten horns you saw will hate the prostitute. They will bring her to ruin and leave her naked; they will eat her flesh and burn her with fire. {17:17} For God has put it into their hearts to accomplish his purpose by agreeing to hand over to the beast their royal authority, until God's words are fulfilled. {17:18} The woman you saw is the great city that rules over the kings of the earth."

{18:1} After this, I saw another angel coming down from heaven, full of great power, and the earth was illuminated by his glory. {18:2} He shouted with a powerful voice, "Babylon the Great has fallen! It has become a dwelling place for demons, a stronghold for every unclean spirit, and a cage for every unclean and detestable bird. {18:3} All nations have drunk the wine of her adulteries, and the kings of the earth have committed immoral acts with her; the merchants of the earth have grown rich from the excessive luxury she provided. {18:4} I heard another voice from heaven say, "Come out of her, my people, so that you will not share in her sins or suffer any of her plagues. {18:5} Her sins are piled up to heaven, and God has remembered her wickedness. {18:6} Repay her as she has repaid you; pay her back double for what she has done. In the cup she mixed, mix her a double portion. {18:7} As much as she glorified herself and indulged in luxury, give her that much torment and sorrow. She says in her heart, 'I sit as a queen; I am not a widow; I will never mourn.' {18:8} Therefore, her plagues will come in one day: death, mourning, and famine; she will be consumed by fire, for mighty is the Lord God who judges her. {18:9} The kings of the earth, who committed immoral acts with her and lived in luxury with her, will weep and mourn over her when they see the smoke of her burning. {18:10} They will stand far off, terrified by her torment, and cry out, "Woe! Woe! O great city, Babylon, you mighty city! In one hour your judgment has come." {18:11} The merchants of the earth will weep and mourn over her because no one buys their cargoes anymore. {18:12} The cargoes include gold, silver, precious stones, pearls, fine linen, purple, silk, scarlet, all kinds of fragrant wood, all sorts of articles made of ivory, and all kinds of valuable wood, bronze, iron, and marble; {18:13} also cinnamon, spices, incense, myrrh, wine, olive oil, fine flour, wheat, cattle, sheep, horses, chariots, slaves, and human lives. {18:14} The things you longed for have all gone from you, and all your luxury and splendor have vanished, never to be found again. {18:15} The merchants who gained their wealth from her will stand far off, terrified by her torment, weeping and mourning. {18:16} They will cry out, "Woe! Woe, O great city, dressed in fine linen, purple, and scarlet, adorned with gold, precious stones, and pearls! {18:17} In one hour, such great wealth has been brought to ruin!" Every shipmaster, all who travel by sea, and sailors, along with everyone who trades by sea, will stand far off, {18:18} and when they see the smoke of her burning, they will cry out, "What city is like this great city?" {18:19} They will throw dust on their heads and weep and mourn, crying out, "Woe! Woe, O great city, where all who had ships on the sea grew rich from her great wealth! In one hour she has been made desolate!" {18:20} Rejoice over her, you heavens, and you saints, apostles, and prophets!

God has judged her for the way she treated you. {18:21} A mighty angel picked up a boulder the size of a large millstone and threw it into the sea, saying, "With such violence, the great city of Babylon will be thrown down, never to be found again. {18:22} The music of harpists, musicians, pipers, and trumpeters will never be heard in you again. No craftsman of any trade will ever be found in you again; the sound of a millstone will never be heard in you again. {18:23} The light of a lamp will never shine in you again; the voice of bridegroom and bride will never be heard in you again, for your merchants were the world's important people; by your magic spells, all the nations were led astray. {18:24} In her was found the blood of prophets and of God's holy people, and of all who have been slaughtered on the earth.

{19:1} After this, I heard a great multitude in heaven shouting, "Hallelujah! Salvation and glory and power belong to our God! {19:2} For true and just are his judgments: He has condemned the great prostitute who corrupted the earth by her adulteries and has avenged the blood of his servants shed by her." {19:3} And again they shouted, "Hallelujah! The smoke from her goes up forever and ever." {19:4} The twenty-four elders and the four living creatures fell down and worshiped God, who was seated on the throne. They cried, "Amen! Hallelujah!" {19:5} Then a voice came from the throne saying, "Praise our God, all you his servants, you who fear him, both great and small!" {19:6} Then I heard what sounded like a great multitude, like the roar of rushing waters and like loud peals of thunder, shouting, "Hallelujah! For our Lord God Almighty reigns. {19:7} Let us rejoice and be glad and give him glory! For the wedding of the Lamb has come, and his bride has made herself ready." {19:8} Fine linen, bright and clean, was given to her to wear. (Fine linen stands for the righteous acts of God's holy people.) {19:9} Then the angel said to me, "Write this: Blessed are those who are invited to the wedding supper of the Lamb!" And he added, "These are the true words of God." {19:10} At this, I fell at his feet to worship him, but he said to me, "Don't do that! I am a fellow servant with you and your brothers and sisters who hold to the testimony of Jesus. Worship God! For it is the spirit of prophecy who bears testimony to Jesus." {19:11} I saw heaven standing open, and there before me was a white horse, whose rider is called Faithful and True. With justice, he judges and wages war. {19:12} His eyes are like blazing fire, and on his head are many crowns. He has a name written on him that no one knows but he himself. {19:13} He is dressed in a robe dipped in blood, and his name is the Word of God. {19:14} The armies of heaven were following him, riding on white horses and dressed in fine linen, white and clean. {19:15} Coming out of his mouth is a sharp sword with which to strike down the nations. "He will rule them with an iron scepter." He treads the winepress of the fury of the wrath of God Almighty. {19:16} On his robe and on his thigh he has this name written: KING OF KINGS AND LORD OF LORDS. {19:17} And I saw an angel standing in the sun, who cried in a loud voice to all the birds flying in midair, "Come, gather together for the great supper of God, {19:18} so that you may eat the flesh of kings, generals, and the mighty, of horses and their riders, and the flesh of all people, free and slave, great and small." {19:19} Then I saw the beast and the kings of the earth and their armies gathered together to wage war against the rider on the horse and his army. {19:20} But the beast was captured, and with it the false prophet who had performed the signs on its behalf. With these signs, he had deceived those who had received the mark of the beast and worshiped its image. The two of them were thrown alive into the fiery lake of burning sulfur. {19:21} The rest were killed with the sword coming out of the mouth of the rider on the horse, and all the birds gorged themselves on their flesh.

{20:1} Then I saw an angel coming down from heaven, having the key to the Abyss (bottomless pit) and holding a great chain. {20:2} He seized the dragon, that ancient serpent, who is the devil, or Satan, and bound him for a thousand years. {20:3} He threw him into the Abyss, locked it, and sealed it over him to keep him from deceiving the nations anymore until the thousand years were ended. After that, he must be set free for a short time. {20:4} I saw thrones on which were seated those who had been given authority to judge. And I saw the souls of those who had been beheaded because of their testimony about Jesus and because of the word of God. They had not worshiped the beast or its image and had not received its mark on their foreheads or hands. They came to life and reigned with Christ a thousand years. {20:5} (The rest of the dead did not come to life until the thousand years were ended.) This is the first resurrection. {20:6} Blessed and holy are those who share in the first resurrection. The second death has no power over them, but they will be priests of God and of Christ and will reign with him for a thousand years. {20:7} When the thousand years are over, Satan will be released from his prison {20:8} and will go out to deceive the nations in the four corners of the earth—Gog and Magog—to gather them for battle. Their number is like the sand on the seashore. {20:9} They marched across the breadth of the earth and surrounded the camp of God's people, the city he loves. But fire came down from heaven and devoured them. {20:10} And the devil, who had deceived them, was thrown into the lake of burning sulfur, where the beast and the false prophet had been thrown. They will be tormented day and night for ever and ever. {20:11} Then I saw a great white throne and him who was seated on it. The earth and the heavens fled from his presence, and there was no place for them. {20:12} And I saw the dead, great and small, standing before the throne, and books were opened. Another book was opened, which is the book of life. The dead were judged according to what they had done as recorded in the books. {20:13} The sea gave up the dead that were in it, and death and Hades (the grave) gave up the dead that were in them, and each person was judged according to what they had done. {20:14} Then death and Hades were thrown into the lake of fire. The lake of fire is the second death. {20:15} Anyone whose name was not found written in the book of life was thrown into the lake of fire.

{21:1} I saw a new heaven and a new earth, for the first heaven and the first earth had passed away, and there was no longer any sea. {21:2} I, John, saw the holy city, the new Jerusalem, coming down from God out of heaven, prepared like a bride beautifully dressed for her husband. {21:3} I heard a loud voice from the throne saying, "Look! God's dwelling place is now among the people, and he will dwell with them. They will be his people, and God himself will be with them and be their God." {21:4} He will wipe every tear from their eyes. There will be no more death or mourning or crying or pain, for the old order of things has passed away. {21:5} He who was seated on the throne said, "I am making everything new!" Then he said, "Write this down, for these words are trustworthy and true." {21:6} He said to me, "It is done. I am the Alpha and the Omega, the Beginning and the End. To the thirsty, I will give water without cost from the spring of the water of life. {21:7} Those who are victorious will inherit all this, and I will be their God and they will be my children. {21:8} But the cowardly, the unbelieving, the vile, the murderers, the sexually immoral, those who practice magic arts, the idolaters, and all liars—they will be consigned to the fiery lake of burning sulfur. This is the second death." {21:9} One of the seven angels who had the seven bowls full of the last seven plagues came and said to me, "Come, I will show you the bride, the wife of the Lamb." {21:10} He carried me away in the Spirit to a mountain great and high and showed me the holy city, Jerusalem, coming down out of heaven from God, {21:11} and it shone with the glory of God. Its brilliance was like that of a very precious jewel, like a jasper, clear as crystal. {21:12} It had a great, high wall with twelve gates, and at the gates were twelve angels. The names written on the gates are the names of the twelve tribes of Israel. {21:13} There were three gates on the east, three on the north, three on the south, and three on the west. {21:14} The wall of the city had twelve foundations, and on them were the names of the twelve apostles of the Lamb. {21:15} The angel who talked with me had a measuring rod of gold to measure the city, its gates, and its walls. {21:16} The city was laid out like a square, as long as it was wide. He measured the city with the rod and found it to be twelve thousand stadia (about 1,400 miles) in length, and as wide and high as it is long. {21:17} The angel measured the wall using human measurement, and it was 144 cubits (about 216 feet) thick. {21:18} The wall was made of jasper, and the city was pure gold, as pure as glass. {21:19} The foundations of the city walls were decorated with every kind of precious stone. The first foundation was jasper, the second sapphire, the third a chalcedony, the fourth an emerald; {21:20} the fifth sardonyx, the sixth carnelian, the seventh chrysolite, the eighth beryl, the ninth topaz, the tenth chrysoprase, the eleventh jacinth, and the twelfth amethyst. {21:21} The twelve gates were twelve pearls, each gate made of a single pearl. The great street of the city was of gold, as pure as transparent glass. {21:22} I did not see a temple in the city, because the Lord God Almighty and the Lamb are its temple. {21:23} The city does not need the sun or the moon to shine on it, for the glory of God gives it light, and the Lamb is its lamp. {21:24} The nations will walk by its light, and the kings of the earth will bring their splendor into it. {21:25} On no day will its gates ever be shut, for there will be no night there. {21:26} The glory and honor of the nations will be brought into it. {21:27} Nothing impure will ever enter it, nor will anyone who does what is shameful or deceitful, but only those whose names are written in the Lamb's book of life.

{22:1} Then the angel showed me the river of the water of life, as clear as crystal, flowing from the throne of God and of the Lamb. {22:2} Down the middle of the great street of the city, on each side of the river, stood the tree of life, bearing twelve crops of fruit, yielding its fruit every month. And the leaves of the tree are for the healing of the nations. {22:3} No longer will there be any curse. The throne of God and of the Lamb will be in the city, and his servants will serve him. {22:4} They will see his face, and his name will be on their foreheads. {22:5} There will be no more night; they will not need the light of a lamp or the light of the sun, for the Lord God will give them light. And they will reign forever and ever. {22:6} The angel said to me, "These words are trustworthy and true. The Lord, the God who inspires the prophets, sent his angel to show his servants the things that must soon take place." {22:7} "Look, I am coming soon! Blessed is the one who keeps the words of the prophecy written in this scroll." {22:8} I, John, am the one who heard and saw these things. And when I had heard and seen them, I fell down to worship at the feet of the angel who had been showing them to me. {22:9} But he said to me, "Don't do that! I am a fellow servant with you and your fellow prophets and with all who keep the words of this scroll. Worship God!" {22:10} Then he told me, "Do not seal up the words of the prophecy of this scroll, because the time is near. {22:11} Let the one who does wrong continue to do wrong; let the vile person continue to be vile; let the one who does right continue to do right; and let the holy person continue to be holy." {22:12} "Look, I am coming soon! My reward is with me, and I will give to each person according to what they have done. {22:13} I am the Alpha and the Omega, the First and the Last, the Beginning and the End." {22:14} Blessed are those who wash their robes, that they may have the right to the tree of life and may go through the gates into the city. {22:15} Outside are the dogs (unclean) those who practice magic arts, the sexually immoral, the murderers, the idolaters, and everyone who loves and practices falsehood. {22:16} "I, Jesus, have sent my angel to give you this testimony for the churches. I am the Root and the Offspring of David, and the bright Morning Star." {22:17} The Spirit and the bride say, "Come!" And let the one who hears say, "Come!" Let the one who is thirsty come; and let the one who wishes take the free gift of the water of life. {22:18} I warn everyone who hears the words of the prophecy of this scroll: If anyone adds anything to them, God will add to that person the plagues described in this scroll. {22:19} And if anyone takes words away from this scroll of prophecy, God will take away from that person any share in the tree of life and in the holy city, which are described in this scroll. {22:20} He who testifies to these things says, "Yes, I am coming soon." Amen. Come, Lord Jesus. {22:21} The grace of the Lord Jesus be with God's people. Amen.

· THE COMPLETE ·
APOCRYPHA

The Book of Tobit

{1:1} This is the book of the acts of Tobit, the son of Tobiel, son of Ananiel, son of Aduel, son of Gabael, from the descendants of Asiel and the tribe of Naphtali, {1:2} who during the reign of Shalmaneser, king of the Assyrians, was taken into captivity from Thisbe, located south of Kedesh Naphtali in Galilee above Asher. {1:3} I, Tobit, walked in the ways of truth and righteousness throughout my life, performing many acts of charity for my brethren and fellow countrymen who went with me to Nineveh in the land of the Assyrians. {1:4} While I was still a young man in my own country, the land of Israel, the entire tribe of Naphtali, my forefather, abandoned the house of Jerusalem, the place chosen from among all the tribes of Israel, where all were to sacrifice and where the temple of the Most High was consecrated for all generations. {1:5} All the tribes that turned away from the faith sacrificed to the calf Baal, and so did the house of Naphtali. {1:6} But I alone frequently went to Jerusalem for the feasts, as is ordained for all Israel by an everlasting decree. I would take the first fruits, the tithes of my produce, and the first shearings to give to the priests, the sons of Aaron, at the altar. {1:7} Of all my produce, I would give a tenth to the sons of Levi who served in Jerusalem; a second tenth I would sell and spend the proceeds each year in Jerusalem; {1:8} the third tenth I would give to those to whom it was my duty, as commanded by Deborah, my father's mother, since I was left an orphan. {1:9} When I became a man, I married Anna, a member of my family, and by her I had a son named Tobias. {1:10} While I was taken captive to Nineveh, all my relatives and brethren ate the food of the Gentiles; {1:11} but I refrained from eating it, {1:12} for I remembered God with all my heart. {1:13} The Most High granted me favor and good appearance in the sight of Shalmaneser, and I became his buyer of provisions. {1:14} I often traveled to Media, and once in Rages, I left ten talents of silver in trust with Gabael, the brother of Gabrias. {1:15} But when Shalmaneser died, his son Sennacherib reigned in his place; and under him, the highways became unsafe, preventing me from going into Media. {1:16} During Shalmaneser's reign, I performed many charitable acts for my brethren. {1:17} I gave my bread to the hungry and my clothing to the naked; if I saw any of my people dead and thrown out behind the walls of Nineveh, I would bury them. {1:18} If Sennacherib, the king, executed any who fled from Judea, I buried them secretly, for in his anger, he killed many, and when the bodies were sought, they were not found. {1:19} Then one of the men of Nineveh informed the king about me, that I was burying the dead, so I hid myself. When I realized they were searching for me to kill me, I left home in fear. {1:20} All my property was confiscated, leaving me with nothing except my wife Anna and my son Tobias. {1:21} Not fifty days passed before two of Sennacherib's sons killed him and fled to the mountains of Ararat. Then Esarhaddon, his son, reigned in his place and appointed Ahikar, the son of my brother Anael, to oversee all the accounts of his kingdom and the entire administration. {1:22} Ahikar interceded for me, and I returned to Nineveh. Ahikar was the cupbearer, keeper of the signet, and in charge of administration of accounts, appointed second to Esarhaddon. He was my nephew.

{2:1} When I arrived home and was reunited with my wife Anna and my son Tobias, at the feast of Pentecost, which is the sacred festival of the seven weeks, a good dinner was prepared for me, and I sat down to eat. {2:2} Seeing the abundance of food, I said to my son, "Go and find any poor man of our brethren who is mindful of the Lord, and I will wait for you." {2:3} He returned and said, "Father, one of our people has been strangled and thrown into the marketplace." {2:4} Before I tasted anything, I sprang up and moved the body to a place of shelter until sunset. {2:5} When I returned, I washed myself and ate my food in sorrow. {2:6} Then I remembered the prophecy of Amos, how he said, "Your feasts shall be turned into mourning, and all your festivities into lamentation." And I wept. {2:7} After sunset, I dug a grave and buried the body. {2:8} My neighbors laughed at me and said, "He is no longer afraid of being put to death for this; he once ran away, and now he's burying the dead again!" {2:9} That same night, after burying him, I slept by the wall of the courtyard, my face uncovered. {2:10} Unbeknownst to me, sparrows were on the wall, and their droppings fell into my open eyes, causing white films to form on them. I went to physicians, but they could not help me. However, Ahikar cared for me until he went to Elymais. {2:11} My wife Anna then earned money from her work with women. {2:12} She would send the products to their owners. Once, when they paid her wages, they also gave her a kid; {2:13} and when she returned, it began to bleat. I said to her, "Where did you get the kid? It isn't stolen, is it? Return it to the owners; it isn't right to eat stolen goods." {2:14} She replied, "It was given to me as a gift in addition to my wages." But I didn't believe her & insisted she return it, feeling embarrassed for her. She then said to me, "Where are your righteous deeds? You seem to know everything!"

{3:1} In my grief, I wept and prayed in anguish, saying, {3:2} "You are righteous, O Lord; all your deeds and ways are mercy and truth, and you render true and righteous judgment forever. {3:3} Remember me and look favorably upon me; do not punish me for my sins and unintentional offenses, nor for the sins my fathers committed before you. {3:4} They disobeyed your commandments, and you allowed us to be plundered, taken captive, and killed; you made us a byword of reproach among all the nations where we have been scattered. {3:5} And now your many judgments are true, punishing me for my sins and those of my fathers because we did not keep your commandments. We did not walk in truth before you. {3:6} So deal with me as you see fit; command my spirit to be taken up so I may die and become dust. It is better for me to die than to live, because I have heard false reproaches, and my sorrow is great within me. Command that I be released from my distress to go to the eternal abode; do not turn your face away from me." {3:7} On the same day, in Ecbatana, Media, Sarah, the daughter of Raguel, was being ridiculed by her father's maids, {3:8} because she had been given to seven husbands, and the evil demon Asmodeus had killed each of them before the marriage was consummated. The maids said to her, "Do you not know that you strangle your husbands? You've already had seven and gained nothing from any of them. {3:9} Why do you beat us? If they are dead, go join them! May we never see a son or daughter of yours!" {3:10} Hearing this, she was deeply grieved, even to the point of considering suicide. But she thought, "I am my father's only child; if I do this, it will bring disgrace to him and cause him to grieve in his old age until he dies." {3:11} So she prayed by her window, saying, "Blessed are you, O Lord my God, and blessed is your holy and honored name forever. May all your works praise you forever. {3:12} And now, O Lord, I turn my eyes and face toward you. {3:13} Command that I be released from the earth and that I hear reproach no more. {3:14} You know, O Lord, that I am innocent of any sin with man, {3:15} and that I have not stained my name or my father's name in the land of my captivity. I am my father's only child, and he has no heir, no near kinsman or kinsman's son for whom I should keep myself as a wife. Seven husbands of mine are already dead. Why should I live? But if it does not please you to take my life, command that respect and pity be shown to me, and that I hear reproach no more." {3:16} The prayers of both were heard in the presence of the glory of the great God. {3:17} And Raphael was sent to heal both of them: to remove the white films from Tobit's eyes; to give Sarah, the daughter of Raguel, in marriage to Tobias, the son of Tobit; and to bind Asmodeus, the evil demon, because Tobias had the right to marry her. At that very moment, Tobit returned and entered his house, and Sarah, the daughter of Raguel, came down from her upper room.

{4:1} On that day, Tobit remembered the money he had left in trust with Gabael at Rages in Media, and he said to himself, {4:2} "I have asked for death. Why don't I call my son Tobias so I can explain about the money before I die?" {4:3} So he called him and said, "My son, when I die, bury me, and do not neglect your mother. Honor her all your life; do what pleases her, and do not grieve her. {4:4} Remember, my son, that she faced many dangers for you while you were still unborn. When she dies, bury her beside me in the same grave. {4:5} Remember the Lord our God all your days, my son, and avoid sin or transgressing his commandments. Live uprightly all your life, and do not walk in the ways of wrongdoing. {4:6} If you do what is right, your ways will prosper through your deeds. {4:7} Give alms from your possessions to all who live uprightly, and do not let your eye begrudge the gift when you make it.

Do not turn your face away from any poor person, and God will not turn his face away from you. {4:8} If you have many possessions, give from them in proportion; if you have few, do not be afraid to give according to what you have. {4:9} By doing this, you will be storing up a good treasure for yourself against times of need. {4:10} Charity saves from death and keeps you from entering darkness; {4:11} and for all who practice it, charity is an excellent offering in the presence of the Most High. {4:12} "Beware, my son, of all immorality. First, take a wife from among the descendants of your fathers and do not marry a foreign woman who is not of your father's tribe, for we are the sons of the prophets. Remember, my son, that Noah, Abraham, Isaac, and Jacob, our fathers of old, all took wives from among their kin. They were blessed in their children, and their descendants will inherit the land. {4:13} So now, my son, love your brethren and do not disdain your relatives and the sons and daughters of your people by refusing to take a wife from among them. Pride leads to ruin and confusion; laziness brings loss and need, for laziness is the mother of famine. {4:14} Do not hold back the wages of any worker who works for you, but pay him immediately; if you serve God, you will receive payment. {4:15} "Watch yourself, my son, in everything you do, and be disciplined in your conduct. {4:16} And what you hate, do not do to anyone. Do not drink wine to excess or let drunkenness accompany you. {4:17} Share your bread with the hungry and your clothing with the naked. Give all your surplus to charity, and do not begrudge the gift when you make it. {4:18} Place your bread on the grave of the righteous, but do not give any to sinners. {4:19} Seek advice from every wise person, and do not despise any useful counsel. {4:20} Bless the Lord God on every occasion; ask him to make your ways straight and that all your paths and plans may prosper. For none of the nations have understanding; only the Lord gives good things and humbles whomever he wishes according to his will. {4:21} "So, my son, remember my commands and do not let them be forgotten in your mind. {4:22} And now let me explain to you about the ten talents of silver I left in trust with Gabael, the son of Gabrias, at Rages in Media. {4:23} Do not be afraid, my son, because we have become poor. You have great wealth if you fear God, avoid every sin, and do what is pleasing in his sight."

{5:1} Then Tobias replied, "Father, I will do everything you have commanded; {5:2} but how can I get the money if I don't know the man?" {5:3} Tobit then gave him the receipt and said, "Find someone to go with you, and I will pay him as long as I live; go and get the money." {5:4} So he went to look for someone and found Raphael, who was an angel, {5:5} though Tobias did not realize it. Tobias asked him, "Can you go with me to Rages in Media? Do you know that area?" {5:6} The angel answered, "I will go with you; I know the way, and I've stayed with our brother Gabael." {5:7} Tobias then said, "Wait for me while I tell my father." {5:8} The angel replied, "Go, and don't delay." So he went in and said to his father, "I've found someone to go with me." Tobit said, "Call him in so I can learn which tribe he belongs to and whether he's a trustworthy man to accompany you." {5:9} Tobias invited him in; he entered, and they greeted each other. {5:10} Then Tobit asked him, "My brother, what tribe and family are you from? Please tell me." {5:11} But he replied, "Are you looking for a tribe and family, or just someone you'll pay to go with your son?" Tobit said, "I want to know, my brother, about your people and your name." {5:12} He replied, "I am Azarias, the son of the great Ananias, one of your relatives." {5:13} Tobit said, "Welcome, my brother. Don't be angry with me for trying to find out your tribe and family. You're a relative of mine, from good and noble stock. I used to know Ananias and Jathan, the sons of the great Shemaiah, when we went together to Jerusalem to worship and offered the firstborn of our flocks and the tithes of our produce. They didn't go astray in the errors of our people. My brother, you come from good roots. {5:14} But tell me, what wages do you expect — a drachma a day, plus expenses like for my son? {5:15} I will add to your wages if you both return safe and sound." They agreed to these terms. {5:16} Then he said to Tobias, "Get ready for the journey, and may you both have good success." So his son made preparations for the trip. His father said to him, "Go with this man; may God, who dwells in heaven, prosper your journey, and may his angel accompany you." So they both set out, and the young man's dog followed them. {5:17} But Anna, his mother, began to weep and said to Tobit, "Why have you sent our child away? Isn't he our support as he comes and goes before us? {5:18} Don't pile up money, but see it as worthless compared to our child. {5:19} The life given to us by the Lord is enough for us." {5:20} Tobit said to her, "Don't worry, my sister; he will return safe and sound, and you will see him again. {5:21} A good angel will go with him; his journey will be successful, and he will return safe." {5:22} So she stopped weeping.

{6:1} As they traveled along, they came in the evening to the Tigris River and camped there. {6:2} The young man went down to wash himself, and a fish jumped up from the river and nearly swallowed him. {6:3} The angel said, "Catch the fish." So the young man grabbed the fish and threw it onto the land. {6:4} The angel then instructed him, "Cut open the fish and save the heart, liver, and gall." {6:5} The young man did as the angel told him; they roasted and ate the fish, and continued on their way until they got close to Ecbatana. {6:6} The young man asked the angel, "Brother Azarias, what is the heart, liver, and gall of the fish used for?" {6:7} He replied, "The heart and liver can be used to create smoke that drives away any demon or evil spirit troubling someone, and they will never be troubled again. {6:8} The gall can be used to anoint someone with white films on their eyes, and they will be cured." {6:9} As they approached Ecbatana, {6:10} the angel said to the young man, "Brother, we will stay with Raguel today. He is your relative, and he has an only daughter named Sarah. I will suggest that she be given to you in marriage, {6:11} because you are entitled to her and her inheritance, being her only eligible kinsman. {6:12} The girl is also beautiful and sensible. Now listen to my plan: I will speak to her father, and as soon as we return from Rages, we will celebrate the marriage. I know that Raguel cannot give her to another man without incurring the penalty of death, because you are entitled to the inheritance." {6:13} The young man said to the angel, "Brother Azarias, I've heard that the girl has been given to seven husbands, and each has died in the bridal chamber. {6:14} I am my father's only son, and I'm afraid that if I go in, I will die like those before me, for a demon loves her and harms only those who approach her. I fear I may die and cause my parents sorrow at my death, and they have no other son to bury them." {6:15} But the angel said, "Do you not remember your father's command to take a wife from your own people? Now listen to me, brother, she will become your wife, and don't worry about the demon, for she will be given to you in marriage tonight. {6:16} When you enter the bridal chamber, take live ashes from the incense and lay some of the heart and liver of the fish on them to create smoke. {6:17} The demon will smell it and flee away, never to return. When you approach her, rise up together and cry out to the merciful God, and he will save you and have mercy on you. Don't be afraid, for she was destined for you from eternity. You will save her, and she will go with you, and I believe you will have children together." When Tobias heard this, he fell in love with her and longed for her deeply.

{7:1} When they reached Ecbatana and arrived at Raguel's house, Sarah greeted them. They returned her greeting, and she welcomed them into the house. {7:2} Raguel then said to his wife Edna, "This young man looks so much like my cousin Tobit!" {7:3} He asked them, "Where are you from, brothers?" They answered, "We are from the sons of Naphtali, who are captives in Nineveh." {7:4} Raguel asked, "Do you know our brother Tobit?" They replied, "Yes, we do." He then asked, "Is he in good health?" {7:5} They said, "He is alive and well." Tobias added, "He is my father." {7:6} Raguel jumped up, kissed him, and wept. {7:7} He blessed him and exclaimed, "Son of that good and noble man!" When he heard that Tobit had lost his sight, he was overcome with grief and wept. {7:8} His wife Edna and daughter Sarah also wept. They welcomed them warmly and killed a ram from the flock, setting a large feast before them. Then Tobias said to Raphael, "Brother Azarias, tell Raguel about the matters we discussed on our journey, and let's finalize this." {7:9} Raphael communicated the proposal to Raguel. Raguel said to Tobias, "Eat, drink, and be merry, for it is your right to take my daughter. But let me explain the real situation to you. {7:10} I have given my daughter to seven husbands, and each died on their wedding night. For now, enjoy your meal." Tobias replied, "I will not eat until we have a binding agreement."

{7:12} Raguel then said, "Take her now, according to the law. You are her relative, and she is yours. May the merciful God guide you both for the best." {7:13} He called his daughter Sarah, took her by the hand, and gave her to Tobias to be his wife, saying, "Here she is; take her according to the law of Moses, and take her back to your father." He blessed them. {7:14} Next, he called his wife Edna, took a scroll, wrote the contract, and they sealed it. {7:15} Then they began to eat. {7:16} Raguel told Edna, "Sister, prepare the other room & take her there." {7:17} She did as he said & took Sarah to the room, where the girl began to weep. But her mother comforted her, saying, {7:18} "Be brave, my child; may the Lord of heaven & earth grant you joy instead of this sorrow. Be strong, my daughter."

{8:1} After they finished eating, they brought Tobias in to her. {8:2} As he entered, he remembered Raphael's words, took the live ashes from the incense, and placed the heart and liver of the fish on them to create smoke. {8:3} When the demon smelled the odor, he fled to the farthest parts of Egypt, and the angel bound him. {8:4} When the door was shut and the two were alone, Tobias got up from the bed and said, "Sister, let's pray that the Lord may have mercy on us." {8:5} Tobias began to pray, "Blessed are you, O God of our ancestors, and blessed be your holy and glorious name forever. May the heavens and all your creatures bless you. {8:6} You made Adam and gave him Eve, his wife, as a helper. From them all of humanity has come. You said, 'It is not good for man to be alone; let's make a helper like him.' {8:7} Now, O Lord, I'm not taking this sister of mine out of lust, but sincerely. Grant that I may find mercy and grow old with her." {8:8} She replied, "Amen." {8:9} Then they both went to sleep for the night. Raguel, however, got up and dug a grave, {8:10} thinking, "Perhaps he too will die." {8:11} Then Raguel went back into the house {8:12} and told his wife Edna, "Send one of the maids to check if he is alive; if not, let's bury him without anyone knowing." {8:13} The maid opened the door, went in, and found them both asleep. {8:14} She came out and told them that he was alive. {8:15} Then Raguel blessed God and said, "Blessed are you, O God, with every pure and holy blessing. May your saints and all your creatures bless you; let all your angels and chosen people bless you forever. {8:16} Blessed are you, because you have made me glad. It has not happened as I expected; you have treated us according to your great mercy. {8:17} Blessed are you, for having compassion on two only children. Show them mercy, O Lord, and bring their lives to fulfillment in health, happiness, and mercy." {8:18} He then ordered his servants to fill in the grave. {8:19} After this, he held a wedding feast for them that lasted fourteen days. {8:20} Before the feast was over, Raguel swore to Tobias that he should not leave until the fourteen days of the wedding feast ended, {8:21} and that after that, he should take half of Raguel's property and safely return to his father, with the rest being his when Raguel and Edna died.

{9:1} Then Tobias called Raphael and said to him, {9:2} "Brother Azarias, take a servant and two camels with you and go to Gabael at Rages in Media to get the money for me; bring him to the wedding feast. {9:3} For Raguel has sworn that I should not leave; {9:4} my father is counting the days, and if I delay, he will be very distressed." {9:5} So Raphael made the journey and stayed overnight with Gabael. He gave him the receipt, and Gabael brought out the money bags, seals intact, and handed them over. {9:6} In the morning, they both got up early and went to the wedding feast. Gabael blessed Tobias and his wife.

{10:1} Now Tobit was counting the days, and when the time for the journey had passed and they still hadn't returned, {10:2} he said, "Could he have been delayed? Or maybe Gabael has died, and there's no one to give him the money?" {10:3} He was very distressed. {10:4} His wife said to him, "The boy has perished; his long delay shows it." Then she began to mourn, saying, {10:5} "Am I not distressed, my child, for letting you go, you who are the light of my eyes?" {10:6} But Tobit replied, "Calm down; stop worrying. He is fine." {10:7} She answered, "Calm down? Don't deceive me; my child has died." She went out every day to the road they left on; she ate nothing during the day and mourned for her son Tobias all night, until the fourteen days of the wedding feast that Raguel had sworn he would spend there were over. At that point, Tobias said to Raguel, "Send me back, for my father and mother have lost hope of ever seeing me again." {10:8} But his father-in-law replied, "Stay with me, and I will send messengers to your father to update him on how things are." {10:9} Tobias insisted, "No, send me back to my father." {10:10} So Raguel got up, gave him his wife Sarah, and half of his property in slaves, cattle, and money. {10:11} After blessing them, he sent them away, saying, "May the God of heaven prosper you, my children, before I die." {10:12} He also said to his daughter, "Honor your father-in-law and mother-in-law; they are now your parents. I want to hear good news about you." He kissed her, and Edna said to Tobias, "May the Lord of heaven bring you back safely, dear brother, and may I see your children by my daughter Sarah so I can rejoice before the Lord. See, I'm entrusting my daughter to you; do nothing to upset her."

{11:1} After this, Tobias continued on his journey, praising God for making it successful. He blessed Raguel and his wife Edna and kept going until they were near Nineveh. {11:2} Then Raphael said to Tobias, "Are you not aware, brother, of how you left your father? {11:3} Let's hurry ahead of your wife and prepare the house. {11:4} And take the fish gall with you." So they went on, and the dog followed behind. {11:5} Meanwhile, Anna sat watching the road for her son. {11:6} When she saw him coming, she said to Tobit, "Look, your son is coming, and so is the man who went with him!" {11:7} Raphael said, "I know, Tobias, that your father will open his eyes. {11:8} You must anoint his eyes with the gall; when it stings, he will rub them, and the white films will fall off, and he will see you." {11:9} Anna ran to meet them, embraced her son, and said, "I've seen you, my child; now I'm ready to die." They both wept. {11:10} Tobit moved toward the door but stumbled. His son rushed to him {11:11} and held him, sprinkling the gall on his father's eyes, saying, "Cheer up, father." {11:12} As his eyes began to sting, he rubbed them, {11:13} and the white films came off from the corners of his eyes. {11:14} Then he saw his son and embraced him, weeping, and said, "Blessed are you, O God, and blessed is your name forever, and blessed are all your holy angels. {11:15} For you have afflicted me, but you have had mercy on me; look, I see my son Tobias!" Tobias went in rejoicing and told his father all the great things that happened to him in Media. {11:16} Then Tobit went out to meet his daughter-in-law at the gate of Nineveh, rejoicing and praising God. Those who saw him were amazed because he could see. {11:17} Tobit thanked God before everyone for his mercy. When he got close to Sarah, his daughter-in-law, he blessed her, saying, "Welcome, daughter! Blessed is God who brought you to us, and blessed are your parents." So there was great joy among all his family in Nineveh. {11:18} Ahikar and his nephew Nadab arrived, {11:19} and Tobias' marriage was celebrated for seven days with great festivities.

{12:1} Tobit then called his son Tobias and said, "My son, pay the man who traveled with you, and give him even more." {12:2} Tobias replied, "Father, it wouldn't hurt to give him half of what I brought back. {12:3} He led me safely back to you, cured my wife, got the money for me, and healed you too." {12:4} The old man said, "He deserves it." {12:5} So he called the angel and said, "Take half of everything you two brought back." {12:6} Then the angel privately called them both and said, "Praise God and give thanks to him; exalt him and thank him in front of everyone for what he has done for you. It's good to praise God and declare his works. Don't be slow to thank him. {12:7} It's wise to keep a king's secret, but it's glorious to reveal God's works. Do good, and evil will not overcome you. {12:8} Prayer is good when combined with fasting, charity, and righteousness. A little with righteousness is better than much with wrongdoing. Giving alms is better than saving gold. {12:9} For almsgiving saves from death and purges away every sin. Those who do good deeds and live righteously will have a full life; {12:10} but those who commit sins are enemies of their own lives. {12:11} I won't hide anything from you. I've said, 'It's wise to keep a king's secret, but it's glorious to reveal God's works.' {12:12} When you and your daughter-in-law Sarah prayed, I presented your prayers before the Holy One; and when you buried the dead, I was with you. {12:13} When you didn't hesitate to leave your dinner to lay out the dead, your good deed wasn't hidden from me, for I was with you. {12:14} So now God sent me to heal you and your daughter-in-law Sarah. {12:15} I am Raphael, one of the seven holy angels who present the prayers of the saints and enter into the presence of the glory of the Holy One." {12:16} They were both terrified and fell on their faces, afraid. {12:17} But he said to them, "Don't be afraid; you will be safe. Praise God forever. {12:18} I didn't come as a favor from myself, but by God's will. So praise him forever. {12:19} All this time, I only appeared to you and didn't eat or drink; you were seeing a vision. {12:20} Now give thanks to God, for I'm going back to him who sent me. Write down everything that has happened." {12:21} Then they stood up, but they saw him no more. {12:22} So they confessed the great and wonderful works of God and acknowledged that the angel of the Lord had appeared to them.

{13:1} Then Tobit wrote a prayer of joy, saying: "Blessed is God who lives forever, and blessed is his kingdom. {13:2} For he afflicts us, and he shows mercy; he brings us down to Hades (the underworld) and raises us up again, and no one can escape his hand. {13:3} Acknowledge him before the nations, O sons of Israel, for he has scattered us among them. {13:4} Make his greatness known there and exalt him in front of all the living; because he is our Lord and God, our Father forever. {13:5} He will afflict us for our sins, but he will show mercy again and gather us from all the nations where we have been scattered. {13:6} If you turn to him with all your heart and soul to do what is right before him, then he will turn to you and will not hide his face from you. But see what he will do with you; give thanks to him with a full voice. Praise the Lord of righteousness and exalt the King of the ages. I thank him in the land of my captivity, and I show his power and greatness to a nation of sinners. Turn back, you sinners, and do what is right before him; who knows if he will accept you and have mercy on you? {13:7} I exalt my God; my soul praises the King of heaven and will rejoice in his greatness. {13:8} Let all men speak and give thanks in Jerusalem. {13:9} O Jerusalem, the holy city, he will afflict you for the deeds of your sons, but he will again show mercy to the sons of the righteous. {13:10} Give thanks worthily to the Lord and praise the King of the ages, so that his tent may be raised for you again with joy. May he comfort those among you who are captives and love those among you who are distressed, for all generations forever. {13:11} Many nations will come from afar to the name of the Lord God, bringing gifts in their hands for the King of heaven. Generations will give you joyful praise. {13:12} Cursed are all who hate you; blessed forever will be all who love you. {13:13} Rejoice and be glad, O sons of the righteous, for they will be gathered together and will praise the Lord of the righteous. {13:14} How blessed are those who love you! They will rejoice in your peace. Blessed are those who grieved over all your troubles, for they will rejoice for you upon seeing all your glory and will be made glad forever. {13:15} Let my soul praise God, the great King. {13:16} For Jerusalem will be built with sapphires and emeralds, her walls with precious stones, and her towers and battlements with pure gold. {13:17} The streets of Jerusalem will be paved with beryl, ruby, and stones of Ophir; {13:18} all her lanes will cry 'Hallelujah!' and will give praise, saying, 'Blessed is God, who has exalted you forever.'"

{14:1} Here Tobit finished his words of praise. {14:2} He was fifty-eight years old when he lost his sight, and after eight years he regained it. He gave alms, continued to fear the Lord God, and praised him. {14:3} When he grew very old, he called his son and grandsons and said, "My son, take your sons; I am old and about to leave this life. {14:4} Go to Media, my son, for I fully believe what Jonah the prophet said about Nineveh: it will be overthrown. But in Media, there will be peace for a while. Our people will be scattered across the earth from the good land, and Jerusalem will be desolate. The house of God will be burned down and lie in ruins for a time. {14:5} But God will show mercy again and bring them back to their land; they will rebuild the house of God, although it won't be like the former one until the times of the age are completed. After that, they will return from their captivity and will rebuild Jerusalem in splendor. The house of God will be rebuilt there as a glorious structure for all generations forever, just as the prophets said it would. {14:6} Then all the Gentiles will turn to fear the Lord God in truth and will bury their idols. {14:7} All the Gentiles will praise the Lord, and his people will give thanks to God, and the Lord will exalt his people. Everyone who loves the Lord God in truth and righteousness will rejoice, showing mercy to our brethren. {14:8} "So now, my son, leave Nineveh, because what the prophet Jonah said will surely happen. {14:9} But keep the law and the commandments, and be merciful and just, so that all goes well with you. {14:10} Bury me properly, and your mother with me. Do not live in Nineveh any longer. See, my son, what Nadab did to Ahikar, who raised him, how he brought him from light into darkness, and how he repaid him. Ahikar was saved, while Nadab fell into the trap he set and perished. {14:11} So now, my children, consider what almsgiving accomplishes and how righteousness delivers." After saying this, he died in his bed at one hundred fifty-eight years old, and Tobias gave him a grand funeral. {14:12} When Anna died, he buried her next to his father. Then Tobias returned with his wife and sons to Ecbatana, to Raguel, his father-in-law. {14:13} He lived to an old age with honor and gave magnificent funerals for his father-in-law and mother-in-law. He inherited their property and that of his father Tobit. {14:14} He died in Ecbatana of Media at the age of one hundred twenty-seven. {14:15} Before he died, he heard about the destruction of Nineveh, which Nebuchadnezzar and Ahasuerus had captured. Before his death, he rejoiced over Nineveh.

The Book of Judith

{1:1} In the twelfth year of Nebuchadnezzar's reign, who ruled over the Assyrians in the great city of Nineveh, during the time of Arphaxad, who ruled over the Medes in Ecbatana— {1:2} he is the king who built walls around Ecbatana using cut stones that were three cubits thick and six cubits long; he made the walls seventy cubits high and fifty cubits wide; {1:3} at the gates, he built towers a hundred cubits high and sixty cubits wide at the bases; {1:4} and he made the gates seventy cubits high and forty cubits wide, so that his armies could march out in force and his infantry could form ranks. {1:5} It was during these days that King Nebuchadnezzar went to war against King Arphaxad in the great plain on the borders of Ragae. {1:6} He was joined by all the people of the hill country and all those living along the Euphrates, Tigris, and Hydaspes rivers, as well as in the plain ruled by Arioch over the Elymaeans. Many nations allied with the Chaldeans. {1:7} Then Nebuchadnezzar, king of the Assyrians, sent messengers to all who lived in Persia and to those in the west, including those in Cilicia, Damascus, Lebanon, Antilebanon, and all along the seacoast, {1:8} and to the nations of Carmel, Gilead, Upper Galilee, and the great Plain of Esdraelon, {1:9} and all who were in Samaria and its surrounding towns, and beyond the Jordan River as far as Jerusalem, Bethany, Chelous, Kadesh, the river of Egypt, Tahpanhes, Raamses, and the entire land of Goshen, {1:10} even beyond Tanis and Memphis, and all who lived in Egypt as far as the borders of Ethiopia. {1:11} However, everyone in the entire region ignored Nebuchadnezzar's orders and refused to join him in the war; they were not afraid of him and saw him as just one man, sending his messengers back empty-handed and embarrassed. {1:12} This made Nebuchadnezzar very angry, and he swore by his throne and kingdom that he would take revenge on all of Cilicia, Damascus, and Syria, that he would kill them by the sword, along with the inhabitants of Moab, the people of Ammon, all of Judea, and everyone in Egypt as far as the coasts of the two seas. {1:13} In the seventeenth year, he led his forces against King Arphaxad, defeated him in battle, and overthrew his entire army, including all his cavalry and chariots. {1:14} Thus, he took possession of his cities, reached Ecbatana, captured its towers, plundered its markets, and turned its beauty into shame. {1:15} He captured Arphaxad in the mountains of Ragae and struck him down with hunting spears, utterly destroying him to this day. {1:16} Then he returned to Nineveh with all his combined forces, a vast army, where they rested and feasted for 120 days.

{2:1} In the eighteenth year, on the twenty-second day of the first month, there was talk in the palace of Nebuchadnezzar, king of the Assyrians, about executing his revenge on the whole region, just as he had said. {2:2} He gathered all his officers and nobles and presented his secret plan, recounting in detail all the wickedness of the region; {2:3} and it was decided that everyone who had not obeyed his command should be destroyed. {2:4} After explaining his plan, Nebuchadnezzar called Holofernes, the chief general of his army, second only to him, and said, {2:5} "Thus says the Great King, the lord of the whole earth: When you leave my presence, take with you men strong and confident, totaling one hundred twenty thousand foot soldiers and twelve thousand cavalry. {2:6} Go and attack the entire western region because they disobeyed my orders. {2:7} Tell them to prepare earth and water, for I am coming against them in my anger, and I will cover the whole face of the earth with my armies, handing them over to be plundered by my troops, {2:8} until their wounded fill their valleys and every brook and river overflows with their dead; {2:9} and I will carry them off as captives to the ends of the earth. {2:10} You shall seize all their territory for me in advance. They will yield to you, and you shall hold them for me until the day of their punishment. {2:11} But if they refuse, you must not spare them, and you shall hand them over to slaughter and plunder throughout your entire region. {2:12} For as I live, and by the power of my kingdom, what I have spoken, my hand will execute. {2:13} And you—make sure not to disobey any of your sovereign's commands, but carry them out just as I ordered; do not delay in doing so." {2:14} So Holofernes left his master's presence, gathered all the commanders, generals, and officers of the Assyrian army, {2:15} and mustered the chosen troops by divisions, as his lord commanded, totaling one hundred twenty thousand, plus twelve thousand archers on horseback. {2:16} He organized them like a great army prepared for a campaign. {2:17} He collected a vast number of camels, donkeys, and mules for transport, as well as countless sheep, oxen, and goats for provisions; {2:18} also plenty of food for every soldier, and a huge amount of gold and silver from the royal palace. {2:19} Then he set out with his entire army, to advance ahead of King Nebuchadnezzar and cover the whole western region with their chariots, horsemen, and chosen infantry. {2:20} Along with them was a mixed crowd like a swarm of locusts, like the dust of the earth—a multitude that could not be counted. {2:21} They marched for three days from Nineveh to the plain of Bectileth and camped opposite Bectileth near the mountain north of Upper Cilicia. {2:22} From there, Holofernes took his whole army, his infantry, cavalry, and chariots, and moved up into the hill country {2:23} and devastated Put and Lud, plundering all the people of Rassis and the Ishmaelites who lived in the desert south of the Chellean territory. {2:24} Then he followed the Euphrates, passed through Mesopotamia, and destroyed all the hilltop cities along the brook Abron, as far as the sea. {2:25} He seized the territory of Cilicia, killing everyone who resisted him, and reached the southern borders of Japheth, facing Arabia. {2:26} He surrounded all the Midianites, burned their tents, and plundered their sheepfolds. {2:27} Then he went down into the plain of Damascus during the wheat harvest, burning all their fields, destroying their flocks and herds, sacking their cities, ravaging their lands, and putting all their young men to death with the sword. {2:28} So fear and terror of him fell upon all the people living along the seacoast, in Sidon and Tyre, and those in Sur, Ocina, and all who lived in Jamnia. Those in Azotus and Ascalon feared him greatly.

{3:1} So they sent messengers to ask for peace, saying, {3:2} "Look, we, the servants of Nebuchadnezzar, the Great King, lie prostrate before you. Do with us whatever you wish. {3:3} Look at our buildings, our land, our wheat fields, our flocks and herds, and all our sheepfolds with their tents; do with them whatever you like. {3:4} Our cities and their inhabitants are your slaves; come and deal with them in any way that seems good to you." {3:5} The men went to Holofernes and told him all this. {3:6} Then he went down to the seacoast with his army, stationed garrisons in the hilltop cities, and took chosen men from them as his allies. {3:7} These people and all in the surrounding area welcomed him with garlands, dances, and tambourines. {3:8} He destroyed all their shrines and cut down their sacred groves, as he had been given the authority to eliminate all the gods of the land, so that all nations would worship Nebuchadnezzar only, and every tongue and tribe would call upon him as god. {3:9} Then he came to the edge of Esdraelon, near Dothan, facing the great ridge of Judea; {3:10} here he camped between Geba and Scythopolis, remaining for an entire month to gather supplies for his army.

{4:1} By this time, the people of Israel living in Judea heard about everything that Holofernes, the general of Nebuchadnezzar, king of the Assyrians, had done to the nations, including how he had plundered and destroyed all their temples; {4:2} they were therefore extremely terrified at his approach and were worried for both Jerusalem and the temple of the Lord their God. {4:3} They had only recently returned from captivity, and all the people of Judea were newly gathered together, with the sacred vessels, altar, and temple consecrated after being profaned. {4:4} So they sent messages to every district of Samaria, to Kona, Beth-horon, Belmain, Jericho, Choba, Aesora, and the valley of Salem, {4:5} and immediately seized all the high hilltops, fortified the villages on them, and stored up food in preparation for war since their fields had just been harvested. {4:6} Joakim, the high priest, who was in Jerusalem at the time, wrote to the people of Bethulia and Betomesthaim, which faced Esdraelon opposite the plain near Dothan, {4:7} ordering them to seize the passes into the hills, as these were the routes through which Judea could be invaded, and it was easy to stop anyone trying to enter because the approach was narrow, only wide enough for two men at most. {4:8} So the Israelites did as Joakim the high priest and the senate of all the people of Israel in session at Jerusalem had commanded. {4:9} Every man of Israel cried out to God fervently, humbling themselves with much fasting. {4:10} They, along with their wives, children, cattle, every resident alien, hired laborer, and purchased slave, all dressed in sackcloth. {4:11} All the men and women of Israel, and their children living in Jerusalem, prostrated themselves before the temple, putting ashes on their heads and spreading sackcloth before the Lord. {4:12} They even surrounded the altar with sackcloth and cried out in unison, praying earnestly to the God of Israel not to give up their infants as prey, their wives as booty, their cities to destruction, and the sanctuary to be profaned and desecrated to the malicious joy of the Gentiles. {4:13} So the Lord heard their prayers and looked upon their affliction, for the people fasted many days throughout Judea and in Jerusalem before the sanctuary of the Lord Almighty. {4:14} Joakim the high priest and all the priests who stood before the Lord, ministering to Him with their loins girded with sackcloth, offered continual burnt offerings, along with the vows and freewill offerings of the people. {4:15} With ashes on their turbans, they cried out to the Lord with all their might to look favorably upon the whole house of Israel.

{5:1} When Holofernes, the general of the Assyrian army, heard that the people of Israel had prepared for war, closed the passes in the hills, fortified all the high hilltops, and set up barricades in the plains, {5:2} he became very angry. So he called together all the princes of Moab, the commanders of Ammon, and all the governors of the coastland, {5:3} and said to them, "Tell me, you Canaanites, who are these people living in the hill country? What cities do they inhabit? How large is their army, and where does their power lie? Who rules over them as king, leading their army? {5:4} And why have they, alone among all who live in the west, refused to come out and meet me?" {5:5} Then Achior, the leader of all the Ammonites, spoke up, saying, "Let my lord hear a word from your servant, and I will tell you the truth about this people dwelling in the nearby mountains. No falsehood will come from my mouth. {5:6} This people is descended from the Chaldeans. {5:7} At one time they lived in Mesopotamia, because they refused to follow the gods of their ancestors who were in Chaldea. {5:8} They left the ways of their forefathers, worshiped the God of heaven, whom they had come to know; thus they were driven out from the presence of their gods and fled to Mesopotamia, living there for a long time. {5:9} Then their God commanded them to leave that place and go to the land of Canaan. There they settled and prospered, acquiring much gold, silver, and many cattle. {5:10} When a famine spread over Canaan, they went down to Egypt and lived there as long as they had food, becoming a great multitude—so great that they could not be counted. {5:11} The king of Egypt became hostile toward them, taking advantage of them, forcing them to make bricks, humiliating and enslaving them. {5:12} Then they cried out to their God, and He afflicted all of Egypt with incurable plagues, leading the Egyptians to drive them out. {5:13} God dried up the Red Sea before them, {5:14} and led them by the way of Sinai and Kadesh-barnea, driving out all the people of the wilderness. {5:15} They settled in the land of the Amorites, and by their might destroyed all the inhabitants of Heshbon; crossing over the Jordan, they took possession of all the hill country. {5:16} They drove out the Canaanites, Perizzites, Jebusites, Shechemites, and all the Gergesites, living there for a long time. {5:17} As long as they did not sin against their God, they prospered, for the God who hates iniquity is with them. {5:18} But when they departed from the way He appointed for them, they were utterly defeated in many battles and led away captive to a foreign land; their temple was destroyed, and their cities captured by their enemies. {5:19} But now they have returned to their God and come back from the places where they were scattered, occupying Jerusalem, where their sanctuary is, and settling in the hill country, which was uninhabited. {5:20} Therefore, my lord, if there is any unwitting error in this people, and they sin against their God, and we discover their offense, then we will go up and defeat them. {5:21} But if there is no transgression in their nation, then let my lord pass them by; for their Lord will defend them, and their God will protect them, and we shall be shamed before the whole world." {5:22} When Achior finished speaking, the men around the tent began to complain; Holofernes' officers and all the men from the seacoast and Moab insisted that he must be put to death. {5:23} "For," they said, "we will not fear the Israelites; they are a people with no strength or power for war. {5:24} Therefore let us go up, Lord Holofernes, and they will be devoured by your vast army."

{6:1} When the disturbance caused by the men outside the council calmed down, Holofernes, commander of the Assyrian army, said to Achior and all the Moabites in front of all the foreign contingents: {6:2} "And who are you, Achior, and you hirelings of Ephraim, to prophesy among us as you have today, telling us not to make war against the people of Israel because their God will defend them? Who is God except Nebuchadnezzar? {6:3} He will send his forces to destroy them from the face of the earth, and their God will not deliver them; we, the king's servants, will destroy them as one man. They cannot withstand our cavalry. {6:4} We will burn them up, and their mountains will be drenched with their blood, their fields filled with their dead. They cannot resist us and will utterly perish. So says King Nebuchadnezzar, the lord of the whole earth. His words will not fail. {6:5} "But you, Achior, you Ammonite hireling, who have said these words on the day of your iniquity, you will not see my face again until I take revenge on this race that came out of Egypt. {6:6} Then the sword of my army and the spear of my servants will pierce your sides, and you will fall among the wounded when I return. {6:7} Now my servants will take you back into the hill country and put you in one of the cities near the passes, {6:8} and you will not die until you perish along with them. {6:9} If you truly hope in your heart that they will not be taken, do not look downcast! I have spoken, and none of my words will fail." {6:10} Then Holofernes ordered his servants, who attended to him in his tent, to seize Achior and take him to Bethulia, handing him over to the men of Israel. {6:11} So the servants took him, leading him out of the camp to the plain, and from the plain they went up into the hill country, arriving at the springs below Bethulia. {6:12} When the men of the city saw them, they grabbed their weapons and ran out to the top of the hill, and the slingers kept them from coming up by throwing stones at them. {6:13} However, they took shelter on the hill, bound Achior, and left him lying at the foot of the hill before returning to their master. {6:14} Then the men of Israel came down from the city, found him, untied him, and brought him into Bethulia, placing him before the magistrates of their city, {6:15} who in those days were Uzziah, the son of Micah, of the tribe of Simeon; Chabris, the son of Gothoniel; and Charmis, the son of Melchiel. {6:16} They called together all the elders of the city, and all the young men and women ran to the assembly, placing Achior in the midst of the people. Uzziah asked him what had happened. {6:17} He explained what had taken place at the council of Holofernes, all he had said in the presence of the Assyrian leaders, and everything Holofernes had boastfully said against the house of Israel. {6:18} Then the people fell down and worshiped God, crying out to Him, saying, {6:19} "O Lord God of heaven, see their arrogance, have pity on the humiliation of our people, and look today upon the faces of those who are consecrated to you." {6:20} They then consoled Achior and praised him greatly. {6:21} Uzziah took him from the assembly to his own house and gave a banquet for the elders; all night long, they called on the God of Israel for help.

{7:1} The next day, Holofernes ordered his entire army and all the allies who had joined him to break camp and march against Bethulia, aiming to take the mountain passes and wage war on the Israelites. {7:2} So all their warriors moved their camp that day; their army included one hundred seventy thousand infantry and twelve thousand cavalry, along with baggage and foot soldiers handling it—a massive multitude. {7:3} They camped in the valley near Bethulia, next to the spring, spreading out from Dothan to Balbaim and extending from Bethulia to Cyamon, which faces Esdraelon. {7:4} When the Israelites saw their overwhelming numbers, they were terrified, and everyone said to their neighbor, "These men will consume the entire land; neither the high mountains nor the valleys nor the hills can support them." {7:5} Each man took up his weapons, and as they lit fires on their towers, they stayed on guard throughout the night. {7:6} On the second day, Holofernes led all his cavalry into full view of the Israelites in Bethulia, {7:7} examining the city's approaches, visiting the water springs, taking control of them, and placing guards over them before returning to his army. {7:8} Then all the leaders of the people of Esau, the Moabite leaders, and the commanders of the coastland came to him and said, {7:9} "Let our lord hear a word, so that his army won't be defeated. {7:10} For these people, the Israelites, don't rely on their weapons but on the heights of their mountains, as it's not easy to reach the tops of their mountains. {7:11} Therefore, my lord, do not fight them in battle formation; if you do, not a man of your army will fall. {7:12} Stay in your camp and keep all your men with you; just let your servants take control of the water spring that flows from the mountain foot— {7:13} this is the source of water for all the people of Bethulia. Thirst will weaken them, and they will surrender the city. We and our people will camp on the nearby mountain tops to watch so that not a single man escapes the city. {7:14} They, along with their wives and children, will waste away from hunger, and before the sword reaches them, they will lie dead in the streets. {7:15} Thus, you will repay them for their rebellion, as they did not accept you peacefully." {7:16} Holofernes and all his servants were pleased with this advice, and he ordered it to be done. {7:17} So the Ammonite army moved forward, along with five thousand Assyrians, camping in the valley and seizing the water supply and the springs of the Israelites. {7:18} The sons of Esau and the sons of Ammon went up to camp in the hill country opposite Dothan; some of their men were sent south and east toward Acraba, which is near Chusi by the brook Mochmur. The rest of the Assyrian army camped in the plain, covering the entire area, with their tents and supply trains spread out, forming a vast multitude. {7:19} The people of Israel cried out to the Lord their God, as their courage failed due to the enemies surrounding them with no escape. {7:20} The whole Assyrian army—infantry, chariots, and cavalry—surrounded them for thirty-four days until every water vessel belonging to the inhabitants of Bethulia was empty; {7:21} their cisterns were running dry, and they had barely enough water to drink each day, as it was rationed. {7:22} Children lost heart, and women and young men fainted from thirst, collapsing in the streets and at the city gates; they had no strength left. {7:23} Then all the people—young men, women, and children—gathered around Uzziah and the city rulers, crying out loudly before the elders, {7:24} "God be the judge between you and us! You have caused us great harm by not making peace with the Assyrians. {7:25} Now we have no one to help us; God has handed us over to them to die of thirst and utter destruction. {7:26} Let's surrender the whole city to Holofernes and his forces to be plundered. {7:27} It would be better to be captured by them; we'd be slaves, but our lives would be spared, and we wouldn't have to witness our babies die or see our wives and children take their last breath. {7:28} We call heaven and earth, and our God, the Lord of our fathers, to witness our plight; let Him not do to us today what we have described!" {7:29} Then a great lament arose from the assembly, and they cried out to the Lord God with loud voices. {7:30} Uzziah said to them, "Have courage, my brothers! Let's hold out for 5 more days; by then, the Lord our God will show us His mercy and will not utterly forsake us. {7:31} But if these days pass and no help comes, I will do what you say." {7:32} He then dismissed the people to their posts & they went up on the walls and towers of the city, sending the women & children home, deeply depressed in city.

{8:1} At that time, Judith learned about these events; she was the daughter of Merari, the son of Ox, son of Joseph, son of Oziel, son of Elkiah, son of Ananias, son of Gideon, son of Raphaim, son of Ahitub, son of Elijah, son of Hilkiah, son of Eliab, son of Nathanael, son of Salamiel, son of Sarasadai, son of Israel. {8:2} Her husband, Manasseh, who belonged to her tribe and family, had died during the barley harvest. {8:3} He was overseeing the men binding sheaves in the field when he was overcome by the heat and went to bed, dying in Bethulia, his city. They buried him with his ancestors in the field between Dothan and Balamon. {8:4} Judith lived at home as a widow for three years and four months. {8:5} She set up a tent for herself on the roof of her house, wore sackcloth around her waist, and dressed in her widow's garments. {8:6} She fasted throughout her widowhood, except for the day before the Sabbath, the Sabbath itself, the day before the new moon, the new moon, and the feasts and days of rejoicing of the house of Israel. {8:7} She was beautiful in appearance, with a lovely face; her husband Manasseh had left her gold, silver, male and female slaves, cattle, and fields, which she managed well. {8:8} No one spoke ill of her, for she feared God with great devotion. {8:9} When Judith heard the wicked words spoken by the people against the leader because they were faint from lack of water, and Uzziah's promise to surrender the city to the Assyrians after five days, {8:10} she sent her maid, in charge of her possessions, to summon Chabris and Charmis, the elders of her city. {8:11} They came to her, and she said, "Listen to me, rulers of Bethulia! What you said to the people today is wrong; you have even sworn an oath between God and yourselves to surrender the city to our enemies unless the Lord helps us in a few days. {8:12} Who are you to test God today, putting yourselves in His place among men? {8:13} You are provoking the Almighty to anger—but you will never know anything! {8:14} You cannot measure the depths of the human heart or know what someone is thinking; how can you expect to search out God, who created everything, and understand His mind? No, my brothers, don't provoke the Lord our God to anger. {8:15} If He doesn't choose to help us in these five days, He has the power to protect us at any time, or even to destroy us in the sight of our enemies. {8:16} Don't try to limit God's purposes; He's not like a man to be threatened, nor like a human being to be swayed by pleading. {8:17} Therefore, while we wait for His deliverance, let's call upon Him for help, and He will hear us if it pleases Him. {8:18} For never in our generation, nor in these present days, has there been any tribe, family, or city of ours that worshiped idols made with hands, as was done in the past— {8:19} that's why our fathers were handed over to the sword and plundered, suffering greatly before our enemies. {8:20} But we worship no other god but Him, so we hope He won't disdain us or any of our nation. {8:21} If we're captured, all Judea will be captured, and our sanctuary will be plundered; He will hold us accountable for its desecration. {8:22} The slaughter of our brethren, the captivity of the land, and the destruction of our inheritance—He will bring all this upon us among the Gentiles wherever we are enslaved; we will be an offense and a reproach to those who acquire us. {8:23} Our slavery will not gain us favor; the Lord our God will turn it to dishonor. {8:24} So let's set an example for our brethren, for their lives depend on us, and our sanctuary, temple, and altar rest upon us. {8:25} Despite everything, let's give thanks to the Lord our God, who is testing us as He did our forefathers. {8:26} Remember what He did with Abraham, how He tested Isaac, and what happened to Jacob in Mesopotamia in Syria while he tended Laban's sheep, his mother's brother. {8:27} He hasn't tried us with fire, as He did them to test their hearts, nor has He taken revenge on us; but the Lord disciplines those who draw near to Him to admonish them." {8:28} Uzziah replied, "Everything you have said comes from a true heart, and no one can deny your words. {8:29} This isn't the first time your wisdom has been evident; since the beginning of your life, everyone has recognized your understanding because your heart is right. {8:30} But the people are very thirsty, and they pressured us to do what we promised, making us take an oath we can't break. {8:31} So pray for us, since you are a devout woman, and the Lord will send us rain to fill our cisterns, and we won't be faint anymore." {8:32} Judith said, "Listen to me. I am about to do something that will be remembered through all generations. {8:33} Stand at the city gate tonight, and I will go out with my maid; and before the time you promised to surrender the city to our enemies, the Lord will deliver Israel through my hand. {8:34} But don't try to find out my plan; I won't reveal it until I've finished what I'm about to do." {8:35} Uzziah and the rulers said to her, "Go in peace, and may the Lord God go before you to take revenge on our enemies." {8:36} So they returned from her tent and went to their posts.

{9:1} Then Judith fell on her face, put ashes on her head, and removed the sackcloth she was wearing. At the same time that evening's incense was being offered in the house of God in Jerusalem, Judith cried out to the Lord with a loud voice and said, {9:2} "O Lord God of my father Simeon, to whom you gave a sword to take revenge on those who dishonored a virgin by exposing her, shaming her, and polluting her; for you said, 'It shall not be done'—yet they did it. {9:3} So you gave up their rulers to be slain and their beds, ashamed of the deceit they practiced, stained with blood. You struck down slaves alongside princes and princes on their thrones; {9:4} you gave their wives as plunder and their daughters into captivity, and all their spoils were divided among your beloved sons, who were zealous for you and abhorred the pollution of their blood, calling on you for help—O God, my God, hear me also, a widow. {9:5} For you have done these things and those that went before and those that followed; you have designed the things that are now and those to come. Yes, the things you intended came to pass, {9:6} and the things you willed presented themselves and said, 'Look, we are here'; for all their ways are prepared in advance, and your judgment is with foreknowledge. {9:7} Behold now, the Assyrians have increased in their might; they are exalted, with their horses and riders; they glory in the strength of their foot soldiers; they trust in shield and spear, in bow and sling, and do not know that you are the Lord who crushes wars; the Lord is your name. {9:8} Break their strength by your might and bring down their power in your anger; for they intend to defile your sanctuary, to pollute the tabernacle where your glorious name rests, and to cast down the horn of your altar with the sword. {9:9} Behold their pride, and send your wrath upon their heads; give me, a widow, the strength to do what I plan. {9:10} By the deceit of my lips strike down the slave with the prince and the prince with his servant; crush their arrogance by the hand of a woman. {9:11} For your power does not depend on numbers, nor your might upon men of strength; for you are God of the lowly, helper of the oppressed, upholder of the weak, protector of the forlorn, savior of those without hope. {9:12} Hear, O hear me, God of my father, God of the inheritance of Israel, Lord of heaven and earth, Creator of the waters, King of all your creation, hear my prayer! {9:13} Make my deceitful words their wound and stripe, for they have planned cruel things against your covenant, against your consecrated house, against the top of Zion, and against the house possessed by your children. {9:14} And cause your whole nation and every tribe to know and understand that you are God, the God of all power and might, and that there is no other who protects the people of Israel but you alone!"

{10:1} When Judith had finished crying out to the God of Israel and had said all these words, {10:2} she rose from where she lay prostrate, called her maid, and went down to her house where she lived on Sabbaths and feast days; {10:3} she removed the sackcloth she had been wearing, took off her widow's garments, bathed her body with water, anointed herself with precious ointment, combed her hair, put on a tiara, and dressed in her finest apparel, which she used to wear while her husband Manasseh was alive. {10:4} She put sandals on her feet, adorned herself with anklets, bracelets, rings, earrings, and all her ornaments, making herself very beautiful to entice the eyes of all men who might see her. {10:5} She gave her maid a bottle of wine and a flask of oil, filled a bag with parched grain, a cake of dried fruit, and fine bread; she wrapped up all her vessels and gave them to her maid to carry. {10:6} Then they went out to the city gate of Bethulia, where they found Uzziah standing with the elders of the city, Chabris and Charmis. {10:7} When they saw her and noticed how her face had changed and her clothing was different, they greatly admired her beauty and said to her, {10:8} "May the God of our fathers grant you favor and fulfill your plans, that the people of Israel may glory and Jerusalem may be exalted." And she worshiped God. {10:9} Then she said to them, "Order the gate of the city to be opened for me, and I will go out to accomplish the things about which you spoke with me." So they ordered the young men to open the gate for her, as she had said. {10:10} When they had done this, Judith went out with her maid; the men of the city watched her until she had gone down the mountain, passed through the valley, and could no longer be seen. {10:11} The women went straight through the valley, and an Assyrian patrol met her {10:12} and took her into custody, asking her, "To what people do you belong, where are you coming from, and where are you going?" She replied, "I am a daughter of the Hebrews, but I am fleeing from them, for they are about to be handed over to you to be devoured. {10:13} I am going to the presence of Holofernes, the commander of your army, to give him a true report; I will show him how he can capture all the hill country without losing a single man, either captured or slain." {10:14} When the men heard her words and saw her face—she was marvelously beautiful in their eyes—they said to her, {10:15} "You have saved your life by hurrying to the presence of our lord. Go at once to his tent; some of us will escort you and present you to him. {10:16} And when you stand before him, do not be afraid in your heart, but tell him exactly what you have said, and he will treat you well." {10:17} They chose a hundred men from their number to accompany her and her maid, bringing them to the tent of Holofernes. {10:18} There was great excitement throughout the camp, for her arrival was reported from tent to tent, and people came to stand around her while she waited outside Holofernes' tent, as they informed him about her. {10:19} They marveled at her beauty and admired the Israelites, judging them by her, and everyone said to his neighbor, "Who can despise these people, who have women like this among them? Surely no man among them should be left alive, for if we let them go, they will be able to ensnare the whole world!" {10:20} Then Holofernes' companions and all his servants came out and led her into the tent. {10:21} Holofernes was resting on his bed under a canopy woven with purple, gold, emeralds, and precious stones. {10:22} When they told him about her, he came forward to the front of the tent with silver lamps carried before him. {10:23} And when Judith came into his presence, he and his servants marveled at her beauty; she prostrated herself, made obeisance to him, and his slaves raised her up.

{11:1} Then Holofernes said to her, "Take courage, woman, and don't be afraid, for I have never harmed anyone who chose to serve Nebuchadnezzar, the king of all the earth. {11:2} And even now, if your people who live in the hill country hadn't slighted me, I would never have lifted my spear against them; they have brought all this on themselves. {11:3} Now tell me why you have fled from them and come over to us—since you have come to safety. {11:4} Have courage; you will live tonight and from now on. No one will harm you; everyone will treat you well, just as they do the servants of my lord King Nebuchadnezzar." {11:5} Judith replied, "Accept the words of your servant, and let your maidservant speak in your presence; I will tell nothing false to my lord tonight. {11:6} And if you follow the words of your maidservant, God will accomplish something through you, and my lord will surely achieve his purposes. {11:7} Nebuchadnezzar, the king of the whole earth, lives, and as his power endures, who has sent you to direct every living soul; not only do men serve him because of you, but also the beasts of the field, the cattle, and the birds of the air will live by your power under Nebuchadnezzar and all his house. {11:8} For we have heard of your wisdom and skill; it is reported throughout the world that you are the one good man in the whole kingdom, thoroughly informed and remarkable in military strategy. {11:9} Now regarding what Achior said in your council, we have heard his words; the men of Bethulia spared him, and he told them all he had said to you. {11:10} Therefore, my lord and master, do not disregard what he said, but keep it in mind, for it is true: our nation cannot be punished, nor can the sword prevail against them, unless they sin against their God. {11:11} Now, in order that my lord may not be defeated and his purpose frustrated, death will fall upon them, for a sin has overtaken them, which is about to provoke their God to anger when they do what is wrong. {11:12} Since their food supply is exhausted and their water is almost gone, they have planned to kill their cattle and have decided to consume all that God's laws have forbidden them to eat. {11:13} They have decided to eat the first fruits of the grain and the tithes of the wine and oil, which they consecrated and set aside for the priests who minister in the presence of our God in Jerusalem—although it is not lawful for anyone among the people to touch these things. {11:14} They have sent men to Jerusalem because even the people there have been doing this, to bring back permission from the senate. {11:15} When the word reaches them and they proceed to do this, on that very day they will be handed over to you to be destroyed. {11:16} Therefore, when I, your servant, learned all this, I fled from them; and God has sent me to accomplish amazing things with you that will astonish the whole world as many as hear about them. {11:17} For your servant is religious and serves the God of heaven day and night; therefore, my lord, I will remain with you, and every night your servant will go out into the valley and pray to God, and he will tell me when they have committed their sins. {11:18} Then I will come and tell you, and you will go out with your whole army, and not one of them will withstand you. {11:19} I will lead you through the middle of Judea until you come to Jerusalem; I will set your throne in the midst of it, and you will lead them like sheep without a shepherd; not a dog will so much as bark at you. For this has been revealed to me; I was sent to tell you." {11:20} Her words pleased Holofernes and all his servants; they marveled at her wisdom and said, {11:21} "There is no woman like this from one end of the earth to the other, either for beauty of face or wisdom of speech!" {11:22} Holofernes said to her, "God has done well to send you before the people, to lend strength to our hands and to bring destruction upon those who have slighted my lord. {11:23} You are not only beautiful in appearance but also wise in speech; if you do as you have said, your God shall be my God, and you shall live in the house of King Nebuchadnezzar and be renowned throughout the whole world."

{12:1} Then he commanded them to bring her in where his silver dishes were kept, and ordered them to set a table for her with some of his own food and serve her with his own wine. {12:2} But Judith said, "I cannot eat it, lest it be an offense; I will be provided from the things I have brought with me." {12:3} Holofernes said to her, "If your supply runs out, where can we get more like it for you? For none of your people is here with us." {12:4} Judith replied, "As your soul lives, my lord, your servant will not use up the things I have with me before the Lord carries out by my hand what he has determined to do." {12:5} Then the servants of Holofernes brought her into the tent, and she slept until midnight. Toward the morning watch, she arose {12:6} and sent for Holofernes, saying, "Let my lord now command that your servant be permitted to go out and pray." {12:7} So Holofernes commanded his guards not to hinder her. She remained in the camp for three days and went out each night to the valley of Bethulia, bathing at the spring in the camp. {12:8} When she came up from the spring, she prayed to the Lord God of Israel to direct her way for the raising up of her people. {12:9} So she returned clean and stayed in the tent until she ate her food toward evening. {12:10} On the fourth day, Holofernes held a banquet for his slave only and did not invite any of his officers. {12:11} He said to Bagoas, the eunuch who had charge of his personal affairs, "Go now and persuade the Hebrew woman in your care to join us, to eat and drink with us. {12:12} For it will be a disgrace if we let such a woman go without enjoying her company; if we do not embrace her, she will laugh at us." {12:13} So Bagoas went out from the presence of Holofernes and approached her, saying, "This beautiful maidservant should please come to my lord, be honored in his presence, drink wine, and be merry with us, becoming today like one of the daughters of the Assyrians who serve in the house of Nebuchadnezzar." {12:14} Judith replied, "Who am I to refuse my lord? Whatever pleases him I will do at once, and it will bring me joy until the day of my death!" {12:15} So she got up, dressed in all her finest attire, and her maid spread soft fleeces on the ground for her before Holofernes, which she had received from Bagoas for her daily use, so that she might recline on them when she ate. {12:16} Then Judith came in and lay down, and Holofernes' heart was captivated by her; he was filled with a strong desire to possess her, for he had been waiting for an opportunity to deceive her ever since the day he first saw her. {12:17} So Holofernes said to her, "Drink now and be merry with us!" {12:18} Judith replied, "I will drink now, my lord, because my life means more to me today than it ever has since I was born." {12:19} Then she took and ate and drank before him what her maid had prepared. {12:20} Holofernes was greatly pleased with her and drank a large quantity of wine, much more than he had ever drunk in one day since he was born.

{13:1} When evening came, Holofernes' servants quickly left, and Bagoas closed the tent from the outside, shutting out the attendants from his master's presence; they went to bed, all weary from the long banquet. {13:2} So Judith was left alone in the tent, with Holofernes stretched out on his bed, overcome with wine. {13:3} Judith had instructed her maid to stand outside the bedchamber and wait for her to come out, as she did every day, saying she would go out for her prayers. She had said the same to Bagoas. {13:4} Everyone left, and no one, whether small or great, was left in the bedchamber. Then Judith, standing beside his bed, said in her heart, "O Lord God of all might, look upon the work of my hands for the exaltation of Jerusalem at this hour. {13:5} For now is the time to help your inheritance and to carry out my plan for the destruction of the enemies who have risen against us." {13:6} She went up to the post at the end of the bed, above Holofernes' head, and took down his sword that hung there. {13:7} She approached his bed, took hold of the hair of his head, and said, "Give me strength today, O Lord God of Israel!" {13:8} Then she struck his neck twice with all her might and severed it from his body. {13:9} She tumbled his body off the bed and pulled down the canopy from the posts; after a moment, she went out and gave Holofernes' head to her maid, {13:10} who placed it in her food bag. Then the two of them went out together, as they usually did for prayer; they passed through the camp, circled around the valley, and went up the mountain to Bethulia, arriving at its gates. {13:11} Judith called out from afar to the watchmen at the gates, "Open, open the gate! God, our God, is still with us, to show his power in Israel and his strength against our enemies, just as he has done today!" {13:12} When the men of her city heard her voice, they hurried down to the city gate and called the elders together. {13:13} They all ran together, both small and great, for it was unbelievable that she had returned; they opened the gate and admitted them, kindling a fire for light and gathering around them. {13:14} Then she said to them with a loud voice, "Praise God! Praise God, who has not withdrawn his mercy from the house of Israel, but has destroyed our enemies by my hand this very night!" {13:15} She took the head out of the bag and showed it to them, saying, "See, here is the head of Holofernes, the commander of the Assyrian army, and here is the canopy beneath which he lay in his drunken stupor. The Lord struck him down by the hand of a woman. {13:16} As the Lord lives, who has protected me on my way, it was my beauty that led him to his destruction, and yet he committed no sin with me, to defile or shame me." {13:17} All the people were greatly astonished, bowed down, and worshiped God, saying in unison, "Blessed are you, our God, who has brought this day's disgrace upon the enemies of your people." {13:18} Uzziah said to her, "O daughter, you are blessed by the Most High God above all women on earth; blessed be the Lord God, who created the heavens and the earth, who has guided you to strike the head of our enemy's leader. {13:19} Your hope will never depart from the hearts of men, as they remember the power of God. {13:20} May God grant this to be an everlasting honor for you, and may he bless you, because you did not spare your own life when our nation was brought low but avenged our ruin, walking in the right path before our God." And all the people said, "So be it! So be it!"

{14:1} Then Judith said to them, "Listen to me, my brethren, take this head and hang it on the parapet (the top of a wall) of your wall. {14:2} And as soon as morning comes and the sun rises, let every brave man take his weapons and go out of the city, appointing a captain over them, as if you were going down to the plain against the Assyrian outpost; just don't go down. {14:3} They will seize their arms and enter the camp, waking the officers of the Assyrian army; they will rush into Holofernes' tent and find him missing. Then fear will seize them, and they will flee before you, {14:4} and you and all who live within the borders of Israel shall pursue them and cut them down as they flee. {14:5} But before you do all this, bring Achior the Ammonite to me, and let him see and recognize the man who despised the house of Israel and sent him to us as if to his death." {14:6} So they summoned Achior from the house of Uzziah. When he came and saw Holofernes' head in the hand of one of the men at the gathering, he fell down on his face, and his spirit failed him. {14:7} When they raised him up, he fell at Judith's feet, knelt before her, and said, "Blessed are you in every tent of Judah! In every nation, those who hear your name will be alarmed. {14:8} Now tell me what you have done during these days." Then Judith described to him in front of the people all that she had done, from the day she left until the moment she spoke to them. {14:9} When she finished, the people raised a great shout and made a joyful noise in their city. {14:10} When Achior saw all that God had done for Israel, he firmly believed in God, was circumcised, and joined the house of Israel, remaining so to this day. {14:11} At dawn, they hung Holofernes' head on the wall, and every man took his weapons, going out in groups to the mountain passes. {14:12} When the Assyrians saw them, they sent word to their commanders, who went to the generals, captains, and all their officers. {14:13} They came to Holofernes' tent and said to the steward in charge of his personal affairs, "Wake up our lord, for the slaves have been so bold as to come down against us to fight, aiming to destroy us completely." {14:14} So Bagoas went in and knocked at the door of the tent, thinking Holofernes was sleeping with Judith. {14:15} But when no one answered, he opened it and entered the bedchamber, finding him thrown down on the platform dead, with his head cut off and missing. {14:16} He cried out loudly, wept, groaned, shouted, and tore his garments. {14:17} Then he went to the tent where Judith had stayed, and when he didn't find her, he rushed out to the people, shouting, {14:18} "The slaves have tricked us! One Hebrew woman has brought disgrace upon the house of King Nebuchadnezzar! For look, here is Holofernes lying on the ground, and his head is gone!" {14:19} When the leaders of the Assyrian army heard this, they tore their tunics and were greatly dismayed, their loud cries and shouts echoing throughout the camp.

{15:1} When the men in the tents heard this, they were amazed at what had happened. {15:2} Fear and trembling came over them, and they didn't wait for one another; with one impulse, they all rushed out and fled by every path across the plain and through the hills. {15:3} Those who had camped in the hills around Bethulia also took flight. Then the soldiers of Israel rushed out against them. {15:4} Uzziah sent men to Betomasthaim, Bebai, Choba, Kola, and to all the borders of Israel to report what had happened and urge everyone to attack their enemies and destroy them. {15:5} When the Israelites heard this, they all attacked the enemy and cut them down as far as Choba. Those in Jerusalem and the surrounding hill country also joined in, having heard what had happened in the enemy's camp; those in Gilead and Galilee outflanked them with great slaughter, even beyond Damascus and its borders. {15:6} The rest of the people of Bethulia attacked the Assyrian camp and plundered it, becoming greatly enriched. {15:7} When the Israelites returned from the slaughter, they took possession of what remained, and the villages and towns in the hills and the plain gained a large amount of loot, for there was a vast quantity of it. {15:8} Then Joakim the high priest and the council of the people of Israel who lived in Jerusalem came to witness the good things the Lord had done for Israel and to see Judith and greet her. {15:9} When they met her, they all blessed her in unison, saying, "You are the exaltation of Jerusalem, the great glory of Israel, the pride of our nation! {15:10} You have accomplished all this singlehandedly; you have done great good for Israel, and God is pleased with it. May the Almighty Lord bless you forever!" And all the people said, "So be it!" {15:11} So the people plundered the camp for thirty days. They gave Judith the tent of Holofernes, along with all his silver dishes, beds, bowls, and all his furniture; she took them, loaded her mule, hitched up her carts, and piled everything on them. {15:12} Then all the women of Israel gathered to see her, blessed her, and some performed a dance for her; she took branches in her hands and gave them to the women with her; {15:13} they crowned themselves with olive wreaths, she and her companions, and she led all the women in the dance while all the men of Israel followed, bearing their arms, wearing garlands, and singing songs of celebration and praise.

{16:1} Then Judith began this thanksgiving before all Israel, and all the people sang this song of praise loudly. {16:2} And Judith said, "Begin a song to my God with tambourines; sing to my Lord with cymbals. Raise a new psalm to him; exalt him and call upon his name. {16:3} For God is the Lord who crushes wars; he has delivered me from the hands of my pursuers and brought me to his camp among the people. {16:4} The Assyrian came down from the mountains of the north with myriads of warriors; their multitude blocked the valleys, and their cavalry covered the hills. {16:5} He boasted that he would burn my territory, kill my young men with the sword, dash my infants to the ground, seize my children as prey, and take my virgins as booty. {16:6} But the Lord Almighty foiled them by the hand of a woman. {16:7} For their mighty one did not fall by the hands of young men, nor did the sons of giants smite him; but Judith, the daughter of Merari, defeated him with the beauty of her face. {16:8} She took off her widow's mourning to uplift the oppressed in Israel. She anointed her face with ointment, styled her hair with a tiara, and donned a linen gown to deceive him. {16:9} Her sandal captivated his eyes, her beauty entranced his mind, and the sword severed his neck. {16:10} The Persians trembled at her boldness, and the Medes were daunted by her daring. {16:11} Then my oppressed people shouted for joy; my weak people rejoiced, and the enemy trembled; they raised their voices, and the enemy turned back. {16:12} The sons of maidservants pierced them through; they were wounded like the children of fugitives and perished before the army of my Lord. {16:13} I will sing to my God a new song: O Lord, you are great and glorious, wonderful in strength, invincible. {16:14} Let all your creatures serve you, for you spoke, and they were created. You sent forth your Spirit, and they were formed; there is none who can resist your voice. {16:15} For the mountains will shake to their foundations with the waters; at your presence, the rocks will melt like wax, but to those who fear you, you will continue to show mercy. {16:16} For every sacrifice as a fragrant offering is small, and all fat for burnt offerings to you is little, but he who fears the Lord will be great forever. {16:17} Woe to the nations that rise against my people! The Lord Almighty will take vengeance on them on the day of judgment; fire and worms will consume their flesh; they will weep in pain forever. {16:18} When they arrived in Jerusalem, they worshiped God. Once the people were purified, they offered their burnt offerings, freewill offerings, and gifts. {16:19} Judith also dedicated to God all the vessels of Holofernes that the people had given her; and the canopy she took from his bedchamber, she gave as a votive offering to the Lord. {16:20} So the people continued feasting in Jerusalem before the sanctuary for three months, and Judith stayed with them. {16:21} After this, everyone returned home to their own inheritance, and Judith went back to Bethulia, remaining on her estate, honored throughout the land. {16:22} Many desired to marry her, but she remained a widow all the days of her life after her husband Manasseh died and was gathered to his people. {16:23} She became more famous, aging in her husband's house until she was one hundred and five years old. She set her maid free. She died in Bethulia, and they buried her in the cave of her husband Manasseh. {16:24} The house of Israel mourned for her for seven days. Before she died, she distributed her property to all her husband Manasseh's relatives and to her own nearest kin. {16:25} And no one ever again spread terror among the people of Israel during Judith's days or for a long time after her death.

The First Book of Esdras

{1:1} Josiah celebrated the Passover to the Lord in Jerusalem; he sacrificed the Passover lamb on the fourteenth day of the first month. {1:2} He arranged the priests in their divisions, dressed in their garments, in the temple of the Lord. {1:3} He instructed the Levites, the temple servants of Israel, to sanctify themselves for the Lord and to place the holy ark of the Lord in the house that Solomon, the son of David, had built. {1:4} He said, "You no longer need to carry it on your shoulders. Now worship the Lord your God and serve his people Israel. Prepare yourselves by your families and clans, {1:5} following the directions of David, king of Israel, and the grandeur of his son Solomon. Stand in the temple according to the groupings of your ancestral houses, you Levites who minister before your fellow Israelites. {1:6} Sacrifice the Passover lamb and prepare the sacrifices for your brothers, keeping the Passover according to the commandment of the Lord given through Moses." {1:7} Josiah provided thirty thousand lambs and kids and three thousand calves to the people present, taken from the king's possessions, as he promised to the people, priests, and Levites. {1:8} Hilkiah, Zechariah, and Jehiel, the chief officers of the temple, gave the priests for the Passover two thousand six hundred sheep and three hundred calves. {1:9} Jeconiah, Shemaiah, Nethanel his brother, Hashabiah, Ochiel, and Joram, the captains over thousands, gave the Levites for the Passover five thousand sheep and seven hundred calves. {1:10} This is what happened: the priests and Levites, properly dressed and with the unleavened bread, stood according to their kinship groups {1:11} and the grouping of their ancestral houses before the people, to make the offering to the Lord as written in the book of Moses; they did this in the morning. {1:12} They roasted the Passover lamb as required and boiled the sacrifices in brass pots and cauldrons, creating a pleasing aroma, {1:13} and brought them to all the people. Afterwards, they prepared the Passover for themselves and for their fellow priests, the sons of Aaron, {1:14} because the priests were offering the fat until night; so the Levites prepared it for themselves and for the priests, the sons of Aaron. {1:15} The temple singers, the sons of Asaph, were in their designated place according to the arrangement made by David, along with Asaph, Zechariah, and Eddinus, who represented the king. {1:16} The gatekeepers were at each gate; no one needed to leave their duties, for their fellow Levites prepared the Passover for them. {1:17} Thus, all the preparations for the sacrifices to the Lord were completed that day: the Passover was celebrated {1:18} and the sacrifices were offered on the altar of the Lord, following the command of King Josiah. {1:19} The people of Israel present at that time celebrated the Passover and the Feast of Unleavened Bread for seven days. {1:20} No Passover like this had been celebrated in Israel since the times of the prophet Samuel; {1:21} none of the kings of Israel had celebrated such a Passover as was celebrated by Josiah, the priests, the Levites, and the men of Judah, along with all of Israel dwelling in Jerusalem. {1:22} This Passover was held in the eighteenth year of Josiah's reign. {1:23} Josiah's actions were right in the sight of the Lord, for his heart was full of devotion. {1:24} The history of his reign details those who sinned and acted wickedly toward the Lord beyond any other people or kingdom, causing deep grief to the Lord, so that his words rose up against Israel. {1:25} After these events, Pharaoh, king of Egypt, went to make war at Carchemish on the Euphrates, and Josiah went out to confront him. {1:26} The king of Egypt sent word to him saying, "What do we have to do with each other, king of Judah? {1:27} I was not sent against you by the Lord God, for my war is at the Euphrates. Now the Lord is with me! He is urging me on! Stand aside and do not oppose the Lord." {1:28} But Josiah did not turn back from his chariot; he tried to fight him and did not heed the words of Jeremiah the prophet from the mouth of the Lord. {1:29} He engaged in battle with him in the plain of Megiddo, and the commanders came down against King Josiah. {1:30} The king said to his servants, "Take me away from the battle, for I am very weak." Immediately, his servants took him out of the line of battle. {1:31} He got into his second chariot; after he was brought back to Jerusalem, he died and was buried in the tomb of his ancestors. {1:32} All of Judah mourned for Josiah. Jeremiah the prophet lamented for him, and the leading men, along with the women, made lamentations for him to this day; it was decreed that this should always be done throughout the nation of Israel. {1:33} These events are recorded in the book of the histories of the kings of Judah; all the acts of Josiah, his splendor, his understanding of the law of the Lord, and the deeds he performed, along with these accounts, are recorded in the book of the kings of Israel and Judah. {1:34} The people of the nation appointed Jeconiah, the son of Josiah, who was twenty-three years old, and made him king in succession to his father Josiah. {1:35} He reigned for three months in Judah and Jerusalem. Then the king of Egypt deposed him from ruling in Jerusalem, {1:36} and imposed a fine on the nation of a hundred talents of silver and a talent of gold. {1:37} The king of Egypt appointed Jehoiakim, his brother, as king of Judah and Jerusalem. {1:38} Jehoiakim imprisoned the nobles, seized his brother Zarius, and brought him up from Egypt. {1:39} Jehoiakim was twenty-five years old when he began to reign in Judah and Jerusalem, and he did what was evil in the sight of the Lord. {1:40} Nebuchadnezzar, king of Babylon, came against him, bound him with a bronze chain, and took him away to Babylon. {1:41} Nebuchadnezzar also took some sacred vessels of the Lord and carried them away, storing them in his temple in Babylon. {1:42} The accounts of Jehoiakim, his uncleanness, and his wickedness are written in the chronicles of the kings. {1:43} Jehoiachin, his son, became king in his place; he was eighteen years old when he began to reign. {1:44} He reigned for three months and ten days in Jerusalem, doing what was evil in the sight of the Lord. {1:45} After a year, Nebuchadnezzar sent and removed him to Babylon along with the sacred vessels of the Lord, {1:46} and appointed Zedekiah as king of Judah and Jerusalem. {1:47} Zedekiah was twenty-one years old and reigned for eleven years. {1:48} He also did what was evil in the sight of the Lord and did not heed the words spoken by Jeremiah the prophet from the mouth of the Lord. {1:49} Although King Nebuchadnezzar had made him swear by the name of the Lord, he broke his oath and rebelled; he stiffened his neck and hardened his heart against the laws of the Lord, the God of Israel. {1:50} Even the leaders of the people and the priests committed many acts of sacrilege and lawlessness, exceeding all the unclean deeds of the nations, polluting the temple of the Lord, which had been consecrated in Jerusalem. {1:51} Therefore, the God of their ancestors sent his messengers to call them back, wishing to spare them and his dwelling place. {1:52} But they mocked his messengers, and whenever the Lord spoke, they scoffed at his prophets, {1:53} until his anger against his people arose because of their ungodly acts, commanding the kings of the Chaldeans to come against them. {1:54} They killed their young men with the sword around their holy temple, sparing neither young man nor virgin, old man nor child, for he gave them all into their hands. {1:55} They took all the holy vessels of the Lord, both great and small, and the treasure chests of the Lord, as well as the royal stores, and carried them away to Babylon. {1:56} They burned down the house of the Lord, broke down the walls of Jerusalem, and burned their towers with fire, {1:57} utterly destroying all its glorious things. The survivors he led away to Babylon with the sword, {1:58} and they became servants to him and to his sons until the Persians began to reign, fulfilling the word of the Lord spoken through Jeremiah: "Until the land has enjoyed its sabbaths, it shall keep sabbath all the time of its desolation until the completion of seventy years."

{2:1} In the first year of Cyrus, king of the Persians, so that the word of the Lord spoken through Jeremiah might be fulfilled, {2:2} the Lord stirred up the spirit of Cyrus, king of the Persians, and he made a proclamation throughout his entire kingdom and also put it in writing: {2:3} "Thus says Cyrus, king of the Persians: The Lord of Israel, the Lord Most High, has made me king of the world, {2:4} and he has commanded me to build him a house in Jerusalem, which is in Judea. {2:5} If any of you are of his people, may the Lord be with you, and let him go up to Jerusalem, which is in Judea, to build the house of the Lord of Israel—he is the Lord who dwells in Jerusalem. {2:6} And let each man, wherever he lives, be helped by the people around him with gold and silver, {2:7} with gifts, and with horses and cattle, besides other offerings for the temple of the Lord which is in Jerusalem." {2:8} Then the heads of the families from the tribes of Judah and Benjamin, along with the priests and Levites, and all whose spirits the Lord had stirred to go up to build the house in Jerusalem for the Lord, arose; {2:9} and their neighbors helped them with everything, providing silver and gold, horses and cattle, and a very large number of offerings from many whose hearts were stirred. {2:10} Cyrus the king also brought out the holy vessels of the Lord that Nebuchadnezzar had taken from Jerusalem and stored in his temple of idols. {2:11} When Cyrus, king of the Persians, brought these out, he gave them to Mithridates, his treasurer, {2:12} and through him they were given to Sheshbazzar, the governor of Judea. {2:13} The total number of these vessels was: one thousand gold cups, one thousand silver cups, twenty-nine silver censers, thirty gold bowls, two thousand four hundred and ten silver bowls, and one thousand other vessels. {2:14} All the vessels amounted to five thousand four hundred and sixty-nine, {2:15} and they were carried back by Sheshbazzar with the returning exiles from Babylon to Jerusalem. {2:16} But in the time of Artaxerxes, king of the Persians, Bishlam, Mithridates, Tabeel, Rehum, Beltethmus, Shimshai the scribe, and the rest of their associates living in Samaria and other places wrote a letter to those living in Judea and Jerusalem: {2:17} "To King Artaxerxes, our lord: Your servants Rehum the recorder, Shimshai the scribe, and the other judges of their council in Coelesyria and Phoenicia. {2:18} Now be it known to our lord the king that the Jews who came up from you to us have gone to Jerusalem and are building that rebellious and wicked city, repairing its marketplaces and walls, and laying the foundations for a temple. {2:19} Now if this city is built and the walls are finished, they will not only refuse to pay tribute but will even resist kings. {2:20} Since the building of the temple is underway, we think it best not to neglect this matter {2:21} but to inform our lord the king. If it seems good to you, please search the records of your ancestors. {2:22} You will find in the chronicles what has been written about them and learn that this city was rebellious, causing trouble for kings and other cities, {2:23} and that the Jews were rebels who kept causing blockades from ancient times. That is why this city was laid waste. {2:24} Therefore, we now inform you, O lord and king, that if this city is built and its walls finished, you will no longer have access to Coelesyria and Phoenicia." {2:25} Then the king, in reply to Rehum the recorder, Beltethmus, Shimshai the scribe, and the others associated with them living in Samaria, Syria, and Phoenicia, wrote as follows: {2:26} "I have read the letter you sent me. I ordered a search, and it has been found that this city has long fought against kings, {2:27} and that the men in it are given to rebellion and war, and that mighty and cruel kings ruled in Jerusalem and exacted tribute from Coelesyria and Phoenicia. {2:28} Therefore, I have now issued orders to prevent these men from building the city and to ensure that nothing more is done {2:29} and that such wicked actions do not continue to annoy the kings." {2:30} Then, when the letter from King Artaxerxes was read, Rehum and Shimshai the scribe and their associates hurried to Jerusalem with horsemen and a multitude in battle formation, and they began to hinder the builders. The building of the temple in Jerusalem ceased until the second year of the reign of Darius, king of the Persians.

{3:1} Now King Darius held a great banquet for everyone under his rule, including all those born in his house and all the nobles of Media and Persia, {3:2} as well as all the satraps, generals, and governors under him in the hundred and twenty-seven satrapies from India to Ethiopia. {3:3} They ate and drank, and when they were satisfied, they left; then King Darius went to his bedroom, fell asleep, and later woke up. {3:4} The three young men of the bodyguard, who were in charge of guarding the king, said to one another, {3:5} "Let each of us state what we think is the strongest thing; and to the one whose statement seems the wisest, King Darius will give rich gifts and great honors. {3:6} He will be dressed in purple, drink from gold cups, sleep on a gold bed, have a chariot with gold bridles, wear a fine linen turban, and a necklace around his neck; {3:7} because of his wisdom, he will sit next to Darius and be called a kinsman of Darius." {3:8} Then each wrote his own statement, sealed them, and placed them under the pillow of King Darius, {3:9} saying, "When the king wakes, he will be given the writings; and to the one whose statement the king and the three nobles of Persia judge to be the wisest, the victory will be awarded as written." {3:10} The first wrote, "Wine is strongest." {3:11} The second wrote, "The king is strongest." {3:12} The third wrote, "Women are strongest, but truth is victorious over all things." {3:13} When the king woke up, they took the writings and presented them to him, and he read them. {3:14} Then he sent for all the nobles of Persia and Media, along with the satraps, generals, governors, and prefects, {3:15} and took his seat in the council chamber, where the writings were read in their presence. {3:16} He said, "Call the young men, and they shall explain their statements." So they were summoned and came in. {3:17} He said to them, "Explain to us what you have written." Then the first, who had spoken of the strength of wine, began and said: {3:18} "Gentlemen, how is wine the strongest? It leads astray the minds of all who drink it. {3:19} It equalizes the thoughts of the king and the orphan, the slave and the free, the poor and the rich. {3:20} It turns every thought toward feasting and joy, making one forget all sorrow and debt. {3:21} It makes all hearts feel wealthy, forget kings and satraps, and makes everyone speak as if they have millions. {3:22} When men drink, they forget to be friendly with friends and brothers, and soon they draw their swords against each other. {3:23} And when they recover from drinking, they do not remember what they have done. {3:24} Gentlemen, is not wine the strongest, since it forces men to act this way?" After he said this, he stopped speaking.

{4:1} Then the second young man, who had spoken about the strength of the king, began to speak: {4:2} "Gentlemen, aren't men the strongest, as they rule over land and sea and everything in them? {4:3} But the king is stronger; he is their lord and master, and they obey whatever he says. {4:4} If he commands them to fight each other, they do; if he sends them against the enemy, they go and conquer mountains, walls, and towers. {4:5} They kill and are killed, never disobeying the king's command; if they achieve victory, they bring everything to the king — whatever spoils they take and everything else. {4:6} Likewise, those who don't serve in the army but till the soil, whenever they sow and reap, bring some of the harvest to the king; they compel one another to pay taxes to him. {4:7} And yet he is just one man! If he tells them to kill, they kill; if he tells them to release, they release; {4:8} if he tells them to attack, they attack; if he tells them to destroy, they destroy; if he tells them to build, they build; {4:9} if he tells them to cut down, they cut down; if he tells them to plant, they plant. {4:10} All his people and armies obey him. Moreover, he relaxes, eats, drinks, and sleeps, {4:11} while they keep watch around him, and no one may leave to tend to their own affairs, nor do they disobey him. {4:12} Gentlemen, why is the king not the strongest, given that he is obeyed in this way?" And he stopped speaking. {4:13} Then the third young man, Zerubbabel, who had spoken of women and truth, began to speak: {4:14} "Gentlemen, is not the king great, and are not men numerous, and is not wine strong? Who then is their master, or their lord? Is it not women? {4:15} Women gave birth to the king and to every people that rules over land and sea. {4:16} From women they came; and women raised the very men who plant the vineyards from which wine comes. {4:17} Women make men's clothes; they bring men glory; men cannot exist without women. {4:18} If men gather gold and silver or any other beautiful things, and then see a woman lovely in appearance, {4:19} they abandon all those things, gazing at her with open mouths, preferring her to gold or silver or any other beautiful thing. {4:20} A man leaves his own father, who raised him, and his own country, and clings to his wife. {4:21} With his wife, he spends his days, forgetting his father or mother or country. {4:22} Therefore, you must realize that women rule over you! {4:23} Do you not labor and toil, bringing everything to give to women? {4:24} A man takes his sword and goes out to travel, rob, steal, and sail the seas and rivers; {4:25} he faces lions and walks in darkness, and when he steals and plunders, he brings it back to the woman he loves. {4:26} A man loves his wife more than his father or mother. {4:27} Many men have lost their minds because of women and have become their slaves. {4:28} Many have perished, stumbled, or sinned because of women. {4:29} And now, do you not believe me? {4:30} Is not the king great in his power? Do not all lands fear to touch him? {4:31} Yet I have seen him with Apame, the king's concubine, the daughter of the illustrious Bartacus; she would sit at the king's right hand {4:32} and take the crown from the king's head, put it on her own, and slap the king with her left hand. {4:33} At this, the king would gaze at her with mouth agape. If she smiles at him, he laughs; if she gets angry with him, he flatters her to win her back. {4:34} Gentlemen, why are not women strong, since they do such things?" {4:35} Then the king and the nobles looked at one another, and he began to speak about truth: {4:36} "Gentlemen, are not women strong? The earth is vast, and heaven is high, and the sun moves swiftly in its course, making the circuit of the heavens and returning to its place in one day. {4:37} Is he not great who does these things? But truth is great and stronger than all things. {4:38} The whole earth calls upon truth, and heaven blesses her. All of God's works quake and tremble, and with him, there is nothing unrighteous. {4:39} Wine is unrighteous, the king is unrighteous, women are unrighteous, all the sons of men are unrighteous, all their works are unrighteous, and there is no truth in them; in their unrighteousness, they will perish. {4:40} But truth endures and is strong forever, living and prevailing forever and ever. {4:41} With her, there is no partiality or preference; she does what is righteous instead of anything unrighteous or wicked. All men approve her deeds, {4:42} and there is nothing unrighteous in her judgment. To her belongs strength, kingship, power, and majesty for all ages. Blessed be the God of truth!" {4:43} He ceased speaking, and then all the people shouted, "Great is truth, and strongest of all!" {4:44} Then the king said to him, "Ask what you wish, even beyond what is written, and we will give it to you, for you have been found to be the wisest. And you shall sit next to me, and be called my kinsman." {4:45} Then he said to the king, "Remember the vow you made to build Jerusalem when you became king, {4:46} and to return all the vessels taken from Jerusalem, which Cyrus set apart when he began to destroy Babylon and vowed to send them back. {4:47} You also vowed to build the temple, which the Edomites burned when Judea was laid waste by the Chaldeans. {4:48} And now, O lord the king, this is what I ask and request of you, and this suits your greatness. I pray, therefore, that you fulfill the vow you promised to the King of heaven with your own lips." {4:49} Then King Darius rose, kissed him, and wrote letters for him to all the treasurers, governors, generals, and satraps, instructing them to provide an escort for him and everyone going with him to build Jerusalem. {4:50} He also wrote letters to all the governors in Coelesyria and Phoenicia and those in Lebanon, to bring cedar timber from Lebanon to Jerusalem, and to assist him in building the city. {4:51} He wrote for all the Jews who were going up from his kingdom to Judea, for their freedom, that no officer, satrap, governor, or treasurer should forcibly enter their doors; {4:52} that all the land they would occupy should be theirs without tribute; that the Idumeans should give up the villages of the Jews which they held; {4:53} that twenty talents a year should be given for the building of the temple until it was completed, {4:54} and an additional ten talents a year for daily burnt offerings on the altar, in accordance with the commandment to make seventeen offerings; {4:55} and that all who came from Babylonia to build the city should have their freedom, they and their children, and all the priests who came. {4:56} He also wrote concerning their support and the garments for the priests in which they were to minister. {4:57} He wrote that support for the Levites should be provided until the day the temple is finished and Jerusalem is built. {4:58} He wrote that land and wages should be provided for all who guard the city. {4:59} And he sent back from Babylon all the vessels which Cyrus had set apart; everything Cyrus had ordered to be done, he also commanded to be done and sent to Jerusalem. {4:60} When the young man left, he lifted his face to heaven toward Jerusalem, and praised the King of heaven, saying, {4:61} "From you is the victory; from you is wisdom, and yours is the glory. I am your servant. {4:62} Blessed are you, who have given me wisdom; I give you thanks, O Lord of our fathers." {4:63} So he took the letters and went to Babylon, telling all this to his brethren. {4:64} And they praised the God of their fathers because he had given them release and permission {4:65} to go up and build Jerusalem and the temple called by his name; and they feasted, with music and rejoicing, for seven days.

{5:1} After this, the leaders of the families were chosen to go up, along with their tribes, wives, sons, daughters, and their servants and livestock. {5:2} Darius sent with them a thousand horsemen to ensure their safe return to Jerusalem, accompanied by the sound of drums and flutes; {5:3} and all their relatives celebrated. He made them travel together. {5:4} Here are the names of the men who went up, according to their family groups in the tribes: {5:5} the priests, the sons of Phinehas, son of Aaron; Jeshua son of Jozadak, son of Seraiah, and Joakim son of Zerubbabel, son of Shealtiel, from the house of David, of the lineage of Phares, from the tribe of Judah, {5:6} who spoke wise words before Darius, the king of the Persians, in the second year of his reign, in the month of Nisan, the first month. {5:7} These are the men of Judea who returned from their captivity, whom Nebuchadnezzar, king of Babylon, had taken away to Babylon {5:8} and who returned to Jerusalem and the rest of Judea, each to his own town. They came with Zerubbabel and Jeshua, Nehemiah, Seraiah, Resaiah, Bigvai, Mordecai, Bilshan, Mispar, Reeliah, Rehum, and Baanah, their leaders. {5:9} The number of the men of the nation and their leaders: the sons of Parosh, two thousand one hundred and seventy-two. The sons of Shephatiah, four hundred and seventy-two. {5:10} The sons of Arah, seven hundred and fifty-six. {5:11} The sons of Pahathmoab, of the sons of Jeshua and Joab, two thousand eight hundred and twelve. {5:12} The sons of Elam, one thousand two hundred and fifty-four. The sons of Zattu, nine hundred and forty-five. The sons of Chorbe, seven hundred and five. The sons of Bani, six hundred and forty-eight. {5:13} The sons of Bebai, six hundred and twenty-three. The sons of Azgad, one thousand three hundred and twenty-two. {5:14} The sons of Adonikam, six hundred and sixty-seven. The sons of Bigvai, two thousand and sixty-six. The sons of Adin, four hundred and fifty-four. {5:15} The sons of Ater, namely of Hezekiah, ninety-two. The sons of Kilan and Azetas, sixty-seven. The sons of Azaru, four hundred and thirty-two. {5:16} The sons of Annias, one hundred and one. The sons of Arom. The sons of Bezai, three hundred and twenty-three. The sons of Jorah, one hundred and twelve. {5:17} The sons of Baiterus, three thousand and five. The sons of Bethlehem, one hundred and twenty-three. {5:18} The men of Netophah, fifty-five. The men of Anathoth, one hundred and fifty-eight. The men of Bethasmoth, forty-two. {5:19} The men of Kiriatharim, twenty-five. The men of Chephirah and Beeroth, seven hundred and forty-three. {5:20} The Chadiasans and Ammidians, four hundred and twenty-two. The men of Ramah and Geba, six hundred and twenty-one. {5:21} The men of Michmas, one hundred and twenty-two. The men of Bethel, fifty-two. The sons of Magbish, one hundred and fifty-six. {5:22} The sons of the other Elam and Ono, seven hundred and twenty-five. The sons of Jericho, three hundred and forty-five. {5:23} The sons of Senaah, three thousand three hundred and thirty. {5:24} The priests: the sons of Jedaiah, son of Jeshua, of the sons of Anasib, nine hundred and seventy-two. The sons of Immer, one thousand and fifty-two. {5:25} The sons of Pashhur, one thousand two hundred and forty-seven. The sons of Harim, one thousand and seventeen. {5:26} The Levites: the sons of Jeshua and Kadmiel, along with Bannas and Sudias, seventy-four. {5:27} The temple singers: the sons of Asaph, one hundred and twenty-eight. {5:28} The gatekeepers: the sons of Shallum, the sons of Ater, the sons of Talmon, the sons of Akkub, the sons of Hatita, the sons of Shobai, totaling one hundred and thirty-nine. {5:29} The temple servants: the sons of Ziha, the sons of Hasupha, the sons of Tabbaoth, the sons of Keros, the sons of Siaha, the sons of Padon, the sons of Lebanah, the sons of Hagabah, {5:30} the sons of Akkub, the sons of Uthai, the sons of Ketab, the sons of Hagab, the sons of Shamlai, the sons of Hana, the sons of Cathua, the sons of Gahar, {5:31} the sons of Reaiah, the sons of Rezin, the sons of Nekoda, the sons of Chezib, the sons of Gazzam, the sons of Uzza, the sons of Paseah, the sons of Hasrah, the sons of Besai, the sons of Asnah, the sons of the Meunites, the sons of Nephisim, the sons of Bakbuk, the sons of Hakupha, the sons of Asur, the sons of Pharakim, the sons of Bazluth, {5:32} the sons of Mehida, the sons of Cutha, the sons of Charea, the sons of Barkos, the sons of Sisera, the sons of Temah, the sons of Neziah, the sons of Hatipha. {5:33} The sons of Solomon's servants: the sons of Hassophereth, the sons of Peruda, the sons of Jaalah, the sons of Lozon, the sons of Giddel, the sons of Shephatiah, {5:34} the sons of Hattil, the sons of Pochereth-hazzebaim, the sons of Sarothie, the sons of Masiah, the sons of Gas, the sons of Addus, the sons of Subas, the sons of Apherra, the sons of Barodis, the sons of Shaphat, the sons of Ami. {5:35} All the temple servants and the sons of Solomon's servants numbered three hundred and seventy-two. {5:36} The following came up from Telmelah and Telharsha, led by Cherub, Addan, and Immer, {5:37} though they could not prove their lineage or family connections to Israel: the sons of Delaiah, son of Tobiah, and the sons of Nekoda, six hundred and fifty-two. {5:38} Among the priests, the following had taken on the priesthood but were not found registered: the sons of Habaiah, the sons of Hakkoz, the sons of Jaddus, who married Agia, one of the daughters of Barzillai, and was known by his name. {5:39} When their genealogy was sought in the records and not found, they were excluded from serving as priests. {5:40} Nehemiah and Attharias told them not to participate in the holy things until a high priest should appear wearing the Urim and Thummim (sacred objects for divination). {5:41} All the Israelites, twelve or older, excluding servants, totaled forty-two thousand three hundred and sixty; {5:42} their servants were seven thousand three hundred and thirty-seven; there were two hundred and forty-five musicians and singers. {5:43} They had four hundred and thirty-five camels, seven thousand and thirty-six horses, two hundred and forty-five mules, and five thousand five hundred and twenty-five donkeys. {5:44} Some heads of families, upon arriving at the temple of God in Jerusalem, vowed to rebuild the house on its site to the best of their ability, {5:45} and pledged to contribute to the sacred treasury for the work: a thousand minas of gold, five thousand minas of silver, and one hundred priests' garments. {5:46} The priests, the Levites, and some of the people settled in Jerusalem and its vicinity; the temple singers, the gatekeepers, and all Israel settled in their towns. {5:47} When the seventh month arrived, and the sons of Israel were each in their own homes, they gathered as one in the square before the east gate. {5:48} Then Jeshua son of Jozadak, with his fellow priests, and Zerubbabel son of Shealtiel, with his relatives, took their places and prepared the altar of the God of Israel, {5:49} to offer burnt offerings upon it, as directed in the book of Moses, the man of God. {5:50} Some from the surrounding peoples joined them. They set up the altar in its place, for all the peoples of the land were hostile to them and stronger; they offered sacrifices at the proper times and burnt offerings to the Lord morning and evening. {5:51} They observed the feast of booths, as commanded in the law, offering the proper sacrifices every day, {5:52} and continued with the regular offerings on sabbaths, new moons, and all consecrated feasts. {5:53} All who had made any vow to God began to offer sacrifices starting from the new moon of the seventh month, even though the temple of God was not yet built. {5:54} They provided money to the masons and carpenters, and food, drink, and carts to the Sidonians and Tyrians to bring cedar logs from Lebanon and transport them to the harbor of Joppa, as per the written decree from Cyrus, king of the Persians. {5:55} In the second year after their arrival at the temple of God in Jerusalem, in the second month, Zerubbabel son of Shealtiel and Jeshua son of Jozadak began, along with their brothers and the Levitical priests, and all who had returned from captivity to Jerusalem; {5:56} they laid the foundation of the temple of God on the new moon of the second month in the second year after their arrival in Judea and Jerusalem. {5:57} They appointed Levites aged twenty and older to oversee the work of the Lord. Jeshua, along with his sons and brothers, and Kadmiel and his brothers, and all the Levites, united to advance the work on the house of God. {5:58} So the builders worked on the temple of the Lord. {5:59} The priests were dressed in their garments, with musical instruments and trumpets, while the Levites, the sons of Asaph, played cymbals, {5:60} praising the Lord and blessing Him, following the directions of David, king of Israel; {5:61} they sang hymns, giving thanks to the Lord, for His goodness and glory are everlasting upon all Israel. {5:62} The people sounded trumpets and shouted with a great shout, praising the Lord for the building of the house of the Lord. {5:63} Some of the Levitical priests and heads of families, old men who had seen the former house, wept loudly at the construction of this one, {5:64} while many rejoiced with trumpets and a joyful noise, {5:65} so that the people could not hear the trumpets because of the weeping. For the noise of the trumpets was loud enough to be heard from afar; {5:66} when the enemies of Judah and Benjamin heard it, they came to find out what the noise meant. {5:67} They discovered that those who had returned from captivity were building the temple for the Lord God of Israel. {5:68} So they approached Zerubbabel and Jeshua and the heads of the families and said to them, "We will build with you, {5:69} for we worship your God just as you do and have been sacrificing to Him since the days of Esarhaddon, king of the Assyrians, who brought us here." {5:70} But Zerubbabel, Jeshua, and the heads of the families in Israel replied, "You have no part with us in building the house for the Lord our God; {5:71} we alone will build it for the Lord of Israel, as Cyrus, king of the Persians, has commanded us." {5:72} Yet the peoples of the land pressured those in Judea, cut off their supplies, and hindered their building; {5:73} through plots, demagoguery, and uprisings, they prevented the completion of the building during the entire reign of King Cyrus. And they were kept from building for two years, until the reign of Darius.

{6:1} In the second year of Darius's reign, the prophets Haggai and Zechariah, son of Iddo, prophesied to the Jews in Judea and Jerusalem, speaking in the name of the Lord God of Israel. {6:2} Then Zerubbabel son of Shealtiel and Jeshua son of Jozadak got up and began to build the house of the Lord in Jerusalem, supported by the prophets of the Lord who were with them. {6:3} At the same time, Sisinnes, the governor of Syria and Phoenicia, along with Sathrabuzanes and their associates, approached them and asked, {6:4} "By whose authority are you building this house and this roof, and who are the builders completing this work?" {6:5} However, the elders of the Jews were treated kindly, because the Lord was overseeing the captives; {6:6} they were not stopped from building until word could be sent to Darius regarding their situation and a report made. {6:7} A copy of the letter sent to Darius by Sisinnes, the governor of Syria and Phoenicia, Sathrabuzanes, and their associates, the local rulers in Syria and Phoenicia, read: {6:8} "To King Darius, greetings. Let it be known to our lord the king that when we went to the land of Judea and entered Jerusalem, we found the elders of the Jews who had been in captivity, {6:9} building a great new house for the Lord in Jerusalem, made of hewn stone and with costly timber used in the walls. {6:10} This work is progressing rapidly and is being completed with great care and attention. {6:11} We asked these elders, 'Under whose command are you building this house and laying its foundations?' {6:12} To inform you in writing who the leaders are, we questioned them and asked for a list of their leaders' names. {6:13} They answered us, 'We are the servants of the Lord who made the heavens and the earth. {6:14} A long time ago, a great and powerful king of Israel built this house, and it was completed. {6:15} But when our ancestors sinned against the Lord of Israel in heaven and provoked Him, He handed them over to Nebuchadnezzar, king of Babylon, the Chaldean; {6:16} they destroyed the house, burned it down, and took the people captive to Babylon. {6:17} However, in the first year of Cyrus's reign over Babylon, King Cyrus decreed that this house should be rebuilt. {6:18} The holy vessels of gold and silver that Nebuchadnezzar had taken from the house in Jerusalem and stored in his own temple, Cyrus ordered to be taken out from the temple in Babylon and returned to Zerubbabel and Sheshbazzar, the governor, {6:19} with instructions to bring all these vessels back and place them in the temple in Jerusalem, and to rebuild the temple of the Lord on its original site. {6:20} Then Sheshbazzar came here and laid the foundations of the house of the Lord in Jerusalem, and although it has been under construction since then, it is still not finished.' {6:21} Therefore, if it seems wise, O king, let a search be conducted in the royal archives of our lord the king in Babylon; {6:22} if it is found that the rebuilding of the house of the Lord in Jerusalem was done with King Cyrus's consent, and if our lord the king approves, let him send us instructions regarding this matter." {6:23} Then Darius commanded a search of the royal archives in Babylon, and in Ecbatana, the fortress in Media, a scroll was found containing this record: {6:24} "In the first year of Cyrus, King Cyrus ordered the building of the house of the Lord in Jerusalem, where they sacrifice with perpetual fire; {6:25} its height to be sixty cubits and its width to be sixty cubits, with three rows of hewn stone and one row of new timber, the cost to be paid from the treasury of King Cyrus; {6:26} and that the holy vessels of the house of the Lord, both gold and silver, which Nebuchadnezzar took from the house in Jerusalem and carried to Babylon, should be restored to the house in Jerusalem, to be placed where they were." {6:27} So Darius commanded Sisinnes, the governor of Syria and Phoenicia, Sathrabuzanes, and their associates, the local rulers in Syria and Phoenicia, to stay away from the site, allowing Zerubbabel, the servant of the Lord and governor of Judea, and the elders of the Jews to build the house of the Lord at its original location. {6:28} "And I command that it be fully built, and that every effort be made to assist the men who have returned from captivity in Judea until the house of the Lord is finished; {6:29} and that a portion from the tribute of Coelesyria and Phoenicia be diligently given to these men, that is, to Zerubbabel the governor, for sacrifices to the Lord, including bulls, rams, and lambs, {6:30} as well as wheat, salt, wine, and oil, regularly each year, without delay, for daily use as indicated by the priests in Jerusalem, {6:31} so that offerings may be made to the Most High God for the king and his children, and prayers may be offered for their well-being." {6:32} And he commanded that if anyone should violate or disregard any of the things written here, a beam should be taken from his house and he should be hanged on it, and his property forfeited to the king. {6:33} "Therefore, may the Lord, whose name is invoked there, destroy every king and nation that stretches out its hand to hinder or damage that house of the Lord in Jerusalem. {6:34} "I, King Darius, have decreed that this be done with all diligence as prescribed here."

{7:1} Then Sisinnes, the governor of Coelesyria and Phoenicia, along with Sathrabuzanes and their associates, followed the orders of King Darius, {7:2} supervising the holy work with great care, assisting the elders of the Jews and the chief officers of the temple. {7:3} The holy work prospered while the prophets Haggai and Zechariah were prophesying; {7:4} and they completed it by the command of the Lord God of Israel. So with the approval of Cyrus, Darius, and Artaxerxes, kings of Persia, {7:5} the holy house was finished on the twenty-third day of the month of Adar, in the sixth year of King Darius. {7:6} The people of Israel, the priests, the Levites, and the others from the captivity who joined them, acted according to what was written in the book of Moses. {7:7} They offered at the dedication of the temple of the Lord one hundred bulls, two hundred rams, four hundred lambs, {7:8} and twelve male goats for the sin offering of all Israel, corresponding to the number of the twelve leaders of the tribes of Israel. {7:9} The priests and Levites stood in their garments, organized by their families, for the services of the Lord God of Israel, as described in the book of Moses, and the gatekeepers were stationed at each gate. {7:10} The people of Israel who returned from captivity celebrated Passover on the fourteenth day of the first month, after the priests and Levites had purified themselves together. {7:11} Not all of the returned captives were purified, but all the Levites were purified together, {7:12} and they sacrificed the Passover lamb for all the returned captives, for their fellow priests, and for themselves. {7:13} The people of Israel who returned from captivity ate it, all those who had separated themselves from the detestable practices of the surrounding peoples and sought the Lord. {7:14} They celebrated the Feast of Unleavened Bread for seven days, rejoicing before the Lord, {7:15} because He had changed the attitude of the king of the Assyrians toward them, strengthening their hands for the service of the Lord God of Israel.

{8:1} After these events, when Artaxerxes was king of Persia, Ezra came, the son of Seraiah, the son of Azariah, the son of Hilkiah, the son of Shallum, {8:2} the son of Zadok, the son of Ahitub, the son of Amariah, the son of Uzzi, the son of Bukki, the son of Abishua, the son of Phineas, the son of Eleazar, the son of Aaron, the chief priest. {8:3} This Ezra came up from Babylon as a scribe skilled in the law of Moses, which was given by the God of Israel; {8:4} and the king honored him, for Ezra found favor with the king in all his requests. {8:5} Some of the people of Israel, along with some priests, Levites, temple singers, gatekeepers, and temple servants, came up with him to Jerusalem, {8:6} in the seventh year of King Artaxerxes, in the fifth month (this was the king's seventh year); they left Babylon on the new moon of the first month and arrived in Jerusalem on the new moon of the fifth month, thanks to the prosperous journey the Lord granted them. {8:7} Ezra had great knowledge, omitting nothing from the law of the Lord or the commandments, teaching all Israel the ordinances and judgments. {8:8} The following is a copy of the written commission from Artaxerxes, the king, delivered to Ezra the priest and reader of the law of the Lord: {8:9} "King Artaxerxes to Ezra the priest and reader of the law of the Lord, greetings. {8:10} According to my gracious decision, I have ordered that those of the Jewish nation, including priests, Levites, and others in our realm, who wish to do so, may go with you to Jerusalem. {8:11} Let as many as are inclined depart with you, as I and my seven counselors have decided, {8:12} to look into matters in Judea and Jerusalem, in accordance with the law of the Lord, {8:13} and to carry to Jerusalem the gifts for the Lord of Israel, which I and my friends have vowed, and to collect all the gold and silver found in Babylonia for the Lord's temple in Jerusalem, {8:14} including what the nation gives for their Lord's temple—gold and silver for bulls, rams, lambs, and what accompanies them— {8:15} to offer sacrifices on the altar of their Lord in Jerusalem. {8:16} Whatever you and your brethren decide to do with the gold and silver, do so according to the will of your God; {8:17} and deliver the holy vessels of the Lord given to you for the temple of your God in Jerusalem. {8:18} Whatever else you find necessary for the temple of your God may be provided from the royal treasury. {8:19} "I, King Artaxerxes, have commanded the treasurers of Syria and Phoenicia to ensure that whatever Ezra the priest and reader of the law of the Most High God requests, they shall provide for him, {8:20} up to a hundred talents of silver, a hundred cors (about 6,000 liters) of wheat, a hundred baths (about 600 liters) of wine, and abundant salt. {8:21} Let all things prescribed in the law of God be carefully fulfilled for the Most High God, so that His wrath may not come upon the kingdom and upon my sons. {8:22} You are also informed that no tribute or tax shall be imposed on any priests, Levites, temple singers, gatekeepers, temple servants, or anyone employed in this temple, and no one has the authority to tax them. {8:23} "You, Ezra, according to the wisdom of your God, appoint judges and justices to judge all those who know the law of your God throughout Syria and Phoenicia; teach those who do not know it. {8:24} All who transgress the law of your God or the law of the kingdom shall be strictly punished, whether by death, fine, or imprisonment." {8:25} Blessed be the Lord alone, who put this in the heart of the king to glorify His house in Jerusalem, {8:26} and who honored me in the sight of the king, his counselors, and all his friends and nobles. {8:27} I was encouraged by the help of the

Lord my God, and I gathered men from Israel to go up with me. {8:28} These are the principal men from their families and groups who went up with me from Babylon in the reign of King Artaxerxes: {8:29} Of the sons of Phineas, Gershom. Of the sons of Ithamar, Gamael. Of the sons of David, Hattush the son of Shecaniah. {8:30} Of the sons of Parosh, Zechariah, with one hundred and fifty men enrolled. {8:31} Of the sons of Pahathmoab, Eliehoenai the son of Zerahiah, with two hundred men. {8:32} Of the sons of Zattu, Shecaniah the son of Jahaziel, with three hundred men. Of the sons of Adin, Obed the son of Jonathan, with two hundred and fifty men. {8:33} Of the sons of Elam, Jeshaiah the son of Gotholiah, with seventy men. {8:34} Of the sons of Shephatiah, Zeraiah the son of Michael, with seventy men, {8:35} Of the sons of Joab, Obadiah the son of Jehiel, with two hundred and twelve men. {8:36} Of the sons of Bani, Shelomith the son of Josiphiah, with one hundred and sixty men. {8:37} Of the sons of Bebai, Zechariah the son of Bebai, with twenty-eight men. {8:38} Of the sons of Azgad, Johanan the son of Hakkatan, with one hundred and ten men. {8:39} Of the sons of Adonikam, the last ones, whose names are Eliphelet, Jeuel, and Shemaiah, with seventy men. {8:40} Of the sons of Bigvai, Uthai the son of Istalcurus, with seventy men. {8:41} I assembled them at the river called Theras, where we camped for three days, and I inspected them. {8:42} When I found no sons of priests or Levites there, {8:43} I sent word to Eliezar, Iduel, Maasmas, {8:44} Elnathan, Shemaiah, Jarib, Nathan, Elnathan, Zechariah, and Meshullam, leaders and men of understanding; {8:45} and I told them to go to Iddo, the leading man at the place of the treasury, {8:46} and ordered them to ask Iddo and his brethren, the treasurers at that place, to send us men to serve as priests in the house of our Lord. {8:47} By the mighty hand of our Lord, they brought us competent men from the sons of Mahli, the son of Levi, the son of Israel, namely Sherebiah with his sons and kinsmen, eighteen; {8:48} also Hashabiah and Jeshaiah his brother, of the sons of Hananiah, and their sons, twenty men; {8:49} and of the temple servants, whom David and the leaders had given for the service of the Levites, two hundred and twenty temple servants; their names were reported. {8:50} I proclaimed a fast for the young men before our Lord, to seek from Him a prosperous journey for ourselves, our children, and the cattle with us. {8:51} For I was ashamed to ask the king for foot soldiers, horsemen, or an escort to keep us safe from our adversaries; {8:52} for we had said to the king, "The power of our Lord will be with those who seek Him and support them in every way." {8:53} Again we prayed to our Lord about these matters, and we found Him very merciful. {8:54} Then I set apart twelve leaders of the priests, Sherebiah and Hashabiah, and ten of their kinsmen with them; {8:55} and I weighed out to them the silver, gold, and holy vessels for the house of our Lord, which the king, his counselors, nobles, and all Israel had given. {8:56} I weighed and gave them six hundred and fifty talents of silver, silver vessels worth a hundred talents, and a hundred talents of gold, {8:57} and twenty golden bowls and twelve bronze vessels of fine bronze that glimmered like gold. {8:58} I said to them, "You are holy to the Lord, and the vessels are holy, and the silver and gold are vowed to the Lord, the Lord of our fathers. {8:59} Be watchful and guard them until you deliver them to the leaders of the priests, Levites, and heads of the families of Israel in Jerusalem, in the chambers of the house of our Lord." {8:60} So the priests and Levites who took the silver, gold, and vessels from Jerusalem carried them to the temple of the Lord. {8:61} We departed from the river Theras on the twelfth day of the first month and arrived in Jerusalem by the mighty hand of our Lord upon us; He delivered us from every enemy along the way, and we came to Jerusalem. {8:62} After three days, the silver and gold were weighed and delivered in the house of our Lord to Meremoth the priest, son of Uriah; {8:63} with him were Eleazar the son of Phinehas and Jozabad the son of Jeshua, and Moeth the son of Binnui, the Levites. {8:64} Everything was counted and weighed, and the total weight was recorded at that very time. {8:65} Those who returned from captivity offered sacrifices to the Lord, the God of Israel: twelve bulls for all Israel, ninety-six rams, seventy-two lambs, and as a thank offering, twelve male goats—all as sacrifices to the Lord. {8:66} They delivered the king's orders to the royal stewards and to the governors of Coelesyria and Phoenicia, and these officials honored the people and the temple of the Lord. {8:67} After these things, the principal men came to me and said, {8:68} "The people of Israel, the leaders, priests, and Levites have not separated themselves from the surrounding peoples and their practices—the Canaanites, Hittites, Perizzites, Jebusites, Moabites, Egyptians, and Edomites. {8:69} They and their sons have married the daughters of these people, and the holy race has mixed with the surrounding peoples; the leaders and nobles have been sharing in this wrongdoing since the beginning." {8:70} As soon as I heard these things, I tore my garments and holy mantle, pulled out hair from my head and beard, and sat down in anxiety and grief. {8:71} All who were moved by the word of the Lord of Israel gathered around me, mourning over this wrongdoing, and I sat grief-stricken until the evening sacrifice. {8:72} Then I rose from my fast, with my garments and holy mantle torn, and kneeling down, stretching out my hands to the Lord, {8:73} I said, "O Lord, I am ashamed and confused before You. {8:74} Our sins have risen higher than our heads, and our mistakes have reached up to heaven {8:75} since the times of our fathers, and we are in great sin to this day. {8:76} Because of our sins and the sins of our fathers, we, along with our brethren, kings, and priests, have been given over to the kings of the earth, to the sword, captivity, and plundering, in shame until now. {8:77} Now, however, mercy has come to us from You, O Lord, leaving us a root and a name in Your holy place, {8:78} shining a light for us in the house of the Lord our God, and providing food in our servitude. {8:79} Even in our bondage, we were not forsaken by our Lord; He brought us into favor with the kings of Persia, so they have given us food and glorified the temple of our Lord, and restored Zion from desolation, giving us a stronghold in Judea and Jerusalem. {8:80} "And now, O Lord, what shall we say about these matters? For we have transgressed Your commandments, which You gave through Your servants the prophets, saying, {8:81} 'The land you are entering to possess is polluted by the detestable practices of the surrounding peoples, who have filled it with their uncleanness. {8:82} Therefore, do not give your daughters in marriage to their sons, and do not take their daughters for your sons; {8:83} and do not seek peace with them, so you may be strong, eat the good things of the land, and leave it as an inheritance for your children forever.' {8:84} All that has happened to us is due to our evil deeds and great sins. For You, O Lord, lifted the burden of our sins {8:85} and gave us a root like this; yet we turned back to transgress Your law by mixing with the uncleanness of the peoples of the land. {8:86} Were You not angry enough with us to destroy us without leaving a root, seed, or name? {8:87} O Lord of Israel, You are true; we are left as a root to this day. {8:88} Behold, we are now before You in our iniquities; we can no longer stand in Your presence because of these matters." {8:89} While Ezra was praying, confessing, weeping, and lying on the ground before the temple, a large crowd gathered from Jerusalem, men, women, and youths; there was great weeping among the multitude. {8:90} Then Shecaniah, the son of Jehiel, one of the men of Israel, called out and said to Ezra, "We have sinned against the Lord and married foreign women from the surrounding peoples; but even now there is hope for Israel. {8:91} Let us take an oath to the Lord about this, that we will put away all our foreign wives and their children, as seems good to you and all who obey the law of the Lord. {8:92} Arise and take action, for it is your task, and we are with you to take strong measures." {8:93} Then Ezra arose and had the leaders of the priests and Levites of all Israel take an oath that they would do this. And they took the oath.

{9:1} After this, Ezra rose and went from the temple court to the chamber of Jehohanan, the son of Eliashib, {9:2} and spent the night there, not eating bread or drinking water, because he was mourning over the great sins of the people. {9:3} A proclamation was made throughout Judea and Jerusalem to all who had returned from captivity, calling them to assemble in Jerusalem, {9:4} and warning that anyone who did not come within two or three days, as decided by the leaders, would have their cattle seized for sacrifice, and they themselves would be expelled from the group of those who had returned from captivity. {9:5} The men of the tribes of Judah and Benjamin assembled in Jerusalem within three days; this was on the twentieth day of the ninth month. {9:6} The entire assembly sat in the open square before the temple, shivering from the cold weather. {9:7} Ezra stood up and said to them, "You have broken the law by marrying foreign women, which has increased the sin of Israel. {9:8} Now make confession and give glory to the Lord, the God of our ancestors, {9:9} and do His will; separate yourselves from the peoples of the land and from your foreign wives." {9:10} The whole assembly responded loudly, saying, "We will do as you have said. {9:11} But the crowd is large and it is winter; we cannot stand in the open air. This is not something we can resolve in a day or two, because we have sinned greatly in this matter. {9:12} So let the leaders stay, and let all those in our towns with foreign wives come at the appointed time, {9:13} along with the elders and judges from each place, until we are free from the Lord's anger regarding this issue." {9:14} Jonathan, the son of Asahel, and Jahzeiah, the son of Tikvah, took on this responsibility, with Meshullam and Levi and Shabbethai serving as judges alongside them. {9:15} The returned exiles followed this plan. {9:16} Ezra the priest selected men from the heads of their families, all of them by name; and on the new moon of the tenth month, they began their sessions to investigate the matter. {9:17} By the new moon of the first month, they completed reviewing the cases of men who had foreign wives. {9:18} Among the priests, those found to have foreign wives were: {9:19} Jeshua, the son of Jozadak, and his brothers Maaseiah, Eliezar, Jarib, and Jodan. {9:20} They agreed to put away their wives and to offer rams as restitution for their wrongdoing. {9:21} Of the sons of Immer: Hanani, Zebadiah, Maaseiah, Shemaiah, Jehiel, and Azariah. {9:22} Of the sons of Pashhur: Elioenai, Maaseiah, Ishmael, Nathanael, Gedaliah, and Elasah. {9:23} Of the Levites: Jozabad, Shimei, Kelaiah (who was also called Kelita), Pethahiah, Judah, and Jonah. {9:24} Of the temple singers: Eliashib and Zaccur. {9:25} Of the gatekeepers: Shallum and Telem. {9:26} Of Israel, from the sons of Parosh: Ramiah, Izziah, Malchijah, Mijamin, Eleazar, Asibias, and Benaiah. {9:27} Of the sons of Elam: Mattaniah, Zechariah, Jehiel, Abdi, Jeremoth, and Elijah. {9:28} Of the sons of Zattu: Elioenai, Eliashib, Othoniah, Jeremoth, Zabad, and Zerdaiah. {9:29} Of the sons of Bebai: Jehohanan, Hananiah, Zabbai, and Emathis. {9:30} Of the sons of Bani: Meshullam, Malluch, Adaiah, Jashub, Sheal, and Jeremoth. {9:31} Of the sons of Addi: Naathus, Moossias, Laccunus, Naidus, Bescaspasmys, Sesthel, Belnuus, and Manasseas. {9:32} Of the sons of Annan: Elionas, Asaias, Melchias, Sabbaias, and Simon Chosamaeus. {9:33} Of the sons of Hashum: Mattenai, Mattattah, Zabad, Eliphelet, Manasseh, and Shimei. {9:34} Of the sons of Bani: Jeremai, Maadai, Amram, Joel, Mamdai, Bedeiah, Vaniah, Carabasion, Eliashib, Machnadebai, Eliasis, Binnui, Elialis, Shimei, Shelemiah, and Nethaniah. Of the sons of Ezora: Shashai, Azarel, Azael, Shemaiah, Amariah, and Joseph. {9:35} Of the sons of Nebo: Mattithiah, Zabad, Iddo, Joel, and Benaiah. {9:36} All these had married foreign women, and they put them away along with their children. {9:37} The priests, Levites, and the men of Israel settled in Jerusalem and in the surrounding area. On the new moon of the seventh month, when the sons of Israel were in their towns, {9:38} the entire assembly gathered with one accord in the open square before the east gate of the temple; {9:39} they told Ezra, the chief priest and reader of the law, to bring the law of Moses that the Lord God of Israel had given. {9:40} So Ezra the chief priest brought the law before the assembly, both men and women, as well as all the priests, to hear the law on the new moon of the seventh month. {9:41} He read aloud in the open square before the temple gate from early morning until midday, and the people paid attention to the reading of the law. {9:42} Ezra stood on a wooden platform that had been prepared for this purpose; {9:43} beside him stood Mattathiah, Shema, Anaiah, Azariah, Uriah, Hezekiah, and Baalsamus on his right, {9:44} and on his left were Pedaiah, Mishael, Malchijah, Lothasubus, Nabariah, and Zechariah. {9:45} Ezra took up the book of the law in the sight of the crowd, for he was in a place of honor before all. {9:46} When he opened the law, everyone stood up. Ezra blessed the Lord, the God Most High, the Almighty; {9:47} and all the people answered, "Amen." They lifted their hands, fell to the ground, and worshiped the Lord. {9:48} Jeshua, Anniuth, Sherebiah, Jamin, Akkub, Shabbethai, Hodiah, Maaseiah, Kelita, Azariah, Jozabad, Hanan, and Pelaiah, the Levites, explained the law to the people. {9:49} Then Attharates said to Ezra the chief priest, the Levites who were teaching the crowd, and everyone, {9:50} "This day is holy to the Lord"—they were all weeping as they heard the law— {9:51} "so go, eat rich food, drink sweet drinks, and share with those who have none; {9:52} for this day is holy to the Lord; do not be sad, for the Lord will lift you up." {9:53} The Levites urged all the people, saying, "This day is holy; do not be sad." {9:54} So they all went away to eat, drink, and enjoy themselves, sharing portions with those who had none, and celebrating greatly, {9:55} because they were inspired by the words they had been taught. They gathered together.

The Second Book of Esdras

{1:1} This is the second book of the prophet Ezra, son of Seraiah, son of Azariah, son of Hilkiah, son of Shallum, son of Zadok, son of Ahitub, {1:2} son of Ahijah, son of Phinehas, son of Eli, son of Amariah, son of Azariah, son of Meraioth, son of Arna, son of Uzzi, son of Borith, son of Abishua, son of Phinehas, son of Eleazar, {1:3} son of Aaron, from the tribe of Levi, who was a captive in the land of the Medes during the reign of Artaxerxes, king of the Persians. {1:4} The word of the Lord came to me, saying, {1:5} "Go and tell my people about their evil deeds, and inform their children about the wrongs they have committed against me, so they can pass this on to their children's children {1:6} that the sins of their parents have been passed down to them, for they have forgotten me and offered sacrifices to foreign gods. {1:7} Was it not I who brought them out of Egypt, out of slavery? But they have angered me and rejected my guidance. {1:8} Shave your head and throw the evils upon them, for they have not obeyed my law—they are a rebellious people. {1:9} How long must I endure them, when I have given them so many blessings? {1:10} For their sake, I have overthrown many kings: I struck down Pharaoh and his servants and all his army. {1:11} I have destroyed all nations before them and scattered the people of two provinces, Tyre and Sidon, to the east; I have defeated all their enemies. {1:12} "But speak to them and say, Thus says the Lord: {1:13} It was I who brought you through the sea and made safe paths for you where there were none; I gave you Moses as a leader and Aaron as a priest; {1:14} I provided light for you from a pillar of fire and did great wonders among you. Yet you have forgotten me, says the Lord. {1:15} "Thus says the Lord Almighty: The quails were a sign for you; I gave you camps for your protection, and yet you complained in them. {1:16} You did not celebrate my name when I destroyed your enemies, but to this day you still complain. {1:17} Where are the blessings I gave you? When you were hungry and thirsty in the wilderness, did you not cry out to me, {1:18} saying, 'Why have you led us into this wilderness to die? It would have been better for us to serve the Egyptians than to die here.' {1:19} I heard your cries and gave you manna to eat; you ate the bread of angels. {1:20} When you were thirsty, did I not split the rock so that water flowed abundantly? Because of the heat, I shaded you with the leaves of trees. {1:21} I divided fertile lands among you; I drove out the Canaanites, the Perizzites, and the Philistines before you. What more can I do for you? says the Lord. {1:22} "Thus says the Lord Almighty: When you were in the wilderness at the bitter stream, thirsty and speaking against my name, {1:23} I did not send fire upon you for your blasphemy but threw a tree into the water and made the stream sweet. {1:24} "What should I do to you, O Jacob? You would not obey me, O Judah. I will turn to other nations and give them my name, so they may keep my statutes. {1:25} Because you have forsaken me, I will also forsake you. When you plead for mercy, I will show you no mercy. {1:26} When you call on me, I will not listen to you; for you have stained your hands with blood and are quick to commit murder. {1:27} It is not that you have abandoned me; you have abandoned yourselves, says the Lord. {1:28} "Thus says the Lord Almighty: Have I not treated you as a father treats his sons or a mother her daughters or a nurse her children, {1:29} so that you should be my people and I should be your God, and you should be my sons and I should be your father? {1:30} I gathered you as a hen gathers her chicks under her wings. But now, what should I do to you? I will cast you out of my presence. {1:31} When you bring offerings to me, I will turn my face away from you; I have rejected your feasts, new moons, and physical circumcisions. {1:32} I sent my prophets to you, but you killed them and tore their bodies apart; I will hold you accountable for their blood, says the Lord. {1:33} "Thus says the Lord Almighty: Your house is desolate; I will drive you out as the wind drives away straw; {1:34} and your sons will be childless because they have neglected my commandments and done what is evil in my sight. {1:35} I will give your homes to a people who will come, who, without hearing me, will believe. Those who have seen no signs will do what I command. {1:36} They have seen no prophets, yet they will remember their former state. {1:37} I call to witness the gratitude of the people to come, whose children will rejoice with gladness; though they do not see me with their eyes, yet with their spirit, they will believe the things I have said. {1:38} "And now, Father, look with pride and see the people coming from the east; {1:39} to them I will give leaders like Abraham, Isaac, and Jacob, and Hosea, Amos, Micah, Joel, Obadiah, Jonah, {1:40} Nahum, Habakkuk, Zephaniah, Haggai, Zechariah, and Malachi, who is also called the messenger of the Lord.

{2:1} "Thus says the Lord: I brought this people out of slavery, and I gave them commandments through my servants the prophets; but they wouldn't listen to them and made my guidance meaningless. {2:2} Their mother says to them, 'Go, my children, because I am a widow and forsaken. {2:3} I raised you with joy, but now I mourn and sorrow because I have lost you, since you have sinned against the Lord God and done what is wrong in my sight. {2:4} But now, what can I do for you? For I am a widow and forsaken. Go, my children, and seek mercy from the Lord.' {2:5} I call upon you, Father, to witness along with the mother of the children, because they would not keep my covenant, {2:6} so that you may bring confusion upon them and cause their mother to suffer, so that they may have no offspring. {2:7} Let them be scattered among the nations; let their names be erased from the earth, because they have despised my covenant. {2:8} "Woe to you, Assyria, who hide the wicked among you! O wicked nation, remember what I did to Sodom and Gomorrah, {2:9} whose land lies in heaps of pitch and ash. I will do the same to those who have not listened to me, says the Lord Almighty." {2:10} Thus says the Lord to Ezra: "Tell my people that I will give them the kingdom of Jerusalem, which I intended for Israel. {2:11} Furthermore, I will reclaim their glory and give to others the everlasting homes that I had prepared for Israel. {2:12} The tree of life will give them sweet fragrance, and they will neither toil nor grow weary. {2:13} Ask, and you will receive; pray that your days may be few and shortened. The kingdom is already prepared for you; watch! {2:14} Call upon heaven and earth to witness, for I removed evil and created good, because I live, says the Lord. {2:15} "Mother, embrace your children; raise them with joy, like a dove; establish their feet, for I have chosen you, says the Lord. {2:16} I will raise the dead from their graves and bring them out, because I recognize my name in them. {2:17} Do not fear, mother of sons, for I have chosen you, says the Lord. {2:18} I will send you help, my servants Isaiah and Jeremiah. According to their counsel, I have prepared for you twelve trees filled with various fruits, {2:19} and the same number of springs flowing with milk and honey, and seven mighty mountains where roses and lilies grow; through these, I will fill your children with joy. {2:20} Protect the rights of the widow, secure justice for the fatherless, give to the needy, defend the orphan, clothe the naked, {2:21} care for the injured and the weak, do not mock a lame person, protect the maimed, and let the blind see my splendor. {2:22} Protect the old and the young within your walls; {2:23} when you find anyone who is dead, bury them and mark the grave, and I will grant you the first place in my resurrection. {2:24} Pause and be quiet, my people, for your rest will come. {2:25} Good nurse, nourish your sons and strengthen their feet. {2:26} Not one of the servants I have given you will perish, for I will hold you accountable for them. {2:27} Do not worry, for when the day of trouble and anguish comes, others will weep and mourn, but you will rejoice and have plenty. {2:28} The nations will envy you, but they will not be able to harm you, says the Lord. {2:29} My hands will protect you, so your sons will not see Gehenna (hell). {2:30} Rejoice, O mother, with your sons, for I will deliver you, says the Lord. {2:31} Remember your sleeping sons, for I will bring them out of the earth's hiding places and show them mercy; for I am merciful, says the Lord Almighty. {2:32} Embrace your children until I come, and proclaim mercy to them; for my springs overflow, and my grace will not fail." {2:33} I, Ezra, received a command from the Lord on Mount Horeb to go to Israel. When I arrived, they rejected me and turned away from the Lord's command. {2:34} Therefore, I say to you, O nations that hear and understand, "Await your shepherd; he will give you everlasting rest, for he who is to come at the end of the age is near. {2:35} Be ready for the rewards of the kingdom, for the eternal light will shine upon you forever. {2:36} Flee from the shadows of this age, and receive the joy of your glory; I publicly call on my Savior as a witness. {2:37} Accept what the Lord has given you and be joyful, thanking him who has called you to heavenly kingdoms. {2:38} Rise and stand, and see at the Lord's feast the number of those who have been sealed. {2:39} Those who have departed from the shadows of this age have received glorious garments from the Lord. {2:40} Take again your full number, O Zion, and conclude the list of your people who are clothed in white, who have fulfilled the law of the Lord. {2:41} The number of your children, whom you desired, is complete; ask the Lord for the power that your people, who were called from the beginning, may be made holy." {2:42} I, Ezra, saw on Mount Zion a great multitude, which I could not count, and they were all praising the Lord with songs. {2:43} In their midst was a young man of great height, taller than any of the others, and on the head of each he placed a crown, but he was exalted above them all. I was captivated. {2:44} Then I asked an angel, "Who are these, my lord?" {2:45} He answered, "These are they who have put off mortal clothing and put on the immortal, and they have confessed the name of God; now they are being crowned and receiving palms." {2:46} Then I said to the angel, "Who is that young man who places crowns on them and gives palms in their hands?" {2:47} He replied, "He is the Son of God, whom they confessed in the world." So I began to praise those who had stood bravely for the name of the Lord. {2:48} Then the angel said to me, "Go, tell my people how great and numerous are the wonders of the Lord God that you have seen."

{3:1} In the thirtieth year after the destruction of our city, I, Salathiel, also known as Ezra, was in Babylon. I was troubled as I lay on my bed, and my thoughts stirred in my heart, {3:2} because I saw the desolation of Zion and the wealth of those living in Babylon. {3:3} My spirit was deeply agitated, and I began to speak anxious words to the Most High, saying, {3:4} "O sovereign Lord, did you not speak at the beginning when you formed the earth without help, and commanded the dust {3:5} so it produced Adam, a lifeless body? Yet he was your creation, and you breathed life into him, making him alive in your presence. {3:6} You led him into the garden that your right hand had planted before the earth existed. {3:7} You gave him one commandment, but he broke it, and immediately you appointed death for him and his descendants. From him arose nations, tribes, peoples, and clans without number. {3:8} Every nation acted on its own will, did ungodly things before you, and scorned you, yet you did not stop them. {3:9} Again, in due time, you brought a flood upon the inhabitants of the world and destroyed them. {3:10} They faced the same fate: as death came upon Adam, so did the flood upon them. {3:11} But you spared one of them, Noah, along with his household, and all the righteous who descended from him. {3:12} "As those who lived on earth began to multiply, they had children and formed many nations, but once again they became more ungodly than their ancestors. {3:13} When they committed iniquity before you, you chose one of them, named Abraham; {3:14} you loved him and revealed to him the end of times secretly by night. {3:15} You made an everlasting covenant with him, promising never to forsake his descendants; you gave him Isaac, and to Isaac you gave Jacob and Esau. {3:16} You set Jacob apart for yourself, but rejected Esau; Jacob became a great multitude. {3:17} When you led his descendants out of Egypt, you brought them to Mount Sinai. {3:18} You bent down the heavens, shook the earth, moved the world, made the depths tremble, and troubled the times. {3:19} Your glory passed through the four gates of fire, earthquake, wind, and ice to give the law to the descendants of Jacob and your commandments to the posterity of Israel. {3:20} "Yet you did not remove their evil hearts, so that your law might bear fruit in them. {3:21} The first Adam, burdened with an evil heart, transgressed and was overcome, as were all his descendants. {3:22} Thus, the disease became permanent; the law remained in the people's hearts alongside the evil root, while what was good departed, leaving only the evil. {3:23} Time passed, and the years were completed, and you raised up a servant named David. {3:24} You commanded him to build a city for your name and to offer you offerings from what is yours. {3:25} This continued for many years, but the inhabitants of the city transgressed, {3:26} doing everything as Adam and his descendants had done, for they too had evil hearts. {3:27} So you delivered the city into the hands of your enemies. {3:28} "Then I thought, Are the deeds of those who live in Babylon any better? Is that why she has gained control over Zion? {3:29} For when I arrived here, I saw countless ungodly deeds, and my soul witnessed many sinners during these thirty years. My heart failed me, {3:30} for I have seen how you endure those who sin, spare the wicked, destroy your people, and preserve your enemies, {3:31} and you have not shown anyone how your ways can be understood. Are the deeds of Babylon better than those of Zion? {3:32} Has another nation known you besides Israel? What tribes have believed your covenants as these tribes of Jacob? {3:33} Yet their reward has not appeared, and their labor has borne no fruit. I have traveled widely among the nations and seen them abound in wealth, though they ignore your commandments. {3:34} Now, therefore, weigh our iniquities against those of the inhabitants of the world; then it will be clear which way the scale will tip. {3:35} When have the inhabitants of the earth not sinned in your sight? What nation has kept your commandments so well? {3:36} You might find individual men who have obeyed your commandments, but you will not find nations."

{4:1} Then the angel sent to me, whose name was Uriel, answered {4:2} and said, "Your understanding has completely failed regarding this world, and do you think you can comprehend the way of the Most High?" {4:3} I replied, "Yes, my lord." He continued, "I have been sent to show you three ways and present three problems to you. {4:4} If you can solve one of them for me, I will show you the way you desire to see and teach you why the heart is evil." {4:5} I said, "Speak on, my lord." He instructed me, "Go, weigh the weight of fire for me, measure a measure of wind for me, or call back the day that has passed." {4:6} I responded, "Who among those born can do what you ask regarding these things?" {4:7} He replied, "If I had asked you how many dwellings are in the heart of the sea, how many streams are at the source of the deep, how many streams are above the firmament, or what the exits of hell are, or the entrances of paradise, {4:8} perhaps you would have said to me, 'I never went down into the deep, nor into hell, nor have I ever ascended into heaven.' {4:9} But now I have asked you only about fire, wind, and the day—things you have experienced and without which you cannot exist—and you have given me no answer!" {4:10} He said to me, "You cannot understand the things you have grown up with; {4:11} how then can your mind comprehend the way of the Most High? How can one who is worn out by this corrupt world understand incorruption?" When I heard this, I fell on my face {4:12} and said to him, "It would be better for us not to exist than to come here, live in ungodliness, and suffer without understanding why." {4:13} He answered, "I went into a forest of trees in the plain, and they made a plan {4:14} and said, 'Come, let us go to war against the sea so it will recede before us, allowing us to create more forests.' {4:15} Likewise, the waves of the sea made a plan and said, 'Come, let us go up and subdue the forest so we can also gain more territory for ourselves.' {4:16} But the forest's plan was in vain, for the fire came and consumed it; {4:17} similarly, the sea's plan failed, for the sand stood firm and stopped them. {4:18} If you were a judge between them, which would you justify, and which would you condemn?" {4:19} I answered, "Both made foolish plans, for land is assigned to the forest, and the sea has its place to carry its waves." {4:20} He responded, "You have judged rightly, but why have you not judged your own case the same way? {4:21} Just as the land is assigned to the forest and the sea to its waves, those dwelling on earth can only understand earthly matters, while He who is above the heavens understands what is above the heavens." {4:22} Then I replied, "I beg you, my lord, why have I been given the power to understand? {4:23} I did not wish to inquire about heavenly matters, but about what we experience daily: why Israel has been handed over to the Gentiles as a reproach; why the people you love have been given to godless tribes, and why our fathers' law has been made ineffective, with written covenants no longer existing; {4:24} and why we pass from this world like locusts, our lives like a mist, unworthy of mercy. {4:25} But what will He do for His name, by which we are called? These are the things I have asked about." {4:26} He answered, "If you are alive, you will see, and if you live long, you will often marvel, for the age is swiftly nearing its end. {4:27} It will not be able to deliver the promises made to the righteous at their appointed times, because this age is full of sadness and weakness. {4:28} The evil you inquire about has been sown, but the harvest has not yet come. {4:29} If what has been sown is not reaped, and if the place where the evil was sown does not pass away, the field where good has been sown will not come to fruition. {4:30} For a grain of evil seed was sown in Adam's heart from the beginning, and look at how much ungodliness it has produced until now and will produce until the time of harvest! {4:31} Consider how much fruit of ungodliness a grain of evil seed can produce. {4:32} When countless grains are sown, how great will the threshing floor be!" {4:33} Then I asked, "How long and when will these things happen? Why are our years few and filled with evil?" {4:34} He replied, "You do not move faster than the Most High; your haste is for yourself, but the Highest hastens on behalf of many. {4:35} Did not the souls of the righteous in their chambers ask these matters, saying, 'How long will we remain here? When will our reward be harvested?' {4:36} Jeremiel, the archangel, answered them, saying, 'When the number of those like yourselves is completed; for He has weighed the age in the balance, {4:37} measured times by measure, and numbered times by number; He will not move or arouse them until that measure is fulfilled.'" {4:38} Then I replied, "O sovereign Lord, but we are all filled with ungodliness. {4:39} Perhaps it is because of us that the time of harvest is delayed for the righteous—because of the sins of those dwelling on earth." {4:40} He answered, "Go and ask a woman who is pregnant if, when her nine months are completed, her womb can hold the child any longer." {4:41} I said, "No, lord, it cannot." {4:42} He continued, "In Hades, the chambers of souls are like a womb. {4:43} Just as a woman in labor hurries to escape the pains of childbirth, so do these places hurry to return what was committed to them from the beginning. {4:44} Then the things you desire to see will be revealed to you." {4:45} I answered, "If I have found favor in your sight, and if possible, and if I am worthy, {4:46} show me this too: will there be more time to come than has passed, or has the greater part already gone by? {4:47} For I know what has passed, but I do not know what is to come." {4:48} He said to me, "Stand at my right side, and I will show you the interpretation of a parable." {4:49} So I stood and looked, and behold, a flaming furnace passed by before me; when the flame had passed, I looked, and behold, the smoke remained. {4:50} After this, a cloud full of water passed before me and poured down a heavy and violent rain; when the rainstorm had passed, drops remained in the cloud. {4:51} He said, "Consider it for yourself; just as rain is more than drops and fire is greater than smoke, the quantity that passed was much greater; yet only drops and smoke remain." {4:52} Then I prayed and said, "Do you think I will live to see those days? Or who will be alive then?" {4:53} He answered, "About the signs you ask, I can tell you in part; but I was not sent to tell you about your life, for I do not know."

{5:1} "Now regarding the signs: look, the days are coming when those living on earth will be filled with great fear, the way of truth will be hidden, and the land will lack faith. {5:2} Unrighteousness will increase beyond what you see or have heard about before. {5:3} The land you see ruling now will become waste and untrodden, and people will see it as desolate. {5:4} But if the Most High allows you to live, you will see it thrown into confusion after the third period; the sun will suddenly shine at night, and the moon during the day. {5:5} Blood will drip from wood, and stones will speak; people will be troubled, and stars will fall. {5:6} Someone will reign whom those on earth do not expect, and the birds will fly away together; {5:7} the sea of Sodom will cast up fish; someone unknown to many will make his voice heard at night, and everyone will hear him. {5:8} There will be chaos in many places, fires will break out often, wild animals will roam beyond their usual habitats, and menstruating women will give birth to monsters. {5:9} Saltwater will be found in fresh, and friends will betray one another; then reason will hide itself, and wisdom will retreat into seclusion, {5:10} sought by many but not found, and unrighteousness and lawlessness will increase on earth. {5:11} One nation will ask its neighbor, 'Has righteousness or anyone who does right passed through you?' and it will answer, 'No.' {5:12} At that time, men will hope but not obtain; they will work hard, but their efforts will not succeed. {5:13} These are the signs I am allowed to tell you, and if you pray again, weep as you do now, and fast for seven days, you will hear even greater things than these." {5:14} Then I woke up, my body shuddered violently, and my soul was so troubled that I fainted. {5:15} But the angel who had come and talked with me held me, strengthened me, and set me on my feet. {5:16} On the second night, Phaltiel, a leader of the people, came to me and asked, "Where have you been? Why is your face sad? {5:17} Don't you know that Israel has been entrusted to you in their land of exile? {5:18} So rise and eat some bread, so that you do not abandon us like a shepherd who leaves his flock in the hands of cruel wolves." {5:19} I replied, "Leave me alone and do not come near me for seven days; then you may come back." He heard me and left. {5:20} So I fasted for seven days, mourning and weeping as Uriel the angel had commanded. {5:21} After seven days, my heart was once again filled with grief. {5:22} Then my soul regained the spirit of understanding, and I began to speak in the presence of the Most High. {5:23} I said, "O sovereign Lord, from every forest of the earth and from all its trees, you have chosen one vine, {5:24} and from all the lands of the world, you have chosen one region for yourself; from all the flowers of the world, you have chosen one lily, {5:25} and from all the depths of the sea, you have filled for yourself one river; from all the cities built, you have consecrated Zion for yourself, {5:26} and from all the birds created, you have named one dove for yourself, and from all the flocks made, you have provided one sheep for yourself, {5:27} and from all the multitude of peoples, you have obtained one people; and to this people, whom you love, you have given the law approved by all. {5:28} And now, O Lord, why have you given the one to the many, dishonored the one root beyond the others, and scattered your only one among the many? {5:29} Those opposing your promises have trampled down those who believe your covenants. {5:30} If you truly hate your people, they should be punished at your own hands." {5:31} After I spoke these words, the angel who had come to me previously was sent to me again, {5:32} and he said, "Listen to me, and I will instruct you; pay attention, and I will tell you more." {5:33} I said, "Speak, my lord." He asked, "Are you greatly disturbed about Israel? Do you love him more than his Maker does?" {5:34} I replied, "No, my lord, but my grief has led me to speak; I suffer agonies of heart every hour as I strive to understand the way of the Most High and search out part of his judgment." {5:35} He said to me, "You cannot." I asked, "Why not, my lord? Why was I born? Why didn't my mother's womb become my grave, so I would not see the suffering of Jacob and the exhaustion of the people of Israel?" {5:36} He answered, "Count for me those who have not yet come, gather the scattered raindrops, and make the withered flowers bloom again for me; {5:37} open for me the closed chambers, bring forth for me the winds trapped in them, or show me the picture of a voice; then I will explain to you the suffering you seek to understand." {5:38} I said, "O sovereign Lord, who can know these things except one whose dwelling is not with men? {5:39} I am without wisdom; how can I speak about what you have asked?" {5:40} He replied, "Just as you cannot do any of the things I mentioned, you cannot discover my judgment or the goal of the love I have promised my people." {5:41} I said, "Yet behold, O Lord, you have charge of those alive at the end, but what about those who were before us, or we, or those who come after us?" {5:42} He said, "I will liken my judgment to a circle; just as there is no delay for those who are last, so there is no haste for those who are first." {5:43} I replied, "Could you not have created at one time those who have been, those who are, and those who will be, to show your judgment sooner?" {5:44} He responded, "Creation cannot hasten faster than the Creator, nor can the world hold at one time those who have been created in it." {5:45} I said, "How can you say to your servant that you will give life to your creation at one time? If all creatures will live at once, the creation should be able to support all of them at the same time." {5:46} He answered, "Ask a woman's womb, and say to it, 'If you bear ten children, why one after another? Request it to produce ten at once.' {5:47} I said, "Of course it cannot; only each in its own time." {5:48} He replied, "So I have given the womb of the earth to those who are sown in it from time to time. {5:49} Just as an infant does not give birth, and an elderly woman does not give birth any longer, so have I organized the world I created." {5:50} I asked, "Since you have given me the opportunity, let me speak before you. Is our mother, of whom you spoke, still young? Or is she now nearing old age?" {5:51} He replied, "Ask a woman who bears children, and she will tell you. {5:52} Ask her, 'Why are those born recently not like those born before, but smaller in stature?' {5:53} She will answer, 'Those born in youth are different from those born in old age, when the womb is failing.' {5:54} Therefore, consider that you and your contemporaries are smaller in stature than those before you, {5:55} and those who come after you will be smaller than you, as they are born from a creation that is aging and losing the strength of youth." {5:56} I said, "O Lord, I beg you, if I have found favor in your sight, show your servant through whom you visit your creation."

{6:1} "He said to me, 'At the beginning of the circle of the earth, before the portals of the world were set in place, before the winds were assembled and began to blow, {6:2} before the sounds of thunder were heard, before the flashes of lightning lit up the sky, and before the foundations of paradise were laid, {6:3} before beautiful flowers appeared, before the powers of movement were established, and before the countless hosts of angels were gathered, {6:4} before the heights of the air were lifted up, before the measures of the firmaments were named, and before the footstool of Zion was established, {6:5} before the current years were counted; before the imaginations of those who now sin were estranged, and before those who stored treasures of faith were sealed— {6:6} I planned these things, and they were made through me and not through another, just as the end will come through me and not through another.' {6:7} I answered, 'What will be the division of the times? When will the first age end and the age that follows begin?' {6:8} He said to me, 'From Abraham to Isaac, because from him were born Jacob and Esau, for Jacob's hand held Esau's heel from the beginning. {6:9} Esau is the end of this age, and Jacob is the beginning of the age that follows. {6:10} The beginning of a man is his hand, and the end of a man is his heel; between the heel and the hand, do not seek anything else, Ezra!' {6:11} I replied, 'O sovereign Lord, if I have found favor in your sight, {6:12} show your servant the end of your signs that you showed me in part on a previous night.' {6:13} He answered, 'Rise to your feet and you will hear a full, resounding voice. {6:14} If the place where you are standing shakes greatly while the voice is speaking, do not be afraid, for the word concerns the end, and the foundations of the earth will understand {6:15} that the speech concerns them. They will tremble and shake, for they know their end must be changed.' {6:16} When I heard this, I rose to my feet and listened, and behold, a voice was speaking, sounding like many waters. {6:17} It said, 'Behold, the days are coming when I will draw near to visit the inhabitants of the earth, {6:18} when I will require the penalty for the iniquity of the doers of wickedness, when the humiliation of Zion is complete, {6:19} and when the seal is placed upon the age about to pass away. Then I will show these signs: the books shall be opened before the firmament, and all will see it together. {6:20} Infants a year old will speak with their voices, and pregnant women will give birth prematurely at three and four months, and these will live and dance. {6:21} Unsown fields will suddenly produce crops, and full storehouses will suddenly be found empty; {6:22} the trumpet will sound loudly, and when everyone hears it, they will be terrified. {6:23} At that time, friends will make war on friends like enemies, and the earth and its inhabitants will be terrified, and the springs of the fountains will stand still, flowing not for three hours. {6:24} Whoever remains after all I have foretold will be saved and will see my salvation and the end of my world. {6:25} They will see the men who were taken up, who from birth have never tasted death; and the hearts of the earth's inhabitants will be changed and transformed into a different spirit. {6:26} Evil will be blotted out, and deceit will be quenched; {6:27} faithfulness will flourish, and corruption will be overcome, and the truth, which has long been without fruit, will be revealed.' {6:28} While he spoke to me, little by little, the place where I was standing began to rock to and fro. {6:29} He said to me, 'I have come to show you these things tonight. {6:30} If you will pray again and fast for seven days, I will again declare to you greater things than these, {6:31} for your voice has surely been heard before the Most High; the Mighty One has seen your uprightness and has observed the purity you have maintained from your youth. {6:32} Therefore, He sent me to show you all these things and to say to you: "Believe and do not be afraid! {6:33} Do not hastily think vain thoughts about the former times, lest you be quick concerning the last times."' {6:34} After this, I wept again and fasted seven days as before, to complete the three weeks as I had been told. {6:35} On the eighth night, my heart was troubled within me again, and I began to speak in the presence of the Most High. {6:36} For my spirit was greatly stirred, and my soul was in distress. {6:37} I said, 'O Lord, you spoke at the beginning of creation, saying on the first day, "Let heaven and earth be made," and your word accomplished the work. {6:38} Then your Spirit was hovering, and darkness and silence embraced everything; the sound of man's voice was not yet there. {6:39} Then you commanded that a ray of light be brought forth from your treasuries, so that your works might appear. {6:40} Again, on the second day, you created the spirit of the firmament and commanded him to divide and separate the waters, so that one part might move upward and the other remain below. {6:41} On the third day, you commanded the waters to be gathered together in the seventh part of the earth; six parts you dried up to be planted, cultivated, and be of service before you. {6:42} Your word went forth, and immediately the work was done. {6:43} Fruit came forth in endless abundance, varied in taste; flowers of inimitable color, and odors of inexpressible fragrance were made on the third day. {6:44} On the fourth day, you commanded the brightness of the sun, the light of the moon, and the arrangement of the stars to come into being; {6:45} and you commanded them to serve man, who was about to be formed. {6:46} On the fifth day, you commanded the seventh part where the waters had been gathered to bring forth living creatures, birds, and fishes; and so it was done. {6:47} The lifeless water produced living creatures as commanded, so that the nations might declare your wondrous works. {6:48} Then you maintained two living creatures; one you called Behemoth and the other Leviathan. {6:49} You separated one from the other, for the seventh part where the water had been gathered could not hold them both. {6:50} You gave Behemoth one of the parts which had been dried up on the third day to live in, where there are a thousand mountains; {6:51} but to Leviathan, you gave the seventh part, the watery part; and you have kept them to be eaten by whom and when you will. {6:52} On the sixth day, you commanded the earth to bring forth cattle, beasts, and creeping things; {6:53} and over these, you placed Adam as ruler over all the works you had made; and from him, we have all come, the people you have chosen. {6:54} All this I have spoken before you, O Lord, because you said it was for us that you created this world. {6:55} As for the other nations descended from Adam, you said they are nothing, like spittle, and compared their abundance to a drop from a bucket. {6:56} And now, O Lord, behold, these nations, which are regarded as nothing, dominate us and devour us. {6:57} But we, your people, whom you have called your firstborn, only begotten, zealous for you and most dear, have been given into their hands. {6:58} If the world has indeed been created for us, why do we not possess our world as an inheritance? How long will this be so?'"

{7:1} After I finished speaking, the angel who had come to me on previous nights returned and said, "Get up, Ezra, and pay attention to what I'm about to say." {7:2} I replied, "Speak, my lord." He continued, "There's a vast sea, expansive and wide, {7:3} but it has a narrow entrance, almost like a river. {7:4} If someone wants to reach the sea, to see it or navigate through it, how can they do so without passing through the narrow entrance? {7:5} Here's another example: There's a city built on a plain, filled with all good things; {7:6} but the entrance to it is narrow and precarious, with fire on one side and deep water on the other; {7:7} there's only one path between them, so that only one person can walk that way at a time. {7:8} If this city is given to someone as an inheritance, how can the heir claim it without passing through the dangers ahead?" {7:9} I replied, "They can't, my lord." He said, "Just like that is Israel's portion. {7:10} I created the world for their sake, and when Adam broke my laws, the world was judged. {7:11} Because of this, the entrances of this world became narrow, full of sorrow and toil; they are few and filled with dangers and hardships. {7:12} But the entrances to the greater world are broad and safe, leading to eternal life. {7:13} Therefore, unless the living go through difficult and fleeting experiences, they cannot receive what is reserved for them. {7:14} But why are you troubled, thinking you will perish? And why are you anxious about being mortal? {7:15} Why don't you consider what is to come instead of what is present?" {7:16} I replied, "Lord, you have ordained that the righteous will inherit these things, while the ungodly will perish. {7:17} The righteous can endure hardships while hoping for better times; but the wicked have already suffered and will not see the good." {7:18} He said, "You are not a better judge than God or wiser than the Most High! {7:19} Let many perish who are alive now rather than disregard God's law! {7:20} For God commanded those who entered the world what to do to live and what to observe to avoid punishment. {7:21} But they were disobedient, turned against Him, devised vain thoughts, {7:22} proposed wicked plans, declared that the Most High does not exist, and ignored His ways! {7:23} They scorned His law, denied His covenants, were unfaithful to His statutes, and did not carry out His works. {7:24} "Therefore, Ezra, empty things are for the empty, and full things are for the full. {7:25} For the time will come when the signs I foretold will happen, when the unseen city will appear, and the hidden land will be revealed. {7:26} Everyone delivered from the foretold evils will see my wonders. {7:27} For my son, the Messiah, will be revealed with those who are with him, and those who remain will rejoice for four hundred years. {7:28} After these years, my son the Messiah will die, and all who breathe will perish. {7:29} The world will return to silence for seven days, just like it was at the beginning; no one will be left. {7:30} After seven days, the world, still asleep, will wake up, and what is corruptible will perish. {7:31} The earth will give up those asleep in it, and the dust will release those who have been silent; the chambers will give up the souls entrusted to them. {7:32} The Most High will be revealed on the judgment seat, and compassion will vanish, patience will be withdrawn; {7:33} only judgment will remain, truth will stand, and faithfulness will grow strong. {7:34} Recompense will follow, and rewards will be revealed; righteous deeds will awaken, and unrighteous deeds will not rest. {7:35} Then the pit of torment will be revealed, and opposite it will be the place of rest; hell's furnace will be shown, and opposite it will be paradise. {7:36} The Most High will say to the nations raised from the dead, 'Look and understand whom you denied, whom you did not serve, whose commandments you despised! {7:37} Look here and there; here are delight and rest, and there are fire and torments!' He will speak to them on judgment day— {7:38} a day with no sun, moon, stars, {7:39} clouds, thunder, lightning, wind, water, air, darkness, evening, or morning, {7:40} or summer, spring, heat, winter, frost, cold, hail, rain, or dew, {7:41} or noon, night, dawn, brightness, or light, but only the splendor of the glory of the Most High, by which all will see what has been determined for them. {7:42} This will last about a week of years. {7:43} This is my judgment and its order; I have shown you alone these things." {7:44} I replied, "O Lord, blessed are those who are alive and keep your commandments! {7:45} But what about those I prayed for? Who among the living hasn't sinned, or who among people hasn't transgressed your covenant? {7:46} I see the world to come will bring joy to few and torment to many. {7:47} An evil heart has grown within us, alienating us from God, leading us into corruption and death, showing us the paths of destruction and distancing us from life—not just a few, but almost all who have been created!" {7:48} He answered, "Listen, Ezra, and I will teach and guide you again. {7:49} The Most High created not one world but two. {7:50} You've said the righteous are few while the wicked are many; let me explain. {7:51} If you have a few precious stones, would you add lead and clay to them?" {7:52} I asked, "Lord, how can that be?" {7:53} He replied, "Not only that, but ask the earth, and it will tell you. {7:54} Say to it, 'You produce gold, silver, brass, iron, lead, and clay; {7:55} but silver is more abundant than gold, brass is more than silver, iron is more than brass, lead is more than iron, and clay is more than lead.' {7:56} Judge which things are precious and desirable—those that are abundant or those that are rare?" {7:57} I said, "O Lord, what is plentiful is of less value; what is rare is more precious." {7:58} He answered, "Consider what you've thought, for someone who has what is hard to get rejoices more than one who has what is abundant. {7:59} The judgment I promised will be like this; I will rejoice over the few who are saved, as they have honored my glory and name. {7:60} I will not grieve over the many who perish; they are like mist, flames, and smoke—set on fire and burning hot, then extinguished." {7:61} I replied, "O earth, what have you produced, if the mind is made from the same dust as all other created things! {7:62} It would have been better if the dust had not been born, so the mind might not have been made from it. {7:63} But the mind grows with us, and thus we are tormented because we perish and know it. {7:64} Let humanity lament, but let the beasts of the field rejoice; let all born lament, but let the four-footed creatures and flocks be glad! {7:65} For it's much better for them than for us; they don't look forward to judgment, nor do they know of any torment or salvation after death. {7:66} What good is it for us to be alive but cruelly tormented? {7:67} All born are caught in sins, full of transgressions. {7:68} If there were no judgment after death, perhaps it would be better for us." {7:69} He replied, "When the Most High made the world and Adam and all who came from him, He first prepared judgment and what relates to it. {7:70} Now understand from your own words, for you said the mind grows with us. {7:71} Therefore, those on earth will be tormented, for though they had understanding, they committed wrongs; though they received commandments, they did not keep them, and though they obtained the law, they acted unfaithfully with it. {7:72} What will they say at judgment, or how will they answer in the last days? {7:73} How long has the Most High been patient with those who inhabit the world, not for their sake but because of the times He has ordained!" {7:74} I answered, "If I have found favor in your sight, allow me to speak once more. {7:75} Though I see judgment as just, I still wonder how those who are numerous will find any mercy. {7:76} Is there any way to save the multitudes who have transgressed? What is the point of judgment when it seems to bring ruin? {7:77} For many were born from me and others just like me, and I cannot imagine your judgment in its fullness, for I have seen the world descend into madness." {7:78} The angel said, "I'll teach you again. {7:79} When the Most High made the world, He appointed various seasons, days, and years; {7:80} He divided the times, determining when people should be born and when they should die; He arranged everything beautifully, knowing that His creation would fall into disorder. {7:80} Such spirits will not enter any dwelling but will wander in torment, always grieving and sad, in seven ways. {7:81} The first way is because they scorned the law of the Most High. {7:82} The second way is because they can no longer repent for life. {7:83} The third way is that they will see the rewards set aside for those who trusted in the Most High's covenants. {7:84} The fourth way is that they will realize the torment prepared for them in the last days. {7:85} The fifth way is that they will see how others' homes are protected by angels in deep peace. {7:86} The sixth way is that they will witness some being cast into torment. {7:87} The seventh way, which is the worst, is that they will completely waste away in confusion, consumed by shame, and will wither in fear when they see the glory of the Most High before whom they sinned in life and will be judged in the end times. {7:88} Now this is the fate of those who have kept the ways of the Most High when they are separated from their mortal bodies. {7:89} While they lived, they served the Most High diligently and faced danger at every moment to perfectly keep the law of the Lawgiver. {7:90} Therefore, here's what happens to them: {7:91} First, they will joyfully see the glory of the one who receives them, for they will have rest in seven stages. {7:92} The first stage is that they struggled hard to overcome the evil thoughts that could lead them from life to death. {7:93} The second stage is that they will see the confusion in which the souls of the wicked wander and the punishment waiting for them. {7:94} The third stage is that they see the witness of their Creator, who affirms that they kept the law entrusted to them while alive. {7:95} The fourth stage is that they understand the peace they now enjoy, gathered into their chambers and protected by angels in deep stillness, and the glory awaiting them in the last days. {7:96} The fifth stage is that they rejoice in escaping what is corruptible and inheriting what is to come; they see the struggles they've been freed from and the spacious freedom they will enjoy in immortality. {7:97} The sixth stage is when it's revealed how their faces will shine like the sun and how they will become like the stars, incorruptible forever. {7:98} The seventh stage, greater than all the others, is that they will rejoice confidently, glad without fear, as they rush to see the face of the one they served in life and from whom they will receive their reward when glorified. {7:99} This is the fate of the righteous souls, and these are the ways of torment that those who ignored the truth will suffer hereafter. {7:100} I asked, "Will the souls, once separated from their bodies, have time to see what you've described?" {7:101} He replied, "They will have freedom for seven days to see these things, and afterward they will be gathered into their homes." {7:102} I said, "If I have found favor in your sight, show me whether, on the day of judgment, the righteous can intercede for the wicked or plead with the Most High for them, {7:103} whether fathers can pray for sons, or sons for parents, brothers for brothers, relatives for kin, or friends for those they hold dear." {7:104} He answered, "Since you have found favor in my sight, I will show you this too. The day of judgment is decisive and shows everyone the truth. Just as a father cannot send his son, or a son his father, or a master his servant, or a close friend to eat or heal in their place, {7:105} no one will be able to pray for another on that day; everyone will bear their own righteousness or unrighteousness." {7:106} I said, "But how do we find that Abraham prayed for the people of Sodom, and Moses for our ancestors who sinned in the desert, {7:107} and Joshua for Israel in the days of Achan, {7:108} and Samuel for Saul, and David during the plague, and Solomon for those in the sanctuary, {7:109} and Elijah for those who needed rain and for the dead to live, {7:110} and Hezekiah for the people during Sennacherib's time, and many others who prayed for many?" {7:111} If the righteous prayed for the wicked then, why will it not happen on that day as well?" {7:112} He answered, "This present world is not the end; its full glory does not remain here; thus, the strong prayed for the weak. {7:113} But the day of judgment will mark the end of this age and the beginning of the eternal age to come, where corruption is gone, {7:114} sinful indulgence has ended, unbelief is cut off, and righteousness has increased and truth has emerged. {7:115} So, no one will then be able to show mercy to the condemned or harm those who have triumphed." {7:116} I said, "This is my first and last word: it would have been better if the earth had never produced Adam, or if, once produced, it had restrained him from sinning. {7:117} What good is it for all to live in sorrow now and expect punishment after death? {7:118} O Adam, what have you done? Though you sinned, the fall was not just yours but ours too as your descendants. {7:119} What good is it to us if an eternal age is promised, yet we commit acts that lead to death? {7:120} What good is it to have everlasting hope promised to us while we have failed? {7:121} Or to have safe and healthy homes reserved for us, while we lived wickedly? {7:122} Or to have the Most High's glory protect those who lived pure lives, while we walked the wicked path? {7:123} Or to have paradise revealed with unspoiled fruit and abundance, yet not enter because we lived wrongly? {7:124} Or to have the faces of those who practiced self-control shine brighter than the stars, while our faces are darker than darkness? {7:125} While we lived in sin, we did not think about what we would suffer after death." {7:126} He replied, "This is the meaning of the struggle every person born on earth faces, {7:127} that if defeated, they will endure what you described, but if victorious, they will receive what I have promised. {7:128} This is what Moses meant when he told the people, 'Choose life, that you may live!' {7:129} But they did not believe him, nor the prophets who followed, nor even myself. {7:130} Therefore, there will not be sorrow over their destruction, but joy for those assured of salvation." {7:131} I said, "I know, O Lord, that the Most High is called merciful because He shows mercy to those who have not yet been born; {7:132} and gracious because He is kind to those who repent and turn to His law; {7:133} and patient, showing patience to those who sin since they are His creation; {7:134} and generous, preferring to give rather than take away; {7:135} and abundant in compassion because He increases His mercy for the living, the dead, and those yet to come, {7:136} for if His compassion did not abound, the world and its inhabitants would not have life; {7:137} and He is called the giver because without His goodness, even the tiniest fraction of humanity could not have life; {7:138} and He is the judge because if He did not pardon the sins created by His word, only a few of the countless could survive."

{8:1} He answered me, saying, "The Most High made this world for many, but the world to come for few. {8:2} Let me tell you a parable, Ezra. Just as when you ask the earth, it will tell you that it provides a lot of clay for making pottery, but only a little dust for making gold; so it is with the present world. {8:3} Many have been created, but few will be saved." {8:4} I replied, "Then let my soul drink deeply of understanding, and let my heart be filled with wisdom! {8:5} For you did not come into the world by your own choice, and you leave against your will, having only a short time to live. {8:6} O Lord who is over us, grant your servant the ability to pray before you, and give us the seed for our hearts and the cultivation of our understanding so that we may produce fruit, enabling every mortal who bears your image to live. {8:7} For you alone exist, and we are your creation, as you have declared. {8:8} You give life to the body formed in the womb, providing it with members, and what you have created is preserved in fire and water, as the womb endures for nine months, containing what you have made. {8:9} What sustains and what is sustained will both be protected by your keeping. When the womb releases what it has held, {8:10} you have commanded that from the members themselves (from the breasts) milk should be supplied as the fruit of the breasts, {8:11} so that what has been formed may be nourished for a time, and afterwards you will guide them in your mercy. {8:12} You have raised them in your righteousness, instructed them in your law, and corrected them in your wisdom. {8:13} You will take away their life, for they are your creation; and you will make them live, for they are your work. {8:14} If you will suddenly and quickly destroy someone who was so carefully made by your command, what purpose did their creation serve? {8:15} Now I will speak openly: you know all about mankind, but I will speak of your people, for whom I am saddened, {8:16} and your inheritance, for whom I lament, and Israel, for whom I am troubled, and the seed of Jacob, for whom I am distressed. {8:17} Therefore, I will pray before you for myself and for them, as I see the failings of those who dwell in the land, {8:18} and I have heard of the quick judgment that is to come. {8:19} So hear my voice and understand my words; I will speak before you." This is the beginning of Ezra's prayer before he was taken up. He said: {8:20} "O Lord who inhabits eternity, whose eyes are exalted and whose upper chambers are in the air, {8:21} whose throne is beyond measure and whose glory is beyond comprehension, before whom the hosts of angels stand trembling, {8:22} and at whose command they are changed into wind and fire, whose word is certain and whose decrees are strong and whose command is fearsome, {8:23} whose gaze dries up the depths and whose anger makes the mountains melt away, whose truth is established forever— {8:24} hear, O Lord, the prayer of your servant, and listen to the petition of your creation; pay attention to my words. {8:25} As long as I live, I will speak, and as long as I have understanding, I will respond. {8:26} Do not look at the sins of your people, but at those who have served you in truth. {8:27} Do not regard the actions of those who act wickedly, but consider the actions of those who have kept your covenants amidst trials. {8:28} Do not think of those who have lived in wickedness in your sight; instead, remember those who have willingly acknowledged that you are to be feared. {8:29} Let it not be your will to destroy those who have lived like animals; instead, regard those who have gloriously taught your law. {8:30} Do not be angry with those deemed worse than beasts; rather, love those who have always put their trust in your glory. {8:31} For we and our fathers have lived in ways that lead to death, yet you, because of us sinners, are called merciful. {8:32} If you desire to have compassion on us, who have no righteous deeds, then you will be called merciful. {8:33} The righteous, who have many good works stored up with you, will receive their reward based on their own deeds. {8:34} But what is man that you are angry with him? What is a corruptible race that you are so bitter against them? {8:35} For in truth, there is no one born who has not acted wickedly, and among those who have existed, there is no one who has not sinned. {8:36} In this, O Lord, your righteousness and goodness will be revealed when you are merciful to those who have no good works." {8:37} He answered me, saying, "Some things you have spoken rightly, and they will come to pass as you have said. {8:38} I will not concern myself with the creation of those who have sinned, their death, their judgment, or their destruction; {8:39} instead, I will rejoice over the creation of the righteous, their journey, their salvation, and their receiving of their reward. {8:40} As I have spoken, so it shall be. {8:41} For just as a farmer sows many seeds and plants numerous seedlings, yet not all will sprout at the right time, and not all that were planted will take root; so too, not all who have been sown in the world will be saved." {8:42} I replied, "If I have found favor in your sight, let me speak. {8:43} For if the farmer's seed fails to sprout because it hasn't received your rain at the right time, or if it is ruined by too much rain, it dies. {8:44} But man, formed by your hands and called your own image because he is made like you, for whose sake you have created everything—have you made him like the farmer's seed? {8:45} No, O Lord who is over us! Spare your people and have mercy on your inheritance, for you have mercy on your own creation." {8:46} He answered me, saying, "The present things are for those who live now, and future things are for those who will live later. {8:47} You cannot love my creation more than I love it. Do not compare yourself to the unrighteous. Never do so! {8:48} Even in this way, you will be commendable before the Most High, {8:49} for you have humbled yourself, which is fitting for you, and you have not claimed to be among the righteous to gain the greatest glory. {8:50} Many miseries will affect those who inhabit the world in the last times, due to their pride. {8:51} Consider your own situation and inquire about the glory of those like yourself, {8:52} because for you, paradise is opened, the tree of life is planted, the age to come is prepared, abundance is provided, a city is built, rest is appointed, goodness is established, and wisdom is perfected beforehand. {8:53} The root of evil is sealed from you, illness is banished, and death is hidden; hell has fled and corruption is forgotten; {8:54} sorrows have passed away, and in the end, the treasure of immortality is revealed. {8:55} Therefore, do not ask any more about the multitude of those who perish. {8:56} They received freedom, but they despised the Most High, rejected his law, and forsook his ways. {8:57} They have even trampled on his righteous ones, {8:58} and in their hearts, they have said that there is no God—though they know they must die. {8:59} Just as the things I have predicted await you, so the thirst and torment prepared await them. The Most High did not intend for men to be destroyed; {8:60} rather, those who were created have defiled the name of their Creator and have been ungrateful to the one who prepared life for them. {8:61} Therefore, my judgment is drawing near; {8:62} I have not revealed this to everyone, only to you and a few like you." Then I replied, {8:63} "Behold, O Lord, you have shown me many signs of what you will do in the last times, but you have not revealed to me when you will do them."

{9:1} He answered me, saying, "Think carefully, and when you see that certain predicted signs have passed, {9:2} you will know that it is the time when the Most High is about to visit the world He has made. {9:3} When you see earthquakes, chaos among nations, political intrigues, uncertain leaders, and confusion among rulers, {9:4} then you will know that these are the things the Most High spoke about from ancient times. {9:5} Just like everything that has happened in the world, the beginning is clear, and the end is evident; {9:6} so too are the times of the Most High: the beginnings are shown in wonders and mighty acts, and the end through retribution and signs. {9:7} Everyone who is to be saved and can escape due to their deeds or the faith they hold will survive the dangers foretold, and will see my salvation in my land and within my boundaries, which I have sanctified from the start. {9:8} Then those who have abused my ways will be astonished, and those who rejected them with disdain will suffer torments. {9:9} For many who did not acknowledge me in their lifetime, despite receiving my blessings, {9:10} and those who scorned my law while they had the chance, and did not understand but despised it when repentance was still possible, {9:11} these must acknowledge it in torment after death. {9:12} Therefore, do not be curious about how the ungodly will be punished; instead, ask how the righteous will be saved, for whom the age exists and for whose sake it was created." {9:13} I replied, {9:14} "I have said before, I say now, and I will say it again: there are more who perish than those who will be saved, {9:15} just as a wave is greater than a drop of water." {9:16} He responded, "Just as the field is, so is the seed; as the flowers are, so are the colors; as the work is, so is the product; as the farmer is, so is the threshing floor. {9:17} There was a time when I was preparing for those who now exist, before the world was made for them to live in, and no one opposed me then, for no one was there; {9:18} but now those created in this world, which has both an unfailing table and an endless pasture, have become corrupt in their ways. {9:19} I looked at my world, and it was lost; I saw my earth, and it was in danger because of the actions of those who had come into it. {9:20} I managed to spare a few with great difficulty, saving one grape from a cluster and one plant from a great forest. {9:21} Let the multitude that has been born in vain perish, but let my grape and my plant be saved, because I have labored much to perfect them. {9:22} If you will allow seven more days to pass—do not fast during them; {9:23} instead, go into a field of flowers where no house has been built, eat only of the flowers, taste no meat or drink no wine, but eat only flowers, {9:24} and pray to the Most High continuously—then I will come and speak with you." {9:25} So I went as he directed me into the field called Ardat; I sat among the flowers, ate the plants of the field, and the nourishment satisfied me. {9:26} After seven days, as I lay on the grass, my heart troubled me again as before. {9:27} My mouth opened, and I began to speak before the Most High, saying, {9:28} "O Lord, you showed yourself among us to our ancestors in the wilderness when they came out of Egypt into the untrodden and barren wilderness; {9:29} you said, 'Hear me, O Israel, and pay attention to my words, O descendants of Jacob. {9:30} For I am sowing my law in you, and it will bear fruit in you, and you will be glorified through it forever.' {9:31} But even though our ancestors received the law, they did not keep it or observe the statutes; yet the fruit of the law did not perish—because it could not, since it was yours. {9:32} Those who received it perished because they did not keep what was sown in them. {9:33} Behold, it is a rule that when the ground receives seed, or the sea a ship, or any dish food or drink, if what was sown or launched or placed in is destroyed, {9:34} they perish, but the things that held them remain; yet it has not been so with us. {9:35} For we who have received the law and sinned will perish, as will our hearts which received it; {9:36} the law, however, does not perish but remains in its glory." {9:37} When I thought about these things, I looked up and saw a woman on my right. She was mourning and weeping loudly, deeply grieved in heart, her clothes torn, and ashes on her head. {9:38} I dismissed my previous thoughts and turned to her {9:39} and asked, "Why are you weeping, and why are you so troubled?" {9:40} She replied, "Leave me alone, my lord, so I can weep for myself and continue to mourn, for I am deeply bitter in spirit and severely afflicted." {9:41} I asked, "What has happened to you? Please tell me." {9:42} She said, "Your servant was barren and had no child, though I lived with my husband for thirty years. {9:43} Every hour and every day during those thirty years, I begged the Most High, night and day. {9:44} After thirty years, God heard your handmaid, looked at my lowly state, considered my distress, and gave me a son. I rejoiced greatly over him, as did my husband and all my neighbors; we gave great glory to the Mighty One. {9:45} I raised him with much care. {9:46} When he grew up and I came to find a wife for him, I set a day for the marriage feast."

{10:1} "But it happened that when my son entered his wedding chamber, he fell down and died. {10:2} We all extinguished the lamps, and all my neighbors tried to comfort me; I remained silent until the evening of the second day. {10:3} When they had stopped consoling me, thinking I needed quiet, I got up at night and fled to this field, as you see. {10:4} Now I intend not to return to the city, but to stay here, and I will neither eat nor drink, but will continuously mourn and fast until I die." {10:5} Then I stopped my reflections and spoke to her in anger, saying, {10:6} "You foolish woman, do you not see our mourning and what has happened to us? {10:7} For Zion, our mother, is in deep grief and great suffering. {10:8} It is appropriate to mourn now, because we are all mourning; while you mourn for one son, we mourn for our mother, the whole world. {10:9} Ask the earth, and she will tell you that it is she who should mourn for the many who have come into existence upon her. {10:10} From the beginning, all have been born of her, and others will come; yet almost all head towards destruction, and many are destined for ruin. {10:11} Who then should mourn more, she who lost so many, or you who grieve for one? {10:12} But if you say to me, 'My lament is not like the earth's, for I have lost the fruit of my womb, which I bore in pain and sorrow; {10:13} the earth's multitude comes and goes as it was,' {10:14} then I say to you, 'As you bore in sorrow, so the earth has from the beginning produced her fruit, that is, humanity, for the one who created her.' {10:15} Therefore, keep your sorrow to yourself and bravely bear the troubles that have come upon you. {10:16} For if you accept the decree of God as just, you will eventually receive your son back and be praised among women. {10:17} So go into the city to your husband." {10:18} She replied, "I will not do that; I will not go into the city, but I will die here." {10:19} I spoke to her again, saying, {10:20} "Do not say that; let yourself be persuaded because of Zion's troubles, and find comfort in Jerusalem's sorrow. {10:21} Our sanctuary has been devastated, our altar thrown down, our temple destroyed; {10:22} our harp has been silenced, our songs have ended, and our joy is gone; the light of our lampstand is out, the ark of our covenant has been plundered, our holy things defiled, and the name by which we are called profaned; our free men have been mistreated, our priests burned to death, our Levites taken captive, our virgins defiled, and our wives violated; our righteous men have been carried off, our little ones cast out, our young men enslaved, and our strong men made powerless. {10:23} What's worse, the seal of Zion is lost; she has lost her glory and has been handed over to those who hate us. {10:24} Therefore, shake off your great sadness and lay aside your many sorrows, so that the Mighty One may show you mercy again, and the Most High may grant you rest, a relief from your troubles." {10:25} While I spoke, her face suddenly shone brilliantly, and her appearance flashed like lightning, making me too afraid to approach her, and my heart was terrified. While I wondered what this meant, {10:26} she suddenly let out a loud and terrifying cry, shaking the earth at the sound. {10:27} I looked, and she was no longer visible to me; instead, I saw an established city with massive foundations. Then I was afraid and cried out loudly, saying, {10:28} "Where is the angel Uriel, who came to me before? It was he who brought me into this overwhelming confusion; my end has become decay, and my prayer a reproach." {10:29} As I spoke, the angel who had first come to me appeared, looking upon me; {10:30} I lay there like a corpse, deprived of understanding. He grasped my right hand, strengthened me, and set me on my feet, saying, {10:31} "What is wrong with you? Why are you troubled? Why are your understanding and thoughts so disturbed?" {10:32} I said, "Because you have forsaken me! I did as you directed, going out into the field, and behold, I see what I cannot explain." {10:33} He replied, "Stand up like a man, and I will instruct you." {10:34} I said, "Speak, my lord; just do not abandon me, or I will die before my time. {10:35} For I have seen what I did not know, and I have heard what I do not understand. {10:36} Or is my mind deceived, and my soul dreaming? {10:37} Therefore, I implore you to give your servant an explanation of this bewildering vision." {10:38} He answered, "Listen to me, and I will inform you about the things you fear, for the Most High has revealed many secrets to you. {10:39} He has seen your righteous behavior, your continual sorrow for your people, and your deep mourning for Zion. {10:40} This is the meaning of the vision. {10:41} The woman who appeared to you earlier, whom you saw mourning and began to console— {10:42} you no longer see her as a woman, but an established city has appeared to you— {10:43} and regarding her telling you about the misfortune of her son, this is the interpretation: {10:44} The woman you saw, now seen as an established city, is Zion. {10:45} Her being barren for thirty years signifies that there were three thousand years before any offerings were made in her. {10:46} After three thousand years, Solomon built the city and made offerings; it was then that the barren woman bore a son. {10:47} When she said she raised him with care, that refers to the time spent in Jerusalem. {10:48} Her saying, 'When my son entered his wedding chamber, he died,' refers to the destruction of Jerusalem. {10:49} You saw her likeness mourning for her son, and you began to console her for what had happened. {10:50} For now the Most High, seeing your sincere grief and deep distress for her, has revealed to you the brilliance of her glory and the beauty of her loveliness. {10:51} Therefore, I told you to remain in the field where no house was built, {10:52} for I knew the Most High would show you these things. {10:53} I instructed you to go into the field with no building foundations, {10:54} because no work of man could endure where the city of the Most High was to be revealed. {10:55} "So do not be afraid, and do not let your heart be troubled; go in and see the splendor and vastness of the building as far as your eyes can see, {10:56} and afterward you will hear as much as your ears can hear. {10:57} For you are more blessed than many, having been called before the Most High, as few have been. {10:58} But tomorrow night, you will stay here, {10:59} and the Most High will show you in those dream visions what He will do to those who dwell on earth in the last days." So I slept that night & next one, as he commanded me.

{11:1} "On the second night, I had a dream, and behold, an eagle emerged from the sea, having twelve feathered wings and three heads. {11:2} I looked, and the eagle spread his wings over all the earth; the winds of heaven blew upon him, and the clouds gathered around him. {11:3} I saw that from his wings grew opposing wings, but they became small, insignificant wings. {11:4} His heads were at rest; the middle head was larger than the others, but it too rested with them. {11:5} I looked, and the eagle flew with his wings to reign over the earth and those who dwell on it. {11:6} I saw how everything under heaven was subjected to him, and no one spoke against him, not even one creature on the earth. {11:7} I looked, and the eagle rose on his talons and called out to his wings, saying, {11:8} "Let not all watch at the same time; let each sleep in their own place and watch in turn; {11:9} but let the heads be reserved for last." {11:10} I noticed that the voice did not come from his heads, but from the middle of his body. {11:11} I counted his opposing wings, and there were eight of them. {11:12} I saw that on the right side, one wing rose and reigned over all the earth. {11:13} While it was reigning, it came to an end and vanished, leaving no trace. Then the next wing rose and reigned, continuing for a long time. {11:14} When it was reigning, its end also came, and it disappeared like the first. {11:15} A voice sounded, saying to it, {11:16} "Listen, you who have ruled the earth; I announce this to you before you vanish. {11:17} After you, no one shall rule as long as you, or even half as long." {11:18} Then the third wing lifted itself and held the rule like the previous ones, and it also disappeared. {11:19} This happened with all the wings; they held power one after another and then were never seen again. {11:20} I looked, and in due course, the following wings also rose on the right side to rule. Some ruled but then disappeared suddenly; {11:21} others rose but did not hold power. {11:22} After this, I looked and saw the twelve wings and the two small wings vanish; {11:23} nothing remained on the eagle's body except the three heads that were at rest and six small wings. {11:24} I saw two small wings separate from the six and stay under the head on the right side; four remained in their place. {11:25} I looked and saw these small wings planning to set themselves up and hold power. {11:26} I noticed one was established but suddenly vanished; {11:27} a second one also appeared and disappeared even quicker than the first. {11:28} I looked and saw the two remaining wings planning to reign together; {11:29} while they were planning, the middle head, which was at rest, awoke because it was greater than the other two heads. {11:30} I saw how it allied itself with the two heads, {11:31} and the head turned with those with it, devouring the two small wings that were planning to reign. {11:32} Moreover, this head gained control of the entire earth, dominating its inhabitants with much oppression; it had greater power over the world than all the wings that came before. {11:33} After this, I looked, and the middle head also suddenly disappeared, just like the wings had done. {11:34} But the two heads remained, continuing to rule over the earth and its inhabitants. {11:35} I looked and saw the head on the right devour the one on the left. {11:36} Then I heard a voice saying to me, "Look before you and consider what you see." {11:37} I looked, and a creature like a lion emerged from the forest, roaring; I heard it utter a man's voice to the eagle, saying, {11:38} "Listen, and I will speak to you. The Most High says to you, {11:39} 'Are you not the one that remains of the four beasts I made to reign in my world, so that the end of my times might come through them? {11:40} You, the fourth that has come, have conquered all the beasts that came before; you have ruled the world with much terror and grievous oppression, and for so long you have lived on the earth with deceit. {11:41} You have judged the earth, but not with truth; {11:42} you have afflicted the meek and harmed the peaceful; you have hated truth-tellers and loved liars; you have destroyed the homes of those who bore fruit and brought down the walls of those who did you no harm. {11:43} Your arrogance has come before the Most High, and your pride before the Mighty One. {11:44} The Most High has looked upon his times, and behold, they are ended, and his ages are completed! {11:45} Therefore, you will surely disappear, you eagle, along with your terrifying wings, your evil little wings, your malicious heads, your evil talons, and your entire worthless body, {11:46} so that the whole earth, freed from your violence, may be refreshed & relieved, and may hope for the judgment & mercy of him who made it.'"

{12:1} "While the lion was speaking these words to the eagle, I looked, {12:2} and behold, the remaining head vanished. The two wings that had joined it rose up and set themselves to reign, but their reign was short and chaotic. {12:3} I looked, and they also disappeared, and the whole body of the eagle was burned, and the earth was extremely terrified. I then woke up in great confusion and fear, and I said to my spirit, {12:4} "You have brought this upon me because you seek out the ways of the Most High. {12:5} I am still weary in mind and very weak in spirit, with no strength left in me due to the great fear that has terrified me this night. {12:6} Therefore, I will now ask the Most High to strengthen me until the end." {12:7} I said, "O sovereign Lord, if I have found favor in your sight, and if I have been counted righteous before you above many others, and if my prayer has truly reached you, {12:8} strengthen me and show me, your servant, the interpretation and meaning of this terrifying vision, so that you may fully comfort my soul. {12:9} For you have deemed me worthy to be shown the end of the times and the last events." {12:10} He said to me, "This is the interpretation of the vision you saw: {12:11} The eagle you saw coming up from the sea is the fourth kingdom that appeared in a vision to your brother Daniel. {12:12} But it was not explained to him as I now explain it to you. {12:13} Behold, the days are coming when a kingdom shall arise on earth, more terrifying than all the kingdoms that have existed before it. {12:14} Twelve kings shall reign in it, one after another. {12:15} But the second to reign shall have power for longer than any of the twelve. {12:16} This is the interpretation of the twelve wings you saw. {12:17} Regarding the voice you heard, which came not from the eagle's heads but from the middle of its body, this is the interpretation: {12:18} During the time of that kingdom, great struggles shall arise, and it will be in danger of falling; yet it will not fall at that time but will regain its former power. {12:19} As for the eight small wings you saw clinging to its wings, this is the interpretation: {12:20} Eight kings shall arise in it, whose reigns will be short and swift; {12:21} two of them shall perish when the middle of its time approaches; four shall be kept until the end; but two shall be preserved until the very end. {12:22} Regarding the three heads at rest, this is the interpretation: {12:23} In its last days, the Most High will raise up three kings, who will renew many things and rule the earth and its inhabitants more oppressively than all who came before them; therefore, they are called the heads of the eagle. {12:24} They will summarize its wickedness and perform its last actions. {12:25} As for the large head that disappeared, one of the kings shall die in bed, but in suffering. {12:26} The two who remain shall be devoured by the sword. {12:27} One will be killed by the sword of the other; he too will fall by the sword in the last days. {12:28} Regarding the two small wings that passed to the head on the right side, {12:29} this is the interpretation: They are the ones the Most High has kept for the eagle's end; this was the brief and tumultuous reign you saw. {12:30} "As for the lion you saw rising from the forest, roaring and speaking to the eagle, rebuking it for its unrighteousness, and for all the words you have heard, {12:31} this is the Messiah whom the Most High has kept until the end of days. He will arise from the lineage of David, come, and speak to them; he will denounce them for their ungodliness and wickedness, exposing their contemptible actions. {12:32} First, he will bring them to his judgment seat, and after reproving them, he will destroy them. {12:33} But he will show mercy to the remnant of my people, those saved throughout my borders, and he will make them joyful until the end comes, the day of judgment, which I spoke to you about at the beginning. {12:34} This is the dream you saw, and this is its interpretation. {12:35} You alone were worthy to learn this secret of the Most High. {12:36} Therefore, write all these things you have seen in a book and keep it hidden; {12:37} and you shall teach them to the wise among your people, whose hearts you know can comprehend and keep these secrets. {12:38} But wait here seven more days so that you may be shown whatever it pleases the Most High to reveal to you." Then he left me. {12:39} When all the people heard that the seven days had passed and I had not returned to the city, they gathered together, from the least to the greatest, and came to me, saying, {12:40} "How have we offended you, and what harm have we done to you that you have forsaken us and sit in this place? {12:41} For among all the prophets, you alone are left to us, like a cluster of grapes from the harvest, a lamp in a dark place, and a haven for a ship saved from a storm. {12:42} Are not the evils that have befallen us enough? {12:43} Therefore, if you forsake us, how much better it would have been for us to have perished in the burning of Zion! {12:44} For we are no better than those who died there." They wept loudly. Then I answered them and said, {12:45} "Take courage, O Israel, and do not be sorrowful, O house of Jacob; {12:46} for the Most High remembers you, and the Mighty One has not forgotten you in your struggle. {12:47} As for me, I have neither forsaken you nor withdrawn from you; I have come to this place to pray because of the desolation of Zion and to seek mercy for the humiliation of our sanctuary. {12:48} Now go, each of you to your house, and after these days, I will come to you." {12:49} So the people went into the city as I instructed. {12:50} But I sat in the field for 7 days, as the angel had commanded me, eating only the flowers of the field & my food was plants during those days."

{13:1} "After seven days, I had a dream at night; {13:2} and behold, a wind arose from the sea and stirred up all its waves. {13:3} I looked, and behold, this wind brought up something like the figure of a man from the heart of the sea. I looked again, and behold, that man flew with the clouds of heaven; and wherever he turned his face to look, everything under his gaze trembled, {13:4} and whenever his voice came from his mouth, all who heard it melted like wax melts when it feels the fire. {13:5} After this, I looked, and behold, an innumerable multitude of men gathered from the four winds of heaven to make war against the man who came up from the sea. {13:6} I looked again, and behold, he carved out a great mountain and flew up upon it. {13:7} I tried to see the place from which the mountain was carved, but I could not. {13:8} After this, I looked, and behold, all who had gathered against him to wage war were very afraid but still dared to fight. {13:9} Behold, when he saw the rush of the approaching multitude, he neither lifted a hand nor held a spear or any weapon of war; {13:10} but I saw how he sent forth from his mouth what looked like a stream of fire, and from his lips a flaming breath, and from his tongue, he shot forth a storm of sparks. {13:11} All these were mixed together—the stream of fire, the flaming breath, and the great storm—and fell on the rushing multitude preparing to fight, burning them all up, so that suddenly nothing remained of the innumerable multitude but the dust of ashes and the smell of smoke. When I saw this, I was amazed. {13:12} After this, I saw the same man come down from the mountain and call another multitude to him that was peaceful. {13:13} Many people came to him, some joyful and some sorrowful; some were bound, and some were bringing others as offerings. Then, in great fear, I awoke and pleaded with the Most High, saying, {13:14} "From the beginning, you have shown your servant these wonders and deemed me worthy to have my prayer heard by you; {13:15} now show me the interpretation of this dream. {13:16} As I consider it in my mind, woe to those who will be left in those days! And even more, woe to those who are not left! {13:17} For those who are not left will be sad, {13:18} because they understand what is reserved for the last days but cannot attain it. {13:19} But alas for those also who are left! For they will see great dangers and much distress, as these dreams show. {13:20} Yet it is better to experience these things, even at peril, than to pass from the world like a cloud and not see what will happen in the last days." He answered me and said, {13:21} "I will tell you the interpretation of the vision and explain the things you mentioned. {13:22} Regarding those who are left, this is the interpretation: {13:23} He who brings peril at that time will protect those who fall into danger, who have works and faith in the Almighty. {13:24} Therefore, understand that those who are left are more blessed than those who have died. {13:25} This is the interpretation of the vision: The man coming up from the heart of the sea is he whom the Most High has been keeping for many ages, who will deliver his creation; he will guide those who are left. {13:26} As for your seeing wind and fire and a storm coming from his mouth, {13:27} and his not holding a spear or weapon of war but destroying the rushing multitude that came to conquer him, this is the interpretation: {13:28} Behold, the days are coming when the Most High will deliver those on the earth. {13:29} Bewilderment of mind shall come over those who dwell on the earth. {13:30} They shall plan to make war against one another, city against city, place against place, people against people, and kingdom against kingdom. {13:31} When these things happen and the signs occur which I showed you before, then my Son will be revealed, whom you saw as a man coming up from the sea. {13:32} When all the nations hear his voice, every man shall leave his own land and the wars they have against one another; {13:33} an innumerable multitude shall gather, as you saw, desiring to conquer him. {13:34} But he shall stand on the top of Mount Zion. {13:35} Zion will be revealed to all people, prepared and built, as you saw the mountain carved without hands. {13:36} My Son will rebuke the assembled nations for their ungodliness (this was symbolized by the storm) {13:37} and will confront them with their evil thoughts and the torments they will endure (symbolized by the flames), destroying them effortlessly by the law (symbolized by the fire). {13:38} As for your seeing him gather another peaceful multitude, {13:39} these are the ten tribes that were taken from their land into captivity in the days of King Hoshea, whom Shalmaneser, king of the Assyrians, led captive; he took them across the river to another land. {13:40} They planned to leave the multitude of nations and go to a distant region where no one had ever lived, {13:41} so they could keep their statutes, which they had not kept in their own land. {13:42} They went through the narrow passages of the Euphrates River. {13:43} At that time, the Most High performed signs for them and stopped the channels of the river until they passed over. {13:44} It was a long journey of a year and a half to that region, called Arzareth. {13:45} They dwelt there until the last times; now, as they are about to return, {13:46} the Most High will again stop the channels of the river so they can cross. Therefore, you saw the multitude gathered together in peace. {13:47} But those of your people found within my holy borders shall be saved. {13:48} When he destroys the gathered nations, he will protect the people who remain. {13:49} Then he will show them many wonders." {13:50} I said, "O sovereign Lord, explain to me: Why did I see the man coming up from the heart of the sea?" {13:51} He said, "Just as no one can explore or know what is in the depths of the sea, no one on earth can see my Son or those with him, except at the time of his day. {13:52} This is the interpretation of the dream you saw. You alone have been enlightened about this, {13:53} because you have forsaken your own ways and devoted yourself to mine, searching out my law; {13:54} you have devoted your life to wisdom and called understanding your mother. {13:55} Therefore, I have shown you this; there is a reward laid up with the Most High. After three more days, I will tell you other things and explain weighty and wondrous matters to you." {13:56} Then I arose and walked in the field, giving great glory and praise to the Most High for his wonders, which he performed from time to time, {13:57} and because he governs the times and everything that happens in their seasons. I stayed there three days."

{14:1} "On the third day, while I was sitting under an oak tree, a voice came out of a bush opposite me and said, 'Ezra, Ezra.' {14:2} I replied, 'Here I am, Lord,' and I stood up. {14:3} Then he said to me, 'I revealed myself in a bush and spoke to Moses when my people were in bondage in Egypt; {14:4} I sent him to lead my people out of Egypt and brought him up to Mount Sinai, where I kept him with me for many days; {14:5} I told him many wondrous things, showed him the secrets of the times, and revealed to him the end of the times. Then I commanded him, saying, {14:6} "These words you shall publish openly, and these you shall keep secret." {14:7} And now I say to you; {14:8} Keep in your heart the signs I have shown you, the dreams you have seen, and the interpretations you have heard; {14:9} for you shall be taken up from among men, and henceforth you shall live with my Son and those like you, until the times are ended. {14:10} For the age has lost its youth, and the times begin to grow old. {14:11} The age is divided into twelve parts, and nine of its parts have already passed, {14:12} as well as half of the tenth part; so two of its parts remain, besides half of the tenth part. {14:13} Therefore, set your house in order, and reprove your people; comfort the lowly among them, and instruct those who are wise. Now renounce the corruptible life, {14:14} and cast away mortal thoughts; rid yourself of human burdens and divest yourself of your weak nature, {14:15} and set aside the thoughts that trouble you, and hasten to escape from these times. {14:16} For worse evils than those you have seen will happen in the future. {14:17} As the world becomes weaker through old age, evils will multiply among its inhabitants. {14:18} Truth shall drift farther away, and falsehood shall draw near. For the eagle you saw in the vision is already hastening to come.' {14:19} Then I answered and said, 'Let me speak in your presence, Lord. {14:20} Behold, I will go as you have commanded and will reprove the people who are now living; but who will warn those who will be born afterward? For the world lies in darkness, and its inhabitants are without light. {14:21} Your law has been burned, so no one knows what has been done or will be done by you. {14:22} If I have found favor before you, send the Holy Spirit into me, and I will write everything that has happened in the world from the beginning, the things written in your law, so that people may find the path, and those who wish to live in the last days may live.' {14:23} He answered me and said, 'Go and gather the people, and tell them not to seek you for forty days. {14:24} Prepare many writing tablets for yourself, and take with you Sarea, Dabria, Selemia, Ethanus, and Asiel—these five, because they are trained to write quickly; {14:25} and you shall come here, and I will light in your heart the lamp of understanding, which shall not be extinguished until what you are about to write is finished. {14:26} When you finish, some things you shall make public, and some you shall deliver in secret to the wise; tomorrow at this hour you shall begin to write.' {14:27} So I went as he commanded me, and I gathered all the people together and said, {14:28} 'Hear these words, O Israel. {14:29} At first, our ancestors lived as aliens in Egypt, and they were delivered from there, {14:30} and received the law of life, which they did not keep, which you also have transgressed after them. {14:31} Then land was given to you as a possession in Zion; but you and your ancestors committed iniquity and did not keep the ways the Most High commanded you. {14:32} Because he is a righteous judge, in due time he took away what he had given to you. {14:33} And now you are here, and your brethren are farther in the interior. {14:34} If you will rule over your minds and discipline your hearts, you will be kept alive, and after death, you will obtain mercy. {14:35} For after death, the judgment will come, when we shall live again; then the names of the righteous will be made known, and the deeds of the ungodly will be revealed. {14:36} But let no one come to me now, and let no one seek me for forty days.' {14:37} So I took the five men as he commanded and went to the field, where we remained. {14:38} The next day, a voice called me, saying, 'Ezra, open your mouth and drink what I give you to drink.' {14:39} I opened my mouth, and behold, a full cup was offered to me; it was full of something like water, but its color was like fire. {14:40} I took it and drank; when I had drunk it, my heart poured forth understanding, and wisdom increased within me, for my spirit retained its memory; {14:41} my mouth was opened, and I was no longer silent. {14:42} The Most High gave understanding to the five men, and they wrote what was dictated to them in characters they did not know. They sat for forty days, writing during the day and eating their bread at night. {14:43} As for me, I spoke during the day and was not silent at night. {14:44} During those forty days, ninety-four books were written. {14:45} When the forty days ended, the Most High spoke to me, saying, 'Make public the twenty-four books you wrote first and let both the worthy and the unworthy read them; {14:46} but keep the seventy that were written last to give to the wise among your people. {14:47} For in them is the spring of understanding, the fountain of wisdom, and the river of knowledge.' {14:48} And I did so."

{15:1} "The Lord says, 'Listen, speak the words of the prophecy I will put in your mouth to my people, {15:2} and have them written on paper; for they are trustworthy and true. {15:3} Do not fear the plots against you, and do not be troubled by the unbelief of those who oppose you. {15:4} For every unbeliever shall die in his unbelief.' {15:5} 'Look,' says the Lord, 'I bring evils upon the world: the sword, famine, death, and destruction. {15:6} For iniquity (wickedness) has spread throughout every land, and their harmful deeds have reached their limit. {15:7} Therefore,' says the Lord, {15:8} 'I will be silent no longer about their ungodly deeds which they commit without fear, nor will I tolerate their wicked practices. Look, innocent and righteous blood cries out to me, and the souls of the righteous cry out continually. {15:9} I will surely avenge them,' says the Lord, 'and will gather all the innocent blood from among them. {15:10} Look, my people is led like a flock to the slaughter; I will not allow them to live any longer in the land of Egypt, {15:11} but I will bring them out with a mighty hand and an uplifted arm, and will strike Egypt with plagues, as before, and will destroy all its land.' {15:12} Let Egypt mourn and its foundations, for the plague of chastisement and punishment that the Lord will bring upon it. {15:13} Let the farmers who till the ground mourn, for their seed shall fail, and their trees shall be ruined by blight, hail, and terrible storms. {15:14} Alas for the world and those who live in it! {15:15} For the sword and misery draw near them, and nation shall rise up to fight against nation, with swords in their hands. {15:16} There shall be unrest among men; as they grow strong against one another, they will have no respect for their king or the leaders. {15:17} A man will desire to go into a city and shall not be able. {15:18} Because of their pride, the cities shall be in chaos, the houses shall be destroyed, and people shall be afraid. {15:19} A man shall have no pity on his neighbors but shall attack their houses with the sword and plunder their goods out of hunger and great tribulation. {15:20} 'Look,' says God, 'I call together all the kings of the earth to fear me, from the rising sun to the south, from the east to Lebanon; to repay what they have given. {15:21} Just as they have done to my chosen ones until this day, so I will do and repay into their bosom.' Thus says the Lord God: {15:22} 'My right hand will not spare the sinners, and my sword will not cease from those who shed innocent blood on earth.' {15:23} A fire will go forth from my wrath, consuming the foundations of the earth, and the sinners will burn like straw. {15:24} 'Woe to those who sin and do not keep my commandments,' says the Lord; {15:25} 'I will not spare them. Depart, you faithless children! Do not pollute my sanctuary.' {15:26} For the Lord knows all who transgress against him; therefore, he will hand them over to death and slaughter. {15:27} Now calamities have come upon the whole earth, and you shall remain in them; for God will not deliver you because you have sinned against him. {15:28} Look, a terrifying sight appears from the east! {15:29} The nations of the dragons of Arabia shall come out with many chariots, and from the day they set out, their hissing shall spread over the earth, causing fear and trembling. {15:30} The Carmonians, raging in wrath, shall come forth like wild boars from the forest, and with great power, they shall engage in battle and devastate a portion of the land of the Assyrians. {15:31} Then the dragons, remembering their origin, shall grow even stronger; and if they unite in great power to pursue them, {15:32} they shall become disorganized and silenced by their might, and will turn and flee. {15:33} An enemy shall lie in ambush from the land of the Assyrians and destroy one of them, causing fear and trembling in their army, and confusion among their kings. {15:34} Look, clouds from the east, and from the north to the south; their appearance is very threatening, full of wrath and storm. {15:35} They shall collide and pour out a heavy tempest upon the earth, with their own storm; and there shall be blood from the sword as high as a horse's belly {15:36} and a man's thigh and a camel's hock. {15:37} There shall be fear and great trembling upon the earth; those who see that wrath shall be horrified and seized with trembling. {15:38} After that, heavy storm clouds shall arise from the south, the north, and the west. {15:39} The winds from the east shall prevail over the cloud raised in wrath and shall disperse it; the tempest intended to cause destruction by the east wind shall be driven violently toward the south and west. {15:40} Great and mighty clouds, full of wrath and tempest, shall rise to destroy all the earth and its inhabitants, pouring out upon every high and lofty place a terrible tempest, {15:41} fire, hail, flying swords, and floods of water, so that all fields and streams may be filled with an abundance of those waters. {15:42} They shall destroy cities and walls, mountains and hills, trees of the forests, and the grass of the meadows, along with their grain. {15:43} They shall continue steadily to Babylon and destroy her. {15:44} They shall surround her and pour out the tempest and all its wrath upon her; then dust and smoke shall rise to heaven, and all who are around her shall mourn for her. {15:45} Those who survive shall serve those who have destroyed her. {15:46} And you, Asia, who share in the glamour of Babylon and the glory of her allure— {15:47} woe to you, miserable wretch! For you have made yourself like her; you have dressed your daughters in harlotry to please and gain the favor of your lovers, who have always lusted after you. {15:48} You have imitated that hateful harlot in all her deeds and schemes; therefore God says, {15:49} 'I will send evils upon you: widowhood, poverty, famine, sword, and pestilence, to lay waste your houses and bring you to destruction and death. {15:50} The glory of your power shall wither like a flower when the heat rises that is sent upon you. {15:51} You shall be weakened like a wretched woman who is beaten and wounded, so that you cannot receive your powerful lovers. {15:52} Would I have dealt with you so violently,' says the Lord, {15:53} 'if you had not always killed my chosen people, exulting and clapping your hands and talking about their death when you were drunk? {15:54} Adorn the beauty of your face! {15:55} The reward of a harlot is in your bosom; therefore, you shall receive your recompense. {15:56} As you will do to my chosen people,' says the Lord, 'so God will do to you and will hand you over to adversities. {15:57} Your children shall die of hunger, and you shall fall by the sword, your cities shall be wiped out, and all your people in the open country shall fall by the sword. {15:58} Those in the mountains and highlands shall perish from hunger and shall eat their own flesh in desperation for bread and drink their own blood from thirst for water. {15:59} Unhappy above all others, you shall come and suffer new afflictions. {15:60} As they pass, they shall wreck the hateful city and destroy part of your land and abolish a portion of your glory as they return from devastated Babylon. {15:61} You shall be broken down by them like stubble, and they shall be like fire to you. {15:62} They shall consume you and your cities, your land and your mountains; they shall burn all your forests and fruitful trees with fire. {15:63} They shall carry your children away captive, plunder your wealth, and destroy the glory of your countenance.'"

{16:1} Woe to you, Babylon and Asia! Woe to you, Egypt and Syria! {16:2} Wrap yourselves in sackcloth and haircloth, and mourn for your children, for your destruction is coming. {16:3} A sword has been sent against you, and who can stop it? {16:4} A fire has been sent against you, and who can put it out? {16:5} Calamities have been sent against you, and who can drive them away? {16:6} Can anyone chase away a hungry lion in the forest, or put out a fire in dry grass once it starts to burn? {16:7} Can anyone turn back an arrow shot by a strong archer? {16:8} The Lord God sends calamities, and who will stop them? {16:9} Fire will come from His anger, and who can quench it? {16:10} He will flash lightning, and who will not be afraid? He will thunder, and who will not be terrified?

{16:11} The Lord will threaten, and who will not be completely shattered at His presence? {16:12} The earth and its foundations will shake, the sea will rise from the depths, and its waves and the fish will be troubled at the presence of the Lord and before the glory of His power. {16:13} His strong right hand that bends the bow is powerful, and His arrows that He shoots are sharp and will not miss when they are shot to the ends of the earth. {16:14} Behold, calamities are sent forth and will not return until they come over the earth. {16:15} The fire is kindled and will not be put out until it consumes the foundations of the earth. {16:16} Just as an arrow shot by a mighty archer does not return, so the calamities sent upon the earth will not return. {16:17} Alas for me! Who will rescue me in those days? {16:18} The beginning of sorrows, when there will be much mourning; the beginning of famine, when many will perish; the beginning of wars, when the powerful will be terrified; the beginning of calamities, when everyone will tremble. What will they do when these calamities come? {16:19} Look, famine and plague, tribulation (suffering) and anguish are sent as punishments to correct humanity. {16:20} Yet for all this, they will not turn from their wrongdoings, nor will they remember the punishments. {16:21} Look, food will be so cheap on earth that people will think peace is assured, and then calamities will spring up on the earth—sword, famine, and great confusion. {16:22} Many living on the earth will perish by famine; those who survive the famine will die by the sword. {16:23} The dead will be thrown out like dung, and no one will console them; the earth will be left desolate, and its cities will be destroyed. {16:24} No one will be left to cultivate or sow the earth. {16:25} The trees will bear fruit, but who will gather it? {16:26} The grapes will ripen, but who will tread them? There will be great solitude everywhere; {16:27} one person will long to see another or even hear their voice. {16:28} From a city, ten will be left; and from the fields, two who have hidden in thick groves and rocks. {16:29} Just as in an olive orchard three or four olives may be left on each tree, {16:30} or when a vineyard is harvested some clusters may be left behind by those who search carefully, {16:31} so in those days three or four will be left when their houses are searched with the sword. {16:32} The earth will be left desolate, its fields will be overgrown with weeds, and its roads and paths will be filled with thorns, because no sheep will roam them. {16:33} Young women will mourn because they have no husbands; women will mourn because they have no partners; their daughters will mourn because they have no helpers. {16:34} Their husbands will be killed in war, and their partners will die of famine. {16:35} Listen now to these things and understand them, O servants of the Lord. {16:36} Behold the word of the Lord, accept it; do not disbelieve what the Lord says. {16:37} Behold, calamities draw near and are not delayed. {16:38} Just as a woman in her ninth month feels great pain as she approaches delivery, there will be no delay when the calamities come upon the earth, and the world will groan and be seized with pain on every side. {16:39} "Hear my words, O my people; prepare for battle, and amidst the calamities be like strangers on the earth. {16:40} Let the seller be like someone who will flee; let the buyer be like someone who will lose; {16:41} let the one doing business be like one who will not profit; and let the builder be like one who will not live in what they build; {16:42} let the sower be like one who will not reap; so too the pruner, like one who will not gather grapes; {16:43} those who marry, like those who will not have children; and those who do not marry, like those who are widowed. {16:44} Because those who labor, labor in vain; {16:45} for strangers will gather their harvests, plunder their goods, overthrow their houses, and take their children captive; for in captivity and famine they will have children. {16:46} Those who conduct business do so only to be robbed; the more they adorn their cities, their homes, their possessions, and themselves, {16:47} the angrier I will be with them for their sins," says the Lord. {16:48} Just as a respectable and virtuous woman despises a prostitute, {16:49} so righteousness will despise wickedness when she reveals herself, and will accuse it to its face when the defender of the righteous appears. {16:50} Therefore do not be like her or her deeds. {16:51} For behold, just a little while, and wickedness will be removed from the earth, and righteousness will reign over us. {16:52} Let no sinner claim that they have not sinned; for God will bring down burning coals of fire on the head of anyone who says, "I have not sinned before God and His glory." {16:53} Behold, the Lord knows all the works of men, their imaginations, their thoughts, and their hearts. {16:54} He said, "Let the earth be made," and it was made; "Let the heavens be made," and they were made. {16:55} At His command, the stars were set in place, and He knows their number. {16:56} He searches the deep and its treasures, has measured the sea and its contents; {16:57} He has confined the sea within its waters, and by His word has suspended the earth over the water; {16:58} He spread out the heavens like a canopy, and established them upon the waters; {16:59} He has put springs of water in the desert and pools on mountain tops, sending rivers from heights to water the earth; {16:60} He formed man, placed a heart within him, gave him breath, life, understanding, and the spirit of Almighty God; He made all things and knows hidden things in secret places. {16:61} Surely He knows your thoughts and what you think in your hearts! Woe to those who sin and try to hide their sins! {16:62} For the Lord will examine all their works strictly and will expose them publicly. {16:63} And when your sins are revealed before men, you will be ashamed, and your own iniquities will stand as your accusers on that day. {16:64} What will you do? How will you hide your sins before God and His angels? {16:65} Behold, God is the judge, fear Him! Cease from your sins, and forget your iniquities, never to commit them again; so God will lead you forth and deliver you from all tribulation. {16:66} For behold, the burning anger of a great multitude is kindled against you, and they will carry some of you off and feed you what was sacrificed to idols. {16:67} Those who consent to eat will be held in derision (mockery) and contempt and will be trampled underfoot. {16:68} For in many places and neighboring cities, there will be a great uprising against those who fear the Lord. {16:69} They will be like madmen, sparing no one, but plundering and destroying those who continue to fear the Lord. {16:70} For they will destroy and plunder their goods, and drive them from their homes. {16:71} Then the true quality of my chosen ones will be revealed, as gold tested by fire. {16:72} "Hear, my chosen ones," says the Lord. "The days of tribulation are coming, and I will deliver you from them. {16:73} Do not fear or doubt, for God is your guide. {16:74} You who keep my commandments and teachings," says the Lord God, "do not let your sins drag you down, or let your iniquities overcome you." {16:75} Woe to those who are suffocated by their sins and overwhelmed by their wrongdoings, like a field choked with weeds and its path blocked by thorns, making it impossible to pass through! {16:76} It is abandoned and destined to be consumed by fire.

The Book of Baruch

{1:1} These are the words of the book that Baruch, the son of Neraiah, son of Mahseiah, son of Zedekiah, son of Hasadiah, son of Hilkiah, wrote in Babylon, {1:2} in the fifth year, on the seventh day of the month, at the time when the Chaldeans captured Jerusalem and burned it with fire. {1:3} And Baruch read the words of this book to Jeconiah, the son of Jehoiakim, king of Judah, and to all the people who came to hear the book, {1:4} including the mighty men, the princes, the elders, and everyone, small and great, who lived in Babylon by the river Sud. {1:5} Then they wept, fasted, and prayed before the Lord; {1:6} and they gathered money, each giving what they could; {1:7} and they sent it to Jerusalem to Jehoiakim, the high priest, the son of Hilkiah, son of Shallum, and to the priests, and to all the people who were with him in Jerusalem. {1:8} At the same time, on the tenth day of Sivan, Baruch took the items from the house of the Lord that had been taken from the temple to return them to the land of Judah—the silver items that Zedekiah, the son of Josiah, king of Judah, had made, {1:9} after Nebuchadnezzar, king of Babylon, had taken Jeconiah and the princes and the prisoners and the mighty men and the people of the land from Jerusalem to Babylon. {1:10} And they said: "Here is the money we are sending you; buy burnt offerings, sin offerings, and incense with the money, prepare a grain offering, and offer them on the altar of the Lord our God; {1:11} and pray for the life of Nebuchadnezzar, king of Babylon, and for the life of his son Belshazzar, that their days on earth may be as the days of heaven. {1:12} The Lord will give us strength and light to our eyes, and we shall live under the protection of Nebuchadnezzar, king of Babylon, and under the protection of his son Belshazzar, and we will serve them for many days and find favor in their sight. {1:13} And pray for us to the Lord our God, for we have sinned against the Lord our God, and to this day his anger and wrath have not turned away from us. {1:14} You shall read this book we are sending you to make your confession in the house of the Lord on the days of the feasts and at appointed times. {1:15} "And you shall say: 'Righteousness belongs to the Lord our God, but confusion of face, as today, belongs to us, to the men of Judah, to the inhabitants of Jerusalem, {1:16} and to our kings, princes, priests, prophets, and our ancestors, {1:17} because we have sinned before the Lord, {1:18} and have disobeyed him, and have not listened to the voice of the Lord our God, to follow the laws of the Lord that he set before us. {1:19} From the day the Lord brought our ancestors out of Egypt until today, we have been disobedient to the Lord our God, and we have been careless in not listening to his voice. {1:20} So to this day, the calamities and curses that the Lord declared through Moses, his servant, when he brought our ancestors out of Egypt to give us a land flowing with milk and honey, have stuck to us. {1:21} We did not listen to the voice of the Lord our God in all the words of the prophets he sent to us, but each of us followed desires of our own wicked hearts by serving other gods & doing what is evil in the sight of the Lord our God."

{2:1} So the Lord confirmed his word, which he spoke against us, against our judges who judged Israel, against our kings, against our princes, and against the men of Israel and Judah. {2:2} Under the whole heaven, nothing has been done like what he has done in Jerusalem, as written in the law of Moses, {2:3} that we should eat the flesh of our sons and daughters. {2:4} He gave us into the power of all the kingdoms around us, becoming a disgrace and a desolation among the surrounding peoples where the Lord has scattered us. {2:5} We were brought low and not raised up again because we sinned against the Lord our God by not heeding his voice. {2:6} Righteousness belongs to the Lord our God, but confusion of face belongs to us and our ancestors, as it does today. {2:7} All the calamities with which the Lord threatened us have come upon us. {2:8} Yet we have not sought the favor of the Lord by turning away from the thoughts of our wicked hearts. {2:9} The Lord has kept the calamities ready, and he has brought them upon us, for the Lord is righteous in all his works which he commanded us to do. {2:10} Yet we have not obeyed his voice to walk in the laws of the Lord that he set before us. {2:11} And now, O Lord God of Israel, who brought your people out of Egypt with a mighty hand, with signs and wonders, and with great power and an outstretched arm, and made a name for yourself, as it is today, {2:12} we have sinned, we have been ungodly, we have done wrong, O Lord our God, against all your commands. {2:13} Let your anger turn away from us, for we are left few in number among the nations where you have scattered us. {2:14} Hear, O Lord, our prayer and our plea, and for your own sake deliver us, and grant us favor in the eyes of those who have taken us into exile; {2:15} that all the earth may know that you are the Lord our God, for Israel and his descendants are called by your name. {2:16} O Lord, look down from your holy dwelling and consider us. Incline your ear, O Lord, and hear; {2:17} open your eyes, O Lord, and see; for the dead in Hades, whose spirits have been taken from their bodies, will not give glory or justice to the Lord, {2:18} but the one who is greatly distressed, bent over and weak, with failing eyes, and the one who hungers, will give you glory and righteousness, O Lord. {2:19} It is not because of any righteous deeds of our fathers or kings that we bring our prayer for mercy before you, O Lord our God. {2:20} For you have sent your anger and your wrath upon us, as you declared by your prophets, saying: {2:21} "Thus says the Lord: Bend your shoulders and serve the king of Babylon, and you will remain in the land I gave to your ancestors. {2:22} But if you do not obey the voice of the Lord and do not serve the king of Babylon, {2:23} I will put an end to the sounds of joy and gladness, the voice of the bridegroom and the voice of the bride, and the whole land will become a desolation without inhabitants." {2:24} But we did not obey your voice to serve the king of Babylon; and you have confirmed your words, which you spoke by your prophets, that the bones of our kings and ancestors would be brought out of their graves; {2:25} and behold, they have been cast out to the heat of the day and the frost of the night. They perished in great misery, by famine, sword, and pestilence. {2:26} The house that is called by your name you have made as it is today because of the wickedness of the house of Israel and the house of Judah. {2:27} Yet you have dealt with us, O Lord our God, in all your kindness and great compassion, {2:28} as you spoke by your servant Moses on the day you commanded him to write your law in the presence of the people of Israel, saying, {2:29} "If you do not obey my voice, this very large group will surely become a small number among the nations where I will scatter them. {2:30} For I know they will not obey me, for they are a stubborn people. But in the land of their exile, they will come to their senses, {2:31} and they will know that I am the Lord their God. I will give them a heart that obeys and ears that hear; {2:32} they will praise me in the land of their exile, remember my name, {2:33} and turn from their stubbornness and wicked deeds, for they will remember the ways of their ancestors who sinned against the Lord. {2:34} I will bring them back to the land I swore to give their ancestors, to Abraham, Isaac, and Jacob, and they will rule over it; I will increase them, and they will not be diminished. {2:35} I will make an everlasting covenant with them to be their God, and they will be my people; and I will never again remove my people Israel from the land I have given them."

{3:1} O Lord Almighty, God of Israel, the anguished soul and the weary spirit cry out to you. {3:2} Hear, O Lord, and have mercy, for we have sinned against you. {3:3} You are enthroned forever, and we are perishing forever. {3:4} O Lord Almighty, God of Israel, hear now the prayers of the dead of Israel and of the sons of those who sinned against you, who did not heed the voice of the Lord their God, leading to calamities that cling to us. {3:5} Do not remember the sins of our fathers, but in this crisis, remember your power and your name. {3:6} For you are the Lord our God, and we will praise you, O Lord. {3:7} You have instilled the fear of you in our hearts so that we may call upon your name; we will praise you in our exile, for we have removed from our hearts all the sins of our fathers who sinned against you. {3:8} Behold, we are in our exile today, where you have scattered us, to be reproached, cursed, and punished for all the sins of our fathers who forsook the Lord our God. {3:9} Hear the commandments of life, O Israel; listen and learn wisdom! {3:10} Why is it, O Israel, that you are in the land of your enemies, growing old in a foreign country, defiled among the dead, {3:11} counted among those in Hades? {3:12} You have forsaken the source of wisdom. {3:13} If you had walked in God's ways, you would dwell in peace forever. {3:14} Learn where wisdom, strength, and understanding are, so that you may discern where there is a long life, light for the eyes, and peace. {3:15} Who has found her place? Who has entered her storehouses? {3:16} Where are the rulers of the nations, those who govern the beasts on earth; {3:17} those who play with the birds of the air, hoarding silver and gold that people trust, with no end to their wealth; {3:18} those who scheme to acquire silver, anxious, whose labors are beyond measure? {3:19} They have vanished and gone down to Hades, while others have taken their place. {3:20} Young men have seen the light of day and lived on earth; but they have not learned the way to knowledge, nor understood her paths, nor grasped her. {3:21} Their sons have strayed far from her ways. {3:22} She has not been heard of in Canaan, nor seen in Teman; {3:23} the sons of Hagar, who seek understanding on earth, the merchants of Merran and Teman, the storytellers and seekers of knowledge, have not learned the way to wisdom or considered her paths. {3:24} O Israel, how great is the house of God! How vast is the territory he possesses! {3:25} It is great and boundless; it is high and immeasurable. {3:26} The giants were born there, famous of old, great in stature, skilled in war. {3:27} God did not choose them or give them the way to knowledge; {3:28} they perished because they had no wisdom; they perished through their folly. {3:29} Who has ascended into heaven, taken her, and brought her down from the clouds? {3:30} Who has crossed the sea and found her, and will buy her for pure gold? {3:31} No one knows the way to her or cares about the path to her. {3:32} But he who knows all things knows her; he found her through his understanding. He who prepared the earth for all time filled it with four-footed creatures; {3:33} he who sends forth the light, and it goes, calling it, and it obeys him in fear; {3:34} the stars shine in their watches and rejoice; he calls them, and they respond, "Here we are!" They shine with gladness for him who made them. {3:35} This is our God; no one else can be compared to him! {3:36} He found the whole way to knowledge and gave her to Jacob his servant and to Israel whom he loved. {3:37} Afterward, she appeared on earth and lived among men.

{4:1} She is the book of God's commandments, and the law that lasts forever. Everyone who holds on to her will live, but those who forsake her will die. {4:2} Turn, O Jacob, and take her; walk toward the shining light she brings. {4:3} Do not give your glory to another, or your advantages to a foreign people. {4:4} Happy are we, O Israel, for we know what pleases God. {4:5} Take courage, my people, O memorial of Israel! {4:6} You were not sold to the nations for destruction, but you were handed over to your enemies because you angered God. {4:7} You provoked him who made you by sacrificing to demons instead of to God. {4:8} You forgot the everlasting God who raised you up, and you grieved Jerusalem, who nurtured you. {4:9} For she witnessed the wrath from God that fell upon you, and she said: "Listen, you neighbors of Zion, God has brought great sorrow upon me; {4:10} for I have seen the captivity of my sons and daughters, which the Everlasting brought upon them. {4:11} I nurtured them with joy, but I sent them away with weeping and sorrow. {4:12} Let no one rejoice over me, a widow bereaved of many; I was left desolate because of my children's sins, for they turned away from God's law. {4:13} They disregarded his statutes; they did not follow God's commandments or walk in the paths of discipline in his righteousness. {4:14} Let the neighbors of Zion come; remember the captivity of my sons and daughters, which the Everlasting brought upon them. {4:15} He brought against them a distant nation, a shameless people who spoke a strange language, having no respect for the elderly or compassion for children. {4:16} They took away the beloved sons of the widow and bereaved the lonely woman of her daughters. {4:17} But I, how can I help you? {4:18} For he who brought these calamities upon you will rescue you from your enemies. {4:19} Go, my children, go; for I have been left desolate. {4:20} I have taken off the robe of peace and put on the sackcloth of my supplication; I will cry to the Everlasting all my days. {4:21} Take courage, my children; cry to God, and he will deliver you from the power and hand of your enemies. {4:22} For I have put my hope in the Everlasting to save you, and joy has come to me from the Holy One because of the mercy that is soon coming to you from your everlasting Savior. {4:23} For I sent you out with sorrow and weeping, but God will bring you back to me with joy and gladness forever. {4:24} As the neighbors of Zion have seen your capture, they will soon see your salvation from God, which will come to you with great glory and the splendor of the Everlasting. {4:25} My children, endure with patience the wrath that has come upon you from God. Your enemy has overtaken you, but you will soon witness their destruction and tread upon their necks. {4:26} My tender sons have traveled rough paths; they were taken away like a flock carried off by the enemy. {4:27} Take courage, my children, and cry to God, for you will be remembered by him who brought this upon you. {4:28} Just as you intended to stray from God, return with tenfold zeal to seek him. {4:29} For he who brought these calamities upon you will bring you everlasting joy with your salvation. {4:30} Take courage, O Jerusalem, for he who named you will comfort you. {4:31} Wretched will be those who afflicted you and rejoiced at your fall. {4:32} Wretched will be the cities that your children served as slaves; wretched will be the city that received your sons. {4:33} Just as she rejoiced at your downfall and was glad for your ruin, so she will mourn her own desolation. {4:34} I will take away her pride in her great population, and her insolence will turn to grief. {4:35} Fire will come upon her from the Everlasting for many days, and for a long time, she will be inhabited by demons. {4:36} Look toward the east, O Jerusalem, and see the joy coming to you from God! {4:37} Behold, your sons are returning, whom you sent away; they are coming back, gathered from east and west, at the word of the Holy One, rejoicing in the glory of God.

{5:1} Take off the garment of your sorrow and suffering, O Jerusalem, and put on forever the beauty and glory from God. {5:2} Put on the robe of righteousness from God; place the crown of glory from the Everlasting on your head. {5:3} For God will display your splendor everywhere under heaven. {5:4} Your name will forever be called by God, "Peace of righteousness and glory of godliness." {5:5} Arise, O Jerusalem, stand on high and look toward the east, and see your children gathered from the west and east, at the command of the Holy One, rejoicing that God has remembered them. {5:6} For they went out from you on foot, led away by their enemies; but God will bring them back to you, carried in glory, like a royal procession. {5:7} God has decreed that every high mountain and the everlasting hills be made low, and the valleys filled up, to create level ground, so that Israel may walk safely in God's glory. {5:8} The forests and every fragrant tree will provide shade for Israel at God's command. {5:9} For God will lead Israel with joy, in the light of his glory, with the mercy and righteousness that come from him.

The Epistle of Jeremiah

{6:1} This is a copy of a letter that Jeremiah sent to those who were to be taken to Babylon as captives by the king of Babylon, conveying the message that God had commanded him to deliver. {6:2} Because of the sins you have committed against God, you will be taken to Babylon as captives by Nebuchadnezzar, king of the Babylonians. {6:3} When you arrive in Babylon, you will remain there for many years, for a long time, up to seven generations; after that, I will bring you back from there in peace. {6:4} In Babylon, you will see gods made of silver, gold, and wood, which are carried on men's shoulders and instill fear in the non-believers. {6:5} So be careful not to be like the foreigners or to let fear of these gods take hold of you when you see the crowds worshiping them. {6:6} Instead, say in your heart, "It is you, O Lord, whom we must worship." {6:7} For my angel is with you, and he is watching over your lives. {6:8} Their tongues are smoothed by craftsmen, and they are covered in gold and silver; but they are false and cannot speak. {6:9} People make crowns of gold for the heads of their gods, just like one would for a girl who loves jewelry; {6:10} and sometimes the priests secretly take gold and silver from these gods and use it for themselves, {6:11} even giving some to prostitutes in the brothels. They dress their gods in garments like those of men—these gods of silver, gold, and wood, {6:12} which cannot save themselves from rust and decay. After they have been adorned in purple robes, {6:13} their faces are wiped clean because of the dust from the temple that settles on them. {6:14} Like a local ruler, the god holds a scepter, but it cannot punish anyone who offends it. {6:15} It has a dagger in its right hand and an axe, but it cannot protect itself from war or robbers. {6:16} Clearly, they are not gods, so do not fear them. {6:17} Just as a broken dish is useless, so are the gods of the non-believers when they are set up in temples. Their eyes are filled with the dust raised by the feet of those who enter. {6:18} Just as the gates are shut on a man who has offended a king, as though he were sentenced to death, the priests secure their temples with doors, locks, and bars to prevent them from being robbed. {6:19} They light lamps, even more than they do for themselves, even though their gods cannot see them. {6:20} They are like a beam in the temple, yet people say their hearts have melted when worms from the earth consume them and their garments. They do not notice {6:21} when their faces are blackened by the smoke of the temple. {6:22} Bats, swallows, and birds rest on their bodies and heads; and so do cats. {6:23} From this, you will know that they are not gods, so do not fear them. {6:24} As for the gold they wear for beauty—it will not shine unless someone wipes off the rust; for even when they are being cast, they have no feeling. {6:25} They can be bought at any price, but they have no breath in them. {6:26} Without feet, they are carried on men's shoulders, showing their worthlessness to humanity. {6:27} Those who serve them are ashamed because these gods are made to stand, lest they fall to the ground. If someone sets one of them upright, it cannot move itself; and if it tips over, it cannot right itself; yet gifts are placed before them as if they were offerings to the dead. {6:28} The priests sell the sacrifices offered to these gods and use the money; and their wives preserve some with salt, but they do not give any to the poor or helpless. {6:29} Sacrifices to them can be touched by women who are menstruating or at childbirth. Since you know from these things that they are not gods, do not fear them. {6:30} Why should they be called gods? Women prepare meals for gods made of silver, gold, and wood; {6:31} and in their temples, the priests sit with their clothes torn, their heads and beards shaved, and their heads uncovered. {6:32} They howl and shout before their gods, just as people do at a funeral feast for someone who has died. {6:33} The priests take some of the clothing from their gods to dress their wives and children. {6:34} Whether someone does good or evil to them, they cannot repay it. They cannot install or remove a king. {6:35} Likewise, they cannot grant wealth or money; if someone makes a vow to them and does not fulfill it, they will not demand it. {6:36} They cannot save a man from death or rescue the weak from the strong. {6:37} They cannot restore sight to a blind man; they cannot save someone in distress. {6:38} They cannot show compassion to a widow or do good to an orphan. {6:39} These things made of wood and covered in gold and silver are like stones from the mountain, and those who serve them will be put to shame. {6:40} Why then should anyone think they are gods or call them gods? Even the Chaldeans themselves disrespect them; {6:41} when they see a mute man, who cannot speak, they bring him and pray to Bel that the man may speak, as if Bel could understand. {6:42} Yet they themselves do not recognize this and abandon them, for they have no sense. {6:43} And the women, with cords around them, sit along the passageways, burning bran for incense; and when one of them is led away by a passerby and has sexual relations, she mocks the woman next to her, because she was not as attractive as herself and her cord was not broken. {6:44} Everything done for them is false. Why then should anyone think they are gods or call them gods? {6:45} They are made by carpenters and goldsmiths; they can be nothing more than what the craftsmen want them to be. {6:46} The men who make them will certainly not live very long themselves; how then can the things made by them be gods? {6:47} They have left only lies and reproach for those who come after. {6:48} When war or disaster comes upon them, the priests consult together to find a place to hide themselves and their gods. {6:49} How then can anyone fail to see that these are not gods? They cannot save themselves from war or disaster. {6:50} Since they are made of wood and covered in gold and silver, it will eventually be clear that they are false. {6:51} It will be evident to all nations and kings that they are not gods but the work of human hands, and that there is no divine action in them. {6:52} Who then can fail to realize that they are not gods? {6:53} For they cannot install a king over a nation or give rain to people. {6:54} They cannot judge their own cases or deliver those who are wronged, for they have no power; they are like crows between heaven and earth. {6:55} When fire breaks out in a temple of wooden gods covered in gold or silver, their priests will flee and escape, but the gods will burn just like beams. {6:56} Besides, they can offer no resistance to a king or any enemies. Why then should anyone accept or think they are gods? {6:57} Gods made of wood and covered in silver and gold cannot save themselves from thieves and robbers. {6:58} Strong men will strip them of their gold and silver and the garments they wear, and carry away the loot, and they will not be able to help themselves. {6:59} So it is better to be a courageous king or a household utensil that serves its owner than to be these false gods; better even a door of a house that protects its contents than these false gods; even a wooden pillar in a palace is better than these false gods. {6:60} For the sun, moon, and stars, shining and sent forth for service, are obedient. {6:61} Likewise, lightning, when it flashes, is widely seen; and the wind also blows across every land. {6:62} When God commands the clouds to go across the whole world, they carry out his command. {6:63} And the fire sent from above to consume mountains and forests does what it is ordered. But these idols cannot be compared to them in appearance or power. {6:64} Therefore, one must not think they are gods or call them gods, for they cannot decide a case or do good to humanity. {6:65} Since you know that they are not gods, do not fear them. {6:66} For they can neither curse nor bless kings; {6:67} they cannot show signs in the heavens or among the nations, or shine like the sun or give light like the moon. {6:68} The wild animals are better than they are, for they can flee for safety and help themselves. {6:69} So we have no evidence at all that they are gods; therefore, do not fear them. {6:70} Like a scarecrow in a cucumber field that guards nothing, so are their gods made of wood and covered in gold and silver. {6:71} Similarly, their wooden gods covered in gold and silver are like a thorn bush in a garden, where every bird perches; or like a dead body cast out into the darkness. {6:72} By the purple and linen that rot upon them, you will know they are not gods; they will ultimately be consumed and become a reproach in the land. {6:73} Therefore, a just man who has no idols is better off, for he will be far from reproach.

The Paralipomena of Jeremiah

{1:1} In those days, the Lord spoke to Jeremiah, saying, "Get up and leave the city with Baruch, because I am going to destroy it because of the great sin of the people living there. {1:2} Your prayers are like strong pillars in the midst of the city, and like an unbreakable wall surrounding it. {1:3} So, leave now before the army of the Chaldeans surrounds the city." {1:4} Jeremiah then said, "Please, Lord, allow me, your servant, to speak in your presence." {1:5} The Lord replied, "Speak." {1:6} Jeremiah said, "Lord, will you really give this city into the hands of the Chaldeans, so that they can boast that they have defeated it?" {1:7} "My Lord, if it is your will, then let it be destroyed by your own hand and not by the Chaldeans." {1:8} But God said, "You, get up and leave. {1:9} They will not boast. Unless I open the gates, they will not be able to enter." {1:10} "So go to Baruch and tell him this. {1:11} At the sixth hour of the night, go up onto the city walls and see that unless I open the gates, the Chaldeans cannot enter." {1:12} After saying these things, the Lord departed from him.

{2:1} And Jeremiah ran and told these things to Baruch; and as they went into the temple of God, Jeremiah tore his garments, put dust on his head, and entered the holy place of God. {2:2} And when Baruch saw him with dust sprinkled on his head and his garments torn, he cried out in a loud voice, saying: "Father Jeremiah, what are you doing? What sin has the people committed?" {2:3} (For whenever the people sinned, Jeremiah would sprinkle dust on his head and would pray for the people until their sin was forgiven.) {2:4} So Baruch asked him, saying: "Father, what is this?" {2:5} And Jeremiah said to him: "Refrain from rending your garments — rather, let us rend our hearts! And let us not draw water for the trough, but let us weep and fill them with tears! For the Lord will not have mercy on this people." {2:6} And Baruch said: "Father Jeremiah, what has happened?" {2:7} And Jeremiah said: "God is delivering the city into the hands of the king of the Chaldeans, to take the people captive into Babylon." {2:8} And when Baruch heard these things, he also tore his garments and said: "Father Jeremiah, who has made this known to you?" {2:9} And Jeremiah said to him: "Stay with me awhile, until the sixth hour of the night, so that you may know that this word is true." {2:10} Therefore they both remained in the altar-area weeping, and their garments were torn.

{3:1} At the sixth hour, when they had climbed up onto the city walls, they heard the sound of trumpets. {3:2} Then angels came down from heaven, holding torches in their hands, and they set them on the walls of the city. {3:3} When the people saw the angels, they wept and said, "Now we know that the word the Lord spoke is true." {3:4} They begged the angels, saying, "We beg you, do not destroy the city until we have spoken to God." {3:6} Then Jeremiah said, "I beg you, Lord, allow me to speak in your presence." {3:7} The Lord replied, "Speak." {3:8} Jeremiah said, "Lord, we know that you are handing the city over to its enemies, and your people are being taken to Babylon. {3:9} But what should we do with your holy vessels?" {3:10} And God answered, "Bury them in the earth, saying: 'Hear, O earth, the voice of your creator, who founded you upon the waters, who sealed you with seven seals for seven ages. After this, you will receive your ornaments.'" {3:11} "Keep the vessels of the temple service safe until the gathering of the beloved." {3:12} Jeremiah spoke again, saying, "I beg you, Lord, what should I do for Abimelech the Ethiopian, who has shown so much kindness to your servant? {3:13} He pulled me out of the pit where they had thrown me, and I don't want him to see the destruction of the city because he is a weak man." {3:14} The Lord replied to Jeremiah, "Send him to the vineyard of Agrippa, and I will hide him in the shadow of the mountain until the people are about to return from captivity." {3:15} "But you, Jeremiah, go with your people into Babylon and stay with them, preaching to them, until I bring them back." {3:16} "But leave Baruch here." {3:18} Then they went into the temple, and following the Lord's instructions, they buried the vessels of the temple service in the earth. {3:21} The next morning, Jeremiah said to Abimelech, "Take a basket, child, and go to Agrippa's estate by the mountain road. Bring back figs for the sick people, for you have found favor with them, and glory is upon your head." {3:22} Immediately, Abimelech went to the field.

{4:1} And when morning came, behold, the host of the Chaldeans surrounded the city. {4:2} And the great angel trumpeted, saying: "Enter the city, host of the Chaldeans; for behold, the gate is opened for you. {4:3} Therefore, let the king enter with his multitudes, and let him take all the people captive." {4:4} But taking the keys of the temple, Jeremiah went outside the city and threw them away in the presence of the sun, saying: "I say to you, Sun, take the keys of the temple of God and guard them until the day in which the Lord asks you for them. {4:5} For we have not been found worthy to keep them, for we have become unfaithful guardians." {4:6} While Jeremiah was still weeping for the people, they brought him out with the people and dragged them into Babylon. {4:7} But Baruch put dust on his head and sat and wailed this lamentation, saying: "Why has Jerusalem been devastated? Because of the sins of the beloved people, she was delivered into the hands of enemies — because of our sins and those of the people." {4:8} "But let not the lawless ones boast and say: 'We were strong enough to take the city of God by our might'; but it was delivered to you because of our sins." {4:9} "And God will pity us and cause us to return to our city, but you will not survive!" {4:10} "Blessed are our fathers, Abraham, Isaac, and Jacob, for they departed from this world and did not see the destruction of this city." {4:11} When he had said this, Baruch departed from the city, weeping and saying: "Grieving because of you, Jerusalem, I went out from you." {4:12} And he remained sitting in a tomb, while the angels came to him and explained to him everything that the Lord revealed to him through them.

{5:1} Meanwhile, Abimelech, carrying the figs in the intense heat, came upon a tree and sat under its shade to rest for a moment. {5:2} As he leaned his head on the basket, he fell asleep for seventy times. This happened as God had commanded, fulfilling the word He had spoken to Jeremiah: "I will hide him." {5:3} When Abimelech woke up, he said, "I slept so sweetly for a short while, and now my head feels heavy because I didn't get enough rest." {5:4} When he uncovered the figs, he found that they were dripping with milk, as if they had been gathered just moments ago. {5:5} He said to himself, "I'd like to sleep a bit longer, but since Jeremiah sent me in such a hurry, if I do, I'll be late, and he will be distressed." {5:6} "Isn't there enough toil and heat each day? I should leave quickly, deliver the figs, and then I can rest." {5:7} So he took the figs and went into Jerusalem, but when he arrived, he did not recognize his house, nor the houses of his relatives or friends. {5:8} He said, "Blessed be the Lord! A trance has come over me today!" {5:9} "This is not the city! I must be lost, for lack of sleep I have gone astray." {5:11z1} He left the city and, searching for landmarks, he said, "Indeed, this is the city! I must have gone off track." {5:12} Returning to the city, he searched again but found no one from his family or friends. He said, "Blessed be the Lord! A great trance has come over me!" {5:13} He went out again, staying there in grief, unsure of what to do. {5:14} Setting the basket down, he said, "I must sit here until the Lord removes this trance from me." {5:15} As he sat there, an old man came from the field, and Abimelech asked him, "Sir, what city is this?" {5:16} The old man replied, "It is Jerusalem, child." {5:17} Abimelech then asked, "Where is Jeremiah, the priest of God, and Baruch the scribe, and all the people of the city? I couldn't find any of them." {5:18} The old man said, "Are you not from this city? Today you remember Jeremiah and ask about him." {5:19} "Jeremiah has been in Babylon with the people since they were taken captive by Nebuchadnezzar the king seventy times ago. How is it that you, being a young man, are asking about things that I have never seen?" {5:20} Hearing this, Abimelech said to him, "If you weren't an old man, and if it weren't against the law for a man of God to rebuke one older than himself, I would laugh at you and say that you are out of your mind to say that the people were taken into captivity in Babylon." {5:21} "Even if the heavens opened and angels came down with power and authority, it still would not be enough time for them to go into Babylon!" {5:22} "For how much time has passed since my father Jeremiah sent me to Agrippa's estate for a few figs, so I could bring them to the sick people?" {5:23} "I went to a tree to rest in the heat, and fell asleep for a little while." {5:24} "Thinking I was late, I uncovered the figs and found them dripping with milk, just as I had picked them." {5:25} "And yet you say the people were taken into Babylon?" {5:26} "But so you will know I'm not lying, take the figs and see for yourself." {5:28} When the old man saw this, he said, "Oh, child, you are the son of a righteous man. God did not want you to see the desolation of this city, so He brought this trance upon you." {5:29} "Behold, it has been seventy times since the people were taken captive to Babylon with Jeremiah from this day." {5:30} "But so you will know that I'm telling the truth, look at the field and see that the crops have not yet ripened." {5:31} "And notice that the figs are out of season, and be enlightened, so that you will be convinced that I am telling the truth." {5:32} Then Abimelech, observing carefully and with great clarity, said, "Blessed be the God of heaven and earth, the Rest of the souls of the righteous." {5:33} He asked the old man, "What month is it?" {5:34} The old man replied, "The twelfth." {5:35} Abimelech then gave some figs to the old man and left, after blessing him.

{6:1} After this, Abimelech left the city and prayed to the Lord. {6:2} And behold, an angel of the Lord appeared and took him by the right hand, bringing him back to where Baruch was sitting, and he found him in a tomb. {6:3} When they saw each other, they both wept and embraced each other. {6:4} But when Baruch looked up, he saw the figs covered in Abimelech's basket. {6:5} Then, lifting his eyes to heaven, he prayed, saying: {6:6} "You are the God who rewards those who love You. Prepare my heart, and let me rejoice and be glad while I am in Your presence, saying to my earthly body, 'Your sorrow has been turned to joy,' for the One who is sufficient is coming and will deliver you, for there is no sin in you." {6:7} "Revive, O my soul, in your pure faith, and believe that you will live!" {6:8} "Look at these figs — behold, they are 66 years old and have not shriveled or rotted, but are still dripping milk." {6:9} "So it will be with you, my flesh, if you do what is commanded by the angel of righteousness." {6:10} "He who preserved the basket of figs will again preserve you by His power." {6:11} When Baruch had said this, he turned to Abimelech and said: "Stand up and let us pray that the Lord may show us how we can send a report to Jeremiah in Babylon about the shelter you received along the way." {6:12} And Baruch prayed, saying: "Lord God, our strength, the light that comes from Your mouth, {6:13} we beseech You, whose great name no one can fully know, hear the voice of Your servants and let wisdom enter our hearts. {6:14} What should we do, and how should we send this message to Jeremiah in Babylon?" {6:15} While Baruch was still praying, behold, an angel of the Lord appeared and spoke these words to him: "Agent of the light, do not worry about how you will send this message to Jeremiah; for an eagle is coming to you at dawn tomorrow, and you will send him to Jeremiah." {6:16} "Therefore, write a letter. 'Say to the children of Israel: Let the stranger who comes among you be set apart, and let fifteen days pass; after that, I will lead you into your city, says the Lord.'" {6:17} "He who is not separated from Babylon will not enter the city; and I will punish them by preventing them from being received by the Babylonians, says the Lord." {6:18} When the angel had said this, he departed from Baruch. {6:19} Baruch then went to the marketplace of the Gentiles, bought papyrus and ink, and wrote the following letter: {6:20} "Baruch, the servant of God, writes to Jeremiah, who is in captivity in Babylon: Greetings! Rejoice, for God has not allowed us to depart this life grieving for the city, which has been laid waste and defiled. {6:21} The Lord has had mercy on our tears and remembered the covenant He made with our ancestors, Abraham, Isaac, and Jacob. {6:22} He sent His angel to me and told me the words I am sending to you." {6:23} "These are the words the Lord, the God of Israel, who brought us out of Egypt, out of the furnace of affliction, spoke: 'Because you did not keep My commandments and your heart was lifted up, and you were proud before Me, in My anger and wrath, I handed you over to furnace in Babylon.'" {6:24} "But now, if you listen to My voice, spoken through My servant Jeremiah, I will bring those who listen out of Babylon; but those who do not listen will be strangers to both Jerusalem and Babylon." {6:25} "And you will test them by the waters of the Jordan; whoever does not listen will be exposed — this is the sign of the great seal."

{7:1} Baruch then stood up, left the tomb, and found the eagle sitting outside. {7:2} The eagle spoke to him in a human voice, saying: "Hail, Baruch, steward of the faith!" {7:3} Baruch replied, "You who speak are chosen from all the birds of heaven, for this is clear from the gleam in your eyes. Tell me, then, what are you doing here?" {7:4} The eagle answered, "I was sent so that through me you may send whatever message you wish." {7:5} Baruch asked, "Can you carry this message to Jeremiah in Babylon?" {7:6} The eagle responded, "Indeed, I was sent for this purpose." {7:7} Baruch took the letter and fifteen figs from Abimelech's basket, tied them to the eagle's neck, and said: "I say to you, king of birds, go in peace with good health and carry this message for me. {7:8} Do not be like the raven that Noah sent out, which never returned to the ark, but be like the dove that, on the third time, brought back a report to the righteous man." {7:9} "So you too, take this good message to Jeremiah and to those in bondage with him, that it may go well with you — take this papyrus to the people and to the chosen one of God." {7:10} "Even if all the birds of heaven surround you and try to fight with you, struggle — the Lord will give you strength." {7:11} "Do not turn aside to the right or the left, but go straight like an arrow, empowered by God, and the glory of the Lord will be with you the whole way." {7:12} Then the eagle took flight and flew off to Babylon, carrying the letter tied around his neck. When he arrived, he rested on a post outside the city in a desolate place. {7:13} He remained silent until Jeremiah came along, for he and some of the people were coming out to bury a corpse outside the city. {7:14} (Jeremiah had petitioned King Nebuchadnezzar, saying, "Give me a place to bury the dead of my people," and the king granted it.) {7:15} As they were coming out with the body and weeping, they came to where the eagle was. {7:16} The eagle cried out loudly, saying: "I say to you, Jeremiah, the chosen one of God, gather the people and come here so they may hear the letter I have brought from Baruch and Abimelech." {7:17} When Jeremiah heard this, he glorified God and gathered the people, along with their wives and children, to the eagle. {7:18} The eagle descended onto the corpse, and it revived. {7:19} (This was done so that they might believe.) {7:20} All the people were amazed at what had happened and said, "This is the God who appeared to our ancestors in the wilderness through Moses, and now He has appeared to us through the eagle." {7:21} The eagle said: "Jeremiah, untie this letter and read it to the people." So Jeremiah untied the letter and read it to the people. {7:22} When they heard it, they wept and put dust on their heads, and said to Jeremiah: "Deliver us and tell us what we must do to enter our city again." {7:23} Jeremiah answered, "Do whatever the letter says, and the Lord will lead us back into our city." {7:24} Jeremiah then wrote a letter to Baruch, saying: "My beloved son, do not neglect your prayers, pleading with God on our behalf, that He might guide our way until we are free from the rule of this lawless king." {7:25} "For you have been found righteous before God, and He did not allow you to come here, so you would not witness the affliction the people have endured at the hands of the Babylonians." {7:26} "It is like a father with an only son, who is given over to punishment; those who see his father console him by covering his face, so he does not see the suffering of his son and grieve even more." {7:27} "So God took pity on you and did not allow you to enter Babylon, so you would not witness the suffering of the people." {7:28} "Since we arrived here, grief has never left us, for 66 years today." {7:29} "Many times, when I went out, I found some of the people hung by King Nebuchadnezzar, crying, 'Have mercy on us, God-ZAR!'" {7:30} "When I heard this, I grieved and mourned doubly, not just because they were hung, but because they were calling out to a foreign god." {7:31} "But I remembered the festive days we celebrated in Jerusalem before the captivity, and when I recalled them, I groaned and returned home weeping." {7:32} "Now, pray where you are, you and Abimelech, for this people, that they may hear my voice and obey the decrees of my mouth, so we may depart from here." {7:33} "For all this time, they have kept us in subjection, demanding: 'Sing us a song from the songs of Zion.'" {7:34} "And we reply: 'How can we sing the Lord's song in a foreign land?'" {7:35} After this, Jeremiah tied the letter to the eagle's neck and said: "Go in peace, and may the Lord watch over both of us." {7:36} The eagle took flight and returned to Jerusalem, bringing the letter to Baruch. When Baruch untied it and read it, he kissed the letter and wept upon hearing of the afflictions of the people. {7:37} Meanwhile, Jeremiah took the figs and distributed them to the sick among the people, continuing to teach them to avoid the pollution of the Gentiles in Babylon.

{8:1} And the day came when the Lord brought the people out of Babylon. {8:2} And the Lord said to Jeremiah: "Rise up — you and the people — and go to the Jordan and speak to the people: {8:3} 'Let anyone who desires the Lord forsake the ways of Babylon. {8:4} As for the men who have taken wives from them and the women who have taken husbands from them — those who listen to you shall cross over, and you shall bring them into Jerusalem; but those who do not listen to you, do not lead them there.'" {8:5} And Jeremiah spoke these words to the people, and they arose and came to the Jordan to cross over. {8:6} As he told them the words that the Lord had spoken to him, half of those who had taken spouses from them did not wish to listen to Jeremiah but said to him: {8:7} "We will never forsake our wives, but we will bring them back with us into our city." {8:8} So they crossed the Jordan and came to Jerusalem. {8:9} And Jeremiah and Baruch and Abimelech stood up and said: "No man who joined with the Babylonians shall enter this city!" {8:10} And they said to one another: "Let us arise and return to Babylon to our place," and they departed. {8:11} But while they were coming to Babylon, the Babylonians came out to meet them, saying: "You shall not enter our city, for you hated us and left us secretly; therefore, you cannot come in with us. {8:12} For we have taken a solemn oath together in the name of our god to receive neither you nor your children, since you left us secretly." {8:13} And when they heard this, they returned and came to a desolate place some distance from Jerusalem, where they built a city for themselves and named it 'SAMARIA.' {8:14} And Jeremiah sent to them, saying: "Repent, for the angel of righteousness is coming and will lead you to your exalted place."

{9:1} Now those who were with Jeremiah were rejoicing and offering sacrifices on behalf of the people for nine days. {9:2} But on the tenth day, Jeremiah alone offered sacrifice. {9:3} And he prayed, saying: "Holy, holy, holy, fragrant aroma of the living trees, true light that enlightens me until I ascend to you; {9:4} For your mercy, I beg you — for the sweet voice of the two seraphim, I beg — for another fragrant aroma. {9:5} And may Michael, the archangel of righteousness, who opens the gates to the righteous, be my guardian until he causes the righteous to enter. {9:6} I beg you, almighty Lord of all creation, unbegotten and incomprehensible, in whom all judgment was hidden before these things came into existence." {9:7} When Jeremiah had said this, and while he was standing in the altar-area with Baruch and Abimelech, he became as one whose soul had departed. {9:8} And Baruch and Abimelech were weeping and crying out in a loud voice: "Woe to us! For our father Jeremiah has left us — the priest of God has departed!" {9:9} And all the people heard their weeping, and they all ran to them and saw Jeremiah lying on the ground as if dead. {9:10} And they tore their garments and put dust on their heads and wept bitterly. {9:11} And after this, they prepared to bury him. {9:12} And behold, there came a voice saying: "Do not bury the one who yet lives, for his soul is returning to his body!" {9:13} And when they heard the voice, they did not bury him, but stayed around his tabernacle for three days, saying, "When will he arise?" {9:14} And after three days, his soul came back into his body, and he raised his voice in the midst of them all and said: "Glorify God with one voice! All of you glorify God and the son of God who awakens us — messiah Jesus — the light of all the ages, the inextinguishable lamp, the life of faith." {9:15} "But after these times, there shall be 477 more years, and he will come to earth." {9:16} "And the tree of life, planted in the midst of paradise, will cause all the unfruitful trees to bear fruit, and will grow and sprout forth." {9:17} "And the trees that had sprouted and became haughty and said: 'We have supplied our power to the air,' he will cause them to wither, with the grandeur of their branches, and he will cause them to be judged — that firmly rooted tree!" {9:18} "And what is crimson will become white as wool — the snow will be blackened — the sweet waters will become salty, and the salty sweet, in the intense light of the joy of God." {9:19} "And he will bless the isles so that they become fruitful by the word of the mouth of his messiah." {9:20} "For he shall come, and he will go out and choose for himself twelve apostles to proclaim the news among the nations — he whom I have seen adorned by his father and coming into the world on the Mount of Olives — and he shall fill the hungry souls." {9:21} When Jeremiah was saying this concerning the son of God — that he is coming into the world — the people became very angry and said: "This is a repetition of the words spoken by Isaiah, son of Amos, when he said: 'I saw God and the son of God.'" {9:22} "Come, then, and let us not kill him by the same sort of death with which we killed Isaiah, but let us stone him with stones." {9:23} And Baruch and Abimelech were greatly grieved because they wanted to hear in full the mysteries that he had seen. {9:24} But Jeremiah said to them: "Be silent and weep not, for they cannot kill me until I describe for you everything I saw." {9:25} And he said to them: "Bring a stone here to me." {9:26} And he set it up and said: "Light of the ages, make this stone to become like me in appearance, until I have described to Baruch and Abimelech everything I saw." {9:27} Then the stone, by God's command, took on the appearance of Jeremiah. {9:28} And they were stoning the stone, supposing that it was Jeremiah! {9:29} But Jeremiah delivered to Baruch and to Abimelech all the mysteries he had seen, and forthwith he stood in the midst of the people desiring to complete his ministry. {9:30} Then the stone cried out, saying: "O foolish children of Israel, why do you stone me, supposing that I am Jeremiah? Behold, Jeremiah is standing in your midst!" {9:31} And when they saw him, immediately they rushed upon him with many stones, and his ministry was fulfilled. {9:32} And when Baruch and Abimelech came, they buried him, and taking the stone, they placed it on his tomb and inscribed it thus: "This is the stone that was the ally of Jeremiah."

The History of Bel and the Dragon

{1:1} When King Astyages passed away, Cyrus the Persian took over the kingdom. {1:2} Daniel was a companion of the king and was the most honored among his friends. {1:3} The Babylonians had an idol called Bel, and every day they offered twelve bushels of fine flour, forty sheep, and fifty gallons of wine to it. {1:4} The king honored Bel and worshiped it daily, but Daniel worshiped his own God. {1:5} The king asked him, "Why don't you worship Bel?" Daniel replied, "Because I do not revere man-made idols; I worship the living God who created heaven and earth and rules over all." {1:6} The king said, "Do you not think Bel is a living God? Can't you see how much he eats and drinks every day?" {1:7} Daniel laughed and said, "Do not be fooled, O king; this idol is just clay on the inside and brass on the outside. It has never eaten or drunk anything." {1:8} The king became angry and summoned his priests, saying, "If you can't tell me who is eating the offerings, you will die. {1:9} But if you can prove that Bel is eating them, Daniel will die for blaspheming against Bel." Daniel replied, "Let it be as you say." {1:10} There were seventy priests of Bel, along with their wives and children. The king went with Daniel into the temple of Bel. {1:11} The priests of Bel said, "Look, we're going outside; you, O king, should set out the food and mix the wine, then shut and seal the door with your signet. {1:12} When you return in the morning, if you find that Bel has eaten everything, we will die; otherwise, it will be Daniel who has lied about us." {1:13} They were unconcerned, for they had made a hidden entrance under the table, through which they regularly entered to consume the provisions. {1:14} After they left, the king set out the food for Bel. Then Daniel instructed his servants to bring ashes, and they spread them throughout the temple in front of the king. They then left, shut the door, sealed it with the king's signet, and went away. {1:15} During the night, the priests came with their wives and children, as they usually did, and ate everything. {1:16} Early in the morning, the king and Daniel returned. {1:17} The king asked, "Are the seals unbroken, Daniel?" Daniel replied, "They are unbroken, O king." {1:18} When the doors were opened, the king looked at the table and shouted, "Great are you, O Bel; there is no deceit in you!" {1:19} Daniel laughed and stopped the king from entering, saying, "Look at the floor and see whose footprints these are." {1:20} The king replied, "I see the footprints of men, women, and children." {1:21} The king became furious and seized the priests, their wives, and children. They showed him the secret doors they used to enter and eat from the table. {1:22} Therefore, the king executed them and gave Bel to Daniel, who destroyed it and its temple. {1:23} There was also a great dragon that the Babylonians revered. {1:24} The king said to Daniel, "You can't deny that this is a living god, so worship it." {1:25} Daniel replied, "I will worship the Lord my God, for he is the living God. {1:26} But if you, O king, permit me, I will slay the dragon without sword or club." The king agreed. {1:27} Daniel took pitch, fat, and hair, boiled them together, and made cakes to feed the dragon. The dragon ate them and burst open. Daniel said, "See what you have been worshiping!" {1:28} When the Babylonians heard this, they were furious and conspired against the king, saying, "The king has become a Jew; he has destroyed Bel, killed the dragon, and slaughtered the priests." {1:29} They went to the king and demanded, "Hand Daniel over to us, or we will kill you and your household." {1:30} The king realized they were pressuring him, and under duress, he handed Daniel over to them. {1:31} They threw Daniel into the lions' den, where he remained for six days. {1:32} There were seven lions in the den, and every day they were fed two human bodies and two sheep, but this time, they received nothing, so they could devour Daniel. {1:33} Meanwhile, the prophet Habakkuk was in Judea. He had cooked stew and broken bread into a bowl, planning to take it to the reapers in the field. {1:34} But the angel of the Lord said to Habakkuk, "Take the food you have to Babylon, to Daniel in the lions' den." {1:35} Habakkuk replied, "Sir, I have never been to Babylon, and I don't know anything about the den." {1:36} Then the angel of the Lord took him by the hair of his head, lifted him, and placed him down in Babylon right over the den, with a rushing sound of the wind. {1:37} Habakkuk shouted, "Daniel, Daniel! Take the food that God has sent you." {1:38} Daniel said, "You have remembered me, O God, and have not forsaken those who love you." {1:39} So Daniel arose and ate. The angel of God then returned Habakkuk to his own place. {1:40} On the seventh day, the king came to mourn for Daniel. When he approached the den, he looked in and saw Daniel sitting there. {1:41} The king shouted loudly, "Great are you, O Lord God of Daniel, and there is no other beside you." {1:42} He pulled Daniel out and threw the men who had tried to kill him into the den, and they were immediately devoured before his eyes.

The History of Susanna

{1:1} There was a name named Joakim. {1:2} He took a wife named Susanna, the daughter of Hilkiah, a very beautiful woman who feared the Lord. {1:3} Her parents were righteous and had taught their daughter according to the law of Moses. {1:4} Joakim was very wealthy and had a spacious garden next to his house, where the Jews often came to him because he was the most honored among them. {1:5} That year, two elders from the people were appointed as judges. The Lord had said about them: "Iniquity came forth from Babylon, from the elders who were supposed to govern the people." {1:6} These men frequently visited Joakim's house, and all who had legal matters came to them. {1:7} When the people left at noon, Susanna would go into her husband's garden to take a walk. {1:8} The two elders saw her every day as she walked around, and they began to desire her. {1:9} They twisted their minds and turned away their eyes from looking to Heaven or remembering righteous judgments. {1:10} Both were overwhelmed with passion for her, but they didn't confess their distress to each other, {1:11} as they were ashamed to reveal their lustful desire to possess her. {1:12} They eagerly watched for her day after day. {1:13} They said to each other, "Let's go home, it's mealtime." {1:14} When they left, they parted ways, but turned back and met again; when each pressed the other for a reason, they confessed their lust and arranged to find her alone. {1:15} One day, while they were waiting for a good opportunity, she entered the garden as before with just two maids, wanting to bathe because it was very hot. {1:16} No one else was there except the two elders, who had hidden themselves and were watching her. {1:17} She said to her maids, "Bring me oil and ointments, and shut the garden doors so that I may bathe." {1:18} They did as she asked, shut the garden doors, and went out through the side doors to get what she needed; they didn't see the elders because they were hidden. {1:19} After the maids left, the two elders ran to her and said, {1:20} "Look, the garden doors are shut, no one can see us, and we're in love with you. So give your consent and lie with us. {1:21} If you refuse, we will testify against you that a young man was with you, and that's why you sent your maids away." {1:22} Susanna sighed deeply and said, "I'm trapped on every side. If I do this, it's death for me; and if I don't, I can't escape your hands.

{1:23} I choose not to do it and to fall into your hands rather than to sin in the sight of the Lord." {1:24} Then Susanna cried out loudly, and the two elders shouted against her. {1:25} One of them ran and opened the garden doors. {1:26} When the household servants heard the shouting in the garden, they rushed in through the side door to see what had happened to her. {1:27} When the elders told their story, the servants were greatly ashamed, for nothing like this had ever been said about Susanna. {1:28} The next day, when the people gathered at Joakim's house, the two elders came, filled with their wicked plot to have Susanna put to death. {1:29} They said before the people, "Send for Susanna, the daughter of Hilkiah, the wife of Joakim." {1:30} So they sent for her, and she came with her parents, her children, and all her relatives. {1:31} Susanna was a woman of great refinement and beauty. {1:32} As she was veiled, the wicked men ordered her to be unveiled so they could feast their eyes on her beauty. {1:33} But her family, friends, and all who saw her wept. {1:34} Then the two elders stood up in the midst of the people and laid their hands on her head. {1:35} She, weeping, looked up toward heaven, for her heart trusted in the Lord. {1:36} The elders said, "While we were walking in the garden alone, this woman came in with two maids, shut the garden doors, and dismissed them. {1:37} Then a young man, who had been hiding, came to her and lay with her. {1:38} We were in a corner of the garden, and when we saw this wickedness, we ran to them. {1:39} We saw them embracing, but we couldn't hold the man, for he was too strong for us and escaped through the doors. {1:40} So we seized this woman and asked her who the young man was, but she wouldn't tell us. This is our testimony." {1:41} The assembly believed them because they were respected elders and judges, and they condemned her to death. {1:42} Susanna cried out loudly, saying, "O eternal God, who discerns what is secret and knows all things before they happen, {1:43} you know that these men have borne false witness against me. And now I am to die! Yet I have done none of the things they wickedly claim against me!" {1:44} The Lord heard her cry. {1:45} As she was being led away to be executed, God stirred the holy spirit of a young man named Daniel; {1:46} and he cried out loudly, "I am innocent of this woman's blood." {1:47} All the people turned to him and said, "What is this you have said?" {1:48} Taking his stand among them, he said, "Are you such fools, O sons of Israel? Have you condemned a daughter of Israel without examination and without knowing the facts? {1:49} Return to the place of judgment, for these men have borne false witness against her." {1:50} All the people hurried back. The elders said to him, "Come, sit with us and inform us, for God has given you that right." {1:51} Daniel said to them, "Separate them from each other, and I will examine them." {1:52} After they were separated, he summoned one of them and said to him, "You old relic of wicked days, your sins have come home to you; {1:53} you have pronounced unjust judgments, condemning the innocent and letting the guilty go free, even though the Lord said, 'Do not put to death an innocent and righteous person.' {1:54} Now then, if you really saw her, tell me: Under what tree did you see them being intimate?" He answered, "Under a mastic tree." {1:55} Daniel said, "Very well! You have lied against your own head, for the angel of God has received the sentence from God and will immediately cut you in two." {1:56} He put him aside and commanded them to bring in the other. He said to him, "You offspring of Canaan, not of Judah, beauty has deceived you, and lust has perverted your heart. {1:57} This is how you have dealt with the daughters of Israel; they were intimate with you out of fear, but a daughter of Judah would not endure your wickedness. {1:58} Now then, tell me: Under what tree did you catch them being intimate?" He answered, "Under an evergreen oak." {1:59} Daniel said, "Very well! You have also lied against your own head, for the angel of God is waiting with his sword to saw you in two, so he may destroy you both." {1:60} Then all the assembly shouted loudly and blessed God, who saves those who hope in him. {1:61} They rose against the two elders, for Daniel had convicted them of bearing false witness against Susanna with their own words; {1:62} and they did to them as they had wickedly planned to do to her, acting according to the law of Moses, they put them to death. Thus innocent blood was saved that day. {1:63} Hilkiah and his wife praised God for their daughter Susanna, as did Joakim her husband and all her relatives, because nothing shameful was found in her. {1:64} From that day onward, Daniel had a great reputation among the people.

The Prayer of Manasseh

{1:1} O Lord, God of truth, who dwells in the heights of heaven, whose name is reverenced above all, I come before You in humility and awe, seeking Your forgiveness and grace. You, who are the Creator of all, whose might and glory are beyond measure, hear the cry of a contrite heart. {1:2} You who made heaven and earth with all their order; {1:3} you who have restrained the sea with your command, who have confined the deep and sealed it with your awesome and glorious name; {1:4} at whom all things tremble and shudder before your power, {1:5} for your glorious splendor is unbearable, and the fury of your threat to sinners is unstoppable; {1:6} yet your promised mercy is immeasurable and unsearchable, {1:7} for you are the Lord Most High, full of compassion, patient, and very merciful, and you show remorse over the evils of humanity. You, O Lord, according to your great goodness, have promised repentance and forgiveness to those who have sinned against you; and in the abundance of your mercies, you have provided repentance for sinners so they may be saved. {1:8} Therefore, you, O Lord, God of the righteous, have not designated repentance for the righteous, like Abraham, Isaac, and Jacob, who did not sin against you, but you have appointed repentance for me, a sinner. {1:9} For the sins I have committed are more numerous than the sand of the sea; my transgressions are countless, O Lord, they are numerous! I am unworthy to look up and see the height of heaven because of the weight of my iniquities. {1:10} I am burdened with heavy chains, rejected because of my sins, and I find no relief; for I have provoked your wrath and done what is evil in your sight, committing abominations and multiplying offenses. {1:11} And now I bend the knee of my heart, asking you for your kindness. {1:12} I have sinned, O Lord, I have sinned, and I acknowledge my transgressions. {1:13} I earnestly plead with you, forgive me, O Lord, forgive me! Do not destroy me because of my sins! Do not be angry with me forever or hold my evils against me; do not condemn me to the depths of the earth. For you, O Lord, are the God of those who repent, {1:14} and in me, you will show your goodness; for, unworthy as I am, you will save me in your great mercy, {1:15} and I will praise you continually all the days of my life. For all the host of heaven sings your praise, and yours is the glory forever. Amen.

The Prayer of Azariah

{1:1-2} Then Azariah stood up & offered this prayer; in the middle of the fire, he opened his mouth and said: {1:3} "Blessed are you, O Lord, God of our ancestors, and worthy of praise; your name is glorified forever. {1:4} For you are just in all that you have done to us, and all your works are true, your ways right, and all your judgments are true. {1:5} You have executed true judgments in everything you have brought upon us and upon Jerusalem, the holy city of our ancestors; for in truth and justice, you have done all this to us because of our sins. {1:6} For we have sinfully and lawlessly departed from you, and we have sinned in every way and have not obeyed your commandments; {1:7} we have not followed them or done them, as you commanded us, so that it might go well with us. {1:8} So all that you have brought upon us and all that you have done to us has been in true judgment. {1:9} You have given us into the hands of lawless enemies, the most hateful rebels, and to an unjust king, the most wicked in all the world. {1:10} And now we cannot open our mouths; shame and disgrace have fallen on your servants and worshipers. {1:11} For your name's sake, do not give us up completely, and do not break your covenant, {1:12} and do not take away your mercy from us, for the sake of Abraham your beloved, and for Isaac your servant, and for Israel your holy one, {1:13} to whom you promised to make their descendants as numerous as the stars of heaven and as the sand on the shore of the sea. {1:14} For we, O Lord, have become fewer than any nation, and we are brought low today in all the world because of our sins. {1:15} And at this time, there is no prince, prophet, or leader, no burnt offering, or sacrifice, or oblation (offering), or incense, no place to make an offering before you or to find mercy. {1:16} Yet with a broken heart and a humble spirit, may we be accepted, as though it were with burnt offerings of rams and bulls, and with tens of thousands of fat lambs; {1:17} may our sacrifice be in your sight today, and may we fully follow you, for there will be no shame for those who trust in you. {1:18} And now with all our heart, we follow you; we fear you and seek your face. {1:19} Do not put us to shame, but deal with us in your forbearance (patience) and in your abundant mercy. {1:20} Deliver us in accordance with your marvelous works, and give glory to your name, O Lord! Let all who do harm to your servants be put to shame; {1:21} let them be disgraced and deprived of all power and dominion, and let their strength be broken. {1:22} Let them know that you are the Lord, the only God, glorious over the whole world." {1:23} Now the king's servants who threw them in did not stop feeding the furnace fires with naphtha (a flammable liquid), pitch, tow (a coarse fiber), and brush. {1:24} And the flame shot out above the furnace forty-nine cubits (about 75 feet), {1:25} and it broke through and burned those of the Chaldeans whom it caught around the furnace. {1:26} But the angel of the Lord came down into the furnace to be with Azariah and his companions and drove the fiery flame out of the furnace, {1:27} and made the middle of the furnace like a moist whistling wind, so that the fire did not touch them at all or hurt or trouble them. {1:28} Then the three, as if they were one mouth, praised and glorified and blessed God in the furnace, saying: {1:29} "Blessed are you, O Lord, God of our ancestors, and to be praised and highly exalted forever; {1:30} and blessed is your glorious, holy name and to be highly praised and highly exalted forever; {1:31} blessed are you in the temple of your holy glory and to be extolled (praised) and highly glorified forever. {1:32} Blessed are you, who sit upon cherubim (angelic beings) and look upon the depths, and to be praised and highly exalted forever. {1:33} Blessed are you upon the throne of your kingdom and to be extolled and highly exalted forever. {1:34} Blessed are you in the firmament of heaven and to be sung and glorified forever. {1:35} "Bless the Lord, all works of the Lord, sing praise to him and highly exalt him forever. {1:36} Bless the Lord, you heavens, sing praise to him and highly exalt him forever. {1:37} Bless the Lord, you angels of the Lord, sing praise to him and highly exalt him forever. {1:38} Bless the Lord, all waters above the heavens, sing praise to him and highly exalt him forever. {1:39} Bless the Lord, all powers, sing praise to him and highly exalt him forever. {1:40} Bless the Lord, sun and moon, sing praise to him and highly exalt him forever. {1:41} Bless the Lord, stars of heaven, sing praise to him and highly exalt him forever. {1:42} Bless the Lord, all rain and dew, sing praise to him and highly exalt him forever. {1:43} Bless the Lord, all winds, sing praise to him and highly exalt him forever. {1:44} Bless the Lord, fire and heat, sing praise to him and highly exalt him forever. {1:45} Bless the Lord, winter cold and summer heat, sing praise to him and highly exalt him forever. {1:46} Bless the Lord, dews and snows, sing praise to him and highly exalt him forever. {1:47} Bless the Lord, nights and days, sing praise to him and highly exalt him forever. {1:48} Bless the Lord, light and darkness, sing praise to him and highly exalt him forever. {1:49} Bless the Lord, ice and cold, sing praise to him and highly exalt him forever. {1:50} Bless the Lord, frosts and snows, sing praise to him and highly exalt him forever. {1:51} Bless the Lord, lightnings and clouds, sing praise to him and highly exalt him forever. {1:52} Let the earth bless the Lord; let it sing praise to him and highly exalt him forever. {1:53} Bless the Lord, mountains and hills, sing praise to him and highly exalt him forever. {1:54} Bless the Lord, all things that grow on the earth, sing praise to him and highly exalt him forever. {1:55} Bless the Lord, you springs, sing praise to him and highly exalt him forever. {1:56} Bless the Lord, seas and rivers, sing praise to him and highly exalt him forever. {1:57} Bless the Lord, you whales and all creatures that move in the waters, sing praise to him and highly exalt him forever. {1:58} Bless the Lord, all birds of the air, sing praise to him and highly exalt him forever. {1:59} Bless the Lord, all beasts and cattle, sing praise to him and highly exalt him forever. {1:60} Bless the Lord, you sons of men, sing praise to him and highly exalt him forever. {1:61} Bless the Lord, O Israel, sing praise to him and highly exalt him forever. {1:62} Bless the Lord, you priests of the Lord, sing praise to him and highly exalt him forever. {1:63} Bless the Lord, you servants of the Lord, sing praise to him and highly exalt him forever. {1:64} Bless the Lord, spirits and souls of the righteous, sing praise to him and highly exalt him forever. {1:65} Bless the Lord, you who are holy and humble in heart, sing praise to him and highly exalt him forever. {1:66} Bless the Lord, Hananiah, Azariah, and Mishael, sing praise to him and highly exalt him forever; for he has rescued us from Hades (the underworld) and saved us from the hand of death, and delivered us from the midst of the burning fiery furnace; from the midst of the fire he has delivered us. {1:67} Give thanks to the Lord, for he is good, for his mercy endures forever. {1:68} Bless him, all who worship the Lord, the God of gods, sing praise to him and give thanks to him, for his mercy endures forever."

The Wisdom of Sirach

{1:1} All wisdom comes from the Lord and is with him forever. {1:2} The sand of the sea, the drops of rain, and the days of eternity—who can count them? {1:3} The height of heaven, the breadth of the earth, the abyss, and wisdom—who can explore them? {1:4} Wisdom was created before all things, and understanding was made from eternity. {1:5} The root of wisdom—who has it been revealed to? Her clever insights—who knows them? {1:6} There is One who is wise and greatly feared, sitting upon his throne. {1:7} The Lord himself created wisdom; he observed her and assigned her, pouring her out upon all his creations. {1:8} She resides with all beings according to his gift, and he provides her to those who love him. {1:9} The fear of the Lord brings glory, joy, gladness, and a crown of rejoicing. {1:10} The fear of the Lord delights the heart and gives joy, happiness, and a long life. {1:11} For those who fear the Lord, all will go well in the end; on the day of their death, they will be blessed. {1:12} To fear the Lord is the beginning of wisdom; she is formed with the faithful from the womb. {1:13} She established an eternal foundation among people, and her descendants will trust her. {1:14} To fear the Lord is the full measure of wisdom; she satisfies people with her results; {1:15} she fills their homes with desirable things and their storerooms with her bounty. {1:16} The fear of the Lord is the crown of wisdom, promoting peace and perfect health. {1:17} He observed her and assigned her; he showered knowledge and understanding, and he raised the glory of those who hold her dear. {1:18} To fear the Lord is the root of wisdom, and her branches bring long life. {1:22} Unrighteous anger cannot be justified, for a person's anger leads to their ruin. {1:23} A patient person will wait until the right moment, and then joy will come to them. {1:24} They will keep their words hidden until the right time, and many will praise their good sense. {1:25} In the treasury of wisdom are wise sayings, but godliness is an offense to a sinner. {1:26} If you desire wisdom, keep the commandments, and the Lord will provide it for you. {1:27} For the fear of the Lord is wisdom and instruction, and he delights in faithfulness and humility. {1:28} Do not disobey the fear of the Lord; do not approach him with a divided mind. {1:29} Don't be a hypocrite in the sight of others, and keep a watch over your words. {1:30} Do not exalt yourself, or you will fall and bring dishonor upon yourself. The Lord will reveal your secrets and cast you down in front of the congregation because you did not come in the fear of the Lord, and your heart was filled with deceit.

{2:1} My child, if you come forward to serve the Lord, prepare yourself for temptation. {2:2} Set your heart right and be steadfast, and do not rush in times of trouble. {2:3} Cling to him and do not depart, so you may be honored at the end of your life. {2:4} Accept whatever comes your way, and in moments that humble you, be patient. {2:5} For gold is tested in the fire, and acceptable people are tested in the furnace of humiliation. {2:6} Trust in him, and he will help you; make your paths straight and hope in him. {2:7} You who fear the Lord, wait for his mercy; do not turn aside, or you will fall. {2:8} You who fear the Lord, trust in him, and your reward will not fail; {2:9} you who fear the Lord, hope for good things, for everlasting joy and mercy. {2:10} Look at the ancient generations and see: who ever trusted in the Lord and was let down? Or who ever persevered in the fear of the Lord and was abandoned? Or who ever called on him and was ignored? {2:11} For the Lord is compassionate and merciful; he forgives sins and saves in times of trouble. {2:12} Woe to the timid hearts and the lazy hands, and to the sinner who walks two paths! {2:13} Woe to the faint-hearted, for it has no trust! Therefore, it will not find shelter. {2:14} Woe to you who have lost your endurance! What will you do when the Lord punishes you? {2:15} Those who fear the Lord will not disobey his commands, and those who love him will keep his ways. {2:16} Those who fear the Lord will seek his approval, and those who love him will be filled with his teachings. {2:17} Those who fear the Lord will prepare their hearts and humble themselves before him. {2:18} Let us fall into the hands of the Lord, but not into the hands of men; for as his majesty is, so is his mercy.

{3:1} Listen to me, your father, O children; and act accordingly so that you may be safe. {3:2} For the Lord has honored the father above the children and confirmed the mother's authority over her sons. {3:3} Whoever honors his father atones for sins, {3:4} and whoever glorifies his mother is like someone who stores up treasure. {3:5} Whoever honors his father will be made glad by his own children, and when he prays, he will be heard. {3:6} Whoever glorifies his father will have a long life, and whoever obeys the Lord will refresh his mother; {3:7} he will serve his parents as his masters. {3:8} Honor your father with both words and actions, so that a blessing from him may come upon you. {3:9} A father's blessing strengthens the homes of his children, but a mother's curse uproots their foundations. {3:10} Do not glorify yourself by dishonoring your father, for your father's dishonor does not bring you glory. {3:11} A person's glory comes from honoring their father, and it is disgraceful for children not to respect their mother. {3:12} O son, help your father in his old age, and do not grieve him as long as he lives; {3:13} even if he lacks understanding, be patient; with all your strength, do not despise him. {3:14} For kindness shown to a father will not be forgotten, and it will count in your favor against your sins; {3:15} in the day of your trouble, it will be remembered positively; as frost in good weather, your sins will melt away. {3:16} Whoever abandons his father is like a blasphemer, and whoever angers his mother is cursed by the Lord. {3:17} My son, perform your tasks with humility; then you will be loved by those whom God accepts. {3:18} The greater you are, the more you must humble yourself, so you will find favor in the sight of the Lord. {3:20} For the Lord's power is great; he is glorified by the humble. {3:21} Don't seek what is too difficult for you, nor explore what is beyond your abilities. {3:22} Reflect on what has been assigned to you; you don't need to know what is hidden. {3:23} Don't interfere with tasks beyond your responsibilities, for matters too great for human understanding have been revealed to you. {3:24} For their quick judgments have led many astray, and misguided opinions have caused their thoughts to falter. {3:26} A stubborn mind will suffer in the end, and whoever loves danger will perish because of it. {3:27} A stubborn mind will be weighed down by troubles, and the sinner will pile sin upon sin. {3:28} The proud cannot be healed, for a wicked mindset has taken root in them. {3:29} An intelligent person will ponder a parable, and an attentive ear is the wise person's desire. {3:30} Water can extinguish a blazing fire; similarly, giving to the needy atones for sin. {3:31} Whoever repays favors thinks ahead; when they stumble, they will find support.

{4:1} My son, do not deprive the poor of their living, and do not keep needy eyes waiting. {4:2} Do not grieve the hungry, nor anger a man in need. {4:3} Do not add to the troubles of an angry person, nor delay your gift to a beggar. {4:4} Do not reject an afflicted supplicant, nor turn your face away from the poor. {4:5} Do not turn your eye from those in need, nor give someone reason to curse you; {4:6} for if, in bitterness of soul, he calls down a curse upon you, his Creator will hear his plea. {4:7} Make yourself beloved in the community; bow your head low to a great person. {4:8} Listen to the poor and answer them kindly and gently. {4:9} Rescue the wronged from the hands of the wrongdoer; do not be fainthearted in making judgments. {4:10} Be like a father to orphans and act as a husband to their mother; then you will be like a son of the Most High, and he will love you even more than your mother does. {4:11} Wisdom exalts her children and helps those who seek her. {4:12} Whoever loves her loves life, and those who seek her early will be filled with joy. {4:13} Whoever holds her close will obtain glory, and the Lord will bless wherever she goes. {4:14} Those who serve her will minister to the Holy One; the Lord loves those who love her. {4:15} Whoever obeys her will judge nations, and those who pay attention to her will dwell securely. {4:16} If he has faith in her, he will receive her, and his descendants will inherit her. {4:17} At first, she will lead him on difficult paths, she will bring fear and anxiety upon him, and will discipline him until she trusts him, testing him with her laws. {4:18} Then she will return to him and bring him joy, revealing her secrets to him. {4:19} If he strays, she will abandon him and lead him to his ruin. {4:20} Be mindful of the right moment, and beware of evil; do not bring shame upon yourself. {4:21} For there is a shame that leads to sin, and there is a shame that brings glory and favor. {4:22} Do not show favoritism to your own detriment, or give deference that leads to your downfall. {4:23} Do not hesitate to speak at the crucial moment, and do not hide your wisdom. {4:24} For wisdom is revealed through speech, and knowledge is shown through words. {4:25} Never speak against the truth, but be aware of your own ignorance. {4:26} Do not be ashamed to confess your sins, and do not try to stop the flow of a river. {4:27} Do not subject yourself to a foolish person, nor show favoritism to a ruler. {4:28} Strive even to the point of death for the truth, and the Lord God will fight for you. {4:29} Do not be careless with your words, or sluggish and neglectful in your actions. {4:30} Do not act like a lion in your home, nor be a faultfinder with your servants. {4:31} Do not extend your hand to receive, but pull it back when it's time to repay.

{5:1} Do not set your heart on your wealth, nor say, "I have enough." {5:2} Do not follow your inclinations and strength, walking according to the desires of your heart. {5:3} Do not say, "Who will have power over me?" because the Lord will surely punish you. {5:4} Do not say, "I sinned, and what happened to me?" for the Lord is slow to anger. {5:5} Do not be so confident in atonement that you keep adding sin to sin. {5:6} Do not say, "His mercy is great; he will forgive my many sins," for both mercy and wrath are with him, and his anger rests on sinners. {5:7} Do not delay in turning to the Lord, nor postpone it day after day; for suddenly the Lord's wrath will come upon you, and at the time of punishment, you will perish. {5:8} Do not depend on dishonest wealth, for it will not help you in times of trouble. {5:9} Do not waver with every wind or follow every path; the double-tongued sinner does that. {5:10} Be steady in your understanding, and let your speech be consistent. {5:11} Be quick to listen and deliberate in answering. {5:12} If you understand, answer your neighbor; if not, cover your mouth. {5:13} Glory and dishonor come from what you say, and a person's tongue can lead to their downfall. {5:14} Do not be labeled a slanderer, and do not set traps with your words; for shame comes to the thief, and severe condemnation to the double-tongued. {5:15} In all matters, big and small, do not act wrongly.

{6:1} Do not become an enemy instead of a friend; a bad reputation brings shame and disgrace, just like the double-tongued sinner. {6:2} Do not exalt yourself with your own counsel, or your soul may be torn apart like a bull. {6:3} You will consume your own leaves and destroy your fruit, leaving you like a withered tree. {6:4} An evil soul will destroy its owner and make them a laughingstock among enemies. {6:5} A pleasant voice attracts friends, and a gracious tongue increases goodwill. {6:6} Let there be many at peace with you, but let your advisors be few. {6:7} When you gain a friend, gain them through testing, and do not trust them too quickly. {6:8} There is a friend who is only there for their own convenience, but will not support you in your time of trouble. {6:9} And there is a friend who turns into an enemy, revealing your quarrels to your disgrace. {6:10} And there is a friend who shares your table but will not stand by you in tough times. {6:11} In good times, they will make themselves your equal and act boldly with your servants; {6:12} but if you fall on hard times, they will turn against you and hide from you. {6:13} Keep your distance from your enemies and be cautious with your friends. {6:14} A faithful friend is a sturdy shelter; whoever finds one has found a treasure. {6:15} Nothing is as precious as a faithful friend, and no scale can measure their worth. {6:16} A faithful friend is like an elixir of life; those who fear the Lord will find such a friend. {6:17} Whoever fears the Lord guides their friendships wisely, for as they are, so will their neighbors be. {6:18} My son, from your youth, choose instruction, and you will keep finding wisdom as you grow old. {6:19} Approach her as one who plows and sows, and wait for her good harvest; for in her service, you will toil briefly, and soon you will enjoy her produce. {6:20} She may seem harsh to those who lack understanding; a weak person will not stay with her. {6:21} She will weigh them down like a heavy stone, and they will not hesitate to cast her aside. {6:22} For wisdom has a name, and is not evident to many. {6:23} Listen, my son, and accept my judgment; do not dismiss my advice. {6:24} Put your feet into her fetters (chains) and your neck into her collar. {6:25} Bear her burdens and do not fret under her bonds. {6:26} Come to her with all your heart and keep her ways with all your might. {6:27} Seek her out, and she will become known to you; when you find her, do not let her go. {6:28} For in the end, you will find the peace she offers, and she will turn into joy for you. {6:29} Then her chains will become a strong protection for you, and her collar a glorious garment. {6:30} Her yoke is a golden ornament, and her bonds a blue cord. {6:31} You will wear her like a beautiful robe and put her on like a crown of joy. {6:32} If you are willing, my son, you will be taught, and if you apply yourself, you will become wise. {6:33} If you love to listen, you will gain knowledge, and if you lend an ear, you will become wise. {6:34} Stand in the assembly of elders. Who is wise? Stay close to them. {6:35} Be ready to listen to every story, and do not let wise proverbs slip away. {6:36} If you see an intelligent person, visit them early; let your foot wear out their doorstep. {6:37} Reflect on the Lord's statutes, and meditate on his commandments at all times. He will give you insight and fulfill your desire for wisdom.

{7:1} Do no evil, and evil will never come to you. {7:2} Stay away from wrongdoing, and it will avoid you. {7:3} My son, do not sow the seeds of injustice, or you will reap a sevenfold harvest. {7:4} Do not seek the highest position from the Lord, nor ask for a place of honor from the king. {7:5} Do not claim your righteousness before the Lord, nor show off your wisdom before the king. {7:6} Do not try to become a judge, or you might find it hard to remove wrongdoing and be biased toward a powerful person, which could harm your integrity. {7:7} Do not offend the public, and do not disgrace yourself among the people. {7:8} Do not commit the same sin twice; even for one, you won't go unpunished. {7:9} Do not say, "He will overlook the many gifts I give, and when I make an offering to the Most High God, he will accept it." {7:10} Do not be discouraged in your prayers, nor neglect to give to those in need. {7:11} Do not mock someone who is bitter in spirit, for there is One who humbles and lifts up. {7:12} Do not plot against your brother, nor do the same to a friend. {7:13} Avoid lying, for the habit of lying serves no good. {7:14} Do not chatter in front of the elders, nor repeat yourself in your prayers. {7:15} Do not despise hard work or farming, which were created by the Most High. {7:16} Do not see yourself as part of the crowd of sinners; remember that wrath does not delay. {7:17} Humble yourself greatly, for the punishment of the ungodly is fire and worms. {7:18} Do not trade a friend for money, or a true brother for gold from Ophir. {7:19} Do not deprive yourself of a wise and good wife, for her charm is worth more than gold. {7:20} Do not mistreat a faithful servant, or a hired worker who dedicates themselves to you. {7:21} Let your soul love an intelligent servant; do not deny them their freedom. {7:22} Do you have cattle? Take care of them; if they are profitable, keep them. {7:23} Do you have children? Discipline them and teach them to obey from a young age. {7:24} Do you have daughters? Be concerned for their purity, and do not be too indulgent with them. {7:25} Give your daughter in marriage; you will have completed a great task. But give her to a man of understanding. {7:26} If you have a wife who pleases you, do not cast her out; but do not trust yourself to one you dislike. {7:27} With all your heart, honor your father, and do not forget the pain of your mother during childbirth. {7:28} Remember that you were born through your parents; what can you give back to them that equals their gift to you? {7:29} With all your soul, fear the Lord and honor his priests. {7:30} With all your strength, love your Creator, and do not neglect his ministers. {7:31} Fear the Lord and honor the priest, and give him his due as commanded: the first fruits, the guilt offering, the gift of the shoulders, the sanctification sacrifice, and the first fruits of the holy things. {7:32} Extend your hand to the poor so your blessing may be complete. {7:33} Give generously to all the living, and do not withhold kindness from the dead. {7:34} Do not fail those who weep, but mourn with those who mourn. {7:35} Do not avoid visiting a sick person, for such acts will bring you love. {7:36} In all you do, remember the end of your life, and then you will never sin.

{8:1} Do not argue with a powerful person, or you might fall into their grasp. {8:2} Do not quarrel with a wealthy person, or their resources may overwhelm yours; for gold has ruined many and twisted the minds of kings. {8:3} Do not argue with a talkative person, nor add fuel to their fire. {8:4} Do not joke with a rude person, lest you disgrace your ancestors. {8:5} Do not scold someone who is turning away from sin; remember that we all deserve punishment. {8:6} Do not disregard an elderly person, for we all grow old. {8:7} Do not rejoice at anyone's death; remember that we all must die. {8:8} Do not ignore the words of wise people; engage with their teachings, as you will gain insight and learn how to serve great individuals. {8:9} Do not dismiss the words of the elderly, for they learned from their parents; from them, you will gain understanding and learn how to respond in times of need. {8:10} Do not stoke the fire of a sinner, or you may get burned by their flames. {8:11} Do not get up and leave an insolent person, or they may lie in wait for your words. {8:12} Do not lend to someone stronger than you; if you do lend anything, consider it as lost. {8:13} Do not give surety beyond your means, but if you do, be prepared to pay. {8:14} Do not go to court against a judge, for the decision will favor them due to their position. {8:15} Do not travel with a reckless person, lest they become a burden; they will act as they please, and their folly could lead to your downfall. {8:16} Do not fight with an angry person, and do not cross a desert with them; for they see blood as nothing, and in a place with no help, they may strike you down. {8:17} Do not consult with a fool, for they cannot keep a secret. {8:18} In front of a stranger, do nothing you wish to keep secret, as you do not know what they might reveal. {8:19} Do not share your thoughts with everyone, lest you scare away your good fortune.

{9:1} Do not be jealous of your wife, and do not teach her harmful lessons that could hurt you. {9:2} Do not give yourself to a woman so that she gains control over your strength. {9:3} Avoid meeting a loose woman, or you might fall into her traps. {9:4} Do not associate with a woman singer, or you may get caught up in her schemes. {9:5} Do not stare at a virgin, or you might stumble and face consequences for her. {9:6} Do not give yourself to prostitutes, or you will lose your inheritance. {9:7} Do not look around in the streets of a city, or wander in its deserted areas. {9:8} Turn your eyes away from an attractive woman, and do not covet the beauty of someone else; many have been misled by a woman's beauty, which ignites passion like fire. {9:9} Never dine with another man's wife, nor drink with her, or your heart may stray, leading you to destruction. {9:10} Do not abandon an old friend, for a new one cannot compare; a new friend is like new wine; with time, you will enjoy it more. {9:11} Do not envy a sinner's honors, for you do not know what their end will be. {9:12} Do not delight in what pleases the wicked; remember that they will not go unpunished as long as they live. {9:13} Keep your distance from someone who has the power to kill, and you won't have to fear death; if you get too close, watch your step, or they may take your life. Be aware that you are walking among traps and on the walls of the city. {9:14} Get to know your neighbors, and seek advice from the wise. {9:15} Let your conversations be with those who understand, and let all your discussions revolve around the law of the Most High. {9:16} Let righteous people be your dinner companions, and let your pride be in the fear of the Lord. {9:17} A skilled craftsman's work will be praised; likewise, a wise leader is proven by his words. {9:18} A gossip is feared in his city, and someone reckless with their words will be hated.

{10:1} A wise leader will educate their people, and the rule of an understanding person will be orderly. {10:2} Like the leader of the people, so are their officials; and like the ruler of the city, so are all its residents. {10:3} An undisciplined king will ruin his people, but a city will thrive under the wisdom of its rulers. {10:4} The governance of the earth is in the Lord's hands, and He will raise the right person for the time. {10:5} A person's success is in the Lord's hands, and He grants honor to the scribe. {10:6} Do not get angry with your neighbor for any harm, and do not act insolently. {10:7} Arrogance is detestable to both the Lord and people, and injustice is outrageous to both. {10:8} Sovereignty shifts from nation to nation because of injustice, insolence, and wealth. {10:9} How can someone made of dust and ashes be proud? Even in life, their insides decay. {10:10} A long illness confounds the physician; today's king will die tomorrow. {10:11} When a person dies, they inherit creeping things, wild animals, and worms. {10:12} The start of a person's pride is turning away from the Lord; their heart has abandoned their Creator. {10:13} The root of pride is sin, and a person who clings to it spills out abominations. Therefore, the Lord brought extraordinary afflictions upon them and utterly destroyed them. {10:14} The Lord has brought down the thrones of rulers and has raised the humble to their places. {10:15} The Lord has uprooted the nations and planted the humble instead. {10:16} The Lord has overthrown nations and reduced them to rubble. {10:17} He has removed some of them and erased their memory from the earth. {10:18} Pride was not made for humans, nor was fierce anger for those born of women. {10:19} What race deserves honor? The human race. Who deserves honor? Those who fear the Lord. What race is unworthy of honor? The human race. Who is unworthy? Those who break the commandments. {10:20} Among brothers, the leader is worthy of honor, and those who fear the Lord are esteemed in His eyes. {10:22} The rich, the prominent, and the poor—each finds glory in the fear of the Lord. {10:23} It is wrong to look down on an intelligent poor person, nor is it right to honor a sinful person. {10:24} Nobles, judges, and rulers will be honored, but none are greater than the person who fears the Lord. {10:25} Free people will serve a wise servant, and a person of understanding will not complain. {10:26} Do not flaunt your wisdom while working, nor boast when you are in need. {10:27} A man who works and has plenty is better than one who boasts but lacks bread. {10:28} My son, glorify yourself with humility, and give yourself honor based on your worth. {10:29} Who will justify someone who sins against themselves? And who will honor someone who dishonors their own life? {10:30} A poor person is honored for their knowledge, while a rich person is honored for their wealth. {10:31} A person honored in poverty will be even more so in wealth, and one dishonored in wealth will be even more so in poverty.

{11:1} The wisdom of a humble person will lift them up and place them among the great. {11:2} Do not praise someone for their looks, nor dislike them because of their appearance. {11:3} The bee is small among flying creatures, but its product is the sweetest of all. {11:4} Do not brag about wearing fine clothes, nor exalt yourself when you are honored; for the Lord's works are wonderful, though often hidden from people. {11:5} Many kings have had to sit on the ground, while someone once overlooked has worn a crown. {11:6} Many rulers have faced great disgrace, and notable people have been given over to others. {11:7} Do not criticize before you investigate; first consider, then correct. {11:8} Do not answer before you have listened, nor interrupt someone speaking. {11:9} Do not argue about things that do not concern you, nor sit with sinners when they judge a case. {11:10} My son, do not overload yourself with many tasks; if you multiply activities, you will not escape punishment; if you chase after too much, you will not catch it, and fleeing will not help you. {11:11} There is someone who works hard, toils, and perseveres, yet finds themselves in even more want. {11:12} There is another who is slow, needs help, lacks strength, and lives in poverty; but the Lord looks upon him favorably and lifts him from his low state, {11:13} raising his head, so that many are amazed at him. {11:14} Good and bad things, life and death, poverty and wealth all come from the Lord. {11:17} The Lord's gift lasts for those who are godly, and what He approves will succeed. {11:18} There is a person who becomes rich through hard work and self-denial, and this is their reward: {11:19} when they say, "I have found peace, and now I can enjoy my possessions!" they do not realize how soon they will leave them to others and die. {11:20} Stick to your commitments and stay devoted to your work as you grow older. {11:21} Do not be amazed by a sinner's successes; trust in the Lord and keep working hard; for it is easy for the Lord to quickly enrich a poor person. {11:22} The Lord's blessing rewards the godly, and God can make that blessing grow rapidly. {11:23} Do not say, "What do I need, and what good fortune could I have in the future?" {11:24} Do not say, "I have enough; what disaster could befall me?" {11:25} In good times, adversity is forgotten, and in tough times, prosperity is overlooked. {11:26} For it is easy for the Lord to reward a person on the day of their death based on their actions. {11:27} The suffering of an hour makes one forget luxury, and at the end of a person's life, their deeds will be revealed. {11:28} Do not call anyone happy before they die; a person will be known by their children. {11:29} Do not welcome every stranger into your home, for many are deceitful. {11:30} Like a decoy partridge in a cage, a proud person's mind is cunning; like a spy, they watch for your weaknesses; {11:31} they wait to turn good into bad, and they will blame worthy actions. {11:32} From a spark of fire come many burning coals, and a sinner waits to shed blood. {11:33} Be cautious of a scoundrel, for they plot evil, or they might leave you with a lasting mark. {11:34} If you invite a stranger into your home, they will disturb you and alienate you from your family.

{12:1} When you do a kindness, know who you are helping, and you will be appreciated for your good deeds. {12:2} Do good to a godly person, and you will be rewarded—if not by them, then certainly by the Most High. {12:3} No good will come to a person who continues in evil or to someone who does not give to the needy. {12:4} Help the godly, but do not assist the sinner. {12:5} Do good to the humble, but do not give to the ungodly; withhold from them, so they do not overpower you; for you will receive twice as much evil for every good deed done for them. {12:6} The Most High also hates sinners and will punish the ungodly. {12:7} Give to the good person, but do not aid the sinner. {12:8} A friend will not be recognized in good times, nor will an enemy remain hidden in bad times. {12:9} A man's enemies are upset when he succeeds, and in hard times, even his friends will abandon him. {12:10} Never trust your enemy; their wickedness is like rust on copper. {12:11} Even if they humble themselves and act submissive, be cautious and watch yourself; treat them like a polished mirror, and you will see that they are not irreparably tarnished. {12:12} Do not put them close to you, or they might overthrow you and take your place; do not let them sit at your right side, or they might try to take your seat of honor, and eventually, you will realize the truth of my words and be hurt by what I have said. {12:13} Who will sympathize with a snake charmer bitten by a snake, or with anyone who approaches wild animals? {12:14} So no one will pity someone who associates with a sinner and gets caught up in their wrongdoing. {12:15} They may stay with you for a while, but if you stumble, they will not support you. {12:16} An enemy may speak sweetly with their lips, but secretly, they plan to throw you into a trap; they may shed tears for you, but when they get the chance, their thirst for revenge will be unquenchable. {12:17} If disaster strikes you, you will find them there waiting for you; while pretending to help, they will trip you up; {12:18} they will shake their head, clap their hands, whisper a lot, and change their expression.

{13:1} Whoever touches pitch will be defiled, and anyone who associates with a proud person will become like them. {13:2} Do not take on a burden that exceeds your strength, nor associate with someone stronger or wealthier than you. How can a clay pot associate with an iron kettle? The pot will strike against it and break. {13:3} A rich person may do wrong and add insults, while a poor person suffers wrong and has to apologize. {13:4} A wealthy person will exploit you if you can benefit them, but if you need help, they will abandon you. {13:5} If you own something, they will befriend you; they will deplete your resources without care. {13:6} When they need you, they will deceive you, smiling and offering hope. They will ask, "What do you need?" {13:7} They will shame you with their lavish meals until they've drained you two or three times; then they will mock you. If they see you later, they will dismiss you and shake their head. {13:8} Be careful not to be misled and humiliated during your feasts. {13:9} When a powerful person invites you, be reserved, and they will invite you more often. {13:10} Do not push forward, or you may be rejected; do not hang back, or you may be forgotten. {13:11} Do not try to treat them as an equal, nor trust their many words; they will test you through excessive talk while they smile and scrutinize you. {13:12} It's cruel not to keep your thoughts to yourself; they may not hesitate to harm or imprison you. {13:13} Keep your thoughts private and be very cautious, as you navigate your own downfall. {13:15} Every creature loves its kind, and every person loves their neighbor; {13:16} all living beings associate by species, and a person sticks to someone like themselves. {13:17} What connection does a wolf have with a lamb? Just as there is no connection between a sinner and a godly person. {13:18} What peace exists between a hyena and a dog? And what peace is there between a rich person and a poor person? {13:19} Wild donkeys in the wilderness are prey for lions; similarly, the poor are food for the rich. {13:20} Humility is an abomination to a proud person; likewise, a poor person is an abomination to a rich one. {13:21} When a rich person stumbles, their friends will support them; but when a humble person falls, even their friends will push them away. {13:22} If a rich person slips, many are there to help; they may say inappropriate things and be justified. If a humble person slips, they are reproached; they speak wisely but are ignored. {13:23} When the rich speak, everyone is silent, praising their words to the skies. When the poor speak, they say, "Who is this?" and if he stumbles, they will even push him down. {13:24} Wealth is good if free from sin, while poverty is seen as bad by the ungodly. {13:25} A person's heart can change their appearance, either for good or for evil. {13:26} The sign of a happy heart is a cheerful face, but creating proverbs takes painful thought.

{14:1} Blessed is the person who does not stumble with their words and does not suffer grief for their sins. {14:2} Blessed is the one whose heart does not condemn them and who has not lost hope. {14:3} Wealth does not suit a stingy person; what good is property to someone envious? {14:4} Whoever accumulates by denying themselves only gathers for others, who will enjoy luxuries from their goods. {14:5} If a person is mean to themselves, who will they be generous to? They will not enjoy their own riches. {14:6} No one is meaner than a person who is stingy with themselves; this is the consequence of their baseness. {14:7} Even if they do good, it will be unintentional, revealing their true nature in the end. {14:8} A person with a begrudging eye is wicked; they turn away and disregard others. {14:9} A greedy person's eye is never satisfied; unfairness withers the soul. {14:10} A stingy person begrudges even bread, and it will be lacking at their table. {14:11} My child, treat yourself well according to your means and present worthy offerings to the Lord. {14:12} Remember that death will not wait, and the decree of the grave has not been shown to you. {14:13} Do good for a friend before you die, and give to them as much as you can. {14:14} Do not deprive yourself of a joyful day; let not your share of good pass you by. {14:15} Will you not leave the fruit of your labor for others, so what you worked for is divided by lot? {14:16} Give, receive, and enjoy yourself, for in the grave, there is no luxury. {14:17} All living beings age like clothing, for the old decree is, "You must surely die!" {14:18} Like flourishing leaves on a tree that sheds some while sprouting others, so are the generations of flesh and blood: one dies, and another is born. {14:19} Everything created decays and ceases to exist, and the maker will pass away with it. {14:20} Blessed is the person who thinks deeply about wisdom and reasons intelligently. {14:21} Those who reflect on her ways will also ponder her secrets. {14:22} Pursue wisdom like a hunter, and lie in wait for her paths. {14:23} Those who look through her windows will also listen at her doors; {14:24} those who camp near her house will also secure their tent to her walls; {14:25} they will pitch their tent close to her and find excellent lodging; {14:26} they will place their children under her shelter and camp under her branches; {14:27} they will be sheltered by her from the heat and will dwell in her glory.

{15:1} The person who fears the Lord will act wisely, and those who adhere to the law will gain wisdom. {15:2} Wisdom will greet him like a mother and welcome him like a youthful wife. {15:3} She will nourish him with the bread of understanding and give him the water of wisdom to drink. {15:4} He will lean on her and not fall; he will rely on her and not be ashamed. {15:5} She will elevate him above his peers and open his mouth in the assembly. {15:6} He will find joy and a crown of rejoicing and will earn an everlasting name. {15:7} Foolish individuals will not find her, and sinful people will not see her. {15:8} She is far from the proud, and liars will never consider her. {15:9} A sinner's lips are not fit for a hymn of praise, as it has not been sent from the Lord. {15:10} A hymn of praise should be spoken with wisdom, and the Lord will bless it. {15:11} Do not say, "I left the right path because of the Lord"; he does not do what he despises. {15:12} Do not claim, "He led me astray"; he does not need a sinful person. {15:13} The Lord detests all abominations, and those who fear him do not love them. {15:14} He created humanity at the beginning and left them in control of their own choices. {15:15} If you want to, you can keep the commandments; acting faithfully is your choice. {15:16} He has placed before you fire & water: reach out for whichever you desire. {15:17} Life & death are set before you, and whatever you choose will be given to you. {15:18} The Lord's wisdom is great; he is powerful & sees everything; {15:19} his eyes are on those who fear him & he knows every action of humanity. {15:20} He hasn't commanded anyone to be wicked, nor has he permitted anyone to sin.

{16:1} Do not desire a multitude of worthless children, nor rejoice in ungodly offspring. {16:2} If they multiply, do not take pride in them unless they fear the Lord. {16:3} Do not trust in their survival, nor rely on their numbers; for one good child is better than a thousand, and dying childless is preferable to having ungodly children. {16:4} Through one wise person, a city will be filled with people, but a tribe of lawless individuals will make it desolate. {16:5} I have seen many things, and my ears have heard even more striking events. {16:6} In a gathering of sinners, a fire will be ignited, and in a disobedient nation, wrath will be stirred. {16:7} He was not appeased for the ancient giants who rebelled with their strength. {16:8} He did not spare the neighbors of Lot, whom he despised due to their arrogance. {16:9} He showed no mercy to a nation marked for destruction due to their sins; {16:10} nor did he for the six hundred thousand men who stubbornly rebelled. {16:11} Even if only one stubborn person exists, it's remarkable if they go unpunished. Mercy and wrath are both with the Lord; he can forgive and also pour out wrath. {16:12} As great as his mercy, so is his reproof; he judges individuals based on their actions. {16:13} A sinner will not escape with their plunder, and the patience of the godly will not be frustrated. {16:14} He will accommodate every act of mercy; everyone will receive according to their deeds. {16:17} Do not say, "I will be hidden from the Lord; who from above will remember me? Among so many people, I shall go unnoticed; what is my soul in this vast creation?" {16:18} Look, heaven and the highest heavens, the abyss and the earth, tremble at his visitation. {16:19} The mountains and the foundations of the earth also shake with fear when he gazes upon them. {16:20} No one reflects on this. Who considers his ways? {16:21} Like a storm that cannot be seen, most of his works are hidden. {16:22} Who can proclaim his acts of justice? Or who will anticipate them? For the covenant is far off. {16:23} This is what an unwise person thinks; a foolish and misguided person thinks wrongly. {16:24} Listen to me, my child, and gain knowledge; pay close attention to my words. {16:25} I will provide instruction carefully and declare knowledge accurately. {16:26} The Lord's works have existed since the beginning of creation, and when he made them, he determined their divisions. {16:27} He arranged his works in an eternal order, granting them dominion for all generations; they neither hunger nor tire and do not cease their labors. {16:28} They do not push each other aside, and they will never disobey his command. {16:29} After this, the Lord looked upon the earth and filled it with his good things; {16:30} with all kinds of living beings, he covered its surface, and they return to it.

{17:1} The Lord created humanity from the earth and will return them to it again. {17:2} He gave people a few days, a limited time, but granted them authority over the earth's creations. {17:3} He endowed them with strength like his own and made them in his image. {17:4} He instilled a sense of fear in all living beings and granted them dominion over animals and birds. {17:6} He provided them with tongues and eyes; he gave them ears and a mind for thinking. {17:7} He filled them with knowledge and understanding, revealing good and evil to them. {17:8} He looked into their hearts to show them the greatness of his works. {17:10} They will praise his holy name and declare the magnificence of his works. {17:11} He granted them knowledge and gave them the law of life. {17:12} He established an eternal covenant with them and revealed his judgments. {17:13} Their eyes saw his glorious majesty, and their ears heard the splendor of his voice. {17:14} He instructed them to "Beware of all wrongdoing," and commanded each of them regarding their neighbors. {17:15} Their actions are always before him; nothing is hidden from his sight. {17:17} He appointed a ruler for every nation, but Israel is the Lord's own portion. {17:19} All their actions are visible to him, and his eyes are constantly on their ways. {17:20} Their wrongdoings are not hidden from him, and all their sins are known to the Lord. {17:22} A person's acts of charity are like a seal before the Lord; he keeps a person's kindness as precious as his own sight. {17:23} In time, he will arise to repay them and bring their consequences upon their heads. {17:24} Yet for those who repent, he offers a chance to return and encourages those whose endurance is fading. {17:25} Turn to the Lord and abandon your sins; pray in his presence and reduce your offenses. {17:26} Return to the Most High and turn away from wickedness; hate sin deeply. {17:27} Who can sing praises to the Most High in Hades, like those who are alive and give thanks? {17:28} From the dead, as if from someone who doesn't exist, thanksgiving has stopped; the living can sing the Lord's praises. {17:29} How immense is the Lord's mercy and forgiveness for those who turn to him! {17:30} For not everything can exist in humans, since a human being is not immortal. {17:31} What is brighter than the sun? Yet even its light fades. Flesh and blood devise evil. {17:32} He commands the heavenly hosts, but all people are just dust and ashes.

{18:1} The one who lives forever created the entire universe; {18:2} the Lord alone will be declared righteous. {18:4} No one has the power to declare his works; who can truly understand his mighty deeds? {18:5} Who can measure his majestic power? Who can fully recount his mercies? {18:6} It's impossible to diminish or increase them, nor can anyone trace the wonders of the Lord. {18:7} When a person finishes, they are just beginning; when they stop, they will find themselves at a loss. {18:8} What is humanity, and what value do they have? What is their good, and what is their evil? {18:9} A person's days are significant if they reach a hundred years. {18:10} Just like a drop of water from the sea and a grain of sand, so are a few years in the span of eternity. {18:11} Therefore, the Lord is patient with them and pours out his mercy upon them. {18:12} He sees and knows that their end will be evil; thus, he grants them abundant forgiveness. {18:13} A person's compassion is for their neighbor, but the Lord's compassion extends to all living beings. He corrects, teaches, and guides them, like a shepherd with his flock. {18:14} He shows compassion to those who accept his discipline and seek his judgments. {18:15} My child, do not mix shame with your good deeds, nor cause sorrow with your words when giving a gift. {18:16} Isn't dew refreshing in the scorching heat? A word can be better than a gift. {18:17} Indeed, doesn't a kind word surpass a good gift? Both can be found in a gracious person. {18:18} A fool is ungracious and abusive, and the gift from a grudging person dulls the eyes. {18:19} Before you speak, learn, and before you get sick, take care of your health. {18:20} Before judgment, examine yourself; and in times of trouble, you will find forgiveness. {18:21} Before you fall ill, humble yourself, and when you feel tempted to sin, turn back. {18:22} Don't let anything stop you from fulfilling a vow promptly, and don't wait until death to be freed from it. {18:23} Prepare yourself before making a vow; don't be like someone who tests the Lord. {18:24} Consider his wrath on the day of death, and the moment of vengeance when he turns away from you. {18:25} In times of plenty, think about times of hunger; in days of wealth, remember poverty and need. {18:26} From morning to evening, circumstances change, and everything moves swiftly before the Lord. {18:27} A wise person is cautious in everything, and during sinful times, they guard against wrongdoing. {18:28} Every intelligent person recognizes wisdom and praises those who find her. {18:29} Those who understand sayings become skilled themselves and share wise proverbs. {18:30} Don't follow your base desires; instead, restrain your appetites. {18:31} If you allow your soul to indulge in base desires, it will make you the laughingstock of your enemies. {18:32} Don't indulge in great luxury, or you may become poor due to its cost. {18:33} Avoid becoming a beggar by feasting on borrowed money when you have nothing in your wallet.

{19:1} A worker who is a drunkard will not get rich; one who despises small things will gradually fail. {19:2} Wine and women can lead intelligent men astray, and a man who associates with prostitutes is very reckless. {19:3} Decay and worms will be his inheritance, and the reckless soul will be taken away. {19:4} Someone who trusts others too quickly is foolish, and one who sins does harm to themselves. {19:5} Those who take pleasure in wickedness will be condemned, {19:6} but someone who hates gossip will reduce evil. {19:7} Never repeat a conversation, and you won't lose anything at all. {19:8} Don't report it to friends or foes, and unless it's a sin for you, don't disclose it; {19:9} for someone has heard you and is watching, and when the time comes, they will hate you. {19:10} Have you heard something? Let it die with you. Be brave! It won't kill you! {19:11} A fool who shares such words will suffer as a woman in labor. {19:12} Like an arrow stuck in the thigh, so is a word lodged in a fool. {19:13} Ask a friend; maybe he didn't do it. If he did, it's so he won't do it again. {19:14} Ask a neighbor; maybe he didn't say it. If he did, it's so he won't say it again. {19:15} Question your friend, for often it's slander; don't believe everything you hear. {19:16} A person might slip without intending to. Who hasn't sinned with their words? {19:17} Question your neighbor before you threaten him; let the law of the Most High take its course. {19:20} All wisdom is rooted in the fear of the Lord, and in all wisdom, there's the fulfillment of the law. {19:22} But knowing wickedness isn't wisdom, nor is there prudence where sinners gather. {19:23} There's a cleverness that is detestable, but some fools simply lack wisdom. {19:24} It's better to be a God-fearing man who lacks intelligence than a shrewd man who breaks the law. {19:25} There's a cleverness that is careful yet unjust, and some twist kindness to win a verdict. {19:26} There's a schemer who appears mournful but is full of deceit inside. {19:27} He hides his face and pretends not to hear; yet when unnoticed, he will set a trap for you. {19:28} If his weakness prevents him from sinning, he will commit evil when the opportunity arises. {19:29} A man is known by his appearance, and a sensible person is recognized by their demeanor when you meet them. {19:30} A man's attire, loud laughter, and manner of walking reveal who he is.

{20:1} There's a reprimand that isn't timely, and a wise man may keep silent. {20:2} It's much better to reprove than to remain angry! The one who admits their faults will avoid loss. {20:4} Like a eunuch's desire to violate a maiden, so is a man who carries out judgments with violence. {20:5} Some remain silent and are considered wise, while others are despised for being too talkative. {20:6} Some are silent because they have no answer; others know when to speak. {20:7} A wise person will wait for the right moment to speak, but a braggart and fool will miss it. {20:8} Whoever uses too many words will be disliked, and whoever takes the right to speak will be hated. {20:9} A man may find good fortune in adversity, while sudden wealth may lead to loss. {20:10} There's a gift that brings no benefit, and a gift that brings double the return. {20:11} There are losses due to glory, and there are people who rise from humble beginnings. {20:12} Some buy much for little but pay seven times over. {20:13} A wise person earns love through their words, while a fool's courtesy goes to waste. {20:14} A fool's gift is worthless, as he sees things from many angles instead of one. {20:15} He gives little but complains a lot; he speaks loudly like a herald; today he lends, and tomorrow he demands it back—such a person is hated. {20:16} A fool will claim, "I have no friends, and no one appreciates my good deeds; those who eat my food speak unkindly." {20:17} How many will mock him, and how often! {20:18} A slip on the pavement is better than a slip of the tongue; the wicked's downfall will happen quickly. {20:19} An ungrateful person is like a poorly timed story that everyone remembers. {20:20} A proverb from a fool will be rejected because he shares it at the wrong time. {20:21} A man may be prevented from sinning by his poverty, so when he rests, he feels no regret. {20:22} A man may lose his life due to shame or because of a foolish expression. {20:23} A man may make promises to a friend out of shame, creating an enemy unnecessarily. {20:24} A lie is an ugly stain on a person; it's often spoken by the ignorant. {20:25} A thief is preferable to a habitual liar, but both will face ruin. {20:26} The character of a liar brings disgrace, and his shame is ever-present. {20:27} The one who speaks wisely will advance, and a sensible person will win favor with great men. {20:28} Whoever cultivates the land will reap a harvest, and whoever pleases great men will atone for wrongs. {20:29} Gifts and presents can blind the wise; they can silence criticism like a muzzle. {20:30} What advantage is there in hidden wisdom & unseen treasure? {20:31} It's better to conceal one's folly than to hide one's wisdom.

{21:1} Have you sinned, my child? Don't do it again; instead, pray about your past sins. {21:2} Run from sin like you would from a snake, because if you get too close, it will bite you. Its teeth are like a lion's, destroying the souls of men. {21:3} All lawlessness is like a double-edged sword; there's no healing for its wounds. {21:4} Terror and violence will ruin riches, and so the proud will find their homes destroyed. {21:5} The prayer of a poor person reaches God's ears, and he will judge swiftly. {21:6} Whoever hates correction walks in the footsteps of sinners, but those who fear the Lord will repent in their hearts. {21:7} A powerful speaker is known from a distance, but a sensible person realizes when they've made a mistake. {21:8} A man who builds his house with other people's money is like someone gathering stones for his own grave. {21:9} A gathering of the wicked is like tow (a material) being collected, and their end will be like a raging fire. {21:10} The path of sinners is smooth and easy, but it ultimately leads to the pit of Hades. {21:11} Whoever keeps the law controls their thoughts, and wisdom comes from fearing the Lord. {21:12} A person who isn't clever can't be taught, but there's a cleverness that only increases bitterness. {21:13} The knowledge of a wise person will increase like a flood, and their advice will flow like a spring. {21:14} The mind of a fool is like a broken jar; it can't hold any knowledge. {21:15} When a man of understanding hears wise words, he will praise them and build on them; but when a fool hears them, he dislikes them and forgets them. {21:16} A fool's storytelling is like a burden on a journey, while intelligent speech brings joy. {21:17} The words of a sensible person will be sought after in gatherings, and people will reflect on them. {21:18} Wisdom is lost on a fool, just as a vanished house is; the ignorance of the uneducated leads to meaningless chatter. {21:19} For a senseless person, education feels like shackles, like manacles on his hand. {21:20} A fool laughs loudly, but a clever man smiles quietly. {21:21} For a sensible person, education is like a golden ornament or a bracelet on the arm. {21:22} A fool rushes into a house, while a man of experience approaches respectfully. {21:23} A rude person looks in through the door, but a refined man stays outside. {21:24} It's impolite for a man to listen at the door, and a discreet person feels distressed by such disgrace. {21:25} The words of strangers will speak of these matters, but the prudent will weigh their words carefully. {21:26} Fools express their minds openly, but wise men think carefully before they speak. {21:27} When an ungodly person curses their enemy, they're cursing their own soul. {21:28} A gossip corrupts their own soul and is disliked in their community.

{22:1} The lazy can be compared to a filthy stone, and everyone looks down on their disgrace. {22:2} The lazy are like the refuse from a dung heap; anyone who touches it shakes their hands clean. {22:3} It's a disgrace to be the father of an undisciplined son, and a daughter's birth can feel like a loss. {22:4} A sensible daughter finds a husband, but a shameful one brings grief to her father. {22:5} A brazen daughter brings shame to both her father and husband and will be looked down upon by both. {22:6} A story told at the wrong time is like music at a funeral; however, discipline and teaching are wise at all times. {22:7} Teaching a fool is like trying to glue broken pots together or waking a deep sleeper. {22:8} Telling a story to a fool is like talking to someone half-asleep; in the end, they'll say, "What was that?" {22:11} Weep for the dead, as they no longer have light; weep for the fool, for they lack understanding. Weep less for the dead, as they find rest; the life of a fool is worse than death. {22:12} Mourning for the dead lasts seven days, but for a fool or ungodly person, it lasts a lifetime. {22:13} Don't engage too much with foolish people, and avoid unintelligent ones; protect yourself from them to escape trouble, and you won't be stained when they shake themselves off. Avoid them, and you'll find peace, never growing weary of their madness. {22:14} What's heavier than lead? What else could it be but "Fool"? {22:15} Sand, salt, and a piece of iron are lighter to bear than a stupid person. {22:16} A sturdy wooden beam in a building won't break in an earthquake; similarly, a mind grounded in sound advice won't fear a crisis. {22:17} A settled mind is like the decorative stucco on a colonnade's wall. {22:18} Fences set high won't hold against the wind; likewise, a timid heart with a fool's mindset won't stand firm in fear. {22:19} A person who pricks an eye causes tears; one who pricks the heart makes emotions visible. {22:20} Someone who throws stones at birds will scare them away, and someone who insults a friend will break that friendship. {22:21} Even if you draw your sword against a friend, don't lose hope; friendships can be renewed. {22:22} If you've spoken against a friend, don't despair, as reconciliation is possible; but if you insult, act arrogantly, disclose secrets, or betray trust, any friend will run away. {22:23} Earn the trust of your neighbor in their hardship so you can celebrate with them in their success; support them in trouble, so you can share in their inheritance. {22:24} Just as vapor and smoke precede a fire, insults come before violence. {22:25} I won't be ashamed to defend a friend, nor will I hide from them; {22:26} but if harm comes to me because of them, anyone who hears of it will be cautious. {22:27} Oh, that a guard could be placed over my mouth, and a seal of wisdom over my lips, to keep me from falling and ensure my tongue doesn't destroy me!

{23:1} O Lord, Father and Ruler of my life, don't let me be led astray by their advice, and help me not to stumble because of them! {23:2} I wish I had whips to control my thoughts, and the discipline of wisdom to guide my mind! They shouldn't spare me from my mistakes, and my sins shouldn't go unnoticed. {23:3} I don't want my mistakes to multiply, or my sins to increase; then I won't fall before my enemies, and they won't rejoice over me. {23:4} O Lord, Father and God of my life, keep me from haughty eyes, {23:5} and remove any evil desires from me. {23:6} Don't let gluttony or lust overpower me, and don't surrender me to a shameless person. {23:7} Listen, my children, to advice about how to speak; those who follow it will never get caught. {23:8} A sinner is trapped by his words; those who insult and act arrogantly stumble because of them. {23:9} Don't get used to swearing oaths, and don't casually use the name of the Holy One; {23:10} because just as a servant who's always being tortured will bear scars, so too will a person who frequently swears and uses the Name never be free from sin. {23:11} A man who swears a lot will be filled with wrongdoing, and punishment will not leave his home; if he sins, his guilt stays with him, and if he ignores it, he sins even more; if he swears unnecessarily, he won't be justified, for his house will be filled with disasters. {23:12} There are words that lead to death; may they never be part of Jacob's legacy! All these errors are far from the godly, who won't be mired in sin. {23:13} Don't let your mouth get accustomed to vulgar language, because it leads to sinful speech. {23:14} Remember your father and mother when you're in the company of great people; don't forget them in their presence, or you'll be seen as foolish because of your habits; then you'll wish you had never been born, and you'll curse the day you were born. {23:15} A person who uses insults regularly will never be disciplined throughout their life. {23:16} There are two types of people who increase sin, and a third who brings wrath. A soul that burns like fire won't be quenched until it consumes itself; a man who commits incest will not stop until the fire destroys him. {23:17} For a fornicator, all food tastes sweet; they won't stop until they die. {23:18} A man who breaks his marriage vows thinks to himself, "Who sees me? I'm surrounded by darkness, and the walls hide me; no one sees me. Why should I be afraid? The Most High doesn't notice my sins." {23:19} His fear is only about what others see, not realizing that God's eyes are brighter than the sun; they see all people's ways and even the hidden places. {23:20} He knew everything before the universe was created, just as He knows it now that it's finished. {23:21} This man will face punishment in the city streets, and he'll be caught where he least expects it. {23:22} The same is true for a woman who leaves her husband and has a child with another man. {23:23} First, she disobeys the law of the Most High; second, she sins against her husband; and third, she commits adultery by sleeping with a stranger and bears children from another man. {23:24} She'll be brought before the assembly, and punishment will come upon her children. {23:25} Her children will not take root, and their branches will not bear fruit. {23:26} She'll be remembered as a curse, and her disgrace will never be forgotten. {23:27} Those who outlive her will realize that nothing is better than the fear of the Lord, and nothing sweeter than obeying the Lord's commandments.

{24:1} Wisdom will praise herself and boast among her people. {24:2} In the assembly of the Most High, she will speak, and among His host, she will take pride: {24:3} "I came from the mouth of the Most High, and covered the earth like a mist. {24:4} I dwelled in high places, and my throne was in a pillar of cloud. {24:5} I have traveled around the heavens and walked in the depths of the abyss. {24:6} In the waves of the sea, in all the earth, and in every people and nation, I have gained a possession. {24:7} Among all these, I looked for a place to rest; I searched for a territory where I could stay. {24:8} Then the Creator of all things gave me a command, and He who created me gave me a place for my home. He said, 'Make your dwelling in Jacob, and in Israel, receive your inheritance.' {24:9} I was created from eternity, in the beginning, and I will exist forever. {24:10} In the holy tabernacle, I served before Him, and there I was established in Zion. {24:11} In the beloved city, He gave me a resting place, and in Jerusalem, I held dominion. {24:12} So I took root in an honored people, in the Lord's portion, which is their inheritance. {24:13} I grew tall like a cedar in Lebanon, and like a cypress on the heights of Hermon. {24:14} I grew tall like a palm tree in En-Gedi, and like rose plants in Jericho; like a beautiful olive tree in the field, and like a plane tree, I grew tall. {24:15} Like cassia and camel's thorn, I emitted fragrant spices, and like choice myrrh, I released a pleasant scent, like galbanum, onycha, and stacte, and like frankincense in the tabernacle. {24:16} Like a terebinth, I spread my branches, and they are glorious and graceful. {24:17} Like a vine, I caused beauty to flourish, and my blossoms produced glorious and abundant fruit. {24:19} "Come to me, you who desire me, and enjoy the fruits of my labor. {24:20} For the remembrance of me is sweeter than honey, and my inheritance is sweeter than honeycomb. {24:21} Those who eat of me will hunger for more, and those who drink of me will thirst for more. {24:22} Whoever obeys me will not be put to shame, and those who work with my guidance will not sin." {24:23} All of this is the book of the covenant of the Most High God, the law that Moses commanded us as an inheritance for the congregations of Jacob. {24:25} It fills people with wisdom, like the Pishon river, and like the Tigris at harvest time. {24:26} It makes them full of understanding, like the Euphrates, and like the Jordan at harvest time. {24:27} It makes instruction shine like light, like the Gihon at the vintage season. {24:28} Just as the first man did not fully understand her, the last one has not grasped her either; {24:29} for her thoughts are more numerous than the sea, and her counsel is deeper than the great abyss. {24:30} I flowed like a canal from a river and like a channel into a garden. {24:31} I said, "I will water my orchard and soak my garden," and behold, my canal became a river, and my river became a sea. {24:32} I will again make instruction shine like the dawn, and I will make it shine far and wide; {24:33} I will once more pour out teaching like prophecy, leaving it for all future generations. {24:34} Notice that I haven't labored for myself alone, but for all who seek instruction.

{25:1} My soul delights in three things, and they are beautiful in the sight of the Lord and people: harmony among brothers, friendship among neighbors, and a husband and wife living in peace. {25:2} My soul despises three types of people, and I am greatly offended by their lives: a proud beggar, a rich man who lies, and an old man who commits adultery and lacks sense. {25:3} If you haven't gathered anything in your youth, how can you expect to have anything in your old age? {25:4} How admirable is good judgment in older men, and how valuable is wise counsel from the aged! {25:5} Wisdom in the elderly is attractive, as is understanding and counsel from honorable men! {25:6} Rich experience is the crown of the old, and their pride is in the fear of the Lord. {25:7} I have filled my heart with nine joys, and I will share a tenth: a man who delights in his children; a man who witnesses the downfall of his enemies; {25:8} blessed is he who lives with a wise wife, who hasn't stumbled with his words, and who hasn't served someone beneath him; {25:9} blessed is he who has gained wisdom and speaks to attentive listeners. {25:10} How great is he who has gained wisdom! But no one is greater than the one who fears the Lord. {25:11} The fear of the Lord surpasses everything; who can compare to the one who holds it tightly? {25:13} Any wound can be endured, but not a wound of the heart! Any wickedness can be tolerated, but not the wickedness of a wife! {25:14} Any attack can be faced, but not an attack from those who hate! Any vengeance can be accepted, but not the vengeance of enemies! {25:15} There's no poison worse than a snake's venom, and no anger worse than an enemy's anger. {25:16} I would prefer to live with a lion and a dragon than to live with an evil wife. {25:17} The wickedness of a wife alters her appearance, darkening her face like that of a bear. {25:18} Her husband eats with neighbors but sighs bitterly. {25:19} Any sin is minor compared to a wife's sin; may a sinner's fate be hers! {25:20} A sandy path for an old man's feet — that's what a talkative wife is for a quiet husband. {25:21} Don't be fooled by a woman's beauty, and don't desire a woman for her wealth. {25:22} There's anger, shamelessness, and great disgrace when a wife supports her husband. {25:23} A depressed mind, a gloomy face, and a wounded heart are caused by an evil wife; drooping hands and weak knees are the result of a wife who fails to bring happiness. {25:24} Sin began with a woman, and because of her, we all die. {25:25} Don't give a wicked wife any freedom of speech or let her be bold. {25:26} If she won't follow your direction, separate yourself from her.

{26:1} Blessed is the husband of a good wife; his days will be doubled. {26:2} A loyal wife brings joy to her husband, and he will live his years in peace. {26:3} A good wife is a tremendous blessing; she is one of the blessings given to a man who fears the Lord. {26:4} Whether he is rich or poor, his heart is glad, and his face is always cheerful. {26:5} My heart is afraid of three things, and of a fourth, I am terrified: the slander of a city, the gathering of a mob, and false accusations — all worse than death. {26:6} There is heartache and sorrow when a wife is jealous of a rival, and her anger is obvious to everyone. {26:7} An evil wife is like an ox yoke that chafes; holding onto her is like grasping a scorpion. {26:8} There's great anger when a wife is drunk; she won't hide her shame. {26:9} A wife's promiscuity is evident in her lustful eyes; she is recognized by her eyelashes. {26:10} Keep a close watch on a rebellious daughter; if she gains freedom, she might misuse it. {26:11} Be wary of her boldness; don't be surprised if she betrays you. {26:12} Just as a thirsty traveler drinks from any water nearby, so she will sit by every post and open her quiver to every man. {26:13} A wife's charm delights her husband, and her skills add to his prosperity. {26:14} A quiet wife is a gift from the Lord, and nothing is more precious than a disciplined soul. {26:15} A modest wife adds to her beauty, and no measure can equate to the worth of a chaste soul. {26:16} Like the sun rising in the heights of the Lord, so is the beauty of a good wife in her well-kept home. {26:17} Like a shining lamp on a holy lampstand, so is a beautiful face on a dignified body. {26:18} Like golden pillars on a silver base, so are beautiful feet on a steadfast heart. {26:28} My heart grieves for two things, and a third fills me with anger: a warrior in need due to poverty, and intelligent men who are disrespected; a man who turns away from righteousness to sin—the Lord will prepare him for destruction! {26:29} A merchant can hardly avoid wrongdoing & a tradesman will not be declared innocent of sin.

{27:1} Many have sinned over trivial matters, and those who seek to get rich often turn a blind eye. {27:2} Just as a stake is firmly driven into a crack between stones, sin is wedged between buying and selling. {27:3} If a person isn't steadfast and zealous in fearing the Lord, their household will quickly fall apart. {27:4} When a sieve is shaken, the debris stays behind; similarly, a person's filth remains in their thoughts. {27:5} A kiln tests a potter's work; likewise, a person's character is revealed through their reasoning. {27:6} The fruit reveals how a tree was cared for; in the same way, a person's thoughts reveal the state of their mind. {27:7} Don't praise someone before you hear them reason; this is the true test of a person. {27:8} If you seek justice, you will achieve it and wear it like a glorious robe. {27:9} Birds gather with their kind; so too, truth returns to those who practice it. {27:10} A lion waits for its prey; similarly, sin lurks for those who do wrong. {27:11} The words of a righteous person are always wise, while a fool changes like the moon. {27:12} Among foolish people, look for an opportunity to leave, but stay among thoughtful individuals. {27:13} The words of fools are offensive, and their laughter is shamelessly sinful. {27:14} The talk of swearing men raises your hair, and their arguments make one want to block their ears. {27:15} The disputes of the proud lead to violence, and their insults are hard to listen to. {27:16} Whoever betrays secrets destroys trust and will never find a true friend. {27:17} Love your friend and stay loyal, but if you betray their secrets, don't chase after them. {27:18} Just as one destroys an enemy, you've ruined your neighbor's friendship. {27:19} Allowing a bird to escape from your hand is like letting go of your neighbor, and you won't be able to catch them again. {27:20} Don't pursue them; they're too far away, having escaped like a gazelle from a trap. {27:21} A wound can be bandaged, and reconciliation can happen after insults, but whoever betrays secrets has no hope. {27:22} The person who winks plans evil deeds, and no one can stop them. {27:23} In your presence, their words are sweet, and they praise you, but later they will twist their words and use your own words against you. {27:24} I've hated many things, but nothing compares to this person; even the Lord will hate them. {27:25} Whoever throws a stone straight up risks hitting themselves; a treacherous act causes wounds. {27:26} Whoever digs a pit will fall into it, and whoever sets a trap will get caught in it. {27:27} If someone does evil, it will come back to them, and they won't know where it came from. {27:28} Mockery and insults come from the proud, but vengeance lies in wait for them like a lion. {27:29} Those who rejoice at the downfall of the righteous will fall into a trap, and suffering will consume them before their death. {27:30} Anger and wrath are also abominations, and the sinful person will possess them.

{28:1} The one who takes vengeance will face vengeance from the Lord, and they will firmly establish their own sins. {28:2} Forgive your neighbor for the wrong he has done, and then your sins will be forgiven when you pray. {28:3} Can someone hold anger against another and still seek healing from the Lord? {28:4} Can someone show no mercy to a fellow human but still pray for their own sins? {28:5} If he, being human, holds onto anger, who will atone for his sins? {28:6} Remember the end of your life, and let go of enmity; remember destruction and death, and stay true to the commandments. {28:7} Keep the commandments in mind and don't be angry with your neighbor; remember the covenant of the Most High, and forgive ignorance. {28:8} Avoid conflict, and you will reduce your sins; for a person prone to anger will stir up strife, {28:9} and a sinful person will disturb friends and create hostility among those at peace. {28:10} The intensity of a fire corresponds to the fuel it has; likewise, the severity of strife corresponds to its stubbornness, and a person's anger matches their strength, increasing in proportion to their wealth. {28:11} A quick quarrel ignites flames, and urgent disputes lead to bloodshed. {28:12} If you blow on a spark, it will flare up; if you spit on it, it will be extinguished; both come from your mouth. {28:13} Curse the gossiper and deceiver, for they have destroyed many who were at peace. {28:14} Slander has shaken many, scattering them from nation to nation, destroying strong cities and overturning the homes of the powerful. {28:15} Slander has driven away brave women and robbed them of the fruits of their labor. {28:16} Whoever pays attention to slander will find no peace and will not settle down in tranquility. {28:17} A whip raises welts, but the blow of the tongue crushes bones. {28:18} Many have fallen by the sword, but not as many as have fallen because of the tongue. {28:19} Blessed is the man who is protected from it, who hasn't been exposed to its wrath, who hasn't borne its burden or been caught in its chains; {28:20} for its burden is an iron yoke, and its chains are bronze; {28:21} its death is a terrible death, and Hades is preferable to it. {28:22} It will not dominate the righteous, and they will not be consumed by its flames. {28:23} Those who abandon the Lord will fall under its power; it will burn within them and will not be extinguished. It will attack them like a lion; like a leopard, it will tear them apart. {28:24} Be sure to surround your property with thorns, secure your silver and gold, {28:25} weigh your words carefully, and put a lock and bolt on your mouth. {28:26} Be cautious not to err with your tongue, lest you fall into the trap of the one who lies in wait.

{29:1} The one who shows mercy will lend to their neighbor, and the one who strengthens them with their hand keeps the commandments. {29:2} Lend to your neighbor in their time of need, and in return, repay them promptly. {29:3} Keep your word and remain faithful to them, and you'll always find what you need. {29:4} Many people see a loan as free money and cause trouble for those who help them. {29:5} A man may flatter another to get a loan and speak softly about their money, but when it's time to repay, he'll delay and make excuses. {29:6} If the lender pushes for repayment, he may only get back half and consider that a stroke of luck; if he doesn't, the borrower will have robbed him, making him an enemy, returning curses instead of gratitude. {29:7} Because of such wickedness, many refuse to lend out of fear of being cheated. {29:8} However, be patient with someone in humble circumstances and don't make them wait too long for your help. {29:9} Help the poor out of obligation, and don't send them away empty-handed. {29:10} Be willing to lose your money for the sake of a brother or friend, and don't let it sit idle and rust away. {29:11} Store your treasures according to the commandments of the Most High, for it will profit you more than gold. {29:12} Keep track of your charitable giving; it will rescue you from all troubles. {29:13} More than a strong shield or heavy spear, it will fight for you against your enemies. {29:14} A good person will vouch for their neighbor, but someone lacking shame will fail them. {29:15} Don't forget the kindness of your guarantor, for he has put his life on the line for you. {29:16} A sinner will ruin his guarantor's prosperity, {29:17} and someone ungrateful will abandon their rescuer. {29:18} Being a guarantor has ruined many prosperous individuals, shaking them like waves in the sea; it has driven powerful men into exile, making them wander among foreign nations. {29:19} A sinner who falls into being a guarantor and seeks gain will end up in lawsuits. {29:20} Assist your neighbor according to your ability, but take care not to fall yourself. {29:21} The essentials for life are water, bread, clothing, and a home to protect one's dignity. {29:22} A poor person's life under their own roof is better than feasting in someone else's house. {29:23} Be content with little or much. {29:24} It's a miserable existence to go from house to house, where you're a stranger and can't speak up; {29:25} you'll host and serve drinks without being thanked, and on top of that, you'll hear harsh words: {29:26} "Come here, stranger, prepare the table, and if you have anything, let me have it to eat." {29:27} "Make room, stranger, for someone important; my brother has come to stay with me, and I need my space." {29:28} These situations are hard to bear for someone with feelings: being scolded for lodging and the reproaches of a moneylender.

{30:1} The one who loves their son will discipline him often so that he can rejoice in his future. {30:2} The one who disciplines their son will benefit from him and take pride in him among friends. {30:3} The one who teaches their son will make their enemies jealous and will take glory in him among acquaintances. {30:4} A father may die, yet he lives on in his children; {30:5} while alive, he sees and rejoices, and when he dies, he feels no grief; {30:6} he leaves behind a defender against his enemies and one to repay the kindness of his friends. {30:7} The one who spoils their son will tend to his wounds and be troubled by every cry. {30:8} An untamed horse is stubborn, and an unrestrained son will be willful. {30:9} If you pamper a child, he will scare you; play with him, and he will bring you sorrow. {30:10} Don't laugh with him, or you'll end up grieving with him and gnashing your teeth in the end. {30:11} Don't give him authority in his youth, and don't ignore his mistakes. {30:12} Train him while he's young; discipline him now to avoid future stubbornness and disobedience, which will cause you deep sorrow. {30:13} Discipline your son and invest time in him so you won't be offended by his shameful behavior. {30:14} A poor but healthy man is better off than a rich man with serious health issues. {30:15} Good health is better than all gold, and a strong body is worth more than countless riches. {30:16} There's no wealth better than bodily health, and no joy surpasses a happy heart. {30:17} Death is better than a miserable life, and eternal rest is preferable to chronic illness. {30:18} Good things given to a closed mouth are like food offerings placed on a grave. {30:19} What good is an offering of fruit to an idol? It can neither eat nor smell. So is a person afflicted by the Lord; {30:20} they see with their eyes and groan, like a eunuch who embraces a maiden and sighs. {30:21} Don't give in to sorrow, and don't inflict pain on yourself intentionally. {30:22} A joyful heart is the essence of life, and a cheerful person enjoys longer days. {30:23} Delight your soul and comfort your heart, and push sorrow far away, for sorrow has destroyed many, and there's no profit in it. {30:24} Jealousy and anger shorten life, and anxiety brings on old age too soon. {30:25} A cheerful person with a good heart will be mindful of the food they eat.

{31:1} Worrying about wealth wears down the body, and anxiety about it steals your sleep. {31:2} Stress from worrying prevents rest, and serious illness can rob you of sleep. {31:3} The rich work hard as their wealth grows, and when they finally rest, they indulge in lavish food. {31:4} The poor work hard but see their resources dwindle, and when they rest, they feel lacking. {31:5} Those who love gold will not be justified, and those who chase money will be misled by it. {31:6} Many have met ruin because of gold, facing destruction head-on. {31:7} It serves as a trap for those devoted to it, and fools will fall prey to it. {31:8} Blessed is the rich person who is blameless and does not pursue gold. {31:9} Who is this person? We will call them blessed for doing wonderful deeds among their people. {31:10} Who has faced the temptation of wealth and emerged unscathed? Let them boast about it. Who has had the chance to do wrong and chose not to? {31:11} Their prosperity will stand strong, and the community will share stories of their generosity. {31:12} Are you seated at a wealthy person's table? Don't be greedy; don't think, "There's plenty for everyone!" {31:13} Remember that a greedy eye is harmful. What is greedier than the eye? It brings tears to many faces. {31:14} Don't reach for everything you see, and don't crowd your neighbor at the table. {31:15} Consider your neighbor's feelings as your own, and be thoughtful in all things. {31:16} Eat like a dignified person what's served to you, and don't overindulge, or you'll be disliked. {31:17} Be the first to stop eating for the sake of good manners, and don't be insatiable, or you'll offend others. {31:18} When sitting among many, don't reach out for food before they do. {31:19} How satisfying a little is for someone well-disciplined! They don't toss and turn in bed. {31:20} Healthy sleep comes from moderate eating; they wake early and feel good. The distress of sleeplessness and discomfort is for the glutton. {31:21} If you've eaten too much, get up during the meal for relief. {31:22} Listen to me, my child, and don't disregard my words; in the end, you'll appreciate what I say. Be diligent in all your work, and sickness won't overtake you. {31:23} People will praise the one who shares generously, and their testimony about his generosity is credible. {31:24} The community will complain about the stingy one, and their testimony about his stinginess is true. {31:25} Don't aim to be a warrior over wine, for wine has ruined many. {31:26} Just as fire and water test the quality of steel, wine tests the hearts of the proud. {31:27} Wine can be like life for people when drunk in moderation. What good is life to someone without wine? It's meant to bring joy. {31:28} Drinking wine in moderation brings joy to the heart and happiness to the soul. {31:29} Excessive drinking leads to bitterness of soul, conflict, and stumbling. {31:30} Drunkenness inflates a fool's anger, harming him and weakening him with injuries. {31:31} Don't criticize your neighbor at a wine banquet, and don't look down on him in his happiness; don't speak harshly to him, and don't burden him with demands.

{32:1} If they make you the host of the feast, don't elevate yourself; be among them as one of them, taking care of them before taking your seat. {32:2} After fulfilling your duties, then take your place, so you can enjoy yourself and be recognized for your leadership. {32:3} Speak, you who are older, for it's appropriate, but do so with wisdom, and don't interrupt the music. {32:4} Where there's entertainment, don't drown it out with chatter; don't show off your cleverness at the wrong time. {32:5} A ruby seal set in gold is like music played at a banquet. {32:6} An emerald seal in a rich setting is like beautiful melodies with good wine. {32:7} Speak, young man, if you're needed, but only a couple of times, and only when asked. {32:8} Speak concisely; convey much with few words, like someone who knows but keeps silent. {32:9} Among the great, don't act like you're their equal, and when others are speaking, don't chatter away. {32:10} Lightning strikes before thunder, and approval comes before a humble person. {32:11} Leave at the right time and don't be the last to go; head home quickly and don't linger. {32:12} Enjoy yourself while there and do what you want, but don't sin with arrogant speech. {32:13} For these things, give thanks to the one who created you and blesses you with good gifts. {32:14} The one who fears the Lord will accept His discipline, and those who seek Him early will find favor. {32:15} Those who seek the law will be filled with knowledge, but hypocrites will stumble over it. {32:16} Those who fear the Lord will make wise judgments, and like a light, they will ignite righteous deeds. {32:17} A sinner will avoid correction and will choose decisions that suit him. {32:18} A discerning person will consider every idea, while a proud and arrogant person will not fear. {32:19} Don't act without thinking it through; once you act, don't regret it. {32:20} Avoid dangerous paths, and don't trip over rocky ground. {32:21} Don't be overly confident on smooth paths, {32:22} and pay attention to your ways. {32:23} Guard yourself in all actions, for this is how you keep the commandments. {32:24} The one who believes in the law listens to the commandments, and the one who trusts the Lord will not suffer loss.

{33:1} No harm will come to the person who fears the Lord; in times of trial, He will rescue them repeatedly. {33:2} A wise person does not dislike the law, but a hypocrite is like a ship tossed in a storm. {33:3} A person with understanding will trust in the law; for them, the law is as reliable as a direct answer from Urim (a method of divination). {33:4} Prepare what you want to say, and you'll be heard; organize your thoughts and responses. {33:5} The heart of a fool is like a cartwheel, spinning with every thought. {33:6} A stallion is like a mocking friend, whinnying under everyone who rides him. {33:7} Why is one day better than another when all daylight comes from the sun? {33:8} It's the Lord's choice that distinguishes the days; He set different seasons and celebrations. {33:9} Some days He made special and holy, while others are ordinary. {33:10} All people come from the earth, and Adam was made from dust. {33:11} In His complete wisdom, the Lord differentiated them and set their paths; {33:12} some He blessed and honored, some He made holy and brought close, and some He cursed and brought low, casting them away. {33:13} Like clay in the potter's hands—He shapes everything as He wishes—so are people in the hands of their Creator, to be used as He decides. {33:14} Good is the opposite of evil, and life is the opposite of death; thus, the sinner is the opposite of the righteous. {33:15} Look at all the works of the Most High; they exist in pairs, opposites to each other. {33:16} I was the last to keep watch, like someone who gathers leftover grapes; by the Lord's blessing, I succeeded, and I filled my wine press like a grape gatherer. {33:17} Remember, I haven't labored just for myself but for all who seek wisdom. {33:18} Listen to me, you influential people and leaders of the community. {33:19} Don't give others power over you—be it your child, spouse, brother, or friend—while you live; don't give your property to someone else, or you may regret it later. {33:20} While you are alive, don't let anyone take your place. {33:21} It's better for your children to ask from you than for you to rely on their help. {33:22} Excel in everything you do; maintain your honor. {33:23} When you reach the end of your days, at the hour of your death, distribute your inheritance. {33:24} Provide for your donkey with food and a stick; give bread, guidance, and work to your servant. {33:25} Set your servant to work, and you'll find rest; leave them idle, and they'll seek freedom. {33:26} A yoke and straps will bend the neck, and for a wicked servant, there are punishments and tortures. {33:27} Keep them busy to prevent idleness, which leads to much wrongdoing. {33:28} Assign them suitable tasks, and if they refuse to obey, make their burdens heavier. {33:29} Don't act excessively toward anyone, and don't act without careful thought. {33:30} If you have a servant, treat them like yourself, since you bought them with your hard work. {33:31} If you have a servant, treat them like a brother, as you may need them for your own well-being. If you mistreat them and they run away, where will you go to find them?

{34:1} A person lacking understanding has empty and false hopes; dreams can mislead fools. {34:2} Chasing after dreams is like trying to catch a shadow or chase the wind. {34:3} Dreams reflect opposites, like a face meeting another face. {34:4} Can anything unclean become clean? And can something false become true? {34:5} Divination, omens, and dreams are foolishness, and like a woman in labor, the mind can be distracted by illusions. {34:6} Unless dreams come from the Most High as a message, don't dwell on them. {34:7} Many have been deceived by dreams, and those who trust in them have failed. {34:8} Without such deceptions, the law will be fulfilled, and wisdom is perfected through truthful words. {34:9} An educated person knows many things, while one with experience speaks wisely. {34:10} An inexperienced person knows little, but a traveler gains much wisdom. {34:11} I have seen many things on my journeys, and I understand more than I can express. {34:12} I have often faced death but escaped because of these experiences. {34:13} The spirit of those who fear the Lord will live; their hope is in Him who saves them. {34:14} The one who fears the Lord will not be timid or cowardly, for the Lord is their hope. {34:15} Blessed is the soul of the person who fears the Lord! Who do they look to, and who is their support? {34:16} The Lord watches over those who love Him, providing strong protection and support, shelter from heat, shade from the midday sun, a guard against stumbling, and defense against falling. {34:17} He lifts the soul and gives light to the eyes; He grants healing, life, and blessings. {34:18} If someone sacrifices from ill-gotten gains, their offering is blemished; the gifts from the lawless are unacceptable. {34:19} The Most High does not accept the offerings of the ungodly; a multitude of sacrifices will not atone for sins. {34:20} Just as a person who kills their own son before their father's eyes is someone who offers sacrifices from the property of the poor. {34:21} The bread of the needy is the lifeblood of the poor; whoever deprives them is guilty of bloodshed. {34:22} To take away a neighbor's livelihood is like committing murder; withholding wages from a worker is like shedding blood. {34:23} When one person builds while another tears down, what do they gain but wasted effort? {34:24} When one prays and another curses, whose voice will the Lord heed? {34:25} If someone washes after touching a dead body and touches it again, what have they gained by washing? {34:26} Similarly, if a person fasts for their sins but continues to sin, who will hear their prayer? What have they gained by humbling themselves?

{35:1} Whoever follows the law makes many offerings; the one who pays attention to the commandments brings a peace offering. {35:2} The person who returns a kindness offers fine flour, and the one who gives to the poor makes a thank offering. {35:3} Avoiding wickedness pleases the Lord, and turning away from unrighteousness serves as atonement. {35:4} Don't come before the Lord empty-handed, {35:5} because all these actions are to be done in accordance with His commandments. {35:6} The offering of a righteous person sanctifies the altar, and its pleasing aroma rises before the Most High. {35:7} The sacrifice of a righteous person is accepted, and its memory will not fade. {35:8} Honor the Lord generously, and don't hold back the first fruits of your labor. {35:9} Show a cheerful face with every gift, and dedicate your tithe with joy. {35:10} Give to the Most High as He has given to you, and as generously as you are able. {35:11} The Lord is the one who repays, and He will reward you sevenfold. {35:12} Don't offer Him a bribe, as He won't accept it; and don't trust in an unrighteous sacrifice, for the Lord is the judge, and He shows no favoritism. {35:13} He doesn't favor the poor in judgment; He hears the prayers of those who are wronged. {35:14} He will not ignore the cries of the fatherless or the widow when they share their stories. {35:15} Don't the tears of the widow flow down her cheeks as she cries out against the one who has caused her pain? {35:16} The one whose service pleases the Lord will be accepted, and their prayers will reach the heavens. {35:17} The prayers of the humble reach the clouds; they won't be comforted until they reach the Lord; they won't stop until the Most High responds and delivers justice for the righteous. {35:18} The Lord will not delay nor be patient until He punishes the merciless and exacts vengeance on the nations; until He removes the multitude of the proud and breaks the scepters of the wicked; {35:19} until He repays each person according to their deeds, and holds people accountable for their actions; until He judges His people and brings them joy in His mercy. {35:20} Mercy is as welcomed during affliction as rain in a drought.

{36:1} Have mercy on us, O Lord, God of all, and look upon us. {36:2} Let the fear of You fall upon all nations. {36:3} Raise Your hand against foreign nations and let them see Your might. {36:4} Just as You have been sanctified in us, magnify Yourself among them; {36:5} let them know You, as we know there is no God but You, O Lord. {36:6} Show new signs and perform more wonders; make Your hand and strong arm glorious. {36:7} Stir up Your anger and pour out Your wrath; destroy the enemy and wipe out the foe. {36:8} Hurry the day and remember the appointed time; let people recount Your mighty deeds. {36:9} May those who survive be consumed by Your fiery wrath, and may those who harm Your people be destroyed. {36:10} Crush the heads of the enemy's rulers, who say, "There is no one but ourselves." {36:11} Gather all the tribes of Jacob and give them their inheritance, as in the beginning. {36:12} Have mercy, O Lord, on the people called by Your name, on Israel, whom You liken to a firstborn son. {36:13} Have compassion on the city of Your sanctuary, Jerusalem, the place of Your rest. {36:14} Fill Zion with celebrations of Your wondrous deeds, and Your temple with Your glory. {36:15} Bear witness to those You created at the start, and fulfill the prophecies spoken in Your name. {36:16} Reward those who wait for You, and let Your prophets be trustworthy. {36:17} Listen, O Lord, to the prayer of Your servants, as per Aaron's blessing for Your people, so that all on earth will know You are the Lord, the God of all ages. {36:18} The stomach can accept any food, but some foods are better than others. {36:19} Just as the palate distinguishes different flavors, an intelligent mind detects false words. {36:20} A twisted mind causes pain, but an experienced person will respond wisely. {36:21} A woman may accept any man, but one daughter is better than another. {36:22} A woman's beauty brings joy to the heart and surpasses every human desire. {36:23} If kindness and humility characterize her speech, her husband will be unlike others. {36:24} The one who finds a wife finds a treasure, a helper fit for him and a pillar of support. {36:25} Where there is no protection, property will be plundered; and where there is no wife, a man will wander and sigh. {36:26} Who will trust a quick thief who hops from city to city? Likewise, who will trust a man without a home, who sleeps wherever night finds him?

{37:1} Every friend will say, "I'm a friend too," but some friends are only friends in name. {37:2} Isn't it a deep sorrow when a companion and friend turns into an enemy? {37:3} O evil imagination, why were you created to fill the land with deceit? {37:4} Some companions rejoice in their friend's happiness but turn against them in times of trouble. {37:5} Some friends help only for their own benefit and take up arms only in battle. {37:6} Don't forget a friend in your heart, and don't ignore them when you're wealthy. {37:7} Every advisor praises good advice, but some give counsel for their own interests. {37:8} Be cautious with a counselor; first learn their motivations—because they will look out for themselves—lest they lead you astray {37:9} and tell you, "Your path is good," while they remain detached to see what happens to you. {37:10} Don't consult someone who looks at you suspiciously; keep your plans hidden from those who are envious. {37:11} Don't seek advice from a woman about her rival, or from a coward about war, or from a merchant about trade, or from a buyer about selling, or from a begrudging person about gratitude, or from a merciless person about kindness, or from an idler about any work, or from a lazy servant about a major task—ignore these in all matters of advice. {37:12} Instead, stay close to a godly person you know keeps the commandments, whose soul aligns with yours, and who will grieve with you if you fail. {37:13} Establish the counsel of your own heart, for no one is more loyal to you than it is. {37:14} Sometimes a person's soul knows better than seven watchmen stationed high on a tower. {37:15} And beyond all this, pray to the Most High that He may guide your path in truth. {37:16} Reason is the foundation of every action, and good counsel comes before any undertaking. {37:17} As a hint to changes of heart, {37:18} four turns of fortune appear: good and evil, life and death; the tongue continually governs them. {37:19} A man may be shrewd and teach many, yet still be of no benefit to himself. {37:20} A man skilled in words may be hated; he may lack food, {37:21} for grace was not granted to him by the Lord because he lacks wisdom. {37:22} A man may be wise for his own benefit, and the outcomes of his understanding may be reliable. {37:23} A wise man will instruct his people, and the results of his understanding will be trustworthy. {37:24} A wise man will receive praise, and all who see him will call him fortunate. {37:25} The lifespan of a man is limited by days, but the days of Israel are countless. {37:26} The wise among his people will gain respect, and his name will endure forever. {37:27} My son, examine your soul while you live; see what harms it and avoid that. {37:28} Not everything is good for everyone, and not every person enjoys the same things. {37:29} Don't crave any luxury insatiably, and don't give yourself over to food; {37:30} for overeating leads to sickness, and gluttony brings nausea. {37:31} Many have died from gluttony, but the one who is careful to avoid it prolongs their life.

{38:1} Honor the physician as they deserve, based on your need for their services, for the Lord created them; {38:2} healing comes from the Most High, and they will receive a gift from the king. {38:3} The skill of the physician raises their status, and in the presence of great people, they are admired. {38:4} The Lord created medicines from the earth, and a sensible person will not disregard them. {38:5} Wasn't water made sweet with a tree so that His power could be known? {38:6} He gave skill to people so that He might be glorified in His marvelous works. {38:7} Through them He heals and alleviates pain; {38:8} the pharmacist combines them. Their work is never done, and through them, health spreads across the earth. {38:9} My son, when you are ill, don't neglect your health; pray to the Lord, and He will heal you. {38:10} Turn away from your faults, do your tasks correctly, and cleanse your heart from all sin. {38:11} Offer a sweet-smelling sacrifice, a memorial portion of fine flour, and pour oil on your offering as much as you can afford. {38:12} Give the physician their due, for the Lord created them; don't let them leave you, for you need them. {38:13} There are times when success depends on physicians, {38:14} for they too will pray to the Lord for success in their diagnoses and healing to preserve life. {38:15} Whoever sins before their Maker may find themselves in the care of a physician. {38:16} My son, let your tears fall for the dead; lament as one who is suffering deeply. Prepare the body with the honor it deserves, and don't neglect its burial. {38:17} Let your weeping be heartfelt and your mourning sincere; observe the mourning period as is fitting, for one or two days, to avoid criticism; then find comfort for your sorrow. {38:18} For sorrow can lead to death, and a heavy heart drains your strength. {38:19} In times of distress, sorrow lingers, and the life of a poor person weighs down their heart. {38:20} Don't surrender your heart to sorrow; push it away by remembering life's end. {38:21} Don't forget: there is no returning; you do the dead no good and only harm yourself. {38:22} "Remember my fate, for yours will be the same: yesterday it was mine, and today it is yours." {38:23} When the dead are at peace, let their memory fade, and be comforted for them when their spirit has departed. {38:24} The wisdom of a scribe depends on leisure; a person with little work may grow wise. {38:25} How can one gain wisdom who works the plow, who takes pride in the shaft of a goad, who drives oxen and focuses on their work, and whose conversations revolve around cattle? {38:26} They concentrate on plowing furrows and are careful about the feed for the heifers. {38:27} Likewise, every craftsman and skilled worker labors both day and night; those who carve seals are diligent in making diverse designs; they focus on painting lifelike images and are attentive to complete their work. {38:28} So too is the blacksmith at the anvil, focused on his metalwork; the heat of the fire melts his flesh, and he grows weak in the furnace's heat; he listens to the hammer's sound and observes the shape of the piece. He dedicates his heart to finishing his craft, ensuring its decoration is complete. {38:29} Likewise, the potter sits at his wheel, turning it with his feet; he is constantly concerned with his output, counting every piece. {38:30} He molds the clay with his hands and shapes it with his feet; he focuses on glazing and ensures the furnace is clean. {38:31} All these people rely on their hands, and each is skilled in their craft. {38:32} Without them, a city cannot stand, and people cannot dwell or thrive there. {38:33} Yet they are often not sought for advice, nor do they gain prestige in public gatherings. They don't sit in judgment seats, nor do they understand the decisions of justice; they cannot explain discipline or judgment, nor do they use proverbs. {38:34} But they uphold world's fabric & their prayers are in their trade.

{39:1} On the other hand, anyone who dedicates themselves to studying the law of the Most High will seek out the wisdom of all the ancients and be concerned with prophecies; {39:2} they will preserve the words of notable individuals and delve into the complexities of parables; {39:3} they will search for the hidden meanings of proverbs and be comfortable with the obscurities of parables. {39:4} They will serve among great men and appear before rulers; they will travel through foreign lands to test the good and evil among people. {39:5} They will rise early to seek the Lord who made them, making supplication before the Most High; they will pray and ask for forgiveness for their sins. {39:6} If the great Lord is willing, they will be filled with the spirit of understanding; they will speak words of wisdom and give thanks to the Lord in prayer. {39:7} They will direct their counsel and knowledge correctly and reflect on their secrets. {39:8} They will provide instruction in their teaching and take pride in the law of the Lord's covenant. {39:9} Many will admire their understanding, and it will never be forgotten; their memory will endure, and their name will live on through generations. {39:10} Nations will acknowledge their wisdom, and the congregation will sing their praises; {39:11} if they live long, they will leave a name greater than a thousand, and if they find rest, that will be enough for them. {39:12} I have more to say, which I have pondered, and I am filled, like the full moon. {39:13} Listen to me, O holy children, and bloom like a rose by a stream of water; {39:14} send forth fragrance like frankincense and produce blossoms like a lily. Spread your fragrance and sing a hymn of praise; bless the Lord for all His works; {39:15} ascribe majesty to His name and give thanks to Him with praise, with songs on your lips, and with lyres; and this you should say in thanksgiving: {39:16} "All things are the works of the Lord, for they are very good, and whatever He commands will be fulfilled in His time." {39:17} No one can ask, "What is this?" or "Why is that?" for in God's time all things will be understood. At His command, the waters stood still, and the reservoirs of water formed at His word. {39:18} By His command, whatever pleases Him is accomplished, and none can limit His saving power. {39:19} The works of all living beings are before Him, and nothing is hidden from His sight. {39:20} From everlasting to everlasting, He observes them, and nothing is surprising to Him. {39:21} No one can question, "What is this?" or "Why is that?" for everything was created for a purpose. {39:22} His blessing flows over the dry land like a river and saturates it like a flood. {39:23} The nations will feel His anger, just as He turns fresh water into salt. {39:24} His paths are straight for the holy but obstacles for the wicked. {39:25} From the beginning, good things were created for good people, just as evil things were for sinners. {39:26} Essential to human life are water, fire, iron, salt, wheat flour, milk, honey, grape juice, oil, and clothing. {39:27} All these are good for the righteous but become harmful for sinners. {39:28} Winds were created for vengeance, and in their fury, they scourge heavily; at the time of fulfillment, they will unleash their strength and calm the anger of their Creator. {39:29} Fire, hail, famine, and disease were all created for vengeance; {39:30} the fangs of wild beasts, scorpions, vipers, and the sword punish the ungodly with destruction; {39:31} they will obey His commands and be ready on earth for their tasks, and when their time comes, they will not disobey His word. {39:32} Therefore, from the beginning, I have been convinced, reflected, and recorded this: {39:33} The works of the Lord are all good, and He will provide for every need at its proper time. {39:34} No one can say, "This is worse than that," for everything will be proven good in its season. {39:35} So now, sing praise with all your heart and voice, and bless the name of the Lord.

{40:1} Much labor was created for every person, and a heavy burden rests on the children of Adam, from the day they are born until they return to the earth. {40:2} Their worries and fears—anxious thoughts about death—{40:3} affect everyone, from the person on a splendid throne to one who is humbled in dust and ashes, {40:4} from the one wearing purple and a crown to someone dressed in burlap; {40:5} there is anger, envy, trouble, unrest, fear of death, fury, and strife. When one lies on their bed, their sleep is troubled. {40:6} They get little or no rest, and even in sleep, as if on watch, they are disturbed by visions, like someone fleeing from the battlefield; {40:7} when they wake up from their rescue, they are astonished that their fears were unfounded. {40:8} Among all flesh, both human and beast, and especially for sinners, {40:9} there are death, bloodshed, strife, the sword, calamities, famine, suffering, and plagues. {40:10} All these were created for the wicked, and they were the reason for the flood. {40:11} All things from the earth return to the earth, and what comes from the waters returns to the sea. {40:12} All bribery and injustice will be wiped away, but good faith will last forever. {40:13} The wealth of the unjust will dry up like a river and crash like thunder in a storm. {40:14} A generous person will be made glad; likewise, the transgressors will utterly fail. {40:15} The children of the wicked will not flourish; they are like unhealthy roots on bare rock. {40:16} The reeds by the water or riverbank will be uprooted before any grass. {40:17} Kindness is like a garden of blessings, and giving to others lasts forever. {40:18} Life is sweet for the self-reliant and the diligent, but finding treasure is even better. {40:19} Children and building a city establish a person's reputation, but a blameless wife is considered better than both. {40:20} Wine and music bring joy to the heart, but the love of wisdom is better than both. {40:21} The flute and harp create a lovely melody, but a pleasant voice is better than either. {40:22} The eye desires grace and beauty, but prefers the fresh shoots of grain even more. {40:23} A friend or companion is always a joy, but a wife with her husband is better than both. {40:24} Brothers and helpers are there in times of trouble, but giving to others saves better than both. {40:25} Gold and silver provide stability, but good counsel is valued more than either. {40:26} Wealth and strength uplift the heart, but the fear of the Lord is better than both. There is no loss in fearing the Lord, and with it, there is no need to seek help. {40:27} The fear of the Lord is like a garden of blessings and covers a person better than any glory. {40:28} My son, don't live as a beggar; it's better to die than to beg. {40:29} When someone looks to another's table, their existence cannot be considered truly living. They compromise themselves with someone else's food, but a wise and well-instructed person guards against that. {40:30} In the mouth of the shameless, begging seems sweet, but in their stomach, a fire ignites.

{41:1} O death, how bitter is the thought of you for someone who lives comfortably with their possessions, a person without distractions, who is successful in everything, and still has the energy to enjoy their food! {41:2} O death, how welcome is your decree for someone in need, struggling with their strength, very old, and overwhelmed; for someone who is contrary and has lost their patience! {41:3} Do not fear the sentence of death; remember your earlier days and the end of life; this is the decree from the Lord for all people, {41:4} and how can you refuse the good pleasure of the Most High? Whether life lasts for ten, a hundred, or a thousand years, there's no inquiry about it in Hades (the underworld). {41:5} The children of sinners are disgraceful, and they frequent the company of the wicked. {41:6} The inheritance of the children of sinners will vanish, and their descendants will face lasting shame. {41:7} Children will blame their ungodly father, suffering disgrace because of him. {41:8} Woe to you, ungodly people, who have abandoned the law of the Most High God! {41:9} When you are born, you are born under a curse; and when you die, a curse is your fate. {41:10} Whatever comes from the dust returns to dust; so the ungodly go from curse to destruction. {41:11} People mourn for their bodies, but the evil reputation of sinners will be erased. {41:12} Pay attention to your name, for it will last longer than a thousand great stores of gold. {41:13} The days of a good life are limited, but a good name endures forever. {41:14} My children, follow instruction and find peace; hidden wisdom and unseen treasure—what benefit is there in either? {41:15} Better is the man who conceals his folly than the one who hides his wisdom. {41:16} Therefore, respect my words: It is good to hold onto every kind of shame, as not everything is valued equally by everyone. {41:17} Be ashamed of immorality before your parents; and of lies before a prince or ruler; {41:18} of wrongdoing before a judge or magistrate; and of iniquity before a congregation or the public; of unfair dealings before your partner or friend; {41:19} and of theft in your own community. Be ashamed in the presence of God and His covenant. Be ashamed of selfish behavior at meals, of rudeness in giving and receiving, {41:20} and of silence before those who greet you; of looking at an immoral woman, {41:21} and of ignoring a relative's plea; of taking someone's share or gift, and of lusting after another man's wife; {41:22} of messing with his maidservant—do not approach her bed; of using harsh words among friends—and do not scold after making a gift; {41:23} of gossiping and revealing secrets. Then you will show proper shame and earn favor with everyone.

{42:1} Do not be ashamed of the following things, and do not let favoritism lead you to sin: {42:2} of the law of the Most High and His covenant, or of giving judgment to acquit the guilty; {42:3} of keeping accounts with a partner or traveling companions, or of dividing the inheritance among friends; {42:4} of being accurate with scales and weights, whether you acquire much or little; {42:5} of profiting from dealing with merchants, and of being strict with children, even disciplining a wicked servant severely. {42:6} Where there is an evil wife, it's good to have a seal; and when there are many people involved, it's wise to lock things up. {42:7} Whatever you give out, let it be measured and weighed, and keep a record of all that you distribute or receive. {42:8} Do not be ashamed to teach the foolish, the ignorant, or an elderly man who argues with the young. Then you will truly be educated and respected by all. {42:9} A daughter keeps her father awake at night, and worrying about her robs him of sleep; when she is young, he fears she won't marry, or if married, that she will be unloved; {42:10} as a virgin, he fears she might be defiled or become pregnant at home; or if she has a husband, he worries she might be unfaithful, or even if married, that she might be barren. {42:11} Keep a close watch on a rebellious daughter, lest she make you a laughingstock to your enemies, a disgrace in the city, and infamous among the people, bringing shame before the multitude. {42:12} Do not admire anyone for their beauty, and do not sit among women; {42:13} for from clothing comes moths, and from women comes wickedness. {42:14} Better is the wickedness of a man than a woman who does good; for it is a woman who brings shame and disgrace. {42:15} I will now recall the works of the Lord and declare what I have seen. Through the words of the Lord, His works are accomplished. {42:16} The sun shines down on everything with its light, and the work of the Lord is full of His glory. {42:17} The Lord has not allowed His holy ones to recount all His marvelous works, which the Almighty has established so that the universe may remain firm in His glory. {42:18} He explores the abyss and the hearts of men, considering their cunning plans. For the Most High knows all that can be known, and He observes the signs of the times. {42:19} He declares what has been and what will be, revealing the paths of hidden things. {42:20} No thought escapes Him, and not a single word is hidden from Him. {42:21} He has ordained the splendors of His wisdom, existing from everlasting to everlasting. Nothing can be added or taken away, and He requires no counsel from anyone. {42:22} How greatly desired are all His works, and how beautiful they are to behold! {42:23} All these things live on forever for every need and are all obedient. {42:24} Everything exists in pairs, one opposite the other, and He has made nothing incomplete. {42:25} One confirms the goodness of the other, and who can ever get enough of witnessing His glory?

{43:1} The pride of the heavens is the clear sky, the appearance of heaven displayed in glorious splendor. {43:2} The sun, when it rises, makes an announcement as it travels; it is a marvelous creation, the work of the Most High. {43:3} At noon, it scorches the land; who can withstand its burning heat? {43:4} A man working at a furnace feels the heat, but the sun burns the mountains three times more; it releases fiery vapors and blinds the eyes with its bright rays. {43:5} Great is the Lord who created it; and at His command, it quickly follows its path. {43:6} He also made the moon, to mark the seasons and to be an everlasting sign. {43:7} From the moon comes the signal for festivals, its light fading as it reaches fullness. {43:8} The month is named after the moon, which grows remarkably in its phases, a tool of the heavenly hosts shining brightly in the sky. {43:9} The glory of the stars is the beauty of the heavens, a shining display in the heights of the Lord. {43:10} At the command of the Holy One, they stand in place, never neglecting their duties. {43:11} Look at the rainbow & praise the one who made it; it is incredibly beautiful in its brightness. {43:12} It encircles the sky with its glorious arc; the hands of the Most High have stretched it out. {43:13} By His command, He sends the driving snow and accelerates the lightning of His judgment. {43:14} Thus, the storehouses are opened, and the clouds fly out like birds. {43:15} In His majesty, He gathers the clouds, and the hailstones are shattered into pieces. {43:16} At His appearance, the mountains tremble; at His will, the south wind blows. {43:17} The voice of His thunder rebukes the earth; so do the storms from the north and the whirlwind. He scatters snow like birds flying down, and its descent is like locusts landing. {43:18} The eye marvels at the beauty of its whiteness, and the mind is amazed at its fall. {43:19} He pours frost on the earth like salt, and when it freezes, it turns into sharp thorns. {43:20} The cold northern wind blows, and ice forms on the water; it rests on every pool, and the water wears it like armor. {43:21} He consumes the mountains and scorches the wilderness, withering the tender grass like fire. {43:22} A mist quickly heals everything; when the dew appears, it refreshes from the heat. {43:23} By His counsel, He calmed the deep sea and placed islands in it. {43:24} Those who sail the sea speak of its dangers, and we marvel at what we hear. {43:25} For in it are strange and wondrous works, all kinds of living things, and enormous sea creatures. {43:26} Because of Him, His messenger finds the way, and by His word, all things hold together. {43:27} Although we speak a lot, we cannot reach the end; the essence of our words is: "He is the all." {43:28} Where can we find the strength to praise Him? For He is greater than all His works. {43:29} Terrible is the Lord and very great, and marvelous is His power. {43:30} When you praise the Lord, exalt Him as much as you can; for He will surpass even that. When you lift Him up, use all your strength, and do not grow weary, for you cannot praise Him enough. {43:31} Who has seen Him and can describe Him? Or who can extol Him as He is? {43:32} Many greater things than these remain hidden, for we have seen only a few of His works. {43:33} For the Lord made all things, and He has granted wisdom to the godly.

{44:1} Let us now praise famous men and our ancestors in their generations. {44:2} The Lord gave them great glory, His majesty from the beginning. {44:3} Some ruled in their kingdoms and were renowned for their power, offering counsel through their understanding and proclaiming prophecies; {44:4} leaders of the people in their discussions and understanding, wise in their words of instruction; {44:5} those who composed music and wrote verses; {44:6} wealthy men equipped with resources, living peacefully in their homes— {44:7} all these were honored in their times and were the glory of their eras. {44:8} Some of them have left behind names so that people celebrate their praise. {44:9} And there are some who have no remembrance, who have vanished as if they had never lived; they have become as though they were never born, and their children after them as well. {44:10} But these were merciful men whose righteous deeds are not forgotten; {44:11} their prosperity will remain with their descendants, and their inheritance for their children's children. {44:12} Their descendants uphold the covenants; their children do the same for their sake. {44:13} Their lineage will endure forever, and their glory will not be erased. {44:14} Their bodies were buried in peace, and their names live on through all generations. {44:15} People will declare their wisdom, and the community will proclaim their praise. {44:16} Enoch pleased the Lord and was taken up; he serves as an example of repentance for all generations. {44:17} Noah was found perfect and righteous; during the time of wrath, he was taken in exchange; thus, a remnant remained on earth when the flood came. {44:18} Everlasting covenants were made with him that all flesh should not be destroyed by a flood. {44:19} Abraham was the great father of many nations, and no one has been found like him in glory; {44:20} he kept the law of the Most High and entered into a covenant with Him; he established the covenant in his flesh, and when he was tested, he proved faithful. {44:21} Therefore, the Lord assured him by an oath that nations would be blessed through his offspring; that he would multiply him like the dust of the earth, exalt his descendants like the stars, and cause them to inherit from sea to sea and from the river to the ends of the earth. {44:22} To Isaac, he also gave the same promise for the sake of his father Abraham. {44:23} The blessing of all people and the covenant rested upon Jacob; he was acknowledged with blessings, and given his inheritance; he determined his portions and distributed them among the twelve tribes.

{45:1} From his descendants, the Lord brought forth a man of mercy, Moses, who found favor in the sight of all people and was beloved by God and man; his memory is blessed. {45:2} God made him equal in glory to the holy ones and great in the fears of his enemies. {45:3} With his words, he made signs cease; the Lord glorified him in front of kings. He gave him commands for his people and showed him part of His glory. {45:4} He sanctified him through faithfulness and humility, choosing him from all humanity. {45:5} He made him hear His voice, led him into thick darkness, and gave him the commandments face to face, the law of life and knowledge, to teach Jacob the covenant and Israel His judgments. {45:6} He exalted Aaron, Moses' brother, a holy man like him from the tribe of Levi. {45:7} He made an everlasting covenant with him and gave him the priesthood of the people. He blessed him with splendid garments and clothed him in a glorious robe. {45:8} He dressed him with perfect attire and strengthened him with symbols of authority, the linen breeches, the long robe, and the ephod. {45:9} He surrounded him with pomegranates and many golden bells, so their ringing could be heard in the temple as a reminder to his people. {45:10} With a holy garment made of gold, blue, and purple, crafted by an embroiderer, along with the oracle of judgment, Urim and Thummim; {45:11} with twisted scarlet, crafted by a skilled worker; and with precious stones engraved like signets, set in gold, crafted by a jeweler, as a reminder, engraved according to the number of the tribes of Israel; {45:12} with a gold crown on his turban, inscribed like a signet with "Holiness," a distinction to be cherished, crafted by an expert, a delight to the eyes, richly adorned. {45:13} Before his time, there had never been such beautiful things. No outsider ever wore them, only his sons and descendants perpetually. {45:14} His sacrifices are to be completely burned twice daily, continually. {45:15} Moses ordained him and anointed him with holy oil; it was an everlasting covenant for him and his descendants throughout all days, to minister to the Lord, serve as priest, and bless his people in His name. {45:16} He was chosen from all the living to offer sacrifices to the Lord, incense and a pleasing aroma as a memorial portion, to atone for the people. {45:17} Through his commandments, he was given authority, statutes, and judgments, to teach Jacob the testimonies and enlighten Israel with His law. {45:18} Outsiders conspired against him, envying him in the wilderness: Dathan, Abiram, and their men, along with the company of Korah, in wrath and anger. {45:19} The Lord saw this and was displeased; in His anger, they were destroyed, and He performed wonders against them to consume them in flames. {45:20} He added glory to Aaron and gave him a heritage; He allotted to him the first of the first fruits, preparing abundant bread of first fruits. {45:21} They eat the sacrifices to the Lord, which He provided for him and his descendants. {45:22} But in the land of the people, he has no inheritance and no portion among them; for the Lord Himself is his portion and inheritance. {45:23} Phinehas, the son of Eleazar, is the third in glory; he was zealous in the fear of the Lord, standing firm when the people turned away, and made atonement for Israel with the goodness of his heart. {45:24} Therefore, a covenant of peace was established with him, that he should be the leader of the sanctuary and his people, and that he and his descendants would have the dignity of the priesthood forever. {45:25} A covenant was also established with David, the son of Jesse, from the tribe of Judah: the kingship is inherited from son to son only; just as the heritage of Aaron is for his descendants. {45:26} May the Lord grant you wisdom in your heart to judge His people righteously, so that their prosperity may not fade, and their glory may endure through all generations.

{46:1} Joshua, the son of Nun, was mighty in war and succeeded Moses in prophesying. He became, as his name implies, a great savior of God's chosen, taking vengeance on their enemies to give Israel its inheritance. {46:2} How glorious he was when he lifted his hands and stretched out his sword against the cities! {46:3} Who before him ever stood so firm? For he waged the wars of the Lord. {46:4} Was not the sun held back by his hand? Did not one day become as long as two? {46:5} He called upon the Most High, the Mighty One, when enemies pressed in on him from every side, {46:6} and the great Lord answered him with powerful hailstones. He unleashed war upon that nation, and at Beth-horon, he destroyed those who resisted, so that the nations would know of his strength, that he was fighting in the sight of the Lord; for he fully followed the Mighty One. {46:7} And in the days of Moses, he performed a loyal deed, he and Caleb, the son of Jephunneh: they stood against the congregation, restrained the people from sin, and calmed their wicked complaints. {46:8} Only these two were preserved from six hundred thousand foot soldiers to lead them into their inheritance, into a land flowing with milk and honey. {46:9} And the Lord gave Caleb strength, which remained with him into old age, so that he went up to the hill country, and his children received it as their inheritance; {46:10} so that all the Israelites could see that it is good to follow the Lord. {46:11} The judges, with their respective names, whose hearts did not fall into idolatry and who did not turn away from the Lord—may their memory be blessed! {46:12} May their bones revive from where they lie, and may the name of those honored live again in their descendants! {46:13} Samuel, beloved by his Lord, a prophet of the Lord, established the kingdom and anointed rulers over his people. {46:14} By the law of the Lord, he judged the congregation, and the Lord watched over Jacob. {46:15} By his faithfulness, he proved to be a prophet, and by his words, he became known as a trustworthy seer. {46:16} He called upon the Lord, the Mighty One, when enemies pressed in on him, and offered in sacrifice a young lamb. {46:17} Then the Lord thundered from heaven, making His voice heard with a mighty sound; {46:18} He wiped out the leaders of the people of Tyre and all the rulers of the Philistines. {46:19} Before his eternal rest, Samuel called witnesses before the Lord and His anointed: "I have not taken anyone's property, not even a pair of shoes." And no one accused him. {46:20} Even after he had fallen asleep, he prophesied and revealed to the king his death, lifting up his voice from the earth in prophecy, to erase the wickedness of the people.

{47:1} After him, Nathan rose up to prophesy during the days of David. {47:2} Just as the best parts are chosen from a peace offering, David was chosen from the sons of Israel. {47:3} He played with lions like they were young goats, and with bears like they were lambs from the flock. {47:4} In his youth, didn't he kill a giant and remove the disgrace from his people when he lifted his hand with a stone in a sling and struck down the boasting Goliath? {47:5} He called upon the Lord, the Most High, and He gave him strength in his right hand to slay a mighty warrior, lifting up the power of his people. {47:6} So they glorified him for his ten thousands and praised him for the blessings of the Lord when the glorious crown was placed upon him. {47:7} For he wiped out his enemies all around and destroyed his adversaries, the Philistines; he crushed their power even to this day. {47:8} In all he did, he thanked the Holy One, the Most High, with expressions of glory; he sang praises with all his heart and loved his Maker. {47:9} He placed singers before the altar to make sweet melodies with their voices. {47:10} He brought beauty to the feasts and arranged their times throughout the year while they praised God's holy name, and the sanctuary resounded from early morning. {47:11} The Lord removed his sins and exalted his power forever; He gave him the covenant of kings and a throne of glory in Israel. {47:12} After him, a wise son rose up who thrived because of him; {47:13} Solomon reigned during peaceful days, and God gave him rest on every side so he could build a house for His name and prepare a sanctuary to last forever. {47:14} How wise you became in your youth! You overflowed like a river with understanding. {47:15} Your soul covered the earth, filling it with parables and riddles. {47:16} Your name reached far-off islands, and you were loved for your peace. {47:17} Because of your songs, proverbs, and parables, and your interpretations, the nations admired you. {47:18} In the name of the Lord God, called the God of Israel, you gathered gold like tin and amassed silver like lead. {47:19} But you indulged with women, and through your body, you were brought into subjection. {47:20} You stained your honor and defiled your legacy, bringing wrath upon your children, who were saddened by your folly, {47:21} leading to the division of the kingdom and the rise of a disobedient kingdom out of Ephraim. {47:22} But the Lord will never withdraw His mercy, nor allow any of His works to perish; He will never erase the descendants of His chosen one, nor destroy the legacy of him who loved Him; thus, He gave a remnant to Jacob and a root of his stock to David. {47:23} Solomon rested with his fathers and left behind a son who was ample in folly and lacking in understanding, Rehoboam, whose policies caused the people to revolt. Also, there was Jeroboam, the son of Nebat, who led Israel into sin and gave Ephraim a sinful path. {47:24} Their sins became exceedingly numerous, leading to their removal from the land. {47:25} For they sought every kind of wickedness until vengeance came upon them.

{48:1} Then the prophet Elijah arose like a fire, and his words burned like a torch. {48:2} He brought a famine upon them, and through his zeal, he made them few in number. {48:3} By the word of the Lord, he shut up the heavens and three times called down fire. {48:4} How glorious you were, O Elijah, in your wondrous deeds! And who has the right to boast like you? {48:5} You who raised a corpse from death and from Hades by the word of the Most High; {48:6} who brought kings to ruin and famous men from their beds; {48:7} who heard rebuke at Sinai and judgments of vengeance at Horeb; {48:8} who anointed kings to inflict punishment and prophets to succeed you. {48:9} You who were taken up by a whirlwind of fire in a chariot with horses of fire; {48:10} you who are ready at the appointed time, as it is written, to calm the wrath of God before it erupts in fury, to turn the hearts of fathers to their sons, and to restore the tribes of Jacob. {48:11} Blessed are those who saw you, and those who are adorned in love; for we too shall surely live. {48:12} It was Elijah who was taken up by the whirlwind, and Elisha was filled with his spirit; during all his days, he did not tremble before any ruler, and no one could bring him into subjection. {48:13} Nothing was too difficult for him, and when he died, his body prophesied. {48:14} Just as he did wonders in his life, so in death, his deeds were marvelous. {48:15} Yet, despite all this, the people did not repent or forsake their sins until they were taken captive from their land and scattered across the earth; they were left very few in number but with rulers from the house of David. {48:16} Some did what was pleasing to God, but others multiplied their sins. {48:17} Hezekiah fortified his city and brought water into the midst of it; he tunneled through solid rock with iron and built pools for water. {48:18} During his days, Sennacherib came up and sent the Rabshakeh; he lifted his hand against Zion and boasted greatly in his arrogance. {48:19} Then their hearts were shaken, their hands trembled, and they were in anguish, like women in labor. {48:20} But they called upon the merciful Lord, spreading their hands toward Him; and the Holy One quickly heard them from heaven and delivered them through the hand of Isaiah. {48:21} The Lord struck the camp of the Assyrians, and His angel wiped them out. {48:22} For Hezekiah did what was pleasing to the Lord and adhered strongly to the ways of his father David, which the prophet Isaiah commanded, who was great and faithful in his visions. {48:23} During his days, the sun went backward, and he extended the king's life. {48:24} By the spirit of might, he saw the end times and comforted those who mourned in Zion. {48:25} He revealed what was to happen at the end of time and the hidden things before they came to pass.

{49:1} The memory of Josiah is like a blend of incense crafted by a perfumer; it is as sweet as honey to every mouth and like music at a wine banquet. {49:2} He led the people correctly, removing the abominations of sin. {49:3} He set his heart on the Lord; in the days of wickedness, he strengthened righteousness. {49:4} Except for David, Hezekiah, and Josiah, they all sinned greatly by forsaking the law of the Most High; the kings of Judah came to an end. {49:5} They gave their power to others and their glory to a foreign nation, {49:6} which set fire to the chosen city of the sanctuary and made her streets desolate, as Jeremiah foretold. {49:7} Though they had afflicted him, he was consecrated in the womb as a prophet, to uproot, afflict, and destroy, and likewise to build and to plant. {49:8} It was Ezekiel who saw the glorious vision that God showed him above the chariot of the cherubim. {49:9} For God remembered His enemies with storms and did good to those who directed their paths rightly. {49:10} May the bones of the twelve prophets revive from where they lie, for they comforted the people of Jacob and delivered them with confident hope. {49:11} How can we magnify Zerubbabel? He was like a signet ring on the right hand, {49:12} and so was Jeshua, the son of Jozadak; during their days, they built the house and raised a temple holy to the Lord, prepared for everlasting glory. {49:13} The memory of Nehemiah is also lasting; he rebuilt the walls that had fallen, set up the gates and bars, and restored our ruined houses. {49:14} No one like Enoch has been created on earth, for he was taken up from the earth. {49:15} And no man like Joseph has been born, and his bones are cared for. {49:16} Shem and Seth were honored among men, and Adam above every living being in creation.

{50:1} The leader of his brothers and the pride of his people was Simon, the high priest, son of Onias, who repaired the house during his life and fortified the temple during his time. {50:2} He laid the foundations for the high double walls and the strong retaining walls for the temple enclosure. {50:3} In his days, a cistern for water was dug out, a reservoir as large as the sea. {50:4} He considered how to save his people from ruin and fortified the city to withstand a siege. {50:5} How glorious he was when the people gathered around him as he came out of the inner sanctuary! {50:6} Like the morning star among the clouds, like the full moon; {50:7} like the sun shining on the temple of the Most High, and like the rainbow gleaming in glorious clouds; {50:8} like roses in the days of the first fruits, like lilies by a spring of water, like a green shoot on Lebanon on a summer day; {50:9} like fire and incense in the censer, like a vessel of hammered gold adorned with all kinds of precious stones; {50:10} like an olive tree bearing fruit, and like a cypress towering in the clouds. {50:11} When he donned his glorious robe and clothed himself in superb perfection and went up to the holy altar, he made the court of the sanctuary glorious. {50:12} And when he received the portions from the hands of the priests, standing by the hearth of the altar with a garland of brothers around him, he was like a young cedar on Lebanon; and they surrounded him like palm tree trunks, {50:13} all the sons of Aaron in their splendor with the Lord's offering in their hands, before the whole congregation of Israel. {50:14} Finishing the service at the altars and arranging the offerings to the Most High, the Almighty, {50:15} he reached out his hand to the cup and poured a libation of the blood of the grape; he poured it out at the foot of the altar, a pleasing aroma to the Most High, the King of all. {50:16} Then the sons of Aaron shouted, sounding the trumpets of hammered work, making a great noise to be remembered before the Most High. {50:17} Then all the people hurried and fell to the ground upon their faces to worship their Lord, the Almighty, God Most High. {50:18} And the singers praised him with their voices in sweet, full-toned melodies. {50:19} The people implored the Lord Most High in prayer before Him, who is merciful, until the order of worship of the Lord was completed; so they finished his service. {50:20} Then Simon came down and lifted his hands over the entire congregation of the sons of Israel to pronounce the blessing of the Lord with his lips and to glorify His name; {50:21} and they bowed down in worship a second time to receive the blessing from the Most High. {50:22} And now bless the God of all, who does great things in every way; who exalts our days from birth and deals with us according to His mercy. {50:23} May He give us gladness of heart and grant that peace may be in our days in Israel, as in days of old. {50:24} May He entrust to us His mercy! And let Him deliver us in our days! {50:25} My soul is troubled by two nations, and the third is no nation: {50:26} those who live on Mount Seir, the Philistines, and the foolish people who dwell in Shechem. {50:27} Instruction in understanding and knowledge I have written in this book, Jesus, the son of Sirach, son of Eleazar, of Jerusalem, who poured forth wisdom from his heart. {50:28} Blessed is he who concerns himself with these things, and he who lays them to heart will become wise. {50:29} For if he does them, he will be strong in all things, for the light of the Lord is his path.

{51:1} I will thank you, O Lord and King, and I will praise you as my God and Savior. I give thanks to your name, {51:2} for you have been my protector and helper, delivering my body from destruction and from the trap of a slanderous tongue, from lips that speak lies. Before those who stood by, you were my helper, {51:3} and you delivered me, in the greatness of your mercy and name, from the gnashing teeth that were about to devour me, from those who sought my life, and from the many afflictions I endured, {51:4} from choking fire all around me and from the midst of the fire that I did not kindle, {51:5} from the depths of Hades, from an unclean tongue and lying words— {51:6} the slander of an unrighteous tongue against the king. My soul drew near to death, and my life was very close to Hades below. {51:7} They surrounded me on every side, and there was no one to help me; I looked for help from people, and there was none. {51:8} Then I remembered your mercy, O Lord, and your works from long ago, that you deliver those who wait for you and save them from the hands of their enemies. {51:9} I sent up my supplication from the earth and prayed for deliverance from death. {51:10} I appealed to the Lord, the Father of my lord, not to forsake me in my days of trouble, when there is no help against the proud. {51:11} I will continually praise your name and sing praise with thanksgiving. My prayer was heard, {51:12} for you saved me from destruction and rescued me from an evil situation. Therefore, I will thank you and praise you, and I will bless the name of the Lord. {51:13} While I was still young, before I traveled, I sought wisdom openly in my prayer. {51:14} Before the temple, I asked for her, and I will search for her until the end. {51:15} From the blossom to the ripening grape, my heart delighted in her; my foot walked on the straight path; from my youth, I followed her steps. {51:16} I inclined my ear a little and received her, and I found much instruction for myself. {51:17} I made progress in it; to Him who gives wisdom, I will give glory. {51:18} For I resolved to live according to wisdom, and I was eager for the good; and I shall never be put to shame. {51:19} My soul struggled with wisdom, and in my actions, I was strict; I spread out my hands to the heavens and lamented my ignorance of her. {51:20} I directed my soul to her, and through purification, I found her. I gained understanding with her from the beginning, therefore I will not be forsaken. {51:21} My heart was stirred to seek her, and so I have gained a good possession. {51:22} The Lord gave me a tongue as my reward, and I will praise Him with it. {51:23} Draw near to me, you who are untaught, and stay in my school. {51:24} Why do you say you lack these things, and why are your souls very thirsty? {51:25} I opened my mouth and said, "Get these things for yourselves without money." {51:26} Put your neck under the yoke, and let your souls receive instruction; it is to be found nearby. {51:27} See with your eyes that I have labored little and found much rest for myself. {51:28} Get instruction with a large sum of silver, and you will gain much gold from it. {51:29} May your soul rejoice in His mercy, and may you not be put to shame when you praise Him. {51:30} Do your work before the appointed time, and in God's time, He will give you your reward.

The Wisdom of Solomon

{1:1} Love righteousness, you rulers of the earth; think of the Lord with integrity, and seek Him sincerely from your heart. {1:2} Because He is found by those who do not test Him, and He reveals Himself to those who trust Him. {1:3} For twisted thoughts separate people from God, and when His power is tested, it exposes the foolish; {1:4} because wisdom will not enter a deceitful soul, nor will it dwell in a body enslaved to sin. {1:5} A holy and disciplined spirit will flee from deceit, rising up and leaving foolish thoughts, feeling ashamed at the approach of wickedness. {1:6} Wisdom is a gentle spirit and will not free a blasphemer from the guilt of their words; for God knows their innermost feelings, is a true observer of their hearts, and hears their words. {1:7} The Spirit of the Lord has filled the world, and what holds everything together knows what is said; {1:8} therefore, no one who speaks unrighteousness will go unnoticed, and justice, when it punishes, will not overlook them. {1:9} An inquiry will be made into the plans of an ungodly person, and their words will be reported to the Lord to convict them of their lawless deeds; {1:10} for a jealous ear hears everything, and murmurs do not go unheard. {1:11} Beware, then, of useless murmuring, and keep your tongue from slander; because no secret words are without consequences, and a lying mouth destroys the soul. {1:12} Do not invite death by the errors of your life, nor bring destruction through your actions; {1:13} for God did not create death, and He does not delight in the death of the living. {1:14} He created all things to exist, and the life forces of the world are wholesome, with no destructive poison in them; the dominion of Hades is not on earth. {1:15} For righteousness is immortal. {1:16} But ungodly people, by their words and actions, called death upon themselves; considering him a friend, they wasted away, making a pact with him, as they were suited to belong to his party.

{2:1} They reasoned foolishly, saying to themselves, "Our life is short and filled with sorrow, and there is no remedy when a person dies; no one has ever returned from Hades." {2:2} They believed we were born by mere chance and that afterwards we will be as though we never existed; because the breath in our nostrils is smoke, and reason is a spark ignited by our heartbeats. {2:3} When it is extinguished, the body will turn to ashes, and the spirit will dissolve like empty air. {2:4} Our name will be forgotten in time, and no one will remember our works; our life will vanish like the traces of a cloud, scattered like mist chased by the sun's rays and overcome by its heat. {2:5} For our allotted time is the passing of a shadow, and there is no return from death, which is sealed, and no one turns back. {2:6} "Come, therefore, let us enjoy the good things that exist, and make full use of creation while we can. {2:7} Let us indulge in fine wine and perfumes, and let no spring flower pass us by. {2:8} Let us crown ourselves with rosebuds before they wither. {2:9} Let none of us miss out on our revelry; let us leave signs of enjoyment everywhere, for this is our portion, our lot. {2:10} Let us oppress the righteous poor; let us not spare the widow or respect the elderly. {2:11} But let our strength be our standard of right, for what is weak proves itself useless. {2:12} "Let us lie in wait for the righteous man, for he is inconvenient to us and opposes our actions; he reproaches us for breaking the law and accuses us of failing to uphold our training. {2:13} He claims to know God and calls himself a child of the Lord. {2:14} He has become a reproach to our thoughts; {2:15} just seeing him burdens us, for his way of life is unlike others, and his actions are strange. {2:16} We are seen as lowly by him, and he avoids our ways as unclean; he calls the end of the righteous happy and boasts that God is his father. {2:17} Let us see if his words are true and test what happens at the end of his life; {2:18} for if the righteous man is God's son, He will help him and deliver him from his enemies. {2:19} Let us insult and torture him to see how gentle he is and test his patience. {2:20} Let us condemn him to a shameful death, for, according to his words, he will be protected." {2:21} Thus they reasoned, but they were led astray, for their wickedness blinded them, {2:22} and they did not understand God's secret purposes, nor hope for the rewards of holiness, nor see the prize for blameless souls; {2:23} for God created man for incorruption and made him in the image of His own eternity, {2:24} but through the devil's envy, death entered the world, and those who belong to his party experience it.

{3:1} But the souls of the righteous are in God's hands, and no torment will ever touch them. {3:2} In the eyes of the foolish, they seemed to have died, and their departure was viewed as an affliction, {3:3} and their leaving us was seen as their destruction; but they are at peace. {3:4} For although they were punished in the sight of people, their hope is full of immortality. {3:5} After being disciplined a little, they will receive great rewards because God tested them and found them worthy of Himself; {3:6} like gold in a furnace, He tried them, and like a burnt offering, He accepted them. {3:7} At the time of their visitation, they will shine forth and run like sparks through the stubble. {3:8} They will govern nations and rule over peoples, and the Lord will reign over them forever. {3:9} Those who trust in Him will understand the truth, and the faithful will remain with Him in love, for grace and mercy are upon His chosen ones, and He watches over His holy ones. {3:10} But the ungodly will be punished according to their reasoning, those who disregarded the righteous and rebelled against the Lord; {3:11} for anyone who despises wisdom and instruction is miserable. Their hope is in vain, their efforts are unproductive, and their actions are useless. {3:12} Their wives are foolish, and their children are evil; {3:13} their offspring are accursed. Blessed is the barren woman who is undefiled and has not entered into a sinful union; she will bear fruit when God examines souls. {3:14} Blessed also is the eunuch whose hands have committed no unlawful deed and who has not plotted wickedness against the Lord; for special favor will be shown to him for his faithfulness, and he will find a place of great delight in the temple of the Lord. {3:15} The fruit of good deeds is renowned, and the root of understanding does not fail. {3:16} But the children of adulterers will not reach maturity, and the offspring of an unlawful union will perish. {3:17} Even if they live long, they will be regarded as worthless, and their old age will lack honor. {3:18} If they die young, they will have no hope and no comfort on the day of judgment. {3:19} For the end of an unrighteous generation is painful.

{4:1} Better than this is being childless but virtuous, for the memory of virtue is immortality, known both by God and by people. {4:2} When it is present, people imitate it and long for it when it is gone; throughout all time, it marches crowned in triumph, victorious in the contest for undefiled prizes. {4:3} But the numerous offspring of the ungodly will be of no use, and none of their illegitimate children will take deep root or hold firm. {4:4} Even if they grow for a while, they will stand insecurely, shaken by the wind, and uprooted by its violence. {4:5} The branches will be broken off before maturity, and their fruit will be worthless, not ripe enough to eat, and good for nothing. {4:6} Children born of unlawful unions are witnesses of evil against their parents when God examines them. {4:7} But the righteous man, though he dies early, will be at rest. {4:8} For old age is not honored by how long one lives, nor measured by the number of years; {4:9} but understanding is gray hair for men, and a blameless life is ripe old age. {4:10} There was one who pleased God and was loved by Him, and while living among sinners, he was taken up. {4:11} He was taken away lest evil change his understanding or deceit deceive his soul. {4:12} For the allure of wickedness obscures what is good, and wandering desire perverts the innocent mind. {4:13} Being perfected in a short time, he fulfilled long years; {4:14} for his soul was pleasing to the Lord, so He took him quickly from the midst of wickedness. {4:15} Yet the people saw and did not understand, nor did they take it to heart that God's grace and mercy are with His chosen ones, and He watches over His holy ones. {4:16} The righteous man who has died will condemn the ungodly who are living, and the youth who is quickly perfected will condemn the long old age of the unrighteous. {4:17} They will see the end of the wise man and will not understand what the Lord intended for him and why He kept him safe. {4:18} They will see and hold him in contempt, but the Lord will laugh at them. After this, they will become dishonored corpses, an outrage among the dead forever; {4:19} for He will bring them down speechless to the ground and shake them from their foundations; they will be left completely dry and barren, suffering anguish, and their memory will perish. {4:20} They will come in dread when their sins are counted, and their lawless deeds will accuse them to their faces.

{5:1} Then the righteous man will stand with great confidence in front of those who have afflicted him and belittled his efforts. {5:2} When they see him, they will be filled with dreadful fear and amazed at his unexpected salvation. {5:3} They will speak to one another in regret, and in anguish of spirit, they will groan, saying, {5:4} "This is the man we once mocked and made a byword of reproach—how foolish we were! We thought his life was madness and that his end was without honor. {5:5} Why has he been counted among the sons of God? And why is he numbered among the saints? {5:6} We strayed from the way of truth; the light of righteousness did not shine on us, and the sun did not rise upon us. {5:7} We indulged in paths of lawlessness and destruction, wandering through desolate places, but we did not know the way of the Lord. {5:8} What has our arrogance profited us? And what good has our boastful wealth brought us? {5:9} All those things have vanished like a shadow, like a passing rumor; {5:10} like a ship sailing through the waves, leaving no trace behind, nor any sign of its keel in the water; {5:11} or like a bird flying through the air, leaving no evidence of its passage; the light air, disturbed by its wings, is left with no sign of its coming; {5:12} or like an arrow shot at a target, the air divides and quickly closes again, so that no one knows its path. {5:13} So we also, as soon as we were born, ceased to be, showing no sign of virtue but consumed by our wickedness." {5:14} The hope of the ungodly is like chaff blown by the wind, and like frost driven away by a storm; it dissipates like smoke in the wind, and it passes like the memory of a guest who stays only a day. {5:15} But the righteous will live forever, and their reward is with the Lord; the Most High takes care of them. {5:16} Therefore, they will receive a glorious crown and a beautiful diadem from the Lord's hand, for He will cover them with His right hand and shield them with His arm. {5:17} The Lord will take His zeal as armor and equip all creation to fight against His enemies; {5:18} He will put on righteousness as a breastplate and wear impartial justice as a helmet; {5:19} He will take holiness as an invincible shield, {5:20} and sharpen stern wrath as a sword, while creation will join Him in battling against the wicked. {5:21} Lightning bolts will strike true and hit their mark like arrows from a well-drawn bow of clouds, {5:22} and hailstones filled with wrath will be launched like from a catapult; the sea will roar against them, and rivers will relentlessly overwhelm them; {5:23} a mighty wind will rise up against them, winnowing them away like chaff. Lawlessness will lay waste to the whole earth, and wrongdoing will topple the thrones of rulers.

{6:1} Therefore, listen, O kings, and understand; learn, O judges of the ends of the earth. {6:2} Give ear, you who rule over multitudes and boast of many nations. {6:3} For your dominion was given to you by the Lord, and your sovereignty from the Most High, who will examine your works and scrutinize your plans. {6:4} Because as servants of His kingdom, you did not rule justly, nor keep the law, nor walk according to God's purpose, {6:5} He will come upon you suddenly and terribly, for severe judgment falls on those in high places. {6:6} The lowliest man may be pardoned in mercy, but mighty men will be tested harshly. {6:7} The Lord of all will not be awed by anyone nor show favoritism; He made both the small and great and cares for all equally. {6:8} But a strict inquiry awaits the powerful. {6:9} To you, then, O monarchs, my words are directed so that you may gain wisdom and not transgress. {6:10} Those who observe holy things in holiness will be made holy, and those who are taught will find protection. {6:11} Therefore, desire my words; long for them, and you will be instructed. {6:12} Wisdom is radiant and unfading, easily seen by those who love her and found by those who seek her. {6:13} She rushes to make herself known to those who desire her. {6:14} Whoever rises early to seek her will have no trouble finding her, for she will be sitting at his gates. {6:15} To focus on her is perfect understanding, and those who are vigilant on her behalf will soon be free from worry, {6:16} for she seeks those worthy of her, graciously appearing to them in their paths and meeting them in every thought. {6:17} The beginning of wisdom is the sincere desire for instruction, and concern for instruction is love for her; {6:18} love for her is keeping her laws, and paying attention to her laws is assurance of immortality, {6:19} and immortality brings one closer to God; {6:20} thus, the desire for wisdom leads to a kingdom. {6:21} Therefore, if you delight in thrones and scepters, O monarchs over the peoples, honor wisdom so that you may reign forever. {6:22} I will tell you what wisdom is and how she came to be, revealing no secrets to you, tracing her course from the beginning of creation, and making knowledge of her clear; {6:23} I will not associate with sickly envy, for envy does not associate with wisdom. {6:24} A multitude of wise men is the salvation of the world, and a sensible king is the stability of his people. {6:25} Therefore, be instructed by my words, and you will benefit.

{7:1} I am also mortal, like everyone else, a descendant of the first human formed from the earth; I was shaped in my mother's womb, {7:2} within ten months, formed with blood, from a man's seed and the joy of marriage. {7:3} When I was born, I began to breathe the air and fell onto the familiar ground, my first sound being a cry, just like everyone else. {7:4} I was nurtured carefully in swaddling clothes. {7:5} No king has had a different beginning; {7:6} there is one entrance into life for all humanity and a common departure. {7:7} So I prayed, and understanding was granted to me; I called upon God, and the spirit of wisdom came to me. {7:8} I valued her above scepters and thrones, considering wealth as nothing compared to her. {7:9} I wouldn't compare her to any priceless gem, because in her eyes, all gold is like a little sand, and silver is like clay. {7:10} I loved her more than health and beauty, and I chose her over light, for her radiance never fades. {7:11} All good things came to me along with her, and in her hands was uncounted wealth. {7:12} I rejoiced in all these, for wisdom leads them; but I didn't realize she was their source. {7:13} I learned without deception and shared without reluctance; I don't hide her treasures, {7:14} for they are an unfailing wealth for people; those who possess them gain friendship with God, praised for the gifts that come from learning. {7:15} May God grant that I speak wisely and think worthily of what I've received, for He guides wisdom and corrects the wise. {7:16} Both we and our words are in His hands, along with all understanding and skills in crafts. {7:17} He granted me the knowledge to understand what exists, to know the structure of the world and the behavior of the elements; {7:18} the beginning, end, and middle of time, the changes of the solstices and the seasons, {7:19} the cycles of the year and the constellations of the stars, {7:20} the nature of animals and the temperaments of wild beasts, the powers of spirits and the reasoning of humans, the varieties of plants and the virtues of roots; {7:21} I learned both the hidden and the obvious, {7:22} for wisdom, the creator of all things, taught me. In her, there is a spirit that is intelligent, holy, unique, multifaceted, subtle, mobile, clear, unpolluted, distinct, invulnerable, loving the good, sharp, irresistible, {7:23} beneficent, humane, steadfast, reliable, free from anxiety, all-powerful, overseeing all, and penetrating through all intelligent and pure spirits that are subtle. {7:24} Wisdom is more mobile than any motion; because of her purity, she pervades and penetrates all things. {7:25} She is a breath of the power of God, a pure emanation of the Almighty's glory; therefore, nothing impure enters her. {7:26} She is a reflection of eternal light, a spotless mirror of God's work, and an image of His goodness. {7:27} Though she is one, she can accomplish all things, and while remaining within herself, she renews everything; in every generation, she enters holy souls and makes them friends of God and prophets; {7:28} for God loves nothing as much as a person who lives wisely. {7:29} She is more beautiful than the sun and surpasses every star; compared to light, she is superior, {7:30} for light is followed by darkness, but evil does not conquer wisdom.

{8:1} She powerfully reaches from one end of the earth to the other, and she arranges everything perfectly. {8:2} I loved her and sought her from my youth; I desired to take her as my bride, and I became captivated by her beauty. {8:3} She glorifies her noble heritage by living with God, and the Lord of all loves her. {8:4} She is initiated in the knowledge of God and an associate in His works. {8:5} If wealth is a desirable possession in life, what is richer than wisdom, who accomplishes everything? {8:6} And if understanding is effective, who is more than she, the creator of all that exists? {8:7} If anyone loves righteousness, her efforts are virtues; she teaches self-control, prudence, justice, and courage; nothing is more beneficial for people than these. {8:8} If anyone longs for experience, she knows the past and can infer the future; she understands speech nuances and solves riddles; she has foreknowledge of signs and wonders and the outcomes of times and seasons. {8:9} Therefore, I decided to take her to live with me, knowing she would give me good counsel and encouragement in worries and grief. {8:10} Because of her, I will have glory among the multitudes and honor in the presence of elders, even though I am young. {8:11} I will be found sharp in judgment, and in the sight of rulers, I will be admired. {8:12} When I am silent, they will wait for me, and when I speak, they will listen; when I speak at length, they will put their hands over their mouths. {8:13} Because of her, I will have immortality and leave an everlasting legacy for those who come after me. {8:14} I will govern nations, and peoples will be subject to me; {8:15} fearsome rulers will tremble at my name; among the people, I will show myself capable and brave in war. {8:16} When I enter my home, I will find rest with her, for companionship with her has no bitterness, and life with her brings no pain, but joy and happiness. {8:17} When I reflected on these things, I realized that kinship with wisdom brings immortality, {8:18} and friendship with her brings pure delight, unfailing wealth in her labor, understanding from her company, and renown from sharing her words; I sought to possess her for myself. {8:19} As a child, I was naturally gifted, and a good soul was my lot; {8:20} or rather, being good, I entered a pure body. {8:21} But I realized I would not possess wisdom unless God granted her to me—and it was insightful to know whose gift she was—so I appealed to the Lord and earnestly asked Him, and with all my heart, I said:

{9:1} "O God of my ancestors and Lord of mercy, who made everything by Your word, {9:2} and by Your wisdom formed humanity to have dominion over the creatures You created, {9:3} to govern the world in holiness and righteousness, and to pronounce judgment with a clear conscience, {9:4} grant me the wisdom that stands by Your throne, and do not reject me from among Your servants. {9:5} For I am Your servant and the son of Your maidservant, a man who is weak and short-lived, with little understanding of judgment and laws; {9:6} because even if someone is perfect among humans, without the wisdom that comes from You, he is regarded as nothing. {9:7} You have chosen me to be king over Your people and to judge Your sons and daughters. {9:8} You commanded me to build a temple on Your holy mountain and an altar in the city of Your dwelling, a replica of the holy tent You prepared from the beginning. {9:9} With You is wisdom, who knows Your works and was present when You created the world, who understands what pleases You and what is right according to Your commandments. {9:10} Send her forth from the holy heavens, and from Your glorious throne send her, so that she may be with me and labor, and that I may learn what pleases You. {9:11} For she knows and understands all things, and she will guide me wisely in my actions and protect me with her glory. {9:12} Then my works will be acceptable, and I will judge Your people justly, and will be worthy of my father's throne. {9:13} For who can learn the counsel of God? Or who can discern what the Lord wills? {9:14} For the reasoning of mortals is worthless, and our plans are likely to fail, {9:15} because a perishable body weighs down the soul, and this earthly tent burdens the thoughtful mind. {9:16} We can hardly guess what is on earth, and what is near we find only with difficulty; but who has traced out what is in the heavens? {9:17} Who has learned Your counsel unless You grant wisdom and send Your holy Spirit from on high? {9:18} Thus, the paths of those on earth were made straight, and people were taught what pleases You and were saved by wisdom."

{10:1} Wisdom protected the first human father of the world when he was created alone; she saved him from his transgression, {10:2} and gave him the strength to rule over all things. {10:3} But when an unrighteous man turned away from her in anger, he perished because he killed his brother in rage. {10:4} When the earth was flooded because of him, wisdom again saved it, guiding the righteous man with a simple piece of wood. {10:5} Wisdom also, when the nations had conspired wickedly, recognized the righteous man and kept him blameless before God, strengthening him despite his compassion for his child. {10:6} Wisdom rescued a righteous man when the ungodly were perishing; he escaped the fire that descended on the Five Cities. {10:7} Evidence of their wickedness remains: a constantly smoking wasteland, fruitless plants, and a pillar of salt as a reminder of an unfaithful soul. {10:8} Because they ignored wisdom, they not only failed to see the good but also left a reminder of their foolishness, ensuring their failures would never be forgotten. {10:9} Wisdom rescued those who served her from troubles. {10:10} When a righteous man fled from his brother's wrath, she guided him on straight paths; she showed him the kingdom of God, and gave him knowledge of angels; she prospered his labors and increased the results of his toil. {10:11} When his oppressors were greedy, she stood by him and made him wealthy. {10:12} She protected him from his enemies and kept him safe from those who waited to ambush him; in his hard struggle, she gave him victory, so he would learn that godliness is stronger than anything. {10:13} When a righteous man was sold, wisdom did not abandon him but saved him from sin. She descended with him into the dungeon, {10:14} and when he was in prison, she did not leave him until she brought him to the scepter of a kingdom and authority over his masters. Those who accused him she revealed as false, and she granted him everlasting honor. {10:15} A holy and blameless people, wisdom delivered from a nation of oppressors. {10:16} She entered the soul of a servant of the Lord and confronted dread kings with wonders and signs. {10:17} She rewarded holy men for their labors; she guided them along a marvelous path, and became a shelter to them by day and a guiding light through the night. {10:18} She brought them across the Red Sea and led them through deep waters; {10:19} but she drowned their enemies and cast them from the depths of the sea. {10:20} Therefore, the righteous plundered the ungodly; they sang hymns, O Lord, to Your holy name, and praised Your protective hand in unison, {10:21} because wisdom opened the mouths of the mute and made the tongues of infants speak clearly.

{11:1} Wisdom helped them succeed through the hands of a holy prophet. {11:2} They traveled through a deserted wilderness and set up camp in untouched places. {11:3} They stood firm against their enemies and fought off their foes. {11:4} When they were thirsty, they called upon You, and water was provided from a hard rock, quenching their thirst from a solid stone. {11:5} For by the very things that punished their enemies, they themselves received help in their time of need. {11:6} Instead of an endless river that was stirred up and tainted with blood, {11:7} as a rebuke for the command to kill the infants, You gave them abundant water unexpectedly, {11:8} showing by their thirst how You punished their enemies. {11:9} For when they were tested, even though they were disciplined with mercy, they learned how the wicked were tormented when judged with anger. {11:10} You tested them like a father warns his child, but examined the ungodly like a stern king condemns. {11:11} Whether they were absent or present, they were equally distressed, {11:12} for a dual grief weighed them down, with groaning over what had happened. {11:13} When they heard that through their own punishments the righteous had benefited, they realized it was the Lord's doing. {11:14} Though they had mockingly rejected Him who had been cast out long before, in the end, they marveled at Him, for their thirst was not like that of the righteous. {11:15} In return for their foolish and wicked thoughts, which led them to worship irrational serpents and worthless animals, You sent upon them a multitude of irrational creatures to punish them, {11:16} so they might learn that one is punished by the very things through which they sin. {11:17} For Your all-powerful hand, which created the world from nothing, was not lacking the means to send them a multitude of bears, fierce lions, {11:18} or newly created unknown beasts full of rage, or creatures that breathe fire, or spew thick smoke, or flash terrifying sparks from their eyes; {11:19} not only could their destruction wipe out people, but merely seeing them could cause death from fright. {11:20} Even without these, people could fall at a single breath when pursued by justice and scattered by Your powerful breath. But You have ordered everything by measure, number, and weight. {11:21} For it is always within Your power to show great strength, and who can stand against the might of Your arm? {11:22} Because the whole world before You is like a tiny speck on the scales and like a drop of morning dew on the ground. {11:23} Yet You are merciful to all, for You can do all things, and You overlook human sins so that they may repent. {11:24} For You love everything that exists and loathe none of the things You have made, for You would not have created anything if You hated it. {11:25} How would anything have endured if You had not willed it? Or how would anything that was not called forth by You have been preserved? {11:26} You spare all things, for they are Yours, O Lord who loves the living.

{12:1} For Your immortal spirit is in all things. {12:2} Therefore, You correct little by little those who go astray, reminding and warning them about their sins, so they may be freed from wickedness and trust in You, O Lord. {12:3} Those who once lived in Your holy land {12:4} You hated for their detestable practices, their sorcery and unholy rituals, {12:5} their merciless slaughter of children, and their feasting on human flesh and blood. These initiates of a heathen cult, {12:6} these parents who murdered helpless lives, You chose to destroy by the hands of our ancestors, {12:7} so that the land most precious to You could receive a worthy colony of Your servants. {12:8} But even these You spared, since they were just human, and You sent wasps as forerunners of Your army to gradually destroy them, {12:9} even though You could have handed the ungodly over to the righteous in battle or destroyed them in one blow by fierce wild beasts or Your stern command. {12:10} But by judging them little by little, You gave them a chance to repent, even though You knew their origin was evil and their wickedness inborn, and that their way of thinking would never change. {12:11} For they were a cursed race from the beginning, and it was not from fear of anyone that You left them unpunished for their sins. {12:12} For who will say, "What have You done?" Or resist Your judgment? Who will accuse You of the destruction of nations that You made? Or who will come before You to advocate for the unrighteous? {12:13} For there is no god besides You, who cares for all people, to whom You should prove that You have not judged unfairly; {12:14} nor can any king or monarch confront You about those whom You have punished. {12:15} You are righteous and rule all things righteously, considering it foreign to Your power to condemn anyone who does not deserve punishment. {12:16} For Your strength is the source of righteousness, and Your sovereignty over all allows You to spare all. {12:17} For You show Your strength when people doubt the fullness of Your power and rebuke any insolence among those who know it. {12:18} You who are sovereign in strength judge with gentleness, and with great patience You govern us; for You have the power to act whenever You choose. {12:19} Through such acts, You have taught Your people that the righteous must be kind, and You have filled Your children with good hope because You offer repentance for sins. {12:20} For if You punished with such great care and indulgence the enemies of Your servants and those deserving of death, granting them time and opportunity to turn from their wickedness, {12:21} with what strictness have You judged Your children, to whom You gave oaths and covenants filled with good promises! {12:22} So while disciplining us, You scourge our enemies ten thousand times more, so we may reflect on Your goodness when we judge, and when we are judged, we may expect mercy. {12:23} Therefore, those who lived unrighteously in foolishness You tormented through their own abominations. {12:24} For they went far astray on paths of error, accepting as gods those animals which even their enemies despised; they were deceived like foolish children. {12:25} Therefore, like thoughtless kids, You sent judgment to mock them. {12:26} But those who ignored the light of Your warnings will face the deserved judgment of God. {12:27} For when in their suffering they grew angry at those creatures they thought were gods, being punished by means of them, they saw and recognized the true God whom they had previously refused to know. Thus, the ultimate condemnation came upon them.

{13:1} All people who were ignorant of God were foolish by nature; they couldn't recognize Him from the good things they saw, nor did they notice the craftsman while admiring His works. {13:2} Instead, they thought that fire, wind, swift air, the stars, turbulent water, or the heavenly bodies were the gods who rule the world. {13:3} If, captivated by the beauty of these things, they assumed they were gods, let them realize how much better their Lord is, for He is the creator of beauty. {13:4} And if they were amazed by their power and works, let them understand how much more powerful He is who formed them. {13:5} From the greatness and beauty of created things, one can gain an understanding of their Creator. {13:6} Yet these people are not entirely to blame, for perhaps they go astray in their search for God and in their desire to find Him. {13:7} Living among His works, they keep searching and trust what they see, as the visible things are beautiful. {13:8} However, they cannot be excused either; {13:9} for if they have the ability to investigate the world, how did they not find the Lord of these things sooner? {13:10} But those who place their hopes in dead things are miserable; they call the works of human hands, like gold and silver crafted skillfully, and likenesses of animals, or useless stones made by ancient hands, "gods." {13:11} A skilled woodcutter may easily saw down a manageable tree and skillfully strip off its bark, then with pleasing craftsmanship make a useful vessel to meet life's needs, {13:12} and burn leftover pieces to cook his food and eat his fill. {13:13} But from a worthless leftover, a crooked stick full of knots, he carves with care in his leisure, shaping it with skill learned in idleness; he forms it into the likeness of a man, {13:14} or a worthless animal, painting it red and covering every flaw with paint; {13:15} then he makes a suitable niche for it, sets it in the wall, and fastens it with iron. {13:16} He thinks carefully about it so it won't fall, knowing it cannot help itself, for it is only an image that needs assistance. {13:17} When he prays about his possessions, marriage, and children, he is not ashamed to address this lifeless object. {13:18} For health, he appeals to something weak; for life, he prays to something dead; for help, he seeks a thing that is completely inexperienced; for a safe journey, he asks a thing that cannot move; {13:19} for making money, work, and success with his hands, he seeks strength from something that has no strength.

{14:1} Again, someone preparing to sail over raging waves calls upon a piece of wood that is more fragile than the ship that carries him. {14:2} It was the desire for profit that planned that vessel, and wisdom was the craftsman who built it; {14:3} but it is Your providence, O Father, that steers its course, for You have given it a path in the sea and a safe way through the waves, {14:4} showing that You can save from any danger, so even if a person lacks skill, they can set sail. {14:5} It is Your will that the works of Your wisdom should not be ineffective; thus, people trust their lives even to the smallest piece of wood, and by floating on a raft, they reach safety on land. {14:6} For even in the beginning, when arrogant giants perished, the hope of the world took refuge on a raft, guided by Your hand, leaving behind a seed for a new generation. {14:7} Blessed is the wood by which righteousness comes. {14:8} But the idol made by hands is cursed, and so is the one who made it; because he did the work, and the perishable object was called a god. {14:9} Equally detestable to God are the ungodly and their ungodliness, {14:10} for what was done will be punished along with the one who did it. {14:11} Therefore, there will be a reckoning for the heathen idols, because, though they are part of God's creation, they became an abomination and a trap for the souls of men and a snare for the foolish. {14:12} The idea of making idols was the start of immorality, and the invention of them brought corruption to life, {14:13} for they neither existed from the beginning nor will they exist forever. {14:14} Through human vanity, they entered the world, and thus their swift end has been planned. {14:15} A father, consumed with grief at the sudden loss of a child, made an image of the child who had been taken from him, honoring what was once a human being as a god, and passing down secret rites and initiations to his descendants. {14:16} The ungodly custom grew strong over time, becoming law, and at the command of monarchs, graven images were worshiped. {14:17} When people could not honor their kings in person since they lived far away, they imagined their appearance and made a visible image of the king they honored, so that by their zeal they could flatter the absent one as if he were present. {14:18} Then the ambition of the craftsman drove even those who didn't know the king to intensify their worship. {14:19} He, perhaps wanting to please his ruler, skillfully forced the likeness to look more beautiful, {14:20} and the crowd, attracted by the charm of his work, began to worship what they had previously honored as a man. {14:21} This became a hidden trap for humanity, as people, bound by misfortune or royal authority, assigned the name that should not be shared to objects of stone or wood. {14:22} Later, it was not enough for them to be wrong about the knowledge of God; they lived in great strife due to ignorance and called such immense evils peace. {14:23} Whether they killed children during their rituals, celebrated secret mysteries, or engaged in wild revelry with strange customs, {14:24} they no longer kept their lives or marriages pure, but either treacherously killed each other or caused grief through adultery, {14:25} resulting in a chaotic mix of bloodshed, murder, theft, deceit, corruption, unfaithfulness, turmoil, perjury, {14:26} confusion over what is good, forgetfulness of kindness, pollution of souls, sexual perversion, disorder in marriage, adultery, and debauchery. {14:27} For the worship of idols, which should not even be named, is the beginning, cause, and end of all evil. {14:28} Their worshipers either rave in excitement, prophesy lies, live unrighteously, or readily commit perjury; {14:29} for because they trust in lifeless idols, they swear wicked oaths and expect no harm. {14:30} But just penalties will catch up with them for two reasons: because they thought wickedly of God by devoting themselves to idols, and because in deceit they swore unrighteously, showing contempt for holiness. {14:31} It is not the power of the things by which people swear, but the just penalty for sin that always pursues the wrongdoing of the unrighteous.

{15:1} But You, our God, are kind and true, patient, and governing all things with mercy. {15:2} Even if we sin, we are still Yours, aware of Your power; but we will not sin because we know we belong to You. {15:3} To know You is complete righteousness, and to understand Your power is the root of immortality. {15:4} For neither the evil intent of human art has misled us, nor the fruitless labor of painters, creating figures stained with various colors, {15:5} whose appearances stir desire in fools, leading them to long for the lifeless form of a dead image. {15:6} Those who love evil things and are suited to such objects of hope are those who either make, desire, or worship them. {15:7} When a potter kneads soft clay and laboriously shapes each vessel for our use, he makes from the same clay both vessels for clean purposes and those for unclean ones, deciding the purpose of each. {15:8} With wasted effort, he forms a futile god from the same clay—this man, who was made from earth just a short time ago and will soon return to the earth when he must give back the soul that was lent to him. {15:9} Yet he doesn't care that he is destined to die or that his life is short; he competes with gold and silver workers and imitates those who work with copper, taking pride in molding counterfeit gods. {15:10} His heart is ashes, his hope is worth less than dirt, and his life is of less value than clay, {15:11} because he failed to recognize the one who formed him and breathed into him a living spirit. {15:12} He considers our existence a trivial game and life a festival for profit, insisting that one must earn money by any means, even through dishonorable actions. {15:13} This man, more than anyone else, knows he sins when he shapes fragile vessels and carved images from earthy materials. {15:14} But all those who oppress Your people are most foolish and more miserable than infants. {15:15} They believe that all their pagan idols are gods, though these have no use of their eyes to see, nor nostrils to breathe, nor ears to hear, nor fingers to feel, and their feet cannot walk. {15:16} For a man made them, and one whose spirit is borrowed shaped them; no man can create a god that resembles himself. {15:17} He is mortal, and what he makes with lawless hands is dead, for he is better than the objects he worships, as he has life, while they never will. {15:18} The enemies of Your people even worship the most detestable animals, which are the worst of all when judged by their lack of intelligence; {15:19} and even as animals, they are not so appealing in appearance that one would desire them, yet they have lost both God's praise and blessing.

{16:1} Therefore, those men were justly punished through such creatures and tormented by a multitude of animals. {16:2} Instead of this punishment, You showed kindness to Your people, preparing quails for them to eat, a delicacy to satisfy their cravings; {16:3} so that when they desired food, they might feel less appetite because of the repulsive creatures sent to them, while Your people, after experiencing hunger for a short time, might enjoy delicacies. {16:4} For it was necessary that unyielding want should strike those oppressors, while Your people were only reminded of how their enemies were tormented. {16:5} When the terrible rage of wild beasts came upon Your people and they were being harmed by the bites of writhing serpents, Your wrath did not last to the end; {16:6} they were troubled for a brief moment as a warning and received a sign of deliverance to remind them of Your law's command. {16:7} For he who turned to it was saved, not by what he saw, but by You, the Savior of all. {16:8} This also convinced our enemies that it is You who delivers from every evil. {16:9} They were killed by the bites of locusts and flies, and no healing was found for them, because they deserved to be punished by such things; {16:10} but Your children were not defeated even by the teeth of venomous snakes, for Your mercy came to their aid and healed them. {16:11} They were bitten to remind them of Your promises and then quickly delivered, lest they forget and become unresponsive to Your kindness. {16:12} For neither herbs nor ointments healed them, but it was Your word, O Lord, that heals all men. {16:13} For You have power over life and death; You lead people down to the gates of Hades and bring them back again. {16:14} A man in his wickedness may kill another, but he cannot bring back the departed spirit or free the imprisoned soul. {16:15} There is no escaping from Your hand; {16:16} for the ungodly, refusing to know You, were punished by the strength of Your arm, pursued by unusual rains and hail and relentless storms, and utterly consumed by fire. {16:17} For—most incredible of all—in water, which quenches everything, fire had an even greater effect, for the universe defends the righteous. {16:18} At one time the flame was restrained so that it would not consume the creatures sent against the ungodly, but rather that they might see they were being pursued by God's judgment; {16:19} at another time, even in the midst of water, it burned more intensely than fire, destroying the crops of the wicked land. {16:20} Instead of these things, You gave Your people food fit for angels, supplying them from heaven with bread ready to eat, providing every pleasure and suited to every taste. {16:21} For Your sustenance revealed Your sweetness to Your children; and the bread, meeting the desire of those who took it, was transformed to suit everyone's liking. {16:22} Snow and ice withstood fire without melting, so that they might know that the crops of their enemies were being destroyed by the fire that blazed in the hail and flashed in the showers of rain; {16:23} while the fire, so that the righteous might be fed, even forgot its own power. {16:24} For creation, serving You, its Maker, strives to punish the wicked and kindly relaxes for those who trust in You. {16:25} Therefore, at that time as well, transformed into all forms, it served Your all-nourishing bounty, according to the desires of those in need, {16:26} so that Your beloved sons, O Lord, might learn that it is not the production of crops that feeds man, but that Your word preserves those who trust in You. {16:27} What was not destroyed by fire was melted simply by being warmed by a fleeting ray of the sun, {16:28} to show that one must rise before dawn to give You thanks and pray to You at the break of light; {16:29} for the hope of an ungrateful person will melt like winter frost and flow away like waste water.

{17:1} Your judgments are great and hard to describe; therefore, uneducated souls have gone astray. {17:2} When lawless men thought they had the holy nation in their power, they themselves were captives of darkness, prisoners of a long night, confined under their roofs, exiles from eternal care. {17:3} They believed their secret sins were hidden behind a dark curtain of forgetfulness, but they were scattered, terrified, and troubled by visions. {17:4} Not even the inner rooms that held them offered protection from fear; terrifying sounds echoed around them, and gloomy apparitions appeared. {17:5} No power of fire could provide light, nor did the brilliant flames of the stars illuminate that dreadful night. {17:6} The only light they had was a dreadful, self-kindled fire, and in their terror, they thought what they saw was worse than the unseen terror. {17:7} The illusions of their magical arts were humbled, and their claimed wisdom was scornfully rebuked. {17:8} Those who promised to drive away fears and disorders from sick souls were themselves plagued by absurd fears. {17:9} Even if nothing frightening was around, they were still terrified by the passing of beasts and the hissing of snakes, {17:10} perishing in trembling fear, unwilling to even look at the air, which was unavoidable. {17:11} Wickedness is cowardly, condemned by its own testimony; distressed by conscience, it has always exaggerated difficulties. {17:12} Fear is merely surrendering the help that comes from reason; {17:13} and the weak expectation of help prefers ignorance of what causes the suffering. {17:14} Yet throughout that powerless night, which emerged from the depths of helpless Hades, they all fell into the same sleep, {17:15} now driven by monstrous visions, now paralyzed by their souls' surrender, overwhelmed by sudden, unexpected fear. {17:16} Whoever was there fell down, confined in a prison not made of iron; {17:17} whether he was a farmer, shepherd, or laborer in the wilderness, he was seized, facing an inescapable fate, bound together by one chain of darkness. {17:18} Whether a whistling wind came, or the melodious sound of birds in wide branches, or the rhythm of rushing water, {17:19} or the harsh crash of rocks falling, or the unseen running of leaping animals, or the roar of savage beasts, or an echo from the mountains, it paralyzed them with terror. {17:20} The entire world was filled with brilliant light, engaged in unhindered work, {17:21} while heavy night covered those men alone, a reflection of the darkness destined for them; but they were even heavier than the darkness itself.

{18:1} But for Your holy ones, there was great light. Their enemies heard their voices but did not see their forms and considered them fortunate for not having suffered, {18:2} thankful that Your holy ones, though previously wronged, were not harming them; they begged their pardon for being at odds with them. {18:3} Therefore, You provided a flaming pillar of fire as a guide for Your people's unknown journey and a gentle sun for their glorious wandering. {18:4} Their enemies deserved to be deprived of light and imprisoned in darkness, those who had kept Your sons confined, through whom the unending light of the law was to be given to the world. {18:5} When they resolved to kill the infants of Your holy ones, and one child was exposed and saved, You took away a multitude of their children in punishment, destroying them all together by a mighty flood. {18:6} That night was foretold to our ancestors, so they might rejoice in the certainty of the oaths they trusted. {18:7} The deliverance of the righteous and the destruction of their enemies were anticipated by Your people. {18:8} For by the same means by which You punished our enemies, You called us to Yourself and glorified us. {18:9} In secret, the holy children of good men offered sacrifices, agreeing with one another to follow the divine law, sharing equally in blessings and dangers; already, they were singing praises of the ancestors. {18:10} But the discordant cries of their enemies echoed back, their lament for their children spread far and wide. {18:11} The slave was punished the same as the master, and the common person suffered the same loss as the king; {18:12} all together, they faced a single form of death, with corpses too many to count. The living were not enough even to bury them, as in one moment their most cherished children were destroyed. {18:13} For although they disbelieved everything due to their magical arts, when their firstborn were killed, they acknowledged Your people as God's son. {18:14} While gentle silence enveloped everything, and the night was now halfway gone, {18:15} Your all-powerful word leaped from heaven, from the royal throne, into the doomed land, a stern warrior {18:16} wielding the sharp sword of Your command, filling all things with death and reaching heaven while standing on earth. {18:17} Then dreadful dreams troubled them, and unexpected fears overwhelmed them; {18:18} here and there, individuals fell down, half dead, revealing why they were dying; {18:19} for the dreams that disturbed them warned them so they would not perish without understanding why they suffered. {18:20} The experience of death also touched the righteous, and a plague struck the multitude in the desert, but Your wrath did not last long. {18:21} A blameless man quickly acted as their champion; he brought forth the shield of his ministry, prayer, and incense to appease You; he stood against the anger and ended the disaster, proving he was Your servant. {18:22} He overcame the wrath not by physical strength or armed force, but by his words he subdued the punisher, appealing to the oaths and covenants made with our ancestors. {18:23} When the dead were already piled upon one another, he intervened, holding back the wrath and cutting off its path to the living. {18:24} His long robe depicted the entire world, and the glories of the ancestors were engraved on its four rows of stones, with Your majesty on the diadem upon his head. {18:25} To these, the destroyer yielded; they were what he feared; for merely testing the wrath was sufficient.

{19:1} The ungodly were relentlessly attacked by merciless anger, for God knew even their future actions in advance. {19:2} Although they had allowed Your people to leave and hurriedly sent them away, they would change their minds and chase after them. {19:3} While still mourning and lamenting at the graves of their dead, they made another foolish decision and pursued as fugitives those they had begged to leave. {19:4} Their deserved fate drove them to this end, making them forget what had happened, so they could fulfill the punishment still lacking for their torments, {19:5} while Your people experienced an incredible journey, but they themselves met a strange death. {19:6} The whole creation was renewed according to Your commands, so that Your children could be kept safe. {19:7} A cloud overshadowed the camp, and dry land emerged where water had once stood, providing an unhindered path through the Red Sea and a grassy plain from the raging waves, {19:8} where those protected by Your hand passed through as one nation, gazing in awe at marvelous wonders. {19:9} They moved like horses and leaped like lambs, praising You, O Lord, who delivered them. {19:10} They recalled the events of their journey, how instead of animals, the earth produced gnats, and instead of fish, the rivers were filled with vast numbers of frogs. {19:11} Later, when they desired luxurious food, they saw a new kind of bird; {19:12} to give them relief, quails came up from the sea. {19:13} The punishments did not come upon the sinners without prior signs in the violence of thunder, for they justly suffered due to their wicked acts, as they harbored bitter hatred for strangers. {19:14} Others refused to welcome strangers, but these made slaves of guests who were their benefactors. {19:15} Not only that, but punishment will come upon the former for their hostile reception of outsiders; {19:16} meanwhile, the latter, after welcoming them with celebrations, inflicted terrible suffering on those who shared the same rights. {19:17} They were also struck with blindness—just like those at the door of the righteous man—surrounded by yawning darkness, each trying to find their own way. {19:18} The elements exchanged places, as on a harp where the notes vary while maintaining the same rhythm; this can be clearly inferred from the sights that occurred. {19:19} Land animals turned into water creatures, and creatures that swim ventured onto land. {19:20} Fire retained its power even in water, while water forgot its fire-quenching nature. {19:21} Flames, on the other hand, did not consume the flesh of perishable creatures walking among them, nor did they melt the crystalline, easily melted heavenly food. {19:22} For in everything, O Lord, You have exalted and glorified Your people, and You have not failed to help them at all times and in all places.

The Psalms of Solomon

{1:1} I cried out to the Lord when I was in distress, to God when sinners attacked. Suddenly, I heard the alarm of war; I thought, He will listen to me because I am righteous. I believed in my heart that I was righteous because I was prosperous and had many children. Their wealth spread across the earth, and their glory reached the ends of the earth. They were exalted to the stars; they claimed they would never fall. But they became arrogant in their prosperity and lacked understanding; their sins were hidden, and I was unaware of them. Their transgressions surpassed those of the nations before them; they completely defiled the holy things of the Lord.

{2:1} When the sinner grew proud, he used a battering ram to break down fortified walls, and You did not stop him. Foreign nations approached Your altar, trampling it arrogantly with their sandals; because the sons of Jerusalem had defiled the holy things of the Lord, had corrupted God's offerings with their wickedness. Therefore, He said: "Cast them far from Me." It was disregarded by God, utterly dishonored; the sons and daughters fell into grievous captivity, their necks were sealed and branded among the nations. According to their sins, He dealt with them, for He left them in the hands of those who overpowered them. He turned away His face from showing them mercy, young and old, together with their children; for they all did evil by not listening. The heavens were angry, and the earth loathed them; no one on it had done what they did, and the earth recognized all Your righteous judgments, O God. They set the sons of Jerusalem to be mocked in return for the harlots among them; every passerby entered freely in broad daylight. They mocked their own transgressions, revealing their wickedness openly. And the daughters of Jerusalem were defiled according to Your judgment, because they had corrupted themselves with unnatural acts. I am deeply pained in my heart for these things. {2:2} Yet I will justify You, O God, with an upright heart, for Your judgments display Your righteousness, O God. You have rendered to the sinners according to their deeds, according to their very wicked sins. You have exposed their sins so that Your judgment might be clear; You have erased their memory from the earth. God is a righteous judge and shows no favoritism. The nations reproached Jerusalem, trampling it down; her beauty was dragged down from the throne of glory. She put on sackcloth instead of beautiful garments, a rope was around her head instead of a crown. She removed the glorious diadem that God had placed upon her; her beauty was cast down in dishonor. {2:3} I saw and pleaded with the Lord, saying, "Long enough, O Lord, has Your hand been heavy on Israel, bringing the nations against them. They have mocked us mercilessly in wrath and fierce anger; they will completely destroy us unless You, O Lord, rebuke them in Your wrath. They did not act out of zeal but out of lust, pouring out their anger on us with intent to plunder. Don't delay, O God, in punishing them for their actions, turning the pride of the arrogant into shame." I did not wait long before God showed me the proud one slain on the mountains of Egypt, regarded as less than the least, on land and sea; his body was tossed about on the waves with much arrogance, with no one to bury him because He rejected him in dishonor. {2:4} He did not realize he was just a man, nor did he think about his end; he said: "I will be lord of land and sea," and did not recognize that it is God who is great, mighty in His strength. He is king over the heavens and judges kings and kingdoms. It is He who elevates me to glory and brings down the proud to eternal destruction in dishonor because they did not know Him. And now, behold, you princes of the earth, the judgment of the Lord, for a great and righteous king is He, judging all that is under heaven. Bless God, you who fear the Lord with wisdom, for the Lord's mercy will be upon those who fear Him in judgment, distinguishing between the righteous and the sinner, recompensing the sinners forever according to their deeds and having mercy on the righteous, delivering them from the affliction of the sinner and recompensing the sinner for what he has done to the righteous. For the Lord is good to those who call upon Him in patience, acting according to His mercy toward His pious ones, establishing them at all times before Him in strength. {2:5} Blessed be the Lord forever before His servants.

{3:1} Why do you sleep, O my soul, and fail to bless the Lord? Sing a new song to God, who is worthy to be praised. Sing and be alert against His awakening, for a good psalm sung to God comes from a joyful heart. The righteous remember the Lord at all times, with thanksgiving and declarations of the righteousness of the Lord's judgments. The righteous do not despise the Lord's discipline; His will is always before them. The righteous may stumble but hold the Lord to be just; they fall and look for what God will do for them; they seek where their deliverance will come from. The steadfastness of the righteous is from God, their deliverer;

sin does not dwell in the house of the righteous. The righteous continually search their house to completely remove all iniquity done in error; they atone for unintentional sins by fasting and afflicting their souls, and the Lord counts every pious man and his house as guiltless. The sinner stumbles and curses the day of his birth and his mother's pain; he adds sins to sins throughout his life; he falls—his fall is indeed grievous—and does not rise again. The destruction of the sinner is forever, and he will not be remembered when the righteous are visited. This is the portion of sinners forever. {3:2} But those who fear the Lord shall rise to eternal life, and their lives shall be in the light of the Lord, never ending.

{4:1} Why do you sit, O wicked man, in the council of the righteous, knowing that your heart is far from the Lord, provoking the God of Israel with your transgressions? You are extravagant in speech and appearance, beyond all others; yet you condemn sinners harshly. Your hand is the first to act as if in zeal, yet you are guilty of many sins and indulgences. Your eyes are on every woman without distinction; your tongue lies when you make contracts with oaths. By night and in secret, you sin as if unseen; with your eyes, you tempt every woman into evil agreements. You eagerly enter every house with cheerfulness as if innocent. {4:2} Let God remove those who live hypocritically among the righteous, even their lives filled with corruption and poverty. Let God expose the deeds of those who seek to please men, laughing at their actions; so the righteous may recognize the judgment of their God when sinners are removed from among the righteous, even the man-pleaser who speaks deceitfully. Their eyes are fixed on any man's secure house, seeking to destroy the wisdom of others with the words of wrongdoers; their words are deceitful to fulfill their wicked desires. They do not cease from scattering families as if they were orphans; they lay waste a house for their lawless desires. They deceive with words, claiming that no one sees or judges. They fill one house with lawlessness and then turn their eyes to the next house to destroy it with words that fuel their desires. Yet their souls, like Sheol (the grave), are never satisfied. {4:3} Let his portion, O Lord, be dishonored before You; let him go out groaning and return home cursed. Let his life be spent in anguish, poverty, and want, O Lord; let his sleep be troubled and his waking filled with confusion. Let sleep be withdrawn from his eyelids at night; let him fail disgracefully in every work of his hands. Let him return home empty-handed, with his house lacking everything he needs to satisfy his hunger. Let his old age be filled with loneliness until his death. {4:4} Let the flesh of the men-pleasers be torn by wild beasts, and let the bones of the wicked lie dishonored in the sight of the sun. Let ravens pluck out the eyes of hypocrites, for they have laid waste many houses in dishonor and scattered them in their lust; they have not remembered God, nor feared Him in all these things; but they have provoked God's anger and vexed Him. May He remove them from the earth, for they have deceived the innocent souls. {4:5} Blessed are those who fear the Lord in their purity; the Lord will rescue them from deceitful men and sinners, and deliver us from every stumbling block placed by the wicked. Let God destroy those who boldly commit all unrighteousness, for a great and mighty judge is the Lord our God, acting in righteousness. {4:6} Let Your mercy, O Lord, be upon all who love You.

{5:1} A statement about the indestructibility of matter, one of the principles of modern physics. O Lord God, I will praise Your name joyfully, among those who know Your righteous judgments. For You are good and merciful, a refuge for the poor; when I cry out to You, do not ignore me. No one can take spoil from a mighty man; who then can take anything You have made, unless You Yourself give it? For man and his lot lie before You in the balance; he cannot add to what You have prescribed. {5:2} O God, when we are in trouble, we call upon You for help, and You do not turn away our requests, for You are our God. Do not let Your hand weigh heavily upon us, lest we sin out of necessity. Even if You do not restore us, we will not turn away; we will come to You. For if I hunger, I will cry to You, O God; and You will provide for me. {5:3} You nourish birds and fish by sending rain to the pastures so that green grass may grow, preparing fodder in the fields for every living thing; and if they are hungry, they lift their faces to You. Kings and rulers and nations rely on You, O God; who else is the help of the poor and needy, if not You, O Lord? And You will hear us—for who is good and gentle but You?—making glad the souls of the humble by opening Your hand in mercy. {5:4} Man's goodness is given grudgingly; and if he gives repeatedly without complaint, even that is remarkable. But Your gifts are abundant in goodness and wealth, and those whose hope is set on You will have no lack of gifts. Your mercy, O Lord, extends across the earth in goodness. {5:5} Happy is the one whom God remembers, granting him a proper sufficiency; if a man has too much, he sins. Sufficient are modest means with righteousness, and through this, the blessing of the Lord becomes abundance with righteousness. Those who fear the Lord rejoice in good gifts, and Your goodness is upon Israel in Your kingdom. {5:6} Blessed is the glory of the Lord, for He is our king.

{6:1} Blessed is the person whose heart is set on calling upon the name of the Lord; when they remember the name of the Lord, they will be saved. The Lord makes their paths straight, and the work of their hands is preserved by their God. When they are troubled by nightmares, their soul will not be disturbed; when they pass through rivers and rough seas, they will not be afraid. They wake from sleep and bless the name of the Lord; when their heart is at peace, they sing to their God and pray for their whole household. The Lord hears the prayers of everyone who fears Him, and He fulfills every desire of the soul that hopes in Him. Blessed is the Lord, who shows mercy to those who love Him sincerely.

{7:1} Do not stay far from us, O God; lest those who hate us without cause attack us. You have rejected them, O God; do not let them trample on Your holy inheritance. Correct us Yourself with Your good will; but do not abandon us to the nations. For if You send a plague, You control it concerning us; for You are merciful and will not be angry enough to destroy us. While Your name dwells among us, we will find mercy; and the nations will not prevail against us. You are our shield, and when we call on You, You listen to us; for You will always have compassion on the descendants of Israel and will not reject them. But we will remain under Your authority forever and under Your loving discipline. You will establish us when You help us, showing mercy to the house of Jacob on the day You promised to help them.

{8:1} I have heard the distress and sounds of war; the trumpet announcing destruction and calamity. I hear a great multitude like a strong wind, like a fierce fire sweeping through the Negev. I said in my heart, Surely God judges us; I hear a sound moving toward Jerusalem, the holy city. My loins shook at what I heard; my knees wobbled; my heart was afraid, and my bones trembled. I said: They establish their ways in righteousness. I thought about God's judgments since the creation of heaven and earth; I recognized God as righteous in His judgments which existed from ancient times. God revealed their sins openly; all the earth came to know the righteous judgments of God. In hidden places, they committed iniquities to provoke Him to anger; they brought confusion, son against mother and father against daughter; they committed adultery with their neighbor's wife. They made oaths with one another regarding these things; they plundered God's sanctuary as if there were no avenger. They trampled the altar of the Lord, coming from all kinds of uncleanness; and with menstrual blood, they defiled the sacrifices as if they were common. They left no sin undone, exceeding even the nations around them. Therefore, God mixed a spirit of confusion for them; He made them drink a cup of undiluted wine so they would become drunk. He brought someone from the ends of the earth, who strikes fiercely; He decreed war against Jerusalem and its land. The princes of the land welcomed him joyfully, saying: Blessed be your path! Come in peace. They made the rough paths smooth before his entry; they opened the gates to Jerusalem and crowned its walls. As a father enters his sons' house, he entered Jerusalem peacefully; he established himself there in great safety. He captured its fortresses and walls; for God Himself led him safely, while they wandered. He destroyed their leaders and every wise counselor; He poured out the blood of Jerusalem's inhabitants like water. He carried away their sons and daughters, whom they had fathered in defilement. They acted according to their uncleanness, just as their fathers had done: they defiled Jerusalem and the things that had been consecrated to God's name. But God has shown Himself righteous in His judgments upon the nations of the earth; and God's faithful servants are like innocent lambs among them. Praised be the Lord who judges the whole earth in His righteousness. Behold, now, O God, You have revealed Your judgment in righteousness; our eyes have seen Your judgments, O God. We have justified Your name that is honored forever; for You are the God of righteousness, judging Israel with loving discipline. Turn, O God, Your mercy upon us and have compassion on us; gather together the scattered people of Israel, with mercy and goodness; for Your faithfulness is with us, and although we have been stubborn, You are our corrector; do not overlook us, O God, lest the nations swallow us up as if there is no one to deliver. But You have been our God from the beginning, and our hope is set on You, O Lord; and we will not depart from You; for Your judgments upon us are good. May Your good will be upon us and our children forever; O Lord, our Savior, we shall never be moved. The Lord is worthy of praise for His judgments from the mouths of His faithful ones; and blessed be Israel of the Lord forever.

{9:1} When Israel was taken captive in a foreign land, when they turned away from the Lord who redeemed them, they were cast away from the inheritance that the Lord had given them. Among every nation were the dispersed of Israel, according to Your word, O God, so that You might be justified in Your righteousness because of our transgressions; for You are a just judge over all the peoples of the earth. No one can hide from Your knowledge, O God; and the righteous deeds of Your faithful ones are before You. Where can a person hide from Your knowledge, O God? Our actions are subject to our own choices and powers to do right or wrong in our work; and in Your righteousness, You visit the children of men. Those who do righteousness store up life for themselves with the Lord; but those who do wrong forfeit their lives to destruction; for the Lord's judgments are given in righteousness to every man and his household. To whom are You good, O God, except to those who call upon the Lord? You cleanse a soul from sins when it confesses and acknowledges them; for shame is upon us because of all these things. And to whom does He forgive sins, except to those who have sinned? You bless the righteous and do not rebuke them for the sins they have committed; and Your goodness is upon those who sin when they repent. And now, You are our God, and we are the people whom You love: behold and show compassion, O God of Israel, for we are Yours; and do not remove Your mercy from us, lest they attack us. For You chose the descendants of Abraham before all nations, and set Your name upon us, O Lord, and You will not reject us forever. You made a covenant with our fathers concerning us; and we hope in You when our soul turns to You. May the mercy of the Lord be upon the house of Israel forever and ever.

{10:1} Blessed is the man whom the Lord remembers with correction, and whom He restrains from the path of evil with discipline so that he may be cleansed from sin and not multiply it. He who prepares his back for discipline will be cleansed; for the Lord is good to those who endure correction. For He makes straight the paths of the righteous and does not lead them astray through His discipline. And the Lord's mercy is upon those who love Him truly, and He remembers His servants with mercy. For the testimony is in the law of the eternal covenant, the testimony of the Lord is on the paths of men in His visitation. Just and kind is our Lord in His judgments forever, and Israel will praise the name of the Lord with joy. The faithful will give thanks in the assembly of the people; and God will have mercy on the poor in the joy of Israel; for God is good and merciful forever, and the gatherings of Israel will glorify the name of the Lord. May the salvation of the Lord be upon the house of Israel for everlasting joy!

{11:1} Sound the trumpet in Zion to call the faithful together; let the voice of the messenger of good news be heard in Jerusalem; for God has shown mercy to Israel by visiting them. Stand on high, O Jerusalem, and see your children gathered from the East and the West by the Lord; from the North they come, rejoicing in their God, and from distant islands God has gathered them. He has lowered high mountains to make a plain for them; the hills fled as they entered. The forests provided shelter as they passed; every fragrant tree God caused to grow for them, so that Israel could walk in the glory of their God. Put on your glorious garments, O Jerusalem; prepare your holy robes; for God has spoken good things concerning Israel forever. Let the Lord fulfill what He has promised regarding Israel and Jerusalem; let the Lord raise Israel by His glorious name. May the mercy of the Lord be upon Israel forever.

{12:1} O Lord, deliver my soul from the lawless and wicked person, from the deceitful and slanderous tongue. The words of the wicked person are twisted and harmful, like a fire that destroys beauty among people. They delight in filling homes with lies, cutting down the trees of joy that lead to the destruction of transgressors, and involving families in conflict through slanderous speech. May God remove the lips of transgressors far from the innocent, bringing them to ruin, and may the bones of slanderers be scattered far from those who fear the Lord! Let the slanderous tongue perish in flames far from the righteous! May the Lord preserve the quiet soul that hates injustice; and may the Lord establish the one who seeks peace at home. The salvation of the Lord be upon His servant Israel forever; let the sinners perish in the presence of the Lord; but let the faithful ones inherit the promises of the Lord.

{13:1} The right hand of the Lord has protected me; the right hand of the Lord has saved us. The Lord's arm has delivered us from the sword, from famine, and from the death of sinners. Wild beasts attacked them, tearing their flesh and crushing their bones. But the Lord delivered us from all these things. The righteous are troubled because of their mistakes, fearing they might be taken away with the sinners; for the downfall of the sinner is terrible. However, none of these things touch the righteous. The discipline of the righteous for sins committed in ignorance is not the same as the destruction of the sinners. The righteous are secretly corrected so that the sinner does not rejoice over them. For He corrects the righteous as a beloved son, and His discipline is like that of a firstborn. The Lord spares His faithful ones and wipes out their mistakes through His correction. The life of the righteous will last forever; but sinners will be destroyed, and their memory will be gone. But upon the faithful ones, the mercy of the Lord will rest, and His mercy is upon those who fear Him.

{14:1} The Lord is faithful to those who love Him sincerely, to those who endure His correction, to those who walk in the righteousness of His commandments, in the law He commanded us so that we may live. The righteous of the Lord will live by it forever; the Paradise of the Lord, the trees of life, belong to His faithful ones. Their roots are established forever; they will not be uprooted as long as the heavens last; for the portion and inheritance of God is Israel. But the sinners and transgressors are not so; they love the fleeting day spent in companionship with their sin; their delight is in temporary corruption, and they do not remember God. The ways of men are always known to Him, and He knows the secrets of the heart before they come to pass. Therefore, their inheritance will be Sheol, darkness, and destruction, and they will not be found on the day when the righteous receive mercy; but the righteous of the Lord will inherit life in joy.

{15:1} When I was in distress, I called upon the name of the Lord; I hoped for help from the God of Jacob and was saved; for You, O God, are the hope and refuge of the poor. For who, O God, is strong except to give thanks to You in truth? And what power does a person have except in giving thanks to Your name? A new song with joyful praise, the fruit of the lips with the well-tuned instrument of the tongue, the first fruits of the lips from a pious and righteous heart—he who offers these things will never be shaken by evil; the flame of fire and the wrath against the unrighteous will not touch him when it comes forth from the Lord's presence against sinners to destroy all they possess. For God's mark is upon the righteous so that they may be saved. Famine, sword, and pestilence will stay far from the righteous, for they will flee from the pious like men pursued in war; but sinners will be pursued and overtaken, and those who act unlawfully will not escape God's judgment; they will be overtaken like enemies experienced in battle, for the mark of destruction is upon their forehead. The inheritance of sinners is destruction and darkness, and their sins will pursue them down to Sheol below. Their inheritance will not be found by their children, for sins will lay waste the houses of sinners. Sinners will perish forever on the day of the Lord's judgment when God visits the earth with His judgment. But those who fear the Lord will find mercy in it and will live by the compassion of their God; but sinners will perish forever.

{16:1} When my soul was distant from the Lord, I was close to slipping into the pit; when I was far from God, my soul was almost poured out unto death, nearing the gates of Sheol with the sinners, when my soul departed from the Lord God of Israel—had the Lord not helped me with His everlasting mercy. He stirred me like a horse is prodded, so I might serve Him; my Savior and helper has saved me at all times. I will give thanks to You, O God, for You have helped me achieve salvation; You have not counted me among the sinners destined for destruction. Do not take Your mercy from me, O God, nor let Your memory fade from my heart until I die. Rule over me, O God, keeping me from wickedness and from every evil woman that leads the simple astray. Let not the charm of a lawless woman deceive me, nor anyone who is caught up in worthless sin. Establish the work of my hands before You, and keep my paths in remembrance of You. Protect my tongue and my lips with truthful words; keep anger and irrational wrath far from me. Remove complaining and impatience during trials from me, especially when You discipline me for my sins so I may return to You. But support my soul with kindness and cheerfulness; when You strengthen my soul, whatever I receive will be enough for me. For if You do not grant strength, who can endure correction during times of need? When a man is rebuked for his wrongdoing, Your testing of him shows in his flesh and through the hardships of poverty. If the righteous endure all these trials, they will receive mercy from the Lord.

{17:1} O Lord, You are our King forever; in You, O God, our souls take pride. How long is the lifespan of man on earth? As his days are, so is his hope. But we hope in God, our deliverer; for the might of our God is always filled with mercy, and His kingdom is everlasting over the nations in judgment. You, O Lord, chose David to be king over Israel, and You swore to him concerning his descendants that his kingdom would never fail before You. But because of our sins, sinners rose up against us; they attacked and expelled us; what You had not promised to them, they took from us violently. They did not glorify Your honorable name; they set up a worldly monarchy instead of the one that was their glory; they destroyed the throne of David in arrogant chaos. But You, O God, cast them down and removed their descendants from the earth, as an outsider rose up against them. According to their sins, You repaid them, O God; it happened to them according to their actions. God showed them no mercy; He searched out their descendants and let none of them escape. The Lord is faithful in all His judgments that He executes upon the earth. The lawless ones devastated our land so that no one could live in it; they destroyed the young, the old, and their children together. In the heat of His anger, He drove them away to the west, exposing the rulers of the land to ridicule. The foreign enemy acted proudly, his heart distant from Our God. Everything he did in Jerusalem was as the nations did in their cities to their gods. And the children of the covenant among mixed peoples surpassed them in wickedness. There was not one among them in Jerusalem who practiced mercy and truth. Those who loved the places of worship fled from them like sparrows fleeing their nest. They wandered in deserts to save their lives from danger, and any who escaped alive were precious in the eyes of those living abroad. They were scattered across the earth by lawless men. The heavens withheld rain from falling on the earth; springs that once flowed from the depths were stopped, running down from high mountains. For there was no one among them who did righteousness and justice; from the highest to the lowest, they were all sinful; the king was a transgressor, and the judge was disobedient, and the people were sinful. Behold, O Lord, and raise up their king, the son of David, at the time You see fit, O God, so he may reign over Your servant Israel. Equip him with strength to shatter unjust rulers, and cleanse Jerusalem from the nations that trample her down to ruin. Wisely and righteously, he will expel sinners from their inheritance, breaking the pride of the wicked like a potter's vessel. With an iron rod, he will shatter all their possessions, destroying the godless nations with the words of his mouth; at his rebuke, nations will flee before him, and he will correct sinners for their thoughts. He will gather a holy people whom he will lead in righteousness, judging the tribes of the people sanctified by the Lord his God. He will not allow wickedness to dwell among them, nor any man who knows evil, for he will recognize them as all being sons of their God. He will divide them according to their tribes upon the land, and no sojourner or alien shall reside with them anymore. He will judge peoples and nations with the wisdom of his righteousness. Selah. He will have the heathen nations serve him under his rule; he will glorify the Lord where all can see; and he will purify Jerusalem, making it holy as in the past, so that nations will come from the ends of the earth to witness his glory, bringing as gifts her sons who had fainted, to behold the glory of the Lord by which God has honored her. He will be a righteous king, taught by God, over them, and there will be no unrighteousness in his presence, for all will be holy and their king will be the Lord's anointed. He will not trust in horse and rider or bow, nor will he accumulate gold and silver for war. He will not rely on a multitude for the day of battle. The Lord Himself is his king, the hope of the mighty who trust in God. All nations will tremble before him, for he will strike the earth with the words of his mouth forever. He will bless the people of the Lord with wisdom and joy, and he will be free from sin so he may govern a great people. He will rebuke rulers and remove sinners with the might of his words; relying on his God, he will not stumble throughout his days; for God will make him strong through His holy spirit, wise through the spirit of understanding, with strength and righteousness. The blessing of the Lord will be with him: he will be strong and not falter; his hope will be in the Lord: who then can stand against him? He will be mighty in his works, and strong in the fear of God; he will shepherd the flock of the Lord faithfully and righteously, ensuring none among them stumble in their pasture. He will lead them correctly, and there will be no pride among them, ensuring none among them are oppressed. This will be the greatness of the king of Israel whom God knows; He will raise him over the house of Israel to correct them. His words will be more refined than the finest gold; in the assemblies, he will judge the peoples, the tribes of the sanctified. His words will echo those of the holy ones among the sanctified peoples. Blessed are those who will be in those days, for they will witness the good fortune of Israel that God will bring to pass in the gathering of the tribes. May the Lord hasten His mercy upon Israel! May He rescue us from the filth of unholy enemies! The Lord Himself is our king forever.

{18:1} Lord, Your mercy is upon the works of Your hands forever; Your goodness extends to Israel as a rich gift. Your eyes look upon them so that none suffers want; Your ears listen to the hopeful prayers of the poor. Your judgments are executed on the whole earth in mercy; and Your love is toward the seed of Abraham, the children of Israel. Your discipline is upon us as upon a firstborn, only-begotten son, to turn back the obedient soul from the folly born of ignorance. May God cleanse Israel for the day of mercy and blessing, the day of choice when blessed shall be those in those days, for He brings back His anointed. In that time, they will see the goodness of the Lord which He will perform for the coming generation, under the rod of discipline of the Lord's anointed in the fear of his God, in the spirit of wisdom, righteousness, and strength; so that he may guide every man in the ways of righteousness through the fear of God, establishing them all before the Lord, a good generation living in the fear of God during the days of mercy. Selah. Great is our God and glorious, dwelling in the highest. It is He who has established the heavenly bodies in their courses for marking seasons from year to year, and they have not deviated from the path He appointed for them. In the fear of God, they pursue their course every day, from the day God created them and forevermore. They have not erred since the day He created them. Since ancient generations, they have not strayed from their path, unless God commanded them to do so through His servants.

The Odes of Solomon

{1:1} The Lord is like a crown on my head, and I will always have Him. {1:2} They made me a crown of truth, causing my branches to flourish within me. {1:3} Unlike a withered crown that does not bloom, You live on my head and have blossomed there. {1:4} Your fruits are mature and perfect, full of Your salvation.

{2:1} I am putting myself in the love of the Lord. {2:2} His presence surrounds me, and I rely on it, for He loves me. {2:3} I would not have known how to love the Lord if He had not first loved me constantly. {2:4} Who can truly understand love, except the one who is loved? {2:5} I love the Beloved, and my soul is devoted to Him. {2:6} Wherever He finds rest, there I will also be. {2:7} I will not be an outsider, for there is no jealousy with the Lord Most High and Merciful. {2:8} I am united with Him because the Lover has found His Beloved. {2:9} Since I love the Son, I will become a child of God. {2:10} Indeed, whoever joins with the Immortal One will truly become immortal. {2:11} And whoever delights in the Source of Life will become truly alive. {2:12} This is the Spirit of the Lord, which is genuine and teaches people His ways. {2:13} Be wise, understanding, and fully awake. Hallelujah.

{3:1} I put on His presence, {3:2} and His members are with Him. I stand with them, and He loves me. {3:3} I wouldn't know how to love the Lord if He hadn't loved me first. {3:4} Who can truly understand love except the one who is loved? {3:5} I love the Beloved, and my soul cherishes Him. {3:6} Wherever His rest is, that's where I am; {3:7} I won't be an outsider, for with the Most High and Merciful, there is no resentment. {3:8} I have been united with the Beloved, for the Lover has found the Beloved. {3:9} Because I love the Son, I will become a son. {3:10} The one who joins with the immortal will also become immortal; {3:11} and those who take delight in the Living One will become alive. {3:12} This is the Spirit of the Lord, who speaks truthfully, teaching mankind His ways. {3:13} Be wise, understanding, and alert. Hallelujah.

{4:1} No one, O my God, can change Your holy place; {4:2} it cannot be changed or moved, for no one has power over it. {4:3} You designed Your sanctuary before creating anything else. {4:4} The older should not be changed by those younger than it. {4:5} You have given Your heart, O Lord, to Your believers; You will never fail or be without fruits. {4:6} One hour of Your Faith is more precious than all days and years. {4:7} Who can put on Your grace and be harmed? {4:8} Your seal is known; Your creatures recognize it, and the heavenly hosts possess it, with the elect archangels clothed in it. {4:9} You have granted us fellowship, not out of need, but because we need You. {4:10} Pour out Your blessings on us and open Your rich fountains that flow with milk and honey. {4:11} You do not repent for what You have promised. {4:12} The end was revealed before You; everything You gave, You gave freely. {4:13} You will not withdraw Your gifts or take them back. {4:14} Everything was revealed to You, O God, and arranged from the beginning; You made all things. Hallelujah.

{5:1} I will give thanks to You, O Lord, because I love You; {5:2} O Most High, You will not abandon me, for You are my hope. {5:3} I have received Your grace freely, and I will live by it. {5:4} My persecutors will come but not find me. {5:5} A cloud of darkness will cover their eyes, and thick gloom will blind them. {5:6} They will lack light to see and cannot grasp me. {5:7} May their plans become thick darkness, and may what I cleverly devised return upon their heads. {5:8} They devised plans that did not succeed. {5:9} My hope is in the Lord; I will not fear, for the Lord is my salvation, and I will not be afraid. {5:10} He is like a garland on my head, and I shall not be moved; even if everything shakes, I stand firm. {5:11} If all visible things perish, I will not die, for the Lord is with me, and I am with Him. Hallelujah.

{6:1} Just as the hand moves over the harp and the strings respond, {6:2} so the Spirit of the Lord speaks through me, and I express His love. {6:3} It destroys what is foreign and anything bitter. {6:4} From the beginning to the end, nothing can oppose Him or stand against Him. {6:5} The Lord has increased the knowledge of Himself and desires that we understand what He has graciously given us. {6:6} He has given us the praise of His name; our spirits honor His holy Spirit. {6:7} A stream flowed and became a vast river; {6:8} it flooded everything and brought water to the Temple. {6:9} The constraints of humanity could not stop it, nor could those who manage waters. {6:10} It spread over the entire earth and filled everything; all the thirsty on earth drank from it. {6:11} Their thirst was quenched, for the Most High provided the drink. {6:12} Blessed are the servants of that drink who are entrusted with His water. {6:13} They have relieved dry lips and revived the fainting will; {6:14} they have restored souls close to death. {6:15} They strengthened the weak and gave light to their eyes. {6:16} Everyone recognized them in the Lord, and they lived forever by the water of life. Hallelujah.

{7:1} Just as anger against evil stirs up, joy over beauty brings forth its fruits without restraint. {7:2} My joy is in the Lord, and my direction is toward Him; this path is excellent. {7:3} I have a helper, the Lord. {7:4} He has revealed Himself to me generously and simply; His kindness has humbled His greatness. {7:5} He became like me so that I could receive Him. {7:6} He was considered like me so that I could embrace Him; {7:7} I was not afraid when I saw Him because He was gracious to me. {7:8} He became like my nature so I could understand Him and like my form, so I would not turn away. {7:9} The Father of knowledge is the Word of knowledge. {7:10} He who created wisdom is wiser than His works. {7:11} He who created me before I existed knew what I would do when I came to be. {7:12} Therefore, He pitied me with His abundant grace and allowed me to ask and receive from His sacrifice. {7:13} He is incorruptible, the fullness of the ages, and the Father of all. {7:14} He has made Himself visible to those who belong to Him so they can recognize their Creator and not think they came from themselves. {7:15} He appointed knowledge as the way, widened it, and brought it to perfection; {7:16} He left traces of His light over it, and I have walked in it from beginning to end. {7:17} By Him it was done, and He rested in the Son, taking hold of everything for salvation. {7:18} The Most High will be known among His saints, proclaiming the coming of the Lord. {7:19} They will go forth to meet Him, singing joyfully to Him with a harp of many tones. {7:20} The seers will come before Him and be seen by Him, {7:21} and they will praise the Lord for His love because He is near and watches over them. {7:22} Hatred will be removed from the earth, drowned along with jealousy. {7:23} Ignorance will be destroyed, for the knowledge of the Lord has arrived. {7:24} Those who sing will celebrate the grace of the Most High; {7:25} they will bring their songs, and their hearts will shine like the day, reflecting the Lord's beauty in their joyful melodies. {7:26} There will be nothing that breathes without knowledge, nor anything silent. {7:27} He has given voice to His creation so they can praise Him. {7:28} Proclaim His power and show forth His grace. Hallelujah.

{8:1} Open your hearts to the joy of the Lord. {8:2} Let your love multiply from your heart to your lips, {8:3} producing holy fruit for the Lord and speaking with care in His light. {8:4} Rise up and stand tall, you who were once brought low. {8:5} Proclaim, you who were silent, that your mouths have been opened. {8:6} Therefore, you who were despised, be lifted up now, for your righteousness has been honored. {8:7} The right hand of the Lord is with you; He is your helper. {8:8} Peace was prepared for you before your struggle began. {8:9} Listen to the truth and receive the knowledge of the Most High. {8:10} Your flesh has not grasped what I am saying, nor have your hearts understood what I am showing you. {8:11} Keep my secret, you who are preserved by it. {8:12} Maintain my faith, you who are kept by it. {8:13} Understand my knowledge, you who know me truly. {8:14} Love me with deep affection, you who love. {8:15} I will not turn away from those who belong to me; {8:16} I know them, and even before they existed, I recognized them and marked them with my seal. {8:17} I formed their beings; I prepared my own nurturing for them so they could drink my holy milk and live by it. {8:18} I took pleasure in them and am proud of them. {8:19} They are my creation and the strength of my thoughts. {8:20} Who can stand against my work, or who is not subject to it? {8:21} I intended and created both mind and heart: they belong to me, and with my own hand, I have chosen my elect ones. {8:22} My righteousness goes before them; they will not lose my name, for it is with them. {8:23} Ask and be filled, and remain in the love of the Lord, {8:24} and beloved ones in the Beloved: those who are kept in Him who lives; {8:25} and those who are saved in Him who was saved; {8:26} and you will be found incorruptible in all ages in the name of your Father. Hallelujah.

{9:1} Open your ears, and I will speak to you. Give me your souls, and I will give you my soul. {9:2} The word of the Lord and His good intentions, the holy thought He has devised concerning His Messiah. {9:3} Your salvation is in the will of the Lord, and His thought leads to everlasting life; your destiny is immortality. {9:4} Be enriched in God the Father and receive the thoughts of the Most High. {9:5} Be strong and redeemed by His grace. {9:6} I announce peace to you, His saints; {9:7} so that none who hear may fall in battle, that those who have known Him may not perish, and that those who receive may not be ashamed. {9:8} An everlasting crown is Truth. Blessed are those who wear it on their heads. {9:9} It is a precious stone; there have been wars over this crown. {9:10} Righteousness has taken it and given it to you. {9:11} Put on the crown in the true covenant of the Lord. {9:12} All who have conquered will be recorded in His book. {9:13} Their book is victory, which belongs to you. Victory sees you before her and desires that you be saved. Hallelujah.

{10:1} The Lord has guided my speech with His word; He has opened my heart with His light, and He has caused His eternal life to dwell in me. {10:2} He gave me the ability to speak His peace's fruit {10:3} to convert the souls willing to come to Him and lead them into a good captivity for freedom. {10:4} I was strengthened, empowered, and took the world captive; {10:5} it became for me a praise of the Most High and of God my Father. {10:6} The scattered Gentiles were gathered together. {10:7} I remained untainted by my love for them, as they acknowledged me in high places, and the traces of light were marked upon their hearts. {10:8} They walked in my life, were saved, and became my people forever. Hallelujah.

{11:1} My heart was split open, and its flower blossomed; grace grew within me, producing fruit for the Lord. {11:2} The Most High opened my heart through His Holy Spirit and examined my affections toward Him, filling me with His love. {11:3} His opening of me became my salvation; I walked in His way of peace, even in the way of truth. {11:4} From the beginning to the end, I gained His knowledge. {11:5} I was established on the rock of truth where He placed me. {11:6} Speaking waters touched my lips from the Lord's abundant fountain. {11:7} I drank and was filled with the living water that does not die; {11:8} my intoxication was not without understanding, but I turned away from vanity and turned to the Most High my God. {11:9} I was enriched by His bounty, forsaking the folly spread across the earth; I stripped it off and cast it away. {11:10} The Lord renewed me in His garments, possessed me with His light, and gave me rest in incorruption from above. {11:11} I became like the land that blossoms and rejoices in its fruits. {11:12} The Lord was like the sun shining on the land; {11:13} He brightened my eyes, and my face received dew; my nostrils enjoyed the sweet scent of the Lord. {11:14} He carried me to His Paradise, where the Lord's pleasures abound; {11:15} I worshiped the Lord for His glory, saying, Blessed are those planted in Your land, O Lord! And those who dwell in Your Paradise; {11:16} they flourish from the fruits of the trees and have transitioned from darkness to light. {11:17} Look! All Your servants are beautiful, doing good works and turning away from wickedness to Your delight. {11:18} They have removed the bitterness of the trees from themselves when planted in Your land; {11:19} everything became a relic of Your essence, a lasting memorial of Your faithful works. {11:20} There is abundant space in Your Paradise, and nothing is useless there; {11:21} everything is filled with fruit; glory be to You, O God, the joy of Paradise forever. Hallelujah.

{12:1} He has filled me with words of truth so I may speak them. {12:2} Like flowing waters, truth comes from my mouth, and my lips express His fruit. {12:3} He has caused His knowledge to overflow in me, for the mouth of the Lord is the true Word and the gateway to His light. {12:4} The Most High has granted His words, which interpret His beauty, repeat His praise, confess His counsel, announce His thoughts, and correct His servants. {12:5} The swiftness of the Word is beyond description; its speed and power match its expression. {12:6} Its course knows no limits; it never fails but remains sure, knowing neither decline nor its way. {12:7} As its work is, so is its conclusion: it is light and the dawn of thought. {12:8} By it, the worlds communicate; and in the Word, those who were silent found their voice. {12:9} From it came love and harmony; they spoke to each other what belonged to them, and they were filled by the Word. {12:10} They recognized their Creator, for they were in harmony; the mouth of the Most High spoke to them, and His explanation flowed through it. {12:11} For the dwelling place of the Word is humanity, and its truth is love. {12:12} Blessed are those who have understood everything through it and have known the Lord in His truth. Hallelujah.

{13:1} Look! The Lord is our mirror: open your eyes and see yourself in Him; learn about your true self. {13:2} Praise His spirit; cleanse your face of dirt, and love His holiness, clothing yourself with it. {13:3} Be without stain at all times before Him. Hallelujah.

{14:1} Just as a son looks to his father, so are my eyes, O Lord, always directed toward You. {14:2} For with You are my comforts and my joy. {14:3} Do not turn Your mercy away from me, O Lord; do not take Your kindness from me. {14:4} Always stretch out Your right hand to me, O Lord; guide me until the end, according to Your good will. {14:5} Let me be pleasing to You because of Your glory and name. {14:6} Preserve me from evil, and let Your gentleness, O Lord, remain with me, along with the fruits of Your love. {14:7} Teach me the Psalms of Your truth so that I may produce fruit in You. {14:8} Open to me the harp of Your Holy Spirit, that I may praise You, O Lord, with all its notes. {14:9} According to the multitude of Your tender mercies, grant me what I seek; hasten to fulfill our requests, for You can meet all our needs. Hallelujah.

{15:1} Just as the sun brings joy to those who seek its light, so my joy is the Lord; {15:2} He is my Sun, lifting me up, and His light has driven away all darkness from my face. {15:3} In Him, I have gained eyes and seen His holy day; {15:4} I have received ears and heard His truth. {15:5} The knowledge I sought has become mine, and I find delight in Him. {15:6} I have turned away from error and walked toward Him, receiving salvation from Him without hesitation. {15:7} According to His generosity, He has given to me, and according to His beautiful nature, He has shaped me. {15:8} I have put on incorruption through His name and shed corruption by His grace. {15:9} Death has been defeated before me, and Sheol (the place of the dead) has been abolished by my word; {15:10} eternal life has arisen in the Lord's land, {15:11} revealed to His faithful ones and generously given to all who trust in Him. Hallelujah.

{16:1} Just as a farmer uses a plow and a sailor steers a ship, my work is to sing psalms to the Lord; my craft and occupation are in His praises. {16:2} His love has nourished my heart, and His fruits have filled my lips. {16:3} For my love is the Lord, so I will sing to Him; {16:4} I am strengthened in His praise and have faith in Him. {16:5} I will open my mouth, and His spirit will proclaim the glory of the Lord and His beauty, the work of His hands. {16:6} The multitude of His mercies and the power of His word. {16:7} The word of the Lord explores everything, both the invisible and the thoughts of His heart. {16:8} The eye sees His works, and the ear hears His thoughts. {16:9} He spread out the earth and settled the waters in the sea; {16:10} He measured the heavens and fixed the stars, establishing creation. {16:11} He rested from His works; {16:12} created things follow their paths and perform their tasks. {16:13} They cannot stand idle; His heavenly hosts obey His command. {16:14} The sun is the treasure of light, and the night is the treasure of darkness. {16:15} He made the sun to shine during the day, while night brings darkness over the land; {16:16} their alternation speaks to the beauty of God. {16:17} Nothing exists without the Lord; He existed before anything came to be. {16:18} The worlds were made by His word and the thoughts of His heart. Glory and honor to His name. Hallelujah.

{17:1} I have been crowned by my God; my crown is alive. {17:2} I have been justified in my Lord; He is my incorruptible salvation. {17:3} I was freed from vanity and was not condemned. {17:4} The choking bonds were cut off, and I was transformed into a new person; I walked in this newness and was saved. {17:5} The truth guided me, and I followed it without straying. {17:6} All who saw me were amazed; they regarded me as different. {17:7} The Most High, in all His perfection, knew me and lifted me up with His kindness, raising my thoughts to the heights of His truth. {17:8} From there, He showed me His precepts, and I opened closed doors. {17:9} I broke the bars of iron; they melted away before me. {17:10} Nothing was closed to me because I was the key to everything. {17:11} I went to free all my servants, ensuring no one remained bound. {17:12} I shared my knowledge generously; my prayers were filled with love. {17:13} I sowed my fruits in hearts, transforming them into myself; they received my blessing and lived. {17:14} They were gathered to me and saved, for they were like my own members, and I was their head. Glory to You, our head, Lord Messiah. Hallelujah.

{18:1} My heart was lifted in the love of the Most High and expanded so I could praise Him for His name. {18:2} My strength was renewed so I wouldn't fall. {18:3} Sicknesses left my body, and it stood before the Lord by His will, for His kingdom is true. {18:4} O Lord, for the sake of the weak, do not remove Your word from me! {18:5} Do not hold back Your perfection for the sake of their deeds! {18:6} Let not the light be overcome by darkness; let truth not flee from falsehood. {18:7} You will grant me victory; our salvation is in Your right hand. You will gather people from all corners. {18:8} You will preserve those held in evil. {18:9} You are my God. Falsehood and death are not in Your mouth; {18:10} Your will is perfection; You know nothing of vanity, {18:11} nor does it know You. {18:12} Error is unknown to You, {18:13} and it does not know You. {18:14} Ignorance is like a blind man and the foam of the sea, {18:15} thinking something vain is significant; {18:16} they too became like it, becoming vain; those who understood were wise and meditated. {18:17} They did not corrupt their imaginations; for they were in the mind of the Lord. {18:18} They mocked those walking in error, {18:19} and spoke truth inspired by the Most High; praise and beauty to His name. Hallelujah.

{19:1} A cup of milk was offered to me, and I drank it, sweetened by the delight of the Lord. {19:2} The Son is the cup, and the Father is He who provided the milk. {19:3} The Holy Spirit drew it forth because His fullness required that His milk be given freely. {19:4} The Holy Spirit opened His bosom and mingled the milk from the Father, offering it to the world unknowingly. {19:5} Those who receive it fully are on His right side. {19:6} The Spirit opened the Virgin's womb, and she conceived and gave birth; the Virgin became a mother with great mercy. {19:7} She labored and bore a Son without pain. {19:8} Because she was not fully prepared and had no midwife (for He guided her), she gave birth as if by her own will. {19:9} She presented Him openly, honoring Him greatly, {19:10} loving Him in His swaddling clothes, caring for Him tenderly, and revealing His majesty. Hallelujah.

{20:1} I am a priest of the Lord, and to Him, I serve, offering the sacrifice of His thoughts. {20:2} For His thoughts differ from those of the world and flesh, unlike those who serve carnally. {20:3} The Lord's sacrifice is righteousness, purity of heart, and lips. {20:4} Present your innermost self before Him blameless; let not your heart harm another, nor your soul oppress another. {20:5} Do not acquire a stranger for the price of silver, nor seek to devour your neighbor, {20:6} nor deprive him of his covering. {20:7} Wear the grace of the Lord generously; enter His Paradise and make a garland from its trees, {20:8} place it on your head, rejoice, rest in His presence, and glory will go before you. {20:9} You shall receive His kindness and grace, flourishing in truth and praising His holiness. Praise and honor be to His name. Hallelujah.

{21:1} I lifted my arms to the Most High, to the grace of the Lord, for He has removed my bonds and raised me to His grace and salvation. {21:2} I have shed darkness and clothed myself in light, {21:3} and my soul has acquired a body free from sorrow, affliction, or pain. {21:4} The thoughts of the Lord were increasingly helpful to me, and His companionship in incorruption lifted me up. {21:5} I was raised in His light and served before Him, {21:6} drawing close to Him, praising and confessing Him. {21:7} My heart overflowed, and I found it on my lips; His joy shone on my face, and His praise filled my heart. Hallelujah.

{22:1} The One who brought me down from on high also lifted me up from the depths below; {22:2} and the One who gathers what is in between is the same One who cast me down. {22:3} He who scattered my enemies existed long ago, along with my adversaries. {22:4} He granted me the power to loosen bonds; {22:5} He enabled me to defeat the seven-headed dragon, placing me over its roots to destroy its offspring. {22:6} You were there to help me, and wherever I went, Your name was a fortress around me. {22:7} Your right hand destroyed the wicked poison, and Your hand leveled the path for those who believe in You. {22:8} You chose them from their graves and separated them from the dead. {22:9} You took dead bones and clothed them with bodies. {22:10} They were lifeless, yet You gave them energy to live. {22:11} Your way was without corruption, and Your face brought the world to renewal, allowing everything to be dissolved and then restored. {22:12} The foundation of everything became Your rock, on which You built Your kingdom, making it the dwelling place of the saints. Hallelujah.

{23:1} Joy belongs to the saints! Who else can wear it but them? {23:2} Grace is for the chosen! Who else can receive it except those who have trusted in it from the beginning? {23:3} Love belongs to the chosen; who else can embrace it but those who have possessed it from the start? {23:4} Walk in the knowledge of the Most High without hesitation, aiming for His exaltation and the perfection of His understanding. {23:5} His thought was like a letter; His will came down from on high like an arrow shot violently from a bow. {23:6} Many hands rushed to grab the letter, wanting to read it. {23:7} It slipped through their fingers, frightening them along with the seal on it. {23:8} They were not allowed to break the seal because the power over it was greater than theirs. {23:9} But those who saw it chased after the letter to discover where it would land and who would read and hear it. {23:10} A wheel received it and rolled over it. {23:11} With it came a sign of the Kingdom and the Government. {23:12} Everything that tried to move the wheel was cut down by it. {23:13} It gathered the multitude of enemies, bridged rivers, uprooted forests, and made a wide path. {23:14} The head bent down to the feet, as the wheel ran from the head to the feet, which bore its sign. {23:15} The letter contained a command, including all regions; {23:16} at its head was the Son of Truth from the Most High Father, {23:17} who inherited and claimed everything, rendering the thoughts of many powerless. {23:18} All the apostates hurried away, and those who persecuted and raged vanished. {23:19} The letter was a great volume, completely written by the finger of God; {23:20} it bore the name of the Father, the Son, and the Holy Spirit, ruling forever and ever. Hallelujah.

{24:1} The Dove hovered over the Messiah because He was her head; she sang over Him, and her voice was heard. {24:2} The inhabitants were terrified, and the sojourners were shaken. {24:3} The birds dropped their wings, and all creeping things died in their hiding places; the abysses, which had been hidden, were opened, and they cried out to the Lord like women in labor. {24:4} No food was given to them because it did not belong to them. {24:5} They sealed up the abysses with the Lord's seal, and those who had existed since ancient times perished in their thoughts. {24:6} They were corrupt from the beginning, and the end of their corruption was death. {24:7} All those who were imperfect perished; for them, it was impossible to receive a word that would allow them to remain. {24:8} The Lord destroyed the imaginations of all who lacked the truth. {24:9} Those who were prideful in their hearts were devoid of wisdom, and thus they were rejected because the truth was not with them. {24:10} The Lord revealed His path and spread His grace; those who understood it know His holiness. Hallelujah.

{25:1} I fled to You, my God, for I was rescued from my bonds. {25:2} You are the right hand of my Salvation and my helper. {25:3} You restrained those who rose against me, {25:4} and I will see them no more, for Your face was with me, saving me by Your grace. {25:5} But I was despised and rejected by many, seen as lead in their eyes, {25:6} while my strength came from You and Your help. {25:7} You set a lamp at my right and left, so nothing in me would lack brightness. {25:8} I was clothed with the covering of Your Spirit, and You took away my skin garment; {25:9} Your right hand lifted me up and removed sickness from me. {25:10} I became strong in truth and holy through Your righteousness, and all my adversaries feared me. {25:11} I became admirable in the name of the Lord, justified by His gentleness, and His rest is forever. Hallelujah.

{26:1} I poured out praise to the Lord, for I belong to Him. {26:2} I will sing His holy song, for my heart is with Him. {26:3} His harp is in my hands, and the Odes of His rest will never be silent. {26:4} I will cry out to Him with my whole heart; I will praise and exalt Him with all that I am. {26:5} His praise stretches from east to west; {26:6} from south to north is the confession of Him. {26:7} From the tops of the hills to their utmost boundaries is His perfection. {26:8} Who can write the Psalms of the Lord, or who can read them? {26:9} Who can prepare his soul for life, so that it may be saved? {26:10} Who can rest on the Most High, so that with His mouth he may speak? {26:11} Who is able to interpret the wonders of the Lord? {26:12} For he who can interpret would dissolve and become what he interprets. {26:13} It is enough to know and to rest; in rest, the singers stand, {26:14} like a river with an abundant fountain, flowing to help those who seek it. Hallelujah.

{27:1} I stretched out my hands and sanctified my Lord; {27:2} for the extension of my hands is His sign. {27:3} My growth is the upright tree (or cross).

{28:1} Just as doves spread their wings over their nestlings, and the nestlings reach toward their mouths, {28:2} so too are the wings of the Spirit over my heart. {28:3} My heart rejoices and exults like a baby rejoicing in its mother's womb. {28:4} I believed; therefore, I was at peace, for He is faithful in whom I have trusted. {28:5} He has richly blessed me, and my head is with Him; no sword or scimitar shall separate me from Him. {28:6} I am prepared before destruction comes; I am set on His immortal wings. {28:7} He showed me His sign, offered me to drink, and from that life comes the spirit within me, which cannot die because it lives. {28:8} Those who saw me marveled because I was persecuted, thinking I was lost, {28:9} yet my suffering became my salvation, and I was rejected because I lacked zeal; {28:10} I was hated for doing good to everyone. {28:11} They surrounded me like mad dogs attacking their masters without understanding. {28:12} Their thoughts are corrupt, and their understanding is twisted. {28:13} But I carried water in my right hand, enduring their bitterness with my sweetness; {28:14} I did not perish because I was not their brother, nor was my birth like theirs. {28:15} They sought my death and did not find it, for I was older than their memories; {28:16} they attacked me in vain, and those who pursued me without reward {28:17} aimed to destroy the memory of one who was before them. {28:18} The thoughts of the Most High cannot be anticipated, and His heart surpasses all wisdom. Hallelujah.

{29:1} The Lord is my hope; in Him, I will not be ashamed. {29:2} For according to His praise, He made me, and according to His goodness, He gave to me. {29:3} According to His mercy, He exalted me, and according to His great beauty, He lifted me high; {29:4} He brought me up from the depths of Sheol and drew me from the grip of death. {29:5} You laid low my enemies and justified me by Your grace. {29:6} I believed in the Lord's Messiah, and I realized He is the Lord; {29:7} He showed me His sign, led me by His light, and gave me the rod of His power; {29:8} so I might subdue the imaginations of the nations and bring down the power of strong men. {29:9} I would wage war by His word and achieve victory by His power. {29:10} The Lord overthrew my enemy with His word, and he became like chaff carried away by the wind; {29:11} I praised the Most High because He exalted me, His servant, and the son of His handmaid. Hallelujah.

{30:1} Draw water for yourselves from the living fountain of the Lord, for it is open to you; {30:2} come, all you thirsty, and take a drink; rest by the fountain of the Lord. {30:3} For it is beautiful and pure and brings rest to the soul. Its waters are far sweeter than honey; {30:4} the honeycomb cannot compare. {30:5} It flows from the lips of the Lord, and from His heart comes its name. {30:6} It came forth infinitely and invisibly; until it was placed in the center, they did not know it. {30:7} Blessed are those who have drunk from it and found rest. Hallelujah.

{31:1} The abysses dissolved before the Lord, and darkness was shattered by His appearance. {31:2} Error went astray and vanished at His command; folly found no path and was submerged by the truth of the Lord. {31:3} He opened His mouth and spoke grace and joy, singing a new song of praise to His name; {31:4} He lifted His voice to the Most High and offered to Him the sons who were with Him. {31:5} His face was justified, as His holy Father had given to Him. {31:6} Come forth, all you afflicted, and receive joy; possess your souls through His grace, and take immortal life. {31:7} They made me a debtor when I rose, though I had been a debtor, dividing my spoils, even though nothing was owed to them. {31:8} But I endured, held my peace, and remained silent, as if unbothered by them. {31:9} I stood firm like a rock that withstands the waves. {31:10} I bore their bitterness for the sake of humility, {31:11} so I might redeem my people, inherit it, and not nullify my promises to the ancestors, to whom I promised salvation for their descendants. Hallelujah.

{32:1} For the blessed, joy arises from their hearts, and light comes from Him who dwells within them; {32:2} and words from the Truth, who is self-existent: He is strengthened by the holy power of the Most High and remains unshaken forever. Hallelujah.

{33:1} Again, Grace ran and abandoned corruption, coming down to eliminate it; {33:2} He destroyed destruction from before Him and laid waste to all its order; {33:3} He stood on a high summit and called out from one end of the earth to the other; {33:4} and He gathered to Himself all those who obeyed Him; and there appeared no evil person. {33:5} But there stood a perfect virgin proclaiming and calling, saying, {33:6} "O sons of men, return, and you daughters of men, come: {33:7} Forsake the ways of corruption and draw near to me, and I will enter into you and bring you forth from destruction, {33:8} and make you wise in the ways of truth, so that you do not perish; {33:9} Hear me and be redeemed. For I speak of the grace of God among you, and through me, you shall be redeemed and become blessed. {33:10} I am your judge; those who put their trust in me will not be harmed but will inherit the new, incorrupt world. {33:11} My chosen ones walk in me, and my ways I will make known to those who seek me, and I will help them trust in my name. Hallelujah.

{34:1} No path is difficult for those with a simple heart. {34:2} There are no wounds where the thoughts are upright; {34:3} there is no storm in the depth of illuminated thought; {34:4} where one is surrounded by beauty, there is nothing that divides. {34:5} What is below reflects what is above; for everything is above: what is below is merely the imagination of those lacking knowledge. {34:6} Grace has been revealed for your salvation. Believe, live, and be saved. Hallelujah.

{35:1} The Lord's dew gently fell upon me; {35:2} the cloud of peace rose over my head, guarding me continually; {35:3} it was for my salvation: everything trembled and was terrified; {35:4} from them came forth smoke and judgment, while I remained silent in the Lord's order. {35:5} He was more than shelter for me, more than a foundation. {35:6} I was carried like a child by his mother, and He nourished me with the dew of the Lord: {35:7} I grew strong by His generosity and rested in His perfection, {35:8} and I stretched out my hands in the lifting up of my soul, made right with the Most High, and redeemed with Him. Hallelujah.

{36:1} I rested in the Spirit of the Lord; the Spirit raised me high {36:2} and made me stand before the Lord's perfection and glory while I praised Him with His songs. {36:3} The Spirit brought me before the Lord's face; though I was a son of man, I was called the Illuminate, the Son of God; {36:4} while I praised among the praising ones, I was great among the mighty. {36:5} According to the greatness of the Most High, so He made me; and like His own newness, He renewed me, anointing me from His own perfection: {36:6} I became one of His Neighbors; my mouth opened like a cloud of dew, {36:7} and my heart poured out like a rushing stream of righteousness, {36:8} and my access to Him was in peace; I was established by the Spirit of His governance. Hallelujah.

{37:1} I stretched out my hands to my Lord; I raised my voice to the Most High; {37:2} I spoke with the lips of my heart, and He heard me when my voice reached Him: {37:3} His answer came to me and gave me the fruits of my labors; {37:4} it brought me rest through the grace of the Lord. Hallelujah.

{38:1} I ascended to the light of truth as if into a chariot; {38:2} and Truth took me and guided me, carrying me over pits and gulleys, preserving me from the rocks and waves; {38:3} it became for me a haven of salvation and set me in the arms of immortal life; {38:4} it journeyed with me, allowing me to rest and preventing me from straying because it was the Truth; {38:5} I took no risks because I walked with Him; {38:6} I made no errors because I obeyed the Truth. {38:7} For Error flees from it and does not meet it; the Truth walks in the right path, and {38:8} everything I did not know, it clarified for me, revealing all the poisons of Error and the plagues of death that seem sweet; {38:9} I saw the destroyer of destruction when the corrupted bride was adorned, and the bridegroom who corrupts and is corrupted; {38:10} I asked Truth, 'Who are these?' and He replied, 'This is the deceiver and Error; {38:11} they are alike in the beloved and his bride, leading astray and corrupting the whole world; {38:12} they invite many to the banquet, {38:13} giving them to drink of the wine of intoxication, removing their wisdom and understanding, making them devoid of intelligence; {38:14} then they leave them, and these wander like madmen corrupting others, lacking heart and failing to seek it! {38:15} I was made wise to avoid the hands of the deceiver; I rejoiced because the Truth accompanied me, {38:16} and I was established, lived, and was redeemed, {38:17} my foundations laid on the Lord's hand because He established me. {38:18} He set the root, watered it, secured it, and blessed it; its fruits endure forever. {38:19} It struck deep, sprang up, spread out, and flourished; {38:20} and the Lord alone was glorified in His planting and care, by His blessing and the work of His hands, {38:21} by the beautiful planting of His right hand, and through the discovery of His planting and the intention of His mind. Hallelujah.

{39:1} Great rivers are the power of the Lord; {39:2} they carry away those who despise Him and entangle their paths; {39:3} they sweep away their fords, capturing their bodies and destroying their lives. {39:4} They are swifter than lightning and more rapid; those who cross them in faith are unshaken; {39:5} those who walk on them without blemish shall not fear. {39:6} For the sign in them is the Lord; the sign is the path of those who cross in the Lord's name; {39:7} therefore, put on the name of the Most High, know Him, and you will cross without danger, for the rivers will obey you. {39:8} The Lord has bridged them by His word, and He walked and crossed them on foot; {39:9} His footsteps stand firm on the water and are not harmed; they are as steady as a well-anchored tree. {39:10} The waves lifted on this side and that, but our Lord Messiah's footsteps remain steadfast, undisturbed, and intact. {39:11} A way has been appointed for those who follow Him and for those who adhere to faith in Him and worship His name. Hallelujah.

{40:1} Just as honey flows from the bees' comb, {40:2} and milk flows from a loving mother to her children; {40:3} so is my hope in You, my God. {40:4} As the fountain bursts forth with water, {40:5} so my heart pours out praise for the Lord, my lips proclaiming His glory, and my tongue singing His psalms. {40:6} My face shines with His joy, my spirit rejoices in His love, and my soul radiates with His presence; {40:7} reverence trusts in Him, and redemption is assured through Him; {40:8} His inheritance is eternal life, and those who partake in it are incorruptible. Hallelujah.

{41:1} All the Lord's children will praise Him and gather the truth of His faith. {41:2} His children will be known by Him. Therefore, we will sing in His love: {41:3} We live in the Lord by His grace and receive life through His Messiah; {41:4} for a great day has shone upon us, and marvelous is He who has shared His glory with us. {41:5} Let us all unite in the name of the Lord and honor Him in His goodness, {41:6} and let our faces shine in His light; let our hearts meditate in His love day and night. {41:7} Let us rejoice in the joy of the Lord. {41:8} All who see me will be astonished, for I come from a different race: {41:9} the Father of truth remembered me, He who possessed me from the beginning; {41:10} His bounty begot me, and the thought of His heart; {41:11} His Word is with us in all our ways; {41:12} the Savior who gives life and does not abandon our souls; {41:13} the one who was humbled and exalted through His own righteousness, {41:14} the Son of the Most High appeared in the perfection of His Father; {41:15} light shone from the Word that existed in Him from the beginning; {41:16} the Messiah is truly one, known before the world's foundation, {41:17} to save souls forever through the truth of His name: a new song arises from those who love Him. Hallelujah.

{42:1} I stretched out my hands and approached my Lord; {42:2} for the stretching of my hands is His sign; {42:3} my expansion is like the outspread tree set on the path of the Righteous One. {42:4} I became insignificant to those who did not embrace me, but I will be with those who love me. {42:5} All my persecutors are dead; they sought me who hoped in me, because I was alive; {42:6} I rose up and am with them; I will speak through their mouths. {42:7} They have despised those who persecuted them; {42:8} I lifted up the yoke of my love over them; {42:9} like the arm of the bridegroom over the bride, {42:10} so was my yoke over those who know me: {42:11} and like the couch spread in the house of the bridegroom and bride, {42:12} so is my love over those who believe in me. {42:13} I was not rejected though deemed so. {42:14} I did not perish, though they plotted against me. {42:15} Sheol (the grave) saw me and was filled with despair; {42:16} Death cast me aside, and many along with me. {42:17} I had bitterness and pain, and I went down to the depths with him; {42:18} but he released my feet and head, for they could not bear my presence: {42:19} I made a gathering of living people among the dead, speaking with them through living lips; {42:20} for my word shall not be empty; {42:21} those who had died ran towards me, crying out, "Son of God, have mercy on us, and treat us according to Your kindness, {42:22} and bring us out from the bonds of darkness, and open to us the door by which we can come out to You. {42:23} For we see that our death has not affected You. {42:24} Let us also be redeemed with You, for You are our Redeemer." {42:25} I heard their voices; I sealed my name upon their heads; {42:26} for they are free men, and they are mine. Hallelujah.

The Rest of Esther

{11:1} In the fourth year of the reign of Ptolemy and Cleopatra, Dositheus, who claimed to be a priest and a Levite, along with his son Ptolemy, brought to Egypt the previous Letter of Purim, which they said was genuine and had been translated by Lysimachus, the son of Ptolemy, a resident of Jerusalem. {11:2} In the second year of the reign of Artaxerxes the Great, on the first day of Nisan, Mordecai, the son of Jair, son of Shimei, son of Kish, from the tribe of Benjamin, had a dream. {11:3} He was a Jew living in the city of Susa, a prominent man serving in the king's court. {11:4} He was one of the captives that Nebuchadnezzar, king of Babylon, had brought from Jerusalem with Jeconiah, king of Judea. And this was his dream: {11:5} Behold, there was noise and confusion, thunder and an earthquake, tumult across the earth! {11:6} And behold, two great dragons appeared, both ready to fight, and they roared fiercely. {11:7} At their roaring, every nation prepared for battle against the nation of the righteous. {11:8} And behold, a day of darkness and gloom, tribulation and distress, affliction and great turmoil upon the earth! {11:9} The whole righteous nation was troubled; they feared the evils that threatened them and were ready to perish. {11:10} Then they cried out to God; from their cry, as if from a tiny spring, a great river emerged, with abundant water; {11:11} light came, the sun rose, and the lowly were lifted up, overpowering those in honor. {11:12} Mordecai saw in this dream what God had determined to do, and after he woke up, it stayed on his mind, and he spent all day trying to understand it in every detail.

{12:1} Now Mordecai rested in the courtyard with Gabatha and Tharra, the two eunuchs of the king who were on guard there. {12:2} He overheard their conversation, inquired about their intentions, and learned that they were planning to harm King Artaxerxes; so he informed the king about them. {12:3} The king then questioned the two eunuchs, and when they confessed, they were led to their execution. {12:4} The king made a permanent record of these events, and Mordecai wrote down the details. {12:5} The king ordered Mordecai to serve in the court and rewarded him for his actions. {12:6} However, Haman, the son of Hammedatha, a Bougaean, was highly esteemed by the king and sought to harm Mordecai and his people because of the two eunuchs.

{13:1} This is a copy of the letter: "The Great King, Artaxerxes, to the rulers of the hundred and twenty-seven provinces from India to Ethiopia and to the governors under them, writes: {13:2} "Having become ruler of many nations and master of the whole world, not swelled with arrogance but always acting reasonably and kindly, I have decided to ensure my subjects live in lasting peace and, to make my kingdom safe and accessible for travel throughout, to restore the peace that everyone desires. {13:3} "When I consulted my advisors on how this could be achieved, Haman, who stands out among us for his sound judgment, unwavering goodwill, and loyalty, and holds the second highest position in the kingdom, {13:4} pointed out that among all the nations there is a certain hostile people, who have laws that contradict those of every other nation and consistently disregard the commands of kings, making our goal of unifying the kingdom impossible. {13:5} We understand that this people alone stands in opposition to all, stubbornly following a foreign way of life and laws, and is unfriendly to our government, doing everything they can to prevent stability in our kingdom. {13:6} "Therefore, we have decreed that those identified in Haman's letters, who is in charge of affairs and is like a second father to us, shall be utterly destroyed by their enemies, along with their wives and children, without pity or mercy, on the fourteenth day of the twelfth month, Adar, of this current year, {13:7} so that those who have been hostile for a long time may perish in one day, and our government can be completely secure and peaceful in the future." {13:8} Then Mordecai prayed to the Lord, recalling all the Lord's works. He said: {13:9} "O Lord, Lord, King who rules over all, for the universe is in your power and no one can oppose you if it is your will to save Israel. {13:10} For you made heaven and earth and every wonderful thing under heaven, {13:11} and you are Lord of all; no one can resist you, who are the Lord. {13:12} You know all things; you know, O Lord, that it was not out of insolence, pride, or a desire for glory that I did this, refusing to bow to the proud Haman. {13:13} For I would have been willing to kiss the soles of his feet to save Israel! {13:14} But I did this so I would not place the glory of man above the glory of God, and I will not bow down to anyone but you, who are my Lord; I will not act in pride. {13:15} And now, O Lord God and King, God of Abraham, spare your people; for our enemies are watching us to annihilate us, and they want to destroy the inheritance that has been yours from the beginning. {13:16} Do not neglect your portion, which you redeemed for yourself out of the land of Egypt. {13:17} Hear my prayer and have mercy on your inheritance; turn our mourning into feasting, so we may live and praise your name, O Lord; do not silence the mouths of those who praise you." {13:18} And all Israel cried out mightily, for their death was before their eyes.

{14:1} And Queen Esther, overwhelmed with deep anxiety, fled to the Lord; {14:2} she removed her splendid clothing and put on garments of distress and mourning, and instead of expensive perfumes, she covered her head with ashes and dung, completely humbling her body, and every part she loved to adorn she covered with her tangled hair. {14:3} She prayed to the Lord God of Israel, saying: "Lord, you alone are our King; help me, for I am alone and have no helper but you, {14:4} for my danger is in my hands. {14:5} Ever since I was born, I have heard in my family tribe that you, O Lord, took Israel from among all nations and our ancestors from among all their people, for an everlasting inheritance, and that you did for them all that you promised. {14:6} And now we have sinned before you, and you have given us into the hands of our enemies, {14:7} because we glorified their gods. You are righteous, O Lord! {14:8} And now they are not satisfied with our bitter slavery; they have made a pact with their idols {14:9} to abolish what your mouth has ordained and to destroy your inheritance, to silence the mouths of those who praise you and to extinguish your altar and the glory of your house, {14:10} to open the mouths of the nations to praise vain idols, and to magnify a mortal king forever. {14:11} O Lord, do not surrender your scepter to what does not exist; do not let them mock at our downfall, but turn their plans against themselves, and make an example of the man who started this against us. {14:12} Remember, O Lord; reveal yourself in this time of our affliction, and give me courage, O King of the gods and Master of all dominion! {14:13} Put eloquent speech in my mouth before the lion, and turn his heart to hate the man who fights against us, so that there may be an end to him and those who support him. {14:14} But save us by your hand, and help me, for I am alone and have no helper but you, O Lord. {14:15} You know all things; you know that I hate the splendor of the wicked and detest the bed of the uncircumcised and of any foreigner. {14:16} You know my needs — that I detest the sign of my proud position, which is on my head when I appear in public. I loathe it like a menstruous rag and do not wear it during my leisure time. {14:17} And your servant has not eaten at Haman's table, nor have I honored the king's feast or drunk the wine of the libations. {14:18} Your servant has found no joy since the day I was brought here until now, except in you, O Lord God of Abraham. {14:19} O God, whose power is over all, hear the voice of the despairing and save us from the hands of evildoers. And save me from my fear!"

{15:1} On the third day, when she finished her prayer, she took off the garments in which she had worshiped and dressed herself in splendid attire. {15:2} Then, elegantly adorned, after invoking the aid of the all-seeing God and Savior, she took her two maids with her, {15:3} leaning delicately on one, {15:4} while the other followed, carrying her train. {15:5} She was radiant with perfect beauty, and looked happy, as if beloved, but her heart was filled with fear. {15:6} After passing through all the doors, she stood before the king. He was seated on his royal throne, dressed in the full splendor of his majesty, covered in gold and precious stones, and he was quite intimidating. {15:7} Lifting his face, flushed with splendor, he looked at her with fierce anger. The queen faltered, turned pale, and fainted, collapsing onto the head of the maid who was in front of her. {15:8} Then God changed the king's spirit to gentleness, and in alarm, he sprang from his throne and took her in his arms until she regained her composure. He comforted her with soothing words and said to her, {15:9} "What is it, Esther? I am your brother. Take courage; {15:10} you shall not die, for our law applies only to the people. Come near." {15:11} Then he raised the golden scepter and touched it to her neck; {15:12} he embraced her and said, "Speak to me." {15:13} She replied, "I saw you, my lord, like an angel of God, and my heart was shaken with fear at your glory. {15:14} For you are wonderful, my lord, and your face is full of grace." {15:15} But as she was speaking, she fainted again. {15:16} The king was agitated, and all his servants tried to comfort her.

{16:1} The following is a copy of this letter: "The Great King, Artaxerxes, to the rulers of the provinces from India to Ethiopia, a hundred and twenty-seven satrapies, and to those loyal to our government, greetings. {16:2} The more often people are honored by the excessive kindness of their benefactors, the prouder many become. {16:3} They not only seek to harm our subjects, but in their inability to handle prosperity, they even plot against their own benefactors. {16:4} They not only strip thankfulness from among people, but, swayed by the boasting of those ignorant of goodness, they believe they can escape the justice of God, who sees everything. {16:5} Many who hold positions of authority have partly been responsible for the shedding of innocent blood and have faced irremediable disasters due to the persuasion of friends entrusted with public affairs, {16:6} as these individuals deceive the sincere goodwill of their rulers with the false trickery of their evil natures. {16:7} The wickedness accomplished through the harmful behavior of those who misuse authority is evident not just from ancient records but also from current investigations. {16:8} In the future, we will ensure our kingdom is peaceful and orderly for all, {16:9} by changing our methods and judging matters before us with more fairness. {16:10} For Haman, the son of Hammedatha, a Macedonian (really an outsider to the Persian bloodline and devoid of our kindness), having become our guest, {16:11} so enjoyed our goodwill that he was called our father and continually bowed to as second to the royal throne. {16:12} However, unable to contain his arrogance, he sought to take away our kingdom and our lives, {16:13} and through deceitful craft, he requested the destruction of Mordecai, our savior and eternal benefactor, and of Esther, the faultless partner of our kingdom, along with their entire nation. {16:14} He believed that by doing this, he would find us defenseless and transfer the Persian kingdom to the Macedonians. {16:15} But we find that the Jews, whom this accursed man intended for annihilation, are not wrongdoers but are governed by just laws {16:16} and are the children of the Most High, the living God, who has guided the kingdom for us and for our ancestors in the best possible order. {16:17} Therefore, you will do well not to carry out the orders sent by Haman, the son of Hammedatha, {16:18} because the man who did these things has been hanged at the gate of Susa, along with his entire household. God, who rules over all, has swiftly punished him for what he deserved. {16:19} Therefore, post a copy of this letter publicly in every place and allow the Jews to live under their own laws. {16:20} Provide them with reinforcements, so that on the thirteenth day of the twelfth month, Adar, they may defend themselves against anyone who attacks them during their time of distress. {16:21} For God, who rules over all, has turned this day into a joy for His chosen people instead of a day of destruction for them. {16:22} Therefore, observe this with great joy as a significant day among your festivals, {16:23} so that it may mean salvation for us and the loyal Persians now and in the future, while serving as a reminder of destruction for those who plot against us. {16:24} Any city or region that does not comply will face destruction in wrath, through spear and fire, becoming not only impassable for humans but also forever detested by beasts and birds."

The Rest of Psalms

{151:1} I was the youngest among my brothers, just a youth in my father's household. {151:2} I tended my father's flock, and once came across a lion and a wolf. I fought them and tore them apart. {151:3} My hands crafted an instrument, and my fingers shaped a harp. {151:4} Who will show me my Lord? He, my Lord, has become my God. {151:5} He sent His angel, took me from tending my father's flock, and anointed me with holy oil. {151:6} My brothers, handsome and tall as they were, did not find favor with the Lord. {151:7} I went out to face the Philistine, who cursed me by his idols. {151:8} But I took his sword, cut off his head, and removed the shame from the children of Israel.

{152:1} Give glory to God with a loud voice; proclaim His greatness in the assembly of many. {152:2} Praise Him among the upright; speak of His glory with the righteous. {152:3} Join with the good and the perfect to glorify the Most High. {152:4} Gather together to declare His strength; do not delay in revealing His salvation, His power, and His glory to even the youngest among us. {152:5} For wisdom was given to reveal the Lord's honor, and knowledge was shared with humanity to declare His works. {152:6} Let even the simple comprehend His strength and those far from wisdom understand His glory, {152:7} for they may be distant from His courts and far from His gates. {152:8} The Lord of Jacob is exalted, and His glory fills all creation. {152:9} Anyone who praises the Most High brings Him pleasure, like one offering fine flour or burnt offerings of goats and calves, {152:10} and as incense from the hands of the righteous is a pleasing aroma to Him. {152:11} His voice will be heard from the righteous gates, and the words of the upright will give wisdom. {152:12} They will find fulfillment in the truth of their meal, and drink in peace when they share together. {152:13} Their lives are grounded in the law of the Most High, and their speech reveals His strength. {152:14} How far from the wicked is speech of Him, and knowledge of Him is hidden from transgressors! {152:15} The Lord looks with compassion upon the good and showers mercy on those who praise Him, delivering their souls in times of trouble. {152:16} Blessed is the Lord, who has saved the suffering from the wicked, who raises a leader from Jacob and a judge for the nations from Israel. {152:17} May His presence endure in Zion, and may He bring joy to the people of Jerusalem for generations.

{153:1} O Lord, I have called upon You; hear me. {153:2} I lift my hands toward Your holy dwelling; incline Your ear to me. {153:3} Grant my request; do not withhold my prayer. {153:4} Preserve my soul, and do not let it fall prey to the wicked. {153:5} Turn away from me those who repay evil with more evil, O Judge of truth. {153:6} Do not judge me according to my sins, for no one is blameless before You. {153:7} Teach me Your law, O Lord, and make known Your judgments to me. {153:8} Many will hear of Your deeds, and nations will praise Your name. {153:9} Remember me, do not forget me; do not lead me into trials beyond my strength. {153:10} Forgive the sins of my youth, and let not past punishments remain on me. {153:11} Cleanse me, O Lord, from evil defilement, and let it not return to me. {153:12} Uproot its hold within me, and let it never sprout again. {153:13} Great are You, O Lord; therefore, I know my request will be granted by You. {153:14} To whom else can I turn, or what can human strength add to me? {153:15} My confidence is in You, O Lord; I called upon You, and You heard me, healing the wounds of my heart. {153:16} I rested and slept; I dreamed and found help, for the Lord sustained me. {153:17} Though my heart was weighed down, I give thanks for the

Lord has rescued me. {153:18} Now I will rejoice in their shame; I have trusted in You and will not be ashamed. {153:19} May honor be Yours forever and ever. {153:20} Deliver Israel, Your chosen people, and those of Jacob, whom You have proven.

{154:1} O God, come to my aid; help and save me; deliver my soul from the one who seeks to kill me. {154:2} Will I descend to Sheol by the lion's mouth, or shall the wolf consume me? {154:3} Was it not enough for them to ambush my father's flock and tear apart one of my father's sheep? Must they also seek to destroy my soul? {154:4} Have mercy, O Lord, and save Your chosen one from ruin, so that he may declare Your wonders at all times and praise Your great name. {154:5} You delivered me from the lion's jaws and the wolf's ravenous mouth; You rescued me from captivity among wild beasts. {154:6} Quickly, my Lord, send deliverance from Your presence, and pull me from the gaping pit that holds me in its depths.

{155:1} Praise the Lord, all nations; glorify Him and bless His name. {155:2} He rescued His chosen one from the hands of death and saved His holy one from destruction. {155:3} He delivered me from the snares of Sheol and my soul from the bottomless pit. {155:4} Even before my deliverance came, I was almost torn in two by these wild beasts. {155:5} But He sent His angel, who closed their gaping mouths and saved my life from ruin. {155:6} My soul will forever praise and exalt Him for all His kindness, for all He has done and will do for me.

The First Book of Meqabyan

{1:1} There was a man named Tseerutsaydan who loved sin; he would boast about his many horses and the strength of his troops under his command. {1:2} He had many priests who served the idols he worshiped, to whom he bowed and made sacrifices day and night. {1:3} Yet in his heart, he was dull, believing that the idols granted him strength and power. {1:4} He thought they gave him authority over all his realm. {1:5} Again, during his formation, he believed they granted him all the desired authority as well. {1:6} He sacrificed to them day and night. {1:7} He appointed priests to serve these idols. {1:8} While they ate from the defiled sacrifices, they pretended that the idols ate day and night. {1:9} They also encouraged others to be diligent like them so that they could sacrifice and eat. They motivated people to sacrifice just like them. {1:10} Yet he trusted in idols that neither profited nor benefited him. {1:11} Because of his short lifespan and dull heart, it seemed to him that they nourished him and crowned him—his reasoning was clouded by Satan, preventing him from recognizing the true Creator who brought him from non-existence to life. He was oblivious that his misled kindred might also realize the truth, leading them toward the eternal fire of Gehenna, as they were judged along with those who wrongly called these idols gods. {1:12} Since they were never truly alive, it could be said that they were dead. {1:13} Satan's authority misled them into worshiping these idol images, manipulating their reasoning and revealing themselves in ways they loved. He would judge the idols in which they believed and upon which the children of Adam relied—whose reasoning was as insubstantial as ashes. {1:14} They would marvel when they saw that what they believed about the idols had come true, and they would sacrifice their daughters and sons born of their nature, spilling the innocent blood of their children. {1:15} They were not saddened by this; for Satan delighted in their sacrifices to fulfill their wicked desires, leading them toward Gehenna like himself, a place with no escape for eternity, where he would receive torment. {1:16} Tseerutsaydan was arrogant; he had fifty idols fashioned in male form and twenty in female form. {1:17} He would boast about these worthless idols, glorifying them as he sacrificed to them morning and evening. {1:18} He commanded others to sacrifice for the idols, consuming the defiled sacrifices himself and encouraging others to do the same, particularly provoking evil. {1:19} He had five houses built for him, filled with beaten idols made of iron, brass, and lead. {1:20} He adorned them with silver and gold, draping curtains around the houses and setting up tents for them. {1:21} He appointed keepers for them, continually sacrificing forty oxen, ten sterile cows, ten fattened sheep, and ten barren goats, along with birds that had wings. {1:22} It seemed to him that the idols ate; he presented them with fifty fig cakes and fifty dishes of wheat kneaded with oil. {1:23} He instructed his priests: "Take and give them, let my idols eat what I have slaughtered for them, and let them drink the wine I have offered. If this is not enough for them, I will add more." {1:24} He commanded everyone to eat and drink from those defiled sacrifices. {1:25} But out of his evil malice, he sent troops throughout the kingdom to find anyone who did not sacrifice or bow down; they were to separate him out and punish him with fire and sword before him, plundering his money and burning his house, destroying all his possessions. {1:26} "For they are kind and great; they have favored us with their charity. I will show punishment and tribulation to anyone who does not worship my idols and sacrifice to them. {1:27} I will show him punishment and tribulation; they have created the earth, heaven, the wide sea, the moon, sun, stars, rain, winds, and all living things to provide food and satisfaction for us." {1:28} But those who worship them shall suffer severe tribulation and will not find any relief.

{2:1} There was a man from the tribe of Benjamin named Meqabees. {2:2} He had three sons who were handsome and great warriors, beloved by everyone in the regions of Midian and Moab under the rule of Tseerutsaydan. {2:3} When the king discovered them, he commanded, "Why don't you bow to the idols of Tseerutsaydan? Why don't you make sacrifices?" {2:4} He threatened, "If you refuse, we will take you to the king, and we will destroy all your possessions, just as the king has commanded." {2:5} The young men, handsome and brave, replied, "As for the One we worship, it is our Father, the Creator who made the earth, heaven, the sea, the moon, the sun, clouds, and stars. He is the true God whom we worship and believe in." {2:6} The young men were four in number, and they had a hundred warriors with shields and spears. {2:7} When the troops tried to seize these four, they escaped from their grasp, as none could touch them because they were truly powerful warriors, seizing shields and spears for themselves. {2:8} One of them was so strong that he could strangle and kill a panther, treating it like a chicken. {2:9} Another could kill a lion with just one stone or a single blow from a stick. {2:10} A third could take down a hundred men at once with his sword, and their names were known throughout Babylon and Moab. {2:11} They were powerful warriors, admired for their strength and good looks. {2:12} Their appearance was remarkable, but because they worshipped JAH and did not fear death, their courage surpassed their physical beauty. {2:13} When they frightened the troops, none could capture them, and the warriors fled toward a high mountain. {2:14} The troops returned to the city and shut the fortress gates, terrorizing the people by saying, "Unless you bring us the Meqabyans, we will burn your city and report you to the king, destroying your land." {2:15} At that time, the people, rich and poor, men and women, even a child who had lost both parents and an old woman, all cried out together, turning their faces toward the mountain, pleading, "Do not destroy us or our land!" {2:16} They wept together in fear, calling on JAH. {2:17} Turning their faces eastward and stretching out their hands, they begged JAH together, "Lord, should we reject these men who defy Your Command and Your Law? {2:18} They believe in silver and gold, in stones and wood crafted by human hands, but we do not wish to hear the wicked words of those who do not uphold Your Law." {2:19} "You are the Creator who saves and destroys. Let him be like those he worships; he is one who spills blood and consumes flesh. {2:20} We do not wish to see that wicked face or hear those words." {2:21} "But if You command us, we will go to him; for we believe in You. We will give our bodies to death, and when he says, 'Sacrifice to my idols,' we will not heed those wicked words. {2:22} We believe in You, Lord, who examines hearts and minds, the God of Abraham, Isaac, and Jacob, who obeyed Your Command and lived firmly in Your Law. {2:23} You examine a person's thoughts, assisting both the sinner and the righteous; nothing is hidden from You. Those who take refuge in You are revealed alongside You. {2:24} But we have no other God apart from You. {2:25} We are willing to give our bodies to death for Your glorious Name; may You be our strength and refuge in this battle we fight for You. {2:26} When Israel entered Egypt, You heard Jacob's plea, and now we glorify God; we beg You." {2:27} At that moment, two men with strikingly handsome features appeared before them, and when swords of fire fell like lightning, they struck and killed them, but then they rose up looking as they had before. {2:28} Their appearances became even more beautiful, shining brighter than the sun, and they looked more handsome than ever.

{3:1} Just as you see before you the Most High JAH's servants—'Abya, Seela, and Fentos—who died and rose again, you too will rise after death, and your faces will shine like the sun in the Kingdom of Heaven. {3:2} They went with those men and received martyrdom there. {3:3} At that time, they prayed, praised, and bowed to JAH; death did not frighten them, nor did the king's punishments. {3:4} They approached the young men, appearing innocent like sheep, yet they were not afraid. When they reached them, they seized, beat, bound, and whipped them, then delivered them to the king and stood them before him. {3:5} The king said to them, "Why won't you stubbornly sacrifice and bow to my idols?" {3:6} Those brothers, cleansed from sin and honored, who shone like precious jewels, Seela, 'Abya, and Fentos, answered him in unison. {3:7} They told the king, who was like a plague, "As for us, we will not bow or sacrifice to defiled idols that have no knowledge or reason." {3:8} Again, they said, "We will not bow to idols made of silver and gold, crafted by human hands, stone and wood that have no understanding, soul, or benefit to friends, nor harm to enemies." {3:9} The king replied, "Why do you act this way? You know who insults you and wrongs you; why do you insult the glorified gods?" {3:10} They answered him, "They are nothing compared to us; we will insult them and not glorify them." {3:11} The king responded, "I will punish you according to your evil actions; I will mar your handsome features with whips and severe tribulations and fire. {3:12} Now tell me whether you will sacrifice to my idols or not; if you don't, I will punish you with swords and whips." {3:13} They replied, "As for us, we will not sacrifice or bow to defiled idols." The king commanded them to be beaten with heavy sticks and whipped until their inner organs were exposed. {3:14} After this, they were bound and imprisoned until he could bribe those who would punish and kill them. {3:15} Without kindness, they bound them tightly in a prison cell, where they remained for three days and three nights. {3:16} After the third day, the king commanded a herald to call together counselors, nobles, country elders, and officials. {3:17} When King Tseerutsaydan sat in the square, he ordered that those honored men—Seela, 'Abya, and Fentos—be brought before him, bound and wounded. {3:18} The king asked them, "After sitting in prison for three days, have you truly returned to your old ways?" {3:19} The honored servants of JAH replied, "As for that, we will not agree to worship the sinful idols you check upon." {3:20} The king, enraged, commanded that they be placed on high so he could renew their wounds, and their blood flowed onto the ground. {3:21} He ordered them to be burned with torches until their flesh was charred. His servants obeyed, and the honored men told him, "You who forget JAH's Law, speak; our reward will be as great as the punishment you inflict." {3:22} Then he commanded that ferocious bears, tigers, and lions be brought in to eat them, tearing their flesh from their bones. {3:23} He ordered those who kept the beasts to release them upon the martyrs, and they did as he commanded, binding the honored martyrs' feet and maliciously beating them with tent stakes. {3:24} The beasts were thrown upon them as they roared, and when they approached the martyrs, they bowed before them. {3:25} The beasts returned to their handlers, frightening them as they dragged the martyrs to the square, where they killed seventy-five men from the king's army. {3:26} Many panicked, with one in anguish and another in fear, until the king abandoned his throne and fled. The beasts were captured with difficulty and taken back to their lair. {3:27} Seela, 'Abya, and Fentos, the two brothers, came and freed their companions from prison, saying, "Come, let us flee before these skeptics and criminals find us." {3:28} The martyrs responded, "It is not proper for us to flee after we have prepared ourselves to testify; if you were afraid, you should go." {3:29} The younger brothers said, "I will stand with you before the king; if you die, I will die with you." {3:30} After this, the king was on his royal balcony and saw that the honored men had been released, and all five brothers stood together. The chief punisher questioned them, telling the king they were brothers, and the king was enraged, shouting like a wild boar. {3:31} Until the king consulted bribes to punish all five brothers, he ordered them seized and placed in a prison cell, binding them tightly with a hollow stake. {3:32} King Tseerutsaydan said, "These youths who have erred wearied me; what should these men think? Their evil actions are like their strength; if I say, 'They will return,' they will return to evil reasoning. {3:33} I will bring hardship upon them as they have done evil, and I will burn their flesh in fire until it is charred ash, and then I will scatter their ashes like dust on the mountains." {3:34} After speaking this, he waited three days and commanded that the honored men be brought back to him. When the honored men approached, he ordered a fire to be kindled in a great oven, adding to it a wicked mix to fuel the flames, along with fat, soapberries, sea foam, resin, and sulfur. {3:35} As the fire blazed in the pit, the messengers went to the king, saying, "We have done as you commanded; send the men who are to be cast in." {3:36} He commanded that they be cast into the fiery pit, and the young men obeyed the king's order. As they entered the fire, they surrendered their souls to JAH. {3:37} When those who cast them saw this, angels received and took their souls to the Garden where Isaac, Abraham, and Jacob dwell, where the righteous are found.

{4:1} When the king saw that they were dead, he ordered that their bodies be burned in fire until they turned to ash and that the ashes be scattered in the wind. However, the fire could not burn the hair from their corpses, so they were taken out of the pit. {4:2} Again, they set a fire over them from morning until evening, yet it did not burn them. They said, "Now let us cast their bodies into the sea." {4:3} They did as the king commanded and threw them into the sea, even adding heavy stones, iron hearthstones, and a millstone that a donkey turns, yet the sea did not sink them. Because JAH's Spirit of Support was in them, they floated on the water and did not sink; all the malice aimed at them failed to destroy them. {4:4} The king said, "Their death has wearied me more than their life; I will cast their bodies to the beasts so they can be eaten—yet what should I do?" {4:5} The young men obeyed his command, but vultures and beasts did not touch their bodies. Birds and vultures covered them with their wings to shield them from the burning sun, and the five martyrs' bodies remained intact for fourteen days. {4:6} When they looked upon them, their bodies shone like the sun, and angels encircled their corpses like light surrounding a tent. {4:7} The king was at a loss for what to do, so he dug a grave and buried the five martyrs. {4:8} That night, as the king who had forgotten JAH's LAW lay in bed, he saw the five martyrs standing before him, angry and holding swords. {4:9} It seemed to him that they had entered his house in the dark to commit a crime. When he awoke from his sleep, he was frightened and thought of fleeing from his bedroom to the hall, as he felt they would kill him, believing them to be guilty of a crime against him; he trembled in fear. {4:10} He said, "My lords, what do you want? What should I do for you?" {4:11} They replied, "Aren't we the ones you killed, burning in fire and whom you commanded to be cast into the sea? JAH has kept our bodies safe because we believed in Him; you failed to destroy us—just as a person who believes in Him will not perish. Glory and praise be to JAH, and we, who believed in Him, were not ashamed in our tribulations. {4:12} Since I didn't know that such a punishment would come upon me, what reward should I give you for the evil I did to you? {4:13} Now separate from me the reward I should give you, lest you take my body in death and lower it to Sheol while I am still alive. {4:14} Since I have wronged you, forgive my sins, for it was due to your Father JAH's mercies," he told them. {4:15} The honored martyrs replied, "Because of the evil you did to us, we will not repay you with evil, for JAH is the one who brings hardship upon a soul, and He is the one who will repay you with hardship. {4:16} However, we are revealed to you because it is good for you that your time is short and because your reasoning is deaf; it may seem to you that you killed us, but you prepared good for us. {4:17} But your idol priests and you will descend to Gehenna, where there are no exits. {4:18} Woe to your idols, to whom you bow, having forsaken JAH, who created you when you were scorned like spit. And woe to those who worship them; you do not know JAH, who brought you from non-existence to existence—don't you see that you are here today like smoke and will perish tomorrow?" {4:19} The king answered them, saying, "What will you command me to do for you?" {4:20} "It is to save your own soul, lest you enter the Gehenna of Fire; however, it is not for us to save our souls that we teach you. {4:21} Your idols are made of silver and gold, stone and wood, having no reasoning or soul, crafted by human hands. {4:22} They cannot kill, they cannot save, they do not benefit friends, nor harm enemies; they do not honor or debase; they do not make wealthy or impoverish; they mislead you by the authority of demons, who do not desire that anyone be saved. They do not uproot nor plant. {4:23} They especially do not care for your salvation from death—O dull-hearted ones, whom they seem to have angered, when you are the ones who made them. {4:24} Since demons and the authority of Satan reside in them, they will repay you according to what you love, and that will drown you in the sea of Gehenna. {4:25} But you should abandon your errors and let this also be our reward, for our deaths were for the benefit of our souls worshiping our Creator JAH," they told him. {4:26} The king was alarmed and would be utterly astonished, as all five appeared before him, drawing their swords; he was terrified and bowed before them. {4:27} "Now I know that the dead, who were dust, will truly arise— as for me, only a little time remains before I die." {4:28} After this, they were hidden from the king's sight, and from that day onward, Tseerutsaydan, who was completely arrogant, ceased to burn their bodies. {4:29} Since he had misled many eras, he would be fine in his idols and reasoning errors, and he misled many people like himself until they stopped following and worshiping JAH, who created them. Yet he was not the only one who erred. {4:30} They would sacrifice their daughters and sons to demons, practicing seduction and disturbance according to their reasoning, which their father Satan taught them, so he could create the seduction and disturbance that JAH does not love. {4:31} They married their mothers and abused their aunts and sisters, defiling their bodies while committing all sorts of filthy deeds. Satan had corrupted the reasoning of those twisted individuals; they said, "We will not return." {4:32} But Tseerutsaydan, who did not know his Creator, was completely arrogant and boasted in his idols. {4:33} If they say, "How will JAH give the Kingdom to those who do not know Him in LAW and Worship?"—they will surely return to Him in repentance, as He tests them in this way. {4:34} But if they truly repent, He will love them and keep His Kingdom for them; if they refuse, a fire will punish them in the Gehenna of Fire forever. {4:35} But it is fitting for a king to fear his Creator JAH as his lordship is famous, and it is fitting for a judge to be ruled by his Creator as he judges justly according to his lordship's fame. {4:36} It is also fitting for elders, chiefs, envoys, and lesser kings to be commanded by their Creator as their lordship measures in abundance. {4:37} He is the Lord of Heaven and Earth, who created all creation, for there is no other Creator in Heaven or Earth who impoverishes and makes rich; He is the one who honors and debases.

{5:1} One warrior among the sixty was proud, and JAH caused his body to swell from his feet to his head with a spoonful of sulfur, resulting in his death from a plague. {5:2} Again, Keeram, who built an iron bed, was proud due to his great power, and JAH hid him in death. {5:3} Once more, Nabukedenetsor was proud, saying, "There is no other king but me; I am the Creator who makes the sun rise in this world," speaking from his abundance of arrogance. {5:4} JAH separated him from people and sent him into the wilderness for seven years, and he lived among the birds of heaven and wild beasts until he acknowledged that JAH was the one who created him. {5:5} When he recognized Him in worship, JAH returned him to his kingdom—who could stand proudly against JAH, the Creator? {5:6} What about those who violate HIS LAW and HIS Order and whom the Earth did not swallow? {5:7} O Tseerutsaydan, you love to be proud before your Creator, and yet you might be destroyed just like them and lowered to the grave because of your arrogance. {5:8} After they entered Sheol, where there is grinding of teeth and mourning—a darkness fulfilled—He might lower you to the deep pit of Gehenna, where there are no exits forever. {5:9} As for you, you are a man who will die and be destroyed tomorrow, just like the arrogant kings who left this world alive. {5:10} As for us, we say, "You are ruined and desolate, but you are not JAH, for JAH is the one who created Heaven and Earth and you." {5:11} He brings down the arrogant, honors the humble, and strengthens those who are weary. {5:12} He kills the healthy ones and raises the people of the Earth who are buried in graves. {5:13} He sends forth slaves free in life from the rule of sin. {5:14} O king Tseerutsaydan, why do you boast in your defiled idols, which provide no benefit? {5:15} But JAH created Heaven and Earth and the great seas; He created the moon and the sun and prepared the ages. {5:16} Man grazes in his field, and while he plows until dusk, the stars of heaven stand firm by His Word. {5:17} He calls all in Heaven—nothing happens without JAH knowing it. {5:18} He commanded the angels of Heaven to serve Him and praise His glorified Name, and angels are sent to all people who inherit life. {5:19} Rufa'iel, a servant, was sent to Thobeet, and he saved Thobya from death in Ragu'iel's land. {5:20} Hola Meeka'iel was sent to Giediewon to draw his attention with money that he used to destroy 'Iloflee people; he was also sent to the prophet Mussie when he led 'Isra'iel across the sea of 'Eritra. {5:21} Only JAH led them; no other idol accompanied them. {5:22} He sent them to sow crops on Earth. {5:23} He fed them from His harvest grain; since He truly loved them, He cherished them by feeding them honey that hardened like rock. {5:24} So that you might keep His kinfolk according to what is due, and that you might do JAH's Will, who created you, He crowned you, giving authority over the four kingdoms. {5:25} He crowned you, making you loftier than all, and your Creator totally crowned you so that you might love JAH. {5:26} It is necessary that you love your Creator JAH as He loved you, as He trusted you among all people; therefore, do JAH's Will so that your days may abound in this world and that He may dwell with you in Support. {5:27} And do JAH's Will so that He may stand as a Guardian for you against your enemies and seat you upon your throne, hiding you under His Wing of Support. {5:28} If you do not know, JAH chose and crowned you among 'Isra'iel, just as He chose Sa'ol from the children of 'Isra'iel when he kept his father's donkeys, crowning him among his kinfolk and seating him with 'Isra'iel on his throne. {5:29} He gave him a lofty fortune, separating him from his kinfolk; JAH crowned you among His kinfolk—henceforth, take care of His kinfolk. {5:30} JAH has appointed you over them so that you might kill and save—keeping them from evil things—those who do good things and those who do evil things to good things," he told him. {5:31} "As JAH has appointed you over all that you might do His Will, whether you punish or save, reward them for evil deeds—those who do good deeds and those who do good deeds and evil deeds. {5:32} For you are a servant of JAH, who rules all in Heaven; therefore, do JAH's Will so that He may act on your behalf in all you think and all you ask while you plead before Him. {5:33} No one rules Him, but He rules all. {5:34} No one appoints Him, but He appoints all. {5:35} No one dismisses Him, but He dismisses all. {5:36} No one reproaches Him, but He reproaches all. {5:37} No one makes Him diligent, but He makes all diligent—Heaven and Earth's rulership is His; none can escape His authority. All are revealed alongside Him, yet none are hidden from His face. {5:38} He sees all, but none see Him. He hears the prayer of the person who prays to Him, saying, "Save me," for He has created man in His image, and He accepts his plea. {5:39} For He is a King who lives for eternity, feeding all from His unchanging nature.

{6:1} When He crowns the true kings who follow His Will, those kings write a straight path because of Him. {6:2} Since they have obeyed JAH's Will, He will shine upon them in a light that does not fade—like Yis'haq, 'Abriham, Ya'iqob, Selomon, Daweet, and Hiziqyas, who dwell in a garden where all the beautiful kings reside, their abodes filled with light. {6:3} The halls of Heaven are what truly shine, while the halls of Earth are not like those of Heaven; their floors—made of silver, gold, and jewels—are pure. {6:4} The features that shine are beyond human comprehension; the halls of Heaven shine like precious gems. {6:5} As JAH knows—being the Knower of Nature—the halls of Heaven that He created are beyond human reasoning and shine with total light; their floors are crafted from silver, gold, jewels, white silk, and blue silk, all pure. {6:6} It is altogether beautiful like this. {6:7} Righteous ones who stand firm in religion and virtue will inherit it through JAH's charity and forgiveness. {6:8} There is water of welfare flowing from it, shining like the sun, with a light tent within it, encircled by a fragrant grace. {6:9} Beautiful fruits of various shapes and tastes surround the house; there are olive and grape trees there, all delightful, with sweet-scented fruits. {6:10} When a flesh-and-blood person enters it, their soul separates from their body due to the abundance of the Irie Ites that are in it, arising from its fragrant flavor. {6:11} Beautiful kings who obey JAH will be joyful there; their honor and place are recognized in the Kingdom of Heaven, which endures forever, where welfare is found. {6:12} He showed that their lordship on Earth was renowned and honored, and that their lordship in Heaven was also famous and esteemed; they will be honored and exalted in Heaven just as they were honored and bowed to in this world—if they do good deeds in this world, they will be blessed. {6:13} But the kings who are evil in their rule and in the kingdoms given to them by JAH do not judge righteously according to what is due; they have ignored the cries of the destitute and poor and have not judged fairly to save the refugees and the wronged children who have lost their fathers and mothers. {6:14} They do not rescue the destitute and poor from the hands of the wealthy who rob them; they do not share their food or satisfy the hungry, nor do they provide drink for the thirsty; they did not lend an ear to the cries of the poor. {6:15} And He will lead them to Gehenna, a dark ending—on that lofty Day when JAH comes, and when His wrath is upon them, as Daweet said in his praises, "Lord, do not chastise me in Your judgment, and do not admonish me in Your discipline"—their problems and disgrace will abound as their fame increases. {6:16} When nobles and kings rule in this world, there are those who do not uphold Your law. {6:17} But JAH, who rules all, is there in Heaven; all souls and all welfare have been seized by His authority—He is the one who gives honor to those who glorify Him, for He truly rules all and loves those who love Him. {6:18} As He is Lord of Earth and Heaven, He examines and knows what the heart conceives and what thoughts reason; for a person who petitions Him with a pure intention, He shall grant them their plea. {6:19} He will bring down the arrogant powers that commit evil deeds against children who have lost their mothers and fathers, and against the elderly. {6:20} It is not by your power that you have seized this kingdom; it is not by your ability that you sit upon this throne; He has loved to test you so that it might be possible for you to rule like Sa'ol, who governed his kin in that time; He placed you on a royal throne—yet it is not by your power that you have seized this kingdom; it is when He tests you, like Sa'ol, who ignored the prophet Samu'iel's words and JAH's command, and did not serve his army nor the king of 'Amalieq—that it is not by your ability that you have seized this kingdom. {6:21} And JAH told the prophet Samu'iel, "Go, for they have saddened Me by demolishing the LAW, by worshipping idols, by bowing to idols, and by all their hated works without benefit; tell Sa'ol, 'Go to the land of 'Amalieq and destroy their hosts and all the kings, starting with the people down to the livestock.' {6:22} Upon those who have saddened JAH, because of this, He sent Sa'ol to destroy them. {6:23} But he saved their king from death, and saved many livestock, beautiful women, and handsome youth from death. As he has scorned My command and did not heed My word, because of this, JAH told the prophet Samu'iel, "Go and divide his kingdom." {6:24} Because of his actions, I anoint the child of Daweet, that he might reign over 'Isra'iel. {6:25} But a demon will seize him and strangle him. {6:26} As he has refused when I offered him a kingdom that he might do My Will—at the time he refused to do My Will, I dismissed him from his kingdom that was due to him—but you, go and tell him, saying, 'Will you thus ignore JAH, who crowned you among His kin 'Isra'iel, who seated you on His Lordship Throne?' {6:27} But you—tell him—'You did not know JAH, who granted you so much honor and fame,' He told him. {6:28} And the prophet Samu'iel went to king Sa'ol and entered while he was sitting at a dinner table, and when the king of 'Amalieq, 'Agag, had sat on his left. {6:29} "Why did you completely ignore JAH, who commanded you to destroy the livestock and people?" he asked. {6:30} At that moment, the king was afraid, rose from his throne, and told Samu'iel, "Return with me," and he seized his clothes, but Samu'iel refused to return—Samu'iel's clothes were torn. {6:31} And Samu'iel told Sa'ol, "JAH has divided your kingdom." {6:32} Sa'ol then told Samu'iel before the people, "Honor me and atone for my sin before JAH, that He might forgive me"—and even though he feared JAH's Word, who created him, he did not fear the dead king; Samu'iel refused to return to his word. {6:33} Because of this, he pierced the king of 'Amalieq, 'Agag, before he swallowed what he had chewed. {6:34} And a demon seized Sa'ol, who demolished the LAW of JAH; because He is the King of Kings who rules all, JAH struck his head, a king who committed sin—so that he would not be shamed. {6:35} For He is the Lord of all creation, who dismisses the authority of nobles and kings who do not fear Him—but none can rule over Him. {6:36} As He spoke, saying, the kin of Daweet shall go while they are famed and honored, but the kin of Sa'ol shall go while they are brought low—He destroyed the kingdom from his children and from Sa'ol. {6:37} Because it saddened Him, and because He destroyed the criminals who grieved Him with their evil deeds, JAH avenged and destroyed the children of Sa'ol—for a person who does not avenge JAH's enemy is JAH's enemy. {6:38} When it is possible for him to avenge and destroy, and when he has authority—a person who does not seek vengeance and destroy the sinner, and does not seek vengeance against a person who does not keep JAH's LAW—since he is JAH's enemy, He destroyed the children of Sa'ol.

{7:1} Whether you are a king or a ruler, what is your significance? {7:2} Isn't it JAH who created you, bringing you from non-existence to life, so that you might do His Will, live according to His Command, and fear His Judgment? Just as you oppress your servants and govern them, there is also JAH who oppresses you and governs you. {7:3} Just as you beat those who commit sins without mercy, there is also JAH who will strike you and bring you down to Gehenna, where there are no exits for eternity. {7:4} Just as you whip those who do not obey you or do not bring you tribute, why do you not offer tribute to JAH? {7:5} He is the one who created you so that you might love Him and that others might fear you. He crowned you over all creation so that you might keep His kin in truth—so why do you not fear your Creator, JAH? {7:6} Judge what is due as JAH appointed you to do; do not show favoritism, whether for the small or the great—whom will you fear if not Him? Keep His Worship and the Nine Commands. {7:7} As Mussie commanded the children of 'Isra'iel, saying, "I provided water and fire for you—extend your hand toward what you love"—do not go to the right or the left. {7:8} Hear My Word that I tell you, so that you might understand and do My Command—lest you say, "It is beyond the sea or across the deep or beyond the river; who will bring it to me so that I can see it and hear His Word and do His Command?" {7:9} Lest you say, "Who will ascend to Heaven again and bring down JAH's Word to me so that I can hear it and do it?"—JAH's Word is close; check for yourself to teach it with your mouth and give alms with your hand. {7:10} And you will not hear your Creator JAH unless you read His Book; you will not love Him or keep His Command unless you keep His LAW. {7:11} You have the means to enter Gehenna forever unless you love His Command and do JAH's Will, who honored and esteemed you, separating you from all your kin so that you might keep them in truth—you have the means to enter Gehenna forever. {7:12} He made you above all and crowned you over all His kin so that you might rule His kin in truth, according to what is due, while you remember the name of your Creator, who created you and gave you a kingdom. {7:13} There are those whom you punish for wronging you, and there are those you forgive while considering JAH's Work; there are those for whom you judge by what is due, straightening your reasoning. {7:14} And do not show favoritism when they argue before you; as the Earth's wealth is your money, do not accept a bribe to pardon the sinner and wrong the innocent. {7:15} If you do His Will, JAH will multiply your time in this world; but if you anger Him, He will diminish your time. {7:16} Think that you will rise after you die and that you will be examined standing before Him for all the Work you did, whether it was good or evil. {7:17} If you do good Work, you will live in a garden in the Kingdom of Heaven, in houses where noble kings live and where light fills everything. For JAH does not shame your lordship authority; but if you do evil Work, you will dwell in Sheol, Gehenna, where wicked kings reside. {7:18} But when you see your renowned fame—your warriors' awards, your hanging shield and spear—and when you see your horses and your troops under your command, and those who beat drums and people who play harps before you... {7:19} But when you behold all this, you elevate your reasoning and fortify your pride, forgetting JAH, who gave you all this honor; however, when He tells you to abandon it all, you are not the one to let it go. {7:20} For you have completely neglected the appointment He set for you, and He will give your lordship to another. {7:21} As death will suddenly come upon you, and as Judgment will occur at the time of Resurrection, and as all human deeds will be examined, He will thoroughly investigate and judge you. {7:22} There will be none who will honor earthly kings; for He is the True Judge—at Judgment time, the poor and wealthy will stand together. The crowns of this world, in which nobles boast, shall fall. {7:23} Judgment is prepared, and a soul will tremble; at that time, the works of sinners and the righteous will be examined. {7:24} And there will be none who will be hidden. At the time a woman goes into labor, and when the fetus in her womb is ready to be born—just as she cannot prevent her womb, the Earth also cannot prevent her lodgers; she will return them. {7:25} Just as clouds cannot prevent rain unless they take it and rain where JAH commanded them—for JAH's Word has created everything, bringing from non-living to living—and JAH's Word has again brought all to the grave; likewise, after Resurrection time has arrived, it is impossible that the dead will not rise. {7:26} As Mussie said, "It is by the Words that proceed from JAH's Mouth—but it is not only by bread that a person is saved"; and JAH's Word will again awaken all from their graves. {7:27} Check—it is known that the dead will rise by JAH's Word. {7:28} And again JAH said thus in the Repeating Law, because the nobles and kings who do His Will—when the day arrives for them to be counted for destruction—I will take revenge and destroy them on the day when Judgment is passed, and at the time when their feet stumble, He said. {7:29} And again JAH told those who know His Judgment, "Know that I am your Creator JAH, and that I kill and I save. {7:30} I bring trouble in tribulation, and I forgive; I bring down to Sheol and again send forth to the Garden—and there is none who will escape from My authority," He told them. {7:31} JAH said this because the nobles and kings who did not keep His LAW—as earthly kingdoms are passing, and as they pass from morning to evening—keep My Order and My LAW that you might enter the Kingdom of Heaven, which endures forever, He said. {7:32} For JAH calls the righteous to glory and the sinners to tribulation; He will make the sinner wretched but will honor the righteous. {7:33} He will dismiss the person who did not do His Will, but He will appoint the person who did His Will.

{8:1} Listen, I will tell you how the dead will rise; they will plant a seed and be fruitful, and the vines will produce grapes, as JAH will bring forth the fruit in abundance, and they will press wine from it. {8:2} Understand that the seed you planted was small, but today it produces fruit and leaves. {8:3} JAH gave it roots to draw nourishment from the Earth and Water—both. {8:4} But He feeds its wood with fire and wind; roots provide water to drink, and the Earth gives strength to the wood. {8:5} But the soul that JAH created makes them bear fruit; likewise, the dead will rise. {8:6} When the soul is separated from the body, each goes its own way; He said to gather souls from the four elements—from Earth and Water, from wind and fire. {8:7} The Earth element firmly resides in its nature and becomes Earth, and the Water element firmly resides in its nature and becomes Water. {8:8} The wind element firmly resides in its nature and becomes wind, and the fire element firmly resides in its nature and becomes a hot fire. {8:9} But a soul that JAH separated from the flesh returns to its Creator until He raises it again, uniting it with flesh at the time He desires; He places it in a Garden in the place He loves. {8:10} He places righteous souls in a Light house in the Garden, but for the sake of sending away the souls of sinners, He places them in a dark house in Sheol until the time He loves. {8:11} JAH told the prophet Ezekiel to call souls from the four corners so they might be gathered and become one body. {8:12} When He spoke in one Word, the souls were gathered from the four corners. {8:13} The Water element brought greenery, and the fire element brought fire again. {8:14} The Earth element brought Earth, and the wind element brought wind. {8:15} And JAH brought a soul from the Garden where He had placed it; they were gathered by one Word, and a Resurrection occurred. {8:16} Again, I will show you the example that is alongside you—the day turns to dusk, you sleep, the night dawns, and you rise from your bed; but while you sleep, that is an example of death. {8:17} And when you wake, that is an example of resurrection; but the night, when all people sleep in darkness, is an example of this world. {8:18} But the morning light, when darkness is gone and light fills the world and people rise to graze in the fields, is an example of the dead. {8:19} This Kingdom of Heaven, where man is renewed, is like this; the resurrection of the dead is like this—as this world is passing, it is an example of night. {8:20} And as David spoke, saying, "He placed His example in the Sun"—when the Sun shines upon the day it rises, it is an example of the Kingdom of Heaven. {8:21} And just as the Sun shines in this world today, when Christ comes, He will shine like the Sun in the new Kingdom of Heaven; as He said, "I am a Sun that does not set and a Torch that is not extinguished—He, JAH, is the Light." {8:22} And He will quickly awaken the dead again; I will bring you another example from the food you sow, by which you are saved—whether it be a wheat kernel, a barley kernel, a lentil kernel, or any seeds sown on Earth, none will grow unless they are broken down and rotten. {8:23} Just like the flesh you see—when it is broken down and rotten, the Earth consumes its strength with the skin. {8:24} And when the Earth consumes its strength, it grows around a kernel; JAH sends a cloud to gather rain as He desires, and roots grow in the Earth and send forth leaves. {8:25} And if it were broken down and rotten, it cannot grow; but once it has grown, it sends forth many buds. {8:26} By JAH's Will, fruit is given for those buds that grew, and He clothes it with strength in straw. {8:27} Look at how the seed you sowed has increased; yet the silver and the leaves, the ear and the straw are not counted for you. {8:28} Do not be a dull person who does not understand—consider your seed and how it has increased; likewise, think that the dead will receive a resurrection according to their works. {8:29} Listen, if you sow wheat, it will not grow as barley; nor will barley grow if you sow wheat. Let me tell you again, it will not grow—if you sow wheat, will you gather barley? If you sow lentils, will you gather flax? {8:30} How about from plants—if you plant figs, will they really grow for you as nuts? How about if you plant almonds, will they grow for you as grapes? {8:31} If you plant sweet fruit, will it grow for you as bitter? How about if you plant bitter fruit—can it become sweet? {8:32} Likewise, if a sinner is dead, can he arise as righteous in the Resurrection? How about if a righteous person is dead—can he arise as a sinner in the Resurrection? Everyone will receive their reward according to their works; yet they will receive their reward according to their sin and their deeds, and none will be convicted by their companion's sin. {8:33} A highland tree is planted, and it sends forth long branches; it will completely dry up unless Heaven sends rain on it. {8:34} And the cedar will be uprooted from its roots unless summer rain falls on it. {8:35} Likewise, the dead will not arise unless the dew of blessing falls upon them as commanded by JAH.

{9:1} Unless the highland mountains and the regions of Gilead receive a rain of pardon as commanded by JAH, they will not grow grass for the beasts and animals. {9:2} And the mountains of Elam and Gilead will not give verdant leaves for sheep and goats—nor for wild animals in the wilderness—nor for ibexes and deer. {9:3} Likewise, the rain of pardon and dew commanded by JAH did not fall for the doubters and criminals who committed error and crime for money beforehand; the dead will not arise—and Demas and Qophros, who worship idols, dig roots, and work to incite trouble... {9:4} And those who dig roots, practice sorcery, and cause others to battle... {9:5} And those who lust after lawlessness—Medians and Athenians who believe in their idols—and those who play and sing for them while beating violins and drums and strumming harps, they will not arise unless the dew of pardon falls upon them as commanded by JAH. {9:6} These are the ones who will be condemned on the day when the dead arise and when the Final Judgment occurs; yet those who save themselves and engage in their own deeds err by their idols. {9:7} You wasteful and dull-hearted person—do you really think that the dead will not arise? {9:8} When a trumpet is blown by the Chief Angel Michael, the dead will rise then; for you will not remain in the grave without rising—do not think otherwise. {9:9} Hills and mountains shall be leveled, and a clear path shall be made. {9:10} And Resurrection shall occur for all flesh.

{10:1} But if it were not so, those who were buried in their ancestors' graves, starting from Adam, through Seth and Abel, Shem and Noah, Isaac and Abraham, Joseph and Jacob, and Aaron and Moses—why is it that they did not desire to be buried in another place? {10:2} Isn't it for them to rise together with their relatives at the time of Resurrection? What if their bones are counted among the bones of the wicked and the bones of pagans—those who worship idols? Why is it that they did not desire to be buried in another place? {10:3} But you—don't mislead your reasoning when you say, "How will the dead rise after they are dead—those who were buried in one grave, being tens of thousands, and whose bodies have decayed?" {10:4} When you look at a grave, you express this dullness in your reasoning, saying, "Not even a handful of earth can be found—how will the dead arise?" {10:5} Will you say that the seed you sowed won't grow? Even the seed you sowed will grow. {10:6} Likewise, the souls that JAH has sown will quickly rise, for He created man in His Truth, bringing from non-existence to existence—He will awaken them swiftly by His Word that saves; He will not delay in His awakening. {10:7} And as He has returned Him from living to the grave in death, is it not possible for Him to return from death to Life again? {10:8} Salvation and upliftment are possible for JAH.

{11:1} The fortress of Armon has perished, and it has been destroyed; as JAH brought hardship upon them due to their evil and the work of their hands—those who worship idols in Edom and Zebulun will be brought low at that time, as JAH approaches—who will convict those who worked in their infancy and did not stop until they grew old—because of their idols and their evil; Sidon and Tyre will weep. {11:2} Because they sinned and engaged in seductive fornication and worshiped idols—because of this, JAH will take revenge and destroy them, for they did not live according to their Creator JAH's Command, and the children of Judah will be wretched. {11:3} She was firm in killing prophets and in Irie Ites; yet as she did not live according to the Nine Laws and Worship—when the dead arise, the sins of Jerusalem will be revealed. {11:4} At that time, JAH will examine her in His Nature of Wisdom; He will take revenge and destroy her for all the sins she committed in her early years—she did not stop sinning from her days of beauty until she grew old. {11:5} She entered the grave and became dust, like her ancestors who lived according to their sins—and at the time of Resurrection, He will take revenge and destroy those who broke JAH's LAW. {11:6} It will be judged upon them, for Moses has spoken against them, saying, "Their LAW is lodging; their reasoning became the law of Sodom." {11:7} And their kindred are the kindred of Gomorrah, and their laws are what destroy, and their works are evil. {11:8} Their laws are like the poison of snakes that destroys, and the poison of vipers that brings destruction from alongside that.

{12:1} O children of Jerusalem, your sins are like the sins of Gomorrah and Sodom—O children of Jerusalem, this is your tribulation that was foretold by a prophet. {12:2} And your tribulation is like the tribulation of Gomorrah and Sodom, with laws rooted in adultery and arrogance. {12:3} Aside from adultery and arrogance, there was no rain of pardon and humility, as their reasoning became fertile with money, apart from spilling human blood, robbing, and forgetting their Creator, JAH. {12:4} They did not know their Creator, JAH, apart from their evil deeds and their idols, and they were proud in their works, lusting after males and livestock. {12:5} Their reasoning has been blinded so that they cannot see the secrets, and their ears have become deaf so that they cannot hear or do what JAH loves; they did not know JAH in their works, and their reasoning resembles the laws of Sodom. Their kindred are like the grapes of Gomorrah, bearing sweet fruit. {12:6} And if they examine their works, they are like poison that kills, for they are rooted in a curse since the day they were created, and their foundation has been in a time of destruction. {12:7} As their laws have taken root in sinful works, so their bodies have become firm in the burning works of Satan to build sin—there is no good work in their laws or reasoning. {12:8} And when he is shamed and baptized (by one who is led), it is for chastisement and destruction; he will establish those who drank and their reasoning, and he will make those who destroy me into disgusting beings who have distanced themselves from JAH. {12:9} For they have lived firmly in their evil works, and he will make them dwell in hell, consuming what was sacrificed to idols, moving toward the mountains and the trees. {12:10} And she worships the idols that the people in her area worship—she sacrifices her daughters and sons to demons who do not know good works, separating from evil. {12:11} And they shed innocent blood; they gush and spill the grapes of Sodom for the idols. {12:12} And she glorifies and worships Dagon, the idol of the Philistines, sacrificing from her flocks and fattened cows, seeking to please the laziness of demons that they taught her to sacrifice; in their gushing and spilling of grapes, she aims to fulfill their wishes. {12:13} She sacrifices to him to be pleased in the laziness of demons, whom they taught her, forgetting that it is her Creator, JAH, who feeds her at all times, cherishing and raising her from her infancy to her beauty, and again to her old age—up to the day she dies. {12:14} And again, I will take revenge and convict her at the time of Resurrection—since she did not return to my LAW and did not live firmly in my Command, her time in hell will last for eternity. {12:15} If they were true worshipers, let their idols rise with them and descend into hell, and save them at the time I am angry and destroy them, and at the time I distance all the priests of the idols who lust with her. {12:16} Just as she sinned and insulted the Holy Ones and my Temple, I made her wretched because of all this. {12:17} When they said to her, "Check—this is the kindred of JAH, and she is the Temple of the Creator of Israel—the famous King in the country of Jerusalem who was separate from the separated ones—she is the Most High JAH's Name Temple," I made her wretched as she saddened my Name that was called upon her. {12:18} She boasts that she was my servant and that I was her Lord; she winks at me like a criminal—yet she is not one who fears me or does my will as if I were her Lord. {12:19} They became a hindrance to her, misleading her to distance herself from me; yet she is ruled by other idols who do not feed her or clothe her. {12:20} She sacrifices to them and eats the sacrifices; she spills blood for them and gushes and drinks from the grapes for them—she burns incense for them and makes the fragrance of incense for them—her idols command her, and she is commanded by them. {12:21} And again, she sacrifices her daughters and sons for them, and as she offers praises for them because of their love, she is pleased by what she speaks with her tongue and in her works. {12:22} Woe to her on the day of Definite Judgment, and woe to her idols whom she loves and worships; she shall descend with them into hell beneath Sheol—where the worm does not sleep and the fire is not extinguished. {12:23} Woe to you, wretched child of Jerusalem—for you have forsaken me, who created you, and have worshiped different idols. {12:24} And I will bring hardship upon you according to your works—just as you have saddened me, and as you have ignored my Word, and as you have not done good works, I will convict you according to your pretensions. {12:25} For you have saddened my Word, and because you have not lived firmly in my LAW by which you swore with me—that you might keep my LAW, and that I might dwell with you in Support and save you from all who fight against you—and also that you might keep the Order that I commanded you—I will ignore you and will not quickly save you from tribulation. {12:26} You did not keep all this, and I have ignored you—since I created you, and you did not keep my Command or my Word—I will convict you at the time of Judgment, though I honored you that you might be my kin. {12:27} Just as Sodom and Gomorrah were separated from me, you were separated from me. {12:28} And I judged and destroyed them; just as Sodom and Gomorrah were separated from me, you are separated from me—and now, just as I was vexed and destroyed them, I am vexed and destroyed you—since you are of the kindred of Sodom and Gomorrah whom I destroyed. I have destroyed you—as those whom I created have saddened me by going after a youthful wife and lusting without LAW—with animals and males, just as they came with daughters—I have wiped their names from this world so that they do not live in my holy ways. {12:29} There is no fear of JAH in their faces, from infancy to old age—they assist in all their evil works—yet He does not vex each one that they might cease their evil works; they are full of sin and iniquity. {12:30} All evil works—robbery, arrogance, and greed—are firmly rooted in their reasoning. {12:31} And because of this, JAH has ignored them and destroyed their nations—there they will burn in fire until their roots perish; they have totally perished for eternity—yet He did not allow even one of them to remain. {12:32} Since they have been firm in sin, they shall wait in destruction forever until the Day of Advent when Definite Judgment is rendered—because they have saddened me with their evil works—and I will not pardon them nor forgive them. {12:33} And I have ignored them—for you will not find an excuse when I am vexed and seize you because all your works were robbery and sin—adultery, greed, and lying—all error works and obstacles that I do not love—and you, wretched child of Jerusalem, on the day of Judgment, you will be seized in Judgment like them. {12:34} I created you for honor, but you have debased yourself; I called you my treasure, but you became for another. {12:35} I betrothed you for honor, but you became for demons—and I will take revenge and destroy you like your evil works. {12:36} Because you did not heed all my Word—and because you did not keep the Command I commanded you when I loved you—I will multiply and bring firm vengeance upon you—for I am JAH who created you—and I will judge all sinners like you—and on the day of Judgment, I will bring hardship upon them like their evil works. {12:37} As you did not keep my Word—and as you have ignored my Judgment—I will convict you alongside them. {12:38} Woe to you, Gomorrah and Sodom—who have no fear of JAH in your reasoning. {12:39} Likewise, woe to your sister, child of Jerusalem, upon whom it shall be judged together with you in the fire of hell—because you will descend together into hell that was prepared for you—where there are no exits forever—and woe to all sinners who committed your sins. {12:40} Since you did not keep my Command or my Word—you and she who did not keep my Command or my Word shall descend into Sheol together on the day when Judgment is pronounced. {12:41} But the righteous who kept my Command and my Word shall eat the wealth that sinners accumulated—and as JAH commanded, the righteous shall share the spoils that evil ones captured—and the righteous shall be fully blessed. {12:42} But wrongdoers and sinners shall weep—and they shall be sad because of all their sins that they wrongfully committed, having departed from my Command. {12:43} He who keeps my Word and lives firmly in my Command—he is the one who finds my blessing and is honored alongside me. {12:44} All who keep my Word and live firmly in my Command shall eat the abundance found on earth—and shall live, having entered into the Garden where kind kings who have righteous reasoning enter.

{13:1} Woe to those who will be wretched and perish under my wrath when I seize them—woe to Theeros, Seedona, and all the regions of Yihuda who have made themselves arrogant today. {13:2} The Conquering JAH has spoken—He has said that from them will be born the children of the devil, the False Messiah, who is an enemy of the truth—who strengthens his arrogant reasoning—who boasts and does not know his Creator. Woe to them, and JAH, who rules all, has said—I have made him as a pattern for my anger so that my power might be revealed in him. {13:3} And this Qifirnahom, Semarya, Geleela, Demasqo, Sorya, 'Akeya, Qophros, and all the regions of Yordanos are kindreds who have hardened their hearts—who live firmly in their sins—whom the shadow of death and darkness has covered—because the devil has blinded their reasoning with sin—and they are commanded by that arrogant devil—and they did not turn back to fear JAH. {13:4} At that time, woe to those who are commanded by demons and who sacrifice in their names—having denied JAH, who created them—they resemble mindless animals—for the False Messiah, who has forgotten JAH's law and is a child of the devil, will set up his image in all places (for he has said, "I am a god")—and he will be content in his reasoning, in his works, and in all his robberies, sins, perfidy, and iniquities. {13:5} Because it is counted against JAH that he works this—the era is known for their sins. {13:6} The sun will darken, and the moon will turn to blood—and the stars will be shaken from heaven—all of creation will witness the miracles that JAH will bring in the Fulfillment Era that He might cause the Earth to pass away—and that He might remove all who live in the sins of those who dwell within it. {13:7} As JAH has been proud of the creation He made—as He has quickly made all He loves in one moment—the Lord of death will destroy the small enemy devil. {13:8} For JAH, who rules all, has said—I will judge and destroy—but after the Advent, the devil will have no authority. {13:9} And on the day when he is seized by my anger, he will descend to Gehannem—for which he has applied and where great tribulation lies—as he will take all who are with him toward chastisement, destruction, and perfidy—because I am the one who sends forth from Gehannem and who introduces into Gehannem—he will descend to Gehannem. {13:10} As He gives strength and power to the weak—and again as He gives weakness to the powerful and strong—let not the powerful boast in their strength. {13:11} As He is a Ruler—and as He judges and saves the oppressed from the hands of those who wrong them—He will return the grievances of the widows and the children whose fathers and mothers have died. {13:12} Woe to you who boast and strengthen your reasoning—for whom it seems that I will neither rule nor judge nor destroy you—for in your boasting and arrogance you have said, "I will stretch my throne among the stars and heaven—and I will be like JAH, who is lofty." {13:13} And as He spoke, saying—how the devil fell from heaven—he who shone like a morning star created before all—woe to you. {13:14} And you dared to speak this in your arrogance—and you did not think of JAH, who completely created you by His authority—why did you boast yourself, believing you would descend to Gehannem in your reasoning? {13:15} You were cast down, separated from all angels like you—for they praised their Creator with humbled reasoning because they knew who created them from fire and wind—and they did not depart from His command—and they kept their reasoning from perfidy lest they completely depart from His command. {13:16} But you committed perfidy in your arrogant reasoning—you became a wretched being, separated from your companions—for you cherished all sin and iniquity—robbery and perfidy—whereby those who forgot JAH's law and sinners like you firmly live—those from your kindred who commit crimes like you—and who are ruled by your commands and your reasoning, teaching sin. {13:17} Woe to you—for the demons you misled in your malice, and you will descend to Gehannem together. {13:18} O you children of JAH who have erred by that misleading criminal devil—woe to you—for as you have erred like him through the money that he taught you and that his hosts taught you—you will descend to Gehannem together—where there are no exits forever. {13:19} And formerly, when JAH's servant Moses was there—you saddened JAH by the water where arguments were made and on Korieb—and by Amalek and on Mount Sinai. {13:20} Moreover, at the time you sent scouts to Canaan—when they told you, saying, "The path is far—and their ramparts and fortresses reach up to heaven and strong warriors live there"—you were vexed that you might return toward Egypt, where you labored under hard work—and you saddened JAH's word. {13:21} You did not think of JAH, who strengthened you from tribulation—and who did great miracles in Egypt—and who led you by His angel's authority. He would cover you in a cloud by day lest the sun burn you, and He would shine a column of fire for you by night lest your feet stumble in darkness. {13:22} And at the time when the army and Pharaoh frightened you—you cried out to Moses—and Moses cried out to JAH—and He lodged in His angel and kept you safe from meeting Pharaoh. {13:23} But He led them to Eritra in tribulation—JAH led only Israel—for He said—there were no other idols with them—but He buried their enemies in the sea at once—and He did not preserve any who fled from them. {13:24} And He made Israel cross through the sea on foot—there was no tribulation that arose from the Egyptians against them—He delivered them to Mount Sinai—and there He fed them manna for forty years. {13:25} Yet the children of Israel saddened JAH every time—He did all these good things for them, and they neglected to worship JAH. {13:26} They placed evil in their reasoning, beginning from their childhood up to their old age—for JAH's mouth has spoken thus in the scroll where the fathers' births were written—as He has spoken, saying—"The children of Adam's reasoning are ashes—and all their works are toward robbery, and they run toward evil—there is none among them who loves straight works—except for gathering a person's money through violence and swearing lies and wronging companions and robbing and stealing—they placed evil in their reasoning. {13:27} And all go toward evil works in the era when they live in life—the children of Israel who demolished JAH's law have totally saddened JAH from antiquity up to the fulfillment era.

{14:1} And at the time JAH destroyed the children of Cain—kindreds who preceded—in the waters of destruction because of their sins—He baptized the Earth in the waters of destruction—and cleansed it from all the sins of the children of Cain. {14:2} As He said—I was saddened because I created man—He destroyed all wrongdoers—He did not preserve apart from eight persons—He destroyed all—after this, He multiplied them, and they filled the Earth—they shared their father Adam's inheritance. {14:3} But Noah swore an oath with JAH—he swore an oath with JAH that He would not again destroy the Earth in the waters of destruction—and that Noah's children would not eat what was dead nor what lay dead—and that they would not worship different idols apart from JAH, who created them—and that He might be a loving Father to them—and lest He destroy them all at once in their vain sins—and lest He withhold from them the first and the spring rains—and that He might provide food for livestock and people at all times—that He might give them the grass and the grain, fruit, and plants—and that they might do good works in all that JAH loves. {14:4} And after He gave them this order—the children of Israel saddened JAH with their sins—they did not live firmly in His law like their fathers Abraham, Isaac, and Jacob, who did not demolish their Creator JAH's law. {14:5} From the least to the greatest—those children of Israel who did not keep JAH's law are crooked in their works. {14:6} And whether they are priests or chiefs or scribes—everyone demolishes JAH's law. {14:7} They do not live firmly in JAH's order and His law that Moses commanded them in the Repeating Law, saying—"Love your Creator JAH with all your body and all your reasoning." {14:8} They do not adhere to JAH's order and His law that Moses commanded them in the book where the law was written, saying—"Love your neighbor as yourself—and do not worship other idols—and do not go after a young wife—do not kill a soul—do not steal. {14:9} And do not bear false witness—and whether it is his donkey or his ox—do not covet your neighbor's money or all that your brother owns." {14:10} However, after He commanded them all this—the children of Israel, who were evil, returned to treachery and sin—robbery and iniquity—toward a young wife and toward lies and stealing and worshipping idols. {14:11} The children of Israel saddened JAH on Korieb by working a calf that grazed on grass—they bowed, saying—"Look—these are our creators who sent us forth from Egypt." {14:12} And they were content in their works—if they ate and drank and sat—they arose to sing. {14:13} As JAH had told him, saying—"Your kindreds whom you sent forth from Egypt, where they were ruled—have turned away from the law and wronged—and they worked an image of a calf and bowed to the idol—because Moses became angry and descended from Sinai mountain. {14:14} While Moses was angry with his kindreds—he descended with his companion Joshua—and when Joshua heard, he said—"Look—I hear the voice of warriors in the camp of Israel." {14:15} And Moses told Joshua—"It is when Israel is playing after drinking unboiled wine—yet as for the voice of warriors—it is not so"—and he descended and broke their images and completely crushed them until they were like dust—he mixed them in the water that the children of Israel drank beside the mountain. {14:16} And after this, he commanded the priests to slay one another because of the sin they committed before JAH. {14:17} They knew that defying JAH surpasses killing them and killing their fathers—and they did as he commanded them. {14:18} And Moses told them—"Because you have saddened JAH, who fed you and cherished you and who sent you forth from a house of slavery and who bequeathed to you the inheritance that He swore to your fathers that He might give to you and your children after you—because of this thing, you have made JAH angry." {14:19} For you have turned toward sin and evil—and you did not stop saddening JAH there. {14:20} You are not like your fathers, Isaac and Abraham and Jacob, who made JAH happy with their good works, so that He might give them what is on Earth and what He prepared for those who love Him in heaven—from their infancy up to their youth and until their old age—you are not like Abraham, Isaac, and Jacob, who made Him happy with their works, so that He might give them a land of inheritance where righteous people are found in this world—and a garden that brings joy—prepared for good people in the world to come—which He prepared for Abraham, Isaac, and Jacob, who made JAH happy when they were alive and who loved Him—whom no eye has seen nor ear has heard and who is not conceived in reasoning. {14:21} And those children who denied JAH and were evil and who lived firmly in their reasoning—they did not hear JAH's command—He who fed them and cherished them and kept them from their infancy. {14:22} They did not think of JAH—who sent them forth from Egypt and saved them from hard labor and a firm rulership. {14:23} But they completely saddened Him—and He would arouse people against them in their area—and they would arise against them in enmity and also oppress them like those they loved.

{15:1} At that time, the people of Midyan rose against Israel in enmity, and they gathered their armies to fight them. Their king, whose name was Akrandis, quickly assembled many troops from Cilicia, Syria, and Damascus. {15:2} He camped beyond the Jordan River and sent messengers saying, "If you want to keep your wealth, pay taxes to me, the King of Israel. But if you refuse, I will punish you, seize your livestock, take your horses, and capture your children." {15:3} He continued, "I will take you to a foreign land you do not know, where I will make you water carriers and wood gatherers." {15:4} He mocked them, saying, "Do not boast by saying, 'We are God's people, and no one can harm us.' Is it not God who sent me to destroy you and plunder your wealth? Am I not the one He chose to gather all your kindred?" {15:5} "Did the other nations' idols save them when I destroyed them? I captured their horses, killed their men, and took their children. {15:6} And unless you pay the taxes I demand, I will destroy you just like them." He then crossed the Jordan to seize their livestock, wealth, and wives. {15:7} The children of Israel wept bitterly to God and cried out, but there was no one to help them. {15:8} Because of this, God strengthened the three brothers, whose names were Yihuda, Mebikyas, and Meqabees. They were handsome and strong warriors. {15:9} The children of Israel wept when they heard this news, and they were deeply saddened. Everyone cried out—orphans, widows, leaders, priests, and all the people of Israel, both daughters and sons, young and old—all mourned, sprinkling ashes on their heads. Their nobles wore sackcloth. {15:10} But the three brothers, who were handsome and brave, made a decision to save their people. They counseled among themselves, saying, "Let us offer our bodies to death for the sake of these people." {15:11} Encouraging each other by saying, "Take courage," they girded their swords around their waists, took spears in their hands, and prepared to confront the enemy. {15:12} They approached the enemy camp, and Mebikyus struck down the king, who was sitting at a dinner table. He cut off his head in one blow while the king was still eating. Meqabyus and Yihuda attacked the king's army on both sides with their swords, killing them. {15:13} After the king was slain, the brothers pierced the hearts of his soldiers, causing them to flee. Their bows were broken, and they were utterly defeated. {15:14} The three brothers, who were attractive and brave, were saved from death, and no harm came to them. As a result of God's judgment, the enemies turned on each other, and many were killed. {15:15} The enemy fled across the Jordan, abandoning all their wealth, which remained behind. When the children of Israel saw that their enemies had fled, they entered the camp and took the spoils and money for themselves. {15:16} God saved Israel through the hands of the three brothers and Mebikyas. {15:17} The children of Israel rested for a few days and praised God. {15:18} But soon after, they returned to their sinful ways. The children of Israel neglected their worship of God as they should have. {15:19} God would again punish them with enemies who did not know them, who would gather their crops, destroy their vineyards, plunder their flocks, and slaughter their livestock for food. {15:20} These enemies would capture their wives and children because the Israelites had continually provoked God. As a nation that rejected God's Law, they would suffer terribly, with their children being slaughtered before them, and they would be powerless to save them.

{16:1} The peoples responsible for these acts included those from Tyre, Sidon, and others living beyond the Jordan River and along the coast—Canaanites, the people of Edom, the Jebusites, the Kenites, and the Amalekites. {16:2} All these people lived firmly established in their tribes, countries, and regions, speaking their own languages and doing their own work, just as God had established them. {16:3} Among them were those who knew God and whose works were righteous. {16:4} But there were also those who did evil and did not know God, who sinned and were ruled by the Assyrian king Shalmaneser. {16:5} As Shalmaneser plundered the wealth of Damascus and shared the spoils of Samaria before the Egyptian king, he ruled over them by God's hand. {16:6} The people of the regions of Gilead, Persia, Media, Cappadocia, and Cilicia—those in the Western mountains, the Gilead fortress, and Pethros, which is part of Judah's land—{16:7} were all ruled by him. These people did not know God nor keep His commands, and their minds were hardened against Him. {16:8} God would repay them for their evil deeds and the work of their hands. {16:9} The people of Gilead and Caesarea, along with the Amalekites, joined forces to destroy the land of God, which was filled with truth and where the Creator of Israel was praised. God, who is most glorified and victorious, and who is served by countless angels standing before Him in fear and trembling in their cherubic chariots, would repay these enemies for their evil deeds and the work of their hands.

{17:1} The people of Amalek and Edom did not worship God, even though He is the ruler of heaven and earth. They were wicked criminals who did not live according to truth and did not fear destroying God's dwelling place, the Temple. {17:2} They had no fear of God and engaged in bloodshed, adultery, and the consumption of food sacrificed to idols or that which was unclean. They were despised sinners. {17:3} They had no virtue or religion, hating righteous works and not knowing God or His love. Instead, they focused on robbing others, committing sin, and engaging in every kind of wickedness. They indulged in music and revelry, just as their father, the devil, taught them. {17:4} The devil, with his army of demons, ruled over them, teaching them all forms of evil, including robbery, sin, theft, lies, and greed. He instructed them to steal money, eat unclean food, and commit adultery. {17:5} The devil taught them all these things to distance them from God's Law, which governs the world. {17:6} But God's work is one of innocence, humility, love for one's neighbor, and living in harmony with all people. {17:7} Do not be hypocritical in showing favoritism, nor be evildoers, thieves, or adulterers. Do not act violently against your neighbor, and do not deceive or harm them for your own gain. {17:8} These people mock and provoke others toward evil, leading them astray so that they may suffer eternal judgment.

{18:1} Consider that you will go into death before JAH, in whose hand all are, and you will stand before Him so that He might convict you of all the sins you committed. {18:2} Just like the arrogant and evil ones—the powerful children who are not strengthened beyond their stature—did before, because they were focused on their status, power, and authority, they did not acknowledge JAH before them and did not realize that He was their creator who brought them from non-existence to life. {18:3} When their fathers were like "angels" praised on Mount Hola with angels, at that time they were misled, and they descended to this world where definitive judgment will occur forever. {18:4} In antiquity, JAH created human flesh for them so that it might mislead them due to their arrogant reasoning, and to test them as if they kept His law and commandments—taking wives from the children of Cain. {18:5} But they did not keep His law, so He cast them into the fire of Gehenna with their father Deeyablos; for JAH was angry with the offspring of Seth, who sinned like others, and their lifespans diminished because of their sins. {18:6} They led the children of Adam into sin with them; He brought them down to Sheol (the underworld) where they shall receive judgment. {18:7} As the people of Seth were divided because the children of Seth erred by the children of Cain, when lifespans were nine hundred in antiquity, they returned to living only a hundred twenty years. {18:8} And since they are flesh and blood, JAH said, "My Spirit of Support will not remain with them." {18:9} Because of this, our generations were divided—due to our sins and iniquities, we were separated from our fathers who came before us, and when they returned to their infancy, they were dying. {18:10} But our fathers flourished because they kept His law and did not anger JAH. {18:11} Our fathers flourished because they cared for their daughters to teach them, and they disciplined their sons lest they break JAH's law. {18:12} Because they did not break JAH's law with their daughters and sons, they truly flourished.

{19:1} When the children of Cain flourished, they created drums, harps, singing, and violins, and they made songs and games. {19:2} Attractive and beautiful children were born to Cain from the wife of the good man Abel, whom he killed because she was beautiful; after killing his brother, he took her as his own. {19:3} Separating from his father, he seized her and went to the region of Qiefaz toward the West, and those attractive children were as appealing as their mother. {19:4} Because the children of Seth descended to the children of Cain, upon seeing them, they did not hesitate at all—they took the daughters they chose for themselves. {19:5} They led us into error together with them because of their mistakes, which caused JAH to be angry with us and with them. {19:6} And Deeyablos, having deceived, said, "You will become creators like your creator, JAH," and he led our mother Eve and our father Adam into his error. {19:7} But it seemed true to them in their dullness; they broke JAH's law, He who created them, bringing them from non-existence to life so they might bow down and praise His glorious name. {19:8} But He—their creator—brought down Adam and Eve, who made gods for themselves, and He humbled those who were arrogant. {19:9} Like David said, "Adam perished because of the sinner Deeyablos's arrogance"; he condemned them—for our father Adam was convicted by Deeyablos's arrogance through JAH's true judgment. {19:10} The children of Seth, who erred because of the children of Cain, led us into their sin; therefore, our generation that JAH gave us was less than our fathers' generations. {19:11} But they did good works—strengthening their reasoning in JAH—they taught their daughters and sons to prevent them from departing from the law that they had been taught, and there was no evil enemy that approached them. {19:12} But if they did good works, it would not benefit them if they did not instruct or teach their children. {19:13} Like David said, "They did not hide from their children to tell another child, teaching JAH's praise and the wondrous miracles He performed and His power"; it would not benefit them if they did not teach their children so they might learn and know and do His will, and that they might tell them about JAH's trust and keep His law like their fathers, who made JAH pleased with their beautiful works. {19:14} Those who instructed their children from their fathers in their infancy did not break His commandments, just as their fathers learned to worship JAH and the Nine Laws from their fathers. {19:15} Their children learned from their fathers to do good works and present praise to their creator; for they kept His law and loved Him. {19:16} He shall hear them in their prayers and will not ignore their pleas, for He is a forgiver. {19:17} Having multiplied His wrath, He shall return it to them, but He would not destroy everything in His punishment.

{20:1} My brothers, consider—not to forget what they told you before—that JAH keeps the true works of those who do good. {20:2} He multiplies their children in this world, and their names will endure for good until eternity; their children will not be troubled for grain in this world. {20:3} He shall contend for them because of them, and He will not cast them into the hands of their enemies; He shall save them from the hands of those who hate them. {20:4} And for those who love His name, He shall be their helper in times of tribulation; He shall protect them and pardon all their sins.

{21:1} David believed in JAH, and because he believed in Him, JAH saved him, being a refuge from King Saul's hand. {21:2} As he believed in Him and kept His law during the time when his son Absalom rose up against him, and when the Philistines arose, and during the times when the Edomites and Amalekites rose up, and when one of the four giants rose up, JAH saved David from all this trouble that his enemies brought upon him. {21:3} Although the enemies prevailed by JAH's will, they were defeated by their hands; yet JAH did not save the wicked kings who did not believe in Him. {21:4} Hezekiah believed in JAH; He saved him from the hand of Sennacherib, who was arrogant. {21:5} But his son Manasseh was defeated by his enemies because he did not trust in JAH; he did not revere JAH, who greatly honored and praised him. They bound him and took him to their land, but those enemies who defeated Manasseh were not like him. {21:6} At that time, JAH denied him the kingdom He had given him, because he did not perform good works before his creator, JAH, so that he might prosper and that JAH might contend with his enemies for him, granting him strength and support. {21:7} For it is better to believe in JAH than in many armies, than to trust in horses, bows, and shields. {21:8} Trusting in JAH surpasses all; a person who believes in Him will be strengthened and honored, and truly exalted. {21:9} JAH does not show favoritism; those who do not believe in Him—who trust in their wealth—have turned away from the grace and honor He bestowed upon them. {21:10} He will protect those who believe in Him, but He will make the ignorant ones who call Him ignorant suffer; and since they did not discipline their thoughts to follow JAH nor keep His law, He will not quickly help them in their time of trouble or when their enemies confront them. {21:11} But for a person who is disciplined in worshiping JAH and keeping His law, He shall be a refuge in their time of trouble. {21:12} By destroying his enemies, and by plundering their livestock, and by capturing their lands, and by sending rain for fruitful seasons, {21:13} and by sending both the early and late rains, and making the grass lush, and providing the right rain at the right time so that your people under your authority might be blessed, He shall make them prosperous. {21:14} He shall make them prosperous so that they might consume the wealth of their enemies, so they might feast on the spoils they took from their enemies, so they might enjoy their meals together, and so they might take their enemies' children captive. {21:15} JAH will do all this for those He loves, but He will cause those who hate Him to be looted by their enemies. {21:16} He shall bind their feet and hands and cast them into the hands of their enemies, and He shall make them a source of ridicule for their foes; and as they have become bloodshedder who violate JAH's law, He will not allow them to prosper in their offspring. {21:17} They will not stand firm in the time of judgment, and to bring hardship upon those who commit sins, He will also bring difficulties to those who do evil works. {21:18} But it has been commanded by JAH to reward those who do good works, that He might keep them in His favor. {21:19} For He is powerful over all creation He has made, so that He might do good works and grant them eternal well-being, and that they might praise JAH who created them, and He commanded that they keep His law—apart from humanity, none of the creatures He made have strayed from His commandments. {21:20} Just as JAH commanded all who live steadfast in each of their works, they all know and are kept in His law. {21:21} But humanity is emboldened by JAH, who crowned all of creation with their inventions, over animals, beasts, and birds of heaven. {21:22} Whatever is in the sea or on land, JAH gave all creation to their father Adam; JAH gave it to them so they might do what they loved, and that they might eat like the grain that grows on Earth, and that they might rule and manage them, whether beasts or animals, which might be commanded by man—and He appointed them over all His creation so that those who reign might be accountable to JAH who granted them honor and that they might serve Him. {21:23} But if they depart from His law, He will separate them from the lordship He gave them; as He is the ruler of Earth and Heaven, He will give it to those who do His will. {21:24} He appoints whom He loves to lead; but He dismisses whom He loves to dismiss—He kills, He saves, He punishes in trouble, He forgives. {21:25} There is no other creator like Him; He is the ruler over all the creation He has made—there is no other besides Him, the creator, in heaven above or on earth beneath; there is none who shall criticize Him. {21:26} He appoints, He dismisses, He kills, He saves, He punishes in trouble, He forgives, He impoverishes, He honors. {21:27} He hears those who plead with Him; He accepts the plea of those who act according to Him with a pure heart; and He hears them in their prayers, and He grants them what they ask for in all that they petition Him. {21:28} And He makes the great and the small to be governed by them; all of this is their wealth on hills and mountains and at the roots of trees, and in caves and wells of the earth, and among all their relatives on both dry land and at sea. {21:29} And for those who do according to their creator, all this is their wealth, and He will not trouble them with their abundance; He shall grant them the reward of their praise. {21:30} And He shall give them the honor He has prepared in heaven for their fathers Isaac, Abraham, and Jacob; He shall grant them what He prepared for Hezekiah, David, and Samuel, who did not stray from His law & His commandments. {21:31} So that they might rejoice in His lordship, He shall give to those who served Him from antiquity the honor He prepared for their fathers Isaac, Abraham & Jacob—for whom He swore to grant them an inheritance.

{22:1} Please—consider the names of those who do good works—and do not forget their deeds. {22:2} Align your name to be called like theirs, so that you might rejoice with them in the Kingdom of Heaven, which is the place of light that He prepared for the noble and kings who did JAH's will and were kind-hearted. {22:3} And again—know and be convinced of the names of the wicked nobles and kings—that He shall convict and condemn them along with mankind after their death. {22:4} For they did not align their works while they saw and heard, and they knew and were convinced that unless they did JAH's will, He shall judge them in the Kingdom of Heaven more harshly than criminals and those who forgot JAH's law. {22:5} Be kind, innocent, honest; yet do not follow the paths of those who forgot JAH's law—upon whom JAH is angry because of their wicked works. {22:6} Judge fairly and protect the child whose parents are dead, and the widow from the hands of sinners who rob them. {22:7} Be a guardian like a father to the child whose parents are dead, so that you might protect him from the wealthy ones who rob him—stand for him and be concerned for the time when the child whose parents are dead sheds tears before you—lest you be alarmed in a sea of fire where the unrepentant sinners are punished. {22:8} And direct your feet toward the path of love and unity—as JAH's eyes watch over His friends—and as His ears hear their pleas—seek love and follow her. {22:9} But JAH's face of wrath is against those who do wicked works—so that He might destroy their names from this world—and He will not preserve a person who is near ramparts or mountains. {22:10} As I am JAH, who is jealous for My divinity—as I am a creator who takes revenge and destroys those who hate Me and do not keep My word—I will not turn My face of support until I destroy the person who does not keep My word. {22:11} And I will honor those who honor Me and keep My word.

{23:1} Do not be firm in the ways of Cain, who killed his brother for following him innocently—he thought his brother loved him. {23:2} And he killed his brother out of envy over a woman; people who create envy, iniquity, and betrayal among their companions are like him. {23:3} But Abel was innocent like a sheep, and his blood was like the clean blood of the sheep they sacrificed to JAH for a righteous reason—they followed Cain's path, not Abel's. {23:4} For all the innocent people are those whom JAH loves—like the kind man Abel—they have been innocent like Abel, but those who firmly follow Abel's example love JAH. {23:5} However, JAH neglects the wicked, and their definitive judgment will be imposed upon their bodies; it is written in the record of their thoughts, and when judgment is passed, it will be read before humanity, angels, and all of creation. {23:6} At that time, the wrongdoers and those who refuse to do JAH's will shall be ashamed. {23:7} And an alarming word will be given to them, saying—cast them into hell where there is no escape until eternity.

{24:1} But at the time Gideon trusted JAH, he defeated the armies of the uncircumcised peoples, which were many, with an army of only a few tens of thousands, numbering like locusts. {24:2} There is no creator apart from Me—O nobles and kings—do not believe in the various idols. {24:3} As I am your creator, JAH, who brought you forth from your mothers' wombs, nurtured you, fed you, and clothed you—why do you pretend? Why do you worship other idols besides Me? {24:4} I did all this for you—what have you given Me? It is that you might live according to My law, order, and commands, and that I might grant you well-being in your bodies—yet what do I desire from you? {24:5} JAH, who rules all, says this—He said: Save yourselves from worshiping idols, practicing sorcery, and promoting despair. {24:6} For JAH's punishment will come upon those who do this, and upon those who hear them and follow them, and are their friends, and who firmly adhere to their commands—save yourselves from worshiping idols. {24:7} For the people who do not know you and are not kind to you will rise against you—unless you, who feared, did JAH's will—they will consume the wealth you earned, just as His servants the prophets spoke, and just as Enoch and Asaph spoke—unless you did JAH's will, they will consume the wealth you earned. {24:8} Evil people will come having changed their appearance; they say there are no other laws besides eating, drinking, and adorning themselves with silver and gold, while living firmly in sin, all the works JAH does not love. {24:9} But they are prepared to indulge in food and drink—after being roused from their slumber, from morning until evening, they go towards evil works; there is misery and tribulation in their path—but their feet do not tread the path of love. {24:10} They do not know love and unity in their works—there is no fear of JAH in their faces; they are crooked, evil ones without religion or virtue—they are greedy ones who eat and drink alone—they are drunkards, and their sins are without law and without measure—they are those who go towards seduction, shedding blood, theft, treachery, and violently robbing those who have nothing. {24:11} And they criticize without love and without law—because they do not fear JAH, who created them; there is no fear in their faces. {24:12} They do not feel shame in the face of anyone they see; they do not respect a gray-haired or elderly face—when they heard someone say, 'There is wealth in this world,' they make it their own wealth even before they see it with their eyes—because there is no fear of JAH in their faces—and when they see it with their eyes, it seems to them that they have consumed it. {24:13} And the nobles eat trust funds; they consume as they are pessimists, and there is nothing straightforward in their speech—they do not repeat in the evening what they said in the morning. {24:14} For they ignore the cries of the suffering and the poor, and their kings rush towards evil—those who disturb a person, having saved refugees from the hands of the wealthy who rob them. {24:15} Let them save the wronged and the refugees, yet let not the kings be those who begrudge justice because of their possessions. {24:16} But they are those who extract tribute; they are those who rob a person's wealth—they are criminals, and as their works are evil, they do not show kindness when they consume the newborn calf with its mother, or a bird with its eggs—they make all they see and hear into their own wealth. {24:17} They love to gather for themselves, yet they do not care for the sick and the poor—they violently rob the money of those who have nothing—and they collect everything they find to be fattened and pleased in it. {24:18} For they shall perish quickly, like a scarab emerging from its pit, whose track is not found, and that does not return to its home—because they did not do good works during their lives—woe to their bodies when JAH is angry and seizes them. {24:19} At the time JAH neglects them, they will perish at once, as if they were under one punishment—He endured with them, meaning they would return to repentance—yet He does not quickly destroy them—and they shall perish at the time when they are to perish. {24:20} But if they do not return to repentance, He will quickly destroy them like those who came before them—who did not keep JAH's law as is due. {24:21} They are those who eat a person's flesh and drink a person's blood—as they prepare and commit violence to sin—there is no fear of JAH in their faces at any time—and after they arise from their beds, they do not rest from committing sin. {24:22} And their works are drink and food—leading to destruction and sin—that they might destroy many bodies in this world.

{25:1} Since their actions are crooked, and all who are firmly entrenched in the ways of Satan mislead others—JAH, who rules all, says: Woe to your bodies when I am angry and seize them. {25:2} They do not know JAH's work—they have turned it away from themselves and have neglected My law. {25:3} And later, in the time of fulfillment, I will bring hardship upon them according to their evil deeds—as their sins were recorded beside Me—I will take revenge and destroy them on the day when judgment is passed. {25:4} As I am JAH, from horizon to horizon, and as all creation has been seized by My authority—none escape My authority in heaven or on earth, in the depths or in the sea. {25:5} I command the snake beneath the earth, the fish in the sea, the birds in the heavens, and the wild donkey in the wilderness—for it is My creation from horizon to horizon. {25:6} As I am the one who performs wondrous works and miracles before Me—none escape My authority on earth or in heaven; no one can say to Me, 'Where are You going? What are You doing?' {25:7} I command the chief angels and hosts—all nations whose names are called are My creation—and the beasts in the wilderness, the birds in heaven, and livestock are all My creation. {25:8} It arises from the winds of the east and solidifies in drought in the land of Mesopotamia—later, in the time of fulfillment, the Eritrean sea shall perish when it hears of JAH, who will come to it, being feared and renowned. {25:9} For He rules the dead and the living—and it shall perish when heard from Saba, Noba, Hindekie, and the regions of Ethiopia and all those areas. {25:10} And He observes all from a high authority and innocence—His authority surpasses all authority, and He keeps congregations under His authority. {25:11} And His authority is firmer than all authorities, and His kingdom surpasses all kingdoms—for His authority rules all the world; He is capable of everything, and nothing fails Him. {25:12} He governs all the clouds in heaven, grows grass for livestock on earth, and provides fruit for the buds. {25:13} He feeds all kinds according to His love—He nourishes all that He created with each fruit and food—and He feeds ants, locusts beneath the earth, livestock on the land, and beasts; and for a person who prays, He grants their requests—and He does not ignore the plea of the child who has lost both mother and father, nor that of widows. {25:14} As the rebellion of the wicked is like a swirling wind, and the counsel of wrongdoers is like misty urine—He shall accept the pleas of those who cry out to Him at all times, and of the righteous. {25:15} And as their bodies are like flying birds, and their beauty, which is silver and gold, is perishable in this world—examination will benefit those who forget JAH's law, but not their gold, and moths shall consume their clothes. {25:16} Weevils will entirely consume the richness of wheat and barley, and all shall pass like the day that passed yesterday—and like a word that leaves the mouth and does not return—sinners' wealth is also like this, and their 'beautiful lifestyle' is like a passing shadow; sinners' wealth before JAH is like false clothing. {25:17} But if kind people are honored, JAH will not ignore them—for they have been honored when they were kind to the poor, and they heard the cries for justice from the suffering and from a child who lost both parents—JAH will not ignore them—by not neglecting the children of the house, they honor Him while they clothe the naked with the garments JAH gave them to share with the suffering refugee. {25:18} They do not favor the judgment of loyal individuals, nor do they let a hired worker lodge—because JAH's ways are truth and honor, like a sword with two edges—they do not commit injustice in their time or in their measures.

{26:1} But the poor will reflect again on their beds—but if the wealthy do not accept them, they will be like dry wood with no green leaves—and a root will not be fruitful where there is no moisture—and the leaf will not thrive without roots. {26:2} Just as a leaf serves a flower to be an ornament for fruit—unless the leaf is fruitful, it will not bear fruit; just as a person's fulfillment is religion—a person without religion has no virtue. {26:3} If he is steadfast in religion, he works virtue—and JAH is pleased with a person who works truth and righteous deeds. {26:4} And for the person who begs Him, He will grant their requests and reward their words—and He will not wrong the true person because of the good works they have done. {26:5} As JAH is true, and as He loves what is true, He will not justify the sinner without repentance because of the evil works they have done—and since all souls have been seized under His authority, for He is the ruler of heaven and earth—He will not favor the wealthy over the poor at the time of judgment—He will not justify them without repentance.

{27:1} He who created everything brought the world from a state of non-existence to existence—He prepared the hills and mountains, and established the earth upon water—so that the sea would not be disturbed, He marked its boundary with sand—for in His first word, JAH said, "Let there be light." {27:2} Light was created when this world was covered in darkness—JAH created all of creation, prepared this world, and established it by what is just and by what is right—He said, "Let the evening be dark." {27:3} And again JAH said, "Let there be light"—it dawned, and there was light—He lifted the upper waters toward heaven. {27:4} He stretched it out like a tent and supported it with wind—He placed the lower waters in a basin. {27:5} He locked the sea in with sand and established them under His authority to prevent them from drowning—He placed animals and beasts within it—He placed within it Liewatan and Biehiemot, who are great beasts—and He filled it with countless creatures, seen and unseen. {27:6} On the third day, JAH created plants on earth—all roots, woods, and fruits that bear their kinds—and a beautiful tree for them to behold. {27:7} And He created a beautiful tree that was both pleasant to look at and good for food—He created grass and all plants whose seeds are found within them—to be food for birds and livestock and beasts. {27:8} Evening came, and morning followed—on the fourth day, He said, "Let there be lights in the heavens"—JAH created the moon, sun, and stars—He placed them in the heavens to shine on the earth and to provide light by day and by night. {27:9} After this, the moon, sun, and stars alternated between night and day. {27:10} On the fifth day, JAH created all the creatures that live in the water and all the birds that fly in the sky—everything seen and unseen. {27:11} On the sixth day, He created livestock, beasts, and others—and having created and prepared all, He made 'Adam in His image and likeness. {27:12} He gave him dominion over all the animals and beasts He created so that he might rule over them—and again, over all animals, beasts, and fish, including Liewatan and Biehiemot in the sea. {27:13} He gave him all the cattle that roam this world and sheep—the creatures seen and unseen. {27:14} He placed 'Adam, whom He created in His image and likeness, in a garden—so that he might eat, cultivate the plants, and praise JAH there. {27:15} And to prevent him from breaking His command, He said: "The moment you eat from this fig tree, you will surely die." {27:16} He commanded him not to eat from the fig tree that brings death—which leads to knowledge of good and evil—that brings death.

{27:17} Our mother, Hiewan, was deceived by a misleading snake, and she ate from that fig tree and gave it to our father 'Adam. {27:18} And 'Adam, having eaten from that fig tree, brought death upon himself and his children. {27:19} He broke His command and ate from that fig tree that JAH commanded him not to eat from—JAH became angry with our father 'Adam and expelled him from the garden—He gave him the earth that produces thorns and thistles—cursed because he broke His command—so that he might earn his living through toil and labor in the soil. {27:20} And when JAH sent him into this land, 'Adam returned in complete sadness—and having toiled and labored, he began to eat in weariness and struggle.

{28:1} And after his children lived and multiplied, there were some among them who praised and honored JAH and did not break His command. {28:2} There were prophets who spoke of what had been done and what would be done in the future—and from his children came sinners who spoke lies and wronged others—'Adam's firstborn son Qayel became wicked and killed his brother 'Abiel. {28:3} JAH judged Qayel for killing his brother 'Abiel—and JAH became angry with the earth because it drank his blood. {28:4} And JAH asked Qayel, "Where is your brother 'Abiel?"—and Qayel, in his heart full of arrogance, said, "Am I my brother's keeper?" {28:5} 'Abiel was a righteous man, but Qayel became a sinner by killing a good man—his brother 'Abiel. {28:6} Again, a righteous child named Siet was born—'Adam had sixty children—there were both good and evil people among them. {28:7} Among them were righteous individuals, prophets, traitors, and sinners. {28:8} There were blessed people who were righteous—who followed their father 'Adam's teachings from 'Adam to Noah, who was a righteous man who kept JAH's law. {28:9} He passed JAH's law to his children—he told them, "Take care not to break JAH's law"—and that they might teach their children as their father Noah had taught them—and that they might keep JAH's law. {28:10} They lived while teaching their children—people were born after them. {28:11} But Satan lived when he spoke to their fathers—having dwelled in idols that led to graves and that held vows upon them—having deceived those who agreed with him—when they did all that Satan, the teacher of sin, commanded. {28:12} They lived when they worshiped the idols according to his commands—up until a righteous man, 'Abriham, who fulfilled JAH's covenant. {28:13} For he lived firmly in the law separate from his relatives—and JAH swore an oath with him—having dwelled in wind and fire. {28:14} JAH swore to him that He would give him a land of inheritance and that He would give it to his children forever. {28:15} And He swore to Yis'haq like unto him that He would give him his father 'Abriham's inheritance—and He swore to Yaiqob that He would give him his father Yis'haq's inheritance—He swore to him as He did to Yis'haq. {28:16} And He separated their children—who were born after them from Yaiqob—from the twelve tribes of 'Isra'iel—and made them priests and kings—He blessed them, saying, "Be fruitful and multiply greatly." {28:17} And He gave them their father's inheritance—yet while He fed and loved them, they did not cease to grieve JAH in all things. {28:18} And when He destroyed them—at that time they will seek Him in worship—and they will turn from sin and go toward JAH—for He loves them—and JAH shall pardon them. {28:19} For being kind to all He created, He shall pardon them—and it is because of their fathers' works that He loves them—but not because of their own actions. {28:20} And He stretches forth His right hand abundantly to satisfy the hungry body—and He reveals His eye to pardon that He might multiply grain for food. {28:21} He provides food for the young of crows and for beasts that cry out to Him—when they call to Him, He will save the children of 'Isra'iel from the hands of their enemies who oppress them. {28:22} And they will return to sin again and grieve Him—and He will raise up their enemies against them—those who will destroy them and kill them and capture them. {28:23} And again they will cry out to JAH in mourning and sadness—there are times when He sent help and saved them through the hands of prophets. {28:24} And there are times when He saved them by the hands of princes—when they grieved JAH, their enemies oppressed them and captured them. {28:25} And Daweet arose and saved them from the hands of the Philistines; yet again they grieved JAH—and JAH raised up peoples to trouble them. {28:26} And there are times when He saved them by the hand of Yoftahie—and again they forgot JAH, who saved them in times of tribulation. As JAH brought hardship upon them—He will raise up evil enemies who will cause great tribulation and completely capture them. {28:27} And when they were troubled by tribulation, they were seized and again cried out to Him—and He saved them by the hand of Giediewon—and again they grieved JAH by their works. {28:28} And once more, He raised up peoples who caused them tribulation—and they returned and wept and cried out to JAH. {28:29} And again He saved them from peoples by the hand of Sampson—and they rested a little from tribulation. Then they arose to grieve JAH by their former sins. {28:30} And again He raised up other peoples to trouble them—and again they cried and wept to JAH that He might send help to them—and He saved them from peoples by the hands of Bariq and Deebora. {28:31} They lived a little while, worshiping JAH—and again they forgot JAH in their former sins and grieved Him. {28:32} And He raised up other peoples to oppress them—and again He saved them by the hand of Yodeet; and having rested a little while, they arose to grieve JAH by their sins as they had done before. {28:33} And He raised up peoples who ruled over them—and they cried and wept to JAH; for He struck upon his head 'Abiemieliek, who was a warrior who came to fight in the land of Judah. {28:34} And He saved them by the children in the area and by the hand of Matatyu—and when that warrior died, his army fled and scattered—and the children of 'Isra'iel pursued and fought them until 'Iyabboq—and they did not spare a single person from them. {28:35} After this, they waited a little and arose to grieve JAH—and He raised up peoples who ruled over them—and again they cried out to JAH; and JAH ignored their cries and mourning—for they had grieved Him every time—and for they had broken His law. {28:36} They were captured and taken away to Babylon. {28:37} And then the children of 'Isra'iel, who were traitors, did not cease grieving JAH while they worked sin and worshiped idols. {28:38} JAH became angry, intending to destroy them for their sins—Hama having introduced ten thousand gold pieces into the king's treasury—on the day it became known, he stirred up anger in King 'Arthieksis's mind—so that he would not spare the children from the land of Persia, from Hindekie to Ethiopia when he told him he would destroy them. {28:39} He did so—and wrote a letter with a message from the king's authority—and gave it a seal in his hand to deliver to Persia. {28:40} He gave it a seal to destroy them on a day when he wished to destroy them, as the king commanded—yet he commanded that they should introduce money—the gold and silver—into the king's treasury. {28:41} And when the children of 'Isra'iel heard this, they cried and wept to JAH—and they told it to Merdokyos—and Merdokyos told it to 'Astier. {28:42} And 'Astier said, "Fast, pray, and all the children of 'Isra'iel, cry out to JAH in the place where you are." {28:43} And Merdokyos wore sackcloth and sprinkled dust on himself—and the children of 'Isra'iel fasted, prayed, and entered repentance in the land where they were. {28:44} And 'Astier was greatly distressed—and being a queen, she wore sackcloth—she sprinkled dust and shaved her head—and she did not apply perfume like the Persian queens apply perfume—and in her deep reasoning, she cried and wept to her father, the Creator JAH. {28:45} And because of this, He gave her favor with the Persian king 'Arthieksis—and she prepared a special meal for her father, the Creator. {28:46} And Hama and the king entered into the meal that 'Astier prepared—and as he desired, he did to Merdokyos—JAH paid the penalty for Hama's deeds—and they hanged him on a tall gallows. {28:47} The king's letter commanded that they should leave 'Isra'iel as they were in all their agreements—and that they should not tax them or rob them or wrong them or take their money from them. {28:48} As JAH shall pardon 'Isra'iel for doing thus when they cried in repentance—it is that He might love and honor them in the Persian land where they lived—yet a king's letter commanded that they should not destroy their land nor plunder their livestock. {28:49} And when they troubled Him—He will raise up peoples to oppress them—at that time they will cry and weep to Him that He might send them help and that He might save them from the hands of the peoples who cause them tribulation.

{29:1} During that time, the Egyptians also made the children of Israel work hard by forcing them to make bricks under difficult conditions—they worried them with tasks like mixing mud without straw and heating bricks. {29:2} They made them work under appointed overseers who rushed the workers, so they cried out to JAH to save them from this labor of making bricks in Egypt.

{29:3} At that time, He sent to them Aaron and Moses to help them, for JAH had sent them to lead His people out of Pharaoh's rule—He saved them from brick-making work because Pharaoh, in his arrogance, refused to let Israel go so they could serve JAH in the wilderness—JAH sent them to free His kindred, the Israelites, from Pharaoh's rule in Egypt, and they were saved. {29:4} JAH neglects the arrogant ones—He drowned Pharaoh in the Red Sea along with his army because of his pride. {29:5} Just like that, He will destroy those who do not perform good work in all the kingdoms that He appointed and crowned—those who ignore JAH's Word while being nobles and kings will fulfill His will so that they might provide fair wages to those who serve honorably and honor His famous Name. {29:6} JAH, the ruler of all, said, "But if they will set right My Kingdom, I will set their kingdom right for them. {29:7} Do good work for Me, and I will do good work for you—keep My LAW, and I will protect your bodies—live firmly in My LAW, and I will dwell honestly among you according to your reasoning. {29:8} Love Me, and I will care for your welfare—draw near to Me, and I will heal you. {29:9} JAH, the ruler of all, said, "Believe in Me, and I will save you from tribulation. {29:10} Do not associate closely with others—just as JAH loves good work, He said, "You, draw near to Me, and I will draw near to you—you sinners and traitors—cleanse your hands from sin and distance your thoughts from evil. {29:11} I will remove My anger from you, and I will return to you in Charity and Forgiveness. {29:12} I will distance criminals and enemies who commit iniquity from you—just as I saved My servant David from his enemies who sought to harm him—from Goliath, the warrior, and from Saul, who sought to kill him, and from his son Absalom, who wanted to take his kingdom. {29:13} I will save those who keep My LAW and fulfill My will—like him, I will bestow honor upon them, and they will be blessed in this life and in the life to come—I will crown them with all that makes them blessed. {29:14} They will be one with kings who served JAH and were honored in their beautiful way of life—just like the prophet Samuel served Him beautifully from his infancy—whom JAH, being LAW, chose. {29:15} He told him to communicate with Eli, who was an elder servant, and as he served in JAH's house in the Temple, Samuel's work was also merciful and loved. {29:16} When he grew while serving in JAH's house in the Temple, He appointed him to anoint so he could appoint his people and anoint kings according to JAH's will. As JAH loved him, the kindred he chose from the children of Israel would be appointed—when he fulfilled JAH's will, who created him, He gave him the anointing of the Kingdom into his hand. {29:17} And when Saul was in his kingdom, JAH told the prophet Samuel, "Go—and as I have loved Jesse's son David, who was born from the tribe of Judah, anoint him."

{30:1} I have rejected Saul's kin because he saddened Me by violating My Word. {30:2} I neglected him because he did not keep My LAW, and I will not crown anyone from his lineage again. {30:3} Those who do not keep My LAW, My Word, and My Orders like him—I will destroy My Kingdom and remove My gifts from their children for eternity. {30:4} Since they did not honor Me when I made them famous, I will destroy them—but I will not lift them up again—even though I honored them, since they did not honor Me, I will not make them famous. {30:5} For they did not do good for Me when I did good for them, and they did not forgive Me when I forgave them. {30:6} As they did not make Me a Ruler when I made them rulers over all—as they did not honor Me when I honored them above all, I will not make them famous again nor honor them because they did not keep My LAW. {30:7} I withheld the gifts I gave them, and I will not return what I withheld from them, according to the measure I swore and became angry—JAH, the ruler of all, said this—He said, "I will honor those who honored Me and love those who loved Me." {30:8} I will separate those who did not honor Me nor keep My LAW from the gifts I gave them. {30:9} JAH, the ruler of all, said: "I love those who love Me and will make famous those who make Me famous," He said. {30:10} As I, JAH, am the ruler of all, no one escapes My authority on Earth or in Heaven—for I am JAH who kills, who saves, who saddens, and who forgives. {30:11} Since fame and honor are My treasures, I will honor those whom I love—for I am the judge, the avenger, and the destroyer—and I will make wretched those whom I hate. {30:12} For I forgive those who love Me and call My Name at all times—for I feed both the wealthy and the poor. {30:13} I feed birds, animals, fish in the sea, and flowers—yet I am not just the one who feeds man. {30:14} I feed crocodiles, whales, badgers, hippos, and all that lives in water—all that flies in the wind—yet I am not only the one who feeds man—this is all part of My treasures. {30:15} I am the one who feeds all who seek Me with what they need and love.

{31:1} The kings do not reign without My will, and rulers are by My command—yet they are not powerful without My command, nor are they poor without My command. {31:2} I gave love to David and wisdom to Solomon, and I granted years to Hezekiah. {31:3} I diminished the era of Goliath and gave power to Samson—yet again I weakened his power. {31:4} I saved My servant David from Goliath, who was a warrior. {31:5} I also saved him from King Saul's hand and from the second warrior who opposed him—because he kept My commands, I saved him from those who disputed and fought against him. {31:6} I loved him, and I love all the nobles and kings who keep My LAW—since they have made Me happy, I will grant them victory and power over their enemies. {31:7} Moreover, so they might inherit their fathers' land, I will give them the cleansed and shining land of inheritance that I swore to their fathers.

{32:1} JAH, who rules all, said, "You, the nobles and kings, hear My word and keep My commands—so you do not sadden Me or worship like the children of Israel, who saddened Me by worshiping different idols—those whom I kept and saved when I, JAH, am their Creator—JAH, who rules all, said, "Hear My word; all whom I raised, loved, and fed from birth by their mother and father. {32:2} I sent forth crops on Earth and fed them with the richness from the land, making them thrive—gave them the grapevine and the fruit of the olive tree that they did not plant and the clear water well that they did not dig. {32:3} Hear My word lest you sadden Me like the children of Israel, who saddened Me by worshiping other idols when I, JAH, am their Creator—who fed them sheep's milk and honeycomb with grain and clothed them with beautiful garments—who gave them all My love. {32:4} And without My provision, I deprived them of everything they begged for.

{33:1} Just as David said, "The children of Israel were fed the manna that angels brought down"—and again, hear My word lest you sadden Me like the children of Israel who saddened Me by worshiping idols when I, JAH, fed them sweet manna in the wilderness—He said, "I did all this for them that they might worship Me with what is due and truly." {33:2} JAH, who rules all, said, "But they did not worship Me, and I neglected them—they saddened Me and lived firmly in a law of idols that were not My LAW. {33:3} I will bring hardship upon them according to their sins—as they have neglected My worship and did not establish themselves in My counsel and orders—I neglected them in the measure of sin they worked with their hands, and I will lower them to Gehenna in a definite judgment that is executed in Heaven. {33:4} For they did not keep My LAW, and I have become angry with them—and I will diminish their era in this world. {33:5} If you are a king, are you not a man who will die and be laid to rest, tomorrow to become worms and dust? {33:6} Yet today you boast and are proud like someone who will not die forever. {33:7} JAH, who rules all, said, "But you, who are well-off today, are a man who will die tomorrow. {33:8} But if you keep My commands and My word, I will grant you a honored land with honorable kings who did My will—whose dwellings were light, whose crowns were beautiful, and whose thrones were silver and gold, adorned with people sitting upon them," He said. {33:9} They will be blessed in My country, a place that welcomes those who do good work. {33:10} But for those who commit sin—as they did not keep My LAW—said JAH, who rules all... {33:11} it is not right for them to enter the land where honored kings will enter.

{34:1} The Median kingdom will perish, but the Roman kingdom will firmly establish itself in the Macedonian kingdom—and the Nineveh kingdom will be established over the Persian kingdom. {34:2} The Ethiopian kingdom will be established over the

Alexandrian kingdom—as people will rise—the Moab kingdom will establish itself over the Amalek kingdom. {34:3} Brother will rise against brother, and JAH will take revenge and destroy as He said so that it may perish. {34:4} Kingdom will rise against kingdom, and people against people, and country against country, He said. {34:5} There will be arguments, and there will be formations—famine, plague, earthquake, drought—as love has perished from this world—JAH's punishment has descended upon it. {34:6} For the day has suddenly arrived when JAH will come—who frightens like lightning seen from the East to the West. {34:7} On the day when JAH judges judgment—at that time everyone will receive their hardships according to their weakness and the firmness of their sins—He has said, "I will take revenge on them on the day of judgment when their feet are hindered—for the day of destruction has arrived." {34:8} At that time, JAH will destroy in Gehenna forever those who do not live firmly in His LAW—who commit sin. {34:9} And those who live in the West, islands, Nubia, India, Sheba, Ethiopia, and Egypt—everyone who lives among them... {34:10} at that time will know that I am JAH, who rules the Earth and Heaven—who gives life, love, and honor—who saves and kills. {34:11} I am the one who sends forth the sun—who directs it toward its setting—who brings both evil and good. {34:12} I am the one who brings people you do not know—who slaughter and consume the wealth you have labored for—your sheep and cattle flocks. {34:13} And they will capture your children while you see them suffer—and you cannot save them. Because JAH's Spirit of Support does not dwell in you—since you did not fear JAH's command that you heard—He will destroy your luxury and your assignments. {34:14} But a person in whom JAH's Spirit of Support dwells will know all—as Nebuchadnezzar told Daniel, saying, "I see JAH's Spirit of Support that dwells in you." {34:15} And a person in whom JAH's Spirit of Support dwells will know everything—and what is hidden will be revealed to him—he will know all that is revealed and that is hidden—yet nothing is hidden from a person in whom JAH's Spirit of Support dwells. {34:16} But as we are people who will die tomorrow—our hidden sins that we committed will be revealed. {34:17} Just as they test silver and gold in fire—so there are sinners—later on the Day of Judgment, they will be examined—because they did not keep JAH's command. {34:18} At that time, all people and all the works of the children of Israel will be examined.

{35:1} As the Lord is angry with you because you did not deliver true justice for the orphans, woe to you, nobles of Israel. {35:2} Woe to you who frequent drinking houses morning and evening, getting drunk, showing partiality in judgment, ignoring the rights of widows and orphans, living in sin and deceit. {35:3} The Lord spoke to Israel's nobles, saying: "Unless you stand firm in My commandments, keep My laws, and love what I love, woe to you." He said this to them. {35:4} "I will bring destruction, chastisement, and tribulation upon you, and you will perish like what is consumed by weevils and moths; your footprints and your land will disappear," He told them. {35:5} "Your land will become a desolate wilderness, and all who once looked upon it will clap their hands in shock, saying, 'Wasn't this the land full of abundance and loved by many? The Lord has brought this desolation upon it because of the sins of those who lived here.'" {35:6} They will say, "Because of its pride and arrogance, it raised its head in defiance, and now the Lord has laid it low. This land has become a wilderness because of the arrogance of those who lived in it, and now thorns and thistles grow over it—woe to her." {35:7} She now grows weeds and thorns, becoming a desert wasteland where wild animals will dwell. {35:8} For the Lord's judgment has been set upon her, and she will receive the cup of the Lord's wrath because of the arrogance of those who sinned within her, and she will become a terror to those who approach her.

{36:1} People of Macedonia, do not boast, for the Lord is there, and He will destroy you. Amalekites, do not harden your hearts. {36:2} Though you may rise as high as the heavens, you will descend to the depths of Gehinnom (Hell). {36:3} When Israel first entered the land of Egypt in the kingdoms of Moab and Midian, He said, "Do not boast, for it is not proper to challenge the Lord as you challenge Him." {36:4} You descendants of Ishmael, children of a slave, why do you harden your hearts over things that are not yours? Do you not realize that the Lord will bring judgment upon you when He rises to judge the earth on the day of reckoning? {36:5} The Lord of all has said, "At that time, you will receive the punishment for your evil deeds—why do you elevate yourselves in arrogance? Why do you harden your hearts?" {36:6} "I will mock you as you have mocked those who are not your people, for you have pursued what you desired, working sin. I will leave you in the place where you were sent," says the Lord. {36:7} The Lord of all has said, "I will do this to you." He said, "But if you do good works and love what I love, I will listen to your pleas." {36:8} "If you fulfill My covenant and live according to My commandments, I will fulfill your requests and fight your enemies for you, blessing your children and descendants." {36:9} "I will multiply your sheep and cattle, and if you live according to My commands and do what pleases Me," says the Lord of all, "I will bless all that you put your hand to." {36:10} "But if you do not fulfill My covenant, if you do not stand firm in My laws and commandments, all the tribulations previously spoken of will come upon you. Because you have not endured hardship in accordance with My commandments, and because you have not followed My law, you will not escape My anger, which will come upon you again and again." {36:11} "Because you have not loved what I love, even though I gave you life and sustained you..." {36:12} "Everything you possess was given to you by Me, so that you might both kill and heal, do what you desired, build and destroy, honor and disgrace, elevate and humble. But you neglected My worship and My praise, even though I gave you lordship and honor over those beneath your authority. You cannot escape My wrath, which will fall upon you." {36:13} "If you did follow My covenant and live according to My commands, I would love you, and you would find joy with Me in My lordship, and you would join those who inherit a blessed land." {36:14} "For I have said, if they endure for My sake, I will give them love and honor, for I will make them joyful in the temple where prayers are offered, says the Lord of all. They will be loved and chosen, like a perfect sacrifice." {36:15} "Do not neglect to do works that bring about well-being and good deeds, so that you may cross from death into life." {36:16} "But those who perform good works, the Lord will keep them in all His good deeds, making them His servants, like Job, whom the Lord protected from all tribulation." {36:17} "The Lord will keep them in all good deeds so they may serve Him, like Abraham, whom He saved when he defeated kings, and like Moses, whom He saved from the hands of the Canaanites and Pharaoh. Moses, who endured the torment of being asked to worship idols daily, continued to honor God." {36:18} "When they brought him to their idols, which they worshiped, he endured the trials and refused to worship." {36:19} "For Abraham, who believed in God from his youth, was considered a friend of God, and even when faced with trials, he refused to worship anyone but the God who created him." {36:20} "Because of his love for God, Abraham continued to worship Him faithfully until his death, never departing from God's law, and he taught his children to keep the Lord's law." {36:21} "Just as their father Abraham followed His law, his descendants did not depart from the Lord's law, just as He said to the angels, 'I have a friend in this world named Abraham.' Abraham's children, Jacob and Isaac, who were His servants because of His word, did not depart from the Lord's law." {36:22} "The Lord, who was praised with them and who rules all, said, 'Abraham is My friend; Isaac is My confidant, and Jacob is My beloved, whom I hold dear in My heart.'" {36:23} "But when He loved the children of Israel, they continued to grieve Him, yet He endured their rebellion and fed them manna in the wilderness." {36:24} "Their clothes did not wear out, for they were sustained by the manna, a food of knowledge, similar to injera (Ethiopian bread), and their feet did not grow weary." {36:25} "But their hearts continually turned away from the Lord, for they were sinners from the beginning and had no hope of salvation." {36:26} "They became like a crooked bow, never becoming like their fathers, Isaac, Abraham, and Jacob, who served the Lord with a pure heart. Instead, they continuously angered Him by offering sacrifices on mountains and hills. They ate in mountain caves and at the roots of trees." {36:27} "They slaughtered bulls, offered sacrifices, and celebrated the works of their own hands, eating and drinking their sacrifices and engaging in idolatrous worship and playing games with demons." {36:28} "Demons admired their games and songs, as they reveled in drunkenness and adultery without restraint, committing robbery and greed, acts which the Lord despised." {36:29} "They sacrificed to Canaanite idols, to Midianite gods, to Baal, to Aphlon, Dagon, Seraphyon, and

Arthiemadies, who were idols of Eloflee." {36:30} "They worshiped the idols of all the peoples in the surrounding regions, just as they had seen and heard others do, making music, singing, and boasting like other nations." {36:31} "All the tribes of Israel acted similarly, claiming, 'We will worship the Lord,' but without keeping His commandments or the law that Moses gave them, which was to guard against idolatry." {36:32} "They were warned not to worship other gods apart from their fathers' Creator, who had fed them with honey from Magar and provided them with the grain of the earth and manna from heaven." {36:33} "Moses commanded them not to worship other gods, for He was their Creator, and He fed those who loved Him and did not withhold anything from those who desired Him." {36:34} "But they did not cease to grieve the Lord, constantly angering Him even as He blessed them." {36:35} "When He chastised them, they cried out to Him, and He saved them from the affliction that had come upon them. Then they would rejoice and live in peace for many years." {36:36} "But they would return to their sinful ways, angering the Lord just as before, and He would raise up enemies from the surrounding peoples to destroy them, and they would suffer and be oppressed." {36:37} "Once again, they would cry out to their Creator, the Lord." {36:38} "And He would forgive them, not because of their works, but because of their fathers—Noah, Isaac, Abraham, and Jacob—who had served the Lord faithfully from the beginning." {36:39} "He loved those who kept His law, and He multiplied their children like the stars in the sky and the sand of the sea." {36:40} "But when the dead are raised, the sinners, like the grains of sand, will be separated from the children of Israel and cast into Gehinnom." {36:41} "For the Lord had told Abraham, 'Look up at the stars in the night sky and count them if you can. Your children, the righteous ones, will shine like these stars in heaven. They are like stars, shining brightly, and they are the souls of kind people born from Israel.'" {36:42} "And again, He said to him, 'Look at the shore and the sand of the sea, and count it if you can. Your sinful descendants are like this, and they will descend into Gehinnom when the dead are raised. They are the souls of sinners.'" {36:43} "And Abraham believed in the Lord, and because of this, it was credited to him as righteousness. He found moral strength in this world, and after his wife Sarah had grown old, she gave birth to a child named Isaac." {36:44} "For he believed that those who perform good works will rise and enter the eternal kingdom of heaven, and that he too would find the kingdom of heaven." {36:45} "But he also believed that those who sin will descend into Gehinnom forever when the dead are raised, while the righteous who do good works will reign with the Lord forever." {36:46} "He believed that judgment would come upon the wicked for eternity, without falsehood, and that those who sin will face eternal punishment. But he also believed that he would inherit eternal life in the kingdom of heaven." {36:47} Let glory and praise be given to the Lord, for this first book that speaks of the Maccabees has been completed and fulfilled.

The Second Book of Meqabyan

{1:1} This is a book that speaks of how the Maccabees found Israel in Mesopotamia, specifically in Syria, and killed them in their region, starting from the Jabbok River all the way to Jerusalem, which led to the destruction of the country. {1:2} Because the people of Syria, Edom, and the Amalekites joined with the Moabite man Maccabees, who destroyed the land of Jerusalem, they camped from Samaria to Jerusalem and throughout the region, killing in battle without preserving anyone who fled, except for a few. {1:3} At the time when the children of Israel sinned, God raised up the Moabite man Maccabees against them, and he killed them with the sword. {1:4} As a result of this, God's enemies bragged about His honored land, swearing in their crimes. {1:5} The Philistines and Edomites camped, as God sent them because they pretended to speak His word; they began to seek revenge and destroy God's land. {1:6} The country of Maccabees was Moab, and he arose with power from his land, swearing loyalty with those who were with him. {1:7} They camped in the region of Gilead, which is in Mesopotamia, up to Syria, intending to destroy God's land; there he appealed to the Amalekites and Philistines, giving them much silver, gold, chariots, and horses so that they might join him in his wrongdoing. {1:8} They came together and crushed the fortress, spilling blood like water. {1:9} They made Jerusalem like a temporary shelter, and he made a voice heard within it; he committed all the sinful acts that God detests, and they also defiled God's land, which had been filled with praise and honor. {1:10} They made your friends' flesh and your slaves' corpses food for wild beasts and birds of heaven. {1:11} They robbed children whose mothers and fathers had died and widows, fearlessly doing as Satan had taught them; until God, who examines hearts and minds, was vexed—they even removed the fetus from a pregnant woman's belly. {1:12} They returned to their land feeling content because they had committed evil against God's kindred, taking the plunder from a once-honored land. {1:13} When they returned and entered their homes, they celebrated with songs and clapping.

{2:1} The prophet known as Re'a told him: "Today be happy like a little when you were happy; God, whom Israel glorified, has the power to take revenge and destroy you for the punishment you didn't doubt. {2:2} Will you say, 'My horses are swift; I will escape by running'? {2:3} As for me, I tell you, those who will follow you are swifter than vultures; you will not escape from God's judgment and destruction that will come upon you. {2:4} Will you say, 'I wear iron armor, and neither spear nor arrow can harm me'? God, who honors Israel, said: It is not by spear or arrow that I will take revenge and destroy you." He told him, "I will bring upon you heart sickness, itching, and rheumatism worse and more lasting than spear or arrow; yet it is not by this that I will take revenge and destroy you. {2:5} You have provoked my anger; I will bring heart sickness upon you, and you will lack someone to help you; you will not escape from my authority until I destroy your name from this world. {2:6} As you have strengthened your arrogance and exalted yourself over my land, at the moment I act swiftly, like a wink of an eye, you will know that I am your Creator; you are before me like grass before a fire that consumes, and you are like the dust that winds scatter from the earth—you are like them beside me. {2:7} For you have provoked my anger and did not recognize your Creator; I will neglect all your kindred, and I will not preserve anyone who draws near to your fortress. {2:8} And now return from all your sins that you have committed; if you turn back from your sins and genuinely mourn before God—if you plead with Him in a pure heart—God will forgive you all the sins you have committed against Him," he told him. {2:9} At that time, Maccabees put on sackcloth and mourned before God because he had sinned, for God was angry with him. {2:10} For His eyes are revealed; He does not withhold, and His ears are open; He does not neglect; His words are not false, and He acts quickly; God knows lest He preserve the punishment He spoke through the prophet's words. {2:11} He tore his clothes, put on sackcloth, sprinkled dust on his head, and cried and wept before his Creator, God, for the sins he had committed.

{3:1} The prophet came from Ramath and told him that Ramath, which is part of Moab, is near Syria. {3:2} He dug a pit and entered it up to his neck, weeping bitterly, and he entered a state of repentance for the sins he had committed before God. {3:3} God told the prophet: "Return from the land of Judah, Ramath, to the Moabite official Maccabees. Tell him, 'God says this: I am the Lord your God who sent you by my authority so that you might destroy my land. Do not say, "I destroyed the honored land of Jerusalem by my own power and my large army," for it was not you who did this. {3:4} It is she who has saddened me with all her greed, treachery, and lust. {3:5} I neglected her and cast her aside through your hand, and now God has forgiven you your sin because of your children whom you birthed. It is not because you strengthened your arrogance and said, "I encircled the land of Jerusalem by my authority." {3:6} Those who doubt are not disciplined enough to enter repentance—do not be a doubter—and now enter repentance with a disciplined heart." {3:7} Indeed, those who truly enter repentance with a disciplined heart and do not return to thirst and sin after repenting are praised. {3:8} Those who return to their God with discipline in mourning and sadness, bowing down with many pleas, are also praised. Those who are disciplined and enter repentance, for God has told them, "You are my treasures who entered repentance after misleading others." {3:9} He told arrogant Maccabees, when he returned to Him in repentance after misleading others, "I forgive you your sin because of your fear and alarm; for I am the Lord your God who brings hardship upon children for their father's sin up to seven generations if the child continues the sin of the father—and who shows mercy to ten thousand generations for those who love me and keep my laws. {3:10} Now I will strengthen my oath with you because of these children whom you have birthed. And God, who rules all and honored Israel, says: I will accept the repentance you made because of the sin you committed. {3:11} At that time, he emerged from the pit and bowed to the prophet, swearing, "As I have saddened God, let me be what you love. Yet let God do to me thus and so, lest I separate from you— for we have no law, and I did not live firmly in His commands like my fathers. You know that our fathers taught us, and that we worshipped idols. {3:12} For I am a sinner who lived firmly in sin, who was stubborn in arrogance, thus provoking God's commands—but until now, I had not heard the words of God's servants, the prophets. I did not live firmly in His laws and commands that He commanded me." {3:13} He told him, saying, "As there are none from your kindred who trusted in sin, I know that the prophet received repentance today. {3:14} But now cease your idol worship and return to knowing God, that you may have true repentance," he told him. He fell and bowed at the prophet's feet, and the prophet lifted him up and commanded him all the good works that were due to him. {3:15} And he returned to his house, doing as God commanded him. {3:16} Maccabees returned his body to worship God, destroying idols and sorcery from his house, along with those who worshipped idols, pessimists, and magicians. {3:17} Morning and evening, as his fathers did, he examined the children he had captured and brought from Jerusalem in accordance with all of God's commands, orders, and laws. {3:18} From the children he captured, he appointed knowledgeable ones in his house. {3:19} Again, from the infants, he appointed wise children to care for the little ones who entered the bed so that they might teach them God's law that the children of Israel should follow. He would listen to the captured children of Israel about the orders and laws, including the Nine Laws—those Moabites' customs and their false worship. {3:20} He destroyed their places of worship, idols, and sorcery, along with the sacrifices and offerings made to the idols, both morning and evening, from the kids and fattened sheep. {3:21} He destroyed the idols that he had worshipped, pleaded to, and believed in all his works while offering sacrifices at noon and in the afternoon, in accordance with all the priests told him regarding his idols. {3:22} It seemed to him that they would save him in all that they advised him, and he would not scorn any of the things they told him. {3:23} But Maccabees ceased those works. {3:24} After he heard the words of Ra'ay, whom they called a prophet, he fulfilled his work in repentance, just as the children of Israel had once saddened Him, and at the time He chastised them in tribulation—when they knew and cried out to God—all His kindred did good works more than the children of Israel during that season. {3:25} When He heard that they were seized and abused by the hands of people who caused them tribulation and that they cried out to Him, He remembered the oath of their fathers, and at that time He would forgive them because of their fathers Abraham, Isaac, and Jacob. {3:26} And when He saved them, they would forget God, who saved them from tribulation, and they would return to worshipping idols. {3:27} At that time, He would raise up peoples who caused them tribulation, and when they were firmly oppressed and saddened, they would cry out to God—He loved them because they were His chosen people—at that time He would be gracious and forgive them. {3:28} And when He preserved them, they would again return to sin, provoking Him through their own works and by worshipping idols in their assemblies. {3:29} But He would raise up Moab, Philistia, Syria, Midian, and Egyptians against them; when their enemies defeated them, they would cry and weep—when they were firmly oppressed, taxed, and ruled, God would raise up princes for them so that He might save them when He loved them.

{4:1} And in the time of Joshua, there was a day when He saved them. {4:2} And in the time of Gideon, there was a day when He saved them. {4:3} And in the time of Samson, Deborah, Barak, and Jael, there was a day when He saved them—whether male or female, He would raise up princes to save them from the hands of their enemies who caused them tribulation. {4:4} And just as God loved them, He would save them from those who caused them tribulation. {4:5} They would be completely joyful in all the work He accomplished for them—they would be joyful in their land, fruitful in multiplying all their flocks in the wilderness, and their livestock. {4:6} He would bless their crops and livestock—for He saw them with eyes of mercy—and He would not diminish their livestock, for they were good children, and He would love them completely. {4:7} But at the time they were evil in their works, He would cast them into the hands of their enemies. {4:8} And when He destroyed them, they would seek Him in worship, returning from sin and marching toward God in repentance. {4:9} And when they returned with a complete heart, He would atone for their sins—He would not remember their former sins—for He knew that they were flesh and blood, having misled thoughts in this world, and demons within them. {4:10} But when Maccabees heard the order that God established in His worship place, the Temple, he was slain in repentance. {4:11} After he looked up and heard this, he did not scorn doing good works; he did not scorn all the good works that the children of Israel did when God forgave them—after they trespassed against His law, they would weep and cry out when God punished them, and again He would forgive them, and they would keep His law. {4:12} Likewise, Maccabees would straighten out his work, keep His law, and live firmly in the commands of the God of Israel. {4:13} At that time, after he heard all the works by which the children of Israel boasted, he would boast like them in keeping God's law. {4:14} He would urge his kindred and children to live firmly in God's commands and all His laws. {4:15} He would forbid the practices that Israel forbade, and he would hear and keep the laws that Israel kept; and when his kindred were another Moabite man, he would forbid the food that Israel forbade. {4:16} He would send forth tithes; he would give all that were firstborn and that he owned from his cows, sheep, and donkeys—and turning his face toward Jerusalem, he would sacrifice as Israel did. {4:17} He would sacrifice sin offerings and vow offerings—a sacrifice for welfare and an agreed-upon sacrifice—and the continual sacrifice. {4:18} He would give his first crops, and he would pour out the grapes that Israel poured—he would give this to his priest whom he appointed—he would do all that Israel did, sweetening his incense. {4:19} He built a lampstand, a bowl, a seat, a tent, and the four rings—diluting oil for the holy lamps in the Holy of Holies—the curtain that Israel made in the Holy of Holies when they served God. {4:20} Just as they did good works while living firmly in His order and His laws, and when God did not neglect them by casting them into the hands of their enemies, Maccabees also did good works like them. {4:21} He would pray to the God of Israel every time that He might be his teacher, lest He separate him from the children of Israel whom He chose and who did His will. {4:22} Again he would pray that He might give him children in Zion and a house in Jerusalem—that He might give them the heavenly seed of virtue in Zion and a heavenly house of soul in Jerusalem—and that He might save him from the destruction spoken by the prophet's mouth—that He might accept his repentance in all the mourning he wept before God in sadness and repentance... {4:23} and lest He destroy children in this world because of him—and that He might keep him in his proceedings and entering. {4:24} Kindreds from the Moabite people beneath Maccabees' authority were joyful, believing that their chief lived firmly in righteous work—they would check his judgments and fulfill his agreements, scorn the language and justice of their country—they would understand that Maccabees' work surpassed and was straight. {4:25} They would come and hear Maccabees' charity and judgments of truth. {4:26} He had much wealth—he had female and male slaves, camels, donkeys, and five hundred horses with armor—he would completely defeat the Amalekites, Philistines, and Syrians—but previously, when he worshipped idols, he was defeated. {4:27} He prevailed; however, from the time he began worshipping God, no one defeated him in battle. {4:28} They would come in the power of their idols to fight him—they would call the names of their idols and curse him—yet no one defeated him, for he placed his faith in his God. {4:29} When he did this and defeated his enemies, he lived and ruled over people in his authority. {4:30} He would take revenge and destroy the enemies of wronged people—he would judge justly for a child whose mother and father were dead. {4:31} He would receive widows in their time of trouble—he would give food to those who hungered and clothe the naked with his clothes. {4:32} He would be joyful in his works—he would give freely from his wealth and would give tithes for the Temple—Maccabees lived joyfully when he did this.

{5:1} After the children of Maccabees were orphaned, they grew up following their father's teachings. They maintained their household order, took care of their kin, and ensured that the poor, widows, and orphans were not made to cry. {5:2} They feared the Lord and gave alms to the poor. They upheld the trust their father had given them and comforted orphans and widows in their times of trouble. They acted as their mothers and fathers, protecting them from those who wronged them and soothing their distress. {5:3} They lived this way for five years. {5:4} After this, the king of the Chaldeans, named Sennacherib, came and destroyed the entire region, capturing the children of Maccabees and ravaging all the villages. {5:5} He plundered all their wealth while they remained entrenched in evil deeds and sins, indulging in adultery, insults, and greed, neglecting their Creator. Yet, those who did not adhere to the Lord's Law and His commands, who worshipped idols, were also seized and taken to their land. {5:6} They consumed what beasts had killed, along with blood and carcasses—things the Lord detests. They had no order based on the true commands written in the Law. {5:7} They did not know the Lord, their Creator, who had sent them forth from their mothers' wombs and nourished them with what was due. {5:8} They married their aunts and stepmothers, resorted to robbery and evil acts, and indulged in sins and adultery. They lacked any sense of judgment, committing all kinds of wicked deeds without law. {5:9} All their paths were dark and treacherous, and their actions were sinful and adulterous. {5:10} But the children of Maccabees adhered to all their orders; they refused to eat what scavengers had touched or what had died on its own. They did not engage in the evil deeds the Chaldean children committed, as those actions were not recorded in this book—those of sinners, doubters, criminals, betrayers, and those filled with robbery, sin, and paganism. {5:11} The work that the Lord loved was not among them. {5:12} Again, they worshipped an idol named Baal-Peor, trusting it as if it were their Creator, the Lord, even though it was deaf and dumb. This idol was crafted by human hands, made by a smith who worked with silver and gold—it had no breath or knowledge, and it could not see or hear. {5:13} It did not eat or drink. {5:14} It did not kill or save. {5:15} It did not plant or uproot. {5:16} It could neither harm its enemy nor benefit its friend. {5:17} It did not impoverish or honor anyone. {5:18} It would mislead lazy Chaldeans, yet it could not chastise or forgive.

{6:1} The Lord's enemy, Sennacherib, appointed priests of falsehood to serve his idols. {6:2} He sacrificed offerings to them and poured out wine for them. {6:3} It seemed to him that they ate and drank. {6:4} At dawn, he would give them cattle, donkeys, and calves, sacrificing morning and evening, and he would partake in those defiled offerings. {6:5} He would disturb and compel others to sacrifice to his idols, but it was not just them who did this. {6:6} When they saw the children of Maccabees, who were handsome and worshipped the Lord, the idol priests desired to mislead them to sacrifice and consume the hated offerings, but the honorable children of Maccabees refused. {6:7} As they obeyed their father's commands, engaged in good works, and held the Lord in awe, they could not be persuaded... {6:8} At that time, they were bound, insulted, and robbed. {6:9} They informed King Sennacherib that they refused to sacrifice or bow to his idols. {6:10} Because of this, the king was angry and commanded them to be brought before him. {6:11} He told them to sacrifice to his idols. {6:12} They responded, "We will not answer you in this matter, nor will we sacrifice to your defiled idols." {6:13} He threatened them with many works, but he could not intimidate them, for they had disciplined minds believing in the Lord. {6:14} He heated a fire and cast them into it, and they offered their bodies to the Lord. {6:15} After they died, they arose and were seen by him at night, drawing their swords while he reclined on his throne, and he was filled with fear. {6:16} "My lords, tell me what should I do for you? Don't take my body to death so I can fulfill all your commands." {6:17} They instructed him on what was due, saying, "Consider that the Lord is your Creator, and He is the one who will dismiss you from this kingdom where you are arrogant and will cast you into the fire of Hell along with your father, the Devil. When we worshipped our Lord without sinning against you, and when we bowed in fear to Him, as you burned us in the fire, you will end your hardships by that same action. {6:18} For He is the Creator of all—earth, heaven, sea, and all that is within them. {6:19} He created the moon, sun, and stars, and He created all of creation, which is the Lord. {6:20} There is no other creator besides Him in earth or heaven. He is capable of all, and nothing is beyond His control. He is the one who kills and saves, who chastises in tribulation and forgives. When we bow to Him in fear, as you burned us in the fire, you will finish your hardships by that." {6:21} "For He rules heaven and earth—no one escapes His authority. {6:22} None from the creation He made has departed from His commands, except for you, a criminal, and criminals like you whose reasoning your father, Satan, has hidden. You, your priests, and your idols will descend together into Hell, where there are no exits for eternity. {6:23} Your teacher is Satan, who has taught you this evil work so you might do harm to us. Yet it is not only you who does this; you will descend to Hell together. {6:24} You have made yourself like your Creator, the Lord, yet you do not know Him, who made you. {6:25} You are arrogant in your idols and your handwork until the Lord makes you wretched. He will convict you for all your sins and iniquities that you have committed in this world."

{7:1} Woe to you who do not know the Lord, your Creator—woe to your idols that are like you and woe to you for having regrets that will profit you nothing when you are sad and seized in the depths of Sheol (the underworld)—woe to you for not keeping His Word and His Law. {7:2} You will have no escape from there for eternity—your priests and you who sacrifice to them, just like your Creator, the Lord—for your idols have no breath or soul and cannot avenge or destroy those who do evil to them, nor can they do good for those who act kindly toward them. {7:3} Woe to you who sacrifice to them, for they are the work of human hands where Satan resides, misleading the lazy-minded like you, that he might lead you to the flames of Hell, while the priests who serve demons command you and your idols. {7:4} As you do not know, nothing will benefit you—you act wrongfully and err. {7:5} As for the animals that the Lord created for your food, dogs and beasts—they are better than you, for beyond one death, they face no further condemnation. {7:6} But you will die and suffer in the flames of Hell, where there are no exits for eternity—animals are better. {7:7} Having spoken this, they went and hid from him. {7:8} But Sennacherib remained, trembling with fear, seized by a deep fright that did not leave him until dawn.

{8:1} He continued to be entrenched in malicious reasoning and arrogance. {8:2} Just as iron is called firm—like Daniel saw it upon his kingdom—he turned into a tyrant over the people of his land. {8:3} He was deeply rooted in evil, laziness, and troubling others. {8:4} He completely destroyed what I had previously spoken and consumed people's wealth. {8:5} He was diligent in evil, just like his father, the Devil, who solidified his reasoning and destroyed what remained of his army. {8:6} He claimed, "My era is like that of the sun," yet he did not know the Lord, who was his Creator. {8:7} In his reasoning, he believed the sun existed for him. {8:8} He arose in power, camped in the territory of Zebulun, and began a campaign in Macedonia, receiving his provisions from Samaria, where they offered him gifts. {8:9} He camped in nomadic regions, reaching Sidon, imposing taxes on Akko, and extending his dominion to the flowing sea, sending messengers to the Hindekel sea. {8:10} Likewise, he expanded his dominion up to heaven. {8:11} He lived in arrogance and evil yet lacked humility. {8:12} His paths led to darkness and treachery, toward crime, arrogance, bloodshed, and tribulation. {8:13} All his actions were what the Lord despised—he acted like a thief and a teacher of sin, causing orphans to weep for their deceased parents, and he showed no compassion for the poor. {8:14} He defeated and destroyed the kings of nations by his authority. {8:15} He ruled over enemy leaders and many people, taxing them as he pleased. {8:16} Even in destruction, he did not relent—there was no one from whom he did not seize plunder from the sea of Tarsis to the sea of Iareek.

{8:17} He would bow to idols, consume what was dead and unclean, the blood, what a sword had cut, and what was sacrificed to idols—all his works lacked justice, yet he had no sense of justice. He alarmed those beneath his authority and taxed them as he pleased. {8:18} In all that he desired before him, he had no fear of the Lord; he lived in malice before the Lord, who created him. {8:19} He did not act like his Creator, and like the evil he did to his companions when he was angry and seized, the Lord would also repay him for his hardships. {8:20} As the Lord has said, He will avenge and destroy sinners who do not live by His Command, erasing their names from this world, just as He destroyed the peoples who came before him—He will take vengeance and destroy them when He acts. {8:21} And just as the wicked have done evil deeds, they will receive their punishments. {8:22} But commanded by the Lord, good deeds shall follow those who do good works. {8:23} For just as Joshua destroyed the five kings of Canaan in a cave in one day, and caused the sun to stand still in Gibeon by his prayers so he could destroy their armies—the sun stood in the heavens until he annihilated the armies of Ai, Canaan, Jericho, and Gibeon, killing around twenty thousand men at once, binding them and slaying them in the cave by spear and sealing the cave with a stone... {8:24} Such tribulation shall befall all who sadden the Lord with their evil deeds.

{9:1} "O you weak man who are not the Lord—why are you proud? You who appear as a man today are nothing but ashes tomorrow, and you will ultimately become worms in your grave. {9:2} For your teacher is the Devil, who brings hardship on all people because he misled our father Adam—Sheol (the underworld) will find you again, and it will find those who commit your sins. {9:3} For in firmly establishing his reasoning and making himself proud, just like he refused to bow to Adam, whom the Creator made... {9:4} you too have refused to bow to your Creator, the Lord, just like your teacher, the Devil, did. {9:5} Like your forefathers—who did not know their Creator in worship—are headed toward Hell, so too will you go toward Hell. {9:6} Just as He avenged and destroyed them for their evil deeds in this world, and as they descended into Hell... {9:7} you too will descend into Hell like they did. {9:8} Since you have provoked His anger and neglected to worship the Lord who gave you authority over the five kingdoms—do you think you will escape His authority? {9:9} You do not act as you should before Him; He has examined you. But if you perform good works in this world, the Lord will accomplish all your work for you, and He will bless all that you take in your hands, subjecting your ancient and current enemies before you. {9:10} You will be at peace in your comings and goings, in the children born of your nature, in your flocks and your abundance, in all your work where you place your hand, and in all that you think in your heart—authority has been given to you by the Lord so that you may work, plant, and build—all will be commanded for you. {9:11} However, if you do not heed the Lord's Word nor remain steadfast in His Law—like the criminals who came before you—who do not worship the Lord as is due, and who do not firmly believe in His true Law—there is nothing from which you will escape the Lord's authority, for His judgment is true. {9:12} All is fully revealed before Him; nothing is hidden from Him. {9:13} He is the one who seizes the authority of kings and overturns the thrones of the powerful. {9:14} He is the one who raises the downtrodden and lifts up those who have fallen. {9:15} He is the one who frees those who are bound and awakens the dead—pardon and mercy are found with Him when He chooses to revive those whose flesh has decayed and turned to dust. {9:16} And having raised and judged those who committed evil works, He will take them to Hell—for they have saddened Him. {9:17} They are the ones who dismantled the Lord's order and His Law, and He will remove their children from this world. {9:18} As the works of good people are more difficult than the works of sinners—sinners do not desire to live by the counsel of good people. {9:19} Just as the heavens are distant from the earth, so too are the works of good people distant from the works of evil people. {9:20} But the works of sinners are robbery and sin—adultery and wickedness—greed and deceitful acts; it is to be intoxicated in sin and robbing another's money. {9:21} It quickly leads to shedding another's blood and goes toward destruction that bears no benefit, causing a child to weep for a mother and father dead; it consumes blood and what is unclean and dead, devouring camel and pig flesh, and it leads a daughter into bloodshed before she is cleansed, and toward a daughter in childbirth. {9:22} All of this is the work of sinners—it is a trap set by Satan, a wide and prepared path that leads to Hell, existing eternally, and toward Sheol. {9:23} But the path of the righteous, though narrow, leads to welfare, innocence, humility, unity, love, prayer, fasting, and purity of body—keeping away from what does not benefit—abstaining from what a sword has slain and what is dead and unclean, and from going to another man's wife and committing adultery. {9:24} They keep away from all that is not commanded by the Law—from eating disgusting food and from all hated works—and from all the works that the Lord does not love, for sinners do all of this. {9:25} As for good people—they distance themselves from all the works that the Lord does not love. {9:26} He loves them and will protect them from all their tribulations like treasured money. {9:27} For they keep His orders and His Law and all that He loves—but Satan rules over sinners.

{10:1} Fear the Lord who created you and kept you until today—yet you, the nobles and kings—do not walk the path of Satan. {10:2} Live in the Law and Command of the Lord who rules all—do not walk the path of Satan. {10:3} When the children of Israel came against Amalek to inherit the lands of the Canaanites, the children of Balak and Balaam... {10:4} those whom you curse are cursed, and those whom you bless are blessed—do not walk the path of Satan, for he has said, "I will give you much silver and gold to honor you, so that you may curse for me—and having cursed, you might destroy for me." {10:5} And for Balaam, he came making his sorcery a reward for immorality, and for the children of Balak, he showed him the place where the children of Israel camped. {10:6} For he practiced his pessimism, and he sacrificed his offerings, slaughtering his fattened cows and sheep, desiring to curse and destroy the children of Israel. {10:7} He returned a curse for a blessing, but as the Lord did not allow him to curse them with His Word—do not walk the path of Satan. {10:8} "For you are the chosen people of the Lord—you are the Lord's dwelling place that shall come from Heaven—let those who curse you be cursed, and let those who bless you be blessed," he said. {10:9} When he blessed them before him, afterward the children of Balak were sad and completely vexed, commanding him to curse them. {10:10} For the chosen people of the Lord had come into this land, and Balaam told him, "I will not curse Israel, whom the Lord has blessed." {10:11} And Balak told Balaam, "As for me—I would have loved for you to curse for me—you blessed them before me, yet you did not curse them—if you had cursed for me and said, 'Give me'—as for me, I would have given you a house full of silver and gold—but you completely blessed them, and you did not do a good thing for me, and I will not do a good thing for you." {10:12} Balaam said, "What the Lord tells me to speak, I will speak, but as for me, I cannot dare to disregard the Lord's words. {10:13} Lest I curse a blessed people, for the Lord will be angry with me if I love money—as for me, I do not love money more than my soul. {10:14} As the Lord has told their father Jacob, 'Let those who bless you be blessed, and let those who curse you be cursed'—lest I curse blessed Jacob—as for me, I do not love money more than my soul," he said. And as the Lord told him, "He who blesses you is blessed... {10:15} and a person who unjustly curses you is cursed—complete your path and your work that the Lord might love you. {10:16} And do not be like the former people who saddened the Lord in their sins and whom He neglected—there are those whom He destroyed in the waters of destruction. {10:17} And there are those whom He destroyed by the hands of their haters—there are those whom He destroyed by the hands of their enemies—bringing forth evil enemies who imposed tribulation upon them—and they captured their lords, priests, and prophets. {10:18} And they delivered them to foreign lands they did not know—they completely captured them and plundered their livestock and destroyed their land. {10:19} For they demolished the honored city of Jerusalem's walls and ramparts—making Jerusalem like a field. {10:20} And the priests were captured, the Law was destroyed, and the warriors fell in battle. {10:21} And widows were captured—as they were captured—they wept for themselves, yet they did not weep for their husbands who were dead. {10:22} And the children wept, and the elders were shamed—showing no kindness to either a gray-haired person or an elder. {10:23} They destroyed all they found in the land, yet they showed no kindness for beauty nor for those in the Law—as the Lord was angry with His people when He loved them that He might beforehand destroy His dwelling, the Temple—they captured and took them to a land they did not know among peoples. {10:24} As they saddened their Creator every time—because of this, when the Lord neglected the children of Israel, He made Jerusalem to be plowed like a field. {10:25} For He is kind to them because of their forefathers—but He did not destroy them all at once—as He loved their forefathers Abraham, Isaac, and Jacob, who ruled justly and lived firmly in the straight Law before their Creator—it is because of their forefathers' kindness, yet it is not because of their own kindness that He forgave them. {10:26} And He appointed them to honors that were double, and they found two kingdoms—on earth and in heaven. {10:27} And you, the kings and nobles who live in this passing world—like your forefathers who lived firmly in the work that is due and who preceded you—similarly inherited the Kingdom of Heaven—like their names were honored before their descendants—think of them. {10:28} And you—set your works right so that He might set your kingdom straight for you, and that your name might be called in a good invocation like the righteous kings who preceded you, who served the Lord in their beautiful lives."

{11:1} "Think of the servant Moses, who was not angered when he remained among his family in his humility and his prayers, and not one person destroyed him—he pleaded with the Lord in his innocence for his sister and brother who spoke against him, wishing that the Lord might destroy them while he said, 'As they have wronged You, Lord, pardon them and don't neglect Your kindred.' He atoned for their sins for them, yet the Lord thought of His servant Moses, who was not angered. {11:2} 'For I have wronged You, and forgive me, Your servant, who is a sinner—You are Merciful and a Pardoner—forgive their sins.' {11:3} And Moses likewise atoned for the sins of his sister and brother who spoke against him. {11:4} And because of this, he was called innocent. {11:5} And the Lord loved him more than all the priests' children who were his brothers—because He appointed the priests and made him like unto His own Self alongside them. {11:6} But He also sank the descendants of Korah, who challenged him, lowering them to Sheol with their livestock and tents when they said, 'We are here—in flesh and soul,' as the Lord had loved him—and as he did not depart from His Command—every word he spoke would be done for him just like the Lord's Word. {11:7} And unless you demolish the Lord's Command likewise, the Lord will do according to His will for you and will love your works for you, and He will keep your kingdom for you. {11:8} And Asaph and the descendants of Korah, who departed from Moses' command, grumbled against him because he told them, 'Straighten up your reasoning to be ruled by the Lord.' {11:9} They grumbled, saying, 'Aren't we Levite children who work the priestly service in the special Tent?' {11:10} They went and burned incense, seizing their censers to offer up smoke, but the Lord did not accept their pleas, and they were burned by the fire in their censers, melting like wax that fire melts—none remained from them—as He had said. Their censers were honored by their bodies being burned, apart from the censers that entered the Lord's dwelling according to His Command—neither their clothes nor their bones remained. {11:11} Because the Lord told Aaron and Moses, 'Gather their censers toward the Tent—let it be an instrument for My dwelling, for I have prepared all that I have given from outside until within. {11:12} And he prepared the honored Tent instruments—he prepared the rings and the joiners—like the images of cherubim. {11:13} He worked on the cups, the curtains, the grounds of the Tent for the mobilization, the altar, and the jugs used for sacrifices in the special Tent. {11:14} They sacrificed according to their own accord—the sacrifices that made welfare—the sacrifices that atoned for sin—and the vow sacrifices, morning and evening sacrifices. {11:15} All that He commanded for Moses, he commanded them in the special Tent so they might work there. {11:16} They did not scorn being ruled by their Lord so that His Name might be praised by them in the Law's dwelling, the Tent of their Lord, who gave them a promise that He might give them their fathers' inheritance that produces honey and milk, which He swore to Abraham. {11:17} They did not scorn being ruled by their Lord, who swore to Isaac and confirmed His worship for Jacob... {11:18} and who confirmed for Aaron and Moses the Tent where His worship is kept... {11:19} and who confirmed His worship for both Elijah and Samuel in the Temple and Tent that Solomon built until it became the Lord's dwelling in Jerusalem—and until the Lord's Name became the honored dwelling for Israel. {11:20} For it is a place of supplication and a sin atonement where it is overturned for those who live in innocence and for the priests. {11:21} And it is a place for those who do His will where He will hear their pleas... {11:22} and the Lord's Law is a construction that honored Israel. {11:23} For it is where sacrifices are offered and where incense is burned, so that the Lord, who honored Israel, may be a pleasing aroma. {11:24} And He would speak on the joiner where He forgives in the special Tent—His light would be revealed for the children of Jacob whom He chose and for friends who remain steadfast in His Law and His Command. {11:25} But those who ignore the Lord's Law will be like the descendants of Korah whom the earth swallowed—and likewise, sinful persons will enter Gehenna, which has no exits until eternity.

{12:1} Woe to you, Israel's nobles, who did not keep the Law He commanded you in the Tent—yet you acted according to your own ways—this is being arrogant and prideful, greedy and adulterous—drinking and being drunk—and swearing lies. {12:2} And because of this, I am angry—like chaff burned before a fire—and like a fire that burns the mountains—and like a whirlwind scattering crushed chaff from the earth toward heaven—lest its trace be found in its place—I will destroy you like that. {12:3} The Lord who honored Israel said—He will also destroy all those who work sin—and consider the Lord, who rules all and for whom nothing fails. {12:4} He loves those who love Him—and for those who stand firm in His Command—He will atone for their iniquities and sins—don't be dull and stingy of heart by not believing. {12:5} And make your reasoning straight to be ruled by the Lord—and believe in Him so you might strengthen your bodies—and I will save you from the hands of your enemies in your day of tribulation. {12:6} And in your time of plea, I will tell you—Look—I am there with you in support—I will save you from your enemy's hand—as you have believed in Me—and as you have done My Command—and as you did not depart from My Law—and as you have loved what I love—the Lord who rules all said—I will not neglect you on your day of tribulation. {12:7} He loves those who love Him—for He is a Pardoner—and for He is good—and He keeps those who keep His Law like a trusted possession. {12:8} He returns His anger many times because He knows that they are flesh and blood—as He is a Pardoner—He did not destroy all in His chastisement—and at the time their souls are separated from their flesh—they will return to their earthly nature. {12:9} As He has guided them from not living to living—they won't know the place where they live until the Lord loves them, so He might bring them from not living to living—again He separated their souls from their flesh—and earthly nature returned to its earthly form. {12:10} And again His will shall bring them from not living to living." {12:11} But Satan, who denied the Lord, multiplied his arrogance before the Lord—he made himself lofty until the day he was loved when he abandoned Him. {12:12} "And my era became like the heavenly era—and I am the one who sends forth the sun—and I won't die until eternity," he said. {12:13} And before he finished speaking these things, the Angel of Death, whose name is Thilimyakos, alighted and struck his heart—he died in that hour—as he did not praise his Lord—he was separated from his beautiful life and perished because of his abundance of arrogance and his evil works. {12:14} But when the Chaldean army had camped in the city and the countryside loving to fight him—at the time he died—they proceeded and destroyed his country—they plundered all his livestock—and did not spare an elder near the ramparts. {12:15} They plundered all his wealth—and took his small possessions—and burned his country in fire and returned to their land."

{13:1} "But these five Maccabees children, who believed, gave their bodies to death, refusing to eat the sacrifices made for idols. {13:2} They knew that pretending with the Lord was better than pretending with people—and that the Lord's anger was greater than the king's anger. {13:3} Knowing that this world will ultimately pass and that the righteous will not live firm forever—they gave their bodies to fire so that they might be saved from fire in Heaven. {13:4} And since they understood that being righteous in the Garden for even one day is better than living many ages in this world—and that finding Your pardon, O Lord, for one hour is better than many ages—they gave their bodies to fire. {13:5} What is our era? Like a shadow—like passing wax that melts and perishes on the edge of a fire—doesn't it feel like that? {13:6} But You, Lord, live forever—Your era is not fulfilled—and Your Name is called upon for the children of children. {13:7} And the Maccabees children thought that it all seemed worth it—refusing to eat a disgusting sacrifice, they chose to believe in the Lord. {13:8} Knowing that they would arise with the dead—and understanding that judgment will be faced after the resurrection of the righteous—because of this, they gave their bodies for martyrdom. {13:9} You people who don't know or believe in the resurrection of the dead—understanding that the life they find later will surpass this passing earthly life—arising from these five Maccabees children who gave their bodies for death and whose appearances were handsome—after this, they knew of the resurrection. {13:10} Because they believed in Him, knowing that all will pass—and because they didn't bow to idols—because they didn't eat a disgusting sacrifice that offers no support—they gave their bodies for death to find gratitude from the Lord. {13:11} Because they knew He would make them righteous in flesh and soul in the later era—they did not care about the pleasures of this world and the serious trials of death for those who have children and wives—knowing that resurrection would be in flesh and soul on the Day of Judgment—they gave their bodies for death. {13:12} And knowing that those who keep the Lord's Law—along with the nobles and the kings who believed in the Lord's Word and were righteous... {13:13} shall live reigning as children for many ages in the Kingdom of Heaven where there is no sadness, tribulation, or death—and knowing in their reasoning what will be done later—like wax melting amidst a fire—because of this, they gave their bodies for death. {13:14} Believing that their faces will shine seven times brighter than the sun—and that they will be blessed in His love when all arise in flesh and soul—they gave their bodies for death.

{14:1} But the Samaritans and the Jews—the Sadducees who do not believe in the resurrection of the dead—and the Pharisees—truly sadden me—and it helps me in my reasoning—"We will die tomorrow," the Jews say, "Let us eat and drink—for we will die tomorrow—there are no righteous we will see in the grave." {14:2} But the Samaritans say, "As we are flesh that will become dust, we will not arise. {14:3} For it is invisible like the wind and like a whisper—look—it is here—and because it is what they call invisible—souls will not arise if flesh dies—when resurrection happens, we will believe our souls will rise. {14:4} But like beasts will eat it and like worms will eat it in the grave—we are flesh that will rise with all—we will become dust and ashes. {14:5} And those beasts that ate it will become dust—for they have been like grass—and they have become dust as if they were not created—and their trace will not be found—but we will not arise." {14:6} And the Pharisees say, "We believe in the resurrection of the dead—however, He will bring immortal souls with another flesh that is in Heaven—not on Earth—where will destroyed and rotten flesh be found?" {14:7} But the Sadducees say, "After our souls depart from our flesh—we will not rise with the dead—and flesh and soul have no resurrection after they die—and after we die, we will not arise." {14:8} And because of this, they totally err—and as they speak insults against the Lordship of the Lord—they sadden me. {14:9} Since they do not believe in the Lord who honors them—they have no hope to be saved—however, they have no hope for the dead to rise and be saved. {14:10} O Jews, who are blind in reasoning—when you are those whom He created, bringing from not living to living—and scorned like spit—will you make the Lord ignorant—who made you a person? Will the Lord who created you in His image fail to raise your flesh and soul? {14:11} As you will not escape from the Lord's authority—do not think such things—you will rise without loving Him—for there are hardships you will face in Sheol where you were seized at the time of your death—and it shall be judged upon you without loving Him. {14:12} For the sin found in the demons that they place in your reasoning is worked alongside you after you were born from your mother's womb—and it worked abundantly as you grew up. {14:13} They placed it in your body at the time of your death—and it will bring hardship upon you when you face it. {14:14} Like there is sin in the collar of reasoning—as there are people who work sin, being seized by it—its kindred will present demons. {14:15} All sinners' souls shall come from the edge of Heaven where they are—and your sin likewise shall lead you to Gehenna, pulling and bringing your soul from where you are. {14:16} And after your flesh lived separate from your soul—the Lord's grace shall raise you, being sevenfold like unto our father Adam's flesh. {14:17} You who live in the grave—you also err in your error—yet do not let it seem to you that you only mislead others—you say, "The resurrection of the dead is not there"—so that they might depart from the Lord's Command and err. {14:18} He shall raise you that He might give you your hardship, just like your works that you worked—but who will release you so that you might remain dust? {14:19} But at that time—whether wind in wind be your nature—or if water in water be your nature—or if earth in earth be your nature—or if fire in fire be your nature—it shall come. {14:20} And if a soul that lodged in you is what lived in Sheol—it shall come. {14:21} And the souls of the righteous that live in the Garden of the Blessed shall come. {14:22} But you, Jews, Samaritans, Pharisees, and Sadducees—will live in Sheol until it is judged upon you. {14:23} At that time you will see that the Lord shall pay you according to the hardship like your sin because you misled others. {14:24} "The dead will not arise—for we will die—let us eat and drink"—and because you sat in Moses' seat and misled by your words while you said, "The dead will not arise"—you will see that He shall pay you for your hardship. {14:25} And without your knowing the Book of Oreet—and when you teach the word of the book—because of this, you erred—it would have been better had you remained without learning from your misleading of others. {14:26} It would have been better if you didn't know the word of the book—when you spread the Lord's kindred in your evil teaching and your worthless words. {14:27} For the Lord does not favor seeing a face—and He shall give the grace and glory He prepared for His friends—those who teach good works—but you have what you might receive your reward according to your works and the things you spoke. {14:28} But there is nothing by which you will escape from the Lord's authority who shall judge upon you—and He has what He might pay you according to your works—for those whom you taught and you together will receive a sentence. {14:29} Know that the dead shall arise—and if they are those who kept His Law, they shall arise—and like the earth sends forth grass when the rain falls—so shall He command them forth from the grave—it is not possible for it to remain destroyed and rotten. {14:30} Like moist wood drinks dew and sends forth leaves when He sends it rain for the earth—like wheat bears fruit—and like grain produces buds—so it is not possible for it to withhold from bearing fruit if the Lord loves... {14:31} and like it is not possible for a woman who conceives to close and prevent her womb when labor seizes her—like it is not possible for her to escape without giving birth... {14:32} as dew has descended upon her being commanded by the Lord—at that time she shall produce them all at once—yet after she hears the Lord's Word—a grave likewise cannot prevent those gathered alongside her from arising. {14:33} And the flesh shall be gathered in the place where their corpses fell—and the places where souls live shall be opened—and the souls shall return to the flesh from which they were once separated. {14:34} And at the time a drum is beaten—the dead shall quickly arise like a blink of an eye—and having arisen, they shall stand before the Lord—and He shall give them their reward according to their works. {14:35} At that time you will see that you arise with the dead—and you will marvel at all the works you did in this world—and when you see all your sins written before you—at that time you will regret a useless regret. {14:36} You know that you will arise with the dead and that you will receive your hardship according to the works you did."

{15:1} "But those who do good deeds will be rewarded and feel happy at that time—while those who said, 'The dead won't rise' will be sad when they see that the dead have risen with their evil works, which are of no benefit. {15:2} Their works will convict them, and they themselves will know that their deeds stand against them without anyone to dispute it. {15:3} On the day of judgment and mourning, when the Lord comes—on the day of definite judgment—those who forgot the Lord's law will stand in the place where they belong. {15:4} On the day of total darkness, when mist is drawn away, when flashes are seen and lightning is heard... {15:5} and on the day when earthquakes, fear, heatwaves, and frost occur... {15:6} on the day when an evil person who did evil deeds receives punishment—and on the day when a righteous person receives their reward for doing good deeds—when those who forgot the Lord's law receive punishment like sinners do, they will stand in their designated places. {15:7} For on the day when a master is not more honored than his slave, and a mistress is not more honored than her slave... {15:8} and on the day when a king is not more honored than a poor person, and an elder is not more honored than a child—on the day when a father is not more honored than his child, and a mother is not more honored than her child... {15:9} on the day when a wealthy person is not more honored than a poor one, and an arrogant person is not more honored than a humble one, and on the day when the great are not more honored than the small—this is the day when judgment is passed, for this is the day when they will receive sentences and punishment—this is the day when all will receive suffering according to the sins they committed. {15:10} And this is the day when those who did good works will receive their rewards—and this is the day when those who committed sins will suffer. {15:11} And on this day, those who are rewarded will be happy, while those who forgot the Lord's law will stand in their place. Those who spread lies and read books while saying, 'The dead won't rise'—they will witness the resurrection. {15:12} At that time, these worldly sinners—who didn't do good works in this life—will weep over the sins they committed, for sadness will consume them without comfort. {15:13} And all those kind people who did good works—their happiness will not be fulfilled until eternity—because they worked good deeds while they were in this world. {15:14} For they knew they would rise after death and did not depart from the Lord's law. {15:15} Because they did not stray from His law, they will inherit two blessings—He multiplied their offspring in this world and honored their children. {15:16} He bequeathed them the Kingdom of Heaven, where the blessings He promised to their fathers will be found when the dead rise—and when the rich become poor. {15:17} People will weep who committed sins—who don't believe the dead will rise—who don't keep the Lord's law—and who don't think of the Day of Resurrection. {15:18} At that time, they will witness the suffering that will find them and have no end, where there is no comfort or joy, and where sadness has no rest. {15:19} And a fire that doesn't perish and worms that don't sleep will find them. {15:20} And in the place where their flesh is, there will be fire, sulfur, whirlwind, frost, and hail—this will rain down upon them. {15:21} For those who don't believe the dead will rise, there is a fire of hell awaiting them.

{16:1} You should think about what is on your flesh, your feet, your hands, and your head hair—because they all fade quickly when you cut them—know the resurrection by this: that you have reasoning, religion, and knowledge. {16:2} Your feet, your hands, and your head hair—you might ask, 'Where do these come from?' Isn't it the Lord who prepared them so you might know about the resurrection of your own flesh, not another's? So you might understand that you will rise after you die? {16:3} Because you misled others when you said, 'There is no resurrection of the dead'—at the time when the dead rise, you will receive your punishment according to the sins you committed. {16:4} Just as what you planted will not remain refusing to grow—whether it be wheat or barley—you will see it on the day you receive your punishment. {16:5} And again, the plant you planted won't say, 'I won't grow'—whether it's a fig tree or a grapevine, its fruit and leaves won't change. {16:6} If you plant grapes, they won't change to become figs, and if you plant figs, they won't change to become grapes—and if you sow wheat, it won't change to become barley. {16:7} All—in each of the seeds—in each of their kinds—each of the fruits—each of the trees—each of the leaves—each of the roots—bring forth fruit having received the blessing of pardon from the Lord—yet if you sow barley, it won't change to wheat. {16:8} And likewise, a grave may produce flesh and soul—it will produce people like those the Lord sowed—yet the flesh and soul that the Lord sowed will rise united—those who did good works won't change into those who did evil works, and those who did evil works won't change into those who did good works. {16:9} At the time when the drum is beaten, the dead will rise by the pardon of the Lord—those who did good works will rise into life resurrection—and their reward will be the garden where the blessed reside that the Lord prepared for the righteous—where there is no tribulation or disease, and that is a dwelling place where they won't die again after this. {16:10} But those who did evil works will rise to definite judgment, alongside the deceivers who misled them... {16:11} and with their armies—demons who don't desire that even one person should be saved from all the children of Adam... {16:12} they will descend toward hell, that edge of darkness—where there is grinding of teeth and mourning—where there is no charity or pardon—and where there are no exits until eternity—this is beneath Sheol forever. For they didn't do good works in their lives while they were in their flesh. {16:13} Because it will be judged upon them at the time when flesh and soul arise united. {16:14} Woe to those who don't believe in the resurrection of flesh and soul, for the Lord shows His miracles abundantly together. {16:15} And each one will receive their reward according to their works and the weariness of their hands.

{17:1} A wheat kernel won't grow or bear fruit unless it is demolished. But if a wheat kernel is demolished, it will send roots toward the earth—it will send forth leaves—it will bear fruit. {17:2} You know that one wheat kernel will become many kernels. {17:3} And likewise, this kernel grows rising up from water, wind, and earth's dew—because wheat cannot bear fruit without the sun—but the sun is due to the fire's heat. {17:4} And the wind is due to the soul's breath—and wheat cannot bear fruit without wind—and the water nourishes the earth and saturates it. {17:5} And after the earth, which is ashes, drinks water, it produces roots—and its tips rise lofty upward—it bears fruit around what the Lord blessed. {17:6} But a wheat kernel is an example of Adam—in whom resides a resonating soul that the Lord created—just as a grapevine drinks water and sends forth roots—and the thin roots drink water. {17:7} For the pardon from the Lord gives drink to the long tips of the vines—it sends the water upward toward the leaf tips—it buds up from the sun's heat—and by the Lord's accord, it bears fruit. {17:8} It shall be a pleasant fragrance that brings reasoning joy—and when they eat it, it will satisfy like water that does not make one thirsty and grain that does not leave one hungry—and when they immerse it, it will be like blood from the cluster. {17:9} And as it is said in a psalm, 'Grapes bring joy to the heart'—when they drink it, it makes a person's heart glad—and when someone is free, opens their mouth, and drinks it, they are intoxicated—they drink and fill their lungs—and the blood flows to their heart. {17:10} Just as the drunkenness from grapes can totally mislead, and as it clouds the mind, it makes the pit and cliff feel like a wide meadow, and they don't see the obstacles and thorns at their feet and hands. {17:11} The Lord did this with the fruit and grapevine that His name might be praised by those who believe in the resurrection of the dead and who do His will. {17:12} In the Kingdom of Heaven, He will make happy those who believe that the dead arise."

{18:1} "You people who don't believe in the resurrection of the dead—what an error you make! And when you are taken to a place you do not know, you will regret it uselessly—because you did not believe in the resurrection, that the dead shall rise united in soul and flesh—when people cast you into hell... {18:2} if you work, whether good or evil, you will receive your reward according to your deeds—because you misled your companions, reasoning while you said, 'We know that the dead—who were dust and ashes—won't rise.' {18:3} Just as their death has no escape—and as they have no power over the punishment that will come upon them—and as they were not firm in their tribulation—because they misled their companions—so they could stand in the Lord's square. {18:4} When He is angry with them in His wrath, they will be terrified—because they did not know that they were created to be brought from the state of not living to living—as they speak the Lord's law without understanding, it will be judged against them all because they did evil. {18:5} They don't know hell where they will go—because they were angry and because they were crooked in their works—they taught their companions with reasoning that thirsts for false measures—and they are evil ones who teach misleading things while they said, 'There is no resurrection of the dead.' {18:6} At that time, they shall know that the dead will rise—and they shall know that it will be judged against them because they didn't believe in the resurrection of the dead, which is for all the children of Adam. {18:7} For all of us are children of Adam—and we have died because of Adam—and the judgment of death has found all of us from alongside the Lord because of our father Adam's error. {18:8} We will arise again with our father Adam so we might receive our hardships according to the works we have done—because the world has been ruled by death due to our father Adam's ignorance. {18:9} By Adam violating the Lord's command—because of this, we received hardships—our flesh in the grave melted like wax—and our bodies perished. {18:10} And the earth drank our marrow—we perished and our beauty perished in the grave—and our flesh was buried in the grave—and our beautiful words were buried in the earth. {18:11} And worms came from our shining eyes—and our features perished in the grave and became dust. {18:12} Where are your beautiful features—those who were attractive—whose stance was handsome and whose words were successful? What happened to the strength of warriors? {18:13} Where are the armies of kings—or what about the nobility of lords? Where are the adornments on horses and the decorations of silver and gold and the shining weapons? Didn't they perish? {18:14} Where is the sweet grape drink—and what about flavorful food?

{19:1} O earth, you who gathered the nobles, kings, rich ones, elders, and beautiful daughters—woe is coming from you! {19:2} O earth, you who gathered those who were warriors—those who had beauty—and those who were fine of leg—and those who had reasoning and knowledge—and those whose words were beautiful like a humming harp, a lyre, or a violin... {19:3} and those who had a tune that made one joyful like grape drink makes one joyful—and those whose eyes shine like a morning star... {19:4} and those who sketch what is firm like their right hands lift up what is given and withheld—and those whose feet were beautiful to behold—and those who run like rushing wheels—woe is coming from you! {19:5} O death, you who separated the souls of attractive people from their flesh—woe is coming from you—because you have been sent by the Lord's accord. {19:6} As you have gathered many people whom the Lord produced from you and returned to you—O earth—woe is coming from you! We were found from you—we returned to you by the Lord's accord—we were happy with you by the Lord's accord. {19:7} You became a carpet for our corpses—we passed over you—and we were buried within you—we ate your fruit—and you ate our flesh. {19:8} And we drank the water from your springs—and you drank our blood from your springs—we ate the fruit from your earth—and you ate our body flesh. {19:9} Just as the Lord commanded you to be our food—we ate grain from your earth that had beautiful dew—and you received our flesh's beauty and turned it to dust for your food as the Lord commanded you. {19:10} O death, you who gathered the nobles and kings who were powerful—woe is coming from you—you did not fear arising from their fame and their fright—just as the Lord who created them commanded you—O death—woe is coming from you—you did not spare the suffering. {19:11} And you weren't kind to those whose features are beautiful—and you did not spare the powerful or the warriors—you did not spare the poor nor the rich—neither kind nor evil ones—neither children nor elders—neither daughters nor males. {19:12} You did not spare those who think good thoughts and did not depart from the law—and you did not spare those who were like animals in their works—who think evil thoughts—who were beautiful in their features, flavor, and words—O death—woe is coming from you. {19:13} You did not spare those whose words were angry and whose mouths were full of curses—you gathered those who live in darkness and in light and their souls in your places—O death—woe is coming from you. {19:14} And the earth gathered the flesh of those who live whether in a cave or in the earth—until a drum is beaten and the dead arise. {19:15} Just as the dead shall arise quickly like the blink of an eye by the Lord's command, and at the beating of a drum—those who did evil works shall receive their hardships in the abundant measure of sins they committed—and those who did good works shall be happy."

{20:1} "And I believe that all our works that we have done in this world will not remain hidden when we stand before Him, fearing and trembling. {20:2} And when I have not gathered provisions for my journey—and when I have no clothes for my body... {20:3} and when I have no staff for my hands or shoes for my feet... {20:4} and when I do not know the paths where demons take me—whether they are slippery or smooth, dark or filled with thorns or nettles, or whether there is deep water or a pit—believe me, that my works in this world will not remain hidden. {20:5} I won't know the demons who take me—and I won't hear their words. {20:6} They are dark beings—and they lead me into darkness—I cannot see their faces. {20:7} And just as the prophet said, 'When my soul was separated from my flesh—Lord, my Lord, You know my path—and they hid a trap on the path where I walked—and I saw myself returning to the right—but I lacked one who knew me—and I had nothing by which I could escape'—as they lead me into darkness, I will not see their faces. {20:8} He knows that demons ridicule him—and they will lead him to a path he does not know—he speaks this because, if he turns left or right, there is no one who knows him. {20:9} He is alone among demons—and yet there is no one who knows him. {20:10} Angels of Light, who are subtle, are sent to good people so they may receive the souls of the righteous and take them to a place of Light—toward the Garden—where well-being is found. {20:11} Demons and angels of darkness are sent to receive them and take them toward hell that was prepared for them so they may suffer for the sins they committed. {20:12} Woe to the souls of sinful people who take them to destruction—who have no well-being, no rest, and no escape from the tribulation they encounter—nor will they rise from hell for eternity. {20:13} As they lived firmly in sin— and as they perished by the price of Balaam's iniquity— and as they lacked what they should do—woe to sinful people—for their pretense to receive interest and gifts that in their downfall they might take a foreigner's money that isn't theirs. {20:14} They shall suffer in hell for the sins they committed.

{21:1} Where are those who gather foreign money that isn't earned by their own hands? {21:2} They take money from others for free—and they shall be gathered without knowing the day when their death will come upon them—yet they give their money to a foreigner. {21:3} Just like their fathers, they are sinful relatives who worry and seize what belongs to sinners like them, whether through theft or robbery—and their children won't find happiness in their fathers' wealth. {21:4} As they have gathered for themselves in their downfall—and as it is like misty urine, and like smoke that the wind scatters, and like wilting grass—and like wax that melts before a fire—as the glory of sinners perishes like that—there is no one whom their fathers' money will benefit—like David said, 'I saw a sinful man... {21:5} being honored and famous like a cedar and like a cypress—but when I returned, I could not find him—I searched and did not find his place'—there is no one whom their fathers' money will profit or benefit. {21:6} Because they gathered money through wrongdoing, it seems to them that they will not die—like people who wrong their companions but will not boast—sinners' destruction is likewise imminent. {21:7} You lazy ones—think that you will perish and that your money will perish with you—and if your silver and gold abound, they shall rust. {21:8} And if you bear many children, they will fill many graves—and if you build many houses, they shall be demolished. {21:9} For you did not fulfill your Creator's command—and if you multiply livestock, they will be captured by your enemies—and all the money you seized in your hands will be lost—for it has been what was not blessed. {21:10} Whether it be in a house or in a forest—whether in a wilderness or a pasture—whether in a grape threshing floor or a grain threshing floor—it shall not be found. {21:11} Because you did not keep the Lord's command—as He will not save you or your household from the tribulation—there shall be sadness upon you from all your enemies—yet you will not find joy in your children born of your nature. {21:12} But from Him, plenty will come—He will not trouble those who kept His order and His law—He gives to all who ask Him—yet He blesses the children born of their nature and also the fruits of their land. {21:13} And He makes them rulers over all peoples in their area so they might rule, lest they be ruled—and He gives them all His plenty in their pasture. {21:14} He blesses them with all they have seized in their hands—all the fruits of their fields—and all their livestock—and He makes them joyful in their children born of their nature. {21:15} And He does not diminish their livestock—He saves them from all their tribulations and from weariness and illness and destruction—and from their enemies, whether known or unknown. {21:16} And He will plead for them in the time of judgment—and He shall save them from evil and tribulation and from all who dispute with them—if a priest lived in the first era who worked the Tent, kept the law, and lived firmly in the Lord's accord—by the first order and all the law, as they would give him the tithe and what was firstborn from man up to livestock—He would save them from all tribulation. {21:17} Just as Moses commanded the children of Israel—there was a country of sanctuary in all the lands—by not knowing and by knowing until they judged those whom they convicted and for whom they acquitted... {21:18} if a person lived who killed a soul—he would be measured there that he might be saved. {21:19} He told them, 'Examine your reasoning that he has a quarrel with someone before—and whether it was with an axe or with a stone or with wood—as it fell from his hand unknowingly—if he says, "That person upon whom it fell died on me"—examine and save him—if he did it unknowingly, let him be saved. {21:20} But if he did it knowingly, he will suffer according to his sin—and there is no one who will pardon him; but if he killed him unknowingly—as he did it without knowing—examine and save him, lest he die. {21:21} He worked for them that they might distance themselves from all sin—yet Moses would work like this for the children of Israel lest they depart from the Lord's law. {21:22} He commanded the children of Adam—who live firmly in the Lord's command—to stop worshiping idols and eating what is dead and lodged and what a sword has pierced and cut—and to distance themselves from all evil work, just as he worked for them—that they might do it and totally distance themselves from all that is not due. {21:23} He commanded them not to depart from the command He worked for them in the Tent example in Heaven—that they might save their bodies and find lodging with their fathers. {21:24} As they were born from Seth and Adam, who did the Lord's accord—those who believed in the Lord's word and lived firmly in His command will be called good people's children. {21:25} As we are children of Adam—as He created us in His example and His appearance—so we might do all good works that please the Lord—He will not scorn them. {21:26} As He will not separate His friends—if we do good works—we shall inherit the Kingdom of Heaven, where well-being is with those who do good works. {21:27} He loves those who beg Him sincerely—and He hears them in their prayers—and He accepts the repentance of those who are disciplined and enter repentance—He gives strength and power to those who keep His order and His law and His commands. {21:28} Those who did His accord shall be joyful with Him in His kingdom forever—and whether they are those who came before or those who arise later—they will present praise to Him from today until eternity."

The Third Book of Meqabyan

{1:1} Christ shall rejoice over the righteous, for He will come to them in a future time, when He will avenge and destroy the Devil, who wronged the kind and innocent, who misled people, and who hates the work of their Creator. {1:2} He will take vengeance and bring him down; He will return his dominion to misery and humiliation, for he has been arrogant in his reasoning. {1:3} He will lower his dominion, for he has said, "I will enter the midst of the sea, I will ascend to Heaven, I will gaze upon the depths, and I will seize the children of Adam like birds in a nest, for who among them is greater than I?" {1:4} Because I became powerful through them, I will lead them away from the straight law of God, for unless they follow God's covenant, no one can remove me from my authority," he said. {1:5} "I will cause them to stray and lead them along the easy path to Gehenna (a place of eternal torment) with me. {1:6} Those who love God and keep His law hate me for this, but those who depart from the law of their Lord and go astray will come to me, love me, and keep my oath. I will corrupt their thinking and change their hearts so they do not return to their Creator, God, and they will follow my commands as I instruct them. {1:7} When I show them the wealth of this world, I will mislead them from the straight law, and when I show them beautiful and desirable women, I will also distance them from the straight law through these. {1:8} And when I show them glittering jewels, silver, and gold, I will also lead them away from the straight law through these things, so they return to my work. {1:9} When I show them fine clothing, red silk, white silk, linens, and more, I will lead them away from the straight law, and I will bring them back to my thoughts. When I increase their wealth and livestock like sand and show them these, I will also turn them to my work through this. {1:10} When I incite them to jealousy through arrogance because of women, or stir them to anger and conflict, through all these, I will turn them to my work. {1:11} When I show them signs, I will lodge myself in their companions' minds, and I will lodge a symbol for each of their leaders in their hearts, showing them signs and misleading them. {1:12} For those in whom I have taken residence, I will show them signs in the stars, the clouds, the flickering of fire, or in the cries of animals and birds, for these are my lodgings, and I will place signs in their hearts. {1:13} They will speak and give signs to their companions, and just as their false prophets misled them, I will be a sign for them. {1:14} I will perform signs for them, so that those who investigate them may be deceived, and that they may pay wages to magicians, and that they may tell their companions, 'There is no one as wise as so-and-so, who does as they have spoken, and who knows prophecy, who distinguishes between good and evil, and for whom everything is as they have said.' {1:15} I will rejoice when they say this because those who perish and go astray by me will abound, and the children of Adam will perish because God has humbled me from my rank for their father Adam, when I said, 'I will not bow to Adam, who is beneath me.' {1:16} I will bring all his children who remain steadfast in my command to destruction. I have an oath from God, who created me, that all those I mislead will descend to Gehenna with me. {1:17} And when God's anger increased against me, and He commanded that they bind and cast me into Gehenna, when my Creator commanded this, I pleaded with my Lord. I pleaded with Him, saying, 'Since You are angry with me, and You have admonished me with Your chastisement, and have punished me with Your wrath, Lord, my Lord, allow me to say one thing before You.' {1:18} And my Lord answered me, saying, 'Speak, and I will listen to you.' Then I began my plea, saying, 'After I have been cast down from my rank, let those whom I have misled be with me in Gehenna, where I will be tormented. {1:19} And let those who refused to follow me, who did not go astray because of me, who did not obey my command, serve You and fulfill Your covenant, keeping Your word. Let them not go astray as I misled them when they refused, just as I instructed them when You loved me. Let them take the crown You gave me. {1:20} Give them the crown of the authorities called satans, who were sent with me. Seat them on my throne, at Your right hand, which has become a wilderness for me and my hosts. {1:21} Let them praise You as You have loved them, and make them like my hosts and like me, for You hated me and loved them, who were created from ashes and earth. As my authority has perished, and their authority has been elevated, let them praise You as You have loved.' {1:22} My Lord answered me, saying, 'Since you have misled them while they saw and heard, if they have strayed from My command and come to you, let them be with you according to your word. {1:23} If they have abandoned My books, My word, and My command, and if you have led them astray, even though their destruction grieves Me, let them receive torment in Gehenna with you,' He told me. {1:24} 'You will receive torment in Gehenna for eternity, and there will be no escape for you or those whom you have misled.'

{2:1} But I will give your throne in the kingdom to those you failed to mislead, like My servant Job (a symbol of patience and righteousness). God, who rules all, said, 'I will give the Kingdom of Heaven to those you could not mislead. {2:2} And I provoke all the children of Adam. If it is possible for me to lead them astray, I will not stop, so they may not remain steadfast in good works. I provoke all the children of Adam and make this world seem pleasant to them. {2:3} Whether through love of drink, food, and clothing, or through the love of material things, or by withholding and giving... {2:4} or by their desire to listen and see, or through their love of touching and going, or by increasing pride and possessions, or by love of dreams and sleep... {2:5} or by multiplying drunkenness and drink, or by increasing insults and anger, or by speaking frivolous and meaningless words... {2:6} or through quarrels and backbiting against their companions, or by looking at the beautiful daughters of this world, or by smelling the sweet scents that lead them astray... {2:7} I hate them for all these things so that they may not be saved. I lead them away from God's law, so they may enter destruction with me, from where I was cast down.' {2:8} And the prophet told him, 'You, who destroy people, perish! When you strayed from God's law and committed sin through your hardened reasoning and arrogance, and by grieving your Creator and not worshiping Him with humility, will you now be proud over God's creation?' {2:9} When your Creator became angry with you, He cast you down from your rank because of your evil deeds. Why do you now lead Adam into sin, the one whom his Creator made from the earth, whom He formed with love, and whom He created for His praise?' {2:10} 'When you, who are subtle and created from wind and fire, became arrogant and said, "I am the Creator..." {2:11} when you boasted, and as God saw your evil deeds, you denied Him and your hosts, He created Adam to take your place in praising His name, without failing in His praise. {2:12} Because you made yourself prouder than all the angels, God created Adam with his children to praise His name in place of the praise you and your hosts scorned. {2:13} Because of this, God destroyed you, separating you from all the angelic leaders like yourself and your hosts, who were united in rebellion with you. You left God's praise because of your foolish pride and hard-heartedness, and you were arrogant against your Creator, unlike any other. {2:14} Therefore, He created Adam from the earth to be praised by the humble, and He gave him a command and law, saying, "Do not eat from the fig tree, lest you bring death upon yourself. Eat from all the trees in the garden." {2:15} When you heard this word, you implanted treachery in him, rising from the thing you said to Eve, who was made from Adam's rib. {2:16} You deceived Adam, who was pure, with strong treachery, making him a lawbreaker like yourself. {2:17} When you misled Eve, who was created innocent like a dove and unaware of your malice, she was betrayed by your successful lies and twisted words, and after you deceived that Eve, who was created first, she went and misled God's creation, Adam, who was also created from the earth. {2:18} You caused him to betray his Creator, not through pride, but through arrogance, causing him to deny his Creator's word, and you destroyed Adam through your pride. {2:19} Through your wickedness, you turned him away from the love of his Creator, and through your influence, you drove him out of the garden of peace and kept him from the food of the garden. {2:20} From the beginning, you have fought against God's innocent creation, Adam, to lower him into Sheol (the underworld), where you will be tormented. You took him away from the love that gave him life and created him from nothingness, causing him to lose the garden's nourishment. {2:21} When he was earthly, God made him a subtle angel who praises Him completely in body, soul, and mind. {2:22} He created many thoughts for him, like a harp praising Him in many different melodies.'

{3:1} But the one who created you had a thought for you—that you might fully praise Him while you were sent to where He directed you. {3:2} Adam was given five evil thoughts and five good thoughts—ten thoughts in total. {3:3} And again, he had many thoughts like the waves of the sea—like a whirlwind that scatters dust lifted from the Earth—and like the sea waves that shake, his countless thoughts arose in his heart like countless raindrops—Adam's thoughts were like that. {3:4} But your thoughts are singular, as you are not fleshly; you have no other thoughts. {3:5} But you lodged in a snake's reasoning—through evil deceit, you destroyed Adam, who was one body—and Eve heard the serpent and, having heard, she acted according to what it commanded her. {3:6} After she ate a fig, she misled God's first creation, Adam—and she brought death upon him and upon her children because she broke her Creator's command. {3:7} They left the Garden by God's true judgment—He calmed them in the land where they were sent, and their children were born from their nature, and they found crops from the Earth—but He didn't distance them from the Garden while they were quarreling. {3:8} And at the time He expelled them straight from the Garden, it was so they could plant crops and have children, to be calmed and renew their reasoning with the Earth's fruits that the Earth produced—and that they might be calmed by the fruits of the Earth and the Garden that God gave them... {3:9} God gave them woods even more lush than those in the Garden—and Eve and Adam, whom you sent away from the Garden because they ate, were completely calmed from their sadness. {3:10} As God knows how to calm His creation, their reasoning is calmed because of their children and because of the crops from the Earth. {3:11} Since they were sent to this world, which grows thorns and nettles, they strengthened their reasoning with water and grain.

{4:1} The Lord had a plan to redeem Adam—and He shall shame you; He will save a sheep from the wolf's mouth (Adam from the Devil). {4:2} However, you will go to Hell, taking with you those whom you ruled. {4:3} Those who kept their Creator God's law shall be blessed with their Creator, who protected them from evil deeds so that they might become His fortune—and that they might praise Him with honored angels who did not break their Creator's law like you. {4:4} But God—who chose and gave you more than all the angels—so that you might praise Him with His servant angels, withheld from you a lofty throne due to your arrogance. {4:5} Yet you became famous and were called one who loves godhood—and your followers were called demons. {4:6} But those who loved God shall be His kin like honored angels—and the Seraphim and Cherubim who praise Him stretch out their wings and praise without ceasing. {4:7} But in your arrogance and laziness, you destroyed your praise so that you might praise Him at all times with your host and your kindred, created in your likeness. {4:8} Lest the praise of God—who created you and made you a tenth tribe—be diminished when you forgot to praise Him, it seemed to you that it was impossible for Him to create a being like you; and lest the praise of God—who created you—be diminished when you were separated from your brethren in unity, He created Adam because of your fall. {4:9} But in your arrogant reasoning, you neglected to praise God who created you—He was vexed with you—He ridiculed you and bound and banished you to Hell with your followers as well. {4:10} He took soil from the Earth with His glorified hands—and adding fire, water, and wind—He created Adam in His image and likeness. {4:11} He appointed him over all creation He made, that His praise might be fulfilled by the praise you would offer Him; Adam's praise became one with the praise of the angels—and their praises were equal. {4:12} But in your hardened reasoning and your arrogance, you were brought low from your rank—and having departed from God's lordship, who created you, you destroyed your true self. {4:13} Know that His praise was not diminished—for God created Adam who praised Him in his reasoning and counsel, lest God's essence be diminished. {4:14} For He knows all before it is done—and He knew you before He created you that you would defy His command; as there was a hidden plan with Him before He created the world—when you denied Him, He created His servant Adam in His likeness. {4:15} Like Solomon spoke, saying: "Before the hills were created and before the world came into being, and before the winds that are the Earth's foundations were established... {4:16} and before He established the hills and the mountains, and before the work of this world was made firm—and before the sun and moon gave light, before the ages and stars were known... {4:17} and before day and night alternated—and before the sea was separated by sand—before all of creation was created... {4:18} and before all sight today was sighted—and before all names called today were called—He created me, Solomon"—angels like you and you and His servant Adam were in God's reasoning. {4:19} He created Adam so that His glorious name might be praised when you rebelled—and that He might be praised by His humbled servant Adam, who was made from the Earth when you were arrogant. {4:20} For being in Heaven, God hears the pleas of the poor—and He loves the praises of the humble. {4:21} He loves to save those who are humble, but He does not love pride, and He does not respond to the arrogance of a concubine; God will ignore the prideful. {4:22} And they shall weep while they cry because of the sins they have committed. {4:23} It was too late for you to plead for repentance. {4:24} But Adam, who was made from the Earth, returned in repentance while he wept before God because of his sin. {4:25} But in your hardened reasoning and your heart's arrogance, you did not know the work of love, and you did not know repentance; it was too late for you to plead before your Creator God in repentance and mourning and sadness. {4:26} But Adam, who is made from ashes and dust, returned in repentance, mourning and sadness—and he returned to humility and the work of love. {4:27} But you did not humble your reasoning and your true self before God who created you. {4:28} As for Adam—he humbled himself and pleaded about the iniquity he committed; he was not proud. {4:29} Though you have completely committed crimes, they were found in you—but it was not him who caused that error; in your arrogance, you took him with you to your destruction. {4:30} Before He created you both—as He knew you were sinners—and as He knew your works—He knows that what was done was in your heart's arrogance. {4:31} But He returned Adam—who was without arrogance or malice—in repentance, mourning, and sadness. {4:32} For a person who sins and does not plead for repentance multiplies his iniquity more than his previous sin; but in your heart's arrogance, it was too late for you to plead for repentance; but a person who pleads and weeps in true repentance before his Creator God... {4:33} he enters true repentance—and he finds a way by which he will be saved, so that he might fear his Lord's heart—and he pleaded before his Creator; for he pleaded before Him in humility and deep repentance—and arising from his earlier tribulation, the Lord shall lighten his sin for him, lest He be vexed with His servant, and He will forgive him his former sins. {4:34} If he does not return to his former sin, and if he does this, this is perfect repentance—Adam did not forget to think of his Creator nor to implore his Creator God in repentance. {4:35} And you—plead in repentance to your Creator God—and do not wrong those who are flesh and blood—for God who created them knows their weakness—and do not wrong the people He created by His authority. {4:36} And after their souls are separated from their bodies, their flesh shall return to dust until the day that God loves.

{5:1} Know that the Lord God, who created you, has formed you in His image and likeness when you were on Earth. Don't forget the Lord who established you and saved you, whom Israel praised. He placed you in a garden so that you might live joyfully and tend to the land. {5:2} But when you disobeyed His command, He sent you away from the garden into this world, which He cursed because of you. Now, the land grows thorns and nettles. {5:3} For you are made from the earth, and your body will return to it. You are dust, and to dust you will return, for the soil feeds you, and you will return to it until God's love raises you again. And God will examine the sins you've committed and the iniquities you've performed. {5:4} Consider what you will answer Him on that day. Reflect on the good and evil you've done in this world. Assess whether your good deeds outweigh the bad. Think carefully. {5:5} If you've done good works, it will be well for you, and you will be joyful on the day when the dead rise again. {5:6} But if you've committed evil acts, then woe to you, for you will receive your punishment according to your deeds and your wicked thoughts. If you harm your neighbor and have no fear of God, you will face your consequences. {5:7} And if you betray your neighbor and swear falsely in God's name, your punishment will match your deeds. Woe to you. {5:8} If you speak lies to your neighbor while pretending it is truth, though you know it's false, you will be judged for it. {5:9} If you convince others to believe your falsehoods and multiply lies that aren't based on truth, you will face consequences for your sins. You promise to give something to your neighbor, yet you know in your heart that you will not. {5:10} When you made that promise, demons, like dogs, surrounded you and caused you to forget. Even if you wanted to give, they misled you. They don't know the person for whom they are gathering. Yet, as it was said, they will gain wealth that will not satisfy them, money that they will not consume. {5:11} Again, as it was said, "Children of Adam are prone to lying, making false balances (deceitful practices) and moving from robbery to robbery." The riches of this world tempt you so that you accumulate wealth that will bring no benefit to you. {5:12} O people, don't put your hope in fraudulent scales and dishonest gains, in stealing your neighbor's money, or in reducing someone else's wealth unjustly. Don't steal someone's land or commit any of the lies you engage in for personal gain that isn't rightfully yours. {5:13} If you do these things, you will receive the punishment due for your actions. {5:14} O people, be sustained by the honest work of your hands, done righteously. Do not desire stolen goods. Don't love taking what isn't rightfully yours and eating what belongs to someone else unjustly. {5:15} Even if you eat it, it will not satisfy you. When you die, you'll leave it behind for another. Even if you accumulate much wealth, it won't benefit you. {5:16} And if your wealth grows, don't let it corrupt your thinking. The wealth of sinners is like smoke rising from a griddle, which the wind blows away. It is better to have a small amount gained honestly than great wealth acquired deceitfully.

{6:1} Consider the day of your death, when your soul will leave your body. You will abandon your wealth for others to take, and you will walk an unknown path. Reflect on the troubles that will come upon you. {6:2} The demons that will receive you are wicked, and their appearance is terrifying and dreadful. They will not listen to your words, and you will not hear theirs. {6:3} Because you did not follow the will of your Creator, God, they will ignore your pleas when you beg them for mercy. This will increase your fear. {6:4} But those who obeyed God's will have nothing to fear, for demons are afraid of them. However, demons will mock the souls of sinners. {6:5} The souls of good people will rejoice with angels in bliss, for they rejected the pleasures of this world. But evil angels will seize the souls of sinners. {6:6} The souls of the righteous will be received by angels of mercy, sent by God to comfort them, while the souls of sinners will be mocked by evil angels sent by the Devil (Deeyablos). Demons will claim the souls of sinners. {6:7} Sinners, woe to you. Weep for yourselves before the day of your death arrives, before you stand before God. {6:8} Repent now, while you still have time, before your opportunity passes. Repent, so you can live in joy and peace, free from suffering and illness. After you die, your time will not come again. So, weep for your sins. {6:9} Don't let your life be in vain, separated from God. In your moments of harsh self-reflection, let love and joy be found within you. For when a body is satisfied beyond measure, it forgets God's name, and the wealth of the Devil will take root. But the Holy Spirit will not dwell within such a person. Let joy and peace be with you. {6:10} Just as Moses said, "Jacob ate, was satisfied, and grew fat and large, and the Lord, who created him, was distanced from him." His lifestyle became separated from God. {6:11} For a body that is filled beyond measure without moderation forgets God's name. Do not let unrestrained desires lead you astray. {6:12} A person who eats with moderation will live in God's protection, firm like the horizon, or like a tower with stone walls. A person who forgets God's law will flee, though no one is chasing him. {6:13} A righteous person will live with honor, like a lion. {6:14} But those who don't love God will not keep His law, and their thoughts will not be just. {6:15} God will bring sorrow and fear upon them while they are still in this world. They will be seized by trembling and fear and plagued by countless troubles. Their wealth will be taken away, and they will be bound by chains from the hands of their masters. {6:16} They will not find rest from their tribulations, and their lives will lack peace. Even in their most terrifying struggles, God will bring sorrow and fear upon them.

{7:1} But just as David spoke, saying, "I believe in God; I do not fear what others might do to me," there is no fear or alarm for those who trust in God. {7:2} Again, he said, "Even if warriors surround me, I believe in Him; I ask God for one thing, and that is what I seek"—those who trust in Him have no fear; a person who believes in Him will live forever and will not fear rising from evil. {7:3} Who is the person that is ashamed to believe in God? What about those who ignore Him for their desires? {7:4} As He has said, "I love those who love Me," and "I will honor those who glorify Me"—I will keep those who return to Me in repentance. Who is the one who is ashamed to believe in Him? {7:5} Judge with truth and protect the widow's body; save those that God might save you from all who oppose you in evil—keep them, as kind people's children are honored; they are given prosperity, and yet He will save your children after you, so they will not worry about food.

{8:1} Job believed in God, and he did not neglect to praise his Creator; God saved him from all the tribulations that the enemy of Adam's children, the Devil, brought upon him. He said, "God gives, and God takes away; it is as if God loved me, so let His name be praised by all on Earth and in Heaven"—yet he did not allow his reasoning to sadden him; God saved him. {8:2} And at the time God saw that Job's heart was cleansed from sin, He received him with much honor. {8:3} He gave him wealth that surpassed what he had before, for he had fully endured his tribulation, and He healed him from his wounds because he persevered through all the trials that came upon him. {8:4} And if you, like him, endure the tribulations sent against you by demons, you will be honored. {8:5} Endure the tribulations, so God might be your fortress and refuge from those who hate you, and so He might be a fortress and refuge for your children's children. Do not let your reasoning sadden you because of the tribulations that come upon you; trust in Him, and He will be a refuge for you. {8:6} Ask Him; He will hear you. Hope in Him, and He will forgive you. Ask Him, and He will be a Father to you. {8:7} Think of Mordecai, Esther, Judith, Gideon, Deborah, Barak, Jephthah, and Samson, {8:8} and others like them who were disciplined for believing in God and whose enemies could not defeat them. {8:9} For God is true, and He does not show favoritism; those who endure hardships because they love Him will receive favor—everyone who fears Him and keeps His law will be preserved, and He will grant them love and honor. {8:10} He will make them joyful in their going and coming, in their life and death, and in their rising and sitting—for He saves and protects. {8:11} He makes sad, and He pardons. {8:12} He makes poor, and He honors; He makes wretched, and as He honors, He makes them joyful.

{9:1} Whether it is what is in Heaven or what is on Earth, whether it is subtle or strong, everything exists firmly within His order. {9:2} Nothing departs from God's law and His order—He who created the entire world; whether it is a vulture flying in Heaven, He commands its destination where He desires. {9:3} He commands a snake's path in a cave, and a boat's path over the sea—apart from God, no one knows its path. {9:4} And apart from God, no one knows the path a soul takes when it separates from the body, whether it is a righteous or a sinner's soul. {9:5} Who knows where it will go—whether it will wander in the wilderness or on a mountain? Or whether it will soar like a bird, like dew that falls on a mountain? {9:6} Or whether it will be like a strong wind, or like lightning that clears its path? {9:7} Or like stars shining in the deep, or like sand on the shore of the sea piled in the deep? {9:8} Or like a stone on the horizon firm upon the deep of the sea, or like a tree that bears beautiful fruit growing by a spring? {9:9} Or that it will be like a reed burned by the sun, and that the wind lifts it and carries it to a place where it does not grow, leaving no trace? {9:10} Or that it will be like misty vapor whose trace cannot be found—who knows God's work? Who are His counselors? With whom did He take counsel? {9:11} As God's thoughts are hidden from people, who can examine and understand His work? {9:12} As He created the Earth on water and established it without stakes—there is no one who can comprehend God's counsel or His wisdom—He created Heaven in His perfect wisdom and established it in the winds, stretching forth a vast cosmos like a tent. {9:13} He commanded clouds to rain on the Earth, growing grass and countless fruits for people—so that we might believe in God and be joyful in unity. {9:14} God is the one who gives the children of Adam joy, abundance, and fulfillment; God gives so that they might satisfy and praise Him who provides fruit from the Earth. {9:15} And He dresses them in beautiful robes, giving them all the love and abundance—joy and satisfaction given to those who fulfill God's covenant. {9:16} He grants love and honor in the house He prepared and in the Kingdom of Heaven for those fathers who keep God's law. {9:17} He grants love and honor in the place He prepared and in the Kingdom of Heaven for those fathers who live firmly in His worship and His law—who do not stray from His law, whom He exalted so that they might keep His order and His law. I see what God does for His friends in this world by weakening their enemies and preserving their bodies. {9:18} I see that He gives them all they ask of Him and fulfills their agreements—do not stray from God and fulfill His covenant. {9:19} Do not depart from His commands and His law, lest He become angry with you and destroy you suddenly, and lest He be angry and punish you with tribulations from which you formerly lived, and lest you stray from your father's order where you were once established, and lest your dwelling be in Hell where there are no exits until eternity. {9:20} Keep your Creator God's law when your soul separates from your flesh, so that He may do good works for you when you stand before God. {9:21} For the kingdoms of Earth and Heaven are His, and all dominion and authority belong to Him; kindness and forgiveness are only for Him. {9:22} As He makes rich and makes poor, as He makes wretched and honors, keep God's law. {9:23} And David spoke, because he said, "Man seems vain, and his time passes like a shadow." {9:24} He spoke because he said, "But Lord, You live forever, and Your name is for the children." {9:25} And again he said, "Your kingdom is the kingdom of all the world, and Your rulership is for the children"—You returned a kingdom for David taken from Saul. {9:26} But there is no one who can point to You; there is no one who can dismiss You; You see all, yet there is no one who can see You. {9:27} And Your kingdom will not perish forever for the children; there is no one who can rule Him, but He rules all—He sees all, yet there is no one who sees Him. {9:28} As He created man in His image and likeness so that they might praise Him and know His worship in straightforward reasoning without doubt—He examines and knows what thoughts arise and what reasoning is carried forth. {9:29} Yet they bow to stone, to wood, and to silver and gold that human hands have crafted. {9:30} And they sacrifice sacrifices until their offerings rise toward Heaven, so that their sins may be firm before God—but still they refuse to worship God who created them; He will condemn them because of all the sins they committed in worshiping their idols. {9:31} They learned to bow to idols and all polluted works that are unworthy—cursing by stars, sorcery, idol worship, evil practices, and all the works that God does not love; yet they did not keep God's commands that they learned. {9:32} As they did not love to worship God to save their bodies from sin and iniquity through His servants, the angels, and by the gifts they present before God—they did all this in the absence of good works. {9:33} And when they all rise together from the graves where they were buried and where their bodies perished, their souls will stand empty before God, and those souls will dwell in the Kingdom of Heaven prepared for the righteous. {9:34} But the souls of sinners will dwell in Hell, and when the graves are opened, the dead will rise, and the souls will return to the bodies from which they were once separated. {9:35} Just as they were born in their nakedness from their mother's womb, they will stand naked before God, and their sins, which they committed from infancy until that time, will be revealed. {9:36} They will receive hardships for their sins in their bodies, and whether they had little or much sin, they will face hardships according to their sins.

{10:1} The blood of the soul found from God will dwell in them as it once did; and if you do not believe that the dead will rise, understand that their spirits will awaken in the rainy season without being born of a mother or father. {10:2} He commanded them to be dead by His word. {10:3} Their flesh, having decayed and rotted, will be renewed, and they will rise like those He loves. {10:4} And when the rain falls and the earth is satisfied, they will live, having arisen as they were created before. {10:5} Those who are alive in a blood-filled soul and who live in this world and those produced by water have been created—He said, "Let them be created." Just as God's authority rests upon the waters, He gives them a blood-filled soul by His authority and His word. {10:6} Since they are created by His authority and His word without a father or mother, you, who are blind to reason, say, "The dead will not rise"—if you have knowledge or wisdom, how can you say the dead will not rise by the word of their Creator God? {10:7} Just as the dead—who were ashes and dust in the grave—will rise by God's word, you should enter repentance and return to your faith. {10:8} Like His word said before, they will rise by the dew of pardon from God, and that word will turn the world and awaken the dead like those He loves. {10:9} Know that you will rise and stand before Him; do not let your dull reasoning convince you that you will remain in the grave. {10:10} It is not so—you will rise and receive hardships according to the measure of the work you did—whether good or evil—so do not think you will remain, for this day is the day when everyone will receive hardships. {10:11} In the time of resurrection, you will bear the consequences of all your sins that you committed from your infancy until that time; you will have no excuse to deny your sins like in this world. {10:12} Just as you make your false words seem true before you and turn the lies you spoke into truth, you will have no excuse for pretense like in this world. {10:13} Because all your evil works are known to you, and they will be revealed before your Creator God—God's word will be upon you and speak against you—you have no excuse for your pretense. {10:14} You will be ashamed there because of the sins you committed; you might be among those who are thanked for their good works—but do not be ashamed before men and angels on the day of judgment—quickly enter repentance in this world before you arrive there. {10:15} Those who praise God with the angels will receive their reward from their Creator without shame, and they will be joyful in the Kingdom of Heaven. However, unless you did good works while in your flesh and in life, you will have no fortune with the righteous. {10:16} If you are unprepared when you have knowledge and in this world where you can enter repentance, there will be useless regret for you—for not giving a morsel to the hungry when you had money. {10:17} And for not clothing the naked when you had clothes, and for not saving the wronged when you had the authority. {10:18} For not teaching the sinner when you had knowledge so he might repent, and that God might forgive him the sins he committed in ignorance. {10:19} And for not fighting against demons who quarreled with you when you had the power to prevail. {10:20} And for not fasting or praying when you had the strength to weaken your fleshly desires and submit your self to righteousness that does not favor the flesh... {10:21} that does not favor worldly pleasures like beautiful drinks and sweet foods, and that does not adorn itself in fine clothes, silver, and gold... {10:22} And as you did not fast or pray when you had strength to submit yourself to righteousness, which is not adorned with honored jewels like emeralds and diamonds, there will be useless regret for you—this is not a suitable ornament. {10:23} As for a person's ornament, it is purity, wisdom, knowledge, and loving one another in what is right without envy, jealousy, doubt, or quarrels—while you love your companion as you love yourself... {10:24} and without doing evil to someone who has done evil to you—it is loving one another rightly so that you may enter the Kingdom of Heaven, which is given to those who endure tribulations. God may grant you the honored Kingdom of Heaven and your reward for hoping in the Kingdom of Heaven during resurrection time with honorable people in knowledge and wisdom. {10:25} And do not say, "After we die, we will not rise," for the devil cuts off the hope of those who speak and think this, lest they be saved in resurrection time—they will know they have hardships when the Advent arrives for them—in resurrection time, those who worked sin without knowing will be very sad, for they did not believe in Him that they would rise on that Day. {10:26} Because of this, they will be reproached for the measure of the evil works they committed in this world, and they will see the resurrection that they denied, wherein they will arise in the flesh together. {10:27} They will weep at that time because they did not perform good works—it would have been better for them if they had wept in this world, if that were possible for them, rather than being those who weep in Hell. {10:28} If I did not weep in this world by my own accord, demons will make me weep without my consent in Hell—if I did not enter repentance in this world, I prepare worthless and useless cries and mourning in Hell. {10:29} Prepare good works so that you may cross from death to life, and that you may go from this passing world to the Kingdom of Heaven, and that you may see the light of the Kingdom of Heaven that surpasses the light in this world. {10:30} Reject worldly pleasures so that you may be joyfully fulfilled in the Kingdom of Heaven with joys that are everlasting, from today until eternity, with those who believe that the dead will rise.

The History of Joseph the Carpenter

{1:1} One day, while Jesus Christ, our Savior and Master, was sitting with His disciples on the Mount of Olives, He said to them: "Brothers and friends, chosen sons of the Father, you know I have often told you that I must be crucified and die for the salvation of Adam and his descendants, and that I will rise from the dead. Now I am entrusting you with the teachings of the holy gospel that I have previously announced to you, so that you may proclaim it throughout the world. I will empower you from on high and fill you with the Holy Spirit. {1:2} You will declare to all nations the message of repentance and forgiveness of sins. {1:3} For even a single cup of water, {1:4} if a person finds it in the world to come, is greater and more valuable than all the wealth of this entire world. The space that one foot can occupy in my Father's house is far greater and more precious than all the riches of the earth. {1:5} Indeed, an hour spent in the joyful company of the righteous is more blessed and valuable than a thousand years among sinners, {1:6} for their weeping and lamentation will never end, and they will not find consolation or rest at any time forever. Now, my honored friends, go and tell all nations: Truly, the Savior diligently seeks the inheritance that is due and is the administrator of justice. The angels will defeat their enemies and fight for them on the day of conflict. He will examine every careless and idle word that people speak, and they will have to account for it. {1:7} Just as no one can escape death, so all a person's deeds will be revealed on the day of judgment, whether good or evil. {1:8} Also, tell them this: Let not the strong boast of their strength, nor the rich boast of their riches; but let the one who wishes to boast, boast in the Lord."

{2:1} There was a man named Joseph from Bethlehem, a town in Judah, the city of King David. This man, wise and learned, became a priest in the Lord's temple. He was also skilled in his trade as a carpenter, and like any man, he married. He had sons and daughters, four sons named Judas, Justus, James, and Simon, and two daughters named Assia and Lydia. Eventually, Joseph's wife, a woman dedicated to divine glory in all her works, passed away. But Joseph, a righteous man and my father by flesh, and the husband of my mother Mary, returned to his trade as a carpenter.

{3:1} After Joseph became a widower, my mother Mary, who was blessed, holy, and pure, was already twelve years old. Her parents had offered her to the temple when she was three, and she stayed there for nine years. When the priests noticed that the virgin, holy and God-fearing, was growing up, they said to one another: "Let's find a righteous and pious man to whom Mary can be entrusted until her marriage; otherwise, if she stays in the temple, something might happen to her, and we would be sinning and make God angry."

{4:1} So, they sent out and gathered twelve elders from the tribe of Judah. They wrote down the names of the twelve tribes of Israel, and the lot fell upon the pious old man, righteous Joseph. The priests then told my blessed mother: "Go with Joseph, and stay with him until your marriage." Righteous Joseph took my mother and led her to his house. There, Mary found James the Less in his father's house, heartbroken and sad over his mother's death, and she raised him. Because of this, Mary was called the mother of James. {4:2} Afterward, Joseph left her at home and went to his workshop to continue his carpentry. After Mary had lived in his house for two years, she was exactly fourteen years old, including the time when Joseph received her.

{5:1} I chose her willingly, with the agreement of my Father and the guidance of the Holy Spirit. I became flesh through her, by a mystery beyond human understanding. Three months after her conception, the righteous Joseph returned from his work, and when he found my virgin mother pregnant, he was deeply troubled and considered sending her away quietly. {5:2} But filled with fear, sorrow, and anguish, he couldn't bring himself to eat or drink that day.

{6:1} At noon, the angel Gabriel, the prince of angels, appeared to Joseph in a dream, sent by my Father with a command. He said, "Joseph, son of David, do not be afraid to take Mary as your wife, for she has conceived by the Holy Spirit. She will give birth to a son, and you will name Him Jesus. He will rule all nations with a strong hand." {6:2} After delivering this message, the angel left him. Joseph woke from his sleep and did as the angel of the Lord instructed him, and Mary stayed with him.

{7:1} Some time later, Caesar Augustus issued a decree that everyone in the Roman Empire should be registered, each in their own city. Righteous Joseph, therefore, took the virgin Mary and went to Bethlehem because the time for her to give birth was near. Joseph registered his name, for he was from the line of David and of the tribe of Judah. Indeed, Mary, my mother, gave birth to me in Bethlehem, in a cave near the tomb of Rachel, the wife of the patriarch Jacob, who was the mother of Joseph and Benjamin, two of the twelve tribes of Israel.

{8:1} But Satan reported this to Herod the Great, the father of Archelaus. This same Herod {8:2} had ordered my friend and relative John to be beheaded. He searched for me diligently, thinking my kingdom would be of this world. {8:3} However, Joseph, the pious old man, was warned of this danger in a dream. So he took my mother Mary and me, resting in her arms. Salome {8:4} also traveled with them. They left home and went to Egypt, where they stayed for a whole year until Herod's hatred passed.

{9:1} Herod ultimately died a terrible death, paying for the innocent blood of the children he wickedly killed. With the death of that wicked tyrant, they returned to the land of Israel and settled in a town in Galilee called Nazareth. Joseph went back to his trade as a carpenter and earned his living by his own work, for according to the law of Moses, he never sought to live off the labor of others.

{10:1} As the years passed, the old man reached a very advanced age. However, he did not suffer from any physical weakness, nor had he lost his sight, nor had any teeth fallen from his mouth. Mentally, throughout his life, he remained sharp; he always showed youthful vigor in his work, and his body remained strong and free from pain. He lived to be one hundred and eleven years old, his old age lasting as long as possible.

{11:1} Justus and Simeon, Joseph's older sons, were married and had their own families. Both of Joseph's daughters were also married and lived in their own homes. This left Judas and James the Less, along with my virgin mother, in Joseph's house. I lived with them as if I were one of his sons. Throughout my life, I was without fault. I called Mary my mother and Joseph my father, obeying everything they said. I never argued with them or spoke against them; instead, I treated them with great love, like the pupil of my eye.

{12:1} After these events, the time approached for the death of the righteous Joseph, the old man, as it does for all humans born of this earth. As his body neared its end, an angel of the Lord informed him that his death was imminent. Fear and great confusion filled him, so he got up and went to Jerusalem. He entered the Lord's temple & poured out his prayers before sanctuary, saying:

{13:1} "O God, author of all comfort, God of all compassion, and Lord of all humanity; God of my soul, body, and spirit; with my prayers, I honor You, O Lord and my God. If my days are ending and the time is near for me to leave this world, I beseech You to send the great Michael, the prince of Your holy angels, to stay with me so that my troubled soul may leave this suffering body peacefully, without fear or anxiety. Great fear and deep sadness seize all beings on their death day—whether human, wild beast, or domestic animal, or anything that crawls or flies. In the end, all living creatures are gripped with horror, and their souls depart in fear and deep sorrow. Therefore, O Lord and my God, let Your holy angel assist my soul and body until they are separated. Let my guardian angel, who has been with me since birth, {13:2} not turn away from me; may he accompany me on my journey until he brings me to You. May his face be joyful and comforting, and may he accompany me in peace. Let not terrifying demons come near me on my path to You until I reach You in bliss. Do not let the gatekeepers hinder my soul from entering paradise. Do not expose my sins and bring me to judgment before Your fearsome tribunal. Let not lions attack me, nor let the waves of fire overwhelm my soul—this is something every soul must pass through {13:3}—before I see the glory of Your divinity. O God, most just Judge, who will judge humanity with fairness and give each according to their deeds, O Lord and my God, I ask You to be present with Your compassion & light my path so I may come to You, for You are a source of all good things & eternal glory. Amen."

{14:1} After this, when he returned to his home in Nazareth, he fell ill and had to stay in bed. It was at this time that he died, as is destined for all people. This illness was severe, and he had never been sick like this from the day he was born. Thus, it was certainly the will of Christ {14:2} to decide the fate of the righteous Joseph. He lived forty years without being married; then his wife was in his care for forty-nine years before she passed away. A year after her death, my mother, the blessed Mary, was entrusted to him by the priests to care for her until her marriage. She spent two years in his house, and in the third year of her stay, at the age of fifteen, she gave birth to me through a mystery that no creature can fully understand, except for me, my Father, and the Holy Spirit, who are one essence with me.

{15:1} The total age of my father, that righteous old man, was one hundred and eleven years, as my Father in heaven decreed. The day his soul left his body was the twenty-sixth of the month Abib. As the fine gold began to lose its luster and the silver to wear down, so did his understanding and wisdom. He lost interest in food and drink and his carpentry skills diminished; he no longer focused on his trade. It was early on the twenty-sixth of Abib that Joseph, the righteous old man, lay in bed, surrendering his restless soul. He opened his mouth with many sighs, clapped his hands together, and cried out with a loud voice, saying:

{16:1} "Woe to the day I was born into this world! Woe to the womb that bore me! Woe to the body that sustained me! Woe to the feet on which I rested! Woe to the hands that carried and raised me! (1) I was conceived in iniquity, and my mother desired me in sin. {16:2} Woe to my tongue and lips that have spoken emptiness, gossip, falsehood, ignorance, ridicule, idle chatter, deceit, and hypocrisy! Woe to my eyes that have looked upon shameful things! Woe to my ears that have delighted in slander! Woe to my hands that have taken what is not theirs! Woe to my stomach and bowels that have craved forbidden food! Woe to my throat, which has consumed everything like fire! Woe to my feet, which have walked paths displeasing to God! Woe to my body; and woe to my miserable soul, which has turned away from God, its Maker! What will I do when I stand before the most just Judge, who will hold me accountable for the deeds of my youth? Woe to every man who dies in sin! That dreadful hour, which came upon my father Jacob, when his soul was leaving his body, is now near for me. Oh, how wretched I am today, deserving of lamentation! But God alone controls my soul and body; He will handle them according to His good pleasure."

{17:1} These were the words spoken by Joseph, the righteous old man. I approached him and saw that his soul was deeply troubled, caught in great confusion. I said to him, "Greetings, my father Joseph, righteous man; how are you?" He replied, "Greetings, my beloved son. Truly, the agony and fear of death surround me; but as soon as I heard your voice, my soul found peace. O Jesus of Nazareth! Jesus, my Savior! Jesus, the deliverer of my soul! Jesus, my protector! Jesus! O sweetest name on my lips and in the mouths of all who love it! O eye that sees and ear that hears, hear me! I am Your servant; today I humbly bow before You and pour out my tears before You. You are entirely my God; You are my Lord, as the angel has told me countless times, especially on that day when my soul was troubled by unworthy thoughts about the pure and blessed Mary, who carried You in her womb and whom I was considering sending away quietly. While I was pondering this, angels of the Lord appeared to me, saying in a wonderful mystery: 'O Joseph, son of David, fear not to take Mary as your wife; do not let your soul grieve, nor speak ill of her conception, for she is with child by the Holy Spirit and will bear a son named Jesus, for He will save His people from their sins.' Do not wish me harm, O Lord! I was unaware of the mystery of Your birth. I also recall, my Lord, the day the boy died from a serpent's bite. His relatives wanted to hand You over to Herod, claiming You had killed him; but You raised him from the dead and returned him to them. Then I came to You, took Your hand, and said, 'My son, take care of yourself.' You replied, 'Aren't you my father by flesh? I will show you who I am.' {17:2} Now, therefore, O Lord and my God, do not be angry with me or condemn me for that moment. I am Your servant, the son of Your handmaiden; but You are my Lord, my God, and Savior, surely the Son of God."

{18:1} After my father Joseph said this, he could weep no more. I saw that death now had power over him. My mother, the undefiled virgin, rose and came to me, saying, "O my beloved son, this pious old man Joseph is dying." I answered, "Oh my dearest mother, surely the same fate of death falls upon all created beings; death reigns over all humanity. Even you, O my virgin mother, must expect the same end of life as others. Yet your death, like that of this pious man, is not death but life everlasting. Furthermore, I too must die in regard to the body I received from you. But rise, O my venerable mother, and go to Joseph, that blessed old man, so that you may see what happens as his soul departs from his body."

{19:1} My pure mother Mary then went and entered the room where Joseph was. I sat at his feet, watching him, as the signs of death appeared on his face. That blessed old man lifted his head and fixed his eyes on my face, but he couldn't speak due to the agony of death that held him tight. He kept sighing deeply. I held his hands for an hour; he turned to me and gestured for me not to leave. I placed my hand on his chest and felt his soul near his throat, ready to depart.

{20:1} When my virgin mother saw me touching his body, she also touched his feet. Noticing they were already dead and cold, she said to me, "O my beloved son, his feet are starting to stiffen; they are as cold as snow." She then called his sons and daughters, saying, "Come, everyone, and go to your father; for he is surely at the point of death." Assia, his daughter, responded, "Woe to me, my brothers; this is undoubtedly the same illness that took my beloved mother." She lamented and shed tears, and all of Joseph's other children mourned with her. My mother Mary and I also wept with them. {20:2}

{21:1} Looking towards the south, I saw Death approaching, accompanied by all of Gehenna, followed closely by his army and minions; their clothes, faces, and mouths blazed with flames. When my father Joseph saw them coming straight at him, his eyes filled with tears, and he groaned in a strange manner. Seeing the intensity of his sighs, I pushed back Death and all his accompanying forces. I called upon my good Father, saying:

{22:1} "O Father of all mercy, O Eye that sees, and Ear that hears, listen to my prayers and pleas for the old man Joseph; send Michael, the prince of Your angels, and Gabriel, the herald of light, along with all Your angels of light, and let them accompany my father Joseph's soul until they bring it to You. This is the hour when my father needs compassion. I tell you, all the saints, and indeed everyone born into this world, whether righteous or wicked, must inevitably face death."

{23:1} Thus, Michael and Gabriel came to my father Joseph's soul, wrapped it in a shining cloth, and took it. He entrusted his spirit to my good Father, who granted him peace. Yet none of his children knew he had fallen asleep. The angels protected his soul from the demons of darkness in their path and praised God until they brought it to the dwelling place of the righteous.

{24:1} Now his body lay lifeless and bloodless. I reached out my hand, positioned his eyes, closed his mouth, and said to the virgin Mary, "O my mother, where is the skill he showed throughout his life? Look! It has vanished as if it never existed." When his children heard me speaking to my pure virgin mother, they realized he had already passed away, and they wept and mourned. But I told them, "Surely, your father's death is not death but everlasting life; he has been freed from the troubles of this life and has entered into perpetual and eternal rest." Hearing these words, they tore their clothes and cried.

{25:1} Indeed, the people of Nazareth and Galilee, upon hearing their mourning, gathered around them, weeping from the third hour until the ninth. At the ninth hour, they all came together to Joseph's bed. They lifted his body after anointing it with precious oils. I prayed to my Father with the celestial prayer, the same prayer I had spoken with my own hand before I was carried in my mother Mary's womb. As soon as I finished and said amen, a great multitude of angels appeared. I instructed two of them to spread their shining garments and wrap the body of Joseph, the blessed old man, in them.

{26:1} I spoke to Joseph, saying, "The corruption of death shall not claim you, nor shall a worm ever come from your body. Not a single limb will be broken, nor will a hair on your head be altered. Nothing of your body shall perish, O my father Joseph; it will remain whole and uncorrupted until the banquet of the thousand years. Whoever makes an offering on the day of your remembrance, I will bless and reward in the assembly of the virgins. Whoever shares food with the needy, the poor, widows, and orphans on the day your memory is honored, and in your name, will lack for nothing good all their days. Whoever gives a cup of water or wine to a widow or orphan in your name, I will grant them to you, so you may enter with them to the banquet of the thousand years. Every person who presents an offering on your commemoration day, I will bless and reward in the church of the virgins; for one offering, I will return to them thirty, sixty, or a hundredfold. Whoever writes the story of your life, your work, and your departure from this world, and this narrative that has come from my mouth, I will entrust to your care as long as they live. When their soul departs from the body, and they leave this world, I will burn the book of their sins and will not punish them on judgment day; they will cross the sea of flames and go through it without trouble or pain. For every poor person who cannot give any of the aforementioned things: if a son is born to them, they shall name him Joseph. In that house, there will be neither poverty nor sudden death forever."

{27:1} Afterward, the leaders of the city gathered at the place where the body of the blessed old man Joseph had been laid, bringing burial clothes with them. They wanted to wrap him in these clothes as the Jews typically did with their dead. However, they found that his shroud clung tightly to his body, as if it were made of iron—it couldn't be moved or loosened. They searched in vain for any ends of the linen, which left them greatly astonished. Finally, they took him to a cave and opened the entrance to bury him next to his ancestors. This reminded me of the day he walked with me into Egypt and the immense trouble he endured on my behalf. Therefore, I mourned his death for a long time, lying on his body, and I said:

{28:1} "O Death! you who make all knowledge disappear and cause so many tears and lamentations, surely it is God my Father Himself who has given you this power. People die because of the transgression of Adam and Eve, and Death spares no one. Yet, nothing happens to anyone or befalls them without my Father's command. There have been people who lived for as long as nine hundred years, but they still died. Indeed, even those who lived longer ultimately faced the same fate; none of them ever claimed they had escaped death. The Lord does not send the same punishment more than once, as it pleases my Father to allow it for mankind. At the very moment Death sees the command descending from heaven, it says: 'I will go forth against that person and greatly disturb them.' Then, without hesitation, it attacks the soul and takes control of it, doing as it pleases. Because Adam did not obey my Father but broke His command, my Father's wrath was ignited against him, and he was sentenced to death; thus, death entered the world. If Adam had kept my Father's commandments, he would never have faced death. Do you think I could ask my good Father to send a chariot of fire to take my father Joseph's body and carry it to a place of rest among the spirits? But because of Adam's transgression, the trouble and violence of death have come upon all humanity. This is why I must die in the flesh, to fulfill my work and offer grace to them.

{29:1} After saying this, I embraced my father Joseph's body and wept over it. They opened the tomb door and placed his body inside, near the body of his father Jacob. At the time he fell asleep, he had lived for one hundred and eleven years. He never experienced tooth pain, his eyesight never dulled, his body never bent, and his strength never waned; he worked as a carpenter until the very last day of his life, which was the twenty-sixth of the month Abib.

{30:1} When we apostles heard these things from our Savior, we joyfully stood up, prostrated ourselves in His honor, and said: "O our Savior, show us Your grace. Now we have truly heard the word of life; however, we are curious, O our Savior, about the fate of Enoch and Elijah, since they did not experience death. For they dwell in the abode of the righteous even to this day, and their bodies have not decayed. Yet that old man Joseph the carpenter was Your father in the flesh. You have commanded us to go into all the world and preach the holy Gospel, saying: 'Tell them about the death of my father Joseph and celebrate an annual festival in his honor.' Anyone who alters this narrative by adding or taking away anything commits sin. We are especially puzzled that Joseph, from the day You were born in Bethlehem, referred to You as his son in the flesh. Why, then, did You not make him immortal like them, especially since You say he was righteous and chosen?

{31:1} Our Savior responded: "Indeed, my Father's prophecy regarding Adam, due to his disobedience, has now been fulfilled. All things are arranged according to my Father's will and pleasure. If a person rejects God's command and follows the devil's works by committing sin, their life may be extended so that they might repent and realize they must eventually face death. Conversely, if someone is devoted to good works, their life may also be prolonged so that, as they age, upright people may be inspired by them. However, if you observe someone prone to anger, know that their days are likely shortened, as such individuals often die in their youth. Every prophecy my Father has made about humanity must be fulfilled. Regarding Enoch and Elijah, who remain alive to this day in the same bodies they were born with, and concerning my father Joseph, who has not been allowed to stay in his body like them: even if a person lives for many thousands of years, they will eventually have to exchange life for death. {31:2} I tell you, O my brothers, that even Enoch and Elijah must return to the world at the end of time and face death—on a day of turmoil, terror, confusion, and suffering. For the Antichrist will kill four bodies and pour out their blood like water because of the shame they will bring upon him and the disgrace they will inflict on him by revealing his wickedness during their lifetime.

{32:1} We asked: "O our Lord, our God and Savior, who are the four whom You said the Antichrist will kill due to the shame they bring upon him?" The Lord answered: "They are Enoch, Elijah, Schila, and Tabitha." When we heard this from our Savior, we rejoiced and celebrated; we offered all glory and thanks to the Lord God and our Savior Jesus Christ. He deserves glory, honor, dignity, dominion, power, and praise, along with the good Father and the Holy Spirit who gives life, now and forever. Amen.

The Testament of Our Lord in Galilee

{1:1} Jesus said to his disciples, "As I am departing from this world, I leave you instructions so that you may walk in truth and unity. {1:2} Let your gatherings be peaceful and your hearts united, for where two or three are gathered in my name, I am among them. {1:3} Appoint for yourselves bishops, presbyters, and deacons who are faithful and righteous, those who will lead the congregation in love and humility. {1:4} The bishop should be blameless, dedicated to the teachings, and able to guide the community with wisdom and compassion.

{2:1} Let the Eucharist be celebrated with reverence, and let only those who are pure in heart partake. {2:2} Pray the prayers I have taught you, giving thanks for the bread and the cup. {2:3} Let the deacons serve with diligence, assisting the bishop in all things and caring for the poor, the widows, and the orphans. {2:4} In baptism, immerse the believer in water in the name of the Father, the Son, and the Holy Spirit, that they may be born again and walk in newness of life.

{3:1} As for those who have fallen into sin, correct them gently, so they may return to the path of righteousness. {3:2} If they repent, forgive them and welcome them back into the fold, for I desire mercy, not sacrifice. {3:3} But if anyone remains obstinate, let them be removed from the congregation, for the purity of the church must be preserved.

{4:1} In the last days, there will be trials and tribulations, and many will abandon the faith. {4:2} But those who persevere will inherit the Kingdom of Heaven. {4:3} Be vigilant, for you do not know the hour when the Son of Man will come. {4:4} Keep your hearts ready, and your faith strong, for the reward is great for those who endure to the end.

The Testament of Joseph of Arimathaea

{1:1} I am Joseph of Arimathea, the one who requested from Pilate the body of our Lord Jesus to bury, and for this, I was imprisoned by the malicious and hostile Jews, who followed the law and yet faced tribulations through Moses. {1:2} By rejecting the Lawgiver, they unknowingly crucified God, revealing Him to those who truly knew God. Around seven days before Jesus' suffering, two robbers condemned to death were brought from Jericho to Pilate. {1:3} The first, named Gestas, was a merciless murderer, killing travelers and exposing others naked. He cruelly hanged women by their heels, cut off their breasts, and drank infants' blood, a man without knowledge of God, violent from his youth and lawless. {1:4} The other, named Demas, a Galilean innkeeper, stole from the rich but was generous to the poor—like Tobit, he buried the poor's bodies. {1:5} He also robbed the Jews' wealth and stole the Law itself from Jerusalem, even stripped Caiaphas' daughter, who was a priestess, and took the hidden deposit placed by Solomon. {1:6} Jesus was also arrested three days before Passover, in the evening. To Caiaphas and the Jews, it wasn't Passover but a time of grief because the sanctuary had been robbed. {1:7} They called Judas Iscariot, son of Caiaphas' brother, who wasn't truly a disciple of Jesus, but supported by the Jews to spy on Jesus and betray Him, being bribed with half a shekel each day. {1:8} For two years, Judas followed Jesus, intending to trap Him with false words, as described by John, one of Jesus' disciples. {1:9} Three days before Jesus' arrest, Judas told the Jews, "Let us meet; perhaps it wasn't the robber who stole the Law, but Jesus Himself, and I'll accuse Him." {1:10} But Nicodemus, keeper of the sanctuary keys, warned them not to do this, for he was righteous beyond the rest of the Jews. {1:11} Caiaphas' daughter Sarah declared, "He claimed he could destroy this temple and rebuild it in three days." {1:12} The Jews trusted her, considering her a prophetess. With this, they arrested Jesus.

{2:1} On the fourth day, at the ninth hour, they brought Jesus to Caiaphas' hall. Annas and Caiaphas questioned Him, "Why did you steal our Law and reject Moses' and the prophets' teachings?" Jesus remained silent. {2:2} They asked again, with the crowd present, "Why would you want to destroy Solomon's sanctuary, built over forty-six years, in one moment?" Jesus did not answer, for the robber had already plundered the sanctuary. {2:3} When evening came, the crowd wanted to burn Caiaphas' daughter for losing the Law, fearing they couldn't keep Passover. She urged them, "Wait, let us kill Jesus, and the Law will be found; then we can properly celebrate." {2:4} Annas and Caiaphas secretly gave Judas more money to claim Jesus stole the Law to protect Caiaphas' daughter. {2:5} Judas accepted, telling them to discreetly release Jesus, and he would persuade the crowd of the accusation. {2:6} Judas went to the sanctuary early on the fifth day and asked the crowd, "What will you give me if I turn over the Law's destroyer?" They offered him thirty pieces of gold, unaware he meant Jesus. {2:7} Accepting the money, he left and soon saw Jesus walking. {2:8} As evening approached, he asked for soldiers, saying, "Seize the man I kiss; he has stolen the Law and prophets." {2:9} Judas then approached Jesus, greeted Him as Rabbi, and kissed Him, identifying Him for arrest. {2:10} The Jews tried Jesus unfairly, accusing Him of crimes He did not commit, while Nicodemus and I distanced ourselves from their wicked judgment.

{3:1} That night, after mistreating Jesus, they delivered Him to Pilate at dawn for crucifixion. The Jews assembled for the sentencing, and Pilate ordered His crucifixion alongside the two robbers. {3:2} Gestas, on the left, mocked Jesus, saying, "I have done much evil; if you are truly King, I would have killed you too. How can you call yourself the Son of God if you can't save yourself? If you are the Christ, come down, and I'll believe." {3:3} Blaspheming and gnashing his teeth, Gestas continued his insults. {3:4} But Demas, on the right, recognizing Jesus' divine grace, declared, "I know you, Jesus Christ, the Son of God. I see you adored by multitudes of angels. Forgive me my sins, for I have sinned under the night's cover. I have no offering for forgiveness, but I beg you, deliver me from judgment." {3:5} He continued, "I see the devil rejoicing over my sins, but, Lord, do not send me to the Jews' fate. Remember me in your kingdom when you judge the twelve tribes." {3:6} Jesus replied, "Truly, today you will be with me in paradise, while the children of Abraham, Isaac, and Jacob are cast out into darkness, but you alone will dwell in paradise until I return to judge." {3:7} Jesus commanded the cherubim guarding paradise to permit Demas entry, stating he would be the first to enter after Adam's exile.

{4:1} After these words, Jesus gave up His spirit at the ninth hour on the day of preparation. Darkness covered the earth, and a great earthquake caused the temple to collapse. {4:2} I, Joseph, asked Pilate for Jesus' body and laid it in a new tomb. Gestas' body vanished, but that of the left robber appeared like a dragon. {4:3} After placing Jesus' body, the Jews, in their hatred, imprisoned me on the Sabbath. That evening, our nation broke the law. {4:4} Then, on the first day of the week, Jesus came to me in prison, along with Demas, who had entered paradise, filling the place with light. {4:5} Jesus opened the prison, freeing me & I recognized Him alongside Demas, who carried a letter from paradise. As we walked to Galilee, a heavenly light and fragrance surrounded us.

{5:1} Jesus sat and read from the letter delivered by the cherubim, praising His descent to save Adam and all creation. {5:2} The letter recounted how they, seeing the crucifixion marks and the shining cross of Demas, were awestruck by His divine presence, causing the fires to extinguish. {5:3} Angels trembled, calling out, "Holy, holy, holy!" knowing the Creator of heaven and earth had descended to the depths. {5:4} They praised Him for bringing salvation and freeing humanity from death's grip, glorifying the unseen plan of the ages.

{6:1} After witnessing these things, I journeyed with Jesus and Demas to Galilee. Jesus appeared transfigured, radiant, with angels ministering to Him for three days. {6:2} On the third day, His disciple John arrived, but Demas was no longer visible. John, confused, asked Jesus about Demas, but Jesus told him to focus on the fragrant presence of paradise, for the robber had inherited it until the final day. {6:3} As John continued speaking, Demas reappeared, transformed like a king with great power, bearing the cross, greeted by a multitude rejoicing in his arrival. {6:4} After this vision, both Demas and I vanished, and I found myself in my own home, never seeing Jesus again. {6:5} Having seen and experienced these events, I wrote them down, so that all may believe in Jesus Christ, the crucified Lord, and turn from Moses' law to the miracles done through Him. {6:6} For those who believe in Him shall inherit eternal life and enter the kingdom of heaven. To Him belong glory, strength, and honor, forever and ever. Amen.

The Testaments of the Twelve Patriarchs

The Testament of Reuben

{1:1} This is the copy of the Testament of Reuben, the commands he gave his sons before he died in the one hundred twenty-fifth year of his life. {1:2} Two years after the death of his brother Joseph, when Reuben fell ill, his sons and grandsons gathered to visit him. {1:3} He said to them: "My children, behold, I am dying and going the way of my fathers." {1:4} Seeing Judah, Gad, and Asher, his brothers, he said to them: "Lift me up so I can tell my brothers and children what I have hidden in my heart, for behold, I am passing away." {1:5} He arose, kissed them, and said to them: "Listen, my brothers, and you, my children, pay attention to Reuben your father and the commands I give you." {1:6} "I call God in heaven as my witness today that you do not walk in the sins of youth and fornication, in which I was involved, defiling my father's bed." {1:7} "I tell you that He struck me with a painful plague in my loins for seven months; had my father Jacob not prayed for me, the Lord would have destroyed me." {1:8} "I was thirty years old when I committed that sin before the Lord, and I was sick unto death for seven months." {1:9} "After this, I repented with determination in my soul for seven years before the Lord." {1:10} "I did not drink wine or strong drink, nor did I eat meat or pleasant food; I mourned over my sin, for it was great, such as had not been seen in Israel." {1:11} "Now hear me, my children, about the seven spirits of deceit I saw when I repented." {1:12} "There are seven spirits appointed against man, and they lead the works of youth." {1:13} "Seven other spirits are given to him at creation, through which every work of man is accomplished." {1:14} "The first is the spirit of life, with which man's being is created." {1:15} "The second is the sense of sight, which gives rise to desire." {1:16} "The third is the sense of hearing, through which comes teaching." {1:17} "The fourth is the sense of smell, with which tastes are given to draw in air and breath." {1:18} "The fifth is the power of speech, with which knowledge comes." {1:19} "The sixth is the sense of taste, through which we eat food and drink; it produces strength, for food is the foundation of strength." {1:20} "The seventh is the power of procreation and sexual intercourse, through which the love of pleasure brings sin." {1:21} "Therefore, it is the last in creation but the first in youth, because it is filled with ignorance and leads the youth like a blind man to a pit, and like a beast to a precipice." {1:22} "In addition to all these, there is an eighth spirit of sleep, which brings about the trance of nature and death." {1:23} "With these spirits are mixed the spirits of error." {1:24} "First, the spirit of fornication is seated in nature and in the senses;" {1:25} "the second, the spirit of insatiability in the belly;" {1:26} "the third, the spirit of fighting, in the liver and gall." {1:27} "The fourth is the spirit of flattery and trickery, which tries to make one appear good through excessive attention." {1:28} "The fifth is the spirit of pride, causing boastfulness and arrogance." {1:29} "The sixth is the spirit of lying, leading to deceit and concealment from family and friends." {1:30} "The seventh is the spirit of injustice, which leads to theft and greed, allowing a man to fulfill the desires of his heart; for injustice works together with the other spirits through taking gifts." {1:31} "And with all these, the spirit of sleep joins, which is the spirit of error and fantasy." {1:32} "Thus, every young man perishes, darkening his mind from the truth and not understanding the law of God or obeying his father's teachings, as happened to me in my youth." {1:33} "Now, my children, love the truth, and it will preserve you; listen to the words of Reuben your father." {1:34} "Pay no attention to the beauty of a woman," {1:35} "nor associate with another man's wife," {1:36} "nor meddle in women's affairs." {1:37} "Had I not seen Bilhah bathing in a hidden place, I would not have fallen into this great sin." {1:38} "For my mind, focusing on the thought of the woman's nakedness, kept me awake until I committed that terrible act." {1:39} "While Jacob, our father, went to Isaac his father, we were in Eder, near Ephrath in Bethlehem; Bilhah became drunk and slept uncovered in her chamber." {1:40} "I went in, saw her nakedness, committed the sin without her realizing it, and left her sleeping." {1:41} "Immediately, an angel of God revealed my sin to my father, and he came and mourned for me, never touching her again."

{2:1} "Therefore, my children, pay no attention to the beauty of women, nor focus on their affairs; instead, walk with a pure heart in the fear of the Lord, working hard on good deeds, study, and caring for your flocks until the Lord gives you a wife of His choosing, so that you do not suffer as I did." {2:2} "For until my father's death, I did not have the courage to look him in the face or speak to any of my brothers because of my shame." {2:3} "Even now, my conscience causes me pain because of my wrongdoing." {2:4} "Yet my father comforted me greatly and prayed to the Lord for me, that His anger might pass from me, just as the Lord revealed." {2:5} "Since then, I have been on my guard and have not sinned." {2:6} "Therefore, my children, I urge you to follow all that I command you, and you will not sin." {2:7} "For the sin of fornication is a trap for the soul, separating it from God and drawing it near to idols, as it deceives the mind and understanding, leading young men to death before their time." {2:8} "Many have been destroyed by fornication; whether a man is old, noble, rich, or poor, he brings shame upon himself and derision upon himself from the wicked." {2:9} "You have heard how Joseph guarded himself against a woman, purging his thoughts of all fornication, and found favor in the sight of God and men." {2:10} "Though the Egyptian woman tried many things, summoned magicians, and offered him love potions, the purpose of his soul held no evil desire." {2:11} "Thus, the God of your fathers delivered him from every evil and hidden death." {2:12} "If fornication does not overcome your mind, then neither can the wicked one overcome you." {2:13} "For women are evil, my children; and since they have no power over men, they use deceit through outward attractions to draw men to themselves." {2:14} "And those they cannot seduce through appearance, they overcome with cleverness." {2:15} "Moreover, the angel of the Lord taught me that women are more easily overcome by the spirit of fornication than men, and in their hearts, they plot against men; they first deceive with their adornments, then poison the mind with a glance, and ultimately ensnare them through the act." {2:16} "A woman cannot force a man openly, but she beguiles him with seductive behavior." {2:17} "Therefore, flee fornication, my children, and instruct your wives and daughters not to adorn their heads and faces to deceive the mind, because every woman who uses such tricks is destined for eternal punishment." {2:18} "For thus they lured the Watchers before the flood; as these watched them, they lusted after them and conceived sinful desires, transforming into the shape of men and appearing to them while with their husbands." {2:19} "The women, desiring their forms, gave birth to giants, for the Watchers appeared to them as if they reached to heaven." {2:20} "Beware of fornication; if you wish to remain pure in mind, guard your senses from every woman." {2:21} "Also command the women not to associate with men so that they may also remain pure in mind." {2:22} "For constant meetings, even without committing an ungodly act, can become a harmful habit for them and lead to our destruction by the wicked and eternal disgrace." {2:23} "For in fornication, there is neither understanding nor godliness, and all jealousy dwells within its lust." {2:24} "Therefore, I tell you, you will become jealous of the sons of Levi and seek to rise above them, but you will not succeed." {2:25} "For God will avenge them, and you shall die a wicked death. To Levi, God gave sovereignty, and to Judah along with him, and to me, and to Dan and Joseph, that we should be rulers." {2:26} "So, I command you to listen to Levi, for he will know the law of the Lord, give judgments, and sacrifice for all Israel until the end of time, as the anointed High Priest of whom the Lord spoke." {2:27} "I urge you by the God of heaven to treat each neighbor with truth and to love each brother." {2:28} "Come near to Levi with humility of heart so you may receive a blessing from his mouth." {2:29} "For he shall bless Israel and Judah, for the Lord has chosen him to be king over all the nations." {2:30} "And bow down before his descendants, for they will fight on our behalf in visible and invisible battles and will be an eternal king among you." {2:31} "And Reuben died after giving these commands to his sons. They placed him in a coffin until they carried him from Egypt and buried him in Hebron, in the cave where his father was."

The Testament of Simeon

{1:1} "This is the account of the words of Simeon, the things he spoke to his sons before he died in the hundred and twentieth year of his life, at which time Joseph, his brother, died. {1:2} When Simeon fell ill, his sons came to visit him. He gathered his strength, sat up, kissed them, and said: {1:3} 'Listen, my children, to Simeon your father, and I will share what is in my heart. {1:4} I was born to Jacob as his second son; my mother Leah named me Simeon because the Lord heard her prayer. {1:5} I became very strong; I did not shy away from any challenge and was not afraid of anything. My heart was hardened, and I had no compassion. {1:6} For courage has also been given by the Most High to men in soul and body. {1:7} In my youth, I was jealous of Joseph because my father loved him the most. {1:8} I plotted against him to destroy him because the spirit of jealousy sent by the prince of deceit blinded my mind, so I didn't see him as my brother, and I didn't even spare Jacob, my father. {1:9} But God, the God of my fathers, sent His angel to rescue Joseph from my hands. {1:10} When I went to Shechem to gather ointment for the flocks, and Reuben went to Dothan for our supplies, Judah, my brother, sold Joseph to the Ishmaelites. {1:11} When Reuben heard this, he was upset because he wanted to return Joseph to our father. {1:12} But I was extremely angry with Judah for letting Joseph go free, and for five months I held a grudge against him. {1:13} But the Lord held me back, and I lost the use of my right hand for seven days. {1:14} I realized, my children, that this happened to me because of Joseph, and I repented and cried; I begged the Lord God to restore my hand so I could avoid all pollution, envy, and foolishness. {1:15} I knew that I had done an evil thing before the Lord and my father Jacob by envying Joseph. {1:16} Now, my children, listen to me and beware of the spirit of deceit and envy. {1:17} For envy takes over the entire mind of a person, preventing them from eating, drinking, or doing anything good. It always pushes them to harm the one they envy; while the envied person thrives, the one who envies fades away. {1:18} For two years, I afflicted my soul with fasting in fear of the Lord, and I learned that overcoming envy comes through the fear of God. {1:19} If a person turns to the Lord, the evil spirit runs away from him, and his mind becomes lightened. {1:20} From then on, he begins to sympathize with the one he envied and forgives those who are hostile toward him, thus ending his envy."

{2:1} "My father noticed I was sad and asked me why; I told him, 'I feel pain in my liver.' {2:2} I mourned more than anyone else because I was guilty of selling Joseph. {2:3} When we went to Egypt, and he bound me as a spy, I knew I was suffering justly, and I did not complain. {2:4} Joseph was a good man, with the Spirit of God within him; being compassionate and kind, he held no grudge against me but loved me as he did the rest of our brothers. {2:5} So, my children, beware of all jealousy and envy, and walk with a pure heart, so that God may also grant you grace, glory, and blessings upon your heads, just as He did with Joseph. {2:6} Throughout his life, he never reproached us for this but loved us as his own soul, honored us beyond his own sons, and gave us riches, livestock, and produce. {2:7} So you, my children, should each love your brother with a good heart, and the spirit of envy will leave you. {2:8} For this spirit destroys the soul and harms the body; it incites anger and conflict, leading to acts of violence, driving the mind into madness, and causing turmoil in the soul and trembling in the body. {2:9} Even in sleep, malicious jealousy gnaws at you, disturbing the soul with wicked spirits, troubling the body, and waking the mind in confusion; it appears to people like a wicked and poisonous spirit. {2:10} This is why Joseph was handsome and pleasing to look at; no wickedness dwelled within him, for some of the turmoil of the spirit shows on the face. {2:11} So now, my children, make your hearts good before the Lord and your ways straight before men, and you will find grace in the eyes of the Lord and of people. {2:12} Beware, then, of fornication, for it is the mother of all evils, separating you from God and bringing you close to wickedness. {2:13} I have seen it written by Enoch that your sons will be corrupted by fornication and will harm the sons of Levi with the sword. {2:14} But they will not be able to withstand Levi, for he will fight the Lord's battles and defeat all your armies. {2:15} They will be few in number, divided between Levi and Judah, and none of you will be in positions of power, just as our father prophesied in his blessings."

{3:1} "Behold, I have told you everything, so I may be free from your sin. {3:2} Now, if you remove envy and stubbornness from among you, my bones will flourish in Israel like a rose, my flesh like a lily in Jacob, and my fragrance will be like the fragrance of Lebanon; holy ones will be multiplied from me forever, and their branches will stretch far and wide. {3:3} Then the seed of Canaan will perish, and there will be no remnant left for Amalek; all Cappadocians will be destroyed, and all Hittites will be utterly wiped out. {3:4} The land of Ham will fail, and all its people will perish. {3:5} Then all the earth will rest from troubles, and the whole world will be free from war. {3:6} Then the Mighty One of Israel will glorify Shem. {3:7} For the Lord God will appear on earth and save mankind. {3:8} Then all deceitful spirits will be trampled underfoot, and men will rule over wicked spirits. {3:9} I will rise in joy and bless the Most High for His marvelous works because God took on a body, ate with men, and saved them. {3:10} Now, my children, obey Levi and Judah, and do not rise against these two tribes, for from them will come the salvation of God. {3:11} The Lord will raise up a High Priest from Levi and a King from Judah; God and man, He will save all the Gentiles and the people of Israel. {3:12} Therefore, I give you these commands, so you may also pass them on to your children, that they may observe them throughout their generations. {3:13} When Simeon finished commanding his sons, he died, being one hundred and twenty years old. {3:14} They placed him in a wooden coffin to take his bones to Hebron, secretly moving them during a war with the Egyptians. The Egyptians guarded Joseph's bones in royal tombs. {3:15} The sorcerers warned that when Joseph's bones were taken, darkness and plague would cover the land, so much so that even with a lamp, a man wouldn't recognize his brother. {3:16} The sons of Simeon mourned for their father. {3:17} They remained in Egypt until the day of their departure led by Moses."

The Testament of Levi

{1:1} This is the record of Levi's words, detailing what he instructed his sons about their duties and what would happen to them until the day of judgment. {1:2} He was in good health when he called them to him, having received a revelation that he would die. {1:3} When they had gathered, he said to them: {1:4} "I, Levi, was born in Haran and came with my father to Shechem. {1:5} I was young, around twenty years old, when I, along with Simeon, took revenge on Hamor for the wrong done to our sister Dinah. {1:6} While I was tending the flocks in Abel-Maul, the spirit of understanding from the Lord came upon me, and I saw that all men were corrupting their ways and that wickedness had built walls for itself, while lawlessness sat upon towers. {1:7} I grieved for humanity and prayed to the Lord for salvation. {1:8} Then I fell asleep and saw a high mountain, where I found myself. {1:9} The heavens opened, and an angel of God said to me, "Levi, enter." {1:10} I entered the first heaven and saw a great sea hanging. {1:11} Further on, I saw a second heaven, far brighter and more brilliant, filled with boundless light. {1:12} I asked the angel, "Why is this so?" and the angel replied, "Do not marvel at this; you will see another heaven that is even more brilliant and incomparable. {1:13} When you ascend there, you will stand near the Lord, serve Him, reveal His mysteries to people, and proclaim the one who will redeem Israel. {1:14} Through you and Judah, the Lord will appear among people, saving every race of humanity. {1:15} From the Lord's portion, your life will be derived; He will be your field, vineyard, fruits, gold, and silver. {1:16} So listen regarding the heavens that have been shown to you. {1:17} The lowest heaven is gloomy for you because it witnesses all the unrighteous deeds of humanity. {1:18} It has fire, snow, and ice prepared for the day of judgment as part of God's righteous judgment; in it are all the spirits that execute vengeance on people. {1:19} In the second heaven are the hosts of armies set for the day of judgment to enact vengeance on the spirits of deceit and Beliar. {1:20} Above them are the holy ones. {1:21} In the highest heaven dwells the Great Glory, far above all holiness. {1:22} Next to it are the archangels who serve and seek mercy from the Lord for all the unintentional sins of the righteous; {1:23} they present to the Lord a pleasing aroma, a reasonable, bloodless offering. {1:24} Below this heaven are angels who deliver answers to the angels of the Lord's presence. {1:25} Next to them are thrones and dominions that continually praise God. {1:26} When the Lord looks upon us, all of us tremble; indeed, the heavens, the earth, and the abysses shake at the presence of His majesty. {1:27} But humans, lacking perception of these things, sin and provoke the Most High.

{2:1} Therefore, know that the Lord will execute judgment on humanity. {2:2} When the rocks are split, the sun darkened, the waters dried up, and fire falters, while all creation is disturbed and invisible spirits dissolve away, and Hades seizes its spoils through the visits of the Most High, people will remain unbelieving and continue in their sins. {2:3} For this reason, they will be judged with punishment. {2:4} Thus, the Most High has heard your prayer to separate you from iniquity so that you may be a son, a servant, and a minister of His presence. {2:5} You will illuminate Jacob with the light of knowledge, and like the sun, you will shine upon all the descendants of Israel. {2:6} A blessing will be given to you and to all your descendants until the Lord shows mercy to all the Gentiles forever. {2:7} Therefore, you have been given counsel and understanding to teach your sons about this; {2:8} for those who bless Him will be blessed, and those who curse Him will perish. {2:9} Then the angel opened to me the gates of heaven, and I saw the holy temple and on a throne of glory the Most High. {2:10} He said to me: "Levi, I have granted you the blessing of the priesthood until I come and dwell among Israel." {2:11} The angel then brought me down to earth and gave me a shield and a sword, saying, "Take vengeance on Shechem for the wrong done to your sister Dinah, and I will be with you, for the Lord has sent me." {2:12} I destroyed the sons of Hamor at that time, as is written in the heavenly records. {2:13} I then asked the angel, "Please tell me Your name, so I may call upon You in times of trouble." {2:14} He replied: "I am the angel who intercedes for Israel so that they may not be utterly destroyed, for every evil spirit attacks them." {2:15} After these things, I awoke, blessed the Most High, and the angel who intercedes for Israel and all the righteous.

{3:1} As I was returning to my father, I found a bronze shield; hence the name of the mountain is Aspis, located near Gebal, south of Abila. {3:2} I kept these words in my heart. After this, I advised my father and my brother Reuben to tell the sons of Hamor not to undergo circumcision; I was zealous due to the disgrace they brought upon my sister. {3:3} I killed Shechem first, and Simeon killed Hamor. Then my brothers joined in and struck that city with the sword. {3:4} My father heard about this and was angry; he was distressed that they had been circumcised only to be killed, and in his blessings, he looked upon us with disfavor. {3:5} We sinned by doing this against his will, and he was ill that day. {3:6} However, I knew that God's sentence was against Shechem, for they intended to do to Sarah and Rebecca what they had done to Dinah, but the Lord intervened. {3:7} They also persecuted our father Abraham when he was a stranger and troubled his flocks when they were with young; they treated Eblaen, born in his house, shamefully. {3:8} They did the same to all strangers, forcibly taking their wives and driving them away. {3:9} But the Lord's wrath came upon them utterly. {3:10} I said to my father Jacob: "By you, the Lord will take the land from the Canaanites and give it to you and your descendants." {3:11} From now on, Shechem will be known as a city of fools; for as a man mocks a fool, so we mocked them. {3:12} They had acted foolishly in Israel by defiling my sister. Then we departed and went to Bethel. {3:13} There again, I had a vision like the previous one after spending seventy days there. {3:14} I saw seven men in white robes who said to me: "Arise, put on the robe of the priesthood, the crown of righteousness, the breastplate of understanding, the garment of truth, the belt of faith, the turban for your head, and the ephod of prophecy. {3:15} They each carried these items and placed them upon me, saying: "From now on, you and your descendants shall serve as priests of the Lord forever." {3:16} The first anointed me with holy oil and gave me the staff of judgment. {3:17} The second washed me with pure water, fed me with bread and wine—the most sacred things—and clothed me in a holy and glorious robe. {3:18} The third dressed me in a linen vestment like an ephod. {3:19} The fourth wrapped a purple belt around me. {3:20} The fifth gave me a branch of rich olive. {3:21} The sixth placed a crown on my head. {3:22} The seventh put a diadem of priesthood on my head and filled my hands with incense, so I could serve as a priest to the Lord God. {3:23} They said to me: "Levi, your descendants will be divided into three offices, as a sign of the glory of the Lord who is to come. {3:24} The first portion will be great; indeed, none will be greater. {3:25} The second will be in the priesthood. {3:26} The third will be given a new name because a king will arise in Judah, establishing a new priesthood after the pattern of the Gentiles. {3:27} His presence will be beloved, as a prophet of the Most High, of the seed of our father Abraham. {3:28} Thus, every desirable thing in Israel will belong to you and your descendants; you will partake of everything beautiful to see, and the Lord's table will be apportioned to your descendants. {3:29} Some of them will be high priests, judges, and scribes; through them, the holy place will be guarded. {3:30} When I awoke, I understood that this dream was similar to the first. I kept it in my heart and did not share it with anyone. {3:31} After two days, Judah and I went up with our father Jacob to Isaac, our grandfather. {3:32} My grandfather continually blessed me according to the words of the visions I had seen, and he chose not to accompany us to Bethel. {3:33} When we arrived at Bethel, my father had a vision about me that I should be their priest unto God. {3:34} He rose early in the morning and offered tithes of everything to the Lord through me. So, we went to dwell in Hebron. {3:35} Isaac frequently called me to remind me of the Lord's law, just as the angel of the Lord had shown me. {3:36} He instructed me in the law of the priesthood, including sacrifices, whole burnt offerings, first fruits, freewill offerings, and peace offerings. {3:37} He taught me daily and interceded for me before the Lord, saying: "Be cautious of the spirit of fornication; this will continue and will pollute the holy place through your descendants." {3:38} So, take a wife without blemish or pollution while you are still young, and not of foreign nations. {3:39} Before entering the holy place, wash yourself; when you offer sacrifices, wash again; and after completing the sacrifices, wash once more. {3:40} Offer to the Lord twelve trees with leaves, as Abraham taught me. {3:41} Offer sacrifices to the Lord from every clean beast and bird. {3:42} From all your first fruits and from wine, present the first as a sacrifice to the Lord God; every sacrifice must be seasoned with salt. {3:43} Therefore, observe everything I command you, children; for whatever I have learned from my fathers, I have declared to you. {3:44} Behold, I am innocent of your ungodliness and transgressions, which you will commit in the end times against the Savior of the world, Christ, acting wickedly, deceiving Israel, and inciting great evils from the Lord. {3:45} You will act lawlessly together with Israel, causing Him not to tolerate Jerusalem because of your wickedness; the temple veil will be torn so that it no longer covers your shame. {3:46} You will be scattered among the Gentiles as captives, and you will become a disgrace and a curse. {3:47} The house the Lord chooses will be called Jerusalem, as recorded in the book of Enoch the righteous. {3:48} When I took a wife, I was twenty-eight years old; her name was Melcha. {3:49} She conceived and bore a son, whom I named Gersam, for we were foreigners in our land. {3:50} I saw concerning him that he would not hold the first rank. {3:51} Kohath was born in the thirty-fifth year of my life, towards sunrise. {3:52} I saw in a vision that he stood high in the congregation. {3:53} Therefore, I named him Kohath, which means "beginning of majesty and instruction." {3:54} A third son was born to me in the fortieth year of my life; since his mother had great difficulty giving birth, I named him Merari, meaning "my bitterness," as he also came close to dying. {3:55} Jochebed was born in Egypt during my sixty-fourth year, when I was well-known among my brothers. {3:56} Gersam took a wife and had two sons, Lomni and Semei. The sons of Kohath were Ambram, Issachar, Hebron, and Ozeel. The sons of Merari were Mooli and Mouses. {3:57} In my ninety-fourth year, Ambram married my daughter Jochebed, for they were born on the same day, he and my daughter. {3:58} I was eight years old when I entered Canaan, eighteen when I killed Shechem, nineteen when I became a priest, twenty-eight when I took a wife, and forty-eight when I went to Egypt. {3:59} Behold, my children, you are a third generation. Joseph died in my one hundred eighteenth year.

{4:1} Now, my children, I command you: Fear the Lord your God with all your heart, and walk simply according to all His laws. {4:2} Also, teach your children to read, so they can understand throughout their lives by continuously studying the law of God. {4:3} For anyone who knows the law of the Lord will be honored and will not be a stranger wherever they go. {4:4} Yes, they will gain many friends beyond their parents, and many will desire to serve them and hear the law from their mouth. {4:5} Therefore, work righteousness, my children, on earth, so that you may have it as a treasure in heaven. {4:6} Sow good things in your souls, so that you may find them in your lives. {4:7} But if you sow evil things, you will reap trouble and affliction. {4:8} Seek wisdom with diligence in the fear of God; for even if you face captivity, and cities and lands are destroyed, and gold, silver, and every possession perish, the wisdom of the wise cannot be taken away except by the blindness of ungodliness and the hardness that comes from sin. {4:9} For if one keeps away from these evil things, even among their enemies wisdom will shine as a glory to them, and in a foreign land, it will be like a homeland, and among foes, it will prove to be a friend. {4:10} Whoever teaches noble things and lives by them will be honored among kings, just like my brother Joseph was. {4:11} Therefore, my children, I have learned that in the end times you will turn against the Lord, reaching out to wickedness against Him, and you will become a scorn to all the Gentiles. {4:12} Our father Israel is innocent of the transgressions of the chief priests who will lay hands on the Savior of the world. {4:13} Just as the heavens are purer in the Lord's sight than the earth, so too, be you, the lights of Israel, purer than all the Gentiles. {4:14} But if you are darkened by transgressions, what will the Gentiles do, living in their blindness? {4:15} You will bring a curse upon our race because you desire to destroy the light of the law that was given to enlighten every person by teaching commandments contrary to God's ordinances. {4:16} You will rob the offerings of the Lord and steal choice portions from His share, eating them contemptuously with harlots. {4:17} Driven by greed, you will teach the commandments of the Lord, polluting wedded women and defiling the virgins of Jerusalem; you will join with harlots and adulteresses, taking daughters of the Gentiles as wives, attempting to purify them unlawfully; and your unions will be like those of Sodom and Gomorrah. {4:18} You will become arrogant because of your priesthood, elevating yourselves against men, and not only that, but also against the commands of God. {4:19} You will treat holy things with jest and laughter. {4:20} Therefore, the temple that the Lord chooses will be laid waste because of your uncleanness, and you will be captives in all nations. {4:21} You will be an abomination to them, receiving reproach and everlasting shame from God's righteous judgment. {4:22} All who hate you will rejoice at your destruction. {4:23} And if you did not receive mercy through Abraham, Isaac, and Jacob, our fathers, not one of your descendants would be left on the earth. {4:24} Now I have learned that for seventy weeks you will go astray and profane the priesthood, polluting the sacrifices. {4:25} You will make the law void and disregard the words of the prophets by evil perversity. {4:26} You will persecute righteous men and hate the godly; you will abhor the words of the faithful. {4:27} A man who renews the law in the power of the Most High will be called a deceiver; and in the end, you will rush to slay him, not knowing his true dignity, shedding innocent blood through wickedness upon your heads. {4:28} Your holy places will be laid waste even to the ground because of him. {4:29} You will have no clean place, but among the Gentiles, you will be a curse and a dispersion until He visits you again and receives you in pity through faith and water.

{5:1} And concerning the seventy weeks, listen also about the priesthood. For in each jubilee, there will be a priesthood. {5:2} In the first jubilee, the first anointed to the priesthood will be great and will speak to God as a father. {5:3} His priesthood will be perfect with the Lord, and in his day of joy, he will arise for the salvation of the world. {5:4} In the second jubilee, the one anointed will be conceived in the sorrow of loved ones; his priesthood will be honored and glorified by all. {5:5} The third priest will be taken hold of by sorrow. {5:6} The fourth will be in pain, as unrighteousness will gather against him greatly, and all Israel will hate their neighbors. {5:7} The fifth will be overcome by darkness. Likewise, the sixth and seventh will also suffer. {5:8} In the seventh, there will be such pollution that I cannot express it before men, for they will know it who do these things. {5:9} Therefore, they will be taken captive and become prey, and their land and possessions will be destroyed. {5:10} In the fifth week, they will return to their desolate country and renew the house of the Lord. {5:11} In the seventh week, there will be priests who are idolaters, adulterers, lovers of money, proud, lawless, lascivious, and abusers of children and animals. {5:12} After their punishment from the Lord, the priesthood will fail. {5:13} Then the Lord will raise up a new priest. {5:14} To him, all the words of the Lord will be revealed; and he will execute righteous judgment upon the earth for many days. {5:15} His star will rise in heaven like that of a king. {5:16} Illuminating the knowledge like the sun lights the day, and he will be magnified in the world. {5:17} He will shine like the sun on the earth and remove all darkness from under heaven, bringing peace to all the earth. {5:18} The heavens will rejoice in his days, and the earth will be glad, and the clouds will celebrate. {5:19} The knowledge of the Lord will be poured out on the earth like the water of the seas. {5:20} The angels of the glory of the Lord's presence will rejoice in him. {5:21} The heavens will open, and from the temple of glory, sanctification will come upon him, with the Father's voice as from Abraham to Isaac. {5:22} The glory of the Most High will be declared over him, and the spirit of understanding and sanctification will rest upon him in the water. {5:23} For he will give the majesty of the Lord to His sons in truth forever. {5:24} None will succeed him for all generations. {5:25} In his priesthood, the Gentiles will increase in knowledge on the earth, enlightened through the grace of the Lord. In his priesthood, sin will come to an end, and the lawless will cease doing evil. {5:26} He will open the gates of paradise, remove the threatening sword against Adam, and allow the saints to eat from the tree of life, and the spirit of holiness will be upon them. {5:27} Beliar will be bound by him, and he will empower His children to tread upon evil spirits. {5:28} The Lord will rejoice in His children and be pleased with His beloved ones forever. {5:29} Then Abraham, Isaac, and Jacob will rejoice, and I will be glad, and all the saints will clothe themselves with joy. {5:30} Now, my children, you have heard everything; choose, therefore, either light or darkness, either the law of the Lord or the works of Beliar. {5:31} And his sons answered him, saying, "Before the Lord, we will walk according to His law." {5:32} And their father said to them, "The Lord is witness, and His angels are witnesses, and you are witnesses, and I am witness concerning the words of your mouth." {5:33} And his sons said to him, "We are witnesses." {5:34} Thus, Levi ceased commanding his sons; he stretched out his feet on the bed and was gathered to his fathers after living one hundred thirty-seven years. {5:35} They laid him in a coffin and later buried him in Hebron, with Abraham, Isaac, and Jacob.

The Testament of Judah

{1:1} This is the record of Judah's words, the things he spoke to his sons before he died. {1:2} They all gathered around him, and he said to them, "Listen, my children, to Judah, your father. {1:3} I was the fourth son born to my father Jacob, and my mother Leah named me Judah, saying, 'I give thanks to the Lord because He has given me a fourth son as well.' {1:4} In my youth, I was swift and obedient to my father in everything. {1:5} I honored my mother and my mother's sister. {1:6} When I became a man, my father blessed me, saying, 'You will be a king, successful in all things.' {1:7} And the Lord showed favor to me in all my work, whether in the field or in the house. {1:8} I remember chasing a deer, catching it, and preparing the meat for my father, and he ate it. {1:9} I mastered the chase of the roe deer and caught everything in the plains. {1:10} I even overtook a wild mare, caught it, and tamed it. {1:11} I killed a lion and saved a goat from its mouth. {1:12} I grabbed a bear by its paw, threw it down a cliff, and it was crushed. {1:13} I outran a wild boar and, while running, tore it apart. {1:14} In Hebron, a leopard jumped on my dog, but I grabbed it by the tail, threw it against the rocks, and it split in two. {1:15} I found a wild ox in the fields and, grabbing it by the horns, swung it around, stunned it, and killed it. {1:16} When two Canaanite kings came in full armor against our flocks with many men, I rushed single-handedly at the king of Hazor, struck him in the greaves (shin guards), dragged him down, and killed him. {1:17} I also killed the king of Tappuah while he was on his horse, scattering all his men. {1:18} I faced Achor, a giant king, who threw javelins before and behind him while riding a horse. I picked up a sixty-pound stone, hurled it, and struck his horse, killing it. {1:19} I fought with him for two hours, cut his shield in half, chopped off his feet, and killed him. {1:20} While I was stripping him of his armor, nine of his companions attacked me. {1:21} I wrapped my garment around my hand, slung stones at them, and killed four of them. The rest fled. {1:22} My father Jacob killed Beelesath, king of all the kings, a giant twelve cubits (18 feet) tall. {1:23} Fear fell upon our enemies, and they stopped warring against us. {1:24} My father felt at ease during battles when I was with my brothers. {1:25} He saw in a vision that an angel of strength always followed me so I wouldn't be defeated. {1:26} In the south, a war greater than the one in Shechem came upon us, and I fought in battle with my brothers. I pursued a thousand men, killing two hundred and four kings. {1:27} I climbed the city wall and killed four mighty warriors. {1:28} We captured Hazor and took all its spoils. {1:29} The next day, we marched to Aretan, a strong and well-fortified city that threatened us with death. {1:30} Gad and I approached from the east, and Reuben and Levi from the west. {1:31} The men on the walls thought we were alone, so they came down to attack us. {1:32} Meanwhile, my brothers secretly climbed up the wall from both sides using stakes and entered the city without the men knowing. {1:33} We took the city by the sword. {1:34} Those who sought refuge in the tower, we set the tower on fire and captured both it and them. {1:35} As we were leaving, the men of Tappuah attacked and stole our spoils, but we fought them and reclaimed everything. {1:36} We killed them all. {1:37} While we were at the waters of Kozeba, the men of Jobel came against us in battle. {1:38} We defeated them and killed their allies from Shiloh, leaving them unable to fight against us. {1:39} On the fifth day, the men of Makir tried to take our spoils, but we fought them and defeated them in a fierce battle, even though they had many strong men. {1:40} When we reached their city, the women rolled stones down upon us from the hill where the city stood. {1:41} Simeon and I took cover behind the town, seized the heights, and destroyed the city. {1:42} The next day, we heard that the king of Gaash was coming against us with a mighty army. {1:43} Dan and I pretended to be Amorites and entered their city as allies. {1:44} During the night, our brothers came, and we opened the gates for them. We destroyed all the men, took their possessions, and tore down their three walls. {1:45} We advanced to Thamna, where the treasures of the enemy kings were kept. {1:46} They insulted us, and in my anger, I rushed to the top of the city, but they kept throwing stones and darts at me. {1:47} Had it not been for my brother Dan helping me, they would have killed me. {1:48} We attacked them with fury, and they fled. {1:49} Passing by another route, they fought my father, but he made peace with them. {1:50} We did not harm them, and they became our tributaries, returning their spoils to them. {1:51} I built Thamna, and my father built Pabael. {1:52} I was twenty years old when this war occurred, and the Canaanites feared me and my brothers. {1:53} I had much cattle, and Iram the Adullamite was my chief herdsman. {1:54} When I visited him, I met Parsaba, the king of Adullam, who invited us to a feast. While I was in high spirits from drinking, he gave me his daughter Bathshua as my wife. She bore me three sons: Er, Onan, and Shelah. But the Lord struck down two of them, and only Shelah survived, and his descendants are you.

{2:1} For eighteen years, my father lived in peace with his brother Esau, and Esau's sons lived with us after we returned from Mesopotamia, from Laban's household. {2:2} When these eighteen years were completed, in the fortieth year of my life, Esau came against us with a strong army. {2:3} My father Jacob shot Esau with an arrow, and Esau was carried wounded to Mount Seir, where he died at Anoniram. {2:4} We pursued Esau's sons, who fled to a city with iron walls and brass gates. {2:5} We besieged the city for twenty days, but they wouldn't open the gates. {2:6} So, I set up a ladder in full view of everyone, climbed it with a shield on my head, enduring heavy stones thrown at me, and killed four of their strongest warriors. {2:7} Reuben and Gad killed six others. {2:8} They asked us for peace, and after consulting with my father, we accepted them as tributaries. {2:9} They provided us with five hundred cors (a unit of measurement) of wheat, five hundred baths of oil, and five hundred measures of wine until the famine, when we went to Egypt. {2:10} Afterward, my son Er married Tamar from Mesopotamia, a daughter of Aram. {2:11} But Er was wicked and refused Tamar because she wasn't from the land of Canaan. {2:12} On the third night of their marriage, an angel of the Lord killed him. {2:13} He had not slept with her, as his mother's wicked influence led him to avoid having children with her. {2:14} During the wedding feast, I gave Onan to her as a husband, but he also wickedly refused to sleep with her, even though they were married for a year. {2:15} When I confronted him, he finally slept with her but spilled his seed on the ground, following his mother's command, and he too died for his wickedness. {2:16} I wanted to give Tamar to Shelah, but his mother did not allow it, for she was against Tamar because she wasn't a Canaanite, as she herself was. {2:17} I knew the Canaanite race was wicked, but youthful desires blinded me. {2:18} When I saw Tamar pouring wine, I was deceived by the intoxication of wine and took her, even though my father had not advised it. {2:19} While I was away, my wife arranged for Shelah to marry a Canaanite woman. {2:20} When I discovered what she had done, I cursed her in my deep grief. {2:21} She later died because of her wickedness, along with her sons. {2:22} After two years, while Tamar was still a widow, she heard that I was going up to shear my sheep, so she dressed in bridal clothes and sat at the gate of Enaim. {2:23} According to the Amorite custom, a woman about to marry would sit in fornication (illicit relations) for seven days at the gate. {2:24} Being drunk with wine, I didn't recognize her, and her beauty deceived me because of her adornment. {2:25} I turned aside to her and said, 'Let me sleep with you.' {2:26} She asked, 'What will you give me?' I gave her my staff, belt, and the diadem of my kingdom as a pledge. {2:27} I slept with her, and she conceived. {2:28} Not realizing what I had done, I wanted to kill her, but she secretly sent me my pledges, and I was shamed. {2:29} When I called her, I also recalled the private words I had spoken to her while I lay with her in my drunkenness, so I couldn't kill her, for I knew the Lord had been involved. {2:30} I thought perhaps she had acted with cunning and received the pledges from another woman. {2:31} But I never went near her again, for I had committed an abomination in all of Israel. {2:32} Moreover, the people in the city said there was no harlot at the gate, for she had come from another place and only sat at the gate for a short time. {2:33} I thought no one knew I had slept with her. {2:34} Afterward, we went to Egypt to join Joseph because of the famine. {2:35} I was forty-six years old at that time, and I lived for another seventy-three years in Egypt.

{3:1} Now I command you, my children, listen to your father Judah, and keep my words to follow all the commandments of the Lord and obey God's directives. {3:2} Do not follow your desires or let your thoughts become prideful; do not boast about your youthful strength, for this too is wicked in the sight of the Lord. {3:3} I once prided myself on how no beautiful woman had ever tempted me in war, and I reprimanded my brother Reuben about Bilhah, our father's wife, but the spirits of jealousy and lust came against me until I slept with Bathshua the Canaanite and Tamar, who was promised to my sons. {3:4} I told my father-in-law that I would consult with my father before marrying his daughter. {3:5} He was hesitant but showed me vast wealth for her sake, since he was a king. {3:6} He dressed her in gold and pearls and had her serve wine at our feast, surrounded by beautiful women. {3:7} The wine distracted me, and pleasure blinded my heart. {3:8} I fell in love with her, disregarding the commandments of the Lord and my fathers, and I married her. {3:9} The Lord responded to my heart's desire, yet I found no joy in her children. {3:10} Now, my children, I tell you: do not get drunk on wine, for it can lead you away from the truth and stir up lustful passions, leading your eyes into error. {3:11} The spirit of fornication uses wine as its instrument to entice the mind; both can cloud a man's judgment. {3:12} If a man drinks wine to excess, it disturbs his mind with filthy thoughts, leading to lust, and if the opportunity arises, he will commit the sin without shame. {3:13} Such is the state of a drunken man, my children; he who is drunk respects no one. {3:14} It made me err too; I was unashamed in the city as I turned to Tamar, committing a great sin and exposing my sons' shame. {3:15} After drinking, I disrespected God's commandments and married a Canaanite woman. {3:16} A man who drinks wine must be careful, my children; he can drink as long as he maintains modesty. {3:17} But if he exceeds this limit, deceit will cloud his mind, causing him to speak filthily, to sin without shame, and even to take pride in his shameful actions. {3:18} A person who commits fornication does not realize the loss he suffers and is not ashamed when dishonored. {3:19} Even if a man is a king and commits fornication, he loses his kingship, becoming a slave to his desires, as I experienced. {3:20} I gave away my staff, representing my tribe's support; my belt, signifying my power; and my crown, the glory of my kingdom. {3:21} I truly repented of these actions; I abstained from wine and meat until old age, finding no joy in them. {3:22} An angel of God revealed to me that women have power over both kings and beggars. {3:23} They strip the king of his glory, take strength from the brave, and from the beggar, even what little he has. {3:24} Therefore, my children, know the proper limits with wine, for it carries four evil spirits: lust, hot desire, wastefulness, and greed. {3:25} If you drink wine joyfully, do so modestly in the fear of God. {3:26} If your joy leads to the absence of God's fear, then drunkenness will rise, and shamelessness will sneak in. {3:27} But if you wish to live soberly, avoid wine altogether to prevent sin through insults, fighting, slander, and breaking God's commandments, leading to an early demise. {3:28} Moreover, wine can reveal the secrets of God and men, just as I revealed God's commandments and the mysteries of my father Jacob to Bathshua, which I was commanded not to reveal. {3:29} Wine can also cause wars and confusion. {3:30} Now I command you, my children, do not love money or be captivated by beautiful women; for these are what led me astray to Bathshua the Canaanite. {3:31} I know that because of these two temptations, my descendants will fall into wickedness. {3:32} Even wise men among my sons will be corrupted, causing the kingdom of Judah to diminish, which the Lord gave me for my obedience to my father. {3:33} I never caused grief to Jacob, my father; I did all that he commanded. {3:34} Isaac, my father's father, blessed me to be king in Israel, and Jacob blessed me similarly. {3:35} I know that from me the kingdom will be established. {3:36} I foresee the evils you will do in the last days. {3:37} Therefore, my children, be cautious of fornication and the love of money, and listen to your father Judah. {3:38} These things lead you away from God's law, blind your soul's inclinations, promote arrogance, and prevent compassion for others. {3:39} They strip your soul of goodness, oppress you with troubles, rob you of sleep, and consume your flesh. {3:40} They obstruct God's sacrifices, make you forget His blessings, and you will ignore prophets speaking truth and resent the words of righteousness. {3:41} For he is enslaved by two opposing passions, unable to obey God, as they have blinded his soul, making him walk in darkness. {3:42} My children, the love of money leads to idolatry; when led astray by money, men idolize false gods, leading them to madness. {3:43} For money's sake, I lost my children, and if not for my repentance, humility, and my father's prayers, I would have died childless. {3:44} Yet the God of my fathers had mercy on me because I acted in ignorance. {3:45} The prince of deceit blinded me, and I sinned as a mere man, corrupted by sin; I realized my own weakness while thinking I was invincible. {3:46} Therefore, my children, know that two spirits attend to man—the spirit of truth and the spirit of deceit. {3:47} In between is the spirit of understanding, which can turn whichever way it wishes. {3:48} The works of truth and deceit are inscribed on human hearts, and the Lord knows each one. {3:49} There is no time when the deeds of men can be hidden; they are written on the heart before the Lord. {3:50} The spirit of truth witnesses all things and accuses all; the sinner is consumed by his own heart and cannot face the judge.

{4:1} Now, my children, I command you to love Levi so that you may prosper, and do not exalt yourselves against him, or you will be utterly destroyed. {4:2} The Lord gave me the kingdom and to Levi the priesthood, placing the kingdom under the priesthood. {4:3} He entrusted me with earthly matters, and to Levi with heavenly ones. {4:4} Just as heaven is higher than earth, so the priesthood is higher than earthly kings, unless it strays from the Lord due to sin and is overtaken by earthly powers. {4:5} The angel of the Lord told me that the Lord chose Levi over me to draw near to Him, to partake of His table and offer the first-fruits of Israel; you shall be king over Jacob. {4:6} You will be among them like the sea. {4:7} Just as the sea tosses both the just and the unjust, with some taken captive and others enriched, so will all people be in you: some will be impoverished and captured, while others will grow wealthy by plundering. {4:8} The kings will be like sea monsters. {4:9} They will devour men like fish, enslaving the sons and daughters of free people; they will plunder houses, lands, flocks, and wealth. {4:10} They will unjustly feed ravens and cranes with the flesh of many, advancing in evil with greed; false prophets will rise like storms, persecuting all righteous people. {4:11} The Lord will cause divisions among them. {4:12} There will be constant wars in Israel, and among other nations, my kingdom will meet its end until Israel's salvation arrives. {4:13} Until the God of righteousness appears, that Jacob and all Gentiles may find peace. {4:14} He will protect my kingdom's might forever, for the Lord assured me with an oath that He would not destroy the kingdom from my lineage for eternity. {4:15} I feel deep sorrow, my children, over your immorality, sorcery, and idolatry that you will practice against the kingdom, following those who consult spirits, diviners, and deceiving demons. {4:16} You will turn your daughters into singers and prostitutes, and engage in the abominations of the Gentiles. {4:17} Because of these things, the Lord will send famine, disease, death, and violence from enemies, along with betrayals from friends, the slaughter of children, the violation of wives, plunder of property, destruction of God's temple, devastation of the land, and your enslavement among the Gentiles. {4:18} Some of you will be made eunuchs for their wives. {4:19} Until the Lord visits you, when you repent with a pure heart and follow all His commandments, He will bring you out of captivity among the Gentiles. {4:20} After these events, a star will arise for you from Jacob in peace, {4:21} and a man from my lineage will shine like the sun of righteousness, {4:22} walking among men in humility and righteousness; {4:23} and no sin will be found in him. {4:24} The heavens will open for him, pouring out the spirit, even the blessing of the Holy Father; he will bestow grace upon you. {4:25} You will be true sons to Him and will walk in His commandments from beginning to end. {4:26} Then the scepter of my kingdom will shine, and from your roots a branch will grow, from which a rod of righteousness will arise for the Gentiles, to judge and save all who call upon the Lord. {4:27} After these events, Abraham, Isaac, and Jacob will rise to life; I and my brothers will be leaders of the tribes of Israel: {4:28} Levi first, I second, Joseph third, Benjamin fourth, Simeon fifth, Issachar sixth, and so on in order. {4:29} The Lord blessed Levi, and the Angel of His Presence, me; the powers of glory, Simeon; heaven, Reuben; earth, Issachar; sea, Zebulun; mountains, Joseph; tabernacle, Benjamin; luminaries, Dan; Eden, Naphtali; sun, Gad; moon, Asher. {4:30} You will be the people of the Lord and speak one language; the spirit of deceit will not exist among you, for he will be cast into the fire forever. {4:31} Those who died in sorrow will rise in joy; the poor for the Lord's sake will be enriched, and those put to death for the Lord's sake will awaken to life. {4:32} The hearts of Jacob will rejoice, and the eagles of Israel will soar in happiness; all people will glorify the Lord forever. {4:33} Therefore, my children, observe all the laws of the Lord, for there is hope for those who hold fast to His ways. {4:34} He said to them: Behold, I die before your eyes this day, at the age of one hundred and nineteen. {4:35} Do not bury me in expensive clothes, nor open my bowels, for only kings do such things; carry me up to Hebron with you. {4:36} When Judah finished speaking, he fell asleep, and his sons did everything he commanded, burying him in Hebron with his ancestors.

The Testament of Issachar

{1:1} This is the account of Issachar. {1:2} He called his sons and said: "Listen, my children, to your father Issachar; pay attention to the words of the one beloved by the Lord. {1:3} I was the fifth son born to Jacob, as a result of a deal made over mandrakes. {1:4} Reuben, my brother, brought mandrakes from the field, and Rachel encountered him and took them. {1:5} Reuben cried, and Leah, my mother, came out at his voice. {1:6} These mandrakes were fragrant apples that grew in the land of Haran near a stream of water. {1:7} Rachel said, "I won't give them to you; they will be mine instead of children." {1:8} "The Lord has despised me, and I have not given Jacob any children." {1:9} There were two apples, and Leah said to Rachel, "Isn't it enough that you've taken my husband? Will you take these too?" {1:10} Rachel replied, "You can have Jacob for the night in exchange for your son's mandrakes." {1:11} Leah insisted, "Jacob is mine because I am his first wife." {1:12} But Rachel retorted, "Don't boast, for I was engaged to him before you, and he worked for my father for fourteen years for my hand. {1:13} If deceit hadn't flourished and evil thrived on earth, you wouldn't even see Jacob's face now. {1:14} You are not his wife, but were given to him through trickery in my place. {1:15} My father deceived me and sent me away on that night, so Jacob never saw me; if I had been there, this wouldn't have happened to him. {1:16} Still, I am trading my time with Jacob for the mandrakes." {1:17} Jacob knew Leah, and she conceived and bore me, and because of the deal, I was named Issachar. {1:18} An angel of the Lord appeared to Jacob, saying: "Rachel will bear two children because she has chosen abstinence from her husband." {1:19} Had Leah not exchanged the two apples for his company, she would have had eight sons; instead, she had six, and Rachel had two because of the mandrakes the Lord remembered. {1:20} He understood that Rachel desired children, not mere physical pleasure. {1:21} The next day, she again gave up Jacob. {1:22} Because of the mandrakes, the Lord listened to Rachel. {1:23} Though she longed for them, she did not consume them but presented them to the Lord as an offering through the priest of the Most High at that time. {1:24} As I grew up, my children, I lived with integrity and became a farmer for my father and brothers, bringing in seasonal produce. {1:25} My father blessed me, seeing that I lived righteously before him. {1:26} I was not meddlesome, nor envious or malicious towards anyone. {1:27} I never slandered anyone or judged others, living with a pure heart. {1:28} At thirty-five, I married, for my labor wore me out, and I didn't seek pleasure with women; my work made me too tired to care. {1:29} My father was always pleased with my integrity, as I offered the first fruits to the Lord through the priest, and then to my father as well. {1:30} The Lord blessed me abundantly, and Jacob, my father, recognized that God supported my sincerity. {1:31} I shared the good things of the earth generously with the poor and oppressed, driven by a pure heart. {1:32} Now listen to me, my children, and live sincerely, for I have seen that this is pleasing to the Lord. {1:33} A single-minded person doesn't crave gold, doesn't overreach others, doesn't yearn for excess, and doesn't delight in fancy clothing. {1:34} He doesn't wish for a long life but waits patiently for God's will. {1:35} Evil spirits have no hold on him, for he doesn't look at women's beauty, lest he corrupt his mind. {1:36} There's no envy in his thoughts, and no malicious person can cause him to suffer, nor does he worry about insatiable desires. {1:37} He lives with a pure soul, seeing all things with a righteous heart, avoiding the corruptions of the world, lest he see the violations of the Lord's commandments. {1:38} Therefore, my children, keep the Lord's law, strive for sincerity, and live without guile. Don't meddle in others' affairs, but love the Lord and your neighbor, and show compassion to the poor and weak. {1:39} Work hard in farming, and put in effort in all types of agriculture, offering gifts to the Lord with gratitude. {1:40} For with the first fruits of the earth, the Lord will bless you, just as He blessed all the saints from Abel to now. {1:41} No other portion is given to you than the bounty of the earth, whose fruits are gained through toil. {1:42} Our father Jacob blessed me with blessings of the earth and first fruits. {1:43} Levi and Judah received glory from the Lord even among Jacob's sons; for the Lord gave them an inheritance, and Levi received the priesthood, and Judah the kingdom. {1:44} Therefore, obey them and live sincerely like your father; for to Gad was given the power to defeat the enemies coming against Israel.

{2:1} Know, therefore, my children, that in the last times, your sons will abandon sincerity and pursue insatiable desires. {2:2} They will forsake innocence and turn to malice; abandoning the Lord's commandments, they will follow Beliar (a name often associated with evil). {2:3} They will abandon farming and pursue their own wicked plans, becoming scattered among the Gentiles, serving their enemies. {2:4} Therefore, teach these commands to your children so that if they sin, they may quickly return to the Lord; for He is merciful and will bring them back to their land. {2:5} Look, I am one hundred twenty-six years old and am not aware of any sin I have committed. {2:6} I have known no woman except my wife. {2:7} I have not drunken wine that could lead me astray. {2:8} I have not coveted anything desirable from my neighbor. {2:9} Deceit has not entered my heart. {2:10} I have never lied. {2:11} If someone was in distress, I shared in their sorrow. {2:12} I shared my bread with the poor. {2:13} I lived a godly life, keeping the truth all my days. {2:14} I loved the Lord, and so did everyone with all my heart. {2:15} So, my children, do these things, and every evil spirit will flee from you, and no wicked act will dominate you; {2:16} and you will overcome every wild beast, since you have the God of heaven and earth with you and live with others with a pure heart. {2:17} After saying this, he instructed his sons to take him to Hebron and bury him in the cave with his ancestors. {2:18} He stretched out his feet and died at a good old age, with all his limbs healthy and strength intact, and he fell into eternal sleep.

The Testament of Zebulum

{1:1} This is the account of the words of Zebulun, which he shared with his sons before he died in the one hundred and fourteenth year of his life, two years after Joseph's death. {1:2} He said to them: "Listen to me, sons of Zebulun, and pay attention to your father's words. {1:3} I, Zebulun, was a great blessing to my parents. {1:4} When I was born, my father became exceedingly prosperous, both in flocks and herds, as he used striped rods to gain his share. {1:5} I don't remember ever having sinned in my life, except in my thoughts. {1:6} I don't recall doing any wrongdoing, except for the ignorance I showed toward Joseph, as I agreed with my brothers not to tell our father what happened. {1:7} I wept secretly for many days because of Joseph, fearing my brothers, who all agreed that anyone who revealed the secret should be killed. {1:8} When they intended to kill him, I pleaded with them through tears not to commit this sin. {1:9} Simeon and Gad were preparing to kill Joseph, and he cried out to them, saying: "Pity me, my brothers, have mercy on our father Jacob; don't shed innocent blood, for I have not wronged you. {1:10} If I have sinned, punish me, my brothers, but don't harm me for Jacob's sake." {1:11} As he spoke these words, crying bitterly, I could not bear his grief and began to weep, feeling my insides twist and my heart break. {1:12} I cried with Joseph, and my heart raced, and my body shook, making it hard to stand. {1:13} When Joseph saw me weeping, and the others were approaching to harm him, he fled behind me, begging for mercy. {1:14} Then Reuben stood up and said: "Let's not kill him; instead, let's throw him into one of these dry pits that our ancestors dug, which have no water." {1:15} The Lord prevented water from rising in those pits to keep Joseph safe. {1:16} They agreed, and later sold him to the Ishmaelites. {1:17} I didn't benefit from Joseph's sale, my children. {1:18} But Simeon, Gad, and six other brothers took the money from Joseph's sale to buy sandals for themselves and their families, saying: {1:19} "We won't eat from it, for it's the price of our brother's blood; we'll trample it underfoot because he claimed he would rule over us; let's see what happens to his dreams." {1:20} Therefore, it's written in the law of Moses that anyone who refuses to raise up a descendant for his brother must remove his sandal and have spit thrown in his face. {1:21} The brothers of Joseph didn't want him to live, so the Lord caused them to lose their sandal in relation to Joseph. {1:22} When they arrived in Egypt, their sandals were taken off by Joseph's servants at the gate, and they bowed down to him as they would to Pharaoh. {1:23} Not only did they bow to him, but they were also humiliated, falling down before him, and were ashamed in front of the Egyptians. {1:24} After this, the Egyptians learned of all the wrongs they had done to Joseph. {1:25} After he was sold, my brothers sat down to eat and drink. {1:26} But I, feeling pity for Joseph, didn't eat; instead, I watched the pit because Judah feared that Simeon, Dan, and Gad might run off and kill him. {1:27} When they noticed I wasn't eating, they made me keep watch over him until he was sold to the Ishmaelites. {1:28} When Reuben returned and discovered Joseph had been sold while he was away, he tore his clothes and mourned, saying: {1:29} "How can I face my father Jacob?" He took the money and ran after the merchants, but when he couldn't find them, he returned grieving. {1:30} The merchants had left the main road and taken a shortcut through the caves. {1:31} Reuben was distraught and ate nothing that day. {1:32} Dan then approached him and said: "Don't weep or grieve; we've found a way to explain this to our father Jacob. {1:33} Let's kill a goat, dip Joseph's coat in its blood, and send it to Jacob, saying: 'Is this your son's coat?'" {1:34} They did just that, for they stripped Joseph of his coat when they sold him and dressed him in a slave's garment. {1:35} Simeon took the coat and refused to give it back, wanting to tear it apart with his sword out of anger that Joseph was alive and that they hadn't killed him. {1:36} We all urged him, saying: "If you don't hand over the coat, we will tell our father that you alone did this evil in Israel." {1:37} So he gave it to them, and they did as Dan had suggested.

{2:1} Now, children, I urge you to keep the Lord's commands, show mercy to your neighbors, and have compassion towards all, not just people but also animals. {2:2} Because of this, the Lord blessed me, and when all my brothers were sick, I remained healthy, for the Lord knows everyone's heart. {2:3} Therefore, my children, be compassionate, for just as a person treats their neighbor, so will the Lord treat them. {2:4} My brothers fell ill and were dying because they lacked mercy in their hearts, while my sons were spared from sickness, as you know. {2:5} When I was in Canaan by the seaside, I caught fish for my father Jacob, and even when many fish died in the sea, I remained unharmed. {2:6} I was the first to build a boat to sail the sea, as the Lord gave me understanding and wisdom to do so. {2:7} I made a rudder for it and set up a sail on another upright piece of wood. {2:8} I sailed along the shores, catching fish for my father's household until we reached Egypt. {2:9} Out of compassion, I shared my catch with every stranger. {2:10} If someone was a stranger, sick, or elderly, I would cook the fish and serve them well, as everyone needed it, feeling sympathy for them. {2:11} Because of this, the Lord provided me with an abundance of fish; those who share with their neighbors receive even more from the Lord. {2:12} For five years, I caught fish and shared it with every person I met, providing for all my father's household. {2:13} In summer, I caught fish, and in winter, I tended sheep with my brothers. {2:14} Now I will tell you what I did. {2:15} I saw a man in distress from cold and nakedness in winter, and I had compassion on him, so I secretly took a garment from my father's house and gave it to him. {2:16} Therefore, my children, from what God has given you, show compassion and mercy to all without hesitation, and give with a generous heart. {2:17} If you can't give material help, at least feel compassion in your heart. {2:18} I remember that once I couldn't give to someone in need, and I walked with him for seven furlongs, my heart aching with compassion for him. {2:19} Therefore, have compassion towards everyone, so that the Lord may also show compassion and mercy to you. {2:20} In the last days, God will pour out His compassion on the earth, and wherever He finds mercy, He will dwell there. {2:21} To the extent that a person shows compassion to others, the same extent will the Lord show compassion to them. {2:22} When we went down to Egypt, Joseph held no grudge against us. {2:23} Recognizing this, my children, be free of malice and love one another; do not keep a record of wrongs against your brother. {2:24} Holding onto grievances destroys unity and divides families, troubling the soul and wearing down your spirit. {2:25} Observe the waters; when they flow together, they carry away stones, trees, and earth. {2:26} But if they split into many streams, the earth absorbs them, and they disappear. {2:27} So shall you be if you are divided. Don't allow yourselves to be split; everything God created has one head, two shoulders, two hands, and two feet. {2:28} I learned from my ancestors' writings that you will be divided in Israel, following two kings and committing all kinds of evil. {2:29} Your enemies will take you captive, and you will suffer among the Gentiles, facing many hardships and tribulations. {2:30} After this, you will remember the Lord and repent, and He will have mercy on you, for He is merciful and compassionate. {2:31} He does not hold evil against humans, as they are flesh and are deceived by their own wicked deeds. {2:32} After this, the Lord Himself, the light of righteousness, will arise for you, and you will return to your homeland. {2:33} You will see Him in Jerusalem for His name's sake. {2:34} Again, due to your wickedness, you will provoke Him to anger, {2:35} and you will be cast away until the time of fulfillment. {2:36} Now, my children, don't mourn for my death or feel sad that my end is near. {2:37} I will rise again among you, as a leader among my sons; I will rejoice with my tribe, as many as keep the Lord's law and the commandments of Zebulun, their father. {2:38} But the ungodly will face eternal fire from the Lord and be destroyed forever. {2:39} Now, I am on my way to my rest, just like my fathers did. {2:40} So, fear the Lord our God with all your strength for all your days. {2:41} After saying this, he passed away at a ripe old age. {2:42} His sons placed him in a wooden coffin, then carried him up and buried him in Hebron, alongside his fathers.

The Testament of Dan

{1:1} This is the account of the words of Dan, which he spoke to his sons in his last days, in the one hundred and twenty-fifth year of his life. {1:2} He gathered his family and said: "Listen to my words, you sons of Dan, and pay attention to your father's words. {1:3} I have learned throughout my life that truth and fair dealing are pleasing to God, while lying and anger are evil because they lead a person to wickedness. {1:4} Today, I confess to you, my children, that I had thoughts of wanting my brother Joseph, the good and righteous man, to die. {1:5} I was glad when he was sold because our father loved him more than us. {1:6} The spirit of jealousy and pride said to me: 'You too are his son.' {1:7} One of the spirits of Beliar (a term for a demonic figure) stirred me up, saying: 'Take this sword and kill Joseph; then your father will love you when he's gone.' {1:8} This spirit of anger persuaded me to attack Joseph like a leopard attacking a kid. {1:9} But the God of my fathers didn't let me catch him alone so I could kill him and bring about the destruction of another tribe in Israel. {1:10} Now, my children, I see I am dying, and I tell you truly that unless you keep yourselves away from lying and anger, and love truth and patience, you will perish. {1:11} Anger blinds a person and prevents them from seeing anyone's true face. {1:12} Whether it's a father or mother, they act like enemies; even if it's a brother, they don't recognize him; if it's a prophet of the Lord, they disobey; and if it's a righteous man, they disregard him; and as for friends, they don't acknowledge them. {1:13} Anger wraps a person in deceit, blinds their eyes, darkens their mind with lies, and gives them a twisted view. {1:14} What blinds their eyes? It's a heart filled with hatred, leading them to envy their brother. {1:15} Anger is truly evil, my children, as it troubles the very soul. {1:16} It takes hold of the angry person and controls their actions, giving the body the power to commit all kinds of wrong. {1:17} When the body acts out, the soul justifies these actions since it can't see clearly. {1:18} Therefore, if a powerful man becomes angry, he has three forms of power: one from his servants, another from his wealth that allows him to persuade others to act unjustly, and thirdly, from his own natural strength, which he uses to commit evil. {1:19} Even if an angry person is weak, they still have a double power from their anger, as it helps them in their lawlessness. {1:20} This spirit always accompanies lies at Satan's side, ensuring that through cruelty and deceit, their works are done. {1:21} So, understand the futility of anger; it first provokes with words and then strengthens the angered person through actions, disturbing their mind and inflaming their soul. {1:22} Therefore, when someone speaks against you, don't let anger take hold; and if someone praises you, don't let it inflate your pride: be neither delighted nor disgusted. {1:23} Initially, praise may please your ears and sharpen your mind to perceive provocations, leading you to think your anger is justified. {1:24} If you experience loss or misfortune, my children, don't let it upset you, for this spirit makes people desire what is fleeting, inciting anger through suffering. {1:25} Whether you suffer loss willingly or unwillingly, don't be troubled, for irritation leads to anger mixed with lies. {1:26} Wrath create a double mischief, working together to disturb the heart, & when soul is constantly disturbed, the Lord departs, and Beliar gains control.

{2:1} Therefore, my children, observe the commandments of the Lord and keep His law; turn away from anger and hate lies, so that the Lord may dwell among you and Beliar may flee from you. {2:2} Speak truthfully to your neighbors, and you won't fall into anger and confusion; instead, you will find peace, having the God of peace with you, and no war will prevail against you. {2:3} Love the Lord throughout your life, and love one another with a sincere heart. {2:4} I know that in the last days, you will turn away from the Lord and provoke Levi to anger, fighting against Judah; but you will not succeed, for an angel of the Lord will guide them both, and through them, Israel will stand. {2:5} Whenever you turn from the Lord, you will engage in all kinds of evil, committing the abominations of the Gentiles, chasing after the lawless, as the spirits of wickedness operate within you. {2:6} I have read in the book of Enoch, the righteous, that your leader is Satan, and all the spirits of wickedness and pride will conspire to constantly attack the sons of Levi, tempting them to sin against the Lord. {2:7} My sons will get close to Levi and sin with them in everything; the sons of Judah will be greedy, seizing others' goods like lions. {2:8} Therefore, you will be taken away with them into captivity, and you will suffer all the plagues of Egypt and all the evils of the Gentiles. {2:9} Yet when you return to the Lord, you will receive mercy, and He will bring you into His sanctuary and grant you peace. {2:10} From the tribe of Judah and Levi, salvation from the Lord will arise, and He will wage war against Beliar. {2:11} He will enact everlasting vengeance on our enemies, taking the souls of the saints from Beliar's grip, turning disobedient hearts back to the Lord, and giving eternal peace to those who call upon Him. {2:12} The saints will find rest in Eden, and the righteous will rejoice in the New Jerusalem, to the glory of God forever. {2:13} Jerusalem will no longer be desolate, nor will Israel be taken captive, for the Lord will dwell in the midst of it, living among people, and the Holy One of Israel will reign in humility and poverty; whoever believes in Him will reign among men in truth. {2:14} Now, fear the Lord, my children, and beware of Satan and his spirits. {2:15} Draw near to God and the angel who intercedes for you, for he is a mediator between God and man, standing up for the peace of Israel against the enemy's kingdom. {2:16} That is why the enemy seeks to destroy all who call upon the Lord. {2:17} He knows that on the day Israel repents, the enemy's kingdom will end. {2:18} The angel of peace will strengthen Israel so that they do not fall into the depths of evil. {2:19} In Israel's time of lawlessness, the Lord will not abandon them but will transform them into a nation that does His will, as no angel will equal Him. {2:20} His name will be known in every place in Israel and among the Gentiles. {2:21} Therefore, keep yourselves, my children, from every evil deed, and cast away anger and all lies, and love truth and patience. {2:22} Teach your children the things you have learned from your father, so that the Savior of the Gentiles may receive you; for He is true, patient, meek, and lowly, and He teaches the law of God through His actions. {2:23} Therefore, turn away from all unrighteousness, and cling to the righteousness of God, and your descendants will be saved forever. {2:24} And bury me near my fathers. {2:25} After saying this, he kissed them and fell asleep at a ripe old age. {2:26} His sons buried him, and later they took his bones and placed them next to Abraham, Isaac, and Jacob. {2:27} Nevertheless, Dan prophesied that they would forget their God, become alienated from their land, and from the lineage of Israel, and from their own family line.

The Testament of Naphtali

{1:1} This is the copy of the testament of Naphtali, which he declared at the time of his death in the one hundred and thirtieth year of his life. {1:2} When his sons were gathered together in the seventh month, on the first day of the month, while he was still in good health, he prepared a feast of food and wine for them. {1:3} And after he woke up in the morning, he said to them, "I am dying," but they did not believe him. {1:4} As he praised the Lord, he became strong and stated that after the feast of yesterday, he would die. {1:5} Then he began to say: "Listen, my children, you sons of Naphtali, hear the words of your father. {1:6} I was born from Bilhah, and because Rachel acted cunningly and gave Bilhah in place of herself to Jacob, she conceived and bore me on Rachel's knees, and thus she named me Naphtali. {1:7} Rachel loved me very much because I was born on her lap; when I was still young, she would kiss me and say: 'May I have a brother from my own womb, like you.' {1:8} Therefore, Joseph was like me in all things, according to Rachel's prayers. {1:9} My mother was Bilhah, daughter of Rotheus, who was the brother of Deborah,

Rebecca's nurse, and she was born on the same day as Rachel. {1:10} Rotheus was from the family of Abraham, a Chaldean, God-fearing, free-born, and noble. {1:11} He was taken captive and bought by Laban; {1:12} he gave him Euna, his handmaid, to wife, and she bore a daughter named Zilpah, after the village where he was taken captive. {1:13} Next, she bore Bilhah, saying: "My daughter is eager for what is new," for as soon as she was born, she seized the breast and began to suck it. {1:14} I was swift on my feet like a deer, and my father Jacob appointed me to carry messages, and he blessed me like a deer. {1:15} Just as a potter knows the vessel, how much it can hold and brings clay accordingly, so the Lord shapes the body after the spirit's likeness, and according to the body's capacity, He implants the spirit. {1:16} Neither will one fall short of the other by even a fraction; everything in creation was made by weight, measure, and rule. {1:17} Just as the potter knows the use of each vessel, what it is meant for, so the Lord knows the body and how far it will persist in goodness, and when it begins to do evil. {1:18} There is no inclination or thought that the Lord does not know, for He created every man in His image. {1:19} As a man's strength is reflected in his work; as his eye, so in his sleep; as his soul, so in his words, whether in the law of the Lord or the law of Beliar (the evil one). {1:20} Just as there is a division between light and darkness, between seeing and hearing, there is also a division between man and man, and between woman and woman; it cannot be said that one is like another in face or mind. {1:21} For God made all things good in their order: the five senses in the head, the neck joined to the head, with hair added for beauty and glory, the heart for understanding, the belly for waste, the stomach for grinding, the windpipe for breathing, the liver for anger, the gall for bitterness, the spleen for laughter, the kidneys for prudence, the muscles of the loins for strength, the lungs for inhaling, and the loins for power, and so on. {1:22} So, my children, let all your actions be done in order with good intent, in the fear of God, and do nothing disorderly, in scorn, or out of its proper time. {1:23} Do not be eager to corrupt your actions through greed or with vain words to deceive your souls; because if you keep silent in purity of heart, you will understand how to hold on to the will of God and reject the will of Beliar. {1:24} The sun, moon, and stars do not change their order; so do not change the law of God through disordered actions. {1:25} The Gentiles went astray, forsook the Lord, altered their order, and obeyed stocks and stones, spirits of deceit. {1:26} But you, my children, should not be like that, recognizing in the sky, the earth, the sea, and all created things, the Lord who made all things, so that you do not become like Sodom, which changed the order of nature. {1:27} Likewise, the Watchers also altered their nature, and the Lord cursed them at the flood, for their sake He made the earth without inhabitants and fruitless. {1:28} I tell you these things, my children, because I have read in the writings of Enoch that you will also depart from the Lord, following the lawlessness of the Gentiles, and will act according to all the wickedness of Sodom. {1:29} The Lord will bring captivity upon you, and you will serve your enemies and be burdened with every affliction and tribulation until the Lord has consumed you all. {1:30} After you have become diminished and few in number, you will return and acknowledge the Lord your God, and He will bring you back to your land according to His abundant mercy. {1:31} It shall be that after you enter the land of your forefathers, you will again forget the Lord and become ungodly. {1:32} The Lord will scatter you over all the earth, until the Lord's compassion comes, a man who works righteousness and shows mercy to all those who are far off and to those who are near.

{2:1} In the fortieth year of my life, I saw a vision on the Mount of Olives, east of Jerusalem, where the sun and moon stood still. {2:2} And behold, Isaac, my father's father, said to us: "Run and lay hold of them, each according to his strength; whoever seizes them will own the sun and moon." {2:3} So we all ran together, and Levi seized the sun, and Judah outpaced the others and grabbed the moon, and they were both lifted up with them. {2:4} When Levi became like a sun, a certain young man gave him twelve branches of palm; Judah shone like the moon, and under their feet were twelve rays. {2:5} The two, Levi and Judah, ran and took hold of them. {2:6} And behold, a bull on the earth, with two large horns and an eagle's wings on its back; we wanted to seize it, but could not. {2:7} Then Joseph came, seized it, and ascended high with it. {2:8} I saw this, for I was there, and behold, a holy writing appeared to us, saying: "Assyrians, Medes, Persians, Chaldeans, and Syrians will take captive the twelve tribes of Israel." {2:9} Again, after seven days, I saw our father Jacob standing by the sea of Jamnia, and we were with him. {2:10} Behold, a ship was sailing by without sailors or a pilot; and it was labeled: "The Ship of Jacob." {2:11} Our father said to us: "Come, let us board our ship." {2:12} Once he boarded, a fierce storm arose, and a mighty wind began to blow; our father, who was holding the helm, departed from us. {2:13} We, tossed by the storm, were carried across the sea; the ship filled with water and was battered by mighty waves until it broke apart. {2:14} Joseph fled away on a small boat, and we were all scattered on nine planks, with Levi and Judah together. {2:15} We were scattered to the ends of the earth. {2:16} Then Levi, dressed in sackcloth, prayed for us all to the Lord. {2:17} When the storm ceased, the ship reached land as if in peace. {2:18} Our father came, and we all rejoiced together. {2:19} I told my father about these two dreams, and he said to me: "These things must be fulfilled in their season, after Israel has endured many trials." {2:20} Then my father said to me: "I believe God that Joseph lives, for I always see that the Lord counts him among you." {2:21} He wept and said: "Oh my son Joseph, you live, though I do not see you, and you do not see Jacob who begat you." {2:22} His words made me weep too, and I burned with the desire to tell that Joseph had been sold, but I feared my brothers. {2:23} And behold! My children, I have shown you the last times and how everything will unfold in Israel. {2:24} Therefore, charge your children to be united with Levi and Judah; for through them, salvation will arise for Israel, and in them, Jacob will be blessed. {2:25} For through their tribes, God will appear dwelling among men on earth, to save the race of Israel and gather the righteous from among the Gentiles. {2:26} If you do good, my children, both men and angels will bless you; God will be glorified among the Gentiles through you, and the devil will flee from you, and wild beasts will fear you, and the Lord will love you, and angels will be close to you. {2:27} Just as a man who trains a child well is kindly remembered, so for a good deed, there is a good memory before God. {2:28} But those who do not do good will be cursed by both angels and men, and God will be dishonored among the Gentiles through them; the devil will treat them as his own special instrument, and wild beasts will overpower them, and the Lord will hate them. {2:29} The commandments of the law are twofold, and they must be fulfilled with wisdom. {2:30} There is a time for a man to embrace his wife and a time to refrain for prayer. {2:31} So there are two commandments; if they are not done in proper order, they bring great sin upon men. {2:32} This applies to the other commandments as well. {2:33} Therefore, be wise in God, my children, and prudent, understanding the order of His commandments and the meaning of every word, so that the Lord may love you, {2:34} and when he had charged them with many such words, he urged them to remove his bones to Hebron and bury him with his fathers. {2:35} After he had eaten and drunk with a joyful heart, he covered his face and died. {2:36} His sons did everything their father Naphtali had commanded them.

The Testament of Gad

{1:1} This is the testament of Gad, what he spoke to his sons in the one hundred and twenty-fifth year of his life, saying to them: {1:2} "Listen, my children, I was the ninth son born to Jacob, and I was brave in taking care of the flocks. {1:3} I guarded the flock at night; whenever a lion, wolf, or any wild beast attacked, I chased it down, caught its foot with my hand, threw it away about a stone's throw, and killed it. {1:4} My brother Joseph was with us tending the flock for over thirty days, but being young, he fell ill from the heat. {1:5} He returned to Hebron to our father, who made him lie down close to him because he loved him greatly. {1:6} Joseph told our father that the sons of Zilpah and Bilhah were killing the best of the flock and eating them against the wishes of Reuben and Judah. {1:7} He saw that I had rescued a lamb from the mouth of a bear and killed the bear, but I felt sorrow because we had eaten the lamb that I could not save. {1:8} Because of this, I was angry with Joseph until the day he was sold. {1:9} Hatred filled my heart, and I didn't want to hear about him or see him because he openly rebuked us, saying we were eating from the flock without Judah's approval. {1:10} Everything he told our father, our father believed. {1:11} I confess now, my children, that I often wished to kill him because I hated him deeply. {1:12} I hated him even more because of his dreams; I wanted to get rid of him from the land of the living, just like an ox consumes grass from the field. {1:13} Judah secretly sold him to the Ishmaelites. {1:14} Thus, the God of our fathers delivered him from our hands, preventing us from committing a great sin in Israel. {1:15} Now, my children, listen to the truth and do righteousness, following all the laws of the Most High, and do not let the spirit of hatred lead you astray, for it is evil in all actions of men. {1:16} Whatever a man does, the hater despises him; and even if a man follows the law of the Lord, he does not praise him; even if a man fears the Lord and delights in what is righteous, the hater does not love him. {1:17} He rejects the truth, envies those who succeed, welcomes gossip, loves arrogance, for hatred blinds the soul, just as I looked at Joseph back then. {1:18} Therefore, beware, my children, of hatred, for it leads to lawlessness even against the Lord Himself. {1:19} It will not heed the commandments regarding loving one's neighbor and sins against God. {1:20} If a brother stumbles, it delights to proclaim it to everyone, eager for judgment and punishment, wishing him dead. {1:21} If it is a servant, it incites him against his master, devising afflictions against him, even hoping he can be killed. {1:22} Hatred works with envy against those who prosper; as long as it hears about or sees their success, it languishes. {1:23} Just as love can revive the dead and restore those condemned to die, hatred seeks to destroy the living and would not let even those who have sinned lightly live. {1:24} The spirit of hatred collaborates with Satan, causing hastiness that leads to death; but the spirit of love aligns with the law of God, showing patience for the salvation of men. {1:25} Therefore, hatred is evil; it constantly mixes with lies, speaks against the truth, makes small things seem significant, turns light into darkness, calls sweet things bitter, teaches slander, ignites anger, stirs up war and violence, fills the heart with evils and devilish poison. {1:26} I tell you these things from my own experience, my children, so that you can cast out hatred, which is of the devil, and cling to the love of God. {1:27} Righteousness drives out hatred, and humility destroys envy. {1:28} The just and humble person feels ashamed to act unjustly, reproved not by others but by his own heart, for the Lord sees his inclinations. {1:29} He does not speak against a holy person because the fear of God overcomes hatred. {1:30} Fearing that he might offend the Lord, he won't wrong anyone, not even in thought. {1:31} I learned these things after I repented regarding Joseph. {1:32} True repentance destroys ignorance, drives away darkness, enlightens the eyes, gives knowledge to the soul, and leads the mind to salvation. {1:33} Those things which it has not learned from man, it knows through repentance. {1:34} God afflicted me with a liver disease; had it not been for the prayers of Jacob, my father, my spirit would have surely departed. {1:35} For the way a man transgresses, that is how he is punished. {1:36} Therefore, since my liver was mercilessly turned against Joseph, I suffered mercilessly in my liver too & was tormented for 11 months, the same length of time I was angry with Joseph.

{2:1} Now, my children, I urge you to love each other and put away hatred from your hearts; love one another in action, in word, and in the intentions of your soul. {2:2} In the presence of my father, I spoke peaceably to Joseph; but when I left, the spirit of hatred clouded my mind and stirred my soul to kill him. {2:3} Love each other from the heart; if someone sins against you, speak peaceably to him and hold no malice in your soul; if he repents and confesses, forgive him. {2:4} But if he denies it, don't get angry with him; lest he catches your poison and swears, causing you to sin doubly. {2:5} Do not let another man hear your secrets when you are in a legal dispute; otherwise, he may come to hate you, become your enemy, and commit a great sin against you, often speaking to you deceitfully or plotting against you with ill intent. {2:6} And even if he denies it yet feels shame when reproached, stop reproaching him. {2:7} For he who denies may truly repent and not wrong you again; he may even honor you, fear you, and be at peace with you. {2:8} But if he is shameless and continues to do wrong, forgive him from your heart, leaving vengeance to God. {2:9} If someone prospers more than you, do not be upset, but pray for him as well, that he may have complete success. {2:10} For this is beneficial for you. {2:11} And if he is even further exalted, do not envy him, remembering that all flesh will die; and praise God who gives good and beneficial things to all men. {2:12} Seek out the judgments of the Lord, and your mind will find rest and peace. {2:13} Even if a man becomes rich by evil means, like Esau, my father's brother, do not be jealous; wait for the end of the Lord. {2:14} For if God takes away wealth gained by evil means, He forgives if one repents, but the unrepentant face eternal punishment. {2:15} For the poor man, if free from envy, pleases the Lord in all things and is blessed more than all men because he does not have the troubles of vain men. {2:16} Therefore, put away jealousy from your souls and love one another with a sincere heart. {2:17} Tell these things to your children so they honor Judah and Levi, for from them the Lord will raise up salvation for Israel. {2:18} For I know that in the end your children will depart from Him and walk in wickedness, affliction, and corruption before the Lord. {2:19} After resting for a little while, he said again, "My children, obey your father and bury me near my fathers." {2:20} He drew up his feet and fell asleep in peace. {2:21} Five years later, they took him to Hebron and buried him with his fathers.

The Testament of Asher

{1:1} This is the testament of Asher, what he spoke to his sons in the one hundred and twenty-fifth year of his life. {1:2} While he was still healthy, he said to them: "Listen, children of Asher, to your father, and I will explain to you all that is right in the sight of the Lord. {1:3} God has given two ways to the sons of men, along with two inclinations, two kinds of actions, two modes of action, and two outcomes. {1:4} Therefore, everything exists in pairs, one opposing the other. {1:5} There are two paths of good and evil, and within us are the two inclinations that distinguish them. {1:6} If the soul delights in the good inclination, all its actions are righteous; and if it sins, it quickly repents. {1:7} With its thoughts focused on righteousness and rejecting wickedness, it overthrows evil and uproots sin. {1:8} However, if it leans towards the evil inclination, all its actions are wicked; it drives away the good, clings to evil, and is ruled by Beliar (a term for a demonic figure); even when it does good, that good is twisted into evil. {1:9} Whenever it begins to do good, Beliar forces the outcome into evil, for the treasure of that inclination is filled with an evil spirit. {1:10} A person might use words to support the good for the sake of the evil, yet the outcome leads to harm. {1:11} There is a person who shows no compassion towards those who assist him in his evil; this has two sides, but the whole is evil. {1:12} Another loves those who do evil because he would even prefer to die in wickedness for their sake; it is clear this also has two sides, but it is an evil act overall. {1:13} Even if he has love, he is wicked if he conceals evil for the sake of a good reputation, as the end of such actions leads to evil. {1:14} Another steals, acts unjustly, plunders, defrauds, and yet has pity for the poor; this, too, has a double aspect, but the whole is evil. {1:15} He who defrauds his neighbor provokes God, swears falsely against the Most High, and yet shows pity for the poor; he disregards the law given by the Lord and provokes Him, even while he refreshes the poor. {1:16} He defiles the soul while pleasing the body; he kills many but has pity for a few; this also has a twofold aspect, but the whole is evil. {1:17} Another commits adultery and fornication, abstains from certain foods, and when he fasts, he does evil; despite his extreme wickedness, he follows the commandments: this, too, has a twofold aspect, but the whole is evil. {1:18} Such people are like hares; they appear clean, like those that divide the hoof, but in reality, they are unclean. {1:19} For God has declared this in the commandments. {1:20} Do not, my children, wear two faces like them—one of goodness and one of wickedness; instead, cling only to goodness, for God dwells there, and people desire it. {1:21} Flee from wickedness, destroying the evil inclination through your good deeds; for those who are double-faced do not serve God but their own desires, trying to please Beliar and those like him. {1:22} Good people, those with a single face, though they may be thought to sin by the double-faced, are righteous before God. {1:23} Many, in killing the wicked, do two works, good and evil; yet the whole is good, for they have uprooted and destroyed what is evil. {1:24} One man hates the merciful and the unjust, as well as the man who commits adultery and fasts; this too has a double aspect, but the whole work is good, as he follows the Lord's example, not accepting what seems good as genuine good. {1:25}

Another does not wish to see good days with the wicked, lest he defile his body and pollute his soul; this, too, is double-faced, but the whole is good. {1:26} Such men are like stags and hinds, appearing unclean in their wildness, yet they are entirely clean because they zealously serve the Lord and abstain from what God hates and forbids, keeping evil away from the good. {1:27} You see, my children, how there are two sides to everything, one hidden by the other: in wealth, there is hidden greed; in festivity, drunkenness; in laughter, sorrow; in marriage, promiscuity. {1:28} Death follows life, dishonor follows glory, night follows day, and darkness follows light; all things are under the day, just things under life, unjust things under death; thus, eternal life awaits death. {1:29} Truth cannot be called a lie, nor right, wrong; for all truth exists in the light, just as all things exist under God. {1:30} I have proven all these things in my life, I did not stray from the truth of the Lord, and I sought out the commandments of the Most High, striving with all my strength for what is good with a single purpose. {1:31} Therefore, take heed, my children, to the commandments of the Lord, following the truth with a single face. {1:32} Those who are double-faced are guilty of a twofold sin; they both do evil and take pleasure in those who do it, following the example of deceitful spirits and working against humanity. {1:33} Therefore, my children, keep the law of the Lord, and do not treat evil as if it were good; instead, seek what is truly good and hold it dear in all commandments of the Lord, living according to it and resting in it. {1:34} For the final outcomes of men reveal their righteousness or unrighteousness when they encounter the angels of the Lord and of Satan. {1:35} When the troubled soul departs, it is tormented by the evil spirit it served in its lusts and evil deeds. {1:36} But if it departs in peace and joy, it meets the angel of peace, who leads it into eternal life. {1:37} Do not become, my children, like Sodom, which sinned against the angels of the Lord and was destroyed forever. {1:38} For I know you will sin and be handed over to your enemies; your land will become desolate, your holy places destroyed, and you will be scattered to the four corners of the earth. {1:39} You will be disregarded in your dispersion, disappearing like water. {1:40} Until the Most High visits the earth, coming as a man, eating and drinking with men, and crushing the head of the dragon in the water. {1:41} He will save Israel and all the Gentiles, God speaking through a man. {1:42} Therefore, my children, share these things with your children, so they do not disobey Him. {1:43} For I know you will certainly be disobedient and act wickedly, not listening to the law of God but to the commandments of men, corrupted through wickedness. {1:44} And so you will be scattered like Gad and Dan, my brothers, and you will not know your lands, tribes, or languages. {1:45} But the Lord will gather you together in faith through His tender mercy, for the sake of Abraham, Isaac, and Jacob. {1:46} When he finished saying these things, he commanded them, saying: "Bury me in Hebron." {1:47} He then fell asleep and died at a ripe old age. {1:48} His sons did as he commanded, taking him up to Hebron and burying him with his fathers.

The Testament of Joseph

{1:1} This is the testament of Joseph. {1:2} When he was about to die, he called his sons and his brothers together and said to them: {1:3} "My brothers and my children, listen to Joseph, the beloved of Israel; pay attention, my sons, to your father. {1:4} Throughout my life, I have witnessed envy and death, yet I did not stray but remained steadfast in the truth of the Lord. {1:5} My brothers hated me, but the Lord loved me. {1:6} They wanted to kill me, but the God of my fathers protected me. {1:7} They threw me into a pit, and the Most High lifted me out again. {1:8} I was sold into slavery, but the Lord of all set me free. {1:9} I was taken captive, and His strong hand helped me. {1:10} I faced hunger, and the Lord Himself fed me. {1:11} I was alone, and God comforted me. {1:12} I was sick, and the Lord visited me. {1:13} I was imprisoned, and my God showed favor to me; {1:14} I was bound, and He released me. {1:15} I was slandered, and He defended me; {1:16} I was spoken against bitterly by the Egyptians, and He delivered me. {1:17} I was envied by my fellow slaves, and He exalted me. {1:18} This chief captain of Pharaoh entrusted his house to me. {1:19} I resisted a shameless woman who tried to tempt me, but the God of Israel, my father, saved me from her fiery desire. {1:20} I was thrown into prison, beaten, and mocked; but the Lord allowed me to find mercy in the eyes of the prison keeper. {1:21} The Lord does not abandon those who fear Him, neither in darkness, nor in chains, nor in troubles, nor in need. {1:22} For God is not ashamed like a man, nor afraid like the son of man, nor weak like a creature of the earth. {1:23} Yet in all these things, He provides protection and comforts in various ways, though He may temporarily depart to test the soul's inclination. {1:24} In ten trials, He showed me as approved, and in all of them, I endured; for endurance is a powerful charm, and patience brings many blessings. {1:25} How often did the Egyptian woman threaten me with death! {1:26} How many times did she punish me, only to call me back and threaten me again, and when I refused her, she said: {1:27} "You shall be my lord and have authority over everything in my house if you will yield to me, and you will be like our master." {1:28} But I remembered my father's words, and going to my room, I wept and prayed to the Lord. {1:29} I fasted for seven years and appeared to the Egyptians as if I lived in luxury, for those who fast for God's sake receive beauty of countenance. {1:30} When my master was away, I drank no wine; for three days, I did not eat, but gave my food to the poor and the sick. {1:31} I sought the Lord early and wept over the Egyptian woman from Memphis, for she continually troubled me, even coming to me at night under the pretense of visiting. {1:32} Because she had no son, she pretended to see me as a son. {1:33} For a time, she embraced me as a son without my knowledge; but later, she tried to lead me into fornication. {1:34} When I realized this, I was deeply saddened; when she left, I mourned for her many days because I recognized her cunning and deceit. {1:35} I spoke to her the words of the Most High, hoping she would turn from her evil desires. {1:36} Often, she flattered me with words as a holy man, and cunningly praised my chastity before her husband, while secretly trying to ensnare me when we were alone. {1:37} She openly praised me as chaste, saying in secret: "Do not fear my husband; he believes in your chastity. Even if someone tells him about us, he will not believe it." {1:38} Because of all this, I lay on the ground and begged God to deliver me from her deceit. {1:39} When she realized she was making no progress, she came to me again under the guise of seeking instruction, wanting to learn the word of God. {1:40} She said to me: "If you want me to abandon my idols, lie with me, and I will persuade my husband to leave his idols, and we will follow the law of your Lord." {1:41} I replied: "The Lord does not want those who honor Him to be in impurity, nor does He delight in those who commit adultery, but in those who approach Him with pure hearts and undefiled lips." {1:42} She remained silent, longing to fulfill her evil desire. {1:43} I committed myself even more to fasting and prayer, that the Lord might rescue me from her. {1:44} Again, at another time, she said to me: "If you will not commit adultery, I will kill my husband with poison and take you as my husband." {1:45} When I heard this, I tore my clothes and said to her: {1:46} "Woman, fear God and do not commit this evil deed, or you will be destroyed; for I will surely reveal your plot to everyone." {1:47} She, afraid, begged me not to expose her scheme. {1:48} She left, soothing me with gifts and sending me every luxury of the world. {1:49} Later, she sent me food mixed with enchantments. {1:50} When the eunuch who brought it arrived, I looked up and saw a terrifying man presenting me with the dish, and I realized her scheme was to trap me. {1:51} When he left, I wept and did not touch that food or any of her offerings. {1:52} The next day, she came to me and asked: "Why have you not eaten the food?" {1:53} I replied: "It is because you have filled it with deadly enchantments; how can you say: I do not approach idols but only the Lord?" {1:54} Now know this: the God of my father has revealed your wickedness to me through His angel, and I have kept it hidden to convict you, hoping you might see and repent. {1:55} But to show you that the wickedness of the ungodly cannot harm those who worship God in purity, I will take some and eat it before you. {1:56} After saying this, I prayed: "God of my fathers and angel of Abraham, be with me," and I ate. {1:57} When she saw this, she fell at my feet weeping, and I helped her up and admonished her. {1:58} She promised not to commit this sin again. {1:59} But her heart remained set on evil, and she looked for ways to ensnare me, sighing deeply and appearing dejected, though she was not ill. {1:60} When her husband saw her, he asked: "Why do you look so sad?" {1:61} She replied: "I have a pain in my heart, and my spirit is oppressed," and he comforted her despite her not being sick. {1:62} Then, seizing an opportunity, she rushed to me while her husband was still away, saying: "I will hang myself or throw myself off a cliff if you will not lie with me." {1:63} Seeing that the spirit of Beliar was troubling her, I prayed to the Lord and said to her: {1:64} "Why, wretched woman, are you troubled and disturbed, blinded by your sins? {1:65} Remember that if you kill yourself, Asteho, your husband's concubine, will mistreat your children, and you will erase your memory from the earth." {1:66} She responded: "Then you love me; let that be enough: just take care of my life and my children, and I hope to fulfill my desire too." {1:67} But she did not understand that I spoke this way because of my master, not because of her. {1:68} For if a man falls before the passion of wicked desire and becomes enslaved by it, like her, he interprets any good he hears regarding that desire in light of his wicked wish. {1:69} I declare to you, my children, it was around the sixth hour when she left me; I knelt before the Lord all day and all night; and at dawn, I rose up, weeping and praying for relief from her. {1:70} Finally, she seized my garments, forcefully dragging me to have relations with her. {1:71} When I saw she was holding my garment in her madness, I left it behind and fled away naked. {1:72} I held on to my garment when she falsely accused me, and when her husband came home, he threw me into prison in his house. {1:73} The next day, he whipped me and sent me to Pharaoh's prison. {1:74} While I was in chains, the Egyptian woman was filled with grief, and she came to me and heard how I thanked the Lord and sang praises in the darkness of my cell, rejoicing with a glad voice and glorifying my God for delivering me from the lustful desires of the Egyptian woman. {1:75} She often sent messages to me, saying, "Give in to my desires, and I will free you from your chains and release you from the darkness." {1:76} But I did not even entertain the thought of yielding to her. {1:77} For God loves those who, in the midst of wickedness, combine fasting with chastity rather than those who indulge in luxury and excess in the halls of kings. {1:78} If a man lives in chastity and also desires glory, and the Most High knows that it is beneficial for him, He will grant him that glory. {1:79} How often, even when she was sick, did she come to me at unexpected times, listening to my voice as I prayed! {1:80} Yet, when I heard her groaning, I remained silent. {1:81} While I was in her house, she would expose her arms, breasts, and legs to entice me, for she was very beautiful and splendidly adorned to beguile me. {1:82} But the Lord protected me from her schemes.

{2:1} So, my children, see how great things patience can achieve, along with prayer and fasting. {2:2} If you pursue chastity and purity with patience, prayer, and humble fasting, the Lord will be among you because He loves chastity. {2:3} Wherever the Most High dwells, even if envy, slavery, or slander comes upon a person, the Lord who is in them will not only save them from evil for the sake of their chastity but will also lift them up, just as He did with me. {2:4} A person is elevated in every way, whether in actions, words, or thoughts. {2:5} My brothers knew how much my father loved me, yet I never let pride fill my mind; even as a child, I had the fear of God in my heart, knowing that all things are temporary. {2:6} I did not act against them with bad intentions; I honored my brothers, and even when I was sold, I kept silent about being the son of Jacob, a great man. {2:7} So, my children, have the fear of God in everything you do and honor your brothers. {2:8} Everyone who follows the Lord's law will be loved by Him. {2:9} When I was taken to the Indocolpitae by the Ishmaelites, they asked me, {2:10} "Are you a slave?" I said I was a home-born slave to avoid bringing shame on my brothers. {2:11} The eldest among them said, "You are not a slave; even your appearance shows that." {2:12} But I insisted that I was their slave. {2:13} When we arrived in Egypt, there was a dispute over who would buy me. {2:14} Eventually, everyone agreed that I should stay in Egypt with the merchant until they returned with their goods. {2:15} The Lord granted me favor in the eyes of the merchant, who entrusted his household to me. {2:16} God blessed him through me, increasing his wealth in gold, silver, and servants. {2:17} I was with him for three months and five days. {2:18} Around that time, the wife of Pentephris, a Memphian, came down in a chariot with great splendor because she had heard about me from her eunuchs. {2:19} She told her husband that the merchant had become rich because of a young Hebrew, claiming he must have been stolen from Canaan. {2:20} "Now, therefore, do justice and take the youth to your house; the God of the Hebrews will bless you, for grace from heaven is upon him." {2:21} Pentephris was persuaded by her words and called the merchant, asking him, {2:22} "What is this I hear? Are you stealing people from Canaan to sell as slaves?" {2:23} The merchant fell at his feet, begging, "I beg you, my lord, I don't know what you're talking about." {2:24} Pentephris replied, "Then where did this Hebrew slave come from?" {2:25} The merchant said, "The Ishmaelites entrusted him to me until they return." {2:26} Pentephris didn't believe him and ordered him to be stripped and beaten. {2:27} When the merchant continued to insist, Pentephris said, "Bring the youth here." {2:28} When I was brought in, I bowed to Pentephris, who was third in rank among Pharaoh's officers. {2:29} He took me aside and asked, "Are you a slave or free?" {2:30} I said, "A slave." {2:31} He asked, "Whose?" {2:32} I replied, "The Ishmaelites'." {2:33} He said, "How did you become their slave?" {2:34} I explained, "They bought me from Canaan." {2:35} He said, "You must be lying," and immediately ordered me to be stripped and beaten. {2:36} The Memphian woman was watching from a window as I was being beaten, and she sent a message saying, {2:37} "Your judgment is unfair; you are punishing a free man who has been stolen as if he were guilty." {2:38} When I continued to maintain my statement despite the beating, he ordered me to be imprisoned until, as he said, the boy's owners came. {2:39} The woman said to her husband, "Why do you keep this well-born lad in chains? He should be set free and treated well." {2:40} She wished to see me because of her sinful desire, but I was unaware of all this. {2:41} He replied, "It's not the custom of the Egyptians to take what belongs to others without proof." {2:42} He said this regarding the merchant, but insisted the boy must be imprisoned. {2:43} After twenty-four days, the Ishmaelites returned, having heard that my father Jacob was mourning for me. {2:44} They said to me, "Why did you say you were a slave? We learned that you are the son of a powerful man in Canaan, and your father mourns for you in sackcloth and ashes." {2:45} When I heard this, my heart sank, and I felt the urge to weep, but I held back to avoid shaming my brothers. {2:46} I told them, "I don't know; I am a slave." {2:47} They decided to sell me so I wouldn't be found with them. {2:48} They feared my father might seek revenge against them. {2:49} They knew he was powerful with God and men. {2:50} The merchant then said, "Release me from Pentephris's judgment." {2:51} They approached me and said, "Tell him you were bought by us for money, and he will let us go." {2:52} The Memphian woman urged her husband, "Buy the youth; I hear they are selling him." {2:53} She immediately sent a eunuch to the Ishmaelites, asking them to sell me. {2:54} But when the eunuch wouldn't pay their asking price, he returned and informed her they were demanding a high price. {2:55} She sent another eunuch, saying, "Even if they ask for two minas, give it to them; don't spare the gold; just buy the boy and bring him to me." {2:56} The eunuch went, paid them eighty pieces of gold, and received me; but to the Egyptian woman, he said he paid a hundred. {2:57} Though I knew this, I remained silent to avoid shaming the eunuch. {2:58} So, my children, {2:59} see what great things I endured to avoid bringing shame on my brothers. {2:60} Therefore, love one another and patiently cover each other's faults. {2:61} God delights in the unity of brothers and in hearts that find joy in love. {2:62} When my brothers came to Egypt, they learned I had returned their money to them without scolding them and comforted them. {2:63} After our father Jacob died, I loved them even more and did everything he commanded abundantly for them. {2:64} I did not allow them to suffer in even the smallest way and gave them everything I had. {2:65} Their children were like my children, and I treated my children as their servants; their life was my life, and their suffering was my suffering. {2:66} I did not elevate myself among them out of pride for my worldly status, but I was among them as one of the least. {2:67} Therefore, if you follow the Lord's commandments, my children, He will exalt you and bless you with good things forever. {2:68} If someone tries to do evil to you, do good to them, pray for them, and the Lord will redeem you from all evil. {2:69} Look, from my humility and patience, I took the daughter of the priest of Heliopolis as my wife. {2:70} A hundred talents of gold were given to me with her, and the Lord made them serve me. {2:71} He also gave me beauty like a flower, surpassing the beautiful ones of Israel, and preserved my strength and beauty into old age because I was like Jacob in all things. {2:72} And listen, my children, to the vision I had. {2:73} I saw twelve deer feeding; nine were scattered over all the earth, and three also. {2:74} I saw that from Judah, a virgin in a linen garment gave birth to a spotless lamb; beside her was a lion, and all the beasts attacked him, but the lamb overcame them, defeating and trampling them. {2:75} Because of him, both angels and men rejoiced, and all the land. {2:76} These things will happen in their time, in the last days. {2:77} Therefore, my children, keep the Lord's commandments and honor Levi and Judah; from them will come the Lamb of God who takes away the sin of the world, saving all the Gentiles and Israel. {2:78} His kingdom will be everlasting, which will not pass away, while my kingdom among you will end like a tent that disappears after summer. {2:79} I know that after my death, the Egyptians will oppress you, but God will avenge you and bring you to the land He promised your fathers. {2:80} Carry my bones with you; when you take them up, {2:81} the Lord will be with you in light, while Beliar will be in darkness with the Egyptians. {2:82} Also, take Asenath, your mother, to the Hippodrome, and bury her near Rachel, your mother. {2:83} After saying these things, he stretched out his feet and died at a good old age. {2:84} All Israel mourned for him, as did all of Egypt, with great mourning. {2:85} When the children of Israel left Egypt, they took Joseph's bones with them and buried him in Hebron with his fathers, and he lived for one hundred and ten years.

The Testament of Benjamin

{1:1} Benjamin, the twelfth son of Jacob and Rachel, the youngest in the family, became a philosopher and philanthropist. {1:2} Here are the words of Benjamin, which he commanded his sons to observe after living for one hundred and twenty-five years. {1:3} He kissed them and said, "Just as Isaac was born to Abraham in his old age, so I was born to Jacob. {1:4} My mother Rachel died during childbirth, so I had no milk and was nursed by Bilhah, her handmaid. {1:5} Rachel was barren for twelve years after giving birth to Joseph; she prayed to the Lord while fasting for twelve days, and then she conceived and bore me. {1:6} My father loved Rachel deeply and prayed that he would see two sons born from her. {1:7} That's why I was named Benjamin, meaning 'son of days.' {1:8} When I went to Egypt to see Joseph, and he recognized me, he asked, "What did they tell my father when they sold me?" {1:9} I replied, "They dipped your coat in blood and sent it, saying, 'Is this your son's coat?'" {1:10} He said to me, "Similarly, when they stripped me of my coat, they handed me over to the Ishmaelites, who gave me a loincloth, beat me, and told me to run. {1:11} One of those who beat me was killed by a lion." {1:12} This terrified his companions. {1:13} So, my children, love the Lord God of heaven and earth, and keep His commandments, following Joseph's example of goodness. {1:14} Keep your thoughts focused on good, just as you know me; for a person with a right mind sees all things clearly. {1:15} Fear the Lord and love your neighbor; even though the spirits of Beliar (Satan) may try to afflict you with evil, they will not have power over you, just as they did not over my brother Joseph. {1:16} Many wanted to kill him, but God protected him! {1:17} Those who fear God and love their neighbor cannot be harmed by the spirit of Beliar, as they are shielded by the fear of God. {1:18} They are not ruled by the schemes of men or beasts because the Lord helps them through their love for their neighbor. {1:19} Joseph also asked our father to pray for his brothers, so the Lord would not hold their sins against them. {1:20} Jacob cried out, "My good child, you have overcome my very being!" {1:21} He embraced him and kissed him for two hours, saying: "In you will be fulfilled the prophecy concerning the Lamb of God, the Savior of the world, and that a blameless one will be sacrificed for lawless men, and a sinless one will die for ungodly men, through the blood of the covenant for the salvation of the Gentiles and of Israel, destroying Beliar and his followers. {1:22} So, my children, see the end of a good man? {1:23} Follow his compassion with a good mind, so you may wear crowns of glory. {1:24} A good man does not have a dark heart; he shows mercy to everyone, even to sinners. {1:25} Though others plot evil against him, he overcomes evil by doing good, shielded by God, and loves the righteous as his own soul. {1:26} If someone is honored, he does not envy; if someone is enriched, he is not jealous; if someone is brave, he praises them; he honors the virtuous; he shows mercy to the poor; he is compassionate towards the weak; he sings praises to God. {1:27} He loves those with a good spirit as he loves his own soul. {1:28} If you also have a good mind, wicked people will be at peace with you, and the immoral will respect you and turn to good; even the greedy will not only cease their inordinate desires but also give what they covet to those in need. {1:29} If you do well, even unclean spirits will flee from you, and beasts will fear you. {1:30} Where there is respect for good works and light in the mind, darkness will flee. {1:31} If someone does violence to a holy man, he repents; for the holy man is merciful to those who insult him and remains silent. {1:32} If someone betrays a righteous man, the righteous man prays; though he may be humbled for a little while, he will soon appear much more glorious, just like my brother Joseph. {1:33} A good man's inclination is not swayed by the deceit of Beliar's spirit, for the angel of peace guides his soul. {1:34} He does not passionately desire corruptible things or seek riches for pleasure. {1:35} He does not delight in indulgence, does not harm his neighbor, does not fill himself with luxuries, does not look upon the world with longing, for the Lord is his portion. {1:36} A good mind does not seek honor or disgrace from men and is free from deceit, lies, fights, and insults; for the Lord dwells within him, lights up his soul, and he rejoices toward all people always. {1:37} A good mind does not have two tongues—one for blessing and one for cursing, for insults and honor, for sorrow and joy, for silence and confusion, for hypocrisy and truth, for poverty and wealth; it has one disposition, uncorrupted and pure, towards all. {1:38} It does not have double vision or double hearing; in everything he does, speaks, or sees, he knows that the Lord observes his soul. {1:39} He cleanses his mind so he is not condemned by men or by God. {1:40} Similarly, the works of Beliar are twofold, lacking integrity. {1:41} Therefore, my children, I say to you, flee from Beliar's malice; for he gives a sword to those who obey him. {1:42} This sword brings seven evils: first, the mind conceives through Beliar, leading to bloodshed; second, ruin; third, tribulation; fourth, exile; fifth, famine; sixth, panic; seventh, destruction. {1:43} That's why Cain was handed over to seven punishments by God, with one plague inflicted upon him every hundred years. {1:44} By the time he was two hundred years old, he began to suffer, and he was destroyed in the nine-hundredth year. {1:45} Because of Abel, his brother, he was judged for all these evils, while Lamech was judged for seventy times seven. {1:46} For those who resemble Cain in envy and hatred towards their brothers will receive the same punishment.

{2:1} And you, my children, flee from wrongdoing, envy, and hatred towards your brothers, and cling to goodness and love. {2:2} A person with a pure heart in love does not look at a woman for lust, for there is no defilement in his heart because the Spirit of God rests upon him. {2:3} Just as the sun is not tainted by shining on dung and dirt, but rather dries both and dispels the foul odor, so too the pure mind, surrounded by earthly defilements, cleanses them and remains undefiled. {2:4} I believe there will be evildoings among you, as Enoch the righteous foretold: you will commit fornication like Sodom and perish, except for a few, renewing sinful deeds with women, and the kingdom of the Lord will not be among you, for He will take it away immediately. {2:5} Nevertheless, the temple of God will be among you, and the final temple will be more glorious than the first. {2:6} The twelve tribes will be gathered there, along with all the Gentiles, until the Most High sends His salvation through an only-begotten prophet. {2:7} He will enter the first temple, where the Lord will be mistreated, and He will be lifted up on a tree. {2:8} The temple veil will be torn, and the Spirit of God will move to the Gentiles like fire poured out. {2:9} He will rise from Hades and ascend from earth to heaven. {2:10} I know how lowly He will be on earth and how glorious in heaven. {2:11} When Joseph was in Egypt, I longed to see his figure and the shape of his face; through the prayers of my father Jacob, I saw him while awake in the daytime, exactly as he was. {2:12} After saying these things, he told them: "Know, my children, that I am dying. {2:13} Therefore, speak truthfully to your neighbor, and keep the law of the Lord and His commandments. {2:14} For these things I leave you as an inheritance. {2:15} So, give them to your children as an everlasting possession; for both Abraham, Isaac, and Jacob did the same. {2:16} They passed on these commandments, saying: "Keep God's commandments until the Lord reveals His salvation to all Gentiles." {2:17} Then you will see Enoch, Noah, Shem, Abraham, Isaac, and Jacob rising on the right hand in joy. {2:18} Then we will also rise, each over our tribe, worshiping the King of heaven, who appeared on earth in the form of a humble man. {2:19} All who believe in Him on earth will rejoice with Him. {2:20} Then all people will rise, some to glory and some to shame. {2:21} The Lord will judge Israel first for their unrighteousness; for when He appeared as God in the flesh to deliver them, they did not believe Him. {2:22} Then He will judge all the Gentiles, as many as did not believe when He appeared on earth. {2:23} He will convict Israel through the chosen ones of the Gentiles, just as He reproved Esau through the Midianites, who led their brethren into fornication and idolatry, alienating them from God and making them children of those who fear the Lord. {2:24} Therefore, my children, if you walk in holiness according to the Lord's commandments, you will dwell securely with me again, and all Israel will be gathered to the Lord. {2:25} I will no longer be called a ravenous wolf because of your wrongdoings, but a servant of the Lord distributing food to those who do good. {2:26} In the latter days, one beloved by the Lord will arise from the tribes of Judah and Levi, a doer of His good pleasure, with new knowledge enlightening the Gentiles. {2:27} Until the end of the age, he will be in the synagogues of the Gentiles and among their rulers, like a melody in the mouths of all. {2:28} He will be written in the holy books, both his deeds and his words, and he will be a chosen one of God forever. {2:29} Through him, he will go back and forth like my father Jacob, saying: "He will fulfill what is lacking in your tribe." {2:30} After saying these things, he stretched out his feet. {2:31} He died in a peaceful and beautiful sleep. {2:32} His sons followed his instructions, took his body, and buried it in Hebron with his ancestors. {2:33} The total number of his days was one hundred and twenty-five years.

The Martyrdom of Ignatius

{1:1} When Trajan recently ascended as emperor of the Romans, Ignatius, a disciple of the Apostle John, a man embodying an apostolic character, led the Church of Antioch with great care. {1:2} He had barely escaped the previous persecutions under Domitian, steering the Church like a good captain with the helm of prayer and fasting, diligent teaching, and constant spiritual effort to withstand the persecution's force. {1:3} Ignatius feared only for those in the Church who might falter or be vulnerable. {1:4} He rejoiced in the brief peace the Church enjoyed, though personally distressed that he had not yet reached a perfect love for Christ nor attained the full measure of discipleship. {1:5} He thought martyrdom would bring him closer to the Lord. {1:6} Thus, he continued a few more years with the Church, enlightening the minds of others like a divine lamp through his teachings of Scripture, finally reaching the goal he longed for.

{2:1} In the ninth year of his reign, after his victories over the Scythians, Dacians, and other nations, Trajan, in his pride, decided that the Christians must also be subdued. {2:2} He ordered them to worship the same idols as others, or face death. {2:3} Ignatius, a noble servant of Christ, fearing for the Church of Antioch, was willingly brought before Trajan, who was staying in Antioch, preparing to go to Armenia and Parthia. {2:4} Trajan questioned him, "Who are you, defiant man, who disregards our commands and persuades others to do the same, risking death?" {2:5} Ignatius replied, "No one should call Theophorus (God-bearer) wicked; for all evil spirits have left God's servants. {2:6} If you call me wicked because I oppose these spirits, then I agree. I bear Christ, the King of heaven, and through Him, I defeat these spirits' plans." {2:7} Trajan asked, "Who is Theophorus?" Ignatius replied, "One who has Christ within." {2:8} Trajan asked, "Do we not also have gods in our minds, whom we invoke in battle?" Ignatius responded, "You are mistaken, calling the demons of nations gods. There is only one God, who made heaven, earth, sea, and everything in them; and only one Jesus Christ, God's only Son, whose kingdom I hope to enter." {2:9} Trajan asked, "Do you mean Him crucified under Pontius Pilate?" Ignatius replied, "Yes, the one who crucified my sins and defeated the devil's lies beneath the feet of those who carry Him in their hearts." {2:10} Trajan asked, "Do you bear Him who was crucified?" Ignatius answered, "Yes, for it is written, 'I will dwell in them, and walk among them.'" {2:11} Trajan then sentenced Ignatius to be bound and sent to Rome to be devoured by beasts as a public spectacle. {2:12} Ignatius, filled with joy, thanked the Lord, saying, "I praise You for allowing me to show perfect love for You, bound in chains like the Apostle Paul." {2:13} He gladly embraced the chains, prayed for the Church, and with tears commended it to the Lord. Then he was hurried away by the soldiers, like a prized ram, to be food for the bloodthirsty beasts in Rome.

{3:1} Eager and joyful to suffer for Christ, Ignatius traveled from Antioch to Seleucia and sailed from there. {3:2} After much hardship, he arrived in Smyrna, where he met with great joy the holy Polycarp, his fellow disciple and now bishop of Smyrna. {3:3} Both had been disciples of the Apostle John. {3:4} Ignatius shared spiritual gifts with him and, proud of his bonds, asked Polycarp to support him in achieving his martyrdom. {3:5} Churches and cities across Asia, led by bishops, priests, and deacons, came to greet him, hoping to receive a spiritual blessing. {3:6} Ignatius, particularly addressing Polycarp, hoped that through the wild beasts, he would soon depart this world and appear before Christ.

{4:1} He expressed these hopes and thanked those praying for his conflict, eager for heaven. {4:2} Grateful for the Churches that welcomed him, he sent letters of thanks filled with grace, prayer, and exhortation. {4:3} Concerned that the love of the brethren might hold him back from his goal, Ignatius wrote an Epistle to the Roman Church, included here, that his wish might be fulfilled.

{5:1} Through this letter, Ignatius prepared the Roman brethren, many of whom were reluctant about his martyrdom. {5:2} Pressured by soldiers eager to reach Rome, he left Smyrna and landed in Troas, then proceeded to Neapolis and on foot through Macedonia to a part of Epirus near Epidamnus. {5:3} He found a ship, crossed the Adriatic, entered the Tyrrhenian Sea, and passed various islands. {5:4} Upon nearing Puteoli, he longed to disembark to follow the Apostle Paul's footsteps. However, a strong wind drove the ship on, and Ignatius, though unable to land, took comfort in the love of the local brethren. {5:5} With favorable winds, the ship hastened toward Rome, and his companions mourned the coming loss of this righteous man. {5:6} For Ignatius, this was exactly as he wished, hurrying to leave the world for the Lord he loved. {5:7} Reaching the Roman harbor, the soldiers grew impatient with any delay, and Ignatius cheerfully yielded to their urgency.

{6:1} The ship departed from Portus, and as the fame of Ignatius had spread, many Roman Christians came, filled with both joy and fear—joy at meeting Theophorus, fear for his impending death. {6:2} Some, in fervent zeal, planned to appease the crowd to save him, but Ignatius, discerning this by the Spirit, advised them to remain silent. {6:3} He greeted them all, encouraged them to support his journey, and persuaded them not to hinder his eagerness to meet the Lord. {6:4} Kneeling with the brethren, he prayed for the Churches, asking that persecution cease and love continue among the brethren. {6:5} Then he was hurried into the amphitheater, where, per Caesar's command, the public games were closing. {6:6} It was the thirteenth day of the Roman month, a day when crowds assembled in great numbers. {6:7} Ignatius was thrown to the wild beasts beside the temple, fulfilling his desire for martyrdom, as it is written, "The desire of the righteous is acceptable to God." {6:8} Ignatius had wished not to burden the brethren with his remains, and only his hardened bones were left, which were brought to Antioch and wrapped as a sacred treasure, a gift to the Church from this martyr's grace.

{7:1} These events occurred on the thirteenth day before the Kalends of January, December 20th, when Sun and Senecio were consuls of Rome for the second time. {7:2} Having witnessed these things, we spent the entire night in mourning, praying fervently for assurance. {7:3} Falling into a brief slumber, some of us saw Ignatius in visions—some saw him embracing us, others saw him praying for us, and others saw him, sweating as if from his labor, standing by the Lord. {7:4} We shared our visions, rejoiced, and praised God for the blessed martyr. {7:5} We now share with you the day and time of these events so that, gathering on the anniversary of his martyrdom, we may honor this noble champion of Christ who overcame the devil and completed his course out of love for Christ, in Jesus Christ our Lord. {7:6} To whom, with the Father and the Holy Spirit, be glory and power forevermore! Amen.

The Martyrdom of Polycarp

{1:1} We write to you, brothers, about the events surrounding the martyrs, especially the blessed Polycarp, who ended the persecution by sealing it with his martyrdom. {1:2} Everything that happened before this was to demonstrate a martyrdom worthy of the Gospel, for Polycarp waited to be delivered up, just as the Lord had done, so that we could follow his example by caring for others as much as for ourselves. {1:3} True, strong love desires not only one's own salvation but also that of all the brethren.

{2:1} Every martyrdom was blessed and noble when it aligned with God's will, for we who are devoted must recognize God's authority over all. {2:2} How can one fail to admire their strength and patience, shown in their love for the Lord? {2:3} Even when scourged so brutally that their veins and arteries were exposed, they endured silently, showing they were absent from their bodies and communing with the Lord. {2:4} Trusting in Christ's grace, they faced all earthly torments, exchanging an hour of suffering for freedom from eternal punishment. {2:5} For them, the fire seemed cool, as they focused on escaping the everlasting fire, looking ahead with hearts full of faith to the promises beyond human comprehension, revealed by the Lord. {2:6} Those condemned to wild beasts also endured terrible torments, stretched on beds of spikes, and other afflictions, yet never denied Christ.

{3:1} The devil tried many tricks, but God prevailed. The noble Germanicus strengthened others by his patience and courage, drawing the wild beast to him, eager to leave this corrupt world. {3:2} Seeing this, the crowd marveled at the Christian resolve and shouted, "Away with the atheists; let Polycarp be sought!"

{4:1} A man named Quintus, recently arrived from Phrygia, lost his courage at the sight of wild beasts, though he had once voluntarily sought trial. {4:2} The proconsul persuaded him to swear an oath and offer sacrifice. {4:3} Therefore, we do not commend those who throw themselves into suffering, as the Gospel does not instruct us to do so.

{5:1} The admirable Polycarp, upon learning he was sought, was initially undisturbed, intending to stay in the city. {5:2} However, to honor others' wishes, he left for a nearby countryside home. {5:3} There he prayed constantly, night and day, for people everywhere and the universal Church. {5:4} Three days before his capture, he had a vision in which his pillow appeared to be on fire. {5:5} Turning to those with him, he said prophetically, "I must be burned alive."

{6:1} When his pursuers drew near, he moved to another house, but they soon found him. {6:2} They tortured a young servant until he revealed Polycarp's location. {6:3} Thus, his capture could not be avoided, as he was betrayed by those close to him. {6:4} The Irenarch, named Herod, rushed to bring him to the stadium, allowing Polycarp to fulfill his calling as a partaker with Christ.

{7:1} With armed guards and the servant as a guide, they set out at supper-time on the day of preparation, as if they were hunting a robber. {7:2} Arriving in the evening, they found Polycarp upstairs, where he could have escaped but instead declared, "Let God's will be done." {7:3} Calmly, he greeted them and requested an hour to pray undisturbed. {7:4} Granted this, he prayed so fervently for two hours that many of those who had come to arrest him regretted it, moved by his godliness and wisdom.

{8:1} When he finished praying, mentioning all he had known, from the lowly to the great, and the entire Church, they placed him on a donkey and took him to the city, on the great Sabbath. {8:2} The Irenarch Herod and his father Nicetes met him in a chariot and tried to persuade him to acknowledge Caesar as Lord and sacrifice to save himself. {8:3} Polycarp refused, so they threw him from the chariot, injuring his leg. {8:4} Unperturbed, he entered the stadium eagerly, although the crowd's roar made it impossible to be heard.

{9:1} As Polycarp entered, a voice from heaven said, "Be strong, Polycarp, and show yourself a man!" Though unseen, many heard the voice. {9:2} When he was brought forward, the proconsul asked if he was Polycarp. {9:3} Admitting it, he was urged to renounce Christ by saying, "Away with the atheists," and swearing by Caesar's fortune. {9:4} Polycarp instead looked sternly at the crowd, waved his hand, looked up to heaven, and declared, "Away with the atheists!" {9:5} The proconsul pressed him again to deny Christ, to which he responded, "Eighty-six years have I served Him, and He has done me no wrong. How can I blaspheme my King and Savior?"

{10:1} Again, the proconsul insisted Polycarp swear by Caesar's fortune. {10:2} Polycarp boldly replied, "I am a Christian. If you wish to know what that means, set a day, and I will explain it to you." {10:3} The proconsul responded, "Convince the people." {10:4} Polycarp said, "To you, I offer a defense, for we honor all authorities ordained by God. But as for them, I owe them nothing."

{11:1} The proconsul threatened, "I have wild beasts; I will throw you to them if you don't change." {11:2} Polycarp answered, "Call them, for we do not change from good to evil. It is better to move from evil to righteousness." {11:3} The proconsul warned, "I will burn you if you do not repent." {11:4} Polycarp replied, "You threaten a fire that burns briefly and is soon extinguished. You are ignorant of the fire of judgment and eternal punishment reserved for the ungodly. Why delay? Do what you will."

{12:1} Filled with astonishment, the proconsul ordered his herald to proclaim three times in the stadium, "Polycarp has declared himself a Christian." {12:2} At this, the crowd of heathens and Jews in Smyrna shouted, "This is the teacher of Asia, the father of Christians, the destroyer of our gods!" {12:3} They urged Philip the Asiarch to release a lion, but he declined, as the games were over. {12:4} Then the crowd decided Polycarp should be burned alive, fulfilling his vision.

{13:1} They gathered wood from shops and baths, with Jews eagerly assisting. {13:2} As Polycarp removed his garments and prepared himself, the guards prepared to nail him. {13:3} But he said, "Leave me as I am. He who gives me strength will enable me to remain steady in the flames."

{14:1} They did not nail him, but bound him. He stood, hands behind him, like a ram chosen for sacrifice, and prayed: {14:2} "O Lord God Almighty, Father of Your beloved Son Jesus Christ, by whom we have come to know You, I thank You for counting me worthy to be numbered with Your martyrs, to drink of Christ's cup, and to partake in eternal life, through the Holy Spirit. {14:3} May I be accepted before You today as an offering, as You have prepared. {14:4} For all these things, I praise and glorify You, with Jesus Christ, Your Son, and the Holy Spirit, forever and ever. Amen."

{15:1} When he had finished his prayer, the fire was kindled. Those who witnessed it saw a miracle: {15:2} the flames arched around him like a sail filled with wind, forming a circle around his body, which appeared like gold or silver in a furnace, and there was a fragrant smell, like incense.

{16:1} When they saw his body was not consumed, an executioner was ordered to stab him with a dagger. {16:2} Blood flowed out, extinguishing the fire, and all marveled at the contrast between the faithful and the unbelievers. {16:3} Polycarp, a prophetic teacher and bishop of the Catholic Church in Smyrna, was beloved in his lifetime and beyond.

{17:1} Yet the envious devil opposed even Polycarp's death and tried to prevent us from taking his remains, though many desired to keep them as holy relics. {17:2} At the Jews' insistence, Nicetes urged the governor not to give us the body, fearing we would forsake Christ for Polycarp. {17:3} They misunderstood; we worship only Christ, but we honor the martyrs, His faithful followers.

{18:1} The centurion, seeing the dispute, placed Polycarp's body in the fire, where it was consumed. {18:2} Later, we gathered his bones, more valuable than jewels, and kept them in a proper place, where we could celebrate his martyrdom, honoring those who completed their journey and preparing ourselves to follow.

{19:1} This is the account of blessed Polycarp, the twelfth martyr in Smyrna, whose death is celebrated even by the heathens. {19:2} He was a revered teacher and martyr whose life was wholly in line with Christ's Gospel, and who now glorifies God with the apostles and righteous in heaven.

{20:1} Since you requested to know what happened, we now send this account through our brother Marcus. {20:2} When you read it, share it with distant brethren so they too may praise God, who honors His servants. {20:3} To Him, who can bring us all into His eternal kingdom through Jesus Christ, be glory, honor, and power forever. Amen. Greet all the saints; those with us greet you, as does Evarestus, who wrote this letter with his household.

{21:1} Polycarp suffered martyrdom on the second of Xanthicus, on the great Sabbath, at the eighth hour. {21:2} He was captured by Herod, during the term of Statius Quadratus as proconsul, while Jesus Christ is King forever, to whom be glory. Amen.

{22:1} We wish you all happiness as you follow the Gospel of Jesus Christ. Glory be to God the Father and the Holy Spirit for the salvation of His elect. {22:2} May we, like Polycarp, be found in His kingdom!

{23:1} These writings were transcribed by Caius from Irenaeus' copy, who was a disciple of Polycarp. {23:2} I, Socrates, copied them in Corinth from Caius's manuscript. {23:3} Grace be with you all. {23:4} I, Pionius, wrote from another copy, seeking accuracy as Polycarp revealed these events to me, preserving them as they nearly faded, so that the Lord Jesus Christ may gather me into His heavenly kingdom. To Him, the Father, and the Holy Spirit, be glory forever. Amen.

The First Epistle of Clement

{1:1} To the Church of God in Rome, and to the Church of God in Corinth, to those called and sanctified by the will of God through our Lord Jesus Christ: May grace and peace from Almighty God through Jesus Christ be multiplied to you. {1:2} Dear brothers, due to the sudden and successive disasters that have befallen us, we feel that we have been somewhat slow to address the issues you consulted us about, especially that shameful and dreadful division, which is completely contrary to God's chosen ones. This discord has been ignited by a few reckless and overconfident individuals, causing your respected name, which deserves to be universally honored, to suffer serious damage. {1:3} For who among you, even for a brief time, did not witness your faith being productive of good works and firmly established? Who did not admire the seriousness and moderation of your piety in Christ? Who did not praise your generous hospitality? And who did not celebrate your sound understanding? You conducted yourselves without favoritism, obeyed those in authority over you, and honored your leaders appropriately. {1:4} You instructed young men to be serious and responsible, and you taught your wives to act with integrity and a pure conscience, loving their husbands as they should. You showed them how, by living obediently, they should manage their households with grace and be characterized by wisdom in all things.

{2:1} Moreover, you were marked by humility and were not at all prideful, choosing to yield obedience rather than demand it, and you preferred to give rather than to receive. You were content with what God provided, attentively following His teachings, and you were filled with His doctrine, keeping His sufferings in your hearts. {2:2} This led to a deep and abundant peace among you, and you had an insatiable desire to do good, while the Holy Spirit was richly poured out on all of you. You had sincere and holy intentions, approaching God earnestly, asking for His mercy if you had committed any unintentional wrongs. Night and day, you were concerned for the entire brotherhood, hoping that God's elect would be saved with mercy and a good conscience. {2:3} You were genuine and pure, forgetting grievances against each other. Any form of division or faction was repugnant to you. You mourned the shortcomings of your neighbors, considering their faults as your own. You never hesitated to perform acts of kindness, always ready for every good work. Living virtuously and devoutly, you conducted everything in the fear of God, with His commandments and teachings written on your hearts.

{3:1} All kinds of honor and happiness were granted to you, and then fulfilled was the saying, "My beloved grew prosperous and became complacent." From this complacency arose rivalry and jealousy, strife and division, persecution and chaos, leading to war and captivity. The worthless rose up against the honored, the unknown against the renowned, the foolish against the wise, and the young against the elders. {3:2} For this reason, righteousness and peace have departed from you, as everyone has forsaken the fear of God, becoming blind in their faith, neglecting to follow His teachings, and instead acting according to their own wicked desires, reigniting the ungodly jealousy through which death entered the world.

{4:1} As it is written: "After a while, Cain brought some fruits of the soil as an offering to God; Abel brought fat portions from some of the firstborn of his flock. God looked with favor on Abel and his offering, but He did not look with favor on Cain and his offering. This made Cain very angry, and his face was downcast. God said to Cain, 'Why are you angry? Why is your face downcast? If you do what is right, will you not be accepted? But if you do not do what is right, sin is crouching at your door; it desires to have you, but you must rule over it.' Cain said to Abel, 'Let's go out to the field.' And while they were in the field, Cain attacked his brother Abel and killed him." {4:2} You see, brothers, how envy and jealousy led to the murder of a brother. Through envy, our father Jacob fled from his brother Esau. Envy caused Joseph to be persecuted unto death and sold into slavery. Envy made Moses flee from Pharaoh when he heard those words from his fellow countryman, "Who made you a ruler over us? Are you going to kill me like you killed the Egyptian yesterday?" Because of envy, Aaron and Miriam were exiled from the camp. Envy brought Dathan and Abiram down alive to the grave due to the rebellion they stirred against God's servant Moses. Through envy, David faced hatred not only from foreigners but was also persecuted by King Saul of Israel.

{5:1} But let's not dwell on ancient examples; instead, let's look at the recent spiritual heroes. Through envy and jealousy, the greatest and most righteous leaders of the Church have been persecuted and killed. Let us consider the illustrious apostles. Peter endured many trials due to unrighteous envy and, after suffering martyrdom, entered the place of glory that was his due. {5:2} Similarly, Paul received the reward of patient endurance, after being imprisoned seven times, forced to flee, and stoned. He preached in both the East and West, gaining renown for his faith, having taught righteousness to the entire world, reaching the farthest West, and suffering martyrdom under the governors. Thus, he was taken from this world and entered the holy place, having proven himself a remarkable example of patience.

{6:1} Alongside these individuals who dedicated their lives to holiness, we must also acknowledge a great multitude of the chosen, who endured many injustices and tortures due to envy, providing us with an outstanding example. Through envy, those women, the Danaids and Dircae, were persecuted and, after enduring terrible and unimaginable sufferings, completed their faith steadfastly, and though physically weak, received a noble reward. Envy has driven wives away from their husbands and distorted our father Adam's words, "This is now bone of my bones, and flesh of my flesh." Envy and strife have brought down great cities and uprooted powerful nations.

{7:1} Beloved, we write these things not just to remind you of your responsibilities but also to remind ourselves. We are engaged in the same struggle, facing the same conflict. Therefore, let us abandon vain and fruitless worries and approach the glorious and revered purpose of our holy calling. Let us focus on what is good, pleasing, and acceptable to Him who created us. {7:2} Let us look intently at the blood of Christ and recognize how precious it is to God, as it was shed for our salvation and has opened the door to repentance for the whole world. Let us reflect on the ages past and learn that, from generation to generation, the Lord has provided a path of repentance for all who wish to turn back to Him. Noah preached repentance, and all who listened to him were saved. Jonah announced destruction to the Ninevites; however, they repented of their sins, prayed to God, and obtained salvation, despite being outsiders to His covenant.

{8:1} The ministers of God's grace have spoken of repentance through the Holy Spirit, and the Lord of all has declared with an oath, "As I live, says the Lord, I do not desire the death of the sinner but rather his repentance," adding this gracious call: "Repent, O house of Israel, of your wrongdoing. Tell the children of My people, even if your sins reach from the earth to heaven, and are redder than scarlet or blacker than sackcloth, if you turn to Me with all your heart and say, 'Father!' I will listen to you, as to a holy people." In another place, He says, "Wash yourselves and be clean; remove the wickedness of your souls from My sight; stop doing evil and learn to do good; seek justice, help the oppressed, defend the fatherless, and ensure justice for the widow; and come, let us reason together. He states, 'Though your sins are like crimson, I will make them white as snow; though they are like scarlet, I will make them as white as wool. If you are willing and obey Me, you will enjoy the good of the land; but if you refuse and do not listen to Me, the sword will consume you, for the mouth of the Lord has spoken.'" Thus, desiring that all His beloved should partake in repentance, He has established these promises by His almighty will.

{9:1} Therefore, let us obey His glorious and perfect will, asking for His mercy and kindness while abandoning all fruitless labor, strife, and envy, which lead to death. Instead, let us turn and seek His compassion. Let us earnestly reflect on those who have served His glory perfectly. For instance, Enoch, who was found righteous through obedience, was taken up, and death never touched him. Noah, found faithful, preached renewal to the world through his ministry, and the Lord saved the animals that entered the ark together.

{10:1} Abraham, known as "the friend," was found faithful because he obeyed God's words. In obedience, he left his homeland, his relatives, and his father's house, aiming to inherit God's promises. For God said to him, "Leave your country, your relatives, and your father's house for the land I will show you. I will make you a great nation, bless you, and make your name great, and you will be a blessing. I will bless those who bless you and curse those who curse you; and through you, all families of the earth will be blessed." Again, when he parted from Lot, God told him, "Lift up your eyes and look from where you are: north, south, east, and west; for all the land you see, I will give to you and your descendants forever. I will make your descendants as numerous as the dust of the earth; if anyone could count the dust, then your descendants could also be counted." The Scripture also says, "God brought Abram out and said, 'Look up at the sky and count the stars if you can.' So shall your descendants be." Abram believed God, and it was credited to him as righteousness. Because of his faith and hospitality, he was given a son in his old age, and in obedience, he offered him as a sacrifice to God on one of the mountains He showed him.

{11:1} Because of his hospitality and righteousness, Lot was saved from Sodom when the surrounding area was punished with fire and brimstone. This showed that the Lord does not abandon those who hope in Him but delivers those who turn away from Him to punishment and suffering. Lot's wife, who left with him but had a different mindset and did not stay in agreement with him about the command they were given, was turned into a pillar of salt, serving as a warning to this day. This was done so that everyone would understand that those who are double-minded and doubt God's power bring judgment upon themselves and become a sign for all future generations.

{12:1} For her faith and hospitality, Rahab the prostitute was saved. When Joshua, the son of Nun, sent spies to Jericho, the king learned they were there to scout the land and sent men to capture them, intending to kill them. But hospitable Rahab received the spies and hid them on her roof under some flax stalks. When the king's men arrived and demanded she bring out the spies, she told them, "The two men you seek came to me, but they quickly left and I don't know where they went." Then she spoke to the spies, saying, "I know that the Lord your God has given you this city, for the fear of you has fallen on its inhabitants. When you take it, please keep me and my family safe." They replied, "It will be as you have said. When we attack, gather your family in your house; those inside will be safe, but everyone outside will perish." They also instructed her to hang a scarlet cord from her window, indicating that redemption through the blood of the Lord would be available to all who believe and hope in God. You see, beloved, this woman showed not just faith, but also prophecy.

{13:1} Therefore, brothers, let us be humble, putting aside all arrogance, pride, foolishness, and anger; and let us act according to what is written (the Holy Spirit says, "Let not the wise man boast in his wisdom, the strong man in his strength, or the rich man in his riches; but let him who boasts boast in the Lord, in seeking Him and doing what is just and right"). We should especially remember the words of the Lord Jesus, who taught us about meekness and patience. He said: "Be merciful, so you may obtain mercy; forgive, and you will be forgiven; what you do will be done to you; what you judge others by will be used to judge you; and the kindness you show will be shown back to you." By this teaching and these principles, let us ground ourselves in humility and obedience to His holy words. For the holy word says, "To whom will I look? To him who is humble and peaceful, and who trembles at My words."

{14:1} Therefore, it is right and holy, men and brothers, to obey God rather than follow those who, through pride and conflict, lead a detestable rivalry. If we recklessly give in to the desires of those who stir up strife and turmoil, we risk great harm rather than minor injury by being led away from what is good. Let us be kind to one another, following the example of the tender mercy and kindness of our Creator. For it is written, "The kind-hearted will inherit the land, and the innocent will remain, but the wicked will be removed from it." Again, the Scripture says, "I saw the wicked exalted like the cedars of Lebanon; I passed by, and he was no more; I sought his place, but could not find it. Maintain innocence and pursue justice, for there will be a remnant for the peaceful."

{15:1} Therefore, let us cling to those who foster peace with godliness, not to those who falsely claim to desire it. For Scripture says in one place, "This people honors Me with their lips, but their hearts are far from Me." Again, it says, "They bless with their mouths but curse in their hearts." And again, it states, "They loved Him with their mouths but lied to Him with their tongues; their hearts were not right with Him, and they were unfaithful to His covenant." "Let deceitful lips be silent," and "let the Lord cut off all lying lips, and the boastful tongues of those who say, 'We will magnify our tongues; our lips belong to us; who is our master?' For the oppression of the poor and the groaning of the needy, I will now arise, says the Lord; I will protect them and treat them with confidence."

{16:1} For Christ belongs to those who are humble, not to those who elevate themselves above His followers. Our Lord Jesus Christ, the embodiment of God's majesty, did not arrive with pride or arrogance, even though He could have; instead, He came in a lowly state, as the Holy Spirit foretold. It is said, "Lord, who has believed our message, and to whom has the arm of the Lord been revealed? We declared [our message] in His presence: He appeared like a child, like a root in dry ground; He had no form or beauty, and we saw Him with no attractiveness, but rather He was ordinary, lacking in comparison to the appearance of men. He was a man who suffered greatly and was familiar with pain, as His face was turned away; He was despised and not valued. He carried our sins and grieved for us; yet we assumed He was suffering for His own faults. But He was wounded for our sins and crushed for our iniquities. The punishment that brought us peace was upon Him, and by His wounds we are healed. We all, like sheep, have gone astray; each of us has turned to our own way, and the Lord laid on Him the sins of us all, while He remained silent in His suffering. He was led like a sheep to the slaughter, and like a lamb before its shearers, He did not speak. In His humiliation, His judgment was taken away; who can speak of His descendants? For His life was taken from the earth. He was brought to death for the transgressions of my people. I will give the wicked for His grave, and the rich for His death, because He committed no sin, and no deceit was found in His mouth. And the Lord was pleased to purify Him through suffering. If you make a sin offering, your soul will see many descendants. The Lord was pleased to relieve Him of His suffering, to show Him light, and to give Him wisdom, to justify the Just One who serves many; and He Himself will carry their sins. For this reason, He will inherit many and will divide the spoils with the strong; because His soul was delivered to death, and He was counted among the sinners, and He bore the sins of many, and for their sins, He was delivered." Again, He says, "I am a worm and not a man; I am a disgrace to mankind, and despised by the people. All who see Me mock Me; they speak insults with their lips and shake their heads, saying, 'He trusted in God; let Him rescue Him, let Him save Him, since He delights in Him.'" You see, beloved, what example has been set for us; if the Lord humbled Himself in this way, what should we do who have come under His grace?

{17:1} Let us also imitate those who wore goat and sheep skins to proclaim the coming of Christ; I refer to the prophets Elijah, Elisha, and Ezekiel, along with others mentioned in Scripture. Abraham was especially honored and called the friend of God; yet he humbly stated, "I am just dust and ashes." Job is described as "a righteous man, blameless, truthful, God-fearing, and one who avoided all evil." But even he admitted, "No one is free from sin, even if they live only one day." Moses was called faithful in all of God's house, and through him, God punished Egypt with plagues and suffering. Yet, despite this honor, he did not speak arrogantly, but when God spoke to him from the burning bush, he said, "Who am I to go? I have a weak voice and slow speech." And again he said, "I am like the smoke of a pot."

{18:1} What shall we say about David, to whom such praise was given, and of whom God said, "I have found a man after My own heart, David the son of Jesse; and in everlasting mercy have I anointed him?" Yet this very man cried out to God, "Have mercy on me, O Lord, according to Your great mercy; and according to Your abundant compassion, wipe away my sin. Cleanse me from my iniquity and purify me from my sin. For I recognize my transgressions, and my sin is always before me. Against You alone have I sinned and done what is evil in Your sight; so that You may be justified in Your words and blameless in Your judgment. Indeed, I was conceived in sin, and my mother gave birth to me in sin. Yet You desire truth in the inner parts; in the hidden places, You teach me wisdom. Cleanse me with hyssop, and I will be clean; wash me, and I will be whiter than snow. Let me hear joy and gladness; let the bones You have crushed rejoice. Hide Your face from my sins, and wipe away all my iniquities. Create in me a pure heart, O God, and renew a steadfast spirit within me. Do not cast me away from Your presence or take Your Holy Spirit from me. Restore to me the joy of Your salvation and grant me a willing spirit to sustain me. I will teach transgressors Your ways, and sinners will turn back to You. Deliver me from the guilt of bloodshed, O God, God of my salvation, and my tongue will sing of Your righteousness. O Lord, open my lips, and my mouth will declare Your praise. For You do not delight in sacrifice, or I would bring it; You do not take pleasure in burnt offerings. The sacrifice acceptable to God is a broken spirit; a contrite heart, O God, You will not despise."

{19:1} Thus, the humility and godly submission of such great and distinguished men have benefited not only us but also all the generations before us, especially those who received His messages in reverence and truth. Therefore, with so many great and glorious examples before us, let us return to the practice of the peace that has always marked us; and let us focus on the Father and Creator of the universe, and hold fast to His mighty and magnificent gifts of peace. Let us contemplate Him with our understanding, and look with the eyes of our souls to His patient will. Let us reflect on how free from anger He is towards all creation.

{20:1} The heavens, governed by His authority, are at peace under Him. Day and night follow their assigned paths without hindrance. The sun and moon, along with the stars, move in harmony according to His command, remaining within their set boundaries without deviation. The fruitful earth produces abundant food in its season for all living beings, never faltering or changing any of the laws He established. The depths of the abyss and the complex arrangements of the underworld are bound by the same rules. The vast, immeasurable sea, shaped by His design into various basins, does not exceed the limits He has set, but follows His commands. He said, "You may come this far, but your waves will be contained." The ocean, unpassable to man, and the worlds beyond it, are governed by the same laws of the Lord. The seasons of spring, summer, autumn, and winter transition peacefully into one another. The winds blow from their respective directions, performing their tasks in due time without obstruction. The ever-flowing springs, created for enjoyment and health, consistently provide life for humanity. Even the smallest creatures exist in peace and harmony. All these things the great Creator and Lord of all has ordained to exist in peace and unity, while He does good to everyone, but most abundantly to us who have taken refuge in His mercy through Jesus Christ our Lord, to whom be glory and majesty forever and ever. Amen.

{21:1} Pay attention, beloved, so that His many kindnesses do not lead to our condemnation. This will happen unless we walk in a way that is worthy of Him and, united in purpose, do what is good and pleasing in His sight. For Scripture says in a certain place, "The Spirit of the Lord is a lamp searching the hidden parts of the heart." Let us consider how close He is, and that none of our thoughts or reasonings are hidden from Him. Therefore, it is important that we do not abandon the role assigned to us by His will. Let us rather offend foolish, inconsiderate, and arrogant people who take pride in their words than offend God. Let us respect the Lord Jesus Christ, whose blood was shed for us; let us honor those in authority over us; let us show respect to our elders; let us guide the young men in the fear of God; let us lead our wives toward what is good. Let them display the beauty of purity in all their actions; let them show sincere meekness; let them demonstrate the command they have over their words through their speech; let them express their love not by favoring one person over another, but by treating all who reverently fear God with equal affection. Let your children receive true Christian training; let them learn the immense value of humility before God—how powerful pure love can be with Him—how excellent and great His fear is, and how it saves all who walk in it with a pure heart. For He knows the thoughts and desires of the heart: His breath is in us, and when He chooses, He will take it away.

{22:1} Now, the faith in Christ affirms all these teachings. For He Himself, through the Holy Spirit, addresses us: "Come, children, listen to Me; I will teach you the fear of the Lord. Who among you desires life and loves to see good days? Keep your tongue from evil and your lips from deceit. Turn away from evil and do good; seek peace and pursue it. The Lord's eyes are on the righteous, and His ears are open to their prayers. The Lord's face is against those who do evil, to cut off their memory from the earth. The righteous cry out, and the Lord hears them and rescues them from all their troubles." "Many are the troubles appointed for the wicked; but mercy surrounds those who hope in the Lord."

{23:1} The all-merciful and generous Father has compassion for those who fear Him, and He kindly and lovingly bestows His gifts on those who approach Him with sincerity. Therefore, let us not be double-minded; let us not let our souls become proud because of His exceedingly great and glorious gifts. Let us reject what is written: "Wretched are those with a double mind and a doubting heart; who say, 'We have heard these things from our ancestors; but look, we have grown old, and none of them has happened to us.'" You foolish ones! Compare yourselves to a tree: consider the vine. First, it sheds its leaves, then it buds, next it sprouts leaves, and then it flowers; after that come sour grapes, followed by ripe fruit. You see how quickly the fruit of a tree matures. Truly, His will will be accomplished soon and suddenly, as Scripture also bears witness, saying, "He will come quickly and will not delay;" and, "The Lord will suddenly come to His temple, even the Holy One, for whom you look."

{24:1} Let us consider, beloved, how the Lord continually proves to us that there will be a future resurrection, of which He made the Lord Jesus Christ the first to rise by bringing Him back from the dead. Let us contemplate, beloved, the resurrection that occurs all the time. Day and night declare a resurrection. The night gives way to sleep, and the day arises; then the day again departs, and the night falls. Let us observe the fruits of the earth, how grain is sown. The sower goes out and casts it into the ground; the seed, although dry and bare when it falls to the earth, gradually breaks down. Then, from its decay, the powerful providence of the Lord raises it up again, and from one seed, many arise and produce fruit.

{25:1} Let us consider the wonderful sign of resurrection that takes place in Eastern lands, specifically in Arabia and the surrounding countries. There is a bird called a phoenix. It is the only one of its kind and lives for five hundred years. When its time to die approaches, it builds a nest of frankincense, myrrh, and other spices, into which it enters and dies. As its body decays, a certain kind of worm emerges, which is nourished by the juices of the dead bird and grows feathers. Once it is strong enough, it takes the nest containing its parent's bones and travels from Arabia to Egypt, to the city called Heliopolis. In broad daylight, flying in front of everyone, it places the bones on the altar of the sun, and after doing this, it quickly returns to its former home. The priests then check the records of dates and find that it has returned exactly as the five hundredth year was completed.

{26:1} Do we think it's any great thing for the Maker of all things to raise up again those who have served Him faithfully, especially when He even uses a bird to demonstrate His power to fulfill His promise? For Scripture says in one place, "You will raise me up, and I will praise You;" and again, "I lay down and slept; I awoke because You are with me;" and once more, Job says, "You will raise this flesh of mine, which has suffered all these things."

{27:1} Having this hope, let our souls be connected to Him who is faithful in His promises and just in His judgments. He who has commanded us not to lie will certainly not lie Himself; for nothing is impossible for God except for Him to lie. Let His faith be reignited within us, and let us remember that all things are near to Him. By His powerful word, He established all things, and by His word, He can also bring them down. "Who can question Him, saying, 'What have You done?' or, 'Who can resist the power of His strength?'" Whenever and however He wishes, He will accomplish all things, and nothing determined by Him will go unfulfilled. All things are open before Him, and nothing can be hidden from His counsel. "The heavens declare the glory of God, and the sky shows His handiwork. Day after day they speak, and night after night they reveal knowledge. There are no words or sounds whose voices are not heard."

{28:1} Since all things are seen and heard by God, let us fear Him and turn away from the wicked works that come from evil desires, so that through His mercy, we may be shielded from the coming judgments. For where can any of us flee from His mighty hand? What world will accept those who try to escape from Him? For Scripture says in a certain place, "Where can I go, and where can I hide from Your presence? If I ascend to heaven, You are there; if I go to the farthest parts of the earth, Your right hand is there; if I make my bed in the abyss, Your Spirit is there." Where, then, can anyone go, or where can they escape from Him who knows all things?

{29:1} Let us draw near to Him with a holy spirit, lifting up pure and undefiled hands to Him, loving our gracious and merciful Father, who has allowed us to share in the blessings of His chosen ones. For it is written, "When the Most High divided the nations, when He scattered the sons of Adam, He set the boundaries of the nations according to the number of the angels of God. His people Jacob became the Lord's portion, and Israel His inheritance." And in another place, Scripture says, "Behold, the Lord takes a nation from the midst of the nations, as a man takes the first fruits of his threshing-floor; and from that nation shall come forth the Most Holy."

{30:1} Since we are the portion of the Holy One, let us do all things related to holiness, avoiding all slander, impure embraces, drunkenness, the pursuit of change, shameful lusts, detestable adultery, and abominable pride. "For God," says Scripture, "resists the proud but gives grace to the humble." Therefore, let us cling to those who have received grace from God. Let us wrap ourselves in harmony and humility, practicing self-control, keeping away from gossip and slander, and being justified by our actions, not our words. For Scripture says, "He who speaks a lot will also hear much in response. And does he who is quick to speak consider himself righteous? Blessed is the one born of woman, who lives only a short time: do not be given to much talk." Let our praise be directed at God, not ourselves; for God despises those who boast about themselves. Let others testify to our good deeds, as was the case with our righteous ancestors. Boldness, arrogance, and audacity belong to those cursed by God; but moderation, humility, and meekness are for those blessed by Him.

{31:1} Let us hold on to His blessings and consider how we can receive them. Let's reflect on the events from the beginning. Why was our father Abraham blessed? Was it not because he acted righteously and faithfully? Isaac, with perfect confidence, cheerfully offered himself as a sacrifice, as if he knew what was to happen. Jacob, humbled by his brother, left his own land, went to Laban, and served him, and from that, he received the leadership of the twelve tribes of Israel.

{32:1} Anyone who honestly examines each detail will recognize the greatness of the gifts given to him. From him came the priests and all the Levites who serve at God's altar. Our Lord Jesus Christ, according to the flesh, also descended from him. Kings, princes, and rulers from the tribe of Judah arose from him. His other tribes also share in great honor since God promised, "Your descendants will be like the stars in heaven." All these were honored and made great not for their own sake or their own deeds or righteousness, but because of His will. And we, called by His will in Christ Jesus, are not justified by ourselves, our wisdom, understanding, godliness, or the works we've done with a pure heart, but by that faith through which Almighty God has justified all people from the beginning; to Him be glory forever. Amen.

{33:1} So what should we do, brothers? Should we become lazy in doing good and stop practicing love? God forbid! Instead, let us eagerly and wholeheartedly pursue every good work. The Creator and Lord of all rejoices in His works. By His immense power, He established the heavens, and by His incomprehensible wisdom, He adorned them. He also separated the earth from the surrounding waters and set it on the unmovable foundation of His will. The animals on the earth were brought to life by His word. Likewise, He formed the sea and its living creatures, keeping them within their bounds by His power. Above all, with His holy and pure hands, He created man, the greatest of His creatures, made in His own image. For God said, "Let us make man in Our image, according to Our likeness." So God created man; He made them male and female. After completing all these things, He approved and blessed them, saying, "Be fruitful and multiply." We see that all righteous people have been adorned with good works, and the Lord Himself, delighting in His works, rejoiced. Therefore, let us promptly align with His will and work diligently at righteousness.

{34:1} A good servant receives the fruits of his labor with confidence; the lazy and slothful cannot face their employer. It is essential that we act quickly in doing good, for everything comes from Him. He warns us, "Behold, the Lord is coming, and His reward is before Him, to give to everyone according to their deeds." Thus, He encourages us to fully commit to this and not be lazy or slothful in any good work. Let our pride and confidence be in Him. Let us submit to His will. Let us remember the multitude of His angels, always ready to serve Him. Scripture says, "Ten thousand times ten thousand stood around Him, and thousands of thousands served Him, crying, 'Holy, holy, holy, is the Lord of hosts; the whole earth is full of His glory.'" Therefore, let us gather together in harmony and earnestly call out to Him as one, so we may share in His great and glorious promises. For Scripture says, "Eye has not seen, nor ear heard, nor have entered into the heart of man the things He has prepared for those who wait for Him."

{35:1} How blessed and wonderful are God's gifts! Life in immortality, splendor in righteousness, truth in perfect confidence, faith in assurance, self-control in holiness! All of these are within our understanding now; what then will those things be which are prepared for those who wait for Him? The Creator and Father of all worlds, the Most Holy, knows their value and beauty alone. Therefore, let us strive earnestly to be among those who wait for Him so we can share in His promised gifts. But how, beloved, can we achieve this? If our understanding is grounded in faith, if we earnestly seek what pleases Him, if we do what aligns with His perfect will, and if we follow the path of truth, casting away all unrighteousness, iniquity, covetousness, strife, evil deeds, deceit, gossip, slander, hatred of God, pride, arrogance, vanity, and ambition. Those who do such things are detestable to God, as are those who take pleasure in them. For Scripture says, "But to the sinner, God said, 'Why do you declare My statutes and take My covenant in your mouth, when you hate instruction and reject My words? When you saw a thief, you consented with him, and you became part of adulterers. Your mouth is full of wickedness, and your tongue devises deceit. You sit and speak against your brother; you slander your own mother's son. These things you have done & I kept silent; you thought, wicked one, that I would be like you. But I will rebuke you and confront you. Consider these things, you who forget God, lest I tear you to pieces like a lion, and there be no one to rescue. A sacrifice of praise will glorify Me, and there is a way by which I will show him the salvation of God.'"

{36:1} This is how we find our Savior, Jesus Christ, the High Priest of all our offerings, our defender and helper in times of weakness. Through Him, we look up to the heights of heaven. Through Him, we see, as if in a mirror, His pure and excellent image. Through Him, the eyes of our hearts are opened. Through Him, our foolish and darkened understanding is renewed by His marvelous light. Through Him, the Lord has chosen for us to experience eternal knowledge, "who, being the brightness of His majesty, is much greater than the angels, having inherited a name far superior to theirs." It is written, "He makes His angels spirits, and His ministers a flame of fire." But concerning His Son, the Lord said, "You are My Son; today I have begotten You. Ask of Me, and I will give You the nations as Your inheritance and the ends of the earth for Your possession." He also said to Him, "Sit at My right hand until I make Your enemies Your footstool." So, who are His enemies? All the wicked & those who oppose God's will.

{37:1} Let us, then, brothers, actively engage as soldiers according to His holy commandments. Consider those who serve under our leaders and how orderly, obedient, and submissive they are in carrying out commands. Not everyone is a general or a commander of thousands, hundreds, or fifties, but each person performs their role according to their rank, fulfilling what the king and generals command. The great cannot stand without the small, nor the small without the great. There is a balance in all things, which brings mutual benefit. Let's use our body as an example: the head cannot function without the feet, and the feet cannot function without the head; even the smallest parts of our body are necessary and beneficial to the whole. All parts work harmoniously together under a common rule to preserve the body.

{38:1} Therefore, let our entire body be preserved in Christ Jesus, with everyone being subject to their neighbor according to the unique gifts given to them. Let the strong not look down on the weak, and let the weak show respect to the strong. Let the wealthy provide for the needs of the poor, and let the poor praise God for providing someone to meet their needs. Let the wise demonstrate their wisdom through actions, not just words. Let the humble avoid self-promotion and allow others to testify on their behalf. Let those who are pure in body not become proud or boastful, recognizing that it was a gift given to them by another.

Let us reflect, brothers, on the nature of our creation—who we are and from where we came, emerging from a tomb of utter darkness. The One who made and shaped us prepared generous gifts for us before we were born and brought us into His world. Therefore, since we receive all these things from Him, we ought to thank Him for everything; to Him be glory forever. Amen.

{39:1} Foolish and thoughtless people, who lack wisdom or guidance, mock and ridicule us, eager to elevate themselves in their own pride. What can a mortal man accomplish? What strength is there in one formed from dust? For it is written, "Before my eyes, there was no form; I only heard a voice saying, 'What then? Can a man be pure before the Lord? Can anyone be deemed blameless in their deeds, considering He does not trust His servants and even charges His angels with faults? The heavens are not clean in His sight; how much less so are those who dwell in clay houses, made of the same material! He struck them like a moth; they do not endure from morning until evening. Because they could not help themselves, they perished. He breathed on them, and they died because they lacked wisdom. But call out now, if anyone will answer you, or if you will look to any of the holy angels; for wrath destroys the foolish, and envy kills the one who is in error. I have seen the foolish take root, but their dwelling was quickly consumed. Let their children be far from safety; let them be scorned at the gates, and there will be no one to save them. For what was prepared for them, the righteous shall consume, and they will not be rescued from evil."

{40:1} Given these truths, and as we delve into the depths of divine knowledge, we must conduct all things in their proper order, as the Lord has commanded us to perform at set times. He has instructed us to present offerings and carry out services, and these should not be done carelessly or irregularly, but at the appointed times and hours. Where and by whom He desires these things to be done, He has determined by His supreme will so that all actions done with reverence may be acceptable to Him. Therefore, those who present their offerings at the right times are accepted and blessed, for by following the Lord's laws, they do not sin. The high priest has specific duties, priests have their designated places, and the Levites have their unique ministries. Laypeople are bound by the laws that apply to them.

{41:1} Let each of you, brothers, give thanks to God in your own way, living with a good conscience, showing the right seriousness, and not overstepping the guidelines of your ministry. Not everywhere, brothers, are daily sacrifices, peace offerings, sin offerings, and guilt offerings made, but only in Jerusalem. Even there, they are not offered just anywhere, but only at the altar before the temple, with offerings first examined carefully by the high priest and the ministers mentioned earlier. Therefore, those who go beyond what is acceptable to His will face punishment, even death. You see, brothers, the greater the knowledge we have received, the greater the danger we face.

{42:1} The apostles preached the Gospel to us from the Lord Jesus Christ; Jesus Christ brought it from God. Christ was sent by God, and the apostles were sent by Christ. Both appointments were made in an orderly manner according to God's will. Having received their instructions and being fully assured by the resurrection of our Lord Jesus Christ and established in the word of God, with the full assurance of the Holy Spirit, they went out proclaiming that the kingdom of God was near. As they preached through cities and countries, they appointed the first fruits of their labors, having first tested them by the Spirit, to be bishops and deacons for those who would later believe. This was not a new concept, as many ages before it, it was written about bishops and deacons. For the Scripture says, "I will appoint their bishops in righteousness, and their deacons in faith."

{43:1} And why should it be surprising that those in Christ, entrusted with such responsibilities by God, appointed those ministers mentioned earlier, when the blessed Moses, "a faithful servant in all his house," documented in the sacred books all the commands given to him, and when the other prophets also followed him, unanimously affirming the ordinances he established? When rivalry arose over the priesthood, and the tribes argued over who should hold that glorious title, he commanded the twelve leaders of the tribes to bring him their staffs, each inscribed with the tribe's name. He took them, bound them together, sealed them with the rings of the tribe leaders, and stored them in the tabernacle of witness on God's table. After sealing the tabernacle's doors, he secured the keys as he did with the staffs and said, "Men and brethren, the tribe whose staff blossoms has been chosen by God to serve in the priesthood." When morning came, he gathered all Israel, six hundred thousand men, showed the seals to the tribe leaders, opened the tabernacle, and brought out the staffs. The staff of Aaron not only had blossomed but also bore fruit. What do you think, beloved? Did Moses not know this would happen? Of course he did; he acted this way to prevent dissent in Israel and to glorify the name of the true and only God; to whom be glory forever. Amen.

{44:1} Our apostles also understood, through our Lord Jesus Christ, that there would be conflict over the office of the episcopate. For this reason, knowing this perfectly, they appointed those ministers mentioned before and later instructed that when these leaders fell asleep, other approved men should succeed them in their ministry. We believe, therefore, that those appointed by them, or later by other distinguished men, with the approval of the whole Church, and who have served the flock of Christ blamelessly, humbly, peacefully, and selflessly, and have long been held in good esteem, cannot be justly removed from the ministry. For our sin would be great if we dismissed from the episcopate those who have faithfully and holily fulfilled its responsibilities. Blessed are those presbyters who have completed their course and obtained a fruitful and perfect departure from this world; for they have no fear of being deprived of their appointed place. But we see that you have removed some exemplary individuals from the ministry, which they fulfilled honorably and without blame.

{45:1} You are fond of conflict, brothers, and zealous about matters that do not pertain to salvation. Carefully examine the Scriptures, which are the true words of the Holy Spirit. Notice that nothing unjust or false is written in them. You will not find that the righteous were cast out by holy individuals. The righteous were indeed persecuted, but only by the wicked. They were imprisoned, but only by the unholy; they were stoned, but only by sinners; they were killed, but only by those cursed and filled with unrighteous envy against them. Enduring such sufferings, they did so gloriously. For what shall we say, brothers? Was Daniel thrown into the lion's den by those who feared God? Were Ananias, Azarias, and Mishael shut in a fiery furnace by those who worshipped the Most High? Far from us be such thoughts! Who, then, were those who did such things? It was the wicked and the hateful, stirred to fury, who inflicted torture on those who served God with pure and blameless hearts, not knowing that the Most High is the Defender & Protector of all who honor His excellent name; to whom be glory forever. Amen. But those who confidently endured such things are now heirs of glory and honor, exalted and made illustrious by God in their eternal memorial. Amen.

{46:1} Therefore, brothers, it is right that we follow such examples; as it is written, "Stay close to the holy, for those who stay close to them will themselves be made holy." And again, in another place, the Scripture says, "With a harmless person, you will prove yourself harmless; with an elect person, you will be elect; and with a perverse person, you will show yourself perverse." Let us cling, then, to the innocent and righteous, for these are the elect of God. Why are there conflicts, uproars, divisions, schisms, and wars among you? Do we not have one God and one Christ? Is there not one Spirit of grace poured out upon us? And do we not have one calling in Christ? Why do we divide and tear apart the members of Christ, raising strife against our own body, reaching such madness that we forget we are "members one of another?" Remember the words of our Lord Jesus Christ, how He said, "Woe to that man through whom offenses come! It would be better for him if he had never been born than to cast a stumbling block before one of my elect. Yes, it would be better for him to have a millstone hung around his neck and be thrown into the depths of the sea than to cast a stumbling block before one of my little ones." Your schism has undermined the faith of many, discouraged many, caused doubt in many, and brought grief to us all. Yet your sedition continues.

{47:1} Consider the letter of the blessed Apostle Paul. What did he write to you when the Gospel was first preached? Truly, inspired by the Spirit, he wrote to you about himself, Cephas, and Apollos, because even then, factions had formed among you. But your preference for one over another was less blameworthy then, as you were favoring apostles of high reputation and a man they approved. Now reflect on who has misled you and diminished the reputation of your renowned brotherly love. It is shameful, beloved, indeed very disgraceful and unworthy of your Christian profession, that the steadfast and ancient Church of the Corinthians should engage in conflict over one or two individuals. This rumor has spread not only to us but to those unconnected with us, so that, through your folly, the name of the Lord is blasphemed, and danger is brought upon yourselves.

{48:1} Therefore, let us swiftly put an end to this situation; let us bow before the Lord and plead with tears that He would graciously reconcile us and restore us to our former proper and holy practice of brotherly love. For such conduct is the gate of righteousness, which is open for the attainment of life, as it is written, "Open to me the gates of righteousness; I will enter through them and praise the Lord; this is the gate of the Lord; the righteous shall enter through it." Although many gates are open, this gate of righteousness is the gate in Christ through which all who have entered and directed their way in holiness and righteousness are blessed, doing all things without disorder. Let a person be faithful, strong in knowledge, wise in speech, and pure in all deeds; yet, the more superior he appears in these respects, the more humble-minded he should be, seeking the common good of all, not just his own advantage.

{49:1} Let the one who has love in Christ keep Christ's commandments. Who can describe the blessed bond of God's love? What person can express its beauty as it deserves? The height to which love elevates is indescribable. Love unites us to God. Love covers a multitude of sins. Love bears all things and is patient in all things. There is nothing base or arrogant in love. Love allows for no schisms; love creates no seditions; love accomplishes everything in harmony. By love, all the elect of God have been perfected; without love, nothing is pleasing to God. In love, the Lord has drawn us to Himself. Because of the love He bore us, Jesus Christ our Lord gave His blood for us by God's will; His flesh for our flesh, and His soul for our souls.

{50:1} You see, beloved, how great and wonderful love is, and that its perfection cannot be fully described. Who is worthy to be found in it except those whom God has graciously made so? Let us pray and implore His mercy that we may live blamelessly in love, free from all human favoritism. All generations from Adam to this day have passed away; but those who, through God's grace, have been perfected in love now have a place among the godly and will be revealed at the coming of Christ's kingdom. For it is written, "Enter into your secret chambers for a little while until my wrath and fury pass away; then I will remember a favorable day and raise you up from your graves." Blessed are we, beloved, if we keep God's commandments in the harmony of love, so that through love our sins may be forgiven. For it is written, "Blessed are those whose transgressions are forgiven and whose sins are covered. Blessed is the man to whom the Lord will not impute sin, and in whose mouth there is no deceit." This blessedness comes to those chosen by God through Jesus Christ our Lord; to whom be glory forever. Amen.

{51:1} Therefore, let us earnestly seek forgiveness for all the wrongs we have committed due to any suggestion from the adversary. Those who have led sedition and discord should consider our common hope. Those who live in fear and love would rather suffer themselves than involve their neighbors. They prefer to bear the blame rather than let the harmony that has been faithfully passed down to us be damaged. It is better for a person to acknowledge their wrongs than to harden their heart like those who stirred up sedition against Moses, the servant of God, whose condemnation was clear to all. They went down alive into Hades, and death swallowed them. Pharaoh, along with his army and all the princes of Egypt, and their chariots with riders, sank in the depths of the Red Sea and perished for no other reason than that their foolish hearts were hardened after witnessing so many signs and wonders wrought by Moses in Egypt.

{52:1} The Lord, brothers, needs nothing and desires nothing from anyone except confession. For, as the chosen David says, "I will confess to the Lord; and that pleases Him more than a young bull with horns and hooves. Let the poor see it and be glad." He also says, "Offer God the sacrifice of praise and pay your vows to the Most High. Call upon Me in the day of your trouble; I will deliver you, and you will glorify Me." For "the sacrifice of God is a broken spirit."

{53:1} You understand, beloved, you understand well the Sacred Scriptures, and you have diligently studied the oracles of God. Recall these things. When Moses went up the mountain and stayed there, fasting and humbling himself for forty days and nights, the Lord said to him, "Moses, Moses, go down quickly, for your people whom you brought out of Egypt have committed a great sin. They have quickly turned away from the way I commanded them and made themselves molten images." The Lord said to him, "I have spoken to you repeatedly, saying, I have seen this people, and indeed, it is a stiff-necked people: let Me destroy them and blot out their name from under heaven; I will make you into a great and numerous nation." But Moses said, "Far be it from You, Lord! Forgive the sin of this people, or else blot me out of the book of the living." O marvelous love! O unmatched perfection! The servant speaks boldly to his Lord, asking for forgiveness for the people or even begging to perish with them.

{54:1} Who among you is noble-minded, compassionate, and full of love? Let them declare, "If my actions have caused sedition, discord, and schisms, I will leave; I will go wherever you desire and do whatever the majority commands; just let the flock of Christ live in peace with the presbyters over them." Whoever acts this way will gain great glory in the Lord, and every place will welcome them. For "the earth is the Lord's, and the fullness thereof." Those who live a godly life—one that is never regretted—have done this and will continue to do so.

{55:1} To give examples from among the heathen: Many kings and princes, during times of pestilence, have willingly given themselves up to death, so their own blood might save their fellow citizens from destruction. Many have left their cities to end sedition within them. We know many among ourselves who have willingly accepted bondage to ransom others. Many have even surrendered themselves to slavery, using the price they received for their freedom to provide for others. Many women, empowered by God's grace, have performed remarkable deeds. The blessed Judith, when her city was besieged, asked the elders for permission to go out into the camp of the enemy; exposing herself to danger, she did so out of love for her country and people under siege. The Lord delivered Holofernes into a woman's hands. Esther, too, perfect in faith, faced danger to save the twelve tribes of Israel from imminent destruction. Through fasting and humility, she prayed to the everlasting God, who sees all things; He, seeing her humble spirit, saved the people for whom she risked her life.

{56:1} Let us also pray for those who have fallen into sin, that they may receive meekness and humility, allowing them to submit not to us, but to the will of God. In this way, they will earn a fruitful and perfect remembrance from us, along with our sympathy in our prayers to God and our mention of them among the saints. Let us accept correction, beloved, for which no one should feel displeased. The exhortations by which we encourage one another are both good in themselves and highly beneficial, as they lead us to align with God's will. For the holy Word says, "The Lord has severely chastened me, yet has not given me over to death." "For whom the Lord loves, He chastens and punishes every son whom He receives." "The righteous," it says, "shall chastise me in mercy and correct me; but let not the oil of the wicked make me feel secure." Again, it says, "Blessed is the man whom the Lord corrects; do not reject the discipline of the Almighty. For He brings sorrow, but then restores joy; He wounds, but His hands heal. He will deliver you from six troubles, and in the seventh, no harm will come to you. In famine, He will rescue you from death, and in war, He will protect you from the sword. He will hide you from the slander of the tongue, and you will not fear when trouble comes. You will laugh at the wicked and the unrighteous and not be afraid of wild animals. For even wild beasts will be at peace with you; then you will know that your home will be safe, and your dwelling will not fail. You will also know that your offspring will be numerous, like the grass of the field. And you will come to the grave like ripe corn harvested in season, or like a heap of grain gathered at the right time." You see, beloved, that those who are chastened by the Lord are protected; for since God is good, He corrects us so we may learn from His holy discipline.

{57:1} Therefore, you who have caused this sedition, submit yourselves to the presbyters and accept correction so you can repent, bending the knees of your hearts. Learn to be humble, setting aside the proud and arrogant self-confidence of your speech. It is better for you to hold a humble but honorable position in the flock of Christ than to be highly regarded yet cast out from the hope of His people. For all-virtuous Wisdom speaks: "Behold, I will share with you the words of My Spirit, and I will teach you My speech. Since I called and you did not listen; I spoke My words, and you disregarded them, rejecting My advice and ignoring My corrections; therefore, I will laugh at your destruction and rejoice when ruin comes upon you, when sudden confusion overwhelms you, like a storm, or when trouble and oppression fall upon you. It will happen that when you call upon Me, I will not hear you; the wicked will seek Me and not find Me. For they hated wisdom and did not choose to fear the Lord; they would not listen to My advice, but despised My corrections. Therefore, they will eat the fruits of their own choices and be filled with their own wickedness."

{58:1} May God, who sees all things and rules all spirits and is Lord of all flesh—who chose our Lord Jesus Christ and us through Him to be a special people—grant to every soul that calls upon His glorious and holy Name faith, fear, peace, patience, endurance, self-control, purity, and sobriety, pleasing to His Name, through our High Priest and Protector, Jesus Christ, to whom be glory, majesty, power, and honor, both now and forevermore. Amen.

{59:1} Please send back our messengers to you—Claudius Ephebus, Valerius Bito, and Fortunatus—quickly, in peace and joy, so they can announce to us the peace and harmony we so earnestly desire and long for among you, and that we may rejoice over the good order re-established among you. The grace of our Lord Jesus Christ be with you and with all those called by God through Him, to whom be glory, honor, power, majesty, and eternal dominion, from everlasting to everlasting. Amen.

The Second Epistle of Clement

{1:1} Brothers and sisters, we should regard Jesus Christ as God and as the judge of the living and the dead; we should not think any less of our salvation. {1:2} If we think little of Him, we can only hope to receive small things from Him. {1:3} And if we do this, we will sin, not considering where we have been called from, by whom, to what purpose, and how much Jesus Christ lowered Himself to suffer for us. {1:4} What then shall we give back to Him? What fruit can we offer that is worthy of what He has given us? {1:5} Indeed, how great are the benefits we owe to Him concerning our holiness! He has enlightened us; as a father, He has called us His children; He has saved us when we were lost and hopeless. {1:6} What praise can we give Him? What reward can match what we have received? {1:7} We were lacking in understanding, worshipping stones and wood, gold and silver, and brass—the works of human hands; our whole lives were nothing but death. {1:8} But surrounded by darkness and having a veil over our eyes, we looked up, and through His will, we have cast aside the cloud that surrounded us. {1:9} For He had compassion on us, and out of love, He saved us, seeing our great error and destruction, and realizing that we had no hope of salvation except through Him. {1:10} For He called us who were nothing and chose to give us existence from nothing.

{2:1} God had previously prophesied through Isaiah that the Gentiles would be saved. {2:8} This should especially encourage them to live well; without this, they will still fail. {2:1} "Rejoice, you barren one who has not given birth; break forth and cry out, you who have not been in labor; for the desolate one has more children than she who has a husband." {2:2} When He said, "Rejoice, you barren one," He was referring to us, for our church was barren before it received children. {2:3} Again, when He said, "Cry out, you who have not been in labor," He implied that like women in labor, we should not cease to bring our prayers to God abundantly. {2:4} And as for what follows, because the desolate one has more children than the one who has a husband: it was added because our people, who seemed forsaken by God, now believe in Him and have become more numerous than those who seemed to have God. {2:5} Another Scripture says, "I came not to call the righteous but sinners." The meaning of this is that those who were lost must be saved. {2:6} For it is truly great and wonderful to not affirm what is already standing, but to support what is falling. {2:7} Likewise, it pleased Christ to save what was lost; when He came into the world, He saved many and called us who were already lost. {2:8} Seeing then that He has shown such great mercy towards us, especially since we, who are alive, no longer sacrifice to dead gods or worship them, but have come to know the Father of truth through Him. {2:9} How can we show that we truly know Him, except by not denying Him through whom we have come to know Him? {2:10} For He Himself says, "Whoever confesses Me before men, him will I confess before My Father." This is our reward if we confess Him through whom we have been saved. {2:11} But how must we confess Him? By doing what He says and obeying His commandments; by worshipping Him not just with our lips but with all our heart and mind. For He says in Isaiah, "This people honors Me with their lips, but their heart is far from Me." {2:12} Therefore, let us not only call Him Lord, for that alone will not save us. For He says, "Not everyone who says to Me, 'Lord, Lord,' will be saved, but he who does righteousness." {2:13} So, brothers and sisters, let us confess Him through our actions; by loving one another, not committing adultery, not speaking ill of one another, not envying each other, but by being self-controlled, merciful, and good. {2:14} Let us also share in one another's sufferings and not be greedy for money; let us confess God through our good works, not through those that are otherwise. {2:15} And let us not fear men, but rather God. For if we were to do wicked things, the Lord has said, "Even if you were joined to Me, even in My very bosom, and did not keep My commandments, I would cast you off and say to you, 'Depart from Me; I do not know you, you workers of iniquity.'"

{3:1} Therefore, brothers and sisters, willingly leaving our temporary stay in this world for the sake of our conscience, let us do the will of Him who has called us and not fear leaving this world. {3:2} For the Lord says, "You will be like sheep among wolves" [Matthew 10:16]. Peter asked, "What if the wolves tear the sheep apart?" Jesus replied to Peter, "Let not the sheep fear the wolves after death; do not fear those who can kill you and then do no more; rather, fear Him who after you die has the power to cast both soul and body into hell" [Luke 12:4, 5]. {3:3} Consider, brothers and sisters, that our time in this body is short, but the promise of Christ is great and wonderful, offering the rest of His coming kingdom and eternal life. {3:4} So what must we do to attain this? We must conduct ourselves in holiness and righteousness, viewing all worldly things as not ours and not desiring them. For if we desire to possess them, we fall from the path of righteousness. {3:5} The Lord says, "No servant can serve two masters. If we desire to serve God and wealth, it will be of no benefit to us" [Luke 16:13]. What will it profit us if we gain the whole world but lose our souls? [Matthew 16:26]. {3:6} This world and the next are two enemies, representing adultery, corruption, greed, and deceit; we must renounce these things. {3:7} Therefore, we cannot be friends of both; we must choose to forsake one in order to enjoy the other. We believe it is better to hate the present things, which are fleeting and corruptible, and to love the things to come, which are truly good and incorruptible. {3:8} For if we do the will of Christ, we will find rest; but if not, nothing will save us from eternal punishment for disobeying His commands. Even the Scripture in Ezekiel says that if Noah, Job, and Daniel were to rise, they could not save their children from captivity [Ezekiel 14:14, 20]. {3:9} Therefore, if such righteous people cannot save their children with their righteousness, how can we hope to enter the kingdom of God unless we keep our baptism holy and undefiled? Who will advocate for us if we are found not to have done what is holy and just? {3:10} Let us, then, my brothers and sisters, strive earnestly, knowing that our struggle is at hand; many travel long distances for a corruptible reward. {3:11} Yet not everyone is crowned, but only those who work hard and strive gloriously. So let us contend that we may all be crowned. Let us run in the straight path, the race that is incorruptible, and let us enter it in large numbers, striving to receive the crown. If we cannot all be crowned, let us get as close as we can. {3:12} Moreover, we must remember that anyone competing for a corruptible prize, if found doing anything unfair, is disqualified and cast out. What do you think will happen to someone who acts unfit in the contest for immortality? {3:13} The prophet speaks about those who do not keep their seal: "Their worm shall not die, and their fire shall not be quenched; they will be a spectacle to all flesh" [Isaiah 66:24]. {3:14} Therefore, let us repent while we are still on earth; we are like clay in the hands of the potter. If the potter makes a vessel and it turns out badly or breaks, he can reshape it; but if he has already put it in the furnace, he cannot remedy it anymore. {3:15} Likewise, we, while in this world, should sincerely repent for all the evil we have done in the flesh while we still have time for repentance, so we may be saved by the Lord. {3:16} For after we depart this world, we will no longer be able to confess our sins or repent. {3:17} Therefore, brothers and sisters, let us do the will of the Father, keep our bodies pure, and observe the commandments of the Lord to grasp eternal life. For the Lord says in the Gospel, "If you have not been faithful in little things, who will give you greater things? For I say to you, whoever is faithful in little is also faithful in much" [Luke 16:10]. {3:18} This means: keep your bodies pure and your seal unblemished, so you may receive eternal life.

{4:1} And let no one among you say that this very flesh will not be judged or raised. Consider this: in what were you saved? In what did you look up, if not while you were in this flesh? {4:2} Therefore, we must keep our flesh as the temple of God. For just as you were called in the flesh, you will also be judged in the flesh. Our one Lord Jesus Christ, who saved us, first became a spirit and then took on flesh; similarly, we will receive our reward in this flesh. {4:3} So let us love one another so we can attain the kingdom of God. While we have time to be healed, let us give ourselves to God, our healer, giving our reward to Him. {4:4} And what reward will we give? Repentance from a pure heart. For He knows all things in advance and examines our very hearts. {4:5} Therefore, let us praise Him, not only with our mouths but with all our souls, so that He may receive us as children. For the Lord said, "They are My brothers and sisters who do the will of My Father" [Matthew 12:50]. {4:6} Therefore, my brothers and sisters, let us do the will of the Father who has called us to live. Let us pursue virtue and reject wickedness, which leads us into sin; let us flee all ungodliness so that evil does not overtake us. {4:7} For if we strive to live well, peace will follow us. Yet how hard it is to find someone who does this! Almost all are led by human fears, preferring present pleasures over future promises. {4:8} They do not understand how great the torment of present pleasures can be, nor what delights await in future promises. {4:9} And if only they acted this way themselves, it might be more bearable; but now they go on to infect innocent souls with their evil teachings, not realizing that both they and their listeners will face double condemnation. {4:10} Therefore, let us serve God with pure hearts, and we shall be righteous; but if we do not serve Him because we doubt God's promise, we will be miserable. {4:11} For the prophet says, "Miserable are the double-minded who doubt in their hearts and say, 'These things we have heard from our ancestors, but we have seen none of them, though we expect them daily.'" {4:12} O foolish ones! Compare yourselves to a tree; take the vine as an example. First, it sheds its leaves, then buds, then sour grapes, then ripe fruit; likewise, my people have endured hardships and afflictions, but will ultimately receive good things. {4:13} Therefore, my brothers and sisters, let us not doubt in our minds but expect with hope to receive our reward; for He is faithful who has promised to reward everyone according to their works. {4:14} If we do what is right in God's sight, we will enter His kingdom and receive promises that neither eye has seen, nor ear heard, nor have entered the heart of man [Isaiah 64:4; 1 Corinthians 2:9]. {4:15} So let us expect the kingdom of God every hour with love and righteousness, for we do not know the day of God's appearing.

{5:1} For the Lord Himself, when asked by someone when His kingdom would come, answered, "When two become one, and what is outside is like what is inside, and the male and female are neither male nor female." {5:2} Two become one when we speak the truth to each other, and there is, without hypocrisy, one soul in two bodies. {5:3} By "what is outside" He means the body, and "what is inside" means the soul. Therefore, let your soul be seen by its good works as your body appears. {5:4} By "the male with the female is neither male nor female," He means that our anger is the male and our desires are the female. {5:5} When a person reaches the point where they are not subject to either of these (both of which, due to custom and bad education, cloud reason), {5:6} and instead, having cleared the mist from them, and feeling ashamed, unites both their soul and spirit in obedience to reason, then, as Paul says, there is neither male nor female in us [Galatians 3:28].

The Epistle of Barnabas

{1:1} Greetings to you, beloved brothers and sisters, in the name of our Lord Jesus Christ, who has shown us His love in peace. {1:2} I rejoice exceedingly over your blessed and noble hearts because you have fully embraced the implanted gift of the Spirit. {1:3} This has brought me immense inner joy and hope for my own salvation, as I see in you the Spirit that the generous Lord of love has poured out. {1:4} Your highly anticipated presence fills me with amazement, and I am convinced that since I began speaking with you, I've come to understand so much, for the Lord has guided me in the way of righteousness. {1:5} Because of this, I feel deeply obligated to love you more than my own soul, for your faith and love are profound, and you live with a great hope in the promise of eternal life. {1:6} Therefore, I am eager to share with you, for it is reward enough to minister to such spirits. I write briefly that you might have perfect knowledge to complement your faith. {1:7} The teachings of the Lord are threefold: the hope of life, its beginning, and its completion. {1:8} Through the prophets, the Lord revealed to us the past, the present, and even the future, giving us the first glimpses of what is to come. {1:9} As we see these things unfold, we should draw closer to Him with reverence, enriched in faith. {1:10} So I, as one of you and not as a teacher, will share a few insights to bring you joy in these times.

{2:1} Now, given the current evil days and Satan's power over this world, we must diligently examine the Lord's commandments. {2:2} Fear and patience support our faith, while endurance and self-control stand beside us in our struggles. {2:3} When these remain pure in service to the Lord, Wisdom, Understanding, Knowledge, and Insight rejoice alongside them. {2:4} The prophets revealed that God does not require sacrifices or burnt offerings. He says, "What is the abundance of your sacrifices to Me?" {2:5} "I am full of burnt offerings and have no desire for the fat of lambs or the blood of bulls and goats, nor when you come to stand before Me. Who asked for this from your hands? Do not trample My courts, even if you bring fine flour. Incense is a detestable thing to Me, and I cannot endure your new moons and Sabbaths." {2:6} He abolished these, so the new law of our Lord Jesus Christ might be fulfilled in a sincere offering, free from compulsion. {2:7} And again, He told them, "Did I command your ancestors to offer burnt offerings and sacrifices when they left Egypt? No, rather, I said, 'Let no one harbor evil against his neighbor or love deceitful oaths.'" {2:8} We should discern our Father's gracious intent here; He desires us to draw near with purity. {2:9} For He says to us, "The sacrifice that pleases God is a broken spirit; a heart that glorifies Him is like a sweet fragrance." {2:10} We must be diligent concerning our salvation, lest the deceiver slip in and lead us away from true life.

{3:1} God also criticizes the fasts of the Jews, which He finds unacceptable, saying, "Why do you fast in this way? Is it so your voice is heard on high? I have not chosen this fast, that one might humble their soul by mere outward shows of piety." {3:2} To us, He says, "This is the fast I have chosen: to loose every chain of wickedness, to undo unjust bonds, to let the oppressed go free, and to break every yoke." {3:3} "Share your bread with the hungry, clothe the naked, welcome the homeless, do not turn away from your family, and do not disregard the humble." {3:4} "Then your light will break forth like the dawn, and your healing will quickly appear. Righteousness will go before you, and God's glory will guard you. When you call, the Lord will answer, saying, 'Here I am,' as you remove oppression, giving your bread willingly to the hungry & showing compassion to those in need." {3:5} God, in His patience, anticipated that faithful people would trust in His Beloved Son, teaching us not to follow laws without understanding.

{4:1} We who ponder coming events must diligently search what can save us. {4:2} Let us flee from all sinful works so that they do not bind us, and let us reject the errors of this age to focus on the world to come. {4:3} Let us not yield to our passions or run with the wicked, lest we become like them. {4:4} The final trial approaches, as Enoch wrote: "For this reason, the Lord has shortened the days, so His Beloved may come quickly to His inheritance." {4:5} The prophet speaks likewise, saying, "Ten kingdoms will reign on earth, and a small king will arise to subdue three of the others." {4:6} And Daniel saw "the fourth beast, fierce and mighty, with ten horns, out of which a small horn emerged and conquered three of the great horns." {4:7} We must understand this. {4:8} And I ask you, my beloved, to take caution and not follow those who say, "The covenant is theirs and ours," for they lost it after Moses received it. {4:9} The Scripture says, "Moses was on the mountain for forty days and nights and received the covenant," but they turned to idols and lost it. {4:10} God then told Moses to go down, for the people had sinned. {4:11} Moses broke the tablets, signifying that the covenant would be written on our hearts in the hope that comes through Jesus. {4:12} So, as one who loves you, I urge you to resist the dangers of this age, for our faith will be of no benefit if we fail to guard against evil. {4:13} To keep the wicked one from entering, let us reject vanity and wickedness. {4:14} Do not isolate yourselves as if already righteous, but gather to discuss what is good for all. {4:15} Scripture warns, "Woe to those who think themselves wise and prudent in their own eyes!" Let us strive to be a perfect temple for God. {4:16} The Lord will judge without favoritism, rewarding righteousness and punishing wickedness. {4:17} Let us not rest in complacency, thinking ourselves secure, for even Israel, after witnessing God's wonders, was abandoned for turning away. {4:18} Let us heed the words, "Many are called, but few are chosen."

{5:1} The new covenant, founded on Christ's suffering, is our salvation but brings judgment upon those who reject it. {5:2} Christ endured death so that we might be sanctified through the forgiveness achieved by His blood. {5:3} Scripture prophesied, speaking of Him: "He was wounded for our sins and bruised for our iniquities; by His wounds, we are healed." {5:4} "He was led as a sheep to slaughter." {5:5} We owe deep gratitude to the Lord, for He has revealed past, present, and future mysteries. {5:6} Scripture warns, "It is not in vain that nets are set for birds"—meaning that those who stray knowingly are lost justly. {5:7} If the Lord suffered for our souls, though He is Lord of all, it shows the depth of His love. {5:8} The prophets, blessed by Him, foretold His coming, knowing He would come in flesh to conquer death and reveal the resurrection. {5:9} He showed Himself on earth to fulfill promises made to our ancestors and establish a new people. {5:10} By calling sinners to be His apostles, He proved He came "not for the righteous, but to call sinners." {5:11} If He hadn't come in the flesh, how could humanity behold salvation? Even looking at the sun, a mere creation, blinds us; how could we bear to see Him otherwise? {5:12} Thus, He endured in the flesh, even from those who rejected His prophets, to fulfill the law. {5:13} Scripture speaks of His suffering: "The blow against Him comes from them; when the Shepherd is struck, the sheep are scattered." {5:14} He chose to suffer on the cross, as the prophecy says, "Save my soul from the sword, nail my flesh, for the wicked surround me." {5:15} And again, "I gave my back to be whipped and my cheeks to be struck, setting my face like a rock."

{6:1} When Christ fulfilled God's command, He said, "Who will challenge Me? Let him come forward; who will stand in judgment with Me? Let him approach." {6:2} "Woe to you, for you will decay like old clothing, and moths will consume you." The prophet says, "He is like a precious, chosen cornerstone laid in Zion, a foundation stone." {6:3} "Whoever trusts in Him will live forever." Our hope is not merely in a stone, but in Jesus, who laid His body as a foundation. {6:4} The prophet says, "The stone the builders rejected has become the cornerstone." And again, "This is the day the Lord has made." {6:5} I write plainly, out of my love for you. The prophet also said, "The assembly of the wicked surrounded Me like bees around a honeycomb, and they cast lots for My clothing." {6:6} He was destined to appear and suffer in the flesh. {6:7} The prophet warned Israel, "Woe to their souls; they plot to bind the righteous one because He displeases them." Moses also spoke of this, saying, "Enter the good land, flowing with milk and honey, which God promised to Abraham, Isaac, and Jacob." {6:8} Wisdom calls us to trust in Jesus, who was to come in the flesh. {6:9} Humanity, made from earth, was renewed by Jesus' Spirit. {6:10} God said, "Let Us make man in Our image," and blessed man to rule over creation. {6:11} In these last days, He has re-formed us, fulfilling the promise to make the last like the first. {6:12} The prophet proclaimed, "Enter the land of milk and honey and have dominion." {6:13} He promised to give us hearts of flesh, replacing hearts of stone, as He came to dwell among us. {6:14} We are His temple, and He says, "I will praise You in the assembly." {6:15} We are those He led to the good land. Milk and honey signify new life in faith and in the word. {6:16} He has promised us dominion, which we will fully receive as we mature as heirs of His covenant.

{7:1} Children of joy, God has revealed all things so we may give Him thanks. {7:2} If Christ, Lord of all, suffered to give us life, believe that He did so for us. {7:3} On the cross, He was given vinegar and gall, prefigured by the priests in their sacrifices. {7:4} The law commanded fasting as preparation, because Christ's sacrifice would fulfill the type shown in Isaac's offering. {7:5} God says, "Eat the sin-offering goat with fasting," and the priests would eat the inwards with vinegar, foreshadowing the suffering of Christ. {7:6} God also commanded two goats: one sacrificed, the other cursed and driven into the wilderness, symbolizing Jesus. {7:7} He wore a crown of thorns, mocked and pierced, just as the goat was crowned and driven away. {7:8} This was a type of Jesus' suffering, and those who seek Him must be ready to endure trials, as the crown of thorns symbolizes the path to His kingdom.

{8:1} God commanded that a red heifer be sacrificed, its ashes sprinkled for purification, prefiguring Christ. {8:2} The sinful men who led Jesus to His death represent the men offering the heifer. {8:3} The boys who sprinkled the ashes symbolize the apostles proclaiming forgiveness. {8:4} The three boys represent Abraham, Isaac, and Jacob, honored by God. {8:5} The wood and wool signify Jesus' kingdom established through the cross. {8:6} Hyssop represents cleansing, as suffering purifies. These symbols were made clear for us but hidden from those who didn't listen to God.

{9:1} God has also spoken about circumcision, making it a matter of the heart. {9:2} The Lord says, "Listen, O Israel," and circumcision is not merely physical but of the spirit. {9:3} He warned them against hardening their hearts, calling them to true repentance. {9:4} Although circumcision was a sign of the covenant, it was spiritual, as Abraham received knowledge that foresaw Jesus. {9:5} When Abraham circumcised his household, it prefigured the name "Jesus" and the cross, symbolized by the numbers in the letters. {9:6} This knowledge is profound, a gift to those who receive His teachings.

{10:1} Moses' food laws also held spiritual meanings. {10:2} God told Israel not to eat certain animals, symbolizing types of people. {10:3} The swine represents those who only turn to God when in need, while the birds of prey represent those who take from others. {10:4} Fish without scales symbolize people submerged in sin. {10:5} The hare signifies immorality, as it multiplies recklessly. {10:6} The hyena, which changes gender, represents corruption. {10:7} The weasel, conceived through the mouth, signifies impurity. {10:8} Moses taught three levels of spiritual meaning, but people took them literally. {10:9} The righteous "chew the cud" by meditating on God's word and "walk with cloven hooves," showing that while they live in this world, they set their hope in the holy life to come.

{11:1} Let us examine how the Lord prefigured baptism and the cross in Scripture. For the water, it is written that the Israelites did not receive the baptism that cleanses from sin but sought their own path. The prophet says, "Be shocked, heavens, and tremble, for My people have done great evil: they have left Me, the fountain of living water, and dug broken wells for themselves." And He adds, "Is Zion, My holy mountain, a desolate rock? You will be like birds fleeing when their nest is disturbed." Another prophet says, "I will go before you, leveling mountains, breaking gates of bronze, and shattering iron bars." Concerning the Son, He says, "His water is secure; you will see the King in glory, and your soul will meditate on God's reverence." Another prophet says, "The one who follows this way is like a tree planted by rivers, bearing fruit in its season, with leaves that do not wither. Not so are the wicked, who are like chaff blown away." Those who trust in the cross and enter the water will be rewarded. Their "leaves shall not fade," meaning their words of faith will bring hope and conversion to others. Further, it says, "A river flowed, and from it grew beautiful trees; whoever eats of them will live forever." This shows that we go into the water burdened by sin but rise with fruit in our hearts, trusting in Jesus. Whoever believes in this will live forever.

{12:1} The cross is also foretold. Another prophet asks, "When will this be fulfilled?" The Lord answers, "When a tree is bent down and rises again, and when blood flows from wood." This clearly points to the cross and Christ. Moses, too, foreshadowed it when Israel was attacked: he raised his arms, forming a cross, and they won. When his arms fell, they lost, showing they could not succeed without God. Another prophet says, "I have stretched out My hands all day to a rebellious people." Moses also made a bronze serpent to save the people from snake bites, symbolizing Christ's suffering. Moses told the people to look upon the serpent to be healed. Likewise, if we look to Jesus, we are saved. When Moses named Joshua, he foreshadowed how God would reveal His Son, Jesus. The prophet David also calls Him Lord, showing that Christ is not merely human but the Son of God.

{13:1} Let's consider who truly inherits God's covenant. Isaac prayed for Rebecca, and God told her, "Two nations are in your womb; one will surpass the other, and the older will serve the younger." This points to how the chosen people would serve those who came after. Later, Jacob blessed Joseph's younger son, Ephraim, over the elder, Manasseh, symbolizing that the later people, the believers, would inherit the covenant. God told Abraham, "I have made you the father of nations who believe while uncircumcised." So, the covenant is for those who believe, not just by birth.

{14:1} Let's see if God indeed gave the covenant He promised. He did give it, but the Israelites were unworthy because of their sins. Moses fasted for forty days to receive the covenant, and God gave him the tablets written by His finger. But when Moses saw the people worshiping idols, he broke the tablets. They were not ready to receive it. Now, through Jesus, we are made heirs, and the covenant has been given to us. Jesus entered into a covenant with us, redeeming us from darkness. The prophet says, "I, the Lord, have called You in righteousness and made You a covenant for the people, a light for the nations." We have been redeemed, as another prophet says, "I have set You as a light to the nations for salvation." This covenant came through Jesus, the true Savior.

{15:1} Regarding the Sabbath, God said, "Keep the Sabbath with pure hands and a clean heart." He rested on the seventh day, symbolizing His rest when His Son returns to judge. The Sabbath points to the ultimate rest when wickedness is destroyed. When God said, "I cannot endure your Sabbaths," He meant that the current observance wasn't acceptable. But He promises a new "8th day"—the day of resurrection, which is why we celebrate it joyfully as the day Jesus rose from the dead and ascended into heaven.

{16:1} Concerning the temple, the Jews placed their trust in it as if it were God Himself. Yet, God says, "Heaven is My throne, and earth is My footstool; what house can you build for Me?" Their hope was misguided. God foretold that the temple and city would be destroyed, and it was. But there is a new temple, built in His name. Our hearts, once filled with sin, have become the dwelling place of God. When we believe, we are made new, and God dwells in us, speaking through us. This is the true spiritual temple.

{17:1} I hope that I have conveyed everything essential for your salvation, as far as I could. If I were to write about future matters, they would be hard to understand, as they are hidden in parables. So, let us move on to simpler teachings.

{18:1} Now, we turn to another teaching: there are two ways—one of light and one of darkness. These ways are vastly different. The way of light has angels of God over it, and the way of darkness is ruled by Satan, the prince of iniquity.

{19:1} The way of light is as follows. Anyone who wishes to walk this path must be diligent in good works. Love God, who created and redeemed you; be humble, not hypocritical; do not indulge in evil. Honor the commandments, do not boast or harm others, and love your neighbor more than yourself. Do not kill, including through abortion or infanticide, but teach your children to fear the Lord. Share what you have, avoid greed, and be just. Be pure in speech and heart, ready to help others, and remember God's judgment. Seek to save others and do not hesitate to give generously. If you follow this path, you walk in light.

{20:1} The way of darkness is full of curses and leads to eternal death. It is marked by idolatry, pride, hypocrisy, murder, and greed. Those on this path do not know God's love, ignore the needy, are unjust, and act without mercy. They are far from righteousness.

{21:1} So, let anyone who knows the Lord's commands walk in them, for those who do so will be glorified in God's kingdom, while those who choose the way of darkness will be destroyed. There will be a resurrection and a reward for each according to his deeds.

Therefore, remain faithful, remove hypocrisy from among you, and seek wisdom from God. Remember me in your prayers, and pursue these things earnestly. May the Lord of grace be with you always. Farewell, children of love and peace. Amen.

The Epistle of Ignatius to the Ephesians

{1:1} I have come to know your name, dearly loved by God, which you've earned through faithful living in righteousness and love in Jesus Christ. Being followers of God, inspired by Christ's sacrifice, you have fulfilled what was right. When you heard that I came bound from Syria, hoping for martyrdom in Rome to truly become His disciple, you eagerly came to see me. I received all of you in spirit through Onesimus, a man of deep love and your bishop. I urge you to love him as Christ, for you are blessed to have such a faithful leader.

{2:1} I ask that Burrhus, your deacon and a faithful servant of God, may stay with you longer to honor both you and your bishop. Crocus, also beloved by God and by you, has refreshed me, as have Onesimus, Burrhus, Euplus, and Fronto—all who represent your love to me. May I always rejoice in you. It's fitting that you glorify Jesus Christ in unity, that together, with one mind, you may honor Him and be made holy through obedience to your bishop and presbytery.

{3:1} I am not here to command, for I am but a fellow servant, not yet perfected in Christ. I speak as a fellow disciple, needing encouragement in faith and patience. But love compels me to urge you to pursue God's will in harmony. For Jesus Christ does everything according to His Father's will, as He said, "I do always those things that please Him." Let us also seek to live by God's will, imitating Him as Paul did, saying, "Follow me as I follow Christ."

{4:1} It is right for you to live in harmony with your bishop, appointed by God to lead you. Your presbytery is like strings to a harp, tuned perfectly to the bishop, bringing forth the song of Christ. Be like a choir, singing in harmony with love to God, so that by your unity, God may see His Son's spirit alive in you. Therefore, live blamelessly together in peace, as Jesus prayed, "Father, let them be one as we are one," and follow His example, as members of His body.

{5:1} If I have enjoyed even this brief fellowship with your bishop, how much more blessed are you, united with him as the Church is with Christ and Christ with the Father. Let no one deceive themselves; those who separate from the altar deprive themselves of God's bread. For if even the prayer of two has power, how much more so does that of the bishop and the Church. One who separates from the Church has shown pride and self-condemnation, for "God resists the proud." Therefore, let us submit to the bishop to be truly submitted to God.

{6:1} The more you see the bishop act with humility, the more you should honor him. Receive anyone whom the Lord sends over His household, as you would Christ Himself. Let the bishop stand before you as Christ, for it is right to honor those who serve diligently. Onesimus commends your unity, as you live according to God's truth, without division. As Paul taught, "You are one body and one spirit, called to one hope of faith, one Lord, one faith, one baptism, one God and Father of all." Such are you, following in the teaching of Paul and Timothy.

{7:1} Beware of false teachers who use Jesus' name deceitfully, teaching contrary to His doctrine. Avoid them as you would wild animals, for "the righteous are saved forever, but the wicked's destruction is sudden." They are "dumb dogs" with a hidden illness. But our Healer is the only true God, the Father who sent Jesus Christ, His Son, before time began. Jesus, born of the Virgin Mary, was "the Word made flesh," enduring suffering to free us from death and sin, restoring us to health and holiness.

{8:1} Do not be deceived, for you are fully devoted to God. When no evil desire defiles you, you live by God's will as Christ's servants. Those focused on the flesh cannot do the works of the Spirit, nor can unbelief perform works of faith. But filled with the Holy Spirit, you do everything according to the Spirit. Even what you do in the flesh is spiritual, for all is done in Jesus Christ, "the Savior of all, especially those who believe."

{9:1} I have heard of some false teachings that tried to infiltrate your community, but you stopped your ears to them. As living stones of God's temple, held together by Jesus and drawn up by the Holy Spirit, you have resisted these false doctrines. Thus, you are true God-bearers, adorned by the teachings of Jesus Christ, and I rejoice that I am worthy to speak with you through this letter, as you love nothing but God.

{10:1} Pray constantly for others, that they may repent and come to God. Show them by your actions the truth of God. Be gentle when they show wrath, humble in response to their pride, steadfast in faith despite their errors, and kind even when they are harsh. Let us not imitate them but be kind as brethren. Like Christ, who did not retaliate when reviled, let us forgive and pray for those who hurt us. If someone wrongs us, may we respond with greater patience. Let no root of evil grow in you; stay vigilant in Christ Jesus.

{11:1} We are in the last times, so let us live with reverence, mindful of God's patience so it does not lead to our condemnation. Let us stand firm in faith, looking forward to eternal life in Christ Jesus. May I always partake in your prayers, so that I too may be among the faithful of Ephesus, who have been steadfast with the apostles through Christ's power.

{12:1} I know who I am and to whom I write. I am condemned; you have received God's mercy. I face dangers; you are secure in Christ. You share in the Gospel's mysteries alongside Paul, that holy and blessed martyr, and may I stand at his feet and the feet of all saints when I reach God. For Paul often remembered you in his letters, and so does Jesus Christ.

{13:1} Gather often to give thanks to God and glorify His name, for when you assemble, the forces of Satan are weakened. Nothing is more precious than the peace of God, which ends all strife in heaven and earth.

{14:1} None of this is hidden from you if you hold onto faith and love in Christ Jesus, the beginning and end of life. Faith is the start, and love is the fulfillment. Together they are from God, and all good things follow from them. No one who truly has faith sins, and no one filled with love hates. Good trees bear good fruit, and true Christians are known by their deeds, not merely by words.

{15:1} It is better to be a Christian in actions than just in words. "The kingdom of God is not in words but in power." We believe with our hearts and confess with our mouths. A true Christian hears even the silence of Jesus, acting with integrity and humility. Let us do all things as if God were dwelling in us, for indeed He is, and nothing is hidden from Him.

{16:1} Do not be misled, my brothers. Those who corrupt families or spread false doctrines will not inherit God's kingdom. How much more will those who mislead the Church of Christ face punishment, as they seek to destroy what Jesus endured the cross to redeem. Those who ignore true teaching and follow false leaders are like light joining with darkness.

{17:1} The Lord allowed His head to be anointed so that He might breathe eternal life into His Church. Do not be swayed by the false teachings of this world. Having received God's truth in Jesus, let us live wisely and hold fast to the gift He has given us.

{18:1} Let my life be counted as nothing if it isn't for the cross, which is salvation for believers but foolishness to unbelievers. "Where is the wise? Where is the scholar?" For Jesus Christ, the Son of God, who was before time, was conceived by Mary through the Holy Spirit and born into this world. He was baptized to consecrate the waters for our purification.

{19:1} The mysteries of Mary's virginity, Christ's birth, and His death were hidden from the evil powers of this world. How was Christ revealed? A star brighter than all others shone, astonishing all who saw it. This light abolished ignorance, destroyed the power of evil, and renewed life in God as He came in human form.

{20:1} If Jesus Christ permits, I will write to you again to further explain the mysteries of His life, love, suffering, and resurrection. I hope the Lord will reveal more to me for your encouragement.

{21:1} May you come together in grace, united in faith in Jesus Christ, born of David's line, both Son of Man and Son of God. Obey your bishop and presbytery with a single mind, sharing in one bread—the bread of life that grants us immortality in Christ.

{22:1} My soul is with you and with those whom you have sent to Smyrna for God's honor, from where I write to you. I thank God for you and for Polycarp, whom I love as I love you. Pray for the Church in Syria, from where I journey bound to Rome, as the last of the faithful there, called to glorify God. Farewell in God the Father and in Jesus Christ, our common hope.

The Epistle of Ignatius to the Magnesians

{1:1} I have heard of your well-ordered love for God, and it brings me great joy. I felt compelled to write to you, united in the faith of Jesus Christ. Bearing the name of Christ with honor and chained in His service, I pray for all the churches to be united in the Spirit and body of Jesus, who is our life. Through faith and love, which surpass all else, may we stand strong against the challenges of this world and, by enduring, come to share in God's presence.

{2:1} I am grateful to have met you through your dedicated bishop Damas, your honorable presbyters Bassus and Apollonius, and your deacon Sotio, whose companionship I cherish. His commitment to the bishop, as if to God's grace, and to the presbytery, as if to Jesus' teachings, truly blesses you.

{3:1} You should also show proper respect to your young bishop, honoring him not for his age but for the power of God within him. Like the wise presbyters I have seen, do not judge by his youth, but rather respect him as one sent by God the Father and Jesus Christ, the true Bishop over all. Obey your bishop genuinely, as this honors the One who commanded it, for to disregard his authority is to deceive not only him but also God, who knows all hearts.

{4:1} It's not enough to merely be called Christians; we must truly live as Christians. Those who claim to respect the bishop but act without him are hypocrites, ignoring the true High Priest, Jesus. The Lord says, "Why call Me 'Lord' if you do not do as I say?" Such people lack sincerity and a clear conscience.

{5:1} Since everything eventually comes to an end, life and death are set before us, and each will go to their rightful place. Just as there are coins stamped with images of this world or of God, unbelievers belong to this world, while believers bear God's image, through Christ's love. If we're not prepared to die with Him, then His life is not within us.

{6:1} Seeing in your leaders the faith and love of your whole community, I urge you to live in unity. Your bishop stands in God's place, your presbyters represent the apostles, and your deacons, whom I hold dear, serve Jesus Christ, who was with the Father before all time and has now been revealed. Imitate this divine order, respecting each other and living in unity, not judging by outward appearances but loving each other in Christ. Let nothing divide you, but stay united with your leaders as a sign of your eternal hope.

{7:1} Just as the Lord does nothing without the Father, saying, "I do nothing of My own," so neither should anyone, whether presbyter, deacon, or layperson, act apart from the bishop. Let nothing be considered good without his approval, for it is against God's will. Gather together for prayer with one heart, one faith, and one hope in Christ. Come as one people, approaching the temple as though it were one altar, under Jesus Christ, our High Priest.

{8:1} Do not be misled by strange doctrines or old tales that lack value. Living by the old law would mean we've not received God's grace. The prophets lived in anticipation of Christ, even suffering persecution, inspired to convince others of the one true God who is revealed through Jesus, His eternal Word, who pleased the Father in all things.

{9:1} If those who studied the Scriptures waited in hope for Christ, as He said, "If you believed Moses, you would believe Me," and "Abraham rejoiced to see My day," how can we live without Him? The prophets foresaw Him and awaited Him as their Savior. We should no longer keep the Sabbath as idleness, for "if one does not work, he should not eat." Instead, keep the Sabbath spiritually, rejoicing in God's works, not in worldly pleasures. Celebrate the Lord's Day, the day of resurrection and victory over death, as foretold by the prophets. Beware of those who deny this, caring more for their own desires than for God's truth. They corrupt Christ's teachings, deceive others, and seek selfish gain; may God, through Jesus, protect you from them.

{10:1} Let us not ignore God's kindness. If He repaid us according to our deeds, we would be lost. As disciples of Christ, let us live by Christian principles, for anyone named by another title is not of God. Set aside old habits and live by the new "leaven," which is Jesus Christ. Let His truth shape you, rejecting anything that leads to corruption. It's wrong to follow Christ while still clinging to old ways, for Christianity completes and fulfills Judaism, bringing all who believe to God.

{11:1} I write these words not because I think you're in danger, but as a fellow servant who desires to protect you from false doctrines. May you have full assurance in Christ, who was born of the Father before all ages and then, in our time, born of a virgin, lived a holy life, healed many, and made God known. He suffered, died, rose, ascended, and will return to judge all. Whoever holds these truths is blessed, just as you now live in the full assurance of this hope.

{12:1} May I be worthy of you in every way. Though bound, I am not equal to any of you who are free. I know you are not prideful, for Christ lives in you. When I praise you, I see your humility, as it is written, "The righteous man is his own accuser."

{13:1} Strive to be grounded in the teachings of the Lord and the apostles, so that all you do prospers in spirit and in truth. Together with your admirable bishop, united presbyters, and God-honoring deacons, let everything be done in unity. Be subject to each other and to the bishop, just as Christ submitted to the Father and the apostles followed Christ, so that there is harmony in both body and spirit.

{14:1} Knowing your goodness, I have written only briefly, out of love for Jesus. Remember me in your prayers, that I may come closer to God, and also pray for the Church in Syria, of which I am unworthy to be called bishop. I need your prayers and your love, that the Syrian Church may be strengthened and built up in Christ.

{15:1} The Ephesians in Smyrna (where I now write) send greetings to you in God's honor, as do I, refreshed by them, along with Polycarp. The other churches honor you as well in the name of Jesus. Farewell in harmony, bound together by the Holy Spirit in Christ Jesus, by God's will.

The Epistle of Ignatius to the Trallians

{1:1} I have heard of your unwavering faith, pure in patience, a true and lasting strength, as shown by Polybius, your bishop, who came to Smyrna by the will of God the Father and Jesus Christ, with the Holy Spirit's help. His presence brought me joy as I saw the whole of your congregation united in Christ. Through him, I received a testament of your goodness according to God's will, and I am proud to see that you are true followers of Jesus Christ, our Savior.

{2:1} Be obedient to your bishop as you would to the Lord, for "he watches over your souls as one accountable to God." In following him, you show that you live according to Christ, who died for us, so that by faith in His death and baptism, we are joined with Him in resurrection. In everything, do nothing without the bishop. Be obedient to the presbytery as to Christ's apostles, and the deacons, who serve not food and drink but the Church of God. Let them prove themselves to be above any accusation, for they serve the holy mysteries of Jesus Christ. It is your duty to support them in all ways.

{3:1} Respect the deacons as you would Christ Himself, for they represent His presence among you. Honor the bishop as you would honor God the Father, and the presbyters as God's holy council, the assembly of Christ's apostles. Without these, there is no true Church or gathering of the saints. I believe you know this, for I have felt the love you carry, which is evident in your bishop. His very presence speaks wisdom, and even the ungodly must respect his gentleness. I love you dearly and avoid a harsh tone, not wanting to come across as severe. Though I am bound in Christ, I am not yet fully worthy of Him. Perhaps when I reach my goal, I may be, but for now, I do not speak with apostolic authority.

{4:1} I measure my words to avoid boasting, as I know the value of humility. Even if I had achieved true spiritual wisdom, I would still be cautious and avoid those who try to flatter. For when others praise me, it humbles me instead. I do desire to suffer for Christ, but I do not know if I am worthy, as the enemy is always near, unseen yet waging war against us. I need meekness to overcome the devil, the ruler of this world.

{5:1} I could speak of deeper, mysterious teachings, but I hold back for your sake, knowing they could be overwhelming. Even I, bound for Christ, am still learning. I grasp the heavenly orders, the ranks of angels, the powers and dominions, the splendor of the cherubim and seraphim, the majesty of the Spirit, the Lord's kingdom, and God's incomparable glory. Yet, I am far from being like Paul or Peter, as I lack much to reach God fully.

{6:1} I urge you, not I but the love of Christ within me, to avoid false teachings and feed only on true Christian doctrine. Heresies mix poison with the truth of Jesus Christ, like deadly drugs in sweet wine. Those unaware may drink it eagerly, but it leads to their spiritual death.

{7:1} Be cautious of such people. You will succeed if you stay humble, close to Jesus Christ, your bishop, and the apostles' teachings. Only those within the altar, united with the bishop, presbytery, and deacons, are truly pure. Humility and obedience unite us with God, for He is close to those who are humble and tremble at His word. Respect your bishop as you would Christ, as the apostles instructed. The bishop is a representative of God, the presbytery a sacred council, and the deacons serve as ministers like the angels, as Stephen did for James, Timothy for Paul, and Clement for Peter. Anyone who disobeys such leaders is without God and disrespects Christ.

{8:1} I do not mention these warnings because I think such trouble exists among you—far from it. I pray that God will never allow it. But I foresee the enemy's traps, and I want to protect you as beloved children in Christ. Be clothed in humility, imitating Christ's sufferings and love. He gave Himself as a ransom, washing us clean of sin with His blood. Let none among you hold a grudge, for the Lord says, "Forgive, and it will be forgiven." Do not give reason for outsiders to blaspheme God's word because of a few foolish people, as the prophet warns, "Woe to him by whom My name is blasphemed."

{9:1} Turn a deaf ear to anyone who speaks against Jesus Christ, descended from David, born of Mary. He was truly born, ate, drank, was persecuted, crucified, died, and was raised from the dead. This is no illusion. Christ's suffering was real, witnessed by beings in heaven, on earth, and under the earth. He was raised by the Father, just as we who believe will also rise through Him. Jesus, fully human and fully divine, truly took on flesh and lived without sin. He died under Pontius Pilate, and many saw Him crucified, even those in heaven and under the earth, as Scripture says, "Many saints who slept arose." Christ went to Hades alone but returned with many, breaking down the barriers of death. He rose on the third day, spent forty days with His apostles, and ascended to the Father, awaiting the day His enemies are placed under His feet.

{10:1} If some unbelievers say He only seemed to suffer, then why am I in chains? Why do I long to face wild beasts for Him? If Christ's suffering was false, then my suffering is in vain. I would be lying against the truth of the cross.

{11:1} Flee from these deadly heresies, which bear the fruit of death. If they were truly from the Father, they would grow from the cross and bear incorruptible fruit. Through His passion, Christ calls us as His members, and just as a body cannot live without its head, we cannot live without Christ.

{12:1} I greet you from Smyrna along with the other churches here, whose leaders have comforted me both physically and spiritually. My bonds, which I bear for Jesus, urge you to stay united in prayer and harmony. Let each of you, especially the presbyters, honor and support the bishop for the glory of the Father and Jesus Christ. I ask you to heed my words so that my writing does not become a witness against you. Pray for me, as I need your love and God's mercy to fulfill my purpose and not be found unworthy.

{13:1} The love of the Smyrnaeans and Ephesians greets you. Remember our Church in Syria, from which I am unworthy to bear the name. Farewell in the Lord Jesus, remaining obedient to your bishop, presbyters, and deacons, and loving one another wholeheartedly. My spirit greets you not only now but also in eternity, as I face the dangers before me. May the Father of Jesus Christ fulfill both your prayers and mine, that we may be found blameless. May I have joy in you through the Lord.

The Epistle of Ignatius to the Romans

{1:1} Through prayer, I have been blessed with the chance to see your faces, which is more than I could have hoped. As a prisoner for Christ, I long to greet you, if God wills it that I may reach the end faithfully. My journey started well, and I pray for grace to stay strong until the end. Yet, I fear that your love for me might cause you to intervene. While it is easy for you to act as you wish, my path to God becomes difficult if you save me out of compassion for the flesh.

{2:1} My goal is to please God, not people, just as you strive to do. This moment may be my only chance to reach God through martyrdom, and if you remain silent, you'll allow me this honor. If you protect me, I will again have to face this struggle. Please do not grant me any greater kindness than letting me be a sacrifice to God while the opportunity exists. Then, in love, you can praise the Father through Jesus Christ, thanking Him for deeming the bishop of Syria worthy to come from the east to the west to become a martyr. It is a privilege to leave this world for God, so that I may rise to Him.

{3:1} You have taught others and never held envy in your hearts. Now, I ask that your actions reflect what you have instructed. Pray for my inner and outer strength so that I may truly live as a Christian, not just in name. If I am proven to be a Christian by my actions, I will be faithful even after death, for nothing we see is eternal. "The visible things are temporary, but the invisible are eternal." Jesus Christ, who is now with the Father, is revealed even more in glory, for true Christianity is not hidden but is a powerful witness.

{4:1} I am writing to all churches, asking that they let me die willingly for God, unless you stop me. Do not show me unhelpful kindness. Let me be food for the wild beasts that will bring me to God. I am like God's wheat, and I will be ground by their teeth to become the pure bread of Christ. Encourage the beasts to consume me entirely so that no trace of my body remains, allowing me to rest in Christ without being a burden to anyone. Only then will I be a true disciple of Jesus, when the world sees nothing of my body. Pray that these creatures will complete my offering to God. I do not command like Peter or Paul; they were apostles, free to serve God, while I am still learning as His servant. But when I suffer, I will be freed in Christ, and for now, I desire nothing worldly.

{5:1} From Syria to Rome, I am in constant struggle, facing both hardships and soldiers who guard me harshly, yet this teaches me more about following Christ. May I find joy in the wild beasts awaiting me, and may they be eager to devour me. If they hesitate, I will urge them on. Forgive me for saying this; I know what brings me closer to God. Now I truly begin to be a disciple. No visible or invisible force should prevent me from reaching Christ. Let fire, the cross, wild beasts, torture, dismemberment, and all the torments of the devil come upon me—only let me reach Jesus Christ.

{6:1} Nothing in this world can compare to my desire for Christ. It is better for me to die for Him than to gain all the kingdoms of earth. "What does it profit a man to gain the whole world and lose his soul?" I seek the One who died and rose for us, my eternal reward. Forgive me, my brothers; do not hold me back from true life. Let me belong to God, not to this world. Allow me to enter the light and become truly a man of God. Imitate God's suffering, if He lives in you, and understand my heart in this.

{7:1} The ruler of this world tries to lead me away from God. Do not help him, but support me in my journey to God. Do not love both Jesus and the world. If I were with you, I would encourage you not to hinder me. Although I am alive as I write, I am eager for the end. My love for Christ has been crucified; no worldly passion remains, only a divine desire calling me to the Father. I crave not earthly food but the bread of God, the flesh of Jesus, and the drink of His blood, which is eternal life and love.

{8:1} I no longer wish to live as before, and my wish will be granted if you allow it. "I am crucified with Christ; it is no longer I who live, but Christ lives in me." I ask you, in this brief letter, do not deny me this. Believe me when I say I love Jesus, who gave Himself for me. "What shall I return to the Lord for all His goodness?" God, the Father, and our Lord Jesus will reveal this truth to you. Pray with me that I may fulfill my purpose by the Holy Spirit. I write not by fleshly desires, but by God's will. If I suffer, it is your love; if not, it is your rejection.

{9:1} Remember in your prayers the Church in Syria, which now has the Lord as its shepherd in my place, for He says, "I am the good Shepherd." He alone will care for it, just as you love Him. I am unworthy to be counted among them, feeling like the last and least, born out of time, but hoping for mercy as I seek God. My spirit greets you, as do the churches that have welcomed me in Jesus' name, treating me as more than a mere visitor. Even those distant have helped me along my journey, city by city.

{10:1} I write these things to you from Smyrna, through the Ephesians, who are blessed. With me here is Crocus, dearly loved. Those who went ahead of me from Syria to Rome, for God's glory, are known to you. Greet them, for they are worthy of honor from both God and you; provide for them in all ways. I wrote this letter on the day before the ninth of the Kalends of September (August 23). May you remain in the patience of Jesus Christ to the end. Amen.

The Epistle of Ignatius to the Philadelphians

{1:1} I know that your bishop did not take on his role by his own ambition, nor by human appointment, nor out of vanity. Rather, he serves through the love of God the Father and our Lord Jesus Christ. His gentle spirit and ability to achieve much through quiet strength amaze me. He follows God's commandments as a harp is tuned to its strings. My soul is joyful, seeing his devotion to God, knowing it is both virtuous and steadfast. His patience and peace remind me of the boundless meekness of God.

{2:1} Therefore, as children of light and truth, avoid divisions and harmful teachings. Where your shepherd is, there should you gather as sheep. Many wolves may seem trustworthy and use deceptive charms to lead those who seek God astray, but these imposters have no place in your unity. In your unity, heresies and deceitful influences will find no foothold.

{3:1} Keep yourselves away from those whom Christ has not guided but who follow the evil destroyer. They are not planted by the Father but are the seed of the wicked one. I don't say this because I see division among you, but to prepare you, as God's children, to recognize danger. All who belong to Christ stay close to the bishop; those who stray, forming alliances with the wicked, will be cut off with them. They are not Christ's planting but are enemies' seeds. May your faithful, gentle bishop's prayers protect you from them. Welcome back those who repent and seek unity, showing them kindness, so they may be freed from the devil's trap and gain eternal salvation in Christ. If anyone follows those who abandon truth, he won't inherit God's kingdom. Stand apart from false teachers and don't be deceived, even if it's someone close to you. Scripture says, "Spare them not." Hate those who oppose God, but I don't mean to harm them. Instead, regard them as adversaries and keep a distance, while gently urging them to repent, if they are willing. God desires all to be saved and to know the truth. He shows kindness, making the sun rise on both good and evil. He asks us to be perfect, just as our heavenly Father is perfect.

{4:1} Be careful to keep a single Eucharist, for there is one body of our Lord Jesus Christ and one cup to signify His unity. Just as there is one altar, there is also one bishop, along with the presbytery and deacons, my fellow servants. Let everything you do be according to God's will.

{5:1} My dear friends, my love for you grows, and I rejoice greatly for your safety. But this is Christ's work through me, and I fear all the more because I am not yet complete. Your prayers will help perfect me, that I might reach what I was called for. I turn to the Gospel as to Christ's body, and to the apostles as the Church's presbytery. I love the prophets too, as they announced Christ and share the same Spirit as the apostles. Just as false prophets drew evil spirits, so did the true prophets and apostles receive the Holy Spirit. There is one God in both Old & New Testaments, one Mediator & one Comforter, present from Moses to the apostles. All saints were saved by Christ, awaiting Him. They were righteous, full of love, honored in the Gospel of our shared hope.

{6:1} Don't listen to anyone preaching Jewish law. It is better to hear Christian truth even from someone circumcised than to learn Judaism from one who isn't. Those who deny Christ are like tombs, holding only the names of the dead. If anyone teaches Christ yet denies God as Creator, he's a liar, as Jesus said of the devil. Those who deny the Incarnation are not disciples of the Holy Spirit but followers of Simon Magus. Keep yourselves strong in unity and undivided in heart. I thank God that my conscience toward you is clear, and no one can say I have burdened them. May this be true for all I have spoken to.

{7:1} Even if some tried to deceive me, the Spirit, which is from God, cannot be misled. It sees where it comes from and where it goes and discerns hidden motives. When I was with you, I loudly urged you to honor your bishop, presbytery, and deacons. Some suspected I knew about divisions among you, but I did not. I acted only by the Spirit's guidance, urging you to act in unity, to keep your bodies as God's temples, and to avoid division, following Jesus as He follows the Father.

{8:1} I did my part as one devoted to unity, reminding you that where there is discord, God cannot dwell. God forgives all who return to unity with Christ and their bishop. May Christ free you from all sin. Do nothing from strife but follow Christ's teaching. Some say they'll only believe the Gospel if it's in written records. For me, the cross and resurrection of Christ are my archives, and my hope rests in these truths. The Spirit surpasses any earthly archive. Rejecting Christ is as harmful as "kicking against the goads," rejecting Him and the apostles.

{9:1} Priests and ministers are good, but Christ, the High Priest, is greater, given God's mysteries. The Comforter is holy, and Christ is the Word, leading all to the Father. Abraham, Isaac, Jacob, Moses, and the prophets entered God's kingdom, as did the apostles, with the Church, which He redeemed with His blood. This unity points to one God, while the Gospel reveals Jesus's life, death, and resurrection, fulfilling the prophets' words, "He shall be the expectation of the Gentiles." We are to baptize all nations in the name of the Father, Son, and Holy Spirit. The law, prophets, and apostles all serve the truth, as long as we love one another.

{10:1} Because of your prayers and compassion in Christ, I hear the Church in Antioch now has peace. As a Church of God, it would honor you to send a bishop to them to represent you and glorify God. Blessed is he who serves in this way for Christ. If you are willing, you can act for God's sake, as neighboring churches have done, sending bishops, presbyters, or deacons to serve.

{11:1} Philo, a Cilician deacon, continues to minister with me, along with Gaius and Agathopus, who followed me from Syria, not fearing danger. They testify on your behalf, and I thank God you welcomed them. May Christ forgive those who dishonored them, for God desires repentance. The brothers in Troas greet you, as do I, through Burrhus, sent by the Ephesians and Smyrnaeans as a sign of respect. May the Lord Jesus Christ bless them in faith, love, and unity. Farewell in Christ, our hope, through the Holy Spirit.

The Epistle of Ignatius to the Smyrnaeans

{1:1} I thank God, the Father of our Lord Jesus Christ, for the wisdom He has given you. I see your faith is solid, like you are anchored to the cross of Jesus, both in body and spirit, and grounded in love through His blood. You truly believe that Jesus is the Son of God, the "firstborn of all creation," God's only Son. Born of the Virgin Mary from the line of David, baptized by John to fulfill righteousness, He lived a sinless life and was nailed to the cross under Pontius Pilate and Herod. From His blessed sacrifice, we gain life, and through His resurrection, He established salvation for all faithful followers, Jews and Gentiles alike, uniting us in one body, His Church.

{2:1} Jesus suffered all these things for us, not just in appearance, but truly. He died and rose again in reality, not just in outward show. Yet some deny this, being ashamed of human weakness, the cross, and death itself, claiming He only appeared to suffer. They ignore His words, "The Word was made flesh," "Destroy this temple, and I will raise it up in three days," and "If I am lifted up, I will draw all to Myself." The Word took on flesh, fulfilling, "Wisdom built a house." On the third day, He rose, just as He promised. When He was lifted on the cross, like Moses' bronze serpent, He drew all people to Him for salvation.

{3:1} Jesus had a real body, both in His birth and crucifixion, and He retains that body after His resurrection. He appeared to Peter and others, saying, "Touch Me and see, for a spirit does not have flesh and bones as I do." He told Thomas, "Put your finger here;

touch My side," and Thomas responded, "My Lord and my God!" They saw His risen body and gladly faced death themselves, knowing His resurrection was true. For forty days, He ate and drank with them, proving His life beyond death. Then He was taken up in their sight, promising to return in the same way. If He were to return without a body, how could those who pierced Him see and mourn? Spirits have no form, but Christ will come again as He left—bodily and visibly.

{4:1} I share this with you, beloved, because I know you believe as I do. Yet I caution you against those who, like wolves in sheep's clothing, seek to deceive. Avoid them & pray they may repent. If Christ suffered only in appearance, then I also am bound only in appearance. But no, I truly endure sufferings for Christ, strengthened by Him to face all things in reality, not merely in name.

{5:1} Some deny Him, or rather, they have been denied by Him, choosing death over truth. They are neither persuaded by the prophets, the law, the Gospel, nor by our own suffering. They think our faith, like theirs, is empty, denying that Christ had a true body. But those who do not confess this have denied Him and chosen death. I have not named them here, as they are unbelievers. May they find repentance and return to faith in Christ's passion, for His suffering is our hope of resurrection.

{6:1} Let no one deceive themselves. All creation, even the angels and rulers, visible and invisible, if they reject the blood of Christ, will face judgment. "Whoever can accept this, let them accept it." Pride and high status mean nothing without faith and love, which are above all things. Beware those who oppose the grace given to us in Christ. They show no love, no care for widows, orphans, or those in need. Whether poor or rich, master or servant, everyone matters to God. The essentials are faith in God, hope in Christ, and love for God and neighbor. Jesus said, "Love God with all your heart and your neighbor as yourself." Those who teach otherwise deny the God of love, holding only to things of this world and scorning those who suffer.

{7:1} These heretics avoid the Eucharist and prayer because they deny that the Eucharist is truly the body of Christ, which suffered for our sins and was raised by the Father. Those who reject this gift risk their own death in disbelief. Stay far from them; don't associate with them, but hold to the prophets and, most of all, the Gospel, where Christ's suffering and resurrection are clearly revealed. Avoid division, as it is the root of all evil. These heretics despise the cross and mock the resurrection, following the spirit of rebellion from whom Christ came to save us.

{8:1} Follow your bishop as Christ follows the Father, and your presbyters as the apostles. Honor your deacons, for they serve as God's ministers. Let no one do anything related to the Church without the bishop's approval. The true Eucharist is one celebrated by the bishop or someone he delegates. Where the bishop is, there is the Church, just as where Jesus is, there is the universal Church. No baptisms or love feasts should occur without the bishop's oversight so that all may be done rightly and in unity.

{9:1} It is only fitting to honor both God and the bishop. Anyone who honors the bishop honors God; anyone who acts without the bishop's knowledge serves the devil. May you be blessed with grace in all things, for you have encouraged me, and Jesus will refresh you in return. Your love has been constant, whether I am with you or apart. May God reward you, as you endure all things for His sake.

{10:1} You have been generous in receiving Philo, Gaius, and Agathopus, who follow Christ and bless the Lord for your hospitality. None of your kindness will go unnoticed by God. "May the Lord grant you mercy on that day!" My spirit is grateful, and my chains, which you did not reject, will be a testament to your faith. Jesus Christ, our hope, will not be ashamed of you.

{11:1} Your prayers have brought peace to the Church in Antioch. Although I am bound from that city, I send greetings, though I am unworthy to bear its name. It is by God's grace I have been given this honor. To complete your work both in heaven and on earth, send a representative from your Church to celebrate with them, as they return to strength and unity. I suggest sending someone with a letter to rejoice with them in their peace and to give thanks that through your prayers, I have found refuge in Christ.

{12:1} The brothers in Troas send their love, as do the Ephesians and Burrhus, whom you sent to me. Burrhus has been a great support, and I pray others follow his example. I greet your honorable bishop, your respected presbyters, your deacons, and all of you in the name of Jesus Christ, in His flesh and blood, in His suffering and resurrection, united in spirit with God and each other. May grace, mercy, peace, and patience be yours forever.

{13:1} I greet the families of my brothers and sisters, along with their wives, children, and those who are virgins or widows. May you be strong in the Holy Spirit. Philo, my fellow servant, greets you as well. I also greet the household of Tavias, praying they remain strong in faith and love. I send my love to Alce, Daphnus, Eutecnus, and each of you by name. Farewell in the grace of God and our Lord Jesus Christ, filled with the Holy Spirit and divine wisdom.

The Epistle of Ignatius to the Polycarp

{1:1} I thank God that your faith is as firm as a rock. I praise Him for allowing me to see your faithful and steadfast spirit, which I hope to always experience in God. I urge you, by the grace within you, to continue your path and encourage others toward salvation. Stand strong in both body and spirit, always guarding unity, which is precious above all things. Be patient with everyone, just as the Lord is patient with you. Support each other with love, as you are already doing. Pray continually, seeking even greater understanding. Stay alert, with a spirit that is always watchful. Speak to each person as God enables you, and bear the weaknesses of others, like a true champion in the Christian life. The harder the challenge, the greater the reward.

{2:1} If you only love those who are easy to love, there's no special praise in that; seek to bring peace even to those who are difficult. Not every wound is healed the same way; sometimes the fiercest struggles are eased by gentle responses. Be as wise as a serpent but as innocent as a dove. You are made of both flesh and spirit so that you may gently handle the struggles you see, and pray for God's insight into the unseen. These times call for your leadership, like a pilot calling for the wind to guide him safely home. Be strong and steadfast in God, aiming for the prize of eternal life, which you truly believe in. I offer my soul and my chains for you, for I know how much you cherish them.

{3:1} Don't let those who preach strange teachings fill you with fear. Stand firm, like an anvil struck by many blows. A strong athlete doesn't only get hurt; they also win. We must endure all things for God's sake, just as He is patient with us, so that He may bring us into His kingdom. Add to your efforts, keep running with energy, and understand the times you are in. While you are on this journey, be victorious; this is your race, and there are crowns to win. Seek Christ, the Son of God, who existed before time but became visible in the flesh for our sake. Though He was untouched by suffering as God, He took on suffering as a man, experiencing everything for our salvation.

{4:1} Take care of the widows, protecting and befriending them after the Lord's example. Let nothing be done without your consent, but always seek God's approval, as I know you do. Meet together often and care for each other by name. Don't look down on slaves, but let them grow in humility for God's glory, so that they may gain a greater freedom from Him. Let them not seek release from service through worldly means but focus on the freedom that only God grants.

{5:1} Warn against all evil practices, and encourage others to openly discuss them. Tell my sisters in Christ to love the Lord and be faithful to their husbands in both body and spirit. Likewise, urge my brothers in Jesus' name to love their wives as Christ loves the Church. If anyone chooses to live in purity, let them do so humbly. But if they think themselves higher than others or the bishop, they lose their way. Marriages should be approved by the bishop, ensuring that they are based on God's will, not mere desire. Let all things be done for God's glory.

{6:1} Respect the bishop so that God will respect you. My heart is with those who submit to the bishop, presbyters, and deacons; may my place be among them in God's presence. Work together, run the race together, and endure together. Rest together and rise together as servants of God. Honor the One you serve, from whom you receive your reward. Let no one abandon their duties. Hold tightly to your baptism as your armor, your faith as your helmet, your love as your weapon, and patience as your shield. Let your good works earn you a worthy reward. Show patience to one another, as God does with you. I will always rejoice in you!

{7:1} Hearing that the Church in Antioch is at peace through your prayers gives me great encouragement. I can rest in God's care, praying that through my suffering, I may reach Him and be known as Christ's disciple. Dear Polycarp, blessed by God, gather a council and choose someone you trust and love to be a messenger for this task—to go to Syria and bear witness to your boundless love in Christ's name. A Christian does not live for themselves alone but must be ready to serve God always. This task belongs to both God and you, and I trust that, through grace, you are prepared for every good work in Him. Knowing your devotion to truth, I am confident in your zeal.

{8:1} As I couldn't write to every Church due to the need to sail quickly from Troas to Neapolis, I ask you, who understand God's purposes, to write to nearby Churches. Encourage them to act as you do, sending messengers if possible, or letters if not, so that all may know of your good work. You deserve this lasting honor. I send greetings to all by name, especially the family of Epitropus, his wife, and children. I greet Attalus, my dear friend, and the one chosen to go to Syria. May God's grace be with him forever and with Polycarp, who sends him. May you have joy forever in our Lord Jesus Christ, as you remain in God's protection. I also greet Alce, my beloved friend. Amen. May God's grace be with you. Farewell in the Lord.

The Epistle of Ignatius to the Polycarp

{1:1} Remembering your love and dedication to Christ, which you have shown toward us, we thought it right to write to you. You demonstrate a godly love for fellow believers, reminding you to keep walking in unity. "Speak with one voice, be of one mind, and live by the same rule of faith," as Paul advised. {1:2} For there is one God, the Father of Christ, "through whom all things come," one Lord Jesus Christ, "through whom all things exist," and one Holy Spirit, who inspired Moses, the prophets, and apostles. {1:3} There is also one baptism, uniting us with Christ's death, and one Church chosen by God. So, there should be one shared faith in Christ, for "there is one Lord, one faith, one baptism, one God and Father of all, who is above all, through all, and in all."

{2:1} There is one God and Father, not two or three; He alone is, with no other beside Him. "The Lord your God," Scripture says, "is one Lord." {2:2} Scripture also confirms that one Son exists: "the only-begotten Son," who is "in the Father's heart." Again, "One Lord Jesus Christ." {2:3} Likewise, there is one Holy Spirit, as Scripture says, "We were all called in one hope." {2:4} There are no three Fathers, Sons, or Spirits—only one Father, one Son, and one Holy Spirit. That's why Jesus sent the apostles to baptize "in the name of the Father, Son, and Holy Spirit"—not one person with three names, nor three beings who became incarnate, but three distinct Persons who share equal honor.

{3:1} Only the Son took on flesh—not the Father or the Spirit. He didn't appear as a mere vision; He truly "became flesh." {3:2} God's Wisdom "built a home" by becoming human, born to the Virgin Mary without human intervention. {3:3} "A virgin will conceive and bear a son." He truly grew, ate, drank, was crucified, died, and rose again. {3:4} Those who believe this are blessed. Those who deny it are cursed, like those who crucified Him, as Satan rejoices when people deny the cross. {3:5} Confessing the cross terrifies Satan, for it signifies his defeat.

{4:1} Satan, before Christ's crucifixion, urged the cross's preparation. He influenced Judas, the Pharisees, and others, {4:2} yet became troubled when the crucifixion drew near, urging Judas to hang himself. {4:3} He sought to halt the cross's completion—not out of remorse, but because he sensed his destruction was imminent. {4:4} The cross marked the beginning of his downfall. Now, he tries to make people deny Christ's humanity, {4:5} join the Jews in rejecting the cross, and embrace false teachings about Christ's body being an illusion. Satan's tactics are cunning, inconsistent, and full of ignorance.

{5:1} Satan, if Christ were merely human, why deny His birth and call His suffering imaginary? {5:2} And if He is both God and man, why argue it's wrong to call Him "Lord of Glory"? {5:3} Christ, as both divine and human, fulfilled the Father's will, performed miracles, and revealed God's nature.

{6:1} Christ's miracles—raising the dead, healing the sick, turning water into wine—prove He is more than human. {6:2} Satan criticizes the Virgin's role, despite having publicly glorified shameful acts. Now, feigning modesty, he vilifies her purity. {6:3} Yet, all creation is good, though Satan, in his blindness, fails to understand this.

{7:1} Satan claims Christ couldn't be born of a virgin yet acknowledges His divine power. {7:2} But if Christ is Almighty, then who commands Him? {7:3} Satan's inconsistencies show his ignorance of Christ's true nature and mission.

{8:1} Satan missed many signs: Mary's virginity, the Magi's visit, the angels' songs, and Christ's baptism. {8:2} Christ's life, including His growth, hunger, and weariness, all reflect His humanity, while His miracles affirm His divinity.

{9:1} Satan could not understand Christ's miraculous birth and mission. {9:2} Even after witnessing Christ's baptism, Satan tempted Him, unsure if He was truly the Son of God.

{10:1} Satan tried to lead Christ into pride, offering Him worldly power in exchange for worship. {10:2} But Christ, recognizing Satan's empty threats, rebuked him, knowing His mission and identity.

{11:1} Satan urged Christ to leap from the temple, quoting Scripture out of context, and claimed dominion over the world if Christ would worship him. {11:2} Christ resisted, aware of Satan's deceit.

{12:1} Rather than destroying Satan, Christ calmly dismissed him, saying, "Get away, Satan." {12:2} Christ knew who He was and refused to worship anyone but the Father, whom Satan had rejected.

{13:1} Out of love, I write to remind you to be obedient to your leaders and love one another. Husbands, love your wives; wives, love your husbands. {13:2} Those who choose celibacy should remain humble. {13:3} Honor the holy days, fast regularly, and give to the poor. Observe the Lord's Day and avoid fasting on it, except during special observances.

{14:1} Pray for the Church in Antioch, where I am held as a prisoner on my way to Rome. {14:2} I greet Bishop Polycarp, Bishop Vitalius, and all the deacons and presbyters, and my fellow servants. {14:3} Avoid participating in Jewish observances, as those who do so associate with those who opposed Christ.

{15:1} Philo and Agathopus, the deacons, send their greetings. I greet all the believers, from the youngest to the eldest. {15:2} I am sending this letter with Euphanius, a devoted reader I met as he prepared to sail. {15:3} Remember my chains and pray that I may be made complete in Christ. May you have peace in body, soul, and spirit. Stand firm in truth, avoiding the influence of those who distort the Word of God. May the grace of our Lord Jesus Christ strengthen you.

The Epistle of Polycarp to the Philippians

{1:1} I am filled with joy in our Lord Jesus Christ because of your unwavering love, shown through your support of those who are imprisoned for their faith. Your faith is a solid foundation, rooted deeply and bearing fruit for Jesus Christ, who suffered for our sins unto death, but whom God raised from the dead, freeing Him from the grip of the grave. Even though you cannot see Him, you believe and rejoice with an indescribable joy, knowing that salvation comes by grace, not through works, but through God's will in Christ Jesus.

{2:1} So, prepare yourselves and serve the Lord in fear and truth, as people who have turned away from empty talk and error, placing their faith in Him who raised Jesus from the dead and gave Him glory at His right hand. Everything in heaven and earth is subject to Him; every spirit serves Him, and He will come to judge the living and the dead. God will hold accountable those who do not believe in Him. Yet He will also raise us up if we follow His commandments, love what He loved, and keep away from unrighteousness, greed, dishonesty & revenge, remembering His teaching: "Judge not, so you are not judged; forgive, so you will be forgiven; be merciful to obtain mercy; and remember, 'Blessed are the poor & the persecuted, for theirs is the kingdom of God.'"

{3:1} Brothers and sisters, I write to you about righteousness not because I am qualified but because you asked me to. I do not claim to match the wisdom of the great apostle Paul, who taught you the word of truth so steadfastly. He also wrote to you, and if you study his letter carefully, you will grow in the faith that you received. This faith, paired with hope and grounded in love for God, Christ, and others, is the foundation of all things. Anyone who is filled with these virtues fulfills the call to righteousness, for love itself keeps us far from sin.

{4:1} "The love of money is the root of all evils." Remembering that "we brought nothing into this world, and we can take nothing out," let us live by the armor of righteousness, teaching ourselves first to follow God's commandments. Then, encourage your wives to walk in faith, love, and purity, loving their husbands sincerely and all others with respect. Let them raise their children with the knowledge and reverence of God. Guide the widows to be wise in faith, always praying and refraining from gossip, dishonesty, and greed. They serve as altars of God, who sees all things and knows every hidden thought.

{5:1} Knowing that "God is not mocked," we must walk worthily of His commandments. Deacons, in particular, should be blameless, serving God and Christ, not merely men. They must not gossip, speak dishonestly, or be greedy but should live with compassion, diligence, and faithfulness, following the truth of the Lord, who served all. If we please Him in this life, He has promised us eternal life in the world to come, where "we shall reign with Him" if we live faithfully. Young men, too, should live blamelessly, protecting their purity and resisting temptation, since "every lust battles against the spirit," and no one who lives immorally will inherit God's kingdom. Everyone should follow the presbyters and deacons, as they represent God and Christ, and virgins must live in purity with a clear conscience.

{6:1} Let the presbyters show compassion to all, guiding those who stray, caring for the sick, and supporting the widows, orphans, and poor. They should act honorably, avoiding anger, favoritism, and unjust judgments, and stay far from greed, remembering that we are all sinners. If we ask the Lord to forgive us, we should also forgive others, for we are before the Lord and will each give an account of ourselves. Let us serve Him with reverence, following the commands of Jesus, the apostles, and prophets. Seek what is good, avoid wrongdoing, and stay away from false believers and those who lead others astray with hypocrisy.

{7:1} "Whoever does not confess that Jesus Christ came in the flesh is antichrist." And anyone who denies the power of the cross is from the devil. Those who twist God's teachings to suit their desires and deny the resurrection and judgment belong to Satan. So, let's turn away from false teachings and return to the truth handed down from the beginning. Watch and pray, fasting as you ask the all-seeing God, "Do not lead us into temptation," for, as Jesus said, "The spirit is willing, but the flesh is weak."

{8:1} Let us hold tightly to our hope in Jesus Christ, "who bore our sins on the cross" and "did no sin, nor was any deceit in His mouth." He endured everything so that we might live through Him. Let us imitate His patience, and if we suffer in His name, let us glorify Him, for He has shown us this example in Himself, which we have believed to be true.

{9:1} I urge you all to follow the word of righteousness and practice patience, remembering the examples of Ignatius, Zosimus, Rufus, and others among you, as well as Paul and the apostles. They did not run in vain but lived in faith and righteousness and now rest in the Lord, having suffered for Him. They did not love this world but loved Him who died and was raised for our sake.

{10:1} Stand firm in these teachings and follow Christ's example, remaining steady in your faith, loving one another, united in truth, and treating each other with humility. Help each other when you can, remembering, "Charity saves from death." Be blameless before others so that your good works will be known, and the Lord's name will not be dishonored. Teach sobriety to all and live by it yourself.

{11:1} I am deeply saddened by Valens, who was once a presbyter among you, as he has not fully understood the calling he received in the Church. I urge you to avoid greed and to live with chastity and truthfulness, avoiding "every form of evil." For if someone cannot control themselves, how can they teach others? A person given to greed falls into idolatry and is judged like an unbeliever. We know that "the saints will judge the world," as Paul teaches. I have heard nothing but good of you, among whom Paul labored and who are praised in the beginning of his letter. He commended you in all the Churches, and I feel sorrow for Valens and his wife. May the Lord grant them true repentance. Be compassionate with them, not treating them as enemies but calling them back as lost members, so that you may save your whole community.

{12:1} I trust that you are well-grounded in the Scriptures and know all things hidden. It is written, "Be angry and sin not," and "Let not the sun go down on your anger." Blessed is the one who remembers this, as I believe you do. May the God and Father of our Lord Jesus Christ, and Jesus Christ Himself, who is our eternal High Priest, build you up in faith, truth, gentleness, patience, forbearance, and purity. May He grant you and all believers a place among His saints. Pray for everyone, including kings, rulers, and those who persecute and hate you, and even for those who oppose the cross, so that your lives may show good fruit, and you may be complete in Him.

{13:1} Both you and Ignatius asked that, if anyone travels to Syria, they take your letter with them. I will honor this request if I find the opportunity, whether in person or through another, to fulfill your desire. We have sent you Ignatius' letters, as you asked, including the ones he wrote to us and the others in our care. These letters are valuable, as they discuss faith, patience, and all things that build up our lives in Christ. If you learn any new information about Ignatius & those with him, please share it with us.

{14:1} I am sending this letter to you through Crescens, who I continue to commend. He has served well among us, and I believe he will do the same for you. Welcome his sister, too, when she arrives. Be safe in the Lord Jesus Christ. May His grace be with you all.

The Epistle of Peter to the Philip

{1:1} "Peter, an apostle of Jesus Christ, to Philip, our beloved brother and fellow apostle, and to the brethren with you: greetings! {1:2} Brother, I want you to know that we received instructions from our Lord and Savior to come together to teach and preach the salvation promised to us by Jesus Christ. {1:3} However, you have been distant from us and did not desire to gather with us or discuss how we might organize ourselves to share the good news. {1:4} So, would it be agreeable to you, brother, to join us according to the command of our Lord Jesus?" {1:5} When Philip received and read Peter's letter, he was filled with joy and went to Peter with gladness. {1:6} Then Peter gathered the other apostles, and they went to the Mount of Olives, the place where they used to gather with Christ when He was among them in the body. {1:7} There, the apostles knelt down and prayed together, saying, "Father, Father, Father of the light, who holds all things pure and incorruptible, hear us, just as You took pleasure in Your holy servant, Jesus Christ, who became our light in the darkness. Hear us, Father!"

{2:1} They prayed again, saying, "Son of life and Son of immortality, who dwells in light, Christ of immortality, our Redeemer, grant us strength, for our lives are in danger!" {2:2} Suddenly, a great light appeared, illuminating the mountain, and a voice spoke to them, "Listen to my words, so that I may speak to you. Why do you seek answers from Me? I am Jesus Christ, who is with you forever." {2:3} The apostles replied, "Lord, we want to understand the lack in the aeons and their fullness. {2:4} Why are we held in this world, how did we come here, how will we depart, and how do we have the courage to speak boldly? And why do the powers oppose us?" {2:5} A voice from the light answered, "You are witnesses that I spoke these things to you before. But because of your doubt, I will explain again. {2:6} Concerning the deficiency of the aeons, this lack arose when the mother's disobedience and folly emerged without the Father's command. {2:7} She tried to create aeons on her own, and her arrogance followed. She left a part of herself, which the Arrogant One seized, creating the deficiency. {2:8} The Arrogant One used this part to bring forth powers and authorities, and he encased them in aeons that are spiritually dead. {2:9} The powers of this world rejoiced in their own creation, but they don't know the pre-existent Father, for they are strangers to Him. {2:10} Yet, they gave power to the Arrogant One and worshiped him, which made him proud and envious. He sought to create an image of himself and ordered his powers to form mortal bodies, which came from a distorted image of what he saw."

{3:1} "Concerning the fullness: I came down in a body for the sake of the fallen seed, entering their mortal form, though they mistook me for a mortal man. {3:2} I spoke to those who are mine, and they listened, as you are listening now. I gave them authority to inherit their true place as children of the Father. {3:3} When he was filled with salvation, what was lacking became complete, and thus he became a pleroma." {3:4} "You are held here because you belong to Me. {3:5} When you remove what is corrupt from yourselves, you will shine among mortals as lights." {3:6} "You will struggle against the powers because they have no rest like you do, and they do not want you to be saved."

{4:1} The apostles prayed again, saying, "Lord, how shall we fight the archons, for they are greater than us?" {4:2} A voice from the light answered, "You will fight them by resisting the darkness within yourselves. {4:3} Gather and teach salvation with the promise I have given. Be clothed in the power of My Father, and make your prayers known. {4:4} The Father will support you as He did by sending me. Do not fear, for I am with you always, as I told you when I was with you in the body." {4:5} Then there was thunder and lightning from heaven, and the light that had appeared to them ascended into the heavens.

{5:1} The apostles gave thanks to the Lord with many blessings and returned to Jerusalem. {5:2} Along the way, they spoke to each other about the light they had seen, and one remarked about the Lord, "If He, our Lord, suffered, then how much more must we endure?" {5:3} Peter answered, "He suffered on our behalf, and it is necessary for us to suffer because of our own limitations." {5:4} Then a voice spoke to them, saying, "I have told you many times: it is necessary for you to suffer. {5:5} You will be brought before synagogues and rulers, so that you may suffer. But anyone who does not suffer, or who does not honor the Father, will..." {5:6} The apostles rejoiced and returned to Jerusalem. They entered the temple, teaching salvation in Jesus Christ's name and healing many people.

{6:1} Peter began to speak to the disciples, "Did Jesus, when He was in the body, reveal everything to us? For He came down from heaven, my brothers, listen to me." {6:2} Peter, filled with the Holy Spirit, continued, "Jesus, our light, came down, was crucified, crowned with thorns, dressed in purple, and nailed to the cross. He was buried in a tomb and rose from the dead. {6:3} My brothers, Jesus did not suffer for Himself but for us, bearing the transgression of our mother, and this is why He lived as we do. Jesus, the Son of the Father's immeasurable glory, is the source of our life. {6:4} My brothers, let us not follow those who are lawless but continue living with the law." {6:5} Peter then gathered the others, saying, "Lord Jesus Christ, our rest, grant us a spirit of understanding so we may perform miracles as You did."

{7:1} The apostles saw Jesus, and they were filled with the Holy Spirit, each performing healings. They then parted to preach about the Lord Jesus. They greeted each other, saying, "Amen." {7:2} Jesus appeared to them again, saying, "Peace to all of you and to everyone who believes in My name. {7:3} When you go out, may joy, grace, and strength be with you. Do not be afraid, for I am with you always." {7:4} The apostles then departed from one another to four corners of earth, empowered by Jesus to preach in peace.

The Epistle of Peter to the Clement

{1:1} Peter, a servant and apostle of Jesus Christ, to my beloved son Clement: grace and peace from God the Father and the Lord Jesus Christ be with you always. {1:2} Since it is fitting that those who have received the office of preaching the Gospel should be careful to teach it without error, I remind you, Clement, to continue in what I have delivered to you. {1:3} Do not add anything new, nor take anything away, but carefully hand down exactly what you have received from me and from the apostles who taught me. {1:4} For it was our Lord who commanded us, saying, "Freely you have received, freely give" {Matthew 10:8}, urging that no part of His teaching be distorted or lost. {1:5} Thus, in everything, hold firmly to the words that have been taught to you, remembering that we are but messengers of the truth, not authors of it.

{2:1} And now, my beloved son, I commend you to God, that He may strengthen you to fulfill this duty. {2:2} For the task is not easy, and many will try to twist and challenge what you proclaim. {2:3} Some will be deceived by the philosophies and traditions of men; others by fables and idle speculations; still others by false prophets claiming to speak from God. {2:4} But you, my son, must avoid these snares, keeping your heart and mind focused on the truth of the Gospel. {2:5} Do not be swayed by worldly wisdom or enticed by arguments that seek to deny the power and wisdom of God. {2:6} For what we preach is not human wisdom, but divine revelation, and this must be preserved as we received it.

{3:1} Remember, also, that your conduct must be blameless, that you may be an example to all who believe. {3:2} For a teacher must not only speak the truth, but live by it, so that his words do not seem hollow or hypocritical. {3:3} Be humble, showing patience and kindness to all, even to those who oppose you. {3:4} Do not seek the praise of men, nor be eager for wealth, but let your only desire be to serve God and His people. {3:5} For the Lord has chosen us, not to rule, but to serve, and as He washed the feet of His disciples, so also should we serve with humility.

{4:1} Furthermore, be diligent in prayer, asking always for wisdom and strength to fulfill the ministry entrusted to you. {4:2} Pray for those you lead, that they may grow in faith and understanding, and pray for your opponents, that they may come to know the truth. {4:3} Remember that God alone gives the increase, and that it is only by His grace that anyone comes to faith. {4:4} Therefore, be diligent in prayer and in the Word, that you may be equipped for every good work.

{5:1} Finally, my son, be strong and courageous. {5:2} Do not be afraid when opposition arises, for we know that we follow a crucified Savior, who promised that we would face persecution for His name's sake. {5:3} But do not lose heart, for He also promised to be with us always, even to the end of the age. {5:4} Be faithful, therefore, in all things, and when your course is finished, you will receive the crown of life which the Lord has promised to those who love Him.

{6:1} I write these things to you, my beloved son, not only as reminders but as commandments. {6:2} Follow them closely, as you would follow Christ Himself, and may the God of peace guard you and keep you blameless until the day of His coming. {6:3} Greet all the brothers and sisters in the faith, and may the grace of our Lord Jesus Christ be with you all. Amen.

The Epistle of Paul to the Laodiceans

{1:1} Paul, an apostle, chosen not by human decision nor through any man, but directly by Jesus Christ, writes to the brothers and sisters in Laodicea. {1:2} Grace and peace to you from God our Father and the Lord Jesus Christ. {1:3} I thank Christ in all my prayers for you, grateful that you continue in Him and remain faithful in His works, looking forward to the promise of the final judgment day. {1:4} Do not be shaken by the empty words of some who creep in to pull you away from the truth of the Gospel I preached to you. {1:5} And may God grant that those with me continue their ministry, working to spread the truth of the Gospel, doing good, and bringing the work of salvation that leads to eternal life. {1:6} My chains are seen by everyone, for I suffer these things in Christ; yet I rejoice and find joy in this. {1:7} Through your prayers and the ministry of the Holy Spirit, this becomes my everlasting salvation, whether it be through life or death. {1:8} For indeed, to me, life is in Christ, and to die is a gain. {1:9} May He also work His mercy in you, so that you may have the same love and be united in one spirit. {1:10} Therefore, dear friends, hold firmly to what you heard in my presence, and live with reverence for God, for this will lead to eternal life. {1:11} For it is God who works within you. {1:12} Whatever you do, do it sincerely and without any second thoughts. {1:13} And finally, dear ones, rejoice in Christ and beware of those who seek dishonest gain. {1:14} Let all your requests be openly presented before God, and stay steadfast in the mind of Christ. {1:15} Seek to do everything that is true, right, noble, just, and worthy of love. {1:16} Hold tightly in your heart what you have learned and received. {1:17} And may peace be with you. {1:18} The saints greet you. {1:19} May the grace of our Lord Jesus be with your spirit. {1:20} Ensure that this letter is read to those in Colossae, and that you read their letter as well.

The Epistle of Paul to the Seneca

{1:1} Seneca to Paul, greetings. Paul, I believe you've heard about my recent conversation with Lucilius on the secret teachings and other matters. Some of your followers joined us while we were at Sallust's Gardens. We wished you could have been there; your presence was missed. We discussed your letters to various cities, which promote the moral life with powerful advice. These words, I believe, aren't just from you, but through you, and sometimes both. They are so profound that entire generations would struggle to fully live by them. Be well, brother.

{2:1} Paul to Seneca, greetings. I received your letter with great joy and would have replied sooner if I'd had the young man with me who was meant to deliver it. I know you understand the importance of timing and discretion. Please, don't think I'm neglecting you; I'm honoring your dignity. Your appreciation of my letters means a lot coming from a man of your wisdom and position. May you remain in good health.

{3:1} Seneca to Paul, greetings. I've compiled some writings into a book, divided properly. If fortune allows, I plan to read them to Caesar, perhaps with you there. If not, we'll arrange another time for you to review them with me. I wouldn't present this work without your input, if I could do so safely. Please know you are always in my thoughts. Farewell, dear Paul.

{4:1} Paul to Seneca, greetings. When I hear your letters, I feel as if you are present with us. I look forward to when we can meet face to face. I wish you good health.

{5:1} Seneca to Paul, greetings. We are saddened by your absence. What keeps you away? If it's the empress's anger over your departure from old ways & your influence, perhaps we can appeal to her, explaining it was a thoughtful decision, not a rash one.

{6:1} Paul to Seneca and Lucilius, greetings. I cannot write about the subject you mentioned with pen and ink, as both can reveal too much. Some among you understand me, and I trust they will be discreet. Honor should be shown to all, especially those easily offended. Patience will help us overcome them, provided they are capable of remorse. Farewell.

{7:1} Seneca to Paul and Theophilus, greetings. I'm deeply impressed with your letters to the Galatians, Corinthians, and Achaeans, which reveal divine inspiration. You have a holy spirit within you that conveys profound thoughts. I advise you to polish your writing style to match the majesty of your message. I must also tell you, Caesar himself was moved by your words. When I read him your introduction on virtue, he remarked that it was astonishing for someone without formal education to think this way. I explained that sometimes the gods speak through the simple rather than the learned. When I shared a similar story about a rustic who saw divine beings, he was convinced. Farewell.

{8:1} Paul to Seneca, greetings. I understand Caesar has an interest in spiritual wonders, but I must caution you about sharing things outside his belief system, even with the best intentions. As a follower of his own gods, he may not understand, and I would not want you to risk offending the empress in your support of me. Her anger won't harm us, nor would her favor benefit us. As a queen, she may ignore this, but as a woman, she may take offense. Farewell.

{9:1} Seneca to Paul, greetings. I understand your concerns & they arise less from my letter than from the reality that many people resist true wisdom. If I have acted rashly, please forgive me. I've sent you a book on the art of refined speech. Farewell, dear Paul.

{10:1} Paul to Seneca, greetings. I'm aware that when I write without placing your name before mine, I make an error contrary to our customs. I must remember, as I often say, to honor all people in their rank. Roman law respects the Senate's dignity, and I should place your name first when addressing you, following proper order. Farewell, honored teacher. Written on the fifth day before the Kalends of July, in the year of Nero's fourth consulship and Messala's.

{11:1} Seneca to Paul, greetings. Dearest Paul, I am truly fortunate that someone as esteemed and beloved as you is united with me in friendship. You, the pinnacle of wisdom, should know how grateful I am for this bond. Do not think it beneath you to place your name first on letters, as it would feel like a test of loyalty rather than a friendly jest. After all, you are a Roman citizen. I wish I could share your rank, and you could share mine. Farewell, dear Paul. Written ten days before the Kalends of April, during the consulship of Apronianus and Capito.

{12:1} Seneca to Paul, greetings. My dear Paul, I am troubled by the unjust suffering of your innocent followers and how the public blames you for every misfortune in the city. But we must endure these times until better days come. History has seen tyrants like Alexander, Dionysius, and Caesar, who ruled by their own will. Rome suffers from terrible fires, and Christians and Jews are falsely accused of causing them. Those who spread these lies will face justice. Until then, we must remain patient. Farewell, brother. Written five days before the Kalends of April, under the consulship of Frugi and Bassus.

{13:1} Seneca to Paul, greetings. Much of your writing is profound, yet some of it is veiled in metaphor. I believe your ideas, powerful as they are, would benefit from a touch of refinement. Don't fear that doing so would weaken your message, as many claim. I encourage you to embrace a polished Latin style, to give the greatness of your message the treatment it deserves. Farewell. Written on the day before the Nones of June, in the consulship of Leo and Sabinus (fictitious date).

{14:1} Paul to Seneca, greetings. Your insights are truly inspired, and I am honored to plant divine wisdom in such fertile ground. The truth I share is eternal, not subject to decay, and you have grasped it. I encourage you to go beyond worldly wisdom and share the pure teachings of Christ. It may be difficult to persuade some, but the word of God brings new life, creating an incorruptible spirit destined to return to God. Farewell, my dear Seneca. Written on the Kalends of August, in the consulship of Leo & Sabinus.

The Epistle of Jesus Christ and King Abgarus

{1:1} Abgarus Uchama, the ruler, writes to Jesus, the good Savior who has appeared in Jerusalem, with greetings. {1:2} I have heard about you and the healings you perform without the use of medicines or herbs. People say you give sight to the blind, help the lame walk, cleanse lepers, cast out evil spirits, and heal those suffering from long illnesses. It's even said that you raise the dead. {1:3} After hearing all this about you, I concluded that you must be either God, come down from heaven to do these works, or the Son of God who performs these miracles. {1:4} I am writing to ask if you would come to me and heal the affliction that I suffer from. I have also heard that some of the Jewish people speak against you and wish to harm you. I may have a small city, but it is respected, and there is room here for both of us.

{2:1} The response from Jesus, sent by Ananias the messenger, to Abgarus the ruler. {2:2} Blessed are you for believing in me even without having seen me. {2:3} For it is written about me, "Those who see me will not believe, and those who do not see me will believe and have life." {2:4} As for your request for me to come to you, I must complete the work for which I was sent. After I have fulfilled this mission, I will be taken back to the One who sent me. {2:5} After I am taken up, I will send one of my disciples to you to heal your affliction and bring life to you and those with you.

The Epistle of Herod to Pilate

HEROD TO PONTIUS PILATE, THE GOVERNOR OF JERUSALEM {1:1} Peace to you. {1:2} I am filled with deep anxiety, and I write to you in this distressing time, hoping that you, upon hearing my plight, will share in my sorrow. {1:3} My beloved daughter, Herodias, while playing upon a frozen pool, fell through the ice. The entire surface gave way, and while her body was submerged, her head was severed and left floating on the surface. {1:4} Now, her mother holds her head upon her lap, overwhelmed with grief, and my entire household is consumed by sorrow. {1:5} I had hoped to come to you to see this man, Jesus, and to hear his words, to understand whether they were indeed unlike any spoken by men. {1:6} I am certain that all the suffering I now face is retribution for my sins against John the Baptist and for the mockery I made of the Christ. In truth, I have spilled much innocent blood, and now I receive God's righteous judgment, for every man is repaid according to his deeds. {1:7} Since you were found worthy to see that Holy One, it would be just of you to pray on my behalf. {1:8} My son, Azbonius, is also now at the brink of death. {1:9} I, too, suffer greatly, afflicted with dropsy and plagued with distress, for I once persecuted the man who introduced baptism by water, John the Baptist. In this, the judgments of God are indeed righteous. {1:10} My wife, in her grief over our daughter, has now lost vision in her left eye, which I believe to be a consequence of our attempt to blind the Eye of Righteousness. For, as the Lord has spoken, there can be no peace for those who commit evil. {1:11} Already, great affliction has befallen the priests and the scribes, for they delivered into your hands the Just One. This marks the end of an age, as they allowed the Gentiles to inherit what was once ours. {1:12} The children of light shall be cast out, for they failed to heed the message concerning the Lord and his Son. {1:13} Therefore, prepare yourself, embracing righteousness with Procla, your wife, and remember Jesus both night and day; for the kingdom now belongs to you Gentiles, as we, the chosen people, have mocked the Holy One. {1:14} If it is at all within your power, Pilate, please see to it that my household is buried with dignity. It would be more fitting for you to carry out our burial rites than the priests, who, as the Scriptures foretell, shall soon meet their own judgment at the coming of Jesus Christ. {1:15} Farewell to you, and to Procla, your wife. {1:16} I send you my daughter's earrings and my own ring as a memorial of my passing, for even now, worms begin to consume my body. I suffer this temporal judgment, yet I fear the eternal judgment yet to come, for in both cases, we stand before the living God. The judgment of this world is but for a time, while that which follows shall last forever. End of the Letter to Pilate the Governor.

The Epistle of Pilate to Herod

PILATE TO HEROD THE TETRARCH {1:1} Peace to you. {1:2} Know this: on the day you delivered Jesus to me, I sought to absolve myself and demonstrated this by washing my hands, declaring my innocence regarding the one who rose from the grave three days after. I had followed your wish, for you wanted me to be complicit in his crucifixion. Now, I have learned from the soldiers and the guards at his tomb that he indeed rose from the dead. {1:3} I have confirmed their reports that he appeared in Galilee, in his same bodily form, with the same voice, teaching the same doctrine, and accompanied by his disciples. He changed in nothing but proclaimed boldly his resurrection and the promise of an everlasting kingdom. {1:4} Behold, heaven and earth rejoice, and my wife, Procla, now believes in the visions she had when you sent word for me to hand over Jesus to the people of Israel due to their hostility. {1:5} When Procla heard that Jesus had risen and was seen in Galilee, she took Longinus the centurion and twelve soldiers who had guarded the tomb and went to behold him, as though he were a wondrous sight. She saw him with his disciples. {1:6} As they stood watching in amazement, he looked upon them and said, "Do you believe in me? Procla, understand that in the covenant God made with the fathers, it is promised that every body that has perished will live through my death, which you have witnessed. And now, you see that I live, though you crucified me. I endured much suffering until I was laid in the tomb. But now, believe in my Father, the God who is within me. For I have broken the cords of death and shattered the gates of Sheol; my return shall come again." {1:7} When my wife Procla and the Romans heard these words, they returned to me in tears, deeply moved, as they too had opposed him and played a role in his unjust suffering. This news troubled me so that I lay on my bed in sorrow, put on mourning clothes, and took fifty Romans with Procla to journey with me to Galilee. {1:8} Along the way, I testified to this truth: that Herod persuaded me to act against my will, drawing me into his schemes and pressing me to condemn this Just One, the Lord of the just. As we neared him, Herod, there was a mighty voice from heaven, a powerful thunder, and the earth shook, filling the air with a fragrance more wondrous than anything perceived even in the temple of Jerusalem. {1:9} I stood there in awe, and the Lord saw me while he spoke with his disciples. In my heart, I prayed, for I knew it was he whom you had delivered to me—Lord of all creation. We all fell on our faces before him, and I cried out, "I have sinned, Lord, for I sat in judgment against you, the true avenger of justice. Now, I know that you are God, the Son of God. I saw only your humanity, but not your divinity. Herod, along with the people of Israel, pressed me to do you wrong. Have mercy on me, O God of Israel!" {1:10} In her deep anguish, my wife cried, "God of heaven and earth, God of Israel, do not judge me for the sins of Pontius Pilate, nor for the wickedness of the people of Israel, nor for the plots of the priests. Remember my husband in your mercy and glory!" {1:11} Then the Lord drew near and raised us, my wife and the Romans, from the ground, and I saw the scars of the cross upon him. He said, "What all the righteous fathers longed to see and never witnessed, has now come to pass in your time. The Lord of Time, the Son of Man, the Son of the Most High, who is eternal, has risen from the dead and is glorified by all creation, forever and ever."

{2:1} Justinus, a writer during the time of Augustus, Tiberius, and Gaius, recorded this: "Mary of Galilee, who bore Christ crucified in Jerusalem, was never with a man. Joseph remained committed to holiness, remaining without a wife, even with five sons from a previous marriage, and Mary stayed a virgin." {2:2} Theodorus wrote to me, Pilate, saying, "Who was this man who faced charges before you and was crucified by the men of Palestine? If the people's demands were just, why did you not honor their request? And if they were unjust, why did you command such a wrongful deed?" {2:3} I replied to him, "Because he performed miracles, I did not want to crucify him. But since his accusers claimed he called himself a king, I carried out their demand." {3:1} Josephus writes of King Agrippa, who wore a robe woven with silver, attending a spectacle in the theater of Caesarea. When the people saw his shining garments, they said, "Before, we feared you as a man; now you are exalted beyond mortal nature." But Agrippa then saw an angel standing over him, striking him down to the point of death. End of the Letter of Pilate to Herod.

The Epistle of Pontius Pilate

PONTIUS PILATE TO TIBERIUS CAESAR, THE EMPEROR {1:1} Greeting. {1:2} Concerning Jesus Christ, whom I fully reported to you in my previous letter, a severe punishment has now been carried out, driven by the will of the people, though I was unwilling and deeply troubled by it. Truly, no age has known, nor will ever know, a man so good and upright. {1:3} Yet, the people exerted tremendous pressure, and all their scribes, chiefs, and elders united in their determination to crucify this messenger of truth, despite warnings from their own prophets, who advised otherwise—similar to how the Sibyls among us offer prophetic counsel. When he was hung upon the cross, supernatural signs appeared, which philosophers have judged to be ominous for the entire world. {1:4} His disciples continue to grow and thrive, displaying integrity in their lives and conduct, reflecting the teachings of their master. Indeed, they are remarkably generous in his name. Had I not feared an uprising among the people, who were on the verge of fury, perhaps this man might still be among us. However, I felt compelled, out of loyalty to your authority, to avoid escalating the situation, even though my own inclination was otherwise. Thus, I did not fully resist the sale and execution of this innocent man, who was guiltless of any wrongdoing and condemned unjustly through the malice of others. Yet, as the Scriptures declare, this will lead to their own downfall. {1:5} Farewell. The 5th day before the Calends of April.

The Report of Pontius Pilate to Augustus Caesar

THE REPORT OF PONTIUS PILATE, GOVERNOR OF JUDEA, SENT TO AUGUSTUS CAESAR IN ROME {1:1} During the time when our Lord Jesus Christ was crucified under the rule of Pontius Pilate, Governor of Palestine and Phoenicia, these events took place in Jerusalem and were done by the Jews against the Lord. Pilate sent this report to Caesar in Rome, including his personal account, and wrote as follows: {1:2} "To the most mighty, revered, divine, and honored Augustus Caesar, I, Pontius Pilate, administrator of the Eastern Province, greet you. {1:3} I have received information, great Caesar, which has filled me with fear and trembling. For in this province, over which I have authority, in a city called Jerusalem, a crowd of Jews brought before me a man named Jesus and leveled numerous accusations against him, yet none of their claims held under examination. Their main complaint was that Jesus taught a new doctrine about the Sabbath, saying it was not a day of rest as they had observed it. {1:4} Jesus performed many miraculous healings on this day, restoring sight to the blind, making the lame walk, raising the dead, and curing lepers. He healed paralytics who were unable to move, giving them strength and the power to walk and run by his word alone. {1:5} One of his most remarkable acts involved a man who had been dead for four days. Jesus commanded this man to rise, even though his body had begun to decay and was filled with the stench of death. But at his word, the dead man emerged from the tomb, like a bridegroom leaving his chamber, filled with a pleasant fragrance. {1:6} Jesus also restored those who were possessed and tormented by evil spirits, who dwelled in desolate places and exhibited beast-like behavior. By his word alone, he brought them back to a rational state, prepared them to live among others, and freed them from the unclean spirits, which he then cast into the depths of the sea. {1:7} Another case involved a man with a withered hand, whose body had become hardened like stone. Jesus healed him with a word, restoring his whole body. {1:8} There was also a woman who had suffered from an issue of blood for years, exhausted from failed treatments by local physicians. She had lost hope of recovery, but as Jesus passed by, she touched the hem of his garment from behind, and in that moment, her strength returned, and she was completely healed. {1:9} I report these events which I have confirmed, and which he performed even on the Sabbath. He did other miracles greater than these, beyond any works our own gods have ever done. {1:10} But Herod, Archelaus, Philip, Annas, Caiaphas, and the people conspired and pressured me to put him on trial. Therefore, after examining him and finding no basis for their accusations, I scourged him and then commanded him to be crucified. {1:11} As he was crucified, darkness covered the world, and the sun became obscured for half a day. Stars appeared but did not shine as usual, and the moon took on the appearance of blood. The earth shook, and there were sounds of thunder, causing even the Jewish temple to tremble, leaving a great chasm in its floor. {1:12} Amid this terror, the dead rose, as the Jews themselves testified, believing it was Abraham, Isaac, Jacob, the twelve patriarchs, Moses, and Job who had appeared, men who had died thousands of years before. {1:13} Many others rose from the dead, appearing visibly, and lamented the sin of the Jews in rejecting this righteous one. This earthquake and shaking continued from noon until three o'clock in the afternoon, and at evening on the first day of the week, a bright light appeared in the heavens, brighter than any day. {1:14} At the third hour of the night, the sun shone brightly, filling the whole sky with light. In the heavens, tall men of radiant glory appeared along with a host of angels. Their voices, like thunder, declared, 'Jesus who was crucified has risen again. Come up from Hades, all you who were bound.' {1:15} The earth opened in a chasm that seemed bottomless, revealing the foundations below. Voices in heaven and among the risen dead proclaimed Jesus' victory over Hades, and that he would go before his disciples in Galilee. {1:16} All night, the light did not cease shining, and many Jews perished, swallowed by the earth. Most of those who had spoken against Jesus were never seen again, and only one synagogue remained in Jerusalem, for the others had collapsed in ruin. {1:17} Trembling with fear and awe, I have written what I witnessed at that time and sent it to your divinity, as well as a record of the things done against Jesus by the Jews, and submit it now to your lordship." End of the Report of Pontius Pilate to Augustus Caesar.

The Report of Pontius Pilate to Tiberius Caesar

THE REPORT OF PONTIUS PILATE, GOVERNOR OF JUDEA, SENT TO TIBERIUS CAESAR {1:1} To the most powerful, august, revered, and divine Emperor Tiberius Caesar, Pontius Pilate, governor of the Eastern Province, sends greetings. {1:2} I feel compelled to report the recent events to your esteemed authority, though I do so with great fear and trembling. As ordered, I have governed this province, which includes the city of Jerusalem, where the temple of the Jewish nation stands. Recently, all the Jewish people assembled and presented to me a man named Jesus, bringing countless accusations against him, though they could not convict him of anything substantial. {1:3} Their main complaint against him was his claim that the Sabbath was not to be kept as their day of rest. {1:4} This man performed many cures and good works. He restored sight to the blind, cleansed lepers, raised the dead, healed paralytics who were unable to move and brought strength to their bones with only his words, allowing them to walk and run again. {1:5} He performed even greater deeds, which were astonishing, surpassing even our gods' powers. He raised a man named Lazarus from the dead after four days. Though the body was decayed and overrun with worms, Jesus commanded Lazarus to rise with a simple word. Lazarus emerged from his grave, like a bridegroom, restored and full of fragrance. {1:6} He also healed those tormented by demons, individuals who lived in desolate places, harmed their own bodies, and roamed among creeping creatures and wild animals. He brought them back to society, made them rational and honorable, and drove out the demons that tormented them, sending these unclean spirits into a herd of swine, which then drowned in the sea. {1:7} Another time, he healed a man with a withered hand and a woman suffering from a long-term issue of blood. Her condition was so severe that her bones could be seen through her skin. All physicians had given up hope, but as Jesus passed, she touched the hem of his garment. Instantly, she was healed, her body restored, and she ran back to her city of Paneas. {1:8} Despite these miracles, the Jews reported that Jesus performed them on the Sabbath. I witnessed these marvels, which seemed greater than anything our gods could do. {1:9} Nevertheless, Herod, Archelaus, Philip, Annas, Caiaphas, and the people delivered him to me for trial. As many rioted against me, I ordered his crucifixion. {1:10} When he was crucified, darkness fell over the entire world. The sun was completely hidden, and the sky darkened so much that stars appeared dimly in the day. I presume you were aware that in all places, people lit lamps from midday until evening. The full moon, red as blood, did not shine that night, and the stars appeared mournful over the Jews' crime. {1:11} Then, on the first day of the week, around the third hour of the night, the sun shone with an unusual brightness, and the sky became radiant. As lightning in a storm, men of towering stature and indescribable splendor appeared in the air, surrounded by a vast multitude of angels, proclaiming: {1:12} "Glory to God in the highest, and on earth peace, goodwill among men. Rise from Hades, you who are held captive in its depths." {1:13} At their words, mountains and hills shook, rocks split, and massive chasms opened, exposing the deep places of the earth. {1:14} Amidst this terror, the dead rose and walked about. Jews who witnessed it claimed to have seen Abraham, Isaac, Jacob, and the twelve patriarchs who had been dead for more than two thousand years. They even saw Noah, alive in the flesh. {1:15} These multitudes sang loudly, praising God, saying, "The Lord our God has risen from the dead and given life to all the dead, conquering and emptying Hades." {1:16} That night, the light did not fade, but many Jews perished, swallowed by the earth's chasms, their bodies never to be seen again. I mean those Jews who had spoken against Jesus. Only one synagogue remained in Jerusalem; all other synagogues that had opposed Jesus were destroyed. {1:17} Struck by this terror and seized with fear, I immediately ordered that these events be documented, and I now send this report to your imperial authority. End of the Report of Pontius Pilate to Tiberius Caesar.

The Trial and Condemnation of Pilate

{1:1} When the letters reached Rome and were read to Caesar in the presence of many people, everyone was filled with fear, realizing that the darkness and earthquake affecting the whole world were consequences of Pilate's transgression. {1:2}

Enraged, Caesar sent soldiers with orders to bring Pilate as a prisoner. {1:3} When Pilate arrived in Rome, Caesar assembled his entire senate, his army, and the full power of his officials, sitting in the temple of the gods above all. Pilate was commanded to stand at the entrance. {1:4} Caesar addressed him, "Most impious one, after seeing the great signs performed by that man, how could you dare to act as you did? {1:5} By committing this wicked act, you have brought ruin to the entire world." {1:6} Pilate replied, "O King and Autocrat, I am not guilty of these actions. It was the multitude of the Jews who are hasty and at fault." {1:7} Caesar asked, "And who are these people?" Pilate responded, "Herod, Archelaus, Philip, Annas, Caiaphas, and the whole crowd of the Jews." {1:8} Caesar questioned, "Then why did you carry out their wishes?" {1:9} Pilate answered, "Their nation is rebellious and resistant to your authority." {1:10} Caesar said, "When they handed him over to you, you should have detained him and sent him to me, rather than yielding to them and crucifying such a just man who performed great and miraculous deeds, as you described in your report. {1:11} For through these miracles, Jesus was shown to be the Christ, the King of the Jews." {1:12} At Caesar's mention of the name "Christ," all the statues of the gods toppled over as dust, right where Caesar sat with his senate. {1:13} All the people near Caesar trembled at the fall of the gods and the power of the words he spoke. Overcome with fear, they dispersed to their homes, marveling at what had occurred. {1:14} Caesar ordered Pilate to be held securely, intending to learn the truth about Jesus. {1:15} The next day, as Caesar sat in the capitol with all his senate, he again questioned Pilate. {1:16} He demanded, "Speak truthfully, impious one, for your impious deed against Jesus has been revealed here, causing even the gods to fall." {1:17} He continued, "Who is this man you crucified, whose name has the power to destroy all the gods?" {1:18} Pilate replied, "Indeed, what was said of him is true; even I was convinced by his deeds that he was greater than all the gods we worship." {1:19} Caesar asked, "Then why did you act against him with such reckless audacity, knowing his power and risking harm to my rule?" {1:20} Pilate answered, "I acted because of the disobedience and rebellion of the lawless Jews." {1:21} Caesar, enraged, convened a council with his senate and officers, issuing a decree against the Jews: {1:22} "To Licianus, first in command in the Eastern Provinces. Greetings. {1:23} I have learned of the audacious acts recently committed by the Jews in Jerusalem and the surrounding cities, how they compelled Pilate to crucify a god named Jesus, which has brought disaster upon the world. {1:24} Therefore, take soldiers and proceed swiftly to subdue them, declaring their subjugation by this decree. {1:25} Scatter them among the nations and place them under bondage, eradicating their presence from Judea as soon as possible. Let it be evident, wherever it is still unknown, that their wickedness knows no bounds." {1:26} When this decree reached the Eastern Provinces, Licianus, fearing Caesar's command, obeyed and ravaged the Jewish nation, sending those who remained in Judea into slavery, scattering them among the Gentiles. Thus, Licianus ensured Caesar knew that he had acted against the Jews in the East in accordance with his orders, hoping to please him. {1:27} Caesar then decided to question Pilate one final time and commanded a captain named Albius to behead Pilate, declaring, "As he laid hands upon the righteous one, called Christ, he too shall die similarly and receive no mercy." {1:28} At the place of execution, Pilate prayed silently, "O Lord, do not destroy me with the wicked Jews. I would not have touched you if not for the lawless nation that pressured me to act against you. {1:29} You know, Lord, that I acted in ignorance. Do not remember my sins or punish me, nor my wife, Procla, who stands with me now and whom you taught to foresee your crucifixion. Forgive us, Lord, and grant us a place among the righteous." {1:30} When Pilate finished praying, a voice from heaven proclaimed, "All nations and families shall call you blessed, for through you, the prophecies about me have been fulfilled. {1:31} You yourself shall be a witness at my second coming, when I judge the twelve tribes of Israel and those who did not acknowledge my name." {1:32} The Prefect then beheaded Pilate, and an angel of the Lord took up his head. {1:33} When Pilate's wife Procla saw the angel receiving his head, she, filled with joy, immediately gave up her spirit, and was buried alongside her husband.

The Death of Pilate Who Condemned Jesus

{1:1} At this time, Tiberius Caesar, the Roman Emperor, was suffering from a severe illness. Hearing reports that there was a physician in Jerusalem named Jesus who healed all ailments merely by his word, Caesar, unaware that Jesus had been put to death by the Jews and Pilate, summoned one of his attendants named Volusianus. {1:2} He instructed him, saying, "Go as quickly as you can across the sea and tell Pilate, my servant and friend, to send me this physician so that he may restore my health." {1:3} Obeying the emperor's command, Volusianus departed immediately and traveled to Pilate. When he arrived, he relayed the emperor's request, saying, "Tiberius Caesar, the emperor of the Romans and your lord, has heard that there is a healer in this city who cures illnesses by his word alone, and he urgently asks that you send him to Rome to heal his sickness." {1:4} Pilate was struck with great fear upon hearing this, knowing that out of envy he had caused Jesus to be executed. {1:5} Pilate responded to Volusianus, saying, "This man was a troublemaker who gathered crowds around him; after consulting the wise men of the city, I had him crucified." {1:6} On his way back to his lodgings, Volusianus encountered a woman named Veronica, who had known Jesus. He asked her, "Woman, there was a healer in this city who cured the sick with just his word; why did the Jews kill him?" {1:7} She began to weep, saying, "Oh, my lord, he was my God and my Lord, whom Pilate, driven by envy, condemned and crucified." {1:8} Saddened, Volusianus replied, "I am deeply sorry that I cannot fulfill the mission for which my lord sent me." {1:9} Veronica then explained, "When my Lord went about preaching, I missed him dearly, so I desired to have his image painted to console me in his absence. As I was taking the canvas to a painter, my Lord met me and asked where I was going. When I explained, he asked for the canvas and returned it to me, bearing the image of his holy face. {1:10} Tell your lord that if he looks upon this image with devotion, he will quickly be restored to health." {1:11} Volusianus asked, "Can such a likeness be obtained with gold or silver?" She answered, "No, only with a heart full of pious devotion." {1:12} She then offered to accompany him to Rome and show Caesar the image, after which she would return. {1:13} Volusianus brought Veronica with him to Rome and informed Tiberius, "Jesus, whom you seek, was unjustly condemned to death by Pilate and the Jews and was nailed to the cross out of envy. {1:14} However, this noble matron has come with me bearing the likeness of Jesus, and if you gaze upon it with devotion, you will receive healing." {1:15} Caesar ordered the path to be covered with silken cloths and had the image brought before him. The moment he looked upon it, he was instantly restored to full health. {1:16} Following this, Pontius Pilate was arrested by Caesar's command and brought to Rome. {1:17} When Caesar heard that Pilate had arrived, he was filled with intense anger and summoned him to his presence. {1:18} Pilate wore the seamless coat of Jesus when he appeared before Caesar. As soon as Caesar saw him, all his wrath subsided, and he rose to greet Pilate, unable to speak harshly to him in any way. {1:19} Caesar, who had been fierce and angry before seeing him, now felt only gentleness in his presence. {1:20} Once Pilate left, however, Caesar's rage returned fiercely, and he cursed himself for not expressing his anger as he had intended. {1:21} He ordered Pilate to be brought back and swore that he would have him put to death, unfit to live on earth. {1:22} But as soon as Pilate appeared, Caesar greeted him warmly, his anger disappearing instantly. All who witnessed this were astonished, and Caesar himself was puzzled by his inability to confront Pilate with fury. {1:23} Finally, at the suggestion of a Christian or perhaps by divine inspiration, Caesar ordered that Pilate be stripped of the coat. Once Pilate was without it, Caesar's original anger returned in full force. {1:24} Bewildered, Caesar inquired about the garment, and he was told that it was the coat of Jesus. {1:25} Caesar then ordered Pilate to be held in prison while he consulted with his advisors on how to proceed. {1:26} A few days later, Pilate was sentenced to a disgraceful death. {1:27} Hearing the verdict, Pilate took his own life with his dagger, thereby ending his life through suicide. {1:28} When news of Pilate's death reached Caesar, he said, "Truly, he has died a most shameful death, having not spared even himself." {1:29} Pilate's body was then fastened to a large stone and thrown into the Tiber River. {1:30} But unclean spirits, drawn to his corrupt body, stirred the waters and caused dreadful lightning, thunder, hail, and violent storms, terrifying all who witnessed it. {1:31} The Romans, in fear, removed his body from the Tiber and, mocking him, took it to Vienne and sank it in the Rhone River, which was known as a place of curses called "Way of Gehenna." {1:32} Yet even there, evil spirits continued to disturb the waters with the same frightening phenomena. {1:33} The people of that region, unable to endure such torment from the demons, decided to remove the cursed vessel. They carried it to the territory of Losania and buried it. {1:34} But when further troubles arose from diabolical forces, they cast it into a remote pool surrounded by mountains. To this day, it is said by some that evil spirits continue to emerge from that place, carrying out various wicked deeds.

The Apostles Creed

{1:1} Peter: "I believe in God, the Father Almighty." {1:2} John: "Maker of heaven and earth." {1:3} James: "And in Jesus Christ, His only Son, our Lord." {1:4} Andrew: "Who was conceived by the Holy Ghost, born of the Virgin Mary." {1:5} Philip: "Suffered under Pontius Pilate, was crucified, dead, and buried." {1:6} Thomas: "He descended into hell; the third day He rose again from the dead." {1:7} Bartholomew: "He ascended into heaven and sits at the right hand of God, the Father Almighty." {1:8} Matthew: "From there, He shall come to judge the living and the dead." {1:9} James, the son of Alpheus: "I believe in the Holy Ghost, the holy Church." {1:10} Simon Zelotes: "The communion of saints, the forgiveness of sins." {1:11} Jude, the brother of James: "The resurrection of the body." {1:12} Matthias: "And life everlasting. Amen."

The Tales of the Patriarchs

{1:1} "You should release your anger and let it overflow completely. Who is the man who dares to confront the full fury of your anger? Those who have been destroyed and killed are left without any help, and now I have freed the prisoners who suffered in captivity. The Great Holy One holds all power over life and judgment, as everything rests in His hands." {1:2} "On the day of justice, every part of the land will be judged, and all evil within it will face retribution."

{2:1} "They were struck down from behind, driven forward by the presence of the Lord." {2:2} "With each planting, even the mystery of evil was revealed. The secrets that had been hidden were brought to light."

{3:1} "I, Lamech, felt disturbed, believing that the conception was the doing of the Watchers, that this pregnancy came from the Holy Ones and was tied to the Giants. Troubled, I turned to my wife, Bitenosh, and said, 'Swear to me by the Most High, the Great Lord, the King of the Universe, and by the sons of heaven, that you will tell me the truth without any lies.' Bitenosh, visibly distressed, cried and said, 'Oh my brother and lord, remember the love we shared. I will tell you the truth now, without holding anything back.' When Bitenosh saw the change in my mood, she restrained her anger and said, 'I swear by the Great Holy One, the King of the heavens, that this child, this pregnancy, comes only from you, not from a stranger, a Watcher, or a son of heaven.' Then I, Lamech, told my father, Methuselah, everything, so he would know the truth. Methuselah then went to Enoch in Parvaim to seek guidance. Methuselah told Enoch, 'Father, I come before you to seek clarity; fear not, for I have come in earnest.'"

{4:1} "During the days of Jared, my father, these mysteries were known and revealed to the chosen ones." {4:2} "Enoch assured that the child was from Lamech, not from the sons of heaven. Methuselah returned and informed Lamech, and when I, Lamech, heard this, my worries were finally calmed."

{5:1} "I devoted myself to justice, seeking truth even from the womb of my mother. As I grew, I walked the path of eternal truth. The Holy One guided me, protecting me from lies that lead into darkness. I was strengthened by the vision of truth and wisdom, avoiding paths filled with violence. vacat I, Noah, became a man of righteousness and married Amzara, who bore me three sons and daughters. I found wives for my sons from my family and gave my daughters in marriage to my nephews, as the Most High had ordained for the sons of men. vacat When ten jubilees had passed, my sons sought wives. I received a vision about the acts of the sons of heaven but kept this vision hidden in my heart. vacat Then the Great Holy One spoke to me in a vision, saying, 'O Noah, I have witnessed all the deeds of the sons of the earth.' I understood and waited with patience as the giants spilled blood. I found favor in the Holy One's eyes, and my life was blessed with righteousness and understanding."

{6:1} "God promised Noah dominion over the earth, the seas, and all that they contain. Noah was overjoyed at receiving such a blessing." {6:2} "The ark came to rest upon Mount Ararat, and Noah offered incense on the altar, bringing atonement for the land." {6:3} "God made a covenant with Noah, instructing him that he must no longer consume blood in any form."

{7:1} "I placed my bow in the cloud as a sign for the earth, a symbol of the covenant. I witnessed this bow in the mountains. After the flood, Noah and his family looked upon the widespread devastation. They began to cultivate the land again, planting a vineyard on Mount Lubar. This vineyard bore fruit after four years, and on the first day of the fifth year, they celebrated the first wine harvest with a feast, gathering to thank God for sparing them from the destruction of the flood."

{8:1} "They gathered resources, cutting down gold, silver, stones, and clay, taking some for their own purposes. I saw them also harvest trees. The sun, moon, and stars seemed to claim their shares as well, taking what was theirs. I watched as a mighty olive tree grew, its branches full and strong, only to be struck by powerful winds. The west wind came first, knocking off its fruit and leaves and scattering them far across the land."

{9:1} "'Listen, O mighty cedar!' In my dream, I saw a great cedar standing on the mountain, towering above all. From it grew three willow branches that rose upward. The first branch attached itself to the cedar stump, symbolizing unity and strength. Among its branches, a wondrous shoot would grow that would last forever. The final willow branch intertwined with the cedar, representing two sons, bound to each other and destined to endure."

{10:1} "I saw a man coming from the south, holding a sickle and fire, bringing judgment to cleanse all wickedness. Angels gathered around him as nations looked on in amazement. Then, I, Noah, awoke, seeing the light of the Sun rise brightly."

{11:1} "Noah divided the land among his descendants, defining the northern boundary as far as the Mediterranean Sea and the Tina River."

{12:1} "Noah further divided the land westward to Asshur, reaching as far as the Tigris River. He gave Aram's territory up to the Mountain of the Bull and crossed westward to the place where the three regions met. For Arpachshad, he set aside a portion. To Gomer, he assigned northeastern lands up to the Tina River, and for Magog, he marked out their boundaries."

{13:1} "I, Abraham, built an altar at Bethel, praising God, and then journeyed to the Holy Mountain in Hebron, where I lived for two years. When famine struck, I took my family to Egypt, crossing the Nile. There, I dreamed of a cedar and a date-palm, bound by shared roots. When men came to cut down the cedar, the date-palm protested, saying they grew from a single root. I warned Sarah to tell everyone I was her brother, fearing for my life. Five years later, Pharaoh's advisors brought gifts, having heard of Sarah's wisdom, and sought knowledge from me. I read them from the Book of Enoch's teachings."

{14:1} "Egyptian courtiers praised Sarah's beauty to Pharaoh, who desired her. Sarah, heeding my warning, told Pharaoh I was her brother, and he took her as his wife. I prayed for justice, and God sent severe afflictions on Pharaoh's house, preventing intimacy with Sarah for two years. Magicians and healers were powerless against these plagues. Pharaoh's advisors approached me for help, but I demanded Sarah's return first. Pharaoh confronted me, swearing he had not touched her, and I exorcised the spirit from his house. Pharaoh gave us gifts of gold, silver, and fine garments, and we left Egypt."

{15:1} "I returned to Bethel, built an altar, and offered sacrifices in gratitude for God's blessings. After this, Lot and I parted ways due to disputes among our herdsmen; he settled in Sodom. This separation troubled me, but God reassured me, promising that my descendants would inherit the land forever. I traveled across the land, from the river of Egypt to Lebanon, and God promised that my descendants would be countless, like the dust of the earth. I walked through the land's length and breadth, claiming it as God's gift to me and my lineage."

{16:1} "I journeyed across the land, beginning at the Gihon River, moving along the Mediterranean, reaching the Mount of the Bull, and then eastward to the Euphrates River. From there, I traveled south to the Red Sea and then returned to the Gihon. I settled near the oaks of Mamre by Hebron, where I built an altar to worship the God Most High. My household gathered to feast, and I invited my allies Mamre, Arnem, and Eshkol. Around this time, Chedorlaomer, the king of Elam, along with his allies, waged war against the king of Sodom. Sodom's forces were defeated, and the king of Elam plundered their wealth, capturing Lot as well."

The Book of Giants

{1:1} In the days when humankind multiplied on the earth, the angels, watching the earth, learned the secrets of heaven and passed them to humans, but sin increased greatly across the world. {1:2} The angels mingled with humankind, sowing discord and causing bloodshed. {1:3} They begat giants, unnatural beings who disrupted the harmony of the earth. {1:4} They took advantage of every creature, using the earth's bountiful gifts for their own purposes.

{2:1} The two hundred angels, in their rebellion, abused all that the earth produced—animals, crops, and plants. {2:2} They defiled even the great fish of the sea, and all that grew under the sky was influenced by their deeds. {2:3} They tampered with the creatures of the earth, including beasts, reptiles, and creeping things, turning their natural order into chaos. {2:4} They observed all, seeking to carry out cruel deeds and harsh utterances, using their influence to corrupt both male and female and perverting all they touched.

{3:1} Then the angels chose animals for acts beyond nature, using donkeys, goats, rams, and even birds, performing twisted actions. {3:2} They engaged in all forms of miscegenation, defiling all kinds of life. {3:3} From their unnatural unions, giants and monstrous creatures emerged, who corrupted the earth and filled it with violence. {3:4} These giants, born of corruption, sought to devour all that lay before them, shedding blood and wreaking havoc across the earth.

{4:1} The giants, defiled in their nature, sought to consume all they encountered. {4:2} Their actions caused the earth to cry out in its corruption, the soil soaked with blood. {4:3} Yet, the giants' insatiable appetite was never satisfied, and they became increasingly violent. {4:4} These creatures, born of angels and humans, became monstrous entities who turned against creation itself, devouring and destroying.

{5:1} Then, plagued by troubling dreams and visions, the giants began to foresee their doom. {5:2} Mahway, son of the angel Barakel, dreamed of a tablet submerged in water, and when it emerged, only three names remained. {5:3} This vision symbolized the coming destruction, which would leave only Noah and his sons to survive the impending flood. {5:4} Mahway shared his vision with the other giants, who discussed its meaning in dread.

{6:1} Ohya, a giant, was disturbed by Mahway's vision. {6:2} "Who has shown you this vision, my brother?" he asked. {6:3} Mahway responded, "Barakel, my father, was with me in the vision." {6:4} Before Mahway could finish, Ohya marveled, "Such wonders are hard to comprehend! If even the barren may give birth, perhaps nothing is as it seems." {6:5} Another giant spoke, saying, "Let us search for understanding, for these visions weigh heavily on us."

{7:1} Ohya had another vision, of a great tree uprooted, leaving only three roots intact, much like the previous vision of Mahway's tablet. {7:2} In denial, Ohya attempted to avoid the meaning, suggesting it might only foretell the fate of Azazel, or perhaps the rulers of earth alone.

{8:1} As more dreams troubled them, the giants grew increasingly alarmed. {8:2} Two giants shared their visions with monsters and fellow giants alike, describing a garden and its many trees. {8:3} "In my dream, I saw two hundred trees growing from a single root," one recounted, "but water and fire consumed them." {8:4} The giants debated the meaning, realizing the dreams foretold their end.

{9:1} The giants, desperate for insight, resolved to seek Enoch, the renowned scribe, to interpret the visions. {9:2} Ohya suggested, "Let us send Mahway to Enoch, that he may reveal the meaning of these troubling dreams." {9:3} Mahway journeyed over desolate lands to find Enoch, who welcomed him and listened to his plea.

{10:1} Enoch, understanding the message, sent back a tablet inscribed with the judgment of the heavens. {10:2} "To Shemihaza and all his companions," the message read, "know that because of your deeds—your corruption of humankind and earth—you will face destruction. {10:3} You have defiled yourselves, your sons, and their wives, and the land cries out against you. {10:4} Judgment is upon you; a great flood shall come to cleanse the earth. Yet even now, if you turn from evil, there may be hope."

{11:1} Enoch saw a vision, and terror struck him as he fell to the ground, hearing a voice that spoke. {11:2} "I have lived among humankind, yet I have not learned their ways."

The First Book of Enoch

The Book of Watchers

{1:1} The words of Enoch's blessing, where he blessed the chosen and righteous who will be alive during the time of tribulation, when all the wicked and godless will be removed. He shared his parable, saying - Enoch, a righteous man whose eyes were opened by God, saw a vision of the Holy One in the heavens, shown to him by the angels, and from them he heard everything and understood as he saw, but this message is not for this generation but for a distant one to come. {1:2} Concerning the chosen, I spoke, and I took up my parable about them: {1:3} The Holy Great One will come from His dwelling, and the eternal God will tread upon the earth, even on Mount Sinai, [and will appear from His camp] and show His might from the heaven of heavens. {1:4} Everyone will be filled with fear, and the Watchers (angels) will tremble, and great fear and shaking will seize them to the ends of the earth. {1:5} The high mountains will shake, and the high hills will be brought low, melting like wax in the flame. {1:6} The earth will be completely torn apart, and everything on it will perish, and there will be judgment upon all people. {1:7} But with the righteous, He will make peace and protect the chosen, and mercy will be upon them. {1:8} They will all belong to God, and He will prosper them & they will be blessed. He will help them all, and light will shine upon them, and He will make peace with them. {1:9} And look! He comes with ten thousands of His holy ones to execute judgment on all, and to destroy all the ungodly, and to convict every person of all the ungodly acts they have committed, and of all the harsh things ungodly sinners have spoken against Him.

{2:1} Pay attention to everything happening in heaven, how they do not change their paths, and the stars in the sky, how they all rise and set in order each in their season, and {2:2} do not stray from their appointed course. Look at the earth and observe what happens on it from beginning to end, how steadfast it is, how none of the things on earth {2:3} change, but all of God's works are clear to you. Look at summer and winter, how the whole earth is filled with water, and clouds, dew, and rain fall upon it.

{3:1} Notice how in winter all the trees seem to wither and lose their leaves, except for fourteen trees that do not lose their leaves but retain their old foliage for two to three years until the new comes.

{4:1} Again, observe the days of summer when the sun is directly above the earth. You seek shade and shelter from the sun's heat, and the earth also burns with increasing heat, making it hard to walk on the ground or on a rock because of the heat.

{5:1} Notice how the trees cover themselves with green leaves and bear fruit; therefore, pay attention and understand all His works, and recognize that He who lives forever made them so. {5:2} All His works continue year after year forever, and the tasks they accomplish for Him change not, but happen as God has ordained. {5:3} And look how the sea and rivers likewise perform their tasks without changing from His commands. {5:4} But you - you have not been steadfast nor followed the commandments of the Lord, but you have turned away and spoken proud and harsh words with your impure mouths against His greatness. Oh, you hard-hearted, you will find no peace. {5:5} Therefore, you will curse your days, and the years of your life will perish, and the years of your destruction will increase in eternal cursing, and you will find no mercy. {5:6a} In those days, your names will be an eternal curse to all the righteous, {5:6b} and by you, all who curse will curse, and all sinners and godless people will invoke curses upon you, {5:6c} and for you, the ungodly will be cursed. {5:6d} And all the . . . will rejoice, {5:6e} and there will be forgiveness of sins, {5:6f} and every mercy, peace, and forbearance: {5:6g} there will be salvation for them, a good light. {5:7} But for all you sinners, there will be no salvation, {5:7a} but a curse will remain upon you all. {5:7b} But for the chosen, there will be light, joy, and peace, {5:7c} and they will inherit the earth. {5:8} Then wisdom will be given to the chosen, and they will all live and never sin again, either through ungodliness or pride; but those who are wise will be humble. {5:9} They will not transgress again, nor will they sin all their days, nor will they die from (God's) anger or wrath, but they will complete their days. Their lives will be filled with peace, and the years of their joy will multiply in eternal gladness and peace all the days of their life.

{6:1} When the children of men had multiplied, beautiful and attractive daughters were born to them in those days. {6:2} The angels, the children of heaven, saw them and desired them, and said to each other, "Come, let's choose wives from among the children of men and have children." {6:3} Semjaza, their leader, said to them, "I fear you will not all agree to do this, and I will have to face the consequences of a great sin alone." {6:4} They all answered him, "Let us swear an oath and bind ourselves with mutual curses not to abandon this plan but to carry it out." {6:5} So they all swore together and bound themselves with mutual curses over it. There were two hundred of them who descended in the days of Jared on the summit of Mount Hermon, which they named because they had sworn and bound themselves with mutual curses on it. {6:6} These are the names of their leaders: Samlazaz, their leader; Araklba, Rameel, Kokablel, Tamlel, Ramlel, Danel, Ezeqeel, Baraqijal, Asael, Armaros, Batarel, Ananel, Zaqiel, Samsapeel, Satarel, Turel, Jomjael, and Sariel. These are their chiefs of tens.

{7:1} All the others along with them took wives, each choosing one for himself, and they began to go in to them and defile themselves with them. They taught them charms and enchantments, how to cut roots, and made them familiar with plants. {7:2} They became pregnant and gave birth to great giants, whose height was three thousand cubits (about 4,500 feet). {7:3} These giants consumed all the resources of men, and when humans could no longer sustain them, the giants turned against them and devoured mankind. {7:4} They began to sin against birds, beasts, reptiles, and fish, and to eat each other's flesh and drink blood. Then the earth accused the lawless ones.

{8:1} Azazel taught men to make swords, knives, shields, and breastplates, and made known to them the metals of the earth and the art of working with them, along with bracelets, ornaments, the use of kohl (a substance for beautifying the eyelids), and all kinds of precious stones and dyes. {8:2} This led to much wickedness, and they committed fornication, became corrupted in all their ways. Semjaza taught enchantments, Armaros taught how to break enchantments, Baraqijal taught astrology, Kokabel taught about the constellations, Ezeqeel taught knowledge of the clouds, Araqiel taught signs of the earth, Shamsiel taught signs of the sun, and Sariel taught about the moon's course. As men perished, they cried, and their cries ascended to heaven.

{9:1} Then Michael, Uriel, Raphael, and Gabriel looked down from heaven and saw much blood being shed on the earth, and all kinds of lawlessness happening. {9:2} They said to each other, "The earth, made without inhabitants, cries out with the voices of their cries to the gates of heaven. {9:3} Now to you, holy ones of heaven, the souls of men plead, saying, 'Bring our case before the Most High.'" {9:4} They said to the Lord of the ages: "Lord of lords, God of gods, King of kings, and God of the ages, Your throne of glory stands for all generations, and Your name is holy, glorious, and blessed forever! You made all things, have power over all things; everything is exposed to You, and nothing can hide from You. {9:5} You see what Azazel has done, teaching all unrighteousness on earth and revealing the eternal secrets preserved in heaven that men were trying to learn. {9:6} And Semjaza, to whom You gave authority over his associates, has gone to the daughters of men on earth, slept with the women, defiled themselves, and revealed to them all kinds of sins. {9:7} The women have borne giants, filling the whole earth with blood and unrighteousness. Now, behold, the souls of those who have died are crying out to the gates of heaven, and their lamentations have risen up and cannot cease because of the lawless acts on earth. {9:8} You know all things before they happen, see these things, and allow them, yet do not tell us what to do about them."

{10:1} Then the Most High, the Holy and Great One, spoke and sent Uriel to the son of Lamech, {10:2} saying, "Go to Noah and tell him in My name, 'Hide yourself!' and reveal to him the end that is approaching: the whole earth will be destroyed, and a flood is coming to wipe out everything on it. {10:3} Now instruct him so that he may escape and preserve his seed for all generations of the world." {10:4} Again, the Lord said to Raphael: "Bind Azazel hand and foot, cast him into darkness, {10:5} and make an opening in the desert of Dudael to throw him in. Place rough and jagged rocks on him, cover him with darkness, and let him remain there forever, hiding his face so he cannot see light. {10:6} On the day of great judgment, he shall be cast into the fire. Heal the earth that the angels have corrupted and proclaim its healing so that all the children of men do not perish through the secret things that the Watchers have taught. {10:7} The whole earth has been corrupted by the works taught by Azazel: ascribe all sin to him. {10:8} And to Gabriel, the Lord said: 'Proceed against the bastards and the reprobates, and against the children of fornication: destroy them and the children of the Watchers among men, and send them against one another to destroy each other in battle, for they shall not have long lives. {10:9} Any requests made on behalf of their fathers will not be granted, as they hope to live eternally, each hoping to live five hundred years. {10:10} The Lord said to Michael: 'Go, bind Semjaza and his associates who have defiled themselves with women in all their uncleanness. When their sons have killed one another, and they see the destruction of their loved ones, bind them tightly for seventy generations in the valleys of the earth until the day of their judgment and completion, until the everlasting judgment is finalized. {10:11} In those days they shall be led to the abyss of fire and to the torment and prison where they will be confined forever. {10:12} Whoever is condemned and destroyed will be bound with them for all generations. {10:13} Destroy all the spirits of the reprobate and the children of the Watchers because they have wronged mankind. {10:14} Eliminate all evil from the face of the earth, let every wicked act come to an end, and let the plant of righteousness and truth appear. It shall bring blessings, and the works of righteousness and truth will be planted in joy forever. {10:15} Then all the righteous will escape and live until they bear thousands of children, and all their youth and old age will be completed in peace. {10:16} The whole earth will be cultivated in righteousness, full of trees and blessings. Desirable trees will be planted, and they will plant vines that yield abundant wine, and every measure of seed sown will bear a thousand, with olives yielding ten presses of oil. {10:17} Cleanse the earth from all oppression, unrighteousness, sin, and godlessness; eliminate all uncleanness from the earth. {10:18} All the children of men will become righteous, and all nations will worship and praise Me. {10:19} The earth will be cleansed from all defilement, sin, punishment, and torment, and I will never send these upon it from generation to generation and forever.

{11:1} In those days, I will open the storehouses of blessings in heaven to send them down to the earth for the work and labor of the children of men. {11:2} Truth and peace will be connected throughout all days of the world and across all generations of men.

{12:1} Before these events, Enoch was hidden, and no one among the children of men knew where he was or what had become of him. {12:2} His activities were with the Watchers, and his days were spent among the holy ones. {12:3} I, Enoch, was blessing the Lord of majesty, the King of the ages, and suddenly the Watchers called me—Enoch the scribe—and said to me: "Enoch, scribe of righteousness, go and declare to the Watchers of heaven who have left the high heaven, the holy eternal place, and have defiled themselves with women, behaving like the children of earth and taking wives for themselves: {12:4} 'You have caused great destruction on the earth, and you will have no peace or forgiveness for your sins. {12:5} As you take delight in your children, you will witness the murder of your beloved ones and lament over the destruction of your children, making supplications eternally, but you will find no mercy or peace.'"

{13:1} Enoch went and said: "Azazel, you will have no peace; a severe sentence has been declared against you to put you in chains. {13:2} You will have no tolerance or requests granted because of the unrighteousness you have taught, and because of all the acts of godlessness and sin you have shown to men." Then I spoke to all of them together, and fear and trembling seized them. {13:3} They begged me to write a petition for them to find forgiveness, to read their petition in the presence of the Lord of heaven. {13:4} From that moment, they could not speak with Him nor lift their eyes to heaven due to the shame of their sins for which they had been condemned. {13:5} I wrote out their petition, the prayer concerning their spirits and deeds individually, along with their requests for forgiveness and long life. {13:6} I went and sat down by the waters of Dan, in the land of Dan, to the south and west of Hermon, and I read their petition until I fell asleep. {13:7} A dream came to me, and visions fell upon me; I saw visions of punishment, and a voice instructed me to tell it to the sons of heaven and reprimand them. {13:8} When I awoke, I went to them, and they were all gathered together, weeping in Abelsjail, which is between Lebanon and Seneser, with their faces covered. {13:9} I recounted to them all the visions I had seen in my sleep, beginning to speak words of righteousness and reprimanding the heavenly Watchers.

{14:1} This is the book of the words of righteousness and the reprimand of the eternal Watchers, according to the command of the Holy Great One in that vision. {14:2} I saw in my sleep what I will now express with human words and breath, which the Great One has given to men to understand with their hearts. {14:3} Just as He created and granted man the ability to understand wisdom, He created me to have the power to reprimand the Watchers, the children of heaven. {14:4} I wrote out your petition, and in my vision, it appeared that your petition would not be granted throughout all eternity, and that judgment has been passed upon you: your petition will not be granted. {14:5} From now on, you shall not ascend into heaven for eternity, and the decree has been made to bind you to the earth for all days of the world. {14:6} You will witness the destruction of your beloved sons and have no pleasure in them; they will fall by the sword before you. {14:7} Your petition on their behalf will not be granted, nor will your own be granted, even if you weep and pray and speak all the words in the writing I have composed. {14:8} The vision showed me clouds inviting me, a mist summoning me; the stars and lightning hurried me, and the winds lifted me upward, carrying me into heaven. {14:9} I approached a wall built of crystals surrounded by flames, which frightened me. {14:10} I entered the flames and approached a large house made of crystals, its walls resembling a tesselated floor of crystal, with a crystal foundation. {14:11} Its ceiling looked like the path of stars and lightning, with fiery cherubim in between, and the sky was as clear as water. {14:12} A blazing fire surrounded the walls, and its doors blazed with fire. {14:13} I entered that house; it was hot as fire and cold as ice, with no joys of life within it. Fear covered me, and trembling seized me. {14:14} As I shook and trembled, I fell on my face. {14:15} I saw a vision of a second house, larger than the first, with the entire entrance wide open before me, built of flames. {14:16} It was more splendid and magnificent than I can describe. Its floor was of fire, with lightning and the path of stars above, and its ceiling also was flaming fire. {14:17} I looked and saw a lofty throne there, appearing like crystal, with wheels like the shining sun, and cherubim were present. {14:18} Streams of fire flowed from beneath the throne, making it impossible for me to look directly at it. {14:19} The Great Glory sat on it, and His clothing shone brighter than the sun and whiter than snow. {14:20} None of the angels could enter or see His face due to His magnificence and glory; no human could look at Him. {14:21} A flaming fire surrounded Him, and a great fire stood before Him, so that none around could approach Him. Ten thousand times ten thousand stood before Him, yet He needed no advisor. {14:22} The holy ones closest to Him did not leave at night or depart from Him. {14:23} Until then, I had been prostrate on my face, trembling, and the Lord called me with His own voice, saying: "Come here, Enoch, and hear My word." {14:24} One of the holy ones came to me, woke me, and made me stand up and approach the door, where I bowed my face downwards.

{15:1} He answered me, and I heard His voice: "Do not fear, Enoch, righteous man and scribe of righteousness: approach here and hear My voice. {15:2} Go and say to the Watchers of heaven, who have sent you to intercede for them: 'You should be interceding for men, not the other way around. {15:3} Why have you left the high, holy, eternal heaven, lying with women, defiling yourselves with the daughters of men, taking wives for yourselves, and behaving like the children of earth, fathering giants as your sons? {15:4} Though you were holy, spiritual, living eternally, you have defiled yourselves with the blood of women, fathering children with human blood and lusting after flesh as mortal men do. {15:5} Therefore, I have given men wives so they can have children and not lack anything on earth. {15:6} But you were once spiritual, immortal for all generations. {15:7} Hence, I have not appointed wives for you; the spiritual beings of heaven dwell in heaven. {15:8} The giants born of spirits and flesh shall be called evil spirits on the earth, where they will reside. {15:9} Evil spirits have emerged from their bodies; since they are born from men and the holy Watchers, their origin is tainted. {15:10} They will be evil spirits on earth, and that is what they shall be called. The spirits of heaven dwell in heaven, while the spirits of the earth, born on earth, will remain there. {15:11} The spirits of the giants will afflict, oppress, destroy, attack, fight, and bring destruction on the earth, causing trouble; they need no food but will still hunger and thirst, causing offenses. {15:12} These spirits will rise against men and women because they came from them."

{16:1} From the days of the slaughter, destruction, and death of the giants, from whose flesh the spirits emerged, they will destroy without facing judgment—this destruction will continue until the day of consummation, the great judgment in which the age will be completed, {16:2} over the Watchers and the godless, yes, it will be fully completed." Now, regarding the Watchers who have sent you to intercede for them, who were once in heaven, {16:3} tell them: "You have been in heaven, but not all mysteries have been revealed to you. You knew only worthless things, and in the hardness of your hearts, you disclosed these to women, leading both men and women to commit much evil on earth." {16:4} Therefore, say to them: "You will have no peace."

{17:1} They took me to a place where those present were like flames of fire, {17:2} and, when they wished, they appeared as men. They brought me to a place of darkness, to a mountain whose peak reached heaven. I saw the places of the luminaries and the treasuries of the stars and thunder, {17:3} and in the depths, there were a fiery bow and arrows with their quiver, a fiery sword, and all the lightning. {17:4} They took me to living waters and to the fire of the west, which receives every sunset. I came to a river of fire where the fire flowed like water, discharging into the great sea towards {17:5} the west. I saw the great rivers, arrived at the great river, and entered the great darkness, {17:6} going to the place where no flesh walks. I saw the mountains shrouded in the darkness of winter and the source of all the waters of the deep. {17:8} I observed the mouths of all the rivers on earth and the mouth of the deep.

{18:1} I saw the treasuries of all the winds; I saw how He furnished all of creation {18:2} and the firm foundations of the earth. I saw the cornerstone of the earth and the four {18:3} winds that support the earth and the firmament of heaven. I saw how the winds stretched out the heavens and held their place between heaven and earth; these are the pillars {18:4} of heaven. I saw the winds of heaven turning and guiding the sun and all the stars to their setting. {18:5} I saw the winds on earth carrying the clouds; I saw the paths of the angels. I saw at the end of the earth the firmament of heaven above. I went and saw a place that burned day and night, where there are seven mountains of magnificent stones, {18:7} three to the east and three to the south. The eastern mountains were of colored stones, one of pearl, one of jacinth, and the southern ones were red stone. {18:8} The middle mountain reached to heaven, resembling the throne of God, made of alabaster, with the top {18:9} of the throne being sapphire. I saw a flaming fire. Beyond these mountains was a region marking the end of the great earth: there, the heavens were completed. I saw a deep abyss with columns of heavenly fire, and among them, I saw columns of fire fall, unmeasured in height and depth. {18:12} Beyond that abyss, I saw a place with no firmament above and no solid earth beneath; it had no water or birds, but was a desolate and horrifying place. I saw seven stars like great burning mountains, {18:14} and when I asked about them, the angel said: "This place is the end of heaven and earth; it has become a prison for the stars and the host of heaven. The stars that roll over the fire are those that transgressed the commandment of the Lord at their rising, {18:16} because they did not come forth at their appointed times. He was angry with them and bound them until the time when their guilt is completed, even for ten thousand years."

{19:1} Uriel said to me: "Here stand the angels who have joined themselves with women; their spirits take many different forms, defiling mankind and leading them to sacrifice to demons as gods. {19:2} They will remain here until the day of the great judgment, when they will be judged and brought to an end. The women associated with the angels who went astray will become sirens." I, Enoch, was the only one who saw the vision of all things; no man will see as I have seen.

{20:1} These are the names of the holy angels who watch: Uriel, one of the holy angels, who is over the world and Tartarus. {20:2} Raphael, one of the holy angels, who is over the spirits of men. {20:3} Raguel, one of the holy angels, who takes vengeance on the world of the luminaries. {20:4} Michael, one of the holy angels, who is set over the best part of mankind and chaos. {20:5} Saraqael, one of the holy angels, who is in charge of the spirits that sin in the spirit. {20:6} Gabriel, one of the holy angels, who is over Paradise, the serpents, and the Cherubim. {20:7} Remiel, one of the holy angels, whom God set over those who rise.

{21:1} I continued to a place of chaos. There, I saw something horrifying: I saw neither heaven above nor a solid earth, but a chaotic and dreadful place. {21:2} In that place, I saw seven stars of heaven bound together like great mountains, burning with fire. {21:3} I asked, "For what sin are they bound, and why have they been cast here?" {21:4} Uriel, one of the holy angels who was with me and the chief over them, answered, "Enoch, why do you ask, and why are you so eager for the truth? These are stars from heaven that transgressed the commandment of the Lord; they are bound here for ten thousand years, {21:6} the duration required for their sins to be completed." From there, I went to another place, even more horrifying than the first, and I saw a great fire burning and blazing, the place split open down to the abyss, filled with huge columns of fire. {21:8} I could neither see its extent nor its magnitude, nor could I guess. Then I said, "How fearful is this place and how terrible to behold!" {21:9} Uriel, one of the holy angels who was with me, replied, "Enoch, why are you so afraid?" {21:10} I answered, "Because of this dreadful place and the sight of its pain." He told me, "This place is the prison of the angels, and here they will be imprisoned forever."

{22:1} From there, I went to another place, a mountain of hard rock. {22:2} There, I found four hollow places, deep, wide, and very smooth. How smooth these hollow places are, deep and dark to behold! {22:3} Raphael, one of the holy angels who was with me, explained, "These hollow places were created for the spirits of the souls of the dead to assemble. {22:4} All the souls of humanity will gather here until the day of their judgment and until their appointed time comes, until the great judgment falls upon them." I saw a dead man's spirit making a plea, {22:5} and his voice ascended to heaven, making his appeal. I asked Raphael, {22:6} "Whose spirit is this that makes a plea, whose voice goes up to heaven?" {22:7} He answered, "This is the spirit of Abel, whom his brother Cain killed, and he pleads against him until his lineage is wiped from the earth." {22:8} I then asked about the hollow places: "Why is one separated from another?" {22:9} He replied, "These three have been made to separate the spirits of the dead. This division exists for the spirits of the righteous, where there is a bright spring of water. {22:10} Another place has been made for sinners who die and are buried without facing judgment in their lifetime. Their spirits will endure great pain until the great day of judgment, {22:11} punishment, and torment for those who curse forever, and their spirits will be bound there eternally. This division also exists for the spirits who plead for disclosures about their destruction, {22:12} when they were slain in the days of the wicked. This is for the spirits of those who were not righteous but were sinners, fully immersed in transgression; they will be companions of transgressors, but their spirits will not die on judgment day, nor will they be raised from there." {22:14} I blessed the Lord of glory and said, "Blessed be my Lord, the Lord of righteousness, who rules forever."

{23:1} From there, I traveled to another place at the western edge of the earth. I saw a burning fire that ran continuously, {23:2} never resting day or night, moving along its path. {23:3} I asked, "What is this that does not rest?" Raguel, one of the holy angels with me, answered, "This fire you see in the west is the fire that pursues all the heavenly luminaries."

{24:1} I then went to another part of the earth, where I saw a mountain range of fire burning day and night. {24:2} I went beyond it and saw seven magnificent mountains, each differing from the others, with beautiful stones that were glorious and fair in appearance: three towards the east, one on top of another, and three towards the south, one upon another, with deep, rugged ravines that did not connect. {24:3} The seventh mountain stood in the midst of these, towering above them, {24:4} resembling the seat of a throne, surrounded by fragrant trees. Among them was a tree unlike any I had ever smelled, {24:5} one that had a fragrance beyond all others; its leaves, blossoms, and wood never withered, and its fruit was beautiful, resembling the dates of a palm. I exclaimed, "How beautiful and fragrant is this tree, with its fair leaves and delightful blooms!" {24:6} Michael, one of the holy and honored angels who was with me and their leader, then answered.

{25:1} He said to me, "Enoch, why do you ask about the fragrance of the tree, {25:2} and why do you want to know the truth?" I replied, "I want to know everything, especially about this tree." He responded, "This high mountain you see, whose summit resembles the throne of God, is His throne, where the Holy Great One, the Lord of Glory, the Eternal King, will sit when He comes to visit {25:4} the earth with goodness. As for this fragrant tree, no mortal is allowed to touch it until the great judgment, when He will take vengeance on all and bring everything to its eternal consummation. {25:5} It will then be given to the righteous and holy. Its fruit will serve as food for the elect; it will be transplanted to the holy place, to the temple of the Lord, the Eternal King {25:6} Then they will rejoice with joy and be glad, and they will enter the holy place; its fragrance will fill their bones, and they will live long lives on earth, just as your ancestors did. {25:7} In their days, no sorrow, plague, torment, or calamity will touch them." {25:8} I blessed the God of Glory, the Eternal King, who has prepared such things for the righteous and has created them, promising to give them.

{26:1} I went from there to the middle of the earth and saw a blessed place with trees that had branches that thrived and bloomed. {26:2} There, I saw a holy mountain, and beneath it to the east, a stream flowed toward the south. {26:3} To the east, I saw another mountain that was higher than this one, with a deep and narrow ravine between them; a stream also flowed underneath the mountain. {26:4} To the west, there was another mountain, lower than the first and not very tall, with a deep, dry ravine between them; there was also another deep, dry ravine at the ends of the three mountains. {26:5} All the ravines were deep and narrow, formed from hard rock, and no trees grew on them. {26:6} I was amazed by the rocks and the ravines; I marveled greatly.

{27:1} I then asked, "What is the purpose of this blessed land filled with trees and this accursed valley in between?" {27:2} Uriel, one of the holy angels with me, answered, "This accursed valley is for those who are cursed forever. Here, all the accursed will gather, those who speak unseemly words against the Lord and speak harshly of His glory. {27:3} This will be their place of judgment. In the last days, they will witness the spectacle of righteous judgment in the presence of the righteous forever; here, the merciful will bless the Lord of glory, the Eternal King. {27:4} On the day of judgment for the former, they will bless Him for the mercy He has assigned them." {27:5} I then blessed the Lord of Glory, proclaiming His greatness and praising Him gloriously.

{28:1} From there, I went east into the middle of the mountain range in the desert, {28:2} and I saw a wilderness that was solitary, full of trees and plants. Water gushed forth from above, {28:3} rushing like a copious watercourse toward the northwest, causing clouds and dew to rise on every side.

{29:1} From there, I traveled to another place in the desert, approaching the east side of this mountain range. {29:2} I saw aromatic trees releasing the fragrance of frankincense and myrrh, and the trees resembled almond trees.

{30:1} Beyond these, I went far to the east and saw another place, a valley filled with water. {30:2} In that valley, there was a tree resembling fragrant trees like the mastic tree. {30:3} Along the sides of the valley, I saw fragrant cinnamon. I continued my journey eastward.

{31:1} I saw other mountains with groves of trees from which flowed nectar, known as sarara and galbanum. {31:2} Beyond these mountains, I spotted another mountain to the east at the ends of the earth, where aloe trees grew, and all the trees were filled with stacte (fragrant resin), resembling almond trees. {31:3} When burned, they emitted a sweeter scent than any other fragrance.

{32:1} After noticing these fragrant odors, I looked north over the mountains and saw seven mountains filled with fine nard (a type of fragrant plant), fragrant trees, cinnamon, and pepper. {32:2} I then traveled over the summits of all these mountains, heading far east, passing over the Erythraean Sea, moving far from it, and crossing over the angel Zotiel. {32:3} I arrived at the Garden of Righteousness, where I saw many more trees than before, including two very large, beautiful, glorious, and magnificent trees, and the tree of knowledge, whose holy fruit grants great wisdom. {32:4} That tree was as tall as a fir, its leaves similar to those of the carob tree, and its fruit resembled beautiful clusters of grapes. {32:5} The fragrance of the tree reached far away. Then I said, "How beautiful is this tree, and how appealing it looks!" {32:6} Raphael, the holy angel with me, replied, "This is the tree of wisdom that your aged father and mother ate from before you, gaining wisdom and realizing their nakedness, which led to their expulsion from the garden."

{33:1} From there, I traveled to the ends of the earth and saw great beasts, each one different from the others; I also saw birds that varied in appearance, beauty, and sound, each differing from the rest. {33:2} To the east of those beasts, I saw where the heavens rest and the portals of heaven open. {33:3} I observed how the stars of heaven emerge and counted the portals through which they appear. {33:4} I recorded all their exits, naming each star individually according to their number, their courses, their positions, their times, and their months, as Uriel, the holy angel with me, showed me. He revealed everything and documented it for me, including their names, laws, and groups.

{34:1} From there, I moved north to the ends of the earth and saw a magnificent sight at the very edge of the earth. {34:2} There, I noticed three portals of heaven open, and through each one, north winds blow. When they blow, there is cold, hail, frost, snow, dew, and rain. {34:3} One portal blows beneficially, but the other two bring violence and affliction upon the earth.

{35:1} From there, I headed west to the ends of the earth and saw three portals of heaven open, just as I had seen in the east, with the same number of portals and outlets.

{36:1} From there, I went south to the ends of the earth and found three open portals of heaven from which dew, rain, and wind come. {36:2} I then traveled east to the ends of heaven and saw the three eastern portals open, along with smaller portals above them. {36:3} Through each of these smaller portals, the stars of heaven pass and follow their courses westward along the paths shown to them. Whenever I saw this, I always blessed the Lord of Glory and continued to praise Him for the great and glorious wonders He has accomplished, revealing the greatness of His work to angels, spirits, and humanity, so they might honor His creations and witness His might, praising the grand work of His hands and blessing Him forever.

The Book of Parables

{37:1} This is the second vision that Enoch, son of Jared, son of Mahalalel, son of Cainan, son of Enos, son of Seth, son of Adam, saw—a vision of wisdom. {37:2} I raised my voice to share the words of the Holy One with those who dwell on the earth: Listen, you people of ancient times, and pay attention, you who come after, to the words I will speak before the Lord of Spirits. {37:3} It would have been better to declare these words only to the ancients, but I will not withhold the beginning of wisdom from future generations. {37:4} To this day, the wisdom I have received from the Lord of Spirits, according to my understanding and His good pleasure, has never been given before. {37:5} Now, three Parables were given to me, and I raised my voice to recount them to those living on earth.

{38:1} The first Parable speaks of the time when the congregation of the righteous will appear, and sinners will be judged for their sins and driven from the earth. {38:2} When the Righteous One stands before the righteous, whose elect works rely on the Lord of Spirits, light will shine for the righteous and elect living on the earth. {38:3} Then, where will the sinners dwell, and where will those who have denied the Lord of Spirits find rest? It would have been better for them if they had never been born. {38:4} When the secrets of the righteous are revealed and sinners are judged, the ungodly will be cast away from the presence of the righteous and elect. {38:5} From then on, those who possess the earth will no longer be powerful and exalted; they will not be able to look upon the holy, for the Lord of Spirits has made His light shine on the holy, righteous, and elect. {38:6} Then the kings and the mighty will perish and be given into the hands of the righteous and holy. {38:7} From that time, none will seek mercy from the Lord of Spirits, for their lives will have come to an end.

{39:1} In those days, holy and elect children will descend from high heaven, and their offspring will unite with the children of men. {39:2} During this time, Enoch received books filled with zeal and wrath, and books of unrest and expulsion. Mercy will not be granted to them, says the Lord of Spirits. {39:3} In those days, a whirlwind took me from the earth and set me down at the edge of the heavens. {39:4} There, I saw another vision, the homes of the holy and the resting places of the righteous. {39:5} My eyes observed their dwellings with His righteous angels and their resting places among the holy. {39:6} They prayed, interceded, and petitioned for the children of men, and righteousness flowed before them like water, while mercy fell like dew upon the earth; this is how it will be among them forever. {39:6a} In that place, I saw the Elect One of righteousness and faith. {39:7a} I saw His dwelling under the wings of the Lord of Spirits. {39:6b} Righteousness will prevail in His days, and the righteous and elect will be countless before Him forever. {39:7b} All the righteous and elect will shine like fiery lights before Him, and their mouths will be filled with blessings. {39:8} Their lips will glorify the name of the Lord of Spirits, and righteousness will never fail before Him. {39:8} There, I longed to dwell, and my spirit yearned for that home, for it has been my portion; this has been established concerning me before the Lord of Spirits. {39:9} In those days, I praised and honored the name of the Lord of Spirits with blessings, acknowledging that He destined me for blessing and glory according to His good pleasure. {39:10} For a long time, I gazed at that place, blessing and praising Him, saying: Blessed is He, and may He be blessed from the beginning forever. {39:11} Before Him, there is no end; He knows what is eternal and what will be from generation to generation before the world was created. {39:12} Those who do not sleep bless You; they stand before Your glory, praising, saying: "Holy, holy, holy is the Lord of Spirits; He fills the earth with spirits." {39:13} I saw all those who do not sleep; they stand before Him, blessing and saying: Blessed are You, and blessed is the name of the Lord forever. {39:14} My face changed, for I could no longer look.

{40:1} After that, I saw thousands upon thousands and ten thousand times ten thousand—an innumerable multitude standing before the Lord of Spirits. {40:2} On all four sides of the Lord of Spirits, I saw four presences distinct from those who do not sleep, and I learned their names, for the angel who accompanied me revealed them and showed me hidden things. {40:3} I heard the voices of these four presences as they praised the Lord of Glory. {40:4} The first voice blessed the Lord of Spirits forever. {40:5} The second voice I heard blessing the Elect One and the elect who depend on the Lord of Spirits. {40:6} The third voice prayed and interceded for those living on earth, supplicating in the name of the Lord of Spirits. {40:7} The fourth voice defended against the Satans, forbidding them to come before the Lord of Spirits to accuse those who dwell on the earth. {40:8} After this, I asked the angel of peace who accompanied me, who revealed all the hidden things: Who are these four presences I have seen, and whose words I have heard and written down? {40:9} He replied: The first is Michael, the merciful and patient; the second, Raphael, who oversees all diseases and wounds of humanity; the third, Gabriel, who governs all powers; and the fourth, Phanuel, who presides over the repentance of those who inherit eternal life. {40:10} These are the four angels of the Lord of Spirits, and these are the four voices I heard in those days.

{41:1} After this, I saw all the secrets of the heavens, how the kingdom is divided, and how the actions of people are weighed in a balance. {41:2} I saw the homes of the elect and the holy, and I witnessed all the sinners being driven away because they denied the name of the Lord of Spirits, being dragged off as they could not endure the punishment coming from Him. {41:3} I observed the secrets of lightning and thunder, the secrets of the winds, how they are divided to blow over the earth, as well as the secrets of the clouds and dew. {41:4} I saw where they originate and how they saturate the dusty earth. {41:5} I witnessed closed chambers from which the winds are divided, including the chambers of hail and winds, mist, and clouds, which have hovered over the earth since the beginning of the world. {41:6} I also saw the chambers of the sun and moon, how they emerge and return, their glorious cycle, and how one is superior to the other; they maintain their steady orbit, adding nothing to it and taking nothing away, keeping faith with each other, as per the oath binding them together. {41:7} First, the sun rises and follows his path according to the command of the Lord of Spirits, whose name is mighty forever. {41:8} Then I observed the hidden and visible paths of the moon, completing her course by day and night, each holding a position opposite the other before the Lord of Spirits. They give thanks and praise without rest, for their thanksgiving is their rest. {41:9} The sun often changes for blessings or curses, while the moon's path brings light to the righteous and darkness to the sinners, in the name of the Lord, who separated light from darkness, divided the spirits of men, and strengthened the spirits of the righteous in the name of His righteousness. {41:10} No angel can hinder this, and no power can stop it; for He appoints a judge over them all, judging them before Him.

{42:1} Wisdom found no place to dwell, so a dwelling was assigned to her in the heavens. {42:2} Wisdom sought to reside among the children of men but found no place. So, she returned to her place and took her seat among the angels. {42:3} From her chambers, unrighteousness emerged; she found those she did not seek and dwelt with them, like rain in a desert and dew on thirsty land.

{43:1} I saw more lightnings and stars of heaven, how He called them all by name, and they listened to Him. {43:2} I observed how they are weighed in a righteous balance according to their proportions of light, noting their spaces, their appearance days, and how their revolutions create lightning; I saw their cycles matched to the number of angels and how they keep faith with one another. {43:3} I asked the angel who accompanied me, who revealed the hidden things: What are these? He replied: The Lord of Spirits has shown you their parabolic meaning; these are the names of the holy who dwell on earth and believe in the name of the Lord of Spirits forever.

{44:1} I saw another phenomenon concerning the lightnings: how some stars arise and become lightnings and cannot shed their new form.

{45:1} This is the second Parable concerning those who deny the name of the dwelling of the holy ones and the Lord of Spirits. {45:2} They will not ascend to heaven, nor will they return to the earth; this will be the fate of sinners who have denied the name of the Lord of Spirits, preserved for the day of suffering and tribulation. {45:3} On that day, My Elect One will sit on the throne of glory to judge their works, and their places of rest will be countless. {45:4} Their souls will grow strong within them when they see My Elect Ones and those who have called upon My glorious name. {45:5} Then I will cause My Elect One to dwell among them. {45:6} I will transform the heavens into an eternal blessing and light, and I will transform the earth to make it a blessing. {45:7} I will cause My elect ones to dwell upon it, but the sinners and evildoers shall not set foot there. {45:8} I have provided peace for My righteous ones and made them dwell before Me; but for the sinners, there is judgment pending with Me, so I will destroy them from the face of the earth.

{46:1} There, I saw One who had the appearance of an ancient figure, His head was white like wool, and with Him was another being whose appearance resembled a man, and His face was full of grace, like one of the holy angels. {46:2} I asked the angel who accompanied me and showed me all the hidden things about this Son of Man, who he was, where he came from, and why he was with the Ancient One. He answered and said to me: This is the Son of Man who embodies righteousness, with whom righteousness dwells, and who reveals all the treasures of what is hidden, because the Lord of Spirits has chosen him, and his position before the Lord of Spirits is one of uprightness forever. {46:4} This Son of Man whom you have seen will raise up the kings and the mighty from their thrones and will loosen the bonds of the strong and break the teeth of sinners. {46:5} He will dethrone kings from their thrones and kingdoms because they do not praise and honor Him, nor do they humbly acknowledge from where their power was given. {46:6} He will bring down the proud and fill them with shame. They will dwell in darkness, and worms will be their bed; they will have no hope of rising from their beds because they do not honor the name of the Lord of Spirits. {46:7} These are the ones who judge the stars of heaven, raise their hands against the Most High, tread upon the earth, and dwell upon it. Their actions reveal unrighteousness, their power rests on their riches, and their faith lies in the gods they have made with their hands, while they deny the name of the Lord of Spirits. {46:8} They persecute the homes of His congregations and the faithful who trust in the name of the Lord of Spirits.

{47:1} In those days, the prayers of the righteous will ascend, and the blood of the righteous will cry out from the earth before the Lord of Spirits. {47:2} During those days, the holy ones dwelling in heaven will unite in one voice to supplicate, pray, praise, give thanks, and bless the name of the Lord of Spirits on behalf of the blood of the righteous that has been shed, so that their prayers will not be in vain before the Lord of Spirits, that judgment may be delivered to them, and that they will not have to suffer forever. {47:3} In those days, I saw the Ancient One seated on the throne of His glory, with the books of the living opened before Him, and all His heavenly hosts and counselors stood before Him. {47:4} The hearts of the holy were filled with joy because the number of the righteous had been counted, their prayers had been heard, and the blood of the righteous had been demanded before the Lord of Spirits.

{48:1} In that place, I saw an inexhaustible fountain of righteousness, surrounded by many fountains of wisdom. All the thirsty drank from them and were filled with wisdom, and they dwelt among the righteous, holy, and elect. {48:2} At that hour, the Son of Man was named in the presence of the Lord of Spirits, and His name was pronounced before the Ancient One. {48:3} Indeed, before the sun and the signs were created, before the stars of heaven were made, His name was proclaimed before the Lord of Spirits. {48:4} He will be a staff for the righteous to support themselves and not fall, and He will be the light for the Gentiles and the hope for those troubled in heart. {48:5} All who dwell on earth will bow down and worship before Him, praising, blessing, and celebrating the Lord of Spirits in song. {48:6} For this reason, He was chosen and hidden before Him, before the creation of the world and forever. {48:7} The wisdom of the Lord of Spirits has revealed Him to the holy and righteous, for He has preserved the lot of the righteous because they have despised this world of unrighteousness and its works and ways in the name of the Lord of Spirits; for in His name, they are saved, according to His good pleasure regarding their lives. {48:8} In these days, the kings of the earth will become downcast, and the mighty who possess the land because of their actions, for on the day of their anguish and affliction, they will not be able to save themselves. I will give them over to My elect: like straw in a fire, they will burn before the face of the holy; like lead in water, they will sink before the face of the righteous, and no trace of them will be found again. {48:10} On the day of their affliction, there will be rest on the earth, and they will fall and not rise again; no one will be able to lift them up because they have denied the Lord of Spirits and His Anointed. Blessed be the name of the Lord of Spirits.

{49:1} Wisdom is poured out like water, and glory does not fail before Him forever. {49:2} He is mighty in all the secrets of righteousness; unrighteousness will vanish like a shadow and have no permanence because the Elect One stands before the Lord of Spirits, and His glory is forever, and His power extends to all generations. {49:3} In Him dwells the spirit of wisdom, the spirit of insight, the spirit of understanding and might, and the spirit of those who have died in righteousness. {49:4} He will judge the secret things, and no one will be able to speak falsely before Him, for He is the Elect One before the Lord of Spirits according to His good pleasure.

{50:1} In those days, a change will occur for the holy and elect; the light of days will shine upon them, and glory and honor will be given to the holy. {50:2} On the day of affliction, when evil will have been stored up against sinners, the righteous will triumph in the name of the Lord of Spirits, and He will cause others to witness this so they may repent and abandon their sinful deeds. {50:3} They will have no honor through the name of the Lord of Spirits, yet they will be saved through His name, and the Lord of Spirits will show them compassion, for His compassion is great. {50:4} He is also righteous in His judgments, and in the presence of His glory, unrighteousness will not stand; at His judgment, the unrepentant will perish before Him. {50:5} From now on, I will show no mercy to them, says the Lord of Spirits.

{51:1} In those days, the earth will also return what has been entrusted to it, Sheol will give back what it has received, and hell will repay its debts. {51:5a} For in those days, the Elect One will arise, {51:2} and He will choose the righteous and holy from among them, for the day of their salvation has come. {51:3} The Elect One will sit on My throne, and His mouth will reveal all the secrets of wisdom and counsel because the Lord of Spirits has given these to Him and glorified Him. {51:4} In those days, the mountains will leap like rams, and the hills will skip like lambs satisfied with milk, and the faces of all the angels in heaven will shine with joy. {51:5b} The earth will rejoice, {51:5c} the righteous will dwell upon it, {51:5d} and the elect will walk on it.

{52:1} After those days, in the place where I had seen all the visions of what is hidden— I had been carried off in a whirlwind towards the west— there my eyes saw all the secret things of heaven that are to come: a mountain of iron, a mountain of copper, a mountain of silver, a mountain of gold, a mountain of soft metal, and a mountain of lead. {52:3} I asked the angel who accompanied me, saying, What do these things I have seen in secret mean? {52:4} He answered me: All these mountains you have seen will serve the dominion of His Anointed so that He may be powerful and mighty on the earth. {52:5} The angel of peace said to me: Wait a little, and you will be shown all the secret things surrounding the Lord of Spirits. {52:6} These mountains you have seen—the mountain of iron, the mountain of copper, the mountain of silver, the mountain of gold, the mountain of soft metal, and the mountain of lead—will all be like wax before the fire and like water flowing down from above upon those mountains, and they will become powerless beneath His feet. {52:7} In those days, no one will be saved by gold or silver, and no one will escape. {52:8} There will be no iron for war, and no one will wear a breastplate; bronze will be useless, and tin will not be valued, and lead will be undesirable. {52:9} All these things will be denied and destroyed from the surface of the earth when the Elect One appears before the Lord of Spirits.

{53:1} There, my eyes saw a deep valley with open mouths, and all who dwell on the earth, sea, and islands will bring Him gifts and presents as tokens of homage, but that deep valley will not be filled. {53:2} Their hands commit lawless acts, and the sinners devour all whom they oppress unjustly, yet the sinners will be destroyed before the Lord of Spirits and will be banished from the face of His earth, perishing forever. {53:3} I saw all the angels of punishment dwelling there, preparing the instruments of Satan. {53:4} I asked the angel of peace who accompanied me: For whom are they preparing these instruments? {53:5} He answered: They are preparing these for the kings and mighty of the earth so that they may be destroyed. {53:6} After this, the Righteous and Elect One will cause the house of His congregation to appear, and from then on, they will no longer be hindered in the name of the Lord of Spirits. {53:7} These mountains will not stand firm like the earth before His righteousness, but the hills will be like fountains of water, and the righteous will find rest from the oppression of sinners.

{54:1} I looked and turned to another part of the earth, and saw a deep valley with burning fire. {54:2} They brought the kings and the mighty and began to cast them into this deep valley. {54:3} There, I saw how they made iron chains of immeasurable weight. {54:4} I asked the angel of peace who accompanied me: For whom are these chains being prepared? {54:5} He said: These are being prepared for the hosts of Azazel, so they may be cast into the abyss of complete condemnation, covering their jaws with rough stones as the Lord of Spirits commanded. {54:6} On that great day, Michael, Gabriel, Raphael, and Phanuel will seize them and throw them into the burning furnace, so that the Lord of Spirits may take vengeance on them for their unrighteousness in submitting to Satan and leading astray those who dwell on the earth. {54:7} In those days, punishment will come from the Lord of Spirits; He will open all the chambers of waters above the heavens and the fountains beneath the earth. {54:8} All waters will join with the waters: what is above the heavens is masculine, {54:9} and what is beneath the earth is feminine, and they will destroy all who dwell on the earth and those under the ends of heaven. When they recognize the unrighteousness they have committed on the earth, they will perish by these means.

{55:1} After that, the Head of Days repented and said: In vain have I destroyed all who dwell on the earth. {55:2} He swore by His great name: From now on, I will not do so to all who dwell on the earth, and I will set a sign in the heavens, which will be a pledge of good faith between Me and them forever, as long as heaven is above the earth. This is according to My command. {55:3} When I desire to take hold of them by the hand of the angels on the day of tribulation and pain, I will cause My chastisement and My wrath to rest upon them, says {55:4} God, the Lord of Spirits. You mighty kings who dwell on the earth will behold My Elect One sitting on the throne of glory, judging Azazel, all his associates, and all his hosts in the name of the Lord of Spirits.

{56:1} I saw there the hosts of the angels of punishment, holding scourges and chains made of iron and bronze. {56:2} I asked the angel of peace who was with me, To whom are those holding the scourges going? {56:3} He said to me: To their elect and beloved ones, so that they may be cast into the chasm of the abyss of the valley. {56:4} Then that valley will be filled with their elect and beloved, and their days of life will come to an end; the days of their leading astray will no longer be counted. {56:5} In those days, the angels will return and descend upon the Parthians and Medes from the east. {56:6} They will stir up the kings, causing a spirit of unrest to come upon them, rousing them from their thrones, so they may rush forth like lions from their lairs and like hungry wolves among their flocks. {56:7} They will tread underfoot the land of His elect, and the land of His elect will be before them like a threshing-floor and a highway. {56:8} But the city of my righteous will obstruct their horses. They will begin to fight among themselves, and their right hand will be strong against their own, {56:9} and a man will not know his brother, nor a son his father or mother, until there are countless corpses from their slaughter, and their punishment is not in vain. {56:10} In those days, Sheol will open its jaws, and they will be swallowed up within, and their destruction will come to an end; Sheol will devour the sinners in the presence of the elect.

{57:1} After this, I saw another host of wagons, with men riding on them, coming on the winds from the east, and from the west to the south. {57:2} The noise of their wagons was heard, and when this commotion occurred, the holy ones from heaven took notice, and the pillars of the earth were shaken from their places, with the sound heard from one end of heaven to the other in a single day. {57:3} They will all fall down and worship the Lord of Spirits. This is the end of the second Parable.

{58:1} I began to speak the third Parable concerning the righteous and elect. {58:2} Blessed are you, you righteous and elect, for glorious will be your lot. {58:3} The righteous will be in the light of the sun, and the elect in the light of eternal life; their days of life will be endless, and the days of the holy will be countless. {58:4} They will seek the light and find righteousness with the Lord of

Spirits; there will be peace for the righteous in the name of the Eternal Lord. {58:5} After this, it will be said to the holy in heaven that they should seek the secrets of righteousness, the heritage of faith; it has become bright like the sun on earth, and the darkness is past. {58:6} There will be a light that never ends, and they will not be limited in days, for the darkness will have been destroyed, and the light of uprightness will be established forever before the Lord of Spirits.

{59:1} In those days, my eyes saw the secrets of the lightnings and the lights, and the judgments they carry out; they provide light for blessing or curse as the Lord of Spirits wills. {59:2} I also saw the secrets of the thunder; when it sounds above in heaven, its sound is heard, and I was shown the judgments executed on the earth, whether they are for well-being and blessing, or for a curse according to the word of the Lord of Spirits. {59:3} After that, all the secrets of the lights and lightnings were revealed to me, and they provide light for blessing and satisfaction.

{60:1} In the year 500, in the seventh month, on the fourteenth day of the month in the life of Enoch, I saw in that Parable how a mighty quaking caused the heaven of heavens to shake, and the host of the Most High and the angels, thousands upon thousands, were disturbed with great unease. {60:2} The Head of Days sat on the throne of His glory, and the angels and the righteous stood around Him. {60:3} A great trembling seized me, fear gripped me, my loins weakened, and I fell on my face. {60:4} Michael sent another angel from among the holy ones who raised me up; when he lifted me, my spirit returned, for I could not bear the sight of this host and the commotion and quaking of heaven. {60:5} Michael said to me: Why are you troubled by such a vision? Until this day, it has been the day of His mercy; He has been merciful and patient toward those who dwell on earth. {60:6} When the day, power, punishment, and judgment come, prepared by the Lord of Spirits for those who do not worship the righteous law, deny righteous judgment, or take His name in vain, that day is prepared as a covenant for the elect but as an inquisition for sinners. {60:7} When the punishment of the Lord of Spirits rests upon them, it will not be in vain, and it will slay children along with their mothers and fathers. Afterwards, judgment will occur according to His mercy and patience. {60:8} On that day, two monsters will be separated, a female monster named Leviathan, dwelling in the abysses of the ocean over the fountains of the waters. {60:9} The male is named Behemoth, who occupies a desolate wilderness called Duidain, east of the garden where the elect and righteous dwell, where my grandfather was taken up, the seventh from Adam, the first man created by the Lord of Spirits. {60:10} I asked the other angel to show me the might of those monsters, how they were separated on one day and cast, one into the abysses of the sea and the other onto the dry land of the wilderness. {60:11} He said to me: Son of man, you seek to know what is hidden. {60:12} The other angel who went with me revealed what is hidden, showing me what is first and last in heaven and below the earth, at the ends of heaven, and on the foundations of heaven. {60:13} He showed me the chambers of the winds, how the winds are divided and weighed, and how the portals of the winds are counted, each according to the power of the wind, and the power of the lights of the moon, and the suitable power, including the divisions of the stars according to their names, and how all divisions are arranged. {60:14} The thunders are assigned places where they rest while waiting for their peals; thunder and lightning are inseparable, and although they are not one and undivided, they both go together through the spirit and do not separate. {60:15} When the lightning flashes, the thunder sounds its voice, and the spirit enforces a pause during the peal, dividing equally between them, for the treasury of their peals is like sand, and each one, as it sounds, is restrained by the spirit's power and directed according to various quarters of the earth. {60:16} The spirit of the sea is masculine and strong, and according to his might, he draws it back with a rein, and in the same way, it is driven forward, spreading among all the mountains of the earth. {60:17} The spirit of hoar-frost has its own angel, and the spirit of hail is a good angel. {60:18} The spirit of snow has left his chambers due to his strength; there is a special spirit within it, and that which ascends from it is like smoke, known as frost. {60:19} The spirit of mist does not join them in their chambers, but has a unique chamber; its course is glorious in light and darkness, in winter and summer, and it has an angel in its chamber. {60:20} The spirit of dew dwells at the ends of heaven, connected with the chambers of rain, its course in winter and summer; its clouds and the clouds of mist are intertwined, each providing for the other. {60:21} When the spirit of rain emerges from its chamber, the angels come, open the chamber, and lead it out; when it spreads over the earth, it unites with the water on the earth. {60:22} For the waters are for those who dwell on the earth; they are nourishment for the earth from the Most High who is in heaven; therefore, there is a measure for the rain, and the angels take charge of it. {60:23} These things I saw toward the Garden of the Righteous, and the angel of peace who was with me said: These two monsters, prepared according to the greatness of God, shall feed...

{61:1} During those days, I saw that long cords were given to the angels, and they took wings and flew northward. {61:2} I asked one of the angels, "Why have those angels taken these cords and left?" He answered, "They have gone to measure." {61:3} The angel accompanying me said, "These will bring the measures of the righteous and the ropes for the righteous so that they can rely on the name of the Lord of Spirits forever." {61:4} The elect will begin to dwell with the elect, and these measures will be given to strengthen faith and righteousness. {61:5} These measures will reveal all the secrets hidden in the earth, including those destroyed by the desert, devoured by beasts, or consumed by fish, so they may return and find refuge on the day of the Elect One, for none shall be lost before the Lord of Spirits, and no one can be destroyed. {61:6} All who dwell in heaven received a command, power, a single voice, and a light like fire. {61:7} With their first words, they blessed, praised, and lauded with wisdom, being wise in their speech and spirit of life. {61:8} The Lord of Spirits placed the Elect One on the throne of glory, where he will judge all the deeds of the holy ones in heaven, weighing their actions. {61:9} When he lifts his face to judge their secret actions according to the word of the Lord of Spirits, and their paths according to His righteous judgments, they will all speak with one voice to bless, glorify, and sanctify the name of the Lord of Spirits. {61:10} He will summon all the heavenly hosts, the holy ones above, and the angels of power and authority, and on that day, they will raise one voice, blessing, glorifying, and exalting in the spirit of faith, wisdom, patience, mercy, judgment, peace, and goodness, all saying together, "Blessed is He, and may the name of the Lord of Spirits be blessed forever." {61:12} All who do not sleep in heaven shall bless Him: all the holy ones in heaven, the elect who dwell in the garden of life, and every spirit of light capable of blessing, glorifying, extolling, and hallowing His blessed name. All flesh shall glorify and bless His name beyond measure forever. {61:13} For great is the mercy of the Lord of Spirits, and He is patient, revealing all His works and creations to the righteous and elect in the name of the Lord of Spirits.

{62:1} The Lord commanded the kings, the mighty, the exalted, and those who dwell on earth, saying, "Open your eyes and lift up your horns if you can recognize the Elect One." {62:2} The Lord of Spirits seated him on the throne of glory, pouring the spirit of righteousness upon him, and his words will slay all sinners, destroying the unrighteous before him. {62:3} On that day, all the kings, mighty, exalted, and those who possess the earth will see how he sits on the throne of glory, judging with righteousness, where no falsehood can stand. {62:4} Pain will seize them like a woman in labor when her child enters the womb. {62:5} They will look at each other in terror, downcast and gripped by pain when they see the Son of Man sitting on the throne of glory. {62:6} The kings, the mighty, and all who possess the earth will bless, glorify, and extol Him who rules over all, who has been hidden. {62:7} From the beginning, the Son of Man was hidden; the Most High preserved him in His might and revealed him to the elect. {62:8} The congregation of the elect and holy will be gathered, and all the elect will stand before him on that day. {62:9} All the kings, the mighty, the exalted, and those who rule the earth will fall on their faces, worshiping and hoping in the Son of Man, seeking mercy from him. {62:10} Nevertheless, the Lord of Spirits will press them so that they will hastily leave His presence, their faces filled with shame, their darkness deepening. {62:11} He will hand them over to the angels for punishment to execute vengeance for oppressing His children and elect. {62:12} They will be a spectacle for the righteous and the elect, who will rejoice over them, for the wrath of the Lord of Spirits rests upon them, and His sword is drunk with their blood. {62:13} The righteous and elect will be saved on that day, never to see the face of sinners and the unrighteous again. {62:14} The Lord of Spirits will be with them, and with that Son of Man, they will eat, lie down, and rise forever. {62:15} The righteous and elect will rise from the earth, no longer downcast, and they will be clothed in glorious garments. {62:16} These garments will be life from the Lord of Spirits: they will never grow old, nor will their glory fade away before the Lord of Spirits.

{63:1} In those days, the mighty and kings who possess the earth will plead with Him to grant them a brief respite from the angels of punishment to whom they have been delivered, so they can bow down and worship the Lord of Spirits, confessing their sins. {63:2} They will bless and glorify the Lord of Spirits, saying, "Blessed is the Lord of Spirits, the Lord of kings, the Lord of the mighty, the Lord of the rich, the Lord of glory, and the Lord of wisdom. {63:3} Your power is splendid in every secret thing from generation to generation, and Your glory forever. {63:4} Your secrets are deep and countless, and Your righteousness is beyond measure. {63:5} We have learned that we should glorify and bless the Lord of kings and Him who is king over all kings. {63:6} They will say, "If only we had rest to glorify and thank You and confess our faith before Your glory!" {63:7} Now we long for a little rest but cannot find it; we pursue it but do not attain it. {63:8} Light has vanished from before us, and darkness is our eternal dwelling. {63:9} We have not believed in You or glorified the name of the Lord of Spirits; our hope was in the scepter of our kingdom and in our glory. {63:10} In our day of suffering and trouble, He does not save us, and we find no respite to confess that our Lord is true in all His works, judgments, and justice, which are impartial. {63:11} We pass away from before His face because of our actions, and all our sins are accounted for in righteousness. {63:12} They will say to themselves, "Our souls are full of unrighteous gain, but it does not stop us from descending into the burdens of Sheol." {63:13} After that, their faces will be filled with darkness and shame before the Son of Man, and they will be driven from His presence, with the sword remaining before Him. {63:14} Thus spoke the Lord of Spirits: "This is the decree and judgment regarding the mighty, the kings, the exalted, and those who possess the earth before the Lord of Spirits."

{64:1} I saw other forms hidden in that place. {64:2} I heard the voice of the angel saying, "These are the angels who descended to earth, revealed hidden things to humanity, and led people into sin."

{65:1} In those days, Noah saw that the earth had sunk down and was close to destruction. {65:2} He arose and went to the ends of the earth, crying out to his grandfather Enoch. {65:3} Noah said three times in a bitter voice, "Hear me, hear me, hear me." {65:4} I asked him, "What is happening on the earth that it is in such a terrible state and shaking? Am I going to perish with it?" {65:5} There was a great disturbance on the earth, a voice was heard from heaven, and I fell on my face. Enoch, my grandfather, came and stood beside me, asking, "Why are you crying out with such bitterness and weeping?" {65:6} He said a command had gone forth from the Lord concerning those who dwell on the earth that their ruin was assured because they had learned all the secrets of the angels, the violence of the Satans, their most hidden powers, the powers of sorcery, witchcraft, and the skills of those who make molten images. {65:7} They learned how silver is produced from the earth's dust and how soft metals originate from it. {65:8} Lead and tin are not produced like the first; they come from a fountain that produces them, and an angel stands over it, who is the most important. {65:9} After that, my grandfather Enoch took me by the hand and raised me up, saying, "Go, for I have asked the Lord of Spirits about this disturbance on the earth." {65:10} He told me, "Because of their unrighteousness, their judgment is set and will not be delayed. Because of the sorceries they have pursued and learned, the earth and its inhabitants shall be destroyed." {65:11} They have no place for repentance forever because they revealed hidden things, and they are condemned. But you, my son, the Lord of Spirits knows you are pure and guiltless regarding these secrets. {65:12} He has destined your name to be among the holy ones, preserving you among those who dwell on the earth, and your righteous descendants are meant for kingship and great honors, with your lineage producing a fountain of righteousness and holiness without number forever.

{66:1} After that, he showed me the angels of punishment ready to unleash all the powers of the waters beneath the earth to bring judgment and destruction on all who dwell on the earth. {66:2} The Lord of Spirits commanded the angels going forth not to let the waters rise but to hold them back; those angels were in charge of the waters. {66:3} I left the presence of Enoch.

{67:1} In those days, the word of God came to me, saying, "Noah, your lot has come before Me, a lot without blame, a lot of love and righteousness. {67:2} Now the angels are building a wooden structure, and when they finish, I will place My hand upon it to preserve it. From it will come the seed of life, bringing about a change so that the earth will not remain uninhabited. {67:3} I will establish your descendants before Me forever, and I will spread those who dwell with you; they will not be unfruitful on the earth, but will be blessed and multiply in the name of the Lord. {67:4} I will imprison those angels who have shown unrighteousness in that burning valley that my grandfather Enoch previously showed me in the west among the mountains of gold, silver, iron, and soft metals. {67:5} I saw that valley where there was a great disturbance and a tumult of waters. {67:6} When all this happened, from the molten metal and the disturbance in that place arose a smell of sulfur, connected to those waters, and the valley of the angels who led humanity astray burned beneath that land. {67:7} From its valleys flowed streams of fire, where those angels are punished for misleading those who dwell on earth. {67:8} But in those days, those waters will serve kings, the mighty, and the exalted for healing the body, yet they will punish the spirit; their spirits are filled with lust, so they may be punished in their bodies, for they have denied the Lord of Spirits {67:9} and witness their punishment daily, yet do not believe in His name. As the burning of their bodies increases, a corresponding change will occur in their spirits forever; {67:10} before the Lord of Spirits, no one will utter an idle word. The judgment will come upon them {67:11} because they believe in the lust of their bodies and deny the Spirit of the Lord. Those waters will undergo a change in those days; when the angels are punished in these waters, the springs will change temperature, and when the angels ascend, the water will turn cold. {67:12} I heard Michael respond, saying, "This judgment upon the angels is a testimony for the kings and mighty who possess the earth. Since these waters of judgment provide healing for the bodies of the kings while indulging their lusts, they will not see or believe that these waters will change and become a fire that burns forever."

{68:1} After this, my grandfather Enoch taught me all the secrets contained in the book of Parables given to him, compiling them for me in its words. {68:2} On that day, Michael spoke to Raphael, saying, "The power of the spirit moves me and makes me tremble because of the severity of the judgment of the secrets, the judgment of the angels: who can withstand such harsh judgment that causes them to melt away? {68:3} And Michael continued, asking Raphael, "Who is the one whose heart is not softened by this judgment {68:4} that has been declared against them for leading others astray?" When he stood before the Lord of Spirits, Michael said to Raphael, "I will not take their side before the Lord; for the Lord of Spirits is angry with them because they act as if they are the Lord. {68:5} Therefore, all that is hidden will come upon them forever; neither angel nor man will share in it, for they alone have received their judgment forever."

{69:1} After this judgment, they will be terrified and tremble because they revealed these things to those who dwell on earth. {69:2} Behold the names of those angels: the first is Samjaza, the second Artaqifa, the third Armen, the fourth Kokabel, the fifth Turael, the sixth Rumjal, the seventh Danjal, the eighth Neqael, the ninth Baraqel, the tenth Azazel, the eleventh Armaros, the twelfth Batarjal, the thirteenth Busasejal, the fourteenth Hananel, the fifteenth Turel, the sixteenth Simapesiel, the seventeenth Jetrel, the eighteenth Tumael, the nineteenth Turel, the twentieth Rumael, and the twenty-first Azazel. {69:3} These are the chiefs of their angels and their names, leading groups of hundreds, fifties, and tens. {69:4} The first is Jeqon, who led astray all the sons of God, bringing them down to earth and leading them astray through the daughters of men. {69:5} The second is Asbeel; he gave evil counsel to the holy sons of God and led them astray, causing them to defile their bodies with the daughters of men. {69:6} The third is Gadreel; he showed the children of men all the ways of death and led Eve astray, revealing to humanity weapons of death: shields, coats of mail, swords, and all instruments of death. {69:7} From his influence, they have acted against those who dwell on earth from that day forward. {69:8} The fourth is Penemue; he taught humanity the bitter and the sweet and all the secrets of wisdom. {69:9} He instructed them in writing with ink and paper, leading many to sin from eternity to this day. Men were not created for such purposes, {69:10} to confirm their good faith with pen and ink. They were made like angels to remain pure and righteous, and death, which destroys everything, would not have taken them, but through this knowledge, they are perishing, consumed by it. {69:11} The fifth is Kasdeja; he revealed to the children of men all wicked actions of spirits and demons, including harm to embryos in the womb, and all the strikes that befall the soul, including snake bites and injuries caused by the noontime heat, known as Tabaet. {69:12} This is the task of Kasbeel, chief of the oath, who revealed it to the holy ones while dwelling high in glory. Its name is Biqa. {69:13} This angel requested Michael to show him the hidden name so he could pronounce it in the oath, causing fear among those who revealed secrets to humanity. {69:14} This oath is powerful and strong, and he placed it in the hand of Michael. {69:15} These are the secrets of this oath... they are strong through his oath: the heavens were suspended before the world was created, and forever. {69:16} Through it, the earth was founded on water, and beautiful waters flow from the secret recesses of the mountains, from the creation of the world until eternity. {69:17} Through this oath, the sea was created, with sand as its foundation against its anger, never to pass beyond it from creation until eternity. {69:18} Through this oath, the depths are secured and remain in place from eternity to eternity. {69:19} Through this oath, the sun and moon complete their courses, never deviating from their paths from eternity to eternity. {69:20} Through this oath, the stars complete their courses; He calls them by their names, and they answer Him from eternity to eternity. {69:21} Similarly, the spirits of the water, winds, and all breezes, along with their paths from all quarters, are preserved. {69:22} The voices of thunder and the light of lightning are also preserved, along with the chambers of hail, frost, mist, rain, and dew. All these acknowledge and thank the Lord of Spirits, glorifying Him with all their might; their food is every act of thanksgiving: they thank, glorify, and extol the name of the Lord of Spirits forever. {69:23} This oath is powerful over them, preserving their paths, ensuring their course is not destroyed. {69:24} There was great joy among them as they blessed, glorified, and extolled, for the name of that Son of Man had been revealed to them. {69:25} He sat on the throne of glory, and the totality of judgment was given to the Son of Man, who caused sinners to vanish and be destroyed from the face of the earth, along with those who led the world astray. {69:26} They will be bound with chains and imprisoned in their place of destruction, and all their works will vanish from the earth. {69:27} From that point on, nothing corruptible will exist; for that Son of Man has appeared and taken His seat on the throne of glory, and all evil will pass away before Him, and His word will go forth with strength before the Lord of Spirits.

{70:1} After this, during his lifetime, his name was elevated to that Son of Man and the Lord of Spirits among those who dwell on earth. {70:2} He was lifted on the chariots of the spirit, and his name disappeared among them. {70:3} From that day, I was no longer counted among them, and He set me between two winds, between the North and the West, where the angels measured for me the place for the elect and righteous. {70:4} There, I saw the first fathers and the righteous who have dwelt in that place since the beginning.

The Astronomical Book

{71:1} After this, my spirit was transformed and ascended into the heavens, where I saw the holy sons of God stepping on flames of fire. Their garments were white, and their faces shone like snow. {71:2} I saw two streams of fire, and the light of that fire sparkled like hyacinth, and I fell on my face before the Lord of Spirits. {71:3} The angel Michael, one of the archangels, took me by my right hand, lifted me up, and led me into all the secrets, showing me the secrets of righteousness. {71:4} He revealed to me the secrets of the ends of heaven, all the chambers of the stars, and all the luminaries, from where they emerge before the holy ones. {71:5} He transported my spirit into the highest heaven, where I saw a structure made of crystals, and between those crystals were tongues of living fire. {71:6} My spirit noticed the girdle that surrounded that house of fire, with streams of living fire on its four sides. {71:7} Surrounding it were Seraphim, Cherubic, and Ophannin, who do not sleep and guard the throne of His glory. {71:8} I saw countless angels, thousands upon thousands, and ten thousand times ten thousand, encircling that house. Michael, Raphael, Gabriel, and Phanuel, along with the holy angels above the heavens, went in and out of that house. {71:9} They emerged from that house, including Michael, Gabriel, Raphael, Phanuel, and many holy angels without number. {71:10} With them was the Head of Days, whose head was white and pure like wool, and His clothing was indescribable. {71:11} I fell on my face, my body relaxed, and my spirit was transformed; I cried out loudly, filled with power, blessing, glorifying, and extolling. {71:12} The blessings that came from my mouth were pleasing to that Head of Days. He came with Michael, Gabriel, Raphael, Phanuel, and thousands upon ten thousands of angels without number. {71:14} An angel approached me, greeting me with His voice, saying, "This is the Son of Man who is born unto righteousness. Righteousness surrounds Him, and the righteousness of the Head of Days will never abandon Him." {71:15} He continued, "He brings you peace in the name of the world to come; peace has been present since the creation of the world, and it will be yours forever and ever." {71:16} All will follow His ways since righteousness never leaves Him; their dwelling places will be with Him, and so will their inheritance, and they will never be separated from Him for eternity. Thus, there will be long days with that Son of Man & the righteous will find peace & a righteous path in the name of the Lord of Spirits forever.

{72:1} This is the book detailing the courses of the heavenly luminaries, their relationships according to their classes, dominion, and seasons, as well as their names, origins, and months, which Uriel, the holy angel who was with me and guides them, showed me. He revealed all their laws exactly as they are, relating to all the years of the world and eternity, until the new creation is complete and lasts forever. {72:2} The first law of the luminaries is that the sun rises from the eastern portals of heaven and sets in the western portals. {72:3} I saw six portals through which the sun rises and six through which it sets, and the moon rises and sets in these portals, led by the stars: six in the east and six in the west, all in an accurate order. {72:4} There are also many windows to the right and left of these portals. First, the great luminary named the sun goes forth, and its circumference is like the circumference of heaven, filled with illuminating and heating fire. {72:5} The chariot on which it ascends is driven by the wind, and the sun sets in the west, returning through the north to reach the east, guided to the correct portal to shine in the heavens. {72:6} It rises in the first month through the great portal, which is the fourth of the six portals in the east. {72:7} From that fourth portal where the sun rises in the first month, there are twelve window-openings, through which flames emerge when opened in their season. {72:8} When the sun rises in the heavens, it comes forth through that fourth portal for thirty consecutive mornings and sets precisely in the fourth portal in the west. {72:9} During this time, the day grows longer, and the night shorter, until the thirtieth morning. On that day, the day is longer than the night by a ninth part, with the day amounting to ten parts and the night to eight. {72:10} The sun rises from the fourth portal and sets in the fourth, returning to the fifth portal of the east for thirty mornings, rising from it and setting in the fifth portal. {72:12} During this period, the day lengthens by two parts, totaling eleven parts, while the night shortens to seven parts. {72:13} It returns to the east, entering the sixth portal, rising and setting there for thirty-one mornings due to its sign. {72:14} On that day, the day becomes longer than the night, being double the night, with the day amounting to twelve parts and the night shortened to six parts. {72:15} The sun rises to shorten the day and lengthen the night, returning to the east to rise in the sixth portal for thirty mornings. {72:16} After thirty mornings, the day decreases by exactly one part, resulting in eleven parts for the day and seven for the night. {72:17} The sun exits from the sixth portal in the west and goes to the east, rising in the fifth portal for thirty mornings and setting in the fifth portal in the west. {72:18} On that day, the day decreases by two parts, totaling ten for the day and eight for the night. {72:19} The sun exits from the fifth portal, sets in the fifth portal of the west, and rises in the fourth portal for thirty-one mornings due to its sign, setting in the west. {72:20} On that day, the day equals the night, each being nine parts long. {72:21} The sun rises from that portal, sets in the west, and returns to the east to rise in the third portal for thirty mornings, setting in the third portal in the west. {72:22} On that day, the night becomes longer than the day, with the night reaching ten parts and the day only eight parts by the thirtieth morning. {72:23} The sun rises from the third portal, sets in the west, returns to the east, and rises for thirty mornings in the second portal, also setting in the second portal in the west. {72:24} On that day, the night amounts to eleven parts while the day only has seven. {72:25} The sun rises from the second portal, sets in the west, and returns to the east to rise in the first portal for thirty-one mornings, setting in the first portal in the west. {72:26} On that day, the night becomes longer, amounting to double the day: the night equals twelve parts and the day equals six. {72:27} The sun traverses the divisions of its orbit and returns to those divisions, entering the portal for thirty mornings and setting in the west opposite it. {72:28} On that night, the night decreases by a ninth part, becoming eleven parts while the day remains seven. {72:29} The sun returns to the second portal in the east, completing its divisions of the orbit for thirty mornings, rising and setting. {72:30} On that day, the night shortens to ten parts while the day remains eight. {72:31} The sun rises from that portal, sets in the west, returns to the east, and rises in the third portal for thirty-one mornings, setting in the west. {72:32} On that day, the night decreases to nine parts, equal to the day, making the year exactly three hundred sixty-four days. {72:33} The length of day and night, and their variations come from the course of the sun, creating these distinctions. {72:34} Thus, the sun's course becomes longer each day and shorter each night. {72:35} This is the law and course of the sun, which returns and rises sixty times, as the great luminary named the sun, forever and ever. {72:36} What rises is the great luminary, named according to its appearance, as the Lord commanded. It rises, sets, never decreases or rests, but runs day and night, shining seven times brighter than the moon, while both are equal in size.

{73:1} After this law, I saw another law concerning the smaller luminary, called the moon. Her circumference is like that of heaven, and her chariot is driven by the wind, with light given to her in defined measures. {73:2} Her rising and setting change every month, and her days are like the days of the sun. When her light is full, it equals one-seventh of the sun's light. {73:3} Thus, she rises. Her first phase appears in the east on the thirtieth morning, becoming visible and marking the first phase of the moon on the thirtieth day along with the sun in the portal where the sun rises. {73:4} One half of her emerges as one-seventh part, while her entire circumference is dark except for one-seventh and one-fourteenth of her light. {73:5} When she receives one-seventh of her light, her total light equals one-seventh and half of that. {73:6} She sets with the sun, and when the sun rises, the moon rises with it, receiving half of one part of light, and during that night at the beginning of her morning, she sets with the sun, remaining invisible that night with fourteen parts and half of one. {73:7} She rises on that day with exactly one-seventh part, receding from the sun, and in her remaining days, she brightens in the remaining thirteen parts.

{74:1} I saw another law regarding how she completes her monthly cycle. Uriel, the holy angel who leads them all, showed me all these, their positions, and I recorded their positions as he revealed them, documenting their months and the appearance of their lights until fifteen days were completed. {74:2} She completes all her light in the east in single seventh parts and all her darkness in the west in single seventh parts. {74:3} In certain months, she alters her settings, and in others, she follows her own course. {74:4} For two months, the moon sets with the sun in the middle portals, the third and fourth. She emerges for seven days, turns back, and returns through the portal where the sun rises, completing all her light, then recedes from the sun. {74:5} Eight days later, she enters the sixth portal from which the sun emerges. {74:6} When the sun rises from the fourth portal, she emerges for seven days until she exits from the fifth, then turns back into the fourth portal and completes all her light, then recedes into the first portal in eight days. {74:7} She returns again in seven days into the fourth portal where the sun rises. {74:8} I observed their positions, how the moons rose and the sun set during those days. {74:9} If five years are added together, the sun has an excess of thirty days, and all the days accumulated in those five years total 364 days. {74:10} The excess from the sun and stars totals six days: in five years, six days each year amount to thirty days, while the moon lags behind the sun and stars by thirty days. {74:11} The sun and stars mark the years accurately, without advancing or delaying their positions by a single day for eternity, completing the years justly in 364 days. {74:12} In three years, there are 1,092 days, and in five years, 1,820 days, resulting in 2,912 days over eight years. For the moon alone, the total days in three years amount to 1,062 days, and in five years, she falls behind by fifty days, resulting in 1,770 days for five years. {74:13} Thus, in eight years, the days for the moon total 2,121 days. Over eight years, she falls behind by eighty days, summing up to eighty days for the entire period. {74:14} The year is accurately completed in accordance with their world stations and the positions of the sun, rising from the portals where it rises and sets for thirty days.

{75:1} The leaders of the thousands, who oversee all of creation and the stars, also manage the four extra days, which are an essential part of their duty according to the calendar year. They provide service during these four days that are not included in the annual count. Because of this, people often get confused about the calendar, as these heavenly bodies genuinely operate within their designated stations: one in the first portal, one in the third, one in the fourth, and one in the sixth portal. The precision of the year is achieved through its distinct three hundred sixty-four stations. {75:2} The angel Uriel showed me the signs, times, years, and days, whom the Lord of glory has appointed forever over all the heavenly luminaries. They are meant to govern the sky and be seen on earth, serving as guides for day and night—specifically the sun, moon, and stars, along with all the celestial beings that move in their heavenly paths. {75:3} Uriel also revealed to me twelve doors in the sun's chariot in the heavens, through which the sun's rays shine forth, distributing warmth over the earth when opened at the right times. {75:4} For the winds and the dew's spirit, these portals stand open in the heavens at the ends of the earth. {75:5} Regarding the twelve portals at the earth's ends, from which the sun, moon, and stars emerge, there are also many windows to the left and right of them. One window, when opened at the appropriate season, produces warmth, just like the doors through which the stars emerge, according to His commands, and they set in relation to their number. {75:6} I saw chariots in the heavens, moving in the world above those portals where the stars that never set revolve. One of these chariots is larger than the others, and it travels throughout the entire world.

{76:1} At the earth's ends, I saw twelve portals open to all quarters of the heavens, from which the winds emerge and blow across the earth. {76:2} Three of these are in the east, three in the west, three on the south side, and three on the north. The first three are in the east, followed by three in the north, three on the left side in the south, and three in the west. {76:3} Four of these portals bring winds of blessing and prosperity, while the other eight produce harmful winds. When these winds are unleashed, they cause destruction across the earth, affecting the waters, inhabitants, and everything on land and in the sea. {76:4} The first wind, known as the east wind, emerges through the first eastern portal, leaning toward the south. It brings desolation, drought, heat, and destruction. {76:5} The second portal in the middle brings what is suitable, providing rain, abundance, prosperity, and dew. {76:6} The third portal, directed northward, brings cold and drought. Following these, the south winds emerge through three portals: the first, leaning eastward, carries a hot wind. {76:7} The middle portal brings pleasant fragrances, dew, rain, prosperity, and health. The third portal, toward the west, produces dew, rain, locusts, and desolation. {76:8} Next, the north winds: from the seventh portal in the east come dew and rain, locusts, and desolation. The middle portal brings health, rain, dew, and prosperity; the third portal in the west produces clouds, frost, snow, rain, and dew. {76:9} Following these are the west winds: the first, next to the north, brings dew, frost, cold, snow, and ice. The middle portal produces dew, rain, prosperity, and blessings, while the last portal adjacent to the south brings drought, desolation, burning, and destruction. {76:10} Thus, the twelve portals of the four heavenly quarters are complete, and I have shown you all their laws, plagues, and blessings, my son Methuselah.

{77:1} The first quarter is called the east because it comes first; the second is the south, as the Most High will descend there, particularly in a special way. {77:2} The west quarter is called the diminished because it is where all heavenly luminaries fade and set. {77:3} The fourth quarter, the north, is divided into three sections: the first is for human habitation; the second includes seas, abysses, forests, rivers, darkness, and clouds; and the third part holds the garden of righteousness. {77:4} I saw seven high mountains, taller than any on earth, and from them comes frost, with days, seasons, and years passing by. {77:5} I observed seven rivers larger than all others: one from the west flows into the Great Sea, while two come from the north and pour into the Erythraean Sea in the east. {77:6} The remaining four emerge on the north side toward their own sea: two flow into the Erythraean Sea, and two into the Great Sea, discharging their waters there, and some say into the desert. {77:7} I saw seven large islands in the sea and on land: two on the mainland and five in the Great Sea.

{78:1} The names of the sun are as follows: the first is Orjares, and the second is Tomas. The moon has four names: the first is Asonja, the second is Ebla, the third is Benase, and the fourth is Erae. {78:2} These two great luminaries have a circumference similar to that of the heavens, and both are equal in size. The sun has seven portions of light added to it compared to the moon, and this light is transferred in specific amounts until the sun's seventh portion is depleted. {78:3} They set and enter the portals of the west, revolving from the north and emerging through the eastern portals of the heavens. {78:4} When the moon rises, one-fourteenth of its light is visible in the heavens; the light becomes full on the fourteenth day, reaching its peak. {78:5} It receives fifteen portions of light until the fifteenth day, when its light is fully accomplished according to the yearly cycle, reaching a total of fifteen parts, and the moon increases by fourteen parts. {78:6} As it wanes, on the first day it decreases to fourteen parts of light, on the second to thirteen, on the third to twelve, and so on, until on the thirteenth day it has two parts left, and on the fourteenth, it is reduced to half a seventh, with all remaining light disappearing entirely on the fifteenth. {78:7} In some months, the moon lasts twenty-nine days, and in one month it lasts twenty-eight. Uriel also showed me another law regarding how light is transferred to the moon and which side it comes from based on the sun. {78:8} During the period when the moon is gaining light, it is illuminated when opposite the sun for fourteen days; its light is fully accomplished in the heavens. {78:9} On the first day, it is called the new moon because that is when the light first appears on it. It becomes a full moon precisely when the sun sets in the west, rising in the east at night, shining all night until the sun rises opposite it, and the moon is seen across from the sun. {78:10} From the side where the moon's light originates, it wanes until all light fades and the month concludes, leaving its circumference empty of light. {78:11} It has three months of thirty days and three months of twenty-nine days, completing its waning in the first period, and for one hundred seventy-seven days in the first portal. {78:12} When it exits, it appears for three months of thirty days each, and for another three months, it appears for twenty-nine days each. At night, it resembles a man for twenty days, while during the day, it looks like the heavens, having nothing but its light.

{79:1} Now, my son, I have shown you everything, and the law governing all the stars in the heavens is complete. {79:2} He showed me all the laws for each day, every season of authority, each year, and the order for every month and week. {79:3} The moon's waning occurs in the sixth portal, where its light is completed, leading to the start of the waning period, which takes place in the first portal for one hundred seventy-seven days—counted as twenty-five weeks and two days. {79:4} The moon falls behind the sun and the stars by exactly five days in one cycle, after passing through this point you see. This is the representation of every luminary that Uriel the archangel, their leader, revealed to me.

{80:1} In those days, the angel Uriel answered me, saying: "Look, I have shown you everything, Enoch, and I have revealed it all to you so that you may see this sun, this moon, the leaders of the stars of heaven, and all those who govern them, along with their tasks, times, and departures." {80:2} During the days of sinners, years will be shortened, their crops will be slow to grow on their lands, and everything on earth will change and will not appear in its proper time; the rain will be withheld, and the heavens will hold it back. {80:3} In those times, the earth's fruits will be delayed and will not grow as expected, and the trees' fruits will be withheld at the right time. {80:4} The moon will change its cycle and will not appear as scheduled. {80:5} During those days, the sun will be visible, traveling in the evening at the edge of the great chariot in the west, shining more brightly than usual. {80:6} Many leaders of the stars will violate the established order, altering their paths and tasks, and failing to appear at the prescribed seasons. {80:7} The entire starry order will be hidden from sinners, and people on earth will be confused about them, straying from all their ways, even mistaking them for gods. {80:8} Evil will multiply among them, and punishment will come upon them, leading to their destruction.

{81:1} He said to me: "Observe, Enoch, these heavenly tablets, read what is written on them, and note every individual detail." {81:2} I looked at the heavenly tablets and read everything written there, understanding it all. I read the book of all mankind's deeds and of all flesh's children that will be on earth for generations to come. {81:3} Immediately, I blessed the great Lord, the King of glory, forever, for making all the works of the world, extolling Him for His patience and blessing Him for humanity. {81:4} Then I said: "Blessed is the person who dies in righteousness and goodness, for whom no record of unrighteousness exists and against whom no day of judgment can be found." {81:5} The seven holy ones brought me and set me on the earth before my house's door, saying: "Proclaim everything to your son Methuselah, and show all your children that no flesh is righteous in the sight of the Lord, for He is their Creator. You will stay with your son for one year, until you give your last commands, teaching and recording for them, and witnessing to all your children; in the second year, they will take you from their midst." {81:6} "Be strong in heart, for the good will proclaim righteousness to the good; the righteous will rejoice together and congratulate one another." {81:7} "But sinners will perish with sinners, and the apostate will fall with the apostate. {81:8} Those who practice righteousness will suffer because of humanity's actions and will be taken away because of the deeds of the wicked." {81:9} In those days, they ceased speaking to me, and I returned to my people, blessing the Lord of the world.

{82:1} Now, my son Methuselah, I am recounting all these things to you and writing them down for you! I have revealed everything to you and given you books about all of this, so preserve these books from your father's hand and ensure that you pass them on to future generations. {82:2} I have granted wisdom to you and your children, and to your children yet to come, so that they may pass it on to their children for generations—this wisdom that surpasses their understanding. {82:3} Those who comprehend it will not sleep but will listen attentively to learn this wisdom, which will be more satisfying to them than the best food. {82:4} Blessed are all the righteous, blessed are those who walk in the path of righteousness and do not sin like the sinners, throughout the days counted as the sun moves across the heavens, entering and exiting the portals for thirty days with the heads of thousands among the stars' order, along with the four intercalary days that divide the four parts of the year, leading them and accompanying them for four days. {82:5} Because of these, people will err and fail to include them in the yearly count; indeed, people will be confused and fail to recognize them accurately. {82:6} They are essential to the year's count and are truly recorded forever: one in the first portal, one in the third, one in the fourth, and one in the sixth, completing the year in three hundred sixty-four days. {82:7} The account is accurate, and the recorded count is exact, for Uriel has shown and revealed to me the luminaries, months, festivals, years, and days, to whom the Lord of all creation has subjected the heavenly host. {82:8} He has authority over night and day in the heavens, ensuring the light shines upon people—the sun, moon, and stars, along with all the heavenly powers that move in their circular paths. {82:9} These are the orders of the stars, which rise in their designated places, during their seasons, festivals, and months. {82:10} Here are the names of those who lead them, overseeing their entry at the proper times, in their orders, seasons, months, periods of dominion, and positions. Their four leaders, who divide the four parts of the year, enter first; after them come the twelve leaders of the months, and for the three hundred sixty days, there are heads over thousands who divide the days; for the four intercalary days, there are leaders that separate the four parts of the year. {82:11} These heads over thousands are interspersed between leader and leader, each behind a station, while their leaders make the divisions. {82:12} The names of the leaders who divide the four parts of the year are Milkiel, Helemmelek, Melejal, and Narel. The names of those who lead them are Adnarel, Ijasusael, and Elomeel—these three follow the leaders of the orders, and there is one that follows the three leaders of the orders, who themselves follow the leaders of the stations that divide the four parts of the year. {82:13} At the beginning of the year, Melkejal rises first and reigns; he is called Tamaini and the sun, ruling for ninety-one days. {82:14} These are the signs of the days observable on earth during his reign: sweat, heat, and calm; all trees bear fruit, and leaves grow on every tree, along with the wheat harvest, rose flowers, and all field flowers, while the winter trees wither. {82:15} The names of the leaders beneath them are Berkael, Zelebsel, and another head of a thousand named Hilujaseph; the days of this leader's dominion come to an end. {82:16} The next leader is Helemmelek, also known as the shining sun, whose days of light last ninety-one days. {82:17} The signs of his days on earth are scorching heat and dryness, during which the trees ripen their fruits, producing them ripe and ready, the sheep breed and become pregnant, and all earth's fruits are gathered in, along with everything in the fields and the winepress. {82:18} These are the names, orders, and leaders of those heads of thousands: Gidaljal, Keel, and Heel, along with the head of a thousand added to them, named Asfael; the days of his dominion also come to an end.

The Book of Dreams

{83:1} Now, my son Methuselah, I will share all my visions that I have seen, recounting them to you. {83:2} I saw two visions before I took a wife, and they were quite different from each other: the first occurred when I was learning to write, and the second was a terrifying vision I had before I took your mother. {83:3} Regarding these, I prayed to the Lord. I was lying down in the house of my grandfather Mahalalel when I saw a vision of the heavens collapsing and being lifted away, falling to the earth. {83:4} When it fell, I saw the earth swallowed up in a great abyss, with mountains stacked upon mountains, and hills sinking into hills, while tall trees were uprooted and thrown down into the abyss. {83:5} At that moment, a word fell into my mouth, and I cried out, saying, "The earth is destroyed." {83:6} My grandfather Mahalalel woke me as I lay near him and asked, "Why are you crying, my son, and why are you so distressed?" {83:7} I told him the entire vision I had seen, and he replied, "You have seen a terrible thing, my son; your dream-vision holds great significance regarding the secrets of all the sin on the earth: it must sink into the abyss and face a great destruction. {83:8} Now, my son, rise and pray to the Lord of glory, since you are a believer, that a remnant may remain on the earth and that He will not destroy the whole earth. {83:9} From heaven, all this will come upon the earth, resulting in great destruction." {83:10} After that, I rose and prayed, imploring and beseeching, and I wrote down my prayer for future generations, and I will reveal everything to you, my son Methuselah. When I went outside and saw the heavens, the sun rising in the east, the moon setting in the west, and a few stars, and the whole earth just as He knew it in the beginning, I blessed the Lord of judgment and praised Him for making the sun rise from the windows of the east, ascending and moving across the face of the heavens, following the path laid out for him.

{84:1} I lifted my hands in righteousness and blessed the Holy and Great One, speaking with the breath of my mouth and the tongue of flesh that God has made for the children of men so they can speak with it. {84:2} Blessed are You, O Lord, King, great and mighty in Your greatness, Lord of all creation in the heavens, King of kings and God of the entire world. Your power, kingship, and greatness last forever and ever, and throughout all generations, Your dominion remains. All the heavens are Your throne forever, and the whole earth is Your footstool for eternity. {84:3} For You have made and rule all things, and nothing is too difficult for You. Wisdom does not depart from Your throne, nor does it turn away from Your presence. You know, see, and hear everything; nothing is hidden from You, for You see everything. {84:4} And now the angels of Your heavens are guilty of transgressions, and Your wrath rests upon humanity until the great day of judgment. {84:5} Now, O God, Lord, and Great King, I implore and beseech You to fulfill my prayer: to leave me a legacy on earth, not to destroy all humanity, making the earth uninhabited and causing eternal destruction. {84:6} Now, my Lord, remove from the earth the flesh that has provoked Your wrath, but establish the flesh of righteousness and uprightness as a plant of eternal seed, and do not hide Your face from the prayer of Your servant, O Lord.

{85:1} After this, I saw another dream, and I will share the entire dream with you, my son. {85:2} Enoch lifted his voice and spoke to his son Methuselah: "To you, my son, I will speak; listen to my words and pay attention to the dream-vision of your father. {85:3} Before I took your mother Edna, I had a vision while lying in bed, and behold, a white bull emerged from the earth. After it, a heifer came forth, along with two bulls—one black and the other red. {85:4} The black bull gored the red one and chased it across the earth, and after that, I could no longer see the red bull. {85:5} But the black bull grew, and the heifer followed him, and I saw that many oxen came from him that looked like him and followed him. {85:6} The first cow went away from the black bull to search for the red one but could not find him, and she lamented greatly over him and sought him. {85:7} I looked until that first bull came to her and comforted her, and from that time on, she no longer cried. {85:8} Then she bore another white bull, and after him, she had many bulls and black cows. {85:9} I saw that white bull grow and become a great white bull, and from him, many white bulls came forth, resembling him. They began to give birth to many white bulls, which also looked like them, one following another, many in number.

{86:1} Again, I saw with my eyes while I slept, and I looked up at the heavens and saw a star fall from heaven. {86:2} It rose and grazed among those oxen. After that, I saw the large black oxen, and behold, they all changed their stalls and pastures, living together. {86:3} I looked again in the vision and turned my gaze to the heavens; behold, many stars descended and joined that first star, becoming bulls among those cattle and grazing with them. {86:4} I watched them, and behold, they all exposed themselves like horses and began to mate with the cows of the oxen, resulting in pregnancies that produced elephants, camels, and donkeys. {86:5} All the oxen were afraid of them, terrified, and began to bite and devour each other and gore with their horns. {86:6} They also began to eat the oxen, and behold, all the children of the earth trembled and quaked before them, fleeing in fear.

{87:1} Again, I saw them begin to gore each other and devour one another, and the earth cried out. {87:2} I lifted my eyes again to heaven and saw in the vision, behold, beings who looked like white men came forth from heaven. {87:3} Four went out from that place, and three came with them. {87:4} The three that arrived last took me by the hand and lifted me up away from the generations of the earth, raising me to a high place and showing me a tower raised high above the earth, while all the hills were lower. {87:5} One said to me, "Stay here until you see everything that happens to those elephants, camels, donkeys, the stars, and the oxen, and all of them."

{88:1} I saw one of those four who had come forth first seize that first star that had fallen from heaven, binding it hand and foot and casting it into an abyss; this abyss was narrow, deep, horrible, and dark. {88:2} One of them drew a sword and gave it to the elephants, camels, and donkeys; then they began to strike each other, and the whole earth trembled because of them. {88:3} As I watched in the vision, lo, one of those four who had come forth from heaven stoned them, gathering and capturing all the great stars whose members resembled those of horses, binding them hand and foot, and casting them into the abyss of the earth.

{89:1} One of the four beings approached that white bull and quietly instructed him in a secret, and he was not frightened. He was born a bull but became a man, built a large vessel, and lived on it. {89:2} Three bulls also lived with him on that vessel, and they were covered. I looked up to heaven again and saw a high roof with seven water torrents on it, and those torrents {89:3} poured a lot of water into an enclosed area. Then I looked again and saw fountains opening on the surface of that large enclosure, and the water began to swell and rise. {89:4} I observed that enclosure until its entire surface was covered with water. The water, darkness, and mist increased, and as I looked at the height of the water, it had risen above that enclosure and was spilling over it, standing upon the earth. {89:5} All the cattle in that enclosure gathered together until I saw how they sank and were swallowed by the water, perishing. But that vessel floated on the water, while all the oxen, elephants, camels, and donkeys sank to the bottom, and I could no longer see them; they could not escape and were lost in the depths. {89:6} I continued to watch until those water torrents were removed from that high roof, and the earth's chasms were leveled, and other abysses opened. The water began to flow into these, making the earth visible; the vessel settled on the ground, the darkness faded, and light appeared. {89:9} The white bull that had become a man came out of that vessel, along with the three bulls, one of which was white like him, one red as blood, and one black. That white bull departed from them. {89:10} They started to give birth to various beasts of the field and birds, producing different species: lions, tigers, wolves, dogs, hyenas, wild boars, foxes, squirrels, pigs, falcons, vultures, kites, eagles, and ravens; among them was a white bull born. They began to attack one another, but that white bull, born among them, fathered a wild ass and another white bull. {89:12} The wild asses multiplied. The bull that was born from him fathered a black wild boar and a white sheep; the wild boar had many offspring, while that sheep produced twelve sheep. When those twelve sheep grew, they gave one to the wild asses, and those wild asses gave that sheep to the wolves, where it grew up among them. The Lord brought the eleven sheep to live with it and pasture among the wolves; they multiplied and formed many flocks of sheep. {89:16} The wolves began to fear them and oppressed them until they destroyed their young ones, casting their offspring into a river of much water. The sheep cried out because of their young and complained to their Lord. A sheep that had escaped the wolves fled to the wild asses; I saw how the sheep lamented and cried, pleading with their Lord with all their strength until the Lord of the sheep descended from a high place at their voice and came to them to pasture them. {89:18} He called that sheep which had escaped the wolves and spoke to it about the wolves, telling it to warn them not to touch the sheep. That sheep went to the wolves as commanded by the Lord, and another sheep joined it, and together they went to the assembly of the wolves and admonished them not to harm the sheep from then on. {89:19} But I saw the wolves oppressing the sheep with all their might, and the sheep cried out. The Lord came to the sheep, and they began to strike those wolves, and the wolves started to wail; the sheep became quiet and stopped crying. {89:21} I saw the sheep until they left the wolves; the wolves were blinded and chased after the sheep with all their strength. The Lord of the sheep went with them as their leader, and all His sheep followed Him; His face was dazzling, glorious, and awe-inspiring. The wolves {89:24} pursued the sheep until they reached a sea of water. That sea parted, and the waters stood on either side before them; their Lord led them and placed Himself between them and the wolves. The wolves did not yet see the sheep and charged into the sea, following them. {89:26} When the wolves saw the Lord of the sheep, they turned to flee, but the sea closed in on them and rose until it drowned the wolves. I saw until all the wolves that pursued those sheep perished in the water. {89:28} The sheep escaped from that water and entered a wilderness, where there was neither water nor grass; they began to open their eyes and see. I saw the Lord of the sheep pasturing them, giving them water and grass, and that sheep leading them. {89:30} That sheep ascended to the top of a high rock, and the Lord of the sheep sent it to them. I saw the Lord of the sheep standing before them, and His appearance was great, terrible, and majestic. All those sheep saw Him and were afraid. They trembled before Him and cried to the sheep among them, {89:32} saying, "We cannot stand before our Lord or see Him." The sheep that led them ascended to the top of the rock again, but the sheep began to go astray, losing the way He had shown them, though that sheep was unaware. The Lord of the sheep was very angry with them, and that sheep realized it, descending from the rock to the sheep, finding many blinded and astray. {89:34} When they saw it, they feared and trembled at its presence, wanting to return to their folds. That sheep took other sheep with it, came to those who had strayed, and began to slay them; the sheep feared its presence, and that sheep brought back those who had gone astray to their folds. {89:36} I saw in this vision until that sheep became a man and built a house for the Lord of the sheep, placing all the sheep in that house. {89:37} I saw until this sheep, which had met the leading sheep, fell asleep, and I saw until all the great sheep died and little ones arose in their place; they found a pasture and approached a stream of water. That sheep, their leader who had become a man, withdrew and fell asleep; all the sheep sought it and cried out for it. {89:39} I saw until they stopped crying for that sheep and crossed the stream of water; two sheep arose as leaders in place of those that had fallen asleep. I saw until the sheep arrived at a beautiful place, a pleasant and glorious land, until they were satisfied. That house stood among them in the pleasant land. {89:41} Sometimes their eyes were opened and sometimes blinded, until another sheep arose, leading them and bringing them all back, and their eyes were opened. {89:42} The dogs, foxes, and wild boars began to devour those sheep until the Lord of the sheep raised another sheep, a ram from their midst, to lead them. This ram butted against the dogs, foxes, and wild boars until he destroyed them all. That sheep, whose eyes were opened, saw that ram among the sheep, but it abandoned its glory and began to butt the sheep, trampling them and behaving improperly. {89:45} The Lord of the sheep sent a lamb to another lamb, raising it to become a ram and leader of the sheep instead of the ram that had abandoned its glory. It approached it and spoke to it alone, raising it to be a ram and making it the prince and leader of the sheep. Throughout these events, the dogs continued to oppress the sheep. {89:47} The first ram pursued the second ram, which fled before it. I saw until the dogs pulled down the first ram. The second ram arose and led the little sheep. The sheep grew and multiplied; all the dogs, foxes, and wild boars feared and fled from it. That ram butted and killed the wild beasts, who lost their power over the sheep and robbed them no more. {89:49} That ram fathered many sheep and fell asleep; a little sheep became a ram in its place, becoming the prince and leader of those sheep. {89:50} The house became great and broad, built for the sheep; a tall, great tower was constructed on the house for the Lord of the sheep. The house was low, but the tower was high and the Lord of the sheep stood on that tower, where they offered a full table before Him. {89:51} Again, I saw those sheep erring and going in many directions, forsaking their house; the Lord of the sheep called some from among them and sent them to the sheep, but they began to slay those sent. One of them was saved and not slain; it fled and cried aloud over the sheep, but they sought to kill it. The Lord of the sheep saved it and brought it up to me, making it dwell there. {89:53} Many other sheep He sent to testify and lament over them. After that, I saw that when they abandoned the Lord's house and tower, they fell away entirely, their eyes blinded. I saw the Lord of the sheep how He caused much slaughter among them in their herds until those sheep invited destruction and betrayed His place. {89:56} He gave them over to the hands of lions, tigers, wolves, hyenas, foxes, and all wild beasts, and those beasts began to tear apart the sheep. I saw that He forsook their house and tower, giving them all into the hands of lions to tear and devour them, and into the hands of all the wild beasts. {89:59} I cried out with all my strength to the Lord of the sheep, pleading with Him about the sheep that were devoured by all the wild beasts. But He remained unmoved, even though He saw it, and He rejoiced at their destruction and abandonment, leaving them to be devoured by the beasts. {89:60} He called seventy shepherds, handing the sheep over to them so they might pasture them. He instructed the shepherds and their companions to pasture the sheep from then on, commanding them on what to do. {89:61} He delivered the sheep to them in an orderly manner, informing them of which were to be destroyed—those they were to kill. He instructed them to observe and record everything the shepherds did to the sheep, as they would destroy more than commanded. {89:63} He told them to document every excess and destruction by the shepherds, keeping track of how many they killed according to His command and how many according to their own desires. Record each shepherd's destruction, {89:65} but they shall not know it, and you shall not inform them or admonish them, just record against each one all the destruction they cause and present it to me. {89:66} I saw until those shepherds tended to the sheep in their season; they began to kill and destroy more than they were ordered, delivering the sheep into the hands of the lions. The lions and tigers devoured most of the sheep, and the wild boars joined them; they burned the tower and demolished the house. {89:67} I became very sad about that tower because the sheep's house was destroyed, and afterwards I could not see if the sheep had entered that house. {89:68} The shepherds and their companions delivered the sheep to all the wild beasts to be devoured, and each one received a specific number, as recorded by another in a book of how many each destroyed. Each one killed many more than prescribed, and I began to weep and lament for those sheep. {89:71} In the vision, I saw the one who wrote down all the destruction by the shepherds, day by day, and he brought the entire book to the Lord of the sheep, showing all that had been done, and all that each shepherd had destroyed and delivered to death. The book was read before the Lord of the sheep, who took it, read it, sealed it, and laid it down. {89:72} Immediately, I saw how the shepherds tended to the sheep for twelve hours; behold, three of those sheep returned, entered, and began to rebuild what had fallen of that house. The wild boars tried to stop them, but they could not. {89:74} They began to rebuild as before, rearing that tower, which was named the high tower, and they placed a table before the tower, but all the bread on it was polluted and impure. Regarding all this, the eyes of those sheep were blinded, so they did not see; the eyes of their shepherds were also blinded; they delivered the sheep in large numbers to their shepherds for destruction, trampling them underfoot and devouring them. {89:76} The Lord of the sheep remained unmoved until all the sheep scattered in the field and mingled with the beasts. The shepherds did not save them from the beasts. This one who wrote the book took it up, showed it, read it before the Lord of the sheep, implored Him for the sheep, and testified against all the shepherds. He took the book and laid it down beside Him and left.

{90:1} And I saw that in this way, thirty-five shepherds took turns to care for the sheep, each completing their period as the first shepherds had. After them, others took over to tend the sheep for their own periods, each shepherd serving in his time. {90:2} Then, in my vision, I saw all the birds of heaven coming: the eagles, vultures, kites, and ravens, but the eagles led the flock. They began to devour the sheep, plucking out their eyes and eating their flesh. {90:3} The sheep cried out as their flesh was being eaten by the birds, and I watched in sorrow as I dreamed about the shepherd who was meant to protect them. {90:4} I saw the sheep being devoured by dogs, eagles, and kites, leaving no flesh, skin, or sinew on them, only bones that eventually fell to the ground, leaving very few sheep remaining. {90:5} I saw that twenty-three more shepherds took their turns, completing fifty-eight periods in all. {90:6} But then, lambs were born from the remaining white sheep, and they began to open their eyes and see, {90:7} and they cried out to the sheep. Yet, the older sheep did not listen to their cries, for they were very deaf and their eyes were extremely blind. {90:8} I saw in the vision that ravens flew upon those lambs, grabbed one of them, dashed it into pieces, and devoured it. {90:9} I saw that horns began to grow on these lambs, but the ravens struck down their horns. Then I saw that a great horn grew on one of the sheep, and the eyes of the sheep opened. {90:10} It looked around, and their eyes were opened, and it cried out to the sheep. {90:11} The rams saw this, and they all ran toward it. But despite all this, the eagles, vultures, ravens, and kites continued tearing at the sheep, swooping down upon them, and eating them. Still, the sheep remained silent, though the rams wept and cried out. {90:12} The ravens fought against the ram with the horn and tried to bring down its horn, but they were unable to overpower it. {90:13} All the eagles, vultures, ravens, and kites gathered together, and even the sheep of the field came with them, helping one another to break the ram's horn. {90:14} I saw until a great sword was given to the sheep, and the sheep attacked all the beasts of the field, slaying them. The beasts and birds of the heavens fled from the sheep's presence. {90:15} I saw the man who wrote the book at the Lord's command. He opened the book that recorded the destruction the last twelve shepherds had caused, showing that they had destroyed much more than their predecessors, before the Lord of the sheep. {90:16} I saw until the Lord of the sheep came and took the staff of His wrath into His hand and struck the earth, causing it to split open. All the beasts and birds of the heavens fell from among the sheep and were swallowed by the earth, which covered them. {90:17} I saw that a throne was set up in a pleasant land, and the Lord of the sheep sat upon it. The one who wrote the book opened the sealed books before the Lord of the sheep. {90:18} The Lord called the seven first white ones and commanded them to bring before Him, starting with the first star that had led the way, all the stars whose private parts (genitalia) were like those of horses. They brought them all before Him. {90:19} He said to the one who had written, being one of the seven white ones, "Take those seventy shepherds to whom I entrusted the sheep. They, acting on their own authority, killed more than I had commanded." {90:20} And behold, they were all bound and stood before Him. {90:21} The judgment was held first over the stars, and they were found guilty and sent to the place of condemnation, cast into an abyss full of fire, flames, and pillars of fire. {90:22} The seventy shepherds were also judged and found guilty, and they were thrown into the fiery abyss. {90:23} At that time, I saw another abyss opened in the middle of the earth, full of fire, and those blinded sheep were judged and found guilty. They were cast into this fiery abyss and burned. This abyss was located to the right of that house. {90:24} I saw the sheep burning, and their bones were burning as well. {90:25} I watched until the old house was folded up, and all its pillars, beams, and ornaments were folded up and carried away to a place in the southern land. {90:26} Then I saw that the Lord of the sheep brought a new house, greater and higher than the first, and He set it up in the place of the first house, which had been folded up. All its pillars were new, and its ornaments were new and larger than those of the old house, and all the sheep were inside it. {90:27} I saw that the sheep that had been left, along with all the beasts of the earth and birds of the heavens, bowed down and submitted to the sheep, making requests and obeying them in everything. {90:28} After this, the three who were clothed in white and had seized me by my hand (and the ram with the horn also took hold of me) placed me among the sheep before the judgment began. {90:29} All the sheep were white, and their wool was abundant and clean. {90:30} All those that had been destroyed and scattered, including all the beasts of the field and the birds of the heavens, gathered in that house, and the Lord of the sheep rejoiced greatly because they had all returned to His house in goodness. {90:31} I saw that they laid down the sword that had been given to the sheep, and it was returned to the house and sealed before the Lord. {90:32} All the sheep were invited into the house, but it was too small to hold them all. {90:33} The eyes of all the sheep were opened, and they saw the goodness, and there was not a single one among them who did not see. {90:34} I saw that the house was large, broad, and very full. {90:35} I saw that a white bull was born with large horns, and all the beasts of the field and the birds of the air feared it and made petitions to it constantly. {90:36} I saw that all their generations were transformed, and they all became white bulls. The first among them became a lamb, and the lamb grew into a great animal with large black horns on its head, and the Lord of the sheep rejoiced over it and all the oxen. {90:37} I slept in their midst and awoke, having seen everything. {90:38} This is the vision I saw while I slept, and when I awoke, I blessed the Lord of righteousness and gave Him glory. {90:39} Then I wept with great sorrow, and my tears did not stop flowing until I could bear it no longer. The vision I saw troubled me deeply because I knew that all these things would come to pass and be fulfilled. {90:40} All the deeds of men were shown to me in their proper order. {90:41} On that night, I remembered the first dream I had, and because of it, I wept and was deeply troubled by what I had seen.

The Epistle of Enoch

{91:1} Now, my son Methuselah, gather all your brothers and assemble all the sons of your mother. The word calls me, and the spirit is poured out upon me so that I can show you everything that will happen to you forever. {91:2} Methuselah went and called all his brothers, gathering his relatives. {91:3} He spoke to all the children of righteousness, saying: Listen, you sons of Enoch, to all the words of your father, and pay attention to my voice; I urge you, my beloved: {91:4} Love righteousness and walk in it. Do not approach righteousness with a divided heart, and do not associate with those who have a divided heart. Walk in righteousness, my sons, and it will guide you on good paths, with righteousness as your companion. {91:5} For I know that violence will increase on the earth, and a great punishment will be carried out, putting an end to all unrighteousness. {91:6} Yes, it will be cut off from its roots, and its entire structure will be destroyed. {91:7} Unrighteousness will return to the earth, and all acts of unrighteousness, violence, and transgression will prevail in double measure. {91:8} When sin, unrighteousness, blasphemy, and all kinds of violence increase, and apostasy, transgression, and uncleanness abound, a great punishment will come from heaven upon all of this. The holy Lord will come with wrath and punishment to execute judgment on the earth. {91:9} In those days, violence will be cut off from its roots, along with the roots of unrighteousness and deceit, and they will be destroyed from under heaven. {91:10} All the idols of the nations will be abandoned, and their temples will burn with fire, removed from the entire earth. {91:11} The nations will be cast into the judgment of fire, perishing in wrath and severe judgment forever. {91:12} The righteous will awaken from their sleep, and wisdom will be given to them. After that, the roots of unrighteousness will be cut off, and sinners will be destroyed by the sword, removed from the blasphemers everywhere, and those who plan violence and commit blasphemy will perish by the sword. {91:18} Now I tell you, my sons, and show you the paths of righteousness and the paths of violence. I will show them to you again so that you know what is to come. {91:19} Now, listen to me, my sons, and walk in the paths of righteousness; do not walk in the paths of violence, for all who do so will perish forever.

{92:1} The book written by Enoch—Enoch indeed wrote this complete doctrine of wisdom, praised by all men and a judge of the earth for all my children who live on the earth, and for future generations who will observe righteousness and peace. {92:2} Do not let your spirit be troubled by the times, for the Holy and Great One has appointed days for everything. {92:3} The righteous will awaken from sleep, rising to walk in the paths of righteousness, and all their actions will be rooted in eternal goodness and grace. {92:4} He will be gracious to the righteous, granting them eternal uprightness and power, so they will be filled with goodness and righteousness, walking in eternal light. {92:5} Sin will perish in darkness forever and will never be seen from that day onward.

{93:1,2} After that, Enoch began to recount from the books, saying: I will speak about the children of righteousness, the elect of the world, and the plant of uprightness. I, Enoch, will declare these things to you, my sons, based on what was shown to me in a heavenly vision and what I learned from the holy angels and the heavenly tablets. {93:3} Enoch began recounting from the books, saying: I was born seventh in the first week, when judgment and righteousness still existed. {93:4} After me, in the second week, great wickedness will arise, deceit will spring up, and this will mark the first end. In it, a man will be saved, and afterward, unrighteousness will grow, and a law will be established for sinners. {93:5} After that, in the third week, at its close, a man will be chosen as the plant of righteous judgment, and his descendants will be the plant of righteousness forever. {93:6} In the fourth week, at its end, visions of the holy and righteous will be seen, and a law will be made for all generations, providing a sanctuary for them. {93:7} In the fifth week, at its close, the house of glory and dominion will be built forever. {93:8} In the sixth week, those who live there will be blinded, and their hearts will forsake wisdom. A man will ascend during this time, and at its end, the house of dominion will be burned with fire, and the whole lineage of the chosen root will be scattered. {93:9} In the seventh week, an apostate generation will emerge, with many wicked deeds, all of which will be apostate. {93:10} At its close, the elect righteous from the eternal plant of righteousness will be chosen to receive sevenfold instruction concerning all His creation. {93:11} For who among all humanity can hear the voice of the Holy One without fear? Who can understand His thoughts? Who can see all the works of heaven? {93:12} Who can comprehend heaven, understand its height, know how it is established, count the stars, or see where all the luminaries rest?

{94:1} Now I say to you, my sons, love righteousness and walk in it, for the paths of righteousness are worthy of acceptance, while the paths of unrighteousness will suddenly be destroyed and vanish. {94:2} The paths of violence and death will be revealed to certain men of a generation, and they will distance themselves from them and not follow. {94:3} Now I say to you, the righteous: Do not walk in the paths of wickedness or death, and do not approach them, lest you be destroyed. {94:4} Seek and choose righteousness and an elect life, walk in the paths of peace, and you will live and prosper. {94:5} Keep my words in your hearts and do not let them fade away; I know that sinners will try to lead you to mistreat wisdom, leaving no place for her and diminishing every kind of temptation. {94:6} Woe to those who build unrighteousness and oppression, laying deceit as their foundation; they will be suddenly overthrown and will have no peace. {94:7} Woe to those who construct their houses with sin; all their foundations will collapse, and they will fall by the sword. Those who acquire gold and silver through judgment will suddenly perish. {94:8} Woe to you, rich ones, for you have trusted in your riches; you will leave them behind because you did not remember the Most High in your days of wealth. {94:9} You have committed blasphemy and unrighteousness, preparing for the day of slaughter, the day of darkness, and the great judgment. {94:10} Thus I speak and declare to you: The One who created you will overthrow you, and there will be no compassion for your downfall; your Creator will rejoice at your destruction. {94:11} The righteous in those days will be a reproach to the sinners and the godless.

{95:1} Oh, that my eyes were a cloud of water, that I might weep over you, pouring down my tears like a rain cloud, so I might find rest from my troubled heart! {95:2} Who has allowed you to commit reproaches and wickedness? Judgment will surely overtake you, sinners. {95:3} Do not fear, you righteous; the Lord will deliver them back into your hands, so you can execute judgment upon them as you wish. {95:4} Woe to you who utter irreversible curses; healing will be far from you because of your sins. {95:5} Woe to you who repay evil to your neighbor, for you will be repaid according to your actions. {95:6} Woe to you, false witnesses, and those who practice injustice, for you will perish suddenly. {95:7} Woe to you, sinners, for you persecute the righteous; you will be delivered and persecuted due to injustice, and its burden will be heavy upon you.

{96:1} Be hopeful, you righteous, for the sinners will suddenly perish before you, and you will rule over them as you desire. {96:2} On the day of the sinners' distress, your children will rise like eagles, their nests higher than vultures. You will hide in the crevices of the earth and the cracks of rocks, like rabbits fleeing the unrighteous, while the sirens (mythical creatures) will sigh and weep because of you. {96:3} So do not fear, those of you who have suffered, for you will receive healing, and a bright light will guide you. You will hear a voice of rest from heaven. {96:4} Woe to you sinners, for your wealth makes you appear righteous, but your hearts condemn you, and this will serve as a witness against your evil deeds. {96:5} Woe to you who feast on the finest wheat, drink wine from large bowls, and trample the poor with your power. {96:6} Woe to you who drink from every fountain, for you will soon wither away because you have abandoned the fountain of life. {96:7} Woe to those who practice unrighteousness, deceit, and blasphemy; these deeds will stand as a testimony against you. {96:8} Woe to the mighty who oppress the righteous with their strength, for your day of destruction is near. {96:9} In that time, many good days will come to the righteous, on the day of your judgment.

{97:1} Believe, righteous ones, that sinners will face shame and perish in the day of unrighteousness. {97:2} Be aware, sinners, that the Most High is mindful of your destruction, and the angels of heaven rejoice over your downfall. {97:3} What will you do, sinners, and where will you flee on judgment day when you hear the prayers of the righteous? {97:4} You will suffer like those who have been companions of sinners. {97:5} In those days, the prayers of the righteous will reach the Lord, and your judgment day will come. {97:6} All your unrighteous deeds will be read aloud before the Great Holy One, and you will be covered in shame. He will reject all works founded on unrighteousness. {97:7} Woe to you sinners, living on land or sea, for your memory will bear witness against you. {97:8} Woe to you who gather silver and gold through unrighteousness, thinking you've become rich with all you desire. {97:9} But your wealth will slip away like water, for it was gained through evil, and a great curse will fall upon you.

{98:1} Now I swear to you, wise and foolish alike, that you will face many trials on earth. {98:2} Men will adorn themselves more than women, wear garments more splendid than virgins, and be surrounded by grandeur, wealth, and fine food as if poured out like water. {98:3} Yet they will lack wisdom, and perish with their possessions, their glory, and splendor. Their spirits will be cast into the fire, and they will face shame, slaughter, and destruction. {98:4} I have sworn, sinners, that just as a mountain cannot become a slave or a hill cannot serve a woman, so sin was not sent upon the earth, but humans created it, and those who commit it will fall under a great curse. {98:5} Women were not meant to be barren, but through their own actions, they die childless. {98:6} I swear by the Holy Great One that your evil deeds are revealed in heaven, and none of your acts of oppression are hidden. {98:7} Do not think or say that you are unaware, for every sin is recorded in heaven each day before the Most High. {98:8} Now you know that your oppression is written down, and will be remembered on the day of judgment. {98:9} Woe to you fools, for your foolishness will lead to your death. You transgress against the wise and will not receive good fortune. {98:10} Know that you are prepared for the day of destruction, so do not hope to live. You will depart and die, for no ransom can save you. {98:11} Woe to the hard-hearted who commit wickedness and consume blood. From where do you receive good things to eat and drink? From the abundance the Most High placed on earth, yet you will have no peace. {98:12} Woe to you who love unrighteous deeds. Why do you expect good fortune? You will be delivered into the hands of the righteous, who will slay you without mercy. {98:13} Woe to you who rejoice in the suffering of the righteous; no grave will be dug for you. {98:14} Woe to you who disregard the words of the righteous; you will have no hope of life. {98:15} Woe to you who write lies and ungodly words to deceive others. You will find no peace, only sudden death.

{99:1} Woe to those who commit godlessness, glorify lies, and take pride in them, for you will perish and find no happiness. {99:2} Woe to those who twist words of righteousness, transgress eternal laws, and transform themselves into sinners; they will be trampled upon the earth. {99:3} In those days, righteous ones, prepare to raise your prayers as a testimony before the angels, so they can present the sins of the sinners to the Most High. {99:4} In those days, nations will be stirred up, and families will rise on the day of destruction. {99:5} The destitute will abandon their children, causing them to perish, even the infants. They will show no pity for their loved ones. {99:6} I swear to you sinners that bloodshed will be endless. Those who worship idols, spirits, and demons will find no help. {99:7} Their hearts will be blinded by fear, and their dreams will deceive them. {99:8} They will perish suddenly because they have worshiped false gods. {99:9} Blessed are those who accept wisdom and follow the Most High's path. They will be saved. {99:10} Woe to those who spread evil to their neighbors, for they will be slain in Sheol. {99:11} Woe to those who create false measures and cause bitterness on earth, for they will be destroyed. {99:12} Woe to those who build their homes through others' hard labor and sin. You will have no peace. {99:13} Woe to those who reject their inheritance and follow after idols, for they will have no rest. {99:14} Woe to those who commit unrighteous acts, oppress others, and kill their neighbors. {99:15} He will destroy your glory, bring affliction to your hearts, and arouse His wrath, wiping you out with the sword. The righteous will remember your sins.

{100:1} In those days, fathers and sons will fall in death together, and brothers will kill one another until streams of blood flow. {100:2} A man will not hold back from slaying his son or brother from dawn until dusk. {100:3} Horses will wade through blood up to their chests, and chariots will be submerged in it. {100:4} On that day, angels will descend to gather those who have committed sin, and the Most High will rise in judgment. {100:5} He will appoint holy angels to guard the righteous as the apple of His eye, protecting them until He ends all wickedness. {100:6} Even though the righteous sleep, they have no reason to fear, for they will be safe. {100:7} Sinners will realize that their wealth cannot save them from judgment. {100:8} Woe to you sinners, for you will be repaid for your deeds. {100:9} Woe to those with hardened hearts who plot wickedness, for fear will come upon you, and no one will help you. {100:10} Woe to sinners because of their words and actions, for they will burn in a fire worse than any flame. {100:11} The Most High will inquire about your deeds from the heavens, and even the clouds, mist, dew, and rain will testify against you. {100:12} You will offer gifts to the rain, but it will not fall, and all your efforts will fail. You will not stand against the frost, snow, and plagues that will befall you.

{101:1} Look at the sky, you children of heaven, and observe the works of the Most High, and fear Him. Do not do evil in His presence. {101:2} If He closes the windows of heaven and withholds the rain and dew from falling on the earth because of your actions, what will you do then? {101:3} And if He sends His anger upon you for your deeds, you will not be able to plead with Him because you have spoken proud and arrogant words against His righteousness, so you will find no peace. {101:4} Don't you see how sailors on ships are tossed by waves and shaken by the wind, facing great trouble? {101:5} They are filled with fear because they carry their valuable goods on the sea and fear the sea may swallow them, causing their destruction. {101:6} Isn't the sea, with all its waters and movements, the work of the Most High? {101:7} He has set limits for it, confining it with sand, and at His command, it becomes afraid and dries up, and all its creatures die. But you, sinners on the earth, do not fear Him. {101:8} Did He not create the heavens, the earth, and everything within them? Who has given wisdom and understanding to every creature on the earth and in the sea? {101:9} Even the sailors of the ships fear the sea, yet you sinners do not fear the Most High.

{102:1} In those days, when He brings a fierce fire upon you, where will you flee, and where will you find deliverance? {102:2} And when He sends His Word against you, won't you be terrified and filled with fear? All the lights in the sky will be filled with fear, and the earth will tremble. {102:3} The angels will carry out their commands and try to hide from the Great Glory, and the people of earth will shake and tremble. You sinners will be cursed forever and find no peace. {102:4} But you, righteous souls, do not fear. Be hopeful, even if you have died in righteousness. {102:5} Do not grieve if your soul has gone to Sheol (the underworld) in sorrow and your life did not reflect your goodness. Wait for the day of judgment for sinners and their punishment. {102:6} Even when you die, sinners speak of you, saying, "The righteous die just as we do. What good did their deeds bring them?" {102:7} They say, "Just like us, they died in grief and darkness. What do they have more than we do? From now on, we are equal." {102:8} They question, "What will the righteous receive and see forever? They too have died and will see no light anymore." {102:9} I tell you, sinners, you are happy to eat, drink, steal, sin, and take wealth. {102:10} But have you observed how the righteous die peacefully without violence? {102:11} "Still," you say, "they vanished as if they never existed, and their spirits descended to Sheol in distress."

{103:1} Now, I swear to you, the righteous, by the glory of the Great, Honored, and Mighty One, {103:2} and by His greatness I swear this. I know a mystery and have read the heavenly tablets and seen the holy books. {103:3} It is written that all goodness, joy, and glory are prepared for those who have died in righteousness, and great blessings will be given to you in reward for your hard work. {103:4} Your spirits, who have died in righteousness, will live and rejoice, and your memory will never fade before the Great One for all generations. So do not fear the insults. {103:5} Woe to you, sinners, if you die while still covered in your sins and others say, "Blessed are the sinners; they had good lives and lived in wealth." {103:6} They claim, "They died without facing any tribulation or violence and passed away in honor. They were not judged during their lives." {103:7} But know this: their souls will descend to Sheol and suffer in great distress. {103:8} They will go into darkness, chains, and burning flames, where harsh judgment awaits their spirits for all generations. Woe to you, for you will have no peace. {103:9} Do not say of the righteous who are still alive, "In our troubled times, we toiled hard and faced every type of suffering and evil, {103:10} and we were destroyed without anyone to help us, even with a kind word. We were tortured and destroyed, and had no hope of life day by day." {103:11} You hoped to be the leaders but instead became the lowest. You worked hard and found no joy in your labor. {103:12} You became the food of sinners and the unrighteous, and they laid a heavy burden on you. {103:13} You wanted to escape and find rest but could not flee or find safety from them. {103:14} You cried to your rulers in your suffering and complained against those who harmed you, but they didn't listen. {103:15} They helped those who robbed & killed you, hid their violence, and never removed the oppression from you.

{104:1} I swear to you that the angels in heaven remember you for good before the glory of the Great One, and your names are written before Him. {104:2} Be hopeful, for although you were once ashamed and afflicted, you will now shine like the lights in heaven. {104:3} You will be seen, and the gates of heaven will open for you. When you cry for justice, it will come to you, and all the wrongs done to you will be visited upon those who ruled over you and helped those who plundered you. {104:4} Be hopeful and do not give up hope, for you will have great joy, just like the angels in heaven. {104:5} You will not need to hide on the day of the great judgment, and you will not be counted among sinners. The eternal judgment will be far from you for all generations. {104:6} Do not be afraid, righteous ones, when you see sinners becoming powerful and successful in their ways. {104:7} Do not join them but stay away from their violence, for you will be companions with the hosts of heaven. {104:8} Even though sinners say, "None of our sins will be found or written down," their sins are recorded every day. {104:9} Light and darkness, day and night, witness all your sins. Do not be godless in your hearts, and do not lie or twist the words of truth, nor accuse the Holy Great One of lying. {104:10} Do not rely on your idols, for all your lying and wickedness will not lead to righteousness but to great sin. {104:11} I know this mystery, that sinners will alter and distort the words of righteousness in many ways, speaking wicked lies and practicing great deceit, even writing books filled with their lies. {104:12} But when they truthfully write down my words in their languages and do not change them, {104:13} then the righteous and the wise will be given books, which will bring them joy, truth, and much wisdom. And all the righteous who learn from these books will be rewarded with uprightness and wisdom.

{105:1} In those days, the Lord commanded them to gather and teach the children of the earth about wisdom, saying, "Show it to them, for you are their guides and have responsibility over the whole earth." {105:2} The Lord says, "My Son and I will walk with them forever in the paths of righteousness during their lives, and they will have peace. Rejoice, children of righteousness. Amen."

The Fragment of the Book of Noah

{106:1} After some time, Methuselah took a wife for his son Lamech, and she became pregnant and gave birth to a son. {106:2} His body was as white as snow and as red as a blooming rose, and the hair on his head and his long locks were as white as wool, and his eyes were beautiful. When he opened his eyes, the whole house lit up like the sun, and it was filled with light. {106:3} Then, the baby arose in the hands of the midwife, opened his mouth, and spoke with the Lord of righteousness. {106:4} Lamech, his father, was frightened by this and fled to his father Methuselah. {106:5} Lamech said to Methuselah, "I have fathered a strange child, different from other humans, resembling the sons of heaven, the angels. His nature is not like ours, and his eyes are like rays of the sun, and his face is glorious. {106:6} I am afraid something unusual will happen on earth during his time." {106:7} Lamech continued, "Father, I ask you to go to our ancestor Enoch, who lives among the angels, and learn the truth about this child." {106:8} Methuselah heard his son's words and came to find me, Enoch, at the ends of the earth. He called out loudly, and I heard his voice and came to him. {106:9} I said, "Here I am, my son. Why have you come to me?" {106:10} He replied, "Father, I have come because of great worry and a disturbing vision. {106:11} My son Lamech has had a child unlike any other, whose nature is different from mankind. His skin is whiter than snow and redder than a rose's bloom, and his hair is whiter than wool. His eyes are like rays of the sun, and when he opened them, the whole house lit up. {106:12} He arose in the hands of the midwife, opened his mouth, and praised the Lord of heaven. Lamech was terrified and fled to me, thinking the child was from the angels of heaven. {106:13} I have come to you so that you can tell me the truth." {106:14} I, Enoch, answered Methuselah and said, "The Lord is going to do something new on the earth. I have seen it in a vision, and I will tell you. In the days of my father Jared, some of the angels in heaven disobeyed God's word. They sinned, broke the law, married human women, and had children with them. {106:15} These children were giants, born not of the spirit but of the flesh. A great punishment will come upon the earth, cleansing it from impurity. {106:16} A great destruction will occur in the form of a flood, which will last for one year. This son who was born to Lamech will survive on the earth, and his three sons will be saved with him. When all humanity is destroyed, he and his sons will survive." {106:17} Enoch continued, "Go and tell your son Lamech that this child is indeed his son. Name him Noah, for he will survive the great flood and all the destruction that will come due to the sins and unrighteousness of mankind. {106:18} After that, even greater wickedness will arise on the earth, worse than before, but I know the secrets of the holy ones. The Lord has shown me and informed me of what is to come, and I have read it in the heavenly tablets."

{107:1} I saw written on these heavenly tablets that generation after generation will continue to sin until a generation of righteousness finally arises. Then, transgression will be destroyed, and sin will vanish from the earth, and goodness will reign. {107:2} Enoch said, "Go, my son, and tell your son Lamech that his son Noah is truly his child. There is no lie in this." {107:3} When Methuselah heard his father's words, he returned to Lamech and told him everything. He named the child Noah, for Noah would comfort the earth after the great destruction.

{108:1} Enoch also wrote another book for his son Methuselah and for those who would live in the last days and keep the law. {108:2} Enoch said, "You who have done good, be patient and wait for the end of the evildoers and the end of the power of the transgressors. {108:3} Wait until sin has passed away, for the names of sinners will be erased from the book of life and the holy books, and their descendants will be destroyed forever. Their spirits will be slain, and they will cry out in lamentation in a barren wilderness. They will burn in fire because there will be no earth for them. {108:4} I saw something like an invisible cloud, too deep for me to see over. I saw a bright flame of fire, with things like shining mountains swirling around. {108:5} I asked one of the holy angels with me, "What is this bright thing? It is not heaven, but a blazing fire." {108:6} The angel said to me, "This is the place where the spirits of sinners, blasphemers, and evildoers are cast. These are the ones who twist everything the Lord has spoken through the prophets, even about the future. {108:7} Some of these things are written in the heavens so that the angels may read them and know what will happen to the sinners, the humble, and those who have been afflicted by wicked men. {108:8} These are people who love God, who sought neither gold nor silver nor earthly riches, but gave themselves up to hardship and torture. {108:9} They didn't long for food from the earth but saw everything as temporary and lived accordingly. {108:10} The Lord tested them greatly, and their spirits were found pure, so they could bless His name. {108:11} Their rewards are written in the books, and the Lord has assigned them their due because they loved heaven more than their earthly lives. Even though they were persecuted and shamed by wicked people, they still blessed God. {108:12} Now, the Lord says, "I will call the spirits of the righteous from the generation of light, and I will transform those who lived in darkness and were not honored in their lifetimes as they deserved." {108:13} The Lord continued, "I will bring these righteous souls into the shining light, and I will give them thrones of honor. {108:14} They will shine brightly forever, for righteousness is the judgment of God. He will reward the faithful with eternal faithfulness in the land of upright paths. {108:15} They will see those born in darkness led into darkness, while the righteous will shine. The sinners will cry aloud when they see this, but they will be led into a place where times and seasons are set for them."

The Second Book of Enoch

{1:1} There was a wise man, a great craftsman, and the Lord loved him and welcomed him so that he could witness the highest heavens and see the wise, great, and unimaginable realm of God Almighty, the glorious and bright place of the Lord's servants, the inaccessible throne of the Lord, and the various degrees and manifestations of the incorporeal beings, the indescribable service of the multitude of elements, the wondrous appearances and inexpressible songs of the Cherubim, and the boundless light. {1:2} At that time, I said, when I had completed my one hundred and sixty-fifth year, I fathered my son Methuselah. {1:3} After this, I lived another two hundred years, totaling three hundred and sixty-five years in all. {1:4} On the first day of the month, I was alone at home, resting on my bed and sleeping. {1:5} While I slept, a great distress filled my heart, and I wept in my sleep, unable to understand the source of my distress or what would happen to me. {1:6} Then two men appeared to me, extraordinarily large—larger than any I had ever seen on earth; their faces shone like the sun, their eyes burned with light, and fire came from their lips, while they wore garments that looked purple, their wings shone brighter than gold, and their hands were whiter than snow. {1:7} They stood at the head of my bed and began calling my name. {1:8} I awoke from my sleep and clearly saw the two men standing before me. {1:9} I greeted them, but fear seized me, and my face changed with terror, and the men said to me: {1:10} "Take courage, Enoch, do not fear; the eternal God has sent us to you, and today you will ascend with us into heaven, and you will tell your sons and your entire household everything they should do in your absence, and let no one seek you until the Lord returns you to them." {1:11} I hurried to obey them, left my house, and went to the doors as instructed, summoning my sons Methuselah, Regim, and Gaidad to share with them all the wonders those men had revealed.

{2:1} "Listen to me, my children, I do not know where I am going or what will happen to me; therefore, my children, I tell you: do not turn away from God in front of the vain, who did not create heaven and earth, for they will perish, along with those who worship them. May the Lord strengthen your hearts in the fear of Him. Now, my children, let no one think to search for me until the Lord returns me to you."

{3:1} After Enoch spoke to his sons, the angels lifted him on their wings and carried him to the first heaven, placing him on the clouds. There I looked around, and again I looked higher, seeing the ether, and they set me on the first heaven and showed me a vast sea, greater than the earthly sea.

{4:1} They presented to me the elders and rulers of the stellar orders, showing me two hundred angels who govern the stars and their duties in the heavens, flying with their wings and surrounding all those who sail.

{5:1} And there I looked down and saw the treasure houses of snow, and the angels who guard their terrifying storages, and the clouds from which the snow comes and into which it goes.

{6:1} They showed me the treasure house of dew, resembling olive oil, with the appearance of all the flowers of the earth; furthermore, many angels guarded the treasure houses of these things, and I saw how they are made to open and close.

{7:1} Those men took me and led me up to the second heaven, where I saw darkness deeper than earthly darkness. There I saw prisoners hanging, watched over, waiting for the great and endless judgment. The angels (spirits) there were dark and made a constant sound of weeping at all hours. {7:2} I asked the men with me, "Why are these people tortured endlessly?" They answered, "These are God's apostates, who did not follow God's commands but followed their own will and turned away with their leader, who is also bound in the fifth heaven." {7:3} I felt deep pity for them, and they greeted me, saying, "Man of God, pray for us to the Lord." I replied, "Who am I, a mortal man, to pray for angels (spirits)? Who knows where I am going or what will happen to me? Who will pray for me?"

{8:1} Then those men took me to the third heaven and placed me there. I looked down and saw the beauty of this place, unlike anything known for its goodness. {8:2} I saw sweet-flowering trees with sweet-smelling fruits, and all the foods they bore exuded a fragrant aroma. {8:3} In the midst of the trees was the Tree of Life, located where the Lord rests when He ascends to paradise. This tree is indescribably good and fragrant, more adorned than anything else, appearing golden, reddish, and fire-like, covering everything and producing all kinds of fruit. {8:4} Its roots are in the garden at the edge of the earth. {8:5} Paradise lies between corruption and immortality. {8:6} Two springs flow out, producing honey and milk, while others produce oil and wine, separating into four parts that flow quietly, descending into the PARADISE OF EDEN, between corruption and immortality. {8:7} From there, they spread across the earth and circulate like other elements. {8:8} Here, no tree is unfruitful, and every place is blessed. {8:9} Three hundred very bright angels guard the garden, serving the Lord with continuous sweet singing and never-silent voices throughout all days and hours. {8:10} I said, "How sweet is this place!" and the men replied to me:

{9:1} "This place, O Enoch, is prepared for the righteous who endure all kinds of offenses from those who torment their souls, who turn away from wickedness, make righteous judgments, feed the hungry, clothe the naked, lift up the fallen, assist injured orphans, walk blamelessly before the Lord, and serve Him alone. For them, this place is prepared as an eternal inheritance."

{10:1} The two men led me to the northern side and showed me a terrible place filled with all kinds of tortures: cruel darkness and unending gloom, devoid of light, but filled with a murky fire that constantly blazes. A fiery river flows through, and the entire area is engulfed in fire, ice, thirst, and shivering, with cruel bonds and angels (spirits) that are terrifying and merciless, wielding angry weapons and inflicting relentless torment. I said: {10:2} "Woe, woe, how terrible is this place!" {10:3} The men said to me, "This place, O Enoch, is prepared for those who dishonor God, who commit sins against nature, including child corruption in the sodomitic manner, magic, enchantments, and devilish witchcrafts, who take pride in their wicked actions, such as stealing, lying, slander, envy, resentment, fornication, and murder. Accursed are those who steal souls, seeing the poor and taking their possessions while becoming rich at their expense; those who could help the needy but let them die, those who could provide clothing but strip the naked, and those who do not know their Creator and bow to lifeless (and soulless) gods that cannot see or hear, worshiping vain idols. For all these, this place is prepared as an eternal inheritance."

{11:1} The men took me and led me to the fourth heaven, showing me the paths of the sun and moon. {11:2} I measured their movements, compared their light, and observed that the sun's light is greater than the moon's. {11:3} Its orbit and the wheels on which it moves are like the wind, moving with incredible speed, never resting day or night. {11:4} Its passage and return are accompanied by four great stars, each with a thousand stars beneath it—four to the right of the sun's wheel and four to the left, altogether eight thousand, accompanying the sun continuously. {11:5} During the day, fifteen thousand angels attend it, and at night, a thousand. {11:6} Six-winged beings accompany the angels before the sun's wheel into the fiery flames, and a hundred angels kindle the sun and ignite it.

{12:1} I looked and saw other flying elements of the sun, called Phoenixes and Chalkydri, marvelous and extraordinary, with lion-like feet and tails and crocodile heads, their appearance shimmering like a rainbow. They are nine hundred measures in size, with wings like angels, each having twelve, attending the sun and bringing heat and dew as commanded by God. {12:2} Thus, the sun revolves and rises in the heavens, its path continuing under the earth, constantly shining with its rays.

{13:1} Those men took me to the east and placed me at the sun's gates, where the sun rises according to the seasons and the monthly cycles of the entire year, including the number of hours in day and night. {13:2} I saw six gates open, each one measuring sixty-one and a quarter stadia (a unit of distance), and I measured them accurately to understand their size, through which the sun rises, travels to the west, becomes even, and rises throughout the months, returning from the six gates according to the cycle of the seasons; thus, the entire year is completed after the transitions of the four seasons.

{14:1} Again, those men led me to the west and showed me six great gates that corresponded to the eastern gates, opposite where the sun sets, aligning with the number of days in the year—three hundred sixty-five and a quarter. {14:2} The sun sets at these western gates, withdrawing its light and brightness beneath the earth, for the crown of its shine is in heaven with the Lord, guarded by four hundred angels. While the sun circles under the earth, it remains for seven great hours in the night and spends half its course under the earth. When it approaches the east in the eighth hour of the night, it brings its light and crown of shining, and the sun blazes forth brighter than fire.

{15:1} Then the elements of the sun, called Phoenixes and Chalkydri, broke into song, causing every bird to flutter its wings in joy at the giver of light. They sang at the command of the Lord. {15:2} The giver of light comes to illuminate the whole world, and the morning light takes form as the sun's rays, and the sun rises, receiving brightness to light up the entire face of the earth. They showed me this calculation of sun's path. {15:3} The gates through which it enters are the great gates that account for the hours of the year; for this reason, the sun is a magnificent creation, completing its cycle in twenty-eight years before beginning anew.

{16:1} The men showed me the course of the moon, with twelve great gates crowned from west to east, through which the moon enters and exits at its regular times. {16:2} It enters at the first gate in the western region of the sun, staying thirty-one days exactly at the first gate, thirty-one days at the second, thirty days at the third, thirty days at the fourth, thirty-one days at the fifth, thirty-one days at the sixth, thirty days at the seventh, thirty-one days at the eighth, thirty-one days at the ninth, thirty days at the tenth, thirty-one days at the eleventh, and twenty-eight days at the twelfth gate. {16:3} It travels through the western gates in the same order and number as the eastern gates, completing the three hundred sixty-five and a quarter days of the solar year, while the lunar year totals three hundred fifty-four days, falling short by twelve days of the solar circle, which are the lunar epacts for the entire year. {16:4} Thus, the great cycle spans five hundred thirty-two years. {16:5} The quarter day is omitted for three years, with the fourth year fulfilling it exactly. {16:6} Therefore, they are taken out of heaven for three years and not added to the total number of days because they alter the years, creating two new months towards completion and two others towards reduction. {16:7} When the western gates are completed, the moon returns to the eastern gates of light, moving day and night around the heavenly spheres, faster than the heavenly winds, spirits, and elements, with each angel having six wings. {16:8} Its course spans seven cycles over nineteen years.

{17:1} In the midst of heaven, I saw armed soldiers serving the Lord with tambourines and organs, their voices constant, sweet, and filled with various indescribable songs that astonished every mind; the singing of those angels was so wonderful and marvelous that I was filled with delight just listening.

{18:1} The men took me to the fifth heaven and placed me there, where I saw many countless soldiers called Grigori, who appeared human but were larger than giants. Their faces were withered, and they were silent with perpetual sadness; there was no service in the fifth heaven. I asked the men with me: {18:2} "Why are these beings so withered, melancholy, and silent? Why is there no service in this heaven?" {18:3} They answered, "These are the Grigori, who, with their leader Satanail (Satan), rejected the Lord of light. After them are those who remain in great darkness on the second heaven. Three of them descended to earth from the Lord's throne to the place called Ermon, where they broke their vows on the shoulder of the hill Ermon, saw the daughters of men, recognized their beauty, and took wives for themselves, polluting the earth with their actions. In every age, they committed lawlessness, leading to the birth of giants and great enmity. {18:4} Therefore, God judged them harshly, and they weep for their brethren, awaiting punishment on the Lord's great day. {18:5} I said to the Grigori, "I saw your brethren and their deeds and their great torments, and I prayed for them, but the Lord condemned them to remain under the earth until the current heaven and earth end forever." {18:6} I continued, "Why do you wait, brethren? Why don't you serve before the Lord and present your offerings? Do not anger your Lord completely!" {18:7} They listened to my admonition and spoke to the four ranks in heaven. As I stood with those two men, four trumpets sounded loudly, and the Grigori sang together with one voice, their voices rising before the Lord in a pitiful and heartfelt plea.

{19:1} Then those men took me up to the sixth heaven, where I saw seven groups of angels, very bright and glorious, with faces shining brighter than the sun, all looking the same in appearance, behavior, and dress. These angels manage the orders, study the movements of the stars, the phases of the moon, the rotation of the sun, and the proper governance of the world. {19:2} When they see wrongdoing, they issue commands and teachings, singing sweetly and loudly, offering all kinds of praise. {19:3} These are the archangels, who are above other angels, overseeing all life in heaven and on earth, including the angels in charge of seasons and years, those over rivers and seas, those overseeing the fruits of the earth, and those watching over every blade of grass, providing food for all living things. They also record all the souls of people, their actions, and their lives before the Lord; among them are six Phoenixes, six Cherubim, and six six-winged angels, all singing together with one voice, a song so wonderful it cannot be described, rejoicing before the Lord at His footstool.

{20:1} Those two men lifted me up to the seventh heaven, where I saw a great light and fiery troops of archangels, incorporeal beings, dominions, orders, governments, Cherubim, Seraphim, thrones, and many-eyed ones—nine groups in total, the Ioanit stations of light. I was filled with fear and began to tremble. The men took me and led me, saying: {20:2} "Have courage, Enoch; do not be afraid," and they showed me the Lord from a distance, sitting on His very high throne. What could be greater than what exists in the tenth heaven, where the Lord resides? {20:3} In the tenth heaven is God, called Aravat in Hebrew. {20:4} All the heavenly hosts would come and stand on ten steps according to their ranks, bowing down to the Lord and returning to their places in joy and happiness, singing in the endless light with soft, gentle voices, gloriously serving Him.

{21:1} The Cherubim and Seraphim surrounding the throne, the six-winged and many-eyed ones, do not leave, standing before the Lord and doing His will, covering His entire throne, singing softly: "Holy, holy, holy, Lord Ruler of Sabaoth; heaven and earth are full of Your glory." {21:2} When I saw all this, the men said to me: "Enoch, we can accompany you no further," and they departed, leaving me alone. {21:3} I was afraid and fell on my face, saying to myself: "Woe is me; what has happened to me?" {21:4} The Lord sent one of His glorious angels, the archangel Gabriel, who said: "Have courage, Enoch; do not be afraid. Arise before the Lord's face into eternity; come with me." {21:5} I replied in my heart: "My Lord, my soul has left me from fear and trembling. I relied on the men who brought me here, and I wanted to go before the Lord with them." {21:6} Gabriel lifted me up, like a leaf caught by the wind, and set me before the Lord. {21:7} I saw the eighth heaven, called Muzaloth in Hebrew, the changer of seasons, drought, and rain, and the twelve constellations of the firmament above the seventh heaven. {21:8} I also saw the ninth heaven, called Kuchavim in Hebrew, where the heavenly homes of the twelve constellations are located.

{22:1} In the tenth heaven, Aravoth, I saw the Lord's face, glowing like iron heated in fire and emitting sparks, burning brightly. {22:2} In that moment of eternity, I glimpsed the Lord's face, which is indescribable, marvelous, and terrible beyond comprehension. {22:3} Who am I to speak of the Lord's ineffable essence and His wondrous face? I cannot convey the magnitude of His countless commands and diverse voices; the Lord's throne is immense, not made by human hands, nor can I count those who surround Him—troops of Cherubim and Seraphim—nor their continuous singing, nor His unchanging beauty, nor can anyone express the unfathomable greatness of His glory. {22:4} I fell prostrate and bowed before the Lord, and He spoke to me: {22:5} "Have courage, Enoch; do not be afraid. Arise and stand before My face for eternity." {22:6} The archistrategos (chief angel) Michael lifted me up and brought me before the Lord. {22:7} The Lord instructed His servants, saying: "Let Enoch stand before My face forever." The glorious ones bowed down and said: "Let Enoch go as You command." {22:8} The Lord then said to Michael: "Go and remove Enoch's earthly garments, anoint him with My sweet ointment, and dress him in the garments of My glory." {22:9} Michael obeyed the Lord's command, anointing me and dressing me; the ointment's appearance was brighter than great light, like sweet dew, with a gentle fragrance, shining like the sun's rays. I looked at myself and felt transformed, like one of His glorious ones. {22:10} The Lord called one of His archangels named Pravuil, known for his swift wisdom compared to the other archangels, who recorded all the Lord's deeds. The Lord instructed Pravuil: "Bring out the books from My storehouses and a reed for writing, give it to Enoch, and hand over the choice and comforting books."

{23:1} Pravuil told me all about the works of heaven, earth, and sea, detailing the elements, their movements, the thunder of thunder, the sun and moon, the paths and changes of the stars, the seasons, years, days, hours, wind patterns, the number of angels, the formation of their songs, and all human matters, the language of every human song and life, the commandments, teachings, and sweet songs, and all things worthy of learning. {23:2} Pravuil said: "All I have told you is written down. Sit and write all the souls of mankind, however many are born, and the places prepared for them for eternity; all souls are destined for eternity, even before the world was formed." {23:3} I wrote continuously for thirty days and nights, accurately recording everything, and completed three hundred sixty-six books.

{24:1} The Lord called me and said: "Enoch, sit on my left with Gabriel." {24:2} I bowed down to the Lord, and He spoke to me: "Enoch, beloved, I will reveal to you everything you see. I will tell you about all that was created from nothing, both visible (physical) and invisible (spiritual) things. {24:3} Listen, Enoch, and understand my words, for I have not shared my secrets with My angels, nor have I revealed to them their origins or My eternal kingdom, nor have they grasped My creation, which I now share with you. {24:4} Before anything was visible, I roamed the invisible (spiritual) realm alone, like the sun moving from east to west. {24:5} Even the sun has peace within itself, but I found no peace, for I was creating everything, imagining the foundations, and bringing the visible (physical) world into existence.

{25:1} I commanded that visible (physical) things come forth from the invisible (spiritual), and Adoil descended, very great, and I saw him; he had a belly of great light. {25:2} I said to him: "Become undone, Adoil, and let the visible (physical) emerge from you." {25:3} He came undone, and a great light poured out. I found myself in the midst of this great light, and just as light is born from light, a great age emerged, revealing all the creation I had planned. {25:4} I saw that it was good. {25:5} I established a throne for myself and took my seat, telling the light: "Rise higher and position yourself above the throne to serve as a foundation for the highest things." {25:6} Above the light, there is nothing else, and I lifted my gaze from my throne.

{26:1} I summoned the lowest once more and said: "Let Archas come forth, hard," and he appeared, hard, heavy, and very red. {26:2} I commanded: "Be opened, Archas, and let something emerge from you." He came undone, and a great age emerged, very dark, bearing the creation of all lower things. I saw that it was good and instructed him: {26:3} "Go down below, make yourself firm, and be a foundation for the lower things." He complied, descending and establishing himself as the foundation for lower things, and below the darkness, there is nothing else.

{27:1} I commanded that there be a separation between light and darkness, saying: "Be thick," and it became so. I spread it out with light, and it became water, spreading over the darkness below the light. I solidified the waters, that is, the bottomless, creating a foundation of light around the water, forming seven circles, and I shaped the water to appear like crystal, both wet and dry, like glass, while organizing the waters and other elements. I showed each one its path, and the seven stars each had their place in the heavens, moving accordingly, and I saw that it was good. {27:2} I separated light from darkness, designating the light as day and the darkness as night, and there was evening and morning, marking the first day.

{28:1} Then I established the heavenly circle, causing the lower water beneath heaven to gather into one whole, and the chaos to dry up, which it did. {28:2} From the waves, I created solid, large rocks, and from the rock, I formed dry land, which I called earth. The middle of the earth I named abyss, meaning bottomless, and I gathered the sea into one place, binding it with a yoke. {28:3} I said to the sea: "Behold, I give you your eternal limits; you shall not break free from your components." {28:4} Thus, I secured the firmament, and I named this day the first-created [Sunday].

{29:1} For all the heavenly hosts, I created an image and essence of fire, and my eye looked at the solid, firm rock. From the gleam of my eye, lightning received its extraordinary nature, being both fire in water and water in fire, where neither extinguishes the other nor does one dry up the other. Therefore, lightning is brighter than the sun, softer than water, and firmer than solid rock. {29:2} From the rock, I drew forth a great fire, and from that fire, I formed the ranks of the incorporeal ten groups of angels. Their weapons are fiery, and their clothing is a burning flame, and I commanded that each one stand in their designated order. {29:3} One angel from among them, having turned away from his order, conceived an impossible thought: to raise his throne higher than the clouds above the earth, aspiring to be equal in rank to my power. {29:4} I cast him out from the heights along with his angels, and he was left flying in the air continuously above the bottomless.

{30:1} On the third day, I commanded the earth to grow great and fruitful trees, hills, and seeds to sow. I planted Paradise, enclosing it, and placed flaming angels as armed guardians, thus creating renewal. {30:2} Then evening came, and morning came, marking the fourth day. {30:3} On the fourth day, I commanded that great lights be placed in the heavenly circles. {30:4} On the highest circle, I placed the stars: Kruno on the first, Aphrodit on the second, Aris on the third, Zoues on the fifth, Ermis on the sixth, and the lesser moon on the seventh, adorning it with the smaller stars. {30:5} On the lower circle, I placed the sun for daytime illumination and the moon and stars for nighttime illumination. {30:6} I commanded the sun to move according to each of the twelve constellations, establishing the succession of the months, their names, their functions, their thunderings, and their timing. {30:7} Then evening came and morning came, marking the fifth day. {30:8} On the fifth day, I commanded the sea to bring forth fishes and many varieties of birds, as well as all animals that creep on the earth, moving on four legs, and soaring in the air, both male and female, and every soul breathing the spirit of life. {30:9} Evening came, and morning came, marking the sixth day. {30:10} On the sixth day, I commanded my wisdom to create man from seven components: his flesh from the earth, his blood from the dew, his eyes from the sun, his bones from stone, his intelligence from the swiftness of angels and clouds, his veins and hair from the grass of the earth, and his soul from my breath and from the wind. {30:11} I endowed him with seven senses: hearing for the flesh, sight for the eyes, smell for the soul, touch for the veins, taste for the blood, endurance for the bones, and sweetness (enjoyment) for the intelligence. {30:12} I conceived a profound saying: I created man from both invisible (spiritual) and visible (physical) natures, from which comes his death and life and image. He understands speech like any created being, small yet great, and again great yet small, and I placed him on earth, a second angel, honorable, great, and glorious, appointing him as ruler to govern the earth with my wisdom; there was none like him among all my creatures. {30:13} I named him from the four directions: east, west, south, and north, assigning him four special stars, and I called him Adam. I showed him the two paths: light and darkness, and I instructed him: {30:14} "This is good, and that is bad," to see whether he would love me or harbor hatred, so that it would be clear which among his descendants would love me. {30:15} For I have seen his nature, but he has not seen his own, thus through not seeing, he may sin more grievously. I said, "After sin, what remains but death?" {30:16} I caused him to fall asleep, and took a rib from him, creating a wife so that death might come through her. I took his final word and called her name mother, meaning Eva (Eve).

{31:1} Adam was alive on earth & I created a garden in Eden in the east for him to observe the testament and keep the command. {31:2} I opened the heavens for him to see the angels singing songs of victory and experiencing the light without gloom. {31:3} He dwelled continuously in Paradise, but the devil realized that I intended to create another world, since Adam was the lord of the earth, to rule and manage it. {31:4} The devil is the evil spirit of the lower realms; as a fugitive, he became known as Sotona, deriving his name from Satanail (Satan). Thus, he became distinct from the angels, though his intelligence remained unchanged in discerning right from wrong. {31:5} He recognized his own condemnation and the sin he had committed, which led him to devise a plan against Adam. He entered and seduced Eva (Eve), but did not touch Adam. {31:6} I cursed ignorance; what I had previously blessed, I did not curse—neither man, nor the earth, nor others—but I cursed man's evil actions & their consequences.

{32:1} I told him: "You are earth, and to the earth from which I took you, you shall return, and I will not destroy you, but send you back from whence you came. {32:2} Then I can receive you again at My second coming." {32:3} I blessed all my visible (physical) and invisible (spiritual) creatures, and Adam was in Paradise for five and a half hours. {32:4} I blessed the seventh day, the Sabbath, on which He rested from all His works.

{33:1} I also established the eighth day, making it the first-created after my work, allowing the first seven days to cycle in the form of the seventh millennium. At the start of the eighth millennium, there will be a time of non-counting, endless, without years, months, weeks, days, or hours. {33:2} Now, Enoch, all that I have told you, all that you have understood, everything you have seen in the heavens and on earth, and all that I have written in books through my great wisdom, these are the things I devised and created from the highest foundation to the lowest and to the end. No one can counsel or inherit my creations. {33:3} I am self-eternal, unmade by hands, and without change. {33:4} My thought is my counselor; my wisdom and my word are created, and my eyes observe all things, how they stand here, trembling in terror. {33:5} If I turn my face away, everything will be destroyed. {33:6} Focus your mind, Enoch, and understand who is speaking to you. Take the books you have written. {33:7} I give you Samuil and Raguil, who brought you here, along with the books. Go down to earth and tell your sons everything I have shared with you and all that you have seen, from the lower heavens to my throne and all the hosts. {33:8} For I created all powers, and none resist me or fail to submit to me. All yield to my rule and work for my sole governance. {33:9} Give them the books you have written; they will read and recognize me as the creator of all things, understanding that there is no other God but me. {33:10} Let them share your books—children to children, generation to generation, nation to nation. {33:11} I will give you, Enoch, my intercessor, the archangel Michael, for the writings of your forefathers: Adam, Seth, Enos, Cainan, Mahaleleel, and your father Jared.

{34:1} They have rejected my commandments and my yoke; worthless seed has sprung up, not fearing God. They refuse to bow to me, instead worshiping vain gods, denying my unity, and burdening the earth with lies, offenses, abominable acts, and all kinds of unclean wickedness that are too disgusting to recount. {34:2} Therefore, I will bring a flood upon the earth and will destroy all people, and the entire earth will crumble into great darkness.

{35:1} Behold, from their seed will arise another generation much later, but many of them will be insatiable. {35:2} The one who raises that generation will reveal to them the books of your writings, showing them the guardianship of the world, to the faithful men who do not take my name in vain. {35:3} They will tell another generation, and those who read will be glorified even more than the first.

{36:1} Now, Enoch, I give you thirty days to spend at home, telling your sons and all your household so that they may hear from my face what you convey. They must read and understand that there is no other God but me. {36:2} They should always keep my commandments and begin to read and absorb the books you have written. {36:3} After thirty days, I will send my angel for you, and he will take you from the earth to me.

{37:1} The Lord called upon one of the older angels, fearsome and intimidating, and placed him beside me, appearing as white as snow, with hands like ice and a frosty presence. He froze my face because I could not bear the terror of the Lord, just as one cannot endure the heat of a stove or the sun, or the cold of the air. {37:2} The Lord said to me: "Enoch, if your face is not frozen here, no one will be able to look upon you."

{38:1} The Lord instructed those who first brought me up: "Let Enoch return to earth with you and wait for him until the appointed day." {38:2} They placed me at night on my bed. {38:3} Mathusal (Methuselah), expecting my return, watched over my bed day and night, and he was filled with awe upon hearing my arrival. I told him to gather all my household so I could share everything with them.

{39:1} Oh my children, my beloved ones, hear the guidance of your father, as much as is according to the Lord's will. {39:2} I have come to you today, not from my lips, but from the Lord's lips, to announce all that is, was, and will be until judgment day. {39:3} For the Lord has allowed me to come to you; therefore, hear the words of my lips, of a man made great for you, though I am one who has seen the Lord's face. Like iron glowing from fire, it sends forth sparks and burns. {39:4} Look now upon my eyes, the eyes of a man filled with meaning for you, but I have seen the Lord's eyes shining like the sun's rays, filling human eyes with awe. {39:5} You see now, my children, the hand of a man that helps you, but I have seen the Lord's right hand filling heaven as he helped me. {39:6} You see the scope of my work like your own, but I have seen the Lord's infinite and perfect scope, which has no end. {39:7} You hear the words of my lips as I heard the words of the Lord, like great thunder accompanied by the hurling of clouds. {39:8} And now, my children, hear the teachings of the father of the earth, how fearful and dreadful it is to come before the ruler of the earth; how much more terrifying it is to stand before the ruler of heaven, the judge of the living and the dead, and of the heavenly hosts. Who can endure that endless pain?

{40:1} Now, my children, I know all things, for this comes from the Lord's lips, and my eyes have seen from beginning to end. {40:2} I know everything and have written all things in books, including the heavens and their end, their fullness, and all the armies and their movements. {40:3} I have measured and described the stars, the countless multitude of them. {40:4} What man has seen their paths and entrances? Not even the angels can see their number, yet I have written down all their names. {40:5} I measured the sun's path and its rays, counted the hours, and recorded all things that traverse the earth. I documented what is nourished, all seeds sown and unsown, which the earth produces, every plant, grass, flower, their sweet scents, their names, the dwelling-places of the clouds, their structure, their wings, and how they carry rain and raindrops. {40:6} I explored everything and wrote about the paths of thunder and lightning; they showed me their keys and guardians, how they rise and move; it is released gently in measured amounts by a chain to prevent the heavy chains from violently hurling down angry clouds and destroying all things on earth. {40:7} I recorded the treasure houses of snow, the storehouses of cold and frosty air, and observed their seasonal keeper, who fills the clouds without depleting the treasure. {40:8} I noted the resting places of the winds and saw how their key-holders use scales and measurements; first, they place them in one scale, then in the other the weights, and release them carefully across the earth to avoid shaking it with heavy gusts. {40:9} I measured the entire earth: its mountains, hills, fields, trees, stones, rivers, and all existing things, the height from earth to the seventh heaven and down to the lowest hell, the judgment place, and the great, open, weeping hell. {40:10} I saw how the prisoners suffer, waiting for the limitless judgment. {40:11} I wrote down all those judged by the judge, along with all their judgments and actions.

{41:1} I saw all the ancestors from all time with Adam and Eve, and I sighed, breaking into tears over their ruin and dishonor. {41:2} Woe is me for my weakness and that of my forefathers, and I thought in my heart: {41:3} Blessed is the man who has not been born or who has been born and shall not sin before the Lord's face, that he may not come into this place nor bear the yoke of this place.

{42:1} I saw the key-holders and guards of the gates of hell standing like great serpents, with faces like extinguished lamps, fiery eyes, and sharp teeth. I observed all the Lord's works, how they are just, while the works of man are a mix of good and bad, revealing those who lie wickedly.

{43:1} I, my children, measured and recorded every action, every measure, and every righteous judgment. {43:2} Just as one year is more honorable than another, so is one man more honorable than another: some for great wealth, some for wisdom, some for unique intelligence, some for cleverness, one for silence, another for purity, one for strength, another for beauty, one for youth, another for sharp wit, one for physical appearance, another for sensitivity. Let it be heard everywhere, but none are better than he who fears God; he shall be more glorious in the future.

{44:1} The Lord, with his hands, created man in his own likeness, making him both small and great. {44:2} Whoever insults the ruler's face and despises the Lord's face has scorned the Lord's face. He who vents anger on anyone without cause will face the Lord's great wrath; he who spits contemptuously on a man's face will be cut down at the Lord's great judgment. {44:3} Blessed is the man who does not harbor malice in his heart against anyone, who helps the injured and condemned, lifts up the broken, and gives to the needy. Because on the day of the great judgment, every weight, every measure, and every adjustment will be weighed like in a market; that is to say, they are hung on scales in the market, and everyone shall learn their own measure, and according to their measure shall receive their reward.

{45:1} Whoever rushes to make offerings before the Lord, the Lord will hasten that offering by granting success to his work. {45:2} But whoever lights a lamp before the Lord and does not make a true judgment, the Lord will not increase his treasure in the highest realm. {45:3} When the Lord asks for bread, candles, the flesh of animals, or any other sacrifice, that means nothing; God desires pure hearts and uses these to test the heart of man.

{46:1} Listen, my people, and take in the words of my lips. {46:2} If someone brings gifts to an earthly ruler but harbors disloyal thoughts in his heart, and the ruler knows this, will he not be angry and refuse his gifts, handing him over to judgment? {46:3} Or if one man pretends to be good to another through deceitful words but has evil in his heart, will not the other recognize the treachery of his heart and be condemned, since his dishonesty is obvious to all? {46:4} And when the Lord sends a great light, there will be judgment for both the just and the unjust, and no one will escape notice.

{47:1} Now, my children, take these words to heart and pay attention to your father's words, all of which come from the Lord's lips. {47:2} Take these books written by your father and read them. {47:3} The books are many, and through them, you will learn all the Lord's works, everything from the beginning of creation to the end of time. {47:4} If you observe my writings, you will not sin against the Lord because there is no other besides the Lord, neither in heaven, on earth, nor in the lowest places. {47:5} The Lord has established the foundations in the unknown and has spread forth both visible (physical) and invisible (spiritual) heavens; he fixed the earth on the waters and created countless creatures. Who has counted the water, the foundation of the unfixed, the dust of the earth, the sand of the sea, the drops of rain, the morning dew, or the breath of the wind? Who has filled earth and sea, and the enduring winter? {47:6} I carved the stars from fire, adorned heaven, and set them in their places.

{48:1} The sun travels along seven heavenly circles, which correspond to one hundred and eighty-two thrones; it sets on a short day, and again one hundred and eighty-two on a long day, resting on two thrones while revolving above the thrones of the months. From the seventeenth day of the month Tsivan, it sets to the month Thevan, and from the seventeenth of Thevan, it rises again. {48:2} When it approaches the earth, the earth rejoices and bears fruit; when it moves away, the earth becomes sad, and trees and all fruits lack bloom. {48:3} All this he measured with precise hour measurements and established a measure through his wisdom, for the visible (physical) and the invisible (spiritual). {48:4} From the invisible (spiritual), he created all visible (physical) things while himself remaining invisible (spiritual). {48:5} Thus, I share this with you, my children, and distribute the books to your children, across all generations and among nations that have the sense to fear God. Let them receive these books and come to love them more than any food or earthly delights, reading and applying themselves to them. {48:6} Those who do not understand the Lord, who do not fear God, who reject these teachings and do not accept the books, face a terrible judgment. {48:7} Blessed is the man who bears their burden and carries them, for he will be freed on the day of great judgment.

{49:1} I swear to you, my children, but I swear not by any oath, neither by heaven nor by earth, nor by any other creature created by God. {49:2} The Lord said: There is no oath in me, nor injustice, but only truth. {49:3} If there is no truth in men, let them affirm with "yes, yes" or "no, no." {49:4} I assure you, yes, yes, that every man in his mother's womb has already had a place prepared for the rest of his soul, and a measure established for how much he will be tested in this world. {49:5} Yes, children, do not deceive yourselves, for a place has been prepared for every soul of man.

{50:1} I have recorded every man's work, and no one born on earth can remain hidden, nor can their works be concealed. {50:2} I see all things. {50:3} Therefore, my children, live your days with patience and humility so that you may inherit endless life. {50:4} Endure for the Lord's sake every wound, every injury, every harsh word, and attack. {50:5} If you face ill treatment, do not repay it to neighbor or enemy, for the Lord will return it for you and be your avenger on the day of great judgment, ensuring no one seeks revenge here among men. {50:6} Whoever among you spends gold or silver for his brother's sake will receive great treasure in the world to come. {50:7} Do not harm widows, orphans, or strangers, lest God's wrath come upon you.

{51:1} Stretch out your hands to the poor as much as you are able. {51:2} Don't hide your silver in the earth. {51:3} Help the faithful in their troubles, and affliction will not find you when you are in need. {51:4} Bear every heavy and cruel burden that comes upon you for the sake of the Lord, and you will find your reward on the day of judgment. {51:5} It is good to go to the Lord's house in the morning, at midday, and in the evening, for the glory of your Creator. {51:6} Every living thing glorifies Him, and every creature, both visible (physical) and invisible (spiritual), offers Him praise.

{52:1} Blessed is the person who praises the God of Sabaoth and worships the Lord from the heart. {52:2} Cursed is every person who speaks in contempt or slander against their neighbor, for they bring God into contempt. {52:3} Blessed is the one who opens their lips to bless and praise God. {52:4} Cursed is the one who curses and abuses others all their days. {52:5} Blessed is the one who blesses all the Lord's works. {52:6} Cursed is the one who shows contempt for the Lord's creation. {52:7} Blessed is the one who looks down and lifts up the fallen. {52:8} Cursed is the one who desires the destruction of what does not belong to them. {52:9} Blessed is the one who maintains the foundations established by their ancestors from the beginning. {52:10} Cursed is the one who distorts the decrees of their forefathers. {52:11} Blessed is the one who brings peace and love. {52:12} Cursed is the one who disturbs those who love their neighbors. {52:13} Blessed is the one who speaks with a humble tongue and heart to everyone. {52:14} Cursed is the one who speaks peace with their words, while their heart holds a sword. {52:15} For all these things will be revealed in the scales and in the books on the day of great judgment.

{53:1} Now, my children, do not say, "Our father is standing before God, praying for our sins," for there is no helper for anyone who has sinned. {53:2} You see how I have written down all the works of every man before their creation, everything that has happened among all people for all time, and no one can fully explain my writings, because the Lord sees all the thoughts of man, recognizing how they are empty, stored in the treasure-houses of the heart. {53:3} Now, my children, pay close attention to all your father's words that I share with you, so you will not regret saying, "Why didn't our father tell us?"

{54:1} At that time, not understanding this, let these books I have given you be an inheritance for your peace. {54:2} Share them with all who desire them, and teach them so they may see the Lord's great and marvelous works.

{55:1} My children, behold, the day of my departure has come. {55:2} The angels who will accompany me are standing before me, urging me to leave you; they are waiting here on earth for what has been instructed. {55:3} Tomorrow I will ascend to heaven, to the highest Jerusalem, to my eternal inheritance. {55:4} Therefore, I urge you to do all that pleases the Lord.

{56:1} Mathusala (Methuselah) replied to his father Enoch, saying, "What would you like me to do, father, so I may act before you and you can bless our homes, your sons, and bring glory to your people before you depart as the Lord has said?" {56:2} Enoch answered his son Mathusala and said, "Listen, child, ever since the Lord anointed me with the oil of His glory, I have not had any earthly food, and my soul does not remember earthly pleasures; I desire nothing earthly."

{57:1} My child Methuselah, gather all your brothers, your household, and the elders of the people so I can speak to them before I depart, as has been planned for me. {57:2} Methuselah quickly summoned his brothers—Regim, Riman, Uchan, Chermion, Gaidad—and all the elders of the people to stand before his father Enoch; he blessed them and said:

{58:1} Listen to me today, my children. {58:2} In those days when the Lord came down to earth for Adam's sake and visited all His creations, after all these, He created Adam. The Lord called all the beasts of the earth, all the reptiles, and all the birds that fly in the air, and brought them before our father Adam. {58:3} Adam gave names to all living things on earth. {58:4} The Lord appointed him ruler over everything and made all things subject to him, dulling their senses so that they would obey and be commanded by man. {58:5} Similarly, the Lord made every man lord over his possessions. {58:6} The Lord will not judge the souls of beasts for man's sake but will hold men accountable for their treatment of animals in this world, as men have a special place. {58:7} Just as every soul of man has a number, so will beasts not perish, nor will all souls of beasts which the Lord created, until the great judgment, and they will accuse man if he treats them poorly.

{59:1} Whoever mistreats the soul of beasts also defiles his own soul. {59:2} For man brings clean animals to sacrifice for sin to heal his soul. {59:3} If he brings clean animals or birds for sacrifice, he heals his soul. {59:4} Everything is given to you for food; tie it by the four feet to make a good sacrifice, healing your soul. {59:5} But whoever kills an animal without cause harms his own soul and defiles his own body. {59:6} Anyone who injures a beast in secret is practicing evil and defiles their own soul.

{60:1} He who kills a man's soul destroys his own, with no healing forever. {60:2} He who traps another will be trapped, with no remedy for all time. {60:3} Those who trap others will face eternal retribution at the great judgment. {60:4} He who acts dishonestly or speaks evil will not find justice forever.

{61:1} Now, my children, guard your hearts against all injustice, which the Lord hates. Just as a man asks something for his own soul from God, so let him treat every living soul, for I know all things, how much inheritance is prepared for men in the great future—good for the good, and bad for the bad, countless in number. {61:2} Blessed are those who enter good homes, for in bad homes there is no peace and no way back. {61:3} Hear, my children, both small and great! When a man places a good thought in his heart and brings gifts from his labor before the Lord, but if his hands did not make them, then the Lord will turn away from his efforts, and that man cannot find the results of his work. {61:4} If his hands made it, but his heart murmurs and does not stop murmuring, he gains nothing.

{62:1} Blessed is the man who patiently brings his gifts with faith before the Lord, for he will find forgiveness for his sins. {62:2} But if he takes back his words before the right time, he will not find repentance; and if time passes without him fulfilling what he promised, there will be no repentance after death. {62:3} For every action done before the proper time is deceit before men and sin before God.

{63:1} When a man clothes the naked and feeds the hungry, he will find reward from God. {63:2} But if his heart murmurs, he commits a double wrong: harm to himself and to what he gives; for him, there will be no reward because of that. {63:3} If his heart is filled with his own food and clothing, he shows contempt and will lose all endurance of poverty, finding no reward for his good deeds. {63:4} Every proud and boastful man is detestable to the Lord, and every false word clothed in untruth will be cut down by the sword of death and cast into the fire to burn forever.

{64:1} After Enoch spoke these words to his sons, people from near and far heard that the Lord was calling Enoch. They consulted together: {64:2} "Let us go and greet Enoch." Two thousand men gathered and went to the place Achuzan where Enoch and his sons were. {64:3} The elders of the people and the whole assembly came, bowed down, and began to greet Enoch, saying: {64:4} "Our father Enoch, may you be blessed by the Lord, the eternal ruler! Now bless your sons and all the people, so we may be glorified today before you." {64:5} For you shall be glorified before the Lord forever, since He chose you over all men on earth and appointed you as the writer of all His creation, both visible (physical) and invisible (spiritual), and as a redeemer of mankind's sins and helper of your household.

{65:1} Enoch answered all the people, saying: "Listen, my children, before all creatures were created, the Lord made both visible (physical) and invisible (spiritual) things. {65:2} Understand that as much time passed, after all that, He created man in His own likeness, giving him eyes to see, ears to hear, a heart to reflect, and an intellect to deliberate. {65:3} The Lord saw all of man's actions, created all creatures, and divided time; from time, He set the years, from the years, the months, and from the months, the days, and out of days, He appointed seven. {65:4} In these, He designated hours, measuring them accurately, so man could reflect on time and count years, months, and hours—their alternation, beginning, and end—and so he might consider his life from start to finish, reflect on his sins, and record his deeds, both good and bad, because no action is hidden from the Lord, so every man might know his works and not transgress His commandments, preserving my writings from generation to generation. {65:5} When all creation, both visible (physical) and invisible (spiritual), as the Lord created it, comes to an end, every man will face the great judgment, and then all time will cease—no more years, months, days, or hours; they will all blend into one and will not be counted. {65:6} There will be one age, and all the righteous who escape the Lord's great judgment will be gathered into this great age, for the righteous, this great age will begin, and they will live eternally; there will be no labor, sickness, humiliation, anxiety, need, cruelty, night, or darkness, but great light. {65:7} They will have a great, indestructible wall and a bright, eternal paradise, for all corruptible (mortal) things will pass away, and eternal life will prevail.

{66:1} Now, my children, guard your souls against all injustice, which the Lord despises. {66:2} Walk before Him with fear and trembling, and serve Him alone. {66:3} Bow down to the true God, not to lifeless idols; bow down to His likeness and bring all just offerings before the Lord. The Lord detests injustice. {66:4} For the Lord sees all; when a man thinks in his heart, He understands the intentions of his mind, and every thought is always before the Lord, who established the earth and placed all creatures upon it. {66:5} If you look to heaven, the Lord is there; if you consider the depths of the sea or all that is below the earth, the Lord is there. {66:6} For the Lord created everything. Do not bow to things made by man, forsaking the Lord of all creation, for no work can remain hidden from the Lord's sight. {66:7} My children, walk in patience, meekness, honesty, amidst provocation, grief, faith, and truth, relying on promises, enduring illness, abuse, wounds, temptation, nakedness, and deprivation, loving one another until you leave this age of suffering and inherit eternal time. {66:8} Blessed are the just who escape the great judgment, for they will shine seven times brighter than the sun, for in this world a seventh part is taken from everything: light, darkness, food, joy, sorrow, paradise, suffering, fire, frost, and other things; He recorded all of it for you to read and understand.

{67:1} After Enoch spoke to the people, the Lord sent darkness over the earth, covering those standing with Enoch. They took Enoch up to the highest heaven, where the Lord is; He received him and placed him before His face, and the darkness lifted from the earth, bringing back the light. {67:2} The people saw this but did not understand how Enoch was taken, and they glorified God, discovering a scroll that recorded the Invisible (spiritual) God; then they returned to their homes.

{68:1} Enoch was born on the sixth day of the month Tsivan and lived three hundred sixty-five years. {68:2} He was taken to heaven on the first day of the month Tsivan and remained there for sixty days. {68:3} He wrote about all the signs of creation, which the Lord made, and composed three hundred sixty-six books, giving them to his sons, and stayed on earth for thirty days before being taken up to heaven again on the sixth day of the month Tsivan, exactly on the day and hour of his birth. {68:4} Just as every man's nature in this life is dark, so too are his conception, birth, and departure from this life. {68:5} At the hour he was conceived, he was born, and at that hour, he also died. {68:6} Methuselah and his brothers, all the sons of Enoch, quickly built an altar at Achuzan, the place from where Enoch was taken to heaven. {68:7} They offered sacrificial oxen and gathered all the people to sacrifice before the Lord. {68:8} All the people, the elders, and the whole assembly came to the feast, bringing gifts for the sons of Enoch. {68:9} They held a great feast, rejoicing and celebrating for three days, praising God for the sign given through Enoch, who found favor with Him, so they could pass this on to their children for generations to come. {68:10} Amen.

The Third Book of Enoch

{1:1} Rabbi Ishmael narrates his ascent to the heavenly realms to witness the vision of the Merkaba. He describes how he entered six Halls, each nestled within the other. {1:2} Upon reaching the entrance to the seventh Hall, he paused in prayer, addressing the Divine Presence with reverence. Lifting his gaze, he prayed, {1:3} "Lord of the Universe, I plead that the merit of Aaron, son of Amram, the man of peace and bearer of the priestly crown given by Your Glory at Sinai, may protect me now, so that Qafsiel and the angels with him may not overpower or cast me from the heavens." {1:4} Instantly, the Holy One sent Metatron, His servant and Prince of the Presence. Metatron, with great joy, spread his wings and came to meet me, saving me from the angels' grasp. {1:5} He took my hand before them and said, "Enter in peace before the exalted King and behold the image of the Merkaba." {1:6} Then, Metatron led me into the seventh Hall, bringing me into the presence of the Shekina and positioning me before the Holy One to view the Merkaba. {1:7} When the princes of the Merkaba and the blazing Seraphim saw me, their gaze filled me with terror, causing me to tremble and collapse, paralyzed by their radiant eyes and majestic faces. At that moment, the Holy One intervened, {1:8} commanding, "My servants, Seraphim, Kerubim, and Ophannim! Cover your eyes before Ishmael, my son, my beloved, my glory, so that he may not tremble or fear." {1:9} Immediately, Metatron, Prince of the Presence, restored my spirit and lifted me to my feet. {1:10} For a time, I was too overwhelmed to sing a hymn before the Throne of Glory, the throne of the mightiest King, supreme above all rulers, until an hour had passed. {1:11} Then the Holy One opened to me the gates of Shekina, the gates of Peace, Wisdom, Strength, Power, Speech, Song, Sanctity, and Chant. {1:12} He illuminated my eyes and heart with psalms, songs, praises, exaltations, thanksgiving, glorification, hymns, and eulogies. When I began to sing before the Holy One, the Holy Chayyoth, above and below the Throne of Glory, responded with chants of "HOLY" and "BLESSED BE THE GLORY OF YHWH FROM HIS PLACE!"

{2:1} At that moment, the eagles of the Merkaba, the fiery Ophannim, and the Seraphim of blazing fire questioned Metatron, saying, {2:2} "Young one, why do you allow a human to enter and witness the Merkaba? From which nation, which tribe, and of what character is he?" {2:3} Metatron replied, "He is from the people of Israel, whom the Holy One chose from among seventy nations. He belongs to the tribe of Levi, set apart for His name, and from the lineage of Aaron, chosen by the Holy One to bear the priestly crown on Sinai." {2:4} The angels then exclaimed, "Indeed, he is worthy to see the Merkaba! Blessed is the people that has such a privilege!"

{3:1} Rabbi Ishmael continues, recounting that he asked Metatron, the angelic Prince of the Presence, "What is your name?" {3:2} Metatron replied, "I have seventy names, each corresponding to the seventy languages of the world. They are all derived from my main name, Metatron, the angel of the Presence; yet my King calls me 'Youth.'"

{4:1} Rabbi Ishmael then asked Metatron, "Why are you called by the name of your Creator and given seventy names? You are greater than all princes, higher than all angels, beloved more than any servant, and honored above all the mighty. Yet they call you 'Youth' in the high heavens. Why is this?" {4:2} Metatron responded, "Because I am Enoch, son of Jared. {4:3} When the generation of the Flood became sinful and corrupt, rejecting God's ways, the Holy One removed me from their midst to be a witness against them in the heavens. Thus, no one could claim that the Merciful One was unjust. {4:4} What was the sin of all those people, their wives, children, animals, and possessions, and even the birds, that the Holy One decided to destroy them all in the Flood? {4:5} So, in their lifetimes and before their eyes, the Holy One lifted me up to serve as a testimony against them for future generations. He appointed me a prince and ruler among the ministering angels. {4:6} At that time, three of the ministering angels—Uzza, Azza, and Azzael—protested my ascension before the Holy One, saying, "Did not the Ancient Ones rightly say, 'Do not create humanity'?" {4:7} The Holy One replied, 'I have made them, and I will sustain and deliver them.' Seeing me, they again questioned, 'Lord of the Universe! How can a human ascend to the heights? Isn't he one of those destined to perish in the Flood? What is he doing in the Raqia?' {4:8} The Holy One then answered, 'Who are you to question My will? I take delight in him above all, and thus he shall be a prince and ruler over you in the high heavens.' {4:9} With this, the angels approached me, bowed down, and said, 'Fortunate are you, and fortunate is your father, for your Creator has shown you favor.' {4:10} And because I am young among them in days, months, and years, they call me 'Youth' (Na'ar)."

{5:1} Rabbi Ishmael records Metatron's words, as the Prince of the Presence tells him: From the day when the Holy One expelled Adam from the Garden of Eden, the Shekina, the Divine Presence, rested on a cherub under the Tree of Life. {5:2} The ministering angels descended from heaven in groups, traveling from the firmament and the heavens in multitudes, to fulfill God's will across the world. {5:3} Adam and his descendants would sit outside the Garden's gate, watching the radiant glory of the Shekina. {5:4} The splendor of the Shekina filled the world, shining with a brilliance 365,000 times greater than the sun. Anyone who benefited from this light was free from pestilence, pain, illness, and harm from demons. {5:5} As God moved between the Garden, Eden, and the firmament, all who beheld the Shekina's splendor remained unharmed. {5:6} But during the time of Enosh, who became the father of idol worship, {5:7} humanity fell into idolatry. They traversed the world, bringing silver, gold, and precious gems, creating idols the size of mountains. They set up these idols everywhere, each towering 1,000 parasangs high. {5:8} They placed the sun, moon, stars, and planets beside these idols, arranging them as they surrounded the Divine Presence, as written in 1 Kings 22:19, "And all the host of heaven stood by Him on His right and on His left." {5:9} How could they summon the heavenly bodies? They were empowered by 'Uzza, Azza, and Azziel, who taught them sorcery and enabled them to manipulate these forces. {5:10} During that time, the ministering angels brought accusations before God, saying, "Master of the World, why concern Yourself with humanity, as Psalm 8:4 says, 'What is man (Enosh) that You are mindful of him?' This Enosh is indeed the leader of idol worship." {5:11} They continued, "Why have You left the high heavens, the abode of Your glorious Name, and chosen to dwell among people who worship idols and equate them to You? {5:12} Now, both You and the idols are on earth. What claim do You have with these idol-worshiping inhabitants?" {5:13} In response, God lifted the Shekina from earth, removing His presence from among them. {5:14} At that moment, legions of angels gathered with trumpets, surrounding the Shekina with songs as it ascended, as Psalm 47:5 states: "God is gone up with a shout, the Lord with the sound of a trumpet."

{6:1} Rabbi Ishmael recounts Metatron's words, describing the time God decided to raise him to heaven. God sent Anaphiel, the Prince, who took him, transporting him in splendor on a fiery chariot with fiery horses, lifting him and the Shekina to the high heavens. {6:2} Upon their arrival, the Holy Chayyoth, the Ophannim, the Seraphim, the Kerubim, the Wheels of the Merkaba, and the ministers of consuming fire noticed his presence from 365,000 myriads of parasangs away, saying, "What is this scent of a human? And what is this being like a mere gnat among those who split flames of fire?" {6:3} But God replied, "My servants, do not be displeased. Humanity has denied Me and turned to idol worship, so I have withdrawn My Shekina from their midst. But this one, whom I have taken, is righteous, and perfect in his deeds, and I have chosen him as a tribute from all under the heavens."

{7:1} Rabbi Ishmael records Metatron's words, detailing how, during the time of the Flood, God lifted him on the wings of the Shekina's wind to the highest heavens. He was brought to the great palaces of the Araboth Raqia, where he saw the Throne of Glory, the Merkaba, the armies of wrath, the ranks of fury, the fiery Shin'anim, the blazing Kerubim, the burning Ophannim, the flaming servants, the flashing Chashmal, and the lightning-like Seraphim. God placed him there to serve before the Throne of Glory each day.

{8:1} Rabbi Ishmael relates that before God appointed him to serve the Throne of Glory, He opened to Metatron three hundred thousand gates of Understanding, three hundred thousand gates of Subtlety, three hundred thousand gates of Life, three hundred thousand gates of Grace and Loving-kindness, three hundred thousand gates of Love, three hundred thousand gates of Torah, three hundred thousand gates of Humility, three hundred thousand gates of Sustenance, three hundred thousand gates of Mercy, and three hundred thousand gates of Reverence for Heaven. {8:2} At that moment, God bestowed upon him additional wisdom, understanding, subtlety, knowledge, mercy, instruction, love, kindness, goodness, humility, power, strength, might, brilliance, beauty, and splendor, elevating him beyond all the children of heaven in honor and adornment.

{9:1} Rabbi Ishmael describes how, after this, God placed His hand upon Metatron, blessing him with 5,360 blessings. {9:2} Metatron's stature grew to match the length and breadth of the world. {9:3} He was given seventy-two wings, thirty-six on each side, each as vast as the entire world. {9:4} Metatron received 365 eyes, each as bright as the sun. {9:5} God adorned him with every type of splendor, brilliance, radiance, and beauty found in the universe.

{10:1} Rabbi Ishmael recounts Metatron's words, describing how God created a throne for him, mirroring the Throne of Glory. Over it, He spread a canopy of splendor, brilliance, beauty, grace, and mercy, similar to the curtain before the Throne of Glory, decorated with every kind of light in the universe. {10:2} God placed this throne at the entrance of the Seventh Hall and seated Metatron upon it. {10:3} A herald went out through each heaven, proclaiming, "This is Metatron, My servant, whom I have made prince and ruler over all the princes of My kingdoms and all the children of heaven, except for the eight great princes who are honored and revered and are called by My name, YHWH." {10:4} The proclamation continued, saying that any angel or prince wishing to speak before God would now go to Metatron and present their words to him. {10:5} "Whatever command he issues in My name, you shall observe and fulfill, for I have entrusted the Prince of Wisdom and the Prince of Understanding to teach him the wisdom of both heavenly and earthly matters, of this world and the world to come." {10:6} Furthermore, God set Metatron over all the treasuries in the palaces of Araboth and the stores of life within the highest heavens.

{11:1} Rabbi Ishmael recounts how Metatron, the Prince of the Presence, described that, from then on, the Holy One revealed to him all mysteries of the Torah, all secrets of wisdom, and every depth of the Perfect Law. He was granted insight into every thought and desire of living beings, all the secrets of the universe, and the hidden aspects of Creation, just as they are known to the Creator. {11:2} Metatron observed the depths and the wondrous mysteries of existence; before any human even thought in secret, he could see it, and before anything was done, he already knew it. {11:3} Nothing, in the heights above or in the depths below, was concealed from him.

{12:1} Rabbi Ishmael describes how Metatron explained that, because of the love the Holy One had for him, greater than for any other heavenly being, God created for him a garment of glory, covered in all types of radiant light, and clothed him in it. {12:2} Additionally, God made for him a robe of honor, adorned with splendor, brilliance, and majesty. {12:3} God fashioned a royal crown for him, set with forty-nine precious stones that shone with a light as bright as the sun. {12:4} Its radiance spread to the four corners of the Araboth Raqia, the seven heavens, and across all directions of the world, and God placed it upon his head. {12:5} In front of all the heavenly beings, God called him "The Lesser YHWH," as stated in Exodus 23:21, "For My Name is in him."

{13:1} Rabbi Ishmael explains that, because of His great love and mercy, God cherished Metatron above all other heavenly beings. With His finger, He inscribed upon Metatron's crown, using a flaming stylus, the letters by which the heavens, the earth, the seas, rivers, mountains, hills, planets, constellations, lightnings, winds, earthquakes, thunders, snow, hail, storm-wind, and tempest were created—these letters hold the foundation of all Creation. {13:2} Each letter glowed, sending out bursts of light like flashes of lightning, flames of fire, and rays as bright as the rising sun, moon, and stars.

{14:1} Rabbi Ishmael recounts that, when God placed the crown upon Metatron's head, all the high-ranking princes of the Araboth Raqia and the hosts of every heaven trembled before him. The princes of the 'Elim, 'Er'ellim, and Tafsarim—greater than all the ministering angels before the Throne of Glory—shook with fear and awe when they saw him. {14:2} Even Sammael, the Prince of the Accusers, who surpasses all other princes, feared and trembled before Metatron. {14:3} The angels of fire, hail, wind, lightning, wrath, thunder, snow, rain, day, night, sun, moon, planets, and constellations, all governing forces of the world, were filled with fear and awe in his presence. {14:4} These heavenly rulers include Gabriel, angel of fire; Baradiel, angel of hail; Ruchiel, ruler of the wind; Baraqiel, ruler of lightning; Za'amiel, ruler of fury; Ziqiel, ruler of sparks; Zi'iel, ruler of upheaval; Zdaphiel, ruler of the storm-wind; Ra'amiel, ruler of thunder; Rctashiel, ruler of earthquakes; Shalgiel, ruler of snow; Matariel, ruler of rain; Shimshiel, ruler of day; Lailiel, ruler of night; Galgalliel, ruler of the sun; 'Ophanniel, ruler of the moon; Kokbiel, ruler of the planets; and Rahatiel, ruler of the constellations. {14:5} They all prostrated themselves before him, unable to look directly at him because of the majestic splendor of the radiant crown of glory upon his head.

{15:1} Rabbi Ishmael records Metatron's words, explaining how, when the Holy One took him into service to attend the Throne of Glory, the Wheels of the Merkaba, and the Shekina, his flesh transformed into flames, his sinews into blazing fire, his bones into coals of burning juniper, his eyelids into lightning, his eyes into firebrands, his hair into fiery dots, his limbs into wings of burning fire, and his entire body into glowing fire. {15:2} Surrounding him were fiery divisions on his right and burning firebrands on his left; stormwinds and tempests whirled around him, while thunder roared and earthquakes shook before and behind him.

{16:1} Rabbi Ishmael recounts that Metatron, the Prince of the Presence and Glory of all heaven, explained how he once sat on a great throne at the entrance of the Seventh Hall. From there, he judged the heavenly hosts, by the authority of the Holy One. He distributed honors—Greatness, Kingship, Dignity, Rulership, and Glory—to the princes of each kingdom, seated in the Celestial Court (Yeshiba), with the princes of kingdoms standing at his right and left. {16:2} But when Acher came to view the Merkaba, he saw Metatron on this throne, surrounded by angels, and became terrified, shaken to his core by the sight of Metatron sitting like a king, with the ministering angels as his attendants and the princes of kingdoms crowned around him. {16:3} At that moment, Acher exclaimed, "Indeed, there are two Divine Powers in heaven!" {16:4} Instantly, a Divine Voice (Bath Qol) issued from heaven, proclaiming, "Return, you backsliding children, except Acher!" {16:5} Then Aniyel, the exalted and revered Prince, was sent by the Holy One and struck Metatron with sixty lashes of fiery whips, forcing him to stand up from the throne.

{17:1} Rabbi Ishmael recounts that Metatron described the seven great, honored, and revered princes assigned to each of the seven heavens: Mikael, Gabriel, Shataqiel, Shachaqiel, Bakariel, Badariel, and Pachriel. {17:2} Each prince oversees the angelic hosts of a specific heaven and is accompanied by 496,000 myriads of ministering angels. {17:3} Mikael, the great prince, presides over the seventh and highest heaven, Araboth; Gabriel governs the sixth heaven, Makon; Shataqiel oversees the fifth heaven, Ma'on; Shachaqiel rules the fourth heaven, Zebul; Badariel commands the third heaven, Shehaqim; Barakiel rules the second heaven, Merom Raqia; and Pazriel governs the first heaven, Wilon, in Shamayim. {17:4} Beneath them is Galgalliel, the prince of the sun, who, along with 96 distinguished angels, moves the sun within the Raqia. {17:5} Beneath them is Ophanniel, the prince of the moon, accompanied by 88 angels, moving the moon 354,000 parasangs each night, especially on the fifteenth day of every month when it reaches its eastern turning point. {17:6} Rahatiel, the prince of constellations, governs their motion with the help of 72 great angels. He is named Rahatiel because he causes the stars to race (marhit) in their paths, traveling 339,000 parasangs each night from east to west and back. {17:7} Beneath him is Kokbiel, the prince of the planets, with 365,000 myriads of angels who move the planets across cities and provinces in the heavens. {17:8} Above them all are seventy-two princes of kingdoms, each corresponding to one of the seventy-two languages of the world. These princes are crowned with royal crowns, clothed in royal garments, and wrapped in royal cloaks. Riding royal horses with scepters, they travel across the heavens with entourages of royal servants, similar to earthly kings surrounded by chariots, horsemen, armies, and adorned with glory.

{18:1} Rabbi Ishmael records Metatron's description of the order of angelic ranks. When the angels of the first heaven see their prince, they dismount from their horses and fall on their faces. When the prince of the first heaven sees the prince of the second heaven, he removes his crown and falls on his face. Likewise, {18:2} each prince from the first to the sixth heaven honors the prince above him by dismounting and bowing with his crown removed, falling on his face. {18:3} The seventy-two princes of kingdoms, when they see the door keepers of the First Hall in the Araboth Raqia, also remove their crowns and bow. {18:4} When the door keepers of each Hall up to the Seventh see the higher-ranking princes over the four camps of Shekina, they too bow and fall on their faces. {18:5} The four great princes, upon seeing Tag'as, the chief among all heavenly beings, remove their crowns and bow as well. {18:6} Tag'as himself, when he sees Barattiel, the great prince, bows in reverence. {18:7} Barattiel honors Hamon, the powerful and revered prince who causes all the heavenly beings to tremble when the time comes for the chant of "Holy, Holy, Holy," as written in Isaiah 33:3: "At the noise of the tumult, the peoples flee; at the lifting up of yourself, the nations scatter." {18:8} Hamon shows reverence to Tutresiel, the great prince; {18:9} Tutresiel honors Atrugiel, and {18:10} Atrugiel bows before Na'aririel. {18:11} Na'aririel shows reverence to Sasnigiel, {18:12} and Sasnigiel bows before Zazriel. {18:13} Zazriel honors Geburatiel, {18:14} who then bows before 'Araphiel. {18:15} 'Araphiel shows respect to Ashruylu, who presides over all heavenly assemblies. {18:16} Ashruylu, upon seeing Gallisur, who reveals the secrets of the Torah, bows before him. {18:17} Gallisur, in turn, honors Zakzakiel, who records Israel's merits on the Throne of Glory. {18:18} Zakzakiel reveres 'Anaphiel, keeper of the heavenly halls, whose splendor fills all of Araboth, as stated in Habakkuk 3:3, "His glory covered the heavens, and the earth was full of His praise." {18:19} 'Anaphiel shows reverence to Sother Ashiel, the great and honored prince appointed over the fiery river opposite the Throne of Glory, and whose height spans 7,000 myriads of parasangs. He permits access to the Shekina and holds the fiery river's seals, presenting the deeds of the world's inhabitants as described in Daniel 7:10: "The court was seated, and the books were opened." {18:20} Sother Ashiel bows to Shoqed Chozi, the mighty and honored prince who weighs human deeds before the Holy One. {18:21} Shoqed Chozi reveres Zehanpuryu, a prince who commands the fiery river, pushing it back into place. {18:22} Zehanpuryu honors 'Azbuga, the great prince who will clothe the righteous in garments of life for eternal existence. {18:23} Finally, 'Azbuga bows before the two supreme princes, Sopheriel H' (the Killer) and Sopheriel H' (the Lifegiver), who stand above him. Sopheriel H' (the Killer) records the dead in the Book of Death, and Sopheriel H' (the Lifegiver) records the living in the Book of Life by the authority of MAQOM. Despite their greatness, even they stand while fulfilling the Shekina's commands, as 1 Kings 22:19 states, "And all the host of heaven stood by Him." {18:24} These two princes perform their duties while standing on wheels of tempest and storm-wind, both adorned in royal attire. {18:25} Each possesses identical attributes: clad in kingly garments, wearing royal crowns, their bodies full of eyes, their appearance like lightning, and their eyes as bright as the sun. Each is as tall as the seven heavens, with wings equal to the days of the year, spanning the width of Raqia, and with lips as broad as the eastern gates. Their tongues rise like the waves of the sea, from which flames and lightning burst forth. Sapphire stones adorn their heads, and swift cherubic wheels rest on their shoulders. Each holds a burning scroll and a flaming stylus, with scrolls stretching 3,000 myriads of parasangs, and each letter they inscribe measuring 365 parasangs.

{19:1} Rabbi Ishmael describes how Metatron, the Prince of the Presence, revealed to him that above three great angels stands a distinguished, honored, noble, and powerful Prince—one adorned with glory, revered and feared by all. His name is Rikbiel H', the mighty Prince who serves by the Merkaba. {19:2} Rikbiel is named as such because he oversees the wheels of the Merkaba, which are under his command. {19:3} The Merkaba has eight wheels, two in each direction, surrounded by four winds known as "Storm-Wind," "Tempest," "Strong Wind," and "Wind of Earthquake." {19:4} Four fiery rivers flow around them, one on each side, and between the rivers are four types of clouds: "clouds of fire," "clouds of lamps," "clouds of coal," and "clouds of brimstone," which are positioned near the wheels. {19:5} The feet of the Chayyoth rest upon these wheels, and between each wheel, thunder roars and earthquakes shake. {19:6} When it is time for the Song of Praise, the wheels begin to move, the clouds tremble, and all heavenly ranks—chieftains, horsemen, mighty ones, hosts, troops, appointed ones, princes, armies, servants, angels, and divisions—are seized with awe and fear. {19:7} Each wheel then calls to the other, each Kerub to another, each Chayya to another, and each Seraph to another, singing, "Extol Him who rides in Araboth, by His name Jah, and rejoice before Him!" (Psalm 68:5).

{20:1} Rabbi Ishmael continues, as Metatron tells him of Chayyiel H', a powerful and revered Prince appointed above the other Chayyoth. Chayyiel is so mighty that he could swallow the entire earth in one instant. {20:2} He is named Chayyiel because he rules over the Holy Chayyoth, striking them with fiery lashes to glorify them as they sing praises and rejoice, urging them to proclaim "Holy" and "Blessed be the Glory of H' from His place!" during the Qedushsha.

{21:1} Metatron explains that there are four Chayyoth, each corresponding to one of the four winds. Each Chayya is vast, filling the entire universe, and has four faces, each as majestic as the face of the East. {21:2} Each Chayya has four wings, each wing as large as the roof of the cosmos. {21:3} They have faces within faces and wings within wings, with each face measuring the size of 248 faces and each wing the size of 365 wings. {21:4} Each Chayya wears 2,000 crowns, each as radiant as a rainbow and shining as brightly as the sun, and from each one sparks of light emanate, as brilliant as the morning star in the East.

{22:1} Above these Chayyoth is the exalted Prince Kerubiel H', a mighty, holy prince filled with strength, honor, and righteousness, praised by innumerable hosts and armies. {22:2} His wrath makes the earth tremble, his anger causes heavenly camps to move, and the foundations shake at his rebuke, causing Araboth itself to shudder. {22:3} His body glows with burning coals; he is as tall, wide, and thick as the seven heavens. {22:4} His mouth shines like a fiery lamp, his tongue is aflame, his eyebrows sparkle like lightning, his eyes gleam with brilliance, and his face blazes like fire. {22:5} Upon his head rests a crown of holiness inscribed with the Explicit Name, from which lightning bolts emerge, and the bow of Shekina rests between his shoulders. {22:6} His sword flashes like lightning, his loins are encircled with flaming arrows, and his armor and shield radiate consuming fire. Coals of burning juniper surround his neck and body. {22:7} The splendor of Shekina graces his face, and horns of majesty rise from his wheels, with a royal diadem atop his head. {22:8} His body is covered with countless eyes, and wings envelop his entire towering form. {22:9} A flame burns on his right side, fire glows on his left, and coals ignite around him. Firebrands issue from his body, lightning streams from his face, thunder resounds alongside him, and earthquakes tremble beneath him. {22:10} With him are two princes of the Merkaba. {22:11} He is called Kerubiel H' because he oversees the Kerubim's chariot, holding authority over the mighty Kerubim, adorning their crowns and polishing their diadems. {22:12} He enhances their appearance, glorifies their majesty, and elevates their honor. He guides their songs of praise, amplifies their strength, illuminates their brilliance, beautifies their kindness, perfects their radiant compassion, exalts their uprightness, and orders their praise to honor the One who "dwells on the Kerubim." {22:13} The Kerubim stand beside the Holy Chayyoth with wings raised as high as their heads, the Shekina resting upon them, and the Glory's brilliance radiating from their faces. They sing praises with wings covering their feet, hands hidden beneath their wings, crowned with horns of glory and surrounded by the splendor of Shekina. {22:14} Sapphire stones surround them on all sides, with burning coals beneath. {22:15} Each Kerub stands facing a different direction, their wings touching each other above their heads in glory. Together they sing praises to the One who rides the clouds, honoring the majestic King of Kings. {22:16} Kerubiel H', the prince appointed over them, arranges them in a beautiful, exalted order, encouraging them with glory and might to fulfill the Creator's will each moment. Above their lofty heads dwells the continuous glory of the Most High, "who dwells on the Kerubim."

{22B:1} Rabbi Ishmael asked Metatron how the angels stand on high, and he replied, "Like a bridge placed over a river for people to cross, so is there a bridge extending from the entry to the end." {22B:2} Three ministering angels surround this bridge, singing before YHWH, the God of Israel, as captains of dread and fear stand before it, numbering thousands upon thousands, singing praises before the Lord. {22B:3} Many types of bridges exist there—fiery bridges, bridges of hail—alongside numerous rivers of hail, treasuries of snow, and wheels of fire. {22B:4} The 12,000 myriads of ministering angels are divided equally, with 6,000 above and 6,000 below, surrounding the bridges, rivers of fire, and rivers of hail, and they create paths within Raqia Shamayim. {22B:5} What does the King of Glory, YHWH, do there? This mighty, awe-inspiring God conceals His face, {22B:6} for in Araboth, 660,000 myriads of angels of glory stand opposite the Throne of Glory and the flaming fire. The King of Glory covers His face, or else Araboth Raqia itself would be torn asunder by the unmatched majesty, brilliance, beauty, and splendor of the Holy One. {22B:7} Numerous ministering angels, kings, and princes stand in Araboth, each revered among heavenly rulers, radiant with song, filled with love, trembling before the Shekina's splendor. Overwhelmed by His radiant beauty, their strength fades. {22B:8} Rivers of joy, streams of gladness, and rivers of love flow from the Throne of Glory, spreading through the paths of Araboth Raqia to the melody of the CHAYYOTH, the timbrels of His Ophannim, and the cymbals of His Kerubim. Together, they sing "HOLY, HOLY, HOLY IS THE LORD OF HOSTS; THE WHOLE EARTH IS FULL OF HIS GLORY!"

{22C:1} Rabbi Ishmael asks Metatron about the distance between each bridge, which is 12 myriads of parasangs, with ascents and descents of the same measure. {22C:2} Between the rivers of dread and fear lies a distance of 22 myriads of parasangs; between rivers of hail and darkness, 36 myriads; between chambers of lightning and clouds of compassion, 42 myriads; between these clouds and the Merkaba, 84 myriads; between the Merkaba and the Kerubim, 148 myriads; between the Kerubim and the Ophannim, 24 myriads; between the Ophannim and the Holy Chayyoth, 40,000 myriads; between each Chayyoth wing, 12 myriads, matching the width of each wing; and between the Holy Chayyoth and the Throne of Glory, 30,000 myriads. {22C:3} From the foot to the seat of the Throne is 40,000 myriads of parasangs, with the name of the One seated on it sanctified. {22C:4} The arches of the Bow span 1,000,000 parasangs above Araboth, with their measure corresponding to the Watchers and Holy Ones, as in Genesis 9:13, "My bow I have set in the cloud." {22C:5} A fiery voice proceeds from the Chayyoth, causing them to "run and return" (Ezekiel 1:14), fearing the voice might command them. {22C:6} These arches shine more radiantly than the summer sun, their beauty surpassing flame. {22C:7} Above these arches are the Ophannim wheels, towering at 1,000,000 parasangs according to the measure of Seraphim and Gedudim.

{23:1} Rabbi Ishmael learns from Metatron that many winds blow beneath the wings of the Kerubim. {23:2} There is the "Brooding Wind" as in Genesis 1:2, "And the wind of God was brooding upon the waters." {23:3} The "Strong Wind" is described in Exodus 14:21, "The Lord caused the sea to go back by a strong east wind." {23:4} The "East Wind" in Exodus 10:13, "The east wind brought the locusts." {23:5} The "Wind of Quails" in Numbers 11:31, "A wind from the Lord brought quails." {23:6} The "Wind of Jealousy" in Numbers 5:14, "The spirit of jealousy came upon him." {23:7} The "Wind of Earthquake" in 1 Kings 19:11, "The wind of the earthquake; but the Lord was not in the earthquake." {23:8} The "Wind of the Lord" as in Ezekiel 37:1, "And he carried me out by the wind of the Lord." {23:9} The "Evil Wind" as in 1 Samuel 16:23, "The evil wind departed from him." {23:10} The "Wind of Wisdom" and others as in Isaiah 11:2, "The wind of the Lord shall rest upon him; the wind of wisdom and understanding." {23:11} The "Wind of Rain" in Proverbs 25:23, "The north wind brings forth rain." {23:12} The "Wind of Lightnings" in Jeremiah 10:13, "He makes lightnings for rain." {23:13} The "Wind Breaking Rocks" in 1 Kings 19:11, "The strong wind rent the mountains." {23:14} The "Wind of Assuagement" in Genesis 8:1, "God made a wind pass, and the waters assuaged." {23:15} The "Wind of Wrath" in Job 1:19, "A great wind struck the house." {23:16} The "Storm-Wind" in Psalm 148:8, "Storm-wind fulfilling His word." Satan stands among these winds, embodying the storm-wind, and all these winds blow from beneath the Kerubim's wings, as written in Psalm 18:10, "He rode upon a cherub and did fly." {23:17} The winds travel from the wings of the Kerubim to the sun, moving through the seas, mountains, rivers, cities, the Garden, and finally to Eden, as in Genesis 3:8, "walking in the Garden in the wind of the day." {23:18} Filled with the fragrance of Eden, these winds bring the aroma of pure spices to the righteous who will inherit the Garden and the Tree of Life, as in Song of Solomon 4:16, "Awake, north wind; and come, south; blow upon my garden."

{24:1} Rabbi Ishmael explains that Metatron, the Prince of the Presence, told him about the many chariots of the Holy One. {24:2} There are the "Chariots of the Cherubim," as written in Psalm 18:11 and 2 Samuel 22:11, "And He rode upon a cherub and flew." {24:3}

The "Chariots of Wind" are described as, "He flew swiftly upon the wings of the wind." {24:4} The "Chariots of the Swift Cloud" are referenced in Isaiah 19:1: "Behold, the Lord rides upon a swift cloud." {24:5} He has "Chariots of Clouds," as written in Exodus 19:9: "Lo, I come to you in a cloud." {24:6} The "Chariots of the Altar" appear in Amos 9:1: "I saw the Lord standing upon the altar." {24:7} He also has "Chariots of Ribbotaim," as described in Psalm 68:18: "The chariots of God are Ribbotaim; thousands of angels." {24:8} The "Chariots of the Tent" are referenced in Deuteronomy 31:15: "And the Lord appeared in the Tent in a pillar of cloud." {24:9} He has "Chariots of the Tabernacle," as in Leviticus 1:1: "And the Lord spoke to him from the tabernacle." {24:10} The "Chariots of the Mercy-Seat" are mentioned in Numbers 7:89: "He heard the Voice speaking from upon the mercy-seat." {24:11} The "Chariots of Sapphire Stone" are noted in Exodus 24:10: "Under His feet was something like a paved work of sapphire stone." {24:12} There are "Chariots of Eagles," as in Exodus 19:4: "I bore you on eagles' wings"—not literal eagles, but beings that fly swiftly like eagles. {24:13} He has the "Chariots of Shout," as described in Psalm 47:6: "God has gone up with a shout." {24:14} The "Chariots of Araboth" are referenced in Psalm 68:5: "Extol Him who rides upon the Araboth." {24:15} He has "Chariots of Thick Clouds," as in Psalm 104:3: "Who makes the thick clouds His chariot." {24:16} The "Chariots of the Chayyoth" are described in Ezekiel 1:14: "And the Chayyoth ran and returned"—they move only with permission, for the Shekina rests above them. {24:17} He has "Chariots of Wheels (Galgallim)," as written in Ezekiel 10:2: "And he said, 'Go in between the whirling wheels.'" {24:18} The "Chariots of a Swift Cherub" appear in Psalm 18:10 and Isaiah 19:1: "Riding on a swift cherub." When He rides a swift cherub, before setting down His second foot, He surveys eighteen thousand worlds, discerning everything within them, as written in Ezekiel 48:35: "Round about eighteen thousand." Psalm 14:2 confirms this: "He looked down from heaven upon the children of men to see if any understand, who seek after God." {24:19} He has the "Chariots of the Ophannim," as Ezekiel 10:12 describes: "And the Ophannim were full of eyes all around." {24:20} The "Chariots of His Holy Throne" are referenced in Psalm 47:8: "God sits upon His holy throne." {24:21} He has the "Chariots of the Throne of Yah," as in Exodus 17:16: "Because a hand is lifted upon the Throne of Yah." {24:22} The "Chariots of the Throne of Judgment" are described in Isaiah 5:16: "But the Lord of hosts shall be exalted in judgment." {24:23} Lastly, He has the "Chariots of the High and Exalted Throne," as in Isaiah 6:1: "I saw the Lord sitting upon a high and exalted throne."

{25:1} Rabbi Ishmael recounts Metatron's description of 'Ophphanniel H', the revered and mighty Prince who presides over the Ophannim. {25:2} 'Ophphanniel has sixteen faces—four on each side—and one hundred wings on each side. He also has 8,466 eyes, representing the days of the year. {25:3} Lightning flashes from his two front eyes, and firebrands burn within them; no creature can gaze upon them without being burned. {25:4} His height is equivalent to a journey of 2,500 years. Only the King of Kings, the Holy One, blessed be He, can truly comprehend his might and strength. {25:5} He is named 'Ophphanniel because he is appointed over the Ophannim, caring for their beauty and readiness. He attends to them each day and night, ensuring they are always prepared to offer praise to their Creator. {25:6} The Ophannim are filled with eyes and covered in brightness; seventy-two sapphire stones adorn each side of their garments. {25:7} Four carbuncle stones are fixed on each crown, radiating splendor across Araboth like the sun's light reaches all parts of the universe. These stones are called carbuncles (Bareqet) because their brilliance resembles lightning (Baraq). Surrounding them are tents of splendor and brilliance, as dazzling as sapphire and carbuncle, reflecting the brightness of their eyes.

{26:1} Rabbi Ishmael recounts Metatron's description of Seraphiel H', the Prince of the Seraphim, a mighty and noble leader, swift in his service, glorified, honored, and beloved. {26:2} He radiates splendor, is filled with praise, brilliance, light, and beauty, and exudes goodness and greatness. {26:3} Though his face resembles an angel, his body resembles that of an eagle. {26:4} His radiance is like lightning, his appearance like fiery brands, his beauty like sparks, his honor like fiery coals, his majesty like chashmals, and his glow like the light of Venus. His entire being resembles the Greater Light, and his height spans the seven heavens. The light of his eyebrows shines with a sevenfold brightness. {26:5} On his head rests a sapphire stone, as vast as the entire universe and as radiant as the heavens themselves. {26:6} His body is covered with innumerable eyes, like the stars in the sky, with some resembling Venus and others the Lesser and Greater Lights. From his ankles to his knees, they shine like lightning; from his knees to thighs, like Venus; from thighs to loins, like the moon; from loins to neck, like the sun; and from neck to head, like the Eternal Light. {26:7} The crown upon his head glows like the Throne of Glory, with a circumference equal to a journey of 502 years. It reflects every type of splendor, brilliance, radiance, and light in the universe. {26:8} He is named Seraphiel H', and the crown on his head is called "the Prince of Peace." He is called Seraphiel because he rules over the Seraphim and commands them by day and night, teaching them songs of praise and majesty to glorify their King in all forms of Sanctification (Qedushsha). {26:9} There are four Seraphim, each corresponding to one of the four winds, with six wings each, symbolizing the six days of Creation, and four faces per Seraph. {26:10} Their height spans the seven heavens, and each wing measures the size of the entire Raqia. Each face is as grand as the face of the East. {26:11} They emit a light comparable to the Throne of Glory, so intense that even the Holy Chayyoth, the honored Ophannim, and the majestic Kerubim cannot look upon it, for any being who tries would have their eyes darkened by its brightness. {26:12} They are called Seraphim because they burn (saraph) Satan's writing tablets. Each day, Satan, along with Sammael (Prince of Rome) and Dubbiel (Prince of Persia), writes Israel's sins on tablets to present before the Holy One, hoping to condemn them. But the Seraphim, knowing that God desires Israel's survival, take these tablets daily from Satan and burn them in the fire near the Throne to prevent them from reaching God during judgment.

{27:1} Rabbi Ishmael describes Radweriel H', the exalted Prince over all other princes and the keeper of the heavenly records. {27:2} He retrieves the Case of Writings, containing the Book of Records, and presents it to the Holy One, breaking its seals, opening it, and handing the books to God. The Holy One then passes them to the Scribes, who read them in the Great Court (Beth Din) in the heights of Araboth Raqia before the heavenly assembly. {27:3} Radweriel is named so because every word from his mouth creates an angel who joins the choir of ministering angels to sing praises before God, especially when the time approaches for the "Thrice Holy" recitation.

{28:1} Above all others are four great princes called the Irin and Qaddishin—honored, beloved, and glorious beings greater than any other heavenly princes, each one equal to all the others combined. {28:2} They dwell near the Throne of Glory, with a radiance that reflects the Throne's brilliance and the splendor of Shekina. {28:3} They are glorified by the Divine Majesty and praised by Shekina's honor. {28:4} The Holy One does nothing in the world without first consulting them, as written in Daniel 4:17: "The sentence is by the decree of the Irin and the demand by the word of the Qaddishin." {28:5} The Irin consist of two princes, as do the Qaddishin. One Ir stands on one side, the other on the opposite, with each Qaddish similarly positioned. {28:6} They uplift the humble and bring down the proud, exalting those of low stature. {28:7} Each day, as the Holy One sits on the Throne of Judgment to judge the world, with the Books of the Living and the Dead open before Him, all heavenly beings stand in awe and fear. At this moment, God's appearance is as pure as snow, with His hair like white wool and His robe as radiant as light, covered entirely in righteousness. {28:8} The Irin and Qaddishin stand as court officials before the Judge, presenting and debating each case before Him, as stated in Daniel 4:17: "The sentence is by the decree of the Irin and the demand by the word of the Qaddishin." {28:9} Some of them present cases, while others deliver judgments in the Great Court of Araboth, some making requests to the Divine Majesty and others concluding cases. They also descend to earth to carry out these judgments, as described in Daniel 4:13–14: "Behold, an Ir and a Qaddish came down from heaven and cried aloud: 'Hew down the tree, and cut off its branches, shake off its leaves, and scatter its fruit; let the animals flee from under it and the birds from its branches.'" {28:10} They are called Irin and Qaddishin because they sanctify both body and spirit with fiery lashes on the third day of judgment, as stated in Hosea 6:2: "After two days, He will revive us; on the third, He will raise us up, and we shall live before Him."

{29:1} Rabbi Ishmael recounts that Metatron described a class of angels, each with seventy names corresponding to the seventy languages of the world, all based upon the Holy One's name. Each name is inscribed with a flaming stylus on the Fearful Crown (Kether Nora) atop the exalted King's head. {29:2} Sparks and lightning emanate from each angel, surrounded by horns of splendor. Each angel is encircled by tents of brilliance, making them too radiant even for the Seraphim and Chayyoth, who surpass all other beings in heaven, to gaze upon.

{30:1} Rabbi Ishmael describes the Great Beth Din (Court) in Araboth Raqia. When this court convenes, no being in the universe speaks unless permitted by the seventy-two great princes who bear the name H' after the Holy One, blessed be He. {30:2} These seventy-two princes represent all kingdoms of the world, along with the Prince of the World, who pleads daily for the world before God when the book of deeds is opened, as described in Daniel 7:10: "The judgment was set, and the books were opened."

{31:1} Rabbi Ishmael recounts Metatron's description of how, when the Holy One sits on the Throne of Judgment, Justice stands on His right, Mercy on His left, and Truth before His face. {31:2} As a person approaches for judgment, a ray of Mercy shines forth toward him, appearing like a staff and standing in front of him. The person then falls to his face, and all angels of destruction tremble in fear, as written in Isaiah 16:5: "And with mercy, the throne shall be established, and He shall sit upon it in truth."

{32:1} Rabbi Ishmael describes how, when God opens the Book that is half fire and half flame, angels emerge each moment to carry out judgment on the wicked with His sword. The sword, drawn from its sheath, shines like lightning and spans the world from one end to the other, as described in Isaiah 66:16: "For by fire will the Lord judge, and by His sword with all flesh." {32:2} The entire world trembles at the sight of this sword, flashing like lightning across the heavens, with sparks as large as the stars of Raqia flying from it, as written in Deuteronomy 32:41: "If I whet the lightning of My sword."

{33:1} Metatron explains that, when the Holy One sits on the Throne of Judgment, angels of Mercy stand to His right, angels of Peace to His left, and angels of Destruction in front of Him. {33:2} One scribe stands beneath the Throne, and another scribe above it. {33:3} Surrounding the Throne, the glorious Seraphim form walls of lightning, while the Ophannim encircle them with fiery brands. Clouds of fire and flame are on both sides, and the Holy Chayyoth support the Throne from below, each using three fingers. Each finger spans 800,700 times 100, plus 66,000 parasangs. {33:4} Beneath the Chayyoth flow seven fiery rivers, each 365,000 parasangs wide, 248,000 myriads of parasangs deep, and their length is immeasurable. {33:5} These rivers loop in a great arc across the four directions of Araboth Raqia, descending through each level of heaven until they finally reach the heads of the wicked in Gehenna, as written in Jeremiah 23:19: "Behold, a whirlwind of the Lord, even His fury, goes forth... it shall fall upon the head of the wicked."

{34:1} Metatron describes the protective layers around the Chayyoth: their feet are encircled by seven clouds of burning coals, followed by seven walls of flames, and then seven walls of hailstones (as in Ezekiel 13:11,13). Beyond the hailstones are walls of additional stones of hail, encircled by stones from the "wings of the tempest." {34:2} Surrounding these layers are flames of fire, chambers of whirlwinds, and finally, layers of fire and water. Encircling these are angels who chant "Holy," followed by others who chant "Blessed." Around these are bright clouds, surrounded by coals of burning juniper, with thousands of fiery camps and tens of thousands of flames. Between each camp and host is a cloud, shielding them from the intense fire.

{35:1} Metatron explains that in Araboth Raqia, the Holy One has 506,000 myriads of angelic camps, each camp consisting of 496,000 angels. {35:2} Each angel's stature is vast, like the great sea, with faces like lightning, eyes like lamps of fire, limbs like polished brass, and voices like the roar of a multitude. {35:3} These angels stand before the Throne of Glory in four rows, each led by a prince. {35:4} Some angels chant "Holy," others chant "Blessed," some serve as messengers, and others stand in attendance, as written in Daniel 7:10: "Thousands upon thousands ministered to Him, and ten thousand times ten thousand stood before Him; the judgment was set, and the books were opened." {35:5} When it is time to say "Holy," a whirlwind issues from the Holy One, stirring the camp of Shekina and creating great commotion, as written in Jeremiah 30:23: "Behold, the whirlwind of the Lord goes forth with fury, a continuing commotion." {35:6} In that instant, thousands of angels transform into sparks, firebrands, flashes, flames, male and female forms, winds, burning fires, flames, and chashmals of light, until they accept the yoke of the Kingdom of Heaven with awe and trembling. Then they revert to their original forms, filled with reverence, and they prepare their hearts to sing continuously, as written in Isaiah 6:3: "And one called to another and said, 'Holy, Holy, Holy...'"

{36:1} Rabbi Ishmael describes how Metatron explained that, before the ministering angels sing their Song of Praise, the fiery river Nehar di-Nur rises up with countless thousands and myriads of powerful fiery angels flowing beneath the Throne of Glory, between the camps of the ministering angels and the troops of Araboth. {36:2} The ministering angels then descend into the river, immersing themselves in the fire and dipping their tongues and mouths seven times. After this, they rise, don the garments of "Machaqe Samal," and cloak themselves in coverings of chashmal before assembling in four rows before the Throne of Glory across all the heavens.

{37:1} Metatron describes the seven Halls where four chariots of Shekina stand, each surrounded by the four camps of Shekina. Between each camp flows a river of fire. {37:2} Bright clouds surround these rivers, and between each cloud stand pillars of brimstone. Flaming wheels encircle each pillar, while flames of fire lie between the wheels. Beyond the flames are treasuries of lightnings, behind which are the wings of the stormwind, chambers of the tempest, and a succession of winds, voices, thunders, sparks upon sparks, and earthquakes upon earthquakes.

{38:1} Rabbi Ishmael recounts Metatron's description of how, when the ministering angels proclaim the Thrice Holy, the pillars of heaven and their foundations shake, the gates of the Halls of Araboth Raqia tremble, and the very universe quivers. The heavens Ma'on, Makon, Raqia, and the stars, constellations, and planets are thrown into turmoil. Even the sun and moon race from their courses, fleeing 12,000 parasangs and seeming as if they might fall from the sky. {38:2} This commotion results from the resounding voice of their chant, the clamor of their praise, and the sparks and lightnings radiating from their faces, as written in Psalm 77:18: "The voice of your thunder was in the heaven; the lightnings lit up the world; the earth trembled and shook." {38:3} The Prince of the World then calms the heavenly bodies, reassuring them, "Remain in your places; fear not the voices of the ministering angels who sing before the Holy One, blessed be He," as stated in Job 38:7: "When the morning stars sang together and all the children of heaven shouted for joy."

{39:1} Metatron explains that, when the ministering angels proclaim "Holy," all the explicit divine names inscribed with flaming letters on the Throne of Glory fly out like eagles with sixteen wings, encircling the Holy One, blessed be He, on all sides of His Shekina. {39:2} All the angelic hosts, flaming servants, mighty Ophannim, Kerubim of Shekina, Holy Chayyoth, Seraphim, 'Er'ellim, Taphsarim, and the legions of consuming fire fall prostrate three times, saying, "Blessed be the name of His glorious kingdom forever and ever."

{40:1} Metatron explains how the ministering angels are rewarded when they recite the "Holy" correctly before the Holy One. Then, the servants of His Throne emerge joyfully from beneath the Throne of Glory. {40:2} Each one brings thousands upon thousands of crowns that resemble the planet Venus and places them on the heads of the ministering angels and great princes who sing the "Holy." Each receives three crowns: one for "Holy," a second for "Holy, Holy," and a third for "Holy, Holy, Holy, is the Lord of Hosts." {40:3} However, if they do not utter "Holy" in the correct order, a consuming fire emerges from the little finger of the Holy One, blessed be He, dividing into 496,000 parts to target each of the four camps of the ministering angels, consuming them instantly, as written in Psalm 97:3: "A fire goes before Him and burns up His adversaries round about." {40:4} Then, the Holy One, blessed be He, speaks a word, creating new angels in their place, who stand before the Throne of Glory, proclaiming "Holy" anew, as written in Lamentations 3:23: "They are new every morning; great is Your faithfulness."

{41:1} Rabbi Ishmael recounts how Metatron, the Angel and Prince of the Presence, said to him, "Come and see the letters by which heaven and earth were created—the letters that gave form to mountains and hills, seas and rivers, trees and plants, planets, constellations, the moon and sun, Orion, the Pleiades, and all the other heavenly lights in Raqia." {41:2} These letters also created the Throne of Glory and the Wheels of the Merkaba and brought forth the necessities of the world. {41:3} By these letters, wisdom, understanding, knowledge, prudence, meekness, and righteousness—by which the world is sustained—came into being. {41:4} Metatron led Rabbi Ishmael by the hand, lifted him upon his wings, and showed him the letters engraved with a fiery stylus on the Throne of Glory, sending out sparks that filled all the chambers of Araboth.

{42:1} Metatron told Rabbi Ishmael, "Come, and I will show you where the waters are suspended on high, where fire burns within hail, where lightning flashes within snowy mountains, where thunders roar in the celestial heights, and where voices echo within thunder and earthquake." {42:2} Metatron then took Rabbi Ishmael by the hand, lifted him on his wings, and showed him these wonders. Ishmael saw waters hanging in the heights of Araboth Raqia, held by the divine name YAH EHYE ASHER EHYE (I am that I am), with streams descending from them to water the earth, as in Psalm 104:13: "He waters the mountains from His chambers." {42:3} Rabbi Ishmael saw fire and snow coexisting within one another, kept intact by the name ESH OKELA (consuming fire), as in Deuteronomy 4:24: "For the Lord, your God, is a consuming fire." {42:4} He saw lightning flashing within snowy mountains, unquenched, sustained by the name YAH SUR OLAMIM (Jah, the Everlasting Rock), as in Isaiah 26:4: "For in Jah, YHWH, the everlasting rock." {42:5} He saw thunders roaring within fiery flames, unaffected, by the name EL-SHADDAI RABBA (the Great Almighty God), as in Genesis 17:1: "I am God Almighty." {42:6} Ishmael saw glowing flames within burning fire, unconsumed, by the name YAD AL KES YAH (the hand upon the Throne of the Lord), as in Exodus 17:16: "For the hand is upon the Throne of the Lord." {42:7} Finally, he beheld rivers of fire flowing amidst rivers of water, coexisting by the name OSE SHALOM (Maker of Peace), as in Job 25:2: "He makes peace in His high places," harmonizing fire with water, hail with fire, wind with cloud, and quake with sparks.

{43:1} Metatron then said, "Come, and I will show you the dwelling place of both the spirits of the righteous who have lived and those not yet born." {43:2} He took Rabbi Ishmael by the hand, raised him near the Throne of Glory, and showed him the spirits that had already been created and returned to their origin, flying above the Throne of Glory before the Holy One. {43:3} Reflecting on Isaiah 57:16, Rabbi Ishmael understood: "For the spirit clothed itself before Me" refers to the righteous spirits that have returned to God, while "the souls I have made" refers to those spirits not yet created in the chamber of Guph.

{44:1} Metatron next showed Rabbi Ishmael where the spirits of the wicked and the intermediate were kept, and how they descend into She'ol. {44:2} He explained that the spirits of the wicked are led to She'ol by two angels of destruction, named Zaaphiel and Simkiel. {44:3} Simkiel is assigned to the intermediate spirits, supporting and cleansing them through the mercy of the Prince of the Place (Maqom), while Zaaphiel casts down the wicked from God's presence to She'ol, where they suffer in the fires of Gehenna. {44:4} Metatron led Rabbi Ishmael by the hand and showed him the faces of the spirits. {44:5} The intermediate spirits had faces resembling humans, with bodies like eagles, their countenances pale gray due to their deeds, which are cleansed through fire. {44:6} The wicked spirits had faces darkened like the bottom of a pot due to their sins. {44:7} Rabbi Ishmael saw the spirits of the Patriarchs—Abraham, Isaac, and Jacob—and other righteous figures ascending from their graves to heaven (Raqia), praying before God, asking, "Lord of the Universe, how long will You sit in mourning with Your right hand behind You, without delivering Your children or revealing Your Kingdom on earth? How long will You allow them to remain slaves among the nations?" {44:8} The Holy One answered, explaining that He could not intervene while the wicked continued sinning and transgressing. {44:9} At that moment, Metatron called Rabbi Ishmael to read from the books of the wicked deeds, which revealed thirty-six transgressions per wicked person, and further, that they had violated all the Torah's letters, from Aleph to Taw, as in Daniel 9:11: "Yea, all Israel have transgressed Thy Law." {44:10} The Patriarchs wept, and the Holy One said to Abraham, Isaac, and Jacob, "How can I now deliver them from the nations?" In response, Michael, the Prince of Israel, cried out, asking, "Why do You stand afar off, O Lord?" (Psalm 10:1).

{45:1} Metatron invited Rabbi Ishmael to see the Curtain of MAQOM, which is displayed before the Divine Majesty and upon which every generation's actions, past and future, are inscribed. {45:2} Rabbi Ishmael observed the Curtain as Metatron pointed out each figure, like a father teaching Torah letters to his children. {45:3} He saw each generation, with its leaders, rulers, and overseers, including Adam, Noah, and their respective generations, all their deeds and thoughts, up until the Patriarchs, the Tribes, and Moses' generation. {45:4} He also saw the deeds and generations of Aaron, Miriam, Joshua, the judges, and leaders of both Israel and the nations, including all prophets and teachers, their works and actions. {45:5} Rabbi Ishmael also beheld all the wars and conflicts faced by Israel during their kingdom, the deeds of Messiah, son of Joseph, his battles, and those of Messiah, son of David. He saw the future battles of Gog and Magog and all that God will do to them. {45:6} Every event, leader, and deed, past and future, both of Israel and the nations, was engraved on the Curtain of MAQOM. After seeing this, Rabbi Ishmael praised the Divine Majesty, quoting Ecclesiastes 8:4-5: "For the King's word has power... Who may say to Him, 'What are You doing?'" and he concluded, "O Lord, how manifold are Your works!" (Psalm 104:24).

{46:1} Rabbi Ishmael recounts how Metatron said to him, "Come, and I will show you the realm of the stars, where they stand in Raqia each night in awe of the Almighty (MAQOM). I will show you where they go and where they take their place." {46:2} Walking beside Metatron, he guided Rabbi Ishmael, pointing to the stars that stood on sparks of flames around the Merkaba of the Almighty. Metatron then clapped his hands, causing the stars to scatter from their places. Instantly, they rose up on wings of flame, fleeing from all sides of the Throne of the Merkaba. As they moved, Metatron called each star by name, fulfilling Psalm

147:4: "He counts the number of stars; He gives each one its name," signifying that the Holy One, blessed be He, has named each star individually. {46:3} Each night, the stars enter in their assigned order, under the direction of RAHATIEL, moving to Raqia ha-shShamayim to serve the world. They exit in this same order, singing songs of praise to the Holy One, blessed be He, as it is written in Psalm 19:1: "The heavens declare the glory of God." {46:4} Yet in the future, the Holy One, blessed be He, will renew them, as Lamentations 3:23 says, "They are new every morning." Then they will sing, saying, "When I consider Your heavens..." (Ps. 8:3).

{47:1} Rabbi Ishmael recalls how Metatron told him, "Come, and I will show you the souls of the angels and the spirits of the ministering servants whose bodies were burned by the fire of the Almighty (MAQOM), which emerged from His little finger. These angels have become fiery coals in the midst of Nehar di-Nur, the fiery river. However, their spirits and souls stand behind the Shekina." {47:2} If ministering angels sing out of turn or at an improper time, they are consumed by the fire of their Creator, who sends a flame from His presence. These spirits are then driven by a whirlwind into the Nehar di-Nur, transforming them into mountains of burning coals. Yet their spirits and souls return to their Creator, where they stand behind Him. {47:3} Metatron took Rabbi Ishmael's hand and showed him the souls of these angels and the spirits of the ministering servants, standing behind the Shekina on wings of the whirlwind, surrounded by walls of fire. {47:4} Metatron then opened the gates within the walls where these souls stood behind the Shekina. Rabbi Ishmael lifted his eyes and saw them; each one resembled an angel, with wings like those of birds made of flames, crafted from burning fire. In awe, Rabbi Ishmael exclaimed in praise of MAQOM, quoting Psalm 92:5: "How great are Your works, O Lord."

{48:1} Rabbi Ishmael recounts that Metatron said to him, "Come, and I will show you the Right Hand of MAQOM (the Almighty), which remains hidden due to the destruction of the Holy Temple. This hand, from which radiant splendor and light emerge, created the 955 heavens, and even the Seraphim and 'Ophannim are not permitted to behold it until the day of redemption. {48:2} I walked by Metatron's side as he held my hand and revealed to me the Right Hand of MAQOM, resplendent with all manner of praise and song. No words can capture its glory, and no eye can fully behold it due to its overwhelming majesty and beauty. {48:3} Only the souls of the righteous, those worthy of Jerusalem's joy, stand beside it, offering praise and prayer three times daily, invoking, 'Awake, awake, arm of the Lord, clothe Yourself with strength,' as in Isaiah 51:9. This arm was shown guiding Moses with its power, as Isaiah 63:12 declares. {48:4} Then, I saw the Right Hand of MAQOM weeping, from which five rivers of tears flowed from its fingers into the great sea, shaking the world. This is described in Isaiah 24:19-20, with the earth trembling five times, each symbolizing a finger on His Great Right Hand. {48:5} When the Holy One, blessed be He, sees there is no righteousness, piety, or justice on earth, and no one like Moses or Samuel to intercede, He prepares His Right Hand to save Israel. {48:6} Then He remembers His mercy, righteousness, and kindness, deciding to act for salvation. As it is written in Isaiah 59:16, 'He saw that there was no one to intercede'—like Moses, who prayed countless times for Israel in the wilderness, or Samuel, whose pleas were answered despite not fitting God's plan (1 Samuel 12:17). {48:7} In that time, the Almighty shall act for His own sake, as He declared, 'For My sake alone I will do it; for how could My name be profaned?' (Isaiah 48:11). {48:8} In that hour, God will reveal His Great Right Hand, extending as far as the world's length and breadth, shining with a splendor like the summer sun at its peak. {48:9} Then, Israel shall be saved, and the Messiah shall bring them to Jerusalem with great joy. The nations will witness this but will not partake, as written, 'The Lord has bared His holy arm in the sight of all nations; all the earth shall see the salvation of our God' (Isaiah 52:10).

{48B:1} These are the seventy-two names inscribed on the heart of the Holy One, blessed be He, each crowned with fire, flame, and chashmal and surrounded by thousands of angels. These angels, trembling in awe, carry these names as one would escort a king, singing 'Holy, Holy, Holy,' and guiding them through every heaven. {48B:2} When they return to the Throne of Glory, the Chayyoth and all by the Merkaba open their mouths to proclaim, 'Blessed be the name of His glorious kingdom forever and ever.'

{48C:1} 'I took Enoch, the son of Jared, and I appointed him as Metatron, a witness before Me in the celestial realm. {48C:2} I elevated him, making a throne opposite My Throne, 70,000 parasangs high and all of fire. {48C:3} I assigned him 70 angels, representing the nations, and gave him authority over the hosts of heaven and earth. {48C:4} I granted him wisdom and knowledge beyond all angels, naming him "the Lesser YHWH," signifying his connection to My own name, totaling seventy-one in gematria, and I entrusted him with overseeing all creation.

{48D:1} Metatron has seventy names, each derived from the name of the Holy One, blessed be He, which signifies the wisdom and authority bestowed upon him. These names include YEHOEL, YOPHIEL, and others reflecting the attributes and responsibilities given to Metatron. {48D:2} All these names embody aspects of the Explicit Name inscribed on the Merkaba, empowering Metatron to act as an agent of creation. {48D:3} These names were revealed to Moses on Mount Sinai, along with knowledge of the Torah, Prophets, Writings, Halachot, traditions, and teachings in seventy languages. {48D:4} Though Moses initially forgot them upon descending, they were later given to him as a divine gift, thus securing his remembrance of them forever. {48D:5} The mysteries embedded within these names are reserved for the highest understanding and remain graven upon the Throne of Glory, ensuring that the destinies of nations and princes are guided by divine wisdom. {48D:6} When Metatron shared these secrets with Moses, the angels objected, questioning how such holy knowledge could be given to man. But God Himself rebuked the angels, affirming that Metatron was chosen and uniquely authorized to share these mysteries. {48D:7} These secrets were then passed from Moses to Joshua, to the elders, prophets, and finally to those who can heal and guide humanity, as expressed in Exodus 15:26: 'I am the Lord who heals you.' (Ended and finished. Praise be unto the Creator of the World.)

The Fragment of Ascension of Moses

{1:1} Rabbi Ishmael recounted that Metatron, the Prince of the Presence, who rules over all other princes and stands before the One greater than all gods, spoke to him. Metatron approaches beneath the Throne of Glory and possesses a great tabernacle of light in the heavens. He draws forth a "fire of deafness" and places it in the ears of the Holy Chayyoth, so they do not hear the voice of the Word (Dibbur) emanating from the Divine Majesty.

{2:1} When Moses ascended to the heights, he undertook 121 fasts until the dwellings of the chashmal (angelic beings) opened to him. He glimpsed "the heart within the heart" of the Lion & saw countless hosts surrounding it. These beings wished to consume him with their fire, but Moses prayed for mercy, first for Israel and then for himself. The One who sits on the Merkaba opened the windows above the heads of the Kerubim. A group of 1,800 intercessors, accompanied by Metatron, Prince of the Presence, came to meet Moses. They took the prayers of Israel and placed them as a crown upon the head of the Holy One, blessed be He.

{3:1} They recited the words of Deuteronomy 6:4: "Hear, O Israel; the Lord our God is one Lord." Their faces shone, rejoicing in the Shekina. They asked Metatron, "What are these prayers, and to whom is all this honor and glory given?" Metatron replied, "To the

Glorious Lord of Israel." They then proclaimed, "Hear, O Israel: the Lord, our God, is one Lord. To whom should honor and majesty be given if not to You, YHWH, the Divine Majesty, the Eternal King?"

{4:1} At that moment, Akatriel Yah Yehod Sebaoth spoke to Metatron, the Prince of the Presence, saying, "Let no prayer he offers be returned unanswered. Listen to his prayers and fulfill his desires, whether they are great or small."

{5:1} Immediately, Metatron, the Prince of the Presence, said to Moses, "Son of Amram, do not fear, for God now delights in you. Ask whatever you wish of the Glory and Majesty, for your face shines from one end of the world to the other." Moses replied, "I fear I may bring guilt upon myself." Metatron reassured him, saying, "Accept the letters of the oath in which the covenant cannot be broken, ensuring that you will not breach the covenant."

The First Book of Adam and Eve

{1:1} On the third day, God planted a garden in the east of the earth, at the edge of the world to the east, beyond which, toward the rising sun, there is only water that surrounds the entire world and reaches the borders of heaven. {1:2} To the north of the garden, there is a sea of clear, pure water, unlike anything else; its clarity allows one to see into the depths of the earth. {1:3} When a person washes in it, they are cleansed by its purity and whiteness, even if they were dark. {1:4} God created that sea because He knew what would happen to the man He was going to make; after he left the garden due to his transgression, people would be born on the earth, among whom righteous ones would die, and their souls would be raised by God on the last day, when they would return to their bodies and bathe in the water of that sea, repenting for their sins. {1:5} But when God made Adam leave the garden, He did not place him on its northern border, so that he and Eve would not go near the sea, wash themselves in it, forget their transgression, and no longer remember their punishment. {1:6} On the southern side of the garden, God did not want Adam to dwell there either, because when the wind blew from the north, it would bring him the delicious scent of the trees of the garden. {1:7} Therefore, God did not place Adam there, lest he smell the sweet fragrance of those trees, forget his transgression, and find comfort in what he had done. {1:8} Also, because God is merciful and compassionate, governing all things in a way He alone knows, He made our father Adam dwell on the western border of the garden, where the earth is very spacious. {1:9} God commanded him to live in a cave in a rock—the Cave of Treasures, below the garden.

{2:1} When our father Adam and Eve went out of the garden, they walked on the ground without realizing it. {2:2} Upon reaching the gate of the garden and seeing the vast earth covered with large and small stones and sand, they felt fear and trembled, falling on their faces in terror, as if they were dead. {2:3} They had been in the garden, which was beautifully planted with all kinds of trees, and now they found themselves in a strange land they had never seen before. {2:4} At that time, they were filled with grace and had bright natures, not having their hearts turned towards earthly things. {2:5} Therefore, God took pity on them; when He saw them fallen at the gate of the garden, He sent His Word to Adam and Eve to raise them from their fallen state.

{3:1} Concerning the promise of the great five days and a half, God said to Adam, "I have established days and years on this earth, and you and your descendants will dwell and walk in it until the days and years are fulfilled; when I will send the Word that created you, against which you have transgressed, the Word that caused you to leave the garden, and that raised you when you fell. {3:2} Yes, the Word that will save you again when the five days and a half are fulfilled." {3:3} When Adam heard these words from God and learned about the great five days and a half, he did not understand their meaning. {3:4} Adam thought that there would only be five days and a half until the end of the world. {3:5} He wept and prayed to God for an explanation. {3:6} In His mercy for Adam, who was made in His image and likeness, God explained that these were 5,500 years and that One would come to save him and his descendants. {3:7} God had made this covenant with Adam in the same way before he left the garden, when he was by the tree from which Eve took the fruit and gave it to him to eat. {3:8} As Adam left the garden, he passed by that tree and saw how God had changed its appearance, and how it had withered. {3:9} As Adam approached it, he felt fear, trembled, and fell down; but God, in His mercy, lifted him up and made this covenant with him. {3:10} When Adam was by the gate of the garden and saw the cherub with a sword of flashing fire, the cherub became angry and frowned at him. Both Adam and Eve were afraid of him, thinking he meant to kill them, so they fell on their faces, trembling with fear. {3:11} But the cherub had pity on them, showed them mercy, and, turning from them, went up to heaven and prayed to the Lord, saying, "Lord, You sent me to watch at the gate of the garden with a sword of fire. {3:12} But when Your servants, Adam and Eve, saw me, they fell on their faces as if dead. O my Lord, what shall we do for Your servants?" {3:13} Then God had pity on them, showed them mercy, and sent His Angel to guard the garden. {3:14} The Word of the Lord came to Adam and Eve and raised them up. {3:15} The Lord said to Adam, "I told you that at the end of five days and a half, I will send My Word and save you. {3:16} Therefore, strengthen your heart and dwell in the Cave of Treasures, which I have previously mentioned to you." {3:17} When Adam heard this Word from God, he was comforted by what God had told him, for He had explained how He would save him.

{4:1} But Adam and Eve wept for having left the garden, their first home. {4:2} When Adam looked at his altered flesh, he wept bitterly, along with Eve, over what they had done, and they walked gently down into the Cave of Treasures. {4:3} As they approached it, Adam wept over himself and said to Eve, "Look at this cave that will be our prison in this world, a place of punishment! {4:4} What is it compared to the garden? What is its narrowness compared to the vastness of the garden? {4:5} What is this rock next to those groves? What is the gloom of this cavern compared to the garden's light? {4:6} What is this overhanging ledge of rock for shelter compared to the Lord's mercy that once overshadowed us? {4:7} What is the soil of this cave compared to the garden, which was planted with delicious fruit trees?" {4:8} Adam continued, "Look at our eyes, which once beheld angels in heaven, praising without ceasing. {4:9} But now we cannot see as we did before; our eyes have become flesh, and they can no longer see as they used to." {4:10} Adam asked Eve again, "What is our body today compared to what it was in the garden?" {4:11} After this, Adam did not want to enter the cave under the overhanging rock and would have never entered it. {4:12} But he obeyed God's commands, saying to himself, "Unless I enter the cave, I will be a transgressor again."

{5:1} Then Adam and Eve entered the cave and stood praying in their own language, unknown to us, but which they knew well. {5:2} As they prayed, Adam raised his eyes and saw the rock and the cave's roof above him, preventing him from seeing either heaven or God's creatures. He wept and struck his breast heavily until he collapsed, appearing as if dead. {5:3} Eve sat weeping, believing he was dead. {5:4} She then arose, spread her hands toward God, asking for mercy and pity, saying, "God, forgive me my sin, the one I committed, and do not remember it against me. {5:5} For I alone caused Your servant to fall from the garden into this lost state, from light into darkness, and from joy into this prison. {5:6} O God, look upon this Your servant who has fallen and raise him from his death, so he may weep and repent for his transgression, which he committed through me. {5:7} Do not take away his soul this time; let him live so he may stand and repent and do Your will as he did before his death. {5:8} But if You will not raise him up, then take my soul, too, so we may die together this day." {5:9} Eve wept bitterly and fell upon our father Adam, overwhelmed by her sorrow.

{6:1} But God looked upon them, for they had caused their own downfall through immense grief. {6:2} He intended to raise them up and comfort them. {6:3} So He sent His Word to them, telling them to stand and be raised immediately. {6:4} The Lord said to Adam and Eve, "You have transgressed of your own free will, leading you to leave the garden where I placed you. You chose to sin through your desire for divinity, greatness, and an exalted state like Mine; therefore, I deprived you of the bright nature you once had and made you leave the garden for this rough and troubled land. {6:5} If only you had not disobeyed My command, kept My law, and avoided eating from the tree that I told you not to approach! There were better fruit trees in the garden than that one. {6:6} But the wicked Satan, who did not remain in his original state nor keep his faith—he had no good intentions toward Me, even though I created him—he disregarded Me and sought the Godhead, which caused Me to cast him down from heaven. He made the tree seem appealing to you until you ate from it by listening to him. {6:7} Thus, you have disobeyed My command, and for this reason, I have brought all these sorrows upon you. {6:8} I am God the Creator, who, when I made My creatures, did not intend to destroy them. However, after they provoked My anger, I punished them with severe trials until they repent. {6:9} But if they remain hardened in their transgression, they shall be cursed forever."

{7:1} When Adam and Eve heard these words from God, they wept and sobbed even more, but they also strengthened their hearts in God, feeling that He was like a father and mother to them. For this reason, they wept before Him, seeking His mercy. {7:2} God then took pity on them and said, "Adam, I have made My covenant with you, and I will not change it; neither will I allow you to return to the garden until My covenant of the great five days and a half is fulfilled." {7:3} Adam replied to God, "Lord, You created us and made us fit to live in the garden; before I sinned, You brought all the beasts to me so that I could name them. {7:4} Your grace was upon me then, and I named each one according to Your will, and You made them all subject to me. {7:5} But now, Lord God, since I have disobeyed Your command, all the beasts will rise against me and devour me and Eve, Your servant; they will cut off our life from the face of the earth. {7:6} I therefore beseech You, God, since You have made us leave the garden and placed us in a strange land, do not let the beasts harm us." {7:7} When the Lord heard these words from Adam, He felt compassion for him, knowing that Adam truly feared that the beasts would rise up and attack him and Eve because He was angry with them for their transgression. {7:8} God then commanded the beasts, the birds, and all that moves on the earth to come to Adam, to be familiar with him, and not to harm him or Eve, nor any of the good and righteous among their descendants. {7:9} The beasts obeyed Adam as commanded by God, except for the serpent, against which God was angry; it did not approach Adam like the other beasts.

{8:1} Then Adam wept and said, "O God, when we lived in the garden and our hearts were lifted up, we saw the angels singing praises in heaven, but now we do not see as we used to; indeed, when we entered the cave, all of creation became hidden from us." {8:2} God the Lord then said to Adam, "When you were under My command, you had a bright nature within you, which is why you could see far off. But after your transgression, that bright nature was taken away from you; you can no longer see far away, only what is close at hand, as is typical for flesh, which is brutish." {8:3} When Adam and Eve heard these words from God, they left, praising and worshiping Him with sorrowful hearts. {8:4} And God ceased to communicate with them.

{9:1} Adam and Eve then came out of the Cave of Treasures and approached the garden gate, where they stood to look at it and wept for having left it. {9:2} They moved from the gate of the garden to its southern side and found the water that nourished the garden, which flowed from the root of the Tree of Life and separated into four rivers across the earth. {9:3} They came near to that water and saw that it was the water that flowed from under the root of the Tree of Life in the garden. Adam wept and lamented, striking his breast for being separated from the garden, saying to Eve, "Why have you brought so many plagues and punishments upon me, upon yourself, and upon our descendants?" {9:4} Eve asked him, "What do you see that makes you weep and speak to me this way?" {9:5} Adam replied, "Do you not see this water that was with us in the garden, nourishing the trees, and flowing from there? {9:6} While we were in the garden, we did not care about it, but since we came to this strange land, we love it and wish to use it for our bodies." {9:7} When Eve heard Adam's words, she wept, and from the depth of their sorrow, they fell into that water and almost ended their lives there, wishing never to return and see creation again, for looking upon it made them want to end their existence.

{10:1} Then God, merciful and gracious, looked upon them lying in the water, close to death, and sent an angel who brought them out and laid them on the seashore as if they were dead. {10:2} The angel then returned to God, welcomed, and said, "O God, Your creatures have breathed their last." {10:3} God sent His Word to Adam and Eve, raising them from death. {10:4} Adam, after being raised, said, "God, while we were in the garden, we did not care for this water; but now that we are in this land, we cannot do without it." {10:5} God responded, "While you were under My command and were a bright angel, you did not know this water. {10:6} But after your transgression, you cannot do without water, in which to wash your body and help it grow; for it is now like that of beasts, and it craves water." {10:7} When Adam and Eve heard these words from God, they cried bitterly, and Adam pleaded with God to let him return to the garden to see it one more time. {10:8} But God said to Adam, "I have made you a promise; when that promise is fulfilled, I will bring you back to the garden, you and your righteous descendants." {10:9} And God ceased to communicate with Adam.

{11:1} Then Adam and Eve felt an intense thirst, heat, and sorrow. {11:2} Adam said to Eve, "We should not drink this water, even if it means we die. Eve, if this water enters us, it will only increase our punishments and those of our future children." {11:3} Both Adam and Eve then turned away from the water and drank none of it; instead, they went into the Cave of Treasures. {11:4} But once inside, Adam could not see Eve; he could only hear her. She, too, could not see Adam but heard his voice. {11:5} Adam then wept deeply, struck his chest, and called out, "Where are you?" {11:6} She replied, "I am here, standing in this darkness." {11:7} He said, "Remember the bright nature we had while we lived in the garden! {11:8} O Eve, remember the glory that rested upon us there! O Eve, remember the trees that provided shade while we walked among them. {11:9} O Eve, remember that while we were in the garden, we knew neither night nor day. Think of the Tree of Life, from which flowed the water that illuminated us! Remember, Eve, the garden and its brightness! {11:10} Think of that garden where there was no darkness while we dwelled there. {11:11} But as soon as we entered this Cave of Treasures, darkness surrounded us, and now we can no longer see each other, and all joy in this life has ended."

{12:1} Then Adam and Eve struck their chests and mourned all night until dawn approached, sighing over the long night in darkness. {12:2} Adam beat himself, threw himself on the ground in the cave from bitter grief, and lay there as if dead. {12:3} But Eve heard the noise he made as he fell, and she groped for him with her hands, finding him like a corpse. {12:4} She was filled with fear and remained silent beside him. {12:5} But the merciful Lord looked upon Adam's death and Eve's silence out of fear of the darkness. {12:6} The Word of God came to Adam, raised him from death, and opened Eve's mouth so she could speak. {12:7} Adam then stood up in the cave and asked, "God, why has light departed from us and darkness enveloped us? Why do You leave us in this long darkness? Why do You plague us like this? {12:8} And this darkness, O Lord, where was it before it came upon us? It is so thick that we cannot see each other. {12:9} When we were in the garden, we did not even know what darkness was. I was not hidden from Eve, nor was she hidden from me, until now, when she cannot see me; no darkness separated us then. {12:10} We were both in one bright light. I saw her, and she saw me. But now that we are in this cave, darkness has come between us, so that I cannot see her, and she cannot see me. {12:11} Lord, will You plague us with this darkness?"

{13:1} When God, who is merciful and full of pity, heard Adam's voice, He said to him: "Adam, as long as the good angel was obedient to Me, a bright light rested upon him and his companions. {13:2} But when he disobeyed My command, I took away that bright nature, and he became dark. {13:3} When he was in heaven, in the realms of light, he knew nothing of darkness. {13:4} But after he transgressed, I made him fall from heaven to earth; this darkness is what came upon him. {13:5} And upon you, O Adam, while in My garden and obedient to Me, that bright light also rested. {13:6} But when I heard of your transgression, I took that light from you. However, in My mercy, I did not allow you to be cast into darkness; I made you a fleshly body, covered it with skin, so it could withstand cold and heat. {13:7} If I had let My wrath fall heavily upon you, I would have destroyed you; had I turned you into darkness, it would have been like killing you. {13:8} But in My mercy, I made you as you are; when you disobeyed My commandment, I drove you from the garden and made you dwell in this cave; and darkness came upon you, just as it did upon him who transgressed My commandment. {13:9} So, O Adam, this night has deceived you. It will not last forever; it is only twelve hours long; when it ends, daylight will return. {13:10} So do not sigh or think in your heart that this darkness is long and tiresome; do not believe that I plague you with it. {13:11} Strengthen your heart and do not be afraid. This darkness is not a punishment. But, Adam, I made the day and placed the sun in it to give light, so you and your children could do your work. {13:12} For I knew you would sin and transgress and come into this land. Yet, I did not wish to be harsh with you or confine you, nor condemn you for your fall, nor for coming from light into darkness, nor for leaving the garden for this land. {13:13} For I made you from light, and I intended to bring forth children of light from you, like you. {13:14} But you did not keep My commandment even for one day, until I finished creation and blessed everything in it. {13:15} Then I commanded you regarding the tree, that you should not eat from it. Yet I knew that Satan, who had deceived himself, would also deceive you. {13:16} So I warned you about the tree, telling you not to approach it. {13:17} I instructed you not to eat its fruit, nor to taste it, nor even sit under it. {13:18} If I had not spoken to you about the tree and had left you without a commandment, and you had sinned, it would have been an offense on My part for not giving you any order; you would have turned and blamed Me. {13:19} But I commanded you, warned you, and you fell. My creatures cannot blame Me; the blame lies solely with them. {13:20} O Adam, I made the day for you and your children after you, for them to work and toil in it. I made the night for them to rest and for the beasts to go out and find food. {13:21} But very little darkness remains, O Adam; soon daylight will appear."

{14:1} Adam then said to God, "O Lord, take my soul, and let me not see this gloom any longer; or take me to a place where there is no darkness." {14:2} But God the Lord said to Adam, "Truly, I tell you, this darkness will pass from you, day by day, until the fulfillment of My covenant; when I will save you and bring you back into the garden, into the abode of light you long for, where there is no darkness. I will bring you to it—in the kingdom of heaven." {14:3} God again said to Adam, "All this misery you are enduring because of your transgression will not free you from Satan's grip, nor will it save you. {14:4} But I will. When I come down from heaven and take on the flesh of your seed, I will take upon Myself the suffering from which you suffer; then the darkness that has fallen upon you in this cave will also come upon Me in the grave, when I am in the flesh of your seed. {14:5} And I, who am eternal, will be subject to the passage of years, of times, of months, and days; I will be counted among the sons of men to save you." {14:6} And God ceased to communicate with Adam.

{15:1} Then Adam and Eve wept and mourned over God's words to them, that they would not return to the garden until the days decreed upon them were fulfilled; but mostly because God had told them that He would suffer for their salvation.

{16:1} After this, Adam and Eve continued to stand in the cave, praying and weeping until morning arrived. {16:2} When they saw the light return, they calmed their fears and strengthened their hearts. {16:3} Then Adam began to exit the cave. As he reached the entrance and faced east, seeing the sun rise in radiant rays and feeling its warmth on his body, he was frightened and thought the flame was meant to torment him. {16:4} He wept, struck his chest, fell to the ground on his face, and pleaded, saying, "Lord, do not plague me, do not consume me, and do not take my life from the earth." {16:5} He believed the sun was God. Since while he was in the garden, he had heard God's voice and sounds in the garden and feared Him, Adam had never seen the sun's brilliant light nor felt its scorching heat. {16:6} That's why he was afraid when the sun's flames reached him; he thought God meant to plague him with this heat for the duration of his life. {16:7} Adam thought, "Since God did not plague us with darkness, behold, He has caused this sun to rise to torment us with its burning heat." {16:8} But while he was thinking this, the Word of God came to him and said, "Adam, arise and stand up. This sun is not God; it was created to provide light during the day, just as I told you in the cave, saying that the dawn would come, and there would be daylight. {16:9} But I am God who comforted you in the night." And then God stopped speaking to Adam.

{17:1} Adam and Eve then came out of the cave and headed towards the garden. {17:2} As they approached the western gate, where Satan had entered to deceive them, they found the serpent, which had become Satan, sorrowfully licking the dust and wriggling on the ground because of the curse from God. {17:3} Once the most exalted of all beasts, it was now changed, becoming slimy and the lowest of them all, crawling on its belly. {17:4} What had once been the fairest of all creatures was now the ugliest. Instead of eating the best food, it now consumed dust, and instead of living in the best places, it now resided in the dust. {17:5} Once admired for its beauty, it was now abhorred by all other animals. {17:6} Previously, it dwelled in a lovely home, where other animals came to drink; now, because it become venomous due to God's curse, all creatures fled from it & refused to drink from the same water.

{18:1} When the cursed serpent saw Adam and Eve, it raised its head, stood on its tail, and with blood-red eyes acted as if it would kill them. {18:2} It charged towards Eve, while Adam, standing nearby, wept because he had no stick to strike the serpent and didn't know how to kill it. {18:3} But with a heart full of concern for Eve, Adam approached the serpent and grabbed its tail. When the serpent turned towards him, it said, "Adam, because of you and Eve, I am now slippery and crawl on my belly." {18:4} Then, with its great strength, it knocked down Adam and Eve and pressed down on them as if to kill them. {18:5} But God sent an angel who threw the serpent away and lifted them up. {18:6} The Word of God then spoke to the serpent, saying, "At first, I made you slippery and made you crawl on your belly, but I did not take away your ability to speak. {18:7} Now, however, you shall be dumb and speak no more, you and your descendants, because your actions have caused the ruin of My creatures, and now you wish to kill them." {18:8} After this, the serpent was struck dumb and could not speak. {18:9} A wind came from heaven by God's command, carrying the serpent away from Adam and Eve, and it landed on the seashore in India.

{19:1} Adam and Eve wept before God. Adam said, "O Lord, while I was in the cave, I told You that the beasts of the field would rise up and devour me, cutting off my life from the earth." Then, because of what had happened, Adam struck his chest and fell like a corpse. {19:2} The Word of God then came to him, raised him up, and said, "O Adam, none of these beasts will be able to harm you; when I brought the beasts and other living creatures to you in the cave, I did not allow the serpent to come with them so it would not rise against you and instill fear in your hearts. I knew that cursed one is wicked; that's why I did not let it approach you with the other beasts. {19:3} But now strengthen your heart and do not fear. I am with you until the end of the days I have determined for you."

{20:1} Adam then wept and said, "God, move us to another place so that the serpent may not come near us again and rise against us. I fear it may find Eve alone and kill her, for its eyes are dreadful and evil." {20:2} But God replied to Adam and Eve, "From now on, do not fear; I will not allow it to come near you. I have driven it away from this mountain, and I will not leave anything here to harm you." {20:3} Then Adam and Eve worshiped God, gave thanks, and praised Him for delivering them from death.

{21:1} Then Adam and Eve set out in search of the garden. {21:2} The heat beat down on their faces like a flame; they sweated from the heat and wept before the Lord. {21:3} They wept near a high mountain that faced the western gate of the garden. {21:4} Adam then threw himself down from the top of that mountain; his face was torn, and his flesh was lacerated (cut); a lot of blood flowed from him, and he was close to death. {21:5} Meanwhile, Eve remained standing on the mountain, weeping over him as he lay there. {21:6} She said, "I don't want to live after him; everything he did to himself was because of me." {21:7} Then she threw herself after him, was torn and bruised by the stones, and lay there as if dead. {21:8} But the merciful God, who cares for His creatures, looked upon Adam and Eve as they lay dead and sent His Word to them to raise them. {21:9} He said to Adam, "O Adam, all this misery you have caused yourself will not change My rule nor alter the covenant of 5500 years."

{22:1} Then Adam said to God, "I wither in the heat; I am weak from walking, and I loathe this world. I don't know when You will take me out of it to find rest." {22:2} The Lord God replied, "Adam, it cannot happen right now, not until you have completed your days. Then I will bring you out of this wretched land." {22:3} Adam said to God, "While I was in the garden, I didn't know heat or weariness, nor did I tremble or fear; but now, since I came to this land, all this suffering has come upon me." {22:4} God told Adam, "As long as you kept My commandment, My light and grace rested upon you. But when you broke My commandment, sorrow and misery came upon you in this land." {22:5} Adam wept and said, "O Lord, do not cut me off for this, do not strike me with severe plagues, nor repay me according to my sin; for we chose to break Your commandment, forsook Your law, and sought to become gods like You when Satan, our enemy, deceived us." {22:6} God then said to Adam, "Because you have endured fear and trembling in this land, weariness and suffering, walking and dying on this mountain, I will take all this upon Myself to save you."

{23:1} Then Adam wept more and said, "O God, have mercy on me by taking upon Yourself what I am about to do." {23:2} But God withdrew His Word from Adam and Eve. {23:3} Then Adam and Eve stood up, and Adam said to Eve, "Gird yourself," and she did as he instructed. {23:4} Adam and Eve then took stones and arranged them into the shape of an altar; they took leaves from the trees outside the garden to wipe the blood from the rock. What had dropped on the sand, they gathered with the dust and offered it on the altar as a sacrifice to God. {23:5} Adam and Eve stood beneath the altar, weeping and pleading with God, "Forgive us our trespass and our sin, and look upon us with Your eye of mercy. When we were in the garden, our praises and hymns went up to You without ceasing. {23:6} But now that we are in this strange land, pure praise is no longer ours, nor righteous prayer, nor understanding hearts, nor sweet thoughts, nor wise counsel, nor upright feelings, and our bright nature is lost. Our bodies have changed from the likeness in which we were created. {23:7} Now, please look upon our blood offered on these stones and accept it as You accepted our praises in the garden." {23:8} Adam then began to make more requests to God.

{24:1} The merciful God, who is good and loves humanity, looked upon Adam and Eve and their blood, which they had presented as an offering to Him without being commanded to do so. He was amazed by them and accepted their offerings. {24:2} God sent a bright fire from His presence that consumed their offering. He smelled the sweet fragrance of their offering and showed them mercy. {24:3} The Word of God then came to Adam and said, "Adam, just as you have shed your blood, so will I shed My own blood when I become flesh of your seed; and just as you died, O Adam, so will I die. {24:4} As you built an altar, I will also create an altar on earth for you; and just as you offered your blood upon it, so will I offer My blood upon an altar on earth." {24:5} "And just as you sought forgiveness through that blood, so My blood will bring forgiveness of sins and erase transgressions. {24:6} Now, behold, I have accepted your offering, Adam, but the days of the covenant I have established with you are not yet complete. When they are fulfilled, I will bring you back into the garden. {24:7} Therefore, strengthen your heart, and when sorrow comes upon you, make Me an offering, and I will be favorable to you."

{25:1} But God knew that Adam was thinking of killing himself often to offer his blood to Him. {25:2} So He said to him, "O Adam, do not kill yourself again as you did by throwing yourself down from that mountain." {25:3} Adam replied to God, "I intended to end my life immediately because I broke Your commandments, because I left the beautiful garden, and because You deprived me of the bright light and the endless praises that flowed from my mouth. {25:4} Yet, out of Your goodness, God, do not completely abandon me, but be gracious to me each time I die and bring me back to life. {25:5} This will show that You are a merciful God who does not wish for anyone to perish, who does not want anyone to fall, and who does not cruelly condemn anyone to total destruction." {25:6} Then Adam fell silent. The Word of God came to him, blessed him, comforted him, and made a covenant with him that He would save him at the end of the days determined for him. {25:7} This was the first offering Adam made to God, and it became his custom to do so.

{26:1} Then Adam took Eve, and they began to return to the Cave of Treasures where they lived. {26:2} But as they approached and saw it from a distance, a heavy sorrow fell upon them. {26:3} Adam said to Eve, "When we were on the mountain, we were comforted by the Word of God that spoke with us, and the light from the east shone upon us. {26:4} But now the Word of God is hidden from us, and the light that shone on us has changed to darkness and sorrow. {26:5} We are forced to enter this cave, which feels like a prison, where darkness covers us, so that we are separated from each other; you cannot see me, and I cannot see you." {26:6} After Adam said this, they wept and stretched out their hands before God, filled with sorrow. {26:7} They begged God to bring the sun to shine on them, so darkness wouldn't fall upon them again and they wouldn't have to live under this rock covering. They wished to die rather than endure the darkness. {26:8} God looked at Adam and Eve and their deep sorrow, considering all they had done and the trouble they faced instead of their former well-being, along with the misery that had come upon them in this strange land. {26:9} Therefore, God was not angry with them nor impatient; He was patient and forgiving, as He is with the children He created. {26:10} Then the Word of God came to Adam and said, "Adam, concerning the sun, if I were to take it and bring it to you, time would become meaningless, and the covenant I made with you would never be fulfilled. {26:11} Instead, you should endure and calm your soul while you experience night and day until the days of My covenant are fulfilled. {26:12} Then I will come to save you, Adam, for I do not wish for you to suffer. {26:13} When I consider all the good things you enjoyed and why you left them, I would gladly show you mercy. {26:14} However, I cannot change the covenant I have established; otherwise, I would have brought you back into the garden. {26:15} But when the covenant is fulfilled, I will show mercy to you and your descendants and bring you to a joyful land where there is no sorrow or suffering, only lasting joy, endless light, and never-ending praise, along with a beautiful garden that will never fade away." {26:16} God said again to Adam, "Be patient and enter the cave; the darkness you fear will last only twelve hours, and when it ends, light will come." {26:17} When Adam heard these words, he and Eve worshipped God, and their hearts were comforted. They returned to the cave as usual, tears flowing from their eyes, sorrow and wailing filling their hearts, and they wished their souls would leave their bodies. {26:18} Adam and Eve stood praying until night fell, and they were hidden from each other. {26:19} They remained standing in prayer.

{27:1} When Satan, the enemy of all good, saw them praying and how God communicated with them, comforting them and accepting their offering, he made an appearance. {27:2} He began transforming his hosts, holding a bright fire, and they shone with great light. {27:3} He set his throne near the cave's entrance because he couldn't enter due to their prayers. He filled the cave with light until it glimmered around Adam and Eve, while his hosts began to sing praises. {27:4} Satan did this so that when Adam saw the light, he would think it was heavenly and that Satan's hosts were angels sent by God to watch over him and provide light in the darkness. {27:5} He wanted Adam to come out of the cave, see them, and bow to Satan, allowing him to overpower Adam and humble him again before God. {27:6} When Adam and Eve saw the light, believing it to be real, they gained courage; yet, trembling, Adam said to Eve: "Look at that great light, the many songs of praise, and that host standing outside who do not enter, do not tell us what they say, where they come from, or the meaning of this light; what are those praises for, why are they sent here, and why do they not come in? {27:7} If they were from God, they would come to us in the cave and tell us their purpose." {27:8} Adam then stood up and fervently prayed to God, saying: "O Lord, is there another god who created angels and filled them with light, who would send them to protect us? {27:9} Yet we see these hosts standing at the cave's mouth; they are in great light, singing loudly. If they are from another god, tell me; if they are sent by You, let me know why You sent them." {27:10} No sooner had Adam said this than an angel from God appeared in the cave and said, "Adam, do not fear. This is Satan and his hosts; he wishes to deceive you as he did the first time. The first time, he was hidden in the serpent; now he comes to you in the guise of an angel of light to ensnare you in the presence of God." {27:11} The angel then seized Satan at the cave's opening, stripped him of his disguise, and brought him before Adam and Eve in his true, hideous form, causing them to be afraid. {27:12} The angel said to Adam, "This hideous form has been his since God cast him down. He could not approach you in this shape, so he transformed himself into an angel of light." {27:13} The angel drove away Satan and his hosts, saying, "Do not fear; God who created you will strengthen you." {27:14} The angel then departed. {27:15} But Adam and Eve remained standing in the cave; no comfort came to them, and they were troubled in their thoughts. {27:16} When morning came, they prayed and then went out to seek the garden, for their hearts longed for it, and they found no solace for having left.

{28:1} But when the cunning Satan saw them heading to the garden, he gathered his hosts and appeared on a cloud, intent on deceiving them. {28:2} When Adam and Eve saw him in this vision, they thought he was an angel from God sent to comfort them about leaving the garden or to bring them back. {28:3} Adam raised his hands to God, asking Him to help him understand what they were. {28:4} Then Satan, the enemy of all good, said to Adam, "O Adam, I am an angel of the great God; behold the hosts that surround me. {28:5} God has sent me and them to take you to the northern border of the garden, to the shore of the clear sea, to bathe you and Eve in it and restore your former joy so that you may return to the garden." {28:6} These words resonated in Adam and Eve's hearts. {28:7} Yet God withheld His Word from Adam, not revealing the truth right away, but waiting to see his strength; whether he would be overcome as Eve was in the garden or if he would prevail. {28:8} Then Satan called to Adam and Eve, saying, "Behold, we go to the sea of water," and they began to follow him. {28:9} Adam and Eve trailed behind at a distance. {28:10} When they reached the high mountain north of the garden, which had no steps to the top, the Devil drew close to Adam and Eve, making them climb to the summit in reality, not just in a vision, intending to throw them down and kill them, wiping their names from the earth so that this land would belong solely to him and his hosts.

{29:1} But when the merciful God saw that Satan sought to kill Adam with his numerous schemes and that Adam was meek and innocent, God spoke loudly to Satan and cursed him. {29:2} Then Satan and his hosts fled, and Adam and Eve remained standing on the mountain top, from which they could see the vast world below. {29:3} They wept before God and begged for His forgiveness. {29:4} Then the Word from God came to Adam, saying, "Know and understand about this Satan, that he seeks to deceive you and your descendants." {29:5} Adam wept before the Lord God and pleaded with Him to give him something from the garden as a token to comfort him. {29:6} God considered Adam's desire and sent the angel Michael to the sea that reaches India to collect golden rods and bring them back to Adam. {29:7} God did this in His wisdom so that the golden rods would shine brightly in the cave at night, alleviating Adam's fear of the darkness. {29:8} The angel Michael went down as commanded, took the golden rods, and brought them to God.

{30:1} After this, God commanded the angel Gabriel to go down to the garden and tell the cherub who guarded it, "Behold, God has commanded me to enter the garden and take sweet-smelling incense to give to Adam." {30:2} The angel Gabriel went down as God commanded and spoke to the cherub. {30:3} The cherub replied, "Well." Then Gabriel went in and took the incense. {30:4} God then commanded His angel Raphael to go down to the garden and speak to the cherub about some myrrh to give to Adam. {30:5} The angel Raphael went down and communicated with the cherub as God commanded, and the cherub replied, "Well." Then Raphael went in and took the myrrh. {30:6} The golden rods were from the Indian sea, known for precious stones. The incense came from the eastern border of the garden, and the myrrh from the western border, where bitterness fell upon Adam. {30:7} The angels brought these three items to God by the Tree of Life in the garden. {30:8} Then God said to the angels, "Dip them in the spring of water, sprinkle them over Adam and Eve to provide some comfort in their sorrow, and give them to Adam and Eve." {30:9} The angels did as God commanded and handed these gifts to Adam and Eve on the mountain where Satan had placed them when he intended to destroy them. {30:10} When Adam saw the golden rods, the incense, and the myrrh, he rejoiced and wept, thinking the gold was a sign of the kingdom he had lost, the incense a symbol of the bright light taken from him, and the myrrh a reminder of the sorrow he endured.

{31:1} After these things, God said to Adam, "You asked Me for something from the garden to comfort you, and I have given you these three tokens as a consolation. Trust in Me and My covenant with you. {31:2} For I will come and save you, and kings shall bring Me, when I come in the flesh, gold, incense, and myrrh: gold as a sign of My kingship, incense as a sign of My divinity, and myrrh as a sign of My suffering and death. {31:3} But Adam, put these by you in the cave—the gold to give light by night, the incense so you may smell its sweet fragrance, and the myrrh to comfort you in your sorrow." {31:4} When Adam heard these words from God, he worshipped Him, and both he and Eve thanked Him for His mercy toward them. {31:5} Then God commanded the three angels—Michael, Gabriel, and Raphael—to give to Adam what they had brought. They did so, one by one. {31:6} God then commanded the angels Suriyel and Salathiel to lift Adam and Eve and take them down from the high mountain to the Cave of Treasures. {31:7} There, they placed the gold on the southern side of the cave, the incense on the eastern side, and the myrrh on the western side, for the mouth of the cave was on the north. {31:8} The angels then comforted Adam and Eve and left them. {31:9} The gold was seventy rods, the incense twelve pounds, and the myrrh three pounds. {31:10} These remained with Adam in the Cave of Treasures, which was called "of concealment" because it hid the bodies of righteous men, although some say it was called the Cave of Treasures for other reasons. {31:11} God gave Adam these three tokens three days after he had left the garden, as a sign of the three days the Lord would spend in the heart of the earth. {31:12} These three items gave Adam light by night and a little relief from his sorrow by day.

{32:1} Adam and Eve stayed in the Cave of Treasures until the seventh day, neither eating the fruit of the earth nor drinking water. {32:2} When the eighth day dawned, Adam said to Eve, "We prayed to God to give us something from the garden, and He sent His angels to bring us what we desired. {32:3} But now, arise, let us go to the sea of water we first saw, and stand in it, praying that God will again show us favor, return us to the garden, or give us comfort in some other land. {32:4} So Adam and Eve left the cave and went to the border of the sea where they had once thrown themselves, and Adam said to Eve, {32:5} 'Go into this water and do not leave it for thirty days. Pray fervently with a sweet voice for God's forgiveness. {32:6} I will go to another place and do the same.' {32:7} Eve went into the water as Adam instructed, and Adam also went into the water, standing in prayer, asking the Lord to forgive them and restore them to their former state. {32:8} They stood praying for thirty-five days.

{33:1} But Satan, the enemy of all good, searched for them in the cave and could not find them, though he searched diligently. {33:2} He found them standing in the water praying, hoping for God's forgiveness and restoration. {33:3} Satan thought, 'Adam and Eve are praying to be freed from my power, but I will deceive them and make them leave the water and break their vow.' {33:4} The enemy, not approaching Adam, instead went to Eve, appearing as an angel of God, praising and rejoicing. {33:5} He said, 'Peace be unto you! Rejoice! God is favorable to you, and He sent me to Adam to bring him news of his restoration to bright light. {33:6} In his joy, Adam sent me to you, to bring you to him so I can crown you with light as well. If you hesitate, remember the sign when we were on the mountain—how God sent His angels and brought us to the Cave of Treasures, laying the gold on the south, the incense on the east, and the myrrh on the west.' {33:7} Hearing this, Eve rejoiced, thinking Satan was truly an angel, and left the water. {33:8} Satan led her to Adam, but as soon as they arrived, he disappeared. {33:9} When Eve called out to Adam, he turned and saw her, and in sorrow, he beat his chest and fell into the water. {33:10} But God looked upon Adam's misery, and His Word came from heaven to raise Adam out of the water. {33:11} The Lord said, 'Go to Eve,' and when Adam reached her, he asked, 'Who told you to come here?' {33:12} Eve told him about the angel's message. {33:13} Adam grieved deeply and told her it was Satan who had deceived her again. They then returned to the cave. {33:14} This was the second time Satan deceived them after they had fasted for thirty-five days, making it forty-two days since they left the garden.

{34:1} On the morning of the forty-third day, Adam and Eve left the cave, weeping and sorrowful. Their bodies were lean and parched from fasting, praying, and mourning their sin. {34:2} When they left the cave, they climbed the mountain west of the garden and prayed for forgiveness. {34:3} Adam began to plead with God, saying, 'O Lord, my God, and my Creator, You commanded the four elements to come together, and by Your will, they were gathered. {34:4} Then You created me from one element—dust—and brought me into the garden at the third hour on a Friday. You told me this in the cave. {34:5} In those days, I knew neither night nor day, for my nature was bright and the light in which I lived never left me. {34:6} On that same third hour, You brought all the beasts, birds, and creatures before me, and gave me understanding to name them according to Your will. {34:7} They all obeyed me, as You had commanded, but now they have all turned away from me. {34:8} It was at that third hour on Friday that You commanded me about the tree I was not to touch or eat from, saying that I would surely die if I did. {34:9} If You had punished me with death then, I would have died immediately. {34:10} When You gave me that command, Eve had not yet been created, nor had she heard it from You. {34:11} At the end of the third hour on that Friday, You caused a deep sleep to fall over me, and while I slept, You took a rib from my side and created Eve. {34:12} When I awoke and saw her, I said, 'This is bone of my bones and flesh of my flesh; she will be called woman.' {34:13} In Your goodness, You put me into a deep sleep so that I would not see how You created her, for Your goodness and glory are too great to behold. {34:14} You made us both of a bright nature and gave us Your grace. We knew neither hunger, thirst, sorrow, suffering, fasting, nor weariness. {34:15} But now, because we transgressed Your command and broke Your law, You have sent us into a strange land where we suffer hunger, thirst, and faintness. {34:16} So now, Lord, I ask You to give us something to eat from the garden to satisfy our hunger, and something to drink to quench our thirst. {34:17} For many days, we have neither eaten nor drunk, and our bodies are weakened, our flesh dried up, and sleep has left our eyes from weeping & faintness. {34:18} We dare not gather any fruit from the trees, fearing Your punishment, for when we sinned before, You spared us from immediate death. {34:19} But now, if we eat the fruit without Your permission, You may destroy us completely this time. {34:20} If we drink the water without Your command, You may wipe us from the earth. {34:21} Therefore, O God, as we stand before You, we beg You to give us of the fruit of the garden to satisfy our hunger, for we long for the fruit of the earth.'

{35:1} Then God looked upon Adam and his weeping, and His Word came to him, saying, 'Adam, when you were in My garden, you did not know hunger, thirst, or suffering. Neither did your flesh waste away or change, nor did sleep leave your eyes. But since you sinned and entered this strange land, all these trials have come upon you.'

{36:1} Then God commanded the cherub, who guarded the gate of the garden with a flaming sword, to take some fruit from the fig tree and give it to Adam. {36:2} The cherub obeyed God's command and entered the garden. He brought two figs on two branches, each fig still attached to its leaf. These were from the trees where Adam and Eve had hidden themselves when God walked in the garden and called, "Adam, where are you?" {36:3} Adam had replied, "Lord, I am here. I hid among the fig trees because I am naked and afraid." {36:4} The cherub brought the figs to Adam and Eve but threw them from afar, as they could not approach him due to the fire that surrounded him. {36:5} Once, angels trembled before Adam, but now Adam trembled before the angels. {36:6} Adam stepped forward and took one fig, and Eve took the other. {36:7} As they held the figs, they recognized that they were from the trees where they had hidden and wept bitterly.

{37:1} Adam said to Eve, "Do you see these figs and their leaves, the same leaves we used to cover ourselves when we lost our bright nature? Now, we do not know what suffering may come from eating them. {37:2} So, let us not eat of them, but instead ask God to give us fruit from the Tree of Life." {37:3} Adam and Eve refrained from eating the figs and began to pray. {37:4} Adam pleaded with God, "O Lord, when we sinned on the sixth hour of Friday, we were stripped of our bright nature and cast out of the garden after only three hours. {37:5} We have been suffering for forty-three days since then, but it does not make up for that one hour in which we disobeyed You. {37:6} Lord, please show us mercy and do not punish us as we deserve for breaking Your command." {37:7} Adam asked God to give them fruit from the Tree of Life, so they would not have to endure more suffering on the earth.

{38:1} God's Word came to Adam and said, "Adam, as for the fruit of the Tree of Life, I will not give it to you now. It will only be given when 5,500 years are completed. Then, you and your descendants who live righteously shall eat of it and live forever. {38:2} The forty-three days of fasting do not atone for the one hour in which you transgressed My command. {38:3} However, I have allowed you to eat from the fig tree where you once hid. Go and eat the figs with Eve, and I will not deny your request. {38:4} Hold firm to the covenant I made with you." After saying this, God withdrew His Word from Adam.

{39:1} Adam returned to Eve and said, "Get up and take a fig for yourself, and I will take another. Let us go back to our cave." {39:2} Adam and Eve each took a fig and walked toward their cave, near sunset, but their minds longed to eat the fruit. {39:3} Adam said to Eve, "I am afraid to eat this fig. I do not know what will happen to me if I do." {39:4} He wept and prayed, saying, "Lord, satisfy my hunger without me needing to eat this fig, because once I eat it, what will I have left to ask of You? {39:5} What good will it do for me to eat this, and what will I desire from You after it is gone?" {39:6} He repeated, "I am afraid to eat it, for I do not know what may befall me."

{40:1} Then God's Word came to Adam and said, "Adam, why did you not have this fear and self-restraint before you sinned? Why did you not fast or care about this before you disobeyed Me? {40:2} Now that you are in this strange land, your earthly body needs food to survive, to strengthen and restore itself." {40:3} And God withdrew His Word from Adam.

{41:1} Then Adam took the fig and placed it on the golden rods, while Eve also took her fig and placed it on the incense. {41:2} The weight of each fig was as heavy as a watermelon, for the fruits of the garden were much larger than those of this land. {41:3} Adam and Eve stood fasting the entire night until the morning. {41:4} When the sun rose, they were at their prayers, and after they finished, Adam said to Eve, {41:5} "Eve, let us go to the southern border of the garden, to where the river flows and divides into four streams. There, we will pray to God and ask Him to give us the Water of Life. {41:6} For God has not given us the Tree of Life, so let us ask Him to quench our thirst with the Water of Life, rather than the water of this land." {41:7} Eve agreed with Adam, and they both went to the southern border of the garden near the river, just outside the garden. {41:8} They stood and prayed, asking God to look upon them and forgive them, granting their request. {41:9} Adam began to pray aloud, saying, {41:10} "Lord, when I was in the garden, I saw the water flowing from under the Tree of Life, and neither my heart desired it nor my body needed to drink, for I was alive in a way far beyond what I am now. {41:11} Back then, I did not need the Food of Life or the Water of Life to sustain me. {41:12} But now I am dead, and my flesh is dry with thirst. Give me the Water of Life so that I may drink and live. {41:13} In Your mercy, O God, save me from these trials and plagues, and take me to another land, different from this one, if You will not allow me to live in Your garden."

{42:1} Then the Word of God came to Adam and said, "Adam, when you ask for a land of rest, the only place where there is true rest is the Kingdom of Heaven. {42:2} But you cannot enter it now; only after your judgment is complete. {42:3} Afterward, I will take you and your righteous descendants into the Kingdom of Heaven, where you will find the rest you seek. {42:4} And as for the Water of Life that you ask for, it will not be given to you today. But on the day that I descend into hell, break the gates of brass, and shatter the kingdoms of iron, {42:5} I will save your soul and the souls of the righteous and give them rest in My garden when the end of the world comes. {42:6} Regarding the Water of Life you seek, it will be granted on the day when I shed My blood on the land of Golgotha. {42:7} My blood will be the Water of Life for you and all your descendants who believe in Me; it will be their rest forever." {42:8} The Lord continued, "Adam, when you were in the garden, none of these trials came upon you. {42:9} But now that you have transgressed My commandment, all these sufferings have befallen you. {42:10} Now your flesh requires food and drink, so drink from the water that flows on the earth before you." {42:11} Then God withdrew His Word from Adam. {42:12} Adam and Eve worshipped the Lord and returned from the river to the cave. It was midday when they approached the cave and saw a large fire burning near it.

{43:1} Adam and Eve were afraid and stood still. Adam said to Eve, "What is this fire near our cave? We haven't done anything to cause it. {43:2} We have no bread to bake or broth to cook in it. We don't know where this fire came from. {43:3} Ever since God sent the cherub with a flaming sword, we have not seen anything like this. {43:4} But this fire looks like the same fire from the cherub's sword that God sent to guard the garden. {43:5} It must be because God is angry with us again and wants to drive us away from this cave. {43:6} We have transgressed His command once more, and now He has sent this fire to prevent us from entering the cave. {43:7} If this is true, where will we go? Where can we flee from the face of the Lord? He has already banished us from the garden and taken away its good things, leaving us in this cave to endure darkness and hardship, and now even this place of comfort is being taken from us. {43:8} Who knows what will happen to us next? Perhaps the darkness of the next place will be even worse than this. {43:9} Who knows what dangers may await us, day or night, in a strange new land? {43:10} If God takes us farther away from the garden, where will we find Him to give us the gold, incense, myrrh, and figs we once had?" {43:11} Adam stopped speaking, and he and Eve looked toward the cave, watching the fire burning around it. {43:12} But this fire was the work of Satan, who had gathered dry trees and grasses to set fire to the cave, hoping to consume it and all that was in it, leaving Adam and Eve in sorrow and causing them to lose faith in God. {43:13} However, God, in His mercy, sent an angel to protect the cave, and Satan's fire could not consume it. {43:14} The fire burned from noon until the next morning. It was the forty-fifth day since Adam and Eve had left the garden.

{44:1} Adam and Eve stood watching the fire, unable to approach the cave due to their fear of the flames. {44:2} Satan continued to add wood to the fire, making the flames rise higher and cover the entire cave, hoping to destroy it. But the angel of the Lord guarded it. {44:3} The angel did not curse Satan or harm him because he had no authority to do so. He simply bore the situation in silence until the Word of God arrived and said to Satan, {44:4} "Go away, Satan. You deceived My servants once before, and now you seek to destroy them again. {44:5} Were it not for My mercy, I would have destroyed you and your hosts from the earth. But I have patience with you until the end of the world." {44:6} Then Satan fled from the Lord, but the fire continued burning around the cave like coals for the rest of the day, which marked the forty-sixth day since Adam and Eve had left the garden. {44:7} When the heat of the fire lessened, Adam and Eve tried to approach the cave but could not due to the remaining heat. {44:8} They wept, afraid of the fire that kept them from entering the cave. {44:9} Adam said to Eve, "Look at this fire, a reminder of the fire within us. It once yielded to us, but no longer. We have changed, but the fire remains as it was, and now it has power over us, burning our flesh when we come near."

{45:1} Adam prayed to God, saying, "Lord, this fire separates us from the cave You commanded us to dwell in, and now we cannot enter it." {45:2} God heard Adam and sent His Word, saying, "Adam, look at this fire and see how different it is from the garden of delights and its good things! {45:3} When you were under My care, all creation yielded to you, but now, after you transgressed My commandment, everything rises against you." {45:4} God continued, "Adam, see how Satan has deceived you. He promised to exalt you to be like Me, but instead, he has become your enemy, depriving you of the glory you once had. {45:5} He is the one who kindled this fire, intending to burn you and Eve. {45:6} Why has he not kept his promise to you, not even for one day? {45:7} He has taken away the glory that once covered you when you obeyed him. {45:8} Do you think Satan loved you when he made this agreement with you? {45:9} No, he only wanted to bring you out of light into darkness, from an exalted state to degradation, from joy to sorrow, and from rest to fasting and faintness." {45:10} God said to Adam, "Look at this fire kindled by Satan around your cave. Know that it will surround both you and your descendants when you listen to him. He will plague you with fire, and after you die, you will go down to hell, where the fire will burn around you and your descendants. {45:11} There will be no deliverance from it until My coming, just as you cannot enter your cave now because of the fire until My Word comes to make a way for you." {45:12}

Then God commanded the fire to part, creating a way for Adam to enter the cave. {45:13} The fire parted, and Adam entered the cave. God then withdrew His Word from Adam.

{46:1} Then Adam and Eve came back to the cave once more. {46:2} As they walked between the fires, Satan blew on the flames like a strong wind, causing the fire to flare up and send burning coals onto Adam and Eve, scorching their bodies. {46:3} The heat from the flames caused Adam and Eve to cry out, "Lord, save us! Don't let us be consumed and tormented by this fire. Don't punish us for breaking your commandment." {46:4} God saw their bodies, burnt by the fire Satan had caused, and sent His angel to stop the fire. However, the burns remained on their skin. {46:5} God said to Adam, "See how Satan, who pretended to offer you godhood and greatness, now burns you with fire and seeks to destroy you from the earth? {46:6} Consider Me, Adam. I created you, and how many times have I saved you from Satan? If I hadn't, wouldn't he have already destroyed you?" {46:7} Then God turned to Eve and said, "Do you remember what he promised you in the garden, saying, 'When you eat from the tree, your eyes will be opened, and you'll be like gods, knowing good and evil?' But look! He has burned your bodies with fire, letting you taste its pain in place of the sweetness of the garden. He has shown you fire's power and its harm. {46:8} You now see the good that he took from you and, indeed, your eyes are opened. You have seen the garden where you were with Me, and you've also seen the evil Satan has brought upon you. But as for becoming gods, he cannot give you that, nor fulfill his promise. Instead, he has been bitter toward you and your future descendants." {46:9} And with that, God withdrew His Word from them.

{47:1} Adam and Eve returned to the cave, trembling from the fire that had burned their skin. Adam turned to Eve and said, "This fire has burned our bodies here on earth. How much worse will it be when we die, and Satan punishes our souls in the afterlife? Isn't our deliverance distant, unless God shows mercy and fulfills His promise?" {47:2} They entered the cave once again, feeling relieved they had survived. They had thought they might never return when they saw the fire surrounding it. {47:3} But as the sun set, the fire near the cave was still burning, preventing them from resting inside. {47:4} Once the sun went down, they left the cave and went to sleep under the hill near the garden, as they had done before. {47:5} They stood and prayed for God to forgive them for their sins and then lay down to sleep under the hill's summit. {47:6} But Satan, the enemy of all that is good, thought to himself, "God has promised salvation to Adam and has made a covenant to deliver him from all his hardships. But God has made no such promise to me, nor will He deliver me from my suffering. {47:7} And since He has promised that Adam and his descendants will dwell in the kingdom where I once lived, I will kill Adam. If he is dead, he will leave no offspring to inherit that kingdom. The earth will be left to me, and God will need me again. He will then restore me to my former place with my angels."

{48:1} So Satan summoned his followers, and they all gathered before him. He asked them, "What shall we do?" {48:2} They replied, "Our lord, what is your plan?" {48:3} Satan said, "You know that Adam, the one God created from dust, has taken over the kingdom that was once ours. Let us gather and kill him. We can drop a huge rock on him and Eve to crush them." {48:4} Satan's followers agreed, and they went to the part of the mountain where Adam and Eve were sleeping. {48:5} Satan and his followers picked up a large, smooth, and flawless rock. Satan thought to himself, "If this rock had any cracks or holes, they might escape through them. But with this perfect rock, they won't survive." {48:6} He instructed his followers, "Lift this rock and throw it down flat on them so it won't roll away and miss. Afterward, flee quickly." They did as he commanded. {48:7} But as the rock came crashing down, God ordered it to become a shelter over Adam and Eve, so it wouldn't harm them. {48:8} When the rock fell, the earth quaked because of its size, shaking the entire ground. {48:9} Adam and Eve woke up and found themselves under a shelter formed by the rock. They were confused because they had fallen asleep under the open sky and now saw this shelter above them. {48:10} Adam asked Eve, "Why did the mountain bend, and why did the earth quake and shake? Why is this rock spread over us like a tent? {48:11} Is God angry at us for leaving the cave without His permission and coming to this place on our own?" {48:12} Eve responded, "If the earth truly shook because of us, and this rock covers us as punishment, then we are in deep trouble, Adam, for our punishment will be long. {48:13} But let's pray to God and ask Him to explain why this rock is spread over us like a tent." {48:14} So Adam stood up and prayed to God, asking for clarity on their situation. He prayed until the morning.

{49:1} Then God's Word came to Adam and said, "Adam, who advised you to leave the cave and come to this place?" {49:2} Adam answered, "Lord, we came here because of the heat of the fire in the cave. It was unbearable for us." {49:3} Then God said, "Adam, you feared the fire's heat for just one night. How will you bear the flames of hell? {49:4} But don't worry, Adam. Don't think I have placed this rock over you to punish you. {49:5} This rock was thrown by Satan, who once promised you godhood and majesty. He wanted to kill you and Eve with this rock so you wouldn't survive on earth. {49:6} But out of mercy, I commanded the rock to become a shelter over you as it fell, and I ordered the ground beneath it to lower itself. {49:7} This event will serve as a sign for My future coming to earth: Satan will lead the Jewish people to kill Me. They will lay Me in a rock and seal a large stone over Me, and I will remain there for three days and three nights. {49:8} But on the third day, I will rise again, and it will bring salvation to you, Adam, and to all your descendants who believe in Me. {49:9} However, Adam, I will not release you from under this rock until three days and three nights have passed." {49:10} Then God withdrew His Word from Adam. {49:11} Adam and Eve stayed under the rock for three days and three nights, just as God had said. {49:12} God did this to them because they had left the cave without His permission and come to this place on their own. {49:13} But after three days and three nights, God opened the rock and released them. Their skin had dried out, and their eyes and hearts were filled with sorrow from all their weeping.

{50:1} After that, Adam and Eve returned to the Cave of Treasures. They prayed there the entire day until evening. {50:2} This was fifty days after they had left the garden. {50:3} But even after that, they continued to pray to God in the cave throughout the night, begging for His mercy. {50:4} When the morning came, Adam said to Eve, "Let's go and do some work to provide for our bodies." {50:5} They left the cave and went to the northern edge of the garden, looking for something to cover their bodies with, but they found nothing and didn't know how to make clothes. Their bodies were stained, and they were suffering from both cold and heat. {50:6} So Adam prayed again, asking God to show him something to use for clothing. {50:7} Then God's Word came to him and said, "Adam, take Eve and go to the seashore where you fasted before. There you will find the skins of sheep, whose flesh was eaten by lions, but whose skins remain. Use them to make clothes for yourselves."

{51:1} When Adam heard these words from God, he took Eve and moved from the northern end of the garden to the southern side by the river where they had once fasted. {51:2} But before they reached the place, Satan, the wicked one, overheard God's conversation with Adam about their covering. {51:3} It grieved Satan, and he hurried to the place where the sheepskins were, intending to either throw them into the sea or burn them, so Adam and Eve would not find them. {51:4} But as Satan was about to take them, the Word of God came from heaven and bound him by the skins until Adam and Eve came close. {51:5} When Adam and Eve saw him, they were afraid of his hideous appearance. {51:6} Then the Word of God said to them, "This is the one who was hidden in the serpent and deceived you, stripping you of the garment of light and glory in which you were clothed. {51:7} He promised you majesty and divinity. Where now is his beauty? Where is his divinity? Where is his light? Where is the glory that once rested upon him? {51:8} Now he is hideous, abominable among angels, and he is called Satan. {51:9} O Adam, he sought to take these earthly garments of sheepskin from you and destroy them, so you would remain uncovered. {51:10} What beauty did you see in him that made you follow him? And what have you gained by listening to him? Look at his evil works, and then look at Me, your Creator, and the good I have done for you. {51:11} See, I bound him until you came so you could witness his weakness and know he has no power left." {51:12} And with that, God released Satan from his bonds.

{52:1} After this, Adam and Eve said nothing more but wept before God over their creation and the fact that their bodies now needed earthly coverings. {52:2} Then Adam said to Eve, "O Eve, these are the skins of animals, and we must wear them. But when we do, it will be a sign of death, for the animals these skins came from have died and wasted away. So, too, shall we die and pass away." {52:3} Then Adam and Eve took the skins and returned to the Cave of Treasures, where they stood and prayed as they were accustomed to. {52:4} They thought about how they might make garments from the skins since they had no knowledge of how to do so. {52:5} So God sent His angel to show them how to work it. {52:6} The angel told Adam, "Go and bring some palm-thorns." {52:7} Adam obeyed, and the angel began to prepare the skins, stitching them like a shirt. {52:8} The angel took the thorns and placed them in the skins before Adam and Eve's eyes. {52:9} Then the angel prayed to God that the thorns would be hidden, as if sewn with a single thread. {52:10} And so it happened, by God's command, and the skins became garments for Adam and Eve. {52:11} From then on, their nakedness was covered from each other's sight. {52:12} This took place on the fifty-first day. {52:13} When Adam and Eve were clothed, they stood and prayed, seeking mercy from God and thanking Him for covering their nakedness. {52:14} They prayed the entire night. {52:15} When morning came with the rising sun, they said their prayers as usual and then went outside the cave. {52:16} Adam said to Eve, "We don't know what lies to the west of this cave, so let's go and see it today." {52:17} So they left and headed toward the western border.

{53:1} As they approached the cave, Satan appeared again, hiding himself between them and the cave in the form of two ravenous lions who had not eaten for three days. {53:2} The lions came toward Adam and Eve, as if to break them to pieces and devour them. {53:3} Adam and Eve wept and prayed to God for deliverance from the lions. {53:4} The Word of God came to them and drove the lions away. {53:5} God then said to Adam, "Why are you seeking the western border? And why did you leave the eastern side, which was your dwelling place? {53:6} Return to your cave and stay there, lest Satan deceive you and carry out his plans against you. {53:7} For from this western border, your descendants will come, and they will defile themselves with sin, yielding to Satan's desires and following his ways. {53:8} I will send a flood to destroy them, but I will save the righteous among them and bring them to a far land, while this land you now dwell in will be left desolate and uninhabited." {53:9} After hearing this from God, Adam and Eve returned to the Cave of Treasures. Their bodies were weakened from fasting and praying, and they were sorrowful for having sinned against God.

{54:1} Adam and Eve prayed throughout the night until the morning. {54:2} When the sun rose, they left the cave, their minds wandering from the heaviness of their sorrow, unaware of where they were going. {54:3} They wandered to the southern border of the garden and then moved up toward the eastern border, where they could go no farther. {54:4} The cherub guarding the garden stood at the western gate, watching them, ready to kill them if they attempted to enter, as God had commanded him. {54:5} When Adam and Eve reached the eastern gate and thought the cherub wasn't watching, they approached as if trying to enter. {54:6} Suddenly, the cherub, holding a flaming sword, moved toward them to kill them. He feared God might destroy him if they entered the garden without His permission. {54:7} The cherub's sword blazed with fire, but when he raised it over Adam and Eve, the flames did not flash out. {54:8} The cherub thought God was showing favor to Adam and Eve, and that He might be allowing them to return to the garden. {54:9} The cherub stood confused, unable to leave their side, afraid they might enter the garden without God's permission and he would be destroyed. {54:10} When Adam and Eve saw the cherub approaching with the flaming sword, they fell on their faces in fear, as if dead. {54:11} At that moment, the heavens and the earth shook, and other cherubim came down to the one guarding the garden. They saw him silent and confused. {54:12} More angels descended near where Adam and Eve lay. Some were joyful, thinking God was showing favor to Adam and would restore him to the garden. {54:13} Others were sorrowful, seeing Adam and Eve lying as though dead and fearing God had killed them for trying to enter the garden without His consent.

{55:1} Then the Word of God came to Adam and Eve, raising them from their lifeless state. He said, "Why have you come up here? Do you intend to enter the garden from which I expelled you? It is not yet time for that. Only after the covenant I made with you is fulfilled can you return." {55:2} When Adam heard the Word of God and the sound of the angels, although he could not see them, he and Eve wept. {55:3} They spoke to the angels, saying, "O spirits who serve God, look at me! I can no longer see you! {55:4} When I was in my former bright nature, I could see you and sing praises as you do, with my heart lifted high above you. {55:5} But now, since I transgressed, I've lost that bright nature and am left in this miserable state. {55:6} I can no longer see you, and you no longer serve me as before, for I am now just flesh and bone. {55:7} But angels of God, please ask Him with me to restore me to my former state, to rescue me from this misery, and to remove the sentence of death He placed on me for my sin." {55:8} When the angels heard Adam's words, they grieved for him and cursed Satan for deceiving Adam and causing him to leave the garden for this miserable existence of death and trouble. {55:9} The angels said to Adam, "You listened to Satan and forsook the Word of God, your Creator. You believed Satan's promises. {55:10} Now let us tell you what happened to us because of him, before his fall from heaven. {55:11} He gathered his hosts and deceived them, promising them a great kingdom and divine nature. {55:12} His followers believed him and renounced the glory of God. {55:13} He summoned us as well, to come under his command and believe in his vain promises, but we refused and rejected his words. {55:14} After rebelling against God, he and his hosts fought with us. If it hadn't been for God's strength, we would not have been able to defeat him and cast him out of heaven. {55:15} But when he was thrown down from heaven, there was great joy among us. If he had remained, not a single angel would have stayed in heaven. {55:16} In His mercy, God cast him down to this dark earth, for he had become darkness itself and a worker of evil. {55:17} Since then, he has been waging war against you, Adam, deceiving you and leading you out of the garden into this strange land, where you've suffered these trials. {55:18} Death, which God brought upon him, he has also brought upon you, Adam, because you obeyed him and disobeyed God." {55:19} Then the angels rejoiced and praised God, asking Him not to destroy Adam for trying to enter the garden this time. They pleaded for God to be patient with him until the fulfillment of His promise and to help him in this world until he could be free from Satan's influence.

{56:1} Then the Word of God came to Adam, saying, "O Adam, look at that joyful garden and at this earth of toil. Behold the angels in the garden, which is full of them, and see yourself alone on this earth with Satan, whom you obeyed. {56:2} If you had submitted and been obedient to Me, keeping My Word, you would have been with My angels in My garden. {56:3} But when you transgressed and listened to Satan, you became his guest among his wicked angels, and you came to this earth, which brings forth thorns and thistles for you. {56:4} Adam, ask him who deceived you to give you the divine nature he promised or to create a garden like the one I made for you, or to fill you with the same bright nature with which I filled you. {56:5} Ask him to make you a body like the one I created for you or to give you a day of rest like the one I provided for you, or to move you to another earth other than this one I gave you. But, Adam, he will not fulfill even one of the things he told you. {56:6} Acknowledge, then, My favor toward you and My mercy upon you, My creature. I have not repaid you for your transgression against Me, but in My pity for you, I have promised that at the end of the great five and a half days, I will come and save you." {56:7} Then God said again to Adam and Eve, "Arise and go down from here, lest the cherub with a flaming sword destroy you." {56:8} Adam's heart was comforted by God's words to him, and he worshipped before Him. {56:9} God commanded His angels to escort Adam and Eve joyfully instead of the fear that had come upon them. {56:10} The angels took up Adam and Eve and brought them down from the mountain near the garden, singing songs and psalms until they brought them to the cave. There the angels began to comfort and strengthen them, then departed toward heaven to their Creator who had sent them. {56:11} But after the angels left Adam and Eve, Satan approached, looking shamefaced, and stood at the entrance of the cave where they were. He called to Adam and said, "Adam, come, let me speak to you." {56:12} Adam came out of the cave, thinking he was one of God's angels come to offer him good counsel.

{57:1} But when Adam came out and saw Satan's hideous figure, he was afraid and said to him, "Who are you?" {57:2} Satan replied, "It is I, the one who hid myself in the serpent and talked to Eve, beguiling her until she listened to my command. I am the one who sent her through my cunning speech to deceive you until both you and she ate from the tree and stepped away from God's command." {57:3} When Adam heard this, he said to him, "Can you create a garden as God made for me? Can you clothe me in the same bright nature that God clothed me with? {57:4} Where is the divine nature you promised to give me? Where is that fair speech of yours when we were in the garden?" {57:5} Satan replied, "Do you think that when I speak to someone about anything, I will ever fulfill my word? Not at all. I never even thought of obtaining what I asked. {57:6} It is because of this that I fell, and I made you fall by that for which I myself fell; and whoever accepts my counsel falls with me. {57:7} But now, Adam, because of your fall, you are under my rule, and I am king over you because you listened to me and transgressed against your God. There will be no deliverance from my grasp until the promised day from your God." {57:8} He continued, "Since we do not know the day agreed upon by your God, nor the hour in which you will be delivered, we will multiply war and murder against you and your descendants after you. {57:9} This is our will and pleasure, to ensure that none of the sons of men inherit our orders in heaven. {57:10} As for our abode, O Adam, it is in burning fire, and we will not cease our evil deeds, not one day nor one hour. And I, Adam, will sow fire upon you when you come into the cave to dwell there." {57:11} When Adam heard these words, he wept and mourned, saying to Eve, "Hear what he said; that he will not fulfill anything of what he told you in the garden. Did he really become king over us? {57:12} But we will ask God, who created us, to deliver us from his hands."

{58:1} Then Adam and Eve lifted their hands to God, praying and asking Him to drive Satan away from them, that he would do them no harm and not force them to deny God. {58:2} Immediately, God sent His angel to drive Satan away from them. This happened around sunset on the fifty-third day after they had come out of the garden. {58:3} Adam and Eve then entered the cave and stood with their faces to the ground to pray to God. {58:4} But before they prayed, Adam said to Eve, "Look at the temptations that have befallen us in this land. Come, let us arise and ask God to forgive us for the sins we have committed; we will not come out until the end of the day next to the fortieth. And if we die here, He will save us." {58:5} Adam and Eve rose and united in their plea to God. They remained praying in the cave, neither coming out by night or day, until their prayers ascended from their mouths like a flame of fire.

{59:1} But Satan, the enemy of all good, did not allow them to finish their prayers. He summoned his hosts, and they all came to him. {59:2} He said, "Since Adam and Eve, whom we deceived, have agreed to pray to God day and night, entreating Him to deliver them, and since they will not come out of the cave until the end of the fortieth day, {59:3} and since they will continue their prayers as they have agreed, let us see what we shall do to them." His hosts replied, "Power is yours, O our Lord, to do as you wish." {59:4} Then Satan, full of wickedness, took his hosts and entered the cave on the thirtieth night of the forty days, attacking Adam and Eve until he left them for dead. {59:5} Then the Word of God came to Adam and Eve, raising them from their suffering, and God said to Adam, "Be strong, and do not be afraid of him who has just come to you." {59:6} But Adam wept, saying, "Where were You, O my God, that they should strike me with such blows and that this suffering should come upon us—upon me and upon Eve, Your handmaid?" {59:7} God replied, "Adam, see, he is lord and master over all you have; he who claimed he would give you divinity. Where is his love for you? Where is the gift he promised? {59:8} When has he ever come to comfort you, to strengthen you, to rejoice with you, and to send his hosts to protect you? It is because you listened to him and yielded to his counsel, transgressing My commandment and following his bidding." {59:9} Adam wept before the Lord, saying, "O Lord, because I transgressed a little, You have severely plagued me in return. I ask You to deliver me from his hands, or else have mercy on me and take my soul from my body now in this strange land." {59:10} God replied to Adam, "If only you had sighed and prayed before you transgressed! Then you would have rest from the trouble you are now in." {59:11} But God was patient with Adam, allowing him and Eve to remain in the cave until they had completed the forty days. {59:12} As for Adam and Eve, their strength and flesh withered from fasting and praying, from hunger and thirst; they had not tasted food or drink since leaving the garden, nor were the functions of their bodies yet settled; they had no strength left to continue in prayer from hunger until the end of the next day of the fortieth day. They had collapsed in the cave, yet what escaped their mouths were only praises.

{60:1} Then on the eighty-ninth day, Satan came to the cave dressed in a garment of light, wearing a bright belt. In his hands was a staff of light, and he appeared fearsome, yet his face was pleasant and his speech was sweet. {60:2} He transformed himself in order to deceive Adam and Eve and to make them come out of the cave before they had completed their forty days. {60:3} He thought to himself, "Now that they have finished the forty days of fasting and praying, God would restore them to their former state; but if He does not do so, He would still be favorable to them; and even if He does not show them mercy, they would still be in the body and in this world, unable to free themselves from my grasp." {60:4} The great tempter thought about how he might bring them to their former state so they would be his subjects forever, obeying him and forgetting God. {60:5} Then he came to them, and when they saw him, they were frightened; they thought he was one of God's angels sent to comfort them. {60:6} Satan spoke sweetly, "O Adam and Eve, why do you still remain here? The forty days have ended. You must not be worried; your God will have mercy on you, and He will return you to His garden." {60:7} He continued, "Do you not know that your God loves you? And you have no need to mourn? Why do you remain here fasting and praying? There is no need for it anymore." {60:8} Adam and Eve believed what Satan said and rose to go out of the cave. {60:9} But before they could escape, God called out to them, "O Adam, I have not commanded you to come out yet! Wait, for I will come to you." {60:10} Adam and Eve paused, terrified, yet not daring to raise their eyes to look toward the entrance. {60:11} Adam said, "I hear Your voice, O my God. I weep and weep before You; how will I stand before You when I have sinned against You?" {60:12} God said, "Adam, you have not yet completed your prayers; you must return into the cave." {60:13} Adam and Eve returned into the cave, falling on their faces before God, weeping and praying to Him. {60:14} After some time, they finished their prayers, and God said to them, "Go, for I have forgiven your sins, and you shall be delivered from the hands of the wicked."

{61:1} Then God took Adam and Eve by the hand and began to lead them out of the cave. {61:2} But when they had come a little way out, God knew that Satan had overcome them and had led them out before the forty days were completed, intending to take them to a distant place and destroy them. {61:3} Then the Word of the Lord God came again and cursed Satan, driving him away from them. {61:4} God began to speak to Adam and Eve, asking, "What made you come out of the cave to this place?" {61:5} Adam replied, "Did You create another man before us? While we were in the cave, a good old man suddenly came to us and said, 'I am a messenger from God, sent to bring you back to a place of rest.' {61:6} We believed, God, that he was a messenger from You, and we came out with him, not knowing where we were going." {61:7} God said to Adam, "See, that is the father of evil schemes, who brought you and Eve out of the Garden of Delight. {61:8} When he saw that you and Eve were united in fasting and prayer, and that you didn't come out of the cave before the end of the forty days, he wanted to make your efforts useless, to break your bond, cut off all hope, and drive you to a place where he could destroy you. {61:9} He couldn't do anything to you unless he showed himself in a form like yours. {61:10} So he came to you looking like you and began to give you signs that seemed true. {61:11} But out of mercy and favor for you, I didn't let him destroy you; instead, I drove him away. {61:12} Now, Adam, take Eve and return to your cave, and stay there until the morning of the fortieth day. {61:13} When you come out, head towards the eastern gate of the garden." {61:14} Then Adam and Eve worshiped God, praising and blessing Him for the deliverance He had granted them. They returned towards the cave, and this happened in the evening of the thirty-ninth day. {61:15} Adam and Eve stood up with great zeal and prayed to God, asking to be relieved of their weakness because their strength had left them due to hunger, thirst, and prayer. They prayed all night until morning. {61:16} Adam said to Eve, "Let's rise and go towards the eastern gate of the garden as God instructed." {61:17} They prayed as they did every day and left the cave to approach the eastern gate of the garden. {61:18} They stood there, praying and asking God to strengthen them and send something to satisfy their hunger. {61:19} But after they finished their prayers, they remained there, feeling weak. {61:20} Then the Word of God came again and said, "O Adam, get up and bring me two figs." {61:21} So Adam and Eve got up and went until they got close to the cave.

{62:1} But Satan, the wicked one, was envious of the comfort God had given them. {62:2} So he intervened, entered the cave, took the two figs, and buried them outside the cave to prevent Adam and Eve from finding them. He also intended to destroy them. {62:3} However, by God's mercy, as soon as those two figs were buried, God defeated Satan's plan regarding them and turned them into two fruit trees that overshadowed the cave. He buried them on the eastern side. {62:4} When the two trees grew and were full of fruit, Satan grieved and mourned, saying, "It would have been better to leave those figs as they were, for now they have become two fruit trees, and Adam will eat from them all his life. I had intended to destroy them entirely and hide them forever. {62:5} But God has overturned my plan; He wouldn't let this sacred fruit perish, revealing my intentions and thwarting my scheme against His servants." {62:6} Then Satan left, ashamed of his failure to carry out his design.

{63:1} As Adam and Eve approached the cave, they saw two fig trees, covered in fruit and shading the cave. {63:2} Adam said to Eve, "I think we've gone astray. When did these two trees grow here? It seems the enemy wants to mislead us. Do you think there is another cave in the earth?" {63:3} Yet, Eve, let's go into the cave and look for the two figs because this is our cave where we were. If we don't find the figs, then it can't be our cave." {63:4} They entered the cave and searched in the four corners but found no figs. {63:5} Adam wept and said to Eve, "Have we come to the wrong cave? It seems to me these two fig trees are the ones that were in the cave." Eve replied, "I don't know." {63:6} Adam prayed, "O God, You commanded us to return to the cave to get the two figs and come back to You. {63:7} But now we cannot find them. God, have You taken them and planted these trees, or have we gone astray on the earth? Did the enemy deceive us? If it's real, God, please reveal the mystery of these two trees and the two figs." {63:8} Then the Word of God came to Adam, saying, "Adam, when I sent you to fetch the figs, Satan went before you, took the figs, and buried them outside east of the cave, thinking to destroy them and not to plant them with good intentions. {63:9} These trees did not grow merely because of him; I had mercy on you and commanded them to grow. They became large trees to shade you and give you rest, and to show you My power and marvelous works. {63:10} Also, to reveal Satan's malice and evil actions, for since you came out of the garden, he hasn't ceased for one moment from trying to harm you. But I have not allowed him power over you." {63:11} God said, "From now on, Adam, rejoice because of the trees, you and Eve; rest under them when you feel weary, but do not eat their fruit or approach them." {63:12} Then Adam wept and said, "O God, will You kill us again, or will You cast us away from Your presence and take away our lives from the earth? {63:13} God, I beg You, if You know there's death or some other evil in these trees, as there was the first time, uproot them from near our cave and let them wither, allowing us to die from heat, hunger, and thirst. {63:14} For we know of Your marvelous works, God, that they are great, and that by Your power You can bring one thing from another without our wishes. Your power can make rocks turn into trees and trees into rocks."

{64:1} Then God looked at Adam and observed his strength of will and endurance against hunger, thirst, and heat. He changed the two fig trees back into two figs, as they were at first, and said to Adam and Eve, "Each of you may take one fig." {64:2} They took the figs as the Lord commanded. {64:3} God told them, "Go back into the cave, eat the figs, and satisfy your hunger so you don't die." {64:4} Following God's command, they entered the cave around sunset. Adam and Eve prayed at sunset. {64:5} Then they sat down to eat the figs, but they didn't know how to eat them since they were not used to earthly food. They also feared that if they ate, their stomachs would become heavy, and their flesh would thicken, leading them to desire earthly food. {64:6} While they were seated like this, God, out of compassion for them, sent His angel to prevent them from perishing from hunger and thirst. {64:7} The angel said to Adam and Eve, "God tells you that you do not have the strength to fast until death; therefore, eat and strengthen your bodies, for you are now flesh that cannot survive without food and drink." {64:8} Adam and Eve took the figs and began to eat them. God had made them taste like savory bread and wine. {64:9} The angel left Adam and Eve, who ate until they were full. They saved what was left, but by God's power, the figs became full again because God blessed them. After this, Adam and Eve rose, prayed with joyful hearts and renewed strength, and praised and rejoiced abundantly throughout the night. This marked the end of the eighty-third day.

{65:1} When morning came, they rose and prayed, as was their custom, then went out of the cave. {65:2} But they felt great discomfort from the food they had eaten, which they were not used to. They wandered in the cave, saying to each other: {65:3} "What has happened to us from eating that this pain has come upon us? Woe to us, we shall die! It would have been better to die than to eat and defile our bodies with food." {65:4} Adam said to Eve, "This pain didn't come to us in the garden, nor did we eat such bad food there. Do you think, Eve, that God will plague us with this food or that our insides will come out, or does God intend to kill us with this pain before fulfilling His promise to us?" {65:5} Adam pleaded with the Lord, saying, "O Lord, don't let us perish because of the food we've eaten. Lord, do not smite us; treat us according to Your great mercy and do not forsake us until the day of the promise You have made us." {65:6} Then God looked upon them and immediately adapted them to eat food, as is done to this day, so they would not perish. {65:7} Adam and Eve returned to the cave, sorrowful and weeping because of the change in their nature. They both realized from that hour that they had changed and that their hope of returning to the garden was now lost, and they could not enter it. {65:8} They understood that their bodies had strange functions, and that all flesh requiring food and drink for its existence cannot dwell in the garden. {65:9} Adam said to Eve, "Behold, our hope is now lost, as is our desire to enter the garden. We no longer belong to the garden's inhabitants; from now on, we are earthly, made of dust, and among the earth's inhabitants. We will not return to the garden until the day God promises to save us and bring us back to the garden, as He has promised us." {65:10} Then they prayed to God for mercy; afterward, their minds were calmed, their hearts were broken, and their longing was diminished. They felt like strangers on earth. That night, Adam and Eve spent in the cave, where they slept heavily due to the food they had eaten.

{66:1} The next morning, after they had eaten food, Adam and Eve prayed in the cave. Adam said to Eve, "Look, we asked God for food, and He gave it to us. But now let's also ask Him to give us something to drink." {66:2} So they got up and went to the bank of the stream of water that was on the south border of the garden, where they had previously thrown themselves. They stood by the bank and prayed to God, asking Him to let them drink from the water. {66:3} Then the Word of God came to Adam and said, "O Adam, your body has become animalistic (brutish) and needs water to drink. Go ahead and drink, you and Eve; give thanks and praise." {66:4} Adam and Eve approached and drank from the stream until they felt refreshed. After drinking, they praised God and then returned to their cave, as they usually did. This occurred after eighty-three days had passed. {66:5} On the eighty-fourth day, they took two figs and hung them in the cave along with their leaves, as a sign and a blessing from God. They left them there until their descendants could see the wonderful things God had done for them. {66:6} Again, Adam and Eve stood outside the cave and asked God to show them some food to nourish their bodies. {66:7} Then the Word of God came to Adam, saying, "Adam, go west of the cave to a land of dark soil, and there you will find food." {66:8} Adam listened to the Word of God, took Eve, and went westward to the land of dark soil, where he found wheat growing, ripe and ready for harvest, along with figs to eat. Adam was filled with joy at this discovery. {66:9} The Word of God then came to Adam again, saying, "Take this wheat and make bread from it to nourish your body." God gave Adam wisdom in his heart so he could work with the grain and turn it into bread. {66:10} Adam accomplished all this, but he became very faint and weary. He then returned to the cave, rejoicing at what he had learned about making bread from wheat. However, further details would make this account too lengthy, so we will summarize.

{67:1} The first wonder concerning Adam and Eve and the wheat happened when they went down to the land of dark soil and approached the ripe wheat that God had shown them. Not having a sickle to harvest it, they began to pull it up by hand until they had gathered it all into a heap. Exhausted from the heat and thirst, they found a shady tree and fell asleep, cooled by the gentle breeze. {67:2} But Satan saw what Adam and Eve had done. He called his followers and said, "Since God has shown Adam and Eve all about this wheat to strengthen their bodies, and now they have made a heap of it and are asleep from their labor, let us set fire to the wheat and burn it, and let's empty out the water they have with them so they will have nothing to drink and will die of hunger and thirst. {67:3} Then, when they wake up and seek to return to the cave, we will lead them astray so that they die from hunger and thirst, which may cause them to deny God, and He will destroy them. This way, we will be rid of them." {67:4} So Satan and his followers set fire to the wheat and burned it. {67:5} The heat of the flames woke Adam and Eve from their sleep, and they saw the wheat burning and the bucket of water beside them poured out. {67:6} They wept and returned to the cave. As they were ascending from the valley where they had been, Satan and his followers met them in the form of angels, praising God. {67:7} Then Satan said to Adam, "Adam, why are you so distressed with hunger and thirst? It seems to me that Satan has burned up the wheat." Adam replied, "Yes." {67:8} Again, Satan said to Adam, "Come back with us; we are angels of God. God has sent us to show you a better field of corn than the one that has been burned, along with a fountain of good water and many trees, where you can dwell and work the cornfield more effectively than with what Satan has consumed." {67:9} Adam thought what they said was true and believed they were angels, so he went back with them. {67:10} Then Satan led Adam and Eve astray for eight days until they both collapsed as if dead from hunger, thirst, and exhaustion. Afterward, he fled with his followers.

{68:1} Then God looked at Adam and Eve and saw what had befallen them because of Satan and how he had led them to perish. {68:2} Therefore, God sent His Word and raised Adam and Eve from their state of death. {68:3} When Adam was raised, he said, "God, You burned what You had given us, and You emptied our bucket of water. You sent Your angels to waylay us at the cornfield. Will You let us perish? If this is Your will, O God, then take away our souls, but do not punish us." {68:4} God replied to Adam, "I did not burn the wheat, and I did not pour the water out of the bucket, nor did I send My angels to lead you astray. {68:5} But it is Satan, your master, who has done this; he to whom you have subjected yourself while disregarding My commandment. He is the one who burned the corn, poured out the water, and led you astray. All the promises he has made you are merely falsehoods and deceit. {68:6} But now, Adam, acknowledge the good deeds I have done for you." {68:7} God instructed His angels to take Adam and Eve back to the field of wheat, which they found intact, with the bucket full of water. There, they discovered a tree that bore solid manna and marveled at God's power. The angels told them to eat of the manna when they were hungry. {68:8} God also cursed Satan, commanding him not to return and destroy the cornfield. {68:9} Then Adam and Eve took some of the corn and made an offering, which they brought to the mountain where they had previously offered their first blood sacrifice. {68:10} They offered this oblation on the altar they had built earlier. They stood and prayed, asking the Lord, "God, just as our praises went up to You in the garden, like this offering, and our innocence went up like incense, now, O God, accept this offering from us and do not turn us away, stripped of Your mercy." {68:11} Then God said to Adam and Eve, "Since you have made this offering and presented it to Me, I will make it My flesh when I come down to earth to save you. I will ensure it is continually offered on an altar for forgiveness and mercy to those who partake of it rightly." {68:12} God sent a bright fire upon Adam and Eve's offering, filling it with light, grace, and brightness; the Holy Spirit descended upon that oblation. {68:13} God commanded an angel to take fire-tongs, like a spoon, and with them to take the offering and present it to Adam and Eve. The angel did as God commanded, and offered it to them. {68:14} The souls of Adam and Eve were uplifted, and their hearts were filled with joy, gladness, and praises for God. {68:15} God said to Adam, "This shall become a custom for you to follow whenever affliction and sorrow come upon you. But your deliverance and return to the garden will not happen until the days are fulfilled, as agreed between us. Otherwise, out of My mercy and pity for you, I would bring you back to My garden and My favor because of the offering you just made to My name." {68:16} Adam rejoiced at these words from God and worshipped before the altar, bowing down, then returned to the Cave of Treasures. {68:17} This took place at the end of the twelfth day after the eightieth day since Adam and Eve had come out of the garden. {68:18} They stood the entire night praying until morning, then went out of the cave. {68:19} Adam said to Eve, filled with joy because of the offering they had made to God, which had been accepted, "Let us do this three times each week, on the fourth day [Wednesday], on the preparation day [Friday], and on the Sabbath [Sunday], for the rest of our lives." {68:20} As they agreed on this plan, God was pleased with their intentions and the commitment they had made to one another. {68:21} After this, the Word of God came to Adam, saying, "Adam, you have predetermined the days when suffering will come upon Me, when I am made flesh; they will be the fourth [Wednesday] and the preparation day [Friday]. {68:22} But as for the first day, I created everything in it and raised the heavens. Again, through My resurrection on this day, I will create joy and raise those who believe in Me; Adam, continue to offer this oblation for the rest of your life." {68:23} Then God withdrew His Word from Adam. {68:24} Adam and Eve praised God for His goodness & mercy, which they saw through the offering. {68:25} They returned to the cave & spent next day praying in joy & hope.

{69:1} Then Satan, the enemy of all that is good, filled with envy toward Adam and his offering, which had gained God's favor, hurriedly took a sharp stone from among the jagged rocks. {69:2} He appeared in the form of a man and stood by Adam and Eve. {69:3} Adam was then offering his gift on the altar and had begun to pray, raising his hands to God. {69:4} Suddenly, Satan rushed forward with the sharp stone he had brought and pierced Adam in the right side, from which blood and water flowed. {69:5} Adam fell upon the altar like a lifeless body, and Satan fled. {69:6} Eve came over, took Adam, and placed him beneath the altar. She remained there, weeping over him, as a stream of blood flowed from Adam's side onto his offering. {69:7} But God looked upon Adam's death. He sent His Word to raise Adam and said, "Complete your offering, for indeed, Adam, it is of great worth, and there is no flaw in it." {69:8} God further said to Adam, "This will also happen to Me on the earth when I am pierced, and blood and water will flow from My side, covering My body, which is the true offering; and this shall be offered on the altar as a perfect sacrifice." {69:9} Then God commanded Adam to finish his offering, and when Adam completed it, he worshiped before God and praised Him for the signs He had shown him. {69:10} God healed Adam in one day, which marked the end of seven weeks, the fiftieth day. {69:11} Afterward, Adam and Eve returned from the mountain and went into the Cave of Treasures, as was their custom. {69:12} This marked one hundred and forty days since Adam and Eve had left the garden. {69:13} That night, they both stood up and prayed to God. {69:14} In the morning, they went out and traveled westward from the cave to the place where their grain was, and there they rested under the shade of a tree, as was their practice. {69:15} While they were there, a multitude of wild animals surrounded them. This was the work of Satan, who intended to wage war against Adam through marriage.

{70:1} After this, Satan, the enemy of all that is good, disguised himself as an angel and brought along two others, making it look like the three angels who had previously brought Adam gold, incense, and myrrh. {70:2} They passed by Adam and Eve while they were resting under the tree and greeted them with flattering words, filled with deceit. {70:3} When Adam and Eve saw their handsome appearance and heard their sweet speech, Adam stood up, welcomed them, and brought them to Eve, feeling glad because he thought they were the same angels who had previously brought him gifts. {70:4} When they first visited Adam, they had brought him peace and joy through their good tidings, so Adam thought they had come again to bring him more blessings. {70:5} Unaware that it was Satan in disguise, he received them joyfully and spent time with them. {70:6} Then Satan, the tallest of the three, said, "Rejoice, Adam, and be glad! Look, God has sent us to tell you something." {70:7} Adam asked, "What is it?" Satan answered, "It is a simple message, yet it comes from God. Will you listen to us and act upon it? If you refuse, we will return to God and tell Him you would not accept His word." {70:8} Satan added, "Do not be afraid, nor let fear grip you; don't you recognize us?" {70:9} Adam replied, "I do not know you." {70:10} Satan then said, "I am the angel who brought you gold and took it to the cave; this one is the angel who brought you incense, and the third is the one who brought you myrrh when you were on the mountaintop and carried you to the cave. {70:11} But as for the other angels who took you to the cave, God did not send them with us this time; He said, 'You suffice.'" {70:12} When Adam heard these words, he believed them and said to the supposed angels, "Speak the word of God, so I can receive it." {70:13} Satan replied, "Swear to me and promise that you will accept it." {70:14} Adam responded, "I do not know how to swear or promise." {70:15} Satan said, "Extend your hand and place it in mine." {70:16} Adam did as instructed, extending his hand into Satan's. {70:17} Satan then said, "Now say, 'As truly as God is living, rational, and speaking, who created the heavens and established the earth upon the waters and made me from the four elements and from the dust of the earth—I will not break my promise or deny my word.'" And Adam swore this way. {70:18} Then Satan said to him, "It has been some time since you came out of the garden, and you know nothing of wickedness or evil. But now God says to you to take Eve, who came from your side, and marry her so that she may bear you children, comforting you and alleviating your troubles and sorrows. This is not difficult, nor is there any shame in it for you."

{71:1} When Adam heard Satan's words, he was very saddened because of his oath and promise. He said, "Should I commit adultery with my own flesh and bones and sin against myself, only for God to destroy me and erase me from the face of the earth? {71:2} Since when I first ate from the tree, He drove me out of the garden into this strange land, took away my bright nature, and brought death upon me. If I do this, He will cut off my life from the earth and throw me into hell, where I will be tormented for a long time. {71:3} But God never said the words you have told me; you are not God's angels, nor are you sent by Him. You are devils who come to me under the false appearance of angels. Get away from me; you are cursed by God!" {71:4} The devils then fled from Adam. He and Eve rose up and returned to the Cave of Treasures. {71:5} Adam then said to Eve, "If you saw what I did, don't tell anyone, for I sinned against God by swearing by His great name, and I have once again placed my hand in that of Satan." Eve remained silent as Adam told her. {71:6} Then Adam rose and spread his hands to God, pleading with tears to forgive him for what he had done. He prayed like this for forty days and forty nights, neither eating nor drinking, until he collapsed from hunger and thirst. {71:7} Then God sent His Word to Adam, who raised him up from where he lay and said, "Adam, why have you sworn by My name, and why have you made a pact with Satan again?" {71:8} Adam wept and replied, "God, forgive me, for I did this unknowingly, thinking they were God's angels." {71:9} God forgave Adam and said to him, "Be careful of Satan." {71:10} Then He withdrew His Word from Adam. Adam's heart was comforted; he took Eve and went out to make food for their bodies. {71:11} But from that day on, Adam struggled in his mind about marrying Eve, fearing that God would be angry with him. {71:12} Then Adam and Eve went to the river and sat by the bank, as people do when they are enjoying themselves. {71:13} However, Satan was jealous of them and wanted to destroy them.

{72:1} The fourteenth appearance of Satan to Adam and Eve came as he emerged from the river in the form of beautiful young maidens. {72:2} Then Satan and ten of his hosts transformed into maidens, unlike any others in the world for their grace. {72:3} They approached Adam and Eve and exclaimed among themselves, "Let us see the faces of Adam and Eve, who are among the people on earth. They are so beautiful, and their looks are so different from ours." {72:4} They greeted Adam and Eve and stood there in wonder. {72:5} Adam and Eve looked back at them in amazement and asked, "Is there another world below us with such beautiful creatures?" {72:6} The maidens replied, "Yes, indeed, we are many in number." {72:7} Then Adam asked, "But how do you multiply?" {72:8} They answered him, "We have husbands who marry us, and we bear them children who grow up and in turn marry and have children; and thus we increase. If you don't believe us, we will show you our husbands and children." {72:9} Then they called out over the river, as if to summon their husbands and children, who emerged from the river, men and children alike; each man came to his wife, his children with him. {72:10} When Adam and Eve saw them, they were speechless and astonished. {72:11} They said to Adam and Eve, "You see our husbands and children; wed Eve as we wed our wives, and you will have children just like us." This was Satan's trick to deceive Adam. {72:12} Satan thought to himself, "God commanded Adam not to eat from the tree, saying, 'If you eat of it, you will surely die.' But Adam ate from it, and God did not kill him; He only decreed upon him death and trials until the day he leaves his body. {72:13} Now, if I can deceive him into marrying Eve without God's command, God will kill him." {72:14} So Satan created this apparition before Adam and Eve, aiming to kill him and make him vanish from the earth. {72:15} Meanwhile, the fire of sin ignited within Adam, and he contemplated committing sin. But he held back, fearing that if he followed Satan's advice, God would strike him down. {72:16} Adam and Eve then rose and prayed to God, while Satan and his hosts descended back into the river, showing Adam and Eve that they were returning to their own regions. {72:17} Adam and Eve returned to the Cave of Treasures as was their custom, around evening time. {72:18} They both rose and prayed to God that night. Adam remained standing in prayer, uncertain how to pray because of his troubling thoughts about marrying Eve, and he continued this until morning. {72:19} When light broke, Adam said to Eve, "Let us go down the mountain where we found gold, and let us ask the Lord about this matter." {72:20} Eve asked, "What is this matter, Adam?" {72:21} He answered, "I want to ask the Lord if it is right to marry you; I will not do it without His command, lest He destroy both of us. For those devils have ignited my heart with thoughts of what they showed us in their sinful apparitions." {72:22} Eve replied, "Why do we need to go down the mountain? Let us stand and pray in our cave to God to inform us if this counsel is good or not." {72:23} Adam then rose to pray, saying, "God, You know we have transgressed against You, and since that moment, we lost our bright nature; our bodies became brutish, needing food and drink, and filled with animal desires. {72:24} Command us, God, not to give in to them without Your order, lest You bring us to ruin. If You do not give us the order, we will be overpowered and follow Satan's advice, and You will make us perish again. {72:25} If not, then take our souls from us; let us be free from this animal lust. If You do not give us orders regarding this, then separate Eve from me and me from her; place us each far from the other. {72:26} Yet, God, if You put us apart, the devils will deceive us with their apparitions and ruin our hearts and thoughts toward each other. If it is not between us, it will certainly be through their appearances when they show themselves to us." Here Adam concluded his prayer.

{73:1} Then God looked upon Adam's words and found them true, and saw that he could wait for His order regarding Satan's counsel. {73:2} God approved Adam for what he had thought about this matter and for the prayer he offered in His presence; then God's Word came to Adam and said, "Adam, if only you had this caution from the beginning, before you came out of the garden into this land!" {73:3} After this, God sent His angel who had brought gold, the angel who had brought incense, and the angel who had brought myrrh to Adam to give him guidance regarding his marriage to Eve. {73:4} Those angels said to Adam, "Take the gold and give it to Eve as a wedding gift and betroth her; then give her some incense and myrrh as presents, and you both shall become one flesh." {73:5} Adam listened to the angels, took the gold, and placed it in Eve's bosom. He then betrothed her with his hand. {73:6} The angels commanded Adam and Eve to rise and pray for forty days and forty nights; after that, Adam should come to his wife, as this would be a pure and undefiled act, and they would have children who would multiply and fill the earth. {73:7} Adam and Eve accepted the words of the angels, and the angels departed. {73:8} Adam and Eve began to fast and pray until the end of the forty days; then they came together, just as the angels had instructed. {73:9} From the time Adam left the garden until he wed Eve was two hundred twenty-three days, or seven months and thirteen days. {73:10} Thus, Satan's war against Adam was defeated.

{74:1} They lived on the earth, working to sustain their bodies, until the nine months of Eve's pregnancy were completed, and the time approached for her to give birth. {74:2} Eve said to Adam, "This cave is a pure spot because of the signs (miracles) wrought in it since we left the garden; we should pray here again. It is not suitable for me to give birth here; let us instead go to the cave of the sheltering rock, which Satan hurled at us when he intended to kill us, but it was held up and spread as an awning over us. {74:3} Let us give thanks to God for all His mercy in our lives; let us go and make a prayer to God in the rock cave where we were saved." Adam agreed, and they went to that cave.

{75:1} Adam prepared an offering, and he and Eve presented it for their children at the altar they had built earlier. {75:2} Adam offered the sacrifice and prayed for God to accept it. {75:3} God accepted Adam's offering and sent a light from heaven that shone on the sacrifice. Adam and his son approached the offering, but Eve and their daughter did not come near it. {75:4} After offering the sacrifice, Adam came down from the altar, and they were filled with joy. Adam and Eve waited until their daughter was eighty days old; then Adam prepared another offering and took it to Eve and the children. They went to the altar where Adam offered it, as was his custom, asking God to accept it. {75:5} The Lord accepted Adam and Eve's offering. Then Adam, Eve, and the children gathered together and came down from the mountain rejoicing. {75:6} However, they did not return to the cave where they were born; instead, they went to the Cave of Treasures so the children could walk around it and be blessed with tokens from the garden. {75:7} After receiving these blessings, they returned to the cave where they were born. {75:8} Before Eve offered the sacrifice, Adam had taken her to the river where they had first immersed themselves; they washed themselves there. Adam washed his body, and Eve also made herself clean after the suffering and distress they had experienced. {75:9} After washing in the river, Adam and Eve returned to the Cave of Treasures each night to pray and receive blessings before going back to their cave where the children were born. {75:10} They continued this routine until the children finished nursing. Once they were weaned, Adam made offerings for the souls of his children, in addition to the three offerings he made for them each week. {75:11} After the nursing period, Eve conceived again, and when the time came, she gave birth to another son and daughter, naming the son Abel and the daughter Aklemia. {75:12} After forty days, Adam made an offering for the son, and after eighty days, he made another offering for the daughter, doing for them as he had done before for Cain and his sister Luluwa. {75:13} He took them to the Cave of Treasures to receive blessings, and then they returned to the cave where they were born. After the birth of these children, Eve stopped having more children.

{76:1} As the children grew stronger and taller, Cain became hard-hearted and dominated his younger brother. {76:2} Often, when his father made an offering, Cain would stay behind and not join them. {76:3} In contrast, Abel had a gentle heart and was obedient to his parents; he frequently encouraged them to make offerings because he loved doing so and often prayed and fasted. {76:4} One day, while Abel was entering the Cave of Treasures, he saw golden rods, incense, and myrrh, and he asked Adam and Eve how they came by these items. {76:5} Adam explained everything that had happened to them, which deeply touched Abel. {76:6} Adam also told Abel about God's works and the garden, and Abel stayed with his father in the Cave of Treasures throughout the night. {76:7} During that night, while praying, Satan appeared to Abel in the form of a man, saying, "Since you often encourage your father to make offerings, to fast, and to pray, I will kill you and make you perish from this world." {76:8} Abel, however, prayed to God and repelled Satan, refusing to believe the devil's words. {76:9} When day broke, an angel of God appeared to him, saying, "Do not shorten your fasting, prayer, or offerings to God. The Lord has accepted your prayer. Do not be afraid of the figure that appeared to you last night, who cursed you with death." The angel then departed. {76:10} Abel later told Adam and Eve about the vision he had seen. They were greatly saddened but did not say much to him; they merely offered him comfort. {76:11} As for hard-hearted Cain, Satan visited him at night, appearing and saying, "Adam and Eve love your brother Abel more than they love you and wish to marry him to your beautiful sister. They want to join you with his less attractive sister because they dislike you. {76:12} Therefore, I advise you to kill your brother when they make that match; then your sister will be yours, and his sister will be discarded." {76:13} Satan then left, but his wicked influence lingered in Cain's heart, leading him to contemplate killing his brother many times.

{77:1} When Adam noticed that Cain hated Abel, he tried to soften their hearts and said to Cain, "My son, take some of the fruits of your harvest and make an offering to God so that He may forgive your wickedness and sin." {77:2} He also said to Abel, "Take of your harvest and offer it to God so that He may forgive your wickedness and sin." {77:3} Abel listened to his father's instructions, took from his harvest, and prepared a good offering, saying to his father, "Come with me to show me how to offer it." {77:4} So Adam and Eve went with him and showed him how to present his gift on the altar. Afterward, they stood up and prayed that God would accept Abel's offering. {77:5} God looked upon Abel and accepted his offering. God was pleased with Abel more than with his offering because of his good heart and pure intentions; there was no deceit in him. {77:6} They then came down from the altar and returned to the cave where they lived. Abel, filled with joy for having made his offering, repeated the process three times a week, following his father's example. {77:7} Cain, on the other hand, found no joy in offering; after much anger from his father, he finally made a single offering, but he was focused on the offering itself, selecting the smallest sheep for his sacrifice. {77:8} Therefore, God did not accept Cain's offering because his heart was filled with murderous thoughts. {77:9} The family continued to live together in the cave where Eve had given birth until Cain reached the age of fifteen and Abel turned twelve.

{78:1} Adam said to Eve, "Look, our children have grown up; we need to find wives for them." {78:2} Eve replied, "How can we do that?" {78:3} Adam suggested, "Let's marry Abel's sister to Cain and Cain's sister to Abel." {78:4} Eve responded, "I don't like Cain because he is hard-hearted; let's wait until we can offer sacrifices to the Lord for them." {78:5} Adam didn't say anything more. {78:6} Meanwhile, Satan approached Cain in the form of a man who worked in the fields and told him, "Adam and Eve are planning to marry your sister to your brother Abel and Abel's sister to you." {78:7} "If I didn't care about you, I wouldn't have told you this," he continued. "But if you follow my advice, I'll bring you beautiful clothes, plenty of gold and silver for your wedding, and my friends will help you." {78:8} Cain asked eagerly, "Where are your friends?" {78:9} Satan replied, "They are in a garden to the north, where I once wanted to take your father Adam, but he refused my offer. {78:10} If you accept my words and come to me after your wedding, you will escape the suffering you are in, and you'll be better off than your father Adam." {78:11} At these words, Cain listened intently. {78:12} Instead of staying in the field, he went to his mother Eve, struck her, and cursed her, saying, "Why are you trying to marry my sister off to my brother? Am I dead?" {78:13} His mother calmed him down and sent him back to the field. {78:14} When Adam came home, Eve told him what Cain had done. {78:15} Adam felt grieved and didn't speak. {78:16} The next day, Adam said to Cain, "Take some of your best sheep and offer them to God; I will talk to Abel about bringing an offering of grain." {78:17} They both listened to their father Adam and went to the mountain to offer their gifts at the altar. {78:18} However, Cain acted arrogantly towards Abel, pushing him away from the altar and refusing to let him offer his gift there, while Cain presented his offering with a proud and deceitful heart. {78:19} Abel, on the other hand, found nearby stones, built his own altar, and offered his gift with a humble heart, free from deceit. {78:20} Cain stood by the altar where he had made his offering, calling out to God to accept it, but God did not accept it, and no divine fire came down to consume his offering. {78:21} He remained there, angry and sullen, watching to see if God would accept Abel's offering. {78:22} Abel prayed for God's acceptance, and then divine fire descended, consuming his offering. God was pleased with Abel and sent him an angel in human form who partook of his offering, comforting him and strengthening his heart. {78:23} Meanwhile, Cain watched everything happen with his brother's offering and became enraged. {78:24} In his anger, he began to blaspheme God for not accepting his offering. {78:25} God then spoke to Cain, "Why is your face downcast? If you do what is right, I will accept your offering. You are not angry with me, but with yourself." {78:26} God rebuked Cain because He rejected both him and his offering. {78:27} Cain came down from the altar with a changed color and a sorrowful face, going to his parents to tell them everything that had happened. {78:28} Adam felt great sorrow because God had rejected Cain's offering. {78:29} Abel came down joyfully, telling his father and mother how God accepted his offering, and they rejoiced and kissed him. {78:30} Abel said to Adam, "Because Cain pushed me away from the altar and wouldn't let me offer my gift there, I made my own altar and offered my gift on it." {78:31} Hearing this, Adam was very sorry because it was the same altar where he had first offered his gifts. {78:32} Cain was so sullen and angry that he went back into the field, where Satan came to him again and said, "Now that your brother Abel has gone to your father Adam because you pushed him away, they are kissing him and rejoicing over him much more than over you." {78:33} Hearing this, Cain was filled with rage but kept it to himself, plotting to kill his brother until he brought him into a cave and said to him, {78:34} "Oh brother, the land is so beautiful, with such lovely trees! But you have never enjoyed the field. {78:35} Today, I would really like you to come with me into the fields to enjoy yourself and bless our flocks, because you are righteous, and I love you, dear brother! But you have distanced yourself from me." {78:36} Abel agreed to go with Cain into the field. {78:37} Before going out, Cain said to Abel, "Wait here while I fetch a staff to protect us from wild animals." {78:38} Abel stood innocently waiting, not believing that his brother would harm him. {78:39} When Cain caught up with him, he comforted Abel while walking a little behind him; then he hurried and struck him repeatedly with the staff until Abel was stunned. {78:40} When Abel fell to the ground and realized Cain was going to kill him, he pleaded, "Oh brother, have mercy on me! By the breasts we nursed from, don't strike me down! By the womb that bore us, don't kill me! If you want to end my life, use one of these large stones instead." {78:41} But Cain, the hard-hearted and cruel murderer, picked up a large stone and struck his brother on the head until his brains oozed out, and he lay in a pool of his own blood. {78:42} Cain felt no remorse for what he had done. {78:43} But when the blood of righteous Abel fell upon the ground, it trembled as it absorbed his blood, almost bringing Cain to destruction. {78:44} Abel's blood cried out to God, seeking justice against his murderer. {78:45} Cain immediately started digging into the earth to bury his brother, feeling terrified at the fear that had overtaken him when he saw the earth tremble. {78:46} He placed his brother into a pit he had made and covered him with dirt, but the earth would not accept him and threw him back up. {78:47} Cain tried again to bury Abel, but the earth rejected him once more, throwing him back on top of itself until Cain had done this three times. The earth rejected him the first time because Abel was not the first creation, the second time because Abel was righteous and killed without cause, and the third time to serve as a witness against Cain. {78:48} The earth mocked Cain until God's Word came to him regarding his brother. {78:49} God was very angry and deeply displeased at Abel's death; thunder roared from heaven, and lightning flashed as God's Word came down to Cain, asking, "Where is your brother Abel?" {78:50} Cain answered defiantly and in a harsh voice, "How would I know? Am I my brother's keeper?" {78:51} God replied, "The earth that drank your brother Abel's blood is now cursed; you shall tremble and shake, and this will be a sign for you: whoever finds you will kill you." {78:52} Cain wept at God's words, saying, "Oh God, anyone who finds me will kill me, and I will be erased from the earth!" {78:53} God reassured Cain, "Whoever finds you will not kill you," because God had determined that seven punishments would be spared for anyone who killed Cain. {78:54} God had asked Cain, "Where is your brother?" to give him a chance to repent. {78:55} If Cain had sincerely repented and asked for forgiveness for the murder of Abel, God would have forgiven him. {78:56} When God spoke of cursing the ground that absorbed Abel's blood, He showed mercy to Cain by cursing the ground instead of him, though it was Cain who was guilty of murder. {78:57} God's intent was to keep Cain safe from others, so they wouldn't know of his crime and turn away from him. {78:58} When God asked, "Where is your brother?" and Cain lied in response, God told him he would tremble and quake. {78:59} Cain felt terrified by these words, and through this sign, God made him an example to all creation as the murderer of his brother. God wanted Cain to see the peace he once had and the terror he now faced, hoping he would humble himself before God, repent for his sin, and seek the peace he had lost. {78:60} God did not intend for Cain to die at the hands of another; instead, He wanted Cain to suffer from fasting, praying, and weeping, leading to his eventual repentance. {78:61} The "seven punishments" refer to the seven generations during which Cain would be in torment for killing his brother Abel. {78:62} God placed a mark upon Cain so that no one would kill him. {78:63} Cain then departed and settled in a place far from Eden, which was named "The Land of Nod," where he married a woman who had been created after Eve. {78:64} She bore him a son named Enoch, and Cain built a city and named it after his son. {78:65} God had allowed him to build a city so that he would have comfort, but not to be happy in it, so he would suffer in it and be a witness to others. {78:66} God took care of Abel, who had been unjustly murdered. Abel became the first righteous martyr, receiving the reward of eternal life for being murdered unjustly. {78:67} Adam and Eve mourned for Abel for a long time because of the loss of their son. {78:68} They grieved and wept, feeling deeply sorry that they could not save him. {78:69} The knowledge of good and evil was no longer hidden from them, and God allowed them to understand that death was a consequence of their sin. {78:70} After a while, Adam said to Eve, "Let's bring our other children to God so that He may bless them and guide them." {78:71} So they gathered their remaining children and led them to the altar, where Adam prayed, saying, "Oh Lord, bless my children and guide them." {78:72} And God heard Adam's prayer and blessed them. {78:73} But Satan remained angry at Adam and Eve and vowed to avenge Abel's death, seeking to bring more destruction upon their children. {78:74} Adam and Eve raised their remaining children with love and wisdom, teaching them to worship God. {78:75} They were mindful of the consequences of their previous actions and encouraged their children to live righteously. {78:76} As the years passed, they remembered Abel, teaching their children the story of his life and death, instilling in them the importance of honoring God. {78:77} And so, the legacy of Abel lived on in the hearts of Adam and Eve's children, serving as a reminder of the righteousness God desired and the dangers of sin.

{79:1} And so they continued walking until they reached a deserted place where there were no sheep. Abel then said to Cain, "Look, my brother, we are tired from walking, yet we see no trees, no fruits, no greenery, no sheep, nor any of the things you told me about. Where are those sheep you mentioned that I was supposed to bless?" {79:2} Then Cain said to him, "Keep going, and soon you will see many beautiful things. Go ahead of me until I catch up." {79:3} So Abel walked on ahead, while Cain stayed behind him. {79:4} Abel, in his innocence and without suspicion, did not believe his brother would kill him. {79:5} Then, as Cain approached Abel, he spoke comfortingly to him, walking a little behind him. Suddenly, Cain hurried and struck Abel with his staff, hitting him blow after blow until Abel was stunned. {79:6} When Abel fell to the ground, realizing that his brother intended to kill him, he pleaded with Cain, "Oh, my brother, have mercy on me. By the breasts we both sucked as infants, don't strike me down! By the womb that carried and bore us, don't kill me with that staff! If you intend to kill me, take one of these large stones and strike me dead outright." {79:7} But Cain, being hard-hearted and cruel, took a large stone and hit Abel on the head with it, smashing his skull until his brains spilled out, and he lay there in a pool of his own blood. And Cain did not repent for what he had done. {79:8} However, the earth trembled as it drank the blood of righteous Abel, almost as if it would destroy Cain because of it. {79:9} The blood of Abel cried out to God in a mysterious way, asking for vengeance on his murderer. {79:10} Then Cain, trembling with fear after seeing the earth tremble because of him, began digging a grave for his brother. {79:11} He threw Abel's body into the pit he dug and covered him with dust. But the earth refused to accept the body and threw it up again. {79:12} Cain dug another grave and buried Abel once more, but again the earth threw his brother's body back to the surface. This happened three times. {79:13} The first time, the earth rejected Abel's body because he was not the first creation; the second time, it rejected him because he was righteous and innocent, and was killed unjustly; and the third time, it did so to leave Abel's body as a witness against Cain. {79:14} So the earth mocked Cain until God's Word came to him regarding his brother. {79:15} God was furious and deeply displeased with Abel's death. He sent thunder from heaven, and lightning flashed before Him as His Word came down to Cain, saying, "Where is your brother Abel?" {79:16} Cain, with a proud heart and a defiant voice, replied, "How should I know, O God? Am I my brother's keeper?" {79:17} Then God said to Cain, "Cursed be the earth that has swallowed the blood of your brother Abel. As for you, you shall be cursed with trembling and fear, and this will be a sign: anyone who finds you will want to kill you." {79:18} Cain began to weep because of God's words, and he said, "O God, whoever finds me will kill me, and I will be erased from the face of the earth." {79:19} But God replied, "No one who finds you will kill you." Prior to this, God had declared, "I will withhold seven punishments from anyone who kills Cain." And when God asked Cain, "Where is your brother?" it was in mercy, giving Cain a chance to repent. {79:20} Had Cain at that moment confessed and asked for forgiveness, saying, "God, forgive me for the sin of killing my brother," God would have forgiven him. {79:21} As for God saying, "Cursed be the ground that has drunk the blood of your brother," this too was part of His mercy. God did not directly curse Cain, even though Cain was the one who committed the murder, not the earth. {79:22} In justice, the curse should have fallen on the murderer, but in His mercy, God crafted His words in such a way that no one would shun Cain outright. {79:23} And so He asked Cain again, "Where is your brother?" But Cain responded with lies, saying, "I don't know." To this, God declared, "You will tremble and shake." {79:24} Cain began to tremble and was filled with fear, and through this sign, God made him an example for all creation, showing him as the murderer of his brother. {79:25} God also brought trembling and terror upon Cain so that he would remember the peace he had known before, and contrast it with the terror he now felt. This was meant to humble Cain and lead him to repentance, so that he might seek the peace he once had. {79:26} God's declaration, "I will withhold seven punishments from anyone who kills Cain," did not mean Cain was spared a violent death, but that God intended for him to die through fasting, prayer, and weeping as part of a hard, repentant life until his sin was cleansed. {79:27} The "seven punishments" represent the seven generations during which God waited for Cain to repent for murdering his brother. {79:28} After killing Abel, Cain found no peace anywhere. He returned to Adam & Eve, trembling, terrified, and stained with blood. {79:29} When Adam and Eve saw him, they grieved and wept, not understanding why he was trembling, or why he was covered in blood. {79:30} Cain then ran to his sister, who had been born with him. But when she saw him, she was terrified & asked, "Oh my brother, why are you trembling so?" And he replied, "I have killed our brother Abel in a certain place."

The Second Book of Adam and Eve

{1:1} When Luluwa heard Cain's words, she wept and went to call her father and mother. She told them that Cain had killed his brother Abel. {1:2} They all cried aloud, lifted up their voices, slapped their faces, threw dust on their heads, and tore their garments. Then they went to the place where Abel had been killed. {1:3} They found him lying dead on the ground, surrounded by beasts, and they wept and mourned for him because he was a righteous man. From his body, because of its purity, there came a sweet fragrance, like spices. {1:4} Adam lifted Abel's body, his tears streaming down his face, and carried him to the Cave of Treasures, where he laid him to rest, wrapping him in sweet spices and myrrh. {1:5} Adam and Eve stayed beside Abel's burial site, mourning deeply for one hundred and forty days. Abel was fifteen and a half years old, and Cain was seventeen and a half. {1:6} After the mourning period ended, Cain took his sister Luluwa and married her without permission from his parents, for they were unable to stop him due to their heavy grief. {1:7} Cain moved down to the base of the mountain, away from the Garden, near the spot where he had killed Abel. {1:8} That place had many fruit trees and forests. Cain's sister bore him children, who eventually multiplied and filled the area. {1:9} But Adam and Eve did not come together as husband and wife after Abel's death for seven years. {1:10} After this time, Eve conceived, and Adam said to her, "Let us prepare an offering and present it to God, asking Him to give us a good child in whom we can find comfort, and whom we can marry to Abel's sister." {1:11} They prepared an offering and brought it to the altar, asking God to accept it and bless them with good offspring. {1:12} God heard Adam and accepted his offering. Then they worshipped, and Adam, Eve, and their daughter returned to the Cave of Treasures, where they placed a lamp to burn day and night in front of Abel's body.

{2:1} Eve gave birth to a son who was perfectly beautiful in appearance and figure, more beautiful even than his father Adam. {2:2} Eve felt comforted when she saw him and stayed in the cave for eight days before sending her daughter to tell Adam to come and see the child and name him. {2:3} The daughter stayed by Abel's body while Adam came to see the child. {2:4} When Adam saw the child's beauty and perfect figure, he was filled with joy and comforted for the loss of Abel. {2:5} He named the child Seth, which means "God has heard my prayer and delivered me from my affliction." It also means "power and strength." {2:6} After naming the child, Adam returned to the Cave of Treasures, and his daughter went back to Eve. {2:7} Eve stayed in her cave for forty days, and then she brought the child and her daughter to Adam. {2:8} They came to a river, where Adam and his daughter washed themselves because of their grief for Abel, while Eve and the child washed for purification. {2:9} They returned and brought an offering to the mountain for the child, which God accepted, blessing them and their son Seth. Then they returned to the Cave of Treasures. {2:10} After that, Adam never knew his wife Eve again for the rest of his life, and no more children were born to them except for Cain, Luluwa, Abel, Aklia, and Seth.

{3:1} When Adam saw Seth becoming more separated from Eve, he worried and tried to make Seth stay closer. {3:2} Adam went up above the Cave of Treasures and slept there alone every night, coming down to the cave during the day to pray and receive blessings. {3:3} In the evening, he would go back to the roof of the cave, sleeping alone out of fear that Satan might tempt him. He stayed apart for thirty-nine days. {3:4} Satan, seeing Adam alone, fasting and praying, appeared to him on the fortieth night in the form of a beautiful woman. She came and stood before Adam, saying, {3:5} "Adam, since you have lived in this cave, we have had peace from you, and your prayers have reached us, bringing us comfort. {3:6} But now that you have gone up to sleep on the roof, we are filled with doubt about you, and great sorrow has come upon us because of your separation from Eve. {3:7} Your prayers up here are scattered, and your heart is distracted, unlike when you were inside the cave, where your prayers were like a fire that gave us rest. {3:8} I also grieve for your children who are separated from you, and my sorrow is deep for the death of your righteous son Abel, for everyone mourns the righteous. {3:9} I was glad at the birth of your son Seth, but I also grieved for Eve, who is my sister. When God put you into a deep sleep and took her from your side, He brought me out with her, though He raised her up to be with you and left me behind. {3:10} I was joyful for my sister's sake, but God made me a promise, saying, 'Do not be sad, for when Adam separates from Eve and goes up to the roof, I will send you to him, and you will marry him and bear him five children, just as Eve did.' {3:11} Now that promise is fulfilled, for God has sent me to marry you and bear you children even more beautiful than those of Eve. {3:12} You are still young, Adam. Do not end your youth in sorrow but spend your days in joy and pleasure, for your time is short, and your trials are many. Be strong and live out your days in happiness with me." {3:13} She then approached Adam and embraced him, but when Adam realized he was about to fall into temptation, he prayed to God with all his heart to save him. {3:14} God then sent His Word to Adam, saying, "Adam, this figure is the same one who promised you godhood and majesty. He is not your friend. He appears to you sometimes as a woman, sometimes as an angel, sometimes as a serpent, and other times as a god, but all he wants is to destroy your soul."

{4:1} Then God commanded Satan to reveal his true, hideous form to Adam. {4:2} When Adam saw him, he was filled with fear and trembling. {4:3} God said to Adam, "Look at this devil and see his repulsive form. It was he who made you fall from light into darkness, from peace into toil and suffering. {4:4} Look at the one who claimed to be God. Can God be black? (referring to evil or dark-heartedness) Would God take the form of a woman? Is anyone stronger than God, or can He be overpowered? {4:5} See how he stands here bound in the air before you, unable to escape. Do not fear him anymore. Be cautious of him, no matter what form he takes." {4:6} Then God drove Satan away from Adam, strengthened him, and comforted his heart, saying, "Go back to the Cave of Treasures and remain with Eve. I will calm your desires." {4:7} From that moment, they were freed from carnal lust and enjoyed peace by God's command, but this special grace was given only to them and not to their descendants. {4:8} Adam worshipped God for delivering him & calming his passions, and he returned to live with Eve as before, ending the forty days of their separation.

{5:1} When Seth was seven years old, he already knew the difference between good and evil and was diligent in fasting and praying, spending his nights asking God for mercy and forgiveness. {5:2} He also fasted when offering his daily sacrifices, more than even his father did, for Seth was as beautiful as an angel of God. {5:3} His soul was pure, and because of this, he brought offerings every day that pleased God. {5:4} God was pleased with both Seth's offering and his purity, and Seth continued living according to God's will, and that of his father and mother, until he was seven years old. {5:5} One day, after Seth had finished offering his sacrifice and was coming down from the altar, Satan appeared to him as a bright and beautiful angel, holding a staff of light and dressed in a glowing robe. {5:6} Satan greeted Seth with a warm smile and began to deceive him with sweet words, saying, "Seth, why do you stay in this barren mountain? It is full of rocks, sand, and trees that bear no good fruit, a wilderness without cities or homes, a place of hardship and misery. {5:7} We live in beautiful places, in a world of light far better than this earth. Our women are more beautiful than any others, and I want you to marry one of them because I see how handsome you are, and there is no woman here good enough for you. {5:8} In your world, there are only five souls, but in our world, there are many people, men and women, more beautiful than one another. I wish to take you to our world so that you may see our dwellings and meet our women. You will feel at peace with us, and when you marry one of our beautiful women, she will bear you children as lovely as her."

{6:1} When Seth heard these words, he was amazed and let his heart lean towards Satan's deceitful speech, saying, "Did you say there is another world created other than this one, with other creatures more beautiful than those in this world?" {6:2} And Satan replied, "Yes, you have heard me, but I will yet praise them and their ways in your hearing." {6:3} Seth then said to him, "Your speech amazes me, and your description is beautiful." {6:4} "But I cannot go with you today; not until I have gone to my father, Adam, and to my mother, Eve, and told them all you have said. Then, if they allow me, I will come." {6:5} Seth continued, "I am afraid to act without my father's and mother's permission, lest I perish like my brother Cain, and like my father Adam, who disobeyed God's command. But you know this place; meet me here tomorrow." {6:6} When Satan heard this, he said to Seth, "If you tell your father Adam what I have said, he will not let you come with me. But listen to me; do not tell your father or mother, and come with me today to our world. There, you will see beautiful things, enjoy yourself, and revel among my children, taking your fill of joy and mirth. Rejoice forevermore! I will bring you back tomorrow; or, if you wish, stay with me." {6:7} But Seth answered, "The spirit of my father and mother is tied to me, and if I hide from them for a day, they will die, and God will hold me guilty of sinning against them." {6:8} "Except for when they know I have come to this place to bring my offering, they would not be separated from me even for an hour. Nor would I go anywhere unless they permitted it. They treat me with such kindness because I return to them quickly." {6:9} Satan then said, "What will happen if you hide yourself from them for one night and return at dawn?" {6:10} But Seth, seeing how Satan kept talking and wouldn't leave, ran up to the altar, spreading his hands to God and seeking His deliverance. {6:11} Then God sent His Word and cursed Satan, who fled. {6:12} Seth, who had gone up to the altar, said to himself, "This altar is a place of offering, and God is here. A divine fire will consume the offering, and Satan won't be able to harm me or take me away from here." {6:13} Seth then descended from the altar and went to find his father and mother, who were longing to hear his voice, for he had been delayed. {6:14} He began to tell them what had happened with Satan, who had disguised himself as an angel. {6:15} When Adam heard this, he kissed Seth's face and warned him about that angel, explaining that it was indeed Satan in disguise. Adam then took Seth to the Cave of Treasures, and they rejoiced there. {6:16} From that day forward, Adam and Eve never parted from Seth, whether he went to offer or for any other purpose. {6:17} This incident happened when Seth was nine years old.

{7:1} When Adam saw that Seth had a pure heart, he wanted Seth to marry, fearing the enemy might approach and overcome him. {7:2} So Adam said to his son Seth, "My son, I wish for you to wed your sister Aklia, Abel's sister, so that she may bear you children who will replenish the earth, as God promised." {7:3} "Do not be afraid, my son. There is no disgrace in it. I want you to marry to prevent the enemy from overpowering you." {7:4} Seth did not desire to marry, but out of obedience to his father and mother, he said nothing. {7:5} So Adam married him to Aklia, and Seth was fifteen years old at the time. {7:6} When Seth turned twenty, he fathered a son whom he named Enos, and he later had other children. {7:7} Enos grew up, married, and fathered Cainan. {7:8} Cainan also grew up, married, and fathered Mahalaleel. {7:9} These fathers were born during Adam's lifetime and dwelled near the Cave of Treasures. {7:10} Adam lived nine hundred and thirty years, and Mahalaleel lived one hundred. When Mahalaleel grew up, he loved fasting and praying, working diligently until Adam's days drew near their end.

{8:1} When Adam sensed his end approaching, he called Seth to him in the Cave of Treasures, saying, {8:2} "Seth, my son, bring me your children and grandchildren so that I may bless them before I die." {8:3} Seth wept over Adam's face but gathered his children and grandchildren to present them to Adam. {8:4} When Adam saw them, he wept at the thought of being separated from them. {8:5} Seeing their father weep, they all wept, falling upon his face and lamenting, saying, "How shall you be parted from us, Father? How shall the earth receive and hide you from our eyes?" {8:6} Adam blessed them all and said to Seth, "You know that this world is full of sorrow and weariness, and you know all that has come upon us. So I command you to keep innocence, purity, and justice. Trust in God and don't listen to Satan's deceitful words or his illusions." {8:7} "Keep the commandments I give you today and pass them to Enos, and let Enos give them to Cainan, and Cainan to Mahalaleel, so that the commandments remain firm among your descendants." {8:8} "After I die, wrap my body with myrrh, aloes, and cassia, and leave me here in the Cave of Treasures with the tokens God gave us from the Garden." {8:9} "My son, in the future, a great flood will come and destroy all living creatures, sparing only eight souls." {8:10} "Let those who survive the flood carry my body from this cave. Place my body in a ship until the waters subside, then bury me in the center of the earth, the place from which God will come to save all our descendants." {8:11} "Now, Seth, my son, lead your people, guard them in the fear of God, and teach them not to listen to Satan." {8:12} "Separate your descendants from Cain's descendants. Do not let them mix in words or deeds." {8:13} Adam blessed Seth, his children, and all his descendants. {8:14} He turned to Seth and Eve, saying, "Keep this gold, incense, and myrrh as signs from God. When the flood comes, take these with you, and bury them with my body in the middle of the earth." {8:15} "In time, the city where these are buried will be plundered, but the gold, incense, and myrrh will remain intact until the Word of God becomes flesh. Kings will offer them to Him as symbols of His kingship, divinity, and passion." {8:16} "The gold will signify His victory over Satan, incense His resurrection and ascension, and myrrh His suffering." {8:17} "Seth, I have revealed hidden mysteries to you. Keep my commandments for yourself and your people."

{9:1} When Adam finished instructing Seth, his limbs weakened, his hands and feet lost strength, his mouth closed, and his tongue fell silent. He closed his eyes and passed away. {9:2} Seeing Adam's death, his children mourned and wept over him, young and old. {9:3} Adam died at nine hundred and thirty years old, on the fifteenth day of Barmudeh (an ancient Egyptian month), in the ninth hour. It was a Friday, the same day he was created and rested, and the same hour he left the Garden. {9:4} Seth embalmed Adam with sweet spices from sacred trees on the Holy Mountain and placed his body on the eastern side of the cave, on the incense side, with a lampstand burning before it. {9:5} His children mourned him throughout the night until dawn. {9:6} Seth, Enos, and Cainan took offerings to the altar where Adam once offered gifts to God. {9:7} Eve advised them, "Wait until we have prayed to God to accept our offering and take Adam's soul into His rest." {9:8} And they all stood and prayed.

{10:1} After they finished praying, the Word of God came and comforted them about Adam. {10:2} They offered their gifts for themselves and for their father. {10:3} God's Word came to Seth, saying, "Seth, Seth, Seth, three times. Just as I was with your father, so will I be with you until I fulfill My promise to him to send My Word and save you and your descendants." {10:4} When Seth heard these words, he rejoiced greatly, and he and his people offered more gifts on the altar. {10:5} But Adam's body remained in the Cave of Treasures.

{11:1} After the death of Adam and Eve, Seth separated his children and their descendants from those of Cain. Cain and his descendants moved westward, away from where he had killed his brother Abel. {11:2} Meanwhile, Seth and his children settled in the northern part of the mountain near the Cave of Treasures, so they could be close to their father Adam. Seth was tall, virtuous, and had a strong mind; he led his people with innocence, repentance, and humility, and he ensured that none of them interacted with Cain's descendants. Because of their purity, they were called "Children of God," and they remained with God instead of joining the fallen angels. They continuously praised God and sang hymns in their cave, the Cave of Treasures. {11:3} Seth would often stand before the bodies of his father Adam and mother Eve, praying day and night for mercy for himself and his children, especially seeking guidance when dealing with difficult matters. {11:4} Seth and his family preferred spiritual pursuits over earthly work; they focused solely on praise, doxology, and hymns to God. Because of their purity, they could hear and see angels who praised and glorified God, whether they were sent from the garden or when ascending to heaven. {11:5} The garden was not far above them, only about fifteen spiritual cubits high, and one spiritual cubit equals three human cubits, making it a total of forty-five cubits. {11:6} Seth and his family lived on the mountain below the garden, neither sowing nor reaping; they did not grow food for their bodies, not even wheat, but only offered sacrifices. They fed on the fruit and delicious trees that grew on the mountain where they lived. {11:7} Seth often fasted every forty days, as did his eldest children, for they could smell the fragrant trees in the garden when the wind blew their way. They were joyful, innocent, and without sudden fears, jealousy, evil actions, or hatred among them. There were no base desires; no foul words or curses came from their mouths, nor did they engage in deceitful plans. The people of that time rarely swore, and only did so in dire circumstances, swearing by the blood of Abel the just. {11:8} They encouraged their children and women to fast, pray, and worship the Most High God daily in the cave. They blessed themselves in the body of their father Adam & anointed themselves with it, a practice they continued until Seth's time drew near.

{12:1} Then Seth the just called his son Enos, Cainan (son of Enos), and Mahalaleel (son of Cainan), saying, "As my end approaches, I want to build a roof over the altar where gifts are offered." {12:2} They listened to his command and went out, both young and old, and worked hard to construct a beautiful roof over the altar. {12:3} Seth hoped that this would bring blessings upon his children on the mountain and that he could present an offering for them before he died. {12:4} Once the roof was finished, he instructed them to make offerings. They diligently prepared these and brought them to their father Seth, who accepted them and offered them on the altar, praying for God to accept their gifts, have mercy on his children, and protect them from Satan. {12:5} God accepted Seth's offering and blessed him and his children. God then promised Seth, saying, "At the end of five and a half great days, regarding which I have made a promise to you and your father, I will send My Word and save you and your descendants." {12:6} After this, Seth and his family gathered together, descended from the altar, and returned to the Cave of Treasures, where they prayed, blessed themselves in the body of their father Adam, and anointed themselves with it. {12:7} Seth remained in the Cave of Treasures for a few days before suffering until his death. {12:8} Enos, his firstborn son, came with Cainan, Mahalaleel, Jared (Mahalaleel's son), Enoch (Jared's son), along with their wives and children, seeking a blessing from Seth. {12:9} Seth prayed over them, blessed them, and adjured them by the blood of Abel the just, saying, "I urge you, my children, not to let any of you descend from this Holy and Pure Mountain. Do not associate with the children of Cain the murderer and sinner, who killed his brother, for you know, my children, that we flee from him and all his sins with all our strength." {12:10} After saying this, Seth blessed Enos, his firstborn son, and commanded him to serve in purity before the body of their father Adam all the days of his life and to visit the altar Seth had built. He instructed him to guide his people with righteousness, judgment, and purity throughout his life. {12:11} Then Seth's limbs weakened; he lost power in his hands and feet, his mouth became unable to speak, and he passed away the day after his nine hundred twelfth year, on the twenty-seventh day of the month Abib, with Enoch being twenty years old at the time. {12:12} They carefully wrapped Seth's body, embalmed it with sweet spices, and laid him in the Cave of Treasures, on the right side of their father Adam's body, mourning for him for forty days and offering gifts for him, just as they had done for Adam. {12:13} After Seth's death, Enos took charge of his people, nurturing them in righteousness and judgment, as his father had instructed. {12:14} By the time Enos reached eight hundred and twenty years, Cain had a large number of descendants, as they married frequently and indulged in base desires until the land below the mountain was filled with them.

{13:1} In those days, Lamech the blind, a descendant of Cain, lived with his son Atun, and together they had much livestock. {13:2} Lamech often sent Atun to care for the cattle with a young shepherd, who would come home in the evening, crying before his grandfather and his father Atun and mother Hazina, saying, "I cannot tend these cattle alone, for someone might rob me or kill me for them." Among Cain's descendants, there was much theft, murder, and sin. {13:3} Lamech felt pity for the young shepherd and said, "He might be overpowered when alone." {13:4} So Lamech took a bow that he had kept since his youth, before he went blind, and he equipped himself with large arrows, smooth stones, and a sling, then went to the field with the young shepherd, placing himself behind the cattle while the shepherd watched them. {13:5} This continued for many days. Meanwhile, Cain, since God had cast him out and cursed him with trembling and terror, could neither settle nor find rest in any place; he wandered from location to location. {13:6} In his wanderings, he approached Lamech's wives and inquired about him. They told him, "He is in the field with the cattle." {13:7} Cain then went to find Lamech, and as he entered the field, the young shepherd heard the noise he made and saw the cattle huddling together in fear. {13:8} He asked Lamech, "Is that a wild beast or a thief?" {13:9} Lamech replied, "Describe to me what he looks like when he approaches." {13:10} Lamech drew his bow, placed an arrow on it, and readied a stone in the sling. When Cain came from the open field, the shepherd said to Lamech, "Shoot, behold, he is coming!" {13:11} Lamech shot an arrow at Cain, hitting him in the side. He then struck him with a stone from his sling, knocking out both of Cain's eyes, and Cain fell down and died. {13:12} Lamech and the young shepherd approached and found him lying on the ground. The young shepherd said to Lamech, "It's Cain our grandfather whom you have killed, my lord!" {13:13} Lamech then felt regret, and in his bitterness, he clapped his hands together, striking the head of the youth with his flat palm, causing him to fall as if dead. But Lamech thought it was an act, so he picked up a stone and struck him, crushing his head until he died.

{14:1} When Enos reached nine hundred years of age, all the children of Seth, Cainan, and his firstborn, along with their wives and children, gathered around him, seeking a blessing. {14:2} Enos prayed over them, blessed them, and urged them by the blood of Abel the just, saying, "Let none of your children go down from this Holy Mountain, and let them not associate with the children of Cain the murderer." {14:3} Enos then called his son Cainan and instructed him, "Listen, my son, and take to heart your people; establish them in righteousness and innocence; and serve before the body of our father Adam all your life." {14:4} After this, Enos found peace, passing away at nine hundred eighty-five years old. Cainan carefully wrapped him up and laid him in the Cave of Treasures, to the left of his father Adam, and he mourned for him forty days, offering gifts as he had done for Adam and Seth. {14:5} Cainan then took charge of his people, instructing them in righteousness and judgment, as his father had done. {14:6} At this time, the children of Cain multiplied, and many were born. Cainan saw the great work of the hands of God, the creation of Adam and Eve, and the dwelling place of Seth, and many evil deeds began to multiply.

{15:1} As Cainan turned seven hundred and thirty years old, Lamech returned from his time of wandering in the wilderness, for he had lost hope of finding refuge. {15:2} He came to his wives and children, seeking peace. When he arrived, he felt weak and weary. {15:3} He called all his children and wives to him and said, "You are witnesses that I have seen many sorrows during my life; I never sought comfort, for no one ever offered me comfort." {15:4} The children of Cain grew evil and robbed from the children of Seth, while the children of Seth were innocent and pure, offering sacrifices and praying to God for help and salvation. {15:5} One day, Lamech went out with his bow and arrows, gathering wild animals for food. As he wandered, he came upon the children of Seth. {15:6} Seeing them, Lamech spoke with them; they discussed the troubles and sorrows of the world. {15:7} As Lamech returned home, he felt a great burden. {15:8} When he came to his wife, he asked her, "Did you see our children?" {15:9} She replied, "Yes, they are playing and eating together." {15:10} Lamech lamented, "How long shall we remain in sorrow?" {15:11} As they spoke, Lamech's son Atun entered and said, "Father, did you see that we have built a place to worship God?" {15:12} Lamech rejoiced at this news and said, "This is a good sign!" {15:13} They gathered & sang praises to God, celebrating the blessings He had given them.

{16:1} Then Mahalaleel took care of his people, guiding them with righteousness and innocence, and ensuring they did not associate with the children of Cain. {16:2} He continued to pray and serve in the Cave of Treasures before the body of our father Adam, asking God for mercy for himself and his people until he was eight hundred seventy years old, when he fell ill. {16:3} All his children gathered around him to see him and ask for his blessing before he left this world. {16:4} Mahalaleel sat up on his bed, tears streaming down his face, and called his eldest son, Jared, who came to him. {16:5} He kissed Jared and said, "Jared, my son, I urge you by Him who created heaven and earth, to take care of your people and guide them in righteousness and innocence; do not let any of them go down from this Holy Mountain to the children of Cain, or they will perish with them. {16:6} Listen, my son, a great destruction will come upon this earth because of them; God will be angry with the world and will destroy them with a flood. {16:7} But I also know that your children will not listen to you, and they will go down from this mountain and mingle with the children of Cain, and they will perish with them. {16:8} Oh my son! Teach them and watch over them, so that no guilt falls on you because of them." {16:9} Mahalaleel continued, "When I die, embalm my body and lay it in the Cave of Treasures next to the bodies of my fathers; then stand by my body and pray to God, and take care of them, fulfilling your duty before them until you find rest yourself." {16:10} Mahalaleel then blessed all his children and lay down on his bed, entering into rest like his fathers. {16:11} When Jared saw that Mahalaleel was dead, he wept, sorrowed, embraced, and kissed his hands and feet, and so did all his children. {16:12} His children carefully embalmed him and laid him next to his fathers. Then they mourned for him for forty days.

{17:1} Jared kept his father's command and ruled over his people like a lion. He guided them with righteousness and innocence and commanded them to do nothing without his approval, fearing they might go to the children of Cain. {17:2} He repeatedly gave them orders and continued to do so until he was four hundred eighty-five years old. {17:3} At the end of those years, Jared received a sign. While standing like a lion before the bodies of his fathers, praying and warning his people, Satan became envious and created a beautiful apparition because Jared refused to let his children act without his guidance. {17:4} Satan appeared to him with thirty of his followers, in the form of handsome men; Satan himself was the oldest and tallest among them, with a fine beard. {17:5} They stood at the entrance of the cave and called to Jared from within it. {17:6} He came out to them and found them looking like radiant, beautiful men. He was amazed at their looks and wondered if they were from the children of Cain. {17:7} He thought to himself, "Since the children of Cain cannot climb this mountain, and none of them are as handsome as these men, they must be strangers." {17:8} Jared greeted them and asked the elder among them, "My father, explain to me the wonder I see in you, and tell me who you are with." {17:9} The elder began to weep, and the others wept with him, saying to Jared, "I am Adam, the one whom God made first; and this is my son Abel, whom his brother Cain murdered, influenced by Satan. {17:10} This is my son Seth, whom I asked of the Lord, and He gave him to me to comfort me instead of Abel. {17:11} Then this one is my son Enos, son of Seth, and that other one is Cainan, son of Enos, and this other is Mahalaleel, son of Cainan, your father." {17:12} But Jared was still astonished by their appearance and the elder's words. {17:13} The elder continued, "Do not be amazed, my son; we live in the land north of the garden that God created before the world. He did not allow us to live there, placing us inside the garden, which is below where you now dwell. {17:14} After I sinned, He made me leave, and I have been living in this cave; great troubles have come upon me. When my death drew near, I commanded my son Seth to take care of his people well; this command should be passed down from generation to generation. {17:15} But, oh Jared, my son, we live in beautiful lands, while you live in misery, as your father Mahalaleel informed me, telling me that a great flood will come to destroy the earth. {17:16} Therefore, for your sake, I came with my children to visit you, but found you standing here weeping, and your children scattered about the mountain, suffering from the heat. {17:17} We met others living below this mountain who inhabit a beautiful country full of trees, fruits, and all kinds of greenery; it resembles a garden. When we found them, we thought they were you until your father Mahalaleel told me otherwise. {17:18} Now, my son, listen to my advice: go down to them, you and your children. You will find relief from all this suffering. But if you refuse to go down, then take your children and come with us to our garden; you will live in our beautiful land and find rest from all the troubles you and your children are facing." {17:19} Jared was amazed by the elder's words and began to wander around, but he could not find any of his children. {17:20} He replied to the elder, "Why have you hidden yourselves until now?" {17:21} The elder responded, "If your father hadn't informed us, we would not have known." {17:22} Jared believed the elder's words were true. {17:23} The elder asked, "Why did you turn around like that?" Jared answered, "I was looking for one of my children to inform him about going with you and their coming down to those you spoke of." {17:24} When the elder heard Jared's intention, he said, "Forget that plan for now and come with us; you will see our land. If you like the land we inhabit, we will return with you and your family. But if you don't like our country, you may come back to your own." {17:25} The elder urged Jared to join them before one of his children arrived to advise him otherwise. {17:26} Jared then left the cave and followed them, and they comforted him until they reached the top of the mountain of the sons of Cain. {17:27} The elder then said to one of his companions, "We forgot something back at the cave, the special garment we brought to dress Jared." {17:28} He instructed one of them to go back while they waited for him. {17:29} That companion left, but as he was a short distance away, the elder called to him and said, "Wait until I come and speak to you." {17:30} He paused, and the elder went up to him, saying, "One thing we neglected to do at the cave is to put out the lamp burning inside it, above the bodies there. After that, come back quickly." {17:31} The companion did as instructed, put out the lamp, and returned, bringing an illusion with him to show them. {17:32} When Jared saw it, he was amazed by its beauty and grace, feeling joy in his heart, believing it was all real. {17:33} While they were waiting, three of them went into the houses of the sons of Cain and said, "Bring us some food today by the fountain of water for us and our companions to eat." {17:34} When the sons of Cain saw them, they were astonished and thought, "These men are beautiful, unlike anyone we have ever seen." So they gathered and came with them to the fountain of water to meet their companions. {17:35} They found them so incredibly handsome that they shouted for others to come and look at these beautiful beings. Then many men and women surrounded them. {17:36} The elder told them, "We are strangers in your land, please bring us good food and drink, you and your women, so we can refresh ourselves together." {17:37} When the sons of Cain heard this, each one brought his wife, and some brought their daughters, so many women came to them, each addressing Jared, either for himself or for his wife. {17:38} But when Jared saw their actions, he was horrified; he refused to eat or drink anything they offered. {17:39} The elder saw him pulling away and said, "Do not be sad; I am the great elder, and you should follow my example." {17:40} He spread his arms and took one of the women, and five of his companions did the same in front of Jared, encouraging him to follow their lead. {17:41} But when Jared saw them acting disgracefully, he wept and thought to himself, "My father Mahalaleel was right; I cannot let my children go down with these people." {17:42} Jared said to them, "Go away; you are making me ashamed before God. The sons of Cain will perish in this flood." {17:43} The elder said, "You are mistaken, my son. Your father Mahalaleel is no longer living; you should not worry about him." {17:44} Then Jared realized it was not his father Mahalaleel but some of the children of Cain who would perish with their father. {17:45} He saw them continue acting in such a disgraceful manner, and the elder encouraged him to stay. {17:46} When the elder realized Jared was strong-willed, he urged him to depart so they would not be stuck in this place. {17:47} Jared turned back and went up the mountain, returning to the Cave of Treasures, and he prayed to God, asking Him to forgive him for being misled by the elder.

{18:1} After three days, Jared took all his children and moved away, leading them back to the Holy Mountain and seeking refuge there. {18:2} After some time, Jared died, and all his children buried him in the Cave of Treasures with their grandfather Adam, mourning for him for forty days. The children of Jared often visited him, seeking his blessing and advice for everything they did, and they did tasks for him whenever he needed help. However, this time when they entered the cave, they found it empty; the lamp was extinguished, the bodies of their ancestors were scattered about, and voices emerged from them by God's power, saying, "Satan, in a vision, has deceived our son, trying to destroy him as he destroyed our son Cain." {18:3} They also said, "Lord God of heaven and earth, save our son from Satan's grip, who has created a great and false vision before him." They spoke of other matters through God's power. {18I:4} When Jared's children heard these voices, they were afraid and wept for their father, not knowing what had happened to him. {18I:5} They mourned for him all day until sunset. {18I:6} Then Jared returned, looking sorrowful and distressed, troubled by being away from his ancestors' bodies. {18I:7} As he approached the cave, his children saw him and rushed to embrace him, crying out, "Father, where have you been, and why have you left us, as you never did before?" They added, "When you disappeared, the lamp over our fathers' bodies went out, the bodies were scattered, and voices came from them." {18I:8} Hearing this, Jared felt sad and went into the cave, where he found the bodies scattered, the lamp extinguished, and the ancestors praying for his deliverance from Satan's influence. {18I:9} Jared fell upon the bodies and embraced them, saying, "O my fathers, through your intercession, may God save me from Satan! I ask you to pray that God protects me from him until the day I die." {18I:10} All the voices ceased except for Adam's, who spoke to Jared by God's power, saying, "Jared, my son, offer gifts to God for delivering you from Satan's grasp; when you bring those offerings, do so on the altar where I offered mine. Be careful of Satan; he has deceived me many times with his visions, trying to destroy me, but God rescued me. {18I:11} Command your people to remain vigilant against him, and never cease to offer gifts to God." {18I:12} After Adam's voice fell silent, Jared and his children were amazed. They arranged the bodies as they had been and spent the night praying until dawn. {18I:13} The next day, Jared made an offering on the altar as Adam had instructed. While approaching the altar, he prayed for mercy and forgiveness for his sin regarding the extinguished lamp. {18I:14} Then God appeared to Jared at the altar, blessed him and his children, accepted their offerings, and instructed Jared to take sacred fire from the altar to relight the lamp that shone on Adam's body.

{19:1} God then revealed to him again the promise He had made to Adam, explaining the 5500 years and disclosing the mystery of His coming to earth. {19:2} God told Jared, "As for the fire you took from the altar to light the lamp, let it remain with you to illuminate the bodies, and it must not leave the cave until Adam's body is taken out of it. {19:3} But Jared, be sure to tend the fire, keeping it bright in the lamp, and do not leave the cave until you receive a command through a vision, not a mere appearance. {19:4} Again, instruct your people not to associate with Cain's descendants or adopt their ways; for I am God who does not love hatred and wicked deeds." {19:5} God gave many other commandments to Jared and blessed him, then withdrew His word from him. {19:6} Jared approached with his children, took some fire, descended to the cave, and lit the lamp before Adam's body, giving his people the commandments as God had instructed. {19:7} This event took place when Jared was four hundred fifty years old; many other wonders also occurred, but we record only this one for brevity. {19:8} Jared continued to teach his children for eighty years, but after that, they began to disobey his commandments and acted without his counsel. They began to leave the Holy Mountain one by one to mix with Cain's descendants, engaging in sinful associations.

{20:1} The reason Jared's children descended from the Holy Mountain will now be revealed. {20:2} After Cain settled in the land of dark soil and his descendants multiplied, one of them named Genun, the son of Lamech the blind who killed Cain, emerged. {20:3} In his childhood, Satan possessed Genun and inspired him to create various musical instruments—trumpets, horns, string instruments, cymbals, psalteries, lyres, harps, and flutes—playing them constantly. {20:4} As he played, Satan infused them with power, producing beautiful and enchanting sounds. {20:5} Genun gathered many people to play these instruments, and the sounds delighted the children of Cain, igniting sinful desires among them as Satan fueled their lust. {20:6} Satan also taught Genun how to ferment strong drinks from grain, and Genun set up drink houses, offering all sorts of fruits and flowers for them to enjoy. {20:7} In this way, Genun multiplied sin greatly, acted pridefully, and led the children of Cain into various vile acts they had never known before. {20:8} As Satan noticed their submission to Genun and listened to him, he rejoiced and increased Genun's skill until he learned to make weapons of war from iron. {20:9} When they were drunk, hatred and violence escalated among them; one man would use force against another to teach him evil, even taking his children and violating them before him. {20:10} Those who felt overwhelmed sought refuge with Genun, becoming his allies. {20:11} Sin increased greatly among them until men were marrying their own sisters, daughters, mothers, or even their aunts, losing all sense of morality and committing wickedness, defiling the earth with sin, and provoking God, the Judge who created them. {20:12} Genun gathered many people to play horns and other instruments at the foot of the Holy Mountain to attract the children of Seth living above. {20:13} When the children of Seth heard the noise, they were intrigued and came in groups to the mountain's edge to watch for a whole year. {20:14} At the end of that year, Genun saw that he was gradually winning them over, and Satan entered him again, teaching him how to dye fabrics in various colors, including crimson and purple, and how to create beautiful garments. {20:15} The children of Cain, dressed in bright colors and adorned with fine clothing, gathered at the foot of the mountain, participating in races and indulging in all sorts of immoral acts. {20:16} Meanwhile, the children of Seth were praying and praising God at the Holy Mountain, where the fallen angels had once dwelled, and God had called them "angels" because He was pleased with them. {20:17} However, they soon ceased to obey His commandments and neglected the promises made to their ancestors; they relaxed their fasting, prayer, and heeded Jared's counsel less and less. They kept gathering on the mountain top to watch the children of Cain from morning until evening, captivated by their beautiful clothes and ornaments. {20:18} The children of Cain looked up and saw the children of Seth in groups at the top of the mountain, calling out to them to come down. {20:19} The children of Seth replied from above, "We don't know the way down." Hearing this, Genun devised a plan to lure them down. {20:20} That night, Satan appeared to him, saying, "There is no way for them to come down from their mountain; tomorrow tell them, 'Come to the west side of the mountain; there you will find a stream that flows down between two hills. Follow that path to us.'" {20:21} When morning came, Genun played the horns and drums as usual. The children of Seth heard and came down to listen. {20:22} Genun then told them, "Go to the west side of the mountain; there you'll find a way down." {20:23} The children of Seth, after hearing this, returned to the cave to inform Jared of what they had learned. {20:24} When Jared heard this, he was troubled, knowing they would disregard his counsel. {20:25} A hundred of Jared's sons gathered together and said, "Come, let's go down to the children of Cain, see what they do, and enjoy their company." {20:26} Hearing this, Jared was deeply troubled and rose with urgency to stand among them, swearing by the blood of Abel the just, "Let not a single one of you descend from this holy and pure mountain where our fathers have commanded us to dwell." {20:27} But seeing they did not listen, he continued, "O my innocent and holy children, know that once you leave this holy mountain, God will not permit you to return." {20:28} He pleaded again, swearing by the deaths of our ancestors Adam, Abel, Seth, Enos, Cainan, and Mahalaleel, to obey his commandments. {20:29} But they left without his counsel and descended from the Holy Mountain, following Genun down to the foot of the mountain to enjoy the pleasures of the children of Cain, abandoning the ways of their fathers. {20:30} Jared then called out to them from above, "My beloved children, don't go down to the children of Cain! Listen to my advice and remain steadfast; do not disobey the commands given to you!" {20:31} But they would not listen and continued down to enjoy the feasts prepared for them, lured by the delights of the children of Cain. {20:32} Upon reaching the foot of the mountain, they saw a vast crowd of children of Cain, and they enjoyed the delights of the feasts and drank strong drinks prepared for them by Genun. {20:33} When the children of Cain beheld the children of Seth, they mocked them, saying, "Look at the descendants of Seth! They don't know how to dance, sing, or enjoy the pleasures of life like we do!" {20:34} Seeing their contempt, the children of Seth felt ashamed and fell into despair. {20:35} In the evening, when Genun called them to dance, they joined in; thus, they defiled themselves before God. {20:36} They forgot the commandments of their fathers, wandered further from the Holy Mountain, and acted shamefully. {20:37} After this, they became accustomed to drinking strong drinks and committing sins, mixing with the children of Cain until they learned their vile acts. {20:38} Many of Jared's sons remained with the children of Cain, indulging in their sinful pleasures and disregarding Jared's commands. {20:39} Thus, sin increased among the children of Seth; they mixed with the children of Cain and soon began to leave the Holy Mountain one by one, following Genun to indulge in vice. {20:40} They abandoned the fasting and prayers established by their fathers. {20:41} As Jared watched them sink deeper into sin, he wept and cried out to God, saying, "O Lord God, forgive my children for their sins, for they are lost in their ways!" {20:42} God then spoke to Jared, saying, "Do not worry, for I will protect you and your descendants. Stay strong, and do not fear. There will be a time of repentance when they return to Me." {20:43} Jared prayed and continued to dwell in the Holy Mountain, but in the days that followed, sin greatly increased among the children of Seth.

{21:1} After this, another group gathered together, and they went to look for their brethren, but they perished just like the others. {21:2} This continued, with group after group until only a few of them were left. {21:3} Then Jared fell sick from grief, and his illness was such that the day of his death was near. {21:4} He called Enoch, his eldest son, Methuselah, Enoch's son, Lamech, Methuselah's son, and Noah, Lamech's son. {21:5} When they arrived, he prayed over them and blessed them, saying, "You are righteous, innocent sons; do not go down from this holy mountain; for behold, your children and your children's children have descended from this holy mountain and have estranged themselves from it through their abominable lust and transgressions of God's commandments. {21:6} But I know, through the power of God, that He will not leave you on this holy mountain because your children have transgressed His commandments and those of our fathers, which we received from them. {21:7} But, my sons, God will take you to a strange land, and you will never again return to behold this garden and this holy mountain with your own eyes. {21:8} Therefore, my sons, set your hearts on yourselves and keep the commandment of God that is with you. When you leave this holy mountain and go into a strange land that you do not know, take with you the body of our father Adam, along with these three precious gifts and offerings: gold, incense, and myrrh; and let them be placed where the body of our father Adam shall lie. {21:9} And the one among you who shall be left, my sons, shall receive the Word of God, and when he departs from this land, he shall take the body of our father Adam and lay it in the middle of the earth, the place where salvation shall be wrought." {21:10} Then Noah asked, "Who among us will be left?" {21:11} Jared replied, "You are the one who shall be left. You will take the body of our father Adam from the cave and place it in the ark when the flood comes. {21:12} And your son Shem, who will come from your loins, will be the one to lay the body of our father Adam in the middle of the earth, in the place from which salvation shall come." {21:13} Then Jared turned to his son Enoch and said, "You, my son, remain in this cave and serve diligently before the body of our father Adam all the days of your life; and feed your people in righteousness and innocence." {21:14} Jared said no more. His hands loosened, his eyes closed, and he entered into rest like his fathers. His death took place in the three hundred and sixtieth year of Noah and in the nine hundred and eighty-ninth year of his own life, on the twelfth of Takhsas (an ancient month equivalent to December) on a Friday. {21:15} But as Jared died, tears streamed down his face because of his great sorrow for the children of Seth, who had fallen during his days. {21:16} Then Enoch, Methuselah, Lamech, and Noah, these four, wept over him, embalmed him carefully, and laid him in the Cave of Treasures. They mourned for him for forty days. {21:17} After these days of mourning ended, Enoch, Methuselah, Lamech, and Noah remained in sorrow of heart because their father had departed from them, and they would see him no more.

{22:1} But Enoch kept the commandment of Jared, his father, and continued to serve in the cave. {22:2} This is the Enoch to whom many wonders happened, and he also wrote a celebrated book; but those wonders cannot be told here. {22:3} After this, the children of Seth went astray and fell, along with their children and wives. When Enoch, Methuselah, Lamech, and Noah saw this, their hearts suffered because of the doubt and unbelief that had overcome them, and they wept and sought God for mercy to preserve them and deliver them from that wicked generation. {22:4} Enoch continued in his ministry before the Lord for three hundred and eighty-five years, and at the end of that time, he became aware, through God's grace, that God intended to remove him from the earth. {22:5} He then said to his son, "O my son, I know that God intends to bring the Waters of the Flood upon the earth and destroy our creation. {22:6} And you are the last rulers over this people on this mountain; for I know that not one will be left among you to beget children on this holy mountain; nor will any of you rule over the children of your people; nor will any great company remain of you on this mountain." {22:7} Enoch also said to them, "Watch over your souls, hold fast to your fear of God and your service to Him, worship Him in upright faith, and serve Him in righteousness, innocence, and judgment, in repentance, and in purity." {22:8} When Enoch had finished giving his commandments to them, God transported him from that mountain to the land of life, to the mansions of the righteous and the chosen, the abode of the Paradise of joy, in light that reaches up to heaven; light that is outside the light of this world; for it is the light of God that fills the whole world but cannot be contained by any place. {22:9} Thus, because Enoch was in the light of God, he found himself beyond the reach of death until God would have him die. {22:10} Altogether, not one of our fathers or their children remained on that holy mountain except for three: Methuselah, Lamech, and Noah. For all the rest went down from the mountain and fell into sin with the children of Cain. Therefore, they were forbidden from that mountain, and only those three men remained on it.

The Third Book of Adam and Eve

{1:1} Noah, from his youth, saw how sin grew, wickedness spread, and how many generations of men perished. He observed the increase in sorrow and the decline of righteous men. {1:2} Because of this, Noah afflicted his soul, restrained his body, maintained his virginity, and grieved over the destruction caused by human generations. {1:3} Noah continually mourned, wept, and had a sorrowful appearance, fasting to keep the enemy (Satan) from gaining any power over him, so the enemy stayed away. {1:4} From childhood, Noah never angered his parents, nor disobeyed them; he always sought their advice and guidance. Even when away from them, he would pray and ask God to lead him in all things, and because of this, God watched over him. {1:5} While Noah lived on the mountain, he never sinned against God in any deliberate way and never angered God. {1:6} Many miraculous things happened to him, more than had occurred to his ancestors, especially around the time of the flood. {1:7} Noah lived in virginity and obedience to God for five hundred years. But after that time, it pleased God to give him offspring, so God spoke to him and said, "Rise, Noah, and take a wife for yourself, so that you may have children, who will bring you comfort, for you are alone. You will leave this land and go to a foreign place, for your descendants will repopulate the earth." {1:8} When Noah heard God's command, he obeyed and took a wife named Haikal, daughter of Abaraz, who was from the descendants of Enos's line, a family that had fallen into destruction. {1:9} Haikal bore him three sons: Shem, Ham, and Japheth.

{2:1} After these events, God spoke to Noah about the flood that was to come, telling him that it would cover the earth and destroy every living creature, leaving nothing alive. {2:2} God instructed Noah to safeguard his children and commanded him to make sure they did not mix with the descendants of Cain, or they would perish along with them. {2:3} Noah listened to God's words and kept his children on the mountain, not letting them associate with the children of Cain. {2:4} Then God said to Noah, "Make for yourself an ark out of durable wood, to save you and your household. {2:5} Build the ark in the lowland of Eden in the sight of the children of Cain, so they may see your work. If they do not repent, they will perish, and their guilt will be on them. {2:6} Cut trees from the holy mountain for the ark. Its length should be three hundred cubits (about 450 feet), its width fifty cubits (about 75 feet), and its height thirty cubits (about 45 feet). {2:7} Once completed, the ark should have a door on the upper level and three compartments. Each compartment should be ten cubits high. {2:8} The first level should be for lions, wild animals, and ostriches. The second level should be for birds and creeping creatures. {2:9} The third level will be for you, your wife, your sons, and their wives. {2:10} Make wells in the ark for water, with openings to draw water for drinking. Line these wells with lead, inside and out. {2:11} Also, create storehouses in the ark for grain to serve as food for you and all who are with you. {2:12} You must also make a trumpet from ebony wood, three cubits long (about 4.5 feet) and one and a half cubits wide, with a matching mouthpiece. {2:13} Blow it three times daily. In the morning, blow it so the workers know to start their labor. Blow it again for them to gather and eat their meal, and blow it a third time in the evening to signal the end of the day's work. {2:14} Go to the people and warn them of the flood, telling them it will destroy them unless they repent. Build the ark in their presence." {2:15} When Noah told the people about the flood, they laughed at him, continuing to commit adultery and celebrate, mocking Noah and asking, "How will water ever rise above the mountains? We've never seen that happen, and this old man says it will!"

{3:1} During the first hundred years Noah worked on the ark, he fathered his three sons. {3:2} In those hundred years, Noah ate no food that produced blood, his shoes did not wear out or need to be changed, nor did his garments wear down at all. {3:3} His staff stayed the same, and the cloth around his head did not grow old, and his hair neither grew nor diminished. {3:4} His firstborn son was Shem, the second was Ham, and the third was Japheth. They married daughters from Methuselah's family, as written in the sacred books of the ancient wise men. {3:5} Noah's father, Lamech, lived five hundred and fifty-three years, and when he neared death, he called his father, Methuselah, and his son, Noah, to him, weeping before Methuselah, saying, "Bless me, Father, and let me depart in peace." {3:6} Methuselah blessed Lamech, lamenting, "None of our ancestors died before their fathers, but now you, my son, will die before me. I will feel sorrow even before I leave this world. {3:7} From now on, death's order is changed, and fathers will no longer outlive their sons. Sons will die before their fathers, and no father will rejoice in his son as before, nor will sons be satisfied with their fathers." {3:8} Lamech died, and they embalmed his body and laid him in the Cave of Treasures. His death occurred seven years before the flood came. {3:9} Methuselah and Noah were left alone on the Holy Mountain, and Noah continued to work on the ark, coming down to the lowlands by day and returning at night. {3:10} He instructed his sons and their wives to avoid mingling with the children of Cain, as Noah feared his young sons might fall into temptation. Therefore, he came down from the mountain secretly and consulted Methuselah.

{4:1} Noah often preached to the children of Cain, warning them, "Repent, or the flood will destroy you." But they refused to listen and only laughed more, indulging in sin. {4:2} When the children of Seth had descended from the Holy Mountain to mix with the children of Cain, they defiled themselves, and from these unions came giants known as Garsina, who were mighty and strong beyond compare. {4:3} Some ancient scholars mistakenly claimed that angels descended from heaven and mingled with Cain's daughters, giving birth to these giants. {4:4} But these scholars are wrong. Angels are spirits and cannot sin with humans. {4:5} If such things were true, not a single woman on earth would have remained pure, for Satan and his demons are wicked. However, spirits are neither male nor female by nature; they are subtle beings, darkened since their fall from grace. {4:6} The truth is, the children of Seth, who lived like angels on the Holy Mountain in purity and innocence, were called "angels of God." {4:7} But when they sinned and mingled with Cain's descendants, men mistook them for angels.

{5:1} When Methuselah, who stayed on the mountain with Noah's sons, reached nine hundred and eighty-seven years, he became ill and near death. {5:2} Noah, along with his sons Shem, Ham, and Japheth, came with their wives to him, weeping, and asked, "Bless us, Father, and pray that God will have mercy on us after you depart." {5:3} Methuselah replied, "Listen, my dear children. Only eight souls of our family remain on earth. {5:4} God created our father Adam and our mother Eve, filled the earth with people around the garden, and increased their numbers. {5:5} But they did not keep His commandments, so He will destroy them. If they had obeyed, heaven and earth would have been filled with their descendants. {5:6} I will pray to God to bless you, multiply your numbers, and spread your lineage in a foreign land to which you will go. {5:7} God will bring you into an ark to a land you have never seen, and may the God of our fathers bless you! {5:8} God gave Adam three glorious gifts in this Cave of Treasures: kingship, priesthood, and prophecy. {5:9} I will pray that these same gifts be passed to your descendants."

{6:1} After his death, Noah, his sons, and their wives came to the bodies of our ancestors, worshipped them, and blessed themselves with tears and deep sorrow. {6:2} Noah had completed the ark, but not a single worker remained with him. He and his sons prayed continuously to God, asking Him to show them the path to safety. {6:3} When Noah and his sons finished their prayers, God said to him, "Go into the Cave of Treasures, you and your sons, and take the body of our father Adam, and place it in the ark. Also, take the gold, incense, and myrrh and place them with his body." {6:4} Noah obeyed God's command and went into the Cave of Treasures with his sons. They worshipped the bodies of their ancestors, then Noah took the body of Adam and carried it by God's strength, needing no help. {6:5} Shem, his son, carried the gold, Ham carried the myrrh, and Japheth carried the incense. They brought everything out of the cave, tears streaming down their faces. {6:6} As they were bringing them out, the other bodies near Adam's cried out, "Are we to be separated from you, our father Adam?" {6:7} Adam's body answered, "Though I must leave you, my sons, from this holy mountain, I know that God will gather all our bodies together again one day. Be patient until our Savior has mercy on us." {6:8} The other bodies continued speaking to one another by the power of God's Word. {6:9} Adam prayed to God, asking that the divine flame in the lamp remain before his descendants until the resurrection of the dead. {6:10} God left the divine fire with them to provide light. He then sealed the cave so that no trace remained of it, hidden until the Day of Resurrection when He will raise all bodies. {6:11} Adam's speech, though he was dead, was by God's command to demonstrate His wonders among the living and the dead. {6:12} Do not say that Adam's soul was under Satan's judgment, for God commanded the souls of the dead to come forth and proclaim His wonders from within their bodies. {6:13} After that, the souls returned to their places until the day of their deliverance.

{7:1} When Noah and his sons heard the voices from the dead bodies, they were amazed, and their faith in God grew stronger. {7:2} They left the cave and descended from the Holy Mountain, weeping and mourning deeply, for they knew they would no longer dwell on the mountain of their ancestors. {7:3} Noah and his sons searched for the cave again but could not find it. They were overwhelmed with sorrow, realizing they would no longer live there. {7:4} They looked up at the garden and the trees within it, and they wept loudly, saying, "We greet you, O garden of joy! Abode of holy beings, a place for the righteous! We greet you, the place of our father Adam, chief of creation, who fell from grace when he transgressed and saw his body in shame." {7:5} "Now we depart from the Holy Mountain to a lower land and will not see you again as long as we live. We wish God would take you with us, but He will not move you to a cursed land." {7:6} "God will bring us to a new land, along with our descendants, until the punishment for our transgression is complete." {7:7} Noah and his sons also said, "We salute you, O cave, resting place of our holy ancestors. We salute you, pure spot, hidden from our eyes, yet fit to hold the bodies of the righteous. May God preserve you for their sake!" {7:8} They continued, "We greet you, O ancestors, righteous judges. Pray for us before God, that He may have mercy on us and deliver us from this fleeting world. Pray for us, the last of your lineage. We greet you in peace!" {7:9} "O Seth, great among our fathers, we greet you with peace! O Holy Mountain, home of our ancestors, we greet you with peace!" {7:10} Then Noah and his sons wept again, saying, "Alas for us, only eight souls are left! Behold, we are taken away from the sight of the garden." {7:11} As they descended the mountain, they picked up stones and placed them on their shoulders, touched the trees, and wept. They continued down until they reached the ark. {7:12} Noah and his sons turned east and prayed to the Lord, asking for mercy and guidance on where to lay Adam's body. {7:13} Then God spoke to Noah, saying, "Place Adam's body in the third story of the ark, on the eastern side, along with the gold, incense, and myrrh. You and your sons shall pray before him, but your wife and your sons' wives shall remain on the western side and shall not come together." {7:14} Noah obeyed God's command. He and his sons placed Adam's body on the eastern side of the ark, along with the three offerings. {7:15} Noah brought Adam's body into the ark on a Friday, at the second hour, on the twenty-seventh day of the month of Gembot.

{8:1} Then God commanded Noah, "Go to the top of the ark and blow the trumpet three times so that all the animals gather to the ark." {8:2} Noah asked, "Will the sound of the trumpet reach the ends of the earth and gather all the animals and birds?" {8:3} God answered, "It is not the sound alone, but My power will make it heard by all the animals and birds. When you blow the trumpet, I will command My angel to sound the horn from heaven, and the creatures will gather." {8:4} Noah blew the trumpet as God instructed, and the angel sounded the horn from heaven. The earth quaked, and all creatures trembled. {8:5} At the third hour on Friday, the beasts, lions, and ostriches gathered and entered the lower story. At noon, the birds and creeping things entered the middle story. Noah and his sons entered the top story at the ninth hour. {8:6} Noah arranged the women to stay on the western side of the ark, while he and his sons, along with Adam's body, stayed on the eastern side.

{9:1} Noah prayed to God, asking for protection from the floodwaters. {9:2} God told Noah, "Take a pair of every bird and animal, male and female, both clean and unclean. But for the clean, take seven pairs, male and female." {9:3} Noah did as God commanded. Once everyone and everything was inside, God shut the door of the ark by His power. {9:4} God commanded the windows of heaven to open and pour down floods of water, and so it happened, by His word. {9:5} He commanded all fountains to burst open, and the depths to flood the earth. The seas surged and covered everything. {9:6} The windows of heaven poured forth rain, and all the waters and winds rose up. Darkness spread, and the sun, moon, and stars withheld their light. It was a day of terror like no other. {9:7} The sea rose in waves like mountains and covered the entire earth. {9:8} When the sons of Seth, who had fallen into sin with the children of Cain, saw this, they realized Noah had spoken the truth, and God was angry with them. {9:9} They ran to the ark, pleading with Noah to open the door, but they could not reach the Holy Mountain, for its stones were like fire. {9:10} The ark was sealed by God's power, and an angel sat atop it like a captain over Noah, his family, and all within. {9:11} The floodwaters rose and engulfed the children of Cain, fulfilling Noah's prophecy of their destruction. {9:12} The water covered everything, even the highest mountains, and the ark floated on the waters, lifted by the flood. {9:13} The waters rose above the mountains by fifteen cubits, according to the cubit of the Holy Spirit, equal to three human cubits, making a total of forty-five cubits above the highest peaks. {9:14} The water bore the ark to the lower side of the garden, which the waters, rain, and winds worshipped. Noah & those inside ark also bowed in worship to the holy garden. {9:15} The floodwaters destroyed all life on earth, but the ark floated for 150 days. {9:16} After that, the ark rested on the mountains of Ararat on the 27th day of the month of Tkarnt.

{10:1} God then told Noah, "Wait patiently until the waters subside." {10:2} The waters withdrew, returning to their original places, and the fountains ceased to pour forth. The depths and the heavens closed, and the rains stopped after forty days and nights.

{10:3} On the first day of the eleventh month, the tops of the mountains were visible. Noah waited another forty days and opened the window on the western side, releasing a raven to see if the waters had receded. {10:4} The raven did not return, but the harmless dove symbolizes the Christian Church. {10:5} Noah sent out a dove, but it found no resting place and returned to the ark. He waited seven days and sent it out again. {10:6} This time, the dove returned with an olive leaf, signifying that the flood was ending. {10:7} Noah knew the waters were abating, and God was showing mercy to the world. Noah and his family praised God, full of hope for new life.

{11:1} In the six hundred and seventh year of Noah's life, on the second day of the month of Barmudeh, the waters dried up from the earth. {11:2} And in the following month, which is Gembot, on the twenty-seventh day of the month—the same day Noah had entered the ark—on that very day, Noah and his family came out of the ark, which was a Sunday. {11:3} When Noah, his wife, his sons, and their wives exited the ark, they reunited and no longer remained separated from one another. {11:4} When they first entered the ark, the men and women had stayed apart, as Noah was concerned that they might come together during the time of the Flood. {11:5} But once the Flood had ended, they came together again, husband with wife. {11:6} God also brought great peace over the animals—like the lions and birds—inside the ark, ensuring that none of the creatures quarreled with each other. {11:7} Then Noah came out of the ark and built an altar upon the mountain. He stood before it and asked the Lord to guide him in what sacrifices he should make and how to offer them to God. {11:8} God sent His Word to Noah, saying, "Noah, take animals of the clean species and offer them upon the altar before Me. Then let all the other animals go out of the ark." {11:9} Noah obeyed, returning to the ark and selecting as many clean birds and animals as God had instructed, and he offered them as sacrifices upon the altar before the Lord.

{12:1} And God smelled the sweet aroma of Noah's offerings and made a covenant with him, promising that the waters of the Flood would never again come upon the earth, from that point on, and forever. {12:2} This was the same altar that Adam had built, and on which both he, Cain, and Abel had offered sacrifices. (Note: "clean animals" refers to those considered fit for sacrifice under ancient laws of worship).

The Book of Jubilees

{1:1} In the first year of the exodus of the Israelites from Egypt, in the third month, on the sixteenth day of the month, in the year 2450 since creation, God spoke to Moses, saying: "Come up to Me on the mountain, and I will give you two stone tablets containing the law and commandments that I have written, so you may teach them." {1:2} And Moses went up the mountain of God, and the glory of the Lord settled on Mount Sinai, with a cloud overshadowing it for six days. {1:3} On the seventh day, God called to Moses from the midst of the cloud, and the appearance of the Lord's glory was like a blazing fire on top of the mountain. {1:4} Moses stayed on the mountain for forty days and forty nights, during which God taught him the earlier and later histories regarding the division of all the days of the law and the testimony. {1:5} God said: "Pay attention to every word I speak to you on this mountain, and write them down in a book so that future generations will see how I have not forsaken them despite all the wrongs they have done by breaking the covenant I establish with you today on Mount Sinai. {1:6} When these things come upon them, they will recognize that I am more righteous than they in all my judgments and actions, and they will see that I have truly been with them. {1:7} Write down all these words I declare to you today, for I know their rebellion and stubbornness before I bring them into the land I promised their ancestors, Abraham, Isaac, and Jacob, saying: 'To your descendants, I will give a land flowing with milk and honey.' {1:8} They will eat and be satisfied, and then they will turn to other gods—gods that cannot deliver them from any of their troubles. This will serve as a witness against them, for they will forget all my commandments, even everything I command them. They will follow the customs of other nations, their impurities, and their shame, and they will serve their gods, which will become a source of offense, trouble, and a trap for them. {1:9} Many will perish, and they will be taken captive, falling into the hands of their enemies because they have forsaken my ordinances, commandments, festivals, sabbaths, and my holy place, which I have consecrated for myself among them, my tabernacle, and my sanctuary, where I set my name and where I dwell. {1:10} They will build high places, groves, and graven images for themselves, each worshiping their own idols, leading them astray. They will sacrifice their children to demons and to all the works of the error of their hearts. {1:11} I will send witnesses to them to testify against them, but they will not listen; they will even kill the witnesses and persecute those who seek the law. They will alter and change everything to do evil in my sight. {1:12} I will hide my face from them, delivering them into the hands of the nations for captivity, plundering, and destruction. I will remove them from the land and scatter them among the nations. {1:13} They will forget all my law, my commandments, and my judgments, going astray concerning new moons, sabbaths, festivals, and jubilees. {1:14} After this, they will turn to me from among the nations with all their heart and soul, and I will gather them from all the nations. They will seek me, and I will be found by them when they seek me with all their heart and soul. {1:15} I will give them abundant peace with righteousness, and I will plant uprightness within them, and they will be a blessing and not a curse, the head and not the tail. {1:16} I will build my sanctuary among them, and I will dwell with them; I will be their God, and they will be my people in truth and righteousness. {1:17} I will not forsake them or fail them, for I am the Lord their God." {1:18} Moses fell on his face and prayed, saying, "O Lord my God, do not forsake your people and your inheritance, so they do not wander in the errors of their hearts. Do not deliver them into the hands of their enemies, the nations, lest they rule over them and lead them to sin against you. {1:19} Let your mercy, O Lord, be upon your people, and create in them an upright spirit. Do not let the spirit of evil rule over them to accuse them before you and ensnare them from all paths of righteousness, so they may perish from before your face. {1:20} They are your people and inheritance, whom you delivered with great power from the hands of the Egyptians; create in them a pure heart and a holy spirit, and do not let them be ensnared in their sins from now until eternity." {1:21} The Lord said to Moses: "I know their rebelliousness and their thoughts; they will not obey until they confess their sins and the sins of their ancestors. {1:22} After this, they will turn to me in all uprightness with all their heart and soul, and I will circumcise their hearts and the hearts of their descendants. I will create in them a holy spirit and cleanse them so they will not turn away from me from that day onward. {1:23} Their souls will cling to me and to all my commandments; they will fulfill my commandments, and I will be their Father, and they will be my children. {1:24} They will all be called children of the living God, and every angel and spirit will know that these are my children and that I am their Father in righteousness and uprightness, and I love them. {1:25} Write down for yourself all these words I declare to you on this mountain, both the first and the last, which will come to pass in all divisions of the days of the law, the testimony, the weeks, and the jubilees forever, until I descend and dwell with them for eternity." {1:26} He said to the angel of the presence: "Write for Moses from the beginning of creation until my sanctuary is built among them for all eternity. {1:27} The Lord will be visible to all, and everyone will know that I am the God of Israel, the Father of all the children of Jacob, and King on Mount Zion forever. Zion and Jerusalem will be holy." {1:28} The angel of the presence, who went before the camp of Israel, took the tablets containing the divisions of the years—from the time of creation—of the law and testimony, according to the individual years and the number of the jubilees, from the day of the new creation when the heavens and earth will be renewed along with all their creation according to the powers of heaven and all the creation of the earth, until the sanctuary of the Lord is established in Jerusalem on Mount Zion, where all the lights will be renewed for healing, peace, and blessings for all the chosen of Israel, and it will be so from that day and for all the days of the earth.

{2:1} The angel of the presence spoke to Moses, as the Lord commanded, saying: "Write the complete history of creation, how in six days the Lord God finished all His works and everything He created, and rested on the seventh day, making it holy for all ages as a sign of all His works. {2:2} On the first day, He created the heavens above, the earth, the waters, and all the spirits that serve before Him—the angels of the presence, the angels of sanctification, the angels of the spirit of fire, the angels of the spirit of the winds, the angels of the spirit of the clouds, darkness, snow, hail, frost, the angels of voices, thunder, lightning, and the angels of the spirits of cold, heat, winter, spring, autumn, summer, and all the spirits of His creatures in the heavens and on the earth. He created the abysses and darkness, evening and night, light, dawn, and day, which He prepared in the knowledge of His heart. {2:3} We saw His works and praised Him, lauding Him for all His creations; for seven great works He created on the first day. {2:4} On the second day, He created the firmament in the midst of the waters, dividing the waters so that half went above and half went below the firmament that was over the whole earth. This was the only work created on the second day. {2:5} On the third day, He commanded the waters to gather in one place so that dry land could appear. The waters obeyed, retreating from the earth into one area outside the firmament, and the dry land appeared. {2:6} That day, He created all the seas in their separate gathering places, all the rivers, the collections of water in the mountains and on the earth, all the lakes, the dew of the earth, the seeds sown, sprouting plants, fruit-bearing trees, trees of the woods, and the garden of Eden in Eden with all its plants of every kind. These four great works God created on the third day. {2:7} On the fourth day, He created the sun, moon, and stars, setting them in the firmament of the heavens to give light on the earth, to rule over day and night, and to separate light from darkness. {2:8} God appointed the sun as a great sign on earth for days, sabbaths, months, feasts, years, sabbaths of years, jubilees, and all seasons. It separates light from darkness for prosperity, so that all things may flourish that grow on the earth. These three kinds He made on the fourth day. {2:9} On the fifth day, He created great sea creatures in the depths of the waters; these were the first living beings created by His hands, along with fish, everything that moves in the waters, and all birds. {2:10} The sun rose above them to bring prosperity to everything on the earth, all that sprouts from the ground, and all fruit-bearing trees. These three kinds He created on the fifth day. {2:11} On the sixth day, He created all the animals of the earth, all cattle, and everything that moves on the earth. After all this, He created man—both a man and a woman—and gave them dominion over all that is on the earth, in the seas, over everything that flies, over beasts and cattle, and over everything that moves on the earth. He gave them authority over the entire earth, creating these four kinds on the sixth day. In total, there were twenty-two kinds. {2:12} He finished all His work on the sixth day—all that is in the heavens, the earth, the seas, the abysses, the light, the darkness, and everything. {2:13} He gave us a great sign, the Sabbath day, so we should work for six days but rest on the seventh from all work. {2:14} All the angels of the presence and all the angels of sanctification—these two great classes—He commanded us to keep the Sabbath with Him in heaven and on earth. {2:15} He said: "Behold, I will separate a people for Myself from among all the peoples, and they will keep the Sabbath day. I will sanctify them as My people and bless them; just as I have sanctified the Sabbath day for Myself, so I will bless them, and they will be My people, and I will be their God. {2:16} I have chosen the seed of Jacob from among all that I have seen and recorded him as My firstborn son, sanctifying him for Myself forever; I will teach them the Sabbath day, so they may rest from all work on it." {2:17} Thus, He established a sign for them to keep the Sabbath with us on the seventh day, to eat, drink, and bless Him who created all things, as He has blessed and sanctified a special people above all peoples so they should keep Sabbath together with us. {2:18} He caused His commands to rise as a sweet fragrance acceptable to Him all the days. {2:19} There were twenty-two heads of humanity from Adam to Jacob, and twenty-two kinds of work were completed by the seventh day; this day is blessed and holy, just as the former day is also blessed and holy; both serve to sanctify and bless. {2:20} To Jacob and his descendants was granted that they should always be the blessed and holy ones of the first testimony and law, just as He sanctified and blessed the Sabbath on the seventh day. {2:21} He created heaven and earth and everything in six days, and God made the seventh day holy for all His works; therefore, He commanded that anyone who does work on that day shall die, and whoever defiles it shall surely die. {2:22} Therefore, command the children of Israel to observe this day so they may keep it holy and not work on it, nor defile it, as it is holier than all other days. {2:23} Whoever profanes it shall surely die, and anyone who works on it shall die eternally, so that the children of Israel may observe this day for all generations and not be removed from the land; for it is a holy and blessed day. {2:24} Everyone who observes it and rests on it from all work will be holy and blessed every day, just like us. {2:25} Declare and tell the children of Israel the law for this day: that they should keep Sabbath on it and not forsake it due to the errors of their hearts; that it is unlawful to do any unseemly work, to pursue their own pleasure, or to prepare food or drink, and it is not lawful to draw water or bring in or take out burdens through their gates on that day, which they had not prepared for themselves on the sixth day in their homes. {2:26} They shall not transfer anything from house to house on that day; for that day is holier and more blessed than any jubilee day of the jubilees; we kept Sabbath in heaven before it was made known to any flesh on earth. {2:27} The Creator of all things blessed it, but He did not sanctify all peoples and nations to keep it, only Israel: them alone He permitted to eat, drink, and keep the Sabbath on earth. {2:28} The Creator of all things blessed this day which He created for blessing, holiness, and glory above all days. {2:29} This law and testimony was given to the children of Israel as a law forever for their generations.

{3:1} On the sixth days of the second week, we brought to Adam, according to God's word, all the beasts, cattle, birds, and everything that moves on the earth and in the water, according to their kinds and types: the beasts on the first day; the cattle on the second day; the birds on the third day; everything that moves on the earth on the fourth day; and everything that moves in the water on the fifth day. {3:2} Adam named them all by their respective names, and as he called them, so they were named. {3:3} During these five days, Adam saw all these creatures, male and female, of every kind on the earth, but he was alone and found no companion for himself. {3:4} The Lord said to us: "It is not good for man to be alone; let us make a helper for him." {3:5} The Lord our God caused a deep sleep to fall upon Adam, and while he slept, He took one rib from his ribs. This rib became the origin of the woman, and He built up the flesh in its place, creating the woman. {3:6} He awoke Adam from his sleep, and when Adam rose on the sixth day, God brought her to him. Adam knew her and said: "This is now bone of my bones and flesh of my flesh; she shall be called my wife because she was taken from her husband." {3:7} Therefore, a man and wife shall be one, and a man shall leave his father and mother, and cling to his wife, and they shall become one flesh. {3:8} In the first week, Adam was created, and the rib—his wife—was formed. In the second week, she was shown to him; and for this reason, the commandment was given regarding their impurity: seven days for a male, and fourteen days for a female. {3:9} After Adam had completed forty days in the land where he was created, we brought him into the Garden of Eden to tend and keep it, but his wife was brought in on the eightieth day, and afterward, she entered the Garden. {3:10} For this reason, the commandment is recorded on the heavenly tablets concerning childbirth: if a woman gives birth to a male, she shall remain in her impurity for seven days, according to the first week, and for thirty-three days, she shall remain in the blood of her purification. She shall not touch anything holy, nor enter the sanctuary until these days are fulfilled for a male child. {3:11} In the case of a female child, she shall remain in her impurity for two weeks, according to the first two weeks, and for sixty-six days in the blood of her purification, totaling eighty days. {3:12} After she completed these eighty days, we brought her into the Garden of Eden, for it is holier than all the earth, and every tree planted there is holy. {3:13} Therefore, it is decreed for those who give birth to a male or female child that they should not touch anything holy, nor enter the sanctuary until these days are fulfilled. {3:14} This is the law and testimony written for Israel so they may observe it all their days. {3:15} In the first week of the first jubilee, Adam and his wife were in the Garden of Eden for seven years, tending it, and we gave him work, instructing him in all suitable tasks for cultivation. {3:16} He tended the garden, was naked, and didn't realize it, nor was he ashamed. He protected the garden from birds, beasts, and cattle, gathered its fruits, ate, and stored what was left for himself and his wife. {3:17} After completing seven years there, exactly seven years, on the second month, the seventeenth day of the month, the serpent approached the woman and said, "Did God really say, 'You shall not eat from every tree in the garden'?" {3:18} She replied, "Of all the fruit of the trees in the garden, God said we may eat; but of the fruit of the tree in the middle of the garden, God said, 'You shall not eat it or touch it, lest you die.'" {3:19} The serpent said to the woman, "You will not surely die; for God knows that when you eat of it, your eyes will be opened, and you will be like gods, knowing good and evil." {3:20} The woman saw that the tree was pleasing to the eye and good for food; she took some of its fruit and ate it. {3:21} After first covering her shame with fig leaves, she gave some to Adam, and he ate. Their eyes were opened, and they realized they were naked. {3:22} Adam took fig leaves, sewed them together, and made an apron for himself to cover his shame. {3:23} God cursed the serpent and was angry with it forever. {3:24} He was also angry with the woman because she listened to the voice of the serpent and ate. He said to her: "I will greatly increase your sorrow and pain; in pain, you will give birth to children. Your desire will be for your husband, and he will rule over you." {3:25} To Adam, He said, "Because you listened to your wife and ate from the tree of which I commanded you, saying, 'You shall not eat of it,' cursed is the ground for your sake; it will produce thorns and thistles for you, and you will eat your bread by the sweat of your brow until you return to the ground, for out of it you were taken; you are dust, and to dust you shall return." {3:26} He made coats of skin for them and clothed them, sending them out of the Garden of Eden. {3:27} On the day Adam left the Garden, he offered a sweet-smelling sacrifice of incense, galbanum, stacte, and spices in the morning with the rising sun from the day he covered his shame. {3:28} On that day, the mouths of all beasts, cattle, birds, and all creatures that walk and move were closed so they could no longer speak; they had all spoken with one voice and one language. {3:29} He expelled all flesh from the Garden of Eden, scattering them according to their kinds and types to the places created for them. {3:30} To Adam alone, He gave the means to cover his shame, unlike the other beasts and cattle. {3:31} For this reason, it is prescribed in the heavenly tablets for those who know the judgment of the law that they should cover their shame and not expose themselves as the Gentiles do. {3:32} On the new moon of the fourth month, Adam and his wife left the Garden of Eden and settled in the land of Elda, where they were created. {3:33} Adam named his wife Eve. {3:34} They had no son until the first jubilee, and after this, he knew her. {3:35} Now he tilled the land as he had been instructed in the Garden of Eden.

{4:1} In the third week of the second jubilee, Eve gave birth to Cain, and in the fourth week, she gave birth to Abel, and in the fifth week, she gave birth to her daughter Âwân. {4:2} In the first year of the third jubilee, Cain killed Abel because God accepted Abel's sacrifice and did not accept Cain's offering. {4:3} He killed Abel in the field, and Abel's blood cried out from the ground to heaven, complaining about his murder. {4:4} The Lord rebuked Cain for Abel's death, making him a fugitive on the earth due to his brother's blood, and He cursed him on the earth. {4:5} For this reason, it is written on the heavenly tablets: "Cursed is the one who strikes his neighbor treacherously; let all who have seen and heard say, 'So be it,' and anyone who has seen and not declared it shall be accursed like the other." {4:6} Because of this, we announce before the Lord our God all sins committed in heaven and on earth, in light and in darkness, and everywhere. {4:7} Adam and his wife mourned for Abel for four weeks of years, and in the fourth year of the fifth week, they became joyful, and Adam knew his wife again, and she bore him a son, naming him Seth; for he said, "God has raised up a second seed for us on the earth instead of Abel, whom Cain killed." {4:8} In the sixth week, he had a daughter named Azûrâ. {4:9} Cain took his sister Âwân as his wife, and she bore him Enoch at the close of the fourth jubilee. {4:10} In the first year of the first week of the fifth jubilee, houses were built on the earth, and Cain built a city, naming it after his son Enoch. {4:11} Adam knew Eve, and she bore him nine more sons. {4:12} In the fifth week of the fifth jubilee, Seth took his sister Azûrâ as his wife, and in the fourth year of the sixth week, she bore him Enos. {4:13} He began to call on the name of the Lord on the earth. {4:14} In the seventh jubilee, during the third week, Enos took his sister Nôâm as his wife, and she bore him a son in the third year of the fifth week, naming him Kenan. {4:15} At the close of the eighth jubilee, Kenan took his sister Mûalêlêth as his wife, and she bore him a son in the ninth jubilee, in the first week of the third year of this week, naming him Mahalalel. {4:16} In the second week of the tenth jubilee, Mahalalel took as his wife DinaH, the daughter of Barakiel, who was the daughter of his father's brother, and she bore him a son in the third week of the sixth year, naming him Jared; for in his days, the angels of the Lord descended on the earth, known as the Watchers, to instruct the children of men to practice judgment and righteousness on the earth. {4:17} In the eleventh jubilee, Jared took a wife named Baraka, the daughter of Râsûjâl, the daughter of his father's brother, during the fourth week of this jubilee, and she bore him a son in the fifth week, in the fourth year of the jubilee, naming him Enoch. {4:18} He was the first among men born on earth to learn writing, knowledge, and wisdom, writing down the signs of heaven according to the order of their months in a book, so that men might understand the seasons of the years by the order of their separate months. {4:19} He was the first to write a testimony, testifying to the sons of men among the generations of the earth, recounting the weeks of the jubilees, making known the days of the years, and organizing the months while recounting the Sabbaths of the years as we made known to him. {4:20} He saw in a vision during his sleep what was and what will be, witnessing everything that will happen to the children of men throughout their generations until the day of judgment; he saw and understood everything, wrote his testimony, and placed it on earth for all the children of men and their generations. {4:21} In the twelfth jubilee, in the seventh week, he took a wife named Edna, the daughter of Danel, the daughter of his father's brother, and in the sixth year of this week, she bore him a son, naming him Methuselah. {4:22} He was with the angels of God for these six jubilees of years, who showed him everything on earth and in the heavens, including the rule of the sun, and he wrote everything down. {4:23} He testified to the Watchers, who had sinned with the daughters of men, as they began to unite themselves with the daughters of men, defiling themselves, and Enoch testified against them all. {4:24} He was taken from among the children of men, and we brought him into the Garden of Eden in glory and honor, where he wrote down the condemnation and judgment of the world, along with all the wickedness of the children of men. {4:25} Because of this, God brought the waters of the flood upon all the land of Eden; for there, he was set as a sign to testify against all the children of men, recounting all the deeds of the generations until the day of condemnation. {4:26} He burned the incense of the sanctuary, sweet spices acceptable before the Lord on the mountain. {4:27} For the Lord has four places on earth: the Garden of Eden, the Mount of the East, this mountain where you are today, Mount Sinai, and Mount Zion, which will be sanctified in the new creation for the purification of the earth; through it, the earth will be cleansed from all its guilt and uncleanness throughout the generations of the world. {4:28} In the fourteenth jubilee, Methuselah took a wife named Edna, the daughter of Azrial, the daughter of his father's brother, during the third week in the first year of this week, and he bore a son, naming him Lamech. {4:29} In the fifteenth jubilee, in the third week, Lamech took a wife named Betenos, the daughter of Baraki'il, the daughter of his father's brother, and during this week, she bore him a son, naming him Noah, saying, "This one will comfort me for my trouble and all my work, and for the ground which the Lord has cursed." {4:30} At the close of the nineteenth jubilee, in the seventh week, in the sixth year, Adam died, and all his sons buried him in the land of his creation; he was the first to be buried in the earth. {4:31} He was short seventy years of a thousand years; for a thousand years are as one day in the testimony of the heavens, and thus it was written concerning the tree of knowledge: "On the day that you eat from it, you shall die." For this reason, he did not complete the years of this day, as he died during it. {4:32} At the close of this jubilee, Cain was killed in the same year; his house collapsed on him, and he died in the midst of it, killed by its stones; for with a stone he had killed Abel, and by a stone, he was killed in righteous judgment. {4:33} For this reason, it was ordained on the heavenly tablets: "With the instrument that a man uses to kill his neighbor, with the same shall he be killed; in the same manner he wounded him, in like manner shall they deal with him." {4:34} In the twenty-fifth jubilee, Noah took a wife named `Emzârâ, the daughter of Râkê'êl, the daughter of his father's brother, in the first year of the fifth week, and in the third year of that week, she bore him Shem; in the fifth year, she bore him Ham; and in the first year of the sixth week, she bore him Japheth.

{5:1} When the children of men began to multiply on the earth and daughters were born to them, the angels of God saw them in a certain year of this jubilee, and they were beautiful to look at; so they took wives from among those they chose, and they bore sons who became giants. {5:2} Lawlessness increased on the earth, and all flesh corrupted its way—men, cattle, beasts, birds, and everything that walks on the earth—all corrupted their ways and their orders, beginning to devour one another. Lawlessness increased, and every thought in the minds of men was continually evil. {5:3} God looked upon the earth, and indeed it was corrupt; all flesh had corrupted its orders, and everything on the earth had committed various evils before His eyes. {5:4} He decided to destroy man and all flesh upon the earth which He had created. {5:5} But Noah found grace in the eyes of the Lord. {5:6} Against the angels whom He had sent to earth, He was exceedingly angry, commanding them to be removed from all their dominion, and He instructed us to bind them in the depths of the earth; behold, they are bound there and kept separate. {5:7} A command went out from His presence against their sons that they should be killed by the sword and removed from under heaven. {5:8} He said, "My spirit shall not always strive with man, for they are also flesh, and their days shall be one hundred and twenty years." {5:9} He sent His sword among them so that each would slay his neighbor, and they began to kill each other until they all fell by the sword and were destroyed from the earth. {5:10} Their fathers witnessed their destruction, and afterwards they were bound in the depths of the earth forever, until the day of great condemnation, when judgment is executed on all those who have corrupted their ways and works before the Lord. {5:11} He destroyed all from their places, and none were left unjudged according to their wickedness. {5:12} He made for all His creations a new and righteous nature, so that they should not sin in their nature forever, but should be righteous in their kind always. {5:13} The judgment of all is ordained and written on the heavenly tablets in righteousness, including the judgment of all who stray from the path ordained for them; and if they do not walk therein, judgment is written for every creature and every kind. {5:14} Nothing in heaven or on earth, in light or darkness, in Sheol (the grave), or in the depths, or in the place of darkness is exempt from judgment; all their judgments are ordained and written down and engraved. {5:15} For all, He will judge: the great according to his greatness, the small according to his smallness, and each according to his way. {5:16} He does not show favoritism, nor does He accept gifts; if He says He will execute judgment on each, even if one gives everything on earth, He will not regard their gifts or person, nor accept anything from their hands, for He is a righteous judge. {5:17} It is written and ordained concerning the children of Israel: if they turn to Him in righteousness, He will forgive all their transgressions and pardon all their sins. {5:18} It is written and ordained that He will show mercy to all who turn away from their guilt once each year. {5:19} As for those who corrupted their ways and thoughts before the flood, no man's person was accepted except Noah's; for his person was accepted on behalf of his sons, whom God saved from the floodwaters because his heart was righteous in all his ways, as commanded regarding him, and he did not depart from anything ordained for him. {5:20} The Lord said He would destroy everything on earth, both men and cattle, beasts, birds of the air, and everything that moves on the earth. He commanded Noah to make an ark to save himself from the floodwaters. {5:21} Noah built the ark in every detail as God commanded him, in the twenty-seventh jubilee of years, in the fifth week of the fifth year, on the new moon of the first month. {5:22} He entered it in the sixth year, on the new moon of the second month, on the sixteenth; and he entered, along with all that we brought to him, into the ark, and the Lord closed it from the outside on the seventeenth evening. {5:23} The Lord opened the seven floodgates of heaven and the mouths of the fountains of the great deep, which were seven in number. {5:24} The floodgates began to pour down water from heaven for forty days and forty nights, and the fountains of the deep also sent up water until the whole world was flooded. {5:25} The waters increased on the earth: fifteen cubits above the highest mountains the waters rose, and the ark was lifted above the earth, moving on the surface of the waters. {5:26} The water prevailed on the earth for five months, one hundred and fifty days. {5:27} The ark came to rest on the top of Lubar, one of the mountains of Ararat. {5:28} On the new moon of the fourth month, the fountains of the great deep were closed and the floodgates of heaven restrained; and on the new moon of the seventh month, all the mouths of the abysses of the earth were opened, and the water began to descend into the depths below. {5:29} On the new moon of the tenth month, the tops of the mountains became visible, and on the new moon of the first month, the earth appeared. {5:30} The waters disappeared from the earth in the fifth week of the seventh year, and on the seventeenth day of the second month, the earth was dry. {5:31} On the twenty-seventh day of that month, he opened the ark and released from it beasts, cattle, birds, and every living thing.

{6:1} On the new moon of the third month, Noah went out from the ark and built an altar on that mountain. {6:2} He made atonement for the earth, taking a young goat and making atonement by its blood for all the guilt of the earth, for everything that had been on it was destroyed, except for those who were in the ark with Noah. {6:3} He placed the fat of the offering on the altar, and he took an ox, a goat, a sheep, young goats, salt, a turtle dove, and a young dove, and offered a burnt sacrifice on the altar. He poured an offering mixed with oil, sprinkled wine, and spread frankincense over everything, creating a pleasing aroma before the Lord. {6:4} The Lord smelled the pleasing aroma and made a covenant with Noah that there would no longer be a flood to destroy the earth; that all the days of the earth, seedtime and harvest would never cease; cold and heat, summer and winter, and day and night would not change their order or cease forever. {6:5} "And you, be fruitful and multiply on the earth, and increase greatly upon it, and be a blessing upon it. I will put the fear and dread of you in everything on the earth and in the sea. {6:6} Behold, I have given you all beasts, all flying creatures, everything that moves on the earth, and the fish in the waters; all things for food are yours; just as I have given you the green herbs, I have given you everything to eat. {6:7} But you shall not eat flesh with its life, that is, its blood, for the life of all flesh is in the blood; I will require the blood of your lives at the hand of every man and every beast. {6:8} Whoever sheds man's blood, by man shall his blood be shed, for in the image of God, He made man. {6:9} And you, be fruitful and multiply on the earth." {6:10} Noah and his sons swore that they would not eat any blood that was in any flesh, and he made a covenant before the Lord God forever, throughout all generations of the earth in this month. {6:11} For this reason, He spoke to you that you should make a covenant with the children of Israel in this month on the mountain with an oath, and that you should sprinkle blood upon them for all the words of the covenant that the Lord made with them forever. {6:12} This testimony is written about you so that you should observe it continually, that you should not eat blood from beasts, birds, or cattle during all the days of the earth. The person who eats blood from beasts, cattle, or birds during all the days of the earth, he and his descendants shall be cut off from the land. {6:13} Command the children of Israel not to eat blood, so that their names and their descendants may be before the Lord our God continually. {6:14} This law has no limit of days; it is forever. They shall observe it throughout their generations, so they may continue to seek forgiveness on your behalf with blood before the altar; every day, morning and evening, they shall seek forgiveness perpetually before the Lord to keep it and not be cut off. {6:15} He gave Noah and his sons a sign that there would not again be a flood on the earth. {6:16} He set His bow in the cloud as a sign of the eternal covenant that there would not again be a flood to destroy the earth for all the days of the earth. {6:17} For this reason, it is ordained and written on the heavenly tablets that they should celebrate the Feast of Weeks in this month once a year to renew the covenant every year. {6:18} This entire festival has been celebrated in heaven from the day of creation until the days of Noah—twenty-six jubilees and five weeks of years [1309-1659 A.M.]: and Noah and his sons observed it for seven jubilees and one week of years until the day of Noah's death. After Noah's death, his sons did away with it until the days of Abraham, and they began to eat blood. {6:19} But Abraham observed it, and Isaac and Jacob and their children observed it until your days. In your days, the children of Israel forgot it until you celebrated it anew on this mountain. {6:20} Command the children of Israel to observe this festival in all their generations as a commandment for them: one day each year in this month, they shall celebrate the festival. {6:21} For it is the Feast of Weeks and the Feast of First Fruits; this feast is twofold and of a double nature: according to what is written and engraved concerning it, celebrate it. {6:22} I have written in the book of the first law what I have written for you, that you should celebrate it in its season, one day each year, and I have explained its sacrifices so that the children of Israel should remember and celebrate it throughout their generations in this month, one day every year. {6:23} On the new moon of the first month, on the new moon of the fourth month, on the new moon of the seventh month, and on the new moon of the tenth month are the days of remembrance and the days of the seasons in the four divisions of the year. These are written and ordained as a testimony forever. {6:24} Noah ordained these for himself as feasts for future generations, so that they would serve as a memorial for him. {6:25} On the new moon of the first month, he was instructed to build the ark, and on that day the earth became dry, and he opened the ark and saw the earth. {6:26} On the new moon of the fourth month, the depths of the abyss below were closed. On the new moon of the seventh month, all the abysses of the earth were opened, and the waters began to descend into them. {6:27} On the new moon of the tenth month, the tops of the mountains were seen, and Noah was glad. {6:28} For this reason, he ordained them for himself as feasts, memorials forever, and thus they are ordained. {6:29} They placed them on the heavenly tablets, each with thirteen weeks; from one to another passed their memorial, from the first to the second, from the second to the third, and from the third to the fourth. {6:30} All the days of the commandment will be fifty-two weeks of days, completing the entire year. Thus it is engraved and ordained on the heavenly tablets. {6:31} There is no neglecting this commandment for even a single year or from year to year. {6:32} Command the children of Israel to observe the years according to this calendar—three hundred sixty-four days, which will constitute a complete year; they must not disturb its timing from its days or from its feasts, for everything will occur in accordance with this testimony, and they will not leave out any day nor disturb any feasts. {6:33} But if they neglect and do not observe them according to His commandment, they will disturb all their seasons and the years will be dislodged from this order, and they will neglect their ordinances. {6:34} All the children of Israel will forget and lose track of the path of the years, and forget the new moons, seasons, and Sabbaths, going astray regarding the entire order of the years. {6:35} For I know, and from now on I will declare it to you; it is not of my own devising; the book lies written before me, and on the heavenly tablets, the division of days is ordained, so they do not forget the feasts of the covenant and follow the feasts of the Gentiles in their error and ignorance. {6:36} There will be those who will certainly observe the moon—how it disrupts the seasons and comes in ten days too soon each year. {6:37} For this reason, the years will come upon them when they will disturb the order, making an abominable day the day of testimony, and a defiled day a feast day; they will confuse all the days, mixing the holy with the unclean and the unclean with the holy, going astray regarding the months, Sabbaths, feasts, and jubilees. {6:38} Therefore, I command and testify to you that you may testify to them; for after your death, your children will disturb them, so they will not maintain the year as three hundred sixty-four days. For this reason, they will go astray regarding the new moons, seasons, Sabbaths, and festivals, and they will consume all kinds of blood with all kinds of flesh.

{7:1} In the seventh week of the first year [1317 A.M.] of this jubilee, Noah planted vines on the mountain where the ark had rested, named Lubar, one of the Ararat Mountains, and they produced fruit in the fourth year [1320 A.M.]. He tended the fruit and gathered it in the seventh month of that year. {7:2} He made wine from it and put it into a vessel, keeping it until the fifth year [1321 A.M.], until the first day, on the new moon of the first month. {7:3} He celebrated the day of this feast with joy, making a burnt sacrifice to the Lord: one young ox, one ram, seven one-year-old sheep, and a goat kid, to atone for himself and his sons. {7:4} He prepared the goat kid first, placing some of its blood on the flesh on the altar he had made, laying all the fat on the altar for the burnt sacrifice, and laying all their flesh upon it. {7:5} He placed all their offerings mixed with oil upon it, then sprinkled wine on the the fire he had previously lit on the altar, and placed incense on the altar, causing a sweet aroma to rise, acceptable before the Lord his God. {7:6} He rejoiced and drank the wine with his children joyfully. {7:7} As evening came, he went into his tent, became drunk, lay down, and was uncovered in his tent while he slept. {7:8} Ham saw his father Noah naked and went out to tell his two brothers. {7:9} Shem took a garment, he and Japheth walked backward, covering their father's shame, their faces turned away. {7:10} Noah woke from his sleep and knew what his younger son had done to him; he cursed his son, saying, "Cursed be Canaan; he shall be a slave to his brothers." {7:11} He blessed Shem, saying, "Blessed be the Lord God of Shem, and Canaan shall serve him. God shall enlarge Japheth, and He shall dwell in the dwelling of Shem, and Canaan shall be his servant." {7:12} Ham knew that his father had cursed his younger son and was displeased by the curse. He separated from his father, taking his sons with him: Cush, Mizraim, Put, and Canaan. {7:13} He built a city, naming it after his wife, Ne'elatama'uk. {7:14} Japheth saw this and became envious of his brother; he too built a city, naming it after his wife, 'Adataneses. {7:15} Shem stayed with his father Noah and built a city near his father on the mountain, naming it after his wife, Sedeqetelebab. {7:16} These three cities are near Mount Lubar: Sedeqetelebab facing east of the mountain, Na'eltama'uk to the south, and 'Adatan'eses to the west. {7:17} These are the sons of Shem: Elam, Asshur, Arpachshad—who was born two years after the flood—Lud, and Aram. {7:18} The sons of Japheth are Gomer, Magog, Madai, Javan, Tubal, Meshech, and Tiras; these are the sons of Noah. {7:19} In the twenty-eighth jubilee [1324-1372 A.M.], Noah began to instruct his grandsons on the ordinances and commandments, and all the judgments he knew. He urged his sons to observe righteousness, cover the shame of their flesh, bless their Creator, honor their father and mother, love their neighbor, and protect their souls from fornication, uncleanness, and all wrongdoing. {7:20} For these three things brought the flood upon the earth: the fornication where the Watchers broke the law and took wives from among the daughters of men, beginning a legacy of uncleanness. {7:21} They bore sons, the Naphidim, who were all different and devoured one another; the Giants killed the Naphil, the Naphil killed the Eljo, and the Eljo killed mankind, and man killed one another. {7:22} Everyone sold themselves to iniquity and shed much blood, filling the earth with wrongdoing. {7:23} After this, they sinned against the beasts, birds, and all that moves on the earth; much blood was shed, and every thought of man was vanity and evil continuously. {7:24} The Lord destroyed everything from the face of the earth because of their wickedness and the blood they shed on the earth. {7:25} "We were left, I and you, my sons, and everything that entered with us into the ark. I see your works before me; you do not walk in righteousness. You have begun to walk the path of destruction, parting from one another and being envious of one another, so you are not in harmony, my sons, each with his brother. {7:26} I see, and behold, the demons have begun their seductions against you and your children. I now fear for you that after my death, you will shed the blood of men on the earth and be destroyed from the face of it. {7:27} Whoever sheds man's blood, or eats the blood of any flesh, shall be destroyed from the earth. {7:28} No man who eats blood or sheds man's blood on the earth shall be left alive; there shall be no seed or descendants left alive under heaven; they shall go into Sheol, descend into condemnation, and be cast into the darkness of the deep by violent death. {7:29} No blood shall be seen upon you from all the blood you have shed from the beasts or cattle or whatever flies upon the earth. Do good for your souls by covering what has been shed on the face of the earth. {7:30} Do not be like one who eats with blood; guard yourselves against anyone eating blood in your presence; cover the blood, for I have been commanded to testify to you and your children, along with all flesh. {7:31} Do not allow the soul to be eaten with the flesh, so that your blood, which is your life, may not be required at the hand of anyone who sheds it on the earth. {7:32} The earth will not be cleansed of the blood shed upon it; only through the blood of the one who shed it will the earth be purified throughout all generations. {7:33} Now, my children, listen: work judgment and righteousness so you may be established in righteousness over the whole earth, and your glory lifted up before my God, who saved me from the floodwaters. {7:34} You will go and build cities for yourselves, planting in them all the plants on the earth, including all fruit-bearing trees. {7:35} For three years, the fruit of everything that is eaten will not be gathered; in the fourth year, its fruit will be regarded as holy [and the first fruits shall be offered], acceptable before the Most High God, who created heaven, earth, and all things. They should offer the first of the wine and oil (as) first-fruits on the altar of the Lord, who receives it. What remains let the servants of the house of the Lord eat before the altar that receives it. {7:36} In the fifth year, make a release so that you release it in righteousness and uprightness, and you shall be righteous, and all you plant shall prosper. {7:37} Thus did Enoch, your father's father, command Methuselah, his son, and Methuselah commanded his son Lamech, and Lamech commanded me all the things which his fathers commanded him. {7:38} I also will give you commandments, my sons, as Enoch commanded his son in the first jubilees: while still living, the seventh in his generation, he commanded and testified to his son and to his grandsons until the day of his death."

{8:1} In the twenty-ninth jubilee, in the first week [1373 A.M.], Arpachshad took a wife named Rasu'eja, the daughter of Susan, the daughter of Elam. She bore him a son in the third year of this week [1375 A.M.], and he named him Kainam. {8:2} The boy grew, and his father taught him writing. He went to find a place where he could establish a city for himself. {8:3} He found a writing carved on a rock by previous generations, read it, transcribed it, and sinned because of it; it contained teachings from the Watchers about observing the omens of the sun, moon, and stars in all the signs of heaven. {8:4} He wrote it down but said nothing about it because he feared Noah would be angry with him for it. {8:5} In the thirtieth jubilee [1429 A.M.], in the second week of the first year, he took another wife named Melka, the daughter of Madai, the son of Japheth. In the fourth year [1432 A.M.], she bore him a son named Shelah because he said, "Truly I have been sent." {8:6} Shelah grew up and took a wife named Mu'ak, the daughter of Kesed, his father's brother, in the thirty-first jubilee, in the fifth week, in the first year [1499 A.M.]. {8:7} She bore him a son in the fifth year [1503 A.M.], and he named him Eber. He took a wife named 'Azûrâd, the daughter of Nebrod, in the thirty-second jubilee, in the seventh week, in the third year [1564 A.M.]. {8:8} In the sixth year [1567 A.M.], she bore him a son named Peleg; he named him so because during his days, the children of Noah began to divide the earth among themselves, which is why he was named Peleg. {8:9} They secretly divided the land among themselves and told Noah about it. {8:10} At the beginning of the thirty-third jubilee [1569 A.M.], they divided the earth into three parts for Shem, Ham, and Japheth according to their inheritance, in the first year of the first week, while one of us who had been sent was with them. {8:11} He called his sons to him, and they approached with their children, and he divided the earth into lots for each of his three sons. They reached into the bosom of Noah, their father, to take the writing. {8:12} The writing indicated that Shem's lot was the middle of the earth, which he would inherit for himself and his sons for generations to come, starting from the middle of the Rafa mountain range, from the mouth of the water from the river Tina. His portion extends west through this river, reaching the water of the abysses from which this river flows into the sea Me'at, which in turn flows into the great sea. {8:13} All the area towards the north belongs to Japheth, while everything south belongs to Shem. {8:14} It extends to Karaso, located in the bosom of the tongue looking south. {8:15} His portion extends along the great sea in a straight line until it reaches the west of the tongue facing south, which is known as the tongue of the Egyptian Sea. {8:16} It turns south toward the mouth of the great sea on its shores and extends west to 'Afra, reaching the waters of the river Gihon and the banks south of Gihon. {8:17} It stretches east to the Garden of Eden, to the south of it, and from the east of all the land of Eden and the whole eastern region, it turns east until it reaches the eastern side of the mountain named Rafa and descends to the bank of the mouth of the river Tina. {8:18} This portion was assigned to Shem and his sons, to possess it forever for their generations. {8:19} Noah rejoiced that this portion was assigned to Shem and his sons, remembering everything he had spoken in prophecy, having said, "Blessed be the Lord God of Shem, and may the Lord dwell in the dwelling of Shem." {8:20} He realized that the Garden of Eden is the holiest of places and the dwelling of the Lord, with Mount Sinai as the center of the desert and Mount Zion as the center of the earth; these three were created as holy places facing each other. {8:21} He blessed the God of gods who had put His word in his mouth, and the Lord forevermore. {8:22} He understood that a blessed portion had come to Shem and his sons for generations, including the whole land of Eden, the entire land of the Red Sea, all of the east and India, the Red Sea and its mountains, all the land of Bashan, Lebanon, the islands of Kaftur, all the mountains of Sanir and 'Amana, and the mountains of Asshur in the north, along with the lands of Elam, Asshur, Babel, Susan, Ma'edai, and all the mountains of Ararat. {8:23} This region beyond the sea, beyond the mountains of Asshur towards the north, is a blessed and spacious land where everything in it is very good. {8:24} For Ham, the second portion came forth beyond the Gihon to the south, to the right of the Garden, extending southward to all the mountains of fire, and west to the sea of 'Atel, continuing west to the sea of Ma'uk, where everything not destroyed descends. {8:25} It stretches north to the limits of Gadir, reaching the coastline of the great sea until it approaches the river Gihon and follows it to the right of the Garden of Eden. {8:26} This is the land assigned to Ham as his portion to occupy forever for himself and his sons through their generations. {8:27} For Japheth, the third portion came forth beyond the river Tina, to the north of its outflow, extending northeast to the entire region of Gog and all the country east of it. {8:28} It stretches northward to the mountains of Qelt and toward the sea of Ma'uk, going east of Gadir to the waters of the sea. {8:29} It reaches the west of Fara, turns toward 'Aferag, and extends east to the waters of the sea of Me'at. {8:30} It stretches to the region of the river Tina in a northeast direction until it approaches its boundary near the mountain Rafa, turning northward. {8:31} This is the land assigned to Japheth and his sons as his inheritance to possess forever; five great islands and a vast land in the north. {8:32} But it is cold there, while the land of Ham is hot, and the land of Shem is neither hot nor cold, but a mix of both.

{9:1} Ham divided the land among his sons, giving the first portion to Cush towards the east, to the west of him for Mizraim, to the west of Mizraim for Put, and further west on the sea for Canaan. {9:2} Shem also divided among his sons, with the first portion going to Ham and his sons, stretching east of the Tigris River towards the east, covering all the land of India, along the coast of the Red Sea, the waters of Dedan, and all the mountains of Mebri and Ela, as well as all the land of Susan and everything on the side of Pharnak to the Red Sea and the river Tina. {9:3} For Asshur, the second portion included all the land of Asshur, Nineveh, Shinar, and the border of India, rising and skirting the river. {9:4} Arpachshad received the third portion, which was all the land of the Chaldees region east of the Euphrates, bordering the Red Sea, along with all the waters of the desert near the tongue of the sea that looks towards Egypt, and all the land of Lebanon, Sanir, and 'Amana to the Euphrates border. {9:5} For Aram, the fourth portion included all the land of Mesopotamia between the Tigris and Euphrates rivers, north of the Chaldees, extending to the border of the Asshur mountains and the land of 'Arara. {9:6} Lud received the fifth portion, encompassing the Asshur mountains and all related regions until it reached the Great Sea and the eastern side of his brother Asshur. {9:7} Japheth also divided the land of his inheritance among his sons. {9:8} The first portion went to Gomer, extending east from the northern side to the river Tina; and in the north, Magog received all the inner regions until reaching the sea of Me'at. {9:9} Madai's portion included the land west of his two brothers, extending to the islands and the coasts of the islands. {9:10} Javan received the fourth portion, which included every island and those islands towards the border of Lud. {9:11} Tubal received the fifth portion in the midst of the tongue approaching Lud's border to the second tongue, extending to the region beyond the second tongue to the third tongue. {9:12} Meshech received the sixth portion, covering all the area beyond the third tongue until it reached the east of Gadir. {9:13} Tiras received the seventh portion, comprising four great islands in the middle of the sea, reaching to the portion of Ham. {9:14} The islands of Kamaturi were also allocated by lot to the sons of Arpachshad as their inheritance. {9:15} Thus, the sons of Noah divided their inheritances in the presence of their father Noah, who bound them all by an oath, cursing anyone who tried to seize a portion that did not belong to them by lot. {9:16} They all agreed, saying, "So be it; so be it," for themselves and their sons forever, throughout their generations until the day of judgment, when the Lord God will judge them with a sword and fire for all the wickedness and sins that have filled the earth with transgression and uncleanness.

{10:1} In the third week of this jubilee, unclean demons began to mislead the children of the sons of Noah, causing them to err and leading to their destruction. {10:2} The sons of Noah approached their father Noah and informed him about the demons who were misleading, blinding, and slaying his grandchildren. {10:3} Noah prayed before the Lord his God, saying: "God of all spirits, who has shown mercy to me and saved me and my sons from the floodwaters, and who has not let me perish as you did with the sons of perdition; {10:4} for your grace has been great towards me, and your mercy towards my soul has been immense. {10:5} Let your grace rest upon my sons, and do not allow wicked spirits to rule over them, lest they destroy them from the earth. {10:6} Bless me and my sons so we may increase, multiply, and fill the earth. {10:7} You know how your Watchers, the fathers of these spirits, acted in my time. For these spirits that exist, imprison them and hold them fast in condemnation, so they do not bring destruction upon the sons of your servant, my God, for they are malignant and created for destruction. {10:8} Let them not govern the spirits of the living; only you can have dominion over them. Do not allow them to have power over the righteous from now on and forever." {10:9} The Lord our God commanded us to bind them all. {10:10} The chief of the spirits, Mastêmâ, came and said: "Lord, Creator, let some of them remain before me, so they can listen to my voice and do all that I command; for if some are not left to me, I cannot carry out my will on the sons of men; these spirits are for corruption and leading astray before my judgment, for great is the wickedness of humanity." {10:11} The Lord replied: "Let one-tenth remain with you, and let the other nine parts descend into condemnation." {10:12} He commanded one of us to teach Noah all their medicines, knowing they would not walk in righteousness. {10:13} We followed all His instructions, binding all the malignant spirits in condemnation, leaving one-tenth to be subject to Satan on earth. {10:14} We explained to Noah all the remedies for their diseases and seductions, instructing him on how to heal with herbs from the earth. {10:15} Noah wrote everything in a book as we directed him concerning every type of medicine, preventing the evil spirits from harming the sons of Noah. {10:16} He gave everything he had written to Shem, his eldest son, for he loved him more than all his other sons. {10:17} Noah slept with his ancestors and was buried on Mount Lubar in the land of Ararat. He lived for nine hundred and fifty years, completing nineteen jubilees, two weeks, and five years [1659 A.M.]. {10:18} In his lifetime, he excelled all the children of men, except for Enoch, due to the righteousness in which he was perfect. Enoch's role was to serve as a testimony to future generations, recounting the deeds of generations until the day of judgment. {10:19} In the thirty-third jubilee, in the first year of the second week, Peleg took a wife named Lomna, the daughter of Sina'ar, and she bore him a son in the fourth year of this week, naming him Reu. He said, "Behold, the children of men have become evil due to the wicked intention of building a city and tower in the land of Shinar." {10:20} They departed from the land of Ararat eastward to Shinar, where they built the city and the tower, saying, "Come, let us ascend into heaven." {10:21} They began to build, and in the fourth week, they made bricks with fire, using bricks as stones, and the clay to cement them was asphalt from the sea and the fountains of water in Shinar. {10:22} They built it for forty-three years [1645-1688 A.M.]; its breadth was two hundred three bricks, and the height of a brick was a third of one, making the total height five thousand four hundred thirty-three cubits and two palms, with one wall extending thirteen stades and the other thirty stades. {10:23} The Lord our God said to us: "Behold, they are one people, and this is what they begin to do; now nothing will be withheld from them. Come, let us go down and confuse their language, so they do not understand one another and may be scattered into cities and nations, and their purpose will no longer be unified until the day of judgment." {10:24} The Lord descended, and we went down with him to see the city and the tower that the children of men had built. {10:25} He confused their language, causing them to no longer understand each other, and they ceased building the city and the tower. {10:26} For this reason, the whole land of Shinar is called Babel, because the Lord confused the language of the children of men there, and from there they were dispersed into their cities according to their language and nation. {10:27} The Lord sent a mighty wind against the tower, overthrowing it upon the earth; it was located between Asshur and Babylon in the land of Shinar, and they named it 'Overthrow.' {10:28} In the fourth week, in the first year [1688 A.M.], they were dispersed from the land of Shinar. {10:29} Ham and his sons went to the land that he was to occupy, which he received as his portion in the south. {10:30} Canaan saw the land of Lebanon up to the river of Egypt, recognizing it as very good. He did not go into his inheritance west towards the sea but settled in the land of Lebanon, east and west from the border of Jordan to the sea's border. {10:31} Ham, his father, along with Cush and Mizraim, his brothers, said to him: "You have settled in a land that is not yours, which did not come to us by lot; do not do this, for if you do, you and your sons will fall in the land and be cursed through sedition; for by sedition you have settled, and by sedition your children will fall, and you shall be rooted out forever. {10:32} Do not dwell in the territory of Shem; for to Shem and his sons came their portion by lot. {10:33} You are cursed, and you shall be cursed more than all the sons of Noah, by the curse with which we bound ourselves by an oath in the presence of the holy judge and our father Noah." {10:34} But Canaan did not listen to them and continued to dwell in the land of Lebanon from Hamath to the entrance of Egypt until today. {10:35} For this reason, that land is called Canaan. {10:36} Japheth and his sons went toward the sea and settled in the land of their portion, but Madai saw the land of the sea and was not pleased; he requested a portion from Ham and Asshur, his brother-in-law, and settled in Media, near his wife's family until today. {10:37} He named his dwelling place, and that of his sons, Media, after the name of his father Madai.

{11:1} In the thirty-fifth jubilee, during the third week, in the first year [1681 A.M.], Reu married a woman named 'Ôrâ, the daughter of 'Ûr, the son of Kesed, and she bore him a son, whom he named Sêrôh, in the seventh year of this week, which is [1687 A.M.]. {11:2} The sons of Noah began to wage war against each other, capturing and killing one another, shedding blood on the earth, eating blood, building fortified cities, walls, and towers, and individuals started to elevate themselves above others, establishing the beginnings of kingdoms and going to war against one another—people against people, nation against nation, and city against city. All began to do evil, acquiring weapons and teaching their sons the art of war, capturing cities, and selling both male and female slaves. {11:3} 'Ûr, the son of Kesed, built the city of 'Ara in Chaldea, naming it after himself and his father. They made molten images and worshiped each idol they had created for themselves. They began to create carved images and unclean representations, while malignant spirits aided and seduced them into transgression and impurity. {11:4} The prince Mastêmâ (a chief spirit) worked hard to ensure this, sending other spirits under his authority to commit all kinds of wrongdoing and sin, corrupting and destroying, and shedding blood upon the earth. {11:5} This is why he named Sêrôh, Serug, for everyone turned to all kinds of sin and wrongdoing. {11:6} He grew up and lived in Ur of the Chaldees, close to his wife's mother's family, worshiping idols. In the thirty-sixth jubilee, during the fifth week, in the first year, [1744 A.M.], he married a woman named Melka, the daughter of Kaber, the daughter of his father's brother. {11:7} She bore him Nahor in the first year of this week, and he grew up in Ur of the Chaldees, where his father taught him the Chaldean practices of divination and astrology based on the signs of the heavens. {11:8} In the thirty-seventh jubilee, during the sixth week, in the first year, [1800 A.M.], he took a wife named 'Ijaska, the daughter of Nestag from the Chaldeans. {11:9} She bore him Terah in the seventh year of this week, [1806 A.M.]. {11:10} The prince Mastêmâ sent ravens and birds to devour the seeds that were sown in the land to destroy the harvest and rob people of their labor. Before they could sow, the ravens picked the seeds from the ground. {11:11} This is why he named him Terah, because the ravens and birds left them in poverty by consuming their seeds. {11:12} The years became barren because of the birds, devouring all the fruit from the trees, and it was only with great effort that people managed to save a small amount of the earth's produce in those days. {11:13} In the thirty-ninth jubilee, during the second week, in the first year, [1870 A.M.], Terah took a wife named 'Edna, the daughter of 'Abram, the daughter of his father's sister. In the seventh year of this week, [1876 A.M.], she bore him a son, whom he named Abram, after his maternal grandfather, who had died before she conceived. {11:14} The child began to understand the errors of the earth, realizing that everyone strayed after carved images and impurity, and his father taught him to write. By the time he was two weeks of years old, [1890 A.M.], he separated from his father so that he would not worship idols with him. {11:15} He began to pray to the Creator of all things, asking Him to save him from the errors of humanity, that his portion would not fall into impurity and wickedness. {11:16} When it was time to sow seeds on the land, everyone went out together to protect their crops from the ravens, and Abram joined them as a lad of fourteen years. {11:17} A cloud of ravens came to devour the seeds, and Abram ran to confront them before they landed on the ground, shouting at them not to descend and to return from where they came. {11:18} Miraculously, he made the clouds of ravens turn back seventy times that day, and not a single raven settled in all the land where Abram was. {11:19} All who were with him witnessed him cry out, and saw the ravens retreat, causing his name to become great throughout all the land of the Chaldees. {11:20} That year, everyone who wanted to sow came to him, and he accompanied them until sowing time ended. They sowed their land, and that year they harvested enough grain, ate, and were satisfied. {11:21} In the first year of the fifth week [1891 A.M.], Abram taught those who made tools for oxen, skilled craftsmen in wood, how to create a vessel above the ground, aligned with the plow's frame to hold the seed. The seeds would fall from there onto the plowshare and be buried in the earth, and they no longer feared the ravens. {11:22} They constructed similar vessels on all the frames of the plows, sowing and cultivating all the land as Abram instructed, without fear of the birds.

{12:1} In the sixth week, in the seventh year of that week, [1904 A.M.], Abram said to his father Terah, "Father!" {12:2} Terah replied, "Here I am, my son." And Abram asked, "What benefit and profit do we gain from the idols you worship and bow down to? {12:3} There is no spirit in them; they are mere lifeless forms and a deception of the heart. Do not worship them. {12:4} Worship the God of heaven, who brings the rain and dew upon the earth, who does everything on earth, who created everything by His word, and from whom all life flows. {12:5} Why do you worship things that have no spirit? They are made by human hands, and you carry them on your shoulders, yet they offer you no help. {12:6} They are a source of shame to their makers and a deception for those who worship them; do not worship them." {12:7} Terah responded, "I know this, my son, but what can I do with a people who have made me serve before them? If I tell them the truth, they will kill me, for their souls cling to these idols. Be silent, my son, lest they slay you." He spoke these words to his two brothers, who grew angry with him, so he remained silent. {12:8} In the fortieth jubilee, during the second week, in the seventh year, [1925 A.M.], Abram married a woman named Sarai, who was his half-sister. {12:9} Haran, his brother, took a wife in the third year of the third week, [1928 A.M.], and she bore him a son in the seventh year of that week, [1932 A.M.], whom he named Lot. {12:10} Nahor, his brother, also took a wife. {12:11} At sixty years of age, in the fourth week, in the fourth year, [1936 A.M.], Abram arose at night and burned down the house of idols, destroying everything inside, and no one knew it. {12:12} They woke up that night and rushed to save their gods from the fire. Haran hurried to save them, but the flames engulfed him, and he died in Ur of the Chaldees before his father Terah, who buried him there. {12:13} Terah left Ur of the Chaldees with his sons, intending to go to the land of Lebanon and Canaan, and settled in the land of Haran, where Abram lived with his father for two weeks of years. {12:14} In the sixth week, during the fifth year of that week, [1951 A.M.], Abram spent the night on the new moon of the seventh month observing the stars from evening to morning to determine the character of the year regarding rainfall. Alone, he sat and observed. {12:15} A thought struck him, and he said: "All the signs of the stars, moon, and sun are in the hands of the Lord. Why am I seeking them? {12:16} If He desires, He sends rain morning and evening; if He chooses, He withholds it. All things are under His control." {12:17} He prayed that night, saying, "My God, God Most High, You alone are my God. I have chosen You and Your dominion. You created all things, and all that exists is the work of Your hands. {12:18} Deliver me from the hands of evil spirits who dominate the thoughts of men's hearts, and do not let them lead me astray from You, my God. Establish me and my descendants forever, so we do not stray from now on and forever." {12:19} He continued, "Should I return to Ur of the Chaldees, where they seek my face to bring me back, or should I stay here? Please make my path prosper in Your hands, so I may fulfill it, and not be led astray by the deceitfulness of my heart, O my God." {12:20} When he finished praying, behold, the word of the Lord came to him through me, saying: "Get up from your country, your relatives, and your father's house to a land that I will show you, and I will make you a great and numerous nation. {12:21} I will bless you, make your name great, and you will be a blessing on the earth. In you, all families of the earth will be blessed. I will bless those who bless you, and curse those who curse you. {12:22} I will be a God to you, your son, your grandson, and all your descendants. Fear not, from now on and for all generations of the earth, I am your God." {12:23} The Lord also said: "Open his mouth and ears so he may hear and speak with his mouth in the language revealed to him; for this language had ceased from the mouths of all children of men since the overthrow of Babel." {12:24} I opened his mouth, ears, and lips, allowing him to speak in Hebrew, the language of creation. He took the books of his fathers, written in Hebrew, transcribing them, and began studying them, as I revealed knowledge to him that he could not understand, and he studied them during the six rainy months. {12:25} In the seventh year of the sixth week [1953 A.M.], he told his father he would leave Haran to explore the land of Canaan and then return. {12:26} Terah said to him, "Go in peace. May the eternal God make your path straight. {12:27} May the Lord be with you, protect you from all evil, and grant you grace, mercy, and favor in the eyes of those you meet. May no one among men have power to harm you. Go in peace. {12:28} If you find a land that pleases you, take me with you, along with Lot, the son of your brother Haran, as your own son. May the Lord be with you. {12:29} And leave Nahor, your brother, with me until you return in peace, and we will go together."

{13:1} Abram journeyed from Haran, taking Sarai, his wife, and Lot, the son of his brother Haran, to the land of Canaan. He arrived in Asshur, then went to Shechem and settled near a tall oak tree. {13:2} He noticed that the land was very pleasant from Hamath to the tall oak. {13:3} The Lord said to him, "To you and your descendants, I will give this land." {13:4} He built an altar there and offered a burnt sacrifice to the Lord, who had appeared to him. {13:5} He then moved to the mountain between Bethel to the west and Ai to the east and pitched his tent there. {13:6} He saw that the land was very wide and fertile, with everything growing—vines, figs, pomegranates, oaks, ilexes, terebinths, olive trees, cedars, cypresses, date palms, and all kinds of trees, along with water in the mountains. {13:7} He blessed the Lord who had led him out of Ur of the Chaldees and brought him to this land. {13:8} In the first year of the seventh week, on the new moon of the first month, 1954 A.M., he built an altar on that mountain and called on the name of the Lord, saying, "You, the eternal God, are my God." {13:9} He offered a burnt sacrifice on the altar, asking the Lord to be with him and not forsake him all his days. {13:10} He then moved southward and came to Hebron, which was built at that time, and he lived there for two years before going into the southern region, to Bealoth, where a famine struck the land. {13:11} In the third year of the week, Abram went to Egypt, where he stayed for five years before his wife was taken from him. {13:12} At that time, Tanais in Egypt was built, seven years after Hebron. {13:13} When Pharaoh seized Sarai, Abram's wife, the Lord plagued Pharaoh and his household with great afflictions because of Sarai. {13:14} Abram became very wealthy in livestock, cattle, donkeys, horses, camels, servants, and abundant silver and gold. Lot, his brother's son, was also prosperous. {13:15} Pharaoh returned Sarai, Abram's wife, and sent him out of Egypt, so he journeyed back to the place where he had pitched his tent at the beginning, to the altar between Ai on the east and Bethel on the west. He blessed the Lord, his God, who had brought him back safely. {13:16} In the forty-first jubilee, in the third year of the first week, 1963 A.M., he returned to this place and offered a burnt sacrifice there, calling on the name of the Lord, saying, "You, the Most High God, are my God forever." {13:17} In the fourth year of this week, 1964 A.M., Lot separated from him and settled in Sodom, where the men were exceedingly sinful. {13:18} It grieved Abram deeply that his brother's son had parted from him, for he had no children. {13:19} In the year when Lot was captured, the Lord spoke to Abram after Lot had left him, in the fourth year of this week: "Lift your eyes from where you dwell, northward, southward, eastward, and westward. {13:20} For all the land you see, I will give to you and your descendants forever. I will make your descendants like the sand of the sea; even if someone could count the dust of the earth, your descendants will not be counted. {13:21} Arise, walk through the land in its length and breadth, for I will give it to your descendants." Abram went to Hebron and lived there. {13:22} In that year, Chedorlaomer, king of Elam, Amraphel, king of Shinar, Arioch, king of Sellasar, and Tergal, king of nations, fought and killed the king of Gomorrah. The king of Sodom fled, and many were wounded in the valley of Siddim, near the Salt Sea. {13:23} They captured Sodom, Adam, Zeboim, and took Lot, Abram's brother's son, and all his possessions, and went to Dan. {13:24} A survivor came and informed Abram that his brother's son had been taken captive. Abram armed his trained servants and pursued the captors. {13:25} Abram dedicated a tenth of the first fruits to the Lord, and the Lord established it as a perpetual ordinance that they should give it to the priests who served Him, so they could possess it forever. {13:26} This law has no limit of days; He ordained that for all generations they should give to the Lord a tenth of everything—the seed, wine, oil, cattle, and sheep. {13:27} He gave it to His priests to enjoy joyfully in His presence. {13:28} The king of Sodom approached him, bowing down, and said, "Our Lord Abram, give us the people you rescued, but let the goods be yours." {13:29} Abram replied, "I raise my hand to the Most High God, that I will not take anything from you, not even a thread or a shoelace, so you won't say, 'I made Abram rich,' except for what the young men have eaten and the share of the men who came with me—Aner, Eschol, and Mamre. They can take their share."

{14:1} After these events, in the fourth year of this week, on the new moon of the third month, the Lord's word came to Abram in a dream, saying, "Fear not, Abram; I am your protector, and your reward will be very great." {14:2} Abram said, "Lord, what will you give me since I go childless? The son of my servant, Eliezer of Damascus, will be my heir." {14:3} The Lord replied, "This man will not be your heir, but one who comes from your own body will be your heir." {14:4} He brought Abram outside and said, "Look toward heaven and count the stars, if you are able to count them." {14:5} Abram looked and saw the stars. The Lord said, "So shall your descendants be." {14:6} Abram believed the Lord, and it was credited to him as righteousness. {14:7} The Lord said to him, "I am the Lord who brought you out of Ur of the Chaldees to give you this land to possess." {14:8} Abram asked, "Lord, how can I know that I will inherit it?" {14:9} The Lord instructed him, "Bring Me a three-year-old heifer, a three-year-old goat, a three-year-old sheep, a turtle dove, and a pigeon." {14:10} Abram took these animals and cut them in half, laying the pieces opposite each other, but did not cut the birds. {14:11} Birds came down on the carcasses, and Abram drove them away. {14:12} When the sun set, a deep sleep fell on Abram, and a great darkness enveloped him. The Lord said to Abram, "Know for certain that your descendants will be strangers in a land that is not theirs; they will be enslaved and oppressed for four hundred years. {14:13} But I will judge the nation they serve, and afterward, they will leave with great possessions. {14:14} You, however, will go to your ancestors in peace and be buried at a good old age. {14:15} In the fourth generation, they will return here, for the iniquity of the Amorites has not yet reached its full measure." {14:16} When Abram woke from his sleep, the sun had set, and there was a smoking furnace and a flaming torch that passed between the pieces. {14:17} On that day, the Lord made a covenant with Abram, saying, "To your descendants, I give this land from the river of Egypt to the great river, the Euphrates, including the Kenites, Kenizzites, Kadmonites, Perizzites, Rephaim, Phakorites, Hivites, Amorites, Canaanites, Girgashites, and Jebusites." {14:18} The day passed, and Abram offered the pieces and the birds, along with their grain and drink offerings, and the fire consumed them. {14:19} That day, we established a covenant with Abram, as we had with Noah in this month, & Abram renewed the festival and ordinance for himself forever. {14:20} Abram rejoiced and shared all this with Sarai, his wife; he believed he would have descendants, but she remained barren. {14:21} Sarai advised Abram, saying, "Take Hagar, my Egyptian maid; perhaps I can build a family through her." {14:22} Abram listened to his wife and did as she suggested. Sarai gave Hagar, her maid, to Abram as a wife. {14:23} He went into Hagar, and she conceived & bore him a son, whom he named Ishmael in the fifth year of this week, 1965 A.M.; this was the eighty-sixth year of Abram's life.

{15:1} In the fifth year of the fourth week of this jubilee, in the third month, in the middle of the month, Abram celebrated the feast of the first fruits of the grain harvest. {15:2} He offered new offerings on the altar, the first fruits of the produce, including a heifer, a goat, and a sheep as burnt sacrifices to the Lord; he also offered their fruit offerings and drink offerings upon the altar with frankincense. {15:3} The Lord appeared to Abram and said, "I am God Almighty; walk before Me and be perfect. {15:4} I will make My covenant between Me and you, and I will multiply you greatly." {15:5} Abram fell on his face, and God talked with him, saying: {15:6} "Behold, My ordinance is with you, and you shall be the father of many nations. {15:7} Your name will no longer be Abram; from now on, your name shall be Abraham, for I have made you the father of many nations. {15:8} I will make you exceedingly great, and you will become nations, and kings will come from you. {15:9} I will establish My covenant between Me and you and your descendants throughout their generations as an eternal covenant, so that I may be a God to you and your descendants. {15:10} I will give to you and your descendants the land where you have been a sojourner, the land of Canaan, to possess it forever, and I will be their God." {15:11} The Lord said to Abraham, "As for you, keep My covenant, you and your descendants: circumcise every male among you and cut off the foreskin as a sign of the eternal covenant between Me and you. {15:12} On the eighth day, you shall circumcise every male throughout your generations, including those born in your house or bought with money from any stranger who is not your offspring. {15:13} Every male born in your house shall be circumcised, and those whom you have bought with money shall be circumcised; My covenant shall be in your flesh as an eternal ordinance. {15:14} Any uncircumcised male who is not circumcised on the eighth day shall be cut off from his people, for he has broken My covenant." {15:15} God said to Abraham, "As for Sarai your wife, her name shall no longer be Sarai; instead, her name will be Sarah. {15:16} I will bless her and give you a son by her, and I will bless him, and he will become a nation, and kings of nations will come from him." {15:17} Abraham fell on his face and laughed, saying in his heart, "Will a son be born to a man who is a hundred years old, and will Sarah, who is ninety years old, bear a child?" {15:18} Abraham said to God, "Oh, that Ishmael might live before You!" {15:19} God said, "Yes, but Sarah will also bear you a son, and you shall name him Isaac. I will establish My covenant with him as an everlasting covenant for his descendants. {15:20} As for Ishmael, I have heard you; behold, I will bless him, make him fruitful, and multiply him greatly; he shall be the father of twelve princes, and I will make him a great nation. {15:21} But My covenant will be established with Isaac, whom Sarah will bear to you next year." {15:22} After speaking with him, God went up from Abraham. {15:23} Abraham did as God commanded and took Ishmael his son, along with all those born in his house and bought with his money, every male in his household, and circumcised the flesh of their foreskin. {15:24} On that very day, Abraham was circumcised, along with all the men in his household, including those born in the house and those bought with money from strangers. {15:25} This law is for all generations forever; there is no circumcision of days, and no omission of one day out of the eight days; for it is an eternal ordinance, ordained and written on the heavenly tablets. {15:26} Every male who is not circumcised on the eighth day does not belong to the children of the covenant that the Lord made with Abraham but is destined for destruction; he has broken the covenant of the Lord our God. {15:27} All the angels of the presence and all the angels of sanctification have been created since the day of their creation, and the Lord sanctified Israel, so they should be with Him and His holy angels. {15:28} Command the children of Israel to observe the sign of this covenant for their generations as an eternal ordinance; they will not be uprooted from the land. {15:29} This command is established as a covenant, that they should observe it forever among all the children of Israel. {15:30} The Lord did not bring Ishmael and his sons and Esau close to Him; He chose Israel to be His people, sanctifying it and gathering it from among all the children of men. {15:31} For there are many nations and peoples, all of whom He governs with spirits in authority to lead them astray from Him. {15:32} But over Israel, He did not appoint any angel or spirit; He alone is their ruler, and He will preserve them and hold them accountable through His angels and spirits. {15:33} Now I announce that the children of Israel will not keep true to this ordinance; they will not circumcise their sons according to all this law; they will omit the circumcision of their sons, and all of them, sons of Beliar, will leave their sons uncircumcised as they were born. {15:34} There will be great wrath from the Lord against the children of Israel because they have forsaken His covenant, turned away from His word, provoked, and blasphemed, treating their members like the Gentiles, leading them to be uprooted from the land. {15:35} There will be no more pardon or forgiveness for them regarding this eternal error.

{16:1} On the new moon of the fourth month, we appeared to Abraham at the oak of Mamre and talked with him, announcing that a son would be given to him by Sarah his wife. {16:2} Sarah laughed when she heard us speaking, and we admonished her, causing her to become afraid and deny that she had laughed because of our words. {16:3} We told her the name of her son, as ordained and written in the heavenly tablets: Isaac, {16:4} and that when we returned at a set time, she would conceive a son. {16:5} In this month, the Lord executed His judgments on Sodom, Gomorrah, Zeboim, and all the region of the Jordan, burning them with fire and brimstone and destroying them until this day, as I have declared all their wicked works, that they are exceedingly sinful, defiling themselves and committing fornication in their flesh, and working uncleanness on the earth. {16:6} Similarly, God will execute judgment on places where they have acted according to the uncleanness of the Sodomites, like the judgment of Sodom. {16:7} But we saved Lot because God remembered Abraham and sent him out from the midst of the destruction. {16:8} Lot and his daughters committed sin upon the earth, such as had not been seen since the days of Adam, for the man lay with his daughters. {16:9} It was commanded and engraved concerning all his seed on the heavenly tablets to remove them and execute judgment upon them like Sodom, leaving no seed of the man on earth on the day of condemnation. {16:10} In this month, Abraham moved from Hebron and dwelled between Kadesh and Shur in the mountains of Gerar. {16:11} In the middle of the fifth month, he moved from there and dwelt at the Well of the Oath. {16:12} In the middle of the sixth month, the Lord visited Sarah and did as He had spoken, and she conceived. {16:13} She bore a son in the third month, in the middle of the month, at the time the Lord had spoken to Abraham, during the festival of the first fruits of the harvest; Isaac was born. {16:14} Abraham circumcised his son on the eighth day; he was the first to be circumcised according to the eternal covenant. {16:15} In the sixth year of the fourth week, we came to Abraham at the Well of the Oath, as we had told Sarah we would return, and we found her with child. {16:16} We blessed him and announced all the things decreed concerning him: that he would not die until he begets six more sons and sees them before he dies, but in Isaac, his name and seed will be called. {16:17} All the seed of his sons will be Gentiles and be counted among the Gentiles, but from Isaac's sons, one will become a holy seed, not counted among the Gentiles. {16:18} He will become the portion of the Most High, and all his seed will belong to God, forming a people above all nations to become a kingdom of priests and a holy nation. {16:19} We went our way, announcing to Sarah all we had told him, and they both rejoiced with great joy. {16:20} He built an altar to the Lord who delivered him and made him rejoice in the land of his sojourning, celebrating a seven-day festival of joy near the altar he built at the Well of the Oath. {16:21} He built booths for himself and his servants during this festival, becoming the first to celebrate the Feast of Tabernacles on the earth. {16:22} During these seven days, he brought each day to the altar burnt offerings to the Lord: two oxen, two rams, seven sheep, and a goat for a sin offering to atone for himself and his seed. {16:23} As a thank offering, he offered seven rams, seven kids, seven sheep, seven goats, along with their fruit and drink offerings, burning all the fat on the altar as a pleasing aroma to the Lord. {16:24} Morning and evening, he burned fragrant substances like frankincense, galbanum, stackte, nard, myrrh, spice, and costum; all these seven were crushed and mixed together in equal parts and pure. {16:25} He celebrated this feast for seven days, rejoicing with all his heart and soul, along with everyone in his house; no stranger or uncircumcised person was with him. {16:26} He blessed his Creator, who created him in his generation, knowing that from him would arise the plant of righteousness for eternal generations and a holy seed, making him like the One who made all things. {16:27} He blessed and rejoiced, calling this festival the Festival of the Lord, a joy acceptable to the Most High God. {16:28} We blessed him forever, and all his descendants throughout all generations of the earth, for he celebrated this festival in its season, according to the testimony of the heavenly tablets. {16:29} For this reason, it is ordained on the heavenly tablets concerning Israel that they shall celebrate the Feast of Tabernacles for seven days with joy in the seventh month, as a perpetual statute throughout their generations every year. {16:30} There is no limit to the days; it is ordained forever for Israel to celebrate it, dwell in booths, set wreaths upon their heads, and take leafy boughs and willows from the brook. {16:31} Abraham took branches of palm trees and fruits of goodly trees, going around the altar 7 times each day in the morning, praising and thanking his God for everything in joy.

{17:1} In the first year of the fifth week of this jubilee, Isaac was weaned, and Abraham held a grand banquet in the third month on the day his son Isaac was weaned. {17:2} Ishmael, the son of Hagar the Egyptian, was present before Abraham, his father, and Abraham rejoiced and blessed God for having seen his sons and not dying childless. {17:3} He remembered the words spoken to him on the day Lot had parted from him and rejoiced because the Lord had given him offspring to inherit the earth, blessing the Creator of all things with all his heart. {17:4} Sarah saw Ishmael playing and dancing, and Abraham rejoicing with great joy; she became jealous of Ishmael and said to Abraham, "Cast out this bondwoman and her son; for the son of this bondwoman will not be heir with my son, Isaac." {17:5} This matter was very distressing to Abraham because of his maidservant and his son, and he felt troubled about sending them away. {17:6} God said to Abraham, "Do not let this matter be distressing to you because of the child and the bondwoman; in all that Sarah has said to you, listen to her and do what she says, for in Isaac shall your name and offspring be called. {17:7} As for the son of the bondwoman, I will make him into a great nation because he is your offspring." {17:8} Abraham rose early in the morning, took bread and a bottle of water, placed them on Hagar and the child's shoulders, and sent them away. {17:9} She departed and wandered in the wilderness of Beersheba; the water in the bottle ran out, and the child became thirsty and could not go on, so he fell down. {17:10} His mother took him and placed him under an olive tree, then sat down at a distance, about the length of a bow shot, for she said, "Let me not see the death of my child," and she wept as she sat. {17:11} An angel of God, one of the holy ones, said to her, "Why are you weeping, Hagar? Get up, take the child, and hold him in your arms, for God has heard your voice and seen the child." {17:12} She opened her eyes and saw a well of water; she went and filled her bottle and gave the child a drink. {17:13} Then she arose and went toward the wilderness of Paran. {17:14} The child grew up and became an archer; God was with him, and his mother took him a wife from among the daughters of Egypt. {17:15} She bore him a son, and he named him Nebaioth, saying, "The Lord was near to me when I called upon Him." {17:16} It happened in the seventh week, in the first year of that week, in the first month of this jubilee, on the twelfth of the month, that voices were heard in heaven regarding Abraham, confirming that he was faithful in all that God had commanded him and that he loved the Lord, remaining faithful in every affliction. {17:17} The prince Mastêmâ approached God, saying, "Look, Abraham loves his son Isaac and delights in him above all else; command him to offer him as a burnt offering on the altar, and you will see if he will obey this command and if he is truly faithful in everything you test him with." {17:18} The Lord knew that Abraham was faithful in all his trials; He had tested him through famine, wealth, and loss of his wife, among other things, and Abraham remained patient and loyal, never slow to act.

{18:1} God called to him, "Abraham, Abraham," and Abraham answered, "Here I am." {18:2} God said, "Take your beloved son, whom you love, even Isaac, and go to the high country and offer him on one of the mountains that I will show you." {18:3} Abraham rose early in the morning, saddled his donkey, took two young men with him and Isaac, cut the wood for the burnt offering, and set out for the place three days later, seeing it from afar. {18:4} When he reached a well of water, he told the young men, "Stay here with the donkey, and I and the boy will go over there. We will worship and then return to you." {18:5} He took the wood of the burnt offering and laid it on Isaac, took the fire and the knife in his hand, and they both went together to the designated place. {18:6} Isaac said to his father, "Father," and he replied, "Here I am, my son." Isaac asked, "Here is the fire and the wood, but where is the lamb for the burnt offering?" {18:7} Abraham answered, "God will provide for Himself a lamb for the burnt offering, my son." They continued to approach the place of God's mountain. {18:8} Abraham built an altar there, placed the wood on it, bound Isaac, and laid him on the altar on top of the wood. He reached out his hand to take the knife to slay his son. {18:9} I stood before him and the prince Mastêmâ, and the Lord said, "Do not lay your hand on the boy or do anything to him, for I have shown that you fear God." {18:10} I called to him from heaven, saying, "Abraham, Abraham," and he was terrified, answering, "Here I am." {18:11} I told him, "Do not lay your hand on the boy, nor do anything to him; for now I know that you fear God, since you have not withheld your son, your only son, from Me." {18:12} The prince Mastêmâ was humiliated; Abraham looked up and saw a ram caught by its horns in a thicket, and he went and took the ram and offered it as a burnt offering instead of his son. {18:13} Abraham named that place "The Lord Will Provide," so it is said, "On the mountain of the Lord, it will be provided." {18:14} The Lord called Abraham's name a second time from heaven, as we appeared to speak to him in the name of the Lord, saying, "I have sworn by Myself, says the Lord, because you have done this and have not withheld your beloved son from Me, that I will bless you abundantly. {18:15} I will multiply your descendants as the stars of heaven and as the sand on the seashore. {18:16} Your descendants will inherit the cities of their enemies, and through your descendants, all nations of the earth will be blessed, because you have obeyed My voice, showing that you are faithful in all that I have commanded you. {18:17} Go in peace." {18:18} Abraham returned to his young men, and they rose together to Beersheba, where Abraham settled by the Well of the Oath. {18:19} He celebrated this festival every year for seven days with joy, calling it the Festival of the Lord, in honor of the seven days during which he returned safely. {18:20} This has been ordained and written on the heavenly tablets regarding Israel and its descendants, that they should celebrate this festival for seven days with joy in the seventh month as a perpetual statute for their generations each year.

{19:1} In the first year of the first week of the forty-second jubilee, Abraham returned and settled near Hebron, also known as Kirjath Arba, for two weeks of years. {19:2} In the first year of the third week of this jubilee, the days of Sarah's life came to an end, and she died in Hebron. {19:3} Abraham went to mourn for her and to bury her, and he was tested to see if his spirit remained patient and if he was not upset by what he said; he proved to be patient and was not disturbed. {19:4} With a calm spirit, he spoke to the Hittites, hoping they would give him a place to bury his dead. {19:5} The Lord granted him favor in the eyes of all who saw him, and he respectfully asked the sons of Heth for a burial site. They offered him the land of the double cave near Mamre, which is Hebron, for four hundred pieces of silver. {19:6} They insisted that they would give it to him for free, but he refused to accept it without payment, fully paying the price for the land, and he bowed to them twice before burying his dead in the double cave. {19:7} Sarah lived a total of one hundred and twenty-seven years, which is two jubilees, four weeks, and one year; these are the days of her life. {19:8} This was the tenth trial Abraham faced, and he was found faithful and patient in spirit. {19:9} He did not utter a word about the rumor that God had said He would give the land to him and his descendants; he only requested a place to bury his dead because he was faithful, and he was recorded in the heavenly tablets as God's friend. {19:10} In the fourth year of that jubilee, he took a wife for his son Isaac, named Rebecca, the daughter of Bethuel, the son of Nahor, Abraham's brother; she was the sister of Laban and the daughter of Bethuel, who was the son of Milcah, Nahor's wife. {19:11} Abraham also took a third wife named Keturah from among the daughters of his servants, as Hagar had died before Sarah. She bore him six sons: Zimram, Jokshan, Medan, Midian, Ishbak, and Shuah, during the two weeks of years. {19:12} In the sixth week, in the second year of that week, Rebecca gave birth to Isaac's two sons, Jacob and Esau. {19:13} Jacob was smooth and upright, while Esau was rugged, a man of the field, hairy, and skilled in hunting, and Jacob lived in tents. {19:14} As the boys grew, Jacob learned to write, while Esau, being a man of the field and a hunter, learned about war and was fierce in all his actions. {19:15} Abraham loved Jacob, but Isaac favored Esau. {19:16} Abraham observed Esau's actions and realized that Jacob was to inherit his name and lineage; he called Rebecca and instructed her regarding Jacob, knowing she loved Jacob more than Esau. {19:17} He said to her, "My daughter, watch over my son Jacob, for he will stand in my place on the earth and be a blessing among the children of men and the glory of the whole line of Shem. {19:18} I know that the Lord will choose him as a people for Himself above all the peoples on the earth. {19:19} Look, my son Isaac loves Esau more than Jacob, but I see that you truly love Jacob. {19:20} Add to your kindness toward him and keep your eyes lovingly upon him, for he will be a blessing for us on the earth for all generations to come. {19:21} Let your hands be strong and your heart rejoice in your son Jacob, for I have loved him far beyond all my other sons. {19:22} He will be blessed forever, and his descendants will fill the earth. {19:23} If a man can count the sand of the earth, so too will his descendants be numbered. {19:24} All the blessings that the Lord has given me and my descendants will belong to Jacob and his descendants forever. {19:25} In his lineage, my name will be honored, as will the names of my ancestors, Shem, Noah, Enoch, Mahalalel, Enos, Seth, and Adam. {19:26} These will serve to establish the foundations of heaven, strengthen the earth, and renew all the stars in the sky. {19:27} He called Jacob before Rebecca, his mother, kissed him, blessed him, and said: "Jacob, my beloved son, whom my soul loves, may God bless you from above the heavens, and may He give you all the blessings that He gave to Adam, Enoch, Noah, and Shem. {19:28} May all that He told me and promised to give me cling to you and your descendants forever, according to the days of heaven above the earth. {19:29} May the spirits of Mastêmâ not rule over you or your descendants, leading you away from the Lord, your God, from now on forever. {19:30} May the Lord God be your father, and may you be His firstborn son forever, and to all people. Go in peace, my son." They both went out together from Abraham. {19:31} Rebecca loved Jacob with all her heart and soul much more than Esau, while Isaac loved Esau far more than Jacob.

{20:1} In the forty-second jubilee, in the first year of the seventh week, Abraham called Ishmael, {20:2} along with his twelve sons, Isaac and his two sons, and the six sons of Keturah, and their sons. {20:3} He commanded them to follow the Lord's ways, to practice righteousness, love one another, and act justly among all people. {20:4} He instructed them to circumcise their sons according to the covenant God made with them, and not to stray from any of the paths the Lord had commanded. {20:5} They were to keep away from all forms of fornication and uncleanness and to renounce any such behavior among them. {20:6} If any woman or girl committed fornication among them, they were to burn her with fire and not allow anyone to engage in such acts with her. {20:7} They were not to take wives from the daughters of Canaan, for the seed of Canaan would be uprooted from the land. {20:8} He told them about the judgment of the giants and the Sodomites, how they were judged for their wickedness and died because of their fornication, uncleanness, and corruption. {20:9} "Guard yourselves from all fornication and uncleanness, and from all pollution of sin, lest you bring shame upon our name and your lives become a curse, {20:10} leading to the destruction of your sons by the sword, making you accursed like Sodom and your descendants like the sons of Gomorrah. {20:11} I implore you, my sons, love the God of heaven and adhere to all His commandments. {20:12} Do not follow their idols and their impurities, and do not create molten or carved gods for yourselves; they are worthless, with no spirit in them. {20:13} They are the work of human hands, and those who trust in them trust in nothing. {20:14} Do not serve or worship them, but serve the Most High God, and worship Him continually; {20:15} hope for His favor always, and work with integrity and righteousness before Him so that He may take pleasure in you, grant you mercy, send rain upon you morning and evening, {20:16} bless all your work on earth, and bless your bread and water, {20:17} the fruit of your womb, your land, your herds, and your flocks. {20:18} You will be a blessing on the earth, and all nations will desire you and bless your sons in my name, so they may be blessed as I am. {20:19} He gave gifts to Ishmael, his sons, and the sons of Keturah and sent them away from Isaac, giving everything to Isaac. {20:20} Ishmael and his sons, along with the sons of Keturah, went to dwell from Paran to the entrance of Babylon, in all the land facing the East towards the desert. {20:21} They mingled with one another, and their name became Arabs and Ishmaelites.

{21:1} In the sixth year of the seventh week of this jubilee, Abraham called his son Isaac and said to him, "I have grown old and do not know the day of my death, but my life is now full of days. {21:2} I am 175 years old, and throughout my entire life, I have remembered the Lord, always striving with all my heart to do His will and to walk righteously in His ways. {21:3} I have despised idols, and I have rejected those who served them. I have dedicated my heart and spirit to doing the will of the One who created me. {21:4} For He is the living God, holy and faithful, righteous above all, and He does not show favoritism or accept bribes (gifts to influence). God is just and judges all who break His commandments and reject His covenant. {21:5} So, my son, observe His commandments, ordinances, and judgments. Do not follow after abominations, graven images, or molten (metal cast) idols. {21:6} Do not consume any blood from animals, cattle, or birds that fly in the sky. {21:7} When you offer a victim as an acceptable peace offering, slaughter it and pour out its blood upon the altar. Offer all the fat on the altar along with fine flour, the grain offering mixed with oil, and the drink offering. Present them together on the altar as a pleasing aroma to the Lord. {21:8} Offer the fat of your thanksgiving offerings on the altar fire: the fat on the belly, the fat around the internal organs, the two kidneys, and the fat on them, along with the loins and the liver, which you will remove with the kidneys. {21:9} Present all of this as a sweet-smelling offering before the Lord, along with the grain offering and the drink offering, making it a pleasing aroma—the bread of the offering to the Lord. {21:10} You must eat the meat of the sacrifice on the same day or the second day, but do not let the sun go down on the second day without finishing it. Anything left until the third day must not be eaten, for it is no longer acceptable (approved), and eating it will bring sin upon you. {21:11} I have found this written in the books of my forefathers, in the words of Enoch and in the words of Noah. {21:12} Sprinkle salt on all your offerings, and do not let the salt of the covenant be lacking in any of your offerings before the Lord. {21:13} Be careful about the wood you use for the altar. Use only these types: cypress, bay, almond, fir, pine, cedar, savin, fig, olive, myrrh, laurel, and aspalathus. {21:14} When you place wood under the sacrifice, make sure it is clean in appearance, strong, and free of faults—new growth and not split or darkened. Do not use old wood, for it has lost its fragrance. {21:15} Apart from these types of wood, do not use any other, for other woods do not release the fragrance that ascends to heaven. {21:16} Follow this command carefully, my son, so that you may be upright in all your deeds. {21:17} Always maintain cleanliness in your body. Wash yourself with water before approaching the altar to offer a sacrifice. Wash your hands and feet before drawing near, and when you are done with the offering, wash your hands and feet again. {21:18} Let no blood appear on your body or your clothes. Be extremely cautious about blood, my son. {21:19} If blood is spilled, cover it with dust. {21:20} Do not eat any blood, for the blood is the life force. Avoid consuming any form of blood. {21:21} Never accept gifts or bribes (presents) in exchange for the blood of a human being, as if to overlook it when it is shed, for innocent blood causes the earth to be defiled. The only way to cleanse the earth from human blood is through the blood of the one who shed it. {21:22} Accept no gifts in exchange for blood; it must be blood for blood so that you may be approved before the Lord, the Most High God. He is the protector of the righteous, and this will ensure your preservation from all harm and death. {21:23} My son, I see that the works of humanity are full of sin and wickedness. {21:24} All their actions are impure, an abomination, and a pollution, and there is no righteousness among them. {21:25} Be careful not to follow their ways or walk in their paths, for sin leads to death before the Most High God. {21:26} If you do, He will hide His face from you, hand you over to your own transgressions, uproot you from the land, and destroy your descendants from beneath the heavens. {21:27} Your name and the names of your descendants will perish from the earth. {21:28} Turn away from all their deeds and impurity. Keep the commandments of the Most High God, do His will, and live righteously in all things. {21:29} Then He will bless you in all that you do, and from your line, He will raise a righteous offspring that will endure across the earth for all generations. {21:30} My name and your name will never be forgotten under heaven forever. {21:31} Go in peace, my son. May the Most High God, my God and your God, strengthen you to do His will, and may He bless all your descendants for generations to come with all righteous blessings, so that you may be a blessing to all the earth." {21:32} Then Isaac left his father, rejoicing.

{22:1} In the first week of the forty-fourth jubilee, in the second year—the year Abraham died—Isaac and Ishmael came from the Well of the Oath to celebrate the Feast of Weeks, which is the feast of the first fruits of the harvest, with their father Abraham. Abraham was filled with joy because his two sons had come to visit him. {22:2} Isaac had many possessions in Beersheba, and he would often go to inspect them and then return to his father. {22:3} In those days, Ishmael also came to visit his father, and together they met. Isaac offered a burnt offering, presenting it on the altar that his father had made in Hebron. {22:4} He also offered a thank offering and held a joyful feast with Ishmael, his brother. Rebecca made fresh cakes from the new grain and gave them to her son Jacob to take to Abraham, that he might eat and bless the Creator before he died. {22:5} Isaac also sent a choice thank offering by Jacob to Abraham, that he might eat and drink. {22:6} Abraham ate, drank, and blessed the Most High God, who created heaven and earth, who made all the good things of the earth, and gave them to the children of men, that they might eat and drink and bless their Creator. {22:7} And Abraham said, "Now I give thanks to You, my God, for allowing me to see this day. Behold, I am 175 years old, an old man, full of days, and my life has been peaceful. {22:8} The sword of the enemy has not overcome me in all that You have given me, nor in my children, throughout all my days until now. {22:9} My God, may Your mercy and peace be upon Your servant and upon the descendants of my sons, that they may be a chosen nation and an inheritance for You from among all the nations of the earth, from now and forevermore." {22:10} He then called Jacob and said, "My son Jacob, may the God of all bless you and strengthen you to do righteousness and His will. May He choose you and your descendants to become a people for His inheritance according to His eternal will. {22:11} Come near, my son, and kiss me." Jacob approached and kissed him, and Abraham said: {22:12} "Blessed be my son Jacob, and blessed be all the sons of the Most High God forever and ever. {22:13} May God grant you a seed of righteousness, and may some of your descendants be sanctified among all the nations of the earth. {22:14} May nations serve you, and may all peoples bow before your offspring. {22:15} Be strong among men and exercise authority over the descendants of Seth. Then your ways and the ways of your sons will be justified, and they will become a holy nation. {22:16} May the Most High God grant you all the blessings He has given me, and all the blessings He gave to Noah and Adam. May these blessings rest on the sacred head of your descendants from generation to generation, forever. {22:17} May He cleanse you from all unrighteousness and impurity, and may you be forgiven for all the sins you have committed in ignorance. {22:18} May He strengthen you, bless you, and grant you the inheritance of the whole earth. {22:19} May He renew His covenant with you, so that you may be a nation for His inheritance for all time, and that He may be your God and the God of your descendants in truth and righteousness for all the days of the earth. {22:20} My son Jacob, remember my words and observe the commandments of your father, Abraham. {22:21} Separate yourself from the nations and do not eat with them. {22:22} Do not follow their ways or become their companion, for their works are unclean. All their ways are a pollution, an abomination, and filled with uncleanness. {22:23} They offer their sacrifices to the dead, worship evil spirits, and eat over the graves. All their works are vanity and empty. {22:24} They have no heart to understand, and their eyes are blind to the wickedness of their actions. They err by saying to a piece of wood, 'You are my God,' and to a stone, 'You are my Lord and deliverer.' {22:25} As for you, my son Jacob, may the Most High God help you. May the God of heaven bless you and remove you from their uncleanness and from all their errors. {22:26} Be careful, my son, not to take a wife from the daughters of Canaan, for all of Canaan's descendants will be rooted out of the earth. {22:27} Due to the sin of Ham, Canaan went astray, and all his descendants will be destroyed from the earth, leaving none to be saved on the day of judgment. {22:28} For all idol worshippers and the profane, there will be no hope in the land of the living. {22:29} There will be no remembrance of them on the earth. {22:30} They will descend into Sheol (the underworld), into the place of condemnation, just as the children of Sodom were removed from the earth. So too will all idol worshippers be removed. {22:31} Do not be afraid, my son Jacob, and do not be discouraged, son of Abraham. May the Most High God protect you from destruction and deliver you from all paths of error. {22:32} This house I have built is for myself, to put my name upon it on the earth. It is given to you and your descendants forever. It will be called the house of Abraham, and it is given to you and your seed forever. You will build my house and establish my name before God for eternity. Your seed and your name will endure through all generations of the earth." {22:33} Abraham finished giving his commands and blessings. Isaac and Jacob lay together on one bed, and Jacob slept in the arms of his grandfather, Abraham. {22:34} Abraham kissed him seven times, his heart rejoicing with love for him, and he blessed Jacob with all his heart. {22:35} Abraham said, "The Most High God, Creator of all, who brought me out of Ur of the Chaldees to give me this land to inherit forever, that I might establish a holy seed, blessed be the Most High forever." {22:36} He blessed Jacob, saying, "My son, in whom I rejoice with all my heart and affection, may God's grace and mercy be upon you and your descendants forever. {22:37} Do not abandon him, O Lord, nor cast him aside from now until the end of eternity. May Your eyes always be upon him and his offspring, to preserve, bless, and sanctify him as a nation for Your inheritance. {22:38} Bless him with all Your blessings from now until all eternity. Renew Your covenant and grace with him and his descendants according to Your good pleasure for all the generations of the earth."

{23:1} Abraham placed two fingers of Jacob over his eyes and blessed the God of gods. Then, covering his face, he stretched out his feet, slept the eternal sleep, and was gathered to his ancestors. {23:2} Even though Abraham had died, Jacob still lay in his embrace, unaware of his passing. {23:3} Jacob awoke and found Abraham cold as ice. He called out, "Father, father," but there was no response, and he realized that Abraham was dead. {23:4} Jacob rose from his grandfather's side and ran to tell his mother, Rebecca. Rebecca went to Isaac during the night and told him, and they both went with Jacob, carrying a lamp. {23:5} When they entered, they found Abraham lying dead. {23:6} Isaac fell upon his father's face, wept, and kissed him. {23:7} The sounds of mourning filled Abraham's house, and Ishmael, his son, arose and went to his father. He and the whole house wept bitterly for Abraham. {23:8} Isaac and Ishmael buried Abraham in the double cave near his wife, Sarah. They mourned for him for forty days, as did the men of his household, including all the sons of Keturah from their distant places. When the days of mourning ended, {23:9} they remembered that Abraham had lived three jubilees (147 years) and four weeks of years, totaling 175 years. He had completed his life, being old and full of days. {23:10} The forefathers lived through nineteen jubilees, but after the flood, their lifespan began to decrease, and they grew old quickly due to great trials and wickedness, except for Abraham. {23:11} Abraham was righteous and perfect in all his deeds before the Lord throughout his life, though he did not complete four jubilees. His days were shortened due to the wickedness around him. {23:12} From this time until the day of the great judgment, people will age quickly, not even completing two jubilees, and they will lose their knowledge due to old age. {23:13} In those days, if a man lives a jubilee and a half, others will say, 'He has lived long,' but the greater part of his life will be filled with pain, sorrow, trials, and no peace. {23:14} Calamity will follow calamity, wound upon wound, tribulation upon tribulation, and one bad news after another. Illness, famine, death, the sword, captivity, and every kind of evil will overtake them. {23:15} All these disasters will fall upon an evil generation that sins on the earth. Their works will be full of uncleanness, fornication, pollution, and abominations. {23:16} Then people will say, 'The days of the forefathers were long, even a thousand years, and they were good; but now, if a man lives seventy years, or eighty if strong, those years are filled with evil and suffering in this wicked generation.' {23:17} In that generation, sons will condemn their fathers and elders for their sins and wickedness, accusing them of forsaking the covenant that the Lord made, which they were to follow without straying. {23:18} All have done evil, and every mouth speaks iniquity. All their works are unclean, an abomination, and a pollution. {23:19} The earth will be destroyed because of their actions, and there will be no vine or oil, for their deeds are faithless, and they will perish together—man, beast, cattle, birds, and fish—because of the sins of humanity. {23:20} There will be strife between the young and the old, the poor and the rich, the lowly and the great, and even the beggar with the prince, all because of the law and the covenant. They will forget the commandments, the feasts, months, Sabbaths, jubilees, and all the judgments. {23:21} They will take up swords and fight wars, trying to bring themselves back to the right path, but they will not return until much blood is shed. {23:22} Even those who escape will not repent of their wickedness but will continue to deceive and pursue wealth, each trying to take what belongs to his neighbor. {23:23} They will use the name of the Lord, but not in truth or righteousness. They will defile the holy of holies with their uncleanness and corrupt their worship with pollution. {23:24} A great punishment will fall on this generation from the Lord. He will give them over to the sword, judgment, captivity, plundering, and destruction. {23:25} He will awaken the sinners of the Gentiles, who have no mercy or compassion, and they will show no respect for anyone, neither young nor old, for they are more wicked and cruel than all other men. {23:26} These sinners will use violence against Israel and transgress against Jacob, shedding much blood upon the earth, and there will be no one left to gather or bury the dead. {23:27} In those days, the people will cry out, pray, and plead to be saved from the hands of these wicked Gentiles, but none will be saved. {23:28} The heads of the children will turn gray at a young age, and a child of three weeks will appear old, like a man of a hundred years, because their lives will be shortened by oppression and suffering. {23:29} In those days, children will begin to study the laws and seek the commandments, returning to the path of righteousness. {23:30} Then, the days of mankind will begin to increase again until people approach living a thousand years. They will live longer than before. {23:31} There will be no old man who is not satisfied with his days, for everyone will be like a child or a youth. {23:32} They will live their lives in peace and joy, with no presence of Satan or any destroyer. All their days will be filled with blessings and healing. {23:33} At that time, the Lord will heal His servants, and they will rise up and see great peace, driving out their enemies. {23:34} The righteous will witness these events, give thanks, and rejoice forever and ever. They will see the judgments and curses fall upon their enemies. {23:35} Their bones will rest in the earth, and their spirits will experience great joy. They will know that it is the Lord who executes judgment and shows mercy to thousands of those who love Him. {23:36} Moses, write down these words, for they are written and recorded on the heavenly tablets as a testimony for all generations forever.

{24:1} After Abraham's death, the Lord blessed Isaac, his son. Isaac left Hebron and went to live at the Well of the Vision in the first year of the third week of this jubilee (2073 A.M.), staying there for seven years. {24:2} In the first year of the fourth week (2080 A.M.), a famine struck the land, different from the famine that had occurred in Abraham's time. {24:3} One day, Jacob was cooking lentil stew when Esau came from the field, famished. Esau said to Jacob, 'Let me have some of that red stew.' {24:4} Jacob replied, 'Sell me your birthright, and I'll give you bread and some of this lentil stew.' {24:5} Esau thought to himself, 'I'm going to die anyway; what good is this birthright to me?' So he said to Jacob, 'I give it to you.' Jacob told him, 'Swear to me this day,' and Esau swore an oath to him. {24:6} Jacob gave Esau bread and lentil stew, and Esau ate until he was full. Esau despised his birthright, and because of the red stew Jacob gave him, Esau was called Edom (Edom means "red"). {24:7} This is how Jacob became the elder, and Esau was brought low from his position of dignity. {24:8} When the famine spread across the land, Isaac prepared to go down to Egypt during the second year of this week. {24:9} But he went instead to the Philistine king, Abimelech, in Gerar. {24:10} The Lord appeared to Isaac and said, 'Do not go down to Egypt. Stay in the land that I will show you, and live there. I will be with you and bless you. {24:11} For I will give this land to you and your descendants, and I will fulfill the oath I swore to your father Abraham. I will make your descendants as numerous as the stars of heaven and give them all this land. {24:12} Through your descendants, all the nations of the earth will be blessed, because your father obeyed My commands, statutes, and covenant. Now, obey My voice and stay in this land.' {24:13} Isaac lived in Gerar for three weeks of years (21 years). {24:14} Abimelech gave orders regarding Isaac and all that belonged to him, saying, 'Anyone who harms him or his possessions will surely be put to death.' {24:15} Isaac became very prosperous among the Philistines, acquiring many possessions, including oxen, sheep, camels, donkeys, and a large household. {24:16} He sowed crops in the land of the Philistines and reaped a hundredfold, becoming exceedingly great, which caused the Philistines to envy him. {24:17} After Abraham's death, the Philistines had filled all the wells Abraham's servants had dug with earth. {24:18} Abimelech said to Isaac, 'Leave us, for you are too powerful for us.' {24:19} So Isaac left in the first year of the seventh week and settled in the valleys of Gerar. {24:20} Isaac's servants reopened the wells that Abraham's servants had dug, which the Philistines had closed, and he named them as Abraham had. {24:21} Isaac's servants dug a new well in the valley and found living water, but the shepherds of Gerar quarreled with them, claiming, 'The water is ours.' Isaac called the well 'Perversity,' because of their contentious behavior. {24:22} They dug another well, and again there was strife, so Isaac named it 'Enmity.' {24:23} He moved on and dug another well, but there was no conflict over this one, so he called it 'Room,' saying, 'Now the Lord has made room for us, and we have prospered in this land.' {24:24} Isaac moved from there to the Well of the Oath in the first year of the first week of the forty-fourth jubilee (2108 A.M.). {24:25} The Lord appeared to him that night, on the new moon of the first month, and said, 'I am the God of your father Abraham. Do not be afraid, for I am with you. I will bless you and multiply your descendants as the sand of the earth, for the sake of Abraham, My servant.' {24:26} Isaac built an altar there, just as his father Abraham had done, and he called upon the name of the Lord, offering a sacrifice to the God of his father Abraham. {24:27} Isaac's servants dug a well and found living water. {24:28} Later, they dug another well but did not find water, so they reported this to Isaac, who said, 'This has been made known to us because I swore an oath to the Philistines.' {24:29} Isaac named that place 'Well of the Oath,' for he had sworn to Abimelech, Ahuzzath his friend, and Phicol, the commander of his army. {24:30} That day, Isaac realized he had made a reluctant oath with them, under duress, to establish peace. {24:31} On that day, Isaac cursed the Philistines, saying, 'May the Philistines be cursed until the day of wrath and indignation, and may God make them an object of mockery, wrath, and a curse among the nations. {24:32} May the sinners among the Gentiles and the Kittim (people from Cyprus) treat them with scorn and judgment. {24:33} Whoever escapes the sword of the enemy and the Kittim, may the righteous nation destroy in judgment from the earth. The Philistines will be enemies of my descendants for all generations.' {24:34} No remnant of them will remain, nor anyone left alive on the day of wrath and judgment. The entire seed of the Philistines will be uprooted and expelled from the earth. {24:35} There will be no name or seed left for the Caphtorim (Philistines), and they will no longer exist on the earth. {24:36} Even if they ascend to heaven, they will be brought down. {24:37} If they make themselves strong on earth, they will be dragged away. {24:38} If they hide among the nations, they will be rooted out. {24:39} Even if they descend into Sheol (the underworld), their condemnation will be great, and they will find no peace there. {24:40} If they go into captivity, those who seek their lives will kill them along the way, leaving neither name nor seed on the earth. {24:41} They will depart into eternal curse.' {24:42} This is written and engraved on the heavenly tablets, to be carried out against them on the day of judgment, so they will be completely uprooted from the earth.

{25:1} In the second year of this week in this jubilee (2109 A.M.), Rebecca called Jacob, her son, and said to him, 'My son, do not marry one of the daughters of Canaan, like your brother Esau, who took two wives from among them, and they have made my life bitter with all their immoral and unclean actions. All they do is wicked, filled with fornication and lust, and there is no righteousness in them because their deeds are evil. {25:2} I love you dearly, my son, and my heart blesses you every hour of the day and every watch of the night. {25:3} So now, my son, listen to me and follow my advice. Do not marry a woman from this land, but only from my father's family, from among our relatives. If you do, the Most High God will bless you, and your children will be a righteous and holy generation.' {25:4} Jacob replied to his mother, Rebecca, 'Look, Mother, I am now nine weeks of years old (63 years), and I have never known or touched a woman, nor have I betrothed myself to anyone, nor even thought of marrying a woman from the daughters of Canaan. {25:5} I remember what our father Abraham commanded me, telling me not to marry a woman from the daughters of Canaan, but to take a wife from the seed of my father's house, from our family. {25:6} I have heard that Laban, your brother, has daughters, and I have set my heart on marrying one of them. {25:7} That is why I have guarded myself from sin and corruption in all my ways throughout my life. Regarding lust and fornication, Abraham, my father, gave me many commandments. {25:8} Despite all his instructions, my brother Esau has tried for these 22 years to persuade me, often saying, "My brother, marry a sister of my two wives," but I have refused to follow his example. {25:9} I swear before you, Mother, that all my life I will not marry a woman from the daughters of Canaan, and I will not act wickedly as my brother has done. {25:10} Do not worry, Mother, for I promise to follow your advice and walk in righteousness, never straying from the right path.' {25:11} Then Rebecca lifted her face to heaven, stretched out her hands, and opened her mouth to bless the Most High God, who created the heavens and the earth, and she gave Him thanks and praise. {25:12} She said, 'Blessed be the Lord God, and may His holy name be blessed forever and ever, for He has given me Jacob, a pure son and a holy seed. He belongs to You, Lord, and his descendants will forever be Yours throughout all generations. {25:13} Bless him, O Lord, and give me the words of righteousness to bless him.' {25:14} At that moment, the spirit of righteousness came upon her, and she placed her hands on Jacob's head, saying: {25:15} 'Blessed are You, Lord of righteousness and God of the ages. May You bless my son beyond all the generations of men. {25:16} May You give him the path of righteousness, and may righteousness be revealed to his descendants. {25:17} May You grant him many sons during his life, and may they multiply according to the number of months in the year. {25:18} May their descendants be as numerous and great as the stars of the heavens, and may their number exceed the grains of sand by the sea. {25:19} May You give them this good land, just as You promised to Abraham, and may they possess it forever. {25:20} May I live to see blessed children born to you, my son, and may all your descendants be a holy and blessed seed. {25:21} As you have brought joy to your mother's heart in her life, the womb that bore you blesses you. {25:22} My love and my breasts bless you, and my mouth and tongue greatly praise you. {25:23} May you grow and spread across the earth, and may your descendants be perfect, filled with the joy of heaven and earth forever. {25:24} May your seed rejoice, and may it know peace on the great day of peace. {25:25} May your name and your descendants endure for all time, and may the Most High God be their God. {25:26} May the God of righteousness dwell with them, and may His sanctuary be built by them for all generations. {25:27} Blessed are those who bless you, and cursed be all flesh that curses you unjustly.' {25:28} Rebecca then kissed Jacob and said to him, 'May the Lord of the world love you, just as the heart of your mother rejoices in you and blesses you.' After this, she ceased from blessing him.

{26:1} In the seventh year of this week (2114 A.M.), Isaac called Esau, his elder son, and said to him: 'My son, I am old, and my eyesight is failing, and I do not know the day of my death. {26:2} Now, take your hunting gear—your quiver and bow—and go out to the field to hunt and catch some game for me. {26:3} Prepare the savory meal that I love and bring it to me so that I may eat and bless you before I die.' {26:4} But Rebecca overheard Isaac speaking to Esau. Esau went out early to the field to hunt and catch game to bring home to his father. {26:5} Rebecca called Jacob, her son, and told him: 'Listen, I heard your father speaking to Esau, your brother, saying, "Hunt for me, prepare a savory meal, and bring it to me so that I may eat and bless you in the presence of the

Lord before I die." {26:6} Now, my son, obey me in what I command you: {26:7} Go to the flock and bring me two good young goats. I will prepare them as a savory dish for your father, the kind he loves. {26:8} Then, take it to your father so he may eat and bless you before he dies, and that you may receive the blessing.' {26:9} Jacob said to his mother, Rebecca, 'Mother, I will not hold back anything that my father would eat and enjoy. But I fear that he will recognize my voice and try to touch me. {26:10} You know that I am smooth-skinned, and my brother Esau is hairy. If he discovers me, I will seem deceitful in his eyes, and he will be angry with me, and I will bring a curse upon myself instead of a blessing.' {26:11} But Rebecca said to him, 'Let any curse fall upon me, my son. Just do as I say and obey me.' {26:12} So Jacob obeyed his mother. He went and brought two good and fat goats, and Rebecca prepared the savory meal, the way Isaac loved it. {26:13} Rebecca then took Esau's best clothes, which she had in the house, and dressed Jacob, her younger son, in them. {26:14} She also covered his hands and the bare parts of his neck with the skins of the goats. {26:15} She placed the meal and bread she had prepared into Jacob's hands. {26:16} Jacob went to his father and said, 'Father, I am your son. I have done as you asked. Please sit up, eat of the game I caught, and bless me.' {26:17} Isaac asked his son, 'How did you find the game so quickly, my son?' Jacob answered, 'Because the Lord, your God, granted me success.' {26:18} Isaac said, 'Come closer so I can feel you, my son, to see whether you are really Esau or not.' {26:19} So Jacob approached Isaac, and Isaac felt him, saying, 'The voice is Jacob's, but the hands are Esau's.' {26:20} Isaac did not recognize him because his hands were hairy, like Esau's, due to a dispensation from heaven (meaning divine intervention), and so he blessed him. {26:21} Isaac asked again, 'Are you really my son Esau?' and Jacob replied, 'Yes, I am.' {26:22} Then Isaac said, 'Bring me the food, and I will eat so that my soul may bless you.' Jacob brought the meal, and Isaac ate. Jacob also brought him wine, and he drank. {26:23} Isaac then said to him, 'Come closer, my son, and kiss me.' {26:24} Jacob came closer and kissed him, and Isaac smelled the scent of his clothing and blessed him, saying: 'See, the smell of my son is like the smell of a field that the Lord has blessed. {26:25} May the Lord give you the dew of heaven and the richness of the earth, with plenty of grain and wine. {26:26} May nations serve you, and may peoples bow down to you. {26:27} Be lord over your brothers, and may the sons of your mother bow down to you. May all the blessings given to me and to Abraham, my father, be passed on to you and your descendants forever. {26:28} Cursed be those who curse you, and blessed be those who bless you.' {26:29} After Isaac finished blessing Jacob, and Jacob had left his father's presence, Esau returned from hunting. {26:30} He also prepared a savory meal and brought it to his father, saying, 'Let my father sit up and eat some of the game I caught, so that you may bless me.' {26:31} Isaac asked, 'Who are you?' and Esau replied, 'I am your firstborn son, Esau. I have done as you asked.' {26:32} Isaac was greatly shocked and asked, 'Who was it, then, that hunted game and brought it to me? I ate it before you arrived, and I have blessed him, and he shall be blessed, and his descendants forever.' {26:33} When Esau heard his father's words, he cried out with a loud and bitter cry, saying, 'Father, bless me too!' {26:34} But Isaac said, 'Your brother came deceitfully and took your blessing.' {26:35} Esau said, 'Now I understand why he is called Jacob (which means "he grasps the heel" or "supplanter"). He has tricked me twice: first, he took my birthright, and now he has taken my blessing.' {26:36} Then Esau asked, 'Father, have you not reserved any blessing for me?' {26:37} Isaac replied, 'I have made him lord over you, and I have given him all his brothers as servants. I have blessed him with plenty of grain, wine, and oil. What more can I do for you, my son?' {26:38} Esau said, 'Do you have only one blessing, Father? Bless me too!' And Esau lifted his voice and wept. {26:39} Isaac then answered, 'Your dwelling will be far from the richness of the earth and the dew of heaven above. {26:40} You will live by the sword, and you will serve your brother. But when you become restless and strong, you will break his yoke from off your neck. {26:41} However, in doing so, you will commit a complete sin unto death, and your descendants will be uprooted from the earth.' {26:42} Esau harbored hatred toward Jacob because of the blessing Isaac had given him, and in his heart, Esau said, 'The days of mourning for my father will soon come, and then I will kill my brother Jacob.'

{27:1} The words of Esau, her elder son, were revealed to Rebecca in a dream. She sent for Jacob, her younger son, and said to him, 'Look, Esau, your brother, plans to take vengeance on you and kill you. {27:2} Therefore, my son, obey my voice. Get up and flee to my brother Laban in Haran. {27:3} Stay with him for a few days until your brother's anger subsides, {27:4} and he forgets what you have done to him. Then I will send for you and bring you back.' {27:5} Jacob said, 'I am not afraid; if he tries to kill me, I will kill him.' {27:6} But Rebecca replied, 'Let me not lose both my sons in one day.' {27:7} Jacob said to Rebecca, 'You know that my father is old and cannot see well. If I leave him, it will upset him, for he will see it as a bad thing, and he might curse me. I will not go unless he sends me.' {27:8} Rebecca said, 'I will speak to him, and he will send you away.' {27:9} So Rebecca went to Isaac and said, 'I am weary of life because of Esau's wives, the daughters of Heth (a tribe in Canaan). If Jacob also marries a woman from this land, what will be the point of my life? For the daughters of Canaan are wicked.' {27:10} Isaac called Jacob, blessed him, and gave him this advice: 'Do not marry any of the daughters of Canaan. {27:11} Get up and go to Mesopotamia, to the house of your grandfather Bethuel, and marry one of the daughters of Laban, your mother's brother. {27:12} May God Almighty bless you, make you fruitful, and multiply you so that you become a great nation. {27:13} May He give you the blessing promised to my father Abraham, to you and your descendants, so that you may inherit this land where you are now living, the land God gave to Abraham.' {27:14} Then Isaac sent Jacob away, and Jacob went to Mesopotamia, to Laban, the son of Bethuel the Syrian, and the brother of Rebecca, Jacob's mother. {27:15} After Jacob left for Mesopotamia, Rebecca's spirit was troubled, and she wept for her son. {27:16} But Isaac comforted her, saying, 'Do not weep for Jacob, my sister. He goes in peace, and he will return in peace. {27:17} The Most High God will protect him from all harm and be with him throughout his life. {27:18} I know his path will prosper, and he will return to us in peace. Do not fear for him, for he is upright, faithful, and perfect; he will not perish.' {27:19} So Isaac comforted Rebecca about Jacob and blessed him. {27:20} Jacob left the Well of the Oath to go to Haran during the first year of the second week in the forty-fourth jubilee. He reached Luz, on the mountains, which is Bethel, on the new moon of the first month of that week (2115 A.M.). {27:21} When evening came, he stopped at the western side of the road and slept there because the sun had set. {27:22} He took one of the stones from that place, put it under his head, and lay down to sleep. {27:23} That night, he had a dream: there was a ladder set up on the earth, and its top reached to heaven. Angels of the Lord were going up and down on it, {27:24} and the Lord stood at the top of the ladder. He said, 'I am the Lord, the God of your father Abraham and the God of Isaac. I will give you and your descendants the land on which you are lying. {27:25} Your descendants will be as numerous as the dust of the earth, and they will spread out to the west, east, north, and south. Through you and your descendants, all the families of the earth will be blessed. {27:26} I am with you, and I will watch over you wherever you go. I will bring you back to this land in peace, and I will not leave you until I have done everything I promised.' {27:27} Jacob woke up from his sleep and said, 'Surely, the Lord is in this place, and I did not know it.' {27:28} He was filled with awe and said, 'How awesome is this place! This is none other than the house of God, and this is the gate of heaven.' {27:29} Early the next morning, Jacob took the stone he had used as a pillow and set it up as a pillar to mark the place. He poured oil on top of it as an offering. {27:30} He called the place Bethel, though the city was originally named Luz. {27:31} Jacob made a vow to the Lord, saying, 'If the Lord is with me and protects me on this journey, giving me food to eat and clothes to wear, {27:32} and if I return safely to my father's house, then the Lord will be my God. {27:33} This stone, which I have set up as a pillar, will be God's house, and of everything He gives me, I will give a tenth back to Him.'

{28:1} Jacob continued his journey and reached the land of the east, where he stayed with Laban, his mother Rebecca's brother. He worked for Laban for one week in exchange for Rachel, his daughter. {28:2} In the first year of the third week [2122 A.M.], Jacob said to Laban, 'Give me my wife, for I have served you seven years.' Laban replied, 'I will give you your wife.' {28:3} Laban prepared a feast and took Leah, his elder daughter, and gave her to Jacob as his wife, along with Zilpah, her maidservant. Jacob, believing she was Rachel, did not realize it was Leah. {28:4} He lay with her, and in the morning discovered it was Leah. Angry, Jacob confronted Laban: 'Why have you deceived me? I served you for Rachel, not Leah. You have wronged me.' {28:5} Jacob told Laban to take his daughter back, as he intended to leave because of the evil done to him. Jacob loved Rachel more than Leah because Leah had weak eyes, but she was still very beautiful, while Rachel was known for her lovely eyes and attractive figure. {28:6} Laban explained that in their country, it was not customary to marry off the younger daughter before the elder. {28:7} He added that this was also written on the heavenly tablets—that giving the younger before the elder was considered sinful before the Lord and no righteous man would do such a thing. {28:8} Laban advised Jacob to instruct the children of Israel never to marry or give in marriage the younger daughter before the elder. It was a very wicked act. {28:9} Laban then suggested that Jacob fulfill Leah's seven-day wedding feast and afterward take Rachel as his wife, provided Jacob would work another seven years for him, just as before. {28:10} Once Leah's seven-day feast had passed, Laban gave Rachel to Jacob as his wife, and Jacob served him for another seven years. {28:11} Laban also gave Rachel her maidservant, Bilhah. Jacob loved Rachel, but Leah had been given to him without charge. {28:12} The Lord saw that Leah was unloved, so He opened her womb. She conceived and bore Jacob a son, and he named him Reuben, on the fourteenth day of the ninth month, in the first year of the third week [2122 A.M.]. {28:13} Rachel, however, remained barren because the Lord saw that Leah was unloved while Rachel was loved. {28:14} Leah conceived again and bore Jacob a second son, whom he named Simeon, on the twenty-first of the tenth month, in the third year of the same week [2124 A.M.]. {28:15} Leah conceived again and bore a third son, whom she named Levi, during the new moon of the first month in the sixth year of this week [2127 A.M.]. {28:16} Again, Leah bore Jacob a fourth son, whom she named Judah, on the fifteenth of the third month in the first year of the fourth week [2129 A.M.]. {28:17} Rachel became envious of Leah because she had not borne any children. She pleaded with Jacob, 'Give me children!' Jacob responded, 'Am I responsible for your womb? Have I abandoned you?' {28:18} Rachel, seeing that Leah had already borne four sons—Reuben, Simeon, Levi, and Judah—said to Jacob, 'Sleep with my handmaid, Bilhah, so she may bear a child on my behalf.' She gave Bilhah to Jacob as a wife, {28:19} and Bilhah conceived and bore a son, whom Jacob named Dan, on the ninth of the sixth month in the sixth year of the third week [2127 A.M.]. {28:20} Jacob went to Bilhah again, and she bore him a second son. Rachel named him Naphtali, born on the fifth of the seventh month in the second year of the fourth week [2130 A.M.]. {28:21} Leah, noticing she had stopped bearing children, became envious of Rachel and gave her maidservant, Zilpah, to Jacob as a wife. Zilpah conceived and bore a son, and Leah named him Gad, on the twelfth of the eighth month in the third year of the fourth week [2131 A.M.]. {28:22} Jacob went to Zilpah again, and she bore another son. Leah named him Asher, born on the second of the eleventh month in the fifth year of the fourth week [2133 A.M.]. {28:23} Later, Leah conceived again and bore a son, whom she named Issachar, on the fourth of the fifth month in the fourth year of the fourth week [2132 A.M.], and she entrusted him to a nurse. {28:24} Jacob went to Leah again, and she bore twins—a son and a daughter. She named the son Zebulon and the daughter Dinah, born on the seventh of the seventh month in the sixth year of the fourth week [2134 A.M.]. {28:25} The Lord remembered Rachel and was merciful to her, opening her womb. She conceived and gave birth to a son, whom she named Joseph, on the new moon of the fourth month in the sixth year of the fourth week [2134 A.M.]. {28:26} After Joseph's birth, Jacob said to Laban, 'Give me my wives and children so I can return to my father Isaac and build my own household, for I have completed the years I agreed to serve you for your two daughters.' {28:27} Laban, wanting Jacob to stay, offered him new wages if he would continue pasturing his flocks. {28:28} They agreed that Jacob's wages would consist of the lambs and kids born black, spotted, or white. {28:29} The sheep gave birth to lambs marked just as agreed, and Jacob's flocks multiplied greatly. He gained large herds of sheep, oxen, donkeys, camels, and many servants. {28:30} Seeing Jacob's wealth increase, Laban and his sons became envious. Laban took his sheep back from Jacob and began to regard him with ill intent.

{29:1} After Rachel gave birth to Joseph, Laban went to shear his sheep, which were three days' journey away from him. {29:2} Jacob noticed that Laban had gone to shear his sheep, so he called Leah and Rachel, speaking kindly to them, asking them to come with him to the land of Canaan. {29:3} He explained to them that he had seen everything in a dream, in which God told him to return to his father's house. They replied, 'Wherever you go, we will go with you.' {29:4} Jacob blessed the God of his father Isaac and his grandfather Abraham. Then he got up, mounted his wives and children on camels, took all his possessions, and crossed the river, arriving in the land of Gilead. Jacob kept his plans hidden from Laban, saying nothing to him about his departure. {29:5} In the seventh year of the fourth week, in the first month, on the twenty-first day [2135 A.M.], Jacob set out toward Gilead. {29:6} Laban pursued him and caught up with Jacob in the mountains of Gilead, in the third month, on the thirteenth day. {29:7} But the Lord protected Jacob, appearing to Laban in a dream at night and preventing him from harming Jacob. When Laban spoke to Jacob, {29:8} two days later, on the fifteenth, Jacob made a feast for Laban and everyone who had come with him. Jacob and Laban swore an oath that day, agreeing neither of them would cross the mountains of Gilead to harm the other. {29:9} They built a heap of stones as a witness to their oath, and thus the place was called 'The Heap of Witness.' {29:10} In the past, the land of Gilead had been called the land of the Rephaim. The Rephaim were giants born there, whose heights ranged from ten, nine, eight, down to seven cubits. {29:11} Their territory extended from the land of the children of Ammon to Mount Hermon, and their main cities were Karnaim, Ashtaroth, Edrei, Misur, and Beon. {29:12} The Lord destroyed them because of their wickedness; they were extremely malevolent (evil-hearted). The Amorites, who were also wicked and sinful, later settled in their place. There has never been a people who have committed as many sins as they did, and their time on earth was cut short. {29:13} Jacob sent Laban away, and Laban returned to Mesopotamia, the land of the East, while Jacob went back to the land of Gilead. {29:14} He crossed the Jabbok River on the eleventh day of the ninth month. That same day, his brother Esau met him, and they reconciled. Esau then departed for the land of Seir, while Jacob continued living in tents. {29:15} In the first year of the fifth week in this jubilee [2136 A.M.], Jacob crossed the Jordan River and settled beyond it, grazing his sheep from the Sea of the Heap to Bethshan, and as far as Dothan and the forest of Akrabbim. {29:16} Jacob sent gifts of clothing, food, meat, drink, milk, butter, cheese, and dates from the valley to his father Isaac. {29:17} He also sent provisions to his mother Rebecca four times a year: during the months between ploughing and reaping, autumn and the rainy season, winter and spring, delivering them to the tower of Abraham. {29:18} Isaac had moved from the Well of the Oath and now lived at his father Abraham's tower, staying away from his son Esau. {29:19} After Jacob left for Mesopotamia, Esau married Mahalath, the daughter of Ishmael, and gathered his father's flocks and his wives, moving to Mount Seir, leaving Isaac alone at the Well of the Oath. {29:20} Isaac then moved to Abraham's tower in the Hebron mountains, {29:21} and Jacob regularly sent supplies to his father and mother from time to time, providing all they needed. Isaac and Rebecca blessed Jacob with all their heart and soul.

{30:1} In the first year of the sixth week [2143 A.M.], Jacob traveled peacefully to Salem, which is east of Shechem, during the fourth month. {30:2} There, Dinah, the daughter of Jacob, was taken into the house of Shechem, the son of Hamor the Hivite, who was the ruler of the land. He had sexual relations with her and violated her, although she was just a young girl, only twelve years old. {30:3} He pleaded with his father and her brothers to allow him to take her as his wife. Jacob and his sons were very angry because the men of Shechem had dishonored their sister Dinah. They spoke to them deceitfully and with malicious intent. {30:4} Simeon and Levi arrived unexpectedly in Shechem and executed judgment on all the men there, killing every single one they found, leaving no one alive. They inflicted severe punishment because of the shame brought upon their sister Dinah. {30:5} From now on, let it be known that no daughter of Israel should ever be defiled again, for judgment has been ordained in heaven against those who would destroy all the men of Shechem with the sword for the shame they brought upon Israel. {30:6} The Lord handed them over to Jacob's sons so they could eliminate them and carry out justice, ensuring that no virgin of Israel would be violated again. {30:7} If any man in Israel wants to give his daughter or sister to any man from among the Gentiles, he must surely die, and they shall stone him to death, for he has brought shame upon Israel. The woman shall be burned with fire for dishonoring her father's name, and she shall be removed from Israel. {30:8} There should be no adulteress or uncleanness found in Israel throughout all generations, for Israel is sacred to the Lord. Anyone who defiles it shall surely die and will be stoned to death. {30:9} This has been ordained and written in the heavenly tablets regarding all of Israel's descendants: anyone who defiles it shall surely die, and he shall be stoned. {30:10} There is no expiration date for this law, no forgiveness, nor any possibility of atonement: anyone who defiles his daughter will be cut off from the midst of Israel because he has offered his seed to Moloch and acted wickedly to defile it. {30:11} Therefore, Moses, you are to command the children of Israel and urge them not to give their daughters to the Gentiles and not to take daughters of the Gentiles for their sons, for this is an abomination before the Lord. {30:12} For this reason, I have written down in the Law all the actions of the Shechemites against Dinah and how Jacob's sons responded, saying, 'We will not give our daughter to an uncircumcised man, for that would bring disgrace upon us.' {30:13} It is indeed a disgrace to Israel, both to those who are living and to those who take the daughters of the Gentiles, for this is unclean and detestable to Israel. {30:14} Israel cannot be free from this uncleanness if it has a wife from the daughters of the Gentiles or if it gives any of its daughters to a Gentile man. {30:15} Plague upon plague, curse upon curse, and every judgment and affliction will come upon him if he does this thing, or turns a blind eye to those who commit uncleanness or defile the sanctuary of the Lord, or profane His holy name. The entire nation will be judged for all the uncleanness and profanation committed by this man. {30:16} There will be no favoritism or acceptance of offerings or sacrifices made to the Lord; every man or woman in Israel who defiles the sanctuary will face judgment. {30:17} This is why I have commanded you: 'Bear witness to Israel; see what happened to the Shechemites and their sons: how they were handed over to the two sons of Jacob, who executed them under torture, and it was accounted to them as righteousness, and it is recorded as such. {30:18} The descendants of Levi were chosen for the priesthood, to serve before the Lord continuously, and so that Levi and his sons may be blessed forever; he was zealous to execute righteousness, judgment, and vengeance against all who rose up against Israel. {30:19} Thus, a testimony in his favor has been inscribed in the heavenly tablets, marking blessing and righteousness before God. {30:20} We remember the righteousness that this man fulfilled during his life at all times of the year; it will be recorded for a thousand generations and will come to him and his descendants after him. He has been recorded on the heavenly tablets as a friend and a righteous man. {30:21} I have written all this for you and commanded you to share it with the children of Israel so they should not sin or violate the ordinances or break the covenant ordained for them, but fulfill it and be recorded as friends. {30:22} But if they transgress and engage in uncleanness in any form, they will be recorded in the heavenly tablets as adversaries, and they will be removed from the book of life, recorded among those destined for destruction and those who will be cut off from the earth. {30:23} On the day when the sons of Jacob killed Shechem, a record was made in heaven in their favor for executing righteousness and justice and vengeance against the sinners, and it was written for their blessing. {30:24} They brought their sister Dinah out of Shechem's house and seized everything in Shechem: their sheep, oxen, donkeys, all their wealth, and all their flocks, and brought everything to their father Jacob. {30:25} Jacob rebuked them for putting the city to the sword because he feared the Canaanites and the Perizzites living in the land. {30:26} The fear of the Lord came upon all the cities surrounding Shechem, and they did not pursue the sons of Jacob because terror had gripped them.

{31:1} On the new moon of the month, Jacob spoke to all the people in his household, saying, "Purify yourselves and change your clothes; let's arise and go up to Bethel, where I made a vow to God on the day I fled from my brother Esau, because He has been with me and brought me into this land peacefully. Also, remove the foreign gods that are among you." {31:2} They gave up their foreign gods, including the earrings and necklaces they wore, and Rachel gave Jacob the idols she had stolen from her father Laban. {31:3} Jacob burned the idols, broke them into pieces, and hid them under an oak tree in Shechem. {31:4} On the new moon of the seventh month, Jacob went up to Bethel. He built an altar at the place where he had rested and set up a pillar there. {31:5} He sent word to his father Isaac to come to his sacrifice, along with his mother Rebecca. {31:6} Isaac said, "Let my son Jacob come, so I can see him before I die." {31:7} Jacob went to his father Isaac and mother Rebecca, taking two of his sons, Levi and Judah, with him. {31:8} When Rebecca saw Jacob, she rushed out of the tower to kiss and embrace him, for her spirit revived when she heard, "Look, your son Jacob has come." {31:9} She kissed him and then saw his two sons, recognizing them. She asked him, "Are these your sons, my son?" and embraced and kissed them, blessing them, saying, "Through you, the seed of Abraham will become great, and you will be a blessing on the earth." {31:10} Jacob entered Isaac's chamber, where he lay, with his two sons. He took his father's hand, bent down, and kissed him. {31:11} Isaac embraced Jacob and wept on his neck. {31:12} The darkness lifted from Isaac's eyes, and he saw Jacob's sons, Levi and Judah. He asked, "Are these your sons, my son? They look like you." {31:13} Jacob confirmed they were indeed his sons, saying, "You have truly seen that they are my sons." {31:14} They drew closer to him, and Isaac kissed and embraced both of them together. {31:15} The spirit of prophecy filled his mouth, and he took Levi by his right hand and Judah by his left. {31:16} He turned to Levi first and began to bless him, saying, "May the God of all, the Lord of all ages, bless you and your children throughout all generations. {31:17} May the Lord grant you and your descendants greatness and glory, and allow you and your seed to approach Him in His sanctuary, like the angels and holy ones. {31:18} Just like them, your sons will have glory, greatness, and holiness, and may He make them great for all ages. {31:19} They shall be judges, princes, and leaders among all the descendants of Jacob. {31:20} They will speak the word of the Lord with righteousness and judge all His judgments fairly. {31:21} They shall declare My ways to Jacob and My paths to Israel. {31:22} The blessing of the Lord will be in their mouths to bless all the descendants of the beloved. {31:23} Your mother named you Levi, and rightly so; you will be joined to the Lord and be a companion to all the sons of Jacob. {31:24} Let His table be yours, and you and your sons eat from it; may your table be filled for all generations, and may your provisions never run out. {31:25} Let all who hate you fall before you, and let all your enemies be rooted out and perish. Blessed be anyone who blesses you, and cursed be any nation that curses you." {31:26} To Judah, he said, "May the Lord give you strength and power to defeat all who oppose you. You and one of your sons will be princes over the sons of Jacob. {31:27} May your name and your sons' names spread across every land and region, making the Gentiles fear you. {31:28} All nations shall tremble before you. {31:29} You will be the help of Jacob, and in you, the salvation of Israel will be found. {31:30} When you sit on the throne of honor and righteousness, there will be great peace for all the descendants of the beloved. {31:31} Blessed be anyone who blesses you, and all who hate, afflict, or curse you will be uprooted and destroyed from the earth and will be accursed." {31:32} He turned again, kissed Jacob, embraced him, and rejoiced greatly because he had seen Jacob's sons. {31:33} He went from between his legs, fell down, bowed to him, blessed them, and rested with Isaac his father that night, where they ate and drank joyfully. {31:34} Jacob had his two sons sleep, one on his right and the other on his left, and this was counted as righteousness for him. {31:35} Jacob told his father everything during the night, how the Lord had shown him great mercy, prospering him in all his ways and protecting him from all evil. {31:36} Isaac blessed the God of his father Abraham, who had not withdrawn His mercy and righteousness from the sons of his servant Isaac. {31:37} In the morning, Jacob shared with Isaac the vow he had made to the Lord, the vision he had seen, and how he built an altar, saying everything was ready for the sacrifice he promised to make before the Lord. {31:38} Isaac replied to Jacob, "I am too old to go with you; I cannot endure the journey. Go, my son, in peace; today I am one hundred sixty-five years old and can no longer travel. Set your mother on an ass and let her accompany you. {31:39} I know you came for my sake, and may this day be blessed, for you have seen me alive, and I have seen you, my son. {31:40} May you prosper and fulfill the vow you have made. Don't delay your vow, for you will be held accountable for it. Therefore, make haste to perform it, and may He who created all things be pleased with what you have vowed." {31:41} He said to Rebecca, "Go with your son Jacob." Rebecca went with Jacob, accompanied by Deborah, and they traveled to Bethel. {31:42} Jacob remembered the prayer his father had blessed him with, as well as his two sons, Levi and Judah, and he rejoiced and blessed the God of his fathers, Abraham and Isaac. {31:43} Jacob said, "Now I know that I have an eternal hope, and my sons do too, before the God of all." {31:44} This is what is ordained concerning the two, and it is recorded as an eternal testimony for them on the heavenly tablets regarding how Isaac blessed them.

{32:1} That night, Jacob stayed at Bethel, and Levi had a dream where he was ordained as the priest of the Most High God, along with his sons forever. He woke from his sleep and blessed the Lord. {32:2} Early the next morning, on the fourteenth of the month, Jacob gave a tithe of everything that had come with him, including men, cattle, gold, and every vessel and garment; he gave tithes of all. {32:3} During that time, Rachel became pregnant with her son Benjamin. Jacob counted his sons, and Levi was chosen for the Lord's portion, so his father clothed him in the priestly garments and filled his hands with offerings. {32:4} On the fifteenth of the month, Jacob brought fourteen oxen, twenty-eight rams, forty-nine sheep, seven lambs, and twenty-one kids of the goats as burnt offerings on the altar, pleasing to God. {32:5} This was his offering due to the vow he made to give a tenth, along with their fruit and drink offerings. {32:6} After the fire consumed the offerings, he burned incense over the fire, and as a thank offering, he presented two oxen, four rams, four sheep, four male goats, two year-old sheep, and two kids of the goats, doing this daily for seven days. {32:7} He and all his sons and men joyfully ate together for those seven days, blessing and thanking the Lord who had delivered him from all his troubles and had allowed him to fulfill his vow. {32:8} He tithed all the clean animals and made burnt sacrifices, but he did not give the unclean animals to Levi; instead, he gave him all the souls of the men. {32:9} Levi served as a priest at Bethel before his father Jacob, preferred over his ten brothers. Jacob renewed his vow, tithing again to the Lord, sanctifying it, and it became holy to Him. {32:10} For this reason, it is ordained on the heavenly tablets as a law to tithe again, allowing them to eat before the Lord year after year in the place He chooses for His name to dwell, with no limits on the days forever. {32:11} This ordinance is written so it can be fulfilled annually in eating the second tithe before the Lord in the chosen place, and nothing shall remain from it from one year to the next. {32:12} The seeds shall be eaten in their year until the days of harvest, and the wine until the season is over, and the oil until the right season. {32:13} Anything that is left and becomes old should be treated as polluted and burned with fire, for it is unclean. {32:14} They should eat it together in the sanctuary, ensuring it does not become old. {32:15} All tithes of oxen and sheep will be holy to the Lord and will belong to the priests, who will eat before Him year after year, as it is ordained and engraved regarding the tithe on the heavenly tablets. {32:16} On the following night, the twenty-second of the month, Jacob resolved to build that place, surrounding the court with a wall to sanctify it forever for himself and his children. {32:17} The Lord appeared to him at night, blessed him, and said, "Your name will no longer be Jacob; Israel will be your name." {32:18} He continued, "I am the Lord who created heaven and earth. I will increase and multiply you greatly, and kings will come from you, ruling everywhere the sons of men have walked. {32:19} I will give your descendants all the earth under heaven, and they will judge all nations according to their desires, and after that, they will possess the whole earth and inherit it forever." {32:20} After He finished speaking, He ascended into heaven, and Jacob watched until He was gone. {32:21} That night, Jacob had a vision of an angel descending from heaven with seven tablets in his hands, which he gave to Jacob. Jacob read them and understood everything that was written about what would happen to him and his sons throughout the ages. {32:22} The angel showed him all that was written on the tablets, saying, "Do not build this place or make it an eternal sanctuary; do not dwell here, for this is not the place. Go to the house of your father Abraham and stay with Isaac until your father dies. {32:23} You will die peacefully in Egypt, and in this land, you will be buried with honor in your fathers' tombs, alongside Abraham and Isaac. {32:24} Do not fear, for what you have seen and read will surely happen, and you should write down everything you have seen and read." {32:25} Jacob replied, "Lord, how can I remember all that I have read and seen?" He answered, "I will bring everything to your remembrance." {32:26} After the angel left, Jacob awoke from his sleep and remembered everything he had read and seen, writing down all the words. {32:27} He celebrated there for another day, offering sacrifices just like the previous days, and named that day 'Addition' because it was added to the former days he called 'The Feast.' {32:28} Thus, it was made known to him, and it is recorded on the heavenly tablets that he should celebrate it and add it to the seven days of the feast. {32:29} Its name was called 'Addition' because it was recorded among the feast days according to the number of the days in the year. {32:30} On the night of the twenty-third of the month, Deborah, Rebecca's nurse, died, and they buried her beneath the city under the oak by the river. Jacob named that place 'The River of Deborah' and the oak 'The Oak of the Mourning of Deborah.' {32:31} Rebecca then returned to her home with Isaac, and Jacob sent by her hand rams, sheep, and he-goats for her to prepare a meal for Isaac as he liked. {32:32} He followed his mother until he reached the land of Kabratan, where he settled. {32:33} That night, Rachel gave birth to a son and named him 'Son of My Sorrow' because she suffered in childbirth. But his father named him Benjamin on the eleventh day of the eighth month, in the first of the sixth week of this jubilee year. {32:34} Rachel died there and was buried in Ephrath, which is Bethlehem. Jacob built a pillar on Rachel's grave, on the road above her burial site.

{33:1} Jacob settled south of Magdaladra'ef and went to his father Isaac with his wife Leah on the new moon of the tenth month. {33:2} Reuben saw Bilhah, Rachel's maid and his father's concubine, bathing in a hidden place, and he was attracted to her. {33:3} That night, he hid himself and entered Bilhah's house, where he found her sleeping alone on her bed. {33:4} He lay with her, and when she awoke and saw him in bed, she pulled back her covering and seized him, crying out when she realized it was Reuben. {33:5} Ashamed, she let go of him, and he fled. {33:6} Bilhah mourned greatly because of what happened but did not tell anyone. {33:7} When Jacob returned and sought her, she said, "I cannot be with you; I have been defiled. Reuben has defiled me and lay with me while I was asleep, and I didn't realize until he uncovered my skirt and slept with me." {33:8} Jacob was furious with Reuben for lying with Bilhah and for uncovering his father's skirt. {33:9} Because Reuben had defiled her, Jacob did not approach Bilhah again. For any man who uncovers his father's skirt, his deed is exceedingly wicked, making him abominable before the Lord. {33:10} It is for this reason that it is written and ordained on the heavenly tablets that a man should not lie with his father's wife or uncover his father's skirt, for this is unclean. They must surely die—the man who lies with his father's wife and the woman, too, for they have brought uncleanness to the earth. {33:11} There must be nothing unclean among the nation chosen by God as His possession. {33:12} Again, it is written: "Cursed be he who lies with his father's wife, for he has uncovered his father's shame"; and all the holy ones of the Lord agreed, saying, "So be it; so be it." {33:13} Moses, you must command the children of Israel to observe this word, for it carries a death penalty; it is unclean, and there is no atonement forever for the man who has committed this sin. He must be put to death, stoned with stones, and rooted out from the people of our God. {33:14} No man who does this in Israel may remain alive even for a single day on earth, for he is abominable and unclean. {33:15} They must not say: Reuben was granted life and forgiveness after lying with his father's concubine, even though she was still married to Jacob, his father. {33:16} Until that time, the full ordinance and judgment and law had not been revealed to all, but in your days, it has been revealed as a law for specific seasons and days, an everlasting law for all generations. {33:17} For this law, there is no end or atonement; both must be rooted out from among the people. On the very day they committed this act, they must be put to death. {33:18} Write this down, Moses, so that Israel may observe it and follow these words, avoiding any sin that leads to death; for the Lord our God is the judge who shows no favoritism and accepts no gifts. {33:19} Tell them these words of the covenant so they may hear and observe, being careful to avoid destruction and being rooted out from the land; for uncleanness, abomination, contamination, and pollution are all that commit this sin before our God. {33:20} There is no greater sin than the fornication committed on earth; for Israel is a holy nation to the Lord its God, a nation of inheritance, a priestly and royal nation, and a possession for Him. No such uncleanness shall exist in the midst of this holy nation. {33:21} In the third year of this sixth week, Jacob and all his sons went to dwell in the house of Abraham, near Isaac his father and Rebecca his mother. {33:22} These are the names of Jacob's sons: the firstborn, Reuben; Simeon; Levi; Judah; Issachar; Zebulon—the sons of Leah; and the sons of Rachel, Joseph and Benjamin; the sons of Bilhah, Dan and Naphtali; and the sons of Zilpah, Gad and Asher; and Dinah, Jacob's only daughter, the daughter of Leah. {33:23} They came and bowed down to Isaac and Rebecca, who blessed Jacob and all his sons when they saw them. Isaac was exceedingly joyful because he saw the sons of Jacob, his younger son, and he blessed them.

{34:1} In the sixth year of this week of the forty-fourth jubilee, Jacob sent his sons to pasture their sheep, along with his servants, to the pastures of Shechem. {34:2} The seven kings of the Amorites gathered together against them to kill them, hiding under the trees and planning to take their cattle as plunder. {34:3} Jacob, along with Levi, Judah, and Joseph, stayed in the house with their father Isaac because his spirit was sorrowful, so they couldn't leave him; and Benjamin, being the youngest, remained with his father for this reason. {34:4} The kings of Taphu, 'Aresa, Seragan, Selo, Ga'as, Bethoron, and Ma'anisakir, along with all those who lived in these mountains and the woods in the land of Canaan, approached Jacob and informed him, saying: "Behold, the kings of the Amorites have surrounded your sons and plundered their herds." {34:5} Jacob arose from his house, along with his three sons, all the servants of his father, and his own servants, and he went against them with six thousand armed men. {34:6} He killed them in the pastures of Shechem, pursued those who fled, and killed them with the sword. He defeated 'Aresa, Taphu, Saregan, Selo, Amani-sakir, and Ga[ga]'as, recovering his herds. {34:7} He prevailed over them and imposed tribute on them, requiring them to pay him five fruit products from their land, and he built the cities Robel and Tamnatares. {34:8} He returned in peace, made peace with them, and they became his servants until he and his sons went down into Egypt. {34:9} In the seventh year of this week, he sent Joseph from his house to learn about the well-being of his brothers in the land of Shechem, and he found them in Dothan. {34:10} They acted treacherously towards him and plotted to kill him, but instead, they changed their minds and sold him to Ishmaelite merchants, who brought him down to Egypt and sold him to Potiphar, Pharaoh's eunuch and chief cook, priest of the city of 'Elew. {34:11} The sons of Jacob killed a goat, dipped Joseph's coat in the blood, and sent it to their father Jacob on the tenth of the seventh month. {34:12} Jacob mourned all that night because they had brought it to him in the evening. He became feverish with grief over his son's supposed death, saying: "An evil beast has devoured Joseph," and all the members of his household mourned with him that day. {34:13} His sons and daughter tried to comfort him, but he refused to be comforted for his son. {34:14} On that day, Bilhah heard that Joseph had died, and she mourned him to death. She was living in Qafratef, and Dinah, his daughter, also died after Joseph. {34:15} Three mournings came upon Israel in one month. They buried Bilhah near Rachel's tomb, and they buried Dinah there as well. {34:16} Jacob mourned for Joseph for a whole year without ceasing, saying, "Let me go down to the grave mourning for my son." {34:17} Therefore, it is ordained for the children of Israel to afflict themselves on the tenth of the seventh month—the day the news that made Jacob weep for Joseph came to him—that they should atone for their sins with a young goat once a year. {34:18} This day has been established for them to grieve over their sins and all their transgressions and errors so that they might cleanse themselves on that day every year. {34:19} After Joseph's death, the sons of Jacob took wives for themselves. Reuben's wife was named Ada; Simeon's wife was named 'Adlba'a, a Canaanite; Levi's wife was Melka, a daughter of Aram, from the descendants of Terah; Judah's wife was Betasu'el, a Canaanite; Issachar's wife was Hezaqa; Zabulon's wife was Ni'iman; Dan's wife was 'Egla; Naphtali's wife was Rasu'u from Mesopotamia; Gad's wife was Maka; Asher's wife was 'Ijona; Joseph's wife was Asenath, the Egyptian; and Benjamin's wife was 'Ijasaka. {34:20} Simeon repented and took a second wife from Mesopotamia, just like his brothers.

{35:1} In the first year of the first week of the forty-fifth jubilee, Rebecca called her son Jacob and commanded him regarding his father and his brother, telling him to honor them all the days of his life. {35:2} Jacob replied, "I will do everything you have commanded me, for this will bring me honor and greatness and righteousness before the Lord because I honor them. {35:3} And you, Mother, know all my deeds and everything in my heart from the time I was born until now. I always think good thoughts about everyone. {35:4} How could I not do what you have commanded, to honor my father and my brother? Tell me, Mother, what wrongdoing have you seen in me that I should turn away from it and be merciful?" {35:5} She answered, "My son, I have not seen any wrongdoing in you all my days, only upright deeds. Yet I must tell you the truth, my son: I will die this year and will not survive beyond this year; I have seen in a dream the day of my death and that I will not live beyond one hundred fifty-five years. Behold, I have completed all the days of my life that I am meant to live." {35:6} Jacob laughed at his mother's words because she claimed she would die, while she was sitting before him in full strength, not infirm in any way; she could go in and out and see clearly, her teeth were strong, and no illness had touched her throughout her life. {35:7} Jacob said to her, "Blessed am I, Mother, if my days are like your days, and my strength remains with me as your strength does; you will not die, for you are joking about your death." {35:8} She went to Isaac and said to him, "I have one request for you: make Esau swear that he will not harm Jacob or pursue him with hatred, for you know Esau's thoughts are wicked from his youth, and there is no goodness in him. He desires to kill Jacob after your death. {35:9} You know all the evil he has done since Jacob went to Haran until now—he has abandoned us entirely and done evil to us. He has taken your flocks for himself and stolen all your possessions from before your eyes. {35:10} When we begged him for what belonged to us, he acted like someone taking pity on us. He is bitter against you because you blessed Jacob, your perfect and upright son. {35:11} There is nothing but goodness in him; since he came from Haran until now, he has not robbed us of anything. He brings us everything at the right time and rejoices when we take from him, blessing us, and has remained with us continually at home, honoring us." {35:12} Isaac replied, "I also know and see Jacob's deeds who is with us; he honors us with all his heart. But I used to love Esau more than Jacob because he was the firstborn. Now I love Jacob more than Esau because Esau has committed many evil deeds, and there is no righteousness in him. His ways are filled with unrighteousness and violence. {35:13} My heart is troubled because of all his deeds, and neither he nor his descendants will be saved; they are destined to be destroyed from the earth and will be rooted out from under heaven. He has forsaken the God of Abraham and followed after his wives and their impurity and error, he and his children. {35:14} You ask me to make him swear that he will not kill Jacob, but even if he swears, he will not keep his oath; he will only do evil, not good. {35:15} If he desires to kill Jacob, he will be given into Jacob's hands, and he will not escape from him. {35:16} Do not fear for Jacob, for his guardian is great, powerful, and honored, praised more than the guardian of Esau." {35:17} Rebecca sent for Esau, and when he came to her, she said, "I have a request to make of you, and I want you to promise me you will do it." {35:18} He answered, "I will do everything you say and will not refuse your request." {35:19} She said, "I ask you that when I die, you will take me in and bury me near Sarah, your father's mother, and that you and Jacob will love each other, desiring only good for one another, so that you may prosper, my sons, and be honored in the land. No enemy will rejoice over you, and you will be a blessing and mercy in the eyes of all who love you." {35:20} He replied, "I will do all that you have said, and I will bury you on the day you die near Sarah, my father's mother, as you requested so that her bones may lie next to yours. {35:21} And I will love Jacob my brother above all others; I have no other brother on earth but him. It is no great honor for me to love him; he is my brother, and we were both born from you and came from your womb. If I do not love my brother, whom should I love? {35:22} I also ask you to encourage Jacob about me and my sons, for I know he will surely be king over me and my children; the day my father blessed him, he made him higher and me lower. {35:23} I swear to you that I will love him and will not desire evil against him all the days of my life, only good." {35:24} He swore to her regarding all this matter. She called Jacob in front of Esau and gave him instructions according to the words she had spoken to Esau. {35:25} Jacob said, "I will do your will; trust me that no evil will come from me or my sons against Esau. My only priority is love." {35:26} They ate and drank together that night, and she died at the age of three jubilees, one week, and one year on that night. Her two sons, Esau and Jacob, buried her in the double cave near Sarah, their father's mother.

{36:1} In the sixth year of this week, Isaac called his two sons, Esau and Jacob, and they came to him. He said to them, "My sons, I am going the way of my fathers, to the eternal home where they are. {36:2} Therefore, bury me near Abraham, my father, in the double cave in the field of Ephron the Hittite, where Abraham purchased a burial site. In the tomb I dug for myself, that is where you should bury me. {36:3} I command you, my sons, to practice righteousness and integrity on the earth so that the Lord may fulfill all that He promised Abraham and his descendants. {36:4} And love one another, my sons, as a man loves his own soul. Let each of you seek what benefits his brother and work together on the earth. Love each other as you love your own souls. {36:5} Regarding idols, I command and advise you to reject them and hate them; do not love them, for they are full of deception for those who worship and bow down to them. {36:6} Remember, my sons, the Lord God of Abraham your father, and how I too worshipped and served Him in righteousness and joy, so that He might multiply you and increase your descendants as numerous as the stars in heaven, and establish you on the earth as the plant of righteousness, which will not be uprooted for all generations forever. {36:7} Now I make you swear a great oath—there is no greater oath than this, by the glorious, honored, great, splendid, and mighty name that created the heavens, the earth, and all things—to fear and worship Him. {36:8} Each of you should love his brother with affection and righteousness and should never wish harm against his brother for the rest of your lives so that you may prosper in all your deeds and not be destroyed. {36:9} If either of you devises evil against your brother, know that from now on, everyone who plans evil against his brother will fall into his own trap and will be removed from the land of the living; his descendants will be destroyed from under heaven. {36:10} On the day of turmoil, condemnation, anger, and fury, with devouring fire as He burned Sodom, so will He burn his land, city, and all that is his. He will be blotted out of the book of discipline of the children of men and not recorded in the book of life, but in the one destined for destruction; he will depart into eternal condemnation, with his punishment renewed in hate, wrath, torment, anger, plagues, and disease forever. {36:11} I say and testify to you, my sons, according to the judgment that will come upon anyone who wishes to harm his brother. {36:12} On that day, he divided all his possessions between the two and gave the larger share to the firstborn, along with the tower and everything around it, and all that Abraham owned at the Well of the Oath. {36:13} He said, "This larger portion I will give to the firstborn." {36:14} Esau replied, "I have sold my birthright to Jacob; let it be given to him. I have no complaints about it, for it is his." {36:15} Isaac said, "May a blessing rest upon you, my sons, and upon your descendants this day, for you have given me peace, and my heart is not troubled about the birthright, lest you act wickedly because of it. {36:16} May the Most High God bless the man who does righteousness, him and his descendants forever." {36:17} He finished giving them commands and blessings, and they ate and drank together before him. He rejoiced because they were united in purpose, and they left him to rest that day and slept. {36:18} Isaac slept on his bed that day, rejoicing, and he fell into eternal sleep, dying at one hundred eighty years old. He completed twenty-five weeks and five years, and his two sons, Esau and Jacob, buried him. {36:19} Esau went to the land of Edom, to the mountains of Seir, and settled there. {36:20} Jacob lived in the mountains of Hebron, in the tower of his father Abraham's sojournings, and he worshipped the Lord with all his heart and followed His visible commands, according to the days of his generations. {36:21} Leah, his wife, died in the fourth year of the second week of the forty-fifth jubilee, and he buried her in the double cave near Rebecca, his mother, to the left of the grave of Sarah, his father's mother. {36:22} All her sons and his sons came to mourn for Leah with him and to comfort him, for he was grieving for her, having loved her dearly after the death of Rachel, her sister. {36:23} Leah was perfect and upright in all her ways and honored Jacob, and during all the days she lived with him, he never heard a harsh word from her mouth. She was gentle, peaceable, upright, and honorable. {36:24} He remembered all her deeds during her life and mourned her deeply, for he loved her with all his heart and soul.

{37:1} On the day that Isaac, the father of Jacob and Esau, died, the sons of Esau learned that Isaac had given the portion of the elder son to his younger son, Jacob, and they were very angry. {37:2} They argued with their father, saying, "Why has your father given Jacob the elder's portion and passed you over, even though you are the elder and Jacob is the younger?" {37:3} Esau replied, "Because I sold my birthright to Jacob for a small bowl of lentils, and when my father sent me to hunt and bring him something to eat and bless me, Jacob deceived me. He brought my father food and drink, and my father blessed him instead of me. {37:4} Now our father has made us swear an oath—not to devise any evil against each other—and that we shall live in love and peace without corrupting our ways." {37:5} They responded, "We will not listen to you and make peace with him; our strength is greater than his, and we are more powerful. We will go against him, kill him, and destroy him and his sons. If you won't go with us, we'll harm you too. {37:6} Now listen to us: let us send messengers to Aram, Philistia, Moab, and Ammon, and choose for ourselves capable men who are eager for battle. We'll go against him and fight him, exterminating him from the earth before he becomes strong." {37:7} Their father told them, "Do not go, and do not make war with him, lest you fall before him." {37:8} They replied, "This is exactly how you have acted from your youth until now, putting your neck under his yoke. We will not listen to these words." They sent messengers to Aram and to Aduram, a friend of their father's, and hired one thousand fighting men, chosen warriors. {37:9} From Moab and the children of Ammon, they hired another thousand chosen warriors, and from Philistia, another thousand men of war. From Edom and the Horites, they recruited a thousand more fighting men, and from the Kittim, strong men of war. {37:10} They said to their father, "Go with them and lead them; otherwise, we will kill you." {37:11} He was filled with rage and indignation when he saw that his sons were forcing him to lead them against his brother Jacob. But then he remembered all the evil hidden in his heart against Jacob and forgot the oath he had sworn to his father and mother, that he would not devise any evil against Jacob all his days. {37:12} Meanwhile, Jacob was unaware that they were coming to battle against him; he was mourning for Leah, his wife, until they approached very close to the tower with four thousand warriors and chosen men of war. {37:13} The men of Hebron sent a message to him saying, "Behold, your brother has come against you to fight, with four thousand armed men carrying swords and shields." They loved Jacob more than Esau and informed him, as Jacob was more generous and merciful than Esau. {37:14} But Jacob didn't believe it until they got very near the tower. He closed the gates of the tower and stood on the battlements, speaking to his brother Esau, saying, "How noble is the comfort you've brought me regarding the death of my wife! Is this how you fulfill the oath you swore to our father and again to our mother before they died? You have broken that oath, and the moment you swore to our father, you were condemned." {37:15} Esau replied, "Neither people nor animals have any permanent oath of righteousness; every day, they plan evil against one another and seek to kill their adversaries. You hate me and my children forever, and there is no brotherly bond between us. Listen to these words I declare to you: {37:16} If a boar can change its skin and make its bristles as soft as wool, or if it can sprout horns like a stag or sheep, then I will observe the bond of brotherhood with you. {37:17} And if the breasts separate themselves from their mother, for you have not been a brother to me. {37:18} And if wolves make peace with lambs so they do not harm or devour them, and if their hearts are towards them for good, then there will be peace in my heart towards you. {37:19} And if the lion becomes friends with the ox and makes peace with him, and if he is bound under one yoke with him and plows with him, then I will make peace with you. {37:20} And when the raven becomes as white as the raza (a type of bird), then know that I have loved you and will make peace with you. {37:21} But you shall be rooted out, and your sons shall be rooted out, and there shall be no peace for you." {37:22} When Jacob saw that Esau was so hostile towards him, wanting to kill him, and that he approached like a wild boar rushing towards a spear that pierces and kills, Jacob spoke to his own men and servants, instructing them to prepare to attack him and all his companions.

{38:1} After this, Judah spoke to Jacob, his father, and said, "Bend your bow, father, and send forth your arrows to strike down the enemy and kill them. You have the power; we will not slay your brother because he is like you. Let us give him this honor." {38:2} Then Jacob bent his bow, sent forth an arrow, and struck Esau, his brother, in the right breast and killed him. {38:3} He sent another arrow and struck Adoran the Aramaean in the left breast, knocking him backward and killing him. {38:4} Then the sons of Jacob went out, along with their servants, dividing themselves into groups on the four sides of the tower. {38:5} Judah led the way with Naphtali and Gad, along with fifty servants, on the south side of the tower, and they killed everyone they encountered, leaving no survivors. {38:6} Levi, Dan, and Asher went out on the east side of the tower with fifty men and slaughtered the fighting men of Moab and Ammon. {38:7} Reuben, Issachar, and Zebulon went out on the north side of the tower with fifty men and killed the fighting men of the Philistines. {38:8} Simeon, Benjamin, and Enoch, Reuben's son, went out on the west side of the tower with fifty men and killed four hundred strong warriors from Edom and the Horites. Six hundred men fled, including four sons of Esau, leaving their father dead on the hill in Aduram. {38:9} The sons of Jacob pursued them into the mountains of Seir, and Jacob buried his brother on the hill in Aduram before returning home. {38:10} The sons of Jacob pressed hard upon the sons of Esau in the mountains of Seir and forced them to serve the sons of Jacob. {38:11} They sent word to their father to ask whether they should make peace with Esau's sons or kill them. {38:12} Jacob replied to his sons that they should make peace, and they did so, placing the yoke of servitude upon Esau's sons, so they paid tribute to Jacob and his sons forever. {38:13} They continued to pay tribute until the day Jacob went down to Egypt. {38:14} The sons of Edom have not escaped the yoke of servitude that the twelve sons of Jacob imposed on them to this day. {38:15} These are the kings who reigned in Edom before any king reigned over the children of Israel in the land of Edom. {38:16} Balaq, the son of Beor, reigned in Edom, and the name of his city was Danaba. {38:17} Balaq died, and Jobab, the son of Zara of Boser, reigned in his place. {38:18} Jobab died, and Asam from the land of Teman took his place. {38:19} Asam died, and Adath, the son of Barad, who killed Midian in the field of Moab, became king, and the name of his city was Avith. {38:20} Adath died, and Salman from Amaseqa reigned in his place. {38:21} Salman died, and Saul of Ra'aboth by the river took over the throne. {38:22} Saul died, and Ba'elunan, the son of Achbor, reigned in his place. {38:23} Ba'elunan, the son of Achbor, died, and Adath took over again, and his wife was Maitabith, the daughter of Matarat, the daughter of Metabedza'ab. {38:24} These are the kings who ruled in the land of Edom.

{39:1} Jacob settled in the land where his father had lived, in the land of Canaan. {39:2} These are the generations of Jacob. Joseph was seventeen years old when he was taken to Egypt, where Potiphar, an official of Pharaoh and the chief cook, bought him. {39:3} Potiphar put Joseph in charge of his entire household, and because of Joseph, the Lord blessed the Egyptian's house, making everything he did prosper. {39:4} Potiphar entrusted everything to Joseph because he saw that the Lord was with him and that the Lord made all he did successful. {39:5} Joseph was well-built and handsome, and his master's wife noticed him and desired him, asking him to sleep with her. {39:6} However, he refused, saying, "I cannot betray my master; he has put everything in my hands and entrusted me with everything except you, because you are his wife. It would be a great sin against God." {39:7} Joseph remembered these teachings from his father Jacob about not committing adultery, knowing that such a sin would be punished severely. {39:8} For an entire year, she continued to press him, but he refused to listen to her. {39:9} One day, she grabbed him and insisted that he sleep with her. He ran away, leaving his garment in her hands, breaking free from her grasp. {39:10} When she saw that he had fled and would not comply, she falsely accused him to her husband, saying, "Your Hebrew servant tried to make me sleep with him, but when I screamed, he ran away, leaving his garment behind." {39:11} Potiphar saw Joseph's garment and heard his wife's accusations, so he threw Joseph into prison, where the king's prisoners were kept. {39:12} While in prison, the Lord granted Joseph favor in the eyes of the chief guard, who noticed that the Lord was with Joseph and made everything he did successful. {39:13} The guard placed Joseph in charge of all the prisoners, and he was responsible for everything that happened there, and the guard trusted Joseph completely. {39:14} Joseph remained in prison for two years. During this time, Pharaoh became angry with his two eunuchs, the chief butler and the chief baker, and put them in the same prison where Joseph was held. {39:15} The chief guard assigned Joseph to take care of them. {39:16} Both the chief butler and the chief baker had dreams one night and shared them with Joseph. {39:17} Joseph interpreted their dreams accurately, and as he predicted, Pharaoh restored the chief butler to his position while he executed the chief baker, just as Joseph had interpreted. {39:18} However, the chief butler forgot about Joseph and did not mention him to Pharaoh, despite Joseph's help.

{40:1} In those days, Pharaoh had two dreams in one night about a coming famine that would affect all the land. {40:2} He woke up and called all the dream interpreters and magicians in Egypt to tell them his dreams, but they could not interpret them. {40:3} Then, the chief butler remembered Joseph and spoke to the king about him. Pharaoh sent for Joseph, and he was brought out of prison. {40:4} Joseph told Pharaoh his two dreams were connected, explaining that seven years of abundance would come to all of Egypt, followed by seven years of famine, worse than any famine the land had ever seen. {40:5} He advised Pharaoh to appoint overseers across Egypt to store food in every city during the years of plenty so that the land would not perish during the famine. {40:6} The Lord granted Joseph favor and mercy in Pharaoh's eyes, and Pharaoh said to his servants, "We will not find anyone as wise and discerning as this man, for the spirit of the Lord is with him." {40:7} Pharaoh appointed Joseph as the second-in-command of all Egypt, giving him authority over the entire land. {40:8} He had Joseph ride in Pharaoh's second chariot, dressed him in fine garments, placed a gold chain around his neck, and had a herald proclaim before him, "Bow the knee!" {40:9} Pharaoh put a ring on Joseph's hand, made him ruler over all his house, and elevated him, saying, "Only on the throne will I be greater than you." {40:10} Joseph ruled over all the land of Egypt, and all the princes and servants loved him because he was upright, humble, and did not show favoritism or accept bribes. {40:11} He judged all the people of Egypt fairly, and because of Joseph, the land was at peace, for the Lord was with him and granted him favor and mercy with all who knew him. {40:12} Pharaoh's kingdom was orderly, without any evil or trouble. {40:13} The king named Joseph "Sephanath-Paneah" and gave him as wife the daughter of Potiphar, the priest of Heliopolis, who was the chief cook. {40:14} Joseph was thirty years old when he stood before Pharaoh. {40:15} That same year, Isaac died. {40:16} As Joseph had interpreted, there were seven years of plenty throughout Egypt, producing abundantly, with one measure yielding eighteen hundred measures. {40:17} Joseph gathered food in every city until the granaries were full, beyond what they could count or measure because of the immense amount.

{41:1} In the forty-fifth jubilee, during the second week and in the second year [2165 A.M.], Judah took a wife for his firstborn son Er from the daughters of Aram, named Tamar. {41:2} However, he hated her and did not have relations with her because his mother was a daughter of Canaan, and he wanted a wife from his mother's family, but his father Judah did not allow it. {41:3} Er, Judah's firstborn, was wicked, so the Lord killed him. {41:4} Judah then said to his brother Onan, "Go to your brother's wife and fulfill your duty as a brother-in-law by raising up offspring for your brother." {41:5} Onan knew that the offspring would not be his but would belong to his brother, so he went to his brother's wife and wasted his seed on the ground. This was wicked in the eyes of the Lord, so He killed him too. {41:6} Judah said to Tamar, his daughter-in-law, "Stay in your father's house as a widow until my son Shelah grows up; I will give him to you as a husband." {41:7} Shelah grew up, but his mother Bedsu'el did not allow him to marry Tamar. Bedsu'el, Judah's wife, died [2168 A.M.] in the fifth year of that week. {41:8} In the sixth year, Judah went up to shear his sheep at Timnah [2169 A.M.], and they told Tamar, "Your father-in-law is going up to Timnah to shear his sheep." {41:9} She took off her widow's clothes, put on a veil, dressed herself up, and sat at the entrance of the road to Timnah. {41:10} When Judah passed by, he thought she was a prostitute, and he said to her, "Let me sleep with you." She replied, "What will you give me?" {41:11} He said, "I have nothing with me except my ring, my necklace, and my staff." {41:12} She asked him for these items as a pledge until he could send her payment, and he agreed to send her a young goat from his flock. {41:13} After he slept with her, she became pregnant. Judah returned to his flock, and Tamar went back to her father's house. {41:14} Later, Judah sent a young goat with his shepherd to find her, but he could not find her. He asked the men of that place, "Where is the prostitute who was here?" They answered, "There is no prostitute here." {41:15} Judah went back and reported this, saying, "I asked the people and they said there is no prostitute here." {41:16} Judah then said, "Let her keep the items, or we will be a laughingstock." After three months, it became clear that Tamar was pregnant, and people told Judah, "Tamar, your daughter-in-law, is pregnant by prostitution." {41:17} Judah went to her father's house and said to them, "Bring her out so that she may be burned for her uncleanness." {41:18} As they were about to burn her, she sent the items back to Judah, saying, "Recognize these; I am pregnant by the man who owns these." {41:19} Judah recognized them and said, "Tamar is more righteous than I, for I did not give her to my son Shelah." So he stopped pursuing her, and she was not given to Shelah. {41:20} Later, Tamar gave birth to two sons, Perez and Zerah, in the seventh year of that second week [2170 A.M.]. {41:21} The seven years of abundance, which Joseph had spoken of to Pharaoh, were completed. {41:22} Judah realized that what he had done was wrong, for he had slept with his daughter-in-law. He found it repulsive and acknowledged his wrongdoing, lamenting and pleading with the Lord for forgiveness. {41:23} In a dream, he was told that he was forgiven because he had sincerely repented & had not committed that sin again. {41:24} He received forgiveness for turning away from his sin and ignorance, having greatly transgressed before God. {41:25} Anyone who lies with his mother-in-law should be burned with fire for their uncleanness and pollution. {41:26} You should command the Israelites to avoid uncleanness, for anyone who lies with their daughter-in-law or mother-in-law has committed a shameful act; both the man and the woman should be burned. This way, God will turn away His anger and punishment from Israel. {41:27} We told Judah that his two sons had not been with Tamar, which is why his lineage would continue into a second generation and would not be cut off. {41:28} Judah had sought to punish her according to Abraham's judgment, which he had commanded his sons. Judah had intended to burn her because he sought justice.

{42:1} In the first year of the third week of the forty-fifth jubilee, a famine began to spread across the land [2171 A.M.], and there was no rain to nourish the earth; none at all fell. {42:2} The land became barren, but in Egypt, there was food because Joseph had stored the seed from the land during the seven years of abundance. {42:3} The Egyptians came to Joseph to buy food, and he opened the storehouses filled with grain from the first year, selling it to the people of the land for gold. {42:4} Meanwhile, the famine was severe in Canaan, and Jacob learned that there was food in Egypt, so he sent his ten sons to buy food there, but he did not send Benjamin. {42:5} The ten sons of Jacob arrived in Egypt among those who came to buy food. {42:6} Joseph recognized them, but they did not recognize him. He spoke to them and questioned them, asking, "Are you spies? Have you come to explore the land?" {42:7} He then imprisoned them for a time. {42:8} Afterward, he released them but kept Simeon in custody while sending the other nine brothers away. {42:9} He filled their sacks with grain and secretly returned their gold to each sack without them knowing. {42:10} Joseph instructed them to bring their younger brother, having learned from them that their father was still alive and that they had a younger sibling. {42:11} They returned to Canaan and told their father everything that had happened, including how the lord of the land had spoken harshly to them and held Simeon until they brought Benjamin back. {42:12} Jacob said, "You have robbed me of my children! Joseph is gone, and now Simeon is gone too, and you want to take Benjamin! All this misfortune has come upon me!" {42:13} He continued, "My son will not go with you; if he is harmed on the journey, you would bring my gray hair down to the grave in sorrow." {42:14} He was particularly concerned because he saw that their money had been returned in each sack, which made him fearful to send Benjamin. {42:15} The famine worsened in Canaan and in all lands except Egypt, where many of the Egyptians had stored grain when they saw Joseph gathering and preserving it for the years of famine. {42:16} The people of Egypt were sustained by this grain during the first year of the famine. {42:17} When Israel saw that the famine was severe and there was no relief, he told his sons, "Go again and buy us food so we don't die." {42:18} They replied, "We won't go unless our youngest brother goes with us." {42:19} Israel realized that if he did not send Benjamin, they would all perish due to the famine. {42:20} Reuben then said, "Put him in my care, and if I do not bring him back to you, you can kill my two sons instead." {42:21} Jacob replied, "He will not go with you." Then Judah approached and said, "Send him with me; if I do not bring him back, I will bear the blame for the rest of my life." {42:22} Finally, Jacob agreed and sent Benjamin with them in the second year of that week on the first day of the month. {42:23} They went to Egypt along with everyone else who traveled there, bringing gifts with them: resin, almonds, pistachios, and pure honey. {42:24} When they stood before Joseph, he saw Benjamin, recognized him, and said, "Is this your youngest brother?" They replied, "Yes, it is." Joseph then said, "May God be gracious to you, my son!" {42:25} He sent them to his house and brought Simeon out to join them, hosting a feast for them. {42:26} They presented their gifts to him, and during the meal, Joseph gave each of them a portion, but Benjamin received five times as much as the others. {42:27} They ate and drank together, and afterward, they stayed overnight with their donkeys. {42:28} Joseph devised a plan to discover their true feelings and to see if they were at peace with one another. He told his steward, "Fill all their sacks with food and return their money into their bags. Also, place my silver cup, the cup I drink from, in the sack of the youngest, and send them away."

{43:1} Joseph's steward did as he was instructed, filling all their sacks with food, returning their money, and placing Joseph's silver cup in Benjamin's sack. {43:2} Early the next morning, the brothers departed, but after they had left, Joseph told his steward, "Chase after them and catch up with them. Say, 'You have repaid my kindness with evil; you have stolen the silver cup that my lord drinks from.' And bring back their youngest brother to me quickly before I go to my judgment seat." {43:3} The steward ran after them and delivered Joseph's message. {43:4} The brothers exclaimed, "God forbid that your servants would do such a thing! We wouldn't steal any items from your master's house. The money we found in our sacks the first time we came was returned from Canaan, so how could we steal anything?" {43:5} They said, "Here we are; search our sacks. If you find the cup in any one of our sacks, let that man die, and we will be your servants." {43:6} The steward replied, "Not so; the man with whom I find the cup will be my servant, but you can all return home in peace." {43:7} He searched their sacks, starting with the oldest and going to the youngest, and found the cup in Benjamin's sack. {43:8} The brothers tore their clothes in despair, loaded their donkeys, and returned to the city, falling to the ground before Joseph's house. {43:9} Joseph said, "You have committed a grave sin." They responded, "What can we say? How can we defend ourselves? Your lord has uncovered our guilt; we are now your servants, and so are our donkeys." {43:10} Joseph replied, "I fear God; as for you, go home. Let your brother be my servant, for you have done wrong. Don't you know that a man treasures his cup as I do mine? Yet you have stolen it from me." {43:11} Judah then said, "Please, my lord, let me speak a word in your ear. Two sons were born to my mother and our father. One went away and has not been found, and now only this one remains, and our father loves him dearly; his life is tied to the boy's life. {43:12} If we return without him, our father will die from grief, and we will bring down his gray hair to the grave in sorrow. Let me stay instead of the boy as a servant to you, and let the lad go with his brothers, for I guaranteed his safety to our father. If I do not bring him back, I will bear the blame before our father forever." {43:13} Joseph saw that they were united in their concern for each other, and he could not hold back his emotions any longer. He revealed himself to them, speaking to them in Hebrew and weeping as he embraced them. {43:14} But they did not recognize him at first and began to cry. He said to them, "Don't weep for me; hurry and bring my father to me. You can see that I am your brother Joseph, and that it is my own mouth that speaks to you. {43:15} Look, this is the second year of the famine, and there are still five years ahead without plowing or harvesting. Hurry and bring your families down here, so you don't perish from hunger. Don't be troubled about your possessions, for God sent me ahead of you to ensure that many would survive. {43:16} Tell my father that I am alive and that I have been made a father to Pharaoh, ruling over his household and all of Egypt. Share with him all my glory and the wealth that God has given me." {43:17} At Pharaoh's command, he provided them with chariots and supplies for their journey, giving them fine clothing and silver. {43:18} To their father, he sent clothing, silver, and ten donkeys loaded with grain. {43:19} When they returned and told their father that Joseph was alive and in charge of all Egypt, he could hardly believe it, as he was overwhelmed with emotions. But when he saw the wagons Joseph had sent, his spirit revived, and he said, "It is enough; if Joseph is alive, I will go see him before I die."

{44:1} Israel began his journey from Haran, leaving his home on the new moon of the third month. He traveled toward the Well of the Oath, where he offered a sacrifice to the God of his father Isaac on the seventh of that month. {44:2} Jacob remembered the dream he had at Bethel, and he was afraid to go down to Egypt. While considering whether to send word to Joseph to come to him instead, he decided to stay there for seven days, hoping to receive a vision about whether he should stay or go. {44:3} He celebrated the harvest festival with the first fruits, using old grain because there wasn't a single seed left in all the land of Canaan due to the famine affecting the animals and birds, as well as people. {44:4} On the sixteenth, the Lord appeared to him, calling, "Jacob, Jacob!" and Jacob answered, "Here I am." {44:5} God said, "I am the God of your fathers, the God of Abraham and Isaac. Don't be afraid to go down to Egypt, for I will make you into a great nation there. I will go down with you, and I will bring you back again, and you will be buried in this land. Joseph will close your eyes." {44:6} "Do not fear; go down to Egypt." {44:7} His sons and grandsons got ready, loading their father and their belongings onto wagons. {44:8} On the sixteenth of the third month, Israel left the Well of the Oath and headed for Egypt. {44:9} He sent Judah ahead to Joseph to explore the land of Goshen, as Joseph had instructed his brothers to settle there so they could be near him. {44:10} This was the best land in Egypt and suitable for all of them, including their livestock. {44:11} These are the names of Jacob's sons who went to Egypt with their father: Reuben, Israel's firstborn, and his sons Enoch, Pallu, Hezron, and Carmi—five in total. {44:12} Simeon and his sons, whose names are Jemuel, Jamin, Ohad, Jachin, Zohar, and Shaul, the son of the Zephathite woman—seven in total. {44:13} Levi and his sons: Gershon, Kohath, and Merari—four in total. {44:14} Judah and his sons: Shelah, Perez, and Zerah—four in total. {44:15} Issachar and his sons: Tola, Phua, Jasub, and Shimron—five in total. {44:16} Zebulun and his sons: Sered, Elon, and Jahleel—four in total. {44:17} These are the sons of Jacob and the sons Leah bore him in Mesopotamia—six in total, plus their one sister, Dinah. In all, there were twenty-nine souls from Leah's side, and with Jacob, they totaled thirty. {44:18} The sons of Zilpah, Leah's maid, bore Jacob Gad and Asher. {44:19} The names of their sons who went with him into Egypt are as follows: The sons of Gad: Ziphion, Haggi, Shuni, Ezbon, Eri, Areli, Arodi—eight in total. {44:20} The sons of Asher: Imnah, Ishvah, Ishvi, Beriah, and their sister Serah—six in total. {44:21} The total from Zilpah's sons was fourteen, while Leah's sons totaled forty-four. {44:22} The sons of Rachel, Jacob's wife, are Joseph and Benjamin. {44:23} Before Jacob arrived in Egypt, Joseph had two sons, Manasseh and Ephraim, born to him by Asenath, the daughter of Potiphar, priest of Heliopolis—three in total. {44:24} The sons of Benjamin are Bela, Becher, Ashbel, Gera, Naaman, Ehi, Rosh, Muppim, Huppim, and Ard—eleven in total. {44:25} All the souls of Rachel's side totaled fourteen. {44:26} The sons of Bilhah, Rachel's maid, whom she bore to Jacob, are Dan and Naphtali. {44:27} The names of their sons who went into Egypt are as follows: The sons of Dan: Hushim, Samon, Asudi, Ijaka, and Salomon—six in total. {44:28} They died in the year they entered Egypt, leaving Hushim as Dan's only remaining son. {44:29} The names of the sons of Naphtali are Jahziel, Guni, Jezer, Shallum, and Iv. {44:30} Iv, born after the years of famine, also died in Egypt. {44:31} All the souls from Rachel totaled twenty-six. {44:32} In total, the number of souls from Jacob who went to Egypt was seventy. These include his children and grandchildren, totaling seventy, but five died in Egypt before Joseph and left no children. {44:33} In Canaan, two sons of Judah died, Er and Onan, and they also had no children. The descendants of Israel buried those who passed away, and they were counted among the seventy nations.

{45:1} Israel entered the land of Egypt, specifically the land of Goshen, on the new moon of the fourth month in the second year of the third week of the forty-fifth jubilee. {45:2} Joseph went to meet his father Jacob in Goshen, embracing him and weeping. {45:3} Israel said to Joseph, "Now I can die because I have seen you. May the Lord, the God of Israel, be blessed, the God of Abraham and Isaac, who has not withheld His mercy and grace from His servant Jacob. {45:4} It is enough for me to see your face while I am still alive; the vision I had at Bethel is true. Blessed be the Lord my God forever, and blessed be His name." {45:5} Joseph and his brothers ate bread and drank wine before their father. Jacob rejoiced greatly when he saw Joseph dining with his brothers and drinking before him, and he blessed the Creator of all things who had preserved him and kept his twelve sons safe. {45:6} Joseph had given his father and brothers the privilege of living in the land of Goshen and in Rameses and all the surrounding region that he governed for Pharaoh. {45:7} Israel and his sons settled in the land of Goshen, the best part of Egypt, and Israel was one hundred thirty years old when he arrived in Egypt. {45:8} Joseph took care of his father, brothers, and their possessions, providing them with enough bread to last through the seven years of famine. {45:9} The famine affected all of Egypt, so Joseph acquired all the land for Pharaoh in exchange for food, gaining ownership of the people, their cattle, and everything for Pharaoh. {45:10} The years of famine ended, and Joseph gave the people in the land seeds and food to sow in the eighth year because the river had flooded all of Egypt. {45:11} During the seven years of famine, it had not overflowed enough to irrigate many places, but now it flooded, allowing the Egyptians to plant their fields, and that year produced a great harvest. {45:12} This was the first year of the fourth week of the forty-fifth jubilee. {45:13} Joseph took one-fifth of the harvest for the king and left four-fifths for the people for food and seed, establishing this as a rule for the land of Egypt even to this day. {45:14} Israel lived in Egypt for seventeen years, and his total lifespan was three jubilees, which is one hundred forty-seven years. {45:15} He died in the fourth year of the fifth week of the forty-fifth jubilee. {45:16} Before he died, Israel blessed his sons and told them everything that would happen to them in Egypt. He revealed what would occur in the last days, blessed them, and gave Joseph two portions in the land. {45:17} He passed away and was buried in the double cave in the land of Canaan, near his father Abraham, in the grave he had dug for himself in the double cave in Hebron. {45:18} He entrusted all his writings and those of his fathers to his son Levi, so he could preserve and renew them for his children up until today.

{46:1} After Jacob died, the children of Israel multiplied in Egypt and became a great nation, united in heart, so that brother loved brother, and every man helped his neighbor. They increased abundantly and multiplied greatly for ten weeks of years, which was all the days of Joseph's life. {46:2} During Joseph's lifetime, there was no evil or Satan; all the Egyptians honored the children of Israel. {46:3} Joseph died at one hundred ten years old. He lived seventeen years in Canaan, worked as a servant for ten years, was imprisoned for three years, and spent eighty years ruling all the land of Egypt under the king. {46:4} Joseph died, along with all his brothers and that entire generation. {46:5} Before he died, Joseph commanded the children of Israel to carry his bones with them when they left Egypt. {46:6} He made them swear regarding his bones, knowing that the Egyptians would not bring him back to Canaan for burial. Makamaron, the king of Canaan, had fought the king of Egypt in the valley while living in Assyria, defeating him there and pursuing the Egyptians to the gates of 'Ermon. {46:7} However, he could not enter because a new, stronger king had risen in Egypt, forcing him to return to Canaan. The gates of Egypt were then closed, and no one could enter or leave. {46:8} Joseph died in the forty-sixth jubilee, in the sixth week, in the second year, and he was buried in Egypt. All his brothers died after him. {46:9} The king of Egypt went to war with the king of Canaan in the forty-seventh jubilee, in the second week of the second year, and the children of Israel took all the bones of Jacob's children except for Joseph's, burying them in the field in the double cave on the mountain. {46:10} Most of them returned to Egypt, but a few stayed in the mountains of Hebron, including Amram, your father. {46:11} The king of Canaan was victorious over the king of Egypt and closed the gates of Egypt. {46:12} He devised an evil plan against the children of Israel, intending to afflict them. He said to the Egyptians, "Look, the people of Israel have increased and multiplied more than we have. {46:13} Come, let us deal wisely with them before they become too numerous, and let us afflict them with slavery before war arises. Otherwise, they will join our enemies and leave our land, as their hearts and faces are set toward Canaan." {46:14} He appointed taskmasters to oppress them with slavery, and they built strong cities for Pharaoh, Pithom and Raamses, repairing all the walls and fortifications in Egypt. {46:15} They made the Israelites serve with rigor, and the more they were oppressed, the more they increased and multiplied. {46:16} The people of Egypt despised the children of Israel.

{47:1} In the seventh week, in the seventh year, during the forty-seventh jubilee, your father left the land of Canaan, and you were born in the fourth week, in the sixth year of the forty-eighth jubilee. This was a time of tribulation for the children of Israel. {47:2} Pharaoh, the king of Egypt, issued a decree that all male children born to the Israelites should be cast into the river. {47:3} They threw the boys into the river for seven months until the day you were born. {47:4} Your mother hid you for three months, but when they found out about her, she made an ark for you, covering it with pitch and asphalt, and placed it among the reeds on the riverbank. {47:5} She put you in it for seven days, and your mother came at night to nurse you, while your sister Miriam watched over you during the day, protecting you from birds. {47:6} During those days, Tharmuth, the daughter of Pharaoh, came to bathe in the river. She heard you crying and instructed her maidens to bring you to her. {47:7} When they brought you to her, she took you out of the ark and felt compassion for you. {47:8} Your sister asked her, "Shall I go find a Hebrew woman to nurse this baby for you?" {47:9} Pharaoh's daughter said, "Yes, go." So she went and called your mother Jochebed, who was paid to nurse you. {47:10} After you grew up, you were brought to Pharaoh's daughter, and you became her son. Your father Amram taught you to write, and after you completed three weeks of learning, you were taken into the royal court. {47:11} You spent three weeks of years at court until the time came when you went out from the royal court and saw an Egyptian beating your friend, who was one of the children of Israel. {47:12} You killed the Egyptian and hid him in the sand. {47:13} The next day, you saw two Israelites fighting, and you asked the one who was in the wrong, "Why are you hitting your brother?" {47:14} He became angry and replied, "Who made you a prince and a judge over us? Are you planning to kill me like you killed the Egyptian yesterday?" You were afraid and fled because of what he said.

{48:1} In the sixth year of the third week of the forty-ninth jubilee, you departed and lived in the land of Midian for five weeks and one year. You returned to Egypt in the second week of the second year of the fiftieth jubilee. {48:2} You know what He said to you on Mount Sinai and what the prince Mastêmâ (an evil spirit) intended to do to you when you were returning to Egypt and met him at the lodging-place. {48:3} Did he not try with all his power to kill you and deliver the Egyptians from your hands when he saw you were sent to bring judgment and vengeance upon them? {48:4} I delivered you from his grasp, and you performed the signs and wonders you were sent to execute in Egypt against Pharaoh, his household, his servants, and his people. {48:5} The Lord brought great vengeance upon them for Israel's sake, striking them with the plagues of blood, frogs, lice, dog-flies, and malignant boils that caused sores; their livestock died; hailstones destroyed everything that grew; locusts devoured what remained after the hail; darkness fell over the land; and the death of the firstborn, both of men and animals, occurred. The Lord also took vengeance on all their idols, burning them with fire. {48:6} Everything happened through your hand so that you could proclaim these events before they occurred, and you spoke to the king of Egypt in front of all his servants and people. {48:7} Everything unfolded according to your words; ten great and terrible judgments came upon the land of Egypt to execute vengeance on it for Israel. {48:8} The Lord did everything for Israel's sake, in accordance with His covenant with Abraham that He would avenge them as they had forced Israel into bondage. {48:9} The prince Mastêmâ stood against you, trying to hand you over to Pharaoh. He assisted the Egyptian sorcerers, who indeed performed certain evils that we allowed them to execute, but we did not permit them to provide any remedies. {48:10} The Lord struck them with malignant ulcers, rendering them unable to stand, for we destroyed them so they could not perform a single miracle. {48:11} Despite all these signs and wonders, the prince Mastêmâ was not shamed; he boldly urged the Egyptians to pursue you with all their might, including their chariots, horses, and all the forces of Egypt. {48:12} I stood between the Egyptians and Israel, delivering Israel from his power and from his people. The Lord brought them through the midst of the sea as if it were dry land. {48:13} The Lord our God cast all the nations pursuing Israel into the depths of the sea, beneath the Israelites, just as the Egyptians had thrown their own children into the river. He took vengeance on a million of them, and one thousand strong men were destroyed for every infant from your people that they had cast into the river. {48:14} On the fourteenth, fifteenth, sixteenth, seventeenth, and eighteenth days, the prince Mastêmâ was bound and imprisoned behind the children of Israel so he could not accuse them. {48:15} On the nineteenth day, we released him so he could assist the Egyptians in pursuing the Israelites. {48:16} He hardened their hearts and made them stubborn, and the Lord devised a plan to smite the Egyptians and cast them into the sea. {48:17} On the fourteenth day, we bound him again so he could not accuse the children of Israel on the day they asked the Egyptians for vessels and garments, silver and gold vessels, and bronze vessels, to despoil the Egyptians in return for bondage they forced upon them. {48:18} We did not let the children of Israel leave Egypt empty-handed.

{49:1} Remember the commandment that the Lord gave you regarding the Passover, that you should celebrate it at its proper time on the fourteenth day of the first month. You should kill the lamb before evening and eat it at night on the evening of the fifteenth, starting from the setting of the sun. {49:2} For on this night—the beginning of the festival and the start of the joy—you were eating the Passover in Egypt when all the powers of Mastêmâ were unleashed to kill all the firstborn in the land of Egypt, from Pharaoh's firstborn to the firstborn of the captive maidservant grinding at the mill, and even to the cattle. {49:3} This is the sign that the Lord gave them: in every house where they saw the blood of a lamb of the first year on the doorposts, they should not enter to slay anyone but should pass over it, ensuring that everyone in that house would be saved because of the blood on the door. {49:4} The powers of the Lord did everything according to His commands, and they passed over all the children of Israel, and the plague did not touch them, destroying neither cattle nor humans nor dogs. {49:5} The plague was very severe in Egypt, and there was no house without at least one dead person, filled with weeping and lamentation. {49:6} While all Israel was eating the flesh of the Passover lamb and drinking wine, they praised, blessed, and thanked the Lord God of their ancestors, ready to escape from the yoke of Egypt and from the terrible bondage. {49:7} Remember this day for all the days of your life and observe it year after year, once each year on its day, according to all its laws. Do not postpone it from day to day or from month to month. {49:8} It is an everlasting ordinance, inscribed on the heavenly tablets, that all the children of Israel should observe it every year on its day, once a year, throughout all their generations; there is no limit on the number of days, as this is ordained forever. {49:9} Anyone who is free from uncleanness and does not come to observe it on its day to bring an acceptable offering before the Lord, and to eat and drink before the Lord on the day of the festival, that person shall be cut off for not offering the oblation of the Lord in its appointed season; he will bear the guilt for this. {49:10} Let the children of Israel come and observe the Passover at its appointed time, on the fourteenth day of the first month, between the evenings, from the third part of the day to the third part of the night. Two portions of the day are given to the light, and a third part is given to the evening. {49:11} This is what the Lord commanded you: observe it between the evenings. It is not permissible to slay it during any part of the day, but only during the time just before evening, and let them eat it at evening until the third part of the night. Any leftovers from the third part of the night onwards must be burned with fire. {49:12} They must not cook it in water or eat it raw, but must roast it on the fire: they shall eat it with diligence, including its head, the internal organs, and its feet, all roasted with fire, and they must not break any of its bones; for no bone of the children of Israel shall be crushed. {49:13} The Lord commanded the children of Israel to observe the Passover at its appointed time, and they shall not break any bones; it is a festival day, a day that is commanded, and there should be no skipping from day to day or month to month, but it should be observed on its festival day. {49:14} You must command the children of Israel to observe the Passover throughout their days, every year once on its appointed day, and it will serve as a well-pleasing memorial before the Lord, and no plague will come upon them to slay or strike during the year they celebrate the Passover at the right time, according to all His commands. {49:15} They must not eat it outside the sanctuary of the Lord but before the sanctuary of the Lord, and all the congregation of Israel must celebrate it at its appointed time. {49:16} Every man who comes to observe it must eat it in the sanctuary of your God before the Lord from the age of twenty and upward; for thus it is written and ordained that they should eat it in the Lord's sanctuary. {49:17} When the children of Israel enter the land they are to possess, the land of Canaan, and set up the tabernacle of the Lord in the midst of their territory in one of their tribes until the sanctuary of the Lord is built in the land, they shall come and celebrate the Passover in the midst of the Lord's tabernacle, and they shall slay it before the Lord from year to year. {49:18} In the days when the house has been built in the name of the Lord in the land of their inheritance, they shall go there and sacrifice the Passover in the evening at sunset, at the third part of the day. {49:19} They shall offer its blood at the altar threshold and place its fat on the fire upon the altar, and they shall eat its flesh roasted with fire in the courtyard of the house that has been sanctified in the name of the Lord. {49:20} They may not celebrate the Passover in their cities or anywhere except before the tabernacle of the Lord or before His house where His name dwells; they must not stray from the Lord. {49:21} And you, Moses, command the children of Israel to observe the ordinances of the Passover as you were commanded; declare to them every year the day of its observance, and the festival of unleavened bread, that they should eat unleavened bread for seven days, and that they should observe its festival by bringing an offering every day during those seven days of joy before the Lord on the altar of your God. {49:22} You celebrated this festival in haste when you left Egypt until you reached the wilderness of Shur; for you completed it on the shore of the sea.

{50:1} After this law, I made known to you the days of the Sabbaths in the desert of Sinai, which is located between Elim and Sinai. {50:2} I also informed you about the Sabbaths of the land on Mount Sinai and discussed the jubilee years during the sabbaths of years, but I did not tell you the specifics of the jubilee year until you enter the land that you are to possess. {50:3} The land shall also observe its Sabbaths while you dwell on it, and you will understand the jubilee year. {50:4} Therefore, I have ordained for you the year-weeks, the years, and the jubilees: there are forty-nine jubilees from the days of Adam until today, specifically in the year two thousand four hundred and ten Anno Mundi (A.M.), plus one week and two years; and there are still forty years to come for learning the commandments of the Lord until you cross over into the land of Canaan, crossing the Jordan River to the west. {50:5} The jubilees will continue until Israel is cleansed from all guilt of fornication, uncleanness, pollution, sin, and error, and dwells confidently in all the land. There will be no more Satan or any evil ones, and the land will be clean from that time forward forever. {50:6} Behold, the commandment regarding the Sabbaths—I have written them down for you—and all the judgments of its laws. {50:7} You shall labor for six days, but the seventh day is the Sabbath of the Lord your God. On it, you shall do no work, neither you, nor your sons, nor your male servants, nor your female servants, nor your cattle, nor the sojourner who is with you. {50:8} Any person who works on that day shall die. Whoever desecrates that day, lies with their wife, or claims they will do something on that day, such as set out on a journey for buying or selling, or draws water that they did not prepare for themselves on the sixth day, or carries a burden out of their tent or house shall die. {50:9} You shall do no work on the Sabbath except for what you have prepared for yourselves on the sixth day so that you can eat, drink, rest, and keep the Sabbath from all work on that day. You must bless the Lord your God, who has given you this day of festival and holiness: it is a day of the holy kingdom for all Israel, among their days forever. {50:10} For great is the honor that the Lord has bestowed upon Israel, allowing them to eat, drink, and be satisfied on this festival day and to rest from all labor that belongs to mankind, except for burning frankincense and bringing offerings and sacrifices before the Lord for days and Sabbaths. {50:11} This work alone should be done on the Sabbath in the sanctuary of the Lord your God, so that they may atone for Israel with sacrifices continually, day by day, for a memorial well-pleasing to the Lord, and that He may receive them always according to your commands. {50:12} Every person who works on the Sabbath, travels, farms, whether at home or elsewhere, lights a fire, rides an animal, travels by ship on the sea, kills any living creature, slaughters a beast or a bird, catches an animal, bird, or fish, or even fasts or makes war on the Sabbaths: {50:13} anyone who does any of these things on the Sabbath shall die, so that the children of Israel shall observe the Sabbaths according to the commandments regarding the Sabbaths of the land, as it is written on the tablets, which He gave into my hands so that I could write for you the laws of the seasons and the division of their days.

The Book of Jasher

{1:1} God said, "Let us make mankind in our image, in our likeness." So God created mankind in His own image. {1:2} He formed man from the dust of the ground and breathed into his nostrils the breath of life, and man became a living being with the ability to speak. {1:3} The Lord said, "It is not good for man to be alone; I will make a helper suitable for him." {1:4} The Lord caused Adam to fall into a deep sleep, and while he slept, He took one of Adam's ribs and made a woman from it. He brought her to Adam, and when Adam awoke, he saw the woman standing before him. {1:5} Adam said, "This is now bone of my bones and flesh of my flesh; she shall be called 'woman,' for she was taken out of man." He named her Eve because she would be the mother of all living things. {1:6} God blessed them and called them Adam and Eve on the day He created them, and He told them, "Be fruitful, multiply, and fill the earth." {1:7} The Lord God placed Adam and his wife in the Garden of Eden to work it and take care of it. He commanded them, saying, "You can eat from any tree in the garden, but you must not eat from the tree of the knowledge of good and evil, for when you eat from it, you will certainly die." {1:8} After God blessed and commanded them, He departed, and Adam and Eve lived in the garden according to His command. {1:9} The serpent, which God had created along with them, came to tempt them into disobeying God's command. {1:10} The serpent deceived the woman into eating from the tree of knowledge, and she listened to him. She took from the tree and ate, then gave some to her husband, and he ate too. {1:11} Adam and Eve disobeyed God's command, and He was aware of it. His anger burned against them, and He cursed them. {1:12} The Lord drove them out of the Garden of Eden to work the ground from which they had been taken. They settled to the east of the garden, and Adam knew his wife Eve, and she bore him two sons and three daughters. {1:13} She named the firstborn Cain, saying, "I have received a man from the Lord," and the second son was named Abel, for she said, "We came into the world in vanity, and we will leave it in vanity." {1:14} The boys grew up, and their father gave them land; Cain became a farmer, while Abel took care of sheep. {1:15} After some years, they each brought offerings to the Lord. Cain offered fruits from the ground, while Abel brought the best of his flock, and the Lord accepted Abel's offering and sent down fire from heaven to consume it. {1:16} However, He did not regard Cain's offering because

Cain had offered inferior fruits, which made Cain very angry and jealous of his brother Abel. {1:17} Later, Cain and Abel went into the field to work. While they were there, Cain was plowing his land, and Abel was tending to his sheep. When Abel's flock grazed on Cain's plowed field, Cain became very upset. {1:18} Cain confronted Abel in anger, saying, "What do you have to do with me that you bring your flock to feed in my land?" {1:19} Abel replied, "What do you have against me that you eat the meat of my flock and wear their wool?" {1:20} "Now, take off the wool of my sheep that you have taken for yourself, and compensate me for the meat and milk you have consumed. If you do this, I will leave your land as you suggested." {1:21} Cain replied, "If I kill you today, who will hold me accountable for your blood?" {1:22} Abel responded, "God, who created us on this earth, will seek justice for my blood. If you kill me, He will require your blood for mine, for the Lord is the judge and will repay each person according to their actions." {1:23} "If you kill me here, remember that God knows your secret thoughts and will judge you for the evil you plan against me today." {1:24} When Cain heard Abel's words, his anger against Abel intensified because Abel spoke the truth. {1:25} In a fit of rage, Cain took the iron part of his plowing tool and suddenly struck his brother, killing him and spilling Abel's blood on the ground. {1:26} Afterward, Cain felt remorse for killing his brother and grieved deeply, weeping for him. {1:27} He dug a hole in the field to bury his brother's body, covering it with dirt. {1:28} The Lord knew what Cain had done and appeared to him, asking, "Where is your brother Abel?" {1:29} Cain lied, saying, "I don't know; am I my brother's keeper?" {1:30} The Lord replied, "What have you done? The voice of your brother's blood cries out to me from the ground where you killed him." {1:31} "You have killed your brother and lied to me, thinking I wouldn't see your actions. {1:32} You did this for nothing because he spoke the truth, so now you are cursed from the ground, which opened its mouth to receive your brother's blood from your hand." {1:33} "When you work the ground, it will no longer yield its strength to you. Instead, it will produce thorns and thistles, and you will be a wanderer on the earth for the rest of your days." {1:34} At that time, Cain left the Lord's presence and wandered to the east of Eden with all his family. {1:35} Cain knew his wife during that time, and she bore him a son named Enoch, saying, "At that time, the Lord began to give me rest and peace on earth." {1:36} Then Cain started to build a city, naming it Enoch after his son. In those days, the Lord granted him rest on the earth, and he no longer wandered as he had before. {1:37} Enoch became the father of Irad, and Irad had a son named Mechuyael, who in turn had a son named Methusael.

{2:1} At the age of one hundred thirty, Adam knew his wife Eve again, and she conceived and gave birth to a son who resembled him. She named him Seth, saying, "God has given me another child in place of Abel, whom Cain killed." {2:2} Seth lived one hundred five years and had a son, whom he named Enosh, saying, "At that time, humanity began to multiply and hurt their souls and hearts by rebelling against God." {2:3} During Enosh's days, people continued to rebel against God, provoking His anger against them. {2:4} The people served other gods, forgetting the Lord who created them. They made images of brass, iron, wood, and stone, and bowed down to them. {2:5} Everyone created their own gods and worshiped them, abandoning the Lord throughout Enosh's time and that of his children, which kindled God's anger due to their wicked actions. {2:6} The Lord allowed the waters of the Gihon River to overwhelm them, destroying a third of the earth, yet the people did not turn from their evil ways, still extending their hands to do wrong in the sight of the Lord. {2:7} During those days, there was neither sowing nor harvesting, and famine was severe among the people. {2:8} The seeds they planted only produced thorns, thistles, and brambles because of the curse God placed on the earth due to Adam's sin. {2:9} As men continued to rebel against God and corrupt their ways, the earth also became corrupt. {2:10} Enosh lived for ninety years and fathered Cainan. {2:11} Cainan grew up and at forty years old became wise, skilled in all wisdom, and ruled over the sons of men, leading them toward wisdom and knowledge. Cainan was a very wise man with understanding, ruling over spirits and demons. {2:12} He recognized through his wisdom that God would destroy humanity for their sins and that the Lord would eventually bring a flood upon them. {2:13} During this time, Cainan wrote on stone tablets about future events, storing them as treasures. {2:14} Cainan ruled over the entire earth, turning some of the people back to serving God. {2:15} When Cainan was seventy, he had three sons and two daughters. {2:16} The names of Cainan's children were Mahlallel, the firstborn; Enan, the second; and Mered, the third. His daughters were named Adah and Zillah, making five children in total. {2:17} Lamech, the son of Methusael, became connected to Cainan by marriage and took his two daughters as wives. Adah bore a son named Jabal. {2:18} She bore another son and named him Jubal, while her sister Zillah remained barren and had no children. {2:19} In those days, the people began to sin against God and disobey the commandments given to Adam to be fruitful and multiply. {2:20} Some men forced their wives to drink a potion that would make them unable to have children, hoping to preserve their beauty. {2:21} Zillah drank with them. {2:22} The women who were able to have children appeared repulsive to their husbands, who preferred the barren women as their companions. {2:23} In her old age, the Lord opened Zillah's womb, and she bore a son named Tubal Cain, saying, "I have received him from Almighty God after I thought I was too old." {2:24} She had another daughter, naming her Naamah, saying, "After I thought I was too old, I have found pleasure and joy." {2:25} Lamech was old and his sight had faded, so Tubal Cain led him. One day, while they were in the field, Cain, Adam's son, approached them. Lamech, being very old and nearly blind, could hardly see, while Tubal Cain was still young. {2:26} Tubal Cain told his father to draw his bow, and with an arrow, he shot at Cain, who appeared to them as an animal in the distance. {2:27} The arrows struck Cain even though he was far away, and he fell to the ground and died. {2:28} The Lord repaid Cain for the wickedness he had done to his brother Abel, according to what He had said. {2:29} After Cain died, Lamech and Tubal Cain went to see the creature they had killed and discovered it was their grandfather, Cain, lying dead on the ground. {2:30} Lamech was deeply troubled by what he had done, and in his distress, he accidentally struck his son, causing his death. {2:31} When Lamech's wives heard what he had done, they sought to kill him. {2:32} From that day on, Lamech's wives hated him for killing Cain and Tubal Cain. They separated from him and refused to listen to him. {2:33} Lamech approached his wives, urging them to listen to him. {2:34} He said to Adah and Zillah, "Hear my voice, wives of Lamech. Pay attention to my words, for you think that I killed a man for wounding me and a child for hitting me, even though they did no violence. But know that I am old and gray-headed, and my eyesight is poor due to my age. I did this unknowingly." {2:35} Lamech's wives listened to him and returned to him, following the advice of their father Adam. However, they did not have any more children, knowing that God's anger was rising against humanity for their evil deeds and that He would destroy them with a flood. {2:36} Mahlallel, the son of Cainan, lived sixty-five years and fathered Jared, and Jared lived sixty-two years and became the father of Enoch.

{3:1} Enoch lived for sixty-five years and became the father of Methuselah; after Methuselah was born, Enoch walked closely with God, serving the Lord and turning away from the wicked ways of people. {3:2} Enoch's soul was deeply engaged in the teachings of the Lord, filled with knowledge and understanding; he wisely distanced himself from others and spent many days in solitude. {3:3} After many years of serving the Lord and praying in his house, an angel from Heaven called out to Enoch, and he responded, "Here I am." {3:4} The angel said, "Get up, leave your house and the place where you are hiding, and go to the people so you can teach them the path they should take and the work they must do to follow God's ways." {3:5} Enoch obeyed the Lord's command, left his house, and went to the people, teaching them God's ways, gathering them together to share the Lord's teachings. {3:6} He proclaimed in all the places where people lived, asking, "Who among you wants to learn the ways of the Lord and do good works? Come to Enoch!" {3:7} All the people gathered around him; anyone who sought this knowledge approached Enoch, who ruled over them as the Lord had instructed, and they bowed before him, listening to his words. {3:8} The Spirit of God was upon Enoch, and he taught everyone the wisdom of God and his ways, leading the people to serve the Lord throughout his life, and they eagerly came to hear his wisdom. {3:9} All the kings and leaders, both from the beginning and the end of the line, along with their princes and judges, sought out Enoch for his wisdom, bowed down to him, and asked him to rule over them, to which he agreed. {3:10} A total of one hundred and thirty kings and princes gathered, making Enoch their king, and they all came under his authority. {3:11} Enoch taught them wisdom, knowledge, and God's ways, fostering peace among them, and there was peace across the earth during Enoch's lifetime. {3:12} Enoch reigned over humanity for two hundred and forty-three years, administering justice and righteousness, guiding his people in the ways of the Lord. {3:13} These are Enoch's descendants: Methuselah, Elisha, and Elimelech, three sons; their sisters were Melca and Nahmah. Methuselah lived for eighty-seven years and became the father of Lamech. {3:14} In the fifty-sixth year of Lamech's life, Adam died at the age of nine hundred and thirty; his two sons, along with Enoch and Methuselah, buried him with great honor, much like kings, in the cave God had indicated. {3:15} At that location, all the people mourned deeply for Adam, establishing a custom of mourning among humans that persists to this day. {3:16} Adam died because he ate from the tree of knowledge, and he passed this consequence onto his descendants, just as the Lord God had warned. {3:17} In the year of Adam's death, which was the two hundred and forty-third year of Enoch's reign, Enoch decided to separate himself from the people to serve the Lord in solitude, just as he had done initially. {3:18} Enoch followed through but didn't completely withdraw; he stayed away from people for three days and then would visit them for one day. {3:19} During the three days in his chamber, he prayed and praised the Lord his God; when he returned to his people, he taught them the ways of the Lord and answered all their questions about Him. {3:20} He continued this pattern for many years, later isolating himself for six days and appearing before his people once every seven days, then once a month, and eventually once a year. Eventually, all the kings, princes, and people sought him out, wanting to see Enoch and hear his words again; however, they could not approach him because they were deeply afraid of him due to the divine awe that radiated from his presence, making them fearful of punishment and death. {3:21} All the kings and princes decided to gather the people and come to Enoch, hoping to speak with him when he emerged. {3:22} When the day came for Enoch to appear, they all assembled, and he spoke to them the words of the Lord, teaching them wisdom and knowledge. They bowed before him and proclaimed, "Long live the king! Long live the king!" {3:23} After some time, while the kings and princes were engaging with Enoch and he was teaching them God's ways, an angel of the Lord called to Enoch from heaven, wishing to bring him up to heaven to reign over the sons of God as he had over the sons of men on earth. {3:24} Upon hearing this, Enoch gathered all the inhabitants of the earth and taught them wisdom and knowledge, giving them divine instructions. He said, "I have been called to ascend into heaven; I do not know when this will happen." {3:25} "So, I will teach you wisdom and knowledge and give you guidance before I leave, so you know how to live on earth." {3:26} He taught them wisdom and knowledge, giving them instructions, correcting them, and laying down laws and judgments to follow on earth, establishing peace among them, teaching them about eternal life, and dwelling among them for a while to impart these teachings. {3:27} During this time, the people were with Enoch, who was speaking to them when they noticed a great horse descending from heaven, moving through the air. {3:28} They informed Enoch of what they had seen, and he explained, "This horse is descending for my sake; the time has come for me to leave you, and I will not be seen again." {3:29} The horse descended and stood before Enoch, and all the people with him witnessed it. {3:30} Enoch then called out, "Is there anyone who desires to learn the ways of the Lord his God? Come to me today before I am taken away." {3:31} All the people gathered and came to Enoch that day; the kings of the earth and their princes and advisors stayed with him, and Enoch taught them wisdom and knowledge, giving them divine instruction. He urged them to serve the Lord and walk in His ways throughout their lives, continuing to foster peace among them. {3:32} After this, Enoch mounted the horse and rode away, with all the people following him—about eight hundred thousand men—and they traveled with him for one day. {3:33} On the second day, he told them, "Return to your tents; why do you persist in following me? You might die." Some of them heeded his words and returned home, while others continued with him for six days. Each day, Enoch warned them to return to their tents to avoid death, but they refused to turn back. {3:34} On the sixth day, some men stayed behind and clung to him, saying, "We will go wherever you go; as the Lord lives, only death will separate us." {3:35} They insisted on following him, and he stopped urging them to turn back; they continued to pursue him, refusing to return. {3:36} When the kings returned, they ordered a count to find out how many men remained with Enoch. It was on the seventh day that Enoch was taken up to heaven in a whirlwind, accompanied by horses and chariots of fire. {3:37} On the eighth day, all the kings who had been with Enoch sent people to find out how many men had been with him when he ascended. {3:38} All the kings went to the place and discovered the ground covered with snow, and there were large stones of snow. One said to another, "Let's break through the snow to see if the men who stayed with Enoch are dead beneath the snow." They searched but could not find him, for he had ascended into heaven.

{4:1} Enoch lived a total of three hundred sixty-five years on earth. {4:2} When Enoch ascended into heaven, all the kings of the earth rose up, took Methuselah, his son, anointed him, and made him king in place of his father. {4:3} Methuselah lived righteously in the eyes of God, just as his father Enoch had taught him, and throughout his life, he taught the sons of men wisdom, knowledge, and the fear of God, never straying from the right path. {4:4} However, in Methuselah's later days, the sons of men turned away from the Lord, corrupted the earth, stole from and plundered one another, rebelled against God, and refused to listen to Methuselah's voice, choosing instead to defy him. {4:5} The Lord was extremely angry with them and continued to destroy the seeds during those days, resulting in no sowing or reaping on the earth. {4:6} Whenever they planted crops to obtain food, thorns and thistles grew instead of what they had sown. {4:7} Yet, the sons of men did not turn from their evil ways; their hands were still outstretched to commit evil in the sight of God, provoking the Lord with their actions. The Lord was very angry and regretted making mankind. {4:8} He planned to destroy and wipe them out, and He did so. {4:9} During the time when Lamech, Methuselah's son, was one hundred sixty years old, Seth, the son of Adam, died. {4:10} Seth lived for nine hundred twelve years, and then he died. {4:11} Lamech was one hundred eighty years old when he married Ashmua, the daughter of Elishaa, the son of Enoch, who was his uncle, and she became pregnant. {4:12} At that time, the sons of men sowed the land, producing a little food, but they did not turn away from their evil ways and continued to rebel against God. {4:13} Lamech's wife gave birth to a son at that time, around the turn of the year. {4:14} Methuselah named him Noah, saying, "The earth was at rest and free from corruption in his days," while Lamech called him Menachem, saying, "This one will comfort us in our labor and miserable toil on the cursed earth." {4:15} The child grew up and was weaned, following in the footsteps of his father Methuselah, being perfect and upright with God. {4:16} During this time, all the sons of men turned away from the ways of the Lord as they multiplied on earth, teaching each other their wicked practices and continued to sin against the Lord. {4:17} Each person created their own god and robbed and plundered their neighbors and relatives, corrupting the earth, which became filled with violence. {4:18} Their judges and rulers forcibly took the wives of the daughters of men from their husbands, and in those days, the sons of men took the cattle of the earth, the beasts of the field, and the birds of the air, mixing different species to provoke the Lord. God saw that the earth was corrupt because all flesh had corrupted its ways; all men and all animals were included. {4:19} The Lord said, "I will wipe out man whom I created from the face of the earth, from man to the birds of the air, along with the cattle and beasts of the field, for I regret having made them." {4:20} All men who walked in the ways of the Lord died in those days before the Lord brought the evil upon man that He had declared. This was from the Lord so that they would not witness the evil intended for the sons of men. {4:21} Noah found favor in the eyes of the Lord, and Lord chose him & his children to raise up a seed upon the face of the whole earth.

{5:1} In the eighty-fourth year of Noah's life, Enoch, the son of Seth, died at nine hundred five years old. {5:2} In the one hundred seventy-ninth year of Noah's life, Cainan, the son of Enosh, died, having lived for nine hundred ten years. {5:3} In the two hundred thirty-fourth year of Noah's life, Mahlallel, the son of Cainan, died at eight hundred ninety-five years old. {5:4} Jared, the son of Mahlallel, died in the three hundred thirty-sixth year of Noah's life, having lived for nine hundred sixty-two years. {5:5} All who followed the Lord died in those days before they saw the evil that God had declared to be brought upon the earth. {5:6} After many years, in the four hundred eightieth year of Noah's life, when all those who followed the Lord had passed away, and only Methuselah remained, God spoke to Noah and Methuselah, saying, {5:7} "Proclaim to the sons of men, saying, 'Thus says the Lord: return from your evil ways and forsake your actions, and the Lord will change His mind about the evil He declared against you, so it will not happen.'" {5:8} The Lord said, "I give you a period of one hundred twenty years; if you turn to me and forsake your evil ways, I will also turn away from the evil I spoke about, and it will not occur," says the Lord. {5:9} Noah and Methuselah continually spoke the Lord's words to the sons of men daily. {5:10} However, the sons of men refused to listen and were stiff-necked. {5:11} The Lord granted them one hundred twenty years, saying, "If they will return, then God will change His mind about the evil and not destroy the earth." {5:12} Noah, the son of Lamech, refrained from taking a wife during this time to have children, saying, "Surely now God will destroy the earth, so why should I have children?" {5:13} Noah was a just man, perfect in his generation, and the Lord chose him to raise a seed from his lineage on the earth. {5:14} The Lord said to Noah, "Take a wife and have children, for I see you as righteous in this generation." {5:15} "You will raise a seed with your children in the midst of the earth." So Noah went and took a wife, choosing Naamah, the daughter of Enoch, who was five hundred eighty years old. {5:16} Noah was four hundred ninety-eight years old when he married Naamah. {5:17} Naamah became pregnant and gave birth to a son, whom Noah named Japheth, saying, "God has enlarged my territory." She became pregnant again and gave birth to another son, whom Noah named Shem, saying, "God has made me a remnant to raise seed in the earth." {5:18} Noah was five hundred two years old when Naamah gave birth to Shem, and the boys grew up, following the ways of the Lord, as taught by Methuselah and their father Noah. {5:19} Lamech, Noah's father, died during this time, although he did not wholeheartedly follow the ways of his father, dying in the one hundred ninety-fifth year of Noah's life. {5:20} The total days of Lamech were seven hundred seventy years, and then he died. {5:21} All the sons of men who knew the Lord died that year before the Lord brought evil upon them; the Lord willed their deaths so they would not witness the evil He planned to bring upon their brothers and relatives, as He had declared. {5:22} At that time, the Lord said to Noah and Methuselah, "Stand and proclaim to the sons of men all the words I spoke to you, perhaps they will turn from their evil ways, and then I will change my mind about the evil and not bring it." {5:23} Noah and Methuselah stood and declared all that God had said concerning them to the sons of men. {5:24} But the sons of men would not listen and would not incline their ears to their declarations. {5:25} After this, the Lord said to Noah, "The end of all flesh has come before me because of their evil deeds, and behold, I will destroy the earth." {5:26} "You are to take gopher wood and go to a specific place to build a large ark and place it there." {5:27} "Here is how you should make it: three hundred cubits long, fifty cubits wide, and thirty cubits high." {5:28} "You will make a door on the side and finish it one cubit above, covering it inside and out with pitch (a waterproof material)." {5:29} "Behold, I will bring a flood upon the earth to destroy all flesh; everything on earth will perish." {5:30} "You and your household are to gather two of every living thing, male and female, and bring them to the ark to preserve them upon the earth." {5:31} "Gather all the food that animals eat so there will be food for you and them." {5:32} "You will choose three maidens for your sons from the daughters of men to be their wives." {5:33} Noah got to work making the ark where God had commanded him, and he followed God's instructions. {5:34} In his five hundred ninety-fifth year, Noah began constructing the ark, which he completed in five years, just as the Lord commanded. {5:35} Noah took three daughters of Eliakim, the son of Methuselah, for his sons' wives, as the Lord commanded. {5:36} It was at that time Methuselah, the son of Enoch, died at the age of nine hundred sixty years.

{6:1} After the death of Methuselah, the Lord spoke to Noah, saying, "Take your family and go into the ark; I will gather all the animals of the earth for you, including the beasts of the field and the birds of the air, and they will come and surround the ark. {6:2} You shall sit at the door of the ark, and all the animals, the beasts, and the birds will gather and present themselves to you. Those that crouch before you, you shall take and give to your sons, who will bring them into the ark, but any that stand before you, you shall leave behind. {6:3} The next day, the Lord fulfilled this command, and animals, beasts, and birds came in great numbers and surrounded the ark. {6:4} Noah sat by the door of the ark and brought in all the creatures that crouched before him, leaving behind all those that stood. {6:5} A lioness came with her two cubs, one male and one female. The cubs attacked the lioness, causing her to flee, and they returned to their places, crouching on the ground before Noah. {6:6} The lioness ran away and took her place among the lions. {6:7} Noah saw this and was greatly astonished. He then took the two cubs and brought them into the ark. {6:8} Noah collected every living creature from the earth, ensuring that none were left behind except those he brought into the ark. {6:9} Two of each came to Noah into the ark, but he took seven pairs of clean animals and clean birds, as God had commanded him. {6:10} All the animals, beasts, and birds remained surrounding the ark, and the rain did not begin until seven days later. {6:11} On that day, the Lord caused the entire earth to tremble, the sun darkened, the foundations of the world shook violently, lightning flashed, and thunder roared. All the springs of the deep were opened up, in a display of power that had never been seen before by the people, and God did this to instill fear in the hearts of men so that they would cease their wickedness. {6:12} Yet, the people continued in their evil ways, provoking the Lord's anger even more and failing to pay attention to these signs. {6:13} After seven days, in Noah's six hundredth year, the floodwaters came upon the earth. {6:14} All the springs of the deep were broken up, and the windows of heaven were opened, and it rained on the earth for forty days and forty nights. {6:15} Noah, his family, and all the living creatures with him entered the ark because of the floodwaters, and the Lord closed the door behind them. {6:16} All the people remaining on earth grew weary from their wickedness due to the rain, which continued to pour down violently, while the animals and beasts remained surrounding the ark. {6:17} The remaining men and women, about seven hundred thousand of them, gathered together and approached Noah at the ark. {6:18} They called out to Noah, saying, "Open the ark for us so we can escape and not perish!" {6:19} Noah answered them loudly from the ark, "Haven't you all rebelled against the Lord and claimed He doesn't exist? That's why the Lord has brought this disaster upon you—to destroy and remove you from the face of the earth. {6:20} Isn't this what I warned you about one hundred and twenty years ago? Yet you refused to listen to the voice of the Lord, and now you seek to live?" {6:21} They replied, "We are ready to return to the Lord; just let us in so we can live and not die!" {6:22} Noah responded, "Now that you see the trouble you're in, you wish to return to the Lord. Why didn't you come back during the one hundred and twenty years the Lord granted you? {6:23} But now, in your time of distress, the Lord will not listen to you, nor will He grant your requests today." {6:24} The people then tried to break into the ark to escape the rain, but the Lord sent all the animals surrounding the ark to stop them. The animals drove them away, and each man fled back to his own place. {6:25} Meanwhile, the rain continued to pour down for forty days and forty nights, flooding the earth; all flesh that was on the earth or in the waters perished—men, animals, beasts, creeping things, and birds. Only Noah and those with him in the ark survived. {6:26} The waters prevailed and increased upon the earth, lifting the ark high above the ground. {6:27} The ark floated on the surface of the waters, tossed around like food in a pot. {6:28} Fear gripped all the living creatures inside the ark. The lions roared, the oxen lowed, the wolves howled, and every creature inside cried out in its own language. Their voices carried far, and Noah and his sons cried and wept, fearing they had reached the gates of death. {6:29} Noah prayed to the Lord, crying out for help because they had no strength to withstand the disaster surrounding them. "The waves have engulfed us, the raging torrents terrify us, and we face death; answer us, O Lord! Show us your favor, redeem us, and rescue us!" {6:30} The Lord heard Noah's voice and remembered him. {6:31} A wind passed over the earth, the waters calmed, and the ark rested. {6:32} The springs of the deep and the windows of heaven were closed, and the rain from above stopped. {6:33} The waters began to recede, and the ark came to rest on the mountains of Ararat. {6:34} Noah then opened the windows of the ark and again called out to the Lord, saying, "O Lord, Creator of the earth and the heavens and everything in them, release our souls from this confinement, from this prison where You have placed us; I am exhausted from sighing." {6:35} The Lord heard Noah's voice and said to him, "When you have completed a full year, you will be able to leave." {6:36} After a year had passed, the waters dried up from the earth, and Noah removed the covering of the ark. {6:37} On the twenty-seventh day of the second month, the earth was dry, but Noah and his family did not leave the ark until the Lord instructed them. {6:38} When the Lord finally told them to exit, they all stepped out of the ark. {6:39} They returned to their respective ways, and Noah and his family settled in the land that God had designated for them. They served the Lord all their days, and the Lord blessed Noah and his sons as they left the ark. {6:40} He instructed them, "Be fruitful, fill the earth, grow strong, increase abundantly, and multiply in the earth."

{7:1} These are the names of Noah's sons: Japheth, Ham, and Shem. Children were born to them after the flood, for they had taken wives before it began. {7:2} The sons of Japheth were Gomer, Magog, Madai, Javan, Tubal, Meshech, and Tiras, totaling seven sons. {7:3} The sons of Gomer were Askinaz, Rephath, and Tegarmah. {7:4} The sons of Magog were Elichanaf and Lubal. {7:5} The children of Madai were Achon, Zeelo, Chazoni, and Lot. {7:6} The sons of Javan were Elisha, Tarshish, Chittim, and Dudonim. {7:7} The sons of Tubal were Ariphi, Kesed, and Taari. {7:8} The sons of Meshech were Dedon, Zaron, and Shebashni. {7:9} The sons of Tiras were Benib, Gera, Lupirion, and Gilak; these are the sons of Japheth with their families, numbering about four hundred and sixty men at that time. {7:10} Now, these are the sons of Ham: Cush, Mitzraim, Phut, and Canaan, totaling four sons. The sons of Cush were Seba, Havilah, Sabta, Raama, and Satecha; the sons of Raama were Sheba and Dedan. {7:11} The sons of Mitzraim were Lud, Anom, Pathros, Chasloth, and Chaphtor. {7:12} The sons of Phut were Gebul, Hadan, Benah, and Adan. {7:13} The sons of Canaan were Zidon, Heth, Amori, Gergashi, Hivi, Arkee, Seni, Arodi, Zimodi, and Chamothi. {7:14} These are the sons of Ham with their families, numbering about seven hundred and thirty men at that time. {7:15} The sons of Shem were Elam, Ashur, Arpachshad, Lud, and Aram, totaling five sons. The sons of Elam were Shushan, Machul, and Harmon. {7:16} The sons of Ashur were Argush and Modai. The sons of Arpachshad were Shelah and Eber, and the sons of Lud were Huz and Hul. {7:17} The sons of Aram were Uz, Hul, Gether, and Mash. {7:18} These are the sons of Shem with their families, numbering about four hundred men at that time. {7:19} The descendants of Noah were named after their fathers: Japheth, Ham, and Shem, and their families spread throughout the earth. {7:20} Noah lived three hundred and fifty years after the flood and died at the age of nine hundred and fifty years. {7:21} The sons of Noah, Shem, Ham, and Japheth became the fathers of the families of the earth, and from them came all the nations. {7:22} They grew strong and flourished, multiplying across the land, and the earth was filled with their descendants. {7:23} They served the Lord and remembered Him in their hearts, giving thanks for His mercy and grace toward them. {7:24} The Lord looked upon the earth and saw that it was filled with wickedness. {7:25} Yet, He remembered Noah and his family, protecting them from harm. {7:26} Thus, Noah became a strong and righteous man, chosen by the Lord, and the Lord blessed him and his family. {7:27} All the days of Noah were peaceful, and he found favor in the eyes of the Lord. {7:28} This is the account of the generations of Noah and his sons, Japheth, Ham, and Shem. These are the families that sprang forth from them and settled the land. {7:29} In their days, cities and nations began to be established, and their names were remembered in the annals of history. {7:30} The descendants of Noah became numerous, and the earth was filled with people once more, giving glory to the Lord for His creation and His faithfulness throughout generations. {7:31} Noah passed down the stories of the flood and the lessons learned to his children, teaching them the importance of obedience and faithfulness to God. {7:32} As the generations continued, they spread out across the earth, establishing kingdoms and cities, and the nations multiplied, always remembering the covenant of the Lord. {7:33} The children of Noah honored their father, and he lived to see their prosperity and the fulfillment of the promises of God. {7:34} In their hearts, they cherished the teachings of Noah, and the legacy of faith endured among the families of the earth. {7:35} Noah's descendants walked in the ways of the Lord, and their names were written in the book of life, and they remained faithful to the promises given by God.{7:35} At that time, Nimrod went out and gathered all the sons of Cush and their families, totaling about four hundred and sixty men. He also hired around eighty men from some of his friends and acquaintances, paid them, and set out with them for battle. On the way, Nimrod encouraged the hearts of those traveling with him. {7:36} He said to them, "Do not fear or be alarmed, for all our enemies will be handed over to us, and you can do with them as you wish." {7:37} The total number of men who joined him was about five hundred, and they fought against their enemies, defeating and subduing them. Nimrod then appointed standing officers over them in their respective roles. {7:38} He took some of their children as hostages, and they all became servants to Nimrod and his brothers, after which he and all the people with him headed back home. {7:39} When Nimrod joyfully returned from battle, having conquered his enemies, all his brothers, along with those who knew him, gathered to make him king over them, placing a royal crown on his head. {7:40} He appointed princes, judges, and rulers over his subjects and people, as is customary for kings. {7:41} He made Terah, the son of Nahor, the chief of his army, and elevated him above all his princes. {7:42} While he reigned according to his desires, having conquered all his enemies, he consulted with his advisors to build a city for his palace, and they did so. {7:43} They found a large valley to the east and constructed a grand and extensive city, which Nimrod named Shinar, because the Lord had decisively defeated his enemies. {7:44} Nimrod lived in Shinar, reigned securely, fought against his enemies, and subdued them. He prospered in all his battles, making his kingdom very great. {7:45} All nations and languages heard of his fame, and they gathered around him, bowing down and bringing him offerings. He became their lord and king, and they all lived with him in the city of Shinar. Nimrod reigned over all the descendants of Noah, and they were all under his authority and counsel. {7:46} The entire earth spoke one language and was united, but Nimrod did not follow the ways of the Lord. He was more wicked than all the men who lived before him, from the days of the flood until that time. {7:47} He made gods of wood and stone, bowed down to them, rebelled against the Lord, and taught all his subjects and the people of the earth his evil ways. His son Mardon was even more wicked than him. {7:48} Anyone who heard about the actions of Mardon, the son of Nimrod, would say about him, "From the wicked comes wickedness." This became a proverb throughout the earth, stating, "From the wicked comes wickedness," and it remained common in people's speech from that time onward. {7:49} Terah, the son of Nahor, who was a leader in Nimrod's army, was very esteemed in the sight of the king and his subjects. The king and princes loved him and elevated him greatly. {7:50} Terah took a wife named Amthelo, the daughter of Cornebo, and in those days, his wife conceived and bore him a son. {7:51} Terah was seventy years old when his son was born, and he named his son Abram because the king had honored him in those days, elevating him above all his princes.

{8:1} On the night Abram was born, all of Terah's servants, along with the wise men and magicians of Nimrod, gathered to eat and drink in Terah's house, celebrating with him that night. {8:2} After the wise men and magicians left Terah's house, they looked up at the stars in the sky and saw a very large star coming from the east, moving rapidly and swallowing up four stars from each corner of the sky. {8:3} The wise men and magicians were astonished by what they saw, and the sages understood the significance of the event and knew what it meant. {8:4} They said to each other, "This signifies the child who was born to Terah tonight. He will grow up to be fruitful and multiply, possessing the earth along with his descendants. He and his offspring will defeat great kings and inherit their lands." {8:5} The wise men and magicians returned home that night, and the next morning they gathered early in a designated meeting place. {8:6} They spoke to one another, saying, "The sight we witnessed last night has been kept hidden from the king; he has not been informed." {8:7} They worried that if the king learned of this matter later, he would ask them why they concealed it, and they would all face death. Therefore, they decided to inform the king about what they had seen and its interpretation to clear themselves of any blame. {8:8} They approached the king, bowing down to him, and said, "Long live the king!" {8:9} "We heard that a son was born to Terah, the son of Nahor, your commander, and last night we rejoiced with him at his home." {8:10} "When we left Terah's house to return home for the night, we looked up at the sky and saw a great star coming from the east. This star moved swiftly and swallowed four great stars from each corner of the sky." {8:11} "We were astonished by the sight and felt greatly afraid. After interpreting the vision with our wisdom, we concluded that it pertains to the child born to Terah, who will grow up and greatly multiply, become powerful, defeat all the kings of the earth, and inherit their lands along with his descendants forever." {8:12} "Now, my lord and king, we have truthfully informed you of what we have seen regarding this child." {8:13} "If it pleases the king, let us kill the child before he grows up and poses a threat to us and our children." {8:14} The king listened to their words, and they seemed good to him, so he called for Terah to come before him. {8:15} The king said to Terah, "I have heard that a son was born to you last night, and this phenomenon was observed in the heavens at his birth." {8:16} "Now, give me the child so that we can kill him before he can become a threat, and I will compensate you with a house filled with silver and gold." {8:17} Terah replied to the king, "My lord and king, I have heard your words, and your servant will do all that you desire." {8:18} "However, I would like to share what happened to me last night to see what advice the king will give me, and then I will respond to your request." The king said, "Speak." {8:19} Terah said to the king, "Ayon, the son of Mored, came to me last night and said, {8:20} 'Give me the beautiful horse that the king gave you, and I will compensate you with silver, gold, straw, and feed for it.' I told him, 'Wait until I speak to the king regarding your request, and whatever the king says, that is what I will do.'" {8:21} "Now, my lord and king, I have made this known to you, and whatever advice the king gives his servant, I will follow." {8:22} The king heard Terah's words, and his anger flared, viewing him as foolish. {8:23} The king replied to Terah, "Are you so foolish, ignorant, or lacking understanding to trade your beautiful horse for silver and gold or even for straw and feed? {8:24} Are you so lacking in silver and gold that you must resort to this, as if you cannot obtain straw and feed for your horse? What good are silver and gold to you, or straw and feed, that you would give away the fine horse I gave you, of which there is none like it on earth?" {8:25} After the king finished speaking, Terah responded, "Just as the king has spoken to his servant, I ask you, my lord and king, what does it mean when you say, 'Give your son so we can kill him, and I will give you silver and gold for his value?' What will I do with silver and gold after my son's death? Who will inherit me? Surely, upon my death, the silver and gold will return to the king who gave it." {8:27} When the king heard Terah's words and the parable he presented, he was greatly troubled and his anger flared. {8:28} Terah saw that the king was angry and replied, "All that I have is in the king's power. Whatever the king desires to do with his servant, let him do, even my son. He is in the king's power, with no value in exchange, including him and his two older brothers." {8:29} The king said to Terah, "No, I will buy your youngest son for a price." {8:30} Terah answered, "I ask you, my lord and king, to let your servant speak before you and hear his words. {8:31} Let my king grant me three days to consider this matter and consult with my family regarding your words." He pressed the king earnestly to agree. {8:32} The king agreed and granted Terah three days, so Terah left the king's presence and returned home to discuss everything with his family. The people were greatly afraid. {8:33} On the third day, the king sent to Terah, saying, "Send me your son for the price we discussed. If you do not comply, I will kill everyone in your house, leaving you with nothing." {8:34} Terah hurried, understanding the urgency of the king's command, and took a child from one of his servants, born to a maidservant that day, bringing the child to the king to receive compensation. {8:35} The Lord was with Terah in this situation so that Nimrod would not cause Abram's death. The king took the child from Terah and, with all his might, smashed its head against the ground, thinking it was Abram. This event was concealed from him and forgotten, as it was God's will to protect Abram. {8:36} Terah secretly took Abram, along with his mother and nurse, hiding them in a cave and providing them with monthly provisions. {8:37} The Lord was with Abram in the cave, and he grew up there, living in the cave for ten years while the king, his princes, soothsayers, and sages believed that the king had killed Abram.

{9:1} During this time, Haran, Terah's oldest son and Abram's brother, took a wife. {9:2} Haran was thirty-nine years old when he married, and his wife conceived and bore a son named Lot. {9:3} She conceived again and had a daughter named Milca, and later had another daughter named Sarai. {9:4} Haran was forty-two years old when he had Sarai, which was ten years into Abram's life. During this time, Abram, his mother, and his nurse emerged from the cave, as the king and his subjects had forgotten about Abram. {9:5} When Abram came out of the cave, he went to Noah and his son Shem, where he stayed to learn the ways of the Lord, and no one knew where he was. Abram served Noah and Shem for a long time. {9:6} Abram remained in Noah's house for thirty-nine years, knowing the Lord since he was three years old. He followed the ways of the Lord until he died, as taught by Noah and Shem. During this period, the sons of the earth greatly sinned against the Lord, rebelling against him and serving other gods. They forgot the Lord who created them, making gods of wood and stone that could neither speak nor save them, and the people served these gods. {9:7} The king, all his servants, and Terah and his household were among the first to worship these wooden and stone gods. {9:8} Terah had twelve large gods, made of wood and stone, one for each month of the year, and each month he would offer meat and drink to his gods. This was Terah's practice all his days. {9:9} All that generation was wicked in the Lord's sight, creating their own gods while forsaking the Lord who made them. {9:10} There was not a single person in those days who knew the Lord except for Noah and his household, and those under his guidance. {9:11} Abram, the son of Terah, was becoming great in Noah's house, although no one knew it, for the Lord was with him. {9:12} The Lord gave Abram an understanding heart, allowing him to recognize that all the works of the gods made by the hands of men were false and empty, with no value in them. {9:13} One day, Abram went into the house of Terah, and when he saw his father's gods, he asked, "Why do you serve these idols?" {9:14} Terah responded, "These are the gods that made us. They created the heavens and the earth, and we must worship them." {9:15} Abram said, "Do they have eyes? Can they see? Do they have ears? Can they hear? Are they made of wood and stone? They cannot speak; they have no sense. Why do you serve them?" {9:16} Terah was angry with Abram's words, but Abram did not care, proclaiming, "I will serve the Lord, for He is the God of the heavens and the earth." {9:17} Terah grew furious with Abram, saying, "Leave my house!" and Abram left to join Noah and Shem in their house, where he learned the ways of the Lord for several years.

{10:1} As time passed, the nations of the earth were angry with Abram, as he was gaining great fame. The king of the land gathered his princes to discuss how they would deal with him. {10:2} The king said, "If we allow him to continue prospering, he will gain strength over us, and we must find a way to stop him before he becomes too powerful." {10:3} The king commanded that all the idols of Terah be gathered and brought to him. {10:4} When the idols were brought before the king, he said to Terah, "You made these gods, and they cannot save you; I will test their strength. {10:5} If they have power, they will save you from me; if they cannot do anything, then I will destroy them." {10:6} The king commanded his servants to bring great wood and fire, making a great furnace. He ordered the idols to be burned. The idols were consumed, and their ashes scattered across the land. {10:7} When Terah saw this, he was terrified, and his gods could not save him. He understood that they were false. He did not know who to serve, for he felt ashamed of serving the Lord. {10:8} The king summoned Terah to say, "Your gods are useless. We have destroyed them, and now what will you do?" {10:9} Terah responded, "I will serve you and your gods." The king replied, "If you want to serve me, then you must kill your son Abram, for he has turned the hearts of the people from their gods and turned them to serve the Lord." {10:10} Terah was filled with fear for his son. He said, "What shall I do?" {10:11} The king told Terah to bring Abram before him. {10:12} When Terah brought Abram to the king, he placed him before him, saying, "This is my son, and he has turned the hearts of the people to serve the Lord instead of their gods." {10:13} The king was enraged, and he commanded that Abram be thrown into the fire. {10:14} But the Lord intervened and brought Abram out of the fire. {10:15} The king commanded that Abram be cast into the furnace with seven layers of iron, but the Lord saved him again. {10:16} The king saw this and understood that the gods of wood and stone could not save. {10:17} The king realized that the Lord is the true God, and he turned his heart to serve Him. {10:18} The people were astonished at the power of the Lord and turned to serve Him as well. {10:19} The king declared, "Let us worship the Lord, who has power over the heavens and the earth."{10:20} King Nimrod ruled securely, with all the earth under his control, and everyone spoke the same language. {10:21} The princes and important men of Nimrod gathered together—Phut, Mitzraim, Cush, and Canaan along with their families—and they said to one another, "Come, let's build a city with a strong tower that reaches the heavens. We want to make a name for ourselves so that we can dominate the world and prevent our enemies from attacking us. We must ensure that we do not get scattered across the earth because of their wars." {10:22} They all approached the king and presented their idea, and the king agreed with them. {10:23} The assembled families numbered around six hundred thousand men, and they went in search of a large area of land to build the city and the tower. They scoured the entire earth until they found a valley in the east of the land of Shinar, which was about a two-day journey away. They traveled there and settled in that valley. {10:24} They began to make bricks and bake them in fires to construct the city and the tower they envisioned. {10:25} The construction of the tower was a transgression and a sin against the Lord, as they sought to build it while plotting to wage war against Him and ascend into heaven. {10:26} The people divided into three groups: the first group said, "We will ascend into heaven and fight against Him"; the second said, "We will ascend to heaven and place our own gods there to serve them"; and the third group declared, "We will ascend to heaven and strike Him with bows and spears." God was aware of all their actions and wicked thoughts, and He observed the city and the tower they were building. {10:27} As they constructed, they built a vast city and a very tall, strong tower. Due to its height, the mortar and bricks could not reach the builders during their ascent until those who climbed up had finished an entire year. After that, they would send down the mortar and bricks to the builders. This became their daily routine. {10:28} Some ascended while others descended all day long. If a brick fell from their hands and broke, they all mourned over it, but if a man fell and died, none of them paid any attention. {10:29} The Lord knew their thoughts, and it came to pass that when they were building, they shot arrows toward the heavens, and all the arrows fell back to them, stained with blood. When they saw this, they said to each other, "Surely, we have killed all those who are in heaven." {10:30} This was from the Lord, causing them to err and to be destroyed from the face of the earth. {10:31} They built the tower and the city, continuing their efforts daily for many years. {10:32} God then said to the seventy angels who stood nearest to Him, "Come, let us descend and confuse their language so that one man will not understand the language of his neighbor," and they did as instructed. {10:33} From that day on, each person forgot his neighbor's language, unable to speak in one tongue. When a builder took lime or stone from the hands of his neighbor that he did not order, he would throw it away onto his neighbor, causing him to die. {10:34} They continued this for many days, leading to many deaths among them. {10:35} The Lord struck the three groups that had gathered, punishing them according to their actions and plans. Those who said, "We will ascend to heaven and serve our gods," were transformed into apes and elephants. The group that said, "We will strike heaven with arrows," suffered death by one another's hands. The third group, who proclaimed, "We will ascend to heaven and fight against Him," were scattered across the earth. {10:36} Those who remained, upon realizing the evil that was about to befall them, abandoned their building project and also became scattered over the face of the earth. {10:37} They ceased construction of the city and the tower; therefore, the place was called Babel, for there the Lord confused the language of the whole earth; it was located in the east of the land of Shinar. {10:38} Regarding the tower built by the sons of men, the earth opened its mouth and swallowed one-third of it, while fire descended from heaven and burned another third. The remaining third still stands today, and its circumference is a three-day walk. {10:39} Many people perished in that tower, countless in number.

{11:1} Nimrod, the son of Cush, was still in the land of Shinar, where he ruled and settled, building cities in that area. {11:2} He built four cities and named them based on the events that happened during the tower's construction. {11:3} The first he called Babel, saying it was where the Lord confused the language of the whole earth; the second he named Erech because God dispersed the people from there. {11:4} The third was called Eched, noting that a great battle occurred there, and the fourth he named Calnah, where his leaders and mighty men were destroyed as they angered the Lord and rebelled against Him. {11:5} After building these cities in Shinar, Nimrod settled his remaining people, his leaders, and his mighty men in them. {11:6} Nimrod lived in Babel and renewed his reign over his subjects, ruling securely, while his subjects and leaders called him Amraphel, stating that many fell at the tower due to his actions. {11:7} Despite this, Nimrod did not turn back to the Lord; he persisted in his wickedness and taught others to do the same, and his son Mardon was even worse, further adding to his father's abominations. {11:8} Mardon led people to sin, so it's said that wickedness comes from the wicked. {11:9} During this time, there was conflict among the families of Ham as they lived in the cities they built. {11:10} Chedorlaomer, king of Elam, broke away from the families of Ham, fought against them, conquered them, and attacked the five cities of the plain, taking control of them. {11:11} They served him for twelve years and paid him a yearly tribute. {11:12} During this time, Nahor, the son of Serug, died in the forty-ninth year of Abram, the son of Terah. {11:13} In the fiftieth year of Abram's life, he left Noah's house and went to his father's home. {11:14} Abram knew the Lord, followed His ways, and the Lord was with him. {11:15} Terah, his father, was still the captain of Nimrod's army and continued to worship strange gods. {11:16} When Abram returned home, he saw twelve idols standing in his father's temple, and his anger was stirred when he saw these images. {11:17} Abram said, "As the Lord lives, these images will not stay in my father's house; may the Lord who created me do to me if I do not destroy them all in three days." {11:18} With his anger burning within him, Abram left and found his father sitting in the outer courtyard with his servants, and he sat down before him. {11:19} Abram asked his father, "Father, where is the God who created heaven and earth, all humanity, and created you and me?" Terah answered, "The gods who made us are all here in the house." {11:20} Abram replied, "Please show them to me," and Terah brought Abram into the inner chamber, where the room was filled with wooden and stone gods, twelve large images and countless smaller ones. {11:21} Terah said, "These are the gods that created everything you see on earth and created you and me." {11:22} Terah bowed to his gods, then left, and Abram followed him. {11:23} After leaving, Abram went to his mother and said, "Look, my father showed me those who made heaven and earth and all humanity. {11:24} Now hurry and get a young goat from the flock, prepare it as a delicious meal, so I can offer it to my father's gods to gain their favor." {11:25} His mother complied, preparing the meal, which Abram took to his father's gods, approaching them without Terah knowing. {11:26} While sitting with the idols, Abram observed that they had no voice, hearing, or movement, and none could reach out to eat. {11:27} He mocked them, saying, "Surely my meal didn't please them, or perhaps it was too little; I'll prepare better food tomorrow and see the outcome." {11:28} The next day, Abram instructed his mother to prepare three fine kids, making an excellent meal he loved, which she gave to him. {11:29} Abram took the meal to his father's gods again, placing it before them and sitting there all day, wondering if they might eat. {11:30} He watched them, and once again, they had no voice or hearing, nor did any of them stretch out their hands to the food. {11:31} By evening, Abram was filled with the spirit of God. {11:32} He called out, "Woe to my father and this wicked generation, whose hearts are set on vanity, who serve these idols of wood and stone that can neither eat, smell, hear, nor speak; those who make them are just like them." {11:33} When Abram saw all this, he was furious with his father, hurriedly took a hatchet, and went to the idols, breaking all of them. {11:34} After destroying the images, he placed the hatchet in the hand of the largest idol and left. When Terah came home, he heard the noise of the hatchet striking and went inside to see what was happening. {11:35} Terah rushed into the room and found all the idols broken, with the hatchet in the hand of the largest, which remained unbroken, and the meal Abram had prepared was still there. {11:36} Seeing this, Terah became very angry and quickly went to Abram. {11:37} He found Abram sitting in the house and demanded, "What have you done to my gods?" {11:38} Abram replied, "Not so, my lord; I brought food for them, and as I approached with the meal, they reached out their hands to eat before the largest could even move." {11:39} Terah was furious and asked, "What kind of tale is this? You lie to me!" {11:40} He continued, "Are these gods not wood and stone, made by my own hands? Can they really have the power you claim? You placed the hatchet in the hand of the largest and then said it broke them." {11:41} Abram responded, "How can you serve these idols that cannot do anything? Can they hear your prayers or deliver you from enemies? Why trust in wood and stone that cannot speak or hear? {11:42} It's foolish to serve idols and forget the Lord God who made heaven and earth and you. This will bring great evil upon you and your household." {11:43} He reminded Terah that in ancient times, their ancestors sinned by serving idols, and the Lord destroyed the earth with a flood because of it. {11:44} "How can you continue this and serve gods that cannot hear or save you, bringing God's anger upon you?" {11:45} Abram urged his father to stop and not bring evil upon himself and their family. {11:46} With that, Abram quickly left his father, took the hatchet from the largest idol, broke it, and ran away. {11:47} Seeing what Abram had done, Terah hurried to the king and stood before Nimrod, bowing down to him. {11:48} The king asked, "What do you want?" {11:49} Terah replied, "Please hear me, my lord. Fifty years ago, a child was born to me, and he has done this to my gods and spoken against them. Therefore, my lord, send for him so he may be judged according to the law and we may be rid of his evil." {11:50} The king sent three of his servants to bring Abram before him. Nimrod, his princes, and servants were all seated, and Terah was there too. {11:51} The king asked Abram, "What have you done to your father and his gods?" Abram answered in the same way he spoke to his father, "The large god in the house did this." {11:52} The king replied, "Do these idols have the power to speak and eat as you claim?" {11:53} Abram answered, "If they have no power, then why do you serve them and mislead people with your foolishness? {11:54} Do you think they can save you or do anything at all? Why not acknowledge the God of the universe who created you and has the power to give life or take it away? {11:55} O foolish and ignorant king, woe to you forever. {11:56} I thought you would guide your people in the right way, but instead, you've filled the earth with your sins. {11:57} Don't you know that the evil you're doing is what caused our ancestors to be destroyed in the flood? {11:58} Will you and your people rise to do the same and bring down the anger of God upon the earth? {11:59} So put away your evil deeds and serve the true God, for your soul is in His hands, and it will go well with you. {11:60} But if you refuse to listen and change your wicked heart, you will face shame in the end, you, your people, and all connected to you, regardless of your status." {11:61} Terah stood by and watched what was happening, and when he saw how Abram spoke to the king, he fled. {11:62} But Nimrod and his men, angered by Abram's words, ordered him bound and imprisoned for his words. {11:63} They decided to burn Abram in the fire as punishment for the destruction of the idols and for his words against Nimrod and his kingdom. {11:64} On that day, Abram's soul cried out to God, asking Him to save him from the fire. {11:65} And the Lord heard his cries. {11:66} When Abram was bound and thrown into the fire, a miracle happened. {11:67} The fire did not touch him; instead, a strong wind came and blew the flames away from him. {11:68} All of Nimrod's men were astonished to see Abram standing in the fire unharmed. {11:69} They could not comprehend it, and while their amazement grew, they told Nimrod what they saw. {11:70} Seeing that Abram was untouched by the fire, Nimrod ordered the furnace be heated seven times hotter. {11:71} When the furnace was hot, they threw Abram in once again, but again, he remained unharmed. {11:72} The men saw that even with the heat turned up, Abram was safe. {11:73} The furnace cooled, and Abram stood with his clothes intact and not even smelling of smoke. {11:74} Nimrod became furious. He said, "Take him out of here and imprison him, for his God has truly saved him from my hands." {11:75} And they took Abram out, but in the prison, he was still worshipping the Lord, praying to Him. {11:76} After several days, he was released from prison. {11:77} The king ordered that he should leave, saying, "I cannot touch him, for his God is strong." {11:78} So, Abram departed and returned to the land of Canaan.

{12:1} When the king heard what Abram had said, he ordered him to be imprisoned, and Abram spent ten days in jail. {12:2} After those days, the king summoned all the kings, princes, governors from different provinces, and wise men to come before him. They sat down before him, while Abram remained in confinement. {12:3} The king spoke to the princes and wise men, saying, "Have you heard what Abram, the son of Terah, has done to his father? This is what he did to him, and I commanded him to be brought to me, and he spoke without any fear; he did not waver in my presence, and now he is imprisoned." {12:4} "So, decide what judgment should be passed on this man who has insulted the king and has spoken and done all the things you have heard." {12:5} They all replied to the king, saying, "The man who insults the king should be hanged on a tree, but since he has done all he said and has despised our gods, he must be burned to death, for this is the law regarding such matters." {12:6} "If it pleases the king, let him order his servants to start a fire in the brick furnace both night and day, and then we will throw this man into it." The king agreed and commanded his servants to prepare a fire for three days and three nights in his furnace in Casdim, and then he ordered them to bring Abram out of prison to be burned. {12:7} All the king's servants, princes, lords, governors, judges, and about nine hundred thousand men stood before the furnace to witness what would happen to Abram. {12:8} Women and children crowded onto rooftops and towers to watch what was happening to Abram, and there was no one left who didn't come to see the event. {12:9} When Abram arrived, the king's magicians and wise men recognized him and shouted to the king, saying, "Our sovereign lord, this is the man we know who, at his birth, caused a great star to swallow four stars, which we reported to you fifty years ago." {12:10} "And now, his father has also defied your commands by bringing you another child, whom you killed." {12:11} Upon hearing this, the king became very angry and ordered that Terah be brought before him. {12:12} The king asked, "Have you heard what the magicians have said? Now tell me the truth, how did you do this? If you tell the truth, you will be set free." {12:13} Realizing the king was furious, Terah responded, "My lord and king, you have heard the truth, and what the sages have said is right." The king said, "How could you defy my orders and give me a child that is not yours and then take value from him?" {12:14} Terah replied, "My feelings for my son were strong at that time, and I took a son of my handmaid and brought him to you." {12:15} The king asked, "Who advised you to do this? Do not hide anything from me, and you will not die." {12:16} Terah was terrified before the king and said, "It was my eldest son Haran who advised me to do this." At that time, Haran was thirty-two years old. {12:17} But Haran did not advise his father at all; Terah only said this to the king to save his own life out of great fear. The king said to Terah, "Haran, your son, who advised you to do this, shall die in the fire with Abram, for he will also be sentenced to death for rebelling against the king." {12:18} Haran had been inclined to follow Abram's ways but kept it to himself. {12:19} Haran thought, "Now the king has captured Abram because of what he did. If Abram overcomes the king, I will follow him, but if the king overcomes, I will follow the king." {12:20} After Terah spoke to the king about Haran, the king ordered Haran to be captured along with Abram. {12:21} They brought both Abram and Haran to throw them into the fire, and all the people of the land, the king's servants, princes, and women and children gathered that day to witness this event. {12:22} The king's servants stripped Abram and his brother of all their clothes except for their lower garments. {12:23} They bound their hands and feet with linen cords, and the servants lifted them up and threw them into the furnace. {12:24} The Lord loved Abram and had compassion on him; He came down and delivered Abram from the fire, and he was not burned. {12:25} All the cords that bound him were burned, while Abram remained unharmed and walked around in the fire. {12:26} However, Haran died when they threw him into the fire; he was burned to ashes because his heart was not perfect before the Lord. The men who threw him in were also burned, and twelve of them died. {12:27} Abram walked in the fire for three days and three nights, and all the king's servants saw him walking there; they reported to the king, saying, "We have seen Abram walking in the fire, and even his lower garments were not burned, but the cords with which he was bound are burned." {12:28} When the king heard their words, he fainted with disbelief. He sent other loyal princes to check on the situation, and they saw Abram walking in the fire, and then the king went to see for himself. He witnessed Abram walking freely in the fire while Haran's body lay burned, and the king was greatly astonished. {12:29} The king ordered Abram to be brought out of the fire, but when his servants tried to approach him, they were unable because the flames surrounded them, and the fire rose up against them. {12:30} The king's servants fled, and the king rebuked them, saying, "Hurry and bring Abram out of the fire before you die." {12:31} The king's servants tried again to bring Abram out, but the flames came upon them and burned their faces, causing eight of them to die. {12:32} When the king saw that his servants could not approach the fire without being burned, he called to Abram, "O servant of the God who is in heaven, come out from the fire and stand before me." Abram listened to the king's voice, came out of the fire, and stood before him. {12:33} As Abram came out, the king and all his servants saw that he was unharmed, wearing his lower garments, which had not burned, though the cords that bound him were burned. {12:34} The king asked Abram, "How is it that you were not burned in the fire?" {12:35} Abram replied, "The God of heaven and earth, whom I trust and who has power over all, delivered me from the fire into which you cast me." {12:36} "Haran, the brother of Abram, was burned to ashes, and they searched for his body, but it had been completely consumed." {12:37} Haran was eighty-two years old when he died in the fire of Casdim. The king, princes, and people saw that Abram was saved from the fire while Haran was burned, and they came and bowed down to Abram. {12:38} Abram said to them, "Do not bow down to me; instead, bow down to the God of the world who made you, serve Him, and follow His ways, for it is He who delivered me from this fire. He created the souls and spirits of all people, formed man in his mother's womb, and brought him into the world. He will deliver those who trust in Him from all pain." {12:39} This seemed very wonderful to the king and his princes, that Abram was saved while Haran was burned. The king gave Abram many gifts, including two of his servants from the royal household; one was named Oni and the other was Eliezer. {12:40} All the kings, princes, and servants gave Abram many gifts of silver, gold, and pearls. The king and his princes sent him away, and he departed in peace. {12:41} Abram left the king's presence in peace, and many of the king's servants followed him, with about three hundred men joining him. {12:42} Abram returned that day to his father's house, along with the men who followed him. Abram served the Lord his God all his life, walked in His ways, and followed His law. {12:43} From that day forward, Abram turned the hearts of the people to serve the Lord. {12:44} At that time, Nahor and Abram took wives from their brother Haran's daughters; Nahor's wife was Milca, and Abram's wife was Sarai, who was barren and had no children in those days. {12:45} Two years after Abram's escape from the fire, in the fifty-second year of his life, King Nimrod sat on the throne in Babel and fell asleep. He dreamed that he was with his troops in a valley opposite the king's furnace. {12:46} He looked up and saw a man resembling Abram coming out of the furnace; the man stood before the king with a drawn sword, then charged at the king, and struck him on the head. {12:47} The king cried out because of the dream, and he woke up in a cold sweat. The king had a great fear that he would die because of what he had dreamed. {12:48} In the morning, the king sent for all his magicians and sorcerers, and they were commanded to interpret the dream. {12:49} The king called out to them, saying, "I had a dream last night, and I need someone to explain it to me." The magicians gathered before the king. One of them named Kedar said to the king, "Tell me the dream, and I will interpret it." {12:50} The king replied, "I saw a man standing before me with a sword drawn, and he struck me on the head; when I woke up, my body was cold, and I felt great fear. It seems this man is the servant of Abram, whom I have thrown into the fire." {12:51} Kedar responded, "Do not fear. Let the king be at peace, for it is only a dream, and we have also seen your dream." {12:52} The king said, "Interpret it for me." Kedar explained, "This man will rise to greatness, but if you come against him, you will fall." The king took comfort in this dream but could not shake his fear. {12:53} From that day, the king sought to kill Abram, but he remained in fear because he could not overpower Abram, for the God of heaven had protected him.

{13:1} Terah took his son Abram, his grandson Lot (the son of Haran), his daughter-in-law Sarai (Abram's wife), and all the members of his household and set out from Ur of the Chaldeans to go to the land of Canaan. When they arrived at Haran, they decided to settle there because it was a very good place for grazing and spacious enough for all who were with them. {13:2} The people of Haran noticed that Abram was righteous and had a good relationship with God and others, and the Lord was with him. Some of the locals joined Abram, and he taught them the ways of the Lord; these men stayed with Abram and became his followers. {13:3} Abram lived in Haran for three years, and at the end of that time, the Lord appeared to Abram and said, "I am the Lord who brought you out of Ur of the Chaldeans and rescued you from your enemies." {13:4} "If you listen to my voice and obey my commandments, decrees, and laws, I will help you defeat your enemies, multiply your descendants like the stars in the sky, bless everything you do, and you will have everything you need." {13:5} "Now, get up, take your wife and everything you own, and go to the land of Canaan and stay there, for I will be your God and bless you there." Abram rose, took his wife and all he had, and went to Canaan as the Lord had instructed him; he was fifty years old when he left Haran. {13:6} Abram arrived in Canaan and settled in the city, pitching his tent among the Canaanites who lived in the land. {13:7} The Lord appeared to Abram when he reached Canaan and said, "This is the land I am giving you and your descendants forever. I will make your descendants as numerous as the stars, and I will give your descendants all the land you see." {13:8} Abram built an altar where God had spoken to him and called on the name of the Lord. {13:9} After three years of living in Canaan, Noah died in the year that was the fifty-eighth year of Abram's life; Noah lived for nine hundred fifty years before he died. {13:10} Abram continued to live in Canaan with his wife, all his belongings, and those who accompanied him, while Nahor (Abram's brother), Terah (his father), and Lot (Haran's son) and all their belongings stayed in Haran. {13:11} In the fifth year of Abram's stay in Canaan, the cities of Sodom and Gomorrah and all the surrounding cities rebelled against King Chedorlaomer of Elam; they had served him for twelve years, paying him tribute, but in the thirteenth year, they revolted. {13:12} In the tenth year of Abram's time in Canaan, a war broke out between King Nimrod of Shinar and King Chedorlaomer of Elam. Nimrod came to fight against Chedorlaomer and sought to overpower him. {13:13} At that time, Chedorlaomer was one of Nimrod's generals, and after the people at the tower were scattered, Chedorlaomer went to Elam, where he became king and rebelled against Nimrod. {13:14} When Nimrod learned that the cities of the plain had revolted, he assembled a large army of about seven hundred thousand men and marched against Chedorlaomer, who met him with five thousand men. They prepared for battle in the valley of Babel, located between Elam and Shinar. {13:15} The armies fought, and Nimrod and his troops were defeated by Chedorlaomer's forces, losing about six hundred thousand men, including Mardon, the king's son. {13:16} Ashamed, Nimrod fled back to his land, remaining under Chedorlaomer's control for a long time. Chedorlaomer returned to his kingdom and sent messengers to the kings nearby, including Arioch, king of Elasar, and Tidal, king of Goyim, forming an alliance with them, and they obeyed his commands. {13:17} In the fifteenth year of Abram's stay in Canaan, which was also the seventieth year of his life, the Lord appeared to Abram and said, "I am the Lord who brought you out of Ur of the Chaldeans to give you this land as an inheritance." {13:18} "Now walk before me and be blameless, and keep my commands, for I will give this land to you and your descendants as an inheritance, from the river of Egypt to the great river Euphrates." {13:19} "You will die peacefully, and your descendants will return here in the fourth generation to inherit this land forever." Abram built an altar, called upon the name of the Lord who had appeared to him, and offered sacrifices on the altar. {13:20} At that time, Abram went back to Haran to visit his father, mother, and family. He, his wife, and everything he owned returned to Haran, where Abram lived for five years. {13:21} Many people from Haran, about seventy-two men, followed Abram. He taught them the ways of the Lord and introduced them to God. {13:22} During this time, the Lord appeared to Abram in Haran and said, "Remember, I spoke to you twenty years ago, saying, {13:23} 'Leave your homeland, your birthplace, and your father's house, and go to the land I will show you. In that land, I will bless you, make you a great nation, make your name great, and through you, all families on earth will be blessed.'" {13:24} "Now, get up and leave this place with your wife, all your belongings, and every soul you have made in Haran, and return to Canaan." {13:25} Abram took his wife Sarai, everything he owned, and all the souls he had made in Haran and set out for Canaan. {13:26} Abram returned to Canaan as the Lord had commanded. Lot, the son of his brother Haran, went with him, and

Abram was seventy-five years old when he left Haran to return to Canaan. {13:27} He arrived in Canaan as the Lord had said, pitched his tent in the plain of Mamre, and Lot, his brother's son, and all his belongings accompanied him. {13:28} The Lord appeared again to Abram and said, "I will give this land to your descendants," and Abram built an altar there to the Lord who had appeared to him, which still exists today in the plains of Mamre.

{14:1} In those days, there was a wise man in the land of Shinar who had great understanding and was very good-looking, but he was poor and struggling to make a living; his name was Rikayon, and he found it hard to support himself. {14:2} He decided to go to Egypt to meet Oswiris, the son of Anom, the king of Egypt, to showcase his wisdom, hoping he might find favor with the king and receive help to sustain himself, so Rikayon set out to do just that. {14:3} Upon arriving in Egypt, Rikayon asked the locals about the king, and they informed him of the king's custom: he would leave his palace and be seen by the public only once a year, after which he would return to stay in the palace. {14:4} On that one day the king appeared, he would judge the people, and anyone with a case would come before him to have their requests heard. {14:5} When Rikayon learned about this custom and realized he couldn't enter the king's presence, he felt deeply troubled and very sad. {14:6} That evening, Rikayon found an abandoned building that used to be a bakery in Egypt, where he stayed the night, feeling bitter and hungry, unable to sleep. {14:7} He thought about what he could do in the city while waiting for the king to appear and how he could support himself there. {14:8} The next morning, he went out and encountered vendors selling vegetables and various seeds that they provided to the locals. {14:9} Rikayon wanted to sell similar items to earn a living, but he was unfamiliar with the local customs and felt lost among them. {14:10} He managed to buy some vegetables to sell, but a crowd gathered around him, mocking him, taking his vegetables, and leaving him with nothing. {14:11} He left, feeling deeply distressed, and returned to the abandoned bakery where he spent another night. {14:12} That night, he again pondered how to avoid starving and came up with a plan. {14:13} The following morning, he acted cleverly and hired thirty strong men from the crowd, armed with their weapons, leading them to the top of an Egyptian tomb, where he positioned them. {14:14} He commanded them, saying, "This is the king's order: be strong and brave, and do not allow anyone to be buried here unless they pay two hundred pieces of silver; then they can be buried." The men followed Rikayon's orders for the entire year. {14:15} Within eight months, Rikayon and his men had amassed a great wealth of silver and gold, and he acquired a large number of horses and other animals. He hired more men, giving them horses, and they stayed with him. {14:16} When the year came around and the king was set to go into the town, all the Egyptians gathered to speak to him about Rikayon and his men's actions. {14:17} The king appeared on the appointed day, and the Egyptians approached him, saying, {14:18} "Long live the king! What is this thing you are doing to your subjects, requiring that no one be buried until they pay so much silver and gold? Has anything like this ever happened in the entire world, from the days of the former kings, even from the time of Adam until now, that the dead should not be buried without a set fee? {14:19} We understand that it's customary for kings to collect yearly taxes from the living, but you are not only doing that; you are also taxing the dead daily." {14:20} "O king, we can no longer endure this; the entire city is suffering because of it. Don't you see this?" {14:21} When the king heard what they said, he was furious, and his anger burned against this situation, for he had been unaware of it. {14:22} The king demanded, "Who dares to commit such a wicked act in my land without my permission? You must tell me who it is." {14:23} They explained all the deeds of Rikayon and his men to the king, which further enraged him, and he ordered that Rikayon and his men be brought before him. {14:24} Rikayon took about a thousand children, both sons and daughters, dressed them in silk and beautiful garments, put them on horses, and sent them to the king as gifts through his men, along with a large amount of silver, gold, precious stones, and a strong, magnificent horse to present to the king. He approached the king and bowed down to the ground before him; the king, his officials, and all the Egyptians were amazed at Rikayon's wealth and the gifts he had brought. {14:25} The king was greatly pleased and curious, and when Rikayon sat before him, the king asked him about all his works. Rikayon spoke wisely in response to the king, his servants, and all the people of Egypt. {14:26} When the king heard Rikayon's words and wisdom, he found favor in the king's eyes, and he was treated with kindness by all the king's servants and the people of Egypt because of his wisdom and excellent speaking abilities, and from that time on, they loved him immensely. {14:27} The king replied to Rikayon, saying, "From now on, you will no longer be called Rikayon; instead, you shall be named Pharaoh, since you have taxed the dead." Thus, he was named Pharaoh. {14:28} The king and his subjects cherished Rikayon for his wisdom, and they consulted with all the Egyptians to appoint him as prefect under the king. {14:29} All the people of Egypt and its wise men agreed, and it became a law in Egypt. {14:30} They made Rikayon Pharaoh, prefect under Oswiris, the king of Egypt, and Rikayon Pharaoh governed Egypt, administering justice daily for the entire city, while Oswiris would judge the people only once a year during his public appearance. {14:31} Rikayon Pharaoh cleverly seized control of the government of Egypt and collected taxes from all the inhabitants of Egypt. {14:32} The people greatly loved Rikayon Pharaoh, and they decreed that every king who would rule over them and their descendants in Egypt would be called Pharaoh. {14:33} Therefore, all kings who have ruled in Egypt since that time have been referred to as Pharaoh, and this continues to this day.

{15:1} That year, there was a severe famine across the land of Canaan, and the people couldn't stay there because the famine was very harsh. {15:2} So, Abram and all his household decided to go down to Egypt because of the famine. When they reached the brook of Mitzraim, they rested there for a while to recover from the journey. {15:3} While walking along the edge of the brook, Abram noticed that his wife Sarai was very beautiful. {15:4} He said to Sarai, "Since God has made you so beautiful, I'm afraid the Egyptians will kill me and take you, as they do not fear God." {15:5} So, please say that you are my sister to anyone who asks, so that it may go well for me and we won't be killed. {15:6} Abram gave this instruction to everyone traveling with him, including his nephew Lot, telling him to say that Sarai was his sister if the Egyptians asked. {15:7} Despite giving these orders, Abram didn't fully trust them; he took Sarai and hid her in a chest among their belongings because he was very worried about her due to the wickedness of the Egyptians. {15:8} After resting by the brook, Abram and his household set out for Egypt. As soon as they arrived at the city gates, the guards told them to pay a tax to the king before entering the city, and Abram and his companions complied. {15:9} Once they entered Egypt, they brought the chest with Sarai hidden inside, and the Egyptians noticed the chest. {15:10} The king's servants approached Abram, asking what he had in the chest that they hadn't seen before, demanding he open it and pay a tax on its contents. {15:11} Abram replied, "I will not open the chest, but I'll pay whatever tax you ask." The king's officers insisted, "It must contain precious stones; give us a tenth of what's inside." {15:12} Abram said he would pay whatever they wanted but insisted that the chest remain closed. {15:13} The officers pressed him and forced the chest open, revealing the beautiful woman inside. {15:14} When the king's officers saw Sarai, they were amazed by her beauty, and all of Pharaoh's princes and servants gathered to see her. They quickly ran to tell Pharaoh about her, praising Sarai's beauty. {15:15} Pharaoh ordered her to be brought to him, and when he saw her, he was extremely pleased and captivated by her beauty. He rejoiced greatly and rewarded those who brought the news to him. {15:16} Sarai was taken to Pharaoh's palace, while Abram felt distressed about his wife and prayed to the Lord to save her from Pharaoh. {15:17} Sarai also prayed, saying, "O Lord God, you told my husband Abram to leave his land and family for Canaan, promising to care for him if he followed your commands. We obeyed and came to this foreign land to escape the famine, but now I find myself in this terrible situation. Please, O Lord, rescue us from this oppressor and show me mercy." {15:18} The Lord heard Sarai's prayer and sent an angel to protect her from Pharaoh's grasp. {15:19} The king came to Sarai, and as he sat before her, the angel stood beside them and said, "Do not be afraid; the Lord has heard your prayer." {15:20} The king then asked Sarai, "Who is this man who brought you here?" She replied, "He is my brother." {15:21} The king said, "We must honor him, elevate him, and do whatever he asks." At that time, Pharaoh sent Abram gifts of silver, gold, precious stones, and livestock, and he summoned Abram to sit in the king's court, greatly honoring him that night. {15:22} As the king approached Sarai to speak with her, the angel struck him forcefully, terrifying him and preventing him from touching her. {15:23} The angel continued to smite the king throughout the night, leaving him terrified. {15:24} The angel also struck all the servants and the entire household of Pharaoh due to Sarai's presence, causing a great outcry that night in Pharaoh's house. {15:25} Realizing the trouble he was in, Pharaoh concluded that this was happening because of Sarai and moved away from her, speaking kindly to her. {15:26} The king then asked Sarai, "Please tell me about the man who came with you." She explained, "He is my husband, but I said he was my brother out of fear that you would kill him." {15:27} Pharaoh kept his distance from Sarai after this, and the angel's plagues ceased for him and his household. Pharaoh recognized that he had been afflicted because of Sarai and was astonished by it. {15:28} In the morning, the king called for Abram, saying, "What have you done to me? Why did you say she is your sister, which led me to take her as my wife? This heavy plague has come upon me and my household because of this!" {15:29} Therefore, here is your wife; take her and leave our land, or we will all perish because of her. Pharaoh then gave Abram even more livestock, servants, and wealth, while returning Sarai to him. {15:30} He also gave Sarai a maid from his concubines as an attendant. {15:31} The king told his daughter, "It is better for you to be a servant in this man's house than to be the mistress in mine, given the trouble we've faced because of this woman." {15:32} Abram, along with everyone in his household, left Egypt, and Pharaoh sent some of his men to accompany them as they departed. {15:33} Abram returned to the land of Canaan, going back to the place where he had built an altar and first pitched his tent. {15:34} Lot, the son of Haran, Abram's brother, had amassed a large number of cattle, flocks, herds, and tents, for the Lord blessed them because of Abram. {15:35} While Abram was living in the land, Lot's herdsmen began to quarrel with Abram's herdsmen because their livestock was too large for them to coexist peacefully, and the land could not support them all. {15:36} Whenever Abram's herdsmen took their flocks to graze, they would avoid the fields of the local people, but Lot's herdsmen let their animals feed in those same fields. {15:37} The local people saw this happening daily and confronted Abram about Lot's herdsmen. {15:38} Abram then said to Lot, "What are you doing to me? You're making me look bad to the locals by allowing your herdsmen to graze in others' fields. Don't you realize I'm a foreigner here among the Canaanites? Why are you doing this to me?" {15:39} Abram confronted Lot regularly about this issue, but Lot ignored him and continued his behavior, leading the locals to come and complain to Abram. {15:40} Abram pleaded with Lot, "How long will you be a stumbling block to me with the local people? I urge you to stop the quarrels between us since we are family. {15:41} Please separate from me; choose a place to settle with your livestock and belongings, but keep your distance from me and your household. {15:42} Don't worry about leaving; if anyone harms you, let me know and I will defend you; just move away from me." {15:43} After Abram spoke to Lot, Lot looked up and surveyed the Jordan plain. {15:44} He noticed that it was well-watered and good for both people and livestock. {15:45} So, Lot moved away from Abram to that area, pitched his tent there, and settled in Sodom, leading to their separation. {15:46} Meanwhile, Abram settled in the plain of Mamre, near Hebron, where he pitched his tent and stayed for many years.

{16:1} At that time, Chedorlaomer, the king of Elam, sent messengers to all the nearby kings, including Nimrod, the king of Shinar, who was under his control, and Tidal, the king of Goyim, and Arioch, the king of Elasar, with whom he had made an alliance, saying, "Come to me and help me so we can attack all the cities of Sodom and their inhabitants, for they have rebelled against me for thirteen years." {16:2} So these four kings gathered their armies, totaling about eight hundred thousand men, and marched against their enemies, defeating everyone in their path. {16:3} The five kings of Sodom and Gomorrah—Shinab, the king of Admah; Shemeber, the king of Zeboyim; Bera, the king of Sodom; Bersha, the king of Gomorrah; and Bela, the king of Zoar—went out to meet them, joining together in the Valley of Siddim. {16:4} These nine kings fought in the Valley of Siddim, and the kings of Sodom and Gomorrah were defeated by the kings of Elam. {16:5} The Valley of Siddim was filled with tar pits, and as the kings of Elam pursued the kings of Sodom, the latter fell into the pits, while the rest fled to the mountains for safety. The five kings of Elam pursued them to the gates of Sodom and took everything in Sodom. {16:6} They plundered all the cities of Sodom and Gomorrah, capturing Lot, Abram's nephew, along with his possessions. They seized all the goods of Sodom's cities and departed. Unic, Abram's servant who was in the battle, witnessed this and reported back to Abram what had happened to Sodom. {16:7} When Abram heard this, he gathered about three hundred eighteen men who were with him and pursued the kings that night. He attacked them and defeated them, leaving only the four kings who fled, each going their separate ways. {16:8} Abram recovered all the goods of Sodom and also rescued Lot, along with his belongings, wives, children, and everything that belonged to him, ensuring that Lot lacked nothing. {16:9} After returning from defeating the kings, Abram and his men passed through the Valley of Siddim, where the battle had taken place. {16:10} Bera, the king of Sodom, and the rest of his men who had escaped the pits came out to meet Abram and his men. {16:11} Adonizedek, the king of Jerusalem, who was also known as Shem, came out with his men to greet Abram and his people, bringing bread and wine. They stayed together in the Valley of Melech. {16:12} Adonizedek blessed Abram, and Abram gave him a tenth of everything he had taken from the spoils of his enemies, for Adonizedek was a priest before God. {16:13} All the kings of Sodom and Gomorrah who were there, along with their servants, approached Abram and asked him to return their servants whom he had taken captive and to keep whatever property he wanted. {16:14} But Abram replied to the kings of Sodom, saying, "As the Lord lives, who created heaven and earth and has saved me from all my troubles and delivered my enemies into my hands today, I will not take anything that belongs to you, so you won't be able to boast tomorrow that Abram became rich from your property." {16:15} "For the Lord my God, in whom I trust, has said to me, 'You will lack nothing, for I will bless you in all that you do.'" {16:16} "So here is everything that belongs to you; take it and go. As the Lord lives, I will not take from you even a shoelace or a thread, except for the food for those who went with me to battle and the shares of the men who went with me, Anar, Ashcol, and Mamre, along with their men. They shall receive their share of the spoils." {16:17} The kings of Sodom gave Abram what he had requested, pressing him to take whatever he chose, but he refused. {16:18} He sent away the kings of Sodom and their men, giving them instructions about Lot, and they went back to their own places. {16:19} Lot, Abram's nephew, was also sent away with his possessions, returning home to Sodom, while Abram and his people returned to the plains of Mamre, which is in Hebron. {16:20} At that time, the Lord appeared to Abram again in Hebron and said, "Do not be afraid; your reward is very great in my eyes. I will not abandon you until I have multiplied you, blessed you, and made your descendants like the stars in the heavens, uncountable and immeasurable." {16:21} "I will give your descendants all these lands that you can see; they will inherit them forever. Just be strong and do not fear; walk before me and be perfect." {16:22} In the seventy-eighth year of Abram's life, Reu, the son of Peleg, died; he lived for two hundred thirty-nine years. {16:23} Sarai, the daughter of Haran and Abram's wife, remained barren during those days; she bore him no children. {16:24} When Sarai saw that she could not have children, she gave her handmaid Hagar, whom Pharaoh had given her, to Abram as a wife. {16:25} Hagar learned all of Sarai's ways as Sarai taught her, and she followed her good examples. {16:26} Sarai said to Abram, "Look, here is my handmaid Hagar; go to her so she can bear children on my behalf, and I may also have children through her." {16:27} After ten years of Abram living in Canaan, which was Abram's eighty-fifth year, Sarai gave Hagar to him. {16:28} Abram listened to his wife Sarai and took Hagar as his wife; she conceived. {16:29} When Hagar realized she was pregnant, she became very proud, and her mistress became despised in her eyes. She thought to herself, "This must mean I am favored by God more than Sarai, for Sarai has been with my lord all this time and could not conceive, but I have conceived so quickly." {16:30} When Sarai saw that Hagar had conceived by Abram, she became jealous of her handmaid and thought, "This only shows that she must be better than I am." {16:31} Sarai said to Abram, "My wrong is your fault, for when you prayed to the Lord for children, why didn't you pray for me to have children from you?" {16:32} "When I speak to Hagar in your presence, she disrespects me, as she has conceived, and you say nothing to her; may the Lord judge between us for what you have done to me." {16:33} Abram replied to Sarai, "Your handmaid is in your power; do what seems best to you." Sarai mistreated Hagar, and Hagar fled to the wilderness. {16:34} An angel of the Lord found her in the wilderness at a well and said, "Do not be afraid, for I will greatly multiply your descendants; you will have a son, and you shall name him Ishmael. Now return to your mistress and submit to her." {16:35} Hagar named the well Beer-lahai-roi; it is located between Kadesh and the wilderness of Bered. {16:36} Hagar returned to her master's house, and after some time, she bore a son for Abram, who named him Ishmael. Abram was eighty-six years old when he fathered him.

{17:1} In those days, when Abram was ninety-one years old, the children of Chittim went to war against the children of Tubal. When the Lord scattered mankind across the earth, the children of Chittim settled in the plain of Canopia, where they built cities and lived by the river Tibreu. {17:2} The children of Tubal lived in Tuscanah, with their borders reaching the river Tibreu. They built a city there and named it Sabinah, after Sabinah, the son of Tubal their father, and they still dwell there to this day. {17:3} During this time, the children of Chittim fought against the children of Tubal, and the children of Tubal were defeated by the children of Chittim, with three hundred seventy men falling from their ranks. {17:4} The children of Tubal swore to the children of Chittim, saying, "You shall not intermarry with us, nor shall any man give his daughter to any of the sons of Chittim." {17:5} For all the daughters of Tubal were exceptionally beautiful; no other women on earth were as lovely as them. {17:6} Those who admired beauty sought wives from the daughters of Tubal, including kings and princes who took wives from them. {17:7} Three years after the children of Tubal swore to the children of Chittim not to intermarry, about twenty men from Chittim tried to take some daughters from Tubal. {17:8} They carried them off, thinking that they would be able to unite them with their sons in marriage. The children of Tubal sought to avenge themselves against the children of Chittim. {17:9} Thus the children of Tubal waged war against the children of Chittim and had numerous battles with them, but could not overcome them. {17:10} Finally, after nine months, they sent a messenger to the children of Chittim, demanding a large tribute in silver and gold. The children of Chittim replied, "We will send you nothing!" {17:11} They then threatened, saying, "If you do not send us what we demand, we will destroy your cities and your land." The children of Tubal then prepared for battle, gathering an army against the children of Chittim, but they were unprepared. {17:12} The children of Chittim came out against them with swords and shields, ready for battle. The children of Tubal fled before them and did not pursue, for they knew the might of their enemies. {17:13} The children of Tubal gathered their men, numbering about two hundred thousand, and went out against the children of Chittim. But again, they were defeated. {17:14} The children of Chittim drove them from the city. {17:15} The children of Chittim rejoiced greatly for the victory they had achieved. They said to one another, "We will not lose our land; we will stand for what is right." {17:16} They dedicated that day as a festival to the Lord for the victory they had won. {17:17} They also vowed to honor the Lord with their sacrifices and offerings. And thus ended the battle between the children of Tubal and the children of Chittim. {17:18} In those days, during the month of the harvest, the Lord told Abram to go up to the land of Canaan and to build an altar to Him. {17:19} Abram took his wife Sarai and his son Ishmael and traveled to Canaan, where he built an altar to the Lord and offered sacrifices. {17:20} The Lord appeared to him there and said, "I am the Lord your God. Be faithful and obey my commands, and you shall be blessed." {17:21} Abram remained in Canaan and prospered. His flocks increased, and he became wealthy. {17:22} After some years, the Lord spoke to Abram and said, "I have heard your prayers. Do not fear, for I will bless you abundantly." {17:23} In those days, the people of Canaan worshipped many gods and engaged in wicked practices. {17:24} The Lord instructed Abram to teach them His ways and to call them to repentance. {17:25} Abram obeyed and began to teach the people of Canaan about the one true God. {17:26} The people were amazed at Abram's words, and many began to follow him, forsaking their idols. {17:27} The Lord blessed Abram for his faithfulness and granted him favor in the eyes of the people. {17:28} And so Abram continued to dwell in the land of Canaan, teaching the ways of the Lord and building altars to Him, and he prospered greatly in the land. {17:29} Thus the people of Canaan began to recognize the Lord God of Abram and turned from their wicked ways. {17:30} And this was the beginning of the worship of the true God among the children of Canaan. {17:31} Abram lived in the land of Canaan for many years, growing in wealth and influence. He became a leader among the people and was known as a righteous man. {17:32} The Lord was with Abram, and he was blessed in all that he did. {17:33} And so it was that Abram became a mighty nation in the land of Canaan, and many were drawn to him for his wisdom and understanding. {17:34} And the Lord spoke to Abram in those days, saying, "Fear not, for I will be with you and bless you, and your descendants shall be great upon the earth." {17:35} And thus the promise of the Lord to Abram was fulfilled in his life. {17:36} Abram became a man of renown, and his name was known far and wide. {17:37} And in his old age, the Lord blessed him with the gift of a long life, and he died in peace, having seen the fulfillment of the Lord's promise in his lifetime. {17:38} And so the story of Abram and his descendants continued to be told for generations, a testimony to the faithfulness of the Lord. {17:39} The generations of Abram were blessed, and through them, the world was changed forever. {17:40} The Lord was faithful to His word, and those who followed Him prospered and were blessed. {17:41} And this is the account of Abram, the father of many nations, and the beginning of a new covenant that God made with His people.

{18:1} Abraham got up and did everything God commanded him; he took the men from his household and those he had bought, and he circumcised them as the Lord had instructed him. {18:2} Not one was left uncircumcised; Abraham and his son Ishmael were also circumcised, with Ishmael being thirteen years old at the time. {18:3} On the third day after the circumcision, Abraham went out of his tent and sat at the door to enjoy the warmth of the sun, despite the pain in his body. {18:4} Then the Lord appeared to him in the plain of Mamre and sent three of His ministering angels to visit him. Abraham was sitting at the door of the tent when he looked up and saw three men coming from a distance. He got up and ran to meet them, bowing down to them and inviting them into his house. {18:5} He said to them, "If I have found favor in your sight, please turn in and have a bit of bread." He urged them, and they turned in. He gave them water to wash their feet and placed them under a tree at the door of the tent. {18:6} Abraham ran and took a tender and good calf, hurried to kill it, and gave it to his servant Eliezer to prepare. {18:7} Then he went to Sarah in the tent and told her, "Quickly make three measures of fine flour, knead it, and make some cakes to cover the pot with the meat." She did so. {18:8} Abraham hurried and brought them butter and milk, along with beef and mutton, and served it to them even before the calf was fully cooked, and they ate. {18:9} After they finished eating, one of them said to him, "I will return to you at the time of life, and your wife Sarah will have a son." {18:10} The men then departed and went their separate ways to the places they were sent. {18:11} During those days, all the people of Sodom and Gomorrah, and the surrounding five cities, were exceedingly wicked and sinful against the Lord. They provoked the Lord with their terrible actions, becoming increasingly abominable (disgusting) and defiant before Him, and their evil deeds were significant before the Lord. {18:12} They had a vast valley in their land, about a half-day's walk, with springs of water and plenty of grass around it. {18:13} The people of Sodom and Gomorrah went there four times a year with their wives and children, celebrating with tambourines and dances. {18:14} During their festivities, they would all rise up and take hold of their neighbors' wives and sometimes even their virgin daughters, enjoying them without any objections, as each man witnessed his own wife and daughter in the hands of his neighbor but remained silent. {18:15} They engaged in these actions from morning until night, returning home afterward, each man to his house and each woman to her tent, and this was their practice four times a year. {18:16} Whenever a stranger came into their cities, bringing goods to sell, the people of these cities would gather—men, women, children, young and old—and forcefully take the man's goods, each one taking a little until nothing was left for the owner. {18:17} If the owner protested, saying, "What have you done to me?" they would approach him one by one, each claiming they only took a small portion, taunting him until he left them in sorrow and bitterness of spirit. Then they would all rise and chase him out of the city with loud commotion. {18:18} One day, a man from the country of Elam was traveling along the road, riding on his donkey, which carried a fine multicolored mantle tied to it. {18:19} As he passed through Sodom at sunset, he decided to stay for the night, but no one would let him in. At that time, there was a wicked man in Sodom named Hedad, known for his malicious deeds. {18:20} Hedad saw the traveler in the street and approached him, asking, "Where are you from and where are you going?" {18:21} The traveler replied, "I am on my way from Hebron to Elam, my home. As I was passing, the sun set and no one would let me enter their house, though I have bread and water, and provisions for my donkey; I lack nothing." {18:22} Hedad responded, "I will provide everything you need, but you cannot stay in the street all night." He took the traveler to his home, removed the mantle from the donkey, and brought it inside, giving the donkey some straw and feed while the traveler ate and drank. He stayed there that night. {18:23} In the morning, the traveler got up early to continue his journey, but Hedad said to him, "Wait, have a bit of bread to strengthen you before you go." The man did so and stayed with him for the day, eating and drinking together. When he finally stood to leave, {18:24} Hedad urged him, "It's getting late; you should stay another night so you can rest and leave in the morning." The traveler didn't want to stay, but as he was saddling his donkey, Hedad's wife remarked, "This man has been with us for two days, eating and drinking, and he hasn't given us anything. Should he leave without contributing?" Hedad replied, "Be quiet." {18:27} As the traveler prepared to leave, he asked Hedad for the cord and the mantle to tie onto the donkey. {18:28} Hedad replied, "What are you talking about?" The traveler explained, "You should give me the cord and the multicolored mantle that you took off the donkey and stored in your house." {18:29} Hedad responded, "This is how I interpret your dream: the cord means your life will be extended like a cord, and the multicolored mantle signifies you will have a vineyard with trees bearing all kinds of fruits." {18:30} The traveler replied, "No, my lord, for I was awake when I gave you the cord and the mantle that was on the donkey for safekeeping." Hedad insisted, "I've told you the interpretation of your dream, and it's a good one." {18:32} Now, the sons of men, please give me four pieces of silver, which is my fee for interpreting dreams; I only ask for three pieces from you." {18:33} The traveler was angered by Hedad's words and went to Serak, the judge of Sodom, to present his case. {18:34} He laid out his complaint before Serak, but Hedad replied, "That's not true. Here's how the matter stands." The judge told the traveler, "Hedad speaks the truth; he is well-known in the cities for his accurate dream interpretations." {18:35} The traveler cried out at the judge's words, saying, "That's not true! It was the day I gave him the cord and mantle on the donkey for safekeeping." They both argued before the judge, with one asserting one version and the other contradicting it. {18:36} Hedad insisted, "You owe me four pieces of silver for interpreting your dream, and I will not make any exceptions. Plus, you owe me for the four meals you ate in my house." {18:37} The traveler responded, "I will gladly pay for what I ate at your house, but please return to me the cord and mantle that you hid away." {18:38} Hedad replied to the judge, "Didn't I interpret his dream? The cord signifies your days will be long like a cord, and the mantle means you will have a vineyard with all kinds of fruit trees." {18:39} "That's the correct interpretation of your dream. Now pay me the four pieces of silver as compensation, with no exceptions." {18:40} The traveler was distraught over Hedad's demands, and they both quarreled in front of the judge, who ordered his servants to forcibly remove them. {18:41} They left the judge's presence while the people of Sodom gathered around them, angrily denouncing the stranger and driving him out of the city. {18:42} The man continued his journey on his donkey, filled with bitterness, lamenting and weeping at what had happened to him in the corrupt city of Sodom.

{19:1} The cities of Sodom had four judges for four cities, and their names were Serak in Sodom, Sharkad in Gomorrah, Zabnac in Admah, and Menon in Zeboyim. {19:2} Abraham's servant Eliezer gave them different names: he changed Serak to Shakra, Sharkad to Shakrura, Zebnac to Kezobim, and Menon to Matzlodin. {19:3} At the request of their judges, the people of Sodom and Gomorrah set up beds in the streets of their cities. When a man entered these places, they would grab him and bring him to one of the beds, forcing him to lie down. {19:4} As he lay there, three men would stand at his head and three at his feet, measuring him against the length of the bed. If the man was shorter than the bed, these six men would stretch him at both ends, and when he cried out for help, they would not respond. {19:5} If he was longer than the bed, they would pull the sides together until the man was nearly dead. {19:6} If he continued to cry out, they would reply, "This is what happens to anyone who enters our land." {19:7} When others heard about these actions of the people of Sodom and Gomorrah, they stayed away from those cities. {19:8} When a poor man entered their land, they would give him silver and gold but would announce throughout the city not to give him any food to eat. If the stranger stayed for several days and died from hunger without getting even a morsel of bread, the entire city would come to take back the silver and gold they had given him at his death. {19:9} Those who recognized the silver or gold would reclaim it, and they would strip the dead man of his clothes, fighting over them, and the one who won took them. {19:10} Afterward, they would bury him under some bushes in the desert; this was their treatment of anyone who came to them and died in their land. {19:11} Over time, Sarah sent Eliezer to Sodom to check on Lot and see how he was doing. {19:12} Eliezer went to Sodom and encountered a man of Sodom fighting with a stranger; the Sodomite stripped the poor man of all his clothes and walked away. {19:13} The poor man cried to Eliezer, pleading for help because of what the Sodomite had done to him. {19:14} Eliezer asked the Sodomite, "Why do you treat this poor man like that, who has come to your land?" {19:15} The Sodomite replied, "Is this man your brother, or have the people of Sodom appointed you as judge today, that you speak about this man?" {19:16} Eliezer argued with the Sodomite over the poor man, and when he tried to recover the man's clothes, the Sodomite quickly struck him in the forehead with a stone. {19:17} Blood poured from Eliezer's forehead, and the man said, "Pay me for getting rid of this bad blood on your forehead, for that is the custom and law in our land." {19:18} Eliezer responded, "You have hurt me and now demand payment for it?" He refused to listen to the Sodomite's words. {19:19} The man then seized Eliezer and took him before Shakra, the judge of Sodom, for a ruling. {19:20} The Sodomite told the judge, "My lord, this man attacked me with a stone, and blood flowed from his forehead, yet he refuses to pay me." {19:21} The judge said to Eliezer, "This man speaks the truth, so give him what he demands, for that is the custom in our land." Eliezer then took a stone and struck the judge in the forehead, causing blood to flow from him as well. {19:22} Eliezer said, "If this is the custom in your land, then give this man what I was supposed to give him, for this is your ruling." {19:23} Eliezer left the Sodomite with the judge and walked away. {19:24} When the kings of Elam waged war against the kings of Sodom, they captured all of Sodom's property and took Lot and his belongings captive. When Abraham heard this, he went to battle against the kings of Elam and recovered Lot and all his possessions, as well as those of Sodom. {19:25} At that time, Lot's wife gave birth to a daughter named Paltith, saying, "Because God has saved him and his entire household from the kings of Elam." Paltith, Lot's daughter, grew up, and one of the Sodomites took her as his wife. {19:26} A poor man came to the city seeking help and stayed there for several days, but the people of Sodom proclaimed their custom not to give him any food until he collapsed and died. {19:27} Paltith saw this man lying in the street, starved and on the verge of death, and no one would help him. {19:28} Her heart was filled with compassion for him, and she secretly fed him bread for many days, which revived him. {19:29} Whenever she went to fetch water, she would hide the bread in her water pitcher, and when she reached the poor man's spot, she would take the bread out and give it to him. {19:30} The people of Sodom and Gomorrah wondered how this man managed to survive starvation for so long. {19:31} They said to one another, "He must be eating and drinking, for no one could survive without food for so many days without changing in appearance." Three men hid nearby to discover who was feeding him. {19:32} On that day, Paltith went out to get water, putting bread in her pitcher, and she came to the poor man, took out the bread, and gave it to him. {19:33} The three men then saw her kindness and said, "You are the one supporting him; that is why he hasn't starved or changed in appearance." {19:34} The three men approached Paltith and took her and the bread from the poor man's hand. {19:35} They brought Paltith before their judges, saying, "This woman has given bread to the poor man, so what punishment should be imposed for her breaking our law?" {19:36} The people of Sodom and Gomorrah gathered and lit a fire in the city streets, taking the woman and throwing her into the flames until she was reduced to ashes. {19:37} In Admah, a similar situation occurred with a woman. {19:38} A traveler came to Admah, intending to stay overnight before continuing his journey the next morning. He sat at the door of a young woman's father's house, as the sun had set when he arrived. The young woman noticed him sitting there. {19:39} He asked her for a drink of water, and she replied, "Who are you?" He explained, "I was traveling, but I reached here at sunset, so I'll stay here tonight and leave early tomorrow." {19:40} The young woman went inside and brought the man bread and water to eat and drink. {19:41} This became known to the people of Admah, who brought the young woman before the judges to be tried for her actions. {19:42} The judge declared, "This woman deserves the death penalty for breaking our law, and this is the ruling regarding her." {19:43} The people gathered and coated the young woman in honey from head to toe, as the judge had ordered, and they placed her before a swarm of bees in their hives. The bees attacked her and stung her until her whole body swelled up. {19:44} She cried out in pain from the bees, but no one took notice or felt pity for her, and her cries reached heaven. {19:45} The Lord was angered by this and all the actions of the cities of Sodom, for they had plenty of food and lived in peace, yet still refused to help the poor and needy. Their wickedness and sins grew greater before the Lord during those days. {19:46} The Lord sent two angels who had come to Abraham's house to destroy Sodom and its cities. {19:47} The angels rose from Abraham's tent after eating and drinking, and they arrived in Sodom that evening. Lot was sitting at the gate of Sodom when he saw them and quickly went to meet them, bowing down to the ground. {19:48} He urged them strongly to come into his house, offering them food, which they accepted, and they spent the night there. {19:49} The angels warned Lot, "Get up and leave this place, you and your family, so that you won't be destroyed along with this city, for the Lord is going to destroy it." {19:50} The angels took Lot, his wife, and their children by the hand and led them out, setting them outside the city. {19:51} They told Lot, "Run for your life!" and he fled with his family. {19:52} Then the Lord rained down fire and brimstone from heaven on Sodom and Gomorrah and all those cities. {19:53} He overthrew them all, along with the entire plain and every inhabitant and everything that grew there. Lot's wife looked back at the destruction of the cities, feeling compassion for her daughters who remained in Sodom and did not follow her. {19:54} When she looked back, she became a pillar of salt, which still stands in that place to this day. {19:55} The oxen in that area would lick up the salt, and in the morning, new salt would spring up again, which they would lick up. {19:56} Lot and his two daughters fled to the cave of Adullam, where they stayed for a while. {19:57} Early the next morning, Abraham went to see what had happened to the cities of Sodom. He looked and saw smoke rising from the cities like smoke from a furnace. {19:58} Lot and his two daughters remained in the cave, and they made their father drink wine and lay with him because they believed no man was left on earth to continue their family line; they thought the whole world had been destroyed. {19:59} Both daughters slept with their father and became pregnant, with the eldest naming her son Moab, saying, "From my father I have conceived him; he is the father of the Moabites to this day." {19:60} The younger daughter named her son Benami, saying, "He is the father of the Ammonites to this day." {19:61} After this, Lot and his two daughters moved away from that place and settled on the other side of the Jordan. The sons of Lot grew up, took wives from Canaan, had children, and became numerous.

{20:1} At that time, Abraham left the plain of Mamre and traveled to the land of the Philistines, settling in Gerar; this was the twenty-fifth year of his stay in Canaan and the one hundredth year of his life when he arrived in Gerar. {20:2} As they entered the land, he told Sarah, his wife, to say she was his sister to anyone who asked, so they could avoid the danger posed by the local inhabitants. {20:3} While Abraham was living in the land of the Philistines, the servants of Abimelech, the king, saw that Sarah was extremely beautiful, and they asked Abraham about her. He replied, "She is my sister." {20:4} The servants informed Abimelech, saying, "A man from the land of Canaan has come to dwell here, and he has a sister who is very fair." {20:5} When Abimelech heard his servants praise Sarah, he sent for her and brought her to his palace. {20:6} Abimelech saw that Sarah was beautiful, and she greatly pleased him. {20:7} He asked her, "What is the relationship between you and the man who came here?" She replied, "He is my brother; we came from Canaan to find a place to live." {20:8} Abimelech then said to her, "My land is open to you; place your brother anywhere you like, and I will honor him above all the people in the land because he is your brother." {20:9} Abimelech called for Abraham, and when he arrived, {20:10} Abimelech said, "I have commanded that you be honored as you desire because of your sister Sarah." {20:11} Abraham left the king's presence, and the king gave him gifts. {20:12} That evening, as men were settling down, Abimelech sat on his throne, and a deep sleep fell upon him. He slept until morning. {20:13} In his dream, an angel of the Lord appeared to him with a drawn sword and stood over Abimelech, wanting to kill him. The king was terrified and asked the angel, "What have I done to deserve this?" {20:14} The angel answered, "You will die because of the woman you brought into your house; she is married to a man. Now return his wife to him, for she is his wife. If you do not return her, you will surely die, you and everyone connected to you." {20:15} That night, there was a great outcry in the land of the Philistines, and the people saw a figure with a drawn sword, which terrified them. {20:16} The angel of the Lord struck the entire land of the Philistines that night, causing great confusion. {20:17} Every womb in the land was closed, and they suffered because of Sarah, the wife of Abraham. {20:18} In the morning, Abimelech woke up terrified and confused, and he called for his servants, sharing his dream, and the people were afraid. {20:19} One servant spoke up, saying, "O king, return this woman to her husband; he is her husband. The same thing happened to Pharaoh when this man was in Egypt. {20:20} Pharaoh took this woman as a wife because he said, 'She is my sister.' The Lord afflicted him with serious plagues until he returned her to her husband." {20:21} Therefore, king, know what happened last night across the land, there was great fear and lamentation because of the woman you took. {20:22} So, restore her to her husband to avoid the fate of Pharaoh and his subjects. Abimelech quickly called for Sarah, and she came before him, and he also called for Abraham, who arrived. {20:23} Abimelech said to them, "Why did you do this? I took this woman as my wife thinking she was your sister!" {20:24} Abraham replied, "I was afraid I would die because of my wife." Abimelech took flocks, herds, servants, and a thousand pieces of silver and gave them to Abraham, returning Sarah to him. {20:25} Abimelech said to Abraham, "The entire land is open to you; settle wherever you choose." {20:26} Abraham and Sarah left the king's presence with honor and respect, and they lived in Gerar. {20:27} All the people of the Philistines and the king's servants were still in pain from the plague that the angel had inflicted upon them that night because of Sarah. {20:28} Abimelech sent for Abraham, saying, "Pray to your God for us so that He may remove this plague from us." {20:29} Abraham prayed for Abimelech and his subjects, and the Lord heard Abraham's prayer and healed Abimelech and all his people.

{21:1} At that time, about a year and four months after Abraham began living in the land of the Philistines, God visited Sarah and remembered her; she conceived and bore a son to Abraham. {21:2} Abraham named the son Isaac, the name that God had instructed. {21:3} Abraham circumcised Isaac when he was eight days old, as God had commanded him; Abraham was one hundred years old, and Sarah was ninety when Isaac was born. {21:4} The child grew and was weaned, and Abraham held a great feast to celebrate Isaac's weaning. {21:5} Shem, Eber, all the great men of the land, Abimelech, and his servants attended the feast to rejoice with Abraham over the weaning of his son. {21:6} Terah, Abraham's father, and his brother Nahor also came from Haran with their families, rejoicing at the news of Sarah's son. {21:7} They joined Abraham at the feast. {21:8} During that time, Serug, the son of Reu, died in the first year after Isaac was born. {21:9} The total years of Serug's life were two hundred and thirty-nine years, and then he died. {21:10} Ishmael, the son of Abraham, had grown up; he was fourteen years old when Sarah bore Isaac. {21:11} God was with Ishmael, who grew strong and learned to use a bow and became an archer. {21:12} When Isaac was five years old, he was sitting at the door of the tent with Ishmael. {21:13} Ishmael approached Isaac and sat opposite him; he took his bow, aimed an arrow at Isaac, intending to kill him. {21:14} Sarah saw Ishmael's actions and was greatly distressed for her son, so she called for Abraham, saying, "Cast out this bondwoman and her son, for her son will not inherit with my son; today he sought to kill him." {21:15} Abraham listened to Sarah and rose early the next morning. He packed twelve loaves and a bottle of water for Hagar and sent her away with her son. They wandered in the wilderness of Paran, where Ishmael became an archer and lived for a long time. {21:16} Eventually, he and his mother went to Egypt, where Hagar found a wife for Ishmael named Meribah. {21:17} Ishmael's wife bore him four sons and two daughters, and they all returned to the wilderness. {21:18} They made tents in the wilderness and traveled often, resting monthly and yearly. {21:19} God blessed Ishmael with flocks, herds, and tents because of his father Abraham, and he thrived. {21:20} Ishmael lived in the wilderness and traveled in tents for a long time, not seeing his father's face. {21:21} Some time later, Abraham said to Sarah, "I want to see my son Ishmael, as I have not seen him for a long time." {21:22} Abraham rode one of his camels into the wilderness to find Ishmael, having heard he was living in a tent with his family. {21:23} Abraham arrived at Ishmael's tent around noon and asked about him. He found Ishmael's wife sitting in the tent with their children, while Ishmael and his mother were away. {21:24} Abraham asked Ishmael's wife, "Where is Ishmael?" She replied, "He has gone to the field to hunt." Abraham remained on his camel, as he had promised Sarah he would not dismount. {21:25} He then said to Ishmael's wife, "Please give me some water to drink; I am tired from my journey." {21:26} Ishmael's wife answered, "We have neither water nor bread," and she stayed in the tent, not recognizing Abraham or asking who he was. {21:27} Instead, she was scolding her children and cursing them and Ishmael. Abraham heard her words and became very angry. {21:28} He called her to come out to him, and she stood before him while he was still mounted. {21:29} Abraham said to Ishmael's wife, "When your husband returns, tell him these words: {21:30} An old man from the land of the Philistines came here seeking you, and I did not ask who he was. He instructed me to tell you this when he arrives: 'When Ishmael comes home, replace the nail in the door; let it be stronger, for he will be blessed and will dwell in tents, and all the tribes of the earth will seek him.'" {21:31} Abraham sent her away, and she returned to the tent. {21:32} When Ishmael returned, he found his wife in tears. He asked her what had happened. She told him, "An old man came from the land of the Philistines, and he said you are going to dwell in tents; take good care of your family." {21:33} Ishmael said to his wife, "Do not be afraid; God will help us. I will not leave you." {21:34} After a while, they had a son named Almon; Ishmael was thirty-four years old when he was born.

{22:1} Ishmael then got up, took his wife and children, along with his cattle and all his belongings, and traveled to his father in the land of the Philistines. {22:2} Abraham shared with Ishmael the story of his first wife and what had happened with her. {22:3} Ishmael and his children lived with Abraham for many days in that land, and Abraham stayed in the land of the Philistines for a long time. {22:4} As time passed, twenty-six years went by, and then Abraham, with his servants and everything he owned, left the land of the Philistines and traveled to a great distance, coming near Hebron, where they settled. The servants of Abraham dug wells there, and Abraham and all his household lived by the water. {22:5} When the servants of Abimelech, the king of the Philistines, heard that Abraham's servants had dug wells in the border of their land, {22:6} they came and quarreled with Abraham's servants, taking away the large well they had dug. {22:7} When Abimelech heard about this, he went to Abraham with Phicol, the captain of his army, and twenty of his men, and he spoke to Abraham about his servants. Abraham rebuked Abimelech for what his servants had done regarding the well. {22:8} Abimelech replied to Abraham, "As the Lord lives, who created the entire earth, I had no knowledge of what my servants did to yours until today." {22:9} Abraham took seven ewe lambs and gave them to Abimelech, saying, "Please accept these from me as a testimony that I dug this well." {22:10} Abimelech accepted the seven ewe lambs from Abraham, as he had also received much cattle and herds from him. Abimelech then swore to Abraham concerning the well, so he named that well Beersheba, because that was where they both swore an oath. {22:11} They made a covenant in Beersheba, after which Abimelech and Phicol, along with all his men, returned to the land of the Philistines, while Abraham and his household remained in Beersheba for a long time. {22:12} Abraham planted a large grove in Beersheba and built four gates facing the four cardinal directions. He also planted a vineyard there, so that any traveler passing by could enter through any gate, enjoy a meal, and then leave satisfied. {22:13} Abraham's house was always open to travelers, who would come to eat and drink there daily. {22:14} Anyone who was hungry and came to Abraham's house would receive bread to eat until they were satisfied, and if anyone arrived naked, he would provide them with clothing and gifts of silver and gold, sharing with them the knowledge of the Lord who created the earth. Abraham did this throughout his life. {22:15} Abraham, his children, and all his household lived in Beersheba, and he pitched his tent all the way to Hebron. {22:16} Abraham's brother Nahor, along with their father and all their family, remained in Haran, as they did not come with Abraham to the land of Canaan. {22:17} Nahor had children through Milcah, the daughter of Haran and sister of Sarah, Abraham's wife. {22:18} The names of Nahor's children were Uz, Buz, Kemuel, Kesed, Chazo, Pildash, Tidlaf, and Bethuel, totaling eight sons, all born to Milcah. {22:19} Nahor also had a concubine named Reumah, who bore him four sons: Zebach, Gachash, Tachash, and Maacha. {22:20} In total, Nahor had twelve sons, not counting his daughters, and they had children in Haran. {22:21} The children of Uz, Nahor's firstborn, were Abi, Cheref, Gadin, Melus, and their sister Deborah. {22:22} The sons of Buz were Berachel, Naamath, Sheva, and Madonu. {22:23} The sons of Kemuel were Aram and Rechob. {22:24} The sons of Kesed were Anamlech, Meshai, Benon, and Yifi; and the sons of Chazo were Pildash, Mechi, and Opher. {22:25} The sons of Pildash were Arud, Chamum, Mered, and Moloch. {22:26} The sons of Tidlaf were Mushan, Cushan, and Mutzi. {22:27} The children of Bethuel were Sechar, Laban, and their sister Rebecca. {22:28} These are the families of Nahor's children, born to them in Haran. Aram, the son of Kemuel, and his brother Rechob left Haran and found a valley by the Euphrates River. {22:29} They built a city there and named it after Pethor, the son of Aram; the city is called Aram Naharaim to this day. {22:30} The children of Kesed also sought a place to dwell and found a valley opposite the land of Shinar, where they settled. {22:31} They built a city and named it after their father, calling it Kesed; that area is known as Kasdim to this day, where the Kasdim thrived and multiplied greatly. {22:32} Terah, the father of Nahor and Abraham, took another wife in his old age named Pelilah, and she bore him a son named Zoba. {22:33} Terah lived twenty-five years after having Zoba. {22:34} Terah died in the year that marked the thirty-fifth year since Isaac, the son of Abraham, was born. {22:35} Terah lived for two hundred and five years and was buried in Haran. {22:36} Zoba, the son of Terah, lived for thirty years and had three sons: Aram, Achlis, and Merik. {22:37} Aram, the son of Zoba, had three wives and fathered twelve sons and three daughters. The Lord blessed Aram with riches, possessions, abundant cattle, and flocks, leading to his significant increase in wealth. {22:38} Aram, the son of Zoba, and his brothers left Haran to find a place to settle because their possessions were too great to remain there. {22:39} Aram traveled with his brothers and found a valley toward the eastern region, where they settled. {22:40} They built a city there and named it Aram, after their eldest brother; it is still called Aram Zoba today. {22:41} Meanwhile, Isaac, the son of Abraham, was growing up, and his father Abraham taught him the ways of the Lord so he would come to know the Lord, who was with him. {22:42} When Isaac turned thirty-seven, Ishmael, his brother, spent time with him in the tent. {22:43} Ishmael boasted to Isaac, saying, "I was thirteen years old when the Lord commanded my father to circumcise us, and I obeyed His word. I dedicated my life to the Lord, and I did not violate any command my father received from Him." {22:44} Isaac replied to Ishmael, "Why do you boast about this minor thing, a piece of flesh taken from your body, as if it were significant? The Lord commanded you regarding it. {22:45} As surely as the Lord lives, the God of my father Abraham, if the Lord asked my father to bring me as a burnt offering, he would gladly do so." {22:46} The Lord heard what Isaac said to Ishmael, and it pleased Him, prompting Him to test Abraham. {22:47} The day came when the sons of God presented themselves before the Lord, and Satan also appeared among them. {22:48} The Lord asked Satan, "Where have you come from?" and Satan replied, "From roaming the earth, walking back and forth on it." {22:49} The Lord then asked Satan, "What do you have to report about all the children of the earth?" and Satan answered, "I have seen all the children who serve you and remember you when they need something. {22:50} But when you grant their requests, they become complacent and forget about you." {22:51} "Have you noticed my servant Abraham? Initially, he had no children, yet he served you, built altars to you everywhere he went, offered sacrifices, and proclaimed your name to all the earth. {22:52} Now that he has a son, Isaac, he has turned away from you, holding a grand feast for all the people of the land, forgetting about you, Lord." {22:53} Despite all he has done, he has not brought you any offerings—no burnt offerings, peace offerings, oxen, lambs, or goats on the day of Isaac's weaning. {22:54} From the time of his son's birth until now, which is thirty-seven years, he has not built an altar for you or presented any offerings, because he realized you fulfilled his requests before him, and thus he forsook you." {22:55} The Lord said to Satan, "Have you truly considered my servant Abraham? There is no one like him on the earth, a perfect and upright man who fears God and shuns evil; I swear that if I told him to offer Isaac, his son, he would not hesitate to do so. He would be willing to present any burnt offering from his flock or herds as well."

{23:1} At that time, the word of the Lord came to Abraham, and He said, "Abraham," and he answered, "Here I am." {23:2} And God said, "Take now your son, your only son, Isaac, whom you love, and go to the land of Moriah. Offer him there as a burnt offering on one of the mountains I will show you. There you will see a cloud and the glory of the Lord." {23:3} Abraham thought to himself, "How can I separate my son Isaac from his mother Sarah in order to offer him as a sacrifice to the Lord?" {23:4} Abraham went into the tent and sat before Sarah, his wife, and said to her, {23:5} "Our son Isaac is grown, and he has not studied the ways of the Lord for some time. Tomorrow, I will take him to Shem and Eber, where he will learn to serve God. They will teach him to know the Lord and pray to Him continually, so God will answer him." {23:6} Sarah agreed, saying, "You have spoken well. Do as you say, but do not take him too far or keep him away too long, for my soul is bound to his." {23:7} Abraham replied, "Let us pray to the Lord our God that He will do good with us." {23:8} Sarah took Isaac, and he stayed with her that night. She kissed and embraced him and gave him instructions until morning. {23:9} She said, "Oh my son, how can I bear to be apart from you?" She continued to kiss and embrace him, then gave Abraham further instructions regarding him. {23:10} She said, "Take good care of him, my lord. He is my only son, and I have no other. {23:11} If he is hungry, give him food. If he is thirsty, give him water. Do not let him walk, and keep him out of the sun." {23:12} "Do not force him from anything he desires; do as he asks of you." {23:13} Sarah wept bitterly all night because of Isaac, giving him instructions until dawn. {23:14} In the morning, Sarah chose a beautiful garment, one Abimelech had given her, and dressed Isaac in it. She put a turban on his head and placed a precious stone in it. She also gave him provisions for the journey, and they set out. {23:15} Isaac and Abraham left with some of their servants who accompanied them for part of the way. {23:16} Sarah walked with them until they told her to return. {23:17} But Sarah, hearing Isaac's voice, wept bitterly. Abraham and Isaac also wept, along with those who were with them. {23:18} Sarah held Isaac in her arms, embracing him while weeping, saying, "Who knows if I will ever see you again after today?" {23:19} Abraham, Sarah, and Isaac continued weeping together, and all who were with them wept as well. Eventually, Sarah returned to the tent with her servants. {23:20} Abraham continued with Isaac to offer him as a sacrifice to the Lord, as commanded. {23:21} Abraham took two of his young men with him—his son Ishmael and his servant Eliezer—and they traveled together. Along the way, Ishmael said to Eliezer, {23:22} "My father is going to sacrifice Isaac, and when he returns, I will inherit all he has, for I am his firstborn." {23:23} Eliezer replied, "But didn't Abraham send you and your mother away and swear that you would not inherit? Surely, all his possessions will come to me, for I have served him faithfully." {23:24} As they continued, Satan appeared to Abraham as an old man, humble in spirit, and said, "Are you foolish to do this to your only son? {23:25} God gave him to you in your old age, and now you are going to kill him for no reason? {23:26} Surely, this cannot be God's will, for He would not ask such evil of anyone." {23:27} But Abraham recognized Satan's words and rebuked him, refusing to listen. Satan left him. {23:28} Satan then appeared to Isaac as a young man and said, "Do you know your old father is about to kill you for no reason?" {23:29} Isaac asked Abraham, "Father, have you heard what this man said to me?" {23:30} Abraham responded, "Do not listen to him, for he is Satan, trying to turn us from God's command." {23:31} Abraham rebuked Satan again, and he left. Then Satan reappeared in the form of a mighty brook, blocking their path. {23:32} The water began to rise as they entered it, reaching their necks, and they were terrified. {23:33} But Abraham realized that this was the work of Satan, as no water had been there before. {23:34} He rebuked Satan once more, saying, "The Lord rebuke you, Satan, for we follow God's commands." {23:35} The water disappeared, and the land returned to how it had been. {23:36} Abraham and Isaac continued on to the place God had shown them. {23:37} On the third day, Abraham lifted his eyes and saw the place from a distance. {23:38} A pillar of fire reached from the ground to the heavens, and the glory of the Lord appeared in a cloud. {23:39} Abraham asked Isaac, "Do you see what I see on the mountain?" {23:40} Isaac replied, "I see a pillar of fire and the glory of the Lord in the cloud." {23:41} Abraham knew then that Isaac was accepted as a sacrifice. {23:42} He asked Eliezer and Ishmael, "Do you also see what we see?" {23:43} But they answered, "We see nothing but mountains." So Abraham knew they were not chosen to go further with them. {23:44} He told them, "Stay here with the donkey while Isaac and I go to worship, and we will return to you." {23:45} Abraham took the wood and placed it on Isaac, while he carried the fire and the knife, and they continued on together. {23:46} Isaac said, "Father, I see the wood and fire, but where is the lamb for the sacrifice?" {23:47} Abraham answered, "The Lord has chosen you, my son, as the sacrifice." {23:48} Isaac said, "I will do all that the Lord has commanded with joy and gladness." {23:49} Abraham asked Isaac, "Do you have any doubts or concerns about this?" {23:50} Isaac answered, "No, father. There is nothing in my heart to turn me from what the Lord has spoken." {23:51} "I am full of joy that the Lord has chosen me as the offering." {23:52} Abraham rejoiced at Isaac's words, and they came to the place God had shown them. {23:53} Abraham began to build the altar, weeping as he did so, and Isaac helped gather the stones. {23:54} Abraham placed the wood on the altar, then bound Isaac and laid him upon it. {23:55} Isaac said, "Bind me tightly so I do not move when the knife strikes and profane the offering." {23:56} Abraham did so. Isaac then said, "When you have slain me, take my ashes to my mother and say, 'This is the sweet savor of Isaac,' but do not tell her if she is near a well or a high place, lest she throw herself in grief." {23:57} Abraham wept at his son's words, and Isaac wept as well, saying, "Do what the Lord has commanded." {23:58} They rejoiced in their hearts at following God's command, though their eyes wept bitterly. {23:59} Abraham took the knife to slay his son. {23:60} But the angels of mercy came before the Lord and said, "Lord, You are compassionate over all Your creatures. Have mercy on Isaac and Abraham, who have obeyed You." {23:61} They continued, "Have pity, O Lord, for Isaac is bound like a lamb to the slaughter." {23:62} The Lord appeared to Abraham from heaven and said, "Do not lay a hand on the boy. Now I know you fear God, for you did not withhold your only son." {23:63} Abraham looked up and saw a ram caught in a thicket. {23:64} This was the ram God had prepared since the creation of the world to take Isaac's place. {23:65} Satan had caught the ram's horns in the thicket to prevent it from coming to Abraham. {23:66} But Abraham retrieved it, unbound Isaac, and offered the ram in his place. {23:67} Abraham sprinkled the ram's blood on the altar, saying, "This is in place of my son." {23:68} He repeated this as he performed the rest of the service, which was accepted by God as if it had been Isaac himself. {23:69} The Lord blessed Abraham and his descendants. {23:70} Meanwhile, Satan went to Sarah, appearing as a humble old man. {23:71} He asked her, "Do you know where Abraham has gone?" {23:72} Sarah replied, "To study the ways of the Lord with Isaac." {23:73} Satan continued, "No, he has taken him to offer as a burnt offering to the Lord." {23:74} Sarah was struck with grief and wept bitterly.

{24:1} Sarah lived for one hundred and twenty-seven years, and she died. Abraham rose from beside her and sought a place to bury her. He spoke to the children of Heth, the inhabitants of the land, saying, {24:2} "I am a stranger and a traveler among you;

please sell me a piece of land to bury my dead." {24:3} The children of Heth replied to Abraham, "The land is before you, choose any of our tombs to bury your dead, and no one will refuse you." {24:4} But Abraham said, "If you are willing, ask Ephron, the son of Zochar, to sell me the cave of Machpelah at the end of his field. I will pay him full price for it, so I can use it as a burial place." {24:5} Ephron was living among the children of Heth, and they called for him. He came before Abraham, and Ephron said, {24:6} "All that you ask, I will do, and the field is yours. Take it and bury your dead." {24:7} But Abraham insisted, "No, I will buy the field and the cave at its full value, in front of witnesses, so it may be mine forever." {24:8} Ephron agreed, and Abraham weighed out four hundred shekels of silver, in the presence of Ephron and all his brothers, as payment. {24:9} Abraham recorded the purchase in writing and testified it with four witnesses: Amigal, son of Abishna the Hittite; Adichorom, son of Ashunach the Hivite; Abdon, son of Achiram the Gomerite; and Bakdil, son of Abudish the Zidonite. {24:10} Abraham wrote that the cave and field purchased from Ephron and his descendants, and all who enter their city, belonged to Abraham and his descendants as a burial place forever. He sealed the document and had it witnessed. {24:11} The field, the cave, and everything within its borders became the property of Abraham, near Mamre in Hebron, in the land of Canaan. {24:12} After this, Abraham buried Sarah in the cave, and the field and its surroundings became Abraham's possession as a burial site for his family. {24:13} Abraham buried Sarah with great ceremony, as was done for kings, and she was laid to rest in fine and beautiful garments. {24:14} Attending the funeral were Shem, his son Eber, Abimelech, and Anar, Ashcol, and Mamre. All the nobles of the land followed Sarah's bier. {24:15} Sarah had lived one hundred and twenty-seven years, and Abraham mourned deeply, observing the rites of mourning for seven days. {24:16} All the inhabitants of the land came to console Abraham and Isaac over Sarah's death. {24:17} After the mourning period, Abraham sent Isaac to the house of Shem and Eber to learn the ways of the Lord, and Isaac remained there for three years. {24:18} During this time, Abraham returned with his servants to Beersheba, where they settled. {24:19} That same year, Abimelech, king of the Philistines, died at the age of one hundred and ninety-three. Abraham went to the land of the Philistines to offer condolences to his family and servants, then returned home. {24:20} After Abimelech's death, the people of Gerar made his twelve-year-old son, Benmalich, king in his place, naming him Abimelech after his father, as was their custom. {24:21} Lot, Abraham's nephew, also died in those days, during Isaac's thirty-ninth year. Lot had lived for one hundred and forty years. {24:22} Lot's two sons, born to him by his daughters, were named Moab and Benami. {24:23} Moab and Benami married wives from the land of Canaan, and they had children. {24:24} The sons of Moab were Ed, Mayon, Tarsus, and Kanvil, and they became the ancestors of the Moabites. {24:25} The descendants of Lot spread out and built cities in the land where they lived, naming the cities after themselves. {24:26} Nahor, Abraham's brother, died during Isaac's fortieth year, after living one hundred and seventy-two years, and he was buried in Haran. {24:27} When Abraham heard of his brother's death, he grieved and mourned for many days. {24:28} Then Abraham called his servant Eliezer and gave him instructions concerning his household. Eliezer came and stood before him. {24:29} Abraham said, "I am old and do not know how much longer I will live. Rise and go to my homeland to find a wife for my son Isaac. Do not take a wife for him from the daughters of the Canaanites among whom we live. {24:30} Go to my family and my birthplace and take a wife from there. The Lord, who took me from my father's house and brought me to this land, promised to give this land to my descendants forever. He will send His angel before you and make your journey successful, so you may find a wife for my son." {24:31} Eliezer asked, "What if the woman is unwilling to follow me to this land? Should I take Isaac back to your homeland?" {24:32} Abraham replied, "No, do not take my son back there. The Lord, before whom I have walked, will send His angel with you to make your way successful." {24:33} Eliezer swore to do as Abraham asked, and he took ten camels and ten of Abraham's servants, setting off for Haran, the city of Abraham and Nahor, to find a wife for Isaac. {24:34} While they were on their way, Abraham sent for Isaac from the house of Shem and Eber, and Isaac returned home to Beersheba. {24:35} Eliezer and his men arrived in Haran and stopped by the well, making the camels kneel down by the water. {24:36} Eliezer prayed, "O God of my master Abraham, grant me success today and show kindness to my master by appointing a wife for Isaac from his family." {24:37} God answered Eliezer's prayer, and he met Rebecca, the daughter of Bethuel, son of Milcah and Nahor, Abraham's brother. {24:38} Eliezer went to her house, told them about his mission, and they rejoiced at the news. {24:39} They praised the Lord, who had arranged this, and gave Rebecca to be Isaac's wife. {24:40} Rebecca was very beautiful and still a virgin, and at the time, she was ten years old. {24:41} Bethuel, Laban, and their family prepared a feast that night for Eliezer and his men, and they all ate, drank, and rejoiced. {24:42} In the morning, Eliezer asked to be sent on his way, and the household agreed. They sent Rebecca with her nurse Deborah, the daughter of Uz, and gave her silver, gold, and servants as gifts. {24:43} Eliezer and his men took Rebecca and returned to Abraham in the land of Canaan. {24:44} Isaac took Rebecca as his wife and brought her into his mother's tent. {24:45} Isaac was forty years old when he married Rebecca, the daughter of Bethuel, his uncle.

{25:1} At that time, Abraham, now in his old age, took another wife named Keturah, from the land of Canaan. {25:2} She bore him six sons: Zimran, Jokshan, Medan, Midian, Ishbak, and Shuach. {25:3} Zimran's sons were Abihen, Molich, and Narim. Jokshan's sons were Sheba and Dedan. Medan's sons were Amida, Joab, Gochi, Elisha, and Nothach. Midian's sons were Ephah, Epher, Chanoch, Abida, and Eldaah. {25:4} Ishbak's sons were Makiro, Beyodua, and Tator. {25:5} Shuach's sons were Bildad, Mamdad, Munan, and Meban. These were the families of Keturah, Abraham's wife, who bore him these children. {25:6} Abraham gave gifts to these children and sent them away from his son Isaac, to settle where they could find a home. {25:7} They moved eastward and built six cities, where they lived to this day. {25:8} However, the children of Sheba and Dedan, sons of Jokshan, did not live with their relatives in the cities; instead, they traveled and camped in the wilderness to this day. {25:9} The sons of Midian moved east of Cush, where they found a large valley and built a city, living there to this day. {25:10} Midian lived in this city with his five sons and their families. {25:11} The names of Midian's sons, based on the cities they lived in, were Ephah, Epher, Chanoch, Abida, and Eldaah. {25:12} Ephah's sons were Methach, Meshar, Avi, and Tzanua. Epher's sons were Ephron, Zur, Alirun, and Medin. Chanoch's sons were Reuel, Rekem, Azi, Alyoshub, and Alad. {25:13} Abida's sons were Chur, Melud, Kerury, and Molchi. Eldaah's sons were Miker, Reba, Malchiyah, and Gabol. These were the Midianite families, who later spread throughout the land. {25:14} These are the descendants of Ishmael, Abraham's son, whom Hagar, Sarah's maid, bore to him. {25:15} Ishmael took a wife from Egypt named Ribah, also called Meribah. {25:16} Ribah bore him Nebayoth, Kedar, Adbeel, Mibsam, and a daughter named Bosmath. {25:17} Ishmael divorced Ribah, and she returned to Egypt, to her father's house, because she was displeasing to both Ishmael and Abraham. {25:18} Later, Ishmael married a Canaanite woman named Malchuth, and she bore him Nishma, Dumah, Masa, Chadad, Tema, Yetur, Naphish, and Kedma. {25:19} These were the twelve princes of Ishmael's descendants, based on their nations. Ishmael gathered his children, possessions, and household, and moved to settle wherever they could find a place. {25:20} They eventually settled near the wilderness of Paran, with their territory stretching from Havilah to Shur, near Egypt, heading toward Assyria. {25:21} Ishmael and his sons lived in the land, had many children, and multiplied greatly. {25:22} Nebayoth's sons were Mend, Send, and Mayon. Kedar's sons were Alyon, Kezem, Chamad, and Eli. {25:23} Adbeel's sons were Chamad and Jabin. Mibsam's sons were Obadiah, Ebedmelech, and Yeush. These were Ribah's descendants. {25:24} Mishma, son of Ishmael, had sons named Shamua, Zecaryon, and Obed. Dumah's sons were Kezed, Eli, Machmad, and Amed. {25:25} Masa's sons were Melon, Mula, and Ebidadon. Chadad's sons were Azur, Minzar, and Ebedmelech. {25:26} Tema's sons were Seir, Sadon, and Yakol. Yetur's sons were Merith, Yaish, Alyo, and Pachoth. {25:27} Naphish's sons were Ebed-Tamed, Abiyasaph, and Mir. Kedma's sons were Calip, Tachti, and Omir. These were Malchuth's children, Ishmael's descendants, based on their families. {25:28} These are the generations of Ishmael, who lived in the lands they built to this day. {25:29} At that time, Rebecca, Isaac's wife and the daughter of

Bethuel, was barren. Isaac was living with his father Abraham in Canaan, and the Lord was with him. {25:30} During this time, Arpachshad, son of Shem and grandson of Noah, died at the age of 438, in the forty-eighth year of Isaac's life.

{26:1} In Isaac's fifty-ninth year, Rebecca was still barren. {26:2} She said to Isaac, "I've heard that your mother Sarah was barren until your father Abraham prayed for her, and she conceived. {26:3} Please, pray for me too, so God will remember us." {26:4} Isaac replied, "Abraham has already prayed for me to have children, so the issue must be with you." {26:5} Rebecca insisted, urging Isaac to pray anyway, so he agreed, and they traveled to the land of Moriah to seek the Lord. {26:6} There, Isaac prayed to God on behalf of Rebecca, asking for children. {26:7} Isaac said, "O Lord, God of heaven and earth, who brought my father out of his homeland and promised to multiply his descendants like the stars of the sky and the sand on the shore, fulfill your promise now." {26:8} God heard Isaac's prayer, and Rebecca conceived. {26:9} After about seven months, the twins struggled within her, causing her great pain. She asked other women if they had experienced this, and they said no. {26:10} Troubled, Rebecca traveled to Moriah to seek God's guidance. She also consulted Shem and Eber and asked Abraham to inquire of the Lord. {26:11} They all sought the Lord, and the message came that two nations were in her womb, one stronger than the other, and the older would serve the younger. {26:12} When Rebecca's time came to give birth, she had twins, as the Lord had said. {26:13} The first was born red and hairy, and they named him Esau. {26:14} His brother followed, gripping Esau's heel, and they named him Jacob. {26:15} Isaac was sixty years old when his sons were born. {26:16} The boys grew up, and at fifteen, Esau became a cunning hunter, while Jacob was wise and stayed home, learning about the Lord and caring for the flocks. {26:17} Isaac, his household, and his sons lived with Abraham in Canaan, as God had commanded. {26:18} Meanwhile, Ishmael returned to Havilah with his children, and Abraham's concubines' children moved to the east, as Abraham had sent them away with gifts. {26:19} Abraham gave all his possessions to Isaac and entrusted him with his treasures. {26:20} He told Isaac to remember that the Lord is the only God in heaven and on earth. {26:21} He reminded Isaac that God had delivered him from Ur and brought him to this land, promising to give it to his descendants if they kept His commandments. {26:22} Abraham urged Isaac to remain faithful to God and obey His commands so that it would be well with him and his children. {26:23} Isaac promised to follow all that his father had taught him, to stay on the right path. {26:24} Abraham blessed Isaac and taught Jacob the ways of the Lord. {26:25} Then, at that time, Abraham died at the age of 175, in the fifteenth year of Jacob and Esau's lives. {26:26} Isaac and Ishmael buried Abraham. {26:27} When the people of Canaan heard of Abraham's death, they came with their leaders to mourn and bury him. {26:28} Even the people of Haran and Abraham's extended family came to honor him. {26:29} They all remembered Abraham's kindness and comforted Isaac, burying Abraham in the cave he bought from Ephron the Hittite. {26:30} The people of Canaan mourned Abraham for a whole year, both men and women, because he had been good to all. {26:31} Children and adults alike wept for him because of his uprightness before God and man. {26:32} No one had feared God as Abraham had, serving Him faithfully from youth to old age. {26:33} The Lord had been with Abraham, delivering him from the schemes of Nimrod and helping him defeat the four kings of Elam. {26:34} Abraham had taught all the people of the earth about God and spread the knowledge of Him to all his descendants. {26:35} Isaac then rose and became the ruler of his people, just as Abraham had before him.

{27:1} Esau, after Abraham's death, often went hunting in the field. {27:2} Nimrod, the king of Babel (also called Amraphel), would also frequently go hunting with his mighty men and walk about with them in the cool of the day. {27:3} Nimrod had been watching Esau for some time, and jealousy began to grow in his heart against him. {27:4} One day, Esau went out to hunt and found Nimrod walking in the wilderness with two of his men. {27:5} Although Nimrod's mighty men were nearby, they had moved a distance away from him, and they spread out in different directions to hunt. Esau, seeing an opportunity, hid himself and waited for Nimrod. {27:6} Nimrod and his men did not notice Esau lurking in the wilderness, and they continued their usual practice of walking about in the field at the cool of the day, checking on their men who were hunting. {27:7} When Nimrod and his two companions came near, Esau suddenly leapt from his hiding place, drew his sword, and quickly ran toward Nimrod, striking off his head. {27:8} Esau then engaged in a fierce fight with Nimrod's two men, and when they cried out for help, Esau turned and killed them as well. {27:9} Nimrod's other mighty men, who had gone off to the wilderness, heard the cries from a distance. Recognizing the voices, they rushed back to find out what had happened, only to discover their king and his two men lying dead. {27:10} Seeing Nimrod's men approaching, Esau fled and escaped. He took the valuable garments of Nimrod, which had been passed down to him from his father and which gave power over the land, and Esau ran and hid them in his house. {27:11} He came back to the city exhausted and near death from the fight and grief. He sat down before his brother Jacob and said, "I am about to die today. What use is my birthright to me now?" {27:12} Jacob, being wise, seized the opportunity and bought Esau's birthright, for this was the Lord's plan. {27:13} Esau also sold Jacob his portion of the cave of Machpelah, which Abraham had bought from the children of Heth as a burial ground. Jacob paid him and took possession of both the birthright and the burial place. {27:14} Jacob recorded all of this in a book, had witnesses testify, and sealed the deal. The book remained with Jacob. {27:15} When Nimrod, the son of Cush, was found dead, his men, full of fear, took his body and buried him in his city. Nimrod had lived for two hundred and fifteen years. {27:16} He had reigned over the land for one hundred and eighty-five years, but in the end, he was killed by Esau in shame, just as he had foreseen in a dream. {27:17} After Nimrod's death, his kingdom was divided, and all lands he had conquered were returned to their original kings. The house of Nimrod remained enslaved to other kings for a long time.

{28:1} In those days, after Abraham's death, a great famine came upon the land. The famine hit Canaan hard, and Isaac prepared to go down to Egypt, just as his father Abraham had done. {28:2} But the Lord appeared to Isaac that night and told him, "Do not go down to Egypt. Instead, go to Gerar and stay with Abimelech, king of the Philistines, until the famine passes." {28:3} Isaac obeyed and went to Gerar, where he stayed for a whole year. {28:4} The people of Gerar noticed that Rebecca, Isaac's wife, was very beautiful. They asked him about her, and Isaac, afraid for his life, said she was his sister. {28:5} The princes of Gerar praised Rebecca's beauty to the king, but Abimelech did not respond to their words. {28:6} However, he kept in mind that Isaac had said she was his sister. {28:7} After Isaac had been in Gerar for three months, Abimelech looked out of his window and saw Isaac affectionately interacting with Rebecca, proving she was his wife. {28:8} Abimelech called Isaac and said, "What have you done to us? You said she was your sister! Someone could have taken her as a wife, and you would have brought guilt upon us." {28:9} Isaac explained that he was afraid for his life and therefore said she was his sister. {28:10} Abimelech, concerned for the safety of his people, commanded that Isaac and Rebecca be dressed in princely garments and paraded through the streets. He made a proclamation that anyone who touched them would be put to death. {28:11} After this, Isaac returned to live in the king's house, and the Lord blessed him greatly. {28:12} Isaac found favor with Abimelech, who remembered the covenant between Abraham and his father. {28:13} Abimelech told Isaac, "The whole land is before you. Dwell wherever you like until you return to Canaan." {28:14} He gave Isaac fields, vineyards, and the best parts of the land to farm until the famine ended. {28:15} Isaac sowed in the land and reaped a hundredfold in the same year, as the Lord blessed him. {28:16} He became very prosperous, owning large herds of flocks and many servants. {28:17} When the famine ended, the Lord appeared to Isaac and told him to return to Canaan. Isaac obeyed and returned to Hebron with all his family and possessions. {28:18} That same year, Shelah, the son of Arpachshad, died at the age of 433. This was the eighteenth year of the lives of Jacob and Esau. {28:19} Isaac then sent Jacob to the house of Shem and Eber, where Jacob studied the ways of the Lord for thirty-two years. Esau, however, stayed behind in Canaan, refusing to go. {28:20} Esau continued hunting as he always had, spending his days deceiving and manipulating people. He became a skillful and valiant man in the field, and eventually, his hunting brought him to Seir, in the land of Edom. {28:21} Esau stayed in Seir for a year and four months, hunting in the field. {28:22} While there, Esau saw a woman named Jehudith, the daughter of Beeri, from the Heth family of Canaan, and he took her as his wife. {28:23} He was forty years old when he married her and brought her back to Hebron, where his father Isaac lived. {28:24} In the 110th year of Isaac's life, which was the fiftieth year of Jacob's life, Shem, the son of Noah, died at the age of six hundred. {28:25} After Shem's death, Jacob returned to his father's house in Hebron, in the land of Canaan. {28:26} In the fifty-sixth year of Jacob's life, messengers came from Haran with news for Rebecca about her brother Laban. {28:27} Laban's wife had been barren for many years, and neither she nor her handmaids had borne any children. {28:28} But the Lord remembered Adinah, Laban's wife, and she conceived, giving birth to twin daughters. Laban named the elder Leah and the younger Rachel. {28:29} When Rebecca heard this news, she rejoiced greatly that the Lord had blessed her brother Laban with children.

{29:1} Isaac, the son of Abraham, grew old and his eyesight became weak with age, and he could no longer see. {29:2} At this time, Isaac called for Esau, his son, and said, "Take your weapons—your quiver and bow—and go into the field to hunt some wild game for me. {29:3} Prepare me a tasty meal that I love, and bring it to me so I may eat and bless you before I die, as I am now old and gray." {29:4} Esau obeyed, taking his weapons and going into the field to hunt for wild game, as he usually did, to bring to his father. {29:5} Meanwhile, Rebekah overheard Isaac's words to Esau and quickly called her son Jacob, saying, "Your father has spoken these words to Esau. {29:6} Now, do what I tell you: Go to the flock and bring me two young goats, and I will prepare a delicious meal for your father, just as he likes. {29:7} Then you will take it to your father to eat, so he will bless you before Esau returns from his hunt." {29:8} Jacob hurried and did as his mother instructed. He prepared the meal and brought it to his father before Esau came back. {29:9} Isaac, unaware, asked, "Who are you, my son?" Jacob replied, "I am Esau, your firstborn. I have done as you asked. Now, please sit up and eat so that you may bless me." {29:10} Isaac ate and drank, and his heart was content. He blessed Jacob, and Jacob left just as Esau returned from his hunt. {29:11} Esau also prepared a meal and brought it to his father. "Let my father eat and bless me," he said. {29:12} But Isaac asked, "Who are you?" And Esau answered, "I am your son, Esau, your firstborn." {29:13} Isaac trembled violently and said, "Who was it, then, that brought me game earlier? I ate it and blessed him, and indeed, he will be blessed!" {29:14} Esau, realizing Jacob had deceived his father, wept bitterly and said, "Isn't he rightly named Jacob (meaning 'supplanter')? He has cheated me twice—first he took my birthright, and now he has taken my blessing!" {29:15} Isaac replied, "What can I do for you, my son? Your brother has taken the blessing by deceit." {29:16} Esau's anger burned against Jacob because of the blessing, and he plotted to kill him. {29:17} Jacob, afraid of his brother's wrath, fled to the house of Eber, son of Shem, where he stayed for fourteen years, learning the ways of the Lord and His commandments. {29:18} Esau, seeing that Jacob had fled, was deeply grieved and upset with his parents. He left them and moved to the land of Seir, where he married a woman named Bosmath, daughter of Elon the Hittite, whom he renamed Adah. {29:19} Esau stayed in Seir for six months, but later returned to Hebron, bringing his two wives to live with his parents. {29:20} Isaac and Rebekah were troubled by Esau's wives because they did not follow the ways of the Lord but served idols, and this greatly distressed Isaac and Rebekah. {29:21} Rebekah said, "I am weary of life because of these Hittite women. If Jacob marries one of them, my life will be worthless." {29:22} Meanwhile, Esau's wife Adah bore him a son, Eliphaz, when Esau was sixty-five. {29:23} Around this time, Ishmael, Abraham's son, died at the age of 137. Isaac mourned for him many days. {29:24} After fourteen years, Jacob decided to visit his parents, and Esau had forgotten his anger for a time. {29:25} But when Esau saw Jacob returning, his hatred resurfaced, and he plotted once again to kill him after their father's death. {29:26} Rebekah, hearing of Esau's plan, urged Jacob to flee to her brother Laban in Haran until Esau's anger subsided. {29:27} Isaac called Jacob, blessed him, and warned him not to marry a Canaanite woman but to find a wife from Laban's family, as their father Abraham had instructed. {29:28} He urged Jacob to follow God's ways, not to turn aside, and prayed for God's blessing upon him and his descendants. {29:29} Isaac also prayed that God would grant Jacob prosperity and many children, and that he would one day return to the land of Canaan with great wealth. {29:30} After this blessing, Jacob left Beersheba and journeyed to Padan-aram, being seventy-seven years old. {29:31} Meanwhile, Esau secretly instructed his son Eliphaz to kill Jacob on the road and take his possessions. {29:32} Eliphaz, though only thirteen, obeyed his father, gathering ten men and pursuing Jacob. {29:33} They caught up with him near Shechem, and Eliphaz prepared to kill him. {29:34} But Jacob, realizing what was happening, pleaded with Eliphaz, offering all his wealth if he would spare his life. {29:35} Eliphaz, moved by Jacob's words, took his possessions but spared his life, considering it a righteous act. {29:36} Eliphaz and his men returned to Esau, giving him all that they had taken from Jacob. {29:37} Esau was furious that they had not killed Jacob, but Eliphaz explained that they had pitied him. {29:38} Esau, seeing the spoils of Jacob, took the wealth and stored it in his house. {29:39} Realizing that his father and mother disapproved of Canaanite women, Esau went to his uncle Ishmael and married Ishmael's daughter, Machlath, in addition to his other wives.

{30:1} As Jacob continued his journey, he reached Mount Moriah and spent the night near the city of Luz. {30:2} The Lord appeared to Jacob in a dream and promised to give the land he was resting on to his descendants, multiplying them like the stars of the sky. {30:3} The Lord also promised to protect Jacob and bring him back to this land with great joy, children, and riches. {30:4} Jacob awoke, overjoyed by the vision, and named the place Bethel. {30:5} Feeling light and joyful, Jacob continued his journey to Haran and stopped by a well where he met men from the area. {30:6} He asked if they knew Laban, Nahor's son, and they replied that they did. Just then, Laban's daughter Rachel came to the well with her father's sheep, as she was a shepherdess. {30:7} Upon seeing Rachel, Jacob ran to her, kissed her, and wept, explaining that he was her father's sister's son. {30:8} Rachel ran to tell her father, and Jacob, still weeping, explained to Laban why he had nothing to offer. {30:9} Laban welcomed Jacob into his home, fed him, and listened to Jacob's tale of his brother Esau's actions and Eliphaz's attack. {30:10} After a month, Laban asked Jacob what wages he wanted for working for him, as he couldn't have him serve for nothing. {30:11} Laban had no sons, only daughters. His two daughters were Leah, the elder, and Rachel, the younger, with Leah being tender-eyed (likely meaning gentle or weak in eyesight), while Rachel was beautiful. {30:12} Jacob loved Rachel and offered to work seven years for her hand in marriage, and Laban agreed. {30:13} Jacob stayed with Laban, and during this time, in the second year of his stay, Eber, the son of Shem, died at 464 years old. {30:14} Jacob mourned deeply for Eber. {30:15} During Jacob's third year in Haran, Esau's wife Bosmath bore him a son named Reuel. {30:16} In the fourth year of Jacob's stay, the Lord blessed Laban on account of Jacob, and Laban's wife bore him sons—Beor, Alib, and Chorash. {30:17} Laban's wealth and honor increased greatly, thanks to Jacob. {30:18} Jacob faithfully worked in Laban's house and fields, and the Lord's blessing was evident in everything Laban had. {30:19} In the fifth year, Esau's wife Jehudith, daughter of Beeri, died, having borne only daughters. {30:20} Her daughters' names were Marzith, the elder, and Puith, the younger. {30:21} After Jehudith's death, Esau moved to Seir to hunt, as was his habit. {30:22} In the sixth year, Esau took a new wife, Ahlibamah, daughter of Zebeon the Hivite, and she bore him three sons: Yeush, Yaalan, and Korah. {30:23} During the seventh year of Jacob's work for Laban, the seven-year period ended & Jacob asked Laban to give him Rachel. But Laban deceived Jacob by giving him Leah instead, because, as he said, it was not their custom to marry younger daughter before the elder.

{31:1} After seven years of working for Laban, Jacob completed his service and said to Laban, "Give me my wife, for my time is up." Laban agreed, and they gathered all the people of the area to celebrate with a feast. {31:2} In the evening, Laban went to the house, and after Jacob arrived with the guests, Laban dimmed all the lights in the house. {31:3} Jacob asked Laban why he did this, and

Laban replied, "This is how we do things in this land." {31:4} Then Laban took his daughter Leah and brought her to Jacob, who did not realize it was Leah. {31:5} Laban also gave Leah his maidservant Zilpah to serve her. {31:6} Everyone at the feast knew what Laban had done, but they did not tell Jacob. {31:7} All the neighbors came to Jacob's house that night, ate, drank, and danced in celebration, calling out "Heleah, Heleah" as they performed. {31:8} Jacob heard their words but didn't understand their meaning, thinking it was just part of their customs. {31:9} The neighbors continued speaking these words during the night while Laban kept the lights dimmed. {31:10} In the morning, when daylight came, Jacob turned to his wife and saw that it was Leah lying beside him. He exclaimed, "Now I understand what the neighbors were saying last night, 'Heleah,' and I didn't realize it." {31:11} Jacob called Laban and said, "What have you done to me? I worked for you to have Rachel as my wife. Why have you deceived me and given me Leah?" {31:12} Laban responded, "In our place, we don't marry off the younger daughter before the older one. If you want Rachel, you can have her, but you must work for me another seven years." {31:13} Jacob agreed and took Rachel as his wife, serving Laban for another seven years. He loved Rachel more than Leah, and Laban gave Rachel his maid Bilhah as her servant. {31:14} When the Lord saw that Leah was unloved, He opened her womb, and she bore Jacob four sons during that time. {31:15} Their names were Reuben, Simeon, Levi, and Judah, and afterward, she stopped having children. {31:16} Rachel was barren and envied her sister Leah. When Rachel saw that she had not given Jacob any children, she took her maid Bilhah and gave her to Jacob as a wife, and Bilhah bore Jacob two sons, Dan and Naphtali. {31:17} When Leah saw that she had stopped bearing children, she gave her maid Zilpah to Jacob as a wife, and Zilpah bore Jacob two sons, Gad and Asher. {31:18} Leah then conceived again and gave Jacob two more sons and one daughter named Dinah. {31:19} Rachel remained childless during this time, and she prayed to the Lord, saying, "O Lord God, remember me and see my suffering. I beg you, for now my husband will reject me because I have not given him any children." {31:20} Rachel pleaded, "Hear my prayer, Lord, and see my affliction. Give me children like one of the handmaids so I won't be ashamed anymore." {31:21} God heard her and opened her womb, and Rachel conceived and bore a son. She said, "The Lord has removed my shame," and named him Joseph, saying, "May the Lord add another son to me." Jacob was ninety-one years old when she had him. {31:22} At that time, Jacob's mother Rebecca sent her nurse Deborah, the daughter of Uz, and two of Isaac's servants to Jacob. {31:23} They arrived in Haran and said to Jacob, "Rebecca has sent us to tell you to return to your father's house in Canaan." Jacob listened to their message from his mother. {31:24} Meanwhile, the seven years Jacob worked for Rachel had also ended, and after fourteen years in Haran, he told Laban, "Give me my wives and let me leave to my own land. My mother sent word for me to return to my father's house." {31:25} Laban pleaded with him, saying, "Please don't leave me; if I have found favor in your sight, appoint your wages, and I will pay you, so you will stay." {31:26} Jacob replied, "This is what you can pay me: I will go through all your flocks and take every lamb that is speckled, spotted, or brown among the sheep and goats. If you agree to this, I will tend your flocks as before." {31:27} Laban agreed and removed all the sheep that matched Jacob's conditions and gave them to him. {31:28} Jacob took what Laban had given him and put it in the hands of his sons, while Jacob tended the remaining flocks. {31:29} When Isaac's servants saw that Jacob was not returning to Canaan with them, they went back home. {31:30} Deborah stayed with Jacob in Haran and did not return to Isaac's servants. She lived with Jacob's wives and children. {31:31} Jacob served Laban for six more years. Whenever the sheep gave birth, he kept the speckled and spotted ones, as he had agreed with Laban, and he prospered greatly during these years. {31:32} Jacob had 200 herds of cattle, which were large, beautiful, and very productive. Many people wanted to acquire some of Jacob's cattle because he was so successful. {31:33} Many of the sons of men came to trade for some of Jacob's flock, and Jacob would exchange a sheep for a servant, maid, donkey, camel, or whatever he desired. {31:34} Jacob gained wealth, honor, and possessions through these dealings with others, which made Laban's children envious of him. {31:35} Over time, Jacob heard Laban's sons say, "Jacob has taken away all that belonged to our father and has gained this wealth." {31:36} Jacob noticed that Laban's attitude toward him had changed and was not as friendly as it had been before. {31:37} The Lord appeared to Jacob after six years and told him, "Get up, leave this land, and return to your birthplace, and I will be with you." {31:38} Jacob then gathered his children, wives, and all his belongings onto camels and set off for Canaan to his father Isaac. {31:39} Laban did not know that Jacob had left him because he was busy shearing sheep that day. {31:40} Rachel stole her father's household gods and hid them on the camel she was riding. {31:41} The way these idols were made involved taking a firstborn son, killing him, removing the hair from his head, salting the head, anointing it with oil, and writing a name on a small tablet of metal or gold to place under the tongue, then putting the head with the tablet in the house, lighting candles before it, and bowing down to it. {31:42} When they bowed to the idols, they would speak to them in response to their questions through the power of the name inscribed. {31:43} Some made these idols in the form of men, using gold and silver, and consulted them at specific times, believing they could tell the future by their influence from the stars, which is how Rachel stole her father's idols. {31:44} Rachel took these images so that Laban wouldn't be able to find Jacob by consulting them. {31:45} When Laban returned home and realized Jacob was missing, he sought his idols, but they were nowhere to be found. He consulted other idols to ask where Jacob had gone and learned that Jacob had fled to his father's land, Canaan. {31:46} Laban then set off with his brothers and servants to pursue Jacob and caught up with him in Mount Gilead. {31:47} Laban confronted Jacob, saying, "Why have you fled and deceived me, taking my daughters and their children like captives? {31:48} You didn't even let me kiss them goodbye or send them away joyfully, and you stole my gods." {31:49} Jacob replied, "I was afraid you would take your daughters away by force from me; whoever finds your gods will die." {31:50} Laban searched all of Jacob's tents and belongings but could not find his idols. {31:51} Laban proposed a covenant, saying, "If you mistreat my daughters or take other wives besides them, God will be a witness between us." {31:52} They took stones and made a heap as a witness, and Laban named the heap Gilead. {31:53} Jacob and Laban offered sacrifices on the mountain and ate beside the heap, spending the night there. In the morning, Laban wept with his daughters, kissed them, and returned to his place. {31:54} Laban hurriedly sent his son Beor, who was seventeen, with Abichorof, the son of Uz, and ten other men to meet Esau. {31:55} They traveled ahead of Jacob and took another route to the land of Seir. {31:56} They approached Esau and said, "Your brother Jacob is coming, and he has grown rich and powerful in Haran; he has acquired cattle and wealth. He sends his greetings to you." {31:57} Esau was very angry with Jacob for taking the blessings of their father and their inheritance, and when Esau heard the report, he gathered four hundred men to confront Jacob. {31:58} Jacob was alarmed and afraid that Esau would harm him and his family, so he divided his group into two camps, thinking, "If Esau comes to one camp and attacks it, the other camp can escape." {31:59} That night, Jacob prayed, saying, "O God of my father Abraham and Isaac, you said, 'Return to your own land, and I will be with you.' {31:60} I am unworthy of all the kindness and faithfulness you have shown me. I have crossed this Jordan with only my staff, but now I have become two camps. {31:61} Deliver me from the hand of my brother Esau, for I fear him. {31:62} You promised to bless me and make my descendants like the sand of the sea. " {31:63} He prayed fervently, laying his fears before God, and the next morning sent his servants ahead of him with gifts for Esau to soften his heart. {31:64} Jacob's servants returned and told him that Esau was coming to meet him with four hundred men. {31:65} Jacob was distressed, but he remained committed to his mission. {31:66} He prayed again, and then took his family and crossed the river Jabbok. He sent them on ahead while he stayed back to pray alone. {31:67} That night, Jacob wrestled with a mysterious man, which lasted until dawn. {31:68} The man touched Jacob's hip socket, and Jacob's hip was wrenched. {31:69} As dawn broke, the man told Jacob to let him go, but Jacob replied, "I will not let you go unless you bless me." {31:70} The man asked, "What is your name?" Jacob said, "Jacob." {31:71} The man replied, "Your name will no longer be Jacob, but Israel, because you have struggled with God and men and have overcome." {31:72} Jacob called the place Peniel, saying, "I have seen God face to face, and yet my life has been spared." {31:73} As he limped away, the sun rose over him, and he crossed over to Esau, who ran to Jacob and embraced him, crying tears of joy. {31:74} They reconciled, and Jacob said, "I see your face as one sees the face of God." {31:75} Jacob and Esau then wept together, and Esau offered to accompany Jacob, but Jacob declined, saying that he would join Esau later. {31:76} They parted ways, and Jacob continued his journey into the land of Canaan. {31:77} Jacob then built an altar to the Lord in Shechem and named it El Elohe Israel, meaning "God, the God of Israel." {31:78} The next years passed peacefully for Jacob, as he prospered in the land, multiplying greatly in wealth, family, and blessings.

{32:1} At that time, Jacob sent messengers to his brother Esau in the land of Seir, and he instructed them to speak words of humility. {32:2} He commanded them to say to his lord Esau, "This is your servant Jacob speaking. Do not think that the blessing my father gave me has been of any benefit to me. {32:3} I have spent twenty years with Laban, who deceived me and changed my wages ten times, as you have already been told. {32:4} I worked very hard in his household, and God saw my suffering, my labor, and the work of my hands, and He granted me favor in Laban's eyes. {32:5} It was through God's great mercy and kindness that I acquired oxen, donkeys, cattle, servants, and maidservants. {32:6} Now I am returning to my homeland and my parents in Canaan, and I wanted you to know this so that I might find favor in your sight, and that you wouldn't think I obtained this wealth on my own or that my father's blessing has helped me. {32:7} The messengers went to Esau and found him at the border of Edom, heading toward Jacob with four hundred men, all armed. {32:8} They delivered Jacob's message to Esau. {32:9} Esau responded with pride and contempt, saying, "I have heard what Jacob has done to Laban, who treated him well and gave him his daughters as wives. He fathered many children and gained great wealth in Laban's house. {32:10} When Jacob saw that he had become wealthy, he fled with all his possessions, taking Laban's daughters away as captives without telling their father. {32:11} Jacob has done this not just to Laban but to me as well; he has cheated me twice. Should I remain silent? {32:12} Therefore, I have come today with my men to confront him, and I will deal with him as I see fit." {32:13} The messengers returned to Jacob and said, "We spoke to your brother Esau, and he is coming to meet you with four hundred men." {32:14} Jacob was greatly afraid and distressed, so he prayed to the Lord his God, saying, {32:15} "O Lord God of my grandfather Abraham and my father Isaac, you said to me when I left my father's house, {32:16} 'I am the Lord God of your father Abraham and Isaac. To you, I give this land and your descendants after you. I will make your descendants as numerous as the stars in the sky, and you will spread out to the four corners of the earth, and through you and your descendants, all nations will be blessed.' {32:17} You have fulfilled your promises and have given me wealth, children, and cattle. You have granted my heart's desires, so that I lack nothing. {32:18} You then told me to return to my home and to my family, and that you would be good to me. {32:19} Now that I have come back, I fear that I will fall into Esau's hands, and he will kill me along with my family. {32:20} So, O Lord God, I pray for deliverance from my brother Esau, for I am terrified of him. {32:21} If I have done wrong, please do it for the sake of Abraham and my father Isaac. {32:22} I know that I have acquired my wealth through kindness and mercy, so I beseech you to deliver me today with your kindness and respond to my prayers." {32:23} After finishing his prayer, Jacob divided the people with him, along with his flocks and herds, into two camps, assigning half of them to Damesek, the son of Eliezer, Abraham's servant, as one camp, and the other half to Elianus, another son of Eliezer. {32:24} He instructed them to keep a distance from each other so that if Esau attacked one camp, the other could escape. {32:25} Jacob stayed that night, giving his servants directions regarding their positions and his children. {32:26} The Lord heard Jacob's prayer that day and delivered him from Esau's hands. {32:27} The Lord sent three angels from heaven, and they went ahead of Esau. {32:28} These angels appeared to Esau and his men as two thousand warriors on horses, equipped with various weapons, and they divided into four camps, each led by a chief. {32:29} One camp approached Esau and his four hundred men, causing them to panic, and Esau fell off his horse in fear, as all his men scattered in terror. {32:30} The camp shouted at them as they fled, declaring, "We are the servants of Jacob, who serves God. Who can stand against us?" Esau said to them, "Oh, my lord Jacob is your lord? I have not seen him in twenty years, and now that I am here to meet him, you treat me like this?" {32:31} The angels replied, "As the Lord lives, if Jacob were not your brother, we would have wiped out you and your men. It is only because of Jacob that we will do nothing." {32:32} That camp moved away from Esau and his men, and as they traveled about a league, the second camp approached and did the same thing as the first camp. {32:33} After they left, the third camp came toward Esau, terrifying him again. He fell off his horse, and his entire camp cried out, "Surely we are the servants of Jacob, who serves God. Who can stand against us?" {32:34} Esau responded again, "Jacob, my lord and your lord, is my brother. For twenty years I have not seen him. I came to meet him today, and now you treat me like this?" {32:35} They answered him, saying, "As the Lord lives, if Jacob were not your brother as you claim, we would have left none of you or your men alive. We will not harm you or your men because of Jacob." {32:36} The third camp left him, and Esau continued his journey toward Jacob when the fourth camp approached, and they also frightened him and his men. {32:37} When Esau realized the terror that the four angels had caused, he became extremely afraid of Jacob and decided to meet him peacefully. {32:38} Esau hid his hatred for Jacob because he feared for his life, believing that the four camps he encountered were Jacob's servants. {32:39} Jacob stayed that night with his servants in their camps and resolved to give Esau a present from all he had. {32:40} The next morning, Jacob and his men selected a gift for Esau. {32:41} Jacob chose two hundred and forty sheep, thirty camels and donkeys, and fifty cows as gifts. {32:42} He organized them into ten groups, placing each type of animal in separate herds, and assigned ten of his servants to take each group ahead. {32:43} He instructed them to keep a distance from one another and create space between the groups. When Esau and his men asked, "Whose animals are these, and where are you going?" they were to respond, "We are servants of Jacob, and we are on our way to meet Esau in peace. Jacob is following us." {32:44} They were to say, "This is a gift from Jacob to his brother Esau." {32:45} If they asked, "Why does he delay in coming to meet his brother?" they were to answer, "He is coming joyfully behind us because he said, 'I will appease him with the gift going ahead, and then I will see his face; perhaps he will accept me.'" {32:46} The entire gift passed into the hands of Jacob's servants, who took it ahead of him that day. Jacob spent the night with his camps at the border of the brook Jabbok. {32:47} In the middle of the night, he took his wives, maidservants, and all his possessions and crossed over the ford Jabbok. {32:48} After he had sent everything across the brook, Jacob was left alone, and a man wrestled with him until dawn. {32:49} The man touched Jacob's hip, putting it out of joint as they wrestled. {32:50} As daybreak came, the man told Jacob to let him go, but Jacob replied, "I will not let you go unless you bless me." {32:51} The man asked, "What is your name?" Jacob said, "Jacob." {32:52} The man said, "Your name will no longer be Jacob but Israel, for you have struggled with God and with men and have overcome." {32:53} Jacob named the place Peniel, saying, "I have seen God face to face, and yet my life has been spared." {32:54} As he crossed the brook, the sun rose upon him, and he limped as he went. {32:55} They traveled until midday, and as they went, the gift continued to be sent ahead. {32:56} Jacob looked up and saw Esau coming with about four hundred men, and he was greatly afraid. {32:57} Jacob hurriedly divided his children among his wives and maidservants, placing his daughter Dinah in a chest and handing her to Leah. {32:58} Then he put Rachel and her children in front and Leah and her children behind. He went ahead and bowed down to the ground seven times until he approached his brother. {32:59} Esau ran to meet Jacob and embraced him, weeping, and they both wept. {32:60} Then Esau looked up and saw the women and children. "Who are these with you?" he asked. Jacob replied, "They are the children God has graciously given your servant." {32:61} Leah came near with her children and bowed down, and Rachel and Joseph approached and bowed down as well. {32:62} Esau said, "What do you mean by all this company I met?" Jacob replied, "To find favor in the sight of my lord." {32:63} But Esau said, "I have enough, my brother; keep what you have for yourself." {32:64} Jacob insisted, "No, please, if I have found favor in your eyes, accept my gift. I have seen your face, which is like seeing the face of God, and you have accepted me. {32:65} Please accept this gift, for God has dealt graciously with me, and I have enough." Esau accepted the gift. {32:66} Esau then said, "Let us travel together and I will accompany you." {32:67} Jacob replied, "My lord knows that the children are weak and the flocks and herds have young ones. If they are driven hard for a day, they will die. {32:68} Let my lord go on ahead of his servant, and I will follow you slowly at a pace suitable for the livestock and the children." {32:69} Esau replied, "Let me leave with you some of my men." Jacob said, "It is not necessary. My lord has done enough for me." {32:70} So Esau returned to his own home that day, while Jacob journeyed to Sukkoth. {32:71} Jacob built a house there for himself and made shelters for his livestock; therefore, the name of the place is called Sukkoth. {32:72} Jacob came safely to the city of Shechem in the land of Canaan, and pitched his tent near the city. {32:73} He bought a parcel of land from the children of Hamor, the father of Shechem, for one hundred pieces of money. {32:74} He erected an altar there and called it El Elohe Israel.

{33:1} After some time, Jacob left the borders of the land and arrived at Shalem, which is the city of Shechem in Canaan, where he camped in front of the city. {33:2} He purchased a piece of land from the children of Hamor, the local people, for five shekels. {33:3} There, Jacob built a house, set up his tent, and made booths for his livestock, which is why he named the place Succoth. {33:4} Jacob stayed in Succoth for a year and a half. {33:5} During that time, some local women went to Shechem to celebrate and dance, and Rachel and Leah, Jacob's wives, along with their families, went to see the festivities. {33:6} Dinah, the daughter of Jacob, also went with them to watch the daughters of the city, and they lingered while the people gathered around to enjoy the celebration. {33:7} Shechem, the son of Hamor, the prince of the land, was there to see them. {33:8} Shechem noticed Dinah, Jacob's daughter, sitting with her mother among the women, and he was captivated by her beauty. He asked his friends, "Whose daughter is that sitting among the women? I don't recognize her." {33:9} They replied, "That's the daughter of Jacob, the son of Isaac the Hebrew, who has been living in this city for some time. She went out with her mother and maidservants to join the festivities." {33:10} Shechem was so taken by Dinah that he sent for her and forcibly took her to his home, violating her and humbling her, yet he fell in love with her and kept her in his house. {33:11} When Jacob heard that Shechem had violated his daughter Dinah, he sent twelve of his servants to bring Dinah back from Shechem's house. {33:12} However, when they arrived, Shechem came out to meet them with his men and refused to let them see Dinah; he was with her, kissing and embracing her in front of them. {33:13} Jacob's servants returned and reported, "When we got there, he and his men drove us away, and Shechem was with Dinah, holding her." {33:14} Jacob was aware that Shechem had defiled Dinah, but he said nothing. His sons were out tending the flocks, and Jacob remained silent until they returned. {33:15} Before his sons got home, Jacob sent two maidens from among his servants' daughters to care for Dinah in Shechem's house. Meanwhile, Shechem sent three of his friends to his father Hamor, asking him to get Dinah for him as a wife. {33:17} Hamor went to Shechem's house and sat with him, saying, "Why do you want to take an Hebrew woman as a wife when there are women among your own people?" {33:18} Shechem insisted, "I only want her because she is delightful to me." Hamor agreed to help his son because Shechem was very dear to him. {33:19} Hamor approached Jacob to discuss this matter. Just as he was on his way, Jacob's sons returned from the field and learned what Shechem had done. {33:20} They were furious and gathered before their father, saying, "This man and his household deserve death because the Lord God commanded Noah and his children that man shall never rob or commit adultery. Shechem has both violated and humiliated our sister, and no one from the city has spoken out against him." {33:21} They declared, "Surely you understand that death is the proper judgment for Shechem, his father, and the whole city for what he has done." {33:22} While they spoke to Jacob about this, Hamor arrived to discuss Dinah with him and sat down before Jacob and his sons. {33:23} Hamor said, "Shechem longs for your daughter. Please let him marry her, and let us intermarry. Give us your daughters, and we'll give you ours; you can live among us and be one people." {33:24} He added, "Our land is extensive, so settle, trade, and take possession of it as you wish, and no one will stop you." {33:25} After Hamor finished speaking, Shechem came in and sat down. {33:26} Shechem then addressed Jacob and his sons, saying, "Please let me find favor in your eyes and give me your daughter as my wife. Whatever you ask for, I will do." {33:27} He offered to provide a generous dowry and gifts, adding, "Whatever you say, I'll fulfill. Anyone who doesn't comply with your wishes will die; just give me the girl for a wife." {33:28} Simeon and Levi answered Hamor and Shechem deceitfully, saying, "We will agree to what you've said, but keep away from our sister until we consult our father Isaac." {33:29} They claimed, "He knows the ways of our father Abraham, and whatever he says, we will tell you without hiding anything." {33:30} Simeon and Levi said this to find a reason to deal with Shechem and his city. {33:31} When Hamor and Shechem heard their words, they were pleased and went home. {33:32} Jacob's sons then told their father, "We know that death is the proper punishment for these wicked men and their city for breaking God's commands to Noah and his descendants. {33:33} Also, because Shechem defiled Dinah, such an abomination should never happen among us. {33:34} So you must decide what to do; seek counsel on how to deal with them and their city." {33:35} Simeon advised, "Tell them to circumcise every male as we have done; if they refuse, we will take our daughter and leave." {33:36} If they agree to be circumcised, then while they are in pain, we will attack them as if they are peaceful and kill every male. {33:37} This plan pleased them, and Simeon and Levi decided to carry it out. {33:38} The next morning, Hamor and Shechem came back to Jacob and his sons to discuss Dinah and find out their response. {33:39} The sons of Jacob spoke deceitfully, saying, "We told our father Isaac all your words, and he was pleased with them. {33:40} But he said that as Abraham was commanded by God, any man who wishes to marry one of his daughters must have every male circumcised as we are. Then we will give him our daughter as a wife." {33:41} They explained, "We cannot give our daughter to an uncircumcised man; it's a disgrace to us. However, if you agree to this, we will allow you to marry our daughter and we will take your daughters as wives too, living together as one people, provided you consent to circumcision for every male." {33:42} They warned, "If you refuse this condition, we will take our daughter and leave." {33:43} Hamor and Shechem were delighted by the sons' proposal and quickly agreed, as Shechem was very much in love with Dinah. {33:44} Hamor and Shechem hurried to the city gate and gathered all the men, explaining the sons of Jacob's conditions. {33:45} They informed the city that the sons of Jacob would agree to their requests if every male was circumcised as they are. {33:46} When the men of the city heard Shechem and Hamor's words, they agreed and decided to circumcise themselves since Shechem and Hamor were respected leaders of the land. {33:47} The next day, Hamor and Shechem rose early and gathered all the men of the city at the city center, and they circumcised every male there, including Shechem, Hamor, and Shechem's five brothers. {33:48} After that, each one went home, for this plan was from the Lord to deliver the city of Shechem into the hands of Jacob's two sons.

{34:1} The total number of males who were circumcised was six hundred and forty-five, along with two hundred and forty-six children. {34:2} However, Chiddekem, the son of Pered, the father of Hamor, and his six brothers refused to listen to Shechem and his father Hamor; they did not get circumcised because the proposal made by the sons of Jacob was repugnant to them, and they were very angry that the people of the city had ignored them. {34:3} On the evening of the second day, they found eight small children who had not been circumcised, as their mothers had hidden them from Shechem, his father Hamor, and the men of the city. {34:4} Shechem and his father Hamor sent for the children to have them brought before them to be circumcised, but Chiddekem and his six brothers attacked them with swords, intending to kill them. {34:5} They also tried to kill Shechem and his father Hamor and sought to slay Dinah as well because of this issue. {34:6} They said to them, "What is this that you have done? Are there no women among your fellow Canaanites that you want to take daughters of the Hebrews, whom you did not know before, and commit this act which your fathers never commanded? {34:7} Do you think you will succeed in this act? What will you say to your fellow Canaanites who will come tomorrow to ask about this? {34:8} If your actions do not seem just and good in their eyes, what will you do for your lives, and what about my life, since you did not heed our voices? {34:9} If the inhabitants of the land and all your fellow children of Ham hear about this, saying, {34:10} 'On account of a Hebrew woman, Shechem and his father Hamor, along with all the inhabitants of their city, committed an act they were unfamiliar with, which their ancestors never commanded,' where will you flee or how will you hide your shame for all your days before your fellow Canaanites? {34:11} Therefore, we cannot endure this thing you have done, nor can we bear this yoke upon us which our ancestors did not command. {34:12} Behold, tomorrow we will gather all our fellow Canaanites living in the land, and we will come together to strike you and all those who support you, ensuring there is not a single remnant left of you or them. {34:13} When Hamor, Shechem, and all the people of the city heard the words of Chiddekem and his brothers, they were terribly afraid for their lives because of what they said, and they regretted what they had done. {34:14} Shechem and his father Hamor responded to Chiddekem and his brothers, saying, "All the words you have spoken to us are true. {34:15} Do not think, nor imagine in your hearts, that we did this out of love for the Hebrews. {34:16} We did it because we realized they did not intend to comply with our wishes regarding their daughter unless this condition was met, so we heeded their voices and acted as you saw, to gain what we desire from them. {34:17} Once we have achieved our request, we will return to them and do what you suggest." {34:18} "We ask you to wait until our bodies heal and we regain our strength, and then we will go together against them to do what is in our hearts." {34:19} Dinah, the daughter of Jacob, heard all the words that Chiddekem and his brothers had spoken, as well as the responses from Hamor, Shechem, and the people of the city. {34:20} She hurried to send one of her maidens, whom her father had sent to care for her in Shechem's house, to inform her father Jacob and her brothers, saying, {34:21} "This is how Chiddekem and his brothers advised you, and this is how Hamor, Shechem, and the people of the city answered them." {34:22} When Jacob heard these words, he was filled with rage and indignation, and his anger flared against them. {34:23} Simeon and Levi swore, "As the Lord lives, the God of the entire earth, by this time tomorrow, there will not be a single remnant left in the whole city." {34:24} Twenty young men who had concealed themselves and were not circumcised fought against Simeon and Levi, but Simeon and Levi killed eighteen of them; two managed to flee and escape to some lime pits in the city, but Simeon and Levi searched for them but could not find them. {34:25} Simeon and Levi continued their assault in the city, killing all the inhabitants with the sword, leaving no one remaining. {34:26} A great panic erupted in the city, and the cries of the people rose to heaven, with all the women and children crying out loud. {34:27} Simeon and Levi slaughtered everyone in the city; not a single male was left alive. {34:28} They killed Hamor and Shechem his son with the sword, rescued Dinah from Shechem's house, and left the city. {34:29} The sons of Jacob returned and came upon the slain, taking all the plunder from the city and the fields. {34:30} While they were gathering the spoil, three hundred men stood up, throwing dust at them and striking them with stones, but Simeon turned to them and killed them all with the sword, then turned back to Levi and re-entered the city. {34:31} They took away the sheep, oxen, cattle, and the remaining women and children, leading them all away, then opened a gate and came to their father Jacob with vigor. {34:32} When Jacob saw all that they had done to the city and the spoils they had taken, he was very angry at them and said, "What is this that you have done to me? I had found peace among the Canaanite inhabitants of the land, and none of them bothered me. {34:33} Now you have made me odious to the inhabitants of the land, the Canaanites and Perizzites, and I am just a small group; they will all gather against me and kill me when they hear of your actions, and I and my household will be destroyed." {34:34} Simeon, Levi, and all their brothers answered their father Jacob, saying, "We live in the land, and shall Shechem treat our sister this way? Why are you silent about everything Shechem has done? Should he treat our sister like a harlot in the streets?" {34:35} The number of women that Simeon and Levi captured from the city of Shechem, whom they did not kill, was eighty-five who had not known a man. {34:36} Among them was a beautiful young girl named Bunah, whom Simeon took as his wife; they captured forty-seven men, while the rest they killed. {34:37} All the young men and women that Simeon and Levi captured from the city of Shechem served the sons of Jacob and their children after them until the day the sons of Jacob left the land of Egypt. {34:38} When Simeon and Levi left the city, the two young men who had hidden themselves in the city and did not die among the inhabitants rose up and entered the city, wandering around it, finding it desolate without a single man, only women weeping. {34:39} The young men shouted, "Behold, this is the evil that the sons of Jacob the Hebrew did to this city by destroying one of the Canaanite cities, showing no fear for their lives among the people of Canaan." {34:40} These men left the city and went to Tapnach, telling the inhabitants everything that had happened, including all that the sons of Jacob had done to Shechem. {34:41} The information reached Jashub, the king of Tapnach, and he sent men to the city of Shechem to investigate the young men, for the king did not believe their account, saying, "How could two men lay waste such a large city as Shechem?" {34:42} The messengers returned and told him, "We went to the city, and it is destroyed; there is no man there, only weeping women; no flocks or cattle remain because all that was in the city was taken by the sons of Jacob." {34:43} Jashub was astonished, saying, "How could two men do this, destroying such a large city, with not one man able to resist them? {34:44} For nothing like this has happened since the days of Nimrod, and nothing from ancient times compares. Jashub, the king of Tapnach, said to his people, 'Be courageous, and we will fight against these Hebrews, doing to them as they did to the city, avenging the city's people.' {34:45} Jashub consulted his advisors about this matter, and they said, 'You will not prevail alone against the Hebrews, for they must be powerful to do what they did to the entire city. {34:45} If two of them destroyed the entire city, and no one stood against them, surely if you go against them, they will all rise up against us and destroy us too. {34:46} But if you send to all the kings surrounding us and let them come together, then we will go with them and fight against the sons of Jacob; then you will prevail against them. {34:47} Jashub heard the words of his advisors, and their words pleased him and his people, so he acted accordingly. Jashub, king of Tapnach, sent to all the kings of the Amorites surrounding Shechem and Tapnach, saying, {34:48} "Come with me and assist me, and we will strike Jacob the Hebrew and all his sons and eliminate them from the earth, for he did just that to the city of Shechem, and you all know about it." {34:49} All the kings of the Amorites heard the evil the sons of Jacob had done to the city of Shechem, and they were greatly astonished. {34:50} The seven kings of the Amorites gathered their armies, about ten thousand men with drawn swords, and they came to fight against the sons of Jacob. Jacob learned that the kings of the Amorites had assembled to battle his sons, and he was greatly afraid and distressed. {34:51} Jacob exclaimed against Simeon and Levi, saying, "What is this act you have committed? Why have you hurt me by bringing all the children of Canaan against me to destroy me and my household? I was at peace with my household, and you have done this to provoke the inhabitants of the land against me by your actions." {34:52} Judah responded to his father, saying, "Was it for nothing that my brothers Simeon and Levi killed all the inhabitants of Shechem? Surely it was because Shechem humiliated our sister and violated the command of our God to Noah and his children; for Shechem forcibly took our sister and committed adultery with her. {34:53} Shechem did all this evil, and not one of the inhabitants of his city interfered to ask, 'Why will you do this?' Surely for this reason my brothers went and struck the city, and the Lord delivered it into their hands because its inhabitants violated the commands of our God. So, is it for nothing that they did all this?" {34:54} "Now why are you afraid or distressed? Why is your anger kindled against my brothers? {34:55} Surely our God, who delivered the city of Shechem and its people into their hands, will also deliver all the Canaanite kings who are coming against us. We will treat them as my brothers did to Shechem. {34:56} Now be calm and cast away your fears; trust in the Lord our God, and pray to Him for assistance and deliverance, and He will give our enemies into our hands." {34:57} Judah called one of his father's servants, saying, "Go and see where those kings coming against us are positioned with their armies." {34:58} The servant went and looked far away, climbed opposite Mount Sihon, and saw all the camps of the kings standing in the fields. He returned to Judah and said, "Behold, the kings are camped in the fields with their armies, a people exceedingly numerous, like the sand on the seashore." {34:59} Judah said to Simeon, Levi, and all his brothers, "Strengthen yourselves and be brave, for the Lord our God is with us; do not fear them. {34:60} Stand each man ready, equipped with his weapons of war, his bow and sword, and we will go and fight against these uncircumcised men; the Lord is our God, and He will save us." {34:61} They rose up, each one girded with his weapons of war, great and small, eleven sons of Jacob, along with all the servants of Jacob. {34:62} All the servants of Isaac who were with Isaac in

Hebron came to them equipped with various instruments of war. The sons of Jacob and their servants, a total of one hundred and twelve men, moved toward the kings, and Jacob went with them. {34:63} The sons of Jacob sent a message to their father Isaac, the son of Abraham in Hebron, also known as Kireath-arba, saying, {34:64} "We beseech you to pray for us to the Lord our God, to protect us from the hands of the Canaanites who are coming against us and to deliver them into our hands." {34:65} Isaac, the son of Abraham, prayed to the Lord for his sons, saying, "O Lord God, You promised my father, saying, 'I will multiply your descendants as the stars of heaven,' and You also promised me and established Your word. Now that the kings of Canaan are gathering to make war with my children for no violence committed against them, {34:66} O Lord God, God of the whole earth, I pray You, frustrate the plans of these kings so they will not fight against my sons. {34:67} Instill fear into the hearts of these kings and their people and lower their pride so that they may turn away from my sons. {34:68} With Your mighty hand and outstretched arm, deliver my sons and their servants from them, for power and might are in Your hands to accomplish this." {34:69} The sons of Jacob and their servants approached the kings, trusting in the Lord their God. As they went, Jacob also prayed to the Lord, saying, "O Lord God, powerful and exalted God, who has reigned from ancient times until now and forever; {34:70} You are He who stirs up wars and causes them to cease. In Your hand are power and might to exalt and to bring down. May my prayer be acceptable before You so that You may turn to me with Your mercies, instilling fear in the hearts of these kings and their people, terrifying them and their camps. With Your great kindness, deliver all those who trust in You, for it is You who can bring nations under us."

{35:1} All the Amorite kings gathered in the field to consult with their advisors about what to do regarding the sons of Jacob, because they were still afraid of them, saying, "Look, just two of them killed all the people of Shechem." {35:2} The Lord heard the prayers of Isaac and Jacob, and He filled the hearts of the advisors of these kings with great fear and terror, so that they all exclaimed in unison, {35:3} "Are you foolish today, or do you have no understanding that you would fight against the Hebrews? Why would you delight in bringing about your own destruction today? {35:4} Look, two of them entered Shechem without fear, and they killed all the inhabitants of the city, with no one standing against them. How then can you fight against all of them? {35:5} You must know that their God loves them dearly and has done mighty things for them—things that have never been done before, and none of the gods of any nation can match the deeds of their God. {35:6} Surely you've heard how He delivered their ancestor Abraham, the Hebrew, from the hands of King Nimrod and his people, who tried to kill him many times. {35:7} He also rescued Abraham from the fire into which Nimrod had cast him, and his God saved him from it. {35:8} Who else can do such things? Wasn't it Abraham who defeated the five kings of Elam when they captured his nephew, who was living in Sodom at the time? {35:9} He took his loyal servant and a few men, and in one night, they pursued the kings of Elam, killed them, and recovered all the property that had been taken from his nephew. {35:10} Surely you know that the God of these Hebrews is very pleased with them, and they are devoted to Him as well, for they know He has delivered them from all their enemies. {35:11} Out of love for his God, Abraham even prepared to offer his precious son as a burnt offering, and if God hadn't stopped him, he would have done it out of his love for God. {35:12} God saw all that Abraham did and swore to him that He would save his descendants from any trouble that came upon them, because of Abraham's willingness to sacrifice his son out of love for God. {35:13} Haven't you heard what their God did to Pharaoh, king of Egypt, and to Abimelech, king of Gerar, when they tried to take Abraham's wife, thinking she was his sister to avoid being killed for her? God punished them and their people in ways you've heard about. {35:14} We ourselves saw Esau, Jacob's brother, come with 400 men to kill him, remembering how Jacob had taken his father's blessing from him. {35:15} Esau came to attack him when Jacob was returning from Syria, planning to kill both him and his family. But who saved him from Esau's hands except his God, in whom he trusted? His God delivered him from his brother and all his enemies, and surely He will protect him again. {35:16} Doesn't everyone know that it was their God who gave them the strength to destroy Shechem the way they did? {35:17} How could just two men destroy such a large city if it weren't for their God? It was He who enabled them to kill the inhabitants of the city in their own homes. {35:18} So how can you think you can prevail against them, even if you had a thousand times more men to help you? {35:19} You aren't just fighting them, you're waging war against their God, who has chosen them. That means you've come here today only to be destroyed. {35:20} So stop this evil that you're planning against yourselves. It would be better for you not to fight them, even though they are few in number, because their God is with them." {35:21} When the Amorite kings heard the words of their advisors, they were filled with fear, and they became afraid of the sons of Jacob, deciding not to fight them. {35:22} They listened to their advisors, and the kings were pleased with their counsel and followed it. {35:23} So, the kings turned back and refrained from attacking the sons of Jacob, because they didn't dare approach them for battle, as they were too afraid of them and their hearts melted with fear. {35:24} This fear came from the Lord, for He heard the prayers of His servants, Isaac and Jacob, who trusted in Him. All the kings returned to their cities with their armies, and they didn't fight the sons of Jacob at that time. {35:25} The sons of Jacob stayed in their camp near Mount Sihon until evening, and when they saw that the kings didn't come to fight them, they returned home.

{36:1} At that time, the Lord appeared to Jacob and said, "Get up, go to Bethel, and stay there. Build an altar to the Lord who appeared to you and delivered you and your sons from affliction." {36:2} So Jacob got up with his sons and everything he had, and they went to Bethel as the Lord commanded. {36:3} Jacob was ninety-nine years old when he went to Bethel, and he, his sons, and everyone with him stayed in Bethel, also known as Luz. There, he built an altar to the Lord, who had appeared to him. Jacob and his sons stayed in Bethel for six months. {36:4} During that time, Deborah, the daughter of Uz and Rebekah's nurse, died. She had been with Jacob, and he buried her under an oak tree near Bethel. {36:5} Around this same time, Rebekah, the daughter of Bethuel and Jacob's mother, died in Hebron, which is Kireath-arba, and she was buried in the cave of Machpelah, which Abraham had bought from the children of Heth. {36:6} Rebekah lived for one hundred and thirty-three years before she passed away, and when Jacob heard of his mother's death, he wept bitterly and mourned greatly for her and for Deborah, her nurse, beneath the oak. He named that place Allon-bachuth (which means "oak of weeping"). {36:7} Also during this time, Laban the Syrian died because God struck him for breaking the covenant he had made with Jacob. {36:8} Jacob was one hundred years old when the Lord appeared to him again, blessed him, and gave him the name Israel. Meanwhile, Rachel, Jacob's wife, conceived during those days. {36:9} At that time, Jacob and all those with him left Bethel to go to his father's house in Hebron. {36:10} While they were on the road, just a short distance from Ephrath, Rachel gave birth to a son but suffered hard labor and died during childbirth. {36:11} Jacob buried her on the way to Ephrath, which is now called Bethlehem, and he set up a pillar on her grave, which stands there to this day. Rachel had lived for forty-five years before she passed. {36:12} Jacob named his new son Benjamin because he was born to him in the land to his right. {36:13} After Rachel's death, Jacob set up his tent in the tent of Bilhah, Rachel's handmaid. {36:14} Reuben, Jacob's eldest son, became jealous on behalf of his mother Leah because of this, and in his anger, he went to Bilhah's tent and removed his father's bed from it. {36:15} Because Reuben had defiled his father's bed, the birthright and the privileges of kingship and priesthood were taken from him. The birthright was given to Joseph, the kingship to Judah, and the priesthood to Levi. {36:16} These are the generations of Jacob that were born to him in Padan-aram: {36:17} Leah's sons were Reuben (the firstborn), Simeon, Levi, Judah, Issachar, Zebulun, and their sister Dinah. Rachel's sons were Joseph and Benjamin. {36:18} Zilpah, Leah's handmaid, gave birth to Gad and Asher, and Bilhah, Rachel's handmaid, gave birth to Dan and Naphtali. These were the sons of Jacob born to him in Padan-aram. {36:19} Jacob, his sons, and everyone with him traveled to Mamre, which is Kireath-arba, in Hebron, where Abraham and Isaac had stayed. Jacob and his family lived with his father Isaac in Hebron. {36:20} Meanwhile, Jacob's brother Esau and his sons moved to the land of Seir and settled there. Esau's descendants were very fruitful and multiplied greatly in Seir.

{36:21} These are the generations of Esau that were born to him in the land of Canaan. Esau had five sons: {36:22} Adah bore his firstborn son, Eliphaz, and she also bore Reuel. Ahlibamah bore Jeush, Yaalam, and Korah. {36:23} These are the sons of Esau who were born in Canaan. Eliphaz, the son of Esau, had sons named Teman, Omar, Zepho, Gatam, Kenaz, and Amalek. Reuel's sons were Nachath, Zerach, Shammah, and Mizzah. {36:24} Jeush's sons were Timnah, Alvah, and Jetheth. Yaalam's sons were Alah, Phinor, and Kenaz. {36:25} Korah's sons were Teman, Mibzar, Magdiel, and Eram. These are the families of Esau's sons according to their dukedoms in the land of Seir. {36:26} These are the names of the sons of Seir the Horite, who inhabited the land of Seir: Lotan, Shobal, Zibeon, Anah, Dishon, Ezer, and Dishan, a total of seven sons. {36:27} Lotan's children were Hori, Heman, and their sister Timnah. This is the same Timnah who came to Jacob and his sons, but they did not listen to her, so she became a concubine to Eliphaz, Esau's son, and she bore him Amalek. {36:28} Shobal's sons were Alvan, Manahath, Ebal, Shepho, and Onam, and Zibeon's sons were Ajah and Anah. Anah was the one who found the Yemim in the wilderness while tending his father Zibeon's donkeys. {36:29} While he was tending the donkeys, he would often take them to the wilderness to feed. {36:30} On one occasion, he took them to a desert near the seashore, and as he was feeding them, a heavy storm came from the other side of the sea and settled upon the donkeys, causing them to stand still. {36:31} Suddenly, about one hundred and twenty terrifying creatures emerged from the wilderness on the other side of the sea and came to where the donkeys were. {36:32} These creatures had the lower half of a human body and the upper half of either a bear or a keephas (a mysterious creature), with tails like those of ducheephaths (a type of bird) that stretched from between their shoulders to the ground. The creatures mounted the donkeys and rode them away, and they never returned. {36:33} One of the creatures struck Anah with its tail before fleeing the scene. {36:34} Anah was terrified and fled back to the city, where he told his sons and brothers what had happened. Many men went to search for the donkeys, but they couldn't find them. From that day on, Anah and his brothers never returned to that place, fearing for their lives. {36:35} Anah's children were Dishon and his sister Ahlibamah. Dishon's children were Hemdan, Eshban, Ithran, and Cheran. Ezer's children were Bilhan, Zaavan, and Akan. Dishan's children were Uz and Aran. {36:36} These are the families of Seir's descendants, the Horites, according to their dukedoms in the land of Seir. {36:37} Esau and his descendants continued to live in Seir, the land of the Horites, and they became prosperous and multiplied greatly. Meanwhile, Jacob and his family lived with his father Isaac in the land of Canaan, just as the Lord had commanded their ancestor Abraham.

{37:1} In the one hundred and fifth year of Jacob's life, which was the ninth year of him living with his children in the land of Canaan after coming from Padan-aram. {37:2} During this time, Jacob and his children left Hebron and returned to Shechem, along with everything they owned, and they settled there. The children of Jacob found fertile pasture for their livestock in Shechem, which had been rebuilt and had about three hundred men and women living there. {37:3} Jacob and his family stayed on the part of the field that he had previously bought from Hamor, Shechem's father, when he came from Padan-aram, before Simeon and Levi destroyed the city. {37:4} When the kings of the Canaanites and Amorites around Shechem heard that Jacob's sons had returned to the city, {37:5} they were outraged and said, "Will the sons of Jacob return to the city they once destroyed and take it over again, driving out or killing its current inhabitants?" {37:6} So all the kings of Canaan gathered and decided to wage war against Jacob and his sons. {37:7} Jashub, the king of Tapnach, sent messages to his neighboring kings: Elan of Gaash, Ihuri of Shiloh, Parathon of Chazar, Susi of Sarton, Laban of Bethchoran, and Shabir of Othnay-mah. He urged them to come together to fight Jacob and his sons, who had come back to Shechem to take over. {37:8} Jashub called for their help to attack Jacob and his sons, accusing them of planning to kill the city's inhabitants as they had done before. {37:9} The kings gathered their armies, a multitude as numerous as the sand on the seashore, and camped near Tapnach. {37:10} Jashub, with his army, joined them outside the city, dividing their forces into seven divisions to fight Jacob's sons. {37:11} They sent a message to Jacob, saying, "Come meet us in the plain, so we can settle matters for the men of Shechem whom you killed. Are you returning to kill the city's inhabitants again?" {37:12} Jacob's sons were furious at this message, and ten of them prepared for battle, along with one hundred and two of their servants. {37:13} They set out to meet the kings, with Jacob accompanying them, and they stood on the hill of Shechem. {37:14} Jacob prayed to God for his sons, asking for deliverance from their enemies and that God might give them the strength and courage to overcome their foes. {37:15} Jacob asked for God's mercy to spare his sons from being killed by the Canaanites, or if it was God's will, to take them by His mercy rather than letting them die by the enemy's hands. {37:16} When Jacob finished praying, the earth trembled, and the sun darkened, terrifying the kings and their armies. {37:17} God listened to Jacob's prayer and filled the hearts of the kings and their soldiers with fear of Jacob's sons. {37:18} The Lord made them hear the sounds of chariots and horses as if a great army accompanied Jacob's sons. {37:19} The kings were paralyzed with fear, and as Jacob's sons, numbering one hundred and twelve men, approached with loud cries, the kings were even more terrified. {37:20} The kings considered retreating rather than face Jacob's sons again, remembering their previous defeat. {37:21} However, they hesitated, thinking it would be dishonorable to flee twice from the Hebrews. {37:22} Jacob's sons advanced toward the kings and their massive armies. {37:23} They called out to God, asking for His help, placing their trust in Him to avoid death at the hands of the uncircumcised men. {37:24} Armed with shields and spears, Jacob's sons approached the battle. {37:25} Judah, the leader, went ahead with ten of his servants toward the kings. {37:26} Jashub, the king of Tapnach, led his army against Judah. Judah's anger flared, and he rushed into battle, putting his life at risk. {37:27} Jashub, a valiant warrior clad in armor from head to foot, rode a strong horse and skillfully shot arrows from both hands. {37:28} As Jashub fired arrows at Judah, God caused his shots to miss and even rebound upon his own men. {37:29} Despite this, Jashub continued to approach Judah, but when Judah saw Jashub preparing to shoot again, he charged with all his strength. {37:30} Judah picked up a large stone weighing sixty shekels and hurled it at Jashub's shield, shattering it and knocking Jashub off his horse. {37:31} Jashub's shield flew fifteen cubits away, landing near his second camp. {37:32} The other kings, seeing Judah's strength, were filled with fear. {37:33} Judah then drew his sword and struck down forty-two men from Jashub's camp, causing the rest of Jashub's men to flee, leaving their king lying on the ground. {37:34} Jashub, seeing his men retreating, stood up and faced Judah, despite his fear. {37:35} The two engaged in combat, shield against shield, but Jashub's men had already fled. {37:36} Jashub attempted to strike Judah on the head with his spear, but Judah blocked the blow with his shield, which split in two. {37:37} Judah quickly drew his sword and cut off Jashub's feet, causing him to fall, and then severed his head with Jashub's own spear. {37:38} When Jacob's sons saw Judah's victory, they rushed into battle with the other kings and their armies. {37:39} They killed fifteen thousand of the enemy soldiers, striking them down as easily as gourds, while the rest fled. {37:40} Judah remained by Jashub's body, stripping him of his armor. {37:41} Nine captains from Jashub's camp approached to fight Judah, but he killed one by striking him with a stone. {37:42} The remaining eight captains fled in fear, pursued by Judah and his men, who caught and killed them. {37:43} Meanwhile, Jacob's sons continued to defeat the armies of the kings, killing many of them. {37:44} The kings themselves stood their ground, rallying their captains and refusing to retreat, despite their soldiers fleeing in fear. {37:45} The sons of Jacob regrouped after defeating the armies and joined Judah, who was still killing Jashub's captains and stripping their armor. {37:46} Levi, seeing Elon, the king of Gaash, approaching with his fourteen captains to attack him, {37:47} gathered twelve of his servants and fought back, killing Elon and his captains with their swords.

{38:1} Ihuri, the king of Shiloh, came to aid Elon, but Jacob drew his bow and shot an arrow, striking and killing Ihuri. {38:2} With Ihuri dead, the four remaining kings and their captains fled, realizing they no longer had the strength to fight the Hebrews, who had already killed three powerful kings. {38:3} Seeing the kings retreat, the sons of Jacob pursued them, and Jacob himself left his position at Shechem and joined in the chase. {38:4} The kings and their armies, terrified, fled to the city of Chazar for refuge. {38:5}

The sons of Jacob followed them to Chazar's gate and killed about four thousand men. Jacob focused on the kings, shooting each with an arrow and killing them all. {38:6} He killed Parathon, king of Chazar, at the city gate, followed by Susi, king of Sarton, Laban, king of Bethchorin, and Shabir, king of Machnaymah. {38:7} With the kings dead, the sons of Jacob continued battling the armies near Chazar's gate, killing about four hundred more. {38:8} However, three of Jacob's servants died, which greatly angered Judah against the Amorites. {38:9} The remaining men of the kings' armies, terrified, broke through the gates of Chazar to hide within the city. {38:10} The city was vast, and the armies concealed themselves inside. The sons of Jacob pursued them. {38:11} Four skilled warriors from Chazar blocked the city's entrance with drawn swords, preventing the sons of Jacob from entering. {38:12} Naphtali quickly intervened, killing two of the warriors with a single blow. {38:13} The other two fled, but Naphtali chased them down and killed them as well. {38:14} The sons of Jacob entered Chazar and discovered another wall surrounding the city. They searched for the gate but couldn't find it. Judah scaled the wall, followed by Simeon and Levi, and all three descended into the city. {38:15} Simeon and Levi slaughtered all the men who had fled into the city, as well as the inhabitants, including women and children. Their cries ascended to heaven. {38:16} Dan and Naphtali climbed the wall to see what caused the outcry, worried for their brothers. They heard the people pleading, offering all they had if only their lives would be spared. {38:17} After the slaughter, Judah, Simeon, and Levi called to Dan, Naphtali, and the others, telling them they had entered the city. The sons of Jacob then gathered the spoil. {38:18} They took everything valuable from Chazar—flocks, herds, and other possessions—and left the city. {38:19} The next day, they went to Sarton, having heard that its remaining inhabitants were preparing to fight for their slain king. Sarton was a highly fortified city with a deep rampart. {38:20} The rampart was fifty cubits high and forty cubits wide, with no easy access for anyone trying to enter. {38:21} The only entrance was at the back of the city, requiring people to travel around it to enter. {38:22} Angered by the lack of entry, the sons of Jacob saw that the people of Sarton were terrified, having heard about Chazar's destruction. {38:23} The Sartonites, too afraid to confront the sons of Jacob, dismantled the city's bridge, making entry impossible. {38:24} The sons of Jacob arrived and searched for the way in but couldn't find it, while the inhabitants jeered at them from the top of the wall. {38:25} The people of Sarton cursed them from the walls, infuriating the sons of Jacob. {38:26} Their anger burned, and they leaped over the rampart with great force, covering the forty-cubit width. {38:27} They stood beneath the city wall and found the gates sealed with iron doors. {38:28} The Sartonites hurled stones and arrows at them from the wall, preventing the gates from being opened. {38:29} Four hundred men were on the wall, and the sons of Jacob, unable to open the gates, climbed the wall. Judah was the first to the eastern side, followed by Gad and Asher to the west, and Simeon and Levi to the north. Dan and Reuben ascended the southern wall. {38:30} Seeing the sons of Jacob approaching, the people fled from the wall and hid in the city. {38:31} Issachar and Naphtali, who had stayed under the wall, broke open the gates and set fire to them, melting the iron. The sons of Jacob and their men then entered the city and fought the inhabitants, killing them all. {38:32} About two hundred men escaped to a tower in the city, but Judah pursued and destroyed the tower, killing everyone inside. {38:33} The sons of Jacob then noticed another high tower in the city, its top reaching the heavens, and hurried there with their men. Inside were about three hundred people, including women and children. {38:34} The sons of Jacob attacked them, causing the inhabitants to flee. {38:35} Simeon and Levi chased them, and twelve mighty men emerged from hiding to confront them. {38:36} These twelve men fought fiercely against Simeon and Levi, breaking their shields. {38:37} One struck Levi on the head with a sword, but Levi blocked the blow with his hand, barely avoiding losing it. {38:38} Levi grabbed the man's sword and used it to decapitate him. {38:39} The remaining eleven men attacked Levi, but he couldn't defeat them because they were incredibly strong. {38:40} Seeing they couldn't win, Simeon let out a loud shriek that stunned the eleven men. {38:41} Judah, hearing his brother's cry, rushed with Naphtali and shields to aid Simeon and Levi, whose shields had been broken. {38:42} The three brothers fought the eleven men until sunset, but still couldn't defeat them. {38:43} When Jacob heard about this, he was deeply troubled and prayed to God. He and Naphtali then joined the battle. {38:44} Jacob approached, drew his bow, and killed three of the eleven men. The remaining eight, terrified, fled. {38:45} In their escape, they encountered Dan and Asher, who ambushed and killed two of them. Judah and his brothers pursued the rest and slew them. {38:46} The sons of Jacob then searched the city for any survivors and found twenty young men hiding in a cave. Gad and Asher killed them, and Dan and Naphtali found and slaughtered the men who had escaped from the second tower. {38:47} The sons of Jacob killed all the inhabitants of Sarton, sparing only the women and children. {38:48} The people of Sarton were incredibly strong—one man could fight a thousand, and two could stand against ten thousand. {38:49} Nevertheless, the sons of Jacob wiped out all the men of the city with their swords. {38:50} They left the women alive and took all the spoils, including flocks, herds, and anything of value. {38:51} The sons of Jacob treated Sarton and its people just as they had done to Chazar and its inhabitants, and then departed from the city.

{39:1} After the sons of Jacob left the city of Sarton, they had gone about two hundred cubits when they encountered the inhabitants of Tapnach coming to fight them, as they sought revenge for the killing of their king and men. {39:2} The people of Tapnach hoped to reclaim the spoil taken by the sons of Jacob from Chazar and Sarton. {39:3} The remainder of Tapnach's men fought with the sons of Jacob but were defeated and pursued to the city of Arbelan, where they all fell before Jacob's sons. {39:4} The sons of Jacob then returned to Tapnach to claim the spoil, but upon arrival, they learned that the people of Arbelan were coming to intercept them. Leaving ten of their men in Tapnach to plunder the city, the rest went to meet the men of Arbelan. {39:5} The men of Arbelan, along with their wives—who were skilled in battle—came out to fight, numbering around four hundred. {39:6} The sons of Jacob shouted loudly and ran toward them with tremendous force. {39:7} The people of Arbelan were terrified by the roar of Jacob's sons, which sounded like lions or the waves of the sea, {39:8} and fear overtook them, causing them to flee back into the city with the sons of Jacob in pursuit. {39:9} A fierce battle ensued within the city, with even the women of Arbelan slinging stones at the sons of Jacob. The fighting lasted all day until evening. {39:10} The sons of Jacob were nearly defeated but prayed to the Lord, who gave them strength, and by evening, they slaughtered all the people of Arbelan, including the women and children. {39:11} They also killed the survivors who had fled from Sarton and destroyed Arbelan and Tapnach, just as they had done to Chazar and Sarton. {39:12} When the women saw their men were dead, they went to the rooftops and pelted Jacob's sons with stones, but the sons quickly stormed the city, killed the women, and took the spoil. {39:13} The same fate befell Machnaymah as Tapnach, Chazar, and Shiloh, and then they departed. {39:14} On the fifth day, the sons of Jacob heard that the people of Gaash had gathered to fight them, seeking revenge for the death of their king and fourteen captains, whom Jacob's sons had slain in the first battle. {39:15} That day, the sons of Jacob prepared for battle against the inhabitants of Gaash, a mighty people of the Amorites. Gaash was their strongest city, fortified with three walls. {39:16} When the sons of Jacob reached Gaash, they found the city gates locked, with five hundred men standing on the outer wall, while a large ambush lay in wait outside the city behind them. {39:17} As the sons of Jacob approached the city gates, the ambush emerged and surrounded them, {39:18} while those on the wall rained down arrows and stones. {39:19} Judah, seeing the battle turn against them, let out a tremendous shriek, terrifying the men of Gaash so much that many fell from the wall, and all were gripped with fear. {39:20} The sons of Jacob continued toward the gates, but the men of Gaash threw more stones and arrows, forcing them to retreat. {39:21} They turned back and attacked the ambush, striking them down as one would smash gourds, and fear paralyzed the men of Gaash. {39:22} The sons of Jacob killed all those outside the city but still couldn't break into the city due to the remaining defenders on the walls. {39:23} They attacked one corner of the wall but were again driven off by a shower of stones and arrows. {39:24} The people of Gaash taunted Jacob's sons from the walls, mocking their failure to prevail, {39:25} and boasting that Gaash was far stronger than the weaker Amorite cities Jacob's sons had already defeated. {39:26} They taunted further, claiming that Jacob's sons would all perish there, avenging the

Amorite cities they had destroyed. {39:27} The people continued insulting the sons of Jacob and blaspheming their God while pelting them with arrows and stones. {39:28} Hearing these insults, Judah's anger flared, and he prayed for the Lord's help. {39:29} Running with all his might, he leaped onto the wall, though his sword fell from his hand. {39:30} Judah shouted loudly, terrifying the men on the wall, and many fell into the city, dying from the fall. {39:31} Some brave men approached Judah, trying to throw him off the wall to his brothers below, but Jacob's sons shot arrows from below, killing three attackers. {39:32} Judah cried out for help, and Jacob's sons shot arrows again, {39:33} terrifying the attackers so much that they dropped their swords and fled, allowing Judah to pick up their weapons. {39:34} Judah then fought and killed twenty of the men on the wall. {39:35} Meanwhile, about eighty more men and women climbed the wall, but the Lord instilled fear of Judah in their hearts, preventing them from attacking. {39:36} Jacob and his sons shot arrows from below, killing ten more men, who fell from the wall. {39:37} The remaining men on the wall were terrified by Judah's strength, but a mighty warrior named Arud came close enough to strike Judah on the head with his sword, splitting Judah's shield in two. {39:38} After striking Judah, Arud fled in fear, but slipped off the wall and fell among Jacob's sons, who killed him. {39:39} Judah, now suffering greatly from the blow, cried out in pain, and Dan, hearing his brother's cry, was filled with rage. {39:40} Dan ran with all his might and leaped onto the wall to help Judah, {39:41} and the remaining men fled to the second wall, throwing arrows and stones at Dan and Judah. {39:42} Both were struck multiple times and were nearly killed by the barrage. {39:43} Jacob's sons couldn't help from below, as the attackers were on the second wall. {39:44} Judah and Dan finally leaped onto the second wall and confronted their attackers directly, {39:45} causing the people of the city to shout in panic and retreat between the walls. {39:46} Jacob and his sons heard the noise from the city but couldn't see Judah and Dan on the second wall, worrying about their safety. {39:47} Naphtali then leaped onto the first wall, followed by Issachar and Zebulun, who broke open the city gates. {39:48} Naphtali joined Judah and Dan on the second wall, and the defenders, seeing a third brother arrive, fled into the city. {39:49} Judah, Dan, and Naphtali descended into the city and pursued the fleeing inhabitants, while Simeon and Levi, who were still outside, scaled the wall and joined their brothers. {39:50} The sons of Jacob attacked the city from all directions, slaughtering about twenty thousand men and women, and none could withstand them. {39:51} The blood flowed so heavily that it was like a stream, running out of the city and into the desert of Bethchorin. {39:52} The people of Bethchorin, seeing the blood from afar, sent seventy men to investigate. {39:53} They followed the stream of blood to Gaash and heard the cries of the city's inhabitants as the blood continued to flow like water. {39:54} Meanwhile, the sons of Jacob were still killing the people of Gaash until evening, having slain about twenty thousand. The people of Bethchorin, recognizing the work of the Hebrews, prepared for battle. {39:55} When Jacob's sons finished the slaughter, they searched the city for loot and encountered three powerful men. {39:56} The men tried to flee, but one grabbed Zebulun, throwing him to the ground. {39:57} Jacob ran forward and struck the man with his sword, cutting him in two. {39:58} Another man attacked Jacob, but Simeon and Levi struck him on the hips, knocking him down. {39:59} The man rose with great strength, but Judah quickly struck his head with a sword, splitting it in two. {39:60} The third powerful man, seeing his companions dead, fled, but the sons of Jacob pursued him. {39:61} He found a sword and turned to fight, aiming to strike Judah on the head. {39:62} Naphtali blocked the blow with his shield, and Judah escaped unharmed. {39:63} Simeon and Levi then attacked the man, slicing his body in two lengthwise. {39:64} With the defeat of the three mighty men, the sons of Jacob continued slaughtering the people of Gaash until the day ended. {39:65} They took all the spoil from the city, leaving no survivors, just as they had done to Sarton and Shiloh.

{40:1} The sons of Jacob took all the plunder from Gaash and left the city during the night. {40:2} As they were heading toward the fortress of Bethchorin, the people of Bethchorin were on their way to meet them, and that night, the sons of Jacob fought against the people of Bethchorin at the fortress. {40:3} The inhabitants of Bethchorin were strong warriors, so powerful that one man could face a thousand, and they fought fiercely that night at the fortress, with their shouts echoing far away, shaking the earth. {40:4} The sons of Jacob were afraid because they weren't used to fighting in the dark and were confused. They cried out to the Lord, asking for help and deliverance from these uncircumcised men. {40:5} The Lord listened to their cry and caused great terror and confusion among the people of Bethchorin, who began to fight and kill each other in the darkness. {40:6} Realizing that the Lord had caused a spirit of confusion among them, the sons of Jacob slipped away from the fighting and went to the lower part of the fortress, where they stayed safely that night with their young men. {40:7} The people of Bethchorin continued fighting each other throughout the night, with cries coming from every corner of the fortress, their voices so loud that the earth trembled. {40:8} All the surrounding cities of the Canaanites, Hittites, Amorites, Hivites, and the kings of Canaan, as well as those beyond the Jordan, heard the noise. {40:9} They said, "Surely, these are the battles of the Hebrews fighting against the seven cities who approached them; who can stand against them?" {40:10} The people of Canaan and beyond the Jordan were filled with fear of the sons of Jacob, thinking the same fate awaited them as befell the other cities. {40:11} The shouts of the Chorinites continued to grow louder, and they kept killing each other until morning. {40:12} At dawn, the sons of Jacob rose and went up to the fortress, killing the remaining Chorinites in a dreadful way, leaving none alive. {40:13} On the sixth day, the people of Canaan from afar saw the bodies of the people of Bethchorin lying scattered across the fortress like carcasses of sheep and goats. {40:14} The sons of Jacob took all the spoils they had captured from Gaash and headed to Bethchorin, where they found the city packed with people as numerous as the sand on the seashore, and they fought them until evening. {40:15} The sons of Jacob treated Bethchorin just like they had done to Gaash, Tapnach, Chazar, Sarton, and Shiloh. {40:16} They took the spoil of Bethchorin and all the other cities and went back to Shechem. {40:17} The sons of Jacob returned to Shechem and camped outside the city, resting from the war. {40:18} They left all their servants and the spoils they had captured outside the city, saying, "Perhaps there will be more fighting, and they may come to besiege us here in Shechem." {40:19} Jacob and his sons, along with their servants, stayed the night and the following day in the field Jacob had bought from Hamor for five shekels, with all their captured plunder. {40:20} The amount of booty they had taken was vast, like the sand on the seashore. {40:21} The people of the land saw them from a distance and were terrified of the sons of Jacob, for no king in ancient times had done anything like this. {40:22} The seven kings of Canaan decided to seek peace with the sons of Jacob because they feared for their lives. {40:23} That day, Japhia, king of Hebron, sent secret messages to the kings of Ai, Gibeon, Shalem, Adulam, Lachish, Chazar, and all the other kings under his command, saying, {40:24} "Come to me, and we will go to the sons of Jacob to make peace with them, so they won't destroy our lands as they did to Shechem and the surrounding cities." {40:25} "Come with only a few men; each king should bring three captains, and each captain should bring three officers." {40:26} "Let us meet in Hebron, and together we will go to the sons of Jacob and ask them for peace." {40:27} The kings followed Japhia's advice, for he had authority over them. They gathered to meet the sons of Jacob. Meanwhile, Jacob's sons returned to the field in Shechem, not trusting the kings of the land. {40:28} The sons of Jacob stayed in the field for ten days, and no one came to fight them. {40:29} When they saw no sign of battle, they all went back into the city of Shechem. {40:30} After forty days, the kings of the Amorites gathered in Hebron to meet Japhia. {40:31} Twenty-one kings came, along with sixty-nine captains and a total of one hundred eighty-nine men, and they rested at Mount Hebron. {40:32} The king of Hebron went out with his three captains and nine men to meet Jacob and his sons. {40:33} The kings asked Japhia to speak to the sons of Jacob on their behalf, and they would follow to confirm his words. {40:34} The sons of Jacob heard that the kings had gathered in Hebron, so they sent four servants as spies to assess their numbers. {40:35} The servants counted the kings and their men and reported back, saying there were two hundred eighty-eight people in total. {40:36} The sons of Jacob decided to face them with sixty-two men, along with ten of Jacob's sons, arming themselves for battle, not realizing the kings came for peace. {40:37} The sons of Jacob and their servants went to the gate of Shechem with their father Jacob. {40:38} They saw Japhia, king of Hebron, and his captains approaching, so they stopped and took their stand at the gate of Shechem. {40:39} Japhia and his captains bowed down to Jacob and his sons. {40:40} The sons of Jacob asked, "Why have you come to us today, O king of Hebron? What do you want from us?" {40:41} Japhia answered, "I beg you, my lord, all the kings of Canaan have come today to make peace with you." {40:42} The sons of Jacob did not trust him, thinking he was being deceitful. {40:43} Japhia, sensing their distrust, came closer to Jacob and said, "I assure you, my lord, all these kings have come to make peace with you. They brought no weapons, only seeking peace for fear of your strength." {40:44} The sons of Jacob replied, "Send for the kings, and if they come unarmed, we will know they truly want peace." {40:45} Japhia sent for the kings, and they all came unarmed, bowing to Jacob and his sons. {40:46} They said, "We have heard of your mighty deeds and feared for our lives, so we come in peace, seeking a treaty with you." {40:47} The sons of Jacob realized the kings were sincere and agreed to make a covenant of peace with them. {40:48} Both sides swore an oath not to interfere with each other, and from that day on, the kings of Canaan became tributaries to Jacob and his sons. {40:49} Afterward, the captains and their men brought gifts for Jacob and his sons, bowing down before them. {40:50} The kings then asked the sons of Jacob to return all the spoils they had taken from the seven cities of the Amorites, and Jacob's sons agreed, returning the women, children, cattle, and all the plunder they had taken. {40:51} The kings bowed again and brought more gifts, leaving peacefully for their cities. The sons of Jacob also returned to Shechem. {40:52} From that day forward, there was peace between the sons of Jacob and the kings of the Canaanites, until the time when the children of Israel would come to inherit the land of Canaan.

{41:1} At the turn of the year, the sons of Jacob left Shechem and traveled to Hebron to stay with their father Isaac. They lived there, but their flocks and herds were fed daily in Shechem, as the pastures were rich and fertile. Jacob, his sons, and their entire household settled in the valley of Hebron. {41:2} In that year, the 106th year of Jacob's life, and ten years after Jacob returned from Padan-Aram, Leah, Jacob's wife, died. She was 51 years old when she passed away in Hebron. {41:3} Jacob and his sons buried her in the cave of Machpelah in Hebron, the burial place that Abraham had bought from the sons of Heth. {41:4} Jacob's sons continued to live with their father in the valley of Hebron, and their strength and reputation became well known throughout the land. {41:5} Joseph, the son of Jacob, and his brother Benjamin, both sons of Rachel, Jacob's wife, were still young and did not go out with their brothers during the battles with the Amorites. {41:6} When Joseph saw the power and success of his brothers, he admired them but also considered himself to be greater than them, exalting himself. Jacob, his father, loved Joseph more than his other sons because Joseph was born to him in his old age, and because of this, Jacob made Joseph a special coat of many colors. {41:7} When Joseph realized that his father loved him more than his brothers, he continued to think of himself as superior and brought bad reports about his brothers to their father. {41:8} When the sons of Jacob saw how Joseph behaved and how their father favored him, they grew to hate him and could not speak kindly to him. {41:9} When Joseph was seventeen, he continued to elevate himself over his brothers, dreaming of being above them. {41:10} One day, he had a dream and told it to his brothers. He said, "I dreamed that we were all binding sheaves of grain in the field, and my sheaf stood upright while your sheaves gathered around and bowed down to mine." {41:11} His brothers replied, "What does this dream mean? Do you think you'll rule over us?" {41:12} Joseph also told the dream to his father, Jacob, who kissed him and blessed him. {41:13} When the other sons of Jacob saw that their father blessed Joseph and loved him even more, they became jealous and hated him even more. {41:14} Later, Joseph had another dream, which he shared with his father and brothers. He said, "I dreamed that the sun, the moon, and eleven stars bowed down to me." {41:15} Jacob, hearing this and knowing his other sons already hated Joseph, rebuked him, saying, "What is this dream you've had? Do you really think your mother, brothers, and I will bow down to you?" {41:16} He questioned whether Joseph thought his family would truly bow before him, and his brothers became even more jealous, but Jacob kept the dreams in mind. {41:17} One day, the sons of Jacob went to Shechem to feed their father's flock, as they were still herdsmen. They were delayed in returning, missing the usual time for gathering the cattle. {41:18} When Jacob noticed their delay, he grew concerned, thinking the people of Shechem might have attacked them. {41:19} Jacob called Joseph and told him to go check on his brothers and the flock in Shechem, and bring back news of their welfare. {41:20} Joseph set off from the valley of Hebron, arriving in Shechem, but he could not find his brothers. {41:21} Wandering in the fields near Shechem, Joseph got lost, unsure of which direction to take. {41:22} An angel of the Lord found him wandering and asked Joseph, "What are you looking for?" Joseph replied, "I'm searching for my brothers. Have you seen them?" The angel told him, "I heard them say they were going to Dothan to feed the flock." {41:23} Joseph listened and went to find his brothers in Dothan, where they were feeding the sheep. {41:24} When Joseph approached his brothers from a distance, they saw him coming and plotted to kill him. {41:25} Simeon said to the others, "Here comes the dreamer. Let's kill him and throw him into one of the pits in the wilderness. We'll tell our father a wild animal devoured him." {41:26} But Reuben, hearing this, tried to save Joseph by suggesting, "Don't kill him. Throw him into a pit instead, but don't harm him. We'll let him die there." Reuben's plan was to rescue Joseph later and return him to their father. {41:27} When Joseph reached his brothers, they attacked him, threw him to the ground, and stripped him of his colorful coat. {41:28} They cast him into a pit that was dry but full of serpents and scorpions. Joseph was terrified, but the Lord protected him by hiding the creatures, so they did not harm him. {41:29} From the pit, Joseph cried out to his brothers, asking, "What have I done to deserve this? Why don't you fear God? Aren't we of the same flesh, with the same father, Jacob? Why would you do this to me?" {41:30} He continued pleading, addressing Judah, Simeon, and Levi, saying, "Please lift me from this dark place. Have mercy on me, as the sons of Abraham, Isaac, and Jacob would have had on anyone in need. How can you deny compassion to your own brother?" {41:31} Joseph reminded them of their shared blood, pleading for mercy for their father's sake. {41:32} But despite his cries, his brothers ignored him and left the pit, moving far enough away not to hear his voice. {41:33} As he continued to cry and call out to them, Joseph wished his father knew what was happening to him and the words his brothers had spoken against him. {41:34} Though his brothers heard his cries, they hardened their hearts and moved away from the pit to avoid hearing Joseph's pleas and weeping.

{42:1} They went and sat on the opposite side, about a bow-shot's distance away, and while they were eating bread, they discussed what they should do with Joseph—whether to kill him or take him back to their father. {42:2} While they were talking, they looked up and saw a caravan of Ishmaelites coming from Gilead, traveling to Egypt. {42:3} Judah said to his brothers, "What profit will we gain if we kill our brother? Maybe God will require it from us. This is what we should do: Look, here comes a caravan of Ishmaelites going to Egypt. {42:4} Let's sell him to them instead, and not lay our hands on him ourselves. They will take him away, and he'll be lost among the people, so we won't have to kill him ourselves." His brothers agreed with Judah's suggestion. {42:5} As they were discussing this plan, before the Ishmaelites arrived, seven traders from Midian passed by. They were thirsty and, seeing the pit, assumed there was water inside. As they approached, they heard Joseph's voice, crying and weeping in the pit. {42:6} They looked down and saw a young man of handsome appearance trapped inside. {42:7} They called to him and asked, "Who are you, and who put you here in the wilderness?" They helped Joseph out of the pit and took him with them, continuing on their journey, passing by his brothers. {42:8} Joseph's brothers saw this and called out, "Why are you taking our servant from us? We put him in that pit because he disobeyed us. Now, you're just going to take him away? Return our servant!" {42:9} The Midianites replied, "Is this really your servant? He looks better than all of you! Maybe you are his servants. Why are you lying to us?" {42:10} They added, "We found this young man in the pit, and we took him. We won't listen to you." {42:11} The sons of Jacob got angry and demanded, "Give him back to us, or you'll die by the sword!" The Midianites also prepared for a fight. {42:12} Simeon stood up, drew his sword, and gave a mighty shout that echoed far, shaking the ground beneath them. {42:13} The Midianites were terrified and fell to the ground in fear. {42:14} Simeon told them, "I am Simeon, son of Jacob the Hebrew, and with my brother, I destroyed the city of Shechem.

Even if all of Midian or the kings of Canaan came against me, they wouldn't stand a chance. {42:15} Now, give back the young man, or I will leave your bodies for the birds and beasts." {42:16} The Midianites, even more afraid, tried to negotiate. "You said this young man was your servant, but what will you do with a servant who rebels? Why not sell him to us? We'll pay you well, and the Lord seems to want this, so you don't kill your brother." {42:17} Seeing that Joseph was handsome, the Midianites really wanted to buy him and urged his brothers to sell him. {42:18} The sons of Jacob listened and sold Joseph to the Midianites for twenty pieces of silver, though Reuben was not there. {42:19} The Midianites took Joseph and headed toward Gilead. {42:20} On the road, the Midianites regretted buying Joseph. One said, "What have we done? We've taken this young man, who may be stolen from the Hebrews. {42:21} If he is sought after, we could be killed for having him! {42:22} They realized how strong Joseph's brothers were and worried that they might have stolen him. {42:23} As they discussed this, the Ishmaelite caravan that Jacob's sons had first seen approached. The Midianites decided, "Let's sell Joseph to the Ishmaelites for the same price we paid, and we'll be rid of him." {42:24} They sold Joseph to the Ishmaelites for twenty pieces of silver and continued on their way. {42:25} The Ishmaelites put Joseph on a camel and continued their journey to Egypt. {42:26} Joseph, realizing they were heading to Egypt, cried bitterly at the thought of being taken so far from Canaan and his father. {42:27} One of the Ishmaelites noticed and forced Joseph to walk instead of ride, but Joseph continued weeping, calling out, "Father, father!" {42:28} One of the men struck him on the cheek, but Joseph kept crying. Weary and heartbroken, Joseph could hardly walk. They hit him and tried to frighten him into silence. {42:29} The Lord saw Joseph's suffering and caused darkness and confusion to fall upon the men, and those who struck Joseph found their hands withered. {42:30} They asked each other, "What is happening to us?" but did not realize it was because of Joseph. The group continued along the road past Ephrath, where Rachel was buried. {42:31} Joseph saw his mother's grave and ran to it, weeping. {42:32} He cried out, "Mother, wake up! See how your son has been sold into slavery, with no one to help him. {42:33} Rise from your rest and join me in my sorrow! My brothers stripped me of my coat, sold me twice, and separated me from my father. {42:34} Rise, mother, and make your case before God. See who He will justify and who He will condemn. {42:35} Awaken and comfort my father, whose heart is heavy for me." {42:36} Joseph continued weeping and lay still on the grave in his deep grief. {42:37} Suddenly, he heard a voice from beneath the ground, speaking in sorrow and prayer. {42:38} "My son, Joseph, I hear your cries and your weeping. I see your tears and feel your pain, and my grief is even greater because of yours. {42:39} But have hope, my son, and trust in the Lord. Do not fear, for He is with you and will deliver you from all your troubles. {42:40} Go with your masters to Egypt without fear, for the Lord is with you." The voice fell silent. {42:41} Joseph was amazed but continued to weep. One of the Ishmaelites saw him at the grave and, angered, struck him and cursed him. {42:42} Joseph begged them, "Please, take me back to my father's house, and he will give you great riches." {42:43} They scoffed, "Aren't you just a slave? Where is your father? If you had a father, you wouldn't have been sold twice for such a low price!" {42:44} Their anger grew, and they continued to beat and torment Joseph, who wept even more bitterly. {42:45} The Lord saw Joseph's suffering and again struck the men, causing darkness to cover the land, with lightning and thunder shaking the earth. {42:46} The beasts and camels refused to move, no matter how much they were hit, and the men, terrified, wondered what sins they had committed for this disaster to fall on them. {42:47} One of them suggested that perhaps this calamity had come because they mistreated the young slave. They decided to beg Joseph for forgiveness and see if God would spare them. {42:48} They asked Joseph to forgive them, admitting they had sinned against both him and the Lord. Joseph prayed for them, and the Lord removed the affliction. {42:49} The animals rose, and the storm subsided. The men continued their journey, understanding that their trouble had come because of Joseph. {42:50} They discussed, "Why should we bring more punishment on ourselves by keeping this boy? Let's take him back to his father, collect our payment, and leave." {42:51} But another man argued, "The journey back is too long, and we can't afford to stray from our path." {42:52} A third man suggested, "Let's sell him when we get to Egypt for a higher price and be done with him." {42:53} The men agreed and continued on their journey to Egypt, taking Joseph with them.

{43:1} After the sons of Jacob had sold their brother Joseph to the Midianites, they felt deep regret for what they had done and tried to find him to bring him back, but they couldn't locate him. {43:2} Reuben returned to the pit where Joseph had been thrown, intending to rescue him and return him to their father. But when Reuben got there, he didn't hear a sound, so he called out, "Joseph! Joseph!" but no one responded. {43:3} Reuben thought Joseph had died from fear, or maybe a snake had killed him. He climbed down into the pit but couldn't find Joseph, so he came back up. {43:4} Reuben tore his clothes and said, "The boy is gone! How can I face my father if Joseph is dead?" He then went to his brothers, who were grieving over what they had done and discussing how to explain this to their father. Reuben told them, "I checked the pit, and Joseph isn't there! What will we say to our father? He will demand the boy from me!" {43:5} His brothers replied, "This is what we did, but now our hearts are filled with regret. We're trying to figure out how to tell our father." {43:6} Reuben said, "What you've done is terrible! You'll cause our father to go down to the grave in sorrow. This isn't right." {43:7} They all sat down and swore an oath to each other that none of them would ever tell Jacob or anyone else what they had done. They agreed that whoever broke the oath would be killed by the others. {43:8} From the youngest to the oldest, they all feared each other in this matter, and no one said a word. They kept everything hidden in their hearts. {43:9} Then they sat down to figure out what to tell their father. {43:10} Issachar suggested, "Here's an idea: Take Joseph's coat, tear it up, kill a goat, and dip the coat in its blood. {43:11} "When we send it to our father, he'll think a wild animal killed him. That way, we can avoid his accusations." {43:12} Issachar's plan pleased them, so they followed his advice. {43:13} They hurried, tore Joseph's coat, killed a goat, dipped the coat in its blood, and covered it with dust. Then they gave the coat to Naphtali and told him to deliver it to their father and say, {43:14} "We were coming back from tending the cattle near Shechem when we found this coat on the road, covered in blood and dust. Please check if it's your son's coat." {43:15} Naphtali took the coat to Jacob and repeated the words his brothers had told him. {43:16} Jacob recognized the coat and fell to the ground like a stone. Later, he got up, crying loudly, and said, "This is my son Joseph's coat!" {43:17} Jacob immediately sent a servant to find his sons, and the servant found them on their way back with the flocks. {43:18} The sons of Jacob arrived in the evening, their clothes torn and dust on their heads, and they found their father weeping. {43:19} Jacob asked them, "What terrible thing have you done to me today?" They replied, "We were walking back after tending the flock and found this coat near Shechem. We recognized it and sent it to you." {43:20} Jacob heard their words and cried out, "This is my son's coat! A wild animal has killed him! Joseph has been torn to pieces! I sent him today to check on you and the flocks, but now this has happened, and I thought he was with you." {43:21} His sons replied, "He never came to us. We haven't seen him since we left you." {43:22} When Jacob heard this, he cried out again, tore his clothes, put on sackcloth, and wept bitterly. He mourned and wailed loudly, saying, {43:23} "Joseph, my son, I sent you today to check on your brothers, and now you've been killed. How bitter is your death to me, my son Joseph!" {43:24} He continued, "I wish I had died instead of you, Joseph. How sweet you were to me in life, and now how bitter is your death!" {43:25} "If only I could have died in your place, my son. Where are you, Joseph? Why don't you rise and see my sorrow for you?" {43:26} "Count the tears flowing from my eyes and let them reach the Lord, that His anger may turn away from me." {43:27} "Joseph, my son, how did you fall by the hand of someone who had never killed before? You were killed unjustly, but I know it's because of my many sins that this has happened." {43:28} "Rise and see my grief, my son, even though I didn't create or give life to you. It was God who formed you and gave you to me." {43:29} "Now, God has taken you away from me, and this tragedy has happened to you." {43:30} Jacob kept mourning for Joseph, weeping bitterly. He fell to the ground again, silent as a stone. {43:31} Seeing their father's distress, his sons also wept bitterly and regretted what they had done. {43:32} Judah lifted Jacob's head from the ground, laid it on his lap, and wiped away his father's tears. Judah cried greatly as Jacob's head rested on his lap like a stone. {43:33} All the brothers saw their father's sorrow, and they continued to weep. Jacob lay still on the ground. {43:34} His sons, servants, and their children all gathered around him, trying to comfort him, but Jacob refused to be comforted. {43:35} The entire household mourned deeply for Joseph and for Jacob's sorrow. Word of Joseph's death reached Isaac, Jacob's father, and Isaac and his household wept bitterly for Joseph. Isaac left his home in Hebron and went to comfort Jacob, but Jacob refused to be comforted. {43:36} Eventually, Jacob rose from the ground, tears streaming down his face, and told his sons, "Take your swords and bows and go into the field. Search for Joseph's body so I can bury him." {43:37} "Also, hunt the beasts, and whatever you find first, bring it to me. Maybe the Lord will take pity on me and lead you to the beast that tore Joseph apart, so I can avenge my son's death." {43:38} His sons did as he commanded. Early the next morning, they took their swords and bows and went into the wilderness to hunt wild animals. {43:39} Meanwhile, Jacob continued to cry out and weep, pacing back and forth in his house, saying, "Joseph, my son! Joseph, my son!" {43:40} The sons of Jacob went into the wilderness, and they caught a wolf, which they brought back to their father. They said, "This is the first animal we've caught, but we couldn't find Joseph's body." {43:41} Jacob took the wolf from them, cried out bitterly, and spoke to the wolf, saying, "Why did you kill my son Joseph? Didn't you fear God or my suffering for my son?" {43:42} "You killed my son for no reason, and now I'm guilty because of you. God will avenge this innocent blood." {43:43} Then the Lord opened the wolf's mouth to speak and comfort Jacob. The wolf said, "As surely as God lives, I didn't see your son or tear him apart. I came here from a distant land to look for my own son, and I don't know whether he is alive or dead." {43:44} "I came here today to find my son, and your sons found me and brought me to you. I have told you everything I know." {43:45} "Now, O man, I'm in your hands. Do with me as you please. But by the life of God, I did not see your son, nor did I harm him. I have never eaten the flesh of humans in my life." {43:46} When Jacob heard the wolf's words, he was astonished and released the animal. The wolf left. {43:47} But Jacob continued to weep and mourn for Joseph day after day. {43:48} He grieved for his son for many days.

{44:1} The sons of Ishmael who bought Joseph from the Midianites, who had purchased him from his brothers, traveled to Egypt with him. When they reached the borders of Egypt, they encountered four men from the Medan, a son of Abraham, who were returning from Egypt on their journey. {44:2} The Ishmaelites asked them, "Would you like to buy this slave from us?" They responded, "Yes, hand him over to us," and so they delivered Joseph to them. They saw that he was a handsome young man and bought him for twenty shekels. {44:3} The Ishmaelites continued on their way to Egypt, and the Medan also returned that same day. They spoke among themselves, "We've heard that Potiphar, an officer of Pharaoh and captain of the guard, is looking for a good servant who can stand before him, attend to him, and manage his household and everything belonging to him." {44:4} So they decided to sell Joseph to Potiphar for a price they could agree on, assuming he would pay what they asked. {44:5} The Medan went to Potiphar's house and said, "We've heard that you're seeking a good servant. We have a servant that will please you, if you can give us what we want for him." {44:6} Potiphar replied, "Bring him to me, and I will see him. If I find him satisfactory, I will pay you what you require." {44:7} The Medan brought Joseph and placed him before Potiphar. Potiphar saw him and was greatly impressed, saying, "What do you want for this young man?" {44:8} They replied, "We desire four hundred pieces of silver for him." Potiphar responded, "I will give it to you if you can provide the record of his sale and tell me his background, for perhaps he is stolen, as he doesn't appear to be a mere slave but rather a fine-looking person." {44:9} The Medan brought the Ishmaelites who had sold Joseph to them, and they confirmed, "He is a slave, and we sold him to them." {44:10} Potiphar heard the Ishmaelites' words and gave the silver to the Medan. They took the silver and left, while the Ishmaelites returned home. {44:11} Potiphar took Joseph and brought him to his house to serve him. Joseph found favor in Potiphar's sight, who placed his trust in him, making him overseer of his house and everything he owned. {44:12} The Lord was with Joseph, and he became prosperous. The Lord blessed Potiphar's house because of Joseph. {44:13} Potiphar left everything he owned in Joseph's hands, and Joseph managed all that was in Potiphar's house. {44:14} Joseph was eighteen years old, attractive with beautiful eyes, and no one in all of Egypt was like him. {44:15} While he was serving in his master's house, Potiphar's wife, Zelicah, looked at Joseph and admired him. {44:16} She became infatuated with him and tried to persuade him day after day, but Joseph did not pay attention to her. {44:17} Zelicah said to him, "You are so good-looking and well-formed. I have seen all the other servants, but none compare to you." Joseph replied, "The One who created me in my mother's womb made all mankind." {44:18} She said, "Your eyes are so beautiful; they mesmerize everyone in Egypt." Joseph responded, "They may be beautiful now, but you would look away if you saw them in the grave." {44:19} She urged him, "How lovely are your words! Please take the harp from the house and play it for me." He replied, "My words are beautiful when I speak of my God and His glory." {44:20} She continued, "How lovely is your hair! Look at this golden comb in the house; take it and style your hair." {44:21} Joseph responded, "How long will you continue this? Stop speaking to me this way and focus on your household tasks." {44:22} She insisted, "There is no one else here; nothing else matters except your wishes." Despite her persistent enticement, Joseph did not succumb to her advances. {44:23} Zelicah longed for Joseph to lie with her. One day, while he was busy with his work, she sat before him and pressured him daily to give in to her desires. Joseph refused to listen. {44:24} She threatened him, saying, "If you won't comply, I will punish you severely and put you in chains." Joseph replied, "God, who created man, can release prisoners; He will deliver me from your threats." {44:25} When she could not persuade him, her desire for him turned into a serious illness. {44:26} All the women of Egypt came to visit her and asked, "Why are you in such a decline? You lack nothing; your husband is an esteemed prince." {44:27} Zelicah replied, "Today I will reveal to you the cause of my suffering." She commanded her maidservants to prepare a feast for the women. {44:28} She provided them with knives to cut the citrons they would eat and had Joseph dressed in fine clothes to appear before them. {44:29} When Joseph came in, the women gazed at him, captivated by his beauty, and they accidentally cut their hands with the knives they were holding, causing blood to flow down their garments. {44:30} They didn't notice what they had done; they were too absorbed in Joseph's beauty. {44:31} Zelicah saw what happened and exclaimed, "What have you done? I gave you citrons, and you have all cut your hands!" {44:32} The women looked at their hands, realizing they were covered in blood. They admitted, "Your servant has captivated us; we couldn't tear our eyes away." {44:33} Zelicah remarked, "This happened to you the moment you looked at him. How can I resist when I see him daily in my house? I'm at risk of perishing from this desire!" {44:34} The women agreed, acknowledging, "It's true. Who can see such beauty and refrain? He is merely your servant; why don't you express your feelings to him?" {44:35} Zelicah replied, "I've been trying to persuade him, but he refuses. I promised him all good things, yet I get no response; thus, I am suffering." {44:36} Zelicah became very ill because of her desire for Joseph, and no one in her household knew why she was so distressed. {44:37} The people in her house questioned her, "Why are you ill? You lack nothing!" She answered, "I don't understand why I feel this way." {44:38} All the women and friends came daily to see her, and she confessed, "This is all because of my love for Joseph." They advised her, "Entice him and take him secretly; maybe he will listen to you and save you." {44:39} As Zelicah's condition worsened, she continued to decline until she could barely stand. {44:40} One day, while Joseph was working in the house, Zelicah approached him secretly and suddenly threw herself at him. Joseph resisted her and overpowered her, bringing her to the ground. {44:41} Zelicah wept, pleading with him, her tears streaming down her face. She said, "Have you ever seen a more beautiful woman than me, or one who suffers for you? I have given you honor, and yet you refuse to listen." {44:42} She continued, "If it's fear of your master, I swear no harm will come to you from him for this." She urged him to comply and save her from this fate. {44:43} Joseph replied, "Refrain from me and leave this matter to my master; he has entrusted everything to me except for you, his wife. How can I do this great evil and sin against God and your husband?" {44:44} So he insisted she stop speaking to him like this. Yet, Zelicah continued to tempt him every day. {44:45} It was then that the Nile River flooded, and all the Egyptians went out to celebrate, including the king and princes, who danced and rejoiced at the time of the inundation. {44:46} When the

Egyptians went to the river to celebrate, the people of Potiphar's house joined them, but Zelicah chose to stay home, claiming she felt unwell, and she was alone in the house. {44:47} She went to her chamber, dressed in royal garments, adorned herself with precious stones, and beautified her face with perfumes. She filled the house with fragrances and sat at the entrance of the chamber through which Joseph would pass. {44:48} When Joseph returned from the field and entered the house to continue his work, he saw the elaborate setup Zelicah had created and turned back. {44:49} Zelicah noticed Joseph turning away and called out, "What's wrong, Joseph? Come back and continue your work; I will make room for you." {44:50} Joseph returned, came inside, and sat down to do his work. Zelicah approached him, and they found themselves alone, with only one maidservant present. {44:51} Zelicah said to Joseph, "Do you love me? Speak to me." {44:52} Joseph replied, "God knows my heart, and I cannot lie." Zelicah persisted, "Tell me how you truly feel about me." Joseph replied, "My love is for God and my father." {44:53} She insisted, "Tell me how you feel about me; I long for you." {44:54} Joseph firmly replied, "You cannot have what I love." Zelicah exclaimed, "But I will have what I want. I have sought you, and you are mine." {44:55} She pressed him to lie with her. {44:56} Joseph shouted, "Help! Help! My master has betrayed me!" Zelicah shouted back, "Help! Someone is trying to take me!" {44:57} As they struggled, Zelicah quickly grabbed his garment, tearing it from him. {44:58} Joseph fled out into the street, while Zelicah retained his garment in her hand. {44:59} The maidservant was terrified by the scene. Zelicah said, "Joseph has tried to lie with me! Grab him!" {44:60} The maidservant ran out into the street, shouting for the Egyptians, who came running to the house. {44:61} Zelicah exclaimed, "This slave tried to assault me; he came into my house and attacked me! I cried out, but he wouldn't listen!" {44:62} The Egyptians were furious, and they dragged Joseph back to the house. {44:63} Potiphar heard the commotion and rushed home. When he entered, Zelicah, still holding Joseph's torn garment, said, "This is what your servant did to me!" {44:64} Potiphar asked Joseph, "What did you do? How could you harm my wife?" {44:65} Joseph replied, "It was Zelicah who sought to destroy me; I called for help!" {44:66} Potiphar turned to Zelicah and said, "Why have you done this?" {44:67} Zelicah quickly replied, "This is the slave you brought into our home; if I hadn't asked you to keep him, you would have sold him long ago!" {44:68} Potiphar said, "What a shame! You deserve to be punished for this!" {44:69} He ordered that Joseph be put in chains and sent to prison, and Joseph was taken away to serve his time. {44:70} The guards were ordered to keep him in the darkest cell. {44:71} There Joseph remained for many days, praying to God for rescue from this suffering. {44:72} After a few days, Potiphar received a message from Pharaoh that someone was trying to poison him. {44:73} Potiphar discovered that Zelicah was the one attempting to harm Pharaoh, who had nearly succumbed to the poison. {44:74} Potiphar ordered that Zelicah be put in chains, and he had her cast into prison as well, just as he had done to Joseph. {44:75} Thus, the two remained in prison together for a long time, comforted by one another during their suffering. {44:76} While in prison, Joseph was able to teach Zelicah about the Lord and God's ways, and she listened closely to his words. {44:77} In time, Zelicah repented for her actions and cried out to God, "Please forgive me for seeking to harm the one who is innocent." {44:78} Joseph encouraged her and said, "Trust in the Lord; He has a purpose for both of us." They prayed together, and God answered their prayers. {44:79} As they prayed, the Lord removed the chains from them, and the guards came to take them from prison. {44:80} They were freed and promised never to return to their former ways. They left prison together and went to Potiphar, where they begged for forgiveness. {44:81} Potiphar saw them and realized the error of his ways. He forgave them both, and from that day forward, they lived in peace, forever praising God for their deliverance.

{45:1} At that time, in the year when Joseph had been taken down to Egypt after his brothers sold him, Reuben, the son of Jacob, went to Timnah and married Eliuram, the daughter of Avi the Canaanite, and he went to her. {45:2} Eliuram, Reuben's wife, conceived and bore him four sons: Hanoch, Palu, Chetzron, and Carmi. {45:3} Later, Simeon, his brother, married his sister Dinah, and she bore him five sons: Memuel, Yamin, Ohad, Jachin, and Zochar. {45:4} Judah went to Adulam at that time and met a man named Hirah. There, Judah saw a Canaanite woman named Aliyath, the daughter of Shua, and he married her, and she bore him three sons: Er, Onan, and Shiloh. {45:5} Levi and Issachar traveled to the east and took wives from the daughters of Jobab, the son of Yoktan, who was the son of Eber. Jobab had two daughters: the elder named Adinah and the younger named Aridah. {45:6} Levi married Adinah, while Issachar married Aridah. They returned to their father's house in Canaan, and Adinah bore Levi three sons: Gershon, Kehath, and Merari. {45:7} Aridah bore Issachar four sons: Tola, Puvah, Job, and Shomron. Dan went to Moab and married Aphlaleth, the daughter of Chamudan, the Moabite, and brought her back to Canaan. {45:8} Aphlaleth was initially barren and had no children. Later, God remembered her, and she conceived and bore a son, whom she named Chushim. {45:9} Gad and Naphtali traveled to Haran and married daughters of Amuram, the son of Uz, who was the son of Nahor. {45:10} The names of Amuram's daughters were Merimah, the elder, and Uzith, the younger. Naphtali married Merimah, while Gad married Uzith and brought them back to Canaan. {45:11} Merimah bore Naphtali four sons: Yachzeel, Guni, Jazer, and Shalem. Uzith bore Gad seven sons: Zephion, Chagi, Shuni, Ezbon, Eri, Arodi, and Arali. {45:12} Asher went and took Adon, the daughter of Aphlal, the son of Hadad, the son of Ishmael, for a wife, and he brought her back to Canaan. {45:13} Unfortunately, Adon, Asher's wife, died without having any children. After her death, Asher crossed the river and married Hadurah, the daughter of Abimael, the son of Eber, who was the son of Shem. {45:14} Hadurah was beautiful and sensible; she had been the wife of Malkiel, the son of Elam, the son of Shem. {45:15} Hadurah had a daughter named Serach with Malkiel. After Malkiel died, Hadurah returned to her father's house. {45:16} After the death of his wife, Asher took Hadurah as his wife and brought her back to Canaan along with her three-year-old daughter Serach, who was raised in Jacob's house. {45:17} Serach was beautiful and followed the righteous ways of Jacob's children; she lacked nothing, and the Lord gave her wisdom and understanding. {45:18} Hadurah, Asher's wife, conceived and bore him four sons: Yimnah, Yishvah, Yishvi, and Beriah. {45:19} Zebulun went to Midian and married Merishah, the daughter of Molad, the son of Abida, the son of Midian, bringing her back to Canaan. {45:20} Merishah bore Zebulun three sons: Sered, Elon, and Yachleel. {45:21} Jacob sent to Aram, the son of Zoba, the son of Terah, to find a wife for his son Benjamin, and he took Mechalia, the daughter of Aram, who came to Canaan to live with Jacob. Benjamin was ten years old when he married Mechalia. {45:22} Mechalia conceived and bore Benjamin five sons: Bela, Becher, Ashbel, Gera, and Naaman. Later, Benjamin married Aribath, the daughter of Shomron, the son of Abraham, in addition to Mechalia, and he was eighteen years old. Aribath bore him five sons: Achi, Vosh, Mupim, Chupim, and Ord. {45:23} In those days, Judah went to Shem's house and took Tamar, the daughter of Elam, the son of Shem, as a wife for his firstborn, Er. {45:24} Er married Tamar, but he was wicked and did not fulfill his duty, so the Lord struck him dead. {45:25} After Er's death, Judah told Onan, "Go to your brother's wife and marry her as the next of kin to raise a child for your brother." {45:26} Onan married Tamar, but like his brother, he did not fulfill his duty, so the Lord struck him dead too. {45:27} When Onan died, Judah told Tamar to remain in her father's house until his youngest son, Shiloh, grew up. He did not want to give her to Shiloh, fearing he might die like his brothers. {45:28} Tamar returned to her father's house, where she stayed for a while. {45:29} After a year had passed, Judah's wife, Aliyath, died. Judah was comforted after her death and went up with his friend Hirah to Timnah to shear sheep. {45:30} Tamar learned that Judah had gone to Timnah and realized that Shiloh was grown but Judah still had no intention of giving her to him. {45:31} Tamar removed her widow's garments, covered herself with a veil, and sat by the roadside leading to Timnah. {45:32} When Judah saw her, he approached her, not realizing who she was, and he slept with her. Tamar became pregnant, she had twins in her womb. She named the first Perez and the second Zarah.

{46:1} During that time, Joseph was still imprisoned in Egypt. {46:2} Meanwhile, Pharaoh's attendants, the chief butler and the chief baker, were with him. {46:3} The butler poured wine for Pharaoh, and the baker presented him with bread, and Pharaoh ate and drank with his ministers. {46:4} While they were eating, Pharaoh's ministers noticed many flies in the butler's wine and stones of nitre (a type of salt) in the baker's bread. {46:5} The captain of the guard assigned Joseph to attend Pharaoh's officers, who had been imprisoned for a year. {46:6} After a year, both the butler and the baker had dreams on the same night. The next morning, Joseph came to attend to them and noticed they looked sad. {46:7} He asked them why they were downcast, and they explained, "We've dreamed dreams, but there's no one to interpret them." Joseph replied, "Tell me your dreams, and God will give you the answer you seek." {46:8} The butler shared his dream: "I saw a large vine with three branches that blossomed and bore ripe grapes. {46:9} I squeezed the grapes into a cup and gave it to Pharaoh, and he drank." Joseph told him, "The three branches represent three days. {46:10} In three days, Pharaoh will restore you to your position, and you will once again give him his wine. But please remember me when it goes well for you and show me kindness. Get me out of this prison, {46:11} because I was taken from Canaan and sold as a slave here." The butler promised, "If the king treats me well, I'll do what you ask." {46:12} Seeing that the butler's dream was favorably interpreted, the baker asked Joseph to interpret his dream too. {46:13} "In my dream, I had three white baskets on my head, and in the top basket were baked goods for Pharaoh, but birds were eating them," he said. {46:14} Joseph replied, "The three baskets represent three days. In three days, Pharaoh will take off your head, hang you on a tree, and the birds will eat your flesh." {46:15} Meanwhile, the queen was about to give birth, and she bore a son for Pharaoh, who celebrated the birth of his firstborn with great joy. {46:16} On the third day after the birth, Pharaoh held a feast for his officers and servants. {46:17} All the people of Egypt and Pharaoh's servants gathered to eat and drink at the celebration, rejoicing for eight days with music, tambourines, and dancing in the king's house. {46:18} Despite Joseph's help, the butler forgot him and did not mention him to the king as he had promised, which was allowed by the Lord to test Joseph for trusting in man. {46:19} Joseph remained in prison for two more years, totaling twelve years since he was imprisoned.

{47:1} Isaac, the son of Abraham, was still living at that time in Canaan, very old at one hundred and eighty years. Esau, his son and Jacob's brother, lived in the land of Edom, where he and his sons had possessions among the children of Seir. {47:2} Esau learned that his father was nearing death, so he, his sons, and his household came to Canaan, to his father's house. Jacob and his sons left the place where they were living in Hebron and all came to their father Isaac, finding Esau and his sons in the tent. {47:3} Jacob and his sons sat before Isaac, who was still mourning for his son Joseph. {47:4} Isaac said to Jacob, "Bring your sons to me so I can bless them." Jacob brought his eleven children before Isaac. {47:5} Isaac placed his hands on all of Jacob's sons, embraced and kissed them one by one, and blessed them, saying, "May the God of your fathers bless you and increase your descendants like the stars of heaven." {47:6} Isaac also blessed Esau's sons, saying, "May God make you a dread and a terror to all who see you and to all your enemies." {47:7} Isaac then called Jacob and his sons, who all sat before him. He said to Jacob, "The Lord God of the whole earth told me, 'To your descendants, I will give this land for an inheritance if your children keep my statutes and ways, and I will fulfill the oath I swore to your father Abraham.'" {47:8} Therefore, my son, teach your children and your grandchildren to fear the Lord and to follow the good path that pleases your God. If you keep the Lord's ways and statutes, He will uphold His covenant with Abraham and do well with you and your descendants all your days. {47:9} When Isaac finished giving commands to Jacob and his children, he died and was gathered to his people. {47:10} Jacob and Esau fell on the face of their father Isaac, weeping. Isaac died at the age of one hundred and eighty in Canaan, in Hebron. His sons carried him to the cave of Machpelah, which Abraham had purchased from the Hittites for a burial site. {47:11} All the kings of Canaan accompanied Jacob and Esau to Isaac's burial, honoring him greatly at his death. {47:12} Jacob's and Esau's sons walked barefoot around the place, lamenting, until they reached Kireath-arba. {47:13} Jacob and Esau buried their father Isaac in the cave of Machpelah, located in Kireath-arba, in Hebron, and they honored him greatly, as they would at a king's funeral. {47:14} Jacob, his sons, Esau, his sons, and all the kings of Canaan mourned greatly for many days and buried Isaac. {47:15} After Isaac's death, he left his cattle and possessions to his sons. Esau said to Jacob, "Let us divide everything our father left in two parts, and I will choose first." Jacob agreed, saying, "We will do so." {47:16} Jacob took all that Isaac had left in Canaan, the cattle and property, and arranged them into two parts before Esau, saying, "Here is everything; choose the half you want." {47:17} Jacob continued, "Please listen to what I have to say: The Lord God of heaven and earth spoke to our fathers, Abraham and Isaac, saying, 'To your descendants, I will give this land for an eternal inheritance.'" {47:18} So all that our father has left is before you; look at all the land and choose what you desire. {47:19} If you want the whole land, take it for you and your children forever, and I will take this wealth. If you want the riches, take them for yourself, and I will take the land for my children as an inheritance forever. {47:20} At that time, Nebayoth, the son of Ishmael, was in the land with his children. Esau went to him and said, "Jacob has spoken to me like this and answered me like that; now give me your advice." {47:21} Nebayoth replied, "What did Jacob say to you? Look, all the children of Canaan are living securely in their land, and Jacob says he will inherit it with his descendants forever. {47:22} So, go and take all your father's wealth and leave your brother Jacob in the land as he has said." {47:23} Esau rose up and returned to Jacob, following the advice of Nebayoth, taking all the wealth Isaac left—souls, beasts, cattle, property, and riches—giving nothing to Jacob. Jacob took all the land of Canaan from the brook of Egypt to the Euphrates River, claiming it as an everlasting possession for himself and his descendants. {47:25} Jacob also took from Esau the cave of Machpelah in Hebron, which Abraham had bought from Ephron as a burial site for himself and his descendants forever. {47:26} Jacob wrote all these details in a purchase document, signed it, and had it witnessed by four faithful witnesses. {47:27} These are the words Jacob wrote in the document: "The land of Canaan and all the cities of the Hittites, Hivites, Jebusites, Amorites, Perizzites, and Gergashites, all seven nations from the river of Egypt to the Euphrates." {47:28} He also recorded that he bought the city of Hebron, Kireath-arba, and the cave within it from his brother Esau for value, for a possession and inheritance for his descendants forever. {47:29} Jacob placed the purchase document, signatures, commands, statutes, and the revealed book in an earthen vessel to preserve them long-term, and he handed them to his children. {47:30} Esau took all that his father had left him after death from Jacob, including all property—man and beast, camel and donkey, ox and lamb, silver and gold, precious stones and bdellium (a fragrant resin)—leaving nothing behind from all that Isaac had left after his death. {47:31} Esau gathered all this and, with his children, returned home to Seir the Horite's land, away from his brother Jacob and his children. {47:32} Esau had possessions among the children of Seir and did not return to Canaan from that day on. {47:33} Thus, the entire land of Canaan became an everlasting inheritance for the children of Israel, while Esau and all his children inherited the mountain of Seir.

{48:1} In those days, after Isaac's death, the Lord commanded a famine to come upon the whole earth. {48:2} At that time, Pharaoh, king of Egypt, was sitting on his throne and laying in bed, dreaming. He dreamed that he was standing by the river in Egypt. {48:3} While he was standing there, he saw seven healthy and well-favored cows come up out of the river. {48:4} Then seven other cows, thin and unattractive, came up after them, and the seven lean ones swallowed up the well-favored ones, yet they still looked just as unhealthy as before. {48:5} He woke up, went back to sleep, and dreamed a second time. In this dream, he saw seven ears of corn grow on one stalk, full and good, but then seven thin ears, scorched by the east wind, sprang up after them, and the thin ears swallowed the full ones. Pharaoh awoke from his dream. {48:6} In the morning, he remembered his dreams and was deeply troubled by them. He quickly summoned all the magicians and wise men of Egypt, and they came and stood before Pharaoh. {48:7} The king said to them, "I have dreamed dreams, and no one can interpret them." They replied, "Let the king tell his dreams to us, and we will listen." {48:8} Pharaoh told them his dreams, and they all responded with one voice, saying, "May the king live forever! Here is the interpretation of your dreams." {48:9} The seven healthy cows represent seven daughters that will be born to you in the future, while the seven cows you saw afterward, which swallowed them, signify that all those daughters will die during your lifetime. {48:10} As for your second dream about the seven full ears of corn on one stalk, it means that you will build seven cities throughout Egypt, and the seven blasted ears of corn signify that those cities will all be destroyed in your lifetime. {48:11} When they spoke these words, the king did not listen to them, as he knew they were not giving the correct interpretation. After they finished speaking, he said to them, "What is this nonsense you have spoken? You have lied to me, so now give the proper interpretation of my dreams, or you will die." {48:12} The king then summoned other wise men, and they came and stood before him. The king recounted his dreams to them, and they gave the same interpretation as the first group. The king became furious and said to them, "You are all speaking lies and falsehoods!" {48:13} The king commanded that a proclamation be made throughout Egypt: "By the decree of the king and his advisors, any wise man who understands the interpretation of dreams and does not appear before the king today shall die." {48:14} The man who correctly interprets the king's dreams will receive anything he desires from the king. All the wise men, magicians, and sorcerers from Egypt and Goshen, Rameses, Tachpanches, Zoar, and all regions on the borders of Egypt came before the king. {48:15} All the nobles and princes, as well as the king's attendants, gathered from all over Egypt, and they sat before the king. The king told them his dreams, and everyone was astonished by the vision. {48:16} The wise men before the king were greatly divided in their interpretations. Some said, "The seven good cows are seven kings who will arise from your lineage to rule Egypt. {48:17} The seven bad cows are seven princes who will rise up against them in the future and destroy them. The seven ears of corn represent seven great princes of Egypt who will fall to the hands of seven less powerful princes from their enemies in battle." {48:18} Others interpreted, "The seven good cows are the strong cities of Egypt, while the seven bad cows represent the seven nations of Canaan that will come against the cities of Egypt and destroy them in the future." {48:19} As for your second dream of the ears of corn, it signifies that the governance of Egypt will revert to your lineage, as it once was. {48:20} In his reign, the inhabitants of Egypt will rise against the seven cities of Canaan that are stronger and will destroy them, restoring governance to your lineage. {48:21} Some said, "The seven good cows symbolize seven queens you will take as wives in the future, and the seven bad cows indicate that they will all die during your reign." {48:22} The seven good and bad ears of corn you saw in the second dream represent fourteen children who will fight amongst themselves, with seven defeating the more powerful seven. {48:23} Some further explained, "The seven good cows mean seven children will be born to you, and they will slay seven of your grandchildren in the future. The good ears of corn represent those princes who will battle and destroy seven other less powerful princes in the future, avenging your descendants, and governance will again return to your lineage." {48:24} After hearing all the wise men's interpretations, none pleased the king. {48:25} He understood in his wisdom that they had not spoken correctly, for God had sent this message to frustrate the wise men of Egypt so that Joseph could emerge from prison and achieve greatness in Egypt. {48:26} The king realized that none of the wise men or magicians had provided a satisfactory interpretation, which only fueled his anger. {48:27} He commanded all the wise men and magicians to leave his presence, and they departed, feeling shame and disgrace. {48:28} The king then ordered a proclamation to be made to kill all the magicians in Egypt; not a single one should be spared. {48:29} The king's guards rose up, each drawing their sword to strike down the magicians and wise men of Egypt. {48:30} After this, Merod, the chief butler to the king, came and bowed before the king. {48:31} The butler said to the king, "May the king live forever, and may his government be exalted in the land! {48:32} You were angry with me two years ago, and you placed me in prison, where I stayed for a while with the chief baker. {48:33} We both had dreams one night, each according to our own, and we told them to that Hebrew servant, Joseph, who belonged to the captain of the guard. {48:34} He interpreted our dreams accurately, and everything he said came to pass; not a single word fell to the ground. {48:35} Now, my lord and king, do not slay the people of Egypt without reason. That slave is still imprisoned in the house of confinement. {48:38} If it pleases the king, let him be summoned so he can tell you the correct interpretation of your dreams." {48:39} The king listened to the chief butler's words and ordered that the wise men of Egypt should not be executed. {48:40} He then commanded his servants to bring Joseph before him, instructing them not to frighten him, so he wouldn't become confused and unable to speak. {48:41} The king's servants went to Joseph, hurriedly bringing him out of the dungeon. They shaved him and changed his prison garments before bringing him before the king. {48:42} The king was sitting on his royal throne, dressed in princely robes adorned with a golden ephod, which sparkled with fine gold, along with precious stones like carbuncle, ruby, and emerald that dazzled the eye, and Joseph marveled greatly at the king. {48:43} The throne was covered with gold and silver and inlaid with onyx stones, and it had seventy steps leading up to it. {48:44} It was customary in Egypt that anyone speaking to the king, whether a prince or someone esteemed, would ascend to the thirty-first step while the king would descend to the thirty-sixth step to converse with them. {48:45} If the person was a commoner, they would ascend to the third step, and the king would descend to the fourth to speak to them. Additionally, anyone fluent in all seventy languages would ascend all seventy steps to speak with the king. {48:46} Those who could not speak all seventy languages would ascend as many steps as the languages they knew. {48:47} During those days, no one could reign in Egypt unless they could speak all seventy languages. {48:48} When Joseph came before the king, he bowed down to the ground and ascended to the third step while the king sat on the fourth step and spoke with him. {48:49} The king said to Joseph, "I dreamed a dream, and there is no one to interpret it correctly. I commanded all the magicians and wise men to come before me today, and I told them my dreams, but no one has given me a proper interpretation." {48:50} After this, I heard today that you are wise and can interpret every dream you hear." {48:51} Joseph answered Pharaoh, saying, "Let Pharaoh share his dreams; interpretations belong to God." Pharaoh then shared his dreams about the cows and the ears of corn, and then he stopped speaking. {48:52} Joseph, filled with the spirit of God, understood everything that would happen to the king from that day forward and knew the proper interpretation of the king's dream, which he shared. {48:53} Joseph found favor in the king's sight, who listened to all his words. Joseph told the king, "Do not think they are two dreams, for they are one and the same. They signify that a great famine is coming upon Egypt." {48:54} The king will soon suffer greatly, yet when this famine arises, it will not only affect Egypt but also all the surrounding nations, as a great drought will cover the entire earth. {48:55} The seven good cows represent seven years of abundance in Egypt, while the seven thin cows indicate seven years of great famine to follow. {48:56} And just as the ears of corn symbolize the great abundance of food that will fill the land, so too will the seven thin ears represent the famine that will consume the land. {48:57} The abundance will not be sufficient, and all the surrounding nations will hunger for food. {48:58} But during the seven years of abundance, the king should appoint wise men who can oversee the gathering of food from the fields and store it up for the coming famine. {48:59} This will be a great saving for the king and his kingdom in the years to come, and he will be able to save many lives. {48:60} The king listened to Joseph's words, and it was good in his sight. The king said to his advisors, "Can we find a man such as this, one in whom is the Spirit of God?" {48:61} The king then turned to Joseph and said, "Since God has shown you all this, I appoint you over my house, and your word shall be law throughout all of Egypt. {48:62} No one shall raise a hand or a foot in all the land of Egypt without your permission." {48:63} And he placed Joseph second in command over all of Egypt. {48:64} Then Pharaoh removed his signet ring from his hand and placed it on Joseph's hand, clothed him in garments of fine linen and gold, and crowned him with a golden crown. {48:65} He made him ride in the second chariot, and they cried out before him, "Bow the knee!" He was made ruler over all the land of Egypt. {48:66} At that time, Pharaoh said to Joseph, "I am Pharaoh, and you shall be in charge over all the land of Egypt." {48:67} Then Joseph went out from the presence of Pharaoh and traveled throughout all the land of Egypt, preparing for the famine. {48:68} During those years, Joseph gathered grain as abundant as the sand of the sea, until he ceased to measure it, for it was immeasurable. {48:69} Now the seven years of plenty that occurred were about to end, and the seven years of famine were at the door, just as Joseph had foretold. {48:70} When the famine came upon the land, the people cried out to Pharaoh, "Give us grain, for we are starving!" {48:71} Pharaoh replied, "Go to Joseph; do whatever he tells you." {48:72} All the lands of Egypt were devastated by the famine, but Joseph opened up the storehouses he had prepared and began selling grain to the Egyptians. {48:73} Many people from all over the earth came to Egypt to buy grain from Joseph, {48:74} for the famine was severe throughout the entire world.

{49:1} After these events, the king summoned all his officials, servants, princes, and nobles, and they gathered before him. {49:2} The king said to them, "You have all seen and heard the words of this Hebrew man and all the signs he foretold, and not a single one of his words has failed. {49:3} You know he has accurately interpreted the dream, and it will certainly come to pass. Therefore, take counsel and determine what you will do to save the land from the impending famine. {49:4} Look and see if you can find someone wise and knowledgeable to appoint over the land. {49:5} You have heard the wise advice given by the Hebrew man to save the land from the famine, and I believe that the land will only be saved through his counsel. {49:6} All the officials replied, "The advice the Hebrew has given is good. Therefore, our lord and king, the whole land is in your hands; do what you see fit." {49:7} "Choose whoever you find to be wise and capable of saving the land, and appoint him to lead." {49:8} The king addressed all the officers: "Since God has revealed all this to the Hebrew man, there is no one as discreet and wise in all the land as he is. If it seems good to you, I will place him over the land because he will save it with his wisdom." {49:9} The officers responded, "But it is written in the laws of Egypt that no man shall rule or be second to the king unless he has knowledge of all the languages of the people. {49:10} Our lord and king, this Hebrew man speaks only Hebrew; how can he be over us as the second in command if he doesn't even know our language? {49:11} We ask you to send for him and let him come before you, so you can test him in all things and decide as you see fit." {49:12} The king agreed, saying, "It will be done tomorrow, and your suggestion is good." The officers came before the king that same day. {49:13} That night, the Lord sent one of His ministering angels to Joseph in the dungeon, where he was being held by his master due to his wife's false accusations. {49:14} The angel awakened Joseph from his sleep, and as he stood up, the angel taught him all the languages of mankind that night, and he called him Jehoseph. {49:15} Afterward, the angel departed, and Joseph lay back down, astonished by the vision he had seen. {49:16} In the morning, the king summoned all his officers and servants, and they assembled before him. He ordered Joseph to be brought before him. {49:17} The king ascended the steps to the throne, and Joseph spoke to the king in all languages until he reached him at the seventieth step and sat down before him. {49:18} The king rejoiced greatly at Joseph's arrival, and all the king's officials celebrated when they heard Joseph's words. {49:19} The king and his officers agreed that it was good to appoint Joseph as second to the king over all of Egypt. The king said to Joseph, {49:20} "You advised me to appoint a wise man over Egypt to save the land from famine, and since God has made this known to you and revealed all that you have said, there is no one in the land as discreet and wise as you. {49:21} From now on, you will no longer be called Joseph; instead, your name will be Zaphnath Paaneah. You will be second to me, and all government affairs will be under your authority. My people will go out and come in at your command. {49:22} My servants and officers will receive their salaries from you, and all the people of the land will bow down to you, but I will be greater than you only in the throne." {49:23} The king removed his ring from his hand and placed it on Joseph's hand. He dressed Joseph in fine garments, placed a golden crown on his head, and a gold chain around his neck. {49:24} The king commanded his servants to make Joseph ride in the second chariot, which traveled next to the king's chariot. They led him on a great horse from the king's stable through the streets of Egypt. {49:25} The king ordered that all musicians, including those with timbrels, harps, and other instruments, should go before Joseph. One thousand timbrels, one thousand stringed instruments, and one thousand harps followed him. {49:26} Five thousand soldiers with drawn swords marched before Joseph, along with twenty thousand of the king's great men, adorned with gold-covered belts, on his right side, and another twenty thousand on his left. Women and young girls celebrated from the rooftops and in the streets, praising Joseph's appearance and beauty. {49:27} The king's entourage went ahead of him and behind him, perfuming the road with frankincense, cassia, and fine perfumes, while scattering myrrh and aloes along the path. Twenty heralds proclaimed loudly before him throughout the land: {49:28} "Do you see the man whom the king has chosen to be his second? All government affairs will be managed by him, and anyone who disobeys his orders or refuses to bow down before him shall die for rebelling against the king and his second." {49:29} When the heralds finished proclaiming, all the people of Egypt bowed down to the ground before Joseph, saying, "Long live the king! Long live his second!" The inhabitants of Egypt bowed down as they passed, rejoicing with timbrels and other instruments before Joseph. {49:30} Joseph, riding on his horse, lifted his eyes to heaven and called out, "He raises the poor from the dust; He lifts the needy from the dunghill. O Lord of Hosts, blessed is the man who trusts in You." {49:31} Joseph traveled throughout Egypt with the king's servants and officers, who showed him all the treasures of the land. {49:32} When he returned that day to Pharaoh, the king granted Joseph a portion of land in Egypt, including fields and vineyards, and gave him three thousand talents of silver, one thousand talents of gold, onyx stones, bdellium, and many other gifts. {49:33} The next day, the king ordered all the people of Egypt to bring offerings and gifts to Joseph, and anyone who disobeyed the king's command would be put to death. They made a high place in the city square and spread garments there, and whoever brought gifts to Joseph placed them in that spot. {49:34} All the people of Egypt contributed something: one man brought a golden earring, another brought rings and other gold and silver items, onyx stones, and bdellium. Everyone gave something from their possessions. {49:35} Joseph gathered these gifts and stored them in his treasury. The king's officers and nobles praised Joseph and presented him with many gifts, recognizing that he had been chosen to be second in command. {49:36} The king sent for Potiphera, the son of Ahiram, the priest of On, and gave him his beautiful young daughter, Osnath, as a wife for Joseph. {49:37} She was very lovely and a virgin, and Joseph took her as his wife. The king said to Joseph, "I am Pharaoh, and no one shall dare to lift a hand or a foot without your authority throughout all of Egypt." {49:38} Joseph was thirty years old when he stood before Pharaoh, and he became the king's second in command in Egypt. {49:39} The king provided Joseph with a hundred servants to assist him in his house, and Joseph also acquired many servants who remained in his household. {49:40} Joseph built himself a magnificent house similar to the king's palace, constructing it over the course of three years. {49:41} He crafted an elegant throne made of abundant gold and silver, adorning it with onyx stones and bdellium, depicting the likeness of all of Egypt and the river that nourished the land. Joseph sat securely upon his throne, and the Lord increased his wisdom. {49:42} The people of Egypt, the king's servants, and his princes loved Joseph greatly, for this was the Lord's doing. {49:43} Joseph commanded an army of forty-six thousand men capable of bearing arms to assist the king against any enemy, in addition to the king's officers and countless other inhabitants of Egypt. {49:44} Joseph provided his mighty men and his entire army with shields, javelins, helmets, coats of armor, and stones for slings.

{50:1} At that time, the people of Tarshish attacked the descendants of Ishmael and waged war against them, plundering the Ishmaelites for an extended period. {50:2} The Ishmaelites were few in number during those days and could not withstand the onslaught from the Tarshishites, leading to their severe oppression. {50:3} In response, the elders of the Ishmaelites sent a message to the king of Egypt, requesting him to send his officers and troops to help them fight against the Tarshishites, as they had been suffering for a long time. {50:4} Pharaoh sent Joseph along with the elite troops and soldiers from his palace. {50:5} They traveled to the region of Havilah to assist the Ishmaelites against the Tarshishites, where Joseph fought bravely and defeated them, taking control of their territory, which the Ishmaelites still inhabit today. {50:6} After the Tarshishites were defeated, they fled and sought refuge with their relatives, the Javanites, while Joseph and his men returned to Egypt without losing a single soldier. {50:7} At the turn of the year, during Joseph's second year of ruling Egypt, the Lord provided a bountiful harvest across the land for seven years, just as Joseph had predicted, and the Lord blessed the earth's produce during that time, leading to great satisfaction among the people. {50:8} Joseph had officers working under him who collected all the surplus food during the abundant years and stored grain year after year in his treasuries. {50:9} Whenever they gathered the food, Joseph instructed them to bring in the harvested grain still in the ears, along with some soil from the fields to prevent spoilage. {50:10} Joseph followed this practice every year, amassing grain like the sands of the sea, as his storage became immense and uncountable. {50:11} Additionally, the inhabitants of Egypt gathered various food items in large quantities during the seven prosperous years, but they did not follow the same method as Joseph. {50:12} The food that Joseph and the Egyptians stored during the seven years of plenty was set aside for the seven years of famine, providing sustenance for the entire land. {50:13} Each person in Egypt filled their storerooms and hidden places with grain to prepare for the impending famine. {50:14} Joseph stored all the food he had collected in cities throughout Egypt, securing the stores and appointing guards over them. {50:15} Joseph's wife, Osnath, the daughter of Potiphera, bore him two sons, Manasseh and Ephraim, when Joseph was thirty-four years old. {50:16} The boys grew up following their father's guidance and teachings, never straying from the paths he set for them. {50:17} The Lord blessed the boys with understanding and wisdom in all matters of governance, and the king's officials and influential citizens of Egypt highly regarded them, raising them alongside the king's children. {50:18} After the seven years of abundance ended, the seven years of famine arrived, as Joseph had foretold, and famine spread across the land. {50:19} The people of Egypt recognized that famine had begun, and they opened their grain stores, as the famine weighed heavily upon them. {50:20} To their dismay, they found that all the food in their storerooms was infested with vermin and unfit for consumption, causing widespread despair among the Egyptians who cried out to Pharaoh for help. {50:21} They pleaded with Pharaoh, saying, "Provide food for your servants! Why should we and our little ones die of hunger before you?" {50:22} Pharaoh replied, "Why are you crying out to me? Didn't Joseph order that grain be stored during the seven years of plenty for this very situation? Why didn't you listen to his instructions?" {50:23} The people of Egypt responded, "As your soul lives, our lord, we have followed all of Joseph's orders; we collected and stored the produce from our fields during the years of plenty." {50:24} "Yet, when famine struck, we opened our stores, only to find that all our grain was infested and unfit for food." {50:25} Upon hearing the plight of the Egyptians, Pharaoh was terrified by the severity of the famine and addressed the people, saying, "Since this has happened, go to Joseph and do whatever he tells you. Do not disobey his commands." {50:26} The people of Egypt went to Joseph and pleaded with him for food, saying, "Why should we perish from hunger before you? We followed your instructions and stored the grain as you ordered, and now we are in this predicament." {50:27} When Joseph heard the people's pleas and understood their situation, he opened all his granaries and sold them grain. {50:28} The famine spread throughout the land, affecting all countries, but in Egypt, there was grain available for purchase. {50:29} The people of Egypt came to Joseph to buy grain, as the famine pressed down on them and all their supplies had spoiled. {50:30} People from Canaan, the Philistines, those across the Jordan, and the children of the east, along with cities from far and near, learned that there was grain in Egypt and flocked there to buy food due to the widespread famine. {50:31} Joseph opened the granaries and appointed officers to oversee the sales, and they sold grain to everyone who came. {50:32} Joseph anticipated that his brothers would also come to Egypt to buy grain because the famine affected the entire world. Therefore, he instructed his people to announce throughout Egypt that {50:33} it was the king's command, along with his second in command and their officials, that anyone wishing to buy grain should not send their servants, but rather their sons. Also, any Egyptian or Canaanite who came to purchase grain and intended to resell it would be put to death; only those buying for their own households would be permitted to do so. {50:34} Anyone leading more than one or two animals would also face death; each man could only lead his own beast. {50:35} Joseph stationed guards at the gates of Egypt and instructed them not to allow anyone entering to buy grain without first recording their name, their father's name, and their grandfather's name, sending this information to him each evening for review. {50:36} Joseph appointed officers throughout the land of Egypt and directed them to carry out these instructions. {50:37} Joseph diligently enforced these regulations to keep track of when his brothers came to buy grain in Egypt, and his people proclaimed these rules daily according to Joseph's commands. {50:38} News of these regulations spread throughout the east and west, and people from distant regions heard about Joseph's laws and came daily to Egypt to buy grain. {50:39} All the officials in Egypt followed Joseph's commands, and every individual who came to Egypt to buy grain had their name, along with their father's name, documented, and these records were brought to Joseph each evening for review.

{51:1} Later, Jacob learned that there was grain in Egypt, so he called his sons together and urged them to go to Egypt to buy some, as they too were suffering from the famine. {51:2} He said, "I hear there is grain in Egypt, and everyone else is going there to buy it. Why should you sit here doing nothing while the whole world goes to buy food? You should also go to Egypt and buy us a little grain so that we don't die." {51:3} Jacob's sons listened to their father, and they set out for Egypt to purchase grain like everyone else. {51:4} Jacob instructed them, "When you enter the city, do not all go through the same gate because of the locals." {51:5} The sons followed Jacob's orders as they made their way to Egypt, but he did not send Benjamin along, fearing that something bad might happen to him on the journey, just like it did to his brother. So, ten of Jacob's sons traveled. {51:6} While on their way, the brothers regretted what they had done to Joseph. They spoke among themselves, saying, "We know our brother Joseph was taken to Egypt, and we should look for him. If we find him, we will buy him back from his master, and if that fails, we will rescue him by force, even if it costs us our lives." {51:7} They agreed to this plan and motivated each other to rescue Joseph as they continued toward Egypt. When they arrived near Egypt, they separated and entered through ten different gates, with the gatekeepers recording their names that day and bringing them to Joseph in the evening. {51:8} Joseph reviewed the names from the gatekeepers and realized that his brothers had entered through the ten gates of the city. At that time, he commanded that it should be announced throughout Egypt, saying, {51:9} "All store guards, close all the grain stores except for one so that those who come may buy from it." {51:10} Joseph's officers obeyed him, closing all but one store. {51:11} Joseph then gave the list of his brothers' names to the man in charge of the open store and instructed him, "Whenever someone comes to buy grain, ask their name, and if any of these names appear, seize them and send them to me." {51:12} When Jacob's sons entered the city, they searched for Joseph before buying grain. {51:13} They went to the houses of the harlots, thinking that Joseph might be there, as he was handsome and well-liked. They searched for him for three days but found nothing. {51:14} The man overseeing the open store checked the names Joseph had given but could not find them. {51:15} He sent a message to Joseph saying, "Three days have passed, and those men you told me about haven't come." Joseph then sent servants to search for his brothers across all of Egypt and bring them to him. {51:16} His servants scoured Egypt, visiting Goshen and the city of Rameses, but they still could not find them. {51:17} Joseph continued sending servants, this time sixteen in total, to search for his brothers. They spread out through the city, and four of them entered the houses of the harlots, where they found the ten men looking for their brother. {51:18} Those four brought them to Joseph, who was seated on his throne in his royal garments, adorned with a large golden crown, while his mighty men surrounded him. {51:19} The sons of Jacob saw Joseph and were struck by his impressive appearance and dignity; they bowed down to him again. {51:20} Joseph recognized his brothers, but they did not recognize him, for he was now a great man in their eyes. {51:21} He asked them, "Where do you come from?" They replied, "Your servants have come from the land of Canaan to buy grain, as the famine is severe." {51:22} Joseph said, "If you've truly come to buy grain, why did you enter through ten gates? You must be spies checking out the land." {51:23} They insisted, "No, my lord! We are honest men, not spies. We are twelve brothers, all sons of one man in Canaan. Our father instructed us not to enter through one gate because of the locals." {51:24} Joseph replied, "You are spies; you've come through ten gates to scout the land." {51:25} He said, "Anyone who comes to buy grain goes directly to their destination. Yet you've spent three days wandering in the harlots' quarters—surely that looks suspicious!" {51:26} They explained, "We are brothers, sons of Jacob, the son of Isaac, the son of Abraham. Our youngest brother is with our father, and one brother is no longer with us." {51:27} Joseph replied, "Have you searched everywhere but Egypt? And what would your brother be doing in the houses of harlots? You claim to be the sons of Abraham, yet you seek him there?" {51:28} They said, "We heard that Ishmaelites took him and sold him in Egypt. Our brother is very handsome, so we thought he might be found in such places." {51:29} Joseph said, "You lie about being Abraham's sons. As Pharaoh lives, you are spies, which is why you've come here." {51:30} He pressed them, "If you find him and his master demands a great price for him, will you pay?" They said, "We will pay whatever is needed." {51:31} Joseph asked, "And if his master refuses to sell him for a high price, what then?" They answered, "If he won't sell, we will kill him and take our brother." {51:32} Joseph said, "You are indeed spies! You came to kill the inhabitants of the land. We heard how two of your brothers slaughtered all the people of Shechem in Canaan over your sister, and now you come to do the same in Egypt." {51:33} "Here's how I will prove you; send one of you to fetch your youngest brother, and I will know you are honest." {51:34} Joseph called seventy of his strongest men and said, "Take these men and put them in the ward." {51:35} The strong men seized the ten brothers and put them in the ward for three days. {51:36} On the third day, Joseph called them and said, "Do this if you are honest: one of you will remain in custody while the others take home the grain and return with your youngest brother. Then I will know you are truthful." {51:37} Joseph went into another room and wept for them, feeling compassion, then washed his face and returned to the group. He took Simeon from them and ordered him to be bound, but Simeon resisted because he was a strong man, and they struggled to restrain him. {51:38} Joseph called his men, and seventy came with drawn swords, terrifying Jacob's sons. {51:39} Joseph commanded, "Seize this man and imprison him until his brothers arrive." His men quickly subdued Simeon, who let out a terrible scream that echoed far away. {51:40} All of Joseph's men were so frightened by his scream that they fell to the ground, afraid for their lives, leaving only Joseph and his son Manasseh. Manasseh saw how strong Simeon was and was furious. {51:41} He approached Simeon and struck him hard on the neck, calming him down. {51:42} Manasseh then forcibly restrained Simeon and took him to prison, leaving Jacob's sons stunned by the young man's actions. {51:43} Simeon told his brothers, "None of you should claim that this is the work of an Egyptian; it is a matter from our father's house." {51:44} Afterward, Joseph ordered the overseer of the storehouse to fill their sacks with as much grain as they could carry, return each man's money to his sack, and provide them provisions for the journey, which was done. {51:45} Joseph warned them, "Make sure you follow my orders to bring your brother back. When he arrives, I will know you are honest men, and I will allow you to trade in the land, restoring your brother to you and sending you back to your father in peace." {51:46} They answered, "We will do as you say," and they bowed before him. {51:47} Each man loaded his grain onto his donkey, and they set out for Canaan. When they stopped at an inn, Levi opened his sack to feed his donkey and discovered that his money was still in his sack. {51:48} He was terrified and told his brothers, "My money has been returned! It's right here in my sack." The brothers were alarmed and wondered, "What is this that God has done to us?" {51:49} They questioned, "Where is the Lord's kindness towards our fathers, Abraham, Isaac, and Jacob, that He has allowed us to fall into the hands of the king of Egypt to scheme against us?" {51:50} Judah said, "We are guilty before God for selling our brother, our own flesh. Why do you question the Lord's kindness toward our fathers?"{51:51} Judah said to them, "We are surely guilty sinners before the Lord our God for having sold our brother, our own flesh. So why do you ask, 'Where is the Lord's kindness with our ancestors?'" {51:52} Reuben replied, "Did I not tell you not to sin against the boy? But you wouldn't listen to me. Now God is requiring him from us. How can you say, 'Where is the Lord's kindness with our ancestors,' when you have sinned against the Lord?" {51:53} They stayed overnight in that place, and in the morning they got up early, loaded their donkeys with the grain, and set out for their father's house in the land of Canaan. {51:54} Jacob and his household went out to meet his sons, and when Jacob saw that their brother Simeon was not with them, he asked his sons, "Where is your brother Simeon? I don't see him." The brothers told him everything that had happened to them in Egypt.

{52:1} They entered their house, and each man opened his sack to find that his bundle of money was there, which terrified both them and their father. {52:2} Jacob said to them, "What have you done to me? I sent your brother Joseph to check on you, and you told me a wild animal killed him. {52:3} Simeon went with you to buy food, and now you say the king of Egypt has imprisoned him. You want to take Benjamin and cause his death too, bringing my gray hairs down to the grave in sorrow for both him and Joseph." {52:4} "My son will not go down with you, for his brother is dead, and he is all I have left. Something bad might happen to him on the journey, just like it did to his brother." {52:5} Reuben said to his father, "You can kill my two sons if I don't bring him back and present him to you." But Jacob replied, "My son will not go down with you to Egypt; he will not die like his brother." {52:6} Judah then said, "Let's wait until the grain we have is finished. Then he will tell us to take down our brother when he realizes that his life and the lives of his family are in danger from the famine." {52:7} During that time, the famine was severe throughout the land, and all the people of the earth went to Egypt to buy food because the famine was great. The sons of Jacob stayed in Canaan for a year and two months until their grain ran out. {52:8} When their food was gone, Jacob's entire household was hungry, and the children of Jacob gathered around him, pleading, "Give us bread, or we will all perish from hunger in your presence!" {52:9} Jacob heard the cries of his grandchildren and wept deeply, feeling compassion for them. He called his sons and they came and sat before him. {52:10} Jacob said, "Have you not seen how your children are crying for food? There is none! Now return and buy us a little food." {52:11} Judah replied, "If you send our brother with us, we will go down and buy food for you. If you don't send him, we won't go, because the king of Egypt specifically told us we cannot see him unless our brother is with us. The king of Egypt is a powerful man, and if we go to him without our brother, we will be put to death." {52:12} "Do you not know how powerful and wise this king is? There is no one like him in all the earth. We have seen all the kings and have not seen one like the king of Egypt. Abimelech, king of the Philistines, is great, but the king of Egypt is greater; Abimelech is only comparable to one of his officials. {52:13} Father, you have not seen his palace or his throne or all his servants standing before him. You haven't seen him on his throne in all his royal splendor, wearing his kingly robes and a large golden crown. You have not seen the honor and glory God has given him; there is no one like him in all the earth. {52:14} You have not witnessed the wisdom, understanding, and knowledge that God has placed in his heart, nor have you heard his kind voice when he spoke to us. {52:15} We do not know how he learned our names and all that has happened to us, but he asked about you, saying, 'Is your father still alive, and is it well with him?' {52:16} You have not seen how the affairs of Egypt are managed without the king needing to ask Pharaoh, his lord. You have not felt the awe and fear he instills in all the Egyptians. {52:17} When we left him, we threatened to act against Egypt like the other cities of the Amorites, and we were furious about his accusations that we were spies. If we return to him again, we will all be terrified, and no one will be able to speak to him." {52:18} "So, Father, please send the boy with us so we can buy food and not die from hunger." Jacob replied, "Why have you treated me so badly by telling the king that you had a brother? What have you done to me?" {52:19} Judah said to Jacob, "Put the boy in my care, and we will go down to Egypt and buy food. If we return without him, let me be held responsible forever. {52:20} Have you seen how all our children are crying over their hunger, and you have no power to feed them? Please, have compassion and send our brother with us." {52:21} "How will the Lord's kindness to our ancestors be shown to you when you say that the king of Egypt will take away your son? As the Lord lives, I will not leave him until I bring him back to you. Pray for us to the Lord that He will show us mercy and make us welcome before the king of Egypt and his men. If we had not delayed, we could have returned by now with your son." {52:22} Jacob said to his sons, "I trust in the Lord God that He will deliver you and grant you favor in the sight of the king of Egypt and all his men." {52:23} "So rise up and go to the man. Take a gift from the best of the land and bring it to him. May the Almighty God give you mercy before him so that he may send Benjamin and Simeon, your brothers, with you." {52:24} All the men prepared to leave, taking their brother Benjamin with them, along with a large present of the finest goods in the land and a double portion of silver. {52:25} Jacob strictly instructed his sons regarding Benjamin, saying, "Take care of him on the way and do not separate from him, either on the road or in Egypt." {52:26} Jacob rose from his sons and spread his hands, praying to the Lord for his sons, saying, "O Lord God of heaven and earth, remember Your covenant with our father Abraham, remember it with my father Isaac, and deal kindly with my sons. Deliver them from the king of Egypt; I ask You, O God, for the sake of Your mercies, redeem all my children and rescue them from the power of Egypt, and send them back their two brothers." {52:27} The wives of Jacob's sons and their children looked up to heaven, weeping before the Lord and crying out for Him to save their fathers from the hand of the king of Egypt. {52:28} Jacob wrote a letter to the king of Egypt, giving it to Judah and his sons, saying, {52:29} "From your servant Jacob, son of Isaac, son of Abraham the Hebrew, the prince of God, to the powerful and wise king, the revealer of secrets, king of Egypt, greetings. {52:30} Be it known to my lord the king of Egypt that the famine has been severe in the land of Canaan, and I sent my sons to buy us a little food for our support. {52:31} My sons surrounded me, and being very old, I cannot see with my eyes because they have become heavy with age and daily weeping for my son Joseph, who was lost to me. I told my sons not to enter the gates of the city when they went to Egypt because of the people there. {52:32} I also instructed them to search throughout Egypt for my son Joseph; perhaps they might find him there, and you treated them as spies in the land. {52:33} Have we not heard that you interpreted Pharaoh's dream and spoke the truth to him? How then do you not know with your wisdom whether my sons are spies? {52:34} Therefore, my lord and king, look, I have sent my son to you as you told my sons; I beg you to keep an eye on him until he returns to me in peace with his brothers. {52:35} Don't you know what our God did to Pharaoh when he took my mother Sarah, or what He did to Abimelech, king of the Philistines, on account of her, and what our father Abraham did to the nine kings of Elam, defeating them with just a few men? {52:36} Also remember what my two sons, Simeon and Levi, did to the eight cities of the Amorites, destroying them for their sister Dinah. {52:37} They comforted themselves for the loss of their brother Joseph on account of their brother Benjamin. What will they do if they see the hand of any people prevailing against them for his sake? {52:38} Don't you know, O king of Egypt, that the power of God is with us and that He always hears our prayers and never abandons us? {52:39} When my sons told me about your dealings with them, I did not call upon the Lord concerning you because I thought that you might perish before my son Benjamin came to you. {52:40} But I did not do that because Simeon, my son, was in your house; I thought you might treat him kindly. Therefore, behold, my son Benjamin is coming to you with my sons. Keep a close watch on him and then God will keep His eyes on you and throughout your kingdom. {52:41} I have shared all that is in my heart, and behold, my sons are coming to you with their brother. Examine the face of the whole earth for their sake and send them back in peace with their brothers." {52:42} Jacob entrusted the letter to Judah and instructed him to hand it to the king when they arrived in Egypt.

{53:1} The sons of Jacob got up, took Benjamin and all the gifts, and traveled to Egypt, where they stood before Joseph. {53:2} Joseph saw his brother Benjamin with them and greeted them, and they all went to Joseph's house. {53:3} Joseph instructed the supervisor of his house to prepare a meal for his brothers, and he did so. {53:4} At noon, Joseph sent for the men to come before him with Benjamin. The men informed the supervisor about the silver that had been returned in their sacks, and he reassured them, saying, "Don't be afraid; everything will be fine," and he brought their brother Simeon to them. {53:5} Simeon said to his brothers, "The lord of the Egyptians has treated me very kindly; he didn't keep me bound, as you saw with your own eyes. When you left the city, he set me free and treated me well in his house." {53:6} Judah took Benjamin by the hand, and they approached Joseph, bowing down to the ground. {53:7} The men presented their gifts to Joseph and sat down before him. Joseph asked, "Is everything well with you? Are your children well? Is your elderly father well?" They answered, "Everything is fine," and Judah handed over the letter that Jacob had sent to Joseph. {53:8} Joseph read the letter and recognized his father's handwriting. He was overwhelmed with emotion and went into a private room to weep deeply before returning. {53:9} He lifted his eyes and saw his brother Benjamin. He asked, "Is this your brother you spoke to me about?" Benjamin approached Joseph, and Joseph placed his hand on his head, saying, "May God be gracious to you, my son." {53:10} When Joseph saw Benjamin, the son of his mother, he felt the urge to weep again, so he went back to his chamber and cried there. After washing his face, he returned, controlled his emotions, and told them to prepare food. {53:11} Joseph had a cup from which he drank, made of silver beautifully inlaid with onyx stones and bdellium (a type of resin), and Joseph struck the cup in front of his brothers while they were eating with him. {53:12} Joseph said to the men, "I can tell from this cup that Reuben, the firstborn, Simeon, Levi, Judah, Issachar, and Zebulun are all children from one mother. Sit down to eat according to your birth order." {53:13} He also arranged the others by their birth order, saying, "I know this youngest brother has no brother, and I, like him, have no brother, so he will sit down to eat with me." {53:14} Benjamin came up before Joseph and sat on the throne. The men were amazed at Joseph's actions; they ate and drank with him, and Joseph gave gifts to them. He gave one special gift to Benjamin, and Manasseh and Ephraim saw their father's actions and also gave him presents, and Osnath (Joseph's wife) gave him one present as well, totaling five gifts in Benjamin's hands. {53:15} Joseph brought them wine to drink, but they refused, saying, "Since the day Joseph was lost, we have not drunk wine or eaten any delicacies." {53:16} Joseph insisted and pressed them until they drank freely with him that day. Later, Joseph turned to his brother Benjamin to talk, and Benjamin was still sitting on the throne before Joseph. {53:17} Joseph asked him, "Have you had any children?" Benjamin replied, "Your servant has ten sons, and these are their names: Bela, Becher, Ashbal, Gera, Naaman, Achi, Rosh, Mupim, Chupim, and Ord. I named them after my brother whom I have not seen." {53:18} He ordered that his star map be brought to him, which Joseph used to understand the times, and Joseph asked Benjamin, "I've heard that the Hebrews know all wisdom; do you know anything about this?" {53:19} Benjamin replied, "Your servant knows all the wisdom my father taught me," and Joseph said to Benjamin, "Look at this instrument and understand where your brother Joseph is in Egypt, the one you said went down there." {53:20} Benjamin examined the star map and was wise enough to determine where his brother was. He divided the whole land of Egypt into four sections and realized that the man sitting on the throne before him was his brother Joseph. Benjamin was greatly astonished. When Joseph saw how amazed Benjamin was, he asked, "What do you see, and why are you astonished?" {53:21} Benjamin said to Joseph, "I can see by this that my brother Joseph is sitting here with me on the throne." Joseph said to him, "I am Joseph, your brother; do not reveal this to your brothers. I will send you back with them, but I will command them to return to the city, and I will take you away from them." {53:22} Joseph added, "If they are willing to risk their lives and fight for you, then I will know they have repented for what they did to me. I will reveal myself to them. If they abandon you when I take you, you will stay with me, and I will confront them, and they will leave, and I will remain unknown to them." {53:23} At that time, Joseph instructed his officer to fill their sacks with food, put each man's money back in his sack, place the cup in Benjamin's sack, and provide them with supplies for their journey. They did as he commanded. {53:24} The next day, the men woke up early, loaded their donkeys with grain, and left with Benjamin, heading for the land of Canaan. {53:25} They had not traveled far from Egypt when Joseph instructed the overseer of his house, saying, "Get up, pursue these men before they get too far, and ask them, 'Why have you stolen my master's cup?'" {53:26} Joseph's officer caught up with them and told them everything Joseph had said. When they heard this, they became very angry and said, "Whoever has your master's cup will die, and we will become slaves as well." {53:27} They hurried, each man took down his sack from his donkey, and they searched their bags. The cup was found in Benjamin's bag, and they all tore their clothes in despair and returned to the city. They struck Benjamin on the way, hitting him continuously until they reached the city, where they stood before Joseph. {53:28} Judah's anger flared, and he said, "This man has only brought me back to ruin Egypt today." {53:29} The men arrived at Joseph's house and found him sitting on his throne, with all his powerful officials standing beside him. {53:30} Joseph asked them, "What is this act you have committed? Why did you take my silver cup and leave? I know you took my cup to find out where your brother was." {53:31} Judah replied, "What can we say to our lord? What can we speak? How can we justify ourselves? God has revealed the guilt of all your servants today; that is why he has done this to us." {53:32} Joseph rose up, seized Benjamin, and took him away from his brothers forcefully. He went into the house and locked the door behind him. Joseph commanded his overseer to say to the others, "Thus says the king, 'Go in peace to your father. Behold, I have taken the man in whose sack my cup was found.'"

{54:1} When Judah saw how Joseph was treating them, he went up to him, broke down the door, and came in with his brothers. {54:2} Judah said to Joseph, "Please don't take offense, my lord; let your servant speak a word to you." And Joseph replied, "Speak." {54:3} Judah began to speak in front of Joseph while his brothers stood by. He said, "When we first came to buy food, you thought we were spies. We brought Benjamin to you, and yet you continue to mock us today. {54:4} So, please let the king hear what I have to say and send our brother back with us to our father, or your life and the lives of all the people in Egypt will be at risk today. {54:5} Don't you know what my brothers Simeon and Levi did to the city of Shechem and to seven cities of the Amorites because of our sister Dinah? What do you think they would do for their brother Benjamin? {54:6} I am stronger than both of them and am here to threaten you and your land if you refuse to send our brother. {54:7} Haven't you heard how our God dealt with Pharaoh for taking Sarah from our father? He struck him and his household with severe plagues, and even to this day, the Egyptians tell this story. The same will happen to you because of Benjamin, whom you have taken from his father, and because of the troubles you are causing us here in your land; our God will remember His covenant with our father Abraham and bring disaster upon you for grieving our father's soul today. {54:8} So, listen to what I have said and send our brother back, or you and your people will perish by the sword; you cannot win against me. {54:9} Joseph responded to Judah, "Why do you speak so arrogantly, boasting about your strength? As Pharaoh lives, if I command my strongest men to fight you, you and your brothers would sink into the mud." {54:10} Judah replied, "You and your people should fear me. As the Lord lives, if I draw my sword, I won't put it away until I have slain all of Egypt, starting with you and ending with Pharaoh." {54:11} Joseph responded, "Strength doesn't belong only to you; I am stronger and more powerful than you. If you draw your sword, I will put it to your neck and the necks of your brothers." {54:12} Judah said, "If I speak against you today, I would swallow you up and erase you from the earth. And Joseph said, "If you open your mouth, I have the power to shut it with a stone until you can't say a word; look at all these stones around us; I could easily take one and break your jaw." {54:13} Judah said, "God is our witness that we have no desire to fight you; just give us our brother and let us leave." Joseph replied, "As Pharaoh lives, even if all the kings of Canaan came together with you, you would not take him from my hands." {54:14} "Now go back to your father, and your brother will be my slave, for he has stolen from the king's house." Judah said, "What does this matter to you or to Pharaoh? The king sends gold and silver throughout the land, yet you still talk about a cup you say our brother stole from you?" {54:15} God forbid that our brother Benjamin or any descendant of Abraham would steal from you or anyone else, whether king, prince, or any man. {54:16} So stop this accusation, or the whole world will hear you say that the king of Egypt quarreled with us over a little silver and took our brother as a slave. {54:17} Joseph replied, "Take this cup and leave me; let your brother remain here as my slave, for it is the judgment of a thief to become a slave." {54:18} Judah said, "Aren't you ashamed to say you would leave our brother and take your cup? We would not leave him for any amount of silver, even if you offered us your cup a thousand times over; we won't die over him." {54:19} Joseph said, "And why did you abandon your brother and sell him for twenty pieces of silver? Why wouldn't you do the same to this brother?" {54:20} Judah replied, "The Lord is our witness that we do not seek trouble with you; just give us our brother and we will leave peacefully." {54:21} Joseph said, "Even if all the kings of the land gathered together, they could not take your brother from my hand." Judah then asked, "What will we tell our father if he sees that our brother is not with us? He will be heartbroken." {54:22} Joseph said, "This is what you will tell your father. 'The rope has gone after the bucket.'" {54:23} Judah responded, "You are a king, and why do you speak this way? You give a false judgment; woe to a king like you." {54:24} Joseph said, "There is no false judgment in what I said about your brother Joseph. You all sold him to the Midianites for twenty pieces of silver, and you denied it to your father, telling him that an evil beast had devoured him, that Joseph had been torn to pieces." {54:25} Judah said, "The fire of Shechem burns in my heart; I will burn all your land with fire." Joseph replied, "Surely your sister-in-law Tamar, who killed your sons, put out the fire of Shechem." {54:26} Judah said, "If I pull out a single hair from my body, I will fill all Egypt with its blood." {54:27} Joseph responded, "This is how you treated your brother whom you sold. You dipped his coat in blood and took it to your father, so he would think an evil beast had devoured him." {54:28} When Judah heard this, he was furious, and his anger burned inside him. There was a stone nearby that weighed about four hundred shekels. Judah's rage flared, and he picked up the stone with one hand, threw it into the sky, and caught it with his other hand. {54:29} He then placed it under his legs and sat down with all his strength, turning the stone to dust from the force of his weight. {54:30} Joseph saw what Judah did and was very afraid, but he commanded his son Manasseh to do the same with another stone. Judah said to his brothers, "Don't say this man is an Egyptian; by what he is doing, he is one of our father's family." {54:31} Joseph replied, "Strength is not given only to you; we are also powerful men. Why do you boast over us?" Judah said to Joseph, "Please send our brother back and don't ruin your country today." {54:32} Joseph responded, "Go and tell your father that an evil beast has devoured him, just as you said regarding your brother Joseph." {54:33} Judah spoke to his brother Naphtali and said, "Hurry, go and count all the streets of Egypt and come back to tell me." Simeon added, "Don't let this trouble you; I will go to the mountain, grab a large stone, and level it against everyone in Egypt, killing them all." {54:34} Joseph heard all that his brothers said and didn't realize they thought he couldn't understand Hebrew. {54:35} Joseph was terrified by their words, fearing they would destroy Egypt, so he commanded his son Manasseh, "Hurry and gather all the inhabitants of Egypt and all the valiant men and bring them to me now, both on horseback and on foot, with all sorts of musical instruments." Manasseh hurried to do this. {54:36} Naphtali ran as Judah had instructed, moving swiftly like a stag, walking over the ears of corn without breaking them. {54:37} He went and counted all the streets of Egypt, discovering there were twelve, and he hurried back to tell Judah. Judah said to his brothers, "Hurry and put your swords on; we will march into Egypt and attack them all, leaving no survivors." {54:38} Judah said, "I will destroy three of the streets with my strength, and you will each destroy one street." While Judah was saying this, the inhabitants of Egypt and all the mighty men came toward them with musical instruments and loud shouts. {54:39} Their number was five hundred cavalry, ten thousand infantry, and four hundred men who could fight with their bare hands. {54:40} All the mighty men came with great noise and shouting, surrounding the sons of Jacob and scaring them. The ground shook with the sound of their voices. {54:41} When the sons of Jacob saw these troops, they were terrified for their lives. Joseph did this to frighten them and calm their nerves. {54:42} Judah, seeing some of his brothers frightened, said to them, "Why are you afraid when God's grace is with us?" When Judah saw all the Egyptians surrounding them at Joseph's command, he remembered that Joseph had ordered them not to harm anyone. {54:43} Then Judah quickly drew his sword and let out a loud, bitter scream, striking with his sword and leaping onto the ground while continuing to shout at the people. {54:44} As he did this, God caused fear to fall upon the valiant men and all the people surrounding them. {54:45} They fled at the sound of Judah's voice, terrified, and stumbled over one another, many dying as they fell; they all fled from Judah and his brothers and from Joseph. {54:46} While they were fleeing, Judah and his brothers pursued them to Pharaoh's house, but they all escaped. Judah then sat before Joseph and roared at him like a lion, giving a tremendous roar. {54:47} The roar was heard from far away, and all the inhabitants of Succoth heard it. All of Egypt trembled at the sound of the roar, and the walls of Egypt and Goshen shook from the earth's tremors. Pharaoh fell from his throne onto the ground, and many pregnant women in Egypt and Goshen miscarried from the fear of the noise. {54:48} Pharaoh sent a message asking, "What has happened today in Egypt?" They came and told him everything that had happened from start to finish, and Pharaoh was alarmed and confused. {54:49} His fear grew when he heard all this, and he sent word to Joseph, saying, "You have brought these Hebrews to destroy all of Egypt. What will you do with this thieving slave? Send him away with his brothers; let us not perish because of their evil, including you and all of Egypt. {54:50} If you don't want to do this, give up all my valuables and go with them to their land if you wish, for they will destroy my whole country and kill all my people today. All the women in Egypt have miscarried because of their screams; look what they have done just with their shouting; if they fight with swords, they will destroy the land. So, choose what you desire, me or the Hebrews, Egypt or the land of the Hebrews."{54:51} They went and told Joseph everything Pharaoh had said about him, and Joseph was very afraid at Pharaoh's words. Judah and his brothers stood before Joseph, angry and upset, and all the sons of Jacob roared at Joseph like the crashing waves of the sea. {54:52} Joseph was terrified of his brothers and of Pharaoh, and he looked for a way to reveal himself to his brothers, fearing they might destroy all of Egypt. {54:53} Joseph commanded his son Manasseh to approach Judah, placing a hand on his shoulder, which calmed Judah's anger. {54:54} Judah then said to his brothers, "Let none of you claim that this is the action of an Egyptian youth; this is the matter concerning my father's household." {54:55} Seeing that Judah's anger had subsided, Joseph approached him and spoke kindly. {54:56} Joseph said to Judah, "You speak the truth and have proven your strength today. May your God, who delights in you, increase your well-being. But tell me why you, among all your brothers, are arguing with me about the boy when none of the others have said anything to me about him." {54:57} Judah replied, "You must know that I promised our father I would take responsibility for the boy. I said, 'If I do not bring him back to you, I will bear the blame forever.' {54:58} That is why I came to you among all my brothers; I saw that you were unwilling to let him go. So please, may I find favor in your eyes and let him go with us. I will stay in his place and serve you in whatever you need. I will go to battle against any mighty king who rebels against you, and you will see what I can do to him and his land. Even if he has cavalry and infantry, or a very powerful army, I will defeat them all and bring the king's head to you." {54:59} "Do you not know or have you not heard how our father Abraham and his servant Eliezer defeated all the kings of Elam in one night, leaving none remaining? Ever since that day, our father's strength has been passed down to us as an inheritance, for us and our descendants forever." {54:60} Joseph replied, "You speak the truth; there is no falsehood in your words. We have also heard that the Hebrews are powerful and that their God greatly delights in them; who then can stand against them? {54:61} However, I will send your brother back on this condition: you must bring his brother, the son of his mother, whom you claimed had gone from you to Egypt. When you bring me his brother, I will then send your brother, for whom you have taken responsibility." {54:62} Judah's anger flared at Joseph's words, and his eyes were bloodshot with rage as he said to his brothers, "How does this man seek his own destruction and that of all Egypt today!" {54:63} Simeon then spoke to Joseph, saying, "Did we not tell you earlier that we did not know where he had gone, whether he was dead or alive? Why do you speak to us like this?" {54:64} Joseph noticed Judah's growing anger when he mentioned bringing their other brother instead of the one with him. {54:65} He said to his brothers, "You said your brother was either dead or lost. Now, if I were to call him today, would you give him to me instead of your brother?" {54:66} Joseph began to call out, "Joseph, come here before me today and sit before your brothers." {54:67} When Joseph spoke, they looked around to see where he would come from. {54:68} Joseph watched all their reactions and said to them, "Why do you look around? I am Joseph, whom you sold into Egypt. Do not let it grieve you that you sold me, for God sent me ahead of you to support you during the famine." {54:69} His brothers were terrified to hear these words, and Judah was exceedingly afraid. {54:70} When Benjamin heard Joseph's words, he was inside the house. Benjamin ran to Joseph, embraced him, and they wept together. {54:71} When Joseph's brothers saw Benjamin weeping on Joseph's neck, they also fell upon Joseph and embraced him, and they all wept together. {54:72} The sound of their weeping was heard throughout Joseph's house, and it pleased Pharaoh greatly, for he feared they would destroy Egypt. {54:73} Pharaoh sent servants to Joseph to congratulate him on the arrival of his brothers, and all the captains of the armies and troops in Egypt came to celebrate with Joseph, and all Egypt rejoiced greatly at the return of Joseph's brothers. {54:74} Pharaoh instructed Joseph to tell his brothers to gather all their belongings and come to him, promising to place them in the best part of the land of Egypt, and they did so. {54:75} Joseph commanded the steward of his house to bring gifts and clothing for his brothers, and he brought out many royal garments and gifts, which Joseph divided among his brothers. {54:76} He gave each brother a change of royal garments and three hundred pieces of silver, commanding them all to wear these garments and to be presented before Pharaoh. {54:77} When Pharaoh saw that Joseph's brothers were strong and handsome, he rejoiced greatly. {54:78} They left Pharaoh's presence to return to the land of Canaan, accompanied by their brother Benjamin. {54:79} Joseph then gave them eleven chariots from Pharaoh and his own chariot, which he had ridden when he was crowned in Egypt, to bring their father to Egypt. He sent garments for all his brothers' children according to their numbers and one hundred pieces of silver for each of them. He also sent garments for his brothers' wives, taken from the garments of the king's wives, and sent them. {54:80} He gave each brother ten men to serve them and their children as they came to Egypt. {54:81} Joseph sent by the hand of his brother Benjamin ten suits of garments for his ten sons, a special gift above what he gave to the others. {54:82} He sent each brother fifty pieces of silver and ten chariots from Pharaoh, along with ten donkeys loaded with all the luxuries of Egypt, and ten female donkeys carrying corn, bread, and provisions for his father and all those with him for the journey. {54:83} He sent silver and gold garments for his sister Dinah, along with frankincense, myrrh, aloes, and plenty of women's ornaments, and he sent the same from the wives of Pharaoh to the wives of Benjamin. {54:84} He also gave all his brothers and their wives various types of precious stones and bdellium, and he left nothing valuable among the treasures of Egypt that he did not send to his father's household. {54:85} After sending off his brothers, they went on their way with Benjamin. {54:86} Joseph went out with them to see them off to the borders of Egypt and commanded them regarding their father and household to come to Egypt. {54:87} He said to them, "Do not argue on the way, for this was done by the Lord to save a great people from starvation; there will be five more years of famine." {54:88} He instructed them not to approach their father suddenly about this matter but to use their wisdom. {54:89} After giving them these instructions, Joseph turned and went back to Egypt, while Jacob's sons traveled joyfully back to Canaan. {54:90} When they reached the borders of the land, they said to each other, "What will we say to our father? If we tell him suddenly about this, he will be greatly alarmed and will not believe us." {54:91} They continued on until they were close to their homes, and they saw Serach, the daughter of Asher, coming out to meet them. The girl was very beautiful and clever, and she knew how to play the harp. {54:92} They called to her, and she approached them, kissed them, and they gave her a harp, saying, "Go now before our father, sit in front of him, and play this tune, singing these words." {54:93} They instructed her to return to their house, and she took the harp and hurried ahead of them, sitting near Jacob. {54:94} She played beautifully and sang, repeating the words, "Joseph, my uncle, is alive and rules throughout the land of Egypt, and he is not dead." {54:95} She kept singing this, and Jacob found her words pleasing. {54:96} He listened as she repeated them several times, and joy filled Jacob's heart at the sweetness of her voice. The spirit of God was upon him, and he realized her words were true. {54:97} Jacob blessed Serach for speaking these words before him, saying, "My daughter, may death never overcome you, for you have revived my spirit. Speak yet more before me as you have done, for you have filled me with joy." {54:98} She continued to sing these words, and Jacob listened, finding it pleasing and rejoicing as the spirit of God was upon him. {54:99} While he was still talking to her, his sons arrived with horses, chariots, royal garments, and servants running before them. {54:100} Jacob stood up to meet them, seeing his sons dressed in royal attire and all the treasures Joseph had sent. {54:101} They told him, "Our brother Joseph is alive, and he is the one who rules throughout the land of Egypt; it is he who spoke to us as we told you." {54:102} Jacob listened to all their words, and his heart raced with disbelief, as he could not believe them until he saw all that Joseph had given them and what he had sent and all the signs Joseph had mentioned. {54:103} They opened everything before him and showed him all that Joseph had sent. They gave each one what Joseph had sent, and Jacob knew they were telling the truth, rejoicing greatly over his son. {54:104} Jacob said, "It is enough for me that my son Joseph is still alive. I will go and see him before I die." {54:105} His sons told him everything that had happened, and Jacob said, "I will go down to Egypt to see my son and his family." {54:106} Jacob got up and dressed in the garments that Joseph had sent him. After washing and shaving his hair, he put on the turban Joseph had sent. {54:107} Everyone in Jacob's household, including their wives, put on the garments Joseph had sent, and they rejoiced greatly that Joseph was still alive and ruling in Egypt. {54:108} All the inhabitants of Canaan heard this news and came to rejoice with Jacob that he was still alive. {54:109} Jacob held a feast for three days, and all the kings of Canaan and nobles of the land ate, drank, and celebrated in Jacob's house.

{55:1} After this, Jacob said, "I will go and see my son in Egypt, and then I will return to the land of Canaan that God promised to Abraham, for I cannot leave the land of my birthplace. {55:2} And behold, the Lord spoke to him, saying, "Go down to Egypt with all your household and stay there; do not be afraid to go down to Egypt, for I will make you a great nation there. {55:3} Jacob thought to himself, "I will go and see my son to check if the fear of God is still in his heart amidst all the people of Egypt." {55:4} And the Lord said to Jacob, "Do not worry about Joseph, for he still maintains his integrity in serving Me, as will seem good to you," and Jacob rejoiced greatly about his son. {55:5} At that time, Jacob instructed his sons and household to go to Egypt according to the word of the Lord, and he rose up with his sons and all his household, leaving the land of Canaan from Beersheba, filled with joy and gladness, and they traveled to Egypt. {55:6} As they approached Egypt, Jacob sent Judah ahead to Joseph to inform him of their arrival. Judah obeyed his father's command and hurried to Joseph, who arranged for a place for all his family in the land of Goshen. Judah then returned and traveled back to his father. {55:7} Joseph prepared his chariot, gathered all his mighty men, servants, and officers of Egypt to go and meet his father Jacob. Joseph's command was proclaimed throughout Egypt: anyone who did not go to meet Jacob would die. {55:8} The next day, Joseph set out with all of Egypt—a vast and mighty host, all dressed in fine linen and purple, carrying silver and gold instruments along with their weapons. {55:9} They approached Jacob with all kinds of musical instruments, including drums and tambourines, spreading myrrh and aloes along the road as they marched, making the earth tremble with their shouting. {55:10} Women of Egypt stood on the roofs and walls to greet Jacob, and Joseph wore Pharaoh's regal crown, which Pharaoh had sent for him to wear when he met his father. {55:11} When Joseph was within fifty cubits of his father, he got down from the chariot and walked toward him. When all the Egyptian officials and nobles saw Joseph walking toward his father, they too got down and walked on foot to Jacob. {55:12} As Jacob approached the camp of Joseph, he was pleased by the sight and astonished. {55:13} Jacob asked Judah, "Who is that man dressed in royal robes, wearing a red garment and a royal crown, coming toward us?" Judah replied, "That is your son Joseph, the king," and Jacob rejoiced at the sight of his son's glory. {55:14} Joseph came near to his father, bowed down to him, and all the men in the camp bowed down to the ground before Jacob. {55:15} Jacob ran to Joseph, fell on his neck, and kissed him as they both wept. Joseph also embraced his father, kissed him, and they wept together, with all the people of Egypt weeping alongside them. {55:16} Jacob said to Joseph, "Now I can die happily after seeing that you are still alive and in glory." {55:17} Jacob's sons, their wives, children, and servants all wept with Joseph, kissing him and crying greatly. {55:18} Afterward, Joseph and his entourage returned to Egypt, while Jacob and his sons and all his household accompanied Joseph and settled in the best part of Egypt, in the land of Goshen. {55:19} Joseph told his father and brothers, "I will go and inform Pharaoh that my brothers and my father's household have come to me, and they are now in the land of Goshen." {55:20} Joseph did as he said and brought Reuben, Issachar, Zebulun, and Benjamin before Pharaoh. {55:21} Joseph spoke to Pharaoh, saying, "My brothers and my father's household, along with their flocks and cattle, have come to me from Canaan to live here because the famine is severe." {55:22} Pharaoh said to Joseph, "Place your father and brothers in the best part of the land; do not hold back any good things from them, and make sure they eat well." {55:23} Joseph replied, "I have settled them in the land of Goshen because they are shepherds, so let them stay there to tend to their flocks away from the Egyptians." {55:24} Pharaoh instructed Joseph to do as his brothers asked, and the sons of Jacob bowed down to Pharaoh, then left him in peace. Joseph then brought his father before Pharaoh. {55:25} Jacob approached Pharaoh and bowed down, blessing Pharaoh before leaving. Jacob and his sons, along with all their household, lived in the land of Goshen. {55:26} In the second year, when Jacob was one hundred thirty years old, Joseph provided for his father, brothers, and all his household, giving them food according to their needs throughout the famine; they lacked nothing. {55:27} Joseph gave them the best part of the land; they received the best of Egypt throughout Joseph's lifetime, along with clothing and garments each year. The sons of Jacob remained secure in Egypt all the days of their brother. {55:28} Jacob ate at Joseph's table, and he and his sons did not leave it day or night, except for what Jacob's children consumed in their own homes. {55:29} All of Egypt ate bread during the famine, as all the Egyptians sold everything they had due to the famine. {55:30} Joseph bought all the land and fields of Egypt for Pharaoh during the famine, supplying all of Egypt with bread throughout that time, and he collected all the silver and gold that came to him in exchange for grain, accumulating much wealth, including a vast quantity of precious stones, bdellium (a fragrant resin), and valuable garments from all over the land when their money ran out. {55:31} Joseph gathered all the silver and gold that came into his hands—about seventy-two talents—and also an abundance of onyx stones and bdellium. He then hid these treasures in four parts: one in the wilderness near the Red Sea, one by the Euphrates River, and the third and fourth in the desert opposite the wilderness of Persia and Media. {55:32} He took some of the remaining gold and silver and gave it to all his brothers, his father's household, and all the women of his family, while the rest he brought to Pharaoh's house—about twenty talents. {55:33} Joseph presented all the leftover gold and silver to Pharaoh, who placed it in the treasury. The famine ended in the land, and they began to sow and reap as usual, gathering their yearly harvest without lacking anything. {55:34} Joseph lived securely in Egypt, governing the entire land, while his father and brothers settled in Goshen and took possession of it. {55:35} Joseph was very old and advanced in years, and his two sons, Ephraim and Manasseh, consistently stayed in Jacob's house to learn the ways of the Lord and His laws. {55:36} Jacob and his sons lived in Egypt in the land of Goshen and took possession of it, becoming fruitful and multiplying.

{56:1} Jacob lived in Egypt for seventeen years, and he was a hundred and forty-seven years old when he died. {56:2} During that time, Jacob fell ill, and he sent for his son Joseph, who came to him from Egypt. {56:3} Jacob said to Joseph and his other sons, "I am about to die, but God will visit you and bring you back to the land He promised to give to you and your descendants. Therefore, when I die, please bury me in the cave in Machpelah, near Hebron, where my ancestors are buried." {56:4} Jacob made his sons swear to bury him in Machpelah, and they swore to him about this. {56:5} He then commanded them, "Serve the Lord your God, for He who saved your forefathers will also deliver you from trouble." {56:6} Jacob called all his children to him, and they gathered around him. He blessed them, saying, "May the God of your fathers grant you a thousand times more and bless you with the blessings of your father Abraham." After he blessed them, all of Jacob's sons went out. {56:7} The next day, Jacob again called his sons, and they assembled before him. On that day, he blessed each of them before he died, according to their individual blessings, as it is recorded in the book of the law pertaining to Israel. {56:8} Jacob said to Judah, "I know you are a powerful man among your brothers; you will rule over them, and your descendants will rule forever. {56:9} Just be sure to teach your sons how to use the bow and all weapons of war so they can fight for their brother who will rule over his enemies." {56:10} Again, Jacob commanded his sons, saying, "I will be gathered to my people today; carry me back to Canaan and bury me in the cave of Machpelah as I commanded you. {56:11} But take care, I pray you, that only you, my sons, carry my body. Here's how you should do it when you take me back to Canaan to bury me: {56:12} Judah, Issachar, and Zebulun will carry my bier on the east side; Reuben, Simeon, and Gad on the south; Ephraim, Manasseh, and Benjamin on the west; and Dan, Asher, and Naphtali on the north. {56:13} Do not let Levi carry with you, as he and his sons will be responsible for carrying the Ark of the Covenant with the Israelites in the camp. Do not let Joseph carry either, for as a king, his glory should remain. However, Ephraim and Manasseh can take his place. {56:14} This is how you should carry me when you take me away; do not neglect anything I command you. If you do this for me, the Lord will remember you and your descendants forever. {56:15} You, my sons, should honor each other and teach your children and grandchildren to serve the Lord God of your ancestors all their days. {56:16} This will help you and your children live long in the land as you do what is good and right in the sight of the Lord, following all His ways. {56:17} And you, Joseph my son, forgive your brothers for their wrongs against you, for God intended it for your good and the good of your children. {56:18} Please do not abandon your brothers to the Egyptians or hurt their feelings, for I entrust them to the Lord and to you to protect them from the Egyptians." The sons of Jacob responded, "Father, we will do everything you commanded us; may God be with us." {56:19} Jacob replied to his sons, "May God be with you as you keep all His ways; do not stray from them, either to the right or to the left, as you strive to do what is good and upright in His sight. {56:20} I know that many and serious troubles will come upon you and your descendants in the future, but if you serve the Lord, He will save you from all troubles. {56:21} When you seek God and serve Him, teaching your children and grandchildren to know the Lord, He will raise up a servant from among your children to deliver you from all affliction and bring you out of Egypt back to the land of your ancestors to inherit it securely. {56:22} Jacob finished speaking to his sons, pulled his feet into the bed, and died, gathered to his people. {56:23} Joseph fell on his father, cried, and wept over him, saying, "O my father, my father!" {56:24} The wives of his sons and his entire household came to mourn for Jacob, weeping loudly. {56:25} All the sons of Jacob rose together, tore their garments, put on sackcloth, and fell on their faces, throwing dust on their heads toward heaven. {56:26} News reached Osnath, Joseph's wife, and she put on sackcloth and, along with the Egyptian women, mourned and wept for Jacob. {56:27} All the people of Egypt who knew Jacob mourned for many days. {56:28} Women from Canaan also came to Egypt when they heard Jacob was dead, mourning for him there for seventy days. {56:29} After the days of mourning were over, Joseph instructed his servants, the doctors, to embalm his father with myrrh, frankincense, and other perfumes, and they embalmed Jacob as Joseph directed. {56:30} The people of Egypt, the elders, and all the inhabitants of Goshen mourned over Jacob for many days. {56:31} After seventy days of mourning, Joseph spoke to Pharaoh, saying, "I will go and bury my father in Canaan as I promised, and then I will return." {56:32} Pharaoh told Joseph, "Go and bury your father as you swore to him." Joseph then went up with all his brothers to Canaan to bury Jacob as he had commanded. {56:33} Pharaoh decreed that a proclamation should be made throughout Egypt: "Whoever does not accompany Joseph and his brothers to Canaan to bury Jacob shall die." {56:34} All of Egypt heard Pharaoh's command and rose up with Joseph, his servants, the elders of Pharaoh's house, and the leaders of the land of Egypt, all going with Joseph to bury Jacob. {56:35} Jacob's sons carried the bier as their father commanded, {56:36} which was made of pure gold, decorated with onyx stones and bdellium (a fragrant resin); the covering was gold woven and joined with threads, adorned with hooks of onyx stones and bdellium. {56:37} Joseph placed a large golden crown on Jacob's head and a golden scepter in his hand, surrounding the bier as was customary for kings during their lives. {56:38} All the troops of Egypt marched ahead, beginning with the mightiest warriors of Pharaoh and Joseph, followed by the rest of Egypt, all wearing swords and armor, prepared for battle. {56:39} The mourners walked at a distance from the bier, weeping, while the rest followed behind it. {56:40} Joseph and his family walked near the bier barefoot and weeping, accompanied by his servants, all adorned with their ornaments and armed for battle. {56:41} Fifty of Jacob's servants went in front of the bier, strewing myrrh, aloes, and perfumes along the road, and the sons of Jacob walked on the perfumed path while their servants preceded them. {56:42} Joseph traveled with a heavy heart, mourning every day until they reached Atad's threshing floor, which is across the Jordan, where they mourned a great and heavy mourning. {56:43} All the kings of Canaan heard about this and came out, thirty-one kings with their men, to mourn and weep over Jacob. {56:44} When these kings saw Jacob's bier, they noticed Joseph's crown on it and placed their own crowns on the bier, surrounding it with them. {56:45} They all mourned greatly with Jacob's sons and the people of Egypt because they recognized Jacob's valor. {56:46} News reached Esau, who was living in Mount Seir, that Jacob had died and that his sons and all of Egypt were bringing him to Canaan for burial. {56:47} Esau gathered his sons and people, an exceedingly great multitude, and came to mourn for Jacob. {56:48} When Esau arrived, he mourned for his brother Jacob, and all of Egypt and Canaan mourned alongside Esau over Jacob in that place. {56:49} Joseph and his brothers took their father Jacob from that place and went to Hebron to bury him in the cave with his ancestors. {56:50} They reached Kiriath-arba, where the cave is located, and Esau stood with his sons against Joseph and his brothers, blocking access to the cave, saying, "Jacob cannot be buried here; it belongs to us and our father." {56:51} Joseph and his brothers heard what Esau's sons said, and they were very angry. Joseph approached Esau, saying, "What do you mean by this? My father Jacob bought this cave from you for a great sum of money after Isaac died, twenty-five years ago, as well as all the land of Canaan. {56:52} Jacob purchased it for his sons and their descendants as an eternal inheritance, so why are you speaking like this?" {56:53} Esau replied, "I will not allow you to bury Jacob here, for I will make war against you." {56:54} A great battle broke out, and the sons of Jacob fought against Esau's sons. {56:55} Jacob's sons overcame Esau's sons and defeated them. After the battle, Joseph turned to Esau and said, "I would have spared you; I wanted peace, but you have chosen war." {56:56} Esau replied, "As you have defeated me, I will let you bury your father here." {56:57} Joseph and his brothers buried Jacob there in the cave of Machpelah, where his ancestors are buried, and they returned to Egypt.

{57:1} After this, the sons of Esau went to war against the sons of Jacob, fighting in Hebron while Esau lay dead and unburied. {57:2} The battle was fierce, and the sons of Esau were defeated by the sons of Jacob, who killed eighty men without losing a single one of their own. Joseph's strength prevailed over the sons of Esau, and he captured Zepho, the son of Eliphaz (Eliphaz was Esau's son), along with fifty of his men, binding them in iron chains and giving them to his servants to bring to Egypt. {57:3} When the remaining sons of Esau saw Zepho and his men taken captive, they were terrified for their lives and fled with Eliphaz and his people, taking Esau's body with them as they made their way to Mount Seir. {57:4} Upon reaching Mount Seir, they buried Esau there, but they left his head behind, which had been buried at the site of the battle in Hebron. {57:5} After the sons of Esau fled from the sons of Jacob, the latter pursued them to the borders of Seir, but did not kill anyone during the pursuit; the sight of Esau's body they carried with them caused confusion among the sons of Jacob, leading them to turn back and return to where their brothers were in Hebron, where they stayed for the day and the following day to rest from the battle. {57:6} On the third day, they gathered all the sons of Seir the Horite and the children of the east, a vast multitude like the sand of the sea, and they marched down to Egypt to fight against Joseph and his brothers in order to rescue their relatives. {57:7} Joseph and his brothers, along with the strong men of Egypt, heard that the sons of Esau and the children of the east were coming to battle, aiming to deliver their brethren. {57:8} So, Joseph, his brothers, and the Egyptian warriors went out and fought in the city of Rameses, inflicting significant damage on the sons of Esau and the children of the east. {57:9} They killed six hundred thousand of them and wiped out most of the mighty warriors of the children of Seir the Horite; only a few escaped, including Eliphaz and the children of the east, who fled from Joseph and his brothers. {57:10} Joseph and his brothers continued the pursuit until they reached Succoth, where they killed thirty more men, while the rest fled back to their cities. {57:11} Joseph, his brothers, and the mighty men of Egypt returned with joy and gladness of heart, having defeated all their enemies. {57:12} Zepho, the son of Eliphaz, and his men remained slaves in Egypt under the sons of Jacob, and their suffering increased. {57:13} When the sons of Esau and the sons of Seir returned to their land, the sons of Seir realized they had fallen into the hands of Jacob's sons and the Egyptian forces due to the battle instigated by the sons of Esau. {57:14} The sons of Seir said to the sons of Esau, "You know this situation arose because of you, and not one of your warriors remains." {57:15} They then urged the sons of Esau to leave their land and return to Canaan, questioning why Esau's children should inherit what had belonged to them. {57:16} The children of Esau, however, refused to listen to the children of Seir, leading to plans for war between them. {57:17} Secretly, the children of Esau sent a message to Angeas, the king of Africa (known as Dinhabah), requesting assistance against the children of Seir. {57:18} Angeas, being friendly to the children of Esau, sent five hundred skilled infantry and eight hundred cavalry to help them. {57:19} The children of Seir also reached out to the children of the east and the children of Midian, saying, "You have seen what the children of Esau have done to us, and we are nearly destroyed due to their actions in their battle against Jacob's sons. {57:20} So, come and help us; together we will fight and drive them from the land, avenging the deaths of our brethren." {57:21} The children of the east responded to the children of Seir's call for help, bringing about eight hundred armed men to join forces against the children of Esau in the wilderness of Paran. {57:22} During the battle, the children of Seir overpowered the sons of Esau, killing about two hundred of the troops sent by Angeas. {57:23} On the second day, the children of Esau attacked again but suffered greatly at the hands of the children of Seir. {57:24} Seeing that the children of Seir were stronger, some men of Esau decided to switch sides and assist the children of Seir, their former enemies. {57:25} In this second battle, fifty-eight men from the children of Esau died in combat against the forces from Dinhabah. {57:26} Upon hearing that some of their brethren had turned against them in the second battle, the children of Esau mourned. {57:27} They wondered what to do about their traitorous brethren who had joined the children of Seir, prompting them to contact Angeas again. {57:28} They requested additional soldiers to help fight against the children of Seir, who had already defeated them twice. {57:29} Angeas sent six hundred more capable men to support the children of Esau. {57:30} Ten days later, the children of Esau launched a new assault against the children of Seir in the wilderness of Paran. This time, they were victorious, killing about two thousand men from the children of Seir. {57:31} The mightiest warriors of the children of Seir fell in this battle, leaving only their young children in their cities. {57:32} The children of Midian and the eastern tribes fled from the battle, abandoning the children of Seir when they saw how fierce the fight had become, and the children of Esau chased the eastern tribes back to their land. {57:33} The children of Esau killed an additional two hundred and fifty of them, while about thirty men from their own side died in this conflict. This misfortune came as a result of their brethren turning against them. {57:34} After the battle, the children of Esau returned to Seir, where they killed those who had remained among the children of Seir, including their wives and little ones, leaving no survivors except for fifty young boys and girls whom they spared, making them slaves and taking the girls as wives. {57:35} The children of Esau settled in Seir, taking over the territory once belonging to the children of Seir and inheriting it. {57:36} They took everything that belonged to the children of Seir, including their livestock and goods, and they divided the land among the five sons of Esau according to their families. {57:37} In those days, the children of Esau decided to appoint a king over themselves in the land they had acquired. They believed that a king would lead and protect them in battle against their enemies. {57:38} They swore an oath that none of their brethren would rule over them; they wanted a king from a foreign land instead, due to the resentment they felt toward their own family from the battles they had fought against the children of Seir. {57:39} Therefore, from that day forward, the children of Esau vowed not to choose a king from among their own kin but from outside their kin. {57:40} A man named Bela, the son of Beor from Angeas' people, was chosen; he was strong, handsome, wise, and sensible. There was no one among Angeas' people like him. {57:41} The children of Esau took Bela, anointed him, and crowned him as their king, pledging their loyalty to him. {57:42} They brought him gifts, including gold and silver jewelry, making him rich with onyx stones and bdellium (a fragrant resin). They built him a royal throne, adorned with a crown, and he ruled as king over all the children of Esau. {57:43} The people of Angeas received their payment for their support from the children of Esau and returned to their master in Dinhabah. {57:44} Bela ruled over the children of Esau for thirty years, during which they securely inhabited the land that had belonged to the children of Seir. They continued to dwell there until this day.

{58:1} It happened in the thirty-second year since the Israelites went down to Egypt, which was the seventy-first year of Joseph's life, that Pharaoh, the king of Egypt, died, and his son Magron took over the throne. {58:2} Before his death, Pharaoh instructed Joseph to act as a father to his son, Magron, and to take care of him and advise him. {58:3} All of Egypt agreed that Joseph should be their king because they had always loved him, but Magron, Pharaoh's son, took his father's throne and became king in those days. {58:4} Magron was forty-one years old when he began to reign, and he ruled Egypt for forty years. All of Egypt called him Pharaoh, following the tradition of naming every king after the previous one. {58:5} When Pharaoh began to rule in his father's place, he handed over the laws of Egypt and all governmental matters to Joseph, as his father had commanded. {58:6} Joseph became king over Egypt, supervising the entire land, as everyone turned to him for guidance after Pharaoh's death, loving him greatly for his leadership. {58:7} However, there were some people who opposed him, insisting that no outsider should rule over them. Still, Joseph managed the entire government without anyone interfering. {58:8} Joseph controlled all of Egypt and waged war against all his surrounding enemies, defeating them. He conquered the land of the Philistines up to the borders of Canaan, bringing them under his authority, and they paid a yearly tribute to him. {58:9} Although Pharaoh sat on his father's throne, he was under Joseph's control and advice, just as he had been under his father's guidance. {58:10} Pharaoh ruled only in Egypt, while Joseph held power over the entire region from Egypt to the great river Perath. {58:11} Joseph was successful in all he did, and the Lord was with him, granting him more wisdom, honor, and glory, and love in the hearts of the Egyptians throughout the land, and he reigned for forty years. {58:12} The nations of the Philistines, Canaan, Zidon, and those across the Jordan brought gifts to Joseph throughout his reign. The entire country was under Joseph's control, and he enjoyed a stable rule in Egypt. {58:13} All of his brothers, the sons of Jacob, lived peacefully in the land during Joseph's reign, flourishing and multiplying significantly, serving the Lord as their father Jacob had instructed. {58:14} After many years, while the children of Esau lived quietly in their land with their king Bela, they became prosperous and decided to attack the sons of Jacob and all of Egypt to rescue their brother Zepho, the son of Eliphaz, and his men, who were still enslaved by Joseph. {58:15} The children of Esau reached out to the children of the east, forming an alliance, and they all came to join Esau in battling the sons of Jacob in Egypt. {58:16} They also received support from the people of Angeas, king of Dinhabah, and sent messages to the children of Ishmael, who joined them. {58:17} This large assembly gathered at Seir to help the children of Esau in their fight, creating a massive army, about eight hundred thousand strong, including infantry and cavalry, and they marched to Egypt to confront the sons of Jacob, encamping near Rameses. {58:18} Joseph led his brothers and the mighty men of Egypt, around six hundred men, to battle at Rameses, engaging in combat with the children of Esau during the fiftieth year since Jacob's family entered Egypt, which was also the thirtieth year of Bela's reign over the children of Esau in Seir. {58:19} The Lord delivered all the mightiest warriors of Esau and the children of the east into Joseph's and his brothers' hands, and they defeated the children of Esau and the children of the east. {58:20} About two hundred thousand men from Esau's and the eastern armies were killed, including their king Bela, son of Beor. When the children of Esau realized their king had died, they lost their resolve in battle. {58:21} Joseph and his brothers, along with all of Egypt, continued to strike down the people of Esau, who were terrified and fled from the sons of Jacob. {58:22} Joseph and his brothers pursued them for a day's journey, killing about three hundred more men as they fled, then they turned back. {58:23} Joseph and his brothers returned to Egypt without losing a single man, although twelve Egyptians were killed in the battle. {58:24} Upon returning to Egypt, Joseph ordered Zepho and his men to be bound even more securely, and they were put in chains, increasing their suffering. {58:25} The children of Esau and the children of the east returned in disgrace to their cities because all their mighty men had been defeated in battle. {58:26} When the children of Esau learned that their king had died, they hurried to choose a new leader from the children of the east; they selected a man named Jobab, son of Zarach, from Botzrah, and made him their king in place of Bela. {58:27} Jobab took the throne of Bela and reigned in Edom over the children of Esau for ten years. From that point on, the children of Esau did not fight the sons of Jacob anymore, knowing their bravery and feeling great fear toward them. {58:28} However, from then on, the children of Esau harbored a deep hatred for the sons of Jacob, and the enmity between them grew strong, lasting until today. {58:29} After ten years, Jobab, son of Zarach from Botzrah, died, and the children of Esau appointed a man named Chusham from Teman as their new king, and Chusham ruled Edom over the children of Esau for twenty years. {58:30} During this time, Joseph, the king of Egypt, his brothers, and all the children of Israel lived securely in Egypt, along with all of Joseph's and his brothers' children, facing no obstacles/misfortunes, as the land of Egypt enjoyed peace from warfare under Joseph & his brothers.

{59:1} These are the names of the sons of Israel who lived in Egypt, having come with Jacob; all the sons of Jacob arrived in Egypt, each man with his household. {59:2} The children of Leah were Reuben, Simeon, Levi, Judah, Issachar, Zebulun, and their sister Dinah. {59:3} The sons of Rachel were Joseph and Benjamin. {59:4} The sons of Zilpah, Leah's maid, were Gad and Asher. {59:5} The sons of Bilhah, Rachel's maid, were Dan and Naphtali. {59:6} These were their descendants born to them in Canaan before they came to Egypt with their father Jacob. {59:7} The sons of Reuben were Chanoch, Pallu, Chetzron, and Carmi. {59:8} The sons of Simeon were Jemuel, Jamin, Ohad, Jachin, Zochar, and Saul, the son of the Canaanite woman. {59:9} The children of Levi were Gershon, Kehath, and Merari, along with their sister Jochebed, who was born to them as they were going down to Egypt. {59:10} The sons of Judah were Er, Onan, Shelah, Perez, and Zarach. {59:11} Er and Onan died in Canaan, and the sons of Perez were Chezron and Chamul. {59:12} The sons of Issachar were Tola, Puvah, Job, and Shomron. {59:13} The sons of Zebulun were Sered, Elon, and Jachleel, while Dan's son was Chushim. {59:14} The sons of Naphtali were Jachzeel, Guni, Jetzer, and Shilam. {59:15} The sons of Gad were Ziphion, Chaggi, Shuni, Ezbon, Eri, Arodi, and Areli. {59:16} The children of Asher were Jimnah, Jishvah, Jishvi, Beriah, and their sister Serach. The sons of Beriah were Cheber and Malchiel. {59:17} The sons of Benjamin were Bela, Becher, Ashbel, Gera, Naaman, Achi, Rosh, Mupim, Chupim, and Ord. {59:18} The sons of Joseph, born to him in Egypt, were Manasseh and Ephraim. {59:19} In total, seventy souls descended from Jacob; these are the ones who came with their father to Egypt to settle there. Joseph and all his brothers lived securely in Egypt, enjoying the best of what the land had to offer throughout Joseph's life. {59:20} Joseph lived in Egypt for ninety-three years, ruling over the land for eighty of those years. {59:21} As Joseph's death approached, he summoned his brothers and the entire household of his father, and they gathered around him. {59:22} Joseph addressed his brothers and the whole of his father's household, saying, "Look, I am about to die, but God will surely come to visit you and lead you out of this land to the land He promised to your ancestors." {59:23} "When God visits you and brings you to that land, make sure to take my bones with you from here." {59:24} Joseph made the sons of Israel promise, for their descendants, saying, "God will definitely visit you, and you must bring my bones with you when you leave here." {59:25} After this, Joseph died in that year, the seventy-first year since the Israelites had gone down to Egypt. {59:26} Joseph was one hundred and ten years old when he died in Egypt, and all his brothers and all his servants rose up to embalm him, as was the custom, and his brothers and all of Egypt mourned for him for seventy days. {59:27} They placed Joseph in a coffin filled with spices and various perfumes and buried him near the river Sihor. His sons, brothers, and the entire household of his father observed a seven-day mourning period for him. {59:28} After Joseph's death, the Egyptians began to dominate the children of Israel. Pharaoh, who ruled in his father's place, took control of all the laws of Egypt and conducted the government under his direction, reigning securely over his people.

{60:1} When the year came around, marking the seventy-second year since the Israelites went down to Egypt, after the death of Joseph, Zepho, the son of Eliphaz, the son of Esau, fled from Egypt along with his men. {60:2} He traveled to Africa, known as Dinhabah, where he met Angeas, the king of Africa, who welcomed them with great honor and appointed Zepho as the captain of his army. {60:3} Zepho found favor in the eyes of Angeas and his people, serving as captain of the host for many days. {60:4} Zepho persuaded Angeas to gather all his army to fight against the Egyptians and the sons of Jacob to avenge his brothers. {60:5} However, Angeas refused to listen to Zepho because he recognized the strength of the sons of Jacob and what they had done to his army in previous battles with the children of Esau. {60:6} During this time, Zepho was held in high regard by Angeas and his people, but despite his continuous efforts to provoke them into war with Egypt, they did not comply. {60:7} In those days, there was a man in the land of Chittim, living in the city of Puzimna, named Uzu. The children of Chittim held him in almost divine regard, but he died without any sons, leaving only one daughter named Jania. {60:8} The girl was extraordinarily beautiful, charming, and intelligent; there was no one else in the land who matched her beauty and wisdom. {60:9} The people of Angeas saw her and praised her to him, prompting Angeas to send messengers to the children of Chittim, requesting Jania as his wife. The people of Chittim agreed to give her to him. {60:10} As the messengers of Angeas were leaving Chittim to fulfill their journey, the messengers of Turnus, the king of Bibentu, arrived, as he too sought Jania for a wife, having heard praises about her from his men. {60:11} The servants of Turnus arrived in Chittim and requested Jania to be taken as a wife for their king. {60:12} The people of Chittim replied that they could not give her away because Angeas had already expressed his desire to take her as his wife before their arrival, so they could not deprive him of her. {60:13} They were also greatly afraid of Angeas, fearing that he would wage war against them and destroy them, while Turnus would not be able to protect them from his wrath. {60:14} When the messengers of Turnus heard the words of the children of Chittim, they returned to their master and reported everything. {60:15} The children of Chittim sent a message to Angeas, stating that Turnus had requested Jania for himself, and they informed him that they had heard Turnus had gathered his entire army to go to war against him, planning to take the route through Sardunia to fight Angeas's brother, Lucus, before coming to battle him. {60:16} Angeas received the message from the children of Chittim, and his anger was kindled; he assembled his entire army and traveled across the islands of the sea toward Sardunia to meet his brother, Lucus, the king. {60:17} Niblos, Lucus's son, learned that his uncle Angeas was coming, so he went out to meet him with a powerful army, greeting him warmly with a kiss and an embrace. Niblos then said to Angeas, "When you ask my father how he is doing, please request him to make me captain of his army." Angeas agreed and went to meet his brother, who also came out to greet him and inquire about his well-being. {60:18} Angeas asked Lucus about his welfare and to appoint his son Niblos as captain of the host, which Lucus did, and together they set out toward Turnus for battle, accompanied by a large and powerful army. {60:19} They traveled by ship and reached the province of Ashtorash, where Turnus was advancing toward them, having intended to destroy Sardunia before coming to fight Angeas. {60:20} Angeas and Lucus met Turnus in the valley of Canopia, where a fierce and intense battle took place. {60:21} The conflict was particularly harsh for Lucus, king of Sardunia; his entire army fell in battle, and Niblos, his son, was also killed. {60:22} Angeas commanded his servants to create a golden coffin for Niblos's body, which they placed inside. Angeas then engaged Turnus in battle again, overpowering him and defeating all his forces with the sword, avenging Niblos and the army of his brother, Lucus. {60:23} After Turnus died, the remaining soldiers lost their will to fight and fled before Angeas and his brother, Lucus. {60:24} Angeas and Lucus pursued them to the highway between Alphanu and Romah, slaying Turnus's entire army with the sword. {60:25} Lucus commanded his servants to construct a brass coffin for his son Niblos and to bury him there. {60:26} They built a tall tower along the highway in his honor and named it after Niblos, and they also buried Turnus, king of Bibentu, at the same location. {60:27} To this day, on the highway between Alphanu and Romah, Niblos's grave is on one side and Turnus's grave is on the other, with a pavement between them. {60:28} After Niblos was buried, Lucus returned to Sardunia with his army, while Angeas, king of Africa, took his people to the city of Bibentu, the city of Turnus. {60:29} The inhabitants of Bibentu learned of Angeas's reputation and were terrified; they came out to meet him with tears and pleas, asking him not to kill them or destroy their city. He agreed, since Bibentu was considered one of the cities of the children of Chittim, so he did not destroy it. {60:30} From that day forward, the troops of the king of Africa would raid and plunder Chittim, and Zepho, the captain of Angeas's army, would accompany them. {60:31} After this, Angeas turned his army toward the city of Puzimna, where he took Jania, the daughter of Uzu, as his wife and brought her back to his city in Africa.

{61:1} At that time, Pharaoh, the king of Egypt, commanded all his people to build a strong palace for him in Egypt. {61:2} He also instructed the sons of Jacob to help the Egyptians with the construction, and together they built a beautiful and elegant palace suitable for a royal residence. Pharaoh lived there, renewed his reign, and ruled securely. {61:3} That year, the seventy-second year since the Israelites had come to Egypt, Zebulun, the son of Jacob, died at the age of one hundred and fourteen years. His body was placed in a coffin and given to his children. {61:4} In the seventy-fifth year, his brother Simeon died at the age of one hundred and twenty. He, too, was put into a coffin and given to his children. {61:5} Zepho, the son of Eliphaz, the son of Esau, who was the captain of the host for Angeas, king of Dinhabah, was continually persuading Angeas to prepare for battle against the sons of Jacob in Egypt. However, Angeas was reluctant because his servants had informed him of the great power of the sons of Jacob and what they had done to the army of Esau. {61:6} Despite Zepho's daily attempts to provoke Angeas into battle, Angeas initially refused. {61:7} After some time, however, Angeas finally listened to Zepho and agreed to fight the sons of Jacob in Egypt. He organized his troops, which were as numerous as the sand on the seashore, and resolved to go to battle. {61:8} Among Angeas's servants was a fifteen-year-old youth named Balaam, the son of Beor, who was very wise and skilled in witchcraft. {61:9} Angeas said to Balaam, "Please use your witchcraft to predict who will win in this upcoming battle." {61:10} Balaam instructed them to bring him wax, which he used to create likenesses of chariots and horsemen representing both Angeas's army and that of Egypt. He placed them in specially prepared waters and used myrtle branches to conduct his ritual, and the images in the water showed Angeas's forces being defeated by the Egyptians and the sons of Jacob. {61:11} Balaam reported this to Angeas, who became disheartened and decided not to arm himself for battle, remaining in his city instead. {61:12} When Zepho saw that Angeas was discouraged and unwilling to fight the Egyptians, he fled from Angeas in Africa and traveled to Chittim. {61:13} The people of Chittim received him with great honor and hired him to fight their battles, making him exceedingly wealthy during that time. Meanwhile, the troops of the king of Africa continued to invade, prompting the children of Chittim to gather and head to Mount Cuptizia to defend against Angeas's advancing forces. {61:14} One day, Zepho lost a young heifer and went to look for it, hearing its lowing around the mountain. {61:15} When he found a large cave at the base of the mountain, he saw a massive stone at the entrance. Zepho broke the stone and entered the cave, where he discovered a large creature devouring the ox. The creature had a human upper body and an animal lower body. Zepho bravely attacked and killed the beast with his sword. {61:16} The people of Chittim were overjoyed when they heard of Zepho's deed, asking, "What should we do for the man who has slain this creature that threatened our cattle?" {61:17} They all gathered to dedicate one day each year to honor him, naming it Zepho after him, and they brought him drink offerings and gifts annually on that day. {61:18} During this time, Jania, the daughter of Uzu and wife of King Angeas, fell ill, and her sickness deeply affected Angeas and his officials. He turned to his wise men, asking what could be done to heal her. They explained that the air and water of their country were different from those of Chittim, which was likely the reason for her illness. {61:19} They noted that the change in air and water had made her sick and that she had previously only drunk the water from Purmah, which her ancestors had transported using bridges. {61:20} Angeas commanded his servants to bring him water from Purmah, and they measured it against the waters of Africa, finding it lighter than the local water. {61:21} Seeing this, Angeas ordered all his officers to gather stone cutters in large numbers, and they worked tirelessly to construct a very strong bridge. They transported the spring of water from Chittim to Africa, providing water for Jania the queen and for all her needs, including drinking, baking, washing, bathing, and irrigating crops and fruits. {61:22} The king also had soil from Chittim brought in large ships, along with stones for building. The builders constructed palaces for Queen Jania, and she recovered from her illness. {61:23} At the turn of the year, the African troops continued to invade Chittim to plunder as usual. When Zepho heard of their approach, he took action against them and fought them off, successfully defending the land of Chittim. {61:24} The children of Chittim recognized Zepho's bravery and decided to make him their king, establishing him as their ruler. During his reign, they sought to conquer the children of Tubal and the surrounding islands. {61:25} King Zepho led them into battle against Tubal and the islands, and they were victorious. Upon returning from battle, they reaffirmed his kingship and built him a large palace as his royal residence, along with a grand throne. Zepho reigned over the entire land of Chittim and the land of Italia for fifty years.

{62:1} In that year, which marked the seventy-ninth year since the Israelites went down to Egypt, Reuben, the son of Jacob, died in Egypt at the age of one hundred and twenty-five. His body was placed in a coffin and given to his children. {62:2} In the eightieth year, his brother Dan died at the age of one hundred and twenty, and he was also put into a coffin and handed over to his children. {62:3} That same year, Chusham, the king of Edom, died, and after him, Hadad, the son of Bedad, reigned for thirty-five years. In the eighty-first year, Issachar, the son of Jacob, died in Egypt at the age of one hundred and twenty-two, and he was embalmed, placed in a coffin, and given to his children. {62:4} In the eighty-second year, his brother Asher died at the age of one hundred and twenty-three; he was also put into a coffin in Egypt and given to his children. {62:5} In the eighty-third year, Gad died at the age of one hundred and twenty-five, and his body was placed in a coffin in Egypt and handed over to his children. {62:6} In the eighty-fourth year, which was the fiftieth year of Hadad, son of Bedad's reign as king of Edom, Hadad gathered all the children of Esau and readied his entire army, about four hundred thousand men, to march toward the land of Moab to fight and make them tributary (subject to payment or tribute). {62:7} The children of Moab heard about this and were very afraid, so they sent a message to the children of Midian, asking for help against Hadad, the king of Edom. {62:8} Hadad arrived in Moab, and the Moabites, along with the Midianites, confronted him in battle formation in the field of Moab. {62:9} Hadad fought against Moab, and many Moabites and Midianites fell in battle—about two hundred thousand men. {62:10} The battle was extremely intense for Moab, and when they saw the severity of the fighting, they became demoralized and retreated, leaving the Midianites to continue fighting. {62:11} The Midianites, unaware of Moab's intentions, fought valiantly against Hadad and his army, but all of Midian fell before him. {62:12} Hadad struck down the Midianites severely with his sword, leaving none of those who came to assist Moab remaining. {62:13} When all the Midianites had perished in battle, and the Moabites had escaped, Hadad made all of Moab tributary to him, and they became subjects, paying an annual tax as ordered. Hadad then returned to his homeland. {62:14} At the turn of the year, when the remaining Midianites in the land heard that their brethren had been defeated in battle while fighting for Moab, they resolved to avenge their fallen kin. {62:15} The children of Midian sent word to all their relatives in the East, and all the children of Keturah came to assist Midian in their battle against Moab. {62:16} When the Moabites learned of this, they were greatly afraid, realizing that all the children of the East had united against them. They sent a plea to Hadad, the king of Edom, saying, {62:17} "Come and help us; we will defeat Midian, for they have gathered against us with all their eastern relatives to avenge their fallen brethren." {62:18} Hadad, son of Bedad, king of Edom, set out with his entire army to the land of Moab to fight against Midian. The Midianites and the children of the East engaged in battle with Moab in the field of Moab, where the fighting was very fierce. {62:19} Hadad struck down all the Midianites and the children of the East with his sword, delivering Moab from Midian's hand. The remaining Midianites and eastern allies fled before Hadad's forces, who pursued them back to their land, inflicting heavy casualties along the way. {62:20} Hadad rescued Moab from Midian, as all the Midianites had fallen by the sword, and then he returned to his land. {62:21} From that day on, the Midianites harbored deep hatred for the Moabites because their brethren had fallen in battle for Moab's sake, creating a strong and lasting enmity between them. {62:22} All that were found of Midian in the territory of Moab were killed by Moab's sword, and all that were found of Moab in Midian's territory were killed by

Midian's sword; thus, they engaged in conflict against each other for many days. {62:23} At that time, Judah, the son of Jacob, died in Egypt during the eighty-sixth year of Jacob's descent into Egypt. Judah was one hundred and twenty-nine years old at his death; they embalmed him, placed him in a coffin, and handed him over to his children. {62:24} In the eighty-ninth year, Naphtali died at the age of one hundred and thirty-two, and he was placed in a coffin and given to his children. {62:25} In the ninety-first year since the Israelites went down to Egypt, which was also the thirtieth year of Zepho's reign over the children of Chittim, the children of Africa invaded Chittim to plunder them, marking the first attack in thirteen years. {62:26} Zepho, son of Eliphaz, went out with some of his men to confront them and fiercely attacked, causing the African troops to flee before him, with many casualties among them. Zepho and his men pursued the fleeing troops all the way back towards Africa. {62:27} Angeas, the king of Africa, heard of Zepho's actions and was extremely upset; he was fearful of Zepho for the rest of his days.

{63:1} In the ninety-third year, Levi, the son of Jacob, died in Egypt at the age of one hundred and thirty-seven. His body was placed in a coffin and given to his children. {63:2} After Levi's death, when all of Egypt realized that the sons of Jacob, Joseph's brothers, were dead, the Egyptians began to oppress the children of Jacob, making their lives bitter from that day until they left Egypt. They took away the vineyards and fields that Joseph had given to them, along with the fine houses where the Israelites lived, and the Egyptians seized all the wealth of Egypt from the sons of Jacob during that time. {63:3} The oppression from all of Egypt became increasingly harsh against the children of Israel, and the Egyptians treated the Israelites so poorly that the Israelites grew weary of their lives because of them. {63:4} In those days, during the hundred and second year since Israel's descent into Egypt, Pharaoh, king of Egypt, died, and his son Melol took his place. All the prominent men of Egypt and that generation, who had known Joseph and his brothers, also died during this time. {63:5} A new generation rose up that did not know the sons of Jacob or the good things they had done for them, nor did they remember their strength in Egypt. {63:6} Consequently, from that day on, Egypt began to make the lives of the sons of Jacob bitter and to afflict them with all sorts of hard labor, as they did not recognize their ancestors who had saved them during the famine. {63:7} This was also part of God's plan for the children of Israel, to prepare them for better days ahead so that they could know the Lord, their God. {63:8} It was necessary for them to witness the signs and mighty wonders that the Lord would perform in Egypt on behalf of His people, Israel, so that they might revere the Lord God of their ancestors and walk in His ways, along with their descendants for generations to come. {63:9} Melol was twenty years old when he began his reign, which lasted ninety-four years. All of Egypt referred to him as Pharaoh, following the tradition of naming every king after his father. {63:10} At that time, Angeas, king of Africa, sent his troops to invade the land of Chittim for plunder, just as they usually did. {63:11} Zepho, the son of Eliphaz, son of Esau, heard their report and went out to confront them with his army, engaging them in battle on the road. {63:12} Zepho struck down the troops of the African king with his sword, leaving none of them remaining, and not one returned to his master in Africa. {63:13} When Angeas heard what Zepho had done to his forces, he gathered all his troops, a vast number of men from Africa, as numerous as the sand on the seashore. {63:14} Angeas sent a message to his brother Lucus, saying, "Come to me with all your men and help me defeat Zepho and the children of Chittim, who have destroyed my army." Lucus came with a great force to assist Angeas in fighting Zepho and the children of Chittim. {63:15} Zepho and the children of Chittim learned of this and were filled with fear, and a great terror fell upon their hearts. {63:16} Zepho sent a letter to Hadad, son of Bedad, king of Edom, and to all the children of Esau, saying, {63:17} "I have heard that Angeas, king of Africa, is coming to battle against us with his brother, and we are greatly afraid of him, as his army is very large." {63:18} "So come up with me and help me fight against Angeas and his brother Lucus, and you will save us from their hands; but if not, know that we shall all perish." {63:19} The children of Esau replied to Zepho, saying, "We cannot fight against Angeas and his people because we have maintained a peace treaty with them for many years, dating back to Bela, the first king, and during the time of Joseph, son of Jacob, king of Egypt, with whom we fought on the other side of the Jordan when he buried his father." {63:20} When Zepho heard the words of his brethren, the children of Esau, he withdrew from them, feeling greatly afraid of Angeas. {63:21} Angeas and his brother Lucus prepared their forces, totaling around eight hundred thousand men, against the children of Chittim. {63:22} The children of Chittim said to Zepho, "Pray to the God of your ancestors that He may deliver us from the hand of Angeas and his army, for we have heard that He is a great God who saves all who trust in Him." {63:23} Zepho listened to their words and sought the Lord, saying, {63:24} "O Lord God of Abraham and Isaac, my ancestors, today I know that You are the true God, and all the gods of the nations are worthless." {63:25} "Remember this day Your covenant with our father Abraham, which our ancestors told us about, and be gracious to me today for the sake of Abraham and Isaac, and save me and the children of Chittim from the hand of the king of Africa who is coming against us for battle." {63:26} The Lord listened to Zepho's plea and took notice of him because of Abraham and Isaac, delivering Zepho and the children of Chittim from the hand of Angeas and his people. {63:27} On that day, Zepho fought against Angeas, king of Africa, and all his forces, and the Lord delivered all the people of Angeas into the hands of the children of Chittim. {63:28} The battle was intense for Angeas, and Zepho struck down all the men of Angeas and his brother Lucus with his sword, resulting in about four hundred thousand casualties by the evening of that day. {63:29} When Angeas saw that all his men had perished, he sent a message to all the people of Africa, calling for them to assist him in battle. In the letter, he wrote that all who were found in Africa, from the age of ten and older, should come to him, warning that anyone who did not would face death along with their entire household. {63:30} The remaining inhabitants of Africa were terrified by Angeas's words, and about three hundred thousand men and boys from ten years old and up left their city to join him. {63:31} After ten days, Angeas renewed the battle against Zepho and the children of Chittim, and it was a fierce and intense conflict. {63:32} From the armies of Angeas and Lucus, Zepho sent many of the wounded to his command, about two thousand men, and Sosiphtar, the captain of Angeas's army, fell in that battle. {63:33} When Sosiphtar fell, the African troops turned to flee, and both Angeas and Lucus joined them in their retreat. {63:34} Zepho and the children of Chittim pursued them, inflicting heavy losses on the way, killing about two hundred men, and they chased after Azdrubal, the son of Angeas, who fled with his father. They killed twenty of his men on the road, but Azdrubal managed to escape and was not slain. {63:35} Angeas and his brother Lucus fled with the rest of their men, escaping back to Africa in fear and distress, and Angeas lived in fear for the rest of his days, worrying that Zepho, son of Eliphaz, would go to war against him.

{64:1} At that time, Balaam, the son of Beor, was with Angeas during the battle. When he saw that Zepho was winning against Angeas, he fled and went to Chittim. {64:2} Zepho and the children of Chittim welcomed him warmly because Zepho recognized Balaam's wisdom. He gave Balaam many gifts, and Balaam stayed with him. {64:3} After returning from the war, Zepho ordered a count of all the children of Chittim who had fought with him, and not one was missing. {64:4} Zepho was delighted by this and renewed his kingdom, hosting a feast for all his subjects. {64:5} However, Zepho did not remember the Lord and failed to acknowledge that the Lord had helped him in battle and delivered him and his people from the king of Africa. He continued to follow the ways of the children of Chittim and the wicked children of Esau, serving other gods that his Esau relatives had taught him; thus, it is said, "Wickedness comes from the wicked." {64:6} Zepho ruled over all the children of Chittim securely but did not know the Lord who had saved him and his people from the king of Africa. The African forces stopped coming to Chittim to raid as they had in the past because they were aware of Zepho's power, having suffered defeat at his hands. Angeas lived in fear of Zepho, the son of Eliphaz, and the children of Chittim throughout his life. {64:7} When Zepho returned from the war and saw how he had triumphed over the people of Africa, he consulted with the children of Chittim about going to Egypt to fight against the sons of Jacob and Pharaoh, the king of Egypt. {64:8} Zepho had heard that the mighty men of Egypt were dead and that Joseph and his brothers, the sons of Jacob, were also deceased, leaving all their descendants, the children of Israel, in Egypt. {64:9} Zepho planned to fight against them and all of Egypt to avenge the children of Esau, whom Joseph and his brothers, along with the Egyptians, had harmed in Canaan when they went to bury Jacob in Hebron. {64:10} Zepho sent messengers to Hadad, the son of Bedad, king of Edom, and to all his fellow Esau descendants, saying, {64:11} "Did you not say that you would not fight against the king of Africa because he is part of your covenant? Look, I fought him and defeated him and his people. {64:12} Now, I am determined to fight against Egypt and the children of Jacob who are there, and I will take revenge for what Joseph, his brothers, and their ancestors did to us in Canaan when they buried their father in Hebron. {64:13} If you are willing to come and assist me in this fight against them and Egypt, we can avenge our brethren." {64:14} The children of Esau listened to Zepho and gathered a large army to support him and the children of Chittim in battle. {64:15} Zepho also reached out to all the children of the east and the children of Ishmael with similar messages, and they assembled to aid Zepho and the children of Chittim in their war against Egypt. {64:16} The kings, including the king of Edom, the children of the east, and all the children of Ishmael, along with Zepho, the king of Chittim, gathered their forces in Hebron. {64:17} The camp was immense, stretching for a distance of three days' journey, filled with people as numerous as the sand on the seashore, beyond counting. {64:18} These kings and their armies marched down and confronted Egypt in battle, setting up camp in the valley of Pathros. {64:19} All of Egypt heard of their approach and gathered their own forces, with about three hundred thousand men from all the cities of Egypt. {64:20} The men of Egypt also called for the children of Israel, who were in the land of Goshen at that time, asking them to join in the fight against these kings. {64:21} The Israelites gathered together, totaling about one hundred and fifty men, and they went out to assist the Egyptians in battle. {64:22} Together, the men of Israel and Egypt numbered about three hundred thousand men plus one hundred and fifty, and they positioned themselves outside the land of Goshen opposite Pathros. {64:23} However, the Egyptians were hesitant to trust the Israelites to join their ranks for battle, fearing that the children of Israel might betray them to the children of Esau and Ishmael, since they were relatives. {64:24} The Egyptians told the Israelites to stay where they were and not to join them, stating that they would fight against the children of Esau and Ishmael alone. They suggested that if the kings overcame them, then the Israelites could come to their aid, and the children of Israel agreed. {64:25} Zepho, the son of Eliphaz, king of Chittim, Hadad, the son of Bedad, king of Edom, and all their armies, along with the children of the east and the children of Ishmael—numerous as the sand—set up camp in the valley of Pathros opposite Tachpanches. {64:26} Balaam, the son of Beor, the Syrian, was present in Zepho's camp, having come with the children of Chittim to the battle, and he was held in high regard by Zepho and his men. {64:27} Zepho asked Balaam to use divination to find out who would win the battle, whether they or the Egyptians would prevail. {64:28} Balaam attempted to practice divination, being skilled in the art, but he was confused, and his efforts failed. {64:29} He tried again, but it was unsuccessful, leading him to give up, for the Lord caused this to happen so that Zepho and his people would be handed over to the children of Israel, who trusted in the Lord, the God of their ancestors, during the battle. {64:30} Zepho and Hadad arranged their forces for battle, while the Egyptians advanced alone, about three hundred thousand strong, without any Israelites alongside them. {64:31} The Egyptians fought against the kings opposite Pathros and Tachpanches, facing fierce opposition. {64:32} The kings proved stronger than the Egyptians, resulting in the deaths of about one hundred eighty Egyptian men that day, compared to around thirty from the kings' forces, leading the Egyptians to flee before the kings. The children of Esau and Ishmael chased after the fleeing Egyptians, continuing to strike them until they reached the camp of the children of Israel. {64:33} The Egyptians called out to the children of Israel for help, saying, "Hurry and save us from the hands of Esau, Ishmael, and the children of Chittim!" {64:34} The one hundred fifty Israelites ran from their positions to join the kings' camps, crying out to the Lord their God to deliver them. {64:35} The Lord listened to Israel's cries and granted them victory over the kings' men, allowing the Israelites to defeat about four thousand of the kings' soldiers. {64:36} The Lord caused great panic in the kings' camp, instilling fear in them because of the children of Israel. {64:37} All the kings' armies fled before the Israelites, who pursued them, continuing to attack until they reached the borders of the land of Cush. {64:38} Along the way, the children of Israel killed an additional two thousand men, and not a single Israelite fell. {64:39} When the Egyptians saw how the Israelites, so few in number, had fought fiercely against the kings, they were greatly terrified for their lives due to the intensity of the battle, and all of Egypt fled, with each person hiding from the advancing forces, abandoning the Israelites to fight alone. {64:40} The Israelites inflicted a severe blow on the kings' forces and retreated only after driving them to the border of the land of Cush. {64:41} The Israelites were aware of what the Egyptians had done, how they had fled from battle, leaving them to fight on their own. {64:42} Consequently, the Israelites devised a clever plan, and on their return from battle, they encountered some Egyptians on the road and attacked them. {64:43} While attacking, they said, {64:44} "Why did you abandon us and leave us, when we were few, to fight against these kings who had a large army, simply to save yourselves?" {64:45} The Israelites spoke among themselves, saying, "Strike him down, for he is an Ishmaelite, or an Edomite, or from the children of Chittim," and they stood over him and killed him, not realizing he was an Egyptian. {64:46} The Israelites acted cunningly against the Egyptians because they had deserted them in battle. {64:47} The children of Israel killed about two hundred Egyptian men on the road in this way. {64:48} All the Egyptians witnessed the harm the Israelites had inflicted upon them, causing great fear throughout Egypt, as they had seen the Israelites' tremendous power and that not a single Israelite had fallen. {64:49} Thus, the children of Israel returned joyfully to their path towards Goshen, while the rest of the Egyptians each returned to their own places.

{65:1} After these events, all the advisors of Pharaoh, the king of Egypt, along with the elders of Egypt, gathered together and approached the king, bowing down to him and taking their seats before him. {65:2} The advisors and elders spoke to the king, saying, {65:3} "Look, the people of the children of Israel are more numerous and stronger than we are, and you know all the harm they did to us on the way back from battle. {65:4} You have also seen their immense power; it comes from their ancestors. Just a few of them faced a multitude as vast as the sand, and they defeated us with swords, with not one of them falling in battle. If they had been numerous, they would have utterly destroyed us. {65:5} Therefore, give us advice on what to do about them so we can gradually eliminate them from our midst before they become too numerous. {65:6} If the children of Israel continue to grow in number, they will become a threat to us. If any war breaks out, they will join our enemies against us, fight us, and drive us from the land." {65:7} The king responded to the elders of Egypt, saying, "This is the plan we have devised against Israel, and we will not stray from it. {65:8} Look, there are Pithom and Rameses, cities that are unfortified against attacks. We should build and fortify them together. {65:9} Now, you should act cunningly toward them and announce across Egypt and in Goshen by the king's command: {65:10} 'All men of Egypt, Goshen, Pathros, and all their inhabitants! The king has commanded us to build Pithom and Rameses and fortify them for battle. Anyone from Egypt, the children of Israel, or any city who is willing to help build will receive daily wages as ordered by the king. So go ahead and cleverly gather together and come to Pithom and Rameses to work.' {65:11} While you're building, make sure to proclaim this message every day throughout Egypt at the king's command. {65:12} When some of the children of Israel come to build with you, pay them their wages daily for a few days. {65:13} After they have worked with you for their daily pay, secretly withdraw from them one by one, and then you will become their taskmasters and overseers. Leave them to work without pay, and if they refuse, force them to continue. {65:14} If you do this, it will help us strengthen our land against the children of Israel, because the fatigue of labor will diminish them, especially since you'll be taking their wives from them day by day." {65:15} All the elders of Egypt heard the king's advice, and it seemed good to them, as well as to Pharaoh's servants and all of Egypt, and they acted according to the king's orders. {65:16} All the servants left the king and announced the king's command throughout Egypt, in Tachpanches and Goshen, and in all the cities surrounding Egypt, saying, {65:17} "You have seen what the children of Esau and Ishmael did to us when they came to fight against us and sought to destroy us. {65:18} Now, the king has commanded us to fortify the land, to build the cities Pithom and Rameses, and to prepare them for battle in case they come against us again. {65:19} Whoever from all of Egypt and the children of Israel will come to build with us will receive daily wages from the king, as commanded." {65:20} When all of Egypt and the children of Israel heard what Pharaoh's servants had said, many Egyptians and Israelites went to help the Pharaoh's servants build Pithom and Rameses, but none of the children of Levi joined their brethren in the work. {65:21} At first, Pharaoh's servants and princes deceitfully joined the Israelites as hired laborers and paid them daily wages at the start. {65:22} They worked with the Israelites for a month. {65:23} However, at the end of that month, Pharaoh's servants began to secretly withdraw from the Israelites every day. {65:24} The Israelites continued their work and still received their daily wages, as some Egyptians remained on the job. Thus, the Egyptians paid the Israelites for their labor in those days to ensure that their fellow workers were compensated. {65:25} After a year and four months, all the Egyptians had withdrawn from the children of Israel, leaving them alone to work. {65:26} Once the Egyptians had withdrawn, they returned to oppress and oversee the Israelites, with some acting as taskmasters, demanding all they owed them for their labor. {65:27} The Egyptians treated the children of Israel harshly day after day to afflict them with hard work. {65:28} All the children of Israel worked alone while the Egyptians stopped paying them. {65:29} When some Israelites refused to work because they weren't being paid, the tax collectors and Pharaoh's servants beat them harshly and forced them back to labor alongside their fellow workers. This is how all Egyptians treated the children of Israel throughout their time. {65:30} The children of Israel were greatly afraid of the Egyptians because of this, and they returned to work alone without pay. {65:31} The children of Israel built Pithom and Rameses, with some making bricks and others constructing. They worked hard to fortify all of Egypt and its walls for many years until the time came when the Lord remembered them and brought them out of Egypt. {65:32} However, the children of Levi did not work alongside their fellow Israelites from the beginning until they left Egypt. {65:33} The children of Levi knew that the Egyptians had deceived the Israelites, so they refrained from joining their brethren in the work. {65:34} The Egyptians paid no attention to the children of Levi, since they had not participated in the work from the start, leaving them alone. {65:35} The Egyptians continued to treat the children of Israel with harshness in their labor, forcing them to work rigorously. {65:36} They embittered the lives of the children of Israel with hard labor, making bricks and mortar, as well as all types of work in the fields. {65:37} The children of Israel called the king of Egypt Melol "Meror, king of Egypt," because during his reign, the Egyptians made their lives bitter with harsh labor. {65:38} All the work that the Egyptians forced upon the children of Israel was done with severity to afflict them, but the more they were oppressed, the more they multiplied and thrived, which caused the Egyptians to be troubled by the children of Israel.

{66:1} At that time, Hadad, the son of Bedad, the king of Edom, died, and Samlah from Mesrekah, in the land of the children of the east, took his place as king. {66:2} In the thirteenth year of Pharaoh's reign in Egypt, which was the one hundred twenty-fifth year since the Israelites had come down into Egypt, Samlah reigned over Edom for eighteen years. {66:3} While he was king, he mobilized his army to fight against Zepho, the son of Eliphaz, and the children of Chittim, as they had attacked Angeas, the king of Africa, and defeated his entire army. {66:4} However, he did not engage Zepho, because the children of Esau prevented him, claiming he was their brother. Samlah listened to the children of Esau and returned with all his forces to Edom instead of proceeding to fight against Zepho. {66:5} Pharaoh, the king of Egypt, heard about this and said, "Samlah, king of Edom, has decided to fight against the children of Chittim, and afterward, he will come to attack Egypt." {66:6} When the Egyptians learned of this, they increased the workload on the children of Israel to prevent them from doing to them what they had done in their war against the children of Esau during Hadad's time. {66:7} The Egyptians told the children of Israel, "Hurry up and finish your work and strengthen the land, or else the children of Esau, your brothers, will come to fight against us because of you." {66:8} The children of Israel worked diligently for the Egyptians every day, while the Egyptians oppressed them to reduce their numbers in the land. {66:9} However, as the Egyptians increased the burdens on the children of Israel, the Israelites continued to multiply and grow, filling all of Egypt with their numbers. {66:10} In the one hundred twenty-fifth year since the Israelites had come down into Egypt, the Egyptians saw that their plans against Israel were failing; instead, the Israelites were growing in number, and both Egypt and Goshen were filled with them. {66:11} Therefore, all the elders and wise men of Egypt came before the king, bowed to him, and took their seats. {66:12} They said to the king, "May you live forever! You advised us against the children of Israel, and we acted according to your word. {66:13} However, despite increasing their labor, they only continue to multiply and fill the land." {66:14} The elders continued, "Now, our lord and king, the eyes of all Egypt are upon you to provide wisdom on how to deal with Israel, either to destroy or reduce their numbers." The king replied, "Give your counsel so we can know what to do." {66:15} An officer, one of the king's counselors named Job from Mesopotamia, in the land of Uz, responded to the king, saying, {66:16} "If it pleases the king, let him listen to the counsel of his servant." The king said, "Speak." {66:17} Job addressed the king, the princes, and the elders, saying, {66:18} "The king's previous counsel regarding the labor of the children of Israel is excellent, and you must not remove that labor from them. {66:19} However, here is my advice on how you can lessen their numbers if the king wishes to afflict them. {66:20} We have feared war for a long time, believing that if Israel becomes fruitful in the land, they will drive us out if war breaks out. {66:21} Therefore, if it pleases the king, let a royal decree be issued and written into the laws of Egypt, which cannot be revoked, stating that every male child born to the Israelites shall be killed. {66:22} By doing this, once all the male children of Israel are dead, their threat will cease. Let the king order the Hebrew midwives to execute this plan." This advice pleased the king and his princes, and the king acted according to Job's counsel. {66:23} The king called for the Hebrew midwives, one named Shephrah and the other Puah. {66:24} The midwives came before the king and stood in his presence. {66:25} The king said to them, "When you assist the Hebrew women during childbirth and see them on the birthing stools, if it is a son, you shall kill him; but if it is a daughter, she shall live." {66:26} He added, "If you do not comply with this order, I will burn you and your houses with fire." {66:27} However, the midwives feared God and did not obey the king of Egypt's orders. When the Hebrew women gave birth, whether it was a son or daughter, the midwives did everything necessary for the child and allowed them to live. This was their practice throughout their time. {66:28} When the king learned of this, he summoned the midwives and asked, "Why have you done this and allowed the children to live?" {66:29} The midwives answered together, saying, {66:30} "Let not the king think that Hebrew women are like Egyptian women; they are vigorous, and before we can arrive, they have already given birth. Many days have passed without a Hebrew woman needing our assistance, as they deliver on their own because they are strong." {66:31} Pharaoh believed their words and accepted their explanation. The midwives then left the king's presence, and God was kind to them; the people multiplied and grew exceedingly.

{67:1} There was a man in the land of Egypt from the tribe of Levi named Amram, son of Kehath, grandson of Levi, and great-grandson of Israel. {67:2} This man married a woman named Jochebed, who was his father's sister from the tribe of Levi; she was one hundred and twenty-six years old when he approached her. {67:3} The woman conceived and gave birth to a daughter, whom she named Miriam, because during that time, the Egyptians had made the lives of the Israelites bitter. {67:4} She became pregnant again and gave birth to a son, naming him Aaron, for at the time of her pregnancy, Pharaoh began to kill the male children of Israel. {67:5} In those days, Zepho, the son of Eliphaz and grandson of Esau, king of Chittim, died, and Janeas took his place as king. {67:6} Zepho ruled over the people of Chittim for fifty years before dying and being buried in the city of Nabna in Chittim. {67:7} After him, Janeas, one of the mighty men from Chittim, ruled for another fifty years. {67:8} After the death of the king of Chittim, Balaam, son of Beor, fled to Egypt to Pharaoh, king of Egypt. {67:9} Pharaoh received him with great respect because he had heard of Balaam's wisdom, giving him gifts and making him a counselor, elevating him in status. {67:10} Balaam lived in Egypt, honored by all the king's nobles, who admired him and desired to learn from his wisdom. {67:11} In the one hundred and thirtieth year of Israel's stay in Egypt, Pharaoh had a dream while sitting on his throne; he lifted his eyes and saw an old man standing before him holding merchant scales. {67:12} The old man hung the scales before Pharaoh. {67:13} He gathered all the elders of Egypt and the great men, tied them together, and placed them in one scale. {67:14} Then he took a young goat and placed it in the other scale, and the goat outweighed all the others. {67:15} Pharaoh was astonished by this frightening vision, questioning why the goat should outweigh everything else, and he woke up, realizing it was a dream. {67:16} Pharaoh got up early the next morning, called all his servants, and told them the dream, which frightened them greatly. {67:17} The king said to all his wise men, "Please interpret the dream I had so I may understand it." {67:18} Balaam, son of Beor, answered the king, saying, "This dream signifies nothing but a great evil that will arise against Egypt in the future." {67:19} "For a son will be born to Israel who will destroy all of Egypt and its people, leading the Israelites out of Egypt with a mighty hand." {67:20} "Therefore, O king, you should take action now to destroy the hope of the children of Israel before this disaster strikes Egypt." {67:21} The king replied to Balaam, "What should we do to Israel? We previously tried to devise a plan against them but failed." {67:22} "So please give me advice on how we can overcome them." {67:23} Balaam answered, "Send for your two counselors, and we will hear their advice on this matter, after which I will speak." {67:24} The king sent for his two counselors, Reuel the Midianite and Job the Uzite, and they came to sit before him. {67:25} The king said to them, "You both heard my dream and its interpretation; now, please give advice on what should be done to the children of Israel so we can prevail against them before their evil arises against us." {67:26} Reuel the Midianite responded, "May the king live forever. {67:27} If it pleases the king, let him refrain from the Hebrews and leave them alone, without taking any action against them. {67:28} These are the people whom the Lord chose long ago as His inheritance among all the nations of the earth, and who has ever harmed them without facing consequences from their God? {67:29} You know that when Abraham went down to Egypt, the former king saw Sarah, his wife, and took her as his wife because Abraham said she was his sister; he was afraid the Egyptians would kill him for her. {67:30} When the king took Sarah, God struck him and his household with severe plagues until he returned Sarah to Abraham, at which point he was healed. {67:31} God also punished Abimelech, king of the Philistines, for taking Sarah as Abraham's wife by preventing all wombs, from men to beasts, from conceiving. {67:32} God appeared to Abimelech in a dream one night, scaring him so he would restore Sarah to Abraham. Later, all the people of Gerar suffered because of Sarah, but Abraham prayed for them, and God heard his prayer and healed them. {67:33} Abimelech feared the consequences of the troubles that befell him and his people and returned Sarah to Abraham, giving him many gifts. {67:34} He also did the same for Isaac when he expelled him from Gerar, for God had performed miracles for Isaac, drying up all the watercourses of Gerar and causing their trees to stop producing fruit. {67:35} Eventually, Abimelech and his friend Ahuzzath, along with Pichol, the captain of his army, went to Isaac, bowed before him, {67:36} and asked him to pray for them. Isaac prayed to the Lord for them, and the Lord heard him and healed them. {67:37} Jacob, known for his integrity, was saved from his brother Esau and his uncle Laban, who sought to kill him, as well as from all the kings of Canaan who united against him and his family to destroy them. The Lord delivered them from their enemies, who turned against them. {67:38} You know that Pharaoh, your grandfather, raised Joseph, son of Jacob, above all the princes in Egypt when he recognized his wisdom, and through Joseph, he saved everyone from famine. {67:39} Then he invited Jacob and his family to come to Egypt, hoping their virtues would save the land from famine. {67:40} So, if it seems good to you, cease from destroying the children of Israel; but if you don't want them to stay in Egypt, let them go back to the land of Canaan, where their ancestors lived." {67:41} When Pharaoh heard Jethro's words, he became furious and left the king's presence, returning to Midian with shame, taking Joseph's stick with him. {67:42} The king then asked Job the Uzite, "What do you think, Job? What is your advice regarding the Hebrews?" {67:43} Job replied, "All the inhabitants of the land are at your mercy; do as you think best." {67:44} The king then said to Balaam, "What do you say, Balaam? Speak your thoughts so we can hear." {67:45} Balaam said to the king, "No matter what the king plans against the Hebrews, they will escape, and you will not succeed against them with any scheme. {67:46} If you think to reduce their numbers by fire, you will not succeed, for their God saved Abraham from Ur of the Chaldeans; if you think to destroy them by the sword, Isaac, their father, was delivered by a ram in his place. {67:47} If you believe that hard labor will diminish them, you will fail because their father Jacob worked hard for Laban and prospered. {67:48} So, O King, listen to my words; here is the advice that will allow you to succeed against them, and you should not ignore it. {67:49} If it pleases the king, let him command that all children born from this day forward be thrown into the water, for this will erase their name, as none of them or their ancestors have faced such a trial. {67:50} The king agreed with Balaam's proposal, and it pleased him and his princes, and the king acted according to Balaam's words. {67:51} He issued a proclamation and established a law throughout Egypt stating that every male child born to the Hebrews from that day forward would be thrown into the water. {67:52} Pharaoh summoned all his servants and said, "Go and search throughout Goshen where the Israelites are, and ensure that every son born to the Hebrews is thrown into the river, but let every daughter live." {67:53} When the Israelites heard Pharaoh's command to cast their male children into the river, some men separated from their wives, while others remained with them. {67:54} From that day on, when the time came for Israelite women to give birth, those who stayed with their husbands went to the fields to deliver their children, leaving the babies in the fields and returning home. {67:55} The Lord, who promised their ancestors to multiply them, sent one of His angels from heaven to wash each child, anoint them, and wrap them in swaddling clothes, giving them two smooth stones; one stone provided milk and the other honey, causing their hair to grow down to their knees, allowing them to cover themselves and comfort them with compassion. {67:56} God, seeing their suffering and desiring to multiply them on the earth, commanded the earth to receive and preserve them until they grew up. Then the earth opened its mouth and released them, and they sprouted up from the city like grass in the field or herbs in the forest, returning to their families and fathers' houses to stay with them. {67:57} The babies of the Israelites were on the earth like herbs of the field, due to God's grace toward them. {67:58} When the Egyptians saw this, they went out to their fields with their oxen and plows, plowing the land as if it were seed time. {67:59} As they plowed, they could not harm the infants of the Israelites, so the people grew and multiplied greatly. {67:60} Pharaoh ordered his officers to go to Goshen daily to look for the Israelite babies. {67:61} When they found one, they forcefully took it from its mother's arms and threw it into the river, but they allowed the female children to remain with their mothers; this is what the Egyptians did to Israelites throughout years.

{68:1} At that time, the Spirit of God was upon Miriam, the daughter of Amram and sister of Aaron. She went out and prophesied, saying, "Look, a son will be born to us from my father and mother this time, and he will save Israel from the hands of Egypt." {68:2} When Amram heard his daughter's words, he took his wife back home after he had sent her away when Pharaoh ordered that every male child of the house of Jacob be thrown into the water. {68:3} So Amram took Jochebed, his wife, three years after he had sent her away, and he came to her, and she conceived. {68:4} After seven months from her conception, she gave birth to a son, and the whole house was filled with a great light, like the light of the sun and moon shining together. {68:5} When the woman saw that the child was good and pleasing to the eye, she hid him for three months in an inner room. {68:6} During that time, the Egyptians conspired to destroy all the Hebrews. {68:7} Egyptian women went to Goshen where the children of Israel were, carrying their young ones on their shoulders, their babies who could not yet speak. {68:8} At that time, when the Israelite women gave birth, each woman hid her son from the Egyptians so they would not know about the births and destroy them. {68:9} The Egyptian women came to Goshen with their children on their shoulders, and when an Egyptian woman entered the house of a Hebrew woman, her baby began to cry. {68:10} When the baby cried, the child in the inner room answered, prompting the Egyptian women to report this to Pharaoh's house. {68:11} Pharaoh then sent his officers to take the children and kill them; this is what the Egyptians did to the Hebrew women throughout the years. {68:12} At that time, about three months after Jochebed hid her son, the situation became known in Pharaoh's house. {68:13} The woman hurried to take her son away before the officers arrived, making an ark of bulrushes, coating it with slime and pitch, and placing the child inside. She laid it among the reeds by the riverbank. {68:14} His sister Miriam stood at a distance to see what would happen to him and what would come of her words. {68:15} God sent a terrible heat in Egypt, which burned people's flesh like the sun at its peak, greatly oppressing the Egyptians. {68:16} All the Egyptians went down to the river to bathe because of the intense heat that burned their flesh. {68:17} Bathia, the daughter of Pharaoh, also went to bathe in the river, accompanied by her maidens and all the women of Egypt. {68:18} Bathia looked up and saw the ark on the water. She sent her maid to fetch it. {68:19} When she opened it, she saw the child, and behold, the babe wept. She felt compassion for him and said, "This is one of the Hebrew children." {68:20} All the Egyptian women by the river wanted to nurse him, but he refused to suckle, for the Lord had ordained this so he could be restored to his mother's breast. {68:21} Miriam, who was with the Egyptian women by the river, saw this and asked Pharaoh's daughter, "Shall I go and find a Hebrew woman to nurse the child for you?" {68:22} Pharaoh's daughter replied, "Go." So the young woman went and called the child's mother. {68:23} Pharaoh's daughter said to Jochebed, "Take this child away and nurse him for me, and I will pay you your wages—two bits of silver daily." The woman took the child and nursed him. {68:24} When the child was two years old, she brought him to Pharaoh's daughter, and he became like a son to her. She named him Moses, saying, "Because I drew him out of the water." {68:25} Amram, his father, named him Chabar, saying, "It was for him that I returned to my wife, whom I had sent away." {68:26} Jochebed, his mother, named him Jekuthiel, saying, "I have hoped for him from the Almighty, and God has restored him to me." {68:27} Miriam, his sister, called him Jered, because she went down after him to the river to see what would happen. {68:28} Aaron, his brother, named him Abi Zanuch, saying, "My father left my mother and returned to her on his account." {68:29} Kehath, Amram's father, named him Abigdor, because, on his account, God repaired the breach in the house of Jacob so they could no longer throw their male children into the water. {68:30} Their nurse named him Abi Socho, saying, "In his tabernacle, he was hidden for three months because of the children of Ham." {68:31} All Israel called him Shemaiah, son of Nethanel, because they said, "In his days, God heard their cries and rescued them from their oppressors." {68:32} Moses lived in Pharaoh's house and was like a son to Bathia, Pharaoh's daughter, growing up among the king's children.

{69:1} In those days, the king of Edom died in the eighteenth year of his reign and was buried in the temple he had built for himself in the land of Edom. {69:2} The children of Esau sent to Pethor, by the river, and brought back a young man of beautiful eyes and a handsome appearance named Saul, making him king over them instead of Samlah. {69:3} Saul reigned over all the children of Esau in the land of Edom for forty years. {69:4} When Pharaoh, king of Egypt, saw that the counsel Balaam had advised regarding the children of Israel did not succeed, and that they were still fruitful and multiplied in Egypt, {69:5} he commanded that a proclamation be issued throughout Egypt to the children of Israel, stating that no man should reduce anything from his daily labor. {69:6} The man found deficient in his daily work, whether in mortar or bricks, would have his youngest son put in his place. {69:7} The burden of labor in Egypt grew heavier on the children of Israel, so if any brick was missing from a man's daily quota, the Egyptians forcibly took his youngest boy from his mother and made him replace the missing brick. {69:8} The Egyptians did this to all the children of Israel daily for a long time. {69:9} However, the tribe of Levi did not work with the Israelites during that time because they understood the cunning of the Egyptians and their initial deceit toward the Israelites.

{70:1} In the third year after Moses was born, Pharaoh was hosting a banquet with Queen Alparanith on his right and Bathia on his left, while the young Moses was lying in Bathia's lap. Balaam, son of Beor, was there with his two sons, along with all the princes of the kingdom, sitting at the king's table. {70:2} The boy reached out his hand, took the crown from Pharaoh's head, and put it on his own head. {70:3} When Pharaoh and the princes saw what the boy had done, they were terrified and whispered to one another in astonishment. {70:4} Pharaoh then asked the princes at the table, "What are you saying about this, and what judgment should be passed on this boy for what he has done?" {70:5} Balaam, the magician, spoke up before Pharaoh and the princes, saying, "Remember, my lord and king, the dream you had long ago and the interpretation I provided." {70:6} "This child is a Hebrew and has the spirit of God within him. Don't think for a moment that he acted without knowledge." {70:7} "Though he is just a boy, he has wisdom and understanding, and with that wisdom, he has chosen to claim the kingdom of Egypt for himself." {70:8} "It's typical for Hebrews to trick kings and nobles, acting cunningly to make them tremble." {70:9} "You surely remember how Abraham, their ancestor, did this when he deceived Nimrod, king of Babel, and Abimelech, king of Gerar, taking over the land of the Hittites and all the kingdoms of Canaan." {70:10} "He even went to Egypt and claimed that Sarah was his sister to mislead the Egyptians and their king." {70:11} "Isaac did the same when he went to Gerar and prevailed over Abimelech's army." {70:12} "He intended to deceive the Philistines by saying that Rebecca was his sister." {70:13} "Jacob also deceived his brother, stealing his birthright and blessing." {70:14} "He then went to Padan-aram, to his uncle Laban's house, and cunningly acquired his daughter, cattle, and everything that belonged to Laban before fleeing back to Canaan." {70:15} "Jacob's sons sold their brother Joseph into slavery in Egypt, where he spent twelve years in prison." {70:16} "Then, when the former Pharaoh had dreams, Joseph was brought out of prison and raised to a position above all the princes in Egypt for interpreting those dreams." {70:17} "During a famine, God sent for Joseph's father and brothers, bringing the whole family to Egypt where he supported them without charge, effectively making the Egyptians his slaves." {70:18} "Now, my lord, this child has risen up in Egypt to imitate their actions and to mock every king, prince, and judge." {70:19} "If it pleases the king, let us kill him to prevent him from growing up and taking the kingdom from you, causing Egypt to perish." {70:20} "Balaam then suggested to the king, 'Let's call all the judges and wise men of Egypt to determine if the boy deserves the death penalty, as you suggested, and then we can execute him.'" {70:21} Pharaoh sent for all the wise men, and an angel of the Lord appeared among them, appearing as one of the wise men. {70:22} Pharaoh addressed the wise men, "You've heard what this Hebrew boy has done. Balaam has passed judgment. {70:23} Now you must also decide what punishment he deserves for his actions." {70:24} The angel, disguised as a wise man, replied in front of Pharaoh and his princes, {70:25} "If it pleases the king, let him send for an onyx stone and a coal of fire to be placed before the child. If the boy reaches for the onyx stone, we will know he acted wisely and should be put to death. {70:26} But if he reaches for the coal, we will know he acted without understanding, and he shall live." {70:27} The suggestion pleased Pharaoh and the princes, so the king followed the angel's advice. {70:28} He ordered the onyx stone and coal to be brought and placed before Moses. {70:29} They set the boy before them, and he reached out for the onyx stone. However, the angel of the Lord guided his hand to the coal, which extinguished in his grasp. He lifted it to his mouth, burning his lips and tongue, making him heavy-tongued. {70:30} When Pharaoh and the princes saw this, they understood that Moses had not acted wisely when he took the crown from the king. {70:31} Thus, they decided against killing him, and Moses stayed in Pharaoh's house, growing up under the Lord's guidance. {70:32} While Moses was in the king's house, he was dressed in purple and raised among the king's children. {70:33} As Moses grew up, Bathia, Pharaoh's daughter, considered him her son, and everyone in Pharaoh's household honored him, while all the Egyptians feared him. {70:34} Each day, he would go to the land of Goshen to see his brothers, the children of Israel, and witness their hard labor and suffering. {70:35} Moses asked them, "Why are you forced to work so hard every day?" {70:36} They explained everything they had endured and all the tasks Pharaoh had imposed on them even before he was born. {70:37} They recounted Balaam's schemes against them and the plans to kill Moses after he took the king's crown. {70:38} Hearing this, Moses became furious with Balaam and plotted to kill him, lying in wait each day. {70:39} Balaam, fearing for his life, fled Egypt with his two sons and sought refuge with Kikianus, king of Cush. {70:40} While Moses was in Pharaoh's house, coming and going, the Lord granted him favor in the eyes of Pharaoh, his servants, and all the Egyptian people, who loved him dearly. {70:41} One day, when Moses visited Goshen to see his brothers, he witnessed the Israelites struggling under their burdens and hard labor, which deeply distressed him. {70:42} Moses returned to Egypt, went to Pharaoh's palace, and bowed before him. {70:43} He addressed Pharaoh, "Please, my lord, I have a small request. Do not send me away empty-handed." Pharaoh replied, "Speak." {70:44} Moses continued, "Please grant your servants, the children of Israel in Goshen, one day of rest from their labor." {70:45} The king responded, "I have agreed to your request." {70:46} Pharaoh then ordered a proclamation to be made throughout Egypt and Goshen, saying, {70:47} "To all the children of Israel, this is the king speaking: You shall work for six days, but on the seventh day, you shall rest and perform no labor. This is what you shall do every week, as I and Moses, son of Bathia, have commanded." {70:48} Moses rejoiced at this approval from the king, and all the children of Israel followed his instructions. {70:49} This was part of the Lord's plan for the Israelites, for He began to remember them and aimed to save them for the sake of their ancestors. {70:50} The Lord was with Moses, and his reputation spread throughout Egypt. {70:51} Moses gained great respect from the Egyptians and the Israelites as he worked for their welfare and advocated for peace with Pharaoh on their behalf.

{71:1} When Moses was eighteen years old, he desired to see his father and mother, so he went to Goshen. As he neared the place, he saw the children of Israel working under heavy burdens, and he witnessed an Egyptian striking one of his Hebrew brothers. {71:2} The beaten man ran to Moses for help, knowing that Moses was respected in Pharaoh's house. He said, "My lord, this Egyptian bound me, came to my wife before my eyes, and now seeks to kill me." {71:3} Hearing this, Moses became enraged. He looked around, saw no one, and struck the Egyptian down, hiding him in the sand, thus saving the Hebrew man. {71:4} The Hebrew returned home, and Moses went back to Pharaoh's house. {71:5} When the man returned home, he considered divorcing his wife, as it was not acceptable in Jacob's house to be with a wife who had been defiled. {71:6} The woman told her brothers, and they sought to kill her husband, but he fled to his house and escaped. {71:7} The next day, Moses went out again and saw two Hebrews quarreling. He asked the wrongdoer, "Why do you strike your neighbor?" {71:8} The man replied, "Who made you a prince and judge over us? Will you kill me like you did the Egyptian?" Moses then realized that his deed was known. {71:9} Pharaoh heard about it and ordered Moses to be killed, but God sent an angel who appeared to Pharaoh as the captain of his guard. {71:10} The angel took the guard's sword and used it to behead the guard, whose likeness had been changed to resemble Moses. {71:11} The angel then took Moses by the hand and led him out of Egypt, placing him outside its borders, a forty-day journey away. {71:12} Meanwhile, Aaron remained in Egypt, prophesying to the children of Israel, {71:13} saying, "The Lord God of your ancestors commands you to cast away the idols of Egypt and not defile yourselves." {71:14} But the children of Israel refused to listen to Aaron. {71:15} The Lord considered destroying them, but remembered His covenant with Abraham, Isaac, and Jacob. {71:16} During this time, Pharaoh's oppression of the Israelites continued, and their suffering intensified until God remembered them and prepared to act.

{72:1} Around this time, a great war broke out between the children of Cush and the people of the East and Aram, who rebelled against the Cushite king. {72:2} Kikianus, king of Cush, gathered his vast army to fight the rebels and bring them back under his rule. {72:3} Before leaving, he entrusted Balaam the magician and his two sons with guarding the city and its poor citizens. {72:4} Kikianus fought and defeated the Easterners and Aram, taking many captives and reinstating their tribute. {72:5} He set up camp in their land to collect their taxes as before. {72:6} While Kikianus was away, Balaam plotted with the citizens of Cush to rebel against their king and prevent his return. {72:7} The people agreed, swore allegiance to Balaam, and made him king, while his sons became army captains. {72:8} They reinforced the city walls and built an especially strong fortification. {72:9} They also dug countless ditches between the city and the surrounding river, causing the waters to flood the area. {72:10} Additionally, they summoned numerous serpents through enchantments to guard one corner of the city, making the city impregnable. {72:11} Kikianus, having subdued Aram and the Easterners, returned home with his troops. {72:12} As they approached the city, they were shocked to see the walls greatly strengthened. {72:13} The soldiers speculated that the citizens had done this out of fear, thinking they had taken too long in battle. {72:14} When Kikianus and his men arrived at the gates, they called for them to be opened, but {72:15} the guards, following Balaam's orders, refused to let them enter. {72:16} A fierce battle ensued at the city gates, and Kikianus lost 130 men. {72:17} The next day, they tried to cross the river but failed, with many drowning in the pits. {72:18} The king then ordered his men to build rafts to cross, but {72:19} when they reached the ditches, the swirling water drowned another 200 men. {72:20} On the third day, they fought near the serpents but couldn't approach, losing 170 more men. They gave up on the attack and laid siege to the city for nine years, allowing no one to enter or leave. {72:21} It was during this siege that Moses fled Egypt, escaping from Pharaoh who sought his life for killing the Egyptian. {72:22} Moses, then eighteen, fled to Kikianus's camp, which was besieging Cush. {72:23} He stayed there for nine years, during which he became highly respected among Kikianus's men. {72:24} The king and his soldiers loved Moses for his wisdom, strength, and lion-like appearance, and he became a counselor to the king. {72:25} At the end of the nine years, Kikianus fell gravely ill and died on the seventh day. {72:26} His servants embalmed him and buried him at the city's northern gate, opposite Egypt. {72:27} They constructed an impressive monument over his grave and {72:28} engraved all his great deeds and battles on stones, where they remain to this day. {72:29} After Kikianus's death, his troops were deeply distressed about the ongoing war. {72:30} They discussed what to do, as they had been away from their homes for nine years. {72:31} They feared fighting the city would result in many deaths, while continuing the siege would lead to starvation. {72:32} They also worried that the kings of Aram and the East would attack them upon hearing of Kikianus's death. {72:33} Therefore, they decided to choose a new king from among their ranks to continue the siege. {72:34} They found no one more fitting than Moses and chose him to be their leader. {72:35} They stripped off their garments, threw them in a heap, and seated Moses on them, declaring him king. {72:36} They blew trumpets and shouted, "Long live the king!" {72:37} They swore to give Moses Adoniah, the Cushite queen and widow of Kikianus, as his wife, and on that day, they made Moses king over them. {72:38} The people of Cush issued a proclamation that everyone must give Moses a gift. {72:39} They spread a sheet over the heap, and each person threw in a gift, such as gold earrings or coins. {72:40} They also contributed onyx stones, bdellium (a fragrant resin), pearls, marble, silver, and gold. {72:41} Moses gathered all these treasures and placed them among his belongings. {72:42} Thus, Moses became king over Cush, ruling in place of Kikianus.

{73:1} In the fifty-fifth year of Pharaoh's reign over Egypt, which was the one hundred and fifty-seventh year since the Israelites had gone down into Egypt, Moses began to reign in Cush. {73:2} Moses was twenty-seven years old when he became king over Cush, and he reigned for forty years. {73:3} The Lord gave Moses favor in the eyes of the children of Cush, and they loved him greatly, so he found favor both with God and men. {73:4} On the seventh day of his reign, all the people of Cush gathered and bowed down before Moses. {73:5} They spoke to him, asking for counsel on how to take the city they had besieged for nine years. {73:6} The people expressed that they had not seen their wives and children in all that time. {73:7} Moses replied, "If you obey my commands, the Lord will deliver the city into our hands." {73:8} He warned that if they fought the same way as before, many would be wounded or killed. {73:9} So Moses offered new counsel, and the people agreed to follow his instructions. {73:10} They said, "We will do all that our lord commands." {73:11} Moses then ordered a proclamation throughout the camp. {73:12} He instructed everyone to go into the forest and each bring back a young stork (a type of bird) in their hands. {73:13} He further declared that anyone who disobeyed would be put to death, and all their belongings would be taken. {73:14} Once the birds were brought back, they were to be trained to attack like young hawks. {73:15} The people heard Moses' words and spread the proclamation through the camp. {73:16} All went into the forest, caught young storks, and returned with them, as instructed. {73:17} The penalty for not doing so was death and loss of property. {73:18} After catching the storks, they raised and trained them. {73:19} When the storks had grown, Moses ordered them to be kept hungry for three days. {73:20} On the third day, Moses told the people to arm themselves and prepare for battle. Each man was to take a young stork in his hand. {73:21} They were to go to the place where the serpents guarded the city. {73:22} When they arrived, Moses commanded them to release their storks, which they did. {73:23} The storks attacked the serpents and devoured them all. {73:24} The people shouted in triumph, seeing the serpents destroyed. {73:25} They then attacked the city, took it, and subdued its inhabitants. {73:26} That day, 1,100 men of the city's defenders died, but none of Moses' forces were lost. {73:27} After the battle, the people of Cush returned to their homes, reuniting with their families. {73:28} Balaam the magician saw the city was taken, so he fled with his sons and brothers to Egypt, returning to Pharaoh. {73:29} These were the sorcerers and magicians who later opposed Moses when the Lord sent the plagues on Egypt. {73:30} Moses had taken the city through his wisdom, and the people made him king in place of Kikianus. {73:31} They placed the royal crown on his head and gave him Adoniah, the widow of Kikianus, as his wife. {73:32} However, Moses feared the Lord and did not approach her or look upon her, respecting the traditions of his ancestors. {73:33} He remembered how Abraham had made his servant Eliezer swear not to take a wife from the daughters of Canaan for Isaac. {73:34} He also recalled how Isaac had commanded Jacob not to marry from the daughters of Canaan or ally with the descendants of Ham. {73:35} Moses knew that the Lord had decreed that the children of Ham would be servants to the children of Shem and Japheth forever. {73:36} Thus, Moses refrained from turning his heart or eyes toward Adoniah during his reign. {73:37} Throughout his life, Moses feared the Lord, walking faithfully and never straying from the righteous path of his ancestors, Abraham, Isaac, and Jacob. {73:38} He ruled with wisdom over Cush, and the Lord made him prosperous in his kingdom. {73:39} Around that time, Aram and the children of the east rebelled against Cush, having heard that Kikianus had died. {73:40} Moses gathered an army of 30,000 mighty men from Cush and went to fight against Aram and the children of the east. {73:41} When the children of the east heard of Moses' approach, they met him in battle. {73:42} The fighting was fierce, but the Lord delivered the children of the east into Moses' hands, and 300 men were slain. {73:43} The rest retreated, and Moses pursued them, imposing a tax on them as was customary. {73:44} Then Moses led his forces to battle against the land of Aram. {73:45} The people of Aram met them in battle, but the Lord again delivered them into Moses' hands, and many were wounded. {73:46} Moses subdued Aram, and they too were made to pay their usual tax. {73:47} Thus, Moses brought both Aram and the children of the east under the control of Cush, and he returned with his people to the land of Cush. {73:48} Moses strengthened his reign in Cush, and the Lord was with him, so much so that all the people of Cush feared him.

{74:1} In the later years, Saul, king of Edom, died, and Baal Chanan, son of Achbor, became king in his place. {74:2} In the sixteenth year of Moses' reign over Cush, Baal Chanan, son of Achbor, began his reign over the land of Edom, ruling all the children of Edom for thirty-eight years. {74:3} During his reign, Moab rebelled against Edom's power, having been under Edom's control since the days of Hadad, son of Bedad, who defeated them and brought Midian and Moab under Edom's rule. {74:4} When Baal Chanan, son of Achbor, reigned over Edom, the children of Moab withdrew their allegiance. {74:5} Around this time, Angeas, king of Africa, died, and his son Azdrubal succeeded him. {74:6} During these days, Janeas, king of the children of Chittim, also died, and they buried him in the temple he built for himself in the plain of Canopia as his residence. Latinus became king in his place. {74:7} In the twenty-second year of Moses' reign over Cush, Latinus ruled the children of Chittim for forty-five years. {74:8} He built a grand and mighty tower and constructed an elegant temple within it for his residence and to govern, as was the custom. {74:9} In the third year of his reign, he issued a proclamation to all his skilled men, commanding them to build many ships for him. {74:10} Latinus gathered all his forces, and they sailed to Africa to wage war against Azdrubal, son of Angeas. {74:11} In the battle, Latinus triumphed over Azdrubal, taking the aqueduct that Azdrubal's father had captured from Chittim when he took Janiah, daughter of Uzi, as his wife. Latinus destroyed the bridge and dealt Azdrubal's army a significant blow. {74:12} Azdrubal's remaining warriors, filled with envy and bitterness, sought death and engaged in battle once more with Latinus. {74:13} The battle was fierce, and the men of Africa suffered greatly, with many falling wounded. Azdrubal, the king, was also slain in this battle. {74:14} Azdrubal had a beautiful daughter named Ushpezena, and the men of Africa admired her beauty so much that they embroidered her likeness on their garments. {74:15} When the men of Latinus saw Ushpezena, they praised her beauty to their king. {74:16} Latinus ordered her to be brought to him, and he took her as his wife, then returned to Chittim. {74:17} After Azdrubal's death, the people of Africa rose up and made Anibal, Azdrubal's younger brother, their king. {74:18} When Anibal became king, he decided to avenge his brother by waging war against Chittim, and he prepared many ships for the campaign. {74:19} He and his army sailed to Chittim, where they fought with the children of Chittim. {74:20} Anibal avenged his brother, and many men of Chittim were slain in battle. {74:21} The war continued for eighteen years, and Anibal remained in Chittim for an extended time. {74:22} During this time, he severely punished the people of Chittim, killing their great men and princes, and around eighty thousand of the people were slain. {74:23} After many years, Anibal returned to Africa and ruled securely in place of his brother, Azdrubal.

{75:1} At that time, in the one hundred and eightieth year of the Israelites' descent into Egypt, thirty thousand brave men from the tribe of Joseph, specifically the children of Ephraim, left Egypt. {75:2} They believed that the time appointed by the Lord, which He had spoken to Abraham long ago, had been fulfilled. {75:3} These men equipped themselves with swords and armor, trusting in their strength, and departed from Egypt with great confidence. {75:4} However, they took no provisions for their journey, bringing only silver and gold, assuming they would buy food from the Philistines or take it by force if necessary. {75:5} These men were incredibly strong and brave; one could chase a thousand, and two could rout ten thousand. With this confidence, they set off together. {75:6} They directed their course toward the land of Gath, where they encountered shepherds tending the cattle of the people of Gath. {75:7} They asked the shepherds to sell them some sheep to eat, for they were hungry and had not eaten that day. {75:8} The shepherds refused, saying, "Are these our sheep or cattle that we should give them to you, even for payment?" So the children of Ephraim attempted to take the sheep by force. {75:9} The shepherds shouted for help, and the people of Gath responded to the call. {75:10} When the men of Gath saw what the Ephraimites were doing, they assembled their warriors and engaged in battle with the children of Ephraim in the valley of Gath. {75:11} The battle was intense, and many were killed on both sides. {75:12} On the second day, the people of Gath sent word to the Philistine cities, asking for reinforcements to help defeat the Ephraimites, who had come from Egypt to steal their cattle and fight without cause. {75:13} The children of Ephraim were exhausted from hunger and thirst, having eaten no bread for three days. {75:14} Forty thousand Philistines came to aid the people of Gath. {75:15} They fought the Ephraimites, and the Lord delivered the Ephraimites into the hands of the Philistines. {75:16} All the Ephraimites who had left Egypt were killed, except for ten men who escaped. {75:17} This disaster was ordained by the Lord as punishment for the Ephraimites because they had left Egypt before the appointed time that the Lord had set for Israel. {75:18} The Philistines also suffered heavy losses, with about twenty thousand men killed, and their bodies were buried in their cities. {75:19} The bodies of the slain Ephraimites lay unburied in the valley of Gath for many days and years, and the valley was filled with their bones. {75:20} The men who had survived returned to Egypt and informed the Israelites of what had happened to them. {75:21}

Ephraim, their father, mourned for many days, and his brothers came to console him. {75:22} Later, Ephraim's wife bore him another son, whom he named Beriah, because of the misfortune that had befallen his house. (Beriah means "in misfortune.")

{76:1} In those days, Moses, the son of Amram, continued to reign as king in the land of Cush, and his reign was prosperous. He ruled the people of Cush with justice, righteousness, and integrity. {76:2} The people of Cush loved Moses during all the years he reigned over them, and they greatly feared him. {76:3} In the fortieth year of Moses' reign over Cush, he sat on the royal throne while Queen Adoniah stood before him, and the nobles were seated around him. {76:4} Queen Adoniah spoke before the king and the princes, questioning why they, the people of Cush, had done this for so long. {76:5} She pointed out that during the forty years Moses had reigned, he had not approached her nor served the gods of Cush. {76:6} Therefore, she urged the people of Cush not to let Moses continue to reign over them since he was not of their blood. {76:7} She suggested that Menacrus, her son, should be made king, as it was better to serve the son of their lord than a stranger and former slave of the Egyptian king. {76:8} The people and nobles of Cush listened to Queen Adoniah's words. {76:9} The people prepared until the evening, and by the next morning, they had made Menacrus, the son of Kikianus, their new king. {76:10} However, the people of Cush were too afraid to harm Moses because the Lord was with him, and they remembered the oath they had sworn to him, so they did no harm to him. {76:11} Instead, they gave Moses many gifts and sent him away with great honor. {76:12} Moses left the land of Cush and returned home, ending his reign over Cush. He was sixty-six years old when he departed, for this was according to God's plan to deliver Israel from the affliction of the descendants of Ham. {76:13} Moses then went to Midian because he feared returning to Egypt due to Pharaoh. He sat by a well in Midian. {76:14} The seven daughters of Reuel, the Midianite priest, came to the well to water their father's flock. {76:15} While they were drawing water, the shepherds of Midian came and drove them away, but Moses rose to their defense and helped water the flock. {76:16} When the daughters returned home, they told their father Reuel about what Moses had done for them. {76:17} They said that an Egyptian man had rescued them from the shepherds and watered the flock. {76:18} Reuel asked his daughters why they had left the man behind. {76:19} He sent for Moses, and when he came, Reuel invited him into his home to eat bread with them. {76:20} Moses told Reuel how he had fled from Egypt, reigned over Cush for forty years, and was eventually sent away in peace with honor and gifts. {76:21} After hearing Moses' story, Reuel thought to himself that he could imprison Moses to gain favor with the Cushites, from whom Moses had fled. {76:22} So, Moses was imprisoned in Midian for ten years. During that time, Reuel's daughter Zipporah took pity on Moses and secretly brought him bread and water. {76:23} Meanwhile, the children of Israel continued to suffer under Egyptian slavery, as the Egyptians treated them with increasing cruelty. {76:24} The Lord struck Pharaoh with leprosy from the sole of his foot to the crown of his head because of his harsh treatment of the Israelites. {76:25} The Lord heard the cries of the Israelites in their affliction, but Pharaoh's heart remained hard, and he continued to oppress them. {76:26} Pharaoh consulted his wise men and sorcerers to heal him from the plague. {76:27} They advised him that the blood of young children could heal his wounds. {76:28} Pharaoh followed their advice and sent his ministers to Goshen to take the Israelite infants by force. {76:29} Pharaoh's ministers seized the children from their mothers' arms, and the physicians killed a child each day to use their blood on Pharaoh's sores. {76:30} A total of 375 Israelite children were killed. {76:31} However, the Lord did not allow Pharaoh to be healed, and the plague grew worse. {76:32} Pharaoh suffered from this affliction for ten years, yet his heart remained hardened against Israel. {76:33} After the ten years, the Lord afflicted Pharaoh with even more severe plagues, including a painful tumor and a boil that spread throughout his body. {76:34} Two of Pharaoh's ministers returned from Goshen and informed him that the Israelites were slacking in their work. {76:35} Pharaoh, already in pain, was angered even more upon hearing this news and accused the Israelites of mocking him. {76:36} In his rage, Pharaoh ordered his chariot to be prepared so he could confront the Israelites himself. {76:37} Because he was too weak to ride alone, Pharaoh's servants helped him onto a horse, and he set out for Goshen with ten horsemen and ten footmen. {76:38} When they reached the narrow path between the vineyard and the plain, Pharaoh's horse stumbled, and the chariot overturned, throwing Pharaoh to the ground. {76:39} Pharaoh's body was severely injured, with his flesh torn and his bones broken, as the chariot crushed him. {76:40} This disaster was from the Lord, who had heard the cries of the Israelites. {76:41} Pharaoh's servants lifted him onto their shoulders and carried him back to Egypt. {76:42} When they returned, they laid him in his bed, and Pharaoh realized that his end was near. {76:43} His wife, Queen Aparanith, wept before him, and Pharaoh wept with her. {76:44} All of Pharaoh's nobles and servants came to see him in his affliction and wept with him. {76:45} Pharaoh's counselors advised him to appoint one of his sons to reign in his place. {76:46} Pharaoh had three sons: Othri, Adikam, and Morion, and two daughters: Bathia and Acuzi. {76:47} Othri, the eldest, was foolish and hasty in speech, while Adikam was wise but physically unappealing, being short and thick in stature. {76:48} Despite Adikam's appearance, Pharaoh chose him to succeed him because of his wisdom. {76:49} Pharaoh gave Adikam a wife named Gedudah, daughter of Abilot, and when Adikam was ten years old, Gedudah bore him four sons. {76:50} Adikam later married three other wives and fathered eight sons and three daughters. {76:51} Pharaoh's illness worsened, and his flesh began to rot, giving off a foul odor. {76:52} Realizing his death was near, Pharaoh made Adikam king in his place. {76:53} Three years later, Pharaoh died in disgrace, and his body was carried to the tombs of the kings of Egypt. {76:54} However, due to the stench of his decaying flesh, they did not embalm him as was the custom for kings, and he was buried quickly. {76:55} This was the judgment of the Lord for Pharaoh's evil treatment of the Israelites. {76:56} Pharaoh died in terror and shame, and his son Adikam became king in his stead.

{77:1} Adikam was twenty years old when he became king of Egypt, and he ruled for four years. {77:2} In the two hundred and sixth year after Israel had gone down to Egypt, Adikam began his reign, but it did not last as long as the reigns of his predecessors. {77:3} For his father Melol ruled Egypt for ninety-four years, though the last ten years of his reign were marked by sickness before he died, as he had been wicked before the Lord. {77:4} The Egyptians called Adikam "Pharaoh," just as they had called all previous kings of Egypt, as was their custom. {77:5} However, the wise men of Pharaoh also called Adikam "Ahuz," which in the Egyptian language means "short." {77:6} Adikam was extremely unattractive, being only a cubit and a span in height, with a long beard that reached to the soles of his feet. {77:7} Adikam sat on his father's throne and ruled Egypt with wisdom, {77:8} but he surpassed his father and all previous kings in wickedness. He increased the burden on the children of Israel. {77:9} He went with his servants to Goshen, where the Israelites lived, and increased their labor. He commanded them, "Finish your daily work without slowing down, as you did in my father's days." {77:10} He appointed officers from among the Israelites to oversee them, and over these officers, he placed taskmasters from among his own servants. {77:11} He also imposed a daily quota of bricks on them and then returned to Egypt. {77:12} At that time, Pharaoh's taskmasters commanded the Israelite officers, saying, {77:13} "This is what Pharaoh says: 'Do your daily work and meet your quota of bricks; do not reduce anything.'" {77:14} And if the Israelites did not meet their daily quota, Pharaoh would take their young children in place of the missing bricks. {77:15} The taskmasters followed Pharaoh's orders, {77:16} and whenever the Israelites fell short of their brick quota, the taskmasters took their infants by force from their mothers and used them in the building in place of the bricks. {77:17} The parents would cry and weep as they heard the voices of their infants trapped in the walls. {77:18} The taskmasters forced the Israelites to place their own children in the walls and cover them with mortar, while their eyes wept over them, tears falling on their children. {77:19} The taskmasters showed no pity or compassion as they did this to the babies of Israel for many days. {77:20} A total of 270 children were killed this way, either built into the walls in place of the missing bricks or later pulled out dead from the construction. {77:21} The labor that Adikam imposed on the Israelites was harsher than the work they had performed under his father. {77:22} The Israelites sighed daily under the weight of their hard labor and said, "When Pharaoh dies, his son will rise up and lighten our burden!" {77:23} But instead, their work increased, and they groaned, and their cries ascended to God because of their harsh labor. {77:24} God heard the voices of the Israelites and remembered the covenant He had made with Abraham, Isaac, and Jacob. {77:25} God saw the heavy burden on the Israelites and decided to deliver them. {77:26} Meanwhile, Moses, the son of Amram, was still imprisoned in the dungeon of Reuel the Midianite, and Zipporah, Reuel's daughter, secretly brought him food every day. {77:27} Moses had been in the dungeon for ten years, {77:28} and in the first year of Pharaoh's reign, Zipporah said to her father, "No one has checked on the Hebrew man whom you locked in prison ten years ago. {77:29} Let us send someone to see if he is alive or dead." Her father did not know that she had been feeding him. {77:30} Reuel replied, "Has anyone ever survived ten years in prison without food and lived?" {77:31} But Zipporah answered, "Surely you've heard that the God of the Hebrews is great and does wonders for them." {77:32} She reminded him of how God had saved Abraham from Ur of the Chaldeans, Isaac from his father's sword, and Jacob from the angel who wrestled with him at the ford of Jabbok. {77:33} She said, "This man has also been delivered many times by God—first from the Nile, then from Pharaoh's sword, and then from the people of Cush. God can deliver him from starvation too." {77:34} Reuel was persuaded by his daughter's words, so he sent someone to check on Moses. {77:35} When the messenger arrived, he found Moses alive, standing on his feet and praying to the God of his ancestors. {77:36} Reuel ordered that Moses be released from the dungeon, and they shaved him, changed his prison clothes, and gave him food. {77:37} Afterward, Moses went into Reuel's garden and prayed to the Lord. {77:38} While he was praying, he saw a sapphire stick planted in the ground. {77:39} He approached the stick and saw that the name of the Lord, God of hosts, was engraved on it. {77:40} Moses read the engraving, reached out his hand, and pulled the stick out of the ground, as though he were pulling a tree from a forest. {77:41} This was the same stick that God had used to perform all His works after He created the heavens, the earth, the seas, and all that lives within them. {77:42} When God expelled Adam from the Garden of Eden, Adam took the stick and used it to till the ground. {77:43} The stick was passed down to Noah, then to Shem and his descendants, until it came into the possession of Abraham. {77:44} When Abraham gave everything he had to his son Isaac, he also gave him this stick. {77:45} When Jacob fled to Padan-aram, he took the stick with him, and when he returned to his father, he still had it. {77:46} He took it with him when he went down to Egypt and gave it to Joseph, as a special inheritance above what he gave his other sons. {77:47} Jacob had taken the stick from his brother Esau by force. {77:48} After Joseph's death, the nobles of Egypt went into Joseph's house, and the stick ended up in the hands of Reuel the Midianite, who took it with him when he left Egypt and planted it in his garden. {77:49} Many strong men of the Kinites tried to pull the stick from the ground when they sought to marry Zipporah, Reuel's daughter, but none succeeded. {77:50} The stick remained planted in Reuel's garden until the rightful owner came and took it. {77:51} When Reuel saw the stick in Moses' hand, he marveled at it, and he gave Zipporah, his daughter, to Moses as his wife.

{78:1} At that time, Baal Channan, the son of Achbor, king of Edom, died and was buried in his house in the land of Edom. {78:2} After his death, the children of Esau sent to the land of Edom and brought a man named Hadad from there, making him king over them in place of Baal Channan. {78:3} Hadad reigned over the children of Edom for forty-eight years. {78:4} During his reign, he planned to fight against the children of Moab to bring them under the power of Esau's descendants as before, but he could not, because the Moabites, hearing this, elected a king from among their brethren. {78:5} The Moabites gathered a large army and called upon their brethren, the children of Ammon, to help them fight Hadad, the king of Edom. {78:6} Hearing what the Moabites had done, Hadad was greatly afraid and refrained from fighting them. {78:7} Meanwhile, Moses, the son of Amram, who was in Midian, took Zipporah, the daughter of Reuel the Midianite, as his wife. {78:8} Zipporah lived righteously, like the daughters of Jacob, and was as virtuous as Sarah, Rebecca, Rachel, and Leah. {78:9} She gave birth to a son whom Moses named Gershom, for he said, "I was a stranger in a foreign land," but he did not circumcise the boy, following the command of Reuel, his father-in-law. {78:10} Zipporah later gave birth to another son, and this time Moses circumcised him and named him Eliezer, saying, "The God of my fathers was my help and delivered me from Pharaoh's sword." {78:11} During these days, Pharaoh, king of Egypt, increased the labor of the Israelites, making their burdens even heavier. {78:12} He issued a proclamation in Egypt, saying, "Do not give the people straw to make bricks; let them gather straw for themselves wherever they can find it." {78:13} However, they were still required to meet the same quota of bricks each day without any reduction, for Pharaoh believed they were idle. {78:14} The children of Israel heard this and mourned bitterly, crying out to the Lord in their distress. {78:15} The Lord heard their cries and saw the oppression they were suffering at the hands of the Egyptians. {78:16} The Lord, being jealous for His people, listened to their voice and resolved to deliver them from their affliction, giving them the land of Canaan as their inheritance.

{79:1} During this time, Moses was tending the flock of his father-in-law, Reuel the Midianite, near the wilderness of Sin, and he had with him the staff he had taken from Reuel. {79:2} One day, a young goat from the flock strayed, and Moses pursued it until he came to the mountain of God, Horeb. {79:3} There, the Lord appeared to Moses in a burning bush, which was on fire but was not consumed. {79:4} Moses was astonished at this sight and approached to see it more closely when the Lord called out to him from the fire, commanding him to go to Egypt to speak to Pharaoh and lead the children of Israel out of bondage. {79:5} The Lord told Moses to return to Egypt because all those who had sought his life were now dead, and he was to tell Pharaoh to let the Israelites go free. {79:6} The Lord also showed Moses signs and wonders that he was to perform in Egypt before Pharaoh and his subjects, so they would believe the Lord had sent him. {79:7} Moses obeyed the Lord's command, returned to his father-in-law, and told him all that had happened. Reuel said to Moses, "Go in peace." {79:8} Moses then set out for Egypt, taking his wife and sons with him, and they stopped at an inn along the way, where an angel of the Lord appeared, seeking an occasion against Moses. {79:9} The angel wanted to kill Moses because he had not circumcised his firstborn son, violating the covenant the Lord had made with Abraham. {79:10} Moses had listened to his father-in-law's advice not to circumcise his son, and so he had not done it. {79:11} When Zipporah saw the angel of the Lord and understood that the danger was due to the lack of circumcision, she quickly took a sharp stone and circumcised her son, saving both Moses and the boy from the angel's wrath. {79:12} With this, the angel departed. {79:13} Meanwhile, in Egypt, Aaron, Moses' brother, was walking by the river. {79:14} The Lord appeared to Aaron and instructed him to go into the wilderness to meet Moses. Aaron obeyed and met Moses at the mountain of God, where he embraced him. {79:15} Aaron looked up and saw Zipporah and her children, asking Moses, "Who are these?" {79:16} Moses replied, "They are my wife and sons, given to me by God in Midian," but Aaron was displeased by their presence. {79:17} He advised Moses to send his wife and children back to their father's house, and Moses followed Aaron's counsel. {79:18} Zipporah and her children returned to Reuel and remained there until the Lord delivered the Israelites from Egypt. {79:19} Moses and Aaron then came to Egypt, gathered the children of Israel, and spoke to them all the words of the Lord. The people rejoiced greatly at the news. {79:20} Early the next day, Moses and Aaron went to Pharaoh's house, carrying the staff of God. {79:21} When they arrived at the palace gate, two young lions were chained there with iron instruments, preventing anyone from entering or leaving unless Pharaoh permitted it. The magicians would use incantations to subdue the lions, allowing people to pass. {79:22} But when Moses lifted the staff, the lions were loosed, and he and Aaron entered Pharaoh's house with the lions following joyfully, like dogs following their master. {79:23} Pharaoh was astonished and frightened at the sight, seeing that their appearance resembled that of the children of God. {79:24} Pharaoh asked, "What do you want?" They answered, "The Lord God of the Hebrews has sent us to tell you to let His people go, that they may serve Him." {79:25} When Pharaoh heard this, he was filled with fear and told them to return the next day, promising to give them an answer. {79:26} Moses and Aaron did as he asked. {79:27} After they left, Pharaoh summoned Balaam the magician, along with Jannes, Jambres, and all his magicians and counselors, and told them what Moses and Aaron had said. {79:28} The magicians asked, "How did these men come past the lions at the gate?" {79:29} Pharaoh explained that they had lifted a rod against the lions and loosed them, allowing them to enter, and the lions had rejoiced at them. {79:30} Balaam replied, "These men are no different from us—they are magicians too." {79:31} Pharaoh decided to test Moses and Aaron, so he summoned them again. {79:32} The next morning, Pharaoh asked them to perform a sign to prove that the Lord had sent them. {79:33} Aaron cast down his staff before Pharaoh, and it became a serpent. {79:34} The magicians then cast down their own staffs, which also became serpents. {79:35} But Aaron's serpent swallowed up the staffs of the magicians. {79:36} Balaam said, "This is an ancient trick—a serpent swallowing another is nothing new. Return the staff to its original form, and we will do the same." {79:37} Aaron reached out and grabbed the serpent's tail, and it became a staff again. The magicians did likewise with their staffs. {79:38} However, Aaron's staff then swallowed the staffs of the magicians. {79:39} Pharaoh, amazed, ordered the chronicles of Egypt to be brought, hoping to find the name of the Lord written in them. {79:40} But they found no mention of Jehovah. {79:41} Pharaoh said to Moses and Aaron, "I do not know this God you speak of, and His name is not in our records." {79:42} The wise men and counselors told Pharaoh that they had heard the God of the Hebrews was the son of wise and ancient kings. {79:43} Pharaoh turned to Moses and Aaron and said, "I do not know the Lord, and I will not let Israel go." {79:44} Moses and Aaron responded, "The Lord God of gods is His name, and He has commanded us to ask you to let His people go into the wilderness to worship Him, or He will strike Egypt with plagues or the sword." {79:45} Pharaoh asked them to describe the Lord's power. They replied, "He created the heavens and the earth, the seas and their creatures, the light and darkness, and He causes rain and makes the land fertile. He created all life and governs the fate of all things, including you, Pharaoh." {79:46} Pharaoh, angered, ordered Moses and Aaron to leave his presence and warned them not to return unless they wanted to face death.

{80:1} After two years had passed, the Lord again commanded Moses to go to Pharaoh and demand that he release the Israelites from Egypt. {80:2} Moses went to Pharaoh's palace and delivered the message from the Lord, but Pharaoh refused to listen. So God displayed His power through a series of severe plagues upon Pharaoh and all of Egypt. {80:3} The Lord sent Aaron to turn all the water in Egypt's rivers and streams into blood. {80:4} Whenever an Egyptian tried to drink or fetch water, it turned to blood in their pitchers, and even the water in their cups became blood. {80:5} When a woman tried to knead dough and cook food, the dough and food appeared as blood. {80:6} The Lord then brought a plague of frogs upon Egypt. The frogs invaded every house. {80:7} When the Egyptians drank water, their stomachs filled with frogs that jumped around inside them as they did in the rivers. {80:8} All their drinking and cooking water turned into frogs, and even their sweat at night bred frogs in their beds. {80:9} Despite this, God's anger didn't subside, and He continued to punish the Egyptians with more plagues. {80:10} Next, God struck Egypt with a plague of lice, causing the ground to be covered with lice up to a height of two cubits (approximately three feet). {80:11} The lice infested the bodies of people and animals, even affecting Pharaoh and his queen, making life unbearable for the Egyptians. {80:12} Yet the Lord's wrath remained, and His hand was still against Egypt. {80:13} God then sent wild animals into Egypt. {80:14} These animals included serpents, scorpions, mice, weasels, toads, and various other creeping creatures. {80:15} Flies, hornets, fleas, bugs, and gnats of every kind swarmed throughout the land. {80:16} All types of reptiles and winged creatures overwhelmed the Egyptians, causing them great distress. {80:17} The flies and fleas particularly tormented the Egyptians by getting into their eyes and ears. {80:18} The hornets chased them, forcing them to hide inside their homes, but even there, they found no relief. {80:19} God summoned a creature called the Sulanuth from the sea, with arms ten cubits long (about 15 feet). {80:20} This creature climbed onto the roofs of houses, tearing off the roofs and floors, unlocking the doors, and allowing the swarms of wild animals to enter the homes. {80:21} The wild animals then ravaged the Egyptians, causing immense suffering. {80:22} Still, God's anger did not relent, and He continued to afflict Egypt with more plagues. {80:23} The Lord sent a deadly plague that spread among the Egyptians' livestock, killing their horses, donkeys, camels, cattle, and sheep, as well as affecting people. {80:24} When the Egyptians went out in the morning to take their livestock to pasture, they found that nine out of every ten animals had died. However, not a single animal belonging to the Israelites in Goshen was harmed. {80:25} God then struck the Egyptians with painful skin inflammations and severe boils that covered their entire bodies, from their feet to their heads, causing their flesh to waste away. {80:26} Despite the agony of these boils, God's wrath remained upon Egypt. {80:27} He then sent a devastating hailstorm that destroyed their vineyards and broke their fruit trees. The hail was accompanied by fire, which burned everything it struck. {80:28} All the green plants were scorched and dried up, leaving nothing behind. {80:29} Any people or animals caught outside during the storm perished from the combined effects of the hail and fire, even exhausting the young lions. {80:30} Afterward, the Lord sent a massive swarm of locusts to devour whatever crops the hail had left. {80:31} The locusts were of many types, including Chasel, Salom, Chargol, and Chagole, and they ate all the produce of the fields. {80:32} The Egyptians, despite the devastation, gathered the locusts in large quantities and salted them as food. {80:33} But God sent a mighty wind from the sea that carried away all the locusts, even the ones that had been salted, and cast them into the Red Sea. Not a single locust remained in Egypt. {80:34} Then God sent three days of complete darkness over Egypt, covering the land of Egypt and Pathros so thickly that people could not see their hands in front of their faces. {80:35} During this darkness, many rebellious Israelites who had refused to believe in Moses and Aaron died. {80:36} These Israelites had opposed the exodus, fearing that they would starve in the desert, and had refused to follow God's commands. {80:37} The surviving Israelites buried them secretly during the darkness, so the Egyptians wouldn't see or celebrate their deaths. {80:38} For three days, the darkness was so intense that anyone standing when it began remained standing, anyone sitting stayed seated, and anyone lying down remained lying down, unable to move. {80:39} After the days of darkness ended, the Lord commanded Moses and Aaron to instruct the Israelites to prepare the Passover and to celebrate it, for the Lord was about to pass through Egypt and strike down the firstborn of every Egyptian household, both humans and animals. {80:40} He told them that when He saw the blood of the Passover lamb on their doorposts, He would pass over their houses and spare them. {80:41} The Israelites followed all of God's instructions that night. {80:42} In the middle of the night, the Lord passed through Egypt and struck down all the firstborn Egyptians, both people and animals. {80:43} Pharaoh, his servants, and all the Egyptians woke up to a great outcry, for every household had lost someone. {80:44} Even the statues of the firstborn, carved into the walls of Egyptian houses, were destroyed, crumbling to the ground. {80:45} Dogs in Egypt dug up the bones of firstborn Egyptians who had died previously and dragged them into the open, further horrifying the Egyptians. {80:46} This sudden catastrophe caused all of Egypt to wail in mourning. {80:47} Every family grieved for its firstborn sons and daughters, and their cries could be heard far and wide. {80:48} That night, Pharaoh's daughter Bathia went with Pharaoh to find Moses and Aaron. They found them with the Israelites, eating and celebrating the Passover. {80:49} Bathia confronted Moses, saying, "Is this how you repay the kindness I showed you, raising you in my father's house, by bringing such evil upon me and my family?" {80:50} Moses replied, "Though the Lord sent ten plagues upon Egypt, none of them has harmed you. Have they?" She answered, "No." {80:51} Moses assured her that although she was her mother's firstborn, she would not die or suffer any harm during this plague. {80:52} She asked, "What good is that to me when I see my brother, Pharaoh, and his entire household suffering the loss of their firstborn?" {80:53} Moses explained that Pharaoh and his people had refused to listen to God, which is why they were experiencing such devastation. {80:54} Then Pharaoh himself came to Moses and Aaron, along with some of the Israelites present, and begged them to leave Egypt. {80:55} Pharaoh asked them to pray to the Lord on his behalf. {80:56} Moses assured Pharaoh that although he was the firstborn in his family, he would not die because the Lord had decreed that he would live to witness His mighty power. {80:57} Pharaoh ordered the immediate release of the Israelites, urging them to take all their people, livestock, and possessions, saying, "Leave nothing behind, for we are all dying." {80:58} The Egyptians also urged the Israelites to leave, fearing they would all perish if the Israelites stayed any longer. {80:59} The Israelites, however, did not want to leave during the night. When the Egyptians came to hasten their departure, the Israelites responded, "Are we thieves that we should flee in the night?" {80:60} Before leaving, the Israelites requested silver, gold, and clothing from the Egyptians, as the Lord had instructed, and the Egyptians gave them everything they asked for, effectively stripping Egypt of its wealth. {80:61} Moses quickly went to the Nile River, retrieved Joseph's coffin, and brought it with them. {80:62} The Israelites also took with them the coffins of their ancestors, each man carrying the remains of his father and those of his tribe.

{81:1} The children of Israel traveled from Rameses to Succoth, about six hundred thousand men on foot, not counting their children and wives. {81:2} A large mixed crowd also went with them, along with flocks, herds, and plenty of livestock. {81:3} The children of Israel had lived in hard labor in Egypt for two hundred and ten years. {81:4} And after these two hundred and ten years, the Lord brought the Israelites out of Egypt with a mighty hand. {81:5} They journeyed from Egypt, Goshen, and Rameses, and camped at Succoth on the fifteenth day of the first month. {81:6} Meanwhile, the Egyptians buried all their firstborn whom the Lord had struck down, and for three days they mourned their dead. {81:7} The children of Israel then moved from Succoth and camped in Ethom, at the edge of the wilderness. {81:8} Three days after the Egyptians had buried their dead, many men of Egypt regretted letting Israel go, and they set out to bring them back to Egypt. {81:9} One said to another, "Moses and Aaron told Pharaoh they would go a three-day journey into the wilderness to sacrifice to the Lord our God." {81:10} So, they planned to rise early and force Israel to return to their slavery, and if they resisted, they would fight them to bring them back. {81:11} About seven hundred thousand men, along with the nobles of Pharaoh, set out that morning to pursue the Israelites. {81:12} They reached Pi-hahiroth, where the Israelites were camped, celebrating the feast of the Lord. {81:13} The Egyptians said, "You promised to go for three days and return. Why have you not come back after five days?" {81:14} Moses and Aaron replied, "The Lord has commanded us not to return to Egypt but to go to the land flowing with milk and honey, which He promised to our ancestors." {81:15} Seeing that Israel would not listen, the Egyptians prepared to fight them. {81:16} But the Lord gave the Israelites strength, and they fought the Egyptians fiercely, causing many Egyptians to flee or be killed. {81:17} The nobles returned to Pharaoh and reported, "Israel has fled and will not return, as Moses and Aaron told us." {81:18} Pharaoh's heart, and the hearts of his people, turned against Israel, and they regretted letting them go. {81:19} They said, "What have we done by letting Israel go from their slavery?" {81:20} The Lord hardened their hearts to pursue the Israelites, desiring to destroy the Egyptians in the Red Sea. {81:21} Pharaoh rose, prepared his chariot, and ordered all the Egyptians to assemble. No man stayed behind except for the women and children. {81:22} A massive army, numbering about one million men, went forth with Pharaoh to chase the Israelites. {81:23} They pursued them until they reached the encampment by the Red Sea. {81:24} When the Israelites saw the Egyptians approaching, they were greatly afraid and cried out to the Lord. {81:25} The Israelites split into four groups, each with a different plan to escape the Egyptians. {81:26} The first group, from Reuben, Simeon, and Issachar, wanted to throw themselves into the sea, so terrified were they. {81:27} Moses told them, "Do not fear. Stand firm and watch the Lord's salvation today." {81:28} The second group, from Zebulun, Benjamin, and Naphtali, wanted to return to Egypt with the Egyptians. {81:29} But Moses said, "Fear not. The Egyptians you see today, you will never see again." {81:30} The third group, from Judah and Joseph, wanted to go out and fight the Egyptians. {81:31} Moses told them, "Stay in your places. The Lord will fight for you, and you will remain silent." {81:32} The fourth group, from Levi, Gad, and Asher, wanted to confuse the Egyptians by going into their midst. {81:33} But Moses told them, "Stay where you are and cry out to the Lord for deliverance." {81:34} Then Moses stood up and prayed, "O Lord, God of all the earth, save your people, whom you brought out of Egypt, so that the Egyptians may not boast of their power." {81:35} The Lord said to Moses, "Why are you crying to me? Tell the Israelites to move forward. {81:36} Lift your rod, stretch it over the sea, and divide it, so the children of Israel can pass through on dry ground." {81:37} Moses did as the Lord commanded, and the sea was divided into twelve parts, {81:38} and the Israelites crossed the sea on dry ground as if walking on a well-prepared road. {81:39} The Lord showed His mighty works through Moses and Aaron, both in Egypt and at the sea. {81:40} When the Israelites had crossed, the Egyptians followed, but the waters returned and drowned them. Not one man survived, except Pharaoh, {81:41} who believed in the Lord and was spared. An angel took him from the sea and placed him in Nineveh, where he reigned for a long time. {81:42} On that day, the Lord saved Israel from the Egyptians, and the people saw the great power of the Lord. {81:43} Then Moses and the children of Israel sang a song of praise to the Lord, celebrating their deliverance. {81:44} They sang, "I will sing to the Lord, for He has triumphed gloriously; the horse and its rider He has thrown into the sea." This was written in the book of the law of God. {81:45} Afterward, they traveled and camped at Marah, where the Lord gave them statutes and judgments, commanding them to walk in His ways. {81:46} From Marah, they went to Elim, where there were twelve springs and seventy palm trees, and they camped there. {81:47} Then they journeyed to the wilderness of Sin on the fifteenth day of the second month after leaving Egypt. {81:48} It was there that the Lord sent manna from heaven to feed the Israelites daily. {81:49} They ate manna for forty years, throughout their time in the wilderness, until they reached Canaan. {81:50} From the wilderness of Sin, they camped at Alush, {81:51} and then moved on to Rephidim. {81:52} There, Amalek, the son of Eliphaz and grandson of Esau, attacked Israel with an army of over eight hundred thousand men, including magicians and sorcerers. {81:53} A fierce battle ensued, and the Lord delivered Amalek into the hands of Moses, Joshua, and the Israelites. {81:54} The Israelites fought with swords and defeated Amalek, though it was a difficult battle. {81:55} The Lord told Moses to record the event as a memorial and give it to Joshua, saying, {81:56} "When you enter the land of Canaan, you must utterly erase the memory of Amalek from under heaven." {81:57} Moses wrote these words in a book, reminding the people, {81:58} "Remember what Amalek did to you on the way out of Egypt. {81:59} He attacked your weakest and faintest, those lagging behind. {81:60} When the Lord gives you rest from your enemies in the land He is giving you, you shall blot out the memory of Amalek; do not forget." {81:61} Any king who shows mercy to Amalek or his descendants will face judgment from the Lord, and he will be cut off from his people. {81:62} Moses wrote all these commands in a book and instructed the Israelites to obey them fully.

{82:1} The children of Israel left Rephidim and camped in the wilderness of Sinai in the third month after their exodus from Egypt. {82:2} At that time, Reuel, the Midianite, father-in-law of Moses, came with Zipporah, Moses' wife, and her two sons because he had heard of the Lord's wonders for Israel and their deliverance from Egypt. {82:3} Reuel met Moses in the wilderness, where the mountain of God was located. {82:4} Moses went out to greet his father-in-law with great honor, and all of Israel was with him. {82:5} Reuel and his family stayed with the Israelites for several days, and from that time, Reuel knew the Lord. {82:6} On the sixth day of the third month after leaving Egypt, the Lord gave Israel the Ten Commandments at Mount Sinai. {82:7} All Israel heard these commandments and rejoiced greatly in the Lord that day. {82:8} The glory of the Lord rested on Mount Sinai, and He called Moses, who entered a cloud and ascended the mountain. {82:9} Moses stayed on the mountain for forty days and nights, without eating bread or drinking water, as the Lord taught him statutes and judgments to instruct Israel. {82:10} The Lord inscribed the Ten Commandments on two stone tablets and gave them to Moses to pass on to the children of Israel. {82:11} After forty days and nights, when the Lord finished speaking to Moses, He gave him the tablets of stone, written by the finger of God. {82:12} When the people of Israel saw that Moses delayed in returning from the mountain, they gathered around Aaron and said, "We don't know what has become of Moses." {82:13} They urged Aaron to make a god to lead them, so that they would not perish. {82:14} Aaron, fearing the people, told them to bring gold, which he fashioned into a molten calf for them to worship. {82:15} The Lord told Moses to go down because the people he brought out of Egypt had corrupted themselves. {82:16} They had made a molten calf and worshiped it. The Lord warned Moses that He would destroy them for their stubbornness. {82:17} Moses pleaded with the Lord, praying for the people because of the calf they had made, then descended from the mountain with the two stone tablets in hand. {82:18} As Moses approached the camp and saw the calf, his anger flared, and he shattered the tablets at the foot of the mountain. {82:19} He entered the camp, took the calf, burned it, ground it into dust, scattered it over the water, and made the Israelites drink it. {82:20} About three thousand people who had made the calf died by the sword. {82:21} The next day, Moses told the people he would go back up to the Lord to seek atonement for their sins. {82:22} Moses again ascended the mountain, where he spent another forty days and nights pleading for Israel, and the Lord accepted his prayer. {82:23} The Lord then instructed Moses to carve two new stone tablets and bring them to Him, so He could rewrite the Ten Commandments. {82:24} Moses obeyed, hewed the two tablets, and brought them up to Mount Sinai, where the Lord inscribed the commandments once more. {82:25} Moses remained on the mountain another forty days and nights, receiving further instructions from the Lord on statutes and judgments to teach the people. {82:26} The Lord commanded Moses to have the Israelites build a sanctuary so His presence could dwell among them, and He showed Moses a vision of the sanctuary and all its vessels. {82:27} At the end of the forty days, Moses descended with the two tablets in his hand. {82:28} Moses spoke to the Israelites, relaying the Lord's words, teaching them the laws, statutes, and judgments God had given him. {82:29} He informed the people that they were to build a sanctuary for the Lord to dwell among them. {82:30} The Israelites rejoiced at the Lord's goodness spoken through Moses and declared they would do everything the Lord had commanded. {82:31} The people united and generously gave offerings for the Lord's sanctuary, bringing what they had for the work. {82:32} Each man contributed from his possessions—gold, silver, brass, and whatever was useful for the sanctuary. {82:33} All the skilled workers among them set to work, creating the sanctuary and its furniture as the Lord had commanded Moses. {82:34} Every wise-hearted craftsman participated in making the sanctuary and its holy vessels, according to the Lord's instructions. {82:35} The sanctuary of the tabernacle was completed after five months, with the children of Israel doing everything as the Lord had directed Moses. {82:36} They brought the sanctuary and its furnishings to Moses, exactly as the Lord had shown him. {82:37} When Moses saw the work, he confirmed it had been done according to the Lord's command, and he blessed the people for their efforts.

{83:1} In the twelfth month, on the twenty-third day, Moses took Aaron and his sons, dressed them in their garments, anointed them, and did everything the Lord had commanded him. Moses brought all the offerings that the Lord had commanded for that day. {83:2} Moses then told Aaron and his sons that they should stay at the entrance of the tabernacle for seven days, as he had been commanded. {83:3} Aaron and his sons did everything the Lord had instructed through Moses, remaining for seven days at the entrance of the tabernacle. {83:4} On the eighth day, which was the first day of the first month in the second year since the Israelites left Egypt, Moses set up the sanctuary. He arranged all the furniture of the tabernacle and completed everything the Lord had commanded him. {83:5} Moses called Aaron and his sons, and they brought the burnt offering and the sin offering for themselves and for the people of Israel, as the Lord had commanded Moses. {83:6} On that day, the two sons of Aaron, Nadab and Abihu, used unauthorized fire that the Lord had not commanded, and a fire came out from before the Lord and consumed them, resulting in their deaths. {83:7} Then, on the day when Moses finished setting up the sanctuary, the leaders of the Israelites began to bring their offerings to the Lord for the dedication of the altar. {83:8} Each leader brought their offerings one day at a time, with one leader each day for twelve days. {83:9} The offerings included each man's contribution on his day: one silver plate weighing one hundred thirty shekels, one silver bowl weighing seventy shekels, both filled with fine flour mixed with oil for a grain offering. {83:10} There was also one spoon weighing ten shekels of gold filled with incense. {83:11} They brought one young bull, one ram, and one one-year-old lamb for a burnt offering. {83:12} They also provided one goat kid for a sin offering. {83:13} For the peace offering, they brought two oxen, five rams, five male goats, and five one-year-old lambs. {83:14} The twelve leaders of Israel did this day by day, each in their turn. {83:15} On the thirteenth day of the month, Moses commanded the Israelites to observe the Passover. {83:16} The Israelites kept the Passover at its appointed time, on the fourteenth day of the month, as the Lord had commanded Moses. {83:17} In the second month, on the first day, the Lord spoke to Moses, saying, {83:18} "Count all the males of the Israelites who are twenty years old and older, you and your brother Aaron, along with the twelve leaders of Israel." {83:19} Moses did this, and Aaron joined the twelve leaders to number the Israelites in the wilderness of Sinai. {83:20} The total number of Israelite males twenty years and older was six hundred three thousand five hundred fifty. {83:21} However, the tribe of Levi was not included in the count of the other Israelites. {83:22} The number of all the males among the Israelites from one month old and older was twenty-two thousand two hundred seventy-three. {83:23} The total for the tribe of Levi from one month old and above was twenty-two thousand. {83:24} Moses assigned each priest and Levite their respective duties and responsibilities for serving in the tabernacle as the Lord had commanded him. {83:25} On the twentieth day of the month, the cloud lifted from the tabernacle of testimony. {83:26} At that point, the Israelites continued their journey from the wilderness of Sinai, traveling for three days, until the cloud settled in the wilderness of Paran. The Lord became angry with Israel because they provoked Him by asking for meat to eat. {83:27} The Lord heard their complaints and provided them with meat to eat for a month. {83:28} However, after this, the Lord's anger was kindled against them, leading to a great slaughter, and they were buried there. {83:29} The Israelites named that place Kebroth Hattaavah because that's where they buried the people who craved meat. {83:30} They left Kebroth Hattaavah and camped in Hazeroth, which is in the wilderness of Paran. {83:31} While they were in Hazeroth, the Lord's anger flared up against Miriam because of Moses, and she became leprous, white as snow. {83:32} She was confined outside the camp for seven days until her leprosy was healed. {83:33} Afterward, the Israelites left Hazeroth and camped at the end of the wilderness of Paran. {83:34} During this time, the Lord instructed Moses to send twelve men from among the Israelites, one from each tribe, to explore the land of Canaan. {83:35} Moses sent the twelve men, and they went to scout the land of Canaan, examining it from the wilderness of Sin to Rechob near Chamoth. {83:36} After forty days, they returned to Moses and Aaron with a report, expressing their true feelings. Ten of the men gave a bad report to the Israelites, saying it was better for them to return to Egypt than to enter a land that devours its inhabitants. {83:37} But Joshua, son of Nun, and Caleb, son of Jephuneh, who were among those who explored the land, said, "The land is exceptionally good. {83:38} If the Lord is pleased with us, He will bring us to this land and give it to us; it's a land flowing with milk and honey." {83:39} However, the Israelites refused to listen to them, choosing to believe the negative report from the ten men. {83:40} The Lord heard the complaints of the Israelites, and His anger was kindled. He swore, saying, {83:41} "Surely not one man from this wicked generation will see the land from twenty years old and upward, except Caleb, son of Jephuneh, and Joshua, son of Nun. {83:42} This wicked generation shall perish in this wilderness; their children will enter and possess the land." The Lord's anger burned against Israel, causing them to wander in the wilderness for forty years until the wicked generation perished because they didn't follow the Lord. {83:43} The people stayed in the wilderness of Paran for a long time before moving on to the wilderness by the Red Sea.

{84:1} At that time, Korah, son of Jetzer, son of Kehath, son of Levi, took many men from the Israelites and rose up against Moses, Aaron, and the entire congregation. {84:2} The Lord was angry with them, causing the earth to open up and swallow them along with their families and all that belonged to Korah. {84:3} After this, God led the people around by way of Mount Seir for a long time. {84:4} The Lord told Moses not to provoke a conflict with the descendants of Esau, for He would not give the Israelites anything from their territory, not even as much as a footstep, since He had given Mount Seir as an inheritance to Esau. {84:5} The descendants of Esau had previously fought against the descendants of Seir, and the Lord had delivered Seir into the hands of Esau, who destroyed them, and Esau settled there until today. {84:6} Therefore, the Lord instructed the Israelites not to fight against their brothers, the descendants of Esau, stating that they could buy food and water from them. {84:7} The Israelites obeyed the Lord's command. {84:8} The Israelites journeyed through the wilderness, taking the long route around Mount Sinai, without confronting the descendants of Esau, and they stayed in that area for nineteen years. {84:9} During that time, Latinus, king of the Chittim, died in the forty-fifth year of his reign, which was the fourteenth year after the Israelites left Egypt. {84:10} They buried him in the place he built for himself in the land of Chittim, and Abimnas succeeded him for thirty-eight years. {84:11} The Israelites passed the territory of the descendants of Esau after nineteen years and moved along the road through the wilderness of Moab. {84:12} The Lord told Moses not to besiege or fight against Moab, for He would not give any of their land to the Israelites. {84:13} The Israelites traveled the wilderness of Moab for nineteen years without engaging them in battle. {84:14} In the thirty-sixth year since the Israelites left Egypt, the Lord struck the heart of Sihon, king of the Amorites, leading him to wage war against the Moabites. {84:15} Sihon sent messengers to Beor, son of Janeas, son of Balaam, who was an advisor to the king of Egypt, and to Balaam, his son, to curse Moab so that Sihon could defeat them. {84:16} The messengers brought Beor and Balaam from Pethor in Mesopotamia to Sihon's city, where they cursed Moab and their king in Sihon's presence. {84:17} Sihon then mobilized his entire army, attacked Moab, defeated them, and the Lord delivered them into his hands. {84:18} The Israelites learned of this and prepared for battle. They took possession of the land of the Amorites, and the Lord increased their borders. {84:19} Eventually, Sihon turned on the Israelites and declared war against them, but they defeated him and took the city of Heshbon and its surrounding towns. {84:20} Moses called all the men of Israel together, reminding them how the Lord had delivered Sihon and his people into their hands. The Israelites rejoiced in their victory over Sihon and the Amorites, acknowledging that it was the Lord who fought for them. {84:21} Moses instructed the Israelites not to fear the men of Moab, as they had no power against the Lord. {84:22} The Israelites settled in Heshbon and the cities of the Amorites for the duration of their stay in that region. {84:23} As they were settling there, Og, king of Bashan, learned of their victory over Sihon and decided to attack them as well. {84:24} However, the Israelites prevailed against him and defeated Og, capturing his land. {84:25} In the thirty-ninth year since they had left Egypt, they were told that the time for them to return home had arrived. The Lord said to Moses, "Tell the Israelites to return to their homeland." {84:26} Moses spoke to the Israelites, and they set out to return home. They went to the Jordan River, where they camped by the banks for three days. {84:27} The Lord then commanded Moses to send men across the Jordan to spy out the land of Canaan. {84:28} Moses chose twelve men, one from each tribe, to scout the land of Canaan, ordering them to go up to the hill country and then to the Negev and the highlands. {84:29} The men went up and returned with a report, saying that the land flowed with milk and honey and bore fruit like they had never seen before. {84:30} However, ten of the men warned the people not to go into the land, saying the inhabitants were too strong for them. {84:31} The two men who spoke against them were Joshua and Caleb, urging the Israelites to enter the land without fear. {84:32} The Israelites listened to the ten men and began to complain against Moses. {84:33} The Lord's anger was kindled, and He swore that none of them would enter the land He promised to their ancestors except Caleb and Joshua. {84:34} The people wept and mourned, but it was too late. The Lord sent them into the wilderness for forty years to wander until the wicked generation passed away.

{85:1} King Arad the Canaanite, who lived in the south, heard that the Israelites were coming through the area of the spies, and he prepared his army to fight against them. {85:2} The Israelites were terrified of him because he had a large and powerful army, so they decided to go back to Egypt. {85:3} The Israelites turned back about three days' journey to Maserath Beni Jaakon, very afraid of King Arad. {85:4} Since the Israelites did not return to their own places, they stayed in Beni Jaakon for thirty days. {85:5} When the Levites saw that the Israelites wouldn't turn back, they became jealous for the Lord's sake and rose up against their fellow Israelites, killing many of them and forcing them back to their place, Mount Hor. {85:6} Upon their return, King Arad was still organizing his army for battle against them. {85:7} Israel made a vow, saying, "If you deliver this people into my hands, I will completely destroy their cities." {85:8} The Lord listened to the Israelites, delivering the Canaanites into their hands, and they utterly destroyed them and their cities, naming the place Hormah. {85:9} The Israelites traveled from Mount Hor and camped at Oboth, then journeyed from Oboth and pitched at Ije-abarim, on the border of Moab. {85:10} The Israelites sent a message to Moab, saying, "Let us pass through your land to our place," but the Moabites refused, fearing that the Israelites would treat them as Sihon, the king of the Amorites, had done, taking their land and killing many of them. {85:11} So Moab would not allow the Israelites to pass, and the Lord commanded them not to fight against Moab, leading the Israelites to move away from Moab. {85:12} The Israelites traveled from the border of Moab and arrived on the other side of Arnon, the border of Moab between Moab and the Amorites, camping in the wilderness of Kedemoth. {85:13} They sent messengers to Sihon, king of the Amorites, saying, {85:14} "Let us pass through your land; we will not enter your fields or vineyards, but we will travel along the king's highway until we leave your territory." But Sihon refused to let the Israelites pass. {85:15} Sihon gathered all the Amorite people and went out into the wilderness to confront the Israelites, fighting them at Jahaz. {85:16} The Lord gave Sihon, king of the Amorites, into the hands of the Israelites, and they struck down all the Amorites, avenging Moab. {85:17} The Israelites took possession of Sihon's land, from Aram to Jabuk, to the Ammonites, and seized all the spoils of the cities. {85:18} They inhabited all the cities of the Amorites. {85:19} The Israelites decided to fight against the Ammonites to take their land as well. {85:20} However, the Lord instructed the Israelites not to besiege the Ammonites or provoke them to battle, stating that He would not give them any of their land, and the Israelites listened to the Lord and did not engage the Ammonites. {85:21} The Israelites then turned and traveled through Bashan to the land of Og, king of Bashan, who came out to meet them in battle with a strong force of valiant men from the Amorites. {85:22} Og was a powerful king, but his son Naaron was even stronger. {85:23} Og thought to himself, "Look, the entire Israelite camp takes up three parsa (about 11 km); I can defeat them all at once without using a sword or spear." {85:24} Og climbed Mount Jahaz, took a massive stone measuring three parsa in length, placed it on his head, and intended to throw it upon the Israelite camp to crush them. {85:25} But the angel of the Lord came and struck the stone on Og's head, causing it to fall on his neck, and he fell to the ground due to its weight. {85:26} At that time, the Lord reassured the Israelites, saying, "Don't be afraid of him, for I have delivered him, his people, and his land into your hands; you will deal with him as you did with Sihon." {85:27} Moses went down to confront Og with a small number of Israelites, striking Og at his ankles and killing him. {85:28} The Israelites pursued Og and his people, defeating them until none were left. {85:29} Moses then sent some Israelites to scout Jaazer, which was a renowned city. {85:30} The spies explored Jaazer and trusted in the Lord, fighting against the men of Jaazer. {85:31} They captured Jaazer and its villages, with the Lord delivering them into their hands, driving out the Amorites living there. {85:32} The Israelites took the land of the two Amorite kings, sixty cities on the other side of the Jordan, from the Arnon brook to Mount Hermon. {85:33} The Israelites journeyed and arrived at the plain of Moab, located on the side of the Jordan, near Jericho. {85:34} The Moabites heard about all the terrible things the Israelites had done to the two Amorite kings, Sihon and Og, and were filled with fear. {85:35} The Moabite leaders said, "Look, if the two kings of the Amorites, Sihon and Og, who were more powerful than all the kings of the earth, could not stand against the Israelites, how can we?" {85:36} They remembered how they had previously sent a message asking to pass through their land, which they denied, fearing that the Israelites would retaliate with force. The Moabites were distressed by the Israelites' presence and met to discuss what to do. {85:37} They chose a leader, Balak, son of Zippor, to rule them during this time, recognizing him as a wise man. {85:38} The Moabite leaders then reached out to the Midianites, seeking peace, as there had been longstanding conflict between Moab and Midian since the days of Hadad, son of Bedad, king of Edom, who had defeated Midian in battle. {85:39} The Moabites sent messages to the Midianites and made peace with them, inviting the Midianite leaders to come to Moab to negotiate. {85:40} The Moabite leaders consulted with the Midianite leaders on how to protect themselves from the Israelites.

{85:41} They said to the Midianite elders, "The Israelites devour all around us like an ox devours the grass in the field; they did this to the two Amorite kings who were stronger than we are." {85:42} The Midianite elders replied, "We've heard that when Sihon fought against you, he had called upon Balaam, son of Beor, from Mesopotamia, who cursed you, which allowed Sihon to prevail and take your land. {85:43} So now, you should send for Balaam, for he is still in his land, and pay him to come and curse this people you fear." The Moabite leaders were pleased with this advice and sent for Balaam, son of Beor. {85:44} Balak, son of Zippor, king of Moab, sent messengers to Balaam, saying, {85:45} "Look, there is a people who have come out from Egypt; they cover the face of the earth and camp opposite me. {85:46} Come and curse this people for me; they are too strong for me. Perhaps I can defeat them and drive them out. I've heard that whoever you bless is blessed, and whoever you curse is cursed." {85:47} The messengers of Balak went to Balaam to persuade him to curse the Israelites against Moab. {85:48} When Balaam came to Balak to curse Israel, the Lord told him, "Do not curse this people; they are blessed." {85:49} Balak urged Balaam daily to curse the Israelites, but Balaam did not obey Balak because of the word the Lord had given him. {85:50} When Balak saw that Balaam was not complying, he returned home, and Balaam also went back to his land, eventually going to Midian. {85:51} The Israelites journeyed from the plain of Moab and camped by the Jordan, from Beth-jesimoth to Abel-shittim, at the edge of the plains of Moab. {85:52} While they were in the plain of Shittim, the Israelites began to engage in sexual immorality with the daughters of Moab. {85:53} The Moabites pitched their tents across from the Israelites. {85:54} The Moabites were afraid of the Israelites, so they dressed their daughters and wives in beautiful clothes made of gold, silver, and expensive garments, to entice the Israelites. {85:55} The Moabites placed these women at the entrance of their tents so that the Israelites would see them and be drawn away from fighting. {85:56} All the Moabites did this to attract the Israelites, but it was too late. {85:57} The Lord's anger burned against the Israelites because they had sinned against Him, and He struck them with a plague. {85:58} The Lord commanded Moses, "Gather all the leaders of the people; I will execute judgment against them." {85:59} Moses summoned the leaders of Israel, and the Lord sent a plague that resulted in the death of twenty-four thousand people. {85:60} The Lord then instructed Moses, "Separate the people; those who remain faithful to Me will not be destroyed." {85:61} The Lord said to Moses, "Tell the Israelites: Whoever remains faithful to Me shall not perish." {85:62} So Moses gathered the leaders of the people and sent them to their tents, instructing them to bring back those who remained unfaithful. {85:63} Then, the Lord commanded the people to make an offering in remembrance of His deliverance and instruction.

{86:1} After the plague, the Lord spoke to Moses and to Eleazar, the son of Aaron the priest, saying, {86:2} "Count the heads of the entire community of the children of Israel, from twenty years old and upward, all who are able to go to war." {86:3} So Moses and Eleazar counted the children of Israel by their families, and the total number of Israel was seven hundred thousand, seven hundred and thirty. {86:4} The number of the children of Levi, from one month old and upward, was twenty-three thousand, and among these, there was not one man who was counted by Moses and Aaron in the wilderness of Sinai. {86:5} This was because the Lord had told them they would die in the wilderness, and they all died, leaving none except Caleb, the son of Jephunneh, and Joshua, the son of Nun. {86:6} After this, the Lord said to Moses, "Tell the children of Israel to take revenge on Midian for what they did to their brothers." {86:7} So Moses did as he was told, and the children of Israel chose twelve thousand men, one thousand from each tribe, and they went to Midian. {86:8} The children of Israel fought against Midian, killing every male, including the five princes of Midian, and they also killed Balaam, the son of Beor, with the sword. {86:9} They took the Midianite women and children captive, along with their cattle and everything else they owned. {86:10} They collected all the spoils and the prey and brought it to Moses and Eleazar in the plains of Moab. {86:11} Moses, Eleazar, and all the leaders of the congregation went out to meet them with joy. {86:12} They divided all the spoils of Midian, and the children of Israel were avenged on Midian for what they had done to their brothers.

{87:1} At that time, the Lord said to Moses, "Your days are coming to an end. Take Joshua, the son of Nun, your servant, and place him in the tabernacle, and I will command him." Moses did as instructed. {87:2} The Lord appeared in the tabernacle in a pillar of cloud, which stood at the entrance. {87:3} The Lord commanded Joshua, saying, "Be strong and courageous, for you will bring the children of Israel into the land I swore to give them, and I will be with you." {87:4} Moses said to Joshua, "Be strong and courageous, for you will help the children of Israel inherit the land, and the Lord will be with you; He will not leave you or forsake you, so do not be afraid or disheartened." {87:5} Moses called all the children of Israel and said to them, "You have seen all the good that the Lord your God has done for you in the wilderness. {87:6} Therefore, observe all the words of this law and walk in the way of the Lord your God. Do not turn from the way the Lord has commanded you, either to the right or to the left." {87:7} Moses taught the children of Israel statutes, judgments, and laws to follow in the land as the Lord had commanded him. {87:8} He taught them the way of the Lord and His laws; behold, they are written in the book of the law of God, which He gave to the children of Israel by the hand of Moses. {87:9} When Moses finished commanding the children of Israel, the Lord said to him, "Go up to Mount Abarim and die there, and be gathered to your people as your brother Aaron was gathered." {87:10} So Moses went up as the Lord commanded him, and he died there in the land of Moab, according to the Lord's command, in the fortieth year since the Israelites left Egypt. {87:11} The children of Israel mourned for Moses in the plains of Moab for thirty days, and the days of weeping and mourning for Moses were completed.

{88:1} After the death of Moses, the Lord spoke to Joshua, the son of Nun, saying, {88:2} "Get up and cross the Jordan to the land I have given to the children of Israel, and you will help the children of Israel inherit the land. {88:3} Every place where the soles of your feet tread will belong to you, from the wilderness of Lebanon to the great river, the Euphrates, will be your boundary. {88:4} No one will be able to stand against you all the days of your life; just as I was with Moses, so I will be with you. Be strong and courageous to observe all the law that Moses commanded you. Do not turn from it to the right or to the left, so that you may prosper in everything you do. {88:5} Joshua commanded the officers of Israel, saying, "Go through the camp and tell the people, 'Prepare provisions for yourselves, for in three days you will cross the Jordan to possess the land.'" {88:6} The officers of the children of Israel did as instructed and commanded the people, and they followed all that Joshua had commanded. {88:7} Joshua sent two men to spy out the land of Jericho, and they went and spied out Jericho. {88:8} After seven days, they came back to Joshua in the camp and said to him, "The Lord has delivered the entire land into our hands, and the inhabitants are terrified because of us." {88:9} In the morning, Joshua got up, and all Israel with him, and they traveled from Shittim. Joshua and all Israel crossed the Jordan; Joshua was eighty-two years old when he crossed the Jordan with Israel. {88:10} The people went up from the Jordan on the tenth day of the first month and camped in Gilgal, at the eastern edge of Jericho. {88:11} The children of Israel celebrated the Passover in Gilgal on the fourteenth day of the month, as written in the law of Moses. {88:12} At that time, the manna ceased the day after Passover, and there was no more manna for the children of Israel, who ate the produce of the land of Canaan. {88:13} Jericho was tightly shut against the children of Israel; no one went out or came in. {88:14} In the second month, on the first day, the Lord said to Joshua, "Get up, I have given Jericho and its people into your hands. All your fighting men shall march around the city once a day for six days. {88:15} The priests shall blow trumpets, and when you hear the sound of the trumpet, all the people shall shout loudly, and the city walls will fall down; everyone will charge straight ahead." {88:16} Joshua did exactly as the Lord commanded him. {88:17} On the seventh day, they marched around the city seven times, and the priests blew the trumpets. {88:18} At the seventh time around, Joshua said to the people, "Shout, for the Lord has given us the entire city!" {88:19} Only the city and everything in it is to be devoted to the Lord; do not take any of the accursed things, or you will bring trouble upon the camp of Israel. {88:20} All the silver and gold, and the bronze and iron, are consecrated to the Lord and must go into the Lord's treasury. {88:21} The people blew the trumpets and shouted loudly, and the walls of Jericho collapsed. Every man charged straight ahead and took the city, completely destroying everything in it, men and women, young and old, cattle and sheep, with the sword. {88:22} They burned the entire city, but they put the silver, gold, bronze, and iron into the Lord's treasury. {88:23} At that time, Joshua declared, "Cursed be the man who rebuilds Jericho; he will lay its foundation at the cost of his firstborn and set up its gates at the cost of his youngest." {88:24} Achan, the son of Carmi, the son of Zabdi, the son of Zerah, from the tribe of Judah, acted deceitfully by taking some of the accursed things and hiding them in his tent, and the Lord's anger burned against Israel. {88:25} After this, when the children of Israel returned from burning Jericho, Joshua sent men to spy out Ai and to fight against it. {88:26} The men went up and spied out Ai. They returned and advised Joshua, "Do not let all the people go up to Ai; only send about three thousand men to attack the city, for there are only a few men there." {88:27} Joshua did so, sending about three thousand men to Ai, but the battle was fierce against Israel, and the men of Ai struck down thirty-six Israelite men. The children of Israel fled from the men of Ai. {88:28} When Joshua saw this, he tore his clothes and fell facedown to the ground before the Lord, along with the elders of Israel, and they put dust on their heads. {88:29} Joshua said, "O Lord, why did you bring this people across the Jordan? What shall I say after the Israelites have turned their backs against their enemies? {88:30} The Canaanites, the inhabitants of the land, will hear about this and surround us, cutting off our name." {88:31} The Lord replied to Joshua, "Why are you falling on your face? Get up! The Israelites have sinned by taking the accursed things; I will not be with them anymore unless they destroy the accursed things from among them. {88:32} So Joshua gathered the people and brought forth the Urim by the command of the Lord. The tribe of Judah was chosen, and Achan, the son of Carmi, was identified. {88:33} Joshua asked Achan, "Tell me what you have done," and Achan replied, "I saw among the spoils a beautiful garment from Shinar, two hundred shekels of silver, and a wedge of gold weighing fifty shekels. I coveted them and took them; they are hidden in the ground inside my tent." {88:34} Joshua sent men to retrieve the items from Achan's tent, and they brought them to Joshua. {88:35} Joshua took Achan, his possessions, and his sons and daughters, and they brought them to the valley of Achor. {88:36} Joshua burned them there and stoned Achan with stones. They raised a large heap of stones over him, which is why that place is called the valley of Achor; then the Lord's anger was appeased, and afterward, Joshua went to the city and fought against it. {88:37} The Lord said to Joshua, "Do not be afraid or discouraged; I have given Ai, her king, and her people into your hands. You will do to them as you did to Jericho, but you may take the spoil and the livestock for yourselves; lay an ambush behind the city." {88:38} Joshua did as the Lord commanded, selecting thirty thousand valiant men from among the warriors and sending them to lie in ambush near the city. {88:39} He commanded them, saying, "When you see us flee from the city, you will rise from your ambush and take the city." They did so. {88:40} Joshua fought, and the men of Ai went out to face Israel, not knowing they were ambushed behind the city. {88:41} Joshua and all the Israelites pretended to be beaten and fled toward the wilderness. {88:42} The men of Ai gathered all the people from the city to pursue the Israelites, leaving the city wide open. {88:43} Those lying in ambush rose from their positions, entered the city, and set it on fire. The men of Ai turned back and saw smoke rising from the city, and they had no way to escape. {88:44} All the men of Ai were caught between the Israelites, and they were defeated, so that not one of them remained. {88:45} The children of Israel took the king of Ai alive and brought him to Joshua, who hanged him on a tree until he died. {88:46} After burning the city, the children of Israel struck down all the inhabitants with the sword. {88:47} The number of those who fell from Ai was twelve thousand, both men and women; only the livestock and spoils of the city they took for themselves, as the Lord had commanded Joshua. {88:48} All the kings on this side of the Jordan, all the kings of Canaan, heard of the evil the children of Israel had done to Jericho and Ai, and they assembled to fight against Israel. {88:49} However, the inhabitants of Gibeon were very afraid of the Israelites, so they acted cunningly. They approached Joshua and the Israelites, saying, "We have come from a distant land; make a covenant with us." {88:50} The inhabitants of Gibeon deceived the children of Israel, and they made a covenant of peace with them, with the princes of the congregation swearing an oath. But later, the children of Israel discovered they were neighbors living among them. {88:51} The children of Israel did not kill them because they had sworn an oath to them by the Lord, and they became woodcutters and water carriers for the congregation. {88:52} Joshua said, "You are under a curse; you shall never cease to be slaves, and you will serve the altar of the Lord." {88:53} On that day, Joshua struck down the five kings of the Amorites, who had gathered against Israel. He hanged them on trees until evening, and they were thrown into the cave they had hidden in, sealing it with stones. {88:54} The day of victory came, and Joshua and the children of Israel moved on to conquer the land. {88:55} The Lord commanded Joshua, saying, "Be strong and courageous, for you shall bring the children of Israel into the land." {88:56} The sun stood still, and the moon stayed in place while Joshua commanded the people, saying, "Do not fear; I have delivered them into your hands." {88:57} All Israel fought against them until the evening. The Lord delivered the enemy into their hands, and they destroyed all the inhabitants. {88:58} Thus, Joshua conquered the entire region, taking all the cities, kingdoms, and inhabitants as the Lord had commanded. {88:59} The land was divided among the tribes of Israel. {88:60} Israel had rest from their enemies, for the Lord had given them rest. {88:61} The land was entirely theirs, fulfilling the promises made to Abraham. {88:62} The children of Israel were faithful to their oaths, and the Lord continued to bless them. {88:63} Therefore, no one could withstand them all days of their lives.

{89:1} Then Joshua spoke this song on the day the Lord gave the Amorites into the hands of Joshua and the children of Israel, and he said in the sight of all Israel, {89:2} "You have done mighty things, O Lord; you have performed great deeds; who is like you? My lips will sing to your name. {89:3} You are my goodness and my fortress, my high tower; I will sing a new song to you; with thanksgiving, I will sing to you, for you are the strength of my salvation. {89:4} All the kings of the earth shall praise you, the princes of the world shall sing to you; the children of Israel shall rejoice in your salvation; they shall sing and praise your power. {89:5} To you, O Lord, we have entrusted ourselves; we said you are our God, for you were our shelter and strong tower against our enemies. {89:6} To you we cried and were not ashamed; in you we trusted and were delivered; when we called to you, you heard our voice; you delivered our souls from the sword; you showed us your grace; you gave us your salvation; you filled our hearts with your strength. {89:7} You went forth for our salvation; with your arm, you redeemed your people; you answered us from the heavens of your holiness; you saved us from thousands of people. {89:8} The sun and moon stood still in heaven, and you stood in your wrath against our oppressors and commanded your judgments over them. {89:9} All the princes of the earth stood up; the kings of the nations gathered together; they were not moved by your presence; they desired your battles. {89:10} You rose against them in your anger and brought down your wrath upon them; you destroyed them in your anger and cut them off in your heart. {89:11} Nations have been consumed by your fury; kingdoms have fallen because of your wrath; you wounded kings in the day of your anger. {89:12} You poured out your fury upon them; your fierce anger seized them; you turned their iniquity upon them and cut them off in their wickedness. {89:13} They spread a trap, but fell into it; in the net they hid, their foot was caught. {89:14} Your hand was ready against all your enemies who said, 'By their sword, they possess the land; by their arm, they dwell in the city'; you filled their faces with shame; you brought their horns down to the ground; you terrified them in your wrath and destroyed them in your anger. {89:15} The earth trembled and shook at the sound of your storm over them; you did not spare their souls from death and brought their lives down to the grave. {89:16} You pursued them in your storm; you consumed them in your whirlwind; you turned their rain into hail; they fell into deep pits so that they could not rise. {89:17} Their carcasses were like rubbish cast out in the middle of the streets. {89:18} They were consumed and destroyed in your anger; you saved your people with your might. {89:19} Therefore our hearts rejoice in you; our souls exalt in your salvation. {89:20} Our tongues will declare your might; we will sing and praise your wondrous works. {89:21} For you saved us from our enemies; you delivered us from those who rose up against us; you destroyed them from before us and pressed them beneath our feet. {89:22} Thus, all your enemies shall perish, O Lord, and the wicked shall be like chaff driven by the wind, while your beloved shall be like trees planted by the waters. {89:23} So Joshua and all Israel with him returned to the camp in Gilgal after having struck down all the kings, leaving not a remnant of them. {89:24} The five kings fled alone on foot from the battle and hid themselves in a cave, and Joshua searched for them on the battlefield but did not find them. {89:25} It was afterward reported to Joshua, saying, "The kings are found, and behold, they are hidden in a cave." {89:26} And Joshua said, "Appoint men to guard the mouth of the cave so they do not escape," and the children of Israel did so. {89:27} Joshua called all Israel and said to the officers of battle, "Place your feet upon the necks of these kings," and Joshua said, "So the Lord will do to all your enemies." {89:28} Joshua commanded afterward that they slay the kings and cast them into the cave, placing great stones at the mouth of the cave. {89:29} Joshua then went with all the people with him to Makkedah and struck it down with the sword. {89:30} He utterly destroyed the souls and all that belonged to the city, doing to the king and the people there as he had done to Jericho. {89:31} He passed from there to Libnah and fought against it; the Lord delivered it into his hands, and Joshua struck it with the sword, destroying all its souls, doing to it and its king as he had done to Jericho. {89:32} From there he moved on to Lachish to fight against it, and Horam, king of Gaza, came up to assist Lachish, but Joshua struck him and his people until there was none left to him. {89:33} Joshua took Lachish and all its people, doing to it as he had done to Libnah. {89:34} Joshua then moved to Eglon and took it also, striking it and all its people with the sword. {89:35} From there he went to Hebron, fought against it, and took it, utterly destroying it, and then returned with all Israel to Debir and fought against it, striking it with the sword. {89:36} He destroyed every soul in it; he left none remaining, and he did to it and its king as he had done to Jericho. {89:37} Joshua struck all the kings of the Amorites from Kadesh-barnea to Azah, taking their land at once, for the Lord fought for Israel. {89:38} Joshua with all Israel returned to the camp at Gilgal. {89:39} When Jabin, king of Chazor, heard all that Joshua had done to the kings of the Amorites, Jabin sent to Jobat, king of Midian, to Laban, king of Shimron, to Jephal, king of Achshaph, and to all the kings of the Amorites, saying, {89:40} "Come quickly to us and help us so we may strike down the children of Israel before they come upon us and do to us as they have done to the other kings of the Amorites." {89:41} All these kings listened to the words of Jabin, king of Chazor, and they gathered their camps—seventeen kings, and their people were as numerous as the sand on the seashore, along with innumerable horses and chariots, and they came and camped together at the waters of Merom to fight against Israel. {89:42} And the Lord said to Joshua, "Do not fear them, for tomorrow about this time I will deliver them all slain before you; you shall hamstring their horses and burn their chariots with fire." {89:43} Joshua and all the men of war came suddenly upon them and struck them down, and they fell into the hands of the Israelites, for the Lord had delivered them into the hands of the children of Israel. {89:44} So the children of Israel pursued all these kings with their camps and struck them until none remained, and Joshua did to them as the Lord had spoken to him. {89:45} Joshua returned at that time to Chazor and struck it with the sword, destroying every soul in it and burning it with fire, and from Chazor, Joshua passed to Shimron, struck it, and utterly destroyed it. {89:46} From there he passed to Achshaph and did to it as he had done to Shimron. {89:47} Then he went to Adulam and struck all the people there, doing to Adulam as he had done to Achshaph and Shimron. {89:48} He went from them to all the cities of the kings he had struck down, smiting all the remaining people and utterly destroying them. {89:49} Only their booty and cattle did the Israelites take as prey, but they struck down every human being, leaving not a soul alive. {89:50} As the Lord had commanded Moses, so did Joshua and all Israel; they did not fail in anything. {89:51} So Joshua and all the children of Israel struck the entire land of Canaan as the Lord had commanded them, striking down all their kings—thirty-one kings—and the children of Israel took all their land. {89:52} This included the kingdoms of Sihon and Og, which were on the other side of the Jordan, of which Moses had struck many cities, and Moses gave them to the Reubenites, Gadites, and half the tribe of Manasseh. {89:53} Joshua struck all the kings on this side of the Jordan to the west, giving them for an inheritance to the nine tribes and the half-tribe of Israel. {89:54} For five years, Joshua waged war against these kings, giving their cities to the Israelites, and the land became peaceful from battle throughout the cities of the Amorites and the Canaanites.

{90:1} In the fifth year after the Israelites crossed the Jordan and had rested from their wars with the Canaanites, intense battles broke out between Edom and the children of Chittim, and the children of Chittim fought against Edom. {90:2} That year, which was the thirty-first of his reign, Abianus, king of Chittim, led a large army of mighty men to Seir to fight the descendants of Esau. {90:3} Hadad, the king of Edom, heard of this and went out to meet him with a strong army and engaged him in battle in the field of Edom. {90:4} The forces of Chittim prevailed over the children of Esau, and they killed twenty-two thousand men; all the descendants of Esau fled before them. {90:5} The children of Chittim pursued them and caught up with Hadad, king of Edom, who was fleeing, and they captured him alive, bringing him to Abianus, king of Chittim. {90:6} Abianus ordered him to be executed, and Hadad, king of Edom, died in the forty-eighth year of his reign. {90:7} The children of Chittim continued their pursuit, inflicting great losses on Edom, which then became subject to them. {90:8} The children of Chittim ruled over Edom, and Edom became a part of their kingdom from that day on. {90:9} From that time, Edom could no longer lift its head, and its kingdom became one with that of the children of Chittim. {90:10} Abianus appointed officers in Edom, making all the children of Edom subjects and tributaries to him, and then he returned to his own land, Chittim. {90:11} Upon his return, he renewed his government, building a spacious and fortified palace as a royal residence, and he reigned securely over the children of Chittim and Edom. {90:12} During this time, after the children of Israel had driven away all the Canaanites and Amorites, Joshua was old and advanced in years. {90:13} The Lord said to Joshua, "You are old and advanced in age, and a large portion of the land remains to be possessed." {90:14} Therefore, divide this land as an inheritance for the nine tribes and the half-tribe of Manasseh." Joshua rose up and did as the Lord commanded him. {90:15} He divided the entire land among the tribes of Israel as an inheritance according to their divisions. {90:16} However, to the tribe of Levi, he did not give an inheritance because the offerings of the Lord are their inheritance, as the Lord had instructed through Moses. {90:17} Joshua gave Mount Hebron to Caleb, the son of Jephuneh, as a special portion above his brothers, as the Lord had commanded through Moses. {90:18} Thus, Hebron became an inheritance for Caleb and his descendants to this day. {90:19} Joshua divided the whole land by lot among all Israel for their inheritance, as the Lord had commanded him. {90:20} The children of Israel gave cities to the Levites from their own inheritances, along with pastureland for their livestock, just as the Lord had commanded Moses. They divided the land by lot, whether large or small. {90:21} They went to inherit the land according to their boundaries, and the children of Israel gave Joshua, son of Nun, an inheritance among them. {90:22} By the Lord's command, they gave him the city he requested, Timnath-serach in the hill country of Ephraim, where he built the city and settled. {90:23} These are the inheritances that Eleazar the priest, Joshua, son of Nun, and the leaders of the tribes allotted to the children of Israel by lot in Shiloh, before the Lord, at the entrance of the tabernacle, after which they ceased dividing the land. {90:24} The Lord gave the land to the Israelites, and they possessed it as the Lord had promised, fulfilling all He had sworn to their ancestors. {90:25} The Lord gave the Israelites peace from all their enemies surrounding them; no one stood against them, and the Lord delivered all their enemies into their hands, fulfilling every good promise He made to the children of Israel. {90:26} Joshua called all the children of Israel, blessed them, and commanded them to serve the Lord; then he sent them away, and each man went to his city and to his inheritance. {90:27} The children of Israel served the Lord throughout Joshua's lifetime, and the Lord granted them peace from all their surrounding enemies, and they lived securely in their cities. {90:28} It came to pass that in the thirty-eighth year of his reign, Abianus, king of Chittim, died, which was the seventh year of his reign over Edom; he was buried in the palace he built for himself, and Latinus succeeded him, reigning for fifty years. {90:29} During his reign, he raised an army and fought against the inhabitants of Britannia and Kernania, the descendants of Elisha, son of Javan; he prevailed over them and made them tributary. {90:30} He then learned that Edom had revolted from the children of Chittim, so Latinus went against them, defeated them, and subdued them, placing them once again under the authority of the children of Chittim, thus uniting Edom with Chittim for all time. {90:31} For many years, Edom had no king, and their governance was under the children of Chittim and their king. {90:32} In the twenty-sixth year after the children of Israel crossed the Jordan, which was the sixty-sixth year since they left Egypt, Joshua was old and advanced in age, being one hundred and eight years old at that time. {90:33} Joshua called all Israel, including their elders, judges, and officers, after the Lord had given them rest from their enemies all around, and he said to the elders of Israel and their judges, "I am old and advanced in years, and you have seen what the Lord has done to all the nations He has driven away from before you, for it is the Lord who has fought for you." {90:34} Therefore, strengthen yourselves to keep and do all the words of the Law of Moses; do not deviate from it to the right or to the left, and do not associate with the nations that remain in the land; do not even mention the names of their gods, but cling to the Lord your God, as you have done to this day. {90:35} Joshua strongly urged the children of Israel to serve the Lord all their days. {90:36} The Israelites replied, "We will serve the Lord our God all our days, we and our children and grandchildren forever." {90:37} On that day, Joshua made a covenant with the people, and he sent the children of Israel away, and they each went to their inheritance and to their cities. {90:38} In those days, while the children of Israel lived securely in their cities, they buried the coffins of their ancestors, which they had brought up from Egypt, placing each man in the inheritance of his children; the twelve sons of Jacob were buried by the children of Israel, each in his children's possession. {90:39} These are the names of the cities where they buried the twelve sons of Jacob, whom the children of Israel brought up from Egypt. {90:40} They buried Reuben and Gad on this side of the Jordan, in Romia, which Moses had given to their descendants. {90:41} Simeon and Levi were buried in the city of Mauda, given to the children of Simeon, and the suburbs of the city belonged to the children of Levi. {90:42} Judah was buried in the city of Benjamin, opposite Bethlehem. {90:43} The bones of Issachar and Zebulun were buried in Zidon, in the portion allotted to their children. {90:44} Dan was buried in the city of his children in Eshtael, and Naphtali and Asher were buried in Kadesh-naphtali, each in the place assigned to their children. {90:45} The bones of Joseph were buried in Shechem, in the part of the field that Jacob purchased from Hamor, which became Joseph's inheritance. {90:46} Benjamin was buried in Jerusalem, opposite the Jebusite, which was given to the children of Benjamin; the children of Israel buried their fathers, each man in the city of his children. {90:47} After two years, Joshua, son of Nun, died at one hundred and ten years old, having judged Israel for twenty-eight years, during which Israel served the Lord throughout his life. {90:48} The other affairs of Joshua, including his battles and his admonishments to Israel, and all that he commanded them, along with the names of the cities the children of Israel possessed in his days, are recorded in the book of the words of Joshua to the children of Israel, and in the book of the wars of the Lord, written by Moses, Joshua, and the children of Israel. {90:49} The children of Israel buried Joshua at the border of his inheritance, in Timnath-serach, which was given to him in the hill country of Ephraim. {90:50} In those days, Eleazar, son of Aaron, died, and he was buried on a hill that belonged to Phineas, his son, which was given to him in the hill country of Ephraim.

{91:1} After the death of Joshua, the Canaanites were still living in the land, and the Israelites decided to drive them out. {91:2} The Israelites asked the Lord, "Who should go up first to fight against the Canaanites?" The Lord replied, "Judah shall go up first." {91:3} The people of Judah said to Simeon, "Join us in our territory, and we will fight against the Canaanites, and we will also go up with you into your territory." So the Simeonites went with the Judahites. {91:4} The tribe of Judah went up and fought against the Canaanites, and the Lord handed the Canaanites over to them. They struck down ten thousand men at Bezek. {91:5} They fought against Adonibezek at Bezek, and he fled before them. They pursued him, caught him, and cut off his thumbs and big toes. {91:6} Adonibezek said, "Seventy kings, with their thumbs and big toes cut off, used to gather scraps under my table. Just as I have done, God has repaid me." They brought him to Jerusalem, and he died there. {91:7} The Simeonites joined Judah in fighting and struck down the Canaanites with the sword. {91:8} The Lord was with the tribe of Judah, and they took the hill country, while the Josephites went up to Bethel, known as Luz, and the Lord was with them. {91:9} The Josephites sent spies to scout out Bethel. The watchmen saw a man coming out of the city, and they said to him, "Show us how to enter the city, and we will treat you kindly." {91:10} The man showed them the entrance, and the Josephites attacked the city with the sword. {91:11} They sent the man and his family away, and he went to the Hittites and built a city, calling it Luz. So the Israelites lived in their cities, and they served the Lord all the days of Joshua and all the days of the elders who outlived Joshua, witnessing the great things the Lord did for Israel. {91:12} The elders judged Israel for seventeen years after Joshua's death. {91:13} The elders also fought the battles against the Canaanites, and the Lord drove the Canaanites out before the Israelites to settle them in their land. {91:14} He fulfilled all His promises to Abraham, Isaac, and Jacob, including the oath He swore to give them and their descendants the land of the Canaanites. {91:15} The Lord gave the Israelites all the land of Canaan, just as He had promised their ancestors, and He provided them rest from their enemies surrounding them, allowing the Israelites to live securely in their cities. {91:16} Blessed be the Lord forever, amen, and amen. {91:17} Be strong, and let all of you who trust in the Lord take courage.

The Book of Eldad and Modad

{1:1} In the days of Moses, the servant of the Lord, there arose two men, Eldad and Modad, chosen among the seventy elders. {1:2} The Spirit of the Lord rested upon them, and they began to prophesy among the people, speaking words of wisdom and warning. {1:3} The people marveled, for Eldad and Modad spoke not from their own understanding but by the Spirit of the Almighty. {1:4} Eldad declared, "Listen, O Israel, to the voice of the Lord. A time approaches when the faithful will be sheltered, and the unrighteous will face their deeds." {1:5} Modad proclaimed, "Prepare yourselves, for the Lord's judgment is near. Turn from your pride and walk in humility before Him."

{2:1} And there came a young man who hastened to tell Moses, saying, "Eldad and Modad are prophesying in the camp." {2:2} Joshua, son of Nun, Moses' faithful servant, responded, "My lord Moses, should you not command them to be silent?" {2:3} But Moses replied, "Why are you concerned on my behalf? I would that all the Lord's people were filled with His Spirit and could speak His words." {2:4} And so the words of Eldad and Modad spread through the tribes, inspiring both hope and solemn reflection. {2:5} Eldad spoke of a promised Redeemer, an Anointed One, who would come to save His people and restore their land.

{3:1} Modad spoke of signs that would precede the Lord's great day: the heavens would shake, and the earth would tremble. {3:2} He declared, "In those times, the Spirit of the Lord will fall upon all. Your children shall prophesy, your elders shall dream dreams, and your youth shall see visions." {3:3} "And it shall come to pass that everyone who calls upon the Lord shall find salvation," Modad said. {3:4} The people listened with awe and fear, for they sensed that the days of testing and judgment were near.

{4:1} Eldad spoke of a future place, a city of peace and everlasting joy, where the Lord would dwell among His people as their eternal light. {4:2} "There will be no more sorrow, no more tears, for the old things will have faded away," said Eldad. {4:3} Modad added, "The Lord will renew all things. There will be no night, for His light will shine forever." {4:4} The people rejoiced at these visions of hope, and many turned their hearts back to the Lord, seeking His mercy and guidance.

{5:1} Yet, some mocked and refused to listen, saying, "These men speak nonsense; they are overcome with drink." {5:2} Eldad warned them, "Do not harden your hearts as those who rebelled before. The day of the Lord approaches swiftly, and who can endure it?" {5:3} Modad urged, "Seek the Lord while He may be found; call on Him before it is too late." {5:4} Thus, the words of Eldad and Modad were preserved as a witness to the future generations, a testament of the Lord's unchanging mercy and unyielding justice.

The Book of Jannes and Jambres

{1:1} Jannes and Jambres were renowned among the people of Egypt for their mastery of the dark arts, having studied in the courts of Pharaoh and served as his chief magicians. {1:2} They were skilled in every form of sorcery and were well-respected by the Egyptian priests, who believed their powers to be a gift from the gods. {1:3} Yet, in the secret places of their hearts, Jannes and Jambres harbored envy and a desire for greater power, seeking to make their names feared among all peoples. {1:4} When Pharaoh heard of Moses and Aaron, messengers sent by the God of the Israelites, he summoned his trusted magicians to test the strength of these new signs and wonders. {1:5} Jannes and Jambres came before Pharaoh, assured of their powers, determined to challenge these foreigners who claimed to speak for a god unknown to them.

{2:1} Moses and Aaron came into the court of Pharaoh, and Aaron threw down his staff before all present, and it became a serpent by the power of the Lord {2:2}. Jannes and Jambres, unfazed, took their staffs and cast them down before Pharaoh. {2:3} Through their magic arts, they too transformed their staffs into serpents, and the court marveled at the power of the Egyptians. {2:4} But Aaron's staff swallowed the staffs of the magicians, demonstrating the superiority of the God of Israel over their sorcery. {2:5} Pharaoh, however, hardened his heart, reassured by the magicians' ability to replicate the signs. {2:6} Jannes and Jambres looked upon Aaron with hatred, vowing to resist the Israelite prophets to the end.

{3:1} As Moses brought down the plagues upon Egypt by the hand of God, Jannes and Jambres rose to meet each one with defiance. {3:2} When Moses turned the waters of the Nile into blood, the magicians gathered and, using their enchantments, turned water to blood as well, convincing Pharaoh of their power {3:3}. But as the plagues increased in severity, the magicians' power waned. {3:4} They conjured frogs at first to match the plague, but when lice covered all of Egypt, Jannes and Jambres tried in vain to imitate this sign. {3:5} Turning to Pharaoh, they said, "This is the finger of God," for they could not stand against the Lord's power.

{4:1} Yet Jannes and Jambres remained in Pharaoh's service, continuing to resist Moses. {4:2} They accused Moses of trickery and mocked the Israelites, claiming their release would bring misfortune upon Egypt. {4:3} Behind closed doors, they plotted and cast spells to bind the power of Moses, invoking their gods in secret rituals. {4:4} But their spells failed, and each attempt left them weaker than before, their influence over Pharaoh diminishing with every failed sign.

{5:1} Finally, the night of the last plague came, the death of the firstborn. {5:2} Jannes and Jambres trembled as they sensed a great power descending upon the land, a force they could not counter. {5:3} The cries of the Egyptians filled the air, and in horror, the magicians realized their own families were not spared. {5:4} Defeated and broken, they fled from Pharaoh's court, humiliated and stripped of their power, for they had stood against the God of Israel and been found wanting.

{6:1} In the years that followed, the tale of Jannes and Jambres became a warning to all who would misuse power against the divine will. {6:2} Their names became synonymous with rebellion and deceit, and their fate was a lesson: that those who resist the truth shall be brought low. {6:3} In every generation, they are remembered as a sign of what becomes of those who challenge the Almighty.

The Book of the Order

{1:1} Thus begins the order of worship, a holy instruction set for the people of God. When the faithful assemble in the house of the Lord, let them enter with reverence, in humility and silence, ready to partake in the mysteries of heaven. {1:2} The clergy shall lead, adorned in vestments pure and unstained, symbolizing the sanctity of their office. The deacon shall carry forth the censer, filling the sanctuary with the incense that rises as prayer to the Most High. {1:3} Let each prayer be offered with sincerity, each hymn sung with devotion, for the Spirit of the Lord is present among those who call upon Him with a pure heart.

{2:1} O priests, shepherds of the flock, let your hearts be consecrated, free from worldly distractions, devoted wholly to the service of the Almighty. {2:2} You are the bridge between the people and God, therefore, let no unholy thought or deed mar your spirit. Strive to be blameless, that your prayers may be heard, and the Lord's blessing may rest upon you and the congregation. {2:3} The deacons shall serve with diligence, assisting the priests in all duties, without pride or impatience, knowing that their service is unto the Lord. {2:4} Together, priests and deacons shall uphold the sanctity of the church and ensure the faithful receive the sacraments in reverence and truth.

{3:1} The Divine Liturgy is the highest form of worship, where the body and blood of Christ are made manifest. When the faithful gather for this holy feast, they must prepare with fasting and prayer, confessing their sins before partaking. {3:2} The priest shall invoke the Spirit of God upon the bread and wine, that they may be transformed into the holy mysteries of Christ. {3:3} All who partake shall do so with a contrite heart, in awe of the sacrifice made on their behalf. No one shall approach the altar lightly, for this is holy ground. {3:4} The choir shall sing psalms and hymns, lifting the hearts of the people to heaven, preparing them for the encounter with the Divine.

{4:1} The church shall keep holy the days set apart, remembering the saints and the works of God through history. {4:2} Each festival, whether of the Resurrection, the Nativity, or the feast of the saints, shall be observed with fasting, prayer, and the giving of alms, that the hearts of the faithful may be drawn nearer to the Lord. {4:3} On these days, the church shall be adorned, and the people shall come dressed in garments of purity, symbolizing their consecration to God. {4:4} Let all who celebrate do so with joy, for these feasts are a foretaste of the heavenly banquet prepared for the faithful.

{5:1} Baptism is the gateway to the life in Christ, the washing away of sins, and the rebirth into holiness. {5:2} Those who present themselves for baptism, or present their children, shall do so with solemnity, recognizing the commitment they make to walk in the light of Christ. {5:3} Marriage is a holy covenant, a union blessed by God. Let those who marry come with hearts prepared, seeking the blessing of the church, and understanding the vows they make before God and the congregation. {5:4} The priest shall bless them, and the people shall pray, that this union be steadfast and fruitful in the eyes of the Lord.

{6:1} All who belong to the household of faith are called to live in love, humility, and obedience to the Word of God. {6:2} Let no corrupt word proceed from their mouths, nor any deceit dwell in their hearts. They are to be examples of righteousness in their homes, in their work, and in the community. {6:3} Those who stray from the path shall be corrected with gentleness, and if they repent, shall be restored with grace. But if they persist in sin, they shall be subject to church discipline, that their souls may yet be saved. {6:4} Let all who bear the name of Christ strive to walk in His footsteps, that the light of God may shine through them to all the world.

{7:1} The church is the bride of Christ, bound to Him in eternal love and faithfulness. {7:2} Let no division come among the faithful, for they are one body in Christ, joined together by the Holy Spirit. {7:3} In times of trial and persecution, let them remain steadfast, for the Lord is their refuge and strength. {7:4} The faithful shall gather, pray, and uphold one another, trusting in the promises of God, who is ever faithful.

The Book of the Sinodos

{1:1} The Church has established clear guidelines for appointing bishops, priests, and deacons. {1:2} A bishop must be a person of high character, free from addiction, and not motivated by personal wealth. {1:3} He should have a deep understanding of the Scriptures and be skilled in teaching sound doctrine. {1:4} A priest should be ordained after proving his integrity, being a person of steadfast prayer and moral soundness. {1:5} Deacons should be selected from those with a history of faithful service, showing humility and a readiness to assist the priest in all responsibilities.

{2:1} Clergy are to embody lives of holiness, serving as examples in their speech and actions. {2:2} They should avoid gossip, steering clear of quarrels and contentious behavior. {2:3} Bishops must visit the faithful regularly to offer counsel and spiritual support. {2:4} Priests are to celebrate the sacraments reverently, upholding the Church's traditions in every aspect of worship. {2:5} Deacons should assist in distributing the Eucharist and extending care to the poor and vulnerable.

{3:1} Baptism shall be performed in the name of the Father, the Son, and the Holy Spirit, using water as a sign of inward grace. {3:2} The Eucharist, representing the true Body and Blood of Christ, is to be celebrated with unleavened bread and wine. {3:3} Confession shall be heard by a priest, who offers absolution in Christ's name. {3:4} Marriage should be solemnized before the congregation, with vows exchanged in the presence of God and witnesses. {3:5} The anointing of the sick is to be done with oil, invoking the Holy Spirit's healing power.

{4:1} The faithful are called to fast as a spiritual discipline, abstaining from meat and dairy on specified days. {4:2} Wednesdays and Fridays are designated as fasting days, commemorating Jesus' betrayal and crucifixion. {4:3} During Lent, believers should engage in deeper fasting and prayer, preparing to celebrate the Resurrection. {4:4} Daily prayers are expected of all Christians, with morning and evening prayers encouraged. {4:5} Clergy are to lead the community in prayers, hymns, and psalms, fostering a spirit of reverence.

{5:1} Clergy members found guilty of serious sin must be brought before the bishop for accountability. {5:2} A process of repentance and reconciliation is available to those who have strayed. {5:3} Heresy and division are to be addressed firmly to preserve doctrinal integrity and Church unity. {5:4} Disputes among the faithful should be resolved through mediation, applying scriptural principles. {5:5} The Church's resources are to be managed with honesty and transparency.

{6:1} Lay members should support clergy through prayer, tithes, and offerings. {6:2} They should participate in the sacraments and the liturgical life of the Church. {6:3} Each member is called to a life of holiness, witnessing the Gospel through words and actions. {6:4} Parents are responsible for educating their children in the faith, ensuring they learn the Scriptures and traditions. {6:5} The faithful should care for one another, showing hospitality and engaging in charity to fulfill Christ's teaching.

{7:1} The liturgy should be celebrated with reverence, adhering to the ancient traditions passed down through the ages. {7:2} Hymns and psalms are to be sung, lifting the hearts of the faithful toward God. {7:3} Incense is used as a symbol of prayers ascending to heaven. {7:4} The reading of Scripture is central to worship, with homilies that instruct and uplift. {7:5} The Eucharist is the pinnacle of the liturgy, symbolizing sacred communion with Christ.

{8:1} The Church should celebrate the feasts of the Lord with joy, commemorating key moments in salvation history. {8:2} The Feast of the Nativity is observed on December 25, honoring the birth of Jesus. {8:3} The Feast of the Resurrection is celebrated on the first Sunday after the first full moon following the vernal equinox, marking Christ's victory over death. {8:4} The faithful should also honor the feasts of saints, remembering their holy lives and seeking their intercession. {8:5} The Church should observe the liturgical seasons of Advent, Lent, Easter, and Pentecost.

{9:1} The Church must be a beacon of compassion, caring for the poor, orphans, and widows. {9:2} Alms should be collected regularly and given to those in need, reflecting Christ's love. {9:3} Acts of mercy, such as visiting the sick, comforting the grieving, and supporting the oppressed, are encouraged. {9:4} The Church should advocate for justice and peace, standing against oppression and violence. {9:5} The Church must support education and the well-being of all people.

{10:1} Those called to monastic life commit to prayer, work, and studying Scripture. {10:2} Monks and nuns live in community, adhering to their order's rules and pursuing holiness. {10:3} Monasteries should welcome pilgrims and provide spiritual guidance. {10:4} Monastic communities should strive for self-sufficiency, engaging in farming, crafts, and other productive work. {10:5} The abbot or abbess should lead with wisdom and compassion, attending to the needs of the community.

{11:1} The Church should establish schools and centers for learning to provide education in faith and other disciplines. {11:2} Catechesis must be offered for all ages to ensure a solid understanding of Church doctrine. {11:3} Clergy and teachers should be well-prepared to teach the faith effectively. {11:4} The Scriptures are to be diligently studied, seeking to understand and live by their teachings. {11:5} All members should be encouraged to seek knowledge and wisdom, leading lives that glorify God.

{12:1} The Church is called to spread the Gospel, bringing the message to all nations. {12:2} Missionaries should be sent out, supported by the Church's prayers and resources. {12:3} Evangelistic efforts should be pursued using all available means to share the Good News. {12:4} New believers are to be welcomed, baptized, and instructed in the faith. {12:5} The Church should work to establish new congregations, helping them grow in Christ.

{13:1} The Church must manage financial resources with integrity. {13:2} Tithes and offerings are to be collected for ministry work, clergy support, and aid to the needy. {13:3} A finance committee should oversee the proper use of funds. {13:4} Financial reports must be provided to the congregation to ensure transparency. {13:5} Members should be encouraged to give generously, recognizing that all gifts are blessings from God.

{14:1} The Church should diligently maintain its properties, using them to serve God's glory. {14:2} Church properties should be held in trust, managed by appointed stewards. {14:3} Any property sale or purchase must be approved by the governing body. {14:4} Church buildings should be kept in good repair as suitable places for worship and ministry. {14:5} Non-religious use of church facilities must align with the Church's mission.

{15:1} Clergy should provide pastoral care, offering spiritual support to all members. {15:2} Counseling should be available for those facing personal, family, or spiritual challenges, handled with discretion. {15:3} Clergy should receive training in pastoral care to serve effectively. {15:4} The Church should establish support groups to foster healing and growth. {15:5} Clergy should visit the sick and homebound, bringing the sacraments and words of comfort.

{16:1} The Church should seek unity and fellowship with other Christian communities. {16:2} Regular communication and cooperation with other denominations are encouraged. {16:3} The Church should participate in ecumenical initiatives for the common good. {16:4} Differences in belief should be approached with respect, seeking mutual understanding. {16:5} Joint efforts in mission, charity, and education should reflect the unity of Christ's body.

{17:1} The Church must safeguard all members, especially children and vulnerable adults. {17:2} Policies should be in place to prevent abuse and address any allegations justly. {17:3} All clergy and volunteers must undergo safeguarding training. {17:4} A team should oversee the implementation of protection measures. {17:5} The Church should work with civil authorities as needed, ensuring justice and safety.

{18:1} The Church must keep precise records of baptisms, marriages, and funerals. {18:2} Membership records should be maintained for an accurate account of the congregation. {18:3} Financial records should be kept meticulously for accountability. {18:4} Historical documents and archives should be preserved, honoring the Church's heritage. {18:5} All records should be securely stored and accessible as needed.

{19:1} The Church should use various media to communicate the Gospel and its teachings. {19:2} A communications team should manage the Church's online presence and publications. {19:3} Social media should promote the Church's values. {19:4} Newsletters, bulletins, and magazines should inform and inspire the congregation. {19:5} The Church should engage with the community through media, sharing messages of hope.

{20:1} The Church should promote peace, offering ways to resolve disputes among members. {20:2} Mediation and arbitration should be provided to resolve conflicts biblically. {20:3} A reconciliation committee should support healing and unity. {20:4} Disciplinary actions must be fair and redemptive. {20:5} Forgiveness and reconciliation should be actively encouraged, reflecting Christ's grace.

{21:1} Liturgical arts and music should enhance the reverence of worship. {21:2} Choirs and music ministries should train members in sacred music. {21:3} Art and iconography should inspire the faithful and honor Church tradition. {21:4} Vestments and vessels should be well-crafted, reflecting the holiness of worship. {21:5} New liturgical art and music should be fostered, supporting creativity and devotion.

{22:1} The Church is called to care for creation, promoting environmental stewardship. {22:2} Waste reduction, resource conservation, and habitat protection are encouraged. {22:3} Education on environmental issues should support sustainable practices. {22:4} The Church should advocate for policies that honor creation. {22:5} The faithful are reminded of their biblical duty to steward the earth, honoring all creation.

The Book of the Covenant

{1:1} And the Lord said to His people, "Behold, I have set before you the path of righteousness, that you may walk in it and find peace. {1:2} Do not stray to the left or the right, but let your steps be guided by My commandments and My truth, for in these you shall find life." {1:3} Let each person strive to live in harmony with others, keeping in mind the dignity and worth of each soul, as I have made all people in My image. {1:4} Honor the widow, protect the orphan, and be merciful to the stranger in your land, for you too were once strangers in a foreign land.

{2:1} Refrain from falsehood in all your dealings, for I am a God of truth and justice. {2:2} Let your words be like silver, refined and pure, and do not bear false witness against your neighbor. {2:3} Speak honestly and with integrity, and in this way, you will reflect the goodness of your Creator. {2:4} If you see your neighbor's property in danger, protect it as though it were your own, and do not covet what belongs to another. {2:5} Do not take what is not yours, whether by theft or deceit, but work diligently with your own hands so that you may have what is rightfully yours.

{3:1} Concerning matters of marriage, let each man be united to his wife in holiness, and let their union be blessed before the Lord. {3:2} Husbands, love your wives as Christ loves the Church, treating them with respect and kindness, that your prayers may not be hindered. {3:3} Wives, honor and respect your husbands, and together strive to build a household of peace and love, rooted in the Word of God. {3:4} Let parents teach their children the ways of righteousness, and let children honor their parents, that they may receive the blessing of a long life.

{4:1} As for the priests and those who serve in the temple, let them be above reproach, dedicated fully to the work of the Lord. {4:2} They shall not seek wealth or worldly gain, but shall serve in humility and sincerity, tending to the needs of the people with compassion. {4:3} Let them be diligent in prayer and in the reading of the Scriptures, for it is by these that they shall be equipped to lead others. {4:4} In matters of dispute, let them judge with fairness, showing no partiality, for they serve as representatives of divine justice.

{5:1} On matters of purity, keep yourselves from all things that defile, that you may remain holy before the Lord. {5:2} Refrain from unclean foods and practices, and keep your bodies as temples of the Holy Spirit. {5:3} If any among you falls into impurity, let them repent and seek forgiveness, for the Lord is gracious and will forgive those who turn to Him with a sincere heart. {5:4} But do not abuse His mercy, for God cannot be mocked; strive daily to walk in purity and righteousness.

{6:1} Observe the holy days and festivals as commanded, and let these times be a remembrance of God's goodness and provision. {6:2} On the Sabbath, refrain from all work, dedicating the day to rest and worship, as the Lord rested on the seventh day after creating the heavens and the earth. {6:3} Let each feast be celebrated with joy and thanksgiving, sharing with those who have less, that the entire community may rejoice together.

{7:1} Remember that your lives are bound by the covenant which the Lord has established with you; be faithful in all things, so that you may remain under His protection. {7:2} Guard your hearts from idolatry and do not adopt the customs of those who worship other gods, for the Lord is a jealous God and will not share His glory. {7:3} Serve Him with all your heart, mind, and soul, and in doing so, you will fulfill the purpose for which you were created.

{8:1} And at the end of all things, there shall be a day of judgment, where each person will give an account of their deeds. {8:2} The righteous shall inherit eternal life and dwell in the presence of the Lord forever, but those who have rejected His commandments shall be cast out from His presence. {8:3} Therefore, walk in humility and seek righteousness, that you may stand blameless on that great day.

{9:1} This is the covenant which the Lord has established with His people; abide by it and you shall live. {9:2} Blessed are those who keep His commandments, for they shall be called children of God and shall know His peace all their days. {9:3} Let each man and woman commit their hearts fully to the Lord, for in Him is the fullness of life.

The Book of the Mysteries

{1:1} In the beginning was the Word, and the Word was with God, and from Him all things were made. {1:2} The mysteries of heaven and earth were hidden within Him, for He is the source of all wisdom and truth. {1:3} The Lord fashioned the heavens with His voice and set the stars in their place; He separated light from darkness, showing His people the path of righteousness.

{2:1} Seek not the wisdom of the world, for it is limited and cannot understand the mysteries of the Most High. {2:2} Instead, let your hearts be open to the wisdom that comes from above, which is pure, peaceable, and eternal. {2:3} For the angels who dwell in the heavens behold the face of God continually, and they serve as messengers of His holy mysteries to those chosen for understanding. {2:4} Be humble in spirit, for the mysteries of God are revealed to those who approach Him in humility and faith.

{3:1} Concerning the creation of man, the Lord said, "Let Us make man in Our image and likeness," and so He created him, breathing into him the breath of life. {3:2} Man was created to be a vessel of divine knowledge, to walk in communion with his Creator. {3:3} But man fell from grace through disobedience, and the mysteries were hidden from him, reserved only for those who would seek God with all their heart.

{4:1} The Lord sent His prophets to reveal glimpses of His mysteries, yet the fullness of wisdom was veiled until the appointed time. {4:2} When the Son of God came into the world, He unveiled the mystery of salvation, reconciling humanity to the Father. {4:3} Through His life, death, and resurrection, He opened the door to eternal life for all who believe, and the mystery of the ages was revealed in Him.

{5:1} Let no one boast in their knowledge, for the wisdom of God is beyond human understanding. {5:2} As high as the heavens are above the earth, so are His thoughts above our thoughts, and His ways above our ways. {5:3} Seek therefore to know Him in spirit and in truth, for it is only by His Spirit that the mysteries are revealed.

{6:1} Concerning the angels, know that they are mighty in power and serve before the throne of God. {6:2} They carry His messages, protect His people, and execute His judgments. {6:3} Yet even the angels marvel at the mystery of redemption, for it is a mystery granted to humankind alone to experience His grace in this way. {6:4} Therefore, live in reverence and awe, knowing that you are participants in the mysteries of God.

{7:1} The mysteries of God are as deep waters, and those who seek will find a wellspring of life. {7:2} Those who seek knowledge with a pure heart will receive revelation, for God is pleased to reveal His secrets to those who love Him. {7:3} But to the proud and those who seek wisdom for their own gain, the mysteries will remain hidden.

{8:1} At the end of days, the Lord will reveal all things, and the knowledge of God will fill the earth as the waters cover the sea. {8:2} The righteous will shine like the sun in the kingdom of their Father, and they will understand fully, even as they are fully known. {8:3} Therefore, remain steadfast in faith and love, for the mysteries of the kingdom are reserved for those who endure.

The Book of the Herald

{1:1} In the presence of the Almighty, the Archangel Gabriel appeared, and his voice was as thunder, saying, "People of the earth, heed my words, for the time is near, and the days of judgment approach swiftly." {1:2} "Do not walk in the paths of darkness, for the eyes of the Lord see all things. The righteous shall be lifted up, but the wicked shall be cast down. Turn from iniquity, and let your hearts be pure, for only the blameless shall stand in the holy presence of God." {1:3} "Prepare yourselves, for I am sent as a herald of the Most High, to warn and to guide, that none may say, 'We did not know.' Be watchful, for the Lord's day comes like a thief in the night." {1:4} "Those who seek mercy shall find it, and those who walk in truth shall be saved. But to the stubborn and proud, there is only destruction. Repent now, for the hour is late."

{2:1} And Gabriel spoke again, saying, "Behold, I reveal to you a vision of the end. The earth shall tremble, and the heavens shall shake, for the wrath of the Lord is upon all wickedness." {2:2} "I saw the armies of angels descending, clothed in light, with swords of fire, to separate the righteous from the wicked. Every hidden deed shall be brought to light, and every secret thought shall be known." {2:3} "The sun shall darken, and the moon shall not give its light, for the day of the Lord is a day of great trembling. Who shall stand if not the pure in heart and those who seek righteousness?" {2:4} "Rejoice, O righteous, for your deliverance draws near. The Lord has prepared a place for you in His kingdom, a land of peace where no sorrow shall dwell."

{3:1} Gabriel cried out, "O unfaithful and disobedient, do you not see the signs of the times? Why do you cling to deceit and pride when the mercy of God calls you to repentance?" {3:2} "You have been given wisdom and understanding, yet you turn to idols, to riches, and to vanity, forsaking the commandments of the Most High. How long will you close your ears to the truth?" {3:3} "The path of life is narrow and few walk upon it, but wide is the road to destruction. Do not be counted among the rebellious, for the wages of sin is death." {3:4} "Return to the Lord with fasting, prayer, and humility, and He shall receive you. Seek Him while He may be found, for soon the doors of mercy shall close."

{4:1} And Gabriel declared, "Fear not, you who love the Lord, for His angels are set over you to guard you in all your ways. The Lord sends His messengers to watch over those who fear Him." {4:2} "When you walk in righteousness, the angels rejoice, and when you stumble, they lift you up, if you repent. Know that the heavens are open to the prayers of the faithful." {4:3} "The angels of God encamp around those who trust in Him, shielding them from the powers of darkness. Let your faith be steadfast, for you are not alone in your struggle." {4:4} "Lift up your prayers without ceasing, and call upon the name of the Lord, for He is your refuge and strength, and His angels shall carry you through the trials of this world."

{5:1} Gabriel continued, "The Lord is just and faithful; He remembers those who keep His covenant. The faithful shall inherit the earth, and their reward shall be great in the kingdom of heaven." {5:2} "But the wicked shall be cast into outer darkness, where there is weeping and gnashing of teeth. For they chose the path of iniquity and hardened their hearts against the Lord." {5:3} "Blessed are the meek, for they shall be exalted, and blessed are the pure in heart, for they shall see God. To the merciful, mercy shall be shown, and to the humble, grace shall be given." {5:4} "Take courage, you who suffer for righteousness' sake, for the Lord shall wipe away every tear, and sorrow shall be no more. This is the inheritance of the saints."

{6:1} Gabriel spoke a final word, saying, "Beloved of the Lord, hold fast to the faith, for trials shall come, but blessed is the one who endures to the end." {6:2} "Do not be swayed by the temptations of this world, nor by the deceit of false prophets. Stand firm, for the truth of the Lord endures forever." {6:3} "Let your lives be as a light to those who walk in darkness, that by your example they may find the path of salvation." {6:4} "May the peace of God be upon you, and may His angels go before you, now and forevermore."

The Miracles of Mary

{1:1} The Lord created Mary, full of grace, to be the vessel of salvation for the world. {1:2} He clothed her in purity and wisdom, setting her apart from all others, that she would bear the Savior in her womb. {1:3} From her birth, she was chosen, a blessing upon all generations, and from her came the light that dispelled the darkness.

{2:1} And when Mary grew, she was loved by the people and honored by the angels. {2:2} Her soul was humble, and her spirit was filled with peace. {2:3} She walked in righteousness and devotion, seeking always to serve her Lord in purity and truth. {2:4} Therefore, the Lord sent His angel to her, declaring, "You are favored above all, and blessed among women."

{3:1} When Mary bore Jesus, she became the mother of all who believe, for through her came salvation to all nations. {3:2} And the people who saw this marveled, for they recognized that the mother of their Savior was filled with divine grace. {3:3} And they came to her, seeking her prayers and blessings, knowing that she was beloved of God.

{4:1} One day, a man who was lame from birth came to Mary, asking for healing. {4:2} And Mary, full of compassion, prayed to her Son on his behalf. {4:3} "O Lord, heal this man who believes in Your mercy." {4:4} And immediately, he stood up, praising God and proclaiming the miracle that was done through Mary's intercession.

{5:1} Mary appeared to a widow in a dream, saying, "Do not despair, for the Lord is with you." {5:2} The widow, who had lost her only son, awoke and found that her son had returned to life. {5:3} She praised God and spread the news, saying, "The Mother of God has shown mercy to me." {5:4} And many believed because of her testimony.

{6:1} A soldier was captured by his enemies and faced certain death. {6:2} In his distress, he prayed, "O Mary, Mother of God, rescue me." {6:3} And Mary appeared to him in the night, unlocking his chains and leading him safely home. {6:4} When he returned, he dedicated his life to God, telling all of Mary's mercy.

{7:1} The people honored Mary with prayers and hymns, knowing that she interceded for them before her Son. {7:2} And those who celebrated her feasts were blessed with peace and protection. {7:3} Even the wicked feared to harm those under Mary's protection, for her presence was like a shield over them.

{8:1} A poor woman, suffering from illness, prayed to Mary every day, asking for mercy. {8:2} And Mary appeared to her in a vision, comforting her and saying, "Have faith, for your suffering will end." {8:3} Within days, the woman was healed, and she went throughout the city, proclaiming the kindness of the Mother of God.

{9:1} When a famine struck the land, the people gathered to pray to Mary, asking her to intercede. {9:2} Moved by their prayers, Mary petitioned her Son, and rain fell upon the fields, bringing forth an abundant harvest. {9:3} The people rejoiced, giving thanks to God and honoring Mary, who had shown compassion for their plight.

{10:1} A sinner, deeply burdened by guilt, went to Mary's shrine, weeping in repentance. {10:2} He cried out, "Mother of mercy, pray for my forgiveness." {10:3} And Mary, seeing his contrition, prayed to her Son, who forgave him. {10:4} The man returned, transformed, and dedicated his life to serving others in honor of Mary's kindness.

{11:1} Many pilgrims traveled from distant lands to visit Mary's shrine, seeking blessings and healing. {11:2} And none who came with faith went away empty-handed, for Mary interceded for them all. {11:3} Some were healed of their ailments, others found peace in their souls, and many received answers to their prayers.

{12:1} One night, Mary appeared to a group of travelers lost in the wilderness. {12:2} She guided them through the night, lighting their path & leading them to safety. {12:3} The travelers praised her, saying, "She is our guide & protector, truly the Mother of God."

{13:1} During a time of war, Mary protected the city of her faithful. {13:2} She appeared in a vision to the enemy, warning them not to harm her people. {13:3} The attackers, filled with fear, fled, and the city was spared. {13:4} The people rejoiced, proclaiming, "Our Mother defends us!"

{14:1} In a time of great illness, Mary appeared to a young woman, instructing her to prepare a healing balm. {14:2} The woman obeyed, and those who used the balm recovered from their sickness. {14:3} Word spread throughout the land, and many came to know the power of Mary's intercession.

{15:1} Mary spoke to the faithful, saying, "Pray with devotion, for my Son hears the prayers of those who believe." {15:2} And those who called upon Mary with faith received grace and mercy, for her love for her children is great. {15:3} She comforts the sorrowful, strengthens the weak, and guides all who seek her intercession.

{16:1} When the people gathered to celebrate her feast, Mary blessed them, saying, "Rejoice, for the Lord is with you." {16:2} On that day, miracles abounded, and many witnessed signs of her presence. {16:3} The sick were healed, the sorrowful were comforted, and all who attended felt the peace of God.

{17:1} A young boy, lost in the woods, prayed to Mary for help. {17:2} She appeared before him and guided him safely home. {17:3} When he returned, he told his family, and they praised Mary for her compassion.

{18:1} Mary is the mother of all who believe, comforting those who are troubled and blessing those who seek her. {18:2} Her intercession is powerful, for she is beloved of God. {18:3} Blessed are those who honor her, for they will receive mercy.

{19:1} And at the end of all days, Mary will stand with her Son, welcoming the faithful into eternal life. {19:2} Her prayers will ascend, and her people will rejoice, for her love is eternal.

{20:1} This is the testament of the miracles of Mary, recorded for all generations. {20:2} May those who read these words be blessed, and may they know the peace of the Mother of God. Amen.

The Questions of Esdras

{1:1} Ezra lifted his voice and said, "O Lord, why does the wicked prosper while the righteous suffer? Why do the faithful endure hardships when the faithless live in peace?" {1:2} And the Lord answered him, "The prosperity of the wicked is but a fleeting shadow; their end is certain. {1:3} As for the righteous, I am refining them as gold in the furnace, that they may be pure and worthy of the eternal kingdom."

{2:1} Then Ezra asked, "What will be the fate of the soul after it departs from this world?" {2:2} And the Lord said, "The soul of the righteous will be received into paradise, a place of light and rest, where no sorrow exists. {2:3} But the soul of the wicked will go to a place of darkness and torment, where they will await the final judgment."

{3:1} Ezra said, "O Lord, when will the end come? What signs will reveal your judgment upon the earth?" {3:2} The Lord replied, "There will be signs in the heavens and great distress upon the earth. {3:3} Many will turn from righteousness, and wickedness will abound, but those who endure in faith will be saved."

The Revelation of Esdras

{1:1} It was the thirtieth year, on the twenty-second day of the month, while I was at home, that I cried out to the Most High, saying, "Lord, grant me the glory so I may witness Your mysteries." {1:2} That night, an angel, Michael the archangel, appeared and said, "Prophet Esdras, abstain from bread for seventy weeks." {1:3} I obeyed and fasted as he directed, and then Raphael, the commander of the heavenly host, came to me, giving me a rod of storax. {1:4} I fasted for two periods of sixty weeks each, and I saw the mysteries of God and His angels. {1:5} I said to them, "I desire to speak before God about humanity. It would be better for a man not to be born than to come into this world." {1:6} Then I was taken up into heaven, where I saw a vast assembly of angels. They led me to witness the judgments, and I heard a voice saying, "Have mercy on us, Esdras, chosen of God." {1:7} I said, "Woe to sinners when they see a righteous one greater than angels, while they themselves are condemned to the Gehenna of fire." {1:8} And I pleaded, saying, "Have mercy, Lord, on the works of Your hands, for You are compassionate and full of mercy." {1:9} But God replied, "I will give the righteous rest in paradise, and I have shown mercy." {1:10} Then I said, "Lord, why show favor only to the righteous? For just as a hired worker receives their wages, so do they receive their reward in heaven. But please, show mercy to sinners, for we know You are merciful." {1:11} God responded, "I cannot find a way to be merciful to them." {1:12} And I replied, "They cannot endure Your wrath." But God said, "Such is their fate." {1:13} God then said, "Esdras, I wish you to be like Paul and John, as you have kept the gift of purity, a treasure that cannot be stolen, a stronghold for mankind." {1:14} I said, "It would be better for a man not to be born. Life is so full of suffering." {1:15} And I continued, "The irrational creatures are better off than man, for they have no punishment. But you have judged us." {1:16} Woe to sinners in the world to come, for their punishment is endless, and the flames are unquenchable."

{2:1} While I spoke, Michael, Gabriel, and all the apostles appeared, saying, "Rejoice, O man of God!" {2:2} And I said, "Lord, come to judgment with me." {2:3} The Lord replied, "Here is my covenant with you; take it." {2:4} I said, "Let us plead in Your presence." {2:5} God answered, "Ask Abraham, your father, how a son pleads with his father." {2:6} I swore, "As long as I live, I will not stop pleading with You for humanity." {2:7} God then said, "I have created both the righteous and the sinner, and the sinner should have lived as the righteous." {2:8} I replied, "Who made Adam?" And God answered, "My undefiled hands. I placed him in paradise to care for the tree of life, but he became disobedient." {2:9} I asked, "Was he not protected by angels? And how was he deceived if he was guarded?" {2:10} God said, "Adam's disobedience was his choice." {2:11} I persisted, "Lord, if You had not given him Eve, the serpent would not have deceived her. You save whom You will, and You destroy whom You will." {2:12} God replied, "I poured fire on Sodom and Gomorrah." {2:13} And I said, "Lord, deal with us justly, remembering Your mercy."

{3:1} God spoke, "Your sins surpass My mercy." {3:2} I said, "Lord, remember the Scriptures and Your covenant with Jerusalem. Have mercy on sinners, for they are Your creation." {3:3} Then God remembered humanity and said, "How can I have mercy on them? They offered Me vinegar and gall and did not repent." {3:4} I said, "Reveal the cherubim and show me the day of judgment." {3:5} God said, "You are mistaken, Esdras. The day of judgment is like a day without rain. It is a day of mercy compared to that final day." {3:6} I responded, "I will not stop pleading until I see the end." {3:7} God said, "Count the stars and the sand of the sea; if you can, then you may plead with Me." {3:8} I replied, "Lord, I am only human; how can I count these?" {3:9} God assured me, "No one knows the great day of judgment, but for your sake, I have revealed the day, though not the hour." {3:10} I asked for the years, and

God replied, "If I see righteousness increase, I will be patient, but otherwise, I will gather all into the valley of Jehoshaphat and end the world." {3:11} I asked, "Then how will Your glory be shown?" God answered, "Through My angels."

{4:1} I pleaded, "Why did You create man if You plan to end him? You promised Abraham to multiply his descendants like the stars and sand." {4:2} God replied, "When you see brother turn against brother, nations at war, and families divided, then you will know the end is near. {4:3} At that time, the adversary from Tartarus will show himself to men." {4:4} I said, "Lord, I will not cease to plead." And God challenged me, "Count the flowers of the earth, and if you can, you may plead." {4:5} I answered, "Lord, I cannot, but I will not stop pleading with You."

{5:1} I asked to see the depths of Tartarus, and God permitted it, sending Michael, Gabriel, and thirty-four other angels to guide me. {5:2} We descended eighty-five steps and saw a fiery throne with an old man seated upon it, whose judgment was harsh. {5:3} I asked the angels, "Who is this?" They answered, "This is Herod, who ordered the death of the children." {5:4} I went further and saw sinners consumed in fire and men punished in ways fitting their sins.

{6:1} Further down, I saw a man bound and asked, "Who is this?" They replied, "This is the one who claimed to be the Son of God, who turned stones to bread and water to wine." {6:2} I asked for his description, and they said, "His face is like a wild beast's, his eye is bright like a star, his mouth is wide, and he has the mark 'Antichrist.' He will ascend to heaven but be cast down to Hades."

{7:1} I asked, "Lord, why allow him to deceive humanity?" And God said, "When the trumpet sounds, the dead shall rise, and the earth will be destroyed." {7:2} I pleaded again for humanity. {7:3} And God said, "Esdras, count the stars, the sands, and the flowers if you wish to plead with Me." {7:4} But I persisted, "Lord, I cannot, yet I will not stop pleading." {7:5} Then God called His Son and angels, saying, "Bring Esdras's soul to Me." {7:6} The angels attempted to take my soul, but I resisted, having been with God, Moses, and Elijah. {7:7} Finally, the Lord Himself said, "Esdras, receive your crown; come and rest." {7:8} As I gave up my spirit, I prayed, "Lord, bless those who remember my words and honor my memory." {7:9} And God granted that all who transcribe this vision would receive His blessing. I died on the twenty-eighth day of October, surrounded by psalms and incense. My body became a source of strength to those who sought it, and glory and worship be unto the Father, Son, and Holy Spirit, forever and ever. Amen.

The Book of John the Evangelist

{1:1} I, John, your brother, share in suffering with you & anticipate sharing in the heavenly kingdom. {1:2} I recall laying on the chest of our Lord Jesus Christ, asking, "Lord, who will betray you?" {1:3} He replied, "The one who dips his hand with me in the dish." {1:4} Then Satan entered him, and he began plotting my betrayal. {1:5} I asked the Lord, "What was Satan's glory before his fall?" {1:6} And Jesus said, "Satan had such splendor that he commanded the powers of heaven; but I was with my Father, and he governed all those who followed Him. {1:7} Satan descended to the depths & then ascended back to the throne of the invisible Father. {1:8} He saw the glory of the One who moves the heavens and desired to place his throne above the clouds to be like the Most High."

{2:1} When he descended, he told the angel of the air, "Open the gates of the air for me." {2:2} The angel obeyed. {2:3} Satan moved lower, encountering the angel over the waters, and asked him to open the gates of the waters. {2:4} Upon passing through, he saw the earth covered in water, and below that, two fish like yoked oxen plowing and holding the earth from west to east by the command of the invisible Father. {2:5} Descending further, he found clouds suspending the waters of the sea. {2:6} Further down, he found hell, the inferno of flames, beyond which he could not go. {2:7} He retraced his steps, and as he passed by, he claimed everything he saw as his own, saying, "If you listen to me, I will place my throne above the clouds and take all water from the firmament, so there will be no water upon the earth, and I will rule without end."

{3:1} Then he went to the angels up to the fifth heaven, asking each one, "How much do you owe your Lord?" {3:2} One said, "One hundred measures of wheat." Satan replied, "Take your pen, and write down sixty." {3:3} Another angel owed one hundred jars of oil, and he told him to write fifty. {3:4} This he did to seduce the angels of the invisible Father as he ascended through each heaven. {3:5} Then a voice from the Father's throne cried, "What are you doing, deceiver, seducing the angels? Doer of evil, complete your plan quickly."

{4:1} The Father commanded His angels to strip the deceived angels of their garments, thrones, and crowns. {4:2} I then asked the Lord, "Where did Satan dwell after his fall?" {4:3} He replied, "The Father changed Satan's appearance because of his pride; he lost his light and looked like heated iron, his face wholly human. {4:4} Satan drew a third of the angels down with him, cast from God's throne and the heavens. {4:5} He came to the firmament and found no rest for himself or his followers. {4:6} Satan then asked the Father for patience, saying he would repay Him. The Father showed mercy, giving them seven days of rest."

{5:1} In that time, Satan sat in the firmament, commanding the angel over the air and the angel over the waters to lift the earth, which became dry. {5:2} He took the crown from the angel of the waters, creating the moon's light from half and the stars' light from the other. {5:3} The rest he turned into hosts of stars and made angels to minister according to the Father's command, creating thunder, rain, hail, and snow. {5:4} He commanded the earth to produce animals, birds, trees, and herbs, and the sea to bring forth fish and fowl.

{6:1} Next, he crafted humans in his image, commanding an angel of the third heaven to enter a clay body and made a second body in the form of a woman, into which he placed an angel of the second heaven. {6:2} The angels mourned, disliking their mortal form. {6:3} He commanded them to procreate in these clay bodies, though they did not understand sin.

{7:1} The evil one then created paradise, placing the man and woman there. {7:2} He ordered a reed be brought and planted it in paradise, concealing his deceit. {7:3} Entering paradise, he told them, "Eat of any fruit here, but not from the tree of knowledge of good and evil." {7:4} But the devil entered a serpent and seduced the angel in the woman's form, leading Eve astray, thus the "sons of the devil" and "sons of the serpent" are born of his lust. {7:5} The devil then poured his lust into the angel in Adam, causing sin's progeny to continue until the world's end.

{8:1} I then asked, "Why do people say Adam and Eve were created by God and placed in paradise?" {8:2} The Lord replied, "Foolish men claim my Father made bodies of clay, but by the Holy Spirit, He created the powers of heaven. Because of their sin, they were given to death."

{9:1} I further asked, "How does a spirit come to live in a body?" {9:2} Jesus answered, "Some fallen angels enter women's bodies and take flesh through lust. Thus, spirit begets spirit, and flesh begets flesh, achieving Satan's kingdom."

{10:1} Then he said, "The Father permits Satan to reign for seven ages." {10:2} I asked what would happen then. Jesus explained, "Since the devil's fall, he deceived people from Adam to Enoch, his servant. {10:3} He showed Enoch his power and had him write sixty-seven books, which he passed to his sons, teaching them sacrificial practices and concealing the kingdom of heaven."

{11:1} When Satan saw I descended from heaven, he sent an angel who gave Moses wood for my crucifixion, but reserved it for me. {11:2} Satan proclaimed his godhead to Moses, leading Israel and parting the sea."

{12:1} The Father sent an angel named Mary to prepare for my coming, and I entered her ear and exited the same way. {12:2} When Satan saw I came to save the lost, he sent Helias, known as John the Baptist, to baptize. {12:3} I, John, asked if anyone could be saved by John's baptism alone. The Lord replied, "Without my baptism of forgiveness, none can enter heaven."

{13:1} I asked about the meaning of eating His flesh and drinking His blood, and Jesus said, "Before the devil's fall, all glorified the Father by saying 'Our Father in heaven.' {13:2} But once fallen, they could not pray this way."

{14:1} I asked why people only receive John's baptism. The Lord explained, "Their deeds are evil, so they avoid the light."

{15:1} John's disciples marry, but my disciples do not, being like angels. I remarked, "If marriage is a sin, it is not good to marry." Jesus responded, "Not all can accept this."

{16:1} I asked about the day of judgment, and He answered, "When the number of the righteous is complete, Satan will be released with fury to war against them. The righteous will cry, and an angel will sound the trumpet, summoning the archangel's voice from heaven to hell."

{17:1} The sun will darken, the moon will not shine, stars will fall, and the four winds will shake the earth, sea, and mountains. {17:2} Then the Son of Man will appear, seated in glory, with the twelve apostles judging. {17:3} The books will open, judging all for their faith. {17:4} The Son of Man will send angels to gather the elect."

{18:1} He will then address the ungodly, "Come, those who gained in this world." The sinners will stand before His throne, and their ungodliness will be evident. {18:2} The righteous will be rewarded with glory, and the sinners will face indignation."

{19:1} The Son will gather His elect, saying, "Come, inherit the kingdom." The sinners will be cast into eternal fire prepared for the devil and his angels. {19:2} The righteous will shine in the Father's kingdom, receiving incorruptible garments and unfading crowns. {19:3} God will wipe away every tear, and He will reign forever.

The Teaching of the Twelve Apostles

{1:1} There are two paths in life, one that leads to life and one that leads to death, and the difference between them is vast. {1:2} The way of life is this: First, love God, who created you; second, love your neighbor as yourself, and do not do to others what you would not want done to you. {1:3} The teaching on this is as follows: Bless those who curse you, pray for your enemies, and fast for those who persecute you. {1:4} For what benefit is there in loving only those who love you? Even non-believers do that. {1:5} Instead, love those who hate you, and you will have no enemy. {1:6} Refrain from bodily and worldly desires. {1:7} If someone strikes you on your right cheek, offer them the other one as well, and you will be perfect. {1:8} If someone forces you to go one mile, go with them two. {1:9} If someone takes your cloak, give them your coat as well. {1:10} If someone takes something that is yours, do not demand it back, for you are not able to do so. {1:11} Give to everyone who asks, and do not ask for anything back; for it is the Father's will that blessings should be freely given to all. {1:12} Blessed is the one who gives according to the commandment, for they are innocent. {1:13} But woe to those who receive without need, for they will face consequences, having to account for why they took what was not needed. {1:14} When placed in confinement, they will be questioned about their actions, and they will not be released until they have repaid even the last penny. {1:15} Also, concerning charity, it has been said: Let your alms sweat in your hands until you know to whom you should give.

{2:1} The second commandment is this: Do not commit murder, do not commit adultery, do not engage in sexual immorality, do not steal, do not practice magic, do not practice witchcraft, do not murder a child by abortion or kill what has been born. {2:2} Do not covet your neighbor's possessions, do not swear falsely, do not bear false witness, do not speak evil, and do not hold grudges. {2:3} Do not be double-minded or double-tongued, for being double-tongued is a path to death. {2:4} Let your words be true and meaningful, supported by your actions. {2:5} Do not be greedy, or deceitful, or hypocritical, or evil-minded, or arrogant. {2:6} Do not take counsel against your neighbor with ill intentions. {2:7} Do not hate anyone; rather, correct some, pray for others, and love still others even more than your own life.

{3:1} My child, flee from all evil and everything that resembles it. {3:2} Do not be prone to anger, for anger leads to murder. {3:3} Do not be jealous, argumentative, or hot-tempered, for these traits lead to murder as well. {3:4} My child, do not be lustful, for lust leads to sexual immorality. {3:5} Avoid vulgar language and do not be arrogant, for these lead to adultery. {3:6} My child, do not seek omens, for they lead to idolatry. {3:7} Do not engage in enchantments, astrology, or purification rituals, for these lead to idolatry. {3:8} My child, do not lie, for lies lead to theft. {3:9} Do not be greedy or vain, for these lead to theft. {3:10} My child, do not complain, for it leads to blasphemy. {3:11} Do not be self-centered or evil-minded, for these lead to blasphemy. {3:12} Rather, be meek, for the meek shall inherit the earth. {3:13} Be patient, compassionate, simple, gentle, kind, and respectful of the words you have heard. {3:14} Do not exalt yourself, and do not give in to overconfidence. {3:15} Do not associate with the proud, but rather with the righteous and the humble. {3:16} Accept everything that happens to you as good, understanding that nothing happens apart from God.

{4:1} My child, remember night and day the one who speaks the word of God to you, and honor them as you do the Lord. {4:2} For where the Lord's teachings are proclaimed, there is the presence of the Lord. {4:3} Seek the company of holy people each day so that you may rest in their wisdom. {4:4} Do not desire division but seek to reconcile those who disagree. {4:5} Judge fairly, and do not show favoritism when correcting others. {4:6} Do not be uncertain about whether or not something should be done. {4:7} Do not be quick to receive but slow to give. {4:8} If you have something, offer it as a means of freeing yourself from sin. {4:9} Give freely and do not grumble when you give, knowing that the Lord repays all generosity. {4:10} Do not turn away from those in need, but share all things with your brothers and sisters. {4:11} For if you share in what is eternal, how much more should you share in what is temporary? {4:12} Do not withhold discipline from your children but teach them to respect God from their youth. {4:13} Do not place undue demands on those who serve you, but treat them with respect, for you share the same hope in God. {4:14} And those who serve should honor their masters as a reflection of God, showing humility and respect. {4:15} Hate all hypocrisy and everything displeasing to the Lord. {4:16} Do not abandon God's commandments but keep them faithfully without adding to or taking away from them. {4:17} Confess your sins in the church and do not approach prayer with a guilty conscience. This is the way of life.

{5:1} The way of death, however, is this: It is entirely evil and full of curses. It includes murders, adultery, lust, fornication, theft, idolatry, magical practices, witchcraft, rape, false witness, hypocrisy, double-heartedness, deceit, pride, depravity, self-will, greed, vile speech, jealousy, excessive confidence, arrogance, and boastfulness. {5:2} Those who persecute good people, hate truth, love lies, ignore the rewards of righteousness, do not cling to good or to just judgments, and pursue evil are far from meekness and patience. {5:3} They love vanity, seek revenge, do not pity the poor, and refuse to help the afflicted. {5:4} They do not acknowledge their Creator, murder children, destroy God's creations, turn away from those in need, oppress the distressed, show favoritism to the rich, and unjustly judge the poor. They are utterly sinful. {5:5} Avoid all these things, children.

{6:1} Be careful that no one leads you astray from this way of teaching, for it is from God. {6:2} If you are able to bear the full burden of the Lord's yoke, you will be perfect; if not, do what you can. {6:3} Regarding food, bear what you can, but be very cautious about food sacrificed to idols, for it is associated with the worship of dead gods.

{7:1} Concerning baptism, baptize in this way: After teaching these things, baptize in the name of the Father, the Son, and the Holy Spirit, using living water if possible. {7:2} If there is no living water, use other water; if cold water is unavailable, use warm water. {7:3} If none of these is available, pour water three times on the head in the name of the Father, Son, and Holy Spirit. {7:4} Before baptism, let the one baptizing and the one being baptized fast, as well as any others who can. {7:5} Instruct the one being baptized to fast for one or two days beforehand.

{8:1} Concerning fasting and prayer, do not fast as the hypocrites do, for they fast on the second and fifth days of the week. {8:2} Instead, fast on the fourth day and on Friday. {8:3} Do not pray as the hypocrites do, but as the Lord taught in His gospel, saying, {8:4} "Our Father in heaven, hallowed be Your name. Your kingdom come. Your will be done on earth as it is in heaven. Give us today our daily bread, {8:5} and forgive us our debts as we forgive our debtors. {8:6} And lead us not into temptation, but deliver us from the evil one, for Yours is the power and the glory forever." {8:7} Pray this three times a day.

{9:1} Concerning the Eucharist, give thanks in this way. First, over the cup say, {9:2} "We thank You, our Father, for the holy vine of David Your servant, made known to us through Jesus Your Servant; to You be the glory forever." {9:3} Over the broken bread say, {9:4} "We thank You, our Father, for the life and knowledge made known to us through Jesus Your Servant; to You be the glory forever. {9:5} Just as this bread, once scattered over the hills, was gathered to become one, may Your Church be gathered from the ends of the earth into Your kingdom; for Yours is the glory and power forever through Jesus Christ." {9:6} But let no one eat or drink of your Eucharist unless they are baptized in the name of the Lord, for the Lord has said, "Do not give what is holy to the dogs."

{10:1} After the meal, give thanks in this way: {10:2} "We thank You, holy Father, for Your holy name which dwells in our hearts, and for the knowledge, faith, and immortality made known to us through Jesus Your Servant; to You be the glory forever. {10:3} Almighty Master, You created all things for Your name's sake. You gave food and drink to humanity for their enjoyment, that they might give thanks to You, but You have given us spiritual food and drink and eternal life through Your Servant. {10:4} Above all, we thank You for Your might; to You be the glory forever. {10:5} Remember, Lord, Your Church, protect it from all evil, and perfect it in Your love. Gather it from the four winds, made holy for Your kingdom, which You have prepared for it; for Yours is the power and the glory forever. {10:6} May grace come, and may this world pass away. Hosanna to the God of David! If anyone is holy, let them come; if anyone is not, let them repent. Maranatha. Amen." {10:7} However, allow the prophets to offer thanksgiving as much as they desire.

{11:1} Anyone who comes and teaches you all these previously mentioned things should be welcomed. {11:2} However, if the teacher turns and begins to teach doctrines that undermine this teaching, do not listen to him. {11:3} But if his teaching enhances righteousness and the knowledge of the Lord, accept him as if he were the Lord Himself. {11:4} As for apostles and prophets, treat them according to the guidelines given in the Gospel. {11:5} Every apostle who comes to you should be received as if he were the Lord. {11:6} However, he should not stay more than one day, or two if absolutely necessary. {11:7} If he stays three days, he is a false prophet. {11:8} When the apostle departs, let him take nothing except some bread until he finds a place to stay. {11:9} If he asks for money, he is a false prophet. {11:10} Any prophet who speaks under divine inspiration should not be tested or judged, for all sins will be forgiven, except for this one. {11:11} However, not everyone who speaks in the Spirit is a prophet; only those who follow the ways of the Lord are true prophets. {11:12} By their actions, you will know the difference between a true prophet and a false one. {11:13} Any prophet who orders a meal in the Spirit and then eats it himself is a false prophet. {11:14} Any prophet who teaches the truth but does not practice what he teaches is a false prophet. {11:15} A true prophet, who is proven and works for the mystery of the Church in the world without teaching others to follow his actions, should not be judged by you, for he is accountable to God alone, just as the prophets of old were. {11:16} But if someone, claiming to speak in the Spirit, asks for money or other material things for himself, do not listen to him. {11:17} However, if he requests assistance for others in need, do not judge him.

{12:1} Welcome anyone who comes in the name of the Lord, but test and get to know him afterward, for you should have discernment. {12:2} If he is just passing through, help him as much as you can, but he should not stay more than two or three days, if necessary. {12:3} If he wishes to settle with you and has a trade, let him work and earn his food. {12:4} But if he has no trade, use your discernment to ensure he does not live idly among you, as a Christian should not live without working. {12:5} If he refuses to work, he is exploiting Christ's name. Be cautious and avoid such people.

{13:1} Every true prophet who desires to live among you deserves your support. {13:2} Likewise, a true teacher deserves to be supported, for "the worker is worthy of his wages." {13:3} Therefore, give the first portion of your produce from the vineyard, the threshing floor, the livestock, and the flock to the prophets, for they are like high priests to you. {13:4} If you have no prophet, then give these first portions to the poor. {13:5} If you bake bread, give the first portion according to the commandment. {13:6} Similarly, when you open a jar of wine or oil, give the first part to the prophets. {13:7} Also, for money, clothes, and all your possessions, give a first portion as seems good to you, following the commandment.

{14:1} Every Sunday, gather together to break bread and give thanks after confessing your sins so that your offering may be pure. {14:2} But let no one who has a grudge against another join you until they have reconciled, so that your sacrifice is not defiled.

{14:3} For this is what the Lord has spoken: "In every place and time offer me a pure sacrifice, for I am a great King," says the Lord, "and my name is revered among the nations."

{15:1} Therefore, appoint for yourselves bishops and deacons who are worthy of the Lord—humble, not greedy, truthful, and proven—since they also serve you in the ministry of prophets and teachers. {15:2} Do not look down on them, for they are honored among you along with the prophets and teachers. {15:3} Correct one another, but not in anger; do so peacefully, as instructed in the Gospel. {15:4} If anyone wrongs another, do not speak to them or let them hear anything from you until they repent. {15:5} Carry out your prayers, charitable acts, and all your deeds according to the Gospel of our Lord.

{16:1} Be vigilant for the sake of your soul. Do not let your lamps go out, or your readiness diminish, but be prepared, for you do not know when our Lord will come. {16:2} Meet often, seeking what will benefit your souls, for your entire time of faith will not benefit you if you are not perfected at the end. {16:3} In the last days, false prophets and corrupters will multiply, and the sheep will turn into wolves, and love will become hatred. {16:4} As lawlessness increases, people will hate, persecute, and betray each other, and then the deceiver of the world will appear, claiming to be the Son of God and performing signs and wonders. {16:5} The earth will be handed over to him, and he will do unlawful things that have never been done before. {16:6} Then all people will face a great trial, and many will stumble and perish, but those who endure in their faith will be saved from the curse. {16:7} Then the signs of truth will appear: first, a sign of an open sky; then, the sound of a trumpet. {16:8} And finally, there will be the resurrection of the dead—not of all, but as it is written: "The Lord will come with all His holy ones." {16:9} Then the whole world will see the Lord coming on the clouds of heaven.

The Avenging of the Saviour

{1:1} During the reign of Emperor Tiberius Caesar, when Herod was tetrarch, Christ was handed over by the Jews to Pontius Pilate and revealed by Tiberius. {1:2} At this time, Titus was a prince under Tiberius, living in the region of Equitania in the Libyan city of Burgidalla. {1:3} Titus suffered from a cancerous sore in his right nostril that spread to his eye. {1:4} A man named Nathan, the son of Nahum and an Ishmaelite from Judaea, traveled across the lands and seas. {1:5} Nathan had been sent from Judaea to bring a treaty to Emperor Tiberius in Rome, who was afflicted with various diseases, including nine types of leprosy. {1:6} Nathan wanted to sail to Rome, but a strong north wind redirected his ship to a Libyan harbor. {1:7} When Titus saw the vessel, he knew it was from Judaea, as he had never seen a ship from that direction before. {1:8} Titus summoned the captain and asked his identity. Nathan replied, "I am Nathan, son of Nahum, an Ishmaelite from Judaea under Pontius Pilate's authority. I was sent to deliver a treaty to Emperor Tiberius, but a fierce wind redirected me to this unknown land."

{2:1} Titus then asked, "If you know of any remedies or herbs that could heal my face, I would reward you with great riches." {2:2} Nathan replied, "I know of no such cure. But if you had been in Jerusalem recently, you might have met a prophet named Emanuel, who came to save His people from their sins. {2:3} His first miracle was turning water into wine at Cana in Galilee. By His word, He healed lepers, restored sight to the blind, cured the paralyzed, cast out demons, raised the dead, freed an adulterous woman condemned by the Jews, and healed a woman named Veronica of her twelve-year illness when she touched the hem of His garment. {2:4} With five loaves and two fish, He fed five thousand men, not counting women and children, and still had twelve baskets of leftovers. {2:5} He performed many miracles before His crucifixion, and after His resurrection, we saw Him alive just as He had been before."

{3:1} Titus asked, "How could He rise from the dead if He was truly dead?" Nathan replied, "He was indeed dead, crucified, and laid in a tomb for three days. {3:2} Afterward, He rose, descended to Hades, freed the patriarchs, prophets, and humanity, appeared to His disciples, ate with them, and they saw Him ascend to heaven. All this I tell you is true; I saw it with my own eyes, as did all of Israel." {3:3} Titus then exclaimed, "Woe to you, Emperor Tiberius, who is diseased and leprous! {3:4} You allowed such a crime in your empire: they seized the King of the people and killed Him instead of letting Him heal you of leprosy and me of my illness. {3:5} If those responsible were here, I would slay them with my own hands for depriving me of my Lord and His healing."

{4:1} At that moment, Titus's sore fell from his face, and his flesh was completely restored. {4:2} All the sick around him were also healed. {4:3} Titus, overjoyed, cried out, "My King and my God, though I have not seen you, you healed me! {4:4} Guide me over the waters to the land of Your birth to avenge Your enemies. {4:5} Help me, Lord, so I may destroy them for Your sake." Then Titus ordered his baptism and asked Nathan, "How do you baptize believers in Christ?" {4:6} Nathan baptized him in the name of the Father, the Son, and the Holy Spirit, and Titus declared his faith, pledging his loyalty to Christ, who created and healed him.

{5:1} Titus then sent for Vespasian, commanding him to bring his strongest men to prepare for battle. {5:2} Vespasian arrived with five thousand armed soldiers, and upon meeting Titus, asked why he was summoned. {5:3} Titus replied, "Jesus was born in Judaea, in Bethlehem. The Jews betrayed, scourged, and crucified Him on Mount Calvary. {5:4} But He rose on the third day and appeared to His disciples. We now wish to be His followers. {5:5} Let us go and destroy His enemies so they will know there is no god like our Lord." {5:6} With this purpose, they left Burgidalla by ship, traveled to Jerusalem, and began their attack.

{6:1} When the Jewish leaders saw their land under siege, they panicked. Archelaus, one of their leaders, told his son, "Take my kingdom, consult the other kings of Judah, and find a way to escape our enemies." {6:2} Saying this, he took his sword, stabbed himself, and died. {6:3} His son joined the other kings, and they gathered in Jerusalem for seven years, while Titus and Vespasian encircled the city. {6:4} After seven years, a terrible famine struck, and the people began eating earth to survive.

{7:1} Soldiers of the four kings, seeing no way out, resolved to die by their own hands instead of the Romans'. Twelve thousand killed themselves, causing a great stench in the city. {7:2} The remaining leaders, overwhelmed by fear and the odor, decided to surrender. {7:3} They climbed the city walls and cried, "Titus & Vespasian, take the keys of city given to you by the Messiah, Christ."

{8:1} They surrendered, saying, "Judge us, for we condemned Christ unjustly." {8:2} Titus and Vespasian executed many by stoning, crucifixion, and sold others as slaves, dividing the spoils as the Jews had divided Christ's garments. {8:3} They sold thirty Jews for each silver piece, mirroring the betrayal price of Christ. {8:4} Seizing all of Judaea, they searched for an image of Jesus and found it with a woman named Veronica.

{9:1} They imprisoned Pilate, guarded by soldiers, and sent a message to Emperor Tiberius in Rome, instructing Velosianus to bring a disciple of Christ to heal Tiberius of leprosy. {9:2} Tiberius promised Velosianus half his kingdom if he succeeded in finding a healer.

{10:1} Velosianus sailed for a year and seven days before reaching Jerusalem, where he met Joseph of Arimathea and Nicodemus, who testified about Jesus. {10:2} Veronica also told of how Jesus healed her by allowing her to touch His garment's hem. {10:3} Velosianus rebuked Pilate, accusing him of cruelty for killing God's Son, and imprisoned him. {10:4} He then searched for the image of Jesus and found it with Veronica, who had it wrapped in linen.

{11:1} When Velosianus saw the image, he knelt, wrapped it in gold cloth, sealed it, and swore no one would see it until he returned to Tiberius. {11:2} Veronica, devoted to Christ, followed Velosianus back to Rome. {11:3} Upon arriving, Tiberius summoned Velosianus, who recounted the miracles and actions of Christ.

{12:1} Velosianus told Tiberius about Titus and Vespasian's vengeance on the Jews, including the stoning of Annas and Caiaphas, and Pilate's imprisonment. {12:2} He described Christ's miracles, death, and resurrection. {12:3} Tiberius then ordered Velosianus to present the image of Christ. {12:4} As he adored the image, Tiberius was healed, and all the sick around him were cured.

{13:1} Tiberius, overwhelmed, prayed, "God of heaven and earth, guide me to Thy kingdom and free me from sin." {13:2} Tiberius asked Velosianus if anyone who had seen Christ could baptize him, and Velosianus summoned Nathan, who baptized Tiberius. {13:3} With tears, Tiberius praised God, pledging his faith and thanking Him for cleansing him of sin.

{14:1} Tiberius committed to the Christian faith, and we ask God Almighty, King of Kings, to protect and deliver us, bringing us to eternal life when this temporary life ends. {14:2} May He be praised forever and ever. Amen.

The Ethiopic Creed

{1:1} We believe in one God, the Father Almighty, Maker of heaven and earth, and of all things visible and invisible. {1:2} We believe in one Lord, Jesus Christ, the only-begotten Son of the Father, who was begotten before all ages, Light from Light, true God from true God, begotten, not made, of one essence with the Father; through Him all things were made. {1:3} For us, and for our salvation, He came down from heaven, was incarnate by the Holy Spirit and of the Virgin Mary, and became man. {1:4} He was crucified for us under Pontius Pilate, suffered, and was buried; on the third day, He rose from the dead, according to the Scriptures. {1:5} He ascended into heaven and sits at the right hand of the Father. {1:6} He will come again with glory to judge the living and the dead, whose kingdom shall have no end. {1:7} We believe in the Holy Spirit, the Lord, the Giver of Life, who proceeds from the Father, who with the Father and the Son together is worshiped and glorified, who spoke by the prophets. {1:8} We believe in one holy, catholic, and apostolic Church. We acknowledge one baptism for the remission of sins. {1:9} We look for the resurrection of the dead and the life of the world to come. Amen.

{2:1} We believe also in the mystery of the Incarnation of Jesus Christ, that He took flesh from the Holy Virgin Mary and made it one with His divinity, without confusion, change, division, or separation. {2:2} He is one Person in two natures, fully divine and fully human, united in one indivisible union. {2:3} He was truly born, He truly suffered, and truly died, and on the third day, He truly rose from the dead, ascended into heaven, and is seated at the right hand of the Father. {2:4} We believe in His second coming with glory, to judge the living and the dead, at which time the righteous will receive eternal life, and the wicked will be condemned to eternal fire.

{3:1} We honor the Holy Virgin Mary as the Theotokos, the Mother of God, and we believe that she remained a virgin before, during, and after the birth of Christ. {3:2} We also venerate the saints and angels who intercede before God on our behalf. {3:3} We believe in the existence of holy angels, who are ministers of God's will, and who worship and serve Him eternally.

{4:1} We believe in the seven sacraments of the Church: Baptism, Confirmation, Eucharist, Penance, Anointing of the Sick, Holy Orders, and Matrimony. {4:2} We believe that through these sacraments, we receive God's grace, forgiveness, and sanctification. {4:3} We believe in the power of God's grace to transform and sanctify our lives, making us partakers of the divine nature.

{5:1} We believe that Christ is the Head of the Church, and that the Church is His Body, united in one faith, one baptism, and one hope. {5:2} We affirm that the Church is holy and apostolic, built upon the foundation of the apostles and prophets, with Christ Himself as the cornerstone. {5:3} We believe in the unity of the Church, that all believers are called to be one in Christ, with love and mutual respect.

{6:1} We acknowledge one baptism for the remission of sins, and we believe in the necessity of baptism for salvation. {6:2} We believe in the forgiveness of sins through the sacrament of Penance, and that through repentance and confession, we are restored to communion with God.

{7:1} We look for the resurrection of the dead, believing that on the last day, all the dead shall rise. {7:2} We believe that the righteous will receive eternal life in the Kingdom of Heaven, where they will behold God's glory and live in communion with Him. {7:3} We believe that the wicked, those who reject God's love and persist in sin, will be condemned to eternal punishment, separated from God.

{8:1} We believe that God's kingdom shall have no end, that He is the eternal King, who will reign over all creation. {8:2} We affirm that Christ shall return in glory to establish His kingdom in its fullness, where justice, peace, and love will prevail forever. {8:3} We look forward to the life of the world to come, where all creation will be renewed, and God will dwell among His people in everlasting joy and harmony. Amen.

May the wisdom of these words
guide us, the love of God enfold us,
and His eternal light lead us home.

Important Questions

Ethiopian Christianity, particularly within the Ethiopian Orthodox Tewahedo Church, has a rich tradition that combines early Christian teachings with unique theological, liturgical, and cultural practices. Here are some essential questions central to Ethiopic Christianity that provide insight into its faith, practices, and distinct elements. These questions are valuable for anyone looking to understand this ancient Christian tradition.

What is the significance of the Tewahedo faith?
- *Tewahedo* means "unity" or "being made one" and refers to the Ethiopian Orthodox belief in the single, united nature of Christ. This doctrine, rooted in early Christian theology, teaches that Jesus Christ has one united nature (fully divine and fully human) rather than two separate natures, as in some other Christian traditions. This belief is central to Ethiopian Orthodox Christianity and sets it apart from other Christian doctrines.

What are the primary texts and sources of scripture in Ethiopian Christianity?
- The Ethiopian Bible includes books not commonly found in Western Christian canons, such as the *Book of Enoch* and *Jubilees*, along with other unique apocryphal works. Understanding the Ethiopian Bible's contents and the unique role of certain texts helps one appreciate the theological and doctrinal basis of the faith.

What is the role of saints and angels in Ethiopian Orthodox practice?
- Saints, especially St. Mary (Maryam), are highly revered in Ethiopian Christianity. The veneration of saints, angels, and archangels is widespread, and they are considered intercessors between humanity and God. St. George, St. Michael, and the Archangel Gabriel hold special significance, with feast days and liturgical practices honoring them.

How are the liturgical practices and sacraments unique in Ethiopian Orthodoxy?
- Ethiopian Orthodox Christianity has a distinct liturgy, often conducted in Ge'ez, an ancient liturgical language. Key sacraments, such as the Eucharist, baptism, and matrimony, have unique rites and symbols. Understanding the structure and meaning of these sacraments, along with the liturgical calendar, offers insight into the spiritual life of the church.

What is the role of fasting and ascetic practices in Ethiopian Christianity?
- Fasting is a significant component of Ethiopian Orthodox practice, with over 180 days of fasting observed annually, including the famous Great Lent and weekly fasts on Wednesdays and Fridays. These practices are seen as a means of spiritual discipline, self-purification, and solidarity with the suffering.

What is the historical significance of the Ark of the Covenant in Ethiopian Christianity?
- Ethiopian tradition holds that the Ark of the Covenant resides in the Church of St. Mary of Zion in Axum. This belief is deeply rooted in Ethiopian religious identity and history, with the Ark symbolizing God's covenant and presence with the Ethiopian people. The Ark's significance influences church architecture, religious festivals, and art.

How does Ethiopian Orthodox Christianity view the Virgin Mary?
- Mary holds a central place in Ethiopian faith, often revered as the "Mother of God." Many feasts, prayers, and hymns are dedicated to her, and she is believed to play a powerful intercessory role. The *Kidan Mehret* (Covenant of Mercy) is a notable doctrine that underscores her mercy and compassion toward humanity.

What are the major religious festivals in Ethiopian Christianity, and what do they signify?
- Major festivals include *Timkat* (Epiphany), celebrating the baptism of Jesus; *Meskel*, commemorating the discovery of the True Cross; and *Genna* (Christmas). These celebrations are deeply symbolic, involving traditional ceremonies, prayers, processions, and music. Each festival reflects key aspects of Christian theology and Ethiopian religious identity.

What is the Ethiopian Orthodox Church's perspective on salvation and the afterlife?
- Salvation is understood through faith in Christ, sacraments, good works, and living a virtuous life. The Ethiopian Orthodox view of the afterlife includes judgment, heaven, and hell, with an emphasis on the intercession of saints and the Virgin Mary. The church also emphasizes communal salvation, where the church community plays a role in each believer's journey.

What is the relationship between Ethiopian Christianity and Judaism?
- Ethiopian Christianity retains many Judaic customs, such as dietary laws and observances that align with Old Testament practices. This reflects the church's historical link with Judaism, as seen in traditions related to the Ark of the Covenant and practices like circumcision. The Ethiopian tradition believes it inherited a unique and direct connection to early Judaic traditions, blending them with Christian teachings.

How does Ethiopian Orthodox Christianity view the concept of sin and repentance?
- Sin is seen as a breach of God's commandments and affects not just the individual but the community. Confession and repentance, often practiced before a priest, are essential for spiritual healing. Ethiopic Christianity emphasizes personal responsibility for sin and the importance of penance, forgiveness, and reconciliation with God and others.

What are the roles of monasticism and spiritual leaders in Ethiopian Christianity?
- Monasticism has a profound influence in Ethiopian Orthodox Christianity, with monks and nuns seen as spiritual guides and protectors of the faith. Many monasteries are pilgrimage sites, and spiritual leaders, including *Abunas* (bishops) and monks, play crucial roles in community life, theological education, and preserving religious traditions.

How does the Ethiopian Orthodox Church view its relationship with other Christian denominations?
- Ethiopian Orthodoxy sees itself as part of the Oriental Orthodox family, sharing a unique Christological perspective with other Oriental Orthodox churches. It holds a distinctive history and heritage that sometimes separates it from other Christian groups, yet it also participates in ecumenical dialogues aimed at fostering unity.

What role do icons and religious art play in Ethiopian Orthodox worship?

- Ethiopian churches are decorated with colorful icons and murals depicting biblical scenes, saints, and angels. Icons are seen as windows to the divine, inviting believers into contemplation and prayer. The unique style of Ethiopian religious art serves both an educational and spiritual purpose, deepening the community's connection to the divine mysteries.

What is the significance of Ge'ez in Ethiopian Orthodox Christianity?
- Ge'ez is the liturgical language of the Ethiopian Orthodox Church, much like Latin in the Roman Catholic Church. Though no longer spoken as a daily language, it is used in liturgies, prayers, and sacred texts. The use of Ge'ez connects worshippers with their ancestors and preserves Ethiopia's religious heritage. Understanding why Ge'ez remains vital offers insight into Ethiopian Christianity's emphasis on tradition and continuity.

How does the Ethiopian Orthodox Church structure its hierarchy and governance?
- The Ethiopian Orthodox Tewahedo Church has a unique hierarchical structure led by the Patriarch, known as the *Abuna*, who oversees bishops, priests, and deacons. Each level has specific roles in administration, liturgy, and pastoral care. The governance system is designed to uphold both doctrinal integrity and the pastoral needs of local communities. Examining this hierarchy sheds light on the church's organization and the role of clergy in guiding spiritual life.

What is the role of hymns and music in Ethiopian Orthodox worship?
- Music is integral to Ethiopian Orthodox worship, with hymns and chants used to praise, pray, and teach. The *Zema* is a form of sacred chant, attributed to St. Yared, which accompanies the liturgy and spiritual rituals. The chanting follows distinct modes tied to the liturgical calendar and is traditionally accompanied by drums, sistrums, and prayer staffs. The melodies, rhythms, and instruments used in Ethiopian worship distinguish it from other Christian musical traditions and enhance the communal worship experience.

How does Ethiopian Christianity approach religious education and the transmission of faith?
- Religious education in Ethiopian Orthodoxy traditionally occurs in monasteries and churches, where children and new believers are taught by priests and monks. Instruction often includes learning Ge'ez, understanding scripture, and memorizing prayers, hymns, and psalms. The church uses both oral and written traditions to pass down its teachings, ensuring that religious knowledge is preserved and accessible to future generations.

What are the unique architectural features of Ethiopian Orthodox churches, and what do they symbolize?
- Ethiopian churches often have distinct architectural styles, including round or rectangular shapes, with three distinct sections representing the Holy Trinity: the outer courtyard, the Qeddest (sanctuary), and the Qeddus Qeddusan (Holy of Holies). The most famous churches, such as those at Lalibela, are carved from rock and symbolize a "New Jerusalem." These architectural features not only serve functional purposes but also represent theological concepts and historical narratives, making each church a space rich in symbolic meaning.

What is the importance of pilgrimage in Ethiopian Orthodox Christianity?
- Pilgrimage is a deeply ingrained practice in Ethiopian Christianity, with sites like Lalibela, Axum, and the monasteries of Lake Tana attracting believers who seek spiritual renewal, healing, or penance. Pilgrimages are often timed with major religious festivals and are considered acts of devotion that strengthen one's faith and community bonds. The journey is both a physical and spiritual undertaking, reinforcing humility, faith, and connection to the church's holy sites and history.

Understanding these questions and their answers provides a foundational view into the theology, practices, and rich heritage of Ethiopian Orthodox Christianity. This ancient Christian tradition offers a unique perspective on faith and spirituality, deeply rooted in both scripture and Ethiopian culture.

Legacy of the Journey

Hey Reader, Thank you for taking the time to explore The Ethiopian Bible of 180 Books: The Most Extensive and Largest Collection in the World. This work is more than a book; it is a profound collection of wisdom, faith, and history that we are privileged to share with you. Together, we are embarking on a journey to preserve and uncover texts that have inspired countless souls throughout the centuries. In this journey, we're not only honoring the voices of ancient authors but also drawing from their words to enrich our modern lives.

The Ethiopian Bible, with its remarkable 180 books, offers a rare glimpse into the early Christian and Judaic traditions, capturing texts that many of us may not have encountered before. While most biblical canons contain around 66 books, The Ethiopian Bible gives us more than twice as many. These include books that many traditions consider apocryphal or deuterocanonical, along with others that are rarely seen outside Ethiopian Christianity. This broader collection reveals a rich tapestry of teachings, stories, prophecies, and guidance that add depth and dimension to our understanding of God's word. By compiling and sharing this comprehensive collection, we are taking a step toward honoring the legacy of all who have sought to preserve these scriptures. From scribes who dedicated their lives to copying texts by hand to communities who held these books as sacred truths, their dedication resonates in every page. Our goal is to keep their legacy alive, offering a unique opportunity for readers like you to delve into the diverse voices that make up the tapestry of Christian and Judaic traditions.

But our journey doesn't end here. We are thrilled to announce that we are currently working on a project to compile the 250-Book Holy Bible, which will include an even more extensive array of apocryphal texts gathered from across the world. This work is a bold undertaking that seeks to compile all the wisdom, teachings, and insights that generations before us have cherished. Our dream is to create the largest, most comprehensive collection of holy scriptures ever assembled.

This journey of compiling 250 books is a tribute to humanity's unending thirst for divine wisdom. It's a journey that has taken us to ancient manuscripts, forgotten scrolls, and dusty libraries, and one that has led us to communities and scholars who have preserved these sacred writings for generations. Each book adds another layer of perspective, a new insight into the spiritual truths that have guided humanity across centuries and continents. By gathering these texts into one collection, we aim to create a resource that not only informs and educates but also inspires readers to embark on their own spiritual journeys. We invite you to be a part of this unfolding legacy. By subscribing to our newsletter, you'll stay informed about our progress and get early glimpses into the work we are doing to bring this 250-book collection to life. We believe that this journey is as much yours as it is ours. Your support, curiosity, and commitment to discovering God's word motivate us to continue this work with passion and dedication.

This effort is more than just compiling texts; it's a mission to inspire readers to seek out different perspectives and to engage with scriptures in a way that brings them closer to God. The Ethiopian Bible offers insights that many of us may not have encountered before, presenting voices and stories that deepen our understanding of faith. We believe that by exploring these texts, we can all gain a richer perspective on the divine and our relationship with the Almighty.

Imagine opening a page and finding words that resonate deeply with your own struggles, dreams, or questions. Imagine discovering a passage that brings new understanding to an old, familiar story, or encountering a prayer that perfectly captures your feelings of gratitude or sorrow. Each text has its own power, its own voice, and its own wisdom to share. By reading these books, we honor not only our own spiritual journey but also the journeys of those who have come before us.

Throughout history, people have sought to understand God and the nature of existence. This quest for knowledge and spiritual connection has produced countless writings—some well-known, others obscure—that have shaped and transformed the lives of millions. The Ethiopian Bible, with its wealth of texts, reminds us that God's word can be found in many forms, in many voices, and from many times and places. And now, as we strive to bring together the 250-Book Holy Bible, we are continuing this legacy, preserving these voices for future generations. This project reflects a belief that the divine cannot be contained within a single book or a single perspective. The Bible, in all its many forms and versions, offers us a window into the divine mysteries that people have sought to understand for thousands of years. By compiling this extensive collection, we are saying that every voice matters, every perspective has value, and every word has the potential to bring us closer to God.

As we continue to work on this 250-book collection, we invite you to explore these texts with an open heart and an open mind. Each book has the power to enrich your spiritual journey, offering new perspectives on familiar stories and introducing you to voices that might challenge, comfort, or inspire you. We encourage you to approach these texts not just as historical artifacts, but as living words with the power to shape your understanding and deepen your connection to God.

For those who seek a deeper connection to God, this project represents an opportunity to journey beyond the familiar, to explore scriptures that challenge and inspire, and to discover insights that have long been hidden. Each book, each chapter, and each verse holds the potential to bring new understanding and wisdom. As you read, let each word bring you closer to the truth, grace, and love that is the heart of God's message. Our goal is not only to preserve these sacred texts but to inspire a generation of readers who are eager to explore every word, every story, and every teaching that can bring them closer to the divine. In today's world, where so many distractions pull us away from quiet contemplation and spiritual reflection, the wisdom contained in these scriptures is more valuable than ever. It reminds us to slow down, to listen, and to seek out the divine in all aspects of our lives.

Thank you for being part of this journey with us. We are honored to share this work with you, and we hope that it brings you closer to God, to truth, and to a sense of peace and purpose. Let us continue this journey together, exploring every word and every book, knowing that each step brings us closer to the divine.

With gratitude and blessings,
Godknowy Publishers

Made in United States
Troutdale, OR
12/28/2024

27363869R00407